Shadwell  07

HA...

Chestnut, 2001, by ALHAARTH...

Winner of 2,000 Guineas and Champion Stakes in 2004.

NAYEF

Bay, 1998, by GULCH - HEIGHT OF FASHION, by BUSTINO

Multiple Group One Winner.

SAKHEE

Bay, 1997, by BAHRI - THAWAKIB, by SADLER'S WELLS

2001 World Champion.

GREEN DESERT

Bay, 1983, by DANZIG - FOREIGN COURIER, by SIR IVOR

A Supreme Champion Sire.

ACT ONE

Grey, 1999, by IN THE WINGS - SUMMER SONNET, by BAILLAMONT

Champion French Trained Two-Year-Old in 2001.

STORMING HOME

Bay, 1998, by MACHIAVELLIAN - TRY TO CATCH ME, by SHAREEF DANCER

Triple Group One winner.

SHADWELL

STANDING FOR SUCCESS

Contact: RICHARD LANCASTER, JOHNNY PETER-HOBLYN (Mob: 07831 261488)
or LOUISE CHANDLER (Mob: 07736 019910) on +44 (0)1842 755913
e-mail: enquiries@shadwellstud.co.uk www.shadwellstud.co.uk

AGE, WEIGHT & DISTANCE TABLE

Timeform's scale of weight-for-age for the flat

Dist	Age	Jan 1-16	Jan 17-31	Feb 1-16	Feb 17-28	Mar 1-16	Mar 17-31	Apr 1-16	Apr 17-30	May 1-16	May 17-31	June 1-16	June 17-30
5f	4	10-0	10-0	10-0	10-0	10-0	10-0	10-0	10-0	10-0	10-0	10-0	10-0
	3	9—5	9—5	9—6	9—7	9—7	9—8	9—8	9—9	9—9	9—10	9-10	9-11
	2						8—0	8—1	8—3	8—4	8—5	8—6	8—7
6f	4	10-0	10-0	10-0	10-0	10-0	10-0	10-0	10-0	10-0	10-0	10-0	10-0
	3	9—2	9—3	9—4	9—5	9—5	9—6	9—7	9—7	9—8	9—8	9—9	9—9
	2									8—0	8—2	8—3	8—4
7f	4	9-13	9-13	10-0	10-0	10-0	10-0	10-0	10-0	10-0	10-0	10-0	10-0
	3	9—0	9—1	9—2	9—3	9—4	9—4	9—5	9—6	9—6	9—7	9—8	9—8
	2											7-13	8—1
1m	4	9-13	9-13	9-13	9-13	10-0	10-0	10-0	10-0	10-0	10-0	10-0	10-0
	3	8-12	8-13	9—0	9—1	9—2	9—2	9—3	9—4	9—5	9—5	9—6	9—7
	2												
9f	4	9-12	9-12	9-12	9-13	9-13	9-13	9-13	10-0	10-0	10-0	10-0	10-0
	3	8-10	8-11	8-12	8-13	9—0	9—1	9—2	9—2	9—3	9—4	9—5	9—5
	2												
1¼m	4	9-11	9-12	9-12	9-12	9-13	9-13	9-13	9-13	9-13	10-0	10-0	10-0
	3	8—8	8—9	8-10	8-11	8-12	8-13	9—0	9—1	9—2	9—2	9—3	9—4
	2												
11f	4	9-10	9-11	9-11	9-12	9-12	9-12	9-13	9-13	9-13	9-13	9-13	10-0
	3	8—6	8—7	8—8	8—9	8-10	8-11	8-12	8-13	9—0	9—1	9—2	9—2
1½m	4	9-10	9-10	9-10	9-11	9-11	9-12	9-12	9-12	9-13	9-13	9-13	9-13
	3	8—4	8—5	8—6	8—7	8—8	8—9	8-10	8-11	8-12	8-13	9—0	9—1
13f	4	9—9	9—9	9-10	9-10	9-11	9-11	9-11	9-12	9-12	9-12	9-13	9-13
	3	8—2	8—3	8—4	8—5	8—7	8—8	8—9	8-10	8-11	8-12	8-13	9—0
1¾m	4	9—8	9—8	9—9	9—9	9-10	9-10	9-11	9-11	9-12	9-12	9-12	9-13
	3	8—0	8—2	8—3	8—4	8—5	8—6	8—7	8—8	8—9	8-10	8-11	8-12
15f	4	9—7	9—8	9—8	9—9	9—9	9-10	9-10	9-11	9-11	9-11	9-12	9-12
	3	7-13	8—0	8—1	8—2	8—4	8—5	8—6	8—7	8—8	8—9	8-10	8-11
2m	4	9—6	9—7	9—7	9—8	9—9	9—9	9-10	9-10	9-11	9-11	9-11	9-12
	3	7-11	7-12	7-13	8—1	8—2	8—3	8—4	8—5	8—6	8—7	8—8	8—9
2¼m	4	9—5	9—5	9—6	9—7	9—7	9—8	9—9	9—9	9-10	9-10	9-10	9-11
	3	7—8	7—9	7-11	7-12	7-13	8—0	8—2	8—3	8—4	8—5	8—6	8—7
2½m	4	9—3	9—4	9—5	9—6	9—6	9—7	9—7	9—8	9—9	9—9	9-10	9-10
	3	7—5	7—7	7—8	7—9	7-11	7-12	7-13	8—1	8—2	8—3	8—4	8—5

For 5-y-o's and older, use 10-0 in all cases
Race distances in the above tables are shown only at 1 furlong intervals.
For races over odd distances, the nearest distance shown in the table should be used:
thus for races of 1m to 1m 109 yards, use the table weights for 1m;
for 1m 110 yards to 1m 219 yards use the 9f table

**The age, weight and distance table covering July to December
appears on the end paper at the back of the book**

RACEHORSES OF 2006

Price £75.00

60 Years of
Timeform

CONTENTS

3	Introduction
14	2006 Statistics
17	Timeform Champions in Europe
18	The Timeform 'Top Hundred'
20	Explanatory Notes
23	Racehorses of 2006
1192	Errata & Addenda
1193	Promising Horses
1196	Selected Big Races 2006
1220	Timeform 'Top Horses Abroad'
1257	Index to Photographs
1263	Stallion Section
1270	The Champions

The age, weight and distance tables, for use in applying the ratings in races involving horses of different ages, appear on the end papers at the front and back of the book

Compiled and produced by

G. Greetham (Director), C. S. Williams (Managing Editor & Handicapper), J. Ingles (Essays & Editor for pedigrees & 'Top Horses Abroad'), P. Morrell (Essays & Editor), E. K. Wilkinson (Essays & Editor), P. Muncaster (Editor), G. J. McGibbon, D. W. Johnson, S. Molyneux (Handicappers), J. Early, M. A. Powell-Bevan, H. W. J. Bowles (Essays), P. Jupp, J. M. Lynch, A. J. Mealor, J. A. Todd, T. J. Windley (Short Commentaries), S. Wright (pedigrees, database updates), G. Crowther, G. Johnstone (proof checking), H. Brewer, M. Hall, D. Holdsworth, W. Muncaster, A-M. Stevens, R. Todd, C. Wright (Production)

© **Portway Press Limited 2007**   ISBN 978 1 901570 63 2

Racehorses of 2006

Introduction

'A good archer is not known by his arrows, but by his aim.' The sixteenth-century proverb should serve as a reminder of what is at stake for racing when various trials resulting from the long-running City of London police investigations into so-called 'race fixing' finally reach the courts in the autumn of 2007. The high profile names involved—headed by six-times champion jockey Kieren Fallon—ensure that a picture of corruption and chicanery will be splashed across the national media again, to a general public which already largely regards racing as shady.

The police would not be taking things so far unless they believed they had a robust case, but experience shows that arrests are one thing and convictions are another. Whether there will be enough damning evidence, no-one knows. The betting public suspects that things might be wrong in some areas but allegations and innuendo are all that it has to go on at present, and that will not be enough in court. How do you convince a jury that a jockey stopped a horse? Where does conspiracy start and end? The roar of derision will be overwhelming if the cases are shown to have been ill-conceived. One of them involves the so-called Hillside Girl affair at Carlisle in 2003, the two-year-old being pulled up after she was allegedly laid on betting exchanges in the knowledge that she was lame. A Jockey Club inquiry in September 2004 was unable to establish guilt on the main charges, the case virtually collapsing, though three of the four men involved, including Hillside Girl's trainer Alan Berry who now faces criminal charges, were later arrested by City of London police in connection with their own investigations.

The newly-formed Horseracing Regulatory Authority took over the day-to-day policing of racing from the Jockey Club in April and was kept busy with its own various investigations which brought under scrutiny several other big-name jockeys including Jamie Spencer (cleared of the most serious allegations in a bizarre, on-going case involving Mickmacmagoole), Robert Winston and Tony Culhane. Winston, released from bail in July in the City of London police case, and Culhane were among a number of riders on the Flat facing disciplinary hearings of the HRA towards the end of the year, most of them concerned with passing information, not publicly available, to named bookmakers and professional punters. Young jockeys Brian Reilly and Dean Williams were warned off for eighteen months in December (subject to Reilly's appeal) for their part in a scam involving ten horses laid to lose between December 2004 and February 2005; the case also involved bookmaker and racehorse owner Owen Churchill who was warned off for eight years. After nine days of evidence covering thirty-seven races between June 2003 and February 2004, the verdicts in the case involving Robert Winston were announced in mid-February 2007. Winston was suspended from riding for a year, becoming (subject to appeal) the most senior jockey to lose his licence since jump jockey Graham Bradley (currently serving a five-year ban). The most serious charges that Winston stopped horses from winning were dismissed, but he was found guilty of passing information for reward and misleading investigators. Fran Ferris (two years) and Robbie Fitzpatrick and Luke Fletcher (both three years) were warned off in the same case, along with bookmaker Ian Nicholl (at least ten years) and four others whose activities on betting exchanges became a focus of attention. In earlier, unrelated cases, trainer Shaun Keightley lost his appeal in April against a three-year warning off over the running of Red Lancer at Wolverhampton in October 2003, and another trainer David Flood was warned off for two years in March for injecting Mossmann Gorge with bute hours before it was due to run at Newmarket in July 2005.

The decision by the Horseracing Regulatory Authority to ban Kieren Fallon, who is licensed by the Irish Turf Club, and the two other jockeys charged by City of London police, Fergal Lynch and Darren Williams, was controversial. The ban on Fallon applied only to riding in Britain and, along with those of Lynch and Williams, was imposed as soon as criminal charges were brought in early-July, Lynch and Williams being promised compensation by the British Horseracing Board for the period of their enforced absence. Fallon's employers, the Coolmore triumvirate of John Magnier, Michael Tabor and Derrick Smith, stood by him as he continued to profess his innocence. Tabor referred in an interview to aspects of the case being like *Alice in Wonderland*. The famous children's story contains a passage in which the Queen demands 'sentence first, verdict afterwards' and there was a feeling that the banning of Fallon, Lynch and Williams breached the basic tenet of British justice, that of being 'presumed innocent until proven guilty'. However, Fallon's High Court challenge to the decision failed, the judge dismissing a complaint that the HRA should have looked at the evidence on which the Crown Prosecution Service was relying and heard submissions on Fallon's behalf about the weakness of the case against him (the jockey claimed that if an HRA panel had viewed the video evidence of the races involved they would have been satisfied he had done his best to win). The judge, however, concluded that the HRA had been right not to examine evidence 'cherry-picked' by Fallon's legal team from a wider range of material. The judge said that preventing Fallon from 'plying his trade and earning a living' in Britain was a serious matter, but claims that he faced relative destitution were not supported by the evidence submitted. The HRA could not be expected to guess the outcome of the criminal proceedings which, if proven, would 'strike at the heart of racing'. Neither Lynch nor Williams appealed against their riding bans.

If the charges of conspiracy to defraud against Fallon, Lynch, Williams, the warned-off founder of Platinum Racing Miles Rodgers, and seven others, are made to stick, it will reopen arguments about the advent of person-to-person betting exchanges. The British Horseracing Board—set to be transformed in 2007 into a new British Horseracing Authority (incorporating regulatory functions)—united with the big bookmakers in the era of Peter Savill's chairmanship of the BHB to portray the exchanges as providing 'unlimited opportunity for skulduggery' by also allowing punters to lay horses. The biggest exchange Betfair, whose customers are specifically mentioned as being defrauded in some of the charges brought by City of London police, has assisted the racing authorities and the police with their enquiries, providing information about betting patterns.

Betfair evidence to a parliamentary committee on the Gambling Bill in 2003 showed that 1,700 *winners* that year had more than doubled in price, a clear indication that 'drifters' in the market are by no means necessarily 'non-triers'. Monitoring movements on the betting exchanges is unlikely to throw suspicion on horses beaten in strong betting races at the better meetings (a good proportion of the cases investigated to date have focussed on races in the lowest grades where betting interest is smallest). Having sufficient numbers of good stewards and good supporting investigative officers is the only way to protect the integrity of British racing. The Government, which seems to have agreed to the continuation of the Levy Board which has underpinned racing for decades, has to view seriously any whiff of corruption in a sport funded by statutory intervention. Racing also needs to guard its reputation as it looks

4

to halt the sport's falling share of today's much more diverse overall betting market (racing-generated turnover on Betfair accounted for seventy per cent of its business when it began, but can reportedly be as low as thirty per cent nowadays on days with uninspiring programmes). Internet betting has come from nowhere in seven years and the betting exchanges have provided the opportunity for punters to trade at better odds than those available with traditional bookmakers.

The exchanges look likely to prove even more attractive if the new arrangements for determining starting prices introduced on November 1st—using a bigger sample of racecourse bookmakers, including more of those representing off-course operators—continues to increase margins, as it did in its first two months. Average theoretical overrounds went up by approaching twenty per cent per runner. The Government's decision in 2001 to replace betting tax with a tax on bookmakers' gross profits led to an agreement between the off-course bookmakers and the BHB to link payments for the funding of racing to bookmakers' profits on British racing. The racing authorities have a vested interest in seeing those profits maximised—ten per cent is paid to racing at present—and income from the levy (which contributes around sixty per cent of total prize money) ought to rise in line with the projected increase in betting-shop customers' losses. The Levy Board's falling income led to an announcement of a drop in its contribution to prize money of around £7.5m for 2007 (most races at the top end will not be affected) and it accepted a proposal from the bookmakers which will yield an estimated £91m in 2007/8, the same as in 2006/7.

Plans to replace the Levy Board (which has government-appointed members) with a commercial arrangement that would have given the sport financial independence had to be abandoned following a judgement by the European Court of Justice in 2004 that racing could not charge bookmakers worldwide for the use of pre-race data such as runners and riders. Tied up with the BHB's efforts to persuade the Government to reinstate the Levy Board (set to be wound up in 2009) has been the continuing saga over the future of the Tote (now trading off-course as totesport) which has around five per cent of the home market and makes a contribution to racing of over £10m a year, through payments to racecourses and sponsorship. The Home Affairs Select Committee recommended a transfer to racing as long ago as 1991. The BHB asked for ownership of the Tote in 1999, when there was speculation that it might be privatised, but the Racecourse Association—with whom the BHB has been at loggerheads for much of its thirteen-year existence—opposed BHB ownership of the Tote, while the Tote itself proposed that it should be owned by a racing trust. The Government effectively nationalised the Tote in 1993, ostensibly to sell it off at half of an agreed 'fair price'—with a seven-year monopoly on pool betting—to the proposed racing trust, a figure of £50m discussed. Progress has been slow since then, with European state-aid laws proving a stumbling block and the Government shifting its position to 'achieving value for money for the taxpayer, while recognising the racing sector's legitimate interest in the Tote.' It looks as if racing will be paying £400m—an offer made by a consortium of racecourses, major owners and totesport management in December—for something from which it already receives one hundred per cent of the benefits. No figures have been produced to show how this is a good deal for racing, but, having done an about-turn and pleaded with the Government to scrap plans to end the levy system, the turf authorities had no chance of persuading it also to abandon plans to sell the Tote. One consequence will be that the racecourses in the consortium will exert greater influence over the Tote's racecourse pools, with some concern that punters will get worse value.

With the future funding of racing still partly in the melting pot at the end of 2006, opening up overseas markets looks an increasingly important potential source of additional revenue. The year ended with the influential Asian Racing Conference in Dubai focussing on 'co-mingling', the transferring of tote bets taken in one country into pools operated by another (the British and Irish totes have been co-operating and the French pari-mutuel has been betting into the Breeders' Cup pool). There are suggestions for a weekly trifecta, involving several countries and leading to a proposed 'super jackpot'. Co-operation on international 'co-mingling' represents another foot in the door for promoting British racing to a worldwide market. The long-overdue introduction of forty-eight-hour declarations for all British Flat-racing from August paved the way for At The Races and Racing UK to negotiate the showing of British racing around the world, though information on progress was notable by its absence. The new declarations system produced grumbles, most notably from trainers (the National Trainers' Federation took a full page advert in the *Racing Post* airing its opposition), but an initial increase in non-runners was reversed once rules concerning the withdrawal of horses because of the going were tightened, after initially being relaxed to placate trainers. Another by-product of the introduction of forty-eight-hour declarations was the welcome restoration of race cards to many regional evening newspapers which had virtually dropped 'meaningless' lists of five-day declarations over the years from their early editions. The total readership of regional and local newspapers in Britain exceeds that for the national dailies and they offer a valuable source of promotion and a stimulus to betting turnover—to which the prosperity of racing will continue to be directly linked.

International initiatives are likely to include proposals for a twenty-four-hour worldwide racing TV channel showing live racing, though, ironically, another bold international initiative—the World Series Racing Championship—was officially scrapped in the latest season. The series was launched in 1999, framed around the world's top middle-distance races. The series brought enhanced competition, earning its early winners a million-dollar bonus through Emirates sponsorship, and contributed towards achieving wider recognition for horse racing as a global sport. It was claimed that each race in the first few series was watched by a billion viewers round the world, but betting and television rights could not be obtained for the series which eventually ended up being staged without a sponsor, run in 2003, 2004 and 2005 'solely for prestige'. Godolphin gave the series its wholehearted support initially and won the first four editions with Daylami, Fantastic Light (twice) and Grandera, all of whom were campaigned in the spirit intended, but its interest waned after Emirates stopped sponsoring, and after the world's richest race, the Dubai World Cup, was withdrawn from the series.

Godolphin still has adventurous global ambitions, although, after seven successive years as the leading British-based stable in terms of foreign earnings, its successes outside Britain have not been enough to earn that accolade in the past two years. Godolphin had its fourth winner of the Dubai World Cup in **Electrocutionist** and was the leading owner in Britain for the sixth time, though unusually it did not have a Group 1 winner in Britain. The stable made a relatively poor start before its horses found their form in the second half of the season, its ups and downs charted in the essay on **Librettist**, one of Europe's best older milers who completed the Jacques le Marois/Prix du Moulin double. Godolphin's two-year-olds were wintered in Britain, in a change to the usual policy of wintering them in Dubai, but by the start of October only two had been out. Only twenty had run by the end of the year, the entry on **Measured Tempo** looking at the potential of those that reached the racecourse.

Sir Michael Stoute, who trains a string of around one hundred and sixty, was champion trainer in Britain for the ninth time but there was a new champion jockey, Ryan Moore becoming the youngest to win the title since Pat Eddery. Moore forged closer links to the Stoute stable, with Michael Kinane being used more by Ballydoyle after Fallon's ban and Robert Winston, another Stoute regular, missing parts of the season through injury and suspension. Stoute and Moore combined to win the International at York with **Notnowcato**, one of only two domestic Group 1s for the yard, the other achieved by **Peeress** in the Lockinge. Ten of the thirty-one British Group 1s were won by overseas-trained horses, seven of them by Ballydoyle inmates, including **George Washington**, the first successful favourite in the Two Thousand Guineas since Zafonic in 1993. George Washington, who had been the most expensive yearling of his year, had a temperamental side but was superior in merit to run-of-the-mill classic winners, as he showed when avenging his defeat in the Irish Two Thousand Guineas by **Araafa** when the pair met in the Queen Elizabeth II Stakes at Ascot. Third in that race was Sussex Stakes winner **Court Masterpiece**, whose entry reviews developments with the bloodstock empire of Maktoum Al Maktoum after his death early in the year. One of George Washington's stable-companions in the Queen Elizabeth II Stakes, Ivan Denisovich, was at the centre of a storm after Frankie Dettori claimed that Librettist had been deliberately interfered with. Ivan Denisovich's jockey Seamus Heffernan was originally banned for fourteen days under rules governing 'team tactics' but the ban was reduced to six after an appeal found that his mount had not acted as a 'spoiler'. **Alexandrova** landed a second British classic for Ballydoyle when romping home in the Oaks, a victory she followed up in the Irish Oaks before being returned to Britain to complete a notable treble when winning the Yorkshire Oaks. She was below her best when third to the versatile French

Sir Michael Stoute was champion trainer for the ninth time,
but there was a new champion jockey, Ryan Moore, the youngest to take the title since Pat Eddery

Royal Ascot returned home and racegoers packed the new stands,
though getting a clear view of the action was a problem in some parts;
the course announced a £10m programme of remedial work to be carried out in time for the 2007 meeting

three-year-old **Mandesha** in the Prix de l'Opera but stays in training. The Ballydoyle five-year-old **Yeats** dominated the out-and-out staying division, completing the Gold Cup-Goodwood Cup double in splendid style, and **Ad Valorem** was also a Royal Ascot winner for the O'Brien team in the Queen Anne. The rules governing interference cause much less controversy than they used to, but the differences between the guidelines in Britain and in France are highlighted in the essays on Ad Valorem and promoted Poule d'Essai des Pouliches winner **Tie Black**. Fallon was able to defer a careless riding ban incurred in the Queen Anne so that he could ride Derby third **Dylan Thomas** in the Irish Derby. Dylan Thomas had been only his stable's third string at Epsom but he progressed really well, following up victory in the Irish Derby with another top-class performance in the Irish Champion. Excellence in the saddle, displayed to full effect on Dylan Thomas in the Irish Champion, cannot be used as evidence in Fallon's defence in his forthcoming trial but, whatever the outcome, he insists that he has no intention of quitting the saddle. His troubles were compounded when he received a six-month suspension, after failing a drugs test in France, which will keep him out of action in Ireland and France until June 2007.

The Vodafone Derby was one of the most exciting in the history of the race;
Sir Percy (far side) came out best in a four-way photo

The HRA ban in Britain cost Fallon the ride on French-trained **Hurricane Run** in the King George VI and Queen Elizabeth Stakes, a race in which there was no runner from Ballydoyle (something examined in the essay on Dylan Thomas). A lack of three-year-old representation has begun to threaten the King George and the entry on Hurricane Run, who was beaten in all four of his races after Ascot, examines the idea of recreating the triple crown to include the King George as the third leg, while suggesting the race also needs a boost in prize money. Hurricane Run's essay also touches on the cricitism of Ascot's new £200m grandstand. From the top tier, the long-sighted can see Canary Wharf and the developing Wembley stadium, as well as the spires of Oxford on a clear day; unfortunately, the sightlines for those on the steps or seats between the concourse and the lawns provided a less than satisfactory view of the racing, something hopefully being remedied by £10m-worth of improvements before the Royal meeting in 2007. The storm in a teacup over a supposed strong draw bias on the new track is covered in the essay on **Sir Gerard**. Changes made to the Grand Prix de Paris provide Ascot with stiff competition for the presence of the top middle-distance three-year-olds in July. The latest Grand Prix winner **Rail Link**, a stable-companion of Hurricane Run and Coronation Cup winner **Shirocco**, went on to win the Prix de l'Arc de Triomphe (worth nearly twice as much as the King George), beating his two stablemates, among others, in a field that had nothing like the strength in depth of a typical renewal, Rail Link and the supplemented St Leger winner **Sixties Icon** among only four members of the classic crop in the line-up. The good horses missing included Derby winner **Sir Percy**, **Youmzain**, Dylan Thomas, Alexandrova and Mandesha.

The 227th Derby, the most valuable race in Britain, was one of the most action-packed editions in its long history, in terms of drama and the closeness of its finish probably behind only the notorious 'suffragette' Derby of 1913. Encouragingly, the latest edition drew a TV audience of 4.1m for the race, the biggest since the race returned to the BBC in 2001. Sir Percy, a 20,000-guinea foal bought by his trainer for only 16,000 guineas as a yearling, is one of only six Derby winners in the last thirty years to be sold at auction in Britain and Ireland. In a season which had more than its share of 'fairytales', Sir Percy

The latest season had more than its share of 'fairytales'
including Speciosa's victory in the Stan James One Thousand Guineas for the smallish stable of Pam Sly,
the first woman officially credited with training a classic winner in Britain

was not the only big winner to emerge from humble origins. One Thousand Guineas winner **Speciosa**, the first British classic winner officially trained by a woman (Pam Sly), was bought at the Doncaster Breeze Up Sale for only 30,000 guineas. What would she have made had she been offered at the end of her three-year-old days at the December Sales? Sun Chariot winner **Spinning Queen**, runner-up to Speciosa in the Nell Gwyn and sixth to her in the Guineas, made three million guineas, a European record for a filly out of training (details of other records at the sale are recounted in her essay).

The continuing story of **Sergeant Cecil**, bought as a yearling for less than £1,000 'out of a field', saw him progress in pattern-company, his last success coming in France's most important race for out-and-out stayers, the Prix du Cadran. Another British success on Arc weekend came in the Prix de l'Abbaye through **Desert Lord**, who cost only 10,000 guineas at the Newmarket Autumn Sales. Another of the season's top sprinters **Les Arcs** also passed through the same sale-ring, bought as a cast-off from the Gosden stable for 32,000 guineas by Richard Guest for whom he won in minor company and was also beaten almost seventy lengths in a maiden hurdle at Cartmel. Transferred to Tim Pitt as a five-year-old, Les Arcs won the Golden Jubilee Stakes and the July Cup at six, his earnings putting him second behind Sir Percy in the list of money winners in Britain in the latest season. The big sprints had a sharp rise in value to make them more attractive to overseas runners, the Golden Jubilee and Royal Ascot's other major sprint the King's Stand being part of the Global Sprint Challenge, a series which is successfully serving the cause of international racing. Another who landed a big sprint double—the Nunthorpe and the Haydock Sprint Cup—was **Reverence**. He reached the track for the first time as a four-year-old after twice breaking his pelvis in his younger days, his owners deserving credit for persevering.

If the sprinters Desert Lord, Les Arcs and Reverence all made remarkable progress in the latest season, then the irrepressible **Young Mick** and the three-year-old filly **Red Evie** arguably did even better. Young Mick recorded ten wins, starting in a maiden claimer at a 'banded' meeting at Wolverhampton in January and ending in the Cumberland Lodge Stakes at Ascot in September. Red Evie won seven in a row, graduating from Yarmouth maiden company to winning the Matron Stakes at Leopardstown. The Matron is a Group 1 nowadays, part of the significantly upgraded programme introduced for fillies and mares in 2004 to encourage owners of pattern-class fillies to keep them in training at four and beyond. The move has been well received. Cheveley Park Stud, which had another good campaign (and purchased Middle Park winner **Dutch Art** late in the year) did particularly well with its fillies, **Nannina** (Coronation Stakes) and **Confidential Lady** (Prix de Diane) among its three-year-olds that are being kept in training, as incidentally is Peeress. When runner-up to Speciosa, Confidential Lady became the first runner in a classic in Britain for her trainer Sir Mark Prescott, who has held a licence since 1971 (Confidential Lady's Prix de Diane success was his first in a classic anywhere). The older fillies and mares generally had a good year against the colts, **Pride** (Grand Prix de Saint-Cloud and Champion Stakes), **Kastoria** (Irish St Leger) and **Montare** (Prix Royal-Oak) among others who won open Group 1s in major European countries. Another who did so was the splendid **Ouija Board**, successful in the Prince of Wales's Stakes at Royal Ascot. She also got the better of another tough mare, Irish-trained **Alexander Goldrun**, in a memorable finish to the Nassau Stakes at Goodwood. The globe-trotting Ouija Board—who won her second Breeders' Cup Filly & Mare Turf—won seven Group/Grade 1 events in her career and earned over £3.5m, easily a record for a filly or mare trained in Britain.

Another to contest prestigious international races was **Collier Hill** whose victories in the Canadian International and Hong Kong Vase took him to the top of the earnings list for British-trained geldings, with over £2.3m so far. The restricted opportunities for geldings in Europe are discussed on **Corre Caminos**. It was a record year for British-trained winners abroad, with prize-money earnings of £14,975,262, according to figures produced by the International Racing Bureau. The richest pickings were at the Dubai Carnival held in the first part of the year, **David Junior**, who went on to win the Eclipse, winning the Dubai Duty Free, the biggest prize ever won by a British-trained horse. France, Ireland and the United States were the happiest hunting grounds for British-trained horses after Dubai, but David Junior made no impression in the Breeders' Cup Classic in which he and George Washington represented a theoretically strong challenge. David Junior's essay comments on the permissive attitude towards the use of drugs which sometimes creates mistrust of the achievements of American horses. Consolation for the poor effort of David Junior came for his stable when **Red Rocks** won the Breeders' Cup Turf to put trainer Brian Meehan at the top of the list of British trainers by earnings on foreign soil in 2006.

Frankie Dettori performs his trademark flying dismount
after Ouija Board's second win in the Breeders' Cup Filly & Mare Turf,
which helped to boost her earnings to over £3.5m, easily a record for a filly or mare trained in Britain.

If international racing is to thrive, authorities around the world will have to reach concensus on a set of rules governing the use of drugs. Two of the highest profile international performers in 2006, **Takeover Target** and **Deep Impact**, were among horses affected. Global Sprint Challenge winner Takeover Target, bought for about £500 as an unraced four-year-old with knee problems, was the latest Australian horse to challenge successfully for honours in Britain (he won the King's Stand). Unfortunately, he had to be withdrawn from the Hong Kong Sprint after failing a series of tests leading up to the race. Japan's champion Deep Impact, whose hordes of fans resulted in his going off at 2/1-on in the Prix de l'Arc, tested positive for a prohibited substance at Longchamp and was disqualified from third. There was no suggestion of foul play or wrongdoing, however, and Deep Impact afterwards won the Japan Cup and the Arima Kinen, putting up a career-best effort in the last-named on his final appearance. Japanese-trained challengers in Europe are taken much more seriously than they once were, a topic discussed in the essay on **Heart's Cry** who finished third in the King George.

With Ballydoyle's juveniles less dominant, the ante-post markets on the 2007 classics have a rather unfamiliar look. Ballydoyle still has four horses quoted at 20/1 or shorter in the Two Thousand Guineas market at the time of writing, **Holy Roman Emperor**, who in most years would have been good enough to be champion two-year-old, **Mount Nelson**, **Duke of Marmalade** (whose essay summarises the record of the stable's juveniles) and **Eagle Mountain**. Another Irish stable, that of Jim Bolger, has the favourites for the first two classics, the unbeaten **Teofilo** and Prix Marcel Boussac winner **Finsceal Beo**. Teofilo defeated Holy Roman Emperor narrowly in the Dewhurst, the pair putting up performances in the race as good as any in the past twenty years, with the exception of seven-length winner Xaar. Even when its own runners are beaten, the Ballydoyle/Coolmore operation has every chance nowadays of reflected glory through the Coolmore sires (Teofilo is by Galileo),

Veteran trainer Fulke Johnson Houghton, who handled such as Ribocco, Ribero, Habitat, Ile de Bourbon and Rose Bowl in his glory days, handed over to his daughter; Richard Quinn, three times runner-up in the jockeys' championship, also decided to call it a day

a subject taken up in the entry on Racing Post Trophy winner **Authorized**. One of the topics dealt with in the essay on Sixties Icon is the expansion of the Coolmore Stud empire since the mid-'seventies when Vincent O'Brien, John Magnier and Robert Sangster devised the successful strategy of 'buying to make stallions'. Among the two-year-old fillies, **Sander Camillo**, who won the Cherry Hinton in a style reminiscent of Attraction, looked like heading the list of classic prospects until Finsceal Beo emerged. **Passage of Time** was another filly whose clear classic potential was highlighted late on, when winning the Criterium de Saint-Cloud. The highest-earning two-year-old in Europe was a filly, **Miss Beatrix**, who won the inaugural Goffs Million, the richest juvenile race anywhere in the northern hemisphere. Miss Beatrix was one of several runners in sales races in the latest season who also did well in pattern company. She won the Moyglare Stud Stakes, while the promoted winner of the very valuable fillies-only Goffs sales race, **Silk Blossom**, won the Lowther, and **Indian Ink** followed up her win in the Watership Down Sales Race by taking the Cheveley Park. Finsceal Beo herself came sixth in the Goffs Million.

The most notable of the season's retirements were those of Richard Quinn, three times runner-up for the jockeys' title (career details included in the entry of his last winner, Young Mick), and trainer Fulke Johnson Houghton, who is handing over the reins at his Blewbury yard to daughter Eve. Johnson Houghton was the youngest trainer in Britain when he took out a licence at the age of twenty in 1961. Johnson Houghton trained the brothers Ribocco and Ribero, both of whom won the St Leger and the Irish Derby, and he won the King George with Ile de Bourbon. Habitat, Double Form and Rose Bowl were others of note that he trained, while, long after its glory days, the stable won the Dewhurst in 2002 with Tout Seul. Many of Johnson Houghton's big winners were in an era when BBC TV's varied Saturday sports show *Grandstand* was in its heyday. The weekly outside broadcast—in black and white—from a featured race meeting was a prominent part of *Grandstand* which undoubtedly played a part in broadening national interest in the sport. Increased competition for broadcasting rights to major sporting occasions put some of *Grandstand*'s traditional events beyond the reach of the BBC and left holes in its schedules. Viewing preferences began to change, too. The programme was 'no longer punching through in this multi-channel world', in the words of the BBC's director general, and was broadcast for the last time at the end of January 2007, two years short of its half century. At least it enjoyed a longer run than the betting paper *The Sportsman*, which was launched in March and closed in October. Other signs that times are changing came with the announcement in December from its owner Trinity Mirror that the *Racing Post*, having fought off the challenge of *The Sportsman*, was being put up for sale. *Timeform* joined forces with Betfair in November to form a powerful alliance for the new multi-media age. Though it is now a wholly-owned subsidiary of Betfair, *Timeform* will continue on a day-to-day basis much as before, and it retains editorial independence.

In this sixtieth edition of *Racehorses*, the hundred or so essays on the top horses (including all those highlighted in bold in this introduction) set out, as usual, to entertain and inform in equal measure. Along with the extensive photographic coverage, and the essential 'Top Horses Abroad' section, *Racehorses* provides an accurate and authoritative record of the racing year. The wealth of facts, analysis and informed opinion should be of considerable practical value to the punter. Every horse that ran on the Flat in Britain is dealt with individually, along with many of the best foreign horses, the total number of commentaries exceeding 11,000 for the first time.

February 2007

2006 STATISTICS

The following tables show the leading owners, trainers, jockeys, sires of winners and horses on the Flat in Britain during 2006 (Jan 1–Dec 31). The prize money statistics, compiled by *Timeform*, relate to first-three prize money and win money. Win money was traditionally used to decide the trainers' championship until, in 1994, the BHB and the National Trainers' Federation established a championship decided by total prize money as determined by *Racing Post*. The jockeys' championship has traditionally been decided by the number of winners ridden during the year, though since 1997 the Jockeys' Association has recognised a championship that runs for the turf season (Mar–Nov).

OWNERS (1,2,3 earnings)	Horses	Indiv'l Wnrs	Races Won	Runs	%	Stakes £
1 Godolphin	121	51	70	247	28.3	1,513,116
2 Mr Hamdan Al Maktoum	158	66	83	556	14.9	1,199,775
3 Gainsborough Stud	89	37	52	318	16.3	975,908
4 Cheveley Park Stud	59	25	34	192	17.7	907,458
5 Mr A. E. Pakenham	2	1	1	4	25.0	811,711
6 Mrs John Magnier, Mr M. Tabor & D. Smith	5	2	4	10	40.0	762,110
7 Mr K. Abdulla	85	37	49	237	20.6	690,032
8 Mrs Susan Roy	7	4	7	20	35.0	528,178
9 Mr M. Tabor	9	3	3	25	12.0	520,162
10 Sheikh Ahmed Al Maktoum	70	27	39	229	17.0	499.793
11 Mr Willie McKay	8	3	9	43	20.9	499,279
12 Anthony & David de Rothschild	1	1	3	6	50.0	439,457

OWNERS (win money, £½m+)	Horses	Indiv'l Wnrs	Races Won	Runs	%	Stakes £
1 Godolphin	121	51	70	247	28.3	935,411
2 Mr A. E. Pakenham	2	1	1	4	25.0	740,695
3 Mrs John Magnier, Mr M. Tabor & D. Smith	5	2	4	10	40.0	736,096
4 Mr Hamdan Al Maktoum	158	66	83	556	14.9	672,742
5 Gainsborough Stud	89	37	52	318	16.3	619,876
6 Cheveley Park Stud	59	25	34	192	17.7	617,725

TRAINERS (1,2,3 earnings)	Horses	Indiv'l Wnrs	Races Won	Runs	%	Stakes £
1 Sir Michael Stoute	147	79	107	487	21.9	2,837,612
2 M. Johnston	222	112	158	1005	15.7	1,755,651
3 B. W. Hills	167	73	103	734	14.0	1,661,573
4 R. Hannon	198	85	127	1067	11.9	1,633,553
5 A. P. O'Brien, Ireland	46	8	11	74	14.8	1,585,326
6 Saeed bin Suroor	121	51	70	247	28.3	1,513,116
7 M. R. Channon	174	83	127	1027	12.3	1,413,557
8 B. J. Meehan	128	58	74	532	13.9	1,365,779
9 J. Noseda	78	34	47	249	18.8	1,211,153
10 K. A. Ryan	149	69	95	828	11.4	1,192,922
11 E. A. L. Dunlop	113	41	55	437	12.5	1,153,115
12 M. P. Tregoning	72	24	29	210	13.8	1,132,676

TRAINERS (win money, £1m+)	Horses	Indiv'l Wnrs	Races Won	Runs	%	Stakes £
1 Sir Michael Stoute	147	79	107	487	21.9	1,842,588
2 A. P. O'Brien, Ireland	46	8	11	74	14.8	1,247,460
3 M. Johnston	222	112	158	1005	15.7	1,245,734
4 B. W. Hills	167	73	103	734	14.0	1,101,094
5 R. Hannon	198	85	127	1067	11.9	1,043,039

TRAINERS (with 100+ winners)	Horses	Indiv'l Wnrs	Races Won	2nd	3rd	Runs	%
1 M. Johnston	222	112	158	125	110	1005	15.7
2 R. Hannon	198	85	127	128	133	1067	11.9
3 M. R. Channon	174	83	127	121	107	1027	12.3
4 Sir Michael Stoute	147	79	107	75	57	487	21.9
5 B. W. Hills	167	73	103	96	103	734	14.0

JOCKEYS (by winners)	1st	2nd	3rd	Unpl	Mts	%
1 Ryan Moore	182	147	141	704	1174	15.5
2 Jamie Spencer	155	113	98	474	840	18.4
3 Eddie Ahern	140	128	109	779	1156	12.1
4 Robert Winston	136	121	104	620	981	13.8
5 L. Dettori	131	81	73	306	591	22.1
6 N. Callan	129	127	128	644	1028	12.5
7 Seb Sanders	117	105	80	532	834	14.0
8 Richard Hughes	113	95	107	489	804	14.1
9 Paul Hanagan	107	118	101	712	1038	10.3
10 Joe Fanning	108	94	99	637	938	11.5
11 Dane O'Neill	94	93	115	642	944	9.9
12 John Egan	92	80	95	574	841	10.9

Note: Ryan Moore was leading jockey in the turf season with 180 winners

JOCKEYS (1,2,3 earnings)	Races Won	Rides	%	Stakes £
1 L. Dettori	131	591	22.1	3,185,990
2 Ryan Moore	182	1174	15.5	2,549,735
3 Jamie Spencer	155	840	18.4	2,391,577
4 Martin Dwyer	90	862	10.4	1,904,990
5 Richard Hughes	113	804	14.1	1,698,619
6 John Egan	92	841	10.9	1,570,497
7 K. Fallon	27	143	18.8	1,487,174
8 N. Callan	129	1028	12.5	1,415,141
9 Jimmy Fortune	77	660	11.6	1,416,629
10 Michael Hills	69	515	13.3	1,387,191
11 K. Darley	75	604	12.4	1,317,934
12 Robert Winston	136	981	13.8	1,283,903

JOCKEYS (win money, £1m+)	Races Won	Rides	%	Stakes £
1 L. Dettori	131	591	22.1	2,205,299
2 Ryan Moore	182	1174	15.5	1,842,614
3 Jamie Spencer	155	840	18.4	1,665,428
4 Martin Dwyer	90	862	10.4	1,427,565
5 K. Fallon	27	143	18.8	1,257,473
6 John Egan	92	841	10.9	1,237,989
7 Richard Hughes	113	804	14.1	1,156,447

| 8 | K. Darley | | | 75 | 604 | 12.4 | 1,054,464 |
| 9 | Jimmy Fortune | | | 77 | 660 | 11.6 | 1,006,192 |

APPRENTICES (by winners)	*1st*	*2nd*	*3rd*	*Unpl*	*Mts*	*%*
1 James Doyle	73	85	82	517	757	9.6
2 Adam Kirby	58	64	59	497	678	8.5
3 Daniel Tudhope	53	60	24	333	470	11.2
4 Stephen Donohoe	47	32	37	278	394	11.9

Note: Stephen Donohoe was champion apprentice in the turf season with 44 winners

		Races			Stakes
SIRES OF WINNERS (1,2,3 earnings)		Won	Runs	%	£
1	Danehill (by Danzig)	64	463	13.8	1,640,675
2	Mark of Esteem (by Darshaan)	52	562	9.2	1,583,381
3	Sadler's Wells (by Northern Dancer)	41	331	12.3	1,539,791
4	Pivotal (by Polar Falcon)	101	625	16.1	1,224,478
5	Montjeu (by Sadler's Wells)	34	292	11.6	1,201,018
6	Cape Cross (by Green Desert)	60	549	10.9	1,192,219
7	Galileo (by Sadler's Wells)	40	267	14.9	1,072,209
8	Danehill Dancer (by Danehill)	61	606	10.0	1,042,322
9	Indian Ridge (by Ahonoora)	57	423	13.4	1,026,129
10	Dansili (by Danehill)	92	690	13.3	970,745
11	Inchinor (by Ahonoora)	58	583	9.9	951,557
12	Singspiel (by In The Wings)	68	454	14.9	782,510

			Indiv'l	Races	Stakes
SIRES OF WINNERS (win money)		Horses	Wnrs	Won	£
1	Mark of Esteem (by Darshaan)	115	34	52	1,385,822
2	Danehill (by Danzig)	103	43	64	1,045,050
3	Sadler's Wells (by Northern Dancer)	101	34	41	1,033,810
4	Montjeu (by Sadler's Wells)	71	24	34	989,717
5	Indian Ridge (by Ahonoora)	69	34	57	853,448
6	Pivotal (by Polar Falcon)	123	60	101	844,795
7	Cape Cross (by Green Desert)	109	43	60	752,472
8	Danehill Dancer (by Danehill)	130	43	61	727,266
9	Dansili (by Danehill)	112	56	92	708,005
10	Galileo (by Sadler's Wells)	65	27	40	679,225
11	Inchinor (by Ahonoora)	105	37	58	641,543
12	Singspiel (by In The Wings)	92	45	68	517,174

		Races		Stakes
LEADING HORSES (1,2,3 earnings)		Won	Runs	£
1	Sir Percy 3 b.c Mark of Esteem – Percy's Lass	1	3	811,711
2	Les Arcs 6 br.g Arch – La Sarto	6	9	469,764
3	Hurricane Run 4 b.c Montjeu – Hold On	1	2	463,545
4	Notnowcato 4 ch.c Inchinor – Rambling Rose	3	6	439,457
5	Alexandrova 3 b.f Sadler's Wells – Shouk	2	3	419,684
6	Reverence 5 ch.g Mark of Esteem – Imperial Bailiwick	4	8	378,680
7	Ouija Board 5 b.m Cape Cross – Selection Board	2	4	378,567
8	George Washington 3 b.c Danehill – Bordighera	2	3	340,094
9	Sixties Icon 3 b.c Galileo – Love Divine	3	6	325,197
10	Dragon Dancer 3 b.c Sadler's Wells – Alakananda	0	5	297,075
11	Court Masterpiece 6 b.h Polish Precedent – Easy Option	1	4	282,400
12	David Junior 4 ch.c Pleasant Tap – Paradise River	1	2	260,620

HORSE OF THE YEAR
BEST THREE-YEAR-OLD COLT
BEST MILER RATED AT 133
GEORGE WASHINGTON

BEST TWO-YEAR-OLD FILLY RATED AT 118
FINSCEAL BEO

BEST TWO-YEAR-OLD COLT RATED AT 126
TEOFILO

BEST THREE-YEAR-OLD FILLY RATED AT 124
MANDESHA

BEST OLDER FEMALE RATED AT 128
PRIDE

BEST OLDER MALE RATED AT 132
DAVID JUNIOR

BEST SPRINTER RATED AT 127
REVERENCE

BEST MIDDLE-DISTANCE COLT RATED AT 132
RAIL LINK

BEST STAYER RATED AT 128
YEATS

BEST PERFORMANCES IN A HANDICAP IN BRITAIN
BALTIC KING
ran to 120
when winning Wokingham Stakes at Royal Ascot
STRONGHOLD
ran to 120
when second in Royal Hunt Cup at Royal Ascot

BEST PERFORMANCE ON ALL-WEATHER IN BRITAIN
ECHO OF LIGHT
ran to 125
when winning Ladbrokes Summer Mile Stakes at Lingfield

THE TIMEFORM 'TOP HUNDRED'

Here are listed the 'Top 100' two-year-olds, three-year-olds and older horses in the annual. Fillies and mares are denoted by (f).

2 YEAR OLDS

126	Teofilo
125	Holy Roman Emperor
124	Dutch Art
118p	Authorized
118	Eagle Mountain
118	Finsceal Beo (f)
116p	Admiralofthefleet
116p	Sander Camillo (f)
116	Wi Dud
115	Charlie Farnsbarns
114p	Evening Time (f)
114p	Mount Nelson
114p	Soldier of Fortune
114	Battle Paint
114	Caldra
114	Captain Marvellous
114	Doctor Brown
114	Excellent Art
114	Strategic Prince
114§	Conquest
113p	Haatef
113p	Passage of Time (f)
113	Spirit One
113	Vital Equine
112	Magic America (f)
112	Thousand Words
111p	Mythical Kid
110p	Duke of Marmalade
110p	Monzante
110	Indian Ink (f)
110	Medicine Path
110	Rallying Cry
110	Simply Perfect (f)
110	Yellowstone
109p	Adagio
109p	Visionario
109	Dhanyata (f)
109	He's A Decoy
109	Sandwaki
108p	Treat (f)
108	Alzerra (f)
108	Baby Strange
108	Cockney Rebel
108	Dijeerr
108	Hellvelyn
108	Prime Defender
107p	Empire Day
107p	Legerete (f)
107p	Yazamaan
107	Drayton
107	Halicarnassus
107	Kirklees
107	Silk Blossom (f)
107	Strobilus
107	Tobosa

106p	Big Robert
106p	Hamoody
106p	Shane (f)
106	Darrfonah (f)
106	Drumfire
106	Miss Beatrix (f)
106	Regime
106	Sesmen (f)
106	Silca Chiave (f)
105p	Rahiyah (f)
105	Beauty Is Truth (f)
105	Bodes Galaxy
105	Brave Tin Soldier
105	Elhamri
105	Hoh Mike
105	La Presse (f)
105	Market Day (f)
105	Not For Me
105	Red Rock Canyon
104P	Asperity
104p	Arch Swing (f)
104p	Consul General
104p	Sakhee's Secret
104p	Utmost Respect
104+	Fleeting Shadow
104	Big Timer
104	Champlain
104	Chinese Whisper
104	English Ballet (f)
104	Enticing (f)
104	Ferneley
104	Major Cadeaux
104	Rabatash
103p	Chanting (f)
103p	Hurricane Spirit
103p	Supposition (f)
103p	Valbenny (f)
103	Bahama Mama (f)
103	Brazilian Bride (f)
103	Jack Junior
103	Massive
103	Scarlet Runner (f)
103	Striving Storm
102+	Kid Mambo
102	Dubai Builder
102	Eddie Jock
102	Hammers Boy
102	Hucking Hot (f)
102	Invincible Force
102	Silent Waves
102	Vital Statistics (f)

3 YEAR OLDS

133	George Washington
132	Bernardini
132	Rail Link

130	Barbaro
129	Dylan Thomas
129	Sir Percy
128	Araafa
127p	Discreet Cat
125	Sixties Icon
125	Youmzain
124	Mandesha (f)
124	Red Rocks
123	Alexandrova (f)
123	Aussie Rules
123	Balthazaar's Gift
123	Best Name
123	Dandy Man
123	Lateral
123	Stormy River
122	Irish Wells
121p	Hala Bek
121	Marchand d'Or
121	Septimus
120	Amadeus Wolf
120	Gentlewave
120	Killybegs
120	Mulaqat
120	Olympian Odyssey
120	Papal Bull
120	Soapy Danger
120	Tam Lin
119	Dragon Dancer
119	Lord of England
119	Nannina (f)
119	Prince Flori
119	Red Clubs
118	Areyoutalkingtome
118	Biniou
118	Darsi
118	Kentucky Dynamite
118	Road To Love
118	Spinning Queen (f)
118	The Last Drop
118	Visindar
117p	Al Qasi
117p	Desert Authority
117	Best Alibi
117	Dilek
117	Formal Decree
117	Grand Couturier
117	Marcus Andronicus
117	Passager
117	Red Evie (f)
117	Short Skirt (f)
117	Sudan
116p	Daramsar
116	Advanced
116	Arras
116	Art Deco

116 Ask
116 Blue Ksar
116 Confidential Lady (f)
116 Cougar Bay
116 Flashing Numbers
116 Frost Giant
116 Linda's Lad
116 Primary
116 Rajeem (f)
116 Schiaparelli
116 Soar With Eagles
116 Stage Gift
115p Counterpunch
115p Multidimensional
115 Allegretto (f)
115 An Tadh
115 Dark Islander
115 Flashy Wings (f)
115 Galatee (f)
115 Heliostatic
115 Ivan Denisovich
115 Jadalee
115 Price Tag (f)
115 Prince Tamino
115 Rising Cross (f)
115 Speciosa (f)
115 Tusculum
114p Danak
114p Sir Gerard
114 Anna Pavlova (f)
114 Dionisia (f)
114 Jeremy
114 Linas Selection
114 Misu Bond
114 Mountain
114 Strike Up The Band
114 Time On (f)
114 Ugo Fire (f)
113 Beauty Bright (f)
113 Decado
113 Dunelight
113 Fermion (f)
113 Final Verse
113 Germance (f)
113 Nightime (f)
113 Puerto Rico
113 Race For The Stars (f)
113 Smart Enough
113 West of Amarillo
113? Dixie Belle (f)

OLDER HORSES
134 Deep Impact
133 Invasor
132 David Junior
130 Hurricane Run
130 Lava Man
129 Absolute Champion
129 Shirocco
128 Pride (f)
128 Yeats
127 Court Masterpiece

127 Electrocutionist
127 Heart's Cry
127 Iffraaj
127 Reverence
126 Les Arcs
126 Maraahel
126 Moss Vale
126 Notnowcato
126 Takeover Target
125 Ad Valorem
125 Alexander Goldrun (f)
125 Delta Blues
125 Echo of Light
125 Ouija Board (f)
124 Corre Caminos
124 Desert Lord
124 Kastoria (f)
124 Librettist
124 Mountain High
124 Peeress (f)
123 Cherry Mix
123 Collier Hill
123 Enforcer
123 Grey Swallow
123 Laverock
123 Majors Cast
123 Manduro
123 Mustameet
122 Alayan
122 Alfie Flits
122 Arcadio
122 Ashdown Express
122 Blue Monday
122 Day Flight
122 Distinction
122 Egerton
122 Etlaala
122 Mubtaker
122 Ramonti
122 Rob Roy
122 Sleeping Indian
121 Benbaun
121 Caradak
121 Chelsea Rose (f)
121 Krataios
121 Percussionist
121 Quito
121 Steenberg
120 Baltic King
120 Borderlescott
120 Bygone Days
120 Fair Nashwan (f)
120 Hawridge Prince
120 Linngari
120 Notable Guest
120 Osterhase
120 Proclamation
120 Satwa Queen (f)
120 Sergeant Cecil
120 Soviet Song (f)
120 Stronghold
120 Welsh Emperor

120 Wilko
119 Admiral's Cruise
119 Distant Way
119 Geordieland
119 Glamour Puss (f)
119 Home Affairs
119 Irridescence (f)
119 Jack Sullivan
119 Kandidate
119 La Cucaracha (f)
119 Moon Unit (f)
119 Munsef
119 Pivotal Point
119 Policy Maker
119 Presto Shinko
119 Satchem
119 Soldier Hollow
118+ Young Mick
118 Ace
118 Bandari
118 Bellamy Cay
118 Crosspeace
118 Falkirk
118 Floriot (f)
118 Into The Dark
118 Pivotal Flame
118 Reefscape
118 Touch of Land
118 Tungsten Strike
118 Vanderlin
118d The Tatling

EXPLANATORY NOTES

'Racehorses of 2006' deals individually, in alphabetical sequence, with every horse that ran on the Flat in Britain in 2006, plus numerous overseas-trained horses not seen in Britain. For each of these horses is given (1) its age, colour and sex, (2) its breeding, and for most horses, where this information has not been given in a previous Racehorses Annual, a family outline, (3) a form summary giving its Timeform rating at the end of the previous year, followed by the details of all its performances during the past year, (4) a Timeform rating, or ratings, of its merit in 2006 (which appears in the margin), (5) a Timeform commentary on its racing or general characteristics as a racehorse, with some suggestions, perhaps, regarding its prospects for 2007, and (6) the name of the trainer in whose charge it was on the last occasion it ran. For each two-year-old the foaling date is also given.

TIMEFORM RATINGS

The Timeform Rating of a horse is a measure of the *best* form it displayed in the season under review, expressed in pounds and arrived at by the use of handicapping techniques which include careful examination of a horse's running against other horses. Without going into complexities, the scale used for Timeform ratings represents around 3 lb a length at five furlongs, 2 lb a length at a mile and a quarter and 1 lb at two miles. Timeform maintains a 'running' handicap of all horses in training throughout the season, the in-season ratings usually reflecting Timeform's interpretation of a horse's *current* form, as opposed to its *best* form, where the two may be different.

THE LEVEL OF THE RATINGS

The attention of buyers of British bloodstock and others who may be concerned with Timeform ratings as a measure of absolute racing merit is drawn to the fact that at the close of each season the ratings of all the horses that have raced are re-examined. If necessary, the general level of the handicap is adjusted so that all the ratings are kept at the same standard level from year to year. Some of the ratings may, therefore, be different from those in the final issue of the 2006 Timeform Black Book series. The 'Racehorses Annual' figure is the definitive Timeform Rating.

RATINGS AND WEIGHT-FOR-AGE

The reader has, in the ratings in this book, a universal handicap embracing all the horses in training it is possible to weigh up, ranging from tip-top performers, with ratings from 130 to 145, through categories such as high-class, very smart, smart, useful, fairly useful, fair and modest, down to the poorest, rated around the 20 mark. All the ratings are at weight-for-age, so that equal ratings mean horses of equal merit: perhaps it would be clearer if we said that the universal rating handicap is really not a single handicap, but four handicaps side by side: one for two-year-olds, one for three-year-olds, one for four-year-olds and one for older horses. Thus, a three-year-old rated, for argument's sake, at 117 is deemed to be identical in point of 'merit' with a four-year-old also rated at 117: but for them to have equal chances in, say, a mile race in May, the three-year-old would need to be receiving 9 lb from the four-year-old, which is the weight difference specified by the Age, Weight and Distance Tables on the end papers at the front and back of the book.

USING THE RATINGS

A. Horses of the Same Age

If the horses all carry the same weight there are no adjustments to be made, and the horses with the highest ratings have the best chances. If the horses carry different weights, jot down their ratings, and to the rating of each horse add one point for every pound the horse is set to carry less than 10 st, or subtract one point for every pound it has to carry more than 10 st.

B. Horses of Different Ages

Consult the Age, Weight and Distance Tables printed on the end papers at the front and back of the book. Treat each horse separately, and compare the weight it has to carry with the weight prescribed for it in the tables, according to the age of the horse, the distance of the race and the time of the year. Then, add one point to the rating for each pound the horse has to carry less than the weight given in the tables: or, subtract one point from the rating for every pound it has to carry more than the weight prescribed by the tables.

Example (1½ miles on June 30th)

(Table Weights: 5-y-o+ 10-0; 4-y-o 9-13; 3-y-o 9-1)

6 Bay Pearl (10-2)	....	Rating 115	....	subtract 2	113
4 Elshabeeba (9-9)	....	Rating 114	....	add 4	118
5 Regal Charge (9-5)	....	Rating 115	....	add 9	124
3 Inclination (9-2)	....	Rating 120	....	subtract 1	119

Regal Charge (124) has the best chance at the weights,
with 5 lb in hand of Inclination

TURF AND ARTIFICIAL-SURFACE RATINGS

When a horse has raced on turf and on an artificial surface and its form on one is significantly different from the other, the two ratings are given, the one for artificial surfaces set out below the turf preceded by 'a'. Where there is only one rating, that is to be used for races on both turf and artificial surfaces.

NOTE ON RIDERS' ALLOWANCES

For the purposes of rating calculations it should, in general, be assumed that the allowance a rider is able to claim is nullified by his or her inexperience. Therefore, the weight adjustments to the ratings should be calculated on the weight allotted by the handicapper, or determined by the race conditions.

WEIGHING UP A RACE

The ratings tell you which horses in a race are most favoured by the weights; but complete analysis demands that the racing character of each horse, as set out in its commentary, is also studied carefully to see if there is any reason why the horse might be expected not to run up to its rating or indeed, with a lightly raced or inexperienced horse, might improve on it. It counts for little that a horse is thrown in at the weights if it has no pretensions to staying the distance, is unable to act on the prevailing going, or to accommodate itself to the conformation of the track.

There are other factors to consider too. For example, the matter of pace versus stamina: as between two stayers of equal merit, racing over a distance suitable to both. Firm going, or a small field with the prospect of a slowly-run race, would favour the one with the better pace and acceleration, whereas good to soft or softer going, or a big field with the prospect of a strong gallop, would favour the sounder stayer. There is also the matter of the horse's temperament; nobody should be in a hurry to take a short price about a horse which might not put its best foot forward. The quality of jockeyship is also an important factor when deciding between horses with similar chances.

Incidentally, in setting out the various characteristics, requirements and peculiarities of each horse in its commentary, we have expressed ourselves in as critical a manner as possible, endeavouring to say just as much, and no more, than the facts seem to warrant. Where there are clear indications, and conclusions can be drawn with fair certainty, we have drawn them; if it is a matter of probability or possibility we have put it that way, being careful not to say the one when we mean the other; and where real conclusions are not to be drawn, we have been content to state the facts. Furthermore, when we say that a horse *may* not be suited by firm going, we do not expect it to be treated as though we had said the horse *is not* suited by firm going. In short, both in our thinking and in the setting out of our views we have aimed at precision.

THE FORM SUMMARIES

The form summary enclosed in the brackets lists each horse's performances on the Flat during the past year in chronological sequence, showing, for each race, the distance, the state of the going and the horse's placing at the finish.

The distance of each race is given in furlongs, fractional distances being expressed in the decimal notation to the nearest tenth of a furlong. The prefix 'a' signifies a race on an artificial surface (except for 'f' for fibresand at Southwell, and 'p' for polytrack at Kempton, Lingfield, Wolverhampton and some US tracks).

The going is symbolised as follows: f=firm (turf) or fast (artificial surface); m=good to firm, or standard to fast (artificial surface); g=good (turf) or standard (artificial surface); d=good to soft/dead, or standard to slow (artificial surface); s=soft (turf) or slow, sloppy, muddy or wet (artificial surface); v=heavy.

Placings are indicated, up to sixth place, by the use of superior figures, an asterisk being used to denote a win.

Thus [2006 81: 10s* 12f³ 11.7g f11g² Sep 7] signifies that the horse was rated 81 the previous year (if there is no rating it indicates that the horse did not appear in 'Racehorses' for that year). In 2006 it ran four times, winning over 10 furlongs on soft going first time out, then finishing third over 12 furlongs on firm going, then out of the first six over 11.7 furlongs on good going, then second over 11 furlongs on standard going on a fibresand track. The date of its last run was September 7.

Included in the pedigree details are the highest Timeform Annual ratings during their racing careers of the sires, dams and sires of dams of all horses, where the information is available.

Where sale prices are considered relevant F denotes the price as a foal, Y the price as a yearling, 2-y-o as a two-year-old, and so on. These are given in guineas unless prefixed $ (American dollars) or € (euros). Other currencies are converted approximately into guineas or pounds sterling at the prevailing exchange rate. Significant sales after the horse's final outing are mentioned at the end of the commentaries.

THE RATING SYMBOLS

The following may be attached to, or appear instead of, a rating:-

p   likely to improve.

P   capable of *much* better form.

+   the horse may be better than we have rated it.

d   the horse appears to have deteriorated, and might no longer be capable of running to the rating given.

§   unreliable (for temperamental or other reasons).

§§   so temperamentally unsatisfactory as not to be worth a rating.

?   the horse's rating is suspect. If used without a rating the symbol implies that the horse can't be assessed with confidence, or, if used in the in-season Timeform publications, that the horse is out of form.

RACEHORSES OF 2006

Horse	Commentary	Rating

AAHAYSON 2 b.c. (Apr 8) Noverre (USA) 125 – See You Later 98 (Emarati (USA) 74) **99**
[2006 5g* 5m 5m² 5m* 5.5m² 6d² 6d³ Sep 29] 34,000Y: small, sturdy colt: third foal:
half-brother to fairly useful 2004 2-y-o 5f winner Annatalia (by Pivotal): dam, 5f winner
(including at 2 yrs), half-sister to smart performers For Your Eyes Only (up to 1m) and
Peak To Creek (6f/7f winner): useful performer: won minor event at Catterick in June and
nursery at Musselburgh in August: placed 4 other times, third of 28 to Caldra in valuable
sales race at Newmarket final start: best at 5f/6f: acts on good to firm and good to soft
going: races prominently. *K. R. Burke*

AAHGOWANGOWAN (IRE) 7 b.m. Tagula (IRE) 116 – Cabcharge Princess (IRE) **88**
64 (Rambo Dancer (CAN) 107) [2006 71: 6g³ 5m* 5.5g⁴ 6.1f* 6m* 6f* 6f³ 6g* 6m² 5g⁵
6m⁵ 6d Sep 15] sturdy mare: poor mover: fairly useful handicapper: won at Thirsk (twice,
apprentice event on first occasion), Chester and Ayr in July and Thirsk in August: best at
5f/6f: acts on any turf going: tried visored/in cheekpieces: tongue tied: makes running:
reportedly in foal to Avonbridge. *M. Dods*

AAIM TO PROSPER (IRE) 2 br.c. (Mar 22) Val Royal (FR) 127 – Bint Al Balad **95**
(IRE) 63 (Ahonoora 122) [2006 7d⁴ 8.1m³ 8.1m² p8.6g* 8m² p8g² 10d² 10g Nov 12]
75,000Y: leggy colt: half-brother to 3 winners, including smart 5f/6f (at 2 yrs) and 1m
winner Hurricane Alan (by Mukaddamah) and 3-y-o Song of Passion: dam ran twice:
useful performer: won maiden at Wolverhampton in September: best efforts last 2 starts,
4 lengths second to Empire Day in listed race at Newmarket and never-dangerous eighth
to Passage of Time in Criterium de Saint-Cloud: stays 1¼m: acts on polytrack, good to
firm and good to soft ground. *M. R. Channon*

AAMAAQ 3 b.c. Danehill (USA) 126 – Alabaq (USA) 111 (Riverman (USA) 131) **87**
[2006 84: 10g 8m 7m* Jun 20] quite good-topped colt: fairly useful performer: won
maiden at Thirsk in June with plenty in hand: injured after: should prove best up to 1m:
acts on good to firm ground: failed to settle on reappearance: sent to UAE. *J. L. Dunlop*

AARON'S WAY 2 b. or gr.f. (Jan 29) Act One 124 – Always On My Mind 91 (Distant **67**
Relative 128) [2006 6g⁶ 6.1d² Oct 4] 5,000Y: leggy, lengthy filly: fourth foal: half-
sister to 5-y-o Dr Thong: dam, 6f winner, half-sister to smart 6f/7f performer Red Carpet:
fair maiden: second to Doric Charm in minor event at Nottingham: free-going sort, likely
to prove best up to 1m. *A. W. Carroll*

AASTRAL MAGIC 4 b.f. Magic Ring (IRE) 115 – Robanna 60 (Robellino (USA) **71**
127) [2006 83: p7g p7g² p6g 7.1d⁴ p7g² 7m⁶ 8.3f 7m⁴ 6g 7m 8.1d 8d³ p8g p8.6g p8g **a78**
p7g Dec 8] close-coupled filly: fair handicapper nowadays: probably best at 7f: acts on
polytrack, firm and good to soft going: tried in blinkers/cheekpieces. *R. Hannon*

ABACONIAN (IRE) 3 b.c. Danehill (USA) 126 – Double Grange (IRE) (Double **74**
Schwartz 128) [2006 p7g⁶ p8g² p8g* 6.5f Dec 26] eighth foal: half-brother to 3 winners
by Turtle Island, notably smart 5f/6f winner (including at 2 yrs) Lincoln Dancer: dam of
little account in Ireland: fair form: won maiden at Lingfield in March, edging right: left
M. Wallace and off 9 months before well held in allowance race at Santa Anita: stays 1m:
acts on polytrack: has been tongue tied. *R. L. McAnally, USA*

ABANDON (USA) 3 ch.f. Rahy (USA) 115 – Caerless (IRE) 77 (Caerleon (USA) 132) **90 p**
[2006 p12g² p12.2g* f12g² Dec 23] third foal: half-sister to smart 8.2f (at 2 yrs) to 1¾m
winner (including 1½m Caulfield Cup in Australia) Tawqeet (by Kingmambo): dam,
1½m, 1½m winner, half-sister to smart performers Baya (around 1¼m in France) and smart
7f (at 2 yrs) to 1¾m winner Narrative out of sister to Triptych: fairly useful form: won
maiden at Wolverhampton (idled) and handicap at Southwell (by ½ length from Opera
Writer), both in December: should stay 1¾m: capable of better still. *W. J. Haggas*

ABBEY CAT (IRE) 3 b.f. Indian Danehill (IRE) 124 – Catfoot Lane 50 (Batshoof 122) **87**
[2006 70: 8d⁶ 7m* 7d³ 7g 8.5f⁵ 8.1g* 8d Oct 2] rather leggy filly: fairly useful handicapper: won at Newcastle in May and Haydock in September: effective at 7f/1m: acts on
firm and good to soft ground: sold 35,000 gns, sent to USA. *G. A. Swinbank*

ABBEYGATE 5 b.g. Unfuwain (USA) 131 – Ayunli 81 (Chief Singer 131) [2006 –, **a57**
a61: p12.2g p9.5g f8g⁴ p10g⁶ p7g⁵ p9.5g* p10g p8g⁴ 8m p9.5f f11m³ p11g² f12g⁵ p12g³
f11g⁵ Dec 28] strong gelding: modest performer: won banded race at Wolverhampton in
April: effective at 7f to easy 1½m: acts on all-weather, little form on turf: tried blinkered/
in cheekpieces/tongue tied. *T. Keddy*

ABBONDANZA (IRE) 3 b.g. Cape Cross (IRE) 129 – Ninth Wonder (USA) (Forty **82**
Niner (USA)) [2006 68: 10.1g* 10.4m 10.4d Aug 23] lengthy, good-topped gelding:
fairly useful performer: form in 2006 only when winning maiden at Newcastle in May:
failed to settle final start: gelded after: stays 1¼m: pulled up on hurdling debut in October.
J. Howard Johnson

ABBOTTS ACCOUNT (USA) 2 b.g. (Apr 16) Mr Greeley (USA) 122 – Agenda **55**
(USA) (Private Account (USA)) [2006 7g 7.1d 8g Sep 28] rangy gelding: modest
form in maidens, not knocked about: subsequently gelded: should be best up to 1m.
Mrs A. J. Perrett

ABBOTTS ANN 2 b.f. (Feb 10) Marju (IRE) 127 – Anne Boleyn (Rainbow Quest **81**
(USA) 134) [2006 p7g² 6g² 6g⁵ p7.1g* p6g Nov 11] first foal: dam unraced half-sister to
very smart middle-distance performer Annus Mirabilis: fairly useful form: made all in
nursery at Wolverhampton in November: free-going type, may be best kept to 6f/7f: sold
11,000 gns. *B. W. Hills*

ABBY ROAD (IRE) 2 b.f. (Apr 4) Danehill (USA) 126 – Bells Are Ringing (USA) 92 **99**
(Sadler's Wells (USA) 132) [2006 5f² 6m⁴ 5g* 5.2g* 5g⁶ 5d Oct 7] $210,000Y:
good-topped filly: second foal: dam, Irish 2-y-o 7f winner, half-sister to high-class US
performer up to 9f Unbridled's Song: useful performer: won maiden at Ripon in July and
listed event at Newbury (beat Vale of Belvoir by length) in August: respectable sixth to
Wi Dud in Flying Childers Stakes at York: best at 5f: raced on good or firmer ground until
final start (below form): tends to hang left: forces pace. *B. J. Meehan*

ABDU 2 ch.g. (Apr 30) Kyllachy 129 – Better Still (IRE) (Glenstal (USA) 118) [2006 5d **49**
5d³ 5m p6g 6d⁵ f8g Nov 10] sturdy gelding: poor maiden: left M. Easterby prior to final
outing: stays 6f: once refused at stalls. *G. P. Kelly*

ABERDEEN PARK 4 gr.f. Environment Friend 128 – Michelee 58 (Merdon Melody **62 §**
98) [2006 62: p10g p8.6g p10g f8g* p10g p9.5f⁴ 10.2m 8m Sep 20] workmanlike filly:
modest handicapper: won at Southwell (maiden event) in July: stays 1¼m: acts on all-
weather and any turf going: tried in cheekpieces, blinkered nowadays: tends to edge left:
often slowly away: won over hurdles in November (joined Mrs H. Dalton 9,800 gns):
untrustworthy. *Mrs H. Sweeting*

ABERLADY BAY (IRE) 3 ch.f. Selkirk (USA) 129 – Desert Serenade (USA) (Green **62 d**
Desert (USA) 127) [2006 p12g⁶ p12g p10g 8.2d p8g p9.5g p7.1g f7g Dec 12] 3,000
2-y-o: sixth foal: sister to German 6f/7f winner Oasis Song and half-sister to 4-y-o
Muscari and fairly useful French 1m (at 2 yrs) to 13f winner Major Performance (by
Celtic Swing): dam, ran twice, sister to high-class sprinter Sheikh Albadou: modest
maiden at best: may prove best short of 1¼m: visored/blinkered last 3 starts. *T. T. Clement*

ABEURBE CONDITA (IRE) 3 ch.g. Titus Livius (FR) 115 – Avantage Service **70**
(IRE) (Exactly Sharp (USA) 121) [2006 –p: 8s³ 8.1s³ 9.1v³ Oct 9] strong, lengthy colt:
fair maiden: not sure to stay beyond 1m: sold 10,000 gns, joined E. McNamara in Ireland.
E. S. McMahon

ABHISHEKA (IRE) 3 b.f. Sadler's Wells (USA) 132 – Snow Bride (USA) 121 **108**
(Blushing Groom (FR) 131) [2006 68: 8.2m* 10.4m⁵ 10s* 10g* 10d⁴ Nov 4] smallish,
well-made, attractive filly: useful performer: won maiden at Nottingham in May, and
handicaps at Newbury and Windsor (beat Kingsholm readily by 3 lengths) in October:
bandaged forelegs, creditable 1½ lengths fourth to Lake Toya in listed race at last-named
course final start: will stay 1½m: acts on soft and good to firm going. *Saeed bin Suroor*

ABIDE WITH ME (USA) 2 b.c. (Feb 26) Danehill (USA) 126 – Sequoyah (IRE) 113 **88**
(Sadler's Wells (USA) 132) [2006 6.3m 8.5m² 7.5g* 8d⁶ Sep 23] smallish, lengthy colt:
second foal: half-brother to 3-y-o Queen Cleopatra: dam, won Moyglare Stud Stakes and
fourth in Irish Oaks, out of sister to dam of high-class sprinter/miler Dolphin Street and
Irish 2000 Guineas winner Saffron Walden: fairly useful form: won maiden at Tipperary
in September: 12/1, well held in Royal Lodge Stakes at Ascot final start: will stay 1¼m.
A. P. O'Brien, Ireland

A BIG SKY BREWING (USA) 2 b.c. (Mar 19) Arch (USA) 127 – Runalpharun **53 p**
(USA) (Thunder Rumble (USA) 116) [2006 5.1s Oct 25] $6,500F: big, strong colt:

second foal: dam, US maiden, out of half-sister to Derby winner Benny The Dip: 20/1, needed experience in maiden at Nottingham: open to improvement. *T. D. Barron*

A BIT OF FUN 5 ch.g. Unfuwain (USA) 131 – Horseshoe Reef 88 (Mill Reef (USA) – 141) [2006 48: f11g Mar 28] useful-looking gelding: poor performer: stays 11f: form only on fibresand: has looked difficult ride. *J. T. Stimpson* **–**

ABLE BAKER CHARLIE (IRE) 7 b.g. Sri Pekan (USA) 117 – Lavezzola (IRE) (Salmon Leap (USA) 131) [2006 101: 8g Sep 28] useful-looking gelding: useful performer at best: just fairly useful form only outing in 2006: effective at 1m/1¼m: acts on polytrack, firm and good to soft ground: has worn crossed noseband: has edged right. *J. R. Fanshawe* **85**

ABLE MIND 6 b.g. Mind Games 121 – Chlo-Jo 65 (Belmez (USA) 131) [2006 64: 7.9m⁵ 10.2m p8.6g³ 8m² 7.9m² 8.5m* 8g² p9.5m⁵ Oct 14] rather leggy, lengthy gelding: fair handicapper on turf, modest on all-weather: won at Beverley in September: stays 1¼m: acts on polytrack, soft and good to firm going: tried in cheekpieces: carries head awkwardly. *D. W. Thompson* **68**

ABOUNDING 2 b.f. (Mar 2) Generous (IRE) 139 – Ecstasy 81 (Pursuit of Love 124) [2006 5.7f p7g³ 7f 10g⁵ Sep 26] leggy filly: second foal: dam 6.7f (at 2 yrs) and 1¼m winner: modest maiden: will stay 1½m. *R. M. Beckett* **54**

ABOUSTAR 6 b.g. Abou Zouz (USA) 109 – Three Star Rated (IRE) 79 (Pips Pride 117) [2006 50: f6g⁵ f7g f6g⁶ f7g f7g f6g² f5g⁴ Dec 29] tall, leggy gelding: modest performer: stays 6f: acts on fibresand: tried in cheekpieces/blinkers. *M. Brittain* **56**

ABOVE AND BELOW (IRE) 2 b.f. (Mar 31) Key of Luck (USA) 126 – Saramacca (IRE) 54 (Kahyasi 130) [2006 8m 8g⁴ Oct 13] €21,000Y: good-bodied, workmanlike filly: third foal: sister to fairly useful Irish 1½m winner Rajeh: dam Irish 1½m winner: last both starts. *M. Quinn* **–**

ABOYNE (IRE) 3 b.g. Mull of Kintyre (USA) 114 – Never End 74 (Alzao (USA) 117) [2006 69: p8.6g⁴ p10g⁵ 10g 12m 8.2d 10.1m p6g Oct 17] small, sturdy gelding: modest performer at best in 2006: left M. Quinlan after fifth outing: stays 1¼m: acts on polytrack, had form on turf earlier in career: in headgear last 3 starts. *K. F. Clutterbuck* **58 d**

ABRAHAM (IRE) 4 b.g. Orpen (USA) 116 – We've Just Begun (USA) (Huguenot(USA)) [2006 67: f12g⁶ Feb 2] maiden: tailed off in claimer at Southwell only outing in 2006: best effort at 7f on heavy going. *Michael Cunningham, Ireland* **–**

ABRAHAM LINCOLN 2 b.c. (Mar 24) Danehill (USA) 126 – Moon Drop 103 (Dominion 123) [2006 5d⁵ 6s² May 18] useful-looking colt: brother to 2 winners, including useful Irish 2003 2-y-o 5f winner Devil Moon, closely related to useful 1996 2-y-o 6f winner Dancing Drop (by Green Desert) and half-brother to several winners, including useful 5f (at 2 yrs) to 7f winner Moon King (by Cadeaux Genereux): dam, best at 6f, half-sister to dam of smart 7f/1m performer Fa-Eq: improved from debut (listed race) when head second to Sadeek in maiden at York: had setback after: will stay 7f: highly regarded, and still likely to make a smart performer at least. *A. P. O'Brien, Ireland* **98 p**

ABSENT LOVE 2 b. or br.f. (Feb 21) Diktat 126 – Jolis Absent 57 (Primo Dominie 121) [2006 5d.5m⁶ 8.3m Sep 5] leggy, workmanlike filly: has a round action: fourth foal: half-sister to 5-y-o Jolizero and 7f (at 2 yrs)/1m winner Loner (by Magic Ring): dam, 1½m/1¾m winner, also successful over hurdles: modest maiden: should be suited by 1m/1¼m: sent to Spain. *G. G. Margarson* **51**

ABSOLUTE CHAMPION (AUS) 5 b.g. Marauding (NZ) – Beauty Belle (AUS) (Ideal Planet) [2006 5m³ 6g⁵ 6s⁴ 6m* 6m* 6m* Dec 10] first foal: dam, Australian 6.5f to 9f winner, half-sister to dam of high-class Australian performer up to 1¼m Grand Armee: named Genius And Evil in Australia, where won once (Group 2 event) from 8 starts: transferred to Hong Kong after summer 2004, and successful once from 10 outings there in 2004/5: left A. Lee after first outing in 2006: much improved last 3 starts, winning handicap in June, Group 3 handicap in October and Cathay Pacific Hong Kong Sprint in December, all at Sha Tin: wearing cheekpieces, high-class form and impressive when breaking course record in last-named event, beating Silent Witness by 4¼ lengths, bursting clear after edging across to rail: best at 5f/6f: acts on good to firm going, winner on good to soft. *D. J. Hall, Hong Kong* **129**

ABSOLUTELYFABULOUS (IRE) 3 b.f. Mozart (IRE) 131 – Lady Windermere (IRE) (Lake Coniston (IRE) 131) [2006 6v⁵ 8.2s⁵ 10d⁶ 6m* 6m* 6g⁴ 6d⁴ 5m⁴ 6g Sep 16] 100,000F: tall, leggy filly: third foal: dam unraced half-sister to Moyglare Stud Stakes winner Sequoyah out of sister to dam of Dolphin Street and Saffron Walden: useful performer: won handicaps at Naas in June and July: respectable fourth in listed race at **98**

Pontefract (on edge and last to post) seventh outing: below form final start: best at 5f/6f: acts on good to firm and good to soft ground. *D. Wachman, Ireland*

ABSOLUTELYTHEBEST (IRE) 5 b.g. Anabaa (USA) 130 – Recherchee (Rainbow Quest (USA) 134) [2006 80: 13d May 7] good-topped gelding: fairly useful performer at best: well held on only Flat outing in 2006: effective at 1½m/1¾m: acts on polytrack, good to firm and good to soft going: tried visored: none too consistent: won over hurdles in July/September. *J. G. M. O'Shea* —

ABSTRACT ART (USA) 3 ch.g. Distorted Humor (USA) 117 – Code From Heaven (USA) (Lost Code (USA)) [2006 78: p10g* p10g⁶ p8.6g p8.6g⁴ p12g* p12g⁴ 12.1d⁴ 10m* May 15] well-made gelding: fairly useful performer: won maiden in January and handicap in March, both at Lingfield, and handicap at Windsor in May: stays 1½m: acts on polytrack and good to firm going: shaped as if amiss in visor third start: sold 44,000 gns, gelded and joined Venetia Williams. *N. A. Callaghan* **81**

ABSTRACT FOLLY (IRE) 4 b.g. Rossini (USA) 118 – Cochiti 35 (Kris 135) [2006 67: p9.5g⁶ 10m 8d⁵ 7.9m 12f³ 13g⁵ 12.1m 10g⁴ p12.2g* p13.9g⁵ p12.2g⁴ Dec 6] leggy gelding: good mover: fair handicapper: won at Catterick in July and Wolverhampton in September: stays easy 1¾m: acts on polytrack, firm and good to soft going: sometimes blinkered. *J. D. Bethell* **67**

ABUNAI 2 ch.f. (Apr 18) Pivotal 124 – Ingozi 91 (Warning 136) [2006 6g⁶ 5f² 5.1g* 5g* 6m* 6s⁵ Oct 7] small, workmanlike filly: half-sister to several winners, including smart 6f (at 2 yrs) to 1½m winner Tissifer (by Polish Precedent) and smart performer up to 1½m Sir George Turner (by Nashwan), 7f winner at 2 yrs: dam, 7f/1m winner, half-sister to smart 7f/1m performer Inchinor: fairly useful form: won maiden at Bath in July and nurseries at Newmarket in August and Southwell in September: speedy, but bred to stay 1m: acts on firm going, below form only start on soft (listed race). *R. Charlton* **88**

ABWAAB 3 b.g. Agnes World (USA) 123 – Flitteriss Park 62§ (Beldale Flutter (USA) 130) [2006 7d³ 8.1m* 8m 8.3g³ 8.3g⁴ 7m p8g Sep 30] 60,000Y: lengthy gelding: closely related to 2 winners by Emarati, including useful 6f winner (including at 2 yrs) Emerging Market, and half-brother to several winners, including smart 5f (at 2 yrs)/6f winner Atraf (by Clantime) and useful 1992 2-y-o 6f winner Son Pardo (by Petong): dam 1m winner: fairly useful performer: won maiden at Haydock in July, then sold from W. Haggas 48,000 gns: best effort when fourth in handicap at Leicester: stays 8.3f: acts on good to firm ground: tongue tied first 3 starts. *R. F. Johnson Houghton* **88**

ABYLA 2 b.f. (Apr 20) Rock of Gibraltar (IRE) 133 – Animatrice (USA) 115 (Alleged (USA) 138) [2006 7m Aug 31] half-sister to several winners, including useful French 1½m (Prix de Royaumont) winner Sadler's Flag (by Sadler's Wells): dam, French 1m (at 2 yrs) to 1½m (Prix de Malleret) winner and third in Oaks, half-sister to smart French 1½m performer Poliglote: 22/1, not knocked about in maiden at Salisbury: will be suited by 1m/1¼m: should progress. *M. P. Tregoning* **65 p**

ACCA LARENTIA (IRE) 5 gr.m. Titus Livius (FR) 115 – Daisy Grey 46 (Nordance (USA)) [2006 36: 13d⁶ 16g 16m 11.1g⁶ Jul 20] leggy, close-coupled mare: poor maiden: no form in 2006: often in cheekpieces/visor. *Mrs H. O. Graham* —

ACCELERATION (IRE) 6 b.g. Groom Dancer (USA) 128 – Overdrive 99 (Shirley Heights 130) [2006 69§, a59§: f12g 15m f16g³ Dec 19] big gelding: modest handicapper: left R. Allan after second start: best at 2m+: acts on heavy and good to firm ground: usually wears headgear, tried tongue tied: *Karen McLintock* **– § a56 §**

ACCENT (IRE) 3 b.g. Beckett (IRE) 116 – Umlaut (Zafonic (USA) 130) [2006 48p: 10d Sep 25] leggy, lengthy gelding: lightly-raced maiden: well beaten in handicap only outing in 2006: should be suited by at least 1m: sold 8,500 gns. *Sir Mark Prescott* —

ACCOMPANIST 3 b.c. Pivotal 124 – Abscond (USA) 97 (Unbridled (USA) 128) [2006 7g 10d² 10.5m² 9.9g² 10m⁴ 10d 8.3g* Oct 16] 47,000F, 100,000Y: rather unfurnished colt: second foal: dam, 1¼m winner who stayed 1½m, out of US Grade 2 1½m winner Lemhi Go: fairly useful performer: won maiden at Windsor in October by ¾ length from Tennis Star: stays 10.5f: acts on good to firm and good to soft going: visored/blinkered last 2 starts: sold 52,000 gns. *J. H. M. Gosden* **81**

ACCORDELLO (IRE) 5 b.m. Accordion – Marello (Supreme Leader 123) [2006 12g⁴ 12.1d³ 14.1d² 16.1m 17.1d⁵ 16v Oct 25] first foal: dam high-class staying hurdler: useful form in bumpers: fair maiden on Flat: should stay beyond 1¾m: acts on good to soft ground: fairly useful winner over hurdles in November. *K. G. Reveley* **66**

ACCORDING TO PETE 5 b.g. Accordion – Magic Bloom (Full of Hope 125) [2006 10m 10d 10d³ Oct 4] good-topped gelding: useful bumper winner: fair maiden on Flat: **72**

will be suited by 1½m: acts on good to soft going: ridden by 7-lb claimer all 3 starts: fairly useful hurdler, successful in October. *J. M. Jefferson*

ACCUMULUS 6 b.g. Cloudings (IRE) 112 – Norstock 52 (Norwick (USA) 125) [2006 10m Sep 5] rangy gelding: modest form in bumpers: 100/1, well beaten in maiden at Leicester on Flat debut: fair hurdler, successful in October. *Noel T. Chance* —

ACE BABY 3 b.g. First Trump 118 – Mise En Scene 85 (Lugana Beach 116) [2006 70: 9.1v Oct 9] neat gelding: fair performer at 2 yrs: off 16 months, well beaten only outing in 2006: stays 6f: acts on soft going: tried in cheekpieces. *K. J. Burke* —

ACECE 2 b.c. (Mar 6) Muthahb (IRE) – Berry Brook 37 (Magic Ring (IRE) 115) [2006 f8g⁵ p8.6g Dec 27] second foal: dam twice-raced half-sister to useful performer up to 1½m Star of Light: much better effort in maidens when 9¼ lengths fifth to Mardi at Southwell on debut. *M. Appleby* **56**

ACE CLUB 5 ch.g. Indian Rocket 115 – Presently 48 (Cadeaux Genereux 131) [2006 52: f7g⁴ f7g f6g f6g f7g f6g⁶ f6g⁴ f6g³ 6m 7.6g p6g f6m⁵ f6g⁶ f6g³ p6g f6g⁴ f6g* Dec 29] angular gelding: modest performer: left J. Hetherton after ninth start: won banded race at Southwell in December: effective at 5f to 7f: acts on all-weather, firm and soft ground: usually wears headgear: unreliable. *M. J. Attwater* **– §** **a54 §**

ACE (IRE) 5 b.h. Danehill (USA) 126 – Tea House 107 (Sassafras (FR) 135) [2006 125: 10d² 12g⁴ 10m 8m² 10f⁶ 10m⁵ 8m³ 7g Dec 24] big, close-coupled horse: high-class performer in 2005: just smart form in 2006, in frame on 3 of first 4 starts, length second to Alayan in Mooresbridge Stakes at the Curragh, 4¾ lengths fourth to Shirocco in Coronation Cup at Epsom and head second to Mustameet in International Stakes at the Curragh: respectable sixth to The Tin Man in Arlington Million next time: left A. O'Brien in Ireland, below form last 2 outings: effective at 1m to 1½m: acts on firm and soft going: sometimes visored: often early/quietly to post (went freely at Epsom): usually races prominently (acted as pacemaker when last of 5 in Irish Champion Stakes at Leopardstown sixth appearance), and took strong hold second/third outings. *S. Seemar, UAE* **118**

ACE OF HEARTS 7 b.g. Magic Ring (IRE) 115 – Lonely Heart 101 (Midyan (USA) 124) [2006 110: 8m 9m 10g² 8m 8.1m² 8g⁶ 8m² 8s 9d 8g Oct 13] short-backed gelding: smart handicapper: best efforts in 2006 when second at Redcar (Zetand Gold Cup, ½ length behind Chantaco) and Sandown (totescoop6 Stakes, beaten 1¼ lengths by Hinterland) third/fifth starts: well below form last 3 outings: best at 1m/1¼m: acts on fibresand, firm and soft going: free-going sort: tough and genuine. *C. F. Wall* **110**

ACHEEKYONE (IRE) 3 b.g. Indian Ridge 123 – Tafrah (IRE) 71 (Sadler's Wells (USA) 132) [2006 85: 8m² 8m⁴ 10s 8g² Jul 6] well-made gelding: useful performer: best effort when 1¼ lengths second to Illustrious Blue in handicap at Newbury final start: gelded after: may prove best short of 1¼m: acts on polytrack, soft and good to firm ground: often takes good hold. *B. J. Meehan* **101**

ACKNOWLEDGEMENT 4 b.g. Josr Algarhoud (IRE) 118 – On Request (IRE) 53 (Be My Guest (USA) 126) [2006 70: 11.6f⁶ 10m⁶ 10g⁴ 12.1m 11.5m² 14.1d² 12s² Oct 21] well-made gelding: fair maiden: stays 1¾m: acts on polytrack, soft and good to firm going: blinkered (ran well) last 3 starts: sold 40,000 gns, joined C. Llewellyn. *D. R. C. Elsworth* **79**

ACOMB 6 b.g. Shaamit (IRE) 127 – Aurora Bay (IRE) (Night Shift (USA)) [2006 92, a81: p7g p6g p7g 7m 7m 7m⁶ 7f p7g Jul 26] good-bodied gelding: handicapper: just fair form at best in 2006: effective at 7f/1m: acts on polytrack, good to firm and good to soft going: occasionally carries head awkwardly: often makes running. *Mrs L. Richards* **69 d**

ACORAZADO (IRE) 7 b.g. Petorius 117 – Jaldi (IRE) 75 (Nordico (USA)) [2006 47, a67: p8g p9.5g f11g p8g p8.6g⁶ Feb 24] quite good-topped gelding: fair at best: little form in 2006: sometimes wears headgear. *C. P. Morlock* **–**

ACOSTA 2 b.c. (Mar 28) Foxhound (USA) 103 – Dancing Heights (IRE) 80 (High Estate 127) [2006 7g 8.1m 8d Sep 27] workmanlike colt: modest form final start in maidens (tried blinkered). *Dr J. R. J. Naylor* **56**

ACROBATIC (USA) 3 ch.c. Storm Boot (USA) – Alvernia (USA) (Alydar (USA)) [2006 79: 8d⁸ 8.3m⁵ 8.1g⁴ p10g* p10g* p11g* p10g² 10d³ 10.5d* Nov 6] well-made colt: useful performer: progressed well, winning maiden at Bath in April, handicaps at Kempton in June, July and September, and listed race at Le Croise-Laroche (made all, beat Sureyya a neck) in November: good efforts when placed in handicaps at Kempton (got in poor position) and Newmarket (third to Rampallion) between last 2 wins: stays 11f: acts on polytrack and good to soft going: sent to Saudi Arabia. *R. Charlton* **107**

ACROPOLIS (IRE) 5 b.g. Sadler's Wells (USA) 132 – Dedicated Lady (IRE) 101 – (Pennine Walk 120) [2006 115: 12d 16.1m Jul 1] strong, sturdy gelding: good walker, but has a short, unimpressive action in faster paces: formerly very smart: left A. O'Brien before reportedly lame on hurdling debut in January: well below form in listed event at Ascot and Northumberland Plate (Handicap) at Newcastle in 2006: gelded after: probably stays 13f: acts on soft and good to firm going: tongue tied on 3-y-o reappearance (successful): has run in snatches/wandered. *J. Howard Johnson*

ACT FRIENDLY (IRE) 3 b.f. Sadler's Wells (USA) 132 – Ozone Friendly (USA) 91 107 (Green Forest (USA) 134) [2006 86: 10.1m* 12s⁶ p10g⁵ Nov 9] leggy filly: fairly useful performer, lightly raced: landed odds easily in maiden at Newcastle in July: good fifth in handicap at Lingfield final outing: stays 1¼m: acts on polytrack and soft going, probably on good to firm: has left Godolphin. *Saeed bin Suroor*

ACTIVE ACCOUNT (USA) 9 b. or br.g. Unaccounted For (USA) 124 – Ameritop – (USA) (Topsider (USA)) [2006 53, a62: p9.5g f11g⁶ f8g f8g f8g Jun 3] has reportedly had breathing operation: no form in 2006: wears blinkers/cheekpieces. *J. R. Holt*

ACTIVE ASSET (IRE) 4 ch.g. Sinndar (IRE) 134 – Sacristy 54 (Godswalk (USA) 92 130) [2006 84: 10.1m 10.5g* 10d 10g³ 10.5g 9.8m³ 10.1m* 10m³ 9.8d³ 9.9m 10d 10.1d 10.5g² 10.4s Oct 6] good-topped gelding: fairly useful handicapper: won at Haydock in April and Newcastle in July: stays 11f: acts on firm and good to soft ground: usually held up: sold 23,000 gns. *M. R. Channon*

ACTIVE AUDIENCE (IRE) 3 b.f. Fasliyev (USA) 120 – Luisa Demon (IRE) (Bara- 39 thea (IRE) 127) [2006 58: 5d 6m f6g⁴ 6.9f⁶ 5.9g 7.1m 7m f7m f7g Nov 2] small filly: poor maiden nowadays: tried blinkered. *A. Berry*

ACTIVIST 8 ch.g. Diesis 133 – Shicklah (USA) 106 (The Minstrel (CAN) 135) [2006 67 69: p16.5g⁶ p13.9g* p12.2g Feb 3] leggy, lengthy gelding: fair performer: won seller at Wolverhampton in January: stays 16.5f: acts on polytrack, firm and good to soft going: wears cheekpieces: usually held up. *D. Carroll*

ACTIVO (FR) 5 b.g. Trempolino (USA) 135 – Acerbis (GER) (Rainbow Quest (USA) 93 134) [2006 95: p10g⁵ p10g⁴ 10s 9m 10.5g p12g p10g² p10g⁶ p10g Dec 20] good-bodied gelding: fairly useful handicapper: creditable efforts at Lingfield second/seventh starts: should stay 1½m: acts on polytrack and good to soft ground: very slowly away on reappearance. *S. Dow*

ACTODOS (IRE) 2 ch.c. (Feb 18) Act One 124 – Really Gifted (IRE) (Cadeaux 80 Genereux 131) [2006 7g⁴ 7.1m⁶ 8d² Sep 27] €22,000F, 8,000Y: big colt: third foal: dam unraced half-sister to useful performer up to 1m Misterah: fairly useful maiden: second to Ladies Best at Salisbury: stays 1m. *B. R. Millman*

ACT SIRIUS (IRE) 2 ch.g. (Mar 2) Grand Lodge (USA) 125 – Folgore (USA) 83 81 (Irish River (FR) 131) [2006 8v 9s* Sep 24] 145,000F, 150,000Y: fourth foal: half-brother to smart 7f (at 2 yrs)/1m winner Excelsius (by Dr Devious) and winner up to 1½m in Italy by Mtoto: dam, 2-y-o 7f/7.5f winner in Italy, half-sister to smart performer up to 1½m Fanjica: fairly useful form: won maiden at Musselburgh in September, dictating: gelded after: will probably stay 1½m: raced on soft/heavy going. *J. Howard Johnson*

ACTS OF GRACE (USA) 3 b.f. Bahri (USA) 125 – Rafha 123 (Kris 135) [2006 10d⁶ 109 10g² 10f* 9.9m⁵ 12g* 12s* 10s⁶ Oct 22] small, leggy filly: half-sister to several at least useful winners, including very smart sprinter Invincible Spirit (by Green Desert), smart 7.6f (at 2 yrs) to 1¾m winner Sadian (by Shirley Heights) and smart 11f winner Aquarius (by Royal Academy), who stayed 2m: dam, 6f (at 2 yrs) to 11.5f winner, including Prix de Diane: useful performer: won maiden at Pontefract in July, listed race at Chantilly in August and Princess Royal PricewaterhouseCoopers Stakes at Ascot (by 1¼ lengths from Gower Song) in September: respectable sixth to Floriot in Premio Lydia Tesio at Rome final outing: was better at 1½m than shorter: acted on firm and soft going: had worn crossed noseband: stud. *J. L. Dunlop*

ACUZIO 5 b.g. Mon Tresor 113 – Veni Vici (IRE) (Namaqualand (USA)) [2006 64: 66 10.9s p8.6g⁵ 12m* 10.5m* 12.3g² 12f⁵ 12f⁴ 12.6g* 14.1f⁶ 12.1m⁵ 12.3m⁴ 15.9m 13.4f³ 12d³ Oct 2] sturdy, compact gelding: fair handicapper: won at Musselburgh in June and Warwick (hung left) in July: stays easy 13.4f: acts on polytrack, firm and good to soft going: effective with/without blinkers/cheekpieces: tried tongue tied. *W. M. Brisbourne*

ADAGE 3 b.f. Vettori (IRE) 119 – Aymara 85 (Darshaan 133) [2006 71: 10.2g 9d⁶ 12g 64 9.7f 13.1m 10.5g⁶ 11.8d⁵ 11.9d³ Oct 19] lengthy, quite good-topped filly: modest maiden: stays 1½m: acts on good to firm and good to soft going: tongue tied last 4 starts. *David Pinder*

ADAGIO 2 br.c. (Apr 7) Grand Lodge (USA) 125 – Lalindi (IRE) 80 (Cadeaux **109 p**
Genereux 131) [2006 7m* 7d Oct 14]

Understandably, Teofilo cemented his place at the head of the Guineas and
Derby betting when maintaining his unbeaten record in the Dewhurst, but there
were other classic prospects who should not be overlooked in what was a strong
renewal. Of those who chased home Teofilo, the most striking trial for Epsom was
run not by the others to make the frame but by Adagio, who finished in the pack.
By the same sire as 2000 Derby winner Sinndar, and, like him stoutly bred on the
dam's side, Adagio could hardly be expected to excel over seven furlongs in the
Dewhurst, but he still showed near-smart form in defeat, beaten just over four
lengths into seventh. His effort was all the more praiseworthy given his inexperience, the fact that he had gone in his coat and that his rider left him alone once the
leaders started to quicken away. Adagio was among the outsiders at Newmarket,
at 25/1 in a field of fifteen. He had gone off third favourite at 11/2 when making
his debut in a maiden over the same course and distance less than a month earlier
and he looked a good prospect that day too, going on with Tybalt over a furlong out
and responding well as the pair came five lengths clear, Adagio getting home by a
short head.

		Chief's Crown	Danzig
	Grand Lodge (USA)	(b 1982)	Six Crowns
	(ch 1991)	La Papagena	Habitat
Adagio		(br 1983)	Magic Flute
(br.c. Apr 7, 2004)		Cadeaux Genereux	Young Generation
	Lalindi (IRE)	(ch 1985)	Smarten Up
	(b 1991)	Soemba	General Assembly
		(b 1983)	Seven Seas

Adagio is by the Dewhurst and St James's Palace Stakes winner Grand
Lodge, who stayed a mile and quarter, and out of a two-mile winner. A strong,
lengthy colt, Adagio must have caught the eye at the sales as he made 100,000
guineas as a foal and twice that at the Newmarket October Sales as a yearling.
His pedigree is not particularly eye-catching, at least not close up in the family. His
dam the fairly useful Lalindi, a winner at nine furlongs before being stepped
up in trip, became temperamental, refusing to race once. Lalindi is a half-sister to
the dam of the very smart mile-and-a-quarter performer Compton Admiral, winner
of the Eclipse, and the smart mile- to mile-and-a-quarter winner Summoner, shock

Snap On Equipment Solutions EBF Maiden Stakes, Newmarket—
newcomers Adagio (No.1) and Tybalt have the finish to themselves

winner of the Queen Elizabeth II Stakes in 2001 when acting as a pacemaker. Adagio is Lalindi's fourth foal. Her fifth, a filly by Cape Cross, was knocked down for 340,000 guineas as a yearling at the Newmarket October Sales shortly after Adagio's debut. Lalindi's first foal was Arvada (by Hernando), a useful mile-and-a-quarter winner in France as a two-year-old and a Grade 2 mile-and-a-half winner in America at three. Adagio should be well suited by a mile and a quarter plus as a three-year-old when he is likely to make his mark in the classic trials before possibly doing so in the classics as well (freely available at 33/1 for the Derby at the time of writing). He acts on good to firm and good to soft ground. *Sir Michael Stoute*

ADALAR (IRE) 6 br.g. Grand Lodge (USA) 125 – Adalya (IRE) (Darshaan 133) [2006 49, a43: f7g⁵ p9.5g⁴ May 2] poor performer: stays 1¼m: acts on all-weather, good to firm and good to soft going: tried in headgear: tongue tied in 2006. *P. W. D'Arcy* — a47

ADANTINO 7 b.g. Glory of Dancer 121 – Sweet Whisper 63 (Petong 126) [2006 78: p6g² p6g⁴ p6g³ 6g 6m* p7g² p6g 5.7g* p6g⁵ 6m* 5f 6m⁵ p7g Sep 5] compact gelding: fairly useful handicapper: won at Windsor (apprentices) in April, Bath in June and Lingfield in July: effective at 6f/7f: acts on all-weather, firm and good to soft going: blinkered: waited with: tough. *B. R. Millman* 88

ADAPTATION 2 b.f. (Mar 30) Spectrum (IRE) 126 – Key Academy 103 (Royal Academy (USA) 130) [2006 6f² 6f* 6m* 6g⁴ 7s⁶ 6s Nov 20] 18,000Y: good-bodied filly: third foal: half-sister to 3-y-o Razed: dam, 1½m winner (later successful in USA), half-sister to Lancashire Oaks/US Grade 1 9f/1¼m winner Squeak: fairly useful performer: won maiden in June and nursery in July, both at Hamilton: off 3 months, good fourth in nursery at Newmarket: bred to be suited by 1m+: acts on firm going (below form in listed events on soft). *M. Johnston* 88

ADARILA (IRE) 5 b. or br.m. Mujadil (USA) 119 – Adalya (IRE) (Darshaan 133) [2006 65: p9.5g⁵ 7s 9g⁶ 10g 11.9m⁵ 12m⁵ 13f Aug 11] fourth foal: half-sister to 3 winners, including 1½m to 2m winner Adalpour (by Kahyasi): dam lightly-raced sister to disqualified Oaks winner Aliysa: modest performer: fifth in handicap at Wolverhampton on reappearance: stays 1½m: acts on polytrack, good to firm and good to soft going. *James Leavy, Ireland* 53 a57

ADDICTIVE 2 b.f. (Mar 31) Averti (IRE) 117 – Shadow Bird 70 (Martinmas 128) [2006 6f 6g* 6m 7m 6.5s 8.3d Oct 9] 4,000F, 9,000Y: tall, quite good-topped filly: half-sister to several winners, including useful 1996 2-y-o 6f winner Shadow Lead (by Midyan), later successful in Hong Kong, and fairly useful 7f/1m winner Air of Esteem (by Forzando): dam 11.5f to 13f winner: fair performer: won maiden at Epsom in July: little impact in nurseries: should stay 7f/1m: acts on good to firm going. *S. C. Williams* 69

totesport Chester Cup (Handicap)—
Admiral, under a good tactical ride from John Egan, caps a fine start to Tim Pitt's training career;
Vinando (blinkers), Greenwich Meantime (left) and Dancing Bay give chase

ADEJE PARK (IRE) 3 ch.f. Night Shift (USA) – Iyandas (ITY) (Love The Groom **95**
(USA) 123) [2006 81: 6g⁵ 7.1g* 8ᵤ 8m 7.6m⁶ p8g⁴ p7g³ a7.5g⁴ Nov 23] quite good-
topped filly: useful performer: won handicap at Warwick in May: good efforts last 3
starts, fourth to Goetot in listed race at Deauville final one: stays 1m: acts on all-weather,
raced only on good/good to firm ground on turf: sold 41,000 gns. *P. W. Chapple-Hyam*

ADELFIA (IRE) 3 ch.f. Sinndar (IRE) 134 – Adaiyka (IRE) 110 (Doyoun 124) [2006 **83**
61p: 10g⁵ 12g³ p12g* p12g Sep 6] plain, leggy filly: has a fluent action: fairly useful
performer: won maiden at Kempton in August: ran as if amiss in handicap there next
time: stays 1½m: raced only on polytrack and good ground. *Sir Michael Stoute*

ADIOS (GER) 7 b.g. Lagunas – Aerope (Celestial Storm (USA) 132) [2006 11.9g **–**
Sep 22] successful 3 times up to 11f in Germany at 3/4 yrs for H. Blume: soundly beaten
in handicap at Haydock, only outing in 2006. *P. D. Niven*

ADMIRAL COMPTON 5 ch.g. Compton Place 125 – Sunfleet 59 (Red Sunset 120) **69**
[2006 74, a79: p10g p10g⁴ p10g p8g 9.7f 9.2m⁵ 10.1m⁶ 8.3g 9m p8g p10g 8d Sep 27] **a77 d**
lengthy gelding: fair handicapper: below best after second start: stays easy 1¼m: acts on
polytrack and firm going: often wears headgear: sold 9,000 gns. *J. R. Boyle*

ADMIRAL (IRE) 5 b.g. Alhaarth (IRE) 126 – Coast Is Clear (IRE) 60 (Rainbow Quest **95**
(USA) 134) [2006 82: 18.7m* 16d⁶ 20m Jun 20] rangy, good sort: fluent mover: useful
handicapper: 28/1, won totesport Chester Cup in May by 1¼ lengths from Vinando, dictating pace: creditable sixth to Toldo at Ascot next time, but suffered slight tendon strain
when in rear in Ascot Stakes final outing: effective at 1¼m to 2¼m: acts on firm and good
to soft going: has worn crossed noseband/had 2 handlers: stays in training. *T. J. Pitt*

ADMIRALOFTHEFLEET (USA) 2 b.c. (Feb 15) Danehill (USA) 126 – Rafina **116 p**
(USA) (Mr Prospector (USA)) [2006 7g 7m* 7m³ 8d* Sep 23]
Making a name as a two-year-old at Ballydoyle is not easy. Even for those
who take high rank among Aidan O'Brien's youngsters, competition for the lime-
light each season tends to be fierce. Since Desert King gave O'Brien his first
Group 1 winner as a trainer in the National Stakes in 1996, only the Cheveley Park
Stakes at Newmarket has eluded the yard among the Group 1 events for juveniles
in Europe. In that time, among other prizes, O'Brien has collected three Middle
Park Stakes and four Racing Post Trophies, while there have been eight successes
in the Phoenix Stakes, four in the Moyglare Stud Stakes and a further five in the
National Stakes in Ireland, along with three Prix Mornys and seven versions of
what is now called the Prix Jean-Luc Lagardere. It is easy to see how, in particular,
those successful in lesser pattern company as juveniles can be overshadowed,
but O'Brien's latest winner of the Royal Lodge Stakes at Ascot, Admiralofthefleet,
could be dangerous to ignore as a three-year-old. Royal Lodge winners have had
a poor record at three since 1996 winner Benny The Dip went on to success in
the Derby, but Admiralofthefleet already looks comfortably better than O'Brien's
two previous winners of the race, Royal Kingdom and Mutinyonthebounty, both of
whom failed to win as three-year-olds. Indeed, Admiralofthefleet is the best Royal
Lodge winner for some years and a good prospect for 2007.
Although he improved with every run, it took a step up to a mile for
Admiralofthefleet to show his worth. In three races over seven furlongs, he won

*Juddmonte Royal Lodge Stakes, Ascot—Admiralofthefleet (No.3) proves well suited by the step up in trip
and wins going away from Medicine Path, Kirklees and Champlain (right)*

a maiden at Gowran in June on his second start before finishing two lengths third of seven behind Halicarnassus in the Superlative Stakes at Newmarket's July meeting. On the strength of those efforts, Admiralofthefleet started only fifth in the betting for the seven-runner Group 2 Juddmonte Royal Lodge Stakes at Ascot in September behind the promising Gold Option, favourite at 7/2 in an open market after the late withdrawal of Halicarnassus due to the testing ground. In a well-run race, Admiralofthefleet had to be put under pressure only briefly to win, forced to wait for a run before being angled wide two furlongs out, then sweeping through to beat Medicine Path going away by two and a half lengths, with Kirklees two lengths further away in third. The third home upheld the form when successful in the Gran Criterium at Milan next time, and the runner-up finished third to Authorized in the Racing Post Trophy on his next outing, doing enough to suggest Admiralofthefleet is not far behind Authorized. The winning time for the Royal Lodge was also good, relatively speaking the best on the card, Admiralofthefleet returning a timefigure of 0.58 fast, equivalent to a timerating of 115.

Admiralofthefleet (USA) (b.c. Feb 15, 2004)	Danehill (USA) (b 1986)	Danzig (b 1977)	Northern Dancer
			Pas de Nom
		Razyana (b 1981)	His Majesty
			Spring Adieu
	Rafina (USA) (b 1994)	Mr Prospector (b 1970)	Raise A Native
			Gold Digger
		Coup de Folie (b 1982)	Halo
			Raise The Standard

Admiralofthefleet is a product of the occasional breeding association between Coolmore and the Niarchos family. His dam Rafina was a maiden in France, finishing placed at up to around a mile, but she is from a fine family, several of whom excelled in the Niarchos colours. Rafina's dam Coup de Folie, who won the Prix d'Aumale, is also the dam of the Prix Morny and Prix de la Salamandre winners Machiavellian and Coup de Genie, both also by Mr Prospector, as well as the Prix Jacques le Marois winner Exit To Nowhere and Hydro Calido, successful in the Prix d'Astarte. Machiavellian was also runner-up in the Two Thousand Guineas, and Coup de Genie, the dam of Prix Marcel Boussac winner Denebola and grandam of Prix de l'Arc de Triomphe winner Bago, was third in the One Thousand Guineas. Neither was tried beyond a mile, but Exit To Nowhere stayed a mile and a quarter, finishing fourth in the Arlington Million. Admiralofthefleet should be better suited by a mile and a quarter than a mile, and shapes as though he will probably stay a mile and a half. His sire Danehill was a sprinter-miler, but he has been responsible for all sorts at stud, including the mile-and-half performers Tiger Hill, Desert King and Dylan Thomas and the Gold Cup winner Westerner, as well as Distinction, another good performer over long distances. A rather leggy, quite good-topped colt, Admiralofthefleet has yet to race on extremes of ground, but acts on good to firm and good to soft. Seemingly a genuine sort, there should be another good prize in him. *A. P. O'Brien, Ireland*

ADMIRAL SAVANNAH (IRE) 2 b.g. (Apr 15) Dilshaan 119 – Valmarana (USA) 51 – (Danzig Connection (USA)) [2006 7f⁴ 7.5m 8v Sep 2] little form. *T. D. Easterby*

ADMIRAL'S CRUISE (USA) 4 b.c. A P Indy (USA) 131 – Ladies Cruise (USA) **119** (Fappiano (USA)) [2006 101: 10g⁶ 12m* 12d⁴ 12f* 12f³ 13.3d* 11g³ Sep 15] big, strong,

The Sportsman Newspaper Geoffrey Freer Stakes, Newbury—Admiral's Cruise hangs right as he holds off Guadalajara, Munsef (striped cap) and Self Defense (third right)

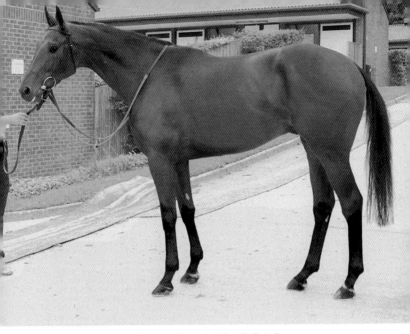

Mr Joe L. Allbritton's "Admiral's Cruise"

close-coupled colt: progressed into smart performer in 2006, winning minor event (by 3 lengths from Palomar) in May and listed event (by 4 lengths from Ouninpohja) in July, both at Newmarket, and The Sportsman Newspaper Geoffrey Freer Stakes at Newbury (beat Guadalajara by ½ length) in August: below-form third to Blue Monday in Arc Trial at Newbury final start, hanging left: stays 13f: acts on firm and soft going: has worn crossed noseband. *B. J. Meehan*

ADOBE 11 b.g. Green Desert (USA) 127 – Shamshir 116 (Kris 135) [2006 63, a58: p9.5g p9.5g 8f⁴ 8.1f* 8m 8.2f⁶ 8.1f 8.3f 8m 10.2f 8m 10.9d p10g Oct 29] small, stocky gelding: modest performer: won amateur handicap at Warwick in June: stays 9.5f: acts on all-weather, firm and good to soft going: tongue tied earlier in career: often claimer ridden: usually held up. *W. M. Brisbourne* **64 a53**

ADONITA 2 b.f. (Jan 30) Singspiel (IRE) 133 – Anna Palariva (IRE) 108 (Caerleon (USA) 132) [2006 8.2d Nov 1] medium-sized, lengthy filly: fifth foal: half-sister to smart French 1m/1¼m winner Advice and fairly useful 7.5f to (in USA) 8.5f winner Anglo Saxon (both by Seeking The Gold): dam, won Prix d'Aumale (ran only at 2 yrs), out of Park Hill Stakes winner Anna of Saxony: 13/2, well-held tenth in maiden at Nottingham: has left Godolphin. *Saeed bin Suroor* **–**

ADOPTED HERO (IRE) 6 b.g. Sadler's Wells (USA) 132 – Lady Liberty (NZ) (Noble Bijou) [2006 14v Sep 2] strong, good-bodied gelding: useful performer at best: won Mijas Cup in Spain on only Flat outing in 2004: below form at Nad Al Sheba and in Spain in 2005: well beaten in handicap only outing on Flat in 2006: stays 15f: acts on polytrack/sand and soft going, ran creditably but gave impression uneasy on good to firm: tried blinkered: fairly useful hurdler. *J. Howard Johnson* **–**

ADRAAJ (USA) 3 b. or br.f. Sahm (USA) 112 – Hachiyah (IRE) 91 (Generous (IRE) 139) [2006 8.2m⁴ 10.1d* 9.7g⁶ 10s² 12d⁴ p10g Nov 9] leggy filly, on weak side at present: fourth foal: half-sister to useful 6f (at 2 yrs) and 1m winner Nasij (by Elusive Quality) and fairly useful UAE 1¼m/11f winner Musaayer (by Erhaab): dam 1¼m winner: fairly **88**

useful performer: very mulish at stall, won maiden at Newcastle in May: best effort when second in handicap at Newbury fourth outing: stays 1¼m: acts on soft going: visored/blinkered last 3 starts: has carried head awkwardly. *E. A. L. Dunlop*

AD VALOREM (USA) 4 b.c. Danzig (USA) – Classy Women (USA) (Relaunch **125** (USA)) [2006 117: 7s⁶ 8m* 8s⁵ 8f³ 8f Nov 4]

The rules governing interference certainly cause much less controversy than they used to. In years gone by, rule 153 rendered disqualification automatic for horses whose jockeys were found guilty of a riding offence. The effects were sometimes ludicrous, with damage done to the integrity of racing each time a travesty of justice was perpetrated. In the 1974 running of the Queen Anne Stakes, for example, the first three, Confusion, Gloss and Royal Prerogative, were all disqualified for interference, and their riders suspended for four days after what the *Bloodstock Breeders' Review* called 'a disgraceful brawl'. The race was awarded to Brook who had been beaten about seven lengths into fourth and really had no right being promoted to first. The latest edition of the Queen Anne provided an example of the working of the present rules. Edging left inside the final furlong, the strongly-ridden Irish-trained four-year-old Ad Valorem hampered the favourite Peeress who, as a consequence, caused interference to eventual runner-up Court Masterpiece, squeezed and denied room to make his challenge. Peeress was already held by the winner when she suffered interference (and lost more ground) and Court Masterpiece didn't look as if he was going to get the better of Ad Valorem either, though he would have finished much closer to the winner than the length and a half he was beaten (Proclamation finished a neck further behind Court Masterpiece in third with Peeress fourth). The Royal Ascot stewards, holding an inquiry under rule 171(iii) into possible interference, took fifteen minutes before concluding that Ad Valorem's rider had caused 'considerable interference' and was guilty of careless riding 'in that Fallon had allowed his mount to drift left-handed towards the rail.' Fallon failed to straighten his mount and did not put his whip down until after the interference. He got a four-day suspension but, because 'the interference had not improved Ad Valorem's placing', the stewards ordered the placings to remain unaltered.

Under the existing rules, winners in Britain are rarely disqualified, the benefit of any doubt always going to the first past the post. The Horseracing Regulatory Authority is reportedly set to review the interference rules in the light of criticism of the stewards' guidelines, which some believe are nurturing an attitude among jockeys that they can get away with foul play, in the knowledge that their mounts are unlikely to be disqualified. There are concerns about safety if a 'win-at-all-costs' culture becomes prevalent. It is just and fair that disciplinary matters are now, in nearly all circumstances, treated separately from matters concerning the equity of the result. Interference has to have an effect on the result of a race before a horse

Queen Anne Stakes, Royal Ascot—Ad Valorem hampers eventual fourth Peeress (No.9) and runner-up Court Masterpiece as he edges left, while Proclamation has a clear run

Mrs John Magnier & Mr R. W. Ingham's "Ad Valorem"

can be disqualified, which is as it should be. However, jockeys who cause interference must be dealt with by fines or suspensions of a severity appropriate to the offences. Any review of the rules should examine whether the current scale of penalties provides a strong enough deterrent. Because the ban was no longer than four days, Ad Valorem's jockey was able to apply successfully to have it deferred because it clashed with a Group 1 event, the Irish Derby (which he won on Dylan Thomas). The big races need the top jockeys but, when a jockey commits an offence in a Group 1 race like the Queen Anne, should he be allowed to defer a ban? The incentive for winning a championship race is bigger than for any other and sanctions to discourage transgressing the rules should arguably be proportionately stronger.

The form of the latest Queen Anne was the worst in four renewals since it was elevated to Group 1 status and it provided Ad Valorem with his first success since his two-year-old days when he gained a Group 1 victory in the Middle Park Stakes. Ad Valorem's performance at Newmarket made it plain that speed rather than stamina was going to be his biggest asset, but he never got the opportunity to race over sprint distances again. His best efforts at three came when second to Shamardal in the St James's Palace Stakes and third to Proclamation in the Sussex Stakes, held up at York and then, with no obvious front runner in the field, sent on at Goodwood. Ad Valorem did not reappear until the Royal meeting as a three-year-old and he was seen out only once at four before the Queen Anne, when well below his best in the Gladness Stakes at the Curragh in early-April. The steady tempo of the Queen Anne played into the hands of Ad Valorem whose superiority was exaggerated by the bare result after the interference suffered by Court Masterpiece, who went on to win the Sussex, and Peeress. Ad Valorem was well below form when fifth—two places behind Peeress—under much more testing conditions in the Prix Jacques le Marois at Deauville in August. That turned out to be the last time Ad Valorem raced in Europe. A respectable third, giving weight all round, in the Woodbine Mile (in which he reportedly lost a shoe) earned Ad Valorem a final racecourse appearance in the Breeders' Cup Mile at Churchill Downs. It was his second successive appearance in the race and he weakened in the final furlong and a half to finish thirteenth of fourteen (ninth of twelve the previous year).

		Northern Dancer	Nearctic
	Danzig (USA)	(b 1961)	Natalma
	(b 1977)	Pas de Nom	Admiral's Voyage
Ad Valorem (USA)		(b or br 1968)	Petitioner
(b.c. 2002)		Relaunch	In Reality
	Classy Women (USA)	(gr 1976)	Foggy Note
	(b 1988)	Aironlass	Proud Clarion
		(b 1979)	Classic Perfection

The smallish, strong, good-topped Ad Valorem was not the only son of Danzig (who died in 2006) to be successful at Royal Ascot. Soapy Danger won the Queen's Vase over two miles but he is most unusual for Danzig, whose progeny have exhibited much more speed than stamina. The average distance of races won by Danzig's offspring at three and above is just under a mile. Danzig's retirement at the age of twenty-seven after the 2004 covering season followed a decline in his fertility. His final crop of yearlings, which numbered twenty-seven, included Dijeerr's 9.2 million-dollar brother, purchased by Sheikh Mohammed at Keeneland the month before Dijeerr won the Horris Hill, and Coolmore's most expensive purchase at the same sale, a 5.2 million-dollar three-parts brother to Beresford Stakes winner Albert Hall (by Danzig's son Danehill). Ad Valorem's dam Classy Women was a Grade 3 winner on turf over eight and a half furlongs (also placed in Grade 1 company on dirt) who once set a track record for an extended five furlongs on turf at Hollywood Park. She has bred five other winners, including Ad Valorem's brother Designer, who finished third in the Middle Park. Classy Women had to be put down in 2006 because of chronic lameness, after producing her final foal, a colt by Forestry; there is also a yearling filly by Stravinsky. Ad Valorem, who sometimes had two handlers in the paddock, stayed a mile and, despite the protestations of his connections that he was 'a different horse on fast ground', showed his form on soft and good to firm going. He has been retired and, after standing at Coolmore for the 2007 northern hemisphere season at a fee of €15,000, will cover at Woodlands Stud, New South Wales, during the Australian breeding season, in a deal similar to that which saw Grand Lodge (a grandson of Danzig) shuttle between the two studs. *A. P. O'Brien, Ireland*

ADVANCED 3 b.c. Night Shift (USA) – Wonderful World (GER) (Dashing Blade 117) **116**
[2006 101: 7g³ p7g² 6d³ 6d² Oct 28] good-topped, attractive colt: smart performer: left R. Charlton 115,000 gns and off 4½ months after second outing: very good efforts last 2 starts, 1¼ lengths third to Fonthill Road in Ayr Gold Cup and ½-length second to New Girlfriend in Prix de Seine-et-Oise at Maisons-Laffitte: best at 6f: acts on polytrack, firm and good to soft going: tongue tied last 2 outings at 2 yrs (reportedly had breathing problem final one): has worn crossed noseband. *K. A. Ryan*

ADVANCEMENT 3 b.g. Second Empire (IRE) 124 – Lambast 70 (Relkino 131) [2006 **74**
6g² p7g f6g* 7.5m² 8d Aug 20] tall gelding: seventh foal: closely related to 5-y-o Philharmonic and half-brother to 2 winners: dam, maiden who stayed 1½m, sister to useful performer up to 1½m My Lamb: fair performer: won maiden at Southwell in July: free-going sort, but stays 7.5f: acts on fibresand and good to firm going: reared and unseated rider second outing. *R. A. Fahey*

ADVENTURESS 3 b.f. Singspiel (IRE) 133 – Arriving 105 (Most Welcome 131) **94**
[2006 7g⁴ 10.2g* 10d⁶ 8m 8.1g 8.1m³ p8g² Sep 30] lengthy filly: sister to useful 7f/1m winner Attune and half-sister to 2 winners, including 4-y-o Asharon: dam 1¼m to 11.4f winner: fairly useful performer: won maiden at Bath in May: good efforts when placed in handicaps at Sandown and Kempton last 2 starts: stays 1¼m: acts on polytrack and good to firm going: blinkered last 3 outings. *B. J. Meehan*

ADVERSANE 2 ch.c. (Feb 28) Alhaarth (IRE) 126 – Cragreen (Green Desert (USA) **65 p**
127) [2006 7s 7d p7g⁶ Nov 22] 45,000Y: angular, useful-looking colt: has a moderate,

quick action: fourth foal: half-brother to winners in Italy (including at 2 yrs) by Medicean and Diktat: dam, Italian 2-y-o 7f winner, out of Italian Group 2 7f winner Croda Alta: easily best effort in maidens when sixth at Kempton final outing: should be suited by 1m+: type to do better in handicaps. *J. L. Dunlop*

AEGEAN DANCER 4 b.g. Piccolo 121 – Aegean Flame 86 (Anshan 119) [2006 69: **87** f6g f5s³ 5m⁴ 5f⁵ 6f 5f² 5m² 5f* 5f⁴ 5f* Aug 15] close-coupled, quite good-topped gelding: reportedly suffered stress fractures at 2 yrs: fairly useful handicapper: won at Carlisle in July and August: effective at 5f/6f: acts on firesand and firm going: sometimes slowly away: has hung/flashed tail/carried head awkwardly. *B. Smart*

AEGEAN MIST 6 ch.m. Prince Sabo 123 – Dizzydaisy 57 (Sharpo 132) [2006 p5.1g **–** 6d Aug 2] lightly-raced maiden: no form in 2006, leaving M. Mullineaux after reappearance. *B. P. J. Baugh*

AEGEAN PEARL (USA) 3 b.f. Lemon Drop Kid (USA) 131 – Reluctant Diva **69** (Sadler's Wells (USA) 132) [2006 p10g⁵ p10g⁴ 12g⁴ p10g⁶ Aug 13] $150,000Y: lengthy, angular filly: third foal: half-sister to winner in USA by Phone Trick: dam ran twice in USA: fair maiden: stayed 1½m: dead. *J. H. M. Gosden*

AEGEAN PRINCE 2 b.c. (Feb 28) Dr Fong (USA) 128 – Dizzydaisy 57 (Sharpo 132) **80 p** [2006 7f³ 6d p7g* Oct 17] compact, close-coupled colt: half-brother to 1½m winner Aegean Sunrise (by Deploy) and 1998 2-y-o 5f winner Aegean Flame (by Anshan): dam maiden who stayed 6f: fairly useful form: won maiden at Lingfield in October: will stay 1m: should improve further. *R. Hannon*

AEGIS (IRE) 2 b.g. (Apr 28) Beckett (IRE) 116 – Silver Spoon (IRE) (College Chapel **79** 122) [2006 6m 6m 7.1m⁵ 8d² p8g³ Oct 6] 26,000Y: unfurnished gelding: fourth foal: brother to 2005 2-y-o 5f and 7f winner in Italy: dam lightly-raced maiden: fair form: placed in nurseries at Goodwood and Lingfield (blinkered, gelded after): stays 1m: acts on polytrack, good to firm and good to soft going. *B. W. Hills*

AERONAUT 3 b.g. Averti (IRE) 117 – Roufontaine 85 (Rousillon (USA) 133) [2006 –: **–** 6.1m 10f⁴ 10m Sep 8] little sign of ability: tried tongue tied. *J. M. Bradley*

AEROPLANE 3 b.c. Danehill Dancer (IRE) 117 – Anita At Dawn (IRE) 77 (Anita's **111** Prince 126) [2006 72: 7g* 7s⁴ 8m 7m* 7d Oct 14] medium-sized, compact colt: smart performer: reportedly cracked pelvis on only outing at 2 yrs: won maiden at Newmarket in April and minor event at Southwell (beat Dickensian by 2 lengths) in September: respectable fourth to Jeremy in listed race at Newmarket, but well held in St James's Palace Stakes at Royal Ascot and Challenge Stakes at Newmarket (sweating) otherwise: should stay 1m: acts on soft and good to firm going. *P. W. Chapple-Hyam*

AFADAN (IRE) 8 br.g. Royal Academy (USA) 130 – Afasara (IRE) (Shardari 134) **–** [2006 76: p12.2g p12g p12g p12g f12g³ p12.2g May 8] rangy gelding: no form in 2006: sometimes tongue tied/visored: often slowly away. *J. R. Jenkins*

AFFILIATION (IRE) 2 b.f. (Jan 27) Danehill Dancer (IRE) 117 – Latin Beauty (IRE) **–** (Sadler's Wells (USA) 132) [2006 7m 6m Sep 16] 30,000Y: neat filly: first foal: dam unraced half-sister to July Cup winner Owington: green and in rear in maidens. *R. Hannon*

AFFIRMED NATIVE (USA) 3 ch.f. Machiavellian (USA) 123 – Affirmed Ambi- **–** ence (USA) (Affirmed (USA)) [2006 6s⁴ 6g 7m⁶ p7g Nov 6] 25,000Y, 23,000 2-y-o: half-sister to several winners abroad: dam, 5f and (at 2 yrs) 5.5f winner in USA, half-sister to dam of very smart performer up to 1¼m Zoman: little impact in maidens/ listed race in Germany: sold 18,000 gns and left A. Trybuhl, well held in banded race at Kempton final outing: should stay 7f: tried blinkered. *J. A. Osborne*

A FOOT IN FRONT 2 b.g. (Apr 17) Sugarfoot 118 – Scoffera 63 (Scottish Reel 123) **–** [2006 6.1g 6s 7f 7g Sep 27] no form: tried visored. *N. Tinkler*

AFRAD (FR) 5 gr.g. Linamix (FR) 127 – Afragha (IRE) 88 (Darshaan 133) [2006 103: **–** 20m Jun 20] smallish, leggy gelding: useful handicapper: ran poorly in Ascot Stakes only Flat outing in 2006: won over fences in December. *N. J. Henderson*

AFRICAN BLUES 3 ch.g. College Chapel 122 – Pearl Dawn (IRE) 91 (Jareer (USA) **– §** 115) [2006 –§: 10m 7m p10g Dec 13] temperamental and of no account. *M. R. Hoad*

AFRICAN CONCERTO (IRE) 3 b.c. Mozart (IRE) 131 – Out of Africa (IRE) 98 **67 d** (Common Grounds 118) [2006 66: p6g p8g p6g p7g*dis p7g⁴ p6g 7m⁶ 6g p6g 5m p6g p6g⁶ p7g p8g Dec 15] leggy colt: fair performer at best: first past post in claimer at Lingfield (claimed £8,000, failed dope test and disqualified) in March: left Ernst Oertel and returned to former trainer after eighth outing: stays 7f: acts on polytrack and firm going. *S. Kirk*

AFRICAN DREAM 5 b.g. Mark of Esteem (IRE) 137 – Fleet Hill (IRE) 99 (Warrshan **106** (USA) 117) [2006 112: p10g⁴ p10g p10g⁵ Apr 15] rather leggy, good-topped gelding: only useful nowadays: best effort in 2006 when fifth of 6 to Simple Exchange in listed event at Kempton final outing: stays 10.3f: acts on polytrack and soft going: visored (well held) second start. *J. Noseda*

AFRICAN GIFT 4 b.f. Cadeaux Genereux 131 – African Light 65§ (Kalaglow 132) **76** [2006 70: p6g p6g 6.1m p7.1g* p7.1g 6g* 6m p7.1g³ Jul 17] tall filly: fair handicapper: won at Wolverhampton and Ayr in June: stayed easy 7f: acted on polytrack and soft going: sometimes hung left: dead. *J. G. Given*

AFRICAN SAHARA (USA) 7 br.h. El Gran Senor (USA) 136 – Able Money (USA) **76** (Distinctive (USA)) [2006 86: p10g f8g⁵ p12.2g⁶ p10g p10g 10s⁶ p12g p10g Jul 29] close-coupled, good-topped horse: fairly useful at best: was effective at 1m/easy 1¼m: acted on all-weather, firm and good to soft going: tried in cheekpieces/visored: tongue tied: usually held up: usually claimer ridden: was tough: dead. *Miss D. Mountain*

AFRICAN STAR 5 b.g. Mtoto 134 – Pass The Rose (IRE) (Thatching 131) [2006 47: **39** 7m p7g p7g May 15] workmanlike gelding: poor maiden: seems to stay 11f: acts on all-weather and firm going: tried in cheekpieces. *J. M. Bradley*

AFRIC STAR 2 b.f. (Apr 18) Woodborough (USA) 112 – America Star (Norwick **46** (USA) 125) [2006 p5g 5s³ 5.1d⁵ 5m⁶ 6.1s⁴ 6f Jun 19] close-coupled filly: half-sister to 5f/ 6f winner Napier Star (by Inca Chief): dam unraced: poor maiden. *P. D. Evans*

AFTER THE SHOW 5 b.g. Royal Applause 124 – Tango Teaser (Shareef Dancer **84** (USA) 135) [2006 80: f5g² 5.1s⁶ p5g³ p5g⁶ p5g² 5d² p6g⁶ 5s p6g p5g⁴ Dec 5] useful-looking gelding: fairly useful handicapper: at least respectable efforts when in frame in 2006: effective at 5f/6f: acts on all-weather, soft and good to firm going: tends to hang left: held up of late. *Rae Guest*

AFTER YOU 3 b.f. Pursuit of Love 124 – Los Alamos 73 (Keen 116) [2006 84p: 7m⁵ **92** 8d* 8m 8.1g 8d Sep 23] rangy filly: fairly useful performer: won minor event at New-market in May by 1¾ lengths from Metropolitan Man: well held in listed races last 3 starts: stays 1m: acts on polytrack, good to firm and good to soft going: often makes running. *B. W. Hills*

AGAINST THE GRAIN 3 b.g. Pivotal 124 – Oh Hebe (IRE) 74 (Night Shift (USA)) **91** [2006 7d* 7.1m³ 7m 8g Jul 28] 45,000Y: good-bodied gelding: fourth foal: half-brother to useful 2002 2-y-o 5f/6f winner Devious Boy (by Dr Devious), later Grade 2 9f winner in USA, and 4-y-o Special Lad: dam, 7f winner, half-sister to smart performers Leporello (at 1¼m) and Poppy Carew (at 1¼m/1½m): fairly useful form: won maiden at Newmarket (beat Villa Sonata 3½ lengths) on debut in May: found little and well below form last 2 starts: bred to stay 1m, but has plenty of speed: sold 11,000 gns in October. *M. Johnston*

AGENT ELEVEN (IRE) 3 b.g. Desert Story (IRE) 115 – Elizabethan Air 55 (Elegant **–** Air 119) [2006 10m May 3] 125/1 and backward, well held in maiden at Pontefract. *B. J. McMath*

AGE OF KINGS (USA) 4 b.g. Kingmambo (USA) 125 – Everhope (USA) (Danzig **66 d** (USA)) [2006 83: p7g p8.6g p8.6g 10.2d p12.2g 10d May 29] smallish, attractive geld-ing: on the downgrade: tried blinkered. *A. B. Haynes*

AGGBAG 2 b.g. (Apr 30) Fath (USA) 116 – Emaura 61 (Dominion 123) [2006 5m⁵ 5g **57** 6m³ 5.2g³ p5g² 6f p6f p6g* p6g p7.1m p7.1m⁵ p6m⁴ f6g³ p6g f6g³ Dec 23] strong gelding: modest performer: claimed from M. Wallace £6,000 fifth start: won claimer at Wolverhampton in August: stays 7f: acts on polytrack and good to firm going: badly hampered and unseated rider penultimate start. *B. P. J. Baugh*

AGGI MAC 5 b.m. Defacto (USA) – Giffoine 79 (Timeless Times (USA) 99) [2006 54: **–** f11m Oct 31] close-coupled, good-topped mare: modest maiden: well held only outing in 2006: stays 11f: acts on all-weather and good to firm ground: tried blinkered. *N. Bycroft*

AGGRAVATION 4 b.g. Sure Blade (USA) 130 – Confection (Formidable (USA) 125) **78** [2006 70, a72: p7g p8g² p8g* p7g p8g² p8g³ p8g p8g⁵ 8.3f* 8.3f* 8m 8.3g³ 9g⁴ 8.5d 7.5m 8.3s⁴ Oct 2] neat gelding: fair handicapper: won at Lingfield in March and Windsor (2) in June: stays 9f: acts on polytrack, firm and good to soft ground: tried visored, effective tongue tied or not: waited with. *D. R. C. Elsworth*

AGGRESIVE 2 ch.g. (Apr 2) Zilzal (USA) 137 – Frankie Fair (IRE) 73 (Red Sunset **71**
120) [2006 p5g⁵ p6g³ p6g p5g 6m p7g 6d⁴ Oct 9] fourth foal: half-brother to 6-y-o Fair
Spin: dam 7f/1m winner: fair maiden: left Ernst Oertel after sixth start: should stay 7f/
1m: sold 10,000 gns. *D. K. Ivory*

AGILETE 4 b.g. Piccolo 121 – Ingerence (FR) (Akarad (FR) 130) [2006 77: p7.1g p6g **68**
p7g p10g p9.5g 8m f12g³ 10g 10m 10.9f⁵ 12f⁴ 11.5f f12g³ 10.1m⁶ 11.7m³ p12.2m* 10m²
10.9d 10.5g² 11g⁵ p12g⁵ Oct 17] workmanlike gelding: fair performer: trained fifth/sixth
starts only by R. Harris: won selling handicap at Wolverhampton (left J. Boyle) in September: stays 1½m: acts on all-weather and firm going: tried tongue tied/in cheekpieces/
blinkered: sometimes slowly away. *J. Pearce*

AGITATOR 2 b.g. (Apr 28) Lujain (USA) 119 – Forum Girl (USA) 79 (Sheikh Albadou **54 p**
128) [2006 p6g³ Oct 28] third foal: half-brother to 7f (at 2 yrs) and 1¼m winner Stagecoach Ruby (by Bijou d'Inde): dam 7f winner: 40/1, third in maiden at Wolverhampton:
will stay 7f: should progress. *Mrs G. S. Rees*

AGNES GIFT 3 b.f. Agnes World (USA) 123 – Evocatrice 91 (Persepolis (FR) 127) **–**
[2006 p8g Aug 9] half-sister to several winners abroad, including useful French 1¼m/
1½m winner Edouna (by Doyoun): dam, French 2-y-o 7f winner who stayed 1¼m, out of
top-class filly up to 1½m Northern Trick: 66/1, seventh to Changing Wind in maiden at
Kempton, travelling well to 2f out. *Jamie Poulton*

AGNES PEARL 3 b.f. Agnes World (USA) 123 – Paris Babe 94 (Teenoso (USA) 135) **–**
[2006 f6g⁶ 7m Aug 5] 5,200F, 19,000Y: lengthy filly: fourth foal: half-sister to 6f (at
2 yrs)/7f winner Ashtree Belle (by Up And At 'em): dam 6f winner: behind in seller and
maiden. *B. Smart*

AHAZ 4 b.g. Zaha (CAN) 106 – Classic Faster (IRE) (Running Steps (USA) 79) [2006 **–**
39: 10f Sep 18] quite good-topped gelding: poor maiden: stays at least 7f: acts on fibresand and good to firm going: tried in blinkers/cheekpieces at 2 yrs. *J. F. Coupland*

AHLAWY (IRE) 3 b.g. Green Desert (USA) 127 – On Call 103 (Alleged (USA) 138) **83**
[2006 p8g 8d⁴ 7m* 9.9f⁶ 8.3m⁶ Jul 8] €105,000Y: fourth foal: brother to 1¼m winner
Optimal and half-brother to fairly useful 1½m to 15f winner One Off (by Barathea) and
useful 9f to 1½m winner Oblique (by Giant's Causeway): dam 1½m to 2m winner: fairly
useful performer: won maiden at Yarmouth in May: creditable sixth in handicaps after:
bred to be well suited by 1¼m+: sold 8,000 gns in October, then gelded. *L. M. Cumani*

AHMEDY (IRE) 3 b.g. Polish Precedent (USA) 131 – Nawaji (USA) 45 (Trempolino **81**
(USA) 135) [2006 80: p10g³ 8m⁴ 12g 10m 9.7f⁴ 10m³ 8m⁴ 10g 9.7m* 10g p10g⁵ Oct 20]
sparely-made gelding: fairly useful handicapper: won at Folkestone in September: should
stay 1½m: acts on polytrack, firm and good to soft going: sometimes slowly away: sold
42,000 gns, joined J. Quinn, and won over hurdles in December. *M. R. Channon*

AI HAWA (IRE) 3 b.f. Indian Danehill (IRE) 124 – Arabian Princess (Taufan (USA) **65**
119) [2006 57: 8d³ 7g⁵ 8.3g² 10.9m⁵ 8f² 8.5m Jul 19] closely related to Irish 1½m winner
Desert Kite (by Flying Spur) and half-sister to several winners, including fairly useful
Irish 1¼m to 1½m winner Master Cooper (by Kahyasi): dam Irish 2-y-o 7f winner: fair
maiden handicapper: ran in Britain first 4 starts in 2006 (placed at Redcar and Hamilton):
best form at 1m: acts on firm going, probably on good to soft: ran well in cheekpieces
fifth start. *E. Tyrrell, Ireland*

AILSA 4 b.f. Bishop of Cashel 122 – Mindomica 63 (Dominion 123) [2006 6d⁵ 5m 6g⁶ **57**
p7.1g 7.2g 5s 7m⁶ 9d² p8g Oct 29] good-topped filly: sixth living foal: half-sister to
3 winners, including 5f/6f (latter at 2 yrs) winner Molotov (by Efisio) and 11f winner
Minstrel Hall (by Saddlers' Hall): dam, 7f winner (including at 2 yrs), half-sister to Fred
Darling winner/Oaks fourth Sueboog, herself dam of very smart 1m/1¼m performer Best
of The Bests: modest maiden: stays 9f: acts on good to soft going. *C. W. Thornton*

AIMEE VIBERT 4 b.f. Zilzal (USA) 137 – Rose Vibert (Caerleon (USA) 132) [2006 **76**
72: p10g p10g² 10.2g⁶ 11.5m* 12m* 12g⁶ Aug 17] useful-looking filly: fair handicapper:
won at Lingfield and Pontefract in July: stays 1½m: acts on polytrack and good to firm
ground. *W. R. Swinburn*

AINAMAA (USA) 2 b.f. (Mar 19) Lemon Drop Kid (USA) 131 – Khibrah (IRE) 107 **68**
(Lahib (USA) 129) [2006 7f 7.5g³ Aug 27] good-bodied filly: second foal: dam 1m/1¼m
winner: 3¾ lengths third in maiden at Beverley: will stay 1¼m: sold 32,000 gns, sent to
USA. *E. A. L. Dunlop*

AINTNECESSARILYSO 8 ch.g. So Factual (USA) 120 – Ovideo 58 (Domynsky **52**
110) [2006 64, a53: f7g² f7g p7g f6g⁶ 6m p7g f6g Nov 28] workmanlike gelding: modest

performer: effective at 5f to 7f: acts on all-weather, firm and soft ground (yet to race on heavy): tried blinkered, wears cheekpieces. *J. M. Bradley*

AIR BISCUIT (IRE) 3 b.f. Galileo (IRE) 134 – Surprise Visitor (IRE) (Be My Guest **84** (USA) 126) [2006 62: 8.2d⁴ 8m 7d p7g p7g³ p8g⁶ 8m* 10g* 10m* 8.3d² 10d Nov 4] fairly useful handicapper: won at Brighton in August and apprentice events at Lingfield and Pontefract in September: stays 1¼m: acts on polytrack, good to firm and good to soft ground: tongue tied nowadays. *C. F. Wall*

AIRBOUND (USA) 3 ch.g. Fusaichi Pegasus (USA) 130 – Secrettame (USA) (Secre- **77** tariat (USA)) [2006 p8g³ f8g² f8g⁴ 8g 8.3m⁵ 10.1m⁵ 10d⁵ p12.2g* p12g p10g Oct 20] $225,000Y: closely related/half-brother to numerous winners, notably smart performer up to 1m Lion Cavern (6f/7f winner at 2 yrs) and US Grade 1 9f winner Gone West (both by Mr Prospector): dam, 6f to 9f winner in USA, half-sister to Known Fact: fair performer: won handicap at Wolverhampton in August: stays 1½m: acts on all-weather: sold 10,000 gns, joined H. Dunlop, then gelded. *M. Johnston*

AIRBUSS (IRE) 3 b.c. Mozart (IRE) 131 – Kardelle 79 (Kalaglow 132) [2006 71p: p8g **89** 8.1s² 8.5g* 10.1m⁶ 9s⁴ 8g⁵ 8m³ 8.2m* Jul 29] close-coupled, attractive colt: fairly useful handicapper: won at Epsom in April and Nottingham in July: should be suited by 1¼m: acts on soft and good to firm going: sent to UAE. *M. R. Channon*

AIREDALE LAD (IRE) 5 b.g. Charnwood Forest (IRE) 125 – Tamarsiya (USA) **52** (Shahrastani (USA) 135) [2006 51: 7d⁶ 12g 10.1d² 8.2s³ 7.9m 8.5g 10f Sep 20] leggy gelding: modest maiden: stays 10.5f: acts on fibresand, firm and soft ground: tried in cheekpieces. *R. M. Whitaker*

AIRGUSTA (IRE) 5 b.g. Danehill Dancer (IRE) 117 – Ministerial Model (IRE) 94 **–** (Shalford (IRE) 124§) [2006 60: p13.9g Jan 4] close-coupled gelding: modest performer: stays 2m: acts on polytrack: well held in cheekpieces only Flat outing in 2006: modest hurdler, successful in June/August. *C. P. Morlock*

AIR OF SUPREMACY (IRE) 5 gr.g. Royal Applause 124 – Lap of Luxury 107 **–** (Sharrood (USA) 124) [2006 56: 8.1g Jul 5] has a quick action: disappointing maiden: tried in cheekpieces/blinkers/tongue strap. *J. L. Spearing*

AITCH (IRE) 3 b.f. Alhaarth (IRE) 126 – Sevi's Choice (USA) (Sir Ivor (USA) 135) **–** [2006 8.3m Apr 24] 55,000F: third foal: half-sister to 2003 2-y-o 5f winner Dontstopthe-music (by Night Shift): dam German 1¼m winner: 66/1, last in maiden at Windsor, soon ridden in rear. *J. Noseda*

AITUTAKI (IRE) 2 b.g. (May 11) Lend A Hand 124 – Amber Fizz (USA) (Effervesc- **62** ing (USA)) [2006 6m⁶ 6s 7.5m Sep 13] unfurnished gelding: modest form in maidens. *T. D. Easterby*

AIZEN MYOO (IRE) 8 b.g. Balla Cove 119 – Fly In Amber (IRE) (Doubletour **73** (USA)) [2006 12s² p12.2g Dec 2] blinkered, much better effort on Flat when second in claimer at Tramore (subsequently left N. Meade in Ireland): very slowly away in maiden at Wolverhampton: modest winning hurdler. *Seamus Fahey, Ireland*

AJAAN 2 br.c. (Mar 6) Machiavellian (USA) 123 – Alakananda 92 (Hernando (FR) 127) **87 p** [2006 7m⁵ 8.3s* Oct 2] 80,000Y: smallish colt: second foal: half-brother to 3-y-o Dragon Dancer: dam, won around 1½m, half-sister to dual Champion Stakes winner Alborada and smart 1½m performer Albanova: much improved from debut when winning maiden at Windsor in October by 1¼ lengths from Vanquisher, patiently ridden: will be suited by 1¼m/1½m: useful prospect. *H. R. A. Cecil*

AJHAR (USA) 2 b.c. (Jan 30) Diesis 133 – Min Alhawa (USA) 108 (Riverman (USA) **85** 131) [2006 8m² 8.1g² 8s² Oct 10] strong, compact colt: half-brother to 3 winners, includ- ing useful 1¼m/1½m winners Mutasallil (including in UAE, by Gone West) and Nuzooa (by A P Indy): dam 7f (at 2 yrs) and 1¼m winner, half-sister to 1000 Guineas winner Harayir: fairly useful maiden: runner-up all 3 starts, beaten 3½ lengths by Sunshine Kid at Newbury final one: will stay 1¼m/1½m. *M. P. Tregoning*

AJIGOLO 3 ch.c. Piccolo 121 – Ajig Dancer 86 (Niniski (USA) 125) [2006 107: 5m 6m **101** 6g 5f 5.1g Aug 15] tall, good-topped colt: useful performer: not at best at 3 yrs, form only when twelfth in Golden Jubilee Stakes at Royal Ascot and last of 7 in Hackwood Stakes at Newbury (dictated long way) second/third starts: raced only at 5f/6f: acts on good to firm going: tried visored: has got on edge/been on toes. *M. R. Channon*

AKAREM 5 b.h. Kingmambo (USA) 125 – Spirit of Tara (IRE) 106 (Sadler's Wells **117** (USA) 132) [2006 110: 12m⁵ 12.1d* 12d² 20m 14g⁴ 14g³ 12g³ 14g⁵ 12d⁵ 12s Oct 21] strong, angular horse: smart performer: won listed races at Hamilton (handicap, by neck from Ouninpohja) and Ascot (sweating, beat Frank Sonata by 4 lengths) in May: ran well when third of 5 to Jadalee in listed event at Goodwood sixth start, but below form after: stays 1¾m (pulled hard in Gold Cup at Royal Ascot fourth start): acts on heavy and good to firm going: tried tongue tied: has worn crossed noseband. *K. R. Burke*

AKASH (IRE) 6 b.g. Dr Devious (IRE) 127 – Akilara (IRE) 87 (Kahyasi 130) [2006 –: 10d May 26] well-made gelding: one-time useful performer: no form since 2004: tried blinkered. *Miss J. Feilden* — —

AKIMBO (USA) 5 b.h. Kingmambo (USA) 125 – All At Sea (USA) 124 (Riverman (USA) 131) [2006 111: 10m⁵ 8m 8g 6m⁴ 8d⁵ Sep 29] quite attractive horse: smart performer for H. Cecil at 4 yrs: only useful in 2006, best effort when seventh to Mustameet in listed race at the Curragh third start: best at 7f/1m: unraced on extremes of going on turf, never going with any fluency only start on all-weather: coltish on 2005 reappearance (when also sweating/edgy) and on second outing (last in Queen Anne Stakes at Royal Ascot) in 2006. *James Leavy, Ireland* **104**

AKINOLA (IRE) 5 ch.g. Lil's Boy (USA) 109 – Miss Margaux (IRE) 68 (Royal Academy (USA) 130) [2006 85: 7s³ 8s⁶ 10g 7s f8g⁴ p9.5g⁴ f8g Dec 23] only fair handicapper in 2006, leaving E. Griffin in Ireland after third start: stays 9.5f: acts on polytrack and heavy going: tongue tied once: tried in cheekpieces/blinkers: unreliable. *K. A. Ryan* **76 §**

AKIYAMA (IRE) 2 b.g. (Mar 31) Traditionally (USA) 117 – Dark Albatross (USA) 89 (Sheikh Albadou 128) [2006 7d³ 8s⁴ 7s² Oct 10] €13,000F, €55,000Y: second foal: dam, 2-y-o 6f winner who stayed 1¼m, out of US Grade 1 1¼m winner Rossard: fair maiden: in frame all 3 starts: will stay 1¼m: raced on going softer than good. *J. Howard Johnson* **74**

AKONA MATATA (USA) 4 b.c. Seeking The Gold (USA) – Oh What A Dance (USA) (Nijinsky (CAN) 138) [2006 75: p8g* p8g² 7m⁴ 9m⁴ 8.5g⁵ 8m³ 7m a8f² Dec 21] tall, angular colt: useful performer: won maiden at Kempton in March and handicap at Yarmouth (beat Surwaki 1¼ lengths, despite hanging left) in April: good efforts when in frame in handicaps after, including at Royal Ascot in Hunt Cup (2 lengths third to Cesare) and, having left C. Brittain and off over 5 months after penultimate start, Nad Al Sheba: effective at 9f, but may prove best at 7f/1m: acts on polytrack/dirt, raced only on good or firmer going on turf. *D. Watson, UAE* **99**

AKRAM (IRE) 4 b.g. Night Shift (USA) – Akdariya (IRE) 103 (Shirley Heights 130) [2006 103+: 8.3m⁵ Jul 1] useful performer in 2005, when trained by J. Oxx in Ireland: last of 5 behind Librettist in listed race at Windsor only Flat outing in 2006: best effort at 8.5f: raced only on good/good to firm going. *Jonjo O'Neill* **93**

AKRITAS 5 b.g. Polish Precedent (USA) 131 – Dazzling Heights 99 (Shirley Heights 130) [2006 p16g p16g 12d⁴ 12d 12m p16g⁴ 15m⁵ 12.1m Sep 1] quite useful-topped gelding: fairly useful performer: well below form last 5 starts: effective at 1½m to 2m: acts on good to firm and good to soft going: blinkered last 2 starts: tried tongue tied: has looked none too keen. *P. F. I. Cole* **83 d**

ALAGHIRAAR (IRE) 2 b.c. (Feb 5) Act One 124 – Tarsheeh (USA) 53 (Mr Prospector (USA)) [2006 7d Oct 28] rangy colt: on weak side at 2 yrs: second foal: dam twice-raced half-sister to smart 7f to 9f performer Haami out of smart half-sister to Derby winner Erhaab: 25/1, green when mid-field in 19-runner maiden at Newmarket: should progress at 1¼m+. *J. L. Dunlop* **67 p**

ALAMBIC 3 gr.f. Cozzene (USA) – Alexandrine (IRE) 78 (Nashwan (USA) 135) [2006 –p: 12.1f⁶ 12g² 12m* 12f* 14.1f* 13g* 14.1m* 14m³ 14g* 16.2m³ Sep 4] big, strong filly: fairly useful handicapper: much improved and won 6 of 8 starts in July/August, at Musselburgh (2), Folkestone, Yarmouth (2) and Hamilton: beat Cool Customer by 3 lengths at Musselburgh for last victory: also ran well final outing: stays 2m: acts on firm ground: tends to wander/idle in front. *Sir Mark Prescott* **88**

ALAN THE AUSSIE 3 b.g. Rossini (USA) 118 – In Ernest (IRE) (Forest Wind (USA) 111) [2006 f8g 11.5m 8.3m 11.5f Jul 6] no form. *G. Prodromou* —

ALARM CALL 3 b.f. Mind Games 121 – Warning Bell 88 (Bustino 136) [2006 –: f7g f7g Apr 4] poor maiden: tried blinkered. *T. D. Easterby* **33**

ALASIL (USA) 6 b.g. Swain (IRE) 134 – Asl (USA) 114 (Caro 133) [2006 10.2m* 10d⁶ p10g p9.5g⁶ p12.2g⁴ p9.5g Dec 2] good-topped gelding: fair nowadays: unraced on Flat in 2004/5 (modest hurdler): won seller at Chepstow in September: stays 1½m: acts on polytrack, raced mainly on ground firmer than good on turf. *R. J. Price* **72**

ALASOUN (IRE) 3 b.c. Kalanisi (IRE) 132 – Alasana (IRE) (Darshaan 133) [2006 63p: 10d⁵ 11.5m⁴ 11.9m² 11.5f² Jul 6] quite good-topped colt: fairly useful maiden: stays **81**

1½m: acts on firm ground: visored (ran creditably) final start: withdrawn after refusing to enter stall on intended debut: sold 16,000 gns in October. *Sir Michael Stoute*

ALAVANA (IRE)   2 b.f. (Mar 1) Kyllachy 129 – Grey Galava 64 (Generous (IRE) 139)   **53** [2006 5g 6f⁶ 6m 5f⁴ 6d Sep 15] €26,000Y: sixth foal: half-sister to several winners, including 6-y-o Millagros and 4-y-o Madhavi: dam 1¾m winner: modest form third start only. *D. W. Barker*

ALAYAN (IRE)   4 b.c. Sri Pekan (USA) 117 – Alaya (IRE) 89 (Ela-Mana-Mou 132)   **122** [2006 118: 8.9m 12m² 12m⁶ 10d* May 1] very smart performer: ran at Nad Al Sheba first 3 starts in 2006, creditable 1¾ lengths second to Oracle West in Dubai City of Gold in March: career-best effort when winning High Chaparral EBF Mooresbridge Stakes at the Curragh in May by a length from Ace, making much of running: stayed 1½m: acted on heavy and good to firm ground: raced prominently: game: reportedly retired after fracturing a sesamoid later in May: sent to Slovakia. *J. Oxx, Ireland*

ALBERT EINSTEIN (IRE)   2 b.c. (Apr 20) Danehill (USA) 126 – Sunset Cafe (IRE)   **94 p** 68 (Red Sunset 120) [2006 6s⁵ 7s² 7s² Oct 30] 550,000Y: eighth foal: brother to useful Irish 1m winner Albertinelli, closely related to smart 1999 2-y-o 5f/6f (Cheveley Park) winner Seazun (by Zieten) and half-brother to 2 winners, including useful Irish 2003 2-y-o 6f winner Mahogany (by Orpen): dam, Irish 1½m winner, sister to smart middle-distance performer Beeshi: progressive form: still green when ¾-length second of 5 to Confuchias in Killavullan Stakes at Leopardstown final start, losing lead when swerving right over 1f out: will stay 1m: capable of better still. *A. P. O'Brien, Ireland*

ALBERTS STORY (USA)   2 b.g. (Feb 1) Tale of The Cat (USA) 113 – Hazino (USA)   **52** (Hazaam (USA) 113) [2006 6s⁴ 6m⁵ 6m Aug 9] rather leggy, lengthy gelding: modest form in maidens: gelded after final start. *R. A. Fahey*

ALCAZAR (IRE)   11 b.g. Alzao (USA) 117 – Sahara Breeze 85 (Ela-Mana-Mou   **116** 132) [2006 118: 15.5d⁶ 18d² 20m⁶ Oct 1]

'It's never easy training an eleven-year-old. If it was, there would be loads of them in training.' Although Alcazar failed to win for Hughie Morrison during the latest season, the feats achieved with him during a long and troubled career remain astonishing, and provide ample testimony to the patience and skill of his long-time trainer. Despite reportedly suffering a fractured pelvis on three occasions and a leg fracture, as well as having trouble with his tendons and suffering with broken blood vessels, Alcazar was nursed back to the track time after time, winning twelve of his thirty-one starts and earning over £400,000 in prize money. The twelfth and final success came in 2005 when, at the age of ten, Alcazar became the joint oldest horse (along with Yavana's Pace, a horse who similarly had his problems with injury) to win a Group 1 when defeating Reefscape by a neck in the Prix Royal-Oak at Longchamp.

Unraced at two, Alcazar developed into a smart performer at three when trained by John Dunlop, winning on four occasions, including a listed event at Doncaster. He missed the next two seasons, before returning from an absence of thirty-four months to win a useful handicap at Newmarket at 25/1 on his first start for Morrison in October 2001. Alcazar didn't get to the racecourse in 2002, but he remained sound long enough in 2003 to manage two races in a month. A win in the listed 'Further Flight' Stakes at Nottingham was followed by a controversial success in the Sagaro Stakes at Ascot. Alcazar beat Savannah Bay by a neck for the latter win, only for the places to be reversed as Alcazar's rider Micky Fenton had hit the runner-up over the head with his whip in the closing stages. The decision was, however, overturned on appeal a couple of weeks later. Alcazar continued performing to a decent level over the next two seasons before winning a second Sagaro Stakes at its temporary home of Lingfield in 2005. He was raced in France for the last three races of that campaign, winning the Prix Kergorlay at Deauville before finishing runner-up in the Prix du Cadran at Longchamp. Alcazar had been placed in the two previous runnings of the Prix Royal-Oak, and didn't need to improve on those efforts to add the Royal-Oak after his second in the Cadran. Alcazar was seen out three times in the latest season, running particularly well, and showing himself to have retained most of his ability, when a length second to Sergeant Cecil in the Doncaster Cup at York before finishing only sixth behind the same rival in the Prix du Cadran at Longchamp.

The workmanlike Alcazar, who was best held up, stayed two and a half miles and, although he acted on good to firm, was usually raced on ground softer than good. He had run well when sweating and tended to be bandaged. He has been retired. *H. Morrison*

ALCHARINGA (IRE) 4 b.g. Ashkalani (IRE) 128 – Bird In Blue (IRE) 57 (Bluebird (USA) 125) [2006 57: p6g Nov 7] strong gelding: modest maiden at best, lightly raced: barely stays 6f: acts on polytrack and good to firm going. *T. J. Etherington* —

ALCHEMIST MASTER 7 b.g. Machiavellian (USA) 123 – Gussy Marlowe 118 (Final Straw 127) [2006 83: 7g 8.2m⁶ 8f⁵ 7.9g 8.5g⁶ p7.1g Jul 17] leggy, quite good-topped gelding: fairly useful performer: claimed from R. Whitaker £10,000 before final start (fell): was best at 7f/1m: acted on all-weather, firm and good to soft going: wore cheekpieces most starts at 5 yrs: dead. *C. R. Dore* **81**

ALCYON (IRE) 3 b.c. Alhaarth (IRE) 126 – West of Eden (Crofter (USA) 124) [2006 p10g² 10m³ 9.8m* 10m³ Jul 13] €55,000F, €25,000Y: leggy, useful-looking colt: half-brother to several winners, including smart 6f (at 2 yrs)/7f winner Tempting Fate (by Persian Bold) and useful 1m (at 2 yrs)/1¼m winner Clapham Common (by Common Grounds): dam unraced: fairly useful form: won maiden at Ripon in June: good third to Formal Decree in quite valuable handicap at Newmarket final outing: not certain to stay beyond 1¼m: acts on polytrack and good to firm ground: sent to Hong Kong, and renamed Industrial Express. *E. A. L. Dunlop* **93**

ALDERNEY (USA) 2 b.f. (Mar 3) Elusive Quality (USA) – Adonesque (IRE) 106 (Sadler's Wells (USA) 132) [2006 6m* 6m⁵ 7d Sep 30] well-made filly: second foal: dam, Irish 9f/1¼m winner, half-sister to smart 6f/7f performer Danehill Dancer: fairly useful form: won maiden at York in June by 4 lengths: much too free as failed to pro- **93**

gress, fifth to Sander Camillo in Cherry Hinton Stakes and only seventh in listed race (favourite), both at Newmarket: bred to stay 7f: edgy, exuberant sort. *M. A. Jarvis*

AL DHAHAB (USA) 3 b.f. Seeking The Gold (USA) – South of Saturn (USA) 91 – (Seattle Slew (USA)) [2006 57: 10m p12g 11.5m Jul 12] strong filly: maiden: little form since debut at 2 yrs. *C. E. Brittain*

ALECIA (IRE) 2 gr.f. (Feb 2) Keltos (FR) 132 – Ahliyat (USA) 55 (Irish River (FR) **71** 131) [2006 6m⁵ 6g Aug 26] €14,000Y: good-bodied filly: fifth foal: half-sister to 3 winners, including fairly useful Irish 1½m winner Allude (by Darshaan) and 2003 2-y-o 5f winner Truly Wonderful (by Highest Honor): dam, 8.5f winner, half-sister to smart 1½m/1¾m winner Artillery out of half-sister to disqualified Oaks winner Aliysa: 3½ lengths fifth in maiden at Newbury: stiff task in sales race at the Curragh other start: will stay 1m. *C. G. Cox*

ALEKHINE (IRE) 5 b.g. Soviet Star (USA) 128 – Alriyaah 73 (Shareef Dancer (USA) **81** 135) [2006 p10g⁴ p9.5g p10g p10g⁵ p8g p12g 9.7f² 9.2m⁴ 9m² 10m 9.7m p10g p10g* **a75** Nov 1] strong, lengthy gelding: fairly useful handicapper on turf, fair on all-weather: won at Kempton in November: good second at Goodwood ninth start: stays 1¼m: acts on polytrack and firm ground: often wears cheekpieces. *J. R. Boyle*

ALERON (IRE) 8 b.g. Sadler's Wells (USA) 132 – High Hawk 124 (Shirley Heights **77** 130) [2006 78: p13.9g 11.1m* 13.8g⁴ 12m⁶ 12m⁶ 10.1m⁶ 12.3m Aug 25] tall gelding: fair handicapper: won at Hamilton in May: effective at 1¼m, barely stays 2m: acts on dirt/fibresand, soft and good to firm going: usually wears cheekpieces: tried visored/tongue tied: has hung/found little: won over hurdles in September. *J. J. Quinn*

ALESSANDRIA 3 b.f. Sunday Silence (USA) – Tereshkova (USA) 113 (Mr Prospec- **100** tor (USA)) [2006 92p: p12g* 12m 11.9g Jul 8] leggy filly: useful form: reportedly threw a splint early in 2006: impressive winner of minor event at Kempton (by 1¾ lengths from Park Esteem, eased) in May: below that level in Ribblesdale Stakes at Royal Ascot and Lancashire Oaks at Haydock after: stays 1½m: acts on polytrack. *E. A. L. Dunlop*

ALESSANO 4 ch.g. Hernando (FR) 127 – Alessandra 101 (Generous (IRE) 139) [2006 **102** 86: 11g 12d⁴ 11.6f* 14m* 14.8d* 13.1d⁴ 12s³ 12g² Oct 12] workmanlike gelding: useful handicapper: progressed well in 2005, winning at Windsor and Sandown in July and Newmarket (beat Duty by 6 lengths) in August: best other effort when good neck second to Counterpunch at Newmarket: effective at 1½m, will stay 2m: acts on polytrack, firm and good to soft going: tried in cheekpieces, usually blinkered: sometimes wanders: reliable. *G. L. Moore*

ALEVIC (IRE) 2 ch.c. (Apr 6) Tendulkar (USA) 114 – Aster Fields (IRE) 50 (Common – Grounds 118) [2006 p6g 7.5f p7.1m Oct 9] compact colt: no form: tried visored. *J. R. Norton*

ALEVISIA (FR) 3 gr.f. Emperor Jones (USA) 119 – Alminieh (FR) (Highest Honor – (FR) 124) [2006 8g p12g Jun 29] €3,000Y: first foal: dam third at 9f from 2 starts in France: little form: trained by S. Gourdain in France at 2 yrs: tried blinkered. *Noel T. Chance*

ALEXANDER ALLIANCE (IRE) 3 b.f. Danetime (IRE) 121 – Geht Schnell (Fairy **80** King (USA)) [2006 106p: 8s 6f⁵ Jul 14] big, lengthy filly: useful form when winning listed race at the Curragh in 2005: refused to settle when tenth of 13 in 1000 Guineas at Newmarket on reappearance (also tended to hang) and only fifth of 6 when favourite for minor event at Fairyhouse over 2 months later (reportedly clinically abnormal): should prove best short of 1m. *T. Stack, Ireland*

ALEXANDER GOLDRUN (IRE) 5 b.m. Gold Away (IRE) 125 – Renashaan **125** (FR) (Darshaan 133) [2006 12m⁵ 10.5v² 10g* 9.9m² 10m³ 8d³ 10m Dec 10]
　　　　Three of the best European racemares seen in recent years were all retired on the same weekend. Pride, Ouija Board and Alexander Goldrun bowed out at Hong Kong's international meeting in December. Pride went out in a blaze of glory in the Hong Kong Cup, while Ouija Board missed her intended swansong in the Hong Kong Vase after stiffness was detected in a foreleg. Alexander Goldrun's career also ended in anticlimax as she came home well beaten behind Pride. It was Alexander Goldrun's third visit to Sha Tin for an event she won as a three-year-old. That victory in the Hong Kong Cup was Alexander Goldrun's second in Group 1 company, following a success in the Prix de l'Opera at Longchamp on Arc day. Ouija Board went for the Arc itself that year, finishing third to Bago. Alexander Goldrun didn't come across Ouija Board as a four-year-old either, though she met

Pride twice at that age, finishing behind her in both the Champion Stakes at New-market and the Hong Kong Cup, Pride finishing second each time and Alexander Goldrun eighth. As tough as she was, Alexander Goldrun didn't keep her form so well as a four-year-old as she did at three, though she won two more Group 1s, the Pretty Polly Stakes at the Curragh and the Nassau Stakes at Goodwood, the last-named followed by an excellent third to Oratorio and Motivator in the Irish Champion before her form fell away.

Alexander Goldrun met Ouija Board in the first of three encounters in the latest season in the Dubai Sheema Classic at Nad Al Sheba in March. Neither was suited by being held up, the way things unfolded, and they finished out of the places behind Heart's Cry, Alexander Goldrun a place behind Ouija Board in fifth on the only outing of her career over as far as a mile and a half. Alexander Goldrun was still below form when going down by seven lengths to Arc winner Hurricane Run in a three-horse race for the Tattersalls Gold Cup at the Curragh at the end of May. Back at the Curragh in early-July, however, Alexander Goldrun returned to her best to record a second consecutive win in the Audi Pretty Polly Stakes, bringing her total of Group 1 victories to five. The four-year-old Chelsea Rose made her work hard, Alexander Goldrun leading over a furlong out and holding on by a neck, with Red Bloom and Tropical Lady making it a one, two, three, four for the mares and older fillies, ahead of Queen Cleopatra and Ardbrae Lady, the placed fillies in the Irish One Thousand Guineas. Alexander Goldrun had taken in the Falmouth Stakes at Newmarket before Goodwood the previous year, but she wasn't seen out between the Pretty Polly and the Nassau as a five-year-old. That race featured a memorable meeting with Ouija Board who had been busy since the Sheema Classic, running four times and gaining her fifth Group 1 win in the Prince of Wales's Stakes at Royal Ascot. Alexander Goldrun and Ouija Board fought out a pulsating finish to a vintage Nassau, recording the best performances in the race since it was upgraded to Group 1 in 1999. Alexander Goldrun looked in tremendous shape but ran into

Audi Pretty Polly Stakes, the Curragh—Alexander Goldrun (right) wins it for the second year running; Chelsea Rose pushes her all the way, while Red Bloom is third and Tropical Lady (star on cap) fourth

Ouija Board at her very best, going down by a short head after leading narrowly for much of the last two furlongs as the pair went at it hammer and tongs. Alexander Goldrun's performance was better than that when winning the race the previous year, the form at least as good as any shown in her career. She repeated her third of the previous year in the Irish Champion Stakes at Leopardstown (Ouija Board came second), but was well below form in the Sun Chariot Stakes at Newmarket (behind Spinning Queen) and the Hong Kong Cup at Sha Tin on her last two starts, bringing a fine career to a close. Alexander Goldrun's five Group 1 wins came in four different countries and she has thoroughly earned her retirement to the paddocks which she begins with a visit to Galileo.

Alexander Goldrun (IRE) (b.m. 2001)	Gold Away (IRE) (ch 1995)	Goldneyev (b or br 1986)	Nureyev / Gold River
		Blushing Away (ch 1987)	Blushing Groom / Sweet Revenge
	Renashaan (FR) (b 1989)	Darshaan (br 1981)	Shirley Heights / Delsy
		Gerbera (ch 1984)	Lyphard / Greenway

The medium-sized, sturdy Alexander Goldrun is by the high-class miler Gold Away out of the useful Darshaan mare Renashaan who won at up to nine furlongs. The pick of Renashaan's four other winners—she was also represented in the latest season by the fair Irish maiden Rio (by Namid)—is the smart miler Medicis (by Machiavellian), who finished second in the Poule d'Essai des Poulains and the Prix de la Foret. Alexander Goldrun's sire and dam both carried the Wertheimer colours, as did the most famous member of the family, the Prix de l'Arc de Triomphe, Prix Royal-Oak and Prix du Cadran winner Gold River, who appears on both sides of Alexander Goldrun's extended pedigree, as the dam of Gold Away's sire Goldneyev and as a half-sister to the dam of Alexander Goldrun's great grandam Greenway, one of the fastest two-year-olds of 1980. Renashaan was sold by the Wertheimer brothers, carrying Alexander Goldrun, for 30,000 guineas at the December Sales in 2000, before Medicis reached the racecourse. Renashaan changed hands for 640,000 guineas, in foal to Pivotal, at the same venue two months after Alexander Goldrun won the Prix de l'Opera. The Pivotal colt should be due to make his racecourse debut in the next season, with a Sadler's Wells filly to follow. Renashaan's two-year-old Shadowy Figure (by Machiavellian) was in training with Saeed bin Suroor but wasn't seen out. Alexander Goldrun has given her siblings plenty to live up to. Probably best at a mile and a quarter, and effective on any going, she was thoroughly game and genuine. Interestingly, Ouija Board was ridden by eight different jockeys in the course of her career while Alexander Goldrun had the same jockey throughout hers, partnered in all her races—usually held up—by Kevin Manning, number one at the Bolger stable for a decade.
J. S. Bolger, Ireland

ALEXANDER SAPPHIRE (IRE) 5 gr.m. Pennekamp (USA) 130 – Beautiful **54** France (IRE) (Sadler's Wells (USA) 132) [2006 60: p16.5g f16g f16g³ Feb 5] modest performer: stays 2m: acts on fibresand: tried tongue tied/in cheekpieces/blinkered. *N. B. King*

ALEXANDER TANGO (IRE) 2 ch.f. (Apr 28) Danehill Dancer (IRE) 117 – House **101** In Wood (FR) (Woodman (USA) 126) [2006 7m* 7g³ 7m⁵ 8d Sep 23] 56,000F: well-made filly: second foal: dam unraced half-sister to Prix Niel winner Housamix: useful form: won maiden at the Curragh in July: improvement when third to Gaudeamus in Debutante Stakes at Leopardstown and fifth to Miss Beatrix in Moyglare Stud Stakes at the Curragh. 9/1, only seventh of 8 in Fillies' Mile at Ascot: should stay 1m. *T. Stack, Ireland*

ALEXANDROVA (IRE) 3 b.f. Sadler's Wells (USA) 132 – Shouk 94 (Shirley **123** Heights 130) [2006 114: 10.4d² 12g* 12m* 12d* 10m³ Oct 1]
Wide-margin winners of the Oaks aren't necessarily good news for the sport. The relatively high number of clear-cut successes in the race over the years, more than in any other classic, might be taken to suggest the Oaks is in rude health. However, they have often served only to expose a lack of strength in depth among

those taking part in the second fillies' classic, particularly of late. The average winning performance in the Oaks has been in steady decline—judged by Timeform ratings—since the race enjoyed something of a golden age in the 'eighties. During that period, seven-length winner Blue Wind, twelve-length winner Sun Princess, six-length winner Oh So Sharp, five-length winner Unite and four-length winner Diminuendo (it measured five lengths on the photo finish strip) all put up high-class performances or better in running out impressive winners. Since then, Salsabil (five lengths), Jet Ski Lady (ten lengths), Lady Carla (nine lengths), Ouija Board (seven lengths) and the latest winner Alexandrova (six lengths) have continued the trend of the race being won by clear margins, yet, among them, Salsabil alone has put up a high-class performance in the process, an achievement matched in the recent period only by User Friendly, a three-and-a-half-length winner, two years after Salsabil, in 1992.

In most renewals of the Oaks, only a handful of fillies prove capable of running to much more than useful form over Epsom's stiff mile and a half. Indeed, the average performance among those finishing in the first six of late is lower than for the equivalent runners in the first fillies' classic, the One Thousand Guineas over a mile. The Guineas is still a significant Oaks trial for those thought likely to have the stamina, but relatively few realistic candidates tend to emerge from the handful of middle-distance events staged as stepping stones to Epsom. Alexandrova is most unusual among recent winners of the Oaks in having been beaten in a middle-distance trial. Indeed, the vast majority of Oaks winners to have come through the middle-distance trials in recent years have run out most decisive winners of their final race beforehand. There were extenuating circumstances for Alexandrova's defeat. Starting at 2/1-on in the Musidora Stakes at York in mid-May, following heavy ante-post support for Epsom on the strength of her home-work, she looked as though the race would bring her on and ran that way. Hampered soon after the start, Alexandrova led under hands and heels over a furlong from home, only to falter, going down by a length and a quarter to Short Skirt.

Despite her defeat, Alexandrova's two-year-old record, which included a short-head second to Nannina in the Fillies' Mile at Newmarket on her final start, still looked the strongest form on offer for Epsom, with the possible exception of the doubtful stayer Speciosa, supplemented for the Oaks after her all-the-way success in the One Thousand Guineas. With her breeding suggesting she would relish the mile and a half, Alexandrova was a strong favourite for the Vodafone Oaks on the day, starting at 9/4. Her position at the head of the betting had strengthened when ante-post gamble Galatee, also a supplementary entry, had been withdrawn unexpectedly with a high white cell count a few days beforehand. In her absence, in a field of ten, Short Skirt started joint second favourite at 9/2 alongside her stable-companion Riyalma, a decisive winner of the Pretty Polly Stakes at Newmarket last time out. Speciosa was at 5/1 with Cheshire Oaks winner Time On at 7/1 and Guilia,

Vodafone Oaks, Epsom—Alexandrova sweeps into the lead as Rising Cross stumbles; Short Skirt (noseband) takes third ahead of Speciosa (partially hidden by winner)

runner-up in a listed event at Newbury, at 8/1, the only other runner at shorter than 33/1. Conditions had dried out considerably from the soft ground prevalent earlier in the week, but, in a well-run race, Alexandrova was the only runner still galloping strongly at the finish. Ridden with a deal of confidence by Kieren Fallon, Alexandrova was second last on the turn, but came with a sweeping run down the outside to quicken right away in the final two furlongs, increasing the margin between herself and the rest all the way to the line as 33/1-shot Rising Cross got the better of Short Skirt by a length and a quarter for second, despite a bad stumble inside the last furlong. The front-running Speciosa faded into fourth, half a length further behind.

Following Reams of Verse in 1997, Ramruma in 1999 and Ouija Board in 2004, Alexandrova was a fourth winner in the Oaks for her rider. She was a third Oaks winner for her trainer Aidan O'Brien, previously successful in the race with Shahtoush in 1998 and Imagine in 2001. Interestingly, the emergence of Ballydoyle as a significant influence on the Oaks has coincided with a downturn in the fortunes in the event for racing's other superpower, the Maktoum family, certainly compared to their unprecedented run of success in the 'eighties and the first half of the 'nineties. During that period, Sheikh Mohammed won the race four times, with Oh So Sharp, Unite, Diminuendo and Intrepidity, while the promoted Snow Bride, Salsabil, Jet Ski Lady, Balanchine and Moonshell also carried Maktoum colours of some description to success. By contrast, in the last eleven years, only Kazzia, successful for Godolphin in 2002, and Eswarah in 2005, have done so.

Recent years have also brought a decline in the subsequent fortunes of Oaks winners, eight of the last twelve failing to score again as three-year-olds and none of them managing a success outside races for their own sex. Perhaps mindful of the blank drawn by Virginia Waters after her One Thousand Guineas success in the same colours in 2005, Coolmore supremo John Magnier expressed caution about Alexandrova's future immediately after the Oaks, saying 'She's done what she was meant to do, so we'll be careful with her from now.' There is, however, a well-trodden path available to Oaks winners after Epsom, and Alexandrova did race on, enhancing her reputation in the process. She was entered in the Eclipse but continued to do her racing against her own sex. Only five took her on in the Darley Irish Oaks at the Curragh in July when, in the continued absence of Galatee, she started at 2/1-on, despite the presence of Guineas runner-up Confidential Lady, a 5/1-shot after her success in the Prix de Diane. The only other Irish-trained runner was 200/1-shot Flyingit. The race took place on ground firmer than Alexandrova had tackled previously but, again confidently ridden by Fallon, held up in last place, Alexandrova passed her rivals readily as the field bunched two furlongs from home, and, switched to the far rail, galloped on strongly to beat Ribblesdale Stakes runner-up Scottish Stage by four lengths with Rising Cross in third, a length closer than at Epsom.

Darley Irish Oaks, the Curragh—
Alexandrova is again much too good for Rising Cross, the pair split by Scottish Stage

Darley Yorkshire Oaks, York—the confidently-ridden Alexandrova is again impressive;
Short Skirt, Allegretto and the partially-obscured Exhibit One battle it out for the minor placings

Alexandrova was the eleventh filly to complete the Anglo/Irish Oaks double, the others Masaka, Altesse Royale, Juliette Marny, Fair Salinia, Blue Wind, Unite, Diminuendo (dead heated), User Friendly, Ramruma and Ouija Board. Fair Salinia, Diminuendo, User Friendly and Ramruma went on to win the Yorkshire Oaks as well, User Friendly and Ramruma after the race was opened up to older fillies and mares in 1991. Alexandrova became only the fifth to complete the same Group 1 Oaks treble, doing so with the minimum of fuss. Again facing only five rivals in the Darley-sponsored event at York, she was backed from 6/4-on to 9/4-on, attracting several bets of £35,000 and more. Among her opponents, the French four-year-old Shamdala was also a Group 1 winner after her success in the Gran Premio di Milano in June, but Alexandrova outclassed the field from start to finish. Ridden in customary style by Michael Kinane, standing in for the suspended Fallon, she was soon going well, held up, and cruised through to take command in the closing stages, this time proving three and a half lengths too good for Short Skirt, with another three-year-old Allegretto in third and Shamdala tailed off.

User Friendly rounded off her three-year-old season by winning the St Leger and finishing a close second in the Arc. Although tackling a mile and three quarters promised to pose her no problems, Alexandrova was never entered in the Leger. Instead, she was dropped back to a mile and a quarter for the first time since the Musidora Stakes, passing up the chance to tackle the colts in the Arc in favour of easier pickings on the same Longchamp card in the Prix de l'Opera. The race featured a clash with France's leading three-year-old filly Mandesha, who had missed the classics at home but had been considered for the Arc after capping a fine winning run with victory in the Prix Vermeille on the course last time out. Alexandrova was preferred in the betting, starting a shade of odds on. She managed only third, but, back under firmer conditions at the shorter trip, was anything but disgraced as the race went, having a fair amount to do off the turn before storming home to be nearest at the finish under Fallon, going down by three quarters of a length and two and a half lengths to Mandesha and Satwa Queen. Alexandrova was mooted as a possible for the Breeders' Cup Filly & Mare Turf afterwards, but reportedly came back sore from France and was retired for the season.

As John Magnier said after Epsom, Alexandrova, who cost 420,000 guineas at the Newmarket October Yearling Sales, was bred to win the Oaks. Following Salsabil, Intrepidity, Moonshell and Imagine, she is the fifth Oaks winner by Sadler's Wells, putting him alongside the late-nineteenth and early-twentieth century stallion St Simon as the joint most successful sire of winners of the race, one ahead of Hyperion. As his record in the Oaks suggests, Sadler's Wells, who also had the distinction of siring the first three in the race in Imagine's year, has been a strong influence for stamina. There is plenty of stamina on the dam's side of Alexandrova's pedigree as well. Her dam Shouk, who gained her one success in a maiden over an extended mile and a quarter and was placed over a mile and a half, is out of the seven-furlong winner Souk, dam of Golden Quest, runner-up in the Goodwood Cup in 2005. Souk is also the dam of Puce, a smart middle-distance stayer and dam

49

of Pukka, another smart middle-distance performer, as well as the Lancashire Oaks winner Pongee. Alexandrova is the second Oaks runner out of her dam. Her first was the Oaks sixth Magical Romance (by Sadler's Wells's son Barathea), who was sold, in foal to Pivotal, at the December Sales in 2006 for 4.6m guineas, a European record for any thoroughbred bought at auction. Magical Romance, who failed to train on after winning the Cheveley Park Stakes as a juvenile, produced a filly foal later in December over three weeks prematurely. Shouk's first foal Grand Wizard (by Grand Lodge) gained his only success over a mile and a quarter and Saree, a sister to Magical Romance, was a two-year-old winner over seven furlongs.

			Northern Dancer	Nearctic
	Sadler's Wells (USA)		(b 1961)	Natalma
	(b 1981)		Fairy Bridge	Bold Reason
Alexandrova (IRE)			(b 1975)	Special
(b.f. 2003)			Shirley Heights	Mill Reef
	Shouk		(b 1975)	Delsy
	(b 1994)		Souk	Ahonoora
			(b 1988)	Soumana

The precedent for Oaks winners staying in training is less encouraging than the record of Ouija Board at four and five might suggest. User Friendly went on to win the Grand Prix de Saint-Cloud as a four-year-old, but neither Intrepidity, Balanchine, Moonshell, Lady Carla nor Ramruma, the other recent Oaks winners kept in training, managed a single success at the same age. Judged on her Longchamp effort, Alexandrova seems unlikely to prove so versatile as Ouija Board over middle distances at four. Alexandrova has shown her best form at a mile and a half and will stay further. Alexandrova has yet to encounter extremes of ground, but there is little to choose between her efforts on good to firm going and good to soft, though she has given the impression of not being altogether at home on a firmish surface. A smallish, leggy, attractive filly, a good walker but not the best of movers in her faster paces, showing a short, unimpressive action, Alexandrova progressed into a very smart performer from two to three, in some ways belying her physical stature. Game and genuine, as well as consistent, she is usually held up and has a good turn of foot. *A. P. O'Brien, Ireland*

ALEXIAN 3 b.g. Almushtarak (IRE) 122 – Rough Guess (IRE) 52 (Believe It (USA)) **75**
[2006 p7.1g p8.6g³ p8.6g³ 10.9g³ 12.6g³ 10.3g⁶ 10.9m⁴ 12s p13.9g³ p12g p13.9g⁴ **a72**
p12g* Dec 15] 3,500F, £1,300Y: neat gelding: half-brother to winner in Italy by Cyrano
de Bergerac: dam placed at 5f at 2 yrs: fair performer: left R. Hollinshead 17,000 gns after
seventh start: won maiden at Kempton in December: stays 1¾m: acts on polytrack and
good to firm going. *D. W. P. Arbuthnot*

ALEXIA ROSE (IRE) 4 b.f. Mujadil (USA) 119 – Meursault (IRE) (Salt Dome **–**
(USA)) [2006 74: p6g p5.1g f5g⁴ f6g² f6g⁴ 6v 6g 5d 5g 5m 5v Oct 31] leggy, lengthy **a69**
filly: fair handicapper on all-weather, had form on turf earlier in career: effective at 5f/
6f: acts on all-weather, firm and soft going: tends to wander/flash tail: sold 2,000 gns.
A. Berry

ALFIE FLITS 4 b.g. Machiavellian (USA) 123 – Elhilmeya (IRE) 94 (Unfuwain **122**
(USA) 131) [2006 12s* 8.2g² 12m* 10m³ 12s 11.6d* Nov 4] 15,500 3-y-o: tall, good-
topped gelding: second foal: dam, won at 10.5f from 2 starts, out of useful Irish 1m/9f
winner Awayed: smart performer in bumpers, winning 3 from 4 in 2005/6: very smart on
Flat: won maiden at Thirsk in May and listed races at Pontefract (by 2½ lengths from
Camrose) in June and Windsor (best effort when beating Orcadian by 5 lengths, travelling
strongly throughout before readily asserting inside final 2f) in November: stays 1½m:
acts on soft and good to firm going. *G. A. Swinbank*

ALFIE LEE (IRE) 9 ch.g. Case Law 113 – Nordic Living (IRE) 53 (Nordico (USA)) **–**
[2006 46: 5f 5d 5m Jul 24] compact, well-made gelding: poor performer: raced mainly at
5f: acts on fibresand and firm going: tried in headgear: tongue tied. *D. A. Nolan*

ALFIE NOAKES 4 b.g. Groom Dancer (USA) 128 – Crimson Rosella 54 (Polar **95**
Falcon (USA) 126) [2006 94: 10.3m⁵ 12s³ 12m* 12m p16g Jul 15] tall, useful-looking
gelding: useful handicapper: won at Epsom (beat Gavroche by neck) in June: creditable
efforts other starts on turf in 2006: upped markedly in trip, well below form at Lingfield
final outing: best at 1¼m/1½m: acts on soft and good to firm going: held up. *Mrs
A. J. Perrett*

ALFIE TUPPER (IRE) 3 ch.g. Soviet Star (USA) 128 – Walnut Lady 91 (Forzando **88**
122) [2006 79p: 8g³ 7.1m³ 8m 8.3g⁶ 7g 8d Sep 26] leggy, attractive gelding: fairly useful
performer: saddle slipped and unseated rider third start: below form after: not sure to stay
beyond 1m: acts on good to firm ground: free-going sort, usually waited with. *S. Kirk*

ALFONSO 5 ch.g. Efisio 120 – Winnebago 63 (Kris 135) [2006 91: p8.6g⁴ f8g* f8s⁴ 8s **78**
7.1g³ 8.1g 7.2d⁵ 7.2m⁴ 7.2m⁵ 9.2g³ p7.1m Sep 2] good-bodied gelding: has a round **a87**
action: fairly useful on all-weather, fair on turf: won handicap at Southwell in February:
should stay 1¼m: acts on fibresand, soft and good to firm going: often blinkered: none
too consistent. *I. Semple*

ALFREDIAN PARK 2 ch.g. (Mar 10) Bertolini (USA) 125 – Ulysses Daughter (IRE) **77 p**
88 (College Chapel 122) [2006 p8.6g* Dec 29] 15,000Y: second foal: brother to 3-y-o
Come Out Fighting: dam 2-y-o 5.7f winner: 7/2, won maiden at Wolverhampton in December by 1¼ lengths from Snow Dancer, despite looking green: should improve. *S. Kirk*

ALFRESCO 2 b.g. (Feb 20) Mtoto 134 – Maureena (IRE) (Grand Lodge (USA) 125) **59 p**
[2006 6m 7s Oct 10] useful-looking gelding: modest form in maidens 3 months apart:
subsequently gelded: will be suited by 1m/1¼m: open to improvement. *Pat Eddery*

ALFRIDINI 5 ch.g. Selkirk (USA) 129 – Vivre En Paix (Nureyev (USA) 131) [2006 **71**
78: p7g⁴ p10g* p10g 8.3g⁵ 9m 8.2s Oct 18] well-made gelding: fair handicapper: won **a77**
at Lingfield (made all) in January: stays easy 1¼m: acts on polytrack and good to firm
going: blinkered on debut: sold 14,000 gns in October. *D. R. C. Elsworth*

ALF TUPPER 3 b.g. Atraf 116 – Silvery 67 (Petong 126) [2006 66: 12d⁴ 9m 11.5f 8g **62**
Sep 14] tall, rangy gelding: modest maiden: will be best short of 1½m: acts on good to
firm and good to soft going: sold 12,000 gns. *M. H. Tompkins*

ALGARADE 2 b.f. (Feb 9) Green Desert (USA) 127 – Alexandrine (IRE) 78 (Nashwan **77 p**
(USA) 135) [2006 f8g² p8g* Dec 20] second foal: half-sister to 3-y-o Alambic: dam,
1¼m to 13f winner, half-sister to very smart 1¼m performer Last Second (dam of 3-y-o
Aussie Rules) and to dams of Alborada/Albanova and Yesterday/Quarter Moon: fair
form: confirmed debut promise when winning maiden at Kempton in December by length
from Vincennes (pair well clear), making all: will stay 1¼m: sure to continue to progress.
Sir Mark Prescott

ALGHARB 4 b. or br.g. Mujahid (USA) 125 – Actress 73 (Known Fact (USA) 135) **96**
[2006 89: p6g³ 6m 6m 6g³ a6f³ Dec 21] good-topped gelding: useful performer: gelded,
improved to win handicap at Kempton in May: back to form when third in similar event
at Goodwood in August: left W. Haggas, below form final outing: effective at 6f/7f: acts
on polytrack and good to firm going. *A. Manuel, UAE*

ALGOL 2 b.g. (Feb 21) Kyllachy 129 – Heckle 47 (In The Wings 128) [2006 5g⁵ 5f³ 6m² **89**
6m* 6d* 6d³ 6s* Oct 6] 41,000F, 50,000Y: good-bodied gelding: fourth foal: dam, ran 3
times in Britain, later 7f winner in Germany: fairly useful performer: gelded after third
start: won maiden at Catterick in July and nurseries at Ripon in August and York (18 ran)
in October: should stay 7f: acts on soft going, probably on firm: races prominently: sold
100,000 gns, sent to Hong Kong. *J. Howard Johnson*

Celebrated Artist Piran Strange Paints For Sparks Stakes (Serlby), Windsor—
Alfie Flits caps a fine first season on the Flat; Orcadian is his nearest pursuer

ALGORITHM 4 b.f. Danehill Dancer (IRE) 117 – Dominelle 74 (Domynsky 110) **43**
[2006 6g 7f 7.1f 8f f8g 6f³ 6g Jul 22] stocky filly: unimpressive mover: poor maiden:
should stay 1m: acts on firm and good to soft going: blinkered last 2 starts. *T. D. Easterby*

ALHAAJES (USA) 3 b.g. Bahri (USA) 125 – Mamlakah (IRE) 104 (Unfuwain (USA) **91 §**
131) [2006 –p: 12m³ 10.3d³ 10d² 10m² 8m³ Jul 30] rangy gelding: fairly useful maiden:
somewhat flattered when third to Art Deco in Dee Stakes at Chester second start: beaten
in maidens after, twice starting odds on: stays 1½m: one to avoid: sold 20,000 gns in
October, then gelded and sent to Australia. *B. W. Hills*

ALHAITHAM (USA) 3 b.c. Storm Cat (USA) – Bint Salsabil (USA) 110 (Nashwan **91**
(USA) 135) [2006 91: 7g³ 7m 10g⁴ 9m 8m⁶ 8m² 9m* 10m Sep 12] angular, quite attractive colt: fairly useful performer: landed odds in maiden at Redcar in August: likely to
prove best short of 1¼m: raced only on good/good to firm going: tongue tied last 4 starts:
has looked untrustworthy: sold 13,000 gns. *J. L. Dunlop*

AL HAZIM (IRE) 3 b.c. Danehill (USA) 126 – Dathiyna (IRE) (Kris 135) [2006 70: **81**
9.7f 9.9m* p10g⁴ 10g Sep 26] good-topped colt: fairly useful performer: best effort when
winning handicap at Salisbury in August: stays 1¼m: acts on polytrack and good to firm
going: sold 22,000 gns. *L. M. Cumani*

ALI BRUCE 6 b.g. Cadeaux Genereux 131 – Actualite (Polish Precedent (USA) 131) **83**
[2006 81, a87: p7g f7g g7g³ f8s p8g³ p7g⁵ f8g Dec 14] big gelding: fairly useful performer, better on all-weather than turf: left G. L. Moore after sixth start: effective at 6f to
1m: acts on all-weather, good to firm and good to soft going: sometimes wears cheekpieces: sometimes slowly away. *P. A. Blockley*

ALICE AMELIA 3 b.f. Alhaarth (IRE) 126 – Wondrous Maid (GER) (Mondrian **–**
(GER) 125) [2006 50: p6g p12g Aug 23] poor maiden: bred to stay 7f+: reportedly had
breathing problem final outing. *C. R. Egerton*

ALICE HOWE 2 b.f. (Mar 31) Vettori (IRE) 119 – Peacock Alley (IRE) 98 (Salse **–**
(USA) 128) [2006 f8g p8g p9.5g Dec 9] second foal: dam 7f winner who stayed 1m: little
form. *W. R. Muir*

ALICE WHO (IRE) 2 ch.f. (May 17) Spectrum (IRE) 126 – Princesse Sharpo (USA) **–**
(Trempolino (USA) 135) [2006 5s⁴ 5.1d Apr 11] €3,500Y, resold 800Y: seventh foal:
half-sister to 3 winners in Ireland, including useful 9f winner East Tycoon (by Bigstone) and 1¾m winner Keithara (by Entrepreneur): dam French maiden: last both starts.
J. S. Moore

ALI D 8 b.g. Alhijaz 122 – Doppio 62 (Dublin Taxi) [2006 70: 7m 8f⁵ 8m³ 8.1m 8m 8m⁴ **69**
8m⁶ 8g³ 10m 10f p10g⁶ Nov 1] sturdy gelding: fair handicapper: stays 10.5f: acts on fibresand, soft and good to firm ground: tried in cheekpieces: usually held up. *G. Woodward*

ALISDANZA 4 b.f. Namaqualand (USA) – Enchanting Eve 67 (Risk Me (FR) 127) **57**
[2006 59: 9.8m² 9.2m³ 8.3m³ 9.2g⁵ 8.3m⁴ 9f⁶ 11s³ 14g² 14.1m 12d³ f16g⁶ Dec 12] quite
lightly-made filly: modest maiden: left G. A. Swinbank prior to final outing: stays 1¾m:
acts on firm going: has shown signs of temperament. *N. Wilson*

ALISTAIR JOHN 3 b.g. Komaite (USA) – Young Rosein 74 (Distant Relative 128) **59**
[2006 –: 6d 7f p6m* f6g p6g Nov 20] modest performer: easily best effort when winning
maiden at Wolverhampton in October: stays 6f: acts on polytrack: tried tongue tied.
Mrs G. S. Rees

ALITTLEBITLEFT (IRE) 2 ch.c. (Mar 4) Danehill Dancer (IRE) 117 – Sifaara **91**
(IRE) (Caerleon (USA) 132) [2006 7m 7.1m 6m p7.1g³ p8.6g² p7.1g* p8g* p8g² p7.1g³
Dec 29] 52,000Y: good-topped colt: fifth foal. half-brother to fairly useful 6f (at 2 yrs)
and 1¼m winner Mark of Zorro (by Mark of Esteem) and 7f (at 2 yrs) to 1½m winner Mr
Midasman (by Entrepreneur): dam, ran twice in France, out of very smart 7f to 9f winner
Royal Touch: fairly useful performer: improved to win nursery at Wolverhampton in
November and minor event at Lingfield (beat Autograph Hunter 7 lengths) in Decem-
ber: will stay 1¼m: raced on polytrack and good to firm going: blinkered last 4 starts.
R. Hannon

ALITTLERISKIE (IRE) 2 ch.f. (Mar 22) Rossini (USA) 118 – Riskie Things 62 **48**
(Risk Me (FR) 127) [2006 p5g 5s* 5g 6.1s⁵ 6m⁴ p5g 5.1d³ 5m⁴ 5.1f Aug 8] 4,200Y: quite
good-topped filly: third foal: half-sister to fairly useful 2002 2-y-o 5f/6f winner Notty
Bitz (by Darnay), later successful abroad: dam 5f/6f winner, including at 2 yrs: poor
performer: won seller at Warwick in April: stays 6f: acts on soft and good to firm going:
blinkered last 3 starts. *J. S. Moore*

ALKHABAR (USA) 3 b.c. Kingmambo (USA) 125 – Ashraakat (USA) 105 (Danzig   –
(USA)) [2006 –p: 8.2g 10s Oct 18] very big, lengthy colt: well beaten in maidens, looking
most irresolute on reappearance: sold 12,000 gns, sent to Saudi Arabia. *J. L. Dunlop*

AL KHALEEJ (IRE) 2 b.c. (Mar 7) Sakhee (USA) 136 – Mood Swings (IRE) 77   **85 p**
(Shirley Heights 130) [2006 6s p6g* 6s⁵ Oct 6] 130,000Y: good-bodied colt: type to carry
condition: half-brother to several winners, including Irish 7f (at 2 yrs)/1m winner Best
Side (by King's Best) who stayed 1½m, and 2000 2-y-o 6f winner Hurricane Floyd
(by Pennekamp), both useful: dam 2-y-o 6f winner: fairly useful form: won maiden at
Wolverhampton (flashed tail) in July: never-nearer fifth of 18 in nursery at York: will stay
7f/1m: should do better still. *E. A. L. Dunlop*

ALL ABOUT HIM (USA) 3 ch.g. Mt Livermore (USA) – Inscrutable Dancer (USA)   –
(Green Dancer (USA) 132) [2006 7g 6m 6f⁶ 5m 5.1m Aug 28] no form. *N. I. M. Rossiter*

ALL A DREAM 4 br.f. Desert Story (IRE) 115 – Alioli (Nishapour (FR) 125) [2006 –,   –
a81: p12.2g p9.5g Feb 6] fair handicapper: stays 12.2f: acts on all-weather, no form both   **a72**
starts on turf. *Mrs L. Williamson*

ALL BLEEVABLE 9 b.g. Presidium 124 – Eve's Treasure (Bustino 136) [2006 49,   –
a55: f14g⁵ f16g f16g⁵ Jan 17] sturdy gelding: modest performer: stays 2¼m: acts on   **a50**
fibresand and good to soft going. *Mrs S. Lamyman*

ALL CLUED UP (IRE) 3 b.f. King Charlemagne (USA) 120 – Clunie 84 (Inchinor   **54**
119) [2006 6.1g 5g³ 5f³ f6g⁵ p5.1g 5s p5.1g p6g p5g⁵ f5g³ f5g Nov 28] leggy filly: third
foal: half-sister to 1m winner Poker (by Hector Protector) and fairly useful 2004 2-y-o 6f
winner Propellor (by Pivotal), both later successful abroad: dam 6f winner, including at
2 yrs: modest maiden: may be best at 5f: acts on all-weather and firm ground. *Rae Guest*

ALLEGRETTO (IRE) 3 ch.f. Galileo (IRE) 134 – Alleluia 117 (Caerleon (USA) 132)   **115**
[2006 76P: 11.4m⁶ 12.1m* 11.9g* 12d³ 13.9d³ Sep 8] strong filly: smart performer: won
maiden at Chepstow in June and bet365 Lancashire Oaks at Haydock (late into paddock
and on edge, beat Local Spirit by 3 lengths) in July: further improvement when third
at York in Yorkshire Oaks (beaten 4¼ lengths by Alexandrova) and Park Hill Stakes
(2 lengths behind Rising Cross): barely stays 1¾m: acts on good to firm and good to soft
going: reportedly finished lame on reappearance: stays in training. *Sir Michael Stoute*

ALLEVIATE (IRE) 2 br.f. (Feb 9) Indian Ridge 123 – Alleluia 117 (Caerleon (USA)   **64 p**
132) [2006 p7g⁶ p7.1g p8.6g⁶ Nov 7] second foal: half-sister to 3-y-o Allegretto: dam,
1¼m to 2¼m (Doncaster Cup) winner, half-sister to very smart 1¼m performer Last
Second (dam of 3-y-o Aussie Rules) and to dams of Alborada/Albanova and Yesterday/
Quarter Moon: first form in maidens when sixth to Maraca at Wolverhampton final
outing: will be well suited by 1¼m/1½m: likely to prove different proposition in 3-y-o
handicaps. *Sir Mark Prescott*

bet365 Lancashire Oaks, Haydock—the fast-improving Allegretto runs on strongly ahead of Local Spirit

ALLEXINA 4 ch.f. Barathea (IRE) 127 – Grecian Bride (IRE) (Groom Dancer (USA) **111**
128) [2006 12g 10d² 12f³ Jun 18] tall, lengthy filly: third foal: half-sister to 7-y-o Champain Sands: dam unraced half-sister to very smart 11f to 13f winner Gamut out of half-sister to dam of North Light: smart performer: successful in 3 listed events, including at Navan and the Curragh in 2005: respectable seventh in John Porter Stakes at Newbury on reappearance then good 3½ lengths second to Galatee in Blue Wind Stakes at Naas: below-form third to Sina Cova in Noblesse Stakes at Cork final outing: stays 1½m: acts on soft ground. *J. Oxx, Ireland*

ALLISON'S ART (IRE) 2 b.f. (Apr 16) Rock of Gibraltar (IRE) 133 – Ibtikar (USA) **67**
63 (Private Account (USA)) [2006 6m 8.2g⁴ Sep 26] leggy, close-coupled filly: half-sister to several winners, including 1998 2-y-o 7f winner Just Name It (by Miswaki), later successful in USA: dam, staying maiden, closely related to US Grade 1 9f/1¼m winner and Kentucky Derby runner-up Desert Wine and half-sister to dam of Fasliyev and grandam of Les Arcs: fair form in maidens at Yarmouth and Nottingham: probably stays 1m: sold 52,000 gns, sent to USA. *N. A. Callaghan*

ALL IVORY 4 ch.c. Halling (USA) 133 – Ivorine (USA) (Blushing Groom (FR) 131) **109**
[2006 102: 7g⁵ 7m 7d* 8s Oct 6] strong colt: useful performer: best effort in 2006 when successful in valuable totesport.com Handicap for second year running, beating Fullandby by 1¼ lengths at Ascot in September: should prove at least as effective at 1m as 7f: acts on good to firm and good to soft going: wandered seventh outing/swerved right ninth at 3 yrs: sold 180,000 gns, sent to UAE. *R. Charlton*

ALL OF ME (IRE) 2 b.c. (Feb 8) Xaar 132 – Silk Point (IRE) (Barathea (IRE) 127) **80**
[2006 8.2s p7g⁴ p7g² p7.1g* Dec 31] 47,000F, 52,000Y: good-topped, quite attractive colt: first foal: dam unraced out of smart performer up to 1¼m Scimitarra, herself half-sister to top-class sprinter Double Form: fairly useful performer: improved to win maiden at Wolverhampton final start by short head from Soft Morning, getting up late on after carrying head high and hanging left: stays 7f: acts on polytrack: also hung left on debut. *T. G. Mills*

ALLORO 2 ch.c. (Jan 23) Auction House (USA) 120 – Minette 55 (Bishop of Cashel **63**
122) [2006 5.1g 6s⁴ 7.1m 7.1d p8g Nov 8] compact colt: modest maiden: should stay 1m. *D. J. S. ffrench Davis*

ALLOUETTE 3 b.f. Largesse 112 – Alo Ez 100 (Alzao (USA) 117) [2006 49: 9.2f 9m **–**
10.1f 14.1g Aug 24] poor maiden. *W. J. H. Ratcliffe*

ALL QUIET 5 b.m. Piccolo 121 – War Shanty 66 (Warrshan (USA) 117) [2006 86: p8g **87**
p8g⁵ 8.3f³ 8.3m⁴ 7m³ 8.3g³ 7m³ 8m³ p8g⁴ p8g³ Dec 4] leggy mare: fairly useful handicapper: in frame last 8 starts: effective at 7f/1m: acts on polytrack, firm and good to soft ground: usually held up: reliable. *R. Hannon*

ALL RISE (GER) 4 b. or br.f. Goofalik (USA) 118 – Astica (GER) (Surumu (GER)) **?**
[2006 10.5s⁴ 10.3g⁴ 10d 10.1g Aug 16] sister to 3 winners in Germany, including smart 1¼m/1½m performer Acambaro, and half-sister to 2 winners there: dam German 7f/1m

winner: unraced prior to 2006: fourth in maidens at Hanover and Krefeld: left A. Wohler in Germany, well beaten in handicap at Yarmouth final outing. *Ian Williams*

ALLROUNDTHEOUTSIDE 2 ch.g. (Feb 24) Tomba 119 – Misty Goddess (IRE) 63 **56** (Godswalk (USA) 130) [2006 7.1m 8.1m p7g 8.3g 8.2s f6g Nov 28] sturdy gelding: modest maiden: seems to stay 1m: blinkered final outing. *P. R. Chamings*

ALL SQUARE (IRE) 6 ch.g. Bahhare (USA) 122 – Intricacy 65 (Formidable (USA) **44** 125) [2006 p10g p16g Jun 29] poor maiden: left L. Young in Ireland after final 4-y-o start: unraced on Flat in 2005: probably stays 1¼m: acts on polytrack, firm and soft going: tried blinkered/tongue tied: winning hurdler. *R. A. Farrant*

ALL STAR (GER) 6 b.g. Lomitas 129 – Alte Garde (FR) (Garde Royale 120) [2006 82: 20s⁵ May 18] angular gelding: fairly useful performer: well held only start on Flat in 2006: probably better around 2m than 2½m, at least when conditions are testing: acts on soft and good to firm going: has worn blinkers: won over fences in November. *N. J. Henderson*

ALL TALK 2 b.f. (Apr 8) Muhtarram (USA) 125 – Bron Hilda (IRE) 50 (Namaqualand **46** (USA)) [2006 p5g 5s⁵ 5f⁶ p5g⁴ p5.1g⁶ 6f⁵ 6f Jul 6] third foal: dam, maiden, stayed 7f: poor maiden: left I. Wood after seventh start: stays 6f: acts on polytrack and firm ground. *Mrs C. A. Dunnett*

ALL THAT AND MORE (IRE) 4 ch.c. Unfuwain (USA) 131 – Ideal Lady (IRE) **102** (Seattle Slew (USA)) [2006 92: 10.1g* 10.1g 12m 9.9m Aug 1] leggy colt: useful performer: won 4 of first 5 starts, including handicap at Epsom (made all to beat Impeller by 2½ lengths) in April: disappointing after: stays 1¼m: acts on good to firm ground: sold 21,000 gns, sent to UAE. *B. W. Hills*

ALL THE GOOD (IRE) 3 ch.c. Diesis 133 – Zarara (USA) (Manila (USA)) [2006 **101** 79p: 10.2d⁶ 10d 12g⁴ p16g² 14g⁴ 12g⁴ 14d⁶ Nov 3] close-coupled colt: useful handicapper: won at Newmarket in September and Musselburgh (beat Piety by 2 lengths) in November: best at 1¾m/2m: acts on polytrack, raced only on good/good to soft going on turf. *G. A. Butler*

ALLY MAKBUL 6 b.m. Makbul 104 – Clarice Orsini (Common Grounds 118) [2006 – f7g Dec 12] modest performer in 2004: missed 2005: tailed off only outing in 2006: best form at 6f to 8.5f: acts on all-weather, raced only on good/good to firm ground on turf. *Ian Emmerson*

ALL YOU NEED (IRE) 2 b.g. (Mar 27) Iron Mask (USA) 117 – Choice Pickings **80** (IRE) (Among Men (USA) 124) [2006 6f³ 6f² 5d Sep 29] €11,000Y, 10,000 2-y-o: rather leggy gelding: first foal: dam unraced out of half-sister to dam of 5-y-o Grey Swallow: fairly useful maiden: twice placed at York: found little final start: will stay 7f: acts on firm going. *R. Hollinshead*

ALMAH (SAF) 8 b.m. Al Mufti (USA) 112 – Jazz Champion (SAF) (Dancing Champ **80** (USA)) [2006 12g⁵ 15.9m³ 21m 16.1d⁴ Aug 12] big mare: fairly useful handicapper: unraced on Flat in 2005: creditable efforts first 2 starts in 2006: stays 2m: acts on good to firm going: wears blinkers nowadays: has looked tricky ride. *Miss Venetia Williams*

ALMANSHOOD (USA) 4 b. or br.g. Bahri (USA) 125 – Lahan 117 (Unfuwain (USA) **81** 131) [2006 77: p9.5g² p9.5g 10d 9.8m p10g p10g Dec 16] big, good sort: fluent mover: fairly useful performer on all-weather, formerly fair on turf: stays 1¼m: acts on polytrack, good to firm and good to soft going: tried blinkered/visored (looked temperamental): gelded after second outing. *P. L. Gilligan*

ALMATY EXPRESS 4 b.g. Almaty (IRE) 113§ – Express Girl 75 (Sylvan Express **66** 117) [2006 66: p5.1g² p5.1g f5g p5.1g* p5.1g³ p5g³ 5g⁵ 5g 5m p5.1m 5s p5.1g⁶ p5.1g⁵ **a72** p6g³ p5.1g² Dec 31] smallish gelding: fair handicapper: won at Wolverhampton in February: best at 5f: acts on polytrack and any turf going: wears blinkers/cheekpieces: often makes running. *J. R. Weymes*

ALMERITA (GER) 3 b.f. Medicean 128 – Averna (Heraldiste (USA) 121) [2006 100: **110** 8v* 8v² 11d* 10g³ 9f⁵ 10s Oct 22] fifth foal: half-sister to 2 winners, including useful German 11f/1½m winner Aviane (by Winged Love): dam unraced: smart performer: won minor event at Dusseldorf at 2 yrs, listed race at Cologne in April and Henkel Preis der Diana at Dusseldorf (by neck from Karavel) in June: creditable efforts when 2 lengths second to Lolita in German 1000 Guineas at Dusseldorf, 1½ lengths third to Lord of England in Grosser Dallmayr-Preis at Munich and 1¾ lengths third to Ready's Gal in Grade 2 Canadian Stakes at Woodbine: below form in E. P. Taylor Stakes at Woodbine final start: stayed 11f: acted on any going: visits Galileo. *W. Hickst, Germany*

ALMISQ (USA) 5 ch.m. Diesis 133 – Inscrutable Dancer (USA) (Green Dancer (USA) – 132) [2006 46: p10g Nov 27] poor maiden: tried blinkered/in cheekpieces. *Miss D. Mountain*

ALMIZAN (IRE) 6 b.g. Darshaan 133 – Bint Albaadiya (USA) 108 (Woodman (USA) **69** 126) [2006 82: 12d 12m³ 12.6m⁶ p16g⁵ Dec 15] leggy, angular gelding: fair handicapper: stays 21f: acts on polytrack, firm and soft going: tried visored at 4 yrs, blinkered last 4 starts: won over hurdles in November. *G. L. Moore*

ALMONDILLO (IRE) 2 b.g. (Mar 27) Tagula (IRE) 116 – Almond Flower (IRE) – (Alzao (USA) 117) [2006 7.1m Jul 7] strong, stocky gelding: 16/1, reportedly lost action (tailed off) in maiden: subsequently gelded. *C. F. Wall*

ALMORA GURU 2 b.f. (Mar 15) Ishiguru (USA) 114 – Princess Almora 88 (Pivotal **58** 124) [2006 5g 6s 5f⁴ 5.1g⁵ 5.1f⁶ 5m² 5m⁶ 5m Sep 11] 4,000Y: close-coupled filly: first foal: dam, 6f winner, half-sister to useful performer up to 2m Rada's Daughter: modest maiden: raced at 5f/6f: acts on firm and soft going. *W. M. Brisbourne*

ALMOWJ 3 b.g. Fasliyev (USA) 120 – Tiriana (Common Grounds 118) [2006 64: p6g **61** p8g⁶ 7m⁵ p8g 8m p8.6g² 7g⁶ 7m 7.1g 8m f7g⁶ p8g p6g⁶ f7g⁵ Dec 28] sturdy gelding: modest maiden: stays 8.6f: acts on polytrack and good to firm ground, probably on fibresand: tried blinkered/in cheekpieces: hung left third start. *C. E. Brittain*

ALMUDO (IRE) 2 b.g. (Mar 19) Almutawakel 126 – Doubleuceeone 52 (Compton – Place 125) [2006 8.1m 8.1m Sep 7] last in maidens. *B. Palling*

ALNWICK 2 b.g. (Apr 19) Kylian (USA) – Cebwob 85 (Rock City 120) [2006 p6g 7m **57** 7g p7.1m Oct 2] close-coupled gelding: modest maiden. *P. D. Cundell*

ALOCIN (IRE) 3 b.g. Titus Livius (FR) 115 – Poker Dice (Primo Dominie 121) [2006 **74** 75: 7v 7s 5.8m⁵ 6d 6s 8.2s Oct 18] €50,000Y: third foal: half-brother to useful Irish 6f winner Cheddar Island (by Trans Island): dam unraced daughter of Flying Childers Stakes winner Poker Chip: fair maiden: left John Quinn in Ireland €2,500, well beaten both starts in Britain: stays 1m: acts on soft and good to firm going: tried blinkered/in cheekpieces: inconsistent. *A. D. Brown*

ALONE IT STANDS (IRE) 3 b.g. King Charlemagne (USA) 120 – Golden Concorde – (Super Concorde (USA) 128) [2006 7d 5s Aug 19] compact gelding: well held in maidens at Galway and Ripon. *D. Nicholls*

ALONG THE NILE 4 b.g. Desert Prince (IRE) 130 – Golden Fortune 102 (Forzando **93** 122) [2006 84: 8.1g² 8.1f 8m* 8m 7f 8d 9.9g² 10g 10m² 10.4s Oct 6] strong, lengthy gelding: fairly useful handicapper: won at Newcastle in June: good efforts when runner-up after: stays 1¼m: best form on good/good to firm ground: tongue tied nowadays: held up: none too consistent. *K. G. Reveley*

ALONSO DE GUZMAN (IRE) 2 b.g. (May 14) Docksider (USA) 124 – Addaya – (IRE) (Persian Bold 123) [2006 6m p6g 5.1g Oct 17] well held in maidens: should be suited by 7f/1m. *J. R. Boyle*

ALOVERA (IRE) 2 ch.f. (Feb 6) King's Best (USA) 132 – Angelic Sounds (IRE) (The **93** Noble Player (USA) 126) [2006 6g* 8g⁴ 7d Sep 30] €70,000F, €320,000Y: leggy, attractive filly: sister to 4-y-o Army of Angels and half-sister to several winners, including Irish 5f winner Alegranza (by Lake Coniston) and 1999 2-y-o 5f winner Seraphina (by Pips Pride), both useful: dam, Irish 2-y-o 5f winner, half-sister to very smart 6f/7f performer Mount Abu: fairly useful form: won maiden at Windsor (beat Blue Echo by short head) in August: better form when 3½ lengths fourth of 5 in Prix d'Aumale at Chantilly: only ninth in listed race at Newmarket final start (softer ground), weakening: stays 1m. *M. R. Channon*

ALPAGA LE JOMAGE (IRE) 4 b.g. Orpen (USA) 116 – Miss Bagatelle 70 **– §** (Mummy's Pet 125) [2006 84§, a68§: f6g* p7.1g² p7.1g⁴ p6g⁴ f6g f5g⁵ p6g³ p6g² f6g⁵ **a71 §** p6g 5.9g May 18] lengthy, quite good-topped gelding: fair performer: won handicap at Southwell in January: stays easy 7f: acts on all-weather, firm and soft ground: tried in blinkers/cheekpieces: tends to hang/carry head high: not one to trust. *M. J. Polglase*

ALPES MARITIMES 2 b.g. (Jan 26) Danehill Dancer (IRE) 117 – Miss Riviera 103 **82** (Kris 135) [2006 7m 7.1m⁵ 8m² 10d⁴ Oct 2] big, good-bodied gelding: fourth foal: half-brother to 1½m winner Super Cannes (by Alzao): dam, 2-y-o 6f winner (later best at 7f/ 1m), half-sister to useful winners Miss Riviera Golf (at 1m) and Miss Corniche (up to 1¼m): fairly useful maiden: twice in frame at Pontefract: will prove best up to 1¼m. *G. Wragg*

ALPHA JULIET (IRE) 5 b.m. Victory Note (USA) 120 – Zara's Birthday (IRE) 71 –
(Waajib 121) [2006 14.1f Jun 24] leggy mare: poor maiden: missed 2005: showed
nothing only 5-y-o start: should stay 1½m. *C. J. Teague*

ALPHUN (IRE) 4 b.g. Orpen (USA) 116 – Fakhira (IRE) 83 (Jareer (USA) 115) [2006 –
60: f11g Dec 28] lightly-raced maiden: virtually refused to race final 3-y-o outing: well
beaten only outing in 2006: tried visored. *G. A. Swinbank*

ALPINE HIDEAWAY (IRE) 13 b.g. Tirol 127 – Arbour (USA) 76 (Graustark) [2006 –
53: 8.5m Aug 16] good-topped gelding: modest performer: well held only outing on Flat
in 2006: tried blinkered/visored, usually wears cheekpieces. *J. S. Wainwright*

ALPINE REEL (IRE) 5 b.g. Danehill Dancer (IRE) 117 – Alpine Flair (IRE) (Tirol **102**
127) [2006 88p: p8.6m² p9.5g³ p9.5m* p10g² p10g* p12.2s⁴ Dec 15] useful handicapper,
lightly raced: progressed again in 2006, winning at Wolverhampton (by 2½ lengths
from Del Mar Secret) in November and Kempton (by head from Fusili) in December:
creditable fourth to Sweet Indulgence at Wolverhampton final start: stays 1½m: acts on
polytrack and good to firm ground. *W. R. Swinburn*

ALQAAB (USA) 3 b.g. Silver Hawk (USA) 123 – Guerre Et Paix (USA) (Soviet Star **92**
(USA) 128) [2006 11g 10.2g⁵ 10m* 12g Jun 28] $500,000Y: strong, heavy-topped geld-
ing: third foal: half-brother to winner in USA by Quiet American: dam, useful French
2-y-o 1m winner (later successful in USA), half-sister to useful 1¼m winner Freedom
Flame: fairly useful form: much improved to win maiden at Lingfield in May: beaten
long way out on handicap debut final outing (gelded after): should stay 1½m: raced only
on good/good to firm going: sold 80,000 gns, joined N. Meade in Ireland. *M. P. Tregoning*

ALQAAYID 5 b.g. Machiavellian (USA) 123 – One So Wonderful 121 (Nashwan **66 §**
(USA) 135) [2006 51§: f11g⁶ f12g p10g⁵ p10g² p9.5g⁴ p10g p10g 11g² 10m² 9.5d² 10.5g⁵ **a56 §**
9g²ᵈ 9d p12g Oct 29] sturdy gelding: fair maiden on turf, modest on all-weather: stays
1¼m: acts on polytrack and good to firm going: tried blinkered: ungenuine. *P. W. Hiatt*

AL QASI (IRE) 3 b.c. Elnadim (USA) 128 – Delisha (Salse (USA) 128) [2006 8m⁶ **117 p**
p6g* 6f* 6d² 6s* 6d* Sep 22] 28,000F, 37,000Y: good-topped, attractive colt: fifth foal:
half-brother to winners up to 9f/1¼m in Italy by Victory Note and Be My Guest: dam,
German 1m winner, half-sister to very smart Hong Kong 1m/1¼m performer Olympic
Express: smart form: unraced at 2 yrs: progressed well in 2006, winning maiden at
Lingfield and handicap at York in July and handicaps at Ripon (by 4 lengths from Greek
Renaissance) in August and Ascot (beat Burning Incense 2 lengths) in September: will
prove as effective at 5f as 6f: acts on polytrack, firm and soft going: raced freely and
tended to hang left on debut: likely to progress further. *P. W. Chapple-Hyam*

AL RAAHI 2 b.c. (Mar 26) Rahy (USA) 115 – Nasmatt 96 (Danehill (USA) 126) [2006 **72**
7.1m⁶ 7f⁵ 7.2m² 7.5g² 7m p8g 8s Oct 21] compact colt: second foal: dam, 2-y-o 6f winner,
closely related to smart 1998 2-y-o sprinter Bint Allayl and smart performer up to 7f
Kheleyf: fair maiden: second at Ayr and Beverley (nursery): stays 1m: acts on polytrack
and firm going: sold 12,000 gns. *M. R. Channon*

AL RAYANAH 3 b.f. Almushtarak (IRE) 122 – Desert Bloom (FR) (Last Tycoon 131) **70**
[2006 62: p7g f8g* 10s⁵ 8m⁵ 8m⁵ 12v⁴ 8m² 10d 8.2f* 8f³ 10.1f⁴ 7m⁵ 8m² 8.1d⁴ 7d³ 7d⁵
8d⁴ Oct 27] fair performer: won maiden at Southwell in February and seller at Nottingham in July: stays 1¼m: acts on fibresand, firm and soft going: sometimes slowly away:
has hung: reportedly lost tooth in stall penultimate outing. *G. Prodromou*

ALSADAA (USA) 3 b.g. Kingmambo (USA) 125 – Aljawza (USA) 86 (Riverman **79**
(USA) 131) [2006 87p: 8d⁶ 8m⁴ p7g Oct 15] close-coupled, quite attractive gelding: fair
maiden: gelded after second start: stays 1m: acts on good to firm ground: tongue tied at
3 yrs: very coltish on reappearance, on toes next time: sold 5,000 gns, joined M. Easterby.
J. H. M. Gosden

AL SHEMALI 2 ch.c. (Mar 14) Medicean 128 – Bathilde (IRE) 102 (Generous (IRE) **97 p**
139) [2006 7.1m 7s* Oct 10] 110,000Y: good-bodied colt: fourth foal: half-brother to
5-y-o Tungsten Strike and fairly useful 2000 2-y-o 7f winner Baillieston (by Indian
Ridge): dam, 10.4f winner who was suited by 1½m, half-sister to smart French performers up to around 1½m Hijaz and Crimson Quest: much improved from debut (hampered)
to win maiden at Newcastle in October by ¾ length from Gemology (pair 11 lengths
clear), merely pushed out: will be well suited by 1¼m/1½m: already useful, and sure to
go on and win more races. *Sir Michael Stoute*

ALTAR (IRE) 2 b.c. (Apr 18) Cape Cross (IRE) 129 – Sophrana (IRE) (Polar Falcon **77**
(USA) 126) [2006 7g⁶ 7.1g⁴ 8.1d Sep 13] €44,000F, 40,000Y: good-topped colt: fourth
foal: half-brother to Irish 9.5f winner Jemmy's Flame (by Grand Lodge): dam French

9.5f/10.5f winner: fair maiden: fourth to Big Robert at Sandown: should stay 1m/1¼m. *R. Hannon*

ALTAY 9 b.g. Erins Isle 121 – Aliuska (IRE) 70 (Fijar Tango (FR) 127) [2006 9.9g* 12s* **87** Sep 22] tall gelding: has a round action: fairly useful handicapper: missed 2005: won both starts in 2006, at Beverley and Ascot (amateurs, leader broke down final 1f): effective at 1¼m to 13f: acts on polytrack, firm and soft going: tried in cheekpieces: usually races prominently. *R. A. Fahey*

ALTENBURG (FR) 4 b.g. Sadler's Wells (USA) 132 – Anna of Saxony 111 (Ela- **88** Mana-Mou 132) [2006 –: 10d⁵ 10g² 10d³ 12g² 14m⁵ 13.3g³ p12g³ Sep 18] good-topped gelding: good walker: fairly useful maiden: placed 5 times in 2006: stays 1¾m: unraced on extremes of going: has shown signs of temperament. *Mrs N. Smith*

ALTERNATIVE 2 ch.c. (Mar 25) Dr Fong (USA) 128 – Oatey 68 (Master Willie 129) **87** [2006 5.1d² 5.1d* 5d 5g⁵ 5m³ 5d⁶ 5g* Dec 17] 20,000Y: smallish, attractive colt: fourth living foal: half-brother to 5-y-o Jomus: dam, 5f winner, half-sister to 1½m to 2m per- former Hateel and winner up to 11.5f Munwar, both smart: fairly useful performer: won maiden at Bath in April: stiff task in Cornwallis Stakes at Ascot (respectable 9 lengths sixth to Alzerra) sixth start before sold from R. Beckett 33,000 gns: won minor event at Dos Hermanas in December: will stay at least 6f: yet to race on extremes of going. *J. Calderon, Spain*

ALTESSA (IRE) 3 b.f. Desert Style (IRE) 121 – Savona (IRE) 70 (Cyrano de Bergerac **–** 120) [2006 7m⁶ Jun 30] 5,500Y: fourth foal: half-sister to 2001 2-y-o 6f winner London Follies (by Danehill Dancer): dam, maiden, should have stayed 7f: 10/1, well beaten in maiden at Newcastle, slowly away. *E. J. Alston*

AL THARIB (USA) 2 b.c. (Mar 28) Silver Hawk (USA) 123 – Ameriflora (USA) **87 p** (Danzig (USA)) [2006 7m³ 7d³ Sep 29] $475,000Y: strong, well-made colt: brother to 3 winners, notably high-class Japanese performer up to 12.5f Grass Wonder and smart US Grade 1 9f winner Wonder Again, and half-brother to 2 winners in USA: dam unraced sister to US Grade 1 9f winner Tribulation, herself dam of smart winner up to 11f Coshoc- ton (by Silver Hawk): promising third in maidens, behind Dijeerr at Leicester and Desert Dew at Newmarket (still green): will stay at least 1¼m: sure to progress further and win races at 3 yrs. *Sir Michael Stoute*

ALTILHAR (USA) 3 b.g. Dynaformer (USA) – Al Desima 93 (Emperor Jones (USA) **86** 119) [2006 76+: 8.3g 12g 10m 11.6m 11.5m² 10m* 10m* 10g⁴ Sep 12] robust gelding: fairly useful handicapper: improved to win at Brighton (edged left) in August and San- down in September: stays 11.5f: acts on polytrack and good to firm going: blinkered last 4 starts: won over hurdles in November. *G. L. Moore*

ALTITUDE DANCER (IRE) 6 b.g. Sadler's Wells (USA) 132 – Height of Passion **–** (Shirley Heights 130) [2006 –: 16f⁶ Jun 13] smallish gelding: fair handicapper in 2004: well held both subsequent starts on Flat: blinkered once at 2 yrs: dead. *A. Crook*

ALUCICA 3 b.f. Celtic Swing 138 – Acicula (IRE) 96 (Night Shift (USA)) [2006 p7.1g **–** Feb 10] third foal: half-sister to 2003 2-y-o 5f/6f seller winner Raphoola (by Raphane): dam 2-y-o 5f/6f winner who stayed 7f: 100/1, slowly away and always behind in maiden at Wolverhampton. *D. Shaw*

ALUGAT (IRE) 3 b.g. Tagula (IRE) 116 – Notley Park 71 (Wolfhound (USA) 126) **78** [2006 71: 5g⁴ 6m 5m 5f⁴ 5m² 5d* 5m³ 5s⁴ 5d³ 5d* 5s* 5d Nov 3] sturdy gelding: fair handicapper: won at Musselburgh in August and Catterick (2) in October: best form at 5f: acts on soft and good to firm going: tried visored, usually wears cheekpieces nowadays: usually races up with pace. *Mrs A. Duffield*

ALUJAWILL (IRE) 3 b.c. Erhaab (USA) 127 – El-Libaab 84 (Unfuwain (USA) 131) **–** [2006 p10g 10.2m 10s Oct 18] well held in maidens. *J. G. M. O'Shea*

ALWARIAH 3 b.f. Xaar 132 – Signs And Wonders 75§ (Danehill (USA) 126) [2006 61: **63** f6g⁵ 10d⁶ 7f⁵ p7g 7f³ 5f⁶ 6f 6d³ 6m⁴ 6g Sep 14] smallish, lengthy filly: modest maiden: stays 7f: acts on firm and good to soft going. *C. E. Brittain*

ALWAYS A STORY 4 b.g. Lake Coniston (IRE) 131 – Silk St James (Pas de Seul **43** 133) [2006 7f 6m⁵ 7f f7g Nov 2] lightly-raced maiden: poor form: blinkered final outing. *Miss D. Mountain*

ALWAYS BAILEYS (IRE) 3 ch.g. Mister Baileys 123 – Dubiously (USA) (Jolie Jo **73** (USA)) [2006 81: 8f⁴ 10.1m⁴ 10g 11m⁶ 12d² 11.8d⁴ p12.2s* Dec 14] tall gelding: fair performer: claimed from M. Johnston £10,000 after sixth start: barely stays 1½m: acts on firm and good to soft ground: failed to handle track at Epsom second start: often looks hard ride. *T. Wall*

ALWAYS BEST 2 b.g. (Apr 11) Best of The Bests (IRE) 122 – Come To The Point **70** (Pursuit of Love 124) [2006 7f 7.1m 7m* 7m 7m 8f² 10g³ 8.3g³ p8.6g Nov 3] 7,000Y: tall gelding: third foal: half-brother to 4-y-o The Pen: dam, unraced, out of half-sister to 2000 Guineas winner Tirol: fair performer: won maiden at Leicester in July: placed 3 times in nurseries: stays 1¼m: acts on firm going: jinked right/unseated debut: gelded after final start. *M. Johnston*

ALWAYS EMIRATES (USA) 3 b.c. Danzig (USA) – Country Belle (USA) 108 **77** (Seattle Slew (USA)) [2006 87: 6f² 7m Jun 15] strong, well-made colt: just fair maiden in 2006, reportedly suffered from breathing problem in latter): stays 7f: best effort on good to firm going: has left Godolphin. *Saeed bin Suroor*

ALWAYS ESTEEMED (IRE) 6 b.g. Mark of Esteem (IRE) 137 – Always Far (USA) **103 d** (Alydar (USA)) [2006 104d: p8.6g⁴ p8.6g³ p8.6g³ 8s 8.1g p7g⁵ May 23] big, lengthy gelding: useful performer: creditable efforts in frame at Wolverhampton first 3 starts, 2 lengths third to Nayyir in minor event on second occasion: well below form last 3 outings, in claimer on final one: best around 1m: acts on polytrack, firm and good to soft ground: wears blinkers/cheekpieces: usually races prominently: tends to hang: unreliable. *K. A. Ryan*

ALWAYS FRUITFUL 2 b.c. (Apr 22) Fruits of Love (USA) 127 – Jerre Jo Glanville **90** (USA) (Skywalker (USA)) [2006 6g* 6d² 6m³ 7m Jun 24] angular, quite good-topped colt: has a fluent action: brother to 2005 2-y-o 7f winner Fruit Salad and half-brother to several winners, including 5-y-o Parkview Love: dam US 2-y-o 6f winner: fairly useful form: won maiden at Ripon in May: placed in minor event at Pontefract and listed race at Epsom (third to Sadeek): favourite, only seventh in Chesham Stakes at Royal Ascot: will stay 1m+. *M. Johnston*

ALWAYS SPARKLE (CAN) 2 ch.c. (Jun 10) Grand Slam (USA) 120 – Dancing All **60** Night (USA) (Nijinsky (CAN) 138) [2006 8.1m 7.1d Sep 16] better run in maidens second start (dictated). *B. Palling*

ALWAYS STYLISH (IRE) 3 b.g. Nashwan (USA) 135 – Kafezah (FR) 93 (Penne- **53** kamp (USA) 130) [2006 11.5f⁵ p13g⁵ Sep 29] modest form in maidens at Yarmouth (very green) and Lingfield: sold 7,500 gns. *M. Johnston*

ALWAYS TURN LEFT (IRE) 3 b.f. King's Theatre (IRE) 128 – Light-Flight (IRE) **66 ?** (Brief Truce (USA) 126) [2006 40+: p8g 8m⁵ 11.6m 10f⁴ Sep 18] good-topped filly: modest maiden: seemingly easily best effort on second outing: should stay 1¼m+: acts on good to firm going: wandered final start. *H. S. Howe*

ALZARMA 4 b.g. Alzao (USA) 117 – Skimra 91 (Hernando (FR) 127) [2006 55: f8g³ **55** f7g⁶ p7.1g f7g 10.2g May 2] smallish, lightly-made gelding: modest maiden: stays 1m: acts on all-weather and any turf going: tried in cheekpieces/blinkered. *J. Gallagher*

ALZERRA (UAE) 2 b.f. (Feb 24) Pivotal 124 – Belle Argentine (FR) 113 (Fijar Tango **108** (FR) 127) [2006 6d³ 6m* 6m² 6m⁵ 5.2g³ 5d* 5d* Oct 7] useful-looking filly, unfurnished at 2 yrs: has a quick action: sixth foal: half-sister to useful 2003 2-y-o 6f/7f winner Matloob (by Halling) and 1m winner Saaryeh (by Royal Academy): dam, French 1m winner (including at 2 yrs) who stayed 10.5f, out of half-sister to high-class French middle-distance performer Lovely Dancer: useful performer: won maiden at Haydock in June, listed race at Ayr (by 1¼ lengths from Holdin Foldin) in September and Willmott Dixon Cornwallis Stakes at Ascot in October, in last-named beating Hoh Mike by 1¾ lengths, soon niggled in rear but taking control over 1f out: also 5 lengths second to Sander Camillo in Cherry Hinton Stakes at Newmarket third start: will stay 7f, probably 1m: acts on good to firm and good to soft going: sent to UAE. *M. R. Channon*

AMA DE CASA (USA) 2 ch.f. (Mar 28) Grand Slam (USA) 120 – Gold Ransom **64** (USA) (Red Ransom (USA)) [2006 6g⁴ p6g⁵ p5g⁴ p5.1g² Nov 25] $122,000Y, $270,000 2-y-o: third foal: sister to winner in USA and half-sister to winner there by Marquetry: dam unraced: modest maiden: may prove better at 6f than 5f: tongue tied last 2 starts: sold 10,000 gns, sent to USA. *J. Noseda*

AMADEUS WOLF 3 b.c. Mozart (IRE) 131 – Rachelle (IRE) (Mark of Esteem (IRE) **120** 137) [2006 118: 8m 6m⁵ 6m⁴ 6.5g³ 5s² 6s³ 5m⁵ Oct 1] good-topped, attractive colt: impresses in appearance: very smart performer: successful 3 times in 2005, including in Middle Park Stakes at Newmarket: stamina stretched when seventh to George Washington in 2000 Guineas at Newmarket on reappearance: returned to sprinting, best efforts when length fourth to Les Arcs in July Cup at Newmarket, 2 lengths second to Reverence

Duddy McDonald Heeney Irish National Stud's "Amadeus Wolf"

in Nunthorpe Stakes at York, 1½ lengths third to same rival in Sprint Cup at Haydock and 2¼ lengths fifth to Desert Lord in Prix de l'Abbaye at Longchamp: effective at 5f/6f: acts on soft and good to firm going: has had 2 handlers. *K. A. Ryan*

AMANDA CARTER 2 b.f. (Mar 18) Tobougg (IRE) 125 – Al Guswa 98 (Shernazar – 131) [2006 7g 8m Sep 21] 18,000Y: leggy filly: half-sister to several winners, including useful 7f (at 2 yrs) to 1½m winner Tough Leader (by Lead On Time) and fairly useful 1¼m to 2¼m winner King Flyer (by Ezzoud): dam Irish 1m (at 2 yrs) and 1¼m winner: no show in maidens. *R. A. Fahey*

AMANDA'S LAD (IRE) 6 b.g. Danetime (IRE) 121 – Art Duo 86 (Artaius (USA) **52** 129) [2006 57: f5g f5g* f5g* f6g f5s f5g 5.2f 5f 5m 6m⁶ 5m⁶ 5g 5d f6g f5g f6g f5g³ **a63** Dec 29] tall gelding: modest performer, better on all-weather than turf: won 2 banded races at Southwell in January: effective at 5f to 7f: acts on all-weather, firm and good to soft going: often races prominently/looks none too keen. *M. C. Chapman*

AMARETTO VENTURE 2 b.f. (Apr 22) Tobougg (IRE) 125 – Cc Canova (Millkom – 124) [2006 5m 7d 6m Sep 11] 10,000Y: leggy filly: second foal: dam unraced half-sister to useful 6f/7f performer Marbella Silks: behind in maidens. *J. J. Quinn*

AMAZIN 4 b.g. Primo Dominie 121 – Aegean Blue (Warning 136) [2006 87: p8.6g p6g⁶ **72** p7g p8.6g⁴ p8.6g p8g⁵ 7d 7g³ May 1] tall gelding: fair performer: stays 8.6f: acts on polytrack, firm and good to soft going: usually blinkered/in cheekpieces nowadays: often races freely: tends to be slowly away: sold 4,000 gns. *N. P. Littmoden*

AMAZING CHARLIE (IRE) 3 b.f. King Charlemagne (USA) 120 – Amazonian **61** (CAN) (Geiger Counter (USA)) [2006 7g⁵ 7f⁵ 10f³ 11g 8g* 7v 11v³ 8g⁶ Dec 3] sturdy filly: third foal: half-sister to minor winner in USA by Matty G: dam won 12 races in Canada from 6f to 8.5f: modest form in maidens for Mrs A. Perrett first 3 starts: won minor event at Madrid in October: stays 11f: acts on any ground. *Ms J. Bidgood, Spain*

AMAZING KING (IRE) 2 b.c. (May 19) King Charlemagne (USA) 120 – Kraemer **63**
(USA) (Lyphard (USA) 132) [2006 7m 6m⁶ 7.1d⁵ 8g⁶ Oct 13] rather leggy colt: modest
maiden: should stay 1m: best run on good to soft going. *W. G. M. Turner*

AMAZING REQUEST 2 b.c. (Apr 8) Rainbow Quest (USA) 134 – Maze Garden **85**
(USA) (Riverman (USA) 131) [2006 7d² 7.1m* 8m⁴ Oct 8] compact, good-topped,
attractive colt: sixth foal: half-brother to 6-y-o Roman Maze and 10.5f (in France)/15f
winner Crossed Wire (both by Lycius): dam useful French 1m winner: fairly useful form:
confirmed debut promise when winning maiden at Chepstow in September: favourite,
only fourth in minor event at Bath: should be suited by 1m/1¼m. *R. Charlton*

AMBER GLORY 3 b.f. Foxhound (USA) 103 – Compton Amber 78 (Puissance 110) **65**
[2006 72: f6g⁴ p6g⁴ f6g⁵ f5g³ 5.1s⁵ 5g 5v⁶ 6s 5d f6g f6g p6g f5g³ Dec 28] close-coupled
filly: fair performer: stays 6f: acts on all-weather and heavy going: usually wears cheek-
pieces/blinkers: normally races up with pace. *K. A. Ryan*

AMBER ISLE 2 b.g. (Apr 1) Weet-A-Minute (IRE) 106 – Cloudy Reef 57 (Cragador **66**
110) [2006 p6m³ p7.1g⁴ p7.1g³ Dec 1] half-brother to several winners, including 3-y-o
Ochre Bay and 6-y-o Gilded Cove: dam, maiden, raced only around 5f: fair maiden:
claimed from R. Hollinshead £6,000 after debut: stays 7f. *D. Carroll*

AMBER NECTAR TWO 6 b.g. Bluegrass Prince (IRE) 110 – Another Batchworth
72 (Beveled (USA)) [2006 49: f6g p6g Mar 27] poor performer nowadays: best at 5f/6f:
acts on polytrack, soft and good to firm going: usually blinkered: tried in tongue tie/
cheekpieces. *A. G. Newcombe*

AMBERSONG 8 ch.g. Hernando (FR) 127 – Stygian (USA) 73 (Irish River (FR) 131) **48**
[2006 45: p13.9g⁴ p16.5g⁵ p12g p12g⁴ 11.6m Jul 24] strong, angular gelding: poor performer: stays 14.8f: acts on all-weather and firm ground: tried visored: sometimes slowly
away. *A. W. Carroll*

AMBER SPIRIT 3 ch.f. Zaha (CAN) 106 – Classic Faster (IRE) (Running Steps –
(USA) 79) [2006 –: f8g Jan 11] little sign of ability. *Peter Grayson*

AMBER VALLEY 2 b.f. (Mar 31) Foxhound (USA) 103 – Amber Mill 96 (Doulab **88**
(USA) 115) [2006 5.2m⁴ 5g* 5s² 6m³ 6m 6s⁵ 6d Sep 16] leggy filly: half-sister to several
winners, including useful 5f to 6.5f winner (including at 2 yrs) Golden Nun (by Bishop
of Cashel) and fairly useful 6f (at 2 yrs)/1m winner Iskander (by Danzero): dam 5f/6f
winner, including at 2 yrs: fairly useful performer: won maiden at Haydock in April:
improvement when second to Gilded in listed event at York and third to Brazilian Bride
in Swordlestown Stud Sprint Stakes at Naas, but lost her form after (tailed off in cheekpieces final start): best at 5f/6f: acts on soft and good to firm going. *K. A. Ryan*

AMBROSIANO 2 b.g. (Apr 29) Averti (IRE) 117 – Secret Circle (Magic Ring (IRE) **68**
115) [2006 6g⁶ p6g⁵ 7g 5.7m⁶ p7.1m⁵ Oct 2] 21,000Y, 16,000 2-y-o: sturdy gelding: fifth
foal: closely related to German 7f/1m winner Secret Affair (by Piccolo) and half-brother
to useful 7f winner Secret Place (by Compton Place): dam unraced half-sister to high-
class 1m/1¼m performer Bijou d'Inde: fair maiden: probably stays 7f: gelded after final
start. *Miss E. C. Lavelle*

AMEEQ (USA) 4 b. or br.g. Silver Hawk (USA) 123 – Haniya (IRE) 92 (Caerleon **88**
(USA) 132) [2006 76: p10g* p10g* p10g⁶ 10g⁶ 12m⁴ 11.6m⁶ Jul 1] quite good-topped gelding:
fairly useful performer: won maiden at Lingfield in February and handicap at Kempton in
March: good efforts in handicaps next 2 starts: gelded after final outing (found little):
stays 1½m: acts on polytrack, good to firm and good to soft going: tried tongue tied: fairly
useful hurdler, successful in September. *G. L. Moore*

AMELIE BROWN (IRE) 2 b.f. (Jan 18) Dr Fong (USA) 128 – Presentation (IRE) 98 **53**
(Mujadil (USA) 119) [2006 5g 6v⁵ 5m⁴ 5m 6s Aug 28] 12,000F, €25,000Y: close-coupled
filly: second foal: dam 2-y-o 5f winner: modest maiden: best effort at 5f: tried blinkered:
sent to Spain. *N. Tinkler*

AMELIORE (IRE) 3 b.f. Dansili 127 – Common Consent (IRE) 68 (Common –
Grounds 118) [2006 –: 7s 7g 5f 7m 6f p10g p8g Dec 15] close-coupled filly: no form.
S. Woodman

AMERICAN SPIN 2 ch.c. (May 17) Groom Dancer (USA) 128 – Sea Vixen 87 (Mach- **81 p**
iavellian (USA) 123) [2006 7d³ Oct 28] 5,500F, 24,000 2-y-o: useful colt: second
foal: half-brother to fairly useful French winner around 6f Worchester (by Spinning
World): dam, half (at 2 yrs) and 1m winner from 3 starts, closely related to 3-y-o Nannina:
12/1, length third of 19 to Mr Napper Tandy in maiden at Newmarket (wandered/flashed
tail): will be suited by 1m: will improve. *B. J. Meehan*

AMES SOUER (IRE) 3 b.f. Fayruz 116 – Taispeain (IRE) 86 (Petorius 117) [2006 46: **48** f5g⁶ f7g Dec 12] leggy filly: poor maiden. *D. Carroll*

AMICUS MEUS (IRE) 2 b.c. (Mar 15) Danehill Dancer (IRE) 117 – Top Brex (FR) **70** (Top Ville 129) [2006 7.2d⁶ 7.2v² Oct 28] €85,000F, 14,000 2-y-o: tall, useful-looking colt: fifth foal: half-brother to 2004 2-y-o 7f winner Easy Mover (by Bluebird): dam French 1½m winner: better effort in maidens at Ayr when second to Bayonyx: will stay 1m. *A. Bailey*

AMIR ZAMAN 8 ch.g. Salse (USA) 128 – Colorvista (Shirley Heights 130) [2006 –, **64** a76d: f12g⁴ f12g Jan 17] big, strong, lengthy gelding: modest handicapper: effective at 1½m to 2m: acts on all-weather, firm and good to soft ground: visored both starts at 8 yrs: tends to race freely. *J. R. Jenkins*

AMISACT 4 b.f. Zaha (CAN) 106 – Valise 52 (Salse (USA) 128) [2006 7m p12g Jul 1] **–** fourth foal: dam sprint maiden: well held in 2 sellers. *D. J. S. ffrench Davis*

AMNESTY 7 ch.g. Salse (USA) 128 – Amaranthus (Shirley Heights 130) [2006 67, a–: **62** p10g³ p10g 9.7d⁴ p10g³ p10g May 15] lengthy gelding: modest performer: stays 1¼m: **a55** acts on polytrack, heavy and good to firm going: wears blinkers: of suspect temperament. *G. L. Moore*

AMONGST AMIGOS (IRE) 5 b.g. Imperial Ballet (IRE) 110 – Red Lory 87 (Bay **68** Express 132) [2006 79: 8v 7m 8.5g 6.5s 7v 8d f8g p9.5g Nov 16] fair performer: left B. Potts in Ireland after second start: stays 1¼m: acts on any turf going: blinkered last 6 starts, at Southwell and Wolverhampton last 2. *Thomas Cleary, Ireland*

AMORADA 3 b.f. Pursuit of Love 124 – Duena (Grand Lodge (USA) 125) [2006 48: **–** p8.6g p8g Feb 7] quite good-topped filly: little solid form: visored final outing. *H. Morrison*

AMORIST (IRE) 4 b.g. Anabaa (USA) 130 – Moivouloirtoi (USA) 106 (Bering 136) **–** [2006 60+, a77: p10g* Jan 28] fairly useful handicapper: improved form when winning **a86** by 3½ lengths from Red Birr at Lingfield in January, making all: stays 1¼m: acts on all-weather and heavy going: sold 80,000 gns in February, pulled up both starts over hurdles for J. Howard Johnson. *Sir Mark Prescott*

AMOUR MULTIPLE (IRE) 7 b.g. Poliglote 121 – Onereuse (Sanglamore (USA) **–** 126) [2006 12s Oct 6] fairly useful performer for Mme C. Head-Maarek in France in 2003, winning minor event and handicap at Maisons-Laffitte: well held only outing on Flat since (fairly useful hurdler, winner in December): stays 11f: acts on heavy ground. *S. Lycett*

AMRON HILL 3 b.g. Polar Prince (IRE) 117 – Maradata (IRE) 68 (Shardari 134) **62** [2006 p9.5g p12g 7d p9.5g⁶ p8.6g⁵ p9.5g⁵ p9.5g Dec 21] workmanlike gelding: modest maiden: stays 9.5f: acts on polytrack. *R. Hollinshead*

AMWAAL (USA) 3 b.c. Seeking the Gold (USA) – Wasnah (USA) 96 (Nijinsky **93** (CAN) 138) [2006 76: 9.9m 8s 8d* Oct 2] strong, rangy colt: fairly useful performer: improved form when winning maiden at Pontefract (by 7 lengths) in October: stays 1m: acts on good to soft ground. *J. L. Dunlop*

AMWELL BRAVE 5 b.g. Pyramus (USA) 78 – Passage Creeping (IRE) 75 (Persian **57** Bold 123) [2006 58, a69: p12.2g³ p13g³ f12g² p12g 12d⁵ p12g⁵ f11g⁴ p13.9g⁶ p12g³ p12g **a72** 12f³ 12g⁴ p12g⁶ p16g p16g⁴ p12g³ f14g² p12g² p13.9g⁶ Dec 31] rather leggy gelding: fair performer on all-weather, modest on turf: effective at 1½m to 2m: acts on all-weather, soft and firm ground: tried visored/tongue tied. *J. R. Jenkins*

AMYGDALA 3 b.f. Royal Applause 124 – Touch And Love (IRE) (Green Desert **60** (USA) 127) [2006 67: p7g p6g³ p8.6g⁵ 5m⁶ 7m Jul 26] leggy filly: modest maiden: stays 7f: acts on polytrack and good to soft going: wore cheekpieces final outing: tried tongue tied: covered by Lucky Story, sent to Italy. *M. Botti*

AMY LOUISE (IRE) 3 ch.f. Swain (IRE) 134 – Mur Taasha (USA) 108 (Riverman **87** (USA) 131) [2006 75: 7m⁴ 7m 8d⁴ 7m 6d 7.2v* 7.2v* Oct 28] close-coupled filly: fairly useful performer: won maiden at Newcastle in June and handicaps at Ayr (2) in October (latter by 5 lengths): stays 1m: acts on heavy and good to firm ground. *T. D. Barron*

ANASENA 3 b.f. Anabaa (USA) 130 – Bolsena (USA) (Red Ransom (USA)) [2006 **54** 10g⁵ 12m⁴ 10.9g⁵ Jul 7] 17,000Y: first foal: dam unraced daughter of champion US older mare Waya: modest form in maidens first 2 starts: stays 1½m. *G. G. Margarson*

ANATOLIAN PRINCE 2 b.c. (Apr 3) Almutawakel 126 – Flight Soundly (IRE) 78 **67** (Caerleon (USA) 132) [2006 7m 8g⁶ p7.1g Oct 30] 35,000Y: strong, good-topped colt, type to carry condition: has a quick action: half-brother to several winners, including useful German 5f/6f (at 2 yrs) winner Elli (by Polar Falcon) and Irish/Spanish 1m/9f winner All Woman (by Groom Dancer): dam 2-y-o 6f winner: fair form in maidens: stays 1m. *J. M. P. Eustace*

ANCHOR DATE 4 b.c. Zafonic (USA) 130 – Fame At Last (USA) 98 (Quest For Fame 127) [2006 81: 6m p6g 6.1g p7.1g p7.1g Nov 7] lengthy colt: fairly useful handicapper at best: on downgrade: stays 1m: acts on polytrack, firm and good to soft going: tongue tied: sold 4,600 gns. *D. Shaw*   **69 d**

ANCIENT SITE (USA) 2 ch.c. (May 4) Distant View (USA) 126 – Victorian Style 88 (Nashwan (USA) 135) [2006 p8.6g6 p8.6m p7.1g6 Dec 31] well held in maidens. *B. P. J. Baugh*   **–**

AND AGAIN (USA) 3 b.f. In The Wings 128 – Garah 107 (Ajdal (USA) 130) [2006 56p: 8.3d3 10m* 9.9f5 11.6m5 9.8s2 10m6 11.9g* Oct 13] sturdy filly: fairly useful performer: won maiden at Lingfield in June and handicap at Brighton in October: stays easy 1½m: acts on firm and soft ground: sold 35,000 gns. *J. R. Fanshawe*   **83**

AND I 3 b.f. Inchinor 119 – Fur Will Fly 66 (Petong 126) [2006 69: 7s4 p6g3 p6g2 p6g Jul 19] tall filly: has scope: fair maiden: not sure to stay beyond 7f: acts on polytrack and soft going: wore cheekpieces third outing (failed to impress with attitude). *M. P. Tregoning*   **73**

ANDORRAN (GER) 3 b.g. Lando (GER) 128 – Adora (GER) (Danehill (USA) 126) [2006 60: 8g 11.1f 10m 14.1g Aug 24] close-coupled gelding: maiden handicapper: little form in 2006. *A. Dickman*   **–**

ANDRE CHENIER (IRE) 5 b.g. Perugino (USA) 84 – Almada (GER) (Lombard (GER) 126) [2006 75: 11.1m 12.4d 12.1m6 13.1g4 Jun 23] modest performer on Flat nowadays: stays 1½m: acts on soft going. *P. Monteith*   **64**

ANDRONIKOS 4 ch.c. Dr Fong (USA) 128 – Arctic Air 79 (Polar Falcon (USA) 126) [2006 111§: 7s3 6m 6s4 6d5 6s 6d4 p7g6 p7g Dec 3] lengthy colt: smart performer: back to best when 1¼ lengths fifth of 23 to Fonthill Road in Ayr Gold Cup (Handicap): creditable fourth to Rising Shadow in listed event at Windsor before below form at Lingfield last 2 outings: free-going sort, best at 6f: acts on firm and soft going: usually tongue tied: has run well when sweating: looked temperamental final 3-y-o start: inconsistent. *P. F. I. Cole*   **114 §**

ANDURIL 5 ch.g. Kris 135 – Attribute 69 (Warning 136) [2006 87: p8.6g p9.5g p10g3 p8.6g 8.1g5 8g 10m p8g 8.1g p8.6g 8g* 8.1m 10d p8.6m5 p10g6 p9.5g f8g2 Dec 14] workmanlike gelding: fairly useful handicapper: left I. McInnes after second start: won at Ayr in August: stays 1¼m: acts on all-weather, firm and soft ground: usually blinkered/in cheekpieces: races freely: held up, and tends to find little. *Miss M. E. Rowland*   **80 §**

ANEWSHADE 2 b.f. (May 13) Vettori (IRE) 119 – On Shade 44 (Polar Falcon (USA) 126) [2006 8.1v6 7.5m Sep 13] 1,000Y: workmanlike filly: second foal: dam disappointing maiden: well beaten in maidens. *N. Tinkler*   **–**

ANFIELD DREAM 4 b.g. Lujain (USA) 119 – Fifth Emerald 54 (Formidable (USA) 125) [2006 76, a82: p5g f6g p6g f5g* 6d 5d p6g p5g 6.1s5 f5g2 p5.1g f5g p6g Dec 20] close-coupled gelding: fairly useful handicapper on all-weather, fair on turf: won at Southwell in February (gelded after): effective at 5f, barely stays 7f: acts on all-weather, soft and good to firm going. *J. R. Jenkins*   **71 a88**

ANGARIC (IRE) 3 ch.g. Pivotal 124 – Grannys Reluctance (IRE) 63 (Anita's Prince 126) [2006 68: 6d2 7.1m* 7.1d2 7.5g* 8.3m2 7.5f2 7f 6d 7s6 p7.1g4 Oct 29] neat gelding: fairly useful handicapper: won at Musselburgh and Beverley in May: stays 1m: acts on polytrack, firm and good to soft ground. *B. Smart*   **86**

ANGELETTA 2 b.f. (Jan 22) Vettori (IRE) 119 – Supreme Angel 85 (Beveled (USA)) [2006 f5g 5d4 6s3 6m2 6g3 7.1m5 7.6f3 8.3d4 8s5 8.5g Dec 10] strong, workmanlike filly: first foal: dam 5f (including at 2 yrs)/6f winner: fair maiden: in frame 6 times, including in nurseries: left E. McMahon 18,000 gns before final outing: stays 1m: acts on soft and good to firm ground: edgy sort. *E. R. Freeman, Canada*   **71**

ANGELINA BANKES 3 b.f. Observatory (USA) 131 – Cloche Call 52 (Anabaa (USA) 130) [2006 58: p8.6g3 p7.1g2 p7.1g6 Feb 17] sturdy filly: modest performer: stays 8.6f: acts on polytrack and good to firm ground: reportedly finished lame final start. *R. A. Harris*   **55**

totepool Silver Bowl (Handicap), Haydock—Anna Pavlova runs on gamely to land this valuable handicap from Sir Gerard (No.6) and Kalankari

ANGELINE 3 b.f. Atraf 116 – Pawsible (IRE) 52 (Mujadil (USA) 119) [2006 9.8m Jun 7] leggy filly: second foal: dam 15f winner: 100/1, last in maiden at Ripon, very slowly away. *H. Alexander* —

ANGELOFTHENORTH 4 b.f. Tomba 119 – Dark Kristal (IRE) 66 (Gorytus (USA) 132) [2006 76: 5v⁶ 5d⁶ 6.1m 5d⁴ 5m⁵ 5m 5m⁴ p5.1g 6m 6g 5d f6g Oct 12] leggy filly: fair performer: left J. Bethell after third start: best at 5f: acts on heavy and good to firm going: tried blinkered: none too consistent. *C. J. Teague* **67**

ANGEL RIVER 4 ch.f. Bold Edge 123 – Riviere Rouge (Forzando 122) [2006 55: p8.6g⁶ 7m p9.5g p8.6g p7g p7g⁴ 10d 8m⁵ p7g 8m p8g³ 8m 7.6g p7g p7g⁵ p8g Dec 18] quite good-topped filly: poor performer nowadays: effective at 6f to 1m: acts on all-weather and good to firm going: usually wears headgear. *J. Ryan* **46**

ANGEL SPRINTS 4 b.f. Piccolo 121 – Runs In The Family 69 (Distant Relative 128) [2006 98: 5s⁴ 6m 5g 6m 6d⁵ Oct 19] good sort: just fairly useful handicapper in 2006: left B. R. Millman after second start: best at 5f/6f: acts on firm and soft going. *C. J. Down* **89**

ANGEL VOICES (IRE) 3 b.f. Tagula (IRE) 116 – Lithe Spirit (IRE) 74 (Dancing Dissident (USA) 119) [2006 81: 8d² p7g 7s⁴ 7m³ Aug 5] good-bodied filly: has a moderate, quick action: fair maiden: below form after reappearance, hanging left final start: stays 1m: acts on good to firm and good to soft ground. *K. R. Burke* **74**

ANGIE AND LIZ (IRE) 3 b.f. Spectrum (IRE) 126 – Mary Magdalene 78 (Night Shift (USA)) [2006 57: p6g³ p5.1g* Feb 10] modest performer: won handicap at Wolverhampton in February: should stay 7f: acts on all-weather. *Peter Grayson* **61**

ANGUS NEWZ 3 ch.f. Compton Place 125 – Hickleton Lady (IRE) 64 (Kala Shikari 125) [2006 85: 6d* 6g² 5.1g⁵ 6.1s* 6s⁵ 6f 5m* 6m 6g 5g 6.1m 5g* 6g 5g⁴ Oct 12] plain, lengthy filly: useful performer: further progress in 2006, winning minor event at Leicester in April and listed races at Nottingham in May, Sandown (by 2 lengths from Dixie Belle) in June and Hamilton (beat Nidhaal by ½ length, racing in group of 2 on stand side) in September: creditable fourth to Mecca's Mate in handicap at Newmarket final outing: raced only at 5f/6f: acts on soft and good to firm going: effective visored or not: looks ungainly, tending to hang/carry head high. *M. Quinn* **103**

ANIMATED 2 b.g. (Mar 8) Averti (IRE) 117 – Anita Marie (IRE) (Anita's Prince 126) [2006 5d⁵ 5m 5m p7.1g⁶ Dec 22] 8,000Y, resold 29,000Y: well-grown, close-coupled gelding: third foal: half-brother to 6-y-o Shava: dam, ran twice, sister to 9-y-o Trinculo: fair form in maidens: gelded and left D. Nicholls before well held final start. *A. J. McCabe* **65**

ANNABELLE JA (FR) 3 b.f. Singspiel (IRE) 133 – Alamea (IRE) (Ela-Mana-Mou 132) [2006 89: 10d 8m⁴ Jul 22] leggy, good-topped filly: fairly useful performer at 2 yrs: better effort in 2006 when respectable fourth in handicap at Newmarket: should stay 1¼m: acts on polytrack: on toes and sweated up on reappearance. *D. R. C. Elsworth* **79**

ANNALS 4 b.f. Lujain (USA) 119 – Anna of Brunswick 78 (Rainbow Quest (USA) 134) **47** [2006 –: p9.5g 5v 7d p8.6g⁶ p7.1g f7g 8m 7.9m Aug 7] quite good-topped filly: poor performer nowadays: probably stays 8.6f: tried in headgear. *R. C. Guest*

ANNAMBO 6 ch.g. In The Wings 128 – Anna Matrushka (Mill Reef (USA) 141) [2006 **82** 84: 11.5m⁴ 14g 14.8m³ Jun 24] smallish, lengthy gelding: unimpressive mover: fairly useful handicapper: effective at 1½m to 16.5f: acts on polytrack, firm and good to soft going: often visored before 2005: signs of temperament. *D. Morris*

ANNA PAVLOVA 3 b.f. Danehill Dancer (IRE) 117 – Wheeler's Wonder (IRE) 43 **114** (Sure Blade (USA) 130) [2006 91: 8s² 8.1s* 10g⁶ 12s* 13.9d² 12s* 10g² Oct 12] tall, leggy, quite good-topped filly: smart performer: improved again in 2006, winning tote-sport Silver Bowl (Handicap) at Haydock (beat Sir Gerard by neck) in May and listed events at York (beat Bunood 3 lengths in Galtres Stakes) in August and Ascot (beat Trick Or Treat 5 lengths in Harvest Stakes, despite veering left) in October: also ran well when second in Park Hill Stakes at York (beaten ¾ length by Rising Cross) and in listed event at Newmarket (beaten 1¼ lengths by Innocent Air) fifth/final outings: stays 1¾m: acts on soft and good to firm going: quirky (tends to hang), but tough. *R. A. Fahey*

ANNE BONNEY 2 b.f. (Mar 28) Jade Robbery (USA) 121 – Sanchez 77 (Wolfhound **58 p** (USA) 126) [2006 p8g⁶ Oct 23] 30,000 2-y-o: fourth foal: sister to winner in Japan and half-sister to French 15f winner Red Mantilla (by Timber Country): dam, Irish maiden who stayed 9f, closely related to high-class miler Starborough and half-sister to Canadian International winner Ballingarry and Racing Post Trophy winner Aristotle: 9/2, led going way when sixth in maiden at Lingfield: sold 46,000 gns: will do better. *E. J. O'Neill*

ANNIA FAUSTINA (IRE) 2 ch.f. (May 9) Docksider (USA) 124 – Benguela (USA) **60** 76 (Little Current (USA)) [2006 7.1m p7g⁴ p8g⁴ Dec 8] €5,500Y: close-coupled filly: closely related to winner in USA by Diesis (dam of US Grade 1 9f winner Honor In War) and half-sister to several winners, including 1m winner Naif (by Storm Bird) and 1½m winner Lady Angola (by Lord At War), both fairly useful: dam 1m/11f winner in USA: modest maiden: should be suited by 1m+. *J. L. Spearing*

ANNIBALE CARO 4 b.g. Mtoto 134 – Isabella Gonzaga 75 (Rock Hopper 124) [2006 **–** 90: p12g⁶ 12g Jul 13] good topped gelding: fairly useful handicapper in 2005: well held both starts in 2006: sold 12,500 gns, joined G. Tuer. *Sir Mark Prescott*

ANNIES VALENTINE 3 b.f. My Best Valentine 122 – Shashi (IRE) 79 (Shaadi **–** (USA) 126) [2006 –: 8m⁵ 10.9m 10.2m 10d f16g Nov 15] little form. *J. Gallagher*

ANNUAL EVENT (IRE) 2 ch.f. (Mar 29) Traditionally (USA) 117 – Elayoon (USA) **66** 76 (Danzig (USA)) [2006 7f⁶ 8.1m³ 7.2d Sep 15] €18,000F, €22,000Y: strong, angular filly: first foal: dam, second in 6f maiden at 2 yrs (only start), closely related to smart sprinter Mutamayyaz out of 1000 Guineas third Ajfan: fair maiden: third at Chepstow second start: stays 1m: sold 7,000 gns. *E. J. O'Neill*

A NOD AND A WINK (IRE) 2 b.f. (Apr 17) Raise A Grand (IRE) 114 – Earth Char- **53** ter 60 (Slip Anchor 136) [2006 6g 5g⁵ 5g⁵ p7g⁴ p8g³ p8g² Dec 2] €3,000F, €5,000Y: half-sister to several winners, including 5-y-o Inchloss: dam maiden who should have stayed beyond 6f: modest maiden: stays 1m: acts on polytrack. *R. Hannon*

ANOTHER BOTTLE (IRE) 5 b.g. Cape Cross (IRE) 129 – Aster Aweke (IRE) 87 **105** (Alzao (USA) 117) [2006 106: 8m⁴ 8m 7m 9d Sep 30] angular, round-barrelled gelding: type to carry condition: useful handicapper: creditable fourth of 25 to Forgery in Spring Cup at Newbury, easily best effort in 2006: stays 1¼m: acts on firm and good to soft ground: usually held up: joined P. Nicholls. *R. Charlton*

EBF Galtres Stakes, York—
Anna Pavlova is a decisive winner from Bunood (left), Gower Song (centre) and Cresta Gold (right)

ANOTHER CON (IRE) 5 b.m. Lake Coniston (IRE) 131 – Sweet Unison (USA) **59**
(One For All (USA)) [2006 –, a58: p16g² p16.5p⁴ p12.2g³ p12.2g⁶ 10.2f* 10.2m* 10.9m*
11.5m⁴ 10f⁵ 12m Aug 4] modest handicapper: claimed from A. Hales after third start:
won at Bath (2 ladies events) in June and Warwick in July: was effective at 1¼m to easy
2m: acted on polytrack and firm going: tried in cheekpieces/visor: dead. *P. A. Blockley*

ANOTHER FAUX PAS (IRE) 5 b.m. Slip Anchor 136 – Pirie (USA) (Green Dancer **69**
(USA) 132) [2006 80: p8g p10g⁴ Apr 23] sturdy mare: just fair performer in 2006: stays
1¼m: acts on polytrack, firm and good to soft ground: has wandered: sold 48,000 gns in
November. *B. G. Powell*

ANOTHER GENEPI (USA) 3 br.f. Stravinsky (USA) 133 – Dawn Aurora (USA) **73**
(Night Shift (USA)) [2006 76: p8g³ 7m² 8.1m 7f⁵ 7m⁵ 7m⁵ p8.6g⁴ Sep 16] angular filly:
fair maiden: acts on polytrack and firm ground: often pulls hard: has sweated,
and suspect temperament. *J. W. Hills*

ANOTHER GLADIATOR (USA) 3 br.c. Danzig (USA) – Scarab Bracelet (USA) **63**
(Riverman (USA) 131) [2006 7m 8g⁴ 8s p8.6g⁵ p7.1g Dec 28] $65,000Y: big, strong colt:
third foal: half-brother to fairly useful 6f winner El Rey Del Mambo (by Kingmambo):
dam, 8.5f winner in USA, out of US Grade 1 9f winner Chain Bracelet: modest maiden:
stays 8.6f: acts on polytrack and good to firm going. *K. A. Ryan*

ANOTHER MISTRESS 4 b.f. Slip Anchor 136 – Mellow Miss 61 (Danehill (USA) **–**
126) [2006 –: p16g Jan 18] no sign of ability. *R. M. Flower*

ANOTHER TRUE STORY 2 b.c. (Jan 19) Piccolo 121 – Lost In Lucca 72§ (Inchinor **89**
119) [2006 5m 5f* 5g 5m* 5.1m² Oct 8] 12,000F, 26,000Y: third foal: half-brother to
German 6.5f/1m winner Lusty Lad (by Lujain): dam, untrustworthy 1m winner, half-
sister to Lowther Stakes winner Jemima: fairly useful performer: won maiden at Windsor
in July and nursery at Goodwood in September: good second to Vaunt in nursery at Bath
final start: will stay 6f: raced on good going or firmer: sold 38,000 gns. *R. Hannon*

ANOUSA (IRE) 5 b.g. Intikhab (USA) 135 – Annaletta 89 (Belmez (USA) 131) [2006 **–**
82: 14g 16.2f 12m Aug 5] strong, stocky gelding: type to carry condition: fairly useful
performer at 4 yrs: well held in 2006: tried visored: sold 1,000 gns, then gelded.
P. Howling

ANS BACH 3 b.g. Green Desert (USA) 127 – Bezzaaf 97 (Machiavellian (USA) 123) **101**
[2006 89: p8g p7g 8s⁵ 7m³ 7.1m² 7.1m* p8g² Sep 2] smallish, strong, compact gelding:
useful handicapper: won at Sandown (by short head from Scrummage) in July: good neck
second to Killena Boy in valuable event at Kempton final outing, finishing fast: stays
easy 1m: acts on polytrack, soft and good to firm going: tried visored, usually wears
cheekpieces: has worn crossed noseband: held up: sent to UAE. *M. A. Jarvis*

ANSWER BACK 2 b.f. (Feb 23) Redback 116 – Martha P Perkins (IRE) 51 (Fayruz **51**
116) [2006 p5.1g p5.1g 5.3m 5.1d⁶ 5.1s⁶ f6g Nov 15] 800F: neat filly: second foal: dam,
maiden, form only at 5f at 2 yrs: modest maiden. *Miss J. R. Tooth*

AN TADH (IRE) 3 b.c. Halling (USA) 133 – Tithcar 67 (Cadeaux Genereux 131) [2006 **115**
95: 7s 7d⁵ 7m* 7m* 8g⁵ 6m⁵ 6g³ Sep 16] €20,000Y: fifth foal: brother to fairly useful 1m
winner Chetak: dam, maiden effective at 5f to 7f, half-sister to high-class middle-distance
stayer Zindabad: smart performer: improved in 2006, winning minor event at Naas and
4-runner Ballycorus Stakes at Leopardstown (made all, beat Lord Admiral by 1½
lengths), both in June: blinkered, good 1¼ lengths third to Beauty Bright in Renaissance
Stakes at the Curragh final outing: effective at 6f/7f: acts on good to firm and good to soft
ground: often makes running. *G. M. Lyons, Ireland*

ANTHEA 2 b.f. (Feb 16) Tobougg (IRE) 125 – Blue Indigo (FR) (Pistolet Bleu (IRE) **66**
133) [2006 7m 7.1m² p8g² 7.1m⁴ 6.1g⁶ Sep 16] leggy filly: third foal: half-sister to useful
2005 2-y-o 1m/8.5f (latter in USA) winner Genre (by Orpen): dam, French maiden, out
of half-sister to Breeders' Cup Classic winner Arcangues: fair maiden: in frame at Warwick (2) and Lingfield: barely stays 1m: acts on polytrack and good to firm going: tends
to wander. *B. R. Millman*

ANTHEMION (IRE) 9 ch.g. Night Shift (USA) – New Sensitive (Wattlefield 117) **67**
[2006 67d: 8.3d 7.9m 8.3f 7.9m 9.2m³ 8.3g⁴ 8m³ 9.1m⁵ 9.2m² 8m* Aug 17] good-topped
gelding: fair handicapper: good second at Hamilton prior to winning apprentice event at
Musselburgh in August: effective at 1m/9f: acts on fibresand, firm and good to soft going:
often makes running. *Mrs J. C. McGregor*

ANTHILL 2 b.f. (Mar 16) Slickly (FR) 128 – Baddi Heights (FR) (Shirley Heights 130) **–**
[2006 6m Aug 6] 2,200F: fourth foal: half-sister to French 1¼m/11f winner Eklektos (by

Bahhare): dam fairly useful French 9f/1¼m winner: 66/1, behind in maiden at Newbury. *I. A. Wood*

ANTICA (IRE) 3 ch.f. Raise A Grand (IRE) 114 – Travel Tricks (IRE) (Presidium 124) **99** [2006 79+: 6d* 6m⁴ 7d² 8s³ 6g⁵ 7d Sep 24] smallish, angular filly: useful performer: won handicap at Ripon in April by 1¼ lengths from Bentong, edging left: below form after, including in listed company: stays 7f: acts on soft going: sent to Oman. *M. H. Tompkins*

ANTIGONI (IRE) 3 ch.f. Grand Lodge (USA) 125 – Butter Knife (IRE) (Sure Blade **74** (USA) 130) [2006 70: 7g² 8.1g⁵ 8m⁵ p7g 7m 7f⁴ Sep 18] quite good-topped filly: fair maiden: stays 1m: acts on polytrack and firm going: visored final start: often slowly away. *A. M. Balding*

ANTIQUE (IRE) 4 ch.f. Dubai Millennium 140 – Truly Generous (IRE) 104 (Generous (IRE) 139) [2006 109: p8g Oct 26] sparely-made filly: half-sister to 8-y-o Nawamees: dam, French 1¼m winner who stayed 12.5f, half-sister to very smart French middle-distance performer Modhish out of Irish 1000 Guineas winner Arctique Royale: useful performer: won twice in France in 2005, including listed race at La Teste: left A. Fabre and off 14 months, well held in listed race at Lingfield only start at 4 yrs: stays 1¼m: raced only on polytrack and going softer than good (acts on heavy): has left Godolphin. *Saeed bin Suroor*

ANTLEY COURT (IRE) 4 ch.g. Tagula (IRE) 116 – Changed Around (IRE) (Doulab **60** (USA) 115) [2006 60: f11g⁴ p12.2g⁵ Jan 21] modest maiden: barely stays 1½m: acts on all-weather: reportedly finished lame final start. *R. Hollinshead*

ANTON CHEKHOV 2 b.c. (Feb 28) Montjeu (IRE) 137 – By Charter 104 (Shirley **98 p** Heights 130) [2006 8d³ 9d* Nov 5] 625,000Y: half-brother to several winners, including 1¼m and 1½m winner Private Charter (by Singspiel) and 1¼m to 1¾m winner First Charter (by Polish Precedent), both smart: dam 2-y-o 7f winner who seemed to stay 1½m, daughter of Time Charter: 7½ lengths third to Consul General in maiden at Cork: deal of improvement when winning listed race at Leopardstown in November by 4½ lengths from Star Inside under forceful ride, making running and never challenged in straight: hung badly left home turn on debut: will be suited by 1½m: sure to improve again. *A. P. O'Brien, Ireland*

ANTRIM ROSE 2 b.f. (Jan 26) Giant's Causeway (USA) 132 – Aunty Rose (IRE) 103 **58** (Caerleon (USA) 132) [2006 p8.6g p8g p8g⁵ Dec 20] first foal: dam, 2-y-o 7f winner (stayed 8.5f), half-sister to very smart 7f/1m performer Bin Rosie: modest form in maidens, fifth to Algarade at Kempton. *J. H. M. Gosden*

ANYBODY'S GUESS (IRE) 2 b.g. (Apr 29) Iron Mask (USA) 117 – Credibility 65 **–** (Komaite (USA)) [2006 6s 6m 7g Sep 27] no show in maidens. *J. S. Wainwright*

A ONE (IRE) 7 b.g. Alzao (USA) 117 – Anita's Contessa (IRE) 68 (Anita's Prince 126) **–** [2006 71: 7.1m 8.1g Jul 5] rather leggy gelding: fair performer in 2005: well held both 7-y-o starts: stays 1¼m: acts on any turf going: front runner. *H. J. Manners*

AONINCH 6 ch.m. Inchinor 119 – Willowbank 66 (Gay Fandango (USA) 132) [2006 **68** 74: 12g May 18] lengthy mare: fair handicapper: best at 1¼m/1½m: acts on polytrack, firm and soft ground: free-going sort: has hung/found little: usually held up: consistent. *Mrs P. N. Dutfield*

APACHE CHANT (USA) 2 b. or br.c. (Apr 1) War Chant (USA) 126 – Sterling Pound **–** (USA) (Seeking The Gold (USA)) [2006 7g 8g Sep 28] tall, rather leggy colt: has a moderate, quick action: behind in maidens at Leicester and Newmarket (blinkered): sold 17,000 gns, joined A Carroll. *E. A. L. Dunlop*

APACHE DAWN 2 ch.g. (Mar 21) Pursuit of Love 124 – Taza (Persian Bold 123) **83 p** [2006 7m⁶ 7.1d² p7.1g³ Oct 8] big, good-topped gelding: half-brother to 3 winners, including 5-y-o Go Solo: dam, no form, half-sister to very smart middle-distance performer Apache: fairly useful maiden: placed at Warwick and Wolverhampton (gelded after): will be suited by 1m/1¼m: has hung right: has scope and should progress further as 3-y-o. *B. W. Hills*

APACHE DREAM (IRE) 2 ch.f. (May 11) Indian Ridge 123 – Blanche Dubois **80** (Nashwan (USA) 135) [2006 6m 6m 6d* 6d Oct 27] 220,000Y: half-sister to several winners, including 3-y-o Noble Gent and 6-y-o Middlemarch: dam unraced half-sister to Irish 2000 Guineas winner Indian Haven (by Indian Ridge): fairly useful form: won maiden at Windsor in October: 9/2, seemed amiss in listed race at Newmarket final start: will be suited by 7f/1m. *B. J. Meehan*

GLS Partnership's "Appalachian Trail"

APACHE FORT 3 b.g. Desert Prince (IRE) 130 – Apogee 113 (Shirley Heights 130) – [2006 p10g p9.5g⁶ p7.1g Dec 9] well held in maidens. *T. Keddy*

APACHE NATION (IRE) 3 b.g. Fruits of Love (USA) 127 – Rachel Green (IRE) 46 **69** (Case Law 113) [2006 66: 7m 8s³ 9m* 8f 9m³ 11f⁴ 7.9g⁴ 10.1m 10.5v⁴ 8v* 8s* 8.2s⁵ 8d⁶ Oct 27] good-bodied gelding: fair handicapper: won at Musselburgh in June and Ayr (2) in September: stays 9f: acts on heavy and good to firm going. *M. Dods*

APACHE POINT (IRE) 9 ch.g. Indian Ridge 123 – Ausherra (USA) 106 (Diesis 133) **67** [2006 71, a49: f8g 11g⁵ 8m 10.1m⁶ 10s⁴ 10.1g³ 10m⁵ 9f* 9d³ 8.5m* 8d 10s² 9s 10.1s **a–** Oct 10] rather leggy gelding: fair performer on turf, poor on all-weather: won handicap at Redcar in July and claimer at Beverley in August: stays 1¼m: acts on any turf going: sometimes races freely: usually waited with. *N. Tinkler*

APACHE SCOUT (IRE) 2 ch.g. (Mar 5) Indian Ridge 123 – Salee (IRE) 102 (Caer- **?** leon (USA) 132) [2006 5.1g 5g³ 6g⁵ Dec 24] 150,000Y: first foal: dam, 1¼m to (in France) 12.5f winner, half-sister to smart sprinter Almaty out of half-sister to 2000 Guineas/Champion Stakes winner Haafhd: sold from R. Beckett 16,500 gns after debut (early speed in maiden at Bath): third and fifth in minor events at Dos Hermanas last 2 starts. *I. A. Diaz, Spain*

A PEACEFUL MAN 2 b.g. (Apr 9) Tipsy Creek (USA) 115 – My Hearts Desire (Dep- **58 p** loy 131) [2006 6g 6d Nov 4] third foal: dam, little form, half-sister to useful performer up to 1½m Prince of My Heart: mid-field in maidens at Newmarket (hampered) and Windsor (not knocked about): subsequently gelded: looks capable of better. *B. W. Hills*

APERITIF 5 ch.g. Pivotal 124 – Art Deco Lady 51 (Master Willie 129) [2006 –: 8s 7g⁴ **77** 7d² 8d⁴ p7g⁶ 7g* 8m 6d 8g Sep 27] strong, good sort: fair handicapper: won at Catterick in May: has won at 1m, probably best up to 7f: acts on soft and good to firm going, probably on polytrack: inconsistent. *D. Nicholls*

APETITE 4 ch.g. Timeless Times (USA) 99 – Petite Elite 47 (Anfield 117) [2006 –: 6m 5.9g 7g May 29] close-coupled gelding: no form since 2 yrs: blinkered last 2 starts: sometimes slowly away. *N. Bycroft* —

APEX 5 ch.g. Efisio 120 – Royal Loft 105 (Homing 130) [2006 93d: 6g 7f 6d⁵ 5.9g⁴ 6g f7g⁶ f6g 5.9g⁵ 6d 6g 6s³ 6s Sep 28] leggy, angular gelding: has a short, round action: fair handicapper: on the downgrade: effective at 6f to 1m: acts on polytrack (seemingly not fibresand), soft and good to firm going: tried blinkered/in cheekpieces: sometimes slowly away: held up: has found little. *N. Tinkler* **72 d**

APHORISM 3 b.f. Halling (USA) 133 – Applecross 117 (Glint of Gold 128) [2006 p9.5g⁶ 10m 9.9m³ 12.1d⁵ 14g³ f12g* f12g⁴ Dec 21] smallish, leggy filly: half-sister to several winners, notably stayer Invermark (by Machiavellian) and 1½m/1¾m performer Craigsteel (by Suave Dancer), both very smart: dam, 1¼m to 13.3f winner, stayed in Park Hill Stakes: fair performer: won maiden at Southwell in December: stays 1¾m: acts on fibresand, good to firm and good to soft going: unbalanced off final turn at Wolverhampton on debut. *J. R. Fanshawe* **74**

APHRODISIA 2 b.f. (Apr 23) Sakhee (USA) 136 – Aegean Dream (IRE) 97 (Royal Academy (USA) 130) [2006 8m Sep 19] 45,000Y: good-topped filly: second foal: dam, 8.5f to 1¼m winner, half-sister to smart 1¼m/11f winner Shagraan: 33/1, burly and green in maiden at Newmarket: type to progress. *S. C. Williams* **– p**

APOLLO FIVE 2 ch.g. (Feb 2) Auction House (USA) 120 – Dazzling Quintet 73 (Superlative 118) [2006 5.5d³ 5.7g* p7.1g⁵ Jul 13] 9,000Y: first foal: dam 5f winner, including at 2 yrs: fairly useful form: won maiden at Bath in June: shaped as if stamina stretched in minor event following month: gelded after: may prove best at 5f/6f. *D. J. Coakley* **84**

APPALACHIAN TRAIL (IRE) 5 b.g. Indian Ridge 123 – Karinski (USA) (Palace Music (USA) 129) [2006 105: p8.6g⁴ p8.6g³ p8.6g² 7.1g 7m² 7m 7m⁴ 8g³ 6s* 6d Sep 16] sturdy gelding: smart performer: won listed event at Newmarket (by 2 lengths from Assertive) in August: several at least creditable efforts otherwise, including in Buckingham Palace Stakes (handicap, neck second to Uhoomagoo) and International Stakes (fourth to Dabbers Ridge), both at Ascot, and Ayr Gold Cup (seventh to Fonthill Road) fifth/seventh/final outings: effective at stiff 6f to 8.6f: acts on polytrack, soft and good to firm going: tried visored, usually blinkered: waited with. *I. Semple* **113**

APPLE ANNIE 4 b.f. Benny The Dip (USA) 127 – Aneen Alkamanja (Last Tycoon 131) [2006 37: 10f 10d Oct 4] no form since debut at 2 yrs. *M. E. Sowersby* **–**

APPLE BLOSSOM (IRE) 2 b.f. (Apr 12) Danehill Dancer (IRE) 117 – Silk (IRE) (Machiavellian (USA) 123) [2006 6.1g Sep 26] first foal: dam unraced out of useful performer up to 1¼m Dances With Dreams, herself half-sister to very smart performer up to 1½m in France/USA Dark Moondancer: 8/1, very green in maiden at Nottingham. *G. Wragg* **–**

APPLE WOOD 6 b.g. Woodborough (USA) 112 – Appelania 63 (Star Appeal 133) [2006 49: f7g Jan 29] poor maiden: stays 1m: acts on fibresand, heavy and good to firm going: tried blinkered/tongue tied. *Denis P. Quinn, Ireland* **–**

APPLY DAPPLY 3 b.f. Pursuit of Love 124 – Daring Destiny 113 (Daring March 116) [2006 67p: 6v* 7m² f6g 7.1d 6.1s² Oct 25] tall, useful-looking filly: fairly useful performer: won maiden at Pontefract in April: back to form in handicap at Nottingham final start: should prove better suited by 7f than 6f: acts on heavy and good to firm going: ran poorly when sweating penultimate outing. *H. Morrison* **81**

APPRECIATED 3 b.f. Most Welcome 131 – Align 69 (Petong 126) [2006 58: f7g⁵ Feb 14] maiden: bred to stay 1m: blinkered sole start at 3 yrs. *W. J. Haggas* **–**

APRES SKI (IRE) 3 b.g. Orpen (USA) 116 – Miss Kinabalu 50 (Shirley Heights 130) [2006 –: f6g⁶ p6g p7g 8m f8g⁴ 8m* 8m* p8g* p8.6m⁴ 8.2s Oct 18] fair handicapper: won at Yarmouth (2, first a selling event, left J. Hills 5,800 gns) in August and Lingfield in September: bolted to start and well below form final outing (gelded after): stays 1m: acts on all-weather and good to firm going: upset in stall and withdrawn ninth intended outing. *J. F. Coupland* **73**

APRIL ATTRACTION (FR) 4 b.f. Mark of Esteem (IRE) 137 – April Lee (USA) (Lyphard (USA) 132) [2006 14.1g p12.2g 11.9d Oct 19] half-sister to 3 winners abroad, including French winner around 1¼m April Raheen (by Lyphard): dam French 9.5f/ **–**

1½m and hurdles winner: fair performer when trained in France by H-A. Pantall, winning 2 handicaps at La Teste in 2005: well beaten in Britain: stays 1½m: acts on soft going: tongue tied final outing. *C. J. Down*

APRIL FOOL 2 ch.g. (Apr 1) Pivotal 124 – Palace Affair 113 (Pursuit of Love 124) **61** [2006 7g 6d 8.2d⁶ Nov 1] close-coupled, compact gelding: modest form in maidens: gelded after. *J. A. Geake*

APRIL SHANNON 4 b.f. Tipsy Creek (USA) 115 – Westering 54 (Auction Ring **–** (USA) 123) [2006 –: p12.2g p12.2g Mar 3] of no account. *J. E. Long*

APSARA 5 br.m. Groom Dancer (USA) 128 – Ayodhya (IRE) (Astronef 116) [2006 71: **75** 9.9f 9.8m 9.9f⁴ 8m³ 8f* 8.5s* 9.2m³ 9.8s³ 10.5s⁴ 10f³ 10g 12d⁵ Oct 3] compact mare: fair handicapper: won at Pontefract in July and Beverley in August: effective at 1m/1¼m: acts on firm and soft going: tried visored/in cheekpieces: more genuine nowadays than in past. *G. M. Moore*

APSIS 5 b.h. Barathea (IRE) 127 – Apogee 113 (Shirley Heights 130) [2006 118: 8s* **117** 8m* 8m Jul 23] smart performer, lightly raced: won listed race at Longchamp (by 1½ lengths from Ridaar) in April and Prix du Chemin de Fer du Nord at Chantilly (by ¾ length from Turtle Bowl) in June: rare poor effort in Prix Messidor at Maisons-Laffitte final start: effective at 1m/1¼m: acted on heavy and good to firm going: held up: reliable: retired, and to stand at Haras de la Hetraie, France, fee €2,000. *A. Fabre, France*

APT TO RUN (USA) 3 b.c. Aptitude (USA) 128 – Tufa 78 (Warning 136) [2006 71: **76** p10g 10d² 10v² 9.7f³ 9.9g⁴ 10f³ Jul 8] tall colt: fair maiden: stays 1¼m: acts on firm and good to soft going (below form on heavy): blinkered last 5 starts: consistent: sold 31,000 gns later in July, joined M. Murphy in Ireland. *E. A. L. Dunlop*

AQALEEM 2 b.c. (Mar 17) Sinndar (IRE) 134 – Dalayil (IRE) (Sadler's Wells (USA) **86** 132) [2006 7d³ 8g² Sep 15] lengthy colt, unfurnished as 2-y-o: fifth foal: half-brother to fairly useful 7f winner Maghazi (by Fasliyev): dam unraced close relative to 1995 champion 2-y-o/very smart performer up to 1¼m Alhaarth: fairly useful form: third in maiden and second in minor event (won by Teslin, Authorized third), both at Newbury: will stay 1¼m/1½m. *M. P. Tregoning*

AQMAAR 2 b.c. (Feb 29) Green Desert (USA) 127 – Hureya (USA) 82 (Woodman **91** (USA) 126) [2006 7m* 7m³ 7d² Sep 27] angular colt: second foal: half-brother to 3-y-o Estiqraar: dam, 1m winner, half-sister to very smart performer up to 1¼m Muqbil out of half-sister to high-class miler Bahri: fairly useful form: won maiden at Newbury in July: placed in minor events at Lingfield and Salisbury (second to Tembanee), racing freely: will stay 1m. *J. L. Dunlop*

AQUA 4 b.f. Mister Baileys 123 – Water Well 96 (Sadler's Wells (USA) 132) [2006 f11s **51** 7.1g 8.5f 8d 8m⁵ 7.9m 7.5f 6f 6g 9d 9.8d⁵ 10f 9s* 9d f8g 9.1v⁵ Oct 28] seventh foal: half-sister to 3 winners, including fairly useful 5f/6f winner Soaked (by Dowsing): dam 7.6f winner out of high-class sprinter Soba: well held in bumpers: modest performer: 50/1, easily best effort when winning seller at Musselburgh in September: should stay 1¼m: acts on soft ground: tried blinkered: has twice refused to enter stall. *P. T. Midgley*

AQUILEGIA (IRE) 2 b.f. (Apr 14) Desert Style (IRE) 121 – Pyatshaw (Common **72** Grounds 118) [2006 6m 6s⁴ 5m⁴ 5d⁵ 5.2d² 5.1d* Nov 1] leggy filly: third foal: half-sister to Italian 2004 2-y-o 5f winner by Revoque: dam unraced: fair performer: won maiden at Nottingham in November: best at 5f: acts on soft and good to firm going: tends to start slowly. *E. S. McMahon*

ARAAFA (IRE) 3 b.c. Mull of Kintyre (USA) 114 – Resurgence (Polar Falcon **128** (USA) 126) [2006 103: 8m⁴ 8v* 8m* 8m⁵ 8d² 8f Nov 4]

'. . . they fly so high, nearly reach the sky, then . . .' Like the pretty bubbles blown in the song, Araafa could only fly so high. Although, in the end, he was not the champion miler, he had a spell mid-way through the season when he looked as though he could be. Shouldering aside George Washington in the Irish Two Thousand Guineas and then making the most of the latter's absence from the St James's Palace Stakes, Araafa produced his best again in the Queen Elizabeth II Stakes in the autumn, only to have his bubble burst by his old rival. After one more run in the Breeders' Cup Mile, Araafa was retired to stud with the record of a high-class miler, good enough to be champion some years but not quite the best around in 2006.

Araafa's reappearance raised no great expectations for the season ahead, but, in hindsight, he was perhaps less forward than some of his rivals in the Two

Boylesports Irish 2000 Guineas, the Curragh—
Araafa readily turns the tables on George Washington; Decado and Yasoodd are next

Thousand Guineas in early-May. Confirmed a definite runner only a few days beforehand after missing an intended outing in the Free Handicap, he started at 66/1 in a field of fourteen, but improved on his two-year-old form, which had been only useful, to be a never-nearer fourth, beaten three quarters of a length for third behind Olympian Odyssey, who was two and a half lengths and a length and a half behind the first two, George Washington and Sir Percy. With George Washington at 7/4-on, Araafa was a 12/1-shot for the Boylesports Irish Two Thousand Guineas at the Curragh three weeks after Newmarket on the last Saturday in May, though he had reportedly worked impressively in his final gallop beforehand. Under an enterprising ride from Alan Munro, he turned the form round to some tune in the contrasting ground, showing better form still. Never far off the steady pace, Araafa was sent for home under three furlongs out as the field came centre to stand side in the heavy ground and kept on strongly under pressure to hold the swerving George Washington by two lengths, with second favourite Decado another length away in third and Yasoodd a further length back in fourth. Araafa was a first classic winner for his jockey since Generous in 1991 and he took the ride only after a two-day ban was deferred. Araafa was a first classic winner for his forty-three-year-old Newmarket-based trainer Jeremy Noseda, a licence-holder since 1998.

George Washington returned injured from the Curragh and, in his absence, Araafa started a heavily-backed favourite for the St James's Palace Stakes on the opening day of the Royal meeting, going off at 2/1, despite getting warm and on edge beforehand. In a field of eleven, the French-trained Stormy River was second favourite at 7/2 after his first defeat of the season, a close third to George Washington's stable-companion Aussie Rules in the Poule d'Essai des Poulains. On Ascot's

St James's Palace Stakes, Royal Ascot—
Araafa improves again and wins in good style from the grey Stormy River and Ivan Denisovich

Saleh Al Homaizi & Imad Al Sagar's "Araafa"

revamped track and back on much firmer going, Munro rode another copybook race as Araafa ran out a clear-cut winner. Soon second as the Ballydoyle pacemaker Arabian Prince raced clear, Araafa was sent on shortly after the turn and was a good four lengths up at one point, holding Stormy River by two lengths with Ivan Denisovich and Marcus Andronicus, stable-companions of George Washington, third and fourth, a length and three quarters and three quarters of a length further away. Following Black Minnaloushe in 2001 and Rock of Gibraltar in 2002, Araafa was the third horse in six years to complete the Irish Two Thousand Guineas/St James's Palace Stakes double.

With Aussie Rules in the line-up this time, a further opportunity to pull together the form of the colts' classics at a mile came in the Sussex Stakes at Goodwood in August. In the continued absence of George Washington, Araafa's connections sensed that the mantle as the season's best miler was in reach for Araafa, his jockey billing the race as 'Araafa's chance to become champion'. Starting favourite at 11/10, with Aussie Rules only fifth best at 8/1, Araafa finished a place behind his fellow three-year-old in fifth, beaten three and a half lengths behind the six-year-old winner Court Masterpiece. In a strongly-run race, Araafa paid the price for being taken on for the lead by Echo of Light, but, more significantly as it turned out, he was reported to have wrenched an ankle. Araafa recovered in time to be among the entries for the Prix du Moulin at Longchamp in the first week in September, but missed the race to wait for the Queen Elizabeth II Stakes at Ascot later in the month in which he was ridden by Christophe Soumillon, deputising for regular partner Alan Munro, who had been suspended from riding with health problems. Araafa was no match for an on-song George Washington, but showed himself superior to any other miler in Europe apart from the winner, leading for much of the last two furlongs before going down by a length and a quarter. Araafa finished closer to the winner than at Newmarket and reversed Sussex Stakes form with Court Masterpiece, who was two lengths further back in third. Araafa was among the five-day entries for the Champion Stakes the following month, but connections passed up the opportunity to see what Araafa could do at a mile and a quarter in favour of a crack at the Breeders' Cup Mile at Churchill Downs in November. Araafa started favourite, but could manage only ninth of fourteen on the firmest ground he tackled, beaten just over five lengths.

Araafa (IRE) (b.c. 2003)	Mull of Kintyre (USA) (b 1997)	Danzig (b 1977)	Northern Dancer
			Pas de Nom
		Retrospective (b 1992)	Easy Goer
			Hay Patcher
	Resurgence (b 1998)	Polar Falcon (b or br 1987)	Nureyev
			Marie d'Argonne
		Fearless Revival (ch 1997)	Cozzene
			Stufida

A tall, lengthy, good sort with a quick action, Araafa was much the most expensive yearling from the first crop of his sire Mull of Kintyre sold in 2004, making 150,000 guineas at the Tattersalls October Sales, having been sold for 48,000 guineas as a foal. He is much the best horse sired by Gimcrack winner Mull of Kintyre among his two crops of racing age. Not surprisingly, he is also easily the best produce of his dam, the unraced Resurgence. Araafa is her second foal. The first Ragged Glory (by Foxhound) was a minor winner abroad and her third Blue Monkey (by Orpen) showed only fair form in maidens as a two-year-old in the latest season. Resurgence's main claim to fame before Araafa came along was that she is a sister to Pivotal, winner of the Nunthorpe Stakes and a leading sire. Like Pivotal, Araafa will stand in Newmarket, where he will be covering at the Plantation Stud at £15,000, October 1st terms. Raced only at seven furlongs and a mile, he showed comfortably his best form at the longer trip and would probably have stayed a mile and a quarter. A genuine sort, though inclined to sweat and become edgy in the preliminaries on occasions, he acted on heavy and good to firm ground. *J. Noseda*

ARABELLAS HOMER 2 b.f. (Feb 17) Mark of Esteem (IRE) 137 – Rush Hour (IRE) **49** (Night Shift (USA)) [2006 p7.1g⁵ 7.5d⁴ 7.5m⁶ 8f f6g p7.1g p8.6g⁴ p9.5g p8.6s⁵ Dec 13] smallish, close-coupled filly: second foal: half-sister to 4-y-o Lincolneurocruiser: dam unraced: poor maiden: left Miss J. Camacho after fourth start: seems to stay 9.5f: acts on all-weather and good to soft going. *Mrs N. Macauley*

ARABIAN BREEZE 3 b.f. Muhtarram (USA) 125 – Dominie Breeze (Primo Dominie **44** 121) [2006 p6g 8.3g³ p8.6g Sep 11] first foal: dam unraced half-sister to useful hurdler Tramantano (by Muhtarram): poor maiden: stays 8.3f: reportedly suffered from breathing problem final outing. *M. Mullineaux*

ARABIAN GULF 2 b.c. (Feb 8) Sadler's Wells (USA) 132 – Wince 117 (Selkirk **73 p** (USA) 129) [2006 7d Oct 28] well-made colt: second foal: brother to very smart 1¼m/ 1½m (Yorkshire Oaks) winner Quiff: dam, 6f (at 2 yrs) to 1m (1000 Guineas) winner, half-sister to very smart performer up to 1½m Ulundi: 8/1 and backward, 4¼ lengths seventh of 19 to Mr Napper Tandy in maiden at Newmarket, not knocked about: will be suited by 1¼m/1½m: will do better. *Sir Michael Stoute*

ARABIAN MOON (IRE) 10 ch.g. Barathea (IRE) 127 – Excellent Alibi (USA) **58** (Exceller (USA) 129) [2006 60: 10.2d⁴ 11.6f 10m⁴ 11.6m⁵ 16.2f⁴ 11.9f² Aug 9] leggy, quite good-topped gelding: easy mover: modest performer: effective at 1½m to 2f: acts on polytrack and firm going: tried in blinkers/visor: held up: often finds little: won over hurdles in November. *R. Brotherton*

ARABIAN PRINCE (USA) 3 b.c. Fusaichi Pegasus (USA) 130 – Add (USA) (Spec- **112** tacular Bid (USA)) [2006 103: 8v 8m 8g 8d 8m² 8d³ Aug 20] tall, rather leggy, close-coupled colt: smart performer: best efforts when ¾-length second to Danak in listed race at Cork and 1¾ lengths third to King Jock in Desmond Stakes at Leopardstown last 2 starts: shaped as though he'd have run well in listed race at the Curragh third outing but persistently short of room and eased: well beaten in Group 1 company other starts, including as pacemaker in St James's Palace Stakes at Royal Ascot second outing: stays 1m: acts on soft and good to firm ground: joined D. Watson in UAE. *A. P. O'Brien, Ireland*

ARABIAN SEA (IRE) 3 b.c. Sadler's Wells (USA) 132 – Teggiano (IRE) 108 (Mujta- **79** hid (USA) 118) [2006 81: p10g² 10s p8g⁶ Jun 7] leggy colt: fair maiden: below form last 2 starts: stays 1¼m: acts on polytrack, good to firm and good to soft going: blinkered final outing: sold 5,000 gns, joined G. Bridgwater. *C. E. Brittain*

ARABIAN TIGER 3 b.c. Singspiel (IRE) 133 – Um Lardaff (Mill Reef (USA) 141) **67**
[2006 10m 9.9m⁵ 11m 11.6d Oct 9] half-brother to several winners, including useful 2001
2-y-o 6f winner Mr Sandancer (later 1m winner in Sweden, by Zafonic) and fairly useful
7f (at 2 yrs)/1¼m winner Expensive Taste (by Cadeaux Genereux): dam, French 11f/1½m
winner, sister to Shirley Heights: fair maiden: form only when fifth in maiden at Beverley: should stay 11f: reportedly lost action third outing: sold 6,000 gns. *P. W. Chapple-
Hyam*

ARABIAN TREASURE (USA) 2 br.f. (May 18) Danzig (USA) – Very Confidential **64 p**
(USA) (Fappiano (USA)) [2006 6g⁴ Sep 28] $270,000Y: strong, good-bodied filly: has
a fluent, quick action: sister to fairly useful 9f and 1½m winner Barcardero, closely
related to 2 winners, including fairly useful 1¾m winner High Tension (by Sadler's
Wells), and half-sister to 2 winners abroad: dam, US maiden, half-sister to US Grade 1
9f/1¼m winner Awe Inspiring: 3/1, encouraging fourth to Dream Scheme in maiden at
Newmarket: will be well suited by 1m/1¼m: sure to progress. *Sir Michael Stoute*

ARABIAN WORD 2 ch.c. (Feb 22) Diesis 133 – Duchcov 101 (Caerleon (USA) 132) **68**
[2006 7.1m 7.1d⁵ 8d⁴ Oct 19] 40,000F, €240,000Y: neat, useful-looking colt: first foal:
dam 1¼m winner in Britain/USA: fair form in maidens: should be well suited by 1m/
1¼m: sold 20,000 gns. *Sir Michael Stoute*

ARABIE 8 b.g. Polish Precedent (USA) 131 – Always Friendly 111 (High Line 125) **§§**
[2006 81: p9.5g 10m 10.5g p8.6m p8.6g f8g Nov 20] lengthy, angular gelding: fairly
useful handicapper at 7 yrs: thoroughly ungenuine in 2006 (left I. Williams after third
outing), refusing to race on four occasions: tried blinkered: banned from racing at HRA
inquiry in December. *Peter Grayson*

ARBELLA 4 ch.f. Primo Dominie 121 – Kristal Bridge 75 (Kris 135) [2006 77: p12.2g* **106**
13.4d³ 11.9s* May 27] tall, good-topped filly: useful performer, lightly raced: has reportedly had splint problems: won maiden at Wolverhampton (by 6 lengths from Fyvie) in
April and 5-runner listed race at Haydock (by neck from Aunt Julia) in May: creditable
7½ lengths third of 5 to The Whistling Teal in Ormonde Stakes at Chester: barely
stays 13.4f: acts on polytrack, yet to encounter heavy ground but acts on any other turf.
W. R. Swinburn

ARCADIO (GER) 4 b.c. Monsun (GER) 124 – Assia (IRE) (Royal Academy (USA) **122**
130) [2006 117: 9.5s* 11s* 8g* 10g⁵ 8g³ 8g⁵ Oct 14] very smart performer: won listed
race at Hanover in April, Grosser Mercedes-Benz-Preis at Baden-Baden (best effort, by
2 lengths from Day Flight) in May and pferdewetten.de-Trophy at Cologne (by neck from
stable-companion Soldier Hollow) in June: below form last 3 starts: ideally suited by
further than 1m and stays 11f: acts on soft ground. *P. Schiergen, Germany*

ARCANGELA 3 b.f. Galileo (IRE) 134 – Crafty Buzz (USA) (Crafty Prospector **–**
(USA)) [2006 51: 10m p12.2g 16.1g Sep 27] lengthy filly: maiden: little form at 3 yrs.
J. G. Given

ARCHDUKE FERDINAND (FR) 8 ch.g. Dernier Empereur (USA) 125 – Lady **90**
Norcliffe (USA) (Norcliffe (CAN)) [2006 –: p16g² 15d⁴ 20m p16g p16g* p16.5g³ Nov 6]
strong, close-coupled gelding: just fairly useful handicapper nowadays: won at Lingfield
in October: best at 2m+: acts on polytrack, firm and soft ground: has worn cheekpieces:
often races freely: none too consistent. *A. King*

ARCHERFIELD LINKS (USA) 3 b. or br.g. Brahms (USA) 118 – Georgian Bay **96**
(USA) (Storm Cat (USA)) [2006 84: p8g* 8m 8.3f⁴ p7f³ Oct 14] tall gelding: useful
performer: won handicap at Kempton (beat Scot Love readily by ¾ length) in April:
had excuses next 2 outings (saddle reportedly slipped on latter), then gelded and left
N. Callaghan: third in optional claimer at Keeneland final start: stays 1m: acts on polytrack and good to soft going: has shown quirks: held up. *P. L. Biancone, USA*

ARCH FOLLY 4 b.g. Silver Patriarch (IRE) 125 – Folly Fox (Alhijaz 122) [2006 65: **67**
p16g⁴ 16g⁵ 16.2g⁵ 18m³ 17.2m² 16.2f* p16g 16.2m p13.9g p12.2m p13.9g Nov
20] close-coupled gelding: fair performer: won claimer at Chepstow (claimed from
J. Portman £10,000) in July: left I. Williams after eighth outing: stays 2¼m, may prove
best at shorter: acts on polytrack and firm going: in cheekpieces last 2 starts. *R. J. Price*

ARCHIDONA (FR) 3 b.f. Bluebird (USA) 125 – Gembira (USA) (Alysheba (USA)) **43**
[2006 p10g p8.6g³ p8.6g 10g⁴ 9.9g⁵ 12.5s 11.8g* Nov 11] sister to French 2002 2-y-o 1m
winner Arevalo and half-sister to 2 winners, including 1m winner Keeper's Lodge (by
Grand Lodge): dam, second at 1m at 2 yrs in France, half-sister to very smart performer
up to 1¼m Two Timing: trained by C. Laffon-Parias in France at 2 yrs, winning claimer
at Le Croise-Laroche: poor form in Britain in 2006 (left M. Quinn after fifth outing),

before winning similar event at Machecoul in November: stays 11.8f: acts on heavy going, probably on polytrack: tried blinkered/visored. *E. Danel, France*

ARCHIE BABE (IRE) 10 ch.g. Archway (IRE) 115 – Frensham Manor (Le Johnstan 123) [2006 59: 10d² 12.4m⁵ 11.8d 11.1d Sep 25] workmanlike gelding: modest handicapper: stays 1½m: acts on heavy and good to firm ground: tried in cheekpieces: sometimes looks ungenuine: successful over hurdles in October and fences in December. *J. J. Quinn* — **62**

ARCHIESTOWN (USA) 3 b.g. Arch (USA) 127 – Second Chorus (IRE) (Scenic 128) [2006 8g⁴ 8m⁴ 10g Jun 1] 26,000Y: tall, angular, quite attractive gelding: second foal: dam once-raced half-sister to useful dam of St Leger winner Rule of Law: fairly useful form in maidens: lethargic and green, best effort when 6¾ lengths fourth to Secret World in newcomers race at Newmarket: gelded after final start: should stay 1¼m. *J. L. Dunlop* — **81**

ARCHIMBOLDO (USA) 3 ch.g. Woodman (USA) 126 – Awesome Strike (USA) 84 (Theatrical 128) [2006 80: p8.6g⁶ p8.6g p12g³ 12.1d⁵ p12g⁵ p12.2g³ 11.7f⁶ p12.2g⁶ p16.5g³ Jul 13] strong gelding: fair performer: stays easy 2m: acts on polytrack and firm ground: tried blinkered: tends to carry head high: ungenuine: winning juvenile hurdler. *T. Wall* — **77 §**

ARCHIPENKO (USA) 2 b.c. (May 30) Kingmambo (USA) 125 – Bound (USA) (Nijinsky (CAN) 138) [2006 7g 7v² 7s* Oct 30] brother to 3-y-o Soar With Eagles and closely related/half-brother to several winners, including fairly useful Irish 7f winner Septimus Severus (by Seeking The Gold) and US 1m minor stakes winner Limit (by Cox's Ridge): dam, minor 1m stakes winner, closely related to Nureyev and half-sister to dam of Sadler's Wells: progressive form in maidens: beaten ¾ length by stable-companion Spanish Harlem in 22-runner event at the Curragh before making all at Leopardstown week later, drawing clear to beat Honoured Guest 6 lengths: will stay 1¼m: sure to improve further. *A. P. O'Brien, Ireland* — **97 p**

ARCHIRONDEL 8 b.g. Bin Ajwaad (IRE) 119 – Penang Rose (NZ) (Kingdom Bay (NZ)) [2006 71: p9.5g⁴ p12.2g 9.9g⁵ May 13] smallish gelding: modest handicapper: effective at 9f to 1½m: acts on polytrack and any turf going: sometimes races freely/finishes weakly: usually held up. *N. Wilson* — **58**

ARCHIVIST (IRE) 3 b.c. Kalanisi (IRE) 132 – Mill Rainbow (FR) (Rainbow Quest (USA) 134) [2006 –: p10g p12.2g p12.2g 12g p12.2g 10.1m Sep 13] signs of a little ability: tongue tied final start. *M. Blanshard* — **–**

ARCH OF TITUS (IRE) 2 ch.c. (Feb 25) Titus Livius (FR) 115 – Cap And Gown (IRE) 81 (Royal Academy (USA) 130) [2006 p7.1g⁴ 7d² 7.5m² 8s⁴ Sep 28] 16,000Y: lengthy colt: fourth foal: half-brother to 5.5f winner in Norway by Charnwood Forest: dam, 1m winner, half-sister to smart performer up to 1½m Papering: fair maiden: second at Newcastle and Beverley: stamina stretched in nursery final start: will prove best short of 1m. *M. L. W. Bell* — **77**

ARCH REBEL (USA) 5 b.g. Arch (USA) 127 – Sheba's Step (USA) (Alysheba (USA)) [2006 –: 10s* 10d⁴ 8d* 8g² 10g⁶ 8d² 8g² 10m⁴ 10s* Oct 30] smart performer: improved in 2006, winning listed races at the Curragh (by 4½ lengths from Tolpuddle) in April and Leopardstown in May (by ½ length from Hard Rock City) and October (comfortably, by 3 lengths from Bon Nuit): also ran well when beaten ¾ length by King Jock in Desmond Stakes at Leopardstown sixth start: best at 1m/1¼m: acts on soft and good to firm ground: wore cheekpieces/blinkers last 2 outings: held up. *N. Meade, Ireland* — **114**

ARCH SWING (USA) 2 b.f. (Mar 26) Arch (USA) 127 – Gold Pattern (USA) (Slew O' Gold (USA)) [2006 6m* 7g* Sep 16] $55,000F, €45,000Y: fifth foal: half-sister to 1m winner in Japan by Swain: dam, 6.5f to 8.5f winner in USA, out of US Grade 1 9f winner Pattern Step: useful form: won maiden in August and C. L. Weld Park Stakes (beat Silk Dress by 4½ lengths) in September, both at the Curragh: will stay 1m: should go on improving. *J. Oxx, Ireland* — **104 p**

ARCTIC COVE 5 b.g. Vettori (IRE) 119 – Sundae Girl (USA) 75 (Green Dancer (USA) 132) [2006 69: p13.9g 10.5m 14.1f 14.1g Aug 3] modest handicapper: stays 1¾m: acts on polytrack, firm and good to soft going. *M. D. Hammond* — **60**

ARCTIC DESERT 6 b.g. Desert Prince (IRE) 130 – Thamud (IRE) (Lahib (USA) 129) [2006 83: p8g* p8g⁵ p8g³ 7d⁴ 7m⁵ p8g³ 7.1m⁶ p6g⁴ 6m³ 7m 5.7m p8g² p7g² Nov 15] big, good-topped gelding: impresses in appearance: fairly useful handicapper: won at Lingfield in January: left A. Balding 15,000 gns before final start: free-going sort, but stays easy 8.6f: acts on polytrack, firm and good to soft going: tried visored/tongue tied: sometimes slowly away/looks none too keen, and to treat with caution. *Miss Gay Kelleway* — **83 §**

ARCTIC WINGS (IRE) 2 b.c. (Mar 29) In The Wings 128 – Arctic Hunt (IRE) (Bering 136) [2006 8g p8.6g² p8.6g⁵ Nov 18] rather leggy, dipped-backed colt: second foal: closely related to 3-y-o Narvik: dam, useful French 1m to 1¼m winner (including 9f at 2 yrs), half-sister to smart French 1¼m/1½m performer Trumbaka: fair form in maidens: will stay 1¼m. *W. R. Muir* **75**

ARCULINGE 3 b.f. Paris House 123 – Calamanco 71 (Clantime 101) [2006 64: p6g⁵ 6f⁵ 6g² 6f 6g⁵ 6m⁵ 7m³ 6d 7.1m p7g Oct 23] leggy filly: modest maiden: will prove best at 5f/6f: acts on polytrack and firm going. *M. Blanshard* **59**

ARDASNAILS (IRE) 4 b.g. Spectrum (IRE) 126 – Fey Lady (IRE) (Fairy King (USA)) [2006 –: p9.5g May 5] no form. *K. G. Wingrove* **–**

ARDBRAE LADY 3 b.f. Overbury (IRE) 116 – Gagajulu 75 (Al Hareb (USA) 123) [2006 93: 7s⁵ 7d² 8v² 10g⁶ 9.5d³ 7.5g⁴ 9m² 8m 10s⁶ 8d 7d⁴ Nov 5] 20,000Y: strong filly: sixth foal: half-sister to 3 winners, including 4-y-o Obe Gold and 6-y-o Beneking: dam 2-y-o 5f winner: useful performer: won maiden at Gowran in 2005: creditable efforts when placed at 3 yrs, including when 6 lengths second to Nightime in Irish 1000 Guineas at the Curragh, third to Race For The Stars in Denny Cordell Stakes at Gowran, and neck second to Blessyourpinksox in listed event at the Curragh third/fifth/seventh outings: stays 9.5f: acts on heavy and good to firm going: blinkered final start. *J. G. Murphy, Ireland* **102**

ARDEA BRAVE (IRE) 4 gr.f. Chester House (USA) 123 – Afto (USA) (Relaunch (USA)) [2006 72: f8g⁴ p8g p10g³ 9.7d p9.5g⁴ p9.5g 11.9m⁴ p12g² 12m² 11.5m* p12.2f* p12g* p13g⁶ p12.2g³ Nov 18] half-sister to 3 winners in USA: dam US Grade 2 7f winner: fairly useful handicapper: left Ms C. Hutchinson in Ireland before return: won at Lingfield and Wolverhampton in August, and Kempton (apprentices, again making all) in September: stays 1½m: acts on all-weather, soft and good to firm going: tried in tongue tie/cheekpieces, in latter nowadays. *M. Botti* **83**

ARDENNES (IRE) 2 b.g. (Jan 26) Jade Robbery (USA) 121 – Ribbon Glade (UAE) (Zafonic (USA) 130) [2006 p6g⁶ Dec 8] 10,000 2-y-o: first foal: dam, unraced half-sister to smart French 1¼m/1½m (in UAE) winner Broche, out of Flaxen Pistol half-sister to Preakness/Belmont winner Risen Star: tongue tied, 11 lengths sixth to Buckie Massa in maiden at Wolverhampton: should improve. *M. Botti* **– p**

ARDENT PRINCE 3 b.g. Polar Prince (IRE) 117 – Anthem Flight (USA) (Fly So Free (USA) 122) [2006 60: f8g Jun 3] tall gelding: modest maiden: best effort at 7f on polytrack. *Mrs H. Dalton* **53**

ARDGLASS (IRE) 4 b.g. Danehill Dancer (IRE) 117 – Leggagh Lady (IRE) 76 (Doubletour (USA)) [2006 67: p12.2g 10.2g May 17] maiden: well held both starts in 2006: tried blinkered/in cheekpieces. *Mrs P. Townsley* **–**

ARDKEEL LASS (IRE) 5 ch.m. Fumo di Londra (IRE) 108 – Wot-A-Noise (IRE) (Petorius 117) [2006 57: f5g⁴ f6s p7.1g⁵ f6g 6f* 6.1m 5.1f 5.3m Aug 22] leggy, lengthy mare: modest performer: successful in 4-runner handicap at L'Ancresse in Guernsey in May: left P. D. Evans after sixth start: effective at 5f/6f: acts on all-weather, firm and good to soft going: tried visored/in cheekpieces: sold £850. *R. A. Harris* **55**

ARDMADDY (IRE) 2 b.g. (Apr 25) Generous (IRE) 139 – Yazmin (IRE) 94 (Green Desert (USA) 127) [2006 p7g⁵ p8g⁵ Oct 23] modest form in maidens at Lingfield (polytrack): gelded after: stays 1m. *J. A. R. Toller* **63**

ARENA'S DREAM (USA) 2 gr. or ro.g. (Apr 25) Aljabr (USA) 125 – Witching Well (IRE) (Night Shift (USA)) [2006 5m⁴ 7d² 7.2d² 7g⁴ Sep 27] $8,500Y, 11,000 2-y-o: rather leggy, angular gelding: sixth foal: half-brother to 3 winners in USA: dam unraced: fairly useful maiden: clear of remainder when second at Newcastle and Ayr: hampered final start: will stay 1m. *R. A. Fahey* **81**

AREYOUTALKINGTOME 3 b.c. Singspiel (IRE) 133 – Shot At Love (IRE) 79 (Last Tycoon 131) [2006 98: p7g³ 8g⁴ 10m² 10f* 9.9f 7m² 8f³ p8.6g⁵ p7g* p7g* p7g* p6g* Dec 16] rather leggy, quite good-topped colt: smart performer: successful in maiden at Brighton in July: progressed really well late in year, winning handicaps at Lingfield in October, November and in December (2), on final occasion showing fine turn of foot under largely hand riding to beat Qadar by length: has won at 1¼m, effective at 6f: acts on polytrack and firm going. *C. A. Cyzer* **118**

ARFINNIT (IRE) 5 b.g. College Chapel 122 – Tidal Reach (USA) 68 (Kris S (USA)) [2006 53: p6g 5.7f 5m 6g p5g Oct 29] good-topped gelding: has a quick action: poor performer: stays 6f: acts on firm and soft going (below form all 3 starts on polytrack): usually wears headgear. *Mrs A. L. M. King* **45**

ARGENT 5 b.g. Barathea (IRE) 127 – Red Tiara (USA) 60 (Mr Prospector (USA)) – [2006 52: 10g Jun 23] sturdy gelding: modest performer: well held in handicap at Ayr only 5-y-o outing: stays 1¼m: acts on fibresand and any turf going: usually wears cheekpieces: tried tongue tied. *Miss L. A. Perratt*

ARGENT DANSEUR 2 b.g. (Mar 10) Lujain (USA) 119 – Perfect Pirouette (JPN) 72 **42** (Warning 136) [2006 5m⁴ 5d⁵ 6g⁵ 5m⁴ Jun 10] tall, close-coupled gelding: poor maiden: in cheekpieces/visor after debut. *B. S. Rothwell*

ARGENTINE (IRE) 2 b.c. (Apr 5) Fasliyev (USA) 120 – Teller (ARG) (Southern **84** Halo (USA)) [2006 5d³ 5g⁴ 5m* 6f² 6m⁵ p6g³ Oct 23] 18,000Y: strong, lengthy colt: has scope: half-brother to winners in South Africa by Spaceship and Gold Press: dam winner in South Africa: fairly useful performer: won maiden at Carlisle in July: placed 2 of 3 starts in nurseries (hung right other one): will prove best kept to 5f/6f: acts on polytrack, firm and good to soft going: sold 32,000 gns. *M. Johnston*

ARGONAUT 6 ch.g. Rainbow Quest (USA) 134 – Chief Bee 89 (Chief's Crown – (USA)) [2006 –: 17.2s Apr 11] smallish, quite good-topped gelding: useful performer at 4 yrs: lightly raced and no form on Flat after: sold 1,200 gns. *P. Bowen*

ARIAN'S LAD 5 b.g. Prince Sabo 123 – Arian Da 81 (Superlative 118) [2006 60: p7g⁴ **58** p7.1g⁴ 7.1d⁴ 6.1d 7f⁶ 6.1m² p7.1g Jul 11] leggy gelding: modest maiden: stays 7f: acts on polytrack, firm and good to soft going: often races up with pace: refused to enter stall intended eighth outing. *B. Palling*

ARIESANNE (IRE) 5 ch.m. Primo Dominie 121 – Living Legend (ITY) (Archway – (IRE) 115) [2006 31: f6g³ f5g f6g* f6g² f7g f6g 7.2g 6m⁶ Jul 4] lengthy, workmanlike **a55** mare: modest on all-weather, poor on turf: made all in banded race at Southwell in January: stays 6f: acts on fibresand: wore cheekpieces final start. *A. C. Whillans*

ARIODANTE 4 b.g. Groom Dancer (USA) 128 – Maestrale (Top Ville 129) [2006 –: **75** 8d 10.1m⁵ 10.1m³ 10g 12m⁴ 14.1f⁴ 11.6f⁶ 11.9f* 12.6m p16.5g⁶ p12g⁴ Dec 20] smallish gelding: fair handicapper: won at Brighton in August: stays 1½m: acts on polytrack and firm ground. *J. M. P. Eustace*

ARISEA (IRE) 3 b.f. Cape Cross (IRE) 129 – Castelfranca (IRE) (Scenic 128) [2006 –: – p5.1g f5g 5.9g 9.3m Aug 7] lengthy filly: little form: visored/in cheekpieces last 3 starts. *R. C. Guest*

ARISTI (IRE) 5 b.m. Dr Fong (USA) 128 – Edessa (IRE) 104 (Tirol 127) [2006 64: **61 d** p16g p16.5g 15s⁴ 21.6d 14.1m f14g⁵ p16.5g p16.5f p16g⁶ Aug 30] angular mare: modest performer: below form after third start: stays 2¼m: acts on polytrack and heavy going: tried blinkered in France, usually wears cheekpieces. *M. Quinn*

ARISTOFILIA 3 b.f. Bahhare (USA) 122 – Noble Story 61 (Last Tycoon 131) [2006 **62** 75: p6g⁴ 6m⁵ 7f⁸ 8.3m 8.2g 8m p6g⁵ Oct 6] just modest maiden in 2006: should stay 1m: acts on polytrack and firm ground: sold 4,000 gns, sent to Iran. *P. F. I. Cole*

ARKADIA HONEY 3 ch.f. Tomba 119 – Arkadia Park (IRE) (Polish Precedent (USA) – 131) [2006 59: 6g 5.1g May 2] small, sturdy filly: modest maiden at 2 yrs: well held in handicaps in 2006. *J. L. Spearing*

ARKHOLME 5 b.g. Robellino (USA) 127 – Free Spirit (IRE) (Caerleon (USA) 132) – [2006 70: p7g⁶ p10g Jul 22] useful-looking gelding: just fair performer in 2005: well held both Flat starts in 2006: usually blinkered. *A. M. Hales*

ARMADA 3 b.g. Anabaa (USA) 130 – Trevillari (USA) (Riverman (USA) 131) [2006 **78** p8g² p9.5g* Jul 1] 70,000Y: leggy, quite good-topped gelding: brother to 2 winners, notably smart French/US sprinter/miler Tsigane, and closely related/half-brother to several winners in France, including 11.5f winner Trillari (by Lure): dam, French maiden sister to Prix Saint-Alary winner Treble, out of half-sister to Triptych: fair form in maidens: confirmed debut promise when comfortably winning at Wolverhampton in July by length from Beldon Hill: stayed 9.5f: twice refused to enter stall: joined W. Haggas. *Sir Michael Stoute*

ARMAGNAC 8 b.g. Young Ern 120 – Arianna Aldini (Habitat 134) [2006 86: 5g **66** May 13] tall, good-topped gelding: unimpressive mover: fairly useful handicapper at best: shaped as if needing further than 5f sole outing at 8 yrs: stays 7f: acts on firm and soft ground: tried in cheekpieces at 5 yrs: occasionally slowly away/pulls hard: held up: none too reliable. *M. A. Buckley*

ARMANATTA (IRE) 5 b.m. Spectrum (IRE) 126 – Via Verbano (IRE) 105 (Caerleon **70** (USA) 132) [2006 80: p8.6g 8v 7.5s⁵ 8g 10m 7g⁴ 10.2m⁵ 9s* 7v⁶ 14s⁶ Oct 30] third foal: sister to 2001 2-y-o 7f winner Solid Gold and 1m to 1½m winner Addario, both fairly useful in Ireland, latter also 7f winner in USA: dam Irish 6f (at 2 yrs) to 1m winner: sold from J. Bolger €15,000 after final 3-y-o start: fair handicapper in 2006, winning at Ballinrobe in October: below form in Britain on first and seventh outings: effective at 7f to 1½m: acts on heavy and good to firm ground: blinkered (below form) once at 3 yrs: sold €16,000. *Mrs A. M. O'Shea, Ireland*

ARMATORE (USA) 6 b.g. Gone West (USA) – Awesome Account (USA) (Lyphard (USA) 132) [2006 –, a63: p9.5g p12.2g Jun 22] maiden: well beaten both starts in 2006: often wears cheekpieces. *E. R. Oertel*

ARM CANDY (IRE) 3 br.f. Nashwan (USA) 135 – Bedara 93 (Barathea (IRE) 127) **101** [2006 93+: 7.6m² 10d 8.1m 7d² 8.1g⁶ 7g⁴ 8d* p10g Nov 18] leggy, unfurnished filly: useful performer: creditable efforts when in frame in 2006 prior to best effort when winning handicap at Newmarket (by 3 lengths from Rio Riva) in October: well held in listed race at Lingfield final outing: probably needs further than 7f nowadays, and stays 1m well: acts on good to firm and good to soft ground: sold 65,000 gns, sent to USA. *J. A. R. Toller*

ARMIGERENT (IRE) 2 b.c. (Mar 30) In The Wings 128 – Roses From Ridey (IRE) **97 ?** 78 (Petorius 117) [2006 7.5f² 6f² 6m² 7m⁴ 7g⁵ 6d⁶ 7d Sep 19] €27,000Y: small colt: fourth foal: dam twice-raced half-sister to very smart 1¼m to 1½m performer Kutub: maiden: appeared to show useful form when 3 lengths second to Strategic Prince in July Stakes at Newmarket third start: best run otherwise (mostly highly tried) when fourth to Satulagi in listed event at Ascot next outing: will stay 1m+: acts on firm and good to soft going: sold 67,000 gns, sent to Austria. *M. Johnston*

ARMILLARY 2 b.f. (Jan 12) Soviet Star (USA) 128 – Marliana (IRE) (Mtoto 134) **–** [2006 6g 7.1m 6m Sep 19] big, strong filly: second foal: half-sister to 2005 2-y-o 6f winner Zambach (by Namid): dam, French 2-y-o 6f winner, out of useful French sprinter Mahalia: little impact in maidens. *Mrs A. J. Perrett*

ARMINIUS (IRE) 3 b.g. Shinko Forest (IRE) – Tribal Rite 95 (Be My Native (USA) **100** 122) [2006 95p: 8.3g³ 8d 7s³ 8d 7g⁵ Oct 13] sturdy gelding: useful performer: gelded after second outing: good efforts when 4 lengths third to Quito in listed event at York and fifth to King's Caprice in handicap at Newmarket third/final starts: effective at 7f/1m: raced on good going or softer (acts on soft): visored second start (refused to settle): sold 110,000 gns, sent to UAE. *R. Hannon*

ARMS ACROSSTHESEA 7 b.g. Namaqualand (USA) – Zolica 60 (Beveled (USA)) **–** [2006 53: f8g May 2] leggy gelding: modest performer: well beaten in seller only 7-y-o outing: tried blinkered/visored, usually wears cheekpieces. *J. Balding*

ARMY OF ANGELS (IRE) 4 ch.g. King's Best (USA) 132 – Angelic Sounds (IRE) **117** (The Noble Player (USA) 126) [2006 105: 7d* 8s* 8d² Oct 28] big, strong gelding: smart performer: out of first 2 only once in 8 outings: gelded, improved to win first 2 starts in 2006, handicaps at Newmarket (by 5 lengths from Skhilling Spirit) in September and York (by 1½ lengths from Wavertree Warrior) in October: just respectable second to stable-companion Blue Ksar in listed event at Newmarket final outing: not sure to stay beyond 1m: acts on soft and good to firm going: tongue tied first 5 starts (prior to 2006): has worn crossed noseband. *Saeed bin Suroor*

ARNIE DE BURGH 4 br.c. Amfortas (IRE) 115 – Align 69 (Petong 126) [2006 66: **77** p7.1g* p7g³ p7.1g* p7.1g⁵ p7.1g 6m⁴ 7.1g May 22] smallish, close-coupled colt: fair handicapper: won at Wolverhampton in January and February: stays 7f: acts on polytrack and good to firm going: often tongue tied at 3 yrs. *D. J. Daly*

ARNIE'S JOINT (IRE) 2 b.g. (Apr 15) Golan (IRE) 129 – Green Green Grass 56 **68** (Green Desert (USA) 127) [2006 5.5d* 6d p6g 6m⁶ Sep 22] 5,000Y: close-coupled gelding: first foal: dam maiden who stayed 6f: fair performer: won maiden at Warwick in May: off 3 months, well held in varied events after (gelded subsequently): should stay at least 6f. *N. P. Littmoden*

ARPETCHEEO (USA) 4 b. or br.c. Deputy Minister (CAN) – Lizanne (USA) (Theat- **–** rical 128) [2006 59: 8.2s 10.2m Jun 3] maiden: well held in handicaps both starts in 2006. *D. Carroll*

ARRAN SCOUT (IRE) 5 b.g. Piccolo 121 – Evie Hone (IRE) 69 (Royal Academy **61** (USA) 130) [2006 75: p8.6g⁵ Mar 25] big, strong gelding: modest performer nowadays: never dangerous in handicap at Wolverhampton only Flat start in 2006: should stay 1¼m: acts on all-weather, firm and soft ground: tried blinkered/in cheekpieces. *T. G. McCourt, Ireland*

ARRAS (GER) 3 ch.c. Monsun (GER) 124 – Avocette (GER) (Kings Lake (USA) 133) **116**
[2006 11g* 10.5m³ Jun 4] fourth foal: brother to useful German 7f (at 2 yrs) and 11f
(Preis der Diana) winner Amarette and half-brother to 2 winners in Germany, including
1¼m/11f winner Anavera (by Acatenango): dam German 9f listed winner: easy winner
of minor events at Saint-Cloud at 2 yrs and Bordeaux in May: plenty of improvement
(smart form) when just under length third to Darsi in Prix du Jockey Club at Chantilly
final start, leading after home turn and worn down only well inside final 1f: stays 11f: acts
on soft and good to firm going: stays in training. *A. Fabre, France*

ARRIVEE (FR) 3 bl.f. Anabaa (USA) 130 – Quiet Dream (USA) (Seattle Slew (USA)) **93**
[2006 9v³ 7d* 7m 7.5s⁶ 8d⁴ Oct 18] good-topped filly: third foal: half-sister to French
12.5f winner Latest Dream (by Grand Lodge): dam, French 1¼m winner, half-sister to
high-class US Grade 1 1¼m winner Dare And Go: fairly useful performer: won minor
event at Compiegne in March: below form afterwards in Fred Darling Stakes at Newbury
and minor events at Maisons-Laffitte and (after 5-month break) Deauville: should stay
1m: acts on good to soft ground: sold 45,000 gns. *A. Fabre, France*

ARRY DASH 6 b.g. Fraam 114 – Miletrian Cares (IRE) 67 (Hamas (IRE) 125§) [2006 **77**
89: p9.5g 8.1m p8.6m 10g 10d³ p10g⁵ Nov 11] small gelding: just fair handicapper in
2006: effective at 1m/1¼m: acts on all-weather, firm and soft ground (yet to race on
heavy): usually visored nowadays: held up. *M. J. Wallace*

ARSAD (IRE) 3 b.f. Cape Cross (IRE) 129 – Astuti (IRE) 84 (Waajib 121) [2006 49: **62**
10g p10g f11g* 14.1m 14g 12d⁵ 9.9g⁶ 9.9m² 11.9d p12g⁴ p12g⁶ f12g³ p13.9g² Dec 31] **a69**
good-topped filly: fair handicapper on all-weather, modest on turf: won at Southwell in
June: stays 1¾m: acts on all-weather and good to firm going. *C. E. Brittain*

ART DECO (IRE) 3 ch.c. Peintre Celebre (USA) 137 – Sometime (IRE) (Royal Acad- **116**
emy (USA) 130) [2006 91: 10.3d* 10.5m⁴ 12m⁵ Jul 14] rather leggy, close-coupled colt:
smart performer: much improved when winning Cheshire Regiment Dee Stakes at
Chester in May by neck from Ivy Creek: ran well after when length fourth to Darsi in Prix
du Jockey Club at Chantilly and when 3¼ lengths fifth to Rail Link in Grand Prix de Paris
at Longchamp: met with minor setbacks after: stays 1½m: acts on soft and good to firm
going: stays in training. *C. R. Egerton*

ART ELEGANT 4 b.g. Desert Prince (IRE) 130 – Elegant (IRE) (Marju (IRE) 127) **76 §**
[2006 75: p7.1g² p8.6g² p8g³ 7g 7.9m* 7.5f³ 7f⁶ 8m 8d 8d 10d 8v Oct 22] useful-looking
gelding: fair performer: won claimer at Carlisle in June: left G. A. Swinbank 9,000 gns
after seventh outing, below form subsequently: stays 9f: acts on polytrack, firm and good
to soft going: tried in cheekpieces/blinkered: ungenuine. *T. G. McCourt, Ireland*

ART EYES (USA) 4 ch.f. Halling (USA) 133 – Careyes (IRE) (Sadler's Wells (USA) **114**
132) [2006 116+: 16.4s⁴ 12m² 12f⁵ 14f² 14g⁴ 13.9d Sep 8] quite lightly-made filly: smart
performer: creditable efforts in 2006 when in frame at Goodwood, namely minor event
(1¾ lengths second to Balkan Knight), Lillie Langtry Fillies' Stakes (neck second to
Tartouche) and listed event (fourth behind Jadalee): ran poorly in Park Hill Stakes at York
final outing: probably stays 2m: acts on firm and soft going: often races prominently.
D. R. C. Elsworth

*Cheshire Regiment Dee Stakes (sponsored by the Elifar Foundation), Chester—
Art Deco (right) holds off the fast-finishing Ivy Creek*

ART GALLERY 2 ch.c. (Mar 17) Indian Ridge 123 – Party Doll 108 (Be My Guest **55 p**
(USA) 126) [2006 7d 6d⁵ p7g Nov 22] 75,000Y, 90,000 2-y-o: rangy colt: has scope:
half-brother to several winners, including French sprinters Titus Livius (smart) and
Bahama Dream (useful), both by Machiavellian: dam French 5f (at 2 yrs) to 1m winner:
not knocked about in maidens: will do better. *G. L. Moore*

ART HISTORIAN (IRE) 3 b.g. Barathea (IRE) 127 – Radhwa (FR) (Shining Steel **61**
123) [2006 63: p9.5m 8.2v³ p12.2g³ p13.9g p12.2g⁵ p13.9g Dec 11] tall, good sort: has a
round action: modest maiden: stays 1½m: acts on polytrack, soft and good to firm ground:
blinkered final 2-y-o start. *T. J. Pitt*

ARTHURS DREAM (IRE) 4 b.g. Desert Prince (IRE) 130 – Blueprint (USA) (Sha- **51**
deed (USA) 135) [2006 69: 10.2d 11.7d 10.2g 8f 7.1f 7.1m Sep 1] modest maiden: stays
11f: acts on good to soft ground: tried visored/in cheekpieces: sometimes slowly away:
has looked none too genuine. *A. W. Carroll*

ARTHUR'S EDGE 2 b.g. (Apr 18) Diktat 126 – Bright Edge 102 (Danehill Dancer **–**
(IRE) 117) [2006 7.1m 6m Sep 16] close-coupled gelding: well held in maidens.
B. Palling

ARTHURS LEGACY 4 b.g. Josr Algarhoud (IRE) 118 – Loch Clair (IRE) 53 **61**
(Lomond (USA) 128) [2006 –: p8g p10g p10g Mar 22] lightly-raced maiden: modest
form last 2 starts: raced only on polytrack. *J. A. R. Toller*

ARTIE 7 b.g. Whittingham (IRE) 104 – Calamanco 71 (Clantime 101) [2006 91: 5d 6g **–**
May 10] big, good-topped gelding: fairly useful handicapper at 6 yrs: well below form in
2006: effective at 5f/6f: acts on any going: tried blinkered. *T. D. Easterby*

ARTIE'S SON (IRE) 3 b.g. Mull of Kintyre (USA) 114 – Eurolink Virago (Charmer **59**
123) [2006 5g⁵ 7g 5g⁴ p5.1g² p6g 7.9g 5.9m⁵ Aug 7] €18,000Y, 11,500 2-y-o: strong **a68**
gelding: seventh foal: half-brother to 3 winners, including fairly useful 7f/9f winner
Eurolink Rooster (by Turtle Island): dam unraced half-sister to smart 7f/1m performer
Eurolink Thunder: fair maiden on all-weather, modest on turf: stays 6f: raced only on
polytrack and good/good to firm ground: sold 1,500 gns. *T. D. Easterby*

ARTIFICIAL 2 ch.g. (Mar 22) Bertolini (USA) 125 – Exclusive Davis (USA) (Our **–**
Native (USA)) [2006 6m Jun 29] 20/1, behind in maiden at Newcastle (gelded after).
T. D. Easterby

ARTIMINO 2 b.c. (Apr 28) Medicean 128 – Palatial 101 (Green Desert (USA) 127) **90 p**
[2006 6.1g⁵ 7.1m* 7d² Sep 24] sturdy, lengthy colt: second foal: dam 7f winner, including
at 2 yrs: fairly useful form: won maiden at Warwick in September: again shaped well
when second to Just Dust in nursery at Ascot: will be suited by 1m: type to go on improving, and should make a useful handicapper. *J. R. Fanshawe*

ART INVESTOR 3 b.g. Sinndar (IRE) 134 – Maid For Romance 71 (Pursuit of Love **75**
124) [2006 81p: 12g⁶ 12d⁵ 9.9g 10m⁶ p10g⁴ f12g² p12.2g² Dec 2] strong, stocky gelding:
fair maiden: stays 1½m: acts on polytrack and good to firm ground: carried head high
fourth start. *D. R. C. Elsworth*

ARTISTIC LADY 3 br.f. Jade Robbery (USA) 121 – Noble Lily (USA) (Vaguely **69**
Noble 140) [2006 –p: 11.9m⁴ 12m⁵ Jun 25] quite attractive filly: fair maiden: best effort
when fourth at Brighton on reappearance: stays 1½m: acts on good to firm ground: carried head awkwardly final start: sold 46,000 gns in July, sent to South Africa. *M. A. Jarvis*

ARTISTIC LIASON 2 ch.f. (Apr 24) Auction House (USA) 120 – Homeoftheclassics **55**
48 (Tate Gallery (USA) 117) [2006 p6g Jul 12] sixth foal: half-sister to 2 winners abroad,
including French 11f to 12.5f winner Aguindari (by Puissance): dam ran twice: 22/1,
green when seventh in maiden at Kempton. *G. C. H. Chung*

ARTISTIC STYLE 6 b.g. Anabaa (USA) 130 – Fine Detail (IRE) 93 (Shirley Heights **92 §**
130) [2006 102§: p10g 10.3m 10g 8m 10s⁶ 10.4s Oct 6] rather leggy gelding: fairly useful
handicapper nowadays: best effort in 2006 when ninth in Zetland Gold Cup at Redcar
third start: stays 1½m: has won on good to firm going, best efforts on softer than good:
reluctant both starts in visor: sometimes races freely: unreliable. *B. Ellison*

ARTIST'S MUSE (USA) 3 b.f. Royal Academy (USA) 130 – Atelier (Warning 136) **68**
[2006 12f⁴ 11.8m⁵ 12m⁶ p12g⁶ p10g Dec 30] good-topped filly: fourth foal: dam unraced
out of sister to Commander In Chief and half-sister to Warning and Deploy: form in
maidens only on first 2 starts: left Mrs A. Perrett 12,000 gns after next outing: may prove
best short of 1½m. *M. S. Saunders*

ARTISTS TOUCH (IRE) 3 b.g. Alhaarth (IRE) 126 – Alla Marcia (IRE) 64 (Marju   – (IRE) 127) [2006 –: p9.5g Jan 27] well held in maidens. *N. P. Littmoden*

ART MAN 3 b.g. Dansili 127 – Persuasion 79 (Batshoof 122) [2006 6f 8d^5 9.7f^2 10f^4 **77** Jul 4] 20,000F, 56,000Y: big gelding: fourth foal: half-brother to 3 fairly useful winners, including 7f/1m winner Nellie Melba (by Hurricane Sky) and 4-y-o Solarias Quest: dam 1¼m/1½m winner: fair maiden: best effort when head second at Folkestone (edged right): stays 9.7f: acts on firm going: slowly away first 2 outings: reportedly finished lame final start (carried head high/tended to hang) in July. *Mrs A. J. Perrett*

ART MARKET (CAN) 3 ch.g. Giant's Causeway (USA) 132 – Fantasy Lake (USA)   **90** (Salt Lake (USA)) [2006 95: p7g 7g^4 8m 7d^6 6s 7m Sep 7] rangy gelding: fairly useful performer: creditable fourth to Racer Forever in listed race at Epsom: well below form after: should stay 1m: acts on good to firm going: tried blinkered/tongue tied. *P. F. I. Cole*

ART MODERN (IRE) 4 ch.g. Giant's Causeway (USA) 132 – Sinead (USA) (Irish   **84** River (FR) 131) [2006 84: 10m^2 10d Sep 13] lengthy gelding: fairly useful performer: easily better effort in 2006 when creditable second in handicap at Newmarket: stays 1¼m: acts on polytrack, good to firm and good to soft going: blinkered 3 times at 3 yrs. *G. L. Moore*

ART MUSEUM (USA) 3 b.c. Storm Cat (USA) – Totemic (USA) (Vanlandingham   **107** (USA)) [2006 111p: 8d* 7d 8v^3 Oct 23] good-topped colt: useful performer, lightly raced: won minor event at Cork on reappearance in September by a length from Absolute Image: still green, mid-field behind Sleeping Indian in Challenge Stakes at Newmarket next time: stays 1m: below form on heavy ground: sent to USA. *A. P. O'Brien, Ireland*

ART OF POKER (IRE) 2 b.c. (Mar 21) Almutawakel 126 – Poker Dice (Primo Dom-   – inie 121) [2006 7s p7g Oct 17] good-topped, attractive colt: behind in maidens: sold 5,500 gns. *B. W. Hills*

ARTURIUS (IRE) 4 b.c. Anabaa (USA) 130 – Steeple (Selkirk (USA) 129) [2006 92:   **106 d** p10g* p12.2g* p10g 8v 12v 12m 8.5d Aug 1] well-made colt: useful performer at best: improved to win handicaps at Lingfield (by 1½ lengths from Red Spell) in February and Wolverhampton (beat Dunaskin by 4 lengths) in March: well below form after, including in Winter Derby at Lingfield and Duke of Edinburgh Stakes at Royal Ascot: stays 1½m: acts on polytrack and good to soft going. *P. J. Rothwell, Ireland*

ARTZOLA (IRE) 6 b.m. Alzao (USA) 117 – Polistatic 53 (Free State 125) [2006 52:   **60** p10g p10g^3 p11g* p12g* p12g* Dec 13] good-bodied mare: modest performer: won banded races at Kempton (2) in November and Lingfield in December: stays easy 1½m: acts on polytrack and good to firm going. *C. A. Horgan*

ARYAAMM (IRE) 3 b.f. Galileo (IRE) 134 – Zibilene 101 (Rainbow Quest (USA)   **94** 134) [2006 8.3f^4 p8g^6 10.3m^3 10m* 12s^6 10g Oct 12] 360,000Y: good-bodied filly: second foal: half-sister to smart French 6f (at 2 yrs) and 7.5f winner Mathematician (by Machiavellian): dam, 1½m winner, half-sister to Barathea and Gossamer: fairly useful performer: made all to win maiden at Leicester in September by 3 lengths from Hotel du Cap, carrying tail awkwardly: bred to stay 1½m: acts on firm going, sent to USA. *M. A. Jarvis*

ARZAAG 3 b.g. Bertolini (USA) 125 – Como (USA) 95 (Cozzene (USA)) [2006 p6g^3 **77** p6g^5 p6g^3 6g^6 5m^4 5.1m^4 p6g^6 p6g* 7m Jul 20] 10,500 2-y-o: workmanlike gelding: first foal: dam 6f winner: fair performer: won claimer at Wolverhampton in June: should stay 7f: acts on polytrack: blinkered last 2 starts: gelded, then sent to Bahrain. *D. M. Simcock*

ASAATEEL (IRE) 4 br.g. Unfuwain (USA) 131 – Alabaq (USA) 111 (Riverman   **70** (USA) 131) [2006 74: p10g 9.9d p10g 10g 10d^2 10m* 8.3s 10s p10g Nov 15] sturdy gelding: fair handicapper: won at Brighton in May: stays 1¼m: acts on soft and good to firm going: usually in headgear nowadays: flashes tail/tends to wander. *G. L. Moore*

ASAAWIR 3 b.f. Royal Applause 124 – Triple Joy 104 (Most Welcome 131) [2006 97:   **97** 7s^5 Apr 15] strong, lengthy filly: useful performer: creditable 1 length fifth to Kamarins- kaya in 1,000 Guineas Trial Stakes at Leopardstown only outing in 2006 (reportedly found to have chipped a knee): should stay 1m: acts on soft and good to firm going: not straightforward: sold 170,000 gns in July. *M. R. Channon*

ASARABACCA (FR) 3 ch.f. Halling (USA) 133 – All Our Hope (USA) 96 (Gulch   **59** (USA)) [2006 p10g^5 p12g Feb 25] third foal: dam, 8.5f winner, closely related to Noosh- man out of Knoosh, both smart performers up to 1½m: better effort in maidens when fifth to Soho Square at Lingfield on debut, running green: sold 1,500 gns in July. *E. A. L. Dunlop*

ASBURY PARK 3 b.c. Primo Valentino (IRE) 116 – Ocean Grove (IRE) 84 (Fairy King **68** (USA)) [2006 69: p9.5g 10.9g⁴ 11.6m 10d Oct 4] good-topped colt: fair maiden: left E. McMahon before final start: stays easy 11f: best efforts on good going. *M. R. Bosley*

ASCOT LADY (IRE) 3 ch.f. Spinning World (USA) 130 – Life At The Top 107 **85 d** (Habitat 134) [2006 a6.5g 7.5d a6.5g⁶ 7.5d⁶ 8v 7g 6g⁴ 5s² 6g⁴ 5.5d³ 5g 5g 6g 6.1d Oct 18] 4,500F, €34,000Y: quite good-topped filly: half-sister to 3 winners, including smart 7f (at 2 yrs) to 9f (in Ireland) winner Tiger Shark (by Chief's Crown) and useful 7f (at 2 yrs)/ 1m winner Primus Inter Pares (by Sadler's Wells): dam, 2-y-o 6f/7f winner who stayed 1¼m, also successful in USA at 4 yrs: fairly useful performer: won maiden and minor event at Angers at 2 yrs: had several trainers in France, leaving R. Chotard before below form in handicaps in Britain last 4 starts: best efforts at 5f/6f: acts on good going. *J. Balding*

ASHAAWES (USA) 3 b.c. Kingmambo (USA) 125 – Crown of Crimson (USA) 109 **106** (Seattle Slew (USA)) [2006 98: 10f* 10.1d* 10d⁵ Sep 16] tall, angular colt: useful performer, lightly raced: won minor events at Leicester (by 1½ lengths from Humungous, making all) in July and Epsom (beat Classic Punch by 1¼ lengths, helping dictate pace) in August: ran poorly in listed race at Ayr (reportedly finished slightly lame) final start: not sure to stay much beyond 1¼m: acts on firm and good to soft going. *Saeed bin Suroor*

ASHARON 4 b.g. Efisio 120 – Arriving 105 (Most Welcome 131) [2006 85§: p7g p7g **73 §** p8g a10g* Oct 15] sturdy gelding: just fair handicapper nowadays: well held first 3 starts in 2006: sold from C. Brittain 1,500 gns, won minor event at Gran Canaria in October: stays 1¼m: acts on polytrack and good to firm going, probably on soft: tried blinkered: held up: unreliable. *B. Rama, Spain*

ASHBURNHAM (IRE) 3 b.f. Intikhab (USA) 135 – Blu Tamantara (USA) (Miswaki **–** (USA) 124) [2006 46, a63: p6g Feb 1] workmanlike filly: maiden: well held only outing at 3 yrs: has reportedly bled. *N. I. M. Rossiter*

ASHDOWN EXPRESS (IRE) 7 ch.g. Ashkalani (IRE) 128 – Indian Express 61 **122** (Indian Ridge 123) [2006 117: 6g 5m 6m⁴ 6m³ 6g⁶ 6.5g 6m² 6g Oct 13]
The sight of the white blaze of Ashdown Express appearing late on the scene in listed and pattern-race sprints has become a very familiar one over the past five seasons. Yet during that time his distinctive head hasn't often been the first one to reach the line, his last outright victory coming in the 2003 Bentinck Stakes at Newmarket. An edgy sort who often sweats up and is taken early to post, Ashdown Express races too freely if allowed to stride on from the start, so his rider's job is to settle him in rear and try to conserve his energy. That brings its own problems, of course, and goes some way to explaining why Ashdown Express' wins-to-runs ratio since his juvenile days is anything but impressive for one of his ability. A steadily-run race, in which he is prone to being left poorly positioned when the pace quickens, usually works against Ashdown Express; the tactics can also lead to his meeting trouble, whichever way the race is run. In other words, things need to drop just right. The 2003 Bentinck remains Ashdown Express' sole pattern-race success, but he does have a host of other good efforts to his name in such events, notably when placed in the July Cup in 2004 (at 100/1) and again in the latest season.
Ashdown Express clearly wasn't considered a sprinter by his connections when he started out, campaigned more in accordance with his pedigree—he's by the high-class miler Ashkalani out of a mare who won at a mile and a mile and a quarter. The last of his three wins as a two-year-old came in a minor event run over a mile at Newmarket, but he hasn't tackled that far since finishing last of nine in the German Two Thousand Guineas, six furlongs the trip at which he's done the vast majority of his racing. All four of his wins in the last five years have come at six, in a listed event at Newbury and minor event at Yarmouth prior to the Bentinck, and in a listed race at Goodwood almost two years after that, though he had to share the spoils with Moss Vale on the last-named course. In the Bentinck, Ashdown Express was followed home by Royal Millennium, Colonel Cotton and The Tatling, all of whom were also still racing in 2006, though only Ashdown Express showed he was still as good as ever, that on his third successive appearance in the July Cup at Newmarket. A neck second to Frizzante in 2004, Ashdown Express finished sixth to Pastoral Pursuits in 2005 and third behind Les Arcs and Iffraaj, beaten a head and three quarters of a length, in the latest running, in which he produced a fine run from halfway. It was the high point of the 2006 campaign for Ashdown Express, though he did run creditably when making the frame on two other occasions,

Mr W. J. P. Jackson's "Ashdown Express"

finishing around three lengths fourth to Les Arcs in the Golden Jubilee Stakes at Royal Ascot, and a neck second to Tax Free in the listed race at Goodwood for which he had dead-heated in 2005.

		Soviet Star	Nureyev
	Ashkalani (IRE)	(b 1984)	Veruschka
Ashdown Express (IRE)	(ch 1993)	Ashtarka	Dalsaan
(ch.g. 1999)		(gr 1987)	Asharaz
	Indian Express	Indian Ridge	Ahonoora
	(ch 1991)	(ch 1985)	Hillbrow
		Bazaar Promise	Native Bazaar
		(b 1985)	Woodland Promise

Ashdown Express, who cost IR 33,000 guineas as a foal and IR 50,000 guineas as a yearling, has picked up almost £340,000 in prize money, his seven wins remarkably accounting for less than a quarter of that total. The third foal of Indian Express, who is a sister to the useful six- and seven-furlong performer Cheyenne Spirit, Ashdown Express is a half-brother to several winners, including the smart mile- to mile-and-a-quarter winner Hoh Buzzard and Tajneed, both by Alhaarth, the latter successful in a one-mile maiden at Galway in 2006. Ashdown Express, a sturdy, lengthy individual, acts on firm and good to soft going, and has finished well held on soft and heavy. He was below form when blinkered on his final start as a three-year-old, after which he was gelded. *C. F. Wall*

ASHES (IRE) 4 b.f. General Monash (USA) 107 – Wakayi 87 (Persian Bold 123) [2006 **77** 76, a70: p6g⁶ p5.1g⁴ p6g⁵ p6g² p6g³ p6g² 5v² p5.1g* 5m p6g² 5g 5.7d⁴ p5.1g⁵ 5m* 6m 5m² 5m 5s 5d 5s 5d Nov 3] good-topped filly: fair handicapper: won at Wolverhampton in April and Hamilton in June: best at 5f/6f: acts on polytrack, heavy and good to firm going: blinkered (well beaten) once. *K. R. Burke*

ASHES REGAINED 3 b.c. Galileo (IRE) 134 – Hasty Words (IRE) 103 (Polish Patriot (USA) 128) [2006 89p: 8.3g Oct 16] maiden: promising fourth at Newmarket only 2-y-o start: favourite, better than bare result at Windsor on return year later, losing ground at start (swerved left) and eased having had every chance 2f out. *B. W. Hills*   **?**

ASHFORD CASTLE (IRE) 3 b.g. Mujadil (USA) 119 – Lonely Heart 101 (Midyan (USA) 124) [2006 7.1g 8m 7d⁶ Oct 3] big, good-topped gelding: well held in maidens. *B. J. Meehan*   **–**

ASHMAL (USA) 2 b.f. (Apr 7) Machiavellian (USA) 123 – Alabaq (USA) 111 (Riverman (USA) 131) [2006 7d Oct 28] angular filly: fourth foal: half-sister to 3-y-o Aamaaq and 4-y-o Asaateel: dam, 7f (at 2 yrs) to 1¼m winner, daughter of Salsabil: 20/1, needed experience in maiden at Newmarket. *J. L. Dunlop*   **–**

ASHN THUNDER 2 ch.c. (Mar 21) Thunder Gulch (USA) 129 – Ashford Castle (USA) (Bates Motel (USA)) [2006 8.3g² 8.2s⁵ 7d Oct 28] 75,000Y: strong, deep-girthed colt: third foal: half-brother to 3-y-o Aspasias Tizzy: dam, 6f to 8.5f (including minor stakes) winner in USA, half-sister to US Grade 1 2-y-o 6f/9f winner Strategic Maneuver: fair maiden: second at Hamilton on debut, best effort: will stay 1½m. *M. Johnston*   **74**

ASHOVER ROCK (IRE) 2 b.g. (Jan 8) Danetime (IRE) 121 – Ascoli (Skyliner 117) [2006 6m May 10] tailed off in maiden at Newcastle. *I. W. McInnes*   **–**

ASHSTANZA 5 gr.g. Ashkalani (IRE) 128 – Poetry In Motion (IRE) 76 (Ballad Rock 122) [2006 –: p12.2g³ f14g p13.9g Nov 22] smallish, well-made gelding: modest maiden: stays 1½m: acts on all-weather, little form on turf: tried in cheekpieces/blinkers: has found little. *R. D. E. Woodhouse*   **53**

ASH THE CASH (IRE) 4 b.g. High Roller (IRE) 102 – Angela's Pet (IRE) (Ridgewood Ben 113) [2006 –: f8g Jan 3] well held in maiden/claimer at Southwell. *K. F. Clutterbuck*   **–**

ASHWELL ROSE 4 b.f. Anabaa (USA) 130 – Finicia (USA) (Miswaki (USA) 124) [2006 –: p12g p12.2g⁶ 16g p13.9g⁵ f12g Jul 31] close-coupled filly: poor maiden. *R. T. Phillips*   **47**

ASIAN ALLIANCE (IRE) 5 ch.m. Soviet Star (USA) 128 – Indian Express 61 (Indian Ridge 123) [2006 p10g p12.2g Dec 23] €38,000Y: closely related to 7-y-o Ashdown Express and half-sister to 2 winners, including smart 1m (including at 2 yrs) to 1¼m Hoh Buzzard (by Alhaarth): dam 8.5f/1¼m winner: modest maiden on Flat: trained by W. Mullins in Ireland at 3 yrs: unraced on Flat in 2005 (won over hurdles): should stay 1½m: acts on soft going, probably on polytrack: wore cheekpieces final outing. *K. A. Ryan*   **57**

ASIAN HEIGHTS 8 b.h. Hernando (FR) 127 – Miss Rinjani 83 (Shirley Heights 130) [2006 –: 12m³ 12f⁵ 12d³ Aug 18] leggy, quite attractive horse: had a quick action: one-time very smart performer, suffered numerous problems and was very lightly raced: useful form in 2006, seemingly best effort when fifth of 8 to Crosspeace in listed race at Goodwood: stayed 13.4f: acted on heavy and good to firm going: had awkward head carriage: sold 54,000 gns, and to stand at Knockboy House Stud, Co Cork, Ireland. *G. Wragg*   **103**

ASK 3 b.c. Sadler's Wells (USA) 132 – Request 87 (Rainbow Quest (USA) 134) [2006 8g³ 10m² 12.1m⁴ 12m 13.9s² 13.9g⁴ Sep 9] angular, quite attractive colt: first foal: dam, second at 1¼m from 2 starts, half-sister to very smart 1½m/1¾m performer Blueprint and smart 1¼m winner Fairy Godmother: smart performer: won maiden at Chepstow in June by 7 lengths: reportedly returned lame next time: upped in trip and tongue tied, further marked improvement at York last 2 starts, short-head second to Trick Or Treat in Melrose Stakes (Handicap) and 3¾ lengths fourth to Sixties Icon in St Leger (wandered): stays 1¾m: acts on soft and good to firm going. *Sir Michael Stoute*   **116**

ASK DON'T TELL (IRE) 2 b.f. (Feb 4) Indian Rocket 115 – Cladantom (IRE) 70 (High Estate 127) [2006 p5.1g* 5.1m 6.1d⁴ 6m⁵ p6g 6g⁶ p5.1g⁵ p5g⁶ 7d* Oct 19] 5,000Y: strong, quite attractive filly: third foal: sister to 4-y-o Fizzlephut: dam 7f winner: fair performer: won maiden at Wolverhampton in April and nursery at Brighton in October: stays 7f: acts on polytrack, good to firm and good to soft going: has hung/flashed tail: sold 6,500 gns, sent to Sweden. *T. G. Dascombe*   **67**

ASK JENNY (IRE) 4 b.f. Marju (IRE) 127 – Waltzing Matilda (Mujtahid (USA) 118) [2006 67: 6m 6.5d 6v 5v p6g Dec 20] €3,000Y: second foal: dam no form: fair maiden   **49**

handicapper at best, poor in 2006: left J. Burns, well beaten at Lingfield final start (wore cheekpieces): stays 6f: acts on good to firm and good to soft ground. *Patrick Morris, Ireland*

ASK NO MORE 3 b.g. Pyramus (USA) 78 – Nordesta (IRE) 72 (Nordico (USA)) **76** [2006 p7g* p7.1g³ 7m p7g p8.6m⁶ p8.6g³ p7.1g Dec 27] 3,800Y: fifth foal: half-brother to winner in Greece by Shaamit: dam 2-y-o 5f winner: fair performer: won maiden at Lingfield in June: stays 8.6f: acts on polytrack: blinkered last 3 starts: inconsistent. *P. L. Gilligan*

ASK THE CLERK (IRE) 5 b.g. Turtle Island (IRE) 123 – Some Fun (Wolverlife 115) **80** [2006 81: 7d 8d³ 7d⁶ 8.3m² 9m³ Jun 23] close-coupled gelding: fairly useful performer: stays 1m: acts on any turf going: tried in cheekpieces/blinkers earlier in career: held up. *Mrs P. Sly*

ASK YER DAD 2 b.g. (Feb 20) Diktat 126 – Heuston Station (IRE) 72 (Fairy King **64** (USA)) [2006 5m⁶ 6m³ 6m p8g p8g⁴ Nov 24] strong, lengthy gelding: modest maiden: stays 1m: wore cheekpieces final outing. *Mrs P. Sly*

ASLEEP AT THE BACK (IRE) 3 b.g. Halling (USA) 133 – Molomo 104 (Barathea **59** (IRE) 127) [2006 10d 10s f11g⁴ f12g⁴ f16g² Dec 28] modest maiden: reportedly had breathing problem on debut: stays 2m: acts on fibresand: tried tongue tied. *J. G. Given*

ASMARADANA 3 b.g. Groom Dancer (USA) 128 – Nsx 74 (Roi Danzig (USA)) **–** [2006 48: f6g Apr 3] good-topped gelding: poor maiden: bred to be suited by at least 1m. *P. F. I. Cole*

AS ONE DOES 2 b.c. (Apr 21) Lujain (USA) 119 – Night Over Day 57 (Most Welcome **83 d** 131) [2006 5g⁵ 6d* 6f³ 7g 6d 6g Sep 17] 20,000Y: strong, close-coupled colt: fifth foal: half-brother to fairly useful Italian 1m to 1¼m winner Mrs Seek (by Unfuwain): dam Irish maiden who stayed 9f: fairly useful performer: won maiden at Hamilton in May: third of 4 to Dubai's Touch in minor event at Pontefract next time, but lost form after: best at 5f/6f: acts on firm and good to soft going: sold 8,000 gns. *K. A. Ryan*

ASPASIAS TIZZY (USA) 3 b. or br.f. Tiznow (USA) 133 – Ashford Castle (USA) **85** (Bates Motel (USA)) [2006 10g³ 12f* 12g 13.8m² 12d 11.9s⁶ Sep 1] tall, rangy filly: second foal: half-sister to 8.5f (including minor stakes) winner in USA, half-sister to US Grade 1 2-y-o 6f/9f winner Strategic Maneuver: fairly useful performer: won maiden at Thirsk in May by 7 lengths: creditable effort in handicaps after only when second at Catterick: stays 13.8f: acts on firm going, well below form on ground softer than good: sold 17,000 gns. *M. Johnston*

ASPEN FALLS (IRE) 3 ch.f. Elnadim (USA) 128 – Esquiline (USA) (Gone West **78** (USA)) [2006 78: 7m⁴ p7g⁴ 8.1m 7.5f 7m⁵ Jul 26] well-made filly: fair handicapper: should stay 1m: acts on polytrack and firm going: hung right third outing. *Sir Mark Prescott*

ASPERITY (USA) 2 b.c. (Mar 5) War Chant (USA) 126 – Another Storm (USA) **104 P** (Gone West (USA)) [2006 7.1d² 8g* Sep 28]
Hundreds of two-year-olds each season put up promising performances in maiden races, but only a handful even come close to achieving the level of form shown by Asperity in winning one at Newmarket in September. Asperity started odds on at Newmarket on the strength of an encouraging debut in a five-runner minor event over seven furlongs at Sandown earlier in the month, when he had come clear of the remainder in going down by a neck to the more experienced Duke of Tuscany, receiving 7 lb. With the run behind him, he dismissed his fourteen rivals with ease, stepped up to a mile at Newmarket, virtually turning the race into a solo effort. Drawn towards the centre of the track, he raced wide of the remainder and made all, responding well when given the office two furlongs out and storming away to beat Life by five lengths. The runner-up disappointed next time, but third-placed Palamoun upheld the form, and Asperity's timefigure was useful, enough to back up the impression that he is a smart colt in the making, sure to win races in better company.

Asperity is bred well enough to win just about anything. His sire War Chant was trained in North America, where he won the Breeders' Cup Mile as a three-year-old. War Chant has yet to hit the heights as a stallion, but he has produced smart horses on both sides of the Atlantic from his first three crops, including Karen's Caper, winner of the Nell Gwyn Stakes and runner-up in both the Corona-tion Stakes at Royal Ascot and the Queen Elizabeth II Challenge Cup at Keeneland

NGK Spark Plugs Maiden Stakes, Newmarket—
Asperity looks a smart prospect as he goes clear after making all down the centre

in America, where she was a Grade 3 winner in 2006 after leaving Asperity's trainer, John Gosden. War Chant's best representative in Britain in 2006 was the smart sprinter Tawaassol, though besides Asperity he was also responsible for a smart juvenile for the same stable in Rallying Cry. Asperity's dam Another Storm raced only at two, winning over eight and a half furlongs and finishing second in Grade 3 company at the same trip. Another Storm's dam Storm Song fared even better as a two-year-old, winning the Breeders' Cup Juvenile Fillies. Storm Song failed to train on at three, despite finishing a promoted third in the Kentucky Oaks over nine furlongs, but there is every reason to expect Asperity to continue to go the right way.

	War Chant (USA) (b 1997)	Danzig (b 1977)	Northern Dancer / Pas de Nom
Asperity (USA) (b.c. Mar 5, 2004)		Hollywood Wildcat (b 1990)	Kris S / Miss Wildcatter
	Another Storm (USA) (b 1999)	Gone West (b 1984)	Mr Prospector / Secrettame
		Storm Song (b 1994)	Summer Squall / Hum Along

A close-coupled, quite attractive colt, Asperity raced exuberantly at Newmarket and isn't sure to stay much beyond a mile judged on his running style, though he should get a mile and a quarter on pedigree. He showed a markedly round action on his two starts as a juvenile which were on good ground or softer. *J. H. M. Gosden*

ASSERTIVE 3 ch.c. Bold Edge 123 – Tart And A Half 83 (Distant Relative 128) [2006 **111** 106: 7m³ 6m* 6d² 6m 7m⁴ 7m³ 6.5g 6s² 7g 6d⁴ Sep 24] angular, good-topped colt: smart performer: won listed race at Lingfield in May by 1¼ lengths from Kingsgate Prince: mostly creditable efforts after, including when placed in Betfair Cup (Lennox) at Goodwood (4¼ lengths, third to Iffraaj) and listed race at Newmarket (2 lengths second to Appalachian Trail) and when 2½ lengths fourth to Red Clubs in Diadem Stakes at Ascot on final outing: stays 7f: acts on soft and good to firm ground. *R. Hannon*

ASSET (IRE) 3 b.g. Marju (IRE) 127 – Snow Peak (Arazi (USA) 135) [2006 96p: p8g* **110** 8m 7m² Jun 21] tall, rather leggy, good-topped gelding: improved into a smart performer

*intercasino.co.uk Easter Stakes, Kempton—Asset shows a fine turn of foot
in a race run for the first time on polytrack; Royal Power and Dubai Typhoon are next to finish*

in 2006: won listed race at Kempton (by 3½ lengths from Royal Power) in April: at least
creditable efforts after, in 2000 Guineas at Newmarket (6¾ lengths ninth to George
Washington) and Jersey Stakes at Royal Ascot (2 lengths second to Jeremy, leading
briefly over 1f out): gelded after: effective at 7f/1m: acts on polytrack and good to firm
going: made running at 2 yrs. *R. Hannon*

ASSUMPTION (IRE) 3 b.f. Beckett (IRE) 116 – Native Force (IRE) 82 (Indian Ridge **57**
123) [2006 48: p8g⁵ f8g³ 7s* Mar 28] modest performer: won selling handicap at Folkestone in March: stays 7f: acts on soft going: sold 2,500 gns in July. *S. C. Williams*

ASTARTE 2 b.f. (Mar 18) Slip Anchor 136 – Nanouche (Dayjur (USA) 137) [2006 p8g **–**
Nov 15] sixth foal: half-sister to 5f winner Faiza (by Efisio): dam, ran once, out of outstanding sprinter Habibti: well beaten in maiden at Kempton. *P. R. Chamings*

ASTON LAD 5 b.g. Bijou d'Inde 127 – Fishki 36 (Niniski (USA) 125) [2006 –: 12.4s⁶ **55**
15.8s* Oct 24] modest performer, lightly raced on Flat nowadays: won handicap at
Catterick in October: stays 2m: acts on soft ground: fairly useful hurdler. *M. D. Hammond*

ASTORYGOESWITHIT 3 b.g. Foxhound (USA) 103 – La Belle Mystere 48 (Lycius **47**
(USA) 124) [2006 64: p8g p7.1g 8m p7g f6g⁶ p8.6g f7g² f6g³ Dec 28] close-coupled
gelding: just poor form in 2006: left Mrs L. Featherstone after third start: stays 7f: acts on
all-weather: wears headgear: has hung/found little. *P. S. McEntee*

ASTRAL CHARMER 2 b.g. (Feb 17) Tobougg (IRE) 125 – Blushing Sunrise (USA) **62**
(Cox's Ridge (USA)) [2006 p8g p9.5g⁴ p10g⁴ Nov 29] 8,000F, €30,000Y: fifth living
foal: half-brother to 1m/9f winner Sharp Needle (by Mark of Esteem): dam 6.5f winner
in USA: modest form in maidens: will stay 1½m. *M. H. Tompkins*

ASTROANGEL 2 b.f. (Jan 21) Groom Dancer (USA) 128 – Nutmeg (IRE) 70 (Lake **73 §**
Coniston (IRE) 131) [2006 6f p6g⁴ 5.2f² 6s⁴ 7.1d 6m 6d³ 7d p7.1g Nov 2] neat, leggy
filly: first foal: dam 7f winner: fair maiden: in frame 4 times, twice in nurseries: should be
suited by 7f/1m: acts on polytrack, firm and soft going: tried blinkered: usually slowly
away: not to be trusted. *M. H. Tompkins*

ASTROBELLA 3 ch.f. Medicean 128 – Optimistic 90 (Reprimand 122) [2006 80p: **84**
8.2g 10.4m 11m⁵ 11.6s Oct 2] neat filly: fairly useful handicapper, lightly raced: best
effort on third start: stays 11f: acts on good to firm and good to soft going. *M. H. Tompkins*

ASTROCHARM (IRE) 7 b.m. Charnwood Forest (IRE) 125 – Charm The Stars (Roi **104**
Danzig (USA)) [2006 109: 14m⁴ 12m⁴ 16.1m Jul 1] leggy mare: has a round action:
useful performer: respectable 2¾ lengths fourth to Sirce in listed event at Musselburgh:
well beaten at Pontefract (reportedly in season) and in Northumberland Plate (Handicap)
at Newcastle subsequently: stays 2m: acts on firm and good to soft ground: tried blinkered, better form when not: tends to sweat: usually held up. *M. H. Tompkins*

ASTROLIBRA 2 b.f. (Apr 12) Sakhee (USA) 136 – Optimistic 90 (Reprimand 122) **50**
[2006 8.2s Oct 18] good-topped filly: fourth foal: half-sister to 3-y-o Astrobella: dam
2-y-o 7f winner who stayed 1¼m: reportedly finished lame when mid-division in maiden
at Nottingham. *M. H. Tompkins*

ASTRONOMER ROYAL (USA) 2 b.c. (Apr 7) Danzig (USA) – Sheepscot (USA) **90 p**
(Easy Goer (USA)) [2006 6m² 6m* Aug 6] fourth foal: half-brother to 3 winners abroad,
including US Grade 2 1½m winner Navesink River (by Unbridled): dam, US 6f to 1m
winner, half-sister to US Grade 1 8.5f/9f winner Vicar: shaped well both starts, winning
maiden at Newbury (still green, beat Maker's Mark 2½ lengths) in August: will stay 1m:
useful prospect. *A. P. O'Brien, Ireland*

ASTRONOMIA (NZ) 4 ch.f. King's Best (USA) 132 – Astralita (AUS) (Kenny's Best **106**
Pal (AUS)) [2006 8g⁵ 8m 9.9m⁴ Aug 19] A$280,000Y: tall filly: second foal: dam
Australian 5f/6f winner, including Group 2 event: smart performer at best: won maiden
at Newcastle (in Australia) and handicap at Caulfield in 2005: left Ms G. Waterhouse in
Australia, only useful form in Britain in 2006, off 2 months prior to fourth to Portal in
listed handicap at Goodwood final outing: best form up to 1¼m: acts on soft going:
bandaged behind (weakened tamely in Windsor Forest Stakes at Royal Ascot) second
start: sent to USA. *Saeed bin Suroor*

ASTRONOMICAL (IRE) 4 b.g. Mister Baileys 123 – Charm The Stars (Roi Danzig **–**
(USA)) [2006 88: p12.2g Jul 20] strong, close-coupled gelding: has a quick action: fairly
useful performer: well below form only outing in 2006: should stay at least 1¼m: acts on
firm and soft ground. *Miss S. J. Wilton*

ASTRONOMICAL ODDS (USA) 3 b.g. Miswaki (USA) 124 – Perfectly Polish **73**
(USA) (Polish Numbers (USA)) [2006 58: 7m 10m f8g* f8g⁴ Dec 9] $17,000Y: first foal:
dam maiden in USA: fair performer: left W. Browne in Ireland, won amateur handicap at
Southwell in November: stays 1m: acts on fibresand, probably on good to soft going:
tended to hang final outing. *T. D. Barron*

ASTRONOMIC VIEW 2 b.c. (Jan 22) Observatory (USA) 131 – On Tiptoes 107 **82**
(Shareef Dancer (USA) 135) [2006 p6g³ p7g³ 6m Aug 11] 40,000Y: neat colt: half-
brother to several winners, including useful 6f (including at 2 yrs)/7f winner Caballero
(by Cadeaux Genereux): dam 5f (including Queen Mary Stakes) winner: fairly useful
maiden: third at Lingfield first 2 starts: stayed 7f: dead. *E. A. L. Dunlop*

ASTRONOVA 3 ch.f. Bahamian Bounty 116 – Astrolove (IRE) (Bigstone (IRE) 126) **–**
[2006 56: p7.1g f8g 7f 6f⁵ Jul 18] neat filly: maiden: no form at 3 yrs. *M. H. Tompkins*

ASTURIAS 2 b.f. (Feb 1) Anabaa (USA) 130 – Halcyon Daze 82 (Halling (USA) 133) **63**
[2006 p7g⁵ 7g Sep 30] 25,000Y: sturdy filly: second foal: dam, 11.5f winner, half-sister
to smart 1¾m winner Ashgar out of half-sister to Oaks winner Ramruma: better effort in
maidens when fifth at Kempton on debut: will stay at least 1m. *J. W. Hills*

ASWAN (IRE) 8 ch.g. Ashkalani (IRE) 128 – Ghariba 112 (Final Straw 127) [2006 –, **70 d**
a70: p8.6g p7.1g² f6g p7.1g⁶ 7m⁵ p7.1g³ p6g⁶ p7.1g p5.1g² Jul 3] sturdy gelding: fair
performer: below form after second start: effective at 5f to 1¼m: acts on polytrack and
firm ground, not on softer than good: tried blinkered: wears tongue tie: free-going front
runner: has carried head high/found little. *S. R. Bowring*

ATAKAMA (GER) 6 b.m. Platini (GER) 126 – Athene (GER) (Nebos (GER) 129) **–**
[2006 –: p9.5g f11g 6m 8.2m Jun 23] ex-German-trained maiden: well held for current
stable, including in Britain first 2 starts in 2006. *A. D. Nolan, Ireland*

A TEEN 8 ch.h. Presidium 124 – Very Good (Noalto 120) [2006 51§: f5g⁴ f5g⁴ p6g f6g⁶ **54 §**
f6g² f6g² f5g p6g⁶ f6g⁵ f6g⁴ f6g² p5.1g³ p6g⁴ p5g² p5g⁵ p5g p6g³ p6g⁵ 6f f6g f6g⁵
f6g⁵ p7g p7g⁵ Dec 30] modest performer: effective at 5f to 7f: acts on all-weather, firm
and soft ground: tried blinkered (not since 2001): has carried head high: unreliable.
P. Howling

ATHAR (IRE) 2 ch.c. (Jan 18) Traditionally (USA) 117 – Lady Nasrana (FR) (Al Nasr **83 p**
(FR) 126) [2006 7s³ Oct 10] 16,000F, 57,000Y: workmanlike colt: unfurnished at 2 yrs:
second foal: dam, Belgian 2-y-o 5f winner, half-sister to US Grade 1 9f/1¼m winner
Janet: 8/1, promising close third of 17 to Hollow Ridge in maiden at Newbury, good
speed: likely to improve. *R. Hannon*

ATHBOY NIGHTS (IRE) 4 b.f. Night Shift (USA) – Missing Love (IRE) (Thatching **64**
131) [2006 –: p6g⁴ p6g a6g⁵ Sep 5] sturdy filly: modest maiden: left M. Wallace after
second start and returned to former trainer: stays 6f: acts on polytrack. *A. J. Martin,
Ireland*

ATHEA LAD (IRE) 2 b.g. (Apr 12) Indian Danehill (IRE) 124 – Persian Empress **55 d**
(IRE) 51 (Persian Bold 123) [2006 5s⁶ 6d 6v 7m 8m 6g f8g p8g⁵ p7.1g Dec 28] modest
maiden: below form after second start: left D. Loughnane in Ireland and gelded after sixth
outing: stays 6f: acts on soft ground: tried blinkered. *W. K. Goldsworthy*

ATHENA'S DREAM 3 b.f. Robellino (USA) 127 – Greek Dream (USA) 79 (Distant **63**
View (USA) 126) [2006 67: 6.1m⁶ 6f 7m⁶ 6g 6f² 6g Sep 14] compact filly: modest
maiden: should stay at least 7f: raced only on good ground or firmer. *C. F. Wall*

ATHENEUM (IRE) 2 b.c. (Apr 1) Noverre (USA) 125 – Anno Luce 107 (Old Vic 136) **79**
[2006 6d⁵ 5m⁶ 7g³ 7f⁶ 7f 7m² 7d Oct 19] tall, leggy colt: fifth foal: closely related to
French 1¼m winner Aloof (by Rahy) and half-brother to 2 winners, including Irish 1m

winner Head Waiter (by Lend A Hand): dam, 1½m performer, out of Preis der Diana winner Anna Paola: fair maiden: third at Epsom and second at Catterick (nursery): will stay 1m/1¼m: best efforts on good/good to firm going: sold 10,000 gns. *M. Johnston*

A THOUSAND SMILES (IRE) 4 b.f. Sadler's Wells (USA) 132 – Bluffing (IRE) 102 (Darshaan 133) [2006 76: p12.2g* p13g⁶ Feb 1] leggy filly: fair performer: won maiden at Wolverhampton in January by 8 lengths: creditable sixth in handicap at Lingfield only subsequent outing: stays 1¾m: acts on polytrack and good to soft ground: sometimes races freely: covered by Rakti, sent to France. *M. A. Jarvis* **73**

ATH TIOMAIN (IRE) 3 b.g. Night Shift (USA) – Broken Spirit (IRE) (Slip Anchor 136) [2006 8.3g 8.3g p12g Sep 18] leggy, close-coupled gelding: well held in maidens. *D. J. S. ffrench Davis* **–**

ATLANTIC ACE 9 b.g. First Trump 118 – Risalah (Marju (IRE) 127) [2006 66: p8.6g p8.6g p8.6g⁶ 7g 10.1d May 16] good-topped gelding: fair performer at best: reportedly suffered stress fracture after final outing in 2005 and well held in 2006: usually wears cheekpieces: usually held up. *B. Smart* **–**

ATLANTIC CITY 5 ch.g. First Trump 118 – Pleasuring 68 (Good Times (ITY)) [2006 73: p12g p12g p12g⁶ Dec 20] quite good-topped, attractive gelding: fair performer at best: well held in 2006: has worn cheekpieces/eyeshields: sometimes looks none too keen. *Mrs L. Richards* **–**

ATLANTIC COAST (IRE) 2 b.g. (Jan 27) In The Wings 128 – Reasonably Devout (CAN) (St Jovite (USA) 135) [2006 10d 10.1d p8.6g³ Nov 11] 42,000Y: fourth foal: half-brother to Irish 1¼m winner Extra Gold (by Grand Lodge): dam, 2-y-o 8.5f winner in USA, out of US Grade 1 1¼m winner Castilla: no form in maidens: will be suited by 1¼m+: gelded after final start. *M. Johnston* **–**

ATLANTIC DAME (USA) 2 ch.f. (May 14) Lemon Drop Kid (USA) 131 – While Rome Burns (USA) (Overskate (CAN)) [2006 p7g p8g Oct 20] $150,000Y: sister to winner in Canada and half-sister to 3 winners, notably US Grade 1 2000 2-y-o 1m winner Burning Roma (by Rubiano): dam 6f to 8.5f winner in USA: well held in maidens. *Mrs A. J. Perrett* **–**

ATLANTIC GAMBLE (IRE) 6 b.g. Darnay 117 – Full Traceability (IRE) 53 (Ron's Victory (USA) 129) [2006 58: 13f 16d p9.5g p13.9g³ p13.9g⁴ p12g⁴ p13.9g⁶ f11g⁵ Dec 19] modest maiden: left P. Fahy in Ireland and gelded after second start: stays 1¾m: acts on all-weather and good to firm going: in cheekpieces last 3 outings. *K. R. Burke* **55**

ATLANTIC LIGHT 2 gr.f. (Mar 14) Linamix (FR) 127 – Atlantic Destiny (IRE) 99 (Royal Academy (USA) 130) [2006 7.5g 7m 6d² 6v³ 6d Nov 4] leggy, close-coupled filly: first foal: dam, 2-y-o 6f winner (later sprint winner in USA), half-sister to smart Irish 1¼m performer Make No Mistake: useful form: much improved to win nursery at Catterick in October by 12 lengths: well held turned out quickly under less testing conditions: will stay 1m+: acts on heavy going. *M. Johnston* **95**

ATLANTIC QUEST (USA) 7 b. or br.g. Woodman (USA) 126 – Pleasant Pat (USA) (Pleasant Colony (USA)) [2006 90: p7.1g p9.5g⁴ p8.6g² p9.5g⁶ p8.6g* p8g p8.6g p8g 7.1d⁶ p10g 8.1m⁵ p9.5g p9.5g⁵ p8.6g² p9.5g³ p10g⁴ p9.5g³ Dec 30] rather leggy, close-coupled gelding: fairly useful handicapper: won at Wolverhampton in February: left R. Harris after eleventh start: effective at 7f to 1¼m: acts on polytrack, firm and good to soft going: has been visored, usually wears cheekpieces (effective without): often slowly away: tends to wander/carry head high, but is consistent. *Miss Venetia Williams* **90**

ATLANTIC STORY (USA) 4 b. or br.g. Stormy Atlantic (USA) – Story Book Girl (USA) (Siberian Express (USA) 125) [2006 8f 9.8d 8m⁴ 8.5m⁴ 10g 9.9m⁵ 8.2d p8g* f7g* p8.6g* Dec 1] angular, good-topped gelding: has a short, quick action: fairly useful performer: trained by Saeed bin Suroor at 2 yrs: unraced in 2005: won handicaps at Kempton and Southwell in November and Wolverhampton in December: stays 8.6f: acts on all-weather, firm and good to soft ground: usually tongue tied in 2006: has worn crossed noseband: has carried head high. *M. W. Easterby* **81 +**

ATLANTIC VIKING (IRE) 11 b.g. Danehill (USA) 126 – Hi Bettina 96 (Henbit (USA) 130) [2006 83: a6g² 6g⁵ a6s² a5g⁴ a8.3s a5g⁵ 7g⁶ 5g³ 5f⁵ 5g³ 5m⁴ 5.9g* 5.7m 5.7m 6d p6m p8.6g p7g p7g⁶ p6g⁴ Dec 22] well-made gelding: just fair on turf, modest on all-weather in 2006: placed several times for P. Haley in Spain, including twice at Mijas in January: rejoined former stable after spell in USA: won claimer at Carlisle (left D. Nicholls £8,000) in August: best at 5f/easy 6f: acts on polytrack/sand, firm and soft going: sometimes wears headgear: sometimes wanders: none too consistent. *P. D. Evans* **71 a58**

Mr Jaber Abdullah's "Atlantic Waves"

ATLANTIC WAVES (IRE) 3 b.c. Sadler's Wells (USA) 132 – Highest Accolade 71 **106 +**
(Shirley Heights 130) [2006 102p: 9g* 12m Jun 3] big, angular, good-topped colt: useful
form only 4 starts: won listed Feilden Stakes at Newmarket in April by short head from
unlucky-in-running Olympian Odyssey, showing good attitude and rallying under pressure: below form when fifteenth to Sir Percy in Derby at Epsom only subsequent outing,
quickly losing prominent position 4f out (moved poorly to start): reportedly treated for a
bad quarter crack after: should be well suited by 1¼m/1½m: has worn crossed noseband.
M. Johnston

ATRAAS (IRE) 2 b.g. (Apr 23) King's Best (USA) 132 – Sundus (USA) 80 (Sadler's **83**
Wells (USA) 132) [2006 7g³ 8s⁴ Oct 10] leggy gelding: first foal: dam, 1¼m winner only
start, out of useful close relation to Nayef and half-sister to Nashwan and Unfuwain:
fairly useful form: in frame in maidens at Newbury won by Proponent then Go On Be A
Tiger, not settling in latter: gelded after: likely to stay 1¼m. *M. P. Tregoning*

ATTACCA 5 b.g. Piccolo 121 – Jubilee Place (IRE) 76 (Prince Sabo 123) [2006 57: **63**
7.1v* 7.5f⁵ 7.1m* 7.1g⁶ 7m 7.1f³ 8m⁴ 6.9f 7.2m⁶ 6.9m⁴ 6d 7.1m⁴ 7.2s⁵ Sep 28] tall, quite
good-topped gelding: modest handicapper: won at Musselburgh in March and May:
stays easy 1m: acts on any turf going: effective in headgear earlier in career: not one to
trust implicitly. *J. R. Weymes*

ATTACK MINDED 5 ch.g. Timeless Times (USA) 99 – French Ginger 66 (Most **–**
Welcome 131) [2006 –: 10f 10d⁶ Aug 13] no form. *L. R. James*

AT THE BAR 3 ch.c. Compton Place 125 – Miss Tress (IRE) 67 (Salse (USA) 128) **–**
[2006 55d: 6.1m p7.1g 7m Jun 29] small, leggy colt: maiden: no form in 2006: tried
blinkered. *A. J. Chamberlain*

AT THE HELM (IRE) 4 b.f. Docksider (USA) 124 – Good Reference (IRE) 84 (Ref- **60**
erence Point 139) [2006 60: p9.5g⁴ p8g² p9.5g⁵ 10.1g p9.5g 10m p10g³ 8f⁴ p10g* p10g
a14g* Dec 17] €11,000Y: fifth foal: half-sister to 3 winners, including fairly useful 2003

2-y-o 7f winner Dark Empress (by Second Empire) and 1m to 1¾m winner The Fairy Flag (by Inchinor): dam 7f (at 2 yrs) and 1m winner: modest performer: left J. Burns in Ireland after 3 yrs: won seller at Lingfield in September and (after sold from W. Knight 7,000 gns) minor event at Gran Canaria in December: stays 1¾m: acts on polytrack/sand and firm ground: has flashed tail. *B. Rama, Spain*

AT THE MONEY 3 b.g. Robellino (USA) 127 – Coh Sho No 59 (Old Vic 136) [2006 **77** 58: f11g³ 11g² 14.1m* 14d² 15d* 16d³ f14g³ f16g² Nov 15] close-coupled gelding: fair handicapper: won at Nottingham in May and Warwick in October: stays 1½m and stays 2m: acts on fibresand, heavy and good to firm going. *J. M. P. Eustace*

ATTICUS TROPHIES (IRE) 3 b.g. Mujadil (USA) 119 – Nezool Almatar (IRE) **64** (Last Tycoon 131) [2006 72: p6g 6m 6g⁴ 7d 8.3m p9.5s³ p10g p10g Dec 30] sturdy gelding: modest maiden: left K. McAuliffe after fifth start: stays 9.5f: acts on polytrack, best turf efforts on good going: often wears cheekpieces/blinkers. *Ms J. S. Doyle*

ATTILA'S PEINTRE 2 b.g. (Feb 20) Peintre Celebre (USA) 137 – Atabaa (FR) (Ana- **–** baa (USA) 130) [2006 8s Oct 7] big, useful-looking gelding: second foal: dam, useful French 1m and 9.5f winner, out of smart French performer up to 12.5f Alma Ata: 40/1, burly and green in maiden at York: sold £2,600. *P. C. Haslam*

ATTILA THE HUN 7 b.g. Piccolo 121 – Katya (IRE) 93 (Dancing Dissident (USA) **50** 119) [2006 46: p6g⁴ 5.9m 6f 6f⁶ 6f 6m Aug 10] modest maiden: best at 6f: acts on poly-track and good to firm ground: tried visored/in cheekpieces. *F. Watson*

ATTISHOE 4 b.f. Atraf 116 – Royal Shoe (Hotfoot 126) [2006 –: p10g 7m Jun 4] no **–** form. *Miss B. Sanders*

ATTITUDE ANNIE 3 b.f. Josr Algarhoud (IRE) 118 – Eclectic (Emarati (USA) 74) **–** [2006 58: p6g⁴ p7g⁵ p7g⁵ p7g⁶ p7g 5.5g p6g⁶ p5g² 6g p7g Nov 6] modest maiden: **a58** effective at 5f to 7f: acts on polytrack, no form on turf. *S. Dow*

ATTORNEY 8 ch.g. Wolfhound (USA) 126 – Princess Sadie 86 (Shavian 125) [2006 **–** 76, a72: f6g f6g f6s⁶ f6g Apr 3] attorneying: fair performer: successful 9 times in 2005: well held in 2006, leaving N. Berry after reappearance: tried blinkered/visored, not since 2004: usually races up with pace. *P. D. Evans*

ATWIRL 3 b.f. Pivotal 124 – Amidst 86 (Midyan (USA) 124) [2006 8.1g 7d 10m p10g **67 +** 7.9g² p7g² p7g* Oct 23] angular filly: sixth foal: half-sister to fairly useful 7f winner Aploy (by Deploy) and 1m winner Ago (later successful in Spain, by Rudimentary): dam 6f (at 2 yrs) and 1m winner: fair performer: won banded race at Kempton in October: effective at 7f/1m: acts on polytrack: tried blinkered, visored last 2 starts. *D. J. Daly*

AUBURNDALE 4 b.g. Mind Games 121 – Primitive Gift 38 (Primitive Rising (USA) **–** 113) [2006 10.1g 12.4m 8d Aug 20] well held in claimer/maidens: left K. Reveley after debut. *A. Crook*

AUBURN LODGE (IRE) 5 ch.m. Grand Lodge (USA) 125 – Hadawah (USA) 68 **37** (Riverman (USA) 131) [2006 54: p6g 11.9g 7f⁵ 8f Jul 6] poor maiden: well held at Wolverhampton on reappearance: stays 1½m: acts on firm and soft going: tried blinkered/in cheekpieces. *J. J. Lambe, Ireland*

AUCTION BOY 2 b.g. (Apr 29) Auction House (USA) 120 – Away Win 50 (Common **64 d** Grounds 118) [2006 5.1g⁵ 5.1g 5.7f⁶ p5.1g f7g Nov 14] modest maiden: form only on debut. *B. Palling*

AUCTIONEERSCOUK (IRE) 2 g.rg. (Mar 1) Desert Style (IRE) 121 – Diamond **–** Waltz (IRE) (Linamix (FR) 127) [2006 p5g 5d Apr 6] no show in maidens: tried visored: dead. *P. D. Evans*

AUCTION OASIS 2 b.f. (Mar 5) Auction House (USA) 120 – Shining Oasis (IRE) 73 **68** (Mujtahid (USA) 118) [2006 5g 6.1g² 6.1f⁶ 6m* p6g Nov 7] 1,800Y: first foal: dam, 7f winner at 2 yrs, out of half-sister to smart middle-distance performer Top Class: fair performer: runner-up in maiden at Chepstow second start: won seller at Lingfield in August: should prove as effective at 5f as 6f: raced on good or firmer going on turf: once withdrawn (unruly stalls). *B. Palling*

AUCTION ROOM (USA) 3 b.f. Chester House (USA) 123 – Didina 115 (Nashwan **90** (USA) 135) [2006 80: 11.4m 10m³ 10.4m 12f⁴ Jul 27] leggy, lengthy filly: fairly useful performer: stays 11.4f: acts on good to firm and good to soft ground: folded tamely last 2 starts (sweating and edgy final one): quirky: sold 100,000 gns in November. *B. W. Hills*

AUCTION TIME 2 b.f. (Mar 23) Auction House (USA) 120 – Sontime 65 (Son Pardo **57** 107) [2006 5.1d³ 5g* 5d⁶ 6f Jul 2] first foal: dam 2-y-o 5f/6f winner: modest form:

claimed from B. Palling £6,000 debut: won claimer at Thirsk (left D. Carroll £7,000) in April: best effort at 5f. *J. L. Spearing*

AUDIENCE 6 b.g. Zilzal (USA) 137 – Only Yours 113 (Aragon 118) [2006 107: 8s⁵ 8m 98 9m 8.1s³ 8g³ 8g² 8.1m* 8s 8d 8g 8d Oct 28] big, good-topped gelding: useful handicapper: won at Haydock in August by 1¼ lengths from Banknote: below form after: probably stays 9f: acts on firm and soft going: tried blinkered, effective with/without cheekpieces: has sweated: usually held up. *J. Akehurst*

AUDIT (IRE) 2 b.g. (Jan 24) Fusaichi Pegasus (USA) 130 – Amethyst (IRE) 111 75 § (Sadler's Wells (USA) 132) [2006 7m² 7m⁶ 8.3d² 10.1d³ Oct 18] 70,000Y: big, rangy gelding: somewhat unfurnished at 2 yrs: has a quick action: third foal: dam, Irish 6f (at 2 yrs) and 7f winner (also second in Irish 1000 Guineas), sister to 2000 Guineas winner King of Kings: fair maiden: placed 3 of 4 starts (visored other one): gelded after: stays 1¼m: ungenuine. *Sir Michael Stoute*

AUENMOON (GER) 5 ch.g. Monsun (GER) 124 – Auenlady (GER) (Big Shuffle 78 (USA) 122) [2006 9.8v⁴ 9.1v² Oct 9] trained by E. Groschel, successful 4 times around 1¼m in Germany: fairly useful hurdler: better effort in handicaps on Flat in Britain when second at Ayr: stays 1¼m: acts on heavy going: has worn blinkers. *P. Monteith*

AUENTRAUM (GER) 6 br.g. Big Shuffle (USA) 122 – Auenglocke (GER) (Surumu 66 (GER)) [2006 58: f6g² f7g⁶ p6g* p6g* p7g* p6g 5s p5.1g⁴ p6g p6g p6g Dec 30] fair performer: won banded races at Wolverhampton (2) in March and Kempton in April: left K. McAuliffe after eighth start and C. Dore after ninth one: best up to 7f: acts on all-weather and good to soft going: usually wears blinkers/cheekpieces: sometimes slowly away/finds little. *Ms J. S. Doyle*

AUGUSTINE 5 b.g. Machiavellian (USA) 123 – Crown of Light 112 (Mtoto 134) 86 [2006 71: f7g² p9.5g* f8g³ p10g⁵ p9.5g⁵ p10g² p9.5g² p12.2g² f12g p10g² p10g² 10.2d* 9.9d* 10d³ 9.8v² 12d³ 9.9f² 12m⁵ 9.9g 9.8d⁴ 9.9m³ 10g² 10d² 11.7m Aug 20] close-coupled gelding: fairly useful handicapper: won at Wolverhampton (amateurs) in January and Bath and Beverley in April: stays 1½m: acts on any going: blinkered final outing: tough and consistent. *P. W. Hiatt*

AUGUSTUS JOHN (IRE) 3 gr.c. Danehill (USA) 126 – Rizerie (FR) 98 (Highest Honor (FR) 124) [2006 64p: p7.1m⁶ Nov 8] first foal: dam, 2-y-o 7f winner who stayed 1¼m, half-sister to smart French winner up to 9f (Prix Jean Prat) Rouvres: modest form in maidens at 2 yrs, leaving A. O'Brien in Ireland 65,000 gns after final outing: slowly away only outing in 2006: will be suited by at least 1m. *T. J. Pitt*

AUGUSTUS LIVIUS (IRE) 3 b.g. Titus Livius (FR) 115 – Regal Fanfare (IRE) 94 48 (Taufan (USA) 119) [2006 –: f7g⁵ f7g 7d⁴ 9.8m⁴ 8.3d³ 8f 9.8m 8d Aug 28] workmanlike a35 gelding: poor maiden: barely stays 9.8f: acts on good to firm and good to soft going: tried in cheekpieces. *W. Storey*

AUNTIE MAME 2 b.f. (Mar 6) Diktat 126 – Mother Molly (USA) 78 (Irish River (FR) 51 131) [2006 p8g⁶ Dec 16] second foal: dam, temperamental maiden, best effort at 6f at 2 yrs: never dangerous when sixth to Colchium in maiden at Kempton, rearing as stall opened. *D. J. Coakley*

AUNT JULIA 4 b.f. In The Wings 128 – Original (Caerleon (USA) 132) [2006 106: 106 10d⁶ 11.9s² 12s 12s⁶ Oct 7] leggy, quite good-topped filly: useful performer: ran creditably in 2006 only when neck second to Arbella in 5-runner listed race at Haydock: should stay beyond 1½m: acts on soft and good to firm going: sold 92,000 gns. *R. Hannon*

AUNTY EURO (IRE) 4 b.f. Cape Cross (IRE) 129 – Alexander Goddess (IRE) 90 (Alzao (USA) 117) [2006 87: p10g⁴ 8.7d 10d 10m² 10m 10.5f* 8m 9.5d p9.5g p10g Dec 20] fairly useful performer: won handicap at Down Royal in June: below form after, in Britain last 2 starts: stays 10.5f: acts on polytrack and firm going. *Patrick Morris, Ireland*

AUREATE 2 ch.c. (Feb 6) Jade Robbery (USA) 121 – Anne d'Autriche (IRE) 75 (Rain- 81 p bow Quest (USA) 134) [2006 7.1s² 7m³ 8s³ p8.6g* Nov 24] big, rangy colt, unfurnished at 2 yrs: fourth foal: brother to 3-y-o Austrian: dam, 11.5f winner, half-sister to very smart 1¼m/1½m winner Annaba: fairly useful performer: placed in maidens before winning similar event at Wolverhampton in November by 1¼ lengths from Snow Dancer: will be suited by 1¼m/1½m: should make a better 3-y-o. *M. Johnston*

AURORA JANE (FR) 3 ch.f. Distant View (USA) 126 – Alto Jane 89 (The Minstrel 69 (CAN) 135) [2006 60: p7g³ 8.2g⁶ 10.3g² 9.7f 10.2f⁶ Jul 27] fair maiden handicapper: stays 10.3f: acts on polytrack, best turf efforts on good going: dropped out tamely last 2 outings. *B. W. Hills*

AUSONE 4 b.f. Singspiel (IRE) 133 – Aristocratique 71 (Cadeaux Genereux 131) [2006 **63** p12g⁵ p12g Sep 18] 58,000F: tall, good-topped filly: fourth foal: half-sister to 3 winners, including smart 1m (at 2 yrs) and 1¼m winner Arcalis (by Lear Fan) and 2001 2-y-o 5f winner Noble Academy (by Royal Academy): dam, Irish sprint maiden, half-sister to useful 6f/7f winner Royal Loft: modest form in bumper/hurdles: better effort in maidens when fifth at Lingfield. *Miss J. R. Gibney*

AUSSIE BLUE (IRE) 2 b.c. (Mar 15) Bahamian Bounty 116 – Luanshya 78 (First **–** Trump 118) [2006 5m 6s Oct 6] strong colt: good mover: green and in rear in maidens. *R. M. Whitaker*

AUSSIE CRICKET (FR) 2 gr.f. (Mar 27) Verglas (IRE) 118 – Coup de Colere (FR) **71** (Pistolet Bleu (IRE) 133) [2006 5.7f⁴ 8.1m² p8.6g² 8.3d p9.5m² p9.5g³ Nov 16] €25,000Y: second foal: dam French 12.5f and 15.5f winner: fair maiden: second at Chepstow and Wolverhampton (2): free-going sort, but should stay 1¼m/1½m: refused to enter stalls intended debut. *D. J. Coakley*

AUSSIE RULES (USA) 3 gr.c. Danehill (USA) 126 – Last Second (IRE) 121 **123** (Alzao (USA) 117) [2006 105: 8g⁵ 8g* 10.5m 10m⁴ 8m⁴ 8g⁴ 8f* Nov 4]

Aidan O'Brien mounted his strongest challenge numerically on the Gainsborough Poule d'Essai des Poulains, a race he had won with Landseer in 2002 when responsible for three of the field. This time O'Brien had four representatives, remarkably all sired by Danehill, and was rewarded with a one, two, Aussie Rules just getting the better of Marcus Andronicus, while stablemates Ivan Denisovich and James Joyce, who acted as pacemaker, finished seventh and last of eleven respectively. That Kieren Fallon was on board pinpointed Aussie Rules as his stable's number one contender, and he did have plenty to recommend him going into a renewal which looked no better than average. Aussie Rules had progressed well at two after making a successful debut in a maiden at the Curragh on his final start that season, putting up a game performance when winning the Somerville Tattersall Stakes at Newmarket by a short head from Killybegs. And he had shaped better than the result suggested on his reappearance in the main trial for the Poule d'Essai des Poulains, the Prix de Fontainebleau, also run at Longchamp. Aussie Rules finished fourth in that race to Stormy River, though was demoted a place for causing some interference as he edged right in the straight. Aussie Rules had five lengths to find if he were to turn the tables on Stormy River, who started at odds on for the Poule d'Essai des Poulains, yet there were good reasons for thinking that Aussie Rules would at least make a closer race of it this time around. Stormy River had had the benefit of a recent run when the pair met for the first time, and he also benefited from racing handily in a steadily-run race, whereas Aussie Rules was waited with at the back of the field.

Paddock inspection before the Poule d'Essai des Poulains revealed that Aussie Rules, who looked very well, had clearly derived plenty of benefit from his first run of the season, and his performance in the race itself confirmed as much. Aussie Rules was given a fine ride by Fallon who kept him to the rail throughout, possibly with his mount's tendency to edge right in mind. Things were a bit tight around two furlongs out, but Fallon stuck to his guns and when a gap appeared just

Gainsborough Poule d'Essai des Poulains, Longchamp—Aussie Rules bursts through on the rail to collar stablemate Marcus Andronicus (No.6) and the grey Stormy River; West of Amarillo (No.5) is fourth

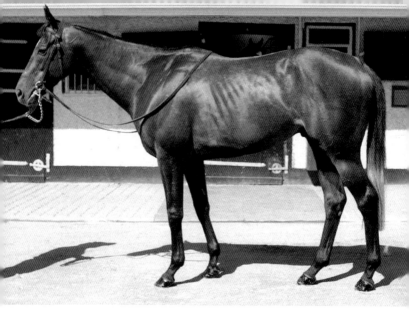

Mrs J. Magnier, Mr M. Tabor and Mr F. Salman's "Aussie Rules"

inside the final furlong, as the leader Stormy River drifted away from the rail, Aussie Rules was able to take full advantage. Quickening to the front shortly after, Aussie Rules had half a length to spare over Marcus Andronicus at the line, with Stormy River a head further back in third. It was to be Aussie Rules's only win of the season in Europe, but he did add to that success when sent to the States in October for the Grade 1 Shadwell Turf Mile at Keeneland. Even though North America's top turf miler Aragorn wasn't among his eight rivals, Aussie Rules still had stiff opposition to overcome, and in winning by a length and three quarters from Remarkable News he showed improved form. Fitted with a visor for the first time and also administered with salix (formerly lasix), he quickened clear in the straight after being held up just behind a fair pace. Both Miesque's Approval, who dead-heated for fourth, and seventh-placed Silent Name turned the tables on Aussie Rules in the Breeders' Cup Mile at Churchill Downs a month later, the former winning it in good style. Aussie Rules, visored again, was never dangerous and finished eighth, having been boxed in when looking to make an effort early in the straight.

Aussie Rules had four outings between his wins, the first two of which were over a mile and a quarter. Attempting to emulate the previous year's Poule d'Essai des Poulains winner Shamardal, who had followed up in the Prix du Jockey Club, Aussie Rules managed only seventh to Darsi at Chantilly, not really shaping as though it was the longer distance that accounted for his below-par run. He did reproduce his Longchamp form next time when a length and three quarters fourth to David Junior in the Coral-Eclipse at Sandown, though the trip looked far enough for him even with the emphasis on speed. With Johnny Murtagh taking over from Kieren Fallon, who had been banned the previous day from riding in Britain by a special panel of the Horseracing Regulatory Authority, Aussie Rules made headway under pressure to dispute the lead approaching the final furlong but then hung right and faded as David Junior took his measure. Still second around a hundred yards out, Aussie Rules was overhauled by both Notnowcato and Blue Monday. Aussie Rules also finished fourth on his next two outings, both over a mile, three lengths behind the winner Court Masterpiece in the Sussex Stakes at Goodwood and the same distance behind Librettist in the Prix du Moulin at Longchamp.

	Danehill (USA) (b 1986)	Danzig (b 1977)	Northern Dancer / Pas de Nom
Aussie Rules (USA) (gr.c. 2003)		Razyana (b 1981)	His Majesty / Spring Adieu
	Last Second (IRE) (gr 1993)	Alzao (b 1980)	Lyphard / Lady Rebecca
		Alruccaba (gr 1983)	Crystal Palace / Allara

Last Second, the dam of Aussie Rules, stayed a mile and a quarter well, as she demonstrated when successful in both the Nassau and Sun Chariot Stakes (now a mile event), producing a fine turn of foot on each occasion. She also had the speed to win over six and seven furlongs on her only appearances at two and finished a close second in the Coronation Stakes over a mile on her reappearance at three. Considered fragile, Last Second ran just seven times in three seasons. Retired to stud after disappointing in the Prix Ganay and Nassau Stakes as a four-year-old, Last Second produced two useful winners, both by Darshaan, from four foals prior to Aussie Rules, namely Approach and Intrigued, each of whom stayed a mile and a half. Her sixth foal is the unraced two-year-old Bold Glance, a Kingmambo colt owned by Godolphin who was the most expensive yearling sold in Europe in 2005, fetching 1,250,000 guineas. Last Second is a very well-bred mare, a half-sister to seven winners including smart performers Alleluia, successful in the 2001 Doncaster Cup and dam of the latest Lancashire Oaks winner Allegretto, and Arrikala, an unlucky third in the 1992 Irish Oaks, and the useful mile-and-a-half listed winner Alouette. The last-named is the dam of Albanova and Alborada (and grandam of Derby runner-up Dragon Dancer), while another half-sister, the maiden Jude, is the dam of two more Group 1-winning mares in Quarter Moon and Yesterday. Aussie Rules's grandam Alruccaba raced only as a two-year-old, winning a six-furlong maiden at Brighton. The next dam Allara, another who was lightly raced, won over seven furlongs in the French Provinces and is a half-sister to the dams of Aliysa and Nishapour. Aussie Rules, medium sized and close coupled, has raced only on good or good to firm going, apart from when finishing fourth to Sir Percy on soft ground at Goodwood on his second start at two, on that occasion not going with any fluency from an early stage. He is to stand at Coolmore Stud in Ireland at a fee of €15,000.
A. P. O'Brien, Ireland

AUSTRIAN (UAE) 3 ch.c. Jade Robbery (USA) 121 – Anne d'Autriche (IRE) 75 **98** (Rainbow Quest (USA) 134) [2006 90p: 10s 10d Nov 4] useful performer, lightly raced: trained by M. Johnston at 2 yrs: not discredited when in mid-field in handicaps at Newbury (met trouble) and Windsor late in 2006: should be suited by 1¼m/1½m: joined S. Seemar in UAE. *Saeed bin Suroor*

AUTHENTICATE 4 b.f. Dansili 127 – Exact Replica (Darshaan 133) [2006 69: 11.8m **64** 9f⁵ 12m⁶ Aug 4] tall filly: modest performer: effective at 7f to 9f: acts on polytrack, firm and good to soft going: sold 3,500 gns in November. *E. J. O'Neill*

AUTHORITY (IRE) 6 b.g. Bluebird (USA) 125 – Persian Tapestry 70 (Tap On Wood **80** 130) [2006 80: 10d³ 12m⁵ 12g Aug 19] rangy, good sort: fair performer, lightly raced: stays 1¼m: acts on polytrack, good to firm and good to soft going: hung left second start. *Lady Herries*

AUTHORIZED (IRE) 2 b.c. (Feb 14) Montjeu (IRE) 137 – Funsie (FR) (Saum- **118 p** arez 132) [2006 8g³ 8s* Oct 21]
For the big owners most closely associated with Coolmore, the monumental scale of the stallion operation there and the fact that five of the top seven sires in Europe in earnings—Danehill, Danehill Dancer, Sadler's Wells, Montjeu and Galileo—either stand or used to stand at the stud provides every chance of reflected glory even when their own runners lose. In the latest covering season, the four active members of the list above and other Coolmore sires of Group 1 winners, Rock of Gibraltar, Mull of Kintyre, Peintre Celebre and Spinning World, covered

Racing Post Trophy, Newbury—away from its usual home but conditions, as so often for this race, are testing; Authorized makes light of them and pulls away from Charlie Farnsbarns, Medicine Path, Eagle Mountain (striped sleeves) and Thousand Words (partially obscured)

more than a thousand mares, which is in line with previous seasonal tallies. No fewer than twelve Group 1 or Grade 1 events in which Mrs John Magnier, Michael Tabor and/or Derrick Smith had at least one runner fell to a horse by a Coolmore stallion in the latest season. The most notable examples were Sixties Icon leading home a Galileo-sired one, two, three in the St Leger, Araafa (by Mull of Kintyre) beating George Washington in the Irish Two Thousand Guineas, Teofilo (by Galileo) seeing off Holy Roman Emperor in the National Stakes and Dewhurst Stakes, Pride (by Peintre Celebre) accounting for Hurricane Run in the Grand Prix de Saint-Cloud and Champion Stakes and last, but by no means least, Authorized (by Montjeu) having odds-on Eagle Mountain back in fourth in the Racing Post Trophy. If all goes well with Authorized—as a strong, good-topped colt he looks the type to train on—the owners of colts trained at Ballydoyle may be forced to seek consolation in the face of defeat by Authorized, as well as by Teofilo.

Lightly-raced horses are not uncommon among the contenders for the Racing Post Trophy and Motivator won the race in 2004 with just one outing, a victory in a maiden race at Newmarket, behind him. However, no maiden had won before Authorized did so, and the fact that he lined up for the race rather than in the alternative of a maiden event at Leicester—and the fact that his trainer Peter Chapple-Hyam bought his yearling half-brother at auction a fortnight earlier—suggested he was held in some esteem. Just over a month beforehand he had shaped promisingly in a minor event with a fine tradition of producing above-average runners, the Haynes, Hanson & Clark Stakes at Newbury. Starting fourth favourite in a field of seven, Authorized travelled strongly from the start and edged ahead over two furlongs out until lack of full fitness told and he was not knocked about in finishing third to Teslin. That run marked him down as a colt to follow, but he still had a lot on his plate in the Racing Post Trophy. The track was different to usual, as Newbury was a substitute due to the redevelopment of Doncaster, but the ground was typically testing, if not quite so testing as the official heavy. Reportedly Chapple-Hyam was in two minds about whether to run Authorized. With easy Beresford Stakes winner Eagle Mountain the obvious favourite, long prices were available about some of the thirteen other runners, including Teslin at 40/1 and Authorized at 25/1. Better-backed contenders included Somerville Tattersall Stakes winner Thousand Words at 7/1, Regime, second in the Goffs Million the previous month, at 15/2 and Royal Lodge Stakes runner-up Medicine Path, a 20/1-shot.

Despite the number of runners, and the fact that some of them required a thorough test of stamina, the Racing Post Trophy was not strongly run throughout, which did little to help Eagle Mountain, a resolute galloper lacking a turn of foot. In contrast, Authorized was ridden like a horse with acceleration. Held up, he was still last with a quarter of a mile to go before making ground smoothly on the outside to get upsides the leader Charlie Farnsbarns over a furlong out. Authorized was soon on top once driven, running on enthusiastically to pass the post a length and a quarter clear of his rival. Medicine Path finished another two lengths adrift, while Eagle Mountain, short of room at a crucial stage and left floundering once the winner quickened, was a neck back in fourth ahead of Thousand Words. The first and second had been among a number entered in the Racing Post Trophy who had also held an entry at the five-day stage in the Horris Hill Stakes, run in the latest season on the same card. The long-standing proximity of these two pattern races for staying two-year-olds was being commented on in these pages as long ago as *Racehorses of 1967* which called it 'a lamentable clash of fixtures that should be easy to avoid with a little planning and foresight.' Some hopes! Though not all the runners in the Racing Post Trophy were able to show their best form for one reason or another, there is no reason to doubt Authorized's ability or promise. The runner-up, who wasn't flagging in the closing stages, was an improving colt who had won a well-contested minor event at Ascot on his most recent start, and the winner's timefigure of 0.69 fast (equivalent to a timerating of 117) was a good one, bettered only by Teofilo, Holy Roman Emperor and Dutch Art among the two-year-olds.

		Montjeu (IRE) (b 1996)	Sadler's Wells (b 1981)	Northern Dancer / Fairy Bridge
Authorized (IRE) (b.c. Feb 14, 2004)			Floripedes (b 1985)	Top Ville / Toute Cy
		Funsie (FR) (b 1999)	Saumarez (b or br 1987)	Rainbow Quest / Fiesta Fun
			Vallee Dansante (b 1981)	Lyphard / Green Valley

Montjeu was something of a rarity among Sadler's Wells's best progeny in being high-mettled with a tendency to sweat up, and he is passing touches of temperament on to a fair proportion of his runners. Not that it hinders them greatly because in many instances he is also passing on his considerable ability. Some of his progeny also seem blessed with his own combination of speed and stamina, and Authorized is an example, his pedigree providing complete confidence in his staying a mile and a half. That makes him an exciting prospect, one who would be worth his place in the Two Thousand Guineas before progressing towards the Derby. His trainer is thinking principally about Epsom, but, despite saying he would not rush Authorized at the start of the year, he added: 'He'll get stronger, and when they get stronger they get faster, so the Guineas wouldn't be out of the question.' Whatever happens at Newmarket, with Teofilo also almost certain to stay the Derby trip Authorized has at least one mountain to climb. However, he should not be underestimated and his career should be fascinating to follow. The pedigree on the dam's side is a good one. Funsie did not race but she is by an Arc winner in Saumarez, who is also maternal grandsire of Derby Italiano winner and Irish Derby runner-up Gentlewave, from a family with no shortage of stamina. The grandam Vallee Dansante foaled eight winners from ten runners, notably Brooklyn's Dance, a smart performer over middle distances and dam of Prix du Jockey Club runner-up Prospect Park, and Krissante, who foaled Grand Criterium winner Okawango. Vallee Dansante was a close relative of Green Dancer, successful in the Observer Gold Cup (a previous incarnation of the Racing Post Trophy) and the Poule d'Essai des Poulains, and a half-sister to the dam of top juvenile Alhaarth. Authorized fetched a lot more as a yearling than his half-brother by Fasliyev referred to above, who sold for 110,000 guineas and now belongs to Cheveley Park Stud. The figure for Authorized was 400,000 guineas, which gave a healthy profit to the vendor who had bought him for 95,000 guineas as a foal. *P. W. Chapple-Hyam*

AUTOGRAPH HUNTER 2 b.g. (Mar 15) Tobougg (IRE) 125 – Kalindi 102 (Efisio **80** 120) [2006 6s f7g* p7g² p8g² Dec 3] 32,000Y: good-bodied gelding: third foal: half-brother to useful Irish 2005 2-y-o 6f/7f winner Abigail Pett (by Medicean) and 4-y-o Mambazo: dam 5f (at 2 yrs) and 7f winner: fairly useful performer: gelded and off nearly 6 months, won maiden at Southwell in November: should stay 1m: acts on all-weather: signs of temperament. *M. Johnston*

AUTOMATION 3 b.f. Tamure (IRE) 125 – Anatomic (Deerhound (USA) 64) [2006 –: **–** 7.5g 6m Jun 21] close-coupled filly: well beaten in 3 maidens: tended to hang on reappearance. *C. W. Thornton*

AUTOUR DU MONDE 2 ch.f. (Mar 20) Spinning World (USA) 130 – Penang Pearl **56** (FR) 106 (Bering 136) [2006 5s 5.9g³ 7f⁵ 7m 5m⁶ Sep 13] 29,000Y: rather leggy filly: third foal: half-sister to 3-y-o Penang Cinta and 2004 2-y-o 5f winner Penang Sapphire (by Spectrum): dam 1m/9f winner: modest maiden: barely stays 7f: tried in blinkers/cheekpieces, once tongue tied. *P. C. Haslam*

AUTUMN STORM 2 b.f. (Feb 4) Auction House (USA) 120 – Cozette (IRE) 49 **58** (Danehill Dancer (IRE) 117) [2006 p5g⁴ p5.1g⁶ p5g⁶ 5m* 5f⁶ p5g⁶ 5.1f⁴ p6g 5.3m⁶ Sep 19] 7,200Y: first foal: dam ran 3 times: modest performer: 66/1, won maiden at Lingfield in June: should stay at least 6f: acts on polytrack and firm going. *R. Ingram*

AUWITESSWEETHEART 4 b.f. Josr Algarhoud (IRE) 118 – Miss Kirsty (USA) 82 **90 d** (Miswaki (USA) 124) [2006 89: 5g* p6g⁵ 5g³ 5m 6g 5.2d⁶ 6d 6g Oct 16] leggy, lengthy filly: fairly useful handicapper: won at Windsor in April: below form last 4 outings: effective at 5f/6f: acts on heavy and good to firm going: once tongue tied: tends to hang left: sold 3,700 gns. *B. R. Millman*

AVALON 4 b.g. Kingmambo (USA) 125 – Lady Carla 122 (Caerleon (USA) 132) [2006 **106** 118: 13.3s³ 21.7m Jun 24] big, strong gelding: smart form in 2005 for A. O'Brien: gelded and just modest form over hurdles prior to respectable 7¼ lengths third of 6 to Distinction in listed event at Newbury on reappearance: should stay 1¾m (long way below form when in rear in Queen Alexandra Stakes over 2¾m at Royal Ascot). *Jonjo O'Neill*

AVANTI 10 gr.g. Reprimand 122 – Dolly Bevan 53 (Another Realm (118) [2006 59: **52** p16g⁶ p12g³ p13.9g Dec 31] smallish, well-made gelding: modest performer: stays 1¾m: acts on polytrack and good to firm going: tried blinkered, often visored nowadays. *Dr J. R. J. Naylor*

AVA'S WORLD (IRE) 2 b.f. (Mar 1) Desert Prince (IRE) 130 – Taibhseach (USA) 94 **79** (Secreto (USA) 128) [2006 p7g 6m* 7d⁴ 6g p7g p6g⁶ Nov 11] 9,500Y: small filly: seventh foal: half-sister to fairly useful 11.6f winner Loch Quest (by Giant's Causeway) and winner in USA by Woodman: dam, Irish 2-y-o 7f winner who probably stayed 1¼m, half-sister to US Grade 1 1¼m winner Mi Selecto: fair performer: won maiden at Catterick in September: below form last 3 starts, possibly amiss first 2: likely to stay 1m: acts on good to firm and good to soft going. *M. Johnston*

AVELIAN (IRE) 3 b.g. Cape Cross (IRE) 129 – Mashoura (Shareef Dancer (USA) **74** 135) [2006 8m⁵ 8m³ 10.3m² 12f⁴ p12g 10f⁵ 11.6d Oct 9] 38,000Y: sturdy gelding: fifth foal: dam, French 1m winner, half-sister to 7-y-o Vanderlin: fair maiden: stays 1½m: acts on firm ground: visored fifth start (said to have had breathing problem), in cheekpieces/tongue tied last 2 outings: hung right on debut (2 handlers in paddock): sold 9,000 gns. *W. J. Haggas*

AVENING 6 br.g. Averti (IRE) 117 – Dependable (Formidable (USA) 125) [2006 6g⁴ 5g **89** 6g² 6d 5s² 6f 6d 6g Nov 7] useful-looking gelding: fairly useful handicapper: won at Deauville in 2005: good second at Maisons-Laffitte and Deauville at 6 yrs: respectable seventh to Munaddam at Folkestone sixth start: best at 5f/6f: acts on firm and soft going: usually blinkered: has had tongue tied. *J. E. Hammond, France*

AVENLEA 5 b.g. Averti (IRE) 117 – Cloudslea (USA) (Chief's Crown (USA)) [2006 **57** 46: p10g p7.1g p6g* 7f Jun 6] modest performer: won maiden claimer at Kempton in April: should have been suited by 7f+: dead. *G. L. Moore*

AVENTURA (IRE) 6 b.g. Sri Pekan (USA) 117 – La Belle Katherine (USA) (Lyphard **61** (USA) 132) [2006 73: 7g³ f8g⁵ p6g³ p7.1g⁵ Jun 22] sturdy, close-coupled gelding: only modest in 2006: stays 8.6f: acts on all-weather, good to firm and good to soft going: races prominently. *S. R. Bowring*

AVERTICUS 2 b.c. (Apr 27) Averti (IRE) 117 – Santa Vida (USA) 64 (St Jovite (USA) **83** 135) [2006 5m³ 5m² 6g* p7.1g Oct 8] leggy, quite attractive colt: second foal: dam maiden who stayed 1½m: fairly useful form: won maiden at Yarmouth in September, making all: only mid-field in nursery over longer trip: may prove best at 5f/6f. *B. W. Hills*

AVERTI STAR 2 b.g. (May 4) Averti (IRE) 117 – Zinzi (Song 132) [2006 6f 6f Jun 22] **49** poor form in maidens: gelded after. *Mrs A. Duffield*

AVERTUOSO 2 b.g. (Jan 24) Averti (IRE) 117 – First Musical 107 (First Trump 118) **93** [2006 5d⁶ 5m* 5d² 5g⁶ 5m 5f² 5f* 5.2g 6s Aug 24] 32,000Y: big, strong gelding: type to carry condition: third foal: half-brother to 5.7f winner Casterossa (by Rossini): dam 5f/6f winner at 2 yrs: fairly useful performer: won maiden at Musselburgh in May and nursery at York (beat Danum Dancer by 1¼ lengths) in July: well beaten in sales races last 2 starts: gelded after: best at 5f: acts on firm and good to soft going. *B. Smart*

AVERY 2 gr.c. (Mar 14) Averti (IRE) 117 – Bandanna 98 (Bandmaster (USA) 97) [2006 **63** 5.1g 5.7g⁶ 5m⁴ 5.1f 6f Sep 18] modest maiden: well held in nurseries last 2 starts: raced at 5f/6f on good and firmer going. *R. J. Hodges*

AVICIA 4 ch.f. Vettori (IRE) 119 – Amarice 85 (Suave Dancer (USA) 136) [2006 64: **–** 11.6m p16g 13.1m Sep 4] maiden: well held in handicaps in 2006. *C. A. Horgan*

AVINA LAUGH 2 ch.f. (Apr 15) Zaha (CAN) 106 – Great Exception 84 (Grundy 137) **69**
[2006 7f 7f² 7g⁴ Aug 18] 800F: half-sister to several winners, including fairly useful
1m and 1½m winner Exclusion and 1¼m winner Exemption (both by Ballad Rock): dam
1½m and 15f winner: fair form in maidens, in frame at Thirsk and Folkestone: should
stay 1¼m+: sold 7,000 gns. *P. W. Chapple-Hyam*

AVIVA 2 b.g. (Jan 10) Noverre (USA) 125 – Evangeline (Sadler's Wells (USA) 132) **78**
[2006 6m³ Jun 18] 30,000F, 60,000Y: big, strong gelding: first foal: dam unraced: 18/1,
fair form in maiden at York: dead. *J. Howard Johnson*

AVOID THE CAT 2 b.c. (Feb 17) Averti (IRE) 117 – Baileys Firecat 67 (Catrail (USA) **61 ?**
123) [2006 6g 6m⁴ p5g 7d Sep 29] maiden: possibly flattered when fourth in slowly-run
minor event at Salisbury: sold 2,000 gns, sent to Sweden. *Mrs A. J. Perrett*

AVONCREEK 2 b.g. (Mar 25) Tipsy Creek (USA) 115 – Avondale Girl (IRE) 73 (Case **53**
Law 113) [2006 5.1d⁵ 5m p6f⁶ 6s p6g Sep 30] close-coupled gelding: modest maiden:
tried in cheekpieces: should prove best at 5f/6f. *B. P. J. Baugh*

AVORIAZ (IRE) 3 gr.c. Desert Prince (IRE) 130 – Abbatiale (FR) 117 (Kaldoun (FR) **88**
122) [2006 9g⁴ 10g⁴ 10g² 10m³ 8d² Oct 2] tall, close-coupled, good-topped colt: fourth
foal: brother to French 11f winner Arlington and half-brother to French 9f winner Apos-
trophe (by Barathea): dam, French 10.5f winner, second in Prix de Diane: fairly useful
form: in frame in minor events at Longchamp first 3 outings for Rodolphe Collet and
in maidens both starts in Britain: stays 1¼m: below form on good to soft going.
L. M. Cumani

AWAKEN 5 b.m. Zafonic (USA) 130 – Dawna 106 (Polish Precedent (USA) 131) [2006 **65**
56: 9.9f⁵ 12m 10.5m⁵ 9.3m* 11.1m* 9f⁴ 9.3f⁵ 9.9g 9.2g Sep 17] fair performer: won
claimers at Carlisle in June and Hamilton in July: stays 11f: acts on firm and good to soft
going: said to have had breathing problem final start. *Miss Tracy Waggott*

AWARDING 6 ch.g. Mark of Esteem (IRE) 137 – Monaiya (Shareef Dancer (USA) **50**
135) [2006 58: p6g p7.1g p6g p7.1g f7g 7g Jun 13] good-topped gelding: modest performer: stays 7f: acts on polytrack and firm going: tried blinkered: visored/tongue tied
nowadays: sometimes slowly away: tends to carry head high. *Dr J. R. J. Naylor*

AWATUKI (IRE) 3 b.g. Distant Music (USA) 126 – Itkan (IRE) (Marju (IRE) 127) **85**
[2006 76: p10g* p10g³ 9.9f² 10.4d 9.9f 10.1d p10g⁵ Dec 20] strong, workmanlike
gelding: fairly useful performer: won maiden at Kempton in March: good placed efforts
in handicaps next 2 starts, but below form after (gelded prior to final outing): stays 1¼m:
acts on polytrack, firm and good to soft ground. *A. P. Jarvis*

AWE 2 b.g. (Mar 14) Muhtarram (USA) 125 – Fleet of Light 94 (Spectrum (IRE) 126) **–**
[2006 6m 7m f8g Nov 10] no form in maidens/claimer. *Mrs C. A. Dunnett*

A WOMAN IN LOVE 7 gr.m. Muhtarram (USA) 125 – Ma Lumiere (FR) (Niniski **63**
(USA) 125) [2006 –: p7g p7g⁴ 7m p7g Jun 15] angular mare: modest nowadays: lightly
raced since 2004: effective at 6f to 1m: acts on polytrack, raced only on good ground
or firmer on turf: free-going sort, usually held up: reportedly bled on reappearance.
Miss B. Sanders

AWWAL MALIKA (USA) 2 b.f. (Feb 8) Kingmambo (USA) 125 – First Night (IRE) **73 p**
102 (Sadler's Wells (USA) 132) [2006 6g² 7d Oct 14] $125,000Y: tall, useful-looking
filly: third foal: dam, 1m and (in USA) 9f winner, closely related to Oaks and Irish Derby
winner Balanchine: fair form: 3½ lengths second to Dream Scheme in maiden at Newmarket: stiff task in Rockfel Stakes there 2 weeks later: will be suited by 1m/1¼m: looks
nervy sort, but should make a better 3-y-o. *C. E. Brittain*

AXIS MUNDI (IRE) 2 b.f. (Mar 13) Titus Livius (FR) 115 – Inventive 84 (Sheikh **–**
Albadou 128) [2006 5d 5m p6g Nov 6] €1,000F, €10,500Y: fourth foal: half-sister to
3-y-o Creative Mind: dam, 5f winner, ran only at 2 yrs: no form in maidens/minor event.
T. J. Etherington

AXIS SHIELD (IRE) 3 b.f. Shinko Forest (IRE) – La Doyenne (IRE) 65 (Masterclass **52**
(USA) 116) [2006 49: f5g* f5g⁵ 5g⁶ 5f⁴ 5f⁴ f5g 5f f6g f5g⁴ Nov 21] leggy filly: modest
performer: won maiden claimer (left J. Portman) in April and banded race in May, both
at Southwell: effective at 5f to 7f: acts on all-weather and firm ground. *M. C. Chapman*

AYALA COVE (USA) 3 ch.f. Mt Livermore (USA) – Kitra (USA) (Woodman (USA) **–**
126) [2006 –: f8g⁴ f8g 9.8m Jul 10] close-coupled filly: little form: tongue tied.
P. C. Haslam

AYAM JANTAN 3 ch.g. Cadeaux Genereux 131 – Madame Est Sortie (FR) (Longleat **61**
(USA) 109) [2006 67: 8m⁵ 8m 8g⁴ 7g⁵ 7.9m³ 6.9m* 7m Aug 31] close-coupled, work-

manlike gelding: modest performer: won handicap at Carlisle in August: probably stays 1m: raced only on good ground or firmer: sold 6,500 gns. *M. Johnston*

AYLMER ROAD (IRE) 4 b.g. Groom Dancer (USA) 128 – Pekan's Pride 84 (Sri – Pekan (USA) 117) [2006 86: 16g 14.1g 12.6m Jun 25] rather leggy gelding: fairly useful at 3 yrs: no form in 2006: stays 1¾m: acts on firm ground: tried blinkered: none too genuine: gelded. *P. F. I. Cole*

AYPEEYES (IRE) 2 b.g. (May 17) King Charlemagne (USA) 120 – Habaza (IRE) 68 **78** (Shernazar 131) [2006 p8.6g* p8.6g³ p9.5s⁴ Dec 14] 4,500Y: fourth foal: half-brother to 4-y-o Killena Boy and 1½m winner Gentle Peace (by Orpen): dam ran 3 times in Ireland: fair form: won maiden at Wolverhampton (by ½ length from Robert The Brave) in October: better form in frame in nurseries there after: will stay 1¼m. *S. Kirk*

AYSGARTH FLYER (IRE) 3 b.g. Soviet Star (USA) 128 – Why Worry Now (IRE) **63** 75 (College Chapel 122) [2006 63: f7g⁶ f7g⁶ f6g f7g Nov 10] modest performer: best efforts at 6f: acts on fibresand and good to firm going: wears cheekpieces/blinkers: sent to Cyprus. *James Moffatt*

AZAHARA 4 b.f. Vettori (IRE) 119 – Branston Express (Bay Express 132) [2006 58d: – 9.8m 10f Jun 23] sturdy filly: fair at 2 yrs: deteriorated after: stayed 1¼m: acted on good to firm going: blinkered final start: dead. *K. G. Reveley*

AZAROLE (IRE) 5 b.g. Alzao (USA) 117 – Cashew 80 (Sharrood (USA) 124) [2006 **112** 115: 7.5m² 8m³ 8.9m³ 8m* p8g³ 8.1m 8g³ 7s⁶ 8v² 9m Sep 16] strong gelding: smart performer: won handicap at Nad Al Sheba in March by ½ length from Proudance: placed after in listed race at Lingfield (below best in tactical event), Jaxx-Pokal at Hamburg (4 lengths third to Lateral) and Oettingen-Rennen at Baden-Baden (1½ lengths second to Notability): well below form final start: stays 1m: acts on polytrack, heavy and good to firm going: tongue tied first 2 outings at 4 yrs: hung right when well below form sixth outing. *J. S. Moore*

AZERLEY (IRE) 3 b.f. Desert Style (IRE) 121 – Miss Indigo 62 (Indian Ridge 123) **59** [2006 6d 8d 6g⁵ f8g 6m³ Jul 25] 10,000Y: quite good-topped filly: first foal: dam maiden half-sister to useful performer up to 1½m Musetta: modest maiden: form only at 6f on good/good to firm ground: tends to hang left. *J. D. Bethell*

AZIME (IRE) 3 b.c. Cape Cross (IRE) 129 – Adjisa (IRE) (Doyoun 124) [2006 59: – 10.9g Apr 17] close-coupled colt: has a short, unimpressive action: modest maiden, lightly raced: tailed off only outing in 2006: stays 9f: sold 1,500 gns, sent to Spain. *C. E. Brittain*

AZIZAM 4 ch.f. Singspiel (IRE) 133 – Perdicula (IRE) (Persian Heights 129) [2006 85: **77** 11g 10m Jun 7] smallish, sturdy filly: fairly useful performer in 2005: better effort (just fair form) in 2006 on first start: should stay 1½m: acts on good to firm going: tongue tied final 3-y-o outing: refused to enter stall once. *P. W. Chapple-Hyam*

AZREME 6 ch.h. Unfuwain (USA) 131 – Mariette 35 (Blushing Scribe (USA) 107) **76** [2006 76d, a57: p9.5g⁵ f8g³ f8g f8g 8.1d² 8d³ May 26] well-made horse: fair performer **a54** on turf, modest on all-weather: won banded race at Southwell in January: stays 1m: acts on all-weather, heavy and good to firm ground: sometimes wears headgear: usually waited with. *P. Howling*

AZURINE (IRE) 3 b.f. Spectrum (IRE) 126 – Flamands (IRE) 92 (Sadler's Wells **72** (USA) 132) [2006 p10g p10g 8g³ 10v⁶ 8f² 8f⁶ 12f⁴ 12f* Jul 28] €28,000Y: sixth foal: half-sister to useful 1½m/1¾m winner Dune (by Desert King) and a winner in Japan by Machiavellian: dam, 1½m/1¾m winner, sister to smart 1¼m performer Casey Tibbs: fair performer: won 4-runner handicap at Thirsk in July, dictating: stays 1½m: acts on firm going: free-going sort. *M. Johnston*

AZYGOUS 3 ch.g. Foxhound (USA) 103 – Flag (Selkirk (USA) 129) [2006 87: p5g **88** 5.2m⁶ p5g 5f³ 5g³ 5.1f* 5m⁴ 5f 5g⁶ 5g³ 5m⁴ Sep 12] neat gelding: fairly useful handicapper: won at Chester in July: best at 5f: acts on polytrack, firm and good to soft going: races prominently. *J. Akehurst*

B

BAAN (USA) 3 ch.g. Diesis 133 – Madaen (USA) (Nureyev (USA) 131) [2006 97: 7g⁶ **102** 10m³ 11.5m³ 12m 12m 10.5m 10s f11g³ p10g⁵ p12.2s Dec 15] small, good-topped geld- **a96** ing: useful performer: several creditable efforts in 2006, including in Classic Trial at Sandown (close third to Primary), Derby Trial at Lingfield (5¼ lengths third to Linda's

Lad) and cantorspreadfair. com Stakes (Handicap) at Goodwood (changed hands 105,000 gns beforehand, eighth to Strategic Mount) final outing: below form last 2 starts: stays 1½m: acts on fibresand, soft and good to firm going: consistent. *M. Johnston*

BAARRIJ 2 ch.f. (Mar 3) Tobougg (IRE) 125 – Bint Albaadiya (USA) 108 (Woodman (USA) 126) [2006 6m 7d⁵ Aug 18] third foal: half-sister to smart 1¼m (including in UAE) winner Remaadd (by Daylami) and 6-y-o Almizan: dam, 6f (including at 2 yrs) winner who probably stayed 7f, out of smart miler Pixie Erin: green, poor form in maidens: sold 7,400 gns, joined K. Burke. *M. R. Channon* **49**

BABA GANOUGE (IRE) 2 ch.f. (Feb 16) Desert Prince (IRE) 130 – Le Montrachet (Nashwan (USA) 135) [2006 p7g Oct 6] 12,000Y: second foal: closely related to winner in New Zealand by Green Desert: dam unraced close relation to smart miler Gold Splash out of Prix Saint-Alary winner Riviere d'Or: 25/1, mid-field in maiden at Lingfield. *B. J. Meehan* **50**

BABA GHANOUSH 4 ch.f. Zaha (CAN) 106 – Vrennan 74 (Suave Dancer (USA) 136) [2006 73p: p8.6g⁵ Nov 14] fair performer, lightly raced: shaped as if in need of run only start in 2006: should stay 1m+: acts on polytrack. *W. Jarvis* **61**

BABCARY 3 b.f. Bertolini (USA) 125 – Midnight Break 78 (Night Shift (USA)) [2006 p8g³ p8g* p10g³ p8g 9.9m² 9.9m* 10m³ 9m⁴ p10g² 10.2f² 10.3f Sep 23] 5,000Y: tall filly: half-sister to 3 winners, including fairly useful 13.3f winner Mac (by Fleetwood) and 7-y-o Bobby Kennard: dam 5f/6f winner: fairly useful performer: won maiden at Lingfield in January and handicap at Goodwood in June: held her form well in handicaps prior to final outing (raced wide at Chester): best at 1m/1¼m: acts on polytrack and firm ground: free-going front runner, wears crossed noseband: reliable. *M. P. Tregoning* **91**

BABE MACCOOL (IRE) 4 ch.g. Giant's Causeway (USA) 132 – Kotama (USA) 96 (Shahrastani (USA) 135) [2006 90: p10g p10g³ 10.1m Sep 13] well-made gelding: fairly useful performer: best effort in 2006 when third in handicap at Kempton: stays 1¼m: acts on polytrack and good to firm ground: sold 46,000 gns. *B. W. Hills* **90**

BABETH (IRE) 3 b.f. Indian Lodge (IRE) 127 – Almond Flower (IRE) (Alzao (USA) 117) [2006 68: f6g³ p8g Jan 11] sturdy filly: modest performer: reportedly finished lame final start: should have been suited by 7f: acted on all-weather and good to soft going: dead. *A. M. Balding* **62**

BABIECA (USA) 2 gr.c. (Feb 11) Tactical Cat (USA) 116 – Secret Mountain (USA) (Mt Livermore (USA)) [2006 7f² 7f* Jul 29] $25,000Y: second foal: dam, ran twice in USA, half-sister to high-class performer up to 1m Mukaddamah: fair form: confirmed debut encouragement when landing odds in maiden at Newmarket: will stay 1m: probably capable of better. *T. D. Barron* **76 p**

BABODANA 6 ch.h. Bahamian Bounty 116 – Daanat Nawal (Machiavellian (USA) 123) [2006 115: 8s⁶ 8.1m² 8s² 8m p8g 8g 9d 7d⁶ 8d⁴ 9d⁶ 8d 8.2d² p10g Nov 18] good-topped horse: smart performer on turf, useful on all-weather: good efforts when second in Sandown Mile (length behind Rob Roy) and listed handicap at York (beaten head by Zero Tolerance): just respectable efforts at best after, including length second of 5 to With Interest in minor event at Nottingham: stays easy 9f: acts on polytrack, heavy and good to firm going: tried infrequently in headgear. *M. H. Tompkins* **115 a99**

BABOOSH (IRE) 5 b.m. Marju (IRE) 127 – Slipper 94 (Suave Dancer (USA) 136) [2006 –: p10g p10g p10g p10g 11.5f* 9.7f 9.9g⁵ 10.2f² 11.9m 10.2m Oct 8] leggy mare: fair handicapper: landed big gamble at Yarmouth in July: stays 11.5f: acts on firm going: tried in cheekpieces. *M. Wigham* **66**

BABY BARRY 9 b.g. Komaite (USA) – Malcesine (IRE) 46 (Auction Ring (USA) 123) [2006 60, a64: p9.5g 7.5f² 8.3m* 8m* 9d² 8m⁶ 7.1m⁴ p8.6g f7g Oct 12] good-topped gelding: modest performer: won seller at Hamilton in July and claimer at Musselburgh in August: left R. Fahey after fifth start: stays 9.5f: acts on all-weather, firm and good to soft going: usually wore headgear earlier in career. *M. J. Attwater* **61**

BABY DORDAN (IRE) 2 b.f. (Apr 5) Desert Prince (IRE) 130 – Three Owls (IRE) 79 (Warning 136) [2006 6m⁶ 6d⁴ 7s Oct 10] third foal: half-sister to useful 2004 2-y-o 5f winner Black Velvet (by Inchinor): dam, 1m winner from 3 starts, half-sister to smart French performer up to around 1¼m Thames: fair maiden: shaped encouragingly at Goodwood first 2 starts (3 months apart): should stay 7f/1m: acts on good to firm and good to soft going, well beaten on soft: joined H. Dunlop. *D. J. Daly* **70**

BABYLON SISTER (IRE) 2 b.f. (Apr 21) Val Royal (FR) 127 – Space Travel (Dancing Dissident (USA) 119) [2006 5d⁵ 5.7f⁵ p7g* p7g 7f 7.1d⁵ 8g³ Dec 31] €51,000Y: half-sister to useful 1997 2-y-o 5f/6f winner Tippitt Boy (by Prince Sabo), later successful **66**

in Germany, and 6f/7f winner Reverie (by Bishop of Cashel): dam unraced out of smart 6f/7f winner Rocket Alert: fair performer: won maiden at Lingfield in June: sold from R. Hannon 9,000 gns before third in minor event at Dos Hermanas final start: stays 1m: acts on polytrack and good to soft going. *J. Valverde, Spain*

BABY STRANGE 2 b. or gr.c. (Apr 27) Superior Premium 122 – The Manx Touch (IRE) 70 (Petardia 113) [2006 5.1g* 6g* 6m 7d⁴ 6s* 6d² Oct 28] 20,000Y: leggy, useful-looking colt: second foal: brother to 3-y-o Mambo Sun: dam 7f/1m winner: useful form: won maiden at Bath and minor event at Ascot in May and listed race at York (beat Hinton Admiral 6 lengths) in October: also in frame in Somerville Tattersall Stakes (not clear run) at Newmarket and Criterium de Maisons-Laffitte (3 lengths second to Captain Marvelous): stays 7f: raced on good or softer ground, bar Royal Ascot (tenth in Coventry Stakes): edgy sort, tends to sweat. *P. A. Blockley* **108**

BACHARACH (IRE) 3 b.g. Indian Lodge (IRE) 127 – Katherine Gorge (USA) (Hansel (USA)) [2006 69: p10g p7.1g 8g 7m 7.2v 10s p8.6g Nov 20] quite good-topped gelding: modest maiden nowadays: stays 7f: acts on good to firm going: tongue tied final start (reportedly bled). *R. F. Fisher* **53**

BACHELOR PARTY (USA) 3 b. or br.c. Brahms (USA) 118 – Fiancee (USA) (Air Forbes Won (USA)) [2006 6m² 7f⁴ 7d* Sep 25] $75,000Y, $250,000 2-y-o: fourth foal: half-brother to 3 winners in USA by Roar, including Grade 1 8.5f runner-up Enjoy: dam unraced: fair form: won maiden at Brighton in September: raced only at 6f/7f: acts on good to firm and good to soft ground: sold 8,000 gns. *J. Noseda* **69**

BACHNAGAIRN 2 b.g. (Mar 4) In The Wings 128 – Purple Heather (USA) 93 (Rahy (USA) 115) [2006 6m⁴ 7g 7.1m 8d⁴ Sep 26] good-topped gelding: third foal: half-brother to fairly useful 7f (at 2 yrs)/1m winner The Coires (by Green Desert) and 3-y-o Gelder: dam, 1¼m winner, out of half-sister to dam of Nashwan, Unfuwain and Nayef: fair maiden: fourth at Newbury and Goodwood (nursery): will stay 1¼m. *R. Charlton* **70**

BACK IN THE RED (IRE) 2 ch.c. (Apr 2) Redback 116 – Fureur de Vivre (IRE) (Bluebird (USA) 125) [2006 5m⁶ 5g 5.7m 5.5m* 5m* 6d⁵ p6g Nov 1] strong colt: modest performer: won nursery at Redcar in September: raced at 5f/6f: acts on good to firm and good to soft ground. *M. Wellings* **62**

BACKSTREET LAD 4 b.g. Fraam 114 – Forest Fantasy 61 (Rambo Dancer (CAN) 107) [2006 60: p12g f14g Nov 21] compact gelding: modest maiden: well beaten both starts on Flat in 2006. *Evan Williams* **–**

BACK TOO BEDLAM 3 b.g. Petoski 135 – Lutine Royal 46 (Formidable (USA) 125) [2006 11g May 30] 66/1, well held in claimer at Redcar. *Mrs S. A. Watt* **–**

BAD BOY AL (IRE) 2 b.g. (Apr 7) Cape Cross (IRE) 129 – Ladycromby (IRE) (Lycius (USA) 124) [2006 6m 7.2g 8v Sep 2] sturdy, lengthy gelding: last in maidens. *D. W. Barker* **–**

BADDAM 4 b.c. Mujahid (USA) 125 – Aude La Belle (FR) 81 (Ela-Mana-Mou 132) [2006 100p: 12g 14.11f⁵ 16d 20m* 21.7m* 16f⁵ 15.9d⁵ 18d³ 20m 18d Oct 14] rather leggy, quite good-topped colt: smart performer: progressed well in 2006, successful at Royal Ascot in 29-runner Ascot Stakes (Handicap) (by 5 lengths from Top The Charts) and Queen Alexandra Stakes (by a neck from Cover Up, becoming first since 1978 to complete the double in same year): creditable fifth to Yeats in Goodwood Cup and good third to Sergeant Cecil in Doncaster Cup at York sixth/eighth outings: stays 2¾m: acts on firm and good to soft going. *M. R. Channon* **114**

BAD HABIT 2 b.c. (Apr 25) Royal Applause 124 – Waft (USA) 67 (Topsider (USA)) [2006 6g 6m Aug 1] unfurnished colt: last in maidens. *M. R. Channon* **–**

Ascot Stakes (Handicap), Royal Ascot—Baddam shows himself a thorough stayer; it's close for second between Top The Charts and Shamayoun (cheekpieces)

*Queen Alexandra Stakes, Royal Ascot—Baddam underlines the point
over an even longer trip four days later, completing a double last achieved by Mountain Cross in 1978;
he gets the better of Royal Ascot regular Cover Up and the blinkered Vinando*

BADOU 6 b.g. Averti (IRE) 117 – Bint Albadou (IRE) 91 (Green Desert (USA) 127) **39**
[2006 –, a45: p7g Dec 13] good-topped gelding: poor performer: stays easy 1m: acts on
all-weather, soft and good to firm going: sometimes wears headgear. *L. Montague Hall*

BA FOXTROT 3 b.g. Foxhound (USA) 103 – Aunt Susan (Distant Relative 128) [2006 **–**
102: 7g 6f May 7] sturdy gelding: useful performer: gelded, well below form in 2006:
best form at 5f/6f: acted on heavy and good to firm going: dead. *M. R. Channon*

BAHAMA MAMA (IRE) 2 b.f. (Mar 5) Invincible Spirit (IRE) 121 – Nassma (IRE) **103**
95 (Sadler's Wells (USA) 132) [2006 5m* 6m* 6m⁶ 5m* 5m³ 5g² 6m⁴ 5d⁴ Oct 7]
17,000F, 40,000Y: good-bodied filly: half-sister to several winners, including useful 6f
(at 2 yrs) to 1m (in UAE) winner Calchas (by Warning) and fairly useful 9f/1¼m winner
Traprain (by Mark of Esteem): dam 1¼m and 13.4f winner: useful performer: won maid-
en at Newmarket in May, minor event at Brighton in June and listed race at Sandown in
July: in frame in pattern events all subsequent starts, best efforts when under length third
to Enticing at Goodwood and 1½ lengths second to Wi Dud in Flying Childers Stakes at
York: reportedly lost action in Mill Reef Stakes next time: will prove best kept to 5f/6f:
raced on good/good to firm going until final start (below form): edgy type: sold 150,000
gns. *J. Noseda*

BAHAMA REEF (IRE) 5 b.g. Sri Pekan (USA) 117 – Caribbean Dancer 71 (Shareef **–**
Dancer (USA) 135) [2006 54d: p7g Jun 15] angular gelding: maiden: well beaten in seller
only outing at 5 years: has run badly in visor/cheekpieces. *B. Gubby*

BAHAMIAN BALLET 4 ch.g. Bahamian Bounty 116 – Plie 75 (Superlative 118) **79**
[2006 77+: 5g p6g² 6m 5m* 5.1g³ 5.7m⁵ 5m² Sep 21] fair performer: won handicap at
Windsor in July: effective at 5f/6f: acts on polytrack and good to firm going.
E. S. McMahon

BAHAMIAN BAY 4 b.f. Bahamian Bounty 116 – Moly 64 (Inchinor 119) [2006 44: **61**
f5g* f6g* 5f 5g* 5d f5g f5g Nov 20] quite good-topped filly: modest performer: won banded
races at Southwell in March and April and handicap at Beverley in August: stays 6f: acts
on fibresand. *M. Brittain*

BAHAMIAN BREEZE 5 b.g. Piccolo 121 – Norgabie 94 (Northfields (USA)) [2006 **64**
63: p6g p6g p6g p5.1g⁴ 5.2m May 11] robust gelding: modest performer: effective at 5f/
6f: acts on polytrack and firm ground: tried visored/in cheekpieces. *D. M. Simcock*

BAHAMIAN DUKE 3 ch.g. Bahamian Bounty 116 – Madame Sisu 47 (Emarati **69**
(USA) 74) [2006 52: f5g⁶ 5m⁴ 5m* 5m* 5g³ 6f⁵ 5g³ 5m³ Sep 21] big, workmanlike
gelding: fair handicapper: won at Carlisle (2) in June: will prove best at 5f/6f: raced only

on good ground or firmer on turf, below form only outing on fibresand: makes running. *K. R. Burke*

BAHAMIAN LOVE 2 br.f. (Mar 18) Bahamian Bounty 116 – Asian Love (Petong **68** 126) [2006 5.1d[6] 5g[6] 6m[3] 6g[4] 6g[4] 6m[3] f6m* p6g[5] Nov 11] strong, good-bodied filly: third foal: half-sister to 3-y-o Silver Chariot: dam unraced: fair performer: made frame 4 times prior to winning maiden at Southwell in October: ran creditably in nursery final start: effective at 5f/6f: acts on all-weather and good to firm going: not straightforward. *B. W. Hills*

BAHAMIAN PIRATE (USA) 11 ch.g. Housebuster (USA) – Shining Through **109** (USA) (Deputy Minister (CAN)) [2006 113: 5.1s[2] 5d 6m[5] 5g[6] 6v[4] 6m[3] 6m[3] 6g[5] 6m[6] 5.1g 5g[3] 5s[6] 6d[5] Sep 25] sturdy gelding: useful performer nowadays: last successful in Nunthorpe Stakes at York in 2004: good efforts in 2006 when third to Beaver Patrol in handicap at Epsom, sixth to Borderlescott in Stewards' Cup at Goodwood and length third to Baltic King in listed race at Beverley sixth/ninth/eleventh outings: below form in handicap at Haydock and minor event at Hamilton (not suited by steady pace) last 2 starts: best at 5f/6f: acts on any going: held up (sometimes slowly away), and takes time to warm up. *D. Nicholls*

BAHAR SHUMAAL (IRE) 4 b.c. Dubai Millennium 140 – High Spirited 80 (Shirley **106** Heights 130) [2006 104: 9g 10g 13.3s[6] 8m[6] 8.1m 12g 8.1m[5] 10.4d 10.1m p9.5g* p10g p10g[3] p12.2s[6] p9.5g* Dec 31] big, good-topped colt: useful handicapper: won at Wolverhampton in October (by 7 lengths from Zato) and December (by short head from Vacation): stays 1½m: acts on polytrack and good to firm going: blinkered nowadays: tried tongue tied. *C. E. Brittain*

BAHHMIRAGE (IRE) 3 ch.f. Bahhare (USA) 122 – Border Mirage (Selkirk (USA) **60** 129) [2006 –: p8.6g p7.1g[6] p8g[3] p10g[6] f7g[4] f7g[6] 7s[3] p6g[6] p7.1g[2] 10m[4] p8.6g[4] 8.2m 8.3d[2] 6.1g[2] p8.6g 8m[4] 6.1f[6] 8.2f 7.1f 5.7f Aug 8] leggy filly: modest maiden on balance: left C. Kellett after fourth outing: likely to prove best at 6f to 1m: acts on all-weather, good to firm and good to soft going: blinkered/visored. *Stef Liddiard*

BAHIA BREEZE 4 b.f. Mister Baileys 123 – Ring of Love 77 (Magic Ring (IRE) 115) **106** [2006 102: 8v 9s[5] 8.5g[5] 8m* 7f[6] 8.1g[2] 8m 9d[3] 8d[3] Oct 28] small, well-made filly: useful performer: won listed race at Pontefract (by ½ length from Mamela) in June: several good efforts otherwise, including in similar event at Sandown (1¼ lengths second to Wasseema), Darley Stakes at Newmarket (3 lengths third to Stage Gift) and listed race at Newmarket (3¼ lengths third to Blue Ksar): stays 9f: acts on firm and soft going. *Rae Guest*

BAHIANO (IRE) 5 ch.g. Barathea (IRE) 127 – Trystero (Shareef Dancer (USA) 135) **109** [2006 104: p6g 8m[5] 6.5m* 6m[3] 6.5g[2] 8m 6m 7m 7m 7g 7d Sep 23] compact gelding: useful handicapper: better on turf than all-weather: won at Nad Al Sheba in February: good efforts when head second to Cartography there and third of 26 to Mutamared at Newmarket fifth/seventh outings: has form up to 8.5f, but possibly best around 6f: acts on polytrack and firm going, below best on softer than good. *C. E. Brittain*

BAHRAIN GOLD (IRE) 6 b.g. Great Commotion (USA) 123 – Hassosi (IRE) (High **53** Estate 127) [2006 54: f8g f7g* f6g[4] 7.2g p6g[4] 5d 6m 7m 6d Aug 13] modest gelding: **a61** better on all-weather than turf: left E. Tyrrell in Ireland €5,800 after final 5-y-o start: won banded race at Southwell in February: stays 7f: acts on all-weather: tried in cheekpieces, usually blinkered nowadays. *N. P. McCormack*

BAIE DES FLAMANDS (USA) 4 b.g. Kingmambo (USA) 125 – Isle de France – (USA) 115 (Nureyev (USA) 131) [2006 81: p12.2s Dec 13] tall, close-coupled, quite good-topped gelding: fairly useful performer: blinkered and tongue tied when well held only Flat outing in 2006: front runner. *Miss S. J. Wilton*

BAILEYS ENCORE 3 b.g. Mister Baileys 123 – Exclusive Life (USA) (Exclusive **74** Native (USA)) [2006 75: 8d[5] 8.5s[3] 10d* 12.1d 10d Sep 16] angular, useful-looking gelding: fair performer: won maiden handicap at Redcar in August: stays 1½m: acts on soft ground: sometimes sweats: sold 21,000 gns. *M. Johnston*

BAILEYS HILIGHT (IRE) 2 b.c. (Apr 27) Kyllachy 129 – Como (USA) 95 **68** (Cozzene (USA)) [2006 5.1s 5d[5] 5.1m[5] 5f[4] 5m Jul 22] 5,000Y: stout-bodied colt: second foal: half-brother to 3-y-o Arzaaq: dam 6f winner: fair maiden: raced at 5f: sold 1,000 gns. *M. Johnston*

BAILEYS HONOUR 4 b.f. Mark of Esteem (IRE) 137 – Kanz (USA) 115 (The **49** Minstrel (CAN) 135) [2006 45, a61: f8g 16g p12g[5] 13f[6] Jun 29] good-bodied filly: poor performer nowadays: stays 1¼m: acts on polytrack. *A. G. Newcombe*

BAILEYS OUTSHINE 2 ch.f. (Feb 26) Inchinor 119 – Red Ryding Hood 83 (Wolf- **73** hound (USA) 126) [2006 6m³ 6m³ 5d* 5.2d Oct 18] small filly: second foal: dam, 5f winner, half-sister to useful 1996 2-y-o sprinter Arethusa: fair form: twice placed before winning maiden at Lingfield in September: poorly drawn in nursery (joint favourite, reportedly had breathing problem): will be best kept to 5f/6f. *J. G. Given*

BAILEYS POLKA 3 b.f. Polish Precedent (USA) 131 – Mistitled (USA) 54 (Miswaki **53** (USA) 124) [2006 66: 8d⁶ 10d p10g 8f⁶ 8m 10.1m 8s Sep 28] good-topped filly: just modest maiden in 2006: best effort (at 2 yrs) at 7f: acts on soft ground: blinkered last 3 starts. *J. G. Given*

BAILIEBOROUGH (IRE) 7 b.g. Charnwood Forest (IRE) 125 – Sherannda (USA) **97** (Trempolino (USA) 135) [2006 92: 8m⁶ 8f⁶ 7m³ 8m⁵ 8.5f 7f² 8m³ 8d* 8g* 8m² 8g Sep 30] quite good-topped gelding: useful performer: left R. Gray after fifth outing: won 2 handicaps at Redcar in August, latter by 3½ lengths from United Nations: effective at 7f to easy 9f: acts on firm and good to soft going: effective visored or not: sometimes slowly away. *B. Ellison*

BAIZICALLY (IRE) 3 ch.g. Galileo (IRE) 134 – Baize 95 (Efisio 120) [2006 69p: **89** 9.2m* 10m⁴ Jun 5] strong gelding: fairly useful form: much improved when winning maiden at Hamilton (by 5 lengths) in May: didn't get run of race when creditable fourth in handicap at Leicester next time: gelded after: stays 1¼m: raced only on good to firm going. *J. A. Osborne*

BAJAN PARKES 3 b. or br.g. Zafonic (USA) 130 – My Melody Parkes 102 (Teenoso **84** (USA) 121) [2006 94p: 6g⁴ 5f⁶ 6g Jul 8] good-topped gelding: fairly useful performer: respectable efforts in handicaps first 2 starts: seemed amiss final outing: will prove best at 5f/6f: acts on firm going. *H. Candy*

BAJAN PRIDE 2 b.g. (Mar 7) Selkirk (USA) 129 – Spry 84 (Suave Dancer (USA) 136) **78 p** [2006 8g 8d³ 8s p8g² Nov 13] well-made gelding: fourth foal: half-brother to 5-y-o Serra-manna: dam 1½m winner from 2 starts: fair maiden: improved form when 1¼ lengths second to Cesc on nursery debut at Lingfield final start, running on: gelded after: will be suited to 1¼m/1½m: acts on polytrack, raced on good or softer going on turf: should do better yet. *R. Hannon*

BAJEEL (IRE) 2 b.c. (Apr 2) Traditionally (USA) 117 – Calypso Grant (IRE) 98 **53** (Danehill (USA) 126) [2006 p5g⁵ Aug 5] 18,000Y, 58,000 2-y-o: fourth foal: half-brother to French 5f winner Calypso Dancer (by Celtic Swing): dam, 1m (including at 2 yrs) winner who stayed 1¼m, sister to smart 1¼m performer Leporello: 7/1, 6 lengths fifth in maiden at Lingfield. *G. A. Butler*

BAKHOOR (IRE) 3 b.f. Royal Applause 124 – First Waltz (FR) 117 (Green Dancer **74 p** (USA) 132) [2006 a7f a7f⁶ a8.5s 6.1f* 6m* Jul 8] half-sister to several winners, including useful 1m winner Atlantic Rhapsody (by Machiavellian) and 4-y-o Gimasha: dam won Prix Morny: well held in UAE when trained by A. Al Raihe: much improved (fair form) to win handicaps at Warwick in June and Leicester in July: best efforts at 6f (bred to stay 7f+): acts on fibre going: tongue tied third outing: capable of better still. *W. Jarvis*

BAKKE 4 b.g. Danehill (USA) 126 – Valagalore 91 (Generous (IRE) 139) [2006 53: **37** p7.1g p7g 8g May 16] tall, rather leggy gelding: poor maiden nowadays: tried blinkered/ tongue tied. *B. I. Case*

BALAKIREF 7 b.g. Royal Applause 124 – Pluck 80 (Never So Bold 135) [2006 86: **85** 5s* 6d* 6.1f 6m 5m³ 6s⁴ 6d 6m⁴ 6d 6m 6.1d⁴ 6.1d⁵ 6v³ Oct 28] quite attractive gelding: fairly useful handicapper, better on turf than all-weather: won at Haydock and Leicester (apprentice event) within 3 days in May: several good efforts after: effective at 5f to 7f: acts on all-weather and any turf going: tried visored (not since 2003): sometimes slowly away: usually held up. *M. Dods*

BALANCED BUDGET 3 b.c. Mark of Esteem (IRE) 137 – Credit-A-Plenty 111 **101** (Generous (IRE) 139) [2006 8m⁶ 10m* 10d⁶ 12m 10m³ 10d⁵ p12g* Sep 18] close-coupled, quite attractive colt: second foal: half-brother to useful 1¼m winner Bridge Loan (by Giant's Causeway): dam, 2-y-o 7f winner who stayed 14.6f (second in Park Hill Stakes), half-sister to very smart 1½m performer Stowaway: useful performer: won maiden at Pontefract in May and handicap at Kempton (beat Royal Jet readily by 1¾ lengths on all-weather debut) in September: stays 1½m: acts on polytrack, good to firm and good to soft ground: has worn crossed noseband: sold 220,000 gns, sent to Saudi Arabia. *J. Noseda*

BALANCE OF POWER 4 b.g. Sadler's Wells (USA) 132 – Cattermole (USA) **86** (Roberto (USA) 131) [2006 89: 10.9g³ 11.7d 12m³ Sep 20] big, good-topped gelding:

fairly useful performer, lightly raced: gelded, creditable efforts in 2006: stays 1½m: acts on good to firm ground: tongue tied at 3 yrs, and final outing: sold 40,000 gns. *R. Charlton*

BALANCHINE MOON 2 ch.f. (Mar 20) Zilzal (USA) 137 – Crescent Moon (Mr **57** Prospector (USA)) [2006 p7g Nov 1] €5,500Y: third foal: dam, placed up to 10.5f in France, out of Oaks and Irish Derby winner Balanchine: 25/1, mid-division in maiden at Kempton. *W. J. Haggas*

BALASHI (USA) 3 b.g. Seeking The Gold (USA) – Via Borghese (USA) 116 (Seattle **60** Dancer (USA) 119) [2006 10d Oct 4] angular gelding: brother to 2 winners abroad and closely related to 2003 2-y-o 6f winner Venetian Pride and 7f winner Pietro Siena (both fairly useful, by Gone West): dam Irish 1m winner and US Grade 2 9f winner: easy to back 7/1 and looking fit, shaped better than bare result when 12½ lengths eighth of 14 in maiden at Nottingham, tiring: will be suited by shorter than 1¼m: sold 6,000 gns, sent to Czech Republic. *Saeed bin Suroor*

BALDOVINA 2 b.f. (May 27) Tale of The Cat (USA) 113 – Baldwina (FR) 111 (Pistolet **73** Bleu (IRE) 133) [2006 p6g² 6f² 7.5m⁵ 8.3m p8g Oct 6] neat filly: first foal: dam French 1¼m/10.5f (Prix Penelope) winner: fair maiden: second at Wolverhampton and Leicester, then fourth to Sweet Wind Music in listed race at Milan: well beaten last 2 starts: should stay 1m. *M. Botti*

BALEARIC STAR (IRE) 5 b.g. Night Shift (USA) – La Menorquina (USA) 65 **60** (Woodman (USA) 126) [2006 76, a64: 8.3g⁴ 8.3f p8g 8.2m⁵ 8.1m⁶ 9g² p10g⁶ Sep 27] strong, close-coupled gelding: modest performer: best around 1m: acts on all-weather and firm going: tried blinkered/visored. *B. R. Millman*

BALEEGH (USA) 3 b.c. Aljabr (USA) 125 – Awtaan (USA) 77 (Arazi (USA) 135) **77** [2006 7f* 8m Jul 15] first foal: dam, 1¾m winner, out of close relative to Nayef and half-sister to Nashwan and Unfuwain: fairly useful form: green, won maiden at Folkestone in June: easy to back, only seventh of 8 in handicap at Salisbury next time, pulling hard and dropping away tamely: should be well suited by 1m+: sold 11,000 gns in October. *M. P. Tregoning*

BALERNO 7 b.g. Machiavellian (USA) 123 – Balabina (USA) 110 (Nijinsky (CAN) **62** 138) [2006 67: p7.1g p7g 7f p8g 7.6m² 8d⁴ p8.6g 7.1m Sep 12] close-coupled gelding: modest performer: left R. Ingram after fourth start: effective at 7f, barely at 1¼m: acts on all-weather, firm and soft going: tried in headgear/tongue tie earlier in career. *Mrs L. J. Mongan*

BALFOUR HOUSE 3 b.g. Wizard King 122 – Tymeera 62 (Timeless Times (USA) **–** 99) [2006 –: p7g p6g 5.1g 7m Jun 29] no form: tried blinkered. *R. A. Harris*

BALIAN 3 b.g. Mujahid (USA) 125 – Imperial Jade 105 (Lochnager 132) [2006 67: 6g **71 §** 6d 5m² 5f² 5.7g 6f² 5m³ 6m³ 6f³ 5g⁴ 5.7m⁶ 5g p6g³ p6g² f6g³ f5g³ f6g Dec 5] fair maiden **a61 §** on turf, modest on all-weather: claimed from G. L. Moore after fourteenth start: should stay easy 7f: acts on all-weather and firm going: blinkers/cheekpieces after reappearance: has failed to go through with effort, and is one to be wary of. *Mrs P. Sly*

BALI BELONY 2 b.f. (Apr 26) Erhaab (USA) 127 – Daarat Alayaam (IRE) (Reference **–** Point 139) [2006 p7.1g p8g Dec 16] half-sister to 3 winners, including 3-y-o Go Amwell and 1¼m/1½m winner Romeo's Day (by Pursuit of Love): dam unraced: well held in maidens and Wolverhampton and Kempton (very slowly away). *J. R. Jenkins*

BALIK PEARLS 3 b.f. Xaar 132 – Miss Mercy (IRE) 62 (Law Society (USA) 130) **83** [2006 76: 6m 7.1m* 7m 8m⁶ Jul 30] tall filly: fairly useful handicapper: best effort when winning at Warwick in July: below form after, rearing and stall opened in latter: stays 7f: acts on polytrack, firm and good to soft going: sometimes blinkered: has looked no easy ride: sold 30,000 gns in October. *N. A. Callaghan*

BALKAN KNIGHT 6 b.g. Selkirk (USA) 129 – Crown of Light 112 (Mtoto 134) **115** [2006 111: 12m⁴ 13.3s² 12m* 12m 13.9f² 16f 16d³ Oct 14] strong, well-made gelding: smart performer: further improvement in 2006, winning minor event at Goodwood (by 1¾ lengths from Art Eyes) in June: also good second to Distinction in listed race at Newbury (beaten a head) and to Linas Selection in listed handicap at York (beaten a length): just respectable third of 7 to Hawridge Prince in Jockey Club Cup at Newmarket final start (bandaged behind): effective at 1½m to 2m: acts on soft and good to firm going: formerly visored. *D. R. C. Elsworth*

BALLARE (IRE) 7 b.g. Barathea (IRE) 127 – Raindancing (IRE) 94 (Tirol 127) [2006 **57** 48: p8.6g p9.5g* p9.5g³ p8.6g³ p8.6g⁵ 7f 7.6m p10g p10g² p8.6g p8.6g Dec 4] good-topped gelding: modest performer: won banded race at Wolverhampton in March: stays

1¼m: acts on polytrack, soft and good to firm ground: tried in cheekpieces, often visored: tongue tied final start. *P. J. Makin*

BALLET BOY (IRE) 2 b.g. (Mar 22) Sadler's Wells (USA) 132 – Happy Landing **54 p** (FR) (Homing 130) [2006 7.1m 7m 6m⁴ Sep 16] 65,000Y: big, strong gelding: closely related to several winners, including US 1992 Grade 1 2-y-o 8.5f winner Creaking Board and smart French sprinter Dyhim Diamond (both by Night Shift), and half-brother to several winners: dam French maiden: green and not knocked about in 3 maidens, within 2 weeks (gelded after): type to progress and do well in middle-distance handicaps at 3 yrs. *Sir Mark Prescott*

BALLET PACIFICA (USA) 3 b.f. Minardi (USA) 119 – Kostroma 116 (Caerleon **104** (USA) 132) [2006 p9.4f* 9.5g³ 10d* 10s³ 9f³ Sep 9] $70,000Y: half-sister to several winners abroad: dam 1m/1¼m performer in Ireland/USA: useful performer: won maiden at Lingfield (only outing for J. Noseda) in February and listed race at Vichy (beat Histoire de Moeurs 1½ lengths) in July: creditable third next 2 starts, to stable-companion Germance in Prix de la Nonette at Deauville and to Vacare in Grade 3 Pucker Up Stakes at Arlington: stays 1¼m: acts on firm and soft going. *J-C. Rouget, France*

BALLIASTA (IRE) 2 b.f. (Jun 5) Grand Lodge (USA) 125 – Obeah 112 (Cure The **57 p** Blues (USA)) [2006 7s⁵ Oct 10] 45,000Y: medium-sized, good-bodied filly: half-sister to several winners, including smart 1m (at 2 yrs)/1½m winner Panama City (by El Gran Senor): dam 7f (at 2 yrs) and 8.5f (at 3 yrs) winner: 20/1, green when 9½ lengths fifth of 16 to Mythical Kid in maiden at Newbury: sure to improve. *B. W. Hills*

BALLINTENI 4 b.c. Machiavellian (USA) 123 – Silabteni (USA) (Nureyev (USA) **85** 131) [2006 p8.6m p9.5g⁴ Oct 28] leggy colt: fairly useful form: better effort in handicaps in 2006 when fourth at Wolverhampton: stays 9.5f: acts on polytrack and soft ground: tongue tied sole start at 2 yrs. *Saeed bin Suroor*

BALLOURA (IRE) 3 b.f. Swain (IRE) 134 – Mowaadah (IRE) 93 (Alzao (USA) 117) **80** [2006 66: 8.1g* 10m⁴ 11.7f³ p12g⁶ 12f⁶ Sep 18] smallish filly: fairly useful performer: won maiden at Warwick in May: good efforts in handicaps next 2 starts: should stay 1½m: acts on firm going. *W. J. Haggas*

BALLROOM DANCER (IRE) 2 b.f. (Apr 29) Danehill Dancer (IRE) 117 – Dwell **77 p** (USA) 96 (Habitat 134) [2006 p7g³ Oct 26] half-sister to several winners, including very smart 5f and (including at 2 yrs) 7f winner Misraah (by Lure) and useful Italian performer up to 1¼m Doowaley (by Sadler's Wells): dam 1m winner: 9/2, strong-finishing 2¼ lengths third of 14 to Dalvina in maiden at Lingfield: sure to improve. *J. Noseda*

BALLYBEG (IRE) 3 b.g. Mujadil (USA) 119 – Sabaniya (FR) (Lashkari 128) [2006 **75** 70: p7g² p7g* p8g 10g³ 11.6m⁵ 11.6g⁵ 10d⁶ 11.6f* p10g⁵ p12.2g p10g p12g p10g Dec 16] close-coupled gelding: has a quick action: fair performer: won handicap at Lingfield (tended to hang) in March and claimer at Windsor (claimed from R. Hannon £12,000) in June: stays 11.6f: acts on polytrack and firm going: often blinkered of late (including for last win): signs of temperament. *R. J. Price*

BALLYBUNION (IRE) 7 ch.g. Entrepreneur 123 – Clarentia 111 (Ballad Rock 122) **65** [2006 69: 5.5d 5.3m 5.7f 5f 5.1f² 5.1f* 6f* 5m⁶ 5.3m⁵ 6.1m 5.1m⁶ Sep 7] strong gelding: fair performer: won handicaps at Chepstow (second outing in 24 hrs) in July and Lingfield in August: effective at 5f to easy 7f: acts on polytrack and firm going (no form on softer than good): tried tongue tied/in headgear. *R. A. Harris*

BALLYCROY GIRL (IRE) 4 ch.f. Pennekamp (USA) 130 – Hulm (IRE) 79 (Mujta- **–** hid (USA) 118) [2006 65: f7g p8g p9.5g⁶ p9.5g 9.2g Jun 21] good-topped filly: fair performer at best: well held in 2006: tried in headgear: none too reliable. *A. Bailey*

BALLYHOOLIGAN (IRE) 3 b.g. Imperial Ballet (IRE) 110 – Cancan Madame **–** (USA) (Mr Prospector (USA)) [2006 –: p6g 6f Jun 30] close-coupled gelding: little form: tried blinkered: sold 3,500 gns, sent to Qatar. *Jamie Poulton*

BALLYHURRY (USA) 9 b.g. Rubiano (USA) – Balakhna (FR) (Tyrant (USA)) [2006 **76** 74, a64: p7.1g⁴ 7.1g⁴ 8m⁴ 9g³ 8m⁴ 10m⁵ 8m² 8g³ 9s⁵ p9.5g² Oct 29] angular gelding: fair **a54** on turf, modest on all-weather: effective at 7f to 9.5f: acts on polytrack and firm ground (seemingly not soft): successful in blinkers earlier in career: held up: tough. *J. S. Goldie*

BALLYMENA 5 b.m. Saddlers' Hall (IRE) 126 – Ace Gunner (Gunner B 126) [2006 **–** 8.1s 10.2m 12.1d⁶ p16.5g 12.1m p16.5g Dec 2] first foal: dam third in 13f bumper: bumper winner: no form on Flat. *R. A. Harris*

BALLYRUSH (IRE) 6 ch.g. Titus Livius (FR) 115 – Mandoline (IRE) (Suave Dancer **49** (USA) 136) [2006 49: p8.6g f8g⁶ f7g⁶ f8g⁴ p5.1g f8g f7g f8g Mar 21] poor performer: stays 9.4f: acts on fibresand and soft going: sometimes wears headgear. *Miss D. A. McHale*

BALLYSHANE SPIRIT (IRE) 2 b.c. (Apr 25) Distant Music (USA) 126 – National- **50** artgallery (IRE) (Tate Gallery (USA) 117) [2006 7d 7.1m 6d³ p7g p7g Dec 19] tall colt: modest maiden: below form in nursery final start: best run at 6f (third in claimer): acts on good to soft ground. *N. A. Callaghan*

BALMONT (USA) 5 b.h. Stravinsky (USA) 133 – Aldebaran Light (USA) (Seattle **103 +** Slew (USA)) [2006 117: 5d 6m⁵ Jun 18] tall, quite good-topped horse: smart performer: awarded Middle Park Stakes at Newmarket at 2 yrs: didn't win again, and below form both starts in 2006, hampered when fifth to Etlaala in listed race at Salisbury final outing: was best at 5f/6f: unraced on heavy going, probably acted on any other turf: had worn crossed noseband: tended to sweat: found little final 4-y-o appearance: to stand at Tara Stud, Co Meath, Ireland, fee €5,000. *J. Noseda*

BALNAGORE 2 b. or br.c. (Feb 28) Tobougg (IRE) 125 – Bogus Mix (IRE) 52 (Lina- **74 +** mix (FR) 127) [2006 7m 7g⁵ 8.1d⁶ 8g⁵ Oct 12] 10,000Y: tall, quite good-topped colt: third foal: half-brother to 2005 2-y-o 7f seller winner Dispol Shabama (by Bahamian Bounty) and winner in Macau by Petong: dam, lightly-raced maiden, bred to stay 1¼m+: fair maiden: never-nearer fifth to Ladies Best in nursery at Newmarket: shapes as if 1¼m/1½m will suit. *J. L. Dunlop*

BALTHAZAAR'S GIFT (IRE) 3 b.c. Xaar 132 – Thats Your Opinion 48 (Last **123** Tycoon 131) [2006 113p: 6d 5m⁴ 6m² 6g⁴ 6.5g 6s Sep 2] tall, good-topped colt: very smart performer: in frame in Prix du Gros-Chene at Chantilly (3¼ lengths fourth to Moss Vale) and Golden Jubilee Stakes at Royal Ascot (best effort when unlucky neck second to Les Arcs, tacking across from wide draw and finishing very strongly) second/third starts: left K. Ryan, below form in Hackwood Stakes at Newbury, Prix Maurice de Gheest at Deauville and Sprint Cup at Haydock after: stays 6f: raced mainly on good/good to firm going (well held both outings on ground softer than good): took strong hold to post on reappearance: reportedly cast in his box and missed July Cup intended fourth outing. *T. R. George*

BALTIC BELLE (IRE) 2 b.f. (Jan 26) Redback 116 – Skerries Bell 71 (Taufan (USA) **82** 119) [2006 5g³ 6s² 6m p6g³ 6m² 6.5s⁵ 7d⁵ 8g³ p7g² Nov 25] 23,000Y: smallish, close-coupled filly: sixth foal: half-sister to 3 winners, including 2004 2-y-o 6f winner Deeday Bay (by Brave Act) and 7-y-o Gone'n'dunnet: dam, Belgian 7f to 9f winner, half-sister to smart sprinter Indian Rocket: fairly useful maiden: placed 6 times, and ran well other starts: stays 7f, not 1m: acts on polytrack, soft and good to firm going. *R. Hannon*

BALTIC GIFT 2 b.f. (May 16) Cadeaux Genereux 131 – Polish Romance (USA) 83 **– p** (Danzig (USA)) [2006 7d Oct 28] neat filly: sixth foal: sister to useful 5f/6f winner (including at 2 yrs) Irresistible: dam, 7f winner, out of US Grade 1 2-y-o 7f/1m winner Some Romance: 20/1, needed experience when thirteenth of 20 in maiden at Newmarket: open to improvement. *M. L. W. Bell*

BALTIC KING 6 b.h. Danetime (IRE) 121 – Lindfield Belle (IRE) 78 (Fairy King **120** (USA)) [2006 117: 6g 5m 6m³ 5m⁶ 6m* 6g⁵ 6.5g 5g* 6d² 6g Oct 13]
The weight-carrying record for the Wokingham Stakes is still held by Boone's Cabin, who in 1975 was successful under top weight of 10-0, 4 lb more than the previous best set by Trappist in 1878. In the essay on Boone's Cabin in *Racehorses of 1975* we said that there wasn't a lot of point in comparing the performances of the two 'since circumstances change through the years and, in any case, so far as the real value of a weight-carrying feat goes everything depends upon the class of the field and the merit of the top weight, which vary from year to year.' Circumstances have continued to change so far as the Wokingham is concerned, and while its latest winner Baltic King put up one of the best handicap performances of the season in triumphing under 9-10, he did so in a race which had a different profile to that of 1975. While so-called heritage handicaps such as the Wokingham have a weight range of 30 lb, the growth of the horse population has resulted in a situation where it is highly unlikely that the weights will extend to anything like that. Before the final declaration for the Wokingham, there were ninety-two horses in the race, spread over a weight range of 43 lb, but restrictions on the size of the field meant that only the first twenty-eight in the handicap to be declared were able to compete. That left a range of just 15 lb, from One Putra on

9-11 to Commando Scott on 8-10. In his year, Boone's Cabin conceded between 4 lb and 34 lb to nineteen rivals.

Baltic King was better than ever at the age of six, as he showed at Royal Ascot, the Wokingham his thirty-sixth start. He had won six of his previous thirty-five, beginning with a maiden at Lingfield on his final appearance at two. Baltic King made up into a smart sprinter the following season, winning a minor event at Leicester and a handicap at Ascot, and he added a valuable handicap at Ascot and a minor event at Beverley at four and a listed race at Windsor at five. The pick of his four efforts leading up to the Wokingham had come just four days earlier, also at Royal Ascot, Baltic King finishing sixth to Takeover Target in the King's Stand Stakes, beaten around a length. Two from well down the field, namely Texas Gold and Fire Up The Band, joined Baltic King in the Wokingham, which looked every bit as competitive as usual beforehand but turned out to be less so due to the supposed effects of the draw. The stand-side runners had the edge in the King's Stand and that trend had continued through the meeting, making it almost inevitable that even the riders of those drawn high in the Wokingham would want to head towards the stand rail. With Baltic King in stall six, that wasn't an issue for his jockey Jimmy Fortune, who rode a much more patient race than he had done in the five-furlong King's Stand, content to stay close to the rail and hope the gaps appeared at the right time. Jamie Spencer had the favourite Firenze even further back early on, but in sharp contrast to Fortune he steered a course from stall one which resulted in his mount having to challenge out wide. Firenze got to the front over a furlong out, hanging left as she did so, Baltic King now being asked for his effort as the field opened up for him but still with around three lengths to make up. The response from Baltic King was impressive, his burst of speed taking him to the front around a hundred yards out and a length and a half clear of Firenze by the line. The previous race on the Royal Ascot card, the Group 1 Golden Jubilee, had been won by Les Arcs, who had finished five places behind Baltic King in the King's Stand. While Baltic King didn't achieve quite enough in the Wokingham to suggest that he would have beaten an improved Les Arcs had he contested the Golden Jubilee instead, he did show that he is well up to winning pattern races. That said, Baltic King was given four opportunities to do so before season's end, but was unable to take advantage of any of them. The closest he came was back at Ascot in September, in the Diadem Stakes, Baltic King running a few pounds below his best in finishing a length and a quarter second to Red Clubs. He did add to his Woking-

Wokingham Stakes (Handicap), Royal Ascot—Baltic King puts up one of the best handicap performances of the year under 9-10; the favourite Firenze, having met trouble, takes second ahead of the veteran Bahamian Pirate (noseband), who does best of David Nicholls' seven runners, and Borderlescott

Thurloe Thoroughbreds VIII's "Baltic King"

ham win in listed company, though, without having to run near top form, when beating Pivotal's Princess a head in the totepool Beverley Bullet Sprint Stakes in August.

			Danehill	Danzig
Baltic King (b.h. 2000)	Danetime (IRE) (b 1994)		(b 1986)	Razyana
			Allegheny River	Lear Fan
			(b 1987)	Allesheny
	Lindfield Belle (IRE) (b 1988)		Fairy King	Northern Dancer
			(b 1982)	Fairy Bridge
			Tecmessa	Home Guard
			(ch 1980)	Two Fast

As a very smart sprinting son of the now deceased Danetime (beaten a head in the Wokingham as a three-year-old), Baltic King, who also looks the part being a strong, lengthy individual, should prove popular with commercial breeders when he is eventually retired to stud. There is speed on his dam's side, too, Lindfield Belle's sole win having come at two in a five-furlong maiden on firm ground at Lingfield. Lindfield Belle, retired to stud after failing to show in a couple of outings as a three-year-old, has produced five other winners, though none remotely in the same league as Baltic King. The latest of her offspring to win a race is the three-year-old Superior Star (by Superior Premium), successful in a nine-furlong handicap at Musselburgh in August. Baltic King's grandam Tecmessa is an unraced sister to the very smart French performer at up to a mile Manjam, who himself finished sixth in the King's Stand in 1980. Baltic King, who has raced only at up to six and a half furlongs, acts on firm and good to soft going, though all of his wins have come on good ground or firmer. He wears a tongue tie, and has been bandaged behind. *H. Morrison*

110

BALTIC PRINCESS (FR) 3 ch.f. Peintre Celebre (USA) 137 – Snow House (IRE) **81**
(Vacarme (USA) 121) [2006 –p: 8d 11.9g⁴ 12f² 12.1m* 15m³ 12d⁴ Jul 22] leggy filly:
fairly useful performer: landed odds in handicap at Hamilton (by 5 lengths) in July: back
to form in similar event at Ripon final start: stays 1½m (not 15f): acts on firm and soft to
soft going. *M. Johnston*

BALTIC RHAPSODY 3 b.f. Polish Precedent (USA) 131 – Rensaler (USA) (Stop **–**
The Music (USA)) [2006 59: p9.5g Jan 16] close-coupled filly: modest maiden in 2005:
in cheekpieces, well held in handicap sole start at 3 yrs: stays 7f: sold 105,000 gns in July.
M. A. Jarvis

BALTIMORE JACK (IRE) 2 b.g. (Feb 17) Night Shift (USA) – Itsibitsi (IRE) (Brief **85**
Truce (USA) 126) [2006 6d⁴ 6m 6d 6s⁴ 7m⁶ 7m⁴ 6g 6v⁴ Oct 31] 23,000F, 28,000Y: good-
topped gelding: second foal: half-brother to 3-y-o Lyndalee: dam unraced half-sister to
smart performer up to 10.5f Siege: fairly useful performer: won maiden at Ayr in June:
ran well several times after, including when eighth of 24 to Danum Dancer in listed
Two-Year-Old Trophy at Redcar seventh start (left R. Whitaker 21,000 gns, then gelded):
acts on soft and good to firm going. *M. W. Easterby*

BALWEARIE (IRE) 5 b.g. Sesaro (USA) 81 – Eight Mile Rock 76 (Dominion 123) **66**
[2006 66: 12.4g⁴ 12g⁶ 12m⁵ 13.1g² 10d 13m⁴ 10f⁴ 10m⁶ 12.1g 11.1d 12.4s⁴ 12s Oct 24]
sturdy gelding: fair handicapper: won at Newcastle in May: stays 13f: unraced on heavy
going, acts on any other: usually wears cheekpieces. *Miss L. A. Perratt*

BALYAN (IRE) 5 b.g. Bahhare (USA) 122 – Balaniya (USA) (Diesis 133) [2006 98: **85**
16m 12d⁵ 14m⁵ 11.5g Jun 28] quite good-topped gelding: fairly useful handicapper nowadays: at least respecable efforts first 3 outings: likely to prove best at 1½m to 2m: acts on
firm and soft going: wore cheekpieces (ran poorly) final outing. *J. Howard Johnson*

BAMALAM 3 br.f. Hunting Lion (IRE) 115 – Dragons Daughter (Mandrake Major 122) **–**
[2006 9.3m 9.8m Jul 10] fourth foal: dam unraced: last in claimer and seller. *C. R. Wilson*

BAMBOO BANKS (IRE) 3 b.g. Indian Lodge (IRE) 127 – Emma's Star (ITY) (Dar- **73 d**
shaan 133) [2006 –: 10d⁴ 10m 11.8d 9.9d⁶ 11.8d⁶ Oct 10] fair maiden: easily best effort
on reappearance: stays 1¼m: acts on good to firm going. *J. L. Dunlop*

BAMZOOKI 4 b.f. Zilzal (USA) 137 – Cavernista 75 (Lion Cavern (USA) 117) [2006 **58 d**
67: f11g³ p12g f11g³ p10g 10.1m 8d 10m 7d Sep 25] on downgrade and just modest
performer in 2006: left D. Daly after third start: stays 11f: acts on fibresand and good to
firm going: sometimes slowly away. *Mrs C. A. Dunnett*

BANANA BELLE 2 b.f. (Apr 29) Josr Algarhoud (IRE) 118 – Scurrilous 56 (Sharpo **–**
132) [2006 p5g f5g⁴ 5g May 8] 1,800Y: fourth foal: dam, sprint maiden, half-sister to
high-class French sprinter Ron's Victory: little form: left P. McEntee after second outing.
A. J. Lidderdale

BAND 6 b.g. Band On The Run 102 – Little Tich (Great Nephew 126) [2006 55, a66: **65**
p8.6g⁶ 8d⁶ 10m p8.6g² p8.6g⁴ f8g² 8.5m³ 8d⁴ 8.2d* p8.6g p9.5g⁴ Nov 27] strong, close-
coupled gelding: fair performer: won handicap at Nottingham in November: effective at
1m to 10.5f: acts on all-weather and any turf going. *E. S. McMahon*

BANDAMA (IRE) 3 b.c. Green Desert (USA) 127 – Orinoco (IRE) 53 (Darshaan 133) **104**
[2006 78p: p8g³ 10d* 10m* 12m³ 12m² 13.9s⁶ 14g⁵ Sep 28] big, lengthy, good sort: useful performer: won maiden at Newbury (pulled hard) in May and handicap at Leicester
(by 1¾ lengths from Quince) in June: very good efforts when third to Linas Selection
in King George V Stakes (Handicap) at Royal Ascot and second to Strategic Mount in
cantorspreadfair.com Stakes (Handicap) at Goodwood: well held after: should stay 1¾m:
acts on polytrack, good to firm and good to soft going. *Mrs A. J. Perrett*

BANDARI (IRE) 7 b.h. Alhaarth (IRE) 126 – Miss Audimar (USA) (Mr Leader **118**
(USA)) [2006 124: 12s³ 10d⁶ 12m 12m⁴ Jul 13] lengthy, angular horse: reportedly had
chip removed from a hind leg after 4-y-o season: very smart performer at best, winning
11 races, 6 of them Group 2/3 events: bit below best in 2006, respectable efforts at Newmarket when 5 lengths third to Shirocco in Jockey Club Stakes and 3½ lengths last of 4 to
stable-companion Soapy Danger in Princess of Wales's Stakes: was best at 1¼m/1½m:
acted on firm and soft going: nervy sort, sometimes sweated up, often wore earplugs in
preliminaries: effective ridden up front, handy or held up: to stand at Peria Stud, Tallow, Co.
Waterford, Ireland, fee €4,000, Oct 1st. *M. Johnston*

BAND OF GOLD 4 ch.f. Spectrum (IRE) 126 – Intellectuelle (Caerleon (USA) 132) **–**
[2006 53: 10.1g Jun 1] modest maiden: well held only 4-y-o outing. *J. Pearce*

BANDOS 6 ch.g. Cayman Kai (IRE) 114 – Lekuti (Le Coq d'Or 101) [2006 64: 7.1f[2] **61**
7.2m 6.9f 7.1m[3] Aug 24] lengthy gelding: modest performer nowadays: stays 1m: acts on
polytrack, firm and soft going: tried in tongue tie, cheekpieces/blinkers: usually races
prominently. *I. Semple*

BANJO BAY (IRE) 8 b.g. Common Grounds 118 – Thirlmere (Cadeaux Genereux **74**
131) [2006 73: p7g* p7g 6m[2] p5.1g 7m[4] 7m 6d[5] 6f* 6f 6g* 6g 6.1m 6d 6m p6s Dec 15]
close-coupled gelding: fair performer: won claimer in March and, having left D. Nicholls
after fifth outing, handicaps in July and August, all at Lingfield: races mainly at 6f/7f:
acts on polytrack, firm and soft going: tongue tied last 6 starts: sometimes gets worked
up/slowly away: none too reliable. *Miss Gay Kelleway*

BANJO PATTERSON 4 b.c. Green Desert (USA) 127 – Rumpipumpy 80 (Shirley **87**
Heights 130) [2006 91: 7m[4] 6m 6d 6m[4] 6m[6] 6f 6m[3] 6g 7d Aug 12] sturdy, attractive
colt: fairly useful handicapper: stays 7f: acts on good to firm going, well below form on
good to soft: tried blinkered/visored: has carried head awkwardly: none too consistent.
G. A. Huffer

BANKNOTE 4 b.c. Zafonic (USA) 130 – Brand (Shareef Dancer (USA) 135) [2006 93: **100**
p8g[2] 8.1s 8.1m* 8.1m[2] p8g[5] Sep 2] smallish, quite good-topped colt: useful handicapper:
won at Haydock (beat Mutawaffer 1½ lengths) in July: creditable efforts both starts after,
second to Audience on same course and fifth to Killena Boy in valuable event at Kempton: stays 8.3f: acts on polytrack and good to firm going, probably not on soft: genuine.
A. M. Balding

BANK ON BENNY 4 b.g. Benny The Dip (USA) 127 – Green Danube (USA) 92 (Irish **74**
River (FR) 131) [2006 67: p16.5g 8m[4] 8d[4] 8.2s[4] p10g* Dec 20] big, strong gelding: fair
handicapper: won at Salisbury (apprentices) in September and Kempton in December:
effective at 1m, stays 16.5f: acts on all-weather and good to soft going. *P. W. D'Arcy*

BANTRY BERE (IRE) 2 b.c. (May 8) Distant Music (USA) 126 – Tirana (USA) **67**
(Fappiano (USA)) [2006 p6g[6] 6d p7g[3] p8g[4] p7g[4] Dec 4] 11,000 2-y-o: half-brother to
several winners, including French 1997 2-y-o 1m winner True (by Common Grounds):
dam French 1¼m/11f winner: fair maiden: made frame last 3 starts, including in nursery
final outing: stays easy 1m: acts on polytrack. *J. R. Best*

BARACHOIS GAUDY 4 br.f. Nomination 125 – Barachois Princess (USA) 62 (Bara- **52**
chois (CAN)) [2006 –: p8g[6] p8g p10g 7s[4] p7g 8m 8m Jun 15] modest maiden: should **a43**
prove as effective at 1m as 7f: acts on soft ground: blinkered final outing. *Mrs N. Smith*

BARANOOK (IRE) 5 b.g. Barathea (IRE) 127 – Gull Nook 120 (Mill Reef (USA) **66**
141) [2006 –: p12.2g[3] 16v Oct 25] strong gelding: fair maiden: stayed easy 1½m: acted
on polytrack: tried in cheekpieces: dead. *D. J. Wintle*

BARATARIA 4 ch.g. Barathea (IRE) 127 – Aethra (USA) 89 (Trempolino (USA) 135) **59**
[2006 72: 8.2s 8.3d 8v 8.5m 8d[2] 9.1v Oct 28] quite good-topped gelding: modest maiden
nowadays: should stay 1¼m: acts on heavy going. *R. Bastiman*

BARATHEA BLAZER 7 b.g. Barathea (IRE) 127 – Empty Purse (Pennine Walk 120) **92**
[2006 8d 10s 18d 10d p13g[4] p13g Dec 22] sturdy, good-bodied gelding: useful performer
at 4 yrs: missed 2004/5: only fairly useful on return: stays 15f: acts soft and good to firm
ground, probably on polytrack: usually races prominently. *K. McAuliffe*

BARATHEA DREAMS (IRE) 5 b.g. Barathea (IRE) 127 – Deyaajeer (USA) 64 **84**
(Dayjur (USA) 137) [2006 89: 8s 8.1m 8.1d[3] 8f[3] p8.6g p8g[5] 9g 8.1g Aug 25] strong, **a74**
lengthy gelding: fairly useful handicapper on turf, fair on all-weather: stays 1¼m: acts on
polytrack, firm and soft going: often makes running. *J. S. Moore*

BARBARO (USA) 3 b. or br.c. Dynaformer (USA) – La Ville Rouge (USA) (Carson **130**
City (USA)) [2006 110: 9f* a9s* a9f* a10f* a9.5f May 20] second foal: half-brother to
US 9f minor stakes winner Holy Ground (by Saint Ballado): dam, US 6f (at 2 yrs) to 9f
winner (placed in Grade 2 events at 11f), half-sister to US Grade 3 9f winner Green
Alligator: top-class performer: unbeaten in first 6 races (first 3 on turf), namely maiden
at Delaware and valuable non-graded event (Laurel Futurity) at Laurel in 2005, Grade 3
Tropical Park Derby at Calder in January, Grade 3 Holy Bull Stakes in February, Florida
Derby (by ½ length from Sharp Humor) in April, last 2 at Gulfstream, and Kentucky
Derby (presented by Yum! Brands) at Churchill Downs in May: gained widest-winning
margin since 1946 when beating Bluegrass Cat by 6½ lengths in last-named race, travelling well, leading approaching straight and quickening clear: 2/1-on, sustained multiple
fractures to off-hind leg after 1f in Preakness Stakes at Pimlico final outing (underwent
surgery after and eventually had to be put down): stayed 1¼m: acted on sloppy dirt, and
on firm going on turf. *M. R. Matz, USA*

BARBILYRIFLE (IRE) 5 b.g. Indian Rocket 115 – Age of Elegance (Troy 137) – §
[2006 8.3m p8.6g Jun 9] good-topped gelding: no longer of any account. *N. B. King*

BARBIROLLI 4 b.g. Machiavellian (USA) 123 – Blushing Barada (USA) 53 (Blush- **76**
ing Groom (FR) 131) [2006 74: 9.2m³ 11.5m⁵ 10f 10.3m⁴ 10m² 12.3m⁵ 9.9m⁴ 9.2d* 11s³
p10g p9.5g⁵ p9.5g p9.5s⁵ p12.2g³ Dec 27] leggy gelding: fair handicapper, better on turf
than all-weather: won at Hamilton in September: effective at 9f, probably stays 11.5f:
acts on polytrack, firm and soft going: tried tongue tied/visored. *W. M. Brisbourne*

BARBS PINK DIAMOND (USA) 2 b.f. (Apr 18) Johannesburg (USA) 127 – Un- **60**
saddled (USA) (Pancho Villa (USA)) [2006 7m p6g⁶ Oct 5] $125,000Y: half-sister to
several winners in USA, including Grade 3 8.5f winner Peach Flat (by Cari Jill Hajji):
dam 4.5f (at 2 yrs) and 6f winner in USA: modest form in minor event and maiden at
Lingfield. *Mrs A. J. Perrett*

BARE RAMBLER 3 ch.g. Woodborough (USA) 112 – Supreme Rose 95 (Frimley –
Park 109) [2006 6f 6.1m p7g p8g 5.7f Aug 8] smallish, leggy gelding: little sign of ability:
tried blinkered/visored: slowly away on first 2 outings. *Stef Liddiard*

BARGAIN HUNT (IRE) 5 b.g. Foxhound (USA) 103 – Atisayin (USA) (Al Nasr –
(FR) 126) [2006 53?: 14.1f Jun 24] smallish gelding: poor maiden: stays 9f: acts on firm
going: tried in cheekpieces/visor: free-going sort: sometimes hangs right: often races
prominently. *W. Storey*

BAR HUMBUG 2 b.c. (Mar 10) Josr Algarhoud (IRE) 118 – Hi Hoh (IRE) (Fayruz **56**
116) [2006 5m p5.1g² f7g p6m f7g Nov 20] well-made colt: modest maiden: second in
seller: bred to stay 7f/1m: wore cheekpieces last 2 starts. *R. A. Fahey*

BARILOCHE 3 b.c. Benny The Dip (USA) 127 – Bella Lambada 87 (Lammtarra **78**
(USA) 134) [2006 p10g⁶ p9.5g⁴ p9.5g⁴ f12g* p12g⁶ p16g Sep 2] second foal:
half-brother to 1½m winner Bella Miranda (by Sinndar): dam, 10.4f winner from 2 starts,
half-sister to high-class 1¼m performer Stagecraft: fair performer: left J. Gosden 11,000
gns after third start: won handicap at Southwell (5 lengths) in March: stays 1½m: raced
only on all-weather: in headgear after debut: signs of temperament. *J. R. Boyle*

BARKASS (UAE) 2 b.c. (Apr 9) Halling (USA) 133 – Areydha 99 (Cadeaux Genereux **65 p**
131) [2006 p7.1g Oct 30] second foal: dam 2-y-o 5f winner: 16/1, green and hampered
when 6¼ lengths seventh in maiden at Wolverhampton: will progress. *M. P. Tregoning*

BARKING MAD (USA) 8 b. or br.g. Dayjur (USA) 137 – Avian Assembly (USA) –
(General Assembly (USA)) [2006 87d: f16g p12.2g p13.9g Feb 6] lengthy gelding: fairly
useful performer at 7 yrs: well held in 2006: makes running. *C. R. Dore*

BARLEY MOON 2 b.f. (May 24) Vettori (IRE) 119 – Trojan Desert 97 (Troy 137) **67 ?**
[2006 6s p7g 6g³ 6d p8g Dec 16] workmanlike filly: half-sister to several winners, including 1¼m winner Alberkinnie (by Ron's Victory) and 4-y-o Meditation: dam 7f winner,
later successful in US: maiden: possibly flattered when third at Newmarket, only form.
T. Keddy

BARNBROOK EMPIRE (IRE) 4 b.f. Second Empire (IRE) 124 – Home Comforts **54**
(Most Welcome 131) [2006 60: p13.9g p12g 17.2f³ 12.1f⁵ 16.4f 16.2f³ Jul 28] modest
maiden on Flat: left R. Harris prior to final outing: stays 17f: acts on polytrack, firm and
good to soft going: blinkered seventh start at 3 yrs: joined L. Dace, won over hurdles in
August. *B. J. Llewellyn*

BARNDEH (IRE) 3 b.g. Marju (IRE) 127 – Sweetest Thing (IRE) 99 (Prince Rupert **75**
121) [2006 63: 8.1g³ 8.1f² 10m³ 12d Jul 31] well-made gelding: fair maiden handicapper: wearing cheekpieces, creditable placed efforts first 3 starts in 2006: left M. Jarvis
22,000 gns after: stays 1¼m: acts on firm going: seems quirky. *R. McGlinchey, Ireland*

BARNEY BUBBLE (IRE) 5 b.g. Bahhare (USA) 122 – Barnabas (ITY) (Slip Anchor –
136) [2006 f12g Mar 8] modest maiden when trained by D. O'Connell in Ireland at 4 yrs:
showed nothing only start in 2006: probably stays 13f: acts on good to soft going, probably on firm. *K. J. Burke*

BARNEY MCGREW (IRE) 3 b.g. Mark of Esteem (IRE) 137 – Success Story 60 **84 p**
(Sharrood (USA) 124) [2006 7f p7.1g* Dec 9] 25,000F, 25,000Y: seventh foal: half-
brother to 3 winners, including useful 1¼m/1½m winner Film Script (by Unfuwain) and
fairly useful 2001 2-y-o 6f/7f winner National Park (by Common Grounds), later successful in USA: dam, 1¼m winner, out of smart 1¼m performer Starlet: much better effort in
maidens (badly hampered first outing) when winning at Wolverhampton in December
by 3½ lengths from Fairdonna: likely to be well suited by 1m: refused to enter stall on
intended debut (blanketed): open to further improvement. *J. A. R. Toller*

BARNEY'S DANCER 2 b.f. (Mar 18) Iron Mask (USA) 117 – Alcalali (USA) 96 **49** (Septieme Ciel (USA) 123) [2006 f8g⁴ Dec 2] fourth foal: half-sister to 1½m winner Queens Fantasy (by Grand Lodge): dam maiden who stayed 1½m: 33/1, 4¼ lengths fourth of 9 to Letham Island in maiden at Southwell. *J. Balding*

BARODINE 3 ch.g. Barathea (IRE) 127 – Granted (FR) 100 (Cadeaux Genereux 131) **92** [2006 80: 10m² 10.9d* 10d³ 11.9f⁵ 10f⁶ 10d 10s Oct 18] leggy, close-coupled gelding: has a round action: fairly useful performer: won maiden at Warwick in May: ran well in handicaps next 2 starts: stays easy 1½m: acts on firm and good to soft going: sold 38,000 gns, then gelded. *H. R. A. Cecil*

BAROLO 7 b.g. Danehill (USA) 126 – Lydia Maria 70 (Dancing Brave (USA) 140) **116** [2006 120: 16.4s³ 20m 16.4m⁴ 12.5g⁵ 14g² 13.9d⁴ p16g3 Nov 11] strong, close-coupled gelding: smart performer: reportedly fractured pelvis final outing at 6 yrs, easily best effort in 2006 when neck second of 5 to Jadalee in listed race at Goodwood, dictating: well below form in handicap at York (went off too hard) and listed race at Kempton last 2 outings: effective at 1½m and probably at 2m: acts on firm and soft going: wore cheek-pieces last 3 starts. *W. R. Swinburn*

BARON DE HOYLAND 3 b.g. First Trump 118 – Efficacy 62 (Efisio 120) [2006 –: **29** f8g 9.8m f7g f6g p7.1m f6g Nov 28] bad maiden. *J. R. Norton*

BARONESS RICHTER (IRE) 2 b.f. (Apr 24) Montjeu (IRE) 137 – Principium **88 p** (USA) (Hansel (USA)) [2006 8.1m* 8g⁶ Sep 9] 26,000F, 75,000Y: rangy filly: has scope: fifth foal: half-sister to winners abroad by Stravinsky and Grand Lodge: dam unraced half-sister to Prix Saint-Alary winner Nadia: fairly useful form: won maiden at Chepstow in August: 10/1, much improved when 6 lengths sixth of 10 to Simply Perfect in May Hill Stakes at York: will be suited by 1¼m/1½m: should progress further. *R. Hannon*

BARON RHODES 5 b.m. Presidium 124 – Superstream (Superpower 113) [2006 90: **70** 5m 6d⁶ 5.9g⁶ 7m 5f Jun 22] compact mare: fair handicapper nowadays: effective at 5f/6f: acts on firm and soft going: usually wears cheekpieces. *J. S. Wainwright*

BARONS SPY (IRE) 5 b.g. Danzero (AUS) – Princess Accord (USA) 115 (D'Accord **80** (USA)) [2006 66: p9.5g⁶ p8.6g⁵ 8.2g 8f² 7f³ 8.2f* 8.2f³ 8.3f² 8.3d² 7g* 7.1m³ 8.3f³ 8.2s⁶ Oct 25] lengthy gelding: fairly useful handicapper: won at Nottingham in July and Leicester in August: effective at 7f/1m: acts on polytrack, firm and good to soft going: tongue tied at 2 yrs: has flashed tail. *R. J. Price*

BARRY ISLAND 7 b.g. Turtle Island (IRE) 123 – Pine Ridge 80 (High Top 131) [2006 **84 d** p10g* p10g 10g p10g 10g p10g p10g p11g p10g⁴ Dec 20] good-topped gelding: type to carry condition: fairly useful performer: first run since 2004 when winning handicap at Lingfield in February: below form after: effective at 1¼m/1½m: acts on polytrack and firm going: sometimes slowly away: often held up. *D. R. C. Elsworth*

BARRY THE BRAVE 4 b.g. Mujadil 119 – Rakli 84 (Warning 136) [2006 **60** a8.3g a8g⁴ 7m 9.3g 6.9f² 8.5m p7.1m⁶ p9.5g f7g³ Dec 28] won 4 races in Spain at 2/3 yrs: left P. Haley after second start: modest form in Britain: stays 1m: acts on sand/all-weather and firm ground. *M. D. Hammond*

BARSHIBA (IRE) 2 ch.f. (Feb 5) Barathea (IRE) 127 – Dashiba 102 (Dashing Blade **73 P** 117) [2006 p7g² Dec 20] second foal: half-sister to useful 2005 2-y-o 1m winner Doctor Dash (by Dr Fong): dam, 9f/1¼m winner, from family of Irish St Leger winner Oscar Schindler: most encouraging 3 lengths second to Basaata in maiden at Lingfield, losing 10 lengths at start before running on strongly: will stay 1m+: sure to do a lot better. *D. R. C. Elsworth*

BARTON BELLE 4 b.f. Barathea (IRE) 127 – Veronica (Persian Bold 123) [2006 11f⁴ **74** Jun 23] 6,500Y: half-sister to several winners, including useful Irish 1½m winner El Bueno and 1¼m winner Canford (both by Caerleon): dam, winner around 1m in USA, half-sister to useful 1m performer Lady Fairfax: fairly useful bumper winner: slowly away when never-nearer fourth of 7 to Eta Draconis in maiden at Redcar on Flat debut: sold 28,000 gns in October. *G. A. Swinbank*

BARTON SANDS (IRE) 9 b.g. Tenby 125 – Hetty Green (Bay Express 132) [2006 **–** 80, a75: p8g* p10g³ p10g⁶ p10g⁶ p10g⁴ p10g² p8g p10g 8.3g p12g p10g p10g Sep 5] neat **a68** gelding: fair performer nowadays: won seller at Lingfield in January (left Andrew Reid after next start): best at 1m/1¼m: acts on polytrack, firm and good to soft going, well beaten on soft/heavy: tried blinkered/visored: tongue tied nowadays. *E. R. Oertel*

BARZAK (IRE) 6 b.g. Barathea (IRE) 127 – Zakuska 96 (Zafonic (USA) 130) [2006 **57** 42, a70: f6g p8.6g p8.6g p9.5g f7g⁵ f7g⁴ p8g⁶ f6m* f6g⁵ f7g⁵ f7g³ f8g f7g⁶ Dec 28] sturdy gelding: modest performer: won banded race at Southwell in October: effective at 6f to easy 9.5f: acts on all-weather and good to soft ground: usually wears headgear/tongue tie. *S. R. Bowring*

BASAATA (USA) 2 b.f. (Feb 24) Dixieland Band (USA) – Asareer (USA) 71 (Gone **85 p**
West (USA)) [2006 7g³ p7g* Dec 20] good-topped filly: first foal: dam, ran 3 times,
closely related to smart performer up to 1¼m Leo's Luckyman out of half-sister to
dam of Bosra Sham and Hector Protector: fairly useful form: off 3 months, won maiden
at Lingfield in December by 3 lengths from Barshiba: will stay 1m+: a useful prospect.
M. P. Tregoning

BASILIKO (USA) 3 ch.g. Fusaichi Pegasus (USA) 130 – Shootforthestars (USA) **– §**
(Seattle Slew (USA)) [2006 77: 11.6g 12g Jun 30] tall gelding: fair maiden at 2 yrs: well
held in handicaps in 2006, looking very awkward in blinkers in latter: one to treat with
caution. *P. W. Chapple-Hyam*

BASINET 8 b.g. Alzao (USA) 117 – Valiancy 87 (Grundy 137) [2006 49: p9.5g² p9.5g³ **64**
p10g² p9.5g* p9.5g² Mar 4] strong gelding: modest performer: won banded race at Wolverhampton in February: stays 1¼m: acts on all-weather, firm and soft going: usually
wears cheekpieces nowadays: often slowly away/races freely: held up. *J. J. Quinn*

BASKERVILLE 3 b.c. Foxhound (USA) 103 – Miss Up N Go (Gorytus (USA) 132) **98**
[2006 83p: 7.1g* 8.2d* 8.1s⁶ 8m⁶ 10s* Oct 18] quite good-topped, attractive colt: useful
performer: progressed well in 2006, winning maiden at Warwick in April and handicaps at Nottingham in May and October (beat Lake Poet by 2½ lengths): stays 1¼m:
acts on soft and good to firm going: sold 60,000 gns, joined D. Selvaratnam in UAE.
P. W. Chapple-Hyam

BATCHWORTH BEAU 5 ch.g. Bluegrass Prince (IRE) 110 – Batchworth Belle 100 **–**
(Interrex (CAN)) [2006 –: 12.1m Sep 1] workmanlike gelding: poor maiden: well beaten
only Flat start in 2006: won over hurdles (claimed from A. Hales £7,000) in October.
A. M. Hales

BATCHWORTH BLAISE 3 b.g. Little Jim – Batchworth Dancer 67 (Ballacashtal **49**
(CAN)) [2006 6g 7f 7d 6s⁶ p5.1g Oct 14] compact gelding: poor maiden: likely to prove
best at 5f/6f: blinkered last 3 starts. *E. A. Wheeler*

BATCHWORTH FLEUR 3 b.f. Little Jim – Batchworth Belle 100 (Interrex (CAN)) **48**
[2006 p8g p6g p8g p5g⁶ 8.1s 7m 6m⁴ 5f Jul 2] leggy filly: second foal: dam, 5f/6f winner
(including at 2 yrs), became temperamental: poor maiden: probably stays 7f: tried blinkered: reportedly bled fifth and final starts. *E. A. Wheeler*

BATELEUR 2 b.g. (Apr 2) Fraam 114 – Search Party 78 (Rainbow Quest (USA) 134) **85 p**
[2006 6m 5.7f* 6d 6.1g* 6m* Sep 19] good-topped gelding: fifth foal: half-brother to
2004 2-y-o 6f winner Evanesce (by Lujain): dam, second at 1m/1¼m from 3 starts, half-
sister to US Grade 1 1¼m winner Bequest: fairly useful form: won maiden at Bath in July
and nurseries at Nottingham and Newmarket (beat Just Dust by 1¾ lengths, value extra)
in September: should stay 7f/1m: should do better still. *M. R. Channon*

BATHWICK ALICE 3 b.f. Mark of Esteem (IRE) 137 – Ciel de Feu (USA) (Blushing **75**
John (USA) 120) [2006 73: p6g⁴ 5.7d 7.1d³ 7.1s⁵ 7f⁴ Jun 17] leggy, short-backed filly:
fair performer: stays 7f: acts on polytrack, good to firm and good to soft going: races
prominently. *B. R. Millman*

BATHWICK BREEZE 2 ch.c. (Apr 23) Sugarfoot 118 – She's A Breeze 35 (Crofthall **67**
110) [2006 7g 7.1m⁴ p7g Jul 26] 10,500Y: close-coupled colt: eighth foal: half-brother to
3 winners, including 1998 2-y-o 5f winner Dispol Clan (by Clantime) and 7f (including
at 2 yrs) to 1¼m winner Dispol Evita (by Presidium): dam maiden: fair form in maidens:
will stay 1m. *B. R. Millman*

BATHWICK EMMA (IRE) 3 ch.f. Raise A Grand (IRE) 114 – Lindas Delight 54 **69**
(Batshoof 122) [2006 75: 7v⁴ 6d⁵ 8.1d⁶ 5.1m⁶ p7g 8m 7.1m³ 7m³ 7d p7.1g f7g⁵ f6g⁶ **a62**
p8.6g³ Dec 30] leggy filly: fair on turf, modest on all-weather: seems to stay 8.6f: acts on
polytrack, heavy and good to firm going: wore cheekpieces last 2 starts: races prominently: sometimes hangs right. *P. D. Evans*

BATHWICK FANCY (IRE) 2 b.f. (Mar 24) Desert Sun 120 – Fleetwood Fancy **63**
(Taufan (USA) 119) [2006 6s⁵ 7m 7.5m 7d 6.1d⁴ Oct 4] €5,000F, €12,000Y: lengthy filly:
sister to 5-y-o Charnock Bates One and half-sister to several winners, including fairly
useful 6f (at 2 yrs) to 1m winner Al Fahda (by Be My Chief): dam, Irish 2-y-o 5f winner,
later won up to 9f in USA: modest maiden on balance: likely to stay 1m: seemed amiss
third start, tongue tied after. *J. G. Portman*

BATHWICK FINESSE (IRE) 4 b.f. Namid 128 – Lace Flower (Old Vic 136) [2006 **60**
p8g⁵ 8m 7g Aug 25] leggy filly: fair performer at 2 yrs: unraced in 2005: modest form at
best in 2006: stays 1m: acts on soft going. *B. R. Millman*

BATHWICK LETI (IRE) 2 b.f. (Apr 10) Trans Island 119 – Brandon Princess **–**
(Waajib 121) [2006 5.1g Jul 10] fifth foal (a twin): half-sister to fairly useful 2001 2-y-o
5f winner Global Princess (by Dashing Blade): dam unraced: 40/1, needed experience in
maiden at Bath. *A. M. Balding*

BATHWICK PRINCE 3 b.g. Superior Premium 122 – Gay Ming 50 (Gay Meadow **58**
52) [2006 63: p6g⁶ Mar 30] close-coupled gelding: modest maiden: stays 6f: acts on polytrack and soft ground: usually blinkered. *B. R. Millman*

BATHWICK PRINCESS 2 b.f. (Mar 20) Forzando 122 – Gay Ming 50 (Gay **32**
Meadow 52) [2006 p5g 5.1d p7.1g⁴ Jul 28] 3,000Y: seventh foal: sister to winner in
Greece: dam 1¼m winner who stayed 2m: poor maiden. *P. D. Evans*

BATHWICK ROX (IRE) 3 b.g. Carrowkeel (IRE) 106 – Byproxy (IRE) (Mujtahid
(USA) 118) [2006 59: p8.6g 8.1m 10s Oct 2] lengthy gelding: modest maiden at 2 yrs:
well held in 2006, leaving B. R. Millman and off over 7 months after reappearance: wore
headgear 5 of last 6 starts. *P. D. Evans*

BATHWICK STYLE 2 b.f. (May 7) Desert Style (IRE) 121 – Baby Loves 94 **64**
(Sadler's Wells (USA) 132) [2006 5s p5.1g² 5.1d 5.1g p8g³ 8g⁵ 8.1d Oct 13] smallish,
dipped-backed filly: sixth foal: half-sister to 3 winners in France: dam 7f (at 2 yrs) and
1¼m winner: modest maiden: stayed 1m: best efforts on polytrack: dead. *B. R. Millman*

BATSWING 11 b.g. Batshoof 122 – Magic Milly 60 (Simply Great (FR) 122) [2006 **–**
12d Apr 11] quite good-topped gelding: fairly useful handicapper in his day: well held
only Flat start since 2003: tried in cheekpieces/blinkered. *G. L. Moore*

BATTALION (IRE) 3 b.c. Grand Lodge (USA) 125 – The Faraway Tree 113 (Suave **65**
Dancer (USA) 136) [2006 69p: 10m p12g⁶ Sep 18] rather leggy, quite attractive colt: fair
form in maidens: sold 6,000 gns after final start: dead. *Sir Michael Stoute*

BATTLE GREEN LAD 9 b.g. Presidium 124 – Antouna (Clantime 101) [2006 f6g **–**
Nov 15] very lightly raced and no form: tried blinkered/tongue tied. *R. F. Marvin*

BATTLE PAINT (USA) 2 b.c. (Mar 29) Tale of The Cat (USA) 113 – Black Speck **114**
(USA) (Arch (USA) 127) [2006 6.5g* 7g* 7m² Oct 1] big, strong, lengthy colt: first foal:
dam, French 9.5f winner, half-sister to smart performer in USA up to 1½m Dynaformer:
smart form: won newcomers race at Deauville in August and minor event at Longchamp
in September: ran well when 2 lengths second of 9 to Holy Roman Emperor in Prix Jean-
Luc Lagardere at Longchamp final start, leading briefly 2f out: will stay 1m: acts on good
to firm going. *J-C. Rouget, France*

BATTLING MAC (IRE) 8 ch.g. Ashkalani (IRE) 128 – Questing Star 66 (Rainbow **– §**
Quest (USA) 134) [2006 85d: p13g Jan 4] fair handicapper: stays 9.5f: acts on heavy and
good to firm ground: often blinkered, in cheekpieces sole 8-y-o start: has had tongue tied:
has refused to race 3 times (including only outing in 2006) and is one to avoid. *L. A. Dace*

BAUER (IRE) 3 gr.c. Halling (USA) 133 – Dali's Grey (Linamix (FR) 127) [2006 –p: **98 p**
p8.6g 10g* 10.2s² 12g* 13.9f* 11.5m³ 11g* Sep 15] strong colt: progressed into a useful
handicapper, winning at Ayr in May, Newbury in June, York in July and Newbury (beat
Beau Nash by ¾ length, value extra) in September: stays 1¾m: acts on firm going, probably on soft: saddle slipped sixth outing: open to further improvement. *L. M. Cumani*

BAUHAUS (IRE) 5 b.g. Second Empire (IRE) 124 – Hi Bettina 96 (Henbit (USA) **71**
130) [2006 14m⁶ Jun 17] fairly useful performer at 3 yrs, winning maiden at Tramore for
C. O'Brien in Ireland: unraced on Flat in 2005: seemingly not discredited only outing in
Britain: seems to stay 1¾m: often wears cheekpieces. *R. T. Phillips*

BAUHINIA (IRE) 4 b.f. Spectrum (IRE) 126 – Juvenilia (IRE) 55 (Masterclass (USA) 116) **45**
[2006 60: p10g 10g p8.6g Jun 9] leggy filly: just poor maiden in 2006: stays 8.6f: acts on
polytrack, raced only on good ground or firmer on turf: sometimes slowly away: sold
2,000 gns in July, sent to Qatar. *J. A. R. Toller*

BAVARICA 4 b.f. Dansili 127 – Blue Gentian (USA) 96 (Known Fact (USA) 135) **81**
[2006 67: p9.5g² p9.5g⁵ p9.5g² p8.6g p10g* p10g⁴ 8f² 10.1f³ p8g⁴ p9.5m p8.6m* p9.5g²
p8.6g³ p8.6g³ p9.5g² Dec 26] fairly useful handicapper: won at Lingfield in
March and Wolverhampton in October: stays 1¼m: acts on all-weather, raced only on
good going or firmer on turf. *Miss J. Feilden*

BAYBERRY KING (USA) 3 b.c. Lear Fan (USA) 130 – Myrtle 96 (Batshoof 122) **51** [2006 p6g⁴ 8g⁵ 8m⁵ Aug 9] robust colt: modest form in maidens. *J. S. Goldie*

BAY BOY 4 b.g. Tomba 119 – Gay Reign (Lord Gayle (USA) 124) [2006 91: 8v⁴ 7s 7d² **89** 8s 9.5s 10s 7v² 8s 8d p8g p7.1g Dec 31] fairly useful performer: won maiden at Gowran and handicap at Galway in 2005, only successes: below form last 4 starts in 2006, leaving A. Oliver in Ireland prior to final one: stays 7f: acts on heavy and good to firm going. *M. Johnston*

BAYBSHAMBLES (IRE) 2 b.g. (May 2) Compton Admiral 121 – Payvashooz 78 **–** (Ballacashtal (CAN)) [2006 5d 5s 6s Oct 24] no form. *R. E. Barr*

BAYEUX (USA) 5 b.g. Red Ransom (USA) – Elizabeth Bay (USA) 116 (Mr Prospector **116** (USA)) [2006 96: p5.1g³ p6g* p6g* 6m 7m⁴ 6m* 7m⁵ 7.6g 7m² 9f* Nov 3] big, lengthy, attractive gelding: smart handicapper: improved for new trainer, winning at Lingfield in February, Wolverhampton (beat Quito impressively by 3 lengths) in March, Hamilton (by ¾ length from Machinist) in July and Churchill Downs (Grade 3 River City Handicap, beat Lord Admiral by 1½ lengths) in November: ran creditably when fifth to Dabbers Ridge in International Stakes (Handicap) at Ascot and neck second to King's Caprice at Goodwood: effective at 6f to 9f: acts on polytrack and firm going, probably on good to soft: has worn crossed noseband: tried visored: has worn tongue tie (reportedly had breathing problem second 2-y-o start). *G. A. Butler*

BAY HAWK 4 b.g. Alhaarth (IRE) 126 – Fleeting Vision (IRE) 79 (Vision (USA)) **79** [2006 67: 11.6g² 11.6g⁵ 12s p13g* p13g⁵ p16.5g Dec 9] fair performer: won handicap at Lingfield in November: should stay 1¾m+: acts on polytrack and good to soft ground. *B. G. Powell*

BAYLAW STAR 5 b.g. Case Law 113 – Caisson 67 (Shaadi (USA) 126) [2006 96: **83** p9.5g p8.6g³ p8g 7v 7.1g* 7g 8f 8.1m 7.6m 9.2g²ᵈ 9m* 8d 8.3g⁶ 8m p8g 7s 7v Oct 31] sturdy, close-coupled gelding: fairly useful performer: won handicap in April and claimer in August (claimed from K. Ryan £18,000), both at Musselburgh: below form after: stays 9f: acts on all-weather, firm and soft going: visored once in 2003, hasn't worn cheekpieces/blinkers since 2004: usually leads. *I. W. McInnes*

BAYLINI 2 gr.f. (Feb 16) Bertolini (USA) 125 – Bay of Plenty (FR) (Octagonal (NZ) **87** 126) [2006 p6g³ p6f² p7g* p7g³ p7g² Dec 19] 800F: first foal: dam unraced: fairly useful form: won maiden at Lingfield in October: good efforts when placed in nurseries there last 2 starts: stays 7f: raced only on polytrack. *Ms J. S. Doyle*

BAYMIST 4 b.f. Mind Games 121 – Milliscent 49 (Primo Dominie 121) [2006 60d: f6g **41** f5g f5g Feb 26] leggy, quite good-topped filly: poor performer nowadays: will prove best at 5f: acts on soft ground: tried blinkered. *M. W. Easterby*

BAY OF LIGHT 2 b.f. (Feb 16) Fantastic Light (USA) 134 – Lady Bankes (IRE) 69 **78** (Alzao (USA) 117) [2006 6f 7m 7f³ 7.1m² 7.1d⁶ Sep 16] 17,000Y: small filly: sixth foal: half-sister to fairly useful 6f (at 2 yrs) to 1m winner Moten Swing (by Kris) and 4-y-o Danzili Bay: dam, 1¼m winner, half-sister to dam of St Leger winner Rule of Law: fair maiden: placed at Folkestone and Warwick: will stay 1m: acts on firm ground. *P. W. Chapple-Hyam*

BAYONYX (IRE) 2 b.c. (Mar 17) Montjeu (IRE) 137 – Dafariya (IRE) 71 (Nashwan **74 p** (USA) 135) [2006 8m⁵ 10d⁵ 7.2v* Oct 28] 70,000F, €360,000Y: strong colt: second foal: dam, Irish maiden (second at 1m/9f), out of Cork And Orrery winner Dafayna, herself half-sister to 2000 Guineas winner Doyoun: fair form: won maiden at Ayr, finding trip barely adequate, despite conditions: will stay 1½m: acts on heavy ground: should progress at 3 yrs. *J. Howard Johnson*

BAY STORY (USA) 4 b.g. Kris S (USA) – Sweeping Story (USA) (End Sweep (USA)) **110** [2006 107: 12.7g³ 14g² 12.6g⁴ 12g 12g Dec 20] tall gelding: smart performer: trained by M. Johnston at 3 yrs: not seen out until October in 2006, and raced only in Australia: placed in quite valuable handicaps at Flemington, then 2½ lengths fourth to Gallant Guru in Group 3 Queen Elizabeth Stakes on same course and creditable seventh in Sandown Classic at Sandown and C. B. Cox Stakes at Ascot, both Group 2: stays 1¾m: acts on good to firm and good to soft going: blinkered last 6 starts in 2005: has tended to hang/carry head awkwardly. *B. Ellison*

BAYTOWN LULU 3 b.f. Timeless Times (USA) 99 – Judys Girl (IRE) (Simply Great **–** (FR) 122) [2006 53: 6.1s 5.1g 8m 7.1g⁵ 8.3m Jul 26] leggy filly: modest at 2 yrs: no form in 2006. *H. S. Howe*

BAYTOWN PAIKEA 2 b.f. (Apr 30) Primo Valentino (IRE) 116 – Mystical Song 68 **58** (Mystiko (USA) 124) [2006 f5g 5m⁵ 5f 6m² 5.2g* p5g⁴ 5f³ f5g⁶ 5.2f⁴ 5f³ 6f 5g⁴ 5g*

5d[6] 5.1f p5g[5] 5.1d* p5.1g[3] p6g p5.1g[3] p5g Dec 16] 1,000Y: small filly: fourth foal: half-sister to 6f winner (including at 2 yrs) Pardon Moi (by First Trump): dam, sprint maiden, half-sister to sprinters Prince Sabo (very smart) and Millyant (smart): modest performer: won sellers at Yarmouth in June and Windsor in August, and nursery at Nottingham in November: stays 6f, raced mostly at 5f: acts on polytrack, firm and good to soft going: front runner. *P. S. McEntee*

BAYTOWN ROSIE (IRE) 2 ch.f. (Apr 16) Intikhab (USA) 135 – Masaniya (IRE) – (Kris 135) [2006 f5g[6] p5g 5d[4] p6g[6] p6g[4] p8g Dec 18] €1,400F, 1,400Y: dam unraced half-sister to smart Irish 1m/9f winner Masani: little form. *P. S. McEntee*

BAYTOWN VALENTINA 3 b.f. Lugana Beach 116 – Baytown Rhapsody 62 (Emperor Jones (USA) 119) [2006 51: p7g p8.6g f8g[6] p5.1g 6m 5.7f 7.1g[2] 8.2f 7d Aug 13] **44** workmanlike filly: poor performer: left P. Howling after third start: stays 7f: acts on firm going: often in headgear. *R. Brotherton*

BAZELLE 4 ch.f. Ashkalani (IRE) 128 – Dona Royale (IRE) 86 (Darshaan 133) [2006 **82** 85: p8.6g* p8.6g[5] p10g Feb 20] close-coupled filly: fairly useful handicapper: won at Wolverhampton in January: barely stays 11.6f: acts on polytrack and firm going. *D. Shaw*

BAZIL DES FIEFFES (FR) 4 b.c. Le Balafre (FR) 116 – Aprilca (FR) (April Axe – (USA)) [2006 p12g p12g p10g p8g p12g Dec 13] blinkered, little sign of ability in Britain. *J. M. Plasschaert, Belgium*

BAZROY (IRE) 2 b.c. (Mar 10) Soviet Star (USA) 128 – Kunucu (IRE) 94 (Bluebird **94** (USA) 125) [2006 p5g* 5d[3] 5m 5m 5m[3] 6.1m[4] 6g[3] 6m* 6g[3] 6g[3] p6g Oct 21] €7,000Y: good-topped colt: sixth foal: half-brother to 3 winning sprinters, including 6-y-o Raccoon and 4-y-o Rancho Cucamonga: dam 5f winner, including at 2 yrs: fairly useful performer: won maiden at Lingfield in March and minor event at Southwell in September: good third in listed races at the Curragh (3½ lengths behind Brave Tin Soldier) and Redcar (24-runner Two-Year-Old Trophy) ninth/tenth starts: will prove best kept to 5f/6f: tried in visor/blinkers (below form): races prominently: quirky. *P. D. Evans*

BEACON RAMBLER 4 ch.g. Cayman Kai (IRE) 114 – Bunty's Friend (Highlands) – [2006 –: 9.2f 6.9f 8s Aug 13] no sign of ability. *F. Watson*

BEAMSLEY BEACON 5 ch.g. Wolfhound (USA) 126 – Petindia 65 (Petong 126) **51** [2006 47, a55: f6g[4] f5g[3] f6g[4] f5g[4] f5g[5] f11g Dec 28] sturdy gelding: modest performer: best at 5f/6f: acts on all-weather: wears headgear. *S. T. Mason*

BEAR ESSENTIAL 2 ch.g. (Feb 4) Rambling Bear 115 – Adar Jane (Ardar 87) [2006 – f8g Dec 21] no promise in maiden at Southwell. *Mrs P. N. Dutfield*

BEATANI 2 b.f. (Mar 27) Beat All (USA) 120 – Jerpahni 58§ (Distant Relative 128) – [2006 5m p5g May 2] first foal: dam, maiden who stayed 1m, became one to treat with caution: no form. *P. D. Evans*

BEAT THE BULLY 2 b.g. (Apr 29) Ishiguru (USA) 114 – Edgeaway 70 (Ajdal (USA) **54 §** 130) [2006 p5g 6m 5g[4] 5.5m 6.1g 5d[6] p7.1m p6g Nov 25] unfurnished gelding: modest and inconsistent maiden: gelded prior to final outing: best at 5f: acts on good to soft ground: blinkered last 4 starts. *I. A. Wood*

BEAT THE HEAT (IRE) 8 b.g. Salse (USA) 128 – Summer Trysting (USA) 83 (Alleged (USA) 138) [2006 –: 12m Jun 16] lengthy gelding: fairly useful at 6 yrs: well held both outings since: tried blinkered. *Jedd O'Keeffe*

BEAUCHAMP PILOT 8 ch.g. Inchinor 119 – Beauchamp Image 79 (Midyan (USA) – 124) [2006 8.1m 8g Jul 22] big, rather leggy gelding: smart at best: off over 2 years, last in handicaps in 2006 (edgy, dropped away tamely final outing): has worn crossed noseband/been bandaged in front. *G. A. Butler*

BEAUCHAMP STAR 5 ch.m. Pharly (FR) 130 – Beauchamp Cactus 86 (Niniski (USA) 125) [2006 –, a59: f11g* f12g[5] f12g[6] f11s[3] Mar 7] modest performer: won banded **a61** race at Southwell in January: stays 11f: acts on all-weather, firm and soft ground: tried in headgear. *Mrs A. Duffield*

BEAUCHAMP TIGER 4 b.g. Pharly (FR) 130 – Beauchamp Jade 105 (Kalaglow – 132) [2006 71: f12g p9.5g Mar 15] leggy, lengthy gelding: lightly-raced maiden, fair form at best: raced freely and well held in 2006: tongue tied final outing. *J. Parkes*

BEAUCHAMP TRUMP 4 b.g. Pharly (FR) 130 – Beauchamp Kate 61 (Petoski 135) **76** [2006 77: p16g[2] p13g[3] p16.5g 15.4m[6] 14m[4] 12.6m Jun 25] good-topped gelding: fair handicapper: stays 2¼m: acts on polytrack, good to firm and good to soft ground: tried blinkered, usually tongue tied. *G. A. Butler*

BEAUCHAMP TWIST 4 b.f. Pharly (FR) 130 – Beauchamp Cactus 86 (Niniski – (USA) 125) [2006 58: f16g⁶ Feb 5] sparely-made filly: well held both starts on all-weather: usually blinkered/visored: tried tongue tied. *M. R. Hoad*

BEAUCHAMP ULTRA 3 b.f. Compton Admiral 121 – Beauchamp Image 79 (Mid-yan (USA) 124) [2006 p8g p7g p10g Apr 7] seventh foal: half-sister to 8-y-o Beauchamp Pilot: dam, Irish 9f winner, half-sister to useful performer up to 15f Beauchamp Express: little form in maidens/seller at Lingfield. *G. A. Butler*

BEAUCHAMP UNIQUE 3 b.f. Compton Admiral 121 – Beauchamp Jade 105 (Kala-   67 glow 132) [2006 62p: p10g³ p10g⁵ 12.1m⁵ 10m³ 12f 13.8m Sep 16] smallish filly: fair performer: left G. Butler after fourth outing: stays 1¼m: acts on polytrack and good to firm going: wore cheekpieces third outing. *James Moffatt*

BEAUCHAMP UNITED 3 b.g. Compton Admiral 121 – Beauchamp Kate 61 (Peto-   45 ski 135) [2006 77: p12g⁵ 12.6g 10.9g⁴ p11g Dec 22] angular, quite attractive gelding: just poor maiden in 2006: tried blinkered. *B. Palling*

BEAUCHAMP VICEROY 2 ch.c. (Feb 16) Compton Admiral 121 – Compton   92 + Astoria (USA) (Lion Cavern (USA) 117) [2006 p5g² p6f* 6s⁴ 6m p7g² p6s* p6s² p7.1g* Dec 29] tall, close-coupled, good-topped colt: fourth foal: dam unraced out of half-sister to Culture Vulture from family of Polish Precedent and Zilzal: fairly useful performer: won maiden in August, and minor event and 4-runner nursery (beat Dubai Magic 2 lengths) in December, all at Wolverhampton: stays 7f: acts on polytrack and soft going. *G. A. Butler*

BEAUFORT 4 b.g. Yaheeb (USA) 95§ – Royal Blaze (Scallywag 127) [2006 71?:   – 14.1m 11.5m 13.1m p12g p16g p13.9g f12g Nov 21] tall, good-topped gelding: maiden: no form in 2006: refused to enter stall on intended reappearance. *D. K. Ivory*

BEAU JAZZ 5 b.g. Merdon Melody 98 – Ichor 52 (Primo Dominie 121) [2006 –: p10g   45 6g 6.1m 5.3g p6g⁶ p5g⁴ p5g p5g p5g Dec 20] strong gelding: poor maiden: raced mainly at 5f/6f: tried in cheekpieces. *W. de Best-Turner*

BEAU MARCHE 4 b.g. My Best Valentine 122 – Beau Dada (IRE) 66 (Pine Circle   61 (USA)) [2006 63d: p6g p6g 7m⁶ 7m² 6m* 7m 8f² 6f² 7.6m 6g 8m* 7d² 7m² 8m⁵ 8.1m 10f Sep 20] modest performer: won sellers at Leicester in June and Yarmouth (handicap) in August: effective at 6f to 1m: acts on polytrack, firm and good to soft going: wears head-gear nowadays: sometimes makes running. *G. G. Margarson*

BEAUMONT BOY 2 b.g. (Apr 18) Foxhound (USA) 103 – Play The Game 70 (Mum-   62 my's Game 120) [2006 5g⁶ 5g⁵ 6g⁵ 6d Sep 14] leggy, close-coupled gelding: modest form in maidens, seeming green: raced at 5f/6f on good to soft going. *G. A. Swinbank*

BEAUMONT GIRL (IRE) 4 ch.f. Trans Island 119 – Persian Danser (IRE) 69 (Per-   46 sian Bold 123) [2006 55: f12g p12.2g⁴ p12.2g⁴ p12.2m f16g Dec 28] leggy filly: just poor form in 2006: stays 13.8f: acts on polytrack and good to soft ground: tried tongue tied/blinkered. *Miss M. E. Rowland*

BEAUMONT (IRE) 2 b.c. (Mar 31) Xaar 132 – Belsay 68 (Belmez (USA) 131) [2006   – 6f 7d 6.1m Sep 15] good-topped colt: well held in maidens: once tongue tied: sold 7,000 gns, sent to Holland. *M. A. Jarvis*

BEAU NASH (USA) 3 b.g. Barathea (IRE) 127 – Style N' Elegance (USA) (Alysheba   95 (USA)) [2006 91: 8m⁵ 10s⁵ 12m 10m 11m³ 11g² 12s 11.6d Nov 4] big, strong gelding: useful handicapper: best efforts when placed at Goodwood and Newbury (¾-length second to Bauer): should stay 1½m: acts on soft and good to firm going: reportedly lame penultimate start: joined D. Pipe. *P. W. Chapple-Hyam*

BEAU PETITE 2 b.f. (Apr 14) Kyllachy 129 – Beau Dalique (IRE) 66 (Pine Circle   – (USA)) [2006 5m Sep 13] 4,500Y: neat filly: half-sister to several winners, including 9-y-o Smokin Beau and 5-y-o Smokin Joe: dam 6f (at 2 yrs) to 1m winner: 33/1, last in maiden. *T. D. Barron*

BEAU SANCY 2 b.g. (Mar 31) Tobougg (IRE) 125 – Bride's Answer 81 (Anshan 119)   64 § [2006 7f* 7m³ p7.1f⁶ 10g p8.6g⁶ p9.5g² p8.6g* p9.5s⁵ Dec 14] workmanlike gelding: third foal: dam, 1m winner, half-sister to smart sprinter Funfair Wane: modest performer: won seller at Redcar (left J. H. Johnson 11,000 gns) in June and, having left J. Pearce £11,000 after second start, nursery at Wolverhampton in November: stays 9.5f: acts on polytrack and firm ground: tried in cheekpieces/blinkers: ungenuine. *R. A. Harris*

BEAUTIFUL MADNESS (IRE) 2 ch.f. (Apr 9) Shinko Forest (IRE) – Dosha 47   68 (Touching Wood (USA) 127) [2006 6m² 6.1f² 6m 6g³ 6m² p6m Oct 2] €4,200Y: workmanlike filly: first foal: dam, 6f winner, half-sister to high-class miler Air Express: fair maiden: placed 4 of 6 starts: will be suited by 7f: acts on firm ground. *M. G. Quinlan*

BEAUTIFUL MOVER (USA) 4 ch.f. Spinning World (USA) 130 – Dancer's Glam- **48** our (USA) (Danzig Connection (USA)) [2006 65: 10.2m p10g p8.6g⁶ p8g⁶ Dec 13] sturdy filly: poor maiden nowadays: stays easy 1m: acts on polytrack and firm going: tried in cheekpieces. *J. E. Long*

BEAUTIFUL REWARD (FR) 2 ch.f. (Jan 28) Diesis 133 – Toujours Elle (USA) **79 p** (Lyphard (USA) 132) [2006 7d² Oct 3] €90,000Y: big filly: half-sister to 3 winners, including 7f (fairly useful at 2 yrs) and 2m (in Ireland) winner Al Towd (by Kingmambo): dam, maiden, closely related to Irish 1000 Guineas winner Mehthaaf and high-class sprinter Elnadim: 9/1, promising neck second to Hi Calypso in maiden at Leicester: will be suited by 1m/1¼m: sure to progress, and win races. *J. R. Fanshawe*

BEAUTIFUL SOUTH 3 b.f. Forzando 122 – Fly South (Polar Falcon (USA) 126) **–** [2006 52: 7.5g f6g 6m Jul 15] strong filly: maiden: no form in 2006: tried blinkered. *N. Wilson*

BEAUTIFUL SUMMER (IRE) 3 br.f. Zafonic (USA) 130 – Sadler's Song 54 **59** (Saddlers' Hall (IRE) 126) [2006 7m 10f⁴ 7f 9.9m 8s³ Sep 28] second foal: dam maiden who stayed 1½m: modest maiden: probably stays 1¼m: acts on firm and soft going. *R. A. Fahey*

BEAUTY BRIGHT (IRE) 3 b.f. Danehill (USA) 126 – Dietrich (USA) 115 (Storm **113** Cat (USA)) [2006 102: 7s² 8g 8v 7m⁴ 6g² 5f 5m⁶ 6g*⁵ 5m⁶ Oct 1] medium-sized filly: smart performer: improved form when winning Ballygallon Stud Renaissance Stakes at the Curragh in September by 1¼ lengths from Noelani: creditable 2¾ lengths sixth to Desert Lord in Prix de l'Abbaye at Longchamp final outing: best at 5f/6f: acts on soft and good to firm going: has worn crossed noseband. *A. P. O'Brien, Ireland*

BEAUTY IS TRUTH 2 b.f. (Feb 1) Pivotal 124 – Zelding (IRE) 108 (Warning 136) **105** [2006 5d* 5.5m⁴ 6d⁶ 6s⁶ 5.5g* 6d Sep 29] quite good-topped filly: fifth foal: half-sister to French 5f and (including at 2 yrs) 6f winner Deziring (by Desert Prince) and useful 2004 2-y-o 6f and 7.5f winner Where With All (by Montjeu): dam, French 5f winner (including at 2 yrs), half-sister to smart French sprinter Zipping: useful performer: won listed newcomers race at Deauville in July and Prix d'Arenberg at Chantilly (made all to beat Iron Lips by 3 lengths) in September: creditable 3½ lengths seventh of 11 to Indian Ink in Cheveley Park Stakes at Newmarket final outing: speedy, raced at 5f/6f: acts on soft and good to firm ground: hung right third start, blinkered afterwards. *R. Collet, France*

BEAVER PATROL (IRE) 4 ch.g. Tagula (IRE) 116 – Erne Project (IRE) 80 (Project **101** Manager 111) [2006 101: p6g³ 6s 6m* 6m 6g⁴ 6f² 7m 6m 6d p6g⁶ p7g⁵ Oct 26] strong, well-made gelding: useful handicapper: won at Epsom (beat Prince Namid by neck) in June: several creditable efforts in defeat, including on last 2 starts: stays easy 7f: acts on polytrack, firm and soft going. *R. F. Johnson Houghton*

BE BOP ALOHA 4 b.f. Most Welcome 131 – Just Julia (Natroun (FR) 128) [2006 47: **–** p9.5g Jan 4] tall filly: poor maiden: tried in cheekpieces. *John Berry*

BECHARM 2 b.f. (Mar 27) Singspiel (IRE) 133 – Zuleika Dobson 106 (Cadeaux Gene- **68** reux 131) [2006 p7g p7g⁴ Dec 20] first foal: dam, winner, daughter of smart half-sister to very smart French 1½m performer Songlines: better effort (fair form) in maidens when 4½ lengths fourth to Basaata at Lingfield: will be suited by 1m+. *M. A. Jarvis*

BECK 2 ch.g. (Feb 27) Cadeaux Genereux 131 – River Cara (USA) 86 (Irish River (FR) **58** 131) [2006 8.2s p7.1g p7.1g Nov 28] good-bodied gelding: fifth foal: half-brother to 3 winners, including 2002 2-y-o 1m winner Ciel (by Rainbow Quest) and 11.7f winner Rill (by Unfuwain): dam French 2-y-o 1m winner: favourite, shaped much better than result suggests when eighth in maiden at Nottingham on debut, prominent until tiring: little impact in similar events on all-weather after: subsequently gelded. *M. L. W. Bell*

BECKENHAM'S SECRET 2 b.g. (Apr 8) Foxhound (USA) 103 – Berlisee (IRE) **73** (High Estate 127) [2006 p5g6 p5g* 6.1d³ 6f p6g 6m⁴ 7.1g 6m⁶ Sep 19] 9,000Y: smallish, close-coupled gelding: third living foal: half-brother to 3-y-o Divine River: dam, ran once, sister to Chester Vase winner High Baroque: fair performer: won maiden at Kempton in April: patchy form in nurseries: should stay 7f: acts on polytrack, firm and good to soft going: possibly temperamental. *B. R. Millman*

BECKERMET (IRE) 4 b.g. Second Empire (IRE) 124 – Razida (IRE) 106 (Last **114** Tycoon 131) [2006 115: 6g³ 6g⁶ 5m 6d 6m 6m 6m² 6g 7m⁴ 6.1m² 6m 5g 6m³ 6g⁵ 7g Sep 30] close-coupled, rather leggy gelding: smart performer: in-and-out form in 2006, running well when placed in listed race at Newmarket (½-length third to Paradise Isle) on reappearance, Chipchase Stakes at Newcastle (½-length second to Fayr Jag) on seventh start and listed races at Chester (½-length second to The Kiddykid) and Goodwood (close third to Tax Free) on tenth/thirteenth outings: effective at 5f/6f, not 7f: best form on good going or firmer: usually races prominently. *R. F. Fisher*

BECKETT HALL (IRE) 3 ch.c. Beckett (IRE) 116 – Date Mate (USA) (Thorn Dance (USA) 107) [2006 75: p8g⁵ 10m² 10d³ 12m 12g 10m⁵ 9m p10g 8.3g Oct 16] lengthy colt: fair maiden: stays 1¼m: acts on polytrack, good to firm and good to soft going: sold 10,500 gns, sent to Sweden. *R. Hannon*   **75**

BED FELLOW (IRE) 2 b.c. (Apr 17) Trans Island 119 – Moonlight Partner (IRE) 81 (Red Sunset 120) [2006 p7g 7f⁶ 8g⁴ 7m 8.3d* 8s* 10d⁵ Oct 28] €24,000F, 32,000Y: sturdy colt: half-brother to useful 7f/1m winner (latter at 2 yrs) Apache Red (by Indian Ridge) and 2 winners abroad: dam, Irish 5f winner, sister to smart Irish 1½m winner Dancing Sunset: fairly useful performer: won nurseries at Windsor and Newbury in October, hanging both times: stiff task when fifth to Empire Day in listed race at Newmarket: barely stays 1¼m: acts on firm and soft ground: not straightforward. *A. P. Jarvis*   **83**

BEDIZEN 3 b.c. Fantastic Light (USA) 134 – Barboukh 95 (Night Shift (USA)) [2006 8m May 13] 90,000Y: strong, useful-looking colt: eighth foal: half-brother to smart French 1¼m performer Barbola (by Diesis) and fairly useful 1m/1¼m winner Tarboush (by Polish Precedent): dam, 1m winner, out of half-sister to Old Vic: 8/1 and impressive in appearance (had 2 handlers), 13 lengths ninth of 11 to Bold Alaska in maiden at Newmarket, not unduly punished when weakening over 3f out: bred to stay 1¼m+: seemed likely to do better. *Sir Michael Stoute*   **–**

BEDOUIN BLUE (IRE) 3 b.g. Desert Style (IRE) 121 – Society Fair (FR) (Always Fair (USA) 121) [2006 77: 10s³ 10g* p12.2g* 12s⁴ Aug 19] strong gelding: fair handicapper, lightly raced: won at Redcar in April and Wolverhampton in July: stays 1½m: acts on polytrack and soft ground. *P. C. Haslam*   **77**

BEECH GAMES 2 b.g. (Feb 29) Mind Games 121 – Dane Dancing (IRE) 68 (Danehill (USA) 126) [2006 p7.1g⁴ p7g⁴ 8.5g² 8.1m⁶ 8g⁵ p8.6g⁵ p8.6g⁵ p9.5s³ p8.6g³ Dec 23] 56,000Y: third foal: brother to 4-y-o Viking Spirit: dam, 9.4f winner, sister to useful performer up to 1¼m Sundari: fair maiden: second at Beverley and Wolverhampton (nursery): will stay 1¼m: acts on polytrack: blinkered (ran creditably) last 2 starts: looks hard ride. *E. J. O'Neill*   **79**

BEECHSIDE (IRE) 2 b.f. (Mar 12) Orpen (USA) 116 – Tokurama (IRE) (Mtoto 134) [2006 7g 6.5d 5g 5.1d Oct 18] €6,000Y: fourth foal: half-sister to Irish 1½m winner Dee's Angel (by Idris): dam unraced: no form. *W. A. Murphy, Ireland*   **–**

BEE MAGIC 3 ch.g. Magic Ring (IRE) 115 – Miss Bananas 63 (Risk Me (FR) 127) [2006 6g 6.1m May 12] close-coupled gelding: well held in maidens. *C. N. Kellett*   **–**

BEE SEVENTEEN (USA) 3 b.f. Chester House (USA) 123 – Stormy Squab (USA) (Storm Bird (CAN) 134) [2006 75: 7g 6g p7g Jul 12] quite good-topped filly: maiden: well held in handicaps in 2006: blinkered/tongue tied final outing: sent to USA. *P. F. I. Cole*   **–**

BEE STINGER 4 b.g. Almaty (IRE) 113§ – Nest Egg (Prince Sabo 123) [2006 69: p8g* 8.3f* p8g³ 8m⁵ 8f* p8g 7m* p8g p7g p7g p8g² Nov 28] workmanlike gelding: fairly useful handicapper: won at Lingfield in May, Windsor in July, Brighton in August and Folkestone in September: good head second at Lingfield final start: stays 1m: acts on polytrack and firm going: tried blinkered. *I. A. Wood*   **92**

BEFORE YOU GO (IRE) 3 b.g. Sadler's Wells (USA) 132 – Here On Earth (USA) (Mr Prospector (USA)) [2006 84p: p10g² p10g* 10.1g* 11.5m⁴ 12m 10g 10m⁶ 12d⁶ 10s⁵ 10d Nov 4] rather leggy gelding: useful performer: won 3-runner races at Lingfield (handicap) in January and Epsom (minor event, by 1¼ lengths from Hanoona) in April: best effort when length fifth to Book of Music in handicap at Ascot penultimate start: should stay 1½m: acts on polytrack, soft and good to firm ground: visored (below form) sixth/seventh outings: has looked tricky ride: gelded after final appearance. *T. G. Mills*   **107**

BEGINNERS LUCK (IRE) 3 b.f. Key of Luck (USA) 126 – Zara's Birthday (IRE) 71 (Waajib 121) [2006 –: f8g f8g p10g p12.2g f7g f7g² f8g³ f7g* p8.6g f7g 8.3g⁶ 8f 8f⁵ 6m 7.1m⁶ Aug 17] poor performer: won banded event at Southwell in April: stays 8.3f: acts on fibresand and firm going: tried visored. *D. Carroll*   **43 a39**

BEHLAYA (IRE) 5 b.m. Kahyasi 130 – Behera 129 (Mill Reef (USA) 141) [2006 86: 12s 16.1m³ 15.9m² 12g² 12s³ 15.9g³ 16.2m* Sep 4] leggy, sparely-made mare: sister to useful French stayer Bayrika and half-sister to several winners, including smart French   **83**

performer up to 15f Behkara (by Kris): dam, runner-up in Arc, would have been suited by further: fairly useful performer: left L. Cusack in Ireland after reappearance: won handicap at Warwick final outing: stays 2m: acts on heavy and good to firm going. *T. D. Easterby*

BEING THERE 3 b.g. Bien Bien (USA) 125 – Segsbury Belle (Petoski 135) [2006 –p: p10g⁵ p12.2g⁶ 11.9m⁶ 16g⁵ Aug 26] lengthy gelding: modest maiden: seems to stay 1½m: seems to act on polytrack. *P. F. I. Cole* — **60**

BEKONING (IRE) 3 b.c. Beckett (IRE) 116 – Echoing 93 (Formidable (USA) 125) [2006 53?: f8g⁶ p7.1g⁵ p8.6g⁶ f6g* p6g f6g² 7d 7m Sep 12] smallish, plain colt: poor performer: won maiden claimer at Southwell in March: should stay 7f/1m: acts on all-weather. *M. Quinn* — **a47**

BELANAK (IRE) 3 b.c. Sinndar (IRE) 134 – Balanka (IRE) 116 (Alzao (USA) 117) [2006 10g⁴ 10.1g³ 12f* 12d⁶ 12f⁵ Sep 18] seventh foal: half-brother to 3 winners, including very smart 1m (at 2 yrs) to 1½m winner Balakheri (by Theatrical) and French 11f winner Balankiya (by Darshaan): dam, French 1m/1¼m winner, out of half-sister to dam of Prix du Jockey Club winner Bering: fairly useful performer: won maiden at Pontefract in July: best effort in handicap final outing: stays 1½m: acts on firm ground: sold 65,000 gns. *Sir Michael Stoute* — **84**

BEL CANTOR 3 b.c. Largesse 112 – Palmstead Belle (IRE) 79 (Wolfhound (USA) 126) [2006 77d: 6g³ 7f² 6d* 6m 5.9m 6f 5g³ 5.1g⁵ p5.1g⁶ 6.1d* 6.1s* f7g⁶ Nov 10] leggy colt: fairly useful performer: won maiden at Pontefract in May and handicaps at Nottingham (2) in October: will prove best at 5f/6f: acts on polytrack, firm and soft going: front runner. *W. J. H. Ratcliffe* — **90**

BELDON HILL (USA) 3 b.f. Rahy (USA) 115 – Bevel (USA) (Mr Prospector (USA)) [2006 9.8m⁵ p9.5g² 12f³ 10.1f p8.6g p8.6g Oct 30] quite good-topped filly: eighth living foal: sister to fairly useful 1½m winner Heavenly Bay, closely related to 1m/9.4f winner Bevier (by Nashwan) and half-sister to 1¼m winner Payola (by Red Ransom): dam, French 1m winner, out of close relation to Ajdal: fair maiden: should stay 1½m: acts on polytrack: wore cheekpieces (well held) final start: sold 30,000 gns, joined R. Fahey. *C. E. Brittain* — **69**

BELENUS (IRE) 4 ch.c. Dubai Millennium 140 – Ajhiba (IRE) 110 (Barathea (IRE) 127) [2006 109: 8m* 8g* Aug 17] big, strong, rangy, good sort: good mover with a quick, fluent action: smart performer: favourite when successful in 5-runner minor event at Newmarket (by 1¾ lengths from Ace of Hearts) and 11-runner totesport.com Sovereign Stakes at Salisbury, both in August, best effort when beating Notability by 1¼ lengths in latter: effective at 1m to 11f: raced only on good/good to firm going: tongue tied 3 times, including both starts in 2006: sometimes hangs left: has been bandaged in front: has left Godolphin. *Saeed bin Suroor* — **116**

BE LIKE A LION 3 b.f. Hunting Lion (IRE) 115 – Princess Kelly (Prince Daniel (USA)) [2006 63?: 7f 6m Jun 5] close-coupled, sparely-made filly: little form since debut at 2 yrs. *B. Palling* —

BELINDAS DREAM (IRE) 5 b.m. Beneficial 117 – Pretty Beau (IRE) (Beau Charmeur (FR)) [2006 p12.2g⁴ 13m 10s 16f p16g Aug 30] fourth foal: dam lightly raced in Irish bumpers: modest maiden: well held after fourth at Wolverhampton on debut. *Aidan Howard, Ireland* — **54**

BELLABELINI (IRE) 3 b.f. Bertolini (USA) 125 – Bethania 70 (Mark of Esteem (IRE) 137) [2006 64: p6g⁶ 6g 6f 8.1m f8g a7g Sep 30] just poor maiden in 2006: sold from S. Kirk 5,000 gns before final start: should stay 7f: acts on polytrack: tried blinkered. *C. Lorenzo, Spain* — **49**

BELLA BERTOLINI 3 b.f. Bertolini (USA) 125 – Fly Like The Wind 76 (Cyrano de Bergerac 120) [2006 67: 6g 6f 5f p5.1g⁴ p6g Nov 28] just modest maiden in 2006: stays 6f: acts on polytrack: wore cheekpieces last 2 starts. *T. G. Mills* — **53**

BELLA FIORELLA (IRE) 3 b.f. Shinko Forest (IRE) – Phylella (Persian Bold 123) [2006 54: p7.1g⁶ p6g⁶ f6g 11m 9.3m² 9.9m* 9.9f Jul 7] leggy filly: modest performer: left T. Pitt after third start: won handicap at Goodwood in June: stays 1¼m: acts on polytrack and good to firm going. *Miss V. Haigh* — **59**

BELLA MARIE 3 b.f. Kasakov – Onemoretime (Timeless Times (USA) 99) [2006 5s 7m³ 8d⁶ Oct 2] close-coupled filly: fourth foal: dam little form: poor maiden. *L. R. James* — **49**

BELL AMICA 2 gr.f. (Mar 15) Weet-A-Minute (IRE) 106 – Capponicus (IRE) 73 (Woodborough (USA) 112) [2006 p7.1g Jul 28] first foal: dam 2-y-o 5f winner (only season to race): well beaten in seller. *M. J. Attwater* —

BELLAMY CAY 4 b.c. Kris 135 – Trellis Bay 100 (Sadler's Wells (USA) 132) [2006   **118**
111: 12g* 12d* 12m³ 14m* 12.5s⁴ 15.5g² Oct 22] second foal: dam, 1½m winner who
stayed 2m, sister to dam of 5-y-o Reefscape and half-sister to Irish Oaks winner Wemyss
Bight, herself dam of high-class 1¼m/1½m performer Beat Hollow: smart performer:
progressed steadily, winning listed race at Saint-Cloud in April, Prix d'Hedouville at
Longchamp (made all, beat Salutino ¾ length) in May and Prix Maurice de Nieuil at
Longchamp (beat Montare 1½ lengths) in July: best effort when keeping-on short-neck
second to Montare in Prix Royal-Oak at Longchamp final start: stays 15.5f: acts on soft
and good to firm ground: consistent: stays in training. *A. Fabre, France*

BELLANORA 3 b.f. Inchinor 119 – Barberello (IRE) (Bigstone (IRE) 126) [2006 69:   **61 d**
6.1d³ 6.1m p6g 7g 7d 5s 6.1d Oct 13] sturdy filly: modest maiden: below form after
reappearance: stays 6f: acts on good to firm and good to soft going: blinkered/visored last
3 starts: sold 800 gns. *R. F. Johnson Houghton*

BELLAPAIS BOY 2 b.g. (Feb 10) Spectrum (IRE) 126 – Denice 106 (Night Shift   **49**
(USA)) [2006 6g p6g⁴ 7m Aug 8] sturdy gelding: poor form in maidens (gelded after):
bred to stay 1m. *T. D. Easterby*

BELLA PAVLINA 8 ch.m. Sure Blade (USA) 130 – Pab's Choice 61 (Telsmoss 91)   **–**
[2006 64: f12g p13.9g Jan 13] smallish mare: modest performer: well held in 2006: tried
in cheekpieces/visored. *R. A. Harris*

BELLE CHANSON 4 b.f. Kingsinger (IRE) 94 – Tallulah Belle 92 (Crowning Honors   **52**
(CAN)) [2006 50: p10g⁶ p10g⁴ p9.5g Feb 20] leggy filly: modest maiden: stays 1¼m:
acts on polytrack and firm ground: wears headgear. *J. R. Boyle*

BELLE ENCORE 4 b.f. Prince Sabo 123 – Frisson (Slip Anchor 136) [2006 45: p7.1g   **–**
p8g Jan 29] poor maiden: stays 7f: acts on good to firm ground: tried visored. *A. P. Jarvis*

BELLEHURST 2 b.f. (Feb 12) King's Best (USA) 132 – Polish Belle (Polish Precedent   **56**
(USA) 131) [2006 6g 7.1d 6g p7g Nov 15] first foal: dam unraced close relation to smart
sprinter Danehurst: modest form only on second start. *B. J. Meehan*

BELLINI STAR 3 b.g. Fraam 114 – Rewardia (IRE) 66 (Petardia 113) [2006 62: 8.1s⁴   **61 ?**
8f* p7g 7.1m 7.2m Aug 12] leggy gelding: modest performer: won handicap at L'Ancresse (Guernsey) in May: well beaten in claimers last 3 starts: stays 1m: acts on any going:
blinkered/visored last 6 starts: has looked awkward ride. *P. D. Evans*

BELLSBANK (IRE) 3 b.f. Beckett (IRE) 116 – Fag End (IRE) 88 (Treasure Kay 114)   **63 §**
[2006 72: p6g p8.6g⁶ p6g 7m 8.1g 7.2f 6m 7.2v⁵ 7.2v Oct 28] tall, rather leggy filly: only
modest nowadays: stays 7f: acts on heavy and good to firm going: tongue tied once at
2 yrs: reportedly had breathing problem sixth start: sold 1,800 gns. *A. Bailey*

BELLY DANCER (IRE) 4 gr.f. Danehill Dancer (IRE) 117 – Persian Mistress (IRE)   **75**
(Persian Bold 123) [2006 88: p6g p7g p8g Oct 11] workmanlike filly: just fair handicapper in 2006: best at 7f: acts on polytrack (promise on fibresand), good to firm and
good to soft going: sometimes found little at 2 yrs: reportedly struck into final outing.
P. F. I. Cole

BELROSE (IRE) 4 b.f. Robellino (USA) 127 – Blue Bay (GER) (Niniski (USA) 125)   **–**
[2006 –: p8g p10g p10g 8m p8.6g 5.2m p7g Jun 6] no form: blinkered/visored last 2
starts. *Mrs C. A. Dunnett*

BELTANE 8 b.g. Magic Ring (IRE) 115 – Sally's Trust (IRE) 51 (Classic Secret (USA)   **– §**
91) [2006 –§: 9g 8.1m 12d Aug 28] no longer of much account: tried blinkered. *W. de
Best-Turner*

BELTON 4 b.g. Lujain (USA) 119 – Efficacious (IRE) 49 (Efisio 120) [2006 –: 10.1f   **–**
Jul 29] rather leggy, angular gelding: modest at 2 yrs: no form since: very slowly away
only outing in 2006. *Ronald Thompson*

BELVEDERE VIXEN 2 b.f. (Jan 24) Foxhound (USA) 103 – Aunt Susan (Distant   **64**
Relative 128) [2006 7m³ 7f² 7f² 7f7g³ p7.1g⁴ Dec 30] 28,000Y, resold 20,000Y: second
foal: sister to 3-y-o BA Foxtrot: dam no form: modest maiden: left J. Osborne 6,500 gns
and off 4 months after third start: likely to prove as effective at 6f as 7f: acts on all-
weather and firm going: slowly away on debut, edged left next 2 starts. *M. J. Wallace*

BE MY CHARM 3 b.f. Polish Precedent (USA) 131 – Demerger (USA) (Distant View   **62**
(USA) 126) [2006 68: 5.1g 6f 5.7g 6f⁵ 5d² 5g³ 5m 6.1g 5m p7g Nov 6] modest maiden
handicapper: probably stays 6f: acts on firm and good to soft going: ridden by 7-lb claimer nowadays. *M. Blanshard*

BENANDONNER (USA) 3 ch.g. Giant's Causeway (USA) 132 – Cape Verdi (IRE) **88**
126 (Caerleon (USA) 132) [2006 8m⁶ 6f⁴ f6g² 8g³ p8g² p8g³ p8.6g² 10g* 10d² p10g
Oct 20] sturdy gelding: third foal: dam, won 1000 Guineas (also 6f winner at 2 yrs), out
of sister to Breeders' Cup Classic winner Arcangues: fairly useful handicapper: made all
at Nottingham in September: stays 1¼m: acts on polytrack and good to soft going: reared
in stall and withdrawn prior to second intended outing: sold 35,000 gns. *E. A. L. Dunlop*

BENAYOUN 2 b.c. (Feb 5) Inchinor 119 – Sosumi 101 (Be My Chief (USA) 122) [2006 **60**
6d 6d⁵ 8.2s* p8g⁶ Nov 8] well-made colt: first foal: dam, 2-y-o 5f winner who stayed
1¼m, out of half-sister to Eclipse winner Compton Admiral and Queen Elizabeth II
Stakes winner Summoner (by Inchinor): modest performer: won seller at Nottingham in
October: creditable effort in nursery final start: should stay 1¼m: acts on polytrack and
soft going. *M. H. Tompkins*

BEN BACCHUS (IRE) 4 b.g. Bahhare (USA) 122 – Bodfaridistinction (IRE) 77 **57**
(Distinctly North (USA) 115) [2006 53: f12g² 12.1d 12m p16g Nov 6] good-topped gelding: modest performer: left P. Blockley after third start: stays 1½m: acts on all-weather,
best turf run on good going: sometimes blinkered: very slowly away second outing.
P. W. Hiatt

BENBAUN (IRE) 5 b.g. Stravinsky (USA) 133 – Escape To Victory (Salse (USA) **121**
128) [2006 119: 5m² 5m² 5g² 5m² 5m* 6f⁵ 6m³ Dec 10]
    Win one Flying Five Stakes and the chances are you'll win another. At least
that is what the record books suggest. Winning the same pattern race in consecutive
seasons is relatively rare, but since 1991 four different horses have achieved the
feat in the Flying Five at the Curragh. Flowing and Tropical both pulled it off
for trainer Dermot Weld in the early-'nineties, as did Tedburrow for Eric Alston at
the end of the same decade. In the latest season, Benbaun completed back-to-

Ransley, Birks, Hillen's "Benbaun"

back wins in the race, gaining a deserved second success by little more than the skin of his teeth, underlining that he was an improved sprinter again in 2006, having progressed from modest handicaps in his early days.

Benbaun's success at the Curragh cured a bad dose of seconditis. In no way to his detriment, he had finished runner-up on consecutive starts in the Prix du Gros-Chene at Chantilly, the King's Stand Stakes at Royal Ascot, a listed event at the Curragh and the Sprint Stakes at Sandown. He ran almost to the pound each time, beaten two lengths by a top-form Moss Vale on his reappearance in France then losing out by a short head to Takeover Target at Royal Ascot, albeit receiving 5 lb from the winner. Benbaun faced twenty-seven rivals at Royal Ascot, but, with the Nolan & Brophy Auctioneers Flying Five run in close proximity to the Nunthorpe at York, only nine took him on at the Curragh, Osterhase a significant withdrawal due to a poor scope. Without one of Ireland's leading sprinters, Benbaun started a hot favourite at 11/10 after two more good efforts the previous month when beaten a length by Dandy Man at the Curragh and half a length by Pivotal Point, conceding the winner 5 lb, at Sandown. All the same, the race proved no pushover as Benbaun got to Desert Lord, another British-trained runner, only inside the final furlong, battling on well to hold him by a head, the pair five lengths clear. Benbaun and Desert Lord were the only two British-trained runners on show when Benbaun made his final appearance of the season in the Hong Kong Sprint at Sha Tin in December. Benbaun started at 38/1 after finishing a creditable fifth of sixteen to two-and-a-half-length winner Takeover Target in the Sprinters Stakes at Nakayama in Japan in October. Benbaun acquitted himself well at Sha Tin in finishing third, having been only sixth the previous year. Ridden from behind by Jamie Spencer, he was no match for the four-and-a-quarter-length winner Absolute Champion, but kept on well, beaten three quarters of a length by Silent Witness for second.

		Nureyev	Northern Dancer
	Stravinsky (USA)	(b 1977)	Special
	(b 1996)	Fire The Groom	Blushing Groom
Benbaun (IRE)		(b 1987)	Prospector's Fire
(b.g. 2001)		Salse	Topsider
	Escape To Victory	(b 1985)	Carnival Princess
	(b 1995)	Gaijin	Caerleon
		(b 1986)	Resooka

In terms of Europe, Benbaun's performances in 2006 put him behind only the very smart sprinter Soldier's Tale among the produce of his sire, the Nunthorpe Stakes and July Cup winner Stravinsky. With Soldier's Tale and Balmont, another smart sprinter, sidelined for the most part, it was a low-key year for Stravinsky at home, though he was represented in the southern hemisphere by Serenade Rose, winner of the Australian Oaks over a mile and a half and the Arrowfield Stud Stakes, another Group 1 event run over a mile and a quarter. Benbaun's dam Escape To Victory was a seven-furlong winner as a two-year-old in Italy. She has produced two other winners abroad, the fairly useful six-furlong winner in Dubai, Tarfaa Bint Swain (by Swain), and the Hong Kong seven-furlong winner Honest Treasure (by Danehill). Escape To Victory is a half-sister to the high-class mile- to mile-and-a-quarter performer Hawksley Hill. Second in the Breeders' Cup Mile as a five-year-old, Hawksley Hill got better with age, and Benbaun has progressed with each season. He needs to improve only a little more to win a top prize. A useful-looking gelding, effective at five/six furlongs, he acts on firm and good to soft ground, and was withdrawn from the Nunthorpe Stakes at York due to the very soft going. He usually wears blinkers or a visor, and usually races prominently. *M. J. Wallace*

BENBROOK 3 b.c. Royal Applause 124 – Muffled (USA) 67 (Mizaaya 104) [2006 58: **75** 8.5g 8f⁴ 9.9m 10f* 10f* 10.3m² 10g⁴ 9.7m² 8m p10g Oct 11] leggy colt: fair handicapper: won at Nottingham and Leicester in July: stays 10.3f: acts on firm going: races up with pace: sold 28,000 gns, sent to Qatar. *J. L. Dunlop*

BEN CASEY 4 b.g. Whittingham (IRE) 104 – Hot Ice (IRE) 53 (Petardia 113) [2006 **?** 60: f6g f6g a6g⁵ a6g 8m 6g³ 6m⁵ a6g⁴ a6g⁴ a6g⁶ 7g⁶ 6g³ a6g² a6d Dec 17] small, sturdy gelding: modest maiden: sold from B. Smart 3,000 gns after second start: stays 6f: acts on fibresand/dirt and firm going: tried in cheekpieces. *Ms K. Stenefeldt, Sweden*

BENCHMARK 2 b.c. (Apr 29) Mark of Esteem (IRE) 137 – Tarneem (USA) 87 (Zilzal **82 d** (USA) 137) [2006 5m³ 5p5g² 6m⁶ 6g⁴ 7pg p7g Oct 11] 8,500F, 22,000Y: close-coupled colt: half-brother to several winners, including 4-y-o Enforcer and fairly useful 2002 2-y-o 5f winner Lord of The Inn (both by Efisio): dam 1m winner: fairly useful form when placed first 2 starts in maidens: deteriorated after (reportedly bled once): should stay 7f/1m: sold 13,000 gns. *R. Hannon*

BEN CHORLEY 2 gr.g. (May 1) Inchinor 119 – Arantxa 77§ (Sharpo 132) [2006 6g **79 p** 7g* Sep 27] 5,000F, €13,000Y: fifth foal: brother to fairly useful 2002 2-y-o 6f winner Vilas and half-brother to 11.5f winner Vicario (by Vettori): dam, unreliable 6f winner (including at 2 yrs), half-sister to useful Irish performer up to 1¾m Damancher: better for debut (gelded after), won 15-runner maiden at Newcastle by 2 lengths, value extra: will go on progressing. *P. W. Chapple-Hyam*

BENDARSHAAN 6 b.g. Darshaan 133 – Calypso Run (Lycius (USA) 124) [2006 91§: **– §** p13g p16.5g 14.1m⁶ 16.4m⁶ 12d Oct 2] close-coupled gelding: fairly useful handicapper at best: very much on downgrade: left R. Hannon after second outing: sometimes blinkered, tried visored: unreliable. *C. A. Dwyer*

BENEDICT 4 b.g. Benny The Dip (USA) 127 – Abbey Strand (USA) 78 (Shadeed **–** (USA) 135) [2006 103: 8s Mar 25] workmanlike gelding: useful handicapper: much improved in 2005, winning 3 times: reportedly fractured pelvis in Lincoln at Redcar in March: stayed 1¼m: acted on good to firm and good to soft going: dead. *John Berry*

BENEKING 6 b. or br.g. Wizard King 122 – Gagajulu 75 (Al Hareb (USA) 123) [2006 **63** 59: p6g* p7.1g³ p6g⁴ p8g² p6g² p7.1g⁵ p6g³ 6.1d⁵ 7.1m⁵ p8g² p7g Dec 19] rather leggy gelding: modest performer: won banded race at Wolverhampton in January: effective at 6f to 1m: acts on polytrack and good to firm going: tried blinkered, usually wears cheekpieces. *D. Burchell*

BENFLEET BOY 2 gr.g. (Mar 21) Fasliyev (USA) 120 – Nicely (IRE) 94 (Bustino **82 p** 136) [2006 6g⁴ p7g* Sep 6] 34,000F, 38,000Y: third foal: half-brother to French 15f winner Supsonic (by Marju): dam, 1m (at 2 yrs) and 2m winner, out of half-sister to very smart 9f to 1½m performer Terimon: fairly useful form: confirmed debut promise when winning maiden at Kempton by ½ length from Malyana: will stay 1m+: open to more improvement. *B. J. Meehan*

BENJUM 3 ch.g. Benny The Dip (USA) 127 – Boojum 101 (Mujtahid (USA) 118) **–** [2006 –: 12.1s⁶ May 29] big, strong, workmanlike gelding: well held in 3 maidens. *B. I. Case*

BEN KENOBI 8 ch.g. Accondy (IRE) 79 – Nour El Sahar (USA) (Sagace (FR) 135) **– §** [2006 50§: 10.9f 12.1m 11.8g Aug 30] well-made gelding: no form in 2006: ungenuine. *Mrs P. Ford*

BENLLECH 2 b.c. (Feb 25) Lujain (USA) 119 – Four Legs Good (IRE) 58 (Be My **87** Guest (USA) 126) [2006 5.1d 5.1m² 5g⁵ 6.1m 5m 5.1f⁴ 6m⁴ 6d⁴ 7d² p7.1g² p7g* p7.1g* Dec 26] 9,000Y: close-coupled colt: has a rather round action: first foal: dam, maiden, form only at 7f at 2 yrs: fairly useful performer: in frame 6 times (including in nurseries) prior to winning maiden at Kempton in November and minor event at Wolverhampton in December: effective at 5f to 7f: acts on polytrack and firm ground: tried tongue tied. *S. Kirk*

BENNANABAA 7 b.g. Anabaa (USA) 130 – Arc Empress Jane (IRE) (Rainbow Quest **–** (USA) 134) [2006 –, a49: p6g p6g 5d p7.1g May 15] good-topped gelding: poor maiden: stays 6f: acts on polytrack: tried blinkered/in cheekpieces: tongue tied. *S. C. Burrough*

BENNY THE BALL (USA) 5 b. or br.g. Benny The Dip (USA) 127 – Heloise (USA) **58** (Forty Niner (USA)) [2006 f7g p7.1g f8g⁴ p8g 7g f8g³ p10g⁵ Dec 3] big, good-bodied gelding: only modest handicapper nowadays: stays 1¼m: acts on all-weather, raced only on good/good to firm going on turf. *N. P. Littmoden*

BENNY THE BAT 2 gr.c. (May 11) Victory Note (USA) 120 – Little Emily 48 (Zafo- **77** nic (USA) 130) [2006 7m⁵ p8g² 8.3s*⁴ p8.6s* Dec 13] angular, quite good-topped colt: fourth foal: half-brother to fairly useful French 2002 2-y-o 1m winner Fireworks (by Kendor) and 1m (at 2 yrs) and 11f (in France) winner Boxgrove (by Trempolino): dam lightly-raced daughter of Norfolk Stakes winner Petillante: fair performer: won maiden at Wolverhampton in December by 5 lengths from Bewildering, rearing as stall opened and hanging left: stays 1m: seems quirky. *H. Morrison*

BENNY THE BUS 4 b.g. Komaite (USA) – Amy Leigh (IRE) 78 (Imperial Frontier **68** (USA) 112) [2006 75: p8.6g p8.6g p6m² p5.1g⁴ p7.1m⁶ f6g* p6g⁴ Dec 2] strong gelding:

fair performer: won maiden at Southwell in November: stays 7f: acts on all-weather and good to firm ground: sometimes wears cheekpieces: found little fifth start. *Mrs G. S. Rees*

BENNY THE RASCAL (IRE) 4 b.g. Benny The Dip (USA) 127 – Bolshoi Star 65§ – (Soviet Star (USA) 128) [2006 12s⁶ Aug 18] 33/1, well held in maiden at Catterick. *J. Pearce*

BENS GEORGIE (IRE) 4 ch.f. Opening Verse (USA) 126 – Peperonata (IRE) 91 **77** (Cyrano de Bergerac 120) [2006 70: p6g⁴ 5.7d 6g* p6g³ 6m⁵ 6f 6f 6.1m 5.5d p6g Oct 15] fair handicapper: won at Windsor in June: below form after next outing: effective at 6f/7f: acts on polytrack, good to firm and good to soft going. *D. K. Ivory*

BENTLEY 2 b.g. (Mar 20) Piccolo 121 – April Lee 70 (Superpower 113) [2006 5d 5.1s⁶ **50** p5g⁶ 6m 8s p5.1g⁶ f6g⁵ p6g⁶ p7g⁶ f8g⁶ p7.1g⁴ Dec 21] sturdy gelding: modest maiden: should stay 7f: visored last 6 starts. *D. Shaw*

BENTLEY BROOK (IRE) 4 ch.g. Singspiel (IRE) 133 – Gay Bentley (USA) (River- **73 d** man (USA) 131) [2006 84: p8.6g p10g⁶ 10m⁵ p10g⁶ 12s 10d p13.9m⁴ p12.2g⁴ Nov 23] workmanlike gelding: on downgrade and just fair form at best in 2006: seems to stay 1¼m: acts on polytrack, good to firm and good to soft going: tried blinkered, tongue tied final start: usually waited with. *P. A. Blockley*

BENTONG (IRE) 3 b.g. Anabaa (USA) 130 – Miss Party Line (USA) (Phone Trick **110** (USA)) [2006 83p: 6d² 6f* 7s 6f* 6m 6g Aug 19] close-coupled, good-topped gelding: smart handicapper: won at Salisbury (beat Pearly Wey 3 lengths) in May and Redcar (by ½ length from Gallery Girl, despite hanging left) in July: below form last 2 starts, in Stewards' Cup at Goodwood on first occasion: gelded after final outing: likely to prove best at 5f/6f: acts on firm going: free-going sort (also took strong hold to post at Salisbury). *P. F. I. Cole*

BEOWULF 3 b.c. Green Desert (USA) 127 – Ethelinda 111 (Indian Ridge 123) [2006 **70** p9.5g³ p7g 8.1s 6d⁴ 7.1m² 7m 6g⁶ 6g Jun 21] first foal: dam French 7f/1m winner: fair maiden: well held after fifth start: seemed to stay easy 9f: acted on polytrack, good to firm and good to soft going: tried blinkered: reportedly lame second outing, hung left on third: had suspect temperament: sold 6,000 gns in July: dead. *M. Johnston*

BERBATOV 2 b.g. (Mar 14) Alhaarth (IRE) 126 – Neptunalia 70 (Slip Anchor 136) **60** [2006 7.6f 8.2s f8g⁵ Nov 20] big, strong gelding: modest maiden: fifth in minor event final start: bred to stay 1¼m+: acts on fibresand. *Ms Deborah J. Evans*

BERESFORD BOY 5 b.g. Easycall 115 – Devils Dirge 68 (Song 132) [2006 6.1m 6m – Jun 5] close-coupled gelding: maiden: missed 2005, no form in 2006. *J. A. Pickering*

BERGONZI (IRE) 2 ch.c. (Feb 26) Indian Ridge 123 – Lady Windley (Baillamont **80 p** (USA) 124) [2006 7d p7g⁵ p8.6g² Nov 11] €190,000Y: closely related to winner in Italy by Dr Devious and half-brother to several winners, including 6-y-o Our Teddy and useful Irish 7f (at 2 yrs) to 1¼m winner Talwin (by Alhaarth): dam, French 11f winner, out of top-class French middle-distance performer Northern Trick: progressive in maidens, fairly useful form when short-head second to Book of Facts at Wolverhampton, challenging strongly as pair pulled clear: will stay 1¼m+: probably capable of better still. *J. H. M. Gosden*

BERKELEY CASTLE (USA) 2 b.c. (Jan 25) Mizzen Mast (USA) 121 – Bristol **87 +** Channel 113 (Generous (IRE) 139) [2006 7m 7.1g 7g³ Oct 12] strong, heavy-bodied colt: type to carry condition: third living foal: dam, 1m (at 2 yrs) to 1½m winner, closely related to Grand Criterium/Dante winner Tenby: fairly useful form in maidens, never-nearer third to Tredegar at Newmarket: will be well suited by 1¼m/1½m: sold 200,000 gns, sent to USA. *Sir Michael Stoute*

BERKHAMSTED (IRE) 4 b.g. Desert Sun 120 – Accounting (Sillery (USA) 122) **83** [2006 –: p8.6g p12.2g* 8.3g p7g p10g 9.7f 10.1d⁵ p12g⁶ 13.9s 12s p8g² p8.6g³ Dec 6] strong, good-topped gelding: good mover: fairly useful performer: won claimer at Wolverhampton (left J. Osborne) in March: left M. Harris after seventh outing: effective at 1m to 1½m: acts on polytrack and heavy ground, probably on firm: tried visored, blinkered last 2 starts (tongue tied on first occasion). *T. G. Dascombe*

BERMUDA BEAUTY (IRE) 3 b.f. Elnadim (USA) 128 – Believing 74 (Belmez **45** (USA) 131) [2006 56: p6g p5.1g³ p6g⁶ 5.1g 6.1f 6.1f p5.1g 5.1m f6g Nov 28] leggy filly: poor nowadays: stays 7f: acts on polytrack, firm and good to soft going. *J. M. Bradley*

BERNARDINI (USA) 3 b.c. A P Indy (USA) 131 – Cara Rafaela (USA) 117 (Quiet **132** American (USA)) [2006 a6f⁴ a8f* a8f* a9.5f* a9s* a10f* a10f* a10f² Nov 4] fifth foal: closely related to winner in USA by Seattle Slew and half-brother to smart US 5f (at

2 yrs) and 8.5f winner Ile de France (by Storm Cat): dam US Grade 1 8.5f winner at 2 yrs: quickly developed into a top-class performer, winning 6 of his 8 starts, namely maiden at Gulfstream in March, Grade 3 Withers Stakes at Aqueduct in April, Preakness Stakes at Pimlico (beat Sweetnorthernsaint by 5¼ lengths, travelling well under patient handling and striding clear 2f out) in May, Grade 2 Jim Dandy Stakes at Saratoga (by 9 lengths) in July, Travers Stakes at Saratoga (by 7½ lengths from Bluegrass Cat) in August and Jockey Club Gold Cup at Belmont (beat Wanderin Boy by 6¾ lengths, quickening clear in a matter of strides) in October: favourite, length second to Invasor in Breeders' Cup Classic at Churchill Downs final outing, leading before home turn but no answer as winner went past: stayed 1¼m: acted well in sloppy conditions: raced prominently: to stand at Darley Stud, Kentucky, fee $100,000. *T. Albertrani, USA*

BERNARDON (GER) 10 b.g. Suave Dancer (USA) 136 – Bejaria (GER) (Konigs- – stuhl (GER)) [2006 16v Mar 31] formerly smart performer in Germany: modest jumper nowadays (temperamental): showed nothing at Musselburgh on return to Flat. *B. Potts, Ireland*

BERNIE'S BEAU (IRE) 3 br.f. Namid 128 – Otter's Field (IRE) (First Trump 118) – [2006 68: 5g 6d p6m p7.1g p7.1g Nov 27] workmanlike filly: maiden: well held in 2006. *R. Hollinshead*

BERTI BERTOLINI 3 b.g. Bertolini (USA) 125 – Cosmic Countess (IRE) 74 (Lahib – (USA) 129) [2006 60: p6g Mar 30] sturdy gelding: modest maiden at 2 yrs: well held in handicap on only outing in 2006. *T. G. Mills*

BERTIE BEAR 3 b.c. Bertolini (USA) 125 – Philarmonique (FR) (Trempolino (USA) **42** 135) [2006 –: p6g² f7g p6g⁶ 5.7g 7g 7m³ 8.2f 7g 7d 7f 10s Oct 2] poor maiden: stays 7f: blinkered/visored: sometimes tongue tied. *G. G. Margarson*

BERTIES BROTHER 3 ch.g. Forzando 122 – Sweets (IRE) (Persian Heights 129) – [2006 –: p7.1g p7.1g² p6g* p7g⁵ p6g³ p6g³ f7g 6f 5f Jul 25] lengthy gelding: poor **a45** performer: won banded race at Lingfield in February: stays 7f: acts on polytrack, little form on turf. *D. G. Bridgwater*

BERTIE SOUTHSTREET 3 b. or br.g. Bertolini (USA) 125 – Salvezza (IRE) 97 **83** (Superpower 113) [2006 82: 6m⁴ 6m 6f 8m⁶ Aug 16] leggy gelding: fairly useful handicapper: below form after reappearance: will prove best at 5f/6f (pulled hard at 1m): acts on firm going. *J. R. Best*

BERTIE SWIFT 2 b.g. (Apr 13) Bertolini (USA) 125 – Hollybell 87§ (Beveled **70** (USA)) [2006 p5g 6f 5.2f⁴ 6m⁴ 5.5m p6g² Dec 28] sturdy gelding: fair maiden: off nearly 4 months and gelded, second in nursery at Wolverhampton (edged left) final outing: should prove best at 5f/6f. *J. Gallagher*

BERTOLIVER 2 b.c. (Mar 23) Bertolini (USA) 125 – Calcavella 75 (Pursuit of Love **81** 124) [2006 6f 6m⁴ 6g⁶ p7g 6m* 6d 6d² Nov 4] 16,000Y: rather leggy, good-topped colt: second foal: half-brother to 3-y-o Skhilling Spirit: dam, maiden who stayed 7f, half-sister to smart Hong Kong miler Dave's Best: fairly useful performer: won maiden at Newmarket (dictated) in September: good second in nursery at Windsor final start: stays 6f: acts on polytrack, good to firm and good to soft going. *D. K. Ivory*

BERTRADA (IRE) 2 b.f. (Apr 11) King Charlemagne (USA) 120 – Goldenfort Queen **51** (IRE) (Distinctly North (USA) 115) [2006 6m p7g⁴ p7g 6f⁶ Jul 22] €13,000F, €42,000Y: third foal: half-sister to fairly useful 7f winner Twin Peaks and winner in Greece (both by Monashee Mountain): dam unraced half-sister to smart middle-distance performers Suplizi, Hieroglyphic and Cairo Prince: modest maiden: well out of weights only start in nursery: will stay at least 1m. *H. Morrison*

BERT'S MEMORY 2 b.f. (Apr 21) Bertolini (USA) 125 – Meg's Memory (IRE) 59 **69** (Superlative 118) [2006 p5.1g⁶ 6.1f³ 6m 5.5m⁵ 6.1m³ 6d³ 7s⁴ 7v⁴ p7.1g⁵ f8g² f8g³ Dec 21] workmanlike filly, unfurnished at 2 yrs: first foal: dam, who stayed 2m (also won over hurdles), half-sister to useful stayer Bean King: fair maiden: made frame 7 times, including in nurseries: will stay 1¼m+: acts on all-weather and any turf going: wore cheekpieces last 2 starts. *K. A. Ryan*

BERYLUNE (GER) 4 ch.f. Devil River Peek (USA) 117 – Berlanga (GER) (Execu- – tive Pride 127) [2006 8.5g Apr 26] second foal: dam German 7f winner: last in maidens at Bad Doberan (for P. Vovcenko in Germany) and Epsom 9 months apart. *S. Dow*

BESHAIRT 2 b.f. (Apr 4) Silver Wizard (USA) 117 – Irja (Minshaanshu Amad (USA) – 91§) [2006 p7g p7.1g p7g Nov 11] 800 2-y-o: second foal: dam unraced out of half-sister to 1000 Guineas winner Waterloo: no form. *D. K. Ivory*

Skybet York Stakes, York—Best Alibi lands the odds in convincing fashion in a race effectively a reworking of the defunct Scottish Derby; outsider-of-five Hattan is runner-up

BESSEMER (JPN) 5 b.g. Carnegie (IRE) 129 – Chalna (IRE) 83 (Darshaan 133) **84** [2006 81: f7g⁴ p7.1g* p7g 7g⁴ 7g⁵ 7m p6g⁵ 7m² 7.1m 7.6m p7.1f⁶ 9.2g p7.1g p9.5g⁵ p7.1m p7.1g⁵ p7.1g* p7.1g³ Dec 26] rangy gelding: fairly useful performer: won handicap in February and seller in December, both at Wolverhampton: effective at 6f to 1¼m: acts on all-weather, firm and soft ground: usually visored/in cheekpieces: tongue tied earlier in career: waited with. *D. Carroll*

BEST ALIBI (IRE) 3 b.c. King's Best (USA) 132 – Chauncy Lane (IRE) 90 (Sadler's **117** Wells (USA) 132) [2006 106p: 10.4s² 12m⁶ 12g³ 10.4f* Jul 29] big, good-topped colt: has a fluent, round action: smart performer: landed odds in 5-runner Skybet York Stakes at York in July by 2 lengths from Hattan, soon leading: had earlier finished second to Septimus in Dante Stakes (beaten 8 lengths) on same course and had run well when 3¼ lengths sixth to Sir Percy in Derby at Epsom (stayed on well from off pace) and 5 lengths third to Dylan Thomas in Irish Derby at the Curragh (kept on after being ridden more prominently): stays 1½m: acts on firm and soft going: joined Godolphin. *Sir Michael Stoute*

BEST DOUBLE 3 ch.f. Compton Place 125 – Bestemor 60 (Selkirk (USA) 129) [2006 **72** 72: p6g² p5g² p5g⁶ 5f⁵ p6g⁴ 6g⁴ 5m⁴ Jul 26] sturdy filly: fair maiden: effective at 5f to 7f: acts on polytrack and soft going: tried blinkered. *G. A. Butler*

BEST GAME 4 b.g. Mister Baileys 123 – Bestemor 60 (Selkirk (USA) 129) [2006 66: **–** p8.6g Jan 20] quite good-topped gelding: fair performer in 2005: well held only outing in 2006: tried in headgear/tongue tied: races prominently: signs of temperament: sold 6,000 gns in March, sent to Germany. *D. W. Thompson*

BEST GUESS (USA) 3 br.f. Stormin Fever (USA) 116 – Probing (USA) (Brocco **84** (USA) 124) [2006 76: 7.1s* p8g⁴ 8v* 10s⁴ Oct 10] leggy filly: fairly useful handicapper: won at Sandown in May and Thirsk in September: stays 1m: acts on polytrack, raced only on good ground or softer (acts on heavy) on turf: sold 38,000 gns, sent to Saudi Arabia. *P. W. Chapple-Hyam*

BEST LADY (IRE) 3 b.f. King's Best (USA) 132 – Sassenach (IRE) 68 (Night Shift **74** (USA)) [2006 69p: 10m³ 8.3g⁶ 10.2m⁴ Sep 25] rangy filly: fair maiden: stays 1¼m: acts on good to firm and good to soft going: sold 20,000 gns. *B. W. Hills*

BEST LEAD 7 b.g. Distant Relative 128 – Bestemor 60 (Selkirk (USA) 129) [2006 60, **–** a67: p5.1g p5.1g p5.1g Dec 7] leggy gelding: no form in 2006: tried visored, blinkered nowadays. *Ian Emmerson*

BEST NAME 3 b.c. King's Best (USA) 132 – Flawly 106 (Old Vic 136) [2006 106: **123** 10g* 10.5m² 12g 10d* 12m⁴ Oct 1] €165,000Y: strong, lengthy colt: first foal: dam 1¼m/1½m winner in USA/France: very smart performer: beaten short head by Linda's Lad in Prix de Conde at Longchamp only start at 2 yrs: won listed race there on reappearance in April and Prix du Prince d'Orange on same course (very confidently ridden and showing

129

fine turn of foot from rear to beat Champs Elysees ½ length) in September: better effort in between when staying-on ¾-length second to Darsi in Prix du Jockey Club at Chantilly: only eighth in Irish Derby at the Curragh next time: poorly to post, best effort when 5¼ lengths fifth (promoted fourth) to Rail Link in Prix de l'Arc de Triomphe at Longchamp final outing, staying on after being trapped in on rail: stays 1½m: acts on good to firm and good to soft going: joined Godolphin. *R. Collet, France*

BEST OF THE LOT (USA) 4 b.g. Lear Fan (USA) 130 – Aerosilver (USA) (Re-launch (USA)) [2006 10.1m p10g 12.3m³ 14.1m⁴ 11.9g 13.9s Oct 7] fair maiden: trained by R. Pritchard-Gordon in France in 2005: left T. Fitzgerald after second start: stays 1¾m: acts on good to firm and good to soft going: tried blinkered earlier in career. *R. A. Fahey*   **77**

BEST OPTION 2 b.f. (Jan 26) Best of The Bests (IRE) 122 – B'Elanna Torres 66 (Entrepreneur 123) [2006 f7g⁶ Dec 23] first foal: dam, maiden who should have been suited by 1m+, out of half-sister to Irish Oaks winner Princess Pati: 33/1, slowly away in maiden at Southwell: will be suited by 1m+. *W. R. Muir*   **–**

BEST PORT (IRE) 10 b.g. Be My Guest (USA) 126 – Portree 82 (Slip Anchor 136) [2006 74, a51: 16m⁶ 13.9m 16.2f 14.1f² 14.1d 16.2g⁴ 14.1m Sep 11] lightly-made gelding: modest handicapper: best form at 1¾m/2m: acts on polytrack, firm and good to soft going: tried in cheekpieces: held up. *J. Parkes*   **58**

BEST PROSPECT (IRE) 4 b.g. Orpen (USA) 116 – Bright Prospect (USA) (Miswaki (USA) 124) [2006 92: 10g 10m⁵ 9.9g 12m* 12m⁴ 12d 10.5s⁶ 10s² 10.4s 10s* 10d⁴ Nov 4] big, lengthy gelding: useful handicapper: won at Newmarket in July and Newbury (impressive when beating Red Admiral by 2 lengths) in October: good close fourth to Folio at Windsor final start: stays 1½m: acts on soft and good to firm going: tongue tied last 4 starts. *M. Dods*   **103**

BEST SELECTION 2 ch.f. (Mar 31) Inchinor 119 – Manila Selection (USA) (Manila (USA)) [2006 p7g p7g⁵ Dec 20] 19,000Y: fourth foal: half-sister to 3 winners, including 3-y-o Danski and 5-y-o Insubordinate: dam unraced: better effort (fair form) in maidens at Lingfield when 5¼ lengths fifth to Basaata. *A. P. Jarvis*   **65**

BEST WARNING 2 br.f. (Apr 10) Best of The Bests (IRE) 122 – Just Warning (Warning 136) [2006 p7g 7d 7.6f Sep 23] 800 2-y-o: third foal: half-sister to 4-y-o Young Mick: dam, well beaten only start, half-sister to very smart 6f to 1m performer Young Ern: well held in maidens. *J. Ryan*   **–**

BEST WOMAN 2 b.f. (Mar 31) Best of The Bests (IRE) 122 – Business Woman (Primo Dominie 121) [2006 5d* 5d⁵ 5m 5f 6f 9.5g⁶ Nov 18] second foal: dam little sign of ability: poor performer: won claimer at Thirsk (left M. Easterby £9,000) in May: stays 9.5f: acts on polytrack and good to soft ground. *P. Howling*   **49**

BETHANYS BOY (IRE) 5 ch.g. Docksider (USA) 124 – Daymoon (USA) (Dayjur (USA) 137) [2006 66, a80: p12.2g* f12g⁵ f12s⁶ 10d f11g² Dec 19] close-coupled gelding: fairly useful handicapper on all-weather, fair at best on turf: won at Wolverhampton in January: left B. Ellison 7,000 gns and off 8 months after fourth start: stays 1¾m: acts on all-weather, soft and good to firm going. *A. M. Hales*   **–**   **a84**

BETSEN (IRE) 4 b.g. Namid 128 – St Clair Star (Sallust 134) [2006 82: 7v 6g 5m 5f⁵ 5m 6m³ 5d⁵ 5.1g 5s 5m 5s Oct 24] rangy gelding: won maiden at Cork on debut in 2005: sold from D. Gillespie in Ireland after final 3-y-o outing: just fair form in handicaps in 2006: stays 6f: acts on firm going: sometimes tongue tied: sold 500 gns. sent to Denmark. *D. Nicholls*   **71**

BETTER OFF RED (USA) 2 b. or br.f. (Apr 29) Red Ransom (USA) – Unending Love (USA) (Dixieland Band (USA)) [2006 p6g 6g 6m Aug 11] $35,000Y: sturdy filly: half-sister to several winners in USA: dam unraced sister to US Grade 1 9f runner-up Rampart Road: little form in maidens. *B. J. Meehan*   **–**

BETTY OXO 2 b.f. (Apr 3) Mind Games 121 – Kildine (IRE) (Common Grounds 118) [2006 p6g⁴ Dec 23] third foal: dam French maiden who stayed 1¼m: 40/1, slowly away and soon behind when last in minor event at Wolverhampton. *B. P. J. Baugh*   **–**

BETWEEN FRIENDS 4 b.f. Slip Anchor 136 – Charisse Dancer 52 (Dancing Dissident (USA) 119) [2006 –: f8g Jan 3] little sign of ability: tried in cheekpieces. *A. Berry*   **–**

BEVERLEY BEAU 4 b.g. Inchinor 119 – Oriel Girl 65 (Beveled (USA)) [2006 61: p6g⁶ p6g⁶ p6g p6g² p5g⁴ p6g 6m³ p5g⁶ p5g⁶ 6m⁴ 6f* 5f⁴ 6m 5f² 5.2f⁶ 6f 5m 6m p5.1m p6g⁴ p6g p6g³ Dec 13] leggy gelding: modest performer, better on turf than all-weather: won claimer at Hamilton in June: stays 6f: acts on polytrack and firm going: tried in cheekpieces: none too consistent. *Mrs L. Stubbs*   **61**   **a55**

BEVERLEY BELL 3 b.f. Bertolini (USA) 125 – Lowrianna (IRE) 50 (Cyrano de Ber- –
gerac 120) [2006 p6g p6g 6d Apr 21] 21,000Y: leggy filly: sixth foal: half-sister to 3
winners, including useful 5f (at 2 yrs)/6f winner Simianna (by Bluegrass Prince) and 6f
to 7.5f winner Bodfari Anna (by Casteddu): dam 2-y-o 5f winner: well held in maidens:
tried in cheekpieces. *Miss J. A. Camacho*

BEVERLEY HILLS (IRE) 3 gr.f. Mozart (IRE) 131 – Attachment (USA) (Trempo- –
lino (USA) 135) [2006 –: 6m 5.9m Aug 7] close-coupled filly: no form in maidens/
handicap. *J. Howard Johnson*

BEVERLEY POLO (IRE) 3 br.c. Prince Sabo 123 – Justfortherecord (Forzando 122) –
[2006 61: 5v⁶ 7.5d 6g 5.9g f6g Jul 11] sturdy colt: well held after winning 5f maiden
at Newcastle on debut at 2 yrs: acts on good to soft going: blinkered last 3 starts.
M. W. Easterby

BEVERLY HILL BILLY 2 b.g. (Mar 3) Primo Valentino (IRE) 116 – Miss Beverley **82**
(Beveled (USA)) [2006 p7g⁵ p8g² 7.1m* p8g⁴ Oct 6] 8,000Y: leggy gelding: fifth foal:
half-brother to 2002 2-y-o 6f winner Night Games and 4-y-o Missed Turn (both by Mind
Games): dam unraced: fairly useful form: won maiden at Warwick in August: fourth to
Strobilus in nursery at Lingfield final start (gelded after): stays 1m. *A. King*

BEVIER 12 b.g. Nashwan (USA) 135 – Bevel (USA) (Mr Prospector (USA)) [2006 –: –
p12.2g May 8] of little account nowadays. *T. Wall*

BEWILDERING (IRE) 2 b.c. (May 2) Tagula (IRE) 116 – Mystic Belle (IRE) 88 **55 p**
(Thatching 131) [2006 p8.6s² Dec 13] €22,000F, €45,000Y: brother to 4-y-o Toldo and
half-brother to winner in Spain by Mukaddamah: dam 7f winner: 3/1, 5 lengths second
of 6 to Benny The Bat in maiden at Wolverhampton, running on late: will stay 1¼m+:
should improve. *E. J. O'Neill*

BE WISE GIRL 5 ch.m. Fleetwood (IRE) 107 – Zabelina (USA) 57 (Diesis 133) [2006 –
63: p12.2g Mar 25] workmanlike mare: modest handicapper: well held only outing
in 2006: stays 1½m: acts on polytrack, heavy and good to firm going: flashes tail.
A. W. Carroll

BEYOND BELIEF (IRE) 3 b.f. Sadler's Wells (USA) 132 – Adjriyna 82 (Top Ville –
129) [2006 –: 8s p12.2g Nov 6] €35,000Y: closely related to 1m/11f (latter in France)
winner Adjiram (by My Guest) and half-sister to 3 winners, including smart Irish
1m winner Adjareli (by Nishapour) and useful 1½m winner Adjawar (by Ashkalani):
dam 8.5f winner: little sign of ability, including in handicap at Wolverhampton. *Charles
O'Brien, Ireland*

BEYOND THE CLOUDS (IRE) 10 b.g. Midhish 109 – Tongabezi (IRE) 75 (Sher- **61**
nazar 131) [2006 76: 6g 5f 5g 5m⁴ 5f 5d 5m Aug 8] big gelding: modest handicapper
nowadays: mostly well held in 2006: best at 5f (all wins)/easy 6f: acts on firm and good
to soft going: tried in visor/cheekpieces: sometimes slowly away. *J. S. Wainwright*

BHUTAN (IRE) 11 b.g. Polish Patriot (USA) 128 – Bustinetta 89 (Bustino 136) [2006 **53**
p12g³ p10g⁵ p12.2g⁶ p12g 8m⁵ p12.2g 16.4f Jul 13] lengthy gelding: only modest nowadays: effective at 1¼m to 17.5f: acts on all-weather/any turf going: visored once: held up,
and often finds little. *J. J. Best*

BIANCA SFORZA 4 b.f. Anabaa (USA) 130 – Caterina Sforza (Machiavellian (USA) –
123) [2006 p8g Jun 28] second foal: half-sister to Italian 7.5f winner Beatrice d'Este (by
Mark of Esteem): dam Italian 9f winner who stayed 11f: fairly useful performer: won
maiden at Rome at 2 yrs: creditable efforts in listed races at Milan first 2 starts in 2005:
sold from E. Borromeo 3,000 gns in February, showed nothing on British debut (tongue
tied, said to have had breathing problem): stays 9f: acts on soft and good to firm going.
D. Shaw

BIBI HELEN 4 b.f. Robellino (USA) 127 – Tarry 65 (Salse (USA) 128) [2006 11.9m **45 §**
May 31] sturdy filly: temperamental maiden (twice bolted to post): dead. *W. M. Brisbourne*

BICOASTAL (USA) 2 ch.f. (Mar 9) Gone West (USA) – Ocean Queen (USA) (Zilzal **101**
(USA) 137) [2006 5m² 6d* 6m 7m² 8m⁵ Oct 1] $425,000Y: big, strong filly: sixth foal:
half-sister to 3 winners, including fairly useful 1¼m winner Sea Gift (by A P Indy): dam,
US Grade 3 9f winner, half-sister to Queen Mary/Fred Darling winner Dance Parade:
useful form: won maiden at Newmarket in May: off 2 months, much improved last 2
starts (blinkered), neck second of 10 to Sesmen in Prestige Stakes at Goodwood and 6½
lengths fifth of 13 to Finsceal Beo in Prix Marcel Boussac at Longchamp: stays 1m: yet
to race on extremes of going. *B. J. Meehan*

BIDABLE 2 b.f. (Apr 8) Auction House (USA) 120 – Dubitable 59 (Formidable (USA) **61**
125) [2006 6.1m³ 5.7m p7.1g⁵ p7.1g⁴ Nov 14] half-sister to winner up to 1¼m in Italy by
Merdon Melody: dam maiden who stayed 1½m: modest form in maidens: will stay 1m+:
acts on polytrack and good to soft ground. *B. Palling*

BIDDERS ITCH 2 b.f. (Feb 9) Auction House (USA) 120 – Sharp Ego (USA) (Shar- **–**
pen Up 127) [2006 6v 5m 5m⁶ 6s⁵ Aug 19] close-coupled filly: half-sister to several
winners, including fairly useful 6f winner Ego Night (by Night Shift): dam Irish 5f
winner: last all starts. *A. Berry*

BID FOR FAME (USA) 9 b. or br.g. Quest For Fame 127 – Shroud (USA) (Vaguely **73**
Noble 140) [2006 71: f16g* p12.2g* p13.9g Mar 6] leggy, lengthy gelding: fair handicapper: won at Southwell and Wolverhampton on consecutive days in February: unseated
rider final outing: effective at 1½m to 16.5f: acts on all-weather and firm going: tried
blinkered/in cheekpieces earlier in career. *J. Pearce*

BID FOR GLORY 2 ch.c. (Jan 24) Auction House (USA) 120 – Woodland Steps 86 **90**
(Bold Owl 101) [2006 6m* 7m² 8m³ 8s⁴ Oct 16] 17,000Y: close-coupled, good-topped
colt: has a quick action: half-brother to several winners by Merdon Melody, including
5f (at 2 yrs) to 6.8f winner Blackpool Mamma's and 1¼m winner Platinum Pirate: dam,
2-y-o 7f winner, sister to useful sprinter Amron: fairly useful form: won maiden at
Newmarket in July: improvement after, placed in 2 nurseries and 7¼ lengths fourth to
Sweet Lilly in listed race at Pontefract: stays 1m: acts on soft and good to firm going.
H. J. Collingridge

BID FOR GOLD 2 b.c. (Apr 30) Auction House (USA) 120 – Gold And Blue (IRE) **78**
(Bluebird (USA) 125) [2006 6m 5g4 5m⁵ 5f⁴ 6m³ 6s Oct 6] 26,000Y: compact colt: half-
brother to several winners, including 6f (at 2 yrs) to 9f winner Blue Star (by Whittingham) and 4-y-o Westbrook Blue: dam lightly-raced Irish maiden: fair maiden: in frame 3
times, including nursery: will prove best kept to 5f/6f: acts on firm ground. *Jedd O'Keeffe*

BIENHEUREUX 5 b.g. Bien Bien (USA) 125 – Rochea 67 (Rock City 120) [2006 71: **71**
p10g⁵ 11g⁵ f12g* 10g p12g* 11.8g⁵ p12g² p13.9m³ p13.9g p12.2g⁵ f11g⁵ p12g f14g³
f12g⁶ Dec 27] workmanlike gelding: fair handicapper: won at Southwell (hung right)
in July and Kempton in August: effective at 1½m to 2m: acts on all-weather and good
to firm going: tried in cheekpieces (below form), often visored/tongue tied. *Miss Gay
Kelleway*

BIG BAD BILL (IRE) 6 gr.g. Entrepreneur 123 – Chamonis (USA) 101 (Affirmed **–**
(USA)) [2006 f12g May 2] well held in claimer on Flat debut. *P. T. Midgley*

BIG BRADFORD 5 b.g. Tamure (IRE) 125 – Heather Honey (Insan (USA) 119) [2006 **60 §**
78: 7m 7.1m 10m 6m⁶ 6g 6.9f⁴ 7m 8.5m Sep 13] sturdy gelding: has a quick, fluent
action: modest performer nowadays: claimed from W. Muir after third outing: best at
6f/7f: acts on polytrack, firm and good to soft going: often wears headgear: ungenuine.
R. A. Fahey

BIGGIN HILL (IRE) 3 b.c. Alzao (USA) 117 – Fire of London 78 (Shirley Heights **58**
130) [2006 9.9g 8.1m 10.5g Sep 22] smallish, sturdy colt: seemingly amiss on debut:
backward, modest form when ninth in maiden at Warwick next time: well held in seller at
Haydock final outing: should be suited by 1¼m+: tongue tied last 2 starts: sold 800 gns.
H. R. A. Cecil

BIG HASSLE (IRE) 4 b.c. Namid 128 – Night After Night (Night Shift (USA)) [2006 **79**
6v 5d Apr 21] big, strong colt: fairly useful winner at 2 yrs: missed 2005: much better
effort in 2006 (bled on reappearance) when eighth in handicap at Thirsk: should stay 6f.
D. Nicholls

BIG MOMENT 8 ch.g. Be My Guest (USA) 126 – Petralona (USA) (Alleged (USA) **89**
138) [2006 104d: 18.7m 11.6d⁶ Nov 4] leggy, good-topped gelding: has a short, round
action: just fairly useful form in handicaps in 2006: stays 18.7f: acts on firm and soft
going: tried in cheekpieces: held up, and usually travels strongly. *Mrs A. J. Perrett*

BIG MYSTERY (IRE) 5 b.m. Grand Lodge (USA) 125 – Mysterious Plans (IRE) **48**
(Last Tycoon 131) [2006 53: p8g⁵ p7g Feb 13] poor performer: stays 9.5f: acts on polytrack: blinkered in 2006. *S. C. Williams*

BIG PLAYER 2 b.c. (Mar 22) Noverre (USA) 125 – Maxizone (FR) (Linamix (FR) **77**
127) [2006 7d* 8g⁵ a6.8g* Dec 3] 15,000Y: lengthy, good-topped colt: third foal: dam
unraced out of half-sister to Prix Jacques le Marois winner Miss Satamixa: fair form: won
maiden at Folkestone in August and (after sold from W. Haggas 22,000 gns) minor event
at Taby in December: raced freely when fifth in nursery at Yarmouth in between: probably stays 1m. *B. Bo, Sweden*

BIG RALPH 3 ch.g. Mark of Esteem (IRE) 137 – Wish Me Luck (IRE) 100 (Lycius **52**
(USA) 124) [2006 p7.1g Dec 21] €10,000Y: third foal: half-brother to 2002 2-y-o 6f
winner Evelyn One (by Alhaarth) and 2003 2-y-o 6f winner Desert Grass (by Green
Desert), both fairly useful in Ireland: dam, Irish 2-y-o 6f winner, half-sister to useful 7f/
1m winner Sir Effendi: behind in bumper in November: seventh of 10 in maiden at
Wolverhampton following month. *M. Wigham*

BIG ROBERT 2 b.c. (Feb 27) Medicean 128 – Top Flight Queen 82 (Mark of Esteem **106 p**
(IRE) 137) [2006 7g² 7.1g* 8m² 7d⁵ Sep 29] 25,000Y: close-coupled colt: second foal:
dam, 1¼m winner, half-sister to smart 1¼m to 1½m winner Sacrament: useful form: won
maiden at Sandown in August: improved efforts when 1¼ lengths second to Caldra in
listed race at Goodwood and 3¼ lengths fifth (not clear run) to Thousand Words in Somerville Tattersall Stakes at Newmarket: should do better still over 1¼m/1½m. *W. R. Muir*

BIG SMOKE (IRE) 6 gr.g. Perugino (USA) 84 – Lightning Bug (Prince Bee 128) **–**
[2006 –: p12g p11g Nov 6] rather leggy gelding: lightly raced and no form since 2004:
tried in blinkers/cheekpieces/tongue tied: none too genuine. *J. C. Tuck*

BIG TIMER (USA) 2 ch.g. (Feb 25) Street Cry (IRE) 130 – Moonflute (USA) 82 (The **104**
Minstrel (CAN) 135) [2006 6f* 6g* 7d* a8f Oct 14] $15,000Y: tall, close-coupled, good-
topped gelding: half-brother to numerous minor winners in USA: dam 2-y-o 6f winner:
useful form: unbeaten first 3 starts, namely maiden at Ayr in July, and minor event at
Ripon and Symphony Group Acomb Stakes at York (beat Gweebarra by 2½ lengths) in
August: tailed-off last of 10 behind Scat Daddy in Champagne Stakes at Belmont on dirt
debut final start: bred to stay 1m, but free-going sort. *I. Semple*

Mr David McKenzie's "Big Timer"

BIJLI (IRE) 3 gr.g. Key of Luck (USA) 126 – More Magnanimous (King Persian 107) **70**
[2006 –: 7s 6f³ 6f³ f6g² Jul 11] good-bodied gelding: fair maiden, lightly raced: probably
stays 7f: acts on fibresand, firm and soft going: sold 6,000 gns later in July. *J. Noseda*

BIJOU DAN 5 ch.g. Bijou d'Inde 127 – Cal Norma's Lady (IRE) 87 (Lyphard's Special **64**
(USA) 122) [2006 60, a72: p9.5g⁶ p8.6g⁵ f7g* f7g⁶ p8.6g p8.6g p8.6g² p8.6g* 8v³ f7g⁴ **a77**
p8.6g* p8.6g* p8.6g 9.1m² 7.2g³ p8.6g 9.2g p8.6g⁵ p8.6g p8.6g p8.6g⁶ Dec 18] angular,
close-coupled gelding: fair on all-weather, modest on turf: won sellers at Southwell in
February and (having left I. Semple after fifth start) Wolverhampton in April, and handicaps at Wolverhampton in June/July: stays 9.5f: acts on all-weather, good to firm and
good to soft going: wears headgear. *W. G. Harrison*

BIJOUTERIE 2 ch.f. (Mar 5) Tobougg (IRE) 125 – Branston Gem 59 (So Factual **64**
(USA) 120) [2006 5.1m³ 5g May 29] 11,000Y: lengthy filly: second foal: half-sister to
3-y-o The Terrier: dam, maiden best at 5f at 2 yrs, out of half-sister to very smart 1m/
1¼m performer Desert Deer and smart 6f/7f performer Branston Abby: good speed when
2¼ lengths third in maiden at Nottingham: awkward in and from stalls other start.
G. A. Swinbank

BILLANROY (IRE) 3 ch.g. Inchinor 119 – Charm The Stars (Roi Danzig (USA)) **–**
[2006 62: 10g 10m 14m Jun 16] strong, workmanlike gelding: maiden: well held, including in handicaps, in 2006: blinkered final start: gelded after. *M. H. Tompkins*

BILL BENNETT (FR) 5 b.g. Bishop of Cashel 122 – Concert (Polar Falcon (USA) **70 §**
126) [2006 62, a58: f16g⁶ f12g* f11g 10.9s 12d* 14.1d⁵ 15.8g 14s⁶ 10d 13.9s 15d⁵ 12s **a58 §**
f14g⁶ Nov 21] small, stocky gelding: fair on turf, modest on all-weather: won banded race
at Southwell in February and apprentice handicap at Folkestone in April: stays 2m: acts
on all-weather and soft going, probably on firm: blinkered/tongue tied once at 2 yrs:
inconsistent and not one to trust. *J. Jay*

BILLICH 3 ch.c. Observatory 131 – Pomponette (USA) (Rahy (USA) 115) **90**
[2006 79: p9.5g² p9.5g³ 11.5f* p12g⁶ 12d 11.8f³ 10.2f⁴ 12f p16g⁴ p16.5g* p16.5g*
p16.5g⁴ Dec 9] good-topped colt: fairly useful performer: won maiden at Yarmouth in
July and handicaps at Wolverhampton (2) in November: stays easy 2m: acts on polytrack
and firm ground: has been mulish at start/run in snatches: withdrawn at start third
intended outing. *E. J. O'Neill*

BILLY BATHWICK (IRE) 9 ch.g. Fayruz 116 – Cut It Fine (USA) (Big Spruce **45**
(USA) [2006 10m 8m 10.2m 10.2m⁴ Sep 1] smallish, close-coupled gelding: poor
handicapper: stays easy 1½m: acts on firm and soft going: tried blinkered/in cheekpieces.
J. M. Bradley

BILLY BLING (IRE) 3 b.g. Enrique 121 – Shewillifshewants (IRE) (Alzao (USA) **57**
117) [2006 70: p6g⁶ p5g³ p6g⁴ p6g* 5.7d 7.1d⁶ 6g May 18] fair performer on all-weather, **a68**
modest on turf: won handicap at Lingfield in April: bred to stay beyond 6f: acts on
polytrack, probably on good to soft going: sold 1,800 gns in October, sent to Sweden.
R. Hannon

BILLY DANE (IRE) 2 b.g. (Apr 16) Fayruz 116 – Lomalou (IRE) (Lightning Dealer **92**
103) [2006 6d⁶ 7.5f² 7m² p7.1f* 6s p7.1g⁴ Oct 8] €26,000F, 30,000Y: strong, lengthy
gelding: fourth foal: half-brother to 6f winner Mr Hullabalou and 4-y-o Princely Vale
(both by Princely Heir): dam unraced: fairly useful performer: won nursery at Wolverhampton in August: good fourth (after trouble) in nursery there final start: stays 7.5f: acts
on polytrack and firm going: has looked tricky ride: sold 52,000 gns. *B. J. Meehan*

BILLY ONE PUNCH 4 b.g. Mark of Esteem (IRE) 137 – Polytess (IRE) (Polish **76**
Patriot (USA) 128) [2006 68: 7d 7m 6g 8.3g⁵ 9.7f* 10f² 10.3m² 8.9f* 8.3g 9.7m⁴ 10f⁶
10.1s Oct 10] strong, good-bodied gelding: fair handicapper: won at Folkestone in June
and York in July: stays 10.3f: acts on firm and soft going. *G. G. Margarson*

BILLY RED 2 ch.g. (Feb 23) Dr Fong (USA) 128 – Liberty Bound 85 (Primo Dominie **72**
121) [2006 5g⁴ 5f p6g⁴ 5.2g 6m⁴ p6g³ p5g⁵ Nov 9] 21,000Y: lengthy gelding: first foal:
dam, 5f winner, half-sister to 5-y-o Majestic Missile: fair maiden: in frame 4 times: will
prove best kept to 5f/6f: acts on polytrack and good to firm going: tried visored: sometimes looks ungenuine (hung left final start). *J. R. Jenkins*

BILLY RUFFIAN 2 ch.g. (Apr 28) Kyllachy 129 – Antonia's Folly 64 (Music Boy **69**
124) [2006 5g p6g⁶ 5d⁵ 6v⁵ p5.1g* f5g⁵ p6g³ Dec 28] 20,000Y: half-brother to several
winning sprinters, including 6-y-o Coranglais: dam 2-y-o 5f winner: fair performer: won
nursery at Wolverhampton in December by 2 lengths from Kilvickeon: stays easy 6f: acts
on polytrack. *T. D. Easterby*

134

BILLY'S BROTHER 4 ch.g. Wolfhound (USA) 126 – Chili Lass (Chilibang 120) – [2006 –: p9.5g Jan 23] no form: blinkered final outing. *M. A. Buckley*

BILLY WIZZ (IRE) 3 b.g. Namid 128 – Mareha (IRE) 95 (Cadeaux Genereux 131) **48** [2006 p6g p6g p5g⁶ p8g p7.1g Apr 22] poor maiden: visored (well held) last 2 starts. *A. M. Balding*

BINANTI 6 b.g. Bin Ajwaad (IRE) 119 – Princess Rosananti (IRE) (Shareef Dancer **95** (USA) 135) [2006 95: p8.6g p7g p7g* p7g³ p8g³ 8.1m 7.1d² 7s³ 8m 7m³ 7g³ 7m 7m 8m³ 7d 7.1g² p8g 7m Sep 9] smallish, useful-looking gelding: useful handicapper: won at Kempton (by head from Tanforan) in March: at least creditable efforts when placed after: stays 8.6f: acts on all-weather, firm and soft going: effective blinkered/visored or not: consistent. *P. R. Chamings*

BINGO ONE (IRE) 3 b.f. Mujahid (USA) 125 – Barque Bleue (USA) (Steinlen 127) [2006 65: 6g 8d Aug 28] fair performer at 2 yrs: off 11 months, well below best in 2006: stays 6f: raced only on good/good to soft going: refused to enter stall intended final outing in September. *W. J. H. Ratcliffe*

BINIOU (IRE) 3 b.c. Mozart (IRE) 131 – Cap Coz (IRE) 110 (Indian Ridge 123) [2006 **118** 6g² 5g³ 5m 6.5g³ 7d⁴ 6g⁴ 5d* 6.5g 7g⁶ 5m³ 5m⁴ Oct 1] leggy colt: second foal: dam, French 2-y-o 5.5f and 7f winner, half-sister to smart performer up to 1m Josr Algarhoud and smart French 5f performer Sainte Marine: smart performer: won minor event at Vichy at 2 yrs: improved in 2006, winning listed race at Deauville in August by ½ length from Abundance: in frame at Longchamp in Prix du Petit Couvert (1¾ lengths third to Majestic Missile) and Prix de l'Abbaye (best effort, 2 lengths fourth to Desert Lord) last 2 starts, finishing well both times: best at 5f/6f: acts on good to firm and good to soft ground: sold €180,000 on eve of final outing: has joined R. Cowell. *R. Collet, France*

BINNION BAY (IRE) 5 b.g. Fasliyev (USA) 120 – Literary 79 (Woodman (USA) **61** 126) [2006 58: f7g⁶ p6g p7g p7g² p6g p7g* p7g* p7g Dec 18] tall, useful-looking gelding: modest performer: blinkered, won banded races at Kempton (wandered) and Lingfield in December: effective at 5f to easy 1m: acts on all-weather, good to firm and good to soft going: usually wears headgear. *J. J. Bridger*

BINOCULAR 2 ch.c. (Feb 19) Observatory (USA) 131 – Well Beyond (IRE) 101 **72 p** (Don't Forget Me 127) [2006 6m⁴ Sep 22] angular colt: half-brother to several winners, including 6f (at 2 yrs) to 8.5f (US Grade 3 event) winner Out of Reach and 1996 2-y-o 6f winner who stayed 7f Well Warned (both useful, by Warning): dam 5f (at 2 yrs) to 1m winner out of sister to dam of Zafonic: 7/1, fit but green when 4¼ lengths fourth to Longquan in maiden at Haydock: will stay 1m: will do better. *B. W. Hills*

BIN RAHY (IRE) 3 ch.c. Rahy (USA) 115 – Belle Genius (USA) 111 (Beau Genius **88** (CAN)) [2006 72p: p10g⁶ 8d² 8.1d* 8.1s⁴ 10.4m⁴ 10m 10m² 10.3m² Aug 25] strong, lengthy colt: type to carry plenty of condition: fairly useful handicapper: won at Chepstow in May: stays 10.4f: acts on polytrack, firm and good to soft going: made running last 2 starts: consistent: joined D. Selvaratnam in UAE. *M. R. Channon*

BINT IL SULTAN (IRE) 4 b.f. Xaar 132 – Knight's Place (IRE) 72 (Hamas (IRE) **46 d** 125§) [2006 53: 12m² 9.9f⁵ 12g 11s 11.7m⁶ 10f⁶ Sep 18] poor maiden: stays 1½m: acts on good to firm going: on downgrade. *W. M. Brisbourne*

BINT ROYAL (IRE) 8 ch.m. Royal Abjar (USA) 121 – Living Legend (USA) **54** (Septieme Ciel (USA) 123) [2006 64, a48: p6g f8g p7.1g⁶ p7.1g 7f 5f 5.9m 7.2g Jun 23] **a50** close-coupled, workmanlike mare: modest handicapper: finds 5f barely adequate, stays 1m: acts on all-weather, firm and good to soft going: tried in headgear, often visored: none too reliable. *Miss V. Haigh*

BINTY 4 b.f. Prince Sabo 123 – Mistral's Dancer (Shareef Dancer (USA) 135) [2006 57: p5.1g 6.1f 5m 6f 7m p6g Oct 23] close-coupled filly: modest performer in 2005: no form in 2006. *A. J. Chamberlain*

BIRBALINI 3 b.f. Bertolini (USA) 125 – La Birba (IRE) 44 (Prince of Birds (USA) 121) [2006 p8.6g p8g 8m⁶ 12g Aug 18] 900 2-y-o: first foal: dam, maiden, form only at 6f at 2 yrs: no form. *P. J. McBride*

BIRDIE BIRDIE 2 b.f. (Mar 19) Superior Premium 122 – Cautious Joe 73 (First **51** Trump 118) [2006 5m⁶ 6d³ 6s² 5m Sep 11] 800Y: strong filly: second foal: sister to 2005 2-y-o 5f/6f winner Magnolia Blossom: dam 5f (at 2 yrs) and 1m winner: modest maiden: placed in sellers: bit slipped final start: stays 6f. *R. A. Fahey*

BIRD OVER 4 b.f. Bold Edge 123 – High Bird (IRE) (Polar Falcon (USA) 126) [2006 **92** 89: 6g³ p6g* 6d 6f 6g 6g Jul 28] sparely-made filly: fairly useful handicapper: won at

Kempton in May: well below form after: stays 6f: acts on all-weather, good to firm and good to soft going. *R. M. Beckett*

BIRDWATCH 8 b.g. Minshaanshu Amad (USA) 91§ – Eider 80 (Niniski (USA) 125) – [2006 –: f14g Apr 10] little form on Flat: fair hurdler. *K. G. Reveley*

BIRKSIDE 3 ch.g. Spinning World (USA) 130 – Bright Hope (IRE) 84 (Danehill (USA) **86** 126) [2006 63: 8.3g² p8.6f⁶ 10.5g⁵ 8d p10g² Nov 11] lengthy, well-made gelding: fairly useful performer: best effort on final start: barely stays 10.5f: acts on polytrack, raced only on good/good to soft going on turf: tongue tied last 2 outings: joined B. Powell. *W. R. Swinburn*

BIRKSPIEL (GER) 5 b.h. Singspiel (IRE) 133 – Beaute (GER) (Lord Udo (GER)) **112** [2006 109: 11s* 12s³ 12d 12d Sep 24] angular horse: half-brother to several winners in Germany, notably very smart 10.5f to 1½m (including Deutsches Derby) winner Belenus (by Lomitas): dam German 7f/1m winner: smart performer: good efforts in 2005 when fourth to Collier Hill in Gerling-Preis at Cologne and neck second to Saldentigerin in Baden-Wurttemberg Trophy at Baden-Baden: left A. Wohler in Germany, won Grosser Preis der Bremer Wirtschaft at Bremen in April by 2½ lengths from Bailamos: ran as if amiss in listed event/Cumberland Lodge Stakes at Ascot last 2 outings: stays 1½m: acts on heavy going: has worn crossed noseband. *S. Dow*

BIRTHDAY STAR (IRE) 4 b.g. Desert King (IRE) 129 – White Paper (IRE) (Marig- **57** nan (USA) 117) [2006 60, a65: p10g p10g³ p12g p12g⁶ p12.2g* 14.1d p12g² p12.2g⁵ **a68** p12g p12.2g⁵ p12g³ p12.2g² 12d⁵ Oct 2] close-coupled gelding: fair handicapper on all-weather, modest on turf: landed gamble at Wolverhampton in March: stays 1½m: acts on polytrack, good to firm and good to soft ground: blinkered (raced freely) final start at 3 yrs. *W. J. Musson*

BISAAT (USA) 3 b.f. Bahri (USA) 125 – Tabrir (IRE) (Unfuwain (USA) 131) [2006 – 10.2m Sep 25] 11,000 2-y-o: first foal: dam unraced sister to 1000 Guineas winner Lahan: 66/1, always behind in maiden at Bath, flashing tail. *M. S. Saunders*

BISH BASHER (IRE) 2 ch.g. (Mar 11) Zilzal (USA) 137 – Gentle Dame 75 (Kris – 135) [2006 10.2m p8.6g Nov 7] behind in maidens. *P. A. Blockley*

BISHOP AUCKLAND (IRE) 2 b.g. (Mar 22) Docksider (USA) 124 – Chancel – (USA) 60 (Al Nasr (FR) 126) [2006 7s 8d Nov 3] well held in maidens. *Mrs A. Duffield*

BISHOPS FINGER 6 b.g. Bishop of Cashel 122 – Bit of A Tart (Distant Relative 128) **64** [2006 55, a69: p10g* p10g³ p10g p10g⁴ p8g p10g p10g 10m* p10g 10m 9g³ p10g² **a69** Sep 27] fair performer: all 6 wins at Lingfield, including in claimer in January and seller in July: stays 1¼m: acts on all-weather and good to soft going: has worn visor, blinkered nowadays: sometimes slowly away: none too genuine. *Jamie Poulton*

BITTER CHILL 3 b.c. Agnes World (USA) 123 – Azula 80 (Bluebird (USA) 125) – [2006 78, a65: 8m f6g⁶ 6g Aug 23] sturdy, compact colt: third in maiden at Newbury on debut as 2 yrs: mostly well held since. *H. Morrison*

BJORLING 5 ch.g. Opening Verse (USA) 126 – Pola Star (IRE) (Un Desperado (FR) – 125) [2006 –: f7g Jan 24] little sign of ability: tried in cheekpieces/tongue tie. *M. J. Gingell*

BLACK BEAUTY 3 br.c. Diktat 126 – Euridice (IRE) 66 (Woodman (USA) 126) **85** [2006 –: p8g⁶ p7g³ 9.7s⁴ 9.7m* 8.5g* 11m⁴ 10m² 9.7f² 10m⁴ 9.9g 10m⁵ 8d⁴ Sep 26] fairly useful handicapper: won at Folkestone in April and Beverley in May: barely stays 11f: acts on polytrack, firm and soft going: sold 70,000 gns. *M. G. Quinlan*

BLACK CHARMER (IRE) 3 b.c. Black Minnaloushe (USA) 123 – Abla (Robellino (USA) 127) [2006 106: 7.1m⁶ 7.1s⁶ 6d p7g Oct 26] good-bodied colt: useful performer at 2 yrs: off 13 months (reportedly cracked a cannon bone and suffered an abscess): well held form in 2006: bred to stay at least 1m: acts on firm and soft going: makes running. *M. Johnston*

BLACK CHIEF (SWE) 5 br.g. Be My Chief (USA) 122 – La Creole (USA) (Best – Turn (USA)) [2006 p8g 10f 11.6g Aug 14] winner 3 times at Taby in 2004: lightly raced since and well held in 3 handicaps (tongue tied) in Britain: stays 1¼m: acts on dirt: usually blinkered/visored. *R. A. Kvisla*

BLACKCOMB MOUNTAIN (USA) 4 b. or br.f. Royal Anthem (USA) 135 – Ski – Racer (FR) (Ski Chief (USA) 115) [2006 16.2m⁶ Jul 2] leggy filly: fair maiden at 2 yrs: missed 2005, and tailed off on return. *M. F. Harris*

BLACK FALCON (IRE) 6 ch.g. In The Wings 128 – Muwasim (USA) (Meadowlake (USA)) [2006 80, a87: p9.5g p8.6g p9.5g f8g³ Dec 27] rather leggy, quite attractive gelding: fairly useful handicapper: stays 10.5f: acts on polytrack and firm going: well beaten only try in visor: sometimes slowly away: often looks ungenuine. *P. T. Midgley*   **80 §**

BLACKHEATH (IRE) 10 ch.g. Common Grounds 118 – Queen Caroline (USA) 67 (Chief's Crown (USA)) [2006 81: p6g⁶ 5d 5m 6d² 6d³ 6f⁴ 6m* 5m⁴ 5f 5g³ 6m 5d² 5m Sep 21] barrel-shaped gelding: type to carry condition: fluent mover: fairly useful handicapper: won at York (raced alone stand rail) in June: best at 5f/6f: acts on firm and good to soft going, probably on soft: tried blinkered/tongue tied: often early to post: sometimes reluctant to enter stall: usually travels strongly. *D. Nicholls*   **83**

BLACK JADE 3 b.c. Averti (IRE) 117 – Rivermead (USA) (Irish River (FR) 131) [2006 53: 6g⁶ p6g May 8] compact colt: maiden: below form in 2006, including in cheekpieces: raced at 5f/6f. *M. A. Jarvis*   **53**

BLACKMAIL (USA) 8 b.g. Twining (USA) 120 – Black Penny (USA) (Private Account (USA)) [2006 73: p13g³ p10g⁶ p16g p13g² p12g p13g p10g 11.9g⁴ 10m 11.9m⁴ 12g⁶ 10.1g* 12m⁴ 11.9f³ p8g⁶ 10g 11.9m 16d p10g² p12g p12g p10g* Dec 20] sturdy gelding: fair handicapper: won apprentice event at Epsom in July and, having left Miss B. Sanders after fifteenth outing, claimer at Lingfield in December: probably best at 1¼m to easy 1¾m: acts on polytrack, firm and good to soft going: tried tongue tied/visored, usually blinkered (not last 4 starts): finished lame thirteenth start: patiently ridden. *P. Mitchell*   **69**

BLACK MOGUL 2 b.g. (May 3) Robellino (USA) 127 – Brilliance 74 (Cadeaux Genereux 131) [2006 6g⁵ 6g Aug 25] well held in maidens, then gelded. *W. R. Muir*   **–**

BLACK MOMA (IRE) 2 b.f. (Mar 31) Averti (IRE) 117 – Sareb (FR) (Indian Ridge 123) [2006 5m⁴ 5f* 5g² 5g* 5m² Sep 11] 10,500Y: close-coupled, attractive filly: second foal: dam, ran once, out of useful winner up to 7.5f Prends Ca: fair performer: won maiden at Leicester in July and nursery at Sandown in August: also second in nurseries at Newmarket and Folkestone: speedy, raced at 5f on good ground or firmer. *R. Hannon*   **76**

BLACK OVAL 5 b.m. Royal Applause 124 – Corniche Quest (IRE) 74 (Salt Dome (USA)) [2006 58§, a42§: 5m⁵ 6m 6f³ 6d 6m 5m 5g 5d⁴ p6g² p6g² p7g⁴ Dec 30] quite good-topped mare: modest performer: effective at 5f to 7f: acts on polytrack, firm and good to soft ground: tried visored: ungenuine. *S. Parr*   **63 §**

BLACK ROCK (IRE) 2 ch.c. (May 20) Rock of Gibraltar (IRE) 133 – Biraya (Valiyar 129) [2006 6d⁴ p7g² Sep 2] €410,000Y: strong, good-topped colt: powerful galloper with a long stride: closely related to fairly useful Irish 2003 2-y-o 6f/7f winner Maroochydore (by Danehill) and half-brother to several winners, including smart Hong Kong winner up to 9f Bowman's Crossing (by Dolphin Street), also 7f winner at 2 yrs in Ireland: dam unraced: promising fourth in maiden at York and second in minor event at Kempton (short-headed by Water Mill): will stay 1m: useful prospect, sure to win races. *M. A. Jarvis*   **91 p**

BLACK SEA PEARL 3 b. or br.f. Diktat 126 – Made of Pearl (USA) 107 (Nureyev (USA) 131) [2006 65: 7.1s 8m⁴ p9.5g 6d* p7g p7.1g² p7.1s³ f8g⁴ Dec 21] fair handicapper: won at Yarmouth in October: stays 1m: acts on all-weather, good to firm and good to soft going. *P. W. D'Arcy*   **72**

BLACKTOFT (USA) 3 b. or br.g. Theatrical 128 – Black Truffle (USA) (Mt Livermore (USA)) [2006 –: p8.6g³ f8g³ 10m 8.5g³ 8m⁴ 8.3m⁴ 9m⁵ p7g⁶ 7.1m p9.5m⁴ p10g* p11g³ p12g² Dec 5] big, unfurnished gelding: fair handicapper: left E. Dunlop after sixth start: won at Lingfield in October: stays 1½m: raced only on all-weather and good/good to firm going. *S. C. Williams*   **78**

BLACKWATER STREAM (IRE) 2 b.c. (Jan 5) Shinko Forest (IRE) – Lady Eberspacher (IRE) 68 (Royal Abjar (USA) 121) [2006 6g 6f 5m³ 6d 6.1g 7.1d⁵ Oct 13] 2,800Y: good-bodied colt: second foal: half-brother to 3-y-o Indian Lady: dam, sprint maiden, half-sister to useful performer up to 1m Voile: modest maiden on balance: well held in nurseries: should stay 7f: acts on firm ground: sold 5,500 gns. *Mrs P. N. Dutfield*   **63 +**

BLADES GIRL 3 ch.f. Bertolini (USA) 125 – Banningham Blade 94 (Sure Blade (USA) 130) [2006 84: 7.1m 7m³ 7m³ 7f⁶ 7.1m² 7m* 7d⁵ Sep 24] big, leggy filly: has a fluent action: useful handicapper: won at Southwell in September by 4 lengths from Mobsir, dictating: respectable fifth to Makderah in listed race at Ascot final outing: stays 7f: acts on firm and good to soft going: usually wears cheekpieces: has been blanketed for stall entry (refused to enter once): game. *K. A. Ryan*   **100**

BLAENAVON 4 b.f. Cadeaux Genereux 131 – One of The Family 73 (Alzao (USA) **43**
117) [2006 57: p10g⁶ p10g p8g Feb 13] poor maiden: stays 1¼m: raced mostly on polytrack. *D. W. P. Arbuthnot*

BLAISE HOLLOW (USA) 4 b.g. Woodman (USA) 126 – Castellina (USA) (Danzig –
Connection (USA)) [2006 96: 10.4d 10g 10s⁶ 11g 12d Sep 30] well-made gelding: useful
handicapper at 3 yrs: well held in 2006: has worn crossed noseband: sold 20,000 gns,
joined J. McConnell in Ireland. *R. Charlton*

BLAKE HALL LAD (IRE) 5 b.g. Cape Cross (IRE) 129 – Queen of Art (IRE) 74 –
(Royal Academy (USA) 130) [2006 54d: p10g Jan 7] lengthy, plain gelding: no form
since early in 2005: tried blinkered/tongue tied. *P. S. McEntee*

BLAKESHALL BOY 8 b.g. Piccolo 121 – Giggleswick Girl 67 (Full Extent (USA) –
113) [2006 –: p7g Dec 30] rather leggy, quite attractive gelding: handicapper: lightly
raced and little show after 2003: tried visored. *A. J. Chamberlain*

BLAKESHALL HOPE 4 ch.g. Piccolo 121 – Elite Hope (USA) 84 (Moment of Hope **49**
(USA)) [2006 56: p9.5g⁶ Nov 20] smallish, workmanlike gelding: modest maiden: stays
8.6f: acts on polytrack and good to firm going: tried visored. *A. J. Chamberlain*

BLAKESHALL QUEST 6 b.m. Piccolo 121 – Corniche Quest (IRE) 74 (Salt Dome **61**
(USA)) [2006 52, a58: f6g f6g² f6g* f6g f6s f5g f6g* 5.1d⁴ 5.5g⁵ p5.1g³ p5g² p7g f6g³
p6g f6g² f6g⁴ f6g* Dec 12] compact mare: modest performer: won banded race in
February, claimer in April and banded race in December, all at Southwell: effective at 5f
to easy 7f: acts on all-weather and good to soft going: visored/blinkered: races up with
pace: none too reliable. *R. Brotherton*

BLAKESHALL ROSE 2 b.f. (Mar 12) Tobougg (IRE) 125 – Giggleswick Girl 67 **38**
(Full Extent (USA) 113) [2006 5.1g p5.1g⁴ 6.1g 5m f6g p5.1g⁵ p7.1g Nov 24] angular
filly: sixth foal: half-sister to fairly useful 5f winner (including at 2 yrs) Blakeshall Boy
(by Piccolo) and 5f (at 2 yrs) to 1m winner Beauty of Dreams (by Russian Revival): dam
5f/6f winner (latter at 2 yrs): poor maiden. *A. J. Chamberlain*

BLANC VISAGE 3 b.g. Tomba 119 – Trinity Hall 67 (Hallgate 127) [2006 p9.5g⁵ **67 d**
p8.6g⁶ p8.6g² f7g⁵ p8.6g² p9.5g p8.6g⁶ p12.2g p12.2g p9.5g p13.9g p10g Dec 8] fair
maiden at best: stays easy 1½m: usually races prominently. *Mrs H. Sweeting*

BLANDFORD FLYER 3 b.g. Soviet Star (USA) 128 – Vento Del Oreno (FR) 67 –
(Lando (GER) 128) [2006 65?: 8.2m 8d p10g Oct 15] smallish, well-made gelding:
fifth in maiden at Lingfield at 2 yrs: well held in handicaps since: should stay 1m.
W. R. Swinburn

BLAZING HEIGHTS 3 b.g. Compton Place 125 – Harrken Heights (IRE) (Belmez **87**
(USA) 131) [2006 74: 5d⁵ 5g² 5g⁴ 5m² 5g² 5.1f² 6f⁶ 5d⁴ 5.1m 5d 5s⁴ 5d* Nov 3] unfurnished gelding: fairly useful handicapper: won at Musselburgh (ridden more prominently
than usual) in November: will prove best at 5f/6f: acts on firm and soft going: sometimes
slowly away. *J. S. Goldie*

BLEND 3 b.f. Zafonic (USA) 130 – Bonash 110 (Rainbow Quest (USA) 134) [2006 10d⁵ **73**
10.2g³ p12g³ Nov 9] fifth living foal: sister to useful 1998 2-y-o 7f winner Bionic and
half-sister to 5-y-o Day Flight: dam, French 1m (Prix d'Aumale at 2 yrs) to 1½m (Prix de
Malleret) winner: fair form in maidens, best effort when 5-length third to Shout at Lingfield final start, finding little: stud. *J. H. M. Gosden*

BLESSED PLACE 6 ch.g. Compton Place 125 – Cathedra (So Blessed 130) [2006 68: **77**
6g 5m³ 5.2m 5.7m² 6g⁴ p6g* 5m³ p6g² 5m* 5m⁵ 5.2d³ 5g³ 5m³ 5.7m p5.1g⁴ p6g³ p5.1g **a69**
p6g p6g p6g Dec 22] leggy gelding: fair handicapper: made all at Wolverhampton and
Pontefract in July: stays 6f: acts on all-weather, firm and soft going: tried in cheekpieces/
blinkers: often tongue tied: races prominently: tough. *D. J. S. ffrench Davis*

BLESSINGS COUNT (USA) 3 ch.f. Pulpit (USA) 117 – Topicount (USA) (Private **63**
Account (USA)) [2006 10g 9.8g⁵ May 10] $100,000F, $150,000Y: good-bodied filly:
sister to minor winner in USA and half-sister to several winners in USA: dam US Grade 2
9f winner: modest form in maidens at Newbury and Ripon, 8¾ lengths fifth to Grain of
Truth on latter course: sent to USA. *E. A. L. Dunlop*

BLISSFULLY 2 b.f. (Apr 18) Kyllachy 129 – Bliss (IRE) 75 (Statoblest 120) [2006 6f –
5f⁶ 6.1d Oct 4] 19,000Y: sturdy filly: fourth foal: half-sister to 6f (including at 2 yrs)
winner Blofeld (by Royal Applause): dam 2-y-o 5f winner: well held all starts. *S. Parr*

BLISSPHILLY 4 b.f. Primo Dominie 121 – Majalis 79 (Mujadil (USA) 119) [2006 –: –
10f 6v f5g⁶ Dec 27] leggy, quite good-topped filly: little form: tried blinkered/visored.
M. Mullineaux

BLITHE 2 b.f. (Feb 5) Pivotal 124 – Pious 74 (Bishop of Cashel 122) [2006 6m³ 7g⁴ 7g² **91 p** 6s³ 7d* Sep 30] quite good-topped filly: first foal: dam, 6f (including at 2 yrs) winner, out of half-sister to smart 5f sprinter Ya Malak: fairly useful form: progressed well, winning 17-runner nursery at Newmarket in September by 1½ lengths, looking to have bit in hand: stays 7f: acts on soft ground, probably good to firm: failed to handle track at Epsom second start: looks capable of better again. *W. J. Haggas*

BLOCKLEY (USA) 2 b.c. (Mar 19) Johannesburg (USA) 127 – Saintly Manner **52 ?** (USA) (St Jovite (USA) 135) [2006 p7.1g⁵ p8.6g Dec 27] $37,000Y: fourth foal: dam, 1m/8.5f winner in USA, out of Italian Group 1 1¼m winner Azzurrina: seemingly modest form in maidens at Wolverhampton. *Ian Williams*

BLUE ALABAMA (IRE) 3 b.f. Ashkalani (IRE) 128 – Alabama (IRE) (Bluebird **63 d** (USA) 125) [2006 10s 9m 8m 8m 9f 12g⁴ 13d p13.9g Nov 20] third foal: half-sister to Irish 2003 2-y-o 1m/8.5f winner Alabama Blues (by Desert King): dam unraced grand-daughter of Arc winner Allez France: modest maiden at best: well held at Wolverhampton final outing: best effort at 1m: tried tongue tied. *Seamus G. O'Donnell, Ireland*

BLUE ARMY (IRE) 3 ch.g. Titus Livius (FR) 115 – Trojan Tale (USA) (Critique **54** (USA) 126) [2006 38: p8g⁵ p8g 8d⁴ 8.1g 8g p9.5g p8.6g⁵ p10g Jul 19] modest maiden on balance: stayed 1m: acted on polytrack and good to soft going: tried blinkered/in cheek-pieces: dead. *Jane Southcombe*

BLUE AURA (IRE) 3 b.g. Elnadim (USA) 128 – Absent Beauty (IRE) 74 (Dancing **80** Dissident (USA) 119) [2006 83p: 5.7d⁵ 5m³ 5g 6g⁵ 6g 5g* 5m 6d Sep 27] strong gelding: fairly useful handicapper: won at Windsor in August: raced only at 5f/6f: acts on good to firm and good to soft going: blinkered last 3 starts: gelded after. *R. Charlton*

BLUE AWAY (IRE) 8 b. or br.g. Blues Traveller (IRE) 119 – Lomond Heights (IRE) **72** (Lomond (USA) 128) [2006 79: 15.4m 15d 13.3m 16m 14.1g⁵ 16.2m⁴ 16m⁴ Sep 10] close-coupled gelding: fair handicapper: best around 2m: acts on firm and good to soft going, some promise on fibresand: rejoined P. Hughes in Ireland. *S. Kirk*

BLUE BAJAN (IRE) 4 b.g. Montjeu (IRE) 137 – Gentle Thoughts 73 (Darshaan 133) **110** [2006 87+: 10g² 10g³ 12m* 11.6m⁵ 10m* 10g⁴ 10m 10s* 9d² p10g² Nov 18] tall, quite good-topped gelding: smart performer: won handicaps at Folkestone in June and New-market (carried head high) in August, and minor event at Ascot (beat Zaif by 1¼ lengths, going away) in September: good efforts when second last 2 starts, beaten 4 lengths by Formal Decree in Cambridgeshire (Handicap) at Newmarket then short head by Nayyir in listed race at Lingfield: effective at 9f to 1½m: acts on polytrack, soft and good to firm going: blinkered once (below form) at 3 yrs: sometimes sweats/edgy (has still run well): held up. *Andrew Turnell*

BLUE BAMBOO 2 b.f. (Apr 18) Green Desert (USA) 127 – Silver Bandana (USA) **67** (Silver Buck (USA)) [2006 6m 6g⁶ 6m⁴ 5.1g⁴ Oct 17] 65,000Y: strong, close-coupled filly: second foal: half-sister to 3-y-o Silver Dip: dam, 1m/8.5f winner in USA (including minor stakes), out of sister to Park Hill winner Quay Line: fair maiden: better at 6f than 5f and should stay further. *Mrs A. J. Perrett*

BLUE BEACON 3 b.f. Fantastic Light (USA) 134 – Blue Duster (USA) 118 (Danzig **64** (USA)) [2006 68: p7.1g² f6g³ p7.1m 6s p7g p9.5g³ p9.5g⁶ p10g⁵ p9.5g Dec 21] neat filly: modest maiden: stays 1¼m: acts on polytrack: blinkered last 2 starts. *K. A. Ryan*

BLUEBELLE DANCER (IRE) 2 b.f. (Mar 11) Danehill Dancer (IRE) 117 – Spring **70** To Light (USA) 93 (Blushing Groom (FR) 131) [2006 5d 6g 6m³ p7.1g Nov 2] €54,000F, 64,000Y: rangy filly: has scope: half-sister to several winners, including 3-y-o Stolen Light and useful Irish 1995 2-y-o 6f winner Catch A Glimpse (by Gulch): dam 6f/7f win-ner: better than bare result (seventh) in nursery: should stay 7f. *W. R. Muir*

BLUEBERRY TART (IRE) 4 b.f. Bluebird (USA) 125 – Tart (FR) 76 (Warning 136) **65** [2006 76, a72: p9.5g p10g 9m 7f 10s Sep 30] sturdy filly: fair maiden: left J. Eustace after **a52** second start: stays 9.5f: acts on all-weather, good to firm and good to soft going: tried blinkered/in cheekpieces. *J. F. O'Shea, Ireland*

BLUEBOK 5 ch.g. Indian Ridge 123 – Blue Sirocco (Bluebird (USA) 125) [2006 85: **90** 5.1s 5g⁴ 5m² 5s 5.2g⁴ 5m* 5.7f⁵ 5g⁴ 5.5m² 5.2f* 5f⁵ 5f⁴ 5m⁵ 5g⁵ 5m⁴ 5.2m* 5.1m⁵ Oct 8] compact gelding: fairly useful handicapper: won at Musselburgh in June, and Yarmouth in July and September: best at 5f: acts on firm going (well below form on soft): often tongue tied (effective without): races prominently. *J. M. Bradley*

BLUE CHARM 2 b.g. (Mar 29) Averti (IRE) 117 – Exotic Forest 66 (Dominion 123) **84** [2006 7g³ p6g* p7g³ Dec 20] 3,200F, 10,500Y: half-brother to 3 winners, including 8-y-o Threezedzz and 5-y-o Smoothly Does It: dam 1m winner: fairly useful performer:

won maiden at Kempton in December by 3 lengths from Go Imperial: only third of 4 in minor event there next time: should prove as effective at 7f as 6f. *S. Kirk*

BLUE DANIELLE (IRE) 3 ch.f. Blue Ocean (USA) 87 – Imco Lucent (ITY) (Barn – Five South (USA) 76) [2006 –: p7.1g p6g p7.1g Feb 3] last all 4 starts. *A. D. Brown*

BLUE ECHO 2 b.f. (Feb 16) Kyllachy 129 – Mazarine Blue 65 (Bellypha 130) [2006   **96** 5f⁵ 6g² 5m* 6d³ 6d* Oct 27] strong, deep-girthed filly: good walker: half-sister to several winners, including smart 7f (at 2 yrs) to 9f winner Putra Pekan (by Grand Lodge) and smart performer up to 9f in USA Sapphire Ring (by Marju), 6f winner in Britain at 2 yrs: dam, 5f winner, half-sister to smart sprinter Rich Charlie: useful form: developed well, winning maiden at Sandown in September and 11-runner listed race at Newmarket (battled well to beat La Presse by short head) in October: will prove best kept to 5f/6f: acts on good to firm and good to soft going: races prominently. *M. A. Jarvis*

BLUE EMPIRE (IRE) 5 b.g. Second Empire (IRE) 124 – Paleria (USA) 77 (Zilzal   **71** (USA) 137) [2006 76: f8g* f8g⁵ p7.1g p8g⁴ p8g p7g 8m⁶ p8g f8g⁴ 7.5f² 7.5f³ 8f⁶ 7.6m⁴ 8.3f³ 8.2m* 8.3d 7.5g 7.1m p7g p7g f8g² p8.6g Dec 23] leggy gelding: fair handicapper: won at Southwell in January and Nottingham in July: stays 8.3f: acts on all-weather and firm going: wore cheekpieces (raced too freely) once: races prominently. *C. R. Dore*

BLUE HEDGES 4 b.c. Polish Precedent (USA) 131 – Palagene (Generous (IRE) 139)   **63** [2006 62: p10g p10g* p12g³ p10g² 9.7d⁵ 8m 10.1g p10g⁵ 10.1m² 10.9m 10m⁴ 12d   **a71** p13.9g* p12g³ p13.9g* Nov 27] big, workmanlike colt: fair handicapper on all-weather, modest on turf: won at Lingfield in January and 2 amateur events at Wolverhampton in November: stays easy 1¾m: acts on polytrack, firm and good to soft going. *H. J. Collingridge*

BLUE HILLS 5 br.g. Vettori (IRE) 119 – Slow Jazz (USA) 106 (Chief's Crown (USA))   **67** [2006 69: f16g² f16g² f14g³ f16g² f16g⁴ p16.5g* f14g⁵ p16.5g² p16.5g f14g p16.5g⁶ p13.9g Dec 31] tall gelding: fair handicapper: won at Wolverhampton in February: stays 2m: acts on all-weather, firm and good to soft going: sometimes wears visor/cheekpieces: usually ridden up with pace. *P. W. Hiatt*

BLUE JAVA 5 ch.g. Bluegrass Prince (IRE) 110 – Java Bay (Statoblest 120) [2006 78,   **84** a62: 7.1d² 7g* 7s⁴ 7m* 7m 7g⁴ 7g 7d 7s 7d⁵ Oct 28] smallish gelding: fairly useful handicapper: won at Salisbury (apprentices) in May and Goodwood in June: best at 7f: acts on polytrack and good to firm going: visored (ran poorly) final 4-y-o start. *H. Morrison*

BLUE JET (USA) 2 b.g. (Apr 17) Black Minnaloushe (USA) 123 – Clickety Click – (USA) (Sovereign Dancer (USA)) [2006 8s 7v Oct 31] leggy, close-coupled gelding: well held in maidens (testing ground). *R. M. Whitaker*

BLUE KNIGHT (IRE) 7 ch.g. Bluebird (USA) 125 – Fer de Lance (IRE) (Diesis 133)   **74 d** [2006 75: f6g⁵ p6g² p6g* p6g⁵ p7.1g⁶ p7.1g 7v 6g p6g 6d 5f 6f⁴ 7f 6d⁵ 5.9g³ 5m⁵ 6m⁶ 6d⁴ 6s⁵ 5g p5.1m p5.1g p6g p6g p6g Dec 30] big, lengthy gelding: fair handicapper: won at Wolverhampton in January: well below form after fifth outing: left D. Nicholls after tenth outing, D. Carroll after twenty-second: effective at 5f to 7f: acts on all-weather, soft and good to firm going: tried in cheekpieces, usually visored/tongue tied. *P. Howling*

BLUE KSAR (FR) 3 b.c. Anabaa (USA) 130 – Delicieuse Lady (Trempolino (USA)   **116** 135) [2006 10m⁴ 16m 10m² 9m* 8d* Oct 28] €320,000Y: big, close-coupled colt: third foal: half-brother to smart French 9f (at 2 yrs) and 1½m (Prix du Jockey Club) winner Blue Canari (by Acatenango): dam, won up to 9f in Scandinavia, out of smart French performer up to 12.5f Savoureuse Lady, herself half-sister to Mtoto: smart performer: won newcomers race at Deauville (for R. Collet) and fourth in Prix Thomas Byron at Saint-Cloud (for A. Fabre) at 2 yrs: further progress in 2006, winning minor event at Newbury in September and listed race at Newmarket (best effort when beating stable-companion Army of Angels by 2½ lengths, dictating) in October: creditable ½-length second to another stable-companion Desert Authority in minor event at Southwell on third start: stays 1¼m, best form at 1m/9f: acts on good to firm and good to soft going: tongue tied: has worn crossed noseband. *Saeed bin Suroor*

BLUE LINE 4 gr.f. Bluegrass Prince (IRE) 110 – Out Line 98 (Beveled (USA)) [2006   **58** 67: p7g⁵ 8m⁵ 7g 7f⁴ p7g⁴ 10m 7.6m 7.6g 7g⁶ 8m Sep 20] lengthy filly: fair maiden: stays   **a65** 7f: acts on polytrack and firm ground: sometimes visored. *M. Madgwick*

BLUE MADEIRA 2 b.g. (Jan 31) Auction House (USA) 120 – Queen of Scotland   **81** (IRE) 75 (Mujadil (USA) 119) [2006 5g 6v* 6m² p7g³ 7.1g⁵ Aug 26] 5,000Y: fourth foal: half-brother to 3-y-o Vice Admiral: dam 7f winner: fairly useful performer: won maiden at Ayr in May: also ran well when placed in minor event at Yarmouth (second to Vital

Equine) and nursery at Kempton: will probably stay 1m: yet to race on firm going, acts on any other turf, and polytrack. *Mrs L. Stubbs*

BLUE MAEVE 6 b.g. Blue Ocean (USA) 87 – Louisville Belle (IRE) 71 (Ahonoora **84** 122) [2006 72, a64: p5.1g p7.1g³ 6m 5g⁵ 5f² 5f⁶ 5f⁵ 6m* 6f* 5m* 6m* 5d³ 5m³ 5m 6d 5s p7.1g⁵ p6g Nov 14] sturdy gelding: fairly useful handicapper: won at Hamilton and Pontefract in July, and Pontefract and Ayr in August: barely stays 7f: acts on all-weather, firm and good to soft going: tried in headgear: makes running. *A. D. Brown*

BLUE MAK 2 b.g. (Mar 30) Makbul 104 – Washm (USA) (Diesis 133) [2006 p7.1g p6g **–** 7g Aug 4] leggy gelding: no form: tried visored. *D. Shaw*

BLUE MISTRAL (IRE) 2 ch.f. (Mar 1) Spinning World (USA) 130 – Blue Sirocco **67** (Bluebird (USA) 125) [2006 6m 6m 6d 6m⁴ p7g 6f³ 6d Oct 3] 56,000Y, 110,000 2-y-o: medium-sized, well-made filly: fourth foal: half-sister to 3-y-o Johannes, 4-y-o Zamboozle and 5-y-o Bluebok: dam once-raced half-sister to smart middle-distance stayers Azzilfi and Khamaseen: fair maiden: best form at 6f on ground firmer than good: signs of temperament. *W. J. Knight*

BLUE MONDAY 5 b.g. Darshaan 133 – Lunda (IRE) 60 (Soviet Star (USA) 128) **122** [2006 117+: 9.8d² 9.9s* 10d³ 10m⁴ 10m³ 10.4d³ 11g* 12s⁴ Oct 22] good-bodied gelding: very smart performer: won listed race at Goodwood (by 3 lengths from Mountain High) in May, steadily-run La Coupe at Longchamp (beat Annenkov by a head) in June and Dubai Duty Free Arc Trial at Newbury (beat Tam Lin by ¾ length) in September: creditable efforts in between, fourth to I'm So Lucky in Wolferton Handicap at Royal Ascot, 1¾ lengths third to David Junior in Eclipse Stakes at Sandown and never-nearer third (beaten 3 lengths) to Notnowcato in International Stakes at York: just respectable fourth to Collier Hill in Canadian International at Woodbine final outing: effective at 9f to 11f, should stay 1½m: yet to race on heavy going, acts on any other turf. *R. Charlton*

BLUE MONKEY (IRE) 2 b.c. (Apr 24) Orpen (USA) 116 – Resurgence (Polar Falcon **69** (USA) 126) [2006 5g³ 6g p7g⁴ Oct 6] 30,000F, 60,000Y: lengthy colt: third foal: half-brother to 2 winners, notably 3-y-o Araafa: dam unraced sister to very smart sprinter Pivotal: fair form in maidens, in frame at Leicester and Lingfield: stays 7f. *M. L. W. Bell*

BLUE MOON HITMAN (IRE) 5 ch.g. Blue Ocean (USA) 87 – Miss Kookaburra **60** (IRE) 44 (Namaqualand (USA)) [2006 59: p5.1g* p5.1g⁶ p5.1g p5.1g p5.1g p5.1g⁴ f5g May 16] small gelding: modest performer: won claimer at Wolverhampton in January: best at 5f: acts on all-weather, firm and good to soft going: tried in cheekpieces/blinkered: usually races prominently: has awkward head carriage. *R. Brotherton*

BLUE OPAL 4 b.f. Bold Edge 123 – Second Affair (IRE) 85 (Pursuit of Love 124) **–** [2006 63: f12g⁶ f14g⁵ f14g² f11g f12g⁵ 12m f12m* f12g⁶ f12g² f12g⁶ Dec 29] modest **a57** performer: won banded race at Southwell in October: barely stays 1¾m: acts on fibresand: effective with/without cheekpieces. *Miss S. E. Hall*

BLUE PATRICK 6 gr.g. Wizard King 122 – Great Intent (Aragon 118) [2006 79: **83 d** p8.6g³ p9.5g* f8g⁶ p8.6g⁴ p9.5g² 10.9g 8d Apr 25] rather leggy gelding: fluent mover: fairly useful performer: won handicap at Wolverhampton in January: left K. Ryan, tailed off last 2 starts: stays 9.5f: acts on all-weather and firm going: has worn cheekpieces (not since 2004): free-going sort. *P. A. Blockley*

Dubai Duty Free Arc Trial, Newbury—Blue Monday (right) is too strong for the three-year-old Tam Lin, both showing very smart form as they pull clear of Admiral's Cruise

BLUE POWER (IRE) 5 b.g. Zieten (USA) 118 – La Miserable (USA) (Miswaki **53**
(USA) 124) [2006 49, a62: f5g² f5g³ f5g f6g⁴ f6g f5g⁶ Mar 21] well-made gelding:
modest performer: was best at 5f: acted on all-weather, firm and good to soft ground: tried
visored/blinkered: dead. *K. R. Burke*

BLUE QUIVER (IRE) 6 b.g. Bluebird (USA) 125 – Paradise Forum 78 (Prince Sabo **–**
123) [2006 49, a65: p9.5g p8.6g³ p10g p10g p8.6g Dec 29] fair handicapper on all- **a65**
weather, modest at best on turf: stays 8.6f: acts on polytrack: usually slowly away.
C. A. Horgan

BLUE ROCKET (IRE) 2 ch.f. (Apr 5) Rock of Gibraltar (IRE) 133 – Champagne **92**
Girl 67 (Robellino (USA) 127) [2006 6m* 6.1m² 6d Sep 29] €96,000Y: close-coupled
filly: half-sister to several winners, including smart 5f/6f winner (including at 2 yrs) Hal-
mahera (by Petardia): dam, 2-y-o 5f winner, half-sister to useful sprinter Deep Finesse:
fairly useful form: won maiden at Haydock in August: second to Pretty Majestic in minor
event at Chester, then highly tried in Cheveley Park Stakes (ninth of 11) at Newmarket:
will prove best at 5f/6f. *T. J. Pitt*

BLUES IN THE NIGHT (IRE) 3 ch.g. Bluebird (USA) 125 – Always True (USA) **88**
67 (Geiger Counter (USA)) [2006 71: 7s p6g² 6m* 6g² 7m² 7d Oct 28] strong gelding:
fairly useful handicapper: won at Haydock in August: good second at Leicester and
Newbury after: stays 7f: acts on polytrack and good to firm going: tongue tied (below
form) final start. *P. J. Makin*

BLUE SKY THINKING (IRE) 7 b.g. Danehill Dancer (IRE) 117 – Lauretta Blue **92**
(IRE) (Bluebird (USA) 125) [2006 p10g 10.5g³ Apr 29] tall, rather leggy gelding: useful
performer at best: missed 2005 (reportedly had joints pin-fired): fairly useful form in
handicaps in 2006: should stay 1½m: acts on polytrack, firm and good to soft
going: has been bandaged in front: often hangs left: held up. *K. R. Burke*

BLUE SPINNAKER (IRE) 7 b.g. Bluebird (USA) 125 – Suedoise (Kris 135) [2006 **105**
109d: 8s 8v³ 10.4d* 10m 10.4f 10.4d 10.4g 9d 8d 10d Nov 4] sturdy gelding: useful handicapper: won at York in May by ½ length from Look Again (pair 13 lengths clear): below
that level after: worth a try at 1½m: probably acts on any going: held up. *M. W. Easterby*

BLUE TOMATO 5 b.g. Orpen (USA) 116 – Ocean Grove (IRE) 84 (Fairy King **98**
(USA)) [2006 82, a90: 6f³ 7.1d p6g 5m 6m² 6m* 6m* 6m² 6f³ 6f 6g⁵ 6m 6m³ 6f⁵
p6g Sep 30] lengthy, useful-looking gelding: impresses in appearance: useful performer:
won handicaps at Goodwood (apprentices) and Newcastle in June and Haydock (beat
Knot In Wood by 2½ lengths) in July: good third at York and Yarmouth (minor event)
after: effective at 6f to 1m: acts on polytrack and firm going: tried tongue tied: often wore
cheekpieces in 2005. *J. M. Bradley*

BLUE TRAIN (IRE) 4 b.g. Sadler's Wells (USA) 132 – Igreja (ARG) 101 (Southern **–**
Halo (USA)) [2006 83: 8.3g Apr 10] rangy gelding: fairly useful performer, lightly raced:
well held only Flat outing in 2006: tried tongue tied. *Jonjo O'Neill*

BLUE TROJAN (IRE) 6 b.g. Inzar (USA) 112 – Roman Heights (IRE) (Head For **93**
Heights 125) [2006 88: 8.3g³ 8g⁵ 8.1d 8.3f 7.1m* 8m⁴ 7g⁵ 7f* 8m³ 7.1g Aug 17] lengthy
gelding: fairly useful handicapper: won at Chepstow in June and Leicester in July: good
third at Ascot next outing: best at 7f/1m: acts on all-weather, firm and good to soft going:
blinkered (below form) once: quirky (sometimes edges left) and dropped out nowadays.
S. Kirk

BLU MANRUNA 3 ch.c. Zaha (CAN) 106 – Vrennan 74 (Suave Dancer (USA) 136) **66**
[2006 66: 9s 8.1m⁵ 7g 7m⁵ 8.5g³ 10m⁵ 8m⁴ 8.1m 8d 8.3g 7g p10g⁴ p10g² Dec 22] leggy
colt: fair maiden: stays 1¼m: acts on polytrack, good to firm and good to soft going:
usually wears blinkers/cheekpieces. *J. Akehurst*

BLUSHING HILARY (IRE) 3 ch.f. City On A Hill (USA) 114 – Trinida (Jaazeiro **78**
(USA) 127) [2006 71: p8.6g³ 10d³ 12.1g⁴ 9.2f⁴ 12m⁵ 12.1m³ 10.5g⁵ p13.9m⁴ Oct 9]
strong filly: fair maiden handicapper: barely stays easy 1¾m: acts on polytrack, good to
firm and good to soft ground: usually visored/in cheekpieces: found little sixth start: often
makes running. *Miss J. A. Camacho*

BLUSHING LIGHT (USA) 3 b. or br.g. Mt Livermore (USA) – Swan River (USA) **66**
(Hennessy (USA) 122) [2006 p7g 6f⁵ p6g³ p7g Jul 12] $62,000F, 75,000Y: second foal:
half-brother to winner in USA by Artax: dam unraced close relative to very smart 6f/7f
performer Catrail: fair maiden: should be suited by 7f. *M. A. Magnusson*

BLUSHING PRINCE (IRE) 8 b.g. Priolo (USA) 127 – Eliade (IRE) 82 (Flash of **47 §**
Steel 120) [2006 12m 10.1d⁵ p12.2g⁶ Dec 27] lightly raced and only poor on Flat nowa-

days: stays 9.4f: acts on all-weather and heavy ground: usually tongue tied: won over hurdles in October. *R. C. Guest*

BLUSHING RUSSIAN (IRE) 4 b.g. Fasliyev (USA) 120 – Ange Rouge (Priolo (USA) 127) [2006 60: p8.6g f8g p7.1g⁴ p7.1g f8g f8g⁵ Dec 29] useful-looking gelding: modest performer: stays 1m: acts on all-weather and good to firm going: tried in cheekpieces: has looked wayward. *J. M. Bradley* **55**

BLUSHING THIEF (USA) 3 ch.c. Cat Thief (USA) 126 – Blushing Princess (USA) (Crafty Prospector (USA)) [2006 p8g⁶ p8g⁶ p7g³ f6g* p6g* 6g p6g⁵ p6g² p6g Jul 12] $27,000Y, 30,000 2-y-o: strong, lengthy colt: fourth foal: half-brother to 2 winners in USA, including Grade 3 6f winner First Blush (by French Deputy): dam ran once in USA: fairly useful performer: won maiden at Southwell (by 9 lengths) and handicap at Kempton, both in March: best form at 6f: acts on all-weather: blinkered last 2 starts (very good effort first occasion): hung right third outing: sold 20,000 gns. *W. Jarvis* **89**

BLYTHE KNIGHT (IRE) 6 ch.g. Selkirk (USA) 129 – Blushing Barada (USA) 53 (Blushing Groom (FR) 131) [2006 109, a114: 8s* 8m 10m³ 8s⁴ 8m 8s⁴ 8d³ 9d Sep 30] quite good-topped gelding: has a round action: useful performer: won 30-runner William Hill Lincoln (Handicap) at Redcar in March by ¾ length from Royal Island: creditable efforts in frame in handicaps at York (fourth to Smart Enough) and Ayr (length third to Vicious Warrior) sixth/seventh outings: raced in disadvantaged group when twelfth to Formal Decree in Cambridgeshire (Handicap) at Newmarket final outing: stays 1½m, raced mainly at 1m/1¼m: acts on polytrack, firm and soft going: has worn headgear: used to be held up, generally ridden more in touch in 2006: useful hurdler. *J. J. Quinn* **107**

BLYTHE SPIRIT 7 b.g. Bahamian Bounty 116 – Lithe Spirit (IRE) 74 (Dancing Dissident (USA) 119) [2006 72, a81: f6g p5.1g⁵ p5.1g⁴ f6g³ f5g⁶ p7.1g³ p6g f6g⁶ Dec 29] lengthy gelding: only modest in 2006: has form at 1m, but races mainly at 5f/6f nowadays: acts on all-weather, firm and soft ground: sometimes wears blinkers/cheekpieces/tongue tie. *R. A. Fahey* **57**

BOANERGES (IRE) 9 br.g. Caerleon (USA) 132 – Sea Siren 68 (Slip Anchor 136) [2006 61, a51+: f5g⁴ f5g* f6g³ p6g f5g² p6g⁵ p5.1g p6g⁴ f5g² f5g⁵ p5.1g* 6m* 5.3m 5f* p6g⁵ 5.3m⁴ 6d Jul 9] smallish, strong gelding: fair performer: won banded race at Southwell in January, claimer at Wolverhampton and seller at Brighton in April, and handicap at Hamilton in June: effective at 5f/easy 6f: acts on all-weather, firm and good to soft going: tried in headgear (not since 2004). *J. M. Bradley* **66**

William Hill Lincoln (Handicap), Redcar—not at its usual venue but the race is as competitive as ever, Blythe Knight is all out to hold off Royal Island (spots) on his first start for present connections; Capable Guest (second left) finishes well for third ahead of Zero Tolerance (partially hidden by winner)

BOB

BOBANSHEIL (IRE) 2 b.f. (Feb 22) Dushyantor (USA) 123 – Bobanlyn (IRE) 76 **66**
(Dance of Life (USA)) [2006 8.5g⁶ 8g 9s⁶ 10d Oct 2] €17,000Y: strong, lengthy filly:
closely related to fairly useful Irish stayer Great Guns (by Deploy), 9f winner at 2 yrs, and
half-sister to winner up to 1½m in Italy by Kris: dam 6f (at 2 yrs) to 1½m winner: fair
form when seventh in maiden at Pontefract final start: highly tried second outing.
J. S. Wainwright

BOB BAILEYS 4 b.g. Mister Baileys 123 – Bob's Princess 69 (Bob's Return (IRE) **59**
123) [2006 –: f8g f8g⁶ f8g⁵ f8g³ p8.6g* p8.6g² p10g p8.6g Jul 11] modest performer:
won banded race at Wolverhampton in April: stays 8.6f, probably not 1¼m: acts on all-
weather: tried in cheekpieces, blinkered last 5 starts. *P. R. Chamings*

BOBBISH 2 b.g. (Mar 9) Best of The Bests (IRE) 122 – Bella Bianca (IRE) 78 (Barathea **75**
(IRE) 127) [2006 7.1m 7g⁶ p7g⁴ 7f³ 7g* 7m² Aug 6] tall gelding: first foal: dam, 6f
winner, out of half-sister to smart 1m to 1¼m winner Bustan: fair performer: won nursery
at Newmarket in July (raced alone): placed both other starts in nurseries: will stay 1m:
acts on firm going, probably polytrack: sold 30,000 gns. *N. A. Callaghan*

BOBBY CHARLES 5 ch.g. Polish Precedent (USA) 131 – Dina Line (USA) 60 **88**
(Diesis 133) [2006 91: p10g³ p10g³ 10v 10.1g 9.9f⁵ f11g⁴ p10g³ Dec 8] good-topped
gelding: fairly useful handicapper: stays 1½m, at least as effective at 1¼m: acts on all-
weather, firm and soft going. *Dr J. D. Scargill*

BOBBY KENNARD 7 b.g. Bobinski 115 – Midnight Break 78 (Night Shift (USA)) **68**
[2006 65: p16.5g⁵ p16.5g* Feb 3] fair performer: won selling handicap at Wolverhampton in February: stays 2m: acts on all-weather and good to soft ground: carries head
awkwardly. *J. A. Osborne*

BOBBY ROSE 3 b.g. Sanglamore (USA) 126 – Grown At Rowan 75 (Gabitat 119) **72**
[2006 p8g p8g p8g⁴ p7g⁴ 7m³ 6g⁴ 6.1d² 6.1d p6g² p7g p6g³ p6g² p6g Dec 22] half-brother
to moody 7f winner Twoforten (by Robellino) and Irish 1¼m winner Wild Zing (by
Jupiter Island): dam 7f winner: fair maiden: effective at 6f/7f: acts on polytrack, good to
firm and good to soft going. *D. K. Ivory*

BOBERING 6 b.g. Bob's Return (IRE) 123 – Ring The Rafters (Batshoof 122) [2006 **55**
49: p8.6g* p9.5g⁵ Dec 29] strong gelding: modest performer: won banded event at Wolverhampton in December: effective at 8.6f to 1½m: acts on all-weather. *B. P. J. Baugh*

BOBSKI (IRE) 4 b.g. Victory Note (USA) 120 – Vivid Impression (Cure The Blues **90**
(USA)) [2006 86: p7g⁶ 6m³ 7f³ 7.1d 7m 6m⁵ 7.1g p6g⁶ p7g* Nov 13] good-topped
gelding: fairly useful performer: won at Lingfield in November: effective at 6f/7f: acts on
polytrack and firm going: blinkered fourth start: often slowly away. *G. A. Huffer*

BOBSLEIGH 7 b.g. Robellino (USA) 127 – Do Run Run 75 (Commanche Run 133) **66**
[2006 75: p16g⁴ 15d⁶ 18m 16.2g⁶ 14m⁶ 14.1m⁵ 12.1m⁶ 14.1g p16g³ 16.4m⁴ 17.2m⁵ p16g
Oct 1] leggy, useful-looking gelding: fair handicapper: stays 21f: acts on polytrack, firm
and soft going: tried blinkered/in cheekpieces: has run well when edgy: usually makes
running: signs of temperament. *H. S. Howe*

BOB'S YOUR UNCLE 3 br.g. Zilzal (USA) 137 – Bob's Princess 69 (Bob's Return **73**
(IRE) 123) [2006 55: p10g⁴ f11g 10g* 11g⁴ 11.5m* 11.6d* 12f⁴ 11.6f 11.6g² p12g 14.1d
11.6d Oct 9] leggy gelding: fair performer: won claimer at Windsor in April and handicaps at Lingfield and Windsor in June: stays 11.6f: acts on polytrack, good to firm and
good to soft going: patiently ridden: sometimes hangs. *J. G. Portman*

BODDEN BAY 4 b.g. Cayman Kai (IRE) 114 – Badger Bay (IRE) 67 (Salt Dome **68**
(USA)) [2006 63: f7g p7g² p7.1g² p7g 5.9m* p6g³ 6f 6.9m 6m 5s 7d* f6g* f6g* f7g
Dec 5] fair performer: won handicaps at Carlisle in June and Leicester (selling event) in
October, and handicap and claimer (left D. Carroll) at Southwell in November: stays 7f:
acts on all-weather, good to firm and good to soft going: tried in cheekpieces/visor at
2 yrs: has run well when sweating: races prominently. *Miss Gay Kelleway*

BODES GALAXY (IRE) 2 b.c. (May 5) Marju (IRE) 127 – Prima Centauri (USA) **105**
(Distant View (USA) 126) [2006 6m⁵ p6g⁴ 5.7m* 6f* 6f² 6d³ p6g 5d Oct 7] €205,000Y,
26,000 2-y-o: compact, useful-looking colt: second foal: dam, ran twice in France,
closely related to smart French 7f/1m performer Etoile Montante: useful performer: won
maiden at Bath in June and nursery at Pontefract (beat Dhanyaa by length) in July: good
head second to Hamoody in Richmond Stakes at Goodwood and 3¼ lengths third to
Conquest in Gimcrack Stakes at York in August: disappointing in other pattern events last
2 starts: best at 5f/6f: acts on polytrack, firm and good to soft going: front runner: sold
140,000 gns, sent to USA. *N. P. Littmoden*

144

BODFARI DREAM 5 ch.m. Environment Friend 128 – Al Reet (IRE) 92 (Alzao — (USA) 117) [2006 –: p13.9g f12g Mar 8] close-coupled mare: of little account. *M. Mullineaux*

BOGAZ (IRE) 4 b.g. Rossini (USA) 118 – Fastnet (Forzando 122) [2006 73, a65: f7g **48** 10.9s 8.1d 8m 7d⁴ 8m p7g⁵ f8m p7g Dec 6] smallish, robust gelding: only poor in 2006: stays 1m: acts on fibresand and firm going: tried in cheekpieces/visored: none too consistent. *Mrs H. Sweeting*

BOGSIDE KATIE 2 b.f. (Mar 15) Hunting Lion (IRE) 115 – Enchanting Eve 67 (Risk **48** Me (FR) 127) [2006 6f⁴ 6m 7g 6.5d p6s⁵ f5g⁶ Dec 23] fourth foal: half-sister to 5-y-o Red Romeo and to a winner in France/Germany by Case Law: dam 5f (at 2 yrs) to 1m winner who stayed 1¼m: poor maiden: left A. Oliver in Ireland, seemingly best effort when 6¼ lengths fifth to Pixie Ring at Wolverhampton penultimate start. *G. M. Moore*

BOISDALE (IRE) 8 b.g. Common Grounds 118 – Alstomeria 61 (Petoski 135) [2006 **44** 61: p5.1g f6g f6g f6g p6g f6g p6g f6g Dec 28] workmanlike gelding: only poor in 2006, leaving S. Keightley after fourth outing, K. Morgan after fifth: effective at 6f/7f: acts on all-weather, soft and good to firm going: tried tongue tied. *P. S. Felgate*

BOLCKOW 3 b.g. Marju (IRE) 127 – Stamatina (Warning 136) [2006 60p: 7m⁴ 7g **63** 8.5g⁵ p12.2g³ 10f 9.9m⁵ 8.1m⁴ 8.5m⁵ 10f⁴ 11g⁶ 9.1v⁵ f11g⁹ p13.9g p12.2g³ Dec 23] tall gelding: modest performer: won maiden claimer at Southwell (left K. Ryan) in November: stays 1½m: acts on all-weather and firm going. *J. T. Stimpson*

BOLD ABBOTT (USA) 2 b.c. (Mar 22) Mizzen Mast (USA) 121 – Ms Isadora (USA) **85** (Miswaki (USA) 124) [2006 7m 7m 7m² 7d³ Aug 18] $90,000Y: lengthy, good-topped colt: has a quick action: third foal: half-brother to winner in USA by Royal Academy: dam, 6f to 9f winner in USA, half-sister to US Grade 3 2-y-o 8.5f winner Bibury Court: fairly useful maiden: placed behind Furnace then Gold Option at Newmarket last 2 starts: will stay 1m. *Mrs A. J. Perrett*

BOLD ACT (IRE) 4 b.g. Brave Act 119 – Banco Solo (Distant Relative 128) [2006 73: **92** p8g⁵ 8.2d³ 8.3f² 10g² 8.3g* 10g³ 8.9s² Oct 7] good-bodied gelding: fairly useful handicapper: won at Windsor in August: good efforts last 2 starts: not sure to stay beyond 1¼m: acts on polytrack, firm and soft going: sold 82,000 gns. *H. Candy*

BOLD ADVENTURE 2 ch.g. (Apr 13) Arkadian Hero (USA) 123 – Impatiente **47 p** (USA) (Vaguely Noble 140) [2006 7m 6m 6g Aug 30] good-bodied gelding: backward and not knocked about in maidens: will do better, probably at 1¼m/1½m. *W. J. Musson*

BOLD ALASKA (IRE) 3 b.g. Cape Cross (IRE) 129 – Dramatic Entry (IRE) 68 **86** (Persian Bold 123) [2006 8m* 8d⁶ May 26] €70,000Y, resold 180,000Y: good-bodied gelding: fifth foal: half-brother to winning sprinters in Norway by Emarati and Perugino: dam, 6f winner in Sweden (including at 2 yrs), half-sister to very smart sprinter Royal Millennium: in fine shape, won maiden at Newmarket in May by 1¾ lengths from Smart Enough: below form in minor event there only subsequent start: not bred to stay beyond 1m: bandaged on fore joints: sold only 8,000 gns in October. *E. A. L. Dunlop*

BOLD APACHE (IRE) 2 ch.c. (May 5) Rock of Gibraltar (IRE) 133 – Velvet Moon **82** (IRE) 108 (Shaadi (USA) 126) [2006 7g 7m³ 8v³ Sep 21] half-brother to several winners, including top-class 9f to 10.4f winner (including Dubai World Cup) Moon Ballad (by Singspiel) and useful 1m winner Velvet Lady (by Nashwan): dam, 6f (at 2 yrs, including Lowther Stakes) to 1¼m winner, half-sister to very smart performer up to 2m Central Park: fairly useful maiden: third at Gowran and Listowel after debut (listed race): stays 1m. *A. P. O'Brien, Ireland*

BOLD ARGUMENT (IRE) 3 ch.g. Shinko Forest (IRE) – Ivory Bride 86 (Domyn- **76** sky 110) [2006 59: p6g⁵ 6.1m⁴ f6g² 7.1m 6f⁶ 6m⁶ 7d 7m 6d Oct 9] big, lengthy gelding: fair handicapper: won at Windsor in July: below form last 3 starts, then gelded: best form at 6f: acts on firm ground (tongue tied, didn't look totally at ease on fibresand third outing). *Mrs P. N. Dutfield*

BOLD ARROW 4 b.g. Bold Fort 100 – Jubilee Belle (Bell Ringer 82) [2006 –: 11.7f — Jun 11] no sign of ability: visored on debut. *B. J. Llewellyn*

BOLD BOBBY BE (IRE) 2 br.c. (Mar 29) Bob Back (USA) 124 – Fantasy Girl (IRE) **71 +** 55 (Marju (IRE) 127) [2006 7d 7g⁵ Oct 12] angular, quite good-topped colt: has a quick action: sixth foal: brother to smart 7f (at 2 yrs) to 10.5f winner Big Bad Bob and half-brother to fairly useful Irish 7f winner Woodland Dream (by Charnwood Forest): dam, maiden who stayed 1½m, half-sister to smart 1¼m/1½m performer Persian Lightning: better effort in maidens at Newmarket when never-nearer fifth of 16 to Tredegar: will be suited by 1¼m/1½m. *J. L. Dunlop*

BOLD BROWNIE 4 b.f. Almaty (IRE) 113§ – Polly So Bold (Never So Bold 135) – [2006 –: p7g 10m 11.7m Aug 25] neat filly: little sign of ability: tried in cheekpieces. *Miss Z. C. Davison*

BOLD CHEVERAK 4 b.g. Bold Edge 123 – Curlew Calling (IRE) 51 (Pennine Walk 53 120) [2006 71: f6g 6m p5g 5.3m 5.2m 6m p6g p10g Sep 5] leggy gelding: only modest performer in 2006: effective at 6f/easy 7f: acts on all-weather, good to firm and good to soft going: has been slowly away. *Mrs C. A. Dunnett*

BOLD CROSS (IRE) 3 b.g. Cape Cross (IRE) 129 – Machikane Akaiito (IRE) (Per- 67 sian Bold 123) [2006 71: 7.1g 8.2m⁵ 8.2s 8.3m⁵ 7g Jun 15] leggy gelding: fair maiden handicapper: stays 1¼m: acts on soft and good to firm ground. *E. G. Bevan*

BOLD CRUSADER 3 b.c. Cape Cross (IRE) 129 – Tee Cee 77 (Lion Cavern (USA) 98 117) [2006 84p: f8g³ Nov 10] sturdy colt: useful performer, lightly raced: off nearly 13 months, much improved when close third to Nevada Desert in handicap at Southwell on only outing in 2006: stays 1m: has worn crossed noseband: joined E. Charpy in UAE. *Saeed bin Suroor*

BOLD DIKTATOR 4 b.g. Diktat 126 – Madam Bold (Never So Bold 135) [2006 78: 85 8.3g 8.1m 8f* 7.6f* 8.1m⁶ 8m 8m⁵ p10g⁶ 7g p7g p8.6g* Dec 30] strong gelding: fairly useful handicapper on turf, fair on all-weather: won at Bath and Lingfield in June and Wolverhampton (first outing after leaving W. Muir 15,000 gns) in December: stays 8.6f: acts on polytrack and firm going: effective with or without blinkers. *T. G. Dascombe*

BOLD FINCH (FR) 4 b.g. Valanour (IRE) 125 – Eagle's Nest (FR) 62 (King of – Macedon 126) [2006 f8g p7g p8g Aug 2] ex-French-trained gelding: no form. *K. O. Cunningham-Brown*

BOLD HAVANA 4 b.f. Bold Edge 123 – Isle of Sodor 63 (Cyrano de Bergerac 120) – [2006 –: f6g Jan 26] well beaten in 3 maidens. *T. T. Clement*

BOLD HAZE 4 ch.g. Bold Edge 123 – Melody Park 104 (Music Boy 124) [2006 74: 64 6m 6m 6g⁴ f6g 6m² 6s 7d² 8.2d Nov 1] big, good-bodied gelding: modest handicapper: stays 7f: acts on good and good to firm going: visored last 4 starts: tends to edge left: inconsistent. *Miss S. E. Hall*

BOLD INDIAN (IRE) 2 b.g. (Feb 25) Indian Danehill (IRE) 124 – Desert Gift 69 73 (Green Desert (USA) 127) [2006 6d 6v p7.1g³ p7.1g³ p7.1g³ Dec 28] €12,000Y: sixth foal: half-brother to 3-y-o Dune Melody: dam, Irish maiden, placed from 5f to 7f: fair maiden: left J. Burns in Ireland and gelded, good placed efforts at Wolverhampton last 3 starts, close third to Play Straight on final one: will stay 1m: acts on polytrack and good to soft going: looked less than straightforward last 2 starts. *I. Semple*

BOLDINOR 3 b.g. Inchinor 119 – Rambold 72 (Rambo Dancer (CAN) 107) [2006 71 d p6g* p6g⁵ 8d p6g⁵ p7.1g 5.7g² 6f 8m 7.1d p7g p6m p8g Nov 11] second foal: dam 6f winner, including at 2 yrs: fair performer: won maiden at Wolverhampton in Feb- ruary, ducking right and unseating rider after post: left W. Swinburn after third outing: well below form last 6 starts: effective at 5.7f, should stay 7f: acts on polytrack: hangs and looks hard ride. *N. E. Berry*

BOLD LOVE 3 ch.f. Bold Edge 123 – Noor El Houdah (IRE) 61 (Fayruz 116) [2006 47 47: p6g f6g 8.2d 7g 7g* 7d f7g⁵ f6g p6g f7g⁵ f6g² Dec 28] workmanlike filly: poor performer: won claimer at Leicester (left J. Bethell) in August: stays 7f: acts on all- weather, probably on good to firm going: in cheekpieces/blinkered last 2 starts: looked none too keen fourth outing. *J. Balding*

BOLD MAGGIE 4 ch.f. Bold Edge 123 – Vera's First (IRE) 69 (Exodal (USA)) [2006 – 52, a40: f5g p5.1g p6g May 2] maiden: no form in 2006. *J. A. Pickering*

BOLD MARC (IRE) 4 b.g. Bold Fact (USA) 116 – Zara's Birthday (IRE) 71 (Waajib 88 121) [2006 92: 6m⁶ 5d³ 5f 5s⁴ 5m³ 5g 5f 5g⁴ 6d 8.1d⁶ 7.2v⁴ 7s* 7s² 7v² f8g² p8.6g⁵ Nov 16] leggy, good-topped gelding: fairly useful handicapper: won at Catterick in October by 6 lengths, making all: good placed efforts next 3 starts: stays 1m: acts on all- weather and any turf going: tried visored, in cheekpieces last 5 starts. *K. R. Burke*

BOLD MEDICEAN 3 b.g. Medicean 128 – Bird of Time (IRE) 75 (Persian Bold 123) – [2006 8d 8.1m 11f⁶ 8.5f Jul 18] tall, good-topped gelding: well held in maidens and apprentice handicap: gave trouble once loaded on second outing. *T. P. Tate*

BOLD MINSTREL (IRE) 4 br.g. Bold Fact (USA) 116 – Ponda Rosa (IRE) 66 (Case 87 Law 113) [2006 82: 5m⁵ 5m 5m 5g* 5g⁶ 5.2m³ 5.1f p5g³ Nov 11] good-bodied gelding: fairly useful handicapper: won at Windsor in August: barely stays 5.7f: acts on polytrack, good to firm and good to soft going. *M. Quinn*

BOLD NEVISON (IRE) 2 b.c. (Apr 15) Danehill Dancer (IRE) 117 – La Pieta (IRE) **62**
96 (Spectrum (IRE) 126) [2006 7g 7v p7.1g⁶ f8g Dec 21] seemingly best effort in
maidens when sixth at Wolverhampton. *B. Smart*

BOLD PHOENIX (IRE) 5 b.g. Dr Fong (USA) 128 – Subya 107 (Night Shift (USA)) **66**
[2006 55: f8g² p9.5g* f8g* p9.5m p8g p10g p9.5g Dec 21] sturdy gelding: fair performer:
won banded races at Wolverhampton in February and Southwell in April: stays 9.5f:
acts on all-weather, soft and good to firm going: effective blinkered or not: has hung.
B. J. Curley

BOLD PIONEER (USA) 3 b.g. Pioneering (USA) – Uber Alyce (USA) (Bold Forbes **–**
(USA)) [2006 –: p8g p8g 11.5m 9.9m Jun 23] little form. *C. P. Morlock*

BOLD SAXON (IRE) 2 ch.c. (Jan 18) Desert Sun 120 – Sirdhana 79 (Selkirk (USA) **70**
129) [2006 7s p7g⁵ p7.1s² Dec 13] €17,000Y: strong, lengthy colt: second foal: dam
second over 1m in Italy at 2 yrs on only start: fair form in maidens, head second to Putra
Laju at Wolverhampton: will be suited by 1m. *M. D. I. Usher*

BOLD TIGER (IRE) 3 b.g. Bold Fact (USA) 116 – Heart of The Ocean (IRE) 73 **48**
(Soviet Lad (USA)) [2006 72d: 7m 6f 7.1g⁵ 8d 6m⁵ 5f 8d Aug 21] just poor maiden in
2006: left D. Nicholls after second start: tried blinkered. *Miss Tracy Waggott*

BOLD TRUMP 5 b.g. First Trump 118 – Blue Nile (IRE) 70 (Bluebird (USA) 125) **57**
[2006 44+: p9.5g p8.6g⁴ p9.5g⁶ f8g⁵ f11g⁵ f12g* f14g⁵ 12.1m f16g³ Dec 28] leggy
gelding: modest performer: won maiden claimer at Southwell in May: stays 1½m: acts on
all-weather: tried in visor/cheekpieces/tongue tie. *Mrs N. S. Evans*

BOLLIN BILLY 4 b.g. Mind Games 121 – Bollin Ann 72 (Anshan 119) [2006 69: p6g* **72**
p6g⁴ p7.1g Jan 21] rather leggy gelding: fair handicapper: won at Lingfield in January:
was effective at 5f/6f: acted on polytrack, firm and soft going: tried blinkered/visored:
dead. *R. Brotherton*

BOLLIN DEREK 3 gr.c. Silver Patriarch (IRE) 125 – Bollin Magdalene 55 (Teenoso **83**
(USA) 135) [2006 –: f11g² 11g* 12m* 12v* 11.8d² 12s² 14g³ 13.9s* Oct 7] big, strong
colt: has a moderate, quick action: progressed into a fairly useful handicapper, winning
at Southwell in April, Pontefract and Ripon in May and York in October: will stay 2m:
has won on good to firm going, better form on good or softer (acts on heavy): tends to
race in snatches, but has made running. *T. D. Easterby*

BOLLIN DOLLY 3 ch.f. Bien Bien (USA) 125 – Bollin Roberta 75 (Bob's Return **72**
(IRE) 123) [2006 –: 8.5f⁵ 9.8g⁶ 12f² 12g³ 10d³ 12.1m⁵ 8d³ 10s⁶ Oct 16] good-topped
filly: fair maiden: stays 1½m: acts on firm and good to soft ground: reluctant to enter stall
on second outing and refused to enter third intended appearance: usually makes running.
T. D. Easterby

BOLLIN EDWARD 7 b.g. Timeless Times (USA) 99 – Bollin Harriet (Lochnager **75**
132) [2006 68: 7d⁷ 7.2d* 7.5f⁶ 7.5f p7.1g⁶ p7.1m p7.1g f8g Dec 14] good-bodied **a–**
gelding: fair handicapper: won at Thirsk in May and Ayr in June: stays 7.5f: acts on firm
and soft going, no form on all-weather: sometimes wears headgear. *K. A. Ryan*

BOLLIN FELIX 2 br.c. (Apr 23) Generous (IRE) 139 – Bollin Magdalene 55 (Teenoso **49 p**
(USA) 135) [2006 7f⁶ 7.5d⁶ 7d⁶ 10g Sep 26] close-coupled, useful-looking colt: seventh
foal: half-brother to 3 winners, including useful 1¼m/1½m winner Bollin Nellie (by
Rock Hopper) and 3-y-o Bollin Derek: dam, staying maiden on Flat, winner over hurdles:
poor form in maidens/nursery: bred to be suited by 1½m+: should do better as a 3-y-o.
T. D. Easterby

BOLLIN FERGUS 2 br.c. (Apr 28) Vettori (IRE) 119 – Bollin Harriet (Lochnager 132) **?**
[2006 6s⁴ 6m⁶ 6g Sep 27] half-brother to several winners up to 7f, including fairly useful
sprinters Bollin Harry (by Domynsky) and Bollin Rita (by Rambo Dancer): dam unraced:
signs of ability in maidens, though flattered on debut. *T. D. Easterby*

BOLLIN FIONA 2 ch.f. (Feb 2) Silver Patriarch (IRE) 125 – Bollin Nellie 98 (Rock **–**
Hopper 124) [2006 8v 8.1g Sep 23] first foal: dam 1¼m/1½m winner: behind in maidens:
sold 2,200 gns. *T. D. Easterby*

BOLLIN FRANNY 2 br.c. (Mar 29) Bertolini (USA) 125 – Bollin Ann 72 (Anshan **72 d**
119) [2006 5f⁵ 5m² 5m* 5.1f⁵ 5m⁶ 6d⁶ 5d⁵ Aug 31] third foal: half-brother to 4-y-o Bollin
Billy: dam, 5f winner, half-sister to St Leger winner Bollin Eric and smart sprinter Bollin
Joanne: fair performer: won maiden at Ripon in June: below form in nurseries last 4
starts, in blinkers final one: best at 5f: acts on firm going. *T. D. Easterby*

BOLLIN FREDDIE 2 ch.g. (Mar 10) Golden Snake (USA) 127 – Bollin Roberta 75 – (Bob's Return (IRE) 123) [2006 6m 7f⁴ 7.5m Aug 16] little form in maidens: sold 3,200 gns. *T. D. Easterby*

BOLLIN MICHAEL 4 b.c. Celtic Swing 138 – Bollin Zola 90 (Alzao (USA) 117) 77 [2006 60: p9.5g f6g⁴ 7d 10g 8g⁵ 8.2s* 8.1s p8.6g Jun 22] tall, good-topped colt: fair performer: won apprentice maiden handicap at Nottingham in May: should stay 1¼m: acts on soft going: blinkered last 4 starts: jinked violently right on home bend on reappearance: dropped away tamely last 2 starts: of suspect temperament. *T. D. Easterby*

BOLLIN THOMAS 8 b.g. Alhijaz 122 – Bollin Magdalene 55 (Teenoso (USA) 135) 72 [2006 78: 14.1s⁵ 14g 11.1m⁶ May 11] strong gelding: fair handicapper: effective at 1½m to 2m: acts on heavy and good to firm going: has worn blinkers/cheekpieces: usually races prominently: sometimes hangs. *R. Allan*

BOLLYWOOD (IRE) 3 ch.g. Indian Rocket 115 – La Fille de Cirque 49 (Cadeaux 56 Genereux 131) [2006 59: p7g² p7g* p7.1g p8g⁶ p7g p8g 6g 6.1d p7g 6f 6g 7m 5m 7m⁴ **a70 d** 7.6g⁶ 6g⁴ 6d 5g p8g² p8g⁶ p10g⁴ p10g p8g p8g p8g Dec 18] fair performer at best: won claimer at Lingfield (claimed from M. Jarvis £14,000) in January: left M. Hoad after fifth outing: stays easy 1¼m: acts on polytrack and good to firm going: tried blinkered/in cheekpieces. *J. J. Bridger*

BOLODENKA (IRE) 4 b.g. Soviet Star (USA) 128 – My-Lorraine (IRE) 77 (Mac's 107 Imp (USA) 116) [2006 92: 8m² 8m 8.5m* 7g⁴ 8s² 10.4g⁴ 9d Sep 30] leggy, useful-looking gelding: useful handicapper: progressed in 2006, winning twice in 4 days at Galway in August (beat Dynamo Dancer 2 lengths in valuable race on second occasion): good efforts in frame at York next 2 starts, 2½ lengths second of 17 to Smart Enough then 1¾ lengths fourth of 11 to Rohaani: run best ignored in Cambridgeshire at Newmarket final outing, poorly drawn: stays 1¼m: acts on polytrack, soft and good to firm going. *R. A. Fahey*

BOLSHOI BALLET 8 b.g. Dancing Spree (USA) – Broom Isle 74 (Damister (USA) 48 123) [2006 –: p12.2g f12g p12.2g⁵ 16g² 16m f16g⁴ p16.5g f16g Dec 12] quite good-topped gelding: poor nowadays: left R. Fahey after fifth start: stays 2m: acts on all-weather, heavy and good to firm going: usually wears headgear: sometimes finds little. *Miss J. E. Foster*

BOLTON HALL (IRE) 4 b.g. Imperial Ballet (IRE) 110 – Muneera (USA) 67 (Green 74 Dancer (USA) 132) [2006 83: 8.2s 8d 8g 10f 7.5f 8d 7g³ 9.3f² 9.2m* 8m⁴ 8g⁵ 8d⁵ Sep 14] strong, angular gelding: fair handicapper: won at Hamilton in August: stays 9f: acts on firm going: edgy sort: sometimes races freely. *R. A. Fahey*

BOLUISCE (IRE) 3 ch.f. Zilzal (USA) 137 – No Islands (Lomond (USA) 128) [2006 48 p7g p8g Feb 22] 1,700Y, 5,000Y: half-sister to 3 winners, including 1m (at 2 yrs) and 2m winner Medelai (by Marju): dam ran once: better effort in maidens at Lingfield final outing: should stay 1¼m: sold 800 gns in July. *M. H. Tompkins*

BOMBARDIER BUSH (IRE) 3 b.g. Desert Prince (IRE) 130 – Fantasy Girl (IRE) 76 55 (Marju (IRE) 127) [2006 7s⁵ May 20] lengthy, good-bodied gelding: fifth foal: half-brother to smart 7f (at 2 yrs) to 10.5f winner Big Bad Bob (by Bob Back) and fairly useful Irish 7f winner Woodland Dream (by Charnwood Forest): dam, maiden who stayed 1½m, half-sister to smart 1¼m/1½m performer Persian Lightning: 9/1 from 20/1, though green and better for race, 6 lengths fifth of 12 to Master Pegasus in maiden at Newbury, starting slowly but getting hang of things at finish. *J. L. Dunlop*

BOMBER COMMAND (USA) 3 b.g. Stravinsky (USA) 133 – Parish Manor (USA) 71 + (Waquoit (USA)) [2006 84: p8g³ 7m⁵ 8.1g 8s p8.6m⁶ p7g⁴ p7g p8g² p7g* p8g³ Dec 22] **a104** big, workmanlike gelding: useful handicapper on all-weather, fair on turf: won at Kempton in November and December (beat Wavertree Warrior by neck): good length third to Orchard Supreme at Lingfield final start: stays 1m: acts on polytrack: tends to idle. *J. W. Hills*

BO MCGINTY (IRE) 5 ch.g. Fayruz 116 – Georges Park Lady (IRE) (Tirol 127) 92 [2006 95: f6g 7v⁶ p6g 6g 6g 6m 6s⁵ 6g⁴ 5m 6m² 5f* 5f⁴ 5m³ 5m 5m⁶ 5m 5d 5.1f⁴ 5s⁶ Oct 16] good-topped gelding: fairly useful handicapper: won at Beverley in June: also ran well tenth, twelfth and thirteenth outings: best at 5f/6f: acts on firm going, probably on soft: wears headgear nowadays: almost unseated at start ninth outing. *R. A. Fahey*

BONA DEA (GER) 3 br.f. Tertullian (USA) 115 – Bejaria (GER) (Konigsstuhl (GER)) – [2006 p8g Feb 7] half-sister to several winners in Germany, notably smart 6f (at 2 yrs) to 1m winner Bernardon (by Suave Dancer): dam German 7.5f/1m winner: well held both starts at 2 yrs for C. Von Der Recke: showed little in seller at Lingfield on British debut. *G. L. Moore*

BOND ANGEL EYES 3 b.f. Dr Fong (USA) 128 – Speedybird (IRE) 71 (Danehill **57** (USA) 126) [2006 62: 6g⁴ 6f 6m 10d⁴ 9.9g 7m 8s Sep 28] modest maiden: likely to prove best at 7f/1m: acts on firm and good to soft going (tailed off on soft): tried in cheekpieces/visor (ran poorly). *G. R. Oldroyd*

BOND BECKS (IRE) 6 ch.g. Tagula (IRE) 116 – At Amal (IRE) (Astronef 116) [2006 **63** 64: 5f³ 6m 5f⁴ 5m* 5m² 5m 5s 5d Oct 3] big, lengthy gelding: reportedly tubed: modest handicapper nowadays: won at Ayr in July, making all: best at 5f: acts on firm going: headstrong. *B. Smart*

BOND BOY 9 b.g. Piccolo 121 – Arabellajill 97 (Aragon 118) [2006 95: 5d⁶ 6g 5s* 5s³ **95** 5m 6f⁴ 5f⁵ 6d 5d⁴ 5s⁵ 5d⁶ Nov 3] sturdy gelding: useful handicapper: won at Thirsk in May: good third at Haydock next start: needs a test at 5f nowadays, and stays 6f: acts on fibresand and any turf going: blinkered/visored nowadays: has raced freely: usually held up. *B. Smart*

BOND CASINO 2 b.f. (Mar 27) Kyllachy 129 – Songsheet 74 (Dominion 123) [2006 **54** 5g⁵ 6m Sep 11] 28,000F, 30,000Y: good-bodied filly: fourth foal: half-sister to fairly useful 2002 2-y-o 5f/6f winner Monsieur Boulanger (by Compton Place): dam best at 5f: modest form in maidens (backward). *G. R. Oldroyd*

BOND CITY (IRE) 4 b.g. Trans Island 119 – Where's Charlotte 53 (Sure Blade (USA) **114** 130) [2006 104: 5m² 5m 5m 5.1m⁵ 6m 5d* 5.4g 5m⁴ 5g² Oct 12] strong, neat gelding: smart performer: won handicap at Epsom (by ½ length from Cape Royal) in August: good short-head second of 11 to Mecca's Mate in similar event at Newmarket final start: effective at 5f/easy 6f: acts on polytrack, firm and soft going: usually ridden prominently. *B. Smart*

BOND CRUZ 3 b.g. King's Best (USA) 132 – Arabis 88 (Arazi (USA) 135) [2006 52?: **–** f8g 8.3d 7g 10f f8g Jul 11] sturdy gelding: modest maiden at 2 yrs: little form in 2006: left B. Smart after second outing: pulled up hard. *G. R. Oldroyd*

BOND DIAMOND 9 gr.g. Prince Sabo 123 – Alsiba 68 (Northfields (USA)) [2006 71: **72** 8.5d² p8.6g⁴ 7d⁶ 8.2g² 8g⁴ 8.9m 8f² 8.1g 7f² 7.5m⁴ 7g³ 6g 8d Sep 14] strong, lengthy gelding: fair handicapper: effective at 7f, stays easy 1¼m: acts on all-weather, firm and good to soft going: tried in cheekpieces: sometimes slowly away: tends to carry head awkwardly: sometimes races freely: held up. *P. T. Midgley*

BOND FREE SPIRIT (IRE) 3 br.f. Shinko Forest (IRE) – Sawaki 71 (Song 132) **54** [2006 54 7f⁶ 7m⁴ 6m Sep 11] €13,000Y: rather leggy filly: half-sister to several winners, including fairly useful 5f (at 2 yrs) to 1m winner Norfolk Reed (by Thatching): dam 7f winner: modest maiden: never dangerous on handicap debut final start: probably stays 7f: raced only on ground firmer than good. *G. R. Oldroyd*

BOND MILLENNIUM 8 ch.g. Piccolo 121 – Farmer's Pet 90 (Sharrood (USA) 124) **–** [2006 59: p9.5g p9.5g Mar 20] sturdy gelding: fairly useful performer in his prime: was effective at 1m/1¼m: acted on all-weather, firm and soft going: had raced freely/found little: waited with: joined B. Pollock over hurdles: dead. *B. Smart*

BOND PLATINUM CLUB 2 ch.f. (Mar 9) Pivotal 124 – Highland Rowena 59 **59 p** (Royben 125) [2006 5d³ Oct 3] 26,000Y: half-sister to several winners, including smart 5f winner (including at 2 yrs) Lord Kintyre (by Makbul) and useful 5f winner Crofters Ceilidh (by Scottish Reel): dam sprinter: 14/1, green when 5½ lengths third to Luscivious in maiden at Catterick: open to improvement. *B. Smart*

BOND PLAYBOY 6 b.g. Piccolo 121 – Highest Ever (FR) (Highest Honor (FR) 124) **74** [2006 –: 7g 7g 7g p6g³ p6g² p7.1g 6s p6m² f6g⁵ p6g⁴ p5.1g³ p6g* Dec 30] good-bodied gelding: fair handicapper: won at Wolverhampton in December: best up to 7f: acts on all-weather, good to firm and good to soft going: usually wears headgear: effective held up/ridden prominently. *G. R. Oldroyd*

BOND PUCCINI 4 b.g. Piccolo 121 – Baileys By Name 66 (Nomination 125) [2006 **53** 51: 5d p5.1g⁵ f6g Nov 22] good-bodied gelding: modest maiden: stays 6f: acts on poly-track, soft and good to firm going: tried in cheekpieces. *G. R. Oldroyd*

BOND SEA BREEZE (IRE) 3 b.f. Namid 128 – Gold Prospector (IRE) 78 (Spec- **–** trum (IRE) 126) [2006 5s 5d 7m Sep 16] €10,000Y: well-made filly: second foal: half-sister to 6f winner Eden Star (by Soviet Star): dam Irish maiden who stayed 1m: well held in maidens. *G. R. Oldroyd*

BOND SILVER STRAND (IRE) 3 b.f. Trans Island 119 – Miss Game Plan (IRE) (Hector Protector (USA) 124) [2006 7m 8.2g 8d Oct 2] 2,700Y: tall, workmanlike filly: first foal: dam unraced: no sign of ability. *P. D. Niven* —

BONGOALI 4 b.f. Fraam 114 – Stride Home 78 (Absalom 128) [2006 57: p12.2m f16g f14g⁶ p11g³ p9.5g Nov 27] leggy, close-coupled filly: poor performer nowadays: stays 11f: acts on all-weather and any turf going. *Mrs C. A. Dunnett* **48**

BONNABEE (IRE) 4 b.f. Benny The Dip (USA) 127 – Samhat Mtoto 64 (Mtoto 134) [2006 68: p10g* Jan 14] strong filly: fair handicapper: won at Lingfield in January, sole start in 2006: stays 1½m: acts on polytrack and good to firm ground. *C. F. Wall* **71**

BONNE D'ARGENT (IRE) 2 b.f. (Apr 28) Almutawakel 126 – Petite-D-Argent 91 (Noalto 120) [2006 7d⁴ Oct 28] €16,000Y: small, sturdy filly: half-sister to several winners, including 5-y-o Winged d'Argent and useful stayer Mana d'Argent (by Ela-Mana-Mou): dam 6f (at 2 yrs) and 7f winner: 100/1, soon well placed when 6¼ lengths fourth of 20 to Measured Tempo in maiden at Newmarket: should stay 1¼m+. *J. R. Boyle* **76**

BONNE DE FLEUR 5 b.m. Whittingham (IRE) 104 – L'Estable Fleurie (IRE) 76 (Common Grounds 118) [2006 88: p5.1g⁵ p6g p5.1g⁵ 5d⁴ 5m* 5g 6g 5m³ 5m 5m p6g⁴ p5.1g⁴ p5.1g² p6g Dec 18] small, strong mare: fair handicapper nowadays: won at Redcar in May: effective at 5f/6f: acts on polytrack, firm and good to soft ground: tried visored, usually blinkered: races prominently. *B. Smart* **78**

BONNET O'BONNIE 2 br.f. (May 17) Makbul 104 – Parkside Prospect 65 (Piccolo 121) [2006 6g Aug 24] second foal: dam 2-y-o 5f/6f winner: 50/1, needed experience in maiden at Redcar. *J. Mackie* —

BONNIE BELLE 3 b.f. Imperial Ballet (IRE) 110 – Reel Foyle (USA) 77 (Irish River (FR) 131) [2006 9.9g⁶ 10.2m 8.3g⁴ Oct 16] 1,600Y: half-sister to several winners, including 6f/7f winner Soldier Point (by Sabrehill) and 5f (at 2 yrs) to 1m winner Unshaken (by Environment Friend): dam 2-y-o 5f winner: modest maiden: best effort at 1m on good ground. *J. R. Boyle* **64**

BONNIE PRINCE BLUE 3 ch.g. Tipsy Creek (USA) 115 – Heart So Blue (Dilum (USA) 115) [2006 93: 8m⁴ 8s⁵ 8m 8.1m⁴ 8d² 8.1m⁴ 8s 8m Oct 8] quite attractive gelding: has scope: useful handicapper: best effort when 3 lengths second to Shumookh at Pontefract: below form last 2 outings (gelded after final one): stays 1m: acts on good to firm and good to soft going. *B. W. Hills* **95**

BON NUIT (IRE) 4 b.f. Night Shift (USA) – Pray (IRE) (Priolo (USA) 127) [2006 112: p8g 9s⁴ 8m 9.9m 10s³ 10s² Oct 30] smallish, good-topped filly: just useful performer in 2006: creditable efforts when 1¾ lengths fourth to Violet Park in Dahlia Stakes at Newmarket and 6 lengths seventh to Soviet Song in Windsor Forest Stakes at Royal Ascot second/third starts and, having left G. Wragg, when 2¼ lengths third to Mountain at Fairyhouse and 3 lengths second to Arch Rebel at Leopardstown in listed races last 2: stays 1¼m: acts on good and good to firm going: has been bandaged off-hind joint. *Mrs J. Harrington, Ireland* **102**

BONNY SCOTLAND (IRE) 2 b.f. (Apr 12) Redback 116 – Muckross Park 41 (Nomination 125) [2006 5g 5m³ 5m 5f 6f 7g⁶ 7m p7.1g Dec 27] workmanlike filly: seventh foal: half-sister to 6-y-o No Time and to winners abroad by Petardia and Mac's Imp: dam sprint maiden: poor maiden: often slowly away. *I. W. McInnes* **47**

BONUS (IRE) 6 b.g. Cadeaux Genereux 131 – Khamseh 85 (Thatching 131) [2006 104: p7g* 7m⁵ 6.3g² Jul 2] big, strong, angular gelding: useful performer: won handicap at Lingfield (by short head from dead-heaters Red Spell and San Antonio) in January: good head second of 25 to Taqseem in valuable handicap at the Curragh final outing, clear of remainder: stays easy 7f: acts on polytrack and firm going: tried in cheekpieces/visor/tongue tie: often lethargic in preliminaries. *G. A. Butler* **106**

BON VIVEUR 3 b.g. Mozart (IRE) 131 – Fantazia 100 (Zafonic (USA) 130) [2006 69: 7m 8.1s 8.3m* 9.9m³ 11.6m⁴ 10m* 10m⁴ 10g⁶ 10m³ Sep 8] close-coupled, good-topped gelding: fair handicapper: won at Windsor in June and July (dictated): stays 1¼m (seemingly not 11.6f): acts on good to firm ground: wore cheekpieces last 5 starts: sold 45,000 gns, joined P. Hobbs. *R. Hannon* **77**

BOO 4 b.g. Namaqualand (USA) – Violet (IRE) 77 (Mukaddamah (USA) 125) [2006 103: p10g² p10g⁵ p10g⁴ p12.2g⁶ p8.6g⁶ p10g p10g 8.1m 10.4f³ 10m⁵ 10.5m 10.4g 10m p9.5g⁵ Dec 31] quite good-topped gelding: useful performer: ran creditably first 7 outings in 2006, and when third of 20 to Fairmile in John Smith's Cup (Handicap) at York and fifth of 6 in minor event at Ascot: stays 1¼m: acts on polytrack, best turf efforts on **100 a103**

good ground or firmer: often visored, wore cheekpieces/looked unenthusiastic penultimate start. *K. R. Burke*

BOOGIE BOARD 2 b.f. (Jan 19) Tobougg (IRE) 125 – Royal Gift (Cadeaux Genereux **52**
131) [2006 p6g⁵ Jun 10] 6,000Y: third foal: half-sister to 4-y-o Savoy Chapel: dam
unraced half-sister to useful 1¼m/1½m winner Mojalid: 16/1, fifth in maiden at Wolverhampton, outpaced. *M. J. Attwater*

BOOGIE DANCER 2 b.f. (Feb 27) Tobougg (IRE) 125 – Bolero (Rainbow Quest **68**
(USA) 134) [2006 6m 7m 7f 8.1m³ 7d p8.6g³ Nov 3] 5,000Y, resold 3,500Y: good-topped
filly: third foal: dam unraced out of Irish Oaks winner Bolas: fair maiden: third at Chepstow and Wolverhampton (nursery): likely to stay 1¼m: none too reliable. *H. S. Howe*

BOOGIE MAGIC 6 b.m. Wizard King 122 – Dalby Dancer 71 (Bustiki) [2006 50: **55**
p7g⁶ p8g⁶ p7g p9.5g* p10g⁴ p10g⁵ 8.3f 8.3m f8g Jul 7] good-topped mare: modest
performer: left T. Clement, won banded race at Wolverhampton in May: effective at 7f,
barely stays 11.6f: acts on polytrack, soft and good to firm going: tried in cheekpieces:
held up of late. *T. Keddy*

BOOGIE STREET 5 b.h. Compton Place 125 – Tart And A Half 83 (Distant Relative **103**
128) [2006 117: 5m 5m 5m 5m 5m³ Sep 5] big, lengthy, good-topped horse: smart
performer at best: successful 5 times during career, 4 of them listed races: useful form
first and final starts in 2006, running moody race when 5½ lengths third to Tax Free in
minor event at Leicester in latter: was best at 5f: acted on firm going: blinkered once:
wore tongue tie earlier in career: had worn crossed noseband: speedy front runner: to
stand at Acrum Lodge Stud, Co Durham, fee £1,000. *R. Hannon*

BOOKIESINDEX BOY 2 b.c. (Apr 30) Piccolo 121 – United Passion 74 (Emarati **73 §**
(USA) 74) [2006 5s⁶ 5f 5m⁵ p6g³ 5.2g f5g³ᵈ p5.1g² p6m⁵ p5.1g* p5.1g² Nov 10]
13,000Y: strong, good-topped colt: second foal: dam 5f winner: fair performer: won
maiden at Wolverhampton in October: creditable second in minor event there next time,
hanging markedly right: best at 5f: acts on all-weather and soft going: usually blinkered:
wayward. *J. R. Jenkins*

BOOKMAN (IRE) 4 b.g. Barathea (IRE) 127 – Literary 79 (Woodman (USA) 126) **66**
[2006 p9.5g⁵ p10g 6d 10.1m a7g² 6v Sep 22] fair maiden: trained by P. Mooney in Ireland
first 2 starts, next 2 by P. Haslam: may prove best at 7f/1m: best form on polytrack/sand:
tongue tied first 4 starts. *Ms I. Monaghan, Ireland*

BOOK OF DAYS (IRE) 3 b.f. Barathea (IRE) 127 – Beeper The Great (USA) (Whad- **–**
jathink (USA)) [2006 8.3g p8.6g p9.5g Dec 11] fifth foal: closely related to 5-y-o Corran
Ard and fairly useful 11f winner Phamedic (both by Imperial Ballet) and half-sister to
winner abroad by Red Ransom: dam unraced half-sister to Prix Marcel Boussac winner
Tropicaro: never dangerous in maidens. *R. M. Beckett*

BOOK OF FACTS (FR) 2 ch.g. (Apr 1) Machiavellian (USA) 123 – Historian (IRE) **84**
(Pennekamp (USA) 130) [2006 8.2s p8.6g* p8g³ Nov 28] strong gelding: first foal: dam,
French 10.5f winner, half-sister to Dubai World Cup winner Street Cry (by Machiavellian): fairly useful form: won maiden at Wolverhampton in November by short head from
Bergonzi (pair clear): similar form when third in nursery at Lingfield next time: likely to
be suited by 1¼m: acts on polytrack. *M. Johnston*

BOOK OF MUSIC (IRE) 3 b.c. Sadler's Wells (USA) 132 – Novelette (Darshaan **107**
133) [2006 86p: 10s⁴ 10m² 13.4g 10m³ 10s* 11.6d³ Nov 4] strong, close-coupled colt:
useful performer: won handicap at Ascot (beat dead-heaters Great Plains and Illustrious Blue a neck) in October: also ran well when placed in similar events at Sandown
(¾-length second to Dansili Dancer), Pontefract (third to Corran Ard) and Windsor (2¾
lengths third to Group Captain in November Stakes): should stay 1½m: acts on soft and
good to firm going: sent to UAE. *Sir Michael Stoute*

BOOM OR BUST (IRE) 7 ch.g. Entrepreneur 123 – Classic Affair (USA) 66 (Trempolino (USA) 135) [2006 10.2f Jul 27] no longer of any account: wears headgear. *Miss
K. M. George*

BOOT 'N TOOT 5 b.m. Mtoto 134 – Raspberry Sauce 65 (Niniski (USA) 125) [2006 **84**
86+: p12g p10g⁵ p10g³ p12g 10.9f⁶ 14.1g 11.5m² 14m 11.9f⁶ 11.7f* p12g⁴ p13g Oct 15]
tall, sparely-made mare: fairly useful handicapper: won at Bath in September: stays 1½m:
acts on polytrack and firm going (below form both outings on soft): none too reliable.
C. A. Cyzer

BOPPYS DANCER 3 b.g. Clan of Roses – Dancing Mary 59 (Sri Pekan (USA) 117) **58**
[2006 5s 7m⁶ 8d⁶ 8.2v p10g f11g² Dec 28] close-coupled gelding: modest maiden: stays
11f: acts on fibresand: blinkered final outing: very slowly away on debut. *P. T. Midgley*

*Vodafone Stewards' Cup (Handicap), Goodwood—the far-side runners are in control,
with Borderlescott improving again to lead home Mutamared (rail), Firenze (stripes, white cap),
Excusez Moi (partially obscured by Firenze) and Tax Free (No.1)*

BOPPYS DREAM 4 ch.f. Clan of Roses – Laurel Queen (IRE) 76 (Viking (USA)) **42**
[2006 51: 6.1d⁵ p7.1m⁶ p8.6g f6g Dec 28] small, strong filly: poor maiden nowadays:
stays 1m: probably acts on all-weather, unraced on extremes of ground on turf.
P. T. Midgley

BOPPYS PRIDE 3 ch.c. Clan of Roses – Joara (FR) (Radetzky 123) [2006 –: 7m³ **65**
9.1v* p12g² p12.2g³ Nov 23] fair performer: won handicap at Ayr in October: good
placed efforts after: stays 1½m: acts on polytrack and heavy ground. *R. A. Fahey*

BOQUILOBO 3 b.g. Rainbow Quest (USA) 134 – Moonlight Paradise (USA) 111 **68**
(Irish River (FR) 131) [2006 75: 12g⁶ 11g⁶ 10m 9.9f³ Jul 8] tall gelding: has scope: fair
maiden: best effort in 2006 when third in handicap at Beverley: stays 1¼m: acts on firm
ground, yet to race on softer than good: sold 14,000 gns later in July. *M. Johnston*

BORDELLO 3 b.g. Efisio 120 – Blow Me A Kiss 72 (Kris 135) [2006 7g 8.3d³ 8.2g **74**
Sep 26] tall, close-coupled gelding: third foal: brother to fairly useful 2003 2-y-o 5f
winner Farewell To Arms (later successful in USA): dam, maiden who stayed 1¼m, out
of half-sister to very smart middle-distance performer Apache: fair maiden: best effort
when third at Windsor: stays 1m: acts on good to soft going. *B. W. Hills*

BORDER ARTIST 7 ch.g. Selkirk (USA) 129 – Aunt Tate (Tate Gallery (USA) 117) **72**
[2006 63: p6g p6g p7.1g³ p7g p6g p7g⁵ p7g p6g² p6g³ p6g 7m⁴ 7m² 7f² 8m² 8.5g² 8f² **a68**
7m³ 7f* 7g* 7g 7m⁶ 8g² p8g⁶ 7d p8g⁴ 7g f7g⁴ p8.6g Dec 23] well-made gelding: fair
performer, better on turf than all-weather: left B. Powell £8,000, won handicaps at
Yarmouth in July and August: stays 8.5f: acts on all-weather, firm and good to soft going:
tried blinkered/in cheekpieces: usually held up. *J. Pearce*

BORDER EDGE 8 b.g. Beveled (USA) – Seymour Ann (Krayyan 117) [2006 76§: **74**
p8g* p10g p10g p8g 7s 8.1d⁶ 8.3g 7f⁴ 7m 7m 8f 9g² 8.5d² 8m* 8.1m 9.7f⁶ 12s 11s² 8d*
p10g³ p13g p10g⁴ p8g⁵ Nov 28] sturdy, close-coupled gelding: fair handicapper: won at
Lingfield in January, Salisbury in August and Brighton in October: effective at 1m to 11f:
acts on all-weather, firm and soft going: tried blinkered/visored: often races prominently.
J. J. Bridger

BORDERLESCOTT 4 b.g. Compton Place 125 – Jeewan 82 (Touching Wood (USA) **120**
127) [2006 106: 6s⁵ 6m⁴ 6m² 6m* 6d² 5.5d⁶ 6g² Oct 13] strong, close-coupled gelding:
very smart performer: significant improvement again in 2006, winning handicap at York
(made all to beat Rising Shadow ½ length) in May and 27-runner Vodafone Stewards'
Cup at Goodwood (by neck from Mutamared) in August: further progress 2 of next 3
starts (raced on unfavoured side at Chantilly in between): length second of 23 to Fonthill
Road in Ayr Gold Cup (made virtually all on stand side) and short-head second of 14 to
Bygone Days in Bentinck Stakes at Newmarket (hung left): should prove as effective at
5f as 6f: acts on firm and soft going: genuine and consistent, and a credit to connections.
R. Bastiman

BORDER MUSIC 5 b.g. Selkirk (USA) 129 – Mara River 86 (Efisio 120) [2006 90, **91**
a110: p7.1g* p6g* 7g6 7g 6m² 6m² 6m Jun 20] big gelding: smart on all-weather, fairly **a115**

useful on turf: has won 6 from 8 on polytrack, including minor events at Wolverhampton (by 3½ lengths from Kamanda Laugh) in March and Kempton (by neck from Presto Shinko) in April: good second in handicaps at Windsor and Goodwood: best at 6f/7f: acts on polytrack, firm and good to soft going: blinkered: travels strongly, but sometimes finds little. *A. M. Balding*

BORDER NEWS 3 ch.c. Selkirk (USA) 129 – Flit (USA) 72 (Lyphard (USA) 132) **74** [2006 11g p8.6g² 8m* 9g 8m 10d Sep 29] well-made colt: brother to smart 6f (at 2 yrs) and 1m (1000 Guineas) winner Wince (dam of Yorkshire Oaks winner Quiff), and half-brother to 3 winners, including very smart 8.5f to 1½m winner Ulundi (by Rainbow Quest): dam, 1¼m winner, sister to smart performer up to 1¼m Skimble: fair performer: fortunate winner of maiden at Newmarket in July, left in front when leader's saddle slipped: left H. Cecil, well below form in claimers afterwards: best effort at 1m: acts on good to firm going: blinkered last 2 starts. *T. Clout, France*

BORDER TALE 6 b.g. Selkirk (USA) 129 – Likely Story (IRE) 94 (Night Shift (USA)) **75 d** [2006 79: p12.2g p13.9g³ 14m 12g 15m p16.5m⁶ Nov 21] strong gelding: fair handicapper: well below form last 4 starts: stays 1¾m: acts on all-weather, soft and good to firm going: tried visored/tongue tied/in cheekpieces: has had breathing problems. *James Moffatt*

BOREAL APPLAUSE 2 b.f. (Feb 20) Royal Applause 124 – Rabwah (USA) 66 **88** (Gone West (USA)) [2006 6.1f* 6m³ 7d 6d⁵ p6g² Nov 22] close-coupled filly: first foal: dam, ran once, out of May Hill winner Mamlakah: fairly useful form: won maiden at Nottingham in July: below form in listed races third/fourth starts: good 1¼ lengths second in nursery at Kempton final outing: should stay 7f: acts on polytrack and firm ground. *E. A. L. Dunlop*

Border Rail & Plant Limited's "Borderlescott"

BOREANA 3 ch.f. Nashwan (USA) 135 – Aliena (IRE) (Grand Lodge (USA) 125) **73**
[2006 8.3m 10m 7m³ 8m 8m 8d Sep 14] second foal: dam French/US 2-y-o 7f/1m winner:
fair maiden: well below form in handicaps last 3 starts, leaving P. Chapple-Hyam after
fourth outing and N. Callaghan after fifth: should be suited by 1m+: acts on good to firm
going. *Jedd O'Keeffe*

BOREHAN 3 b.c. Agnes World (USA) 123 – Crime Ofthecentury 80 (Pharly (FR) 130) **108**
[2006 84: 5g* 6m* 6s* 6m Jun 17] big, good-topped colt: useful performer: progressed
well to win first 3 starts in 2006, namely maiden at Thirsk in April and handicaps at
Haydock and Newmarket (by 1¾ lengths from Signor Peltro) in May: folded tamely in
William Hill Trophy (Handicap) at York final outing (dismounted after line, reportedly
sore): will prove best at 5f/6f: acts on good to firm ground: has worn crossed
noseband: joined D. Selvaratnam in UAE. *M. A. Jarvis*

BORN DANCING 2 b.f. (Mar 26) Groom Dancer (USA) 128 – Birthday Venture 65 **–**
(Soviet Star (USA) 128) [2006 p7g 6d Sep 26] third foal: half-sister to 4-y-o Born To Be
Bold: dam 7f to 1¼m winner: well held in maidens, once tongue tied. *J. G. Portman*

BORN FOR DIAMONDS (IRE) 4 b.f. Night Shift (USA) – Kirri (IRE) (Lycius **36**
(USA) 124) [2006 47: f6g 6g 6g 8f⁶ 6m 7f 5s⁶ 7m Sep 16] well-made filly: poor maiden:
tried visored. *R. E. Barr*

BORN TO BE BOLD 4 ch.c. Bold Edge 123 – Birthday Venture 65 (Soviet Star **72**
(USA) 128) [2006 80: 6g 6d 6m⁵ 6f⁴ 6f⁵ Jul 10] fair handicapper: stayed 6f: acted on firm
and good to soft going: dead. *R. Hannon*

BORN WEST (USA) 2 b. or br.c. (Feb 7) Gone West (USA) – Admirer (USA) (Private **70**
Terms (USA)) [2006 p8.6g p8.6g³ p8g Dec 1] $120,000Y: second foal: brother to win-
ner in USA: dam, ran 3 times in USA, closely related to US Grade 3 9f winner Party
Manners out of US Grade 2 9f winner Duty Dance: easily best effort in maidens when
third at Wolverhampton on second start: will be suited by 1¼m: raced only on polytrack.
P. W. Chapple-Hyam

BORN WILD (GER) 3 b.f. Sadler's Wells (USA) 132 – Borgia (GER) 124 (Acate- **79**
nango (GER) 127) [2006 68p: 10g⁶ f11g² 14.1d* Aug 21] rangy filly: fair performer:
upped in trip, improved to win maiden handicap at Yarmouth (by 4 lengths) in August:
stays 1¾m: acts on all-weather and good to soft going. *Sir Michael Stoute*

BORODINSKY 5 b.g. Magic Ring (IRE) 115 – Valldemosa 81 (Music Boy 124) [2006 **57**
62: 7g 7d 7m 6.9f⁶ 7.1d⁴ 6g 6.9f 6m f7g⁴ f7g Dec 28] heavy-topped gelding: modest
performer: effective at 6f to 9f: acts on firm and soft going. *R. E. Barr*

BORSCH (IRE) 4 b.g. Soviet Star (USA) 128 – Cheese Soup (USA) (Spectacular Bid **–**
(USA)) [2006 –: 8g 10v 7.1d 7.2m Aug 12] no sign of ability: tried blinkered. *Miss
L. A. Perratt*

BORZOI MAESTRO 5 ch.g. Wolfhound (USA) 126 – Ashkernazy (IRE) 60 (Salt **64**
Dome (USA)) [2006 f5g² p6g f5s p5.1g 5.1m 5.5d 5.3m⁶ 5f⁴ 5.3m 5f 5g 5m f5m* f5g
p5.1g⁴ f5g⁶ Dec 28] small gelding: modest performer: missed 2005: claimed from
J. Spearing on reappearance: won banded race at Southwell in October: effective at 5f/6f:
acts on all-weather and firm going: wears headgear: races prominently. *M. Wellings*

BOSCHENDAL (IRE) 2 b.f. (Apr 7) Zamindar (USA) 116 – My Lass 91 (Elmaamul **–**
(USA) 125) [2006 6g⁵ 6d p7.1g Nov 14] strong filly: fourth foal: half-sister to 5-y-o
Mac Love: dam 1½m winner: green and little impact in maidens: tongue tied final start.
J. W. Hills

BOSCOBEL 2 ch.c. (Mar 1) Halling (USA) 133 – Dunnes River (USA) 84 (Danzig **91 p**
(USA)) [2006 p7g* Nov 22] second foal: half-brother to smart US 8.5f winner Crested
(by Fantastic Light), 1m winner in Britain at 2 yrs: dam, 1m winner only start, half-sister
to 5-y-o Bayeux: 9/2 and green, impressive when winning 11-runner maiden at Kempton
by 3 lengths from Silmi, carrying head awkwardly under pressure initially before getting
hang of things and powering clear: will be suited by 1m+: sure to improve, and looks a
useful prospect at least. *M. Johnston*

BOSSET (USA) 3 ch.f. Stravinsky (USA) 133 – Kadwah (USA) 80 (Mr Prospector **104**
(USA)) [2006 7s* 8f² 8m* 7g³ 7d 8f³ Dec 9] $80,000Y: tall, good-topped filly: has scope:
closely related to fairly useful UAE 7.5f to 9f winner Mustafhel (by Wolfhound) and
half-sister to 3 winners, including 7f/1m winner Awaamir and 6f (at 2 yrs) and 1m winner
Khassah (both useful, by Green Desert): dam 1m/1¼m winner: useful performer: won
maiden at Newbury in May and handicap at Newmarket (by 1½ lengths from Leningrad)
in July: good third after in handicap at Newbury (¾ length behind Jamieson Gold) and

non-graded stakes at Hollywood (blinkered on first start after leaving J. Noseda, beaten 2¼ lengths by Captive Melody): stays 1m: acts on firm and soft going. *Kathy Walsh, USA*

BOSS MAK (IRE) 3 ch.g. Shinko Forest (IRE) – Lucky Achievement (USA) (St Jovite (USA) 135) [2006 55: p8g 7m 9.8g 11.5m p16.5g Jul 13] unfurnished gelding: modest maiden: well held in handicaps on last 3 outings: should be suited by 1m+: tried in cheekpieces. *V. Smith* **55**

BOTHAM (USA) 2 b. or br.c. (Mar 9) Cryptoclearance (USA) – Oval (USA) (Kris S (USA)) [2006 6m p7g 5.1d⁶ Nov 1] good-topped colt: poor form in maidens. *T. J. Pitt* **49**

BOTTEEN 3 br.c. Singspiel (IRE) 133 – Abyaan (IRE) 106 (Ela-Mana-Mou 132) [2006 89p: 11.5m May 13] well-made colt: fairly useful winner in 2005: broke leg in Derby Trial at Lingfield only 3-y-o outing: should have been suited by 1¼m/1½m: dead. *M. P. Tregoning* **–**

BOTTOMLESS WALLET 5 ch.m. Titus Livius (FR) 115 – Furry Dance (USA) (Nureyev (USA) 131) [2006 55: 7g 8.2m 6.9f 7m 8s Aug 13] big mare: maiden: well held in 2006: tried in cheekpieces/visored. *F. Watson* **–**

BOUBOULINA 3 b.f. Grand Lodge (USA) 125 – Ideal Lady (IRE) (Seattle Slew (USA)) [2006 91p: 7g⁵ 7g² 7.1m 6g p7g³ p8g Oct 26] quite good-topped filly: useful performer: best effort when length third to Ceremonial Jade in handicap at Lingfield: below form in listed race there final start: stays 7f: acts on polytrack, best efforts on turf on good going: free-going sort: sold 120,000 gns. *E. A. L. Dunlop* **97**

BOUCHEEN 3 b.g. Foxhound (USA) 103 – Anytime Baby 56 (Bairn (USA) 126) [2006 41: p7.1g f5g p8.6g⁶ f7g³ 8.1m 9.9g⁴ 10m 7f² 9d p8.6g⁵ p9.5g³ f8g Dec 12] modest maiden: may prove best short of 1¼m: acts on all-weather, firm and good to soft going: sometimes races prominently. *Ms Deborah J. Evans* **51**

BOULE D'OR (IRE) 5 b.h. Croco Rouge (IRE) 126 – Saffron Crocus 83 (Shareef Dancer (USA) 135) [2006 113: 8.9m⁴ 8.9m 8.9g³ 8.9m⁴ 10m⁴ 10m² 10d² 8.5m² 10m⁶ 10.1g³ p8g Jul 15] tall, quite good-topped horse: good walker: smart performer: several creditable efforts in 2006, including when runner-up in Brigadier Gerard Stakes at Sandown (beaten 1¼ lengths by Notnowcato) and Diomed Stakes at Epsom (beaten neck by Nayyir) seventh/eighth starts: stays 1¼m: acts on polytrack, firm and good to soft going: has refused to settle (has worn crossed noseband) and idled: slowly away last 3 outings, well below form last 2: usually waited with: tough: sent to USA. *J. Akehurst* **115**

BOULEVIN (IRE) 6 b. or br.g. Perugino (USA) 84 – Samika (IRE) (Bikala 134) [2006 –: f16g 12.1d* 10g⁵ 12.6g p13.9m Oct 2] good-topped gelding: modest performer: left D. Hassett in Ireland prior to reappearance: best effort when winning apprentice handicap at Chepstow in May: stays 1½m: acts on good to soft ground. *R. J. Price* **54**

BOUMSONG (IRE) 3 b.g. Fasliyev (USA) 120 – Festive Season (USA) (Lypheor 118) [2006 51: 5.9g⁵ 9m 8f 7.9m 9.3m Aug 7] rather unfurnished gelding: poor maiden nowadays: best effort at 5f: acts on soft going: tried blinkered/visored. *R. C. Guest* **39**

BOUNDLESS PROSPECT (USA) 7 b.g. Boundary (USA) 117 – Cape (USA) (Mr Prospector (USA)) [2006 89, a82: f8s⁶ 8s⁵ 10.1m⁵ 8.1g⁴ 8g* 8m⁵ 8m 7m 8f 8.2s f8g* f8g⁴ f8g⁶ Dec 27] lengthy gelding: fairly useful handicapper on turf, just fair on all-weather nowadays: won at Yarmouth in June and Southwell in November: effective at 1m/1¼m: acts on polytrack, firm and soft going: sometimes slowly away: free-going type, held up. *Miss Gay Kelleway* **92 a78**

BOUQUET 4 b.f. Cadeaux Genereux 131 – Bayadere (USA) 61 (Green Dancer (USA) 132) [2006 71: 10d³ 12m⁵ 11.9m⁶ 10.6⁶ Oct 2] tall, quite attractive filly: fair maiden handicapper: left J. Fanshawe 14,000 gns after third start: barely stays 1½m: acts on good to firm and good to soft going: looked none too keen once at 2 yrs. *Francis Ennis, Ireland* **74**

BOURNONVILLE 3 b.g. Machiavellian 123 – Amellnaa (IRE) 86 (Sadler's Wells (USA) 132) [2006 –: p8.6g f7g p10g 6.1m 7m 8.3d 7f⁶ 11.5d p8g⁵ p13.9g⁶ Nov 6] rather leggy gelding: poor maiden: left J. Ryan after sixth start: tried tongue tied/in cheekpieces. *M. Wigham* **43**

BOUZOUKI (USA) 3 b. or br.g. Distant Music (USA) 126 – Pamina (IRE) (Perugino (USA) 84) [2006 69: p6g p7g Jul 19] rather leggy gelding: modest maiden: stays 8.6f: raced only on polytrack and good ground. *W. R. Swinburn* **61**

BOWING 6 b.g. Desert Prince (IRE) 130 – Introducing 78 (Mtoto 134) [2006 p12.2g p8.6g Mar 25] leggy, lengthy gelding: ungenuine maiden: missed 2005: well held both 6-y-o starts: tried in cheekpieces. *J. L. Spearing* **– §**

BOW

BOWLANDER 3 ch.g. Zaha (CAN) 106 – Lambeth Belle (USA) (Arazi (USA) 135) – [2006 –: p6g Mar 6] no sign of ability. *Miss K. M. George*

BOWLED OUT (GER) 4 b.f. Dansili 127 – Braissim (Dancing Brave (USA) 140) 75 [2006 76: p10g⁶ 12d 12m 11.8m⁴ p12.2g² p12.2g³ 12m 10g² 12d⁴ p12g p9.5m³ p10g² p9.5g² p9.5g Dec 1] close-coupled filly: fair handicapper: effective at 9.5f to easy 1½m: acts on polytrack, good to firm and good to soft going: tried blinkered/in cheekpieces. *P. J. McBride*

BOWL EM OVER 2 ch.f. (Jan 23) Primo Valentino (IRE) 116 – Clansinge 55 (Clan- 54 time 101) [2006 5d⁵ 5m 5s⁶ 5f² 5f⁴ 5m* 5f⁴ 5m Sep 11] 4,800Y: workmanlike filly: first foal: dam 2-y-o 5f winner: modest performer: won seller at Catterick in July: raced at 5f: acts on firm and good to soft going: often wears cheekpieces. *M. E. Sowersby*

BOWL OF CHERRIES 3 b.g. Vettori (IRE) 119 – Desert Nomad 56 (Green Desert 67 (USA) 127) [2006 45: 8m⁴ 8m 10m 10d f7g³ f8g* p8g* p8g² p8g² Dec 18] compact geld- ing: fair performer: improved late in year, winning banded race at Southwell in November and handicap at Kempton in December: stays 1m: acts on all-weather and good to firm going: tried in cheekpieces, blinkered last 5 starts. *I. A. Wood*

BOWMAN'S BOY (IRE) 2 b.g. (Mar 16) Golan (IRE) 129 – Haut Volee (Top Ville – 129) [2006 6m 6f⁶ 7m Aug 6] workmanlike gelding: well held in maidens. *M. W. Easterby*

BOWNESS 4 b.f. Efisio 120 – Dominio (IRE) 99 (Dominion 123) [2006 84: 6g 5g⁵ 5d³ 81 p7.1g 5m Aug 16] strong, compact filly: fairly useful performer: flattered when third in listed event at Ayr third start: poor efforts in handicaps both starts after: effective at 5f/6f: acts on polytrack, firm and good to soft ground. *J. G. Given*

BOW WAVE 4 b.g. Danzero (AUS) – Moxby (Efisio 120) [2006 81: p7g 7.1d 8d 7.1m – Jun 16] good-topped gelding: fairly useful performer at 3 yrs: well held in 2006: visored final outing. *H. Candy*

BOXHALL (IRE) 4 b.g. Grand Lodge (USA) 125 – March Hare 60 (Groom Dancer 80 (USA) 128) [2006 80: 11.5m 13.3m⁵ 14m² 14.1m² 15.9g⁶ 16.2d 18d Oct 14] rangy gelding: fairly useful handicapper: probably stays 2m: acts on firm going, below form on good to soft: effective tongue tied or not: sold 14,000 gns. *W. R. Swinburn*

BOY DANCER (IRE) 3 ch.g. Danehill Dancer (IRE) 117 – Mary Gabry (IRE) (Kris 70 135) [2006 48+: 5d 7.1m⁵ 8m³ 7.2v⁵ 5.9m* 6m 5.9g² 5.9m 7.2g⁵ 8v Sep 14] strong, stocky gelding: fair handicapper: won at Carlisle in June: effective at 6f to 1m: acts on good to firm going: has run well when sweating: sometimes slowly away. *D. W. Barker*

BOYSIE BRIGADOR (USA) 3 ch.g. Gone West (USA) – Summer Voyage (USA) – (Summer Squall (USA)) [2006 6m 7f⁵ 11.9f Aug 9] fifth in minor event at Taby at 2 yrs: tongue tied, no form in Britain: sold 20,000 gns. *R. A. Kvisla*

BRABAZON (IRE) 3 b.c. In The Wings 128 – Azure Lake (USA) (Lac Ouimet 81 (USA)) [2006 66p: 9.7s 11.6m² 11.6m² 11.6g 14m Jun 16] quite good-topped, attractive colt: fairly useful maiden: good efforts when second in handicaps at Windsor in April/ May: should stay 1¾m: acts on good to firm ground: sold 35,000 gns in July. *R. Charlton*

BRABINGER (IRE) 3 b.g. Xaar 132 – Particular Friend 88 (Cadeaux Genereux 131) – [2006 –: 10.2f Sep 9] no sign of ability. *B. G. Powell*

BRACE OF DOVES 4 b.g. Bahamian Bounty 116 – Overcome (Belmez (USA) 131) 61 [2006 73: 8m⁵ May 5] quite good-topped gelding: fair handicapper at best: shaped as if in need of run when below form only outing at 4 yrs: stays 1m: acts on fibresand, firm and soft going: sold 2,500 gns in August. *T. D. Barron*

BRACKLINN 4 b.f. Deploy 131 – Blane Water (USA) 93 (Lomond (USA) 128) [2006 73 73: 10m³ 10m³ 10f² Aug 10] compact filly: fair handicapper: stays easy 1¼m: acts on polytrack and firm going: sold 5,500 gns. *J. R. Fanshawe*

BRADDOCK (IRE) 3 b.c. Pivotal 124 – Sedna (FR) (Bering 136) [2006 7v* 8.2d* 75 Apr 22] 125,000Y: close-coupled colt: second foal: half-brother to winner in Denmark by Bachir: dam French 10.5f winner: won both starts, namely maiden at Southwell in March and handicap at Nottingham in April: stays 1m: acts on heavy ground. *T. D. Barron*

BRAGADINO 7 b.g. Zilzal (USA) 137 – Graecia Magna (USA) 109 (Private Account 59 (USA)) [2006 58: p8g⁵ 7f 7f⁴ 7g 8d⁶ 8d Sep 29] close-coupled, quite good-topped geld- ing: modest handicapper: left L. Woods after fourth start: stays 9f: acts on polytrack and any turf going: well held in blinkers/visor: sometimes tongue tied. *Padraig O'Connor, Ireland*

156

BRAHMINY KITE (USA) 4 b.g. Silver Hawk (USA) 123 – Cope's Light (USA) **105** (Copelan (USA)) [2006 113: 12m⁴ 12.1d⁶ 11.9g 8m a9f⁴ a8g a10f³ Dec 22] big, angular gelding: just useful performer at 4 yrs: sold from M. Johnston 85,000 gns and off 5 months after third outing: best effort of 2006 when 3½ lengths third to Singing Poet in listed race at Jebel Ali final start: stays 1½m: acts on dirt, good to firm and good to soft going: visored once in 2005 and on third 4-y-o outing. *R. Bouresly, UAE*

BRAINY BENNY (IRE) 2 b.c. (Jan 7) Barathea (IRE) 127 – Sonachan (IRE) 73 (Dar- **90** shaan 133) [2006 6g⁴ 8v⁶ p8g* p8g² 8g³ p8g 8.5d³ Nov 25] 18,000F, 58,000Y: big, rangy colt: has a quick action: first foal: dam Irish 1¾m winner: fairly useful form: won maiden at Kempton (hung left) in September: placed after in well-contested nurseries at Ling- field then Newmarket and non-graded Laurel Futurity at Laurel (first start after leaving N. Callaghan, 9 lengths third to Strike A Deal): will stay 1¼m: acts on polytrack: pulled too hard sixth outing. *W. I. Mott, USA*

BRAMANTINO (IRE) 6 b.g. Perugino (USA) 84 – Headrest (Habitat 134) [2006 79: 12m 12.4g 13.1g 13.8s Oct 14] strong, lengthy gelding: fair handicapper at 5 yrs: well beaten in 2006: often wears headgear. *T. A. K. Cuthbert*

BRAMCOTE LORNE 3 b.g. Josr Algarhoud (IRE) 118 – Dreamtime Quest **67** (Blakeney 126) [2006 56: 8m 8.1g⁵ 8g⁴ 12.1g⁵ 11.1f³ 14m² 12f 16g⁵ p12g 12.4s 13.9g **a59** p12g⁴ p16g⁴ Nov 28] stocky gelding: fair maiden on turf, modest on all-weather: stays 1¾m: acts on polytrack and firm going. *S. Parr*

BRANDYWELL BOY (IRE) 3 b.g. Danetime (IRE) 121 – Alexander Eliott (IRE) **81** 73 (Night Shift (USA)) [2006 87: p5g 5.1f 6.1s 5g 5f³ 5m⁶ 5g⁶ 6g² 6m 6m⁶ p6g⁴ p6g p6g² **a88** p6g⁵ p5g⁶ Dec 10] close-coupled gelding: fairly useful handicapper, better on all-weather than turf: best at 5f/6f: acts on polytrack and firm going: sometimes wears headgear (in- cluding last 3 starts). *D. J. S. ffrench Davis*

BRANSTON TIGER 7 b.g. Mark of Esteem (IRE) 137 – Tuxford Hideaway 102 (Cawston's Clown 113) [2006 69+: f6g Dec 23] rangy gelding: fair performer: off 22 months, well beaten only outing in 2006: blinkered/visored. *Ian Emmerson*

BRAVE AMBER 2 ch.f. (Mar 10) Soviet Star (USA) 128 – Be Brave (FR) (Green – Forest (USA) 134) [2006 6g 7m Jul 15] second foal: dam, 1¼m to 15.5f winner in France, also won over hurdles in Britain: well beaten in maidens. *M. Blanshard*

BRAVE BEAR 4 br.f. Bold Edge 123 – Sarah Bear (Mansingh (USA) 120) [2006 69: **67** 5v⁵ Mar 31] good-topped filly: fair handicapper: probably best at 5f: acts on any turf going: blinkered: races prominently: sold 5,000 gns in November. *T. D. Easterby*

BRAVE DANE (IRE) 8 b.g. Danehill (USA) 126 – Nuriva (USA) 100 (Woodman **73** (USA) 126) [2006 53: p10g* p10g* 10.2g⁵ 10.2d 10g p8g Aug 9] lengthy, angular geld- ing: fair performer: won 2 banded races at Kempton in May: stays 1¼m: acts on polytrack and any turf going: tried blinkered: carries head high: often slowly away: held up. *A. W. Carroll*

BRAVE FIGHT 3 b.g. Kalanisi (IRE) 132 – Baalbek 76 (Barathea (IRE) 127) [2006 78: **83** 10m p8g² p8g p10g Sep 2] fairly useful maiden handicapper: good second at Kempton in July: well beaten after: should stay 1¼m: acts on polytrack and firm going: sold 10,000 gns, sent to Qatar. *A. King*

BRAVE HIAWATHA (FR) 4 b.g. Dansili 127 – Alexandrie (USA) 114 (Val de – L'Orne (FR) 133) [2006 12m Jul 15] fairly useful performer: best effort when winning minor event at Chantilly in 2005: left A. de Royer-Dupre in France 28,000 gns, last in handicap at Salisbury sole start in Britain: stays 10.5f. *J. A. B. Old*

BRAVE QUEST (IRE) 2 b.g. (Apr 3) Indian Danehill (IRE) 124 – Mill Rainbow (FR) **56** (Rainbow Quest (USA) 134) [2006 p6f 7.1m 8d Sep 27] big gelding: modest maiden: seems to stay 1m. *C. J. Down*

BRAVE TIN SOLDIER (USA) 2 b.c. (Mar 30) Storm Cat (USA) – Bless (USA) (Mr **105** Prospector (USA)) [2006 6m² 6d² 6g* 6d⁵ Sep 29] big, strong colt: type to carry condi- tion: has a quick action: second foal: brother to 9f winner in Japan: dam unraced sister to Kentucky Derby winner Fusaichi Pegasus: useful form: second in maidens at Goodwood and York then improved to win 10-runner listed race at the Curragh (beat Invincible Force by 2½ lengths) in September: 9/2, creditable 5¾ lengths fifth of 6 to Dutch Art in Middle Park Stakes at Newmarket, rallying: will be suited by 7f/1m. *A. P. O'Brien, Ireland*

BRAVO MAESTRO (USA) 5 b.g. Stravinsky (USA) 133 – Amaranthus (USA) **103** (Kingmambo (USA) 125) [2006 78, a85: p8.6g* p10g* p10g³ p8g p8.6g* p10g⁶ p8g⁵ **a111** p10g⁴ 9m 10g⁶ 12m 10.4f² 10.5m³ 13.9d p12g⁴ 10m 8.5f Nov 24] tall, leggy gelding:

smart on all-weather, useful on turf: won handicaps at Wolverhampton and Lingfield in January and Wolverhampton (beat Divine Gift 1¾ lengths) in March: good efforts after at Lingfield in Winter Derby (sixth to Sri Diamond) and Kempton in Rosebery Stakes (Handicap) and September Stakes (fourth to Kandidate both times): also ran well in several turf handicaps, including when ¾-length second to Fairmile in John Smith's Cup at York and third to Dansili Dancer in valuable event at Haydock: sold from N. Littmoden 105,000 gns, in Citation Handicap at Hollywood final outing: stays 1½m: acts on polytrack and firm going: blinkered last 2 starts: not straightforward. *B. D. A. Cecil, USA*

BRAVURA 8 ch.g. Never So Bold 135 – Sylvan Song (Song 132) [2006 60: p16g⁶ p16g⁶   **61**
Feb 28] modest performer, raced mainly on all-weather nowadays: stays easy 2m: acts on polytrack and good to firm ground: effective blinkered or not. *G. L. Moore*

BRAZILIAN BRIDE (IRE) 2 b.f. (Jan 24) Pivotal 124 – Braziliz (USA) 70 (King-   **103**
mambo (USA) 125) [2006 5d⁴ 6m* 6m⁴ 7m⁴ Aug 27] third foal: half-sister to Irish 6f winner Brazilian Sun (by Barathea): dam, Irish maiden who stayed 1m, half-sister to dam of Dolphin Street and Saffron Walden: useful performer: won maiden at Naas in April and Swordlestown Stud Sprint Stakes there (by 2 lengths from Gee Kel) in June: better form afterwards when fourth at the Curragh in 7-runner Phoenix Stakes (beaten 2¼ lengths by Holy Roman Emperor) and 12-runner Moyglare Stud Stakes (length behind Miss Beatrix): stays 7f. *K. Prendergast, Ireland*

BREAKER MORANT (IRE) 4 b.c. Montjeu (IRE) 137 – Arcade (Rousillon (USA)   **79**
133) [2006 –: 8d² 8.2v 7f⁴ 8f* 7g* 7m* 9m* 9d 8m 7s p7.1g Oct 29] half-brother to several winners, including smart Montecastillo (by Fairy King) and useful Kalamunda (by Royal Academy), both 7f/1m winners in Ireland: dam, Irish 5f winner, half-sister to smart pair Orientor (sprinter) and Yeast (at 7f to 1¼m): fair handicapper: improved when completing 4-timer in July and August at Bellvestown, Roscommon (2) and Ballinrobe: left A. McGuinness in Ireland after ninth start: good seventh at Wolverhampton final outing: effective at 7f to 9f: acts on polytrack and firm going: blinkered. *Patrick Morris, Ireland*

BREAKING SHADOW (IRE) 4 br.g. Danehill Dancer (IRE) 117 – Crimbourne 83   **87**
(Mummy's Pet 125) [2006 87: 7g³ 7.2g² 7g³ 6m 7g 7m⁴ 7f 7f⁵ 7.1m 7d⁴ 7g 7.5g² 7.1s³ 8.9s⁴ 8.2s 7d³ Oct 28] close-coupled gelding: fairly useful handicapper: made frame 9 times in 2006: stays 9f: acts on soft and good to firm going: tried blinkered/in cheekpieces. *T. D. Barron*

BREAK 'N' DISH 2 b.g. (Apr 10) Montjoy (USA) 122 – Ship of Gold 78 (Glint of   **–**
Gold 128) [2006 p8g 8.3g Oct 16] leggy gelding: tailed off both starts. *B. R. Johnson*

BREAN DOT COM (IRE) 2 b.g. (Apr 5) Desert Sun 120 – Anna Elise (IRE) 106   **62**
(Nucleon (USA) 94) [2006 6m f7g⁵ Dec 14] sturdy gelding: better effort in maidens 4 months apart when mid-field at Haydock (hung left) on debut: still green next time: should stay 1m. *Mrs P. N. Dutfield*

BRECKLAND BOY 2 b.g. (Apr 17) City On A Hill (USA) 114 – Sea Idol (IRE) 65   **–**
(Astronef 116) [2006 5d⁴ 6m⁶ p6g 6g⁵ 6m⁶ p5.1g Sep 11] good-topped gelding: little form: tried in cheekpieces/visor. *Mrs C. A. Dunnett*

BREEDER'S FOLLY 4 b.f. Mujahid (USA) 125 – Wynona (IRE) 89 (Cyrano de   **–**
Bergerac 120) [2006 42: p9.5g Mar 27] poor maiden: well held only outing in 2006. *T. J. Fitzgerald*

BREEZE IN (IRE) 3 b.g. Houmayoun (FR) 114 – Breeze Up 66 (Coquelin (USA) 121)   **51**
[2006 –: 9m⁶ 6m⁵ 5d f6g Dec 29] leggy-raced maiden: left C. Swan in Ireland, modest form in banded race at Southwell on British debut final start. *R. A. Fahey*

BREEZEWAY (IRE) 2 b.f. (Feb 5) Grand Lodge (USA) 125 – Puck's Castle 92   **70**
(Shirley Heights 130) [2006 6m 7m 7.1d³ 8s p8.6g Dec 23] €340,000Y: deep-girthed filly: has a quick action: sixth foal: half-sister to 3 winners, including Irish 1½m winner Down Mexico Way (by Sadler's Wells) and 5f winner (including at 2 yrs) Emerald Peace (by Green Desert), both useful: dam, 1m winner (ran only at 2 yrs), half-sister to Cheveley Park winner Embassy out of Cheveley Park winner Pass The Peace: fair maiden: third to Elusive Flash at Warwick, easily best effort: should stay 1m. *B. J. Meehan*

BRENDAN'S SURPRISE 4 b.g. Faustus (USA) 118 – Primrose Way 59 (Young   **–**
Generation 129) [2006 58: p9.5g 21.7m Jun 24] modest maiden: well held both starts in 2006: tried blinkered/visored. *K. J. Burke*

BRENIN GWALIA 2 ch.c. (Mar 27) Arkadian Hero (USA) 123 – Princess Aurora 58   **71**
(Prince Sabo 123) [2006 p7.1g² 6g² 7f³ 5.5m³ 5m² p5g² 5d³ Oct 8] 3,500Y: strong, lengthy colt: second foal: dam sprint maiden: fair maiden: placed all 7 starts, 3 in nurse-

ries: may prove best at 5f/6f: acts on polytrack and firm going: sold 25,000 gns, sent to USA. *D. M. Simcock*

BRENNIE (IRE) 5 ch.m. Grand Lodge (USA) 125 – Brentsville (USA) (Arctic Tern (USA) 126) [2006 53: f16g³ Jan 3] close-coupled mare: modest maiden: stays 16.5f: acts on all-weather and firm going: usually visored/in cheekpieces. *V. Smith* **53**

BRET MAVERICK (IRE) 2 b.g. (Mar 28) Josr Algarhoud (IRE) 118 Shady Street (USA) (Shadeed (USA) 135) [2006 7d p8.6f³ 8.3d⁵ Sep 25] modest maiden: stays 8.6f. *J. R. Weymes* **60**

BREUDDWYD LYN 8 br.g. Awesome 73 – Royal Resort 57 (King of Spain 121) [2006 p12g Mar 22] poor maiden in 2003: last in seller only outing on Flat since. *D. Burchell* **–**

BRIANNIE (IRE) 4 b.f. Xaar 132 – Annieirwin (IRE) 94 (Perugino (USA) 84) [2006 53: 11.9m Apr 30] modest maiden: stays 1½m: acts on polytrack and good to firm ground: tried blinkered/in cheekpieces: hung markedly/looked far from keen on 3-y-o reappearance. *P. Butler* **–**

BRIANNSTA (IRE) 4 b.g. Bluebird (USA) 125 – Nacote (IRE) (Mtoto 134) [2006 93: 6g 6g 6g 6d p6g* p6g* p5.1g³ Dec 7] lengthy, quite attractive gelding: fairly useful handicapper: left M. Channon, won handicaps at Wolverhampton in October and November: effective at 5f to 7f: acts on polytrack, good to firm and good to soft ground: tried visored: effective ridden prominently or held up. *C. G. Cox* **87**

BRIARWOOD BEAR 2 ch.g. (Apr 29) Woodborough (USA) 112 – Bramble Bear 72 (Beveled) [2006 5g 6m p7.1g⁴ p7.1g Dec 21] second foal: dam, 5f (including at 2 yrs)/6f winner, half-sister to smart sprinter Rambling Bear: gelded, easily best effort when fourth to Leonard Charles in maiden at Wolverhampton: stays 7f: acts on polytrack. *M. Blanshard* **59**

BRIDEGROOM 4 b.g. Groom Dancer (USA) 128 – La Piaf (FR) (Fabulous Dancer (USA) 124) [2006 –: 8d 8m p8.6g⁶ 10f p8g⁵ p12g⁴ 9.9m* 9.9d⁵ 10.2m⁶ Oct 8] modest performer: left Lady Herries after fourth outing: won handicap at Beverley in September: stays easy 1½m: acts on polytrack, good to firm and good to soft going: tried in cheekpieces/visor: sold 22,000 gns. *D. R. C. Elsworth* **62**

BRIDESHEAD (IRE) 3 b.c. Danehill (USA) 126 – Kanmary (FR) 117 (Kenmare (FR) 125) [2006 10g Apr 18] strong, well-made colt: half-brother to several winners, notably Breeders' Cup Sprint winner Lit de Justice and 2000 Guineas/Derby third Colonel Collins (both by El Gran Senor) and Racing Post Trophy winner Commander Collins (by Sadler's Wells), later stayed 1½m: dam, French 2-y-o 5f (Prix du Bois) winner, stayed 9f: 10/1 and burly, well held in maiden at Newmarket, green and off bridle some way out. *A. P. O'Brien, Ireland* **–**

BRIDE TO BE (USA) 3 b.f. Dixie Union (USA) 121 – Leading The Way (USA) (Septieme Ciel (USA) 123) [2006 p10g³ 8.1g 11.8m 9.9f 8g³ p10g p10g 9.7d⁴ Aug 23] third foal: half-sister to winner in USA by Theatrical: dam unraced out of US Grade 2 7f/8.5f winner Fit To Lead: fair maiden: stays 1m (seemingly not 1¼m): sold 800 gns in November. *C. E. Brittain* **73**

BRIDGE IT JO 2 gr.f. (Feb 27) Josr Algarhoud (IRE) 118 – T G'S Girl 57 (Selkirk (USA) 129) [2006 5g 5m³ p5g⁴ 5.1g* 6f⁵ 5.1f² 5.2g⁴ 6m⁵ 5d⁵ Sep 15] 7,500Y: good-topped filly: third foal: half-sister to 3-y-o Calypso King: dam maiden who should have stayed 7f: fairly useful performer: won maiden at Nottingham in June: best efforts sixth/seventh starts, second to Not For Me in minor event at Chester and fourth to Abby Road in listed race at Newbury: best at 5f: acts on firm going. *Miss J. Feilden* **91**

BRIDGET'S TEAM 2 b.f. (Apr 29) Elnadim (USA) 128 – Overcome (Belmez (USA) 131) [2006 5d³ 7f⁵ p7.1g f6g* f6g² f6g³ p7.1g⁶ Dec 30] 8,000Y: third foal: half-sister to 4-y-o Brace of Doves: dam, German 1¼m winner, out of half-sister to German Derby winners Orofino and Ordos: modest performer: won nursery at Southwell in November: claimed from P. Haslam after next start: stays 6f: acts on fibresand: tongue tied last 2 starts. *D. G. Bridgwater* **58**

BRIDGEWATER BOYS 5 b.g. Atraf 116 – Dunloe (IRE) 54 (Shaadi (USA) 126) [2006 83, a70: f8g p9.5g⁴ p8.6g* p9.5g³ p8.6g* p8.6g p8.6g p8.6g³ 8.5g* 8.2g⁴ 8.9m p8.6g³ 9.3g p10g p9.5g² Dec 9] lengthy gelding: fair handicapper: won at Wolverhampton (twice) in February and Beverley in May: stays easy 9.5f: acts on all-weather, firm and soft ground: wears headgear: tried tongue tied: usually races prominently nowadays. *K. A. Ryan* **74**

BRIEF ENGAGEMENT (IRE) 3 br.f. Namid 128 – Brief Fairy (IRE) (Brief Truce (USA) 126) [2006 p5g Dec 10] €2,000Y: second foal: half-brother to fairly useful 2004 2-y-o 6f winner Sir Anthony (by Danehill Dancer): dam Italian 5f (at 2 yrs) and 7f winner: 16/1 and green, slowly away and always behind in maiden at Kempton. *T. D. McCarthy*   –

BRIEF GOODBYE 6 b.g. Slip Anchor 136 – Queen of Silk (IRE) 93 (Brief Truce (USA) 126) [2006 84: 8.1m⁵ 10.5g² 10g 10f* 10m³ 10d⁶ 10g⁶ 10.5g* Sep 22] quite good-topped gelding: fairly useful handicapper: won at Windsor in July and Haydock in September: should stay 1½m: acts on firm and good to soft going: held up: sometimes slowly away/finds little. *John Berry*   **89**

BRIEF HISTORY 3 ch.c. Galileo (IRE) 134 – Take Liberties 110 (Warning 136) [2006 8s 10m 12g a12g² a13.3g³ a8.6g⁵ a12g Nov 18] big, strong colt: fourth foal: half-brother to winners abroad by Hennessy and Gone West: dam, French 2-y-o 6f winner, best at 1¼m: fair maiden: sold from H. Candy 16,000 gns after third start: placed in minor event at Taby and handicap at Jagersro afterwards: stays 13.3f: acts on dirt. *C. Hederud, Sweden*   **66**

BRIEF PASSING (IRE) 7 b.h. Karaar 74 – Rose The Brief (IRE) (Barry's Run (IRE) 48) [2006 p13g Sep 29] 66/1, well beaten on debut in maiden at Lingfield. *Luke Comer, Ireland*   –

BRIEF STATEMENT (IRE) 4 b.g. Desert Prince (IRE) 130 – Brief Sentiment (IRE) 96 (Brief Truce (USA) 126) [2006 63: 9.2m⁶ 11.9s⁵ 10g* 10d⁶ 12g⁵ 12m* 17.5d 12s Sep 22] strong gelding: fair performer: won handicaps at Ayr in June and Goodwood in August: looked sure to win amateur event at Ascot in September when breaking down final 1f: stayed 1½m: acted on good to firm and soft going: wore visor/cheekpieces final 3 starts: dead. *W. M. Brisbourne*   **67**

BRIERLEY LIL 2 ch.f. (Mar 29) Intikhab (USA) 135 – Pooka 65 (Dominion 123) [2006 5.5d 6m 6m 7f p7.1g⁴ Dec 27] 22,000Y: half-sister to several winners, including 3-y-o Rydal Mount and 4-y-o Dove Cottage: dam placed at 5f at 2 yrs: poor maiden: fourth in nursery at Wolverhampton. *J. L. Spearing*   **46**

BRIERY BLAZE 3 b.f. Dansili 127 – Sabonis (USA) 68 (The Minstrel (CAN) 135) [2006 63: 8.2g 6.9m 5.9g³ 5d Sep 25] plain filly: modest maiden: may prove best at 6f: acts on polytrack. *Mrs K. Walton*   **60**

BRIERY LANE (IRE) 5 ch.g. Tagula (IRE) 116 – Branston Berry (IRE) 86 (Mukaddamah (USA) 125) [2006 60: 6d² 6m⁵ 7g 6g* 6m⁴ 7m 6d³ 6g² 6s 6.1s p7.1g⁴ Nov 3] lengthy gelding: fair handicapper: won amateur maiden event at Redcar in May: stays easy 7f: acts on polytrack, firm and good to soft going: wears cheekpieces nowadays: sold 6,400 gns. *Mrs K. Walton*   **71**

BRIGADORE 7 b.g. Magic Ring (IRE) 115 – Music Mistress (IRE) 55 (Classic Music (USA)) [2006 82: 6g 5g 5.7s² 5.7g³ 6g⁵ 5g⁶ p6g 5f 5f 6f⁶ 5m⁵ 5m 6g⁶ 5.5d* 5d⁶ 6s⁴ 6d⁵ 7d⁶ Oct 18] small, good-quartered gelding: fair handicapper: won at Warwick in September: stays 6f: acts on any turf going: usually held up: has been slowly away. *J. G. Given*   **71**

BRIGADORE (USA) 3 gr. or ro.c. Sandpit (BRZ) 129 – Mersey 123 (Crystal Palace (FR) 132) [2006 –: 10g⁵ 11f* 12g 14m⁵ 14g⁶ Aug 17] angular, unfurnished colt: fairly useful performer: won maiden at Redcar in June: best effort in handicaps after when fifth to Doctor Scott at Sandown: stays 1¾m: acts on firm going. *W. R. Muir*   **83**

BRIGHT 3 ch.g. Mister Baileys 123 – Razzle Dazzle (IRE) (Caerleon (USA) 132) [2006 –: p8.6g f8g f11g f11g Dec 9] little form: left Miss J. Feilden after second start. *Robert Gray*   –

BRIGHT DANCE 2 b.f. (Jan 16) Groom Dancer (USA) 128 – Illumination 101 (Saddlers' Hall (IRE) 126) [2006 p7g 7.6f⁵ 7g Aug 18] 11,000F: second foal: sister to winner abroad up to 1¼m: dam 1¼m winner: little form in maidens: will be suited by 1¼m. *L. M. Cumani*   –

BRIGHTLING (IRE) 2 b.f. (Mar 12) Gorse 116 – Brightside (IRE) 99 (Last Tycoon 131) [2006 p5g⁶ Aug 5] half-sister to 3 winners, including smart Hong Kong 6f to 1m winner Dave's Best (by Bishop of Cashel) and useful 5f to 1m winner Miss George (by Pivotal): dam 2-y-o 1m winner who stayed 1½m: 3/1 but very green when sixth in maiden at Lingfield: gave trouble stalls intended next start: likely to progress. *Jamie Poulton*   **– p**

BRIGHT MOON 2 b.f. (Mar 15) Compton Place 125 – Mashmoon (USA) 80 (Habitat 134) [2006 6m p6g² 7f⁶ 7m* 7m⁶ 7d³ 7d Sep 30] smallish, compact filly: half-sister to several winners, including winner around 1m Talathath (by Soviet Star) and 1m to 1½m winner Gurrun (by Dansili), both fairly useful: dam, 6f (at 2 yrs) and 1m winner, half-sister to very smart French middle-distance filly Galla Placidia: fairly useful performer: **80**

won nursery at Salisbury in August: will stay 1m: acts on polytrack, firm and good to soft going. *R. Hannon*

BRIGHT SPARKY (GER) 3 ch.g. Dashing Blade 117 – Braissim (Dancing Brave (USA) 140) [2006 47: 7.9g 14.1g Aug 24] big, good-topped gelding: poor maiden: should stay beyond 6f: tongue tied both starts at 3 yrs. *M. W. Easterby* –

BRIGHT SUN (IRE) 5 b.g. Dcscrt Sun 120 – Kcalbra Lady (Petong 126) [2006 77: 9.9d 10m 9g⁴ 9.8m* 10.3g 9.8m⁶ 10f² 10.1m⁴ 8.9f⁴ 9.8g p8.6g⁵ 10f* 10g Sep 30] good-topped gelding: fair handicapper, better on turf than all-weather: won at Ripon in June and Redcar in September: stays easy 1½m: acts on firm and good to soft going: tongue tied: free-going sort, often makes running. *N. Tinkler* **77**

BRIGYDON (IRE) 3 b.g. Fasliyev (USA) 120 – Creme Caramel (USA) 88 (Septieme Ciel (USA) 123) [2006 p8.6g⁵ 7.1m⁵ Aug 28] 60,000Y: compact gelding: third foal: half-brother to 2003 2-y-o 7f winner Monte Bianco (by King of Kings), later successful in USA, and 4-y-o Soft Focus: dam, 2-y-o 7f winner, half-sister to smart performer up to 1m Robellation: better effort in maidens (fair form) when fifth at Warwick final start: will be suited by drop to 6f: open to further improvement. *J. R. Fanshawe* **70 p**

BRING IT ON HOME 2 b.c. (Feb 19) Beat Hollow 126 – Dernier Cri 63 (Slip Anchor 136) [2006 7f 9m Sep 20] well held in maidens. *G. L. Moore* –

BRISK BREEZE (GER) 2 ch.f. (Apr 12) Monsun (GER) 124 – Bela-M (IRE) 106 (Ela-Mana-Mou 132) [2006 7m³ 7d⁵ Aug 25] €38,000Y: close-coupled, good-topped filly: has a fluent action: fourth foal: sister to German 11f winner Beau Cadeau and half-sister to useful German 1¼m/11f winner Beau Chapeau (by Spectrum): dam German 1¼m winner: fair form in maidens at Newmarket, rallying fifth to Golden Dagger in latter: will improve further at 1¼m/1½m. *H. R. A. Cecil* **76 p**

BROADFIELD LADY (IRE) 6 ch.m. Perugino (USA) 84 – Dama de Noche (Rusti-caro (FR) 124) [2006 6g⁴ a5s⁶ a6s* a5g⁴ 6d p5.1g 5v f5g Nov 21] half-sister to 3 winners in Italy: dam Italian 7f (at 2 yrs) and 9f winner: no form in Ireland in 2004: won handicap at Mijas in February: well held all 4 starts in Britain: best at 5f/6f: acts on sand, best turf effort on good going: wore cheekpieces last 2 starts. *E. J. Creighton* **?**

BROADWAY CALLING 3 ch.g. Dr Fong (USA) 128 – Manhattan Sunset (USA) 76 (El Gran Senor (USA) 136) [2006 53p: p8g p8g 11s Aug 13] modest maiden: left A. Balding 2,500 gns after second start: bred to stay 1¼m+: acts on polytrack. *M. E. Sowersby* **63**

BROCATELLO (IRE) 3 b.g. Sadler's Wells (USA) 132 – Brocatelle 65 (Green Desert (USA) 127) [2006 9.9m³ 8.1s² p12g Nov 9] third foal: half-brother to winner in Japan by Machiavellian: dam highly-raced half-sister to high-class miler Barathea (by Sadler's Wells): fair form when placed in maidens at Beverley and Haydock: forced wide throughout at Lingfield final outing: gelded after: should stay 1½m: acts on soft and good to firm ground: blinkered. *M. Johnston* **68**

BROCKHOLE (IRE) 4 gr.g. Daylami (IRE) 138 – Free Spirit (IRE) (Caerleon (USA) 132) [2006 75d: p12.2g⁴ p12.2g⁵ p12g² 10.9s 14m May 4] smallish gelding: fair maiden on all-weather, modest on turf: stays 1½m: acts on polytrack: tried in cheekpieces. *J. G. Given* **50 a74**

BROGHILL 2 ch.c. (Mar 1) Selkirk (USA) 129 – Mystify 104 (Batshoof 122) [2006 7m* 7d³ Oct 7] useful-looking colt: second foal: dam, 7f and (in USA) 8.5f winner, half-sister to Lancashire Oaks and US Grade 1 9f/1¼m winner Squeak: fairly useful form: won maiden at Newmarket (made most to beat Broomielaw by 1¾ lengths) in September: 3¾ lengths third of 8 to Charlie Farnsbarns in well-contested minor event at Ascot, held up and still green: will stay 1m: will do better still. *J. H. M. Gosden* **93 p**

BROGUE LANTERNS (IRE) 4 ch.f. Dr Devious (IRE) 127 – Landrail (USA) 63 (Storm Bird (CAN) 134) [2006 88: a8.3s p8.6g f8g Dec 21] €10,000Y: half-sister to 1m to 1¼m winner in Hong Kong by Sri Pekan: dam maiden best up to 1¼m: fairly useful performer at 2/3 yrs for T. Hogan in Ireland: well held in 2006: stays 9.5f: acts on heavy going. *E. J. Creighton* –

BROKEN SPUR (FR) 3 b.c. Bahri (USA) 125 – Aerleon Jane 89 (Caerleon (USA) 132) [2006 78: p7g³ p7g⁵ 7.1g⁶ p7g 7f 7d Oct 3] fair performer: should stay easy 1m: acts on polytrack and good to firm going: tongue tied last 3 starts: sold 800 gns. *B. W. Hills* **76**

BRONCO'S FILLY (IRE) 2 b. or br.f. (Feb 23) Val Royal (FR) 127 – Lady Esther (IRE) 75 (Darnay 117) [2006 5.1d 5f 7m Aug 11] 1,500Y: sparely-made filly: first foal: dam Irish 1¼m winner: well held in sellers. *J. G. M. O'Shea* –

BRONTE'S HOPE 2 ch.f. (Apr 6) Gorse 116 – General Jane (Be My Chief (USA) **67 p**
122) [2006 p6g⁵ Jun 28] 7,500Y: second foal: dam, ran 4 times, half-sister to smart sprinter Venture Capitalist: 7/2, 2¾ lengths fifth to Zahour Al Yasmeen in maiden at Kempton,
smooth headway briefly: should progress. *M. P. Tregoning*

BRONX BOMBER 8 ch.g. Prince Sabo 123 – Super Yankee (IRE) (Superlative 118) **56**
[2006 50: f7g⁴ f7g⁶ Feb 5] leggy gelding: modest performer: best at 6f/7f: acts on all-
weather, on heavy: tried tongue tied: usually blinkered. *Dr J. D. Scargill*

BRONZE DANCER (IRE) 4 b.g. Entrepreneur 123 – Scrimshaw (Selkirk (USA) **81**
129) [2006 70: 12g² 13.8g³ 13f² 16f⁵ 13m* 13g³ 13.8m* 13.8v⁶ Oct 31] lengthy gelding:
fairly useful handicapper: won at Hamilton in July and Catterick in August: stays
easy 13.8f: acts on firm and soft going: carries head awkwardly: sometimes hangs left.
G. A. Swinbank

BRONZE STAR 3 b.f. Mark of Esteem (IRE) 137 – White House 84 (Pursuit of Love **73**
124) [2006 58p: 8.1m⁴ p8g p10g² p10g* p12g⁴ Dec 20] good-topped filly: fair performer:
won handicap at Kempton in December: stays 1¼m: acts on polytrack. *J. R. Fanshawe*

BRONZO DI RIACE (IRE) 2 b.c. (Mar 19) Montjeu (IRE) 137 – Afreeta (USA) **–**
(Afleet (CAN)) [2006 7g p8.6g Sep 16] well held in maidens. *K. A. Ryan*

BROOMIELAW 2 ch.c. (Mar 24) Rock of Gibraltar (IRE) 133 – Peony 108 (Lion **86 p**
Cavern (USA) 117) [2006 7m² Sep 19] 190,000Y: close-coupled, good-topped colt:
third foal: half-brother to smart 1¼m/11f winner Unfurled (by Unfuwain) and 3-y-o
Synonymy: dam, French 7f (including at 2 yrs) and 1m winner, runner-up in Poule
d'Essai des Pouliches: 6/1, promising 1¾ lengths second of 11 to Broghill in maiden at
Newmarket, running on well, not unduly knocked about: will stay 1m+: sure to progress
and win races. *E. A. L. Dunlop*

BROSNA CRY (IRE) 2 b.c. (Apr 14) Street Cry (IRE) 130 – Wedding Gift (FR) 108 **86 p**
(Always Fair (USA) 121) [2006 7s 7v p7.1g* Nov 28] €48,000Y: fifth foal: half-brother
to fairly useful French winners up to 1m Wana Doo (by Grand Slam) and Sky Gift (by
Stravinsky): dam French 2-y-o 7f/1m winner who stayed 10.5f: well held in maidens
at Cork and the Curragh first 2 starts: much improved when winning similar event at
Wolverhampton in November by 3½ lengths from First Bloom, coming back on bridle
entering straight and quickly clear: likely to be suited by 1m+: acts on polytrack: should
do better still. *James G. Burns, Ireland*

BROTHER CADFAEL 5 ch.g. So Factual (USA) 120 – High Habit 79 (Slip Anchor **48**
136) [2006 52: f14g⁶ f14g⁴ Jan 31] strong gelding: poor performer: stays 2m: acts on
fibresand and good to soft going: tried tongue tied/in cheekpieces. *John A. Harris*

BROUGHTON BUZZER 5 b.m. Rudimentary (USA) 118 – Broughtons Lure (IRE) **54**
55 (Archway (IRE) 115) [2006 59: 10d² f8g Jul 7] lengthy mare: modest performer: stays
1¼m: acts on fibresand and good to soft ground. *A. G. Newcombe*

BROUGHTONS FOLLY 3 b.f. Groom Dancer (USA) 128 – Cressida (Polish Prece- **76**
dent (USA) 131) [2006 10m p12g⁴ 10s p10g⁶ p12g* p12g³ Dec 5] 3,000Y: lengthy filly:
second foal: half-sister to 4-y-o Strathtay: dam ran twice: fair performer: won handicap at
Lingfield in November: stays 1½m: acts on polytrack. *W. J. Musson*

BROUGHTONS REVIVAL 4 b.f. Pivotal 124 – Ella Lamees 61 (Statoblest 120) **55**
[2006 p10g Jul 5] third foal: half-sister to 5-y-o Mugeba: dam 6f winner: ninth of 14 to
Millistar in maiden at Kempton, steady headway from rear. *W. J. Musson*

BROUGHTON TREASURE 3 b.f. Bahamian Bounty 116 – Quite Happy (IRE) 78 **–**
(Statoblest 120) [2006 43: p8.6g Jun 9] poor maiden: likely to stay 6f. *W. J. Musson*

BROUHAHA 2 b.c. (Apr 10) Bahhare (USA) 122 – Top of The Morning 56 (Keen 116) **65**
[2006 8m 7g 6d⁵ Oct 27] 800F: big, well-made colt: fourth foal: dam, maiden likely to
have proved best up to 1¼m, half-sister to useful performer up to 1¼m Whitefoot: fair
form in maidens at Newmarket: free-going sort, but bred to stay 1m/1¼m. *Miss Diana
Weeden*

BRUNELLESCHI 3 ch.g. Bertolini (USA) 125 – Petrovna (IRE) 78 (Petardia 113) **78**
[2006 80: 5.2m⁵ 6m⁴ 5g⁶ 5f 5g⁵ 6f⁶ p6g 5g p6g Oct 8] strong, compact gelding: has a
quick action: fair handicapper: below form after third outing: probably stays 6f: acts on
polytrack, firm and soft going: tried visored. *P. L. Gilligan*

BRUNSTON CASTLE 6 b.g. Hector Protector (USA) 124 – Villella (Sadler's Wells **–**
(USA) 132) [2006 –: f11g Jan 24] no form after 2003: sometimes tongue tied.
A. W. Carroll

BRUT 4 b.g. Mind Games 121 – Champenoise 64 (Forzando 122) [2006 70, a56: 5g³ 6d **73** 7g 5f* 5g⁵ 6m 5m 5m³ 5m⁵ 5m 6d 5s 6f 5g⁵ 5d³ Oct 3] lengthy, good-topped gelding: fair handicapper: won at Catterick in June: stays easy 7f, races mostly at 5f/6f: acts on fibresand, firm and soft going: tried visored/in cheekpieces. *D. W. Barker*

BRYNRIS 2 gr.g. (Apr 30) Perryston View 114 – Isle of Mull (Elmaamul (USA) 125) **35** [2006 p5g p5.1g 6g p7.1g p7.1g⁵ Dec 27] poor maiden: gelded and left W. Turner after third start. *Mrs G. S. Rees*

BUACHAILL DONA (IRE) 3 b.g. Namid 128 – Serious Contender (IRE) (Tenby **101 p** 125) [2006 78: 6d* 5f* 5f² 5d* 6d⁶ Sep 22] quite good-topped gelding: useful form: won maiden at Thirsk in April and handicaps at Catterick in July and York (beat Terentia by head) in August: not discredited when sixth to Al Qasi in handicap at Ascot final outing, racing freely: has won over 6f, may prove best at 5f: acts on firm and good to soft going: sort to do well at 4 yrs. *D. Nicholls*

BU ALI (USA) 3 b.f. Silver Hawk (USA) 123 – Mantua (Mtoto 134) [2006 48: 10m **–** 11.5m 11.6d 16g Aug 4] €25,000Y: third foal: dam, German 9.5f winner, half-sister to Breeders' Cup Sprint winner Elmhurst: maiden: no form in 2006, leaving H. Rogers in Ireland after reappearance: tried blinkered. *B. W. Duke*

BUBBLING FUN 5 b.m. Marju (IRE) 127 – Blushing Barada (USA) 53 (Blushing **55** Groom (FR) 131) [2006 71: p9.5g 10m 10.9m 12.1g⁶ p13.9g⁶ 12.1m 10g 10.2m⁶ p13.9g⁶ p9.5g⁶ p12.2g Dec 27] leggy, quite good-topped mare: modest handicapper nowadays: seems to stay easy 1¾m: acts on polytrack, firm and good to soft going: tongue tied once: temperament under suspicion. *T. Wall*

BUCCELLATI 2 ch.c. (Apr 28) Soviet Star (USA) 128 – Susi Wong (IRE) (Selkirk **86** (USA) 129) [2006 6f 7.1m* 8g² Oct 12] 25,000Y: close-coupled, quite attractive colt: fourth foal: half-brother to 3 winners, including useful 1½m winner (including in Scandinavia) La Petite Chinoise (by Dr Fong) and fairly useful 1¼m winner Hope An Glory (by Nashwan): dam German 1m winner: fairly useful form: won maiden at Warwick in August: good second of 16 to Ladies Best in nursery at Newmarket: stays 1m. *A. M. Balding*

BUCHAREST 3 b.g. Barathea (IRE) 127 – Zorleni (Zafonic (USA) 130) [2006 89: p7g **70** p7g⁶ 6d p7g 6m 7d 6m 8.1m* 8d f8g f8g f8g Dec 27] workmanlike gelding: fair handicapper: easily best effort in 2006 when winning at Haydock in August: stays 1m: acts on firm going: got loose and completed circuit of course before win on debut at 2 yrs. *M. Wigham*

BUCKIE MASSA 2 ch.c. (Mar 17) Best of The Bests (IRE) 122 – Up On Points 97 **77** (Royal Academy (USA) 130) [2006 6g⁶ 7m 6d 7d p6g² p7g⁵ p6g* Dec 8] 18,000Y: goodtopped colt: second foal: half-brother to 3-y-o Zafantage: dam 2-y-o 7f winner: fair performer: won maiden at Wolverhampton (jinked right after line and unseated rider) in December: should stay 1m: acts on polytrack. *S. Kirk*

BUCKLE AND HYDE 3 ch.f. Foxhound (USA) 103 – Step On Degas 69 (Super- **56** power 113) [2006 51: 6.1g 6.1f 8.3d⁵ p7g⁴ 7.1m p7g p8g Oct 29] lengthy filly: modest maiden: stays 7f: acts on polytrack, best effort on turf on good going: in cheekpieces final outing. *Mrs A. L. M. King*

BUCKS 9 b.g. Slip Anchor 136 – Alligram (USA) 61 (Alysheba (USA)) [2006 84: 14m³ **73** 11.6g³ 11.7m Aug 20] quite good-topped gelding: fair handicapper nowadays: effective at 1¼m to easy 2m: acts on all-weather, firm and soft going: waited with. *Ian Williams*

BUCKTHORN 2 ch.c. (Mar 10) Lomitas 129 – Emma Peel 113 (Emarati (USA) 74) **56** [2006 7d Oct 28] 65,000Y: sturdy colt: third foal: half-brother to Norwegian 7f (at 2 yrs)/ 1m (Norsk 1000 Guineas) winner Females Fun (by Diktat): dam 5f and (including at 2 yrs) 6f winner: 100/1 and backward, fourteenth of 19 in maiden at Newmarket. *G. Wragg*

BUDDIES GIRL (IRE) 2 b.f. (Feb 26) Golan (IRE) 129 – Moonlight (IRE) 69 (Night **77 d** Shift (USA)) [2006 6d² 6m³ 6m⁴ 7m⁵ 7.1g⁴ 6.5s p7g² 6d p7g Nov 11] 15,000Y: big, strong filly: fourth foal: half-sister to 6f (at 2 yrs) and 1¼m winner in Italy by Xaar: dam, maiden who stayed 1¼m, half-sister to useful performers Duty Paid (best at 7f/1m) and Lady Miletrian (should have stayed 1¼m): fair maiden: made frame 5 times, once in nursery: likely to stay 1m: acts on polytrack, good to firm and good to soft going: races prominently: sold 12,000 gns. *R. Hannon*

BUDDY BROWN 4 b.g. Lujain (USA) 119 – Rose Bay 64 (Shareef Dancer (USA) **–** 135) [2006 –: f8g 9.8v 10d 11.5f⁴ 8g Sep 27] smallish, close-coupled gelding: little form since 2004. *J. Howard Johnson*

BUDDY MAN (IRE) 8 ch.g. Shalford (IRE) 124§ – Helen Belle (IRE) 59 (Parliament **72**
117) [2006 74: 8v⁵ 7s 8.5s* 9d⁴ 9m⁴ 9m 10g f8g Dec 23] fair handicapper: successful 5
times in Ireland, including at Killarney in May: well held at Southwell final outing: stays
1¼m: acts on soft and good to firm going: tongue tied. *Patrick Martin, Ireland*

BUDS DILEMMA 2 b.f. (Mar 23) Anabaa (USA) 130 – Lady Thynn (FR) (Crystal **–**
Glitters (USA) 127) [2006 6.1g Aug 4] 16,000F, 30,000Y: closely related to 6-y-o Cayman Breeze and half-sister to several winners, including useful 2001 2-y-o 1¼m winner
Stage By Stage (by In The Wings): dam French 12.5f winner: hung left and well beaten in
maiden. *I. W. McInnes*

BUKIT FRASER (IRE) 5 b.g. Sri Pekan (USA) 117 – London Pride (USA) 106 (Lear **67**
Fan (USA) 130) [2006 p12g⁶ 10.1m 14.1s 11g³ 12.1f⁶ p16g 11.5m⁵ 16.2m Aug 28] leggy,
quite good-topped gelding: fair handicapper nowadays: missed 2005: barely stays 14.4f:
acts on good to firm going, probably on firm: tried tongue tied: often soon off bridle.
P. F. I. Cole

BULBERRY HILL 5 b.g. Makbul 104 – Hurtleberry (IRE) 87 (Tirol 127) [2006 53: **56**
f12g² f12g² f12g³ f14g³ f14g⁶ f12g f16g* f14g f16g⁵ f16g* Dec 12] modest performer:
won banded races at Southwell in October and December: stays 2m: acts on all-weather,
probably on firm ground. *R. W. Price*

BULL RUN (IRE) 5 ro.g. Daylami (IRE) 138 – Bulaxie 110 (Bustino 136) [2006 **–**
11.6d⁶ Nov 4] unraced at 2 yrs: won both starts at 3 yrs when trained by D. Loder, showing smart form on second occasion: off 30 months (reportedly injured a foreleg in May
2004), no show in listed event at Windsor only start in 2006: should stay 1½m: acts on
soft going. *Saeed bin Suroor*

BULLSEYE 4 b.g. Polish Precedent (USA) 131 – Native Flair 87 (Be My Native (USA) **48**
122) [2006 54: p12g⁶ p10g p10g⁵ 12f f14g 10.2f⁶ Jul 27] robust gelding: modest maiden **a63**
on all-weather, poor on turf: left A. Jarvis after third start: stays 1¼m: acts on polytrack,
probably on firm going: tried blinkered/visored. *J. R. Boyle*

BULWARK (IRE) 4 b.c. Montjeu (IRE) 137 – Bulaxie 110 (Bustino 136) [2006 99+: **109 §**
12g⁵ 18.7m⁶ 16.2f* 16.1m p16g³ 16f 15.9d⁴ 16d⁴ 16d² Oct 14] good-bodied colt: useful
performer: improved again in 2006, and won quite valuable handicap at Haydock in June
by ½ length from Colloquial: at least creditable efforts after, running well when fourth to
easy winner Hawridge Prince in listed event at Ascot and 6 lengths second to same rival
in Jockey Club Cup at Newmarket last 2 starts: stays easy 2¼m: acts on polytrack, firm
and soft going: blinkered nowadays: tends to carry head awkwardly/wander under pressure: looks ungenuine, but is consistent. *Mrs A. J. Perrett*

BUNDEROS (IRE) 2 b.f. (May 15) Areion (GER) 115 – Bundheimerin (GER) (Ordos **–**
(GER)) [2006 7g Sep 30] €8,500 2-y-o: half-sister to several winners in Germany,
including winner up to 1½m Bad Harzburger (by Northjet): dam unraced: tailed off in
maiden. *Mrs A. Duffield*

BUNDY 10 b.g. Ezzoud (IRE) 126 – Sanctuary Cove (Habitat 134) [2006 65: 6v 5.9g 6g² **62**
p7.1g⁶ Jun 22] smallish, leggy gelding: modest performer nowadays: effective at 6f/7f:
acts on heavy and good to firm going: blinkered once at 3 yrs: usually held up. *M. Dods*

BUNGIE 2 gr.g. (May 28) Forzando 122 – Sweet Whisper 63 (Petong 126) [2006 5s⁵ 7m **64**
6m 5d⁴ 5d⁶ p5.1g* f5g⁴ Dec 21] leggy, useful-looking gelding: modest performer: won
maiden at Wolverhampton in December, jinking left when leading early in straight: may
prove best at 5f: acts on polytrack and good to soft ground. *Ms Deborah J. Evans*

BUNOOD (IRE) 3 b.f. Sadler's Wells (USA) 132 – Azdihaar (USA) 81 (Mr Prospector **106**
(USA)) [2006 97p: 10s² 12m 12s² 12s³ 12s Oct 7] tall, lengthy, unfurnished filly: useful
performer, lightly raced: second in listed races at Newmarket (beaten 2½ lengths by
Riyalma) and York (best effort when 3 lengths behind Anna Pavlova) reappearance/third
outing: respectable third to Acts of Grace in Princess Royal Stakes at Ascot next time but
ran poorly in listed race there final start: stayed 1½m: acted on soft going: reportedly
suffered bruised foot after reappearance: visits Green Desert. *J. L. Dunlop*

BUON AMICI 5 b.m. Pivotal 124 – Supreme Rose 95 (Frimley Park 109) [2006 47: f8g **–**
Feb 5] lightly-raced maiden: well held only outing in 2006. *W. J. Musson*

BURGUNDY 9 b.g. Lycius (USA) 124 – Decant 68 (Rousillon (USA) 133) [2006 83: **80**
p12g p10g⁵ p12g⁶ 11g 10d p12g⁵ p10g p10g* 10.1g 10.1g⁶ p10g³ 10.1g² p10g³ p10g⁶
p10g⁵ p10g p11g⁶ p12g⁶ p12g* p10g⁶ Dec 20] smallish gelding: fairly useful handicapper: won at Kempton in June (apprentices) and December: stays 1½m: acts on polytrack, firm and soft going: wears headgear: often slowly away, and held up. *P. Mitchell*

BURHAAN (IRE) 4 b.c. Green Desert (USA) 127 – Arjuzah (IRE) 110 (Ahonoora 122) [2006 75: p8g p8g 6f p7.1g5 p6g p7.1g p6g p6g5 p6g2 p6g3 p6g2 p7g* Dec 30] sturdy colt: modest performer nowadays: won handicap at Lingfield in December: stays 8.6f: acts on polytrack and good to firm ground: tried visored: sometimes tongue tied. *J. R. Boyle* — **a63**

BURLEY FIREBRAND 6 b.g. Bahamian Bounty 116 – Vallauris 94 (Faustus (USA) 118) [2006 66: 7.2d2 7d3 8.5d 8d 8s p7g Nov 25] quite good-topped gelding: fair handicapper: effective at 7f to 1½m: acts on good to firm going, good to soft and fibresand (well held at Kempton on polytrack debut final outing): tried blinkered/visored. *Michael McElhone, Ireland* **65**

BURLEY FLAME 5 b.g. Marju (IRE) 127 – Tarsa 81 (Ballad Rock 122) [2006 90: 7d Apr 6] sturdy, angular gelding: useful handicapper on all-weather, fairly useful on turf at 3/4 yrs: ran as if needing outing sole start in 2006: visored nowadays: none too consistent. *J. G. Given* —

BURLINGTON FAYR (IRE) 2 ch.f. (Mar 17) Fayruz 116 – Fair Princess 83 (Efisio 120) [2006 5d5 6g2 6g6 7g5 6d 7.1m5 6s* 5m3 6d Oct 3] 3,000Y: workmanlike filly: second foal: dam 6f winner: modest performer: won seller at Ripon in August: best at 5f/ 6f: acts on soft and good to firm going: sold 2,600 gns, sent to Spain. *N. Tinkler* **57**

BURNBANK (IRE) 3 ch.c. Danehill Dancer (IRE) 117 – Roseau 75 (Nashwan (USA) 135) [2006 67: p7g2 8.5g2 10.1m5 Jun 3] lengthy colt: fair maiden: good efforts last 2 starts: likely to prove best up to 1¼m: raced on polytrack and good/good to firm ground. *W. Jarvis* **77**

BURNINGFOLD BABE 2 b.f. (Mar 9) Muhtarram (USA) 125 – Laser Light Lady (Tragic Role (USA)) [2006 5.1m f7g6 p6g2 p8g f7g p7.1g Dec 7] fourth foal: half-sister to 2005 2-y-o 5f seller winner My Lady Valentine (by Bahamian Bounty): dam, well beaten on Flat, winning selling hurdler: modest form only on third start: should stay 7f/1m: blinkered (raced freely) final start. *P. Winkworth* **56**

BURNING INCENSE (IRE) 3 b.g. Namid 128 – Night Scent (IRE) 85 (Scenic 128) [2006 73p: p5g6 6g2 6m2 6g3 6d* 6g2 6m3 6g* 6d 6d2 Sep 22] big, strong gelding: useful handicapper: progressed well in 2006 (including physically), winning at Windsor in June and Newmarket (by 1¼ lengths from Mutamarres) in August: best effort when 2 lengths second to Al Qasi at Ascot final outing: gelded after: best at 6f: acts on good to firm and good to soft going: blinkered last 3 starts. *R. Charlton* **106**

BURNING MOON 5 b.g. Bering 136 – Triple Green 69 (Green Desert (USA) 127) [2006 –: 14.1s 10d 8m Jun 23] leggy, useful-looking gelding: fairly useful winner at 3 yrs: lightly raced and no form after: tried visored. *J. Ryan* —

BURNLEY AL (IRE) 4 ch.g. Desert King (IRE) 129 – Bold Meadows 80 (Persian Bold 123) [2006 67: p8g* p8.6g5 p8.6g2 p6.6g p8g p9.5g 8d6 8.1m5 9g2 9.2m3 8m2 8d4 8.3m2 8.3m* 8m3 9.2g* 9m2 9.2g5 10.5g p8.6m p9.5g5 p9.5s p8.6g6 p8.6g4 Dec 29] close-coupled gelding: fair performer: won handicap at Lingfield in January and, having been claimed from R. Fahey after thirteenth outing, 2 claimers at Hamilton in August: left A. Berry after twentieth outing: stays 1¼m: acts on polytrack (well held on fibresand), soft and good to firm going: usually wears headgear: tough. *Peter Grayson* **72**

BURNTOAKBOY 8 b.g. Sir Harry Lewis (USA) 127 – Sainte Martine (Martinmas 128) [2006 16s2 11.9g2 14m2 20m 16d 16g5 Aug 17] leggy gelding: fairly useful hurdler: similar level of form when runner-up first 3 starts on Flat: well below that form after, in Ascot Stakes fourth start: stays 2m: acts on soft and good to firm going. *Michael Cunningham, Ireland* **80**

BURNT OAK (UAE) 4 b.g. Timber Country (USA) 124 – Anaam 81 (Caerleon (USA) 132) [2006 f11g4 12g4 12s* Aug 18] quite good-topped gelding: won 2 of his 4 starts in bumpers during winter: fairly useful form: best effort when winning maiden at Catterick in August: stays 1½m: acts on soft going: has been bandaged fore joints. *C. W. Fairhurst* **85**

BURNT ORANGE (IRE) 3 b.g. Agnes World (USA) 123 – Orange Walk (IRE) 88 (Alzao (USA) 117) [2006 7s 7g 5f6 6f 6d 6.1d Oct 13] sturdy gelding: little form: tried blinkered. *T. D. McCarthy* —

BURTON ASH 4 b. or br.f. Diktat 126 – Incendio (Siberian Express (USA) 125) [2006 75: p8g2 f7g4 p8g6 7.5f 8.2s4 8m* 8.2m 8g Sep 14] tall, angular filly: fair handicapper: won (for first time) at Pontefract in June: probably stays 1¼m: acts on polytrack, firm and good to soft going: effective with or without headgear: races prominently. *J. G. Given* **66**

BUSCADOR (USA) 7 ch.g. Crafty Prospector (USA) – Fairway Flag (USA) (Fairway Phantom (USA)) [2006 73: p8.6g p12.2g³ p10g p9.5g³ p9.5g p9.5g³ p9.5g* p9.5g⁵ 12g⁴ 10.5s 12.3g p9.5g* p9.5s³ p9.5g³ Dec 22] fair handicapper on all-weather, modest on turf: won at Wolverhampton in March and November: stays easy 1½m: acts on all-weather, soft and good to firm ground: races prominently: none too consistent. *W. M. Brisbourne* **52 a70**

BUSH BREAKFAST 2 b.c. (Feb 27) Averti (IRE) 117 – Basbousate Nadia 92 (Wolfhound (USA) 126) [2006 5.1s³ 5m³ 5m³ 5m 6.1m p5g Sep 30] 18,500Y: first foal: dam, 2-y-o 5f winner, out of half-sister to smart 7f/1m performer Gothenberg: fair maiden: third first 3 starts, below form last 3: should stay 6f: sold 3,500 gns, sent to Spain. *P. Winkworth* **70**

BUSINESS TRAVELLER (IRE) 6 ch.g. Titus Livius (FR) 115 – Dancing Venus 61 (Pursuit of Love 124) [2006 15s 17.2s Apr 11] strong, close-coupled gelding: maiden handicapper: tried blinkered/visored: tongue tied both starts in 2006: won over hurdles in May. *R. J. Price* **–**

BUSSEL (USA) 2 ch.f. (Feb 10) Royal Academy (USA) 130 – Reigning Princess (USA) (Storm Boot (USA)) [2006 7g 6d³ p6g* f6g* Dec 21] 45,000Y: strong, good-bodied filly: second foal: dam 6.5f winner in USA: fair form: won maiden at Kempton in November and claimer at Southwell (4 ran) in December: may prove best at 5f/6f: acts on polytrack: races prominently. *W. J. Haggas* **76**

BUSTAN (IRE) 7 b.g. Darshaan 133 – Dazzlingly Radiant 81 (Try My Best (USA) 130) [2006 p10g 10g 8m² 8m 10.4f⁶ 10m 8g⁴ 8m 9m⁶ 9d 8g 8.2d⁴ Nov 1] strong gelding: useful performer: missed 2005: some creditable efforts in handicaps in 2006, including neck second to Grey Boy at Ripon, sixth to Fairmile in John Smith's Cup at York and fourth to Prince of Thebes at Ascot third/fifth/seventh outings: effective at 1m to 1½m: acts on polytrack and firm going: blinkered (raced freely) once at 5 yrs: carried head awkwardly ninth start: none too consistent. *G. C. Bravery* **105**

BUSTER HYVONEN (IRE) 4 b.g. Dansili 127 – Serotina (IRE) 73 (Mtoto 134) [2006 76: 10m⁶ p10g⁴ 12m² 11m* 12m 10g² Oct 13] well-made gelding: fairly useful handicapper: won at Goodwood in August: stays 1½m: raced only on all-weather and good/good to firm going: game: won over hurdles in November. *J. R. Fanshawe* **80**

BUSTIN JUSTIN (USA) 3 b.c. Forestry (USA) 121 – Designatoree (USA) (Alysheba (USA)) [2006 6m* 7m* 7m* 6g Oct 13] $100,000Y, $485,000 2-y-o: lengthy, good-topped colt: half-brother to several winners, including US Grade 3 1m winner Voice of Destiny (by Mane Minister): dam, US maiden, half-sister to Breeders' Cup Sprint winner Very Subtle: useful form: successful first 3 starts, namely in maiden at Newbury in June and handicaps at Newmarket in July (hung left) and August (further improvement when beating Ceremonial Jade by 1½ lengths, making all): not discredited when ninth to Bygone Days in Bentinck Stakes at latter course final outing: should prove as effective at 6f as 7f: raced on good/good to firm ground: has worn rope halter for stall entry. *J. Noseda* **104**

Igloos Bentinck Stakes, Newmarket—Bygone Days (right) just gets up to beat Borderlescott (second left), with Tax Free and the winner's stable-companion, Great Britain (white cap), between the pair

BUSY MAN (IRE) 7 b.g. Darnay 117 – Make Or Mar 84 (Daring March 116) [2006 **59** p10g p8g p7g³ p7g⁶ f7s p10g³ p10g p8g⁵ 10m p10g⁶ p10g p10g² Oct 29] tall, rather leggy gelding: failed to complete in 5 Irish points: well beaten in bumper/novice hurdles: modest maiden: stays 1¼m: acts on polytrack. *J. R. Jenkins*

BUSY SHARK (IRE) 3 gr.g. Shinko Forest (IRE) – Felicita (IRE) 97 (Catrail (USA) **65** 123) [2006 68: p9.5g³ Jan 16] good-topped gelding: fair maiden: stays 9.5f: acts on polytrack and good to firm going: sold 7,000 gns in July, joined Miss S. Collins in Ireland. *M. R. Channon*

BUTLERS BEST 2 b.g. (Apr 9) Best of The Bests (IRE) 122 – Evening Charm (IRE) **63** (Bering 136) [2006 8.1g 8.1d p8.6g⁶ Nov 23] 5,000 2-y-o: strong gelding: third foal: half-brother to useful 1m (at 2 yrs)/1½m winner Hello It's Me (by Deploy): dam French maiden: gelded, best effort in maidens when sixth at Wolverhampton final start: stays 8.6f: acts on polytrack. *E. J. O'Neill*

BUTTERFLY BUD (IRE) 3 b.g. Lend A Hand 124 – Rathbawn Realm (Doulab **69** (USA) 115) [2006 65: 6f³ p6g 6.1f² 5f⁶ 6g⁶ 5g 6d³ 6d Oct 18] useful-looking gelding: fair maiden: stays 6f, possibly not 7f: acts on firm and good to soft ground. *J. O'Reilly*

BUXTON 2 b.c. (May 6) Auction House (USA) 120 – Dam Certain (IRE) 61 (Damister **–** (USA) 123) [2006 p7g Sep 6] half-brother to 3 winners, including 4-y-o Nan Jan: dam 7f to 9f winner: 20/1, needed experience in maiden at Kempton. *R. Ingram*

BUY ON THE RED 5 b.g. Komaite (USA) – Red Rosein 97 (Red Sunset 120) [2006 **81** 89: 6g 6d 6f⁵ p6g⁴ 6g³ 6m 6g⁴ 6f⁴ p6g 6m⁵ p6g³ p7g p7g⁴ p6g³ p6s² p7.1g* Dec 31] tall, **a89** quite good-topped gelding: fairly useful handicapper: won at Wolverhampton final start: stays 7f: acts on polytrack and firm going: tried blinkered, wore cheekpieces (all good efforts) last 3 outings. *W. R. Muir*

BUZBURY RINGS 2 b.g. (Apr 22) Piccolo 121 – Mory Kante (USA) (Icecapade **56** (USA)) [2006 5g May 18] half-brother to several winners, including 9-y-o Pagan Prince and 5-y-o Sforzando: dam German 7f/1m winner: 25/1, faded into seventh in maiden at Salisbury won by Strategic Prince: gelded after: looked sure to improve. *A. M. Balding*

BUZ KIRI (USA) 8 b.g. Gulch (USA) – White Corners (USA) (Caro 133) [2006 50d: **–** p16g⁶ Jan 18] smallish, sturdy gelding: poor performer: well held only outing in 2006: tried blinkered/visored, sometimes tongue tied: usually held up. *A. W. Carroll*

BUZZIN'BOYZEE (IRE) 3 ch.f. Monashee Mountain (USA) 115 – Las Bela 75 **67** (Welsh Pageant 132) [2006 61: f6g⁴ p6g³ p6g³ p6g p7g⁶ p6g* p6g³ f6g³ 7f* 6g⁵ 6.1d⁵ 6f³ p7.1g⁵ p7g p7.1g³ p7.1g⁴ p7.1g Dec 28] angular filly: fair performer: won seller at Wolverhampton in March and handicap at Catterick in April: stays 7f: acts on polytrack and firm ground, probably on good to soft: tried visored. *P. D. Evans*

BYANITA (IRE) 2 b.f. (Apr 2) Anita's Prince 126 – Byliny (IRE) (Archway (IRE) 115) **–** [2006 p7g 6g p7.1m p6g⁵ Dec 11] half-sister to winning sprinter in Italy by Monashee Mountain: dam unraced: no form. *B. Palling*

BYGONE DAYS 5 ch.g. Desert King (IRE) 129 – May Light 62 (Midyan (USA) 124) **120** [2006 109: 6.5m³ 6m² 6d 6.5m² 6d* 6g* Oct 13] quite attractive gelding: very smart performer: placed in handicaps at Nad Al Sheba 2 of first 4 starts in 2006: left I. Mohammed and off 6½ months, improved form when winning minor event at Hamilton (by ¾ length from Fonthill Road) in September and Igloos Bentinck Stakes at Newmarket (did well to come from off pace when beating Borderlescott by short head) in October: stays 6.5f: acts on soft and good to firm going: has turn of foot. *Saeed bin Suroor*

BYO (IRE) 8 gr.g. Paris House 123 – Navan Royal (IRE) 61 (Dominion Royale 112) **–** [2006 67, a74: f5g² p5.1g² f5g* p5.1g² f5g⁵ p6g² f5g³ p6g f6g³ p6g 5.2m 6d p5.1g⁶ **a67** Jul 20] smallish, workmanlike gelding: fair performer: won banded race at Southwell in February: best at 5f/easy 6f: acts on all-weather and probably on any going when last showed form on turf: visored (below form) once: usually races prominently: sold £820 in December. *P. Howling*

BYRON 5 b.h. Green Desert (USA) 127 – Gay Gallanta (USA) 112 (Woodman (USA) **117** 126) [2006 117: 7d² 7d Oct 14] strong, quite attractive horse: good mover: smart performer: showed he retains all his ability when length second to Stronghold in Supreme Stakes at Goodwood on reappearance in September: seemingly amiss in Challenge Stakes at Newmarket only other start in 2006: was best at 6f/7f: acted on good to firm and good to soft going: usually tongue tied: to stand at Kildangan Stud, Ireland, fee €7,000. *Saeed bin Suroor*

BYRON BAY 4 b.c. My Best Valentine 122 – Candarela 41 (Damister (USA) 123) **91**
[2006 81: p9.5g⁵ f8g* p7.1g* 8v² 7.1m⁶ 6v 7f² 8f⁴ 8.3g⁵ 7m⁵ 7.2d f8g⁵ p9.5g⁶ Dec 31] **a95**
tall, leggy colt: useful performer on all-weather, fairly useful on turf: won handicaps at
Southwell in February (hung left) and Wolverhampton in March: respectable efforts at
best after: effective at 7f to 1¼m: acts on all-weather and any turf going: below form in
cheekpieces sixth start at 3 yrs: races prominently: has carried head high/weakened
tamely. *I. Semple*

BY STORM 3 b.f. Largesse 112 – Polar Storm (IRE) 76 (Law Society (USA) 130) [2006 **55**
40: p8g 8m² 8m 7m 10d* p10g p12g Nov 25] modest performer: won selling handicap at
Nottingham in October: stays 1¼m: acts on good to soft and good to firm going. *John
Berry*

BY THE EDGE (IRE) 2 b.f. (Mar 29) Shinko Forest (IRE) – Magic Annemarie (IRE) **–**
75 (Dancing Dissident (USA) 119) [2006 7f 6m 5d⁶ Aug 29] strong, good-bodied filly:
fourth foal: sister to 3-y-o How's She Cuttin': dam Irish 5f/6f winner: little form in
maidens. *T. D. Barron*

BY THE RIVER 2 b.g. (Feb 6) Zamindar (USA) 116 – Baby Bunting 63 (Wolfhound **–**
(USA) 126) [2006 6.1m Sep 15] strong, heavy-topped gelding, type to carry condition:
22/1, very green in maiden at Nottingham: gelded after. *P. Winkworth*

C

CAAN 3 b.g. Averti (IRE) 117 – Bellifontaine (FR) (Bellypha 130) [2006 65d: p8g f8g **–**
p6g Feb 13] close-coupled gelding: maiden: no show in 2006: tried visored/in cheekpieces: has looked ungenuine. *D. K. Ivory*

CABINET (IRE) 2 b.c. (Mar 7) Grand Lodge (USA) 125 – Passe Passe (USA) 78 (Lear **96 p**
Fan (USA) 130) [2006 7d² p7g* Oct 26] 85,000Y: fourth foal: half-brother to fairly
useful 1¼m and 1½m winner Magic Instinct (later winner in Australia, by Entrepreneur)
and 3-y-o Ryedale Ovation: dam, maiden who stayed 1½m, sister to smart 1¼m to 1¾m
winner Windermere: confirmed debut promise when winning maiden at Lingfield by 3½
lengths from Sea Land, forging clear once in full stride: will be suited by 1¼m/1½m:
already useful, and sure to go on to better things. *Sir Michael Stoute*

CABOPINO LAD (USA) 4 b.g. Comic Strip (USA) 115 – Roxanne (USA) (Wood- **–**
man (USA) 126) [2006 –: p9.5g f8g Mar 14] of no account. *Miss Tracy Waggott*

CABOURG (IRE) 3 b.g. Danehill (USA) 126 – Loire Valley (IRE) (Sadler's Wells **65**
(USA) 132) [2006 81: 10m 7m⁵ p7g 7m 9s⁵ 8d⁴ p8.6g⁴ f8g⁶ f8g p8.6g³ Dec 29] close-
coupled gelding: fair maiden: sold from C. Egerton 1,500 gns after third outing: stays
8.6f: acts on polytrack, firm and good to soft ground: tried blinkered. *R. Bastiman*

CABRILLO (IRE) 5 b.m. Indian Rocket 115 – Cerosia (Pitskelly 122) [2006 –: f8g **–**
f12g Jan 19] no sign of ability: tongue tied last 2 starts. *John A. Quinn, Ireland*

CABRIOLE 3 b.f. Dansili 127 – Arabesque 100 (Zafonic (USA) 130) [2006 6f 6.1g **52 §**
6m³ 6m p6g⁶ 5s³ 5.7m Sep 25] compact filly: second foal: closely related to smart 6f
winner (including at 2 yrs) Camacho (by Danehill): dam, 6f winner, out of Cheveley Park
winner Prophecy: modest maiden on balance: stays 6f: acts on polytrack and good to firm
ground: ungenuine: sold 35,000 gns. *H. R. A. Cecil*

CACTUS KING 3 b.g. Green Desert (USA) 127 – Apache Star 96 (Arazi (USA) 135) **91**
[2006 81p: 7s⁵ 8.3g³ 7m⁶ 10m³ 8g p9.5g p9.5m Nov 9] big, strong gelding: fairly useful **a81 +**
performer: stays 1¼m: acts on polytrack, soft and good to firm ground: slowly away final
outing. *J. H. M. Gosden*

CADEAUX DES MAGES 6 b.g. Cadeaux Genereux 131 – On Tiptoes 107 (Shareef **72 d**
Dancer (USA) 135) [2006 p8.6g 8d p8.6g 9s p9.5g Oct 29] deep-girthed gelding: fairly
useful performer at 3 yrs: unraced in 2004/5: fair form at best in 2006: should stay beyond
1m: acts on good to firm and good to soft ground: blinkered final outing. *J. G. Given*

CADEAUX DU MONDE 2 ch.c. (Jan 29) Cadeaux Genereux 131 – La Mondotte **85**
(IRE) 66§ (Alzao (USA) 117) [2006 6g 6m⁴ p6g p6g⁴ 6d² 7m⁴ 6m² 6d³ Oct 9] 42,000Y:
rather leggy, attractive colt: second foal: dam 11f winner out of half-sister to dam of
Pilsudski: fairly useful maiden: in frame 6 times, best run when second of 20 to Cheap
Street in sales race at Newmarket fifth start: stays 7f: unraced on extremes of turf going,

below form on all-weather: blinkered (didn't settle) final start: sold 24,000 gns, sent to USA. *E. J. O'Neill*

CADI MAY 2 b.f. (May 6) Fasliyev (USA) 120 – Sound of Sleat (Primo Dominie 121) –
[2006 5g 6.1g 7m Aug 6] 6,000Y: tall, leggy filly: third foal: dam unraced half-sister to smart French miler Soft Currency: well held in maidens. *W. M. Brisbourne*

CADWELL 2 b.c. (Apr 18) Pivotal 124 – Sur Les Pointes (IRE) 62 (Sadler's Wells **56 p**
(USA) 132) [2006 7.5d 8m⁴ 7s Oct 10] 23,000Y, 45,000 2-y-o: strong, good-bodied colt: first foal: dam, ran once in Ireland, sister to useful Irish performer up to 1¾m Family Tradition: better than bare result in maidens, showing good speed: could well prove best at 5f/6f: type to improve and do well in 3-y-o handicaps. *D. Nicholls*

CAERNARVON (IRE) 2 b.g. (May 21) King's Best (USA) 132 – Reloy (USA) 119 **71**
(Liloy (FR) 124) [2006 p7.1g⁵ p8.6g Nov 11] brother to 3-y-o Marmota and half-brother to several winners, including 1994 2-y-o 5f/6f winner Loyalize (by Nureyev) and Irish 1¼m winner Relish (by Sadler's Wells), both useful: dam won 10.5f Prix de Royaumont and US Grade 1 9f/1¼m events: better effort in maidens at Wolverhampton when fifth on debut: took strong hold next time (reportedly suffered breathing problem): should stay 1m. *M. A. Jarvis*

CAERPHILLY GAL 6 b.m. Averti (IRE) 117 – Noble Lustre (USA) 71 (Lyphard's **51**
Wish (FR) 124) [2006 59: f7g³ Jan 17] modest performer: stays 1m: acts on fibresand and any turf going: free-going sort: usually races prominently. *P. L. Gilligan*

CAJ (IRE) 2 b.f. (Apr 4) Tagula (IRE) 116 – Notley Park 71 (Wolfhound (USA) 126) **56**
[2006 5g⁵ 5d p5.1g 5g⁴ 5m² 5.2f⁵ 5.2g³ 5g² 5m 5.3m Sep 19] €14,500Y: smallish, workmanlike filly: fifth foal: sister to 3-y-o Alugat and half-sister to 2 winners, including 4-y-o Knot In Wood: dam, maiden who stayed 7f, half-sister to smart sprinter Notley: modest maiden: placed in sellers: raced at 5f: acts on firm going: tail flasher. *M. Quinn*

CALABASH COVE (USA) 2 ch.c. (Jan 18) Rahy (USA) 115 – I Need A Holiday **79 p**
(USA) (Nureyev (USA) 131) [2006 p7.1g² Oct 30] first foal: dam unraced out of useful winner up to 1¼m Island of Silver: 2/1, encouraging 1½ lengths second to Phoenix Tower in maiden at Wolverhampton, wide and green throughout: will do better. *Saeed bin Suroor*

CALABAZA 4 ch.g. Zaha (CAN) 106 – Mo Stopher 47 (Sharpo 132) [2006 70: 6d 6m³ **75**
6g⁴ 6m 6.1g 6.1s Oct 25] strong gelding: fair performer: should stay 7f: acts on good to firm ground: often blinkered/in cheekpieces. *W. Jarvis*

CALAMARI (IRE) 4 ch.f. Desert King (IRE) 129 – Mrs Fisher (IRE) 94 (Salmon **63 d**
Leap (USA) 131) [2006 63: 9.9f³ 8.3d 7m⁶ 9.2g⁶ 8f p8g p8.6g Nov 20] heavy-topped filly: reportedly underwent wind operation in 2005: modest maiden: well below form after third outing: stays 1¼m: acts on firm going: tried tongue tied, blinkered final outing. *Mrs A. Duffield*

CALATAGAN (IRE) 7 ch.g. Danzig Connection (USA) – Calachuchi 74 (Martinmas **73**
128) [2006 73, a75: 14g⁴ 15.8g² 12m 16.1m³ Aug 9] short-backed gelding: fair handicapper: stays 2m: acts on polytrack, good to firm and good to soft going: races freely/prominently: useful chaser, won in October and December. *J. M. Jefferson*

CALCULATING (IRE) 2 b.c. (Feb 24) Machiavellian (USA) 123 – Zaheemah (USA) **– p**
96 (El Prado (IRE) 119) [2006 8g Sep 28] $225,000Y: strong, heavy-bodied colt: second foal: dam 1m winner: 33/1, burly and green in maiden at Newmarket (tongue tied): should do better. *J. H. M. Gosden*

CALCUTTA 10 b.h. Indian Ridge 123 – Echoing 93 (Formidable (USA) 125) [2006 **99**
101: 9g 8m 8.1f 8.2m² 8g⁴ 8.1m⁶ 8g 7f³ 8m Sep 13] smallish, sturdy horse: carried condition: smart performer at his best, winner of 13 of his 101 races, including Porcelanosa Handicap at Doncaster in 1999, 2001 and 2004: useful in 2006, best efforts in handicaps at Nottingham (½-length second to Samuel Charles) and Salisbury (fourth to Sew'n'So Character) in June: stayed easy 9f: acted on dirt, firm and good to soft going: tried blinkered: sometimes swished tail/looked less than keen, and was usually produced late: to stand at Louella Stud, Leicestershire, fee £700. *B. W. Hills*

CALCUTTA CUP (UAE) 3 br.g. Jade Robbery (USA) 121 – Six Nations (USA) **73**
(Danzig (USA)) [2006 p10g⁵ 11.8d 10.9d³ 16f⁶ 12.1m 8g 12.4s⁵ 12d² Nov 3] lengthy gelding: closely related to useful 7f (at 2 yrs) to 1¼m (in UAE) winner Asood (by Machiavellian) and half-brother to UAE 9f winner Outside Centre (by Benny The Dip): dam, French 10.5f winner, sister to multiple US Grade 1 winner up to 1¼m Chief's Crown: fair maiden: left M. Johnston 11,000 gns and gelded after fourth start: stays easy 1½m: acts on good to soft going, probably on polytrack: signs of temperament. *Karen McLintock*

£250000 Tattersalls October Auction Stakes, Newmarket—Caldra (nearer camera) runs on too strongly for Tobosa; Aahayson (near side) takes third ahead of Passified (far side) and Chataway is fifth

CALDRA (IRE) 2 b.g. (Mar 28) Elnadim (USA) 128 – Lady Rachel (IRE) 75 (Priolo (USA) 127) [2006 6s² 6m⁴ 7g* 7.1g² 8m* 6d* 8s* Oct 7] 14,000Y: sturdy, close-coupled gelding: third foal: half-brother to useful Irish 6f (at 2 yrs) to 1m winner Kestrel Cross (by Cape Cross): dam 1¼m/1½m winner: smart performer: gelded after second start: most progressive subsequently, winning 4 of last 5 starts (second in Solario Stakes other one), namely maiden at Salisbury, listed race at Goodwood, 28-runner £250000 Tattersalls October Auction Stakes (beat Tobosa by ½ length, pair clear) at Newmarket and Les Ambassadeurs Club Autumn Stakes at Ascot, in last-named beating Kid Mambo by 5 lengths (8 ran): reportedly underwent surgery later in October after suffering a condylar fracture of off-fore: effective at 6f to 1m, likely to stay 1¼m: acts on soft and good to firm going: a credit to connections. *S. Kirk* **114**

CALFRAZ 4 b. or br.g. Tamure (IRE) 125 – Pas de Chat (Relko 136) [2006 55: 14.1m⁶ 18s⁴ Oct 16] leggy gelding: modest maiden handicapper: stays 2¼m: acts on soft and good to firm ground: held up. *M. D. Hammond* **54**

CALIBAN (IRE) 8 ch.g. Rainbows For Life (CAN) – Amour Toujours (IRE) (Law Society (USA) 130) [2006 –: p16.5m Nov 21] lengthy gelding: modest handicapper at best: off 16 months, no impact on return: stays 19f: acts on fibresand and firm ground: tried visored: races freely: inconsistent. *Ian Williams* **–**

CALIFORNIA LAWS 4 b.g. Pivotal 124 – Noor El Houdah (IRE) 61 (Fayruz 116) [2006 69: 6g⁵ p6g⁶ f8g* p7.1g⁵ 7.2g⁴ 7.1s* 8.3g⁵ 8g 7.2v⁶ f7g* f6g* Dec 21] strong, lengthy gelding: fairly useful handicapper on all-weather, fair on turf: improved in 2006, winning at Southwell in July, Haydock in September and Southwell in November and December: effective at 6f to 1m: acts on all-weather, soft and good to firm going. *T. D. Barron* **77 a89**

CALLAHAN (FR) 2 gr.g. (Feb 26) Verglas (IRE) 118 – Late Night (FR) (Night Shift (USA)) [2006 7m f7g Nov 20] well beaten in maiden/seller. *Ms Deborah J. Evans* **–**

CALLISTO MOON 2 b.g. (Mar 1) Mujahid (USA) 125 – Nursling (IRE) 57 (Kahyasi 130) [2006 5.2m⁴ p6g² 6.1m⁶ p7g⁶ 8d p8.6g³ p8.6m² p8.6g⁵ p8.6g² Nov 28] 3,000Y: close-coupled gelding: first foal: dam, ran 3 times at 1¼m/1½m, out of half-sister to Park Hill winner Eva Luna, herself dam of St Leger winner Brian Boru: fair maiden: left R. Curtis after fourth start: creditable efforts last 4 outings: will stay 1¼m: acts on polytrack and good to firm going: tried blinkered. *P. A. Blockley* **71**

CALL ME GEORGE 3 ch.c. Rainbow Quest (USA) 134 – Coretta (IRE) 118 (Caerleon (USA) 132) [2006 –: 10d 11.5m⁶ 14.1g* 14.1m² 14.1m⁴ 16.2f² Jul 8] big, close-coupled colt: fair performer: won handicap at Redcar in May: good second twice after: should stay beyond 2m: acts on firm going: sold 20,000 gns later in July. *M. Johnston* **75**

CALL ME MAX 4 b.g. Vettori (IRE) 119 – Always Vigilant (USA) 85 (Lear Fan (USA) 130) [2006 88: 7m p7g 10f⁶ p8g 9.5s⁶ Oct 6] lengthy, quite attractive gelding: fairly useful performer: left E. Dunlop 18,000 gns after fourth start: stays easy 1¼m: acts on polytrack, firm and good to soft ground: tried visored. *Eoin Doyle, Ireland* **80**

CALL ME ROSY (IRE) 2 ch.f. (Feb 5) Shinko Forest (IRE) – Fanciful (IRE) (Mujtahid (USA) 118) [2006 6g 6f² p6m⁴ p7.1g p6g Nov 15] €22,000Y, 30,000 2-y-o: sturdy, workmanlike filly: closely related to 5-y-o Queenstown and half-sister to 3 winners, including 2004 2-y-o 6f winner Heres The Plan (by Revoque): dam ran once at **69**

2 yrs in Ireland: fair maiden: twice in frame at Wolverhampton: should stay 7f: acts on polytrack. *C. F. Wall*

CALL ME WAKI (USA) 3 ch.f. Miswaki (USA) 124 – S S Capote (USA) (Capote (USA)) [2006 73: 7.1g⁴ 7f⁴ 6m⁴ 6m* Aug 5] leggy, workmanlike filly: fair performer: won maiden at Windsor in August, hanging left: stays 7f: acts on firm going: races prominently. *A. M. Balding* **74**

CALL MY BLUFF (FR) 3 b.g. Highest Honor (FR) 124 – Baino Bluff (Be My Guest (USA) 126) [2006 12d 12g² 12d p10g² p8.6g⁵ Dec 18] €72,000Y: brother to several winners in France, notably smart miler Take Risks: dam French 1m winner: fair maiden: best efforts when second at Lyon Villeurbanne (penultimate start for Mme M. Bollack-Badel in France) and Kempton: stays 1½m: acts on polytrack. *Rae Guest* **71**

CALL MY NUMBER (IRE) 3 b.g. Grand Lodge (USA) 125 – Screen Idol (IRE) 86 (Sadler's Wells (USA) 132) [2006 88: p8g⁵ 7.5f² 7.5g⁶ 6m³ 7g Jul 6] strong, attractive gelding: fairly useful performer: good short-head second to Sir Gerard in handicap at Beverley second start: should stay 1m: acts on polytrack and firm going: sold 30,000 gns later in July, gelded, and sent to Bahrain. *M. R. Channon* **83**

CALLOFF THE SEARCH 2 b.g. (Apr 25) Piccolo 121 – Unchain My Heart 70 (Pursuit of Love 124) [2006 5.1d³ 5m⁴ 6m f8g p7.1g Dec 27] rather leggy, close-coupled gelding: first foal: dam 7f/1m winner: modest maiden: below form after second start: may prove best at 5f: acts on good to firm and good to soft ground: tried in cheekpieces: lost action third outing. *W. G. M. Turner* **63 d**

CALLWOOD DANCER (IRE) 2 ch.f. (Mar 23) Danehill Dancer (IRE) 117 – Ahdaab (USA) 73 (Rahy (USA) 115) [2006 5f³ 6f² p8.5f⁴ p6.5f³ p7f³ Nov 17] €100,000Y: second foal: closely related to 2005 2-y-o 5f winner Walklikeanegyptian (by Danehill): dam, maiden who may have proved best at 1¼m/1½m, half-sister to Queen Elizabeth II Stakes winner Maroof: in frame in maidens at Windsor (2, then left B. Hills) and Woodbine (3): should stay 1m: acts on polytrack and firm going. *R. L. Attfield, Canada* **73**

CALMING WATERS 3 ch.c. Dr Fong (USA) 128 – Faraway Waters 102 (Pharly (FR) 130) [2006 p8g p8g² p10g² Nov 13] fifth foal: half-brother to 4-y-o Something Exciting: dam, 2-y-o 6f winner who probably stayed 1½m, out of sister to smart performer up to 14.6f Shining Water, herself dam of Tenby: fair maiden: similar form when second at Lingfield: stays easy 1¼m: raced only on polytrack. *D. W. P. Arbuthnot* **79**

CALUSA LADY (IRE) 6 ch.m. Titus Livius (FR) 115 – Solas Abu (IRE) 82 (Red Sunset 120) [2006 46: p7g⁶ Dec 13] smallish, lengthy mare: poor maiden: effective at 6f/ easy 7f: acts on polytrack, firm and soft going: tried visored/tongue tied. *J. A. Geake* **42**

CALYPSO KING 3 gr.g. Agnes World (USA) 123 – T G'S Girl 57 (Selkirk (USA) 129) [2006 90: 6g 6.1f 6.1s 6m 7m 6g p7g p6g² p6g Oct 6] tall, quite good-topped gelding: fairly useful handicapper: will prove best kept to 5f/6f: acts on polytrack and firm ground: edgy sort: looked awkward fifth outing. *J. W. Hills* **86**

CALZAGHE (IRE) 2 ch.g. (May 25) Galileo (IRE) 134 – Novelette (Darshaan 133) – [2006 7g 8m p8.6g⁴ Nov 11] good-topped gelding: little sign of ability. *A. M. Balding*

CAME BACK (IRE) 3 ch.c. Bertolini (USA) 125 – Distant Decree (USA) (Distant View (USA) 126) [2006 –p: p6g³ p6g⁴ p6g* p6g 5.3m p6g* p6g p6g³ p6s⁵ Dec 15] fair performer: won maiden in February and seller in October, both at Lingfield: raced mainly over 6f on polytrack: reportedly finished lame seventh outing. *J. A. Osborne* **72**

CAMEO STORY 3 b.f. Spectrum (IRE) 126 – Alpine Park (IRE) 87 (Barathea (IRE) 127) [2006 6v 5m 8f⁵ 8d⁴ p8.6g f7g p7.1g Dec 21] 10,000Y: first foal: dam, 2-y-o 6f winner in Britain (later successful at 5.5f in Norway), half-sister to useful sprinter Pakhoes: modest maiden: stays 1m: acts on firm and good to soft going, little form on all-weather. *A. Oliver, Ireland* **50 a–**

CAMISSA 2 b.f. (Mar 28) Averti (IRE) 117 – Ambitious 98 (Ardkinglass 114) [2006 5g² 5m⁵ 5g* 5s p6g Jun 7] tall, quite good-topped filly: second foal: dam 5f/6f winner: fair performer: won maiden at Windsor in May: stiff tasks after in listed race at York and minor event at Kempton: should prove best at 5f/6f. *D. K. Ivory* **74**

CAMPANILE 3 ch.f. Zilzal (USA) 137 – High Barn 72 (Shirley Heights 130) [2006 75p: 8m p8.6g³ 10g Aug 19] lengthy filly: modest maiden: bred to be suited by 1¼m+: acts on good to soft ground: withdrawn after getting loose prior to third intended outing: sold 4,000 gns in October. *J. R. Fanshawe* **57**

CAM

CAMP ATTACK 3 b.g. Fleetwood (IRE) 107 – Queen of Tides (IRE) 62 (Soviet Star **60** (USA) 128) [2006 10m 10f 10g p10g p12g⁶ 10m⁴ p10g⁵ p12g² p10g³ p12g Dec 22] modest maiden: stays easy 1½m: acts on polytrack and good to firm ground. *S. Dow*

CAMPBELLS LAD 5 b.g. Mind Games 121 – T O O Mamma's (IRE) 50 (Classic **62** Secret (USA) 91) [2006 48: f8g 12m⁶ 9.3m⁵ 9g⁴ 9.2m⁶ 8.3g⁶ 11s⁴ f11g p12.2g² Nov 14] big gelding: modest maiden: effective at 1m to 1½m: acts on all-weather, soft and good to firm going: tried in cheekpieces/blinkers. *Mrs G. S. Rees*

CAMPBELTOWN (IRE) 3 b.c. Mull of Kintyre (USA) 114 – Jallaissine (IRE) **87** (College Chapel 122) [2006 97: p7g⁵ p8g⁶ 6s 6g 6m 5m 5.1f 5.1m 6d Oct 19] strong, good-bodied colt: type to carry condition: just fairly useful at best in 2006, leaving E. O'Neill 21,000 gns after third start: should stay beyond 6f: acts on polytrack, good to firm and good to soft going: tried in cheekpieces. *R. A. Harris*

CAMP COMMANDER (IRE) 7 gr.h. Pennekamp (USA) 130 – Khalatara (IRE) **–** (Kalaglow 132) [2006 –: p7.1g p8.6g p7.1g Jan 30] rather leggy horse: useful in his day: no form in 4 races since 2004: usually tongue tied. *C. R. Dore*

CAMPEON (IRE) 4 b.g. Monashee Mountain (USA) 115 – Arctic Lead (USA) (Arctic **60** Tern (USA) 126) [2006 71, a62: p5g⁴ 5.3m 5.5d 5.1s⁶ 5.3m p5g 5f 5m⁴ 5.1m f5m³ p5.1g⁴ p5g p5g p5.1g³ f5g⁵ f6g⁴ Dec 29] good-bodied gelding: just modest performer in 2006: effective at 5f to easy 7f: acts on all-weather, firm and soft going: tried in headgear: sometimes races freely/wanders. *J. M. Bradley*

CAMPO BUENO (FR) 4 b.c. Septieme Ciel (USA) 123 – Herba Buena (FR) (Fabu- **99 d** lous Dancer (USA) 124) [2006 a6.5g⁵ a6.5g* 6v* 5.5v⁵ 7.6d³ 6s 7.1s⁵ 6g 6d⁴ 5s⁶ p6g Nov 16] €25,000Y: second living foal: dam, French 2-y-o 1m winner, half-sister to useful 7f/1m winner Volontiers: useful performer: won 3 times at 2 yrs, including in listed race at Deauville: successful early in 2006 in minor events at Cagnes-sur-Mer and Maisons-Laffitte: left X. Nakkachdji in France after fifth start: just fairly useful form at best in Britain: best up to 6.5f: acts on heavy going and all-weather: tried blinkered: often makes running. *A. Berry*

CAMPS BAY (USA) 2 b.c. (Mar 5) Cozzene (USA) – Seewillo (USA) (Pleasant Col- **74** ony (USA)) [2006 7.1g 7m⁵ 8.3d³ Oct 10] $130,000Y: rangy colt: half-brother to several winners, including useful French/US 1m/9f winner Perfect Copy (by Deputy Minister): dam, US Grade 3 9f winner, half-sister to Arlington Million/Japan Cup winner Golden Pheasant: fair form in maidens, including fifth to Adagio at Newmarket: stays 1m. *Mrs A. J. Perrett*

CAMROSE 5 ch.g. Zafonic (USA) 130 – Tularosa (In The Wings 128) [2006 106: 12s² **106** 12m⁵ 12m² 12d² 12.3m³ 12d 11.6d³ Nov 4] good-bodied gelding: useful performer: good efforts in 2006 when placed, including in listed event at Pontefract (2½ lengths second to Alfie Flits), minor event at Newmarket (¾-length second to Perfectperformance) and listed event at Chester (third to Foxhaven) third/fourth/fifth outings: best around 1½m: acts on soft and good to firm going: blinkered: doesn't always impress with attitude (tends to carry head high/run in snatches): gelded after final outing. *J. L. Dunlop*

CANADIAN DANEHILL (IRE) 4 b.c. Indian Danehill (IRE) 124 – San Jovita **78** (CAN) 71 (St Jovite (USA) 135) [2006 68: f6g p5.1g³ p6g⁴ p7.1g* p5.1g* p5.1g p5g² 6m² 5.1s 5m² 6f 5g⁵ 6m³ 5m² 5f 6f 5g⁵ 6.1g 5d f6g³ p5g⁶ Dec 3] big, lengthy colt: fair handicapper: won at Wolverhampton in January and February: effective at 5f to 7f: acts on all-weather, firm and soft going: effective with or without cheekpieces: has looked none too keen. *R. M. H. Cowell*

CANARY DANCER 4 b.f. Groom Dancer (USA) 128 – Bird of Time (IRE) 75 **46** (Persian Bold 123) [2006 46: f7g f6g⁵ f6g f5g⁶ Feb 23] strong, lengthy filly: poor maiden: stays 1m: acts on all-weather and firm ground: sometimes wears cheekpieces/blinkers. *Miss Z. C. Davison*

CANARY GIRL 3 br.f. Primo Valentino (IRE) 116 – Cumbrian Concerto 44 (Petong **41** 126) [2006 –: 7m 7m p8.6g 8f⁵ 8m 7f 10d p6m⁴ Oct 9] poor maiden: stays 1m: acts on polytrack and firm going. *Mrs C. A. Dunnett*

CANARY ISLAND (IRE) 4 b.g. Polar Falcon (USA) 126 – Yellow Trumpet 75 (Pet- **–** ong 126) [2006 70: p5g 5.3f 5.3m p6g 6f Jul 22] fair performer at 3 yrs: no show in 2006. *J. M. Bradley*

CAN CAN STAR 3 br.c. Lend A Hand 124 – Carrie Can Can 73 (Green Tune (USA) **70** 125) [2006 7.5f³ p8.6g 7f³ 8m⁵ 9.9m⁶ 9.8s³ 10g⁴ p10g Oct 15] first foal: dam 9.4f winner: fair maiden: stays 1¼m: acts on firm and soft going: blinkered final outing: has raced freely: sold 11,000 gns, joined A. Carroll. *J. G. Given*

172

CANDARLI (IRE) 10 ch.g. Polish Precedent (USA) 131 – Calounia (IRE) (Pharly **67**
(FR) 130) [2006 p12.2g⁴ p12.2g⁴ p16g⁴ Feb 28] fair maiden: stays 2m: acts on polytrack.
D. R. Gandolfo

CANDLE 3 b.f. Dansili 127 – Celia Brady 62 (Last Tycoon 131) [2006 10m² p10g* 11m **92**
12g² 11.7f 14g² 12d Oct 27] close-coupled, quite attractive filly: unfurnished at present:
half-sister to 3 winners, including fairly useful 1¼m and 11.7f winner Clarisse (by Salse),
later successful abroad, and 5-y-o Colloquia: dam, 1m winner, half-sister to Warrsan,
Luso, Needle Gun and Cloud Castle: fairly useful performer: won maiden at Kempton in
June: good second after in handicaps at Salisbury and Haydock: stays 1¾m: acts on
polytrack, best efforts on turf on good going. *H. Candy*

CANDY ANCHOR (FR) 7 b.m. Slip Anchor 136 – Kandavu 87 (Safawan 118) [2006 **–**
46: p7.1g p9.5g p12.2g May 5] lengthy mare: poor maiden: well held in 2006: often
blinkered nowadays, tried tongue tied. *R. E. Peacock*

CANDYLAND (IRE) 2 b.f. (Feb 7) Bubble Gum Fellow (JPN) 120 – Capoeira (USA) **64**
(Nureyev (USA) 131) [2006 5.2d⁶ p6g p6g⁵ 5f² 5.3f² 5g⁶ Aug 31] good-topped filly: has
scope: third foal: dam French 1m winner: modest maiden: second at Windsor and Brighton (3-runner nursery): should stay 7f/1m: acts on polytrack, firm and good to soft going.
M. R. Channon

CANINA 3 b.f. Foxhound (USA) 103 – Fizzy Fiona (Efisio 120) [2006 70, a68: p5.1g² **69**
p6g² p7.1g³ p6g* p6g³ p7g p7g p5.1g 5.1s 6s⁶ p6g p6g Nov 23] tall filly: fair performer:
won maiden at Wolverhampton in February: stays 7f: acts on polytrack and heavy
ground. *Ms Deborah J. Evans*

CANKARA (IRE) 3 b.f. Daggers Drawn (USA) 114 – Suddenly 86 (Puissance 110) **–**
[2006 p9.5g p8.6g p6g p8g f8g Dec 28] 20,000Y: third foal: half-sister to 2004 2-y-o
6f/7f winner Sudden Dismissal (by Inchinor) and Irish 1m winner Sudden Silence (by
Kris), both fairly useful: dam 2-y-o 7f winner: little form: often slowly away. *D. Carroll*

CANNI THINKAAR (IRE) 5 b.g. Alhaarth (IRE) 126 – Cannikin (IRE) 82 (Lahib **–**
(USA) 129) [2006 p6g 10.2f Jun 17] angular gelding: maiden: last both starts in 2006:
tried in cheekpieces. *P. Butler*

CANNON FIRE (FR) 5 ch.h. Grand Lodge (USA) 125 – Muirfield (FR) (Crystal **–**
Glitters (USA) 127) [2006 18m Jun 3] fair form at 2 yrs: unplaced in maiden at Cologne
only outing in 2004 when trained in Germany: unraced on Flat in 2005: won over hurdles
prior to well held only Flat outing in 2006: should stay 2m+: acts on firm going. *Evan
Williams*

CANNYGO (IRE) 3 b.g. Brave Act 119 – Cannylass (IRE) 43 (Brief Truce (USA) 126) **–**
[2006 –: f8g Jan 17] last in maidens at Lingfield and Southwell (blinkered). *R. M. Flower*

CANTABILLY (IRE) 3 b.g. Distant Music (USA) 126 – Cantaloupe (Priolo (USA) **76**
127) [2006 67: p8g³ 8.3g 8.2s³ 8.3g 8.2s² 8.1s 8.3d⁶ 10f² 10.1m* 12m⁴ 9.9m⁵ 9m **a82**
p9.5m* p10g* 10s⁵ p10g⁴ Oct 20] close-coupled gelding: fairly useful handicapper on
all-weather, fair on turf: won at Epsom in July, and Wolverhampton and Lingfield in October: stays 1½m: acts on polytrack, firm and soft going: sold 30,000 gns, then gelded.
M. R. Channon

CANTABRIA 3 br.f. Dansili 127 – Valencia 79 (Kenmare (FR) 125) [2006 98: 7m² 7f³ **108**
8m⁶ 7d⁴ 7d.4 a8.5f* Dec 6] neat filly: useful performer: improved form when placed first 2
starts in 2006, in Fred Darling Stakes at Newbury (beaten short head by Nasheej) and Oak
Tree Stakes at Goodwood (1½ lengths third to Red Evie, repeatedly short of room): well
below form in listed races 2 of next 3 starts, then left Sir Michael Stoute: won allowance
race at Hollywood in December by 4¼ lengths: stays 8.5f: acts on Cushion Track, firm
and good to soft going. *R. J. Frankel, USA*

CANTARNA (IRE) 5 ch.m. Ashkalani (IRE) 128 – Lancea (IRE) (Generous (IRE) **69**
139) [2006 75: f8g 8.2d 8.1s p8.6g⁴ 8.3f* 8.3d³ 10g Aug 30] rather sparely-made mare:
fair handicapper: won at Leicester in July: stays 8.6f: acts on polytrack, firm and good to
soft going. *J. Mackie*

CANTIQUE (IRE) 2 b.f. (May 12) Danetime (IRE) 121 – Bethania 70 (Mark of **65**
Esteem (IRE) 137) [2006 6m⁶ 5.7f 5.1m³ p6g³ 6f p7.1m² p7.1g³ p7.1m⁵ p6s⁴ Dec 15]
€2,000F, 9,000Y: second foal: dam, maiden (best form at 7f), half-sister to Middle Park
winner Fard: fair maiden: placed 4 times, in seller sixth start (left R. Beckett £6,000):
stays 7f: acts on polytrack and firm going: tended to hang final outing. *A. G. Newcombe*

CANTRIP 6 b.m. Celtic Swing 138 – Circe 73 (Main Reef 126) [2006 66: 11.9m 11.9m **57**
12f⁵ 12m 11.5m⁵ 11.6f 14.1g p12g Dec 6] sparely-made mare: modest handicapper: left

173

Miss B. Sanders after seventh start: stays 1¾m: acts on firm and good to soft going, probably on polytrack: tried blinkered/tongue tied: usually races prominently: none too consistent. *S. Dow*

CANVAS (IRE) 3 b.f. Dansili 127 – Sampan (Elmaamul (USA) 125) [2006 47: 10m 8m — p6g 8f 7g Aug 2] little form. *Miss Z. C. Davison*

CANYOUWIN 3 b.f. Inchinor 119 – Tharwa (IRE) 63 (Last Tycoon 131) [2006 –: p8g⁶ **65** p10g³ 10m 12m⁵ 16g² Aug 26] angular filly: fair maiden handicapper: best effort final start: stays 2m: acts on polytrack: sold 10,000 gns. *J. H. M. Gosden*

CAPABLE GUEST (IRE) 4 b. or br.g. Cape Cross (IRE) 129 – Alexander Confranc **102** (IRE) 73 (Magical Wonder (USA) 125) [2006 102: p8g* 8s³ 8m 8f 8m 8.1m⁴ 8g³ 8f⁶ 10.4g⁶ 9d Sep 30] rather leggy, attractive gelding: useful handicapper: won at Lingfield (by neck from Sew'n'So Character) in February: good efforts in frame at Sandown (2½ lengths fourth to Hinterland, forced to wait for gap) and Newbury (close third to Salinja) sixth/seventh starts: stays 1¼m: acts on polytrack, firm and soft going: tried blinkered/ visored at 3 yrs: held up. *M. R. Channon*

CAPAHOUSE 2 b.g. (Jan 22) Auction House (USA) 120 – Perecapa (IRE) 44 (Arch- — way (IRE) 115) [2006 7g Aug 23] last in maiden at Leicester. *B. Palling*

CAPANIA (IRE) 2 br.f. (Mar 24) Cape Cross (IRE) 129 – Gentle Papoose (Comman- **54 p** che Run 133) [2006 p7g Nov 11] €20,000Y: half-sister to 2 winners, including fairly useful 1998 2-y-o 5f/6f winner Cheyenne Gold (by Anita's Prince), later successful in USA: dam poor Irish maiden: 33/1, in need of experience when 7¾ lengths eighth of 14 to Sell Out in maiden at Kempton, slowly away and late headway not knocked about: should do better. *J. W. Hills*

CAPANNINA 2 ch.f. (Feb 1) Grand Lodge (USA) 125 – Mauri Moon 104 (Green **72** Desert (USA) 127) [2006 5m⁴ 6f³ p7.1g* 7m⁴ 7m³ 8m Sep 21] good-topped, attractive filly: first foal: dam, 6f (at 2 yrs) to 1m winner, half-sister to useful French 1¼m per- former All Glory: fair performer: won maiden at Wolverhampton (hung right) in July: in frame 4 of 5 other starts, twice in nurseries: should stay 1m: acts on polytrack and firm going: looks none too keen. *J. Noseda*

CAPE 3 b.f. Cape Cross (IRE) 129 – Rubbiyati 56 (Cadeaux Genereux 131) [2006 6.1m³ **101 p** 6.1g* 6s* 6g* Sep 28] good-bodied filly: fourth foal: half-sister to 1m and 9.6f winner Alsyati (by Salse): dam, 1m winner at 4 yrs (only season to race), half-sister to high-class miler Air Express: reportedly injured in late-2005: useful form: progressed well in 2006, winning maiden at Nottingham in June, and handicaps in August (by head from Stanley Goodspeed) and September (beat Misphire by ¾ length), both at Newmarket: bred to be suited by 7f/1m, though clearly not short of speed (has good turn of foot): will do better still. *J. R. Fanshawe*

CAPE COLUMBINE 4 b.f. Diktat 126 – Cape Merino 103 (Clantime 101) [2006 106: **105** 6g 6.1s³ 7.1g³ 8m Jul 12] big, strong filly: type to carry condition: impresses in appear- ance: useful performer: back up in trip, respectable 2½ lengths third to Quito in listed race at Haydock: stiff task, last of 7 in Falmouth Stakes at Newmarket only subsequent start: stays 1m, but could well prove best at 7f: acts on firm and good to soft going: has been bandaged behind: sold 130,000 gns in November. *D. R. C. Elsworth*

CAPE COURIER (IRE) 3 b.g. Cape Cross (IRE) 129 – Russian Countess (USA) 104 — (Nureyev (USA) 131) [2006 –: p6g 8m Jun 6] close-coupled gelding: little form: tried in cheekpieces. *I. W. McInnes*

CAPE DANCER (IRE) 2 b.f. (Apr 12) Cape Cross (IRE) 129 – Yankee Dancer 62 **66** (Groom Dancer (USA) 128) [2006 7.2g³ 7f⁴ 7g⁵ 6d 7m⁶ Sep 12] €44,000F, 20,000Y, 29,000 2-y-o: sturdy, workmanlike filly: fluent mover: second foal: sister to useful 2005 2-y-o 6f/7f winner Yankee George: dam maiden who probably stayed 1¾m: fair form in maidens: well held in sales race and nursery: will stay 1m+. *J. S. Wainwright*

CAPE DIAMOND (IRE) 3 b.g. Cape Cross (IRE) 129 – Jemalina (USA) 52 (Trem- **70** polino (USA) 135) [2006 71: p7.1g² 8.3g 10f⁴ 10g⁵ p10g* 11.9g⁶ p10g Oct 20] leggy, **a83** quite good-topped gelding: fairly useful handicapper on all-weather, fair on turf: best effort when winning apprentice event at Lingfield in September: stays 1¼m: acts on polytrack and firm going: has looked lazy/quirky: sold 21,000 gns. *W. R. Swinburn*

CAPE FREE 2 ch.f. (Mar 24) Mark of Esteem (IRE) 137 – Cape Cod (IRE) 62 (Unfu- **51 ?** wain (USA) 131) [2006 f6m⁴ p7g⁵ Nov 13] first foal: dam maiden sister to useful 7f/1m winner Abeyr: seemingly modest form when last of 5 in claimer at Lingfield second start. *E. F. Vaughan*

CAPE GIGI (IRE) 3 b.f. Cape Cross (IRE) 129 – L'Accolade (IRE) (Seattle Dancer (USA) 119) [2006 43: p8g Jan 3] maiden: blinkered, well held only 3-y-o outing. *B. J. Meehan* —

CAPE GOLD (IRE) 3 b.g. Cape Cross (IRE) 129 – Filigree (Salse (USA) 128) [2006 77d: 8m 8s 7g p8.6g Jun 9] close-coupled gelding: fair maiden at best at 2 yrs: well beaten in 2006: tried blinkered. *R. A. Fahey* —

CAPE GREKO 4 ro. or gr.g. Loup Sauvage (USA) 125 – Onefortheditch (USA) 79 (With Approval (CAN)) [2006 100: 8g 8d p8.6g p7g² p8g⁵ p7g Dec 15] tall, good-bodied gelding: fairly useful performer nowadays: fractured a knee after final outing at 2 yrs then reportedly injured after final start in 2005: creditable efforts in handicaps at Kempton fourth/fifth starts: should stay 1¼m: acts on polytrack and firm ground: visored last 4 outings. *A. M. Balding* **94**

CAPE HAWK (IRE) 2 b.g. (Feb 20) Cape Cross (IRE) 129 – Hawksbill Special (IRE) (Taufan (USA) 119) [2006 7d⁶ Sep 29] €47,000F, €92,000Y: strong, well-made gelding: eighth foal: half-brother to several winners, including 6f winner Zietunzeen (by Zieten) and 3-y-o Choosy: dam unraced: 14/1 and burly, 6¼ lengths sixth of 14 to Supersonic Dave in maiden at Newmarket: capable of better. *R. Hannon* **73 p**

CAPE JASMINE (IRE) 2 b.f. (Apr 15) Danehill (USA) 126 – Oumaldaaya (USA) 111 (Nureyev (USA) 131) [2006 6m 6m Sep 22] €320,000Y: quite well-topped filly: half-sister to 3 winners, including useful 1m/1¼m winner Ayun (by Swain) and smart 7f (at 2 yrs) to 9f winner Haami (by Nashwan): dam, 7f (at 2 yrs) and 1¼m (Italian Group 2 event) winner, half-sister to Derby winner Erhaab: well held in maidens 3 months apart (lame on debut). *J. Howard Johnson* —

CAPE LATINA 3 b.f. Cape Cross (IRE) 129 – Latina (IRE) (King's Theatre (IRE) 128) [2006 42: p7g p7g p6g⁶ p10g⁵ p8.6g 8m⁶ Aug 22] sturdy filly: poor maiden: probably stays easy 1¼m: acts on good to firm going: carried head high final start: sold 800 gns, sent to Spain. *J. R. Best* **38**

CAPEL ISLAND (USA) 2 ch.f. (Feb 13) Royal Academy (USA) 130 – Fight The Question (USA) (Fit To Fight (USA)) [2006 8.1m Aug 28] $15,000Y, €60,000Y: eighth foal: half-sister to 3 winners abroad: dam unraced: 14/1, needed experience (very slow start) in maiden at Chepstow. *R. Hannon* —

CAPE MAYA 3 gr.f. Cape Cross (IRE) 129 – Incatinka 63 (Inca Chief (USA)) [2006 10d⁶ 8m 10m⁶ 8.5g⁶ 8.5g Aug 3] leggy filly: fourth foal: half-sister to French 1¼m winner Vieri (by Pelder): dam lightly-raced maiden: fair maiden: stays 1¼m: acts on good to firm and good to soft ground. *B. J. Meehan* **67**

CAPE OF LUCK (IRE) 3 b.c. Cape Cross (IRE) 129 – Fledgling 76 (Efisio 120) [2006 87: p7g 7m* p8g p10g p8g Dec 30] smallish, well-made colt: fairly useful performer: won handicap at Newmarket in June: stays 1m: acts on polytrack and good to firm going: tends to edge left. *P. Mitchell* **93**

CAPE OF STORMS 3 b.c. Cape Cross (IRE) 129 – Lloc 79 (Absalom 128) [2006 p7g³ 7v p6g 6.1m 6m 8.3m³ 6.9m⁶ 8.1m⁵ p10g 8g f7g Dec 5] 120,000F: compact colt: fifth foal: half-brother to fairly useful 5f (at 2 yrs) to 1m winner Aimee's Delight (by Robellino): dam, 5f winner (including at 2 yrs), half-sister to July Cup winner Compton Place: fair maiden: left M. Channon after seventh start: stays 1m: acts on polytrack and good to firm going. *R. Brotherton* **70 d**

CAPE PRESTO (IRE) 3 b.c. Cape Cross (IRE) 129 – Samhat Mtoto 64 (Mtoto 134) [2006 89: 8m 7s 7g 10m 8g⁶ 8.3g 8m p7.1m⁵ p6g* p6g² p6g⁶ Dec 3] strong, deep-girthed colt: has a quick action: fairly useful performer: left R. Hannon 13,000 gns after third start: won handicap at Wolverhampton in November: has won over 1m, may prove best at shorter: acts on polytrack and good to firm ground: visored last 5 outings: races prominently. *Mrs C. A. Dunnett* **86**

CAPE ROYAL 6 b.g. Prince Sabo 123 – Indigo 86 (Primo Dominie 121) [2006 105: p5g 5.1s⁵ 5.2m 5g² 5.1f 5s 5s⁵ 5m 5m⁴ 5f³ 5m⁶ 5m p5g⁵ 5m 5m⁴ 5d² 5s* 5.4g 5f² 5g⁶ 5d 5.1m³ 5g⁶ 5s Oct 14] good-bodied gelding: useful handicapper: made all at Haydock (beating Kenmore a neck) in September: several other creditable efforts in 2006, including 1¼ lengths second to The Jobber at Leicester and around a length third to Intrepid Jack at Bath in September/October: stays 5.6f: acts on polytrack, firm and soft going: often wears blinkers/tongue tie: sometimes slowly away, otherwise races prominently. *J. M. Bradley* **102**

CAPE RUNAWAY (IRE) 2 b.f. (Feb 23) Cape Cross (IRE) 129 – Secrets of Honour (Belmez (USA) 131) [2006 p6g 7f⁴ Aug 15] 19,000F: sister to 4-y-o Gibraltar Bay and **54**

half-sister to 3 winners, including fairly useful 1m winner Another Secret (by Efisio): dam unraced half-sister to high-class sprinter Mr Brooks: green and not knocked about in maidens: will be suited by at least 1m. *L. M. Cumani*

CAPE SCHANCK 2 b.g. (Mar 15) Observatory (USA) 131 – Sally Gardens 60 (Alzao (USA) 117) [2006 p7g² p7.1g³ 7m² 7g⁶ p8.6m² Sep 2] 12,000Y: close-coupled gelding: second foal: dam 2-y-o 7f seller winner: fairly useful maiden: placed 4 of 5 starts (stiff task at Ascot other occasion), second to Majuro in minor event at Wolverhampton final one: stays 8.6f: sent to Hong Kong, where renamed Embraces. *Jane Chapple-Hyam* — **82**

CAPE SECRET (IRE) 3 b.g. Cape Cross (IRE) 129 – Baylands Sunshine (IRE) (Classic Secret (USA) 91) [2006 59: 11.6g³ 11.8d³ 14m* 14g* 14.8m* 13.9s Aug 24] leggy gelding: fairly useful performer: improved in 2006, making all in handicaps at Goodwood in June, and Haydock and Newmarket in July: stays 15f: acts on good to firm and good to soft going, poor effort on soft final start. *R. M. Beckett* — **92**

CAPE SYDNEY (IRE) 3 b.f. Cape Cross (IRE) 129 – Lady At War (Warning 136) [2006 –: f6g 6d 5.9g⁵ 8.3g 7m² 6g 7m* 7.1d⁵ Oct 8] good-topped filly: poor performer: won maiden at Catterick in September: stays 7f: unraced on extremes of going on turf. *D. W. Barker* — **47**

CAPE THEA 2 b.f. (Mar 4) Cape Cross (IRE) 129 – Pasithea (IRE) 101 (Celtic Swing 138) [2006 p7.1g² Nov 17] 14,000Y: second foal: dam, 7f (at 2 yrs) to 1½m winner, half-sister to 6-y-o Somnus: 10/1, promising debut when ½-length second of 11 to Giant Slalom in maiden at Wolverhampton: should improve. *W. R. Swinburn* — **71 p**

CAPE VELVET (IRE) 2 b.f. (Jan 27) Cape Cross (IRE) 129 – Material Lady (IRE) 74 (Barathea (IRE) 127) [2006 6g 6.1m² Sep 15] €28,000Y: angular filly: first foal: dam, Irish maiden who stayed 1¼m, half-sister to useful Irish performer up to 9.5f Dolmur: much better run in maidens when 2 lengths second to Tobermory at Nottingham: will stay 1m/1¼m. *J. W. Hills* — **80**

CAPE WIN (IRE) 3 b.g. Cape Cross (IRE) 129 – Monarchy (IRE) (Common Grounds 118) [2006 72: 8.3d³ p8.6g² 7f² 8g⁶ Jun 30] fair maiden: stays 8.6f: acts on polytrack, firm and good to soft ground: wore cheekpieces last 3 starts: free-going sort: sold 9,000 gns in July. *W. J. Haggas* — **68**

CAPISTRANO 3 b.g. Efisio 120 – Washita (Valiyar 129) [2006 68p: 8.1s⁶ 9.8g* 10.2s⁵ 10d Oct 10] close-coupled gelding: fair performer: best effort when making successful handicap debut at Ripon in May: left B. Hills 30,000 gns and gelded prior to shaping as if amiss final outing: should stay 1½m: acts on polytrack. *Mrs P. Sly* — **79**

CAPITALISE (IRE) 3 b.g. City On A Hill (USA) 114 – Prime Interest (IRE) (Kings Lake (USA) 133) [2006 –: p9.5g 8g⁵ 8f 9.9m⁶ 10.1f⁶ 14.1f⁵ 11.5f 8d p13.9g² p13.9g⁴ p16.5g² Dec 29] modest maiden on Flat (winning juvenile hurdler): stays 2m: acts on polytrack and firm ground: tried blinkered/tongue tied. *V. Smith* — **55 a61**

CAPITAL LASS 3 b. or br.f. Forzando 122 – Fair Test 95 (Fair Season 120) [2006 55: p5g 5d 5g p8g f7g* p7.1g⁵ f6g⁶ f7g⁴ f7g* Dec 28] compact filly: modest performer: left M. Wallace after reappearance and D. Simcock (former trainer) after third start: won banded races at Southwell in November and December: stays 7f: acts on all-weather and good to firm going. *D. K. Ivory* — **61**

CAPPANRUSH (IRE) 6 gr.g. Medaaly 114 – Introvert (USA) (Exbourne (USA) 125) [2006 p12.2g⁶ Feb 6] always behind in maiden at Wolverhampton on Flat debut: modest winning hurdler. *A. Ennis* — **–**

CAPPED FOR VICTORY (USA) 5 b.g. Red Ransom (USA) – Nazoo (IRE) 99 (Nijinsky (CAN) 138) [2006 –: 5s 9g May 30] good-topped gelding: fairly useful performer at 3 yrs: no form since. *W. S. Cunningham* — **–**

CAPRICHO (IRE) 9 gr.g. Lake Coniston (IRE) 131 – Star Spectacle (Spectacular Bid (USA)) [2006 100d: 6g⁵ 6g 6g 7m⁶ 8m³ 8m 6.1d 8.2s Oct 18] tall gelding: smart handicapper in prime, just fairly useful nowadays: well below form last 3 starts: effective at 6f, and probably stays 1m: acts on firm and soft going: tried in cheekpieces: sometimes finds little. *J. Akehurst* — **83 d**

CAPRICORN RUN (USA) 3 br. or b.c. Elusive Quality (USA) – Cercida (USA) (Copelan (USA)) [2006 87: 8d Oct 2] well-made colt: fairly useful form in 3 runs at 2 yrs: off 12 months, well held in handicap at Pontefract sole 3-y-o outing: should stay 1m: acts on good to firm ground: has worn crossed noseband. *Saeed bin Suroor* — **–**

CAPRIOLLA 3 b.f. In The Wings 128 – Seren Quest 90 (Rainbow Quest (USA) 134) [2006 9.7d³ 10g 8.2m 11.6m 11.8d⁵ May 30] leggy, close-coupled filly: seventh foal: — **55**

closely related to 2 winners, including smart 1¼m to 11.6f winner Saddler's Quest (by Saddlers' Hall) and half-sister to 2 winners, including useful 1m (at 2 yrs) to 12.5f winner Seren Hill (by Sabrehill). dam 1¼m winner: modest maiden on balance: should be suited by 1½m+: tried blinkered. *P. F. I. Cole*

CAPTAIN BOLSH 3 b.g. Tagula (IRE) 116 – Bolshoi Star 65§ (Soviet Star (USA) 128) [2006 60, a63: 8.2d 7f⁴ p8.6g⁴ 8.5m 12f³ 10m p10g 10.1n p7.1g Dec 14] strong, workmanlike gelding: modest maiden handicapper: stays 1½m: acts on polytrack and firm ground: visored third/fourth starts. *J. Pearce* — **59 a49**

CAPTAIN DARLING (IRE) 6 b.g. Pennekamp (USA) 130 – Gale Warning (IRE) (Last Tycoon 131) [2006 45, a67: p8g p8.6g⁴ p7.1g⁶ p8g p7g f7s⁴ p7.1g* p8.6g⁵ p8g* p7g⁶ p7.1g³ 7d p7.1g f8g³ Dec 14] big gelding: fair performer: won handicaps at Wolverhampton in July and Kempton (apprentices) in August: effective at 7f, barely at 1¼m: acts on all-weather, firm and good to soft going: tried in headgear: has worn tongue tie: has edged left/raced freely: usually makes running. *R. W. Price* — **– a70**

CAPTAIN GENERAL 4 br.c. In The Wings 128 – Sea Quest (IRE) (Rainbow Quest (USA) 134) [2006 67: 11.5m* 14m⁵ 12g 11.5m p12g* p13g* Oct 15] fair performer: won handicaps at Yarmouth in May and Lingfield in September and October: will probably stay 2m: acts on polytrack and good to firm going. *J. A. R. Toller* — **78**

CAPTAIN HURRICANE 4 b.g. Desert Style (IRE) 121 – Ravine 81 (Indian Ridge 123) [2006 –: 6s 5m May 6] tall, leggy gelding: smart performer at 2 yrs: no form since: blinkered final outing: free-going sort: held up: has been early/led to post. *P. W. Chapple-Hyam* — **–**

CAPTAIN JACKSPARRA (IRE) 2 b.c. (Apr 17) Danehill (USA) 126 – Push A Venture 58 (Shirley Heights 130) [2006 6m⁴ 7.2g³ 6s⁶ Sep 4] 62,000Y, 90,000 2-y-o: quite attractive, dipped-backed colt: fifth foal: brother to 3 winners and half-brother to winner by King of Kings, all in Australia: dam, third at 7f, half-sister to dam of Rock of Gibraltar (by Danehill): fair form in maidens, third to Massive at Ayr second start, and better than bare result at Newcastle (travelled strongly) final one: will prove best up to 7f: should make a better 3-y-o. *K. A. Ryan* — **73 p**

CAPTAIN MARGARET 4 b.f. Royal Applause 124 – Go For Red (IRE) (Thatching 131) [2006 73: p12.2g³ p12g⁴ p13g⁴ p10g⁴ p12g² p10g* 10.1m³ p12g³ 10m² p10g p10g p12.2g Nov 10] well-made filly: fairly useful handicapper: won at Lingfield in March: good efforts when placed next 3 starts: effective at 1¼m to 13f: acts on polytrack and firm going: has worn tongue tie/cheekpieces: consistent. *J. Pearce* — **81**

CAPTAIN MARVELOUS (IRE) 2 b.c. (Apr 19) Invincible Spirit (IRE) 121 – Shesasmartlady (IRE) (Dolphin Street (FR) 125) [2006 5g³ 5.1m* 6m² 6m 7m⁵ 6.1g² 6m* 6d³ 6d* Oct 28] €56,000F, €100,000Y: well-made, quite attractive colt: third foal: half-brother to 3-y-o Hero Worship and 1m winner in USA by Royal Applause: dam Irish maiden half-sister to useful Irish performer up to 1m Dashing Colours: smart performer: won maiden at Chester in May, nursery at Newbury in September and 8-runner Criterium de Maisons-Laffitte in October, in last-named making all to beat Baby Strange by 3 lengths: also ran well when 3¼ lengths third of 6 to Dutch Art in Middle Park Stakes at Newmarket eighth start: should stay 7f: acts on good to firm and good to soft going: used to look quirky, but became more straightforward with experience. *B. W. Hills* — **114**

Criterium de Maisons-Laffitte, Maisons-Laffitte—Captain Marvelous records a third win for British stables since the race was shortened in 2001; Baby Strange completes a British-trained 1,2 ahead of Iron Lips

CAPTAIN NEMO (USA) 2 b.g. (Feb 21) Officer (USA) 120 – Macarena Macarena (CAN) (Gone West (USA)) [2006 6g⁵ 7.1d 6s³ Oct 16] $13,000Y: useful-looking gelding: fourth living foal: half-brother to 3 winners in USA/Italy: dam, 6.5f winner in North America, half-sister to very smart US Grade 1 1½m winner Sligo Bay and smart stayer Wolfe Tone, an excellent family: fair form in maidens, staying-on third at Pontefract: gelded after: should be suited by 7f/1m. *T. D. Barron* **70**

CAPTAIN OATS (IRE) 3 b.g. Bahhare (USA) 122 – Adarika (Kings Lake (USA) 133) [2006 71: 11s p9.5g p9.5g⁴ f11g⁶ Dec 1] fair maiden at 2 yrs: left A. Mullins in Ireland and off 12 months, below form in 2006: stays 8.5f: acts on firm going: wore cheekpieces final 2-y-o outing. *Mrs P. Ford* **–**

CAPTAIN SMOOTHY 6 b.g. Charmer 123 – The Lady Captain (Neltino 97) [2006 –: f11g Oct 12] little form. *M. J. Gingell* **–**

CAPTAIN TORRANCE (IRE) 3 b.g. Titus Livius (FR) 115 – Gay's Flutter 78 (Beldale Flutter (USA) 130) [2006 58p: 7m 8.1s 6m 6.1m 5.1g⁴ 6m Jun 15] quite good-topped gelding: fair maiden: effective at 5f/6f: looked difficult ride final outing. *P. W. Chapple-Hyam* **67**

CAPTAIN XAAR (FR) 3 b.c. Xaar 132 – Rabea (USA) 61 (Devil's Bag (USA)) [2006 –p: p7g⁴ p7.1g² 8m⁶ May 13] close-coupled colt: fair maiden: should stay 1m: acts on polytrack: sent to Singapore. *J. R. Fanshawe* **72**

CAPTIVATE 3 ch.f. Hernando (FR) 127 – Catch (USA) (Blushing Groom (FR) 131) [2006 55: p10g f12g⁵ 12d f8g 8g 9.9g 10m⁴ 12s p12g² p13.9g² p12g p13.9g* p13.9g Dec 8] modest performer: left M. Polglase after sixth start: won banded event at Wolverhampton in December: stays 1¾m: acts on all-weather and good to firm going: usually wears blinkers/cheekpieces: none too consistent. *A. J. McCabe* **55**

CARABINIERI (IRE) 3 b.g. Danehill Dancer (IRE) 117 – Cartuccia (IRE) (Doyoun 124) [2006 9.2f 10.1m⁴ 6m Aug 5] best effort in maidens when fourth at Newcastle second start: dead. *J. Barclay* **53**

CARACCIOLA (GER) 9 b.g. Lando (GER) 128 – Capitolina (FR) (Empery (USA) 128) [2006 16d May 27] angular gelding: useful winner around 1½m in 2001 in Germany for P. Rau: well beaten in handicap at Ascot only Flat start since: useful hurdler nowadays. *N. J. Henderson* **–**

CARADAK (IRE) 5 b.h. Desert Style (IRE) 121 – Caraiyma (IRE) 84 (Shahrastani (USA) 135) [2006 121: 7m* 7d³ 8m* 7m* 8g³ Oct 14] **121**

Whilst not hitting the jackpot as they did when acquiring Daylami from the same source in 1997, Godolphin will surely be more than happy with the deal struck over another colt who had already shown very smart form for the Aga Khan. Caradak didn't show any improvement for his new owners, but he did win three races, including his first at Group 1 level.

Caradak was not seen out at two but raced ten times for John Oxx in Ireland during the next two seasons. He won a maiden at Galway and a listed event at Cork at three, and then progressed very well at four, when successful in a listed race and

totesport Celebration Mile, Goodwood—in a muddling race,
Caradak holds Killybegs (No.5) as George Washington (third right) gets going too late;
pacemaker River Tiber (rail) fades into fourth ahead of Soviet Song (extreme right) and Rob Roy

Prix de la Foret Casino Barriere de Biarritz, Longchamp—a three-way photo
as Caradak edges ahead of dead-heaters Linngari (noseband) and Welsh Emperor (left);
Stormy River (right) is staying on well for fourth, in front of New Girlfriend (hoops) and Gwenseb (rail)

the Emirates Airline Minstrel Stakes, both at the Curragh, and the Desmond Stakes at Leopardstown. On his final start for the Aga Khan, Caradak was beaten a head in the Group 1 Prix de la Foret at Longchamp, a race in which he was to go one better twelve months later. Caradak had had three runs for Godolphin before then. After landing the odds in a minor event at Newbury in July, he failed to do the same in the Hungerford Stakes there the following month, finishing only third to Welsh Emperor. Eight days later Caradak turned up at Goodwood for the totesport Celebration Mile, but this time the Two Thousand Guineas winner George Washington was the centre of attention in what was a notably strong race for a Group 2. George Washington was one of three three-year-olds in the six-runner field, along with his pacemaker River Tiber and the Craven Stakes winner Killybegs, and he started at 6/5-on. Second favourite at 3/1 was Soviet Song, runner-up in the Sussex Stakes over the course and distance on her previous start, with Caradak at 6/1 and Sussex Stakes third Rob Roy at 7/1. With River Tiber more or less ignored in a clear lead—he was at least ten lengths ahead at one stage—the Celebration Mile turned into a tactical race, one in which Caradak and Killybegs were best placed when it began in earnest. Caradak, the first to set off after the pacemaker, took over from him a furlong out and held on by a short head from Killybegs, the pair a length and a quarter ahead of third-placed George Washington, who was never nearer following a slow start.

There was nothing of George Washington's quality in the line-up for the Prix de la Foret at the end of September, though it was a much stronger contest numerically than the Celebration Mile, fourteen runners the biggest field for the race since the same number contested the 1987 edition, which was won by Soviet Star. The majority in the latest edition were three-year-olds, including the Prix Jean Prat winner Stormy River and Prix Maurice de Gheest winner Marchand d'Or. That pair were sent off first and second favourites respectively, just ahead of Caradak. Older horses filled the first three places in a steadily-run race in which first and last were separated only by around five lengths. As at Goodwood, Caradak benefited from a good ride from Frankie Dettori, who soon had his mount in a handy position from an unfavourable draw as Welsh Emperor dictated, Linngari also close up. The trio were involved in a tremendous battle from over a furlong out and Caradak just prevailed, having a short neck to spare over Welsh Emperor and Linngari, who dead-heated for second, with Stormy River three quarters of a length back in fourth. Caradak was a little below his best on his only subsequent appearance, when third of eight to Ramonti in the Premio Vittorio di Capua at Milan.

Godolphin's "Caradak"

Caradak (IRE) (b.h. 2001)	Desert Style (IRE) (b 1992)	Green Desert (b 1983)	Danzig
			Foreign Courier
		Organza (b 1985)	High Top
			Canton Silk
	Caraiyma (IRE) (b 1992)	Shahrastani (ch 1983)	Nijinsky
			Shademah
		Caraniya (br 1986)	Darshaan
			Callianire

     Caradak is by the very smart six-furlong and seven-furlong winner Desert Style, who enjoyed a very successful Arc weekend, his daughter Mandesha, also a product of the Aga Khan's studs, winning the Prix de l'Opera the day after Caradak's triumph. The dam Caraiyma showed fairly useful form for John Oxx as a three-year-old, her only season to race, carrying the Aga Khan's colours to victory in a nine-furlong maiden at Tipperary. Caradak is the fourth foal out of Caraiyma and her third winner, following the useful Irish six-furlong winner Carallia (by Common Grouds) and the fair mile-and-a-half winner Caraman (by Grand Lodge), the latter also a fairly useful two-mile hurdler. Caraiyma is a sister to the smart Irish middle-distance performer Cajarian out of the fairly useful winner at up to a mile and a half Caraniya, herself a daughter of Callianire, successful over an extended seven furlongs in France at two and a granddaughter of top racemare Apollonia. Caradak has raced only at seven furlongs and a mile to date, and he is unlikely to be tried over further. He is equally effective at both distances. A strong, useful-looking horse who has been bandaged behind, the game and consistent Caradak acts on firm and good to soft going. *Saeed bin Suroor*

CARAGH MIA (IRE) 4 b.f. Desert Prince (IRE) 130 – Decant 68 (Rousillon (USA) 133) [2006 80: 8.5s 9m 8m p7g p8.6g⁶ p8g⁵ p10g p12.2s⁶ Dec 13] close-coupled filly: **59**

modest form at best in 2006: left Ms F. Crowley in Ireland after third outing: stays 8.6f: acts on polytrack and good to firm going: blinkered (free but ran respectably) final 3-y-o start. *G. G. Margarson*

CARAMAN (IRE) 8 ch.h. Grand Lodge (USA) 125 – Caraiyma (IRE) 84 (Shahrastani (USA) 135) [2006 69: p12.2g* p16.5g² 12m p13.9g² p12.2g⁵ 12.1d⁴ 11.9g Sep 22] quite good-topped horse: fair performer: won maiden at Wolverhampton in January: in-and-out form after: stays easy 2m: acts on polytrack and good to soft ground: fairly useful hurdler, successful in October. *J. J. Quinn* **72 a76**

CARCINETTO (IRE) 4 b.f. Danetime (IRE) 121 – Dolphin Stamp (IRE) (Dolphin Street (FR) 125) [2006 53: p6g p6g⁵ p5.1g p6g⁵ p6g 7g 5.1f* 5.7f² 5.1m² 5m² 5s p5.1g³ p6g* p5.1g⁴ p6g⁶ p6g² p6g³ Dec 30] angular filly: fair performer: won claimer at Bath in July and, having been claimed from B. Palling £6,000 after eighth start, seller at Lingfield in November: stays 6f: acts on polytrack and firm ground: tried visored/in cheekpieces: sometimes flashes tail, but is consistent. *P. D. Evans* **67**

CARDINAL VENTURE (IRE) 8 b.g. Bishop of Cashel 122 – Phoenix Venture (IRE) 69 (Thatching 131) [2006 104: f8g⁴ f7g⁶ p8g p9.5g² 8s 10.4d 10.3m 9d⁵ 7m p7.1g Oct 29] big, strong, close-coupled gelding: fairly useful performer: below form after second start: probably stays 9.5f: acts on all-weather (best on fibresand), firm and soft going: tried blinkered, often wears cheekpieces nowadays: usually makes running. *K. A. Ryan* **93 d**

CAREER GIRL (USA) 2 b.f. (Feb 26) Theatrical 128 – Dubai Spirit (USA) (Mt Livermore (USA)) [2006 6m 7.1m⁵ 8.2m 7d Oct 3] smallish, unfurnished filly: first foal: dam, French 1m winner, out of half-sister to Arazi: fair maiden: fifth of 14 at Warwick, clearly best effort: should stay at least 1m. *E. A. L. Dunlop* **67**

CAREFREE 2 b.f. (Feb 5) Medicean 128 – Hertha (Hernando (FR) 127) [2006 p7.1g⁵ p8g⁶ Dec 20] 5,500F: second foal: dam, won up to 1½m in Scandinavia, out of half-sister to high-class 1¼m/1½m performer Storming Home: some promise both starts in maidens, not at all knocked about when sixth at Kempton: remains likely to do better. *W. J. Haggas* **59 p**

CAREFREE GIRL 3 b.f. Josr Algarhoud (IRE) 118 – Double Fault (IRE) 54 (Zieten (USA) 118) [2006 –: p9.5g p8g Feb 7] little sign of ability: tried blinkered. *E. A. Wheeler* **–**

CARESSED 3 b.f. Medicean 128 – Embraced 103 (Pursuit of Love 124) [2006 8.2m² 7.5g* 8m* 8m* Jun 15] quite good-topped filly: has a fluent action: first foal: dam, 1m winner (including at 2 yrs), half-sister to very smart 1½m performer Nowhere To Exit and 5-y-o Cesare: fairly useful and progressive form: won maiden at Beverley in May and handicaps at Newmarket in June and Salisbury (beat Usk Poppy by head, doing well to get up once switched) in July: slightly lame after: bred to stay 1¼m, though not short of speed: raced only on good ground or firmer: blanketed for stall entry: tends to edge right: had looked open to further improvement. *J. R. Fanshawe* **92**

CARIBBEAN CORAL 7 ch.g. Brief Truce (USA) 126 – Caribbean Star 81 (Soviet Star (USA) 128) [2006 95: 5.1f 5m⁶ 5m 6f³ 5f³ 5.5m* 6.1f⁴ 5f² 6f 5m⁶ 5d⁶ 5.1m* 5f 5.1m Oct 8] strong, good sort: useful handicapper: won at Warwick (by neck from Bluebok) in July and Chester (by ½ length from Handsome Cross) in September: effective at 5f/easy 6f: acts on firm and good to soft going: usually visored/in cheekpieces: tends to carry head awkwardly: has found little: waited with. *J. J. Quinn* **98**

CARIBBEAN DANCER (USA) 4 b.f. Theatrical 128 – Enticed (USA) (Stage Door Johnny (USA)) [2006 76: f12g⁴ Dec 27] good-topped filly: fair performer: off 17 months, below form on only outing in 2006 (all-weather debut): stays 1½m: acts on good to firm and good to soft going: blinkered nowadays: usually makes running. *M. Johnston* **68 +**

CARIBBEAN NIGHTS (IRE) 3 b.g. Night Shift (USA) – Caribbean Knockout (IRE) (Halling (USA) 133) [2006 –, a65: 8f 6g 6m Aug 9] big, good-bodied gelding: modest maiden: stays 1m: acts on fibresand and firm ground: blinkered final start: sold 2,500 gns. *T. D. Easterby* **52**

CARIBBEAN PEARL (USA) 4 b.f. Silver Hawk (USA) 123 – Ras Shaikh (USA) 105 (Sheikh Albadou 128) [2006 85p: 11.5m² Mar 29] big, strong filly: fairly useful performer: reportedly split a pastern at 2 yrs: good effort only outing in 2006, when 5 lengths second to Young Mick in handicap at Yarmouth: stayed 1½m: acted on good to firm and good to soft ground: stud. *C. E. Brittain* **86**

CARILLON (IRE) 2 ch.f. (Feb 9) Desert Prince (IRE) 130 – Steeple (Selkirk (USA) 129) [2006 6m² 7m² 6m* Sep 11] good-topped filly: fourth foal: half-sister to 4-y-o Arturius and French 1m/9.5f winner Royal Puck'r (by Bering): dam, French 9f winner, **79**

closely related to smart performers around 1m Soprano and Enharmonic: progressive form, winning 15-runner maiden at Redcar (beat Emaara by 1½ lengths) in September: effective at 6f, but bred to be suited by 1m+: sold 34,000 gns, sent to Saudi Arabia. *M. Johnston*

CARK 8 b.g. Farfelu 103 – Precious Girl 76 (Precious Metal 106) [2006 48§, a55§: **50 §** p5.1g⁵ f5g p5.1g Dec 4] sturdy gelding: modest performer: left J. Balding after second start: best at 5f: acts on all-weather and any turf going: tried visored/in cheekpieces, blinkered final start: races prominently: unreliable. *T. J. Pitt*

CARLBURG (IRE) 5 b.g. BaratIREa (IRE) 127 – Ichnusa 83 (Bay Express 132) [2006 **–** f7g p8g Nov 6] smallish, close-coupled gelding: fair maiden at best: missed 2005: well beaten both starts in 2006: tried blinkered. *Mrs C. A. Dunnett*

CARLITOS SPIRIT (IRE) 2 ch.g. (Feb 5) Redback 116 – Negria (IRE) (Al Hareb **66** (USA) 123) [2006 p5g⁴ 5g⁵ 6m⁶ 6f 7m⁵ 7.1d⁴ Sep 16] 33,000Y: sixth foal: half-brother to 3 winners, including 2002 2-y-o 5f winner Melrose Place (by Danetime) and 5f (at 2 yrs)/ 6f winner Church Mice (by Petardia), both fairly useful: dam German 2-y-o 6f winner: fair maiden: fourth in nursery at Warwick final start (blinkered): stays 7f: acts on poly-track, firm and good to soft going: tends to wander: gelded after final start. *B. R. Millman*

CARLOMAN 3 ch.g. King Charlemagne (USA) 120 – Jarrayan 64 (Machiavellian **67** (USA) 123) [2006 63: 8s 8.2g⁴ p8g² 8.1g² 8.5m⁴ 8.5g 8m⁶ p8g Oct 5] leggy gelding: fair performer on turf: won maiden handicap at Epsom in July: stays 8.5f: acts on polytrack and good to firm ground: blinkered last 5 starts, tongue tied final one: races prominently: hung left (reportedly had breathing problem) seventh outing: sold 3,000 gns. *R. M. Beckett*

CARLOTAMIX (FR) 3 gr.c. Linamix (FR) 127 – Carlitta (USA) (Olympio (USA)) **108** [2006 113p: 8g⁶ 8g² 10s⁵ 8s² Nov 22] smart at 2 yrs when unbeaten in 3 starts, notably Criterium International at Saint-Cloud: disappointing in 2006, second in listed race at Deauville (beaten short head by Kersimon) and minor event at Saint-Cloud: fifth of 6 to Multidimensional in Prix Guillaume d'Ornano at Deauville in between, then sold from A. Fabre €175,000: stayed 1m: acted on soft ground: to stand at Haras d'Ayguemorte, France *N. Clement, France*

CARLTON SCROOP (FR) 3 ch.g. Priolo (USA) 127 – Elms Schooldays (Emarati **66** (USA) 74) [2006 –: p10g* 11g³ p10g² 14.1g⁴ Aug 25] stocky gelding: fair performer: improved form in blinkers in 2006, winning banded race at Kempton in April: effective at 1¼m to 1¾m: acts on polytrack: refused to enter stall prior to third and fourth intended outings. *J. Jay*

CARMENERO (GER) 3 b.g. BaratIREa (IRE) 127 – Claire Fraser (USA) (Gone West **84** (USA)) [2006 81: 7.1g² 7g 7.1m⁵ 7m² 8g 7m⁶ 7f 7.1m⁵ 7.1m⁶ 7m p7g² p7g⁶ Oct 21] sturdy, close-coupled gelding: fairly useful handicapper: creditable efforts when runner-up in 2006: stays 7f: acts on polytrack and firm going, seemingly not on softer than good: tried in cheekpieces: reportedly bled once. *W. R. Muir*

CARNIVORE 4 ch.g. Zafonic (USA) 130 – Ermine (IRE) 86 (Cadeaux Genereux 131) **83** [2006 59: 7.1f* 6.9f³ 7m* 7d² 7.1m² 7m⁶ 7g* Sep 15] tall gelding: fairly useful handi-capper: won at Musselburgh in June, Newcastle in August and Newbury in September: stays 7f: acts on firm and good to soft going, probably on fibresand. *T. D. Barron*

CARPETING 3 b.g. Alhaarth (IRE) 126 – Wigging 96 (Warning 136) [2006 –: p7.1g **56** p10g 8m³ 8g 10m Jul 8] close-coupled gelding: modest maiden: stays 1m: acts on good to firm going: visored last 3 starts: sold 4,000 gns, sent to Belgium. *D. Morris*

CARPET RIDE 4 ch.g. Unfuwain (USA) 131 – Fragrant Oasis (USA) 113 (Rahy **61 d** (USA) 115) [2006 71: p10g 10g⁵ p12g⁶ 12.1d 8.1f p8.6g 11.6m 8m Aug 19] strong, good-bodied gelding: modest performer at best nowadays: stays 1½m: acts on polytrack and good to firm going: tried in headgear (looked none too keen in visor)/tongue tied: sold £1,700. *B. G. Powell*

CARR HALL (IRE) 3 b.g. Rossini (USA) 118 – Pidgeon Bay (IRE) 66 (Perugino **60** (USA) 84) [2006 67: 10g⁵ 9.9f⁵ 8d 8.5g⁴ 7.5f³ 6.9m⁴ 7.5g⁶ Aug 31] tall gelding: modest maiden: stays 1¼m: acts on firm and good to soft going: sold 6,000 gns. *T. D. Easterby*

CARRIE MCCURRY (IRE) 2 b.f. (Apr 13) Fath (USA) 116 – Simply Devious **71** (IRE) (Dr Devious (IRE) 127) [2006 7s⁶ p6g² f5g⁴ Dec 23] €4,500Y: first foal: dam un-raced out of half-sister to smart winner up to 11f Annie Edge, herself the dam of Selkirk: easily best effort in maidens when neck second to Teasing at Wolverhampton, wandering and clear of remainder: should stay 7f. *Patrick Martin, Ireland*

CARRIETAU 3 b.g. Key of Luck (USA) 126 – Carreamia 62 (Weldnaas (USA) 112) **52**
[2006 69d: 8.2m 6.1f 9.8m² 10.1m⁵ 9.8d² Aug 29] big, heavy-topped gelding: modest
maiden: stays 1¼m: acts on good to firm and good to soft going: tried blinkered: edgy
type, withdrawn after injuring rider intended debut: claimed £6,000 after final outing,
joined F. Murtagh and fair winner over hurdles. *J. G. Given*

CARRY ON DOC 5 b.g. Dr Devious (IRE) 127 – Florentynna Bay 61 (Aragon 118) **65**
[2006 68: p8.6g p8g p9.5g p8g p8g Mar 24] compact gelding: fair handicapper: stays
8.5f: raced only on all-weather/good going or firmer on turf: free-going sort: very slowly
away penultimate start. *E. R. Oertel*

CARSON'S SPIRIT (USA) 2 ch.c. (Jan 30) Carson City (USA) – Pascarina (FR) **82**
(Exit To Nowhere (USA) 122) [2006 5.1d* 6m p7g 7d⁶ Sep 27] €40,000Y: deep-girthed
colt: second foal: dam useful French 2-y-o 7.5f/1m winner: fairly useful performer: won
maiden at Bath in April: mid-field in Coventry Stakes at Royal Ascot next start, but below
form last 2 in nursery and minor event (blinkered): should stay 7f. *W. S. Kittow*

CARTIMANDUA 2 b.f. (Apr 2) Medicean 128 – Agrippina 99 (Timeless Times (USA) **81 p**
99) [2006 6m² Jul 14] big, good-bodied filly: second foal: half-sister to 3-y-o Terentia:
dam 2-y-o 7f winner: 10/1, 2 lengths second of 7 to Medley in maiden at Newmarket:
open to improvement. *E. S. McMahon*

CARTOONIST (IRE) 3 ch.g. Fruits of Love (USA) 127 – Verusa (IRE) (Petorius 117) **58**
[2006 58: 10.5g³ 12.1g p12.2g p12g Jun 29] strong gelding: modest maiden: should stay
beyond 10.5f. *A. King*

CARWELL (IRE) 2 ch.f. (Feb 23) King's Best (USA) 132 – Lady Kestrel (USA) **73 p**
(Theatrical 128) [2006 7f* 7d² Oct 10] first foal: dam unraced out of half-sister to high-
class sprinter Committed: fair form: won maiden at Thirsk in July: off 3 months, 1¾ lengths
second of 3 to Majuro in minor event at Leicester, heavily eased once held: will stay 1m:
sold 50,000 gns, sent to USA: should still do better. *M. Johnston*

CASABLANCA MINX (IRE) 3 b.f. Desert Story (IRE) 115 – Conspire (IRE) 81 **81**
(Turtle Island (IRE) 123) [2006 63: p7g³ p8g* p8.6g* p8g* p8.6g* p10g p8g⁵ 8.3m
p10g p7.1g⁵ Dec 23] lengthy filly: fairly useful performer: won handicap at Lingfield
and claimer at Wolverhampton (claimed from Mrs H. Sweeting £9,000) in January, and
claimer at Lingfield (claimed from J. Boyle £14,000) and handicap at Wolverhampton in
February: barely stays easy 1¼m: acts on polytrack and firm ground. *N. P. Littmoden*

CASALESE 4 ch.g. Wolfhound (USA) 126 – Little Redwing 37 (Be My Chief (USA) **–**
122) [2006 –: 9.8d Aug 29] no form: tried blinkered. *M. D. Hammond*

CASHBAR 5 b.m. Bishop of Cashel 122 – Barford Sovereign 72 (Unfuwain (USA) 131) **–**
[2006 –: p10g Mar 17] tall, leggy mare: fairly useful performer at 3 yrs: well beaten since.
J. R. Fanshawe

CASHCADE (IRE) 2 br.g. (Apr 3) Raise A Grand (IRE) 114 – Cotton Grace (IRE) 62 **72**
(Case Law 113) [2006 5.1g 6.1m⁵ 6g 8m 8d Sep 26] €7,000Y: third foal: dam, Irish
maiden (best effort at 7f on 2-y-o debut), half-sister to useful Irish 1m/1¼m performer
Saying Grace: fair maiden: should have stayed 1m: tried blinkered: dead. *A. M. Balding*

CASHEL BAY (USA) 8 b.g. Nureyev (USA) 131 – Madame Premier (USA) (Raja **–**
Baba (USA)) [2006 p8g 16d Nov 5] leggy gelding: one-time fairly useful performer,
lightly raced since 2001: well beaten at 8 yrs, including in handicap at Kempton: seems to
stay 1¾m: acts on soft and good to firm going: tried blinkered. *Luke Comer, Ireland*

CASHEL MEAD 6 b.m. Bishop of Cashel 122 – Island Mead 86 (Pharly (FR) 130) **94**
[2006 72: p5.1g* p5.1g f5g⁶ f6s⁴ p5.1g⁵ f5g⁴ p5g* 5.1m⁵ 5.2m³ 5.5d² 5.7d* 5.1s* 5s* 5g*
5.7g p5g⁴ 5m 5f 5.2m³ 5m 5.2d* 5d* 5s 5g 5.1m Oct 8] leggy mare: fairly useful handicapper: winner 8 times in 2006, at Wolverhampton (amateurs) in January, Kempton in
April, Bath, Nottingham and Goodwood in May, Sandown in June and Newbury and
Newmarket in August: effective at 5f/6f: acts on all-weather, soft and good to firm going:
used to wear blinkers (not since third outing): often fractious in stall/slowly away: tough.
J. L. Spearing

CASHEMA (IRE) 5 b.m. Cape Cross (IRE) 129 – Miss Shema (USA) 81 (Gulch **–**
(USA)) [2006 41: 7.1v 8g⁶ 9g Jul 3] leggy, lengthy mare: maiden: well held in 2006: tried
in cheekpieces/visor/tongue tie. *D. R. MacLeod*

CASHIER 4 gr.c. Alhaarth (IRE) 126 – Cashew 80 (Sharrood (USA) 124) [2006 102: **107**
8m* 8.1m⁵ 9m May 13] quite attractive colt: good walker: had a short, unimpressive
action: useful handicapper: won at Nad Al Sheba (by 1¾ lengths from Desert Destiny) in

February: at least respectable efforts both starts after: should have stayed 1¼m: acted on good to firm and good to soft going: had worn crossed noseband: dead. *J. H. M. Gosden*

CASH ON (IRE) 4 ch.g. Spectrum (IRE) 126 – Lady Lucre (IRE) 73 (Last Tycoon 131) – § [2006 77§: p12g⁶ May 23] good-topped gelding: fair performer: well held only outing on Flat at 4 yrs (won over hurdles in August): visored final 3-y-o outing (reluctant to race): one to treat with caution. *Miss K. M. George*

CASONOVA (IRE) 3 b.g. Trans Island 119 – Sherna Girl (IRE) (Desert Story (IRE) 47 115) [2006 f6g 7f 8d 5.9m⁶ 7.5f Jun 22] big, strong, workmanlike gelding: poor maiden handicapper: should be suited by 7f/1m: acts on good to firm going. *T. D. Easterby*

CASPIAN ROSE 3 b.f. Paris House 123 – Caspian Morn 63 (Lugana Beach 116) [2006 38 –: 7d p8g f6m f6g⁴ Nov 15] compact filly: poor maiden. *M. J. Attwater*

CASSIARA 2 gr.f. (Jan 31) Diktat 126 – Heaven-Liegh-Grey 90 (Grey Desire 115) 82 [2006 5d³ 5g⁴ 5s³ 5g⁶ 6m 6d³ 7d Sep 8] 8,000Y: tall, lengthy, leggy filly: has a quick action: half-sister to several winners, including fairly useful 1m/9f winner French Connection (by Tirol): dam best at 5f: fairly useful maiden: made frame 4 times, including listed race at York (third to Gilded) third start: ran poorly in nursery there final start: stays 6f: acts on soft going. *J. Pearce*

CASSIE'S CHOICE (IRE) 2 b.f. (Feb 8) Fath (USA) 116 – Esteraad (IRE) 90 (Cade-70 aux Genereux 131) [2006 6f⁴ 6g³ 6f² 7g² 7d⁵ Oct 3] €16,500Y: good-topped, close-coupled filly: third foal: half-sister to 5-y-o Noora and 2004 2-y-o 7f winner Caitlin (by Intikhab): dam 2-y-o 6f winner who stayed 1¼m: fair maiden: placed 3 times: likely to stay 1m: acts on firm and good to soft going. *B. Smart*

CASTANO 2 br.g. (Apr 15) Makbul 104 – Royal Orchid (IRE) 74 (Shalford (IRE) 124§) 74 [2006 5.1s³ 5.1f² 5m² 5d Sep 29] 12,500Y: fifth foal: half-brother to 5f/6f winner Mad-die's A Jem (by Emperor Jones) and 5-y-o Imtalkinggibberish: dam maiden who stayed 7f: fair maiden: second to Conquest at Nottingham and to Oldjoesaid at Sandown: raced at 5f: acts on firm going: gelded after final start. *B. R. Millman*

CASTANZA 4 b.f. Bachir (IRE) 118 – Sylhall (Sharpo 132) [2006 74, a49: f8g² f7g f7g 45 f8g 7g f8g⁴ f8g May 16] workmanlike filly: poor performer: stays 1m: acts on fibresand and soft ground: visored/blinkered last 3 starts. *M. Wellings*

CASTARA BAY 2 b.c. (Mar 29) Sakhee (USA) 136 – Mayaro Bay 108 (Robellino 85 (USA) 127) [2006 6g 7f³ 7m³ p8g⁵ p10g² Nov 25] smallish, sturdy colt: second foal: dam 6f (at 2 yrs) to 1m winner: fairly useful maiden: improved form when ½-length second to Montalembert in minor event at Lingfield final start: stays 1¼m: acts on polytrack, raced only on good ground or firmer on turf: coltish on debut. *R. Hannon*

CAST IN GOLD (USA) 2 b.f. (Feb 28) Elusive Quality (USA) – Crystal Crossing 90 (IRE) 99 (Royal Academy (USA) 130) [2006 7m² 7m² 7g² p7g² p7g* Oct 21] big filly: has scope: fifth foal: half-sister to high-class 7f (at 2 yrs) to 14.6f (St Leger) winner Rule of Law (by Kingmambo): dam, 2-y-o 6f winner, sister to smart performer up to 8.5f Circle of Gold: fairly useful form: runner-up first 3 starts, on third in minor event at Newbury (short-headed by Darrfonah), then won maiden at Lingfield by 2½ lengths: will probably stay 1m. *B. J. Meehan*

CASTLE HOWARD (IRE) 4 b.g. Montjeu (IRE) 137 – Termania (IRE) (Shirley 99 Heights 130) [2006 12s² 13.1g⁴ 14m 12d⁵ 14v 11.6d⁴ Nov 4] 115,000F: rather leggy geld-ing: second foal: dam French maiden who stayed 13f: useful performer: won minor event at Chantilly in 2005: left A. Fabre 32,000 gns, creditable efforts in handicaps first 2 starts in 2006: stays 15f: acts on soft ground. *W. J. Musson*

CASTLESHANE (IRE) 9 b.g. Kris 135 – Ahbab (IRE) 81 (Ajdal (USA) 130) [2006 – 80: 10m Aug 9] big, strong gelding: useful handicapper at best: lightly raced on Flat since 2003, well held only outing in 2006: blinkered (raced freely) twice: usually forces pace: fair hurdler. *S. Gollings*

CASUAL AFFAIR 3 b.g. Golden Snake (USA) 127 – Fontaine Lady 41 (Millfontaine 71 114) [2006 7.1m⁴ 8f⁶ 8.2g³ p9.5g³ p8.6g p8.6g p6g⁵ p6g² Dec 7] fifth foal: half-brother to fairly useful 7f winner (at 2 yrs) and 1m winner Juste Pour L'Amour (by Pharly): dam 5f/ 6f winner: fair maiden: stays 9.5f: raced only on polytrack and on good ground or firmer. *E. J. O'Neill*

CASUAL GLANCE 4 b.f. Sinndar (IRE) 134 – Spurned (USA) 91 (Robellino (USA) 102 127) [2006 96: 14.1s 16m⁵ 20m 16g³ 13.4g³ Aug 26] leggy filly: useful performer: good efforts when fifth to Cover Up in Sagaro Stakes at Lingfield and third to New Guinea at Chester second/final outings: stays 2m: acts on soft and good to firm going. *A. M. Balding*

CATABOUND (USA) 3 b. or br.g. Black Minnaloushe (USA) 123 – Castellina (USA) **58 d**
(Danzig Connection (USA)) [2006 53: 6f 8.2g 9.9m 5.7g 7g Aug 17] close-coupled,
quite good-topped gelding: modest maiden at best: sold 2,400 gns, sent to Denmark.
B. R. Millman

CATBANG (IRE) 3 b.c. Zafonic (USA) 130 – Silky Dawn (IRE) 100 (Night Shift **78**
(USA)) [2006 67p: 8.2m² 8m² 10f 8.3d p7.1g* Jun 30] quite good-topped colt: has scope:
fair handicapper: won at Wolverhampton in June: stays 1m: acts on polytrack and good to
firm going. *N. A. Callaghan*

CATCH THE CAT (IRE) 7 b.g. Catrail (USA) 123 – Tongabezi (IRE) 75 (Shernazar **72**
131) [2006 87, a49: 5d 5m 5f³ 5m² 5m 5f⁶ 5f 5m 5d⁶ 5m* 5d 5g 6s⁵ 6v Oct 23] well-made **a–**
gelding: fair handicapper on turf, poor on all-weather: won at Hamilton in August: left
R. Gray after twelfth start: effective at 5f/6f: acts on fibresand and any turf going: usually
wears headgear: sometimes slowly away: races prominently: reportedly returned lame
twice in 2006. *Samuel Murphy, Ireland*

CAT DE MILLE (USA) 2 b. or br.c. (May 14) Stormin Fever (USA) 116 – De Mille **86 p**
(USA) 88 (Nureyev (USA) 131) [2006 7d⁵ 8.1d* Oct 13] $35,000Y, 42,000 2-y-o: work-
manlike colt: fifth foal: half-brother to winner in USA by Pleasant Tap: dam, 1¼m winner
on only outing, closely related to useful Irish 1m winner Chanzi: fairly useful form:
confirmed debut promise when winning 14-runner maiden at Warwick (beat Strikeen 1¼
lengths): will be suited by 1¼m: should do better still. *P. W. Chapple-Hyam*

CATEGORICAL 3 b.g. Diktat 126 – Zibet 90 (Kris 135) [2006 82: 6g 7m⁶ 8s³ 7d **81**
10.3m 12.1m 13.8v⁵ Oct 31] leggy gelding: fairly useful performer: left J. Toller after
third start: stays 1m: acts on fibresand and soft going: looked none too keen on reappearance: fair winning hurdler. *K. G. Reveley*

CATE WASHINGTON 3 b.f. Superior Premium 122 – Willisa 67 (Polar Falcon **44**
(USA) 126) [2006 –: 6.1d p7g 6g 6.1f⁶ 6g f6g Dec 28] leggy filly: poor maiden. *Mrs
L. Williamson*

CATHERINE MEDICI 3 ch.f. Medicean 128 – Fine Honor (FR) (Highest Honor **57 d**
(FR) 124) [2006 p7g² 6g f8g 8f 8m p7g Oct 23] second foal: dam French 1¼m winner:
modest form on debut only: tried visored: bred to stay 1m. *R. M. H. Cowell*

CATHERINES CAFE (IRE) 3 b.f. Mull of Kintyre (USA) 114 – Wisecrack (IRE) **68 d**
(Lucky Guest 109) [2006 72: p6g 6g³ 5.1g 6f 7.1m 7g⁶ 8.1m 7d p10g Oct 23] good-
bodied filly: modest performer: well below form after second outing: stays 7f: acts on
good to firm and good to soft going: tried visored. *Mrs P. N. Dutfield*

CATHERINISKI (IRE) 4 b.f. Danetime (IRE) 121 – Choralli 44 (Inchinor 119) [2006 **–**
–: f7g⁶ f8g Apr 10] no form: dead. *P. A. Blockley*

CATIVO CAVALLINO 3 ch.g. Bertolini (USA) 125 – Sea Isle 73 (Selkirk (USA) **66 d**
129) [2006 73: p6g 5m 6m p6g 7m p10g 8m 16g p12g p12g Nov 24] lengthy gelding: fair
maiden: left Julian Poulton after reappearance: best form at 5f, bred to stay further: acts
on polytrack and good to soft ground: in cheekpieces (tailed off) once. *Jamie Poulton*

CATLIVIUS (IRE) 2 ch.f. (Mar 24) Titus Livius (FR) 115 – Cat's Tale (IRE) (Catrail **66**
(USA) 124) [2006 5m⁴ 5g⁴ 6g⁵ 6v⁶ f5g² f6g⁴ Dec 21] quite good-topped filly: has a
quick action: second foal: dam ran twice in France: fair maiden: below form last 3 starts,
including in claimer: should stay 6f: acts on good to firm going: wore cheekpieces last 3
outings, also tongue tied final one: sometimes hangs right. *K. A. Ryan*

CAT SIX (USA) 2 b.f. (Mar 1) Tale of The Cat (USA) 113 – Hurricane Warning (USA) **54 p**
(Thunder Gulch (USA) 129) [2006 6.1g Sep 26] $140,000F, $190,000Y: second foal:
dam unraced half-sister to US Grade 2 9f winner Recoup The Cash: 11/1, eighth of 15 in
maiden at Nottingham, tiring and hanging left: open to improvement. *B. J. Meehan*

CATSKILL 4 ch.g. Inchinor 119 – Manhattan Sunset (USA) 76 (El Gran Senor (USA) **78**
136) [2006 75: p8g 10.1m* 9.7f³ 10.1g 10g⁶ 8d p10g Oct 20] lengthy gelding: fair handicapper: won at Yarmouth in May: stays 1¼m: acts on firm going: tried in cheekpieces:
sold 16,000 gns. *E. F. Vaughan*

CATSPRADDLE (USA) 3 ch.f. High Yield (USA) 121 – Beaux Dorothy (USA) **76**
(Dehere (USA) 121) [2006 74: 8.5g p6g 6f* 5m 6m³ 6g 6.1g p6g⁶ p5.1g⁶ p6g Dec 2] **a70**
workmanlike filly: fair handicapper: won at Windsor in June: best at 5f/6f: acts on firm
going: races up with pace (pulled hard once held up). *R. Hannon*

CATWEASEL 2 ch.g. (Mar 31) Auction House (USA) 120 – Gracious Imp (USA) (Imp **44**
Society (USA)) [2006 p5g 5f 6v⁴ 6.1s 10.1d Oct 18] poor maiden: left W. Turner after
fourth start: tried in tongue strap/visor. *L. A. Dace*

CAUGHT YOU LOOKING 2 b.f. (Mar 18) Observatory (USA) 131 – Corndavon **70 p**
(USA) 95 (Sheikh Albadou 128) [2006 6d⁶ p6g⁴ Nov 6] 46,000Y: fourth foal: half-sister
to 3 winners, including smart 2003 2-y-o 5f/6f winner Nevisian Lad (by Royal Applause)
and 3-y-o Woodnook: dam 6f winner: promising efforts in maidens at Windsor and
Wolverhampton, better effort when 4¾ lengths fourth to Penny Post, poorly placed into
straight and not knocked about: will stay 7f: likely to improve again. *W. R. Swinburn*

CAUSTIC WIT (IRE) 8 b.g. Cadeaux Genereux 131 – Baldemosa (FR) (Lead On **79**
Time (USA) 123) [2006 81: p6g p5.1g p6g p7g 6m 6.1d p5.1g² 6g 5.7f* 6f* p6g 5.7m **a70**
6m² 6f 6g* 7.1f³ 7.6m 6g² 7g³ 5.7m⁴ p6g* 6m⁶ p6m⁵ 6g p6g⁶ p6g⁵ Dec 30] leggy, quite
good-topped gelding: fair handicapper, better on turf than all-weather: won at Bath and
Windsor in June, Epsom in July and Wolverhampton in August: effective at 5f to 7f: acts
on all-weather, firm and soft going: usually wears cheekpieces nowadays: races prominently: tough. *M. S. Saunders*

CAVA BIEN 4 b.g. Bien Bien (USA) 125 – Bebe de Cham 75 (Tragic Role (USA)) **57 §**
[2006 73d: 16g⁴ 16d³ 15.8s Oct 24] angular gelding: modest handicapper nowadays:
stays 2m: acts on firm and good to soft going: tried blinkered: won twice over hurdles in
July: ungenuine. *B. J. Llewellyn*

CAVALLINI (USA) 4 b. or br.g. Bianconi (USA) 123 – Taylor Park (USA) (Sir Gay- **85**
lord) [2006 91: 9.9g 10m 13.3g 12m⁵ 12m Sep 20] tall gelding: fairly useful performer:
stays 11.6f: acts on good to firm going: none too consistent. *G. L. Moore*

CAVALLINO (USA) 6 br.g. Joyeux Danseur (USA) 123 – Krypto Katie (USA) (Cryp- **95**
toclearance (USA)) [2006 105: 16g 14.8d⁵ Aug 25] useful performer: winner of 10 races,
all at Taby, including minor event/2 handicaps in 2005: tongue tied, little impact in
handicaps at Ascot and Newmarket both starts in Britain: effective at 1½m, stays 2¼f: all
but one of his wins on dirt. *R. A. Kvisla*

CAVALLO DI FERRO (IRE) 2 b.g. (Feb 17) Iron Mask (USA) 117 – Lacinia 107 **70**
(Groom Dancer (USA) 128) [2006 p6g p6g* 7.1g Aug 26] €11,000Y: sixth foal: half-
brother to 1¼m winner who stayed 1¾m Maxilla (by Lahib): dam Irish 6f (at 2 yrs) and
11f winner: fair form: won maiden at Kempton in June, dictating: off 2 months, well held
in nursery: should stay 7f/1m. *J. R. Boyle*

CAVALRY GUARD (USA) 2 ch.g. (Feb 18) Officer (USA) 120 – Leeward City **83 §**
(USA) (Carson City (USA)) [2006 6m² 6g² 7f⁴ 7d Oct 10] $132,000F, $180,000Y,
$200,000 2-y-o: good-topped gelding: first foal: dam maiden in USA: maiden: fairly
useful form when second to Cockney Rebel at Newmarket on debut: went wrong way,
looking temperamental (tried visored): gelded after final start. *H. R. A. Cecil*

CAVALRY TWILL (IRE) 2 b.c. (Mar 6) Alhaarth (IRE) 126 – Blue Mantle (IRE) 79 **70**
(Barathea (IRE) 127) [2006 p8.6g p8.6g² Nov 18] 52,000Y: first foal: dam, 1m to 1½m
winner (latter in Ireland), half-sister to useful Italian performer up to 1½m Antonio-
castiglione: much better effort in maidens when 1¾ lengths second to Peregrine Falcon at
Wolverhampton, still looking shade green. *P. F. I. Cole*

CAVAN GAEL (FR) 4 b.g. Dansili 127 – Time Will Show (FR) (Exit To Nowhere **–**
(USA) 122) [2006 73, a61: p9.5g 8m f8g p10g² p9.5f⁵ 8d p8.6g p10g Sep 27] leggy geld- **a63**
ing: modest maiden nowadays: gelded after seventh start: stays 1¼m: acts on all-weather
and soft going: free-going sort: has bled on more than one occasion: none too reliable:
sold 1,000 gns. *P. Howling*

CAVENDISH 2 b.g. (Apr 15) Pursuit of Love 124 – Bathwick Babe (IRE) 71 (Sri Pekan **–**
(USA) 117) [2006 6d p6g 6m f8g f8g⁶ Nov 10] little form. *J. M. P. Eustace*

CAVE OF THE GIANT (IRE) 4 b.g. Giant's Causeway (USA) 132 – Maroussie **72**
(FR) 115 (Saumarez 132) [2006 14.1m³ 14.1d Sep 27] leggy, close-coupled gelding: fair
maiden: unraced on Flat in 2005: should be suited by at least 1½m: has sweated: gave
trouble and withdrawn intended third 4-y-o outing. *T. D. McCarthy*

CAVEWARRIOR 3 b.g. Arkadian Hero (USA) 123 – Lyna (Slip Anchor 136) [2006 –, **82**
a82: p6g⁴ a5g⁶ a8.7g² Sep 5] strong, useful-looking gelding: fairly useful performer: sold
from J. Noseda 4,000 gns and off 6 months after reappearance: second in minor event at
Jagersro final start: stays 8.7f: acts on polytrack/dirt. *F. Reuterskiold, Sweden*

CAVIAR HEIGHTS (IRE) 2 b.c. (May 10) Golan (IRE) 129 – Caviar Queen (USA) **50**
(Crafty Prospector (USA)) [2006 6s 7.1d⁶ Nov 3] better run in maidens when sixth at
Musselburgh: will stay 1m/1¼m. *Miss L. A. Perratt*

CAV OKAY (IRE) 2 gr.g. (Apr 27) Fasliyev (USA) 120 – Dane's Lane (IRE) (Danehill **99**
(USA) 126) [2006 5.2m* 5.1m² 5v² 5m³ 5m 5.2g 5m Aug 1] €22,000F, €35,000Y: close-

coupled, quite attractive gelding: has a fluent, easy action: eighth foal: half-brother to several winners, including 7f/1m winner (including at 2 yrs) Hoh Steamer, later successful in USA, and 9f winner Peruvia (both fairly useful, by Perugino): dam unraced: useful performer: impressive winner of maiden at Newbury (by 5 lengths) in April: best effort when 2¾ lengths third to 11 to Dutch Art in Norfolk Stakes at Royal Ascot fourth start: below form after, tried once in blinkers: all speed (forces pace), and raced at 5f, mainly on good going or firmer: none too reliable. *R. Hannon*

CAVORT (IRE) 2 ch.f. (Jan 30) Vettori (IRE) 119 – Face The Storm (IRE) 72 (Barathea (IRE) 127) [2006 5g 5g² 6s* 6g⁶ 7m 8d Sep 26] 12,000Y: leggy, quite attractive filly: first foal: dam 1m winner at 2 yrs (only season to race): fair performer: won maiden at Goodwood in May: well held in nurseries last 2 starts: should stay 1m: acts on soft going. *Pat Eddery* **75**

CAYMAN BREEZE 6 b.g. Danzig (USA) – Lady Thynn (FR) (Crystal Glitters (USA) 127) [2006 71, a62: p6g³ p7.1g⁵ p7g⁵ 7m 6.1m⁵ 6f 6f⁵ 6m⁵ 7m⁶ 6g 6.1m⁶ 6m⁴ p6g* p7g⁵ p6g⁶ p6g³ Dec 20] smallish, sturdy gelding: modest performer nowadays: won apprentice handicap at Lingfield in October: effective at 6f/7f: acts on all-weather, raced mainly on good ground or firmer on turf (acts on firm): tried in visor/cheekpieces: has looked none too keen. *J. M. Bradley* **63**

CAYMAN CALYPSO (IRE) 5 ro.g. Danehill Dancer (IRE) 117 – Warthill Whispers 59 (Grey Desire 115) [2006 57: p13.9g⁴ Jan 4] tall gelding: modest performer: stays 2m: acts on all-weather, good to firm and good to soft going: tried visored/blinkered. *Mrs P. Sly* **55**

CAYMAN KING 4 b.g. Cayman Kai (IRE) 114 – Distinctly Laura (IRE) (Distinctly North (USA) 115) [2006 59: p6g⁵ f6g⁶ May 9] modest maiden: stays 6f: acts on fibresand raced only on good to firm ground on turf: blinkered final outing. *R. Craggs* **54**

CAYMAN MISCHIEF 6 b.m. Cayman Kai (IRE) 114 – Tribal Mischief 61 (Be My Chief (USA) 122) [2006 48: p6g p5.1g p5.1g Apr 28] poor maiden: best around 5f: acts on good to soft ground: blinkered final outing. *James Moffatt* **–**

CAYMANS GIFT 6 ch.g. Cayman Kai (IRE) 114 – Gymcrak Cyrano (IRE) 61 (Cyrano de Bergerac 120) [2006 64: f12g 12.4g³ 12.4m² 14.1g³ 13d⁴ 13f 15m³ 15m⁶ 14m Aug 24] modest maiden handicapper: stays 15f: acts on soft and good to firm going: wore cheekpieces last 2 starts: took strong hold sixth start: sold 800 gns. *A. C. Whillans* **64**

CD EUROPE (IRE) 8 ch.g. Royal Academy (USA) 130 – Woodland Orchid (IRE) 64 (Woodman (USA) 126) [2006 94: 7m⁵ 6d³ p6g* Jun 2] lengthy gelding: carries little condition: has reportedly had sinus problems: fair performer nowadays: won sellers at Redcar in May and Wolverhampton in June: best at 6f/7f: acts on polytrack, firm and soft going: tried in cheekpieces/blinkers: held up. *G. A. Swinbank* **74**

CD FLYER (IRE) 9 ch.g. Grand Lodge (USA) 125 – Pretext (Polish Precedent (USA) 131) [2006 85: 6d 7d 6d Jul 9] lengthy, angular gelding: good walker: fairly useful performer at 8 yrs: well held in handicaps in 2006: tried in visor/cheekpieces: held up: reportedly bled once at 8 yrs. *R. C. Guest* **–**

CECCHETTI (IRE) 3 b.f. Imperial Ballet (IRE) 110 – Quiver Tree 68 (Lion Cavern (USA) 117) [2006 51: p7g p6g f8g⁵ p7.1g⁶ p8g² 8.3d p8.6g⁶ 7.1g Jul 5] modest maiden: stays 1m: acts on polytrack (little show on turf): has raced freely: often slowly away. *Mrs H. Sweeting* **– a53**

CEDARLEA (IRE) 2 ch.g. (Mar 9) Shinko Forest (IRE) – Baileys First (IRE) 74 (Alzao (USA) 117) [2006 6m² 5g² 7s³ Oct 14] €8,000F, €13,500Y: sixth living foal: half-brother to 2004 2-y-o 7f seller winner Uredale (by Bahhare) and winners abroad by Salse and Spectrum: dam, maiden (best at 7f to 1¼m), half-sister to very smart 1m/1¼m performer Candy Glen: fair form in maidens, placed all 3 starts: gelded after: stays 7f. *R. A. Fahey* **72**

CELEBRATION SONG (IRE) 3 b.g. Royal Applause 124 – Googoosh (IRE) 77 (Danehill (USA) 126) [2006 84: p8g³ 7m³ 8.3g p8g Sep 18] quite good-topped gelding: fairly useful performer: good third in 2006 in handicaps at Kempton and Yarmouth: unseated rider soon after start at Kempton final outing: stays easy 1m: acts on polytrack, firm and soft ground (yet to race on heavy). *W. R. Swinburn* **88**

CELESTIAL HALO (IRE) 2 b.c. (May 7) Galileo (IRE) 134 – Pay The Bank 81 (High Top 131) [2006 7d⁵ Aug 22] 40,000Y: rather leggy, useful-looking colt: half-brother to several winners, including about 5f (at 2 yrs) to 7f winner My Branch (by Distant Relative) and fairly useful 1½m winner Banco Suivi (by Nashwan): dam 2-y-o 1m winner who stayed 1¼m: 25/1, promise in face of stiff introduction when 6¼ lengths **86 p**

fifth of 7 to Big Timer in Acomb Stakes at York, green and soon behind: will be suited by 1¼m/1½m: should improve and win races. *B. W. Hills*

CELTIC CARISMA 4 b.f. Celtic Swing 138 – Kathryn's Pet 92 (Blakeney 126) [2006 **65** 61: 14.1s 16g* 16.1d 15.8g 14.1f⁵ 16.1m 12d 13.8s Oct 14] strong filly: fair handicapper: won at Southwell in April: stays 2m: acts on firm ground, seemingly not on softer than good. *K. G. Reveley*

CELTIC CHANGE (IRE) 2 br.c. (Mar 7) Celtic Swing 138 – Changi (IRE) (Lear Fan **70** (USA) 130) [2006 7g⁴ 7d⁴ Aug 28] 22,000F, 22,000Y: good-topped colt: first foal: dam French 9.5f winner: fourth in maidens, much better run on debut at Thirsk: wandered next time (softer ground): will stay 1¼m+. *M. Dods*

CELTICELLO (IRE) 4 b. or br.g. Celtic Swing 138 – Viola Royale (IRE) 90 (Royal **–** Academy (USA) 130) [2006 94: p10g 8.1g Sep 22] leggy gelding: fairly useful performer at 3 yrs: well beaten both starts in 2006: tried in cheekpieces. *Mrs H. Dalton*

CELTIC EMPIRE (IRE) 3 b.g. Second Empire (IRE) 124 – Celtic Guest (IRE) (Be **43** My Guest (USA) 126) [2006 –: f11g 12g 12.4d p12.2g f14g⁵ Nov 2] workmanlike gelding: poor maiden: stays 1¾m: acts on fibresand. *Jedd O'Keeffe*

CELTIC JIG (IRE) 3 b.g. Celtic Swing 138 – Ceide Dancer (IRE) 79 (Alzao (USA) **–** 117) [2006 9s 12f⁵ 12s May 20] well beaten in maidens: tried blinkered. *T. D. Easterby*

CELTIC MEMORIES (IRE) 2 ch.f. (Apr 23) Selkirk (USA) 129 – Memories (IRE) **59 p** 95 (Don't Forget Me 127) [2006 7.5g⁵ Aug 27] fourth foal: half-sister to winner in USA by Gone West: dam, US Grade 2 1½m winner, half-sister to 4-y-o Scorpion: 40/1, soon lot to do when fifth of 12 in maiden at Beverley: likely to progress. *M. W. Easterby*

CELTIC MILL 8 b.g. Celtic Swing 138 – Madam Millie 99 (Milford 119) [2006 118, **113** a107+: 5m 6m⁴ 5m 6m³ 5m⁴ 5m 6m* 5g* 5.2m 5g⁵ Sep 28] tall, leggy gelding: smart performer: won minor event at Windsor (by 1¼ lengths from Andronikos) in August and listed Scarbrough Stakes at York (by ¾ length from Orientor) in September: also ran well when third to Fayr Jag in Chipchase Stakes at Newcastle and fifth to Fantasy Believer in listed event at Newmarket: effective at 5f/6f: acts on all-weather, firm and good to soft going: usually wears cheekpieces: normally front runner: good servant to connections. *D. W. Barker*

CELTIC SHADOW (IRE) 4 b.g. Celtic Swing 138 – Shabby Chic (USA) 114 (Red **–** Ransom (USA)) [2006 –: 12m 10.1m May 10] rather leggy gelding: no form: tried tongue tied. *K. G. Reveley*

CELTIC SPA (IRE) 4 gr.f. Celtic Swing 138 – Allegorica (IRE) (Alzao (USA) 117) **75** [2006 80: 8.2s 8d 7g 9d⁵ 8.3m 7.1m³ 8.3m⁵ 7.1f* 6.9g* 8.1m³ 6g 8d 7.2v p8.6g⁵ p8g **a62** p8.6g Dec 23] small, leggy filly: fair handicapper on turf, modest on all-weather: left Mrs P. Dutfield after fourth outing: won at Chepstow in July and Carlisle in August: needs further than 6f, and stays 1m: acts on polytrack, firm and soft going. *P. D. Evans*

CELTIC SPIRIT (IRE) 3 ch.g. Pivotal 124 – Cavernista 75 (Lion Cavern (USA) 117) **90** [2006 8d⁶ 8.1s* p10g² 10g* 10.5g³ 10d³ Oct 9] leggy gelding: third foal: half-brother to 6f winner Capetown Girl (by Danzero): dam, maiden who should have stayed 1¼m, half-sister to smart stayer Give Notice: fairly useful performer: won maiden at Chepstow in May and handicap at Sandown in August: creditable third in handicaps at Haydock and Windsor after: will stay 1½m: acts on polytrack and soft going. *R. M. Beckett*

CELTIC STAR (IRE) 8 b.g. Celtic Swing 138 – Recherchee (Rainbow Quest (USA) **57** 134) [2006 –: p12.2g³ May 15] tall gelding: modest handicapper, lightly raced on Flat in recent years: stays 1½m: acts on polytrack and good to soft ground: sometimes wears headgear. *Mrs L. Williamson*

CELTIC STEP 2 br.c. (Mar 10) Selkirk (USA) 129 – Inchiri 108 (Sadler's Wells (USA) **86** 132) [2006 7.1g 7m* 8s³ 7s* 8s⁵ Oct 21] 100,000Y: big colt: second foal: dam, 1¼m/ 1½m winner, out of half-sister to smart performer up to 1m Inchinor: fairly useful performer: won maiden at Leicester in September and nursery at Catterick in October: ran creditably both other starts in nurseries: bred to stay beyond 1m, but has raced freely: acts on soft and good to firm going: blinkered last 2 starts: difficult ride. *M. Johnston*

CELTIC SULTAN (IRE) 2 b.c. (Apr 5) Celtic Swing 138 – Farjah (IRE) (Charnwood **92** Forest (IRE) 125) [2006 6g² 6m* 7g³ 7g 6s Oct 7] €48,000F, €62,000Y: sturdy colt: second foal: dam French 2-y-o 5.5f winner: fairly useful form: won maiden at Haydock in July: ran well next 2 starts (despite going freely), third to Dubai's Touch in listed race at Newbury and seventh to Vital Equine in Champagne Stakes at York: stays 7f: acts on good to firm going, well beaten on soft. *T. P. Tate*

CELTIC SUNSET (IRE) 3 b.f. Celtic Swing 138 – Hishmah 79 (Nashwan (USA) –
135) [2006 f8g Feb 2] €15,000F, €56,000Y: third foal: dam 7.5f winner, sister to useful
performer up to 1½m Mubkera: 10/1, slowly away and took strong hold when behind in
maiden at Southwell. *M. A. Jarvis*

CELTIC THUNDER 5 b.g. Mind Games 121 – Lake Mistassiu 86 (Tina's Pet 121) **63**
[2006 77: p7.1g p6g p7.1g 6f⁶ 5f² 6g* 6ᵤ 6d p7.1m Nov 8] good-topped gelding: modest
handicapper nowadays: won apprentice event at Haydock in July: best at 5f/6f: acts on
polytrack, firm and good to soft going: sometimes blinkered. *T. J. Etherington*

CELTIQUE 4 b.f. Celtic Swing 138 – Heart's Harmony (Blushing Groom (FR) 131) **85**
[2006 80: p8.6g p8g p8g p10g p8g p12g* 11.6m² 10m* 10g³ 12m* 12g Aug 19] leggy,
good-topped filly: fairly useful handicapper: won at Lingfield in June and Newmarket in
July and August: stays 1½m: acts on polytrack, firm and good to soft going: tried visored/
blinkered: has hung/found little. *M. Wigham*

CEMGRAFT 5 b.m. In The Wings 128 – Soviet Maid (IRE) (Soviet Star (USA) 128) **59**
[2006 49: f16g f11g f11g p12g² p16.5g⁶ 14.1m² 12.1f* p12g p16g Aug 30] big, strong, lengthy
mare: modest handicapper: won amateur event at Chepstow in July: effective at 1½m,
probably at 2m: acts on polytrack and firm going: tongue tied nowadays: in cheekpieces
last 6 starts: held up. *A. J. Lidderdale*

CENTAURUS 4 br.c. Daylami (IRE) 138 – Dandanna (IRE) 97 (Linamix (FR) 127) –
[2006 115: 11.6d Nov 4] tall, lengthy colt: has had shins fired: has a powerful, round
action: smart performer at 3 yrs: well held in listed event at Windsor only start in 2006:
barely stays 1¾m: raced only on good/good to soft ground: tongue tied at 3 yrs. *Saeed bin
Suroor*

CENTENARY (IRE) 2 b.g. (Mar 17) Traditionally (USA) 117 – Catherinofaragon **71**
(USA) (Chief's Crown (USA)) [2006 7m⁵ 7f³ 7m² 7m³ 7.5g⁶ 8d³ 9m⁴ 8g* 8s Oct 16]
€21,000Y: neat gelding: fifth living foal: half-brother to fairly useful 2001 2-y-o
7f winner Lucayan Legacy (by Persian Bold) and 1m/8.5f winner Catstreet (by Catrail):
dam unraced: fair performer: claimed from J. Howard Johnson £12,000 third start: won
maiden at Newcastle in September: best form up to 1m on good ground or firmer: sold
26,000 gns. *J. S. Wainwright*

CENTREBOARD (USA) 2 gr. or ro.f. (Feb 14) Mizzen Mast (USA) 121 – Corsini 88 **72**
(Machiavellian (USA) 123) [2006 5m² 6m⁶ 5.1m² Aug 25] fourth foal: half-sister to 2004
2-y-o 7f winner Corcoran and 1¼m/1½m winner Corsican Native (both useful, by Lear
Fan): dam, 2-y-o 7f winner, out of close relative to dam of Zafonic: fair maiden: second
at Lingfield and Bath (favourite but too free in between): should stay 7f/1m. *R. Charlton*

CENTREOFATTENTION 3 b.f. Groom Dancer (USA) 128 – Centre Court 74 **34**
(Second Set (IRE) 127) [2006 6g 7m 6d 7f 6.1f 8f Jul 28] 2,200Y: leggy filly: fourth foal:
half-sister to unreliable 2002 2-y-o 5f seller winner Service (by College Chapel): dam
2-y-o 5f winner: poor maiden: tried in cheekpieces. *Mrs A. Duffield*

CEREBUS 4 b.f. Wolfhound (USA) 126 – Bring On The Choir 87 (Chief Singer 131) **69**
[2006 73: f6g f6g p6g⁶ f6g⁶ f6g Dec 23] strong, close-coupled filly: fair performer:
effective at 5f to 7f: acts on all-weather, firm and soft going: effective blinkered or not.
A. J. McCabe

CEREDIG 3 b.g. Lujain (USA) 119 – Anneli Rose 56 (Superlative 118) [2006 66p: **63**
5.1g³ 5.3m⁵ 5m 5m 5.1g 5m² p6m³ p5.1g³ p6g p5g³ Nov 11] tall gelding: modest maiden:
can be headstrong, and barely stays easy 6f: acts on polytrack, raced only on good/good
to firm going on turf: tried blinkered, tongue tied last 4 starts. *W. R. Muir*

CEREMONIAL JADE (UAE) 3 b.g. Jade Robbery (USA) 121 – Talah 87 (Danehill **100**
(USA) 126) [2006 8.5f* 7m² 7s p7g* p7g* Oct 6] 10,000 2-y-o: good-topped gelding:
second foal: dam, French 7.5f winner, sister to smart performer up to 1m Firth of Lorne
out of 1000 Guineas runner-up Kerrera, herself half-sister to very smart 6f to 1m performer Rock City: useful and progressive form: won maiden at Beverley (hung left in
front) in June and handicaps at Kempton (by 3½ lengths from Sant Elena) in September
and Lingfield (tongue tied and heavily backed, beat Rochdale by head) in October: stays
8.5f: acts on polytrack and firm going: has been bandaged forelegs. *M. Botti*

CERIS STAR (IRE) 2 b.g. (Feb 20) Cadeaux Genereux 131 – Midsummernitedream –
(GER) 43 (Thatching 131) [2006 6g 7.1m 7.1m Sep 7] rangy gelding: little form: gelded
after final start. *B. R. Millman*

CERTAIN CIRCLES (USA) 3 b.c. King Cugat (USA) 122 – Daily Special (USA) **70**
(Dayjur (USA) 137) [2006 78: p8g⁶ a6s⁴ a8g⁴ 8f⁶ 9g⁶ 6.5f⁶ Aug 23] smallish, strong
colt: fair performer: left A. Balding after reappearance and W. Wofford after third out-

ing: should stay 1m: raced only on polytrack/dirt and good ground or firmer. *M. E. Casse, Canada*

CERTAIN JUSTICE (USA) 8 gr.g. Lit de Justice (USA) 125 – Pure Misk 55 **79** (Rainbow Quest (USA) 134) [2006 82: f6g f7g 7m* 8.2g³ 6g² 7g³ Aug 23] rather leggy gelding: fair performer: won minor event at Leicester in July: held form well after: effective at 6f to 1m: acts on fibresand, soft and good to firm going: tried blinkered, has worn cheekpieces. *Stef Liddiard*

CERULEAN ROSE 7 ch.m. Bluegrass Prince (IRE) 110 – Elegant Rose 72 (Noalto **71** 120) [2006 78: 5g 6.1m⁵ 5.7d 5s² 6.1d² 5.2m 5.5g 6f 5.1f⁵ 5g* 5.1m³ 5.5d 6d⁶ p6m Nov 21] workmanlike mare: fair handicapper: won at Sandown in August: effective at 5f/6f: acts on firm and soft going: tried blinkered/tongue tied at 3 yrs. *A. W. Carroll*

CESARE 5 b.g. Machiavellian (USA) 123 – Tromond 94 (Lomond (USA) 128) [2006 **116** 104: 8s 8m* p8g 7.1m* 7g⁵ Sep 15] deep-girthed gelding: smart performer: won 30-runner Royal Hunt Cup at Royal Ascot (by neck from Stronghold) in June and minor event at Warwick (beat Mostashaar by 1¾ lengths, coasting home) in August: very good fifth of 13 to Sleeping Indian in listed race at Newbury final outing: effective at 7f, should stay 1¼m: acts on polytrack, soft and good to firm going. *J. R. Fanshawe*

CESAR MANRIQUE (IRE) 4 ch.g. Vettori (IRE) 119 – Norbella (Nordico (USA)) **74** [2006 77: 5g² 5.7s⁴ 5.7g 5.2m² 6g³ 6s 5.7m 6d⁶ 6g p7g f8g⁶ Dec 9] leggy gelding: fair handicapper: left B. Hills, below form in cheekpieces last 2 starts: stays 6f: acts on firm and soft going: blinkered final outing at 3 yrs: held up. *A. E. Jones*

CESC 2 b.c. (Mar 9) Compton Place 125 – Mana Pools (IRE) 76 (Brief Truce (USA) 126) **95** [2006 5.1d 5f 5m⁶ 6m³ 7m* p7.1f² p8g p8g* p7g* p8g* Dec 8] 10,000Y: first foal: dam, 1m to 1¼m winner, half-sister to useful French 1m winner Miss Chryss: useful performer: won nurseries at Newbury in August and Lingfield (2) in November, and 4-runner minor event at Kempton (beat Alittlebitleft by 2½ lengths) in December: stays 1m: acts on polytrack and good to firm ground. *P. J. Makin*

CETSHWAYO 4 ch.g. Pursuit of Love 124 – Induna (Grand Lodge (USA) 125) [2006 **66** 60: 10m 14.1d p10g* 11g Sep 30] big gelding: fair performer: won seller at Lingfield in September: stays 1¼m: acts on polytrack and good to firm going: reportedly bled when tailed off second start. *J. M. P. Eustace*

CEZZARO (IRE) 8 ch.g. Ashkalani (IRE) 128 – Sept Roses (USA) (Septieme Ciel **–** (USA) 123) [2006 49: 13.8f⁵ Jun 9] compact gelding: poor performer: stays 12.6f: acts on any turf ground, little form on all-weather: tried visored/in cheekpieces: tongue tied once at 6 yrs: usually races prominently. *T. A. K. Cuthbert*

Royal Hunt Cup (Handicap), Royal Ascot—Cesare gives James Fanshawe his second win in the race in four years; Stronghold (rail) is a gallant runner-up under 9-8, with Akona Matata third and Hinterland (right) fourth; Mine (right of group), first home on the far side, is only eighth

Cheveley Park Stud's "Cesare"

CHACO (IRE) 3 b.c. Cape Cross (IRE) 129 – Carotene (CAN) (Great Nephew 126) – [2006 –: 8v 7.5v 8d 12s p12g Dec 6] strong colt: little form, including in visor at Kempton final start: often tongue tied. *Niall Moran, Ireland*

CHAIRMAN BOBBY 8 ch.g. Clantime 101 – Formidable Liz 66 (Formidable (USA) 66 125) [2006 –: 5g 6d 5g 5f 5m³ 5.9m² 6f⁵ 6g³ 5m* 5m³ 5m² 5m³ 6m² 5d⁴ 5g Sep 27] smallish, sturdy gelding: fair performer: won claimer at Catterick in July: effective at 5f/ 6f: acts on all-weather, firm and good to soft going: wears cheekpieces nowadays: usually races prominently. *D. W. Barker*

CHAIRMAN RICK (IRE) 4 b.g. Danehill Dancer (IRE) 117 – Come Together 68 62 (Mtoto 134) [2006 61: f8g f7g f8g p9.5g f7g⁵ 6m* 6g 6m 6m Jun 21] modest performer a45 on turf, poor on all-weather: won apprentice claimer at Redcar in May: effective at 6f, seemingly at 9f: raced only on good going or firmer on turf: tried visored: very slowly away final start. *D. Nicholls*

CHAKA ZULU 9 b.g. Muhtarram (USA) 125 – African Dance (USA) (El Gran Senor – (USA) 136) [2006 69: p16.5g Feb 17] sturdy gelding: fair handicapper: broke down only 9-y-o outing: stayed 15f: acted on fibresand, firm and good to soft going: tried visored/ tongue tied in 2001: held up: dead. *D. W. Thompson*

CHALENTINA 3 b.f. Primo Valentino (IRE) 116 – Chantilly Myth 81 (Sri Pekan 80 (USA) 117) [2006 66: 10g⁵ 8.2m² 7m⁵ 7f² 7f* 7d² 8.3f p8g p8.6g⁴ Dec 30] leggy filly: a63 fairly useful performer on turf, modest on all-weather: won maiden at Yarmouth in July: ran well in handicap next time: left H. Cecil 4,000 gns before final start: best form at 7f: acts on firm and good to soft going. *P. Howling*

totesport.com Heritage Handicap, Beverley—Champions Gallery improves again to beat Pearly King (rail), with Noble Gent (partially obscured) third and Formal Decree fourth

CHALICE WELCOME 3 b.g. Most Welcome 131 – Blue Peru (IRE) 48 (Perugino (USA) 84) [2006 –: p6g² p7.1g p6g³ p7g p7.1g⁶ p8.6g⁴ Dec 4] poor maiden: left J. Supple after fourth outing: stays 8.6f: acts on polytrack: tried blinkered/visored. *C. F. Wall* **46**

CHALLIS (IRE) 2 b.c. (Feb 14) Barathea (IRE) 127 – Chalosse (Doyoun 124) [2006 p8g⁵ p7g⁴ Dec 20] third foal: half-brother to French 2004 2-y-o 5.5f to 1m winner Faussaire (by Fasliyev): dam, French maiden who stayed 1½m, closely related to high-class French performer up to 10.5f Creator: better effort in maidens at Lingfield when fourth to Danehillsundance, running on strongly when hampered 1f out: will stay 1m: open to further improvement. *J. Noseda* **69 p**

CHAMPAGNE CRACKER 5 ch.m. Up And At 'em 109 – Kiveton Komet 71 (Precocious 126) [2006 74: 5v³ 5d 5m 5f⁶ 5f⁶ 6v⁶ Oct 9] big, strong mare: fair handicapper: best at 5f: acts on firm and good to soft going: very slowly away fourth start. *I. Semple* **71**

CHAMPAGNE MOMENT 3 ch.f. Perryston View 114 – Ashleen (Chilibang 120) [2006 48: p7g⁶ 7m p5.1g p6g 8.2d May 19] big filly: modest maiden: stays 7f: acts on polytrack and good to firm ground: wore cheekpieces final start. *V. Smith* **55**

CHAMPAGNE PERRY 2 ch.g. (Mar 16) Perryston View 114 – Ashleen (Chilibang 120) [2006 p5g 6m⁶ 7m 6f Jul 24] little form. *V. Smith* **–**

CHAMPAGNE ROSSINI (IRE) 4 b.g. Rossini (USA) 118 – Alpencrocus (IRE) (Waajib 121) [2006 54: f8g 7g 7f Jul 28] workmanlike gelding: poor maiden nowadays: stays 1m: acts on fibresand and good to firm going. *M. C. Chapman* **41**

CHAMPAGNE SHADOW (IRE) 5 b.g. Kahyasi 130 – Moet (IRE) 72 (Mac's Imp (USA) 116) [2006 79‡: p12g³ p12g⁴ p16g⁴ p12g* p16g³ p16g⁵ p13.9g⁴ p12g* p12g² 12s* p13.9f³ 12s p13.9g² p16.5g³ p16.5g³ Dec 9] fairly useful performer: won claimer in March and seller in June, both at Lingfield, and, having been claimed from G. L. Moore £6,000, amateur handicap at Catterick in August: stays 16.5f: acts on polytrack and soft going: effective blinkered or not: refused to race on 4-y-o return. *K. A. Ryan* **86**

CHAMPAIN SANDS (IRE) 7 b.g. Green Desert (USA) 127 – Grecian Bride (IRE) (Groom Dancer (USA) 128) [2006 61: 8d 8m² 8d 8.3f⁵ 7.9m⁴ 8.1g⁴ 6.9f* 8m* 8.3d⁴ 8g⁴ 9.2d Sep 25] smallish gelding: fair handicapper: won at Carlisle in July and Thirsk in August: best at 6.9f to 1m: acts on all-weather, firm and good to soft going: tried visored/blinkered/tongue tied. *E. J. Alston* **74**

CHAMPERY (USA) 2 b.c. (Apr 9) Bahri (USA) 125 – Ice Ballet (IRE) 103 (Nureyev (USA) 131) [2006 6m* 7.5f* 8g³ Aug 25] good-topped colt: fifth foal: half-brother to fairly useful Irish 8.5f winner Frost Fair (by Indian Ridge): dam, French 1m/9f winner, sister to smart French/US performer up to 9f Fadeyev: useful form: won maiden at Newcastle (beat Algol 2 lengths) and 4-runner minor event at Beverley (by 3 lengths from Billy Dane) in July: further progress when 1¾ lengths third behind Streets Ahead and **97**

Eddie Jock in listed race at Salisbury final start, setting only steady pace: will stay 1¼m: raced on good ground or firmer. *M. Johnston*

CHAMPION LION (IRE) 7 b.g. Sadler's Wells (USA) 132 – Honey Bun 51 (Unfu- **60** wain (USA) 131) [2006 66: p12.2g³ p12g⁴ f12g³ 11v* f12g⁴ 15.8d⁶ 15.8g⁶ May 9] strong, close-coupled gelding: fluent performer: modest performer, better on all-weather than turf: won seller at Southwell (by 7 lengths) in March: claimed from J. Boyle after fifth start: barely stays 1¾m: acts on all-weather, heavy and good to firm going: sometimes slowly away: usually waited with. *James Moffatt*

CHAMPIONS GALLERY 3 b.c. Dansili 127 – Pure (Slip Anchor 136) [2006 96p: **105** 7.6d⁵ 9s⁵ 8m 8m* 8g 9.9g* 9m* Dec 26] big, strong colt: useful performer: improved in 2006, winning handicaps at Ascot in July, Beverley (by length from Pearly King) in August, and, having left D. Elsworth, Sha Tin in December: stays 1¼m: acts on good to firm going, probably on soft. *A. Schutz, Hong Kong*

CHAMPIONSHIP POINT (IRE) 3 b.c. Lomitas 129 – Flying Squaw 102 (Be My **112** Chief (USA) 122) [2006 106: 11g* 12m 12d 13.9g 9.9m³ 9d Oct 14] sturdy colt: smart performer: won listed Predominate Stakes at Goodwood in May impressively by 4 lengths from Sienna Storm, eased: below that level at Epsom in Derby (stirred up in paddock and took too strong a hold when eleventh to Sir Percy, reportedly very stiff after) and at York in Great Voltigeur Stakes and St Leger (ninth to Sixties Icon) next 3 starts: respectable neck third to Imperial Stride in listed event back at Goodwood penultimate outing, then poor effort in Darley Stakes at Newmarket: should be suited by 1½m, though probably finds 1¾m too far: yet to race on heavy going, acts on any other. *M. R. Channon*

CHAMPION'S WAY (IRE) 4 b.c. Namid 128 – Savage (IRE) 98 (Polish Patriot **52** (USA) 128) [2006 6d p8.6g⁵ p8.6g Dec 18] modest maiden: stays 8.6f: acts on polytrack. *B. R. Millman*

CHAMPLAIN 2 b.c. (Jan 21) Seeking The Gold (USA) – Calando (USA) 110 (Storm **104** Cat (USA)) [2006 6s³ 7m* 7m 8d⁴ 8s² Oct 16] well-made, attractive colt: fluent mover: third foal: half-brother to 4-y-o Sovereignty: dam, 2-y-o 7f/1m (May Hill Stakes) winner, out of Oaks winner and St Leger runner-up Diminuendo: useful performer: won listed Chesham Stakes at Royal Ascot by 2 lengths from Country Song: reportedly had sore shins after next start (off 2 months), then good 4¾ lengths fourth to Admiralofthefleet in Royal Lodge Stakes at Ascot and 1¾ lengths second to Sweet Lilly in listed event at Pontefract: will stay 1¼m/1½m: acts on soft and good to firm going: highly strung sort, has run well when looking stirred up: sent to UAE. *M. A. Jarvis*

CHANCELLOR (IRE) 8 ch.h. Halling (USA) 133 – Isticanna (USA) 96 (Far North **103 §** (CAN) 120) [2006 107d: p10g 10.1g* 10g 10m 11.6d Nov 4] strong, lengthy horse: one-time smart performer, useful nowadays: won Vodafone Rose Bowl (Handicap) at Epsom (by ¾ length from Look Again) in June, easily best effort of 2006: left E. Oertel after fourth outing: best around 1¼m: below form on firm going, acts on any other turf, probably on polytrack: tried in cheekpieces: usually tongue tied: refused to race once at 6 yrs: untrustworthy: joined Mrs C. Bailey. *D. K. Ivory*

Vodafone Rose Bowl (Handicap), Epsom—
Chancellor (noseband) clicks on the right day to take this valuable prize from Look Again;
Kings Quay (rail) is caught for third by the strong-finishing Star of Light (extreme left)

CHANGE COURSE 2 b.f. (Feb 19) Sadler's Wells (USA) 132 – Orford Ness 107 **– p**
(Selkirk (USA) 129) [2006 7f Aug 3] big, good-topped filly: fifth foal: closely related to
6-y-o Weightless, and half-sister to fairly useful French 7.5f to 10.5f winner Castle Rising
(by Indian Ridge) and 4-y-o Home Affairs: dam, won Prix de Sandringham, also 1m winner at 2 yrs: 10/1, not knocked about in mid-field in maiden at Goodwood won by Cumin:
will do better. *Sir Michael Stoute*

CHANGING WIND (USA) 3 br. or b.c. Storm Cat (USA) – Miss Caerleona (FR) 106 **89**
(Caerleon (USA) 132) [2006 p8g* p11g6 Sep 1] good-bodied colt: fifth foal: brother to
winner in USA and half-brother to 2 winners, including smart 7f/1m winner (including in
USA) Karen's Caper (by War Chant): dam useful French/US 8.5f to 10.5f winner: fairly
useful form: green, won maiden at Kempton in August by 1¼ lengths from Country
Escape: tongue tied, not discredited when sixth in handicap there only other outing: probably stays 11f: joined M. Al Muhairi in UAE. *Saeed bin Suroor*

CHANGIZ 3 b.g. Foxhound (USA) 103 – Persia (IRE) (Persian Bold 123) [2006 –: 10d4 **51**
10m May 12] sturdy gelding: modest maiden: stays 1¼m: acts on good to soft ground.
J. A. Geake

CHANNEL CROSSING 4 b.g. Deploy 131 – Wave Dancer 76 (Dance In Time **57**
(CAN)) [2006 56: p9.5f 8m 16.1s 11.1d 12d2 f11g3 p12g f14g Nov 2] sturdy gelding: **a46**
modest maiden on turf, poor on all-weather: stays 1½m: acts on all-weather, good to firm
and good to soft ground: wore cheekpieces last 4 starts. *W. M. Brisbourne*

CHANTACO (USA) 4 b.g. Bahri (USA) 125 – Dominant Dancer 97 (Primo Dominie **103**
121) [2006 91: 10g3 10m2 10g* 10.1g 12m 10.4f5 12g 10m Sep 16] close-coupled gelding: useful handicapper: improved in 2006, winning Zetland Gold Cup at Redcar (by ½
length from Ace of Hearts) in May: ran well next 4 starts, including when fifth to Fairmile
in John Smith's Cup at York: well held in valuable event at Newbury final outing: gelded
after: barely stays 1½m: acts on polytrack, firm and soft going. *A. M. Balding*

CHANT DE GUERRE (USA) 2 b.f. (May 7) War Chant (USA) 126 – Fatwa (IRE) **62**
95 (Lahib (USA) 129) [2006 7g6 6g Aug 30] $25,000Y: close-coupled filly: second foal:
dam, 6f winner, out of close relative to high-class miler Maroof: modest form in maidens,
better effort debut: sold 4,000 gns, joined H. Dunlop. *P. Mitchell*

CHANTELLE'S DREAM 4 ch.f. Compton Place 125 – Polar Peak 41 (Polar Falcon **60 §**
(USA) 126) [2006 57: p6g p5.1g p6g2 p6g p5g5 p5g p6g* 6.1m p6g4 5f 5.7f2 6m 6g 5.7m
Aug 20] rather leggy, close-coupled filly: modest performer: won seller at Lingfield in
April (mulish beforehand): stays easy 6f: acts on polytrack and firm going: sometimes
blinkered/tongue tied: often slowly away: none too reliable. *Ms J. S. Doyle*

CHANTEUSE NOIRE (USA) 3 b.f. War Chant (USA) 126 – Galeta (ARG) (South- **67**
ern Halo (USA)) [2006 69: 8m 8m2 6d3 5m4 5f3 6m* Aug 5] close-coupled, attractive
filly: fair performer: won maiden at Hamilton (by 5 lengths) in August: effective at 5f to
7f: acts on firm going: visored after reappearance: sold 22,000 gns, sent to Saudi Arabia.
J. Noseda

CHANTILLY BEAUTY (FR) 4 b.f. Josr Algarhoud (IRE) 118 – Lysabelle (FR) **103**
(Lesotho (USA) 118) [2006 105: 7m2 8m 6g 6m Nov 5] big filly: useful performer:
creditable length second to Echelon in Chartwell Fillies' Stakes at Lingfield (looked
tricky ride) on reappearance: respectable effort when eighth to Soviet Song in Windsor
Forest Stakes at Royal Ascot next time (hampered briefly over 1f out): below form last
2 starts: best at 7f/1m: acts on firm going, below form on softer than good and dirt:
blinkered: has had tongue tied/worn cheekpieces. *Rupert Pritchard-Gordon, France*

CHANTING (USA) 2 b.f. (Apr 6) Danehill (USA) 126 – Golden Reef (USA) (Mr **103 p**
Prospector (USA)) [2006 6m5 6m* 6g* Jul 19] half-sister to fairly useful 1¼m winner
Murjana (by Pleasant Colony) and several winners in North America: dam, US Grade 2
2-y-o 6f winner, second in Grade 1 2-y-o 7f event: progressive form: won maiden at
Leopardstown (by 1½ lengths from Duke of Marmalade) in June and 6-runner listed race
there in July, latter by 1¼ lengths from Miss Beatrix, quickening well to lead inside final
1f: will stay 7f: likely to progress further. *D. Wachman, Ireland*

CHAPELIZOD (IRE) 3 b.g. Raphane (USA) 102 – Fulminus Instar (IRE) (Classic **53**
Secret (USA) 91) [2006 38: 5m 7m5 7f6 8f6 8m 6v3 5v4 p5.1g6 Dec 8] modest maiden
handicapper: below form at Wolverhampton final start: best up to 7f: probably acts on
any ground on turf. *L. McAteer, Ireland*

CHAPTER (IRE) 4 ch.g. Sinndar (IRE) 134 – Web of Intrigue 66 (Machiavellian **74 d**
(USA) 123) [2006 76: 10m3 10f 8f 9.9s6 8.1m3 9g 8.1m6 9m Sep 10] rather leggy gelding:

fair handicapper: below form after reappearance: stays 1¼m: acts on firm going: in cheekpieces/blinkered last 6 starts. *Mrs A. L. M. King*

CHARANNE 3 b.f. Diktat 126 – Mystique (Mystiko (USA) 124) [2006 –: 5.7m 6m p6m⁶ p7.1m Nov 21] no form in maidens. *J. M. Bradley* —

CHARLES DARWIN (IRE) 3 ch.c. Tagula (IRE) 116 – Seymour (IRE) 78 (Eagle Eyed (USA) 111) [2006 92: 6d⁴ 6f 5.1g 6g³ 7m³ 6m 6m² 6m* 6g⁵ 6s² 6d³ 5d³ p5.1g⁴ Oct 29] well-made colt: useful handicapper: won at Ascot in July by neck from Third Set: good efforts when in frame last 4 starts: effective at stiff 5f to 7f: acts on polytrack, firm and soft going: consistent. *M. Blanshard* 95

CHARLES PARNELL (IRE) 3 b.g. Elnadim (USA) 128 – Titania (Fairy King (USA)) [2006 73: 5.1g³ 6f* 6f 6m 7.2v 6.1g² 6s⁴ 6g² p6g⁶ p6g⁴ Nov 14] leggy gelding: fairly useful performer: won maiden at Redcar in June: twice good second in handicaps after: likely to prove best at 5f/easy 6f: acts on polytrack, firm and soft going. *M. Dods* 83

CHARLES STREET LAD (IRE) 3 b.g. Mull of Kintyre (USA) 114 – Tropicana (IRE) (Imperial Frontier (USA) 112) [2006 56: p7g 6g p7g 6d 10.2m Sep 7] lengthy gelding: maiden: poor form in 2006: probably stays 7f: tried tongue tied: not straightforward (unseated rider and bolted before start on reappearance). *M. R. Bosley* 46

CHARLEY'S AUNT (IRE) 3 ch.f. King Charlemagne (USA) 120 – Dane's Lady (IRE) 75 (Danehill (USA) 126) [2006 61: p6g* p5.1g p6g⁶ p5.1g Jul 17] modest performer: improved to win claimer at Wolverhampton (claimed from N. Littmoden £9,000) in January: left J. Boyle £6,000 after second outing (reportedly finished lame): stays 6f: raced only on polytrack. *Mrs C. A. Dunnett* 63

CHARLEYS SPIRIT 2 ch.f. (Apr 24) Presidium 124 – Frilly Front 82 (Aragon 118) [2006 5m Jun 21] first foal: dam 5f winner, including at 2 yrs: 12/1, behind in maiden at Ripon. *T. D. Barron* —

CHARLIE BEAR 5 ch.h. Bahamian Bounty 116 – Abi 84 (Chief's Crown (USA)) [2006 66: p6g³ p6g⁵ p6g⁵ p6g 7m* 7.1d⁵ 7f⁵ 7m⁴ 7f³ 8m* 7.6d⁴ 7.1m⁶ 8d Sep 27] tall horse: fair handicapper: won at Yarmouth in April and Salisbury in July (amateurs): effective at 6f to 1m: acts on polytrack, firm and good to soft going: withdrawn after bolting intended twelfth start. *Miss Z. C. Davison* 66

CHARLIE COOL 3 ch.c. Rainbow Quest (USA) 134 – Tigwa 68 (Cadeaux Genereux 131) [2006 93: 8m³ 8.1m* 10m² 9d p10g³ Nov 18] lengthy, good-topped colt: smart performer: won handicap at Haydock (by ½ length from Count Trevisio) in August: good ¾-length second to Pinpoint in valuable event at Newbury next time: below-form eighth in Cambridgeshire at Newmarket penultimate start, then creditable third to Nayyir in listed race at Lingfield: stays 1¼m: acts on polytrack and good to firm and good to soft going: held up. *W. J. Haggas* 110

CHARLIE DELTA 3 b.g. Pennekamp (USA) 130 – Papita (IRE) 77 (Law Society (USA) 130) [2006 78: 6m 6.1g* 6m⁴ 6g⁶ p6g³ p6g 6d² 6g 6s⁴ p6g³ 5s⁴ 6v⁴ p6g p6g p7.1g⁴ p6g⁵ f6g³ f5g² Dec 27] close-coupled gelding: fairly useful handicapper: won at Nottingham in June: needs good start at 5f and stays 7f: acts on all-weather, heavy and good to firm going: wore cheekpieces last 2 starts. *D. Carroll* 88

CHARLIE FARNSBARNS (IRE) 2 b.c. (May 20) Cape Cross (IRE) 129 – Lafleur (IRE) 75 (Grand Lodge (USA) 125) [2006 6g² 6m* 7m⁵ 7d 7d* 8s² Oct 21] €105,000Y: good-topped colt: third foal: half-brother to a minor 1m winner in Italy by Efisio: dam lightly-raced half-sister to Oaks third Crown of Light: smart performer: won maiden at Newmarket in June and well-contested minor event at Ascot in October: further marked improvement when 1¼ lengths second of 14 to Authorized in Racing Post Trophy at Newbury, always prominent: likely to stay 1¼m: acts on and good to firm going: tends to hang right: ran poorly only try in blinkers. *B. J. Meehan* 115

CHARLIE GEORGE 5 ch.g. Idris (IRE) 118 – Faithful Beauty (IRE) (Last Tycoon 131) [2006 48: 8m 11.1m Aug 5] sparely-made gelding: poor maiden: stays 9f: acts on good to firm going. *P. Monteith* 34

CHARLIE KENNET 8 b.g. Pyramus (USA) 78 – Evaporate 51 (Insan (USA) 119) [2006 77: 10g⁴ 10d 10d* p10g⁵ p10g p10g 10g Aug 21] strong, close-coupled gelding: fair performer on turf, modest on all-weather: won handicap at Leicester in May: stays easy 1½m: acts on all-weather, soft and good to firm going. *Mrs H. Sweeting* 77 a62

CHARLIES GIRL (IRE) 2 ch.f. (May 18) Trans Island 119 – Indian Charm (IRE) 70 (Indian Ridge 123) [2006 5s 7m p5.1g Jun 22] 2,000Y: second foal: sister to winning sprinter in Italy: dam Irish maiden who stayed 6f: little form. *M. J. Attwater* —

CHARLIE TANGO (IRE) 5 b.g. Desert Prince (IRE) 130 – Precedence (IRE) 88 **65** (Polish Precedent (USA) 131) [2006 63: 11g³ 10d 8v 10f Jun 23] leggy gelding: fair performer: well held after reappearance: effective at 1m to 11f: acts on polytrack and firm ground: tried blinkered/visored/tongue tied: won over hurdles in August. *D. W. Thompson*

CHARLIE TIPPLE 2 b.g. (Feb 9) Diktat 126 – Swing of The Tide 75 (Sri Pekan **77 p** (USA) 117) [2006 6m⁶ 6m* 7m 7m³ Sep 6] 8,000Y: big, good-topped gelding: first foal: dam, 1m/9f winner, became unreliable: fair form: won 15-runner maiden at Newcastle in June by 2½ lengths: better run in nurseries when strong-finishing third at Southwell (gelded after): will be suited by 1m: raced on good to firm going: type to improve and do well in handicaps at 3 yrs. *T. D. Easterby*

CHARLIE TOKYO (IRE) 3 b.g. Trans Island 119 – Ellistown Lady (IRE) (Red **92** Sunset 120) [2006 80: 10.4d⁶ 10.1m 9.9g⁶ 12.1m² 11m⁴ 10d² 10d* 9.1v² 10d Nov 4] good-bodied gelding: good walker: fairly useful handicapper: won at Windsor in October, carrying head high and hanging right: also ran well in 2006 when runner-up: effective at 9f to 1½m: acts on heavy and good to firm going: blinkered/visored last 4 starts. *R. A. Fahey*

CHARLOTTEBUTTERFLY 6 b.m. Millkom 124 – Tee Gee Jay 63 (Northern **53** Tempest (USA) 120) [2006 7m³ 6g 7m p7g⁶ p7g p6g p6g² Dec 13] good-topped mare: missed 2005: poor performer nowadays: stays 7f: acts on all-weather and good to firm going: tried visored. *P. J. McBride*

CHARLOTTE GREY 2 gr.f. (Apr 10) Wizard King 122 – Great Intent (Aragon 118) **64** [2006 a5g³ a5.5g² a6g³ a6.5g⁴ 7f⁴ p7g p6.8g p6m⁵ f7g² p6g* p6s* p6g² Dec 23] 3,000Y: eighth foal: sister to 6-y-o Blue Patrick and 3-y-o Par Excellence, and half-sister to winner in Greece by Mind Games: dam once-raced sister to smart sprinter Argentum: modest performer: in frame at Mijas first 4 starts for R. Smith in Spain: won maiden and nursery (beat Suntan Lady by head) at Wolverhampton in December: stays 7f: acts on all-weather, probably on firm going. *C. N. Allen*

CHARLOTTE VALE 5 ch.m. Pivotal 124 – Drying Grass Moon 66 (Be My Chief **84 d** (USA) 122) [2006 81: 13.8d² 12g² 13d⁵ 13.8g² 12m⁴ 13.1g 13.1s³ 12s 13.8v² Oct 31] leggy, plain mare: fairly useful handicapper: below form after fifth start: stays 13.8f: acts on firm and soft going: sometimes hangs left. *M. D. Hammond*

CHARLTON 3 b.g. Inchinor 119 – Sabina 87 (Prince Sabo 123) [2006 92: 7v² p8g p7g **78** 8.3g 8.3d 8m 7d² 7.1m⁵ 7.1d Oct 13] close-coupled gelding: fair performer: should stay 1m: acts on polytrack, heavy and good to firm going: sometimes visored, including last 4 starts. *T. G. Mills*

CHARMING ESCORT 2 ch.g. (Apr 11) Rossini (USA) 118 – Iktizawa (Entrepreneur **66 p** 123) [2006 p8g⁵ Sep 30] first foal: dam unraced: 66/1, 14¼ lengths last of 5 in useful minor event won by Rallying Cry at Kempton: open to improvement. *T. T. Clement*

CHARMING PRINCESS 3 b.f. Primo Valentino (IRE) 116 – Via Dolorosa (Chad- **52** dleworth (IRE) 103) [2006 –: f7g 6g⁵ 5.9m 5f 6.1f Jul 8] left P. Midgley, form only when fifth in maiden at Catterick: last all other outings in 2006. *J. S. Wainwright*

CHARNOCK BATES ONE (IRE) 5 b.m. Desert Sun 120 – Fleetwood Fancy (Tau- **58** fan (USA) 119) [2006 62: p12.2g p9.5g⁶ Feb 10] angular mare: has a quick action: modest handicapper nowadays: stays 1¼m: acts on polytrack, soft and good to firm going: tried visored, in cheekpieces last 2 starts: sometimes slowly away. *J. J. Quinn*

CHART EXPRESS 2 b.c. (Feb 18) Robellino (USA) 127 – Emerald Angel (IRE) (In **–** The Wings 128) [2006 5m 7d Sep 29] strong, workmanlike colt: last in maidens. *P. Howling*

CHART OAK 3 b.g. Robellino (USA) 127 – Emerald Angel (IRE) (In The Wings 128) **62** [2006 p8.6g³ p9.5g⁵ p12.2g⁴ Dec 22] modest maiden: gelded and off 9 months after debut: has hung left. *P. Howling*

CHASING A DREAM 3 b.f. Pursuit of Love 124 – Preening 62 (Persian Bold 123) **72** [2006 78p: 8.3m 8g p8g³ p8.6g⁵ p9.5g² p8.6g² p9.5g² p9.5g² Dec 11] fair maiden: runner-up at Wolverhampton last 4 starts: stays 9.5f: acts on polytrack: hung left on reappearance: reportedly bled fifth outing. *B. W. Hills*

CHASING MEMORIES (IRE) 2 b.f. (Apr 12) Pursuit of Love 124 – Resemblance **67** (State Diplomacy (USA)) [2006 7d⁵ 7.5m³ f7g² f8g⁶ p7.1g⁴ f8g f7g³ p7.1g⁴ Dec 28] 3,800Y: sturdy filly: fourth foal: closely related to 2003 2-y-o 7f winner Annie Harvey (by Fleetwood): dam tailed off only start: fair maiden: barely stays 7.5f: acts on all-weather: hung right fifth start: blinkered (ran creditably) final outing. *B. Smart* —

CHASTITY (IRE) 2 b.f. (Mar 28) Dilshaan 119 – Fanny Bay (IRE) 76 (Key of Luck (USA) 126) [2006 6m³ Jul 18] €21,000Y: first foal: dam lightly-raced sister to smart sprinter Miss Emma: 16/1, beaten almost 20 lengths when third of 4 in minor event at Newcastle. *N. Tinkler* —

CHATAWAY 2 b.g. (Feb 29) Mujahid (USA) 125 – Copy-Cat 60 (Lion Cavern (USA) 117) [2006 6g³ 6m* 6d⁵ Sep 29] 35,000Y: sturdy gelding: second foal: half-brother to 3-y-o Gilt Linked: dam maiden half-sister to smart sprinter Averti: useful form: promising debut at Newbury (third behind Traffic Guard and Prime Defender), then won maiden at Goodwood in August by length from Brave Tin Soldier, flashing tail: 6/1, fifth of 28 to Caldra in sales race at Newmarket, again impressing with speed: will prove best at 5f/6f: sent to Hong Kong. *B. J. Meehan* 95

CHATEAU (IRE) 4 ch.g. Grand Lodge (USA) 125 – Miniver (IRE) (Mujtahid (USA) 118) [2006 6d⁶ 8.5f 6m⁶ 7g* 8m⁶ Jun 3] well held in 3-y-o bumpers: fair form on Flat: improved when winning seller at Redcar in May: should be suited by 1m/1¼m: sold 5,500 gns in October, joined M. Sowersby. *G. A. Swinbank* 69

CHATEAU NICOL 7 b.g. Distant Relative 128 – Glensara (Petoski 135) [2006 97: p6g p6g⁴ p7g p6g p6g 7s⁵ p7g p6g p8g Dec 19] well-made gelding: fairly useful handicapper: well held last 3 starts: best at 6f/7f: acts on all-weather, heavy and good to firm going: often visored/blinkered: tends to hang left. *B. G. Powell* 87 d

CHATER KNIGHT (IRE) 5 b.g. Night Shift (USA) – Neat Dish (CAN) 90 (Stalwart (USA)) [2006 71+: f12g⁴ f12g³ f12g⁴ f14s³ p12.2g* p12.2g⁴ p13.9g⁵ p12.2g⁵ p8.6g Jul 3] fair performer: left M. Hammond after fourth start: won apprentice seller at Wolverhampton in April: below form subsequently: stays 1½m: raced only on all-weather in Britain: in blinkers/cheekpieces last 5 outings. *R. A. Harris* 67 d

CHATILA (USA) 3 b.f. Red Ransom (USA) – Silvester Lady 108 (Pivotal 124) [2006 94: 10.1m Sep 13] quite attractive filly: fairly useful performer at 2 yrs: in need of race, never dangerous in listed race at Yarmouth only 3-y-o outing: should stay at least 1¼m: acts on good to firm going. *J. H. M. Gosden* —

CHATSHOW (USA) 5 br.g. Distant View (USA) 126 – Galanty Show 76 (Danehill (USA) 126) [2006 82: 5m⁶ 5f 5g 5.1s⁵ 5.7s 6g 5m 5.7m* 5.3g⁵ 6g² p6g³ p5.1m⁴ p6g⁶ Dec 18] leggy gelding: fair handicapper: left D. Carroll after fifth outing and G. Bridgwater after seventh: won apprentice event at Bath in September: best at 5f/6f: acts on all-weather, firm and soft going: tongue tied once: tough. *A. W. Carroll* 75

CHEAP N CHIC 3 ch.f. Primo Valentino (IRE) 116 – Amber Mill 96 (Doulab (USA) 115) [2006 79: 5g⁶ 6m May 6] lengthy filly: fair performer: stays 6.5f: raced only on poly-track and good or firmer going: blinkered once. *T. D. Easterby* 79

CHEAP STREET 2 ch.c. (Apr 26) Compton Place 125 – Anneliina 80 (Cadeaux Genereux 131) [2006 6m 5.7m³ 6f² 5m⁴ 6m* 6d* 6m 6g² Oct 13] 12,000Y: smallish, compact colt: third foal: half-brother to 3-y-o Piccostar: dam maiden who stayed 7f: fairly useful performer: generally progressive, winning maiden at Windsor and 20-runner sales race at Newmarket in August, and nursery at Newmarket in October: likely to stay 7f: yet to race on soft/heavy going, acts on any other: tough. *J. G. Portman* 90

CHECK TOU 2 b.f. (Apr 11) Inchinor 119 – Dramraire Mist 73 (Darshaan 133) [2006 5g⁴ p5.1g 7g Aug 18] €8,000Y: second foal: dam maiden who stayed 1¼m: modest form in maidens: sold 500 gns. *P. A. Blockley* 57

CHEEKY CHI (IRE) 5 b.m. Desert Style (IRE) 121 – Grey Patience (IRE) (Common Grounds 118) [2006 44: p12.2g p6g⁵ f6g Apr 7] small mare: poor performer: effective at 5f to 7f: acts on polytrack and soft ground: often wears headgear: tongue tied final start. *P. S. McEntee* 40

CHEENEY BASIN (IRE) 8 ch.g. King's Signet (USA) 110 – Gratclo 65 (Belfort (FR) 89) [2006 –: f6g f5g f8g f7g f6g f6g f6g Apr 4] fairly useful in his day: little form since 2002. *M. C. Chapman* —

CHEERY CAT (USA) 2 b. or br.g. (Apr 17) Catienus (USA) 115 – Olinka (USA) (Wolfhound (USA) 126) [2006 7m 7.2d³ 7g 7s p8.6m Oct 31] rather leggy, close-coupled gelding: modest maiden: should stay 1m: acts on polytrack and good to soft going: gelded after final start. *D. W. Barker* 63

CHEESE 'N BISCUITS 6 b.m. Spectrum (IRE) 126 – Bint Shihama (USA) 78 (Cadeaux Genereux 131) [2006 71, a87: p7g⁵ Jan 4] fair performer: not discredited in handicap 79

at Lingfield only 6-y-o start, very slowly away: effective at 7f/1m: acts on polytrack, heavy and good to firm going: usually wears cheekpieces: sold 32,000 gns in November. *M. Wigham*

CHELSEA CHELSEA 3 ch.c. Medicean 128 – Shoshone (Be My Chief (USA) 122) **69** [2006 66: p8g⁵ p10g Oct 11] good-bodied colt: fair maiden: should be suited by 1½m: acts on polytrack: tongue tied both starts at 3 yrs: sold 15,000 gns, sent to Belgium. *P. F. I. Cole*

CHELSEA ROSE (IRE) 4 ch.f. Desert King (IRE) 129 – Cinnamon Rose (USA) 96 **121** (Trempolino (USA) 135) [2006 119: 10d³ 8m² 10g² 9.9m⁴ 10m² 12.5m Sep 30] lengthy, good-bodied filly: very smart performer: best effort in 2006 when neck second to Alexander Goldrun in Pretty Polly Stakes at the Curragh third start: respectable efforts next 2 outings when fourth to Ouija Board in Nassau Stakes at Goodwood and 3 lengths second of 4 to Mustameet in Royal Whip Stakes at the Curragh: below form in Prix de Royallieu at Longchamp final start: effective at 1m to 1½m: acts on good to firm ground, not discredited on soft: none too consistent. *C. Collins, Ireland*

CHELSEY JAYNE (IRE) 3 b.f. Galileo (IRE) 134 – Lady Lahar 106 (Fraam 114) **–** [2006 57: 10m 16.1g Sep 27] lengthy filly: maiden: well held in handicaps in 2006: bred to be suited by further than 1m: acts on heavy and good to firm ground. *M. R. Channon*

CHENEY HILL 3 b.g. Compton Place 125 – Catriona 75 (Bustino 136) [2006 52p: 5f² **75** 5.1s* 5f³ 6g⁶ 5.2m 5g⁵ 6.1d Oct 4] useful-looking gelding: fair performer: won maiden at Bath in May: below form last 4 starts: likely to prove best at 5f: acts on firm and soft going: visored sixth outing: sold 7,000 gns. *H. Candy*

CHERIE'S DREAM 2 b.f. (Apr 15) Silver Wizard (USA) 117 – Last Dream (IRE) 80 **57 p** (Alzao (USA) 117) [2006 6.1g⁵ Sep 26] sixth foal: half-sister to 3 winners abroad, including useful 8.5f winner Last Cry (by Peintre Celebre): dam, Irish 1½m winner, half-sister to Grand Criterium winners Lost World and Fijar Tango, latter also high class up to 1½m: 11/1, 5¼ lengths fifth of 15 in maiden at Nottingham, running on: will do better at 1m+. *D. R. C. Elsworth*

CHERISHED NUMBER 7 b.g. King's Signet (USA) 110 – Pretty Average 40 (Sky- **65** liner 117) [2006 78: p12.2g⁶ p9.5g p9.5g⁴ p8.6g² p10g² p10g⁵ p8.6g p10g 12g Jul 13] workmanlike gelding: fair performer: claimed from I. Semple after fourth start: stays 1¼m: acts on all-weather and any turf going: usually wears headgear: sometimes slowly away: fair hurdler. *A. M. Hales*

CHEROKEE NATION 5 br.g. Emperor Jones (USA) 119 – Me Cherokee 48 (Persian **59** Bold 123) [2006 –, a84: p7g² p7.1g p6g⁶ p6g³ 7f p6g³ 6m⁶ 5m p6g Jul 11] tall **a70** gelding: fair performer on all-weather, modest on turf: best up to 7f: acts on polytrack, raced only on ground firmer than good on turf: tried in cheekpieces/blinkers, visored final outing: sold 4,000 gns. *P. W. D'Arcy*

CHEROKEE VISION 3 b.g. Primo Valentino (IRE) 116 – Me Cherokee 48 (Persian **62** Bold 123) [2006 59: p8g p8.6m p8.6g f8g Nov 20] modest maiden: probably stays 8.6f: acts on polytrack: well held in cheekpieces/blinkers last 2 starts. *Miss T. Spearing*

CHERRI FOSFATE 2 b.g. (Apr 29) Mujahid (USA) 125 – Compradore 82 (Mujtahid **80 d** (USA) 118) [2006 5g² p6g⁴* 6m 8m 6v⁵ p6m⁵ f6g² f6g² Dec 21] second foal: dam, 5f (at 2 yrs) to 7f winner, half-sister to smart performer up to 14.6f Mazuna: fairly useful form on debut, then won maiden at Kempton in May: off 4 months, well below form on return, including in cheekpieces/visor: stays 6f: acts on polytrack. *W. G. M. Turner*

CHERRY MIX (FR) 5 gr.h. Linamix (FR) 127 – Cherry Moon (USA) (Quiet **123** American (USA)) [2006 120: 12m 13.9s⁶ 12m⁶ 12g* 10.4d⁶ 12g³ 10m* Nov 5]
That Cherry Mix should be used as a pacemaker for Electrocutionist in the latest King George VI and Queen Elizabeth Stakes is some indication of how far his stock had fallen in less than two years. A half-length second to Bago in the Prix de l'Arc de Triomphe at Longchamp on his final start at three, when trained by Andre Fabre, Cherry Mix subsequently joined Godolphin, who must have had high hopes that the colt would continue to play a leading role in the top races at around a mile and a half. However, Cherry Mix proved unable to recapture his Arc form and his career hasn't developed as might have been expected. But it hasn't been all doom and gloom. Far from it. Cherry Mix might no longer be a major player on the main stage, but he has had his triumphs elsewhere, with two Group 1 victories in Italy and one in Germany.

Rheinland-Pokal der Sparkasse KolnBonn, Cologne—Cherry Mix, released from pacemaking, wins a good prize; Fracas pips Collier Hill (noseband) for second in a clean sweep for the visitors

Cherry Mix's first Group 1 win came in the Gran Premio del Jockey Club at Milan in October, 2005, the only occasion he reached a place in six outings that season. His performances in his two runs immediately before he was selected for pacemaking duties suggested that he could find it hard to fulfil even that role effectively in 2006. Cherry Mix was well held in the Dubai City of Gold at Nad Al Sheba on his reappearance, the third time in three starts, including on dirt, that he has failed to do himself justice at the track. It was a similar story when he was stepped up to a mile and three quarters in the Yorkshire Cup at York, beaten before stamina became an issue, having had plenty of use made of him. Although last of six behind Hurricane Run, Cherry Mix did run a more encouraging race in the King George, not headed until after two furlongs out, albeit having set just a steady pace. It was, therefore, no great surprise to see him return to winning ways on his next start, in the Rheinland-Pokal der Sparkasse KolnBonn at Cologne in August, especially as it was a weak race by Group 1 standards. The six home-trained runners had shown no better than smart form, and the three overseas challengers filled the first three places, Cherry Mix winning by four lengths from close-finishers Fracas and Collier Hill. Only one of Cherry Mix's three remaining races was over a mile and a half, that when attempting to repeat his victory in the Gran Premio del Jockey Club Italiano. He managed only third this time around but did run creditably, beaten a length and a half by Laverock. A mile and a quarter had looked to be on the short side for Cherry Mix when he came sixth of seven behind Notnowcato in the International at York on his previous start, but he showed himself effective at the trip, admittedly in a much less taxing race, on his final outing. Cherry Mix had nine rivals in the Premio Roma in November, but none had shown form in the latest season which quite matched that achieved by Cherry Mix at Cologne, his rivals including German challenger Soldier Hollow, who had won the two previous runnings. With Soldier Hollow and most of the others not at their best, Cherry Mix had things very much his own way, making the running and going clear in the final furlong to win by four lengths from Hattan.

Cherry Mix (FR) (gr.h. 2001)	Linamix (FR) (gr 1987)	Mendez (gr 1981)	Bellypha
			Miss Carina
		Lunadix (gr 1972)	Breton
			Lutine
	Cherry Moon (USA) (b 1995)	Quiet American (b 1986)	Fappiano
			Demure
		Datsdawayitis (b 1989)	Known Fact
			Baton Twirler

Cherry Mix is the first foal of Cherry Moon, a winner four times in North America at up to eight and a half furlongs, including in a listed handicap. Cherry

Moon's second foal, also by Linamix, is the three-year-old colt Moon Mix, a useful winner at a mile and a quarter and a mile and a half in France before being sold for €235,000 at the Arc sale. Their two-year-old sister Cherryxma was seventh in a newcomers race at Longchamp in the autumn. Incidentally, Moon Mix was also employed as a pacemaker in the latest season, for the Derby favourite Visindar in the Prix Greffulhe. Cherry Mix, a small, quite attractive individual, acts on heavy and good to firm going, and he usually wears a tongue tie. *Saeed bin Suroor*

CHERUB (GER) 6 b.g. Winged Love (IRE) 121 – Chalkidiki (GER) (Nebos (GER) 129) [2006 p10g Apr 15] useful performer at 2/3 yrs when trained by A. Schutz in Germany: unraced on Flat in 2004/5 (useful hurdler in meantime): tongue tied, well held in handicap on return: stays 11f: acts on heavy ground: tried blinkered: won over fences in October. *Jonjo O'Neill* —

CHERVIL 2 b.f. (Feb 7) Dansili 127 – Nashmeel (USA) 121 (Blushing Groom (FR) 131) [2006 5f³ p6g* 6m⁴ 6m Sep 19] close-coupled filly: closely related to very smart French/US 1m to 1¼m winner Light Jig (by Danehill) and half-sister to numerous winners, including smart French miler Battle Dore (by Sanglamore): dam French 1m winner who stayed 1¼m: fairly useful performer: won maiden at Lingfield in July: creditable fourth of 5 to Wid in minor event at Haydock (raced alone) next time: seemed ill-at-ease at Brighton final start: will stay 1m: sold 85,000 gns. *Mrs A. J. Perrett* — 80

CHESHIRE PRINCE 2 br.g. (Apr 2) Desert Prince (IRE) 130 – Bundle Up (USA) (Miner's Mark (USA) 120) [2006 5.1m 6m* 6m⁴ 6g 6m⁶ 6.1m⁵ 7m⁵ 7m⁴ 7.1d² 8.3d Oct 9] 5,000Y: close-coupled gelding: second foal: half-brother to French 11.5f/11½m winner Ut Majeur (by Brahms): dam, ran twice in USA, closely related to smart French 1987 2-y-o Balawaki: fair performer: won seller at Yarmouth in May: held form well after, short-head second in nursery at Warwick ninth start: should stay 1m: acts on good to firm and good to soft going. *W. M. Brisbourne* — 67

CHESS BOARD 3 b.c. Vettori (IRE) 119 – Cruinn A Bhord 107 (Inchinor 119) [2006 59p: 14.1m 11.9m* Jun 15] leggy colt: fair performer: best effort when winning handicap at Brighton in June: should stay 1¾m: acts on good to firm ground: sold 30,000 gns in July, joined P. Hobbs and fair winner over hurdles. *Sir Mark Prescott* — 67

CHEVELEY FLYER 3 ch.g. Forzando 122 – Cavern Breeze (Lion Cavern (USA) 117) [2006 54+: p7g⁶ p8g⁵ 8.1g 8m 7f 10g p16g⁶ Nov 28] modest maiden: below form after reappearance: stays 1m: acts on polytrack and heavy going: tried visored: winning juvenile hurdler. *J. Pearce* — 59 d

CHEVEME (IRE) 2 b.f. (May 15) King Charlemagne (USA) 120 – Warusha (GER) (Shareef Dancer (USA) 135) [2006 6g 6m 7.1m⁶ Aug 28] 12,000Y, 19,000 2-y-o: lengthy filly: fourth foal: half-sister to 3 winners, including fairly useful 2005 2-y-o 1m winner Economic (by Danehill Dancer): dam, German 7f to 9.5f winner, half-sister to dam of Nassau Stakes winner Zahrat Dubai: modest maiden: out of depth in Albany Stakes second start: will stay 1m. *B. W. Duke* — 57

CHEVIOT HEIGHTS 3 b.f. Intikhab (USA) 135 – Cheviot Hills (USA) (Gulch (USA)) [2006 72: 9.8g⁴ 11f* 9.8s 8.1g⁴ 12.1m p8.6g p8.6g p8.6g Nov 25] smallish filly: fair maiden: left Mrs A. Perrett after second outing and S. Williams after fifth one: stays 1¼m: acts on polytrack, good to firm and good to soft going: tried in cheekpieces. *J. S. Goldie* — 65

CHIA (IRE) 3 ch.f. Ashkalani (IRE) 128 – Motley (Rainbow Quest (USA) 134) [2006 69: p8g p8g⁵ p8g⁴ 8.3m 8.1d 8.3f⁵ 7f³ p8.6f p8g² p8.6g² p9.5g³ p8.6g² Dec 18] leggy filly: fair maiden handicapper: stays easy 9.5f: acts on all-weather and firm ground: tried visored/in cheekpieces: has raced freely. *D. Haydn Jones* — 72

CHIAVE 2 ch.c. (Mar 4) Medicean 128 – Fearless Revival 102 (Cozzene (USA)) [2006 7d Oct 28] close-coupled colt: brother to winner in Denmark and half-brother to several winners, notably very smart sprinter Pivotal (by Polar Falcon): dam 2-y-o 6f/7f winner who stayed 1¼m: 20/1, last in maiden at Newmarket: sold 4,500 gns, sent to Denmark. *M. A. Jarvis* —

CHICAMIA 2 b.f. (Mar 17) Kyllachy 129 – Inflation 68 (Primo Dominie 121) [2006 6m 6s Oct 16] 8,500Y: close-coupled filly: fourth foal: half-sister to 5-y-o Global Achiever: dam sprint maiden: well beaten in maidens. *M. Mullineaux* —

CHICHEROVA (IRE) 3 b.f. Soviet Star (USA) 128 – Ruby Rose 55 (Red Ransom (USA)) [2006 50: f8g⁴ f8g³ f8g² 8g f7g p12.6g⁵ Dec 28] poor maiden handicapper: left — 48

T. D. Barron before final start: stays 1m: acts on fibresand and good to firm going: sometimes slowly away. *W. M. Brisbourne*

CHICKADO (IRE) 5 b.m. Mujadil (USA) 119 – Arcevia (IRE) 85 (Archway (IRE) – 115) [2006 –, a61: p7.1g⁶ f7g p7.1g¹ f8g⁴ p6g f6g* f6g p7.1g⁶ f7g² f7g³ f7g f7g³ **a60** p7.1g f7g⁵ f7g Dec 21] angular mare: modest performer: won seller at Southwell in April: stays 1m: acts on all-weather, firm and good to soft going: usually wears cheekpieces: has hung/found little. *D. Haydn Jones*

CHICKEN SOUP 4 br.g. Dansili 127 – Radiancy (IRE) 77 (Mujtahid (USA) 118) **97** [2006 72: f8g⁴ f8g* p8.6g 7.6m² 8f² 7.6m* 8.1m 7m p7.1m p9.5g* Dec 30] leggy gelding: useful handicapper: won at Southwell (left D. Carroll after next start) in January, Chester in August and Wolverhampton (heavily backed, plenty of improvement when beating Kildare Sun impressively by 5 lengths) in December: stays 9.5f: acts on all-weather, firm and soft going: visored (below form) penultimate start. *T. J. Pitt*

CHIEF ARGENT (IRE) 3 b.g. Robellino (USA) 127 – Running Tycoon (IRE) 62 **66** (Last Tycoon 131) [2006 58: 10.1d⁴ May 16] compact gelding: fair maiden: not knocked about sole start at 3 yrs: gelded after: stays 1¼m: raced only on good to soft ground. *J. Howard Johnson*

CHIEF COMMANDER (FR) 3 br.g. Commands (AUS) – Neeran (USA) (Fast Play **101** (USA)) [2006 76: p7.1g* p7.1g² 7.5d² p8g⁶ 8.3g² 8g⁴ 8s³ 8g 7s 7m⁶ Sep 6] tall, good-topped gelding: useful performer: landed odds in maiden at Wolverhampton (hung left) in January: better form after on turf, notably in minor event at Windsor (1¼ lengths second to Upper Hand), Mehl-Mulhens-Rennen at Cologne (2 lengths equal-fourth to Royal Power) and listed event at Saint-Cloud (third to Indianski): well below form last 3 starts: stays 1m: acts on polytrack and soft going. *Jane Chapple-Hyam*

CHIEF EDITOR 2 b.g. (Apr 6) Tomba 119 – Princess Zara (Reprimand 122) [2006 **87** f5g* 5g³ 5d* 5s² May 26] 9,000Y: strong, well-made gelding: fourth foal: brother to 4-y-o Chief Scout: dam unraced: fairly useful form: won maiden at Southwell in April and minor event at York in May: improved again when 3 lengths second of 6 to Sonny Red in listed event at Goodwood final start (sweating/edgy, gelded after): will probably stay 6f/ 7f: raced on fibresand and good or softer going. *M. J. Wallace*

CHIEF EXEC 4 b.g. Zafonic (USA) 130 – Shot At Love (IRE) 79 (Last Tycoon 131) – [2006 71, a90: p7g* p7g³ p6g³ p7g p7g p7g⁵ p7g² p7g p6g 7.1f p7g p6g⁵ p6g p7g p10g³ **a91** Nov 28] leggy gelding: fairly useful handicapper on all-weather: pulled up only start on turf in 2006: won at Lingfield in January: best form around 7f: acts on polytrack and good to firm ground: tried visored: looked temperamental (soon off bridle) eleventh start. *C. A. Cyzer*

CHIEF OPERATOR (USA) 2 b.c. (Mar 29) Elusive Quality (USA) – Crimson Con- **85** quest (USA) 85 (Diesis 133) [2006 6g* p6g⁴ Oct 11] half-brother to several winners, including very smart 6f (at 2 yrs) to 1¼m winner Crimplene (by Lion Cavern) and smart 1¼m/1½m winner Dutch Gold (by Lahib): dam 2-y-o 6f winner who probably stayed 1¼m: fairly useful form: won 15-runner maiden at Newcastle in September, unextended by 2 lengths: odds on, only fourth to Resplendent Alpha in muddling minor event at Lingfield, racing freely: will stay 1m. *Saeed bin Suroor*

CHIEF SCOUT 4 br.g. Tomba 119 – Princess Zara (Reprimand 122) [2006 89: 7.2g **87** 8.1s⁵ 8g⁴ 9.2m* 9.8g⁶ 10g⁴ 9.2d 9.1v* 9.1v⁴ Oct 28] big, strong gelding: fairly useful handicapper: won at Hamilton in July and Ayr (by 5 lengths) in October: probably stays 1¼m: acts on heavy and good to firm ground: usually races prominently: has run well when sweating: joined Mrs S. Bradburne. *I. Semple*

CHIFF CHAFF 2 ch.f. (Feb 7) Mtoto 134 – Hen Harrier 94 (Polar Falcon (USA) 126) **59** [2006 7d p8g p8g⁶ Nov 5] sturdy filly: sixth foal: sister to fairly useful 1½m/1¾m winner King Eider and half-sister to 2 winners, including useful 1¼m winner Woodcracker (by Docksider): dam 7f (at 2 yrs) to 1¼m winner: modest form in maidens: will be suited by 1¼m/1½m. *M. L. W. Bell*

CHIFNEY RUSH (IRE) 3 b.f. Grand Lodge (USA) 125 – Don't Rush (USA) 93 – (Alleged (USA) 138) [2006 p10g 10.2g⁴ Jul 10] half-sister to 3 winners, including French 2003 2-y-o 6f winner Just For Chance (by Danehill) and 1m winner Reine de Neige (by Kris), both useful: dam, 1½m winner, half-sister to dam of Fantastic Light: well held in maidens at Kempton and Bath: will be suited by 1½m: sold twice, most recently for 35,000 gns in November. *B. W. Hills*

CHILDISH THOUGHTS 2 b.f. (Mar 14) River Falls 113 – Simmie's Special 75 – (Precocious 126) [2006 p7g p8g⁶ p7g p7.1g Dec 27] half-sister to 2001 2-y-o 5f winner

Sarrego (by Makbul) and 6-y-o Hiccups: dam 5f/6f winner: well held in maidens/nursery. *Mrs Norma Pook*

CHILLIN OUT 4 ch.c. Bahamian Bounty 116 – Steppin Out 63 (First Trump 118) **44** [2006 49: p6g p7.1g⁶ p7g p6g 6m Aug 10] poor maiden: seems to stay 7f: form only on polytrack: has raced freely. *W. Jarvis*

CHILLIPETALS 3 br.f. Averti (IRE) 117 – Island Mead 86 (Pharly (FR) 130) [2006 –: – p8.6g Jun 26] little sign of ability. *J. Balding*

CHILLY CRACKER 4 ch.f. Largesse 112 – Polar Storm (IRE) 76 (Law Society **52** (USA) 130) [2006 69: 6f⁵ 5d⁵ 5.7m Sep 25] quite good-topped filly: modest handicapper nowadays: effective at 5f to 7f: acts on all-weather and any turf going: usually races up with pace. *John Berry*

CHILSDOWN 3 b.g. Mozart (IRE) 131 – Goodwood Blizzard 97 (Inchinor 119) [2006 – 72: 7m 9.8m 6m 7m f8g Nov 14] strong, close-coupled gelding: fair maiden at 2 yrs: well held in 2006. *Ronald Thompson*

CHIMES AT MIDNIGHT (USA) 9 b.h. Danzig (USA) – Surely Georgie's (USA) **49 §** (Alleged (USA) 138) [2006 f14g 13.3m 12f⁴ 12m p16g p16g⁵ 14g 10s 16s Oct 8] well-made horse: one-time smart performer: missed 2005: just poor form in 2006 (first 6 starts in Britain): stays 14.6f: acts on firm and good to soft going: often blinkered: not one to rely on (often set very stiff tasks). *Luke Comer, Ireland*

CHINA CHERUB 3 ch.f. Inchinor 119 – Ashlinn (IRE) 86 (Ashkalani (IRE) 128) **78** [2006 6.1g³ 6f* 6m² 7m⁴ 6m* 6m⁵ 6d³ 7s Oct 10] lengthy filly: first foal: dam, 2-y-o 7f winner who stayed 1m, half-sister to smart French 1¼m performer Alloway: fair performer: won maiden at Lingfield in June and handicap at Salisbury in August: seems to be suited by 1m, but has plenty of speed: acts on firm and good to soft ground. *H. Candy*

CHINALEA (IRE) 4 b.g. Danetime (IRE) 121 – Raise-A-Secret (IRE) (Classic Secret **81** (USA) 91) [2006 84: 6g 6g³ 6g³ 6d 5m² 6f 5g³ 5m⁶ 5f² 6f 5m 5d⁶ 5.3d³ 5s³ 6g Oct 16] rather leggy gelding: fairly useful handicapper: best at 5f/6f: acts on firm and soft going: wears cheekpieces nowadays: tried tongue tied: effective held up or racing prominently: consistent. *C. G. Cox*

CHINA PEARL 3 ch.g. Benny The Dip (USA) 127 – Seek The Pearl 91 (Rainbow – Quest (USA) 134) [2006 74: 11.6d 14.1m Aug 27] useful-looking gelding: fair maiden at 2 yrs: last both outings in 2006 (reportedly finished lame final start): stays 1m. *John Berry*

CHINESE WHISPER (IRE) 2 b.c. (Mar 20) Montjeu (IRE) 137 – Majinskaya (FR) **104** 110 (Marignan (USA) 117) [2006 7g⁴ 8.5d* 7.5v² 8g³ Oct 15] 570,000Y: sixth foal: half-brother to several winners, including useful Irish 2002 2-y-o 6f winner Danaskaya (by Danehill) and 3-y-o Modeerooch: dam, French 1m/1¼m winner, half-sister to dam of very smart French sprinter Kistena: useful form: won maiden at Galway in September: second in listed race at Tipperary, then much improved when length third of 11 to Kirklees in Gran Criterium at Milan: will stay at least 1¼m: raced on good or softer going. *A. P. O'Brien, Ireland*

CHINGFORD (IRE) 2 ch.f. (Apr 5) Redback 116 – Beverley Macca 73 (Piccolo 121) **64** [2006 6m 5g⁶ 5m p5g² p5g p6g⁵ 6.5s Sep 22] 12,000Y: strong filly: first foal: dam, 5f (including at 2 yrs) winner, half-sister to very smart 5f to 1m winner Airwave: modest maiden: effective at 5f/6f: best form on polytrack. *D. W. P. Arbuthnot*

CHINGOLA 4 b.f. Atraf 116 – Sulaka (Owington 123) [2006 –: f7g Jan 24] good- – bodied filly: no form: dead. *R. M. Whitaker*

CHIN WAG (IRE) 2 b.g. (Feb 5) Iron Mask (USA) 117 – Sweet Chat (IRE) (Common **87** Grounds 118) [2006 6m* 6m³ 6g* 6m 6m⁵ Sep 16] 19,500F, €40,000Y: workmanlike gelding: second foal: dam showed little in 3 starts: fairly useful performer: won maiden at Leicester in June and minor event at Newmarket (by ½ length from Dickie Le Davoir) in July: disappointing in pattern company last 2 starts: likely to stay 7f: races prominently: sold 24,000 gns, gelded, joined K. Burke. *E. S. McMahon*

CHIP LEADER 2 ch.g. (Mar 14) Kyllachy 129 – Scundes (IRE) (Barathea (IRE) 127) **68 d** [2006 5g p5g⁶ 5.1d⁵ 5m 7m 6d p5g Oct 5] sturdy, workmanlike gelding: fair maiden: well below form after third start: sold 3,000 gns. *R. Hannon*

CHIP N PIN 2 b.f. (Mar 2) Erhaab (USA) 127 – Vallauris 94 (Faustus (USA) 118) [2006 – 7.5f⁵ Jun 27] 3,500Y: half-sister to several winners, including fairly useful 1m to 1¼m winner Whitsbury Cross (by Cape Cross) and 7f/1m winner Mystic Ridge (by Mystiko): dam 1¼m winner: needed experience in maiden at Beverley. *T. D. Easterby*

CHIRACAHUA (IRE) 4 ch.g. Desert Prince (IRE) 130 – Irish Celebrity (USA) (Irish   **41**
River (FR) 131) [2006 f7g⁴ p8.6g 9m⁵ f6g⁶ 8d 8.5f⁴ 8v Sep 21] strong gelding: poor
maiden: left B. Smart after fourth start: stays 7f: acts on fibresand: blinkered fourth
outing. *C. Hennessy, Ireland*

CHISELLED (IRE) 4 b.g. Rossini (USA) 118 – Con Dancer (Shareef Dancer (USA)   **52**
135) [2006 66: 6d p5.1g³ 5g⁵ May 22] deep-girthed gelding: modest maiden nowadays: likely to prove best at 5f: acts on good to firm going: tongue tied final 2-y-o start.
K. R. Burke

CHISOM 3 b.g. Averti (IRE) 117 – Cinder Hills 72 (Deploy 131) [2006 63: f5g f8g   **–**
Apr 27] compact gelding: maiden: little form since debut at 2 yrs. *M. W. Easterby*

CHIVALROUS (IRE) 2 b.c. (Mar 25) Danehill (USA) 126 – Aspiration (IRE) 73   **97**
(Sadler's Wells (USA) 132) [2006 6g⁴ 6.3m³ 7d² 6m² 7m³ 7v* Sep 21] 300,000Y: fourth
foal: half-brother to 3 winners, including French 1m/9f winner Open Way (by Giant's
Causeway) and Irish 1m winner Great Hope (by Halling), both fairly useful: dam, Irish
1¼m winner, sister to Irish Derby runner-up Sholokhov: useful performer: won maiden
at Listowel in September: placed previous 4 starts, including ½-length third to Regional
Counsel in Anglesey Stakes and 3 lengths second to Rabatash in Round Tower Stakes,
both at the Curragh: will stay 1m: yet to race on firm going, acts on any other.
A. P. O'Brien, Ireland

CH.JIMES (IRE) 2 b.g. (Mar 11) Fath (USA) 116 – Radiance (IRE) 54 (Thatching 131)   **94 d**
[2006 5.1s* 5d² 6g³ 6m 6g 5m⁵ 6g 5s⁴ 7s Oct 21] €16,000F, 18,000Y: close-coupled
gelding: has a round action: seventh foal: closely related to 7f/1¼m winner Freecom Net
(by Zieten) and half-brother to fairly useful Irish 2001 2-y-o 5f/7f winner Barriance (by
Charnwood Forest): dam lightly-raced half-sister to 7-y-o Bustan: fairly useful performer
at best: won maiden at Nottingham in April: good efforts next 2 starts, placed in listed
race at the Curragh (second to Drayton) and minor event at Ascot: below form after:
best at 5f/6f on good or softer ground: blinkered once: gelded after final start. *K. R. Burke*

CHOCOLATE BOY (IRE) 7 b.g. Dolphin Street (FR) 125 – Kawther (Tap On Wood   **50**
130) [2006 70, a63: p16.5g⁶ p16g⁵ p12g p10g p10g 11.9m² p12g⁵ 11.6m 11.9f³ Aug 9]   **a55**
modest performer: stays easy 2m: acts on polytrack and firm going: tried in cheekpieces,
usually blinkered. *G. L. Moore*

CHOCOLATE CARAMEL (USA) 4 b.g. Storm Creek (USA) – Sandhill (BRZ)   **96**
(Baynoun 128) [2006 92: 12s⁵ p12g* 14m Jun 23] tall gelding: useful handicapper: best
effort when winning at Lingfield in June by ¾ length from Dower House: well below
form at Goodwood final start: stays 1¾m (possibly not 2m): acts on polytrack and soft
ground, probably on good to firm. *Mrs A. J. Perrett*

CHOOKIE HAMILTON 2 ch.g. (Mar 19) Compton Place 125 – Lady of Windsor   **73**
(IRE) 73§ (Woods of Windsor (USA)) [2006 7.2d 7.2m⁴ 8.3m³ 8.1v 9s⁴ 7.1d³ p8.6g*
f8g* p8.6g² Dec 23] second foal: half-brother to 3-y-o Chookie Windsor: dam ungenuine
7f/1m winner: fair performer: won claimer at Wolverhampton in November and 4-runner
nursery at Southwell in December: barely stays 9f: acts on all-weather, soft and good to
firm ground. *I. Semple*

CHOOKIE HEITON (IRE) 8 br.g. Fumo di Londra (IRE) 108 – Royal Wolff (Prince   **108**
Tenderfoot (USA) 126) [2006 114: 6m⁴ 5g 5m⁶ 6m Jun 24] strong, lengthy gelding:
useful performer nowadays: best run in 2006 when sixth to Handsome Cross in valuable
handicap at Musselburgh (said to have lost both front shoes): soon behind in Wokingham
final start (suffered slight tendon injury): best at 5f/6f: acts on firm and good to soft going,
below form on soft: has had joints bandaged. *I. Semple*

CHOOKIE WINDSOR 3 b.g. Lake Coniston (IRE) 131 – Lady of Windsor (IRE) 73§   **61**
(Woods of Windsor (USA)) [2006 56: 9p5.5g 7fg f8g² p8.6g³ f10g p12g 10m 10.2f 8m⁶
8f⁵ f12g⁴ 10m⁴ 12.1m p10g 10s Oct 2] modest performer: left I. Semple, won claimer at
Lingfield in February: left M. Saunders after twelfth start: stays easy 1¼m: acts on all-
weather and firm ground: tried in cheekpieces, visored last 2 starts. *R. M. Stronge*

CHOOSY (IRE) 3 b.f. Kalanisi (IRE) 132 – Hawksbill Special (IRE) (Taufan (USA)   **88**
119) [2006 93: p8g Apr 1] close-coupled filly: fairly useful performer: not discredited
when seventh in listed race at Kempton only 3-y-o outing: stays 1m: acts on polytrack
and soft going: sold 26,000 gns in November. *R. Hannon*

CHORD 2 ch.g. (Feb 1) Pivotal 124 – Choirgirl 106 (Unfuwain (USA) 131) [2006 7m   **61**
8.2s Oct 18] good-topped, angular gelding: second foal: dam, 2-y-o 7f winner who stayed
1¼m, half-sister to very smart 1m/1¼m winner Chorister: behind in maidens at Newmarket and Nottingham (favourite): subsequently gelded. *Sir Michael Stoute*

CHOREOGRAPHIC (IRE) 4 b.g. Komaite (USA) – Lambast 70 (Relkino 131) **50**
[2006 52: 5d 7.1d² 5s 7m³ 8d⁵ Oct 8] workmanlike gelding: modest maiden: barely stays
1m: acts on firm and soft going, well held on fibresand: tried blinkered/in cheekpieces.
R. A. Fahey

CHOREOGRAPHY 3 ch.g. Medicean 128 – Stark Ballet (USA) (Nureyev (USA) **81**
131) [2006 56: 7v³ 7m⁵ 9.8m 7.1d⁴ 6d⁵ 7.1m* 6g* 8m⁴ Aug 31] sturdy gelding: fairly
useful performer: won handicaps at Musselburgh and Hamilton in August: likely to prove
best at 6f/7f: acts on good to firm and good to soft going. *D. Nicholls*

CHORISTAR 5 ch.g. Inchinor 119 – Star Tulip 99 (Night Shift (USA)) [2006 64: **66**
p9.5g⁶ p8.6g³ f8g⁵ p8.6g 8.3f 10m³ 9.9g* 10.9m² 9.9m⁴ Sep 19] fair handicapper: won
maiden apprentice event at Beverley in August: stays 11f: acts on polytrack and firm
going. *J. Mackie*

CHORUS BEAUTY 5 b.m. Royal Applause 124 – Happy Lady (FR) 72 (Cadeaux **–**
Genereux 131) [2006 –: p8g p6g p6g⁶ p7.1g f7g⁶ 8g⁵ 5.7f Jun 17] fair winner in 2004:
little form since. *N. I. M. Rossiter*

CHOYSIA 3 b.f. Pivotal 124 – Bonica 56 (Rousillon (USA) 133) [2006 92: 5g 6m⁶ 7s⁵ **77 §**
6g⁵ 6m⁵ 5f⁴ 6m 8d 7g 6s³ Oct 24] leggy, workmanlike filly: fair performer nowadays:
stays 6f: acts on firm and soft going: edgy sort: often slowly away: one to treat with
caution. *D. W. Barker*

CHRIS CORSA 3 b.g. Mark of Esteem (IRE) 137 – Risque Lady 109 (Kenmare (FR) **–**
125) [2006 79: 8d⁶ 8m 8g Aug 19] close-coupled gelding: fair performer at 2 yrs: well
held in handicaps in 2006: should stay 1m: acts on good to soft going. *M. L. W. Bell*

CHRISJEN 4 ch.f. Wolfhound (USA) 126 – Chadwick's Ginger (Crofthall 110) [2006 **–**
11f⁵ 8d⁵ 8g 9.9g 10m Sep 11] neat filly: second foal: dam, maiden on Flat, unreliable
winning hurdler/chaser: flattered on Flat debut: no form after. *M. W. Easterby*

CHRISTA BEE 3 b.f. Groom Dancer (USA) 128 – Beleza (IRE) (Revoque (IRE) 122) **77 §**
[2006 79: 5.1f 6.1s⁶ 5f 5f 5f⁵ Jul 19] leggy, good-topped filly: fair performer: well below
form after reappearance: bred to stay beyond 6f: acts on fibresand and firm going: tried in
cheekpeices (virtually refused to race)/blinkered: also looked reluctant fourth outing: one
to treat with caution. *A. Berry*

CHRISTALINI 2 b.g. (Apr 27) Bertolini (USA) 125 – Jay Tee (IRE) (Charnwood **82**
Forest (IRE) 125) [2006 6m⁵ 7g⁶ 7d⁴ 8g Oct 17] close-coupled gelding: first foal: dam
unraced: fairly useful maiden: 2 lengths fourth to Tembanee in minor event at Salisbury:
stays 7f. *J. C. Fox*

CHRISTIAN BENDIX 4 ch.g. Presidium 124 – Very Good (Noalto 120) [2006 54: **–**
f6g³ f6g⁵ f6g⁶ f6g* f6g² f6g* f6g f6g 6m f7g⁴ 6.1m f7g f7g f6g⁴ f6g³ p6g f6g Dec 29] **a58**
strong gelding: modest performer: won banded race in January and handicap in February,
both at Southwell: probably stays 7f: acts on all-weather: tried in cheekpieces. *P. Howling*

CHRISTMAS PLAYER (USA) 3 b. or br.f. Theatrical 128 – Christmas Gift (USA) **77**
(Green Desert (USA) 127) [2006 64: p10g⁶ p9.5g* p8.6g⁶ a8.5f⁵ Dec 27] unfurnished
filly: fair performer: best effort when winning maiden at Wolverhampton in March:
reportedly finished lame next time, then left J. Gosden and off 7½ months: should stay
1¼m: acts on polytrack. *A. J. Sciametta, jnr, USA*

CHRISTMAS TART (IRE) 2 b.f. (Mar 25) Danetime (IRE) 121 – Missish (Mum- **74**
my's Pet 125) [2006 5s⁴ 5.2d⁴ 5v* 5m 6f p5.1g³ 6m 6s Oct 6] smallish, quite attractive
filly: has a quick action: half-sister to several winners, including smart 5f to 7f (including
at 2 yrs) winner Andreyev (by Presidium): dam unraced: fair performer: won maiden at
Sandown in May: seemingly best run when seventh of 15 to Gilded in Queen Mary Stakes
at Royal Ascot next time: best at 5f: acts on heavy and good to firm going: in cheekpieces/
visor last 2 starts: sent to France. *V. Smith*

CHRISTMAS TRUCE (IRE) 7 b.g. Brief Truce (USA) 126 – Superflash (Superla- **71**
tive 118) [2006 p12g p16.5g⁶ p8g² p7g⁵ p9.5g p9.5g⁵ p8g* p7g p8g p10g⁶ 8m* 10m² **a66**
8.3g⁶ 9.7f p10g 10m³ 9g 8m² 8.1m 9.7m⁶ 8d 8d p10g p10g² p10g⁵ Dec 30] good-topped
gelding: fair performer: won seller at Lingfield in April and handicap at Brighton in May:
effective at 1m to 13f: acts on all-weather, heavy and good to firm going: usually wears
headgear: has looked none too keen: inconsistent. *Ms J. S. Doyle*

CHRONOMATIC 3 gr.g. Mister Baileys 123 – Sky Red 75 (Night Shift (USA)) [2006 **74**
80: 9s² 7g⁵ 10v² p12g* 12.1m 16g 13.9s⁶ 12g³ Oct 13] tall, leggy gelding: fair performer:
won maiden at Lingfield in June: stays 1½m: acts on polytrack, heavy and good to firm
going: sold 28,000 gns. *M. H. Tompkins*

CHRYSANDER 4 b.g. Cadeaux Genereux 131 – Jumairah Sun (IRE) 98 (Scenic 128) **105**
[2006 112: 8s 9.8d³ 8s 8.5m 8.1m Jul 8] big, close-coupled gelding: useful performer:
easily best efforts in 2006 when 4 lengths third to Profit's Reality in minor event at Ripon
and seventh to Nayyir in Diomed Stakes at Epsom (visored), second/fourth outings:
stays 1¼m: acts on heavy and good to firm going: sold 65,000 gns in July, and gelded.
M. R. Channon

CHUNKY BELL 3 b.c. Easycall 115 – Lady Susan (Petong 126) [2006 46: 5m⁶ 5m **45**
Jun 5] lengthy, heavy-topped colt: poor maiden: raced only at 5f/6f. *P. T. Midgley*

CHUNKY'S CHOICE (IRE) 2 b.g. (Apr 12) Key of Luck (USA) 126 – Indian Imp **74**
(Indian Ridge 123) [2006 8g 7d Oct 28] 37,000F, 115,000Y: close-coupled gelding: fifth
foal: half-brother to 2 winners, including useful 8.5f to 1½m winner Telemachus (by
Bishop of Cashel): dam unraced half-sister to very smart 1½m/1¾m performer Mons: fair
form when mid-field in maidens at Newmarket: gelded after: will be suited by 1¼m/
1½m. *J. Noseda*

CHURCHTOWN 2 b.g. (Mar 3) Kyllachy 129 – Manhattan Diamond 54 (Primo **–**
Dominie 121) [2006 p6g p8.6g p6g Dec 8] well held in maidens at Wolverhampton.
K. R. Burke

CIAO (IRE) 3 b.f. Imperial Ballet (IRE) 110 – White Squall (Caerleon (USA) 132) **85**
[2006 75: 6d² 8.5s* 11v⁶ 8m 9m 7m Aug 3] smallish, quite attractive filly: first foal: dam,
unraced, out of sister to smart French performer up to 13.5f Whitehaven: fairly useful
performer: won maiden at Killarney in May: well held in listed handicap at Royal Ascot
fourth start: stays 11f: acts on heavy going. *John Joseph Murphy, Ireland*

CICADA (IRE) 2 b.g. (Jan 20) Tendulkar (USA) 114 – Artic Ocean (IRE) (Spectrum **–**
(IRE) 126) [2006 6v 7m Jun 20] tailed off in maidens. *J. R. Weymes*

CICCONE 3 ch.f. Singspiel (IRE) 133 – Untold Riches (USA) 94 (Red Ransom (USA)) **67**
[2006 59: 8.2m⁶ 8.3m 7m³ 7f⁴ 7m⁶ p7g⁵ p8g p12g⁵ p12g² p10g⁴ p10g⁶ p10g* Dec 30]
strong filly: fair performer: claimed from W. Jarvis after sixth start: won seller at
Lingfield in December: probably stays easy 1½m: acts on polytrack and firm going: has
worn cheekpieces, including for win. *G. L. Moore*

CIMYLA (IRE) 5 b.g. Lomitas 129 – Coyaima (GER) 100 (Night Shift (USA)) [2006 **113**
113+: p8.6g* a10g⁴ p10g⁵ p8.6m* Nov 21] good-topped gelding: smart performer:
reportedly fractured a pastern after final 3-y-o start: won minor events at Wolverhampton
in January (by short head from Hard To Explain) and November (beat Speedy Sam by 4
lengths on first start for 8 months): also ran well when fifth to Sri Diamond in Winter
Derby at Lingfield: stays 1¼m: acts on polytrack, soft and good to firm going: hung left,
including final start: tried to bite a rival on 4-y-o reappearance: waited with. *C. F. Wall*

CINAMAN (IRE) 2 b.g. (Apr 29) Key of Luck (USA) 126 – Madame Nureyev (USA) **–**
(Nureyev (USA) 131) [2006 8.1g Sep 23] small gelding: behind in maiden at Haydock:
gelded after. *R. F. Fisher*

CINDER MAID 4 b.f. Piccolo 121 – Bella Helena (Balidar 133) [2006 –: f8g Jan 31] **–**
very lightly raced and no form. *J. G. Portman*

CINDERS SPARK 3 b.f. Groom Dancer (USA) 128 – Oriel Girl 65 (Beveled (USA)) **–**
[2006 8.2v p7g Dec 4] 1,500Y: compact filly: third foal: half-sister to 4-y-o Beverley
Beau: dam 5f (at 2 yrs) to 7f winner: well held in maiden at Nottingham and claimer at
Lingfield. *G. L. Moore*

CINDERTRACK 3 b.g. Singspiel (IRE) 133 – Beading 82 (Polish Precedent (USA) **83**
131) [2006 74: f8g³ p8g⁵ 7.1m³ 7f* 7m* 7.1m³ 7f⁵ p7g⁶ p7g Sep 29] fairly useful on **a75**
turf, fair on all-weather: won handicaps at Brighton (by 5 lengths) and Catterick in July:
effective at 7f, should stay 1¼m: acts on all-weather and firm going: sold 14,000 gns.
J. A. Osborne

CINEMATIC (IRE) 3 b.g. Bahhare (USA) 122 – Eastern Star (IRE) (Sri Pekan (USA) **77**
117) [2006 76: 8.2d 7f⁵ 6d p8g⁴ Aug 13] tall, leggy gelding, unfurnished at 2 yrs: fair
performer: at least respectable efforts in handicaps in 2006, leaving M. Tompkins after
third start: stays 1m: acts on polytrack, firm and good to soft ground: usually slowly
away: gelded after final outing. *J. R. Boyle*

CINQUANTE CINQ (IRE) 2 b.f. (Mar 27) Danehill (USA) 126 – Castilian Queen **69 p**
(USA) 82 (Diesis 133) [2006 6m⁶ Sep 16] leggy, attractive filly: seventh foal: sister to
fairly useful 7f winner Three Secrets and half-sister to 2 winners, notably very smart 5f
winner (including at 2 yrs) Carmine Lake (by Royal Academy): dam, 2-y-o 6f winner, out

of Breeders' Cup Mile winner Royal Heroine: 20/1, 6¼ lengths sixth of 16 to Thunder Storm Cat in maiden at Newbury, prominent going freely: will do better. *B. J. Meehan*

CIRCLE OF LOVE 2 b.f. (Mar 29) Sakhee (USA) 136 – Claxon 110 (Caerleon (USA) 132) [2006 7m³ 8m³ Sep 19] leggy, close-coupled filly: third foal: half-sister to useful 7f (at 2 yrs) and 11.5f winner Cassydora (by Darshaan): dam, 1m (including at 2 yrs) and 1¼m (including Premio Lydia Tesio) winner, half-sister to smart 1¼m winner Bull Run: fairly useful form when third in maidens at Newbury and Newmarket (2½ lengths behind Light Shift): refused to enter stalls in between: will stay 1¼m/1½m. *J. L. Dunlop* **86**

CIRCLE OF TRUTH 2 b.g. (Mar 23) Makbul 104 – Jade's Girl (Emarati (USA) 74) [2006 p5g 5.1d⁶ p5g² p5.1g³ 5f⁵ Jun 12] modest maiden: placed in claimers: raced at 5f. *W. G. M. Turner* **58**

CIRCUIT DANCER (IRE) 6 b.g. Mujadil (USA) 119 – Trysinger (IRE) (Try My Best (USA) 130) [2006 95d: f7g 6m* p6g* 6d 6f² 6m³ 6f 6g² 6f⁴ 5g² 5.1m⁶ 5d 5.1f* Sep 23] tall gelding: fairly useful handicapper: won at Catterick (apprentices) in April, Kempton (awarded race) in May and Chester in September: effective at 5f to easy 7f: acts on polytrack, firm and soft going: tried cheekpieces at 5 yrs: has been slowly away. *D. Nicholls* **94**

CIRCUMSPECT (IRE) 4 b.g. Spectrum (IRE) 126 – Newala 61 (Royal Academy (USA) 130) [2006 –: 10s f8g³ Oct 12] strong, lengthy gelding: maiden: no form since 2 yrs: tried tongue tied. *P. C. Haslam* **–**

CIRCUS DANCE 9 b.h. Sadler's Wells (USA) 132 – Dance By Night 84 (Northfields (USA)) [2006 p10g Nov 11] well-made horse: smart performer at best, third to Holding Court in Prix du Jockey Club at Chantilly in 2000 when trained by A. Fabre in France: first outing since 2001, tailed off in handicap at Kempton in November: stays 1½m: best on going softer than good: tried blinkered/tongue tied. *Luke Comer, Ireland* **–**

CIRCUS POLKA (USA) 2 br.c. (Feb 2) Stravinsky (USA) 133 – Far Wiser (USA) (Private Terms (USA)) [2006 p7g* f8g* Dec 27] $40,000F, 27,000Y: first foal: dam unraced half-sister to US Grade 3 9.5f winner Secret River: fairly useful form: successful both starts, namely minor event at Kempton (beat Tokyo Jo by 2½ lengths) and 4-runner nursery at Southwell (still green and again took strong hold, beat Eau Good readily by 2½ lengths despite wandering): stays 1m: tongue tied: capable of better still. *P. F. I. Cole* **82 p**

CITA VERDA (FR) 8 b.m. Take Risks (FR) 116 – Mossita (FR) (Tip Moss (FR)) [2006 8v⁴ Mar 31] heavy-bodied mare: fair handicapper at 5 yrs: well held only outing on Flat since. *P. Monteith* **–**

CITELLE (IRE) 3 ch.f. City On A Hill (USA) 114 – La Rochelle (IRE) 80 (Salse (USA) 128) [2006 60: 10.9g⁵ 11.6m 10m⁴ f11g³ 11.7f⁴ f12g⁶ Jul 7] stocky filly: fair performer: stays 11f: acts on fibresand and good to firm going: tongue tied: sold £700 in October. *Mrs P. N. Dutfield* **65**

CITHOGUE (IRE) 3 ch.f. Machiavellian (USA) 123 – Another Dancer (FR) 114 (Groom Dancer (USA) 128) [2006 –p: 10.2g⁵ Oct 17] well held in maidens at Lingfield and Bath 12 months apart. *J. R. Fanshawe* **–**

CITOYEN (IRE) 2 ch.g. (Mar 23) City On A Hill (USA) 114 – La Doyenne (IRE) 65 (Masterclass (USA) 116) [2006 5s 5d 5f 7f⁵ Jun 13] lengthy gelding: no form. *Ronald Thompson* **–**

CITRUS CHIEF (USA) 2 b.c. (Jan 31) Lemon Drop Kid (USA) 131 – Tricky Indy (USA) (A P Indy (USA) 131) [2006 8.1m 7.6f p8.6g f8g⁶ Nov 28] modest maiden: soon off bridle in nursery final outing. *R. A. Harris* **61**

CITY AFFAIR 5 b.g. Inchinor 119 – Aldevonie 75 (Green Desert (USA) 127) [2006 p10g p16g Oct 23] modest maiden at best: unraced on Flat in 2005: upped in trip and well held in 2006: often wears blinkers/cheekpieces. *J. G. M. O'Shea* **–**

CITY BHOY 2 b.c. (Feb 17) Ishiguru (USA) 114 – Magic Moment 63 (Magic Ring (IRE) 115) [2006 5.3f⁶ 7f 5m⁵ Jul 29] modest maiden: best effort at 5f: sold 2,500 gns, sent to Spain. *T. G. Dascombe* **55**

CITY FOR CONQUEST (IRE) 3 b.f. City On A Hill (USA) 114 – Northern Life (IRE) (Distinctly North (USA) 115) [2006 82: p5.1g* 5g 5.2m 5.1f⁵ 5g⁵ 5m⁴ 5f⁴ 5m 5g⁵ 5d³ p5.1g* p5.1g⁴ p6g p5.1g⁵ p5g³ p5.1s² p5g p6g Dec 28] compact filly: fair performer: won claimer in March and handicap in September, both at Wolverhampton: left K. Burke after twelfth outing: probably best at 5f: acts on polytrack and firm going: usually visored/blinkered: quirky (tends to find little). *T. J. Pitt* **77**

CITY MINX 4 b.f. Almaty (IRE) 113§ – Marie's Crusader (IRE) (Last Tycoon 131) – [2006 p8.6g 8.3g⁶ 10.1m f8g⁵ f11g⁵ f11g f11g Dec 29] unfurnished filly: fifth foal: dam unraced half-sister to smart 1m to 1½m performer Noble Patriarch: poor maiden: claimed from D. Morris £3,000 after fourth start. *S. R. Bowring*

CITY MISS 3 br.f. Rock City 120 – Miss Pigalle 55 (Good Times (ITY)) [2006 5s 6d – 7m Sep 16] 800Y: first foal: dam 7f winner: well held in maidens: withdrawn (unruly at start) once. *Miss L. A. Perratt*

CITY OF MANCHESTER (IRE) 4 b.g. Desert Style (IRE) 121 – Nomadic Dancer – (IRE) 52 (Nabeel Dancer (USA) 120) [2006 f11g³ f11g p8.6g f12g Jan 31] well held in bumper: no form in maidens/banded race: left D. Nicholls, successful over hurdles in April (for P. Haslam) and November (for B. Leavy, joined M. Allen 8,000 gns). *D. Nicholls*

CITY OF TRIBES (IRE) 2 b.c. (Feb 23) Invincible Spirit (IRE) 121 – Yellow Trum- **94** pet 75 (Petong 126) [2006 5f* 5m 5g⁴ 6g⁵ Sep 17] 22,000F, 19,000Y, 110,000 2-y-o: small, quite attractive colt: second foal: half-brother to 4-y-o Canary Island: dam, 2-y-o 5f winner, sister to sprinter Petula and half-sister to 7f performer Naahy, both useful: fairly useful performer: won maiden at Tipperary (beat Rabatash and Miss Beatrix) in June: well held in Norfolk Stakes at Royal Ascot next start, but ran creditably last 2, in listed races at Tipperary and the Curragh: may prove best at 5f. *G. M. Lyons, Ireland*

CITY OF TROY 3 ch.c. Grand Lodge (USA) 125 – Arazena (USA) (Woodman (USA) **108** 126) [2006 105p: 8g 10.3d⁴ 8m³ Aug 5] big, strong, good sort: has a quick action: good walker: useful performer: disappointed first 2 starts on return (in Craven Stakes at New-market and Dee Stakes at Chester): tongue tied, best effort when length third to Prince of Light in listed event at Goodwood final start, never nearer after troubled passage: should stay 1¼m: acts on good to firm going: looks to have questionable attitude (has swished tail preliminaries/looked reluctant at stall), carrying head awkwardly at Goodwood: sent to Hong Kong. *Sir Michael Stoute*

CITY WELL 3 b.g. Sadler's Wells (USA) 132 – City Dance (USA) (Seattle Slew **74** (USA)) [2006 p12g³ p12.2g* Mar 3] 55,000Y: closely related to several winners, includ-ing useful 7f winner Clematis and smart Irish 5f and (at 2 yrs) 6f winner Black Rock Desert (both by Danzig), and half-brother to 2 winners: dam, 8.5f minor stakes winner in USA, sister to US Grade 1 9f/1¼m winner Slew City Slew: fair form: confirmed debut promise when winning maiden at Wolverhampton (by 5 lengths) in March, but not seen out again: subsequently gelded. *M. Johnston*

CLAPPERS (IRE) 2 b.f. (Feb 17) Royal Applause 124 – Cashmere 86 (Barathea (IRE) – 127) [2006 6.1m 5g Aug 17] quite good-topped filly: first foal: dam, won around 7f, half-sister to Irish 1000 Guineas winner Classic Park, herself dam of Derby runner-up Walk In The Park: no show in maidens: sold 1,100 gns, sent to Israel. *T. D. Easterby*

CLARA ALLEN (IRE) 8 b.m. Accordion – Deeco Valley (IRE) (Satco (FR) 114) **106** [2006 90: 11m* 12m⁶ 14m³ 18d⁶ 16s³ 16d³ Nov 5] useful performer: improved in 2006, winning handicap at Killarney in July: good efforts last 4 starts, including when sixth to Sergeant Cecil in Doncaster Cup at York, close third to Iktitaf in Irish Cesarewitch at the Curragh and third to Lounaos in handicap at Leopardstown: stays 2¼m: acts on firm and soft going. *J. E. Kiely, Ireland*

CLARE HILLS (IRE) 3 b.f. Orpen (USA) 116 – Morale (Bluebird (USA) 125) [2006 **89** 94: p5g 6m⁵ 5m⁵ 5d⁴ 5g Sep 17] leggy filly: fairly useful performer: creditable efforts in listed races third/fourth starts: best at 5f: acts on good to firm and good to soft ground, probably on polytrack: in cheekpieces last 4 outings: tends to hang right: sold 65,000 gns. *K. R. Burke*

CLARET AND AMBER 4 b.g. Forzando 122 – Artistic Licence (High Top 131) **84** [2006 91: p7.1g⁶ p8.6g p8g⁵ p8.6g 8m² 8.5f* p8.6g⁶ 8.5s⁶ 7.1m⁶ Aug 17] sturdy gelding: has a quick action: fairly useful handicapper: won at Beverley in July: should stay easy 1¼m: acts on polytrack, firm and soft going (unraced on heavy) tends to take time to warm to task: effective with or without blinkers. *R. A. Fahey*

CLARRICIEN (IRE) 2 br.g. (Feb 21) Key of Luck (USA) 126 – Tango Two Thousand **80** (IRE) 84 (Sri Pekan (USA) 117) [2006 8.1m 8.3g* 10d Oct 28] €24,000F, 27,000Y: compact gelding: second foal: half-brother to Irish 1¼m and 13f winner Tango Foxtrot (by Foxhound): dam 1m winner: fairly useful form: still green when winning maiden at Hamilton (beat Ashn Thunder 3 lengths) in September: eased as if amiss in listed race at Newmarket: should stay 1¼m/1½m: gelded after final start. *E. J. O'Neill*

CLASSIC BLUE (IRE) 2 b.f. (Apr 4) Tagula (IRE) 116 – Palace Blue (IRE) (Dara **60** Monarch 128) [2006 7f 5.1d p7.1g Nov 17] 4,000Y: compact filly: sister to 6-y-o Tagula Blue and half-sister to winners abroad by Digamist and Paris House: dam unraced: seemingly best effort in maidens when eighth at Wolverhampton final start, never dangerous. *E. J. O'Neill*

CLASSIC ENCOUNTER (IRE) 3 b.g. Lujain (USA) 119 – Licence To Thrill 83 **98** (Wolfhound (USA) 126) [2006 99: 5m p5g 5d p5.1g p5g³ Dec 10] rather leggy, quite attractive gelding: useful handicapper: ran creditably in 2006 only on second/final starts, not clear run when third to Harry Up at Kempton in latter: will prove best at 5f: acts on polytrack and good to firm going: goes early to post: has carried head high. *D. M. Simcock*

CLASSIC EVENT (IRE) 5 ch.g. Croco Rouge (IRE) 126 – Delta Town (USA) (San- **–** glamore (USA) 126) [2006 64: 16m⁵ Jun 7] tall, close-coupled gelding: unimpressive mover: maiden handicapper: well held only outing on Flat in 2006: fair hurdler, successful in October. *T. D. Easterby*

CLASSIC HALL (IRE) 3 b.f. Saddlers' Hall (IRE) 126 – Classic Mix (IRE) 72 (Clas- **–** sic Secret (USA) 91) [2006 8.2m Sep 15] sturdy filly: second foal: dam, Irish 8.5f to 1½m winner, also won over hurdles: 16/1, always behind in maiden at Nottingham, slowly away and very green. *S. Kirk*

CLASSIC PUNCH (IRE) 3 b.g. Mozart (IRE) 131 – Rum Cay (USA) 75 (Our Native **104** (USA)) [2006 83p: 10m* 12g 12m 10.1d² 10m 14§ Sep 28] big, rangy gelding: useful performer: won maiden at Windsor in June by neck from Ask: ran well next 3 starts, in Irish Derby at the Curragh (ninth to Dylan Thomas), BGC Stakes (Gordon) at Goodwood (seventh to Sixties Icon) and minor event at Epsom (1¼ lengths second to Ashaawes): below form last 2 outings (gelded after final one): should stay 1¾m: acts on good to firm and good to soft ground. *D. R. C. Elsworth*

CLASSIC SIREN (IRE) 2 br.f. (Feb 1) Fath (USA) 116 – Vino Veritas (USA) 72 **–** (Chief's Crown (USA)) [2006 p6g Oct 5] €12,000F, €24,000Y: fourth foal: half-sister to Irish 1½m winner Nora Chrissie (by Bahhare) and winner in Italy up to 1¼m by Efisio: dam, ran twice, half-sister to very smart Hong Kong 1m/1¼m performer Bullish Luck: green and in rear in maiden: sold 500 gns. *J. W. Hills*

CLAUDIA MAY 5 gr.m. Cloudings (IRE) 112 – Princess Maxine (IRE) 68 (Horage **–** 124) [2006 9.2d⁴ 8m⁶ 11.1m 12m 8m Jul 25] third foal: dam 7f/1m winner: no form. *Miss Lucinda V. Russell*

CLAWS 3 b.f. Marju (IRE) 127 – Paws (IRE) 72§ (Brief Truce (USA) 126) [2006 8.7d **63** 10.2d 8m 6f* 7d⁴ f6g p7.1g* p7g³ Dec 19] first foal: dam Irish 6.5f winner: modest performer: won handicap at Fairyhouse in July and, having left G. Lyons in Ireland after fifth start, banded event at Wolverhampton in December: stays 7f: acts on polytrack, firm and good to soft ground. *A. J. Lidderdale*

CLEAR IMPRESSION (IRE) 4 b.f. Danehill (USA) 126 – Shining Hour (USA) 104 **103** (Red Ransom (USA)) [2006 86: 5.1g³ 6.1s⁴ 6f³ 5d² Jul 9] smallish, good-quartered filly: useful performer: best efforts when 1½ lengths third in listed events at Bath (behind Indian Maiden) and Haydock (behind Paradise Isle): just respectable second to Free Roses in similar event at Ayr final start: stays 6f: acts on firm and soft going. *S. C. Williams*

CLEARING SKY (IRE) 5 gr.m. Exploit (USA) 117 – Litchfield Hills (USA) (Relau- **64** nch (USA)) [2006 64: p6g p5.1g p6g³ p5g⁵ p5.1g 5g² 5f³ 5m 6g* 5m 6.1g p7g p6g Dec 5] strong mare: modest handicapper: won at Newmarket in August: effective at 5f to 7f: acts on polytrack and firm going: wore cheekpieces final start: usually races prominently. *J. R. Boyle*

CLEAR PICTURE 3 ch.f. Observatory (USA) 131 – Defined Feature (IRE) 91 (Na- **–** beel Dancer (USA) 120) [2006 8m Jun 9] 22,000Y: fourth foal: half-sister to 1m winner Ranny (by Emperor Jones) and 4-y-o Tacid: dam 2-y-o 5f/6f winner: 100/1 and green, well held in maiden at Goodwood. *A. P. Jarvis*

CLEAR SAILING 3 b.g. Selkirk (USA) 129 – Welsh Autumn 107 (Tenby 125) [2006 **87** 9.7d³ 10d* Oct 4] big, strong gelding: fourth foal: half-brother to useful 1m (at 2 yrs)/9f winner Rainwashed Gold (by Rainbow Quest): dam, French 1m winner (including at 2 yrs), half-sister to very smart 7f/1m performer Tillerman: fairly useful form: confirmed debut promise when winning maiden at Nottingham in October by ½ length from Red Gala, pair clear: carries head high (wears net muzzle). *Mrs A. J. Perrett*

CLEAR VISION 3 b.f. Observatory (USA) 131 – Claxon 110 (Caerleon (USA) 132) **64** [2006 71p: p10g³ p12g³ p13g³ Dec 22] modest maiden: probably stays easy 1½m: took strong hold final outing. *Mrs A. J. Perrett*

CLEAVER 5 ch.g. Kris 135 – Much Too Risky 87 (Bustino 136) [2006 72: 10.2d 10s **83**
9.8m p12g⁴ 12.1g⁴ 11.9g⁶ 11.1d* 12.4s* 10d* Nov 1] leggy, quite good-topped gelding:
fairly useful handicapper: won at Hamilton (apprentices) in September, Newcastle in
October and Nottingham in November: stays 1½m: acts on polytrack and soft ground:
usually held up: has looked tricky ride/ungenuine. *Lady Herries*

CLEIDE DA SILVA (USA) 2 gr.f. (Mar 13) Monarchos (USA) 129 – Sage Cat (USA) **73**
(Tabasco Cat (USA) 126) [2006 7m² p7g³ Sep 27] $44,000Y, $250,000 2-y-o: lengthy,
good-topped filly: has scope: second foal: half-sister to winner in USA by Crafty Prospector: dam 6f winner from 2 starts in USA: placed in maidens at Yarmouth (second to
Jaasoos) and Lingfield: will be suited by 1m. *J. Noseda*

CLEOBURY 2 b.f. (Mar 29) Superior Premium 122 – Nine To Five 64 (Imp Society **46**
(USA)) [2006 5.1s⁴ 5.7f⁶ 5.1f Jun 17] 8,500Y: second foal: sister to 3-y-o Trombone Tom:
dam, 5f winner, ran only at 2 yrs: poor form in minor event/maidens at Bath. *M. Meade*

CLEVELAND 4 b.g. Pennekamp (USA) 130 – Clerio 108 (Soviet Star (USA) 128) **68**
[2006 65: 7.1d 7.1m p7.1m f7g* f7g* f7g³ p7.1g Dec 26] lengthy gelding: fair performer:
won seller and banded race at Southwell in November: stays 7f: acts on fibresand and
good to firm going: has looked difficult ride. *R. Hollinshead*

CLEVELAND WAY 6 b.g. Forzando 122 – Fallal (IRE) 47 (Fayruz 116) [2006 –, a46: **52**
f7g⁵ f7g f7g⁴ f6g f7g f6g⁴ f6g Apr 10] good-topped gelding: modest performer: effective
at 5f to 7f: acts on all-weather and firm going: tried blinkered/visored: races up with pace:
inconsistent. *D. Carroll*

CLEWER 2 b.f. (Apr 14) Bahamian Bounty 116 – Polisonne (Polish Precedent (USA) **59**
131) [2006 p6g³ p6g 7m 5.1m³ 5.1f⁴ 5.7m Sep 25] 1,000F: half-sister to 3 winners, including Irish 1m winner Disobey (by Machiavellian): dam, 2-y-o 5f winner in Belgium,
close relative of Cheveley Park Stakes winner Regal Rose: modest maiden: in frame
3 times, including only nursery start: best at 5f/6f: acts on polytrack and firm going.
P. A. Blockley

CLICHE (IRE) 2 b.f. (Jan 25) Diktat 126 – Sweet Kristeen (USA) 69 (Candy Stripes **92 p**
(USA) 115) [2006 7m⁴ 7d³ 7d³ Sep 19] €50,000F, €165,000Y: angular, quite good-
topped filly: first foal: dam, 7f winner, half-sister to useful 1m/1¼m performer Ras
Shaikh: progressive form: in frame in maidens at Newmarket, then 1½ lengths third of
27 to demoted Wait Watcher in valuable sales race at the Curragh, finishing strongly
(weaved through from last place): will be suited by 1m: useful prospect, sure to win races.
Sir Michael Stoute

CLIMATE (IRE) 7 ch.g. Catrail (USA) 123 – Burishki 49 (Chilibang 120) [2006 –§: **72**
7g p7.1m⁴ 7.2v³ p7.1g* p9.5g* p8.6g f7g³ Dec 21] strong, compact gelding: fair
performer nowadays: won handicap and claimer within 24 hrs in October, both at
Wolverhampton: effective at 7f to easy 1¼m: acts on polytrack and any turf going: tried
blinkered/visored, in cheekpieces last 4 starts: hasn't always impressed with attitude:
joined R. Hollinshead. *K. A. Ryan*

CLINET (IRE) 4 b.f. Docksider (USA) 124 – Oiche Mhaith 74 (Night Shift (USA)) **110**
[2006 104: 7.5m* 8m* 8.9m 8f² 8f Nov 26] good-topped filly: smart performer: improved in 2006, winning handicap in January and listed race (by 2¼ lengths from Brindisi) in
February, both at Nad Al Sheba: last in Jebel Hatta there on third outing: off nearly 8
months (reportedly due to large cut to a hind leg), good head second to Beautyandthebeast
in Grade 2 Las Palmas Handicap at Santa Anita in October: not entirely discredited when
eleventh to Price Tag in Matriarch Stakes at Hollywood final outing: best at 7f/1m: acts
on polytrack and firm going. *J. W. Hills*

CLIPPER HOY 4 ch.g. Bahamian Bounty 116 – Indian Flag (IRE) 39 (Indian Ridge **70**
123) [2006 75: p6g p5g⁴ 5.1s 5g p5g p5g⁶ Apr 26] fair performer: best at 5f: acts on all-
weather: sometimes looks none too keen. *Mrs H. Sweeting*

CLOANN (IRE) 4 b.f. Danetime (IRE) 121 – Rustic Lawn (Rusticaro (FR) 124) [2006 **58 §**
64§: p5.1g⁵ p6g⁵ p7g² p7.1g⁴ p7g 6m p7g May 23] quite good-topped filly: modest
performer: stays 7f: acts on polytrack and firm going: wears headgear: not one to trust.
E. A. Wheeler

CLOSE TO YOU (IRE) 3 b.c. Shinko Forest (IRE) – Maritana (USA) (Rahy (USA) **111**
115) [2006 108: p8g* 8m May 6] lengthy, quite attractive colt: smart performer: good
walker: won listed race at Lingfield (by ¾ length from Kingsgate Prince) in April: respectable tenth to George Washington in 2000 Guineas at Newmarket only subsequent
start, outpaced 2f out before rallying: stays 1m: unraced on soft/heavy going, acts on any
other turf going and on polytrack: genuine. *T. G. Mills*

CLOUD ATLAS (IRE) 3 b.g. Monashee Mountain (USA) 115 – Blue Sioux 69 **77** (Indian Ridge 123) [2006 77: 6s² p7g 8m p8g p8g* 8m 7m p7.1g⁴ Sep 30] leggy, quite attractive gelding: fair handicapper: won apprentice event at Kempton in August: stays easy 1m: acts on polytrack and soft going: sold 15,000 gns. *S. Kirk*

CLOUDED LEOPARD (USA) 2 b.f. (Mar 28) Danehill (USA) 126 – Golden Cat **81** (USA) 102 (Storm Cat (USA)) [2006 p7g³ p7g Nov 11] fifth foal: sister to useful 2003 2-y-o 5f winner Celtic Cat, later successful at 6f in Hong Kong, and closely related to 3-y-o Mozie Cat: dam Irish 1m winner (stayed 1¼m) out of Irish St Leger winner Eurobird: much better run in maidens when third to Cast In Gold at Lingfield on debut. *J. H. M. Gosden*

CLUB CAPTAIN (USA) 3 b.g. Red Ransom (USA) – Really Fancy (USA) (In Reality) [2006 –p: 7m Apr 25] big gelding: well held in minor event/maiden. *G. A. Butler* –

CLYTHA 2 ch.f. (Apr 23) Mark of Esteem (IRE) 137 – India Atlanta (Ahonoora 122) **57** [2006 7m 8g 7d⁵ Oct 19] close-coupled, quite good-topped filly: has a fluent action: halfsister to several winners, including smart 5.7f (at 2 yrs) to 1m winner Ventiquattrofogli (by Persian Bold): dam unraced: modest form in maidens only on final start. *M. L. W. Bell*

CNOC MOY (IRE) 2 b.c. (Apr 5) Mull of Kintyre (USA) 114 – Ewar Sunrise 67 – (Shavian 125) [2006 p7.1g Oct 30] behind in maiden. *C. F. Wall*

COALITE (IRE) 3 b.g. Second Empire (IRE) 124 – Municipal Girl (IRE) 53 (Mac's **65** Imp (USA) 116) [2006 72: 6d⁴ 5g 6g 7g⁵ 7g³ 6f⁶ 7.5f 6.1f 7.5f 5m Aug 8] compact gelding: fair handicapper: stays easy 7f: acts on good to firm going: tried blinkered/in cheekpieces. *A. D. Brown*

COALPARK (IRE) 3 b.f. Titus Livius (FR) 115 – Honey Storm (IRE) 73 (Mujadil **79** (USA) 119) [2006 79: 8d 8m 8.3m⁴ 10.5m⁶ 9d⁵ 7.9f* 8g² p9g* 10f p9.5m p8g Oct 23] rather leggy filly: fair handicapper: won at Carlisle in August and Kempton in September: stays 1m: acts on polytrack, firm and good to soft going: tongue tied nowadays: sold 15,000 gns. *M. Johnston*

COASTAL BREEZE 3 b.c. Fasliyev (USA) 120 – Classic Design (Busted 134) [2006 **56** p6g p6g⁶ p7g² Feb 4] modest form in maidens: stays 7f. *J. W. Hills*

COASTAL COMMAND 2 b.g. (Feb 28) Sakhee (USA) 136 – Zenith 88 (Shirley **62 p** Heights 130) [2006 p7g⁴ Dec 15] ninth foal: half-brother to 3 winners, including useful 1¼m winner Spinning Top (by Alzao) and 7f/9f (in USA) winner Daytime (by Danehill): dam 2-y-o 8.5f winner out of smart miler Soprano: 9/1 and reluctant at stall, 5¼ lengths fourth to Messiah Garvey in maiden at Kempton, running on from rear not knocked about after short of room 2f out: should do better. *R. Charlton*

COBRA KING (IRE) 2 b.c. (Apr 23) Dilshaan 119 – Oiche Mhaith 74 (Night Shift – (USA)) [2006 8.1d p8g Oct 23] compact colt: well held in maidens: sold 3,500 gns. *P. Winkworth*

COCKATOO (USA) 3 b.c. Dynaformer (USA) – Enticed (USA) (Stage Door Johnny **64** (USA)) [2006 61p: p12g 11m⁶ p13g³ Sep 29] heavy-topped colt: modest maiden: left J. Gosden 40,000 gns before reappearance: stays 13f: acts on polytrack: in cheekpieces (best effort) final outing. *G. L. Moore*

COCKNEY REBEL (IRE) 2 b.c. (Mar 16) Val Royal (FR) 127 – Factice (USA) 78 **108** (Known Fact (USA) 135) [2006 6m* 6s² 7g³ Sep 9] 15,000F, 30,000Y: tall, leggy colt: closely related to Irish 2000 2-y-o 7f winner Factice Royal (by Royal Academy) and halfbrother to several winners, including 7f (at 2 yrs, in Ireland) to 1½m (in Spain) winner Mejhar (by Desert Prince): dam Irish 2-y-o 5f winner: useful form: won maiden at Newmarket in July: improved both starts after at York, second of 19 to Doctor Brown in valuable sales race and ½-length third of 8 to Vital Equine in Champagne Stakes (edged ahead briefly): will stay 1m. *G. A. Huffer*

COCOBEAN 2 b.g. (Mar 7) Josr Algarhoud (IRE) 118 – Aker Wood 86 (Bin Ajwaad – (IRE) 119) [2006 p8.6g Nov 18] 40/1, tailed off in claimer at Wolverhampton. *M. Appleby*

COCONUT MOON 4 b.f. Bahamian Bounty 116 – Lunar Ridge (Indian Ridge 123) **86** [2006 68: 5g 5m p5.1g* 5.1g³ 5m² 5.1m⁵ 5f² 5m 5f 5.1g* 5.1m 5g Sep 17] smallish filly: fairly useful handicapper: won at Wolverhampton in June and Chester in August: best at 5f: acts on polytrack and firm going. *E. J. Alston*

COCONUT QUEEN (IRE) 2 b.f. (Apr 14) Alhaarth (IRE) 126 – Royal Bounty (IRE) **70** 80 (Generous (IRE) 139) [2006 6f⁴ 7.5m³ 7m⁶ 8m 7d² Oct 3] €14,000Y: fifth foal: half-sister to 3-y-o Harvest Queen and fairly useful 6f winner Generous Gesture (by Fasliyev): dam, 7.5f winner (ran only at 2 yrs), out of smart half-sister to smart French stayer Sought Out (dam of Derby winner North Light): fair performer: won maiden at Catterick in August: good head second to Laurentina in nursery there final start: should stay 1m: acts on firm and good to soft going. *Mrs A. Duffield*

COCONUT SQUEAK 4 b.f. Bahamian Bounty 116 – Creeking 65 (Persian Bold 123) **101** [2006 105: 6s 7g 7m⁴ 6.1s⁵ 8.5g⁶ Jun 2] lengthy filly: useful performer: respectable efforts in 2006 only when 1½ lengths fourth to Echelon in Chartwell Fillies' Stakes at Lingfield and 2¾ lengths sixth to same filly in Princess Elizabeth Stakes at Epsom (sweating and early to post): effective at 6f to easy 8.5f: acts on polytrack, good to firm and good to soft ground, well held on soft/heavy: usually visored: races prominently. *Stef Liddiard*

CODA AGENCY 3 b.g. Agnes World (USA) 123 – The Frog Lady (IRE) 52 (Al Hareb **67** (USA) 123) [2006 58: p10g³ p12g⁶ p10g⁵ p10g³ 10.2g⁵ 10.9m⁵ 11.7g 10m⁶ p10g³ 17.2g² p16g³ p16g² Nov 28] strong gelding: fair maiden: stays 17f: acts on polytrack and good to firm ground. *D. W. P. Arbuthnot*

CODEWORD (IRE) 2 gr.c. (Feb 7) Dansili 127 – Spinamix 67 (Spinning World **88** (USA) 130) [2006 6f* 6g⁴ 7m² 7d 7d⁵ p7g³ Oct 15] €56,000F, €140,000Y: rather leggy, close-coupled colt: first foal: dam disappointing maiden: fairly useful performer: won maiden at York in July: placed after in minor events at Southwell and Lingfield (close third to Ekhtiaar) third/final starts: will stay 1m: acts on polytrack, firm and good to soft going: forces pace: has run well when sweating: sold 55,000 gns, sent to USA. *M. Johnston*

Mr Phil Cunningham's "Cockney Rebel"

COEUR COURAGEUX (FR) 4 b.g. Xaar 132 – Linoise (FR) 108 (Caerwent 123) **96**
[2006 107: 6m 6s 7.1m 7m Jul 1] tall, rather leggy gelding: useful performer: not so good
in 2006 (unseated leaving stall on reappearance), making little impact in handicaps: stays
1m: best effort on good going: tried tongue tied. *D. Nicholls*

COEUR DE LIONNE (IRE) 2 b.g. (Feb 1) Invincible Spirit (IRE) 121 – Lionne **80**
(Darshaan 133) [2006 p8g⁶ p8g² 8d² Sep 27] 78,000F, 145,000Y: sturdy gelding: fourth
foal: half-brother to 3 winners, notably 3-y-o Jadalee: dam unraced close relation to 3-y-o
Sir Percy: fairly useful form in maidens: runner-up at Kempton and Salisbury (beaten ¾
length by Spume): will probably prove best up to 1m. *R. Charlton*

COFFIN DODGER 3 ch.f. Dracula (AUS) 121 – Karakul (IRE) 78 (Persian Bold 123) **53**
[2006 –: p8g p10g⁴ p8.6g p8g 8.2d 10d³ p12.2g² 11.5m² p12g 11.5f² 14.1f 11.5f⁶ 10.1m*
10.1g 10.1m 10.1m 10d⁶ 11.5d⁵ f12g² f12g p12g³ Dec 1] angular filly: modest performer:
won claimer at Yarmouth in August: stays 1½m: acts on all-weather, firm and good to soft
going: tried in headgear: usually claimer ridden. *C. N. Allen*

COLCHIUM (IRE) 2 br.f. (Feb 20) Elnadim (USA) 128 – Dog Rose (SAF) (Fort **76**
Wood (USA) 117) [2006 5f⁶ 5.1g³ 5.1g 8g² 8g⁶ 8g² p8g* Dec 16] lengthy, good-bodied
filly: second foal: dam, Group 2 winner at 1m in South Africa, half-sister to Group 1
winner at 1m/9f here: fair performer: placed 3 times (including in nursery) prior to
winning maiden at Kempton in December by short head from Miss Saafend Plaza: stays
1m: acts on polytrack, raced mainly on good going on turf. *H. Morrison*

COLD CLIMATE 11 b.g. Pursuit of Love 124 – Sharpthorne (USA) 91 (Sharpen Up **–**
127) [2006 64: p8g Jan 11] lengthy gelding: modest performer: well beaten only outing in
2006: tried visored: usually held up. *Bob Jones*

COLDITZ (IRE) 2 ch.g. (Apr 18) Noverre (USA) 125 – West Escape 95 (Gone West **77**
(USA)) [2006 6s 6m² 6.1m 7.1m⁶ p7g 7m* 7g³ 7m 8d² 8d Sep 16] smallish, attractive
gelding: fourth foal: half-brother to 3 winners, including fairly useful 2003 2-y-o 5f/6f
winner Cape Trafalgar (by Cape Cross) and 4-y-o New England: dam, 1m winner, closely
related to smart 6f/7f performer Cartography: fair performer: won seller at Catterick (left
M. Channon 12,500 gns) in July: good second in nursery at Newcastle ninth start, gelded
after final one: stays 1m: acts on good to firm and good to soft going. *D. W. Barker*

COLD QUEST (USA) 2 b.c. (Apr 19) Seeking The Gold (USA) – Polaire (IRE) 108 **90**
(Polish Patriot (USA) 128) [2006 7g* p7g³ Sep 2] good-topped colt: first foal: dam, Irish
7f (including at 2 yrs) and 1¼m winner, later successful in USA: fairly useful form: won
17-runner maiden at Leicester in August: close third in minor event at Kempton 10 days
later, hampered briefly by winner Water Mill: will be suited by 1m/1¼m. *J. H. M. Gosden*

COLD TURKEY 6 b.g. Polar Falcon (USA) 126 – South Rock 102 (Rock City 120) **102**
[2006 102: p12g⁴ p12.2g⁵ p13g* p16g* 18.7m 12d⁴ 18d 11.6d p12g² Nov 18] sturdy
gelding: useful handicapper: won at Lingfield in March and Kempton (Queen's Prize for
second year running, beat Valance easily by 1¾ lengths) in April: effective at 1½m, and
stays 2¼m with emphasis on speed (well held in Cesarewitch seventh start): acts on polytrack, firm and soft ground: free-going sort: held up: tough and consistent. *G. L. Moore*

COLE (IRE) 3 b.g. Distant Music (USA) 126 – Dark Albatross (USA) 89 (Sheikh **–**
Albadou 128) [2006 52: 7.2d 6m 8f Jul 28] sturdy gelding: poor mover: form only in
maiden on debut at 2 yrs: dead. *J. Howard Johnson*

COLEORTON DANCER 4 ch.g. Danehill Dancer (IRE) 117 – Tayovullin (IRE) 65 **106**
(Shalford (IRE) 124§) [2006 105: 6v² 7m⁴ 7g 6s 6d 6d⁴ 6s Oct 7] leggy, quite good-
topped gelding: useful handicapper: good efforts in 2006 when in frame, notably fourth
of 23 to Fonthill Road in Ayr Gold Cup on penultimate start (not clear run, stayed on
strongly): stays easy 7f: acts on heavy and good to firm going: tried blinkered: wore
cheekpieces last 2 starts. *K. A. Ryan*

COLEORTON DANE 4 gr.g. Danehill Dancer (IRE) 117 – Cloudy Nine (Norton **–**
Challenger 111) [2006 78d: f12g Jan 2] big, lengthy gelding: fair performer at best: well
below form since third 3-y-o start: tried blinkered. *K. A. Ryan*

COLERIDGE (AUS) 7 ch.g. Yeats (USA) – Coco Cheval (AUS) (Zephyr Bay (AUS)) **81**
[2006 6g² 7g⁵ 6g⁴ 8.2g*⁷ 7.1m 7g p8g⁶ p7g p8g² p8.6g⁵ Dec 18] well-made gelding: won
4 of his 33 races when trained in Australia, including handicaps at Muswellbrook and
Bunbury in 2005: left M. Lane, fairly useful form on British debut when winning handicap at Nottingham in August: in-and-out form after: effective at 5f to 1m: tried blinkered:
has raced freely. *B. G. Powell*

COLINCA'S LAD (IRE) 4 b.g. Lahib (USA) 129 – Real Flame (Cyrano de Bergerac **71**
120) [2006 74?: 10m⁶ 10s 10f p8g⁴ 8.5d³ 9m⁴ 9.7f³ Sep 18] tall gelding: fair maiden: left

J. Ryan after third start: stays 1¼m: acts on polytrack, firm and good to soft going: tends to edge right. *T. T. Clement*

COLINETTE 3 b.f. Groom Dancer (USA) 128 – Collide 102 (High Line 125) [2006 **57** –p: 10g 9.9g⁶ 11.6g 10s Oct 18] leggy filly: modest maiden. *H. Candy*

COLISAY 7 b.g. Entrepreneur 123 – La Sorrela (IRE) (Cadeaux Genereux 131) [2006 **114** 111, a105: 8.9m⁴ 8m⁴ p10g 8m² 10m⁵ Aug 6] sturdy gelding: smart performer: best **a100** efforts in 2006 when fourth in handicap at Nad Al Sheba second start and very good ½-length second to Forgery in Spring Cup (Handicap) at Newbury (wandered in front): effective at 1m/1¼m: acts on firm and good to soft going: tried in visor/cheekpieces prior to 2006: sold 16,000 gns in July. *Mrs A. J. Perrett*

COLLATERAL DAMAGE (IRE) 3 b.c. Orpen (USA) 116 – Jay Gee (IRE) 93 **94** (Second Set (IRE) 127) [2006 83: 7g 7.6d² 7s* 8d⁵ 8s³ 8d⁶ 8d² 8s³ Oct 28] big, strong colt: fairly useful handicapper: won at York in May: stays 1m: acts on heavy and good to firm ground: consistent. *T. D. Easterby*

COLLECT 4 b.f. Vettori (IRE) 119 – Ring Fence 74 (Polar Falcon (USA) 126) [2006 **60 §** 70: 8m 9.7f⁶ f12g Jul 7] leggy, lengthy filly: ungenuine maiden: only modest form in 2006: stays 1¼m: acts on good to firm and good to soft going: blinkered last 2 starts, refusing to race second occasion: refused to enter stall once at 3 yrs. *M. H. Tompkins*

COLLEGE LAND BOY 2 b.g. (Mar 5) Cois Na Tine (IRE) 101 – Welcome Lu 45 **68** (Most Welcome 131) [2006 6m⁶ Aug 11] compact gelding: second foal: dam, 7f/1m winner, seemed to stay 2m: 66/1, staying-on sixth to Blue Rocket in maiden at Haydock. *J. J. Quinn*

COLLEGE QUEEN 8 b.m. Lugana Beach 116 – Eccentric Dancer 47 (Rambo Dancer **42** (CAN) 107) [2006 63: p5.1g p5g p5.1g 5f 5g⁴ p5g p5g⁶ Dec 18] strong mare: poor performer: effective at 5f/6f: acts on firm and good to soft going: sometimes wears headgear: tried tongue tied: usually races up with pace. *S. Gollings*

COLLEGE REBEL 5 b.m. Defacto (USA) – Eccentric Dancer 47 (Rambo Dancer **56** (CAN) 107) [2006 39: f11g² f11g⁵ f11g³ p13.9g⁵ p12.2g³ f12g⁵ f14g 15.8g³ 15.8g⁴ 17.1m⁵ 17.2m p16.5g Jul 28] tall mare: modest maiden: stays 17f: acts on all-weather and good to firm ground. *J. F. Coupland*

COLLEGE SCHOLAR (GER) 2 ch.c. (Apr 11) Dr Fong (USA) 128 – Colina (GER) **96** (Caerleon (USA) 132) [2006 6m⁴ 6f* 6s* 6g⁵ 6d* Oct 27] €30,000Y: lengthy, quite good-topped colt: third foal: half-brother to German 9.5f winner Colatina (by Winged Love) and French 1½m winner Cabari (by Vettori): dam German 11f winner: useful form: developed well, winning maiden at Folkestone and nursery at Newmarket in August, and minor event at Newmarket (beat Dream Scheme 1¼ lengths) in October: raced at 6f, bred to stay much further: acts on firm and soft going: genuine. *M. R. Channon*

COLLETTE'S CHOICE 3 b.f. Royal Applause 124 – Brilliance 74 (Cadeaux Gene- **67** reux 131) [2006 48: 8g 9.3m² 12.1f³ 12f* 14g⁵ 12f⁶ Jul 19] strong, good-bodied filly: fair handicapper: won at Pontefract in July: stays 1½m, seemingly not 1¾m: raced only on good going or firmer on turf. *R. A. Fahey*

COLLIER HILL 8 ch.g. Dr Devious (IRE) 127 – Polar Queen 76 (Polish Preced- **123** ent (USA) 131) [2006 120: 12m⁶ 12m² 12m 14g² 12g³ 14.1m² 12g* 12s* 12m* Dec 10]

Persian Punch was the first British-trained gelding to take his total earnings past the million-pound mark. In the process, he beat Teleprompter's long-standing record, a record that stood for so long because the £428,571 he earned when winning the Arlington Million at Chicago put him a distance clear at the top. That was in 1985 when all Group 1 events in Europe were closed to geldings and Tele-prompter's connections were forced to look to America where there was no such discrimination. Teleprompter had won the Queen Elizabeth II Stakes at Ascot the previous year, but it was a Group 2 event at the time which, along with other similar races, had been open to geldings only for five years (Teleprompter was only the sixth gelding to win a Group 2 in Britain). Teleprompter was a top-class racehorse at his best, rated 130, and his splendid career hastened a welcome relaxation in the illogical big-race ban on high-class geldings by the European authorities. Geldings are generally campaigned for longer than entires and allowing them to compete in the very best races increases competition, and often helps to provide a guide to the relative merits of different crops, as well as adding to the entertainment. Geldings

Pattison Canadian International Stakes, Woodbine—
Collier Hill (far side) holds off Go Deputy in a tight finish

should be eligible for every race open to entires, but, even now, they remain barred from some top races, the current position outlined in the essay on Corre Caminos.

If Teleprompter's connections had their race planning somewhat forced upon them, the enterprising connections of the latest horse to head the British-trained geldings' earnings list have acted very much through choice. Travelling top horses long distances, to different countries and climates, is more straightforward, and therefore more readily undertaken, than it was in Teleprompter's day when the Breeders' Cup, for example, was in its infancy and there were considerably fewer prestigious international races than nowadays. Collier Hill, trained in Richmond, North Yorkshire, as was Teleprompter, wouldn't have been able to amass over £2.3m in prize money without leaving Britain. He isn't so good a racehorse as Teleprompter but has reaped a rich harvest in well-endowed races abroad, winning in seven different countries in all, including Britain. Collier Hill didn't race outside Britain until he was six when he landed the biggest prize of his career up to that point with a short-head win from fellow British challenger Foreign Affairs in the Stockholm Cup International at Taby, worth £29,740. The Scandinavian middle-distance horses were vulnerable to smart visitors from Britain—Collier Hill's most important wins before that had come in the Old Newton Cup at Haydock in 2003 and a listed rated stakes at Hamilton in 2004—and there was still no real inkling that Collier Hill might develop into a globe-trotter of such distinction. Sent for the Dubai Carnival in the spring as a seven-year-old, Collier Hill showed further improvement to win a handicap at 20/1 at Nad Al Sheba on his first start and excelled himself when third at 40/1 in the Dubai Sheema Classic on the last of his three appearances. Back in Europe, he won the Group 2 Gerling-Preis at Cologne and the Irish St Leger at the Curragh, his first Group 1. An attack of sesamoiditis—Collier Hill has been prone to trouble with his joints for much of his career—put paid to a tilt at the Melbourne Cup.

By the time Collier Hill reappeared as an eight-year-old, he had changed hands at the Newmarket Autumn Sales for 97,000 guineas, purchased by a new partnership which includes one of his former part-owners. The new partnership well and truly hit the jackpot when Collier Hill earned six times his sale price (more than doubling his career earnings) for finishing second in the much-boosted Dubai Sheema Classic in March, starting at 22/1 and beaten four and a quarter lengths by Heart's Cry, ahead of South African-trained Falstaff and other notable Anglo-Irish challengers Ouija Board and Alexander Goldrun. There was much more to come, though Collier Hill took time to find his very best form again after being given a three-month break, the pick of his summer efforts a close second to Kastoria in the Curragh Cup and to Wunderwood in a minor conditions event at Salisbury, on both occasions giving weight away (he was twice hit across the face with the winning rider's whip at Salisbury).

A very ambitious three-country autumn tour got off to a successful start with a second win in the Stockholm Cup International at Taby, Collier Hill proving much too good for his Scandinavian rivals, winning by nine lengths from Binary File, like Collier Hill a former inmate of the Gosden stable. Collier Hill bypassed the Irish St Leger and the Melbourne Cup, being sent instead for the Pattison Canadian International in October and the Cathay Pacific Hong Kong Vase in December. Amazingly, he picked up both, earning £645,161 at Woodbine and £521,910 at Sha Tin, winning by a nose on each occasion, looking booked for second in Canada until rallying splendidly against the Man o' War Stakes runner-up Go Deputy and then producing another sterling effort in Hong Kong to hold off the unlucky-in-running Kastoria (who had been down the field on soft in the Canadian International after winning the Irish St Leger). European-trained horses enjoyed a one, two, three in the Hong Kong Vase, French-trained Shamdala finishing a length behind Kastoria after the short-priced British-trained ante-post favourite Ouija Board was a late absentee through injury. Collier Hill, whose own participation had been in some doubt until two days before because of dehydration, had certainly

Cathay Pacific Hong Kong Vase, Sha Tin—Collier Hill takes another big international prize,
this time holding on from the Aga Khan pair, the unlucky Kastoria (right)
and Shamdala (noseband, virtually obscured on left)

come a long way since making a successful racecourse debut in a bumper at Catterick as a four-year-old (he had been bought unnamed by his trainer for 3,000 guineas at Ascot as a three-year-old when known as Dr Freeze). The same stable's Alfie Flits made an excellent start to his career on the Flat in the latest season, having also begun in bumpers.

				Lorenzaccio
	Dr Devious (IRE)	Ahonoora		Helen Nichols
	(ch 1989)	(ch 1975)		
Collier Hill		Rose of Jericho		Alleged
(ch.g. 1998)		(b 1984)		Rose Red
	Polar Queen	Polish Precedent		Danzig
	(b 1992)	(b 1986)		Past Example
		Rain Date		Rainbow Quest
		(b 1987)		Roussalka

The pedigree of the strong Collier Hill, who is a poor mover, is of only academic interest and was dealt with fully in last year's Annual. His sire, the Derby winner Dr Devious, now stands in Italy after beginning his stud career in Japan before having a spell in Ireland at Coolmore. Collier Hill's dam Polar Queen, a winner over seven furlongs, has had only one other winner, a colt by Selkirk called Sicamous who is a winner in Slovakia. The game, genuine and consistent Collier Hill is effective at a mile and a half to two miles and acts on soft and good to firm going. He is set to begin his 2007 tour of exotic racing locations with a third crack at the Sheema Classic in March. *G. A. Swinbank*

COLLOQUIAL 5 b.g. Classic Cliche (IRE) 128 – Celia Brady 62 (Last Tycoon 131) **97**
[2006 96: 16d 16.2f² p16g⁶ 16d Oct 27] sparely-made gelding: useful handicapper: good second to Bulwark in quite valuable event at Haydock second start: not disgraced next outing (only second run on all-weather): should be suited by further than 2m: acts on firm and good to soft ground: visored last 3 outings. *H. Candy*

COLLOSEUM 5 b.g. Piccolo 121 – Trig Point (Rudimentary (USA) 118) [2006 57: **–**
p7.1g p7.1g p7.1g Mar 20] good-topped gelding: modest performer at best: well held in 2006: tried blinkered: none too reliable. *T. J. Etherington*

COLLUSION (FR) 3 ch.g. Zafonic (USA) 130 – Chantereine (USA) (Trempolino **57**
(USA) 135) [2006 8m p8g 8s May 27] big, good-bodied gelding: modest form in maidens first 2 starts: withdrawn after refusing to enter stall prior to intended third outing: gelded after. *Pat Eddery*

COLMAR SUPREME 3 b.f. Woodborough (USA) 112 – Child Star (FR) 58 (Belly- **63**
pha 130) [2006 75: p8g p7g³ a8.3g* a8g 10.5g May 7] lengthy filly: unimpressive mover: fair performer at best: claimed from R. Hannon £12,000 second outing: won minor event at Mijas in February: left C. Bjorling after next start: stays 8.3f: acts on polytrack/sand and good to soft ground. *O. Rodriguez, Spain*

COLONEL BILKO (IRE) 4 b.g. General Monash (USA) 107 – Mari-Ela (IRE) 60 **– §**
(River Falls 113) [2006 64§: f7g² p8.6g⁵ p9.5g f8g² f11s⁴ f8g 9.9d p12g p6g p7g p8g⁶ **a58 d**
p8g⁴ p8g Dec 18] modest performer: left Miss S. Wilton after seventh outing: stays 1¼m, probably not 11f: acts on all-weather, soft and good to firm going: tried in blinkers/tongue tie/cheekpieces: has started slowly: tends to hang: unreliable. *J. J. Bridger*

COLONEL COTTON (IRE) 7 b.g. Royal Applause 124 – Cutpurse Moll 76 (Green **79 d**
Desert (USA) 127) [2006 92: f6g f5g p6g 5m⁴ 6m 5m⁴ 5f³ 5m⁴ 6g⁶ 5f 5s 5d 5s p7g
Nov 11] good-topped gelding: just fair handicapper in 2006: left D. Nicholls after third start: below form last 6 outings: best at 5f/6f: acts on firm and soft going, little form on all-weather: usually blinkered/visored: no easy ride, sometimes slowly away. *R. A. Fahey*

COLONEL FLAY 2 ch.c. (Mar 15) Danehill Dancer (IRE) 117 – Bobbie Dee 93 (Blak- **76**
eney 126) [2006 7.1m² 6d 8s Oct 10] 10,000Y: good-topped colt: fifth foal: half-brother to 1¾m winner In Deep (by Deploy): dam, maiden who should have stayed 1½m, also third over hurdles: fair maiden: second at Sandown on debut, easily best effort: should stay at least 1m: once refused at stalls. *Mrs P. N. Dutfield*

COLONEL KLINK (IRE) 2 b.c. (May 5) Monashee Mountain (USA) 115 – Persian **–**
Velvet (IRE) (Distinctly North (USA) 115) [2006 6m 7f⁶ 6d Sep 29] no form. *J. S. Moore*

COLORADO RAPID (IRE) 2 b.c. (Apr 13) Barathea (IRE) 127 – Rafting (IRE) 87 **84 p**
(Darshaan 133) [2006 7.1m² Sep 7] 25,000Y, 40,000 2-y-o: third foal: half-brother to German 1¼m winner Ruffian Reef (by Singspiel): dam, 1½m winner, half-sister to smart

performer up to 2¼m Lear White: 12/1, neck second to Amazing Request in maiden at Chepstow, always prominent: will do better, particularly at 1¼m/1½m. *M. Johnston*

COLOR MAN 2 b.g. (Mar 24) Rainbow Quest (USA) 134 – Subya 107 (Night Shift (USA)) [2006 p7g 7m 7f⁵ Jul 22] poor form in maidens (slowly away), then gelded. *Mrs A. J. Perrett* — **48**

COLORUS (IRE) 3 b.g. Night Shift (USA) – Duck Over 72 (Warning 136) [2006 92: 6.1f 6g 6f 6d⁶ 5d 7d 7m⁶ 5s Oct 6] stocky, good sort: fair handicapper: seems to stay 6f: acts on fibresand, good to firm and good to soft going: in headgear 4 of last 5 starts: temperament under suspicion. *R. A. Fahey* — **78**

COLOURPOINT (USA) 3 b. or br.f. Forest Wildcat (USA) 120 – Farrfesheena (USA) 89 (Rahy (USA) 115) [2006 81d: 5.1d 7d May 28] medium-sized, good-topped filly: fairly useful form at 2 yrs: has regressed since: tried in blinkers/cheekpieces: sold 30,000 gns in November. *C. E. Brittain* — **–**

COLTCHESTER (IRE) 3 b.g. Tagula (IRE) 116 – Eveam (IRE) 88 (Mujadil (USA) 119) [2006 65+: p8g⁵ p8g Apr 12] lightly-raced maiden: blinkered (well held) final start: has been slowly away/looked none too keen. *Peter Grayson* — **50**

COLTON 3 b.g. Zilzal (USA) 137 – Picot 76 (Piccolo 121) [2006 69: 6g⁶ 7g 8d 8m* 10.1g* 8m³ 10g 8g⁴ p8.6g⁴ Oct 30] tall, close-coupled gelding: fair handicapper: won at Pontefract and Yarmouth in August: stays easy 1¼m: acts on polytrack and good to firm going. *J. M. P. Eustace* — **78**

COLUMBUS (IRE) 9 b.g. Sadler's Wells (USA) 132 – Northern Script (USA) 95 (Arts And Letters (USA)) [2006 16v⁵ Oct 25] fair in maidens at 3 yrs in Ireland for A. O'Brien: well held only Flat outing since 2002: tried blinkered: has carried head high. *Jennie Candlish* — **–**

COLWAY RITZ 12 b.g. Rudimentary (USA) 118 – Million Heiress (Auction Ring (USA) 123) [2006 57: 12m⁵ 12f² 14.1f 12f³ Jul 5] big, strong gelding: good mover: poor handicapper nowadays: effective at 1¼m to 13.8f: acts on firm and good to soft going: tried blinkered/in cheekpieces: held up. *W. Storey* — **49**

COMEINTOTHESPACE (IRE) 4 b.g. Tagula (IRE) 116 – Playa Del Sol (IRE) (Alzao (USA) 117) [2006 73: p8.6g p8.6g⁴ p9.5g 12g 10.2m p8.6g 8.1g³ 8.2f⁵ 8.1m 8f 9g⁶ Sep 12] quite good-topped gelding: modest performer nowadays: left A. Bailey after reappearance, J. Osborne after fourth start: stays 1¼m: acts on polytrack and firm going: tried blinkered/in cheekpieces: very slowly away third outing. *Miss Victoria Roberts* — **54**

COME ON 7 b.g. Aragon 118 – All On 68 (Dunbeath (USA) 127) [2006 50: p9.5g f8g p7.1g May 5] good-bodied gelding: maiden: no form in 2006. *J. Hetherton* — **–**

COME ON JONNY (IRE) 4 b.g. Desert King (IRE) 129 – Idle Fancy 79 (Mujtahid (USA)) [2006 113: 12s 11.6d Nov 4] close-coupled gelding: smart and game handicapper in 2005: off 11 months (reported in May to have suffered from ulcers) and gelded: well held both outings in 2006: often front runner. *R. M. Beckett* — **–**

COME OUT FIGHTING 3 b.c. Bertolini (USA) 125 – Ulysses Daughter (IRE) 88 (College Chapel 122) [2006 95: p5g⁴ 5f 6m² 5f 6g* 6g³ 7m³ 6d Sep 22] compact colt: useful performer: won handicap at Ascot in August by 2 lengths from Didn't We: good third after in similar race at Newmarket (to Burning Incense) and minor event at Southwell (2¾ lengths behind Aeroplane): best at 6f/7f: acts on polytrack and good to firm going, well below form on softer than good: has worn crossed noseband. *P. A. Blockley* — **100**

COME TO DADDY (IRE) 4 ch.g. Fayruz 116 – Forgren (IRE) (Thatching 131) [2006 –: 8.1m 12g Jul 6] strong gelding: maiden: no form since 2004. *F. Jordan* — **–**

COME WHAT AUGUSTUS 4 b.g. Mujahid (USA) 125 – Sky Red 75 (Night Shift (USA)) [2006 52: 11.6m Jun 5] lightly-raced maiden: well held only outing in 2006. *R. M. Stronge* — **–**

COME WHAT JULY (IRE) 5 b.g. Indian Rocket 115 – Persian Sally (IRE) (Persian Bold 123) [2006 71, a93d: f14g⁶ f8g f11g⁶ p12.2g p13.9g⁶ p10g p10g p12.2g³ p12.2g Dec 23] compact gelding: only modest in 2006: left Mrs N. Macauley after third start: stays 1¾m: acts on all-weather, good to firm and good to soft going: sometimes wears headgear. *D. Shaw* — **a52**

COME WHAT MAY 2 b.f. (Mar 17) Selkirk (USA) 129 – Portelet 91 (Night Shift (USA)) [2006 5d 5.1s³ Oct 25] 50,000Y: big filly: has scope: sister to 4-y-o Etlaala and 7-y-o Selective, and half-sister to 2 other winners: dam 5f winner out of half-sister to smart middle-distance stayer Braashee: better effort in maidens when third to Dramatic Turn at Nottingham: will be suited by 6f/7f: open to more improvement. *Rae Guest* — **67 p**

COMICAL ERRORS (USA) 4 b.g. Distorted Humor (USA) 117 – Fallibility (USA) **54** (Tom Rolfe) [2006 53: 12m³ 14.1d 16g² Aug 14] compact, quite attractive gelding: modest maiden: stays 2m: acts on good to firm and good to soft ground: tried in cheekpieces/tongue tie. *P. C. Haslam*

COMIC TALES 5 b.g. Mind Games 121 – Glorious Aragon 88 (Aragon 118) [2006 45: **47** f6g p5.1g⁵ p5.1g⁶ f5g f5g f5g² p5.1g² p5.1g⁴ 6m f5g³ f5g p5g p5.1g p6g³ p6g f6g⁵ Dec 27] good-topped gelding: poor maiden: probably stays 7f: acts on all-weather and good to firm going: tried blinkered/in cheekpieces: often starts slowly. *M. Mullineaux*

COMMANDER WISH 3 ch.c. Arkadian Hero (USA) 123 – Flighty Dancer (Pivotal **–** 124) [2006 71d: 7f p8g p13.9g Nov 6] stocky colt: fair form when third in maiden second 2-y-o start: well held since. *P. Howling*

COMMANDO SCOTT (IRE) 5 b.g. Danetime (IRE) 121 – Faye 79 (Monsanto (FR) **99** 121) [2006 92: p8.6g 8s⁴ 7d² 6d² 7.1m³ 7.2g* 6s 6v* 7g 6m 6m 6s³ 6d⁶ 7.2d³ 7f³ 7d Sep 30] good-topped gelding: useful performer: won 2 handicaps at Ayr in May, latter by 1¾ lengths from Rising Shadow: probably best at 6f/7f: acts on any turf going. *I. W. McInnes*

COMMAND RESPECT 3 b.f. Commands (AUS) – The Blade (GER) 101 (Sure **–** Blade (USA) 130) [2006 –: 10m 8m 7d Sep 25] well held in maidens: visored final start. *E. F. Vaughan*

COMMA (USA) 2 b.f. (Feb 12) Kingmambo (USA) 125 – Flute (USA) 124 (Seattle **88** Slew (USA)) [2006 8.2g⁶ 7s² 7d Oct 28] well-made filly: second foal: dam, US Grade 1 9f/1¼m winner, out of half-sister to dam of Racing Post Trophy/St Leger winner Brian Boru: fairly useful maiden: best run, shaping well, when second to Magic Echo at Newcastle, quickening 6 lengths clear before tiring and headed close home: didn't take eye before final start: bred to be suited by 1m+, but not short of speed: raced on good ground or softer. *Sir Michael Stoute*

COMMENTARY 3 b.f. Medicean 128 – Eloquent 94 (Polar Falcon (USA) 126) [2006 **84** 87: 8m⁴ Jun 20] leggy filly: fairly useful performer: off 8 months and favourite, not discredited in handicap at Thirsk only outing in 2006: stays 1m: acts on good to firm and good to soft going: has started slowly. *W. J. Haggas*

COMMITMENT LECTURE 6 b.m. Komaite (USA) – Hurtleberry (IRE) 87 (Tirol **74** 127) [2006 71: 8d⁸ 8.2d⁸ 8.2g 9.1g 8d⁴ 8m⁴ 8.3g⁶ 8v 8g⁵ Sep 27] smallish mare: fair handicapper: won at Thirsk in April and Nottingham in May: stays 9f: acts on heavy and good to firm going, below form on all-weather: tongue tied: held up. *M. Dods*

COMMON PURPOSE (USA) 2 b.g. (Feb 15) Elusive Quality (USA) – Kithira 106 **74 p** (Danehill (USA) 126) [2006 p7g³ Oct 26] first foal: dam, French/US 6f (at 2 yrs) and 1m winner, half-sister to Prix de Psyche winner Tenuous: 10/1, 5 lengths third of 14 to Cabinet in maiden at Lingfield, fading: should progress. *J. H. M. Gosden*

COMMON WORLD (USA) 7 ch.g. Spinning World (USA) 130 – Spenderella (FR) **116 d** (Common Grounds 118) [2006 115: 8s 7s* 6d⁵ 8s 10d⁴ 8s³ 8d⁶ 9d 8g 7.5v 8.5s⁶ Oct 14] rather leggy, quite attractive gelding: smart performer: won Castlemartin & La Louvière Studs Gladness Stakes at the Curragh in April by 6 lengths from Mustameet: respectable fourth to Notnowcato in Brigadier Gerard Stakes at Sandown fifth outing: well below form last 5 starts: effective at 7f to 1¼m: acts on soft and good to firm going (though all wins on softer than good), well held on dirt: tried in blinkers/cheekpieces. *T. Hogan, Ireland*

COMPETITOR 5 b.h. Danzero (AUS) – Ceanothus (IRE) 61 (Bluebird (USA) 125) **–** [2006 –, a62: p10g² p10g⁵ p10g p10g⁶ p12g* p10g³ p10g* p12g³ p10g 9.7f 10.2m p12g **a69** p10g³ Dec 30] fair performer: won sellers at Lingfield in March and April: stays 1½m: acts on polytrack and good to firm ground: usually wears headgear: sometimes tongue tied: has run as if amiss/suffered breathing problems. *J. Akehurst*

COMPOSING (IRE) 2 b.f. (Feb 22) Noverre (USA) 125 – Aqaba 65 (Lake Coniston **71 p** (IRE) 131) [2006 8d³ Sep 27] first foal: dam, maiden who should have stayed 1m, half-sister to smart performers Lady of Chad (won Prix Marcel Boussac) and Alcazar (stayer): 25/1, encouraging 4¼ lengths third in maiden at Salisbury: should do better. *H. Morrison*

COMPROMIZNOTENSION (IRE) 3 br.g. Key of Luck (USA) 126 – Music Khan **84** (Music Boy 124) [2006 82p: 7m² 7m⁵ 5g⁶ 8s* 8v³ 8d* 8v* Oct 28] good-topped gelding: fairly useful performer: left M. Jarvis 9,000 gns after third start: won maiden at Newcastle in September and claimer at Pontefract and handicap at Ayr in October: stays 1m: acts on heavy and good to firm ground: fractious in stall and possibly amiss third start (wore cheekpieces): makes running. *I. Semple*

COMPTON BAY 6 b.g. Compton Place 125 – Silver Sun 83 (Green Desert (USA) **47** 127) [2006 –, a43: f7g 7f⁵ 6.9m 7s⁶ f7m Oct 31] leggy, plain gelding: poor maiden: tried blinkered. *M. Brittain*

COMPTON BOLTER (IRE) 9 b.g. Red Sunset 120 – Milk And Honey 102 (So **116 d** Blessed 130) [2006 118: p10g p10g 12g 13.4d⁴ 10m 10m Jul 30] smallish gelding: had a quick action: smart performer at best: won 12 races in his career, 7 of them listed events, including Churchill Stakes at Lingfield on 3 occasions, and Group 3 Arc Trial at Newbury: far from discredited when close seventh of 8 behind Grand Passion in minor event at Lingfield 2006 reappearance, but well below best after: was effective at 1¼m to 13.4f: acted on dirt/polytrack, firm and soft going: occasionally visored/blinkered: effective tongue tied or not: reported in August to have been retired due to tendon trouble. *G. A. Butler*

COMPTON CHARLIE 2 b.c. (Mar 12) Compton Place 125 – Tell Tale Fox (Tel Quel **67** (FR) 125) [2006 6d 6d⁵ f7g² Nov 14] €26,000 2-y-o: first foal: dam French 2-y-o 5f/7f winner: best effort in maidens when 1¾ lengths fifth of 16 to Edge Closer at Windsor, hanging badly right 1f out. *J. G. Portman*

COMPTON CLASSIC 4 b.g. Compton Place 125 – Ayr Classic 74 (Local Suitor **67** (USA) 128) [2006 55: p6g p5.1g* p5.1g² 5m⁶ 5g² 5m 5m⁶ 6m 5d* 5m⁴ 5m 5d⁶ 5s⁵ 5s* 5d³ 6v² 5d² p5.1g Nov 18] good-bodied gelding: fair performer: won banded race at Wolverhampton in April and handicaps at Ayr in July (amateurs) and September: best at 5f: acts on polytrack, heavy and good to firm going: usually wears cheekpieces. *J. S. Goldie*

COMPTON COMMANDER 8 ch.g. Barathea (IRE) 127 – Triode (USA) 105 (Sharpen **– §** Up 127) [2006 13.8g 15.8g 14.1f 14.1m Aug 31] useful-looking gelding: fairly useful performer in 2003, lightly raced and mostly well held since: tried blinkered/visored: ungenuine. *E. W. Tuer*

COMPTON COURT 4 b.g. Compton Place 125 – Loriner's Lass 80 (Saddlers' Hall **77 §** (IRE) 126) [2006 75: p10g³ 10d² 9m 10m³ 8.3g⁴ 9m Sep 10] fair maiden: effective at 1m/ 1¼m: acts on polytrack, unraced on extremes of going on turf: has carried head high/ looked wayward: sold 15,000 gns. *A. M. Balding*

COMPTON DRAGON (USA) 7 ch.g. Woodman (USA) 126 – Vilikaia (USA) 125 **61** (Nureyev (USA) 131) [2006 67: 8.3d 10.1m⁶ Jun 30] compact gelding: modest performer: stays 1¼m: acts on polytrack and good to firm going, probably on soft: usually wears headgear: has worn tongue tie: edgy sort: often slowly away. *R. Johnson*

COMPTON DRAKE 7 b.g. Mark of Esteem (IRE) 137 – Reprocolor 114 (Jimmy **81** Reppin 131) [2006 90, a85: p12.2g⁴ Jan 30] big, good-topped gelding: fairly useful handicapper: stays 1½m: acts on all-weather, good to firm and good to soft ground: tried blinkered earlier in career: usually tongue tied (not on only start in 2006): held up. *G. A. Butler*

COMPTON EARL 6 ch.g. Efisio 120 – Bay Bay 101 (Bay Express 132) [2006 –: p6g **–** Mar 20] strong gelding: fair winner at 3 yrs for G. Butler: well held subsequently: was sometimes tongue tied: dead. *J. J. Lambe, Ireland*

COMPTON ECLAIRE (IRE) 6 ch.m. Lycius (USA) 124 – Baylands Sunshine **66 §** (IRE) (Classic Secret (USA) 91) [2006 62§: p16g 15.8d 16g² 13.9m* 14.1f² 16.2m⁴ 14m⁴ 14.1g⁶ 17.1d⁶ 14.1m 14.1m³ Sep 11] good-topped mare: fair handicapper: won apprentice event at York in June: stays 2m: acts on all-weather and firm going: blinkered/ visored: held up: ungenuine: sold 1,500 gns. *B. Ellison*

COMPTON ECLIPSE 6 ch.g. Singspiel (IRE) 133 – Fatah Flare (USA) 121 (Alydar **72** (USA)) [2006 76: p8.6g* p8.6g⁵ p8.6g 10f 8m² 10g 8.5g 7s Sep 30] leggy gelding: fair **a76** handicapper: landed gamble at Wolverhampton in February: best around 7f/1m: acts on polytrack and firm ground: has been blinkered/tongue tied: sometimes carries head high. *J. J. Lambe, Ireland*

COMPTON EXPRESS 3 gr.f. Compton Place 125 – Jilly Woo 60 (Environment **49** Friend 128) [2006 49: p8g p8g 7f p7g p10g p10g Dec 22] poor maiden. *Jamie Poulton*

COMPTON FIELDS 2 b.g. (Apr 25) Compton Place 125 – Julia Domna (Dominion **75** 123) [2006 5g 5m* 5f³ 5.5m⁴ 6.1g Sep 15] useful-looking gelding: half-brother to 3 winners, including smart 7f (including at 2 yrs) to 1¼m winner Vintage Premium (by Forzando) and 4-y-o Jalissa: dam, no form, half-sister to smart 7f/1m performer Norwich: fair performer: won maiden at Warwick in July: in frame 2 of 3 starts in nurseries (below form in visor other one): should prove best kept to 5f/6f: raced on good going or firmer: suspect temperament: sold 18,000 gns. *R. Charlton*

COMPTON FLYER 3 ch.c. Compton Admiral 121 – Elegantissima 57 (Polish Pre- –
cedent (USA) 131) [2006 ?: p7g 7f 6.1d 5m 10.9m Jul 2] close-coupled colt: maiden: well
held in 2006: tried in cheekpieces. *J. M. Bradley*

COMPTON LAD 3 b.g. Compton Place 125 – Kintara (Cyrano de Bergerac 120) [2006 **51**
51: 5m 5m⁵ 5m 5d 5m³ 5g 5m p5.1g 5d Oct 8] modest maiden: should stay 6f: acts on
all-weather, soft and good to firm ground: tried in cheekpieces/tongue tie. *D. A. Nolan*

COMPTON MICKY 5 ch.g. Compton Place 125 – Nunthorpe 79 (Mystiko (USA) **49**
124) [2006 63: f8g 7m 8.5g f6m f7g⁶ f6g⁵ Dec 28] strong gelding: poor performer nowadays: stays 7f: acts on all-weather, firm and soft ground: tried blinkered/in cheekpieces:
somewhat wayward. *R. F. Marvin*

COMPTON PLUME 6 ch.g. Compton Place 125 – Brockton Flame 72 (Emarati **67**
(USA) 74) [2006 76: 7d 5g 7g 5m 6f 6g* 6m⁴ 6m⁶ 6f⁴ Sep 20] strong, lengthy gelding:
fair handicapper: won ladies event at Thirsk in August: best at stiff 5f/6f: acts on firm
ground: usually blinkered/visored at 3 yrs. *M. W. Easterby*

COMPTON'S ELEVEN 5 gr.g. Compton Place 125 – Princess Tara 85 (Prince Sabo **107**
123) [2006 107: 6.5m* 6.5m² 6.5g⁴ p6g⁴ 7g 7g 7m 7m² 7m 7d² 7g² 7m⁵ 7d 7d³ Sep 30]
good-topped gelding: useful handicapper: won at Nad Al Sheba in January: good efforts
when short-head second to Paper Talk at Newmarket and Illustrious Blue at Goodwood
tenth/eleventh outings: effective at 5f (given test) to 7f: acts on polytrack, firm and good
to soft going: sometimes carries head high/edges left: tough. *M. R. Channon*

COMPTON SPECIAL 2 ch.f. (Feb 20) Compton Place 125 – Spectina 92 (Spectrum **46**
(IRE) 126) [2006 p6g p7.1g Dec 1] 14,000Y: first foal: dam, maiden best at 7f/1m,
half-sister to dam of smart performer up to 1½m Summitville: poor form in maidens at
Wolverhampton, carrying head awkwardly latter start. *J. G. Given*

COMPTONSPIRIT 2 ch.f. (Feb 20) Compton Place 125 – Croeso Cynnes 70 (Most –
Welcome 131) [2006 p6g Dec 30] 3,000F: fifth foal: dam 5f and (including at 2 yrs) 6f
winner: 66/1 and green, niggled along when hitting rail and unseating rider 2f out in
3-runner minor event at Wolverhampton. *B. P. J. Baugh*

COMPTON VERNEY 2 b.c. (May 25) Compton Admiral 121 – Gipsy Princess 65 **46**
(Prince Daniel (USA)) [2006 5f 6m⁵ 7f⁶ 7.5f⁶ Jul 8] close-coupled colt: poor maiden:
tried blinkered. *M. W. Easterby*

COMRADE COTTON 2 b.c. (May 6) Royal Applause 124 – Cutpurse Moll 76 **51**
(Green Desert (USA) 127) [2006 p6g p5.1g⁶ Dec 22] brother to 7-y-o Colonel Cotton
and half-brother to several winners, including useful 6f winner Cyclone Connie (by Dr
Devious) and fairly useful 7f (at 2 yrs) and 1½m winner Lola Sapola (by Benny The Dip):
dam 7f winner: slowly away and never dangerous in maidens at Kempton (better effort)
and Wolverhampton. *N. A. Callaghan*

CONFIDE (IRE) 4 ch.g. Namid 128 – Confidential 60 (Generous (IRE) 139) [2006 **77**
64: 7d³ 8d 7g* 7.9m² 7m⁴ 7.2m* 7d Aug 12] big, workmanlike gelding: fair performer:
improved and won maiden at Catterick in June and handicap at Ayr in July: should also
have won handicap at Carlisle on fourth start, rider banned for easing prematurely: barely
stays 1m: acts on firm and good to soft going: sold 11,000 gns. *G. A. Swinbank*

CONFIDENT 2 b.f. (May 16) Machiavellian (USA) 123 – Sweet Willa (USA) (Assert –
134) [2006 p8g f8g Dec 9] eighth foal: closely related to US Grade 3 9f winner Under-
mine (by Miner's Mark) and half-sister to 3 winners there: dam, 6f winner in USA, half-
sister to Grade 1 winners Willa On The Move (8.5f) and Will's Way (9f/1¼m): well held
in maidens at Kempton and Southwell. *M. A. Jarvis*

CONFIDENTIAL LADY 3 b.f. Singspiel (IRE) 133 – Confidante (USA) 95 **116**
(Dayjur (USA) 137) [2006 108: 8s² 8v⁶ 10.5m* 12m⁵ 10d⁵ 10s² Oct 22]
    A chapter devoted solely to Confidential Lady wouldn't be unrealistic
should Sir Mark Prescott ever get round to writing his memoirs. The master of
Heath House has had several better performers in his care since taking out a licence
in 1971, including other fillies such as the dual Champion Stakes winner Alborada,
Albanova, who won three Group 1s in Germany, and the Nassau and Sun Chariot
Stakes winner Last Second. Yet it was Confidential Lady who made history by
becoming Prescott's first runner in a classic in Britain, when contesting the One
Thousand Guineas at Newmarket in May; and again when giving her trainer his
first classic success, in the Prix de Diane Hermes at Chantilly just over a month
later.

Except for a disappointing effort on her final two-year-old start, Confidential Lady had progressed rapidly in her first season and won four races, including the Prix du Calvados at Deauville. The form she had shown there, and also when a head second to Nasheej in the Sweet Solera Stakes at Newmarket on her previous outing, didn't leave her with too much to find to make an impact in the One Thousand Guineas on her seasonal reappearance. Confidential Lady's trainer was clearly more than satisfied that she had made the necessary improvement, and she didn't let him down, running really well to finish two and a half lengths second to Speciosa. Usually a front runner at two, Confidential Lady was closest to the all-the-way winner throughout at Newmarket. She looked to have a good opportunity to go one better just three weeks later, in the Irish One Thousand Guineas at the Curragh, and was sent off favourite, but her supporters knew their fate when, after leading from the off, she was headed by the eventual six-length winner Nightime after two furlongs out, weakening into sixth. It is possible that Confidential Lady was unsuited by the heavy ground at the Curragh, though conditions weren't that much more testing than they had been at Deauville, or at Newmarket come to that. The suggestion that her rider Seb Sanders overdid things in front seems wide of the mark given that the winner was never that far behind her; and the theory that the race came too soon for her after Newmarket was put to bed when, just two weeks later, she triumphed at Chantilly.

The Prix de Diane attracted a larger-than-average field of sixteen and had an open look to it. There wasn't a filly with outstanding claims going into the race, the unbeaten Prix Saint-Alary winner Germance starting favourite. Racing over a distance two and a half furlongs further than she had tackled previously, Confidential Lady was ridden much more patiently than in her earlier races, not moving onto the heels of the leaders until early in the straight, having improved her position by sticking to the rail turning in. Soon switched outside, Confidential Lady responded most gamely to strong pressure to take the lead off Germance entering the final furlong, and went on to beat that filly by a length and a half. The only other challenger from outside France, Queen Cleopatra, was a nose further back in third. Confidential Lady was the first classic winner bred by the Cheveley Park Stud to race in the stud's colours—Entrepreneur was bred by them but raced in Michael Tabor's colours when winning the Two Thousand Guineas in 1997, and Russian Rhythm was bought by Cheveley Park Stud as a yearling before being successful in the One Thousand Guineas in 2003. Confidential Lady provided a second victory in a classic for her rider, successful on Bachelor Duke in the 2004 Irish Two Thousand Guineas. Confidential Lady's win came at a price for Sanders, though, as he received an eight-day ban for his use of the whip. The stewards found that Sanders had hit his mount on thirty-two occasions, four times the limit stated in the French rules. Prescott, reporting that Confidential Lady had returned home none the worse for

Prix de Diane Hermes, Chantilly—Confidential Lady gives Sir Mark Prescott his first classic winner;
Germance and Queen Cleopatra (rail) come next, ahead of Mussoorie (hooped cap),
Alix Road (No.4) and Mauralakana

Cheveley Park Stud's "Confidential Lady"

her exertions, was of the opinion that the stewards had misjudged the number of times the filly was hit, but Sanders did not appeal, even though his ban included all five days of Royal Ascot. Confidential Lady made three more appearances kept to Group 1 company. She didn't run much of a race in the first of them, beaten before stamina became an issue when stepped up to a mile and a half in the Irish Oaks at the Curragh. Given a three-month break, she finished a respectable fifth to Pride in the Champion Stakes at Newmarket and a good second to the German filly Floriot, beaten a length and a quarter, in the Premio Lydia Tesio at Rome.

	Singspiel (IRE) (b 1992)	In The Wings (b 1986)	Sadler's Wells
			High Hawk
		Glorious Song (b 1976)	Halo
Confidential Lady (b.f. 2003)			Ballade
	Confidante (USA) (b 1995)	Dayjur (br 1987)	Danzig
			Gold Beauty
		Won't She Tell (b 1984)	Banner Sport
			Won't Tell You

Confidential Lady, the fourth foal of Confidante, is a half-sister to a couple of fairly useful seven-furlong winners by Machiavellian, namely Crown Counsel and Registrar. Confidante was also successful at that trip, in a maiden at Thirsk and a handicap at Sandown on her first two starts at three, though she showed her best form when second in a listed event over a mile at Ascot later that season. She is a half-sister to several winners including the smart Wind Cheetah and the 1992

Solario Stakes winner White Crown, and is a daughter of Won't She Tell, a multiple winner in North America who stayed at least nine furlongs; Won't She Tell is closely related to Affirmed. The good-topped Confidential Lady, a thoroughly genuine filly who acts on soft and good to firm ground, stays in training, but will be another valuable addition to the Cheveley Park Stud's already impressive-looking list of broodmares when the time comes. *Sir Mark Prescott*

CONFUCHIAS (IRE) 2 b c Cape Cross (IRE) 129 – Schust Madame (IRE) 46 **96** (Second Set (IRE) 127) [2006 7g³ 6d* 7s* Oct 30] 160,000F, 90,000 2-y-o: third foal: half-brother to Irish 2003 2-y-o 6f/7f winner Little Whisper (by Be My Guest) and 2004 2-y-o 7f winner Secret Pact (by Lend A Hand), both fairly useful: dam, Irish 1½m winner, half-sister to smart performers Sweet Lady (won up to 9f in Italy/USA) and Late Parade (Italian sprinter): useful form: won 20-runner maiden at Naas in October and 5-runner Killavullan Stakes at Leopardstown (by ¾ length from Albert Einstein) later in month: should stay 1m: acts on soft ground. *Francis Ennis, Ireland*

CONGESTION CHARGE 3 b.f. Diktat 126 – Overdrive 99 (Shirley Heights 130) **72** [2006 p10g⁵ 11.5m² 14.1d⁴ 14m Jun 16] closely related to useful 1½m/2m (Queen's Vase) winner Endorsement (by Warning) and half-sister to 3 winners, including 6f (including at 2 yrs) winner (later stayed 1½m) Zugudi (by Night Shift): fair maiden: stays 1½m: acts on good to firm ground: sold 62,000 gns in July. *E. A. L. Dunlop*

CONGRESSIONAL (IRE) 3 b.f. Grand Lodge (USA) 125 – Gilah (IRE) (Saddlers' **69** Hall (IRE) 126) [2006 80: 8.3g p8g 8d⁵ Sep 25] good-topped filly: just fair handicapper in 2006: stays 1m: carried head awkwardly final start. *M. A. Jarvis*

CONJECTURE 4 b.g. Danzig (USA) – Golden Opinion (USA) 127 (Slew O' Gold **79** (USA)) [2006 81: 5m⁵ 5m 5m³ 5m⁵ 5.2f² 5.2m⁴ 5m 5.2m⁶ 5f⁶ 5g 5s² 5d⁶ p6g⁶ Nov 23] fair handicapper nowadays: best at 5f: acts on polytrack, firm and soft ground: tried blinkered/visored: tends to edge left: races up with pace. *R. Bastiman*

CONJUROR 5 b.g. Efisio 120 – Princess Athena 119 (Ahonoora 122) [2006 90: p7g⁵ **81** Mar 25] fairly useful performer: reportedly returned with a badly bruised pedal bone after only outing in 2006: stays 7f: acts on firm and good to soft going: tongue tied nowadays. *A. M. Balding*

CONKERING (USA) 3 ch.g. Horse Chestnut (SAF) 119 – Nunbridled (USA) (Un- **87** bridled (USA) 128) [2006 82: 8d* 10f 10.5s 10d⁴ Oct 4] lengthy, good-topped gelding: fairly useful performer, lightly raced: won maiden at Ripon in April: stays 1¼m: acts on good to soft going: sold 105,000 gns. *J. R. Fanshawe*

Killavullan Stakes, Leopardstown—Confuchias (left) finds a solution to the problems posed by Ballydoyle representatives Albert Einstein and Frederick Ozanam (striped sleeves)

CONNECT 9 b.g. Petong 126 – Natchez Trace 52 (Commanche Run 133) [2006 108, a–: 6m 6m⁵ 6m 6m 6f³ 5m 6m 5.1g⁵ 6d³ 6m 5.4g 6f 5d⁵ 5g p6g⁵ p6g* Nov 16] strong, lengthy gelding: unimpressive mover: useful handicapper on turf, fairly useful on all-weather: won at Wolverhampton final start, ridden closer to pace than usual: effective at 5f/easy 6f: acts on all-weather, firm and good to soft going: wears blinkers/visor: sometimes hangs: usually held up. *M. H. Tompkins* **101 a89 +**

CONNOTATION 4 b.f. Mujahid (USA) 125 – Seven Wonders (USA) (Rahy (USA) 115) [2006 80: p8.6g³ p7.1g⁵ p7.1g p8.6g 7g 8d p7.1g p10g p7.1g 8f⁵ p9.5g⁴ p8g Dec 5] leggy filly: fairly useful handicapper: left P. Chapple-Hyam after second start, below best subsequently: stays 9.5f: acts on polytrack and firm ground: tried visored/blinkered: flashes tail under pressure, one to treat with caution. *A. G. Newcombe* **80 d**

CONNY NOBEL (IRE) 2 gr.g. (Apr 4) Marju (IRE) 127 – Beauharnaise (FR) (Linamix (FR) 127) [2006 p7g p8g⁵ p7.1g² Dec 22] easily best effort in maidens when 5 lengths second to Regal Riband at Wolverhampton: should stay 1m: tongue tied. *R. A. Kvisla* **64**

CONQUEST (IRE) 2 b.c. (Feb 12) Invincible Spirit (IRE) 121 – Aguinaga (IRE) 76 (Machiavellian (USA) 123) [2006 5s² 6s⁵ 5m² 5.1f* 6d* 6d⁶ Sep 29] €80,000F, 135,000Y: strong, good-topped colt: has scope: has a fluent, quick action: second foal: dam, Irish 12.5f winner, half-sister to very smart 6f/7f performer Iktamal and smart French performer up to 12.5f First Magnitude: smart performer: improvement in blinkers after first 2 starts, second in Windsor Castle Stakes at Royal Ascot prior to winning maiden at Nottingham in July and Scottish Equitable Gimcrack Stakes at York (beat Wi Dud by ¾ length, despite trouble) in August: 5/1, tailed-off last of 6, seeming to take little interest, in Middle Park Stakes at Newmarket (reportedly lost action and thought to have got tongue over bit) final start: should stay 7f: unraced on heavy going, acts on any other turf: looks ungenuine. *W. J. Haggas* **114 §**

CONRAD 3 b.g. Royal Applause 124 – Milly-M (Cadeaux Genereux 131) [2006 78: 7g³ 6m 5f⁵ 6m* 6g 6s 8d³ 8d Oct 27] 100,000F: long-backed gelding: first foal: dam unraced daughter of smart 5f performer Millyant: fair performer: in frame in maidens at 2 yrs for D. Wachman in Ireland: won handicap at Pontefract in August: stays 8.5f: acts on soft and good to firm ground: tried in cheekpieces (reported to have lost action)/blinkers: gelded after final outing. *R. A. Fahey* **77**

CONSENT 3 ch.f. Groom Dancer (USA) 128 – Preference (Efisio 120) [2006 –p: 9m Jun 3] strong filly: maiden: well beaten in handicap only outing in 2006. *A. Dickman* **–**

CONSERVATION (FR) 3 b.c. Green Desert (USA) 127 – Lightly Dancing (FR) (Groom Dancer (USA) 128) [2006 62p: 8.1s³ 8m⁴ 10.2g³ 10m² 11.7g 10.3m⁴ 11m² 11.6s³ 10d² 10s² Oct 18] big colt: fair maiden: stays 11.6f, at least as effective at shorter: acts on soft and good to firm going: sold 48,000 gns, joined N. Gifford. *P. W. Chapple-Hyam* **79**

Scottish Equitable Gimcrack Stakes, York—
the strongly-ridden Conquest wins a substandard renewal from Wi Dud (noseband) and Bodes Galaxy

Highclere Thoroughbred Racing XXXVIII's "Conquest"

CONSERVATIVE 3 b. or br.g. Pivotal 124 – Happy Omen (Warning 136) [2006 6d² **74** 8m² p7g³ p7g Nov 15] 50,000Y: second foal: dam once-raced half-sister to Middle Park winner First Trump: fair maiden: left W. Haggas after second start: stays 1m: acts on polytrack, good to firm and good to soft ground: slowly away on debut. *P. G. Murphy*

CONSIDERTHELILIES (IRE) 3 b.f. Mull of Kintyre (USA) 114 – Gilding The **–** Lily (IRE) 58 (High Estate 127) [2006 50: 7m 6g 8.3m 8d 8v Sep 14] sturdy filly: maiden: little form in 2006: tried in cheekpieces. *Miss L. A. Perratt*

CONSIDINE (USA) 5 b.g. Romanov (IRE) 119 – Libeccio (NZ) (Danzatore (CAN) **–** 120) [2006 75: 21.7m Jun 24] big, workmanlike gelding: fair performer: flattered eighth in steadily-run Queen Alexandra Stakes at Royal Ascot only Flat outing in 2006: stays at least 2m: acts on polytrack, firm and soft going: has worn crossed noseband: won over hurdles in August: sold 6,500 gns in October. *C. J. Mann*

CONSONANT (IRE) 9 ch.g. Barathea (IRE) 127 – Dinalina (FR) (Top Ville 129) **75** [2006 93: p10g² p10g⁵ p10g⁶ 10.9g 10.2g 9.7f 10g² 9.9g³ 8m 9g³ 10m⁴ 8.3f⁵ p8.6g² **a87** p9.5g² p9.5m⁶ p9.5g p10g p9.5g Dec 30] sturdy, lengthy gelding: fairly useful handicapper on all-weather, fair on turf: below form last 4 starts (brought down second occasion): stays 1¼m: acts on all-weather, firm and soft going: tried visored: tends to hang. *D. G. Bridgwater*

CONSTABLE BURTON 5 b.g. Foxhound (USA) 103 – Actress 73 (Known Fact **–** (USA) 135) [2006 64, a72: 10f p8.6g Jul 28] big, workmanlike gelding: fair handicapper at best: well held both starts in 2006: tried visored/blinkered: usually races prominently: sold 17,000 gns in October. *Mrs A. Duffield*

CONSTABLES ART 3 b.g. Royal Applause 124 – Social Storm (USA) (Future Storm **49** (USA)) [2006 10.1m 12.1m² 10s Oct 2] strong gelding: poor form in sellers: stays 1½m: blinkered last 2 outings. *N. A. Callaghan*

bet365 Old Newton Cup (Handicap), Haydock—Consular is too tenacious for the irresolute Ouninpohja

CONSTANT CHEERS (IRE) 3 b.g. Royal Applause 124 – Juno Marlowe (IRE) 100 **64**
(Danehill (USA) 126) [2006 62: 8.2d 10.2g4 p10g 11.9m5 p12g Jun 29] sturdy gelding:
modest maiden: stays 1¼m: tried visored/in cheekpieces. *W. R. Swinburn*

CONSTRUCTOR 5 b.g. So Factual (USA) – Love And Kisses 70 (Salse (USA) **–**
128) [2006 70: 7.6m Jul 29] maiden handicapper: well held only outing in 2006: sold
3,500 gns in October. *C. A. Cyzer*

CONSUELITA 3 b. or br.f. Singspiel (IRE) 133 – Green Rosy (USA) (Green Dancer **–**
(USA) 132) [2006 8.3m 9.9g5 10f 8.3m p9.5s Dec 13] half-sister to several winners, including French/US 7f (at 2 yrs) to 1½m winner Majorien (by Machiavellian) and French
9f (at 2 yrs) to 1½m winner America (by Arazi), both smart: dam French 1½m winner:
little form: bred to stay 1½m. *B. J. Meehan*

CONSULAR 4 br.g. Singspiel (IRE) 133 – Language of Love 63 (Rock City 120) [2006 **106**
100: 10.4d 12m3 12m 11.9g* 12g4 13.9d Aug 23] lengthy, useful-looking gelding: useful
handicapper: won bet365 Old Newton Cup at Haydock in July by length from Ouninpohja: creditable fourth to Young Mick at Ascot next time: stays 1½m (well held over
1¾m in Ebor at York final start): acts on good to firm going: races prominently: sold
240,000 gns, sent to UAE. *M. A. Jarvis*

CONSUL GENERAL 2 b.c. Selkirk (USA) 129 – West Dakota (USA) (Gone West **104 p**
(USA)) [2006 8d* 10g Nov 12] third foal: half-brother to 4-y-o Great Plains and 3-y-o
Rapid City: dam useful French 1m winner: won 18-runner maiden at Cork in September
by 7 lengths from Eyshal, powering clear after leading 2f out: not entirely discredited
when seventh of 13 to Passage of Time in Criterium de Saint-Cloud next time: should
stay 1¼m: should do better yet. *D. K. Weld, Ireland*

CONTACT DANCER (IRE) 7 b.g. Sadler's Wells (USA) 132 – Rain Queen (Rain- **90**
bow Quest (USA) 134) [2006 99: 18.7m 13d6 18d Oct 14] leggy gelding: useful handicapper in 2005: form (fairly useful) in 2006 only when sixth of 7 at Hamilton: sweated
up badly when well held in Chester Cup (only outing for C. Swann in Ireland) and
Cesarewitch at Newmarket: stays at least 2¼m: has won on good to firm going, best on
good or softer (acts on heavy): wore cheekpieces on reappearance: sold 16,000 gns,
joined P. Bowen. *M. Johnston*

CONTEMPLATION 3 b.c. Sunday Silence (USA) – Wood Vine (USA) (Woodman **67**
(USA) 126) [2006 14.1d2 11.9s4 7m2 p9.5m5 10s Oct 16] third live foal: brother to useful
2001 2-y-o 6f (including Cherry Hinton Stakes) winner Silent Honor: dam unraced half-
sister to useful French 1½m winner Maeander out of sister to Miesque: fair maiden: left
M. Johnston after second outing (folded tamely): stays 9.5f: acts on polytrack, probably
on good to firm and good to soft going. *G. A. Swinbank*

CONTENTED (IRE) 4 b.g. Orpen (USA) 116 – Joyfullness (USA) (Dixieland Band **59**
(USA)) [2006 62, a66: p10g p10g p7g f7g2 p7g4 f6g2 9.7d f7g2 8.1d3 7m p8g Jun 29] fair **a66**
maiden handicapper: effective at 6f, seems to stay 1¼m: acts on all-weather and good to
soft going: usually wears cheekpieces nowadays: looked none too keen fourth outing.
Mrs L. C. Jewell

CONTENTIOUS (IRE) 2 b.f. (Feb 13) Danetime (IRE) 121 – Serious Contender **59 p**
(IRE) (Tenby 125) [2006 5.1m Aug 25] 26,000 2-y-o: fourth foal: half-sister to 5-y-o Fox
Covert and 3-y-o Buachaill Dona: dam unraced: 4/1, good speed (hampered) in maiden at
Bath: open to improvement. *D. M. Simcock*

CONTENTIOUS (USA) 2 b.f. (Mar 16) Giant's Causeway (USA) 132 – Illicit (USA) **77 p**
(Mr Prospector (USA)) [2006 7.1d⁴ 7s² Oct 10] second foal: dam unraced half-sister to
very smart US performer up to 1¼m Smuggler out of Breeders' Cup Distaff winner Inside
Information: in frame in minor event at Salisbury and maiden at Newbury (3 lengths
second of 16 to Mythical Kid): will stay 1m: should do better. *J. L. Dunlop*

CONTINENT 9 ch.g. Lake Coniston (IRE) 131 – Krisia (Kris 135) [2006 102§: 6s 6m⁶ **100 §**
6s 5m³ 5m⁴ 6m 6m 6s 6d 7.2d² 6g Sep 23] angular gelding: one-time very smart
performer: useful nowadays: good efforts when in frame in handicaps at Epsom (third
to Desert Lord in 'Dash'), Newcastle (fourth to Peace Offering) and Ayr (second to
Glenbuck): effective at 5f to 7f: acts on firm and soft ground: has worn tongue tie: visored
once at 6 yrs: often slowly away: usually held up: unreliable. *D. Nicholls*

CONTRA MUNDUM (USA) 3 ch.g. Giant's Causeway (USA) 132 – Speak Softly **81**
To Me (USA) (Ogygian (USA)) [2006 p8g 10d³ 11.9m⁵ Jun 4] quite good-topped gelding: fifth foal: half-brother to winner in USA by Danehill: dam unraced half-sister to dam
of Poule d'Essai des Poulains winner Green Tune and Cheveley Park Stakes winner Pas
de Reponse: best effort in maidens when third to Bandama at Newbury: stays 1¼m: acts
on good to soft ground: slowly away first 2 outings: sold 6,000 gns in August.
B. J. Meehan

CONTROVENTO (IRE) 4 b.f. Midhish 109 – La Maya (IRE) 54 (Scenic 128) [2006 **69**
13m 9g 8.7f 8g 6m 6m 6m 7m 6g 8d 6v⁴ 5d* 6v 5v* 5d p6g Nov 18] fourth foal: dam
maiden who stayed 2m: fair handicapper: won twice at Navan (first one apprentice
race) in October: seemed to run well at Musselburgh penultimate outing: best at 5f: acts
on heavy ground, well held on polytrack: in blinkers/cheekpieces after first 2 starts.
E. Tyrrell, Ireland

CONVALLARIA (FR) 3 b.f. Cape Cross (IRE) 129 – Scarlet Davis (FR) (Ti King **–**
(FR) 121) [2006 7g 8m May 13] €27,000Y, 20,000 2-y-o: sturdy filly: sixth foal: half-
sister to French 2001 2-y-o 9f winner Settima (by Septieme Ciel): dam unraced: well held
in maidens at Newmarket. *G. Wragg*

CONVERTI 2 b.c. (Jan 26) Averti (IRE) 117 – Conquestadora 98 (Hernando (FR) 127) **60**
[2006 6f 7.1m p8g Sep 6] first foal: dam, 13f to 2m winner, half-sister to smart performer
up to 1½m Saddler's Quest: modest form in maidens. *P. F. I. Cole*

CONVINCE (USA) 5 ch.g. Mt Livermore (USA) – Conical 63 (Zafonic (USA) 130) **71**
[2006 81: 5.7f⁵ 5m 6g³ 7.1f 5.1f³ 6g 6g⁵ 5.2m⁶ 5.1m 5.5d 7d² 8.2d⁶ Nov 1] tall, close-
coupled gelding: fair handicapper: effective at 5f to 7f: acts on firm ground, probably
on good to soft: tried in cheekpieces: has carried head awkwardly: none too consistent.
J. M. Bradley

CONVIVIAL SPIRIT 2 b.g. (Apr 30) Lake Coniston (IRE) 131 – Ruby Princess **64**
(IRE) 70 (Mac's Imp (USA) 116) [2006 5m⁶ p6f³ 5g² 6d 5.2d p6g⁴ Nov 1] 5,000Y:
workmanlike gelding: fourth foal: half-brother to 5-y-o Red Sovereign and 6f (at 2 yrs)/
7f winner Merely A Monarch (by Reprimand): dam second over 5f at 2 yrs on soft ground:
modest maiden: in frame 3 times, in nursery final outing: effective at 5f/6f: tongue tied
last 2 starts. *E. F. Vaughan*

COOKIE CUTTER (IRE) 4 b.f. Fasliyev (USA) 120 – Cut The Red Tape (IRE) 75 **71**
(Sure Blade (USA) 130) [2006 67: f6g² p5.1g³ f6g* p6g³ Jan 30] fair performer: won
maiden at Southwell in January: effective at 5f/6f: acts on all-weather, good to firm and
good to soft going: sometimes wears cheekpieces/blinkers: sold 22,000 gns in November.
K. R. Burke

COOKIES QUIFF (IRE) 2 b.g. (Feb 22) Iron Mask (USA) 117 – Amy G (IRE) 52 **54**
(Common Grounds 118) [2006 5.1g³ 5.2f⁴ 7m 6m⁶ 5m Sep 13] leggy gelding: modest
maiden, raced mostly in sellers: stays 6f. *J. S. Moore*

COOLAW (IRE) 3 b.f. Priolo (USA) 127 – Cool Gales 85 (Lord Gayle (USA) 124) **–**
[2006 8g p12g⁶ p12.2g⁶ Dec 2] half-sister to several winners, including 9-y-o What-A-
Dancer: dam maiden who probably stayed 1½m: little form in maidens, leaving Ms
F. Crowley in Ireland after debut: blinkered last 2 outings. *G. G. Margarson*

COOL BATHWICK (IRE) 7 b.g. Entrepreneur 123 – Tarafa 93 (Akarad (FR) 130) **–**
[2006 –: p9.5g p12.2g 10.2d 12.1d 18m f12g Jul 31] useful-looking gelding: fair handicapper at best: no form since 2004: tried tongue tied/in headgear. *G. H. Yardley*

COOL BOX (USA) 2 b.c. (Apr 18) Grand Slam (USA) 120 – Frigidette (USA) (It's **90** Freezing (USA) 122) [2006 6m³ 7g⁶ 6m⁵ p7.1g³ p6g* Nov 11] $85,000Y: tall, good-topped colt: half-brother to several winners in USA, including 2000 Grade 2 2-y-o 9f winner Windsor Castle (by Lord Carson): dam US 6f to 1m winner: fairly useful performer: improved to win nursery at Lingfield in November: will prove best up to 7f: acts on polytrack and good to firm going. *Mrs A. J. Perrett*

COOL CUSTOMER (USA) 3 b.c. Gone West (USA) – Radu Cool (USA) (Carni- **100** valay (USA)) [2006 79: p8g6 11.8d* p12g* 12s² 11s² 11.6m* 11m⁴ 14g² 14.1g⁴ 13d² 12g³ Oct 12] compact, attractive colt: has a fluent, round action: useful performer: won maiden at Leicester in April, and handicaps at Kempton in May and Windsor in July: good efforts in handicaps after, neck second to Macorville at Hamilton penultimate start: stays 1¾m: acts on polytrack, soft and good to firm going: visored (raced freely/hung) final outing: edged right eighth start: held up: sent to UAE. *E. A. L. Dunlop*

COOL EBONY 3 br.g. Erhaab (USA) 127 – Monawara (IRE) 73 (Namaqualand **86** (USA)) [2006 72?: 12g⁵ 14.1m 10g³ 10m⁵ 8g⁴ 8.1f* 8f* 8g² 8s 8m Oct 8] sturdy, angular gelding: fairly useful handicapper: won at Haydock in July and Bath in August: good second at Thirsk next time: best efforts at 1m: acts on firm going. *M. Dods*

COOLEYCALL STAR (IRE) 5 b.g. Foxhound (USA) 103 – Ozwood (IRE) (Royal **46** Academy (USA) 130) [2006 51: f7g p6g³ p8.6g f6g Mar 21] poor maiden: stays 1m: acts on all-weather: usually wears headgear: tried tongue tied in 2004. *A. G. Juckes*

COOL HUNTER 5 ch.g. Polar Falcon (USA) 126 – Seabound 65 (Prince Sabo 123) **90** [2006 89: 10g 10g* 9.8v 10.5g p10g 12.3m⁴ 12m Sep 16] lengthy gelding: fairly useful handicapper: won at Windsor in May: stays easy 1½m: acts on good to firm and good to soft going: inconsistent: sold 16,000 gns, joined R. C. Guest. *W. R. Swinburn*

COOL ISLE 3 b.f. Polar Prince (IRE) 117 – Fisher Island (IRE) 59 (Sri Pekan (USA) **51** 117) [2006 55: p8.6g⁵ f7g³ f8g³ f8g² p7g⁶ f8g⁴ f11g f8g p12.2g⁵ p12g 10.1f² 11.9f⁵ **a59** 10.1g* 9.8d p12.2m² 10.1m 12.1m* p12g f12g³ p13.9g p12.2g* p12.2s⁵ p12.2g⁴ Dec 18] close-coupled filly: modest performer: left K. Ryan after fourth start: won claimer at Yarmouth in August and sellers at Beverley in September and Wolverhampton in November: stays 1½m: acts on all-weather and firm going: wears blinkers (tried in cheekpieces). *P. Howling*

COOL PANIC (IRE) 4 b.g. Brave Act 119 – Geht Schnell (Fairy King (USA)) [2006 **94 ?** 99: p7g 7m 8s⁵ 7g 7d 7g Aug 19] close-coupled, quite good-topped gelding: fairly useful handicapper nowadays: easily best effort of 2006 on second outing: best at 6f/7f: acts on soft and good to firm going: gelded after final start. *M. L. W. Bell*

COOL SANDS (IRE) 4 b.g. Trans Island 119 – Shalerina (USA) (Shalford (IRE) **59** 124§) [2006 62, a68: f6g⁵ p6g⁵ p7g* 7d⁶ 7d 7g 6d⁴ p6g 6s p6m p7.1g p7g p10g f7g* **a69** p7g² f8g⁵ Dec 27] strong gelding: fair handicapper on all-weather, modest on turf: won at Lingfield in March and Southwell in December: best at 6f/7f: acts on all-weather, soft and good to firm going: visored. *D. Shaw*

COOL STING (IRE) 3 b.g. Bluebird (USA) 125 – Honey Bee (Alnasr Alwasheek **74** 117) [2006 72: p6g p5g³ p5g² p6g* 5.7d p6g⁶ p6g 7m⁴ 8g⁶ 8m⁶ 7m⁵ 7f 7f³ 7m⁶ 8m³ 7m⁴ p6g* 6d p6g⁶ p6g⁵ p7.1g p6g⁶ Dec 22] leggy gelding: fair performer: won maiden at Lingfield in April and (having left A. Balding after sixteenth outing) seller at same track in October: left P. McEntee before final start: stays 7f: acts on polytrack and good to firm ground: often wears headgear nowadays: tongue tied penultimate start. *M. G. Quinlan*

COOL TIGER 3 ch.g. Vettori (IRE) 119 – Juvenilia (IRE) 55 (Masterclass (USA) 116) **64** [2006 8m⁴ p8g 6d 7f p10g f6g* f6g p6g* Dec 18] 1,000 3-y-o, resold £4,600 3-y-o: fifth foal: half-brother to 6-y-o Riquewihr: dam third at 7f both starts: modest performer: won banded races at Southwell in November and Kempton in December: stays 6f: acts on all-weather and good to firm ground. *P. Howling*

COOPERSTOWN 3 ch.g. Dr Fong (USA) 128 – Heckle 47 (In The Wings 128) [2006 **87** 8d³ 8d² Oct 2] 37,000F, €140,000Y: good-bodied gelding: third foal: dam, ran 3 times in Britain, later 7f winner in Germany: green, better effort in maidens at Pontefract when ¾-length third to Mosharref, despite tending to wander: will be suited by 1¼m. *J. Howard Johnson*

COPERNICAN 2 ch.g. (Mar 25) Hernando (FR) 127 – Wonderful World (GER) **54 p** (Dashing Blade 117) [2006 p8g p8g⁶ p7g Sep 27] 80,000Y: big, lengthy, good-topped gelding: second foal: half-brother to 3-y-o Advanced: dam, German 7f winner, sister to smart German 1¼m/11f performer Winning Dash: not knocked about in maidens, all in

September, and gelded after: type to do better in 3-y-o handicaps at 1¼m/1½m. *Sir Mark Prescott*

COPPER KING 2 ch.g. (Feb 12) Ishiguru (USA) 114 – Dorissio (IRE) 75 (Efisio 120) **78**
[2006 5.5d 5.1d³ 6f⁶ 6f 5.5m⁶ 5.5m 7.1d* p8.6m⁵ p7.1g² p7.1g* p7.1g p7g⁴ Dec 19]
30,000F, 20,000Y: good-bodied gelding: second foal: dam 1m winner: fair performer:
won claimer at Warwick (left A. Balding £8,000) in October and nursery at Wolverhampton (dead-heated with Stoneacre Gareth in 4-runner event) in November: stays 8.6f: acts
on polytrack and good to soft ground: visored sixth/seventh starts. *P. D. Evans*

COPPERMALT (USA) 8 b.g. Affirmed (USA) – Poppy Carew (IRE) 110 (Danehill **51**
(USA) 126) [2006 54: p13g³ p13g 12f Jun 30] modest maiden on Flat: stays 2m: acts on
polytrack and firm going, possibly not on soft/heavy: has been reluctant at stall: won over
hurdles in September and November. *R. Curtis*

COPPINGTON MELODY (IRE) 3 b.f. Ordway (USA) 117 – Chorus (USA) (Darshaan 133) [2006 10.2m 10.2g⁶ p9.5g p16.2m p16g Dec 15] €7,500F, €7,000Y: **61**
fourth foal: half-sister to minor winner in USA by Boundary: dam ran once in USA: modest maiden: easily best effort on fourth outing: stays 2m: acts on polytrack. *B. W. Duke*

COPPLESTONE (IRE) 10 b.g. Second Set (IRE) 127 – Queen of The Brush (Averof **54 §**
123) [2006 16g³ 13.1g 16g Jul 3] tall gelding: poor handicapper: stays 2m: acts on firm
and good to soft going: tried visored/tongue tied, wears cheekpieces nowadays: ungenuine: won over fences in August. *A. C. Whillans*

COQUET ISLAND 3 ch.g. Alhaarth (IRE) 126 – Abir 73 (Soviet Star (USA) 128) **–**
[2006 72: f5g⁶ 5d 6m May 4] leggy gelding: maiden: no form in 2006. *G. M. Moore*

COQUIN D'ALEZAN (IRE) 5 ch.g. Cadeaux Genereux 131 – Nwaahil (IRE) **72**
(Nashwan (USA) 135) [2006 72: f6g⁵ p6g⁵ p7g Apr 12] fair maiden: stays easy 7f: raced
only on all-weather. *W. Jarvis*

CORANGLAIS 6 ch.g. Piccolo 121 – Antonia's Folly 64 (Music Boy 124) [2006 71: **60**
6f 6g 5.7s 5s⁵ 6g 5.7f 5.7m⁶ 6m 6m⁴ 5d⁵ Aug 20] compact gelding: good walker: modest
handicapper: effective at 5f to easy 7f: acts on polytrack, firm and soft ground: wears
blinkers/cheekpieces. *J. M. Bradley*

CORA PEARL (IRE) 3 b.f. Montjeu (IRE) 137 – Castara Beach (IRE) 74 (Danehill **51**
(USA) 126) [2006 –: f7g 12d⁶ 12m⁴ 14.1m⁶ 12.1g May 31] good-topped filly: modest
maiden: may prove best short of 1½m. *M. J. Polglase*

CORDAGE (IRE) 4 ch.g. Dr Fong (USA) 128 – Flagship 84 (Rainbow Quest (USA) **–**
134) [2006 69: p8.6g 8m 11.1m⁶ 8f p13.9g f8g p13.9g Nov 27] close-coupled gelding:
fair performer at best: well held in 2006, leaving Karen McLintock after fourth start: tried
in cheekpieces/visor/tongue tie. *J. A. Pickering*

CORDELIA 3 b.f. Green Desert (USA) 137 – Bint Zamayem (IRE) 95 (Rainbow Quest **71**
(USA) 134) [2006 6v⁶ 7d⁵ 7m⁵ 5f² 5.1f⁴ 5.7m 6d⁵ p7g² p7g² p6g² Nov 14] good-bodied
filly: seventh foal: sister to useful Irish 6f (at 2 yrs)/7f winner Sweet Deimos and half-sister to 7.5f winner Queenie (by Indian Ridge) and 2002 2-y-o 1m winner Rumbalara
(by Intikhab), both fairly useful: dam, 1¼m winner, half-sister to smart French miler
Rouquette: fair maiden: stays 7f: acts on polytrack, firm and good to soft going: temperament under suspicion: sold 32,000 gns. *B. W. Hills*

CORDIER 4 b.g. Desert Style (IRE) 121 – Slipper 94 (Suave Dancer (USA) 136) [2006 **–**
75: p12.2g⁶ p12.2g* f12s³ 10m 12d⁶ May 26] fairly useful performer: won handicap at **a85**
Wolverhampton in February: stays 1½m: acts on all-weather, lightly raced and no form
on turf: races up with pace. *J. Mackie*

CORDWAIN 2 b.g. (Apr 17) Lomitas 129 – Goodie Twosues 91 (Fraam 114) [2006 8m **83**
10.1d² 10d⁴ Oct 28] 72,000Y: sturdy gelding: first foal: dam, 2-y-o 6f winner who stayed
8.5f, became one to treat with caution: fairly useful form: blinkered and much improved
after debut, second in maiden at Yarmouth and fourth (to Empire Day) looked none too
keen in listed event at Newmarket: stays 1¼m: sold 26,000 gns, sent to Denmark.
J. H. M. Gosden

CORKY (IRE) 5 br.g. Intikhab (USA) 135 – Khamseh 85 (Thatching 131) [2006 85, **85 §**
a73: f8g p8g p9.5g⁴ p9.5g p8.6g 7s² 8.2s 8d 8g⁶ 8.2d 7s 8.1s³ May 27] sturdy gelding: **a73 §**
fairly useful handicapper on turf, fair on all-weather: stays 9.5f: acts on polytrack and
heavy ground: tried visored/blinkered: often very slowly away, and one to treat with caution: sold 4,500 gns in October. *I. W. McInnes*

CORLOUGH MOUNTAIN 2 ch.c. (Feb 7) Inchinor 119 – Two Step 60 (Mujtahid **71 p**
(USA) 118) [2006 p6g² p7g² p8g⁵ Dec 19] 11,000F, 56,000Y: third foal: brother to 3-y-o

Smooch and half-brother to winner in Greece by Singspiel: dam 5f/7f winner: similar form all starts in maidens, still green when fifth at Lingfield (stumbled after 2f and wandered under pressure): stays 1m: raced only on polytrack: should make a better 3-y-o. *N. A. Callaghan*

CORMORANT WHARF (IRE) 6 b.g. Alzao (USA) 117 – Mercy Bien (IRE) 63 (Be **76** My Guest (USA) 126) [2006 76: p7g p10g 8m⁶ 10.2g* 12d² 10m⁶ 10f² 12g⁵ 9.7m⁵ 12s³ p12g² Nov 13] well-made gelding: fair handicapper: won ladies race at Bath in May: left G. L. Moore after tenth start: stays 1½m: yet to race on heavy going, acts on any other turf and polytrack: tried tongue tied/in headgear earlier in career: often ridden by Miss J. Powell. *T. E. Powell*

CORNELL PRECEDENT 2 ch.c. (May 15) Polish Precedent (USA) 131 – Sham- **58** wari (USA) 63 (Shahrastani (USA) 135) [2006 8v 7.2d⁵ 7s⁶ Oct 10] smallish, shallow-girthed colt: modest form in maidens: gives impression 1¼m/1½m will suit: raced on going softer than good. *J. J. Quinn*

CORN FLOWER (USA) 2 b.f. (Feb 6) Seeking The Gold (USA) – Lilium 111 (Nash- **60 p** wan (USA) 135) [2006 7s⁵ Oct 10] second foal: dam, 7f (at 2 yrs) and 1½m winner, half-sister to Middle Park Stakes winner Lujain and smart sprinter Botanical (both by Seeking The Gold): odds on, 6¼ lengths fifth in maiden at Newcastle, travelling well but fading (testing ground): will probably do better. *Saeed bin Suroor*

CORNUS 4 ch.g. Inchinor 119 – Demerger (USA) (Distant View (USA) 126) [2006 **77 §** 102§: p6g⁶ f6g p7g⁵ p7g p5.1g p6g 5f 5m 5.7m⁶ p6g⁴ 6.1g⁴ 6.1d 7s Oct 14] smallish, **a87 §** sturdy, attractive gelding: fairly useful handicapper: left M. Polglase after sixth outing, J. Osborne after eleventh: stays 6f: acts on polytrack (well held both outings on fibre-sand), soft and good to firm going: unreliable. *A. J. McCabe*

CORONADO FOREST (USA) 7 b.g. Spinning World (USA) 130 – Desert Jewel **45** (USA) (Caerleon (USA) 132) [2006 55: p8g p8g p8g Apr 3] poor performer nowadays: barely stays 1¼m: acts on all-weather, no recent form on turf: tried in blinkers/cheek-pieces. *M. R. Hoad*

CORONADO'S GOLD (USA) 5 ch.g. Coronado's Quest (USA) 130 – Debit My **57** Account (USA) (Classic Account (USA)) [2006 –: p10g p8.6g⁵ Feb 24] won in US in 2004: modest form in Britain: tried in cheekpieces. *W. R. Swinburn*

CORONATION FLIGHT 3 b.f. Missed Flight 123 – Hand On Heart (IRE) 62 **54** (Taufan (USA) 119) [2006 –: 9.8g 9.2d⁵ 7m 7.9m³ 10m⁵ 9.3m⁶ 8d² 7m⁵ 8d³ 9d³ 7.2v³ Oct 28] angular filly: modest maiden: probably stays 1¼m: acts on good to firm and good to soft going. *F. P. Murtagh*

CORONATION QUEEN 3 b.f. Pivotal 124 – Coffee Ice 92 (Primo Dominie 121) **–** [2006 –p: 9s May 25] tall filly: little impact in maidens at Newbury and Goodwood. *S. Kirk*

CORRAN ARD (IRE) 5 b.g. Imperial Ballet (IRE) 110 – Beeper The Great (USA) **95** (Whadjathink (USA)) [2006 8.1m* 10m* 10m* Sep 21] leggy gelding: useful handi-capper, lightly raced: left Mrs J. Harrington in Ireland and off nearly 2 years prior to reappearance: won at Sandown in April (Flat/Jump Jockeys event) and June and at Ponte-fract (further improvement when beating Along The Nile a head) in September: stays 1¼m: acts on good to firm ground. *Evan Williams*

CORRE CAMINOS (FR) 4 b.g. Montjeu (IRE) 137 – Dibenoise (FR) (Kendor **124** (FR) 122) [2006 114: 10g² 10.5d* 9.3d⁵ 10m⁶ 10g³ Sep 22]

Geldings are still barred from some of the top races in Europe but the list has grown shorter over the years. Only seven Group 1s are still closed in Britain —the Two Thousand Guineas, Derby, St Leger, St James's Palace, Middle Park, Dewhurst and Racing Post Trophy—and four in Ireland—the Two Thousand Guineas, Derby, Phoenix Stakes and National Stakes. The restrictions in Britain and Ireland are in line with an edict by the European Pattern Committee that races open to colts but restricted to two-year-olds or three-year-olds must exclude geldings. The banned Group 1s in France number eleven. The Poule d'Essai des Poulains, Prix Jean Prat, Prix du Jockey Club, Grand Prix de Paris, Morny, Jean-Luc Lagardere, Criterium International and Criterium de Saint-Cloud are closed under the European Pattern Committee's archaic ruling, which reflects pre-judices against geldings on the grounds that they have been 'artificially improved' (a remark that applies equally to other surgical procedures that result in horses being 'able to do what they could not have done otherwise'). The French authorities

Prix Ganay - Grand Prix Air Mauritius, Longchamp—Corre Caminos turns the tables on Manduro (No.3); Royal Highness is second and Pride only fourth

still exercise their discretion in persisting with a ban on geldings in three Group 1 races that are not restricted to one age group, the Jacques le Marois, Moulin and Prix de l'Arc. A number of others were belatedly opened up in 2001, including the Prix Ganay - Grand Prix Air Mauritius at Longchamp, the first Group 1 of the European season and a race that often sees the return of some of the top older middle-distance performers.

The distinction of becoming the first gelding to win the Ganay fell to Corre Caminos. Castration is normally performed to make colts without potential breeding value easier to handle and more effective as racehorses—'Good stallions make better geldings'—but the well-bred Corre Caminos, who cost €200,000 as a yearling, was reportedly gelded as a two-year-old because his action was impeded by over-sized testicles. He was backward into the bargain and didn't see a racecourse until he was three when he won a newcomers event at Saint-Cloud and the Prix du Prince d'Orange at Longchamp from five starts. None of the seven who lined up for the Prix Ganay at the end of April had won at Group 1 level. Arc winner Hurricane Run was sent instead for the Tattersalls Gold Cup at the Curragh the following month, his stable relying at Longchamp on the ex-German four-year-old Manduro who had just held the fast-finishing Corre Caminos in the Prix d'Harcourt over the same course three weeks earlier. Corre Caminos turned the tables in no uncertain manner, quickening clear in tremendous fashion in the final furlong, after being ridden much closer to the pace than in the Harcourt. Five lengths was the margin of victory over the previous year's Prix de Malleret winner Royal Highness, who held on to second by three quarters of a length from Manduro, with Pride fourth and Montare fifth. Corre Caminos provided his trainer, who has a string of around forty at Chantilly, with his first Group 1 winner. The Ganay was easily the highlight of the season for Corre Caminos who didn't repeat the form in three later appearances, fifth (three places behind Manduro) when odds on for the Prix d'Ispahan at Longchamp in May, sixth of seven when 33/1 in the Prince of Wales's Stakes at Royal Ascot and a not-discredited third, coming out the best horse at the weights, when again odds on in La Coupe de Maisons-Laffitte in September. Corre Caminos evidently has his quirks and he spoiled his chance in the d'Ispahan by pulling too hard, while at Royal Ascot his rider never seemed able to really get at him in the straight as he persistently edged in behind his rivals and found himself short of room after being waited with.

Corre Caminos (FR) (b.g. 2002)	Montjeu (IRE) (b 1996)	Sadler's Wells (b 1981)	Northern Dancer Fairy Bridge
		Floripedes (b 1985)	Top Ville Toute Cy
	Dibenoise (FR) (gr 1993)	Kendor (gr 1986)	Kenmare Belle Mecene
		Boreale (b 1981)	Bellypha Princesse Tora

The tall, quite good-topped Corre Caminos is not alone among the leading progeny of Montjeu in having his quirks. Issues of temperament are not, however, preventing Montjeu's offspring from excelling on the racecourse. The victories of Corre Caminos and another typical Montjeu in Montare (Prix Royal-Oak) brought the number of individual Group 1 winners from Montjeu's first crop to five (discounting the Singapore Derby won by ex-Irish Falstaff), only one short of the six achieved by his sire Sadler's Wells with his first crop. Montjeu's fee was reduced for his second season, and further reduced for his third. Three of Montjeu's three-year-olds won at Royal Ascot—Papal Bull (King Edward VII Stakes), Mont Etoile (Ribblesdale) and Snoqualmie Boy (Hampton Court Stakes)—and, among the two-year-olds, Authorized emulated Motivator by winning the Racing Post Trophy. Motivator's achievements at two saw Montjeu's star in the ascendancy again and, after Hurricane Run and Scorpion (Grand Prix de Paris and St Leger) joined Derby winner Motivator as Group 1 winners at three, Montjeu was being labelled the natural successor to his sire, a title for which, after his achievements in 2006, Galileo is now vying. Corre Caminos is the fourth foal of the unraced Dibenoise, and was followed by the smart Racinger (by Spectrum) who gave her a second winner on the Flat in France. Dibenoise is a half-sister to the smart sprinter-miler River of Light, while the grandam of Corre Caminos, Boreale, finished second in the Poule d'Essai des Pouliches. The great grandam of Corre Caminos, Princesse Tora (a daughter of Dewhurst winner and Irish Oaks runner-up Torbella), was a half-sister to Sussex Stakes winner Carlemont and to Cambrienne, a one-time record-priced European yearling who became an influential broodmare (great grandam of Derby winner Dr Devious and of Queen Elizabeth II Stakes winner Markofdistinction). The tall, quite good-topped Corre Caminos has been raced only at around a mile and a quarter and he acts on soft going. He is usually held up and has worn a crossed noseband. *M. Delzangles, France*

CORRECT TIME (IRE) 3 b.c. Danetime (IRE) 121 – Solo Symphony (IRE) 67 **69** (Fayruz 116) [2006 58: p6g⁵ p5g* p5.1g⁴ p5g⁴ p6g³ Mar 4] fair handicapper: won at Lingfield in January: effective at 5f/easy 6f: acts on polytrack and good to firm going: hung third start: sent to Singapore. *N. P. Littmoden*

CORRIB ECLIPSE 7 b.g. Double Eclipse (IRE) 122 – Last Night's Fun (IRE) (Law **101** Society (USA) 130) [2006 104: 21.7m⁵ 18d⁵ Sep 14] good-topped gelding: useful performer: creditable 2¾ lengths fifth to Baddam in Queen Alexandra Stakes at Royal Ascot: ran as if amiss at Pontefract only subsequent outing: stays 2¾m: acts on polytrack, firm and good to soft going. *Ian Williams*

CORRIB (IRE) 3 b.f. Lahib (USA) 129 – Montana Miss (IRE) 80 (Earl of Barking **78** (IRE) 119) [2006 81: 8.1d 7f p7.1g² p7.1g* 7d p7.1g p6g⁶ p7.1g Dec 1] leggy filly: fair handicapper: won at Wolverhampton in July: stays 7f: acts on polytrack and good to firm going. *B. Palling*

CORRIDOR CREEPER (FR) 9 ch.g. Polish Precedent (USA) 131 – Sonia Rose **115** (USA) (Superbity (USA)) [2006 114: 5.2m² 5m 5g* 5s³ 5m 5m 5m 5f 5d 5.4g 6m⁵ 5g⁴ 5d 5g 5s³ Oct 14] smallish gelding: smart performer: won minor event at Beverley in May by ½ length from Sierra Vista: best other effort in 2006 when good second to Green Manalishi in handicap at Newbury on reappearance: has form at 6f, best at 5f: acts on firm and soft going: tried blinkered/tongue tied, wears cheekpieces: races prominently. *J. M. Bradley*

CORRUCASECO 2 b.f. (Mar 20) Bertolini (USA) 125 – Konica 57 (Desert King **–** (IRE) 129) [2006 6f p7.1g Jun 30] €5,500Y: first foal: dam, maiden who should have stayed 1¼m, half-sister to useful performers Abeyr (7f/1m winner) and Boojum (2-y-o 6f/7f winner): last in sellers: sold £1,800 in August. *M. D. I. Usher*

CORTESIA (IRE) 3 ch.f. Courteous 120 – Cecina 100 (Welsh Saint 126) [2006 55p: **90** 10g* 11.4m 12s 10d Oct 9] good-topped filly: fairly useful performer, lightly raced: won maiden in April: best effort when ninth in listed race at Chester next time: should stay 1½m: acts on good to firm ground, well below form on softer than good. *P. W. Chapple-Hyam*

CORTINA 3 b.f. Cigar 68 – Dorothea Sharp (IRE) 50 (Foxhound (USA) 103) [2006 p7g **–** 11f⁵ f11g 12m⁶ 12.1g Aug 1] 6,000Y: good-topped filly: first foal: dam, maiden, stayed 7f: no sign of ability: tried blinkered/tongue tied. *J. Jay*

CORUM (IRE) 3 b.c. Galileo (IRE) 134 – Vallee Des Reves (USA) (Kingmambo **96** (USA) 125) [2006 –p: 10m* 10m⁶ 12g² 14g 10d Nov 4] strong, good-bodied colt: useful performer, lightly raced: won maiden at Sandown in June: best effort when second to Sweet Indulgence in handicap at Newmarket: stays 1½m: acts on good to firm going (well held both starts on softer than good): sold 32,000 gns, joined Mrs K. Waldron. *J. H. M. Gosden*

CORVIGLIA 3 b.f. Nashwan (USA) 135 – Ski Run 112 (Petoski 135) [2006 9.9d⁵ 10d Oct 4] lightly-made filly: first foal: dam 1½m and 2m winner: well held in maidens. *J. R. Fanshawe* —

COSIMO PRIMO 2 b.g. (Mar 25) Medicean 128 – Cugina 99 (Distant Relative 128) [2006 6m 7s 6d Nov 4] workmanlike gelding: well held in maidens: bred to stay 1¼m+. *J. A. Geake* —

COSMIC DESTINY (IRE) 4 b.f. Soviet Star (USA) 128 – Cruelle (USA) (Irish River (FR) 131) [2006 66: p5g 5.3m⁵ 5.1m 5.2m⁵ 5.3m³ 5m⁶ 5m³ 5.1g⁴ 5.2f p5g* 5.5d 5m⁵ 5.3d⁵ p5.1m p6m⁶ p5.1g⁵ p5g Dec 3] smallish filly: fair handicapper: won at Lingfield in July: free-going sort, best at 5f: acts on polytrack and good to firm going, probably on good to soft: reared at start twelfth outing: finds little. *E. F. Vaughan* **64 §** **a68 §**

COSMIC GIRL 3 b.f. Gorse 116 – Lotus Moon (Shareef Dancer (USA) 135) [2006 7g 7.1g 7m Jul 29] 5,000F: close-coupled filly: sixth foal: half-sister to several winners, including 1½m winner Luna Flight (by Ela-Mana-Mou): dam unraced daughter of very smart 7f to 9f winner in Britain/USA Asteroid Field: well held in maidens: sold 2,000 gns in October. *H. Candy* —

COSMIC MESSENGER (FR) 3 ch.g. Septieme Ciel (USA) 123 – Bonnie And Howard (USA) (Fly So Free (USA) 122) [2006 11.8m 8.3g p12g⁵ 16d Sep 26] modest maiden: pulled up final outing. *L. A. Dace* **56**

COSMOPOLITAN LADY 2 b.f. (Mar 22) Kyllachy 129 – Sunflower Seed 70 (Mummy's Pet 125) [2006 5g⁶ 6m² 6g³ 6g³ 5.2f² 5m⁴ 5g² 5m* 5s 8f Dec 31] 10,000F, 19,000Y: sparely-made filly: has a quick action: half-sister to 3 winners, including fairly useful 7f/1m winner Strathmore Clear (by Batshoof): dam maiden who stayed 1½m: fair performer: in frame 6 of 7 starts prior to winning nursery at Catterick in September: sold 40,000 gns and left D. Simcock before final outing: will prove best at 5f/6f: acts on firm going: usually forces pace. *J. M. Cassidy, USA* **79**

COSTUME 2 b.f. (Feb 15) Danehill (USA) 126 – Dance Dress (USA) 110 (Nureyev (USA) 131) [2006 7m³ Jun 24] good-bodied filly: first foal: dam, French 7f to 10.5f (Prix Fille de l'Air) winner, out of half-sister to dam of Poule d'Essai des Pouliches winner Matiara: 3/1, 2 lengths third of 8 to dead-heaters Halicarnassus and Norisan in maiden at Newmarket, travelling smoothly: should improve. *J. H. M. Gosden* **78 p**

COTE D'ARGENT 3 b.g. Lujain (USA) 119 – In The Groove 127 (Night Shift (USA)) [2006 83: 8m Apr 21] tall, leggy gelding: fairly useful performer at 2 yrs: well held in handicap at Newbury only outing in 2006: should stay 1m: acts on soft ground: withdrawn after refusing to enter stall intended second start: sold 3,000 gns, and gelded. *M. Johnston* —

COTSWOLD TRAVELLER 2 br.f. (Feb 11) Hunting Lion (IRE) 115 – Perfect Partner (Be My Chief (USA) 122) [2006 5g 5g May 1] stocky filly: second foal: half-sister to 6f seller winner Molly Dancer (by Emarati): dam unraced half-sister to smart sprinter Funfair Wane: mid-field in maidens at Warwick in spring. *T. G. Dascombe* **50**

COTTINGHAM (IRE) 5 b.g. Perugino (USA) 84 – Stately Princess 70 (Robellino (USA) 127) [2006 50: f8g⁶ p9.5g* p10g² 10.1m² 10.1g* p9.5g* 9.2m² 10.1m* 10m³ 9.3g⁶ Aug 3] workmanlike gelding: fair performer: left M. Chapman after reappearance, won banded race at Wolverhampton in May and handicaps at Yarmouth and Wolverhampton in June and Newcastle in July: stays 1¼m: acts on all-weather, firm and soft going: reliable: joined R. Lee and showed fair form over hurdles. *T. D. Barron* **75**

COTTON EASTER 5 b.m. Robellino (USA) 127 – Pluck 80 (Never So Bold 135) [2006 59, a55: p10g 13.1s* 12.1d f11m⁵ f12g Nov 10] good-topped mare: modest performer: won handicap at Bath in May: stays 13f: acts on all-weather and heavy ground: tongue tied: sometimes slowly away. *Mrs A. J. Bowlby* **58** **a44**

COTTON EYED JOE (IRE) 5 b.g. Indian Rocket 115 – Cwm Deri (IRE) (Alzao (USA) 117) [2006 59: f12g* f14g* f16g³ f14g* f16g⁵ 12g⁶ 13d³ 13.9s⁴ f14g³ 11.5g⁴ 16m⁵ p13.9f⁵ Aug 30] lengthy, good-topped gelding: fairly useful performer: easy winner of banded events (2) and handicap, all at Southwell in January: stays 13¾m, seemingly not 2m: acts on fibresand and soft going: tends to hang left. *G. A. Swinbank* **80**

COUGAR BAY (IRE) 3 b.c. Daylami (IRE) 138 – Delimara (IRE) (In The Wings 128) [2006 78: 12m² 9m* 10m 12g 10.5m⁴ 8g³ 10m² Sep 9] €47,000F: small, lengthy colt: fourth foal: half-brother to 2 winners, including French 15f winner Marlengo (by Octagonal): dam maiden French 1m winner who stayed 1¼m: smart performer: trained by Ms F. Crowley at 2 yrs: won maiden at Leopardstown in June: ran well when 3¼ lengths fourth to Mulaqat in Rose of Lancaster Stakes at Haydock fifth start, and particularly so **116**

when head second to Frost Giant in Kilternan Stakes at Leopardstown final outing: best form at 1¼m: raced mainly on good/good to firm ground: blinkered second to sixth starts (has looked difficult ride). *D. Wachman, Ireland*

COUNCELLOR (FR) 4 b.g. Gilded Time (USA) – Sudden Storm Bird (USA) (Storm Bird (CAN) 134) [2006 83: f6g³ f8g³ p7g p6g* p7.1g⁴ p6g⁶ 8.3g⁴ Apr 10] big, strong gelding: fairly useful handicapper: won at Wolverhampton in March: effective at 6f to 8.5f: acts on all-weather, good to firm and good to soft ground: free-going sort: carries head awkwardly/looks hard ride: gelded. *Stef Liddiard*　**88**

COUNCIL MEMBER (USA) 4 b.c. Seattle Slew (USA) – Zoe Montana (USA) (Seeking The Gold (USA)) [2006 110: p7g² Oct 21] lengthy, quite attractive colt: smart performer at best: neck second to Mostashaar in steadily-run minor event at Lingfield (all-weather debut) only outing in 2006, slowly away and racing wide: stays 7f: acts on polytrack and firm ground, below form on softer than good: usually races prominently, and acted as pacemaker fourth 3-y-o outing. *Saeed bin Suroor*　**107**

COUNSEL'S OPINION (IRE) 9 ch.g. Rudimentary (USA) 118 – Fairy Fortune 78 (Rainbow Quest (USA) 134) [2006 112: p10g³ p10g 10.1g⁵ 10.3f² 10.1g 10g 12d 10s Oct 7] big gelding: smart performer: good efforts in 2006 at Lingfield first 2 starts (close seventh to Sri Diamond in Winter Derby on second occasion) and at Chester (3 lengths second of 4 to Maraahel in Huxley Stakes) fourth outing: well below form last 4 starts: effective at 1¼m/1½m: acts on all-weather, soft and firm going: sometimes early to post/ slowly away: takes strong hold, and held up. *C. F. Wall*　**110 d**

COUNTBACK (FR) 7 b.g. Anabaa (USA) 130 – Count Me Out (FR) (Kaldoun (FR) 122) [2006 59: p13.9g³ p16.5g² f16g⁴ p12.2g⁴ p13g⁵ f11g⁴ p12.2g Dec 23] modest maiden: stays 16.5f: acts on all-weather: has worn cheekpieces: consistent. *A. W. Carroll*　**61**

COUNT BORIS 5 b.g. Groom Dancer (USA) 128 – Bu Hagab (IRE) (Royal Academy (USA) 130) [2006 72: 10.9s⁶ 14.1s 10.9d Oct 13] angular gelding: modest handicapper: stays 1½m: acts on soft and good to firm going: held up. *J. A. Geake*　**57**

COUNT CEPRANO (IRE) 2 b.c. (Mar 17) Desert Prince (IRE) 130 – Camerlata (Common Grounds 118) [2006 p6g⁴ p6g* p7g² Oct 21] first foal: dam unraced half-sister to Middle Park Stakes winner Primo Valentino: progressive form: readily won maiden at Lingfield in September: looked unlucky when beaten by head in nursery there (winner Market Day got first run): likely to stay 1m: raced on polytrack: will go on improving. *W. R. Swinburn*　**94 p**

COUNT COUGAR (USA) 6 b.g. Sir Cat (USA) 118 – Gold Script (USA) (Seeking The Gold (USA)) [2006 64, a71: f6g p5.1g p5.1g p7.1g² f6s⁵ f5g* p7.1g f7g⁴ f6g* p6g p5.1g p6g f7g⁴ p6g p6g⁶ f6g⁴ Dec 23] sturdy gelding: poor walker and mover: fair handicapper: won at Southwell in April and May: effective at 5f to easy 7f: acts on all-weather, firm and soft ground: tried blinkered/in cheekpieces earlier in career: races prominently. *S. P. Griffiths*　**74**

COUNTDOWN 4 ch.g. Pivotal 124 – Quiz Time 90 (Efisio 120) [2006 86: p5.1g² p6g⁵ p6g 5d² 5g 6m 6m⁵ 6m² 6d 7.1s³ 6.1d⁴ 7s³ 7v³ Oct 31] close-coupled gelding: fairly useful handicapper: left Miss J. Camacho after seventh start: won at Catterick in October: stays 7f: acts on polytrack and any turf going: usually blinkered/visored for previous trainer. *T. D. Easterby*　**89**

COUNTERFACTUAL (IRE) 3 br.g. Key of Luck (USA) 126 – Wakayi 87 (Persian Bold 123) [2006 8m⁵ 7m⁶ 8g 8g Aug 14] good-topped gelding: modest maiden: probably stays 1m: withdrawn after bolting on intended debut: said to have had breathing problem final outing. *B. Smart*　**64**

COUNTERPUNCH 3 ch.g. Halling (USA) 133 – Evil Empire (GER) 108 (Acatenango (GER) 127) [2006 11m* 11.6s* 12g** Oct 12] second foal: dam German 7f (at 2 yrs) and 1½m winner: smart form in only 3 starts: won maiden at Goodwood in September and handicaps at Windsor (beat Wannabe Posh 5 lengths with plenty to spare) and New-market (impressively by neck from Alessano, pair clear) in October: will stay 1¾m: capable of better still. *Saeed bin Suroor*　**115 p**

COUNTESS CARMINE 3 b.f. Royal Applause 124 – Red Ryding Hood 83 (Wolf-hound (USA) 126) [2006 68: 8.5d 6g May 30] angular, lengthy filly: has a round action: maiden: well beaten in 2006. *P. C. Haslam*　**–**

COUNTESS MAJELLA (IRE) 2 b.f. (Apr 2) Grand Lodge (USA) 125 – Mrs Moonlight (Ajdal (USA) 130) [2006 7s p7.1g⁴ Dec 22] half-sister to 3 winners, including smart 7f (at 2 yrs)/1m winner Soviet Flash (by Warning) and 4-y-o Play Me: dam unraced half-sister to 1½m performer Jupiter Island and 1983 2-y-o Precocious, both high class:　**53 p**

modest form in maidens at Leopardstown (trained by C. Collins) and Wolverhampton (fourth to Regal Riband): should progress. *E. J. O'Neill*

COUNTING HOUSE (IRE) 3 ch.g. King's Best (USA) 132 – Inforapenny 111 (Deploy 131) [2006 71p: 10g 10m 12g⁴ 12g² 12m⁵ Jul 30] good-bodied gelding: fairly useful maiden: should stay 1¾m: raced only on good/good to firm going: sold 55,000 gns in October, and gelded. *R. Charlton*   **85**

COUNT KRISTO 4 br.g. Dr Fong (USA) 128 – Aryadne (Rainbow Quest (USA) 134) [2006 81: 10m* 10m⁶ 11.9g⁵ 11.8m 11.9m⁵ Aug 10] tall, leggy gelding: fair handicapper: won at Nottingham in May: stays 1½m: acts on good to firm going: tried in cheekpieces: hung right third start: sold 20,000 gns. *C. G. Cox*   **79**

COUNTRY AFFAIR (USA) 3 ch.c. Vettori (IRE) 119 – Nany's Affair (USA) 57 (Colonial Affair (USA) 126) [2006 80: p7g⁵ p8.6g Apr 10] lightly-raced maiden: left J. Quinn in Ireland after 2 yrs: just fair form in 2006: stays 8.6f: acts on polytrack. *P. R. Webber*   **69**

COUNTRY ESCAPE 3 b.g. Zafonic (USA) 130 – Midnight Allure 85 (Aragon 118) [2006 8m³ p8g² 8s⁴ 8.1d* p8.6m* Oct 2] 10,000Y, 7,000 2-y-o: second foal: half-brother to fairly useful 2004 2-y-o 5f winner Midnight Tycoon (by Marju): dam, 1m winner, sister to smart sprinter Midnight Escape: fairly useful performer: won handicaps at Warwick in September and Wolverhampton (edged right) in October: acts on polytrack and good to firm and good to soft going: joined J. O'Neill. *C. F. Wall*   **88**

COUNTRY PURSUIT (USA) 4 ch.g. Theatrical 128 – Jade Flush (USA) 117 (Jade Hunter (USA)) [2006 88+: p13g² p12g* 12s³ p12g⁶ 11.6d f14g⁴ p12g p13g³ Dec 22] leggy gelding: fairly useful handicapper: won at Lingfield in April: seems to stay 1¾m: acts on polytrack (probably on fibresand), soft and good to firm going: has twice looked quirky in blinkers, including last 2 starts. *C. E. Brittain*   **93**

COUNTRY SONG (USA) 2 b.c. (Mar 17) Fusaichi Pegasus (USA) 130 – Eliza (USA) (Mt Livermore (USA)) [2006 5s* 7.5f* 7m² Jul 29] close-coupled, quite attractive colt: half-brother to several winners in USA/Japan: dam US Grade 1 8.5f winner, including Breeders' Cup Juvenile Fillies: useful form: won maiden in May and minor event in June, both at Tipperary: second of 11 to Champlain in listed Chesham Stakes at Royal Ascot (fractious beforehand): blinkered when respectable sixth to Teofilo in another listed race at Leopardstown final start: will be suited by 1m: sold privately, and joined J. Noseda. *D. Wachman, Ireland*   **98**

COUNTRYWIDE BELLE 3 b.f. Josr Algarhoud (IRE) 118 – Dancing Bluebell (IRE) 79 (Bluebird (USA) 125) [2006 76d: p6g² p7.1g³ p8.6g* p8.6g⁵ p8.6g² Mar 15] close-coupled, workmanlike filly: has a fluent action: modest performer: won seller at Wolverhampton in February: stays 8.6f: acts on all-weather: wears cheekpieces/blinkers: races prominently: consistent. *K. A. Ryan*   **58**

COUNTRYWIDE LUCK 5 b.g. Inchinor 119 – Thelma (Blakeney 126) [2006 81: p12g* p12.2g² p16g p13g⁵ Feb 25] big, rather leggy gelding: fairly useful handicapper: won at Lingfield in January: stays 13f: acts on polytrack and good to firm going, well held on softer than good: tried blinkered. *N. P. Littmoden*   **83**

COUNTRYWIDE STYLE (IRE) 2 b.c. (Mar 8) Xaar 132 – Nautical Light (Slip Anchor 136) [2006 8.1g⁵ 7.1m Aug 28] quite good-topped colt: seemingly better effort in maidens when last of 5 at Sandown. *N. P. Littmoden*   **59 ?**

COUNT THE TREES 3 ch.f. Woodborough (USA) 112 – Numerate 69 (Bishop of Cashel 122) [2006 –: p8.6g⁴ p10g³ f11s⁵ 10.2g 9.9g 10m f11g⁶ Dec 29] modest maiden: stays 1¼m: acts on polytrack. *W. G. M. Turner*   **– a51**

COUNT TREVISIO (IRE) 3 b.c. Danehill (USA) 126 – Stylish (Anshan 119) [2006 83: 9m* 10f³ 8.1m² 8g Oct 13] lengthy colt: useful handicapper: won at Sandown (beat Heaven Knows by neck) in June: good placed efforts next 2 starts, making most when ½-length second to Charlie Cool at Haydock: barely stays 1¼m: acts on firm going: tends to flash tail. *Saeed bin Suroor*   **104**

COUNTYOURBLESSINGS 2 br.f. (Feb 28) Lujain (USA) 119 – To The Woods (IRE) 86 (Woodborough (USA) 112) [2006 5g p6g p7.1g 5m⁵ 5.1m 5g⁶ Aug 26] 6,800Y: close-coupled filly: first foal: dam 5f (at 2 yrs) and 7f winner who became unreliable: little form: left J. Portman after third start. *I. A. Wood*   **–**

COUP D'ETAT 3 ch.g. Diktat 126 – Megdale (Waajib 121) [2006 95: 8s 8m 10m 10m⁴ 10m³ 9.9m 9m⁶ 10g 11g⁵ Sep 15] good-topped colt: fairly useful handicapper: stays 1¼m: acts on good to firm going: sold 12,500 gns. *J. L. Dunlop*   **92**

COURAGEOUS DOVE 5 gr.g. Overbury (IRE) 116 – Mazzelmo 67 (Thethingabout- –
itis (USA) 106) [2006 –: f11g Feb 5] leggy gelding: no sign of ability. *A. Bailey*

COURAGEOUS DUKE (USA) 7 b.g. Spinning World (USA) 130 – Araadh (USA) **105**
70 (Blushing Groom (FR) 131) [2006 108: 10m⁵ 10m 10m 10.4f 10m⁵ 10m Sep 16]
close-coupled, quite good-topped gelding: useful handicapper: below par at Nad Al
Sheba early in 2006, but not far from best when eighth to Fairmile in John Smith's Cup at
York (poorly drawn) and fifth to Road To Love at Ascot fourth/fifth outings: stays 10.5f:
acts on firm going: visored (ran poorly) final outing: held up: sold 26,000 gns. *J. Noseda*

COURT MASTERPIECE 6 b.h. Polish Precedent (USA) 131 – Easy Option **127**
(IRE) 115 (Prince Sabo 123) [2006 122: a8g⁶ 8s³ 8m² 8m* 8d³ 8f 7f Dec 17]
 Court Masterpiece's thirty-two-race career is set to be extended after his expected retirement to stud was postponed in favour of another campaign, beginning
at the 2007 Dubai International Carnival. Court Masterpiece finished seventh of
eighteen behind Daiwa Major in the Group 1 Mile Championship at Kyoto in November and ninth of seventeen to top 2005 two-year-old Fusaichi Richard when
favourite for the Group 2 Hanshin Cup the following month. He wasn't beaten that
far in either race, by around four lengths and three lengths respectively, but he failed
to trouble the principals after being waited with, and the form was below that which
he had shown in Europe. Presumably the main reason for his taking part in these
contests was to show him off to the Japanese, since he was expected to be retired to
stud there. The plan backfired but, in an era when information about the achievements of virtually any above-average thoroughbred is readily accessible, breeders
in Japan were surely already fully aware that Court Masterpiece was tough, consistent and high class. He had won the Prix de la Foret as a five-year-old and proved
better than ever at six, when his success in the Sussex Stakes established him as the
top older miler in Europe. A fine achievement for any horse, let alone one who, like
Court Masterpiece, had fractured a hind ankle as a three-year-old.
 Apart from the Japanese excursions, Court Masterpiece's latest season
followed pretty much the normal path for a miler of his ability in Europe, taking in
all four Group 1 races in Britain open to older horses. He started off abroad, though,
in the Godolphin Mile on dirt at Nad Al Sheba in March in which he finished a
never-dangerous sixth of ten to the Japanese six-year-old Utopia. Perhaps the
artificial surface did not suit him, since Jack Sullivan beat him decisively, but it is
worth noting that he had run pretty well on polytrack in 2005. The Lockinge Stakes
at Newbury in May did not show Court Masterpiece to full advantage either as he
came home just over five lengths third to Peeress, the soft going almost certainly
taxing his stamina. Three fine runs on less testing ground followed, starting in the
Queen Anne Stakes at Royal Ascot. The tempo was steadier than in the Lockinge,
which suited Court Masterpiece, who travelled best of all through the race towards
the rear. He made his challenge along the rail but had his momentum interrupted
when Ad Valorem went left in the final furlong, Court Masterpiece losing out by a
length and a half to the Irish colt. Without the interference Court Masterpiece would

Cantor Spreadfair Sussex Stakes, Goodwood—Court Masterpiece is a decisive winner of this
clash of the generations from another six-year-old Soviet Song (blaze); Rob Roy (far side) takes third
from Aussie Rules (second right) as favourite Araafa fades into fifth in front of Echo of Light

Gainsborough Stud's "Court Masterpiece"

have finished closer but it is doubtful whether he would have won. The stewards supported this interpretation, leaving Ad Valorem as the winner while suspending his rider Kieren Fallon for four days for careless riding.

The form of the Queen Anne was at least as good as anything Court Masterpiece had achieved before, and even better was to follow in the Cantor Spreadfair Sussex Stakes at Goodwood six weeks later. Ad Valorem was an absentee but the opposition was hot enough to leave Court Masterpiece only fourth choice in the betting behind short-priced favourite Araafa, winner of the Irish Two Thousand Guineas and St James's Palace Stakes; Godolphin's supplementary entry Echo of Light, recently successful in the Summer Mile on the all-weather at Lingfield; and Soviet Song, who had won the Windsor Forest Stakes at Royal Ascot but nonetheless appeared not quite so good as in previous years. The other runners were Aussie Rules, winner of the Poule d'Essai des Poulains, Rob Roy, successful in the betfred.com Mile at Sandown but below form in the Lockinge last time, and rank outsider Vanderlin. Echo of Light set too strong a gallop for his own good and for the good of those in immediate pursuit, notably Araafa. The result was that when Court Masterpiece, held up as usual, began to make ground halfway up the straight he was challenging runners near the end of their tether. Allowing for that, Court Masterpiece was still impressive in bursting clear a furlong out, soon having the race won. Soviet Song made some headway but at the line she was still two lengths adrift of the eased Court Masterpiece. Rob Roy was a further half a length away while Araafa, who finished slightly lame, was only fifth. In passing, the most recent six-year-old winner of the Sussex before Court Masterpiece was Noalcoholic in 1983. Araafa was in better form when he and Court Masterpiece met again in the Queen Elizabeth II Stakes at Ascot in September, Court Masterpiece still running a creditable race to be three and a quarter lengths third to George Washington, especially as his effort was delayed and George Washington and Araafa had flown by the time he got clear.

Court Masterpiece (b.h. 2000)	Polish Precedent (USA) (b 1986)	Danzig (b 1977)	Northern Dancer / Pas de Nom
		Past Example (ch 1976)	Buckpasser / Bold Example
	Easy Option (IRE) (ch 1992)	Prince Sabo (b 1982)	Young Generation / Jubilee Song
		Brazen Faced (ch 1975)	Bold And Free / Maurine

Court Masterpiece's pedigree was discussed in detail in *Racehorses of 2005* and there is little to add. His sire Polish Precedent had another Group 1 winner in Darsi, successful in the Prix du Jockey Club, his three-year-old half-brother Easy Air (by Zafonic) won a seven-furlong handicap at Lingfield in April and finished second in the Britannia Handicap at Royal Ascot, and his smart dam Easy Option, also responsible for Prix de Saint-Georges winner Maybe Forever (also by Zafonic), produced a filly foal by Cape Cross in May. As a postscript, it is worth reporting developments with the bloodstock of Maktoum Al Maktoum, owner-breeder of Court Masterpiece, who died in January. Like Laverock when he won the Prix d'Ispahan, Court Masterpiece raced in the colours of the late Sheikh's Gainsborough Stud Management Ltd. The company's assets, including two studs in Kentucky, two in Ireland and the principal base at Newbury, plus around twenty stallions and getting on for two hundred mares, were transferred into the ownership of Sheikh Mohammed's Darley operation in three stages ending at the turn of the year. Like Topsy, Darley grows with each passing year, and presumably trickier to manage efficiently given the number of mares—including the new arrivals, the tally is around eight hundred worldwide. That makes the decision to cull only fourteen mares at the December Sales slightly surprising. As regards action on the racecourse, Darley bloodstock adviser John Ferguson didn't give a lot away when quoted as follows: 'Everything will merge but things will remain the same. On the racing side there will still be Gainsborough horses but they will be managed by Darley. There are still a few details to be ironed out, but from next year there will be a Gainsborough identity, although it will be part of the same entity—on the racecourse you will see no change.' For the record, Laverock ran in Sheikh Mohammed's colours when successful in the Gran Premio del Jockey Club in October. Court Masterpiece is likely to start off carrying the colours of Sheikh Mohammed's son Sheikh Rashid as a seven-year-old, though will still be under the ownership of Darley. Court Masterpiece, a lengthy, angular horse who shows traces of stringhalt, is effective at seven furlongs and a mile and acts on polytrack, good to firm and good to soft going, probably on soft. *E. A. L. Dunlop*

COURT OF APPEAL 9 ch.g. Bering 136 – Hiawatha's Song (USA) (Chief's Crown (USA)) [2006 78, a84: p12.2g⁶ f12g⁵ 12g 12.4g 12g⁵ 13.8f* 12.3g⁴ 12f* 12.6m⁵ 12m⁴ 12s² 12s² Oct 14] lengthy gelding: fair performer: won seller at Catterick and ladies handicap at Ripon, both in June: stays 1¾m: acts on fibresand and any turf going: visored once, often wears cheekpieces: usually tongue tied: reportedly had breathing problem second start. *B. Ellison* **77**

COURT ONE 8 b.g. Shareef Dancer (USA) 135 – Fairfields Cone (Celtic Cone 116) [2006 47: 16g Jul 3] small, leggy gelding: shows knee action: poor performer: well held only outing in 2006: visored once in 2003: sometimes slowly away. *R. E. Barr* **–**

COUSTEAU 3 ch.c. Spinning World (USA) 130 – Wavy Up (IRE) (Brustolon 117) [2006 85: 8g⁵ p8g² 10.3d⁵ 8d* 7m Jun 21] tall, good-topped colt: has a short, unimpressive action: useful performer: creditable fifth in Craven Stakes at Newmarket on reappearance: won maiden there in May: best effort when 4 lengths seventh to Jeremy in Jersey Stakes at Royal Ascot final outing, dictating: free-going sort (probably best when allowed to stride on), and may prove best short of 1¼m: acts on polytrack, soft and good to firm going: has carried head awkwardly: sold 17,000 gns, joined A. Mullins in Ireland. *P. W. Chapple-Hyam* **103**

COUSTOU (IRE) 6 b.g. In Command (IRE) 114 – Carranza (IRE) (Lead On Time (USA) 123) [2006 67: p12g Sep 27] lengthy, good-topped gelding: fair handicapper: always behind only Flat outing in 2006: sometimes wears cheekpieces/blinkers. *R. M. Stronge* **–**

COVE MOUNTAIN (IRE) 4 br.f. Indian Danehill (IRE) 124 – Nordic Pride (Horage **68** 124) [2006 70: 8d⁴ 8.5d² 10s 8g p10g p10g⁶ p10g² p13g⁴ p9.5g Dec 26] €14,000Y: half-sister to 3 winners in Ireland, including useful 7f (at 2 yrs) to 1¼m winner Identify (by Persian Bold): dam Irish 2-y-o 6f winner: fair maiden handicapper: left J. Coogan in Ireland after fourth start: stays 1¼m: acts on polytrack, raced only on good ground or softer (acts on heavy) on turf: tried blinkered: none too consistent. *S. Kirk*

COVER UP (IRE) 9 b.g. Machiavellian (USA) 123 – Sought Out (IRE) 119 (Rainbow **114** Quest (USA) 134) [2006 114: 16m* 16.4s 21.7m² 16f Aug 3] close-coupled, quite good-topped gelding: smart performer: as good as ever in 2006, winning Hesmonds Stud Sagaro Stakes at Lingfield in May by a head from Tungsten Strike: easily best effort after when good neck second to Baddam (rec. 12 lb) in Queen Alexandra Stakes at Royal Ascot (won race in 2002 and 2003, and also runner-up in 2005): stays 2¾m: acts on firm and good to soft going, seemingly not on soft/heavy: visored once at 3 yrs: has raced lazily/flashed tail: usually patiently ridden. *Sir Michael Stoute*

COW GIRL (IRE) 2 b.f. (Apr 6) King's Best (USA) 132 – Reveuse de Jour (IRE) 79 **58** (Sadler's Wells (USA) 132) [2006 6m Jul 21] 16,000Y, resold 16,500Y: compact filly: seventh foal: half-sister to several winners including 3-y-o Grand Jour and Irish 1m winner who stayed 1½m Day Ticket (by Mtoto): dam, maiden (should have been well suited by further than 7f), out of Coronation Stakes winner Magic of Life: 33/1, twelfth of 15 in maiden at Newbury. *A. M. Balding*

COY JOY (IRE) 2 b.f. (Feb 28) Tagula (IRE) 116 – Be Prepared (IRE) (Be My Guest **–** (USA) 124) [2006 5d May 13] 3,200Y: sixth foal: half-sister to 2 winners, including fairly useful 7f (at 2 yrs) to 2m winner Look First (by Namaqualand): dam unraced: well held in claimer. *M. Dods*

COYOTE CREEK 2 b.g. (Mar 22) Zilzal (USA) 137 – High Barn 72 (Shirley Heights **70** 130) [2006 7f⁶ 8g⁴ 8.1d³ Oct 13] 20,000Y: good-bodied gelding: second foal: dam, maiden who should have stayed 1¾m+, half-sister to smart 1½m/13f winner and Gold Cup third Compton Ace out of Irish St Leger winner Mountain Lodge: fair form in maidens, third to Cat de Mille at Warwick final start: gelded after: will benefit from 1¼m/ 1½m. *E. F. Vaughan*

CRACKLEANDO 5 ch.g. Forzando 122 – Crackling 57 (Electric 126) [2006 –: 17.5d **–** Sep 15] close-coupled gelding: fair handicapper at 3 yrs: no form both Flat outings since: winning hurdler. *Mrs J. C. McGregor*

CRAFTY FOX 3 b.g. Foxhound (USA) 103 – Surrealist (ITY) (Night Shift (USA)) **60** [2006 p6g⁴ p7g p6m 6f³ f6g p6m⁴ p6g f7m* p6g Nov 5] well-made gelding: modest performer: won maiden claimer at Southwell in October: stays easy 7f: acts on all-weather and firm going: tried visored (below form): carried head high fourth start. *A. P. Jarvis*

CRAGGANMORE CREEK 3 b.g. Tipsy Creek (USA) 115 – Polish Abbey (Polish **68** Precedent (USA) 131) [2006 54p: p10g⁵ p9.5g 8m 12m 10m f11g⁶ 11.5m 11.5d p11g³ f12g* f14g⁴ f12g⁴ Dec 14] tall gelding: fair performer: improved to win banded race at Southwell in November: stays 1½m: acts on all-weather: blinkered last 4 starts: inconsistent. *D. Morris*

CRAGG LASS (IRE) 2 b.f. (Mar 5) King Charlemagne (USA) 120 – Mepa Discovery **–** (USA) (Clever Trick (USA)) [2006 p6m p7.1g⁶ p7.1g Dec 31] €8,000F, €3,200Y: sixth foal: closely related to useful French sprinter Melkior (by Neverneyev): dam French 6f/ 7f winner: last in minor events/maiden, all at Wolverhampton. *A. Berry*

CRAIC SA CEILI (IRE) 6 b.m. Danehill Dancer (IRE) 117 – Fay's Song (IRE) 84 **–** (Fayruz 116) [2006 64: p7.1g Jan 5] leggy mare: modest handicapper at 5 yrs: well held only outing in 2006: sometimes wears cheekpieces/blinkers: held up: has found little. *M. S. Saunders*

CRAIG Y NOS 2 ch.f. (Apr 16) Auction House (USA) 120 – Thabeh 57 (Shareef **–** Dancer (USA) 135) [2006 6f⁴ Jul 3] half-sister to 7f/1m winners Jamestown and Melody Queen (both by Merdon Melody), latter subsequently useful up to 1¼m in North America: dam irresolute 1m maiden: tailed off in minor event. *A. Berry*

CRAIL 6 b.g. Vettori (IRE) 119 – Tendency 77 (Ballad Rock 122) [2006 76, a90: p9.5g **–** p10g 8m p12g p8.6g³ 8d⁶ p8.6g Sep 11] workmanlike gelding: fairly useful handicapper **a81** on all-weather: stays 1¼m: acts on polytrack and on soft and good to firm going when last showed form on turf in 2005: sometimes looks awkward ride. *C. F. Wall*

CRANWORTH BLAZE 2 b.f. (Mar 20) Diktat 126 – Julietta Mia (USA) 72 **–** (Woodman (USA) 126) [2006 5g 6m 5d Oct 3] 3,600F, 3,700Y: lengthy filly: fifth foal:

half-sister to 5f winner Ivory Venture (by Reprimand): dam 2-y-o 7f winner: little form in maidens. *T. J. Etherington*

CRATHORNE (IRE) 6 b.g. Alzao (USA) 117 – Shirley Blue (IRE) (Shirley Heights 130) [2006 70: 12g⁴ 12m⁴ 14m⁵ 14g³ Aug 31] deep-girthed gelding: fair handicapper: won at Musselburgh in May: effective at 1½m to 2m: acts on firm and soft going: wore cheekpieces in 2004: held up: fairly useful hurdler. *M. Todhunter* **73**

CRAZY BEAR (IRE) 3 ch.f. King Charlemagne (USA) 120 – Specifiedrisk (IRE) (Turtle Island (IRE) 123) [2006 62: f8g² f11g³ p9.5g⁴ p8.6g² Apr 29] fair maiden: stays 11f: acts on all-weather: joined T. George. *K. A. Ryan* **71**

CREAMBISCUIT 3 ch.g. Cadeaux Genereux 131 – Star Ridge (USA) (Storm Bird (CAN) 134) [2006 59: p6g 6f Jun 6] maiden: well held in handicaps in 2006: should stay 6f: sent to Singapore. *N. P. Littmoden* **–**

CREAM OF ESTEEM 4 b.g. Mark of Esteem (IRE) 137 – Chantilly (FR) (Sanglamore (USA) 126) [2006 52: 12d Oct 8] smallish, stocky gelding: maiden: well held only outing in 2006: usually tongue tied. *M. Todhunter* **–**

CREATIVE MIND (IRE) 3 b.f. Danehill Dancer (IRE) 117 – Inventive 84 (Sheikh Albadou 128) [2006 81: p7g⁴ 8s⁶ 8m⁵ 7.5g² 7f² 6g⁵ 7m* 7f⁵ 7m² 6.5g² Oct 1] close-coupled filly: fairly useful performer: won handicap at Lingfield in July: probably best up to 7.5f: yet to race on heavy going, acts on any other turf and polytrack: front runner. *E. J. O'Neill* **88**

CREDENTIAL 4 b.c. Dansili 127 – Sabria (USA) (Miswaki (USA) 124) [2006 72: 8.1m 10s 7.9m² 8.3f 10d 8.2d⁴ Nov 1] sturdy colt: modest maiden: stays 1m, seemingly not 1¼m: acts on good to firm and good to soft ground. *John A. Harris* **63**

CREDIT (IRE) 5 b.g. Intikhab (USA) 135 – Tycooness (IRE) 80§ (Last Tycoon 131) [2006 85: f11g⁶ f12g p12.2s⁶ Dec 13] big, good-topped gelding: has a quick, fluent action: just fair performer nowadays: stays 1½m: acts on good to firm ground, seemingly on polytrack. *Jennie Candlish* **78**

CREDIT SLIP 2 b.c. (Apr 17) Slip Anchor 136 – Credit-A-Plenty 111 (Generous (IRE) 139) [2006 8m 8s 8.2d Nov 1] useful-looking colt: third foal: half-brother to 1¼m winner Bridge Loan (by Giant's Causeway) and 3-y-o winner Balanced Budget, both useful: dam, 2-y-o 7f winner who stayed 14.6f (second in Park Hill Stakes), half-sister to very smart 1½m performer Stowaway: modest form in maidens: will be suited by 1¼m/1½m: should do better. *J. L. Dunlop* **52 p**

CREE 4 b.g. Indian Ridge 123 – Nightitude 93 (Night Shift (USA)) [2006 76, a60: 6m 5.7s 6.1d 7m⁵ 6.1m⁶ 5.9m³ 6f² 6m² 6f 6g 6.1m² 6m 6d³ f6g⁴ p6g² p7.1g² p6g* p6g* p6g² Dec 22] close-coupled, quite good-topped gelding: fair performer: won banded race at Kempton and handicap at Lingfield, both in December: effective at 6f/7f: acts on polytrack and any turf going: tried blinkered: free-going sort, has found little. *W. R. Muir* **69**

CREME BRULEE 3 b.f. College Chapel 122 – Balinsky (IRE) 55 (Skyliner 117) [2006 64p: p6g² p6g⁴ 6.1g 6d p7.1m p6g² p6g* p6g Dec 22] leggy filly: fair performer: won maiden at Wolverhampton in December: stays 6f: acts on polytrack. *C. R. Egerton* **66**

CRESTA GOLD 3 b.f. Halling (USA) 133 – Fleet Hill (IRE) 99 (Warrshan (USA) 117) [2006 70: 10.3f⁶ 11.9m* 11.5g* 11.9m⁴ 12m² 14f⁴ 12s⁴ 14g³ p13g⁴ Oct 26] leggy filly: useful performer: won maiden at Haydock and handicap at Carlisle (by 5 lengths from Lucayan Dancer) in June: better form after, including when ½-length second to Quenched in listed race at Newmarket, and fourth in Lillie Langtry Stakes at Goodwood (length behind Tartouche) and listed event at Lingfield (beaten 3 lengths by High Heel Sneakers) on sixth/final outings: stays 1¾m: acts on polytrack and firm going, probably on soft: races prominently: consistent. *A. Bailey* **107**

CRIME SCENE (IRE) 3 b.g. Royal Applause 124 – Crime (USA) (Gulch (USA)) [2006 87p: 8m* 10g³ 10.4m² 8m 10m 12g 10d² 12d 12m* 10m 11.8d³ Oct 3] tall gelding: developed into a useful handicapper: won at Musselburgh in May and Southwell (by ½ length from Trick Or Treat) in September: good third to Green Room at Leicester final outing: stays easy 1½m: acts on good to firm and good to soft going: sometimes hangs/looks less than straightforward: has run well when sweating: sent to UAE. *M. Johnston* **105**

CRIMINAL ACT (USA) 3 b.c. Bahri (USA) 125 – Captive Island 116 (Northfields (USA)) [2006 91: 10g³ 10m⁵ 10s May 20] well-made, quite attractive colt: has a quick action: fairly useful performer: stays 1¼m, though likely to prove at least as effective at 1m: acts on good to firm and good to soft going, below form on soft: sold 40,000 gns in July, joined Miss S. Finn in Ireland. *B. W. Hills* **94**

CRIMSON BOW (GER) 4 ch.f. Night Shift (USA) – Carma (IRE) (Konigsstuhl – (GER)) [2006 42: f11g Jan 24] sturdy filly: poor maiden: should stay 1½m. *J. G. Given*

CRIMSON FLAME (IRE) 3 b.g. Celtic Swing 138 – Wish List (IRE) 98 (Mujadil **73 d** (USA) 119) [2006 78: p12g⁴ 8.3m⁴ 8s⁶ 8.1g⁵ 8.1m 8g 8.1f⁶ 9.3f⁵ 8.1m⁶ 7f² 8m⁶ 7.1m² 8m 8m⁴ 8m 8m f8g p13.9g Dec 31] smallish, lightly-made gelding: has a quick action: fair maiden: below form last 6 starts, leaving M. Channon 11,000 gns after sixteenth outing: effective at 7f, and should stay 1¼m: acts on firm going: sometimes visored: sometimes looks none too keen. *A. J. Chamberlain*

CRIMSON KING (IRE) 5 ch.g. Pivotal 124 – Always Happy 75 (Sharrood (USA) **93** 124) [2006 f6g³ f6g* f7g* Apr 27] progressive form: 5-length winner of maiden in February and handicap in April, both at Southwell, eased late when accounting for 11 rivals in latter: stays 7f: twice failed stall tests in 2005. *T. T. Clement*

CRIMSON MONARCH (USA) 2 b.c. (Apr 28) Red Ransom (USA) – Tolltally **73 §** Light (USA) (Majestic Light (USA)) [2006 7m 8d⁶ 8.3d⁴ Oct 10] $165,000Y: sturdy colt: sixth foal: half-brother to 2 winners in USA by Dixie Brass: dam, maiden in USA, half-sister to dam of US Grade 1 9f/1¼m winner Riskaverse: fair form in maidens, looking temperamental. *Mrs A. J. Perrett*

CRIMSON SILK 6 ch.g. Forzando 122 – Sylhall (Sharpo 132) [2006 5d³ 6g 6s 6d 5s **97 d** Oct 16] strong, heavy-topped gelding: useful performer: unraced in 2005: easily best effort in 2006 when ½-length third to Trinculo in handicap at Beverley: effective at 6f/7f: acts on good to firm and good to soft going: sometimes wears headgear. *B. Smart*

CRIMSON YEAR (USA) 4 ch.f. Dubai Millennium 140 – Crimson Conquest (USA) – 85 (Diesis 133) [2006 6m 10m May 13] workmanlike filly: half-sister to several winners, including very smart 6f (at 2 yrs) to 1¼m winner Crimplene (by Lion Cavern) and smart 1¼m/1½m winner Dutch Gold (by Lahib): dam 2-y-o 6f winner who probably stayed 1¼m: behind in maidens. *C. E. Brittain*

CRIPSEY BROOK 8 ch.g. Lycius (USA) 124 – Duwon (IRE) 55 (Polish Precedent **87** (USA) 131) [2006 86: 13d 14.1s⁵ 14.1g² 14.1g 16f⁴ 10.1m² 12m 10.1f² 10g² 10d⁴ 10.5g Sep 22] tall gelding: fairly useful handicapper: effective at 1¼m, probably stays 2m: acts on firm and good to soft going: sometimes tongue tied: claimer ridden nowadays: free-going sort, patiently ridden. *K. G. Reveley*

CRISTOFORO (IRE) 9 b.g. Perugino (USA) 84 – Red Barons Lady (IRE) (Electric **105** 126) [2006 103: p12g³ 10m⁵ 12m Feb 16] big, good-topped gelding: useful handicapper: good close third to Polygonal at Lingfield in January: below form at Nad Al Sheba both subsequent starts: effective at 1¼m to 14.6f: unraced on heavy going, acts on any other turf/all-weather: sometimes slowly away. *B. J. Curley*

CRITICAL STAGE (IRE) 7 b.g. King's Theatre (IRE) 128 – Zandaka (FR) (Doyoun **70** 124) [2006 60: 16m p16g² Dec 15] sturdy gelding: fair performer: stays 2m: acts on all-weather, good to firm and good to soft ground: usually held up: won over hurdles in August and December. *J. D. Frost*

CRITIC (IRE) 3 b.g. Fasliyev (USA) 120 – Scruple (IRE) (Catrail (USA) 123) [2006 **80** 85: p7.1g* p7g⁴ 7d⁶ 8g 8.3m⁴ 7m⁴ 6m p7g Sep 5] tall, quite good-topped gelding: fairly **a85** useful performer: won maiden at Wolverhampton in January: eased as if amiss last 2 starts: stays 7.5f: acts on polytrack and good to firm ground: visored sixth/seventh starts: sold 16,000 gns. *M. L. W. Bell*

CROCODILE BAY (IRE) 3 b.g. Spectrum (IRE) 126 – Shenkara (IRE) 79 (Night – Shift (USA) 93) [2006 93: 7.1m 7.1m p10g Dec 8] good-topped, attractive gelding: has a quick action: fairly useful performer at 2 yrs: well held in 2006. *C. Llewellyn*

CROCODILE DUNDEE (IRE) 5 b.g. Croco Rouge (IRE) 126 – Miss Salsa Dancer **116** 64 (Salse (USA) 128) [2006 10.4f³ 11.6g* 11g⁵ Sep 15] good-topped gelding: smart performer: missed 2005: reportedly suffered bout of colic in spring: nearly as good as ever when winning listed race at Windsor in August by head from Khyber Kim: below form behind Blue Monday in Arc Trial at Newbury only subsequent outing, finding little: stays 1½m: acts on polytrack, good to firm and good to soft going: held up: game and consistent: sold 190,000 gns, joined J. Howard Johnson and gelded. *L. M. Cumani*

CROCODILE KISS (IRE) 4 b.f. Rossini (USA) 118 – Pipe Opener 58 (Prince Sabo **52** 123) [2006 52: f8g² f8g f8g⁵ 8g⁴ 11g a8.8g⁴ a8.8g⁵ a10.5g³ 10g Sep 17] modest maiden: left J. Osborne after third start, P. Haley after fifth: stays 10.5f: acts on all-weather/sand and firm going: blinkered final outing in Britain. *H. Lopez, Spain*

241

CROCODILE STAR (USA) 3 b. or br.g. Woodman (USA) 126 – Rhumba Rage **55** (USA) (Nureyev (USA) 131) [2006 53: p9.5g⁵ p10g p8.6g² f8g⁵ 11g⁴ 8g 6.5g³ 10g* 11d⁵ 8.8g* 11f 10g⁶ a9g* 11v Nov 26] modest performer: left J. Osborne after fourth start: won seller at Madrid in May (final start for P. Haley), handicap there in June and minor event at Sanlucar in August: stays 11f: acts on polytrack/sand, good to firm and good to soft ground: blinkered last 2 starts in Britain. *E. Olgado, Spain*

CROESO BACH 2 b.f. (May 31) Bertolini (USA) 125 – Croeso-I-Cymru 96 (Welsh **–** Captain 113) [2006 5.7m 5.1g Oct 17] third foal: half-sister to useful 5f/5.7f winner Croeso Croeso (by Most Welcome): dam 5f/6f winner: well held in maidens. *J. L. Spearing*

CROFT (IRE) 3 b.g. Mull of Kintyre (USA) 114 – Home Comforts (Most Welcome **63** 131) [2006 65: 8.1s 7.1g 8.2m⁶ 7g 8m² 9.9m 8m⁵ p12g Sep 5] strong, good-bodied gelding: modest maiden: left J. Hills after fifth start: stays 1m: acts on good to firm going: none too consistent. *R. M. Stronge*

CROOKHAVEN 3 b.g. Dansili 127 – My Mariam 79 (Salse (USA) 128) [2006 77: **95** 8.7d⁴ 8.2d² 8v 10m* 10m 14d 9v Sep 22] 15,500Y: sixth foal: half-brother to 3 winners, including fairly useful Irish 1½m winner In The Ribbons (by In The Wings) and 5-y-o Yashin: dam, 6f winner at 2 yrs, sister to Moyglare Stud Stakes winner Bianca Nera: useful performer: won minor event at Roscommon in June by 2 lengths from Sandton City: very stiff task, flattered when eighth in Irish 2000 Guineas at the Curragh time before: well held last 3 starts, in listed race at Royal Ascot first occasion: stays 1¼m: acts on heavy and good to firm going. *John Joseph Murphy, Ireland*

CROON 4 b.g. Sinndar (IRE) 134 – Shy Minstrel (USA) (The Minstrel (CAN) 135) **86** [2006 82p: 14.1f³ p12g* p12g⁴ 14.1g⁴ 12m* 12g⁵ 12d⁶ Aug 28] close-coupled gelding: fairly useful handicapper: won at Lingfield in May and Epsom in July: stays 1¾m: acts on polytrack and firm ground: refused to enter stall on intended reappearance: gelded, and joined Mrs Caroline Bailey. *H. Morrison*

CROSBY HALL 3 b.g. Compton Place 125 – Alzianah 102 (Alzao (USA) 117) [2006 **–** 87: 6m 6m 5g 6g 6d 7d Aug 21] sturdy, attractive gelding: fairly useful form at 2 yrs: well held in handicaps (tongue tied) in 2006: gelded after final outing. *N. Tinkler*

CROSBY JEMMA 2 ch.f. (Mar 21) Lomitas 129 – Gino's Spirits 98 (Perugino (USA) **48** 84) [2006 6g 6m 8m⁶ Sep 21] 14,000Y: unfurnished filly: second foal: dam, 9f/1¼m winner, later Grade 3 1m winner in USA: poor maiden. *J. R. Weymes*

CROSBY MILLIE 2 gr.f. (Feb 22) Linamix (FR) 127 – Calling Card (Bering 136) **57** [2006 7d 7.6f⁵ 8v⁵ Oct 9] 16,000Y: second foal: half-sister to Italian 9f winner by Daylami: dam useful French 10.5f winner: modest maiden: will stay 1¼m. *J. R. Weymes*

CROSBY VISION 3 b.c. Agnes World (USA) 123 – Aegean Blue (Warning 136) **77** [2006 78: 7.5f⁵ 7m⁴ 8d 8m² 8g 8g⁶ Aug 31] quite good-topped colt: fair handicapper: stays 1m: acts on good to firm going. *J. R. Weymes*

CROSSBOW CREEK 8 b.g. Lugana Beach 116 – Roxy River 38 (Ardross 134) [2006 **90** 12g⁶ p12g* p12g Sep 18] rangy, good-bodied gelding: useful hurdler/smart chaser (successful twice in October): first season on Flat in 2006, easily best effort when winning maiden at Lingfield in August by 5 lengths from Falpiase: pulled hard final start: stays 1½m: acts on polytrack. *M. G. Rimell*

CROSS CHANNEL (USA) 3 ch.f. Giant's Causeway (USA) 132 – Sterling Pound **97** (USA) (Seeking The Gold (USA)) [2006 98p: p8g⁵ 11.5m⁴ 10g⁵ p7f³ Oct 19] tall filly: easy mover: useful performer: hinted at temperament in 2006 (edgy in paddock first 2 starts), best effort when 3½ lengths fifth to Princess Nada in listed race at Newbury (pulled hard) third appearance (final one for E. Dunlop): third in allowance race at Keeneland final outing: stays 1¼m: acts on polytrack and good to firm going: has had fore joints bandaged: blinkered second outing. *C. Clement, USA*

CROSSING THE LINE (IRE) 2 b.g. (Apr 15) Cape Cross (IRE) 129 – Tropical **63 p** Zone (Machiavellian (USA) 123) [2006 6.1m 5.7m p6g Sep 29] 95,000Y: fourth foal: half-brother to French 2003 2-y-o 1m winner Tropical Mark (by Mark of Esteem): dam, unraced half-sister to smart French winner up to 1¼m The Scout, out of Prix Marcel Boussac winner Tropicaro: mid-field in sprint maidens within 15 days in September, and gelded after: likely to thrive over 1m+ at 3 yrs. *Sir Mark Prescott*

CROSS MY MIND 4 b.g. Cape Cross (IRE) 129 – Dynamic Dream (USA) 87 (Dyna- **92** former (USA)) [2006 90: 8m² 7d³ 8s 7d⁶ 8g p9.5g Oct 28] deep-girthed gelding: fairly useful handicapper: effective at 7f/1m: acts on polytrack, good to firm and good to soft going. *T. Keddy*

CROSS MY SHADOW (IRE) 4 b.g. Cape Cross (IRE) 129 – Shadowglow (Shaadi (USA) 126) [2006 56, a47: f8g p7g Oct 29] quite good-topped gelding: maiden: well held in 2006: blinkered final 2-y-o start: tongue tied: sent to France. *M. F. Harris*   **–**

CROSS OF LORRAINE (IRE) 3 b.g. Pivotal 124 – My-Lorraine (IRE) 77 (Mac's Imp (USA) 116) [2006 9.2d³ 8d⁴ p7.1m² f5g² p6g* p7.1g² Dec 27] 3,200 3-y-o: compact gelding: fifth foal: half-brother to fairly useful but unreliable 5f winner (including at 2 yrs) Izmail (by Bluebird) and 4-y-o Bolodenka: dam, Irish 5f/6.5f winner, half-sister to smart Irish sprinter Catch The Blues: fair performer: won maiden at Wolverhampton in December, making all: best at 6f/7f: acts on polytrack: blinkered: looked none too keen on debut. *I. Semple*   **75**

CROSSPEACE (IRE) 4 b.c. Cape Cross (IRE) 129 – Announcing Peace (Danehill (USA) 126) [2006 116+: 12d⁶ 12m 10m³ 14.1s⁵ 10g³ 13.3s⁴ 10.1g 10m³ 10m⁴ 10.1g⁴ 9.9m* 12f* 10s p12g² 9.9m² 12d Sep 24] sturdy, good-topped colt: smart performer: successful twice within 4 days at Goodwood in August, in quite valuable handicap (from Tabadul) and listed race (beat Foxhaven), both by neck: good second in September Stakes at Kempton (beaten 1¼ lengths by Kandidate) and Select Stakes at Goodwood (beaten neck by Pictavia, edged right), both in September: best at 1¼m/1½m: acts on polytrack and any turf going: tends to run in snatches. *M. Johnston*   **118**

CROSS THE LINE (IRE) 4 b.g. Cape Cross (IRE) 129 – Baalbek 76 (Barathea (IRE) 127) [2006 80: p8g² p7g³ 7s² 8g⁴ 6g⁵ p8g* p8g² 7d p8g² p8g* 8g p8g² Oct 15] big gelding: useful handicapper on all-weather, fairly useful on turf: won at Kempton in July and September (beat Norton by 1¾ lengths): good second at Lingfield final start: effective at 7f, should stay 9f: acts on polytrack, soft and good to firm ground: consistent. *A. P. Jarvis*   **87** **a95**

CROW'S NEST LAD 2 b.c. (Mar 11) Komaite (USA) – Miss Fit (IRE) 87 (Hamas (IRE) 125§) [2006 6m 5m³ 5f* Jul 28] strong, workmanlike colt: second foal: dam 5f/6f winner (including at 2 yrs): fair form: improved with experience and won maiden at Thirsk in July: should prove best at 5f/6f: raced on going firmer than good. *T. D. Easterby*   **77**

Favourites Racing's "Crosspeace"

CROW WOOD 7 b.g. Halling (USA) 133 – Play With Me (IRE) 73 (Alzao (USA) 117)   **94**
[2006 107: p10g⁶ 10m 10g 12m 12m 11.9g 12m³ 13.1d² 12d Sep 30] strong, close-coupled gelding: just fairly useful performer in 2006, seemingly best effort when 2¼ lengths sixth to Grand Passion in minor event at Lingfield: effective at 1¼m, probably at 1¾m: acts on fibresand, firm and good to soft going, possibly not on soft: usually races handily: useful hurdler, successful in November. *J. J. Quinn*

CRUISE DIRECTOR 6 b.g. Zilzal (USA) 137 – Briggsmaid 70 (Elegant Air 119)   **92**
[2006 93: 12d⁶ 12s⁴ 12m 10m 13.3g Aug 18] heavy-topped gelding: fairly useful handicapper: below form after second start: stays 1½m: acts on all-weather and soft going: held up. *Ian Williams*

CRUMBS OF COMFORT (USA) 2 b.f. (Feb 10) Pulpit (USA) 117 – British Col-   **85**
umbia (Selkirk (USA) 129) [2006 p6g* 6m⁵ 7m² 7d p8g Oct 20] $60,000Y: big, strong filly: second foal: half-sister to 2005 2-y-o 7.5f winner in France Becky Moss (by Red Ransom): dam, French maiden, half-sister to useful performer up to 1¼m Heart of Darkness: fairly useful form: won maiden at Wolverhampton in July: best effort when second in nursery at Yarmouth: should stay 1m: sent to USA. *L. M. Cumani*

CRUSADER'S GOLD (FR) 3 b.g. Lujain (USA) 119 – Rain And Shine (FR) 78   **60**
(Rainbow Quest (USA) 134) [2006 66: 6f 8s 7g⁶ p5.1g³ p6g⁴ p6g³ 5g⁶ p5.1g p6m Oct 9] strong gelding: modest maiden: may prove best at 6f/7f: acts on polytrack, firm and good to soft going: usually races prominently: slowly away eighth outing: tried visored/ blinkered: sold 6,000 gns. *T. D. Easterby*

CRUSH ON YOU 3 b.f. Golden Snake (USA) 127 – Mourir d'Aimer (USA) (Trem-   **55**
polino (USA) 135) [2006 44: f7g* f8g f7g 7.1s⁴ 8.2d f7g 8.1m² 7.1g 8.3m² 7.9g 9.9g 7f* 7d p8.6g⁴ f8g⁴ f8g³ Dec 29] leggy, close-coupled filly: modest performer: won sellers at Southwell in January and Leicester in September: stays 8.6f: acts on all-weather, firm and soft going. *R. Hollinshead*

CRUSOE (IRE) 9 b.g. Turtle Island (IRE) 123 – Self Reliance 72 (Never So Bold 135)   **63 d**
[2006 –, a64: f8g f6g f7g f8g³ f8g⁶ f7g³ f8g f8g³ f8g³ p7.1g⁴ f8g* p9.5g f7s⁶ f8g* f11g³ f8g² f7g f8g⁴ f8g p9.5g f7g f7g f8g f8g f8g f8g Dec 29] small gelding: modest performer: won banded races at Southwell in February and March: ended year out of form: effective at 1m to 11f: acts on all-weather, lightly raced and no form on turf after 3 yrs: tried in cheekpieces/tongue tie, usually blinkered. *A. Sadik*

CRUX 4 b.g. Pivotal 124 – Penny Dip 86 (Cadeaux Genereux 131) [2006 58, a48: p9.5g   **–**
Jan 23] rather leggy gelding: modest maiden on turf, poor on all-weather: well held only outing in 2006. *C. W. Thornton*

CRYFIELD 9 b.g. Efisio 120 – Ciboure 74 (Norwick (USA) 125) [2006 63: f8g Jan 24]   **–**
big, good-bodied gelding: modest performer: well held only outing in 2006: sometimes visored. *N. Tinkler*

CRY PRESTO (USA) 2 b.g. (Feb 22) Street Cry (IRE) 130 – Sabaah Elfull 75 (Kris   **85 §**
135) [2006 7m 7g 8m³ 8g⁴ 8d⁵ 8s p8g² p9.5s⁶ Dec 14] 60,000Y, 43,000 2-y-o: stocky gelding: half-brother to 4-y-o Oh Dara and UAE 6f/7f winner Outlaw (by Danehill): dam, 5f winner who stayed 7.5f, closely related to smart French sprinter Pole Position: fairly useful maiden: seemed to run well in listed event second start: creditable short-head second of 4 to Solid Rock in nursery at Lingfield penultimate start: stays 1m (well held over 9.4f final start): acts on polytrack: tried blinkered, tongue tied last 2 starts: unreliable. *R. Hannon*

CRYPTIC CLUE (USA) 2 b.g. (Mar 12) Cryptoclearance (USA) – Nidd (USA) 112   **55**
(Known Fact (USA) 135) [2006 6s 5.7m 6m⁴ 8f 6v⁶ f5g² f8g³ f5g⁵ f6g Dec 23] good-topped gelding: modest maiden: left Mrs A. Perrett 13,000 gns after second start: stays 1m: acts on fibresand and good to firm ground. *D. W. Chapman*

CRYSTAL AIR (IRE) 3 b.f. Distant Music (USA) 126 – Columbian Sand (IRE)   **80**
(Salmon Leap (USA) 131) [2006 71: p10g a6f* a6g* a6g⁴ 8g⁵ a8s* a6d* a8g Nov 19] fair performer: left Miss J. Feilden after reappearance, won minor event at Jagersro and handicap at Taby in August and minor events at Taby in October/November: stays 1m (raced freely at 1¼m on reappearance): acts on dirt and good to soft going: refused to enter stall second intended outing. *O. Strenstrom, Sweden*

CRYSTAL ANNIE 3 b.f. Namaqualand (USA) – Crystal Canyon 59 (Efisio 120)   **52**
[2006 8.2m 8.2g⁵ p8.6g Oct 8] first foal: dam sprint maiden: form only when fifth in maiden at Nottingham: will stay 1¼m. *Mrs H. Dalton*

CRYSTAL BAY (IRE) 3 b.f. Carrowkeel (IRE) 106 – Cajo (IRE) (Tirol 127) [2006 –:   **–**
5f 5.9g 9.1v Oct 9] of no account. *A. Berry*

CRYSTAL GAZER (FR) 2 b.f. (Apr 1) Elnadim (USA) 128 – Chrysalu 102 (Distant **77** Relative 128) [2006 p5g² p5g² 5.2d³ 6m* 6.1m⁶ 7d⁴ 6m Sep 16] €37,000Y: strong, good-bodied filly: fifth foal: half-sister to French 1¼m/11f winner Track Show (by Unfuwain): dam French 1m winner: fair performer: won maiden at Goodwood in June: best at 5f/6f: acts on polytrack, good to firm and good to soft going. *R. Hannon*

CRYSTAL ICE (IRE) 2 br.f. (Mar 26) Lahib (USA) 129 – Chalfont (IRE) 71 (Com- **56** mon Grounds 118) [2006 p5.1g 5.1m⁶ 6m⁶ Jun 27] 800F, 1,000Y: leggy filly: first foal: dam, maiden, stayed 1m: maiden: sixth at Chester second start, only form (modest). *Mrs L. Williamson*

CRYSTAL KA (FR) 4 b.g. Northern Crystal 114 – Kahuna Magic (FR) (Dancing **–** Spree (USA)) [2006 p10g Jan 14] ex-Belgian gelding: won claimer at Le Croise-Laroche in 2004: left A. Hermans, well held on British debut: stays 9f. *M. R. Hoad*

CRYSTAL MYSTIC (IRE) 4 b.g. Anita's Prince 126 – Out On Her Own (Superlative **58** 118) [2006 63: p7.1g⁴ 6m 6.1m⁶ 6.1d 6.1d⁵ 6g p6g Oct 23] leggy gelding: modest performer: effective at 6f/7f: acts on polytrack, soft and good to firm going: blinkered first three 2-y-o starts. *B. Palling*

CRYSTAL PLUM (IRE) 2 ch.f. (Apr 30) Rock of Gibraltar (IRE) 133 – State Crystal **67** (IRE) 114 (High Estate 127) [2006 7f 7g⁵ p7g Sep 5] leggy, close-coupled filly: half-sister to several winners, including useful 2003 2-y-o 7f winner Crystal Curling (by Peintre Celebre), 1¼m winner True Crystal and 3-y-o Malakiya (both fairly useful and by Sadler's Wells): dam 7f (at 2 yrs) and 1½m (Lancashire Oaks) winner: fair maiden: fifth at Leicester, easily best effort: free-going sort, but likely to stay at least 1m. *B. W. Hills*

CRYSTAL PRINCE 2 b.c. (May 3) Marju (IRE) 127 – Crystal Ring (IRE) 83 (Kris **–** 135) [2006 8s 8.2s Oct 25] strong, good-bodied colt: behind in maidens (soft ground). *T. P. Tate*

CUBAN NIGHT 2 b.g. (Mar 26) Zaha (CAN) 106 – No Candles Tonight 74 (Star **–** Appeal 133) [2006 8d Sep 27] last in maiden: bred to stay 1¼m+. *D. J. S. ffrench Davis*

CUCCINELLO (IRE) 3 b.f. Makbul 104 – Costa Verde 77 (King of Spain 121) [2006 **–** –: 5.9g 7g May 29] seems of little account. *K. W. Hogg, Isle of Man*

CUESTA CANYON (IRE) 3 b.g. Indian Ridge 123 – Perfect Plum (IRE) 113 (Dar- **46** shaan 133) [2006 39: p5.1g f8g² f7g 9m⁴ 9.9g³ 7g p6g⁶ f7g Nov 21] leggy gelding: poor maiden: left M. Polglase after sixth start: stays 1¼m: acts on all-weather: tried blinkered. *A. J. McCabe*

CULACHY FOREST 2 b.g. (May 17) Kyllachy 129 – Abscond (USA) 97 (Unbridled **–** (USA) 128) [2006 7g 7s Oct 10] well beaten in maidens (tongue tied debut). *N. Tinkler*

CULCABOCK (IRE) 6 b.g. Unfuwain (USA) 131 – Evidently (IRE) (Slip Anchor **47** 136) [2006 10d 15m⁶ 15m⁴ 16.1s³ Sep 4] lightly raced on Flat and only poor nowadays: stays 2m: acts on soft and good to firm ground. *Miss Lucinda V. Russell*

CULROY 2 b.g. (Mar 23) Fath (USA) 116 – Folly Finnesse 80 (Joligeneration 111) **–** [2006 7g Sep 27] sixth foal: half-brother to 3 winners, including 2000 2-y-o 5f/6f winner Quantum Lady (by Mujadil): dam, 6f (at 2 yrs) to 10.8f winner, half-sister to useful sprinter Westcourt Magic: 50/1, not knocked about in maiden at Newcastle. *N. Tinkler*

CULTURED 5 b.m. Danzero (AUS) – Seek The Pearl 91 (Rainbow Quest (USA) 134) **–** [2006 60: 10.9s Apr 4] tall mare: maiden: well held only outing in 2006. *Mrs A. J. Bowlby*

CULTURE QUEEN 3 b.f. King's Best (USA) 132 – Cultured Pearl (IRE) 72 (Lamm- **91** tarra (USA) 134) [2006 81+: 7m Apr 22] medium-sized, quite good-topped filly: fairly useful performer, lightly raced: good seventh to Nasheej in Fred Darling Stakes at Newbury on only outing in 2006, short of room 2f out: should have stayed 1m: acted on good to firm ground: stud. *M. P. Tregoning*

CUMBERLAND ROAD 3 ch.g. Efisio 120 – Thatcher's Era (IRE) 57 (Never So Bold **–** 135) [2006 60: p8.6g⁶ 7m p8.6g⁵ Dec 30] workmanlike gelding: maiden: well held in 2006, leaving P. Haslam after reappearance: barely stays 7f: acts on polytrack and good to firm ground. *C. A. Mulhall*

CUMBRIAN KNIGHT (IRE) 8 b.g. Presenting 120 – Crashrun (Crash Course 128) **70** [2006 72: p16.5g* p12.2g p16.5g 13m 14.1f⁴ 12s p13.9g⁵ p13.9g² Nov 27] fair handicapper: won amateur event at Wolverhampton in January: stays 2m: acts on polytrack, best turf effort on good ground: usually amateur ridden. *J. M. Jefferson*

CUMIN (USA) 2 ch.f. (Jan 23) Fusaichi Pegasus (USA) 130 – User Cat (USA) (Storm **100** Cat (USA)) [2006 6m² 7m⁶ 7f² 7f* 7m³ 8m Oct 1] $600,000Y: well-grown, close-coupled, quite attractive filly: has a quick action: second foal: dam unraced out of Oaks and St Leger winner User Friendly: useful performer: shaped well first 3 starts, including in listed Chesham Stakes (sixth) at Royal Ascot, then much improved to win 15-runner maiden at Goodwood by 7 lengths in August: better run in pattern events after when 1¾ lengths third of 10 to Sesmen in Prestige Stakes at Goodwood, again making running: should stay 1m: raced on going firmer than good. *B. W. Hills*

CUMMISKEY (IRE) 4 b.g. Orpen (USA) 116 – Ansariya (USA) 83 (Shahrastani **100** (USA) 135) [2006 f6g* f6g² f6g* f7g³ f6g³ p7g³ p8.6g p6g⁴ 8f⁴ 11f³ 8.5f* 8f⁵ Oct 11] lengthy, attractive gelding: useful performer: reportedly split a pastern and unraced in 2005: successful in maiden at Southwell in January, minor event there (beat Wessex by 1½ lengths) in February, and, having left J. Osborne after eighth outing, non-graded event at Golden Gate Fields in September: stays 8.5f: acts on all-weather and firm going: blinkered (ran creditably) eighth start: has flashed tail under pressure. *J. M. Cassidy, USA*

CUNEGONDE 3 ch.f. Observatory (USA) 131 – Brave Princess 70 (Dancing Brave **50** (USA) 140) [2006 –: 8m 8m 10d 8.5m⁴ 10f 8m² 10.9m Sep 4] modest maiden: stays 1m: acts on good to firm ground. *G. L. Moore*

CUPID'S GLORY 4 b.g. Pursuit of Love 124 – Doctor's Glory (USA) 91 (Elmaamul **105 +** (USA) 125) [2006 119: p7g³ Dec 22] rather lengthy, good-bodied gelding: smart performer at best: off 15 months and gelded, shaped encouragingly when 1¼ lengths third of 6 to Vortex in minor event at Lingfield only outing in 2006, making running: stays 1m: acts on polytrack, soft and good to firm going: blinkered on 3-y-o reappearance: has run well when sweating: hung left when successful at Chester in 2005. *Sir Mark Prescott*

CUP OF LOVE (USA) 4 ch.f. Behrens (USA) 130 – Cup of Kindness (USA) (Secre- **70** tariat (USA) 168) [2006 68: p9.5g* p10g p8.6g² Feb 11] close-coupled filly: fair handicapper: won at Wolverhampton in January: stays 1½m: acts on all-weather and firm going: free-going sort. *Rae Guest*

CUPPACOCOA 2 b.f. (Mar 18) Bertolini (USA) 125 – Coffee Time (IRE) 88 (Efisio **70** 120) [2006 5.1m⁴ p5g 5m³ 5.1m* 5.1f* 6d 5.1m⁴ Oct 8] 8,500F, 13,000Y: small filly: first foal: dam thoroughly ungenuine maiden (effective at 5f to 1m): fair performer: won maiden in August and nursery in September, both at Bath: best at 5f: acts on firm and good to soft ground: has given trouble at stalls. *C. G. Cox*

CURRAHEE 2 b.c. (May 21) Efisio 120 – Dixie Favor (USA) 82 (Dixieland Band **–** (USA)) [2006 6m 7s⁶ Oct 10] good-bodied colt: no show in maidens. *Miss J. A. Camacho*

CURRENCY 9 b.g. Sri Pekan (USA) 117 – On Tiptoes 107 (Shareef Dancer (USA) **74** 135) [2006 88: 6s p6g⁶ 5.7g 6m 6m⁵ 6f 6f² 6m⁶ 6g⁶ 6m⁵ 6g 7g⁶ 7.1m 7m Sep 3] sturdy gelding: fair handicapper: stays 7f: acts on polytrack (well below form on fibresand), firm and good to soft going: tried in cheekpieces/blinkers. *J. M. Bradley*

CURSUM PERFICIO 4 b.g. Tagula (IRE) 116 – Simply Sooty 78 (Absalom 128) **81** [2006 81: p8g² 8d p8g⁵ 7g 8.3f² p8.6g⁴ p8g⁶ Oct 11] good-bodied gelding: fairly useful handicapper: stays 8.6f: acts on polytrack and firm going: sold 15,000 gns, joined R. Lee. *W. R. Muir*

CURTAIL (IRE) 3 b.g. Namid 128 – Nipitinthebud (USA) 59 (Night Shift (USA)) **101** [2006 102: 5m 6m 6m 6g p8g⁸ Dec 16] smallish, strong, quite attractive gelding: useful performer: seemingly easily best effort in 2006 when 2¾ lengths last of 4 to Vortex in steadily-run minor event at Lingfield, short of room 2f out and not knocked about: seems to stay 1m: acts on polytrack and good to firm going, probably on soft. *I. Semple*

CURTAIN BLUFF 4 b.g. Dansili 127 – Gayane 125 (Nureyev (USA) 131) [2006 87: **79 §** p7g 7.1m⁵ 7.6f⁵ 7f⁵ 7f² p7.1g* 8.2f⁵ 8m 7g 7m⁴ 7.2v p7.1g³ Sep 30] good-topped **a84 §** gelding: good walker: fairly useful handicapper: won at Wolverhampton in July: stays 8.2f: acts on polytrack, firm and good to soft going: visored nowadays: inconsistent: sent to Sweden. *M. R. Channon*

CURVED AIR (IRE) 4 gr.f. Turtle Island (IRE) 123 – Poetry (IRE) 84 (Treasure Kay **–** 114) [2006 14m Aug 11] fourth foal: dam 7f winner: modest form in bumpers: tailed off in maiden at Lingfield (slowly away) on Flat debut. *Stef Liddiard*

CURZON PRINCE (IRE) 2 b.c. (Feb 5) Mujadil (USA) 119 – Smooth Spirit (USA) **84 p** (Alydar (USA)) [2006 6m⁴ 6g* Aug 16] €26,000F, 45,000Y: quite attractive colt: half-brother to several winners abroad: dam maiden in USA: still green, confirmed Newmarket promise by winning maiden at Yarmouth, beating Dodge City by ¾ length: likely to stay 7f: should make a useful 3-y-o. *C. F. Wall*

CUSIIAT LAW (IRE) 2 b.f. (Feb 28) Montjeu (IRE) 137 – Blush With Love (USA) **58** (Mt Livermore (USA)) [2006 6.1f 8m 8.2s Oct 18] 40,000Y: good-bodied filly: fourth foal: half-sister to 8.5f winner Stonor Lady (by French Deputy): dam, ran twice in USA, out of half-sister to dam of Mark of Esteem: modest form in maidens. *W. Jarvis*

CUSOON 4 b.g. Dansili 127 – Charming Life 88 (Habitat 134) [2006 80: 7m² 8.3f³ **82** 10m* 10m 9g⁴ 8.1m⁶ p10g* p8.6g* p10g* Dec 20] useful handicapper on all-weather, **a100** fairly useful on turf: won at Windsor in July, Lingfield in October, Wolverhampton in November and Lingfield (further improvement when beating Watamu by 2 lengths) in December: stays 1¼m: acts on polytrack and firm going: tried in cheekpieces/blinkers: often slowly away, and has looked wayward, more reliable in 2006. *G. L. Moore*

CUSTODIAN (IRE) 4 b.g. Giant's Causeway (USA) 132 – Desert Bluebell 83 (Kala- **79** glow 132) [2006 p10g² p9.5g* p10g⁵ p10g⁶ 10g* Aug 2] fair performer: won maiden at Wolverhampton in February and handicap at Leicester in August: likely to stay 1½m: withdrawn after refusing to enter stall on intended run. *H. R. A. Cecil*

CUT GLASS 3 ch.f. Fantastic Light (USA) 134 – Shady Point (IRE) 76 (Unfuwain (USA) 131) [2006 62: 7m 7.1g 11.5f⁵ Jul 25] leggy filly: lightly-raced maiden: well beaten in 2006: sold 2,500 gns in October, sent to Iran. *C. E. Brittain*

CUT RIDGE (IRE) 7 b.m. Indian Ridge 123 – Cutting Ground (IRE) 85 (Common **52** Grounds 118) [2006 58: p6g⁶ 5f⁴ 6m 6f⁴ 6.9g³ 8g⁵ 7.1m 7.1d* p7g f7g Nov 21] lengthy mare: modest performer: won banded race at Musselburgh in October: effective at 5f to 7.6f: acts on firm and good to soft going: sometimes wears cheekpieces: free-going sort. *J. S. Wainwright*

CUT THE CAKE (USA) 2 b.f. (May 27) Diesis 133 – Wife For Life (USA) (Dynafor- **77 p** mer (USA)) [2006 8s² Oct 7] rangy filly: has plenty of scope: fourth foal: half-sister to US Grade 1 8.5f (at 2 yrs)/9f winner Hollywood Story (by Wild Rush): dam 7.5f/1m winner in USA: 9/2, 3 lengths second of 13 to Victorian Prince in maiden at York (green, flashed tail): will do better. *J. Noseda*

CUT TO (USA) 3 b.g. Red Ransom (USA) – Bubble Club (USA) (Vanlandingham **–** (USA)) [2006 8.3g p8g 10d p7g Oct 15] well held in maidens, slowly away second outing. *J. Akehurst*

CUYAMACA (IRE) 4 b.f. Desert King (IRE) 129 – Surprise Visitor (IRE) (Be My **68** Guest (USA) 126) [2006 p9.5g³ p8.6g⁴ Feb 27] €80,000F: closely related to useful French 4.5f (at 2 yrs)/5f winner Ziria (by Danehill Dancer) and half-sister to 2 winners, including useful 2003 2-y-o 7f winner Tashkil (by Royal Applause): dam, lightly-raced French maiden, half-sister to dam of very smart miler Swallow Flight: fair form in maidens at Wolverhampton (reportedly finished lame in latter). *C. F. Wall*

CYBER SANTA 8 b.g. Celtic Swing 138 – Qualitair Ridge (Indian Ridge 123) [2006 **–** 55: p12.2g 13f Jun 29] big gelding: modest performer: well held in 2006. *J. Hetherton*

CYCLICAL 4 b.g. Pivotal 124 – Entwine 92 (Primo Dominie 121) [2006 95: 6m 6.1f **88** 7f⁴ p6g³ p7g⁶ Sep 5] good-topped gelding: fairly useful handicapper, lightly raced: seems to stay easy 7f: acts on polytrack and good to firm going, probably on good to soft. *G. A. Butler*

CYFRWYS (IRE) 5 b.m. Foxhound (USA) 103 – Divine Elegance (IRE) (College **59** Chapel 122) [2006 72, a56: p6g⁵ f6s 6.1s f6g p6g⁶ Nov 20] close-coupled mare: mod- est handicapper nowadays: effective at 5.7f to easy 7f: acts on all-weather, good to firm and good to soft ground: tried tongue tied/visored/in cheekpieces: carries head high. *B. Palling*

CYPRUS ROSE 2 br.f. (Apr 11) Whittingham (IRE) 104 – Blackpool Belle 70 (The **54 d** Brianstan 128) [2006 5g⁶ 6g p5g 5f³ 5m⁶ 5.2f⁵ 6f⁶ p5g⁶ p5g Nov 18] half-sister to several winners, notably smart sprinter Croft Pool (by Crofthall): dam sprinter: modest maiden at best: left V. Smith after seventh start. *S. Curran*

D

DAAWEITZA 3 ch.g. Daawe (USA) 103 – Chichen Itza (Shareef Dancer (USA) 135) **82** [2006 67: f8g* p10g⁵ 8.2d 9.8m⁶ 8g² 8m² 8.1f³ p8.6g* 7d² 8m* 8g 8.9s⁶ Oct 7] sturdy gelding: fairly useful performer: improved in 2006, winning maiden at Southwell in January and handicaps at Wolverhampton in July and Redcar in August: stays 9f: acts on all-weather, firm and soft ground: tried in cheekpieces/blinkers at 2 yrs. *B. Ellison*

totesport International Stakes (Handicap), Ascot—Dabbers Ridge caps a good season with his third win, denying Uhoomagoo; Marching Song (black cap) and Appalachian Trail (rail) head the chasing pack

DABBERS RIDGE (IRE) 4 b.c. Indian Ridge 123 – Much Commended 100 (Most **112** Welcome 131) [2006 94: 7d³ 7g* 7.6d* 8s³ 8m 7m* 7s⁵ 7.1s³ Sep 7] lengthy colt: smart performer: much improved form in 2006 and won handicaps at Thirsk in April, Chester (beat Shot To Fame by 5 lengths) in May and Ascot (totesport International Stakes, beat Uhoomagoo by neck) in July: respectable third to Quito in listed race at Haydock final outing: likely to prove best at 6f/7f (tried former trip only on 2-y-o debut): acts on soft and good to firm going: races prominently: reliable. *B. W. Hills*

DAB HAND (IRE) 3 b.g. Alzao (USA) 117 – Deft Touch (IRE) (Desert Style (IRE) **67** 121) [2006 10g 8g⁵ p8.6g⁴ 8.3f 7m² 7f⁵ 8.1m³ p8g* p10g² Oct 15] €10,000F, 15,500Y: **a77** lengthy, good-topped gelding: first foal: dam well beaten only start: fair performer: won maiden at Lingfield in October: best effort final start: stays 1¼m: acts on polytrack and firm ground: hung right fourth start: makes running/races prominently: sold 36,000 gns, joined C. Swan in Ireland. *D. M. Simcock*

DA BOOKIE (IRE) 6 b.g. Woods of Windsor (USA) – Hurgill Lady 62 (Emarati **78** (USA) 74) [2006 68: 8g 9m 9m³ 9f³ 8.5m⁶ 8.5g 7m⁵ 8m³ 8d 8.5g² p8.6g p8g* p8g⁶ p8g p9.5g Dec 7] fair handicapper: left C. Swan in Ireland after tenth start: won at Lingfield in October (final start for P. Blockley): stays 1¼m: acts on polytrack and firm ground. *E. J. Creighton*

DABOY (IRE) 2 b.g. (Mar 11) Indian Danehill (IRE) 124 – Notable Dear (ITY) (Last **61** Tycoon 131) [2006 p7g p8.6g⁶ Nov 28] modest form in maidens at Lingfield and Wolverhampton. *John A. Quinn, Ireland*

DADDY COOL 2 b.c. (Mar 25) Kyllachy 129 – Addicted To Love 73 (Touching Wood **57** (USA) 127) [2006 p6g⁶ p5g³ Aug 5] better effort in maidens (struck into on debut) when third at Lingfield: shapes as if will prove best at 5f. *W. G. M. Turner*

DADO MUSH 3 b.c. Almushtarak (IRE) 122 – Princess of Spain (King of Spain 121) **62** [2006 –: p7g⁶ 8d⁴ 8d* 8.3d⁴ 8m⁶ 7f p7g f8g f8g Dec 9] modest performer: won maiden at **a–** Ripon in July: left T. Clement after sixth start: stays 1m: acts on good to firm and good to soft going, little form on all-weather: tried visored. *G. Prodromou*

DAGOLA (IRE) 5 b.g. Daggers Drawn (USA) 114 – Diabola (USA) (Devil's Bag **55** (USA)) [2006 66: p9.5g p9.5g p10g³ p10g² p9.5g p12g² p12g⁴ p12g p10g* p10g 10.1g Jun 1] quite good-topped gelding: modest performer: won banded race at Kempton in May: stays easy 1½m: acts on polytrack and firm going: tongue tied once: has looked none too keen on occasions. *C. A. Dwyer*

DAHMAN 4 b.g. Darshaan 133 – Nuriva (USA) 100 (Woodman (USA) 126) [2006 86: **79** 11.7f⁶ 10d Oct 4] tall, leggy gelding: fairly useful performer in 2005 (reportedly returned lame final outing that season): better effort in 2006 when fair sixth in handicap at Bath: should stay 1½m: acts on good to firm and good to soft going: soon off bridle: sold 13,000 gns. *Saeed bin Suroor*

DAKOTA RAIN (IRE) 4 br.g. Indian Ridge 123 – Mill Rainbow (FR) (Rainbow **81** Quest (USA) 134) [2006 87: 8v³ 7.2g 8.1m 7.1m² 7m 8d Sep 14] tall gelding: fairly useful handicapper: stays 1m: acts on good to firm ground: usually races prominently. *R. C. Guest*

DALLMA (IRE) 3 b.f. Daylami (IRE) 138 – Play With Fire (FR) (Priolo (USA) 127) **69** [2006 8.2m⁴ 7d⁴ 6g⁶ 8.1g⁶ 10.3f⁶ 8f⁵ p7g⁴ p7g Nov 1] rather leggy, close-coupled filly: fourth foal: half-sister to useful sprinters Coconut Penang (by Night Shift) and Millbag (by Cape Cross): dam French 1½m winner: fair maiden handicapper: stays 1m: acts on good to firm and good to soft going: blinkered (well held) final start. *C. E. Brittain*

DALPE 5 ch.g. Siphon (BRZ) 130 – Double Stake (USA) (Kokand (USA)) [2006 53: **–** 8.3m⁵ 13.3m p8g 8.1m Sep 12] maiden: well held in 2006: tried tongue tied/in cheekpieces. *A. J. Lidderdale*

DALRIATH 7 b.m. Fraam 114 – Alsiba 68 (Northfields (USA)) [2006 –: 12m Aug 4] **–** rangy, angular mare: well held all 3 starts since 2004. *M. C. Chapman*

DALVINA 2 ch.f. (Mar 8) Grand Lodge (USA) 125 – Foodbroker Fancy (IRE) 113 **90 p** (Halling (USA) 133) [2006 p7g² Oct 26] 145,000Y: second foal: half-sister to 3-y-o Soft Centre: dam 6f (at 2 yrs) and 1¼m winner: 12/1, impressive debut in 15-runner maiden at Lingfield (beat Salsa Steps by 1¼ lengths), winning smoothly despite slow start/forced wide: will stay 1¼m: sure to go on and win more races. *E. A. L. Dunlop*

DAMA'A (IRE) 3 b.f. Green Desert (USA) 127 – Lady Miletrian (IRE) 103 (Barathea **85** (IRE) 127) [2006 77p: 8.3m⁴ 8g 7m⁵ p6g* p6g Aug 23] strong, good-bodied filly: type to carry condition: fairly useful performer: won maiden at Kempton in August: best form at 6f: acts on polytrack and good to firm going. *J. H. M. Gosden*

DAMACHIDA (IRE) 7 ch.g. Mukaddamah (USA) 125 – Lady Loire 94 (Wolverlife **88** 115) [2006 101: 6.5m 7.5m a7f 7.5d⁴ p7g a8d³ a8.7g 7g⁶ 12g Jul 9] useful performer: won handicaps at Nad Al Sheba and Ovrevoll in 2005: mostly below form in 2006, last in handicap at Lingfield fifth start after another spell in UAE: stays 1m: acts on dirt and good to firm ground: often tongue tied, tried blinkered: won over hurdles in September. *Ms E. Sundbye, Norway*

DAMBURGER XPRESS 4 b.g. Josr Algarhoud (IRE) 118 – Upping The Tempo **60** (Dunbeath (USA) 127) [2006 68: 10g 10.1m 10.2m⁶ p12g p8g³ f8g³ 8m p8.6g Aug 31] modest maiden: stays 1¼m: acts on polytrack, soft and good to firm ground: tried tongue tied. *D. M. Simcock*

DAME HESTER (IRE) 3 br.f. Diktat 126 – Aunt Hester (IRE) 68 (Caerleon (USA) **92** 132) [2006 79: p8g²* 7g⁴ 7.5f⁴ 7g 7.1m⁵ 8m³ 9.7f* 9m⁵ 9.7g³ 9.9m 10.5d³ 10.8d⁶ Oct 8] €52,000Y: leggy filly: half-sister to several winners, including smart 5f/6f winner Funny Valentine (by Cadeaux Genereux): dam 2-y-o 5f winner: fairly useful performer: left M. Halford in Ireland after final start at 2 yrs: won maiden at Lingfield (despite flashing tail) in February and handicap at Folkestone in July: creditable third in listed race at Toulouse penultimate start: stays 10.5f: acts on polytrack, firm and good to soft ground: blinkered fifth/sixth starts, effective with blinkers. *E. J. O'Neill*

DAMELZA (IRE) 3 b.f. Orpen (USA) 116 – Damezao (Alzao (USA) 117) [2006 84: **78** 8d⁴ 10m⁵ 8s⁴ 8.2g³ 8m⁶ 8f³ p7.1g⁶ 8d⁵ 8.5m Sep 19] lengthy, useful-looking filly: fair handicapper: stays 1m, probably not 1¼m: acts on firm and good to soft ground: tongue tied last 4 starts. *T. D. Easterby*

DAMHSOIR (IRE) 2 b.f. (Mar 17) Invincible Spirit (IRE) 121 – Ceide Dancer (IRE) **55** 79 (Alzao (USA) 117) [2006 5f⁶ 5m p6g p5.1g⁴ Nov 2] €8,000Y: closely related to 2003 2-y-o 1m winner Five Gold (by Desert Prince) and half-sister to 2 winners by Indian Ridge, including 7f winner Prairie Dunes: dam, 8.5f winner, half-sister to Sprint Cup winner Lavinia Fontana: modest maiden: best efforts at 5f. *H. S. Howe*

DAMIKA (IRE) 3 ch.c. Namid 128 – Emly Express (IRE) (High Estate 127) [2006 6g* **93** 7m* 6s⁵ 6m² 6m² 7.1m 6f³ 6d* 6d Sep 22] €30,000F, 22,000Y: strong, good-topped colt: second foal: half-brother to fairly useful French 9.5f to 11.5f winner Quai du Roi (by Desert King): dam French 11.5f winner: won at 5.5f from 4 starts at Mijas at 2 yrs when trained by P. Haley: fairly useful in Britain, winning handicaps at Newcastle and Lingfield in May and Redcar in August: will prove best at 6f/7f: acts on firm and good to soft going. *R. M. Whitaker*

DANAATT (USA) 4 b.f. Gulch (USA) – Agama (USA) 44 (Nureyev (USA) 131) [2006 **–** 39: f7g Jan 24] compact filly: bad maiden: blinkered last 3 starts. *K. R. Burke*

DANAKIL 11 b.g. Warning 136 – Danilova (USA) (Lyphard (USA) 132) [2006 p10g **–** 12g 10.1g Jul 13] small gelding: fairly useful handicapper in 2004: missed 2005 and well held in 2006: visored once. *S. Dow*

DANAKIM 9 b.g. Emarati (USA) 74 – Kangra Valley 56 (Indian Ridge 123) [2006 51§:   **– §**
f5g p6g f5g Mar 21] lengthy, good-quartered gelding: poor performer: no form in 2006:
tried in headgear/tongue tied: ungenuine. *J. R. Weymes*

DANAK (IRE) 3 br.c. Pivotal 124 – Daniysha (IRE) 76 (Doyoun 124) [2006 7m* 9m*   **114 p**
8m* Aug 7] second foal: dam, 7f winner, out of half-sister to smart French 6.5f performer
Danakal: unbeaten in maiden at Gowran and minor event at Fairyhouse (beat Taqseem
4 lengths) in July and listed race at Cork (beat Arabian Prince ¾ length, making virtually
all) in August: had slight setback following month: stays 9f: already smart, and capable
of better still. *J. Oxx, Ireland*

DANAMOUR (IRE) 3 b.g. Dansili 127 – Love And Affection (USA) (Exclusive Era   **84**
(USA)) [2006 78p: 9m⁴ Aug 27] big, good-topped gelding: fairly useful performer,
lightly raced: good fourth in handicap at Goodwood only outing in 2006: stays 9f: raced
only on polytrack and good to firm going: sold 95,000 gns. *M. P. Tregoning*

DANA MUSIC (USA) 2 b.g. (May 17) Silver Hawk (USA) 123 – Inca Princess (USA)   **64**
(Big Spruce (USA)) [2006 p8g 8s Oct 10] compact gelding: half-brother to several
winners, notably very smart German 1¼m/1½m performer Germany (by Trempolino):
dam, Irish 2-y-o 6f winner: mid-field in maidens at Kempton and Newbury: gelded after:
will be suited by 1¼m/1½m. *M. R. Channon*

DANAOS 2 b.g. (Apr 16) Danetime (IRE) 121 – Ionian Secret 56 (Mystiko (USA) 124)   **–**
[2006 6.1g Aug 4] 25/1, early speed in maiden at Nottingham. *J. A. Osborne*

DANAPALI (IRE) 2 b.f. (Apr 23) Danehill (USA) 126 – Taking Liberties (IRE) 57   **73**
(Royal Academy (USA) 130) [2006 7.5f⁴ 7d² 7g⁵ 6s p6g* Nov 25] 65,000Y: sister to
smart Irish 6f (at 2 yrs) and 1m winner Troubadour (later successful in Hong Kong) and
half-sister to several winners, including 4-y-o Eccollo: dam ran once: fair performer: won
maiden at Wolverhampton in November by ½ length from Napoleon Dynamite, making
running: likely to stay 1m: acts on polytrack and good to soft going, probably on firm.
P. J. Prendergast, Ireland

DANAWI (IRE) 3 ch.c. Elnadim (USA) 128 – Just Rainbow (FR) (Rainbow Quest   **71 d**
(USA) 134) [2006 91: p7g² 6g 6.1d⁵ 6d⁶ 6m⁵ 6f³ 6g⁵ 6d⁴ p6g p7g p8g Nov 27] angular,
good-topped colt: fair maiden: below form after reappearance, leaving R. Hannon following ninth start: best at 6f: acts on polytrack and good to soft ground, probably on firm:
tried visored: temperamental, and one to treat with caution. *M. R. Hoad*

DAN BUOY (FR) 3 b.g. Slip Anchor 136 – Bramosia (Forzando 122) [2006 62p: p10g⁴   **79**
8.3g² 10g⁵ 8.3s² Oct 2] tall gelding: fair maiden: stays 1¼m: acts on soft going, probably
on polytrack. *A. King*

DANCE A DAYDREAM 3 b.f. Daylami (IRE) 138 – Dance A Dream 115 (Sadler's   **67**
Wells (USA) 132) [2006 –p: 8.1g 8.2m 11.5m⁶ p10g* 12.1m³ 16d⁴ 16g⁶ Sep 14] leggy
filly: fair performer: won handicap at Lingfield in June, despite hanging: probably stays
2m: acts on polytrack and good to firm going. *J. R. Fanshawe*

DANCEINTHEVALLEY (IRE) 4 b.g. Imperial Ballet (IRE) 110 – Dancing Willma   **–**
(IRE) (Dancing Dissident (USA) 119) [2006 76: 9g 8f 7.5g Aug 27] close-coupled gelding: fair performer at best: well held in 2006: reportedly had breathing problem seventh
3-y-o start. *G. A. Swinbank*

DANCE NIGHT (IRE) 4 b.c. Danehill Dancer (IRE) 117 – Tiger Wings (IRE) (That-   **–**
ching 131) [2006 –: p5g 5g Aug 26] good-bodied colt: useful performer at 2 yrs: lightly
raced and no form since: tried blinkered/tongue tied. *R. Charlton*

DANCE OF DREAMS 2 ch.c. (Apr 12) Johannesburg (USA) 127 – Nunatak (USA)   **67**
(Bering 136) [2006 6g 6m² 7m⁶ Sep 19] 75,000Y: big, good-topped colt: half-brother to
several winners, including French 2001 2-y-o 7f winner Nunatall (by Night Shift), later
Grade 3 8.5f winner in USA: dam French 9f winner: fair maiden: easily best run when
second at Southwell: should stay 7f/1m. *N. P. Littmoden*

DANCE OF LIGHT (USA) 2 b.f. (Apr 4) Sadler's Wells (USA) 132 – Flamelight   **73 P**
(IRE) 71 (Seattle Slew (USA)) [2006 8g⁵ Oct 13] $340,000Y: attractive
filly: second foal: sister to Italian 9f/1¼m winner Fussignac: dam, ran once in Ireland,
half-sister to smart performers up to 1¼m Dr Massini (by Sadler's Wells, became temperamental) and Weigh Anchor: 8/1, lethargic and backward, shaped very well when
3 lengths fifth of 13 to Sam Lord in maiden at Newmarket, finishing strongly from rear
for hand riding: will be suited by 1¼m+: looks capable of much better, and is sure to win
races. *Sir Michael Stoute*

DANCE PARTNER 4 b.f. Danzero (AUS) – Dancing Debut 83 (Polar Falcon (USA)   **105**
126) [2006 95: 10g 10.1m* Sep 13] big, well-made filly: useful performer: won listed

event at Yarmouth in September by ½ length from Gower Song, dictating: stayed 1½m: acted on polytrack and good to firm ground: had worn crossed noseband: dead. *J. H. M. Gosden*

DANCE PARTY (IRE) 6 b.m. Charnwood Forest (IRE) 125 – Society Ball 72 (Law **40** Society (USA) 130) [2006 45: f11g Apr 10] good-topped mare: maiden: lightly raced and only poor nowadays: stays easy 1½m: acts on polytrack, good to firm and good to soft ground: tried blinkered/in cheekpieces. *M. W. Easterby*

DANCER'S SERENADE (IRE) 4 b.g. Almutawakel 126 – Dance Serenade (IRE) **81** 54 (Marju (IRE) 127) [2006 92: 10.5g 10.4d 12g 9.8m 14m⁴ 14m³ 16m* 16.1d³ 16.2d⁶ Sep 16] tall, good-topped gelding: fairly useful handicapper: won at Thirsk in August: stays 2m: acts on soft and good to firm ground. *T. P. Tate*

DANCE SPIEL 2 b.c. (Mar 10) Singspiel (IRE) 133 – Demure (Machiavellian (USA) **90 p** 123) [2006 p7g² Oct 11] 200,000Y: fifth foal: half-brother to smart 6f (at 2 yrs)/1m winner Coy and 6-y-o Presumptive (both by Danehill): dam unraced half-sister to smart 6f/7f performer Diffident: 11/1, promising 2 lengths second of 13 to Tybalt in maiden at Lingfield, going strongly up with pace: sent to USA: will improve and make a useful 3-y-o. *J. Noseda*

DANCE SPIRIT (IRE) 3 ch.g. Namid 128 – Phantom Act (USA) (Theatrical 128) **72** [2006 10d 8m⁴ 7.1g⁵ p8g Aug 9] 13,000Y: first foal: dam, ran once in Ireland, sister to Queen's Vase winner Duke of Venice: fair maiden: probably stays 1m: sold 6,000 gns. *B. J. Meehan*

DANCE TO MY TUNE 5 b.m. Halling (USA) 133 – Stolen Melody 74 (Robellino **82** (USA) 127) [2006 86: 10v³ Apr 4] big, workmanlike mare: fairly useful handicapper: stayed 1½m: acted on any turf going: visored final outing in 2003: held up: sometimes found little: dead. *M. W. Easterby*

DANCE TO THE BLUES (IRE) 5 br.m. Danehill Dancer (IRE) 117 – Blue Sioux **73** 69 (Indian Ridge 123) [2006 73: 5.3m³ 5.2m⁵ 6f 6f 5.7f³ 6.1g³ 6d p7g⁵ p6g Nov 17] leggy mare: fair handicapper: effective at 5f/6f: acts on polytrack and firm going: tried blinkered, usually wears cheekpieces: tended to hang on reappearance. *B. De Haan*

DANCEWITHTHESTARS (USA) 2 b.f. Cryptoclearance (USA) – Sir **– p** Harry's Waltz (IRE) (Sir Harry Lewis (USA) 127) [2006 p7g⁶ Nov 25] half-sister to several minor winners in USA: dam, no form, out of close relative to dam of champion US turf mare Flawlessly: 8/1, 7½ lengths sixth of 11 to Benllech in maiden at Kempton, running on from rear not knocked about: will do better. *J. R. Fanshawe*

DANCE WORLD 6 b.g. Spectrum (IRE) 126 – Dansara (Dancing Brave (USA) 140) **–** [2006 85: p9.5g f12g p12.2g⁶ Dec 26] leggy gelding: fairly useful handicapper at best: well held in 2006. *Miss J. Feilden*

DANCING BAY 9 b.g. Suave Dancer (USA) 136 – Kabayil 75 (Dancing Brave (USA) **110** 140) [2006 110: 14.1s² 18.7m⁴ 21.7m⁶ p16g Jul 15] sturdy gelding: smart performer: creditable efforts in 2006 when second to Frank Sonata in listed race at Nottingham and 1½ lengths fourth to Admiral in Chester Cup (Handicap): bit below form in Queen Alexandra Stakes at Royal Ascot penultimate start (in frame in previous 2 runnings): seemingly amiss at Lingfield (all-weather debut) final outing: stays 2¾m: acts on any going: has been tongue tied (not since 2001): usually held up (has found little/gone in snatches): sometimes edges left. *N. J. Henderson*

DANCING BEAR 5 b.g. Groom Dancer (USA) 128 – Sickle Moon (Shirley Heights **–** 130) [2006 f12g p12g May 25] strong, good-topped gelding: maiden: well held in 2006, leaving Mrs L. Featherstone after reappearance: tried blinkered. *P. S. McEntee*

DANCING BEAUTY (IRE) 4 b.f. Charnwood Forest (IRE) 125 – Viennese Dancer **44** (Prince Sabo 123) [2006 –: 7s 6m p5g⁵ p5g⁶ Dec 20] poor maiden: form only at 5f. *T. T. Clement*

DANCING DAISY (IRE) 2 br.f. (Apr 1) Bold Fact (USA) 116 – Daisy Dancer (IRE) **58** 57 (Distinctly North (USA) 115) [2006 5.7g 5.1f⁵ 5.1g⁵ 5.7f⁵ p6g⁶ 6.1d⁶ Oct 4] 1,800Y: stocky filly: first foal: dam Irish 6.5f winner: modest maiden: raced at 5f/6f: best efforts on good/good to soft going. *Mrs P. N. Dutfield*

DANCING DEANO (IRE) 4 b.g. Second Empire (IRE) 124 – Ultimate Beat (USA) **71** (Go And Go) [2006 69: 5.9g* 7g² 7g⁶ 6d p7.1m 7.5m³ 6s p7.1g f6g Dec 5] good-topped **a–** gelding: fair performer on turf, no solid form on all-weather: won seller at Carlisle in May: effective at 6f/7f: acts on good to firm and good to soft ground: visored: usually races prominently. *R. M. Whitaker*

DANCING DIAMONDS 3 b.f. Agnes World (USA) 123 – Aquaba (USA) (Damascus **54** (USA)) [2006 10.5g p10g 9.9g Aug 31] closely related to 3 winners, including 5f winner (including at 2 yrs) Millstream (by Dayjur) and 1995 2-y-o 6f winner Polska (by Danzig), both useful, and half-sister to 3 winners, including useful Irish 1m/1¼m winner Woodsia (by Woodman): dam, 7f (including at 2 yrs) to 9f winner in USA, including Grade 3 8.5f event: well held in maidens (sold from H-A. Pantall 36,000 gns after debut), seemingly modest form at Lingfield on second outing: returned to France after next start. *D. M. Simcock*

DANCING DUO 2 b.f. (Mar 12) Groom Dancer (USA) 128 – Affaire Royale (IRE) 95 **62** (Royal Academy (USA) 130) [2006 7m 8m 6d⁶ p7.1g* Oct 30] attractive filly: first foal: dam, 2-y-o 7f winner, out of close relative to US Grade 1 1m winner Quiet American: modest form: not knocked about in maidens prior to winning seller at Wolverhampton in October: should stay 1m. *W. J. Haggas*

DANCING FLAME 3 b.f. Groom Dancer (USA) 128 – Catch The Flame (USA) **60** (Storm Bird (CAN) 134) [2006 58: 8d 8.2s 9.3m⁴ 10.3g³ 11.1d⁵ 8.1g 9.3f 8.1m⁴ 10.5g⁴ 9.1v⁶ p9.5g f8g p8.6g³ p12.2g⁵ Nov 24] angular filly: modest maiden handicapper: stays 10.3f: acts on soft and good to firm going: tried in cheekpieces: sold £2,800. *E. J. Alston*

DANCING GRANNY 2 b.f. (May 15) Rock of Gibraltar (IRE) 133 – Euro Empire **74** (USA) 111 (Bartok (IRE) 94) [2006 7.5f³ 7f⁵ 7f² 8g* 8m 8.3d⁵ Oct 9] 26,000Y: useful-looking filly: third foal: half-sister to Irish 5f winner Moving Diamonds (by Lomitas) and a winner in USA by Forestry: dam, 2-y-o 5f to 8.5f winner in USA, also runner-up in Grade 1 1m event: fair performer: won maiden at Musselburgh in August: good fifth in nursery at Windsor final start: stays 1m: acts on firm and good to soft going. *M. L. W. Bell*

DANCING GUEST (IRE) 3 ch.f. Danehill Dancer (IRE) 117 – Saibhreas (IRE) 83 **86** (Last Tycoon 131) [2006 69: 8.3g 7d p7g* 8m³ p8g* p8g² 8d⁴ 7s p8g p8g Sep 30] leggy filly: fairly useful performer: won handicaps at Kempton in June and July: stays 1m: acts on polytrack, good to firm and good to soft going: sold 45,000 gns. *G. G. Margarson*

DANCING JEST (IRE) 2 b.f. (Feb 7) Averti (IRE) 117 – Mezzanine (Sadler's Wells **54** (USA) 132) [2006 6.1d⁵ 6d Oct 27] 31,000Y: good-bodied filly: fourth foal: half-sister to 3 winners, including 6-y-o The Kiddykid and 7f winner World Series (by Almutawakel): dam unraced: better run in maidens when fifth at Warwick on debut. *Rae Guest*

DANCING LYRA 5 b.g. Alzao (USA) 117 – Badaayer (USA) 105 (Silver Hawk **90** (USA) 123) [2006 90: 7v* 8v* 10g⁵ 8.9m⁵ 9.9m 8.1g Sep 22] small, compact gelding: has a quick action: fairly useful handicapper: won at Southwell and Musselburgh in March: effective at testing 7f to 13f: acts on polytrack, heavy and good to firm going: tried tongue tied: patiently ridden: won over hurdles in December. *R. A. Fahey*

DANCING MELODY 3 b.f. Dr Fong (USA) 128 – Spring Mood (FR) (Nashwan **59** (USA) 135) [2006 61: 8.2d⁶ 10m 8.1s 8m 10d 11s Oct 10] lengthy filly: modest maiden: below form after reappearance: stays 1m: acts on good to firm and good to soft ground. *J. A. Geake*

DANCING MOONLIGHT (IRE) 4 b.f. Danehill Dancer (IRE) 117 – Silver Moon **–** (Environment Friend 128) [2006 –: p8.6g p6g f6g 9d f6g Nov 15] of no account. *Mrs N. Macauley*

DANCING MYSTERY 12 b.g. Beveled (USA) – Batchworth Dancer 67 (Ballacash- **79** tal (CAN)) [2006 90, a109: f5g⁴ f5g² p5g⁶ p5.1g⁶ p5g p5g⁵ 5g 5m⁵ 6g 5f 5m 5m² 5m* **a100** 5.3g* p5g⁴ f5g* f5g⁵ Dec 5] close-coupled gelding: useful handicapper on all-weather, fair on turf nowadays: won at Goodwood (apprentices) in September, Brighton in October and Southwell in November: best at 5f: acts on all-weather and any turf: usually blinkered: has spoilt chance by rearing in stall, front runner otherwise. *E. A. Wheeler*

DANCING REVA (IRE) 2 b.g. (Apr 6) Revoque (IRE) 122 – Brave Dance (IRE) **–** (Kris 135) [2006 6m 8g 7g 8d Oct 19] leggy gelding: last in maidens. *J. J. Bridger*

DANCING STORM 3 b.f. Trans Island 119 – Stormswell 56 (Persian Bold 123) [2006 **61** 60: f6g⁶ 7.1g 8.1f* 8.3m⁴ 8m⁵ 8.1m p9.5g Sep 30] modest handicapper: won at Chepstow in July: stays 8.3f: acts on firm ground: in cheekpieces (well held) final outing. *W. S. Kittow*

DANCING VALENTINE 2 b.f. (Jan 16) Primo Valentino (IRE) 116 – Shanuke (IRE) **–** 56 (Contract Law (USA) 108) [2006 p6g Sep 1] close-coupled filly: third foal: dam 1½m seller winner: tailed off in maiden. *L. A. Dace*

DAN DARE (USA) 3 b.g. Dynaformer (USA) – Etheldreda (USA) 64 (Diesis 133) **84** [2006 82p: 10d³ 12m⁵ Jun 18] tall, good-bodied gelding: fairly useful maiden, lightly

raced: best effort when third at Newmarket in May: gelded after next outing: should stay
1½m. *Sir Michael Stoute*

DANDY MAN (IRE) 3 b.c. Mozart (IRE) 131 – Lady Alexander (IRE) 112 (Night **123**
Shift (USA)) [2006 98: 5d² 5m* 5m⁴ 5g* 5s 5.2m³ Sep 16]
  Once again the first pattern-race sprint of the season in Britain, the Palace
House Stakes, was won by a horse with little or no background in pattern events
previously. What was more unusual was that the horse in question, Dandy Man,
was a three-year-old. The last winner of the Palace House to come from this age
group, which receives 4 lb more from the older horses than it should according
to Timeform's weight-for-age scale, had been Yorkies Boy in 1998. Dandy Man
had been raced solely in Ireland and hadn't contested a pattern race before the
Group 3 contest, run at Newmarket on Two Thousand Guineas day. Useful at two
when successful in a maiden at Naas and a listed race at Tipperary from four starts,
Dandy Man had shown even better form on his reappearance, finishing a length
second to smart five-year-old mare Moon Unit in another listed event back at Naas.
Much more was required of Dandy Man in the Stan James Palace House, in which
he was one of only three three-year-olds in a twenty-two-runner field, and the
shortest priced of that trio at 25/1. Although one of those to benefit from racing
handily in the larger group which raced towards the centre, where the pace was that
much stronger, Dandy Man nevertheless took the eye showing speed before being
driven to get on top late on to win by a length and a quarter from Pivotal Flame.
Several of those further behind went on to win even better races, notably fourth-
placed Reverence, who ended the season as the leading sprinter in Europe.
  Dandy Man added only another listed success to his portfolio, but that was
in the King of Beers Stakes (Richard H. Faught Memorial) at the Curragh in July.
In winning that race by a length and half a length from Benbaun and Osterhase,
both previous winners, Dandy Man ran to a level of form bettered only by a handful
of sprinters in Europe during the season. He couldn't match the performance in
three other starts, all in pattern races in Britain, though he would have gone close to
doing so in the King's Stand Stakes at Royal Ascot but for being drawn well away

King of Beers Stakes (Richard H. Faught Memorial), the Curragh—on home ground,
Dandy Man is too fast for Benbaun (visor) and compatriot Osterhase (partially hidden)

from the main action. Dandy Man dead-heated for fourth with Falkirk, only three quarters of a length behind the winner Takeover Target, despite having nothing to race with after going clear of the far-side group at halfway. Soft ground might have been a factor in Dandy Man's very disappointing performance on his penultimate start in the Nunthorpe Stakes at York, for which he started favourite, though he didn't help his cause by failing to settle early on. He was an even warmer order dropped back to Group 3 level for the World Trophy at Newbury, but, while bettering his York effort, was still some way short of his best in finishing third to Dixie Belle. Shortly afterwards, it was announced that Dandy Man had returned home tired and he was retired for the season. There is no reason why he shouldn't return as good as ever and win more races in 2007, when he could well have a similar campaign. While Dandy Man won at six furlongs as a two-year-old, five furlongs is his optimum trip and all of his races at three were at around that distance.

		Mozart (IRE) (b 1998)	Danehill (b 1986)	Danzig
Dandy Man (IRE) (b.c. 2003)				Razyana
			Victoria Cross (b 1983)	Spectacular Bid
				Glowing Tribute
		Lady Alexander (IRE) (ch 1995)	Night Shift (b 1980)	Northern Dancer
				Ciboulette
			Sandhurst Goddess (ch 1986)	Sandhurst Prince
				Paradise Bird

Dandy Man was the last in a long line of winners owned by Alfie McLean, who died a few weeks after the colt's Newmarket triumph. The founder of a book-making chain in Northern Ireland, McClean had had horses with Dandy Man's

Exors of the late A. McLean's "Dandy Man"

trainer Con Collins since the 'sixties, the best of them prior to Dandy Man the 1978 William Hill Futurity winner Sandy Creek. Sadly, Collins, the longest-serving holder of a trainer's licence in Ireland who achieved his biggest win in the 1984 Irish Oaks with Princess Pati, died early in 2007 at the age of eighty-two. Sandy Creek was bought as a yearling for 40,000 guineas, whereas 32,000 guineas was enough to secure Dandy Man twenty-seven years later. His size, or lack of it, might well have counted against Dandy Man in the sales ring—two years on he's still on the smallish side, and compact to boot. His pedigree certainly shouldn't have counted against him. From the only crop of the July Cup and Nunthorpe winner Mozart, Dandy Man is the third foal and third winner out of the smart Lady Alexander, following on from the useful 2004 two-year-old five-furlong winner Alexander Queen (by King's Best) and Alexander Ambition (by Entrepreneur), a fair winner at seven furlongs. The fourth foal, Lady Shanghai (by Alhaarth), showed enough in five races in Ireland in the current season to suggest that she should also win a race or two. Lady Alexander herself, also trained by Collins, gained all three of her wins at two, including in the Anglesey Stakes (by a short head from King of Kings) over six and the Molecomb Stakes over five. However, Lady Alexander showed even better form at three, when runner-up in the Greenlands Stakes and the King George Stakes. Lady Alexander failed to make the frame in her final season in 1999, her best effort when eighth in the King's Stand. Closely related to the useful 1996 Irish two-year-old and six-furlong winner Star Profile, Lady Alexander is a daughter of the useful Irish five- to seven-furlong winner Sandhurst Goddess who also ran at Royal Ascot, finishing unplaced in the 1990 Cork And Orrery. The next dam, Paradise Bird, was a fairly useful two-year-old, successful twice over six furlongs. Like his dam, Dandy Man has won on good to soft going, at Tipperary, but he has put up his best performances on good and good to firm. *C. Collins, Ireland*

DANDYS HURRICANE 3 br.g. Diktat 126 – Bahamian Rhapsody (IRE) 76 (Fairy King (USA)) [2006 9.2d⁴ 8d p7.1m Nov 8] strong, lengthy gelding: easily best effort in maidens at Hamilton on debut, running green and considerably handled. *D. Nicholls* — **57**

DANEBANK (IRE) 6 b.g. Danehill (USA) 126 – Snow Bank (IRE) (Law Society (USA) 130) [2006 61: 14.1d² 14.1m 12s⁴ p13.9g⁴ p13.9g⁴ p13.9g Nov 25] close-coupled gelding: modest performer: stays 1¾m: acts on firm and soft ground: tried visored, usually wears cheekpieces. *J. Mackie* — **64**

DANEBURY HILL 2 b.c. (Feb 28) Danehill (USA) 126 – Mackie (USA) (Summer Squall (USA)) [2006 6m* 6m⁵ 6f⁵ 7.1g³ 7d Sep 29] rather leggy colt: sixth foal: half-brother to 3 winners abroad, including US Grade 2 8.5f winner Mr Mellon (by Red Ransom): dam, US Grade 3 8.5f winner, half-sister to Kentucky Derby winner Sea Hero and to dam of top-class sprinter Mozart (by Danehill): useful performer: won minor event at Yarmouth in May: kept pattern company after: good fifth in both July Stakes at Newmarket and Richmond Stakes at Goodwood and third in Solario Stakes (beaten length behind Drumfire and Caldra) at Sandown: may prove best at 5f/6f: raced on good or firmer ground until final race (found little and eased): tongue tied last 2 starts. *B. J. Meehan* — **97**

DANEHILL DAZZLER (IRE) 4 b.f. Danehill Dancer (IRE) 117 – Finnegans Dilemma (IRE) (Marktingo) [2006 85: p10g⁶ 8.3d² 10m⁶ p10g Sep 3] lengthy filly: fairly useful performer: needs to settle to stay beyond 1m: acts on good to firm and good to soft going, probably on polytrack. *Ian Williams* — **83**

DANEHILL KIKIN (IRE) 2 b.f. (Feb 25) Danehill (USA) 126 – Miletrian (IRE) 113 (Marju (IRE) 127) [2006 6g 6g⁵ Oct 16] strong, long-backed filly: second foal: dam, 9f (at 2 yrs) to 14.6f (Park Hill Stakes) winner, half-sister to very smart 1½m/13f winner Mr Combustible: more promise than bare result in maidens at Newmarket and Windsor, fading and not knocked about: will be suited by 1m+: will do better. *B. W. Hills* — **58 p**

DANEHILL SILVER 2 b.g. (Mar 24) Silver Patriarch (IRE) 125 – Danehill Princess (IRE) 62 (Danehill (USA) 126) [2006 8.1g 8.2s⁴ 8.2d Nov 1] strong, close-coupled gelding: third foal: dam maiden who stayed 7f: fair maiden: fourth at Nottingham, easily best effort: will stay at least 1¼m: acts on soft going. *R. Hollinshead* — **71**

DANEHILL STROLLER (IRE) 6 b.g. Danetime (IRE) 121 – Tuft Hill 92 (Grundy 137) [2006 79: 6f⁵ 5.7g⁶ 6g 5.7m⁵ 6f⁶ f6g 5.7f³ 6m 6m³ 7d⁶ 7g p7g p6g³ p6g⁵ p6g⁶ Dec 22] angular gelding: fair performer: left R. Beckett after sixth outing: effective at 5f/ — **74 a66**

6f: acts on polytrack, good to firm and good to soft going: sometimes wears cheekpieces, blinkered final outing: usually held up. *A. M. Hales*

DANEHILLSUNDANCE (IRE) 2 b.c. (May 7) Danehill Dancer (IRE) 117 – Rosie's Guest (IRE) (Be My Guest (USA) 126) [2006 6s⁴ 6m³ 6m² 6d² p6g³ p7g⁴ p7g* Dec 20] 48,000Y: tall, leggy colt: half-brother to several winners, including 7-y-o Northern Desert and 6-y-o Franksalot: dam Irish maiden: fair performer: won maiden at Lingfield in December: in frame all previous starts, including nursery: stays 7f: acts on polytrack, soft and good to firm going. *R. Hannon* **74**

DANEHILL WILLY (IRE) 4 b.g. Danehill Dancer (IRE) 117 – Lowtown (Camden Town 125) [2006 98: p10g² 10v⁶ 12g 12s³ May 20] big, leggy, lengthy gelding: has a round action: useful handicapper: best effort of 2006 when good second to Ameeq at Kempton: probably stays 1½m: acts on polytrack, soft and good to firm going: visored (found little) once at 3 yrs, ran respectably in cheekpieces last 2 starts: joined Evan Williams. *N. A. Callaghan* **98**

DANELOR (IRE) 8 b.g. Danehill (USA) 126 – Formulate 119 (Reform 132) [2006 93: p12.2g² p9.5g* f12g f12g³ p10g 8.1g p8.6m 10d f8g p10g f7g⁶ f8g f11g⁴ Dec 28] sturdy, good-bodied gelding: fair performer: won claimers at Wolverhampton in January and Southwell (left R. Fahey) in February: well below form after: stays 1½m: acts on all-weather, firm and good to soft going: often visored/wears cheekpieces: free-going sort (has been early to post), and usually races prominently. *D. Shaw* **79 d**

DANESCOURT (IRE) 4 b.g. Danetime (IRE) 121 – Faye 79 (Monsanto (FR) 121) [2006 51: p6g p5.1g 6m 6g May 10] maiden: well held in 2006: tried in cheekpieces, usually blinkered nowadays. *J. M. Bradley* **–**

DANE'S ROCK (IRE) 4 b.g. Indian Danehill (IRE) 124 – Cutting Ground (IRE) 85 (Common Grounds 118) [2006 54: f8g⁶ p9.5g f7g⁵ p8.6g⁴ p8g⁶ Apr 3] modest performer: stays 8.6f: acts on all-weather and firm ground: sometimes wears headgear: not straightforward. *M. S. Saunders* **55**

DANETHORPE (IRE) 3 b.g. Monashee Mountain (USA) 115 – Waroonga (IRE) (Brief Truce (USA) 126) [2006 p6g p6g p5g 5g 8s f5m f6g³ f7g⁶ p8.6g⁶ f7g³ p7g Dec 30] modest maiden: stays 7f: acts on all-weather: visored last 6 starts. *D. Shaw* **53**

DANETHORPE LADY (IRE) 4 b.f. Brave Act 119 – Annie's Travels (IRE) (Mac's Imp (USA) 116) [2006 36: p6g p6g⁵ p6g p6g 6.1m p6g⁵ May 5] poor maiden: raced only at 5f/6f: sometimes visored. *D. Shaw* **42**

DANETIME LADY (IRE) 6 b.m. Danetime (IRE) 121 – Hawattef (IRE) (Mujtahid (USA) 118) [2006 74: p6g Feb 18] fair maiden: best at 6f: acts on firm ground, little form on all-weather in Britain: has worn blinkers/cheekpieces/tongue strap. *Adrian Sexton, Ireland* **–**

DANETIME LORD (IRE) 3 b.g. Danetime (IRE) 121 – Seven Sisters (USA) (Shadeed (USA) 135) [2006 –: p7.1g⁵ p6g² p6g* 5v² p7.1g* 7.5d⁶ 6f⁵ 6f⁵ 6.1m⁴ 6s p7.1g⁵ p6g⁴ Dec 18] compact gelding: fair handicapper: won at Wolverhampton in March and April: stays 7f: acts on polytrack, heavy and good to firm going: wears cheekpieces: usually races prominently. *K. A. Ryan* **77**

DANETIME MUSIC (IRE) 2 b.f. (Mar 24) Danetime (IRE) 121 – Tuesday Morning (Sadler's Wells (USA) 132) [2006 6.1m* 5.2g p6g⁴ p6g Nov 7] 12,000Y: closely related to useful Irish 7f (at 2 yrs)/1m winner Danehill Music (by Danehill Dancer) and half-sister to several winners: dam unraced: fair performer: won maiden at Nottingham in July: good subsequent run only when fourth in nursery at Lingfield: should prove best at 5f/6f: acts on polytrack and good to firm going: sold 22,000 gns, sent to Norway. *M. J. Wallace* **73**

DANETIME PANTHER (IRE) 2 b.c. (Apr 19) Danetime (IRE) 121 – Annotate (Groom Dancer (USA) 128) [2006 6m Aug 11] €10,000Y, 34,000 2-y-o: tall colt: has scope: fifth foal: half-brother to winners abroad by Cape Cross and College Chapel: dam unraced: 50/1, very green when mid-field in maiden at Haydock. *C. Llewellyn* **66**

DANETTIE 5 b.m. Danzero (AUS) – Petite Heritiere 43 (Last Tycoon 131) [2006 64: p8g³ p8.6g p9.5g⁶ p8.6g* p8g Feb 7] modest handicapper: won at Wolverhampton in February: best around 1m: acts on polytrack and good to firm going. *W. M. Brisbourne* **64**

DANEWAY 3 ch.f. Danehill Dancer (IRE) 117 – Scylla 50 (Rock City 120) [2006 55p: p9.5g⁴ f12g⁴ p12g Dec 22] modest maiden: left H. Cecil 4,500 gns before final start: should stay 1¾m: raced only on all-weather: blinkered only outing at 2 yrs (slowly away and raced freely). *P. Howling* **56**

DANGER ALLEY 2 b.c. (Feb 9) Bertolini (USA) 125 – My Girl 39 (Mon Tresor 113) **64**
[2006 6m 6.1m[6] 5m[3] 5.2f* 5g[6] 5.2g* 5m p5g[4] Sep 30] close-coupled colt: modest
performer: won sellers in July (nursery) and August, both at Yarmouth: best at 5f: visored/
blinkered after debut: acts on polytrack and firm ground: races prominently. *E. J. O'Neill*

DANGER BIRD (IRE) 6 ch.m. Eagle Eyed (USA) 111 – Danger Ahead (Mill Reef **–**
(USA) 141) [2006 –, a52: f8g p9.5g Mar 27] leggy mare: modest on all-weather at
best: no form in 2006: tried in cheekpieces: free-going sort: sometimes flashes tail.
R. Hollinshead

DANGERMOUSE 3 b.f. Afternoon Deelites (USA) 122 – Ghost Dance (IRE) (Lure **40**
(USA) 131) [2006 50: p6g f7g f6g May 16] quite good-topped filly: poor maiden: stays
7f: acts on fibresand, soft and good to firm ground. *A. G. Newcombe*

DANGEROUS BUSINESS (IRE) 5 b.m. Entrepreneur 123 – Cachet (IRE) (Warn- **55**
ing 136) [2006 12f p12g[6] 10d 11s Oct 10] €4,000Y: fifth foal: dam unraced half-sister to
smart middle-distance performer Papering: twice in frame in bumpers: modest maiden:
left P. Flynn in Ireland after Flat debut: stays 1½m: acts on polytrack and good to soft
ground: blinkered on debut. *H. Morrison*

DANGEROUS DANCER (IRE) 2 b.f. (May 6) Danehill Dancer (IRE) 117 – Elite **56**
Guest (IRE) (Be My Guest (USA) 126) [2006 7g Sep 15] leggy filly: closely related to
5f (at 2 yrs) to 7f winner Newton and 2005 2-y-o 6f/7f winner Amigoni (both useful
in Ireland, by Danehill) and half-sister to 2 winners in France by Highest Honor: dam,
French 9f winner, half-sister to smart stayer Capal Garmon: 25/1, eleventh of thirteen in
minor event at Newbury. *R. Charlton*

DANGEROUSLY GOOD 8 b.g. Shareef Dancer (USA) 135 – Ecologically Kind **–**
(Alleged (USA) 138) [2006 15d 16v Oct 25] leggy gelding: one-time fair performer:
unraced on Flat in 2004/2005: well beaten in 2006: tried in headgear. *G. L. Moore*

DANGER ZONE 4 b.g. Danzero (AUS) – Red Tulle (USA) 66 (A P Indy (USA) 131) **80**
[2006 79: p10g[4] p10g[2] p12g p10g[6] p10g* p9.5g[6] 7m 9m[4] p10g[3] 9.9g[2] 11g[6] Jul 6] rangy
gelding: fairly useful handicapper: won at Lingfield in February: effective at 7f to 1¼m:
acts on polytrack, firm and good to soft going: visored (carried head awkwardly) once, in
cheekpieces 6 of last 7 starts: sold 30,000 gns later in July. *Mrs A. J. Perrett*

DANIELLA 4 b.f. Dansili 127 – Break Point (Reference Point 139) [2006 74: 6.1m* 6d **86**
6m[4] 7m[5] 6m[2] 6m 6.1m[3] 7d[5] 6g Oct 12] deep-girthed filly: fairly useful performer: won
handicaps at Nottingham in May and Goodwood in June: flattered when 2 lengths third
to Ripples Maid in listed race at Chester and fifth of 8 in Supreme Stakes at Goodwood:
effective at 6f/7f: unraced on extremes of going: in cheekpieces nowadays: often makes
running. *Rae Guest*

DANIELLE'S LAD 10 b.g. Emarati (USA) 74 – Cactus Road (FR) (Iron Duke (FR) **66**
122) [2006 74: p7.1g p8.6g f7s p7.1g 7.1m[3] 7.1m[2] p8.6g 7g 7.1m 7m 5.7m 7d[4] p7g p8.6g **a55**
Dec 11] strong gelding: fair performer on turf, modest on all-weather: effective at 7f to
8.6f: acts on all-weather, heavy and good to firm going: often blinkered, in cheekpieces
final outing: races up with pace: has edged right. *B. Palling*

DANIEL THOMAS (IRE) 4 b.g. Dansili 127 – Last Look (Rainbow Quest (USA) **93**
134) [2006 83: p8g p8g[6] Dec 30] good-topped gelding: has a quick action: fairly useful
performer: reportedly suffered splint problem after sole start in 2005: better effort after
long lay-off when good sixth in handicap at Lingfield: stays 1m: acts on polytrack, soft
and good to firm going. *Mrs A. J. Perrett*

DANISH BLUES (IRE) 3 b.g. Danetime (IRE) 121 – Sing A Song (IRE) 82 (Blues **65**
Traveller (IRE) 119) [2006 –: p8g[2] p8.6g[5] p7g f6g p5g[3] p5g p5.1g[4] p5g[6] 5.1g[3] 6f[3] 7g[4] 7f[4]
6f 7g 6m p6g[4] p6g[5] p6g* p6g Nov 8] fair performer: left R. Flower after reappearance:
won maiden claimer at Kempton (claimed from N. Littmoden) in October: stays 7f: acts
on polytrack and firm ground: often in cheekpieces: has pulled hard/looked wayward.
D. E. Cantillon

DANISH MONARCH 5 b.g. Great Dane (IRE) 122 – Moly 64 (Inchinor 119) [2006 **61**
50: p9.5g p10g 10.2g* 9.7f[4] 10f[6] 10m[5] 10.2f[3] 10.2m[5] 10.2f 9g* Sep 12] leggy gelding:
modest performer: won sellers at Bath in May and Lingfield in September: stays 1¼m:
acts on firm going: blinkered twice in 2005: usually races prominently (waited with at
Lingfield). *David Pinder*

DANISH REBEL (IRE) 2 b.c. (Apr 13) Danetime (IRE) 121 – Wheatsheaf Lady **53**
(IRE) 83 (Red Sunset 120) [2006 f8g[5] f8g Dec 9] modest form in maidens at Southwell.
J. I. A. Charlton

DANJET (IRE) 3 bl.f. Danehill Dancer (IRE) 117 – Jet Lock (USA) (Crafty Prospector (USA)) [2006 86: p7g 5g 6m 6.1g 5s² 5.3g p5g Nov 5] quite good-topped filly: fairly useful performer: left P. D. Evans after third outing: best effort in 2006 when second in handicap at York: best at 5f: acts on polytrack and soft going. *J. M. Bradley* **82**

DANJOE 2 ch.c. (Mar 6) Forzando 122 – Baytown Rhapsody 62 (Emperor Jones (USA) 119) [2006 p8.6g p8.6g p6g Dec 22] well held in maidens. *R. Brotherton* **–**

DANNABELLE (IRE) 6 b.m. Danetime (IRE) 121 – Cerosia (Pitskelly 122) [2006 6m 8m* p8.6g 8m p6g⁵ f6g p8g Nov 27] fair performer on turf, modest on all-weather: won amateur handicap at Goodwood in August by 8 lengths: well below that level after: stays 1m: acts on good to firm going. *John A. Quinn, Ireland* **70 a58**

DANNI DI GUERRA (IRE) 2 b.g. (Mar 28) Soviet Star (USA) 128 – Lina Bella (FR) (Linamix (FR) 127) [2006 5d⁶ 8.3m⁵ 7.2d Sep 15] workmanlike gelding: little form: bred to stay 1¼m+. *P. C. Haslam* **–**

DANNY TEMPLETON (IRE) 2 ch.c. (Apr 2) Namid 128 – Singing Millie (Millfontaine 114) [2006 6g² 6g² Oct 12] €55,000Y: compact colt: half-brother to several winners, including smart 1999 Irish 2-y-o 6f and 8.5f winner Barrier Reef (by Perugino), later successful in Norway up to 1½m: dam, Irish 7f/1m winner, half-sister to dam of Racing Post Trophy winner Seattle Rhyme: promising second in maidens at Yarmouth and Newmarket (15 ran, beaten 3 lengths by Truly Royal), pulling hard both times: will prove best at 5f/6f: sold 145,000 gns, sent to USA: should do better yet. *D. R. C. Elsworth* **82 p**

DANNY THE DIP 3 b.g. Prince Sabo 123 – Ann's Pearl (IRE) 81 (Cyrano de Bergerac 120) [2006 56: 5m⁴ 5.1g⁴ 5.3f⁵ 5.3m³ 5m 5.2m⁴ 5f 5.3f⁵ 5m² 6f 5g 6d 5m 6d p6g Oct 6] tall gelding: modest performer: stays 6f: acts on firm and good to soft going: tried in cheekpieces/blinkered: ungenuine: sold £700. *J. J. Bridger* **61 §**

DANSA QUEEN 3 gr.f. Dansili 127 – Pericardia 60 (Petong 126) [2006 81p: 8.2g 8m³ 10m 8.3g* 8.1d* Sep 13] unfurnished filly: fairly useful handicapper: won at Windsor in August and Sandown (hung right) in September: stays 1m: acts on polytrack, good to firm and good to soft ground: reluctant to post and to enter stall before running poorly third outing. *W. R. Swinburn* **89**

DANSE SPECTRE (IRE) 4 b.f. Spectrum (IRE) 126 – Danse Royale (IRE) 112 (Caerleon (USA) 132) [2006 70p: p10g Jan 25] fair performer, lightly raced: well held only outing in 2006: stays 1¼m: acts on polytrack: withdrawn after unruly in stall prior to intended second outing at 3 yrs: sold 165,000 gns in November. *E. J. O'Neill* **–**

DANSEUSE 2 b.f. (Feb 10) Dr Fong (USA) 128 – Danemere (IRE) 90 (Danehill (USA) 126) [2006 p6g² 6m Jun 23] smallish, strong filly: first foal: dam 2-y-o 6f winner who stayed 1m: fair form: second in maiden at Lingfield and tenth (of 18 to Sander Camillo) in Albany Stakes at Royal Ascot: will stay 1m. *C. E. Brittain* **78**

DAN'S HEIR 4 b.g. Dansili 127 – Million Heiress (Auction Ring (USA) 123) [2006 66: 16g 12.1d 15.8m 15.8d* 18s⁶ p12.2g Dec 16] sturdy gelding: fair handicapper: won at Catterick in October: stays 2m: acts on all-weather, firm and good to soft going: tried visored, usually wears cheekpieces. *P. C. Haslam* **69**

DANSILI DANCER 4 b.g. Dansili 127 – Magic Slipper 97 (Habitat 134) [2006 94: 8s 8m 8m* 8m 10m* 10.5m* 10m⁴ 10m⁴ Sep 16] strong, close-coupled gelding: useful handicapper: reportedly wrong in his back after second start: much improved to win 3 of next 5 races, at Goodwood in June, Sandown in July and Haydock (valuable event, beat Fairmile **107**

totesport.com Stakes (Handicap), Haydock—Dansili Dancer is a convincing winner; Fairmile (left) finishes strongly to deprive Bravo Maestro of second

by 1½ lengths) in August: good fourth to Pinpoint in John Smith's Stakes at Newbury final outing: stays 1¼m: acts on good to firm and good to soft going: below form only start in cheekpieces: usually races prominently. *C. G. Cox*

DANSIL IN DISTRESS 2 b.f. (Apr 24) Dansili 127 – Just Speculation (IRE) 86 (Aho- **59** noora 122) [2006 7f p7g⁶ p8.6m⁵ Nov 21] half-sister to several winners, including useful 1m/1¼m winner The Judge (by Polish Precedent) and 3-y-o Just Observing: dam, 2-y-o 6f winner, half-sister to Gold Cup/Irish St Leger runner-up Tyrone Bridge: modest form in maidens. *S. Kirk*

DANSILVER 2 b.g. (Jan 21) Dansili 127 – Silver Gyre (IRE) 65 (Silver Hawk (USA) **58** 123) [2006 6.1m⁵ 6.1g 5f⁵ 7g² 7.5g 8d⁶ p7.1g² 7s 8.2s p8.6g Nov 18] strong gelding: modest maiden: second in claimer and seller: bred to stay 1¼m/1½m: acts on polytrack and good to firm going. *D. J. Wintle*

DANSIMAR 2 gr.f. (Apr 18) Daylami (IRE) 138 – Hylandra (USA) (Bering 136) [2006 **73** 8d³ 8.3m 9m⁵ Sep 20] 50,000Y: good-topped filly: half-sister to several winners, in- cluding useful French 2000 2-y-o 1m/8.5f winner Hope Town (by Sillery): dam French 1m (at 2 yrs)/9f winner: fair form in maidens, not settling fully: probably stays 9f. *M. R. Channon*

DANSKI 3 b.c. Dansili 127 – Manila Selection (USA) (Manila (USA)) [2006 78p: p8g³ **91** 8s² 8.3m⁵ 8.3f* 8.1m Sep 8] leggy colt: fairly useful performer: won maiden at Windsor in July by 7 lengths from Montpellier: not discredited next time, though said to have had a breathing problem: stays 1m: acts on polytrack and firm going: tends to wander. *P. J. Makin*

DANTE'S DIAMOND (IRE) 4 b.g. Orpen (USA) 116 – Flower From Heaven **65** (Baptism 119) [2006 76: 10s p8.6g p8.6g p9.5g³ p8.6g² p9.5s⁶ Dec 13] strong, lengthy gelding: fair maiden handicapper: stays 9.5f: acts on polytrack, firm and soft going. *G. A. Swinbank*

DAN TUCKER 2 b.g. (Feb 16) Dansili 127 – Shapely (USA) 81 (Alleged (USA) 138) **57** [2006 7m 6g 7d⁶ Aug 28] close-coupled gelding: modest form in maidens, then gelded. *B. J. Meehan*

DANUM 6 b.g. Perpendicular 119 – Maid of Essex 66 (Bustino 136) [2006 46§: f11g **52** f8g⁵ p9.5g² p9.5g² p9.5g³ f8g⁵ p8.6g p8.6g p9.5g Dec 4] strong, deep-girthed gelding: modest maiden: stays 1½m: acts on all-weather, soft and good to firm ground: usually wears cheekpieces: often front runner: unreliable. *R. Hollinshead*

DANUM DANCER 2 ch.c. (Apr 21) Allied Forces (USA) 123 – Branston Dancer **95** (Rudimentary (USA) 118) [2006 5f⁶ 5d⁴ 5m⁵ 5f² 5g 6d 5d* 5g 6g* 6s⁶ Oct 7] 1,000F, 1,000Y: rather leggy, lengthy colt: third foal: brother to winner in Greece: dam unraced: useful performer: much improved fitted with blinkers after sixth start, winning nursery at Beverley in August and 24-runner listed totepool Two-Year-Old Trophy at Redcar (beat Rainbow Mirage 1¾ lengths) in September: also ran well when 4¾ lengths eighth of 9 behind Wi Dud in Flying Childers Stakes at York in between: effective at 5f/6f: acts on good to soft ground (below form on soft final start), probably on firm. *N. Bycroft*

totepool Two-Year-Old Trophy, Redcar—
bargain-buy Danum Dancer takes this very valuable event from Rainbow Mirage and Bazroy

DANUM DIVA (IRE) 2 ch.f. (Jan 11) Danehill Dancer (IRE) 117 – Comprehension –
(USA) 87§ (Diesis 133) [2006 6m 7g Sep 30] 30,000Y: angular filly: fourth foal: sister
to winner in Spain and half-sister to 2 winners, including 4-y-o Kyles Prince: dam 1m
winner (refused to race final start): no show in maidens. *T. J. Pitt*

DANZAR 4 b.g. Danzero (AUS) – Tarf (USA) 92 (Diesis 133) [2006 63: 7f p8.6g⁵ 8.5m **55**
p8.6g f6g f8g Dec 12] modest maiden: stays 8.6f: acts on polytrack and good to firm
going: blinkered final 2 starts. *M. Brittain*

DANZARE 4 b.f. Dansili 127 – Shot of Redemption (Shirley Heights 130) [2006 68: **60**
p8g 10.2f 10f⁴ 8m⁶ p8.6g⁶ 9.7f² 10m 10.1g 9.7f⁵ 8f⁶ 8.1m 8m³ p10g³ Dec 10] modest
handicapper: left Mrs A. Hamilton-Fairley 7,500 gns prior to final outing: stays 1¼m:
acts on polytrack, firm and good to soft ground. *J. L. Spearing*

DANZATRICE 4 b.f. Tamure (IRE) 125 – Miss Petronella (Petoski 135) [2006 –: 10s **65**
12m³ 13.9m 12m⁵ 13m* 15m* 14m⁴ 14g* 17.5d⁴ 13.9s⁴ Oct 7] lengthy, unfurnished
filly: fair handicapper: won at Musselburgh (amateurs), Ayr and Musselburgh again, all
in August: stays 17f: acts on soft and good to firm going. *C. W. Thornton*

DANZIG RIVER (IRE) 5 b.g. Green Desert (USA) 127 – Sahara Breeze 85 (Ela- **81**
Mana-Mou 132) [2006 92: 5g 6g 7g⁴ 7f⁴ 6d 6m 7d⁵ 5g* 6m 6d 6.1g Sep 26] big, good-
bodied gelding: fairly useful handicapper: won at Beverley in August: best at 5f/6f: acts
on firm and soft going: tried visored at 4 yrs: takes keen hold. *D. Nicholls*

DANZILI BAY 4 b.c. Dansili 127 – Lady Bankes (IRE) 69 (Alzao (USA) 117) [2006 –
96: 6d Nov 4] small, sturdy colt: useful performer at 3 yrs: well held in listed event at
Windsor only outing in 2006. *P. W. Chapple-Hyam*

DANZOLIN 5 b.m. Danzero (AUS) – Howlin' (USA) (Alleged (USA) 138) [2006 64: **54**
p8.6g p10g p12.2g⁵ Feb 10] modest maiden: should stay 1½m: acts on polytrack and firm
going. *W. R. Muir*

DA POOCH (IRE) 3 br.f. Key of Luck (USA) 126 – Kinlochewe 102 (Old Vic 136) **59**
[2006 62: 9m 10g 7d 11.9d³ 12s³ 12.5s⁵ p12.2g Nov 6] sixth foal: half-sister to 3 winners,
including fairly useful 6f (including at 2 yrs) winner Statue Gallery (by Cadeaux Genereux) and 5-y-o Pharaoh Prince: dam, 1¼m winner, half-sister to smart 7f/1m performer
Ardkinglass: modest maiden: third at Ballinrobe in October: well held in handicap at
Wolverhampton final start: stays 12.5f: acts on soft ground: tried in cheekpieces.
H. Rogers, Ireland

DAPPLE DAWN (IRE) 3 b.f. Celtic Swing 138 – Lasting Chance (USA) (American **75**
Chance (USA) 117) [2006 8.2v 8m 7m⁶ 8m* 7d* 7d² 7f p8.6g⁴ Dec 18] 48,000Y: second
foal: dam Canadian 6f (at 2 yrs) to 9f (Grade 3) winner: fair handicapper: won at Bellewstown and Tralee in August: left E. Tyrrell in Ireland 14,000 gns and off 3 months
before final outing: stays 8.6f: acts on polytrack, good to firm and good to soft ground.
D. Carroll

DARA MAC 7 b.g. Presidium 124 – Nishara (Nishapour (FR) 125) [2006 61: f8g p9.5g –
8.1g p13.9g Nov 25] rather sparely-made gelding: modest at 6 yrs: no form in 2006: tried
blinkered/in cheekpieces. *M. Scudamore*

DARAMSAR (FR) 3 b.c. Rainbow Quest (USA) 134 – Daryaba (IRE) 121 (Night Shift **116 p**
(USA)) [2006 10s* 12.5g* 12d³ 12.5g* 12s* 10d³ 12g* Oct 15] second foal: half-brother
to useful French 7.5f (at 2 yrs)/1m winner Daryamar (by Machiavellian), later successful
in USA: dam won Prix de Diane and Prix Vermeille: smart performer: won newcomers
race and minor event at Chantilly in May/June, minor event at Deauville and listed race
at Clairefontaine in August and Prix du Conseil de Paris at Longchamp (by neck from
Alix Road, making all) in October: stays 12.5f: acts on soft ground: type to do well at
4 yrs. *A. de Royer Dupre, France*

DARASIM (IRE) 8 b.g. Kahyasi 130 – Dararita (IRE) (Halo (USA)) [2006 –: 18m⁵ –
p16g 21m Aug 2] lengthy, quite good-topped gelding: one-time smart performer: no form
since 2004: blinkered/visored. *M. Johnston*

DARCY'S PRIDE (IRE) 2 b. or br.f. (Feb 15) Danetime (IRE) 121 – Cox's Ridge **47**
(IRE) (Indian Ridge 123) [2006 6m 6m 5d⁶ 5d⁴ Oct 8] €1,500Y: second foal: dam unraced: poor maiden. *D. W. Barker*

DARENEUR (IRE) 6 ch.m. Entrepreneur 123 – Darayna (IRE) (Shernazar 131) [2006 **60**
10.2m² 12.1g⁴ 12.1f⁵ 12.1f Jul 28] modest maiden: missed 2005: stays 1½m: acts on good
to firm going, probably on firm: found little penultimate start. *J. G. M. O'Shea*

DARENJAN (IRE) 3 b.c. Alhaarth (IRE) 126 – Darariyna (IRE) 80 (Shirley Heights 70
130) [2006 10d⁵ 9.9m² 9.9g Aug 25] big, strong colt: has plenty of scope: second foal:
half-brother to French 1¼m winner Dariynia (by King's Best): dam, 1½m/13.4f winner,
half-sister to smart/unreliable stayer Darasim: fair form in maidens first 2 starts: well held
final outing: will be suited by 1½m: wandered second start: sold 14,000 gns in October.
Sir Michael Stoute

DARFOUR 2 b.c. (Apr 20) Inchinor 119 – Gai Bulga 110 (Kris 135) [2006 6m⁶ 7f 7f* 76
8.1v 8.3d Oct 9] 28,000Y, 41,000 2-y-o: lengthy, workmanlike colt: half-brother to useful
1m to 1¼m winner Chivalry (by Mark of Esteem) and fairly useful 1m winner Sword
Arm (by Be My Guest), later successful in USA: dam, 1¼m winner who stayed 1½m,
half-sister to dam of 2000 Guineas winner Footstepsinthesand: fair form: won maiden
at Lingfield in July: more testing conditions when well held in nurseries: should stay 1m/
1¼m: acts on firm going: sold 30,000 gns. *M. Johnston*

DARGHAN (IRE) 6 b.g. Air Express (IRE) 125 – Darsannda (IRE) 86 (Kahyasi 130) 70
[2006 66: 10.9s⁵ 14.1d 12.4m⁴ 11.5m⁴ 12.6m³ 11.5f⁴ 11m* 11.9m⁶ 14.1m³ 11.5m 11s
12s Oct 24] strong gelding: fair handicapper: won at Newcastle in May and Newbury
in July: stays 1¾m: acts on any going: tried tongue tied earlier in career: held up.
W. J. Musson

DARING AFFAIR 5 b.m. Bien Bien (USA) 125 – Daring Destiny 113 (Daring March 87
116) [2006 78: p8.6g p12.2g⁴ 12m 10.5f² 10.5m* 10m 9.8d³ 10.5g⁵ p9.5g* p9.5g³ p9.5g*
Dec 9] good-topped mare: fairly useful handicapper: won at Haydock (tended to wander)
in July and Wolverhampton in November and December: best form around 1¼m: acts on
all-weather, firm and soft going: visored once in 2004. *K. R. Burke*

DARING RANSOM (USA) 4 b.g. Red Ransom (USA) – Young And Daring (USA) 94
(Woodman (USA) 126) [2006 104: 12m⁵ Jan 26] tall, leggy, unfurnished gelding: useful
performer in 2005: visored, respectable fifth in handicap at Nad Al Sheba only outing at
4 yrs: stayed 2m: acted on firm going: dead. *J. Noseda*

DARING YOU 2 b.g. (Apr 22) Mtoto 134 – Sari 83 (Faustus (USA) 118) [2006 6m³ 6f 59
7.1m 7m p7g 8.3g³ Oct 16] modest maiden: stays 8.3f: acts on firm ground: tried blinkered: sent to Belgium. *P. F. I. Cole*

DARK CHAMPION 6 b.g. Abou Zouz (USA) 109 – Hazy Kay (IRE) 77 (Treasure 65
Kay 114) [2006 70: 6g 7g 5f* 5f6m⁶ 5f⁶ 6d 6g 5g 5d* 5f 5g 5d⁴ 5v⁴ Oct 31] good-topped
gelding: fair handicapper: won at Redcar in June and Catterick in September: effective at
5f to 7f: acts on fibresand and any turf going: usually wears headgear. *R. E. Barr*

DARK CHARM (FR) 7 b.g. Anabaa (USA) 130 – Wardara 107 (Sharpo 132) [2006 80
86: 8g 8.1g 7f⁶ 8.2d 8.1s* 8.3m⁵ 9.1g⁵ 8.3m² 9.9m² 10g⁴ 10m* 8g² 10g⁵ 10.5s⁵ Sep 7]
tall, quite good-topped gelding: fairly useful handicapper: won at Haydock in May and
Pontefract (amateur event) in August: stays 1¼m: acts on polytrack, firm and soft going:
effective with or without cheekpieces: often races freely. *R. A. Fahey*

DARK EMOTION 3 b.g. Prince Sabo 123 – Sorrowful (Moorestyle 137) [2006 10d –
10f⁶ 10.5g Sep 22] leggy gelding: no sign of ability. *W. de Best-Turner*

DARK ENERGY 2 br.c. (Mar 8) Observatory (USA) 131 – Waterfowl Creek (IRE) 88 76 p
(Be My Guest (USA) 126) [2006 8d³ Nov 3] 35,000Y, 25,000 2-y-o: fifth living foal:
half-brother to 3 winners, including useful 1¼m winner Maid of Camelot (by Caerleon):
dam, 1m winner, closely related to smart miler Inchmurrin, herself dam of Inchinor: 18/1,
4½ lengths third to Hohlethelonely in maiden at Musselburgh, finishing well: open to
improvement. *B. Smart*

DARKER THAN BLUE 3 b.f. Erhaab (USA) 127 – My Preference (Reference Point 52
139) [2006 p8g⁴ p8.6g 10d 12.6g 10d³ 8.3d⁴ p7g⁵ Jun 15] fifth foal: dam unraced half-
sister to very smart 1989 2-y-o Be My Chief: modest maiden: needs further than 7f, bred
to stay at least 1¼m: blinkered last 3 starts. *B. J. Meehan*

DARK ISLANDER (IRE) 3 br.c. Singspiel (IRE) 133 – Lamanka Lass (USA) 79 115
(Woodman (USA) 126) [2006 93: 7g² p7g³ 8m 8m* 8m⁴ 8f* 9f* 10f Nov 26] rangy,
angular colt: has a quick action: developed into a smart performer, winning handicaps
at Newmarket (beat Dunelight 1¾ lengths) in July and Bath (by 2½ lengths from
Humungous) in September, and Grade 2 Oak Tree Derby at Santa Anita (beat Obrigado
by 1¼ lengths) in October: well below form in Hollywood Derby final outing: bred to
stay 1¼m, though tends to race freely: acts on polytrack, firm and good to soft going.
J. W. Hills

totesport.com Stakes (Handicap), Newmarket—
a bunched finish as Dark Missile (noseband) edges out Mutamarres (visor);
Prince Tamino takes third ahead of Ripples Maid (spotted cap) and Grantley Adams (rail)

DARK MISSILE 3 b.f. Night Shift (USA) – Exorcet (FR) 78 (Selkirk (USA) 129) **100**
[2006 80p: 6f 5s⁴ 5.1g² p6g² 6m* 7f 6g* 6d 6d Sep 16] big, strong filly: useful handicapper: won totesport.com Stakes at Newmarket (by head from Mutamarres) in July and
quite valuable event at Ascot (beat Lady Livius by 1½ lengths, travelling strongly and
readily going clear) in August: well below form in listed race at Pontefract and Ayr Gold
Cup last 2 starts: best at 5f/6f: acts on polytrack and firm going. *A. M. Balding*

DARK MOON 3 b.f. Observatory (USA) 131 – Lady Donatella 57 (Last Tycoon 131) **62**
[2006 49: 8.1g⁶ p8.6g⁵ 7g 7m³ 7.6g* 8m³ p8g⁵ 8m f6g p6g Nov 27] modest handicapper **a48**
on turf, poor on all-weather: won at Lingfield in August: left A. Balding 4,000 gns after
eighth outing: stays 1m: acts on good to firm going: often races prominently. *D. Shaw*

DARK NIGHT (IRE) 3 b.g. Night Shift (USA) – Shamaness (USA) (Darshaan 133) **47**
[2006 –: 9m 8.3g⁵ 12f Jul 3] maiden: form only when fifth in handicap at Hamilton.
D. W. Barker

DARK PARADE (ARG) 5 b.g. Parade Marshal (USA) – Charming Dart (ARG) **61**
(D'Accord (USA)) [2006 61: 12d p16g p12g* 13.9m⁴ p13.9g⁴ p16g² p16g² p12g p16g² **a73**
16d⁶ Sep 26] close-coupled gelding: fair handicapper on all-weather, modest on turf:
won at Lingfield in May: effective at 1½m to 2m: acts on sand/all-weather and good to
firm going: tried blinkered: has looked hard ride. *G. L. Moore*

DARK PLANET 3 ch.g. Singspiel (IRE) 133 – Warning Shadows (IRE) 113 (Cadeaux **68**
Genereux 131) [2006 59: p10g² 9.9f* 11.6g⁶ p10g⁴ p12.2g⁴ 10m p12g⁴ Jul 1] strong
gelding: fair handicapper: won at Beverley in April: stays 1½m: acts on polytrack and
firm going: gelded after final start: sold 12,000 gns in October. *C. E. Brittain*

DARK SOCIETY 8 b.g. Imp Society (USA) – No Candles Tonight 74 (Star Appeal **–**
133) [2006 63: 10g 11.6g⁶ 8m Aug 19] medium-sized, useful-looking gelding: fair at
best: well held in 2006: tried visored. *A. W. Carroll*

DARLING BELINDA 2 ch.f. (Feb 17) Silver Wizard (USA) 117 – Katyushka (IRE) **66**
73 (Soviet Star (USA) 128) [2006 p7g p6g 6d⁵ p5.1g p5.1g³ p6g³ p6s² p6g² Dec 22]
fourth foal: half-sister to 5-y-o Future Deal: dam, 7f winner, out of smart 5f performer
Welsh Note: fair maiden: placed last 4 starts, first 2 in nurseries, final one in cheekpieces:
will stay 7f: acts on polytrack and good to soft going: suspect temperament (tends to
hang). *D. K. Ivory*

DARLING DEANIE (IRE) 4 ch.f. Sinndar (IRE) 134 – Blushing Melody (IRE) 80 **79**
(Never So Bold 135) [2006 77: 11.6m² 14.1g⁵ 12m⁶ 10.5s Sep 1] sturdy, workmanlike
filly: fair handicapper: left D. Elsworth after third start: effective at 11.6f, probably not
1¾m: acts on good to firm and good to soft going. *K. A. Ryan*

DARLING RIVER (FR) 7 b.m. Double Bed (FR) 121 – Oh Lucky Day (Balidar 133) **–**
[2006 p9.5g f8g p12.2g p9.5g Mar 29] fair maiden in 2002: well held since. *R. Brotherton*

DARRFONAH (IRE) 2 b.f. (Apr 14) Singspiel (IRE) 133 – Avila 76 (Ajdal (USA) **106**
130) [2006 p7g⁶ 6m⁵ 6g² 6s³ 7g* 8m² Oct 1] rangy filly: unfurnished at 2 yrs: half-sister
to several winners, including Racing Post Trophy/Dante Stakes winner Dilshaan and
11f to 2m winner Aveiro (both by Darshaan): dam, third at 7f, half-sister to Chester Vase
winner Nomrood: useful performer: placed twice, including in Lowther Stakes at York (3
lengths third to Silk Blossom), prior to winning minor event at Newbury in September:
more improvement when 5 lengths second of 13 to Finsceal Beo in Prix Marcel Boussac
at Longchamp: will stay 1¼m/1½m· acts on soft and good to firm going. *C. E. Brittain*

DARSI (FR) 3 b.c. Polish Precedent (USA) 131 – Darashandeh (IRE) 108 (Dar- **118**
shaan 133) [2006 11g² 12.5d* 10.5m* 12g⁵ Jul 2]
    The Aga Khan and his long-standing French trainer Alain de Royer-Dupre
had been among those opposed to the reduction in distance of the Prix du Jockey
Club from a mile and a half to ten and a half furlongs. But in just the second running
of the 'French Derby' over its new distance, Darsi provided owner and trainer with
their seventh and fifth winners of the race respectively. The trainer again expressed his regret at the Prix du Jockey Club's reduction in distance when discussing
Darsi's chance beforehand, the colt having won at Chantilly on his previous outing
over fully two furlongs further. The shorter trip was one concern, but a greater one
perhaps was the fact that Darsi was going into a classic without having tackled
anything other than minor company. Darsi made his debut at Chantilly the previous
autumn, finishing fifth in a newcomers race, before a six-length win at Lyon-
Parilly. He returned in April, when going down to another of the Aga Khan's colts,
Vison Celebre, over eleven furlongs at Longchamp before successfully stepping up
further in trip at Chantilly in early-May.
    The Aga Khan looked to have a better chance of landing the Derby at
Epsom the same weekend with the Andre Fabre-trained favourite Visindar, while
his stable-companion Linda's Lad was another leading French colt sent to Epsom
in preference to the shorter option at Chantilly. That still left a number of runners
in the fifteen-strong field for the Prix du Jockey Club (under its new sponsor,
Mitsubishi Motors) who had already proved themselves at a much higher level
than Darsi. Ballydoyle's Aussie Rules started favourite (coupled with pacemaker
Hurricane Cat) after his win in the Poule d'Essai des Poulains, attempting the
same double completed by Shamardal the year before, while the three British representatives were Dee Stakes winner Art Deco, the Lingfield Derby Trial runner-up
Hazeymm and the Two Thousand Guineas third Olympian Odyssey. None of the
visitors reached the places though, as Darsi got the better of two colts even more
lightly raced than he.
    Despite the drop in trip, and conditions which placed an emphasis on speed,
Darsi was always travelling well in touch with the leading group and moved into a
more prominent position on the outside from the home turn. With second favourite
Arras taking up the running at that point from Hazeymm, Darsi went in pursuit but
it was only at the end of a good tussle, and in the last fifty yards or so, that Darsi
came out on top, despite Christophe Soumillon dropping his whip in the final

*Prix du Jockey Club Mitsubishi Motors, Chantilly—Darsi gives the Aga Khan a seventh win in the race,
staying on too strongly for Best Name (light colours, dark seams) and Arras (rail);
Art Deco (white sleeves) does best of the foreign-trained challengers in fourth*

furlong. Best Name ran on well to snatch second from Arras three quarters of a length behind the winner, with Art Deco, the slow-starting but strong-finishing Numide, and Irish Wells completing the first half-dozen home (covered by less than two lengths) ahead of Aussie Rules in seventh. The bunched finish was not indicative of a steadily-run race, however. The course record, set by Lypharita in the 1985 Prix de Diane, was lowered by a tenth of a second.

Darsi had taken a big step up in class in his stride which, coupled with the fact that he had still had only five races and that he promised to be at least as effective returned to further, made it reasonable to expect that he would make more of a name for himself at the top level in the rest of the season. But Darsi was seen out only once more, starting second favourite for the Irish Derby (for which he was supplemented) but managing only a never-nearer fifth, seven lengths adrift of Dylan Thomas. Darsi was a substandard winner of the Prix du Jockey Club and certainly well below the level of the Aga Khan's other winners of the race Charlottesville (rated 135), Top Ville (129), Darshaan (133), Mouktar (129), Natroun (128) and Dalakhani (133). The last four of those were also trained by Alain de Royer-Dupre, while Darsi provided Soumillon with his third winner of the Prix du Jockey Club in six years after Anabaa Blue in 2001 and Dalakhani in 2003. Incidentally, the Aga Khan Studs' slogan is 'Success breeds success' and that's certainly the case where their Prix du Jockey Club winners are concerned, Top Ville being out of a mare by Charlottesville and Dalakhani being a son of Darshaan.

		Danzig	Northern Dancer
	Polish Precedent (USA)	(b 1977)	Pas de Nom
	(b 1986)	Past Example	Buckpasser
Darsi (FR)		(ch 1976)	Bold Example
(b.c. 2003)		Darshaan	Shirley Heights
	Darashandeh (IRE)	(br 1981)	Delsy
	(br 1994)	Daralinsha	Empery
		(b 1984)	Darazina

Darsi is by the top-class miler Polish Precedent who died in 2005. Polish Precedent's stud record was not the most consistent, but he did get top-class winners as older horses in Pilsudski and Rakti and, in the latest season, Sussex Stakes winner Court Masterpiece, another by Polish Precedent who has improved with age. Darsi owes his stamina to the dam's side of his pedigree which, in another example of success breeding success, features a couple of the Aga Khan's aforementioned Jockey Club winners. Darsi's dam Darashandeh is by Darshaan and his fourth dam, Djebellina, is by Charlottesville. Darashandeh has had two other winners from three foals prior to Darsi. Darasa (by Barathea) won over eleven furlongs in the French Provinces, while four-year-old Dashtaki (by Night Shift) was successful in a mile handicap at Maisons-Laffitte in the latest season. Their dam's only win came as a two-year-old over a mile and a quarter (at Evry's final meeting before the track closed) and she ran her best races at around the same trip as a three-year-old, finishing second in the Prix Penelope and fourth in the Prix Saint-Alary. Darashandeh was among several useful middle-distance winners (all of them fillies) out of the smart Prix Minerve winner Daralinsha, including the Prix de Royallieu runner-up Daraydala. Djebellina, mentioned above as Darsi's fourth dam, is also the great grandam of the 1999 Prix de Diane and Vermeille winner Daryaba, who in the latest season figured as the dam of another smart three-year-old colt for the Aga Khan, Daramsar, winner of the Prix du Conseil de Paris at Longchamp. Unlike Darsi, Daramsar will be around as a four-year-old. Darsi stayed a mile and a half well and acted on good to firm and good to soft ground without encountering extremes of going. He has been retired to Beechbrook Stud, County Wicklow, Ireland as a jumps stallion. *A. de Royer Dupre, France*

DART ALONG (USA) 4 b.c. Bahri (USA) 125 – Promptly (IRE) 88 (Lead On Time **83** (USA) 123) [2006 81: 6v 7m 6m⁴ 7m² 8.5m⁵ 7g⁶ 7.5g 8g* 8v p7g p8.6g⁵ p9.5g* Dec 2] stocky colt: fairly useful performer: trained by R. Hannon in 2005: won claimer at Tralee in August and, having left M. McCullagh after eighth start, handicap at Wolverhampton in December: stays 9.5f: acts on polytrack and good to firm ground: tongue tied last 2 starts at 3 yrs: effective blinkered or not. *Eoin Doyle, Ireland*

DARTANIAN 4 b.g. Jurado (USA) – Blackpool Mamma's 73 (Merdon Melody 98) – [2006 8.1f p12.2g⁶ Jun 30] leggy gelding: modest performer at 2 yrs: well held both starts since. *M. Scudamore*

DARUMA (IRE) 2 b.g. (Apr 18) Iron Mask (USA) 117 – Mary's Way (GR) 78 (Night **53 §** Shift (USA)) [2006 p5g⁵ 5f 5f⁵ 6g 5.1m⁴ p5.1m Nov 8] strong, heavy-topped gelding: modest maiden: form only at 5f: usually blinkered: seems ungenuine. *Peter Grayson*

DARUSSO 3 ch.g. Daylami (IRE) 138 – Rifada 103 (Fla-Mana-Mou 132) [2006 68: **67** 8.3g⁶ p8.6g Oct 30] leggy gelding: fair maiden: should stay at least 1¼m: acts on soft and good to firm going. *J. S. Moore*

DA SCHADENFREUDE (USA) 2 b. or br.g. (Feb 9) Tale of The Cat (USA) 113 – **61** Conquistas Jessica (USA) (Boundary (USA)) 117) [2006 p7g 7.5m 7.6f Sep 23] big gelding: modest form in maidens. *W. G. M. Turner*

DASHEENA 3 b.f. Magic Ring (IRE) 115 – Sweet And Lucky (Lucky Wednesday 124) **67** [2006 65: p6g² p7.1g³ 6g⁴ 6m 6.1g p6g⁴ 6s p6m³ p7.1s⁶ Dec 14] angular filly: fair handicapper: left M. Polglase after fourth start: stays 7f: acts on polytrack and firm going. *A. J. McCabe*

DASHFA BAILEYS 3 ch.g. Mark of Esteem (IRE) 137 – Dahshah 77 (Mujtahid – (USA) 118) [2006 42: p6g Jan 11] leggy gelding: poor maiden. *C. A. Dwyer*

DASH OF LIME 4 b.f. Bold Edge 123 – Green Supreme (Primo Dominie 121) [2006 **67** 65: f6g p6g⁵ Jan 5] fair performer, lightly raced: not sure to stay much beyond 6f: acts on polytrack and soft ground. *J. Akehurst*

DASH TO THE FRONT 3 b.f. Diktat 126 – Millennium Dash 94 (Nashwan (USA) **88** 135) [2006 81p: p8.6g* 8d² 9.9m 8d Sep 23] useful-looking filly: unfurnished at present: fairly useful performer, lightly raced: won maiden at Wolverhampton in July: good efforts in handicaps next 2 starts: stays 1¼m: acts on polytrack, good to firm and good to soft ground. *J. R. Fanshawe*

DATZNYCE (IRE) 3 b.f. Cape Cross (IRE) 129 – Sharera (IRE) 88 (Kahyasi 130) – [2006 p6g p9.5g p12.2g 8d 6s Oct 20] third foal: dam, 1¼m winner, out of half-sister to Derby winner Shahrastani: well held in maidens: left D. Elsworth after third outing. *M. P. Sunderland, Ireland*

DAUGHTERS WORLD 3 b.f. Agnes World (USA) 123 – Priluki 65 (Lycius (USA) – 124) [2006 48: p8g p6g Oct 29] leggy, useful-looking filly: no form since debut at 2 yrs. *J. R. Best*

DAVAYE 2 b.f. (Mar 13) Bold Edge 123 – Last Impression 69 (Imp Society (USA)) **69** [2006 5g³ 5f⁴ 5m⁵ 5m³ 5m* 6v⁴ Oct 9] leggy, quite good-topped filly: first foal: dam 2-y-o 5f winner: fair performer: won nursery at Musselburgh in August: probably stays 6f: probably acts on any going. *K. R. Burke*

DAVENPORT (IRE) 4 b.g. Bold Fact (USA) 116 – Semence d'Or (FR) (Kaldoun (FR) **90** 122) [2006 91: 8s 8d⁴ p8g⁴ 8s² 8.1d* 10m p8g³ 8g 8m 8.2s f8g⁵ p8g⁴ p9.5g² p9.5g⁴ Dec 28] leggy, close-coupled gelding: fairly useful handicapper: won at Sandown in May: stays easy 9.5f: acts on polytrack and soft going: in cheekpieces (ran to form) last 3 starts: often slowly away: held up. *B. R. Millman*

DAVIDIA (IRE) 3 b.g. Barathea (IRE) 127 – Green Life 63 (Green Desert (USA) 127) **66** [2006 65: p8g³ p10g 8.2d⁵ p8g⁴ 7g² p8g³ 9.9m p7g⁵ p10g⁴ p8.6g Dec 21] well-made gelding: fair maiden handicapper: stays easy 1¼m: acts on polytrack and good to soft ground: tried blinkered. *S. Kirk*

DAVID JUNIOR (USA) 4 ch.c. Pleasant Tap (USA) – Paradise River (USA) **132** (Irish River (FR) 131) [2006 127: 8.9m* 10m⁴ 10m* a10f Nov 4]

    Madness was defined by Einstein as doing the same thing over and over again while continuing to expect a different result. To the lengthy list of top European challengers that have failed to make an impression in the Breeders' Cup Classic can now be added the names of George Washington, the best three-year-old of 2006, and David Junior, the year's best older horse. Arcangues, who started at 1336/10 in 1993, remains the only European-trained winner of the Classic, the richest of the Breeders' Cup races and the one that counts most for the American audience. European stables traditionally mount their strongest challenges for the three Breeders' Cup races run on turf, and for good reason. The pick of the American horses contest the Classic, the two who fought out the finish in the latest edition, four-year-old Invasor and three-year-old Bernardini (the first horse to win

265

Dubai Duty Free Sponsored By Dubai Duty Free, Nad Al Sheba—
the most valuable event ever won by a British-trained horse as David Junior gets the better of
The Tin Man to give Brian Meehan a dream start at his new base Manton

an American classic—the Preakness—for Sheikh Mohammed) having run up sequences, as had the Californian-based five-year-old Lava Man, the trio having won, collectively, sixteen of their eighteen starts in 2006. They dominated the betting, ahead of George Washington and David Junior who were both running on dirt for the only time in their careers. European victories come regularly at the Breeders' Cup, particularly so for British-trained horses nowadays, Ouija Board and David Junior's stable-companion Red Rocks providing a double on turf at the latest meeting. The problems associated with travelling horses long distances and racing them in different climates have been largely overcome, but the unfamiliar dirt surface and the sharp American tracks remain very difficult obstacles to surmount against the best of the home-trained horses. George Washington received a bump from the winner Invasor while making his challenge but found little in the straight and probably didn't get the trip; David Junior, one of only four among sixteen European challengers on the day to run without salix, formerly lasix, failed to take to the surface and was soon behind before eventually being pulled up, reportedly stiff and sore afterwards.

Perhaps the connections of George Washington and David Junior, the last-named trying to defy a four-month absence, took encouragement beforehand from the fact that the venue for the latest Breeders' Cup, Churchill Downs, with its slightly longer straight, probably has one of the dirt tracks in North America that is least unfavourable to the Europeans. Arazi and Sheikh Albadou won the Juvenile and the Sprint there, while Giant's Causeway and Swain both went close in the Classic and Tagel and Eltish reached a place in the Juvenile. There are reports that Churchill Downs, which is set to host the Breeders' Cup for a seventh time in 2008, may—in common with some other American courses—have introduced a synthetic surface on its main track by then (the new polytrack at Keeneland and Turfway Park has been well received, and Hollywood Park, Del Mar, Santa Anita and Arlington are among other courses to have changed or to be changing to a synthetic surface). Whether such changes will benefit the Europeans remains to be seen, but the introduction of more cushioned surfaces should at least remove one of the justifications trotted out for the liberal use of drugs in American racing. The sport in America—where rules on medication differ from state to state—has a long way to go to conform with most other leading racing countries on the use of drugs, its permissive attitude sometimes creating mistrust of American horses on the track. 'There are no great racehorses any more . . . only great vets,' wrote one cynic. Following the furore over the use by some trainers of so-called 'milkshakes' (a subject dealt with in the essay on Shirocco in *Racehorses of 2005*), American racing was hit in 2006 by a number of suspensions for drug offences of some of its most prolific trainers. Five of the top ten trainers by earnings in 2006 had horses who were revealed to have failed dope tests, among them champion trainer Todd Pletcher (lost an appeal against a 45-day suspension), Steve Asmussen (served a six-month suspension) and Richard Dutrow, all of whom were cited for meprivacaine, a drug that can dull pain. The different drug rules from state to state, and the complex guidelines on withdrawal times, make very large stables like those of Pletcher and Asmussen, particularly vulnerable. However, this vexing issue, which has implications for global competition (Brass Hat, Deep Impact and Takeover Target were among those affected in 2006), is not going to go away—and nor should it—until racing agrees internationally, and adheres to, a uniform set of doping rules.

David Junior's connections took the decision to miss good opportunities in Europe so that the horse would be 'fresh' for his Classic bid. Not seen out after winning the Coral-Eclipse at Sandown in July, he was trained specially for the Classic—though no horse had ever won the race after such a long lay-off—and he was not sent to America until six days beforehand, virtually as late as possible. The idea of trying David Junior on dirt in the Dubai World Cup in March had apparently been considered, but the value of the major turf races at the World Cup meeting, the Sheema Classic and the Duty Free, was boosted to five million dollars in the latest season, only a million behind the World Cup itself. David Junior started favourite for the Dubai Duty Free on the strength of a most progressive three-year-old career which had begun with eleventh of nineteen in the Two Thousand Guineas and concluded with a first Group 1 victory, over a strong international field in the Champion Stakes at Newmarket. David Junior carried on where he had left off, matching his Champion Stakes form with a three-and-a-half-length victory in a fifteen-runner line-up at Nad Al Sheba. Fifth turning for home, David Junior quickened ahead in good style over a furlong out and was well on top at the finish, followed home by American-trained front-runner The Tin Man (winner of the Arlington Million later in the year), the home-trained seven-year-old Seihali, another American challenger Host and Hong Kong-based Bullish Luck. As well as

Coral-Eclipse Stakes, Sandown—a second Group 1 of the season for David Junior, who beats Notnowcato (No.5) and Blue Monday (No.1); Aussie Rules (rail) is fourth as Ouija Board (No.6) leaves it too late after meeting trouble; Snoqualmie Boy (mostly hidden) and pacemaker Royal Alchemist are the others in the picture

Roldvale Limited's "David Junior"

putting up the best performance in the Duty Free since its elevation to Group 1 status in 2002, David Junior also got his stable's move from Lambourn to the Sangster family-owned Manton off to a flier. Brian Meehan became the fifth trainer—following Michael Dickinson, Barry Hills, Peter Chapple-Hyam and John Gosden—to occupy Manton since it was purchased by Robert Sangster in the mid-'eighties. David Junior's victory at Nad Al Sheba yielded the biggest first prize ever won by a British-trained horse, £1,714,286 at prevailing exchange rates, a sum which dwarfed the stable's entire earnings in 2005. With the Breeders' Cup Turf victory of Red Rocks bringing in £852,632 and the number of domestic winners going up from forty-three in 2005 to seventy-four in 2006, Meehan certainly made a dream start to the latest chapter in his career.

After missing a clash with Prix de l'Arc winner Hurricane Run in the Tattersalls Gold Cup at the Curragh because of heavy ground, David Junior was seen next at Royal Ascot. His meeting with Dubai World Cup winner Electrocutionist in the Prince of Wales's Stakes was eagerly anticipated, but, in a race which turned into a sprint, both were outshone on the day by the mare Ouija Board. David Junior started a hot favourite but, clearly not at his best and hanging right when first coming under pressure, he managed only fourth, two lengths behind the winner. Connections attributed David Junior's effort to the steadily-run race and they did something about it before his next appearance in the Coral-Eclipse, purchasing Royal Alchemist (third in the Windsor Forest at the Royal meeting) to act as a pacemaker. Ouija Board started 2/1 favourite in a nine-runner field at Sandown, followed in the betting by David Junior at 9/4, the Poule d'Essai des Poulains winner Aussie Rules at 11/2, the very smart Blue Monday at 8/1, the Prince of Wales's fifth Notnowcato at 9/1, and 16/1 bar. David Junior opened at 11/4 on the course after adverse rumours—vehemently denied by his trainer—about his well-being in the days leading up to the race. Those punters who kept faith with David Junior were rewarded with

268

a decisive win. Royal Alchemist didn't set so strong a pace as expected, the tempo only steady early on, but, turning for home last in a well-bunched field, David Junior showed a fine turn of foot (again hanging right) to win by a length and a half and a neck from Notnowcato and Blue Monday, who were followed by Aussie Rules and Ouija Board, the last-named unable to get a clear run until the race was as good as over in a race in which there was no shortage of hard-luck stories, including from the second and third, neither of whom had the best of runs.

David Junior (USA) (ch.c. 2002)	Pleasant Tap (USA) (b 1987)	Pleasant Colony (b or br 1978)	His Majesty
			Sun Colony
		Never Knock (b or br 1979)	Stage Door Johnny
			Never Hula
	Paradise River (USA) (b 1994)	Irish River (ch 1976)	Riverman
			Irish Star
		North of Eden (b 1983)	Northfields
			Tree of Knowledge

The sturdy, close-coupled David Junior improved from three to four, as could have been anticipated from a study of his pedigree. Those on both sides of the family have tended to improve with age. David Junior's sire Pleasant Tap was at his best at five when he won the Jockey Club Gold Cup and the Suburban Handicap and finished second in the Breeders' Cup Classic (he was second to Sheikh Albadou in the Sprint the year before). David Junior's dam Paradise River, who has bred three other winners (her closely in-bred two-year-old Optical Illusion, by Theatrical, ran once for Ed Dunlop in the latest season), ran only at four and ended her racing career still a maiden. She was, however, extremely well bred, a sister to Paradise Creek who also peaked at five when he won the Arlington Million and the Washington International, before finishing third in the Breeders' Cup Turf and second in the Japan Cup. David Junior's grandam North of Eden, a three-parts sister to Irish Derby runner-up and subsequent multiple Grade 1 winner Theatrical and a half-sister to the high-class Japanese performer Taiki Blizzard, was also a maiden but she has bred three Grade 1 winners, Paradise Creek being followed by half-brothers who won Grade 1 events as six-year-olds, Wild Event (Turf Classic) and Forbidden Apple (Manhattan Handicap). David Junior will not have the opportunity to emulate his most notable relatives and add to his achievements on the track. He was sold to the Japan Racing Association after the Eclipse for a sum reportedly in excess of £4m and will stand at the Shizunai Stallion Station in 2007. His sire has had a Japan Cup winner in Tap Dance City who won Japan's richest race as a six-year-old. The genuine David Junior, who acted on good to firm and good to soft going (successful at two on firm), was raced mostly at around a mile and a quarter, but would probably have stayed a mile and a half given the chance. He was held up to make optimum use of his good turn of foot. *B. J. Meehan*

DAVIDS MARK 6 b.g. Polar Prince (IRE) 117 – Star of Flanders (Puissance 110) [2006   **62**
53: p6g² p6g p6g³ f5g p5.1g⁴ p6g p5g⁶ 6m p5g⁴ p7g⁶ 5.2f* 6f 5.2m⁵ 5.7m² p5.1g³ p5g⁴ p5g* Dec 6] modest performer: won handicap at Yarmouth in July and banded event at Kempton in December: best at 5f/6f: acts on all-weather, soft and firm going: tried in headgear/tongue tie. *J. R. Jenkins*

DAVOSKI 12 b.g. Niniski (USA) 125 – Pamela Peach 81 (Habitat 134) [2006 12.6m   **–**
12.1f Jul 28] well held both starts on Flat since 1997. *Dr P. Pritchard*

DAWALEEB (IRE) 3 b.f. Alhaarth (IRE) 126 – Summerhill (Habitat 134) [2006 65:   **61**
7m 8.1g⁶ p7.1m 7f p9.5g Oct 29] sturdy filly: modest maiden: left M. Tregoning following reappearance: well below form after: best effort at 6f: acts on good to firm going: tried visored. *Jane Chapple-Hyam*

DAWARI (IRE) 8 b.g. In The Wings 128 – Dawala (IRE) (Lashkari 128) [2006 f14g   **–**
May 31] close-coupled, attractive gelding: useful performer in 2002: no form both outings in Britain since: has worn visor. *R. Ford*

DAWERA (IRE) 3 b.f. Spinning World (USA) 130 – Dawala (IRE) (Lashkari 128)   **84**
[2006 10m³ 10f* Jul 21] half-sister to 3 useful winners, including 8-y-o Dawari and 1¼m/ 13f winner Darapour (by Fairy King): dam, French 1½m winner, closely related to Prix du Jockey Club winner Darshaan: better effort in maidens when landing odds in 4-runner event at Pontefract in July by 6 lengths from Pochard, soon taking strong hold, making

most and coasting in: would have stayed 1½m: looked potentially useful, but retired to stud. *Sir Michael Stoute*

DAWEYRR (USA) 2 b.c. (May 6) Kingmambo (USA) 125 – With Flair (USA) (Broad **51 p** Brush (USA)) [2006 7.1m Sep 7] $200,000Y: third foal: dam Canadian Grade 3 1¼m winner: 20/1, ran green in maiden at Chepstow: likely to improve. *M. P. Tregoning*

DAWN MYSTERY 2 gr.f. (Mar 8) Daylami (IRE) 138 – Frustration 108 (Salse (USA) – 128) [2006 p8g Dec 1] 31,000Y: sixth foal: half-sister to fairly useful 1¼m winner Star Protector (by Hector Protector) and 1¼m and 2m winner Argentum (by Sillery): dam, 1¼m winner, half-sister to US Grade 1 9f winner Mister Wonderful: 66/1, never dangerous in maiden at Lingfield, slowly away. *Rae Guest*

DAWN SKY 2 b.c. (Jan 28) Fantastic Light (USA) 134 – Zacheta (Polish Precedent **75 p** (USA) 131) [2006 8.2d² Nov 1] 100,000Y: good-bodied colt: first foal: dam unraced half-sister to Prix de l'Arc de Triomphe winner Marienbard: 14/1, encouraging 4 lengths second to Regal Flush in maiden at Nottingham: will be suited by 1¼m/1½m: sure to improve. *M. A. Jarvis*

DAWN'S LAST SHOT (IRE) 4 b.g. Son of Sharp Shot (IRE) 105 – Dawn Star 94 **67** (High Line 125) [2006 –p: 11.8d⁵ 14.1d 12m Aug 27] tall gelding: fair maiden, lightly raced: best effort at 11.8f: acts on good to soft ground. *J. L. Dunlop*

DAWN SPIRIT 3 ch.f. Barathea (IRE) 127 – Samsung Spirit 79 (Statoblest 120) [2006 – 12m³ 14.1d 12m Jun 25] strong, workmanlike filly: fifth foal: half-sister to 3 winners, including useful 5f (including at 2 yrs) winner Mystical Land (by Xaar) and 9f 1¼m winner Graceful Air (by Danzero): dam 6f winner (including at 2 yrs): no form. *J. R. Weymes*

DAWSON CREEK (IRE) 2 ch.c. (Apr 15) Titus Livius (FR) 115 – Particular Friend **52** 88 (Cadeaux Genereux 131) [2006 p6g p7g 8.3s Oct 2] modest form in maidens. *B. Gubby*

DAYBREAKING (IRE) 4 br.c. Daylami (IRE) 138 – Mawhiba (USA) 63 (Dayjur – (USA) 137) [2006 –: p12g p13.9g Feb 6] leggy colt: lightly-raced maiden: well held all 3 starts since 2 yrs. *R. F. Johnson Houghton*

DAY BY DAY 2 ch.f. (Mar 23) Kyllachy 129 – Dayville (USA) 86 (Dayjur (USA) 137) **– P** [2006 6.1d Oct 13] 22,000Y: useful-looking filly: has scope: half-sister to 3 winners, including really useful Irish 5f winner Alexander Ballet (by Mind Games) and 1¼m/1½m winner My Daisychain (by Hector Protector): dam, 6f winner (including at 2 yrs), half-sister to US Grade 1 1¼m winner Spanish Fern: 6/1, lot more promise than bare result (tenth of 13) in maiden at Warwick, green throughout but eye-catching headway before eased: likely to do much better. *B. J. Meehan*

DAY FLIGHT 5 b.h. Sadler's Wells (USA) 132 – Bonash 110 (Rainbow Quest (USA) **122** 134) [2006 122: 10g* 11s² 12m⁴ Jun 24] good-topped horse: has a short, quick action: very smart performer: at least as good as ever in 2006, winning Betfred Gordon Richards Stakes at Sandown in April by length from Notable Guest: respectable efforts after, 2 lengths second to Arcadio in Grosser Mercedes-Benz-Preis at Baden-Baden and 2¼ lengths fourth to Maraahel in Hardwicke Stakes at Royal Ascot (would have finished closer but for being squeezed out when challenging): effective at 1¼m to 13.4f: acts on good to firm ground, raced mostly on good going or softer and acts on soft (below best only outing on heavy): has worn crossed noseband: carries head high/flicks tail under pressure: stays in training. *J. H. M. Gosden*

DAYLAMI DREAMS 2 gr.g. (Mar 11) Daylami (IRE) 138 – Kite Mark 58 (Mark of **69** Esteem (IRE) 137) [2006 7g 8m⁴ 7g Sep 15] 12,000Y: angular gelding: second foal: dam once-raced half-sister to Park Hill Stakes winner Madame Dubois, herself dam of Irish 2000 Guineas winner Indian Haven and grandam of 5-y-o Imperial Stride: fair form in maidens: will benefit from 1¼m/1½m. *J. S. Moore*

DAYLAMI STAR 3 gr.c. Daylami (IRE) 138 – Ascot Cyclone (USA) 93 (Rahy (USA) **93** 115) [2006 84: 12.3m² 14d⁶ May 30] strong colt: fairly useful performer: stays 1½m, not sure to get 1¾m: acts on good to firm and good to soft going: tends to edge left: sold 12,000 gns in October. *J. H. M. Gosden*

DAYLESFORD 3 ch.f. Golden Snake (USA) 127 – Lady Day (FR) (Lightning (FR) – 129) [2006 10.5m⁶ Aug 10] close-coupled filly: half-sister to several winners, including 1995 2-y-o 1m winner who stayed 12.4f Ladykirk (by Selkirk): dam French 9f to 12.5f winner: 40/1 and backward, well held in maiden at Haydock. *I. Semple*

DAYOFF (IRE) 5 gr.m. Daylami (IRE) 138 – Dabtara (IRE) 88 (Kahyasi 130) [2006 **60** 68, a–: p12.2g² p13.9g 12.3g 12m 12f 12.1f⁴ 15m* 12.1f 14.1g⁵ 15m³ Aug 12] modest handicapper: won at Ayr in July: stays 15f: acts on polytrack, firm and good to soft going: usually blinkered/visored. *P. D. Evans*

DAYROSE 3 ch.f. Daylami (IRE) 138 – Blush Rambler (IRE) (Blushing Groom (FR) **94** 131) [2006 54p: 9.9g² 12f² 9.7d* 10.5g* 10d Nov 4] big, long-backed filly: fairly useful performer: won maiden at Folkestone in August and handicap at Haydock in September: should stay 1½m: acts on good to soft going. *Sir Michael Stoute*

DAYS OF MY LIFE (IRE) 3 b.g. Daylami (IRE) 138 – Truly Yours (IRE) (Barathea **96** (IRE) 127) [2006 7s³ 7.1g³ 7m* 7s* 8.3g⁴ 8.5f* 8.3m* 8m⁶ Jun 30] €80,000Y: compact gelding: first foal: dam, French 2-y-o 1m winner, half-sister to Poule d'Essai des Poulains runner-up Catcher In The Rye out of smart French middle-distance performer Truly A Dream: useful performer: won maiden at Folkestone in April, and handicaps at Goodwood in May and Beverley (by 9 lengths) and Leicester (by 2 lengths with plenty to spare from Sharplaw Autumn) in June: will stay 9f: acts on soft and good to firm going: gelded after final outing: sent to Hong Kong, where renamed Young Hero. *R. Charlton*

DAY TO REMEMBER 5 gr.g. Daylami (IRE) 138 – Miss Universe (IRE) 99 (Warn- **100** ing 136) [2006 91: 10g 10g⁴ 10d* 12g³ 10m 9d 10s p12g Oct 21] small, quite attractive gelding: useful handicapper: won at Newmarket in May by 4 lengths from Folio: very good third to Telemachus at the Curragh next time: stays 1½m: acts on soft and good to firm going: reportedly had breathing problem on reappearance in 2005, tongue tied since: has worn crossed noseband: sold 42,000 gns, joined J. J. Quinn: won over hurdles in December. *E. F. Vaughan*

DAY WALKER 4 b.c. Dr Devious (IRE) 127 – Island Race 93 (Common Grounds 118) **102** [2006 114: 10m² 12g⁶ 11d² 11g 9d⁶ 12g³ 12d Sep 29] 35,000Y: third foal: half-brother to 6-y-o Soldier Hollow: dam 6f winner: smart performer at best: won listed race at Hamburg and Furstenberg-Rennen at Baden-Baden in 2005 when trained by A. Schutz: just useful form in 2006 (left M. Hofer in Germany after reappearance): 11 lengths third to Collier Hill in Stockholm Cup International at Taby before well beaten in listed race at Newmarket final start: effective at 1¼m to 1½m: acts on good to firm and good to soft going: tried blinkered. *R. Haugen, Norway*

DAZED AND AMAZED 2 b.c. (Feb 2) Averti (IRE) 117 – Amazed 58 (Clantime **96** 101) [2006 5g³ 5d* 5m⁵ 6m* 6m⁴ 5m⁵ 6f 6s 6m⁶ Sep 16] 52,000Y: compact, well-made colt: second foal: dam, sprint maiden, sister to smart sprinter Bishops Court and half-sister to smart sprinter Astonished: useful performer: won maiden at Newmarket in May and listed race at Newbury in June: ran well after when 3½ lengths fourth of 9 to Strategic Prince in July Stakes at Newmarket and 2¾ lengths fifth of 13 in Molecomb Stakes at Goodwood: well below par last 3 starts (tongue tied final one): will prove best kept to 5f/6f: acts on good to firm and good to soft going. *R. Hannon*

DAZZLER MAC 5 b.g. Komaite (USA) – Stilvella (Camden Town 125) [2006 57: **60** 5.9g 6g³ 6g⁶ 5f⁵ 6g* 8s² 6g⁵ Aug 24] sturdy gelding: modest performer: won apprentice maiden handicap at Thirsk in August: effective at 5f to 1m: acts on firm and soft going: consistent. *N. Bycroft*

DAZZLING BAY 6 b.g. Mind Games 121 – Adorable Cherub (USA) 58 (Halo (USA)) **97 §** [2006 92§: 6g* 6m⁶ 6f 6g 6g 5s Oct 14] big, rather leggy gelding: has a round action: useful handicapper: won at Ripon in May by length from Prince Tum Tum: well held last 4 starts: best at 5f/6f on good or firmer going: effective with/without blinkers: has been reluctant to post/slowly away: unreliable. *T. D. Easterby*

DAZZLING OLIVIA (IRE) 2 b.f. (Apr 9) Tagula (IRE) 116 – Make Hay (Nomina- **42** tion 125) [2006 5g 6m 6s⁵ f7g Nov 14] 6,000Y: strong, good-topped filly: half-sister to 5f winner Mount Park (by Colonel Collins) and winner in Japan by Kefaah: dam unraced: poor maiden. *R. A. Fahey*

DEADLINE (UAE) 2 ch.c. (Mar 7) Machiavellian (USA) 123 – Time Changes (USA) **79** (Danzig (USA)) [2006 6d⁶ 7.1m⁵ 6m² 6s Oct 6] workmanlike colt: third foal: dam use- ful French 1m winner: fair maiden: second to Odin Dawn at Pontefract: well beaten in nursery (testing ground): will stay 1m. *M. Johnston*

DEADSHOT KEEN (IRE) 2 b.g. (Mar 16) Invincible Spirit (IRE) 121 – Madam **84** Waajib (IRE) (Waajib 121) [2006 5g⁴ 5.1g* 6m 6m⁵ p7g³ 7d p7g² 8f⁴ Nov 24] €38,000Y: robust, useful-looking gelding: type to carry condition: third foal: half-brother to 5-y-o Play Master: dam lightly raced at 2 yrs: fairly useful performer: won maiden at Bath in May: good efforts last 2 starts, head second to Ekhtiaar in minor event at Lingfield and, having left B. Meehan, 4¼ lengths fifth (promoted to fourth) to Warning Zone in Grade 3

Generous Stakes (Div 1) at Hollywood: stays easy 1m: acts on polytrack and firm going: blinkered (well held in valuable sales race at the Curragh) sixth outing. *P. Eurton, USA*

DEAR GRACIE (IRE) 3 b.f. In The Wings 128 – Allegheny River (USA) (Lear Fan **80** (USA) 130) [2006 8.2m³ 8.3d² 7.5f² p10g* Aug 2] 42,000Y: half-sister to several winners, including very smart 6f winner (including at 2 yrs) Danetime and useful Irish performer up to 7f Dane River (both by Danehill): dam Irish 7f winner: fairly useful performer: won handicap at Kempton in August: stays 1¼m: acts on polytrack, firm and good to soft going. *J. R. Fanshawe*

DEAR ONE (IRE) 2 b.f. (Apr 28) Montjeu (IRE) 137 – Siamoise (Caerleon (USA) **54** 132) [2006 p5g⁵ p7.1g⁶ Dec 8] €30,000Y: tall, close-coupled filly: fourth foal: half-sister to useful French 7.5f and 1¼m winner Mount Eliza (by Danehill): dam French 1¼m winner: modest form in maidens at Kempton and Wolverhampton. *P. A. Blockley*

DEAR SIR (IRE) 6 ch.g. Among Men (USA) 124 – Deerussa (IRE) (Jareer (USA) 115) **51** [2006 16.4f⁴ 16.2f⁵ 14.1d Aug 12] modest maiden: probably stays 16.4f: acts on firm and good to soft ground. *Mrs P. N. Dutfield*

DEBBIE 7 b.m. Deploy 131 – Elita (Sharpo 132) [2006 53: p12.2g* p13.9g⁵ Mar 27] **55** close-coupled mare: modest performer: won banded race at Wolverhampton in February: stays 1½m: acts on all-weather, soft and good to firm going: tends to race freely. *B. D. Leavy*

DEBORD (FR) 3 ch.c. Sendawar (IRE) 129 – Partie de Dames (USA) (Bering 136) **70** [2006 p7g 8.5g 10.3f 8s⁴ 8.1g* 8m 9.9g p8g 8d Oct 27] €12,000 2-y-o: strong colt: half-brother to French 13f/13.5f winner Party Pro (by King's Theatre): dam unraced half-sister to smart French middle-distance performer Marchand de Sable: fair performer: won handicap at Sandown in June: well held after: should stay 1¼m: acts on soft going. *Jamie Poulton*

DEBS BROUGHTON 4 b.f. Prince Sabo 123 – Coy Debutante (IRE) 58 (Archway **–** (IRE) 115) [2006 47: p9.5g p8g Feb 6] leggy filly: maiden: well held in 2006: tried tongue tied. *W. J. Musson*

DEBUTANTE 3 b.f. Medicean 128 – Throw Away Line (USA) (Assert 134) [2006 8.3g **67** p10g⁶ Sep 30] 80,000Y: half-sister to several winners, including useful French 1½m winner Rebuff (by Kris): dam, minor winner at 4 yrs in USA, half-sister to champion US filly Go For Wand: better effort in maidens when sixth to Woolfall Blue at Kempton: sold 70,000 gns. *L. M. Cumani*

DECADO (IRE) 3 b.c. Danehill Dancer (IRE) 117 – Pirie (USA) (Green Dancer (USA) **113** 132) [2006 81: 7s* 7d* 7d* 8v³ 8m Jun 20] €110,000Y: quite attractive colt: fourth foal: half-brother to 5-y-o Another Faux Pas: dam unraced out of half-sister to dam of Irish Oaks winner Wemyss Bight: smart performer: won at the Curragh in listed race (by 4 lengths from Queen Cleopatra) in April and Rock of Gibraltar EBF Tetrarch Stakes (by 3½ lengths from Sir Xaar) in May: creditable 3 lengths third to Araafa in Irish 2000 Guineas there next time (held when slightly hampered inside final 1f), but well below form behind same rival in St James's Palace Stakes at Royal Ascot (firmer ground) final outing (reportedly coughing after): stays 1m: acts on heavy going. *K. Prendergast, Ireland*

DECCAN EXPRESS (IRE) 2 ch.c. (May 9) Grand Lodge (USA) 125 – Harda Arda **68** (USA) 66 (Nureyev (USA) 131) [2006 7.1m⁶ 7f 7.1m⁴ 8d³ 8s Oct 16] 75,000Y: rather leggy, quite attractive colt: fourth foal: half-brother to winners in USA by Smart Strike and A P Indy: dam, Irish 9f winner, half-sister to smart Irish/US middle-distance performer Phantom Breeze: fair maiden: made frame at Sandown and Newmarket (nursery): likely to stay 1¼m: acts on good to firm and good to soft going: sold 12,500 gns. *R. Hannon*

DECENT (IRE) 3 b.f. Desert Sun 120 – Guyum (Rousillon (USA) 133) [2006 –: 8.5f **–** f7g Nov 21] little form: tried blinkered. *W. J. H. Ratcliffe*

DECENT PROPOSAL 2 b.f. (Mar 13) Montjeu (IRE) 137 – Markova's Dance 64 **– p** (Mark of Esteem (IRE) 137) [2006 7f⁶ Jul 28] 68,000Y: second foal: dam, third at 6f from 3 starts (ran only at 2 yrs), half-sister to smart middle-distance stayers Azzilfi and Khamaseen: 3/1 favourite but needed experience in maiden at Thirsk: can do better. *T. D. Easterby*

DECHIPER (IRE) 4 b. or br.g. Almutawakel 126 – Safiya (USA) (Riverman (USA) **58** 131) [2006 f12g 6m⁴ 6g⁴ 8s² Sep 4] modest maiden: stays 1m: acts on soft going: in cheekpieces (carried head high, but ran creditably) penultimate outing. *R. Johnson*

DECIDER (USA) 3 ch.c. High Yield (USA) 121 – Nikita Moon (USA) (Secret Hello **68**
(USA)) [2006 5g⁵ 6m 6m 6.1f 6g 5.7m⁴ 6m⁵ p6g² f5g* p5g* Dec 20] $100,000Y, 6,500
2-y-o: rangy colt: third foal: half-brother to minor winners in USA by Awesome Again
and Golden Missile: dam ran twice in USA: fair form: improved at end of year, winning
maiden at Southwell in November and handicap at Kempton in December: should be best
kept to 5f/6f: acts on all-weather. *J. M. Bradley*

DECISION DAY 2 b.f. (Apr 12) Groom Dancer (USA) 128 – Indubitable 87 (Sharpo **–**
132) [2006 6d Nov 4] sister to 6-y-o Gold Ring and half-sister to 2 winners, notably
useful 1¼m winner Cugina (by Distant Relative): dam 1¼m winner: 50/1, mid-field in
maiden at Windsor. *J. A. Geake*

DECREE NISI 3 ch.g. Compton Place 125 – Palisandra (USA) (Chief's Crown (USA)) **70**
[2006 68: 9v⁵ 7.9m* 8m⁶ 9.3f⁶ 8m 7.5g² 7f Sep 18] sturdy gelding: fair performer: won
handicap at Carlisle in June: stays 1m: acts on good to firm going: visored last 2 starts.
Mrs A. Duffield

DEE BURGH 2 b.f. (Apr 30) Zaha (CAN) 106 – Glensara (Petoski 135) [2006 6g p6g⁶ **56**
6m Sep 13] 5,000Y: strong, close-coupled filly: fourth foal: half-sister to 3 winners,
including 3-y-o Hypocrisy and 7-y-o Chateau Nicol: dam unraced: modest form in
maidens: will be suited by 7f/1m. *J. Pearce*

DEE CEE ELLE 2 b.f. (Jan 17) Groom Dancer (USA) 128 – Missouri 86 (Charnwood **60 p**
Forest (IRE) 125) [2006 5.1m⁶ 6s 7.1f⁵ 8m⁵ 8s p9.5g* Nov 7] 13,000Y: big, good-topped
filly: first foal: dam, 15f winner, out of half-sister to very smart Hong Kong performer up
to 1½m Indigenous: modest form: won nursery at Wolverhampton in November: will be
suited by 1½m+: should progress further. *M. Johnston*

DEE JAY WELLS 2 b.g. (Mar 15) Ishiguru (USA) 114 – Stravaig (IRE) (Sadler's **72**
Wells (USA) 132) [2006 5g 5g² 6g⁵ 7f² 7m⁴ 5m² 5g 6m⁶ 7d Sep 29] 30,000F: well-made
gelding: third foal: dam unraced half-sister to smart performers up to around 1¼m Lord
of Men and Her Ladyship: fair maiden: runner-up at Sandown (2) and Brighton: effective
at 5f to 7f: acts on firm going: sold 15,000 gns, then gelded. *R. Hannon*

DEEP COVER (IRE) 2 ch.c. (Apr 21) Boundary (USA) 117 – Chibi (USA) (Dyna- **53**
former (USA)) [2006 7.6f p8g p10g⁶ Nov 29] modest maiden. *R. M. Flower*

DEEPER IN DEBT 8 ch.g. Piccolo 121 – Harold's Girl (FR) (Northfields (USA)) **77**
[2006 74, a83: p8.6g* p8.6g 8.1d 7m⁵ 8m⁴ 8.3m* 8.2f² 8.5g⁴ 9m 8m⁵ 8.2s p7g p7g p8g **a83**
p8g Dec 16] deep-girthed gelding: fairly useful handicapper on all-weather, fair on turf:
won at Wolverhampton (apprentices) in January and Windsor in July: stays 1¼m, races
mainly around 1m: acts on all-weather, firm and soft going: tried blinkered/tongue tied
earlier in career: ridden prominently. *J. Akehurst*

DEEP IMPACT (JPN) 4 b.c. Sunday Silence (USA) – Wind In Her Hair (IRE) **134**
114 (Alzao (USA) 117) [2006 128: 15g* 16f* 11d* 12m³ᵈ 12f* 12.5f* Dec 24]
    The 1999 Prix de l'Arc de Triomphe not only had an outstanding winner
in Montjeu, but an outstanding runner-up in El Condor Pasa, who posted the best
performance by a Japanese horse on the international stage when earning a rating
of 136 in failing only by half a length to last home after attempting to make all.
Until the latest season, the only challenger for the Arc from Japan in the interim had
been Tap Dance City who beat only two home in 2004 when trying to pull off the
same tactics. Although Tap Dance City was a Japan Cup winner, like El Condor
Pasa, his trainer had been under no illusions about how his horse compared with the
1999 runner-up. Asked in a television interview beforehand how he thought they
measured up, Tap Dance City's trainer didn't need a great command of English to
get the message across. He signified El Condor Pasa by standing on tiptoe and
reaching up as high as he could, while, to indicate Tap Dance City, he knelt down
on the grass and peered into an imaginary hole in the ground. He would probably
have needed to borrow a step-ladder to convey the standing in his home country of
Japan's latest Arc challenger Deep Impact.
    Deep Impact had been the almost unanimous choice as Japan's horse of the
year in 2005 after becoming only the sixth to complete the country's triple crown,
the first since 1994 and only the second horse to do so with an unbeaten record still
intact. Deep Impact won his first seven starts in all (including his only outing as a
two-year-old) and met with his first defeat on his final three-year-old appearance
when beaten half a length by that year's Japan Cup runner-up Heart's Cry in the
Arima Kinen, in which the winner got first run on him. Three more wins in Japan in

Takarazuka Kinen, Kyoto—Deep Impact books a trip for the Arc,
making light of the conditions to record his tenth win in eleven starts and his fifth Group 1 success

the first half of 2006 took Deep Impact's record to ten from eleven starts. He won the Group 2 Hanshin Daishoten over fifteen furlongs on his reappearance in March, the Group 1 Tenno Sho (Spring) over two miles at Kyoto in April, and the Group 1 Takarazuka Kinen over eleven furlongs at the same course in June. The last of those wins was gained by four lengths, the other two by three and a half. Those were the bare facts of Deep Impact's career so far. However, on top of a near faultless record, he had regularly impressed observers with the manner of his wins, typically gained by being waited with in rear, making his move around the field on the home turn, and then delivering a powerful finish wide in the straight.

With his popularity aided by the superstar status in Japan of his regular rider, Yutaka Take, Deep Impact started at odds on for all his races. In most of his races he was returned at 10/1-on on the Japanese equivalent of the tote, but even that was made to look generous when he completed the triple crown in Japan's St Leger, the Kikuka Sho. On that occasion, punters simply had their stake money returned with no dividend! Deep Impact's reputation for being something out of the ordinary was seemingly backed up by some scientific evidence. The Sport Science Division of the Japan Racing Association's Equine Research Institute undertook a study of Deep Impact's stride pattern in the final furlong of the Kikuka Sho using high-speed video. It was found that his 'overlap' time (the period in a horse's stride when more than one of his feet is in contact with the ground) was much shorter than average, while the length of his diagonal step (the distance between his off-fore and near-hind or near-fore and off-hind when those feet are in contact with the ground) was found to be longer than average. A similar study of the outstanding 1973 American triple crown winner Secretariat had apparently found similar characteristics in his stride pattern.

Judged strictly on form, Deep Impact was harder to pin down prior to the Arc. His string of wins made it easier, in a way, to tell 'how bad he wasn't' rather than how good he was, while he had never faced international competition. There were some encouraging lines of form though, not least those provided by the only horse to have beaten Deep Impact. Heart's Cry had won the world's new joint-richest turf race, the Dubai Sheema Classic in March, by more than four lengths from a field which included accomplished international performers Collier Hill, Ouija Board and Alexander Goldrun. Heart's Cry had then finished a length behind Hurricane Run when third in the King George VI and Queen Elizabeth Stakes at Ascot. Also, in the Tenno Sho in April, Deep Impact was chased home by Lincoln, beaten less than two lengths the previous autumn into fourth behind Alkaased and Heart's Cry in the Japan Cup.

Deep Impact's preparation for the Arc was very different from the path chosen by El Condor Pasa's connections seven years earlier. El Condor Pasa had an entirely French campaign leading to his Arc challenge, finishing second in the Prix d'Ispahan in May before winning the Grand Prix de Saint-Cloud in July and the traditional Arc trial for older horses, the Prix Foy, at Longchamp in September. Deep Impact, on the other hand, arrived in France in August, lodging with Carlos Laffon-Parias at Chantilly. With his trainer, Yasuo Ikee, preferring to go straight to the Arc without a preparatory run, there was considerable interest in Deep Impact's first public appearance at Longchamp, when, three days after the Arc trials had taken place, Deep Impact galloped over the full Arc course in company with his lead horse, Picaresque Coat. All preparations were said to have gone well, and after one of his final pieces of work, Deep Impact's trainer reported 'We don't need to sharpen this great sword any more. I just put it back in the sheath and wait for the raceday so that he will be able to run the race of his life.'

Yutaka Take had won fifteen jockeys' titles in Japan and in 2005 rode more than two hundred winners for the third consecutive year—he was champion again in 2006 with 178 winners. Take also partnered Japan's very first winner in Europe, Seeking The Pearl, in the 1998 Prix Maurice de Gheest, and he rode regularly in France in both 2001 and 2002. But, for all that, it's fair to say that Take enjoys a less exalted reputation in Britain, though that is essentially the result of one ride, when he received bad press for his handling of the leading British contender in the 1994 Arc, White Muzzle. Apparently going against instructions to have his mount handily placed, Take brought White Muzzle with a strong late run from the rear which resulted in a never-nearer sixth. Take's only ride in the Arc since then, third on Sagacity in 2001, had brought no adverse comment. Take's popularity with Japanese fans was a factor in what the French media called 'Impact mania' which hit Longchamp on Arc day. Two thousand Japanese racegoers had swelled the crowd when El Condor Pasa contested the Arc, but the Japanese contingent was

Japan Cup, Tokyo—back on home soil, Deep Impact comes from last to first; Dream Passport is second ahead of Ouija Board

reckoned to be about three times as large this time, the Arc day crowd of 60,400 (boosted by the usual influx of British visitors) reported to be the largest attendance at Longchamp for some time. That figure looks less impressive when compared to the 137,601 racegoers who had packed into Kyoto to see Deep Impact complete the triple crown, more than ten thousand of whom had slept outside the track overnight to guarantee entry! Many of Deep Impact's fans made their presence felt with flags and banners, some of them dressed in his owner's colours of black, blue and yellow, while near-hysteria broke out every time the horse, his rider or his trainer were shown on the screens around the course during the preliminaries. The French authorities had anticipated the influx of Japanese supporters to some extent, providing a help desk and dedicated betting windows, but these were soon overwhelmed. In addition to those who had made the trip to Longchamp, sixteen per cent of the Japanese population was reported to have watched the Arc on television despite the race taking place in the early hours in Japan.

'Impact mania' really made its presence felt on the pari-mutuel. British bookmakers had struggled to find a clear favourite for the Arc, with Deep Impact vying for the position with the two main Andre Fabre-trained contenders Hurricane Run and Shirocco. The nature of pool betting meant there was no such indecision on the pari-mutuel. On Arc day, a total of €4.8 million was bet at the meeting as a whole on course (representing a fifty-five per cent increase on the turnover the year before), but bets on Deep Impact accounted for around a third of that total. The weight of money for Deep Impact was described in the British media as a 'gamble', though perhaps 'unanimous support' would have been a more accurate description of what took place; it was certainly not a gamble of the old-fashioned variety, as British punters would understand it. For a while, it looked as though Deep Impact might start at his usual Japanese odds of 10/1-on. There was incredulity from the British bookmakers' representatives at Longchamp that Deep Impact's supporters should be queuing up to back him at such odds, but they were missing the point. Many of the bets were token ones at the minimum stake, the pari-mutuel tickets to be kept as souvenirs rather than cashed in. In the end, Deep Impact was sent off at 2/1-on (compared to the British industry odds of 9/4), resulting in his rivals going off at much longer odds on the pari-mutuel than with the bookmakers in Britain, most notably Rail Link, an 8/1 chance on industry returns who paid nearly 24/1 on the pari-mutuel.

Deep Impact looked well beforehand, without striking our representatives as being out of the ordinary in appearance, being a rather leggy colt who showed a round action on the way to post. With the ground firmer than the official good, conditions were not far removed from those Deep Impact was used to in Japan, the good run from his travelling companion Picaresque Coat to finish second in the Prix Daniel Wildenstein the day before looking another positive sign. The small field of eight also meant that Deep Impact would be less likely to encounter trouble in running if set, as usual, to make ground from the rear. That was assuming that his customary tactics were to be adopted, though it soon became clear that he was going to race more handily than usual. Take guided Deep Impact off the rail before the turn out of the back straight after he had started to race a little freely behind the pace, but he settled again round the turn behind the leaders Irish Wells and Shirocco. Deep Impact looked to be travelling well when ranging upsides that pair on entering the home straight but, when shaken up, Deep Impact was able only to edge ahead and was soon challenged by Rail Link who got the better of him inside the final furlong, Pride also passing Deep Impact in the closing stages and relegating him to third, beaten a neck and half a length.

It appeared that Deep Impact might have needed the outing after all, the sword maybe not so sharp as his trainer had claimed. That would have been an easier conclusion to reach if Deep Impact's connections had not departed from their usual manner of racing. That's not to criticise Take, who would doubtless have been shown little mercy if Deep Impact had been beaten after being held up well in rear in a race that by Arc standards was not strongly run. Take would certainly have been taken to task if he had met with the sort of trouble in running that Kieren Fallon experienced on Hurricane Run, who finished a place behind him. From a Japanese point of view, anything less than a win was going to be an intense disappointment, but, more objectively, there were good elements to take from Deep

Impact's performance. He fared best of the three who dominated the betting and, while not on a par with the form shown in the Arc by El Condor Pasa, Deep Impact still put up a top-class effort in going down narrowly to a highly progressive three-year-old colt and a high-class mare.

What initially looked an honourable defeat soon became academic when, three weeks later, it was announced that Deep Impact's post-race sample had tested positive for a prohibited substance, Ipratropium. His disqualification was made official in November. How much worse it would have been if he had actually passed the post first. It turned out that during his stay in France, Deep Impact had been treated with a nasal spray to address a breathing problem. It was claimed that the correct guidelines had been followed in using the spray (halting its use before the recommended deadline beyond which there was a risk of a positive result). What might have happened was that Deep Impact's box had become contaminated when he was given the treatment, and he ingested some of the substance at a later date. Deep Impact's trainer bore the financial consequences, being fined €15,000, but there was no suggestion of foul play or any deliberate wrong-doing, though the incident caused embarrassment for Japanese racing. It was the first instance of a horse testing positive in the Arc, but the Arc was the second major international race of the year to be affected after a similar incident in the Dubai World Cup, from which the American gelding Brass Hat was disqualified from second. There was an incident too before the Hong Kong Sprint when likely favourite Takeover Target was withdrawn after testing positive for a banned substance in pre-race checks. The winner of France's most important trotting race, the Prix d'Amerique, was disqualified after failing a drugs test early in the year.

Deep Impact soon had the opportunity to redeem his reputation in front of his home fans in the Japan Cup. The twenty-sixth running of Japan's top international race drew an unusually small field of eleven (none of the previous Japan Cups had had fewer than fourteen runners) and the foreign challenge was particularly light, consisting only of Ouija Board and the Prix de Pomone winner Freedonia. Deep Impact was sent off the 10/3-on favourite, with Heart's Cry (having his first start since Ascot) and Ouija Board next in the betting. Deep

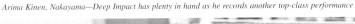

Arima Kinen, Nakayama—Deep Impact has plenty in hand as he records another top-class performance

Impact's customary tactics were re-employed, waiting in last place with Ouija Board just ahead of him. Reaching the home turn, Take asked Deep Impact to improve and he began his move smoothly around the outside of the field, boxing in Ouija Board as he made ground early in the straight and then staying on well down the outside to lead in the final furlong, beating the three-year-old Dream Passport, who had been placed in all three legs of the triple crown, by two lengths. While Ouija Board stayed on well for third, another half a length behind, she was a little below her best and Heart's Cry clearly failed to give his running in beating only one home. Before his retirement to stud, Deep Impact had one more point to prove and atone for his defeat in the Arima Kinen the year before. He did so in convincing fashion at Nakayama on Christmas Eve with what probably amounted to a career-best effort, eased down to beat the Melbourne Cup runner-up Pop Rock by three lengths, with Dream Passport fourth this time, Heart's Cry having been retired after the Japan Cup.

Between the Arc and the Japan Cup, Deep Impact's retirement to stud was announced. He will stand at the Shadai Stallion Station, syndicated for 5.1 billion yen (around £22.5 million), about twice the amount of El Condor Pasa's syndication. Deep Impact had been sold for seventy million yen (just over £300,000) as a foal, his sale coming only a year after the death of his sire Sunday Silence, who dominated the Japanese breeding industry to such an extent that Deep Impact was among an estimated thirty per cent of the Japanese foals of 2002 who had Sunday Silence in their pedigree. Deep Impact was Sunday Silence's sixth Japanese Derby winner and his third winner of the Japan Cup, after Special Week in 1999 (also winner of the Derby the year before) and Zenno Rob Roy in 2004. Heart's Cry will be another of his sons at stud in 2007.

Deep Impact may have been bred in Japan but the female side of his family could not be any more British, stemming as it does from the Royal Studs. His great grandam Highclere won the One Thousand Guineas and Prix de Diane and finished second in the King George VI and Queen Elizabeth Stakes. She bred seven more winners for the Queen, notably Milford and Height of Fashion who were both successful in the Princess of Wales's Stakes. Height of Fashion made even more of a name for herself as a broodmare, though by then she had been sold privately to Hamdan Al Maktoum for whom she produced, among others, Nashwan, Unfuwain and Nayef. Burghclere was another of Highclere's winners (by Busted, sire of Height of Fashion's sire Bustino) but her only success came in a maiden at Sandown over a mile and three quarters. She too was sold before her stud career got under way, and while not so serious a loss to the Royal Studs as Height of Fashion, Burghclere, the grandam of Deep Impact, has now belatedly proved a loss of sorts nonetheless. Unlike Height of Fashion, Burghclere was disposed of at public auction and, as a four-year-old in foal to Final Straw, was sold at the December Sales in 1981 (Height of Fashion an unbeaten two-year-old at the time) for 460,000 guineas. That was short of the new record for a broodmare that had been set earlier in the same session, but Burghclere's price was more than twice the previous record for a broodmare at the December Sales, set just the day before.

			Halo	Hail To Reason
		Sunday Silence (USA) (b or br 1986)	Halo (b or br 1969)	Hail To Reason / Cosmah
Deep Impact (JPN) (b.c. 2002)			Wishing Well (b 1975)	Understanding / Mountain Flower
		Wind In Her Hair (IRE) (b 1991)	Alzao (b 1980)	Lyphard / Lady Rebecca
			Burghclere (b 1977)	Busted / Highclere

The foal Burghclere was carrying turned out to be the smart filly Capo di Monte whose wins included the Pretty Polly Stakes at Newmarket, and she was beaten only a short head in the Sun Chariot Stakes. Burghclere's next foal, Kingsmill, showed high-class form over hurdles when winning the Irish Champion Hurdle but his career was cut short by a fatal fall at Aintree on his next start. Wind In Her Hair proved the most notable of Burghclere's winners. She too won the Pretty Polly Stakes, and, while not quite so good as Capo di Monte (rated 4 lb lower than that filly's 118), she could boast a more impressive race record, which included a second place to Balanchine in the Oaks and a Group 1 win at four in the Aral-

Pokal in Germany. Wind In Her Hair therefore maintained the family's excellent record over middle distances but, surprisingly, Deep Impact is the only one of her five winners to have shown anything in the way of stamina. Deep Impact's elder brother Black Tide gained his biggest win in a Group 2 event over nine furlongs in Japan, while his year-younger brother On Fire (unraced at three) won at the same trip there as a two-year old. Deep Impact's two-year-old half-brother New Beginning (by Agnes Tachyon) has made a good start, winning both his races, including a listed event on the same card as the Arima Kinen. Wind In Her Hair's other winners are the fillies Veil of Avalon (by Thunder Gulch), a useful six- and seven-furlong winner in Britain who later won a Grade 3 event over eight and a half furlongs in the States, and the Japanese six-furlong winner Lady Blond (by Seeking The Gold). Another of Wind In Her Hair's daughters, Glint In Her Eye (a fair maiden by Arazi), is the dam of the latest Jersey Stakes winner Jeremy. Hopefully, Deep Impact will enjoy a longer innings at stud than El Condor Pasa. The 1999 Arc runner-up fell victim to colic aged only seven in 2002, just a month before Sunday Silence's death, and before his first foals had reached the track. *Y. Ikee, Japan*

DEEP PURPLE 5 b.g. Halling (USA) 133 – Seal Indigo (IRE) 93 (Glenstal (USA) 118) [2006 89: 10m 11g Sep 15] tall, leggy gelding: fairly useful performer at 3 yrs: lightly raced since, and well held in 2006: visored final outing. *A. M. Balding* —

DEEP SLEEP 3 b.g. Tipsy Creek (USA) 115 – Tiempo 50 (King of Spain 121) [2006 70: 6g⁵ 8.2s 7g Jun 1] sturdy gelding: maiden handicapper: well held after reappearance: should stay 7f (pulled hard at 1m): sold 1,700 gns in October. *M. H. Tompkins* **60**

DEEPWATER BAY (USA) 3 b.c. Chester House (USA) 123 – Gem Treck (USA) (Java Gold (USA)) [2006 84: p7g* 8s² 10m a8.3s 7m* Dec 2] rather leggy colt: useful performer: won maiden at Kempton in April: good efforts in listed races next 2 starts, at Goodwood (2½ lengths second to Final Verse) and Royal Ascot (4¼ lengths eighth to Snoqualmie Boy): left A. Balding after, and renamed Survey Survey: won handicap at Sha Tin in December: effective at 7f, barely at 1¼m: acts on polytrack, soft and good to firm going. *A. S. Cruz, Hong Kong* **100**

DEER PARK COUNTESS 5 ch.m. Shaddad (USA) 75 – Logani (Domynsky 110) [2006 8.3m 6m 6d Sep 25] first foal: dam no sign of ability over hurdles: no form: tried tongue tied. *D. A. Nolan* —

DEE VALLEY BOY (IRE) 2 b.g. (Apr 17) Val Royal (FR) 127 – Canadian Girl (IRE) 82 (Rainbows Fire (CAN)) [2006 5.9g 7m 8.5g Aug 27] modest form in maidens only on second start: gelded after final outing. *J. D. Bethell* **53**

DEFI (IRE) 4 b.g. Rainbow Quest (USA) 134 – Danse Classique (IRE) 94 (Night Shift (USA)) [2006 90d: p7.1g³ p7.1g p8.6g⁴ 8m³ 8.3f 8.3m⁴ 8m 5.9m⁵ 8.3g* 8.3m* 7.1m 8g p8.6g 8.5f p8.6g⁴ p8.6g Dec 21] good-bodied gelding: fairly useful performer: won handicap in July and claimer in August, both at Hamilton: stays 8.6f: acts on polytrack and firm going: wears cheekpieces/blinkers: tried tongue tied. *I. Semple* **81**

DEFINITE (IRE) 8 b.g. Definite Article 121 – My Gossip (IRE) 68 (Camden Town 125) [2006 –: 12g 11v² 12m³ 12g⁵ 10d 14s p13.9g³ Nov 20] modest maiden: stays 1¾m: acts on polytrack, heavy and good to firm going. *T. G. McCourt, Ireland* **55**

DEFINITELY BLUE 3 b.f. Definite Article 121 – Atmospheric Blues (IRE) 91 (Double Schwartz 128) [2006 9.9g 8.2g Sep 26] sturdy filly: half-sister to 3 winners, including 4-y-o Shaheer: dam, 2-y-o 5f winner, later won in Italy: well beaten in maidens. *C. F. Wall* —

DEGAS ART (IRE) 3 b.g. Danehill Dancer (IRE) 117 – Answer (Warning 136) [2006 88: 10g² 12f* 10s² 12m⁴ 13m³ 10m⁴ 12d* Sep 29] good-topped gelding: has a choppy action: smart performer: much improved in 2006, winning maiden at Salisbury in May and listed event at Newmarket (beat Into The Dark 1¾ lengths) in September, making most each time: also good efforts in frame in listed race at Newmarket (4 lengths second to Red Rocks) and King Edward VII Stakes at Royal Ascot (4¾ lengths fourth behind Papal Bull) third/fourth starts: stays 1½m: acts on firm and soft going: hung right on reappearance: carries head awkwardly: joined J. Howard Johnson, fairly useful form when winning both starts over hurdles. *D. R. C. Elsworth* **112**

DEIRA (USA) 3 b.f. Green Desert (USA) 127 – New Sayyedati (USA) (Shadeed (USA) 135) [2006 64: 10g⁴ 7s 8m⁵ 7m⁵ 8f 7d⁶ p7g Nov 13] compact filly: fair handicapper: won at Wolverhampton in May and Leicester in July: barely stays 1m: acts on polytrack, good to firm and good to soft going. *C. E. Brittain* **79**

DEIRDRE'S DILEMMA (IRE) 4 b.f. Primo Dominie 121 – Sartigila 67 (Efisio – 120) [2006 –: 7m p7g Dec 4] no form. *G. C. Bravery*

DEJEEJE (IRE) 5 ch.g. Grand Lodge (USA) 125 – Christan (IRE) (Al Hareb (USA) – 123) [2006 37: f16g f12g f11g 16g May 22] maiden: no form in 2006: tried in cheekpieces. *D. W. Chapman*

DELAMEAD (IRE) 3 b.g. King of Kings (IRE) 125 – Al Saqiya (USA) 68 (Woodman – (USA) 126) [2006 8d 8.5f 9m May 5] behind in maidens. *B. Ellison*

DELAPORTE 2 ch.f. (Feb 11) Fantastic Light (USA) 134 – Poppadam 87 (Salse (USA) – 128) [2006 6.1m 6g p6g⁴ p8.6g Nov 23] sturdy filly: third foal: sister to winner in USA: dam, 1m winner, half-sister to Irish 1000 Guineas winner Classic Park, herself dam of Derby second Walk In The Park: well beaten in maidens, visored/tongue tied last 2 starts. *M. A. Buckley*

DE LA RUE (USA) 3 b.c. Louis Quatorze (USA) 125 – Primevere (USA) 91 (Irish **84** River (FR) 131) [2006 58p: p9.5g* p10g³ 10d 8m⁶ Sep 12] close-coupled colt: fairly useful performer: won maiden at Wolverhampton in January: stays easy 1¼m: acts on polytrack: raced freely last 3 outings: sold 18,000 gns. *M. G. Quinlan*

DELFINIA 5 b.m. Kingsinger (IRE) 94 – Delvecchia (Glint of Gold 128) [2006 10f Sep – 20] no form. *Miss Tracy Waggott*

DELIGHTFULLY 5 b.m. Definite Article 121 – Kingpin Delight (Emarati (USA) 74) – [2006 54: p12g p12g Dec 6] modest performer: well held both starts in 2006: wears blinkers/cheekpieces nowadays. *Jean-Rene Auvray*

DELLAGIO (IRE) 5 b.h. Fasliyev (USA) 120 – Lady Ounavarra (IRE) (Simply Great **56** (FR) 122) [2006 67: p5.1g⁴ Jul 20] smallish, good-bodied horse: fair performer in 2005: modest form only outing in 2006: effective at 5f/6f: acts on all-weather and firm going: tried in cheekpieces. *R. W. Price*

DELLA SALUTE 4 gr.f. Dansili 127 – Marie Dora (FR) 86 (Kendor (FR) 122) [2006 **82** 83: 8d 8.1m⁶ 7m 8.3f 10m* 10f 10m⁴ 10f² 9g⁵ p10g 11g Sep 15] rather leggy filly: fairly useful handicapper: won at Windsor in July: effective at 1m/1¼m: acts on firm and good to soft going: quirky, and sometimes finds little: sold 12,000 gns. *Miss E. C. Lavelle*

DEL MAR SUNSET 7 b.g. Unfuwain (USA) 131 – City of Angels (Woodman (USA) **82** 126) [2006 86: 10g⁵ 10g⁵ 10d² p12g p9.5g p9.5m² Nov 9] tall, rather leggy gelding: fairly **a88** useful handicapper: stays 1¼m: acts on all-weather and firm going: blinkered (well held) once: has won in cheekpieces: usually held up nowadays. *W. J. Haggas*

DELORAIN (IRE) 3 b.g. Kalanisi (IRE) 132 – Lady Nasrana (FR) (Al Nasr (FR) 126) **54** [2006 –: 10g 10m 11.5m⁴ 12f 12m 14.1d³ 16g³ Sep 14] unfurnished gelding: modest maiden: stays 2m: acts on good to firm and good to soft ground: visored last 5 starts: gelded after. *J. A. R. Toller*

DELTA BLUES (JPN) 5 b.h. Dance In The Dark (JPN) – Dixie Splash (USA) **125** (Dixieland Band (USA)) [2006 117: 11f⁵ 15g³ 16f 12g³ 16g* 12.5f⁶ Dec 24] half-brother to winners in USA and Japan (2): dam, 6f to 8.5f winner in USA, half-sister to useful German stayer Ocean Sea: high-class performer: won Kikuka Sho (Japanese St Leger) in 2004: ran only 3 times at 4 yrs, winning Group 2 event at Nakayama: below form on first 3 starts in 2006, then off course nearly 6 months: good close third to Tawqeet in Caulfield Cup (Handicap) at Caulfield in October before becoming first Japanese-trained winner of a Group 1 in Australia when winning Emirates Melbourne Cup (Handicap) at Flemington in November by short head from stable-companion Pop Rock, leading 2f out and just holding on: fair sixth to Deep Impact in Arima Kinen at Nakayama final outing: stays 2¼m: acts on firm going. *K. Sumii, Japan*

DELTA FORCE 7 b.g. High Kicker (USA) – Maedaley 45 (Charmer 123) [2006 f16g **50** p12g p16.5g 14m 16.2g⁴ 12.1d⁴ 15m⁴ Jun 24] modest performer: missed 2005 reportedly because of a leg injury: effective at 11f to 17f: acts on fibresand and firm ground: tried in cheekpieces: races freely. *P. A. Blockley*

DELTA QUEEN 2 b.f. (Mar 16) Montjoy (USA) 122 – Full of Passion (USA) (Blush- – ing Groom (FR) 131) [2006 5.1m 5d⁵ 5.1g 6m 7s p6g 5.1d Oct 18] close-coupled filly: fifth foal: half-sister to French winners around 11f Majed (by Fijar Tango) and Madmoud (by Siberian Express): dam French maiden: little form. *C. N. Kellett*

DELTA SHUTTLE (IRE) 2 b.c. (Feb 10) Bluebird (USA) 125 – Ibtihal (IRE) 75 **68** (Hamas (IRE) 125§) [2006 6d 7g³ 6s Oct 24] €2,500F, €6,500Y: strong, good-bodied colt: first foal: dam, Irish maiden who stayed 1½m, out of half-sister to high-class middle-distance performer Ibn Bey and Yorkshire Oaks winner Roseate Tern: fair maiden: third of 16 at Newcastle in September: will be suited by 1m+. *K. R. Burke*

DEMATRAF (IRE) 4 gr.f. Atraf 116 – Demolition Jo 89 (Petong 126) [2006 63: p6g **50** p6g p7.1g p7.1g f6g 6m² 6m⁶ Aug 16] compact filly: modest performer: stays 6f: acts on all-weather and good to firm ground. *Ms Deborah J. Evans*

DEMI SEC 3 ch.f. Bahamian Bounty 116 – Veuve (Tirol 127) [2006 p7g Jun 15] 8,000 – 2-y-o: seventh foal: half-sister to 3 winners, including fairly useful 1¾m winner Destination (by Deploy): dam unraced half-sister to smart miler Fizzed: well held in maiden at Lingfield. *Dr J. D. Scargill*

DEMOCRATIC DEFICIT (IRE) 4 b.c. Soviet Star (USA) 128 – Grandiose Idea **114 §** (IRE) 89 (Danehill (USA) 126) [2006 116: 8.9m 7.5m 8m³ 8.1m⁴ 8d 8m Jun 7] strong, good-bodied colt: smart performer on his day: creditable efforts in 2006 when 1¼ lengths third to Mustameet in listed race at Leopardstown and 2¼ lengths fourth to Rob Roy in Mile at Sandown: below form in listed events at Leopardstown last 2 outings: stays 9f: acts on firm and good to soft ground: best recent efforts when tongue tied: sometimes wanders: inconsistent: sold 88,000 gns in December. *J. S. Bolger, Ireland*

DEMOLITION 2 ch.g. (Feb 21) Starborough 126 – Movie Star (IRE) (Barathea (IRE) – 127) [2006 p7g Nov 11] 50/1, tailed off in maiden at Kempton: subsequently gelded. *C. A. Cyzer*

DEMON DOCKER (IRE) 3 ch.c. Docksider (USA) 124 – Green Moon (FR) (Shirley **97** Heights 130) [2006 85p: p8g⁴ 8m⁵ 8g³ 8.3g* 8.1m Sep 8] useful handicapper: won at Leicester in August by 1¼ lengths from Shumookh: not discredited at Sandown final start: will stay 1¼m: acts on polytrack, best effort on turf on good going: sold 32,000 gns, sent to UAE. *P. W. Chapple-Hyam*

DENBERA DANCER (USA) 2 b.c. (Feb 22) Danehill (USA) 126 – Monevassia **60 p** (USA) (Mr Prospector (USA)) [2006 6m⁵ Aug 9] $170,000Y: close-coupled colt: fifth foal: brother to 3-y-o Rumplestiltskin: dam, twice in France, sister to Kingmambo and Miesque's Son and half-sister to East of The Moon, out of Miesque: 6/1, fifth of 15 to Ebn Reem in maiden at Pontefract: likely to improve. *M. Johnston*

DENEUVE 4 b.f. Tomba 119 – Princess Sadie 86 (Shavian 125) [2006 –: 6d 6g 6f⁵ 6f **54** 5s² 6v⁵ 5v f6g f6g Dec 28] half-sister to 8-y-o Attorney: dam 2-y-o 5f winner: modest maiden: left P. Flynn in Ireland, well held in banded events at Southwell both starts in Britain: best at 5f: acts on soft ground, probably on firm: tried in cheekpieces/tongue tie. *M. G. Quinlan*

DENNICK 4 b.g. Nicolotte 118 – Branston Dancer (Rudimentary (USA) 118) [2006 55: **60** p8g³ Jan 11] modest maiden: should stay 1¼m: acts on polytrack and good to firm ground: tongue tied only start in 2006 (ran well): free-going sort: sold 8,000 gns in May. *P. C. Haslam*

DEN'S GIFT (IRE) 2 gr. or ro.g. (May 2) City On A Hill (USA) 114 – Romanylei **74** (IRE) 106 (Blues Traveller (IRE) 119) [2006 6m³ 6d 6g⁴ Oct 16] €27,000F, 34,000Y: sturdy gelding: second foal: dam 6f winner (including at 2 yrs): fair maiden: in frame at Goodwood and Windsor, and twelfth of 28 to Caldra in valuable sales race at Newmarket in between: likely to stay 7f: gelded after final start. *C. G. Cox*

DENTON HAWK 2 b.g. (Apr 16) Mujahid (USA) 125 – Lamasat (USA) (Silver Hawk **58** (USA) 123) [2006 5g⁶ 7m 5f³ 6f³ 5m⁵ 7s⁵ 7.1m⁴ 7m⁴ Sep 5] workmanlike gelding: modest maiden: stays 7f: acts on firm and soft going: tried in cheekpieces. *M. Dods*

DEPRAUX (IRE) 3 br.g. Generous (IRE) 139 – Happy Memories (IRE) (Thatching **70** 131) [2006 p8g⁶ 8.3g³ p9.5g⁴ p12g² f11g³ Dec 9] 28,000Y: third foal: half-brother to fairly useful 6f/7f winner Instant Recall (by Indian Ridge): dam unraced half-sister to smart Irish 1¼m/1½m performer Topanoora: fair maiden: stays 1½m: acts on polytrack: claimed £8,000 after final outing, joined D. McCain Jnr. *W. J. Haggas*

DEPRESSED 4 ch.f. Most Welcome 131 – Sure Care 62 (Caerleon (USA) 132) [2006 **71** 80: p6g p6g⁵ p6g p7g p6g³ 6f 10m⁴ 9.7f⁵ Jul 13] quite good-topped filly: fair handicapper: stays 1¼m: acts on polytrack and good to firm going: tried blinkered/tongue tied, in cheekpieces nowadays: none too consistent. *E. R. Oertel*

DESCARGO 2 ch.f. (May 14) Delta Dancer – Secret Miss 55 (Beveled (USA)) [2006 **49** p6g Nov 24] fifth foal: half-sister to 8-y-o Molly's Secret and 2004 2-y-o 5f winner Smokincanon (by Fumo di Londra): dam 5f winner: 16/1, 8 lengths seventh of 9 to Bussel in maiden at Kempton, taking strong hold after slow start: bred to be suited by 7f+. *C. G. Cox*

DESCARTES 4 b.c. Dubai Millennium 140 – Gold's Dance (FR) (Goldneyev (USA) **98**
114) [2006 p12g* p12g* Oct 21] tall colt: useful maiden: off nearly 2 years, won handicap at
Lingfield in October by length from Transvestite: ran as if amiss in similar event there
later in month: stays 1½m: raced only on polytrack and heavy going. *Saeed bin Suroor*

DESERT AUTHORITY (USA) 3 b. or br.c. War Chant (USA) 126 – Tuzla (FR) **117 p**
121 (Panoramic 120) [2006 8.1m* 10m* Sep 7]
    'Good things come to those who wait'. The Godolphin team may not be the
biggest fans of all things Irish, but the policy with many of their horses could well
have been adopted from the famous Guinness marketing slogan. Godolphin ended
the latest season with a host of lightly-raced types who look capable of going on to
better things, few more so than twice-raced Desert Authority. Not forward enough
to be targeted at the classics, Desert Authority looks like making up for lost time as
a four-year-old. He made up into a smart performer, winning on both his racecourse
appearances, and has more improvement in him.
    Sent off joint favourite for a maiden at Sandown in late-July, a race rendered
weaker with the other joint favourite well beaten, reportedly suffering an irregular
heartbeat, Desert Authority travelled easily under Frankie Dettori as he led over
two furlongs out and beat Mulaazem by a length and a half, value for a winning
margin of around four. The form was boosted when Mulaazem went on to win a
similar event at Haydock next time. Stepped up to a mile and a quarter in a six-
runner minor event at Southwell six weeks later, Desert Authority was seemingly
second choice among Godolphin's three runners, Dettori opting to ride Into The
Dark. Desert Authority's inexperience was still in evidence as he tended to wander
when coming under pressure, but he knuckled down well to overhaul his other
stable-companion Blue Ksar well inside the final furlong, having half a length to
spare at the line, with Into The Dark back in fifth. Desert Authority wasn't raced
again in the latest season, but Blue Ksar went on to win his next two starts, the
second of them a listed event at Newmarket. Third-placed Take A Bow ran another
four times, finishing fourth in three listed races and in the Cambridgeshire.

			Danzig		Northern Dancer
	War Chant (USA)		(b 1977)		Pas de Nom
	(b 1997)		Hollywood Wildcat		Kris S
Desert Authority (USA)			(b 1990)		Miss Wildcatter
(b. or br.c. 2003)			Panoramic		Rainbow Quest
	Tuzla (FR)		(b 1987)		Immense
	(b 1994)		Turkeina		Kautokeino
			(b 1982)		Turquoise Bleue

    Desert Authority is the second foal of his dam and is a half-brother to the
mile-and-a-quarter maiden winner Mambo Princess (by Kingmambo), who later
showed fairly useful form in the States, winning over a mile and a half at Keeneland
in 2005. Tuzla's two-year-old, Tybalt (by Storm Cat), won a seven-furlong maiden
at Lingfield in October. Tuzla was originally trained in France, but had a fine record
in North America where she won the Grade 1 Ramona Handicap at Del Mar over
nine furlongs, before finishing runner-up in the 1999 Breeders' Cup Mile at Gulfstream Park. Desert Authority's sire War Chant went one better in that race at
Churchill Downs the following season. He has done well with the relatively few
runners he has had in Britain, with the John Gosden-trained duo Karen's Caper
(subsequently a Grade 3 winner in the States) and very promising two-year-old
Asperity among the most noteworthy. Desert Authority raced on good to firm going
on both outings and seems likely to stay beyond a mile and a quarter. *Saeed bin
Suroor*

DESERT BOUNTY 3 b.f. Bahamian Bounty 116 – Aldevonie 75 (Green Desert (USA) **–**
127) [2006 54: 6m May 4] good-topped filly: has a quick, unimpressive action: modest
maiden at 2 yrs: last on only outing in 2006. *G. M. Moore*

DESERT CHIEF 4 b.c. Green Desert (USA) 127 – Oriental Fashion (IRE) 110 (Marju **93**
(IRE) 127) [2006 98p: 7g Oct 13] smallish, good-bodied colt: fluent mover: useful performer, winner of both his starts in 2005: respectable eighth in handicap at Newmarket only
outing in 2006: not sure to stay beyond 1m: yet to race on extremes of going. *Saeed bin
Suroor*

DESERT COMMANDER (IRE) 4 b.g. Green Desert (USA) 127 – Meadow Pipit **101** (CAN) 113 (Meadowlake (USA)) [2006 5d* 5s 6m* 6m 6s 6d 6d Sep 16] robust gelding, type to carry condition: useful performer: trained by Saeed bin Suroor at 2 yrs: off over 20 months and gelded, won handicaps at Thirsk (by 3 lengths from Countdown) in April and Ripon (by 2½ lengths from Zidane) in June: well below form after: effective at 5f/6f: acts on good to firm and good to soft going: tongue tied once at 2 yrs. *K. A. Ryan*

DESERT CRISTAL (IRE) 5 ch.m. Desert King (IRE) 129 – Damiana (IRE) (Thatch- **89** ing 131) [2006 89: 8d⁵ p10g² 10d⁵ p12g⁵ 9.9m p12g⁶ 10s Oct 10] sparely-made mare: fairly useful performer: stays easy 1½m: acts on polytrack, soft and good to firm ground: tends to race freely: prominently ridden: not straightforward. *J. R. Boyle*

DESERT DESTINY 6 b.g. Desert Prince (IRE) 130 – High Savannah 77 (Rousillon **109** (USA) 133) [2006 110: 8m² 8m p8.6g⁴ Oct 8] leggy, useful-looking gelding: useful per- former: creditable 1¾ lengths second to Cashier in handicap at Nad Al Sheba: well below form both subsequent starts (off 8 months before final one): best form at 7f/1m: acts on good to firm going, probably on soft: usually visored/tongue tied: signs of temperament. *Saeed bin Suroor*

DESERT DEW (IRE) 2 ch.c. (Mar 23) Indian Ridge 123 – Blue Water (USA) 104 **95** (Bering 136) [2006 7m⁶ 7d* 7s Oct 21] 250,000Y: sturdy colt: has a quick action: fourth foal: brother to smart 1m to 1½m winner Indian Creek and half-brother to fairly useful 1m to 1¼m winner Honorine (by Mark of Esteem): dam French 1¼m/1½m winner: use- ful form: confirmed debut promise when winning maiden at Newmarket (beat Urban Spirit by 1¾ lengths) in September: 8/1, well held in Horris Hill Stakes at Newbury (soft ground): will be suited by 1m/1¼m. *B. W. Hills*

DESERT DREAMER (IRE) 5 b.g. Green Desert (USA) 127 – Follow That Dream **90** 90 (Darshaan 133) [2006 89, a92: p7g⁴ p7g 6g 7m p7g² 7m 7m² p7g 8.3m² 7f* p8g 8m 7.1g³ 6g* 7.1m⁴ 7m 7g⁵ 6d p7.1m⁵ p7g p7g Nov 13] smallish, good-topped gelding: fairly useful performer: won handicap at Brighton in July and claimer at Windsor in Aug- ust: best at 6f/7f: acts on polytrack, firm and good to soft ground: held up. *P. R. Chamings*

DESERT DUST 3 b.g. Vettori (IRE) 119 – Dust 61 (Green Desert (USA) 127) [2006 **50** 62: f6g⁴ p5g³ 8d 7f 6m 5f 5g² 5d p5.1g p6g⁵ f5m² p5g⁴ p5.1g* p5g⁵ p5g³ p5.1g⁵ Dec 8] **a62** modest performer: won banded race at Wolverhampton in November: effective at 5f, should stay 7f: acts on all-weather, best effort on turf on good going: usually wears head- gear. *R. M. H. Cowell*

DESERTED DANE (USA) 2 b.c. (Apr 18) Elusive Quality (USA) – Desertion (IRE) **97 p** 92 (Danehill (USA) 126) [2006 6s³ 5m* Sep 13] €16,000Y, 31,000 2-y-o: small, strong colt: first foal: dam, 6f and 1m winner, sister to Irish 2000 Guineas and Irish Derby winner Desert King: needed debut (third at Newmarket), then impressive winner of maiden at Beverley by 7 lengths, clear by halfway and just kept up to work: will prove best at 5f/6f: bolted intended debut, early/steady to post after: already useful, and will go on to better things. *G. A. Swinbank*

DESERTED ISLAND (IRE) 3 b.f. Desert Style (IRE) 121 – Osprey Point (IRE) **–** (Entrepreneur 123) [2006 –: 7m May 4] good-topped filly: no form. *N. Wilson*

DESERTED PRINCE (IRE) 3 b.g. Desert Prince (IRE) 130 – Pool Party (USA) **57** (Summer Squall (USA)) [2006 70: p10g p8g⁵ 6g p8g 8g 7f⁶ 10.1m³ 8m 10.1m⁴ p10g Sep 5] quite good-topped gelding: modest performer: stays 1¼m: acts on polytrack and good to firm going: tried blinkered/in cheekpieces: tends to race freely. *M. J. Wallace*

DESERT FANTASY (IRE) 7 b.g. Desert King (IRE) 129 – Petite Fantasy 110 (Man- **–** sooj 118) [2006 107: 8m p7.1g May 8] useful performer: well held in 2006: usually tongue tied/blinkered: dead. *M. Meade*

DESERT FLAIR 3 b.f. Desert Style (IRE) 121 – Celtic Cross 100 (Selkirk (USA) 129) **50** [2006 77: p7g⁴ 7g 8.3g Aug 26] well-made filly: maiden: just modest form in 2006: stays 7f: raced only on polytrack and good/good to firm going: sold 3,000 gns in November. *R. Hannon*

DESERT FURY 9 b.g. Warning 136 – Number One Spot 71 (Reference Point 139) **59 §** [2006 43, a54: f8g⁵ f8g⁴ f8g* f8g f8g² f8g* f8g 7.5f 10.1m f8g Jun 3] small gelding: modest performer: won banded races at Southwell in February and March: stays 8.6f: acts on all-weather, soft and good to firm going: usually blinkered, has worn cheekpieces/ tongue tie: virtually refused to race seventh outing. *R. Bastiman*

DESERT GOLD (IRE) 3 b.g. Desert Prince (IRE) 130 – Brief Sentiment (IRE) 96 **91 §** (Brief Truce (USA) 126) [2006 97: 7m⁴ 7m 7g 7f 8.5f⁵ 8v⁵ 8d Nov 5] second foal: dam Irish 2-y-o 7f winner who stayed 1¼m: fairly useful handicapper: left D. Wachman after final 4-y-o outing: gambled on, tailed off at Royal Ascot second start: creditable efforts after only when fifth at Cork and the Curragh: stays 8.5f: acts on any going: formerly tongue tied: often slowly away: needs treating with caution. *A. J. Martin, Ireland*

DESERT HAWK 5 b.g. Cape Cross (IRE) 129 – Milling (IRE) 89 (In The Wings 128)   **59**
[2006 65d: p12.2g⁶ p12.2g² p9.5g* p9.5g³ p9.5g⁴ p12.2s³ p9.5g³ Dec 21] stocky gelding: modest performer: won handicap at Wolverhampton in February: stays 1½m: acts on polytrack and good to firm going: has been blinkered: formerly wayward, but seems reliable nowadays. *W. M. Brisbourne*

DESERT HUNTER (IRE) 3 b.g. Desert Story (IRE) 115 – She-Wolff (IRE) 104 (Pips   **59**
Pride 117) [2006 52: 6d 5m⁵ 5m³ 6m* 6m 5.9m Aug 7] good-topped gelding: modest handicapper: won at Catterick in July: effective at 5f/6f: acts on good to firm and good to soft going. *M. D. Hammond*

DESERT IMAGE (IRE) 5 b.g. Desert King (IRE) 129 – Identical (IRE) (Machiavel-   **72**
lian (USA) 123) [2006 71: p12g p16g³ Oct 11] short-backed gelding: fair handicapper: stayed easy 2m: acted on all-weather and firm going: tried tongue tied: dead. *C. Tinkler*

DESERTINA (IRE) 4 b.f. Spectrum (IRE) 126 – Kayanga (Green Desert (USA) 127)   **55 d**
[2006 58: 5d⁴ 6.1m⁶ 6g⁶ 6m 6.9m 5g Aug 17] good-topped filly: modest performer: below form after reappearance: effective at 5f/6f: acts on fibresand and good to soft ground. *R. M. Whitaker*

DESERT ISLAND DISC 9 b.m. Turtle Island (IRE) 123 – Distant Music (Darshaan   **80**
133) [2006 77, a–: 11.7g* 15d 16s⁴ 12.1s² 12g⁴ 12m⁶ 12m⁵ 14m⁶ Jul 26] sturdy mare: **a–**
fairly useful handicapper: won at Bath in May: effective at 1½m to 2m: acts on any turf going, little recent form on all-weather: usually held up nowadays: tough and game. *Dr J. R. J. Naylor*

DESERT ISLAND MISS 3 b.f. Medicean 128 – Miss Castaway (Selkirk (USA) 129)   **69**
[2006 8.2m p8g 8.3g⁵ p8g⁵ Nov 1] sturdy filly: first foal: dam unraced sister to useful 1m winner Bestam: fair maiden: best effort on polytrack. *W. R. Swinburn*

DESERT JOY 3 gr.f. Daylami (IRE) 138 – Russian Rose (IRE) 82 (Soviet Lad (USA))   **54**
[2006 8m 10m⁶ Sep 8] fourth foal: half-sister to useful 1m (at 2 yrs)/1¼m (Pretty Polly Stakes) winner Hanami (by Hernando): dam 1¼m/17f winner: better effort in maidens when seventh at Salisbury on debut, slowly away and not knocked about: said to have had breathing problem subsequent outing. *D. R. C. Elsworth*

DESERT LEADER (IRE) 5 b.g. Green Desert (USA) 127 – Za Aamah (USA) (Mr   **–**
Prospector (USA)) [2006 69, a90: p9.5g³ p9.5g p12.2g² f12g⁶ p9.5g⁵ p9.5g Dec 30] good   **a84**
sort: fairly useful handicapper on all-weather: stays 1½m: acts on all-weather and good to soft going, probably on good to firm. *W. M. Brisbourne*

DESERT LIGHT (IRE) 5 b.g. Desert Sun 120 – Nacote (IRE) (Mtoto 134) [2006 58:   **–**
p6g³ p6g* p7.1g⁵ p6g f6s p6g* p6g⁴ p6g* p6g³ 5.9g 5s p6g 5s p6m p5.1m⁵ p6g⁶ p6m⁴   **a71**
p6g⁴ p6g⁴ p6g⁴ Dec 22] sturdy gelding: fair performer on all-weather: won handicap at Wolverhampton in February, banded race there in March and handicap at Lingfield in April: effective at 5f to 7f: acts on all-weather, good to firm and good to soft ground: visored. *D. Shaw*

DESERT LIGHTNING (IRE) 4 ch.g. Desert Prince (IRE) 130 – Saibhreas (IRE) 83   **64**
(Last Tycoon 131) [2006 76: p8.6g p8.6g p7.1g p7.1g p8g 7d² 7g² 6m⁵ 7g 8m² 8.3m 8m³ 8.2f⁴ 8d³ 8m⁵ 10.1d² 9.8d 10.1m* 9s² p9.5g⁴ p8.6g⁵ p8.6g p8.6g Nov 25] big gelding: modest performer: won seller at Yarmouth in September: stays easy 1¼m: acts on polytrack, soft and good to firm going: tried visored/in cheekpieces/tongue tied: hangs right. *K. R. Burke*

DESERT LORD 6 b.g. Green Desert (USA) 127 – Red Carnival (USA) 109 (Mr   **124**
Prospector (USA)) [2006 97: p5g³ 5d* 5g 5.1f⁵ 5m* 5.1m² 5f² 5m² 6m⁵ 5m* 6m Dec 10]
  The latest Flat-racing year had more than its share of 'fairytales', none arguably more incredible than the story of Desert Lord, the 10,000-guinea horses-in-
training sale purchase who became a Group 1 winner. Desert Lord started his career
with Group 1 potential—a blue-blooded product of Cheveley Park Stud sent into
training with the Stoute stable—but he proved hard to keep sound. He ran in the
Dewhurst as a two-year-old, albeit well beaten at 50/1, but, after missing his three-
year-old season with a string of problems reportedly including a pelvic injury, a
fractured vertebra and troublesome feet, he was culled at the Autumn Sales after
winning a handicap at Newmarket as a four-year-old. He added a second victory

that season, on the polytrack at Lingfield in December for David Flood, and won at Pontefract as a five-year-old, having left Flood's stable for Alan Berry. Desert Lord seemed fully exposed as no more than a useful handicapper, none too consistent-to boot, but he was much improved in the latest season, progressing after being beaten off a BHB handicap mark of 83 on the all-weather at Kempton in March, to win one of the top sprints in Europe, the Prix de l'Abbaye de Longchamp, from the Nunthorpe and Haydock Sprint Cup winner Reverence, another gelding with a remarkable story.

Desert Lord had a new trainer as a six-year-old, leaving Berry for Kevin Ryan before his reappearance. Desert Lord did nearly all his racing at six furlongs to a mile before becoming a sprinter purely and simply in his time with Berry (his Pontefract win was over five). Ryan refined things even further, Desert Lord being raced mostly at the minimum trip. Victories in a handicap at Musselburgh and in the Vodafone 'Dash' at Epsom confirmed that Desert Lord's natural inclination is to get on with things and his forte is out-and-out speed. Well backed and refitted with blinkers, in which he had been tried earlier in his career, Desert Lord made most at Musselburgh to score in good style. Circumstances conspired against him in his next two races but he was back on song in the Vodafone 'Dash', soon to the fore and showing too much speed for a fairly useful, twenty-runner field, winning by a length and a half from Bond City. Stepped up to listed company in the City Wall Stakes at Chester and then to pattern company in the King George Stakes at Goodwood, Desert Lord came close to adding two more victories, showing fine speed and collared only late on by Tournedos and La Cucaracha respectively, reportedly losing his near-fore shoe at Goodwood where he was aided by the sharp track and a draw near the rail in an eighteen-runner field. Desert Lord came even closer to

Bull & Bell Partnership's "Desert Lord"

bringing off his first pattern win in the Flying Five at the Curragh in August, again attempting to make all and going down by a head to fellow British challenger Benbaun, the pair clear.

Benbaun, along with Golden Jubilee and July Cup winner Les Arcs and King's Stand winner Takeover Target, were among the top sprinters who missed the Prix de l'Abbaye de Longchamp Majestic Barriere for the much more valuable Sprinters Stakes, part of the Global Sprint Challenge, in Japan in early-October. The Abbaye's prize money was boosted in the latest season (Desert Lord won £95,872) though it still lags some way behind the top British sprints. Reverence, who started clear favourite in a fourteen-runner field at Longchamp, earned £147,401 in the Nunthorpe and £170,340 in the Sprint Cup, while the July Cup's first prize was £204,408 and Royal Ascot's two big sprints, the King's Stand and the Golden Jubilee, were worth £113,560 and £198,730 respectively to the winner. Desert Lord started at just over 23/1 for the Prix de l'Abbaye, four times the odds of his stable-companion Amadeus Wolf, who had been placed behind Reverence at York and at Haydock. Longchamp's five-furlong course favours blinding speed, especially when underfoot conditions are on the firm side, as they were for the latest edition. With a tailwind accentuating things further, Desert Lord sprang a surprise, smartly away and making most to hold on by a neck and a short neck from Reverence and Moss Vale, producing a clean sweep for horses trained in the North of England (Amadeus Wolf came fifth). Desert Lord showed once again that he is all speed nowadays and on his only two outings over six furlongs in the latest season, in a listed event at Goodwood and in the Hong Kong Sprint (formerly run over five furlongs), either side of the Prix de l'Abbaye, he was some way below form, leading until weakening on both occasions.

	Green Desert (USA) (b 1983)	Danzig (b 1977)	Northern Dancer
			Pas de Nom
		Foreign Courier (b 1979)	Sir Ivor
Desert Lord (b.g. 2000)			Courtly Dee
	Red Carnival (USA) (b 1992)	Mr Prospector (b 1970)	Raise A Native
			Gold Digger
		Seaside Attraction (b 1987)	Seattle Slew
			Kamar

The lengthy, good-topped Desert Lord is by Green Desert out of the Cherry Hinton winner Red Carnival, a useful performer who showed her form at up to a mile as a three-year-old when she was third in the Nell Gwyn and the Challenge Stakes. Red Carnival is a sister to Golden Attraction, a leading juvenile filly in the States in 1995, and a close relative to the 1998 Florida Derby winner Cape Town. Their dam, Seaside Attraction, won the Kentucky Oaks and their grandam Kamar, winner of the Canadian Oaks, is also the grandam of the top-class middle-distance performer Fantastic Light (Kamar's sister Love Smitten, also a Grade 1 winner, is the dam of Swain). Red Carnival raced for the Cheveley Park Stud/Stoute combination, as did her two other winners, the very smart mile-and-a-quarter performer Carnival Dancer (by Sadler's Wells), who is now one of the Cheveley stallions, and the smart miler Funfair (by Singspiel) who went on to win at Grade 2 level in the States. Desert Lord has form at a mile but is clearly suited by a test of raw speed. He acts on polytrack, firm and good to soft going, usually wears blinkers or cheekpieces and has been bandaged on his fore joints. His transformation is a tremendous credit to his trainer. *K. A. Ryan*

DESERT LOVER (IRE) 4 b.g. Desert Prince (IRE) 130 – Crystal Flute (Lycius (USA) 124) [2006 57: f7g⁶ f7g* f8g* p7.1g* p8.6g³ f7g⁵ p7.1g* f7g 7d⁴ p6g² 8d⁶ 7.1m p7.1g p7.1s Dec 14] close-coupled gelding: fair performer: won banded race at Southwell and handicaps there and at Wolverhampton (2) early in 2006: effective at 6f to 8.6f: acts on all-weather and good to soft ground: tried once in visor. *R. J. Price*   **64 a69**

DESERT MAZE (IRE) 2 ch.g. (May 8) Desert Sun 120 – Allzi (USA) 83 (Zilzal (USA) 137) [2006 6m² 7f⁶ Jul 29] little show in minor event (17 lengths second of 4) and maiden. *J. Wade*   **–**

DESERT MOVE (IRE) 4 b.f. Desert King (IRE) 129 – Campestral (USA) 97 (Alleged (USA) 138) [2006 104: 12m 13.9d 12s Oct 7] close-coupled filly: useful performer in 2005: no form in 2006: held up. *M. R. Channon*   **–**

DESERT OPAL 6 ch.g. Cadeaux Genereux 131 – Nullarbor (Green Desert (USA) 127) [2006 77: p6g⁴ p6g⁵ f6g p5.1g* f6g⁶ f6g 5g² 5.9g⁵ 7g p6g² p6g p6g 5.1g² 6d 6g³ p6g⁴ p6m p7.1g p5.1m² 6d p5.1g* p5.1g³ p5.1g* p5.1g* Dec 12] leggy, good-topped gelding: fair performer: won handicaps in March and (having left D. Chapman after tenth start) November and December (2), all at Wolverhampton: stays 1m, best recent form at 5f/6f: acts on all-weather and soft going: sometimes wears headgear (in cheekpieces last 3 wins). *C. R. Dore*   **79**

DESERT REALM (IRE) 3 b.g. Desert Prince (IRE) 130 – Fawaayid (USA) 92 (Vaguely Noble 140) [2006 94: 8f² 8m 8.1m 8.3g² 10m² 9.9f² 10.4d 8f 10m 10s⁶ Oct 7] good-topped gelding: useful performer: runner-up 4 times in 2006, including in handicaps at Redcar (beaten head by Isidore Bonheur) on reappearance and Goodwood (went down by 5 lengths to stable-companion Road To Love in ladbrokes.com Stakes) sixth start: creditable efforts last 2 outings (gelded after): stays 1¼m: acts on firm going: sometimes wanders: sent to UAE. *M. Johnston*   **104**

DESERT REIGN 5 ch.g. Desert King (IRE) 129 – Moondance (Siberian Express (USA) 125) [2006 80: p10g⁴ p10g⁶ 10d⁶ 9m Jun 9] workmanlike gelding: fair handicapper: finds 1m bare minimum, and should stay 1½m: acts on polytrack, heavy and good to firm going. *A. P. Jarvis*   **73**

DESERT SEA (IRE) 3 b.g. Desert Sun 120 – Sea of Time (USA) (Gilded Time (USA)) [2006 63: 8.3g 8.1s p12.2g* p12g² p16g* p16g* Sep 2] compact gelding: improved into a fairly useful handicapper, winning at Wolverhampton in June, Lingfield in July and Kempton (smoothly by a length from All The Good) in September: stays 2m: acts on polytrack, some promise on turf. *C. Tinkler*   **91**

totesport Cesarewitch (Handicap), Newmarket—Detroit City makes a successful return to the Flat to land a gamble, making Jamie Spencer the first jockey to land the autumn double since 1885; Inchnadamph is placed for the second year running, ahead of Dr Sharp (rail) and Ski Jump, another grey

DESERT SECRETS (IRE) 4 b.f. Almutawakel 126 – Shaping Up (USA) 89 (Storm Bird (CAN) 134) [2006 67: p13g Feb 25] leggy filly: fair maiden: well held only Flat outing in 2006: won over fences in December. *J. G. Portman* —

DESERT SOUL 2 b.c. (Feb 23) Fantastic Light (USA) 134 – Jalousie (IRE) 108 (Barathea (IRE) 127) [2006 6m⁴ 7.1m⁶ 7.1d Sep 16] 85,000Y: tall, good-topped colt: first foal: dam, 10.4f to 1½m winner, half-sister to useful 1993 2-y-o The Deep: fair maiden: best run when sixth at Warwick, still green: reared as stall opened final start: type to improve at 1¼m/1½m. *M. Johnston* **68 p**

DESERT STORM (DEN) 4 br.g. Desert Prince (IRE) 130 – Boss Lady (IRE) 80 (Last Tycoon 131) [2006 73: 13.1m² 16g* 17.2m 16v* Oct 25] leggy gelding: fair handicapper, lightly raced: won at Yarmouth in September and Nottingham in October: stays 2m: acts on heavy and good to firm going: makes running: sold 56,000 gns, joined P. Hobbs. *Rae Guest* **76**

DESIRABLE DANCER (IRE) 2 b.f. (Mar 13) Fath (USA) 116 – Tender Time (Tender King 123) [2006 5.1m 6d p6g p6m⁶ f7g⁶ f6g p8.6g Dec 18] €6,500F, €8,000Y, 11,000 2-y-o: half-sister to several winners, including fairly useful 1994 2-y-o 6f winner Regal Fanfare (by Taufan) and 1m to 15f winner Final Settlement (by Soviet Lad): dam ran twice: poor maiden: tried in blinkers/cheekpieces. *R. A. Harris* **46**

DESPERATE DAN 5 b.g. Danzero (AUS) – Alzianah 102 (Alzao (USA) 117) [2006 94: f5g³ f5g³ f5g* f6g⁶ p5.1g 5s 5g 5.7f³ 5g 5.5m³ 6f 5.2m⁶ Aug 6] quite good-topped gelding: fairly useful handicapper: won at Southwell in January: effective at 5f/6f: acts on all-weather and firm going: often blinkered: sometimes finds little. *J. A. Osborne* **88 a94**

DESPERATION (IRE) 4 b.g. Desert Style (IRE) 121 – Mauras Pride (IRE) (Cadeaux Genereux 131) [2006 81: p12.2g* p10g⁵ p12.2g² p12.2g² p12.2g² p12.2g* p16.5g⁶ 12.3g p13.9g p12.2g Jul 11] good-topped gelding: fairly useful performer: won claimer in January and, having left K. Burke after fourth start, handicap in February, both at Wolverhampton: stays 1½m: acts on all-weather, soft and good to firm going: tried visored/blinkered: tends to edge left, looked none too keen final outing: joined A. J. Martin, Ireland. *B. D. Leavy* **84**

DETENTE 3 b.f. Medicean 128 – Truce (Nashwan (USA) 135) [2006 10m 9.9g⁴ 10d⁴ 12d Oct 27] first foal: dam unraced half-sister to very smart 1½m performer Nowhere To Exit and 5-y-o Cesare: fair maiden: should stay 1½m: sold 7,000 gns. *J. R. Fanshawe* **73**

288

DETONATE 4 b.g. Mind Games 121 – Bron Hilda (IRE) 50 (Namaqualand (USA)) **57**
[2006 64, a55: p5g⁶ p6g f5g⁶ p5g⁵ 5.3m 5.2m⁴ p6g 5.2g³ 5f 5f⁵ p5.1g 5m 5.2f⁵ 6m 5.2m²
p6g³ p7g⁴ Dec 30] leggy, close-coupled gelding: modest maiden: left Mrs C. Dunnett
before penultimate start: stays 7f: acts on polytrack, soft and good to firm going: sometimes in headgear: edgy sort: sometimes slowly away. *Ms J. S. Doyle*

DETROIT CITY (USA) 4 gr. or ro.g. Kingmambo (USA) 125 – Seattle Victory **107**
(USA) (Seattle Song (USA) 130) [2006 86: 18d* Oct 14] big, strong gelding: useful performer: smart juvenile hurdler in 2005/6, winning Triumph Hurdle at Cheltenham and
Anniversary Hurdle at Aintree: won totesport Cesarewitch (Handicap) at Newmarket on
only Flat outing in 2006 by length from Inchnadamph, needing plenty of rousting and
leading inside final 1f: stays 2¼m: acts on all-weather, yet to encounter extremes of going
on turf: visored last 2 starts at 3 yrs, blinkered at Newmarket: high-class form on return to
hurdling, winning in November and December. *P. J. Hobbs*

DEUTSCHLAND (USA) 3 b.g. Red Ransom (USA) – Rhine Valley (USA) 101 (Dan- **88**
zig (USA)) [2006 74: p10g³ f12g² 11.6m³ 10v* May 25] close-coupled, good-topped
gelding: has a quick action: fairly useful performer: won maiden at Ayr in May by 12
lengths from Apt To Run, making all: stays 1½m: acts on heavy and good to firm ground,
some promise on all-weather: wore cheekpieces last 2 outings: sold 70,000 gns, joined
W. Mullins in Ireland, and won over hurdles in December. *M. A. Jarvis*

DEVELOPER (IRE) 3 b.g. Danehill Dancer (IRE) 117 – Via Camp 88 (Kris 135) **67 d**
[2006 70: p5g³ f6g³ p6g³ p5g⁵ p5g 6m 5g p6g f5m f6g f6g Nov 21] fair maiden: below
form after reappearance, leaving T. Mills following eighth outing: should stay 6f: acts on
polytrack, good to firm and good to soft going: often wears headgear. *G. F. Bridgwater*

DEVERON (USA) 3 b. or br.f. Cozzene (USA) – Cruisie (USA) (Assert 134) [2006 **–**
105: a8f⁵ 9.9g⁶ May 6] tall, quite good-topped filly: useful performer at 2 yrs for
C. Brittain: below form in 2006 in UAE 1000 Guineas at Nad Al Sheba (only outing for
I. Mohammed) and listed race at Goodwood (favourite and tongue tied, last of 6): should
be suited by 1¼m: has twice hung right: has left Godolphin. *Saeed bin Suroor*

DEVILFISHPOKER COM 2 ch.g. (Apr 15) Dr Fong (USA) 128 – Midnight Allure **42**
85 (Aragon 118) [2006 5g 5g 5g 5g 5m 6m⁴ 7.5g 7m⁴ p7.1g Dec 27] workmanlike
gelding: poor maiden: tried blinkered. *R. C. Guest*

DEVIL'S BITE 5 ch.g. Dracula (AUS) 121 – Niggle 65 (Night Shift (USA)) [2006 –: **–**
f7m Oct 31] strong, workmanlike gelding: has a round action: fair maiden at 2 yrs: no
form since: often breaks blood vessels, and was banned from racing for a second time at
HRA inquiry in December. *M. C. Chapman*

DEVIL'S ISLAND 4 b.g. Green Desert (USA) 127 – Scandalette (Niniski (USA) 125) **70**
[2006 f8g p8.6g* p8g p10g² p9.5g⁴ 8m⁴ p8g⁴ May 12] tall gelding: fair handicapper:
missed 2005: won at Wolverhampton in January: stayed 1¼m: acted on polytrack: blinkered final outing: dead. *Sir Mark Prescott*

DEVINE DANCER 3 ch.f. Woodborough (USA) 112 – Princess Londis 59 (Interrex **83**
(CAN)) [2006 50: p5g** 5.1d 5.3f* 5g 5m⁵ 5.5m 5f⁶ 5.1f³ 5g 5m² Sep 9] attractive,
compact filly: fairly useful performer: won maiden at Lingfield in March and handicap at
Brighton in May: speedy, and likely to prove best at 5f: acts on polytrack and firm ground:
races prominently: none too consistent. *H. Candy*

DEVON FLAME 7 b.g. Whittingham (IRE) 104 – Uae Flame (IRE) (Polish Precedent **88**
(USA) 131) [2006 86: 5g³ 6g 5.7g² 5.7f* 5m⁴ 6.1f 5.7f⁶ Aug 8] strong gelding: fairly
useful handicapper: won at Bath in June: reportedly lame final outing: possibly at very
best around 6f nowadays: acts on firm and good to soft going. *R. J. Hodges*

DEVONIA PLAINS (IRE) 4 ch.g. Danehill Dancer (IRE) 117 – Marlfield Lake **68**
(Cadeaux Genereux 131) [2006 14.1d 10d 11.6f⁵ p10g f6g³ Jul 31] big gelding: fair
maiden: should be suited by further than 6f: acts on fibresand: visored after debut. *Mrs
P. N. Dutfield*

DEVON RUBY 3 ch.f. Zilzal (USA) 137 – Last Result (Northern Park (USA) 107) **51**
[2006 51: f8g f7g 10d⁴ 5.1g⁵ 5.7f 10f p8g Oct 23] modest maiden at best: left Mrs
A. Duffield after third outing: stays 1m: acts on all-weather, best effort on turf on good
going: tried in cheekpieces/tongue tied. *C. L. Popham*

DEXILEOS (IRE) 7 b.g. Danehill (USA) 126 – Theano (IRE) 114 (Thatching 131) **57**
[2006 55d: p7.1g f7g⁵ f6g⁶ p8g² p8g² p8.6g⁵ f8g³ f8g⁶ p7.1g² f8g⁴ p8.6g² p8.6g⁵ p7g*
p7g⁴ p8g 7.6m⁶ 7m p7.1g p8g³ p7g Dec 18] close-coupled gelding: modest performer:
won banded race at Kempton in May: effective at 6f to 8.6f: acts on all-weather, firm and
soft ground: tried visored/blinkered in past: tongue tied. *David Pinder*

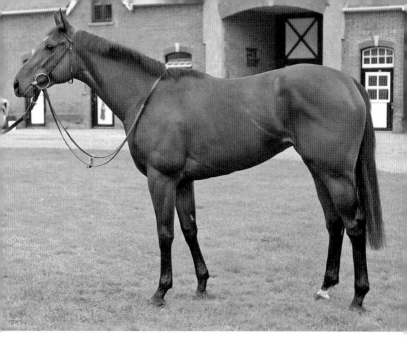

Mrs Sheila Tucker's "Dhanyata"

DEXTROUS 9 gr.g. Machiavellian (USA) 123 – Heavenly Cause (USA) (Grey Dawn **58**
II 132) [2006 48: f12g⁵ f12g³ f11g f12g⁴ f11g⁵ f12g* f11g* f11g⁶ Apr 4] tall gelding:
modest performer: won maiden claimer and banded race at Southwell in March: stays
1½m: acts on fibresand and any turf going: wears cheekpieces: tried tongue tied.
P. T. Midgley

DHANYATA (IRE) 2 b.f. (Apr 27) Danetime (IRE) 121 – Preponderance (IRE) 85 **109**
(Cyrano de Bergerac 120) [2006 6.1g 6m* 6f² 6s⁵ p6g* 6d² 7d⁶ Oct 14] 11,000Y: strong
filly: eighth foal: half-sister to 3 winning sprinters, including smart Guinea Hunter
(by Pips Pride): dam Irish 2-y-o 5f winner: useful performer: won maiden at Newbury in
June and totepool Sirenia Stakes at Kempton (beat La Neige 2 lengths) in September:
more progress when neck second of 11 to Indian Ink in Cheveley Park Stakes at Newmarket sixth start, and better than bare result (stamina stretched) in Rockfel Stakes there
final one: best at 5f/6f: acts on polytrack, firm and good to soft going: sent to USA.
B. J. Meehan

DHAULAR DHAR (IRE) 4 b.c. Indian Ridge 123 – Pescara (IRE) 108 (Common **103**
Grounds 118) [2006 85: p7.1g⁶ 8s 7g⁵ 6g² 7g* 6m 6m⁵ 7m 7m⁴ 7.6g³ 8d 7f² 6d* 6s⁶ 5s*
p5.1g Oct 29] leggy, quite attractive colt: useful handicapper: won at Chester in June and
twice at Catterick in October: best effort when beating Inter Vision by ½ length for last
success: has won over 7f/1m, will prove best at stiff 5f/6f: unraced on heavy going, acts
on any other turf and polytrack: held up: tough and consistent. *J. S. Goldie*

DHEHDAAH 5 b.g. Alhaarth (IRE) 126 – Carina Clare (Slip Anchor 136) [2006 71: **69**
14.1s² 16.1d² 14.1g² Jun 7] angular gelding: fair handicapper: stays 2m: acts on firm and
soft going: blinkered once at 3 yrs: won over hurdles in October. *Mrs P. Sly*

DHEKRAA (IRE) 3 b.f. Fasliyev (USA) 120 – White Heat 67 (Last Tycoon 131) [2006 **102**
92: 5.1g² 6f⁴ 5.1m⁶ 6m Jul 30] rangy, attractive filly: useful performer: ran in listed events
first 3 starts, best effort when neck second to Indian Maiden at Bath on reappearance:

well held in handicap at Ascot final outing, failing to settle: was best at 5f/6f: raced only on good going or firmer: covered by Haafhd (to Southern Hemisphere time), and sent to South Africa. *M. A. Jarvis*

DHURWAH (IRE) 3 b.f. Green Desert (USA) 127 – Bintalbawadi (IRE) 67 (Diesis 133) [2006 p6g 5d⁵ 6s Oct 2] 18,000 2-y-o: first foal: dam, 1m winner on only start, out of half-sister to smart US 6f/7f performer Gold Land: poor form in maidens. *T. Keddy* **47**

DIAFA (USA) 4 b.f. Swain (IRE) 134 – I'm Unapproachable (USA) (Distinctive Pro (USA)) [2006 62: p12.2g p9.5g f12g 10.9s 8m 10f p12g⁵ f12g p12g Nov 27] fifth foal: half-sister to 3 winners in USA: dam unraced: poor maiden: left K. Prendergast in Ireland after final 3-y-o start: stays 1½m: acts on polytrack: tried blinkered. *J. G. M. O'Shea* **49**

DIAMONDBANKER 3 b.c. Banker Mason (USA) 82 – Diamante VII (Damsire Unregistered) [2006 f8g 12m Jun 25] tailed off in 2 maidens. *Jedd O'Keeffe* **–**

DIAMOND DAN (IRE) 4 b.g. Foxhound (USA) 103 – Kawther (Tap On Wood 130) [2006 49: p9.5g³ p10g p12.2g p9.5g* p9.5g⁵ p9.5g⁶ p10g 10m* 10.2f⁵ 10.2m 7.6m³ 8f² 8f² 9g⁶ p8.6g* Aug 31] smallish gelding: modest performer: won banded race at Wolverhampton in March, and handicaps at Brighton in June and Wolverhampton in August: stays 1¼m: acts on polytrack and firm ground: wore cheekpieces third outing. *P. D. Evans* **62**

DIAMOND DE TRIANO (USA) 3 b. or br.f. Forest Wildcat (USA) 120 – Hot Princess 101 (Hot Spark 126) [2006 63: p7.1g 8.2s* 9.3m* 8m⁶ 8.3m² 8.5g 8g Aug 19] tall, good-bodied filly: fairly useful performer: won handicaps at Nottingham in May and Carlisle in June: ran as if amiss last 2 starts: stays 9.3f: acts on heavy and good to firm ground: has given trouble at stall: sent to Australia. *P. W. Chapple-Hyam* **81**

DIAMOND DIGGINS (GER) 4 ch.c. Kendor (FR) 122 – Diana Dancer (FR) (Fabulous Dancer (USA) 124) [2006 81?: 10.9g p9.5g⁵ 10g 7d 8s⁴ May 28] close-coupled colt: maiden: well held in Britain first 3 starts in 2006: left V. Smith and returned to Germany: stays 1¼m: acts on soft ground: tried blinkered. *W. Figge, Germany* **?**

DIAMOND DIVA 2 br.f. (Mar 20) Dansili 127 – Vivianna (Indian Ridge 123) [2006 7g⁵ 6.5s³ p7g* Oct 17] sturdy filly: second foal: half-sister to 3-y-o Kaylianni: dam, French 11f winner, out of champion 3-y-o filly in South Africa Kundalini: fairly useful form: similar efforts in maiden at Newbury and sales race at Ascot (6 lengths third of 22 to Indian Ink), then won maiden at Lingfield by 5 lengths: will stay 1m/1¼m. *J. W. Hills* **86 +**

DIAMOND HERITAGE 4 ch.g. Compton Place 125 – Eccolina 65 (Formidable (USA) 125) [2006 –: 6d f7g f8g 8.2g 6m⁵ 6f⁴ 7.1m 7m 9f 7m 8.2g 7m 7.1d Oct 8] big, strong gelding: modest maiden: stays 7f: acts on firm going: tried tongue tied: often blinkered/in cheekpieces. *S. Parr* **52**

DIAMOND HURRICANE (IRE) 2 b.g. (Apr 9) Mujadil (USA) 119 – Christoph's Girl 50 (Efisio 120) [2006 5d³ 5g* 6.1d⁵ 6.1m* p6g⁴ 6m Sep 19] €6,500Y: small gelding: brother to 2 winners, including 8-y-o Taboor, and half-brother to 3 winners, including 4-y-o Transvestite: dam, Belgian 6f/7f winner, sister to very smart sprinter Hever Golf Rose: fair performer: won maiden at Catterick in May and nursery at Chepstow in August: effective at 5f/6f: acts on good to firm and good to soft ground. *P. D. Evans* **76**

DIAMOND JOSH 4 ch.g. Primo Dominie 121 – Exit 82 (Exbourne (USA) 125) [2006 62: p6g² p6g p6g² p6g p6g⁵ 6m⁵ 5.7f* 6m* 6f⁴ 6f³ 6f⁵ p6m 6m p5.1g³ p6g⁴ p6g p5.1g p6g Dec 30] neat gelding: fair performer: won sellers at Bath and Ripon (apprentices) in June: claimed from P. D. Evans £6,000 prior to final outing: stays 6f: acts on polytrack and firm going: below form in visor/cheekpieces: sometimes makes running. *M. Mullineaux* **68**

DIAMOND KATIE (IRE) 4 b.f. Night Shift (USA) – Fayrooz (USA) 74 (Gulch (USA)) [2006 75: 5d 5m 5f⁵ 5m 6g⁶ 5g 5f⁶ 6g 5g² 6g³ 5.1m 5f 5.7m³ p6g Oct 23] deep-girthed filly: fair handicapper: effective at stiff 5f/6f: acts on firm ground. *N. Tinkler* **66**

DIAMOND LIGHT (USA) 2 ch.f. (Feb 22) Fantastic Light (USA) 134 – Queen of Women (USA) (Sharpen Up 127) [2006 6g³ 6m⁶ 6.1f⁴ 7g² 7m⁴ 7f³ 7.1d 7d² p7g Dec 20] $170,000Y: close-coupled, attractive filly: half-sister to several winners, including US Grade 3 8.5f winner Antoniette (by Nicholas): dam, French 11f winner (later successful in USA), half-sister to high-class miler Mukaddamah: fair maiden: in frame 6 times, 4 in nurseries: left J. Dunlop 44,000 gns before final start: will stay 1¼m+: acts on firm and good to soft going. *M. Botti* **70**

DIAMOND NECKLACE (USA) 2 gr.f. (May 6) Unbridled's Song (USA) 125 – Helsinki (Machiavellian (USA) 123) [2006 8g⁶ 7m Aug 27] $1,150,000F: first foal: half-sister to 3 winners, notably high-class 1m and 10.5f winner Shamardal (by Giant's Causeway), 6f/7f winner at 2 yrs: dam, useful French 1¼m winner, sister to Dubai World **90**

Cup winner Street Cry out of Irish Oaks winner Helen Street: seemingly better effort when 5 lengths tenth of 12 to Miss Beatrix in Moyglare Stud Stakes at the Curragh, making running. *A. P. O'Brien, Ireland*

DIAMONDS AND DUST 4 b.g. Mister Baileys 123 – Dusty Shoes 72 (Shareef **92**
Dancer (USA) 135) [2006 97: 8m 10.3m 7m³ 8.2m³ 8f* 8.1m⁵ 8m 8m p8.6g Dec 21] smallish, close-coupled gelding: fairly useful handicapper: won at Ripon in June: well held after, leaving M. Tompkins 10,000 gns before final start: stays 1m: acts on polytrack, firm and good to soft going: usually blinkered. *N. P. Littmoden*

DIAMOND SHOWER (USA) 3 b.c. Swain (IRE) 134 – Quality Gift (Last Tycoon **79**
131) [2006 10f 9.9g² 10f* Jul 20] leggy, good-topped colt: third foal: half-brother to useful French/US winner (including at 2 yrs) Bright Abundance (by Quiet American) who stayed 1¼m and 2004 2-y-o 6f winner Nightfall (by Rahy): dam, French 11f winner, half-sister to National Stakes winner Manntari: fair form: didn't need to improve to win maiden at Leicester in July: will be suited by 1½m: acts on firm going: sold 10,000 gns in October. *E. A. L. Dunlop*

DIAMOND TYCOON (USA) 2 b.c. (Mar 23) Johannesburg (USA) 127 – Palacoona **84 p**
(FR) 105 (Last Tycoon 131) [2006 8g² Oct 13] $55,000F, 35,000 2-y-o: tall, close-coupled colt: fluent mover: fourth living foal: dam, French/US 1m/9f winner, out of sister to Prix du Jockey Club winner Polytain: 12/1, stirred up (sweated) but shaped well when ¾-length second of 13 to Sam Lord in maiden at Newmarket: should do better. *B. J. Meehan*

DIAMOND WINNIE 3 b.f. Komaite (USA) – Winsome Wooster 71 (Primo Dominie **57**
121) [2006 6d³ 6g⁵ 7g 8.1f Jul 14] compact filly: third living foal: half-sister to 4-y-o Leighton Buzzard: dam 5f (at 2 yrs) to 7f winner: maiden: modest form only on debut: left Mrs A. Duffield after third start: should be suited by 7f+: acts on good to soft ground. *Mrs N. S. Evans*

DIAMOND WORLD 3 b.f. Agnes World (USA) 123 – In A Twinkling (IRE) 74 (Brief **64 ?**
Truce (USA) 126) [2006 –: 6f³ p5g 6g 5.7m Sep 4] quite good-topped filly: modest maiden: stays 6f: acts on firm going. *C. A. Horgan*

DIANE'S CHOICE 3 ch.f. Komaite (USA) – Ramajana (USA) (Shadeed (USA) 135) **95**
[2006 73: p6g² p6g⁵ p5g* p6g⁵ 5d* 5g* 6f² p6g³ Nov 1] improved into a useful performer: won maiden at Lingfield in February and handicaps there and at Leicester in August: good placed efforts after: likely to prove best at 5f/easy 6f: acts on polytrack and heavy ground: often front runner. *J. Akehurst*

DICHOH 3 b.g. Diktat 126 – Hoh Dancer 66 (Indian Ridge 123) [2006 10s p7.1m* **85**
p7.1g² p7g* Dec 10] 6,000Y: heavy-topped gelding: fourth foal: dam, disappointing maiden, half-sister to useful 1987 2-y-o 5f winner Infanta Real: fairly useful form: won maiden at Wolverhampton in November and handicap at Kempton in December: should prove as effective at 6f as 7f: form only on polytrack. *M. A. Jarvis*

DICKENSIAN (IRE) 3 br.c. Xaar 132 – Cappella (IRE) 75 (College Chapel 122) **102**
[2006 103: 7m² 10.4s⁶ Oct 7] rather leggy colt: useful performer: creditable 2 lengths second to Aeroplane in minor event at Southwell on belated reappearance in September: mulish leaving paddock, ran poorly in similar race at York only outing after: should stay beyond 7f: acts on good to firm and good to soft going: visored/tongue tied in 2006: joined E. Charpy in UAE. *Saeed bin Suroor*

DICKIE DEANO 2 b.g. (May 1) Sooty Tern 79 – Chez Bonito (IRE) 49 (Persian Bold **–**
123) [2006 p7g Dec 15] well beaten in maiden. *J. M. Bradley*

DICKIE LE DAVOIR 2 b.g. (Apr 28) Kyllachy 129 – Downeaster Alexa (USA) (Red **87**
Ryder (USA)) [2006 5g⁵ 5s* 5g⁴ 6m 6g² 6m 6.1g⁴ 6s 6s³ Oct 6] 11,000F, 22,000Y: good-topped gelding: half-brother to useful 1996 2-y-o 5f/6f winner Arethusa (by Primo Dominie) and fairly useful 5f winner Red Ryding Hood (by Wolfhound): dam Irish 2-y-o 5f winner: fairly useful performer: won maiden at Haydock in May: several good efforts after, third of 18 to Algol in nursery at York final start (subsequently gelded): effective at 5f/6f: acts on soft going: sometimes visored: edgy sort, has given trouble at stall. *K. R. Burke*

DICKIE'S DREAM (IRE) 3 b.c. Xaar 132 – Swallowtailed Kite (USA) (Silver **76**
Hawk (USA) 123) [2006 63: p8.6g⁴ p9.5g² 12.1d³ p12g⁴ 14g p16.5g⁴ p16.5m⁵ Oct 14] neat colt: fair maiden: stays 2m: acts on polytrack, unraced on extremes of going on turf: sold 15,000 gns. *P. J. McBride*

DICTATION 4 b.f. Diktat 126 – Monaiya (Shareef Dancer (USA) 135) [2006 77: 10m **43**
10m 8.5g 12d 9s p8.6g⁵ f7g Dec 9] €80,000Y: half-sister to several winners, including

useful 7f (at 2 yrs) and 1¼m winner Musetta (by Cadeaux Genereux): dam French winner around 1m: fair performer for D. Weld in Ireland at 3 yrs, winning handicap at Ballinrobe: poor form in 2006, including on all-weather: stays 9f: acts on good to firm ground: usually blinkered, tried in cheekpieces. *Mrs Valerie Keatley, Ireland*

DICTATOR (IRE) 5 ch.g. Machiavellian (USA) 123 – Obsessed 80 (Storm Bird (CAN) 134) [2006 p12.2g³ p13.9g⁴ Mar 6] fair maiden, lightly raced: left J. Oxx in Ireland €29,000 after final 3-y-o start and unraced on Flat in 2005: stays 1¾m: acts on polytrack, unraced on extremes of going on turf: tongue tied all starts. *D. R. Gandolfo* **74**

DICTATRIX 3 gr.f. Diktat 126 – Apennina (USA) (Gulch (USA)) [2006 67p: 7m⁶ 8s⁶ 8.1m 7m 8d Oct 2] leggy filly: fairly useful performer: good sixth to Nasheej in Fred Darling Stakes at Newbury on reappearance: well below that form after: should stay 1m: acts on heavy and good to firm ground: reluctant in preliminaries second outing, mounted on track and early to post next time. *J. M. P. Eustace* **91 ?**

DICTION (IRE) 4 br.f. Diktat 126 – Waft (USA) 67 (Topsider (USA)) [2006 –, a62: f7g f7g f8g⁴ f7s² f7g⁴ f8g* Mar 16] quite good-topped filly: modest performer: won claimer at Southwell in March: stayed 1m: acted on fibresand (possibly not polytrack), no form on turf: usually in cheekpieces/visor of late: in foal to Pastoral Pursuits, sold 12,500 gns in November. *K. R. Burke* **– a60**

DIDACTIC 2 b.g. (Apr 11) Diktat 126 – Scene (IRE) 87 (Scenic 128) [2006 6m p8.6g Sep 16] smallish, sturdy gelding: mid-field in maidens, for J. Osborne on debut (favourite). *A. J. McCabe* **51**

DIDIFON 11 b.g. Zafonic (USA) 130 – Didicoy (USA) 104 (Danzig (USA)) [2006 12.6m 10.2m 10f Jul 8] strong, good sort: lightly raced/little form on Flat since 1999: has worn cheekpieces/blinkers. *Mrs L. J. Young* **–**

DIDNT TELL MY WIFE 7 ch.g. Aragon 118 – Bee Dee Dancer (Ballacashtal (CAN)) [2006 66: p9.5g p10g p10g 10m p10g f7g p8.6g p8g⁴ Dec 15] modest nowadays: left Mrs Lucinda Featherstone after second outing and G. Chung after fourth: stays 9f: acts on all-weather, heavy and good to firm going: tried in headgear: reportedly has bled. *P. S. McEntee* **51**

DIDN'T WE (IRE) 3 b.c. Mujadil (USA) 119 – Non Dimenticar Me (IRE) 63 (Don't Forget Me 127) [2006 75p: p7.1g⁴ p6g* p7g² p7g² p7g² 6g 6m* 6g 6f* 6m⁴ 5.2m² 6g² p6g 5.1m Oct 8] compact colt: improved into a useful performer, winning maiden at Lingfield in January and handicaps there in May and Folkestone in June: largely creditable efforts after: effective at 5f to 7f: acts on polytrack and firm going: usually blinkered/visored, effective when not: jinked leaving stall penultimate outing: usually races prominently: sold 35,000 gns, sent to USA. *T. G. Mills* **96**

DIDOE 7 br.m. Son Pardo 107 – My Diamond Ring 65 (Sparkling Boy 110) [2006 58: 8.1g 10.2g 10m 10.2m³ 8f 10f⁴ 10.2f⁴ 10f⁶ 8m⁴ 9g Sep 12] leggy mare: modest performer: effective at 1m/1¼m: acts on firm ground: often races prominently. *P. W. Hiatt* **53**

DIEGO CAO (IRE) 5 b.g. Cape Cross (IRE) 129 – Lady Moranbon (USA) (Trempolino (USA) 135) [2006 96: 10.1g⁶ 12s⁵ 12s Oct 7] well-made gelding: fairly useful performer nowadays: best effort in 2006 on reappearance: stays 1¼m: acts on good to soft ground. *Mrs N. Smith* **90**

DIG DEEP (IRE) 4 b.g. Entrepreneur 123 – Diamond Quest (Rainbow Quest (USA) 134) [2006 89: 7d p7g p7.1g*' p7g Dec 15] well-made gelding: fairly useful handicapper, lightly raced: won at Wolverhampton in December: should stay 1m: acts on polytrack and good to firm ground. *W. J. Haggas* **88**

DIGGER BOY 3 b.g. King's Best (USA) 132 – Chameleon 79 (Green Desert (USA) 127) [2006 p7g p8g² 7m f8g² p9.5g³ p12.2g⁴ p10g 10.1g² p8.6g Sep 16] 40,000Y: second foal: dam, 7f winner, sister to very smart sprinter Owington: fair maiden: may prove best short of 1½m: acts on all-weather: joined C. Egerton, and gelded. *M. A. Jarvis* **70**

DIGGS LANE (IRE) 2 b.g. (Feb 2) Galileo (IRE) 134 – Desert Bluebell 83 (Kalaglow 132) [2006 7f 7m 7m p7g⁴ 8s p9.5g Nov 7] useful-looking gelding: modest maiden: should stay 1¼m/1½m: best effort on polytrack: blinkered last 3 starts (has looked moody): gelded after final start. *N. A. Callaghan* **55**

DIGITAL 9 ch.g. Safawan 118 – Heavenly Goddess (Soviet Star (USA) 128) [2006 84: 7v³ 6g⁵ 7g 6g 5.7s* 6d 5.7m⁵ 6d 6m 6.1g³ p6g⁶ 6.1d² p6g Nov 3] workmanlike gelding: fairly useful handicapper: won at Bath in May: mainly creditable efforts after: effective at 5.7f to 1m: acts on polytrack and any turf going: sometimes starts slowly: waited with. *M. R. Channon* **80**

Stan James Horris Hill Stakes, Newbury—Dijeerr (light cap) rallies under pressure to pip Mythical Kid; Striving Storm (third left) holds Opera Music for third

DIJEERR (USA) 2 b.c. (Feb 9) Danzig (USA) – Sharp Minister (USA) (Deputy **108** Minister (CAN)) [2006 6g² 7m* 7d² 7s* Oct 21] $500,000Y: sturdy colt: fourth foal: half-brother to winner in USA by Capote: dam, ran twice in USA, sister to very smart French/US performer up to 1½m Flag Down: useful form: won maiden at Leicester in September and Stan James Horris Hill Stakes at Newbury in October, in latter rallying to beat Mythical Kid by short head (pair clear): also ran well when 2½ lengths second to Thousand Words in Somerville Tattersall Stakes at Newmarket in between: will stay 1m: acts on soft and good to firm going: genuine: joined Godolphin. *M. A. Jarvis*

DIK DIK 3 b.g. Diktat 126 – Totom 80 (Mtoto 134) [2006 8d 10m² p8g 10.5v² 10d 12g **65** p12.2g Nov 14] compact gelding: fair maiden: left J. Fanshawe £10,000 after second start: stays 10.5f: acts on heavy and good to firm going: usually visored. *C. N. Allen*

DIKTALEX (IRE) 3 b.f. Diktat 126 – Kingdom Royale (IRE) (Royal Academy (USA) **66** 130) [2006 62: p6g* p6g² f5g² p7.1g f6g² p6g⁵ p6g f6g* f6g² p5.1g² p6g f6g⁴ May 31] big, lengthy filly: fair performer: won seller at Lingfield in January and, having been claimed from W. Turner after second start, handicap at Southwell in April: claimed from M. Attwater after ninth outing: should stay 7f: acts on all-weather and good to soft going: tried visored, tongue tied except fourth outing (virtually refused to race). *C. J. Teague*

DIKTATIT 4 b.f. Diktat 126 – Mystique Smile 78 (Music Boy 124) [2006 50d: 7.1g **– §** 9.1m 8m Aug 17] leggy, close-coupled filly: maiden: very slowly away and well held all starts in 2006: tried visored/blinkered: ungenuine. *R. C. Guest*

DIKTATORIAL 4 br.g. Diktat 126 – Reason To Dance 96 (Damister (USA) 123) [2006 **90** –: p7g p8g 8m⁶ 10.1g⁶ 8g 8m 9m² 9.9g⁵ 11.7m⁴ p12g Oct 21] tall, leggy gelding: has a round action: fairly useful handicapper nowadays: seems to stay 1½m: acts on polytrack, good to soft and good to firm going: tried blinkered, often tongue tied: has been blanketed/attended by expert in stall entry: looked wayward third 3-y-o start: sold 85,000 gns, joined J. Howard Johnson, and gelded. *G. A. Butler*

DIKTATORSHIP (IRE) 3 b.g. Diktat 126 – Polka Dancer 93 (Dancing Brave (USA) **60** 140) [2006 75: 6g 7m p5g 6f 10.1g³ 10.1m² 10.3m⁵ 10d p11g p9.5g p10g Dec 4] good-topped gelding: modest maiden handicapper: left Gay Kelleway after fourth start: stays easy 1¼m: acts on good to firm going: tried blinkered/visored. *E. R. Oertel*

DIL 11 b.g. Primo Dominie 121 – Swellegant 84 (Midyan (USA) 124) [2006 f8g Feb 5] **–** lengthy, good-topped gelding: lightly raced and no form since 2003: tried tongue tied/visored/in cheekpieces. *Mrs N. Macauley*

DILEK (FR) 3 b.c. Sendawar (IRE) 129 – Diyawara (IRE) (Doyoun 124) [2006 10.5d⁵ **117** 10.5d* 9d* 10d* 9d* 8d³ 7m Dec 10] fifth foal: half-brother to fairly useful French 7.5f and (at 2 yrs) 1m winner Diyapour (by Alhaarth) and French 11f winner Dihaila (by Valanour): dam fairly useful French 15f winner: smart performer: won maiden at Maisons-Laffitte and minor event at Longchamp in May, then listed race at Compiegne and Prix Daphnis at Longchamp (had plenty in hand when beating Champs Elysees 2 lengths) in June: creditable 2 lengths third to Stormy River in Prix Jean Prat at Chantilly, then reportedly sold privately and left A. de Royer Dupre in France: off 5 months and

294

renamed Viva Macau, well held in handicap at Sha Tin final outing: stays 10.5f: raced only on good to soft ground in France. *J. Moore, Hong Kong*

DILWIN (IRE) 2 b.g. (Feb 10) Dilshaan 119 – Welsh Harp (Mtoto 134) [2006 7m³ **67** 7.5m⁶ Sep 13] €28,000F, €38,000Y: strong, compact gelding: second foal: dam unraced daughter of smart 5f performer Welsh Note: better run in maidens when third at Catterick: gelded after final start. *D. Nicholls*

DIMASHQ 4 b.f. Mtoto 134 – Agwaas (IRE) (Rainbow Quest (USA) 134) [2006 56: **50** 12.4m 12m 15.8m² 16.2g* 16d 15.8d f12g Nov 10] sparely-made filly: modest performer: won selling handicap at Beverley in August: stays 2m: acts on good to firm and good to soft ground. *Ronald Thompson*

DIMBOOLA 2 b.g. (Feb 10) Averti (IRE) 117 – Mindomica 63 (Dominion 123) [2006 **87** 5d² 5g² 6g³ 5m* 5m 5.1m² 6m² Jul 26] compact gelding: has a quick action: seventh living foal: half-brother to 3 winners, including 6-y-o Molotov and 11f winner Minstrel Hall (by Saddlers' Hall): dam, 7f winner (including at 2 yrs), half-sister to Fred Darling winner/Oaks fourth Sueboog, herself dam of very smart 1m/1¼m performer Best of The Bests: fairly useful performer: won maiden at Ripon in June: good second in minor event at Chester and nursery at Leicester last 2 starts (gelded after): raced at 5f/6f: acts on good to firm going, probably good to soft: in cheekpieces fifth start (stiff task). *B. W. Hills*

DIMELIGHT 3 b.f. Fantastic Light (USA) 134 – Dime Bag 87 (High Line 125) [2006 **74** 69p: 9.9g⁴ 9d² 11m 9.9g² 9.9g 10.2f⁴ 9.9m 8.5m Sep 19] lengthy, quite attractive filly: fair maiden: will stay 1½m (dam 2m winner): acts on good to soft going: blinkered final start: tack slipped when pulled up soon after start on third outing: edgy on fifth start (below form): has raced freely. *D. R. C. Elsworth*

DIMINUTO 2 b.f. (Feb 9) Iron Mask (USA) 117 – Thicket 87 (Wolfhound (USA) 126) **62** [2006 p5g³ f5g³ f5g² p5g⁵ p5g⁵ p5g⁵ 6f³ 6f 5.1g⁶ 6f³ 5.1f* p5g p5.1g⁴ 5g⁴ 5.3m³ f6g³ f5g* f5g* p5.1g⁴ Dec 26] fourth foal: half-sister to 5f winner Baileys Applause (by Royal Applause): dam, 5f winner, ran only at 2 yrs: modest performer: won seller at Bath in August and nurseries (2) at Southwell in December: effective at 5f/6f: acts on all-weather and firm going. *M. D. I. Usher*

DINGAAN (IRE) 3 b.g. Tagula (IRE) 116 – Boughtbyphone 62 (Warning 136) [2006 **95** 81: p6g* p6g* p7g p7g* p7g⁶ 7g⁵ 8m 7m⁵ 6d Sep 22] tall gelding: improved into a useful performer, winning maiden and handicap in January, both at Lingfield, and handicap at Kempton in May: stays 7f: acts on polytrack and firm going: tried in cheekpieces/blinkers: slowly away last 2 outings. *A. M. Balding*

DINNER DANCE 3 b.f. Groom Dancer (USA) 128 – Misleading Lady (Warning 136) **–** [2006 f8g⁶ p7g p8.6g⁶ Mar 15] sister to 4-y-o Dinner Date and half-sister to 5-y-o Lord Mayor: dam, ran twice, sister to smart 1½m performer Little Rock and closely related to 3-y-o Short Skirt: little form: reportedly lost action second outing: blinkered final start: sold 1,000 gns. *W. J. Haggas*

DINNER DATE 4 ch.g. Groom Dancer (USA) 128 – Misleading Lady (Warning 136) **69** [2006 64: 11.5m² p10g* p12g³ 10m p10g p12g p12.2g p12g⁵ p12g p10g Dec 22] rather leggy, quite attractive gelding: fair handicapper: won at Kempton in May: stays easy 1½m: acts on polytrack and good to firm going. *T. Keddy*

DIONISIA (USA) 3 br.f. Tejano Run (USA) 121 – Essie's Maid (USA) (Linkage **114** (USA)) [2006 98: 8m* 8g* 8m⁶ 10m* 11m* 10m⁶ Oct 1] $13,000Y: well-made filly: half-sister to a winner in USA by Cherokee Colony: dam US 6f to 8.5f winner: smart performer: successful 5 times at 2 yrs, including in 2 listed races at both Milan and Rome: also length second of 4 to Lateral in Gran Criterium at Milan: won minor event and listed race at Rome in April, Premio Mario Incisa della Rochetta at Milan (by 3½ lengths from Wickwing) in May and Oaks d'Italia at Milan (best effort, by 6 lengths from Twardowska) in June: left R. Menichetti in Italy and off 3½ months, last of 6 in Prix de l'Opera at Longchamp final start, folding quickly: should stay 1½m: acts on soft and good to firm ground: has had tongue tied. *L. M. Cumani*

DIPPED WINGS (IRE) 3 b.f. In The Wings 128 – Fantasy Wood (IRE) (Charnwood **60** Forest (IRE) 125) [2006 10g 12f⁵ 14.1d⁵ 16d Sep 26] stocky filly: first foal: dam unraced half-sister to useful performers Son of Sharp Shot (stayed 1¾m) and Fantasy Hill (stayer): modest maiden: should stay 2m: sold 3,000 gns, sent to Qatar. *J. L. Dunlop*

DIRECT DEBIT (IRE) 3 b.g. Dansili 127 – Dimple (Fairy King (USA)) [2006 74p: **95** p8g* p10g² 8.1g³ 8m² 8m Jun 22] lengthy, quite attractive gelding: useful performer: won maiden at Lingfield in January: good placed efforts next 3 starts: eased as if amiss final outing (gelded after): stays easy 1¼m: acts on polytrack and good to firm going. *M. L. W. Bell*

DISCO BALL 3 ch.f. Fantastic Light (USA) 134 – Danceabout 110 (Shareef Dancer (USA) 135) [2006 8m 7d⁵ 6m² 6g 6d Oct 3] sturdy filly: has a fluent action: first foal: dam, 7f and 1m (Sun Chariot Stakes) winner, out of sister to Precocious and half-sister to Jupiter Island: fair maiden: best effort at 6f on good to firm going. *G. Wragg* **75**

DISCO DAN 2 b.g. (Mar 16) Danehill Dancer (IRE) 117 – Ghay (USA) 61 (Bahri (USA) 125) [2006 6.1m p6g⁶ 6m* 7g³ 7f⁶ 6m* 6g⁵ Oct 13] 13,000Y: lengthy, good-topped gelding: second foal: dam, ran once, out of close relation to Irish 1000 Guineas winner Enscone: fairly useful performer: won maiden in June and (after gelded) nursery in September, both at Brighton: stays 7f: acts on polytrack and good to firm going. *D. M. Simcock* **85**

DISCO LIGHTS 3 b.f. Spectrum (IRE) 126 – Discomatic (USA) (Roberto (USA) 131) [2006 76, a65: p10g⁴ 10v³ 11.6m 7.5g⁴ 9g³ 9g 9.5d 11.5g 8g⁴ 8d a12g⁴ Dec 24] close-coupled, workmanlike filly: fair maiden: left D. Daly after third outing: stays 1¼m: acts on polytrack and heavy ground. *C. Gourdain, France* **65**

DISCOMANIA 4 b.g. Pursuit of Love 124 – Discomatic (USA) (Roberto (USA) 131) [2006 71: p13g p12.2g⁶ f8g f14g⁵ p10g p12g f11g Dec 29] strong gelding: modest maiden nowadays: left V. Smith after fourth start: stays 1¾m: acts on all-weather and firm ground: tried in cheekpieces, visored/blinkered in 2006. *K. F. Clutterbuck* **50**

DISCO QUEEN (IRE) 2 ch.f. (Mar 31) Night Shift (USA) – Fashion 84 (Bin Ajwaad (IRE) 119) [2006 5d 6g⁴ p6g 7m* 8g² Sep 14] 17,000Y: strong filly: third foal: half-sister to 3-y-o Scot Love: dam, 1m (at 2 yrs)/1¼m winner, closely related to Oaks d'Italia winner Bright Generation: fair performer: good efforts upped in trip last 2 starts (in tongue tie/cheekpieces), winning selling nursery at Leicester in September and second in similar event at Yarmouth (claimed by D. Pipe £6,000): stays 1m. *P. C. Haslam* **65**

DISCORD 5 b.g. Desert King (IRE) 129 – Lead Note (USA) 62 (Nijinsky (CAN) 138) [2006 p8.6g⁶ p9.5g⁴ p12.2g³ p12.2g⁶ f12g 11.9s³ May 26] well held in bumpers/over hurdles: fair maiden: stays 1½m: acts on polytrack and soft ground. *T. H. Caldwell* **71**

DISCOTHEQUE (USA) 3 ch.f. Not For Love (USA) – Disco Darlin' (USA) (Citidancer (USA)) [2006 72: p7g³ p6g³ 5g² 6m 6.1f⁴ 6f² 6g⁵ 6m 7m⁶ 7m⁵ p7g p7g⁴ p7.1g* p9.5s² p8.6g p9.5g³ Dec 29] strong, compact filly: fair performer: won handicap at Wolverhampton in November: stays 9.5f: acts on polytrack and firm going: blinkered final 2-y-o start. *P. Howling* **68**

DISCREET CAT (USA) 3 b.c. Forestry (USA) 121 – Pretty Discreet (USA) 117 (Private Account (USA)) [2006 a8f* a9g* a7f* a8g* a8f* Nov 25] seventh foal: half-brother to 3 winners in USA, including 2002 2-y-o Grade 1 runner-up at 7f/1m Pretty Wild (by Wild Again): dam, US Grade 1 1¼m winner, out of Kentucky Oaks winner Buryyour-belief: high-class form, unbeaten in 6 races: sold privately out of S. Hough's stable after only outing at 2 yrs: successful in 2006 at Nad Al Sheba in minor event (very easily) and Group 2 UAE Derby Sponsored by S & M Al Naboodah Group (by 6 lengths from stable-companion Testimony), both in March, allowance optional claimer at Saratoga (impressively by 11 lengths, having been off for 5 months beforehand, reportedly having suffered from a cough and a temperature) in August, Grade 2 Jerome Breeders' Cup Handicap at Belmont (beat Valid Notebook by 10¼ lengths, cruising away final 2f) in October and Hill 'N' Dale Cigar Mile at Aqueduct (beat Badge of Silver by 3¼ lengths, **127 p**

UAE Derby Sponsored by S & M Al Naboodah Group, Nad Al Sheba—
unbeaten Discreet Cat wins from Testimony and the grey Flamme de Passion;
Uruguayan 'triple crown' winner Invasor (left) is fourth

just nudged clear) in November: will stay 1¼m, but isn't short of speed: a most exciting prospect. *Saeed bin Suroor*

DISGUISE 4 b.g. Pursuit of Love 124 – Nullarbor (Green Desert (USA) 127) [2006 75: **63** p6g⁶ 5f 6g⁵ 6m Jul 18] strong gelding: modest performer nowadays: will prove best at 5f/ 6f: acts on firm going, probably on polytrack: tried tongue tied: reportedly bled final start. *J. J. Quinn*

DISHDASHA (IRE) 4 b.g. Desert Prince (IRE) 130 – Counterplot (IRE) 91 (Last Ty- **–** coon 131) [2006 –, a53: f11g f11g p9.5g³ p12g p9.5g⁵ p10g⁶ May 8] strong, workmanlike **a51** gelding: modest performer: seemingly effective at 6f to 1½m: acts on polytrack, raced only on good ground or firmer on turf: joined Mrs A. Thorpe and won over hurdles in October/November. *C. R. Dore*

DISINTEGRATION (IRE) 2 b.g. (Mar 24) Barathea (IRE) 127 – Leave Me Alone **65 p** (IRE) 95 (Nashwan (USA) 135) [2006 7g 9m⁶ 8.3d⁵ Oct 10] 30,000F, €28,000Y: big, good-bodied gelding: closely related to fairly useful Irish 1½m winner Clearing The Water (by Sadler's Wells) and half-brother to Irish 1¼m winner Go For Glamour (by Sinndar): dam Irish 1m/1¼m winner: fair form in maidens, not knocked about, then gelded: will be suited by 1¼m/1½m: should make a better 3-y-o. *A. King*

DISPOL CHARM (IRE) 4 br.f. Charnwood Forest (IRE) 125 – Phoenix Venture **–** (IRE) 69 (Thatching 131) [2006 –: f6g Jan 19] leggy filly: little form. *D. W. Chapman*

DISPOL FOXTROT 8 ch.m. Alhijaz 122 – Foxtrot Pie 77 (Shernazar 131) [2006 77: **71** 10d⁴ 7g⁶ 9.1v p8.6g Nov 7] close-coupled mare: bad mover: fair performer, better on turf than all-weather: stays 11f: acts on fibresand, best on good ground or softer on turf: has been slowly away/found little/edged right. *D. Nicholls*

DISPOL ISLE (IRE) 4 gr.f. Trans Island 119 – Pictina (Petong 126) [2006 66: f7g* **71** f6g³ f7g⁴ 7.1v⁵ 7g* 8g 7.1g* 7f⁴ 7m 7f 6.9g⁵ 8m 7.1m 8f⁴ 7g 6v³ 6.5g³ Oct 18] leggy, workmanlike filly: fair handicapper: won at Southwell in January, Redcar in April and Musselburgh in May: effective at 6f to 1m: acts on fibresand and any turf going: tried blinkered/visored at 3yrs. *T. D. Barron*

DISPOL KATIE 5 ch.m. Komaite (USA) – Twilight Time (Aragon 118) [2006 90: **81** 7.1g⁵ 7.1m 7d⁶ 6v² 7m⁵ 7.1m 7m 7.2g² 6.9g⁶ 5.9m 5f 6m 6g⁴ 7.5g 7.2v 6s³ 6d 7d Oct 18] tall mare: fairly useful handicapper: effective at 5f to 7.6f: acts on any going: often races prominently. *T. D. Barron*

DISPOL LADY 3 b.f. Foxhound (USA) 103 – River of Fortune (IRE) 68 (Lahib (USA) **–** 129) [2006 45: f5g Apr 4] poor maiden: reportedly bled only 3-y-o outing. *P. T. Midgley*

DISPOL MOONLIGHT (IRE) 2 b.g. (Mar 8) Night Shift (USA) – Kiristina (FR) **–** (Royal Academy (USA) 130) [2006 5g 6m 7f 7m 7g Aug 4] lengthy, rather hollow-backed gelding: little form: tried blinkered. *T. D. Barron*

DISPOL PETO 6 gr.g. Petong 126 – Plie 75 (Superlative 118) [2006 59: 7g 6d⁵ 5.9g **62** f8g* f8g⁵ 9.2m 10.1s 12d⁵ p12.2g⁵ p13.9g f7g⁶ Dec 12] good-quartered gelding: modest performer: won apprentice handicap at Southwell in May: stays easy 1½m: acts on fibresand, soft and good to firm going: usually wears headgear: often races up with pace: has hung right. *R. Johnson*

DISPOL SPLENDID (IRE) 2 ch.f. (Mar 24) Raise A Grand (IRE) 114 – Somers **49** Heath (IRE) 58 (Definite Article 121) [2006 5m⁴ 7f² 7f 6s 7f 7g Sep 27] 3,400Y: sparely-made filly: second foal: dam 2-y-o 6f seller winner: poor maiden: left T. D. Barron after fourth start. *P. T. Midgley*

DISPOL TRULY (IRE) 2 b.f. (Apr 19) Bold Fact (USA) 116 – Beautyofthepeace **47** (IRE) (Exactly Sharp (USA) 121) [2006 6g⁶ 6g⁴ 6m² 7f⁴ f6m⁶ Oct 31] 800Y: half-sister to 3 winners, including 2002 2-y-o 6f to 1m winner Lakelands Lady (by Woodborough) and 1m (including at 2 yrs) to 14.8f winner Windshift (by Forest Wind), both fairly useful: dam unraced: poor maiden: claimed from P. Midgley second start. *A. G. Newcombe*

DISPOL VALENTINE 3 b.f. Whittingham (IRE) 104 – Bint Baddi (FR) (Shareef **39** Dancer (USA) 135) [2006 49?: f6g f7g 7m⁶ 7g⁶ 6.9m 6m 6.1f 7g Aug 2] leggy filly: poor maiden: stays 7f: wore cheekpieces last 3 starts. *P. T. Midgley*

DISPOL VELETA 5 b.m. Makbul 104 – Foxtrot Pie 77 (Shernazar 131) [2006 83: f8g⁴ **72** f8g⁴ 11g 9.9f⁵ 8.3d* 8d⁶ 9.8v 9.2g³ 9.2m 8.3s 10d⁵ p10g Nov 1] good-topped mare: fair handicapper: won jump jockeys event at Hamilton (for second successive year) in May: left T. D. Barron 10,000 gns after ninth start: probably stays 10.3f (all wins around 1m): acts on fibresand and soft ground. *Miss T. Spearing*

DISSITATION (IRE) 3 b.f. Spectrum (IRE) 126 – Park Charger 105 (Tirol 127) [2006 **77**
77: 8d³ 8.5s² 10m⁶ 8m⁶ 8m 8.5s⁵ p8.6g⁴ Nov 11] €65,000Y: sister to useful Irish 6f (at
2 yrs) and 7f winner Rum Charger and half-sister to several winners, including useful
Irish 2002 2-y-o 6f winner Pakhoes (by College Chapel): dam Irish 1m/1¼m winner:
fair maiden: below form at Wolverhampton final start: stays 8.5f: acts on heavy ground,
below form on good to firm: tried blinkered, in cheekpieces last 2 starts. *M. Halford,
Ireland*

DISTANT COUNTRY (USA) 7 b.g. Distant View (USA) 126 – Memsahb (USA) **70**
(Restless Native) [2006 74d, a82d: p8.6g⁶ p7.1g⁴ p7.1g* f7g p8g p8.6g³ p7.1g* p7.1g³
p7g⁶ p8.6g³ p8.6g* p8.6g³ p8.6g 8.5g p7.1g Jun 2] tall, good-topped gelding: fair performer: won sellers in January (sold from R. Harris 5,000 gns) and March and apprentice
claimer in April, all at Wolverhampton: claimed from K. Burke £8,000 after twelfth outing: stays 8.6f: acts on all-weather and firm ground: usually wears cheekpieces/blinkers:
has looked tricky ride/carried head awkwardly: usually held up. *B. D. Leavy*

DISTANT COUSIN 9 b.g. Distant Relative 128 – Tinaca (USA) (Manila (USA)) **–**
[2006 49+, a69: p12g f12g⁵ May 2] quite good-topped gelding: modest performer now- **a52**
adays: stays 14.6f: acts on all-weather, soft and good to firm going: often races freely:
wears headgear: finds little. *M. A. Buckley*

DISTANT DRUMS (IRE) 3 ch.f. Distant Music (USA) 126 – No Hard Feelings (IRE) **64**
86 (Alzao (USA) 117) [2006 –: p7g³ 7m⁴ 8f* p7g 7f Sep 18] workmanlike filly: modest
performer: looked none too straightforward when landing odds in 3-runner maiden
at Brighton in August: stays 1m: acts on polytrack and firm going: sold 1,500 gns, sent to
Qatar. *B. W. Hills*

DISTANT FLASH 2 b.f. (Mar 11) Mujahid (USA) 125 – Fly In Style (Hernando (FR) **56**
127) [2006 5.2f⁵ 6f* 6f 8.3g Oct 16] first foal: dam unraced out of sister to smart
1¼m/1½m performer Run Don't Fly: modest performer: won seller at Yarmouth (left
M. Wallace 8,800 gns) in July: should stay 1m: sold 4,500 gns later in October, sent to
Spain. *G. L. Moore*

DISTANT MIND (IRE) 3 b.f. Distant Music (USA) 126 – Mind Song 53 (Barathea **–**
(IRE) 127) [2006 –: 7m 8d f7g 7f p12.2m Oct 2] close-coupled, unfurnished filly: little
form: tried in cheekpieces. *Mrs C. A. Dunnett*

DISTANT PROSPECT (IRE) 9 b.g. Namaqualand (USA) – Ukraine's Affair (USA) **–**
(The Minstrel (CAN) 135) [2006 97: 20m 21m 16g⁶ Sep 15] close-coupled gelding: useful performer at best: hasn't won on Flat since 2001 Cesarewitch, and well held in 2006:
often sweating. *A. M. Balding*

DISTANT STARS (IRE) 2 ch.f. (Mar 10) Distant Music (USA) 126 – Thirlmere **69**
(Cadeaux Genereux 131) [2006 6d⁵ 6g⁶ 6m⁴ Sep 22] close-coupled filly: half-sister to
several winners, including fairly useful 2004 2-y-o 5f winner Canton (by Desert Style)
and 8-y-o Banjo Bay: dam unraced half-sister to useful 5f performer Power Lake: fair
form in maidens: likely to prove best at 5f/6f. *E. S. McMahon*

DISTANT SUNSET (IRE) 2 b.g. (Apr 18) Distant Music (USA) 126 – Blushing **54 p**
Libra (Perugino (USA) 84) [2006 6m p7g 6m 8f⁶ Sep 20] €12,000F, 20,000Y: first foal:
dam unraced out of half-sister to smart performer up to 1½m Theatre Script: modest
maiden: finished well when sixth of 17 in nursery at Redcar final start (gelded after): will
stay 1¼m: type to do better at 3 yrs. *B. W. Hills*

DISTANT SUN (USA) 2 b.g. (Mar 12) Distant View (USA) 126 – The Great Flora **63 p**
(USA) (Unaccounted For (USA) 124) [2006 p8.6g³ Nov 24] 30,000Y: second foal: dam
6f/6.5f winner in USA, including at 2 yrs: 25/1, seemed green when 6¼ lengths third of
10 to Aureate in maiden at Wolverhampton: sure to improve for experience. *R. Charlton*

DISTANT TIMES 5 b.g. Orpen (USA) 116 – Simply Times 64 (Dodge) [2006 **82**
79§: 7d 6g 5.9g² 6d 6g 6m 5.9m⁶ 6g* 6v* 6v⁶ 8d Nov 5] big, lengthy gelding: fairly
useful handicapper: left T. Easterby 18,000 gns after seventh start: won at the Curragh in
August and Listowel in September: stays easy 7f, best form at 6f: acts on heavy and good
to firm ground: tried visored/blinkered: formerly inconsistent. *L. McAteer, Ireland*

DISTANT VISION (IRE) 3 br.f. Distant Music (USA) 126 – Najeyba 80 (Indian **37**
Ridge 123) [2006 –: 7m³ 8.1m⁶ 10.1m 7m f7g f6g⁵ Nov 15] angular filly: poor maiden:
tried tongue tied/visored. *A. Berry*

DISTANT WAY (USA) 5 b.h. Distant View (USA) 126 – Grey Way (USA) 109 (Coz- **119**
zene (USA)) [2006 112: 8.5m* 9g* 10m* 8m⁵ 8g⁴ 10m³ Nov 5] second foal: dam Italian
1¼m/11f winner: smart performer: won 6 times at 4 yrs, notably in listed races at Rome
and Milan and Premio Ribot at Rome: successful at Rome in April/May in minor event,

listed race (by ¾ length from Ramonti) and Premio Presidente della Repubblica At The Races (strong run close home to beat Soldier Hollow a length): not in same form in autumn, 5¾ lengths third to Cherry Mix in Premio Roma final start: has form up to 1½m (fourth in Derby Italiano in 2004), best at 1m/1¼m: acts on good to firm and good to soft ground. *F. Brogi, Italy*

DISTILLER (IRE) 2 b.g. (Mar 21) Invincible Spirit (IRE) 121 – Bobbydazzle 81   **72**
(Rock Hopper 124) [2006 6m 7d⁵ 7f⁵ 7.1d⁶ 7f³ 7d⁴ Sep 29] 26,000Y: third foal: dam, 1m (including at 2 yrs) winner, half-sister to smart 7f performer Tumbleweed Ridge: fair maiden: stays 7f: acts on firm and good to soft going. *W. R. Muir*

DISTINCTION (IRE) 7 b.g. Danehill (USA) 126 – Ivy Leaf (IRE) 76 (Nureyev   **122**
(USA) 131) [2006 125: 13.3s* 20m³ Jun 22] big, strong, good sort: usually impresses in appearance: very smart performer: won Goodwood Cup in 2005: won 6-runner listed event at Newbury (by head from Balkan Knight, rallying) in May: respectable third to Yeats in Gold Cup (best effort when second in corresponding race in 2005) at Royal Ascot final start: reported in late-July to have suffered a leg injury: stays 2½m: acts on firm and soft going: has wandered/raced freely: reportedly very stiff behind after final 6-y-o start. *Sir Michael Stoute*

DISTINCTIVE LOOK (IRE) 3 b.f. Danehill (USA) 126 – Magnificient Style   **86**
(USA) 107 (Silver Hawk (USA) 123) [2006 80: 10g² 10m⁶ p10g² 9m* 8g⁶ Jul 28] big, good-topped filly: has scope: had a quick, unimpressive action: fairly useful performer: won handicap at Goodwood in June: stiff task, below form in listed race at Ascot final start: stayed 1¼m (possibly found 1m to short final outing): acted on polytrack and good to firm going: tongue tied last 3 starts: stud. *B. J. Meehan*

DISTINCTLY GAME 4 b.g. Mind Games 121 – Distinctly Blu (IRE) 70 (Distinctly   **–**
North (USA) 115) [2006 102: 5m 6m f5g Nov 15] tall, leggy, quite good-topped gelding: useful performer at 3 yrs: reportedly underwent knee surgery prior to reappearance: last all 3 outings in 2006 (said to have bled final one): best at 5f/6f: acts on fibresand, good to firm and good to soft going: tried in cheekpieces/blinkers. *K. A. Ryan*

DISTINCTLY JIM (IRE) 3 ch.g. City On A Hill (USA) 114 – Bucaramanga (IRE)   **62**
(Distinctly North (USA) 115) [2006 58: 8m 7.9m³ 7.5f 8f 7.9m 7.5f⁴ Jul 18] useful-looking gelding: modest maiden: stays 1m: raced only on ground firmer than good: blinkered fifth start. *B. Smart*

DISTINCTLYTHEBEST 6 b.g. Distinctly North (USA) 115 – Euphyllia 70 (Super-   **–**
power 113) [2006 7m Sep 11] strong, lengthy gelding: no sign of ability: tried tongue tied. *F. Watson*

DITTON DANCER 3 ch.f. Danehill Dancer (IRE) 117 – Dubai Lady 78 (Kris 135)   **–**
[2006 68: 10.3g 8.1f Jul 16] rather leggy, lengthy filly: fair performer at 2 yrs: last both starts in 2006. *J. J. Quinn*

DIUM MAC 5 b.g. Presidium 124 – Efipetite 54 (Efisio 120) [2006 66: 8d⁴ 10.1m* 9g*   **84**
9.9f⁶ 11.5g⁶ 10.1d² 10g³ 10.1s* 10s* Oct 16] leggy gelding: improved into a fairly useful handicapper, winning at Newcastle and Redcar in May, and Newcastle and Pontefract in October: stays 1¼m: acts on firm and soft going: tried blinkered: tended to hang left sixth start: held up. *N. Bycroft*

DIVALINI 2 ch.f. (Feb 23) Bertolini (USA) 125 – Divine Grace (IRE) (Definite Article   **–**
121) [2006 5m p6g 6g Oct 16] 58,000Y: second foal: half-sister to smart German 6f (including at 2 yrs)/7f winner Electric Beat (by Shinko Forest): dam ran twice: behind in maidens. *J. Akehurst*

DIVERSE FORECAST (IRE) 2 b.g. (Apr 27) Fasliyev (USA) 120 – Motley (Rain-   **–**
bow Quest (USA) 134) [2006 7f 7m 5d Aug 20] close-coupled gelding: last in maidens. *Mrs P. Sly*

DIVINE GIFT 5 b.g. Groom Dancer (USA) 128 – Child's Play (USA) (Sharpen Up   **104**
127) [2006 104: p8.6g² p10g 10.1g³ 10.3m* 8m 10.4f 10m⁶ Jul 29] good-topped gelding: has a quick action: useful handicapper: back to best when winning at Chester (by 1¼ lengths from Nice Tune, dictating) in May: below form after: best form at 1¼m: acts on polytrack, firm and good to soft going: blinkered fifth start: races prominently: successful over hurdles in August. *K. A. Ryan*

DIVINE LOVE (IRE) 2 b.f. (Feb 10) Barathea (IRE) 127 – Darling (Darshaan 133)   **78**
[2006 8.1m p7g⁵ p8g² Oct 20] 85,000Y: first foal: dam unraced close relation of useful 1½m performer Shemozzle: fair maiden: easily best effort when ¾-length second to Frag-rancy at Lingfield: will stay 1¼m. *E. J. O'Neill*

Burns Farm Racing's "Dixie Belle"

DIVINE RIGHT 2 ch.f. (Mar 16) Observatory (USA) 131 – Grail (USA) (Quest For **84**
Fame 127) [2006 6g* 6m Jul 12] 100,000Y: sturdy, medium-sized filly: third foal: dam,
French 1½m winner, half-sister to smart performer up to 1m Three Valleys, out of half-
sister to outstanding broodmare Hasili: fairly useful form: won maiden at Goodwood by
3½ lengths in June: 28/1 and stiff task when seventh of 10 behind Sander Camillo in
Cherry Hinton Stakes at Newmarket, showing inexperience: will stay at least 1m: looked
capable of better. *B. J. Meehan*

DIVINE RIVER 3 b.f. Lujain (USA) 119 – Berliese (IRE) (High Estate 127) [2006 **77**
10g* 10m6 p10g6 7m 9m p12g3 11g6 14g6 Sep 28] 14,000Y: angular filly: fourth foal:
dam, ran once, sister to Chester Vase winner High Baroque: fairly useful performer: won
maiden at Newbury in April: just respectable efforts at best after: stays 1½m (possibly
found stamina stretched at 1¾m): raced only on polytrack and good/good to firm going:
slowly away sixth outing. *A. P. Jarvis*

DIVINE SPIRIT 5 b.g. Foxhound (USA) 103 – Vocation (IRE) 74 (Royal Academy **76**
(USA) 130) [2006 89, a78: 5d 6g4 6g* 5m4 5g3 6m 5m 5d2 6m 5m 5m6 5g 6d6 5s 5d5
Sep 25] leggy gelding: fair handicapper: won at Catterick in June: effective at 5f/6f: acts
on polytrack, firm and good to soft going: probably on soft: sometimes wears cheek-
pieces/blinkers. *M. Dods*

DIVINE WHITE 3 ch.f. College Chapel 122 – Snowy Mantle 54 (Siberian Express **58**
(USA) 125) [2006 61: p6g 6f 5.1g5 6f3 6.1f4 5.5g 7.1f2 p7g6 Aug 11] lengthy, leggy filly:
modest maiden handicapper: effective at 6f/7f: acts on polytrack and firm going, probably
on heavy: wore cheekpieces final start: races prominently. *Mrs A. J. Perrett*

DIVISIVE 3 b.f. Alhaarth (IRE) 126 – Hakkaniyah 84 (Machiavellian (USA) 123) **58**
[2006 50: p8.6g p10g 8.1m5 8d 8d6 Oct 18] compact filly: modest maiden: left M. Blanshard after second start: stays 8.6f: acts on polytrack, good to firm and good to soft going:
hung left second 2-y-o outing: sold 2,500 gns. *G. Wragg*

300

DIVO NERO (IRE) 3 br.c. Black Minnaloushe (USA) 123 – Backgammon Becky **61**
(USA) (Irish River (FR) 131) [2006 p6g⁵ 7m 7m⁵ Jul 29] modest form in maidens: bred
to be suited by 1m+: sold 5,000 gns in October. *L. M. Cumani*

DIXIE BELLE 3 b.f. Diktat 126 – Inspiring (IRE) (Anabaa (USA) 130) [2006 94: 6f **113 ?**
5m² 5d⁵ 5.1g⁶ 5m² 5.2m* Sep 16] tall, leggy filly: smart performer: 50/1, seemingly
much improved form when winning Dubai International Airport World Trophy at
Newbury (by length from Excusez Moi, making running and virtually unchallenged) in
September: second in listed race at Sandown (behind Angus Newz) and minor event at
Leicester (to Tax Free) previously: seems better at 5f than 6f: acts on good to firm ground:
tongue tied: slowly away fourth outing, reluctant to go to post at Newbury. *M. G. Quinlan*

DIXIELAND BOY (IRE) 3 b.g. Inchinor 119 – Savannah Belle 84 (Green Desert **77**
(USA) 127) [2006 p8g⁵ 8.3f⁴ 7g⁴ 8d² p7.1m² p8g p7.1g² Dec 22] 8,000Y: strong, good-
bodied gelding: second foal: half-brother to Italian 6.5f to 1m winner by Second Empire:
dam, 2-y-o 5f winner, out of Ribblesdale winner Third Watch: fair maiden: stays 1m: acts
on polytrack and good to soft going, probably on firm. *P. J. Makin*

DIXIE STORM (USA) 3 b.c. Dixieland Band (USA) – Sweetheart (USA) (Mr Pros- **80 ?**
pector (USA)) [2006 8g⁵ p7g⁶ 7d Oct 3] angular, good-topped colt: second foal: brother
to useful 2001 2-y-o 7f winner Sweet Band, later successful in USA: dam, 5f (at 2 yrs in
France) and 7f (in USA) winner, out of US Grade 1 8.5f/9f winner Gorgeous, herself half-
sister to dam of Fantastic Light: easily best effort (fairly useful form) when fifth in
newcomers race at Newmarket: tongue tied final outing: sold 7,500 gns. *A. M. Balding*

DIYSEM (USA) 2 b.c. (Feb 5) Johannesburg (USA) 127 – Technicolour (IRE) 79 **89**
(Rainbow Quest (USA) 134) [2006 6g² 6m* 8g⁵ p8g⁴ Sep 30] $57,000Y, 30,000 2-y-o:
tall colt: fifth foal: half-brother to winners abroad by Boundary and Pulpit: dam, 2-y-o 7f
winner from 2 starts (should have stayed at least 1¼m), out of very smart French performer up to 9f Grecian Urn: fairly useful form: second to Wait Watcher at Newmarket,
then won maiden at Lingfield in September: ran respectably in minor events after: barely
stays 1m. *B. J. Meehan*

DIZZY DREAMER (IRE) 3 b.f. Spinning World (USA) 130 – Divine Prospect (IRE) **103**
75 (Namaqualand (USA)) [2006 77: 7g 5m⁶ 6g* 6.1m⁶ 6.1m⁶ Nov 20] tall, leggy filly: useful
performer: reportedly had breathing operation in winter: best effort when winning
handicap at Leicester (by 2 lengths from Blues In The Night) in August: sixth in listed
races at Chester (seemed not to handle track) and Maisons-Laffitte (made most, not entirely discredited) last 2 starts: should stay 7f: acts on good to firm going. *P. W. Chapple-
Hyam*

DIZZY FUTURE 4 b.g. Fraam 114 – Kara Sea (USA) 70 (River Special (USA)) [2006 **54**
62: p12.2g p13.9g⁵ p13.9g Dec 11] good-topped gelding: modest maiden: left B. Llewellyn after reappearance: stays 1¾m: acts on all-weather and good to firm ground: tried
blinkered/in cheekpieces: joined M. Bosley, won over hurdles in September. *M. R. Bosley*

DIZZY IN THE HEAD 7 b.g. Mind Games 121 – Giddy 60 (Polar Falcon (USA) 126) **80**
[2006 81, a73: 6d⁴ 5m* 5m 6f* 5m³ 6f⁶ 5m* 6m 6f 5d 6d Oct 3] leggy gelding: fairly
useful handicapper: won at Hamilton in May, June and July: best at 5f/6f: acts on any
turf going, probably on fibresand: wears headgear: usually front runner: often hangs.
I. Semple

DOCKSIDE DANCER (IRE) 2 b.f. (Apr 9) Docksider (USA) 124 – Kazimiera **–**
(IRE) 77 (Polish Patriot (USA) 128) [2006 5d 6g 6g⁵ Jul 22] 800Y: fifth foal: half-sister
to 3-y-o Revien: dam placed up to 1m: no form: dead. *P. T. Midgley*

DOCOFTHEBAY (IRE) 2 ch.c. (Mar 22) Docksider (USA) 124 – Baize 95 (Efisio **75**
120) [2006 8g² f8g* Nov 2] €35,000Y: sturdy colt: half-brother to several winners, including smart 1m (at 2 yrs)/9f (US Grade 1) winner Singhalese (by Singspiel) and 3-y-o
Baizically: dam 2-y-o 5f winner (later 5f/6f winner in USA): fair form: confirmed debut
promise (runner-up to Duke of Tuscany at Goodwood) when winning maiden at Southwell 3 months later: likely to stay 1¼m. *J. A. Osborne*

DOCTOR BROWN 2 b.g. (Mar 26) Dr Fong (USA) 128 – Molly Brown 95 **114**
(Rudimentary (USA) 118) [2006 6g* 7g² 6s* 6m² Sep 16] 34,000Y: strong, lengthy, good
sort: third foal: half-brother to fairly useful 2004 2-y-o 5f/6f winner Bright Moll (by Mind
Games) and 3-y-o La Fanciulla: dam 5f (at 2 yrs)/6f winner: smart performer: won
maiden at Leicester and 19-runner St Leger Yearling Stakes at York in August, in latter
impressing with speed and beating Cockney Rebel by 1½ lengths: runner-up both other
starts, stamina stretched in minor event at Ascot (7f), and improvement when short-

£300000 St Leger Yearling Stakes, York—in a typically competitive renewal
of this valuable prize, Doctor Brown (rail) sees off Cockney Rebel (right); Prime Defender is third,
ahead of We'll Confer, Dhanyata and Lipocco

headed by Excellent Art in 6-runner Mill Reef Stakes at Newbury: will prove best at
5f/6f: has edged right: joined A. Cruz in Hong Kong, where renamed Helene Brilliant.
B. J. Meehan

DOCTOR DASH 3 ch.g. Dr Fong (USA) 128 – Dashiba 102 (Dashing Blade 117) **89**
[2006 99: 8.1g 8g 8f⁴ 10d Sep 29] tall, close-coupled gelding: easy mover: just fairly useful handicapper at 3 yrs: stays 1m: acts on good to soft ground: raced freely last 2 starts:
sold 28,000 gns, sent to Saudi Arabia. *D. R. C. Elsworth*

DOCTOR DAVID 3 gr.g. Zilzal (USA) 137 – Arantxa 77§ (Sharpo 132) [2006 p8g **65**
p8g⁶ p8g p8g p8g³ p7g Aug 30] fair maiden: best efforts at 1m: raced only on polytrack.
E. R. Oertel

DOCTOR DENNIS (IRE) 9 b.g. Last Tycoon 131 – Noble Lustre (USA) 71 (Lyp- **66**
hard's Wish (FR) 124) [2006 61: f6g* f7g⁵ f6g² f6g f6g² f6s² f6g⁴ f6g p7g 7m 7g f6g⁵ f8g
p6g⁴ f7g Dec 12] good-bodied gelding: fair performer: won handicap at Southwell in
January: effective at 6f/7f: acts on all-weather, firm and soft going: wears headgear: held
up. *J. Pearce*

DOCTOR NED 2 b.g. (Mar 12) Bahamian Bounty 116 – Sangra (USA) 69 (El Gran **– p**
Senor (USA) 136) [2006 6s Aug 26] 46,000Y: quite good-topped gelding: third foal:
dam, maiden, might have proved best up to 7f: 20/1, green and behind in maiden at
Newmarket: gelded after: should progress. *N. A. Callaghan*

DOCTOR'S CAVE 4 b.g. Night Shift (USA) – Periquitum 56 (Dilum (USA) 115) **–**
[2006 74: p7.1g² p7.1g⁵ f6g⁴ p8.6g⁵ p7g p6g⁴ 7.1g⁶ p5g² 6.1m 5.7s p5.1g⁵ p6g p6g **a67**
p6g Oct 23] sturdy, close-coupled gelding: fair performer: effective at 5f to 8.6f: acts
on all-weather, best turf efforts on good going: tried tongue tied, usually blinkered: races
prominently. *K. O. Cunningham-Brown*

DOCTOR SCOTT 3 b.g. Medicean 128 – Milly of The Vally 93 (Caerleon (USA) 132) **96**
[2006 90: 8.1g⁶ 10.1m⁴ 10.4m⁶ 12m⁶ 11.9g⁵ 13m² 14m* 14m 14.1d⁶ 14g 13.1d⁶ Sep 16]
good-bodied gelding: useful handicapper: in good form prior to winning at Sandown
in July: below form last 3 starts (gelded after): stays 1¾m: acts on firm and good to soft
going. *M. Johnston*

DODAA (USA) 3 b.g. Dayjur (USA) 137 – Ra'a (USA) 106 (Diesis 133) [2006 8d **45**
p7.1m f6g p8.6g f7g f6g* Dec 28] workmanlike gelding: poor performer: won banded
race at Southwell in December: stays 6f: acts on fibresand: tried blinkered. *N. Wilson*

DODGE CITY (USA) 2 ch.c. (Feb 9) Gone West (USA) – Djebel Amour (USA) (Mt **101**
Livermore (USA)) [2006 6g⁴ 6g² 6m* 6g Sep 30] good sort: first foal: dam, 1m/8.5f
winner in USA, out of 1000 Guineas winner Sayyedati: useful form: improved to win

302

maiden at Goodwood in September, making all by 5 lengths despite hanging right over to far rail: 11/2, well held (albeit poorly drawn) in listed Two-Year-Old Trophy at Redcar: speedy, and raced at 6f, but bred to stay further: sent to USA. *J. Noseda*

DOLCELLO (IRE) 2 b.f. (Feb 23) Distant Music (USA) 126 – Mugello 96 (Emarati (USA) 74) [2006 6m Aug 5] €11,000Y: fifth foal: half-sister to 2 winners by Revoque, including 6f winner Miss Judgement: dam 2-y-o 5f winner: broke leg in maiden. *Mrs P. N. Dutfield* –

DOLCE MARIA (IRE) 3 b. or br.f. Trans Island 119 – The State of Her (IRE) (Turtle Island (IRE) 123) [2006 51: p5.1g p7.1g⁵ 5.7f Jun 17] maiden: just poor form in 2006, leaving K. Morgan £850 after second start: stays 6f: acts on polytrack and good to firm going: tongue tied final start. *M. R. Bosley* 38

DOLLAR CHICK (IRE) 2 b.f. (Apr 8) Dansili 127 – Dollar Bird (IRE) 103 (Kris 135) [2006 7.5f² 7f* Jul 19] €40,000Y: third foal: half-sister to useful 9.7f winner Higher Love (by Sadler's Wells) and 3-y-o Kentucky Warbler: dam, 2-y-o 1m winner who stayed 1¾m, half-sister to smart French middle-distance stayer Legend Maker, herself dam of 1000 Guineas winner Virginia Waters: fairly useful form: odds on after debut promise, won 4-runner minor event at Catterick by 2½ lengths from Rosbay (idled): will be suited by 1¼m+: capable of better if all is well. *M. Johnston* 82 p

DOLLY 4 b.f. Thowra (FR) – Sweet Symphony (IRE) (Orchestra 118) [2006 –: p8.6g 10.2g p10g⁶ Dec 13] poor maiden: trained by W. Knight on reappearance. *T. G. Dascombe* 45

DOLLY BROWN 3 ch.f. Bertolini (USA) 125 – Birichino (Dilum (USA) 115) [2006 54: f7g 5f Jun 14] lengthy filly: maiden: little form since debut at 2 yrs. *T. D. Easterby* –

DOLLY COUGHDROP (IRE) 2 b.f. (Apr 3) Titus Livius (FR) 115 – Fairy Berry (IRE) (Fairy King (USA)) [2006 5g f6g 5m⁴ 6f² 6m² 6m⁴ 6g⁴ 6s* 6d 6g⁵ 5s⁴ Oct 2] second foal: dam Italian maiden: fair performer: best effort when winning nursery at Catterick in August: will stay 7f: acts on firm and soft going: sold 12,000 gns. *K. R. Burke* 72

DOMART (POL) 6 gr.g. Baby Bid (USA) – Dominet (POL) (Dixieland (POL)) [2006 8.1d May 30] big, lengthy gelding: unraced on Flat in 2005: well beaten only start in 2006. *J. R. Best* –

DOMENICO (IRE) 8 b.g. Sadler's Wells (USA) 132 – Russian Ballet (USA) (Nijinsky (CAN) 138) [2006 70: 11.5m 11.6m 12f 14.8m⁵ 14.1m⁴ p16g³ Dec 18] strong, close-coupled gelding: modest handicapper nowadays: probably stays 2½m: acts on polytrack, soft and good to firm going: tried blinkered at 3 yrs: none too consistent. *J. R. Jenkins* 60

DOMESDAY (UAE) 5 b.g. Cape Cross (IRE) 129 – Deceive 100 (Machiavellian (USA) 123) [2006 9.2g 9s p8.6g⁵ Nov 25] well held in 2 bumpers and all 3 starts on Flat: tried visored. *W. G. Harrison* –

DOMINELLO 3 b.g. Primo Valentino (IRE) 116 – Forever Nellie (Sabrehill (USA) 120) [2006 –: 5s 7m p6m Oct 9] workmanlike gelding: no form in maidens. *R. A. Fahey* –

DOMINO DANCER (IRE) 2 b.g. (Feb 27) Tagula (IRE) 116 – Hazarama (IRE) 91 (Kahyasi 130) [2006 5g³ 6m² 6d⁵ 5.9g* 7m⁵ 6s Aug 24] €32,000F, 55,000Y: quite attractive gelding: fourth foal: dam, Irish 13f winner, half-sister to smart Irish 1¼m/1½m performer Hazarista: fairly useful performer: won maiden at Carlisle (by 8 lengths) in June: stiff task in valuable sales race at York final start (gelded after): likely to stay 1m: acts on good to firm going. *J. Howard Johnson* 87

DOMIRATI 6 b.g. Emarati (USA) 74 – Julia Domna (Dominion 123) [2006 76: p5.1g 5g f6g⁶ f6g May 2] angular gelding: modest performer: effective at 5f/easy 6f: acts on polytrack (probably on fibresand), good to firm and good to soft going: tried blinkered/in cheekpieces. *J. D. Bethell* 60

DONALDSON (GER) 4 b.g. Lando (GER) 128 – Daytona Beach (GER) (Konigsstuhl (GER)) [2006 108: 10.3g*ᵈⁱˢ 12g* 11g⁶ 12g 12g 10m⁶ Nov 5] brother to useful German winner up to 11f Daytona and half-brother to 3 winners in Germany, including useful 9f to 10.5f winner Duke of Hearts (by Halling): dam German 1m (at 2 yrs) to 11f winner: smart performer: first past post in maiden at Baden-Baden at 3 yrs, minor event at Krefeld in May (disqualified, tested positive for banned substance) and Deutschland-Preis der Freunde und Forderer at Dusseldorf (made all at steady pace, beat Schiaparelli ¾ length) in June: disappointing afterwards, gelded prior to final start: stays 1½m: acts on soft going. *P. Rau, Germany* 114

DON AND GERRY (IRE) 5 ch.m. Vestris Abu 105 – She's No Tourist (IRE) (Doubletour (USA)) [2006 p12.2g³ p12.2g 12f⁵ Jul 11] second foal: dam of little account over 67

hurdles in Ireland: dual bumper winner, fair novice hurdler (successful in May): best effort in maidens when third at Wolverhampton: raced only at 1½m: acts on polytrack. *P. D. Evans*

DONA VITORIA 3 b.f. Diktat 126 – Salanka (IRE) 68 (Persian Heights 129) [2006 62: **71 d** 6f³ 7g p7g p8g Nov 24] compact filly: fair maiden: well held after reappearance: should stay 7f: acts on firm ground: sold 24,000 gns. *S. Kirk*

DONEGAL SHORE (IRE) 7 b.g. Mujadil (USA) 119 – Distant Shore (IRE) 71 **47** (Jareer (USA) 115) [2006 45, a65: f8g⁵ f8g f11g Feb 12] rather leggy gelding: poor performer: gelded after final start: effective at 6f to 8.5f: acts on all-weather, heavy and good to firm going: tongue tied/visored. *Jennie Candlish*

DONNA BLINI 3 ch.f. Bertolini (USA) 125 – Cal Norma's Lady (IRE) 87 (Lyphard's **109** Special (USA) 122) [2006 109: 8s 8m 6f² 5m* 5f⁶ 5.2m⁶ 5g Sep 28] strong, lengthy filly: useful performer: successful in Cheveley Park Stakes at Newmarket at 2 yrs: won minor event there (beat Majestic Missile ¾ length) in July: respectable efforts when 1¼ lengths second to La Chunga in Summer Stakes at York and sixth to La Cucaracha in Audi Stakes (King George) at Goodwood (hung right) third/fifth starts: below form otherwise: best at 5f/6f (well beaten in 2000 Guineas on reappearance): acts on firm going: on toes and sweating second outing: races freely: sold 500,000 gns. *B. J. Meehan*

DONNA GIOVANNA 3 b.f. Mozart (IRE) 131 – Chelsea (USA) (Miswaki (USA) **74** 124) [2006 71: p7.1g⁴ p7.1g* p7.1g⁴ p8.6g p7g Oct 11] quite attractive filly: good walker: fair performer: won maiden at Wolverhampton in January: stays 7f: acts on polytrack and firm going: twice blinkered (including for win). *J. A. Osborne*

DONNA'S DOUBLE 11 ch.g. Weldnaas (USA) 112 – Shadha 57 (Shirley Heights **60** 130) [2006 60: 7d* 10d⁵ 10.1m⁴ 10.1d³ 8.3m⁶ 12.4m² 10d* 9.3g⁴ 10.1d⁴ 8d³ 11.1d 12s Oct 14] smallish, workmanlike gelding: modest performer: won seller at Catterick in April and handicap at Ayr in July: effective at 7f to 12.4f: acts on firm and soft going: tried blinkered/visored, wears cheekpieces nowadays: held up. *Karen McLintock*

DONNASPEAR (IRE) 3 b.f. Spectrum (IRE) 126 – Lancea (IRE) (Generous (IRE) **–** 139) [2006 p9.5g p12.2g f11g Dec 14] €13,000F, €21,000Y: fifth foal: half-sister to Irish 6f winner Salishan (by Namid) and 5-y-o Cantarna: dam unraced half-sister to very smart performer up to 1½m Riyadian out of Irish Oaks winner Knight's Baroness: well beaten in all-weather maidens. *J. Mackie*

DON PASQUALE 4 br.g. Zafonic (USA) 130 – Bedazzling (IRE) 105 (Darshaan 133) **–** [2006 74: p8.6g p8.6g f12g p8.6g f7g May 31] smallish gelding: fair maiden at 3 yrs: well held in 2006: tried tongue tied/visored/blinkered: possibly temperamental. *J. T. Stimpson*

DON PELE (IRE) 4 b.g. Monashee Mountain (USA) 115 – Big Fandango (Bigstone **97** (IRE) 126) [2006 92: 6m⁵ 6m* 5m 6.1f 6g 6m p6g² p6g⁶ p6g* p6g² Dec 30] good-bodied gelding: useful performer: won handicap at York in June and claimer at Wolverhampton (claimed from K. Ryan £15,000) in December: best at 6f: acts on polytrack and good to firm going: blinkered final outing at 3 yrs: none too consistent. *D. Carroll*

DON PIETRO 3 b.g. Bertolini (USA) 125 – Silver Spell 54 (Aragon 118) [2006 7m² **90** 8.3d* 8.6g² 10m³ p8.6g f11g 8s² 8m² p9.5m⁵ Nov 9] 14,000Y: tall gelding: fourth foal: half-brother to 8-y-o Warden Warren: dam, 5f winner, sister to smart sprinter Argentum: fairly useful performer: won maiden at Leicester in May: good placed efforts in handicaps after: effective at 1m to 1¼m: acts on polytrack, soft and good to firm ground. *D. J. Coakley*

DONT CALL ME DEREK 5 b.g. Sri Pekan (USA) 117 – Cultural Role 95 (Night **–** Shift (USA)) [2006 95: 18d Oct 14] big, workmanlike gelding: useful handicapper at best: ran as if needing race when mid-field in Cesarewitch at Newmarket only start in 2006: stays 16.5f: acts on all-weather and heavy ground: wore blinkers/eyeshields once in 2004. *J. J. Quinn*

DON'TCALLMEGINGER (IRE) 3 ch.g. Fruits of Love (USA) 127 – Scotia Rose **–** (Tap On Wood 130) [2006 61: 12m May 31] rather leggy, quite good-topped gelding: fair form in maidens at 2 yrs: never a threat in handicap only start in 2006: should stay 1½m. *M. H. Tompkins*

DON'T DESERT ME (IRE) 2 b.g. (Feb 8) Desert Style (IRE) 121 – Eye View (USA) **64** (Distant View (USA) 126) [2006 p8.6g p8.6g⁶ p7.1g⁵ p8g² Dec 20] €65,000Y: first foal: dam unraced out of half-sister to Danehill: fair maiden: second in nursery at Kempton: stays 1m: raced on polytrack. *R. Charlton*

DONT DILI DALI 3 b.f. Dansili 127 – Miss Meltemi (IRE) 100 (Miswaki Tern (USA) **102**
120) [2006 89: a7f⁵ a8f⁶ a9f³ p8g* 9g⁴ 8v May 28] leggy, quite good-topped filly: useful
performer: third in UAE Oaks (3¼ lengths behind Imperial Ice) prior to improved form
when winning listed race at Kempton (by 2 lengths from Song of Silence) in April: creditable fourth to Atlantic Waves in listed race at Newmarket next time: well beaten in Irish
1000 Guineas at the Curragh final outing: reportedly suffered hairline fracture of a tibia
following month: stays 9f: acts on dirt, polytrack, soft and good to firm going. *J. S. Moore*

DON'T MIND ME 3 b.f. Mutamam 123 – Dynamic Dream (USA) 87 (Dynaformer **58**
(USA)) [2006 7d 8m⁶ Jun 18] quite good-topped filly: second foal: half-sister to 4-y-o
Cross My Mind: dam, 2-y-o 7f winner, stayed 1¼m: better effort in maidens (green and
slowly away on debut) when sixth at Salisbury. *T. Keddy*

DON'T PANIC (IRE) 2 ch.c. (Apr 7) Fath (USA) 116 – Torrmana (IRE) (Ela-Mana- **96**
Mou 132) [2006 7m⁴ 6g⁴ 7.1d*⁷ Sep 29] €8,000F, €40,000Y: strong, lengthy colt:
sixth foal: half-brother to 2 winners in Italy, including winner up to 1¼m Dany Girl
(by Daggers Drawn): dam unraced: useful form: won maiden at Warwick in September
by 5 lengths, dictating: 13/2, improvement when 6 lengths eighth of 10 to Thousand
Words in Somerville Tattersall Stakes at Newmarket, still looking green: will stay 1m.
P. W. Chapple-Hyam

DON'T TELL (IRE) 2 ch.f. (Mar 14) Diesis 133 – Alinga (IRE) 91 (King's Theatre **55**
(IRE) 128) [2006 6d May 26] €58,000Y: plain filly: first foal: dam 6f (at 2 yrs) and 8.5f
(in USA) winner: ninth in maiden at Newmarket: dead. *M. L. W. Bell*

DON'T TELL SUE 3 ch.c. Bold Edge 123 – Opopmil (IRE) 68 (Pips Pride 117) [2006 **92**
72: 5.1s³ 5.7d 5m⁶ 5.3m* 5.1m* 5g 5f 6d Jun 26] strong, good-topped colt: fairly useful
handicapper: third at Brighton in May and Chepstow in June: below form after: best
around 5f: acts on polytrack, heavy and good to firm going: very slowly away sixth outing: sold 33,000 gns in July, joined Miss J. Tooth. *B. W. Hills*

DON'T TRY IT ON 2 b.c. (Apr 27) Mujahid (USA) 125 – Branston Berry (IRE) 86 **–**
(Mukaddamah (USA) 125) [2006 5d 6m 6m⁶ Jun 20] lengthy, dipped-backed colt: little
form: dead. *M. W. Easterby*

DONYA ONE 4 b.f. Cadeaux Genereux 131 – Fadhah 65 (Mukaddamah (USA) 125) **41**
[2006 63: f6g p7.1g f7g f8g³ f7g 8.2f Jul 8] poor maiden nowadays: stays 1m: acts on
good to firm ground, probably on all-weather: sold 800 gns, sent to Saudi Arabia. *John
A. Harris*

DOONIGAN (IRE) 2 b.g. (Feb 15) Val Royal (FR) 127 – Music In My Life (IRE) 59 **54 p**
(Law Society (USA) 130) [2006 6d 6d⁶ f7g⁴ Nov 14] €26,000F, 30,000Y: tall gelding:
half-brother to several winners, including 1m (at 2 yrs) to 2¼m winner Galleon Beach
(by Shirley Heights) and Italian 9f to 10.5f winner Musical Score (by Blushing Flame),
both useful: dam maiden who stayed 1m: modest form in maidens: will be suited by
1¼m+: should do better. *A. M. Balding*

DORA EXPLORA 2 br.f. (Jan 22) Vettori (IRE) 119 – Fredora 93 (Inchinor 119) [2006 **88**
6m⁵ 7f* 7.1m⁵ 7d⁶ 8m Sep 19] 3,500F: big, angular, workmanlike filly: second foal: half-
sister to a winner in Germany by Piccolo: dam 7f to 1¼m winner: fairly useful performer:
won maiden at Folkestone in July: better form in listed race at Sandown (fifth to Sudoor)
and Sweet Solera Stakes at Newmarket (last of 6): well beaten in nursery final start:
should stay 1m: acts on firm and good to soft going: sold 30,000 gns. *P. W. Chapple-Hyam*

DORA'S GREEN 3 b.f. Rambling Bear 115 – Compradore 82 (Mujtahid (USA) 118) **57**
[2006 51: p6g⁵ p5g⁵ 5d 5.1g⁶ 7f 6m³ 6g 5.7f p7g f5g⁵ Nov 20] sparely-made filly: modest
maiden: left M. Blanshard after eighth start: stays 6f: best efforts on polytrack and good
to firm ground: wore cheekpieces final outing. *S. W. Hall*

DORELIA (IRE) 3 b.f. Efisio 120 – Dominio (IRE) 99 (Dominion 123) [2006 6g³ 6g³ **86**
p8g* 8g Nov 3] 120,000Y: compact filly: sister to 4-y-o Bowness and half-sister to 2
winners, notably smart 5f performer Dominica (by Alhaarth): dam, best at 5f, half-sister
to smart sprinter Ya Malak out of half-sister to Cadeaux Genereux: fairly useful and
progressive form: won maiden at Lingfield in September: far from discredited in listed
race at Saint-Cloud final outing: stays easy 1m: acts on polytrack. *J. H. M. Gosden*

DORIC CHARM 2 b.f. (Mar 30) Diktat 126 – Cinnamon Lady 77 (Emarati (USA) 74) **92**
[2006 6d² 6s* 6.1d* 6d³ Oct 27] 14,000Y: strong, lengthy filly: third foal: dam 7f winner:
fairly useful form: unextended to make all in maiden at Ayr in September and minor
event at Nottingham in October: further progress when 1¼ lengths third of 11 to Blue
Echo in listed race at Newmarket, rallying: will stay 7f: raced on ground softer than good.
B. Smart

DORIC (USA) 5 ch.g. Distant View (USA) 126 – Doree (USA) 110 (Stop The Music **89** (USA)) [2006 93: 7.2g 6s 7m⁵ 8m 7m Jul 1] tall gelding: fairly useful performer: likely to prove best at 7f/1m: acts on soft and good to firm going: wore cheekpieces final start (below form). *B. Ellison*

DORIES DREAM 2 b.f. (Jan 31) Foxhound (USA) 103 – Milliscent 49 (Primo Domi- **–** nie 121) [2006 5.2m p6g⁵ 5.1m Sep 4] 3,400Y, resold 3,000Y: fourth foal: half-sister to 4-y-o Baymist: dam maiden who stayed 1m: little show in maidens. *Jane Southcombe*

DORN DANCER (IRE) 4 b.f. Danehill Dancer (IRE) 117 – Appledorn 99 (Doulab **71** (USA) 115) [2006 65: 5v* 5d² 6.1m⁴ 6d⁶ 6d⁴ 5.9g 7g³ 6m³ 6.1f⁵ 6d 6d² 5s⁴ 6s⁶ 6.1d⁶ Oct 4] good-topped filly: fair handicapper: won at Musselburgh in March: stays easy 7f: acts on heavy and good to firm going: tried blinkered/in cheekpieces: held up: possibly not the most straightforward. *D. W. Barker*

DORN HILL 4 b.f. Lujain (USA) 119 – Benedicite (Lomond (USA) 128) [2006 55, **43** a47: 6m 6g 6m 7.1m⁶ 8g 7m⁵ Aug 22] close-coupled, quite good-topped filly: poor per- former: stays 7f: acts on polytrack and good to firm ground: often wears cheekpieces: has flashed tail: refused to enter stall intended fifth outing. *D. G. Bridgwater*

DOROTHY'S FRIEND 6 b.g. Grand Lodge (USA) 125 – Isle of Flame (Shirley **103** Heights 130) [2006 16.2f⁶ 16.1m⁴ p16g⁶ 21m⁶ 16g* 13.9d Aug 23] strong, useful-looking gelding: useful handicapper: reportedly suffered leg injury and unraced in 2005: good effort when winning quite valuable event at Ascot (won same race in 2004) in August, beating McEldowney by 4 lengths: ran respectably when fourth to Toldo in Northumber- land Plate at Newcastle and sixth to Key Time at Goodwood second/fourth outings: blinkered, well below form in Ebor at York final start: needs further than 1¾m, and stays 21f: acts on firm going, weakened quickly when below form only outing on polytrack: usually held up: game. *R. Charlton*

DOTTY'S DAUGHTER 2 ch.f. (Apr 4) Forzando 122 – Colonel's Daughter 61 **59** (Colonel Collins (USA) 122) [2006 p5.1g⁴ p5g 5d² 5f⁴ 6g³ 5f⁶ 5.1f⁶ 6s 5g³ 5m² 5.3m* p5.1g* f6g f6g Nov 15] smallish, quite attractive filly: first foal: dam sprint maiden (ran only at 2 yrs): modest performer: successful in sellers at Brighton and Wolverhampton in September: should have won at Thirsk on third outing, eased prematurely (jockey banned for 28 days): best at 5f: acts on all-weather, firm and good to soft going: usually wears headgear: tends to hang left. *Mrs A. Duffield*

DOUBLE AGENT (FR) 3 ch.g. Sinndar (IRE) 134 – Conspiracy 98 (Rudimentary **–** (USA) 118) [2006 8m Apr 22] medium-sized, sturdy gelding: 50/1, burly and green, ran as if amiss when tailed off in maiden at Newbury: sold 1,500 gns in July. *J. L. Dunlop*

DOUBLE BANDED (IRE) 2 b.g. (Mar 13) Mark of Esteem (IRE) 137 – Bronzewing **53** 103 (Beldale Flutter (USA) 130) [2006 7g p7g Nov 11] leggy, sparely-made gelding: modest form in maidens. *J. L. Dunlop*

DOUBLE BAY (USA) 3 b.f. War Chant (USA) 126 – Once To Often (USA) (Raise A **64** Native) [2006 7g 7d⁴ 10g⁵ 10m p12g p10g Dec 16] $30,000Y: rather leggy, quite good- **a–** topped filly: closely related to winner in USA by Pine Bluff and half-sister to several winners there: dam, Canadian 4.5f (at 2 yrs) and 6.5f winner, closely related to Breeders' Cup Sprint third Exclusive Enough: modest maiden: well held in handicaps last 3 starts: may prove best up to 1m. *Jane Chapple-Hyam*

DOUBLE BILL (USA) 2 b. or br.c. (Mar 26) Mr Greeley (USA) 122 – Salty Perfume **61 p** (USA) (Salt Lake (USA)) [2006 6d Aug 23] $18,000Y, 95,000 2-y-o: big, strong, angular colt: closely related to 2 winners in USA by Gone West and half-brother to 2 winners there: dam, US Grade 2 2-y-o 6.5f winner, half-sister to smart performer up to 1m Green Perfume: 6/1, needed race when eighth in maiden at York won by La Presse: should improve. *P. F. I. Cole*

DOUBLE CARPET (IRE) 3 b.g. Lahib (USA) 129 – Cupid Miss (Anita's Prince **67** 126) [2006 60?: p6g 6s 7d² p7g f6g² f7g Dec 5] unfurnished gelding: fair maiden on turf, **a55** modest on all-weather: stays 7f: acts on fibresand and good to soft going. *G. Woodward*

DOUBLE DEPUTY (IRE) 5 b.h. Sadler's Wells (USA) 132 – Janaat 74 (Kris 135) **–** [2006 91: 10g 11.9s Sep 1] smallish, good-bodied horse: fairly useful performer at best, lightly raced: well held both starts in 2006: wore tongue tie and tried visored previously. *J. J. Quinn*

DOUBLE EXPOSURE 2 b.c. (Feb 21) Double Trigger (IRE) 123 – Last Night's Fun **–** (IRE) (Law Society (USA) 130) [2006 10.1d p8g Dec 19] well held in maidens: bred for stamina (brother to 7-y-o Corrib Eclipse). *Jamie Poulton*

DOUBLE HELIX 7 b.g. Marju (IRE) 127 – Totham 84 (Shernazar 131) [2006 p8.6g Mar 27] good-topped gelding: maiden: well held only Flat outing since 2003: tried blinkered/visored: sent to Belgium. *B. P. J. Baugh*   **–**

DOUBLE M 9 ch.g. First Trump 118 – Girton Degree 41 (Balliol 125) [2006 62, a78: p6g p7g p6g p7g⁴ p5g³ p6g p6g⁴ p6g* 5g 5.7f 5.3m⁵ p6g p6g p6g p6g p7g Dec 18] strong, sturdy gelding: modest performer, better on all-weather than turf: won banded event at Kempton in May: effective at 5f to easy 7f: acts on all-weather, firm and good to soft ground: wears visor/blinkers: waited with. *Mrs L. Richards*   **a63**

DOUBLE MYSTERY (FR) 6 ch.g. Starborough 126 – Chene de Coeur (FR) (Comrade In Arms 123) [2006 60: 9.5g² 8m 13f* 13d⁶ 12f⁵ p8.6g Dec 30] smallish, lengthy gelding: fair handicapper: won at Wexford in August: left E. Griffin in Ireland prior to final outing: stays 13f: acts on firm ground, probably on soft: tried blinkered/in cheekpieces: tongue tied at 6 yrs: races prominently. *K. J. Burke*   **66**

DOUBLE OBSESSION 6 b.g. Sadler's Wells (USA) 132 – Obsessive (USA) 102 (Seeking The Gold (USA)) [2006 12v⁴ 12g 16m 16d³ 16s 14m³ 20m 15.8m⁴ 16.2m⁵ Aug 16] compact gelding: one-time smart performer: left M. Johnston and missed 2005: best effort in 2006 (useful form) when third in handicap at Thirsk fourth start: stays 2½m: acts on firm and soft ground: usually blinkered/visored: usually races prominently. *D. Nicholls*   **99 d**

DOUBLE OH SEVEN (IRE) 3 ch.c. Alhaarth (IRE) 126 – Liberi Versi (IRE) (Last Tycoon 131) [2006 65: 7.1m 10f⁵ 8.1m f7g Nov 2] leggy colt: fair maiden at 2 yrs: no show in 2006: tried blinkered/tongue tied. *J. W. Unett*   **–**

DOUBLE PRECEDENT 2 b.f. (Mar 22) Polish Precedent (USA) 131 – Jolies Eaux 73 (Shirley Heights 130) [2006 7f 7d 8.5g Aug 27] 8,000Y: lengthy filly: seventh foal: half-sister to 3 winners, notably very smart 1m (at 2 yrs) to 13f winner Water Jump (by Suave Dancer): dam, maiden, probably stayed 1¼m: no show in maidens. *M. Johnston*   **–**

DOUBLE RANSOM 7 b.g. Bahamian Bounty 116 – Secrets of Honour (Belmez (USA) 131) [2006 62: p10g⁵ p10g 9.2m* 7.9m 9.2g⁵ 8.5m 9d Oct 8] lengthy, good-topped gelding: modest performer: won claimer at Hamilton in May: effective at 1m/1¼m: acts on polytrack, heavy and good to firm ground: tried in cheekpieces, usually wears blinkers. *Mrs L. Stubbs*   **53**

DOUBLE SPECTRE (IRE) 4 b.g. Spectrum (IRE) 126 – Phantom Ring 62 (Magic Ring (IRE) 115) [2006 72: 10d³ 10s⁵ 11m 12g³ 11.6f 9.9m² 10.2m 8.1m* 10d³ Oct 10] smallish, close-coupled gelding: fair handicapper: won at Sandown in September: effective at 1m to 1½m: acts on firm and good to soft going. *Jean-Rene Auvray*   **74**

DOUBLE VALENTINE 3 ch.f. Primo Valentino (IRE) 116 – Charlottevalentina (IRE) 80 (Perugino (USA) 84) [2006 49: p5g 7f⁶ 6m² 6.1f⁶ 5f p6g² p7g Dec 19] modest maiden handicapper: best form at 6f: acts on polytrack and good to firm going. *R. Ingram*   **61**

DOUBLE VODKA (IRE) 5 b. or br.g. Russian Revival (USA) 125 – Silius (Junius (USA) 124) [2006 81: 16.1m Jun 29] leggy gelding: fairly useful handicapper: upped in trip, never dangerous only outing in 2006: effective at 1m to 11f: acts on soft and good to firm going: fairly useful hurdler, won in May and December. *C. Grant*   **–**

DOUBLY GUEST 2 b.f. (Apr 12) Barathea Guest 117 – Countess Guest (IRE) 59 (Spectrum (IRE) 126) [2006 5d 7f³ 7f 8m³ 8s* Oct 16] strong, workmanlike filly: has a round action: first foal: dam, maiden who stayed 7f (ran only at 2 yrs), half-sister to Oaks third Crown of Light: fair performer: won nursery at Pontefract in October: will be suited by 1¼m: acts on firm and good to soft going. *G. G. Margarson*   **74**

DOUBTFUL SOUND (USA) 2 b.c. (Mar 5) Diesis 133 – Roam Free (USA) (Unbridled (USA) 128) [2006 p7.1g² Dec 28] $12,000Y: first foal: dam, ran twice in France, granddaughter of very smart performer up to 1m Interval: 12/1, encouraging neck second to Play Straight in maiden at Wolverhampton, taking good hold in front and headed close home: should improve. *T. D. Barron*   **71 p**

DOUGHTY 4 b.g. Bold Edge 123 – Marquante (IRE) (Brief Truce (USA) 126) [2006 53: f7g f8g p9.5g f8g⁶ Apr 10] maiden: well held in 2006: tried blinkered/tongue tied. *D. J. Wintle*   **–**

DOVE COTTAGE (IRE) 4 b.g. Great Commotion (USA) 123 – Pooka 65 (Dominion 123) [2006 67: 10.9s² p10g⁴ p10g⁴ 10.2m* 10.2m* 10.1g 10d⁴ Sep 13] close-coupled gelding: fair handicapper: won twice at Chepstow in June: stays 11f: acts on polytrack, firm and soft going: tried in cheekpieces: front runner. *W. S. Kittow*   **78**

DOVEDALE 6 b.m. Groom Dancer (USA) 128 – Peetsie (IRE) (Fairy King (USA)) **65**
[2006 69: 12s p16.5g p16.5m Oct 14] lengthy mare: fair performer: stays easy 1¾m: acts
on polytrack, soft and good to firm going. *H. S. Howe*

DOVEDON HERO 6 ch.g. Millkom 124 – Hot Topic (IRE) (Desse Zenny (USA)) **77**
[2006 88d: p13g⁵ p13g* p12.2g⁶ p12g⁵ p12g⁵ p16g² p12g⁵ 12m² 21.7m 12.6m²
16.1m⁶ 12d 14.1m⁵ p12.2f Aug 30] sturdy, close-coupled gelding: fair performer nowadays: won handicap at Lingfield in February: stays 2m: acts on all-weather and firm
going: blinkered: held up: races freely, and is a weak finisher. *P. J. McBride*

DOWER HOUSE 11 ch.g. Groom Dancer (USA) 128 – Rose Noble (USA) 62 (Vagu- **74**
ely Noble 140) [2006 78, a93: p12g⁶ p10g p12g⁵ p12.2g p12g p10g⁴ p12g p12g² p10g **a91**
10.5s⁶ 10g⁶ 10d⁴ 8.2s² p9.5g⁶ p9.5m p9.5g² p12g³ Dec 20] lengthy, rather leggy gelding:
has a fluent, round action: fairly useful handicapper on all-weather, fair on turf: effective
at 1m to easy 1½m: acts on all-weather, firm and soft going: tongue tied: takes good hold:
held up. *Andrew Turnell*

DOWLLEH 2 b.g. (Apr 13) Noverre (USA) 125 – Al Persian (IRE) (Persian Bold 123) **84**
[2006 6d² 5.7g² 6m² 6m⁵ p6g² 6g² 7m⁵ 6d⁴ 5.1m⁵ Oct 8] 53,000F, 45,000Y: good-topped
gelding: sixth foal: half-brother to fairly useful Irish 1m winner Dicharachera (by Mark
of Esteem) and 1m to 10.5f winner in Spain by Suave Dancer: dam, winner in Spain,
half-sister to high-class performer up to 1½m Legal Case: fairly useful performer: runner-
up 5 times prior to winning maiden at Brighton in August: ran creditably in nurseries after
(gelded subsequently): stays 7f: acts on polytrack, good to firm and good to soft going.
M. R. Channon

DOWNBEAT 2 b.c. (Mar 30) Fantastic Light (USA) 134 – Green Charter 77 (Green **64**
Desert (USA) 127) [2006 7m⁶ 7.1m 8.1g⁶ 8s 7d* Nov 4] good-topped colt: fifth foal:
half-brother to 3-y-o Manouche and 2001 2-y-o 7f winner Safe Trip (by Hector Protector): dam, 2-y-o 7f winner, closely related to 1¼m to 2m winner First Charter and half-
sister to middle-distance performer Private Charter, both smart: eye-catching sixth at
Haydock third start in maidens before well held in nursery final outing for J. Dunlop:
blinkered, won maiden at Copenhagen in November: will stay 1¼m/1½m: acts on good
to firm and good to soft going. *Caroline Stromberg, Sweden*

DOWNLAND (IRE) 10 b.g. Common Grounds 118 – Boldabsa 96 (Persian Bold 123) **–**
[2006 73: f7g 7d 7m p7.1g* f7g⁵ 7f p7.1g p8.6g f8g 8g⁶ Aug 14] tall, good sort: modest **a59**
performer: won seller at Wolverhampton in May: best at 7f/1m: acts on all-weather,
heavy and good to firm going: tried blinkered at 4 yrs. *N. Tinkler*

DOWN THE BRICK (IRE) 2 b.g. (Apr 14) Daggers Drawn (USA) 114 – Damezao **64**
(Alzao (USA) 117) [2006 p5g⁶ 7.1g³ p7g 7m⁵ 10g 8.3d Oct 9] close-coupled gelding:
modest maiden on balance: best efforts at short of 1m. *B. R. Millman*

DOWN THE WELL (IRE) 2 b.f. (Apr 3) Mujadil (USA) 119 – Batchelor's Button **82**
(FR) (Kenmare (FR) 125) [2006 5f 5.1m* 5s⁵ p6g⁵ p6g⁴ p5g* 8f⁵ 8f 6f⁶ Dec 13]
€17,000F, €36,000Y: rather leggy filly: half-sister to several winners, including useful
French/US 5f (at 2 yrs) to 1¼m winner Speedfriend (by Unfuwain): dam French 7.5f
winner: fair performer: won maiden at Nottingham in May and nursery at Kempton
(left J. Osborne after) in August: creditable eighth of 12 to Valbenny in Grade 3 Miesque
Stakes at Hollywood on penultimate start: seems to stay 1m: acts on polytrack and firm
going. *J. M. Cassidy, USA*

DOWN TO THE WOODS (USA) 8 ch.g. Woodman (USA) 126 – Riviera Wonder **– §**
(USA) (Batonnier (USA)) [2006 9s Sep 24] tall, angular gelding: well held only Flat outing since 2004: sometimes wears headgear/tongue tie: temperamental. *N. Wilson*

DOYLES LODGE 2 b.g. (Apr 7) Prince Sabo 123 – True Bird (IRE) 63 (In The Wings **71 p**
128) [2006 6f 6d⁴ Oct 9] 4,200Y: fourth foal: half-brother to winner in Spain by Vettori:
dam staying maiden: fair form in maidens at Windsor 2½ months apart, better run when
fourth to Heroes: will stay 7f/1m: should progress. *H. Candy*

DRAGON DANCER 3 b.c. Sadler's Wells (USA) 132 – Alakananda 92 (Hernan- **119**
do (FR) 127) [2006 66p: p10g³ 11g² 12.3f² 12m² 12g⁴ 10m² 12m⁴ 12s⁶ Oct 21]
'They can't all be good horses!'. They can, of course, even in a bunched
finish, but usually they're not, and by season's end Dragon Dancer stood out as the
one horse seemingly flattered by his position, a close second, in one of the tightest
finishes to the Derby, flattered by his proximity at least in relation to third and third.
Whereas Sir Percy had better form beforehand and Dylan Thomas improved afterwards, Dragon Dancer ended the campaign still a maiden after four more starts. He

hasn't won in nine outings in all, and on the balance of his form can be rated no better than smart.

Leaving aside the raising of questions over the level of the overall form, a bunched finish often points to a race run at a false pace to at least some degree. Unusually, the Derby was run at something less than an end-to-end gallop, despite having eighteen runners. In the circumstances, Dragon Dancer was better ridden than most, soon in a good rhythm, racing close up under Darryll Holland, going for home with Dylan Thomas rounding Tattenham Corner and running on strongly to the line, going down by a short head to Sir Percy with Dylan Thomas a head behind him in third and Hala Bek another short head away in fourth. Starting at 66/1, Dragon Dancer would have been the longest-priced Derby winner since Psidium won at the same odds for his trainer's father Harry in 1961. He would also have been the first maiden to win the Derby since Merry Hampton who won the race in 1887 on his racecourse debut. As it was, he made a little piece of history as the first maiden to reach a place since Freefoot, another trained by Harry Wragg who finished third in 1973. Freefoot was still a maiden at the end of his three-year-old season and broke his duck in the John Porter as a four-year-old.

Apart from Epsom, Dragon Dancer came closest to breaking his duck when going down by three quarters of a length to Papal Bull in the Chester Vase on his third start of the season, rallying at the finish after tending to hang right round the

Mr J. L. C. Pearce's "Dragon Dancer"

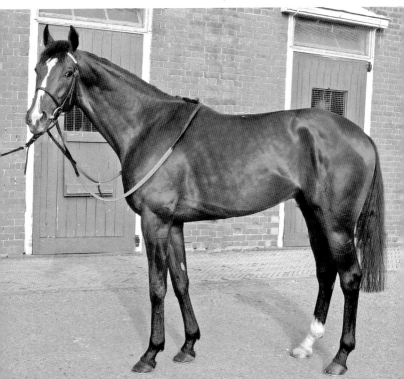

turns. After Epsom, he was never quite the same. Beaten six and a half lengths into fourth in the Irish Derby at the Curragh in July, when he failed to confirm Epsom placings with the winner Dylan Thomas and Derby sixth Best Alibi, he finished runner-up in the Prix Eugene Adam at Maisons-Laffitte later in the month. A mile and a quarter seemed too sharp for him that day and Dragon Dancer ran a better race when fourth of six in the Prix Niel returned to a mile and a half at Longchamp in September, going down by three and a quarter lengths behind close finishers Rail Link and Youmzain, with Papal Bull fifth.

Dragon Dancer (b.c. 2003)	Sadler's Wells (USA) (b 1981)	Northern Dancer (b 1961)	Nearctic / Natalma
		Fairy Bridge (b 1975)	Bold Reason / Special
	Alakananda (br 1998)	Hernando (b 1990)	Niniski / Whakilyric
		Alouette (gr 1990)	Darshaan / Alruccaba

Whether or not he finally wins a good race, Dragon Dancer should find a place at stud given his pedigree. By Sadler's Wells, he is from a much sought-after family, and his yearling sister sold for €2m at the Goffs Million Sale in Ireland in September. His half-brother Ajaan (by Machiavellian), winner of a maiden over a mile in October as a two-year-old, made 80,000 guineas as a yearling, and Dragon Dancer made 200,000 guineas at the same age. Dragon Dancer is the first foal of his dam Alakananda, a half-sister to the dual Champion Stakes winner Alborada and the smart mile-and-a-half performer Albanova. Alakananda's dam Alouette, a winner at a mile and a mile and a half in Ireland, is also impeccably bred. She is a sister to the dam of Oaks runner-up Quarter Moon and Irish One Thousand Guineas winner Yesterday, and a half-sister to the very smart mile-and-a-quarter winner Last Second (dam of Aussie Rules), as well as the smart stayer Alleluia. Alakananda gained her successes at around a mile and a half, showing fairly useful form in winning twice when tried in blinkers. Alouette was also tried in blinkers as was Albanova, but Dragon Dancer has shown few quirks so far except for a high head carriage, a trait not unusual for a son of his sire. Withdrawn from the Arc de Triomphe on firmish going in October, Dragon Dancer's best form has come on firm ground all the same, and he ran his one poor race of the season on soft in the St Simon Stakes at Newbury on his final start, albeit ridden with more restraint than usual that day. A tall, quite good-topped colt, his best efforts have come when ridden up with the pace. *G. Wragg*

DRAGON FLAME (IRE) 3 b.c. Tagula (IRE) 116 – Noble Rocket (Reprimand 122) **63** [2006 5g⁴ 6.1d⁴ 5.1s⁴ 5.1g⁵ p6g 6.1d Oct 13] angular colt: modest maiden: acts on soft going. *M. Quinn*

DRAGON FLOWER (USA) 2 b.f. (Jan 24) Gulch (USA) – Rawabi (Sadler's Wells **79** (USA) 132) [2006 6g² p7g² 7d Oct 3] strong filly: first foal: dam unraced sister to Dewhurst Stakes winner In Command, closely related to smart sprinter Lyric Fantasy and half-sister to very smart sprinter Royal Applause: fair form in maidens, second at Newbury and Kempton (odds on, left with lot to do): well held on softer ground final start: will stay 1m. *B. W. Hills*

DRAGON SLAYER (IRE) 4 ch.g. Night Shift (USA) – Arandora Star (USA) **88** (Sagace (FR) 135) [2006 81: f8g⁶ p8.6g² p12.2g³ p12.2g⁴ p7.1g p8.6g² p8.6g³ 10.1m* **a82** 10.5g³ 10g* 10f³ 9.8d 10g⁵ 10.1m Sep 13] rather leggy gelding: fairly useful handicapper, better on turf than all-weather: won at Yarmouth in March and Newmarket in June: left M. Attwater prior to final outing: stays easy 1½m: acts on all-weather and firm ground: tried in cheekpieces: usually races prominently. *Ian Williams*

DRAMATIC REVIEW (IRE) 4 b.g. Indian Lodge (IRE) 127 – Dramatic Shift (IRE) **50** (Night Shift (USA)) [2006 54: 10.5m⁶ 10g⁶ 9.1v Oct 28] close-coupled gelding: modest maiden handicapper: left P. Haslam after second start: stays 1¼m: acts on heavy and good to firm going: often wears headgear: tongue tied nowadays. *J. Barclay*

DRAMATIC TOUCH 2 b.f. (Mar 31) Royal Applause 124 – Sismique (Warning 136) **49 p** [2006 p6s⁴ Dec 14] second foal: dam, French 1m winner, out of half-sister to high-class performer up to 1½m Wagon Master: 4/1, fourth to Pixie Ring in maiden at Wolverhampton, green and not knocked about: sure to progress. *G. Wragg*

DRAMATIC TURN 2 b.f. (Mar 10) Pivotal 124 – Eveningperformance 121 (Night   **87 p**
Shift (USA)) [2006 6s⁶ 5.1s* Oct 25] good-topped filly: third foal: half-sister to 7f winner
Evening Encore (by Kris): dam, 5f performer, out of half-sister to 2000 Guineas winner
Tirol: encouraging debut at Newbury (sixth to Party), then smoothly won maiden at Not-
tingham by 2½ lengths, value more: will make a useful sprinter. *Mrs A. J. Perrett*

DRAMATICUS 4 b.g. Indian Ridge 123 – Corinium (IRE) 116 (Turtle Island (IRE)   **–**
123) [2006 –: 6m 7d 7s Oct 10] strong gelding: useful at 2 yrs: no form since: tried tongue
tied. *B. Palling*

DRAWBACK (IRE) 3 b.g. Daggers Drawn (USA) 114 – Sacred Heart (IRE) 45 (Cat-   **64**
rail (USA) 123) [2006 57p: f7g* 8.1d 7.1d 7f⁵ 8g 8m 8d p8.6g f8g Nov 14] modest
performer: won claimer at Southwell (claimed from J. Osborne £12,000) in January:
seems to stay 1m: acts on fibresand and firm ground: tried in cheekpieces/blinkers: sometimes slowly away. *R. A. Harris*

DRAWN GOLD 2 b.g. (Apr 28) Daggers Drawn (USA) 114 – Gold Belt (IRE) 61   **69 p**
(Bellypha 130) [2006 6s⁴ Oct 6] workmanlike colt: half-brother to several winners,
including 5f (at 2 yrs)/6f winner Goldeva (by Makbul) and 9.4f to 1½m winner Royal
Cavalier (by Prince of Birds), both useful: dam 1m winner: 11/1 and burly, faded when
fourth to Kafuu in maiden at York: open to improvement. *R. Hollinshead*

DRAWN OUT (IRE) 3 ch.g. Daggers Drawn (USA) 114 – Fastnet (Forzando 122)   **–**
[2006 54: p9.5g f8g f8g⁵ 12m Jul 10] workmanlike gelding: modest maiden at 2 yrs: well
held in 2006: wears headgear. *P. C. Haslam*

DRAYTON (IRE) 2 b. or br.c. (Mar 9) Danetime (IRE) 121 – Exponent (USA)   **107**
(Exbourne (USA) 125) [2006 5v*ᵈⁱˢ 5d* 5v* 6g² 6m⁵ 5g⁵ Aug 24] €18,000F, 15,500Y:
third living foal: half-brother to 4-y-o Exponential: dam unraced: useful performer: first
past post in maiden in March (subsequently disqualified after testing positive) and 2 listed
races in May, all at the Curragh: ran well there behind Holy Roman Emperor in Railway
Stakes (¾-length second) and Phoenix Stakes (fifth): odds on, below-par fifth in listed
event at Tipperary final start: effective at 5f/6f: acts on heavy and good to firm going:
front runner: joined M. de Kock in UAE. *T. Stack, Ireland*

DREAM AGAIN 2 b.f. (May 9) Medicean 128 – Dance A Dream 115 (Sadler's Wells   **65 p**
(USA) 132) [2006 8.2m p7g⁵ Oct 21] good-bodied filly: sixth foal: half-sister to 5-y-o
Elusive Dream and 3-y-o Dance A Daydream: dam, 1m (at 2 yrs) and 11.4f winner who
was second in Oaks, sister to 2000 Guineas winner Entrepreneur and half-sister to
Coronation Stakes winner Exclusive (dam of very smart 7f/1m performer Chic): better
effort in maidens when fifth at Lingfield: will be suited by 1¼m/1½m: should make a
better 3-y-o. *Sir Michael Stoute*

DREAM ALIVE 5 b.g. Unfuwain (USA) 131 – Petite Sonnerie 78 (Persian Bold 123)   **–**
[2006 55: 11.6m 8m Aug 19] leggy gelding: well held both starts in 2006: usually tongue
tied. *S. Curran*

DREAM CATCHER (SWE) 3 b.c. Songline (SWE) 110 – Queen Ida (SWE) (Diligo   **95 ?**
(FR)) [2006 8g 8m³ a12g⁴ 9.8s⁵ p9.5g⁶ Nov 25] Swedish-bred colt: useful performer: ran
only at Taby at 2 yrs, winning maiden and 2 minor events: good 3¾ lengths fourth to Mad
Dog Slew in listed Svenskt Derby at Jagersro third start: better effort in handicaps in
Britain when respectable sixth at Wolverhampton final outing: best effort at 1½m: acts on
dirt and good to firm going: tried tongue tied. *R. A. Kvisla*

DREAM CHAMPION 3 b.c. Fraam 114 – Forest Fantasy 61 (Rambo Dancer (CAN)   **89**
107) [2006 81p: p8g² p8g² 11g² 12.1d² 11g³ 12f* 12g² 12.3m* 14.1f⁴ 12s 12f* Sep 18]
sturdy colt: fairly useful performer: won maiden at Catterick in June and handicaps
at Chester (by 5 lengths) in July and Folkestone (carried head awkwardly) in September:
stays 1½m: acts on polytrack, firm and good to soft going (possibly not on soft): sold
120,000 gns. *M. R. Channon*

DREAM DANCE 3 ch.f. Diesis 133 – Bella Ballerina 90 (Sadler's Wells (USA) 132)   **62**
[2006 8.3d 8.3f Jul 10] sturdy foal: sister to useful 1¼m winner Design Perfection and
half-sister to fairly useful 1¼m winner Ballet Ballon (by Rahy): dam, 9f winner, sister to
high-class 1¼m performer Stagecraft: modest form in maidens at Windsor: slowly away
on debut. *H. Morrison*

DREAM EILE (IRE) 2 b. or br.c. (Apr 19) Mull of Kintyre (USA) 114 – Jayess Elle   **78**
55 (Sabrehill (USA) 120) [2006 6f 6g p6g³ Jul 13] fifth foal: half-brother to 3 winners,
including 3-y-o Smart Ass and 5-y-o Penel: dam maiden: fair maiden: left Patrick Martin
after debut: much improved when third at Wolverhampton: will stay 7f: tried blinkered.
P. D. Deegan, Ireland

DREAM FACTOR (IRE) 3 br.f. Bold Fact (USA) 116 – Bobby's Dream 53 (Reference Point 139) [2006 63: p6g⁴ p6g p7.1g 7m 6.1f Jul 8] stocky filly: modest performer: well below form last 4 starts: stays 7f: acts on all-weather and good to firm going: tried visored. *J. O'Reilly* **51 d**

DREAM FANTASY (IRE) 3 b.g. Baratpea (IRE) 127 – Night Mirage (USA) 80 (Silver Hawk (USA) 123) [2006 99: 10s³ Sep 14] useful performer: ran well only 3-y-o start when third to Krugerrand in handicap at Ayr: stays 1¼m: acts on polytrack, soft and good to firm going. *Sir Mark Prescott* **99**

DREAM FOREST (IRE) 3 b.g. Raise A Grand (IRE) 114 – Theresa Green (IRE) 65 (Charnwood Forest (IRE) 125) [2006 60: p6g³ 6f p7g 7g p7g⁴ 8.1m 8.1m³ 7g p7.1g 10s f8g* f8g⁶ p9.5g p10g⁴ Dec 30] quite good-topped gelding: fair on all-weather, modest on turf: won maiden claimer at Southwell (claimed from Mrs P. Dutfield) in October: stays 1m: acts on all-weather and good to firm going. *M. S. Saunders* **63 a70**

DREAM IMPACT (USA) 5 b.h. Royal Academy (USA) 130 – One Fit Cat (USA) (Storm Cat (USA)) [2006 109: 5m² 6d* 5m² 6g 6m⁴ 5m* 5m* 5f 5s³ 6m Oct 13] $26,000Y: well-made horse: third foal: dam 2-y-o 6f winner in USA: useful performer: won 4 races in 2005, including Gran Premio Citta'di Napoli at Naples: successful in 2006 in minor event at Rome in March and minor event/listed race (for second year running) at Naples in June/July: below form last 3 starts, first of them Audi Stakes (King George) at Goodwood: effective at 5f/6f: acts on soft and good to firm ground: has had tongue tied: sweating/slowly away at Goodwood. *L. Riccardi, Italy* **109**

DREAM LODGE (IRE) 2 ch.c. (Mar 12) Grand Lodge (USA) 125 – Secret Dream (IRE) (Zafonic (USA) 130) [2006 p8g³ 8.1g⁴ p7.1g* 8s⁶ Oct 16] 45,000Y: medium-sized, good-topped colt: first foal: dam unraced half-sister to 5-y-o Gentleman's Deal out of 1000 Guineas winner Sleepytime: fairly useful form: won maiden at Wolverhampton in October: stiff task in listed race at Pontefract final start: should stay 1m. *J. G. Given* **84**

DREAM MASTER (IRE) 3 b.g. Priolo (USA) 127 – Pip's Dream 52 (Glint of Gold 128) [2006 8s 8.2g 10s Oct 18] very tall, good-topped gelding: well held in maidens: slowly away on debut. *J. Ryan* **–**

DREAM MOUNTAIN 3 b.g. Mozart (IRE) 131 – Statua (IRE) 98 (Statoblest 120) [2006 70, a56: 8f 9d 8v 10d² p10g⁶ p12g⁴ Dec 22] useful-looking gelding: fair performer: claimed from M. Johnston after fourth start: probably stays easy 1½m: acts on all-weather, good to firm and good to soft going. *Ms J. S. Doyle* **68 a57**

DREAM OF DUBAI (IRE) 5 b.m. Vettori (IRE) 119 – Immortelle (Arazi (USA) 135) [2006 48: 7.9f⁶ 7f³ 8m⁵ 8d Sep 27] modest maiden: covered by Lujain in spring: stays 1¼m: acts on polytrack and good to firm ground: tried in cheekpieces/blinkered. *P. Mitchell* **61**

DREAM OF PARADISE (USA) 3 ch.f. Atticus (USA) 121 – Scrumptious (USA) (Slew O' Gold (USA)) [2006 56: f8g 10.3f¹¹ 8.5g⁶ 10.3g 8f⁴ 9.9f² 10.1f⁶ 10.3m* 10.1m 10.3m⁶ p9.5g Sep 30] fair handicapper: won at Chester in August: stays 10.3f: acts on fibresand and firm going. *Mrs L. Williamson* **67**

DREAM ON DREAMERS (IRE) 2 b.g. (Apr 22) Iron Mask (USA) 117 – Harifana (FR) (Kahyasi 130) [2006 5g 6g 6s p8.6g Nov 27] well-made gelding: no form. *R. C. Guest* **–**

DREAM PRIZE (IRE) 3 ch.g. Peintre Celebre (USA) 137 – Night Teeny (Platini (GER) 126) [2006 10g⁶ 9.8m* 10m⁴ 12m 12s Oct 6] 43,000F, 170,000Y: good-bodied gelding: fluent mover: first foal: dam, German 1¼m winner, half-sister to Preis der Diana winner Night Petticoat, herself dam of Deutsches Derby winner Next Desert: fairly useful performer: whinnying and swishing tail in paddock, won maiden at Ripon in April: good fourth on handicap debut at Sandown: well beaten both starts after: stays 1¼m: acts on good to firm going: visored final start: sold 9,000 gns, sent to Qatar. *Sir Michael Stoute* **85**

DREAM ROSE (IRE) 3 b.f. Anabaa (USA) 130 – Hiddnah (USA) 105 (Affirmed (USA)) [2006 79: 7g 8m 7.2d² 7f 8f* 8.1f⁶ 8.3m³ 9m 8.5d Aug 28] rangy, lengthy filly: fairly useful handicapper: won at Pontefract in July: below form last 2 starts: stays 1m: yet to race on heavy going, acts on any other: sold 12,000 gns. *M. R. Channon* **80**

DREAM SCHEME 2 b.f. (Feb 24) Machiavellian (USA) 123 – Dream Ticket (USA) 73 (Danzig (USA)) [2006 6g* 6d² Oct 27] good-topped filly: has a quick action: sixth foal: sister to smart French/US 1m/1¼m performer Magic Mission and closely related to French 1m winner Drifting Skies (by Lion Cavern): dam, 7f winner, out of smart half-sister to dam of 4-y-o Deep Impact: good impression when winning maiden at Newmarket by 3½ lengths in September: second to College Scholar in minor event there **91 p**

month later, not run of race and still green: will be suited by 7f/1m: useful performer in the making. *E. A. L. Dunlop*

DREAM SHARED 3 ch.f. Fantastic Light (USA) 134 – Land of Dreams 115 (Cadeaux **71** Genereux 131) [2006 9s p10g⁴ 10.9m⁶ 12g⁵ p13g² 10d Nov 1] leggy, quite attractive filly: third foal: half-sister to 5-y-o Into The Dark and useful Irish 2004 2-y-o 7f winner Only Make Believe (by Selkirk): dam, best at 5f (won Flying Childers and King George Stakes), also 6f winner at 2 yrs: fair maiden: probably stays 13f: acts on polytrack, best effort on turf on good going: flashed tail fifth start: sold 26,000 gns. *E. A. L. Dunlop*

DREAMS JEWEL 6 b.g. Dreams End 93 – Jewel of The Nile 35 (Glenstal (USA) 118) **53** [2006 p12.2g⁶ 10.2m Jun 3] seemingly better effort in maidens when seventh at Chepstow (slowly away): fair winning hurdler. *C. Roberts*

DREAM THEME 3 b.c. Distant Music (USA) 126 – Xaymara (USA) (Sanglamore **105** (USA) 126) [2006 79p: p7g⁸ 7s⁶ 7f⁸ 7d* 7.1m³ 7d Sep 23] big, good-bodied colt: useful performer: won maiden at Kempton in April and handicaps at Goodwood and Leicester (beat Jimmy The Guesser by 3 lengths) in August: good 3¾ lengths third to Cesare in minor event at Warwick penultimate start: below form in valuable handicap at Ascot final start: should stay 1m: acts on polytrack, firm and good to soft going. *B. W. Hills*

DREAM WITNESS (FR) 3 gr.f. Sagamix (FR) 129 – Dial Dream (Gay Mecene **54** (USA) 128) [2006 9.9g⁵ 10m p12g 11.7g 16.2m 11.9f⁴ 11.7m⁴ Aug 25] €45,000Y: half-sister to several winners, including 9-y-o Material Witness and useful French 1½m/ 15f winner Periple (by In The Wings): dam French 9f and 10.5f (listed race) winner: modest maiden: seems to stay 1½m: acts on good to firm going: joined B. Duke, won juvenile hurdle in September. *W. R. Muir*

DRESSED TO DANCE (IRE) 2 b.f. (Feb 16) Namid 128 – Costume Drama (USA) **67** (Alleged (USA) 138) [2006 6m 7d 6g⁴ p7g² p7.1g² Dec 7] €9,000F, 8,000Y: sturdy filly: third foal: half-sister to fairly useful Irish 2-y-o 8.5f winner Widely Accepted (by Mujadil): dam unraced: fair maiden: stays 7f: acts on polytrack. *B. J. Meehan*

DRESS TO IMPRESS (IRE) 2 b.c. (Jan 27) Fasliyev (USA) 120 – Dress Code (IRE) **79** 83 (Baratea (IRE) 127) [2006 5v³ 5.1g² 5f² p5g⁴ p5.1g* p5.1g² p5.1g³ Dec 26] €30,000Y: good-topped colt: first foal: dam, 2-y-o 5f winner, sister to useful performer up to 7f Rag Top: fair performer: in frame all starts prior to winning maiden at Wolverhampton in November by 2 lengths from Ama de Casa: placed in nurseries thereafter: will prove best kept to 5f: acts on polytrack, probably on any turf going: front runner, takes strong hold: consistent. *J. R. Boyle*

DR FLIGHT 4 b.g. Dr Fong (USA) 128 – Bustling Nelly 94 (Bustino 136) [2006 p12g – Jan 28] showed ability in bumpers: tongue tied and in cheekpieces, well held in maiden at Lingfield. *H. Morrison*

DRIFTING GOLD 2 ch.f. (Mar 26) Bold Edge 123 – Driftholme 27 (Safawan 118) **69** [2006 p5.1g² 6.1g⁵ p5.1g² p6g² 6g 5.7m³ p7g⁵ Oct 17] 1,600F, 2,700Y: fourth foal: half-sister to winners abroad by Muhtarram and Petong: dam maiden: fair maiden: placed 4 times, once in nursery: should stay 7f: best efforts on polytrack. *C. G. Cox*

DRINK TO ME ONLY 3 b.g. Pursuit of Love 124 – Champenoise 64 (Forzando 122) **55** [2006 57: p6g* p7.1g f5g p7.1g p6g⁶ 5.9g³ 5.9m⁴ 6f⁶ 7.1g* 7.1d 7.1m Aug 24] sturdy gelding: modest handicapper: won at Wolverhampton in January and Musselburgh in July: stays 7f: acts on polytrack and good to firm going: tried in cheekpieces. *J. R. Weymes*

DR LIGHT (IRE) 2 b.g. (Feb 6) Medicean 128 – Allumette (Rainbow Quest (USA) **55** 134) [2006 p9.5m p8g⁶ Dec 1] still green, much better effort in maidens when sixth to Sweeney at Lingfield second outing: should stay 1¼m. *S. Kirk*

DR MCFAB 2 ch.c. (Feb 12) Dr Fong (USA) 128 – Barbera 54 (Baratea (IRE) 127) **63** [2006 p7.1g p7.1g² Dec 1] 68,000F, 130,000Y: first foal: dam lightly-raced daughter of useful sprinter Premiere Cuvee: better effort in maidens at Wolverhampton when length second to Little Eskimo. *J. A. Osborne*

DR SHARP (IRE) 6 ch.g. Dr Devious (IRE) 127 – Stoned Imaculate (IRE) 73 (Durgam **95** (USA)) [2006 95: 16m 18.7m 13.9s 14g 18s 18d³ 16d* Oct 27] good-topped gelding: useful handicapper: creditable 3 lengths third to Detroit City in Cesarewitch at Newmarket prior to winning 16-runner event there in October by 1¼ lengths from Kayf Aramis: stays 2½m: acts on heavy and good to firm going: races prominently. *T. P. Tate*

DR SYNN 5 br.g. Danzero (AUS) – Our Shirley 84 (Shirley Heights 130) [2006 76: 7s **71** 6m p6g 7m² 7f² 7m 7g 7d 7d Oct 18] tall, good-topped gelding: fair handicapper: best at 6f/7f: acts on firm and soft going: no easy ride: none too consistent. *J. Akehurst*

Iveco Daily Solario Stakes, Sandown—Drumfire (left) makes most to win from Caldra, who catches Danebury Hill (No.2) for second; Norisan (rail) is fourth

DR THONG 5 ch.h. Dr Fong (USA) 128 – Always On My Mind 91 (Distant Relative **83** 128) [2006 86: 8.1f 8.3f p8g⁵ 8m³ 7m* 7g p7g Sep 30] tall, lengthy horse: fairly useful performer: best effort in 2006 when winning handicap at Southwell in September: effective at 7f/1m: acts on polytrack, soft and good to firm going: tried in cheekpieces/ blinkers, sometimes tongue tied (including last 4 starts): free-going sort: sent to USA. *P. F. I. Cole*

DRUM DANCE (IRE) 4 b.g. Namid 128 – Socialite (IRE) (Alzao (USA) 117) [2006 **58** 64: f6g 7g⁶ 6g⁴ 5.9g² 7g³ 6m³ 6d 6g⁴ 5s 7d⁵ Oct 10] sturdy, close-coupled gelding: modest performer: probably best at 5f/6f: acts on firm and soft going: tried in cheekpieces. *N. Tinkler*

DRUMFERGUS BOY (IRE) 4 b.g. Josr Algarhoud (IRE) 118 – Care And Comfort **–** 64 (Most Welcome 131) [2006 16d p13.9g³ p12.2g⁵ Dec 2] little form in maidens. *A. Oliver, Ireland*

DRUMFIRE (IRE) 2 b.c. (Apr 5) Danehill Dancer (IRE) 117 – Witch of Fife (USA) **106** 91 (Lear Fan (USA) 130) [2006 7.5f* 7g² 7.1g* 7d³ 8s Oct 21] €43,000Y: big, lengthy colt: has scope: fifth foal: half-brother to smart 2001 2-y-o 6f winner Ho Choi (by Pivotal), later 1m winner in Hong Kong, and 1m winner Witchcraft (by Zilzal): dam 2-y-o 6f/7f winner: useful performer: won maiden at Beverley in June and 8-runner Iveco Daily Solario Stakes at Sandown (rallied to beat Caldra ½ length) in August: also ran well when neck second to Thousand Words in minor event at Newbury and third of 28 to Miss Beatrix in very valuable sales race at the Curragh: seemed unable to handle testing ground (eased) in Racing Post Trophy final start: should stay 1m: acts on firm and good to soft going. *M. Johnston*

DRUMMING PARTY (USA) 4 b. or br.g. War Chant (USA) 126 – Santaria (USA) **69** (Star de Naskra (USA)) [2006 56: p6g 5.1m² 6.1m³ 6g⁶ 6g² 5.2m* 5g⁵ 5f 5g⁴ 5.7f Sep 9] good-topped gelding: fair handicapper: passed post first at Nottingham (hampered runner-up and subsequently demoted) in May and Newbury in June: effective at 5f/6f: acts on firm going: tongue tied: has no left eye, and tends to hang. *A. M. Balding*

DRUMROLL (IRE) 4 b.g. Diktat 126 – Mystic Tempo (USA) 76 (El Gran Senor **65** (USA) 136) [2006 67: p12g⁵ p8.6g f8g³ f8g³ 8.2s⁶ 8.1f p8.6g Jun 30] fair maiden: stays 9.5f: form only on all-weather: usually wears headgear: sold £2,000. *Miss J. Feilden*

DRURY LANE (IRE) 6 b. or br.g. Royal Applause 124 – Ghost Tree (IRE) 88 (Caer- **57 §** leon (USA) 132) [2006 58§, a–: 5.9m 7.5f 5m 6m⁴ 6m* 7.1d⁵ 7m f6g f6g⁶ f6g Dec 28] tall, leggy gelding: modest performer: won handicap at Catterick in July: best at 6f/7f: acts on firm and good to soft ground: usually blinkered/in cheekpieces: inconsistent. *D. W. Chapman*

DRY ICE (IRE) 4 b.g. Desert Sun 120 – Snowspin 75 (Carwhite 127) [2006 85: p7g⁴ **90** p8g 8m² 8m³ 8m⁶ 7.1g 7.1m 7d² 8m Oct 8] close-coupled gelding: fairly useful handicapper: good second at Goodwood penultimate start: raced mainly over 7f/1m, well worth a try back at 6f: acts on polytrack, firm and good to soft going: blinkered final outing: sold 42,000 gns, sent to Bahrain. *H. Candy*

DUALAGI 2 b.f. (Feb 19) Royal Applause 124 – Lady Melbourne (IRE) 76 (Indian **55** Ridge 123) [2006 5m Sep 8] 16,000Y, 44,000 2-y-o: third foal: dam, 6f winner, half-sister

314

to smart performers Crisos Il Monaco (at 1m/1¼m in Italy) and Gay Burslem (stayed 1m in Ireland): 33/1, mid-field in maiden at Sandown. *J. S. Moore*

DUBAI ACE (USA) 5 b.g. Lear Fan (USA) 130 – Arsaan (USA) 106 (Nureyev (USA) 131) [2006 –: p10g³ p12g² p12g² p12g p16g⁵ 14.8m² 14m⁶ Jul 7] smallish gelding: fair maiden: stays easy 2m: acts on polytrack and good to firm going. *Miss S. West* **72**

DUBAI AROUND (IRE) 3 ch.g. Zinaad 114 – Triple Transe (USA) (Trempolino (USA) 135) [2006 53: 10g⁶ 11.1f⁴ 9m⁶ 10m² 10.1m³ 12.4d 12d³ Sep 5] modest maiden handicapper: stayed 1½m: acted on firm and good to soft going: carried head awkwardly on reappearance: won juvenile hurdle in October: dead. *M. D. Hammond* **61**

DUBAI BUILDER 2 b.c. (Apr 27) Tobougg (IRE) 125 – Roseum 102 (Lahib (USA) 129) [2006 5g 6.1f³ 7m 6d* 6m³ 6d* 7d Oct 14] 2,000F, €17,000Y, 24,000 2-y-o: big, strong colt: second foal: half-brother to 3-y-o Glasshoughton: dam 5f/6f winner: useful performer: reportedly returned with a splint at debut: won nursery at York in August and minor event at Salisbury in September: best effort when 3½ lengths third of 6 to Excellent Art in Mill Reef Stakes at Newbury in between: not discredited in Dewhurst Stakes at Newmarket (tenth of 15) final start: should be suited to 7f/1m: acts on good to firm and good to soft going. *J. S. Moore* **102**

DUBAI DREAMS 6 b.g. Marju (IRE) 127 – Arndilly 75 (Robellino (USA) 127) [2006 –, a67: 12.1m Sep 1] close-coupled gelding: unimpressive mover: fair performer in 2005: well beaten only 6-y-o start: tried tongue tied: usually blinkered/visored: usually races up with pace: has finished weakly. *M. Sheppard* **–**

DUBAI MAGIC (USA) 2 ch.g. (Feb 24) Rahy (USA) 115 – Dabaweyaa 118 (Shareef Dancer (USA) 135) [2006 p6g³ 7.1m 7g* 6m 7f² 8g p7.1g p7g⁵ p7.1g² Dec 29] medium-sized, attractive gelding: brother to fairly useful 5.7f (at 2 yrs) to 7f winner Ascot Cyclone, closely related to useful sprinter Bin Nashwan (by Nashwan) and half-brother to numerous winners, notably smart 1m/1¼m performer Magellan (by Hansel): dam, 7f/1m winner, second in 1000 Guineas: fairly useful performer: won maiden at Salisbury in June: twice second in nurseries after: stays 7f: acts on polytrack and firm going: tongue tied once. *C. E. Brittain* **82**

DUBAI MARINA 2 b.f. (Feb 28) Polish Precedent (USA) 131 – Cape Siren (Warning 136) [2006 7.1d Sep 16] third foal: half-sister to a winner in Sweden by Efisio: dam no form: tailed off in maiden. *F. Jordan* **–**

DUBAI MELODY (USA) 3 ch.f. Woodman (USA) 126 – Dabaweyaa 118 (Shareef Dancer (USA) 135) [2006 63p: 10m² 10f 11.6m Aug 5] leggy, close-coupled filly: fair maiden: weakened quickly last 2 starts: stays 1¼m: raced only on good ground or firmer: sold 120,000 gns. *J. H. M. Gosden* **74**

DUBAI ON 3 b.f. Daylami (IRE) 138 – Cambara 97 (Dancing Brave (USA) 140) [2006 94p: 10s⁴ p10g* Nov 9] tall filly: useful form: trained by M. Tregoning at 2 yrs: best effort when winning handicap at Lingfield in November by head from Lake Shabla: should be suited by 1½m: acts on polytrack and soft ground: has worn crossed noseband: carried head high on reappearance: has left Godolphin. *Saeed bin Suroor* **98**

DUBAI'S FAIRY 2 b.f. (Mar 26) Medicean 128 – Fairy Flight (IRE) 86 (Fairy King (USA)) [2006 5m 6g p7g Oct 21] 36,000F, 87,000Y: sturdy filly: fifth foal: half-sister to 7-y-o Just James: dam Irish 2-y-o 6f winner: little form: sold 20,000 gns, sent to Australia. *R. Hannon* **–**

DUBAI SHADOW (IRE) 2 b.f. (Mar 1) Cape Cross (IRE) 129 – Farista (USA) (Alleged (USA) 138) [2006 6m 7d Aug 25] €70,000F, 40,000Y: fourth foal: half-sister to French winner around 1½m Full Mistery (by Distant View): dam US 8.5f/1¼m winner: modest form in maidens. *C. E. Brittain* **56**

DUBAI'S TOUCH 2 b.c. (Mar 29) Dr Fong (USA) 128 – Noble Peregrine (Lomond (USA) 128) [2006 5d⁶ 6d⁴ 6f* 6f* 6m³ 6f³ 7g²⁵ 7s Oct 21] 27,000F, 115,000Y: strong colt: half-brother to several winners, including smart 1m/9f winner Wannabe Around (by Primo Dominie) and 3-y-o Grantley Adams: dam, Italian 1¼m winner, half-sister to smart performer up to 1¼m Amrak Ajeeb: useful performer: won maiden at Ripon in June, minor event at Pontefract in July and listed race at Newbury (beat Valiance by 1¼ lengths) in August: good third in July Stakes at Newmarket and Richmond Stakes (1½ lengths behind Hamoody) at Goodwood fifth/sixth starts: will stay 1m: acts on firm going, well held on soft final start (Horris Hill Stakes). *M. Johnston* **99**

DUBAI SUNDAY (JPN) 5 b.g. Sunday Silence (USA) – Lotta Lace (USA) (Nureyev (USA) 131) [2006 f12g³ p12.2g 21.7m 10.1f f14g 10m 10g p10g⁴ 10.1m⁵ 12d⁵ Aug 18] **58**

leggy, close-coupled gelding: bumper winner on polytrack: modest maiden on Flat: stays easy 1½m: acts on all-weather: tried blinkered/tongue tied. *P. S. McEntee*

DUBAI TWILIGHT 2 b.c. (Feb 14) Alhaarth (IRE) 126 – Eve 81 (Rainbow Quest (USA) 134) [2006 7g⁴ 7m² Sep 5] 110,000Y: close-coupled, quite good-topped colt: second living foal: dam, 1m winner, half-sister to 6-y-o Putra Kuantan: fairly useful form: fourth to Dubai's Touch in listed race at Newbury and second to Dijeerr in maiden at Leicester: will stay at least 1m. *B. W. Hills*   **88**

DUBAI TYPHOON (USA) 3 ch.c. Thunder Gulch (USA) 129 – Dubian 120 (High Line 125) [2006 10.3d 7g 8m Jun 22] useful-looking colt: fairly useful performer: best effort when 4½ lengths third to Asset in listed race at Kempton on reappearance: well held after: bred to stay 1¼m: acts on polytrack and good to firm going: sold 8,500 gns in October. *C. E. Brittain*   **94**

DUBONAI (IRE) 6 ch.g. Peintre Celebre (USA) 137 – Web of Intrigue 66 (Machiavellian (USA) 123) [2006 54: f8g⁶ Apr 7] leggy gelding: modest handicapper: below form only Flat outing in 2006: occasionally tongue tied. *G. M. Moore*   **–**

DUDLEY DOCKER (IRE) 4 b.g. Victory Note (USA) 120 – Nordic Abu (IRE) 60 (Nordico (USA)) [2006 71: f8g f8g f7g² p7.1g² p8.6g⁶ 7.5f⁴ 8.3f 7g 7d 8g p7.1g⁴ p7.1m* f8g² p7.1g⁴ p6g⁶ f6g⁶ Dec 23] leggy gelding: fair handicapper: won at Wolverhampton in November: stays 1m: acts on all-weather and firm ground: often slowly away. *D. Carroll*   **76**

DUELING B'ANJIZ (USA) 7 b.g. Anjiz (USA) 104 – Stirling Gal (USA) (Huckster (USA)) [2006 a12s⁶ 11g a14g⁵ p16g p16g Dec 18] poor when trained by P. Martin in Ireland in 2002/3: in frame in maiden events in Spain in 2005: unplaced in 2006, including at Kempton last 2 starts: stays 1¾m: acts on firm going and sand: tried in blinkers/cheekpieces/tongue tie. *E. J. Creighton*   **–**

DUEL IN THE SANDS 3 ch.g. Allied Forces (USA) 123 – Kildine (IRE) (Common Grounds 118) [2006 57: p9.5g⁵ p10g f8g⁵ f11g f8g Feb 16] leggy gelding: modest maiden: should stay 1¼m: acts on polytrack and good to firm ground. *D. Shaw*   **51**

DUELLING BANJOS 7 ch.g. Most Welcome 131 – Khadino (Relkino 131) [2006 83: p13g⁶ p12g p12g³ p12g⁵ 10g p10g p12g⁴ p10g³ Dec 20] fair handicapper nowadays: stays 13f: best efforts on all-weather and going softer than good (acts on heavy): versatile tactically. *J. Akehurst*   **73**

DUFF (IRE) 3 b.c. Spinning World (USA) 130 – Shining Prospect (Lycius (USA) 124) [2006 98: 8m³ 8g 7g³ Sep 30] fifth foal: dam unraced half-sister to smart performer up to 1½m Valley of Gold: useful performer: won maiden at Gowran at 2 yrs: good efforts in listed events all 3 starts in 2006, 2¾ lengths third to Danak at Cork, seventh to Ivan Denisovich at the Curragh and 3 lengths third to New Seeker at Redcar: stays 1m: acts on good to firm going. *Edward Lynam, Ireland*   **107**

DUKEDOM 3 gr.c. Highest Honor (FR) 124 – Rose Noble (USA) 62 (Vaguely Noble 140) [2006 8s³ 8.1m² Jun 9] 65,000F, 140,000Y: rather leggy, quite good-topped colt: brother to French 11.5f winner Rugosa and half-brother to 3 winners, including useful 6f/7f (including at 2 yrs) winner Dowager (by Groom Dancer) and 11-y-o Dower House: dam, 11.5f winner, half-sister to high-class performer up to 1¼m Grand Lodge: fairly useful form in maidens at Newmarket (coltish beforehand, shaped with plenty of promise when 1¾ lengths third to Muzher) and Haydock (odds on, on edge and upset in stall, 1½ lengths second to Royal Oath, wandering): likely to be suited by 1¼m: sold 27,000 gns in October, and joined T. McCourt in Ireland. *Sir Michael Stoute*   **82**

DUKE OF MARMALADE (IRE) 2 b.c. (Mar 12) Danehill (USA) 126 – Love Me True (USA) 99 (Kingmambo (USA) 125) [2006 6m² 7g* 7m² Aug 2]   **110 p**

Aidan O'Brien secured his eighth successive trainers' championship in Ireland and won fourteen Group and Grade 1s worldwide. It was noticeable, however, that Ballydoyle's juveniles were less dominant. O'Brien ran fifty-four two-year-olds in a total of one hundred and sixty races. They recorded thirty-one wins, only two each in Britain and France, the remainder in Ireland, which resulted in the stable's strike rate, which had been above 30% in each of the two previous seasons, dropping to 19.4%. This has, in part, resulted in a somewhat unfamiliar look to the ante-post markets for the classics, with horses hailing from other Irish yards more prominently represented, notably Jim Bolger's Teofilo and Finsceal Beo. That said, O'Brien still has a host of interesting prospects for 2007. Holy Roman Emperor is second favourite for the Two Thousand Guineas, whilst, among the stable's smart colts in the making, Duke of Marmalade is available at 20/1 at the time of writing.

Duke of Marmalade was an easy-to-back favourite when making his debut in a six-furlong maiden at Leopardstown in June, and he ran on eye-catchingly to finish second to Chanting, a David Wachman-trained filly, also with Coolmore connections, who went on to win a listed event back over course and distance on her only subsequent outing. Stepped up to seven furlongs just nine days later, Duke of Marmalade landed the odds in an above-average maiden at the Curragh by a neck from Supposition. The Vintage Stakes at Goodwood is one of the few leading two-year-old events that O'Brien has yet to win, perhaps surprisingly given the tradition the race has of producing classic winners, Shamardal and Sir Percy successful in the two most recent years. Duke of Marmalade finished runner-up to Strategic Prince after being sent off the 11/4 favourite in the ten-strong field, despite the stronger claims on form held by several of his opponents. Duke of Marmalade was only really getting going towards the finish, cutting the winner down with every stride as the line came, going down by a neck. Duke of Marmalade returned with a leg injury, but could follow the same route as 2005 Vintage winner, Sir Percy, in going for the Two Thousand Guineas and the Derby. Whether or not he proves fully effective at the Derby trip, he looks sure to improve for a stiffer test of stamina than he faced at Goodwood for all his pedigree doesn't guarantee that he'll stay a mile and a half.

Duke of Marmalade (IRE) (b.c. Mar 12, 2004)	Danehill (USA) (b 1986)	Danzig (b 1977)	Northern Dancer
			Pas de Nom
		Razyana (b 1981)	His Majesty
			Spring Adieu
	Love Me True (USA) (ch 1998)	Kingmambo (b 1990)	Mr Prospector
			Miesque
		Lassie's Lady (b 1981)	Alydar
			Lassie Dear

Duke of Marmalade, a big, strong, well-made colt, who has raced only on good and good to firm ground, is from an excellent family. He is the second foal of the mile winner Love Me True, who was also trained at Ballydoyle and is a sister to winners in Japan and the States and a half-sister to several winners, including the very smart performer at up to a mile and three quarters Shuailaan. Duke of Marmalade's grandam Lassie's Lady won over seven furlongs in the States and is a half-sister to the high-class sprinter-miler Wolfhound and to the dam of AP Indy and Summer Squall. *A. P. O'Brien, Ireland*

DUKE OF MILAN (IRE) 3 ch.g. Desert Prince (IRE) 130 – Abyat (USA) (Shadeed (USA) 135) [2006 78: 8.2d³ 7m⁶ 8.3g³ 8.3g⁶ 7.1m p6g* p6g 6s p6g³ p6g p6g⁶ p6g Dec 1] €60,000Y: fourth foal: half-brother to fairly useful Irish 1¼m winner Indian Belle (by Indian Ridge) and 5-y-o Poetical: dam unraced half-sister to Middle Park Stakes winner Hayil: fair performer: sold from D. Weld in Ireland 13,000 gns after second outing: won apprentice handicap at Lingfield in September: effective at 6f to 8.3f: acts on polytrack and good to soft going: edged left and found little fifth start. *G. C. Bravery* **75**

DUKE OF TUSCANY 2 b.c. (Feb 2) Medicean 128 – Flawless 107 (Warning 136) [2006 6m 7g² 8g* 7.1d* Sep 13] 32,000Y: sturdy, close-coupled colt: fourth foal: dam 2-y-o 7f winner who stayed 1m: useful performer: developed well, winning maiden at Goodwood in August and minor event at Sandown in September, in latter beating Asperity by a neck: stays 1m. *R. Hannon* **100**

DUKES BOND 3 gr.g. Paris House 123 – Glowing Lake (IRE) 54§ (Lake Coniston (IRE) 131) [2006 8g Aug 4] angular gelding: 100/1, well beaten in maiden at Thirsk. *M. E. Sowersby* **–**

DUKESTREET 5 ch.g. Cadeaux Genereux 131 – El Rabab (USA) 70 (Roberto (USA) 131) [2006 79, a?: f6g⁶ Feb 2] fairly useful performer at best: wearing cheekpieces, well below form only Flat outing in 2006: stays 1m: acts on heavy going: joined D. Shaw. *Michael Cunningham, Ireland* **–**

DULCE SUENO 3 b.f. Lahib (USA) 129 – Graceland Lady (IRE) 55 (Kafu 120) [2006 48: 5d² 5g⁶ 5f² 6m² 5m⁵ 6g 6d⁴ Sep 5] modest maiden: should stay 7f: acts on firm and good to soft going. *I. Semple* **63**

DUMARAN (IRE) 8 b.g. Be My Chief (USA) 122 – Pine Needle 89 (Kris 135) [2006 95d: p8.6g⁴ p10g⁶ 10s³ p10g⁵ 10d Nov 1] fairly useful handicapper: stays 10.4f: acts on **81**

polytrack, best turf efforts on good going or softer: visored (below form) twice: sometimes slowly away/pulls hard: usually races up with pace: none too reliable. *W. J. Musson*

DUMAS (IRE) 2 b.c. (Mar 23) Iron Mask (USA) 117 – Bucaramanga (IRE) (Distinctly North (USA) 115) [2006 6g⁶ 6m p7g 6g Sep 30] €24,000F, 20,000Y: unfurnished colt: second foal: dam Italian 7f (at 2 yrs) to 1¼m winner: fair maiden: more promise than bare result (not knocked about) first 3 starts, and stiff task final one in listed Two-Year-Old Trophy at Redcar: should stay 7f: will do better yet. *A. P. Jarvis* **75 p**

DUNASKIN (IRE) 6 b.g. Bahhare (USA) 122 – Mirwara (IRE) (Darshaan 133) [2006 107: p12.2g² p10g 12m³ 11.9g 10.4f 10.4d² 10.4g 10.4s Oct 6] smallish, workmanlike gelding: useful handicapper: patchy form in 2006, though ran well when third to Soulacroix in ladies race and 1¼ lengths second to Topatoo in valuable event, both at York: well held last 2 outings: stays 1½m: acts on polytrack, soft and good to firm ground: sometimes hangs right: races up with pace. *Karen McLintock* **103**

DUNCANBIL (IRE) 5 b.m. Turtle Island (IRE) 123 – Saintly Guest (What A Guest 119) [2006 34: p8g f6g Jan 19] workmanlike mare: maiden: well held in 2006: tried visored/tongue tied. *J. J. Bridger* **–**

DUNDONALD (IRE) 7 ch.g. Magic Ring (IRE) 115 – Cal Norma's Lady (IRE) 87 (Lyphard's Special (USA) 122) [2006 49§, a53§: p7.1g⁶ p7.1g p8.6g Feb 11] big gelding: unreliable performer: well held in 2006: tongue tied: usually wears headgear. *M. Appleby* **– §**

DUNDRY 5 b.g. Bin Ajwaad (IRE) 119 – China's Pearl (Shirley Heights 130) [2006 86: 16g³ 14.1g 17.2m 15d⁶ Oct 13] big, good-topped gelding: fairly useful handicapper: below form after reappearance: stays 2m: acts on polytrack and soft ground: usually wears cheekpieces. *G. L. Moore* **83**

DUNELIGHT (IRE) 3 ch.c. Desert Sun 120 – Badee'a (IRE) (Marju (IRE) 127) [2006 85: 10g³ 8m* 8m 8m² 8g* 8f² 8g³ 9d Sep 30] good sort: good walker: smart performer: much improved in 2006, winning handicaps at Newmarket in May and Ascot (beat Easy Air by 5 lengths) in July: creditable placed efforts next 2 starts, ½-length second to Spectait in totesport Mile at Goodwood and close third to Ivan Denisovich in listed race at the Curragh: didn't take eye, well below form in Cambridgeshire at Newmarket final start: free-going type, best efforts at 1m: acts mainly on good going or firmer (acts on firm): visored last 5 outings: front runner. *C. G. Cox* **113**

DUNE MELODY (IRE) 3 b.f. Distant Music (USA) 126 – Desert Gift 69 (Green Desert (USA) 127) [2006 73: 6d⁶ 7s 7s² 7f³ 7m p7g 7d Oct 28] unfurnished filly: fairly useful performer: good efforts in 2006 only when placed: stays 7f: acts on firm and soft going: wore cheekpieces final start: often held up. *J. S. Moore* **80**

DUNLIN 3 ch.f. Inchinor 119 – Hen Harrier 94 (Polar Falcon (USA) 126) [2006 8.3m 8.2m 9s⁵ 12d Oct 3] strong filly: fifth foal: half-sister to 3 winners, including 1½m/1¾m winner King Eider (by Mtoto) and 1¼m winner Woodcracker (by Docksider), both useful: dam 7f (at 2 yrs) to 1¼m winner: fair maiden: best effort when fifth at Goodwood third outing: should be suited by 1¼m+: acts on good to soft: sold 2,500 gns. *H. Morrison* **68**

DUNN DEAL (IRE) 6 b.g. Revoque (IRE) 122 – Buddy And Soda (IRE) 75 (Imperial Frontier (USA) 112) [2006 79: 5g 6d 5.5d* 5.7s 6d³ 6.1d 6d 6f 6g 6.1m Aug 28] smallish, sturdy gelding: fair handicapper: won at Warwick in May: effective at 5f/6f: acts on fibresand and any turf going: tried tongue tied: sometimes wanders: usually held up. *W. M. Brisbourne* **78**

DUNNETT AGAIN (IRE) 5 b.g. Petardia 113 – Pat Said No (IRE) 59 (Last Tycoon 131) [2006 56, a45: f6g⁴ f7g f8g Apr 4] leggy gelding: poor maiden: gelded after final start: stays 7f: acts on all-weather and good to firm going: visored/blinkered nowadays: has shown signs of temperament. *Mrs C. A. Dunnett* **45**

DURBA (AUS) 6 ch.g. Desert Prince (IRE) 130 – Placate (AUS) (Brief Truce (USA) 126) [2006 15.8d Apr 12] won maiden at 1¼m in 2004 from 6 starts on Flat in Australia: finished lame when well held only outing on Flat in Britain. *R. C. Guest* **–**

DUROOB 4 b.g. Bahhare (USA) 122 – Amaniy (USA) 96 (Dayjur (USA) 137) [2006 79: 14.1d* 12.4g 13.9s⁶ 14m 13.1g⁶ 14.1m² 11.9g⁵ 13.9s⁵ 12s⁵ Oct 21] small, sturdy gelding: fair handicapper: won at Nottingham in April: probably stays 17.5f: acts on good to firm and good to soft going: sold 11,500 gns, joined P. Brady in Ireland. *K. R. Burke* **72**

DUROVA (IRE) 2 b.f. (May 15) Soviet Star (USA) 128 – Taroudannt (IRE) (Danehill (USA) 126) [2006 5f⁵ 5f² 5.1m² 5g² 5m³ 5f² 5m* 5.1f² 5s Oct 14] 20,000 2-y-o: first foal: dam unraced: fair performer: won maiden at Redcar in August, making all: good second **76**

at Chester only start in nursery next time: raced at 5f, mostly on good or firmer going. *T. D. Easterby*

DUSKINESS (FR) 2 b.f. (Jan 26) Kyllachy 129 – Johanita (FR) (Johann Quatz (FR) **73** 120) [2006 5m⁵ 5.1g⁵ p7g⁴ p5.1g⁵ Oct 30] €150,000Y: unfurnished filly: first foal: dam, French 6f (at 2 yrs) and 9f winner, half-sister to useful French miler Green Groom: fair maiden: fourth to Cast In Gold at Lingfield, easily best effort: stays easy 7f: joined S. Seemar in UAE. *M. J. Wallace*

DUTCH ART 2 ch.c. (Mar 18) Medicean 128 – Halland Park Lass (IRE) (Spec- **124** trum (IRE) 126) [2006 5m* 5m* 6s* 6d* Sep 29]

The essay on Bassenthwaite in *Racehorses of 1984* noted that the reputation of the Middle Park Stakes as a true championship event had come under pressure over the previous twenty-five years because of the appearance, or elevation in status, of top tests over further which were better for two-year-olds bred to get a mile or more. The essay added that the winner of the Middle Park Stakes was rarely allotted top weight in the Free Handicap and that few horses bred to stay middle distances won the race. Perhaps it is time for an update. Since 1984, two Timeform champion two-year-old colts, Johannesburg (2001) and Oasis Dream (2002), have won the race but only two winners, Rodrigo de Triano (1991) and Ad Valorem (2004), have gone on to land a Group 1 race over a mile or more after their two-year-old season—Johannesburg won the Breeders' Cup Juvenile over eight and a half furlongs immediately after his Middle Park success. Predictably, specialist sprinters have been much more numerous, with Stalker, Mister Majestic, Gallic League, Royal Applause, Bahamian Bounty, Lujain, Primo Valentino, Oasis Dream, Balmont and Amadeus Wolf all fulfilling that role. Rodrigo de Triano, whose tally at three included the Two Thousand Guineas and Champion Stakes, was the only winner of a major prize at a mile and a quarter, and coincidentally he was trained by Peter Chapple-Hyam, who is also responsible for the latest winner Dutch Art. Dutch Art's prospects of emulating Rodrigo de Triano in the Guineas are open to doubt, while the Champion Stakes must be regarded as virtually out of the question. Dutch Art seems to be very much a modern Middle Park winner, likely to make a top sprinter rather than a miler.

Dutch Art changed hands twice during the year, in the first instance being bought by future British Horseracing Authority chairman Paul Roy and his wife Susan as a replacement for their very smart five-year-old Majors Cast, who broke a leg on the gallops in mid-June. Dutch Art made his debut for his new owners shortly afterwards in the Norfolk Stakes at Royal Ascot, where he went off second favourite on the strength of decisively beating Simply Perfect in a nine-runner minor event at Windsor at the start of June. The Norfolk Stakes favourite was Hoh Mike, successful in two minor events, but he did not enjoy any luck, getting no sort of run after being trapped on the rail. Dutch Art did not break with the alacrity he had shown at Windsor, but once switched outside for a run he made swift headway and forged clear over a furlong out, coming home a length and three quarters ahead of the strong-finishing Hoh Mike, despite idling near the finish. Hoh Mike looked unlucky but by the end of the season there was no doubt which was the better colt. Dutch Art went straight to the Darley Prix Morny at Deauville two months later, a race which lost some of its interest when the Phoenix Stakes winner Holy Roman Emperor was withdrawn because of the soft going. Sandwaki, unbeaten and successful in the Prix du Bois on his latest outing, was a short-priced favourite

Darley Prix Morny, Deauville—Dutch Art gets a pat on the head from Christophe Soumillon as he wins from Magic America (No.7) and Excellent Art

Shadwell Middle Park Stakes, Newmarket—
a second Group 1 for Dutch Art, who runs out a convincing winner from Wi Dud;
Captain Marvelous is third, ahead of Hellvelyn (white cap) and Brave Tin Soldier (partially hidden)

ahead of the only other British runner, National Stakes winner and Railway Stakes third Excellent Art. Dutch Art was third choice and the best of the rest looked to be the first three in the Prix Robert Papin, Boccassini from Germany, Golden Titus from Italy and the filly Magic America. The soft going did not inconvenience Dutch Art in the slightest—he also acts on good to firm—and six furlongs clearly suited him admirably. After travelling easily close to the pace set by Sandwaki, Dutch Art quickened ahead over a furlong out and looked in no danger thereafter, scoring by a length from the fast-finishing Magic America with Excellent Art third, a head further back.

The Shadwell Middle Park Stakes at Newmarket at the end of September was an obvious target for Dutch Art after this, the double having been achieved by Bahamian Bounty and Johannesburg in the previous decade. Only five lined up against Dutch Art, and his odds of 6/5, after opening at evens, perhaps suggests it was uncompetitive. This is hardly fair on Dutch Art since his opponents were a representative collection including the winners of the Coventry Stakes (Hellvelyn), the Flying Childers Stakes (Wi Dud) and Gimcrack Stakes (Conquest) in addition to listed winner Brave Tin Soldier, representing Ballydoyle, and dual scorer Captain Marvelous. There were excuses for Conquest afterwards, but there were no excuses for the others as Dutch Art made them look almost pedestrian. Soon leading or disputing the lead, he did not need subjecting to maximum pressure to stamp his authority on the race leaving the Dip, running on strongly to see off Wi Dud by two lengths with the outsider Captain Marvelous, successful on his next start in the Criterium de Maisons-Laffitte, a length and a quarter away third. Dutch Art's victory produced the third-best timefigure of the year by a juvenile (0.70 fast, equivalent to a timerating of 118), behind only those of Teofilo and Holy Roman Emperor in the Dewhurst Stakes. It was also the best performance, judged on form, in the Middle Park since Bassenthwaite, who was rated 126 after winning by four lengths. That is a considerable compliment to Dutch Art, who changed hands again late in the year, being bought by Cheveley Park Stud, where he will stand after he finishes racing. In the meantime, he will continue running in Mrs Roy's colours.

Dutch Art's sire Medicean—also at Cheveley Park—is shaping well, with Almerita and Nannina also winning Group 1 races. In so far as Medicean, who was not precocious, proved fully effective over a mile and a quarter and is getting progeny who are suited by a mile or more, Dutch Art should have prospects of staying the trip in the Two Thousand Guineas. However, his dam, and more particularly the way Dutch Art himself races, tell a different story. Halland Park Lass, by a fair stamina influence in Spectrum, had a dismal record on the track, failing to finish ahead of any of her forty-seven rivals in two maiden races and a claiming event, twice starting slowly and once pulling too hard for her own good. She was sold for

8,500 guineas at the end of 2002—Dutch Art is her first foal—and 12,000 guineas carrying to Kyllachy at the December Sales in 2005. Not a bad buy as it turned out, since at the same venue in November the resultant foal was sold for 280,000 guineas and Halland Park Lass, in foal to Tobougg, for 710,000 guineas.

Dutch Art (ch.c. Mar 18, 2004)	Medicean (ch 1997)	Machiavellian (b 1987)	Mr Prospector
			Coup de Folie
		Mystic Goddess (ch 1990)	Storm Bird
			Rose Goddess
	Halland Park Lass (IRE) (ch 1999)	Spectrum (b 1992)	Rainbow Quest
			River Dancer
		Palacegate Episode (b 1990)	Drumalis
			Pasadena Lady

Dutch Art, who cost 14,500 guineas as a foal and 16,000 guineas as a yearling, shows no sign of the temperament his dam seemingly possessed, but the Middle Park Stakes in particular confirmed he has speed in abundance. In that respect he resembles his grandam Palacegate Episode, a smart and tough front-running five-furlong specialist who hit the target eleven times including in the Group 3 Premio Omenoni. Speed was also of the essence with Palacegate Episode's brother Another Episode, winner of eleven races and second in the Molecomb Stakes, and with her half-brother Palacegate Jack, whose tally of fifteen races included three listed events. To a mating with Danehill, Palacegate Episode produced King Quantas, successful in Scandinavia where he won the Group 3 Polar Cup over an extended six furlongs. In truth, besides her paternal grandsire Tumble Wind, there are no sprinters or significant influences for speed close up in the third dam Pasadena Lady's family, so the out-and-out speed of her best descendants is an

Mrs Susan Roy's "Dutch Art"

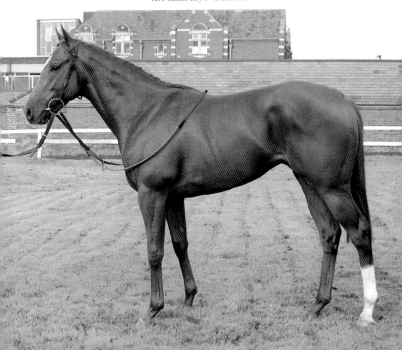

oddity. Indeed, Pasadena Lady was out of a daughter of Irish Oaks winner Silken Glider, who also produced the very smart out-and-out stayer Alciglide. As has been noted in *Racehorses* before, the first Group 1 event over five or six furlongs does not take place until Royal Ascot, with only one race at that level over seven furlongs all season in the Prix de la Foret. The pattern programme provides every incentive for connections of speedy colts to have a go for the early classics and it seems fair to assume Dutch Art will follow that route, since there is little to lose. He may prove capable of showing high-class form at a mile, but sprint distances promise to show him to even better advantage. If he trains on satisfactorily—he is a close-coupled, quite attractive colt—such as Dandy Man, Desert Lord, Les Arcs and Reverence, and whatever the Australians may send over, will have to look to their laurels. *P. W. Chapple-Hyam*

DUTCH KEY CARD (IRE) 5 b.g. Key of Luck (USA) 126 – Fanny Blankers (IRE) (Persian Heights 129) [2006 53, a69: f6g p6g f5g f5g p5.1g p7.1g⁶ 5m⁴ 6m⁶ p5.1g Oct 14] modest performer: trained second/third starts by A. Carroll: has form up to 1m, but probably best at 5f/6f: acts on all-weather and good to firm going: tried tongue tied: blinkered/visored last 6 starts. *C. Smith*   **54**

DUTY FREE (IRE) 2 b.c. (Feb 9) Rock of Gibraltar (IRE) 133 – Photographie (USA) (Trempolino (USA) 135) [2006 8m⁵ 8g⁴ Oct 17] 60,000Y: fourth foal: dam, French maiden, sister to Marcel Boussac winner Juvenia and closely related to very smart French 1m/9f performer In Extremis: shaped promisingly both starts at Bath, fourth to Grey Rover in maiden, going on strongly: will stay at least 1¼m: should do better. *H. Morrison*   **68 p**

DUTY (IRE) 3 b.g. Rainbow Quest (USA) 134 – Wendylina (IRE) (In The Wings 128) [2006 –p: 10m² 11.5m* 11.9f⁴ 13.3g⁴ 14.8d² 14.1g² Sep 14] angular, useful-looking gelding: useful performer: won maiden at Yarmouth in May: in frame in handicaps all 4 starts after, including when 6 lengths second to Alessano at Newmarket and ½-length second to Rationale (pair clear) at Yarmouth (visored): stays 14.8f: acts on firm and good to soft going: hung and flashed tail under pressure third outing: sold 58,000 gns. *Sir Michael Stoute*   **102**

DUXFORD 5 ch.g. Young Ern 120 – Marsara (Never So Bold 135) [2006 61: p8g p8.6g p8g⁶ p8g9.7d 8m p13.9g 10d f8g p7g⁶ p8g 10m Jul 12] modest maiden: stays 1m: acts on polytrack: often wears headgear: sometimes slowly away. *D. K. Ivory*   **– a61**

DVINSKY (USA) 5 b.g. Stravinsky (USA) 133 – Festive Season (USA) (Lypheor 118) [2006 78: 8m⁴ 8.5g 8s 7g⁴ 7.1m² 6m* 7.1m² 6m⁶ 6m 6f³ 7f⁵ 6f 6m⁴ p8g³ p7g 7g p7.1g³ p6g⁴ p7.1m p7g² p6g³ p6g⁴ Dec 22] compact gelding: fairly useful handicapper: won at Pontefract in June: left D. Carroll after eleventh start, S. R. Bowring after fourteenth and M. Allen after nineteenth: effective at 6f, barely stays 1m: acts on polytrack, firm and soft going: tried tongue tied: has worn headgear. *P. Howling*   **83 a78**

DYANITA 3 b.f. Singspiel (IRE) 133 – Dance Clear (IRE) 99 (Marju (IRE) 127) [2006 70: p10g³ 12m 10d⁶ 10m 10.2m p8.6m⁵ p8.6g* p8g⁵ p8.6g³ Dec 18] fair performer on all-weather, fair on turf: won handicap at Wolverhampton (made all) in October: stays 1¼m: acts on polytrack, yet to race on extremes of going on turf: blinkered (ran to form) last 2 starts. *B. W. Hills*   **63 a76**

DYLAN (IRE) 3 b.g. Mull of Kintyre (USA) 114 – Rose of Shuaib (IRE) 68 (Caerleon (USA) 132) [2006 50: f6g f8g f8g* f7g² f8g 8.2d f7g Jun 3] sturdy gelding: modest performer: won banded race at Southwell in March, hanging left: stays 1m: acts on fibresand. *N. Tinkler*   **50**

DYLAN THOMAS (IRE) 3 b.c. Danehill (USA) 126 – Lagrion (USA) 68 (Diesis 133) [2006 102: 10d* 12m³ 12g* 10.4d⁴ 10m* a10f⁴ Oct 7]   **129**

The Irish Derby is the least likely of Europe's three major middle-distance classics to reveal a hitherto-unrecognised champion. Its position in the calendar, coming after the Epsom Derby and the Prix du Jockey Club, means that more is known about the merits of the leading middle-distance three-year-olds when representatives of the crop line up at the Curragh. In forty-five runnings since 1962, when the Irish Derby's prize money was first boosted significantly to raise its international status, thirty-eight of the favourites have started at shorter than 2/1, twenty of them (including Relko, withdrawn not under orders in 1963) at odds on. Fourteen have completed the Derby double at Epsom and the Curragh, though it should be said that the Irish Derby has proved by no means a formality for the

Epsom winner, ten having met with defeat at the Curragh, five at odds on. The Chantilly/Curragh Derby double has been completed only four times, from considerably fewer runners. The Epsom winner has come out on top in four out of five meetings with the Prix du Jockey Club winner at the Curragh, attesting to the fact that more often than not the Derby is harder to win than its French counterpart, the latter now run over ten and a half furlongs. In the absence of Derby winner Sir Percy, the betting on the latest Budweiser Irish Derby was the most open in the race's modern history, despite the presence of the first two from the Prix du Jockey Club, Darsi and Best Name. One of the placed horses from Epsom, Dylan Thomas from the Ballydoyle stable, started 9/2 favourite (Hail The Pirates, an 11/4-shot in 1973, had been the shortest-priced favourite in the period since 1962).

The wide-open look to the Irish Derby reflected the tight finishes to both the Derby and the Prix du Jockey Club, a short head, a head and a short head separating the first four at Epsom and a length and a half covering the first six at Chantilly. Five of the first six in the betting at the Curragh had contested either the Derby (Dragon Dancer, runner-up at 66/1 at Epsom, and sixth-placed Best Alibi joined Dylan Thomas) or the Prix du Jockey Club. The exception was French-trained Gentlewave, the odds-on, four-length winner of the Derby Italiano who was sent off third favourite behind Dylan Thomas and Darsi. Dragon Dancer, Gentlewave and Darsi were among four supplementary entries (at a cost of €100,000). Dylan Thomas was Kieren Fallon's choice from three saddled at the Curragh by Ballydoyle, but few outside his own stable could have anticipated the significant improvement that was manifested. Dylan Thomas won the Irish Derby most decisively, his three-and-a-half-length margin of victory the widest since High Chaparral won by the same margin in 2002, the last time Ballydoyle triumphed in the race. The stable has now won the race four times under Aidan O'Brien with Desert King and Galileo, a four-length winner, preceding High Chaparral.

Winning margins of the order of those recorded by Galileo, High Chaparral and Dylan Thomas are not exceptional for the Irish Derby. St Jovite won by twelve lengths in 1992, the widest winning margin officially recorded in the race since the race became recognised as one of world-wide importance, while Sinndar won by nine, with Shahrastani and Assert both officially returned eight-length winners. Zagreb was successful by six lengths when the second longest-priced winner at 20/1 in the period under review (Weavers' Hall won the 1973 edition at 33/1). The past ten runnings have also seen Prix du Jockey Club winners Dream Well and Montjeu triumph by four and a half lengths and five lengths respectively. With no dedicated pacemakers in the latest edition, the early stages were steadily run, but Dylan Thomas was much more patiently ridden than at Epsom and still had a bit to do from sixth early in the straight. He quickened in fine style, however, and ran on strongly after hitting the front a furlong out. Gentlewave was also held up but was never a threat to the winner, while third-placed Best Alibi ran at least as well as he had at Epsom to finish a length and a half behind the runner-up. Dragon Dancer

Budweiser Irish Derby, the Curragh—Dylan Thomas gives Aidan O'Brien his fourth win in the race;
Gentlewave (right) takes second from Best Alibi with Dragon Dancer (white sleeves) fourth,
Mountain (striped sleeves) sixth and Heliostatic (rail) seventh; fifth-placed Darsi is out of the picture

came a respectable fourth, though below the form he had shown at Epsom, while Darsi and Best Name were never better than mid-division, finishing fifth and eighth respectively in the field of thirteen.

It is usually an advantage to be up with the leaders in a race that is not truly run and Dylan Thomas's rider at Epsom, Johnny Murtagh, was widely credited at the time with riding a particularly good race—as was Darryll Holland on Dragon Dancer—in a Derby run at a tempo which placed more emphasis than usual on speed. Dylan Thomas was moved up to lead a mile from home and kept on well after being sent for home in earnest with Dragon Dancer after rounding Tattenham Corner. Dylan Thomas was only the third string among the Ballydoyle quartet that took part in the Derby. The ill-fated 'stable selected' Horatio Nelson, said to be back to his two-year-old form (four wins and an unlucky second to Sir Percy in the Dewhurst), started 11/2 second favourite behind French-trained Visindar, while the Ballydoyle 'number two' Septimus, an eight-length winner of the Dante, was at 17/2. Dylan Thomas started well-nigh three times those odds, sent off at 25/1 despite winning the Derrinstown Stud Derby Trial, a race with an illustrious list of recent winners, over a mile and a quarter at Leopardstown on his reappearance, ahead of stable-companion Mountain (50/1 at Epsom) and British challenger Youmzain. That form still left Dylan Thomas with something to find to figure in the Derby, though it was a step up on his efforts as a two-year-old which included wins in a maiden at Tipperary and a minor event at Leopardstown, and sixth of seven (three places behind odds-on Septimus) under testing conditions in the Racing Post Trophy on his final start. Those who thought that Dylan Thomas had had the run of the race and might have been flattered at Epsom were proved wrong at the Curragh. A fit Sir Percy—sidelined after returning from Epsom 'stiff and jarred up'—would have had to step up on his Derby form to confirm placings with Dylan Thomas at the Curragh. O'Brien said before the Irish Derby that the galloping, right-handed track at the Curragh might well suit Dylan Thomas better than the undulating, left-handed Epsom course where, contradicting the majority view among the critics, O'Brien thought 'he was left in front earlier than we would have liked and did a little too much too soon.'

Having come through the Irish Derby with flying colours, Dylan Thomas had his sights set on proving himself against the best of the older horses that had stayed in training from the previous season. The King George VI and Queen Elizabeth Stakes at Ascot in July is still usually the most significant race in the British calendar, but it has struggled to attract the leaders of the classic crop in some recent years. Seven Derby winners challenged for the King George in the 'nineties, but only two—Galileo and Kris Kin—have done so in the seven years since. Four Irish Derby winners in the 'nineties went on to Ascot in the same year as their triumph, though there were three French-trained winners in that period, two of whom—Dream Well and Montjeu—were given the traditional French mid-summer break after the Curragh before being returned for an autumn campaign. In 2001, Galileo became the seventh horse, and the first since Generous in 1991, to achieve the feat of winning the Derby at both Epsom and the Curragh and then go on to success in the King George. However, Galileo and Alamshar are the only Irish Derby winners that have run in the King George as three-year-olds in the past seven years. Alamshar also won at Ascot but might have bypassed the race had his owner the Aga Khan not had French-trained Dalakhani in the same year.

There were no three-year-olds in the King George line-up in either 2002 (for the first time since 1969) or in the latest edition, while Irish Derby third Tycoon and Oaks winner Eswarah were the only members of the classic crop in the King George fields of 2004 and 2005. Tycoon is the only runner Ballydoyle has had since Galileo, one reason for not running dual Derby winner High Chaparral in 2002 being that—in hindsight—the team at Ballydoyle felt that Galileo's hard race at Ascot left its mark and prejudiced his late-season campaign (he was beaten in the Irish Champion and the Breeders' Cup Classic). Ballydoyle had a very strong collection of three-year-olds in 2002. Derby runner-up Hawk Wing, who won the Eclipse and would have been a leading candidate for the King George, was, however, aimed at the Juddmonte International at York (which he was eventually forced to miss after contracting a viral infection). Another factor in 2002 may have been that Coolmore, for whom Ballydoyle is the racing arm, had taken a controlling interest in the four-year-old Golan who had won the Two Thousand Guineas and finished second to Galileo in the Derby. Golan won the King George for the Stoute stable and joined the roster at Coolmore at the end of the season. Aidan O'Brien was more explicit about the plans for Dylan Thomas after the latest Irish Derby. 'There are plenty of options but a lot will depend on Hurricane Run [trained in France but bought by Coolmore for a sum rumoured to be around £6m as a three-year-old before he won the Irish Derby],' O'Brien said. 'If he goes for the King George, we might look at the Irish Champion for Dylan Thomas.'

The Irish Champion Stakes had been the next intended outing for High Chaparral after his Irish Derby win, but he was withdrawn on the day with his trainer unhappy with the results of a blood test. The 2004 Irish Derby winner Grey Swallow was put away for the Irish Champion after the Curragh too, while Hurricane Run also waited for the autumn, being tuned up for his successful bid for the Arc in the Prix Niel in September. Dylan Thomas was given a break after the Irish Derby and a relatively late decision was made to run him in the International at the York August meeting, a race won by the stable with Giant's Causeway in 2000 before he went on to victory in the Irish Champion. With more good older horses being kept in training in Europe nowadays, the top open-aged events in the summer and early-autumn are arguably becoming tougher than they used to be for the top three-year-olds at that stage of their development. Giant's Causeway had been the only three-year-old to win the International in its twelve previous runnings and one of only four successful in the Irish Champion in the same period. Odds-on Dylan Thomas was disappointing in a far from vintage International, finishing nearly four lengths behind the winner Notnowcato in fourth (older horses filling the first three places) after racing too freely early on in a race that only began in earnest as the field turned for home. Connections also blamed the good to soft going, though Dylan Thomas had won the Derrinstown Derby Trial under similar conditions.

Dylan Thomas was a different horse two and a half weeks later in the Baileys Irish Champion on good to firm ground at Leopardstown. Kieren Fallon was banned from riding in Britain from early-July onwards by the Horseracing Regulatory Authority after charges of conspiracy to defraud were brought against him, but, having missed the mount on Dylan Thomas at York, he was back on board in the Irish Champion. With the previous year's fourth Ace fulfilling a pacemaking role, Dylan Thomas settled much better than at York and restored his reputation under the firmer conditions with a hard-fought neck victory over Ouija Board. Ouija Board passed Dylan Thomas over a furlong out after he had taken over briefly from his stable companion, but, with Fallon at his strongest, Dylan Thomas battled back on Ouija Board's inner to regain the lead near the line. Fallon was cautioned for misuse of the whip, using it in the banned forehand position, but he explained that Dylan Thomas was hanging and was too close to Ouija Board for him to use his whip correctly. Alexander Goldrun repeated her third from the year before, finishing two and a half lengths behind Ouija Board, while the five-year-old Mustameet,

Baileys Irish Champion Stakes, Leopardstown—
Dylan Thomas (rail) rallies to regain the lead from Ouija Board; Alexander Goldrun is third
for the second year running, ahead of Mustameet (virtually obscured) and Ace

who had fully earned his place with a fine sequence in listed and lesser pattern races, finished fourth of the five runners. The form of the Irish Champion represented further improvement for Dylan Thomas and he looked set to follow in the footsteps of Giant's Causeway by running in the Breeders' Cup Classic, held at Churchill Downs where the last-named had put up a tremendous performance to finish a narrow second to Tiznow. Plans were scrapped, however, after Dylan Thomas flopped when tried on dirt for the first time in the Jockey Club Gold Cup at Belmont Park in early-October. Consideration was reportedly given to switching Dylan Thomas to the Breeders' Cup Turf—in which Hurricane Run was a starter—but it came to nothing and he wasn't seen out again.

	Danehill (USA) (b 1986)	Danzig (b 1977)	Northern Dancer, Pas de Nom
Dylan Thomas (IRE) (b.c. 2003)		Razyana (b 1981)	His Majesty, Spring Adieu
	Lagrion (USA) (ch 1989)	Diesis (ch 1980)	Sharpen Up, Doubly Sure
		Wrap It Up (ch 1979)	Mount Hagen, Doc Nan

The big, strong, lengthy Dylan Thomas is by Danehill who was champion sire in Britain and Ireland posthumously for the second consecutive year. Dylan Thomas was Danehill's biggest money earner, but there were sizeable contributions too from such as Two Thousand Guineas and Queen Elizabeth II Stakes winner George Washington (who was Ballydoyle's representative in the Breeders' Cup Classic), Poule d'Essai des Poulains winner Aussie Rules and the two-year-olds Holy Roman Emperor, Admiralofthefleet and Simply Perfect. The average distance of races won by Danehill's three-year-olds is just over a mile, though his notable

Mrs John Magnier and Mr M. Tabor's "Dylan Thomas"

progeny include the 2004 Derby winner North Light and, among his older horses, the 2005 Gold Cup first and second Westerner and Distinction. While Danehill was a sprinter, the dam of Dylan Thomas, the maiden Lagrion, was not seen out at two and did all her racing at middle distances. She was a sister to Middle Park runner-up Pure Genius and easily her best offspring before Dylan Thomas was the high-class Lowther and Cheveley Park winner Queen's Logic (by Grand Lodge), who won the Fred Darling on her only outing at three and should have stayed a mile, and possibly even further. Among Lagrion's other winners, Tulsa (by Priolo) won at a mile and a quarter and Carlo Bank (by Lahib) was successful at up to a mile and a half in Italy. The grandam of Dylan Thomas, Wrap It Up, never saw a racecourse but is a half-sister to the Lingfield Oaks Trial winner Gift Wrapped, the dam of Royal Lodge winner Reach and of Oaks d'Italia runner-up Wrapping, herself the dam of Yorkshire Oaks and Prix Vermeille runner-up Papering. If the balance of probabilities was at one time slightly against Dylan Thomas's staying the Derby trip, judged purely on his pedigree, such conjecture is irrelevant now that he has proved himself at the distance. He is fully effective at a mile and a quarter to a mile and a half, which gives his connections a wide choice of targets to aim at in the next season. The genuine Dylan Thomas, who incidentally has won all four of the races in which he has been ridden by Fallon (who looks like being out of action for much of 2007), has won on good to soft going but has shown his best form on good or firmer. *A. P. O'Brien, Ireland*

DYNACAM (USA) 3 b.f. Dynaformer (USA) – Najecam (USA) (Trempolino (USA) **89**
135) [2006 82p: 12.3m⁴ 9.9g³ 10.1d³ p12g Sep 18] strong, heavy-bodied filly: fairly useful performer: good third in handicaps at Beverley and Epsom: will stay 1¾m: acts on heavy going: has shown signs of temperament. *Sir Michael Stoute*

DYNAMIC RHYTHM (USA) 3 b.c. Kingmambo (USA) 125 – Palme d'Or (IRE) **77**
111 (Sadler's Wells (USA) 132) [2006 76: 8.1m² 8m Aug 19] strong colt: best effort when 1½ lengths second to Abwaab in maiden at Haydock on belated reappearance: effort best excused following month (not clearest of runs): will stay 1¼m: acts on good to firm ground: sold 22,000 gns, joined G. Brown. *J. Noseda*

DYNAMITE DEANO 3 b.g. Dracula (AUS) 121 – Katy Ivory (IRE) 68 (Night Shift **58**
(USA)) [2006 44: 8.2d 10m f11g p12.2g⁴ f14g Nov 21] modest maiden: stays 1½m: acts on polytrack. *D. K. Ivory*

DYSONIC (USA) 4 b.g. Aljabr (USA) 125 – Atyab (USA) (Mr Prospector (USA)) **39**
[2006 47, a53: f6g p7.1g f7g 5f⁴ p5.1g³ 5m⁶ f6g³ f5g⁵ p5.1g* p5g* Dec 13] angular **a63**
gelding: modest performer on all-weather, poor on turf: left D. Burchell after second start: won banded races at Wolverhampton and Lingfield in December: effective at 5f/6f: acts on all-weather: tried in cheekpieces, visored of late. *J. Balding*

DZESMIN (POL) 4 b.g. Professional (IRE) 73 – Dzakarta (POL) (Aprizzo (IRE)) **87**
[2006 10.1m⁴ 14.8m³ 16.2m 12m* 12d⁶ Sep 30] ex-Polish gelding: won 4 of his 6 starts in Poland in 2005, including 2000 Guineas, Derby and St Leger: fairly useful form in Britain, best effort when winning handicap at Catterick in September: should stay 2m: acts on good to firm going: wore cheekpieces last 3 outings: gelded after final outing. *R. C. Guest*

DZHANI 3 b.g. Singspiel (IRE) 133 – Heuston Station (IRE) 72 (Fairy King (USA)) **–**
[2006 –: p8.6g⁶ 8d p9.5g 8d 7.9g Aug 3] strong gelding: little form: tongue tied final start: sold 2,500 gns, sent to Denmark. *Jedd O'Keeffe*

E

EAGER IGOR (USA) 2 b. or br.g. (Mar 8) Stravinsky (USA) 133 – Danube (USA) **74**
(Green Desert (USA) 127) [2006 6f 6f⁶ 5f² 6d⁵ 6d 7d⁴ Oct 19] 19,000Y: second foal: dam French 7f and 8.5f winner: fair maiden: blinkered, best run when fourth in nursery at Brighton final start: effective at 5f to easy 7f: acts on firm and good to soft going. *R. F. Johnson Houghton*

EAGER LOVER (USA) 2 ch.c. (Feb 13) More Than Ready (USA) 120 – True Love **93**
(USA) (Affirmed (USA)) [2006 5.1d⁴ 7m⁶ 7m⁶ p7f* p8.5f p7f⁶ Nov 18] $16,000Y, resold $20,000Y, resold €120,000Y: tall, good-topped colt: closely related to winner in USA by

Southern Halo and half-brother to several winners abroad: dam 9f winner in USA: fairly useful form: much improved when 6 lengths sixth of 10 to Strategic Prince in Vintage Stakes at Goodwood on third start (then left B. Hills): won maiden at Woodbine in September: below form after, including in Grade 3 Grey Breeders' Cup there next time: stays 7f: acts on polytrack and good to firm going. *R. L. Attfield, Canada*

EAGLE EYE 3 br.g. Capote (USA) – Bitwa (USA) (Conquistador Cielo (USA)) [2006 **71**
p7g⁴ 8m 7m⁵ p8g 6f Jun 9] 25,000Y: tall, rangy gelding: half-brother to several winners in USA: dam 6f to 8.5f winner in USA: fair maiden: well held in 2 handicaps: gelded after: should stay 1m: acts on good to firm going: sold 12,000 gns. *G. Wragg*

EAGLE MOUNTAIN 2 b.c. (Feb 25) Rock of Gibraltar (IRE) 133 – Masskana **118**
(IRE) (Darshaan 133) [2006 6d⁵ 6v* 7g² 7g² 8s* 8s⁴ Oct 21]
Aidan O'Brien has regained his stranglehold on the Juddmonte Beresford Stakes, a race he had won six times in succession prior to John Oxx taking it in 2002 and 2003 with Alamshar and Azamour respectively. O'Brien has now won the last three runnings, the latest with Eagle Mountain who put up the best performance in the race since El Prado, trained by Vincent O'Brien and ridden by Lester Piggott, in 1991. El Prado flopped as a three-year-old, and it has to be said that Aidan O'Brien's previous Beresford winners hardly set the racing world alight in their second season, the Dante winners Saratoga Springs and Septimus turning out the best of them. Eagle Mountain may well enjoy greater success as a three-year-old if he improves for a step up in trip, although he has a long way to go if he's to achieve anything like so much as either Alamshar or Azamour.
Eagle Mountain had four runs before the Beresford in October, winning a maiden at the Curragh in May second time out, then going on to finish runner-up in both the Futurity Stakes there and the Champagne Stakes at York. The form he showed in going down by a head to Teofilo in the Futurity and by half a length to Vital Equine in the Champagne was the best on offer in the Beresford. Of the six who took him on at the Curragh, only Capital Exposure, the winner of a maiden at Leopardstown on his one previous start, and the sole British challenger Silent Waves, a good fourth in the Vintage Stakes at Goodwood last time out, started at single-figure odds. Eagle Mountain was odds on and gave his supporters very little cause for concern. Held up as Silent Waves made the running, Eagle Mountain made his move early in the straight and swept through to lead over a furlong out, soon pulling well clear and eased slightly near the line, where he had seven lengths to spare over Capital Exposure. It was an impressive performance from a colt who had clearly benefited from the step up to a mile, and a testing mile at that, with the ground soft. Five of O'Brien's previous Beresford winners had gone on to contest the Racing Post Trophy, with Saratoga Springs completing the double. Lermontov, Castle Gandolfo, Albert Hall and Septimus were all placed in the Racing Post, a race O'Brien also won with Beresford runner-up Brian Boru. That Eagle Mountain should take the same route was no surprise and, with conditions at Newbury similar

Juddmonte Beresford Stakes, the Curragh—Eagle Mountain shows improved form stepped up in trip, winning by seven lengths from Capital Exposure (right), the grey Silent Waves and Malacara

to those which had prevailed at the Curragh, he was a warm order to follow up. In the event, he could finish only fourth, around three and a half lengths behind Authorized in a race which wasn't truly run and didn't play to his strengths. A resolute galloper who needs time to build momentum, Eagle Mountain, once again patiently ridden, never had much room, rather crowded in the pack and not getting the gaps. Eagle Mountain hasn't reproduced his best on two visits to Britain so far, but he will surely have plenty of opportunities to put that right in 2007.

Eagle Mountain (b.c. Feb 25, 2004)	Rock of Gibraltar (IRE) (b 1999)	Danehill (b 1986)	Danzig
			Razyana
		Offshore Boom (ch 1985)	Be My Guest
			Push A Button
	Masskana (IRE) (b 1988)	Darshaan (br 1981)	Shirley Heights
			Delsy
		Masarika (b 1981)	Thatch
			Miss Melody

Eagle Mountain shapes as though he will stay a mile and a quarter, and possibly further, something which couldn't be guaranteed judged on pedigree. From the first crop of the top-class miler Rock of Gibraltar, whose best other representative is Eagle Mountain's stablemate Mount Nelson, winner of the Criterium International, also over a mile, Eagle Mountain is out of the French nine-furlong and mile-and-a-quarter winner Masskana. Masskana didn't get off the mark until she was four and then won twice more the following year. Four of Masskana's seven earlier foals are winners, and they include two who also showed smart form. Wallace (by Royal Academy) won two races, both over a mile, at three, including a listed event at Ascot; Sulk (by Selkirk) was successful twice at two, notably in the Prix Marcel Boussac, and the following season showed herself effective over as far as nearly two miles when second in the Prix Royal-Oak. Masskana herself is a daughter of the Poule d'Essai des Pouliches winner Masarika and granddaughter of the smart 1972 two-year-old Miss Melody. Eagle Mountain, a rather leggy, close-coupled colt who fetched 220,000 guineas as a yearling, seems unlikely to have the speed to win a Guineas, and there have to be some stamina doubts regarding the Derby. However, the fact that Sulk, also by a good miler, should stay as well as she did is encouraging for Eagle Mountain's prospects of staying a mile and a half. Eagle Mountain has been raced only on good ground or softer, with his wins coming on soft and heavy. *A. P. O'Brien, Ireland*

EAMON AN CHNOIC (IRE) 5 gr.g. Lil's Boy (USA) 109 – Caranina (USA) 85 (Caro 133) [2006 69: p13g f16g 11.6m⁶ 17.2f⁴ p12g 12.6g⁴ 16.4f 12.1f Jul 28] modest maiden handicapper: left J. Bolger in Ireland prior to return: stays 17f: acts on firm going. *B. W. Duke* **57**

EARL COMPTON (IRE) 2 b.c. (May 2) Compton Place 125 – Noble Story 61 (Last Tycoon 131) [2006 6g⁵ 5d p7g Oct 6] modest form in maidens: tried tongue tied. *P. F. I. Cole* **51**

EARL KRAUL (IRE) 3 b.g. Imperial Ballet (IRE) 110 – Bu Hagab (IRE) (Royal Academy (USA) 130) [2006 69: 10g p8g 7f 10s⁴ 10d³ Oct 19] just modest maiden in 2006: stays 1¼m: acts on good to firm and good to soft going: tried in cheekpieces, blinkered last 2 starts. *G. L. Moore* **51**

EARL MARSHAL (USA) 2 b.c. (Mar 14) Kingmambo (USA) 125 – Fairy Godmother 113 (Fairy King (USA)) [2006 7d Oct 28] good-topped colt: third foal: dam, 1¼m winner, half-sister to very smart middle-distance stayer Blueprint: 20/1, green when midfield in maiden at Newmarket won by Spanish Moon: will do better. *Sir Michael Stoute* **65 p**

EARL OF SPECTRUM (GER) 5 b.g. Spectrum (IRE) 126 – Evry (GER) (Torgos) [2006 46: p10g May 15] poor performer: well held only outing on Flat in 2006: won over hurdles in July. *J. L. Spearing* **–**

EARLY EVENING 3 b.f. Daylami (IRE) 138 – Regent Court (IRE) 78 (Marju (IRE) 127) [2006 50p: 8m² 8.3f² 10m* 9.7g* 10.2f⁶ 10.5g Sep 23] leggy filly: progressed into a fairly useful performer, winning maiden at Nottingham in July and handicap at Folkestone in August: should stay 1¼m: raced only on good ground or firmer. *H. Candy* **84**

EARLY PROMISE (IRE) 2 b.f. (Apr 4) Abou Zouz (USA) 109 – Habla Me (IRE) (Fairy King (USA)) [2006 p5g⁴ 6m² p6g² 6f p6g² p5g p7g⁴ Oct 17] sixth foal: sister to **66**

2003 2-y-o 6f winner Pompey Blue and half-sister to 2 winners, including 3-y-o Near-down Beauty: dam Italian 7f winner: runner-up 3 times: best efforts at 6f on polytrack: once refused at stalls. *P. L. Gilligan*

EARTH AND SKY (USA) 3 br.g. Dynaformer (USA) – Earthly Angel (USA) (Crafty Prospector (USA)) [2006 10d Oct 9] $200,000F, $375,000Y: second foal: half-brother to 4-y-o Legally Fast: dam unraced sister to US Grade 2 11f winner Mr Bluebird: 6/1, well held in maiden at Windsor: sold 70,000 gns. *Saeed bin Suroor* —

EARTHLING 5 b.g. Rainbow Quest (USA) 134 – Cruising Height 112 (Shirley Heights 130) [2006 58d: f7g f11g 8m 8m Aug 17] lightly-raced maiden: well held in 2006: tried in cheekpieces. *D. W. Chapman* —

EARTH MASTER (IRE) 3 gr.g. Grand Lodge (USA) 125 – Beautiful France (IRE) (Sadler's Wells (USA) 132) [2006 77: p10g⁵ p10g p8g 12.6g 11.6m p9.5g p10g 8.3d⁶ 8m Sep 4] fair form when winning maiden at Leopardstown at 2 yrs, leaving K. Prendergast in Ireland prior to final start: modest form at best in Britain: best effort at 7f on good ground: has been blinkered, including for win: signs of temperament. *S. Kirk* **63 d**

EASIBET DOT NET 6 gr.g. Atraf 116 – Silvery 67 (Petong 126) [2006 82§: 11.1m³ 12g⁴ 12.1m⁴ 13g⁴ 12.1m⁴ 14m p16.5m³ p13.9g⁶ Oct 30] tall gelding: fair handicapper: stays 2m: acts on all-weather, firm and good to soft going: wears cheekpieces: tried visored/blinkered/tongue tied: irresolute, and usually carries head high: joined Miss L. Russell. *I. Semple* **71 §**

EASTBOROUGH (IRE) 7 b.g. Woodborough (USA) 112 – Easter Girl (Efisio 120) [2006 86, a79: p10g² p12g p16g³ p12g² p16g p12g⁴ p16g 17.2s 16g⁶ 10m² 15d² p12g 13.3m 20m 15m³ 15m⁶ 10m³ 11.6f 21m 12.6m³ 16m⁶ p16g⁶ p13.9g³ p13.9m² Nov 9] close-coupled, quite good-topped gelding: fairly useful handicapper: below form after eleventh start: left B. Powell after nineteenth start, Stef Liddiard after twentieth and I. Wood after twenty-second: effective at 1¼m to easy 2m: acts on all-weather, soft and good to firm going: tried blinkered earlier in career: none too reliable. *J. R. Jenkins* **83 d**

EAST CAPE 9 b.g. Bering 136 – Reine de Danse (USA) 78 (Nureyev (USA) 131) [2006 50: f14g f14g Feb 12] leggy, useful-looking gelding: modest performer at best: well held both starts in 2006: tried visored much earlier in career: sometimes finds little. *N. Tinkler* —

EASTERN ANTHEM (IRE) 2 b.c. (Feb 27) Singspiel (IRE) 133 – Kazzia (GER) 121 (Zinaad 114) [2006 8.2s* Oct 18] leggy, quite good-topped colt: first foal: dam, won 1000 Guineas and Oaks, also 7f/1m winner at 2 yrs: odds on, easy winner of maiden at Nottingham (beat Sagredo by 5 lengths, value double), pushed clear before eased: smart prospect, impeccably bred, and should go on to much better things. *Saeed bin Suroor* **97 P**

EASTERN PLAYBOY (IRE) 2 b.c. (May 18) Desert Sun 120 – Coolaba Princess (IRE) 47 (Danehill (USA) 126) [2006 6f⁵ 6g 7m 6d p5.1g Nov 16] strong, sturdy colt: modest maiden: speedy, and may prove best at 5f: tried in blinkers. *J. Jay* **51**

EASTERN PREMIUM 2 b.f. (Apr 1) Superior Premium 122 – Make Ready 76 (Beveled (USA)) [2006 6m Jun 20] 5,000Y: third foal: half-sister to 2003 2-y-o 1m winner Xpressions (by Turtle Island): dam 5f (at 2 yrs)/6f winner: last in seller: dead. *R. A. Fahey* —

EASTERN PRINCESS 2 b.f. (Apr 23) Almutawakel 126 – Silvereine (FR) (Bering 136) [2006 p6g⁶ 6m⁴ 6g 8g 6f 6g⁶ p7g p6g p6g⁶ p5g⁴ Dec 16] 14,000Y: fourth foal: half-sister to winners in Hungary by Emperor Jones and Groom Dancer: dam French 1½m winner: modest maiden: well below best last 4 starts: should stay 7f/1m: acts on polytrack and firm ground. *J. A. Geake* **59 d**

EASTER OGIL (IRE) 11 ch.g. Pips Pride 117 – Piney Pass (Persian Bold 123) [2006 61, a67: p13g⁶ p16g p12g⁴ p10g 12d Apr 11] lengthy, good-topped gelding: modest performer nowadays: effective at 1m, barely at 13f: acts on polytrack and any turf going: tried in visor/cheekpieces: sometimes soon off bridle/gets behind. *P. G. Murphy* **— a57**

EASTLANDS (IRE) 3 b.g. Imperial Ballet (IRE) 110 – Blue Dream (USA) (Irish River (FR) 131) [2006 10g 8.3d 8f p10g 12g Aug 18] modest maiden: stays 1¼m: acts on polytrack and good to soft ground: slowly away all starts. *Jamie Poulton* **63**

EAST RIDING 6 b.m. Gothenberg (IRE) 117 – Bettynouche 69 (Midyan (USA) 124) [2006 –: p10g Dec 20] tall, leggy mare: maiden: no form since 2004: tried in cheekpieces: has carried head awkwardly. *A. J. Chamberlain* —

EASY AIR 3 ch.c. Zafonic (USA) 130 – Easy Option (IRE) 115 (Prince Sabo 123) [2006 86P: p7g* 76.6d⁴ p7g² 8m² 7m⁵ 8g² 7.6g p7g⁴ Oct 26] lengthy colt: useful handicapper: won at Lingfield in April, landing odds comfortably: good efforts after, including at Royal Ascot (2 lengths second to Sir Gerard in Britannia Stakes) and Lingfield (1¼ **108**

lengths fourth to Areyoutalkingtome) fourth/final outings: stays 1m: acts on polytrack, good to firm and good to soft going: joined Godolphin. *E. A. L. Dunlop*

EASY FEELING (IRE) 4 b.f. Night Shift (USA) – Talena (Zafonic (USA) 130) [2006 – 81, a63: p6g Jan 20] attractive filly: fairly useful at best: well held only outing in 2006: tried in cheekpieces/blinkers. *R. Hannon*

EASY LAUGHTER (IRE) 5 b.g. Danehill (USA) 126 – All To Easy 91 (Alzao   **75** (USA) 117) [2006 76: p12.2g⁴ p12g⁵ 10.2d Apr 11] fair handicapper: stays 1½m: acts on polytrack, firm and good to soft going: effective blinkered or not, well held in visor final start: tongue tied. *A. King*

EASY LOVER 2 ch.f. (Jan 15) Pivotal 124 – Easy To Love (USA) 86 (Diesis 133)   **91** [2006 6g p7g* 7m f7g² p7.1f³ 8g⁴ 8.1v* 8g 7s³ 8d Oct 28] 80,000Y: medium-sized, close-coupled filly: third foal: dam, 11.5f winner, sister to Oaks winner Love Divine, herself dam of 3-y-o Sixties Icon: fairly useful performer: won maiden at Kempton in June and nursery at Haydock in September: ran well several other times, including third to Party in listed event at Newbury ninth start: will stay 1¼m: acts on all-weather and heavy ground. *J. A. Osborne*

EATHIE 4 ch.g. Bluegrass Prince (IRE) 110 – Persian Fortune 53 (Forzando 122) [2006 – –: p8g 8d 11.8d p8.6g 7.1m f6g Jul 11] little form: tried tongue tied/visored. *M. J. Attwater*

EAU GOOD 2 ch.g. (Feb 21) Cadeaux Genereux 131 – Girl's Best Friend 89 (Nicolotte   **86** 118) [2006 6s² 6d³ 6s³ p6g* f5g³ f8g² Dec 27] 32,000Y: first foal: dam 6f (at 2 yrs) and 9.4f winner: fairly useful performer: left M. Johnston and gelded, improved when winning maiden at Wolverhampton in December by 6 lengths from Wee Ellie Coburn: good second in nursery at Southwell final outing: needs further than 5f and stays 1m: acts on all-weather and soft going: blinkered third outing. *M. C. Chapman*

EA (USA) 2 b. or br.c. (Feb 5) Dynaformer (USA) – Enthused (USA) 109 (Seeking The   **77 p** Gold (USA)) [2006 7m⁶ Aug 11] close-coupled colt: second foal: half-brother to fairly useful 2005 2-y-o 6f winner Erytheis (by Theatrical): dam, 2-y-o 6f winner (including Lowther Stakes) who stayed 1m, out of Coronation Stakes winner Magic of Life: 3/1 favourite but very green, 4¼ lengths sixth of 17 to Furnace in maiden at Newmarket: sure to improve. *Sir Michael Stoute*

EAU SAUVAGE 2 ch.f. (Feb 26) Lake Coniston (IRE) 131 – Mo Stopher 47 (Sharpo   – 132) [2006 p7g Dec 15] half-sister to several winners, including 4-y-o Calabaza and 7f winner Robin Sharp (by First Trump): dam maiden: 40/1, always behind in maiden at Kempton. *J. Akehurst*

EBERT 3 b.g. Polish Precedent (USA) 131 – Fanfare 89 (Deploy 131) [2006 70: 8m⁴ 8g⁵   **86** 8m* 8.5g⁴ 8m² 9m³ Aug 27] strong gelding: fairly useful handicapper: won at Salisbury in July: good efforts after: should stay 1¼m: raced only on polytrack and good/good to firm ground. *P. J. Makin*

EBN REEM 2 b.c. (Feb 14) Mark of Esteem (IRE) 137 – Reematna 75 (Sabrehill (USA)   **90** 120) [2006 6m 6s² p6g⁴ 7m² 6m* 6s³ 6d³ Oct 27] good-topped colt: good walker: third foal: half-brother to fairly useful 2004 2-y-o 6f winner Dahteer (by Bachir): dam, disappointing maiden (might have proved best at 7f/1m), half-sister to Derby Italiano winner Morshdi: fairly useful performer: won maiden at Pontefract in August: in frame another 5 starts, third in nursery and minor event at Newmarket last 2: stays 7f: acts on soft and good to firm going: makes running. *M. A. Jarvis*

EBONY LADY 3 br.f. Vettori (IRE) 119 – Keen Melody (USA) 60 (Sharpen Up 127)   **36** [2006 –: 12.1d 11g 10d 11g³ 9.8m⁶ 12.1g 11s Aug 13] compact filly: poor maiden: tried visored/in cheekpieces. *R. M. Whitaker*

EBRAAM (USA) 3 b.c. Red Ransom (USA) – Futuh (USA) 95 (Diesis 133) [2006 74p: **72** 7m 7f² 7m* 7g Oct 13] well-made colt: fair form: won maiden at Catterick in September: raced only at 7f on good ground or firmer: reportedly finished distressed on reappearance: carried head awkwardly second start/found little final outing: sold 16,000 gns. *E. A. L. Dunlop*

EBTIKAAR (IRE) 4 b.c. Darshaan 133 – Jawlaat (USA) 91 (Dayjur (USA) 137) [2006   **106** 100p: 12g⁴ 14.1f* 16d⁵ 21.7m⁴ 16f 15.9d 18d² 18d Oct 14] medium-sized, quite attractive colt: useful performer: won handicap at Salisbury in May by neck from Michabo: met trouble when running creditably at Ascot next 2 starts, including 2½ lengths fourth to Baddam in Queen Alexandra Stakes: below form last 4 outings: stays 2¾m: acts on firm and good to soft going (well held on heavy final 3-y-o outing). *J. L. Dunlop*

Princess Elizabeth Stakes (Sponsored By Vodafone), Epsom—Echelon gains a second pattern-race victory, beating Musicanna (right) and Zayn Zen (dark epaulets)

ECCOLLO (IRE) 4 b.g. Spectrum (IRE) 126 – Taking Liberties (IRE) 57 (Royal **86**
Academy (USA) 130) [2006 –: p8g 10d 8.3m p7g² p8g* p9.5g* p8g* p10g* p8.6g* p8g³
p9.5g Nov 25] tall gelding: fairly useful performer: progressed very well in late-October/
November, winning banded race at Kempton and handicaps at Wolverhampton (2) and
Kempton (2): suffered fatal fall at Wolverhampton: stayed 1¼m: acted on polytrack and
good to firm going: sometimes flashed tail. *T. J. Pitt*

ECHELON 4 b.f. Danehill (USA) 126 – Exclusive 115 (Polar Falcon (USA) 126) [2006 **115**
107: 7m* 8.5g* 8m² 9.9m⁵ Aug 5] sturdy, good sort: good walker/mover: smart
performer: won totepool Chartwell Fillies' Stakes at Lingfield (beat Chantilly Beauty by
length) in May and Princess Elizabeth Stakes (Vodafone) at Epsom (beat Musicanna by
½ length) in June: creditable efforts after when 2 lengths second to Soviet Song in
Windsor Forest Stakes at Royal Ascot and 6½ lengths fifth to Ouija Board in Nassau
Stakes at Goodwood: effective at 7f to 1¼m: best efforts on good/good to firm going: can
take time to find stride: stays in training. *Sir Michael Stoute*

ECHO OF LIGHT 4 b.c. Dubai Millennium 140 – Spirit of Tara (IRE) 106 **125**
(Sadler's Wells (USA) 132) [2006 115: p8g* 8m⁶ 8.9g* 8m* 8f Nov 4]
The term 'flat-track bully' has colloquially come to be associated with
sporting figures unable to transfer impressive records at a lower level to the big
stage; those that produce their best when all is in their favour. Perhaps one of the
most famous examples is from the world of cricket. The highly prolific Graeme
Hick, who recently became the first batsman since Geoff Boycott to score a century of centuries for a single county, was, possibly unfairly, branded with the label
after hitting just six three-figure scores in one hundred and fourteen innings for
England. Thus far in his career, Echo of Light has failed to reproduce his best form
against top opposition. Although he has won each of his three outings in Group 2
and Group 3 company, showing high-class form, Echo of Light has managed to
beat just a single opponent in his three starts in Group 1s, that rival returning amiss.
Echo of Light made a highly encouraging return when winning the Ladbrokes Summer Mile at Lingfield in July on his first outing on polytrack. Dictating
the pace in a clear lead, Echo of Light never looked like being caught in the straight,
beating shorter-priced stablemate Satchem by two and a half lengths to record the
best performance ever on the all-weather. Despite having several others engaged in
the race, Godolphin opted to supplement Echo of Light for the Sussex Stakes at
Goodwood the following month, at a cost of £19,500. Front-running tactics were

Ladbrokes Summer Mile Stakes, Lingfield—
the best performance ever on the all-weather, as Echo of Light and Satchem give Godolphin a 1,2

less well employed, however, Dettori setting an overly-strong pace on Echo of Light, who had the favourite Araafa in close proximity from the start. Neither had anything left for the finish and were readily brushed aside in the closing stages.

Stepped up a furlong in trip, Echo of Light was again able to dominate when getting back to winning ways in the Grahame Stowe Bateson Family Law Unit Strensall Stakes at York, with Dettori, judging things better than at Goodwood, gradually increasing the tempo in the straight, his mount responding well to pressure and beating Stage Gift by two and a half lengths. Back at a mile, Echo of Light won his third race of the campaign when landing the odds in the Prix Daniel Wildenstein Castel Marie-Louise de La Baule at Longchamp on Arc weekend. He again demonstrated his quirky nature, however, hanging left as he got on top inside the final furlong after being ridden with a little more restraint. Echo of Light had two lengths in hand of Japanese-trained Picaresque Coat, but, by the time Dettori

Prix Daniel Wildenstein Castel Marie-Louise de la Baule, Longchamp—
Echo of Light collects his third pattern race of the year despite hanging left;
Deep Impact's travelling companion, Picaresque Coat (left), performs with credit in second

managed to pull him up, he was against the stand rail, after hanging all the way across the wide course. On his final outing of the season, Echo of Light failed to live up to expectations again at the highest level. The shorter-priced of the Godolphin representatives in the Breeders' Cup Mile at Churchill Downs, he found disappointingly little in the straight, finishing last of the fourteen runners.

Echo of Light (b.c. 2002)	Dubai Millennium (b 1996)	Seeking The Gold (b 1985)	Mr Prospector
			Con Game
		Colorado Dancer (b 1986)	Shareef Dancer
			Fall Aspen
	Spirit of Tara (IRE) (b 1994)	Sadler's Wells (b 1981)	Northern Dancer
			Fairy Bridge
		Flame of Tara (b 1980)	Artaius
			Welsh Flame

After Dubawi, Echo of Light can be considered the best of Dubai Millennium's only crop. It remains to be seen whether he can shrug off the 'flat-track bully' tag, but, in any event, he looks sure to pay his way, with the Dubai Carnival set to be the first port of call. Echo of Light, who fetched €1,200,000 as a yearling, is the third well-above-average performer out of his dam Spirit of Tara. Multazem (by Kingmambo) was a useful winner at a mile and nine furlongs in Ireland, while Multazem's brother Akarem showed smart form in winning listed events at Hamilton and Ascot in the latest season, both at a mile and a half. A sister to Salsabil and a half-sister to Marju, the useful Spirit of Tara finished out of the frame just once in seven starts. She won a three-year-old maiden at Galway over a mile and a half and was runner-up in the Blandford Stakes at the Curragh on her final outing. Echo of Light has won at eleven and a half furlongs, but is best at around a mile and a mile and a quarter. He acts on polytrack and good to firm going, and has yet to race on soft or heavy. He was tongue tied for the first three outings of his career, on the third occasion hanging left and running out. An edgy type, the big, well-made Echo of

Godolphin's "Echo of Light"

Light has worn a crossed noseband (he was formerly tongue tied) and been taken early to post. He usually makes the running or races prominently. *Saeed bin Suroor*

ECLIPSE PARK 3 ch.g. Rainbow Quest (USA) 134 – Gino's Spirits 98 (Perugino (USA) 84) [2006 69: p8g⁴ p10g p10g⁴ 11.6g 8.1s 8f p10g Nov 1] fair maiden: well held in handicaps last 4 starts: stays 1¼m: acts on polytrack (no form on turf): tried in cheekpieces. *M. J. McGrath* — **a69**

ECO CENTRISM 2 ch.c. (Jan 28) Selkirk (USA) 129 – Way O'Gold (USA) (Slew O' Gold (USA)) [2006 8g² Sep 14] 52,000Y: strong colt: fifth foal: half-brother to 5-y-o Isidore Bonheur: dam, French maiden, half-sister to smart French 6f/7f performer Crystal Castle: 16/1, tongue tied and green, promising neck second to Paceman in maiden at Yarmouth, soon lot to do: sure to improve. *W. J. Haggas* — **81 p**

EDAARA (IRE) 3 ch.f. Pivotal 124 – Green Bonnet (IRE) (Green Desert (USA) 127) [2006 93p: 7g² 10g⁴ 7d* Oct 3] strong, good sort: fairly useful performer, lightly raced: off 3½ months, won maiden at Leicester in October by 6 lengths from Double Carpet: best up to 1m: yet to race on ground firmer than good. *W. J. Haggas* — **83 +**

EDAS 4 b.c. Celtic Swing 138 – Eden (IRE) 88 (Polish Precedent (USA) 131) [2006 85: 12g 9.9f⁶ 9.9f⁶ 10.1f⁶ 12s⁵ p12.2g² p12.2g⁵ Nov 10] good-topped colt: just fair handicapper in 2006: stays easy 1½m: acts on polytrack, firm and good to soft going: tried visored. *J. J. Quinn* — **73**

EDDIE JOCK (IRE) 2 ch.g. (Apr 29) Almutawakel 126 – Al Euro (FR) 57 (Mujtahid (USA) 118) [2006 6m 6v⁵ 6f* 7m* 7f² 7g* 8g² 7d² Oct 7] 26,000Y: angular, rather lightly-made gelding: third foal: half-brother to 3-y-o Supercast: dam lightly-raced half-sister to high-class miler Air Express: useful performer: gelded after second start: soon thrived, winning maiden at Brighton in June, nursery at Newmarket in July and minor event at Ascot (beat non-staying Doctor Brown by 4 lengths) in August: runner-up last 2 starts, in listed race at Salisbury and minor event at Ascot (2 lengths behind Charlie Farnsbarns): should stay 1m: acts on firm and good to soft going. *M. L. W. Bell* — **102**

EDDIES JEWEL 6 b.g. Presidium 124 – Superstream (Superpower 113) [2006 49: 8.3m 7f 9.9f⁵ 8m 8.5m Aug 16] strong gelding: poor performer: left H. Alexander and returned to former trainer after second outing: effective at 7f to 1½m: acts on polytrack, soft and good to firm going: tried in headgear. *I. W. McInnes* — **41**

EDEN ROCK (IRE) 5 b.g. Danehill (USA) 126 – Marlene-D 57 (Selkirk (USA) 129) [2006 102: 8m⁵ 7m⁵ 8f Aug 4] big, good-bodied gelding: useful handicapper, lightly raced (reportedly had pelvic injury after 2 yrs): easily best efforts in 2006 when fifth in valuable handicaps at Newbury (beaten 2 lengths by Forgery) and Royal Ascot (not clear run when beaten 2½ lengths by Uhoomagood): well held final outing: best at 7f/1m: raced only on good going or firmer: tried tongue tied/in cheekpieces at 4 yrs: got very worked up before well held second outing in 2005. *Pat Eddery* — **102**

EDEN STAR (IRE) 4 b.f. Soviet Star (USA) 128 – Gold Prospector (IRE) 78 (Spectrum (IRE) 126) [2006 50: f7g Jan 3] poor performer: well held only outing in 2006. *D. K. Ivory* — **–**

EDE'S DOT COM (IRE) 2 b.c. (Apr 10) Trans Island 119 – Kilkee Bay (IRE) 61 (Case Law 113) [2006 6d p6g* p6g³ 6m⁴ 6g Oct 13] 9,000F: third foal: dam, placed up to 7f at 2 yrs, half-sister to top-class sprinter Lake Coniston: fairly useful performer: won maiden at Lingfield in July: ran well in frame in nurseries at Wolverhampton and Newmarket next 2 starts: raced on 6f: acts on polytrack and good to firm going. *W. J. Knight* — **81**

EDGE CLOSER 2 b.c. (Mar 25) Bold Edge 123 – Blue Goddess (IRE) 94 (Blues Traveller (IRE) 119) [2006 6d* Nov 4] second foal: dam, 2-y-o 6f winner (won all 3 starts), out of close relative to Yorkshire Oaks winner Hellenic, herself dam of Islington and Greek Dance: 6/1, won maiden at Windsor by ¾ length from Danehillsundance, racing prominently: open to improvement. *R. Hannon* — **76 p**

EDGED IN GOLD 4 ch.f. Bold Edge 123 – Piccante (Wolfhound (USA) 126) [2006 61: p5.1g⁵ p5.1g⁶ p5.1g⁵ p5g⁵ p5g p5.1g⁵ p5.1g⁴ p5.1g* 5g⁴ p5.1g⁶ p5g Jul 26] modest performer: won banded race at Wolverhampton in May: raced only at 5f: acts on polytrack: sometimes finds little: sold 5,000 gns in October. *P. J. Makin* — **60**

EDGE END 2 ch.g. (Apr 12) Bold Edge 123 – Rag Time Belle 34 (Raga Navarro (ITY) 119) [2006 6d⁶ Nov 4] well held in maiden at Windsor. *D. J. S. ffrench Davis* — **–**

EDGEFOUR (IRE) 2 b.f. (May 7) King's Best (USA) 132 – Highshaan (Pistolet Bleu (IRE) 133) [2006 6.1g p7g Oct 21] €98,000F, 40,000 2-y-o: fifth foal: half-sister to 1¼m winner Night Driver (by Night Shift) and French 1½m winner Anna Banana (by Spec- — **–**

trum): dam, French 9f (at 2 yrs) and 10.5f winner, half-sister to 5-y-o Alexander Goldrun: well beaten in maidens. *B. I. Case*

EDGE FUND 4 b.g. Bold Edge 123 – Truly Madly Deeply (Most Welcome 131) [2006 **42** 73: p8.6g p8g p7g⁵ f7g 8.5d 8m 7m 10m⁵ 10m⁵ Jun 27] workmanlike gelding: modest **a52** at best nowadays: stays 1m: acts on polytrack, soft and good to firm going: tried in headgear/tongue tied: sent to Holland. *Miss Gay Kelleway*

EDIN BURGHER (FR) 5 br.g. Hamas (IRE) 125§ – Jaljuli 107 (Jalmood (USA) 126) **63** [2006 63+: p6g⁴ 7m p7.1g³ p8g p7.1g p6g Jun 30] modest performer: should stay 1m: raced mainly on polytrack: tried in cheekpieces. *T. T. Clement*

EDISON 2 ch.c. (Feb 25) Best of The Bests (IRE) 122 – Lanciana (IRE) (Acatenango **81** (GER) 127) [2006 6s⁶ 7f³ 8m⁴ Sep 19] 38,000Y, 47,000 2-y-o: sturdy, compact colt: second foal: half-brother to 3-y-o Lalina: dam, won at around 1¼m in France/Germany, out of half-sister to dam of Deutsches Derby winners Lando and Laroche: fairly useful maiden: made frame at Lingfield and Newmarket (fourth to Empire Day): will stay 1¼m: sold 57,000 gns. *N. P. Littmoden*

EDWARD (IRE) 4 b.g. Namid 128 – Daltak (Night Shift (USA)) [2006 –: p5g⁴ p5g f5g **59** Apr 3] modest maiden: should be suited by 6f+: reportedly bled final outing. *A. P. Jarvis*

EESHEE 3 b.f. Distant Music (USA) 126 – Madame Curie (Polish Precedent (USA) **34** 131) [2006 46: p5.1g p5.1g f5g⁶ f6g f5g⁴ 5m Apr 25] poor maiden: left S. Keightley after fifth outing: visored last 2 starts. *Miss Diana Weeden*

EFFECTIVE 6 ch.g. Bahamian Bounty 116 – Efficacy 62 (Efisio 120) [2006 84, a71: **82** p6g* p6g² p6g³ p5g⁵ 6m 7m p6g Dec 20] lengthy gelding: fairly useful handicapper: won at Lingfield in February: effective at 5f to 7f: acts on all-weather, firm and soft ground: tried visored. *A. P. Jarvis*

EFFECT ME NOT (IRE) 4 b.f. Xaar 132 – Beauty Appeal (USA) (Shadeed (USA) **56** 135) [2006 –: 8.2s 8d 13m 11v⁶ p12.2m Sep 2] fifth foal: half-sister to 3 winners, including 6f to 8.5f winner Beauteous (by Tagula): dam unraced: modest maiden: left D. Gillespie in Ireland, tailed off in selling handicap at Wolverhampton final start: stays 13f: acts on heavy and good to firm ground: wore cheekpieces penultimate outing. *Peter Grayson*

EFFIGY 2 b.c. (May 7) Efisio 120 – Hymne d'Amour (USA) 58 (Dixieland Band **67 p** (USA)) [2006 6s 6d⁴ Nov 4] half-brother to 3 winners, including smart performer up to 1¾m in Britain/USA Chelsea Barracks and fairly useful 2m winner Guard Duty (both by Deploy): dam, lightly raced on Flat and winning hurdler, out of half-sister to Alzao: better run in maidens when fourth at Windsor: should go on improving at 1m+. *H. Candy*

EFIDIUM 8 b.g. Presidium 124 – Efipetite 54 (Efisio 120) [2006 73: 8g³ 8f⁵ 7m⁵ 8f³ **75** 7.9m⁶ 7.1f⁶ 8m 7d⁴ 8g 8f³ 8g³ 7s² 7s Oct 24] small gelding: fair performer: effective at 6f to 1m: acts on fibresand, firm and soft going: sometimes blinkered, including last 6 outings: has been early to post: tough. *M. Bycroft*

EFIMAC 6 b.m. Presidium 124 – Efipetite 54 (Efisio 120) [2006 55: f7g Jan 3] small, **–** plain mare: modest performer: well held only outing in 2006: tried blinkered/visored. *N. Bycroft*

EFISIO PRINCESS 3 br.f. Efisio 120 – Hardiprincess (Keen 116) [2006 7f 6s³ 6.1d* **64** Oct 13] 4,000Y, resold 800Y: good-topped filly: sixth foal: half-sister to 9.4f/1¼m winner Anne-Sophie (by First Trump): dam ran twice: modest form: won maiden at Warwick in October by 1¼ lengths from Tagula Bay: stays 6f. *J. E. Long*

EFISTORM 5 b.g. Efisio 120 – Abundance 62 (Cadeaux Genereux 131) [2006 79: f5g **82** f5g² p5.1g f5g³ f5s* p5g⁴ 5d⁵ 5s⁶ p6g f5g⁵ p5.1g³ f5g p5.1g* Dec 27] smallish, quite **a90** good-topped gelding: fairly useful handicapper: won at Southwell in March and Wolverhampton in December: stays 6f: acts on all-weather and soft ground. *J. Balding*

EFORETTA (GER) 4 ch.f. Dr Fong (USA) 128 – Erminora (GER) (Highest Honor **66** (FR) 124) [2006 –, a56: f11g f7g f11g² p12.2g³ f11g f12g³ f14g* f14g* p16.5g² 18f³ **a72** Jul 29] close-coupled filly: fair performer: won banded race and handicap at Southwell, both in May: stays 2¼m: acts on all-weather and firm ground: blinkered second start. *D. J. Wintle*

EFRHINA (IRE) 6 ch.m. Woodman (USA) 126 – Eshq Albahr (USA) (Riverman **–** (USA) 131) [2006 75: f12g Feb 14] leggy mare: fair handicapper at best: well held only outing in 2006: tried in cheekpieces: usually held up: sold 2,500 gns. *Stef Liddiard*

EGERTON (GER) 5 b.h. Groom Dancer (USA) 128 – Enrica 106 (Niniski (USA) 125) **122** [2006 9.3g* 10d³ᵈ 11g* 12g⁴ 12g⁴ 12g² 12g⁴ 12m⁶ Dec 10] very smart performer: excelled himself when neck second to Warrsan in Grosser Preis von Baden at Baden-Baden in 2004 (missed 2005 with leg injury): successful on return in maiden at Cologne in May and won Idee Hansa-Preis at Hamburg in July by length from Song Writer: very good ½-length second to Youmzain in Preis von Europa at Cologne sixth start: respectable fourth to Laverock in Gran Premio Jockey Club Italiano at Milan before below-form sixth to Collier Hill in Hong Kong Vase at Sha Tin final outing: stays 1½m: acts on soft ground: none too consistent. *P. Rau, Germany*

EGLEVSKI (IRE) 2 b.c. (Feb 14) Danehill Dancer (IRE) 117 – Ski For Gold 76 (Shirley Heights 130) [2006 7g⁵ 7m² 8.2d³ 9m² 10d* Oct 2] good-topped colt: sixth foal: half-brother to 2001 2-y-o 1m winner Ski For Me (by Barathea) and fairly useful 2004 2-y-o 1m winner Alpine Gold (by Montjeu), both of whom stayed 1½m: dam, 2-y-o 7f winner who might have proved best around 1¾m, half-sister to US Grade 1 1¼m winner Bequest: fairly useful form: placed 3 times prior to winning maiden at Pontefract, positively ridden: will stay at least 1½m. *J. L. Dunlop* **83**

EGO TRIP 5 b.g. Deploy 131 – Boulevard Rouge (USA) 71 (Red Ransom (USA)) [2006 72: 12v 12g³ 12.4d⁶ 11.8d 13.1g³ f14g² 12s* Oct 24] close-coupled gelding: fair handicapper: won at Catterick in October: stays 1¾m: acts on fibresand and any turf going: tried visored, blinkered nowadays. *M. W. Easterby* **75**

EGYPTIAN LORD 3 ch.g. Bold Edge 123 – Calypso Lady (IRE) 88 (Priolo (USA) 127) [2006 67: p5g* 5g 5g 5.1m³ 5m p5.1g⁶ 5m³ 5d p6g p5.1m p5.1g p5.1g p5g⁴ Dec 3] workmanlike gelding: fair handicapper on all-weather, modest on turf: won at Lingfield in January: best at 5f: acts on all-weather and good to firm going: usually blinkered/visored: not one to trust. *Peter Grayson* **60 a70**

EIDSFOSS (IRE) 4 b.g. Danehill Dancer (IRE) 117 – Alca Egeria (ITY) (Shareef Dancer (USA) 135) [2006 44: f11g p13g Dec 22] poor maiden: tried visored. *T. T. Clement* **–**

EIJAAZ (IRE) 5 b.g. Green Desert (USA) 127 – Kismah 111 (Machiavellian (USA) 123) [2006 66, a69: p10g p9.5g⁴ p12g⁶ p9.5g⁶ 11.5m 10.2g² 10m 10f⁶ 9g⁶ p8.6g Jul 11] quite attractive gelding: fair performer on all-weather, modest on turf: stays 1¾m: acts on polytrack and firm going: tried in cheekpieces: usually ridden by Kristin Stubbs: has joined G. Harker. *Mrs L. Stubbs* **54 a66**

EILEAN BAN (USA) 3 ch.f. Silver Hawk (USA) 123 – Isla Del Rey (USA) 103 (Nureyev (USA) 131) [2006 98p: 8.1g Aug 26] strong, lengthy filly: useful in 3 races at 2 yrs: reported in February to have fractured a tibia: ran as if amiss in listed race at Sandown only outing in 2006: not sure to stay much beyond 1m: raced on good/good to firm going. *E. A. L. Dunlop* **–**

EISTEDDFOD 5 ch.g. Cadeaux Genereux 131 – Ffestiniog (IRE) 96 (Efisio 120) [2006 115: 6g³ 6d⁶ 5d⁵ 6m 6.5g 6s² 5.2m 6d³ 6g 6d⁵ Nov 4] lengthy, good-quartered gelding: smart performer: best efforts in 2006 when length second to Indian Maiden in Prix de Meautry at Deauville (won race at 4 yrs) and 2¾ lengths third to Bygone Days in minor event at Hamilton on sixth/eighth starts: best form at 6f, though should prove as effective returned to 7f: yet to race on heavy going, acts on any other: blinkered sixth/seventh outings: often held up. *P. F. I. Cole* **115**

EKHTIAAR 2 b.g. (Mar 6) Elmaamul (USA) 125 – Divina Mia 66 (Dowsing (USA) 124) [2006 8m⁶ p7g* p7g* Oct 15] 33,000F, 85,000Y: useful-looking gelding: brother to useful 2001 2-y-o 6f winner Mine Host, later successful at 9f/1¼m in Hong Kong, and half-brother to 3 winners, including useful 7f (at 2 yrs)/1m winner Antediluvian (by Air Express): dam, 2-y-o 6f winner who stayed 11f, out of useful half-sister to Shirley Heights: fairly useful form: won maiden and minor event at Lingfield in October, in latter beating Deadshot Keen cosily by head, still looking green (gelded after): should stay 1m: should do better still. *J. H. M. Gosden* **89 p**

EKTIMAAL 3 ch.g. Bahamian Bounty 116 – Secret Circle (Magic Ring (IRE) 115) [2006 8.3g 8.1m⁶ 8.2m⁴ 7d³ 7d² Oct 18] 34,000F, 130,000Y: tall, good-topped gelding: fourth foal: half-brother to useful 7f winner Secret Place (by Compton Place) and German 7f/1m winner Secret Affair (by Piccolo): dam unraced half-sister to high-class 1m/1¼m performer Bijou d'Inde: fair maiden: stays 1m: said to have had breathing problem on debut: tongue tied last 3 starts: has found little. *E. A. L. Dunlop* **73**

EKTISHAAF 4 b.f. Mujahid (USA) 125 – Tahnee (Cadeaux Genereux 131) [2006 73: p8.6g⁵ p8g p6g⁵ p7g* 7.1g 6.1m p7.1g³ 10d p10g Nov 25] sturdy filly: fair handicapper: won at Lingfield in April: left C. Wall after seventh outing: stays 7f: acts on polytrack and firm going, probably on good to soft. *R. McGlinchey, Ireland* **65**

ELAALA (USA) 4 ch.f. Aljabr (USA) 125 – Nufuth (USA) (Nureyev (USA) 131) **56**
[2006 53: f14g* f16g² Dec 28] neat filly: modest performer: won banded race at Southwell in March: stays 1¾m: acts on fibresand and good to soft going. *B. D. Leavy*

ELA ALEKA MOU 2 ch.f. (Mar 23) Tobougg (IRE) 125 – Miss Grimm (USA) 69 **83**
(Irish River (FR) 131) [2006 6m* 6m² 6m⁶ Aug 5] well-made filly: first foal: dam maiden
out of useful performer up to 1m Gretel: fairly useful performer: won maiden at York in
June (raced alone much of way): no progress after, second in minor event at Haydock and
sixth in nursery at Newmarket: likely to stay 7f. *M. A. Jarvis*

EL ALAMEIN (IRE) 3 ch.g. Nashwan (USA) 135 – El Rabab (USA) 70 (Roberto **74**
(USA) 131) [2006 –p: 11.5m* 11.7f³ 14.1f⁶ p16g² p16g³ Sep 2] big, workmanlike gelding: fair handicapper: won at Yarmouth in June: stays 2m: acts on polytrack and firm
going. *Sir Mark Prescott*

ELATED (IRE) 4 b.g. Erhaab (USA) 127 – Elauyun (IRE) (Muhtarram (USA) 125) **72**
[2006 p10g p12.2g² 11.8d Apr 6] leggy gelding: easily best effort in 3 maidens (fair
form) when second to Marmota at Wolverhampton: found little final outing: stays 1½m.
W. J. Haggas

EL BOSQUE (IRE) 2 b.g. (May 4) Elnadim (USA) 128 – In The Woods 101 (You And **90**
I (USA) 118) [2006 5m 6g* 5.2g⁴ 6m 6g* 6m 6d Sep 29] 23,000Y: leggy, attractive gelding: has a quick action: first foal: dam, 2-y-o 6f winner, later 6f winner in Scandinavia:
fairly useful performer: won maiden at Haydock in July and minor event at Windsor in
August: well below form last 2 starts (gelded after): may prove best kept to 5f/6f: acts on
good to firm ground. *B. R. Millman*

EL CAPITAN (FR) 3 b.g. Danehill Dancer (IRE) 117 – Fille Dansante (IRE) (Dancing **64**
Dissident (USA) 119) [2006 78: 8m 7m⁶ p7g 8.1g³ 10.1m³ 11.6d Oct 9] tall, rather leggy
gelding: modest maiden: stays 1m: acts on polytrack and good to firm ground: tried
blinkered/visored: has hung left/flashed tail. *Miss Gay Kelleway*

EL CHAPARRAL (IRE) 6 b.g. Bigstone (IRE) 126 – Low Line 66 (High Line 125) **69**
[2006 75, a83: p10g 12m⁵ 10f 10m Aug 9] lengthy gelding: fair performer: left **a66**
W. Haggas after reappearance: stays easy 1½m: acts on polytrack and firm ground:
tried in cheekpieces/blinkers (ran poorly): quirky and tends to start slowly/race freely.
F. P. Murtagh

EL COTO 6 b.g. Forzando 122 – Thatcherella 80 (Thatching 131) [2006 99: 8v 8m 10g⁴ **97**
8.9m⁴ 8m 10.4f 8m³ 10s 9.5g p7.1g² p7.1g Dec 31] smallish, good-topped gelding: **a90**
useful handicapper on turf, fairly useful on all-weather: left E. McMahon, good fourth in
Zetland Gold Cup at Redcar third start: in-and-out form after: effective at 7f, and probably stays 10.5f: acts on polytrack, firm and soft going: tried in headgear. *K. A. Ryan*

EL DECECY (USA) 2 b.c. (Apr 11) Seeking The Gold (USA) – Ashraakat (USA) **83**
105 (Danzig (USA)) [2006 7m 7m³ 8d Sep 27] tall colt, unfurnished at 2: yrs: fifth foal:
half-brother to 5-y-o Hezaam and fairly useful 7f winner Ahdaaf (by Bahri): dam, 6f/7f
winner, sister to high-class sprinter Elnadim and closely related to very smart 1m/1¼m
performer Mehthaaf: fairly useful maiden: easily best effort when third to Celtic Step at
Leicester, losing second close home (jockey suspended for dropping hands): may prove
best short of 1m. *J. L. Dunlop*

EL DEE (IRE) 3 br.g. Brave Act 119 – Go Flightline (IRE) 63 (Common Grounds 118) **48**
[2006 43: f11g⁴ 11g⁵ 14.1g 12.1f 12.1g² 11s⁵ Aug 13] strong, close-coupled gelding: **a53**
modest maiden: stays 1½m: acts on fibresand, best effort on turf on good going.
D. Carroll

ELDON ENDEAVOUR 2 b.g. (Apr 20) Hunting Lion (IRE) 115 – La Noisette (Rock **–**
Hopper 124) [2006 6d 5.9g 6m 8.3g Sep 17] last in maidens. *B. Storey*

ELDON OUTLAW 3 b.g. Hunting Lion (IRE) 115 – La Noisette (Rock Hopper 124) **–**
[2006 –: 5m 5m 7.1g Jul 3] little form. *B. Storey*

ELDORADO 5 b.g. Hernando (FR) 127 – Catch (USA) (Blushing Groom (FR) 131) **78**
[2006 85: 11.7d 10g 10s⁴ 12g 9.9g* 11.6f⁴ 11m³ 14.1m² 14m⁵ 11g Sep 15] workmanlike
gelding: fair handicapper: won at Salisbury in June: stays 1¾m: acts on any going: sold
16,000 gns. *S. Kirk*

ELDORI 3 b.f. Vettori (IRE) 119 – Elderberry (Bin Ajwaad (IRE) 119) [2006 –: p7g⁵ 6g **–**
8.3g p8g Oct 23] no form. *M. S. Saunders*

EL DOTTORE 2 b.c. (Feb 18) Dr Fong (USA) 128 – Edouna (FR) (Doyoun 124) [2006 **52 p**
8m Sep 19] unfurnished colt, weak as 2-y-o: second foal: dam, useful French 1¼m/1½m
winner, granddaughter of top-class filly up to 1½m Northern Trick: 20/1 and green, mid-
field in maiden at Newmarket: likely to progress. *M. L. W. Bell*

ELECTRIC STORM 3 b.c. Zafonic (USA) 130 – Rainbow Lake 113 (Rainbow Quest **69**
(USA) 134) [2006 10.2g⁶ 10m 11.7m⁶ Jun 28] strong, close-coupled colt: half-brother
to several winners, including high-class 7.5f (at 2 yrs) to 1½m winner Powerscourt (by
Sadler's Wells) and 13f/1¾m winner Brimming (by Generous) and 5f to 7f winner Kind
(by Danehill), both smart: dam 1¼m/1½m (Lancashire Oaks) winner: easily best effort
in maidens when sixth at Bath on debut: will be at least as effective at 1m as 1¼m: sold
15,000 gns in July. *R. Charlton*

ELECTRIC WARRIOR (IRE) 3 b.g. Bold Fact (USA) 116 – Dungeon Princess **85**
(IRE) 62 (Danehill (USA) 126) [2006 53p: 8.1s p8.6g⁶ 8s 8.1f* 6m* 7m* 7m³ 7.1m⁶
8.1m⁵ 8d⁴ Oct 2] strong, lengthy gelding: fairly useful handicapper: won at Haydock
(edged left/carried head awkwardly), Pontefract and Newcastle in June: bit below best
last 2 starts: effective at 6f to 1m: acts on firm going: tends to race freely. *K. R. Burke*

ELECTRIQUE (IRE) 6 b.g. Elmaamul (USA) 125 – Majmu (USA) 105 (Al Nasr **–**
(FR) 126) [2006 p8g p12g p8g Dec 5] leggy, quite good-topped gelding: fairly useful at
3 yrs: well held in handicaps in 2006: blinkered/visored last 5 starts. *A. J. McCabe*

ELECTROCUTIONIST (USA) 5 b.h. Red Ransom (USA) – Elbaaha 97 (Arazi **127**
(USA) 135) [2006 127: a10f* a10g* 10m² 12m² Jul 29]
        In the decade since the inaugural running of the World Cup, Dubai has made
giant strides towards becoming the chief meeting point for many of the world's top
horses. Since Cigar led home an American one, two, three in the first World Cup,
the raceday of which the World Cup is the centrepiece has itself become the cul-
mination of a ten-week International Racing Carnival, which can justifiably be said
to have attracted horses from all corners of the racing world. In the latest season,
three hundred and fifty horses competed at Nad Al Sheba on World Cup day and
the ten meetings preceding it. They hailed from nineteen different countries, at least
one from each continent, with overseas winners coming from Britain, Turkey,
Macau, Germany, Brazil, South Africa, Saudi Arabia, France, Japan and the United
States. Clearly much of the attraction lies in the value of the races, the World Cup
day prize money itself further enhanced in 2006 by increasing the value of the two
turf races on the card, the Sheema Classic and Duty Free, which became the two
richest turf races ever run.
        Electrocutionist was the fifth winner of the Dubai World Cup for Saeed bin
Suroor (and a fourth for Godolphin) after following a tried and tested route at Nad
Al Sheba, running in Round 3 of the Sheikh Maktoum Bin Rashid Al Maktoum
Challenge on his reappearance, a race won by subsequent World Cup winners
Dubai Millennium and Street Cry (Moon Ballad won Round 2 of the same series)
in recent years. Electrocutionist reproduced the best of his turf form on his first
try on dirt, stretching away to beat the smart Chiquitin by seven lengths. Despite
some pessimism because of his draw in stall one, Electrocutionist was a worthy
favourite for the World Cup. The American challenge was a little less formidable
than usual, with the winner of the Donn Handicap, Brass Hat, seemingly the pick.
Also in the line-up were Japan's leading dirt performer Kane Hekili and British-
trained Maraahel, who finished a close third to Electrocutionist in the Juddmonte
International at York in the previous season. In the event, Electrocutionist needed
to do no more than repeat the form of his trial to win, although he didn't travel
particularly smoothly, bustled along leaving the stalls and then being chased along
four furlongs out. Sixth early in the straight, Electrocutionist stayed on gamely
under sustained pressure in the final two furlongs, getting on top inside the last
furlong and beating Brass Hat by a length and a half. Brass Hat failed a dope test for
the anti-inflammatory drug methylprednisolone, depriving connections of second-
place prize money, despite their insistence that the drug had been given twenty-
eight days before the race, well within the guidelines set out by the Emirates Racing
Association. Wilko, temporarily back with former trainer Jeremy Noseda, for
whom he had won the Breeders' Cup Juvenile in 2004, was promoted to second
after finishing three lengths behind Brass Hat. Kane Hekili appeared to be going
best of all on the home turn but was unable to quicken, finishing fifth before being
promoted after the disqualification. Maraahel came seventh (promoted to sixth).
        As with Dubai Millennium, Electrocutionist reappeared in Europe in the
Prince of Wales's Stakes at Royal Ascot on his return from a three-month absence
after the World Cup, and he looked in fine shape beforehand. He ran with credit

Dubai World Cup Sponsored By Emirates Airline, Nad Al Sheba—the ill-fated Electrocutionist gets on top inside the final furlong; Brass Hat (blinkered) passes the post in second, but fails a dope test and is disqualified, Wilko (rail) being promoted from third

again but was unable to repel the finishing run of Ouija Board, finishing half a length second of the seven runners. Electrocutionist would almost certainly have benefited from setting a stronger pace. It was clear by the time of the King George VI and Queen Elizabeth Stakes back at Ascot in July that Godolphin's runners were generally finding their form after a relatively poor start. Despite a scare on the morning of the race when reportedly stiff, after a suggestion that he'd been cast in his box, Electrocutionist again looked very well in the paddock and moved fluently to post, where he was checked over by a vet. Partly because of the pre-race concerns, Electrocutionist was available at 4/1, behind Hurricane Run (6/5-on) and high-class Japanese performer Heart's Cry (3/1). Also running was Maraahel, who had returned from Dubai in good form, winning at Chester and Royal Ascot. Godolphin ran Cherry Mix, an Arc runner-up, ostensibly as a pacemaker, and turning for home Electrocutionist took over to share the lead with Heart's Cry, both seemingly travelling better than Hurricane Run. Electrocutionist kept on between horses, despite showing a tendency to carry his head awkwardly and hang to the left, resulting in a gap opening up for Hurricane Run who found plenty under strong pressure and eventually won by half a length from Electrocutionist, with a similar distance back to Heart's Cry.

Electrocutionist (USA) (b.h. 2001)	Red Ransom (USA) (b 1987)	Roberto (b 1969)	Hail To Reason Bramalea
		Arabia (b 1977)	Damascus Christmas Wind
	Elbaaha (ch 1994)	Arazi (ch 1989)	Blushing Groom Danseur Fabuleux
		Gesedeh (ch 1983)	Ela-Mana-Mou Le Melody

Electrocutionist was subsequently found to have aggravated an old splint injury during the King George, and ten days afterwards was ruled out of a repeat attempt at the International and out of the Irish Champion Stakes. Connections became concerned that Electrocutionist might have a heart abnormality and, whilst in the care of specialists in Newmarket, he suffered a fatal heart attack in the early hours of September 9th. The quite good-topped, useful-looking Electrocutionist won eight of his twelve career starts, in the process earning over £3m in prize money. He was capable of high-class form both on turf (good to firm and good to soft, unraced on extremes) and dirt, and was effective at a mile and a quarter to a mile and a half. Electrocutionist's pedigree has been covered in previous editions of *Racehorses*, and there is little to add other than that his half-sister Grigorieva (by Woodman) won twice during 2006, on the second occasion in a listed event at Saint-Cloud. Electrocutionist's victory in the Dubai World Cup was another boost for his sire Red Ransom who stands at Darley's Dalham Hall Stud at Newmarket, having been purchased from America principally because of his progeny's good record on turf. Electrocutionist was, ironically, his sire's first Group/Grade 1 winner on dirt. Electrocutionist's dam Elbaaha was led out unsold at the Keeneland January Sale where, in foal to Montjeu, she failed to reach her reserve after being expected to be the top lot. The resultant Montjeu colt set a sale record for a foal of 2.7m dollars at Keeneland's November Sale. *Saeed bin Suroor*

ELECTRON PULSE 3 ch.f. Dr Fong (USA) 128 – Lost In Lucca 72§ (Inchinor 119) [2006 p6g 7.1g 8g⁵ 6g⁵ 6g⁴ 7.2f⁴ Jul 17] 35,000Y: second foal: half-sister to German 6.5f and 1m winner Lusty Lad (by Lujain): dam, untrustworthy 1m winner, half-sister to Lowther Stakes winner Jemima: modest maiden: stays 1m: acts on firm going. *J. S. Goldie*   **59**

ELEGANT TIMES (IRE) 3 b.f. Dansili 127 – Simply Times (USA) 64 (Dodge (USA)) [2006 68: 7m³ 7d 6g² p6g* f6g 7.1d² 7g 7.1m³ p7.1m 7d⁵ 7g Sep 27] sparely-made filly: fair performer: won maiden at Wolverhampton in June: raced only at 6f/7f: acts on polytrack, firm and good to soft going: tried blinkered. *T. D. Easterby*   **68**

EL FARO (FR) 3 b.g. Fantastic Light (USA) 134 – Pagoda (FR) (Sadler's Wells (USA) 132) [2006 60p: 11g 12f 14.1g 11.5m 12m Aug 5] sturdy gelding: lightly-raced maiden: best effort at 11f on good going: joined Alan Fleming in Ireland. *M. R. Channon*   **69**

ELGIN MARBLES 4 b.g. Lujain (USA) 119 – Bold Gem 68 (Never So Bold 135) [2006 76: 6m 6f 6.1d p8g p6g Oct 23] heavy-topped gelding: fairly useful performer at best: no form in 2006: tried blinkered/in cheekpieces/tongue tied. *A. B. Haynes*   **–**

ELHAMRI 2 b. or br.c. (Feb 17) Noverre (USA) 125 – Seamstress (IRE) 72 (Barathea (IRE) 127) [2006 5m⁵ 5s⁶ 5m* 5.2g* 6d⁴ 5g⁵ 5d⁵ Oct 7] 30,000F, 28,000Y: small, strong colt: first foal: dam, 7f (at 2 yrs) and 1m (in USA) winner, sister to useful performer up to 7f Rag Top: useful performer: won maiden at Windsor in April, listed Windsor Castle Stakes at Royal Ascot and Weatherbys Super Sprint at Newbury (beat Ishi Adiva by length, making all) in July: not clear run in Gimcrack Stakes (fourth to Conquest) and Flying Childers (fifth to Wi Dud) at York, but hung left/weakened in Cornwallis Stakes final start: best at 5f, probably on good or firmer going. *S. Kirk*   **105**

Weatherbys Super Sprint, Newbury—top weight Elhamri makes all; Ishi Adiva (left) pips We'll Confer (second left) for the runner-up spot, with El Bosque (tracking first three) taking fourth

ELH

ELHAREER (IRE) 2 ch.f. (Feb 25) Selkirk (USA) 129 – Ellway Star (IRE) 104 (Night **71 p**
Shift (USA)) [2006 p7g³ p7g p5.1g* Dec 22] lengthy filly: third foal: half-sister to 3-y-o
Figaro Flyer: dam 5f (including at 2 yrs) winner, half-sister to smart 7f/1m performers
Corinium and Fa-Eq: fair form in maidens, better than bare result both starts prior to
winning at Wolverhampton by 2½ lengths from Wibbadune, making all: will prove best
at 5f/6f: remains open to improvement. *B. J. Meehan*

EL HOGAR (IRE) 3 ch.g. Namid 128 – Fussing (IRE) (Persian Bold 123) [2006 p7g **–**
Oct 23] 12/1, well held in maiden at Lingfield: sold 2,500 gns. *S. Kirk*

ELIDORE 6 b.m. Danetime (IRE) 121 – Beveled Edge 60 (Beveled (USA)) [2006 76: **69**
10.2d 7.1m 8m 8.1m⁴ 8.1m² 8.1m⁴ 8.1m³ 8.1d 8.2s Oct 18] rangy mare: fair handicapper:
best up to 1m: acts on polytrack and any turf going: visored (weakened quickly) once at
4 yrs: front runner. *B. Palling*

ELIMINATOR 3 ch.g. Observatory (USA) 131 – Effie (Royal Academy (USA) 130) **–**
[2006 70: p9.5g p8.6g 9s⁵ 8.2s 8g 8m⁶ 8g 8.2m 7.5f 7.5f 10m Jul 24] quite good-topped
gelding: regressive maiden: tried in cheekpieces/blinkers. *I. W. McInnes*

ELISHA (IRE) 4 ch.f. Raise A Grand (IRE) 114 – Social Butterfly (USA) (Sir Ivor **55**
(USA) 135) [2006 66: 6m³ 5m⁴ 6f 6g 5g Aug 17] sturdy filly: modest performer: left
A. Mullins in Ireland after second start: stays 6f: acts on firm going: tried in blinkers/in
cheekpieces. *K. A. Ryan*

ELITE LAND 3 b.g. Namaqualand (USA) – Petite Elite 47 (Anfield 117) [2006 44: **51**
10d² 10f 7.9m⁴ 9.8m⁵ 8.5f⁵ 8f⁴ 9.3m⁴ 11s² 14.1g 9.8d Aug 29] close-coupled gelding:
modest maiden: stays 11f: acts on firm and soft going: tried blinkered: gelded after final
start. *N. Bycroft*

ELIZABETH GARRETT 2 b.f. (Mar 2) Dr Fong (USA) 128 – Eleonor Sympson 50 **55**
(Cadeaux Genereux 131) [2006 5s⁴ 5g p5.1g³ 5f⁶ f5g⁵ 6f⁵ 7g p6g Dec 4] leggy, close-
coupled filly: first foal: dam maiden half-sister to useful stayer Random Quest: modest
maiden: best at 5f: tried in cheekpieces. *R. M. H. Cowell*

ELIZABETH STREET (USA) 2 b. or br.f. (May 18) Street Cry (IRE) 130 – Affir- **80**
med Ambience (USA) (Affirmed (USA)) [2006 5f³ 6m p7g² 7d p7.1g Oct 30] 80,000Y:
close-coupled filly: half-sister to several winners abroad: dam, 5f (at 2 yrs) 5.5f
winner in USA, half-sister to dam of very smart performer up to 1¼m Zoman: fairly
useful maiden: second to Guacamole at Kempton: running well when put through rail by
winner (Phoenix Tower) at Wolverhampton final start: stays 7f: best efforts on polytrack.
P. F. I. Cole

ELIZA MAY 2 b.f. (Apr 2) Kyllachy 129 – Elsie Plunkett 92 (Mind Games 121) [2006 **80**
5s* 5g³ 6f⁶ 6.5s 7s Oct 21] 26,000Y: sparely-made filly: second foal: dam 2-y-o 5f
winner: fairly useful performer: won maiden in May: sixth to Hope'n'charity in
listed event at Newmarket following month: below form both starts in autumn: effective
at 5f/6f: acts on firm and soft ground. *K. A. Ryan*

ELKHORN 4 b.g. Indian Ridge 123 – Rimba (USA) 82 (Dayjur (USA) 137) [2006 78: **81**
8.2s p7g 7d p6g 6g⁶ 6m⁴ 6g³ 7g 6d⁶ 6g* 6m* 6f* 5g* 5s Oct 6] leggy gelding: fairly useful handicapper: won 4 times in August/September, all at Redcar: effective at 5f to 7f: acts
on polytrack and firm going: wears headgear (blinkered last 5 starts). *Miss J. A. Camacho*

ELLABLUE 2 ch.f. (Mar 18) Bahamian Bounty 116 – Elabella (Ela-Mana-Mou 132) **62**
[2006 5.1g⁵ p5g p5g⁴ Dec 16] half-sister to several winners, including useful sprinter
Espartero (by Ballad Rock): dam unraced: modest maiden: will probably stay 6f. *Rae
Guest*

ELLA WOODCOCK (IRE) 2 b.g. (Mar 25) Daggers Drawn (USA) 114 – Hollow **61**
Haze (USA) 90 (Woodman (USA) 126) [2006 7.1m 5.1f 5.7m Sep 25] compact gelding:
modest form in maidens: will stay 1m. *J. A. Osborne*

ELLA Y ROSSA 2 ch.f. (May 9) Bertolini (USA) 125 – Meandering Rose (USA) (Irish **51**
River (FR) 131) [2006 5m p6g⁴ 5.1d 5.1m 6.5s f7g⁵ p8g* Dec 18] leggy filly: fourth
foal: dam unraced granddaughter of top-class 1m to 1¼m performer Rose Bowl: modest
performer: won maiden at Kempton in December: stays 1m: acts on all-weather: slowly
away third start. *P. D. Evans*

ELLE NINO 4 b.f. Inchinor 119 – Robellino Miss (USA) (Robellino (USA) 127) [2006 **67 d**
69§: 10m 10g⁶ 14f 12m 10g 9s⁴ p12.2g Nov 18] sparely-made filly: fair maiden handi-

capper: stays 1¼m: acts on polytrack, best effort on turf on good going: blinkered (ran poorly) final 3-y-o outing: not to be trusted. *Patrick Morris, Ireland*

ELLENS ACADEMY (IRE) 11 b.g. Royal Academy (USA) 130 – Lady Ellen 67 **88** (Horage 124) [2006 95: 6g 6g⁵ 6s 5s 6g⁴ 6m⁴ 6m⁶ 6f* 6f⁴ 6g² 6m* 6d⁴ 6d⁴ 6g Sep 23] big, useful-looking gelding: impresses in appearance: fairly useful handicapper: won at Ayr in July and Haydock in August: creditable fourth in Ayr Silver Cup penultimate start: effective at 5f/6f: acts on fibresand, firm and good to soft going: tried blinkered: sometimes slowly away/wanders: reportedly resents whip, and usually ridden with hands and heels nowadays. *E. J. Alston*

ELLENS PRINCESS (IRE) 4 b.f. Desert Prince (IRE) 130 – Lady Ellen 67 (Horage **52** 124) [2006 62: 7d p7.1g 8.3f 8m 8f 8.2m 7.9f Aug 15] tall filly: modest handicapper: stays 1m: acts on firm going, probably on good to soft: twice blinkered (including for win in 2005), tried in cheekpieces: sold €67,000. *J. S. Wainwright*

ELLERAY (IRE) 4 b.f. Docksider (USA) 124 – Saint Ann (USA) 66 (Geiger Counter **–** (USA)) [2006 –: p8.6g Jan 20] no form in 2 maidens (said to have finished lame only outing in 2006). *J. G. Given*

ELLE'S ANGEL (IRE) 2 b.f. (Apr 27) Tobougg (IRE) 125 – Stamatina (Warning **–** 136) [2006 p5g 6m 7m⁶ 8.2g Sep 26] €9,500Y: compact filly: fourth foal: half-sister to fairly useful 1m winner Just A Martian and 3-y-o Bolckow (both by Marju): dam Italian 7f to 9f winner: no show in maidens. *B. R. Millman*

ELLESAPPELLE 3 b.f. Benny The Dip (USA) 127 – Zizi (IRE) 87 (Imp Society **76** (USA)) [2006 66: p8g² 8d⁴ 10m⁴ 9.8g⁵ 11g⁵ 9.3m⁶ 9d⁶ 8.1m² 8d* 7d 8m* 10s 8d⁵ p9.5g p10g Dec 10] leggy filly: fair performer: won handicap at Newcastle in August and claimer at Yarmouth (left K. Burke) in September: stays 1¼m: acts on polytrack, good to firm and good to soft ground: tried visored, blinkered last 2 starts: sometimes slowly away: has looked none too keen. *G. L. Moore*

ELLIES FAITH 2 ch.f. (Feb 17) Sugarfoot 118 – Star Dancer (Groom Dancer (USA) **47** 128) [2006 6g 7f⁶ 6d 5d 6s 7s⁶ 7s⁶ Oct 14] small, sturdy filly: sixth foal: half-sister to 2 winners, including 4-y-o Shatin Leader: dam, tailed off in claimer only start, from family of Irish 1000 Guineas and Yorkshire Oaks winner Sarah Siddons: poor maiden: tried blinkered. *N. Bycroft*

ELLI LEWTIA 3 ch.f. Tomba 119 – Troia (IRE) 54 (Last Tycoon 131) [2006 –: p6g **–** 7m 9.8m f11g p12.2g f16g⁵ Dec 28] leggy filly: little form: tried blinkered. *J. Jay*

ELLINA 5 b.m. Robellino (USA) 127 – Native Flair 87 (Be My Native (USA) 122) **68** [2006 68, a79: 11.6m⁵ Jul 3] workmanlike mare: fair handicapper, better on all-weather **a–** than turf: ran creditably only outing in 2006: stays easy 2m: acts on polytrack, heavy and good to firm going: sold 2,200 gns in October. *J. Pearce*

ELLO LUCKY (IRE) 4 b.f. Key of Luck (USA) 126 – Ellopassoff 69 (Librate 91) **–** [2006 –: 7f 8.2f 10.1f⁶ 8m 11.7m p10g Dec 18] no form: left J. M. Bradley after fifth start. *C. Roberts*

EL MANX SENORITA 2 b.f. (Jan 26) Mind Games 121 – L A Touch 58 (Tina's Pet **–** 121) [2006 p6m p7.1g⁵ Nov 24] second foal: dam 6f (including at 2 yrs) and 7.5f winner: well held in minor events at Wolverhampton. *C. Smith*

ELMASONG 2 ch.f. (Apr 28) Elmaamul (USA) 125 – Annie's Song 69 (Farfelu 103) **42** [2006 p7g p7g 6d 8g p7g p10g⁵ p8g⁶ Dec 8] £450Y: workmanlike filly: second foal: dam 7f winner (including at 2 yrs): poor form. *J. J. Bridger*

ELMS SCHOOLBOY 4 ch.g. Komaite (USA) – Elms Schoolgirl 79 (Emarati (USA) **55** 74) [2006 54: f8g⁶ f8g³ p9.5g f8g p6g³ f6g f7g p7.1g* f8g⁵ p7.1g⁵ p10g p10g⁵ 10f⁶ 10g⁶ p12.2g⁶ 11.9f p10g⁶ f8g³ p8g f7g³ 8g p10g* p8.6g⁵ p8g p8g Dec 18] smallish gelding: modest performer: left J. Eustace after reappearance: won banded races at Wolverhampton in March and Kempton in November: effective at 6f to 12.2f: acts on all-weather and firm ground: usually blinkered: reportedly bled twentieth start: has looked difficult ride. *P. Howling*

ELOPEMENT (IRE) 4 ch.f. Machiavellian (USA) 123 – Melanzane (Arazi (USA) **58** 135) [2006 57: 8.1g³ 10.9d⁵ Oct 13] leggy filly: modest maiden: stays 11f. *W. M. Brisbourne*

ELOQUENT KNIGHT (USA) 4 b. or br.c. Aljabr (USA) 125 – Matinee Mimic **81** (USA) (Silent Screen (USA)) [2006 73: p10g⁴ p10g* p12g³ f12g* p12g² 10.5g 10f p12g⁵ p12g Jul 14] lengthy colt: fairly useful handicapper: won at Lingfield in February and Southwell in March: effective at 1m to easy 1½m: acts on all-weather, firm and good to soft going: tongue tied last 2 starts: races prominently: sold 11,000 gns in October. *W. R. Muir*

ELOQUENT ROSE (IRE) 2 b.f. (Feb 25) Elnadim (USA) 128 – Quintellina 83 **83** (Robellino (USA) 127) [2006 5d* 5f* 5g⁴ 6s⁴ 6g 5s Oct 14] 12,500F, 10,000Y: strong, sturdy filly: type to carry condition: fifth foal: half-sister to 3 winners, including Irish 7f (at 2 yrs) to 1m winner Nutley King (by Night Shift) and 5-y-o Who's Winning: dam, 7f winner, ran only at 2 yrs: fairly useful performer: won maiden at Pontefract in April and minor event at Thirsk in May: off 3 months (reportedly had corn in foot), best run when fourth in nursery at Haydock fourth start: effective at 5f/6f: acts on firm and soft going. *Mrs A. Duffield*

ELOUNDA (IRE) 2 b.f. (Apr 30) Sinndar (IRE) 134 – Gaily Grecian (IRE) (Ela-Mana- **62 p** Mou 132) [2006 7d Oct 28] attractive filly: sixth foal: half-sister to 3-y-o Polish Precedent and 2 winners abroad by Polish Precedent: dam unraced half-sister to dam of Pilsudski: 25/1, faded into mid-field in maiden at Newmarket won by Measured Tempo: likely to improve at 1¼m+. *H. R. A. Cecil*

EL PALMAR 5 b.g. Case Law 113 – Aybeegirl 66 (Mazilier (USA) 107) [2006 69: f7g **61** f8g f7s⁶ f8g² f8g* f7g⁴ f8g f8g⁵ 8.3f 7.1m Jun 16] good-topped gelding: modest performer nowadays: trained on reappearance by J. Pearce: won banded race at Southwell in March: stays 1m: acts on fibresand, heavy and good to firm going: tried in cheekpieces/blinkered: has looked wayward/reared in stall. *M. J. Attwater*

EL POTRO 4 b.g. Forzando 122 – Gaelic Air 65 (Ballad Rock 122) [2006 68: f5g **73 d** p5.1g² f5s⁴ p6g 5m 5.5d 5.1s p5.1g 5m⁶ p6g 7f f5g² p5.1g p6g² p5g f5g² Dec 29] fair performer: on downgrade: left E. McMahon after eighth start: effective at 5f/6f: acts on all-weather, lightly raced on turf. *J. R. Holt*

ELRAFA MUJAHID 4 b.f. Mujahid (USA) 125 – Fancier Bit (Lion Cavern (USA) **–** 117) [2006 81: f8g⁴ p8.6g p9.5g p8.6g⁵ p8.6g² 7s 7d p8g p8g p6g⁵ p8g p7.1g f7g⁴ p10g **a76** p7g* 7m⁶ 6.1m Sep 9] tall filly: fair performer: won handicap at Lingfield in August: effective at 7f/1m: acts on all-weather and good to soft going: sometimes wears blinkers/cheekpieces/tongue tie: has pulled hard/looked difficult ride: often races prominently: reportedly bled eighth outing: sent to Saudi Arabia. *E. R. Oertel*

EL REY ROYALE 4 b.g. Royal Applause 124 – Spanish Serenade 76 (Nashwan **53** (USA) 135) [2006 61: 10m 10.1g 10g 8.2f⁴ 8.3m⁶ 8m 6.9m Aug 7] close-coupled gelding: modest performer: stays 1¼m: acts on good to firm and good to soft going: tried visored. *M. D. Hammond*

ELSIE ALDERMAN 4 b.f. Fumo di Londra (IRE) 108 – Eastwood Heiress (Known **–** Fact (USA) 135) [2006 10.2m 8.3g Aug 23] sixth foal: dam unraced: well beaten in maidens. *J. C. Fox*

ELSIE HART (IRE) 4 b.f. Revoque (IRE) 122 – Family At War (USA) 71 (Explodent **68** (USA)) [2006 74: p9.5g f7g⁴ Feb 23] leggy, quite good-topped filly: fair performer: stays 7f: acts on fibresand and heavy ground. *T. D. Easterby*

ELSINORA 5 b.m. Great Dane (IRE) 122 – Deanta In Eirinn (Red Sunset 120) [2006 –: **–** p8.6g Jan 4] workmanlike mare: modest at 3 yrs, well held both starts since: usually wears headgear. *A. G. Juckes*

ELTANIN (IRE) 2 gr.g. (Mar 27) Linamix (FR) 127 – Housatonic (USA) 59 (Riverman **68** (USA) 131) [2006 8v³ 6s⁶ Oct 6] 50,000Y: angular gelding: brother to 3 winners in France, notably very smart 1m (at 2 yrs)/1½m (Prix Niel) winner Housamix, and half-brother to useful French/US 1m/9f performer Housa Dancer (by Fabulous Dancer): dam 7f winner: fair form in maidens at Thirsk and York (stirred up), good speed. *J. Howard Johnson*

EL TIGER (GER) 5 b.g. Tiger Hill (IRE) 127 – Elea (GER) (Dschingis Khan) [2006 **94 ?** –: p10g* p10g 12d p10g 12m 10.5g 10g p16.5g Nov 27] heavy-topped gelding: smart performer at 3 yrs for P. Schiergen in Germany: form in Britain only when winning handicap at Lingfield in January: stays 1½m: acts on polytrack and soft going: tried in blinkers/cheekpieces. *B. J. Curley*

EL TOREADOR (USA) 2 ch.f. (Mar 30) El Corredor (USA) 123 – Marsha's Dancer **74 p** (USA) (Northern Dancer) [2006 6f Jul 1] $32,000Y, resold $115,000Y: quite good-topped filly: has a fluent action: half-sister to several winners, including useful 6f winner (including at 2 yrs) Two Step Kid (by Gone West): dam 1m/8.5f winner in USA: 33/1, 5 lengths tenth of 11 to Hope'n'charity in listed event at Newmarket: should improve. *G. A. Butler*

ELUSIVE DREAM 5 b.g. Rainbow Quest (USA) 134 – Dance A Dream 115 (Sadler's **103** Wells (USA) 132) [2006 98: 18.7m 16d² 20m p16g² 16g* 14m* 13.9d Aug 23] rangy, useful-looking gelding: useful performer: won listed race at Hamburg (by ¾ length from El Tango) in July and minor event at Galway (very easily, by 14 lengths from Peak of Perfection) in August: blinkered, in rear in Ebor (Handicap) at York final outing: stays 2¼m (seemingly not 2½m): acts on all-weather, firm and soft going: sometimes hangs right: often makes running: genuine: joined P. Nicholls. *Sir Mark Prescott*

ELUSIVE FLASH (USA) 2 b.f. (Apr 15) Freud (USA) 113 – Giana (USA) (Exclusive **85** Era (USA)) [2006 6g⁴ p7g² 7.1d* p8g⁶ 7s Oct 21] good-topped filly: closely related/half-sister to several winners in USA: dam 6f/7f winner in USA: fairly useful performer: won maiden at Warwick in September: better run after when sixth to Strobilus in nursery at Lingfield: stays 1m: acts on polytrack, raced on good or softer going on turf: signs of temperament. *P. F. I. Cole*

ELUSIVE WARRIOR (USA) 3 b.g. Elusive Quality (USA) – Love To Fight (CAN) **74** (Fit To Fight (USA)) [2006 77: p7g⁵ 8.5g 5f⁴ 6f³ 5m 6f⁶ 7f* 7m 7d 8g f6g² p6m f7g* f7g* p7.1g Dec 21] rangy gelding: fair handicapper: won at Brighton (maiden event) in June and (having left Mrs A. Perrett after next start) Southwell (2) in December: stays 7f: acts on fibresand and firm ground: sometimes wears cheekpieces, including for all wins. *R. A. Fahey*

ELUSORY 2 b.c. (Mar 8) Galileo (IRE) 134 – Elude (Slip Anchor 136) [2006 8.2d – Nov 1] sturdy colt: fourth foal: half-brother to 1m winner Baffle (by Selkirk): dam un-raced close relation to smart 1¼m performer Perpendicular out of half-sister to Kris and Diesis: 28/1, needed race (also hampered) in maiden at Nottingham. *J. L. Dunlop*

ELVINA 5 b.m. Mark of Esteem (IRE) 137 – Pharoah's Joy 66 (Robellino (USA) 127) **55** [2006 65: p5.1g 5f 5m p5g 5g⁴ 5d Oct 8] modest performer: best at 5f: acts on all-weather and good to firm going. *A. G. Newcombe*

ELVINA HILLS (IRE) 4 ch.f. Bluebird (USA) 125 – Women In Love (IRE) (Danehill **58** (USA) 126) [2006 60: p7g⁶ p8g 8m p8g p12g Jun 15] modest maiden handicapper: stays 7f: acts on all-weather and good to firm ground: wore cheekpieces final start: looked wayward last 2 outings at 2 yrs. *P. Mitchell*

ELYAADI 2 b.f. (Mar 17) Singspiel (IRE) 133 – Abyaan (IRE) 106 (Ela-Mana-Mou **72 p** 132) [2006 p8g⁴ Oct 20] third foal: sister to fairly useful 2005 2-y-o 1m winner Botteen: dam, 1¼m winner who stayed 12.5f, sister to dam of very smart 1m/9f winner Autumn Glory: 7/2, promising never-nearer fourth to Sunlight in maiden at Lingfield, not knocked about: will do better at 1¼m/1½m. *M. R. Channon*

EMAARA 2 b.f. (Feb 14) Fasliyev (USA) 120 – Shuruk 73 (Cadeaux Genereux 131) **78** [2006 6g³ 6m² 5d² Oct 3] second foal: dam, 2-y-o 6f winner, half-sister to very smart per-former up to 1½m Volochine: fair form first 2 starts in maidens: looks quirky. *J. L. Dunlop*

EMEFDREAM 2 b.g. (Mar 26) Efisio 120 – Alkarida (FR) (Akarad (FR) 130) [2006 **66** 5.1s p5g 5s⁵ 5f³ 5m² 5m⁶ 6d⁵ p6g f6g f6g* p7g⁵ f7g Dec 19] neat gelding: fair performer: won seller at Southwell (sold from K. Ryan) in November: stays 6f: acts on fibresand and firm ground: tried blinkered/in cheekpieces. *Mrs N. Macauley*

EMERALD BAY (IRE) 4 b.g. King's Best (USA) 132 – Belle Etoile (FR) (Lead On **93** Time (USA) 123) [2006 90: 8v² 8g 8f 10d Jun 1] rangy gelding: fairly useful handicapper, quite lightly raced: well below form after reappearance: stays 1¼m: acts on any turf going: races up with pace. *I. Semple*

EMERALD SKY 2 b.f. (Feb 12) Diktat 126 – Dekelsmary 61 (Komaite (USA)) [2006 – f6m p6m p6g⁶ Dec 4] third foal: dam 5f and 7f winner: no show in maidens. *R. Brotherton*

EMERALD WILDERNESS (IRE) 2 b.g. (Apr 10) Green Desert (USA) 127 – **79** Simla Bibi 69 (Indian Ridge 123) [2006 7m⁴ 7.5m² 8.1d³ 8g⁶ Oct 17] 90,000F, 135,000Y: tall, leggy gelding: second foal: half-brother to 3-y-o Ooh Aah Camara: dam, maiden (best effort at 1m on debut), half-sister to smart 7f to 9f performer Gateman: in frame first 3 starts: stays 1m: suspect attitude: gelded after final outing. *M. R. Channon*

EMERGENCY SERVICES 2 b.g. (Mar 13) Foxhound (USA) 103 – Compact Disc **64** (IRE) 48 (Royal Academy (USA) 130) [2006 p5g 5.5d 6s 5.1s² 5g 5.1g 7f⁶ 6f² 7m⁵ 6d²

8.3g* 8.2s² p8g f8g² Nov 10] leggy, close-coupled gelding: modest performer: won seller at Windsor in October: stays 8.3f: acts on firesand, firm and soft going: once blinkered, usually in cheekpieces: sold 5,200 gns. *T. G. Dascombe*

EMILIO 5 b.g. Kris 135 – Easter Moon (FR) (Easter Sun 122) [2006 7.1m 6m 7g 7m⁶ **89** 6m 7.1g p6g p8g Dec 2] sturdy gelding: fairly useful performer: winner of 7 races in Scandinavia, including Danish 2000 Guineas in 2004 and 2 handicaps and minor event at Ovrevoll in 2005, when trained by W. Neuroth in Norway: ran creditably in handicaps in Britain only in ladies event at Ascot fourth start: stays 1m: acts on dirt, good to firm and good to soft going: tongue tied. *R. A. Kvisla*

EMILION 3 ch.f. Fantastic Light (USA) 134 – Riberac 110 (Efisio 120) [2006 51p: 8d⁴ **67** 8.5f⁴ p8.6g⁴ 10f⁴ p11g p10g p12.2g* Dec 22] neat filly: fair performer: left W. Haggas after fourth start: won maiden at Wolverhampton in December: stays 1½m: acts on poly-track and firm going. *W. R. Muir*

EMILY BRONTE 3 gr.f. Machiavellian (USA) 123 – Zafadola (IRE) 112 (Darshaan **101** 133) [2006 100p: p8g² 10m Nov 5] half-sister to useful 5f/6f (latter including at 2 yrs) winner Zelanda (by Night Shift) and fairly useful 1¼m winner Zaman (by Caerleon): dam, Irish 9f/11f winner, third in Irish St Leger: useful form: successful on both starts in 2005 for A. Fabre in France, newcomers race at Longchamp and Prix des Reservoirs at Deauville, latter by a length from Sanaya, making all: off over 12 months (reported to have suffered an injury in April), length second to Mayonga in listed race at Lingfield on return: stiffish task, tailed off in Premio Roma at Rome 10 days later: should stay 1¼m: acts on polytrack and good to firm going: has left Godolphin. *Saeed bin Suroor*

EMILY (FR) 3 b.f. Dansili 127 – Palomelle (FR) 112 (Moulin 103) [2006 64: p6g **–** p8g Apr 3] close-coupled filly: maiden: tongue tied, no form in sellers in 2006. *Mrs L. J. Young*

EMILY'S PET (IRE) 3 ch.g. Raise A Grand (IRE) 114 – Zaola (IRE) 68 (Alzao (USA) **52** 117) [2006 –: p7.1g⁶ 8f 10m⁶ 8.1m⁵ Aug 10] angular gelding: modest maiden: barely stays 1m: acts on polytrack and good to firm going. *B. W. Duke*

EMILY'S PLACE (IRE) 3 b.f. Mujadil (USA) 119 – Dulcinea 73 (Selkirk (USA) **74** 129) [2006 72: 6g p8g² 8.3m³ 6.9m³ p8g 8.1m⁶ 8.1m⁵ 8m p8.6g⁴ p9.5g⁶ p12.2s³ p9.5g⁴ Dec 26] rather leggy filly: fair performer: won claimers at Haydock and Sandown (left M. Tompkins) in August: stays 9.5f: acts on polytrack and good to firm ground: wore cheekpieces last 2 starts: reportedly had breathing problem tenth outing. *J. Pearce*

EMINENCE GIFT 4 b.f. Cadeaux Genereux 131 – Germane 100 (Distant Relative **–** 128) [2006 60: 9.9f 10.1g 9.3m 10g Jun 23] modest at 3 yrs: well held in 2006: tried in cheekpieces. *K. R. Burke*

EMIRATE ISLE 2 b.g. (May 22) Cois Na Tine (IRE) 101 – Emmajoun 69 (Emarati **70** (USA) 74) [2006 6f⁵ 5d Aug 20] good-topped gelding: second foal: dam 5f winner: seem-ingly better run in maidens when fifth (of 6) at Ayr on debut. *J. Wade*

EMIRATES FIRST (IRE) 3 ch.f. In The Wings 128 – Genovefa (USA) 107 (Wood-**77** man (USA) 126) [2006 p9.5g² p9.5g* Nov 10] sister to very smart 1m (at 2 yrs) to 2m winner Mamool and half-sister to 2 winners, including useful French 1999 2-y-o 1m winner Ejlaal (by Caerleon): dam, won 1½m Prix de Royaumont, closely related to smart French 1m/1¼m winner Grafin: fair form: won maiden at Wolverhampton in November by ½ length from Fringe: will stay 1½m: has left Godolphin. *Saeed bin Suroor*

EMIRATES LINE (USA) 3 ch.c. Kingmambo (USA) 125 – Style Setter (USA) **89** (Manila (USA)) [2006 10s* Oct 18] well-made, quite attractive colt: closely related to useful French 2003 2-y-o 5.5f/6f winner Saville Row (by Gone West) and half-brother to several winners, notably 1m (at 2 yrs) and 1½m (Oaks) winner Casual Look and French 1¼m winner Shabby Chic (both smart, by Red Ransom): dam US 1m (including at 2 yrs)/ 8.5f winner: 11/8-on, won maiden at Nottingham by length from Sculastic, travelling smoothly and asserting late on: stays 1¼m: joined E. Charpy in UAE. *Saeed bin Suroor*

EMIRATES SKYLINE (USA) 3 b.c. Sunday Silence (USA) – The Caretaker 113 **104** (Caerleon (USA) 132) [2006 104: 9m² 10.4s³ Oct 7] quite good-topped colt: impresses in appearance: useful performer: good effort when 1½ lengths second to Blue Ksar in minor event at Newbury on belated reappearance, finishing well: odds on, bit below best behind Ofaraby in minor event on soft ground at York following month: should stay at least 1¼m: acts on good to firm and good to soft ground. *Saeed bin Suroor*

EMMA JEAN LAD (IRE) 2 ch.c. (Mar 30) Intikhab (USA) 135 – Swing City (IRE) **47** 58 (Indian Ridge 123) [2006 p5g 6m⁶ Jun 3] poor form in maidens. *J. S. Moore*

EMMA LILLEY (USA) 4 ch.f. Theatrical 128 – Changed Tune (USA) (Tunerup –
(USA)) [2006 53: 16f Jul 31] modest maiden at 3 yrs: tailed off only outing in 2006: tried
visored. *J. G. M. O'Shea*

EMMA'S SURPRISE 2 b.f (Feb 23) Tobougg (IRE) 125 – Selvi (Mummy's Pet 125) **69**
[2006 6g⁴ 6m 8g p6g⁶ p6g⁴ Dec 1] 28,000Y. tall, close-coupled, sparely-made filly:
half-sister to several winners, notably smart sprinter Indian Rocket (by Indian Ridge) and
6-y-o The Bonus King: dam, maiden, best at 6f: fair performer: won maiden at Redcar in
May: stiff task at Royal Ascot next start: off 4 months, little impact in nurseries: should
prove best at 5f/6f: not straightforward. *K. A. Ryan*

EMMA TOLD LIES 2 b.f. (Apr 16) Warningford 119 – Itsanothergirl 77 (Reprimand **59**
122) [2006 f5g 5g⁶ 5f 6v³ 6g³ 6g⁸ 6m⁶ 5g⁵ 6f f7g 5m a8g⁴ Dec 17] 5,000Y: first foal: dam
7f (at 2 yrs) to 10.5f winner: modest performer: won 2 sellers at Thirsk in June: sold from
M. Easterby 1,200 gns before final start: best at 6f: acts on heavy and good to firm going:
quirky. *C. Lorenzo, Spain*

EMOTIVE 3 b.g. Pursuit of Love 124 – Ruby Julie (Clantime 101) [2006 49: p8g² p10g **69**
8.5g⁶ 10m 8d 8.3d* 8.1m* 8.3f p10g⁶ 8.3d² p10g 8.1m p8g 10f³ 8d Sep 27] leggy geld- **a63**
ing: fair performer on turf, modest on all-weather: won claimer at Leicester in May and
apprentice handicap at Warwick in June: stays 8.3f: acts on polytrack, good to firm and
good to soft going: tried blinkered/in cheekpieces: sold 7,600 gns. *I. A. Wood*

EMPEROR CAT (IRE) 5 b.g. Desert Story (IRE) 115 – Catfoot Lane 50 (Batshoof **54**
122) [2006 48: p9.5g⁴ f7g³ p8.6g⁵ p9.5g 8.1g² 12.1f 8.1m 10.2m² f11m f8g Nov 21]
close-coupled gelding: modest performer: stays easy 11f: acts on all-weather and firm
going: tried in headgear. *Mrs N. S. Evans*

EMPEROR'S WELL 7 ch.g. First Trump 118 – Catherines Well 99 (Junius (USA) **65**
124) [2006 70: 9.9g 8.1f p8.6g 10f 9.9f 9.9s² 8.5g 10g² 10f 8.2s⁶ p9.5g Nov 6] well-made
gelding: fair handicapper: stays 1¼m: acts on fibresand, soft and good to firm going: tried
visored, usually blinkered nowadays. *M. W. Easterby*

EMPHASIS 3 ch.f. Pivotal 124 – Matoaka (USA) 92 (A P Indy (USA) 131) [2006 68: **61**
8f⁵ a6g² Dec 10] good-topped filly: fair maiden, lightly raced: sold from Mrs A. Perrett
4,000 gns after reappearance: second in minor event at Taby 6 months later: probably
stays 1m: acts on polytrack/dirt. *C. Hederud, Sweden*

EMPIRE DANCER (IRE) 3 b.g. Second Empire (IRE) 124 – Dance To The Beat 58 **74**
(Batshoof 122) [2006 –: 11.5m⁴ p8.6g² 10g p8.6g* 9.7f⁶ p8g p8.6g p12.2g Nov 10] leggy
gelding: fair performer: won maiden at Wolverhampton in June: stays 9.7f: acts on polytrack and firm going: front runner. *C. N. Allen*

EMPIRE DAY (UAE) 2 ch.c. (Jan 11) Lomitas 129 – Evil Empire (GER) 108 (Acate- **107 p**
nango (GER) 127) [2006 8m* 8s³ 10d* 10g³ Nov 12] medium-sized, quite good-topped
colt: third foal: half-brother to 3-y-o Counterpunch: dam German 7f (at 2 yrs) to 1½m
winner: useful form: won maiden in September and listed race in October, both at Newmarket, in latter forging clear to beat Aaim To Prosper by 4 lengths: creditable 3¾ lengths
third of 13 to Passage of Time in Criterium de Saint-Cloud final start, staying on: will be
suited by 1½m+: acts on soft and good to firm going: joined Godolphin: should make a
smart 3-y-o. *M. Johnston*

EMPOR CASTLE (IRE) 4 b.g. New Frontier (IRE) 110 – Is She A Star (IRE) (Sex- –
ton Blake 126) [2006 p12.2g Dec 2] in cheekpieces, well held in maiden at Wolverhampton on Flat debut. *Adrian Sexton, Ireland*

EMPRESS JAIN 3 br.f. Lujain (USA) 119 – Akhira 90 (Emperor Jones (USA) 119) **105**
[2006 82: 5.2m* 5.1f* 5m 6g⁶ 5f 5g 5g Oct 12] leggy, sparely-made filly: useful performer: won handicaps at Yarmouth (by 5 lengths from Fisola) in April and Chester (beat
Green Park by neck) in May: below form in varied company after: best at 5f: acts on firm
going: has been early to post: speedy front runner. *M. A. Jarvis*

EMPRESS OLGA (USA) 2 br.f. (Apr 1) Kingmambo (USA) 125 – Balistroika (USA) **76**
(Nijinsky (CAN) 138) [2006 p6g² 6m Aug 2] $1,500,000Y: useful-looking filly: has
scope: sister to very smart 6f (at 2 yrs) to 1¼m winner (including 1000 Guineas) Russian
Rhythm and closely related/half-sister to several winners, including 3-y-o Mobaasher
and 4-y-o Perfectperformance: dam unraced half-sister to Cheveley Park winners
Park Appeal and Desirable and to Irish Oaks winner Alydaress: fair form in maidens
at Lingfield (second to Chervil) and Goodwood (hung right throughout): will stay 1m.
E. A. L. Dunlop

EMPTY GESTURE 4 b.g. Cadeaux Genereux 131 – Broken Spectre 65 (Rainbow   –
Quest (USA) 134) [2006 59: 7f p7g Jul 26] lengthy gelding: maiden: no form in 2006
(pulled up reportedly lame on reappearance). *J. R. Best*

EMULATE 2 b.f. (Mar 27) Alhaarth (IRE) 126 – Aquarelle (Kenmare (FR) 125) [2006   **81**
p7g* 7d Sep 30] good-topped filly: sixth foal: half-sister to 3 fairly useful winners, including 9f winner Aqualung (by Desert King) and French 6f to 1m (including at 2 yrs)
winner Coastline (by Night Shift): dam, useful French 2-y-o 1m winner, out of close relative to St Leger winner Toulon: fairly useful form: good impression when winning minor
event at Kempton in September: 11/2, last in listed race at Newmarket: will be suited by
1m+. *B. W. Hills*

ENCHANTING TIMES (IRE) 3 b.f. Danetime (IRE) 121 – Enchanted Isle 47 (Muj-   –
tahid (USA) 118) [2006 62, a49: p8.6g 7m 6.1d 7m 5f Jun 12] small filly: maiden: no
form in 2006: often visored. *D. G. Bridgwater*

ENCHANTMENT 5 b.m. Compton Place 125 – Tharwa (IRE) 63 (Last Tycoon 131)   **91 d**
[2006 –: 5.1g 5.1f 5s³ 5s⁶ 5m 5m 5d 5s⁵ 5f 5s Oct 16] lengthy mare: fairly useful
performer: below form after third outing: speedy, and best at 5f: acts on firm and soft
ground: sometimes wears cheekpieces: usually front runner. *J. M. Bradley*

ENCIRCLED 2 b.f. (Mar 2) In The Wings 128 – Ring of Esteem (Mark of Esteem   **75**
(IRE) 137) [2006 8d 8.2s⁵ p7.1g p8.6m³ p9.5g* Dec 7] 34,000F, 22,000Y: small, well-
made filly: second foal: closely related to 3-y-o Montpellier: dam unraced half-sister to
smart German 1½m performer Catella: fair performer: won maiden at Wolverhampton in
December by 1¼ lengths from Lord Oroko: will stay 1½m: acts on polytrack. *D. Haydn
Jones*

ENCRYPT (IRE) 4 ch.f. Entrepreneur 123 – Just An Illusion (IRE) 79 (Shernazar 131)   **62**
[2006 49: 14.1d³ 14.1g⁵ p16.5g 12s Oct 14] strong filly: modest maiden: stays easy 1¾m:
acts on good to soft ground. *O. Brennan*

ENDIAMO (IRE) 2 ch.g. (Mar 17) Indian Ridge 123 – Aldafra 91 (Spectrum (IRE)   **91**
126) [2006 6s⁴ 6m⁴ 6m⁴ Sep 16] sturdy gelding: first foal: dam, 6f winner (including at
2 yrs), sister/half-sister to useful 7f winners Makfool and Raheibb: fairly useful form:
fourth in maidens at Newbury (2) and Goodwood, off 3 months before final start (gelded
after): will be suited by 7f/1m. *M. P. Tregoning*

ENDLESS NIGHT 3 ch.g. Dracula (AUS) 121 – La Notte 88 (Factual (USA) 108)   **68**
[2006 69p: p7g⁵ 8.2s⁵ 10.2g 8.3m p7g³ 7m² 7g p7g 8m Sep 20] close-coupled gelding:
fair maiden handicapper: stays 1m: acts on polytrack, soft and good to firm going: tried in
cheekpieces/visor/tongue tie. *H. Morrison*

ENDLESS SUMMER 9 b.g. Zafonic (USA) 130 – Well Away (IRE) (Sadler's Wells   **74**
(USA) 132) [2006 92d: 6d³ 5.1d² 5m³ 5g* 5m² 6g 6m* 5.1g 5.7m⁴ 5g* 6d Oct 9] small,
sturdy gelding: had fertility problems at stud: fair performer nowadays: won handicap in
July and claimer in August, both at Haydock, and claimer at Sandown in September: best
at 5f/6f: acts on polytrack, firm and soft going: tried tongue tied: held up: sometimes
carries head awkwardly: has bled. *A. W. Carroll*

ENFIELD CHASE (IRE) 5 b.g. Foxhound (USA) 103 – Melinte (Caerleon (USA)   **91**
132) [2006 90: 6m 7m 6.3g 7m³ 7g³ 7.5f² 6.5d² 7d 7m Sep 9] leggy, lengthy gelding:
fairly useful handicapper: well held at Newmarket on reappearance: stays 7.5f: acts on
firm and good to soft going: tried blinkered/tongue tied/in cheekpieces. *T. Stack, Ireland*

ENFORCER 4 b.c. Efisio 120 – Tarneem (USA) 87 (Zilzal (USA) 137) [2006 116:   **123**
10g⁶ 10g⁴ 12s⁵ 12g³ 12m³ 12m³ 12m⁴ 10.1d⁴ 12g³ Sep 24]
    'Frankie felt that had he not tried to win the Jockey Club we might have
finished third instead of fifth' . . . 'We rode him to finish third [in the Coronation
Cup] and Martin said that had he been a bit braver he would have finished second.'
The reported words of Enforcer's trainer William Muir about the riding of Frankie
Dettori and Martin Dwyer might be said to raise hypothetical questions about the
interpretation of rule 155 of the *Rules of Racing* which lays down that a horse must
be 'given a full opportunity to obtain the best possible placing.' The rule used to say
that a horse had to be 'given a full opportunity to *win*,' but was revised in 2003 to
identify more clearly trainers' responsibilities—widened by the rule change—for
giving adequate instructions to jockeys. The splendidly tough Enforcer faced uphill
work as a four-year-old, his connections enterprisingly setting out their stall to take
the best advantage they could of the weaker than normal fields for the leading
British middle-distance events over the summer. The stated aim was to 'pinch a

slice of the pie', as his trainer put it, and Enforcer did so in the Coronation Cup (third of six to Shirocco, half a length behind runner-up Ouija Board), the Hardwicke Stakes (third of eight to Maraahel), the Princess of Wales's Stakes (third of four to Soapy Danger) and the King George VI and Queen Elizabeth Stakes (fourth of six to Hurricane Run) before then going on to finish third of seven to Youmzain in a good renewal of Germany's final Group 1 of the season, the Preis von Europa at Cologne. Enforcer started at 66/1 in the Coronation Cup and at 50/1 in the King George, and he would have been at long odds in a third Group 1 in Britain, the International at York, but for missing that race because of a last minute foot injury. His one poor effort during the season, when odds on for a minor event won by Ashaawes at Epsom on his penultimate start, can be blamed on an infection in the same foot.

Enforcer had progressed well in a busy campaign as a three-year-old, winning three handicaps at nine furlongs to a mile and a quarter (including the valuable and well-contested one that opens the Derby Day programme) before graduating to minor pattern company and winning the nine-furlong Darley Stakes at Newmarket at the back end. His style of racing—brought with a late run from well back—had suited him in competitive, strongly-run handicaps and had also helped to keep him ahead of the handicapper. However, kept to pattern races as a four-year-old, the tactics were not ideal against better horses, in races that, for the most part, tend not to be run at an end-to-end gallop. Enforcer failed to reach a place, nearest at the finish, in the Prix d'Harcourt at Longchamp or in the Gordon Richards Stakes at Sandown on his first two outings. He did better, stepped up to a mile and a half for the first time, in the Jockey Club Stakes at Newmarket in May, running as well as ever to finish just over five and a half lengths fifth to

D. G. Clarke & C. L. A. Edginton's "Enforcer"

the impressive Shirocco, only half a length behind third-placed Bandari. Enforcer finished much closer to Shirocco in a tactical affair at Epsom, form which he repeated when beaten only a little over a length and a half by Maraahel at Royal Ascot, where he confirmed himself an improved performer, having to be switched wide after having only one behind him turning for home. Enforcer, ridden more prominently, finished slightly closer to the Hardwicke runner-up Mountain High when the pair were a close second and third in the Princess of Wales's Stakes at Newmarket in July. Dropped out again in the King George, Enforcer proved no great threat to the first three, though he was closer to them a furlong out than he was at the line, where he was two and three quarter lengths behind the winner (and a place ahead of Maraahel).

Enforcer (b.c. 2002)	Efisio (b 1982)	Formidable (b 1975)	Forli
			Native Partner
		Eldoret (b 1976)	High Top
			Bamburi
	Tarneem (USA) (b 1993)	Zilzal (ch 1986)	Nureyev
			French Charmer
		Willowy Mood (gr or ro 1982)	Will Win
			Lohagogo

The tall, leggy Enforcer, who has been sent to Saudi Arabia, is by the smart miler Efisio whose fee in a long career at stud was never higher than the £12,000 commanded in his last two seasons (he was put down at the age of twenty-four in the latest season, having been retired from stud duties). Efisio was represented by Attraction and July Cup winner Frizzante in 2004 but was unfashionable for most of his career and did not have anything like the number of mares of most present-day sires with a comparable record. Enforcer's dam Tarneem was a fairly useful miler, though her only victory was in a maiden at Brighton. Enforcer's grandam Willowy Mood won fourteen races in the States, including a Grade 3 event over an extended mile as a two-year-old. Tarneem has bred three other winners, including Enforcer's fairly useful brother the two-year-old five-furlong winner Lord of The Inn. Another of Tarneem's offspring, Kris's Bank (by Inchinor), was successful at up to thirteen and a half furlongs in Italy. Enforcer stays a mile and a half and acts on soft and good to firm going. It bears repeating that he is tough and game. *W. R. Muir*

ENFORD PRINCESS 5 b.m. Pivotal 124 – Expectation (IRE) 59 (Night Shift (USA)) **85** [2006 88: p7g⁵ Mar 2] big, well-made mare: fairly useful performer: respectable effort at Lingfield (all-weather debut) only outing in 2006: stays 1m: acts on soft and good to firm ground, probably on polytrack: blinkered 3 times at 4 yrs. *Miss B. Sanders*

ENGLISH ARCHER 3 b.g. Rock City 120 – Fire Sprite 83 (Mummy's Game 120) **50** [2006 54: 8d⁵ 6g 6m 8d 9d 7.1m 9m⁵ Aug 31] leggy gelding: modest maiden: seems to stay 9f: tried in cheekpieces. *J. R. Weymes*

ENGLISH BALLET (IRE) 2 ch.f. (Feb 6) Danehill Dancer (IRE) 117 – Stage **104** Presence (IRE) 95 (Selkirk (USA) 129) [2006 6m* 7d* 8g² 8d³ 7d⁵ Oct 14] €70,000Y: strong, useful-looking filly: has scope: second foal: half-sister to 3-y-o Spectacular Show: dam, 7f/1m winner, half-sister to useful performers Pakhoes (at 6f) and Rum Charger (Irish 6f/7f winner): useful performer: won maiden at Windsor in July and 6-runner Swynford Paddocks Hotel Sweet Solera Stakes at Newmarket (by length from Princess Taise) in August: ran well next 2 starts, placed behind Simply Perfect in May Hill Stakes at York and Fillies' Mile at Ascot: below best in Rockfel Stakes at Newmarket final start (fifth to Finsceal Beo): yet to race on extremes of going. *B. W. Hills*

ENGLISH CITY (IRE) 3 ch.c. City On A Hill (USA) 114 – Toledana (IRE) (Sure **61** Blade (USA) 130) [2006 62: 7.5d 10d* 9m² 10.3g⁴ p12.2g⁴ 9.3f³ 9.9m³ 10.1m⁴ Aug 9] sturdy colt: modest performer: won seller at Redcar in May: stays 10.3f: acts on firm and good to soft going (well below form both starts on polytrack): joined Mrs L. Normile. *B. Smart*

ENJOY THE BUZZ 7 b.h. Prince of Birds (USA) 121 – Abaklea (IRE) (Doyoun 124) **61** [2006 64, a54: p6g p5.1g p5.1g⁶ f6g p6g 6m 6g⁵ 6.1m² 5s³ 5.3m 5f³ 5f⁶ 5f 5.1m Aug 28] **a45** small, sturdy horse: modest on turf, poor on all-weather: effective at 5f/6f: acts on all-weather, firm and soft going: held up. *J. M. Bradley*

ENJOY THE MAGIC 4 br.f. Namaqualand (USA) – Abaklea (IRE) (Doyoun 124) **59** [2006 p6g p7g 7m 8.3m⁵ 7d* 8.5m Sep 13] half-sister to 7-y-o Enjoy The Buzz: dam unraced: left Miss J. Tooth after third start: won seller at Leicester in August: stays 7f: acts on good to soft going: tried in cheekpieces. *E. J. Alston*

ENJOY THE MOMENT 3 b.g. Generous (IRE) 139 – Denial (Sadler's Wells (USA) 132) [2006 69: 10m⁵ 11.9m* 12m² 12m⁶ 14.1d⁵ Aug 15] sturdy gelding: useful performer: won maiden at Brighton in June: good 3½ lengths second to Linas Selection in King George V Stakes (Handicap) at Royal Ascot next time: stays 1½m: acts on good to firm going, probably on good to soft: has worn crossed noseband and been bandaged hind coronets. *J. A. Osborne* **98**

ENNOBLING 3 b.f. Mark of Esteem (IRE) 137 – Noble Dane (IRE) 79 (Danehill (USA) 126) [2006 62: 8.5g⁶ p10g p8.6g Nov 7] fourth foal: half-sister to 5-y-o Let It Be : dam, 1m winner at 2 yrs (stayed 1½m), sister to smart but ungenuine winner up to 10.5f Amrak Ajeeb: modest maiden, lightly raced: should be suited by 1¼m+: sold 3,000 gns. *E. F. Vaughan* **56**

ENSIGN'S TRICK 2 b.f. (Apr 27) Cayman Kai (IRE) 114 – River Ensign 63 (River God (USA) 121) [2006 f5g 6g³ 6m 6g³ 6g* 6.1m 6.1m⁴ 6d⁴ 6m p7.1g Nov 2] smallish, strong filly: first foal: dam 6f to 1¼m winner: fair performer: won seller at Ripon in July: should stay 7f/1m: acts on good to firm going: unreliable. *W. M. Brisbourne* **72 §**

ENTAILMENT 4 b.g. Kris 135 – Entail (USA) 97 (Riverman (USA) 131) [2006 76: 10d May 26] leggy gelding: fair performer at best: well held only Flat outing in 2006: tried tongue tied. *Miss Gay Kelleway* **–**

ENTHUSIUS 3 b.c. Generous (IRE) 139 – Edouna (FR) (Doyoun 124) [2006 –: 11g Apr 25] lengthy colt: well held in maidens. *M. L. W. Bell* **–**

David Reid Scott & Sangster Family's "English Ballet"

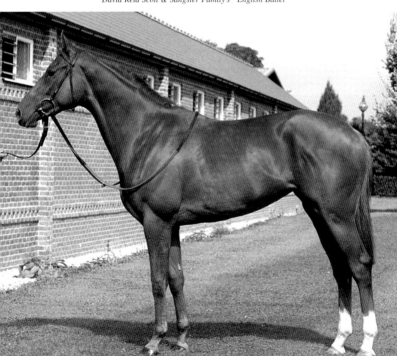

Lael Stable's "Enticing"

ENTICING (IRE) 2 b.f. (Mar 2) Pivotal 124 – Superstar Leo (IRE) 114 (College **104**
Chapel 122) [2006 5g* p5.1g* 5m* 5s 5d³ Oct 7] compact filly: second foal: dam 2-y-o
5f winner (including Flying Childers Stakes): useful performer: won first 3 starts, namely
maiden at Salisbury in June, minor event at Wolverhampton in July and 13-runner Molecomb Stakes at Goodwood (beat Wi Dud by short head, reportedly lost a shoe) in August:
well held against older horses in Nunthorpe Stakes at York next time, but ran creditably
when 3¾ lengths third of 10 to Alzerra in Cornwallis Stakes at Ascot final start: all speed,
and will prove best kept to 5f: acts on polytrack, good to firm and good to soft going.
W. J. Haggas

ENTRANCED 3 b.f. Saddlers' Hall (IRE) 126 – Vent d'Aout (IRE) (Imp Society **69**
(USA)) [2006 75p: p10g 12.1g 12.1m⁵ p12.2g⁵ p12g f14g⁵ Dec 5] lengthy filly: fair
handicapper: races freely, and may prove best short of 1½m: acts on polytrack. *Miss
J. A. Camacho*

ENVISION 3 b.g. Pivotal 124 – Entwine 92 (Primo Dominie 121) [2006 89: 8m 8.1s 8g⁴ **96**
8.5g* 7m* 8m* 8.3g* 8.3g* 8d³ p8g³ Sep 30] smallish gelding: useful performer: won
claimers at Epsom (2) and Salisbury in July and handicaps at Windsor (2) in August,
beating Nanton by 1¼ lengths for last success, hanging right: good third in handicaps
at Ascot (to Supaseus) and Kempton (behind Persian Express) after: stays 8.5f: acts on
polytrack, firm and good to soft going: blanketed for stall entry, and twice withdrawn
when fractious: sold 55,000 gns, joined S. Seemar in UAE. *R. Hannon*

EPICES 4 b.g. Mtoto 134 – French Spice 85 (Cadeaux Genereux 131) [2006 –: 11s 13g **–**
7.5f 7m p8g p10g⁶ Dec 30] maiden: little form since 2 yrs, leaving Sir Mark Prescott after
final start at 3 yrs and J. F. O'Shea in Ireland after fourth in 2006: tried in cheekpieces/
blinkers. *R. Ingram*

EPICUREAN 4 ch.f. Pursuit of Love 124 – Arminda (Blakeney 126) [2006 73: 10d* **71**
8.9m 10f 11.9g 10.1s⁵ 13.8v p12.2g Nov 23] lengthy, quite good-topped filly: fair handi-

capper: won at Pontefract in May: stays 1¼m: acts on soft and good to firm going: blinkered final outing in 2005. *Mrs K. Walton*

EPIDAURIAN KING (IRE) 3 b.g. King's Best (USA) 132 – Thurayya (Nashwan (USA) 135) [2006 f6g⁶ Dec 27] 25/1, reared leaving stall and always behind in maiden at Southwell. *D. Shaw* —

EPINEUSE 3 b.f. Gorse 116 – Four-Legged Friend 101 (Aragon 118) [2006 –: 5f² 5.1g 5g* 5g⁶ p5g p6g Dec 18] modest performer: won selling handicap at Ripon in August: best at 5f: acts on firm ground, no form on polytrack: visored final start. *J. R. Best* **56 a–**

EQUAL AND APPROVED 2 b.c. (Jan 15) Auction House (USA) 120 – Rave On (ITY) 73 (Barathea (IRE) 127) [2006 5m⁴ 5m 7m 6m Aug 30] poor maiden: bred to stay 1m+. *R. Hannon* **49**

EQUATOR 3 ch.g. Observatory (USA) 131 – Fleet River (USA) 93 (Riverman (USA) 131) [2006 p8g⁴ 10.2s⁴ May 22] fifth foal: half-brother to useful French 1m winner Delta (by Zafonic) and French 9f winner Humber (by Bering): dam, 2-y-o 7f winner, half-sister to very smart performer up to 1½m Eltish and smart sprinter Forest Gazelle: better effort in maidens when fourth to Scot Love at Kempton on debut: sold 28,000 gns, joined A. Martin in Ireland. *Mrs A. J. Perrett* **80**

EQUILIBRIA (USA) 4 b.g. Gulch (USA) – Julie La Rousse (IRE) 114 (Lomond (USA) 128) [2006 58: p12g⁶ p12g⁶ 16.4f⁵ 11.9f⁴ 12.1f² 12.1m* 16m p13.9g⁵ Nov 6] modest performer: won handicap at Chepstow in August: effective at 1½m, barely stays 16.4f: acts on all-weather, firm and good to soft ground: tried visored. *G. L. Moore* **59**

EQUULEUS PICTOR 2 br.c. (Apr 10) Piccolo 121 – Vax Rapide 80 (Sharpo 132) [2006 5.1g⁶ 5f³ p5.1g⁵ Sep 11] modest form in maidens, looking difficult ride: raced at 5f. *J. L. Spearing* **64**

ERHGENT SEA 3 gr.g. Erhaab (USA) 127 – Gentle Gypsy 94 (Junius (USA) 124) [2006 –: p10g Mar 27] well beaten in maidens. *T. M. Jones* —

ERIDANI (IRE) 2 ch.f. (Mar 28) Daggers Drawn (USA) 114 – Rorkes Drift (IRE) 55 (Royal Abjar (USA) 121) [2006 p8g p8g p8.6g Dec 29] first foal: dam, Irish maiden, half-sister to smart performer up to 1½m Sobriety: well held in maidens. *M. L. W. Bell* —

ERMINE GREY 5 gr.g. Wolfhound (USA) 126 – Impulsive Decision (IRE) 71 (Nomination 125) [2006 75, a86: p9.5g 8.2s⁵ 10g⁶ 8.1m⁶ 8.2d² 8.1s⁴ 8.3f⁵ 10f² 10f⁵ 8d⁵ 10.9d 8.2d⁵ f8g Nov 15] rather leggy gelding: fair handicapper: stays 1¼m: acts on all-weather, firm and soft going: sometimes wears headgear. *A. W. Carroll* **68 a73**

ERMINE SEA 3 b.g. Rainbow Quest (USA) 134 – Bint Pasha (USA) 126 (Affirmed (USA)) [2006 66p: 11.5m² p12g² 11.9m² 16m³ 12g* 15d⁵ 15m 14d⁵ Nov 3] angular, quite attractive gelding: useful performer: 1¾ lengths third to Soapy Danger in Queen's Vase at Royal Ascot prior to winning maiden at Newbury in July by 1¾ lengths from Altenburg: good 3½ lengths fifth to Getaway in listed race at Deauville next time: better at around 2m than shorter: acts on polytrack, good to firm and good to soft going: blinkered final outing (gelded after): usually races up with pace. *J. H. M. Gosden* **102**

ERNMOOR 4 b.g. Young Ern 120 – Linpac North Moor 69 (Moorestyle 137) [2006 –: p10g⁴ p7g p10g⁶ p9.5g Mar 29] modest maiden, lightly raced: stays easy 1¼m. *J. R. Best* **51**

ERRA GO ON 5 ch.g. Atraf 116 – Pastelle 52 (Tate Gallery (USA) 117) [2006 7d 7m⁶ 7m⁶ 7m 7f 8m⁴ 7.5m⁴ 7.5g* 8d* 6g p6g Dec 3] fairly useful handicapper: left P. Prendergast after fifth start: has won 4 races, including at Tipperary and Tralee in 2006: creditable efforts on all-weather in Britain last 2 starts a day apart: stays 1m: acts on poly-track, firm and good to soft going: tried blinkered. *A. McGuinness, Ireland* **87**

ESCAPE CLAUSE (USA) 3 b.c. Red Ransom (USA) – Promptly (IRE) 88 (Lead On Time (USA) 123) [2006 84p: p7g² 8.1s⁵ 8.2m³ 7.1m³ 8.1m⁴ 8.3g⁴ 10m⁴ p8.6g* Oct 8] big, close-coupled colt: fairly useful performer: in frame all 9 starts, winning maiden at Wolverhampton (hung right) in October: stays 1¼m: acts on polytrack, soft and good to firm going: tried visored: reportedly had irregular heartbeat after poor effort fifth outing: not entirely straightforward: sold 90,000 gns. *Sir Michael Stoute* **84**

ESCAPE ROUTE (USA) 2 b.c. (Feb 17) Elusive Quality (USA) – Away (USA) (Dixieland Band (USA)) [2006 p7g* Oct 20] $170,000Y: first foal: dam, US 6f (including at 2 yrs)/7f winner, out of half-sister to US Grade 3 6f winner Belong To Me: 6/1, good impression when winning maiden at Lingfield by 2½ lengths from Mystic Dancer, going away at finish: will be suited by 1m: useful prospect. *J. H. M. Gosden* **87 p**

ESCAYOLA (IRE) 6 b.g. Revoque (IRE) 122 – First Fling (IRE) 63 (Last Tycoon 131) **91**
[2006 92: 14m³ 20m 16.1m⁶ 16g 16.1d⁵ 15.9m³ p16g⁵ 16d* Nov 3] good-topped gelding:
fairly useful handicapper: left W. Haggas, won at Musselburgh in November by 4 lengths:
stays 2¼m: acts on polytrack, firm and soft going: visored/blinkered: sometimes tongue
tied: tends to hang left: usually held up: largely reliable. *G. F. Tuer*

ESCOBAR (POL) 5 b.g. Royal Court (IRE) 116 – Escola (POL) (Dixieland (POL)) **54**
[2006 55: p10g⁶ p7g p8g³ 10.2f Jun 17] modest form at best in Britain: probably stays
1¼m: tried tongue tied/in cheekpieces: won over hurdles in October. *Mrs P. Townsley*

ESCOFFIER 4 b.g. Entrepreneur 123 – Gooseberry Pie 63 (Green Desert (USA) 127) **63**
[2006 75: p12g 11.9g p12g p12g* p12g⁶ Dec 16] big gelding: modest performer: won
handicap at Kempton in November: stays easy 1½m: acts on polytrack. *Pat Eddery*

ESKIMO NELL 3 b.f. Polar Prince (IRE) 117 – We're Joken 62 (Statoblest 120) [2006 **–**
53: 12.1d 8s f6g May 31] strong filly: modest maiden at 2 yrs: little form in 2006: sold
1,500 gns, sent to Sweden. *T. D. Easterby*

ESKIMO'S NEST 4 b.f. Polar Falcon (USA) 126 – White House 84 (Pursuit of Love **–**
124) [2006 58: p12.2g p10g p7.1g Feb 13] tall, leggy filly: maiden: no form in 2006: tried
visored. *D. Shaw*

ESOTERICA (IRE) 3 b.g. Bluebird (USA) 125 – Mysterious Plans (IRE) (Last **72**
Tycoon 131) [2006 61p: 6d³ 6d 7m³ 7d⁶ 6f⁴ 7f⁴ 8f* 7.1g² 6.9m³ 7.5f² 10m³ 8v 8.5m⁶ Sep
19] useful-looking gelding: fair handicapper: won at Musselburgh in June: stays 1¼m:
acts on firm and good to soft going (well below form on heavy): effective in cheekpieces/
blinkers or not: sold 15,000 gns. *T. D. Barron*

ESPARTANO 2 b.g. (Jan 21) Vettori (IRE) 119 – Talighta (USA) 62 (Barathea (IRE) **87**
127) [2006 5g* 5g* 5m 6g 6d p6g² Oct 23] 12,000Y: tall, good-topped gelding: fourth
foal: half-brother to 2-y-o 5f winners Kuringai (in 2003, by Royal Applause) and Melandre (in 2004, by Lujain) and 3-y-o Forces Sweetheart: dam Irish sprint maiden: fairly
useful performer: won maiden in April and minor event in May, both at Windsor: good
efforts after when eighth of 18 to Elhamri in listed Windsor Castle Stakes at Royal Ascot
third start and second in minor event at Lingfield final one: off 2 months (and gelded)
before penultimate outing: effective at 5f/6f: acts on polytrack and good to firm going.
M. J. Wallace

ESPEJO (IRE) 2 b.g. (Mar 16) City On A Hill (USA) 114 – Beechwood Quest (IRE) **79**
65 (River Falls 113) [2006 7g³ 7.1m³ 7g Sep 27] €17,000Y: lengthy gelding: fourth foal:
half-brother to 4-y-o Union Jack Jackson: dam 2-y-o 5f seller winner: fair maiden: third
at Thirsk and Warwick: will prove as good at 6f as 7f. *K. R. Burke*

ESPERANCE (IRE) 6 ch.g. Bluebird (USA) 125 – Dioscorea (IRE) (Pharly (FR) 130) **46**
[2006 46, a56: p10g p13g Mar 4] good-topped gelding: poor performer: stays 11f: acts
on polytrack, soft and good to firm going: tried in cheekpieces, blinkered nowadays.
J. Akehurst

ESPRIT D'AMOUR (IRE) 2 b.f. (Mar 14) Invincible Spirit (IRE) 121 – Elton Grove **55**
(IRE) (Astronef 116) [2006 5d⁶ 5g³ 5d⁴ 5m⁵ Jun 3] €7,000F, 16,000Y: sixth foal: closely
related to 5-y-o Trysting Grove and half-sister to fairly useful 2002 2-y-o 1m winner La
Muette (by Charnwood Forest): dam French 9f and 10.5f winner: modest maiden: raced
at 5f. *T. D. Easterby*

ESPRIT DE CORPS 4 b.g. Hernando (FR) 127 – Entente Cordiale (USA) (Affirmed **84**
(USA)) [2006 69p: f11g p12.2g p12g 14.1m* 15.8m² 18s* Oct 16] fairly useful performer, lightly raced: gelded and off over 7 months after third start: upped in trip, improved
and won handicaps at Redcar in September and Pontefract (hung left) in October: stays
2¼m: acts on soft and good to firm ground, probably on polytrack: quirky: sold 80,000
gns, joined P. Hobbs. *Sir Mark Prescott*

ESPRIT DE NUIT (IRE) 2 b.g. (Apr 10) Invincible Spirit (IRE) 121 – Night Spirit **48 ?**
(IRE) 78 (Night Shift (USA)) [2006 p5g⁶ p5.1g⁶ Nov 25] seemingly modest form first
start in maidens: should stay 6f. *Mrs A. Duffield*

ESQUILLON 4 b.f. High Estate 127 – Our Aisling 82 (Blakeney 126) [2006 51: f16g⁴ **51**
f16g⁶ 14.1d⁴ 15.8g 14.1f 15.8m⁴ 14.1f⁶ f16g Oct 12] leggy filly: modest maiden: stays
2m: acts on good to soft and good to firm ground: tried in cheekpieces. *S. Parr*

ESQUIRE 4 b.c. Dubai Millennium 140 – Esperada (ARG) (Equalize (USA)) [2006 –: **94**
8.1g⁴ 7d Sep 23] tall, attractive colt: fairly useful performer, lightly raced: much better
effort in handicaps in 2006 when good fourth to Killena Boy at Sandown: stays 1m: best
form on good going: joined A. Al Raihe in UAE. *Saeed bin Suroor*

ESTABLISHMENT 9 b.g. Muhtarram (USA) 125 – Uncharted Waters 68 (Celestial **89**
Storm (USA) 132) [2006 79: p16g* p16g⁴ p16g³ 16s³ 20m 21.7m 16.1m⁴ p16g³ 15.9g*
15.9m² 16d⁵ 16d⁵ p16g Nov 11] smallish, workmanlike gelding: fairly useful performer:
won handicaps at Kempton in April and Chester in August: seems to stay 2¾m: acts on
polytrack, firm and soft going: blinkered twice: sometimes sweats/races freely: held up.
C. A. Cyzer

ESTEEM 3 b.g. Mark of Esteem (IRE) 137 – Please (Kris 135) [2006 p8g 8s 7m p8.6g² **79**
8.3f³ 8g* Aug 14] good-topped gelding: third foal: dam, ran twice (signs of ability), out of
sister to smart middle-distance stayer Spring and close relation of Pentire: fair performer: won on handicap debut at Thirsk in August, tending to edge left: will be suited by
1¼m: acts on polytrack. *W. Jarvis*

ESTEEMED PRINCE 2 b.g. (Feb 9) Mark of Esteem (IRE) 137 – Princess Alaska **62**
(Northern State (USA) 91) [2006 p5g⁵ 6.1d May 19] better run when fifth in maiden at
Kempton on debut: bred to stay 1m: once refused at stalls. *D. Shaw*

ESTHLOS (FR) 3 ch.g. Limnos (JPN) 124 – Cozzie 60 (Cosmonaut) [2006 64: 8.2m² **79**
p9.5m² p8.6g⁴ p8.6g² p8g* Nov 25] strong, workmanlike gelding: fair performer: in
frame all starts, including in handicaps, prior to winning maiden at Kempton in November: stays easy 9.5f: acts on polytrack and good to firm going. *J. Jay*

ESTIMATOR 2 b.c. (Feb 1) Auction House (USA) 120 – Fresh Look (IRE) 64 (Alzao **79 p**
(USA) 117) [2006 p6g* p6g* Dec 28] €15,000F, 15,000Y: sixth foal: half-brother to
Irish 2003 2-y-o 6f winner Euro Route (by Desert Style) and 7-y-o Tuscarora: dam 11.5f
winner: won maiden at Kempton (by 1¼ lengths from Mo) and nursery at Wolverhampton (made most, beat Bertie Swift by length), both in December: should stay 7f: should
improve further. *Pat Eddery*

ESTIQRAAR (IRE) 3 b.c. Alhaarth (IRE) 126 – Hureya (USA) 82 (Woodman (USA) **82**
126) [2006 79: 9s* 10d⁶ Apr 6] leggy colt: has a quick action: fairly useful performer:
won maiden at Redcar (beat Chronomatic readily by 4 lengths) in March: raced too freely
when last in handicap at Leicester 12 days later: should stay 1¼m: acts on soft ground:
carried head high latter 2-y-o start: sold 30,000 gns in July. *J. L. Dunlop*

ESTOILLE 5 b.m. Paris House 123 – Nampara Bay 50 (Emarati (USA) 74) [2006 61: **59**
6v p5.1g f5g* f5g⁵ 5f³ 5m² 5g³ 6g 5d⁵ 5m f6g⁴ f5g f5g Dec 28] leggy mare: modest
performer: won banded race at Southwell in May: effective at 5f/6f: acts on all-weather,
firm and good to soft going: sometimes tongue tied. *Mrs S. Lamyman*

ESTRELLE (GER) 4 ch.f. Sternkoenig (IRE) 122 – Enrica 106 (Niniski (USA) 125) **76**
[2006 80: 16g 13d 12m⁴ 12g⁴ 13.8m² 11d⁵ 10g* Sep 9] leggy filly: fair performer: left
H. Cecil after fifth start (looked none too keen): won maiden at Krefeld in August and
handicap at Hoppegarten in September: stays 13.8f, probably not 2m: acts on good to
firm and good to soft going. *P. Rau, Germany*

ETAAR 4 b.g. Zafonic (USA) 130 – Hawayah (IRE) 68 (Shareef Dancer (USA) 135) **–**
[2006 78: 8d 8g Sep 27] angular gelding: has a quick action: fair performer at best, lightly
raced: left E. Dunlop 6,000 gns, well held in handicaps in 2006. *C. W. Fairhurst*

ETA DRACONIS (IRE) 3 ch.g. Daylami (IRE) 138 – Velvet Moon (IRE) 108 (Shaadi **87**
(USA) 126) [2006 11f* 11.8f⁴ Jul 25] half-brother to 3 winners, including top-class 9f to
10.4f winner (including Dubai World Cup) Moon Ballad (by Singspiel) and useful 1m
winner Velvet Lady (by Nashwan): dam, 6f (at 2 yrs, including Lowther Stakes) to 1¼m
winner, half-sister to very smart performer up to 2m Central Park: won maiden at Redcar
on debut in June by neck from idling Hyperalert, green: tailed off in handicap at Leicester
only subsequent start: gelded, then sold 10,000 gns. *Saeed bin Suroor*

ET DONA FERENTES 3 b.f. Green Desert (USA) 127 – Sister Golden Hair (IRE) **58**
(Glint of Gold 128) [2006 8g 9.5d 8m 10s f6g² Dec 27] €62,000Y: half-sister to several
winners, including useful 7f (in Ireland at 2 yrs)/1m winner Alexis (by Alzao), later
successful in Canada: dam German 2-y-o 1m winner: modest maiden: left W. Browne in
Ireland before creditable effort at Southwell final outing: effective at 6f, seems to stay
9.5f: acts on fibresand. *T. D. Barron*

ETERNAL LEGACY (IRE) 4 b.f. Monashee Mountain (USA) 115 – Tender Time **59**
(Tender King 123) [2006 6d⁴ 6m⁵ 7.5g⁵ f8g 6.9m 7m Aug 31] 6,000Y: half-sister to
several winners, including fairly useful 1994 2-y-o 6f winner Regal Fanfare (by Taufan)
and 1m to 15f winner Final Settlement (by Soviet Lad): dam ran twice: lightly-raced
maiden, modest form: stays 7.5f: acts on good to soft going. *J. Parkes*

ETERNALLY 4 ch.g. Timeless Times (USA) 99 – Nice Spice (IRE) (Common **50**
Grounds 118) [2006 –: f5g² f5g f5g³ f5g³ p5.1g⁵ f5g⁴ p5.1g f5g f5g p5g Dec 18] leggy

gelding: modest performer: best at 5f: acts on fibresand and firm ground: wears cheek-pieces/visor. *R. M. H. Cowell*

ETERNAL PATH (USA) 2 ch.f. (Mar 29) Theatrical 128 – Houdini's Honey (USA) **83 p** 84 (Mr Prospector (USA)) [2006 7d³ Oct 28] useful-looking filly: first foal: dam, 1¼m winner (later successful in US), sister to Machiavellian and to grandam of Bago: 12/1, shaped well when third of 20 to Measured Tempo in maiden at Newmarket, weaving through from rear: will be suited by 1¼m/1½m: useful prospect, sure to win races. *Sir Michael Stoute*

ETIJAHAAT (IRE) 4 b.g. King's Best (USA) 132 – Dance Ahead 81 (Shareef Dancer – (USA) 135) [2006 89d: 7g 12m 8s⁵ 7m 8g 10f Sep 20] angular gelding: fairly useful at best: no form in 2006: tried visored. *C. W. Fairhurst*

ETLAALA 4 ch.c. Selkirk (USA) 129 – Portelet 91 (Night Shift (USA)) [2006 116: **122** 7.1g* 7g* 6d 6m* 6m 7m⁵ 7d⁶ Aug 19] big, good-topped colt: impressed in appearance: very smart performer: won minor event at Warwick in April, and listed races at Leicester (beat Philharmonic ¾ length, edging left) later in month and Salisbury (better than ever when beating same horse by 1¾ lengths) in June: well below form in pattern company all 3 starts after: was effective at 6f/7f: acted on firm going, probably not on softer than good: sometimes bandaged behind/wore net muzzle: dead. *B. W. Hills*

ETOILE D'OR (IRE) 2 ch.f. (Mar 15) Soviet Star (USA) 128 – Christeningpresent **70** (IRE) (Cadeaux Genereux 131) [2006 6m 6g⁵ 7s³ Oct 10] workmanlike filly: third foal: dam unraced out of useful half-sister to smart French miler Rouquette: fair form in maidens: will stay 1m. *M. H. Tompkins*

ETOILE RUSSE (IRE) 3 b.g. Soviet Star (USA) 128 – To The Skies (USA) 89 (Sky **69** Classic (CAN)) [2006 65: 8d 10m² p9.5g Nov 10] big, good-topped gelding: fair maiden handicapper on Flat: stays 1¼m: acts on fibresand and good to firm ground: tongue tied in 2006: races freely. *P. C. Haslam*

ETON (GER) 10 ch.g. Suave Dancer (USA) 136 – Ermione (Surumu (GER)) [2006 **61** 64: p12.2g⁴ p13.9g³ p12.2g Jan 20] strong, close-coupled gelding: modest nowadays: effective at 1¼m/1½m: acts on polytrack, best turf form on good ground or firmer: tried blinkered earlier in career: usually races prominently: inconsistent. *D. Nicholls*

ETTRICK WATER 7 ch.g. Selkirk (USA) 129 – Sadly Sober (IRE) 70 (Roi Danzig **96** (USA)) [2006 103: 8m⁶ 8m 8g Sep 28] strong gelding: useful handicapper: respectable effort in 2006 only on reappearance: best at 7f/1m: acts on firm and soft going, probably on polytrack: tried blinkered, visored nowadays: effective ridden prominently or waited with. *L. M. Cumani*

EULOGIZE 2 b.f. (Feb 20) Pivotal 124 – Tantalize (Machiavellian (USA) 123) [2006 **70** 8.3d³ p8g³ Nov 15] first foal: dam unraced close relative to smart performer up to 1m Dazzle: fair form: third in maidens at Leicester and Kempton (favourite, still green): sold 75,000 gns, sent to USA. *E. A. L. Dunlop*

EURANA 3 ch.f. Mark of Esteem (IRE) 137 – Intervene (Zafonic (USA) 130) [2006 –: **39** 6d 8g⁶ 6.9m⁵ 7.9m 5.9m Aug 7] poor maiden. *Jedd O'Keeffe*

EUROPEAN (ARG) 6 br.g. Nugget Point – Enfeitada (ARG) (Gem Master (USA)) **–** [2006 –: 8.1g 6m 7g 8.3m⁶ Jul 3] useful-looking gelding: little form in Britain, including in claimers: blinkered (took strong hold) final outing. *R. M. Beckett*

EUROPEAN DREAM (IRE) 3 br.g. Kalanisi (IRE) 132 – Tereed Elhawa 75 (Cade- **92** aux Genereux 131) [2006 69: 8.2s² 8g* 8m⁴ 7.6d³ 8.2d³ 8m⁵ 8m³ 8.1m 8.9s Oct 7] close-coupled gelding: fairly useful handicapper: won at Newcastle in May: stays 1m: acts on soft and good to firm going: wore cheekpieces (well held) final outing: fair winning hurdler. *R. C. Guest*

EVA SONEVA SO FAST (IRE) 4 ch.g. In The Wings 128 – Azyaa 101 (Kris 135) **94** [2006 86: 10s 12g p12g⁵ p13g² p12g² p13g² Dec 22] sturdy gelding: has a quick action: fairly useful performer: good second last 3 outings: will stay 1¾m: acts on polytrack and good to firm going. *J. L. Dunlop*

EVEN BOLDER 3 ch.g Bold Edge 123 – Level Pegging (IRE) 48 (Common Grounds **72** 118) [2006 8m p8.6g³ 8g p7.1g p6g² 5m⁴ 6g p5.1g² 6d Oct 9] strong, workmanlike geld-ing: third foal: dam twice-raced sister to smart sprinter Flanders: fair maiden: has form at 1m, likely to prove best at shorter: acts on polytrack and good to firm going. *S. Kirk*

EVEN HOTTER 5 b.m. Desert Style (IRE) 121 – Level Pegging (IRE) 48 (Common **43** Grounds 118) [2006 50: p7g Feb 8] smallish, leggy mare: poor maiden: should stay 1¼m: acts on polytrack. *D. W. P. Arbuthnot*

EVE

EVENING 3 ch.f. Mark of Esteem (IRE) 137 – Kind of Light 83 (Primo Dominie 121) **63**
[2006 8g 8.2m p8.6g⁴ p10g² 10.3m 8.3g⁵ p10g Sep 3] 7,500F: good-topped filly: has a **a75**
quick action: third foal: half-sister to 7f winner Menai Straights (by Alhaarth) and winner
in Norway by Persian Bold: dam 6f and (at 2 yrs) 7f winner: fair maiden on all-weather,
modest on turf: stays 1¼m: acts on polytrack, best effort on turf on good going. *B. W. Hills*

EVENING TIME (IRE) 2 gr.f. (Mar 2) Keltos (FR) 132 – Shadow Casting 72 **114 p**
(Warning 136) [2006 6s* 6s* Oct 8]
    Keltos' stallion career is up and running again, fertility problems in his first
year at stud having led to his being put back into training for a couple of seasons.
He ran fourteen times during 2004 and 2005, and, while unable to recapture the
top-class form he had shown when taking the 2002 Lockinge Stakes, Keltos did
win three races, including a listed event at Saint-Cloud, and was second in the
Challenge Stakes at Newmarket. His fee was only €2,500 when he resumed stallion
duties at Haras des Granges in 2006—it was set at €10,000 when retired to the
Airlie Stud in 2003—but it has been increased to £4,000 for 2007, when Keltos will
be standing at the Chevington Stud in Newmarket. As a result of his problems,
Keltos reportedly had only fourteen foals in his first crop. Encouragingly for his
stallion prospects that small batch included the filly Evening Time. A most impressive winner of both her starts to date, she looks one who could help raise her sire's
profile significantly in the next season.
    Evening Time made her debut in an eighteen-runner maiden at Fairyhouse
in September. Sent off favourite, she took up the running over a furlong out and
finished to such purpose that, by the time she reached the line, her lead had
stretched to nine lengths. With the runner-up Crown Colony having shown fairly
useful form on his previous start, Evening Time was clearly out of the ordinary, and
when she turned out again just eight days later it was for a listed event. The Flame
of Tara European Breeders Fund Stakes at the Curragh attracted twelve fillies but
the betting suggested it was very much a two-horse race, with Evening Time the
favourite at 5/4 and the Aidan O'Brien-trained Theann, fifth in the Cheveley Park
Stakes on her previous outing, at 2/1. As at Fairyhouse the ground was soft, and
once again Evening Time made light of the conditions. Still travelling well when
she joined the leaders over two furlongs out, Evening Time began to get on top
soon after and stayed on well to win by five lengths from Theann. Evening Time
completed a hat-trick at the meeting for her trainer Kevin Prendergast. 'The owner
has told me that she will have to be entered for the Irish One Thousand Guineas,'
said Prendergast afterwards. Already smart and open to further improvement,
Evening Time looks fully capable of making her presence felt in that race, provided
she has the necessary stamina. She will definitely stay seven furlongs, and it is
possible that a mile will prove to be within her compass.

		Kendor	Kenmare
Evening Time (IRE)	Keltos (FR)	(gr 1986)	Belle Mecene
(gr.f. Mar 2, 2004)	(gr 1998)	Loxandra	Last Tycoon
		(b 1991)	Northshiel
	Shadow Casting	Warning	Known Fact
	(b 1993)	(b 1985)	Slightly Dangerous
		Fanciful	Gay Mecene
		(b 1985)	Bold Fantasy

    Keltos stayed a mile well, and Evening Time's dam Shadow Casting was
bred to stay that far, though she showed better form at seven furlongs, including
when winning a maiden at Chepstow on the second of her five starts, all as a three-
year-old. Shadow Casting's three previous winners were certainly best at short of a
mile, though all three were sired by sprinters. Distinctly Dancer (by Distinctly
North) was a smart sprinter in Italy, Lake Andre (by Lake Coniston) a useful winner
over seven furlongs in Ireland, and Mujadil Shadow (by Mujadil) a five- and six-
furlong winner in Italy. Fanciful, the grandam, won over a mile in France and is also
responsible for a couple of other winners including Solar Flight, useful up to a
mile. The next dam Bold Fantasy, who was runner-up in the Irish One Thousand
Guineas, is from a fine family and she has produced a host of winners herself, the
Lowther Stakes winner Kingscote among them. Given her pedigree, it might have
been expected that Evening Time would have fetched more than €28,000 when she
went through the sales ring. What a bargain she looks now! *K. Prendergast, Ireland*

357

EVENS AND ODDS (IRE) 2 ch.c. (Feb 27) Johannesburg (USA) 127 – Coeur de La **96 +**
Mer (IRE) 87 (Caerleon (USA) 132) [2006 6d⁵ 5f* 5.5m 6g⁴ Sep 30] second foal: dam
2-y-o 1m winner: useful form: won maiden at Beverley in July: stiff task in Prix Robert
Papin at Maisons-Laffitte later in month: improvement when fourth of 24 in listed Two-
Year-Old Trophy at Redcar final start: will stay 7f/1m. *K. A. Ryan*

EVENT MUSIC (IRE) 2 ch.f. (Mar 9) Distant Music (USA) 126 – Evening Set (GER) **77**
95 (Second Set (IRE) 127) [2006 6m² 6g* 7d⁴ Oct 20] €46,000Y: second foal: half-sister
to winner abroad by Desert Prince: dam 2-y-o 6f winner: fair form: won maiden at Redcar
in August: good fourth to Smokejumper in valuable sales race at Baden-Baden 2 months
later: stays 7f. *M. R. Channon*

EVER CHEERFUL 5 b.g. Atraf 116 – Big Story 50 (Cadeaux Genereux 131) [2006 **81**
78: p5g* p6g² p7g⁴ p6g⁴ p6g p7.1g p6g p5g⁵ p6g⁵ p6g⁴ p6g⁵ p7.1g⁴ Dec 22] workmanlike gelding: fluent mover: fairly useful handicapper: won at Lingfield in January:
left G. Chung after sixth start: effective at 5f to easy 7f: acts on all-weather, raced only on
good going or firmer on turf: has worn cheekpieces: has raced freely. *D. G. Bridgwater*

EVEREST (IRE) 9 ch.g. Indian Ridge 123 – Reine d'Beaute 97 (Caerleon (USA) 132) **87**
[2006 90: p8.6g⁶ p9.5g² 8s⁶ 8m³ 8m 7m 9d* 8.3m³ Aug 16] strong, deep-girthed gelding: **a81**
type to carry condition: fairly useful performer: won claimer at Redcar in August: stays
9.5f: acts on polytrack and any turf going: sometimes races freely: held up. *B. Ellison*

EVERSDEN (USA) 3 b.c. Red Ransom (USA) – Who Did It And Run (USA) (Polish **69**
Numbers (USA)) [2006 82: 6g 6g 5m 5g 6m 5m⁶ a6.5g Dec 29] strong colt: fair
performer: sold from C. Cox 2,000 gns after sixth start: stays 6f: raced only on good/
good to firm going on turf: in cheekpieces last 2 starts in Britain: possibly temperamental.
N. Minner, Belgium

EVER SPECIAL (IRE) 3 b.g. Fruits of Love (USA) 127 – El Corazon (IRE) (Mujadil **43**
(USA) 119) [2006 –: f8g⁶ f8g 9.8m⁶ 8.3d⁵ 9d Oct 8] big, leggy gelding: poor maiden on
Flat: probably stays 9.8f: acts on good to firm going: won 4 times over hurdles, joining
J. Stimpson 9,100 gns after final Flat start). *P. C. Haslam*

EVERY INCH (IRE) 3 gr.g. Inchinor 119 – African Light 65§ (Kalaglow 132) [2006 **–**
9s⁶ 10m 12s⁶ 12.1f 12f 16.2m Jul 24] rather leggy gelding: no form: mulish at start/ran
wide third outing: dead. *T. D. Easterby*

EVERYMAN 2 gr.c. (Feb 29) Act One 124 – Maid To Dance 62 (Pyramus (USA) 78) **56 §**
[2006 5s³ p5g⁵ 5.1d p6g⁵ 6f⁴ 6f p7.1f Aug 14] well-grown colt: modest maiden: should
stay 7f/1m: tried visored/blinkered: ungenuine. *P. D. Evans*

EVERYMANFORHIMSELF (IRE) 2 b.c. (Jan 12) Fasliyev (USA) 120 – Luisa **95**
Demon (IRE) (Barathea (IRE) 127) [2006 5d* 6.1d² 5g* 6m 5.2g 6m⁵ 6.1g* 6s² 6m³ 7d
Oct 7] 4,000Y: big, strong, good-topped colt: has scope: has quick action: third foal:
dam, Italian 2-y-o 5f/6f winner, half-sister to useful sprinters Fred Bongusto and Atlantic
Viking: useful performer: won maiden at Beverley in April, minor event there in May and
nursery at Nottingham in August: ran well when placed in listed race at Ripon (second to
Stevie Gee) and nursery at Newmarket eighth/ninth starts: best at 5f/6f: acts on soft and
good to firm going: lazy sort, tends to get behind, but is consistent. *J. G. Given*

EVIDENT PRIDE (USA) 3 b.g. Chester House (USA) 123 – Proud Fact (USA) 108 **93**
(Known Fact (USA) 135) [2006 p8g³ 7m³ p6g² p8.6g* p8g* p7g² Dec 10] 9,000 2-y-o:
sixth foal: half-brother to winner in USA by Kris S: dam, French 7f/1m winner, half-sister
to Poule d'Essai des Pouliches winner Houseproud: fairly useful performer, lightly raced:
progressed well in 2006, winning handicaps at Wolverhampton (maiden) in September
and Kempton in November: good second to Dichoh in similar event at Kempton final
outing: stays 8.6f: acts on polytrack: tends to edge left. *B. R. Johnson*

EVITA 2 b.f. (May 15) Selkirk (USA) 129 – Darara 129 (Top Ville 129) [2006 7d Oct 28] **– p**
big, good-bodied filly: half-sister to several winners, most at least smart, including
French 1½m winner Darazari (also Group 1 1¼m winner in Australia) and 1¼m performer Diaghilev (known as River Dancer in Hong Kong), both very smart by Sadler's
Wells: dam, Prix Vermeille winner, half-sister to Darshaan: 33/1 and backward, behind in
maiden at Newmarket: should do better at 1¼m+. *L. M. Cumani*

EVOLUTION EX (USA) 4 b. or br.g. Bahri (USA) 125 – Zoe's Gold (USA) 77 (St **68**
Jovite (USA) 135) [2006 86: 10g 10g 10m 10f⁶ 11.5f³ 10.5m⁵ 10.5g* 12s⁶ p12g Dec 8]
close-coupled gelding: has a short, unimpressive action: just fair in 2006: won stable at
Haydock in September: left K. Burke 4,000 gns prior to final outing: stays 10.5f: acts on
soft and good to firm going: tried visored: races up with pace. *I. W. McInnes*

EVOLVE (USA) 3 ch.f. With Approval (CAN) – Conical 63 (Zafonic (USA) 130) – [2006 7m Apr 21] tall filly: fourth foal: half-sister to 5-y-o Convince and 6f (at 2 yrs)/7f winner Convex (by Nureyev), both fairly useful: dam, maiden in Britain/USA, half-sister to very smart middle-distance performers Wandesta and De Quest: 16/1 and backward in coat, well beaten in maiden at Newbury: sold 7,500 gns in October. *B. W. Hills*

EXCELLENT 3 ch.f. Grand Lodge (USA) 125 – Exclusive 115 (Polar Falcon (USA) **60** 126) [2006 61p: 8.3f Jul 10] strong, lengthy filly: modest form in 2 maidens 9 months apart, still green on only outing of 2006. *Sir Michael Stoute*

EXCELLENT ART 2 b.c. (Feb 25) Pivotal 124 – Obsessive (USA) 102 (Seeking **114** The Gold (USA)) [2006 5g* 5v* 6g³ 6s³ 6m* Sep 16]

The Coolmore triumvirate of John Magnier, Michael Tabor and Derrick Smith have a number of options for the Two Thousand Guineas, with four horses quoted at odds of 20/1 or shorter at the time of writing, including second favourite Holy Roman Emperor. However, in an unusual move which may signal a change of policy, another potential Guineas prospect has been purchased in the shape of Excellent Art. Unlike its main rivals, Godolphin, Coolmore has purchased very few horses in training in recent years. The acquisitions of L'Ancresse and Airwave, who both went into training with Aidan O'Brien, were understandable given their potential as broodmares, whilst Hurricane Run, who continued to be trained by Andre Fabre, was one of the leading sons of Coolmore stallion Montjeu, having already proven himself very smart when Michael Tabor bought him for a rumoured £6m before the Irish Derby. Montjeu himself was also bought by Tabor after his two-year-old campaign. The purchase of the smart juvenile Excellent Art, however, is more intriguing, as he has a long way to go to develop into a serious Guineas contender, his form at least 10 lb shy of what is required at Newmarket in an average year. Should Excellent Art do well enough to make it on to the Coolmore stallion roster, he would be one of the few to take up duties there that has not been sired by another Coolmore stallion. A son of Pivotal, who is part-owned by Sheikh Mohammed, Excellent Art is still a product of the Northern Dancer line.

Excellent Art's previous owner, Matthew Green, has a number of horses in training, mainly with Excellent Art's trainer as a two-year-old Neville Callaghan and with David Elsworth. Excellent Art isn't the first horse to be sold for a significant sum by Green, who sold another Guineas prospect to Paul and Susan Roy in Dutch Art (now owned by Cheveley Park Stud but to continue racing in Mrs Roy's colours). Dutch Art changed hands after he made a winning debut at Windsor. Others sold by Green include part-owned Art Trader, who won twice before being sold to Hong Kong, and Triumph Hurdle prospect Degas Art, bought by Graham

Dubai Duty Free Mill Reef Stakes, Newbury—Excellent Art (rail) confirms the improvement he showed in the Prix Morny and just beats Doctor Brown; Dubai Builder is third ahead of Bahama Mama

Mr Matthew Green's "Excellent Art"

		Polar Falcon	Nureyev
	Pivotal	(b or br 1987)	Marie d'Argonne
	(ch 1993)	Fearless Revival	Cozzene
Excellent Art		(ch 1987)	Stufida
(b.c. Feb 25, 2004)		Seeking The Gold	Mr Prospector
	Obsessive (USA)	(b 1985)	Con Game
	(b or br 1993)	Secret Obsession	Secretariat
		(b or br 1986)	Ann Stuart

Wylie after a listed win on the Flat for David Elsworth. Now in training at Bally-doyle with Aidan O'Brien, Excellent Art was purchased after winning the Dubai Duty Free Mill Reef Stakes at Newbury. For all that the race tends to be over-shadowed by the Middle Park later in the month, it drew a useful field and Excellent Art did well to win. The field was well bunched until approaching the final furlong, with Excellent Art still to be asked for full effort, when Doctor Brown was driven upsides. Excellent Art responded well, despite his rival leaning into him, and held on by a short head, reportedly returning with a spread plate.

Excellent Art had won his first two starts, a maiden at Newmarket in April and a four-runner listed race at Sandown in May, easily landing the odds in the latter contest by nine lengths from Cav Okay. With his trainer of the opinion that Excellent Art needed some give underfoot to be seen at his best, Royal Ascot was missed in favour of the Railway Stakes at the Curragh. Excellent Art was sent off favourite but didn't quite come up to expectations, beaten a little over two lengths into third by Holy Roman Emperor and Drayton. Excellent Art's only other outing came in the Prix Morny at Deauville, where he ran right up to his best, looking the main threat to Dutch Art inside the final furlong, and losing second to Magic America only in the last strides.

Excellent Art cost 76,000 guineas as a yearling and, though the figure that Coolmore paid for him hasn't been disclosed, it will be considerably more than that. Excellent Art has been raced only at up to six furlongs to date, but there is plenty of encouragement on the dam's side to suggest he'll stay seven furlongs at least, and more than likely get a mile. Excellent Art's dam Obsessive showed plenty of speed at two, winning a six-furlong maiden at Yarmouth, and showed at three that she stayed a mile and a quarter, finishing third in the Musidora. Excellent Art is the seventh foal of Obsessive and is a half-brother to four winners, among them the smart stayer Double Obsession (by Sadler's Wells), winner of the Ascot Stakes. Grandam Secret Obsession, a fairly useful mile-and-a-quarter winner, is a half-sister to the King Edward VII Stakes winner Beyton. The lengthy, quite attractive Excellent Art, who has a quick action, showed that he acts on good to firm when winning the Mill Reef, but copes every bit as well with soft/heavy ground. Excellent Art has worn a crossed noseband, but settles well enough to suggest that he will stay as far as his pedigree suggests, with the Guineas a realistic option should new connections opt for that route, though, as has been said, he'll need to improve to take a hand at Newmarket. *N. A. Callaghan*

EXCESSIVE 2 ch.f. (May 3) Cadeaux Genereux 131 – Show Off 56 (Efisio 120) [2006 **66 p** 5d³ 5.1s⁴ Oct 25] compact filly: fourth foal: half-sister to fairly useful 2005 2-y-o 6f winner Bling (by Mark of Esteem) and 7f winner Bluff (by Bluebird): dam sprint maiden (ran only at 2 yrs): in frame in maidens at Lingfield and Nottingham: will be suited by 6f: looks capable of better. *W. Jarvis*

EXCUSEZ MOI (USA) 4 b.c. Fusaichi Pegasus (USA) 130 – Jiving 69 (Generous **112** (IRE) 139) [2006 108: 6d⁶ 7.1g⁴ 7m 6g² 6m⁴ 6s* 6s⁶ 5.2m² 5m Oct 1] tall, quite good-topped colt: smart performer: good efforts when short-head second to Somnus in minor event at Haydock and when close fourth to Borderlescott in Stewards' Cup (Handicap) at Goodwood prior to winning 19-runner William Hill Great St Wilfrid Stakes (Handicap) at Ripon in August by length from Fullandby: creditable length second to Dixie Belle in World Trophy at Newbury penultimate start: missed break, always behind in Prix de l'Abbaye at Longchamp final outing: effective at 5f to 7f: acts on polytrack, dirt, soft and good to firm going: has worn cheekpieces/tongue tie. *C. E. Brittain*

EXECUTIVE PADDY (IRE) 7 b.g. Executive Perk 120 – Illbethereforyou (IRE) **67** (Supreme Leader 123) [2006 p12.2g³ p9.5g⁴ p8.6g⁴ Dec 18] fair form in 3 maidens, only outings on Flat: should prove better around 1½m than shorter: acts on polytrack: fair hurdler, won 3 times in November. *I. A. Wood*

William Hill Great St Wilfrid Stakes, Ripon—
Excusez Moi makes amends for an unlucky run in the Stewards' Cup and holds off the strong-finishing
Fullandby (spots); Ice Planet (checked cap) and Pieter Brueghel (right) also make the frame

EXHIBIT ONE (USA) 4 b.f. Silver Hawk (USA) 123 – Tsar's Pride (Sadler's Wells **114** (USA) 132) [2006 75+: 10m⁴ 10m* 12.5g³ 12d⁴ Aug 23] lengthy filly: fair performer for Sir Michael Stoute at 3 yrs: much improved in 2006, winning Premio Paolo Mezzanotte at Milan in June by 1¼ lengths from Floriot: smart form when in frame in Prix de Pomone at Deauville (keeping-on 3¾ lengths third to Freedonia) and Yorkshire Oaks at York (4½ lengths fourth to Alexandrova): will stay 1¾m: acts on good to firm and good to soft going: tongue tied at 3 yrs. *V. Valiani, Italy*

EXISTENCE 3 b.f. Zafonic (USA) 130 – Nullarbor (Green Desert (USA) 127) [2006 **–** p7.1m f6g f5g p6g⁵ Dec 6] 5,500 3-y-o: fourth living foal: half-sister to 6-y-o Desert Opal and 4-y-o Disguise: dam, French 2-y-o 5.5f winner, half-sister to very smart French/US performer up to 1½m Radevore: little form in maidens. *D. Shaw*

EXIT SMILING 4 ch.g. Dr Fong (USA) 128 – Away To Me (Exit To Nowhere (USA) **77** 122) [2006 67, a64: p6g² p7.1g⁶ p7.1g p8g² p8g p8g⁶ f8g* f8g² 8.1m 8d* f7g 10g⁴ 10d f8g Dec 23] big, good-topped gelding: fair handicapper: left G. Chung, won at Southwell (amateurs) in April and Pontefract in May: stays easy 1¼m: acts on all-weather and good to soft ground: tried visored/blinkered: sometimes races freely: has looked hard ride, unseated rider leaving stall third outing. *P. T. Midgley*

EXIT STRATEGY (IRE) 2 b.g. (Mar 1) Cadeaux Genereux 131 – Black Belt Shop- **63** per (IRE) 82 (Desert Prince (IRE) 130) [2006 6g p7.1g f7g⁶ Nov 13] neat gelding: modest form in maidens. *W. J. Haggas*

EXIT TO LUCK (GER) 5 b.g. Exit To Nowhere (USA) 122 – Emy Coasting (USA) **78** 78 (El Gran Senor (USA) 136) [2006 8g* 8g* 8g⁴ p8.6g² p10g Dec 20] successful in 2005 in maiden at Cologne and 2 handicaps at Bremen, and won handicaps at Bremen and Frankfurt in July: left A. Wohler in Germany, fair form when second in handicap at Wolverhampton on British debut, looking no easy ride: below form next time: stays 8.6f: usually wore blinkers in Germany. *S. Gollings*

EX MILL LADY 5 br.m. Bishop of Cashel 122 – Hickleton Lady (IRE) 64 (Kala **–** Shikari 125) [2006 p6g Mar 30] sturdy mare: modest winner in 2004: missed 2005, and tailed off on return. *W. de Best-Turner*

EXMOOR 4 b.g. Cape Cross (IRE) 129 – Royal Jade 82 (Last Tycoon 131) [2006 83: **85** 6g² 6d 6d* 6m 6s 7g p7g 7s⁶ 6g³ Oct 16] tall gelding: fairly useful handicapper: won at Newbury in May: should stay 7f: acts on polytrack, good to firm and good to soft going: blinkered (ran respectably) final outing: has edged left: sold 22,000 gns, joined A. Al Raihe in UAE. *R. Charlton*

EXMOOR DANCER (IRE) 3 b.f. Mujahid (USA) 125 – Amy G (IRE) 52 (Common **–** Grounds 118) [2006 –: 7g 5.1g 5m⁶ 6m Aug 16] little form. *H. S. Howe*

EXPECTED BONUS (USA) 7 b. or br.g. Kris S (USA) – Nidd (USA) 112 (Known **54** Fact (USA) 135) [2006 –: p10g² p10g² 10.2m⁵ 10.9m 8d p10g p10g p10g⁴ p10g p10g⁴ Dec 22] lengthy gelding: poor walker: modest performer: stays 1¼m: acts on polytrack, firm and good to soft going: tried blinkered, wore cheekpieces last 3 starts: sometimes carries head awkwardly. *Jamie Poulton*

EXPEDIENCE (USA) 2 gr.f. (May 6) With Approval (CAN) – Promptly (IRE) 88 **63** (Lead On Time (USA) 123) [2006 p7g Oct 26] sixth foal: closely related to fairly useful 2002 2-y-o 6f/7f winner To The Rescue (by Cozzene) and half-sister to 3 winners, includ- ing 4-y-o Dart Along and smart 2003 2-y-o 7f/1m winner Fantastic View (by Distant View): dam, 6f and (US minor stakes) 1m winner, out of Nell Gwyn winner Ghariba: 10/1, faded into mid-field in maiden at Lingfield. *Sir Michael Stoute*

EXPENSIVE 3 b.f. Royal Applause 124 – Vayavaig 78 (Damister (USA) 123) [2006 **101** 98: 8m 8.1m³ 10.1f⁵ 8g⁴ 8.1g⁶ Aug 26] close-coupled, good-topped filly: useful perform- er: easily best effort in 2006 when close third to Star Cluster in listed race at Sandown: stays 1m, seemingly not 1¼m: raced mainly on good or firmer going (acts on good to firm). *C. F. Wall*

EXPENSIVE DETOUR (IRE) 2 b.c. (Mar 23) Namid 128 – Sail With The Wind 74 **79** (Saddlers' Hall (IRE) 126) [2006 5 9g³ 6m² 6d Sep 29] 18,500F, 17,000Y: good-topped colt: first foal: dam, Irish 1¼m/1½m winner, half-sister to useful 1¼m winner Shield: fair form: placed in maidens before ninth of 28 to Caldra in valuable sales race at Newmarket: will be suited by 7f/1m. *Mrs L. Stubbs*

EXPERIMENTAL (IRE) 12 b.g. Top of The World 103 – Brun's Toy (FR) (Bruni **58** 132) [2006 –: p8.6g f8g f8g f12g² Dec 29] formerly useful, modest nowadays: stays 1½m: acts on all-weather and any turf going. *John A. Harris*

EXPERT WITNESS (IRE) 3 b.f. Jade Robbery (USA) 121 – Golden Dancer (IRE) **81**
(Sadler's Wells (USA) 132) [2006 9.5v³ 9.5g⁴ 9d* 9g* 9g³ 11g⁵ 8m 10d Nov 4] third foal:
dam unraced sister to smart Irish 1¼m/1½m winner Briolette and half-sister to top-class
1¼m/1½m performer Pilsudski: won maiden at Saint-Malo in May and minor event there
in June: changed hands 50,000 gns after fifth start: left H-A. Pantall in France before
well held in listed race at Windsor on final outing: stays 9f: acts on good to soft ground.
M. R. Channon

EXPLODE 9 b.g. Zafonic (USA) 130 – Didicoy (USA) 104 (Danzig (USA)) [2006 8.1g **57 §**
8g 10g 9d 12s³ p12g Oct 29] modest performer: stays 1½m: acts on soft and good to firm
ground: blinkered last 3 starts: unreliable. *Miss L. C. Siddall*

EXPLOSIVE FOX (IRE) 5 ch.g. Foxhound (USA) 103 – Grise Mine (FR) 121 (Crys- **66**
tal Palace (FR) 132) [2006 68: p12.2g* p12.2g 12g p12.2g Sep 16] fair performer: won
handicap at Wolverhampton in April: below form after (seemingly amiss last 2 starts):
stays 1¾m: acts on polytrack, firm and good to soft going: effective with/without headgear. *S. Curran*

EXPONENTIAL (IRE) 4 b.g. Namid 128 – Exponent (USA) (Exbourne (USA) 125) **–**
[2006 –: p7.1g 6v Apr 4] fair winner at 2 yrs: lightly raced, and well held since: tried in
blinkers. *S. C. Williams*

EXPRESSION ECHO (IRE) 4 b.f. Bahhare (USA) 122 – Bint Alreeys (Polish Pre- **41**
cedent (USA) 131) [2006 59: p9.5g 12f 9.9f 9.9d 12d⁶ Oct 8] sparely-made filly: poor
maiden: should stay 1½m: acts on good to firm going: tried in cheekpieces: has flashed
tail. *A. G. Newcombe*

EXPRESS WILLY 2 b.g. (Apr 21) Hunting Lion (IRE) 115 – Express Girl 75 (Sylvan **–**
Express 117) [2006 5.1f⁴ 6g Jul 22] big, workmanlike gelding: has no near eye: well
beaten in maiden and seller (unseated to post). *J. R. Weymes*

EXPRESS WISH 2 b.c. (Mar 19) Danehill Dancer (IRE) 117 – Waffle On 89 (Chief **62 p**
Singer 131) [2006 7d 7g 7f Sep 29] good-topped, attractive colt: half-brother to several winners, including smart 7f/1m winner Madid (by Cape Cross) and useful 7f winner Desert
Alchemy (by Green Desert): dam 6f and (in France) 6.8f winner: 13/2 and backward,
eleventh of 14, pulling too hard, in maiden at Newmarket: should do better. *J. Noseda*

EXTEMPORISE (IRE) 6 ch.g. Indian Ridge 123 – No Rehearsal (FR) (Baillamont **62**
(USA) 124) [2006 52: f8g⁵ f7g⁶ p7g* May 23] sturdy gelding: fair performer: won
banded race at Kempton in May: stays 8.6f: acts on all-weather and heavy ground: tried
tongue tied. *T. T. Clement*

EXTRA COVER (IRE) 5 b.g. Danehill Dancer (IRE) 117 – Ballycurrane (IRE) **– §**
(Elbio 125) [2006 61§, a57§: f12g f12g³ f12g⁶ Jan 31] modest performer: left Ronald **a58 §**
Thompson after) second start: stays 1½m: acts on all-weather, soft and good to firm
going: has worn visor/blinkers: sometimes slowly away: ungenuine. *Miss V. Scott*

EXTRACTOR 2 b.g. (May 6) Siphon (BRZ) 130 – Tri Pac (IRE) (Fairy King (USA)) **61**
[2006 7f 7g 7f Sep 5] 11,500Y: quite good-topped gelding: fourth foal: dam unraced half-
sister to high-class 7f to 1¼m winner Timarida: modest form second start in maidens.
J. L. Dunlop

EXTRA MARK 4 b.g. Mark of Esteem (IRE) 137 – No Comebacks 70 (Last Tycoon **55**
131) [2006 67: p8g⁶ p7.1g⁶ Jan 9] just modest maiden in 2006: best at 5f/6f: acts on
all-weather and good to soft ground. *J. R. Best*

EXTRAORDINARY (IRE) 3 ch.f. Swain (IRE) 134 – Oumaldaaya (USA) 111 **–**
(Nureyev (USA) 131) [2006 7m Apr 21] 16,000Y: smallish filly: eighth foal: sister to
useful 1m/1¼m winner Ayun and closely related to 2 winners by Nashwan, notably smart
7f (at 2 yrs) to 9f winner Haami: dam, 7f (at 2 yrs) and 1¼m (Italian Group 2 event)
winner, half-sister to Derby winner Erhaab: 18/1, tailed off in maiden at Newbury: sold
7,500 gns in July. *P. W. Chapple-Hyam*

EXTRAVAGANCE 2 b.f. (Feb 10) King's Best (USA) 132 – Meritxell (IRE) **80**
(Thatching 131) [2006 6m² p8g Oct 20] 65,000F, 100,000Y: good-bodied filly: third foal:
sister to 1¼m winner in Norway and to winner in USA by Danehill: dam, French 1½m
winner, half-sister to very smart 1m/1¼m performer Almushtarak: promising 1½ lengths
second to Kaseema in maiden at Yarmouth: favourite, possibly amiss at Lingfield (eased):
should be suited by 1m/1¼m. *L. M. Cumani*

EXTREMELY RARE (IRE) 5 b.m. Mark of Esteem (IRE) 137 – Colourflash (IRE) **74 d**
(College Chapel 122) [2006 82: 6g 6m 6g⁴ 5.7s 5g 6m p5.1g 5.5g 5m⁵ 6f 6.1m 5.5d⁶ 6d
Oct 3] rather leggy mare: fair handicapper: below form after third start: effective at 5f/6f:

363

acts on heavy and good to firm going: tried in cheekpieces: usually races up with pace. *M. S. Saunders*

EYE CANDY (IRE) 5 b.g. Princely Heir (IRE) 111 – Timissa (IRE) 73 (Kahyasi 130) **79**
[2006 74: p13g⁴ p16.5g p12g 17d 14f Sep 10] fair nowadays: below form after reappearance (blinkered, trained second and third starts only by K. Ryan). *Mrs Sandra McCarthy, Ireland*

F

FABINE 2 b.f. (Apr 13) Danehill Dancer (IRE) 117 – Waypoint 95 (Cadeaux Genereux **70**
131) [2006 p7g³ p6g⁴ Nov 17] 75,000Y: fifth foal: half-sister to 2002 2-y-o 5f/5.5f (Prix Robert Papin) winner Never A Doubt (by Night Shift) and 5-y-o Primo Way, both useful: dam, 7f winner, half-sister to smart sprinter Acclamation: favourite, fair form in frame in maidens on polytrack. *B. J. Meehan*

FABRIAN 8 b.g. Danehill (USA) 126 – Dockage (CAN) (Riverman (USA) 131) [2006 **86**
81: 8d p10g⁶ 10m⁶ 8.2d 10d⁶ 8.3f 8.3f 8.1g* 8.1f³ 8.1m² 8m⁴ 10d² 9g² 10g 8.1m² 12m 10d* 7d Oct 28] strong gelding: fairly useful handicapper: won at Chepstow in July and Leicester in October: stays 1¼m: acts on polytrack, firm and good to soft going: tends to hang right: usually races up with pace: tough and consistent. *R. J. Price*

FABULEUX MILLIE (IRE) 2 ch.f. (Mar 2) Noverre (USA) 125 – Flying Millie **82 +**
(IRE) 99 (Flying Spur (AUS)) [2006 5m* 5.2g p6g* Sep 27] rather leggy, quite attractive filly: first foal: dam 5f (at 2 yrs)/6f winner: fairly useful form: won maiden at Windsor in July and nursery at Lingfield (by neck, with bit in hand) in September: too inexperienced in listed race in between: likely to stay 7f. *R. M. Beckett*

FABULOUS EMPEROR (IRE) 4 b.g. Imperial Ballet (IRE) 110 – Al Cairo (FR) **63**
(Vayrann 133) [2006 73d: p12g³ p12g Jan 28] modest maiden, lightly raced: stays 1½m: form only on polytrack: gelded, and joined W. Turner. *Jamie Poulton*

FACCHETTI (USA) 2 ch.c. (Apr 25) Storm Cat (USA) – Twenty Eight Carat (USA) **101**
(Alydar (USA)) [2006 6m⁴ 6m⁴ 5g 6s⁴ 6d⁵ 5d² 5v* Oct 23] sixth foal: half-brother to 2 winners in USA, notably very smart performer up to 1½m A P Valentine (by A P Indy): dam 6.5f/1m winner in USA: fair form at best prior to useful effort when winning 13-runner minor event at the Curragh in October by 9 lengths from Naigani, making all and well clear from 2f out: best effort at 5f on heavy ground: carried head awkwardly on debut. *A. P. O'Brien, Ireland*

FACTUAL LAD 8 b.g. So Factual (USA) 120 – Surprise Surprise 91 (Robellino (USA) **69**
127) [2006 79, a–: p9.5g 11.9g 10m 8.1g 10f* 10f⁴ 10m 10.2m² 10.2m⁴ Sep 7] close-coupled, workmanlike gelding: fair handicapper: won at Brighton (fourth course success) in July: stays 1¼m: acts on all-weather, firm and good to soft going: tried blinkered/in cheekpieces. *B. R. Millman*

FADANSIL 3 b.g. Dansili 127 – Fatah Flare (USA) 121 (Alydar (USA)) [2006 –: 8m **56**
7.1g 10.1m² 11.1g⁶ 8s Sep 28] deep-girthed gelding: modest maiden: stays 1¼m: acts on good to firm going. *J. Wade*

FADE TO GREY (IRE) 2 gr.g. (Apr 28) Aljabr (USA) 125 – Aly McBear (USA) **–**
(Alydeed (CAN) 120) [2006 6g 7m 7f Jun 24] no form. *W. G. M. Turner*

FADEYEV (IRE) 2 b.g. (Feb 26) Imperial Ballet (IRE) 110 – Inga (IRE) 77 (Project **70**
Manager 111) [2006 6f⁴ 7m⁵ 6s² 6g 6m³ 6d Sep 29] €17,000F, €30,000Y: small, workmanlike gelding: second foal: dam Irish 10.5f winner: fair maiden: runner-up at Ripon in August: below form in cheekpieces last 3 starts: will prove best at 5f/6f: acts on soft and good to firm going: sold 5,000 gns. *K. A. Ryan*

FAIR ALONG (GER) 4 b.g. Alkalde (GER) – Fairy Tango (FR) (Acatenango (GER) **92**
127) [2006 69: 12g⁴ 14.1g⁴ 14.1g* 16d⁴ Sep 23] rather leggy, quite good-topped gelding: fairly useful performer: much improved in 2006 and made all in 2 handicaps at Salisbury in August, latter by 8 lengths: seemed not to stay 2m final start: will prove best at 1½m/1¾m: acts on all-weather and good to firm going: raced freely in cheekpieces final 3-y-o start: small hurdler/novice chaser, unbeaten in 3 races over fences in November/December. *P. J. Hobbs*

FAIRDONNA 3 ch.f. Bertolini (USA) 125 – Shamrock Fair (IRE) 77 (Shavian 125) **71**
[2006 8.3g⁵ 8.1m p8g 7.1d p7.1g⁶ p7.1g³ p7.1g² p7.1g² Dec 21] leggy filly: fourth foal: half-sister to 6-y-o Fair Shake: dam 2-y-o 7f winner: fair maiden: stays 8.3f: acts on polytrack, best effort on turf on good going. *D. J. Coakley*

FAIRFIELD PRINCESS 2 b.f. (Jan 25) Inchinor 119 – Cool Question 99 (Polar **85**
Falcon (USA) 126) [2006 5g⁴ p5g* p5g³ 5m⁵ 5.1f² 6f 5m⁶ p5g³ 5.5m³ 5m⁴ 5s² Oct 2]
75,000Y: leggy, quite attractive filly: has a quick action: first foal: dam 5f/6f winner (ran
only at 2 yrs): fairly useful performer: won maiden at Kempton in April: held her form
well after, in frame 6 times, in nurseries last 3 starts: effective at 5f/6f: unraced on heavy
going, acts on any other turf and polytrack: sold 25,000 gns. *N. A. Callaghan*

FAIRGAME MAN 8 ch.g. Clantime 101 – Thalya (Crofthall 110) [2006 59, a34: 5.2g **55**
6m 5.9m 5f 5f 5f 5m 6m³ 6g Aug 5] strong gelding: modest handicapper: best at 5f/6f:
acts on firm and good to soft going: sometimes wears cheekpieces/visor. *J. S. Wainwright*

FAIRLIGHT EXPRESS (IRE) 6 ch.g. Carroll House 132 – Marble Fontaine (La- **70**
fontaine (USA) 117) [2006 11.9m 12.1d³ f11g³ 12m p12.2g⁶ Sep 16] lightly-raced **a52**
maiden on Flat, fair on turf, modest on all-weather: stays 1½m: left Stef Liddiard after
fourth outing: won over hurdles in September. *B. G. Powell*

FAIRLY HONEST 2 br.g. (Apr 10) Alhaarth (IRE) 126 – Miller's Melody 86 (Chief **75**
Singer 131) [2006 6g 7f 7m⁴ p7g³ p8.6g⁵ Nov 23] 24,000Y: leggy, close-coupled gelding:
half-brother to several winners, including 8-y-o Top Dirham and useful German 1¼m/
1½m performer Metaxas (by Midyan): dam disappointing maiden: fair maiden: third
(of 4) in nursery at Lingfield, hanging badly before closing well: will stay 1m: gelded
after final start. *D. R. C. Elsworth*

FAIRMILE 4 b.g. Spectrum (IRE) 126 – Juno Marlowe (IRE) 100 (Danehill (USA) **107**
126) [2006 93: 12g 10.3m p10g* 9.9g² 10.4f* 10.5m² 9d Sep 30] tall gelding: has a quick
action: useful handicapper: further improvement in 2006, winning at Kempton in June
and John Smith's Cup at York (beat Bravo Maestro by ¾ length) in July: looked unlucky
when 1½ lengths second to Dansili Dancer in valuable event at Haydock next start, needing to weave through: run best ignored in Cambridgeshire at Newmarket final outing,
going well in disadvantaged group: should stay 1½m: acts on polytrack, firm and soft
going: sold 280,000 gns, and joined I. Mohammed in UAE. *W. R. Swinburn*

FAIR NASHWAN 4 b.f. Nashwan (USA) 135 – Fairy Sensazione (Fairy King (USA)) **120**
[2006 102: 10d² 10m* 11m⁵ 11m³ 10d* 11d* 12g² 10m Nov 5] first foal: dam Italian 7f
(at 2 yrs) to 9f winner: very smart performer: won 3 times at 3 yrs, including listed race at
Milan, and third at same course in Oaks d'Italia: successful at Milan in 2006 in limited
handicap in May, minor event in September and Premio Federico Tesio (by ½ length from
Groom Tesse) in October: excelled herself when head second to Laverock in Gran Premio
del Jockey Club Italiano there next time: below form in Premio Roma final outing: stays
1½m: acts on good to firm and good to soft ground: has had tongue tied. *B. Grizzetti, Italy*

John Smith's Cup (Handicap), York—
the progressive Fairmile is given a good ride by apprentice Adam Kirby;
they are followed by Bravo Maestro (outside), Boo (second right), Forgery (rail) and Chantaco (diamonds)

FAIRNILEE 2 b.f. (Mar 17) Selkirk (USA) 129 – Fantastic Belle (IRE) 79 (Night Shift **59 p**
(USA)) [2006 p5.1g³ Dec 22] third foal: dam, 6f winner, half-sister to 4-y-o Fantaisiste: dam, 6f winner,
half-sister to smart performer up to 1½m Germano: 9/2, caught the eye when 4½ lengths
third of 6 to Elraheer in maiden at Wolverhampton, losing several lengths at start and
nearest finish, not knocked about: should stay 7f: will improve. *Sir Mark Prescott*

FAIR 'N SQUARE (IRE) 2 b.f. (Apr 26) Fath (USA) 116 – Icefern 88 (Moorestyle **57**
137) [2006 5g 5.1g⁶ 5.1f⁶ 5.3f* 6f⁴ 6m⁴ 5.1f 6d Oct 3] €4,500Y: half-sister to several winners, including useful 1m winner Iamus (by Most Welcome) and fairly useful 2003 2-y-o
5f winner Mac The Knife (by Daggers Drawn): dam sprinter: modest performer: won
maiden at Brighton in June: effective at 5f/6f: acts on firm going: sold 1,800 gns, sent to
Sweden. *J. L. Spearing*

FAIR SHAKE (IRE) 6 b.g. Sheikh Albadou 128 – Shamrock Fair (IRE) 77 (Shavian **75**
125) [2006 84: p9.5g p8.6g 8.3f³ 8.9m 8m⁴ 8d⁵ 7m 7d 7s Oct 14] close-coupled gelding:
fair handicapper: stays 1m: acts on firm and soft ground: usually wears cheekpieces/
visor: sold 9,000 gns. *Karen McLintock*

FAIR SPIN 6 ch.g. Pivotal 124 – Frankie Fair (IRE) 73 (Red Sunset 120) [2006 64d: **56**
10d⁴ 10d 12.3m 16d* 17.1d 16v Oct 25] smallish, sturdy gelding: modest handicapper:
won at Ripon in August: stays 2m: acts on any going: sometimes wears headgear.
M. D. Hammond

FAIRY MONARCH (IRE) 7 b.g. Ali-Royal (IRE) 127 – Cookawara (IRE) (Fairy **57**
King (USA)) [2006 59: p9.5g 9.8m 8.3f⁴ 7.9m 8f⁴ 9.9f 8f 8.5g⁶ 9m³ 8.5m⁶ 9.9m³ 10m⁶
8d* p10g⁴ Oct 29] compact gelding: modest performer: won banded race at Musselburgh
in October: effective at 1m to 1½m: yet to race on heavy going, acts on any other turf, and
polytrack: wears headgear: tried tongue tied earlier in career: has reportedly bled: difficult ride. *P. T. Midgley*

FAIRY SLIPPER 2 b.f. (Apr 5) Singspiel (IRE) 133 – Fairlee Mixa (FR) (Linamix **–**
(FR) 127) [2006 7.5g 8m Sep 21] third foal: dam, French 2-y-o 6f winner (later successful
in USA), sister to very smart French 1¼m/1½m performer Fair Mix: well held in maidens. *Jedd O'Keeffe*

FAIRYTALE OF YORK (IRE) 3 b.f. Imperial Ballet (IRE) 110 – Pekanski (IRE) 90 **–**
(Sri Pekan (USA) 117) [2006 –: 12.1f 10m 12.1g⁶ 10.1m 11s Aug 13] little form: tried
visored. *D. Carroll*

FAITH AND REASON (USA) 3 b.g. Sunday Silence (USA) – Sheer Reason (USA) **90**
110 (Danzig (USA)) [2006 88: p10g⁴ p10g² 11.6m⁵ Jul 17] good-bodied gelding: fairly
useful performer, lightly raced: stays 1¼m: acts on polytrack and good to firm going:
visored (seemingly outbattled) final start: gelded after: sold 32,000 gns in October, and
joined B. Curley. *Saeed bin Suroor*

FAITHISFLYING 4 ch.g. Wolfhound (USA) 126 – Niggle 65 (Night Shift (USA)) **–**
[2006 37§, a48§: f6g⁵ f6g f8g² f6g² f7g³ f8g* p8.6g p8.6g f7g f8g 7.5f Jul 7] workmanlike **a53**
gelding: modest performer: won maiden claimer at Southwell in April: effective at 6f to
1m: acts on all-weather: wears blinkers/cheekpieces. *D. W. Chapman*

FAJR (IRE) 4 b.g. Green Desert (USA) 127 – Ta Rib (USA) 116 (Mr Prospector (USA)) **90**
[2006 62: p8g* p7g* p8g² p8g* p8g* 8m* p7g p8g⁵ 8g³ Sep 28] good-bodied gelding:
fairly useful handicapper: progressed well in 2006, winning at Lingfield in February
(2, left N. King after second occasion), April and May, and Newmarket later in May:
stays 1m: acts on polytrack and good to firm ground: held up and tends to idle in front.
Miss Gay Kelleway

FAKE LEFT 3 ch.c. Foxhound (USA) 103 – Ragged Moon 72 (Raga Navarro (ITY) **–**
119) [2006 p7g p9.5g Oct 28] in rear in maidens at Lingfield and Wolverhampton (blinkered). *B. P. J. Baugh*

FALCON FLYER 2 br.f. (Feb 19) Cape Cross (IRE) 129 – Green Danube (USA) 92 **–**
(Irish River (FR) 131) [2006 p6g 7g 6g Aug 25] 21,000Y: close-coupled filly: half-sister
to several winners, including 4-y-o Bank On Benny: dam 7.6f and 1¼m winner: little
form in maidens. *J. R. Best*

FALCON'S FIRE (IRE) 2 b.c. (Mar 28) Orpen (USA) 116 – Tres Chic (USA) **60**
(Northern Fashion (USA) 114) [2006 6s 7.1d⁵ f7g⁴ Nov 13] modest form in maidens.
Mrs A. Duffield

FALIMAR 2 b.f. (Feb 10) Fasliyev (USA) 120 – Mar Blue (FR) 75 (Marju (IRE) 127) **66**
[2006 p6g 7f³ 7d Aug 13] 28,000Y: rather leggy filly: first living foal: dam, Irish 9f winner, out of half-sister to dam of Westerner: fair maiden: third at York: will prove suited by
1m+. *Miss J. A. Camacho*

FALKIRK (NZ) 6 br.h. Tale of The Cat (USA) 113 – Madam Valeta (NZ) (Palace **118**
Music (USA) 129) [2006 5.5g* 6s 5m⁴ 6m Jul 14] lengthy, good-topped horse: half-
brother to several winners in Australasia, including Group 2 9f winner Mulan Princess
(by Kaapstad): dam Group 3 6f winner in New Zealand and 7f listed winner in Australia:
smart performer: won 8 of his 22 starts, including three Group 2/3 events in 2004:
successful in Group 3 Gilgai Stakes at Flemington in 2005: won listed handicap on same
course in March by short head from Message Bank: shaped well when close equal-fourth
of 28 to Takeover Target in King's Stand Stakes at Royal Ascot on third start, finishing
best of all: ridden far more prominently when below form in July Cup at Newmarket final
outing, tending to hang: was effective at 5f to 6.5f: acted on good to firm and good to soft
going, well held only outing on soft: wore blinkers: tongue tied last 2 starts: moody type:
to stand at Windsor Park Stud, New Zealand, fee NZ$8,000. *Lee Freedman, Australia*

FALLAL PARC 3 ch.g. Tachyon Park 87 – Fallal (IRE) 47 (Fayruz 116) [2006 –: p7g **–**
p7.1g f7g² 7g⁶ f7g⁶ 7.1g 7d a8g² a8g² Nov 1] poor maiden: left M. Harris for seventh **a39**
start: second at Mons last 2 outings (trained by C. Von Der Recke penultimate start only):
stays easy 1m: acts on fibresand. *Mme C. Lenaerrs, Belgium*

FALMASSIM 3 b.c. Mozart (IRE) 131 – Scostes (Cadeaux Genereux 131) [2006 6.1m⁴ **77**
6d⁴ 6m* p6g 6m⁴ 7d⁶ Aug 21] sturdy colt: fourth living foal: half-brother to 2004 2-y-o
1m winner in Italy Famcapii (by Montjeu): dam fairly useful Italian 7f to 9f winner: fair
performer: won maiden at Windsor in July: should stay 7f: acts on good to firm ground,
well beaten on polytrack: sold 18,000 gns. *L. M. Cumani*

FALPIASE (IRE) 4 b.g. Montjeu (IRE) 137 – Gift of The Night (USA) (Slewpy **80**
(USA)) [2006 10.5m³ p12g² 10d⁶ Oct 4] big, good-topped gelding: half-brother to several
winners, notably top-class 1m to 1½m performer Falbrav (by Fairy King): dam French
2-y-o 7.5f winner: fairly useful maiden: blinkered, similar form when placed at Haydock
(wandered) and Lingfield: failed to settle when well below form final outing: stays easy
1½m: acts on polytrack and good to firm going: temperament under suspicion: sold
65,000 gns, joined J. Howard Johnson, then gelded. *L. M. Cumani*

FAMCRED 3 b.f. Inchinor 119 – Sumingasefa (Danehill (USA) 126) [2006 88p: p7g³ **89**
8.2g² 8f p8g⁵ Jul 19] good-topped filly: fairly useful performer: stays 1m: acts on polytrack and good to firm going: sold 12,000 gns in October, joined P. Phelan. *L. M. Cumani*

FAME 6 ch.g. Northern Amethyst 99 – First Sapphire (Simply Great (FR) 122) [2006 –: **74**
p10g 10.1m⁶ 9.9d 10m⁶ 10d May 19] tall, lengthy, angular gelding: fair maiden: left
P. Hobbs after reappearance: stays 1½m: acts on polytrack and good to firm going: tongue
tied last 2 starts. *W. Jarvis*

FAMILIAR AFFAIR 5 b.g. Intikhab (USA) 135 – Familiar (USA) 96 (Diesis 133) **–**
[2006 –: p8.6g f8g p8g Feb 8] leggy, close-coupled gelding: has a rather round action: fair
performer at 3 yrs: lightly raced and well held since: *T. D. Barron*

FAMILIAR TERRITORY 3 br.c. Cape Cross (IRE) 129 – Forever Fine (USA) (Sun- **103**
shine Forever (USA)) [2006 97: 9.9f⁴ 10s³ Aug 26] big, good-topped colt: useful performer, lightly raced: ran well in 2006, fourth to Road To Love in ladbrokes.com Stakes
(Handicap) at Goodwood then 1¾ lengths third to Forroger in handicap at Newmarket
(swished tail): will be suited by 1½m: acts on firm and soft going. *Saeed bin Suroor*

FANCY WOMAN 2 b.f. (May 9) Sakhee (USA) 136 – Fancy Wrap (Kris 135) [2006 **–**
7d Oct 28] 3,000Y: good-topped filly: fifth foal: dam, ran twice, sister to Royal Lodge
Stakes winner Reach: last in maiden at Newmarket. *J. L. Dunlop*

FANCY YOU (IRE) 3 b.f. Mull of Kintyre (USA) 114 – Sunset Park (IRE) 61 (Red **48**
Sunset 120) [2006 54: 8s 8d⁶ 5m 6g p5.1g⁵ Sep 11] good-topped filly: poor maiden:
trained for reappearance only by T. Pitt: should stay 6f: acts on polytrack and soft ground:
tried visored. *A. W. Carroll*

FANGORN FOREST (IRE) 3 b.f. Shinko Forest (IRE) – Edge of Darkness 62 **77**
(Vaigly Great 127) [2006 83, a64+: f7g² p7g p8g⁵ 8.3m p7.1g 7.1d⁴* 7s 8s 7m⁶ 8.3m 7m⁶ **a61**
Jul 21] lengthy, workmanlike filly: fair performer on turf, modest on all-weather: left
K. Ryan after second start: won handicap at Warwick in May: below form after: stays 7f:
acts on all-weather, good to firm and good to soft ground: wears cheekpieces. *R. A. Harris*

FANLIGHT FANNY (USA) 2 b.f. (Feb 20) Lear Fan (USA) 130 – Miss Nureyev **90**
(USA) (Nureyev (USA) 131) [2006 5m² 5.1m* 5d² 5g Sep 8] $13,000Y, 22,000 2-y-o:
compact filly: first foal: dam unraced out of half-sister to US Grade 3 7f winner Devil's
Bride: fairly useful form: won maiden at Chepstow in August: improvement when second
to Not For Me in listed race at York later in month: stiff task in Flying Childers Stakes

there (last of 9) final start: will prove best at 5f/6f: sold 120,000 gns, sent to USA. *P. Winkworth*

FANN (USA) 3 b.f. Diesis 133 – Forest Storm (USA) (Woodman (USA) 126) [2006 69: **83** p8g⁴ p10g⁴ 9.8g² 9d* 9.9g⁶ Jun 13] sturdy filly: fairly useful handicapper: won at Sandown in May: better at 9f/1¼m than 1m: acts on polytrack, firm and good to soft going: free-going sort. *C. E. Brittain*

FANTAISISTE 4 b.f. Nashwan (USA) 135 – Fantastic Belle (IRE) 79 (Night Shift **90** (USA)) [2006 92: p6g* 7g⁶ p6g* 6m 6f 6f⁵ Jul 3] strong, useful-looking filly useful **a103** handicapper on all-weather, fairly useful on turf: better than ever when twice winning impressively at Kempton in April, beating Idle Power by 1¾ lengths in latter: below form last 3 starts, blinkered on final one: stayed 7f: acted on polytrack and firm going: reportedly in foal to Cadeaux Genereux. *P. F. I. Cole*

FANTASTIC ARTS (FR) 6 b.g. Royal Applause 124 – Magic Arts (IRE) 76 (Fairy **–** King (USA)) [2006 15.9g Aug 26] fairly useful performer when trained by Mme J. Laurent-Joye Rossi in France at 2/3 yrs, winning at up to 15f: well beaten only Flat start in Britain: acts on soft going: won over hurdles in November. *Miss Venetia Williams*

FANTASTIC DELIGHT 3 b.f. Fantastic Light (USA) 134 – Putout 69 (Dowsing **–** (USA) 124) [2006 9m Aug 31] half-sister to 3 winning sprinters, including useful 2001 2-y-o 6f winner Rajab (by Selkirk): dam, 5f winner, half-sister to smart French sprinter Pole Position: very green and showed nothing in maiden at Redcar. *G. M. Moore*

FANTASTIC PROMISE (USA) 3 b.f. Fantastic Light (USA) 134 – Extra Fancy **61** (USA) (Danzig (USA)) [2006 p9.5g⁵ p12g⁵ p8g Sep 27] first foal: dam, US 1m/1¼m winner, close relative of US Grade 1 9f/1¼m winner Possibly Perfect and Horris Hill winner Makhlab: modest form in maidens first 2 starts: sent to USA. *J. H. M. Gosden*

FANTASTISCH (IRE) 3 b.f. Fantastic Light (USA) 134 – Alexandra S (IRE) (Sad- **85** ler's Wells (USA) 132) [2006 74: 10g⁴ 8.1m* 8f⁵ 9m Aug 27] lengthy filly: fairly useful performer: best effort when winning handicap at Sandown in June, flashing tail: best form at 1m, though bred to stay further: acts on good to firm ground: refused to enter stall once at 2 yrs. *H. R. A. Cecil*

FANTASY BELIEVER 8 b.g. Sure Blade (USA) 130 – Delicious 51 (Dominion 123) **115** [2006 101: 6m 6s 6m⁶ 6m 7m⁵ 6m 6g³ 6f* 6m⁴ 6f 6f* 6s 6g* 5.4g* 6d 5g* 6g Oct 13] sturdy gelding: smart performer: better than ever at 8 yrs, winning handicaps at Pontefract, Goodwood (2) and York (Ladbrokes Portland, beat One Putra by 3 lengths), and listed event at Newmarket (best effort when beating Prince Tamino by short head) between July/September: never in contention (held up from poor draw) in Bentinck Stakes at Newmarket final start: effective at 5f to 7f: acts on any going: sometimes hangs/carries head awkwardly: usually waited with nowadays. *J. J. Quinn*

Ladbrokes Portland (Handicap), York—in a race transferred from Doncaster, eight-year-old Fantasy Believer shows improved form to beat One Putra (quartered cap), Hogmaneigh (broad white face), Texas Gold (second left), Woodcote (partially hidden by winner) and Treasure Cay (second right)

FANTASY CRUSADER 7 ch.g. Beveled (USA) – Cranfield Charger (Northern State 62
(USA) 91) [2006 63: 10g⁴ p10g* 9m⁵ 9.7f² p8g 10f³ p10g 10f* 9m⁵ 9.7f p9.5g p9.5g
p10g p10g Dec 22] modest performer: won banded race at Kempton in May and handicap
at Brighton in August: stays 1¼m: acts on polytrack and firm going: has worn headgear:
tried tongue tied: none too consistent. *R. M. H. Cowell*

FANTASY DEFENDER (IRE) 4 b.g. Fayruz 116 – Mrs Lucky (Royal Match 117) 57
[2006 60: p8.6g p10g p8g³ 8.3m⁵ 8.1f² 8m⁶ 8f³ 8f⁵ 7.6m* 8f 8m 8m p8g⁶ p7g⁶ p9.5g³ **a54**
p8.6g² p8g⁵ Dec 10] good-topped gelding: modest performer: won handicap at Lingfield
in July: seems to stay easy 9.5f: acts on all-weather, firm and good to soft going: tried in
cheekpieces, visored nowadays. *E. R. Oertel*

FANTASY EXPLORER 3 b.g. Compton Place 125 – Zinzi (Song 132) [2006 52: 96
p5.1g² p5g* 5m² 5m* 5g* 5f* 5d³ 5g Sep 23] rather leggy, good-topped gelding: useful
handicapper: won at Kempton in May, Newmarket (2) in June and Ayr in July: below
form final start, carrying head awkwardly and not finding much: may prove best at 5f:
acts on polytrack, firm and good to soft going. *J. J. Quinn*

FANTASY LEGEND (IRE) 3 ch.g. Beckett (IRE) 116 – Sianiski (Niniski (USA) –
125) [2006 p9.5g p9.5g p12g f12g p12.2s Dec 13] little form: blinkered final outing.
N. P. Littmoden

FANTASY PARKES 2 ch.f. (Apr 17) Fantastic Light (USA) 134 – My Melody Parkes 82 p
102 (Teenoso (USA) 135) [2006 6m* Sep 22] leggy filly: has a fluent action: fifth foal:
half-sister to 3-y-o Bajan Parkes: dam, 5f winner (including at 2 yrs), half-sister to useful
sprinters Summerhill Parkes and Lucky Parkes: 4/1, won 17-runner maiden at Haydock
by ½ length from Mimisel, learning all the time and not needing full drive: sure to progress. *K. A. Ryan*

FANTASY RIDE 4 b.g. Bahhare (USA) 122 – Grand Splendour 79 (Shirley Heights –
130) [2006 12d 10s p9.5g Dec 9] rather leggy, quite attractive gelding: has a markedly
round action: missed 2005 and well held in 2006. *J. Pearce*

FARADAY (IRE) 3 b.c. Montjeu (IRE) 137 – Fureau (GER) (Ferdinand (USA)) [2006 ?
10d⁴ 8g⁶ 11d⁴ 10g³ 11g³ p9.5g Dec 29] third foal: half-brother to 4-y-o Floriot and
German 11/1¼m winner Fantasmatic (by Lomitas): dam German 7f to 8.5f winner: ran
in Italy at 2 yrs, better effort in maidens at Milan when third: third in maidens at Munich
in 2006 for W. Glanz in Germany: no show in handicap on British debut final 3-y-o start:
stays 11f: acts on good to soft going. *B. J. Curley*

FARAFRAN (IRE) 3 b.f. Rainbow Quest (USA) 134 – Sahara Star 95 (Green Desert 55
(USA) 127) [2006 10g Apr 21] small, sparely-made filly: closely related to fairly useful
7.5f/1m winner Star Invader (by Nashwan) and half-sister to several winners, including
smart sprinter Land of Dreams (by Cadeaux Genereux) and useful 1½m winner Edraak
(by Shirley Heights): dam 2-y-o 5f (including Molecomb Stakes) winner: 9/1, 10¾
lengths eighth to Divine River in maiden at Newbury: sent to Australia. *E. A. L. Dunlop*

FARA'S KINGDOM 2 ch.g. (May 1) Groom Dancer (USA) 128 – Kingdom Ruby –
(IRE) 70 (Bluebird (USA) 125) [2006 6g p8.6m Oct 31] well beaten in maidens. *Miss
J. A. Camacho*

FARAWAY ECHO 5 gr.m. Second Empire (IRE) 124 – Salalah 62 (Lion Cavern –
(USA) 117) [2006 –: 13.8s⁵ Oct 14] rather leggy mare: modest handicapper at 3 yrs:
lightly raced and well held on Flat since: ran creditably both tries in visor. *James Moffatt*

FARDI (IRE) 4 b.g. Green Desert (USA) 127 – Shuruk 73 (Cadeaux Genereux 131) 67
[2006 69: 7g 9.9d 12m⁴ 12g 14.1g 14m 12g Jul 3] rather leggy gelding: fair performer:
form in 2006 only on third start: stays 1½m: acts on good to firm going: tried blinkered.
K. W. Hogg, Isle of Man

FAREFIELD LODGE (IRE) 2 b.c. (Jan 18) Indian Lodge (IRE) 127 – Fieldfare 78
(Selkirk (USA) 129) [2006 5.7g 6g² Jun 13] €16,000Y: first foal: dam, French maiden,
half-sister to very smart 7f winner Trade Fair: better effort in maidens (hampered debut)
when neck second to Sans Reward at Salisbury. *C. G. Cox*

FARES (IRE) 2 b.c. (Feb 27) Mark of Esteem (IRE) 137 – Iftitan (USA) (Southern Halo 90
(USA)) [2006 6m⁵ p7g⁵ 7m³ 7.5g⁴ 8.1v⁶ 7d 6g p8g³ p7.1g* p7.1g* p7g² Dec 20] rather
leggy, quite attractive colt: first foal: dam unraced half-sister to US Grade 3 8.5f winner
Silent Greeting: fairly useful performer: won nursery and minor event (hung left) at Wolverhampton within a week in November: good second in minor event at Kempton final
start: stays 1m: acts on polytrack and good to firm going: blinkered last 4 starts: quirky.
C. E. Brittain

FAREWELL GIFT 5 b.g. Cadeaux Genereux 131 – Daring Ditty (Daring March 116) **84**
[2006 82: p8g² p8g* p7g³ p8g⁵ 8d p8g⁴ 8.3f 8m⁴ 8.1m p8g Oct 11] big, good-topped gelding: fairly useful handicapper: won at Lingfield in January: stays 1m: acts on polytrack, soft and good to firm going: has been visored, usually blinkered. *R. Hannon*

FARLEIGH HOUSE (USA) 2 b.c. (Feb 10) Lear Fan (USA) 130 – Verasina (USA) **89**
83 (Woodman (USA) 126) [2006 6m⁵ 7f² 7d² 7f* Sep 5] well-made colt: first foal: dam, second at 1m both starts, out of high-class performer up to 1m Vilikaia: fairly useful form: twice runner-up in maidens at Newmarket (behind Rallying Cry then Gold Option) prior to winning similar event at Lingfield readily by 2 lengths: will stay 1m: acts on firm and good to soft going. *M. H. Tompkins*

FARLEY STAR 2 b.f. (Feb 15) Alzao (USA) 117 – Girl of My Dreams (IRE) 51 (Marju **82 p**
(IRE) 127) [2006 p7g³ 7g* 7d⁶ Sep 24] useful-looking filly: fifth foal: sister to smart 2002 2-y-o 6f/7f (Rockfel Stakes) winner Luvah Girl, later successful in USA: dam 7f winner: fairly useful form: won maiden at Folkestone (beat Blithe by neck) in August: better than bare result (not clear run) in nursery at Ascot: will stay 1m: type to progress further. *R. Charlton*

FARNBOROUGH (USA) 5 b.g. Lear Fan (USA) 130 – Gretel 100 (Hansel (USA)) **62**
[2006 60, a67: p12.2g p10g p9.5g p8.6g² p9.5g p9.5g⁶ p9.5g f12g² p12.2g 14.1d p9.5g⁶ p10g May 23] modest performer: effective at 1m to easy 1½m: acts on all-weather and good to soft ground: tends to edge left. *R. J. Price*

FARNE ISLAND 3 ch.c. Arkadian Hero (USA) 123 – Holy Island 81 (Deploy 131) **66**
[2006 65p: 9.8g 8s 7.5f⁴ 8d⁴ 9m² 8.5f* 9.3f⁴ 8m 8g Aug 14] sturdy colt: fair handicapper: won apprentice event at Beverley in July: below form after: should be suited by 1¼m+ (dam 1¼m/1½m winner): acts on polytrack, firm and good going. *J. J. Quinn*

FARNE ISLE 7 ch.m. Midnight Legend 118 – Biloela 67 (Nicholas Bill 125) [2006 68: **–**
18v 15.8d 12g 11.9m Jul 6] leggy mare: lightly-raced maiden: fair form at best: well held in 2006: tried in cheekpieces/tongue tie. *G. A. Harker*

FAR NOTE (USA) 8 ch.g. Distant View (USA) 126 – Descant (USA) (Nureyev (USA) **–**
131) [2006 61, a71: p6g f6g⁵ f7g³ f7g p6g f6g f6g⁶ Nov 2] sturdy, well-made gelding: **a64**
modest performer: has form at 7f, probably best at 5f/6f: acts on fibresand, firm and good to soft going: tried in cheekpieces: blinkered and tongue tied nowadays: sometimes makes running: none too consistent. *S. R. Bowring*

FARRIERS CHARM 5 b.m. In Command (IRE) 114 – Carn Maire 83 (Northern Pros- **–**
pect (USA)) [2006 71: p9.5g p9.5g Jan 30] well-made mare: fair performer at best: well held in 2006: tried visored. *D. J. Coakley*

FARRINGDON 3 b.g. Sadler's Wells (USA) 132 – Rebecca Sharp 122 (Machiavellian **80**
(USA) 123) [2006 57p: 10m* 10d³ 11.7f Sep 9] fairly useful performer: won maiden at Windsor in July: below form in handicaps after: should be suited by 1½m: acts on good to firm ground: sold 21,000 gns. *M. P. Tregoning*

FAR SEEKING 2 b.c. (Apr 16) Distant Music (USA) 126 – House Hunting (Zafonic **62 p**
(USA) 130) [2006 7g Oct 12] good-bodied colt: has scope: has a quick action: fourth foal: half-brother to winner in Greece by Kahyasi: dam unraced daughter of Poule d'Essai des Pouliches winner Houseproud: 25/1, burly and green, eighth of fifteen in maiden at Newmarket, not knocked about: open to improvement. *Mrs A. J. Perrett*

FASCINATIN RHYTHM 2 br.f. (Apr 11) Fantastic Light (USA) 134 – Marguerite de **70 +**
Vine (Zilzal (USA) 137) [2006 p8g⁵ p8g³ Dec 8] second foal: dam unraced half-sister to dam of Rock of Gibraltar: fair form in maiden/minor event at Kempton: should stay 1¼m. *V. Smith*

FASHION CHIC 3 b.f. Averti (IRE) 117 – Fashion Bride (IRE) (Prince Rupert (FR) **–**
121) [2006 –: p6g p5g Feb 21] little form. *Stef Liddiard*

FASHION DISASTER 3 b.f. Weldnaas (USA) 129 – Give Us A Treat (Cree Song 99) **–**
[2006 p8.6g 6d 5g 5m Jun 5] rather leggy filly: half-sister to 5f (at 2 yrs) to 7f winner Whippasnapper (by Cayman Kai): dam maiden who should have stayed 1m: no sign of ability. *A. Crook*

FASHION MODEL 2 b.f. (May 18) Rainbow Quest (USA) 134 – Gracious Beauty **79 p**
(USA) 67 (Nijinsky (CAN) 138) [2006 7d³ Oct 3] lengthy filly: closely related to useful 1¼m/1½m winner Jazil (by Nashwan) and half-sister to 2 winners, including 11.5f winner who stayed 15f Labeed (by Riverman): dam, maiden who stayed 1¼m, sister to Grade 1 9f/1¼m winner Maplejinsky (dam of champion US older mare Sky Beauty) and

closely related to outstanding sprinter Dayjur: 12/1, close third to Hi Calypso in maiden at Leicester: will do better as a 3-y-o, particularly at 1¼m/1½m. *M. A. Jarvis*

FASHION STATEMENT 2 b.f. (Apr 13) Rainbow Quest (USA) 134 – Shabby Chic (USA) 114 (Red Ransom (USA)) [2006 7f 8.3m* 8v* 10d³ Oct 28] smallish, well-made filly: fourth foal: half-sister to 3-y-o Kerriemuir Lass: dam, French 1¼m winner, sister to Oaks winner Casual Look: fairly useful form: won maiden at Ayr (by 8 lengths) in October: more improvement when third to Empire Day in listed race at Newmarket: will be suited by 1½m+: acts on heavy going, promise on good to firm. *M. A. Jarvis* **89**

FAST BOWLER 3 b.g. Intikhab (USA) 135 – Alegria 94 (Night Shift (USA)) [2006 83p: 6m* 7m 7m⁵ p8g p7g Nov 13] small, heavy-topped gelding: fairly useful performer: off 11 months and gelded, won handicap at Windsor in July: not seen to best advantage after (said to have bled final outing): stays 1m: acts on polytrack and good to firm ground. *J. M. P. Eustace* **87**

FAST FREDDIE 2 b.g. (Feb 23) Agnes World (USA) 123 – Bella Chica (IRE) 95 (Bigstone (IRE) 126) [2006 p5g² p5g³ 5m Aug 1] 34,000F, 35,000Y: lengthy, good-topped gelding: first foal: dam 5f/6f winner at 2 yrs, out of half-sister to smart 6f to 1m winner Pipe Major: fair maiden: twice placed at Lingfield, good speed: off 4 months (and gelded), pulled up lame in Molecomb Stakes at Goodwood: will prove best at 5f. *T. J. Pitt* **75**

FAST HEART 5 b.g. Fasliyev (USA) 120 – Heart of India (IRE) (Try My Best (USA) 130) [2006 107: 5d⁶ p6g 5g⁴ 6g⁶ 5m³ 5m 7.1m 6d p7g⁴ p6g p6g³ p5g⁵ p6g p6g⁵ Dec 28] lengthy, good-bodied gelding: just fairly useful performer in 2006: left B. Meehan after third outing: below form after fifth start, left D. Nicholls after eleventh: best at 5f: acts on polytrack, best turf efforts on good going or firmer: tried blinkered, usually tongue tied: often slowly away: held up. *R. A. Harris* **92 d**

FASTRAC BOY 3 b.g. Bold Edge 123 – Nesyred (IRE) 75 (Paris House 123) [2006 p6g⁶ p5.1g* p5.1g⁶ p5g⁶ Dec 3] £2,200Y: second foal: dam 6f winner: fair performer: won maiden at Wolverhampton in October: effective at 5f: raced only on polytrack. *J. R. Best* **67**

FASUBY (IRE) 2 b.f. (Mar 10) Fasliyev (USA) 120 – Sue's Ruby (USA) (Crafty Prospector (USA)) [2006 p5g 5s⁶ 5.1d 6f 6f⁴ 7.1m⁶ p7.1f 8.1m⁶ 8.1m⁶ 7m Sep 5] €17,500Y: unfurnished filly: fourth foal: half-sister to smart winner Irish 2003 2-y-o 7f winner Forty Grand (by Red Ransom) and winner in USA by Cryptoclearance: dam 2-y-o 6f winner in USA: poor maiden: barely stays 1m: acts on firm and soft ground: tends to wander. *P. D. Evans* **48**

FASYLITATOR (IRE) 4 b.c. Fasliyev (USA) 120 – Obsessed 80 (Storm Bird (CAN) 134) [2006 89: p8g⁴ p8g⁴ 8.2s⁶ 8m² 8d² 9m³ 8.3f⁴ p8.6g³ 8m* Jul 21] close-coupled colt: fairly useful handicapper on all-weather, fair on turf: in good form in 2006, winning at Newmarket in July: effective at 1m/1¼m: acts on all-weather, firm and good to soft going: visored (found little) once at 3 yrs. *D. K. Ivory* **76 a85**

FATEFUL ATTRACTION 3 b.f. Mujahid (USA) 125 – Heavens Above (FR) (Pistolet Bleu (IRE) 133) [2006 61: p7g* p7g³ p8g 7d 7g³ 7f⁴ 7.6g p7g⁵ p6g² p6g⁴ p7g* p7g p7g p7g⁵ Dec 10] leggy filly: fairly useful handicapper on all-weather, modest on turf: won at Lingfield (made all) in February and Kempton in November: stays 7f: acts on all-weather and firm going: blinkered of late. *I. A. Wood* **59 a80**

FATH AND FURIOUTH (IRE) 2 b.g. (Apr 2) Fath (USA) 116 – Bay View 78 (Slip Anchor 136) [2006 5d 5d 6m 8g Sep 14] strong, compact gelding: has a round action: poor maiden. *P. C. Haslam* **38**

FATHOM FIVE (IRE) 2 b.c. (Apr 22) Fath (USA) 116 – Ambria (ITY) (Final Straw 127) [2006 5g* 5g² 5m 6m² 6s⁶ 6g³ 6g Sep 30] strong, compact colt: seventh foal: closely related to winner up to 1¼m in Italy by Perugino: dam 6f winner in Italy: fairly useful performer: won maiden at Musselburgh in May: better form when placed 3 times after, twice in nurseries: should prove best kept to 5f/6f: acts on good to firm ground. *B. Smart* **83**

FAVERSHAM 3 b.g. Halling (USA) 133 – Barger (USA) (Riverman (USA) 131) [2006 10d* 10g⁴ p12g Jun 14] tall, quite good-topped gelding: half-brother to 3 winners, including French 1m/1¼m performer Baya (by Nureyev) and 7f (at 2 yrs) to 1¾m winner Narrative (by Sadler's Wells), both smart: dam, smart French performer around 1¼m, sister to Triptych: fairly useful form: won maiden at Leicester in April: creditable fourth to Linas Selection in handicap at Sandown next time: last in similar event at Kempton final start: should stay 1½m: acts on good to soft going: sold 10,500 gns in July, joined M. Wigham. *M. A. Jarvis* **80**

John Smith's 'Extra Cold' Chipchase Stakes, Newcastle—
Fayr Jag wins his first race in more than two years from Beckermet (right) and Celtic Mill

FAVOURING (IRE) 4 ch.g. Fayruz 116 – Peace Dividend (IRE) (Alzao (USA) 117) **60**
[2006 59: f6g* f6g f8g f7s⁵ f7g* f8g² f7g⁵ f7g² 8m⁵ 7.5f² 7f 8.2f² 7f⁵ 6m³ 5m f6g f8g⁶
f7g⁶ f7g⁵ f7g⁴ f7g² Dec 28] sturdy gelding: modest performer: won maiden claimer
(left R. Fahey) in January and banded race in March, both at Southwell: stays 8.3f: acts
on all-weather, firm and soft going: tried blinkered, usually visored: often forces pace.
M. C. Chapman

FAVOURITA 4 b.f. Diktat 126 – Forthwith 104 (Midyan (USA) 124) [2006 103d: 8g⁵ **92**
12s⁶ May 24] tall, leggy filly: just fairly useful form when fifth in listed race at Goodwood: well held only other start in 2006: stays 1¼m: acts on soft and good to firm ground
(won on firm on debut): tongue tied both 4-y-o starts: edgy sort, has sweated: temperament under suspicion. *J. W. Hills*

FAYR FIRENZE (IRE) 5 b.g. Fayruz 116 – Shillay (Lomond (USA) 128) [2006 54, **51**
a50: p8g⁵ p7g p8.6g⁶ Mar 27] modest performer: stays easy 1m: acts on all-weather and
good to firm going: usually wears headgear. *M. F. Harris*

FAYR JAG (IRE) 7 b.g. Fayruz 116 – Lominda (IRE) 80 (Lomond (USA) 128) [2006 **117**
116: 6d⁴ 6m⁵ 6m 6m* 6m 6g* 5f⁵ 6m⁵ 5s 5g⁴ 6d³ 6g⁵ Oct 13] close-coupled gelding:
usually impresses in appearance: smart performer: as good as ever in 2006, winning John
Smith's 'Extra Cold' Chipchase Stakes at Newcastle (by ½ length from Beckermet) and
Stan James Hackwood Stakes at Newbury (beat Kodiac by neck), both in July: several
creditable efforts after, including in Audi Stakes (King George) at Goodwood (fifth to
La Cucaracha), listed race at York (fourth to Celtic Mill), Diadem Stakes at Ascot (1½
lengths third to Red Clubs) and Bentinck Stakes at Newmarket (fifth to Bygone Days):
effective at 5f/6f (well held both outings at 7f): acts on firm and good to soft going,
possibly not on soft/heavy. *T. D. Easterby*

FAYR SKY (IRE) 3 b.f. Fayruz 116 – Dutosky 80 (Doulab (USA) 115) [2006 68: 5.1d³ **66**
5f 5m 6.1m⁶ 5g Aug 17] quite attractive filly: fair handicapper: effective at 5f to 7f: acts
on firm and good to soft ground: upset in stall and withdrawn intended second outing:
races prominently. *J. J. Quinn*

FAYRZ PLEASE (IRE) 5 ch.g. Fayruz 116 – Castlelue (IRE) (Tremblant 112) [2006 **–**
: 11v⁶ f7g⁶ f5g⁵ 7d f6g⁴ 7f Jun 24] maiden: little form since 2004: tried tongue tied.
M. C. Chapman

FEALEVIEW LADY (USA) 2 b.f. (Feb 9) Red Ransom (USA) – Alice White (USA) **70**
(Thunder Gulch (USA) 129) [2006 p7g p7g p7.1j³ p8.6g³ p8.6s⁴ Dec 15] 19,000 2-y-o:
second foal: dam 8.5f minor winner in USA: fair maiden: in frame at Wolverhampton last
3 starts: likely to stay beyond 8.6f: raced only on polytrack. *H. Morrison*

FEAR TO TREAD (USA) 3 ch.f. Peintre Celebre (USA) 137 – Pleine Lune (IRE) **85**
(Alzao (USA) 117) [2006 77p: 10.2d 10.9m* 11.6m⁶ 11.6m⁶ 12.6m* 12d Oct 27] sturdy
filly: fairly useful performer: won handicaps at Warwick in June (drifted left) and August:
well below form final start: stays 12.6f: acts on good to firm going: sold 15,000 gns.
J. L. Dunlop

FEAST OF ROMANCE 9 b.g. Pursuit of Love 124 – June Fayre (Sagaro 133) [2006 **58**
57d, a66d: f7g² f7g f7g 6m⁵ f7g* f7g⁴ f7g² May 31] sturdy gelding: modest performer:
left C. Dore and rejoined former trainer after third outing: won banded race at Southwell in May: effective at 6f to 1m: acts on all-weather, soft and good to firm going: wears
headgear. *G. A. Huffer*

FEATHERGRASS (IRE) 4 b.f. Fasliyev (USA) 120 – Jamaican Punch (IRE) (Sha- **–**
reef Dancer (USA) 135) [2006 67: p7.1g p8.6g Feb 3] good-bodied filly: fair maiden at
3 yrs: well beaten both starts in 2006. *B. S. Rothwell*

FEATHERLIGHT 2 b.f. (Feb 25) Fantastic Light (USA) 134 – Feathers Flying (IRE) **55**
100 (Royal Applause 124) [2006 6m 7m 7d 8m 8m⁴ p8.6g⁴ f8g³ p9.5g⁴ Nov 18] 41,000Y:
rather leggy, useful-looking filly: first foal: dam 2-y-o 7f winner who stayed easy 1¼m:
modest maiden: claimed after penultimate outing: stays 9.5f: acts on
all-weather and good to firm going: tried blinkered/visored. *J. Jay*

FEED THE METER (IRE) 6 b.m. Desert King (IRE) 129 – Watch The Clock 93 **82**
(Mtoto 134) [2006 86: 10g³ 12m⁶ 14.1s³ 10f Jun 12] big, good-bodied mare: fairly useful
handicapper: below form after reappearance: barely stays 1¾m: acts on soft and good to
firm going: withdrawn having bolted to post intended fourth start. *J. Ryan*

FEELIN FOXY 2 b.f. (Apr 9) Foxhound (USA) 103 – Charlie Girl 70 (Puissance 110) **72 §**
[2006 5g² 5f³ 5s⁶ 5s³ 5m 5g³ 5.2g⁶ p5.1g⁴ p5g³ p5g³ p6g² p5g* Dec 8] 20,000Y: well- **a67 §**
made filly: fourth foal: sister to 2003 2-y-o 7f seller winner Gone To Ground and half-
sister to 4-y-o Josh: dam, 2-y-o 5f winner, out of half-sister to high-class French 1¼m
performer Creator: fair performer, better on turf than all-weather: placed 7 times before
winning maiden at Kempton in December: stays easy 6f: acts on polytrack, firm and soft
going: visored last 4 outings: temperamental. *D. Shaw*

FEELING WONDERFUL (IRE) 2 b.f. (Feb 24) Fruits of Love (USA) 127 – **73 p**
Teodora (IRE) 93 (Fairy King (USA)) [2006 7v* Oct 31] 14,000Y: third foal: sister to
3-y-o Prince of Love: dam untrustworthy 2-y-o 6f winner: 25/1, won maiden at Catterick
in October comfortably by 1¼ lengths from Nota Liberata, despite running green: will be
suited by 1¼m+: should progress. *M. Johnston*

FEELIN IRIE (IRE) 3 b.g. Key of Luck (USA) 126 – Charlotte's Dancer (Kris 135) **65**
[2006 65: 8.2s 8.2d 8g² 8f³ 8m⁴ 7.6f⁵ 8.1m⁴ 8m³ 7.1m² 7.5g³ p6g Nov 8] close-coupled,
workmanlike gelding: fair performer: left N. Tinkler 7,000 gns prior to final outing: stays
1m: acts on firm going: tongue tied first 5 starts at 2 yrs: makes running: often races
freely. *J. R. Boyle*

FEI MAH 4 b.f. Vettori (IRE) 119 – Bluewain Lady 76 (Unfuwain (USA) 131) [2006 –: **–**
7.1g f5g May 9] no form. *J. R. Jenkins*

FEISTY 2 b.f. (Mar 9) Mujahid (USA) 125 – Fifth Edition 66 (Rock Hopper 124) [2006 **63 d**
5d³ 7m p7.1g* 6f* 7m* 8m 8f 7.1d 7d Oct 19] smallish, sturdy filly: first foal: dam, 1½m
winner who stayed 2m, out of close relative to smart middle-distance performer Valley
of Gold: modest performer at best: completed hat-trick in summer in sellers at Wolverhampton and Yarmouth and nursery at Catterick: ran poorly after: should stay 1m: acts
on polytrack and firm going. *Rae Guest*

FELICITOUS 3 b.f. King's Best (USA) 132 – Embassy 114 (Cadeaux Genereux 131) **90**
[2006 77: 6d⁴ 6d⁶ p7g* p8g Nov 5] rather leggy filly: fairly useful performer: won
maiden at Yarmouth in August and handicap at Lingfield in September: below form in
handicap at Lingfield final start: stays 7f: acts on polytrack, unraced on extremes of going
on turf: has left Godolphin. *Saeed bin Suroor*

FELIN GRUVY (IRE) 3 b.f. Tagula (IRE) 116 – Felin Special (Lyphard's Special **–**
(USA) 122) [2006 69: 7s 6.1g 6m Aug 10] lengthy filly: fair maiden at 2 yrs: well held in
2006, reportedly finishing lame final start: should prove best at 5f/6f: acts on good to soft
ground. *R. F. Johnson Houghton*

FEMINIST (IRE) 4 b.f. Alhaarth (IRE) 126 – Miss Willow Bend (USA) (Willow Hour **–**
(USA)) [2006 –, a57: f5g p5.1g⁵ p5.1g⁵ p5.1g³ p5.1g Apr 10] poor performer nowadays: **a46**
likely to prove best at 5f/6f: acts on polytrack: has worn blinkers/cheekpieces: often races
prominently. *J. M. Bradley*

FEN DREAM 2 b.c. (Feb 27) Tobougg (IRE) 125 – Fred's Dream 67 (Cadeaux Gene- **55**
reux 131) [2006 f6g⁴ 7m p6f 6g Aug 30] modest form in maidens: sold 2,500 gns, sent to
Spain. *E. F. Vaughan*

FEN GAME (IRE) 4 b.g. Montjeu (IRE) 137 – Hatton Gardens 96 (Auction Ring **77**
(USA) 123) [2006 75: p13g³ p16g p12g 10m p12g Sep 27] quite good-topped gelding:
fair handicapper: below form after reappearance: stays 13f: acts on polytrack, good to
firm and good to soft ground: sold 18,000 gns. *J. H. M. Gosden*

FEN GUEST 3 b.f. Woodborough (USA) 112 – Crackling 57 (Electric 126) [2006 73p: **62**
p6g p6g* 5.9m 5d p6g Oct 23] modest performer: won maiden at Wolverhampton in July:
should stay 7f: acts on polytrack and good to firm going. *Rae Guest*

FENNERS (USA) 3 ch.g. Pleasant Tap (USA) – Legal Opinion (IRE) (Polish Precedent **59**
(USA) 131) [2006 80: 12m⁶ 12f³ 12.1s⁵ 12.1m 12.4d Aug 28] sturdy gelding: just modest
performer in 2006: left M. Johnston 1,500 gns after reappearance: stays 1½m: acts on
firm going: tongue tied: has looked none too keen: joined M. Easterby, then gelded.
G. P. Kelly

FENTASTIC 3 b.f. Desert Prince (IRE) 130 – Golden Symbol 54 (Wolfhound (USA) **–**
126) [2006 7m p12g p12g⁶ 10.9g 10m⁶ a12g 9d 9g Sep 23] €21,000F, 22,000Y: first foal:
dam maiden who should have stayed 7f: little form: sold from R. Guest 1,500 gns after
fifth start. *Ecurie Prince Rose, Belgium*

FENWICKS PRIDE (IRE) 8 b.g. Imperial Frontier (USA) 112 – Stunt Girl (IRE) **–**
(Thatching 131) [2006 49: f6g p7.1g Jan 28] strong, lengthy gelding: poor performer:
well held in 2006: usually visored/in cheekpieces. *A. Berry*

FEOLIN 2 b.f. (Feb 24) Dr Fong (USA) 128 – Finlaggan 83 (Be My Chief (USA) 122) **75 p**
[2006 7d 8.2m³ 8v⁴ Oct 9] good-bodied filly: half-sister to several winners, notably dual
5f to 7f winner Needwood Blade (by Pivotal), later Grade 3 9f winner in USA, and 3-y-o
Merveilles: dam 11f to 2m winner: fair form in maidens, staying-on third to Treat at Nottingham: well beaten (heavy ground) final start: will be suited by 1¼m/1½m: should
make a better 3-y-o. *H. Morrison*

FEREEJI 2 b.g. (Feb 3) Cape Cross (IRE) 129 – Belle Genius (USA) 111 (Beau Genius **–**
(CAN)) [2006 6g Jul 6] 11/1, well beaten in maiden at Newbury (gelded after).
M. R. Channon

FERMION (IRE) 3 b.f. Sadler's Wells (USA) 132 – Pieds de Plume (FR) (Seattle Slew **113**
(USA)) [2006 79: 9.5s⁶ 10m* 9m² 12m* 12m⁶ Sep 10] big, lengthy filly: fourth foal:
sister to useful 1m (at 2 yrs)/1¼m winner Rave Reviews: dam, second at 1m in France on
only start, half-sister to high-class French 1¼m performer Groom Dancer: smart performer: won handicap at Naas in June and listed race at Newbury (showed good turn of foot to
beat Reunite by 1¼ lengths) in August: held up in steadily-run race when just respectable
staying-on sixth to Mandesha in Prix Vermeille at Longchamp final start, carrying head
awkwardly: will stay 1¾m: acts on good to firm going. *A. P. O'Brien, Ireland*

FERNELEY (IRE) 2 b.c. (Mar 9) Ishiguru (USA) 114 – Amber Tide (IRE) 75 (Pursuit **104**
of Love 124) [2006 7g³ 7m* 7.5m* 7g³ 7d³ Sep 29] €24,000Y, 50,000 2-y-o: neat colt:
second foal: dam, maiden who stayed 1¼m, half-sister to US Grade 2 1m winner Uncharted Haven: useful performer: won maiden at Galway and minor event at Tipperary in
August: more progress when 3¼ lengths third to Teofilo in Futurity Stakes at the Curragh
and 2¾ lengths third to Thousand Words in Somerville Tattersall Stakes at Newmarket:
will stay 1m: acts on good to firm and good to soft ground. *Francis Ennis, Ireland*

FERN HOUSE (IRE) 4 b.g. Xaar 132 – Certain Impression (USA) (Forli (ARG)) **46**
[2006 –: p5g⁵ 5m⁵ 5g² p5g⁶ Oct 29] poor maiden: best efforts at 5f: raced on polytrack
and good/good to firm going. *Peter Grayson*

FERRANDO 4 b.g. Hernando (FR) 127 – Oh So Misty (Teenoso (USA) 135) [2006 –: **65**
p8g⁶ p7g p10g² 11.5m 15.8s³ Oct 24] strong, lengthy gelding: fair maiden: left D. Daly
after fourth start: stays 1¼m: acts on polytrack, and probably on soft and good to firm
going. *G. A. Swinbank*

FERRARA FLAME (IRE) 4 b.f. Titus Livius (FR) 115 – Isolette (Wassl 125) [2006 **–**
63: p8.6g p8.6g p10g 8f Jul 4] modest performer in 2005: well held in 2006: twice
visored. *R. Brotherton*

FERROLI 3 b.g. Efisio 120 – Ordained 66 (Mtoto 134) [2006 –: 7.1g p7.1g 8.2d May **–**
19] lengthy gelding: little form: tried blinkered/in cheekpieces. *J. Balding*

FESTIVE STYLE (SAF) 6 b.m. Fort Wood (USA) 117 – Fanciful (ARG) (Ringaro **91**
(USA)) [2006 7.5m 8m 10m⁶ 8.9d⁶ Feb 24] useful performer at best: successful in maid-

en at Kenilworth in 2003 (runner-up on other 3 starts in South Africa): won Cape Verdi Stakes at Nad Al Sheba in 2004 by 6½ lengths, only success in UAE (rated 104): left S. Seemar after final start in 2005: never dangerous there in 2006, leaving J. Noseda after third start: probably stays 11f: acts on dirt and good to firm going: tried visored. *H. Brown, South Africa*

FESTIVE TIPPLE (IRE) 2 b.c. (Mar 7) Tipsy Creek (USA) 115 – Gi La High 68   **65** (Rich Charlie 117) [2006 5g⁶ p6g p7g Sep 27] fair form second start in maidens: should prove fair at 5f/6f. *P. Winkworth*

FEU D'ARTIFICE (USA) 3 b.g. Stravinsky (USA) 133 – Alashir (USA) (Alysheba   **77** (USA)) [2006 76: p8g³ 8.1s 8.5g⁴ 10m⁴ 12g 9.9g p8g 8.3g² p10g³ Nov 13] tall, rather leggy, close-coupled gelding: has a quick action: fair maiden: stays 1¼m: acts on polytrack and firm going: has looked none too keen, and twice blinkered (below form). *R. Hannon*

FEVER 2 b.c. (Jan 23) Dr Fong (USA) 128 – Follow Flanders 92 (Pursuit of Love 124)   **80** [2006 p7g³ 8.1g³ p8g⁵ Sep 1] 75,000Y: close-coupled colt: first foal: dam, 5f winner (including at 2 yrs), half-sister to high-class sprinter Kyllachy: fairly useful form in maidens, third at Lingfield and Sandown: stays 1m. *R. Hannon*

FICOMA 2 b.f. (Feb 12) Piccolo 121 – Hemaca (Distinctly North (USA) 115) [2006   **75** 5.7f⁴ p7g⁴ 7d³ Oct 3] compact filly: second foal: half-sister to 4-y-o Premier Fantasy: dam unraced: fair form: won maiden at Bath in August: in frame in minor event at Kempton and nursery at Catterick: stays 7f. *C. G. Cox*

FICTIONAL 5 b.h. Fraam 114 – Manon Lescaut 56 (Then Again 126) [2006 101: 5.1g²   **99** 5m 5f⁵ 6s Oct 7] sturdy horse: useful performer: reportedly had a setback in the spring: good 1¾ lengths second to Peace Offering in minor event at Nottingham in August on reappearance: below form after: effective at 5f/6f: acts on good to firm ground, possibly not on softer than good: races prominently. *E. J. O'Neill*

FICTION FACTORY (IRE) 3 b.f. Alzao (USA) 117 – Nordic Way (IRE) (Nordico   **–** (USA)) [2006 54: 10m May 15] half-sister to 11f (in Germany) and 1¾m winner Notte Italiana (by Mtoto) and winner in Turkey by Distinctly North: dam unraced half-sister to very smart miler Swallow Flight: modest form at best in Irish maidens at 2 yrs: left M. Byrne, well held in similar event at Windsor only start in Britain. *J. Pearce*

FIDDLERS CREEK (IRE) 7 b.g. Danehill (USA) 126 – Mythical Creek (USA)   **59** (Pleasant Tap (USA)) [2006 66, a83: p12.2g f8g⁵ 12.4g 12m⁶ 9.2m² 8d 13f⁴ 12m 12m⁶   **a75** Aug 8] quite good-topped gelding: fair on all-weather, modest on turf: effective at 1m to 1½m: acts on all-weather, soft and firm going: often wears cheekpieces/visor: usually tongue tied: inconsistent. *R. Allan*

FIDDLERS FORD (IRE) 5 b.g. Sadler's Wells (USA) 132 – Old Domesday Book 93   **60** (High Top 131) [2006 p16g p16g 20s⁶ 18m⁶ p16g Jul 19] strong, good-bodied gelding: modest handicapper nowadays: missed 2005: stays 2¼m: acts on polytrack and good to firm going: visored on debut, wore cheekpieces final start (lost action, pulled up). *T. Keddy*

FIDDLERS SPIRIT (IRE) 2 b.c. (Mar 22) Invincible Spirit (IRE) 121 – Coco Ricoh   **46** (IRE) (Lycius (USA) 124) [2006 5s⁴ 6m 6m⁵ 7f Sep 5] poor maiden: best effort at 6f: visored (last in nursery) final start. *J. G. M. O'Shea*

FIDDLERS WOOD 3 b.g. Spectrum (IRE) 126 – Tanasie (Cadeaux Genereux 131)   **83 §** [2006 95?: p8g² p8g³ p8.6g* p12g⁵ 10g⁴ 11g⁵ 9s 12m Jun 23] workmanlike gelding: fairly useful performer: won maiden at Wolverhampton in February: well held last 3 starts: stays 1¼m: acts on polytrack and soft going: usually visored, in cheekpieces final outing: none too straightforward: sold 31,000 gns in July. *V. Smith*

FIDELIA (IRE) 2 b.f. (Apr 20) Singspiel (IRE) 133 – Rosse 100 (Kris 135) [2006   **78 p** p7.1g² Dec 1] third foal: half-sister to 7f winner Lasso (by Indian Ridge): dam, 7f winner (stayed 1m), half-sister to very smart 7f/1m performer Rebecca Sharp: neck second to Lacework in maiden at Wolverhampton: should be suited by 1m+: will improve. *G. Wragg*

FIEFDOM (IRE) 4 br.g. Singspiel (IRE) 133 – Chiquita Linda (IRE) (Mujadil (USA)   **91** 119) [2006 99: 8s 8.1m 7.6d⁶ 7m³ 7m* 7.1m⁴ 7m 7f⁶ 7f 7.6m 8d 7.6g 7m³ 7.2d 7d⁵ p7.1m 7s Oct 24] compact gelding: has a quick action: fairly useful handicapper: won at Lingfield in June: effective at 7f to 1¼m: acts on firm and soft going: blinkered tenth/eleventh (raced too freely) outings: has hung left. *I. W. McInnes*

FIELD SPORT (FR) 2 b.c. (Mar 23) Sagamix (FR) 129 – Ewar Empress (IRE) 57 **45** (Persian Bold 123) [2006 p7.1g 7.6f 8g 8g 8.2s Oct 25] good-bodied colt: poor maiden: bred to stay 1¼m/1½m: tried in cheekpieces. *C. E. Brittain*

FIFTY CENTS 2 ch.c. (Mar 15) Diesis 133 – Solaia (USA) 110 (Miswaki (USA) 124) **88 p** [2006 7g² Sep 15] 120,000Y: rangy colt: has scope: third foal: half-brother to smart 1m (at 2 yrs in France) to 1½m (US Grade 2) winner Olaya (by Theatrical): dam 7f (at 2 yrs) and 11.4f winner: 7/2, promising ½-length second in maiden at Newbury, carried left by winner Opera Music: will be suited by 1¼m/1½m: useful prospect, sure to win races. *R. Charlton*

FIGARO FLYER (IRE) 3 b.g. Mozart (IRE) 131 – Ellway Star (IRE) 104 (Night **91** Shift (USA)) [2006 92: p6g² 5g 6.1f³ 6g 6g 5m 5m 5.2f⁵ 6m 6m 6g⁴ 6m p6g² p6g p6g⁴ **a96** p6g p5.1m⁶ p6g* p6g² p6g⁴ Dec 28] sturdy gelding: useful handicapper at best on all-weather, fairly useful on turf: ran well when placed in 2006, winning at Wolverhampton in December: effective at 5f/6f: acts on polytrack and good to firm going. *P. Howling*

FIGARO'S QUEST (IRE) 4 b.g. Singspiel (IRE) 133 – Seren Quest 90 (Rainbow **70** Quest (USA) 134) [2006 65: 12d 11.9m* p12.2g* 12.4m⁴ p12g³ 14.8m 12.6g² 12.6m Aug 28] close-coupled gelding: fair performer: won handicap at Brighton (by 10 lengths) in April and banded race at Wolverhampton in May: effective at 1½m to 2m: acts on polytrack and good to firm going: often blinkered: difficult ride: has joined C. N. Kellett. *P. F. I. Cole*

FIGHTING MOOD 2 b.c. (Apr 29) Mujahid (USA) 125 – Dramatic Mood (Jalmood **51** (USA) 126) [2006 8m 8.3s 8.3g⁴ Oct 16] heavy-bodied colt: modest maiden: will stay 1¼m: sold 8,200 gns, sent to Denmark. *A. M. Balding*

FIGURATIVE (IRE) 4 b.g. Machiavellian (USA) 123 – Marble Maiden 117 (Lead On **62** Time (USA) 123) [2006 –: f12g⁴ f8g² f8g² Feb 16] rangy gelding: modest maiden: best effort at 1m (raced freely over 1½m on reappearance): acts on fibresand. *G. A. Swinbank*

FIKRI 3 b.g. Bertolini (USA) 125 – Welcome Home 55 (Most Welcome 131) [2006 80: **69** p8.6g f6g³ 5m⁵ 5f² p6g Jul 3] 48,000Y: fifth foal: half-brother to useful 7f (at 2 yrs) and 8.5f (in USA) winner Joint Aspiration (by Pivotal): dam, 1½m winner, half-sister to smart sprinter Two Clubs: fair maiden: left K. Prendergast in Ireland 25,000 gns and gelded after 2 yrs: should prove best at 5f/6f: acts on firm and good to soft going, below par on all-weather: blinkered/visored and tongue tied last 3 starts: sold 2,000 gns in October, sent to Germany. *T. J. Pitt*

FILEY BUOY 4 b.g. Factual (USA) 108 – Tugra (FR) (Baby Turk 120) [2006 47, a59: **49** f7g p8.6g 7.5f⁵ 9d 8.5m 8f f7g f11m Oct 31] workmanlike gelding: poor performer: best efforts at 7f/1m: acts on fibresand, firm and good to soft ground: tried visored. *R. M. Whitaker*

FILIOS (IRE) 2 b.c. (Apr 14) Kutub (IRE) 123 – Karlinaxa (Linamix (FR) 127) [2006 **79 p** p8g³ 8g⁴ p8.6m* Oct 31] 33,000Y: leggy, angular colt: half-brother to 3 winners abroad, including French 11f/13.5f winner Coquin de Sort (by Croco Rouge): dam, French maiden who stayed 1¼m, half-sister to smart French performers Karmifira (up to 9f) and Karmousil (stayer): fair form: shaped well in maidens, odds on when winning at Wolverhampton, barely adequate test: will do better, especially at 1¼m/1½m. *L. M. Cumani*

FILLAMEENA 6 b.m. Robellino (USA) 127 – Lotus Moon (Shareef Dancer (USA) **48** 135) [2006 56: f12g f8g⁶ p9.5g Feb 20] poor performer nowadays: stays easy 1¾m: acts on dirt, all-weather and good to soft going: wears headgear nowadays. *P. T. Midgley*

FILLIEMOU (IRE) 5 gr.m. Goldmark (USA) 113 – St Louis Lady 71 (Absalom 128) **–** [2006 –: 11.7m 10.2m p8g Dec 10] quite good-topped mare: maiden: no form since 2004: tried visored. *A. W. Carroll*

FINAL AWARD (IRE) 3 b.f. Grand Lodge (USA) 125 – Never So Fair 65 (Never So **64** Bold 135) [2006 7.5f 8.5f³ 8m⁵ 7m 7m p7g Oct 15] 30,000 2-y-o: half-sister to several winners, including smart 6f (at 2 yrs) to 9f (in USA) winner Circle of Gold and 1996 2-y-o 6f winner Crystal Crossing (both by Royal Academy), latter dam of St Leger winner Rule of Law: dam race maiden: modest maiden: stays 8.5f: raced only on polytrack and ground firmer than good: sold 13,000 gns. *G. M. Moore*

FINAL BID (IRE) 3 b.g. Mujadil (USA) 119 – Dusky Virgin 62 (Missed Flight 123) **59** [2006 65: p8g⁵ p7g 7d p12g⁴ Nov 24] just modest maiden in 2006: best effort at 7f: acts on polytrack and good to soft going: tried blinkered: none too consistent. *M. G. Quinlan*

FINAL CURTAIN 2 b.f. (Feb 5) Royal Applause 124 – Forever Fine (USA) (Sunshine **59** Forever (USA)) [2006 7s⁵ p8g p6g p7g p6s⁵ f6g Dec 23] 30,000F, 45,000Y: half-sister to several winners, including 3-y-o Familiar Territory: dam 2-y-o 4.5f/6f winner in USA: modest maiden: will prove best short of 1m: tongue tied (well held) final outing. *M. A. Magnusson*

FINAL DYNASTY 2 b.f. (Apr 17) Komaite (USA) – Malcesine (IRE) 46 (Auction **80** Ring (USA) 123) [2006 p6f⁴ 5d² p5.1g* 5.1f⁶ 6s³ 6d⁶ Oct 27] good-topped filly: sister to several winners, including useful 2004 2-y-o 5f winner Castelletto and 5-y-o Lake Garda: dam 1m seller winner: fairly useful performer: won maiden at Wolverhampton in September: ran well after, in listed races last 2 starts, third at York and sixth (to Blue Echo) at Newmarket: effective at 5f/6f: acts on polytrack, firm and soft going. *Mrs G. S. Rees*

FINAL ESTEEM 3 ch.g. Lomitas 129 – Fame At Last (USA) 98 (Quest For Fame 127) **67** [2006 12g 9.2f⁵ 8m* 12.1m⁵ 8d 12d Nov 3] 12,000 2-y-o: lengthy, angular gelding: second foal: half-brother to 4-y-o Anchor Date: dam, 2-y-o 7f winner (stayed 11.4f), out of half-sister to smart 1¼m winner Rambushka: fair performer: won maiden at Pontefract in July: should stay 1¼m (seemingly not 1½m): acts on firm ground (below form on good to soft). *I. Semple*

FINALMENTE 4 b.g. Kahyasi 130 – Sudden Spirit (FR) (Esprit du Nord (USA) 126) **107** [2006 83+: 16d⁴ 14s* 12m* 16.1m p16g* 18d Oct 14] good-bodied gelding: useful handicapper: improved in 2006, winning at Newmarket (by length from Quizzene) in May, Folkestone (dead-heated with Blue Bajan) in June and Lingfield (beat Elusive Dream by neck) in July: well held in Cesarewitch at Newmarket final start: should stay beyond 2m: acts on polytrack, soft and good to firm ground. *N. A. Callaghan*

FINAL PROMISE 4 b.g. Lujain (USA) 119 – Unerring (Unfuwain (USA) 131) [2006 **–** 75: 8.2s 10d 8.3g Jun 6] tall, close-coupled gelding: fair handicapper at 3 yrs: well held in 2006: gelded after final start. *J. A. Geake*

FINAL TUNE (IRE) 3 ch.g. Grand Lodge (USA) 125 – Jackie's Opera (FR) (Indian **77** Ridge 123) [2006 65: 7v 6g⁵ 6f⁵ 7.1g⁴ 7m² 8.5m 8.3m* 7m⁶ 8.1m⁴ 10g⁵ p7g* p7.1g² Nov 3] angular gelding: fair performer: won seller at Leicester (left D. Nicholls after) in July and handicap at Lingfield in October: has form at 1¼m, best efforts at 7f: acts on polytrack, firm and good to soft going: slowly away fourth outing. *Miss M. E. Rowland*

FINAL VERSE 3 b.c. Mark of Esteem (IRE) 137 – Tamassos 76 (Dance In Time **113** (CAN)) [2006 104: 8m⁶ 8s* 8d Oct 28] good-topped, attractive colt: has a quick action: smart performer: best effort when 5¾ lengths sixth to George Washington in 2000 Guineas at Newmarket on return, racing freely: odds on, won listed race at Goodwood (by 2½ lengths from Deepwater Bay) in May: off 5 months (reported to have suffered foot injury in mid-June), ran as if amiss in another listed event at Newmarket final start: bred to stay 1¼m: acts on soft and good to firm going: stirred up in preliminaries in 2006, sweating at Goodwood. *Sir Michael Stoute*

FINANCIAL FUTURE 6 b.g. Barathea (IRE) 127 – In Perpetuity 90 (Great Nephew **54** 126) [2006 67: 10.2d⁵ 12.1d⁵ 10.2m 12.1g Jul 5] strong, close-coupled gelding: just modest performer nowadays: stays 1½m: acts on good to firm and good to soft going: tried blinkered/in cheekpieces: usually races prominently. *C. Roberts*

FINANCIAL TIMES (USA) 4 b.g. Awesome Again (CAN) 133 – Investabull (USA) **82** (Holy Bull (USA) 134) [2006 p5g* p5g⁵ 5m⁵ p5g² p6g 5m 5d 5g p5g² p5.1g² p5.1g² Dec 27] strong, attractive gelding: fairly useful performer: missed 2005: won maiden at Lingfield in March, making all: should prove best at 5f: acts on polytrack and good to firm going: tongue tied last 5 outings (good efforts last 3): forces pace. *Stef Liddiard*

FIND IT OUT (USA) 3 b.g. Luhuk (USA) 114 – Ursula (VEN) (Phone Trick (USA)) **–** [2006 56: 9v⁵ 11.6d 12f 9d 12d Sep 1] smallish, strong gelding: modest maiden at 2 yrs: well held in 2006: tried tongue tied: sold 4,000 gns. *T. D. Barron*

FIND ME (USA) 2 ch.g. (Feb 1) Point Given (USA) 134 – Island Jamboree (USA) **75 p** (Explodent (USA)) [2006 8.1g 8.3s p8g³ Oct 23] $17,000Y: strong, angular gelding: half-brother to several winners, notably high-class winner up to 1¼m in Britain and USA Fiji (by Rainbow Quest) and smart 1½m winner Capri (by Generous): dam, won 10 times in USA from 6f to 8.5f, also second in Grade 1 9f event: progressive in maidens, possibly still green (soon off bridle) when third at Lingfield: gelded after: will stay 1¼m: should do better still. *M. Johnston*

FIND THE KING (IRE) 8 b.g. King's Theatre (IRE) 128 – Undiscovered (Tap On **–** Wood 130) [2006 14g 12s 17m p16g p16.5g⁶ f16g⁵ p16.5g Dec 29] sturdy, useful-looking gelding: has a round action: fairly useful handicapper in 2003: missed 2004 and 2005: well held in Ireland after third outing: has worn tongue tie: tried in cheekpieces. *D. W. P. Arbuthnot*

FINE DAY 2 b.f. (Apr 3) Fantastic Light (USA) 134 – Queen's Gallery (USA) 98 (Forty Niner (USA)) [2006 6s⁶ May 24] strong filly: sixth foal: half-sister to 7-y-o Qobtaan and a winner in Greece, both by Capote: dam, French 2-y-o 6.5f winner, closely related to US Grade 1 9f/1¼m winner Marquetry and smart French sprinter Spain Lane: 11/2, green and considerately handled in maiden at Goodwood: sold 13,000 gns in November, sent to USA. *M. P. Tregoning* –

FINE DEED 5 b.g. Kadeed (IRE) – Kristis Girl 76 (Ballacashtal (CAN)) [2006 p9.5g p12.2g Dec 2] well beaten in maidens at Wolverhampton. *Ian Williams* –

FINE LEG 2 b.f. (Apr 7) Lujain (USA) 119 – In A Twinkling (IRE) 74 (Brief Truce (USA) 126) [2006 p5.1g⁵ 5m p6g 7d 6m 8g Sep 14] 1,000Y: leggy filly: second foal: dam maiden who stayed 1¼m: little form: usually tongue tied. *P. J. McBride* –

FINE RULER (IRE) 2 b.g. (Mar 15) King's Best (USA) 132 – Bint Alajwaad (IRE) (Fairy King (USA)) [2006 6m³ 7m Sep 13] tall, leggy gelding: second foal: dam unraced half-sister to 6f/7f winner Material Witness and French 1½m/15f winner Periple, both useful: fair maiden: third to St Philip at Salisbury: possibly amiss other start: gelded after: will stay 1m. *M. R. Channon* 73

FINISHED ARTICLE (IRE) 9 b.g. Indian Ridge 123 – Summer Fashion 84 (Moorestyle 137) [2006 74: p8g p8.6g² 10.2m⁴ 10f³ p12.2g* p12.2f⁵ 12m⁵ p13.9m³ p12.2g f11g p13.9g⁴ p10g p12.2g² Dec 18] workmanlike gelding: fair performer on turf, modest on all-weather: won at Wolverhampton (claimed from W. Musson £7,000) in July: stays easy 1¾m: acts on polytrack, firm and good to soft going: held up. *P. A. Blockley* 76 a64

FINLAY'S FOOTSTEPS 2 ch.g. (Mar 26) Dr Fong (USA) 128 – Bay Shade (USA) 90 (Sharpen Up 127) [2006 6m 6s Aug 19] close-coupled gelding: well beaten in maidens: bred to stay 1m/1¼m. *G. M. Moore* –

FINNEGANS RAINBOW 4 ch.g. Spectrum (IRE) 126 – Fairy Story (IRE) 80 (Persian Bold 123) [2006 58: f11g⁵ f11g 12f⁴ 11.5f⁶ 9.9g⁶ f12g Dec 29] big gelding: modest maiden: stays 1½m: acts on fibresand and good to firm ground: none too consistent. *M. C. Chapman* 56 ?

FINSBURY 3 br. or gr.g. Observatory (USA) 131 – Carmela Owen (Owington 123) [2006 71§: 6m p6g* p6g⁶ p7g* p7g³ p7g⁶ p7.1m⁶ p7.2g p7g³ p7.1g Dec 31] fairly useful handicapper, better on all-weather than turf: won at Kempton in June and July: left C. Wall 21,000 gns after eighth start: stays 7f: acts on polytrack, best effort on turf on good going: looked none too straightforward early in career: held up. *Miss J. Feilden* 89

FINSCEAL BEO (IRE) 2 ch.f. (Feb 19) Mr Greeley (USA) 122 – Musical Treat (IRE) 98 (Royal Academy (USA) 130) [2006 6m* 8g² 7d⁶ 8m* 7d* Oct 14] 118

For much of the season Sander Camillo looked clearly the best of the juvenile fillies, but all that changed in October, when Finsceal Beo emerged from the shadows to put up two eye-catching displays in the space of a fortnight. First came the Prix Marcel Boussac, which she won officially by five lengths, then the Rockfel Stakes, where the margin was three lengths. The style of both victories was striking and the form placed Finsceal Beo firmly at the top of the tree, which wasn't bad for a filly who had made her debut in April and who had been off the track for more than four months afterwards because of a hairline fracture to a cannon bone. Finsceal Beo, a strong, well-made, attractive filly and an excellent walker, one of the most imposing two-year-olds we saw all year, looks sure to train on. She also

Prix Marcel Boussac-Criterium des Pouliches Royal Barriere Deauville, Longchamp—
Finsceal Beo shows a lot of improvement as she draws clear of Darrfonah (striped cap),
Legerete (one off the rail), Poltava (second right) and Bicoastal (blinkers)

'In The Pink' Rockfel Stakes (Sponsored By Owen Brown), Newmarket—
Finsceal Beo confirms herself Europe's top two-year-old filly; Rahiyah (white cap) is second

appears to have an equable temperament, and, assuming no further leg problems intervene, the future looks very bright, perhaps bright enough for her to live up to her august name, which means 'living legend' in Gaelic. One thing is certain. The clash between Finsceal Beo and Sander Camillo in the One Thousand Guineas—the principal classic target for both, given that neither is likely to stay the Oaks trip—is one to anticipate with relish. Finsceal Beo, 4/1 with two of the major firms at season's end, has the edge on form, but Sander Camillo, at around the same odds, has improvement in her.

Given the shrewdness of her trainer Jim Bolger, Finsceal Beo's presence in the line-up for the Prix Marcel Boussac-Criterium des Pouliches Royal Barriere Deauville at Longchamp on Arc day perhaps should have acted as a pointer, though her form was some way below that usually required to win the race. Her debut in a thirteen-runner maiden at Leopardstown on April 23rd was early for a filly of her size and scope, and decidedly early for one who developed into the best of her age and sex. In recent years, only one champion, Morning Pride, a sprinter who did not race after early July, began her career earlier—one day earlier to be precise. Two other speedsters that topped the class, Lemon Souffle and Attraction, started on April 26th and April 29th. Coincidentally, another of the leading two-year-old fillies of 2006 in Ireland, Miss Beatrix, made her debut on March 26th. Starting joint third favourite at Leopardstown, Finsceal Beo accounted for Yario by three quarters of a length but then was off until the start of September when a length second to Numen in a valuable nursery at Tralee under 9-6. Being drawn among the lower numbers in the Goffs Million at the Curragh later in the month did Finsceal Beo no favours but she showed up well to be second in her group on the stand side and sixth of twenty-eight overall behind Miss Beatrix.

Finsceal Beo clearly had ability, but not enough to suggest her odds of 19/1 at Longchamp were particularly generous. All the thirteen runners were winners but only five were trained in France, headed by the favourite Poltava, who had won the Prix d'Aumale. The seven others preferred to Finsceal Beo in the betting were: Legerete, successful in a minor event over the course and distance; dual provincial scorer Bal de La Rose; Rock of Gibraltar's sister Nell Gwyn; and four who had been placed in pattern races, namely Bicoastal and Cumin from Britain, Sugar Baby Love from Germany and Ikat. Newbury minor event winner Darrfonah was at 22/1.

Finsceal Beo's performance was a revelation. Held up in a strongly-run race with the running made by Poltava and Nell Gwyn, Finsceal Beo was always travelling well, accelerated smoothly to hit the front a furlong and a half out and readily drew away. At the line she was clear of the staying-on Darrfonah and Legerete, though the margin looked more like four lengths than five. The race was inaugurated in 1969 and this was the widest winning margin since Hippodamia scored by six lengths in 1973, but it has to be borne in mind that, like a number of contests in France, the Marcel Boussac sometimes develops into a sprint after only a steady early pace, which tends to compress the distances at the finish. In the wake of any major race involving a horse's rising from relative obscurity to win decisively, there

379

is a tendency in some quarters to ignore the evidence of the eyes and use the pejorative term 'fluke'. The fact that Finsceal Beo was available at 12/1 for the One Thousand Guineas after Longchamp indicated perhaps that the bookmakers thought her victory too good to be true, or at least unconvincing without further proof. The doubting Thomases were converted when Finsceal Beo lined up as favourite against thirteen rivals in the 'In The Pink' Rockfel Stakes at Newmarket nearly a fortnight later.

After the Marcel Boussac, Bolger said he didn't particularly want the filly to carry a penalty in any trials in the immediate run-up to the Guineas. But she had to give 4 lb all round in the Rockfel, and Bolger actually told the media: 'We weren't worried about the penalty, as we were viewing this as a Guineas trial.' Seeing a two-year-old Group 1 winner contesting a Group 2 event before the end of the season is not a common occurrence. The shortage of races is one factor, but, presumably more significant with colts at least, is the notion that loss of status through defeat would tend automatically to outweigh any advantage from victory. However, El Prado won the Beresford Stakes carrying a 5-lb penalty for his National Stakes success in 1991 and Whipper won the Criterium de Maisons-Laffitte with no penalty for landing the Prix Morny in 2003. The opposition in the Rockfel hardly looked sufficient to make a 4-lb concession a serious inconvenience to Finsceal Beo, unless the good to soft going proved to suit her less well than the good to firm at Longchamp, or the drop back to seven furlongs caused her any problems. She stood out in a field well up to standard on looks, and consisting mostly of winners, headed by Dhanyata, runner-up in the Cheveley Park Stakes, and English Ballet, successful in the Sweet Solera Stakes before gaining places in the May Hill Stakes and Fillies' Mile. Different tactics were applied but the result was precisely the same. The gallop was slower than in France and Finsceal Beo was ridden closer to the front before being driven clear over two furlongs out and staying on much too strongly for the rest. At the line she was well on top of Sander Camillo's stable-companion Rahiyah, winner of a maiden race at Goodwood, with Puggy, narrowly beaten in a listed race at Newmarket, three and a half lengths further back. The form was of a similar level to the Marcel Boussac, but this time the bookmakers took no chances, one major firm quoting Finsceal Beo as low as 5/2 for the One Thousand Guineas.

Finsceal Beo (IRE) (ch.f. Feb 19, 2004)	Mr Greeley (USA) (ch 1992)	Gone West (b 1984)	Mr Prospector
			Secrettame
		Long Legend (ch 1978)	Reviewer
			Lianga
	Musical Treat (IRE) (ch 1996)	Royal Academy (b 1987)	Nijinsky
			Crimson Saint
		Mountain Ash (b 1989)	Dominion
			Red Berry

Finsceal Beo follows Reel Buddy, successful in the 2004 Sussex Stakes, as the second Group 1 winner for their sire Mr Greeley from only a handful of runners in Europe. His record overall is pretty good but he has had only five per cent stakes winners to foals of racing age, well short of the ten per cent which received opinion considers to be the benchmark for a top sire. With more and more sires internationally covering more and more mares, resulting in more and more foals, the likelihood of any stallion's maintaining a ten per cent figure is growing slimmer. It is a matter of simple arithmetic: the number of stakes races has not increased at a commensurate rate with the size of stallion books. Mr Greeley, who has covered an average of one hundred and forty mares in each of the last four years, may be falling foul of this modern trend. Either way, he is still becoming highly commercial and at the end of 2005 he was moved from Spendthrift Farm to Gainesway, where rightly or wrongly he was described as 'globally influential'. After the move Mr Greeley's fee initially stayed the same at 35,000 dollars but it has more than doubled to 75,000 dollars for the 2007 covering season; he began his career at 10,000 dollars. One of Mr Greeley's yearlings fetched 2.7m dollars in 2005, a two-year-old went for two million dollars in February and, to cap it all, a colt by him fell to a bid of 5.7m dollars from John Ferguson for Sheikh Mohammed at Keeneland in September. Finsceal Beo fetched a lot less than that at Goffs as a yearling, €340,000 to be precise. Like the majority of Mr Prospector's descendants, Mr Greeley was a

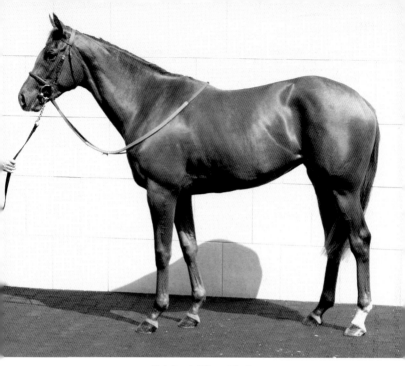

M. A. Ryan's "Finsceal Beo"

sprinter-miler, the winner of three Grade 3 events over six and seven furlongs whose best performance came when a close second to Desert Stormer in the Breeders' Cup Sprint. Mr Greeley is not a noted influence for stamina, with the smart Irish colt Merger an exception in staying a mile and a quarter. In the States, where his daughter Nonsuch Bay won the Mother Goose Stakes over nine furlongs, the average distance of races won by Mr Greeley's offspring is 6.7 furlongs. None of that matters for Finsceal Beo, who clearly stays a mile well, and may get a mile and a quarter in time. The dam, Musical Treat, stayed the latter distance and was useful, winning three times from sixteen starts in Europe and America and finishing second in the Lupe Stakes. Her first foal, the Red Ransom colt Red Riot, won in the Czech Republic. Since producing Finsceal Beo, whom she was carrying when sold for 100,000 dollars at Keeneland, Musical Treat foaled a filly by Barathea who fetched €150,000 as a yearling at Goffs in September. Musical Treat comes from a successful family. Her dam Mountain Ash, who had four other winners at stud, ran twenty-two times for ten wins at up to a mile headed by the Group 3 Premio Royal Mares. The next dam Red Berry, a daughter of One Thousand Guineas and July Cup runner-up Big Berry, finished second in the Cheveley Park Stakes and foaled a total of eight winners. It will be disappointing if Finsceal Beo fails to add further lustre to the family name. *J. S. Bolger, Ireland*

FIONA FOX 2 b.f. (Mar 10) Foxhound (USA) 103 – First Play 59 (Primo Dominie 121) **55** [2006 p6s³ Dec 14] closely related to winners abroad by Emarati and Wolfhound and half-sister to 5-y-o Leah's Pride: dam 6f winner: 16/1, 4 lengths third to Pixie Ring in maiden at Wolverhampton, always prominent: likely to prove best at 5f/6f. *R. Hollins-head*

FIONA'S WONDER 2 b.c. (Mar 12) Inchinor 119 – Wondrous Maid (GER) (Mondrian (GER) 125) [2006 p7g f8g⁶ Dec 21] little sign of ability in maidens. *R. A. Harris* –

FIORE DI BOSCO (IRE) 5 b.m. Charnwood Forest (IRE) 125 – Carabine (USA) (Dehere (USA) 121) [2006 64: f7g⁶ p9.5g⁶ f8g f8g p9.5g* p9.5g³ p12g 10g³ 10f⁵ 9.9f 10.1f⁵ p9.5f 10g Aug 23] tall, rangy mare: modest performer: won banded race at Wolverhampton in March: stays 1¼m: acts on all-weather and firm ground: blinkered once at 4 yrs. *T. D. Barron* **59**

FIRE ALARM 2 b.g. (May 25) Smoke Glacken (USA) 120 – Brandywine Belle (USA) (Trempolino (USA) 135) [2006 5g 6m 6f Jul 21] little form in maidens. *J. J. Quinn* –

FIRE AND RAIN (FR) 3 b.c. Galileo (IRE) 134 – Quatre Saisons (FR) (Homme de Loi (IRE) 120) [2006 103p: 12d⁶ 13.9g 12d Sep 29] strong, good-bodied colt: has a quick action: useful performer: not discredited on belated return at York when 7 lengths sixth to Youmzain in Great Voltigeur Stakes and 11 lengths tenth to Sixties Icon in St Leger (found little): well held in listed race at Newmarket final start: probably stays 1¾m: raced only on good/good to soft ground: sold 40,000 gns. *A. P. O'Brien, Ireland* **107**

FIRED UP (GER) 2 b.c. (Feb 22) Rainbow Quest (USA) 134 – Fantastic Flame (IRE) 79 (Generous (IRE) 139) [2006 p8.6g³ Nov 18] 125,000F: half-brother to 3 winners, including smart 2002 2-y-o 8.5f winner Bahamian Dancer (by Bering, later successful at 9f to 1½m in Hong Kong where called Industrial Success) and fairly useful 1½m winner Flaming Salsa (by Salse): dam, 1¼m winner, sister to smart 1¼m/1½m performer Germano: 2 lengths third to Peregrine Falcon in maiden at Wolverhampton, running on well under hands and heels: will improve. *Saeed bin Suroor* **72 p**

FIRE IN CAIRO (IRE) 2 b.f. (Jan 30) Barathea (IRE) 127 – Ibiza (GER) (Linamix (FR) 127) [2006 6g 7.2g⁵ 8.3m 6d f6g Dec 23] €31,000Y: workmanlike filly: third foal: half-sister to fairly useful 2004 2-y-o 5f winner Spree (by Dansili): dam German 10.5f winner: modest maiden: well below form in nurseries last 2 starts: seems to stay 8.3f. *P. C. Haslam* **59**

FIRENZE 5 ch.m. Efisio 120 – Juliet Bravo 61 (Glow (USA)) [2006 96: 6d³ 6m* 6m² 6m³ 6d 6g* Oct 12] strong, lengthy mare: useful performer: further progress in 2006, winning handicap at Goodwood (by length from Border Music) in June and listed event at Newmarket (by neck from Ripples Maid) in October: good efforts in between when 1½ lengths second of 28 to Baltic King in Wokingham at Royal Ascot and close third to Borderlescott in 27-runner Stewards' Cup at Goodwood: stays 6f: acts on fibresand, good to firm and good to soft going, unraced on extremes: patiently ridden. *J. R. Fanshawe* **109**

FIRE OF LOVE 3 ch.f. Allied Forces (USA) 123 – Princess Minnie (Mistertopogigo (IRE) 118) [2006 p8g³ p8.6g p8g p8g⁵ p7g Nov 11] 35,000Y: second foal: dam unraced half-sister to very smart 1m/1¼m performer Supreme Leader out of half-sister to dam of Pebbles: modest maiden: stays 1m: raced only on polytrack. *N. P. Littmoden* **61**

FIRESONG 4 b.g. Dansili 127 – Leaping Flame (USA) (Trempolino (USA) 135) [2006 81: 8.2s² 8.1m⁴ 8.2d 10m⁶ p8g⁶ 10m Aug 11] big, leggy gelding: has a round action: fairly useful performer: below form after second outing: effective at 1m (given test), and stays 1¼m: acts on firm and soft going: has been early to post: sold 26,000 gns. *Pat Eddery* **80 d**

FIRESTORM (IRE) 2 b.g. (Feb 8) Celtic Swing 138 – National Ballet (Shareef Dancer (USA) 135) [2006 7f⁴ 7.5m⁵ 8.1v⁴ 8s Oct 16] close-coupled gelding: modest maiden: bred to stay 1½m. *C. W. Fairhurst* **57**

FIRE TWO 3 b.c. Cape Cross (IRE) 129 – Reematna 75 (Sabrehill (USA) 120) [2006 81: 8d⁴ 8.5f² 10.1g² 11f² 11m⁵ 12g³ a6f³ Dec 22] compact colt: fairly useful maiden: placed 5 times in 2006, leaving M. Channon before final outing: stays 1½m: acts on firm and good to soft going: below form in visor third start: consistent. *D. J. Selvaratnam, UAE* **87**

FIRE UP THE BAND 7 b.g. Prince Sabo 123 – Green Supreme (Primo Dominie 121) [2006 117: p5g⁵ 6s 6g 5s⁴ 5m 5m 6m 5g Sep 8] lengthy, good-topped gelding: smart performer: largely disappointing in 2006: best effort when fifth in minor event at Lingfield on reappearance: best at 5f/easy 6f: acts on polytrack, firm and good to soft going, possibly not on soft: tried visored: has won when sweating: usually front runner. *D. Nicholls* **112 d**

FIREWORK 8 b.g. Primo Dominie 121 – Prancing 98 (Prince Sabo 123) [2006 64: 5.5d 5.7m 6f 6g³ p6g² p6g³ f6g⁴ p6g p6g³ p6g Dec 13] quite attractive gelding: modest performer: best at 6f: acts on all-weather, firm and soft ground: has worn headgear: often slowly away. *E. A. Wheeler*

FIRST AMONG EQUALS 3 b.f. Primo Valentino (IRE) 116 – Margarets First (Puissance 110) [2006 59: 5m⁶ 5.7g⁶ 5.1g 6.1f 5g⁶ 5g⁵ f5g Nov 21] neat filly: poor performer nowadays: left Miss J. Tooth prior to final start: raced only at 5f/6f: acts on good to firm going: tried blinkered/in cheekpieces. *D. G. Bridgwater* — **39**

FIRST APPROVAL 3 b.f. Royal Applause 124 – Gaijin 97 (Caerleon (USA) 132) [2006 73: 8.5g³ 7s³ 7g* 7m⁶ 7m⁶ p7g p7g Nov 15] leggy, lengthy filly: fair performer: won maiden at Thirsk in June: stays 7f, stamina stretched at 8.5f: acts on polytrack, soft and good to firm going. *B. W. Hills* — **78**

FIRST BLOOM (USA) 2 br.f. (Apr 15) Fusaichi Pegasus (USA) 130 – Shy Princess (USA) 117 (Irish River (FR) 131) [2006 p7.1g² Nov 28] $250,000Y, $250,000 2-y-o: sister to a winner in USA and half-sister to several winners, notably very smart 6f/7f performer Diffident (by Nureyev): dam French 6f to 7f winner: 3½ lengths second to Brosna Cry in maiden at Wolverhampton: likely to progress. *P. F. I. Cole* — **71 p**

FIRST BOY (GER) 7 b.g. Bering 136 – First Smile 104 (Surumu (GER)) [2006 f8g f8g May 31] fair performer: won maiden at Frankfurt at 3 yrs and handicap at Dresden in 2003 when trained by P. Rau in Germany: well held both Flat starts in Britain. *D. J. Wintle* — **–**

FIRST BUDDY 2 ch.g. (Apr 4) Rock of Gibraltar (IRE) 133 – Dance Treat (USA) 115 (Nureyev (USA) 131) [2006 7s p7g² p8g² Nov 29] 28,000Y: rather leggy, close-coupled gelding: fifth foal: half-brother to 3 winners, including 7f winner River Treat (by Irish River) and 1¼m winner Jubilee Treat (by Seeking The Gold), both fairly useful: dam, won La Coupe (1¼m) and Prix de Flore (10.5f), out of half-sister to Derby winner Golden Fleece: fair form: progressed in maidens, 1¼ lengths second to World Spirit at Kempton final outing: gelded after: stays 1m. *W. J. Haggas* — **76**

Jan and Peter Hopper's "Firenze"

FIRST BYTE 3 b.f. Primo Valentino (IRE) 116 – Shark Games (Mind Games 121) – [2006 54, a47: p6g p7.1g p6g[5] p7.1g p10g Feb 28] leggy filly: modest performer at 2 yrs: little form in 2006: tried blinkered, visored nowadays: tongue tied last 3 starts: very slowly away final outing. *Miss D. A. McHale*

FIRST CENTURION 5 b.g. Peintre Celebre (USA) 137 – Valley of Hope (USA)   **76** (Riverman (USA) 131) [2006 10g 10.2d[3] May 30] sturdy gelding: fair performer nowadays: unraced on Flat in 2005: left J. Hills 30,000 gns prior to reappearance: should stay 13f: acts on heavy going, below form on polytrack. *Ian Williams*

FIRST ECLIPSE (IRE) 5 b.m. Fayruz 116 – Naked Poser (IRE) 83 (Night Shift – (USA)) [2006 –: 6f Jul 28] good-topped mare: modest performer at 2 yrs: no form since: blinkered once. *G. Woodward*

FIRST FRIEND (IRE) 5 b.h. Mark of Esteem (IRE) 137 – Bustira (Busted 134) [2006   **76** 10g 10g 10m[6] p10g p8g p7.1m p8g p7g p10g[3] Nov 25] leggy horse: fair performer: won 2 minor events at Gavea in 2005: left D. Guignoni in Brazil after second start: effective at 6.5f to 1¼m: acts on polytrack, raced mainly on good going or softer on turf. *M. Mitchell*

FIRST FROST 2 ch.f. (Apr 27) Atraf 116 – Bless 58 (Beveled (USA)) [2006 p8g Dec 16] second foal: dam 1½m winner: 66/1, well beaten in maiden at Kempton. *M. J. Gingell*

FIRST GENERATION 4 b.g. Primo Dominie 121 – My Cadeaux 93 (Cadeaux Genereux 131) [2006 51: 7.5v 9d 6g 9s f7g p12.2g Dec 18] strong, angular gelding: modest maiden at best: well held in 2006, leaving T. Hogan in Ireland after fourth start: tried tongue tied. *P. D. Evans*

FIRST LOOK (FR) 6 b.g. Acatenango (GER) 127 – First Class (GER) (Bustino 136)   **78** [2006 –: 13d[2] May 7] fair performer: second in handicap at Hamilton sole Flat outing at 6 yrs: will be suited by 2m: acts on heavy ground: fairly useful hurdler/novice chaser. *P. Monteith*

FIRST MATE (IRE) 2 b.c. (May 1) Desert Style (IRE) 121 – Sail Away (GER) (Platini   **79** (GER) 126) [2006 5.9g[4] 6m* 6d[3] 6s[5] Sep 7] lengthy, useful-looking colt: third foal: closely related to useful German 6f/7f winner Shinko's Best (by Shinko Forest) and half-brother to 2005 2-y-o 5f winner Multiple (by Mull of Kintyre), later successful at 1m in USA: dam German 2-y-o 7f winner: fair form: won maiden at Ayr in August: ran creditably in nurseries: speedy, raced at 5f/6f: acts on soft and good to firm going. *M. Johnston*

FIRST ORDER 5 b.g. Primo Dominie 121 – Unconditional Love (IRE) 104 (Polish   **97** Patriot (USA) 128) [2006 p6g p6g 5g p6g[2] 6m[5] 6f[4] 6f 5g[3] 6d p5.1g[3] p6g* f5g p6g[3] Dec 16] big, strong gelding: useful handicapper: unraced in 2005: left Ernst Oertel after eighth start: won at Wolverhampton in November by ½ length from Prince Tum Tum: good third to Areyoutalkingtome at Lingfield final start: effective at 5f/6f: acts on polytrack and firm going: visored last 4 starts: has looked tricky ride. *I. Semple*

FIRST PRINCESS (IRE) 2 b.f. (Feb 26) King's Best (USA) 132 – Try To Catch   **68** Me (USA) (Shareef Dancer (USA) 135) [2006 p6g[4] p7g[4] p7g[5] p7.1g[2] Dec 21] 19,000Y: half-sister to several winners, notably high-class 7f (at 2 yrs) to 1½m winner Storming Home (by Machiavellian): dam French miler: fair maiden: left C. Tinkler, good second in nursery at Wolverhampton final start: has taken good hold, but bred to stay at least 1m: raced only on polytrack. *J. S. Moore*

FIRST RHAPSODY (IRE) 4 b.f. Rossini (USA) 118 – Tinos Island (IRE) (Alzao   **63** (USA) 117) [2006 67: p7.1g 7.1v[4] 7.5f 5.9g 7g* 7f[3] 6g 6.9g 7s[4] Aug 18] good-bodied filly: modest handicapper nowadays: won at Catterick in May: best at 6f/7f: acts on polytrack and any turf going: sometimes slowly away. *T. J. Etherington*

FIRST SHOW 4 b.g. Cape Cross (IRE) 129 – Rose Show (Belmez (USA) 131) [2006   **85** 84: p8g[3] p8.6g 8.3g[2] 8s[3] 8.3f[6] Jun 12] sturdy gelding: fairly useful performer: mainly creditable efforts in 2006, including on final outing (continually denied a run in last 2f): subsequently gelded: may prove best around 1m: acts on soft and firm going. *J. Noseda*

FIRST SLIP 3 b.c. Slip Anchor 136 – Nanouche (Dayjur (USA) 137) [2006 77: p12g   **74** p12g[4] 11m Sep 20] fair maiden: barely stays 1½m: raced mainly on polytrack: blinkered final start: sold 12,000 gns, joined J. O'Neill. *Mrs A. J. Perrett*

FIRST TO CALL 2 ch.c. (Mar 25) First Trump 118 – Scarlett Holly 81 (Red Sunset   – 120) [2006 7g Aug 17] strong, good-bodied colt: behind in maiden at Salisbury. *P. J. Makin*

FIRST VALENTINI 2 b.f. (Feb 14) Bertolini (USA) 125 – Oscietra 72 (Robellino   **56** (USA) 127) [2006 5m 5s[5] 5g[6] 6m[5] 6m[6] 5m 6s 5d[4] 5m 8f 6s 5s Oct 14] 5,600Y: lengthy filly: first foal: dam 9f winner: modest maiden: effective at 5f/6f: acts on good to firm and good to soft ground: tried in blinkers/tongue tie. *N. Bycroft*

FIR TREE 6 b.g. Mistertopogigo (IRE) 118 – Marina's Song (Savahra Sound 111) [2006 53: f8g5 f6g2 f6g6 f6g4 f6g2 6g May 30] tall gelding: modest maiden: effective at 6f to 8.6f: acts on all-weather: tried tongue tied: wore cheekpieces last 2 starts. *S. R. Bowring* **– a50**

FISBERRY 4 gr.c. Efisio 120 – Elderberry (Bin Ajwaad (IRE) 119) [2006 82: 5g2 6g 6.1f 6d Sep 27] fairly useful performer, lightly raced: well held after reappearance: best at 5f/6f: acts on good to firm going: waited with. *M. S. Saunders* **88**

FISBY 5 ch.g. Efisio 120 – Trilby 72 (In The Wings 128) [2006 78: p13.9g Jul 1] sturdy gelding: fair handicapper at best: tailed off only outing in 2006. *K. J. Burke* **–**

FISH CALLED JOHNNY 2 b.g. (Mar 3) Kyllachy 129 – Clare Celeste 73 (Coquelin (USA) 121) [2006 6.1f4 6.1g* 6g3 6s 6m 6g Sep 30] 31,000Y: close-coupled gelding: closely related to useful 7f winner Pizazz (by Pivotal) and half-brother to several winners, including fairly useful 1m/1¼m winner Sovereigns Court (by Statoblest): dam, maiden, best effort at 7f at 2 yrs: fairly useful performer: won maiden at Nottingham in August: creditable effort after only on next start: raced at 6f. *B. J. Meehan* **85**

FISHER BRIDGE (IRE) 3 ch.g. Singspiel (IRE) 133 – Kristal Bridge 75 (Kris 135) [2006 68p: 11.7m2 Aug 20] much better effort in maidens when 5 lengths second at Bath: suffered injury after, then gelded: bred to stay at least 1½m. *W. R. Swinburn* **85**

FISHFORCOMPLIMENTS 2 b.c. (Apr 3) Royal Applause 124 – Flyfisher (USA) (Riverman (USA) 131) [2006 6m2 6m* 6s 7g5 8s Oct 16] 22,000F, 32,000Y: big colt: has scope: fourth foal: brother to 3-y-o Playtotheaudience and half-brother to winner in Japan by Crafty Prospector: dam, placed in USA, half-sister to smart US 6f/7f performer Regal Thunder: useful performer: won maiden at Haydock in August: best effort when 3¼ lengths fifth of 8 to Vital Equine in Champagne Stakes at York (blinkered), but again difficult ride: stays 7f: acts on good to firm going, below form both starts on soft: refused at stall intended debut: suspect temperament. *R. A. Fahey* **99**

FISOLA (IRE) 3 b.f. Fasliyev (USA) 120 – Afisiak 60 (Efisio 120) [2006 80: 5.2m2 5g 5f2 5g 5.2f5 5g3 Aug 7] rather leggy, quite attractive filly: fairly useful performer: creditable efforts when placed in 2006: should stay 6f: raced only on good going or firmer (acts on firm): wore cheekpieces final outing: sold 7,000 gns in October. *C. G. Cox* **80**

FISTRAL 2 b.g. (Apr 23) Piccolo 121 – Fayre Holly (IRE) 57 (Fayruz 116) [2006 6m 7d6 6d p7.1g Oct 30] little form: bred for sprinting: gelded after final start. *M. R. Channon* **–**

FIT TO FLY (IRE) 5 b.g. Lahib (USA) 129 – Maid of Mourne (Fairy King (USA)) [2006 50: p9.5g 7g4 f8g3 10.1d6 8m 8m 10m f12g6 Nov 10] modest performer: left R. C. Guest after seventh outing: stays 1m: acts on all-weather, soft and good to firm going: wears headgear. *C. A. Mulhall* **50**

FITZSIMONS (IRE) 3 b.g. Carrowkeel (IRE) 106 – Our Pet 64 (Mummy's Pet 125) [2006 52: p12g Jun 24] leggy gelding: modest maiden at 2 yrs: well held in seller only outing in 2006: tried in cheekpieces/blinkers. *A. M. Hales* **–**

FIUMICINO 2 b.f. (Apr 22) Danehill Dancer (IRE) 117 – Valhalla Moon (USA) 92 (Sadler's Wells (USA) 132) [2006 7g6 8.1m4 8m4 8m* 8s4 Oct 16] 85,000Y: good-topped filly: first foal: dam, highly tried in 2 starts at 2 yrs, granddaughter of Irish St Leger winner Dark Lomond: fair performer: won nursery at Pontefract in September: stays 1m: acts on soft and good to firm going. *M. R. Channon* **76**

FIVE A SIDE 2 b.c. (Mar 8) Lomitas 129 – Fifth Emerald 54 (Formidable (USA) 125) [2006 7m* 8.2d2 Aug 15] 28,000F: fourth foal: half-brother to 6-y-o Goodbye Mr Bond and 4-y-o Anfield Dream: dam, 1m winner, out of close relation of smart middle-distance filly Valley of Gold: fairly useful form: won maiden at Epsom in July: improvement when second to Sesmen in minor event at Nottingham: will stay 1¼m: should do better still. *M. Johnston* **84 p**

FIVE TWO 3 ch.g. Mark of Esteem (IRE) 137 – Queen's Gallery (USA) 98 (Forty Niner (USA)) [2006 7m3 8m5 7m2 7f 8f 7d 7f2 6s 7s Oct 30] workmanlike gelding: fifth foal: half-brother to 7-y-o Qobtaan and a winner in Greece, both by Capote: dam, French 2-y-o 6.5f winner, closely related to US Grade 1 9f/1¼m winner Marquetry and smart French sprinter Spain Lane: fair maiden: sold from M. Channon 13,500 gns after fifth start: stays 1m: acts on firm ground: tongue tied (ran well) seventh outing. *A. J. Martin, Ireland* **75**

FIVE WISHES 2 b.f. (Mar 29) Bahamian Bounty 116 – Due West 56 (Inchinor 119) [2006 6m6 Aug 10] 25,000Y: smallish, strong filly: second foal: dam, ran 3 times, closely **62 p**

related to useful German stayer Western Devil out of half-sister to smart 7f/1m performer Redback: 100/1 and green (upset in stall), sixth in maiden at Haydock: open to improvement. *M. Dods*

FIZZLEPHUT (IRE) 4 b.g. Indian Rocket 115 – Cladantom (IRE) 70 (High Estate **86** 127) [2006 86: f6g p6g p5.1g⁴ p5.1g⁵ 5g 5g³ 5m 5m² 5g² 5.7g 5m³ 5g⁶ 5.5m 5m 5f 5g p6g **a82** p5.1m p5.1g* p5g p5.1g² p5.1s⁴ p5.1g Dec 27] lengthy gelding: fairly useful handicapper: won at Wolverhampton in November: best at 5f: acts on all-weather and good to firm going: tried in cheekpieces: has flashed tail. *Miss J. R. Tooth*

FIZZY LIZZY 6 b.m. Cool Jazz 116 – Formidable Liz 66 (Formidable (USA) 125) **51 §** [2006 45§: p6g⁴ p6g f8g p7.1g* p7.1g p6g p7.1g³ f7g 7.1m p7g⁶ p7g² Dec 13] dipped-backed mare: modest performer: won banded race at Wolverhampton in March: stays 7f: acts on polytrack (below form on fibresand) and firm going: tried in cheekpieces: inconsistent. *H. E. Haynes*

FLAME CREEK (IRE) 10 b.g. Shardari 134 – Sheila's Pet (IRE) (Welsh Term 126) **93** [2006 11.9g² 12v² p16g p16.5g² f14g* f14g* p12.2g⁵ Dec 26] one-time smart hurdler: not seen on Flat until 2006, fairly useful form when winning handicaps at Southwell in December by 14 lengths and 9 lengths: close second over 16.5f on polytrack, but best efforts at 1¾m on fibresand. *E. J. Creighton*

FLAMED AMAZEMENT 2 b.g. (Feb 13) Hernando (FR) 127 – Alligram (USA) 61 **68 p** (Alysheba (USA)) [2006 10.2m⁴ Sep 25] 28,000Y: closely related to 3-y-o Kyoto Summit and half-brother to 3 winners, including very smart 1m/1¼m winner Kissogram (by Caerleon): dam lightly-raced daughter of top-class miler Milligram: 10/1, fourth in maiden at Bath: sold 50,000 gns, then gelded: should improve. *M. Johnston*

FLAMESTONE 2 b.g. (Feb 4) Piccolo 121 – Renee 55 (Wolfhound (USA) 126) [2006 **58** 5d 5m³ p6g⁵ 6m³ 6g⁵ 7m 6d⁶ 6s Aug 28] close-coupled gelding: modest maiden: effective at 5f/6f: blinkered last 2 starts. *J. D. Bethell*

FLAMING CAT (IRE) 3 b. or br.g. Orpen (USA) 116 – Brave Cat (IRE) (Catrail – (USA) 123) [2006 –: 5.9g 7g Jun 2] tall gelding: little form. *J. Wade*

FLAMINGO GUITAR (USA) 3 ch.f. Storm Cat (USA) – Lotta Dancing (USA) **71** (Alydar (USA)) [2006 10g 7m* Jul 12] sturdy, lengthy filly: has a quick action: fifth foal: sister to 2 winners, including smart US Grade 2 9f winner Fantasticat and half-sister to winner in USA by Pulpit: dam, US Grade 3 8.5f winner, out of US Grade 1 1m winner Lotka: fair form: green on debut at Newmarket: much better effort when winning maiden at Naas nearly 3 months later: likely to prove best short of 1¼m. *D. Wachman, Ireland*

FLAMING SHOT (IRE) 4 b.c. Son of Sharp Shot (IRE) 105 – Brockton Flame 72 – (Emarati (USA) 74) [2006 54: f8g 10f f6m Oct 31] maiden: no form in Britain: tried blinkered/visored. *Jennie Candlish*

FLAMING WEAPON 4 b.g. Unfuwain (USA) 131 – Flame Valley (USA) 112 (Gulch **44** (USA)) [2006 53: f11g p12g Oct 29] good-bodied gelding: poor maiden on Flat: stays 1¼m: acts on good to soft ground. *G. L. Moore*

FLARAN 6 b.g. Emarati (USA) 74 – Fragrance (Mtoto 134) [2006 67: 5.2m 5f 5g 5.2f – p6g Oct 23] smallish, rather dipped-backed gelding: fair performer at best: well held in 2006: tried visored. *J. A. R. Toller*

FLASHING FEET (IRE) 2 b.c. (May 8) Soviet Star (USA) 128 – Delphini (IRE) 69 – (Seattle Dancer (USA) 119) [2006 p8g p9.5g p6g Dec 16] well held, including in seller. *R. Hannon*

FLASHING FLOOZIE 3 ch.f. Muhtarram (USA) 125 – High Habit 79 (Slip Anchor **54** 136) [2006 53p: p9.5g p8g⁵ p10g p7g⁴ p7g⁵ p8g⁵ 10m⁵ f11g 10f 8.1m 10.9m⁴ 10.9g³ 8m 10f³ 7.9f³ 9.9g³ 8s⁵ f7g p8g³ p8.6g⁵ Dec 4] good-topped filly: modest maiden: left M. Harris after fifteenth outing, J. Given before final one: stays 1¼m: acts on polytrack and firm going: tried blinkered/visored. *A. W. Carroll*

FLASHING NUMBERS (USA) 3 b. or br.c. Polish Numbers (USA) – Tanwi 101 **116** (Vision (USA)) [2006 105: a8f⁴ a9f⁶ 10d³ 10m* Jul 23] 60,000, 2-y-o: half-brother to several winners, including Irish 9f winner Sofyaan (by Silver Hawk) and 1¼m to 13f winner Fahs (by Riverman): dam Irish 5f to 1m winner: smart performer, both fairly useful: won newcomers race at Milan before 3 lengths third to Linda's Lad in Criterium de Saint-Cloud at 2 yrs: best effort when winning 5-runner Prix Eugene Adam at Maisons-Laffitte in July by 2 lengths from Dragon Dancer: missed rest of year (reportedly operated on for bout of colic): stays 1¼m: acts on soft and good to firm ground, below form on dirt at Nad Al Sheba first 2 starts: joined J. Noseda. *M. Hofer, Germany*

around 6f, half-sister to Middle Park winner Fard: fair form: won maiden at Lingfield in November: third in nursery there after: will prove best at 5f/6f. *R. Charlton*

FLY BY JOVE (IRE) 3 b.g. Fasliyev (USA) 120 – Flyleaf (FR) (Persian Bold 123) – [2006 –: 5g⁴ p7g⁵ Dec 22] good-topped gelding: no form in 3 outings, leaving A. Balding £1,400, gelded and off 6 months after reappearance. *Jane Southcombe*

FLYING BANTAM (IRE) 5 b.g. Fayruz 116 – Natural Pearl (Petong 126) [2006 91: 74 7v 7d 7.2m⁵ 7m⁵ 6g⁶ 7m² 7.2v⁴ 7s³ 6v p7.1g Dec 23] small, well-made gelding: fair handicapper nowadays: stays 7f: acts on polytrack, firm and soft going: tried in cheekpieces. *R. A. Fahey*

FLYING CLARETS (IRE) 3 b.f. Titus Livius (FR) 115 – Sheryl Lynn (Miller's Mate 85 116) [2006 65: 8g* 8.2s⁵ 8d² 9.8m⁴ 10.4m* 10m⁴ 10.3f⁴ 10.4f³ 12s³ 13.1d 10.5g 12s² 12d⁶ Oct 27] tall, quite good-topped filly: fairly useful handicapper: won at Ripon in May and York in June: creditable efforts when in frame after: stays 1½m: acts on firm and soft going: tried in cheekpieces at 2 yrs: usually takes good hold: saddle slipped tenth outing: tough. *R. A. Fahey*

FLYING DANCER 4 b.f. Danzero (AUS) – Alzianah 102 (Alzao (USA) 117) [2006 44 60, a53: f6g f6g⁴ f6g⁴ p6g p5.1g⁵ 5.7f⁴ 7f 5.7m 5g Sep 13] strong, close-coupled filly: just poor maiden in 2006: probably stays 7f: acts on all-weather and firm ground: tried in cheekpieces/blinkers: sold 5,000 gns. *R. A. Harris*

FLYING DOCTOR 3 b.g. Mark of Esteem (IRE) 137 – Vice Vixen (CAN) (Vice – Regent (CAN)) [2006 54: 9.8m Apr 29] well held only outing in 2006: stays 7.5f: best effort on good going. *G. M. Moore*

FLYING EDGE (IRE) 6 b.g. Flying Spur (AUS) – Day Is Dawning (IRE) (Green 80 Forest (USA) 134) [2006 76, a58: 5.9g p7.1g 6m³ 6.1m⁴ 6m² 6m* 7s p7.1g Nov 3] a– close-coupled gelding: fairly useful handicapper, better on turf than all-weather: won at Catterick in August: best at 6f nowadays: acts on all-weather, firm and soft going: tried blinkered at 3 yrs: sometimes flashes tail: races prominently. *E. J. Alston*

FLYING ENCORE (IRE) 2 b.f. (Apr 26) Royal Applause 124 – Come Fly With Me 82 (Bluebird (USA) 125) [2006 p7g⁴ 7g³ p7g² 8.3g⁴ Oct 16] 26,000Y: unfurnished filly: third foal: half-sister to 2003 2-y-o 7f winner On The Wing (by Pivotal) and Italian 5f winner (including at 2 yrs) by Mind Games: dam, once-raced half-sister to smart 7f/1m winner Madid: fairly useful maiden: in frame all 4 starts, including third to Caldra at Salisbury: probably stays 1m. *W. R. Swinburn*

FLYING GOOSE (IRE) 2 ch.c. (Apr 19) Danehill Dancer (IRE) 117 – Top of The 74 p Form (IRE) 79 (Masterclass (USA) 116) [2006 p7.1g² Nov 3] 110,000Y: fifth foal: half-brother to 5-y-o Glencalvie and 2004 2-y-o 6f winner Top Form (by Almutawakel): dam, 5f (including at 2 yrs)/6f winner, half-sister to useful 5f performer Double Quick: favourite, neck second to Majestic Cheer in maiden at Wolverhampton: will do better. *L. M. Cumani*

FLYING GREY (IRE) 2 gr.c. (May 8) Desert Prince (IRE) 130 – Grey Goddess 117 59 (Godswalk (USA) 130) [2006 6g 6m⁵ 7.1m⁴ 7d p6g p8.6g⁵ f7g⁵ Nov 13] compact colt: modest maiden: barely stays 8.6f: acts on polytrack, good to firm and good to soft going: blinkered final start. *P. A. Blockley*

FLYINGIT (USA) 3 b.f. Lear Fan (USA) 130 – Byre Bird (USA) (Diesis 133) [2006 90 75: 8g⁶ 9m³ 8m² 8m³ 12m⁶ 8d⁶ 9.5s⁵ 10s⁵ 10v³ 10d² p9.5g³ f11g* Dec 14] $45,000Y: fifth live foal: sister to French 7.5f (at 2 yrs)/1m winner Ronnie Gaucho and 1½m winner Bylaw who stayed 15f, both useful, and half-sister to winner in USA by Green Dancer: dam unraced half-sister to US Grade 1 9f winner Roanoke: fairly useful performer: left Thomas Mullins in Ireland after tenth outing: below best both starts in Britain, including when winning maiden at Southwell (pulled hard, wandered and idled markedly) in December: should stay 1½m (out of depth in Irish Oaks fifth start): acts on all-weather and good to firm ground (probably on heavy): blinkered final 2-y-o start: wore cheekpieces last 3 starts: sometimes tongue tied. *K. A. Ryan*

FLYING LION 2 b.f. (Apr 5) Hunting Lion (IRE) 115 – Princess Kelly (Prince Daniel 58 (USA)) [2006 5s⁵ 5s⁶ 5.1d 7m³ 7f* Jun 24] smallish filly: fourth foal: dam unraced: modest performer: won seller at Redcar (joined J. Balding 8,000 gns) in June: will stay 1m. *M. R. Channon*

FLYING NAMID (IRE) 2 b.f. (Apr 9) Namid 128 – Palio Flyer (Slip Anchor 136) – [2006 p6g p6g Aug 11] €5,500Y: seventh foal: half-sister to fairly useful 2000 2-y-o 7f winner Matlock (by Barathea), later successful in USA and a winner in Greece by Indian Lodge: dam unraced: last in maiden/seller. *P. A. Blockley*

FLYING PASS 4 b.g. Alzao (USA) 117 – Complimentary Pass 80 (Danehill (USA) **67**
126) [2006 –: p8.6g p7.1g⁶ p9.5g p10g⁵ p12g 10.2d p10g² p10g p10g May 3] close-
coupled gelding: has a quick action: fair maiden handicapper: barely stays 1½m: acts on
polytrack, firm and probably good to soft going: tried visored/tongue tied/in cheekpieces.
D. J. S. ffrench Davis

FLYING PATRIARCH 5 gr.g. Silver Patriarch (IRE) 125 – Flying Wind 51 (Forzan- **52**
do 122) [2006 f16g⁴ Mar 8] modest maiden: stays easy 2m: acts on fibresand: tried
blinkered. *G. L. Moore*

FLYING PENNE 3 b.f. Pennekamp (USA) 130 – Flying Wind 51 (Forzando 122) **–**
[2006 55: 10d 10m 7f p8g 16.2m 9g 10s 11.8d Oct 10] maiden: little form in 2006, leaving
M. Channon after fourth start. *R. Curtis*

FLYING SPIRIT (IRE) 7 b.g. Flying Spur (AUS) – All Laughter (Vision (USA)) **–**
[2006 76: p12g Mar 2] quite good-topped gelding: fair handicapper in 2005: stays 1½m:
acts on firm and good to soft going (well held on polytrack, including only outing on Flat
in 2006): sometimes wears headgear: races prominently. *G. L. Moore*

FLYING SPUD 5 ch.g. Fraam 114 – Lorcanjo 36 (Hallgate 127) [2006 –: f8g⁵ p12.2g **–**
f7g f8g p9.5g Feb 11] modest performer at best: no form since 2004. *A. J. Chamberlain*

FLYING TACKLE 8 ch.g. First Trump 118 – Frighten The Life (Kings Lake (USA) **56**
133) [2006 59: 5f³ 5f 5f 5f³ 5m⁴ 5m 6g 5.1m² 5s p6g Nov 20] strong, lengthy gelding:
modest performer: effective at 5f/6f: acts on polytrack and any turf going: wears headgear: tends to get behind: sometimes wanders. *I. W. McInnes*

FLYING VALENTINO 2 b.f. (Apr 22) Primo Valentino (IRE) 116 – Flying Romance **83 p**
(IRE) 68 (Flying Spur (AUS)) [2006 5f 6m* Aug 9] €5,000Y: first foal: dam 1½m/13f
winner: very green on debut, then impressive winner of maiden at Newcastle by neck
(had much more in hand), confidently ridden and barely coming off bridle: useful sprinter
in the making. *G. A. Swinbank*

FLYING VENTURE (IRE) 4 b.f. Mujadil (USA) 119 – Angela's Venture (GER) **–**
(Simply Great (FR) 122) [2006 9.7f 8.1d Jun 26] 2,300 2-y-o: sixth foal: half-sister to 2
winners abroad by Waajib: dam 7f winner in Germany: ran as though amiss both starts
(reportedly broke blood vessel when pulled up last time). *B. J. McMath*

FLYING VISITOR 3 b.f. Magic Ring (IRE) 115 – Just Visiting 85 (Superlative 118) **–**
[2006 p8g 10.1d 8.2m 8.1f 7f Aug 15] third foal: dam 2-y-o 5f/6f winner: little form: tried
blinkered. *J. M. P. Eustace*

FLYINGWITHOUTWINGS 7 b.g. Komaite (USA) – Light Slippers (IRE) (Ela- **57**
Mana-Mou 132) [2006 p12g p7g p8g 10.2d⁵ p12g May 15] modest maiden: should stay
1½m: raced only on polytrack and good to soft going. *A. King*

FLYLOWFLYLONG (IRE) 3 b.f. Danetime (IRE) 121 – Jellybeen (IRE) 72 (Petar- **74**
dia 113) [2006 72: p8.6g⁵ 7f⁶ 6.9g 7m 6m² 7.1m⁴ p7.1m³ 6g⁵ 7.2v p8.6g³ p8.6m⁴ Nov 9]
good-topped filly: fair handicapper: stays easy 8.6f: acts on polytrack, soft and good to
firm going (below form on heavy): visored (ran creditably) final outing: hung right
penultimate start. *I. Semple*

FLY MORE 9 ch.g. Lycius (USA) 124 – Double River (USA) (Irish River (FR) 131) **–**
[2006 56, a–: p6g p5g May 15] very big, lengthy gelding: modest performer in 2005,
when often in cheekpieces: well held on all-weather, including both outings in 2006.
J. M. Bradley

FLYOFF (IRE) 9 b.g. Mtoto 134 – Flyleaf (FR) (Persian Bold 123) [2006 f12g f12g **–**
Dec 29] modest in 2003: lightly raced and no form since: wears headgear. *Mrs
N. Macauley*

FLY SO FREE (IRE) 2 b.f. (Apr 9) Fath (USA) 116 – Xania 32 (Mujtahid (USA) 118) **66**
[2006 5d⁴ 5m³ 5g Aug 1] €17,000Y: strong, close-coupled filly: third foal: half-sister to
3-y-o Money Mate and 4-y-o Tiffin Deano: dam maiden: fair maiden: in frame at Thirsk
(minor event) and Ripon: off 3 months, well beaten final start (favourite): likely to prove
best at 5f/6f. *D. Nicholls*

FLY THE WORLD 2 b.f. (Jan 16) Agnes World (USA) 123 – Focosa (ITY) (In The **–**
Wings 128) [2006 8.2m p7g f6g Nov 28] 18,000Y: strong, good-topped filly: first foal:
dam Italian 11f winner: well held in maidens/seller. *A. P. Jarvis*

FLY TIME 2 b.f. (Apr 17) Fraam 114 – Kissing Time 79 (Lugana Beach 116) [2006 5s² **65 d**
5g 5.7f² 5m⁵ 5m⁵ p7g 5.1g² 5.7f³ 5.1m⁵ 5g² 6f p5.1g³ p5.1g p6m p5.1g⁴ p6g Dec 11]
leggy, workmanlike filly: has a quick action: second foal: sister to 3-y-o Fun Time: dam,

5f (including at 2 yrs) winner, half-sister to smart sprinter Acclamation: fair maiden: on downgrade after third outing: claimed from M. Channon seventh start, from H. Manners on twelfth: best form at 5f: acts on polytrack, firm and soft going: ran once in cheek-pieces. *Mrs L. Williamson*

FOCUS GROUP (USA) 5 b.g. Kris S (USA) – Interim 117 (Sadler's Wells (USA) 132) [2006 93: 8v 10.3m³ 10.4d³ 12m 10.4f Jul 15] strong gelding: has reportedly had shins fired: useful handicapper, lightly raced: best effort in 2006 when good third to Divine Gift at Chester second start: probably stays 1½m: acts on firm and good to soft going: often blanketed for stall entry. *J. J. Quinn* **98**

FOCUS STAR 2 ch.g. (Apr 20) Auction House (USA) 120 – Vida (IRE) 70 (Wolfhound (USA) 126) [2006 6v 5g 6f⁵ 5m 7g a6d² Dec 17] little form for J. M. Jefferson first 5 starts: second in maiden at Taby final outing: stays 6f. *J-E. Pettersson, Sweden* **?**

FOLGA 4 b.f. Atraf 116 – Desert Dawn 108 (Belfort (FR) 89) [2006 93: 5d 6g p6g³ 6m² 6m⁴ 6f* 6f* 6m 6m* 6m 6g 6d Aug 20] leggy filly: useful performer: won handicaps at Redcar in June, and Pontefract and Newmarket (by neck from Daniella) in July: well below form after: effective at 5f/6f: acts on polytrack and firm ground. *J. G. Given* **104**

FOLIO (IRE) 6 b.g. Perugino (USA) 84 – Bayleaf 104 (Efisio 120) [2006 85: 10g² 10d² 10f² 9.8m* 10f⁴ 9.9m³ 10.5m⁶ 10.1m² 10.4s 10s³ 10d* Nov 4] rather leggy, useful-looking gelding: useful handicapper: won at Ripon in June and Windsor (beat Rampallion by short head) in November: stays 1¼m: acts on polytrack, unraced on heavy ground but acts on any other turf: usually held up: consistent. *W. J. Musson* **95**

FOLIO (USA) 2 b.c. (Apr 23) Langfuhr (CAN) 124 – Foible (USA) (Riverman (USA) 131) [2006 6m² 6m² 7m 6d 7m⁴ Sep 19] strong, quite attractive colt: fourth foal: closely related to winner in Austria by Belong To Me: dam, French 1m (at 2 yrs) and 1½m winner, half-sister to dam of 1000 Guineas winner Wince: maiden: fairly useful form when second at Leicester and York first 2 starts: well below form after: likely to stay 1m: acts on good to firm going: sold 20,000 gns, sent to USA. *B. W. Hills* **84 d**

FOLK OPERA (IRE) 2 ch.f. (Feb 22) Singspiel (IRE) 133 – Skiphall (Halling (USA) 133) [2006 p7g³ Oct 11] 27,000F, 105,000Y: first foal: dam, fairly useful French maiden who stayed 10.5f, half-sister to smart French/US 1¼m/10.5f winner Skipping: 14/1, third to Tybalt in maiden at Lingfield, taking strong hold: will be suited by 1m/1¼m: sure to improve. *M. A. Jarvis* **80 p**

FOLLINGWORTH (IRE) 3 ch.f. Midhish 109 – Pennine Way (IRE) (Waajib 121) [2006 –: p8.6g 10.1g May 1] compact filly: no form. *A. D. Brown* **–**

FOLLOWING FLOW (USA) 4 b. or br.g. King of Kings (IRE) 125 – Sign Here (USA) (Private Terms (USA)) [2006 79, a86: p8.6g p8.6g* p8g 8.1g⁶ 8.2d⁶ 8.2g p9.5g p8.6g⁴ Dec 21] good-topped gelding: fairly useful handicapper: won at Wolverhampton in March: stays 8.6f: acts on polytrack, soft and good to firm going: sometimes wears cheekpieces: sometimes slowly away: patiently ridden: none too consistent. *R. Hollinshead* **80**

FOLLOW ME IN (IRE) 3 b.f. Elnadim (USA) 128 – Arjan (IRE) 88 (Paris House 123) [2006 47: p6g Jan 6] poor maiden: refused to race only outing in 2006: blinkered final 2-y-o start: one to avoid. *K. R. Burke* **– §**

FOLLOW MY TRAIL (IRE) 3 br.g. Indian Danehill (IRE) 124 – Lady Stalker 57 (Primo Dominie 121) [2006 54: f11g 8.5d 7g Apr 25] useful-looking gelding: maiden: no form in 2006. *B. Smart* **–**

FOLLOW ON 4 b.c. Barathea (IRE) 127 – Handora (IRE) 82 (Hernando (FR) 127) [2006 10.1g⁴ 11.9m⁴ 10f p16g³ 16.1m Jul 13] €32,000Y: rather leggy, quite good-topped colt: first foal: dam Irish 1½m winner: fairly useful maiden: best effort when third in handicap at Kempton: sprained hock final outing: stays 2m: acts on polytrack, best effort on turf on good going. *A. P. Jarvis* **84**

FOLLOW THE BUZZ 2 b.c. (Apr 29) Enjoy The Buzz 64 – Moody Madam (Man Among Men (IRE)) [2006 p7.1g 8.2s Oct 18] angular, heavy-topped colt: tailed off in maidens. *J. M. Bradley* **–**

FOLLOW THE COLOURS (IRE) 3 b.g. Rainbow Quest (USA) 134 – Gardenia (IRE) (Sadler's Wells (USA) 132) [2006 69: 8d² 8.5g³ 8s³ 10.3g 11g p10g* p10g⁶ 9g⁵ p10g Oct 20] neat gelding: fair handicapper: won at Kempton in July: gelded prior to final outing: stays 1¼m: acts on polytrack and soft going. *W. J. Hills* **75**

FOLLOW THE FLAG (IRE) 2 ch.g. (Mar 31) Traditionally (USA) 117 – Iktidar 80 (Green Desert (USA) 127) [2006 6g³ f6g³ 6m² 7f³ 6d Aug 25] 75,000Y: heavy-topped **72**

gelding: sixth foal: half-brother to several winners, including 4-y-o Qadar: dam, maiden who stayed 1m, out of half-sister to Sheikh Albadou: fair maiden: placed first 4 starts, including nursery, and gelded after final one: stays 7f: acts on firm going. *N. P. Littmoden*

FOLLY LODGE 2 ch.f. (May 1) Grand Lodge (USA) 125 – Marika 103 (Marju (IRE) **75** 127) [2006 7m p7g* 7d Sep 30] good-bodied filly: second foal: dam, 6f and 1m winner, half-sister to Oaks fourth Sueboog, the dam of Best of The Bests: fair form: won maiden at Kempton in September: stiff task in listed race at Newmarket final start: will stay 1m. *B. W. Hills*

FONDNESS 3 ch.f. Dr Fong (USA) 128 – Island Story 88 (Shirley Heights 130) [2006 **70** 10g⁵ 10m p12g⁵ 11.6m⁶ p9.5g⁶ Nov 24] third foal: half-sister to fairly useful 1¼m/11f **a–** winner Strategy (by Machiavellian): dam, 1¼m winner who stayed 2m, half-sister to smart winner up to 1½m Arabian Story: fair maiden on turf: left R. Charlton after fourth start: stays 11.6f: acts on good to firm going, little form on polytrack: free-going sort. *D. Carroll*

FONGALONG 2 b.f. (Jan 27) Dr Fong (USA) 128 – Shafir (IRE) 68 (Shaadi (USA) **–** 126) [2006 5.1f 6g p6g⁶ Jul 12] 6,500Y: sturdy filly: half-sister to several winners, including 4-y-o Gallego and 15f winner Toledo Sun (by Zamindar): dam 2-y-o 5f winner: well held all starts: will stay at least 1m. *T. G. Dascombe*

FONGS GAZELLE 2 b.f. (Feb 6) Dr Fong (USA) 128 – Greensand 96 (Green Desert **74** (USA) 127) [2006 5g⁴ 6v³ 6g⁵ 7f² 7.5g 8g³ 8m² 8s² Oct 16] 4,500F, 17,000Y: rangy filly: fourth foal: dam, 2-y-o 6f winner, half-sister to smart performer up to 9.5f in USA Country Garden: fair maiden: placed 5 times, in nurseries last 3 starts: stays 1m: acts on any going: races prominently. *M. Johnston*

FONIC ROCK (IRE) 3 b.f. Zafonic (USA) 130 – Blue Crystal (IRE) 77 (Lure (USA) **63** 131) [2006 –: 12.6g⁶ 12.1f² 12f 11.5f² 12g 13.1m 11.9m 11.5d⁴ Oct 18] quite good-topped filly: modest maiden: stays 1½m: acts on firm ground: visored final outing: sold 8,000 gns. *M. L. W. Bell*

totesport Ayr Gold Cup (Handicap), Ayr—Fonthill Road, runner-up in this race and the Stewards' Cup in 2005, gains a deserved win; the next six home, Borderlescott, Advanced, Coleorton Dancer, Andronikos, Out After Dark (No.9) and Appalachian Trail, are all on the stand side

Mrs Una Towell's "Fonthill Road"

FONT 3 b.g. Sadler's Wells (USA) 132 – River Saint (USA) 73§ (Irish River (FR) 131) **94 p**
[2006 82p: 8d² 10d³ Oct 4] good-bodied gelding: has a round action: fairly useful form:
best effort in maidens when neck second to Peppertree Lane at Ripon (reportedly jarred
up): gelded, just fair third at Nottingham 5½ months later, travelling strongly into contention but not moving that freely at finish: should stay 1¼m: raced only on good to soft
going: should do better yet. *J. R. Fanshawe*

FONTANA AMOROSA 2 ch.f. (Apr 16) Cadeaux Genereux 131 – Bella Lambada 87 **75**
(Lammtarra (USA) 134) [2006 5g 6.1d* 7d Oct 14] 13,000Y: angular, good-topped filly:
third foal: half-sister to 1½m winner Bella Miranda (by Sinndar) and 3-y-o Bariloche:
dam, 10.4f winner from 2 starts, half-sister to high-class 1¼m performer Stagecraft: fair
form: won minor event at Nottingham in May: raced freely/well
beaten in Rockfel Stakes at Newmarket: likely to stay 1m. *K. A. Ryan*

FONTHILL ROAD (IRE) 6 ch.g. Royal Abjar (USA) 121 – Hannah Huxtable (IRE) **113**
(Master Willie 129) [2006 113: 5g⁵ 6d 6s 6d* 6d² 5g⁵ Oct 12] strong gelding: smart
performer: back to best (had reportedly been suffering from back problems) when
winning totesport Ayr Gold Cup in September by length from Borderlescott: creditable
¾-length second of 9 to Bygone Days in minor event at Hamilton next time: respectable
fifth to Mecca's Mate in handicap at Newmarket final outing: effective at 5f/6f: acts on
fibresand, very best turf efforts on good ground or softer: usually waited with: genuine.
R. A. Fahey

FOODBROKER FOUNDER 6 ch.g. Groom Dancer (USA) 128 – Nemea (USA) 97 **78**
(The Minstrel (CAN) 135) [2006 87: 10d 12m 9.9g Jun 28] good-bodied gelding: just fair
handicapper in 2006: stays 1¼m: acts on firm and good to soft ground. *D. R. C. Elsworth*

FOOD FOR THOUGHT 3 b.f. Mind Games 121 – Ladycake (IRE) 71 (Perugino **43**
(USA) 84) [2006 62: 7g f8g³ f12g p8.6g f7g Nov 21] quite good-topped filly: maiden:
just poor form in 2006: stays 1m: acts on fibresand (probably on polytrack) and good to
firm ground: often blinkered/visored. *J. J. Quinn*

FOOLISH GROOM 5 ch.g. Groom Dancer (USA) 128 – Scared (Royal Academy **70**
(USA) 130) [2006 70: 9.9d⁵ 8m 10s⁵ 8.1d² 8.3f³ 8m² 8.1f 8.1m⁵ 8.1m 8.2d Nov 1] quite
good-topped gelding: fair handicapper: stays 1¼m: acts on polytrack, firm and soft going:
tried in cheekpieces/tongue tied, visored of late. *R. Hollinshead*

FOOL ME (IRE) 2 b.c. (Feb 10) Mull of Kintyre (USA) 114 – Dawn's Folly (IRE) 47 **82**
(Bluebird (USA) 125) [2006 5d⁴ 5g* 6g² Aug 7] 34,000Y: strong, stocky colt: fourth
foal: closely related to 5f winner (including at 2 yrs) Red Eagle (by Eagle Eyed) and half-
brother to fairly useful 2002 2-y-o 6f/7f winner Love Is Blind (by Ali-Royal): dam Irish
maiden (probably stayed 7f): fairly useful form: won maiden at Leicester in April: further
progress (after 3-month break) when 4 lengths second to Big Timer in minor event at
Ripon: may prove best kept to 5f/6f. *E. S. McMahon*

FOOTBALL CRAZY (IRE) 7 b.g. Mujadil (USA) 119 – Schonbein (IRE) 60 (Per- **–**
sian Heights 129) [2006 88: 20m Jun 20] lengthy, quite good-topped gelding: fairly useful
handicapper at best: well beaten in Ascot Stakes only Flat outing in 2006: tried blinkered.
P. Bowen

FOOTSTEPSINTHESNOW (IRE) 3 b.f. Medicean 128 – Charlecote (IRE) (Caer- **57**
leon (USA) 132) [2006 6g⁵ 6m 7f⁶ 7d p7g p10g p10g⁶ p12g p10g Dec 30] close-coupled
filly: first foal: dam unraced out of sister to Barathea and Gossamer: modest maiden:
probably stays easy 1¼m: acts on polytrack and good to firm going: sweating (ran poorly)
fourth start. *M. A. Buckley*

FORCED UPON US 2 ch.g. Allied Forces (USA) 123 – Zing (Zilzal (USA) **59**
137) [2006 6g p7.1g* p7.1g⁶ Dec 21] modest form: won seller at Wolverhampton in
September: sixth in nursery there final start: will stay 1m. *P. J. McBride*

FORCE GROUP (IRE) 2 b.c. (Apr 6) Invincible Spirit (IRE) 121 – Spicebird (IRE) **61**
67 (Ela-Mana-Mou 132) [2006 8m 7g p7.1g Nov 3] close-coupled, good-topped colt:
modest form in maidens. *M. H. Tompkins*

FORCES SWEETHEART 3 b.f. Allied Forces (USA) 123 – Talighta (USA) 62 (Bar- **90**
athea (IRE) 127) [2006 76d: p7g 6m 6f 6m 6f 5m 6g* 6d* 6g* 6d* 6s* 6g⁵ 6d p5g⁶ Nov
11] rather leggy, lengthy filly: fairly useful handicapper: won 5 times between August
and October, at Yarmouth (twice), Folkestone, Leicester and Newcastle, last-named by
2½ lengths from Greek Secret: left M. Bell 30,000 gns, below form last 2 outings (stiff
task first occasion): best form at 6f: acts on soft and good to firm going: visored
nowadays: swerved violently right at start second outing. *V. Smith*

FOREFATHERS (USA) 2 b.c. (Feb 20) Gone West (USA) – Star of Goshen (USA) **63 p**
(Lord At War (ARG)) [2006 7m Aug 30] $680,000Y: big colt: fourth foal: half-brother to
winner in USA by Old Trieste: dam, 6.5f to 1m winner in USA, half-sister to US Grade 2
7f winner Powis Castle: 11/4, green throughout when seventh in minor event at Lingfield:
sent to USA: sure to improve. *M. L. W. Bell*

FOREIGN AFFAIRS 8 ch.h. Hernando (FR) 127 – Entente Cordiale (USA) (Affir- **117**
med (USA)) [2006 106: 12m⁵ 14m³ 11.3m* 14g* 16f 12d² Aug 20] rather leggy, good-
topped horse: smart performer: back to best in 2006, winning listed races at Limerick (by
¾ length from Ask Carol) in June and Leopardstown (beat Mkuzi 3 lengths) in July:
creditable 3 lengths second of 5 to Kastoria in similar event at Leopardstown final outing:
effective at 1¼m to 1¾m (went off too quickly in 2m Goodwood Cup fifth start): acts on
fibresand, soft and good to firm going: blinkered once: often makes running: genuine.
Sir Mark Prescott

FOREIGN EDITION (IRE) 4 b.g. Anabaa (USA) 130 – Palacegate Episode (IRE) **89**
111 (Drumalis 125) [2006 93: 6d 6m³ p6g⁵ p6g Nov 16] lengthy, useful-looking gelding:
fairly useful handicapper, lightly raced: stays 7f: acts on polytrack and good to firm
going. *Miss J. A. Camacho*

FOREIGN ENVOY (IRE) 3 ch.g. Grand Lodge (USA) 125 – Soviet Artic (FR) 84§ **62**
(Bering 136) [2006 56p: 7.1g 8.5g⁵ 11m 10.9m⁶ 12g Jun 30] well-made gelding: modest
maiden: stays 11f: raced only on good and good to firm going on turf: sold 4,000 gns in
October, sent to Spain. *B. W. Hills*

FOREIGNER (IRE) 3 b.g. Montjeu (IRE) 137 – Northumbrian Belle (IRE) (Dist- **78**
inctly North (USA) 115) [2006 9.9g⁴ 10m⁵ p12g⁶ p13g Sep 29] €37,000Y, 110,000 2-y-o:
sturdy, close-coupled gelding: third foal: dam unraced half-sister to very smart miler
Revoque: fair maiden: stays 1¼m: acts on good to firm going: failed to settle second/third
outings: sold 5,000 gns. *B. J. Meehan*

FOREIGN LANGUAGE (USA) 3 ch.f. Distant View (USA) 126 – Binary 109 **80**
(Rainbow Quest (USA) 134) [2006 p8g³ p8.6g² p8.6g* Dec 18] 18,000 2-y-o: sister to

useful 1m winner Binary Vision and half-sister to 2 winners, including smart 7f to 9f winner Binary File (by Nureyev): dam, 9f/1¼m winner in France/USA, sister to smart 1½m winner Bequeath: progressive in maidens, fairly useful form when winning at Wolverhampton in December by 4 lengths from Chia: stays 8.6f: raced only on polytrack. *N. A. Callaghan.*

FOR EILEEN 2 b.f. (Mar 4) Dinar (USA) 65 – Dreams of Zena (Dreams End 93) [2006 **50** 5.1d p7.1g³ p8g² p8.6g Dec 31] first foal: dam of little account: modest maiden: trained by D. Burchell debut: placed in sellers after: will prove best up to 1m. *M. G. Quinlan.*

FORELAND SANDS (IRE) 2 b.g. (Mar 11) Desert Sun 120 – Penrose (IRE) 75 – (Wolfhound (USA) 126) [2006 5g 6m 6m Sep 11] behind in maidens, then gelded. *J. R. Best.*

FOREMENTOR 3 b.f. Little Jim – Lizzy Cantle 52 (Homing 130) [2006 p8g p10g – Aug 13] half-sister to 1m and 11f winner Bundaberg (by Komaite) and 6f winner Dryad (by Risk Me): dam 7f winner: well beaten in maidens at Lingfield. *D. K. Ivory.*

FOREPLAY (IRE) 3 b.f. Lujain (USA) 119 – Watch Me (IRE) 106 (Green Desert **86** (USA) 127) [2006 71: p7.1g⁴ 7m² p7g p7.1g³ 7m p7g⁵ 8.3g p7.1g² p7.1g* p7.1g² Dec 23] tall, close-coupled filly: fairly useful handicapper: improved form in cheekpieces last 3 starts, winning at Wolverhampton in November: stays 7f (raced freely at 1m): acts on polytrack and good to firm going. *E. A. L. Dunlop.*

FOREST AIR (IRE) 6 br.m. Charnwood Forest (IRE) 125 – Auriga 73 (Belmez – (USA) 131) [2006 –: 7g 6f Aug 10] workmanlike mare: no form since 2004: tried in cheekpieces. *B. R. Johnson.*

FOREST DANE 6 b.g. Danetime (IRE) 121 – Forest Maid (Thatching 131) [2006 57: **87** p5g² p6g* p6g³ 5.3m* 6m³ p5g³ 5g⁴ 5m* 5g⁵ 5m* 6m² p6g² p5g* 6d p6g⁵ Nov 5] smallish, good-topped gelding: fairly useful performer: much improved in 2006, winning banded race at Kempton and handicap at Brighton in May, and handicaps at Sandown in August and September, and Lingfield in October: effective at 5f/6f: acts on polytrack and firm going. *Mrs N. Smith.*

FORESTELLE (IRE) 3 br.f. Shinko Forest (IRE) – Machudi (Bluebird (USA) 125) **54** [2006 6d⁴ 6d⁶ 7.5g⁶ 6m⁵ f8g Jul 11] €23,000Y: good-topped filly: second foal: closely related to 2004 2-y-o 5f winner Rightprice Premier (by Cape Cross): dam maiden who stayed 7f: modest maiden: reportedly finished lame final outing: stays 7.5f: best effort on good going. *M. Dods.*

FOREST LODGE (IRE) 3 ch.f. Indian Lodge (IRE) 127 – Folkboat (Kalaglow 132) **44** [2006 –: 9s 8m⁵ 9.9g Aug 31] tall filly: poor maiden. *D. R. C. Elsworth.*

FOREST MACHINE 2 b.g. (Apr 24) Largesse 112 – Polar Storm (IRE) 76 (Law **65** Society (USA) 130) [2006 5f⁵ 5m⁴ Aug 31] workmanlike gelding: mid-field in maidens: once refused at stalls. *J. S. Wainwright.*

FOREST OF LOVE 4 br.f. Charnwood Forest (IRE) 125 – Touch And Love (IRE) – (Green Desert (USA) 127) [2006 74: f8g p7.1g p7.1g Mar 25] tall filly: fair performer at best: well held in 2006. *M. W. Easterby.*

FOREVER AUTUMN 3 b.g. Sinndar (IRE) 134 – Photo Call 73 (Chief Singer 131) **58** [2006 10.5m⁶ 11.9m⁵ 10f Jun 19] quite attractive gelding: modest maiden: gelded after final outing: probably stays 1½m. *B. J. Meehan.*

FOREVER ROCKY 3 b.g. Kayf Tara 130 – Song For Jess (IRE) (Accordion) [2006 – –: 10g p8g 8m Jun 28] little form: tried blinkered. *F. Jordan.*

FOREVER THINE 3 ch.f. Groom Dancer (USA) 128 – Indubitable 87 (Sharpo 132) – [2006 10g 9.9g 10d Oct 9] sister to 6-y-o Gold Ring and half-sister to 2 winners, notably useful 1¼m winner Cugina (by Distant Relative): dam 1¼m winner: no sign of ability in maidens. *J. A. Geake.*

FORFEITER (USA) 4 ch.g. Petionville (USA) – Picabo (USA) (Wild Again (USA)) **74** [2006 76: 8v² 8.7d 8d³ 7f 7g 8.5g 9m* a7g³ p8.6g Nov 23] workmanlike gelding: fair performer: won claimer at Ballinrobe in August: left G. Lyons in Ireland before well held in handicap at Wolverhampton final start: stays 9f: acts on fibresand, firm and soft going: often wears headgear. *R. Ford.*

FORGERY (IRE) 4 ch.g. Dr Devious (IRE) 127 – Memory Green (USA) (Green **105** Forest (USA) 134) [2006 93: p8.6g⁴ 8m* 8m 10.4f⁴ Jul 15] strong, well-made gelding: useful handicapper, lightly raced: won 25-runner Bloor Homes Spring Cup at Newbury in April by ½ length from Colisay: good 1¼ lengths fourth to Fairmile in John Smith's

Cup at York final start: suffered injury in late-September: effective at 1m to 10.4f: acts on polytrack, firm and soft going. *G. A. Butler*

FOR LIFE (IRE) 4 b.g. Bachir (IRE) 118 – Zest (USA) (Zilzal (USA) 137) [2006 71§: f6g p8g 7m² 7f⁵ 7m 7.6m 6m⁵ f8g² p6g⁴ p7g f7g⁵ Dec 12] strong, lengthy gelding: modest maiden: stays 1m: acts on all-weather and good to firm ground: tried in cheekpieces/ visored: has been withdrawn after giving trouble on 3 occasions: difficult ride and best treated with caution. *A. P. Jarvis*   **60 §**

FORMAL DECREE (GER) 3 b.g. Diktat 126 – Formida (FR) (Highest Honor (FR) 124) [2006 71: 8g² 8d* 10m* 10m* 9.9g⁴ 10m³ 9d* Sep 30] lengthy, good-topped gelding: smart handicapper: progressed really well, winning at Pontefract in May (reared and lost 10 lengths at start) and June, and Newmarket in July and September (beat Blue Bajan impressively by 4 lengths in totesport Cambridgeshire, showing fine turn of foot to take charge from Dip): effective at 1m, should stay 1½m: acts on good to firm and good to soft going: held up: sold, and joined I. Mohammed in UAE. *G. A. Swinbank*   **117**

FORM AND BEAUTY (IRE) 4 b.c. Orpen (USA) 116 – Formezza (IRE) (Cyrano de Bergerac 120) [2006 64: f12g⁶ Feb 16] form (modest) only on debut at 3 yrs: tried in cheekpieces. *C. Roberts*   **–**

FORMAT 3 b.f. Mark of Esteem (IRE) 137 – Forum 86 (Lion Cavern (USA) 117) [2006 8m 7g Jun 28] big, strong, close-coupled filly: third foal: dam, 7f (at 2 yrs) and 8.5f winner, half-sister to useful performer up to 1¼m Forthwith: slowly away when well beaten in maidens at Salisbury. *A. W. Carroll*   **–**

FORMIDABLE WILL (FR) 4 b.g. Efisio 120 – Shewillifshewants (IRE) (Alzao (USA) 117) [2006 74: f8g p8.6g² 8g f8g* f8g⁴ f8g* f8g⁴ Dec 23] well-made gelding: fair performer: won sellers at Southwell in November and December (sold 10,000 gns from M. Easterby): stays 8.6f: acts on all-weather, best turf effort on good ground (well held on firm): usually in cheekpieces, blinkered/visored last 2 starts: tongue tied nowadays. *D. Shaw*   **77**

FOR NO ONE (IRE) 3 b.g. Mozart (IRE) 131 – Dame Laura (IRE) 100 (Royal Academy (USA) 130) [2006 7.1g⁶ 10g 10g 10f 9.8m Jul 10] modest maiden: probably stays 1¼m: sold 800 gns later in July. *M. Johnston*   **53**

FORREST FLYER (IRE) 2 b.c. (Apr 30) Daylami (IRE) 138 – Gerante (USA) (Private Account (USA)) [2006 8d Nov 3] last in maiden at Musselburgh. *Miss L. A. Perratt*   **–**

FORROGER (CAN) 3 br.c. Black Minnaloushe (USA) 123 – Count On Romance (CAN) (Geiger Counter (USA)) [2006 78: 8d³ 10g⁴ 10s 8.3d⁴ 10s* 10d⁶ Oct 9] tall, close-coupled colt: fairly useful performer: left V. Smith and off 3 months, won handicap at Newmarket in August: ran creditably final outing: stays 1¼m: acts on soft ground (unraced on firmer than good). *M. A. Jarvis*   **84**

FORSTERS PLANTIN 2 ch.f. (Feb 18) Muhtarram (USA) 125 – Ischia 64 (Lion Cavern (USA) 117) [2006 7g 7s Oct 14] first foal: dam, maiden (form only at 7f at 2 yrs), half-sister to smart performers Attache (best around 7f) and Tadeo (5f/6f): well beaten in maidens. *J. J. Quinn*   **–**

FORT AMHURST (IRE) 2 ch.c. (Feb 11) Halling (USA) 133 – Soft Breeze 99 (Zafonic (USA) 130) [2006 8g³ Oct 13] angular, useful-looking colt: fluent mover: second foal: dam, 7f/1m winner, out of very smart Irish sprinter Tropical: 40/1, took eye to post, third to Sam Lord in maiden at Newmarket: likely to improve. *E. A. L. Dunlop*   **81 p**

---

totesport Cambridgeshire (Handicap), Newmarket—
Formal Decree routs his field with a performance rarely seen in such a competitive race, winning by four
lengths from Blue Bajan (noseband), Pinpoint (hooped cap) and Take A Bow (dark colours, fourth left);
Spectait, who raced alone on the far side, finishes in mid-division

FORT CHURCHILL (IRE) 5 b.g. Barathea (IRE) 127 – Brisighella (IRE) (Al Hareb (USA) 123) [2006 p12.2g p12.2g p12g 14.1s 12.4g² 11.5m⁶ 14s⁵ 12.1f² 12.4m* 12m³ 12f* 11.7m⁵ 12d 10d* 11g⁴ 10d³ 10.4s Oct 6] big, good-topped gelding: fairly useful on turf, fair on all-weather: won claimer at Newcastle in June, and handicaps at York in July and Sandown in September: effective at 1¼m to 1¾m: acts on polytrack, firm and soft going: tried in cheekpieces, blinkered/tongue tied nowadays: has carried head awkwardly. *B. Ellison* **88 a76**

FORTHRIGHT 5 b.g. Cadeaux Genereux 131 – Forthwith 104 (Midyan (USA) 124) [2006 80: p10g 10d 10g* 8m⁵ 10f² 12d⁴ 12s³ 8.9s⁵ 10g Oct 16] tall, good sort: fairly useful handicapper: left G. L. Moore after reappearance: won at Newbury (amateurs) in June and Ripon in July: creditable efforts next 2 starts: stays 1½m: acts on polytrack/dirt, firm and soft ground: tried in blinkers/cheekpieces. *A. W. Carroll* **88**

FORTISZAMO 4 b.g. Forzando 122 – Flamingo Times 60 (Good Times (ITY)) [2006 –: p10g p8g May 15] strong, well-made gelding: maiden: well held since 2 yrs: tried visored. *A. W. Carroll* **–**

FORTRESS 3 b.f. Generous (IRE) 139 – Imperial Bailiwick (IRE) 104 (Imperial Frontier (USA) 112) [2006 64: p7.1g⁶ 5g 6.9m⁴ 6g² 5.9g* 5m⁴ p6m Sep 2] fair performer: won handicap at Carlisle in August: likely to prove best at 6f: acts on polytrack and good to firm going: blinkered last 5 starts. *E. J. Alston* **66**

FORTUNATE ISLE (USA) 4 ch.c. Swain (IRE) 134 – Isla Del Rey (USA) 103 (Nureyev (USA) 131) [2006 90+: 8v* 8.1m 9.9g 8s 10m 12d 10s⁴ Oct 21] angular, quite attractive colt: fairly useful handicapper, lightly raced: won at Pontefract in April: creditable efforts at Newbury fifth and final starts: stays 1¼m: probably acts on any going: sweating (well held) second outing: sold 30,000 gns, joined R. Fahey. *B. W. Hills* **93**

FORTUNE ISLAND (IRE) 7 b.g. Turtle Island (IRE) 123 – Blue Kestrel (IRE) 70 (Bluebird (USA) 125) [2006 100: p16g 16d 14m⁶ p16g 21m Aug 2] good-topped gelding: just fairly useful handicapper nowadays: stays 21f: acts on polytrack, soft and good to firm going: visored/tongue tied. *D. E. Pipe* **87**

FORTUNE POINT (IRE) 8 ch.g. Cadeaux Genereux 131 – Mountains of Mist (IRE) 80 (Shirley Heights 130) [2006 –§, a69§: p9.5g p8g⁵ p9.5g p10g⁴ f8g⁵ 10m* 8.5g³ 10f⁶ 10f⁵ Aug 9] strong, angular gelding: fair performer: won claimer at Brighton in June: stays easy 1½m: acts on all-weather and any turf going: tried tongue tied, visored nowadays: usually races prominently: sometimes finds little: unreliable. *A. W. Carroll* **66 § a61 §**

FORTUNES FAVOURITE 6 ch.m. Barathea (IRE) 127 – Golden Fortune 102 (Forzando 122) [2006 52§: p9.5g p10g p9.5g p12g 11m 10d p11g Nov 6] unreliable performer in 2005: little form at 6 yrs. *J. E. Long* **– §**

FORT WORTH (IRE) 2 b.c. (Mar 22) Mull of Kintyre (USA) 114 – Raazi 46 (My Generation 111) [2006 5m⁶ 6s⁴ 6m p7g 6m⁴ 6.1g p6g 6d³ Nov 4] €26,000Y: sturdy, close-coupled colt: third foal: half-brother to 4-y-o Paparaazi: dam maiden who stayed 7f: fair maiden: should stay 7f/1m: acts on soft and good to firm ground, probably polytrack. *B. Gubby* **68**

FORWARD MOVE (IRE) 4 ch.g. Dr Fong (USA) 128 – Kissing Gate (USA) 62 (Easy Goer (USA)) [2006 112: 10m 8.3m⁴ p8.5f² 8f² 8f² Dec 17] big, angular gelding: just useful performer at 4 yrs: sweating: respectable ninth to So Lucky in Wolferton Handicap at Royal Ascot on reappearance: below form in listed race at Windsor 8 days later, then left R. Hannon: gelded and off 3½ months, second in allowance races at Keeneland and Hollywood (2) after: barely stays 1¼m: acts on polytrack, firm and good to soft going. *C. Clement, USA* **106**

FORZARZI (IRE) 2 b.c. (Mar 7) Forzando 122 – Zarzi (IRE) (Suave Dancer (USA) 136) [2006 6g 5d⁶ 6g³ Sep 27] modest maiden: third at Newcastle (100/1, beaten 8 lengths): will stay 1m. *A. Berry* **59**

FOSROC (USA) 4 ch.g. Royal Anthem (USA) 135 – Stellar Blush (USA) (Blushing John (USA) 120) [2006 64d: p12g p16g Aug 30] maiden: well beaten in 2006: tried blinkered/tongue tied. *B. R. Johnson* **–**

FOSSGATE 5 ch.g. Halling (USA) 133 – Peryllys 67 (Warning 136) [2006 67: 9g⁶ 10m* 10.1m⁴ 10.1m² 12g* 12.1d* 12s⁶ p12.2m³ Oct 31] angular gelding: fairly useful handicapper: won at Nottingham in June, and Ripon and Beverley in August: stays 1½m: acts on polytrack, firm and soft going: tried in cheekpieces/visor: tends to hang right but is consistent. *J. D. Bethell* **81**

FOUR AMIGOS (USA) 5 b.g. Southern Halo (USA) – Larentia 58 (Salse (USA) 128) **61 d**
[2006 77: f6g f6g⁶ p5.1g⁴ f6g³ p6g p6g f5s 6v⁵ p7g³ p6g⁴ f6g⁵ f6g f5g f6g Nov 28]
compact gelding: just modest nowadays: left D. Nicholls after eighth outing: stays easy
7f: acts on all-weather and soft ground: tried visored/in blinkers: sold £600. *I. A. Wood*

FOURFOOT BAY (IRE) 2 b.g. (Apr 12) Elnadim (USA) 128 – Zagreb Flyer (Old **76**
Vic 136) [2006 6m⁴ 6m² 7m⁶ p7.1g⁶ Oct 8] €28,000F, 23,000Y: big, strong, good-bodied
gelding: half-brother to 2 winners, including useful Irish 2003 2-y-o 6f/7f winner Venturi
(by Danehill Dancer): dam unraced: fair maiden: free-going sort, better form at 6f than
7f: dead. *J. D. Bethell*

FOUR KINGS 5 b.g. Forzando 122 – High Cut 84 (Dashing Blade 117) [2006 45: f7g **–**
5m 7.2m 5s⁵ 8s Sep 4] good-topped gelding: maiden: has suffered from breathing problems: no form in 2006: tried tongue tied. *R. Allan*

FOUR MIRACLES 2 b.f. (Feb 26) Vettori (IRE) 119 – North Kildare (USA) (Northjet **64**
136) [2006 8m⁶ 7s³ f8g³ Nov 2] 3,000Y: good-bodied filly: half-sister to 2 winners,
including fairly useful 6f (at 2 yrs) to 1¼m winner Flying North (by Distinctly North):
dam unraced half-sister to high-class performer up to 1¾m Fanmore and very smart
performer up to 9f Labeeb: fair form in maidens, third at Newcastle and Southwell: will
stay 1¼m. *M. H. Tompkins*

FOUR PLEASURE 4 ch.f. King's Best (USA) 132 – Please (Kris 135) [2006 59: 10.1g **–**
7m Jun 17] leggy filly: maiden: well held in 2006. *A. M. Hales*

FOURSQUARE FLYER (IRE) 4 ch.g. Tagula (IRE) 116 – Isla (IRE) (Turtle Island **73**
(IRE) 123) [2006 76: 11.8m⁵ 14m⁶ p12.2g² Dec 28] angular gelding: fair maiden: off
nearly 6 months, first past post at Wolverhampton (hung left) final outing: seems to stay
1¾m: acts on polytrack and firm going. *J. Mackie*

FOUR TEL 2 gr.c. (Jan 17) Vettori (IRE) 119 – Etienne Lady (IRE) 67 (Imperial **63 p**
Frontier (USA) 112) [2006 p8g p8.6m³ Oct 31] third foal: brother to 4-y-o Top Man Tee:
dam, 6f winner from 2 starts, half-sister to useful miler Fine Silver: encouragement in
maidens at Lingfield and Wolverhampton (third to Filios): should go on progressing.
J. H. M. Gosden

FOWEY (USA) 2 b. or br.f. (Jan 31) Gone West (USA) – Kumari Continent (USA) 114 **51**
(Kris S (USA)) [2006 p8g³ Dec 10] $250,000Y: first foal: dam US Grade 2 9f winner: 6/1
and green, 8 lengths third to Mr Aviator in maiden at Kempton, slowly away and pushed
along before halfway: will stay beyond 1m. *Sir Mark Prescott*

FOX COVERT (IRE) 5 b.g. Foxhound (USA) 103 – Serious Contender (IRE) (Tenby **47**
125) [2006 57: f5g f6g 7d p6g 5f 6f 6f⁵ 6g⁴ 6m 5.9g⁴ Aug 3] workmanlike gelding: just
poor performer in 2006: effective at 5f/6f: acts on fibresand, firm and good to soft going:
sometimes wears headgear: inconsistent. *D. W. Barker*

FOX FLIGHT (IRE) 3 b.g. Brave Act 119 – Danz Danz (Efisio 120) [2006 –: 9.9g 11g **–**
12f⁵ 12.4m Jun 29] sturdy gelding: no form: tried in cheekpieces. *D. W. Barker*

FOXHAVEN 4 ch.c. Unfuwain (USA) 131 – Dancing Mirage (IRE) 83 (Machiavellian **111**
(USA) 123) [2006 109+: 10m⁶ 12f² 13.9d 12.3m* 12d⁴ 12s Oct 21] smallish, sturdy,
lengthy colt: smart performer: won listed race at Chester in September by ½ length from
Soulacroix: creditable efforts when in frame in similar event at Goodwood (neck second
to Crosspeace) and Cumberland Lodge Stakes at Ascot (fourth to Young Mick): well
below form in St Simon Stakes at Newbury final outing: stays easy 12.3f (stamina
stretched in Ebor over 1¾m): acts on firm and soft going: genuine. *P. R. Chamings*

FOXIES FIRSTGLANCE 2 ch.f. (Jan 16) Zaha (CAN) 106 – Classic Faster (IRE) **–**
(Running Steps (USA) 79) [2006 p6g⁶ 6.1f f5g Jul 31] £600Y: fifth foal: dam Italian 7f
winner, including at 2 yrs: well held in maidens. *R. D. E. Woodhouse*

FOXXY 2 b.f. (Apr 28) Foxhound (USA) 103 – Fisher Island (IRE) 59 (Sri Pekan (USA) **76 d**
117) [2006 f5g⁶ 5f⁵ 6m⁴ 8s* 8s p8.6g f8g⁵ p7.1g⁴ p8.6g⁶ Dec 31] 9,000Y: lengthy filly:
second foal: half-sister to 3-y-o Cool Isle: dam, 1¼m winner, half-sister to useful Irish
performer up to 1½m Smuggler's Song: fair performer at best: won nursery at Ayr in
September: well below form after, including in cheekpieces/blinkers: stays 1m: acts on
soft going. *K. A. Ryan*

FOXY GAMES 2 b.f. (Feb 29) Foxhound (USA) 103 – Manderina (Mind Games 121) **70**
[2006 p6g⁶ 6g² 5.7f³ 6g 5g² 5.1m* 6f² 8f Nov 25] 1,000Y, resold 1,000Y: tall, leggy,
unfurnished filly: second foal: dam well beaten all 3 starts: fair performer: won maiden at
Bath in September: good second in nursery at Leicester next time: left D. ffrench Davis

31,000 gns after: raced only at 5f/6f until very stiff task at 1m: acts on firm going: sometimes slowly away. *B. D. A. Cecil, USA*

FOXY MUSIC 2 b.g. (Apr 6) Foxhound (USA) 103 – Primum Tempus 49 (Primo **49** Dominie 121) [2006 p5.1g p5g p5g p6g p5g p5.1g⁵ p6g² Dec 30] poor maiden: best efforts in nurseries last 2 starts, giving impression should have won when beaten neck by stable-companion Grange Lili in 2-runner event at Lingfield: likely to prove best at 5f/6f: blinkered fourth/fifth starts: tends to hang right. *Peter Grayson*

FRACAS (IRE) 4 b.c. In The Wings 128 – Klarifi 91 (Habitat 134) [2006 116: 12g² 12g **115** 14g⁴ 12s Oct 21] angular, quite good-topped colt: has a round action: smart performer: off 13½ months (reportedly jarred up final 3-y-o outing), creditable 4 lengths second to Cherry Mix in Rheinland-Pokal at Cologne in August: fair fourth to Kastoria in Irish St Leger at the Curragh prior to well held in St Simon Stakes at Newbury (visored): stays 1½m: acts on heavy going. *D. Wachman, Ireland*

FRACTURED FOXY 2 b.f. (Mar 5) Foxhound (USA) 103 – Yanomami (USA) 71 **72** (Slew O' Gold (USA)) [2006 5.1s² 5g² 5m⁴ 6d* 7s* 8d⁵ 7m* 7d² 7s⁵ Oct 14] 4,000Y: compact filly: fifth foal: half-sister to 3 winners, including 5-y-o Mirasol Princess: dam 6f winner: fair performer: won sellers at Redcar and Catterick in August and nursery at Catterick in September: stays 7f: acts on soft and good to firm going. *J. J. Quinn*

FRAGRANCY (IRE) 2 ch.f. (Mar 2) Singspiel (IRE) 133 – Zibet 90 (Kris 135) [2006 **83 p** p8g* Oct 20] second foal: half-sister to 3-y-o Categorical: dam, 7f winner, half-sister to 2000 Guineas fourth Zoning: 10/1, smooth winner of maiden at Lingfield in October by ¾ length from Divine Love, held up travelling easily: will improve. *M. A. Jarvis*

FRANCESCAS BOY (IRE) 3 b.g. Titus Livius (FR) 115 – Mica Male (ITY) (Law **–** Society (USA) 130) [2006 –: 12d Sep 5] rather leggy gelding: no form. *P. D. Niven*

FRANCESCO 2 ch.g. (Mar 14) Vettori (IRE) 119 – Violet (IRE) 77 (Mukaddamah **57** (USA) 125) [2006 8m 7d p8.6m⁵ Oct 31] sturdy gelding: modest form in maidens: gelded after final start. *M. L. W. Bell*

FRANCHOEK (IRE) 2 ch.c. (Apr 29) Trempolino (USA) 135 – Snow House (IRE) **59** (Vacarme (USA) 121) [2006 7g 8.1m 8d Sep 27] mid-field in maidens. *A. King*

FRANK CARTWRIGHT (IRE) 3 b.g. Mull of Kintyre (USA) 114 – Punta Gorda **–** (IRE) (Roi Danzig (USA)) [2006 7.1g 8.3d 6m 9v⁶ 12.1g Aug 1] no form. *A. Berry*

FRANK CROW 3 b.g. Josr Algarhoud (IRE) 118 – Belle de Nuit (IRE) 85 (Statoblest **70** 120) [2006 81: 7.2d 8.9s Oct 7] sturdy, close-coupled gelding: fairly useful at 2 yrs: not at best in 2006: stays 7f: acts on good to soft ground, possibly not on soft. *J. S. Goldie*

FRANKLINS GARDENS 6 b.h. Halling (USA) 133 – Woodbeck 90 (Terimon 124) **117** [2006 117: 15.9d² 15.5m 16d 16d⁵ 12s Oct 21] rather leggy, close-coupled horse: smart performer: virtually pulled up (reportedly suffered 2 hairline fractures) in Melbourne Cup final 5-y-o start: good ½-length second to Sergeant Cecil in Lonsdale Cup at York in August on reappearance: ran as if amiss last 4 starts: effective at 1¾m, barely at 2½m: acts on soft and good to firm going: has been bandaged near-fore joint: goes well fresh: usually front runner. *M. H. Tompkins*

FRANKSALOT (IRE) 6 ch.g. Desert Story (IRE) 115 – Rosie's Guest (IRE) (Be My **79** Guest (USA) 126) [2006 77, a83: p6g⁶ p6g⁴ p6g p6g 6f² 6d* 7m² 7f⁴ 6m⁶ 7.1f⁴ 7.5m⁶ 7g 7.2m² 7.2g 7.1m⁶ p7.1m p7.1s p8.6m³ Dec 22] tall, close-coupled gelding: fair performer: won claimer at Windsor (left Miss B. Sanders) in May: effective at 6f to easy 1m: acts on polytrack, firm and good to soft going: tried blinkered/in cheekpieces: tends to edge left. *I. W. McInnes*

FRANK SONATA 5 b.h. Opening Verse (USA) 126 – Megdale (IRE) 74 (Waajib 121) **115** [2006 119d: 14.1s* 12g⁶ 16d² 12d² 14v 14g⁶ 16d² 12s* 15.5g Oct 22] good-bodied horse: smart performer: won listed races at Nottingham (by 3½ lengths from Dancing Bay) in April and the Curragh (beat Scorpion a length, pair clear) in October: ran poorly in Prix Royal-Oak at Longchamp final outing: effective 1½m (given test) to 2m: best form on ground softer than good, though below form both starts on heavy. *M. G. Quinlan*

FRANK'S QUEST (IRE) 6 b.g. Mujadil (USA) 119 – Questuary (IRE) 63 (Rainbow **–** Quest (USA) 134) [2006 –, a62: p8g p6g p8.6g² p8.6g⁵ p8.6g³ p8g² p8.6g³ p8.6g⁵ p10g **a57** p8.6g⁶ p8g² p8g p8g⁴ Dec 18] sturdy gelding: modest performer: finds 7f a minimum, and stays 1¼m: acts on all-weather, had form on firm and good to soft ground earlier in career. *A. B. Haynes*

FRANKY'N'JONNY 3 b.f. Groom Dancer (USA) 128 – Bron Hilda (IRE) 50 (Nama- **58 d** qualand (USA)) [2006 57: f8g⁴ p8g² p10g⁶ p10g² p8.6g³ f8g³ 7.1s³ 9.8m 8.2d f8g⁶ 8f 6m

7d 7m³ 10d f8g⁶ p8g³ f7g² f8g f7g⁶ Dec 12] modest maiden at best: left J. Pearce after second start, I. Wood after ninth and Mrs C. Dunnett following sixteenth outing: stays 1¼m: acts on all-weather and soft going, probably on good to firm: tried tongue tied/in cheekpieces/visor. *M. J. Attwater*

FRATERNITY 9 b.g. Grand Lodge (USA) 125 – Catawba 98 (Mill Reef (USA) 141) **49**
[2006 66, a70: f8g p8.6g⁴ p6g p9.5g 8.3m p8.6g⁶ p7.1g f6m f7g Nov 2] just poor performer nowadays: has form at 1½m, best at 6f to 8.6f: acts on all-weather and good to soft going: tried blinkered/visored earlier in career: front runner. *J. A. Pickering*

FRATT'N PARK (IRE) 3 b.f. Tagula (IRE) 116 – Bouffant (High Top 131) [2006 64: **71**
8.5g⁵ 8.3g⁴ 6g 8m² 7g* 7m 8.3f 7.1m 7f⁴ 9m⁶ p8g⁵ 10d³ 10s p10g Dec 10] leggy filly: fair handicapper: won at Newbury in June: stays 1¼m: acts on firm and soft going, probably on polytrack. *J. J. Bridger*

FREDA'S CHOICE (IRE) 3 b.f. Shinko Forest (IRE) – Marimar (IRE) (Grand Lodge **60**
(USA) 125) [2006 –: 8v 8m 8.5m² 9.6m⁴ 9s p8g p8.6g* Dec 4] €2,200Y: second foal: dam Italian 1¼m/11f winner: modest performer: left A. Oliver after second start: blinkered, won banded race at Wolverhampton in December: stays 9.6f: acts on polytrack and good to firm going. *Patrick Morris, Ireland*

FREDDY (ARG) 7 ch.h. Roy (USA) – Folgada (USA) (Lyphard's Wish (FR) 124) **–**
[2006 11.6m p16g Jul 15] third foal: dam unraced sister to useful performer up to 1¾m Wishing: successful in 5 of his 6 starts in Argentina in 2002, including 3 Group 1s, namely Estrellas Juvenile and Gran Premio Nacional (Argentine Derby), both at Hipodromo Argentino, and Gran Premio Carlos Pellegrini at San Isidro: left J. Alves and lightly raced in US for D. Burke, well held in 2005 in Grade 3/2 handicaps (blinkered): well beaten both starts in handicaps (tongue tied) in Britain, hanging on first occasion: stays 12.5f: acts on sloppy dirt and firm going on turf. *E. R. Oertel*

FREE ANGEL (USA) 4 b.f. Mystery Storm (USA) – No Makeup (USA) (Proud Truth **73**
(USA)) [2006 68+: p7.1g* p7g² p7g Nov 8] tall, leggy filly: fair performer, lightly raced: won handicap at Wolverhampton in June: should stay 1m: acts on polytrack, raced only on good to firm ground on turf: sold 8,500 gns. *M. Wigham*

FREEDOM AT LAST (IRE) 2 ch.f. (Mar 15) Alhaarth (IRE) 126 – Soubrette (USA) **76**
(Opening Verse (USA) 126) [2006 6m⁴ 6m Aug 2] 60,000Y: useful-looking filly: good walker: has a quick action: third foal: half-sister to French 2004 2-y-o 1m winner Aldo L'Argentin (by Anabaa): dam unraced out of US Grade 2 9f winner Dame Mysterieuse: better/effort in maidens when fourth at Newmarket on debut: will stay 1m. *W. Jarvis*

FREEDONIA 4 b.f. Selkirk (USA) 129 – Forest Rain (FR) (Caerleon (USA) 132) **117**
[2006 12.5s² 12m* 12.5g* 12m⁴ 12f² 12f Nov 26] tall, rather leggy filly: first foal: dam, French 1¼m/11f winner, half-sister to high-class miler Domedriver: smart performer: won maiden at Dieppe in 2005 (off over 10 months afterwards): minor event at Chantilly in June and Prix de Pomone at Deauville (much improved, beat Montare 2 lengths in good style) in August: unlucky fourth to Mandesha in Prix Vermeille at Longchamp next time (short of room much of straight, should have finished second): not discredited last 2 starts when 4½ lengths second to English Channel in Joe Hirsch Turf Classic Invitational at Belmont and seventh to Deep Impact in Japan Cup at Tokyo: stays 12.5f: acts on firm going. *J. E. Hammond, France*

FREELOADER (IRE) 6 b.g. Revoque (IRE) 122 – Indian Sand (Indian King (USA) **94**
128) [2006 94: 8s 8v⁶ 8.1d⁵ 8.1f 7.9g 8d² 8.3g⁴ 10d* p8g³ f8g Dec 2] strong, lengthy gelding: fairly useful handicapper: won at Ayr in September: good third at Kempton next start: best at 1m/1¼m: acts on all-weather, firm and good to soft going. *R. A. Fahey*

FREE OFFER 2 b.f. (Mar 28) Generous (IRE) 139 – Proserpine 95 (Robellino (USA) **79 p**
127) [2006 7m⁴ 7f* Aug 9] close-coupled, quite attractive filly: first foal: dam, 2-y-o 1m winner, half-sister to smart performer up to 1¾m in USA Chelsea Barracks: shaped well in maiden at Newmarket (fourth to Princess Taise), then odds-on winner of 4-runner event at Brighton by 5 lengths: will stay 1¼m/1½m: looks capable of better. *J. L. Dunlop*

FREE ROSES (IRE) 3 b.f. Fasliyev (USA) 120 – Ghanaj (Caerleon (USA) 132) [2006 **96**
75: 6m² 6f* 5d* 5m 5m 5g Sep 17] €105,000Y: second foal: half-sister to Irish 2004 2-y-o 7f winner Perfect Memory (by Nashwan): dam unraced: useful performer: won maiden at Naas (by 8 lengths) in June and listed race at Ayr (easily best effort, beat Clear Impression a length) in July: likely to prove best at 5f/6f: acts on firm and good to soft ground: tongue tied last 2 starts in 2005: lost all chance when rearing start final outing: sold 70,000 gns. *Edward Lynam, Ireland*

FREE SILVER (IRE) 3 b.f. Lujain (USA) 119 – Joonayh 81 (Warning 136) [2006 –: **55** p6g⁶ 6.1m 6.1f⁵ 6g 7.6m p7g p7g⁴ p8g³ p7g³ Nov 6] smallish filly: modest maiden: stays easy 1m: acts on polytrack and firm going. *Miss K. B. Boutflower*

FREE SPEECH 3 b.c. King's Best (USA) 132 – Daring Miss 113 (Sadler's Wells **–** (USA) 132) [?2006 8m Apr 22] unfurnished colt: has a quick action: 9/1, backward and very green (free to post), well beaten in maiden at Newbury, slowly away: sold 13,000 gns, joined John Joseph Murphy in Ireland. *Sir Michael Stoute*

FREE STYLE (GER) 6 ch.m. Most Welcome 131 – Furiella 70 (Formidable (USA) **–** 125) [2006 44, a58: p13g p13g⁵ p12.2g Mar 20] modest on all-weather, poor on turf: **a51** stays 13f: acts on all-weather, good to firm and good to soft ground: said to have bled on reappearance/reportedly amiss final outing. *Mrs H. Sweeting*

FREE TO AIR 3 b.g. Generous (IRE) 139 – Petonica (IRE) 77 (Petoski 135) [2006 73: **88** 11g* 11.6g* 11s³ 12g⁵ 12g 12m⁶ 16g 12s Oct 21] big, good-topped gelding: fairly useful performer: won maiden at Southwell in April and handicap at Windsor in May: stays 1½m: acts on polytrack, soft and good to firm ground. *A. M. Balding*

FREE WHEELIN (IRE) 6 b.g. Polar Falcon (USA) 126 – Farhana 109 (Fayruz 116) **56** [2006 57, a47: 5s⁶ 5m p6g Nov 28] lengthy, useful-looking gelding: modest performer: best at 5f/6f: acts on soft and good to firm ground, little form on all-weather: often slowly away. *T. M. Jones*

FREEZE THE FLAME (GER) 3 b.g. In The Wings 128 – Fantastic Flame (IRE) 79 **58** (Generous (IRE) 139) [2006 61: 7.1g 8.2s 12.1f⁵ 12f⁵ Jul 3] good-topped gelding: modest maiden on Flat: stays 1½m: acts on firm going: blinkered (ran well) final start: fairly useful juvenile hurdler. *C. R. Egerton*

FREGATE ISLAND (IRE) 3 b.g. Daylami (IRE) 138 – Briery (IRE) 66 (Salse (USA) **87** 128) [2006 86: 10.4d 9.8m² 9.9f 8.3m³ Jul 8] tall, angular gelding: fairly useful performer: stays 9.8f: acts on polytrack and good to firm going: hung right on reappearance. *W. J. Haggas*

FREMEN (USA) 6 ch.g. Rahy (USA) 115 – Northern Trick (USA) 131 (Northern Dan- **91** cer) [2006 6m 9g* 8f* 8.5d 9m⁵ 8d⁵ 8f² 8g 8.9s³ Oct 7] big, lengthy, quite good-topped gelding: fairly useful performer: missed 2005: won claimer at Musselburgh and handicap at York in July: stays 9f: acts on firm and soft going: has been bandaged in front: free-going sort. *D. Nicholls*

FRENCHGATE 5 br.g. Paris House 123 – Let's Hang On (IRE) (Petorius 117) [2006 **47** –: 8m³ 8g² 10f 8g p8g⁵ p10g Nov 27] poor maiden: stays 1m: acts on polytrack and good to firm going: visored last 2 starts. *I. W. McInnes*

FRENCH GIGOLO 6 ch.g. Pursuit of Love 124 – French Mist 71 (Mystiko (USA) **–** 124) [2006 f8g Oct 12] sturdy gelding: lightly-raced maiden: well held only outing in 2006. *C. N. Allen*

FRENCH MANNEQUIN (IRE) 7 gr.m. Key of Luck (USA) 126 – Paris Model **67** (IRE) (Thatching 131) [2006 62: 12.3g p12.2g* p16g* 16.2m p13.9m⁶ p16.5g Oct 8] sparely-made mare: fair performer: won amateur seller at Wolverhampton in June and handicap at Kempton in September: effective at 1½m to easy 2m: acts on polytrack and any turf going: blinkered/visored. *P. A. Blockley*

FRENCHMANS LODGE 6 b.g. Piccolo 121 – St Helena (Monsanto (FR) 121) [2006 **–** 52: p7g 7m 7g Jun 13] modest performer: no form in 2006: usually blinkered. *L. A. Dace*

FRENCH OPERA 3 b.g. Bering 136 – On Fair Stage (IRE) 103 (Sadler's Wells (USA) **63** 132) [2006 61: 10.2f⁴ p12g Jul 1] modest maiden, lightly raced: should be suited by 1½m. *J. A. Osborne*

FRESHWINDS 4 ch.g. Bahamian Bounty 116 – La Noisette (Rock Hopper 124) [2006 **62** 46: p5.1g f5g² f5g p5.1g⁶ p5g⁴ f6g p6g⁵ p5g* Dec 18] modest performer: left S. Keightley after fourth start: won banded race at Kempton in December: effective at 5f/6f: raced only on all-weather: wore blinkers last 4 starts. *Miss Diana Weeden*

FRETWORK 2 b.f. (Jan 18) Galileo (IRE) 134 – Celtic Cross 100 (Selkirk (USA) 129) **86** [2006 7d² 7m² 8.2g³ Sep 26] close-coupled, good-topped filly: third foal: half-sister to fairly useful 9f/1¼m winner Maclean (by Machiavellian): dam, 7f winner who stayed 1m, half-sister to smart 1m/1¼m performer Right Approach: fairly useful form in maidens: placed all starts, best effort on debut at Newmarket (second to Passage of Time): will stay 1¼m. *R. Hannon*

FREYA TRICKS 2 b.f. (Jun 3) Noverre (USA) 125 – Trick of Ace (USA) (Clever – Trick (USA)) [2006 8d Nov 3] fifth foal: half-sister to 5-y-o Trickstep and 3-y-o Trick Or Treat: dam, won in USA, half-sister to US Grade 2 1½m winner Prospectress: 16/1, no show in maiden at Musselburgh. *I. Semple*

FRIENDS HOPE 5 ch.m. Docksider (USA) 124 – Stygian (USA) 73 (Irish River (FR) **65** 131)) [2006 69: p9.5g p9.5g² p9.5g² 10.2f³ 10f⁴ 9.9f⁴ 11.1m⁵ 10f* 10m⁶ Aug 22] fair handicapper: won at Brighton in August: stays 11f: acts on all-weather, firm and soft going: often slowly away. *P. A. Blockley*

FRILL A MINUTE 2 b.f. (Apr 13) Lake Coniston (IRE) 131 – Superfrills 54 (Super- – power 113) [2006 6.1m 6g 5.1d 5.1d Nov 1] workmanlike filly: first foal: dam 5f/6f winner: last all starts. *Miss L. C. Siddall*

FRIMLEY'S MATTERRY 6 b.g. Bluegrass Prince (IRE) 110 – Lonely Street 93 **62** (Frimley Park 109) [2006 55: 5.9m 7f⁵ 7.1g 7.5f 8d 6g² 6d* 6g 6m 6m 8d Oct 8] modest handicapper: won at Redcar in August: below form after: effective at 6f/7f: acts on all-weather, firm and good to soft going: tried visored. *R. E. Barr*

FRINGE 3 ch.f. In The Wings 128 – El Jazirah (Kris 135) [2006 10s³ p9.5g² 10.5v⁴ **93** Dec 5] 13,000 3-y-o: fifth foal: closely related to useful 1¼m to 13f (in France) winner Mount Elbrus (by Barathea) and half-sister to 7f winner Christaleni (by Zilzal): dam unraced sister to Prix de Diane winner Rafha: placed in maidens at Nottingham and Wolverhampton (forced very wide) then much improved when 3¾ lengths fourth to Pearl Sky in listed race at Saint-Cloud: stays 10.5f: acts on heavy going. *Jane Chapple-Hyam*

FRISKY TALK (IRE) 2 b.f. (Mar 3) Fasliyev (USA) 120 – Happy Talk (IRE) 74 **82** (Hamas (IRE) 125§) [2006 5g 5g² 5.1m² 5.1g⁴ 5f* 5.1f² 5.2g 5g² 6d⁶ 5m³ p5g* Sep 30] 24,000Y: leggy filly: first foal: dam, Irish 1¼m winner, half-sister to US Grade 3 8.5f winner Storm Dream: fairly useful performer: won maiden at Warwick in June and nursery at Kempton in September: in frame another 6 times: best at 5f: acts on polytrack and firm going: can look awkward under pressure. *B. W. Hills*

FROGS' GIFT (IRE) 4 gr.f. Danehill Dancer (IRE) 117 – Warthill Whispers 59 (Grey – Desire 115) [2006 43: f6g 7g 7f⁶ 8f 10d 9.9f 8m Aug 5] leggy filly: poor maiden: probably stays 1m: acts on firm going. *G. M. Moore*

FROISSEE 2 b.f. (Apr 27) Polish Precedent (USA) 131 – Crinkle (IRE) (Distant **72 d** Relative 128) [2006 6m³ 6.1g⁶ 6d p8g⁵ p8.6g Nov 23] lengthy filly: second foal: closely related to 3-y-o Mr Sandicliffe: dam unraced out of half-sister to very smart Irish 6f/7f performer Desert Style: fair form only when third in maiden at Newmarket on debut: should stay 1m: wore cheekpieces final outing. *N. A. Callaghan*

FROMSONG (IRE) 8 b.g. Fayruz 116 – Lindas Delight 54 (Batshoof 122) [2006 104: **106** p5g⁴ p5g² p6g⁵ 5.2m⁵ 5s⁴ 5m 6m p6g Dec 30] tall, angular gelding: useful performer: good 1¼ lengths second to Qadar in handicap at Lingfield second start: well below form last 3 outings, final one in claimer after lay-off: stays easy 6f: acts on polytrack, soft and good to firm going: has worn cheekpieces/sweated: tried tongue tied. *D. K. Ivory*

FRONTLINEFINANCIER 6 b.g. Bluegrass Prince (IRE) 110 – Bunny Gee (Last **63** Tycoon 131) [2006 61: 15d 16.4f Jul 13] leggy gelding: modest handicapper: stays 17f: acts on polytrack and good to firm ground: said to have finished lame final outing. *N. I. M. Rossiter*

FRONTLINE IN FOCUS (IRE) 2 ch.f. (Apr 21) Daggers Drawn (USA) 114 – **82** Christan (IRE) (Al Hareb (USA) 123) [2006 5f⁴ 5m⁵ 5.2f* 6d⁵ 6f Sep 18] €8,200Y: rather leggy, workmanlike filly: fifth foal: half-sister to fairly useful 2005 2-y-o 5f winner Dusty City (by City On A Hill) and winner in Greece by Mukaddamah: dam, 2-y-o 5f winner in Belgium who stayed 1m, half-sister to very smart miler Sorbie Tower: fairly useful performer: won maiden at Ripon and minor event at Yarmouth (idled) in July: also ran well when fifth in competitive nursery at York: effective at 5f/6f: reportedly bled final start. *K. R. Burke*

FRONT RANK (IRE) 6 b.g. Sadler's Wells (USA) 132 – Alignment (IRE) 98 (Alzao **66** (USA) 117) [2006 62: 13f² 14.1f⁵ Aug 15] strong, good-bodied gelding: lightly-raced maiden on Flat, fair form: should stay 1¾m: acts on fibresand, firm and good to soft going: fairly useful hurdler, won twice in October. *Mrs Dianne Sayer*

FROST GIANT (USA) 3 ch.c. Giant's Causeway (USA) 132 – Takesmybreathaway **116** (USA) 55 (Gone West (USA)) [2006 p9p: 8m 10m* 12f⁵ 10f Nov 26] lengthy, good-bodied colt: smart performer: agitated in preliminaries, below form in 2000 Guineas at Newmarket on reappearance: off 4 months, fully confirmed 2-y-o promise when winning Bruce Betting Kilternan Stakes at Leopardstown in September by head from

Cougar Bay, all out: creditable 6 lengths fifth to English Channel in Joe Hirsch Turf Classic at Belmont next time (would probably have finished second but for being badly hampered): left A. O'Brien in Ireland, below form in Hollywood Derby final outing: stays 1½m: acts on any going. *R. E. Dutrow, jnr, USA*

FROSTY NIGHT (IRE) 2 b.g. (Mar 23) Night Shift (USA) – Abla (Robellino (USA) 127) [2006 7.1m⁴ 7.2d* 8.1g² 7d Sep 19] €51,000F, €120,000Y: well-made gelding: third foal: half-brother to 3-y-o Black Charmer and US 7f/1m minor stakes winner Chenia (by Sahm): dam, well beaten only start, out of Galtres Stakes winner Sans Blague: fairly useful performer: won maiden at Ayr in July: beaten 1¼ lengths by Gold Option in 2-runner race at Sandown (minor event): mid-division in valuable 28-runner sales race at the Curragh final start: gelded after: stays 1m. *M. Johnston*   **86**

FRUITS D'AMOUR (IRE) 2 b.f. (Apr 3) Fruits of Love (USA) 127 – Chatsworth 51 Bay (IRE) (Fairy King (USA)) [2006 6s p7.1g p6g p7.1g 8.6g Dec 18] €3,000Y resold 15,000Y: angular, good-topped filly: sister to 3-y-o Trafalgar Bay and half-sister to winners in Italy by Red Sunset and Dolphin Street: dam unraced: modest form only on second start. *S. Kirk*

FUBOS 5 b.g. Atraf 116 – Homebeforemidnight (Fools Holme (USA)) [2006 p9.5g Jan 20] workmanlike gelding: lightly-raced maiden: well held only outing since 2004: tried visored. *Mrs Lucinda Featherstone*

FUEL CELL (IRE) 5 b.g. Desert Style (IRE) 121 – Tappen Zee (Sandhurst Prince 49 128) [2006 73: 7d 8d 10.1g 8d p9.5g p13.9g Dec 11] compact gelding: only poor in 2006: stays 1¼m: acts on polytrack, good to firm and good to soft going: tried in cheekpieces, usually blinkered: often tongue tied: has raced freely/carried head awkwardly/hung left. *J. O'Reilly*

FUERO REAL (FR) 11 b.g. Highest Honor (FR) 124 – Highest Pleasure (USA) (Fool- ish Pleasure (USA)) [2006 16.2f Jul 28] poor performer: well held all 3 races on Flat since 2000. *R. Brotherton*

FUERTA VENTURA (IRE) 4 b. or br.f. Desert Sun 120 – Cradle Brief (IRE) (Brief – Truce (USA) 126) [2006 102: 14.1s 13m 9.5s May 7] leggy filly: useful performer at 3 yrs: soundly beaten in listed races in 2006, at Nottingham on reappearance: stays 1¾m: acts on heavy and good to firm going: blinkered second start. *K. J. Condon, Ireland*

FUJI (IRE) 2 b.c. (Mar 5) Monashee Mountain (USA) 115 – Yavarro 44 (Raga Navarro 65 (ITY) 119) [2006 7f* p7g⁶ 7m Aug 6] €20,000Y, 82,000 2-y-o: half-brother to useful 5f (at 2 yrs) to 1m winner Pelham (by Archway), later successful in Hong Kong: dam, maiden, stayed 1¼m: fair performer: won maiden at Folkestone in June: well held after in minor event and nursery: will stay 1m: sold 20,000 gns, sent to USA. *M. L. W. Bell*

FUJISAN 2 b.c. (Apr 23) Fuji Kiseki (JPN) – Appreciation (IRE) 64 (Caerleon (USA) 68 132) [2006 5f⁴ p7.1g a6g* Nov 19] second foal: dam, Irish maiden, out of Irish Oaks winner Alydaress: better effort in maidens for M. Johnston when fourth at Beverley on debut: sold 13,000 gns, won similar event at Taby in November: stays 6f. *Y. Durant, Sweden*

FULLANDBY (IRE) 4 b.g. Monashee Mountain (USA) 115 – Ivory Turner (Efisio 106 120) [2006 95: p6g³ 5f 6s 5m⁵ 6m 5m⁵ 6g* 6g⁵ 6s² 6s* 7d² 6g Oct 13] strong gelding: type to carry plenty of condition: useful performer: won handicap at Newmarket in July and minor event at Haydock (beat Charles Darwin by 1¾ lengths) in September: further improvement last 2 starts, 1¼ lengths second to All Ivory in totesport.com Handicap at Ascot and seventh to Bygone Days in Bentinck Stakes at Newmarket: best at 5f to 7f: acts on polytrack, soft and good to firm going: edged right fifth outing (slowly away) and at Haydock. *T. J. Etherington*

FULL AS A ROCKET (IRE) 5 b.g. Foxhound (USA) 103 – Taysala (IRE) (Akarad – (FR) 130) [2006 55: 12f 12s Aug 18] maiden: well beaten in 2006. *D. Nicholls*

FULL HOUSE (IRE) 7 br.g. King's Theatre (IRE) 128 – Nirvavita (FR) (Highest 89 Honor (FR) 124) [2006 14g⁴ 17.1m* 20m⁴ 18d Oct 14] strong, close-coupled, useful- looking gelding: fairly useful performer, lightly raced on Flat in recent years: won handi- cap at Pontefract in June: good fourth to Baddam in Ascot Stakes (Handicap) at Royal Ascot next time: pulled too hard when well held in Cesarewitch final outing: stays 2½m: acts on polytrack and firm going, possibly not on good to soft: tried blinkered earlier in career: has worn crossed noseband: sometimes races freely: useful chaser. *P. R. Webber*

FULL OF PROMISE (USA) 2 b.f. (Apr 4) Street Cry (IRE) 130 – Believe It Beloved 65 p (USA) (Clever Trick (USA)) [2006 p8g⁵ Oct 20] half-sister to numerous winners abroad:

dam 6.5f to 8.5f winner in USA: 33/1, green when fifth to Sunlight in maiden at Lingfield: should progress. *Mrs A. J. Perrett*

FULL OF ZEST 4 ch.f. Pivotal 124 – Tangerine 70 (Primo Dominie 121) [2006 74: **71** p8g⁵ p10g 12s⁶ p12g⁴ 7m 12d p12g³ p10g 10f p16g Nov 28] leggy filly: fair maiden: probably stays easy 1½m: acts on polytrack and soft ground: often wears headgear. *Mrs L. J. Mongan*

FULL SPATE 11 ch.g. Unfuwain (USA) 131 – Double River (USA) (Irish River (FR) **71 d** 131) [2006 77: 6m 6g⁴ 6m 7.1m* 6m 6g⁶ 6f⁵ 6g 6m⁵ 7.1m 7.1m 5.7m⁴ Sep 25] tall, good-topped gelding: fair performer: won claimer at Chepstow in June: below form after: stays 7f: acts on any turf going, lightly raced on polytrack: well held in blinkers/cheekpieces earlier in career: sometimes slowly away: usually held up. *J. M. Bradley*

FULL VICTORY (IRE) 4 b.g. Imperial Ballet (IRE) 110 – Full Traceability (IRE) 53 **84** (Ron's Victory (USA) 129) [2006 73: 8d⁴ 8.1d* 8.3g* 8m p8.6g⁴ p7.1g⁵ 8.3g 8.3g² 7g² 8.1s⁵ 8d⁵ 7s Oct 10] fairly useful handicapper: left T. Doyle in Ireland prior to reappearance: won at Chepstow in May and Windsor in June, hanging left both times: stays 8.6f: acts on polytrack and heavy going: blinkered final 2-y-o start. *R. A. Farrant*

FULVIO (USA) 6 b.g. Sword Dance – One Tuff Gal (USA) (Lac Ouimet (USA)) [2006 **–** 51, a61: p7.1g² p7g* f8g³ p8g⁴ p7g³ p7.1g³ p8.6g³ p7.1m² p7g f8g p7.1g⁵ p8.6g² p7g³ **a64** Dec 30] big gelding: modest performer, better on all-weather than turf: won banded race at Lingfield in February: effective at 6f to easy 8.6f: acts on all-weather, firm and good to soft going: tried blinkered, visored nowadays: consistent. *P. Howling*

FUNFAIR WANE 7 b.g. Unfuwain (USA) 131 – Ivory Bride 86 (Domynsky 110) **96 d** [2006 90§: p6g 6s 6m 5.1g⁴ 5f 6g p7.1g Sep 30] strong, lengthy gelding: has a long stride: useful performer at best nowadays: no form after fourth outing (unseated at start on sixth): best at 5f/6f: acts on polytrack, soft and good to firm ground: has run well when sweating: races prominently: unreliable. *D. Nicholls*

FUN IN THE SUN 2 ch.g. (May 22) Piccolo 121 – Caught In The Rain 66 (Spectrum **–** (IRE) 126) [2006 5.7m 7m 6.1f Jul 28] no form in maidens. *Jane Southcombe*

FUNNY TIMES 5 b.m. Silver Patriarch (IRE) 125 – Elegant City (Scallywag 127) **–** [2006 12v Oct 31] fairly useful bumper winner/fair form over hurdles: well held in maiden at Catterick on Flat debut. *N. G. Richards*

FUN THAI 2 ch.f. (Mar 20) Fraam 114 – Thailand (Lycius (USA) 124) [2006 6m 7f⁴ 7s⁴ **46** 7.1m 8g p9.5g p9.5g p8g p8.6g Dec 18] neat filly: second foal: dam, little form, out of half-sister to 1000 Guineas winner Sayyedati: poor maiden: stays 7f: acts on firm and soft going. *M. R. Channon*

FUN TIME 3 br.f. Fraam 114 – Kissing Time 79 (Lugana Beach 116) [2006 64: 8m 7.1g **60** 6f⁴ 6g⁶ 7.1m f8g⁶ p7g² p8g³ p7g² Dec 18] modest performer: probably stays 1m: acts on polytrack, probably on firm going. *M. R. Channon*

FUN TO RIDE 5 ch.m. Desert Prince (IRE) 130 – Zafaaf 105 (Kris 135) [2006 82: 6d **–** 6g 5s May 20] leggy, useful-looking mare: fairly useful handicapper in 2005: well held in 2006. *M. W. Easterby*

FURBESETA 2 b.f. (Mar 5) Danehill Dancer (IRE) 117 – Fafinta (IRE) (Indian Ridge **69 +** 123) [2006 p7g⁶ p7g³ Nov 11] second foal: dam, Italian 8.5f and 1¼m winner, half-sister to Falbrav: fair form in maidens, staying-on third at Kempton: will be suited by 1m. *L. M. Cumani*

FURMIGADELAGIUSTA 2 ch.c. (Feb 10) Galileo (IRE) 134 – Sispre (FR) (Master **80 p** Willie 129) [2006 7f 7d p8g³ Sep 1] good-topped colt: half-brother to 3 winners in Italy, including smart winner up to 1¼m Fisich and useful winner up to 1½m Fa A Mezz (both by Halling): dam, won up to around 1m in Italy, sister to Gimcrack winner Chilly Billy: fairly useful maiden: much improved when third to Monzante at Kempton: will benefit from 1¼m/1½m: should do better still. *L. M. Cumani*

FURNACE (IRE) 2 b.c. (May 5) Green Desert (USA) 127 – Lyrical Dance (USA) **90** (Lear Fan (USA) 130) [2006 7m* 7.1g 7d³ Sep 27] 130,000Y: leggy, quite attractive colt: sixth foal: closely related to fairly useful Irish 6f winner Lightwood Lady (by Anabaa) and half-brother to useful winner in USA by Diesis: dam, 8.5f winner in USA, half-sister to Pennekamp, Black Minnaloushe and Nasr El Arab: fairly useful performer: won maiden at Newmarket in August: similar form when seventh to Drumfire in Solario Stakes at Sandown and third to Tembanee in minor event at Salisbury: will be suited by 1m. *M. L. W. Bell*

FURTHER OUTLOOK (USA) 12 gr.g. Zilzal (USA) 137 – Future Bright (USA) **73** (Lyphard's Wish (FR) 124) [2006 88: 5d 6d⁴ 5g* 5g* 6f* f6g* 6g⁵ 5g p6m f6g⁴ f6g⁴ **a56** f6g⁶ f7g Dec 28] big, strong gelding: carries condition: fair performer on turf, modest on all-weather nowadays: won seller at Musselburgh in May, and claimers at Hamilton and Folkestone in June and Southwell (left D. Carroll) in July: best at 5f/6f: acts on all-weather and any turf going: sometimes tongue tied/in cheekpieces: sometimes hangs right: races up with pace. *Miss Gay Kelleway*

FUSCHIA 2 b.f. (Mar 2) Averti (IRE) 117 – Big Pink (IRE) (Bigstone (IRE) 126) [2006 **53** p7g Oct 26] third foal: dam unraced half-sister to very smart French 1m/1¼m performer Pink: 40/1, mid-field in maiden at Lingfield. *R. Charlton*

FUSHE JO 2 gr.c. (Apr 23) Act One 124 – Aristocratique 71 (Cadeaux Genereux 131) **83 p** [2006 6d⁵ 7.2d* Sep 15] 65,000Y: tall, rather leggy, useful-looking colt: on weak side: sixth foal: half-brother to 3 winners, notably smart 1m (at 2 yrs) and 1¼m winner Arcalis (by Lear Fan), also smart hurdler: dam, Irish sprint maiden, half-sister to useful 6f/7f winner Royal Loft: fairly useful form: won maiden at Ayr in good style by 3 lengths, still rather green: will stay 1m+: should go on progressing. *J. Howard Johnson*

FUSILI (IRE) 3 ch.f. Silvano (GER) 126 – Flunder (Nebos (GER) 129) [2006 75: **100** p10g* p10g³ p8.6g³ p10g³ p10g⁴ p10g* p12g² 12.1d² 11.4m 11.5m² 12s p13g 10d p10g³ p8.6m⁴ p10g² Dec 8] smallish, close-coupled filly: useful performer: won handicaps at Lingfield in January and March: very good close second in listed race at Lingfield (to Sindirana) and handicap at Kempton (beaten head by Alpine Reel) tenth/final outings: stays 1½m: acts on polytrack, soft and good to firm ground. *N. P. Littmoden*

FUSILLADE (IRE) 6 ch.g. Grand Lodge (USA) 125 – Lili Cup (FR) (Fabulous **–** Dancer (USA) 124) [2006 –: 9.9s Aug 1] sturdy, lengthy gelding: of little account. *A. J. Lockwood*

FUSTAAN (IRE) 2 b.f. (Feb 11) Royal Applause 124 – Alhuoof (USA) 100 (Dayjur **71 p** (USA) 137) [2006 6g⁶ Aug 18] well-made filly: third foal: dam, 2-y-o 6f winner, half-sister to useful dam of 1000 Guineas winner Lahan: 8/1, sixth to Silca Chiave in maiden at Newbury, not unduly punished: should do better. *M. P. Tregoning*

FUTOO (IRE) 5 b.g. Foxhound (USA) 103 – Nicola Wynn 83 (Nicholas Bill 125) **56** [2006 74d: f12g p9.5g p9.5g p13.9g p10g 10m 9.9f 10.1f f11m p10g Dec 18] tall, useful-looking gelding: modest performer nowadays: left G. M. Moore after reappearance: tried visored, often in cheekpieces nowadays. *D. W. Chapman*

FUTUN 3 b.c. In The Wings 128 – Svanzega (USA) (Sharpen Up 127) [2006 83p: 10g* **107** 11.1d² 11.9g* 12f² 10.4d Aug 23] big, strong, close-coupled colt: useful performer: won maiden at Leicester in April and handicap at Haydock (beat Prowess by ½ length) in July: good ½-length second of 4 to Nihal in handicap at York next time, but below form in similar event next time (tongue tied) final outing: stays 1½m: acts on firm and good to soft ground: races freely. *L. M. Cumani*

FUTURE DEAL 5 b.m. First Trump 118 – Katyushka (IRE) 73 (Soviet Star (USA) **62** 128) [2006 72: p10g p8g⁴ p8g 9.9m⁶ 8m p12g Nov 11] strong, workmanlike mare: modest nowadays: stays easy 9.5f: acts on polytrack and good to firm going: has carried head high/been slowly away. *C. A. Horgan*

FUTURE'S DREAM 3 b.g. Bertolini (USA) 125 – Bahawir Pour (USA) (Green **90 d** Dancer (USA) 132) [2006 8.1s* f8g² 9.9g 8.1g 8.9s Oct 7] 36,000F, 105,000Y: fifth foal: half-brother to useful 2002 2-y-o 7f winner Captain Saif (by Compton Place) and winner abroad by Mister Baileys: dam unraced trained in France at 2 yrs (left R. Pritchard-Gordon 40,000 gns): fairly useful performer: best effort when winning maiden on British debut at Haydock in May: most unlucky second in handicap at Southwell next time: well below form last 3 starts: should be suited by 1¼m: acts on soft going, probably on fibresand: wore cheekpieces final outing: gelded after. *K. R. Burke*

FUTURISTIC DRAGON (IRE) 2 b.c. (Feb 1) Invincible Spirit (IRE) 121 – Calvia **– p** Rose (Sharpo 132) [2006 5.1g⁵ Oct 17] £18,000F, 20,000Y, 32,000 2-y-o: sixth foal: half-brother to 1¾m winner Rosewings (by In The Wings): dam unraced close relation to winner up to 1¼m Dusty Dollar and half-sister to winner up to 11f Kind of Hush, both smart: 33/1 and green when mid-division in maiden at Bath: open to improvement. *P. A. Blockley*

FYODOR (IRE) 5 b.g. Fasliyev (USA) 120 – Royale Figurine (IRE) 107 (Dominion **106** Royale 112) [2006 95+: f5g* f5g² p5.1g* p5g² 5.2m 5m 5f 5m⁴ 5.1g³ Aug 15] tall, good- **a117** topped gelding: progressed into a smart performer on all-weather, winning handicaps at Southwell in January and Wolverhampton (beat Qadar by short head with something in hand) in February: also ran well when ½-length second to Les Arcs in minor event at Lingfield fourth outing: best effort on turf when fourth to Machinist in Hong Kong Jockey Club Sprint (Handicap) at Ascot on penultimate start: stays 6f: acts on all-weather and good to firm going (well beaten on softer than good). *W. J. Haggas*

FYVIE 3 ch.f. Grand Lodge (USA) 125 – Island of Silver (USA) 107 (Forty Niner 77 (USA)) [2006 70p: p12.2g² 12m* p10g³ 12g p10g Sep 2] strong, good-bodied filly: fair performer: won maiden at Pontefract (flashed tail/idled) in June: stays 1½m: acts on polytrack and good to firm ground: suspect temperament: sold 22,000 gns. *E. A. L. Dunlop*

G

GABOR 7 b.g. Danzig Connection (USA) – Kiomi 65 (Niniski (USA) 125) [2006 55: – p16.5g Apr 24] tall gelding: well held only Flat outing in 2006: sometimes blinkered: joined Mrs S. Smith, successful over hurdles in June/August. *D. W. Thompson*

GAELIC GAMES (UAE) 3 b.g. Jade Robbery (USA) 121 – Colleen (IRE) (Sadler's 58 Wells (USA) 132) [2006 57: p10g⁶ 9.7m Apr 25] big, good-topped gelding: modest maiden: stayed 1¼m: dead. *P. G. Murphy*

GAELIC PRINCESS 6 b.m. Cois Na Tine (IRE) 101 – Berenice (ITY) (Marouble 89 116) [2006 91, a81: p9.5g 8.3d⁵ 8m⁴ 8m² 10m² 8m 7m² 8f 8.1g² 7m* 7d p8.6g* p8g³ p9.5g³ Dec 11] big, good-bodied mare: fairly useful handicapper: won at Salisbury in August and Wolverhampton in November: effective at 7f to easy 1¼m: acts on all-weather and firm going, probably on good to soft: patiently ridden. *A. G. Newcombe*

GAELIC ROULETTE (IRE) 6 b.m. Turtle Island (IRE) 123 – Money Spinner 55 (USA) 61 (Teenoso (USA) 135) [2006 56: p16.5g p12g⁵ Apr 5] rather leggy mare: modest performer: stays 1¾m: acts on polytrack, best turf form on good going or firmer: often slowly away: fair hurdler, successful in June/July. *J. Jay*

GAGARIN (FR) 6 b.g. Quest For Fame 127 – Good To Dance (IRE) 115 (Groom – Dancer (USA) 128) [2006 12d 10.9d p10g Oct 29] quite good-topped gelding: lightly-raced maiden: no form in 2006. *Miss L. C. Siddall*

GALA CASINO KING (IRE) 3 ch.g. Elnadim (USA) 128 – Fashion Scout (IRE) 60 (Thatching 131) [2006 –: 10.1g⁶ 14.1g⁴ May 29] angular gelding: modest maiden, lightly raced: best effort at 14.1f: sold 5,000 gns in October. *M. Dods*

GALACTIC STAR 3 ch.c. Galileo (IRE) 134 – Balisada 115 (Kris 135) [2006 67P: 81 p 10d² 10s* Oct 18] good-bodied, attractive colt: type to carry condition: best effort in maidens when winning at Nottingham in October by length from Conservation, taking while to warm to task: will stay 1½m: acts on soft going: unseated and bolted before intended reappearance: open to further improvement. *Sir Michael Stoute*

GALA JACKPOT (USA) 3 b. or br.g. Crafty Prospector (USA) – True At Heart 41 (USA) (Storm Cat (USA)) [2006 –: 8d 10.2f 7.5f⁶ Jun 22] poor maiden: should stay 1m: acts on firm going. *W. M. Brisbourne*

GALANDORA 6 b.m. Bijou d'Inde 127 – Jelabna (Jalmood (USA) 126) [2006 49: – f14g⁶ p16g Dec 18] close-coupled mare: poor performer: well held both starts in 2006: formerly tongue tied: usually held up. *Dr J. R. J. Naylor*

GALANTOS (GER) 5 b.g. Winged Love (IRE) 121 – Grey Metal (GER) (Secret 'n 65 Classy (CAN)) [2006 p12.2g f14g* 16g f14g* f14g p16g p16g f16g* Dec 28] leggy gelding: trained by C. Von Der Recke in Germany in 2005, winning maiden at Mulheim and handicap at Cologne: fair form in Britain: won banded races at Southwell in April, Kempton in May and Southwell in December: stays 2m: acts on all-weather and soft ground: blinkered (below form) penultimate outing. *G. L. Moore*

GALA SUNDAY (USA) 6 b.g. Lear Fan (USA) 130 – Sunday Bazaar (USA) (Nureyev 76 (USA) 131) [2006 76: p8.6g* p10g 10.5m⁴ 8.1f⁴ 10f* 9.9f* 10.1f 9.9s* 10.1m* 10g⁴ 10g 10d Oct 10] smallish, well-made gelding: fair performer: won banded race at Wolverhampton in May, and ladies handicaps at Nottingham, Beverley (2) and Yarmouth in July/August: best at 1¼m: acts on polytrack, firm and soft going: usually blinkered nowadays (including for all wins in 2006): sometimes tongue tied (including last 5 starts): sometimes makes running. *M. W. Easterby*

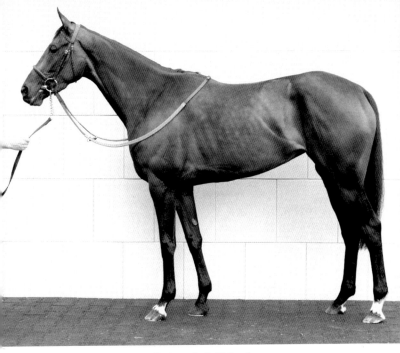

Ennistown Stud's "Galatee"

GALATEE (FR) 3 b.f. Galileo (IRE) 134 – Altana (USA) (Mountain Cat (USA)) [2006 **115**
10d* 9.5s* 10d* 12s⁶ 10s³ Oct 30] €400,000Y: first foal: dam, ran 3 times in France,
half-sister to Breeders' Cup Classic winner Arcangues and to dams of Cape Verdi and
Aquarelliste: smart performer: won first 3 starts in April/May, namely maiden at Naas
(by 9 lengths), listed race at Gowran (beat Helena Molony 2 lengths) and Irish Stallion
Farms EBF Blue Wind Stakes at Naas (best effort, beat Allexina by 3½ lengths): off
nearly 5 months (had been supplemented for Oaks but missed race following persistent
high white blood-cell count), below form in 2 listed races in autumn, third to Arch Rebel
at Leopardstown: should stay 1½m: acts on soft going. *J. S. Bolger, Ireland*

GALAXY BOUND (IRE) 3 b.g. Mark of Esteem (IRE) 137 – Diner de Lune (IRE) **–**
(Be My Guest (USA) 126) [2006 64: p10g p8g p8.6g⁶ p7.1g p7g f6g 6m p8.6g p6g p6g
p7g Dec 6] regressive maiden: often visored. *D. Shaw*

GALAXY OF STARS 2 b.f. (Mar 26) Observatory (USA) 131 – Divine Secret (Her- **60**
nando (FR) 127) [2006 5g⁵ p5.1g⁴ 5d 5.1d² f5g² p5.1g* p6g⁶ p6g⁵ Dec 8] 10,000Y: third
foal: half-sister to useful Italian winner up to 1m Adorabile Fong (by Dr Fong) and 4-y-o
Joyeaux: dam unraced out of sister to smart sprinter Monde Bleu: modest performer: won
nursery at Wolverhampton in November: probably stays 6f: acts on all-weather and good
to soft ground: visored last 3 starts. *D. Shaw*

GALAXY STARS 2 b.g. (Mar 11) Golden Snake (USA) 127 – Moly 64 (Inchinor 119) **72 p**
[2006 p6g* Dec 22] 8,000Y: fourth foal: half-brother to 5-y-o Danish Monarch and 4-y-o
Bahamian Bay: dam lightly-raced half-sister to smart winner up to 1¼m Don Micheletto:
7/1 and tongue tied, won 7-runner maiden at Kempton by neck from Darling Belinda:
should stay 7f: looks capable of better. *P. J. Makin*

GALIBARD (IRE) 3 b.g. Montjeu (IRE) 137 – His Lady (IRE) (Selkirk (USA) 129) **62**
[2006 12f⁶ p12g May 24] strong gelding: modest form at best in maidens: hung right on
debut/slowly away next time: joined J. Rudge, and gelded. *A. M. Balding*

GALIENT (IRE) 3 b.g. Galileo (IRE) 134 – Endorsement 107 (Warning 136) [2006 **107**
64p: 12m* 12.3m* 16m² 13.3d⁵ 13.9g Sep 9] tall, good-topped gelding: fluent mover:
useful performer, lightly raced: won maiden at Newmarket (by 6 lengths from Cougar
Bay) in April and handicap at Chester (beat Daylami Star by length) in May: good 1¼
lengths second to Soapy Danger in Queen's Vase at Royal Ascot next time: last after in
Geoffrey Freer Stakes at Newbury (not discredited despite reportedly banging head in
stall) and St Leger at York (weakened tamely and eased, subsequently gelded): will stay
beyond 2m: acts on good to firm going: sweated at Chester, but calmer at Royal Ascot:
races prominently: has worn crossed noseband. *M. A. Jarvis*

GALINGALE (IRE) 2 b.f. (Apr 23) Galileo (IRE) 134 – Urban Sky (FR) (Groom **67**
Dancer (USA) 128) [2006 7.5g 8.2g⁵ Sep 26] 28,000Y: close-coupled filly: closely
related to winner in Italy by Entrepreneur and half-sister to several winners, including
fairly useful Irish 1¼m winner Sky To Sea (by Adieu Au Roi): dam French 1¼m winner:
better effort in maidens at Nottingham. *Mrs P. Sly*

GALIPETTE 2 b.f. (Feb 9) Green Desert (USA) 127 – Arabesque 100 (Zafonic (USA) **79 p**
130) [2006 6s⁵ Oct 10] strong, compact filly: third foal: closely related to smart 6f winner
(including at 2 yrs) Camacho (by Danehill): dam, 6f winner, out of Chevley Park winner
Prophecy: 7/1, fit but green when 1¼ lengths fifth to Party in maiden at Newbury: open to
improvement. *H. R. A. Cecil*

GALLANTRY 4 b.g. Green Desert (USA) 127 – Gay Gallanta (USA) 112 (Woodman **94**
(USA) 126) [2006 90: 7f² 7.1d 6m 6m 7m⁵ 7f* 7m 6f 7.1m 7m Sep 9] strong gelding:
fairly useful handicapper: won at York in July: well below form last 2 starts: best form at
7f: acts on firm going. *D. W. Barker*

GALLANT SIR 3 ch.c. Grand Lodge (USA) 125 – Gay Gallanta (USA) 112 (Woodman (USA) 126) [2006 10d May 26] strong, lengthy colt: seventh foal: half-brother to
several winners, including 5-y-o Byron and 4-y-o Gallantry: dam, Queen Mary/Cheveley
Park winner, half-sister to very smart Irish performer up to 1¼m Sportsworld: 25/1,
backward and green, tailed off in maiden at Newmarket: sold 2,500 gns in July, sent to
Qatar. *J. R. Fanshawe*

GALLAS (IRE) 5 b.g. Charnwood Forest (IRE) 125 – Nellie's Away (IRE) 72 (Magical **55**
Strike (USA) 114) [2006 57: p12g² p12g⁵ Dec 6] sturdy gelding: modest maiden: stays
easy 1½m: acts on all-weather and good to firm going: effective visored/blinkered or not:
has looked tricky ride. *S. Lycett*

GALLEGO 4 br.g. Danzero (AUS) – Shafir (IRE) 68 (Shaadi (USA) 126) [2006 68: p8g **70**
f8g p8.6g p9.5g² p9.5g* p9.5g* p8.6g 10.9s p9.5g p8.6g 10.2g³ 10.2g⁴ 10.5m* 10m² **a61**
10.2d⁵ 11g 10f* 10.5f⁵ 8.1m 8.1d 12s 10.2m² p9.5m p7g³ p7.1g³ p8.6g p8.6g p10g Dec 3]
strong, close-coupled gelding: fair performer on turf, modest on all-weather: successful
in handicap and banded race at Wolverhampton in March, ladies handicap at Haydock in
June and handicap at Nottingham in July: stays 10.5f: acts on polytrack, firm and good to
soft going: tried blinkered/visored at 2 yrs: often slowly away: tough. *R. J. Price*

GALLERY BREEZE 7 b.m. Zamindar (USA) 116 – Wantage Park 104 (Pas de Seul **–**
133) [2006 80: p12.2g⁴ Jun 30] leggy mare: fairly useful performer at best: said to have
finished lame when well held only outing in 2006: tried in cheekpieces/blinkers: sometimes finds little/hangs. *P. A. Blockley*

GALLERY GIRL (IRE) 3 ch.f. Namid 128 – September Tide (IRE) 58 (Thatching **99**
131) [2006 97: 6m⁴ 6s 6m 5.1f⁴ 6f² 5d 6d 5s Oct 14] big, good sort: useful performer: best
effort in 2006 when ½-length second to Bentong in Summer Sprint (Handicap) at Redcar:
stays 6.5f: acts on firm and good to soft going. *T. D. Easterby*

GALLEY LAW 6 ch.g. Most Welcome 131 – Miss Blitz 83 (Formidable (USA) 125) **58**
[2006 62: f11g³ f12g⁵ f11g⁵ f11g⁶ f11g Dec 5 May 9] sturdy gelding: modest performer: stays
1½m: acts on all-weather and soft ground. *R. Craggs*

GALLILEO FIGARO (USA) 3 b.f. Galileo (IRE) 134 – Temperence Gift (USA) **74**
(Kingmambo (USA) 125) [2006 f11g 14m⁵ 10.3m⁴ 15.9m⁶ 16.1g⁶ 17.2g³ p13.9m⁶
p16.5g² p16.5g⁵ Dec 9] 42,000 2-y-o: first foal: dam unraced out of half-sister to Breeders' Cup Juvenile winner Brocco: fair maiden: barely stays 17f: acts on polytrack and
good to firm going. *W. M. Brisbourne*

GALLOISE (IRE) 2 b.f. (Mar 5) Val Royal (FR) 127 – Spring Daffodil 97 (Pharly **–**
(FR) 130) [2006 8.2s Oct 18] 31,000Y: tall, leggy filly: half-sister to several winners,

including French/Spanish winner up to 13.5f Tunduru (by Croco Rouge) and 1m to 1¼m winner Pantar (by Shirley Heights) both useful: dam Irish 7f/1m winner, later successful in USA: 12/1, burly and green in maiden at Nottingham. *C. G. Cox*

GALLOPING GERTIE 4 b.f. Aragon 118 – Meltonby 67 (Sayf El Arab (USA) 127) **45** [2006 f7g 10.1d f8g 8f 10m 12d Oct 8] fourth foal: dam 6f to 1m winner, including at 2 yrs: form (poor) only on fifth start. *J. Hetherton*

GALLOWAY BOY (IRE) 9 ch.g. Mujtahid (USA) 118 – Supportive (IRE) (Nash- **–** amaa 113) [2006 p6g p5.1g 6f 5g 5g Sep 13] smallish, sturdy gelding: one-time useful performer: unraced in 2005 and little form in 2006: tried in headgear: usually tongue tied. *J. F. Panvert*

GALLOWS HILL (USA) 2 b.g. (Apr 22) Stravinsky (USA) 133 – Verinha (BRZ) **–** (Baronius (BRZ)) [2006 6s⁵ 6m Jun 18] sturdy gelding: well held in maidens at York, then gelded. *R. A. Fahey*

GALWAY GIRL (IRE) 2 b.f. (Mar 22) Namid 128 – Cherry Falls (IRE) 81 (Ali-Royal **–** (IRE) 127) [2006 5g 7s Oct 10] €32,000Y: tall filly: second foal: dam Irish 7f winner (ran only at 2 yrs): 33/1, well held in maidens. *T. D. Easterby*

GAMBLE IN GOLD (IRE) 3 b.f. Monashee Mountain (USA) 115 – Starisa (IRE) **93** (College Chapel 122) [2006 92: 6d² 6f⁴ 7m 6s⁶ 5m³ 7.1m 6g 6g⁶ 6g Oct 12] smallish, quite good-topped filly: fairly useful performer: probably best at 5f/6f: acts on firm and good to soft going: sweating/edgy fourth start: sold 35,000 gns. *R. Hannon*

GAMBLING SPIRIT 4 ch.f. Mister Baileys 123 – Royal Roulette 77 (Risk Me (FR) **82** 127) [2006 66: 10.2d p10g³ 11.9g* 11.6m 11.6m 9.7f* 10.1f* 10m* Aug 11] fairly useful handicapper: won at Brighton in May, Folkestone and Yarmouth in July and Newmarket in August: effective at 9.7f to 13f: acts on polytrack and firm ground. *H. Candy*

GAME BERTIE 3 b.g. Mind Games 121 – Carol Again 48 (Kind of Hush 118) [2006 **–** 5s Aug 19] sparely-made gelding: 28/1 and troublesome in preliminaries, behind in maiden at Ripon: gelded after. *N. Bycroft*

GAME FLORA 5 b.m. Mind Games 121 – Breakfast Creek 63 (Hallgate 127) [2006 **–** 50d: f7g p6g f5g Mar 21] leggy mare: modest performer at best: no form in 2006. *D. Shaw*

GAME LAD 4 b.g. Mind Games 121 – Catch Me 75 (Rudimentary (USA) 118) [2006 **100** 104: 7g³ 8f⁴ 7g 6g Aug 7] big, lengthy gelding: useful handicapper: creditable efforts when in frame at Newmarket and Thirsk: well below form both subsequent outings: very best form at 7f: acts on soft and firm going. *T. D. Easterby*

GAME LADY 2 b.f. (Mar 24) Mind Games 121 – Highland Gait 63 (Most Welcome **67** 131) [2006 5d³ 6d⁶ 6.1m Sep 15] 12,000Y: small, sparely-made filly: first foal: dam, 7f winner who stayed 1¼m, half-sister to 4-y-o King's Gait and smart stayer Bold Gait: fair maiden, given time between runs: stays 6f. *A. Wood*

GAMESTERS LADY 3 br.f. Almushtarak (IRE) 122 – Tycoon Tina 61 (Tina's Pet **–** 121) [2006 84: 10m⁵ 12.3m⁴ 10.3f 10.3m Aug 6] sturdy filly: fairly useful at 2 yrs: well held in handicaps in 2006. *W. M. Brisbourne*

GANDALF 5 b.g. Sadler's Wells (USA) 132 – Enchant 92 (Lion Cavern (USA) 117) **86** [2006 85: 16g² p13.9g³ 16.2m³ 16.2d 13.9s Oct 7] good-topped gelding: fairly useful handicapper: stays 2m: acts on polytrack and good to firm going, possibly unsuited by softer than good: has been slowly away: looked none too keen third start: sold 7,000 gns. *J. R. Fanshawe*

GANDOR (IRE) 3 b.c. Cape Cross (IRE) 129 – Daftiyna (IRE) 74 (Darshaan 133) **97** [2006 66p: 8.5g* 10.3d⁶ 8m 10f³ p12.2f² Aug 30] small, quite attractive colt: useful performer: won maiden at Epsom in April: creditable placed efforts in minor event at Leicester and handicap at Wolverhampton last 2 starts: stays 1½m: acts on polytrack and firm going. *J. H. M. Gosden*

GANYMEDE 5 gr.g. Daylami (IRE) 138 – Germane 100 (Distant Relative 128) [2006 **70** 83§: p12.2g² p12g³ p13.9g p12g 15d 11.6f² 12.6m⁶ 12.6g⁵ 11.1m² 11.6m⁶ p10g³ p12g⁵ p16g⁴ 11.9m⁶ p16g* p16g* p16.5m Nov 21] close-coupled gelding: fair performer: left J. O'Shea after tenth start: won banded races at Kempton in October and November: stays 2m: acts on polytrack, firm and good to soft going: sometimes wears headgear. *Mrs L. J. Mongan*

GAP PRINCESS (IRE) 2 b.f. (Feb 23) Noverre (USA) 125 – Safe Care (IRE) (Caer- **69** leon (USA) 132) [2006 5m³ 5g² 5g³ 6.1g² 6m⁴ 7d Oct 3] 8,500Y: leggy, unfurnished filly:

third foal: half-sister to 3-y-o Hazium: dam unraced half-sister to smart sprinter Lugana Beach and to dam of very smart sprinter The Tatling: fair maiden: placed 4 times, including second to Bateleur in nursery at Nottingham: should stay 7f/1m. *R. A. Fahey*

GARAFENA 3 b.f. Golden Snake (USA) 127 – Eclipsing (IRE) 93 (Baillamont (USA) 124) [2006 10g³ 9.9g² 10g² 10m² Jul 12] good-bodied filly: half-sister to useful performer up to 1½m Vagabond Chanteuse (by Sanglamore), 7f winner at 2 yrs, and fairly useful 1998 2-y-o 6f winner Esteraad (by Cadeaux Genereux): dam 1m winner: fairly useful maiden, placed all starts: will stay 1½m: acts on good to firm going. *Pat Eddery* — **83**

GARDEN SOCIETY (IRE) 9 ch.g. Caerleon (USA) 132 – Eurobird 118 (Ela-Mana-Mou 132) [2006 98: 16d p16.5g⁵ Nov 6] small gelding: useful handicapper at best: well held both outings in 2006: visored once in 2002. *T. T. Clement*

GARHOUD 4 b.g. Grand Lodge (USA) 125 – Puce 112 (Darshaan 133) [2006 53: 17.2s Apr 11] modest performer: well held (in cheekpieces) only Flat run in 2006: blinkered (won) once at 3 yrs. *Miss K. M. George* — **–**

GARIBALDI (GER) 4 ch.g. Acatenango (GER) 127 – Guanhumara (Caerleon (USA) 132) [2006 72: p12.2g⁵ p12g 10m⁴ 9.9g 10.1s p12.2g⁶ p16.5m⁴ Nov 21] rangy gelding: fair performer: left D. Elsworth after fourth start: seems to stay 16.5f: acts on polytrack and good to firm going: tongue tied (ran creditably) final start. *J. O'Reilly* — **74**

GARLOGS 3 b.g. Hunting Lion (IRE) 115 – Fading (Pharly (FR) 130) [2006 55: f5g* f5g* f5g² p5.1g² f5g² 5v* 5.1s³ 5g⁴ p5.1g p5.1g p5.1g Nov 27] close-coupled gelding: fair handicapper: won at Southwell in January and February, and Musselburgh in March: best at 5f: acts on all-weather, heavy and good to firm ground: front runner. *A. Bailey* — **72**

GARPLE BURN 4 b.g. Zaha (CAN) 106 – Skedaddle 57 (Formidable (USA) 125) [2006 65d: p13.9g p10g p16g May 8] leggy gelding: poor maiden: should stay 1½m: wears blinkers/cheekpieces. *J. J. Best* — **47**

GARRULOUS (UAE) 3 b.c. Lomitas 129 – Friendly (USA) (Lear Fan (USA) 130) [2006 10d 10.5m⁵ May 6] modest form in maidens: sold 6,000 gns, joined G. L. Moore. *M. Johnston* — **60**

GARRYA 2 ch.c. (Mar 18) Mark of Esteem (IRE) 137 – Sherkova (USA) (State Dinner (USA)) [2006 7.1m p8g 7d 8g 8.3g a8g Nov 18] good-bodied colt: little form: sold from R. Hannon 3,500 gns before final start. *R. Verheye, Belgium* — **–**

GARSTANG 3 ch.g. Atraf 116 – Approved Quality (IRE) 66 (Persian Heights 129) [2006 56: f6g p6g² p6g² p6g* p6g p6g* p7g* p7g⁵ p7g³ 5d p6g* 6s² p6g⁶ 6g⁴ p6g* 7.1d⁶ 6g p6g Sep 12] rather leggy, workmanlike gelding: fairly useful handicapper: won at Wolverhampton in February and Lingfield in March (2), May and July: stays easy 7f: acts on polytrack, soft and good to firm ground: blinkered: signs of temperament, but generally reliable. *Peter Grayson* — **80**

GARSTON STAR 5 ch.g. Fleetwood (IRE) 107 – Conquista 87 (Aragon 118) [2006 10.2d 11.9g 14.1f 12.6g⁶ 12.1f⁴ 10m⁵ 11.9m 11.9d⁶ Oct 19] good-topped gelding: modest handicapper: missed 2005: acts on firm and good to soft going: front runner: withdrawn (got loose before start) intended seventh outing. *J. S. Moore* — **54**

GARY'S INDIAN (IRE) 3 b.f. Indian Danehill (IRE) 124 – Martino 44 (Marju (IRE) 127) [2006 8.1s 8.2m Sep 15] 5,000F: tall, leggy filly: fourth foal: half-sister to 1m to 13f winner Otago (by Desert Sun): dam, Irish maiden, stayed 13f: well held in maidens. *B. P. J. Baugh* — **–**

GATECRASHER 3 gr.g. Silver Patriarch (IRE) 125 – Girl At The Gate 53 (Formidable (USA) 125) [2006 10m May 15] 66/1 and very green, tailed off in maiden at Windsor. *Pat Eddery* — **–**

GATELAND 3 b. or br.g. Dansili 127 – Encorenous (USA) (Diesis 133) [2006 65: p7g 10m p10g² 13.1m 12.1m Sep 1] fair maiden: left W. Swinburn after third outing: stays easy 1¼m, not 1½m: acts on polytrack. *B. J. Llewellyn* — **67**

GATES OF EDEN (USA) 3 b.f. Kingmambo (USA) 125 – Amethyst (IRE) 111 (Sadler's Wells (USA) 132) [2006 71: 10m 10d 8.1f⁵ Jul 16] fair maiden: free-going sort, likely to prove best around 1m: acts on firm going. *M. L. W. Bell* — **68**

GATTUSO 3 b.g. Zilzal (USA) 137 – Daanat Nawal (Machiavellian (USA) 123) [2006 57, a64: p8g⁴ p8g⁵ 7.5d 8g⁶ p8.6m⁵ p7.1m p6g p8.6g f12g⁵ Dec 21] close-coupled gelding: modest maiden: stays 1m: acts on polytrack, heavy and good to firm going: sometimes slowly away/races freely: none too consistent. *Miss Deborah J. Evans* — **63**

GAUDALPIN (IRE) 4 b.f. Danetime (IRE) 121 – Lila Pedigo (IRE) 62 (Classic Secret (USA) 91) [2006 62: p6g p6g p6g⁶ p6g⁶ p7g⁴ p7g³ p7g² p7g p7g p7g p6g⁵ p5g⁴ f6g⁶ — **53**

Dec 28] workmanlike filly: modest performer: stays 7f: acts on all-weather and soft going: usually tongue tied: in cheekpieces last 2 starts. *E. R. Oertel*

GAUDEAMUS (USA) 2 b.f. (May 23) Distorted Humor (USA) 117 – Leo's Lucky **95**
Lady (USA) (Seattle Slew (USA)) [2006 6d* 7.5f³ 7g* 6.3m⁴ 7g* 7m 8d⁵ Sep 23]
$60,000Y: close-coupled, useful-looking filly: half-sister to several winners, notably
7-y-o Leo's Luckyman and useful 2004 2-y-o 6f winner Leo's Lucky Star (by Forestry):
dam, 6f winner in USA (including at 2 yrs), half-sister to dam of Bosra Sham and Hector
Protector: useful performer: won maiden at Naas in May, listed race at the Curragh in
June and 5-runner Robert H. Griffin Debutante Stakes at Leopardstown (by head from
Dimenticata) in July: ran well last 2 starts, eighth in Moyglare Stud Stakes at the Curragh
and fifth (6½ lengths behind Simply Perfect) in Fillies' Mile at Ascot: stays 1m: acts on
firm and good to soft going. *J. S. Bolger, Ireland*

GAVANELLO 3 br.g. Diktat 126 – Possessive Artiste 73 (Shareef Dancer (USA) 135) **–**
[2006 10m p12g 9.8d 10f 16.1g f14g⁵ Dec 29] little form, including in sellers/banded
race: left W. Swinburn after second start. *M. C. Chapman*

GAVARNIE BEAU (IRE) 3 b.g. Imperial Ballet (IRE) 110 – Mysticism 79 (Mystiko **91**
(USA) 124) [2006 69: p6g⁵ p7g² p6g³ 6g² 5.7d² p6g⁵ 6s* 6d* p6g⁶ 6g 6g⁴ 6m⁴ 6m p6g⁶ **a73**
6d 7d Oct 28] well-made gelding: fairly useful handicapper on turf, fair on all-weather:
won at Haydock and Leicester in May: stays easy 7f: acts on all-weather, soft and good to
firm going. *M. Blanshard*

GAVIOLI (IRE) 4 b.g. Namid 128 – Pamina (IRE) (Perugino (USA) 84) [2006 63: 6m **58**
5.5d 6m 6g² 6f 6m 6.1m Sep 1] big, workmanlike gelding: modest handicapper: best
form at 6f: acts on good to firm and good to soft going: usually tongue tied at 2 yrs,
tried in cheekpieces: bolted to post and hung left on reappearance: none too consistent.
J. M. Bradley

GAVROCHE (IRE) 5 b.h. Docksider (USA) 124 – Regal Revolution 105 (Hamas **106**
(IRE) 125§) [2006 102: p10g⁶ p12.2g³ p13g 12s* 12m² 11.3m⁵ 11.9g 13.4g⁶ 12.3m⁶ 10m **a97**
Sep 16] close-coupled horse: useful performer, better on turf than all-weather: won handicap at Goodwood in May by ¾ length from Nawamees: mostly creditable efforts after,
including when neck second to Alfie Noakes in handicap at Epsom: barely stays 13.4f:
acts on all-weather and any turf going: visored (raced freely) once in 2004: sometimes
slowly away: held up: reliable. *J. R. Boyle*

GAWROSZ (POL) 7 ch.g. Saphir (GER) – Galarda (POL) (Parysow) [2006 p8.6g 16g **48**
f12g⁴ f14g⁶ 11.8d f8g⁵ f12g Jul 7] workmanlike gelding: winner of 11 races in Poland,
including first 2 starts in 2005: poor form in Britain: stays 1½m: acts on fibresand.
G. J. Smith

GAZBOOLOU 2 b.c. (Feb 4) Royal Applause 124 – Warning Star 104 (Warning 136) **80**
[2006 6.1m² 6f² 7.2g² 7f² Sep 18] 42,000Y: half-brother to 3-y-o Speedy Sam, 4-y-o
Sound That Alarm and 3 winners abroad: dam 5f (including at 2 yrs)/6f winner: fairly
useful maiden: runner-up all starts, on final one beaten 1½ lengths by Ready For Spring
at Leicester (minor event): will prove best up to 7f: raced on good going or firmer.
K. R. Burke

GAZE 3 b.f. Galileo (IRE) 134 – Gryada 93 (Shirley Heights 130) [2006 8.2m 10d 10m³ **74**
11.9m⁵ 12f³ p12g p12g⁴ p13.9m⁵ p13.9g Oct 30] 50,000Y: close-coupled filly: half-sister
to several winners, including smart 7f (at 2 yrs) to 1½m winner Grampian (by Selkirk)
and useful 1¼m/1½m winner Guaranda (by Acatenango): dam, 2-y-o 7f/1m winner,
closely related to useful stayer Gondolier: fair maiden: stays easy 1¾m: acts on polytrack
and firm ground: visored fifth (wandered)/sixth outings: sold 20,000 gns. *W. Jarvis*

GEE DEE NEN 3 b.g. Mister Baileys 123 – Special Beat 65 (Bustino 136) [2006 78: **90**
10s² 11.8g³ 12.3m³ 14d³ 12m² 13.9s³ 13.1d³ 14g⁴ 12s⁴ 16d Oct 27] close-coupled, good-
topped gelding: fairly useful handicapper: best efforts at Pontefract and York (third to
Trick Or Treat in Melrose Stakes) fifth/sixth starts: should stay 2m: acts on soft and good
to firm going: visored (well held) final outing (gelded after): consistent. *M. H. Tompkins*

GELDER 3 b.f. Grand Lodge (USA) 125 – Purple Heather (USA) 93 (Rahy (USA) 115) **77 §**
[2006 8d⁵ 8.3m⁵ 8m* 8.1g² 8.3m⁶ 9.8s 8.1d p8.6m² Oct 14] second foal: half-sister to
fairly useful 7f (at 2 yrs)/1m winner The Coires (by Green Desert): dam, 1¼m winner, out
of half-sister to dam of Nashwan, Unfuwain and Nayef: fair performer: enterprisingly
ridden to win maiden at Salisbury in June: should stay 1¼m: acts on polytrack and good
to firm ground, possibly not on soft/good to soft: flashes tail: ungenuine: sold 8,000 gns.
H. Morrison

411

GEM BIEN (USA) 8 b.g. Bien Bien (USA) 125 – Eastern Gem (USA) (Jade Hunter – (USA)) [2006 61, a65: f8g f8g f7s³ f7g⁶ p8.6g⁴ 7.5f 8v⁶ f8g² p8.6g⁵ p7.1g f8g² p8.6g* **a61** p8.6g p8.6g⁴ 6.9m p9.5f⁶ p8.6g³ p8.6g f8g⁴ f8g f7g f7g p8g Dec 18] rather leggy gelding: modest handicapper: won selling event at Wolverhampton in July: effective at 7f to 1¼m: acts on all-weather, soft and good to firm ground: wears blinkers/cheekpieces: tongue tied once at 3 yrs: carries head awkwardly/wanders. *D. W. Chapman*

GEMINI LADY 6 b.m. Emperor Fountain 112 – Raunchy Rita (Brigadier Gerard 144) – § [2006 41§: f12g Feb 5] strong, close-coupled mare: unreliable maiden: well held only outing in 2006: has worn blinkers/cheekpieces. *Mrs J. C. McGregor*

GEMOLOGY (USA) 2 b.c. (Feb 15) Horse Chestnut (SAF) 119 – Miners Girl (USA) **90 p** (Miner's Mark (USA) 120) [2006 7s² Oct 10] $23,000F, €115,000Y: fifth foal: half-brother to a winner in USA by Eastern Echo: dam, 6f winner in USA, sister to smart UAE miler Cherry Pickings: 5/2, promising ¾-length second to Al Shemali (pair well clear) in maiden at Newcastle: sure to go on and win races. *Saeed bin Suroor*

GENARI 3 b.g. Generous (IRE) 139 – Sari 83 (Faustus (USA) 118) [2006 93: 8.1g⁵ **93 d** 11.1d³ 10.1m 8g 9.9f 8m⁶ p7g 8s Sep 22] big, good-topped gelding: fairly useful performer: well below form after second outing: stays 11f: acts on firm and good to soft ground: tried blinkered: gelded after final start. *P. F. I. Cole*

GENAU (IRE) 3 ch.g. Grand Lodge (USA) 125 – Intizaa (USA) 77 (Mr Prospector **70** (USA)) [2006 72: p9.5g³ p8.6g 12d Apr 24] strong, lengthy gelding: fair maiden: ran poorly last 2 starts: should stay 1¼m: sold 5,500 gns, joined Evan Williams. *Mrs L. Stubbs*

GENERAL FEELING (IRE) 5 b.g. General Monash (USA) 107 – Kamadara (IRE) **80 d** (Kahyasi 130) [2006 85: p6g⁴ p7.1g⁴ p6g p7.1g² p7.1g p8g p7.1g 8.1g 6g 7g 7.5f p5.1g p5.1s⁶ p7.1g p6g⁶ Dec 28] good-bodied gelding: fairly useful performer: left S. Kirk after reappearance: below form after fourth outing: effective at 5f to 1m: acts on polytrack, firm and soft going: tried blinkered/tongue tied: sometimes slowly away: held up: none too reliable. *M. Mullineaux*

GENERAL FLUMPA 5 b.g. Vettori (IRE) 119 – Macca Luna (IRE) 78 (Kahyasi 130) **65** [2006 67: p12g⁶ p13g 12d³ 11.8d³ p12g⁴ 11m⁴ p10g 10.9m* 10.9d⁴ p12g Sep 29] close-coupled gelding: fair handicapper: won apprentice event at Warwick in September: best at 1¼m/1½m: acts on all-weather, soft and good to firm going. *C. F. Wall*

GENERAL NUISANCE (IRE) 4 ch.g. General Monash (USA) 107 – Baywood – (Emarati (USA) 74) [2006 –: f11g Jan 12] sturdy gelding: modest maiden at 2 yrs (often blinkered/in cheekpieces): well held both starts since. *A. J. Chamberlain*

GENERATOR 4 ch.g. Cadeaux Genereux 131 – Billie Blue 63 (Ballad Rock 122) **71** [2006 71: f6g² 7g⁴ 10g 10s p8g⁶ p7g* p7g* Dec 8] fair performer, lightly raced: won handicaps at Lingfield in November and Kempton in December: stays easy 1m: acts on all-weather. *Dr J. D. Scargill*

GENERIST 2 b.f. (May 1) Generous (IRE) 139 – Amidst 86 (Midyan (USA) 124) [2006 **55** p5.1g⁶ p6g⁶ 7m⁴ 7.1m⁴ 7f³ 7m⁴ 7s⁶ 8.2s³ p7.1g⁴ f8g p8.6g⁵ Nov 18] 2,500Y: seventh foal: half-sister to 3 winners, including fairly useful 7f winner Aploy (by Deploy) and 3-y-o Atwirl: dam 6f (at 2 yrs) and 1m winner: modest maiden: raced mainly in sellers/claimers: stays 1m: acts on firm and soft going: below form in cheekpieces last 2 starts. *M. J. Attwater*

GENEROSIA 3 b.f. Generous (IRE) 139 – Come On Rosi 77 (Valiyar 129) [2006 52: **72** 8.2m 9.9g⁴ 10d³ 11.9m* 10m 11.6m⁴ Aug 5] big, strong filly: fair handicapper: won at Haydock in July, despite flashing tail: stays 1½m: acts on good to firm going: tongue tied. *A. M. Balding*

GENEROUS JEM 3 b.f. Generous (IRE) 139 – Top Jem 85 (Damister (USA) 123) **62** [2006 10m 12.4s⁴ Oct 10] leggy filly: third foal: half-sister to useful 9f to 1½m winner Polar Jem (by Polar Falcon): dam, 9f/1¼m winner, half-sister to smart performer up to 1½m Polar Red: better effort in maidens when fourth to Grey Outlook at Newcastle, off bridle fair way out: should stay 1¾m. *G. G. Margarson*

GENEROUS LAD (IRE) 3 b.g. Generous (IRE) 139 – Tudor Loom (Sallust 134) **74** [2006 64: 10.9g 10.2g 10m 10.2m p10g* p10g² Dec 20] leggy gelding: fair handicapper: left Miss J. Davis after fourth start: different tactics, improved form to win at Kempton in December, held up: good second there next time: stays 1¼m: acts on polytrack and good to firm going: wore cheekpieces 3 of last 4 starts. *A. B. Haynes*

GENEVIEVE 4 b.f. Mtoto 134 – Eternal Flame 73 (Primo Dominie 121) [2006 8d 7m –
10.1f⁶ Jul 18] seventh foal: half-sister to fairly useful 9.4f and 1¼m winner Diamond
Flame (by Suave Dancer): dam 7f and 8.5f winner: no form. *Mrs C. A. Dunnett*

GENKI (IRE) 2 ch.g. (Jan 30) Shinko Forest (IRE) – Emma's Star (ITY) (Darshaan **79 p**
133) [2006 p7g⁶ 6g² Oct 16] 55,000Y: third foal: dam Italian 8.5f winner: green on debut,
then short-head second to Vitznau in maiden at Windsor, pair going clear: should improve
further. *R. Charlton*

GENOA STAR 3 b.f. Woodborough (USA) 112 – Naval Dispatch (Slip Anchor 136) **45 §**
[2006 44: f8g4 p8g² f8g4 f8g f7g4 p10g Apr 5] poor maiden: stays 1m: acts on all-weather
and good to firm ground: usually wears headgear: often slowly away: temperamental.
T. J. Pitt

GENTIAN 3 ch.f. Generous (IRE) 139 – French Spice 85 (Cadeaux Genereux 131) **61**
[2006 –p: p12.2g* Jun 10] unfurnished filly: modest performer, lightly raced: upped in
trip, improved form to win seller at Wolverhampton very easily on only Flat outing in
2006 (sold 10,000 gns, joined D. McCain Jnr): stays 1½m: acts on polytrack: fair winning
juvenile hurdler. *Sir Mark Prescott*

GENTLE GURU 2 b.f. (Jan 8) Ishiguru (USA) 114 – Soft Touch (IRE) 78 (Petorius **81 +**
117) [2006 6m⁵ 6d² 6.1d* Oct 13] 15,000Y: good-topped filly: second foal: half-sister to
Italian 7.5f/1m winner by Fraam: dam 1m and hurdles winner: fairly useful form in maidens, winning at Warwick: will prove best at 5f/6f. *R. T. Phillips*

GENTLEMAN PIRATE 2 ch.c. (Jan 15) Bahamian Bounty 116 – Verdura 63 (Green **91**
Desert (USA) 127) [2006 5m² 6m³ 6m² 6d² Aug 22] good-topped colt: second foal:
brother to 4-y-o Green Pirate: dam maiden who stayed 9f: fairly useful maiden: placed all
starts, second to Dubai Builder in competitive nursery at York final one: will stay 7f: sent
to Hong Kong. *M. H. Tompkins*

GENTLEMAN'S DEAL (IRE) 5 b.h. Danehill (USA) 126 – Sleepytime (IRE) 121 **95**
(Royal Academy (USA) 130) [2006 f8g* p9.5g* 8s 10.4g 8.1g4 8s⁵ 8d⁴ 10d f8g* Dec 2] **a112**
big, strong, good-topped horse: has an unimpressive, quick action: smart performer on
all-weather, useful on turf: lightly raced (missed 2005): impressive when winning handicaps at Southwell and Wolverhampton in January, and (having been to stud) at Southwell
(much improved to beat Wessex by 6 lengths) in December: stays 1¼m: acts on all-
weather, raced only good ground or softer on turf. *M. W. Easterby*

GENTLEWAVE (IRE) 3 b.c. Monsun (GER) 124 – Saumareine (FR) (Saumarez **120**
132) [2006 10v* 10.5s* 10.5g* 11d² 12g* 12g² Jul 2]

    Reducing the distance of the Prix du Jockey Club to ten and a half furlongs
has made rolling stones out of some of France's leading three-year-olds. Other
Derbys around Europe are now proving more natural homes for French-trained
colts thought likely to be suited by a mile and a half, formerly the distance of the
Prix du Jockey Club. With Hurricane Run finishing strongly into second in the Prix
du Jockey Club in 2005, trainer Andre Fabre was—unusually for him—represented
in the Derby at Epsom and even further afield in the Derby Italiano at Rome in
2006. Favourite Visindar managed only fifth as he performed the better of Fabre's
representatives at Epsom, while Gentlewave was successful in some style in Italy,
making short work of the opposition as he scored by four lengths.

    On what he did in the spring, Gentlewave would have been an obvious
contender for the Prix du Jockey Club had it still been run over a mile and a half.
Unraced as a two-year-old, he was unlucky not to go to the Derby Italiano unbeaten
in four starts. A three-length winner of a minor event at Saint-Cloud on his debut in
March, he proved a length and a half too good for Numide in a listed race on the
course later in the month. Stepping up further in class in the Group 2 Prix Noailles
at Longchamp in April on his first run for new owner Gary Tanaka, Gentlewave
came with a strong late run to beat his stable-companion Bremen a short head.
Gentlewave's only defeat before Rome came in another Group 2, the Prix Hocquart, a traditional trial for the Prix du Jockey Club, run over eleven furlongs at
Longchamp in early-May. Starting odds-on, Gentlewave had just started to assert
when rider Christophe Soumillon dropped his whip, Gentlewave going down only
by a short-neck to Numide. With the rest six lengths and more behind, the Hocquart
performance of Gentlewave still looked a good trial for the Derby Italiano later
in the month and he started odds on in a field of fourteen. Rattle And Hum, winner
of the Italian Two Thousand Guineas, the Premio Parioli, was shortest-priced of

Derby Italiano, Rome—French-trained Gentlewave lands the odds in style;
Yarqus (rail) does the better of the two British-trained challengers in sixth

the home-trained contenders at 9/2, but there was nothing to touch Gentlewave. Running at a mile and a half for the first time, he made his move up the centre of the course and strode clear from a furlong and a half out, chased home by Storm Mountain with the rest well strung out. On the strength of his effort at Rome, Gentlewave was supplemented for the Irish Derby at the Curragh, and more than justified the move. In an open market, he started third favourite at 11/2 behind Derby third Dylan Thomas and Prix du Jockey Club winner Darsi, and finished a clear second of thirteen. Held up again, Gentlewave stayed on strongly once switched off the rail over a furlong out, though never threatening the winner, going down by three and a half lengths to Dylan Thomas, a length and a half in front of Best Alibi in third, with Darsi only fifth. Unfortunately, Gentlewave was found to have suffered a tendon injury the following month, and it was announced in November that he had been retired to the Haras du Thenney in France at a fee of €4,500.

Gentlewave (IRE) (b.c. 2003)	Monsun (GER) (br 1990)	Konigsstuhl (br 1976)	Dschingis Khan
			Konigskronung
		Mosella (b 1985)	Surumu
			Monasia
	Saumareine (FR) (b 1993)	Saumarez (b 1987)	Rainbow Quest
			Fiesta Fun
		Charming Queen (ch 1975)	Habitat
			Charming Fun

Gentlewave's highly successful sire Monsun was well represented in European Derbys in 2006. Apart from Gentlewave, Schiaparelli added to his sire's growing reputation by winning the Deutsches Derby at Hamburg, a race also won by Monsun's best son Shirocco, and Arras was third in the Prix du Jockey Club at Chantilly. Gentlewave, who cost €55,000 at Deauville as a yearling, is a half-

414

brother to three winners in France. They include the useful ten-and-a-half-furlong winner Splendeur (by Desert King), later successful in the States, and the fairly useful winner at around eleven furlongs Sonka (by Desert Prince). Their dam Saumareine, a useful French mile- to mile-and-a-quarter winner, is a half-sister to the American Grade 1 nine-furlong winner Charming Duke. A genuine sort, never out of the first two in six starts, Gentlewave raced only on good ground or softer and stayed a mile and a half well. *A. Fabre, France*

GENUINE CALL 2 b.f. (Mar 14) Tobougg (IRE) 125 – Gena Ivor (USA) (Sir Ivor (USA) 135) [2006 6m⁴ p6g³ p6g* p6g Nov 11] sturdy filly: closely related to fairly useful 1m winner Joint Statement (by Barathea) and half-sister to 3 winners, including 6-y-o Roman Empire: dam 6f to 8.5f winner in USA: fair form: won maiden at Lingfield in October: last in nursery final outing (reportedly finished sore behind): will stay 1m. *C. F. Wall* — **72**

GENUINE SURPRISE (IRE) 4 br.f. Definite Article 121 – Morning Surprise 58 (Tragic Role (USA)) [2006 53: p8.6g Mar 3] maiden: well held only outing in 2006. *A. P. Jarvis* — **–**

GEOJIMALI 4 ch.g. Compton Place 125 – Harrken Heights (IRE) (Belmez (USA) 131) [2006 –: p7.1g p6g² p7.1g² p6g* 6g 5.9g* 5d² 6m² p6g² 6f² 6m* 6g⁵ 6m³ 6d* 5s³ Oct 16] heavy-topped gelding: fairly useful performer: progressed well in 2006, winning banded event at Wolverhampton in May and handicaps at Carlisle later in May and Ayr in July and September, beating Zomerlust by head in Silver Cup on last occasion: effective at stiff 5f to 7f: acts on polytrack, firm and soft going: often slowly away: held up: consistent. *J. S. Goldie* — **91**

GEORDIE DANCER (IRE) 4 b.g. Dansili 127 – Awtaar (USA) 67 (Lyphard (USA) 132) [2006 62§: 7d p7.1g 7.1f 5.9m 5m⁶ 6m 6m⁵ f6g Nov 13] good-bodied gelding: modest and inconsistent handicapper at 3 yrs: little form in 2006. *A. Berry* — **– §**

GEORDIELAND (FR) 5 gr.h. Johann Quatz (FR) – Aerdee (FR) (Highest Honor (FR) 124) [2006 120: 10v⁴ 10g 12m⁴ 16f² 13.9d⁴ 16g Nov 7] strong, close-coupled horse: smart performer: left J-M. Beguigne in France after third outing: good efforts in Britain after, in Goodwood Cup (5 lengths second to Yeats, eased final 1f) and Ebor (Handicap) at York (2 lengths fourth to Mudawin): well below best when eighteenth in Melbourne Cup at Flemington final outing (reportedly bled): effective at 1½m to 2m: acts on any going: normally held up: blinkered second outing. *J. A. Osborne* — **119**

GEORDIE'S POOL 2 b.c. (Apr 15) Dilshaan 119 – Last Result (Northern Park (USA) 107) [2006 p8g⁴ p8g⁶ Nov 8] modest form in maidens. *J. W. Hills* — **61**

GEORGE HENSON (IRE) 2 b. or br.g. (Mar 9) Desert Style (IRE) 121 – Alexandria (IRE) (Irish River (FR) 131) [2006 7d Oct 28] sturdy gelding: 66/1 and backward in maiden at Newmarket: subsequently gelded. *M. H. Tompkins* — **–**

GEORGE'S FLYER (IRE) 3 b.c. Daggers Drawn (USA) 114 – Winged Victory (IRE) 93 (Dancing Brave (USA) 140) [2006 64: p9.5g* p10g 10m 10m⁶ 10.1m 8.5m 12s p9.5g p7g³ f8g p8.6g Dec 21] sturdy colt: fair performer on all-weather, modest on turf: won handicap at Wolverhampton in January: stays 9.5f: acts on all-weather and good to firm going: blinkered. *R. A. Fahey* — **61 a70**

GEORGES PRIDE 2 b.c. (Mar 30) Averti (IRE) 117 – Thaw 74 (Cadeaux Genereux 131) [2006 5.7m 5.1f 5.7m Sep 25] in rear in maidens. *J. M. Bradley* — **–**

GEORGE THE BEST (IRE) 5 b.g. Imperial Ballet (IRE) 110 – En Retard (IRE) 97 (Petardia 113) [2006 71d: f6s f6g 5d⁵ 6d* 5d 7.2d⁶ 6f 6d⁶ 7m 6d⁵ 6g 5d* 6s 6v* 6.1s⁴ Oct 25] workmanlike gelding: fair handicapper on turf, little solid form on all-weather: won at Hamilton in May and September, and Ayr in October: stays 6f: acts on heavy going: tried visored: has been slowly away: ungenuine. *M. D. Hammond* — **71 § a– §**

GEORGE THE SECOND 3 b.c. Josr Algarhoud (IRE) 118 – Pink Champagne (Cosmonaut) [2006 61, a58: p7g³ 7.1s² 6m² 6.1d* 6g p6g* p7g 6g p6g⁶ 6m 5.5d p6m⁵ p6g p6g* p6g Dec 15] leggy colt: fair handicapper: won at Chepstow in May and Lingfield in June and November: stays 7f: acts on all-weather, soft and good to firm going: tried tongue tied. *Mrs H. Sweeting* — **71**

GEORGE WASHINGTON (IRE) 3 b.c. Danehill (USA) 126 – Bordighera (USA) 104 (Alysheba (USA)) [2006 118p: 8m* 8v² 8m³ 8d* a10f⁶ Nov 4] — **133**

Call me George! There is a lot to be said for being familiar. In business, for example, being on first name terms can open doors that otherwise might be shut. In life in general, the sound of our own first name is said to be the sweetest sound an individual can hear. To some, however, familiarity breeds contempt, leading to a lack of proper respect and a blurring of sensible boundaries. Should pupils be allowed to call a teacher by his or her first name? Or should a television audience be heard addressing Prime Minister Blair as Tony in a face-to-face political debate? Ballydoyle has encouraged increasing familiarity with its prospective champions over the years. Names such as Mozart and Stravinsky, which have lent stature and credibility to reputations by association with great figures of the past, have given way to the likes of Horatio Nelson, Dylan Thomas and George Washington in the Coolmore naming convention. If George Washington was meant to live up to his namesake in terms of achievement, he played his part well. In merit, he was worthy of being associated with America's first President, but the fact that he came to be referred to by his first name played a part in softening his image as a roguish champion. Undoubtedly a heavyweight, superior to run-of-the-mill classic winners, champion miler and Timeform's Horse of the Year, inferior only to Hawk Wing and Galileo among those trained by Aidan O'Brien, 'George' or 'Gorgeous George', as he became known, had a temperamental side which shouldn't be clouded by image.

George Washington's name and the remarks of his trainer Aidan O'Brien led to his being attributed with human personality, sections of the media from the outset falling into the trap of using anthropomorphisms. Under the headline, 'Gorgeous George deserves our respect,' the *Racing Post*'s chief correspondent described him as having film-star looks and a politician's ego. The idea that George Washington had an 'ego' stemmed from the comments of his trainer in the spring, and helped create an aura of invincibility. 'Brilliance and arrogance often come together and he is a very arrogant colt. I've never had one with an ego like him. He looks down on everyone and on other horses,' said his trainer at his annual open day. Connections of his Guineas rivals could have been excused for believing they might as well have stayed at home. O'Brien pushed on with the same tack after Newmarket. 'He has developed a real personality. He has a big attitude. He has this attitude that he's absolutely different class to every other horse,' he commented. George Washington's name went hand in hand with the opportunity for connections to build a persona for the horse which excused his wayward tendencies more than might otherwise have been the case, making a virtue of his flaws. Words such as difficult, headstrong and temperamental were studiously avoided by O'Brien where George Washington was concerned. To his credit, George Washington twice lit up the season with his performances, but in terms of his racing character the bottom line was this: he could be reluctant at the stalls, he could be slowly away, he could pull hard and he could hang both ways and carry his head awkwardly under pressure.

George Washington showed flashes of both his brilliance and his waywardness as a two-year-old. Unbeaten in four starts after his debut, including in three pattern races, the last two Group 1s, he had been particularly impressive when running out an eight-length winner of the Phoenix Stakes at the Curragh on his penultimate outing, but had raised doubts about his temperament—and the form of his Phoenix win—when making much heavier weather of the National Stakes on the course on his final start, edging left in front and flashing his tail under pressure. All the same, a strong, good-topped colt with an impressive easy action, George Washington seemed likely to make into a fine-looking three-year-old and add to his already impressive tally of wins if he went the right way. His trainer's comments in the spring underlined his high opinion of him, while raising doubts about his stamina for the stiff mile at Newmarket. 'George Washington is a very special horse. He is very fast and very brilliant with a remarkable action,' O'Brien said prior to his reappearance, adding that George Washington was probably the fastest horse he had trained for the Guineas. 'I'll believe it when I see it,' said O'Brien when asked about George Washington's ability to stay.

Last seen at two when declared for the Dewhurst Stakes at Newmarket, but withdrawn at the eleventh hour due to softish ground, George Washington made his first public appearance as a three-year-old in a racecourse gallop at the Curragh in early-April, a traditional starting point for Ballydoyle classic candidates in the spring. He again made headlines with his antics, jinking left and out through a gap in the running rail on his way to the six-furlong start before cantering with a stable-companion. His behaviour, combined with a paucity of winners for Ballydoyle, saw

Stan James 2000 Guineas Stakes, Newmarket—George Washington is an impressive winner from Sir Percy (right), Olympian Odyssey (striped sleeves) and Araafa (No.2)

George Washington drift briefly from his winter odds of around 2/1 for Newmarket, though there was no lack of market confidence in him for the Stan James Two Thousand Guineas on the day. In a representative field of fourteen, George Washington was backed down to 6/4. There were eight pattern-race winners in opposition, but only the Dewhurst first and second, the unbeaten Sir Percy, a 4/1-shot, and 6/1-chance Horatio Nelson, a stable-companion of the favourite and winner of the Prix Jean-Luc Lagardere at two, were seriously backed against him.

Despite the concerns surrounding the form of the stable, George Washington looked in fine shape at Newmarket. He was attended by a posse of handlers in the paddock, but took most of the preliminaries in his stride, though joined at the start by his trainer and needing to be manhandled into the stalls. In the race, he outclassed the opposition from start to finish. Soon travelling supremely well under Kieren Fallon in a race run at only a fair pace, George Washington cruised through from towards the rear before the Dip as the field began to fan to the far rail and, ridden along, quickly settled matters, showing a fine turn of foot to go clear, despite drifting sharply right with the race won. He scored by two and a half lengths from Sir Percy, who rallied once passed, with the front-running Olympian Odyssey, a 33/1-shot, a length and a half further away in third and another outsider Araafa fourth at 66/1, three quarters of a length further back. Since Zafonic, the last successful favourite, scored by three and a half lengths in 1993, George Washington's winning margin has been bettered only by King's Best, also a three-and-a-half-length winner in 2000. Following King of Kings in 1998, Rock of Gibraltar in 2002 and Footstepsinthesand in 2005, George Washington was a fourth winner of the race for O'Brien (all of them on their reappearance), leaving him one short of Sir Michael Stoute's modern-day record.

If George Washington had taken the preliminaries at Newmarket in his stride for the most part, he was in no mood to co-operate on his return to the winner's enclosure, turning in an almost unique display of temperament for a classic winner, rooting himself to the spot on the walkway to the paddock, refusing to be led forward even when his trainer took the reins, eventually being taken via the pre-paddock but still failing to appear in the designated area, delaying his rider weighing in. 'He didn't want to come in because the other horses had gone the other way,' said O'Brien. 'There was no point getting into an argument. If he pleases us on the track, that's the big thing. Mentally, he's immature and sometimes he doesn't see your point of view, but, after a while, I think he will.' It was the second time George Washington had shown such behaviour, refusing to leave the winner's enclosure on schedule after his victory in the Railway Stakes at the Curragh on his third outing as a two-year-old.

Although connections were keen to excuse him, George Washington is one of several Ballydoyle inmates to have shown a temperamental streak in recent seasons. Among the stable's better horses since 2003, Oratorio, Scorpion, One Cool Cat, Antonuis Pius, Brian Boru, Powerscourt, Yesterday and Hold That Tiger have all exhibited quirks either in their mannerisms or racing style. Only Antonius Pius among them was awarded a Timeform squiggle, symbolising distinct unreliability, his temperament costing him victory in the Poule d'Essai des Poulains and possibly success in the Breeders' Cup Mile as well. All the same, of the others mentioned, none was inclined to run as straight and true from start to finish throughout their careers as some of the Ballydoyle champions of the past. The end of 2003 saw a split between Aidan O'Brien and his long-standing stable-jockey Michael Kinane, replaced for one season by Jamie Spencer, who in turn was succeeded by Kieren Fallon in 2005. Fallon, who had an injury scare two days before Newmarket, partnered King's Best and Golan to success in the Two Thousand Guineas before joining Ballydoyle from Sir Michael Stoute and George Washington was his second for O'Brien following Footstepsinthesand twelve months earlier.

Although the bad habits among some members of the Ballydoyle string have extended well beyond the learning process, learning on the course has always played a bigger part in education at Ballydoyle than in some other yards which regularly have runners in classics. Easy victories by good two-year-olds perhaps result in them learning less than horses of lesser ability might be expected to do. The Ballydoyle approach requires toughness in the make-up of its two-year-olds and George Washington, who made his debut as a two-year-old when third in a Newmarket maiden on Guineas weekend, would almost certainly have been required to demonstrate continued toughness himself at three but for injury on his next outing. After the doubts expressed by his trainer before Newmarket over his ability to stay a mile, there was little talk of the Derby for George Washington—though he was entered for Epsom at a cost of £8,000 in early-April—and he had his next race in the Irish Two Thousand Guineas at the Curragh later in May. Opposed only by Araafa from Newmarket, George Washington seemed to have little to trouble him in a field of eleven made up almost exclusively of home-trained runners, and he started at 7/4-on to become the sixth horse to complete the Anglo-Irish Guineas double, last achieved by Rock of Gibraltar in 2002. One unknown, however, was George Washington's ability to cope with the heavy ground and he came unstuck in the contrasting conditions, Araafa making first run as the field came towards the stand side in the straight before George Washington jinked left inside the final furlong this time, after making much heavier weather of getting into contention than at Newmarket, going down by two lengths to Araafa. In the immediate aftermath of defeat, O'Brien blamed the ground and a slow pace, adding that the race would have 'done the horse's character good'. Two days later it was announced that George Washington had 'pulled some muscles above his hip'.

The injury to George Washington deflected attention from his continued mulish behaviour in the preliminaries at the Curragh, where he left the paddock backwards and was flanked by his three stable-companions on the way to post, again proving tricky at the stalls. On his return at Goodwood in August, he was accompanied by an outrider in the pre-parade before being taken down first, out of order with permission of the stewards. With a 6-lb penalty for his Guineas success in the Group 2 totesport Celebration Mile, and using the race as a stepping stone to the Queen Elizabeth II Stakes at Ascot the following month, George Washington looked in fine shape, despite his three-month absence, and again started favourite, going off at 6/5-on in a field of six. With Fallon now suspended from riding in Britain, George Washington was partnered for the first time by Kinane. O'Brien was guarded over the horse's chance of making a winning return, saying 'ability-wise you just have to hope that everything is still there.' At the weights, George Washington ran several pounds below his best, after making things harder for himself by missing the break, and being the backmarker by a good three lengths as his stable-companion River Tiber established a clear lead ignored by the remainder.

After failing to settle, George Washington looked reluctant to close when finally shaken up, carrying his head awkwardly and hanging left as he made late inroads on the leaders, going down by a length and a quarter to the close-finishers Caradak and Killybegs, the latter only eleventh in the Guineas. O'Brien had stated before-hand that the race would be 'a big learning curve for his jockey' but, after a second successive defeat, he was at his most defensive afterwards, saying 'If you got an injury like he did, you would be hanging more than the left of your head.'

George Washington came close to being given a squiggle in *Timeform* after Goodwood. At the time, taken together, his two most recent performances certainly raised doubts about his trustworthiness. In the end, he escaped the ignominy. As a matter of interest, in the last ten years, only a handful of three-year-olds rated in Timeform's top hundred at the end of the season have received a squiggle, most of them after showing a marked reluctance to race or, as with O'Brien's Antonius Pius, a marked reluctance to go through with their finishing effort. Far more squiggles have been awarded to those lower down the performance scale, but, in general, it seems the upper echelons of the horse population have proved a genuine bunch as three-year-olds, or have been given the benefit of the doubt while their racing character was still being fully established. As a rule as well, where temperament is concerned, consistency of performance has usually been the decisive factor, rather than quirks such as a high head carriage, or a tendency to hang.

With the Goodwood run behind him, it seemed reasonable to expect George Washington to be harder to beat in the Queen Elizabeth II Stakes at Ascot, provided he put his best foot forward, but the question of his temperament dominated the build up to the race. BBC television, which covered the meeting, hired Kelly Marks, a 'horse psychologist', to comment on the horse's antics during the season and on the day. 'Aidan O'Brien has done a wonderful job with George Washington, but he's spinning when he says the horse is arrogant,' she said beforehand, adding 'Arrogance is purely a human trait. An arrogant horse in the wild would get eaten. To me, George Washington looks insecure and immature. He puts his head in the air, which is what a frightened horse does. He runs like a horse lacking confidence, and when he gets hit he doesn't run on, he runs sideways.' Without an outrider this time, though accompanied by another horse in the saddling area, George Washing-ton was on his best behaviour beforehand and produced another top-class perform-

Queen Elizabeth II Stakes, Ascot—George Washington puts up the best performance of the year in Europe; Araafa is a good second ahead of Court Masterpiece (right) and Killybegs

ance. On ground softened by the previous day's rain, though conditions were less testing than at the Curragh, he was backed down to 13/8 favourite in a field of eight. Godolphin's Librettist, the first horse since 1997 to complete the Marois/Moulin double, was next best at 3/1 followed by his stable-companion, the joint-champion miler of 2005 Proclamation, a 5/1 chance. Breaking more quickly than at Goodwood, George Washington tracked Araafa through effortlessly in the straight. Once shaken up, he was soon in control, albeit carrying his head high and edging left as he got on top, hardly touched with the whip. In this third meeting between the pair, George Washington won by a length and a quarter (it looked further) from Araafa, a high-class miler in his own right, with the Sussex Stakes winner Court Masterpiece two lengths further away. It is debatable whether George Washington would have found much more had Kinane put him under the strongest pressure.

On average, the Queen Elizabeth II Stakes has been Europe's top event over a mile for some time, and the roll of honour reads like a who's who of European miling, including, since 1990, those other top-class performers Markofdistinction, Mark of Esteem, Desert Prince, Dubai Millennium, Observatory and Falbrav. George Washington's performance was at least as good as any in the race in that time except for Mark of Esteem's outstanding victory over Bosra Sham in 1996, and it was the best seen on a European racecourse in 2006. Mark of Esteem's jockey Frankie Dettori, who rode all seven winners on the card in 1996, was at the centre of a storm over the running of George Washington's stablemate Ivan Denisovich in the Queen Elizabeth II Stakes. Ivan Denisovich's jockey Seamus Heffernan was banned for fourteen days under the rule governing 'team tactics' after being found guilty of interfering with Dettori's mount Librettist. Ballydoyle ran three horses in the race, including the pacemaker, River Tiber, but claimed that Ivan Denisovich, a 28/1-chance wearing a visor for the first time and a smart horse in his own right, was running on his merits. On appeal, the case against Heffernan under Instruction H1 Pacemakers (Team Tactics), introduced in response to an incident at the Shergar Cup meeting in 2003, was thrown out, the appeal panel concluding that he had not acted as a spoiler, though stopping short of completely exonerating the rider. The panel also found that Heffernan, who raced to the fore on Ivan Denisovich with River Tiber, flanked by Librettist on his outside, did deliberately take a line which had the effect of interfering with Librettist. The panel instead imposed a six-day ban on Heffernan for careless riding. The turnaround, which came against a background of stinging criticism of Dettori's character from O'Brien after Dettori offered the opinion on Caradak at Goodwood that Ballydoyle's pacemaker had gone too fast, came after the production of new evidence from Heffernan's solicitor, including evidence that Ivan Denisovich had been bumped by Araafa in the back straight, causing him to lose his action, and a submission that Heffernan had been looking for better ground. Interestingly, had the original offence been committed in France and the decision upheld, the stewards would have been within their rights to disqualify or demote all the horses in the same, shared ownership as Ivan Denisovich. The action of the appeal panel, however, left British racing's regulations on team tactics needing an overhaul. It needs undertaking quickly as this wasn't the first time Ballydoyle and Godolphin runners had clashed under similar circumstances and it almost certainly won't be the last.

With the sword of Damocles lifted after Ascot, connections went back on the front foot in the battle over George Washington's reputation. Speaking immediately after the race, Aidan O'Brien was effusive in his praise of the colt, saying 'If I say too much people say I'm hyping him, but he's an unbelievably special horse with unbelievable pace, movement and stride and temperament.' Temperament? On the announcement of George Washington's impending retirement, Coolmore manager Christy Grassick also got in on the act. 'We've been lucky enough to stand a lot of champion stallions over the years, but I don't think any of them could match George Washington's range of qualifications,' he said. The onslaught continued after the somewhat surprising announcement at the time that George Washington's final race would come on dirt in the Breeders' Cup Classic at Churchill Downs, as opposed to on turf in the Breeders' Cup Mile for which he had been installed a short-priced favourite after Ascot. Under the headline 'Go get 'em George', O'Brien commented 'We've never had anything like this before', while acknowledging that 'not having raced on dirt will be a big disadvantage.' In preparation,

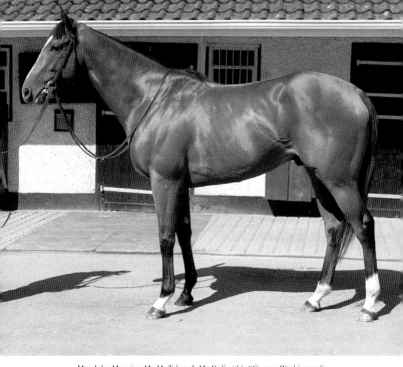

Mrs John Magnier, Mr M. Tabor & Mr D. Smith's "George Washington"

George Washington was to have been given a gallop at Southwell, but that had to be cancelled due to fog at the nearby airport. George Washington limbered up for his final challenge by cantering on the course at Churchill Downs in the days beforehand. His trainer sported a jacket bearing the words 'Gorgeous George' on the back, but the Americans remained unimpressed, pitching 'The Showdown on the Downs' as a clash between The 'Great' Bernadini and The 'Comeback Kid' Lava Man. Starting fourth favourite at 94/10, George Washington beat Lava Man, but he could manage no better than sixth, reluctant to be loaded and only briefly looking as though he might get into the race off the turn where he was bumped by the eventual winner. Hanging left as he faded, George Washington was beaten seven lengths behind Invasor, probably failing to stay. He was the sixth Ballydoyle representative to tackle the Classic since Giant's Causeway, 'The Iron Horse', finished runner-up to Tiznow at Churchill Downs in 2000, and the sixth to finish unplaced, following Galileo and Black Minnaloushe in 2001, Hawk Wing in 2002, Hold That Tiger in 2003 and Oratorio in 2005.

Following Dylan Thomas's disastrous run in the Jockey Club Gold Cup at Belmont in October, George Washington was the second son of Danehill on dirt which Ballydoyle tried to show off to American breeders in 2006. Including George Washington, Coolmore will stand seven sons of Danehill in Ireland in 2007, among them the successful sire Danehill Dancer and Rock of Gibraltar, another winner of the Two Thousand Guineas and, along with George Washington, the joint-highest rated son of their sire. The game and genuine Rock of Gibraltar was a much more straightforward racehorse than George Washington, but there are plenty of examples of quirky performers making good at stud. Red God and Grey Sovereign, both high-class performers given Timeform squiggles, went on to make successful stallions. Sadler's Wells had a high head carriage, while more recently Montjeu showed considerable idiosyncracies as a racehorse before making a flying start as a stallion. Danehill was killed in a paddock accident in 2003 and George Washington is from his penultimate crop, which, as well as Irish Derby winner Dylan Thomas, included another classic winner in Aussie Rules, successful in the Poule d'Essai des Poulains.

George Washington (IRE) (b.c. 2003)	Danehill (USA) (b 1986)	Danzig (b 1977)	Northern Dancer
			Pas de Nom
		Razyana (b 1981)	His Majesty
			Spring Adieu
	Bordighera (USA) (ch 1992)	Alysheba (b 1984)	Alydar
			Bel Sheba
		Blue Tip (b 1982)	Tip Moss
			As Blue

Danehill has sired a string of high-class performers, including such diverse sorts as champion sprinter Mozart and outstanding stayer Westerner. The majority of his offspring have been genuine and George Washington almost certainly gets his quirks from his dam's side. His half-brother Grandera (by Grand Lodge) mixed ability with a dubious temperament, showing a tendency to be edgy, flash his tail, hang and carry his head high, though he was still good enough to win three Group 1 races as a four-year-old, including the Prince of Wales's Stakes and the Irish Champion Stakes, showing high-class form. Other than George Washington, Grandera is much the best produce of his dam Bordighera, a useful winner over thirteen furlongs in France, though Bordighera has produced two other minor winners, Fifty Five (by Lake Coniston) and Ampelio, a brother to Grandera, successful at a mile and a mile and a quarter in Dubai. Wyeth, another brother to Grandera, was unplaced on his only outing as a two-year-old in 2006. A yearling colt by Pivotal out of Bordighera was bought by John Ferguson for Sheikh Mohammed for 1,200,000 guineas at Tattersalls October Yearling Sales.

Wyeth ran in the colours of Lael Stable, owned by Roy and Gretchen Jackson, who bred George Washington and the top-class American colt Barbaro, a six-and-a-half-length winner of the Kentucky Derby in their colours the same day George Washington won the Guineas. George Washington was sold for 1,150,000 guineas at the Tattersalls October Yearling Sales, making him the most expensive yearling of his year in Europe. He turned out to be a bargain. Despite his quirks, George Washington won six of his ten races. He acted on good to firm and good to soft ground and was below form on heavy and on dirt. His best efforts came at six furlongs to a mile. His fee in 2007 at Coolmore, County Tipperary, will be €60,000, well short of the fees commanded by the top Irish-based Coolmore stallions—Sadler's Wells (private), Galileo (€150,000), Montjeu (€125,000) and Danehill Dancer (€115,000)—but twice as much as Arc and King George winner Hurricane Run who was also retired at the end of the latest season. Giant's Causeway, incidentally, was retired in 2000 at IR 100,000 guineas and he is now the leading light at Coolmore's American stud, Ashford, where his fee for 2007 is advertised as 'private'. *A. P. O'Brien, Ireland*

GEORGIE'S LASS (IRE) 7 gr.m. Flemensfirth (USA) 122 – Rongai (IRE) (Commanche Run 133) [2006 –: 10d f12m Oct 31] angular mare: no form. *R. J. Price*   –

GERMANCE (USA) 3 b.f. Silver Hawk (USA) 123 – Gaily Tiara (USA) (Caerleon (USA) 132) [2006 10d* 10.5d* 10d* 10.5m² 10s* 9f⁴ 11f Nov 4] $200,000Y: second foal: dam, Japanese 6f winner, half-sister to useful French performer up to 1½m Aiglonne (by Silver Hawk): smart performer: won newcomers race at Bordeaux at 2 yrs, minor event at Toulouse in March, Prix Penelope at Saint-Cloud (by length from Sanaya) in April, Montjeu Coolmore Prix Saint-Alary at Longchamp (beat same rival ½ length) in May and Darley Prix de la Nonette at Deauville (easily, by 3 lengths from Mysterious Lina) in August: creditable 1½ lengths second to Confidential Lady in Prix de Diane at Chantilly other start in France: bit below best (hampered start) when fourth to Vacare in Queen Elizabeth II Challenge Cup at Keeneland before well held in Breeders' Cup Filly   **113**

Montjeu Coolmore Prix Saint-Alary, Longchamp—Germance extends her unbeaten record to four; Sanaya (left) is runner-up ahead of Alix Road

& Mare Turf at Churchill Downs final start: stayed 10.5f: acted on soft and good to firm going: raced with plenty of zest/sometimes took strong hold: stud. *J-C. Rouget, France*

GERTIE (IRE) 2 b.f. (Mar 12) Redback 116 – Rosalia (USA) 66 (Red Ransom (USA)) –
[2006 p7.1g p6g[4] Dec 4] €4,500Y: second foal: half-sister to winner in Italy by Tipsy Creek: dam maiden who stayed 7.5f: well held in maidens at Wolverhampton. *E. J. Creighton*

GESSECAPADE 4 b.f. Largesse 112 – Muscade (USA) (Spend A Buck (USA)) [2006 –
p9.5g 11.5g[5] Jun 1] half-sister to German 11f to 14.5f winner Mindanao (by General Assembly): dam unraced: well held in bumpers and claimers. *P. S. McEntee*

GETTYSBURG (IRE) 3 b.g. Imperial Ballet (IRE) 110 – Two Magpies 43 (Doulab 54
(USA) 115) [2006 –: 14.1g 10f[6] 13.8m[4] 16g 16.1g Sep 27] strong, close-coupled gelding: modest maiden: stays 13.8f: acts on firm going. *J. Howard Johnson*

GHALLAB 3 b.c. Alhaarth (IRE) 126 – Ta Rib (USA) 116 (Mr Prospector (USA)) 72
[2006 10d 10m 10.9d[4] 12g Jun 15] angular, quite attractive colt: brother to fairly useful 7f winner Khaizarana, closely related to 8-y-o Kabeer and half-brother to 3 winners, including fairly useful 11f winner Mawaheb (by Nashwan): dam 7f/1m (Poule d'Essai des Pouliches) winner: fair maiden: best effort on second start: sold 26,000 gns in July. *E. A. L. Dunlop*

GHOST DANCER 2 ch.c. (Mar 5) Danehill Dancer (IRE) 117 – Reservation (IRE) 77
78 (Common Grounds 118) [2006 6m[5] 6f[2] p6g[4] 5m p5g[6] p7g[2] p7.1g* Oct 8] 32,000Y: good-topped colt: third foal: dam, 7f winner, half-sister to useful performer up to 1½m Fort: fair performer: won nursery at Wolverhampton in October: will stay 1m: acts on polytrack and firm going. *L. M. Cumani*

GHOST STORY (JPN) 3 ch.f. Dance In The Dark (JPN) – Pazienza (IRE) (Arazi 84
(USA) 135) [2006 7m[2] Apr 21] rather leggy, shallow-girthed filly: third foal: half-sister to French 2001 2-y-o 5.5f/6f winner Pazzazz (by Green Desert): dam unraced half-sister to high-class miler Cape Cross out of Cheveley Park winner Park Appeal: 10/1, 2½ lengths second to Silver Touch in maiden at Newbury: sold 26,000 gns in November. *M. A. Jarvis*

GIANT SLALOM 2 b.g. (Mar 24) Tomba 119 – Fallara (FR) (Tropular) [2006 6s² p7g **78 p** p7.1g* Nov 17] 10,000Y: second foal: half-brother to 2004 2-y-o 6f winner Seamless (by Gold Away): dam, French 15f winner, half-sister to useful French winner up to 1½m Home Alone: fair form in maidens, winning at Wolverhampton in November by ½ length from Cape Thea: will stay at least 1m: should do better. *W. J. Haggas*

GIANT'S ROCK (IRE) 4 ch.g. Giant's Causeway (USA) 132 – En Garde (USA) 82 **–** (Irish River (FR) 131) [2006 68: p12.2g Jan 21] sturdy gelding: maiden: well held only outing in 2006: tried blinkered/tongue tied: has looked difficult ride. *B. J. Llewellyn*

GIBBS CAMP 3 b.f. Marju (IRE) 127 – Serengeti Bride (USA) 91 (Lion Cavern (USA) **69** 117) [2006 63: p7g⁶ p10g² p12.2g⁴ 9.7m a11g⁴ a7g* Dec 17] fair performer: sold from E. Dunlop 2,000 gns after fourth start: won minor event at Gran Canaria in December: stays 1¼m: acts on polytrack/sand. *B. Rama, Spain*

GIB (IRE) 2 ch.f. (Feb 28) Rock of Gibraltar (IRE) 133 – Saucy Maid (IRE) 69 (Sure **61 p** Blade (USA) 130) [2006 6g 6m 5.7m⁶ Sep 25] 30,000Y: closely related to fairly useful 2001 2-y-o 6f winner Sophorific (by Danehill) and half-sister to 3 winners, including 11f winner La Mondotte (by Alzao): dam, maiden who stayed 1¼m, half-sister to dam of Pilsudski: modest but progressive form in maidens, off 3 months before staying-on sixth of 15 to Maker's Mark at Bath: will benefit from 7f/1m: should make a better 3-y-o. *B. W. Hills*

GIBRALTAR BAY (IRE) 4 b.f. Cape Cross (IRE) 129 – Secrets of Honour (Belmez **90** (USA) 131) [2006 89: p12g² p16g⁶ Jan 29] lengthy filly: fairly useful handicapper: barely stays easy 2m: acts on polytrack, good to firm and good to soft going: races prominently. *T. G. Mills*

GIBSONS 2 ch.g. (Feb 21) Tipsy Creek (USA) 115 – Amy Leigh (IRE) 78 (Imperial **50** Frontier (USA) 112) [2006 p5g 5.1g p5g 6f f5g² f7g 5.5m p6m f6m² f5g Nov 10] stocky gelding: modest maiden: best efforts at 5f/6f on fibresand: joined P. Blockley. *Mrs P. N. Dutfield*

GIDAM GIDAM (IRE) 4 b.g. King's Best (USA) 132 – Flamands (IRE) 92 (Sadler's **–** Wells (USA) 132) [2006 65: 14.1m May 3] leggy gelding: maiden handicapper: well held in cheekpieces only Flat outing in 2006: tried tongue tied: fairly useful hurdler, winner in October. *J. Mackie*

GIFT AID 3 b.c. Generous (IRE) 139 – Sans Diablo (IRE) (Mac's Imp (USA) 116) **55** [2006 48: p5.1g⁴ 7g⁴ 5.7g⁵ 6d⁵ 7f⁵ p6m² p6g Oct 17] lengthy colt: modest maiden: stays 7f: acts on polytrack and good to soft going: blinkered final start at 2 yrs: sold 10,000 gns, sent to Qatar. *P. J. Makin*

GIFTED FLAME 7 b.g. Revoque (IRE) 122 – Little Lady Leah (USA) (Shareef **78** Dancer (USA) 135) [2006 78: 8.5g⁵ 7.9m³ 8f² 7.9m 9.3f⁴ 7.5g 8d 8g⁴ Sep 27] rangy gelding: fair handicapper: effective at 7f to 9f: acts on firm and good to soft going: tried visored/in cheekpieces: sometimes slowly away/races freely: waited with. *J. J. Quinn*

GIFTED GAMBLE 4 b.g. Mind Games 121 – Its Another Gift 64 (Primo Dominie **98** 121) [2006 98: 6d 6g 6s³ p6g 6m 6d³ 6d² p7g⁵ p7g³ p8.6g³ p7.1g⁴ Dec 31] leggy **a91** gelding: useful handicapper on turf, fairly useful on all-weather: at least creditable efforts in 2006 when placed: effective at 6f to easy 8.6f: acts on polytrack, firm and good to soft ground: tried in cheekpieces, usually blinkered: has high head carriage. *K. A. Ryan*

GIFTED GLORI 3 ch.g. Vettori (IRE) 119 – Azira 45 (Arazi (USA) 135) [2006 50: **48** 7.1m⁶ 7.2v 6m⁵ 5.9m⁴ 6g⁵ Aug 23] sturdy gelding: poor maiden handicapper: stays 7f: acts on good to firm going: joined M. Hammond. *J. J. Quinn*

GIFTED HEIR (IRE) 2 b.c. (Apr 22) Princely Heir (IRE) 111 – Inzar Lady (IRE) **59** (Inzar (USA) 112) [2006 p6g 6g p6g⁵ 7m² 7m 7m 8f³ 8.3g⁵ p7g* Nov 15] small colt: modest performer: won nursery at Kempton in November: barely stays 1m: acts on polytrack and good to firm going. *I. A. Wood*

GIFTED LASS 4 b.f. Bold Edge 123 – Meeson Times 71 (Enchantment 115) [2006 –: **–** 5s p6g³ p5.1m² f5g⁴ p5.1g* p5g⁵ f5g* Dec 28] good-bodied filly: fair performer: won **a72 +** handicap at Wolverhampton and banded race at Southwell, both in December: will prove best at 5f: acts on all-weather: sometimes looks wayward. *J. Balding*

GIFTED MUSICIAN 4 b.g. Sadler's Wells (USA) 132 – Photogenic 93 (Midyan **74** (USA) 124) [2006 80p: 16g 14.1d⁵ 13.9s Oct 7] quite good-topped gelding: just fair performer in 2006, form only when fifth at Salisbury: probably stays 1¾m: acts on heavy and good to firm ground. *J. L. Dunlop*

Queen Mary Stakes, Royal Ascot—Gilded gains her fifth win in a row
at the chief expense of Simply Perfect, Nina Blini and Sparkling Eyes (virtually obscured)

GIFT HORSE 6 ch.g. Cadeaux Genereux 131 – Careful Dancer (Gorytus (USA) 132) **110**
[2006 120: 6d⁵ 6m 6m 5s 5g 5m Oct 1] lengthy, angular gelding: poor mover in slower
paces: smart performer: raced mainly in pattern company in 2006 and not at best,
probably pick of efforts on third start when ninth to Les Arcs in July Cup at Newmarket,
better than bare result in a race not run to suit: stays 6f: acts on good to firm and good to
soft going: usually waited with. *D. Nicholls*

GIGANTICUS (USA) 3 ch.g. Giant's Causeway (USA) 132 – Shy Princess (USA) **105**
117 (Irish River (FR) 131) [2006 89p: 7g³ 8m 8m 8g Sep 28] rangy gelding: useful performer, lightly raced: easily best effort when third to Levera in handicap at Newmarket
on reappearance: likely to prove best at 6f/7f: gelded after final start. *B. W. Hills*

GIG HARBOR 7 b.g. Efisio 120 – Petonica (IRE) 77 (Petoski 135) [2006 –, a105: –
10.1g 10m p8g p12g p12g p12g p12g Nov 5] good-bodied gelding: poor mover: useful at best:
well held in 2006. *Miss E. C. Lavelle*

GIGI GLAMOR 4 b.f. Secret Appeal – Gilboa 48 (Shirley Heights 130) [2006 7m –
10.3m 10d Oct 4] sturdy filly: sister to fairly useful 1m to 10.3f winner Pentagon Lad:
dam lightly-raced close relative of useful stayer Gondolier: well held in maidens.
W. M. Brisbourne

GIGS MAGIC (USA) 3 ch.g. Gulch (USA) – Magic of Love 99 (Magic Ring (IRE) **60**
115) [2006 62, a76: p12g⁶ 8.2s 9.7m 10g 9m⁵ 8.3g* 9m⁴ 10f² 11.5f² 12g⁶ 12.1m² 10g
10.2m⁵ 11.1d³ 11.9d² 9.1v Oct 28] lengthy, good-topped gelding: modest handicapper:
won at Hamilton in June: stays 1½m: acts on polytrack, firm and good to soft going.
M. Johnston

GILDED COVE 6 b.h. Polar Prince (IRE) 117 – Cloudy Reef 57 (Cragador (110) [2006 **78**
84: f5g⁵ f6g p5.1g³ p6g⁵ p6g* p6g⁶ 5.1s² 5s³ p6g⁶ p6g⁴ 6.1m² p6g⁵ 6.1g⁶ 6.1d p6g
p6g* Dec 18] strong horse: reportedly has only one eye: fair performer: won claimer at
Wolverhampton in March, and dead-heated there in amateur handicap in December: stays
6f: acts on all-weather and soft ground, probably on good to firm: sometimes slowly away
and usually held up. *R. Hollinshead*

GILDED (IRE) 2 b.f. (Jan 28) Redback 116 – Tumbleweed Pearl 96 (Aragon 118) **101**
[2006 p5g⁴ 5s* 5g* 5f* 5s* 5m* 6m³ 5.2g⁶ Jul 22] 13,000Y: good-quartered, quite
attractive filly: fourth foal: half-sister to 5-y-o Jasmine Pearl: dam, 6f winner (including
at 2 yrs), half-sister to smart 7f performer Tumbleweed Ridge: useful performer: won 5 in
a row between April/June, namely maiden at Warwick, minor events at Newmarket and
Salisbury, listed race at York and Queen Mary Stakes at Royal Ascot, in last-named
beating Simply Perfect by length (15 ran): best effort when 5 lengths third of 10 to Sander
Camillo in Cherry Hinton Stakes at Newmarket: much better than bare result (sixth of 23)
in Super Sprint at Newbury final start, clear of stand-side group: effective at 5f/6f: acts on
firm and soft going: tough: sold 210,000 gns, sent to USA. *R. Hannon*

GILDED YOUTH 2 b.g. (Apr 24) Gorse 116 – Nisha (Nishapour (FR) 125) [2006 6g **78 p**
6m 7s⁵ Oct 10] lengthy, good-topped gelding: half-brother to 3 winners, including useful
1m winner Bishopric and fairly useful 2004 2-y-o 6f winner The Abbess (both by Bishop

of Cashel): dam lightly-raced maiden: progressive form in maidens, prominent long way when 2¼ lengths fifth of 17 to Hollow Ridge at Newbury: may prove best up to 7f: should do better still. *H. Candy*

GILLIPOPS (IRE) 3 b.f. Xaar 132 – Snoozeandyoulose (IRE) 73 (Scenic 128) [2006 – 72: 8.3g⁵ May 8] leggy filly: fair winner at 2 yrs: poor efforts all 4 starts since. *R. Hannon*

GILT LINKED 3 b.f. Compton Place 125 – Copy-Cat 60 (Lion Cavern (USA) 117) **84** [2006 85: 5m 5g 5g 5.1f Sep 23] tall, lengthy filly: fairly useful performer: ran poorly after reappearance, leaving B. Hills after second start: headstrong, and will be best at 5f: acts on good to firm going. *J. S. Wainwright*

GIMASHA 4 b.f. Cadeaux Genereux 131 – First Waltz (FR) 117 (Green Dancer (USA) **103** 132) [2006 105: 6m⁶ 6g³ 6f 6m 5g² 6m* 5g 5g Sep 28] rangy filly: useful performer: trained by E. Charpy in UAE on reappearance only: won handicap at Lingfield (by short head from Obe Brave) in September: creditable seventh to Fantasy Believer in listed event at Newmarket final start: effective at 5f/6f: acts on firm going: has been early to post: races prominently. *W. Jarvis*

GINGER COOKIE 4 ch.f. Bold Edge 123 – Pretty Pollyanna (General Assembly – (USA)) [2006 47: f8g Apr 4] tall, lengthy filly: poor maiden: well held only outing in 2006. *B. Smart*

GINGER POP 2 ch.g. (Feb 28) Mark of Esteem (IRE) 137 – Norcroft Lady 85 (Muj- **64** tahid (USA) 118) [2006 p6g⁴ p7.1s⁶ Dec 13] first foal: dam 2-y-o 6f winner: better effort in maidens when 2½ lengths fourth to Estimator at Kempton: laboured effort 11 days later. *G. G. Margarson*

GINGER SPICE (IRE) 4 ch.f. Cadeaux Genereux 131 – Pop Queen (Nashwan (USA) **82** 135) [2006 86: 7d p7.1g⁵ 8d* 8.5d⁶ 8d Sep 26] quite good-topped filly: fairly useful hand- icapper: won at Newmarket in August: stays 1m: acts on good to firm and good to soft going: very free penultimate outing: sold 9,000 gns, sent to Saudi Arabia. *W. J. Haggas*

GINGKO 9 b.g. Pursuit of Love 124 – Arboretum (IRE) 83 (Green Desert (USA) 127) **60** [2006 –, a82: p9.5g p10g³ p10g p10g² p12g⁵ p10g² p10g⁴ 10.2d p10g 10.2g⁶ 10m 10.2f² **a82** 10.2m⁶ Jun 28] fairly useful handicapper on all-weather, just modest on turf: effective at 1¼m/1½m: acts on all-weather, firm and good to soft going. *P. R. Webber*

GIN JOCKEY (FR) 3 b.c. Soviet Star (USA) 128 – Singing Lark (FR) (Pampabird **105** 124) [2006 95p: 8g³ 9s⁶ 10s⁵ May 27] tall, close-coupled colt: useful performer: unbeaten in 2 runs at 2 yrs: good 3¾ lengths third to Killybegs in Craven Stakes at Newmarket on reappearance: respectable sixth to Boris de Deauville in Prix de Guiche at Chantilly next time, but well held in listed race at Newmarket (visored) final outing: best effort at 1m, bred to stay further: acts on soft and good to firm going: tends to carry head awkwardly: races prominently. *R. Hannon*

GIOCOSO (USA) 6 b.g. Bahri (USA) 125 – Wing My Chimes (USA) (Flying Paster – (USA)) [2006 89: 8.3g Apr 10] quite good-topped gelding: fairly useful handicapper at best, well held only outing in 2006: probably best when able to dominate. *B. Palling*

GIOVANNI D'ORO (IRE) 2 b.g. (Feb 10) Johannesburg (USA) 127 – Maddie G **63 p** (USA) (Blush Rambler (USA) 119) [2006 7d 8g p6g Nov 6] 160,000F, 270,000Y: rather finely-made, useful-looking gelding: first foal: dam, ran once in USA, half-sister to dam of high-class 7f/1m performer Le Vie dei Colori: behind in maidens at Newmarket (2) and Wolverhampton, raced wide and not knocked about at latter track (gelded after): likely to be suited by 1m+: sort to do better now qualified for handicaps. *N. A. Callaghan*

GIRANDOLA 3 b.g. Observatory (USA) 131 – Honeyspike (IRE) 79 (Chief's Crown **59** (USA)) [2006 65: 5m 6m 6d³ 7d⁶ 6v⁵ 6s⁵ p8g 8.3g p6g⁶ Oct 23] modest maiden: should stay 7f: acts on good to firm and good to soft ground: blinkered (ran poorly) last 2 outings: gelded after. *R. F. Johnson Houghton*

GIRARDII 3 ch.g. Sinndar (IRE) 134 – Armeria (USA) 79 (Northern Dancer) [2006 **68** 59p: 10g 12.6g⁴ 10f² 11.9f² Jul 4] well-made gelding: fair maiden: stays 12.6f: raced only on good ground or firmer: blinkered last 3 outings, finding little final occasion: sold 22,000 gns, joined K. Bailey and gelded. *R. Charlton*

GIUNCHIGLIO 7 ch.g. Millkom 124 – Daffodil Fields (Try My Best (USA) 130) – [2006 68d: f11g⁵ Jan 29] tall gelding: on downgrade and well held only outing in 2006: tried visored at 4 yrs, wore cheekpieces final 6-y-o outing. *W. M. Brisbourne*

GIVE EVIDENCE 2 b.c. (Feb 13) Averti (IRE) 117 – Witness 71 (Efisio 120) [2006 **67** p7g⁶ p7g³ p8g p7.1g⁴ p7g⁶ Dec 4] 25,000Y: first foal: dam, 7f winner, half-sister to smart

1m/1¼m performer Shamrock City: fair maiden: fourth in nursery at Wolverhampton: ran poorly (carried head awkwardly/wandered) final start: stays 7f: has raced freely. *A. P. Jarvis*

GIVE HER A WHIRL 2 b.f. (Feb 18) Pursuit of Love 124 – Peggy Spencer 77 (Formidable (USA) 125) [2006 6g⁶ p6g⁵ Oct 28] leggy, useful-looking filly: sixth foal: closely related to 2002 2-y-o 6f winner Takes Two To Tango (by Groom Dancer) and half-sister to 5-y-o La Cucaracha: dam 6f/7f winner: encouraging sixth to Truly Royal in maiden at Newmarket: odds on, only fifth at Wolverhampton: should yet do better. *B. W. Hills* **63 p**

GIVE IT TIME 3 b.f. Kayf Tara 130 – Startino 111 (Bustino 136) [2006 66p: 10.1g⁵ p9.5g 14.1m 16.1g⁴ 13.8s 16v² f16g³ Nov 15] good-topped filly: fair maiden: stays 2m: acts on polytrack and heavy going: sold 18,000 gns. *J. G. Given* **68**

GIVE ME THE NIGHT (IRE) 3 b.f. Night Shift (USA) – There With Me (USA) 63 (Distant View (USA) 126) [2006 83: a7f³ a8f⁴ a9f⁶ 6.1m 5g³ 5g Sep 28] strong filly: fairly useful performer: creditable efforts in UAE first 3 starts in 2006 for D. Watson: flattered when equal-third to Angus Newz in listed race at Hamilton penultimate start: well beaten in similar event at Newmarket final outing: stays 9f (though all wins at 5f): acts on polytrack/dirt, firm and good to soft ground. *B. Smart* **83**

GIVEN A CHANCE 5 b.g. Defacto (USA) – Milly Molly Mango (Mango Express 106) [2006 55: 16f Jul 31] close-coupled gelding: modest performer at best: well held only outing in 2006. *T. J. Pitt* **–**

GIVEN A CHOICE (IRE) 4 b.g. Trans Island 119 – Miss Audimar (USA) (Mr Leader (USA)) [2006 92: 10g 12s⁶ p12g² 12m 13.1g p8.6g* 8f p10g p12g⁵ p12g Oct 23] big, strong gelding: good mover: fairly useful handicapper: won at Wolverhampton in July: left 2. Given after seventh start: effective at 8.6f to 1½m: acts on polytrack and good to firm ground: visored (below form) seventh outing. *R. A. Fahey* **93**

GIVERNY SPRING 3 b.f. Lujain (USA) 119 – Matisse 65 (Shareef Dancer (USA) 135) [2006 73: p8.6g 8m 8f 8.5m³ 8d² 9d³ 7.1m⁵ Sep 1] big, strong filly: modest maiden: stays 9f: acts on good to firm and good to soft going: raced freely and wandered in front fifth start: once withdrawn (reared over in stall): joined N. Henderson, sold 11,000 gns, then sent to Qatar, where won at 7f. *J. W. Hills* **58**

GIVING 3 br.f. Generous (IRE) 139 – Madiya 73 (Darshaan 133) [2006 87p: p10g² 12m 10g² p10g⁵ 10g p10g⁴ Nov 9] leggy, close-coupled filly: useful performer: good short-head second to Salute Him in handicap at Sandown third start: should stay 1½m (pulled hard when tried): acts on polytrack, yet to race on extremes of going on turf: consistent. *G. Wragg* **98**

GIZMO 3 b.g. Fasliyev (USA) 120 – Sly Baby (IRE) 59 (Dr Devious (IRE) 127) [2006 p8.6g Dec 18] reported in June 2005 to have suffered a stress fracture: 16/1, ran as if amiss in maiden at Wolverhampton on belated debut. *B. Smart* **–**

GIZMONDO 3 ch.g. Lomitas 129 – India Atlanta (Ahonoora 122) [2006 –: p8g p8g⁶ 8g⁶ 10.1f* 10g⁶ Aug 2] fair performer: easily best effort when winning handicap at Yarmouth in July by 5 lengths: stays 1¼m: acts on firm ground: hung left third start. *M. L. W. Bell* **70**

GLAD BIG (GER) 4 b.g. Big Shuffle (USA) 122 – Glady Sum (GER) (Surumu (GER)) [2006 72+: p7g⁴ p8g* p8g² p7g⁴ p8g² p7.1g⁶ p7.1g² p7g³ p8g* 8.3g p8g⁵ p7g⁴ p10g p8.6g Jul 1] rangy gelding: fairly useful performer: won maiden and apprentice handicap at Lingfield in January/February and handicap at Kempton in April: stays 8.6f: acts on polytrack and good to firm ground: held up: sold 28,000 gns in July. *J. A. Osborne* **87**

GLADS IMAGE 4 ch.f. Handsome Ridge 121 – Secret So And So (So Factual (USA) 120) [2006 9.7f⁵ f8g p12.2m Oct 2] little form: left J. Ryan after second start. *S. W. Hall* **–**

GLAMARAAZI (IRE) 3 b.f. Orpen (USA) 116 – Raazi 46 (My Generation 111) [2006 51: 5s³ 5d 7m f6g³ f6g⁴ Nov 20] good-topped filly: fair maiden: should be suited by 7f: best effort on fibresand. *R. A. Fahey* **65**

GLAMIS CASTLE (USA) 3 b.g. Selkirk (USA) 129 – Fairy Godmother 113 (Fairy King (USA)) [2006 p10g³ 10d⁴ Oct 9] second foal: dam, 1¼m winner, half-sister to very smart middle-distance stayer Blueprint: fair form in maidens at Kempton (beaten 3 lengths by Woolfall Blue) and Windsor, still green at latter track: will be suited by 1½m: sold 42,000 gns, and joined C. Swan in Ireland. *Sir Michael Stoute* **76**

GLAMOUR PUSS (NZ) 6 b.m. Tale of The Cat (USA) 113 – Escada (NZ) (Centaine (AUS)) [2006 6g⁴ 6g⁴ 6.5s⁵ 6g² 5m 6m Jun 24] strong, sturdy mare: third foal: half-sister **119**

to 2 winners in Australia, notably Group 2 7f winner Rare Insight (by O'Reilly): dam winning sprinter: smart performer: won 9 of her 26 races, including in 2005 Goodwood Handicap at Morphettville and Salinger Stakes at Flemington, both Group 1, and Group 2 The Age Classic at Flemington: best efforts in 2006 when ¾-length equal-fourth behind Takeover Target in Newmarket Handicap at Flemington on second outing and when close seventh of 28 behind same horse in King's Stand Stakes at Royal Ascot on penultimate start (still carrying winter coat): below form when tenth to Les Arcs in Golden Jubilee Stakes there final outing: stayed 7f: acted on heavy and good to firm going: wore blinkers: raced just off pace: was genuine: visits Redoute's Choice. *D. O'Brien, Australia*

GLARAMARA 5 b.g. Nicolotte 118 – Digamist Girl (IRE) (Digamist (USA) 110) **92**
[2006 96: f5g⁶ f6g² 6v⁶ May 25] big, good-topped gelding: fairly useful handicapper: effective at 6f to 7.5f: acts on fibresand (below form on polytrack), firm and good to soft going (well held on heavy last 2 starts): blinkered (raced freely) once. *A. Bailey*

GLASSHOUGHTON 3 b.g. Dansili 127 – Roseum 102 (Lahib (USA) 129) [2006 74: **83**
7.1g 6m⁴ 6s⁴ 5m* 5g⁵ 5g* 5.1f 5f Aug 4] smallish, angular gelding: fairly useful handicapper: won at Sandown and Carlisle, both in June: best at 5f/6f: acts on soft and good to firm going: tried in cheekpieces/blinkers at 2 yrs, below form in latter: gelded after final outing. *M. Dods*

GLASSON LODGE 4 b.f. Primo Dominie 121 – Petrikov (IRE) (In The Wings 128) **–**
[2006 52: f11g Jan 29] quite good-topped filly: modest performer at best: well held only outing in 2006: usually blinkered/visored: looked unwilling at times at 2 yrs. *A. L. Forbes*

GLEAMING SPIRIT (IRE) 2 b.g. (Mar 10) Mujadil (USA) 119 – Gleam (Green **65**
Desert (USA) 127) [2006 p5.1g⁴ p6m Oct 2] 7,500Y: third foal: dam unraced out of half-sister to smart sprinter Zarani Sidi Anna: better effort in maidens at Wolverhampton when fourth on debut: shapes like a sprinter. *A. P. Jarvis*

GLENARGO (USA) 3 ch.g. Concerto (USA) 114 – Her Gift (USA) (Saint Ballado **66**
(CAN)) [2006 p7.1g³ p7.1g³ p8.6g f7g⁶ 6f² 5.3m⁶ 6m³ p6g p6g⁶ p5.1g* 5f² 5m 5d⁶ p6g **a59**
p6g p5.1g p6g Dec 20] $115,000 2-y-o: fourth foal: brother/half-brother to winners in Puerto Rico: dam unraced: fair on turf, modest on all-weather: left P. Mooney in Ireland after second start: won seller at Wolverhampton in July: below form last 6 starts: effective at 5f/6f: acts on polytrack and firm going: tried tongue tied, in cheekpieces nowadays: races prominently. *R. A. Harris*

GLEN AVON GIRL (IRE) 2 b.f. (Apr 10) Mull of Kintyre (USA) 114 – Sandystones **55**
60 (Selkirk (USA) 129) [2006 5g⁴ 5d⁶ 6.1d⁶ Oct 13] €20,000Y: good-topped filly: fifth foal: closely related to fairly useful 2001 2-y-o 5f winner Sighting (by Eagle Eyed), later successful abroad, and half-sister to ungenuine 5f winner Tatweer (by Among Men): dam, maiden, best effort at 9f: modest form in maidens. *T. D. Easterby*

GLENBUCK (IRE) 3 b.g. Mujadil (USA) 119 – Bryna (IRE) (Ezzoud (IRE) 126) **89**
[2006 76: f7g⁴ 8.2s 7.5d 7d 6m³ 6m⁴ 7d* 7d* p7.1m* 7d* 7.2d* 8m* 7g p9.5g p7.1g⁵ Dec 6] angular, workmanlike gelding: fairly useful performer: won claimer at Newmarket in August and handicaps at Wolverhampton, Catterick and Ayr in September: barely stays 1m: acts on all-weather, soft and good to firm going: usually visored: front runner. *A. Bailey*

GLENCAIRN STAR 5 b.g. Selkirk (USA) 129 – Bianca Nera 107 (Salse (USA) 128) **84**
[2006 72: 6d 6d 5m* 5m² 5g* 5m² 5f 5m 5m 6d 5s p6g 5d³ Nov 3] sturdy, good sort: fairly useful handicapper: won at Musselburgh and Ayr in June: winner at 6f/7f, best form at 5f: acts on all-weather, good to firm and good to soft ground: in cheekpieces last 2 starts: waited with. *J. S. Goldie*

GLENCALVIE (IRE) 5 ch.g. Grand Lodge (USA) 125 – Top of The Form (IRE) 79 **85**
(Masterclass (USA) 116) [2006 87: p8g⁵ p7g⁶ 7m⁴ p8g² p8g 8m 8.3g*¹ 8.3g 8m* 8d Sep 26] strong, well-made gelding: fairly useful handicapper: won at Yarmouth in September: stays 1m: raced mainly on polytrack and good/good to firm going on turf: visored/in cheekpieces. *J. Akehurst*

GLENDALE 5 ch.g. Opening Verse 126 – Kayartis 57 (Kaytu 112) [2006 60: **61**
f8g p9.5g² p10g* p10g³ p10g² p9.5g³ p10g p12g² p10g² 10m³ p10g* Jul 29] big, **a71**
strong, workmanlike gelding: fair performer on all-weather, modest on turf: won banded race in February and handicap in July, both at Lingfield: stays easy 1½m: acts on polytrack and good to firm going: tried in cheekpieces/visor: tends to hang right. *D. K. Ivory*

GLENDENING 3 b.g. Mark of Esteem (IRE) 137 – Mistook (USA) (Phone Trick **?**
(USA)) [2006 57, a61: 8m 5.9g a6.5g² a8.8g⁵ a8.8g² 10g 8.8v 9g 7.5g Dec 17] leggy,

close-coupled gelding: modest maiden: left D. Nicholls after second start: second in 2 minor events at Mijas for new stable: stays 8.8f: acts on polytrack/sand, soft and good to firm going: quirky. *P. Haley, Spain*

GLENMUIR (IRE) 3 b.g. Josr Algarhoud (IRE) 118 – Beryl 77 (Bering 136) [2006 81: 7g 8.1d² 8s⁶ 7.6f* 8s 8m⁶ 8.2s Oct 25] angular, well-made gelding: fairly useful handicapper: won at Chester in July: stays 1m: acts on firm and soft going. *B. R. Millman* **86**

GLEN NEVIS (USA) 2 b. or br.c. (Feb 16) Gulch (USA) – Beating The Buzz (IRE) 96 (Bluebird (USA) 125) [2006 7d³ 8.3d* Oct 10] \$75,000Y, resold \$190,000Y: medium-sized, attractive colt: fifth foal: brother to smart 5f (at 2 yrs) to 1m winner in USA/UAE winner Sleeping Weapon: dam Irish 6f winner: confirmed debut promise at Newmarket (third to Supersonic Dave) when winning maiden at Leicester by length (value 5): sent to UAE: useful prospect. *J. Noseda* **87 p**

GLENREE 5 b.g. Wizard King 122 – The Prussian Queen (Dilum (USA) 115) [2006 62: p8g 8f⁴ 5.5m³ May 14] modest maiden handicapper nowadays: below form at Lingfield on reappearance (left E. Tyrell in Ireland after): stays 8.6f: acts on polytrack and firm going: usually wears blinkers/cheekpieces. *T. J. Bougourd, Jersey* **52**

GLENRIDDING 2 b.g. (Feb 22) Averti (IRE) 117 – Appelone (Emperor Jones (USA) 119) [2006 p8.6g f8g Dec 2] well held in maidens at Wolverhampton and Southwell: gelded after. *J. G. Given* **–**

GLENTAISIE (USA) 3 b.f. Giant's Causeway (USA) 132 – Successfully (USA) (Affirmed (USA)) [2006 p9.5g² p12.2g⁴ p12g⁴ Feb 25] \$110,000Y: fourth foal: closely related to fairly useful Irish 2004 2-y-o 7f winner Full Moon Tonight (by Storm Cat): dam lightly-raced sister to dual champion US turf mare Flawlessly: fair maiden: raced freely, and barely stayed 1½m: covered by Bahamian Bounty, sent to USA. *J. Noseda* **68**

GLEN VALE WALK (IRE) 9 ch.g. Balla Cove 119 – Winter Harvest (Grundy 137) [2006 f11g⁴ f11m f12g⁶ Dec 12] leggy gelding: poor performer: missed 2005: stays 1½m: acts on fibresand, firm and soft going: usually slowly away/races freely/finds little: held up. *Mrs G. S. Rees* **45**

GLENVIEWS BABALOU (USA) 4 ch.f. Deputy Commander (USA) 124 – Hey Baba Lulu (USA) (Silent Screen (USA)) [2006 p6g⁵ p7.1g p7.1g² p8g p7.1g 7.1f Jun 26] \$37,000F: sixth foal: half-sister to 3 winners abroad: dam won 13 races in USA, including Grade 3 9f event: modest maiden: trained by M. O'Toole in Ireland at 3 yrs: stays 7f: acts on polytrack and good to firm going: tried in cheekpieces/blinkers: inconsistent. *Peter Grayson* **54**

GLENVIEWS OLDPORT (USA) 4 ch.f. Old Trieste (USA) 122 – Port Plaisance (USA) (Woodman (USA) 126) [2006 60: p12.2g p8.6g p10g⁵ p10g f8g p9.5g⁵ p10g 10m 7.1d Aug 2] modest maiden: on downgrade: should stay 1½m: acts on polytrack and good to soft ground, well beaten on firmer than good: tried in cheekpieces, blinkered after reappearance. *Peter Grayson* **52 d**

GLENVIEWS YOUNGONE (IRE) 3 b.f. Namid 128 – Baltic Beach (IRE) (Polish Precedent (USA) 131) [2006 68: p6g⁴ p5g p5.1g³ p6g² p5.1g* 5g⁴ 5.1g* 5m 5d⁶ 5f 5f 5d⁶ 5g Sep 23] tall, close-coupled filly: fairly useful performer: won handicaps at Wolverhampton in April and Nottingham (jinked left) in June: raced only at 5f/6f: acts on polytrack, good to firm and good to soft ground: blinkered (below form) second start. *Peter Grayson* **88**

GLIMMER OF LIGHT (IRE) 6 b.g. Marju (IRE) 127 – Church Light 88 (Caerleon (USA) 132) [2006 14m 15.9m Jul 15] leggy gelding: fair handicapper at best: well held both starts on Flat since 2004: tried blinkered. *S. A. Brookshaw* **–**

GLISTENING 4 b.c. Sadler's Wells (USA) 132 – Shining Water 111 (Kalaglow 132) [2006 102: 12m⁶ 12m² 12g³ 13.9d² 12d³ 16g Nov 7] compact, quite attractive colt: smart performer: further progress for new trainer in 2006, particularly good efforts when placed, including in Duke of Edinburgh Stakes (Handicap) at Royal Ascot (head second to Young Mick), Ebor (Handicap) at York (head second to Mudawin) and Cumberland Lodge Stakes at Ascot (3½ lengths third to Young Mick, making running): bit below best when tenth to Delta Blues in Melbourne Cup (Handicap) at Flemington final outing (reportedly had problems settling after arriving in Australia): should stay 2m: acts on good to firm and good to soft going: game. *L. M. Cumani* **112**

GLITTERATI 3 b.f. Observatory (USA) 131 – Stardom (Known Fact (USA) 135) [2006 56p: 7m 7d p7g Oct 23] good-topped filly: lightly-raced maiden: well held in 2006, leaving R. Charlton and off 6 months after reappearance. *J. S. Moore* **–**

GLOBAL ACHIEVER 5 b.g. Key of Luck (USA) 126 – Inflation 68 (Primo Dominie **–** 121) [2006 –, a75d: p5g⁶ p5.1g⁶ p6g³ p6g⁶ f5g² p6g p5.1g⁵ Jul 20] just modest performer **a54** nowadays: effective at 5f to 7f: acts on all-weather, little form on turf: blinkered/in cheek-pieces: tried tongue tied. *G. C. H. Chung*

GLOBAL CHALLENGE (IRE) 7 b.g. Sadler's Wells (USA) 132 – Middle Prospect **72** (USA) (Mr Prospector (USA)) [2006 p12g p16g⁶ 15.4m 16s 14m⁵ p16g⁶ 16m 16d Sep 26] big, rangy gelding: useful winner in 2003: only fair form at best on return to Flat in 2006: should stay 2m: acts on good to firm and good to soft going: tried visored: tends to wander. *P. G. Murphy*

GLOBAL GUARDIAN 3 ch.g. Dr Fong (USA) 128 – Penmayne 95 (Inchinor 119) **–** [2006 55+: p6m f8g 6.8g Nov 26] leggy gelding: maiden: no form in 2006: sold from Mrs G. Rees after second start. *Mrs S. Dysell, Sweden*

GLOBAL GUEST 2 b.c. (Feb 21) Piccolo 121 – By Arrangement (IRE) 60 (Bold **73 §** Arrangement 127) [2006 6g 7.5f³ 7f³ 7f⁵ 7m² 8d 7d p6g Sep 30] 28,000Y: big, quite good-topped colt: fifth foal: brother to useful 7f (at 2 yrs) to 1½m winner Turbo and half-brother to 1½m winner Its Your Bid (by Dilum): dam 1m to 2m winner: fair maiden: second in nursery at Salisbury in August: stays 7.5f: acts on firm going: unreliable: sold 18,000 gns. *M. R. Channon*

GLOBAL STRATEGY 3 b.g. Rainbow Quest (USA) 134 – Pleasuring 68 (Good **65** Times (ITY)) [2006 10d p7.1g⁶ p8.6g Dec 18] 120,000F: half-brother to several winners, including 8-y-o Suggestive and useful French 7.5f to 9f winner (latter at 2 yrs) Rashbag (by Reprimand): dam sprint maiden: best effort in maidens at Naas on debut: left D. Weld in Ireland 13,000 gns, below form at Wolverhampton next 2 starts. *Rae Guest*

GLOBAL TRAFFIC 2 br.c. (Mar 7) Generous (IRE) 139 – Eyes Wide Open 44 **60** (Fraam 114) [2006 p5g p6g⁶ 6m⁵ 7m 8f 7.1d⁶ 8.3g² f8g⁴ f8g⁵ p8.6g² Dec 18] strong colt: modest maiden: second in seller (left P. Cole £6,000) and claimer (blinkered): stays 8.6f: acts on polytrack. *P. D. Evans*

GLOBE 3 b.f. Agnes World (USA) 123 – Hoist (IRE) 75 (Bluebird (USA) 125) [2006 **–** 33: f5g 6f Jul 27] poor maiden. *M. S. Saunders*

GLOBE TREKKER (USA) 4 gr.f. Aljabr (USA) 125 – Amazonia (USA) (Deputy **–** Minister (CAN)) [2006 –: 5d p6g Aug 31] lengthy filly: fair maiden at 2 yrs: no form since: tried blinkered. *Peter Grayson*

GLORIOUS PRINCE (IRE) 2 b.c. (Feb 8) Emperor Jones (USA) 119 – Glorieuse **73** (FR) (Bering 136) [2006 7f 7f³ 6m⁵ 7f² 8g² 7g⁵ 8.3d⁶ Oct 9] 13,500Y: leggy, close-coupled colt: first foal: dam, French maiden, sister to Fillies' Mile winner Glorosia: fair maiden: second in nurseries at Lingfield and Yarmouth in September: stays 1m: acts on firm going, probably good to soft: sold 20,000 gns. *M. G. Quinlan*

GLORIOUS VIEW 2 b.g. (Apr 15) Observatory (USA) 131 – Prime Property (IRE) **–** 60 (Tirol 127) [2006 6m 8v⁵ 8m Sep 21] well beaten in maidens: bred to stay 1¼m+. *M. W. Easterby*

GLORY BE (ITY) 4 ch.f. Dashing Blade 117 – Hasana (USA) (Private Account **52** (USA)) [2006 8.1d 8.2s 10g 11.6m³ 9.7f⁴ 11s 11.7m² f11g² p11g² p12.2g⁴ f14g³ p12g⁵ Nov 27] tall filly: half-sister to useful 7f/1m winner Thihn (by Machiavellian) and winners in Italy by Green Desert and Be My Chief: dam unraced half-sister to very smart miler Magic Gleam: modest maiden: left A. & G. Botti in Italy prior to reappearance: stays 1¾m: acts on all-weather and firm ground: sometimes wears headgear. *J. L. Spearing*

GLOVED HAND 4 b.f. Royal Applause 124 – Fudge (Polar Falcon (USA) 126) [2006 **96** 93: 6d⁴ 6m⁵ 6g² 7m² 7d³ Sep 24] strong filly: useful performer: good efforts when placed last 3 starts, 3½ lengths third to Makderah in listed event at Ascot (sweating and on edge) final one: best at 6f/7f: acts on polytrack, good to firm and good to soft going: has been blanketed for stall entry. *J. R. Fanshawe*

GLOWETTE (IRE) 4 ch.f. General Monash (USA) 107 – Why Not Glow (IRE) **–** (Glow (USA)) [2006 37: p12.2g Apr 25] poor maiden. *I. W. McInnes*

GNILLAH 3 b.f. Halling (USA) 133 – Dimakya (USA) 83 (Dayjur (USA) 137) [2006 **59** –p: p8g⁴ 10m p10g 8.1m⁵ p8g p9.5g⁶ Sep 30] tall, lengthy filly: modest maiden: should be suited by 1¼m+: acts on polytrack and good to firm going: has raced freely. *B. W. Hills*

GO AMWELL 3 b.g. Kayf Tara 130 – Daarat Alayaam (IRE) (Reference Point 139) **58** [2006 49: p8g f8g 8m 11.5m 9.9m⁵ 11.5f p10g p12.2m⁵ p16g p12g² p13.9g* p12g²

f12g³ Dec 29] modest performer: won maiden at Wolverhampton in November: effective
at 1½m, seems to stay 2m: acts on all-weather and good to firm going: tried visored.
J. R. Jenkins

GOBI KING 4 b.g. Desert King (IRE) 129 – Risarshana (FR) (Darshaan 133) [2006 **71**
8.1s⁴ 8.1m⁵ 9.5p⁵ 10.5m³ 11.8d⁶ Aug 13] big, strong gelding: fair maiden: should be
suited by 1½m: dropped away tamely final outing. *L. M. Cumani*

GO DANCING 2 b.f. (Apr 10) Golan (IRE) 129 – Torrid Tango (USA) (Green Dancer **55 p**
(USA) 132) [2006 6g p7g p8.6m Nov 21] 22,000F: strong, well-made filly: closely
related to US Grade 2 7f winner Dancing (by Spectrum), earlier 1m winner in Ireland at
2 yrs, and half-sister to several winners, including 9-y-o Torrid Kentavr: dam lightly-
raced half-sister to dam of Suave Dancer: modest form in maidens: should be suited by
1¼m+: should still do better. *P. W. Chapple-Hyam*

GODFREY STREET 3 ch.g. Compton Place 125 – Tahara (IRE) (Caerleon (USA) **94**
132) [2006 104: 5d 5m 6m 6m 5d 6m 6f 6d⁴ p6g 5d² Oct 7] strong, compact gelding:
fairly useful handicapper: creditable neck second to Woodcote at Ascot final outing:
effective at 5f/easy 6f: acts on polytrack, soft and good to firm going: sold 45,000 gns.
and gelded. *R. Hannon*

GO DUDE 2 b.g. (Apr 17) Mujahid (USA) 125 – Miss Doody 63 (Gorytus (USA) 132) **62**
[2006 6d 7.1d p9.5m⁶ f8g⁴ p8g p8g² f8g² p8.6g⁵ Dec 29] good-topped gelding: modest
maiden: may prove suited by 1¼m: acts on all-weather: tried in cheekpieces/visored.
J. Ryan

GO FIGURE (IRE) 3 ch.g. Desert Prince (IRE) 130 – Interpose (Indian Ridge 123) **89**
[2006 73: p7g* p8g³ p9.5g² 10.2d² 11.6d⁶ 8d² 10d p10g* Oct 20] strong, well-made
gelding: fairly useful handicapper: won at Lingfield in March and October (dead-heat):
stays 1¼m: acts on polytrack, good to firm and good to soft ground: sometimes tongue
tied, including last 5 outings: sold 27,000 gns. *B. J. Meehan*

GO FREE 5 b.g. Easycall 115 – Miss Traxdata (Absalom 128) [2006 53, a57: p13g* **–**
p12.2g Feb 20] modest performer: won banded race at Lingfield in February: tried visored **a56**
at 4 yrs: acts on all-weather, good to soft going: tried visored and good to soft going: tried visored at 4 yrs. *C. J. Down*

GO GARUDA 5 b.g. Air Express (IRE) 125 – Free As A Bird 62 (Robellino (USA) **67**
127) [2006 71: p7g⁵ p8g⁵ p7g³ p7g⁵ p7.1g⁴ p8.6g 8g⁴ Aug 14] good-topped gelding: fair
performer: should stay 1¼m: acts on polytrack, best efforts on turf on good going: tried
tongue tied/in cheekpieces/visored: has run in snatches/carried head awkwardly/edged
left: sold £420. *Miss Gay Kelleway*

GO IMPERIAL (IRE) 2 b.c. (Apr 14) Imperial Ballet (IRE) 110 – Miss Divot (IRE) **64**
67 (Petardia 113) [2006 5.1d p6g p6g² Dec 5] leggy, workmanlike colt: easily best effort
when 3 lengths second of 9 to Blue Charm in maiden at Kempton: should stay 7f: slowly
away last 2 outings. *M. G. Quinlan*

GOING SKINT 3 b.g. Elnadim (USA) 128 – Prospering 50 (Prince Sabo 123) [2006 **57**
f6g⁶ f5g⁵ f6g³ f6g³ Dec 27] best effort in maidens at Southwell on third start: left
T. Easterby and off 9 months after: should stay 7f. *M. Wellings*

GOING STRAIGHT (IRE) 2 b.f. (Feb 9) Princely Heir (IRE) 111 – Easy Going **75**
(Hamas (IRE) 125§) [2006 5g p5g² p5g* 6m² 7g 5.2g 5m⁶ p5g Sep 30] €5,000Y: lengthy
filly: has a quick action: second foal: dam unraced half-sister to smart sprinter Easycall: fair performer: won maiden at Lingfield in May: flattered (dictated) when second to
Sadeek in listed race at Epsom next time: little impact in varied events after: effective at
5f/6f: acts on polytrack and good to firm going: sold 22,000 gns. *I. A. Wood*

GOING TO WORK (IRE) 2 b.f. (Apr 3) Night Shift (USA) – Firesteed (IRE) 91 **58 p**
(Common Grounds 118) [2006 p7g Dec 20] €95,000Y: second foal: half-sister to French
1¼m winner Marillen (by Daylami): dam, French 1m winner, out of half-sister to smart
sprinter Governor General: 16/1, 7½ lengths seventh to Basaata in maiden at Lingfield,
slowly away and taking strong hold then running on under hands and heels: will do better.
D. R. C. Elsworth

GOLANO 6 gr.g. Linamix (FR) 127 – Dimakya (USA) 83 (Dayjur (USA) 137) [2006 **–**
84: p12g Jan 11] rather leggy, quite good-topped gelding: fairly useful handicapper at
best: well held only Flat outing in 2006: usually waited with: tried visored/in cheekpieces.
P. R. Webber

GOLAN WAY 2 b.c. (Feb 6) Golan (IRE) 129 – Silk Daisy 74 (Barathea (IRE) 127) **78**
[2006 6m 5.7m 6m⁵ 6m⁵ 7d² 7d³ p8g⁵ p8.6g* Nov 28] second foal: half-brother to 4-y-o
William's Way: dam 7f/1m winner: fair performer: won maiden at Wolverhampton in

November by short head from Callisto Moon: likely to stay 1¼m: acts on polytrack and good to soft going. *I. A. Wood*

GOLBAND 4 b.f. Cadeaux Genereux 131 – Hatheethah (IRE) (Machiavellian (USA) – 123) [2006 77: f6g 6m 5g 6f p5.1g f5g Dec 28] rather leggy filly: fair handicapper at 3 yrs: left L. Cumani, well held in 2006. *R. F. Marvin*

GOLDA SEEK (USA) 3 b.f. Seeking The Gold (USA) – Golightly (USA) (Take Me 53 Out (USA)) [2006 61d: p9.5g p9.5g Dec 9] leggy, short-backed filly: modest maiden: seems to stay 9.5f: tried in cheekpieces. *B. J. Meehan*

GOLDEN ALCHEMIST 3 ch.g. Woodborough (USA) 112 – Pure Gold 88 (Dilum 79 (USA) 115) [2006 76: 8d 8m 7g³ 8m p7.1g² p7.1f p8.6g³ p8.6g⁶ p8g Dec 4] strong, good-bodied gelding: fair maiden: best form up to 7f: acts on polytrack and good to soft going: tried visored. *M. D. I. Usher*

GOLDEN APPLAUSE (FR) 4 b.f. Royal Applause 124 – Golden Circle (USA) 72 80 (Theatrical 128) [2006 78: 8d 10m 9.7f* 10m⁵ 8.5g³ 8.3g⁵ p8.6g 8m Oct 8] leggy filly: fairly useful handicapper: won at Folkestone in June: stays 9.7f: acts on firm and good to soft going: ran respectably in cheekpieces final outing. *Mrs A. L. M. King*

GOLDEN ARROW (IRE) 3 b.c. Danehill (USA) 126 – Cheal Rose (IRE) 83 (Dr 110 Devious (IRE) 127) [2006 104: 10m² 10d⁵ 8v⁵ 8g⁴ 9.5s⁵ 8.5f* Sep 10] smart performer: creditable 4¼ lengths fifth to Araafa in Irish 2000 Guineas at the Curragh on third outing: won 4-runner minor event at Cork in September by 3½ lengths from Latino Magic: has form at 1¼m: acts on any going: blinkered/visored last 4 starts: sold 260,000 gns, joined I. Mohammed in UAE. *D. K. Weld, Ireland*

GOLDEN ASHA 4 ch.f. Danehill Dancer (IRE) 117 – Snugfit Annie 49 (Midyan 96 (USA) 124) [2006 87: 5d⁴ p6g⁴ 6m⁴ 6s⁶ 6m* 5.3f⁴ Jun 9] leggy, lengthy filly: useful handicapper: won at Folkestone in June by length from Folga: best at 5f/6f: acts on firm and good to soft going: held up. *N. A. Callaghan*

GOLDEN BALLS (IRE) 2 ch.c. (Feb 16) Danehill Dancer (IRE) 117 – Colourful 94 Cast (IRE) 93 (Nashwan (USA) 135) [2006 6g³ 6m⁶ 7.1m³ 7m* 6s 7d⁵ 8m* Oct 8] 40,000F, 100,000Y: neat colt: second foal: half-brother to Irish 1m to 11f winner Morning Glow (by King of Kings): dam Irish 7f winner: fairly useful performer: won maiden at Salisbury in July and minor event at Bath (beat Aaim To Prosper by 3 lengths) in October: stays 1m: acts on good to firm and good to soft going: sold 200,000 gns, sent to USA. *R. Hannon*

GOLDEN BOOT 7 ch.g. Unfuwain (USA) 131 – Sports Delight (Star Appeal 133) 66 d [2006 75: p16.5g p12.2g p12.2g⁴ 16v 14g 14.1d 12.3g 14m p13.9g Nov 17] big, strong gelding: fair handicapper: below form after third start: effective at 1½m to easy 2m: acts on any going: sometimes wears headgear: sometimes slowly away: free-going sort, held up: sold 5,500 gns. *A. Bailey*

GOLDEN CHALICE (IRE) 7 ch.g. Selkirk (USA) 129 – Special Oasis (Green Des- – ert (USA) 127) [2006 86: 8.2s Oct 25] rather leggy, close-coupled gelding: useful winner in 2004: lightly raced since, and well held in handicap only outing in 2006: visored (found little) once at 5 yrs. *P. R. Chamings*

GOLDEN DAGGER (IRE) 2 ch.f. (Apr 15) Daggers Drawn (USA) 114 – Santarene 85 (IRE) 46 (Scenic 128) [2006 7d³ 7d* 6f⁶ 7d6 Sep 30] €9,000F, €31,000Y, resold 16,000Y: big, strong filly: fourth foal: half-sister to 5-y-o Richtee: dam, 1¼m seller winner, half-sister to US Grade 3 1m winner Gino's Spirits: fairly useful form: won maiden at New-market in August: better effort after when sixth to Selinka in listed race at Newmarket final start: will prove suited by 1m/1¼m: acts on good to soft ground. *K. A. Ryan*

GOLDEN DESERT (IRE) 2 b.c. (Mar 27) Desert Prince (IRE) 130 – Jules (IRE) 76 84 (Danehill (USA) 126) [2006 p7g 6m 6.1m² 6d p6m* Nov 9] 42,000Y: strong, lengthy colt: first foal: dam, 7f winner, out of champion US 2-y-o filly (Grade 1 winner at 6f/7f) Before Dawn: fairly useful performer: didn't need to match best (second to Selinka at Nottingham) to win maiden at Wolverhampton final start: should stay 7f. *T. G. Mills*

GOLDEN DIXIE (USA) 7 ch.g. Dixieland Band (USA) – Beyrouth (USA) (Alleged 100 (USA) 138) [2006 94: p6g² 5d p5g² p5g⁶ 6g 5s 5m* 5f² 5m 6.1f 5m³ 6f 5g 6m⁴ 6d 5.1m Oct 8] good-bodied gelding: useful handicapper: better than ever in 2006, and won at York in June by 1¼ lengths from Talbot Avenue: good close third to Machinist in Hong Kong Jockey Club Sprint at Ascot eleventh start: best at 5f/6f: acts on polytrack, firm and good to soft going: wore cheekpieces fourth outing: sometimes edgy/early to post/slowly away: tough. *R. A. Harris*

GOLDEN FOLLY 2 ch.g. (Feb 6) Polish Precedent (USA) 131 – Height of Folly 81 **57 p**
(Shirley Heights 130) [2006 7g p7g f7g⁶ Nov 14] brother to smart 1¼m to 1¾m winner Sarangani and half-brother to several winners, including useful 7.5f (at 2 yrs) to 2m winner Charity Crusader (by Rousillon): dam winning stayer: some promise in maidens, showing his inexperience: will be suited by 1½m+: type to do better. *Lady Herries*

GOLDEN GROOM 3 b.g. Groom Dancer (USA) 128 – Reine de Thebes (FR) 67 **55**
(Darshaan 133) [2006 8.5f 10f⁵ 7f 9.9m 14.1g³ 12d² 16.1g³ Sep 27] modest maiden: stays 2m: acts on firm and good to soft going. *C. W. Fairhurst*

GOLDEN MEASURE 6 b.g. Rainbow Quest (USA) 134 – Dawna 106 (Polish Precedent (USA) 131) [2006 61: f12g Feb 14] good-topped gelding: maiden on Flat: well held only outing in 2006. *G. A. Swinbank*

GOLDEN PROSPECT 2 b.c. (May 7) Lujain (USA) 119 – Petonellajill 73 (Petong **56**
126) [2006 8d p6g⁵ p7g Nov 11] modest form in maidens: should stay 7f. *J. W. Hills*

GOLDEN QUEST 5 ch.g. Rainbow Quest (USA) 134 – Souk (IRE) 98 (Ahonoora **–**
122) [2006 123: 16f 15.9d⁶ Aug 22] strong gelding: made into very smart performer in 2005 (reportedly found to have suffered slab fracture of near-fore knee after final start that season): well held in Goodwood Cup and in Lonsdale Cup at York in 2006: stays 2½m: acts on all-weather, good to firm and good to soft going. *M. Johnston*

GOLDEN RIBBONS 2 ch.f. (Apr 10) Compton Place 125 – Mim 39 (Midyan (USA) **–**
124) [2006 p6g p7g p6g Nov 22] 3,000F, 7,800Y: fourth foal: sister to 6-y-o Kennington: dam, little sign of ability, half-sister to smart 6f/7f performer Norton Challenger: well held in maidens. *J. R. Boyle*

GOLDEN SPECTRUM (IRE) 7 ch.g. Spectrum (IRE) 126 – Plessaya (USA) (Nure- **66**
yev (USA) 131) [2006 64: f8g* f7g³ f8g² p8.6g² f8g* f8g p8.6g³ p7.1g 8m³ p9.5g² 8m 10m p7.1g f8g p8.6g* Dec 27] leggy, quite good-topped gelding: fair performer: won banded races in January (apprentices) and February, both at Southwell, and handicap at Wolverhampton in December: stays 9.5f: acts on all-weather, firm and soft going: wears headgear: tried tongue tied. *R. A. Harris*

GOLDEN SPRITE 3 b.f. Bertolini (USA) 125 – Shalad'or 97 (Golden Heights 82) **71**
[2006 58: p8g 10.2f² 10.2f⁵ 10.2m⁴ 10.2m* p8.6g⁶ f11g Nov 11] workmanlike filly: fair handicapper: won at Bath in October: stays 10.2f: acts on polytrack and firm going: bolted to post once at 2 yrs. *B. R. Millman*

GOLDEN SQUARE 4 ch.g. Tomba 119 – Cherish Me 88 (Polar Falcon (USA) 126) **68**
[2006 52§, a68§: f7g* f8g⁴ f7g 8.1g* 7d⁴ 8.1d f7g 7.6m 7.1f² 7f⁵ Aug 10] workmanlike gelding: fair handicapper: won at Southwell in January and Warwick (apprentices) in May: stays 8.6f: acts on all-weather, firm and good to soft ground: tried in blinkers/cheek-pieces. *A. W. Carroll*

GOLDEN SURF (IRE) 3 b.f. Gold Away (IRE) 125 – Silvery Surf (USA) (Silver **–**
Deputy (CAN)) [2006 6m⁶ Aug 5] 40,000Y: fourth foal: dam unraced half-sister to dam of Poule d'Essai des Poulains winner Green Tune and Cheveley Park winner Pas de Reponse: 8/1, well held in maiden at Windsor, held up and not knocked about. *R. Hannon*

GOLDEN TOPAZ (IRE) 2 b.f. (Apr 6) Bering 136 – Miss Champagne (FR) **63**
(Bering 136) [2006 5f⁶ 7f³ 7.5g⁴ Aug 27] €30,000F, 55,000Y: second foal: half-sister to fairly useful Irish 2005 2-y-o 6f winner Play Misty For Me (by Danehill Dancer): dam unraced sister to useful French 6f/7f performer Stella Berine: modest form in maidens: will stay 1m. *J. Howard Johnson*

GOLD EXPRESS 3 b.g. Observatory (USA) 131 – Vanishing Point (USA) (Caller I D **82 p**
(USA)) [2006 68: 8m 7m 6d* Aug 18] big, strong gelding: fairly useful form: won handicap at Newmarket in August by short head from Al Qasi: gelded after: should stay 7f: should progress again. *W. A. O'Gorman*

GOLD FLAME 3 b.g. Gorse 116 – Uae Flame (IRE) (Polish Precedent (USA) 131) **77**
[2006 7s May 20] tall gelding, unfurnished at present: sixth foal: half-brother to 3 winners by Whittingham, including 6f to 1m (including at 2 yrs) winner Flambe and 7-y-o Devon Flame, both fairly useful: dam unraced out of smart 1¼m performer On The Staff: 20/1, 5 lengths seventh to Bosset in maiden at Newbury, slowly away and not unduly knocked about: suffered minor injury after. *H. Candy*

GOLD GUEST 7 ch.g. Vettori (IRE) 119 – Cassilis (IRE) (Persian Bold 123) [2006 66, **60** a69: 10.2m⁵ 10m Sep 15] leggy gelding: modest performer: effective at 9.5f to 1½m: acts on all-weather, firm and soft going: tried visored, not since 2003: tongue tied last 7 outings in 2005: sometimes slowly away: modest hurdler. *P. D. Evans*

GOLD GUN (USA) 4 b.g. Seeking The Gold (USA) – Possessive Dancer 118 (Shareef **–** Dancer (USA) 135) [2006 100: 13.9d⁶ 16d 12g Oct 12] big, useful-looking gelding: useful performer at best, lightly raced: reportedly suffered hairline fracture of a cannon bone after winning in 2005: well held in 2006. *K. A. Ryan*

GOLDHILL PRINCE 4 b.g. Prince Sabo 123 – Lady Mabel 34 (Inchinor 119) [2006 **55** 64, a70: p7g⁶ p7g p5g p6g³ 6m p6g May 8] useful-looking gelding: modest performer: stays easy 6f: acts on polytrack and firm ground (well beaten only run on soft): wears headgear: often forces pace. *E. R. Oertel*

GOLD HUSH (USA) 2 ch.f. (Jan 17) Seeking The Gold (USA) – Meniatarra (USA) 68 **80 p** (Zilzal (USA) 137) [2006 p7g⁵ p8g² Oct 20] half-sister to smart 2003 2-y-o 1m winner Menokee (by Cherokee Run) and 7f winner Give Him Credit (by Quiet American): dam, ran twice, half-sister to Lammtarra out of Oaks winner Snow Bride: better effort when 1¼ lengths second to Sunlight in maiden at Lingfield: will improve and win races. *Sir Michael Stoute*

GOLD OPTION 2 ch.c. (Mar 1) Observatory (USA) 131 – Minskip (USA) 64 (The **93** Minstrel (CAN) 135) [2006 7m 7d* 8.1g* 8d⁵ Sep 23] good-topped colt: half-brother to several winners, including French/US 1¼m/1½m performer Skipping (by Rainbow Quest) and 3-y-o Innocent Air, both smart: dam, 2-y-o 5f winner, closely related to dam of high-class 1¼m/1½m performer Muhtarram and half-sister to very smart middle-distance performer St Hilarion: fairly useful form: won maiden at Newmarket and 2-runner minor event at Sandown in August: favourite, though stiff task, only fifth (beaten 14 lengths) behind Admiralofthefleet in Royal Lodge Stakes at Ascot: will stay 1¼m. *J. H. M. Gosden*

GOLD RESPONSE 2 ch.g. (Mar 18) Intikhab (USA) 135 – Razor Sharp (Bering 136) **54** [2006 p7.1g p7.1g⁶ 6f 7g f8g p7g p8.6g⁴ p8.6g* Dec 31] workmanlike gelding: modest performer: improved to win seller at Wolverhampton in December: stays 8.6f: acts on polytrack: tried visored. *D. Shaw*

GOLD RING 6 ch.g. Groom Dancer (USA) 128 – Indubitable 87 (Sharpo 132) [2006 **–** 97: 14.8d⁶ 14g Sep 23] leggy, workmanlike gelding: useful handicapper at best: lightly raced on Flat nowadays, well held in 2006. *J. A. Geake*

GOLD SPIRIT (IRE) 2 b.c. (Apr 30) Invincible Spirit (IRE) 121 – Butter Knife (IRE) **97** (Sure Blade (USA) 130) [2006 5d⁶ 5.3f⁴ 5.1m* 5.2g 5m 6d* 6.1g* p6g⁶ 6m⁵ 6g Sep 30] 12,000F, 10,000Y: good-topped colt: eighth foal: half-brother to useful 2003 2-y-o 1¼m winner Uncle Cent (by Peintre Celebre) and winner in Hong Kong by Danehill: dam unraced half-sister to 5-y-o Ace: useful performer: won maiden at Chester in July and 4-runner minor events at Lingfield and Chester (beat Captain Marvelous 3 lengths) in August: also ran creditably in listed company (fifth at Saint-Cloud) ninth start: raced at 5f/6f: usually forces pace: sold 35,000 gns. *E. J. O'Neill*

GOLDSTAR DANCER (IRE) 4 b.c. General Monash (USA) 107 – Ravensdale **–** Rose (IRE) (Henbit (USA) 130) [2006 53: f12g Jan 3] maiden: well held only outing in 2006: tried in cheekpieces (below form). *J. J. Quinn*

GOLO GAL 4 b.g. Mark of Esteem (IRE) 137 – Western Sal 75 (Salse (USA) 128) **–** [2006 71: p9.5g 10s p11g Dec 22] tall, close-coupled gelding: fair maiden at 3 yrs: well held in 2006. *Mrs L. J. Mongan*

GO MO (IRE) 4 br.g. Night Shift (USA) – Quiche 83 (Formidable (USA) 125) [2006 **62** 89: 6g 7s 8.3g 7g 7m 7d Sep 25] quite good-topped gelding: only modest form in 2006: effective at 6f/7f: acts on polytrack, heavy and good to firm going: tried tongue tied in 2005. *S. Kirk*

GONE'N'DUNNETT (IRE) 7 b.g. Petardia 113 – Skerries Bell 71 (Taufan (USA) **76** 119) [2006 80, a75: f6g⁴ p6g f5g³ f6g f5g* p5.1g⁶ f5s² 6m 6g³ 5d p6g 5.2g⁶ p6g 6m³ 5f³ 6m 5m p6g³ 6m⁵ 6g 5.2m⁴ p6g⁶ p6m³ 6g p6g p6m⁵ p5g p5g Dec 20] strong gelding: fair handicapper: won at Southwell in February: best at 5f/6f: acts on all-weather, firm and good to soft going: wears headgear: races prominently. *Mrs C. A. Dunnett*

GONE TOO FAR 8 b.g. Reprimand 122 – Blue Nile (IRE) 70 (Bluebird (USA) 125) **64** [2006 69: 16v³ 16.1d⁶ 14m³ 14m Aug 24] sparely-made gelding: modest handicapper:

stays easy 2m: acts on any turf going: usually blinkered/visored: races up with pace: fairly useful hurdler/chaser. *P. Monteith*

GOOD ARTICLE (IRE) 5 b.g. Definite Article 121 – Good News (IRE) 61 (Ajraas (USA) 88) [2006 48: p7g p10g⁴ p8.6g² p10g² p9.5g p12g p12g³ p12g* p10g⁴ 10m* 10.2m* 10.2f* 9.7f* 10.1s p10g Oct 20] sturdy gelding: blind in near-side eye: fair performer: won seller at Lingfield in July, and handicaps there and at Chepstow (hung left) in August and Bath and Folkestone in September: stays easy 1½m: acts on polytrack and firm going: has worn tongue strap. *D. K. Ivory* — **70**

GOODBYE 2 ch.f. (Apr 8) Efisio 120 – Blow Me A Kiss 72 (Kris 135) [2006 6g Aug 18] strong filly: fourth foal: sister to fairly useful 2003 2-y-o 5f winner Farewell To Arms: dam, maiden who stayed 1¼m, out of half-sister to very smart middle-distance performer Apache: not take eye and green in maiden at Newbury. *B. W. Hills* — **–**

GOODBYE CASH (IRE) 2 b.f. (Apr 28) Danetime (IRE) 121 – Jellybeen (IRE) 72 (Petardia 113) [2006 6m² 6m 6.1g³ 6g⁶ 7.1m³ 7g⁶ p6m 5.1s² 6v* 6d⁵ Nov 4] €11,000Y: small, leggy filly: second foal: sister to 3-y-o Flylowflylong: dam 2-y-o 9.4f winner: fair performer: won nursery at Ayr in October: effective at 5f to 7f: acts on heavy and good to firm going. *P. D. Evans* — **76**

GOODBYE GIRL (IRE) 3 b.f. Shinko Forest (IRE) – Adieu Cherie (IRE) (Bustino 136) [2006 54, a–: f6g 8d 7m f5g⁴ f6g f7g⁴ 7f⁶ 8m 7f 10.1f Jul 25] heavy-topped filly: poor performer: stays 7f: acts on fibresand and firm ground: wears headgear. *Mrs C. A. Dunnett* — **42**

GOODBYE MR BOND 6 b.g. Elmaamul (USA) 125 – Fifth Emerald 54 (Formidable (USA) 125) [2006 94: 10.5g 9.8v* 8.1s² 10g 8.9m* 10m⁵ 8m⁴ 8.1m 8s⁵ 10.4g Sep 9] strong, lengthy gelding: useful handicapper: won at Ripon in May and York in June: also ran well third/sixth starts: needs good test at 1m nowadays: acts on fibresand and any turf going: visored (raced freely) once: waited with: tough. *E. J. Alston* — **98**

GOOD COMPANION (IRE) 3 ch.g. Elnadim (USA) 128 – Broadway Rosie 101 (Absalom 128) [2006 60p: 7m⁶ 6.1g 6m⁶ 6m² 6.1f Jul 15] big, strong gelding: modest maiden: flattered fourth start: probably stays 7f: acts on soft and good to firm going: blinkered (well held) once: temperamental, and has looked tricky ride: gelded after final outing. *J. L. Dunlop* — **59 §**

GOOD EFFECT (USA) 2 ch.c. (Mar 15) Woodman (USA) 126 – River Dreams (USA) (Riverman (USA) 131) [2006 7g p8g³ p8.6g⁴ Nov 24] $40,000F, 30,000Y: strong, useful-looking colt: first foal: dam unraced out of half-sister to high-class miler Last Fandango: fair form in maidens. *A. P. Jarvis* — **66**

GOODENOUGH MOVER 10 ch.g. Beveled (USA) – Rekindled Flame (IRE) (Kings Lake (USA) 133) [2006 93, a97: 6g 7m² 7m 6m 6m⁶ 7.1m 6m 6d Sep 27] rangy gelding: just fairly useful performer in 2006: best at 6f/7f: acts on polytrack, firm and soft going: often races prominently. *Andrew Turnell* — **86**

GOODENOUGH PRINCE 3 b.g. Bluegrass Prince (IRE) 110 – Goodenough Girl (Mac's Imp (USA) 116) [2006 7.1m p10g 8.1m 10d f8g Nov 2] neat gelding: little form. *Andrew Turnell* — **–**

GOOD ETIQUETTE 2 b.g. (Apr 13) Tipsy Creek (USA) 115 – Aliuska (IRE) 70 (Fijar Tango (FR) 127) [2006 6m Sep 21] last in maiden at Pontefract. *Mrs S. Lamyman* — **–**

GOOD INTENTIONS 4 ch.f. Bien Bien (USA) 125 – Level Headed 68 (Beveled (USA)) [2006 11.8d 10.2g p8.6g p13.9g p12.2s p11g⁴ Dec 22] leggy filly: first foal: dam 9.4f to 10.2f winner: poor maiden. *P. W. Hiatt* — **38**

GOOD INVESTMENT 4 b.g. Silver Patriarch (IRE) 125 – Bundled Up (USA) (Sharpen Up 127) [2006 64: 10s⁴ 11g 12s f14g² Dec 29] unfurnished gelding: modest performer: bred to stay 1½m (below form at 1¾m): tried in cheekpieces, blinkered final outing: none too consistent. *Miss Tracy Waggott* — **56**

GOOD LUCK CHIP (IRE) 2 b.f. (Mar 24) Princely Heir (IRE) 111 – Surabaya (FR) (Galetto (FR) 118) [2006 5.1g p6g Oct 28] first foal: dam 2-y-o 1¼m winner in France (where also successful over hurdles): well held in maidens. *I. A. Wood* — **–**

GOODRICKE 4 b.c. Bahamian Bounty 116 – Star 83 (Most Welcome 131) [2006 124: 6m⁴ 7g Sep 30] small, attractive colt: good walker: had a quick action: very smart performer at best: won Sprint Cup at Haydock at 3 yrs, then left D. Loder and off 12 months: well below form in 2006 in minor event at Yarmouth (found little, albeit carried right — **102**

when fourth to Riotous Applause) and listed race at Redcar (off bridle in rear before half-way and failed to respond): was effective at 6f/7f: acted on good to firm and good to soft going (won on soft): usually wore visor, blinkered final start: wore tongue tie: was usually slowly away: to stand at Overbury Stud, Gloucestershire, fee £4,000. *Saeed bin Suroor*

GOOD TURN 3 b.f. Royal Applause 124 – Gracious Gift 96 (Cadeaux Genereux 131) **56** [2006 7m 6f⁶ 6d⁶ 6f Jun 6] lengthy, unfurnished filly: sister to 2004 2-y-o 5f winner Godsend, later successful in USA, and half-sister to 6f winner Instinct (by Zafonic): dam, 6f/7f winner, half-sister to smart performer up to 7f Sharp Prod: modest maiden: stays 6f: acts on firm going: sold 2,500 gns, sent to Sweden. *R. Hannon*

GOOD WEE GIRL (IRE) 4 b.f. Tagula (IRE) 116 – Auriga 73 (Belmez (USA) 131) – [2006 48: p7g Dec 6] leggy filly: poor performer: well held only outing in 2006: tried in cheekpieces, blinkered last 6 starts: sometimes slowly away/looks less than keen. *S. Woodman*

GOODWOOD BELLE 2 b.f. (Mar 9) Soviet Star (USA) 128 – Waif (Groom Dancer – (USA) 128) [2006 6g Jun 6] 26,000Y: fifth foal: half-sister to winners in Italy by Peru-gino (sprinter) and Bigstone (up to 1¼m): dam unraced: behind in maiden at Windsor. *J. L. Dunlop*

GOODWOOD MARCH 3 b.f. Foxhound (USA) 103 – Military Tune (IRE) (Nash- **66** wan (USA) 135) [2006 –: 7g 7m⁴ 8d⁶ 6g⁴ 5.7m² 5m 6s* 6d Oct 27] tall, leggy filly: fair performer: won maiden at Windsor in October: may prove best up to 7f: acts on soft and good to firm ground: hung right fourth outing, ran as if amiss sixth: sold 15,000 gns. *J. L. Dunlop*

GOODWOOD SPIRIT 4 b.g. Fraam 114 – Rechanit (IRE) (Local Suitor (USA) 128) – [2006 90: 7m 7g 6.1f 7f⁶ 6f 7g⁶ p7.1g Oct 28] leggy gelding: fairly useful performer at 3 yrs: well held in 2006: tried in cheekpieces/blinkers. *J. M. Bradley*

GO ON BE A TIGER (USA) 2 br.c. (Jan 25) Machiavellian (USA) 123 – Queen's **98 p** Logic (IRE) 125 (Grand Lodge (USA) 125) [2006 8s* Oct 10] good-topped, attractive colt: has scope: first foal: dam, 5f (at 2 yrs) to 7f winner (unbeaten in 5 starts, including Queen Mary and Cheveley Park Stakes), half-sister to 3-y-o Dylan Thomas: 5/1, fit but green, won maiden at Newbury by 1½ lengths from Yeaman's Hall, going away at finish: will improve and make mark in higher grade. *M. R. Channon*

GO ON GREEN (IRE) 2 b.c. (Mar 28) Kyllachy 129 – Colouring (IRE) 79 (Catrail **76** (USA) 123) [2006 6m² 6m⁴ 7.1m⁴ p7g Sep 27] €53,000F, 55,000Y: third foal: dam 8.5f winner in Ireland: fair maiden: will stay 1m: reportedly had breathing problem second start, tongue tied after. *E. A. L. Dunlop*

GO ON JESSICA (IRE) 2 ch.f. (Feb 28) Soviet Star (USA) 128 – Peig Sayers (IRE) **54** 58 (Royal Academy (USA) 130) [2006 5g² p5g³ 5d 5d³ 6m p6s Dec 14] €9,000Y: unfurnished filly: sixth foal: half-sister to 4-y-o Tharua: dam, Irish maiden (best at 1m at 2 yrs), closely related to very smart stayer Assessor: modest maiden: claimed from P. D. Evans after debut, from D. Nicholls third start (clipped heels/unseated), £8,000 both times: should stay 1m: blinkered final outing. *A. G. Juckes*

GOOSE CHASE 4 b.g. Inchinor 119 – Bronzewing 103 (Beldale Flutter (USA) 130) **76** [2006 71: p8g p5g⁴ p8g⁵ p7g* p7g p7g⁴ p8g⁶ p8g p7g⁴ p8.6g⁶ Dec 21] quite good-topped gelding: fair handicapper: left C. Mann after second start: won at Kempton in April: best at 7f/1m nowadays: acts on all-weather and good to soft going: blinkered second start: has looked no easy ride. *A. M. Hales*

GOOSE GREEN (IRE) 2 b.g. (Feb 28) Invincible Spirit (IRE) 121 – Narbayda (IRE) **69** 68 (Kahyasi 130) [2006 5s³ 5d 5g³ p7g⁴ 7g⁶ p7.1f⁴ 8m* 8.1v⁴ 8m⁵ 7.1d* 8f⁴ 7d 7.1d³ Oct 13] 37,000Y: neat gelding: first foal: dam, ran twice, half-sister to very smart 1¼m/ 1½m winner Narwala: fair performer: won seller at Musselburgh in August and nursery at Warwick in September: stays 1m: acts on polytrack and any turf going. *M. R. Channon*

GORDONSVILLE 3 b.c. Generous (IRE) 139 – Kimba (USA) (Kris S (USA)) [2006 **88** 74p: 11.7m⁴ 12f² 12m⁵ 12d⁴ Aug 12] tall, good-topped colt: fairly useful maiden: good fifth in valuable event on handicap debut at Goodwood third start: bred to stay 1¾m: acts on firm going (well below form on good to soft). *A. M. Balding*

GO RED 2 b.g. (May 20) Best of The Bests (IRE) 122 – Boulevard Rouge (USA) 71 **51** (Red Ransom (USA)) [2006 7m 7f 7.5d⁵ 7.5m 8f Sep 20] close-coupled, workmanlike gelding: modest maiden: bred to stay 1¼m+. *M. W. Easterby*

GORGEOUS BOY (IRE) 4 ch.g. Forzando 122 – Instil (Rudimentary (USA) 118) – [2006 40: f5g p5.1g Jan 5] maiden: well held both starts in 2006. *P. L. Gilligan*

GORGEOUS GIRL 2 b.f. (May 6) Generous (IRE) 139 – Zielana Gora (Polish Prece- 46 dent (USA) 131) [2006 p6g p7g⁶ 7f Jul 13] third foal: dam, no sign of ability, half-sister to smart performers Mon Tresor (up to 7f) and Montendre (sprinter): poor form in maidens. *P. W. D'Arcy*

GORSE 11 b.g. Sharpo 132 – Pervenche (Latest Model 115) [2006 f6g Feb 2] big, strong, lengthy gelding: smart performer at best: successful 8 times, including in 5 pattern races: went to stud, but then reportedly became infertile, and subsequently gelded: only run since 2001, tailed off in minor event at Southwell. *Jamie Poulton*

GO SOLO 5 b.g. Primo Dominie 121 – Taza (Persian Bold 123) [2006 88: 8g 7f 8g² 96 8.3m* 11.5g³ 10.3m³ 12m* 10g* 11m³ 12m² Sep 16] workmanlike gelding: has a quick action: useful handicapper: won at Hamilton in June, and Pontefract and Ayr in August: good efforts when placed at Southwell and Catterick last 2 starts: stays 1½m: acts on firm and good to soft going: usually races prominently: consistent: sold 52,000 gns, joined D. Pipe. *G. A. Swinbank*

GO TECH 6 b.g. Gothenberg (IRE) 117 – Bollin Sophie (Efisio 120) [2006 96: 10v⁵ 92 10m 10.4d⁶ 10g 8.9m 10f* 10.4f 9.9g 11m 10s 10m⁴ 10.4s Oct 6] rather leggy gelding: shows plenty of knee action: fairly useful handicapper: best effort in 2006 when winning at Redcar in June: stays 1½m: acts on polytrack and any turf going: sometimes races freely (pulled too hard second start). *T. D. Easterby*

GOT TO BE CASH 7 ch.m. Lake Coniston (IRE) 131 – Rasayel (USA) 79§ (Bering – 136) [2006 47: 10.5m 9.9g Aug 31] strong, lengthy mare: poor performer nowadays: well held only outing in 2006. *W. M. Brisbourne*

GOURANGA 3 b.f. Robellino (USA) 127 – Hymne d'Amour (USA) 58 (Dixieland 72 Band (USA)) [2006 74p: 9.9g³ p12g⁴ 10m 12d³ 13.1m⁵ 16d Sep 26] fair maiden: credit-able efforts when third in 2006: barely stays 1½m: unraced on extremes of going on turf: sold 6,000 gns. *H. Candy*

GOVERNMENT (IRE) 5 b.g. Great Dane (IRE) 122 – Hidden Agenda (FR) 55 – (Machiavellian (USA) 123) [2006 49: f6g⁴ f7g* 10m f7g⁶ f8g f7g Dec 21] well-made a60 gelding: modest performer on all-weather: won maiden claimer at Southwell in March: stays 7f: acts on fibresand, little form on turf: tried blinkered. *M. C. Chapman*

GOWER 2 b.c. (Feb 11) Averti (IRE) 117 – Alashaan 73 (Darshaan 133) [2006 5m⁶ 5d² 78 5.1g² Oct 17] first foal: dam, lightly-raced maiden (placed at 1½m), half-sister to Prix de l'Abbaye winners Patavellian and Avonbridge (by Averti): fair form in maidens, second at Lingfield and Bath: will prove best at 5f/6f. *R. Charlton*

GOWER SONG 3 b.f. Singspiel (IRE) 133 – Gleaming Water 81 (Kalaglow 132) 107 [2006 65p: 9s⁶ 10f* 10f* 10d* 12g* 12m⁴ 12m 12s³ 10.1m² 12s² Sep 22] workmanlike filly: useful performer: much improved to win handicaps at Brighton (hung right), Windsor (2) and Newmarket in June: even better form in defeat after, including when 3¾ lengths third to Anna Pavlova in listed race at York, and when second in similar event at Yarmouth (beaten ½ length by Dance Partner) and Princess Royal Stakes at Ascot (went down by 1¼ lengths to Acts of Grace): suited by 1½m: acts on firm and soft going: reliable. *D. R. C. Elsworth*

GRACECHURCH (IRE) 3 b.g. Marju (IRE) 127 – Saffron Crocus 83 (Shareef Danc- 85 er (USA) 135) [2006 82: 10s* 10.2d* 10.4d 10.1m 12m 10m 10g⁵ 10g⁴ 10m 10.5s³ 10m⁵ 10g² 10g p10g Oct 20] leggy, useful-looking gelding: fairly useful handicapper: won at Redcar in March and Bath in April: below form last 2 starts: likely to stay 1½m: acts on firm and soft going (yet to race on heavy): sweating fifth start: genuine: sold 32,000 gns, joined R. Hodges. *M. R. Channon*

GRACEFUL FLIGHT 4 gr.f. Cloudings (IRE) 112 – Fantasy Flight (Forzando 122) 47 [2006 47: 6d p6g 6m 6f² 6f 6m Aug 11] close-coupled filly: poor maiden: best efforts at 6f: acts on firm going. *P. T. Midgley*

GRACEFUL STEPS (IRE) 2 b.f. (Feb 1) Desert Prince (IRE) 130 – Ghassak (IRE) 61 78 (Persian Bold 123) [2006 7f 7s⁵ 7v⁵ Oct 31] €42,000Y: sixth foal: half-sister to fairly useful Irish 1¼m/1½m winner Khetaam (by Machiavellian): dam, Irish 11f winner, sister to high-class 1m/1¼m performer Kooyonga: modest form in maidens: will be suited by 1¼m/1½m. *E. J. O'Neill*

GRACIE'S GIFT (IRE) 4 b.g. Imperial Ballet (IRE) 110 – Settle Petal (IRE) (Roi **69** Danzig (USA)) [2006 66: f6g³ 5.7s³ p6g² f6g⁴ 7g⁴ 8m* 7d* p7g⁶ f8g³ Dec 9] compact gelding: fair handicapper: won at Goodwood (claiming event) in September and Yarmouth in October: stays 1m: acts on all-weather, good to firm and good to soft going: slowly away third start: consistent. *A. G. Newcombe*

GRADETIME (IRE) 2 b.f. (Mar 5) Danetime (IRE) 121 – Grade A Star (IRE) (Alzao **80** (USA) 117) [2006 5s² f5g* p5g* 5.5m⁴ May 28] €15,000F, 12,000Y: closely related to winner abroad by Indian Danehill and half-sister to useful 6f (including at 2 yrs) winner March Star (by Mac's Imp) and fairly useful 1¼m winner Jimmy Swift (by Petardia): dam Irish 2-y-o 1m winner: fairly useful form: won maiden at Southwell in April and minor event at Lingfield in May: creditable fourth to Docksil in listed race at Rome later in month: not seen after: speedy front runner, best at 5f. *M. J. Wallace*

GRAFT 7 b.g. Entrepreneur 123 – Mariakova (USA) 84 (The Minstrel (CAN) 135) **63** [2006 68: p10g p8g p10g p10g p10g³ p10g Dec 22] quite good-topped gelding: modest handicapper nowadays: best form at 9f/1¼m: acts on polytrack, firm and soft going: blinkered/wears cheekpieces: sometimes slowly away. *Mrs P. Townsley*

GRAFTON (IRE) 3 b.g. Desert Style (IRE) 121 – Gracious Gretclo 54 (Common **69 d** Grounds 118) [2006 62: p7.1g* p6g 7.5d 6f 6g p6g f8g f7g Dec 5] strong gelding: fair performer: won handicap at Wolverhampton in February: well below form after (left J. Bethell 3,500 gns before final start): stays 7f: acts on polytrack and firm going: blinkered fifth start (none too keen). *J. O'Reilly*

GRAFTY GREEN (IRE) 3 b.g. Green Desert (USA) 127 – Banafsajee (USA) 107 **–** (Pleasant Colony (USA)) [2006 p12.2g⁶ Dec 22] well held in bumpers/maiden at Wolverhampton. *T. H. Caldwell*

GRAHAM ISLAND 5 b.g. Acatenango (GER) 127 – Gryada 93 (Shirley Heights 130) **90** [2006 91: p9.5g⁴ p12.2g⁴ 12.3d May 12] strong, lengthy gelding: has a round action: fairly useful performer: creditable efforts first 2 starts in 2006: stays 1¾m: acts on polytrack and good to firm ground (no form on softer than good): free-going sort: has shown signs of temperament. *G. Wragg*

GRAIN OF TRUTH 3 b.f. Gulch (USA) – Pure Grain 121 (Polish Precedent (USA) **103** 131) [2006 70P: 9.8g* 10g⁶ 10.4m² p10g* 9.9m² 10.1m³ 8d² 10g Oct 12] rangy filly: useful performer: won maiden at Ripon in May and handicap at Lingfield (by 2½ lengths from Nice Tune) in July: good placed efforts in listed races next 3 starts, including when ¾-length third to Dance Partner at Yarmouth: will stay 1½m: acts on polytrack, good to firm and good to soft going: visored last 2 starts: usually held up: joined I. Mohammed in UAE. *Sir Michael Stoute*

GRAMADA (IRE) 4 b.f. Cape Cross (IRE) 129 – Decatur (Deploy 131) [2006 71: **78** p7.1g p9.5g⁴ 10.2d² 9.9f* 11.7g³ 11.9s⁵ 11.6m Jun 5] sturdy, good-bodied filly: fair performer: won handicap at Beverley in April: stays 1½m: acts on polytrack and firm going, probably on soft: races prominently. *P. A. Blockley*

GRAMM 3 b.c. Fraam 114 – Beacon Silver 75 (Belmez (USA) 131) [2006 96: 8f 8d⁶ **82 +** Oct 28] angular, useful-looking colt: fairly useful performer: much the more encouraging effort in 2006 when sixth to Arm Candy in handicap at Newmarket final start, first home on stand side: stays 1¼m: acts on good to soft ground. *L. M. Cumani*

GRAMMATICUS 3 b.c. Zaha (CAN) 106 – Autumn Stone (IRE) (Bigstone (IRE) **–** 126) [2006 –: p6g Feb 11] strong, quite attractive colt: well held in maidens. *K. A. Ryan*

GRANAKEY (IRE) 3 b.f. Key of Luck (USA) 126 – Grand Morning (IRE) 77 (King **63** of Clubs 124) [2006 p6g p8.6g p6g⁵ f6g² p6g³ f6g* f7g³ p7g Dec 19] €5,000F: half-sister to Irish 7f winners Cruiskeen Lawn (by Ashkalani) and Topsy Morning (by Lahib): dam 2-y-o 5f winner: modest performer: won banded event at Southwell in November: stays 7f: raced only on all-weather. *M. G. Quinlan*

GRAN AMOR 3 ch.f. Piccolo 121 – Sunfleet 59 (Red Sunset 120) [2006 12m Apr 25] **–** 11,000F: half-sister to several winners, including 1997 2-y-o 5f winner Pool Music and 7f/1m winner Russian Music (both useful, by Forzando): dam maiden suited by 1¼m: 66/1, always behind in maiden at Folkestone. *P. D. Cundell*

GRANARY GIRL 4 b.f. Kingsinger (IRE) 94 – Highland Blue 55 (Never So Bold 135) **60** [2006 57: p10g p10g p9.5g⁶ p10g p9.5g⁵ p8.6g⁴ p10g³ 10.1g⁶ 8f⁶ p12.2g² 11.5f³ 12m² 9.7f³ 10g* 10.9m⁵ 10m Sep 15] leggy filly: modest performer: won handicap at Leicester in August: stays easy 1½m: acts on all-weather and firm going: races prominently. *J. Pearce*

GRAN CLICQUOT 11 gr.m. Gran Alba (USA) 107 – Tina's Beauty 41 (Tina's Pet **51**
121) [2006 47: p12g 10m 8.3m⁴ 11.6m³ 8m p10g p11g⁶ p12g Dec 13] modest performer **a43**
on turf, poor on all-weather: stays 11.6f: acts on polytrack, raced only on good going or
firmer on turf: tried in cheekpieces at 7 yrs. *G. P. Enright*

GRANDAD BILL (IRE) 3 ch.g. Intikhab (USA) 135 – Matikanehanafubuki (IRE) **–**
(Caerleon (USA) 132) [2006 70: 8m 10m 9.9m Aug 16] rather leggy gelding: poor
mover: fair performer at 2 yrs: well held in handicaps in 2006. *T. D. Easterby*

GRAN DANA (IRE) 6 b.g. Grand Lodge (USA) 125 – Olean (Sadler's Wells (USA) **–**
132) [2006 50: f11g Mar 28] big, strong gelding: poor performer: well beaten only start in
2006: tried in cheekpieces/visor/tongue strap. *G. Prodromou*

GRAND ART (IRE) 2 b.g. (Feb 9) Raise A Grand (IRE) 114 – Mulberry River (IRE) **71**
(Bluebird (USA) 125) [2006 6m⁵ 6m³ 7d⁵ p8g Oct 20] €3,800F, €22,000Y: third foal:
dam Irish maiden: fair maiden: third at Newcastle, easily best effort: should stay 1m:
gelded after final start. *M. H. Tompkins*

GRAND ASSAULT 3 b.g. Mujahid (USA) 125 – As Mustard (Keen 116) [2006 f8g **59**
p9.5g p7g p7.1m⁴ p9.5g p8g² p7g Dec 30] modest maiden: left Mrs L. Featherstone after
second start: stays 1m: raced on all-weather: tried in headgear. *P. S. McEntee*

GRAND CHEROKEE (IRE) 3 gr.c. Fayruz 116 – Divine Apsara (Godswalk (USA) **–**
130) [2006 72: 10s p9.5g Apr 13] strong colt: fair form at 2 yrs: well beaten in 2006: wore
cheekpieces final start. *B. Ellison*

GRAND COURT (IRE) 3 b.f. Grand Lodge (USA) 125 – Nice One Clare (IRE) 117 **52**
(Mukaddamah (USA) 125) [2006 –: 8.3f 7.1m⁴ Aug 10] modest maiden: stays 8.3f: raced
only on good ground or firmer: twice failed stall test in 2005. *A. W. Carroll*

GRAND COUTURIER 3 b.c. Grand Lodge (USA) 125 – Lady Elgar (IRE) (Sadler's **117**
Wells (USA) 132) [2006 11.5g* 10.5g³ 12d⁸ 12m⁴ 12f³ 11d⁴ Sep 24] 3,500Y, €26,000
2-y-o: third foal: half-brother to fairly useful 1¼m winner Sir Edward Elgar (by King's
Best): dam, well beaten in France only start, sister to smart Irish performer up to 1½m
Desert Fox: smart performer: won both outings at 2 yrs, and minor event at Angers in
March then listed race at Bordeaux in May: good efforts next 2 starts, 2¼ lengths fourth
to Rail Link in Grand Prix de Paris at Longchamp and 3½ lengths third to Go Deputy
in Sword Dancer Invitational at Saratoga: left J-C. Rouget in France, below form in
Grade 2 Sky Classic at Woodbine final outing: stays 1½m: acts on firm and soft going.
R. Ribaudo, USA

GRAND DESIGN 4 b.f. Danzero (AUS) – Duende 75 (High Top 131) [2006 62: **64**
p12g² p8g⁶ p10g⁵ p8.6m 8.1m p13g p7g* Oct 15] modest maiden: best effort at 1¼m:
acts on polytrack: sold 15,000 gns. *C. A. Cyzer*

GRAND DIAMOND (IRE) 2 b.c. (Mar 7) Grand Lodge (USA) 125 – Winona (IRE) **62**
120 (Alzao (USA) 117) [2006 7.1m⁵ 8g⁵ 8m Sep 9] €32,000Y: good-bodied colt: fourth
foal: half-brother to winners abroad by Danehill and Rainbow Quest: dam Irish 7f (at
2 yrs) and 1½m (Irish Oaks) winner: mid-field in maidens. *Mrs A. J. Perrett*

GRAND DREAM (IRE) 2 ch.c. (Apr 22) Grand Lodge (USA) 125 – Tamaya (IRE) **– p**
(Darshaan 133) [2006 9m⁶ 8.3d Oct 10] €50,000Y: big, good-topped colt: half-brother to
several winners, including useful Italian 7.5f to 1¼m winner Troppo Oca (by Orpen) and
fairly useful 6f winner Red Opal (by Flying Spur), later successful in France: dam placed
up to 1¼m in France: more promise than bare result in maidens at Redcar and Leicester
(still not wound up), making running: type to do better at 3 yrs. *M. Johnston*

GRANDE CAIMAN (IRE) 2 ch.c. (Apr 4) Grand Lodge (USA) 125 – Sweet Retreat **85 p**
(Indian Ridge 123) [2006 p7.1g p7g⁵ p8g* Dec 19] €65,000Y: second foal: dam, ran 3
times in Ireland, half-sister to dam of Ribblesdale winner Irresistible Jewel out of US
Grade 1 1m winner Aptostar: fairly useful form: confirmed promise of first 2 runs when
winning maiden at Lingfield in December by 2½ lengths from Salford Mill: likely to stay
1¼m: raced only on polytrack: looks capable of better still. *R. Hannon*

GRAND ENTRANCE (IRE) 3 b.g. Grand Lodge (USA) 125 – Alessia (GER) (War- **79**
ning 136) [2006 74: 7.1g² 7m* 8.2g⁴ 7.1m 7m p7g Sep 6] fair performer: won maiden at
Newmarket in July: well below form in handicaps last 3 starts: should stay 1m: acts on
polytrack, firm and good to soft going. *C. R. Egerton*

GRANDE ROCHE (IRE) 4 b.g. Grand Lodge (USA) 125 – Arabian Lass (SAF) (Al **61**
Mufti (USA) 112) [2006 72: p12.2g 8d p10g⁶ 8.3d² 9.8m⁵ 11.1m² 11.1g⁴ Jul 20] good-
topped, attractive gelding: modest maiden: stays 11f: acts on polytrack, good to firm and

good to soft going: tried blinkered: slow to get going: quirky: sold 3,500 gns in October. *G. A. Swinbank*

GRANDE TERRE (IRE) 5 b.m. Grand Lodge (USA) 125 – Savage (IRE) 98 (Polish **65** Patriot (USA) 128) [2006 67: 7g² 8d 8.3m⁵ 7.9m 8.3f⁶ 8f³ 8m⁶ Jul 10] leggy mare: fair handicapper: stays 1m: acts on firm going: wore cheekpieces final start: held up. *R. A. Fahey*

GRAND HEIGHTS (IRE) 2 br.c. (Apr 30) Grand Lodge (USA) 125 – Height of Fan- **76 p** tasy (IRE) 101 (Shirley Heights 130) [2006 7m 7m 7m³ 8d Sep 26] sturdy, good-bodied colt: fourth foal: half-brother to 4-y-o Velvet Heights and 3-y-o Height of Fury: dam, 1¾m/2m winner, half-sister to smart 1¼m/1½m performer Persian Lightning: fair form in maidens: will be well suited by 1½m+: should make a better 3-y-o. *J. L. Dunlop*

GRAND IDEAS 7 br.g. Grand Lodge (USA) 125 – Afrafa (IRE) (Lashkari 128) [2006 **–** –, a66: p7.1g p9.5g Apr 10] maiden: well held both starts in 2006: tried visored. *G. J. Smith*

GRAND JOUR (IRE) 3 b.g. Grand Lodge (USA) 125 – Reveuse de Jour (IRE) 79 **86 d** (Sadler's Wells (USA) 132) [2006 75: p7g* p8.6g* 7.5d p7g p8g p8g 10.3d 8.1m p8g p7g p10g Dec 20] tall gelding: fairly useful performer: won handicaps at Lingfield and Wolverhampton in January: below form after, leaving K. McAuliffe following seventh start and M. Wallace after ninth: stays 8.6f: acts on polytrack and heavy going: sometimes tongue tied: often races prominently. *Ms J. S. Doyle*

GRAND LUCRE 2 b.f. (Mar 3) Grand Slam (USA) 120 – Naughty Crown (USA) 84 **69** (Chief's Crown (USA)) [2006 5m 6.1f⁵ p8g⁴ p8.6f² p7g Sep 12] 16,000Y: unfurnished filly: third foal: sister to winner in USA: dam, 7f winner, half-sister to smart performer up to 1¼m Tahreeb: fair maiden: easily best effort fourth start: stays 8.6f *E. J. O'Neill*

GRANDMA RYTA 4 br.f. Cyrano de Bergerac 120 – Tamara 83 (Marju (IRE) 127) **40** [2006 41: f8g p8g p8.6g p9.5g⁵ f7g Jun 3] close-coupled filly: poor maiden: stays 8.5f. *John Berry*

GRANDMA'S GIRL 4 b.f. Desert Style (IRE) 121 – Sakura Queen (IRE) 52 (Wood- **–** man (USA) 126) [2006 64: 12m 17.2m 14.1g 15.8m⁶ Aug 8] maiden: well held in 2006: in cheekpieces 6 of last 7 starts. *Robert Gray*

GRAND MEMPARI 3 b.f. Grand Lodge (USA) 125 – Mempari (IRE) 102 (Fairy King **–** (USA)) [2006 11.5m 11.5m May 11] 800Y: third foal: dam, Irish 5f and 8.5f winner, out of Prix Vermeille winner Sharaya: tailed off in maidens at Yarmouth. *Mrs C. A. Dunnett*

GRAND OFFICER (IRE) 2 b.g. (Jan 29) Grand Lodge (USA) 125 – Sheer Bliss **–** (IRE) 86 (Sadler's Wells (USA) 132) [2006 8.1m 8m p9.5m p8g⁴ Dec 2] well held in maidens/nursery: bred to stay 1¼m/1½m: tried blinkered. *D. J. S. ffrench Davis*

GRAND OPERA (IRE) 3 b.g. City On A Hill (USA) 114 – Victoria's Secret (IRE) 70 **70** (Law Society (USA) 130) [2006 76: 9.8m³ 10.1d³ 6.9f* Jul 21] angular, good-topped gelding: has a quick action: fair performer: in frame 7 of 8 starts: gelded prior to winning at Carlisle in July: stays 1¼m: acts on firm going, probably on good to soft. *J. Howard Johnson*

GRANDOS (IRE) 4 b.g. Cadeaux Genereux 131 – No Reservations (IRE) 87 (Com- **54** manche Run 133) [2006 58: 8d 7.5f⁶ 8.1m 6g 7g 8.1m 11.7m 9.9d Sep 27] tall gelding: modest maiden: left T. Easterby £2,600 after fifth start: stays 7.5f: acts on firm and soft going: wore cheekpieces final start. *Miss K. M. George*

GRAND PALACE (IRE) 3 b.g. Grand Lodge (USA) 125 – Pocket Book (IRE) 60 **59** (Reference Point 139) [2006 p7g 6g p7.1g⁵ f7g* p9.5g⁶ 8s 8g f14g⁵ f7g⁵ p8g³ p8.6g² Dec 27] modest performer: won handicap at Southwell in June: stays 8.6f: acts on all-weather: visored last 3 starts. *D. Shaw*

GRAND PARROT 3 b.g. Prince Sabo 123 – Silkstone Lady (Puissance 110) [2006 –: **–** 6d 6g 5m p6g Aug 2] sparely-made gelding: little form. *W. de Best-Turner*

GRAND PASSION (IRE) 6 b.g. Grand Lodge (USA) 125 – Lovers' Parlour 83 (Bel- **103** dale Flutter (USA) 130) [2006 113: p8.6g⁶ p10g* p10g² 9.8d⁴ 10d⁵ 10m 8g⁶ 10g 10.4s⁵ **a113** 8.2d³ p10g⁵ Nov 18] good-bodied gelding: smart performer: won minor event at Ling-field in February for second time in 3 years, beating Red Spell ½ length: good ½-length second to Sri Diamond in Winter Derby on same course next start: not at best after: effective at 1m/1¼m: acts on polytrack, firm and good to soft going: waited with. *G. Wragg*

GRAND PLACE 4 b.g. Compton Place 125 – Comme Ca (Cyrano de Bergerac 120) – [2006 6g p6g 7.1d 7m 7.1m Jun 3] leggy, lengthy gelding: fair winner at 2 yrs, missed 2005: well held in 2006: tongue tied final start. *R. Hannon*

GRAND PRAIRIE (SWE) 10 b.g. Prairie – Platonica (ITY) (Primo Dominie 121) – [2006 f16g Feb 2] lightly raced and modest form at best in Britain: blinkered, well held only outing in 2006. *G. L. Moore*

GRAND PRIX 2 ch.c. (Apr 15) Grand Lodge (USA) 125 – Divine Quest 81 (Kris 135) **93** [2006 5.1d³ 5.1g² 5g* 6.1m* 6g⁴ 7g 7m* 7d Oct 7] 20,000Y: good-topped colt: sixth foal: half-brother to several winners, including 3-y-o Zabeel House and 2000 2-y-o 6f winner Ecstatic (by Nashwan), both fairly useful: dam, 7f winner, sister to smart French sprinter Divine Danse and half-sister to very smart 6f to 1m performer Pursuit of Love: fairly useful performer: won maiden at Sandown and minor event at Chepstow in June and nursery at Chester (dictated) in September: stays 7f: acts on good to firm ground: tongue tied last 2 starts: sold 110,000 gns, sent to Bahrain. *R. Hannon*

GRAND REBECCA (IRE) 3 ch.f. Namid 128 – Krayyalei (IRE) 94 (Krayyan 117) – [2006 –: 6m² 7d Oct 3] small filly: little form in maidens. *G. A. Huffer*

GRAND SEFTON 3 br.g. Pivotal 124 – Nahlin (Slip Anchor 136) [2006 64: p8g⁶ 7d **60** f7g Dec 2] rangy gelding: modest maiden: left J. Portman 4,000 gns after second start: stays easy 1m: acts on all-weather. *D. Shaw*

GRAND SHOW 4 b.g. Efisio 120 – Christine Daae 74 (Sadler's Wells (USA) 132) **94** [2006 85: 7g p6g⁵ p6g* p6g* p5.1g⁶ p6g⁴ p6g⁶ Dec 1] strong, good-bodied gelding: fairly useful handicapper, lightly raced: won at Lingfield in September and October: effective at 5f/6f: acts on polytrack and soft going: has taken strong hold. *W. R. Swinburn*

GRAND SILENCE (IRE) 3 ch.g. Grand Lodge (USA) 125 – Why So Silent (Mill **71** Reef (USA) 141) [2006 8.3f⁶ 10m p8g Sep 27] rather leggy gelding: half-brother to several winners, notably 7f (at 2 yrs) to 10.5f winner Leporello and 7f (at 2 yrs) to 1½m winner Poppy Carew, both smart and by Danehill: dam unraced close relative to useful stayer Top Cees: fair form in maidens: best effort second outing (hung left): gelded after: tongue tied final start. *W. R. Swinburn*

GRAND SYMPHONY 2 ch.f. (Jan 30) Zamindar (USA) 116 – Gitane (FR) (Grand – Lodge (USA) 125) [2006 p7g Dec 20] 31,000Y: second foal: dam, French 11f winner, half-sister to useful French 9f/10.5f winner Ghost Dance: 25/1, forced wide when well held in maiden at Lingfield. *W. Jarvis*

GRAND VIEW 10 ch.g. Grand Lodge (USA) 125 – Hemline 77 (Sharpo 132) [2006 **52** 55: p6g p6g³ f6g⁵ p6g⁵ p6g* p6g 6g 5d Oct 8] workmanlike gelding: modest performer: won banded race at Wolverhampton in May: stays 6f: acts on all-weather and any turf going: tried blinkered, wears cheekpieces. *J. R. Weymes*

GRAND WELCOME (IRE) 4 b.g. Indian Lodge (IRE) 127 – Chocolate Box 70 – (Most Welcome 131) [2006 p10g Dec 22] smallish gelding: modest performer: ran in Spain in 2005, winning minor event at Dos Hermanas: tongue tied, well held only outing in 2006: stays 11f: often blinkered. *E. J. Creighton*

GRANGEHURST 2 ch.f. (Jan 25) Inchinor 119 – My Way (IRE) (Marju (IRE) 127) **58** [2006 8.2g 8.3d p7g⁵ Oct 21] 5,000Y: fourth foal: dam unraced half-sister to smart 2-y-o Strategic Prince out of useful sister to Oaks winner Ramruma: modest form in maidens. *Miss J. R. Gibney*

GRANGE LILI (IRE) 2 b.f. (Mar 19) Daggers Drawn (USA) 114 – Lili Cup (FR) **62** (Fabulous Dancer (USA) 124) [2006 p6g² p7g⁵ 5m² p7g p6g f5g² p6g⁴ p8g⁶ f5g³ f6g p5.1g² p6g* Dec 30] €29,000Y: half-sister to several winners, including useful Italian sprinter Uruk (by Efisio) and fairly useful Irish 2001 2-y-o 7f winner Marannatha (by Pursuit of Love): dam unraced: modest performer: landed odds in 2-runner nursery at Lingfield in December by neck from stable-companion Foxy Music: best at 5f/6f: raced mainly on all-weather: often blinkered. *Peter Grayson*

GRANNY PEEL (IRE) 2 b.f. (Feb 8) Redback 116 – Bacchanalia (IRE) 69 (Blues **66 d** Traveller (IRE) 119) [2006 p5g⁵ 5s⁴ 5g* 5g³ 5m² p5.1g* 5d⁵ 5f* 5g² 5m² 6d p5.1g³ p5.1g f6g Nov 28] €12,500Y: close-coupled filly: first foal: dam 2-y-o 7f winner: fair performer at best: won maiden seller at Redcar in April and claimers at Wolverhampton and Leicester in May and Beverley in June: ran poorly last 4 starts (claimed from K. Ryan £6,000 eleventh): raced mostly at 5f: acts on polytrack, firm and good to soft going: wore cheekpieces fifth start. *M. Brittain*

GRANSTON (IRE) 5 b. or gr.g. Revoque (IRE) 122 – Gracious Gretclo 54 (Common **98**
Grounds 118) [2006 94: 8s² p8g² 8f⁵ 8.5g 8.9m² 8.1m⁵ 8m* 8s² p8g³ 8d Sep 23] leggy,
quite good-topped gelding: useful handicapper: won at Thirsk in August: good placed
efforts at Ripon and Kempton next 2 starts: stays 9f: acts on polytrack, firm and soft
going: sometimes races freely (has worn crossed noseband), markedly so in visor final
outing: effective held up or racing up with pace: consistent. *J. D. Bethell*

GRANTLEY 9 b.g. Deploy 131 – Matisse 65 (Shareef Dancer (USA) 135) [2006 105: **105**
a9.5g* a9.5g* a9.5g* p10g 12s³ 10s a9.5g² a9.5g³ Dec 26] useful performer nowadays:
successful at Neuss in 2 minor events and placed there last 2 starts: well held in Winter Derby at Lingfield
fourth start: stays 11f: acts on fibresand/sand and heavy going: was usually visored/
blinkered when trained in Britain earlier in career. *H. Hesse, Germany*

GRANTLEY ADAMS 3 b.g. Dansili 127 – Noble Peregrine (Lomond (USA) 128) **102**
[2006 92: p5g 6m⁵ 6m³ 6g⁶ 6m³ 6m* Sep 10] tall gelding: useful handicapper: won at
Goodwood in September by ½ length from Machinist: also ran well when fifth at
Newmarket (behind Dark Missile in valuable event), and third at Ascot (behind Charles
Darwin) and Lingfield (to Gimasha): effective at 6f/7f: acts on firm and soft going:
consistent. *M. R. Channon*

GRASP 4 b.g. Kayf Tara 130 – Circe 73 (Main Reef 126) [2006 68: 16d 18s 16v³ p16g* **64**
Nov 8] close-coupled gelding: modest performer nowadays: won handicap at Kempton in
November: stays 17f: acts on polytrack and soft ground: often visored/blinkered: usually
tongue tied: races prominently. *G. L. Moore*

GRASSLANDIK 10 b.g. Ardkinglass 114 – Sophisticated Baby 39 (Bairn (USA) 126) **–**
[2006 33: f5g f6g f5g 5f Jun 9] lengthy gelding: little form since 2003: usually wears
headgear. *Miss A. Stokell*

GRATEFUL 3 ch.f. Generous (IRE) 139 – Duende 75 (High Top 131) [2006 –: 7m³ 8g **69**
11.6m 14.1m Jul 29] strong filly: fair maiden: should stay 1m+: blinkered (pulled too
hard) final start. *R. M. Beckett*

GRAVARDLAX 5 ch.g. Salse (USA) 128 – Rubbiyati 56 (Cadeaux Genereux 131) **46 §**
[2006 65d: p9.5g f12g⁴ f11g 17.2f p12.2g p16g⁵ f12g⁵ p16.5g⁶ Jul 28] leggy, quite
good-topped gelding: good mover: one-time fairly useful performer: very much on downgrade, and just poor nowadays: often wears headgear: tried tongue tied: ungenuine.
Miss D. A. McHale

GRAVE MATTERS (USA) 3 b.g. Dynaformer (USA) – Agarita (USA) (Danzig **77**
(USA)) [2006 8.5g 12m³ 11.6f⁵ 10.2g³ 13d⁶ 9.5s p12.2m Oct 31] $100,000Y: first foal:
dam, 7f winner in USA, sister to high-class sprinter Bertolini: fair maiden: sold from
M. Johnston 8,000 gns after fourth start: stays 1½m: acts on firm going: wandered second
outing. *T. G. McCourt, Ireland*

GRAVINSKY (USA) 3 b. or br.c. Theatrical 128 – Prospectress (USA) 87 (Mining **75**
(USA)) [2006 76p: 9.9g³ 10m p10g⁴ 8.3g⁵ Oct 16] tall, leggy colt: first foal: dam, 7f
winner, later Grade 2 1½m winner in USA: fair maiden: barely stays 1¼m: free-going
sort: blinkered last 2 starts: sold 7,000 gns. *Mrs A. J. Perrett*

GRAZE ON 4 b.g. Factual (USA) 108 – Queens Check 69 (Komaite (USA)) [2006 81: **96**
p6g* f6g* p5.1g* p6g* p6g p6g 5g³ 6s 5m⁶ 5f 5.1m* 5m p5g⁶ 5m 5m p5.1g f5g⁴
p6g p5g⁵ Dec 10] lengthy gelding: useful performer: won 5 races in 2006, claimer at
Wolverhampton (claimed from J. Quinn £12,000), and handicaps at Southwell, Wolverhampton (2) and Chester: left R. Harris after fifteenth outing: effective at 5f/6f: acts on
all-weather, soft and good to firm going: usually visored/blinkered: often makes running.
Peter Grayson

GRAZEON GOLD BLEND 3 ch.g. Paris House 123 – Thalya (Crofthall 110) [2006 **92**
91: 5.1f⁶ 5s² 5.1g 5f 6g 6m* 6f⁵ 6m⁵ 6d 5g² Aug 30] big gelding: fairly useful handicapper: won at Ripon in July: creditable second at Leicester final start: effective at 5f/6f:
acts on firm and soft going: visored (seemed not to take to it) fourth start. *J. J. Quinn*

GRAZE ON TOO (IRE) 3 b.f. Rainbow Quest (USA) 134 – Whispering (IRE) 81 **50**
(Royal Academy (USA) 130) [2006 54p: 9.8g 7.5g 9.9f Jul 7] modest maiden: seems to
stay 9.8f: acts on soft ground. *J. J. Quinn*

GRAZIE MILLE 2 b.f. (Mar 25) Bertolini (USA) 125 – Daintree (IRE) 66 (Tirol 127) **61**
[2006 5f 7f 6d² 6.1g p8.6g Nov 3] third foal: half-sister to 3-y-o Sir Douglas and smart
French performer (best around 9f/1¼m) Billy Allen (by Night Shift), 7f winner in Britain

at 2 yrs: dam, 1m winner, half-sister to very smart sprinter The Tatling: modest maiden: form only when second in seller at Redcar (left T. Easterby £6,000). *R. Brotherton*

GREAT AS GOLD (IRE) 7 b.g. Goldmark (USA) 113 – Great Land (USA) (Friend's **70** Choice (USA)) [2006 –: p16.5g 18v* 21.6d³ 20s⁴ 17.1d⁶ 18s³ 16v Oct 25] good-topped gelding: fair handicapper: won at Pontefract in April: stays 21.6f: acts on fibresand, heavy and good to firm going: usually wears cheekpieces: tried blinkered/tongue tied earlier in career: usually held up. *B. Ellison*

GREAT BELIEF (IRE) 4 b.g. Namid 128 – Fairy Lore (IRE) 89 (Fairy King (USA)) **63** [2006 56: 6m⁴ 5f⁵ 5.3m 5f 5m p6g 6m* 5.1m⁵ 6.1m 6g Sep 14] tall, close-coupled gelding: modest maiden event at Yarmouth in August, hanging markedly left: stays 6f: acts on firm going: not straightforward. *T. D. McCarthy*

GREAT BRITAIN 4 b.c. Green Desert (USA) 127 – Park Appeal 122 (Ahonoora 122) **114** [2006 102p: 7g⁶ 6g⁴ 6d³ Nov 4] close-coupled, good-topped colt: smart performer: improved form when 1¾ lengths fourth to stable-mate Bygone Days in Bentinck Stakes at Newmarket, making running: not disgraced when ¾-length third to Rising Shadow in listed event at Windsor final start: has won over 7f, may well prove best at 5f/6f: acts on good to firm and good to soft ground. *Saeed bin Suroor*

GREAT CHIEFTAIN (IRE) 3 b.g. Lend A Hand 124 – Well Wisher (USA) (Sangla- **71** more (USA) 126) [2006 67: 7f³ 8s 7.2d³ 7g² 7.9m³ 8.1f 8.2m⁵ p9.5g⁴ p8.6g⁵ p12.2g 7d⁴ p7.1g f8g⁴ Nov 14] workmanlike gelding: has a round action: fair maiden: best at 7f/1m: acts on polytrack, firm and good to soft going: wore cheekpieces final outing: troublesome at stall at 2 yrs (once failed test) and on second outing: races freely. *R. A. Fahey*

GREAT COMPOSER (IRE) 3 b.g. Mozart (IRE) 131 – Talena (Zafonic (USA) 130) **47** [2006 54: 10d 8.1g 7m³ 8m 10.1d p8.6g f7g Dec 12] poor maiden: claimed from Mrs A. Perrett £6,000 after third start: gelded, left M. Attwater after fifth one: stays 7f: acts on polytrack and good to firm ground: tried blinkered/visored/in tongue tie. *M. Wellings*

GREAT EXPLORER (IRE) 2 b.c. (Feb 7) Indian Danehill (IRE) 124 – Ninth Wond- **58 p** er (USA) (Forty Niner (USA)) [2006 6g⁶ Jun 1] 9,000F, 19,000Y: fourth foal: half-brother to 3-y-o Abbondanza: dam unraced close relation to smart UAE sprinter Conroy out of Rockfel/Nell Gwyn winner Crystal Gazing: 10/1 and green, staying-on sixth in maiden at Yarmouth: will be suited by 1m: should do better. *E. J. O'Neill*

GREAT FOX (IRE) 5 b.h. Foxhound (USA) 103 – Good Enough (IRE) (Simply Great **–** (FR) 122) [2006 87: 5.2m 5m Sep 8] big, strong horse: fairly useful handicapper at best: well held both starts in 2006: tongue tied once at 3 yrs: has shown signs of temperament. *P. L. Gilligan*

GREAT HAWK (USA) 3 b.c. El Prado (IRE) 119 – Laser Hawk (USA) (Silver Hawk **108 p** (USA) 123) [2006 8g 10.5m* 10d⁴ 10.4m⁵ 10m⁵ p10g⁸* Sep 6] $150,000F, $400,000Y: strong, good-topped colt: has a fluent, round action: fifth foal: half-brother to winners in North America by Known Fact and Lord Carson: dam 7f (at 2 yrs)/8.5f winner in USA: useful form: won maiden at Haydock in May and handicap at Kempton (visored, beat Acrobatic by 4 lengths on all-weather debut) in September: will stay 1½m: acts on polytrack, unraced on extremes of going on turf: reportedly lost action fifth outing: smart performer in the making. *Sir Michael Stoute*

GREAT ORATOR (USA) 4 b.g. Bahri (USA) 125 – Verbal Intrigue (USA) (Dahar **83** (USA) 125) [2006 83: 8.2m⁵ 10m² 10g⁶ 8.3g³ a7g³ Dec 17] tall, good-topped gelding: fairly useful maiden: sold from H. Candy 16,000 gns before final start: free-going sort, but stays 1¼m: acts on good to firm and good to soft ground. *C. Lorenzo, Spain*

GREAT PLAINS 4 b.c. Halling (USA) 133 – West Dakota (USA) (Gone West (USA)) **107** [2006 100: 9m⁶ p10g⁵ 9.9g* 10.4f 10.5m⁴ 10m⁵ 10s² Oct 7] compact colt: useful handicapper, lightly raced: won at Salisbury (beat Fairmile by length) in June: creditable efforts last 3 starts, including when equal-neck second to Book of Music at Ascot on final one: stays 1¼m: acts on polytrack, good to soft and good to firm going: has hinted at temperament, but is consistent: sold 155,000 gns, joined E. Charpy in UAE. *Mrs A. J. Perrett*

GREAT SPHINX (USA) 2 b.c. (Apr 6) Giant's Causeway (USA) 132 – Chaposa **93** Springs (USA) 120 (Baldski (USA)) [2006 6g³ 7g5⁸* 8g⁴ 6d⁴ 8s Oct 21] $725,000Y: tall colt: fourth living foal: dam, US Grade 1 7f winner, half-sister to US Grade 1 1m winner You And I: fairly useful performer: won maiden at Tipperary in August: out of depth in Racing Post Trophy at Newbury final start (hung left): stays 1m. *A. P. O'Brien, Ireland*

GREAT TIDINGS 3 b.g. Fantastic Light (USA) 134 – On The Tide 72 (Slip Anchor **76**
136) [2006 –: 10m⁴ 12v³ 14m⁴ 12.1m 16g⁵ 18s p16g Oct 20] good-topped gelding: fair
maiden: stays 1¾m, seemingly not 2m: acts on good to firm going (possibly not on softer
than good): sold 8,000 gns. *M. Johnston*

GREAT VIEW (IRE) 7 b.g. Great Commotion (USA) 123 – Tara View (IRE) (Wassl **83**
125) [2006 66: 9.9g³ 12d* 10m* 10f⁴ 12f⁵ 12d⁴ 11g p12g³ 12s* 11.6d p12g Nov 13] **a76**
lengthy gelding: fairly useful handicapper on turf, fair on all-weather: won at Newmarket
in May, Newbury in June, Epsom in July and at Newbury (ladies) in October: stays easy
13f: acts on all-weather, firm and soft going: wears headgear. *Mrs A. L. M. King*

GRECIANETTE (IRE) 3 b.f. Night Shift (USA) – Alexandria (IRE) (Irish River **57**
(FR) 131) [2006 66: p6g p5g³ p5g³ p7g p7g p8g⁴ 8.1g⁴ 9.7f 10.1m⁵ Aug 27] modest
maiden: left J. Toller 6,000 gns prior to third start (only outing for Gay Kelleway): stays
easy 1m: acts on polytrack and good to soft ground: tried blinkered: hung markedly left
once at 2 yrs. *W. J. Musson*

GRECIAN GOLD (IRE) 4 b.g. Lujain (USA) 119 – Falconera (IRE) (Tirol 127) **76**
[2006 85: 6g³ 8.3m* p8.6g Jul 28] fair performer, lightly raced: won claimer at Leicester
(claimed from C. Cox £12,000) in June: stays 8.3f: raced only on polytrack, good/good to
firm going: slowly away on reappearance. *J. R. Boyle*

GREEK EASTER (IRE) 3 b. or br.f. Namid 128 – Easter Heroine (IRE) 72 (Exactly **80**
Sharp (USA) 121) [2006 7m⁴ 7g³ p10g² 10f³ Jul 11] good-topped filly: fifth foal: half-
sister to useful 2001 2-y-o 5f/6f winner Doc Holiday (by Dr Devious): dam, Irish maiden
who stayed 1¼m, half-sister to useful sprinter Ocker: fairly useful maiden: good short-
head second at Kempton third start: stays 1¼m: acts on polytrack and firm ground: tended
to flash tail final outing. *B. J. Meehan*

GREEK ENVOY 2 br.c. (Mar 24) Diktat 126 – South Shore 102 (Caerleon (USA) 132) **85**
[2006 7g* 7f⁵ 8g Oct 12] 15,000Y: rangy, useful-looking colt: closely related to 15f winner Stonecutter (by Warning) and half-brother to several winners, including useful 7f/1m
winner South Rock (by Rock City): dam, 1¼m/1½m winner, half-sister to very smart 7f/
1m performer Soviet Line: fairly useful form: won minor event at Redcar in August:
better effort after when seventh in well-contested nursery at Newmarket: stays 1m.
T. P. Tate

GREEK GOD 2 b.g. (Feb 19) Grand Lodge (USA) 125 – Cephalonia 103 (Slip Anchor **61**
136) [2006 7.1m 7g 8.3m⁴ 8f 10g Sep 26] good-topped gelding: good walker: modest
maiden: should stay 1¼m/1½m: blinkered (below form) once: gelded after final start.
W. Jarvis

GREEK RENAISSANCE (IRE) 3 b.c. Machiavellian (USA) 123 – Athene (IRE) **108**
83 (Rousillon (USA) 133) [2006 84p: 7s⁶ p6g* p6g² 6s² 6m* 6d² Sep 27] leggy, quite
good-topped colt: useful performer: won maiden at Wolverhampton in June and handicap at Goodwood (could have been more impressive when beating Forest Dane by 5
lengths) in September: good short-head second to Hoh Hoh Hoh in similar event at
Salisbury final start: should prove just as effective at 5f as 6f: acts on polytrack, soft and
good to firm going: sent to UAE. *M. P. Tregoning*

GREEK SECRET 3 b.g. Josr Algarhoud (IRE) 118 – Mazurkanova 63 (Song 132) **77**
[2006 73: 6f* 6m 6m 6g 7.5f⁵ 6.1m⁵ 6m² 5d 6m 6s² 6.1s p7.1g p6g Dec 19] leggy gelding:
fair handicapper: won at Thirsk in May: left T. Easterby 9,000 gns after seventh start:
effective at 5f/6f: acts on firm and soft going: tried in cheekpieces, blinkered final outing:
has looked none too genuine. *J. O'Reilly*

GREEK WELL (IRE) 3 b.c. Sadler's Wells (USA) 132 – Hellenic 125 (Darshaan **67 p**
133) [2006 10m 10f 12s⁴ Aug 18] brother to several at least smart performers, including
1¼m winner Greek Dance and 1¼m/1½m winner Islington, both very smart, and half-
brother to useful 4-y-o Mountain High: dam won Yorkshire Oaks and second
in St Leger: 7/1 second favourite for Derby in January but taken out of race at forfeit stage
in March: fair form in maidens: effort best ignored on debut (badly hampered) in June:
best effort when ninth at Windsor second start: should stay 1½m: tongue tied final outing
(well held, but not knocked about): should still do better. *Sir Michael Stoute*

GREENACRE LEGEND 4 b.g. Faustus (USA) 118 – Alice Holt (Free State 125) **–**
[2006 9.7f⁴ 14.1d⁶ May 19] has shown more temperament than ability in bumper/over
hurdles: well held in 2 maidens on Flat. *D. B. Feek*

GREENBELT 5 b.g. Desert Prince (IRE) 130 – Emerald (USA) (El Gran Senor (USA) **74**
136) [2006 –, a73: f8g³ f8g³ f12g³ f11g* p12.2g² f12s⁴ 12v³ 13.8d 10.5s² 10d 10.5s 8g **a81 d**

10.1s⁶ p8.6g f11g⁶ f11g Dec 5] fairly useful handicapper on all-weather, fair on turf: won at Southwell in February: below form after: stays 1½m: acts on all-weather and heavy going: wore cheekpieces final start. *G. M. Moore*

GREEN COAST (IRE) 3 b.c. Green Desert (USA) 127 – Oriental Fashion (IRE) 110 **82 p** (Marju (IRE) 127) [2006 7m⁵ Sep 11] well-made colt: third foal: brother to useful 7f/1m winner Desert Chief and half-brother to useful 2003 2-y-o 6f/7f winner Oriental Warrior (by Alhaarth): dam, 1m winner (including at 2 yrs), out of close relation to Nayef and half-sister to Nashwan and Unfuwain: 5/1-on and coltish, won maiden at Redcar by 5 lengths from Lottie, barely having to come off bridle: will improve. *Saeed bin Suroor*

GREEN DAY PACKER (IRE) 2 br.g. (Apr 2) Daylami (IRE) 138 – Durrah Green **64** 79 (Green Desert (USA) 127) [2006 6m⁵ 7m 6m p8.6g p7.1g⁶ f7g⁵ Dec 19] 38,000F, 30,000 2 y o: small, sturdy gelding: sixth living foal: half-brother to fairly useful 2000 2-y-o 6f winner Strike The Green (by Smart Strike) and winner in USA by Slew City Slew: dam, Irish 5f winner, from family of Nureyev and Sadler's Wells: modest maiden: stays 7f. *P. C. Haslam*

GREEN FALCON 5 b.g. Green Desert (USA) 127 – El Jazirah (Kris 135) [2006 50: **–** 13f Jun 29] strong, good-bodied gelding: maiden: well held only start in 2006: tried visored/in cheekpieces/tongue tied. *Miss S. E. Forster*

GREEN GINGER 10 ch.g. Ardkinglass 114 – Bella Maggio (Rakaposhi King 119) **–** [2006 –: f8g May 9] no form since 2003: tried visored. *J. T. Stimpson*

GREEN MANALISHI 5 b.g. Green Desert (USA) 127 – Silca-Cisa 93 (Hallgate 127) **107** [2006 107: p5g⁶ 5.1s⁶ 5.2m* 5.1f³ 5s² 5m⁵ 5g⁶ p5g* 5f 5.1g⁴ 5.2m⁵ 5g 5d Oct 7] sturdy gelding: useful performer: won handicaps at Newbury (by 1½ lengths from Corridor Creeper) in April and Lingfield (beat Texas Gold by ¾ length) in July: several creditable efforts in defeat, including in listed event at the Curragh (sixth to Dandy Man) on seventh outing: best at 5f/easy 6f: acts on polytrack, firm and soft going: has hung left: consistent: sold 75,000 gns. *D. W. P. Arbuthnot*

GREENMEADOW 4 b.f. Sure Blade (USA) 130 – Pea Green 98 (Try My Best (USA) **66** 130) [2006 70: 7g 9d 9.7f⁴ 9.7f⁶ 9.7f* 8.3g³ 10.2m³ 10.2f⁶ p8.6m³ Oct 14] workmanlike filly: fair handicapper: won at Folkestone in August: stays 1¼m: acts on polytrack and firm going. *S. Kirk*

GREEN PARK (IRE) 3 b.g. Shinko Forest (IRE) – Danccini (IRE) 78 (Dancing Dissi- **97** dent (USA) 119) [2006 84: 6m 5.1f² 5s* 6s³ 5m⁶ 5m 6m 6g⁶ 5g 5d⁴ 5s Oct 14] useful-looking gelding: useful performer: won handicap at Thirsk in May: creditable third to Skhilling Spirit in listed race at Haydock next time: mostly just respectable efforts after: raced at 5f/6f: acts on firm and soft ground. *R. A. Fahey*

GREEN PIRATE 4 b.g. Bahamian Bounty 116 – Verdura 63 (Green Desert (USA) **67** 127) [2006 68: f6g f6g 6m⁴ 7m² 7d⁵ 7g² 7f⁶ p6g 7f p8g p7.1g³ p8.6g² p8g* p8.6g⁵ p7.1g² Dec 28] leggy, angular gelding: fair performer: claimed from R. Craggs £6,000 after sixth start, left M. Wellings after ninth: won banded event at Lingfield in December: stays 8.6f: acts on polytrack and good to firm going: tried in cheekpieces: sometimes slowly away. *W. M. Brisbourne*

GREEN ROOM (FR) 3 b.f. In The Wings 128 – Scarlet Plume 103 (Warning 136) **106** [2006 60p: 10g⁶ 10m² 10.9m* 12m³ 14m 12g* 11.8d* 12s* Oct 29] leggy filly: useful performer: won maiden at Warwick in June, handicaps at Salisbury (beat Juniper Girl by 1¾ lengths) in August and Leicester (by 2 lengths from Trick Or Treat) in October and listed race at Milan (beat Penelope Star 1¾ lengths) also in October: worth another try at 1¾m: acts on soft and good to firm ground: tends to hang. *J. L. Dunlop*

GREENSLADES 7 ch.h. Perugino (USA) 84 – Woodfield Rose 41 (Scottish Reel 123) **108** [2006 103: 6m 6d⁴ 6m 6g³ 6d p6g Nov 11] big, strong horse: good walker: useful handicapper: showed himself better than ever when winning at Newmarket (beat Idle Power by length) in May: good close third behind same rival at Windsor: well below form both outings after: effective at 6f/7f: acts on polytrack, soft and good to firm going: races close to pace. *P. J. Makin*

GREENWICH MEANTIME 6 b.g. Royal Academy (USA) 130 – Shirley Valentine **102** 104 (Shirley Heights 130) [2006 80: 12g* 16m* 18.7m³ 13.1g* 16.1m³ 13.9d 13.9d⁵ Sep 8] sturdy gelding: useful handicapper: much improved in 2006, winning at Thirsk and Ripon in April and Ayr (beat Lets Roll by 4 lengths) in June: good close third of 20 to Toldo in Northumberland Plate at Newcastle next time: not at best at York last 2 starts, in

Ebor first occasion: best up to 2m: acts on polytrack, good to firm and good to soft going: waited with. *R. A. Fahey*

GREENWICH VILLAGE 3 b.g. Mtoto 134 – D'Azy 91 (Persian Bold 123) [2006 **78** 62: p8g³ p8.6g⁴ 11m³ p12.2g Jul 3] fair maiden: will stay 1½m: acts on polytrack and good to firm ground: gelded after final start. *W. J. Knight*

GREENWOOD 8 ch.g. Emarati (USA) 74 – Charnwood Queen 61 (Cadeaux Genereux **81** 131) [2006 81: p6g p6g³ p6g p7g² p7g 6g⁴ 6m 7m* 6m 7m³ 6m 6m⁴ 7m² 6d³ 7m 7m⁴ 7d **a70** 7s 6.1d⁶ p6g⁴ Nov 8] strong, lengthy gelding: fairly useful handicapper on turf, fair on all-weather: won ladies event at Lingfield in May: stays 7f: acts on all-weather, firm and soft going: formerly blinkered (not since 2003): has worn tongue tie. *P. G. Murphy*

GREMLIN 2 b.g. (Apr 30) Mujahid (USA) 125 – Fairy Free (Rousillon (USA) 133) **78** [2006 5.5d² 6m⁴ 6.1f² 6m² 6d³ Aug 25] 12,000Y: tall, leggy gelding: has a quick action: closely related to 7-y-o Lord of The East and half-brother to a winner in Hong Kong by Pivotal: dam, maiden who stayed 1¼m in Ireland (no form in Britain), half-sister to smart miler Protection: fair maiden: runner-up 3 times, including in nursery at Newmarket: favourite when only respectable third in sales race there final start: will stay 1m: acts on firm and good to soft going. *A. King*

GRENANE (IRE) 3 b.c. Princely Heir (IRE) 111 – Another Rainbow (IRE) 72§ (Rain- **78** bows For Life (CAN)) [2006 70: p6g* p6g p6g Nov 10] fair performer: won handicap at Wolverhampton in January: stays easy 7f: acts on polytrack and firm going. *P. D. Evans*

GRETHEL (IRE) 2 b.f. (Feb 15) Fruits of Love (USA) 127 – Stay Sharpe (USA) **61** (Sharpen Up 127) [2006 6m 6s⁵ 6s⁶ 8d Nov 3] €9,000Y: workmanlike filly: half-sister to numerous winners, including 7f/1m winner Jalaab (by Green Desert) and 1¼m (including at 2 yrs)/1½m winner Takamaka Bay (by Unfuwain), both useful: dam unraced: modest maiden: should stay 1m. *A. Berry*

GREY ADMIRAL (USA) 5 gr.g. Cozzene (USA) – Remarkable Style (USA) 99 **–** (Danzig (USA)) [2006 –: p8.6g p12.2g Jan 28] workmanlike gelding: fair maiden in 2004: little form on Flat since: free-going sort: sent to Italy. *B. R. Johnson*

GREY BOY (GER) 5 gr.g. Medaaly 114 – Grey Perri 103 (Siberian Express (USA) **88** 125) [2006 79: 7g² 7d² 7m* 8m* 7m 8f² f8g p8g Dec 19] tall gelding: fairly useful handi-capper: improved to win at Yarmouth (by 5 lengths) in May and Ripon in June: stays 1m: acts on firm and good to soft going: races prominently. *R. A. Fahey*

GREY COSSACK 9 gr.g. Kasakov – Royal Rebeka (Grey Desire 115) [2006 68: 5g⁴ **61** 6f⁴ 6m 6m Jul 4] leggy, good-topped gelding: modest performer nowadays: best at 6f: acts on any turf going: tried visored at 3 yrs. *Mrs L. Stubbs*

GREY FINALE 4 b.f. Grey Desire 115 – Tanoda 77 (Tyrnavos 129) [2006 f12g Dec 9] **–** sixth foal: dam 5f (at 2 yrs) to 1½m winner: well beaten both starts in bumpers, and on Flat debut. *M. Brittain*

GREYFRIARS ABBEY 2 b.c. (Mar 11) Fasliyev (USA) 120 – Mysistra (FR) (Mach- **67 p** iavellian (USA) 123) [2006 p7g⁵ 7.1d Nov 3] 18,000Y: seventh foal: half-brother to Irish 1½m winner Jug of Punch (by In The Wings) and winner in Italy by Cadeaux Genereux: dam, French 11f winner, out of half-sister to Irish St Leger winner Dark Lomond: promis-ing fifth to Cabinet in maiden at Lingfield: still very green next time: will be suited by 1m/1¼m: should make a better 3-y-o. *M. Johnston*

GREY OUTLOOK 3 ch.f. Observatory (USA) 131 – Grey Galava 64 (Generous (IRE) **73** 139) [2006 70: 7.1g⁵ 9m³ 8g⁴ 10v⁵ 9.9g³ 10.5v⁵ 8v⁴ 10d⁴ 12d³ 12.4s* 16d³ Nov 3] fair performer: won maiden at Newcastle (by 7 lengths) in October: stays 2m: acts on heavy going: tends to race freely: probably temperamental. *Miss L. A. Perratt*

GREY PAINT (USA) 3 gr. or ro.g. El Prado (IRE) 119 – Devil's Art (USA) (Devil's **74** Bag (USA)) [2006 75: 8.1d 10m 12g 11.6d p16g⁴ 14.1m⁴ 14.1g⁵ 14.1g⁶ Aug 25] good- **a79** topped gelding: fair handicapper: may prove best short of 2m: best efforts on polytrack, unraced on extremes of going on turf: tongue tied all starts, visored last 2 runs at 2 yrs: joined D. Pipe. *R. Hannon*

GREY REPORT (IRE) 9 gr.g. Roselier (FR) – Busters Lodge (Antwerp City) [2006 **70** p10g⁶ p12.2g Mar 3] smart novice hurdler in 2003/4: let down by jumping/temperament since and just fairly useful out of novice company over fences: fair form on first of 2 outings on Flat: should be suited by 1½m+. *R. H. Buckler*

GREY ROVER 2 b.c. (May 20) Zilzal (USA) 137 – Island Story 88 (Shirley Heights **79 p** 130) [2006 p7g⁶ 8g* Oct 17] fourth foal: half-brother to fairly useful 1¼m/11f winner

Strategy (by Machiavellian): dam, 1¼m winner who stayed 2m, half-sister to smart winner up to 1½m Arabian Story: showed benefit of debut when winning maiden at Bath in October by ¾ length from Murdoch, making all: will stay 1¼m/1½m: sold 30,000 gns, sent to USA: likely to improve further. *R. Hannon*

GREYSIDE (USA) 3 gr.g. Tactical Cat (USA) 116 – Amber Gold (USA) (Mr Prospector (USA)) [2006 9.2m⁴ 12m⁴ 12s Aug 18] $22,000Y, 52,000 2-y-o: good-topped, quite attractive gelding: first foal: dam unraced: fair maiden: still green, best effort when fourth at York second start: ran poorly at Catterick final outing: should prove suited by 1½m: won juvenile hurdle in October. *J. Howard Johnson* **78**

GREY SWALLOW (IRE) 5 gr.h. Daylami (IRE) 138 – Style of Life (USA) (The Minstrel (CAN) 135) [2006 129: 12f* 10d³ 10.2g Oct 28] close-coupled, good-topped horse: good walker: fluent mover, with quick action: won Irish Derby at the Curragh at 3 yrs and Tattersalls Gold Cup at the Curragh in 2005: still showed very smart form at 5 yrs, and made winning reappearance for fourth consecutive season when beating Brecon Beacon by 5 lengths in Grade 2 Jim Murray Memorial Handicap at Hollywood in May: creditable ½-length third to Cacique in Manhattan Handicap at Belmont following month, staying on well: left D. Weld in Ireland and off 4½ months (reportedly sold for A$4m), last of 12 behind Fields of Omagh in Cox Plate at Moonee Valley final outing: effective at 1¼m/1½m: acts on firm and soft going. *D. Sutton, Australia* **123**

GREYT BIG STUFF (USA) 2 gr.c. (Apr 10) Aljabr (USA) 125 – Dixie Eyes Blazing (USA) 56 (Gone West (USA)) [2006 6g⁴ 6f³ 7m³ 6d f7g* f8g² Nov 20] 27,000Y: big colt: seventh foal: half-brother to 1m winner Johnny Reb (by Danehill) and winners abroad by Barathea and Kris: dam, ran twice, out of sister to dam of Zafonic: fair performer: won maiden at Southwell in October, then left B. Meehan 33,000 gns: odds on, second in minor event there final start: stays 1m: acts on fibresand and firm going: quirky, tried in blinkers. *Miss Gay Kelleway* **76**

GREYTOWN 3 gr.f. Daylami (IRE) 138 – Hawayah (IRE) 68 (Shareef Dancer (USA) 135) [2006 71: p8.6g⁶ 8d Oct 27] quite good-topped filly: fair maiden at 2 yrs: well beaten both starts in 2006: should stay at least 1m: acts on good to firm going. *M. A. Jarvis* **–**

GREY VISION 3 gr.f. Grey Desire 115 – Brief Star (IRE) 49 (Brief Truce (USA) 126) [2006 f6g Nov 15] second foal: dam sprint maiden who ran only at 2 yrs: 8/1 and blinkered, little show in maiden at Southwell. *M. Brittain* **–**

GREZIE 4 gr.f. Mark of Esteem (IRE) 137 – Lozzie (Siberian Express (USA) 125) [2006 57: p7g² p7.1g⁶ p7g² p7g p6g⁴ 7.1g 7m⁶ 7f p7g⁵ 7f⁶ p7g⁵ p7.1g⁵ Nov 20] workmanlike filly: modest handicapper: effective at 7f/1m: acts on all-weather and firm ground. *T. D. McCarthy* **63**

GRIGOROVITCH (IRE) 4 b.c. Fasliyev (USA) 120 – Hasty Words (IRE) 103 (Polish Patriot (USA) 128) [2006 92: 5d 5f⁶ 5g³ 5m 5g 5m² 5f 5.4f³ 5f* 5m Aug 12] neat colt: useful handicapper: best effort when winning at Newcastle (by short head from Malapropism, overcoming trouble to lead on line) in July: best at 5f: acts on polytrack, firm and soft going: sometimes slowly away, and patiently ridden: has carried head awkwardly: tried in cheekpieces: sold 12,000 gns in November. *I. Semple* **100**

GRIMES FAITH 3 b.c. Woodborough (USA) 112 – Emma Grimes (IRE) 54 (Nordico (USA)) [2006 81: p7g² 6g³ 7m³ 6m 6g² 7m³ 6m 6m³ 8g³ 8d² 8g p7g p6g² p6g p6g p7g Dec 15] good-topped colt: useful handicapper: runner-up 4 times in 2006: stays 1m: acts on polytrack, firm and good to soft going. *R. Hannon* **95**

GRIMES GLORY 2 b.c. (May 9) Atraf 116 – Emma Grimes (IRE) 54 (Nordico (USA)) [2006 p7g 7m 5f⁶ 7m⁶ 6m 7m³ 8g³ 8.3g a8g Dec 17] neat colt: modest maiden: placed in selling nurseries: sold from R. Hannon 6,000 gns before final start: stays 8.3f: acts on good to firm going. *T. Ruiz, Spain* **53**

GRINGO 4 gr.g. Alzao (USA) 117 – Glen Falls (Commanche Run 133) [2006 83: 10.9g⁴ 12.3d 10g 12m* 11.9g* 12f² 12g⁶ 12d⁴ Aug 22] strong, stocky gelding: has a round action: fairly useful handicapper: won at Newmarket (very slowly away and hung right) in June and Haydock in July: good fourth at York final start: stays 1½m: acts on firm and soft going: joined J. Howard Johnson, won over hurdles in December. *B. W. Hills* **91**

GRIZEDALE (IRE) 7 ch.g. Lake Coniston (IRE) 131 – Zabeta (Diesis 133) [2006 89§: 7d 6g 6g⁶ 7s⁶ 7m⁴ 7.6f² 7g² 7m⁵ 7.6d³ 7g 7g² 7d 7g 7d Oct 28] strong gelding: fairly useful handicapper: stays 1m: acts on any going: tongue tied: free-going sort: slowly away second outing: reportedly bled final 6-y-o start: unreliable. *J. Akehurst* **85 §**

totesport.com November Stakes (Handicap), Windsor—
a temporary change of venue for the highlight of the final day of the turf season; Group Captain asserts
from Resonate (rail) while Book of Music (star on head) takes third off Castle Howard

GROOMS AFFECTION 6 b.g. Groom Dancer (USA) 128 – Love And Affection (USA) (Exclusive Era (USA)) [2006 –: p12.2g⁴ p16g Mar 27] good-bodied gelding: fairly useful handicapper: seemingly creditable effort at Wolverhampton on reappearance: well held only subsequent start: stays 1½m: acts on soft and good to firm going, probably on polytrack: tried tongue tied (tailed off). *K. A. Morgan* **85**

GROUND PATROL 5 b.g. Ashkalani (IRE) 128 – Good Grounds (USA) (Alleged (USA) 138) [2006 p10g p10g⁵ p12g* p10g 11.7f² p10g Jun 24] good-topped gelding: fair performer: won handicap at Lingfield in February: stays 1½m: acts on polytrack, firm and good to soft going: tried in headgear/tongue tie: sometimes slowly away. *G. L. Moore* **68**

GROUND RULES (USA) 4 b.g. Boundary (USA) 117 – Gombeen (USA) (Private Account (USA)) [2006 81p: p8g p9.5g² p8.6g p8.6g⁵ 7s p8g Apr 1] sturdy gelding: fairly useful performer, lightly raced: in-and-out form in handicaps in 2006: stays 9.5f: acts on polytrack, good to soft and good to firm ground: tried visored: sent to Czech Republic. *V. Smith* **84**

GROUP CAPTAIN 4 b.g. Dr Fong (USA) 128 – Alusha 88 (Soviet Star (USA) 128) [2006 101: 12d 10g 10m* 10.4d³ 12d² 11.6d* p10g Nov 18] lengthy gelding: smart performer: further improvement for new trainer in 2006, winning handicaps at Newmarket (beat Mutawaffer by 2 lengths) in July and Windsor (totesport.com November Stakes by 1¼ lengths from Resonate) in November: also ran well in handicaps at York (third to Topatoo) and Ascot (neck second to Pevensey): respectable seventh to Nayyir in listed race at Lingfield final outing: effective at 1¼m/1½m: acts on polytrack, firm and soft going. *R. Charlton* **110**

GROUP FORCE (IRE) 2 b.f. (Mar 12) Montjeu (IRE) 137 – Allspice (Alzao (USA) 117) [2006 7f⁶ p8g 6d³ 7m 8g* 8m⁶ p8.6g Nov 3] 12,000Y: smallish filly: third foal: half-sister to 4-y-o Zorippi: dam, maiden bred to be suited by 1¼m+, out of half-sister to Last Second and to dam of Alborada, both very smart at 1¼m: modest performer: won selling nursery at Yarmouth in September: will stay 1½m: twice blinkered: no easy ride. *M. H. Tompkins* **56**

GROVE CHERRY (IRE) 3 b.f. City On A Hill (USA) 114 – Kaliningrad (IRE) (Red Sunset 120) [2006 –: p8.6g 7g a6.8g 8g⁴ a6.8g a11g⁵ a8.6g Nov 12] lengthy, quite good-topped filly: little form: sold from M. Tompkins 800 gns after second start: tongue tied final 2-y-o outing. *Madeleine Smith, Sweden* **–**

GRUB STREET 10 b.g. Barathea (IRE) 127 – Broadmara (IRE) 91 (Thatching 131) [2006 –: f12g f16g p13.9g Jun 22] big, lengthy gelding: modest winner at best: no form since 2004: tried tongue tied. *J. Parkes* **–**

GSTAAD (USA) 2 b.c. (Mar 11) Storm Cat (USA) – Cash Run (USA) 119 (Seeking The Gold (USA)) [2006 6m 5g* Sep 16] second foal: brother to a minor winner in USA: dam, Breeders' Cup Juvenile Fillies' winner, half-sister to very smart US Grade 1 7f **88 p**

winner Forestry (by Storm Cat) out of US Grade 1 8.5f winner Shared Interest: 25/1, easily better effort in maidens at the Curragh when winning 21-runner event in September by ½ length from Divert, leading well inside final 1f: sent to USA: likely to improve again. *A. P. O'Brien, Ireland*

GUACAMOLE 2 ch.f. (Mar 2) Inchinor 119 – Popocatepetl (FR) 66 (Nashwan (USA) **84** 135) [2006 7m⁵ p7g⁴ p7g* 8.1v² 8m⁴ 10d⁶ Oct 28] tall, close-coupled filly: first foal: dam maiden who probably stayed 1¾m: fairly useful performer: won maiden at Kempton in July: ran well in frame in nurseries at Haydock and Newmarket: below form in listed race final start: should stay 1¼m: acts on polytrack, heavy and good to firm going. *B. W. Hills*

GUADALAJARA (GER) 5 ch.m. Acatenango (GER) 127 – Guernica (Unfuwain **115** (USA) 131) [2006 116: 20m⁶ 12g* 13.3d² 13.9d⁶ Sep 8] big, rangy mare: good sort: third foal: half-sister to smart German performer up to 1½m Guadalupe (by Monsun): dam unraced half-sister to dual Gold Cup winner Royal Rebel: smart performer: sold from P. Schiergen in Germany €110,000 after final 3-y-o start: much improved in 2005, winning 4 times, including listed race at Lyon-Parilly: placed afterwards in Prix de Pomone at Deauville (unlucky) and Prix de Royallieu at Longchamp: left J-C. Rouget in France 800,000 gns after final 4-y-o outing: better than bare result suggests when sixth of 12 to Yeats in Gold Cup at Royal Ascot on reappearance: comfortable winner of minor event at Newmarket (beat Ouninpohja by 2½ lengths) in July: good ½-length second to Admiral's Cruise in Geoffrey Freer Stakes at Newbury next time: disappointing in Park Hill Stakes at York final start: effective at 1½m, should have stayed 2m: acted on soft going, probably on good to firm: had worn crossed noseband: visits Tiger Hill. *Saeed bin Suroor*

GUADALOUP 4 ch.f. Loup Sauvage (USA) 125 – Rash (Pursuit of Love 124) [2006 **65** 70: p7.1g⁴ 6.9g 6d² 6s p6g⁶ f6g* p6g³ f7g f6g Dec 5] big, lengthy filly: fair performer: won handicap at Southwell in November: stays 7f: acts on all-weather, good to firm and good to soft ground: blinkered/visored last 7 starts. *M. Brittain*

GUADIANA (GER) 4 b.f. Dashing Blade 117 – Gamberaia (IRE) (Konigsstuhl **53** (GER)) [2006 56: p8.6g p8.6g p9.5g f11g⁵ 10d⁵ 10.2f 10f² 11.6m⁴ 10m² 12.1m³ 11.7m* 10.9m p12g* Oct 23] leggy filly: modest performer: won seller at Bath in August and banded event at Kempton in October: stays 1½m: acts on all-weather, firm and good to soft going: usually visored nowadays: very slowly away twelfth start. *A. W. Carroll*

GUANYIN 3 b.f. Zaha (CAN) 106 – Misty Moon (Polar Falcon (USA) 126) [2006 40: **–** f7m p12g Dec 1] sturdy filly: maiden: no form in 2006: tried in cheekpieces/blinkers. *Ms J. S. Doyle*

GUARANTIA 2 ch.f. (Jan 28) Selkirk (USA) 129 – Maskunah (IRE) (Sadler's Wells **92** (USA) 132) [2006 p7g³ 7d³ Sep 30] lengthy filly, unfurnished at 2 yrs: third foal: dam unraced close relative to smart performer up to 1½m Cloud Castle and half-sister to Luso and Warrsan: fairly useful form: third in maiden at Kempton and listed race at Newmarket, in latter tongue tied and much improved when beaten 2 lengths by Selinka, again making running: will probably stay 1¼m/1½m. *C. E. Brittain*

GUEST CONNECTIONS 3 b.g. Zafonic (USA) 130 – Llyn Gwynant 115 (Persian **93** Bold 123) [2006 98: 8m 7d⁴ 7g 7.1m 8m 7.1m⁵ 8m⁶ 8m 7d³ 6m* p6g³ 6d p7g p7g Oct 21] tall, leggy, attractive gelding: fairly useful handicapper: won at Goodwood in August: well below form last 3 starts: best at 6f/7f: acts on good to firm going, probably on good to soft: often visored of late: usually gives trouble at stall (withdrawn once), and very slowly away fourth outing: has looked temperamental: sold 13,000 gns. *M. R. Channon*

GUIDELINE 3 b.g. Diktat 126 – Polisonne (Polish Precedent (USA) 131) [2006 59: f8g **–** 10g Apr 17] big, rangy gelding: modest maiden: well held in 2006: dead. *M. W. Easterby*

GUILDED WARRIOR 3 b.g. Mujahid (USA) 125 – Pearly River 72 (Elegant Air **73** 119) [2006 70: 6g³ p6g³ 6g⁴ 6f⁴ 5.7g p7g⁴ p7.1m⁶ Sep 2] fair performer: stays 7f: acts on polytrack and firm going: tried visored: withdrawn prior to intended fifth outing after getting loose and bolting. *W. S. Kittow*

GUILDENSTERN (IRE) 4 b.g. Danetime (IRE) 121 – Lyphard Abu (IRE) 78 **89** (Lyphard's Special (USA) 122) [2006 92: 6g p6g⁵ 7d³ 8.2g⁵ 6g* 6m 6m* 6d⁶ 6f Sep 18] well-made gelding: fairly useful handicapper: won at Salisbury (ladies) in June and Newmarket in August: effective at 6f to 1m: acts on polytrack, good to firm and good to soft going: often tongue tied: sold 15,000 gns. *H. Morrison*

GUILIA 3 ch.f. Galileo (IRE) 134 – Lesgor (USA) 106 (Irish River (FR) 131) [2006 78p: **106** 10d² 12g⁵ 11.9g⁶ 12s p13g⁵ Oct 26] leggy, light-framed filly: useful performer: good efforts first 2 starts when head second to Scottish Stage in listed race at Newbury (hung left) and 9¾ lengths fifth to Alexandrova in Oaks at Epsom: respectable fifth to High Heel Sneakers in listed event at Lingfield final start: should stay 1¾m: acts on polytrack and good to soft going. *Rae Guest*

GUILTY PLEASURE 2 ch.f. (Feb 25) Inchinor 119 – Idolize 92 (Polish Precedent **50** (USA) 131) [2006 8.2g p8g Oct 20] 18,000Y: lengthy filly: third foal: half-sister to useful 1m winner Golden Feather (by Dr Fong): dam, 1m (at 2 yrs) and 1¼m winner, sister to very smart performer up to 1½m Riyadian out of Irish Oaks winner Knight's Baroness: modest form final start in maidens. *G. C. Bravery*

GUISEPPE VERDI (USA) 2 ch.c. (Feb 25) Sky Classic (CAN) – Lovington (USA) **85** (Afleet (CAN)) [2006 7d 7s p8g* Oct 23] $105,000Y: strong, lengthy colt: fourth living foal: half-brother to 3 winners in USA, including Grade 3 6f winner Savorthetime (by Gilded Time): dam 8.5f winner in USA, including at 2 yrs: fairly useful form: improved to win maiden at Lingfield by 1½ lengths from Hurricane Thomas, pair clear: stays 1m. *J. H. M. Gosden*

GULF EXPRESS (USA) 2 b.c. (May 18) Langfuhr (CAN) 124 – Wassifa 95 (Sure **67 p** Blade (USA) 130) [2006 6m⁶ May 31] $290,000Y: half-brother to several winners, including smart 7f (at 2 yrs)/1m winner Hold To Ransom (by Red Ransom): dam, 11f winner in Britain who later won up to 9f in USA, out of half-sister to Most Welcome: 7/2, very green when last of 6 in minor event at Yarmouth won by Danebury Hill: should improve. *Sir Michael Stoute*

GULF (IRE) 7 ch.g. Persian Bold 123 – Broken Romance (IRE) (Ela-Mana-Mou 132) **–** [2006 110: 12g 12s⁶ May 7] big, strong gelding: smart performer at best: well held in John Porter Stakes at Newbury and Jockey Club Stakes at Newmarket in 2006: tried tongue tied: waited with. *D. R. C. Elsworth*

GULF OF GOLD (USA) 3 br.g. Seeking The Gold (USA) – Borodislew (USA) 118 **71** (Seattle Slew (USA)) [2006 7g⁴ May 6] $280,000Y: lengthy gelding: sixth foal: brother to US Grade 3 9f winner Seeking Slew and closely related to 2 winners, including US Grade 3 6f winner Canadian Frontier (by Gone West): dam, French 6.5f (at 2 yrs)/7f winner, later successful in US Grade 2 8.5f event: 11/10 favourite and tongue tied, 4½ lengths fourth to Illustrious Blue in maiden at Goodwood, not knocked about: gelded after, then left Godolphin. *Saeed bin Suroor*

GULL WING (IRE) 2 ch.f. (Apr 18) In The Wings 128 – Maycocks Bay 100 (Muhtar- **88** ram (USA) 125) [2006 8.3m⁶ 8.2g² p8.6g* Oct 29] good-topped filly: second foal: dam, 1¼m and 1¾m winner, out of half-sister to smart performer up to 2½m Compton Ace: fairly useful form in maidens: second to Shorthand at Nottingham prior to winning at Wolverhampton: will be suited by 1½m+. *M. L. W. Bell*

GUNDULA (IRE) 3 b.f. Singspiel (IRE) 133 – Playgirl (IRE) 77 (Caerleon (USA) **–** 132) [2006 7.1m 10.2m p9.5g f12g Dec 12] smallish filly: first foal: dam, lightly-raced maiden (second at 1¼m), sister to useful performer up to 1½m Drama Class: no form. *D. J. S. ffrench Davis*

GUNNER'S VIEW 2 ch.c. (Apr 19) Medicean 128 – Stark Ballet (USA) (Nureyev **57** (USA) 131) [2006 p7g³ 7g Oct 12] rather leggy, quite attractive colt: has a quick action: modest form in maidens (well backed). *B. J. Meehan*

GUS 3 b.g. Dr Fong (USA) 128 – Tender Moment (IRE) 78 (Caerleon (USA) 132) [2006 **75** 53: p10g⁴ p10g² p10g⁶ Mar 18] strong gelding: half-brother to several winners, including 4-y-o Tucker and fairly useful 6f (at 2 yrs)/7f winner Marlo (by Hector Protector): dam 7f winner: fair maiden: should prove at least as effective at 1m as 1¼m: acts on polytrack: sold 7,500 gns in November. *B. W. Hills*

GUTO 3 b.g. Foxhound (USA) 103 – Mujadilly 43 (Mujadil (USA) 119) [2006 87: 5g* **100** 5.1f 6s² 5m 6m 5d⁶ Aug 23] quite good-topped gelding: useful performer: won handicap at Thirsk in April: good neck second to Skhilling Spirit in listed race at Haydock third start: not at best after: best effort at 6f, but may prove best at 5f: acts on soft and good to firm going, probably on polytrack: races prominently. *K. A. Ryan*

GUTTER PRESS (IRE) 2 b.f. (Feb 7) Raise A Grand (IRE) 114 – Grandel (Owington **51** 123) [2006 p8g 7m⁵ Sep 19] €1,200Y, resold 8,500Y: second foal: half-sister to smart 4-y-o Tax Free: dam unraced: well held in maidens, in blinkers second start: has joined K. Burke. *J. S. Moore*

GWEEBARRA 2 b.c. (Mar 14) Lomitas 129 – Complimentary Pass 80 (Danehill **97** (USA) 126) [2006 6m³ 7m⁵ 7f³ 7m* 7d² 8m⁴ 8d Sep 23] 45,000Y: strong, lengthy colt: fourth foal: half-brother to 3-y-o Spunger: dam, ran twice, closely related to useful sprinter Daawe: useful performer: won maiden at Chester in August: ran well after when second of 7 to Big Timer in Acomb Stakes at York and fourth of 7 to Caldra in listed race at Goodwood: clearly amiss in Royal Lodge Stakes at Ascot final start: will stay 1¼m: acts on firm and good to soft going: sent to USA. *K. A. Ryan*

GWILYM (GER) 3 b.c. Agnes World (USA) 123 – Glady Rose (GER) (Surumu (GER)) [2006 76: 5.7d 5m 5.1m⁵ 5m 5m⁵ 5f⁴ 5m⁴ 5m* 5m² 5g⁵ 5.1m⁴ p6g³ p6g⁵ p5g⁵ p5.1g³ p6g p6g³ Dec 22] compact colt: fair handicapper: won at Sandown in July: will prove best at 5f/easy 6f: acts on polytrack and firm going: blinkered final outing: consistent. *D. Haydn Jones* **76**

GWYLLION (USA) 2 b. or br.f. (Mar 7) Red Ransom (USA) – Lady Angharad (IRE) 95 (Tenby 125) [2006 p6g p7g⁴ Oct 21] $45,000F, €260,000Y: first foal: dam 6f (at 2 yrs) to 1¼m winner: promise in maidens at Lingfield, particularly when eye-catching fourth to Malaath, dropped out and finishing strongly: will go on improving. *J. H. M. Gosden* **71 p**

GYMBOLINI 3 b.f. Bertolini (USA) 125 – Gymcrak Flyer 73 (Aragon 118) [2006 61, a58: p7g Jan 4] modest maiden at 2 yrs: last only start in 2006: sometimes tongue tied: sold 1,400 gns in March. *N. P. Littmoden* **–**

GYPSY ROYAL (IRE) 4 b.f. Desert Prince (IRE) 130 – Menominee (Soviet Star (USA) 128) [2006 54: 7g p7.1g 7f 8g³ 9.8d⁴ 10m f12m f12g Nov 20] leggy filly: poor maiden: stays 1m: acts on good to firm and good to soft ground: tongue tied second outing. *G. Woodward* **47**

GYPSY'S KISS 3 b.g. Cyrano de Bergerac 120 – Reina 24 (Homeboy 114) [2006 –: p9.5g 8.1m Jul 22] leggy gelding: well held in maidens/handicap: has pulled hard: sent to Belgium. *B. P. J. Baugh* **–**

GYRATION (IRE) 2 ch.c. (Apr 10) Spinning World (USA) 130 – Tomori (USA) 106 (Royal Academy (USA) 130) [2006 7s Oct 10] 16/1, last in maiden at Newcastle. *J. G. Given* **–**

GYROSCOPE 2 b.f. (Mar 7) Spinning World (USA) 130 – Far Across (Common Grounds 118) [2006 p7.1g³ Oct 30] €180,000Y: fourth foal: closely related to very smart 6f to 1m winner Arakan (by Nureyev) and half-sister to winner in USA by Mt Livermore: dam unraced: 3/1, needed experience when 2½ lengths third to Phoenix Tower in maiden at Wolverhampton: will do better. *Sir Michael Stoute* **71 p**

H

HAATEF (USA) 2 b.c. (May 11) Danzig (USA) – Sayedat Alhadh (USA) (Mr Prospector (USA)) [2006 6m* 7d⁴ Oct 14] smallish, sturdy colt: fourth living foal: brother to Irish 6f (at 2 yrs)/7f winner Walayef and Irish 6f winner (including at 2 yrs) Ulfah, both useful and half-brother to winner in USA by Deputy Minister: dam, US 7f winner, sister to smart US/UAE 7f winner Kayrawan: won 25-runner maiden at the Curragh in August: 22/1, smart form when 3 lengths fourth of 15 to Teofilo in Dewhurst Stakes at Newmarket 2 months later, going strongly patiently ridden and running on gamely: will stay 1m: open to more improvement, and sure to be a force in some of the leading 3-y-o events. *K. Prendergast, Ireland* **113 p**

HAATMEY 4 b.g. Josr Algarhoud (IRE) 118 – Raneen Alwatar 80 (Sadler's Wells (USA) 132) [2006 –: 10.1m⁴ p12g 12g 13d⁴ 14.1g* 17.1m⁶ 14.8m* 14m 16.2f³ 14.8m⁴ 14.1m 17.5d⁵ 14.1d⁶ p16g³ p16.5g⁶ Dec 29] strong, heavy-topped gelding: fairly useful handicapper: won at Redcar in May and Newmarket in June: below form subsequently, leaving M. Channon 4,500 gns after thirteenth start: probably stays 17f: acts on firm and good to soft going: often visored: temperament under suspicion. *B. G. Powell* **82 d**

HABALWATAN (IRE) 2 b.c. (Mar 10) In The Wings 128 – Mureefa (USA) 73 (Bahri (USA) 125) [2006 6m 7m 7m⁴ p7g p8.6g* p8g* p10g⁴ p8g* Dec 20] compact colt: first foal: dam, 1¼m runner-up from 2 starts, granddaughter of Musidora winner Fatah Flare: fairly useful performer: won nursery at Wolverhampton (looked none too keen early and hung left) and minor event at Lingfield in November, and nursery at Kempton in December: should stay 1½m: raced on polytrack and good to firm ground: blinkered after second start: quirky, no easy ride. *C. E. Brittain* **87**

HABANERO 5 b.g. Cadeaux Genereux 131 – Queen of Dance (IRE) (Sadler's Wells (USA) 132) [2006 93: p12g p9.5g 10.5g p9.5g Nov 2] good-topped, quite attractive gelding: fairly useful at best: well held in 2006: tried tongue tied: front runner. *Miss S. J. Wilton* **–**

HABANUS LIVIUS (IRE) 3 ch.g. Titus Livius (FR) 115 – Wheatsheaf Lady (IRE) 83 (Red Sunset 120) [2006 –: 11v 7.5f⁶ 8.5m⁵ 7m Sep 12] modest maiden: well held in seller at Yarmouth final start: stays 7.5f: acts on firm going. *Joseph Quinn, Ireland* **53**

HABITUAL DANCER 5 b.g. Groom Dancer (USA) 128 – Pomorie (IRE) 67§ (Be My Guest (USA) 126) [2006 69: 21.6d Apr 24] good-bodied gelding: fair handicapper at 3/4 yrs: well held only Flat outing in 2006. *Jedd O'Keeffe* **–**

HABITUAL (IRE) 5 b.g. Kahyasi 130 – Kick The Habit 94 (Habitat 134) [2006 66: p12g⁵ p16g p16g Nov 8] rangy gelding: modest performer on Flat nowadays: acts on polytrack and good to firm going: stays easy 2m: tried in tongue tie. *John A. Quinn, Ireland* **52**

HABSHAN (USA) 6 ch.g. Swain (IRE) 134 – Cambara 97 (Dancing Brave (USA) 140) [2006 86: p8g p8g* 8g² 8.2m⁵ 8.1m* 8.1m* 8.3g² 8.1g⁶ 8m 8g Sep 28] smallish, good-topped gelding: fairly useful handicapper: improved in 2006, winning at Lingfield in March and Warwick and Sandown in July: stays 1m: acts on polytrack, good to firm and good to soft going. *C. F. Wall* **93**

HADAHOO (USA) 2 b.c. (Mar 17) War Chant (USA) 126 – Carly's Crown (USA) (Wild Again (USA)) [2006 7m⁴ 7d² 8v* 8d Sep 26] $150,000Y: fifth foal: closely related to a winner in USA by Belong To Me and half-brother to smart US performer up to 8.5f French Assault (by French Deputy): dam, 6f to 9f winner in US, out of half-sister to Breeders' Cup Juvenile winner Chief's Crown: fairly useful form: shaped well in maidens, winning at Thirsk in September: favourite, only seventh in nursery at Goodwood: stays 1m: yet to race on firm ground, acts on any other. *M. A. Jarvis* **85**

HADATH (IRE) 9 br.g. Mujtahid (USA) 118 – Al Sylah 118 (Nureyev (USA) 131) [2006 50, a73: p7.1g p6g³ p7g³ p6g² p6g⁴ p7g⁶ p7g p7g⁴ p6g⁶ p6g p6g⁴ 6m² 8.1d 7m² p7g⁴ 7m 8f⁴ 8f⁴ 7.6m 7g⁵ 8f* 7m² 8m⁴ 7d⁵ p8g⁶ p6g p8g p8g Dec 5] lengthy gelding: fair performer on all-weather, modest on turf: won apprentice handicap at Brighton in August: effective at 6f to 1m: acts on polytrack and any turf going: usually wears headgear: held up. *B. G. Powell* **60 a70**

HAENERTSBURG (IRE) 4 b.f. Victory Note (USA) 120 – Olivia's Pride (IRE) (Digamist (USA) 110) [2006 42, a46: p8.6g p13.9g f11g Jan 29] sturdy filly: maiden: well held in 2006: tried in cheekpieces/tongue tie. *A. L. Forbes* **–**

HAHNS PEAK 3 b.g. Mujtahid (USA) 125 – Fille Genereux 58 (Cadeaux Genereux 131) [2006 –: p7g p6g 6m 10s p8g Oct 29] little form: tried in cheekpieces. *Mrs A. L. M. King* **–**

HAIBAN 4 b.c. Barathea (IRE) 127 – Aquarela (Shirley Heights 130) [2006 75: 12m 9m 12s 14s p13.9g³ Nov 25] quite good-topped colt: fair maiden at 3 yrs for G. Butler: poor form since: should stay 1¾m: acts on firm and soft ground, probably on polytrack: has been tongue tied. *J. J. Lambe, Ireland* **48**

HAIFA (IRE) 3 ch.f. Spectrum (IRE) 126 – Mrs Fisher (IRE) 94 (Salmon Leap (USA) 131) [2006 76p: p7g p8g f12g⁵ f12g³ Dec 27] lengthy, good-topped filly: fair performer: stays 1½m: acts on fibresand and heavy going: wore cheekpieces final start. *Mrs A. Duffield* **71**

HAIL THE CHIEF 9 b.h. Be My Chief (USA) 122 – Jade Pet 90 (Petong 126) [2006 67, a97: p10g⁴ p8.6g⁵ 7s* 7d* 8.2s* p8g* 8.1m² 8m May 13] rather sparely-made horse: good mover: useful handicapper, better on all-weather than turf: won at Folkestone, Leicester, Nottingham and Kempton (by ¾ length from Granston) in March/April: arguably should have completed 5-timer in race won by Public Forum at Sandown, idling after jockey put whip down: met trouble final start: effective at stiff 7f to 1¼m: acts on dirt, all-weather, soft and good to firm going: has been bandaged in front: effective held up/making running. *R. Hannon* **96 a107**

HAIR OF THE DOG 2 b.c. (Mar 22) Foxhound (USA) 103 – Bebe de Cham 75 (Tragic Role (USA)) [2006 f6g 6f 5m⁶ 7.1m³ 9m² 8f 10d 8s 8.2s⁵ p9.5g⁶ Nov 7] stocky colt: modest maiden: should stay 1¼m/1½m: acts on soft and good to firm going: sold 5,000 gns. *J. G. Given* **55**

HAITI DANCER 3 b.f. Josr Algarhoud (IRE) 118 – Haitienne (FR) (Green Dancer (USA) 132) [2006 64: 7.1s⁶ 8.2d 10m 9.9m³ p10g 10m⁴ 10.2m Aug 28] leggy filly: modest performer: stays 1¼m: acts on soft and good to firm going: visored/in cheekpieces last 3 starts. *C. G. Cox* **64**

HALA BEK (IRE) 3 b.c. Halling (USA) 133 – Place de L'Opera 98 (Sadler's   **121 p**
Wells (USA) 132) [2006 11g* 12m⁴ Jun 3]

The jury is still out on which horse will prove the best to have contested the
Derby in 2006. Sir Percy, Dylan Thomas, Visindar, Sixties Icon and Septimus are
among a strong group from the race due to be kept in training at four, but the pick of
the field, all being well with him, could yet prove to be Hala Bek, who would have
been placed at least at Epsom had he not swerved away his chance when challenging strongly well inside the final furlong. Although finishing fourth, Hala Bek was
beaten only a short head, a head and a short head and his effort was all the more
remarkable in that it came on only his second start, a matter of weeks after his
belated debut. Furthermore, he had an interrupted preparation, which left his
participation in doubt until a few days beforehand.

Lightly-raced winners of the Derby have had contrasting preparations down
the years. 1993 winner Commander In Chief, the last horse to be successful in the
Derby without having run at two, negated his inexperience by managing three races
in four weeks beforehand, winning each of them. Lammtarra, the last horse to win
the Derby with only one race behind him, made a successful debut in a listed race at
Newbury as early as August as a two-year-old. 1973 winner Morston, the only
horse besides Lammtarra to win the Derby on only his second appearance since
Bois Roussel was successful in 1938, was even more of a raw recruit on Derby Day,
having made a winning debut in a maiden at Lingfield less than a month before
Epsom. Considered too backward to race at two, Hala Bek was exercised every day
on the Heath at Newmarket from November. As a result, he knew his job well
enough to make a winning debut in a thirteen-runner maiden over eleven furlongs
at Newbury in late-April, where he went off at 5/4 and beat Dragon Dancer most
impressively by a length and a quarter, the pair pulling six lengths clear of the rest.
Hala Bek was meant to complete his Derby preparation in the Dante Stakes in May,
but he was forced to forego further experience when returning a 'poor scope' a few
days beforehand, ante-post favourite for York at the time. It was to cost him dear at
Epsom. Backed down to 9/1 on Derby Day once given the all clear, Hala Bek
looked very much at home for much of the race, travelling with the same ease he
had at Newbury, but, asked for everything in the closing stages this time, he
swerved sharply right, away from the whip, all but unseating Philip Robinson.
Although his rider quickly regathered the reins, Hala Bek lost some of his momentum, and, despite rallying, he went down narrowly to Sir Percy, Dragon Dancer and
Dylan Thomas. Sir Percy came from a long way back but, all the same, considering
all the work that had been put in, defeat must have been a bitter pill to swallow for
Hala Bek's jockey and his trainer Michael Jarvis, both still without a Derby success
as they reach the veteran stage, though Jarvis had led up Charlottown in 1966. 'He
went and changed his legs or took a funny stride, and it's cost him the race,' said
Robinson afterwards. There was to be no consolation for connections either. Hala
Bek was forced to sit out the Irish Derby due to a recurrence of the throat infection
which troubled him before Epsom, and it was announced in September that he was
to be taken out of training, believed to have suffered a tendon injury. He left
Michael Jarvis but is said to be staying in training as a four-year-old, though at the
time of writing he was still recuperating at a Darley pre-training yard and no firm
plans had been made about his future.

Hala Bek (IRE) (b.c. 2003)	Halling (USA) (ch 1991)	Diesis (ch 1980)	Sharpen Up Doubly Sure
		Dance Machine (b 1982)	Green Dancer Never A Lady
	Place de L'Opera (b 1993)	Sadler's Wells (b 1981)	Northern Dancer Fairy Bridge
		Madame Dubois (ch 1987)	Legend of France Shadywood

Hopefully, more will be seen of Hala Bek as a four-year-old than was seen
of his half-brother Imperial Stride (by Indian Ridge) in his first year for Godolphin
in 2006. Imperial Stride developed into a high-class performer over a mile and a
quarter and a mile and a half for Sir Michael Stoute in 2005, and missed most of the
latest season after surgery on an ankle in February. Imperial Stride is a full brother
to the very smart High Pitched, who won at up to thirteen furlongs, including the

St Simon Stakes. Their dam, the useful mile-and-a-half winner Place de L'Opera, a half-sister to the Irish Two Thousand Guineas winner Indian Haven out of the Park Hill winner Madame Dubois, is also responsible for Zero Tolerance (by Nashwan), a smart miler in 2006. Hala Bek is the fifth foal of Place de L'Opera. The latest of racing age is Dar Es Salaam, a two-year-old by King's Best, in training with Ed Dunlop in 2006. Hala Bek's sire Halling, a dual winner of the Eclipse and the International, will stand at Darley Stud in Newmarket again in 2007 after spending three seasons in Dubai. He has been a fair influence for stamina at stud and his progeny have tended to get better with age, Franklins Gardens winning the York-shire Cup as a six-year-old in 2006. As his form stands, Hala Bek is already good enough to make short work of the opposition at minor pattern level, and being a big, strong, attractive colt—he made 130,000 guineas as a yearling—he should mature into a still more imposing individual at four. His inexperience was there for all to see as he whinnied his way round the paddock at Epsom, and, before being side-lined, he had the potential to go right to the top with more racing. He will prove equally effective at a mile and a quarter as at a mile and a half. *M. A. Jarvis*

HALCYON MAGIC 8 b.g. Magic Ring (IRE) 115 – Consistent Queen 55 (Queen's – Hussar 124) [2006 60, a56: p10g f11g p12.2g⁵ p12.2g 10d 10m 8m 8.1f 8m 8d 8d Oct 8] sturdy gelding: fair performer in his day: little form in 2006: blinkered. *M. Wigham*

HALFWAYTOPARADISE 3 b.f. Observatory (USA) 131 – Always On My Mind 91 **66** (Distant Relative 128) [2006 69: f6g⁶ 6v⁵ 6f p8.6g p7g⁶ 7f² 6g 7.1m 7g² p7g p6g f7g **a56** p7g Dec 18] sturdy filly: fair maiden on turf, modest on all-weather: left M. Bell after fifth start: stays 7f: acts on polytrack, firm and soft going: tried visored, wears cheekpieces nowadays: hung markedly left sixth outing: reportedly had breathing problem next time. *W. G. M. Turner*

HALICARNASSUS (IRE) 2 b.c. (Mar 15) Cape Cross (IRE) 129 – Launch Time **107** (USA) (Relaunch (USA)) [2006 7m* 7m* 7d Oct 14] 35,000Y: rather leggy colt: half-brother to 1m winner Follow My Lead (by Night Shift) and 3 winners in North America: dam, placed in USA, half-sister to high-class Irish/US performer up to 1¼m Executive Pride: useful form: successful at Newmarket on first 2 starts, in maiden (dead-heated with Norisan) in June and 7-runner Weatherbys Superlative Stakes in July, in latter 33/1 and much improved to beat He's A Decoy by ½ length, last to first having gone in snatches: off 3 months, well beaten in Dewhurst Stakes final start: withdrawn from Royal Lodge Stakes at Ascot on similar going previous month: will stay 1m. *M. R. Channon*

HALKERSTON 2 ch.g. (Feb 6) Medicean 128 – Summer Daze (USA) (Swain (IRE) **60 p** 134) [2006 7s Oct 10] 10,000F, 14,000Y: strong, good-bodied gelding: first foal: dam unraced: 25/1, burly and green when mid-field in maiden at Newbury won by Mythical Kid: gelded after: should do better. *C. G. Cox*

Weatherbys Superlative Stakes, Newmarket—in a race run for the first time as a Group 2, Halicarnassus (No.4) stays on strongly from a poor position to foil He's A Decoy; Admiralofthefleet is third

HALLAND 8 ch.g. Halling (USA) 133 – Northshiel 85 (Northfields (USA)) [2006 –: **65** p16g⁶ 20s 14.1g 13.1g⁵ p16.5g⁵ 13.9s³ 18s Oct 16] quite attractive gelding: fair performer **a72** nowadays: probably stays 2¼m: acts on any going: tried in cheekpieces (well beaten) twice: has shown signs of temperament. *T. J. Fitzgerald*

HALLA SAN 4 b.g. Halling (USA) 133 – St Radegund 85 (Green Desert (USA) 127) **86** [2006 74: 10g⁵ 12.1s* 12s⁴ 12m* 12s Oct 6] tall gelding: has a quick action: fairly useful handicapper: won at Beverley in August and Goodwood in September: stays 1½m: acts on soft and good to firm going: effective held up or ridden prominently. *R. A. Fahey*

HALLINGS OVERTURE (USA) 7 b.g. Halling (USA) 133 – Sonata (Polish Pre- **66** cedent (USA) 131) [2006 p8.6g p7.1g p10g 8d 8s⁶ 9m p10g* 8.1m p8g p10g* Dec 3] robust gelding: fair performer: missed 2005: won handicaps at Lingfield in August and December: stays 1¼m: acts on polytrack, probably on soft going. *C. A. Horgan*

HALL OF FAME 2 b.g. (Jan 26) Machiavellian (USA) 123 – Petrushka (IRE) 126 **73** (Unfuwain (USA) 131) [2006 8.2s⁶ 8.2d⁴ p7g⁴ Nov 22] small, attractive gelding: first foal: dam, 7f (including at 2 yrs) to 1½m (including Irish Oaks and Yorkshire Oaks) winner, out of half-sister to Spectrum: fair form in maidens: likely to stay 1¼m/1½m: joined M. Johnston. *Saeed bin Suroor*

HALLUCINATE 4 b.g. Spectrum (IRE) 126 – Swift Spring (FR) 56 (Bluebird (USA) **–** 125) [2006 66: p13.9g Feb 6] leggy gelding: maiden: well below form only outing in 2006. *R. A. Fahey*

HAMAASY 5 b.g. Machiavellian (USA) 123 – Sakha 109 (Wolfhound (USA) 126) **63** [2006 68: 6v 7g⁵ 6m 6m² 5f 6m 6g³ 7m³ 8.5g f6g* Oct 12] quite attractive gelding: modest performer: won banded event at Southwell in October: best at 6f/7f: acts on all-weather, good to firm and good to soft going: twice tongue tied at 2 yrs: visored final 4-y-o outing: races prominently. *D. Nicholls*

HAMILTON HOUSE 2 b.g. (Mar 6) Bahamian Bounty 116 – Grove Dancer 61 **–** (Reprimand 122) [2006 7d Sep 29] strong gelding: backward in maiden at Newmarket: gelded after. *M. H. Tompkins*

HAMMER OF THE GODS (IRE) 6 ch.g. Tagula (IRE) 116 – Bhama (FR) (Habitat **65** 134) [2006 73: p5.1g² p5.1g⁴ p6g² 6.1m⁴ 5.3m³ p6g⁴ 6f³ 0f p6g⁵ p6g⁵ p6g p5g² p6g **a85** Nov 24] strong gelding: poor mover: fairly useful handicapper on all-weather, fair on turf: left Mrs L. Featherstone after third outing: won at Lingfield in June: best at 5f/easy 6f: acts on polytrack and good to firm going: tried visored, blinkered nowadays: tongue tied: effective held up or ridden prominently. *P. S. McEntee*

HAMMERS BOY (IRE) 2 b.c. (Feb 9) Mujadil (USA) 119 – Majesty's Nurse (Indian **102** King (USA) 128) [2006 5d⁴ 6d* 7.5f² 6m 7g⁵ 7m* Aug 5] €40,000F, 25,000Y: close-coupled colt: has a quick action: brother to useful 1m/9f winner in South Africa, UAE and USA Dancal and half-brother to several winners, including fairly useful Irish 1½m winner Sherabi (by Shernazar): dam Irish sprinter: useful performer: won maiden at Leopardstown in May and nursery at Galway in August: well beaten (inadequate test) in Coventry Stakes at Royal Ascot fourth start: will stay 1m: sent to Hong Kong, where renamed Beautiful Dreamer. *T. Stack, Ireland*

HAMOODY (USA) 2 ch.c. (Mar 23) Johannesburg (USA) 127 – Northern Gulch **106 p** (USA) (Gulch (USA)) [2006 6m* 6f* 7d Oct 14] $75,000Y, 210,000 2-y-o: strong, well-

Sterling Insurance Richmond Stakes, Goodwood—
Hamoody (left) lands the odds narrowly from Bodes Galaxy; Dubai's Touch (blaze) is third

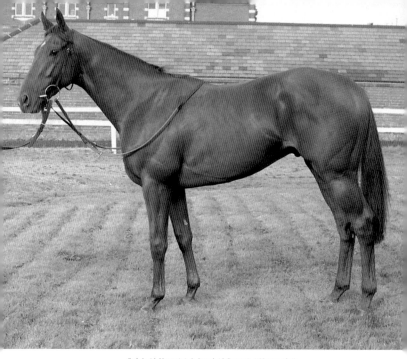

Saleh Al Homaizi & Imad Al Sagar's "Hamoody"

made colt: fluent mover: fifth foal: dam, maiden in USA, half-sister to US Grade 3 8.5f/9f winner Stylish Star: useful form: won minor event at Newmarket in July and 7-runner Sterling Insurance Richmond Stakes at Goodwood (beat Bodes Galaxy by head) in August, racing with plenty of zest both times: 9/1, weakened into rear in Dewhurst Stakes at Newmarket final start: free-going sort, may prove best at 5f/6f: acts on firm ground: probably remains capable of better. *P. W. Chapple-Hyam*

HAMS (USA) 3 b. or br.f. Dixie Union (USA) 121 – Desert Victress (USA) 70 (Desert Wine (USA)) [2006 7.1g² 7m² 7g⁶ May 9] $150,000F: smallish, rather leggy filly: seventh foal: half-sister to 3 winners, including US 1996 Grade 2 2-y-o 6.5f winner Desert Digger (by Mining): dam, maiden in Britain who stayed 1m, later 6f winner in USA: fair maiden: will stay 1m: sold 32,000 gns in July. *M. Johnston*   **67**

HANAZAKARI 5 b.g. Danzero (AUS) – Russian Rose (IRE) 82 (Soviet Lad (USA)) [2006 p10g f16g⁵ Mar 21] poor maiden: tried visored. *J. A. R. Toller*   **41**

HANBRIN BHOY (IRE) 2 b.c. (Feb 1) Cape Cross (IRE) 129 – Sea of Stone (USA) 71 (Sanglamore (USA) 126) [2006 7f⁴ 6s³ p7g* Nov 1] 11,000F, 10,000Y: fourth foal: half-brother to 6-y-o Miss Pebbles and French 9f to 1¼m winner Sea of Luck (by Ezzoud), both fairly useful: dam maiden who stayed 1¾m: fair form, winning maiden at Kempton by a head from Buddies Girl: will be suited by 1m/1¼m. *R. Dickin*   **73 +**

HAND CHIME 9 ch.g. Clantime 101 – Warning Bell 88 (Bustino 136) [2006 63, a68: p7.1g³ p8 6g p7g⁶ p8g p7g² p7g³ p7.1g⁶ p8g⁴ p7g⁵ p7g 7f Jun 6] angular gelding: fair handicapper on all-weather, modest on turf: stays easy 1m: yet to race on heavy going, acts on any other turf/all-weather: sometimes slowly away: free-going sort: has reportedly bled. *E. R. Oertel*   **– a69**

HAND OF DESTINY (USA) 3 ch.g. High Yield (USA) 121 – Special Happening **52**
(USA) (Relaunch (USA)) [2006 54: p8.6g² p8.6g 8g f8g Jul 7] modest maiden: will stay
1¼m: acts on polytrack: tried tongue tied/blinkered. *N. P. Littmoden*

HANDSET (USA) 2 ch.f. (Apr 29) Distant View (USA) 126 – Call Account (USA) **56**
(Private Account (USA)) [2006 8.2g¹ Sep 26] good-topped filly: fifth foal: sister to useful
2002 2-y-o 7f winner Dialing Tone, closely related to fairly useful French 1¼m winner
Home Call (by Chester House) and half-sister to French 1m winner Forest Canopy (by
Forest Wildcat): dam 7f to 8.5f winner in USA: 14/1, poorly to post, faded/hung when
sixth in maiden at Nottingham won by Shorthand. *H. R. A. Cecil*

HANDSOME CROSS (IRE) 5 b.g. Cape Cross (IRE) 129 – Snap Crackle Pop (IRE) **95**
87 (Statoblest 120) [2006 92: p6g p5g 5d 5f² 5g⁴ 5m* 5.1g² 5.1m⁴ 5m² 5f⁶ 5m 6f⁶ 5m⁵
5.1g⁴ 5.1m² 5d 5.1f³ Sep 23] strong gelding: useful handicapper: won GNER Scottish
Sprint Cup at Musselburgh in June by neck from Peace Offering: mostly creditable efforts
after: stays easy 6f: acts on firm going: races up with pace: consistent. *D. Nicholls*

HANDSOME FALCON 2 b.g. (Jan 31) Kyllachy 129 – Bonne Etoile 94 (Diesis 133) **78 p**
[2006 5m* Sep 19] 19,000F: fourth foal: half-brother to French 11f/1½m winner Coming
Home (by Vettori) and French 13f winner Xanthus (by Hector Protector): dam, 1m/1¼m
winner, out of smart middle-distance stayer/US Grade 1 1¼m winner Bonne Ile: 14/1,
overcame greenness to win minor event at Beverley (beat Ice Mountain by neck), getting
up close home: will do better. *R. A. Fahey*

HANEEN (USA) 3 b.f. Bahri (USA) 125 – Tamgeed (USA) 66 (Woodman (USA) 126) **67**
[2006 70: 8d⁶ 9.9m⁴ Jun 16] smallish, leggy filly: fair maiden: seems to stay 1¼m: sold
3,000 gns in July. *J. L. Dunlop*

HANELLA (IRE) 3 b.f. Galileo (IRE) 134 – Strutting (IRE) 95 (Ela-Mana-Mou 132) **79**
[2006 7s 8m⁶ 8.1d² 10.2f* 10m* 12g⁶ Aug 25] €45,000Y, 25,000 2-y-o: seventh foal:
half-sister to smart Irish 7f/1¼m winner Chiming (by Danehill): dam 7f (at 2 yrs) and
1¼m winner: fair handicapper: won at Bath in July and Newbury in August: stays 1¼m:
acts on firm going. *R. M. Beckett*

HANGING ON 2 b.f. (May 13) Spinning World (USA) 130 – Lydia Maria 70 (Dancing **89**
Brave (USA) 140) [2006 7m* 7m p8g³ Oct 20] smallish, workmanlike filly: half-sister to
several winners, including 7-y-o Barolo and 4-y-o Propinquity: dam maiden who stayed
1¼m: fairly useful form: won maiden at Newmarket in August: improvement when
eighth in Prestige Stakes at Goodwood (still green) and third in nursery at Lingfield: will
stay 1¼m. *W. R. Swinburn*

HANG LOOSE 3 b.g. Agnes World (USA) 123 – My Cadeaux 93 (Cadeaux Genereux **70**
131) [2006 68p: p5g⁴ 5f⁶ 6g 6s p7g⁶ p6g⁶ Nov 14] fair maiden: left R. Charlton 20,000
gns after third start: stays 7f: acts on polytrack and good to firm ground· tried blinkered/
in checkpieces: gelded after final outing. *S. W. Hall*

HANNICEAN 2 ch.c. (Apr 9) Medicean 128 – Hannah's Music 85 (Music Boy 124) **76 p**
[2006 7d⁵ Oct 28] big, strong, lengthy colt: fourth foal: half-brother to useful 7f/1m
winner Russian Rhapsody (by Cosmonaut) and fairly useful 6f winner Wax Lyrical (by
Safawan): dam, 5f winner, ran only at 2 yrs: 33/1, promising fifth of 19 to Mr Napper
Tandy in maiden at Newmarket, never far away but green virtually throughout: sure to
improve, and should win races. *M. A. Jarvis*

HANOONA (IRE) 3 ch.f. Zafonic (USA) 130 – Wedoudah (IRE) 80 (Sadler's Wells **94**
(USA) 132) [2006 87: 10.1g² 10d May 19] tall, well-made filly: has scope: fairly useful
performer: creditable second in minor event at Epsom on reappearance: may have been
amiss in listed race at Newbury: seems to stay 1¼m: acts on good to firm ground: highly
strung (has got loose in parade ring/been led to start). *M. R. Channon*

HANSEMELLE (IRE) 4 b.f. Titus Livius (FR) 115 – Handsome Anna (IRE) 67 **63**
(Bigstone (IRE) 126) [2006 72: 8.3m⁴ 7.2d 8.3f 9.2g² 9.2m 7.9f⁴ 12.1g 8.5m 10.5g 9.2d⁶
7.2s² 7.2v⁵ Oct 28] workmanlike filly: modest performer: stays 9f: acts on any turf going:
none too consistent: sold 6,000 gns. *B. Mactaggart*

HANSOMIS (IRE) 2 b.f. (Apr 9) Titus Livius (FR) 115 – Handsome Anna (IRE) 67 **69**
(Bigstone (IRE) 126) [2006 6m⁶ 6m⁵ 7s⁴ 6v² Oct 28] leggy, quite attractive filly: third
foal: sister to 3-y-o The History Man and 4-y-o Hansomelle: dam Irish maiden who probably stayed 8.5f: fair maiden: short-head second in nursery at Ayr: stays 7f: acts on heavy
and good to firm ground. *B. Mactaggart*

HAOIN AN BOTHAR (IRE) 2 b.c. (May 6) Bishop of Cashel 122 – Drefflane Ann **64**
(IRE) (Petorius 117) [2006 7g 7v p6m⁶ p9.5g⁴ Dec 9] sixth foal: dam unraced: modest
maiden: improved form when equal-fourth in claimer at Wolverhampton: blinkered on
debut. *Adrian Sexton, Ireland*

HA'PENNY BEACON 3 ch.f. Erhaab (USA) 127 – Beacon (High Top 131) [2006 9v³ **68**
f11g² p12.2m⁴ 16v Oct 25] closely related to useful 1994 2-y-o 7f/1m winner Indian
Light (by Be My Chief) who stayed 1½m and half-sister to 3 winners, including useful
1¼m and 1¾m winner Maycocks Bay (by Muhtarram): dam unraced half-sister to smart
performer up to 2½m Compton Ace: fair maiden: stays 1½m (seemingly not 2m): acts on
polytrack and heavy going: slowly away on debut. *D. Carroll*

HAPPY AS LARRY (USA) 4 b. or br.g. Yes It's True (USA) 116 – Don't Be Blue **99**
(USA) (Henbane (USA) 91) [2006 85: p7g p7g p6g 8.3m p7.1g⁶ 5.4f 6m p7g p7.1g
p8.6g* p8.6g* p9.5g² p10g² p8g* Dec 30] useful handicapper: left Saeed bin Suroor after
sole 3-y-o start: better than ever in 2006, winning at Wolverhampton in November and
December and Lingfield (by ½ length from Lacework) later in December: stays 1¼m: acts
on polytrack, well held on turf: has worn visor/blinkers/tongue tie. *T. J. Pitt*

HAPPY GO LILY 2 b.f. (Mar 24) In The Wings 128 – Lil's Jessy (IRE) 101 (Kris 135) **83 p**
[2006 p8g* Nov 5] 65,000Y: second foal: closely related to smart Irish 1m winner Paris
Winds (by Galileo): dam, 7f winner (at 2 yrs, and Nell Gwyn Stakes), half-sister to smart
French miler Lone Bid: 12/1, promising debut when winning 12-runner maiden at Lingfield by length from Lacework, held up after slowish start and not hard ridden to assert
final 1f: sure to progress. *W. R. Swinburn*

HAPPY HARRY (IRE) 3 b.g. Raphane (USA) 102 – Zalotti (IRE) 84 (Polish Patriot **–**
(USA) 128) [2006 43: 8.3m 7.9m Jul 8] poor maiden: well held in 2006: blinkered on
reappearance. *B. Storey*

HAPPY LOVE 2 b.f. (Mar 4) Royal Applause 124 – Ivory's Joy 109 (Tina's Pet 121) **55**
[2006 5g Apr 19] 62,000Y: rather leggy, useful-looking filly: second foal: dam 5f/6f
winner, including at 2 yrs: 14/1 and green, weakened in maiden at Newmarket won by
Silk Blossom. *M. Johnston*

HARARE 5 b.g. Bahhare (USA) 122 – Springs Eternal 69 (Salse (USA) 128) [2006 62: **71**
p8.6g³ p8g 10.2m⁵ 10.9f³ 10.2m⁴ 12.1g³ 12.1f p9.5f* p8.6g 8m² p8.6g⁵ p8.6g* Dec 11]
workmanlike gelding: fair handicapper: won at Wolverhampton in August (apprentice
event) and December: effective at 8.6f, barely stays 1½m: acts on polytrack and firm
going: often blinkered nowadays: has found little. *R. J. Price*

HARBOUR HOUSE 7 b.g. Distant Relative 128 – Double Flutter 92 (Beldale Flutter **43**
(USA) 130) [2006 48: p6g p7g Feb 7] leggy gelding: poor performer: effective at 5f to
easy 1m: acts on polytrack and any turf going: tried blinkered/visored (not since 2003).
J. J. Bridger

HARCOURT (USA) 6 b.g. Cozzene (USA) – Ballinamallard (USA) 112 (Tom Rolfe) **68**
[2006 84: p10g 11g 11.7d 11.6m 8d 11s Oct 10] rangy gelding: fair handicapper nowadays: probably stays 1½m: acts on polytrack, soft and good to firm going: tried blinkered.
M. Madgwick

HARD AS IRON 2 b.c. (Mar 15) Iron Mask (USA) 117 – Runs In The Family 69 **64**
(Distant Relative 128) [2006 7g p7g p7g⁶ Nov 11] sturdy, workmanlike colt: modest form
in maidens. *M. Blanshard*

HARD TO CATCH (IRE) 8 b.g. Namaqualand (USA) – Brook's Dilemma 80 **65**
(Known Fact (USA) 135) [2006 80, a76: p7g³ p6g p7g p6g p6g⁶ p5.1g⁶ 6g Jun 6] close-
coupled gelding: fair handicapper, better on turf than all-weather: effective at 5f to 7f:
acts on all-weather, firm and good to soft going: visored once, often blinkered: has been
slowly away. *D. K. Ivory*

HARD TO EXPLAIN (IRE) 3 br.c. Marju (IRE) 127 – Kesh Kumay (IRE) 76 (Dane- **107**
hill (USA) 126) [2006 83: p8.6g² 10d 12m p8.5f⁶ Sep 8] well-made colt: useful performer: easily best effort when short-head second to Cimyla in minor event at Wolverhampton
on reappearance (final outing for E. O'Neill): below form subsequently, including in
King George V Stakes (Handicap) at Royal Ascot on third outing (left L. Cumani after):
should be suited by 1¼m+: acts on polytrack and good to soft going. *R. Baker, Canada*

HARD TOP (IRE) 4 b.g. Darshaan 133 – Well Head (IRE) (Sadler's Wells (USA) 132) **115**
[2006 120: 12s 12m⁵ 12m⁵ 12f⁴ Jul 1] big, lengthy gelding: smart performer, lightly
raced: not quite so good as in 2005, but better than bare result when fifth behind Policy

Maker in Grand Prix de Chantilly (left with lot to do) and Maraahel in Hardwicke Stakes at Royal Ascot (pulled too hard): well below form in listed event at Newmarket final start: gelded after: best form at 1½m: acts on good to firm ground, well beaten both starts on soft. *Sir Michael Stoute*

HARDY NORSEMAN (IRE) 3 b.g. Mull of Kintyre (USA) 114 – Miss Willow Bend (USA) (Willow Hour (USA)) [2006 69: p5g⁵ p6g⁶ p5g² a6g² a6f² a6g* a6g⁵ a6d a6g Dec 3] sturdy gelding: fair performer: sold from W. Jarvis 9,500 gns after third start: won minor event at Jagersro in September: effective at 5f/6f: acts on polytrack/dirt and good to firm ground: tried blinkered. *Madeleine Smith, Sweden* **65**

HARLAND 2 b.c. (Apr 13) Halling (USA) 133 – White Star (IRE) 108 (Darshaan 133) [2006 7d⁵ Oct 10] fourth foal: dam, French 11f/1½m winner, out of US Grade 1 winner at 8.5f to 1¼m White Star Line: 14/1, faded into fifth in maiden at Leicester (raced alone until halfway): should do better. *M. A. Jarvis* **75 p**

HARLESTONE LINN 4 ch.g. Erhaab (USA) 127 – Harlestone Lake 78 (Riboboy (USA) 124) [2006 62: 17.2s 14.1m 17.2f⁶ 16.4f Jul 13] compact gelding: modest maiden handicapper: should be suited by 2¼m+: acts on firm and soft ground. *J. L. Dunlop* **54**

HAROLDINI (IRE) 4 b.g. Orpen (USA) 116 – Ciubanga (IRE) (Arazi (USA) 135) [2006 50: p6g 6m f6g² p6g⁴ p7.1g 6m f7g² p7.1g* f7g² f7g² p7.1g* Dec 28] lengthy gelding: fair performer: won maiden claimer at Southwell in May, and handicap and band-event and handicap at Wolverhampton in December: effective at 5f to 7f: acts on all-weather, good to firm and good to soft going: usually wears cheekpieces. *J. Balding* **– a70**

HARRIETS DREAM 2 b.f. (Mar 6) Foxhound (USA) 103 – Rythm N Time 75 (Timeless Times (USA) 99) [2006 5.1m 5.1g Jun 13] workmanlike filly: third foal: dam 5f winner, including at 2 yrs: broke down fatally second start (well held debut). *Peter Grayson* **–**

HARRINGTON BATES 5 ch.g. Wolfhound (USA) 126 – Fiddling 82 (Music Boy 124) [2006 56: 5d 5g⁶ 6g p6g⁶ 6g 6g 5s⁴ 5d³ 5s⁶ 6v f6g² 5v Oct 31] strong, compact gelding: modest maiden: best at 5f/6f: acts on polytrack, firm and soft going: tried in cheekpieces, often visored. *R. M. Whitaker* **53**

HARRISON'S FLYER (IRE) 5 b.g. Imperial Ballet (IRE) 110 – Smart Pet 77 (Petong 126) [2006 88, a85: 5g 5m 5m 5.2m³ 5g³ 5.1f⁶ 5g⁵ 5.1g³ 5g² 5.2m³ p6g 5m³ 5.3d* 5s 5.3g³ p5.1g p5.1m p5.1g⁴ p5.1g⁶ p6g p6g Dec 30] good-topped gelding: fair handicapper: won at Brighton in September: best at 5f/6f: acts on all-weather, firm and soft going: usually wears headgear: signs of temperament, but generally consistent. *J. M. Bradley* **75**

HARRYS HOUSE 4 gr.g. Paris House 123 – Rum Lass 54 (Distant Relative 128) [2006 68: 5d 5g² 5g⁶ 6v⁵ 5s Oct 24] close-coupled gelding: fair handicapper: likely to prove best at 5f/6f: acts on soft and good to firm ground, probably on firesand: visored last 4 outings at 3 yrs, in cheekpieces last 4 starts: sold 5,200 gns. *J. J. Quinn* **72**

HARRY THE HAWK 2 b.g. (Feb 21) Pursuit of Love 124 – Elora Gorge (IRE) (High Estate 127) [2006 6m 7.5m⁵ 8s Oct 7] quite good-topped gelding: modest form second start in maidens. *T. D. Walford* **63**

HARRY TRICKER 2 b.g. (Mar 13) Hernando (FR) 127 – Katy Nowaitee 112 (Komaite (USA)) [2006 7d Oct 28] good-topped gelding: second foal: dam 1m to 1¼m winner (including Cambridgeshire): 80/1, not knocked about in mid-field in maiden at Newmarket won by Spanish Moon: should progress. *Mrs A. J. Perrett* **71 p**

HARRY UP 5 ch.g. Piccolo 121 – Faraway Lass 94 (Distant Relative 128) [2006 91: f5g p5.1g 5m 5.1g⁶ p6g* 5f⁵ 5f² 6f⁵ 5d 6d p6g p6g p5g* Dec 10] strong gelding: fairly useful handicapper: won at Wolverhampton in July and Kempton in December, latter by ¾ length from Talbot Avenue: effective at 5f/6f: acts on all-weather, firm and soft ground: front runner. *K. A. Ryan* **94**

HART OF GOLD 2 b.g. (Feb 28) Foxhound (USA) 103 – Bullion 85 (Sabrehill (USA) 120) [2006 p5g³ 5.1s⁴ 5g p6g* 7.1f² p7.1g³ 7f⁵ 7m² 6d 7m* 7m² 7m⁵ Sep 16] 8,000Y: good-bodied gelding: fourth foal: half-brother to 3 winners, including 3-y-o Primo Gold and 4-y-o Keresforth: dam 2-y-o 1m winner: fairly useful performer: won maiden at Wolverhampton in June and nursery at Southwell in September: stays 7f: acts on polytrack and firm ground: sometimes edgy, once unseated to post: consistent. *M. J. Wallace* **89**

HARTSHEAD 7 b.g. Machiavellian (USA) 123 – Zalitzine (USA) 98 (Zilzal (USA) 137) [2006 99: 8f⁶ 7g² 8m⁵ 8.9m 8m³ 7f* 7f* 8g⁵ a8g³ Sep 10] tall, leggy gelding: useful handicapper: won at Catterick and Newcastle in July: also ran well when 3½ lengths second to Imperialistic at Catterick and fifth to Prince of Thebes at Ascot second/eighth **103**

starts: respectable third to Maybach in listed race at Taby final start: stays 1m: acts on dirt, firm and good to soft ground: waited with: reliable. *G. A. Swinbank*

HARVEST JOY (IRE) 2 b.f. (Apr 15) Daggers Drawn (USA) 114 – Windomen (IRE) **89** (Forest Wind (USA) 111) [2006 5f⁵ 6s⁴ 6m² 6.1f* 7.1m³ 7m Aug 27] €7,000Y: lengthy, good-bodied filly: third foal: half-sister to 3-y-o Touch of Ivory: dam unraced half-sister to smart Italian performer up to 1¼m Super Bobbina: fairly useful performer: won maiden at Nottingham in July: best run when third to Sudoor in listed race at Sandown: not discredited in Prestige Stakes at Goodwood (seventh of 10) final start: will stay 1m/ 1¼m: acts on firm going: signs of temperament. *B. R. Millman*

HARVEST QUEEN (IRE) 3 ch.f. Spinning World (USA) 130 – Royal Bounty (IRE) **100** 80 (Generous (IRE) 139) [2006 70p: 8.2m⁵ 8.2g* 8m⁵ 7m 8g⁴ 8d⁵ Oct 28] tall, good-topped filly: useful performer: impressive winner of maiden in May and handicap (by 2½ lengths from Famcred) in June, both at Nottingham: good fourth to Rain Stops Play in handicap at Newmarket penultimate start: below par in similar event there final start: bred to stay 1¼m: raced mainly on polytrack and good/good to firm going. *P. J. Makin*

HARVEST WARRIOR 4 br. or gr.g. Mujahid (USA) 125 – Lammastide 93 (Martin- **93 d** mas 128) [2006 91: 8s³ 10v⁴ 8g⁴ 7.2g 8.1s 8.9m 7f 7m⁶ 6g 7g⁶ 7.1s Sep 7] tall, leggy gelding: fairly useful handicapper: creditable third at Redcar on reappearance: below form after: stays 1m (seemingly not 1¼m): acts on soft going: usually blinkered: often slowly away: sold 5,500 gns. *T. D. Easterby*

HASAYAZ (IRE) 3 b.c. Barathea (IRE) 127 – Hasainiya (IRE) 109 (Top Ville 129) **96** [2006 10g 10m³ p12g* p12g² Oct 21] strong, good-bodied colt: half-brother to several winners, including 11f and 13f winner Hasanpour (by Dr Devious) and Irish 9f winner Hasikiya (by Green Desert), both useful: dam Irish 1¼m winner: useful form: won maiden at Kempton (tended to hang left) in May: good second on handicap debut at Lingfield final start: stays 1½m: acts on polytrack, probably on good to firm ground: slowly away first 2 outings: sold 68,000 gns, sent to Spain. *Sir Michael Stoute*

HASSAAD 3 b.g. Danehill (USA) 126 – Ghazal (USA) 103 (Gone West (USA)) [2006 **88** 7s 7m⁵ 8m⁴ 9m⁴ 8m* p8g² p8g* Nov 22] sturdy gelding: first foal: dam, 6f winner (including at 2 yrs), sister to US Grade 3 7f/1m winner Elusive Quality and closely related to smart Irish 1999 2-y-o 5f/6f winner Rossini: fairly useful performer: gelded, won handicaps at Bath in September and Kempton in November: should stay 9f: acts on polytrack and good to firm ground, probably on soft: tried blinkered (seemed reluctant to race on one occasion): tongue tied last 3 starts. *W. J. Haggas*

HATCH A PLAN (IRE) 5 b.g. Vettori (IRE) 119 – Fast Chick 93 (Henbit (USA) 130) **74** [2006 74: p8.6g⁶ 9.7f 11.9g⁶ 10m⁴ 10.2m 11g² 10.1g 11m² 11.6f⁴ 11.6g* 10g⁴ Aug 21] leggy gelding: fair handicapper: won at Windsor in August: stays 1½m: acts on polytrack, best efforts on turf on good ground or firmer: wore cheekpieces final outing at 3 yrs. *Mrs A. J. Hamilton-Fairley*

HATHAAL (IRE) 7 b.g. Alzao (USA) 117 – Ballet Shoes (IRE) 75 (Ela-Mana-Mou **?** 132) [2006 10.5g⁴ a10.5s³ a12s a14g*ᵈⁱˢ f12g⁶ Dec 21] good-topped gelding: has a short, unimpressive action: useful performer for Sir Michael Stoute in 2002: won twice in Spain in 2003 and first past post (disqualified) in minor event at Mijas in April: well held on return to Britain: stays 1¾m: acts on sand, unraced on extremes of going: tried blinkered/ visored. *E. J. Creighton*

HATHERDEN 2 b.g. (Jan 30) Tobougg (IRE) 125 – Million Heiress (Auction Ring **–** (USA) 123) [2006 7.1g 8m Sep 9] robust gelding: no show in maidens. *Miss E. C. Lavelle*

HATHLEN (IRE) 5 b.g. Singspiel (IRE) 133 – Kameez (IRE) 72 (Arazi (USA) 135) **–** [2006 75, a66: p12g p16g Nov 8] leggy gelding: fair handicapper at best, better on turf than all-weather: well held both starts in 2006 (pulled up in latter): usually blinkered: somewhat wayward. *Mrs N. Smith*

HATTAN (IRE) 4 ch.c. Halling (USA) 133 – Luana 101 (Shaadi (USA) 126) [2006 **114** 116: 10m 10m⁴ 10d³ 12m⁴ 10m 10.4f² 10.5m³ 11.6g⁶ 11g⁶ 10m² Nov 5] leggy colt: smart performer: reportedly had a few minor problems early in season, and underwent dental treatment: several creditable efforts in 2006, including in York Stakes at York (second to Best Alibi), Rose of Lancaster Stakes at Haydock (third to Mulaqat) and Premio Roma at Rome (4 lengths second to Cherry Mix) sixth/seventh/final outings: stays 1½m: acts on firm and good to soft going: tends to hang, and sometimes looks quirky. *C. E. Brittain*

HATTON FLIGHT 2 b.c. (Apr 9) Kahyasi 130 – Platonic 79 (Zafonic (USA) 130) **52**
[2006 8m p8g⁶ p9.5g⁴ Nov 11] modest form in maidens. *A. M. Balding*

HAUGHTON HOPE 3 b.g. Daawe (USA) 103 – Kandymal (IRE) 52 (Prince of Birds **–**
(USA) 121) [2006 7.1g 7f 7d p8g p11g Nov 6] good-bodied gelding: well held in maidens/banded races, leaving J. Balding after second start. *T. J. Pitt*

HAULAGE MAN 8 ch.g. Komaite (USA) – Texita 65 (Young Generation 129) [2006 **55**
7.1v 7g⁵ 5f⁴ 6m 5.9m³ 6d⁴ Jul 9] tall gelding: modest handicapper: missed 2005: probably needs further than 5f, and stays 1m: acts on firm and good to soft going: often wears cheekpieces: often slowly away. *Karen McLintock*

HAUT LA VIE 2 b.g. (Mar 25) Josr Algarhoud (IRE) 118 – Spark of Life 63 (Rainbows **–**
For Life (CAN)) [2006 10.2m⁶ 8s 8.2s Oct 25] small, workmanlike gelding: little form, in seller final start. *R. F. Johnson Houghton*

HAVING A BALL 2 b.g. (Feb 5) Mark of Esteem (IRE) 137 – All Smiles 41 (Halling **60**
(USA) 133) [2006 p6g p6g⁵ p7.1g⁵ 7m Sep 6] smallish gelding: modest maiden: will probably stay 1m. *P. D. Cundell*

HAWAII PRINCE 2 b.g. (Feb 23) Primo Valentino (IRE) 116 – Bollin Rita 82 (Rambo **72 d**
Dancer (CAN) 107) [2006 5f 5g⁵ 6m³ 5f 5m Aug 3] 11,000 2-y-o: second foal: dam 6f winner: fair maiden: third to Champery at Newcastle: well held in nurseries (gelded after): stays 6f. *D. Nicholls*

HAWK ARROW (IRE) 4 ch.g. In The Wings 128 – Barbizou (FR) (Selkirk (USA) **63**
129) [2006 72: 11g 15d Oct 13] tall, quite good-topped gelding: modest performer nowadays: stays 11.6f: acts on firm going: has shown signs of temperament: joined G. L. Moore. *Miss S. West*

HAWKIT (USA) 5 b.g. Silver Hawk (USA) 123 – Hey Ghaz (USA) (Ghazi (USA)) **80**
[2006 80, a76: f12g² f11g* f12g³ p12.2g⁴ 9.9d⁶ 10.5g f11g³ 8g² 8.1s⁵ 10d⁵ 10.3g⁶ 9.1g* **a73**
10.3m² 8d⁶ 12.3m⁴ 9.2m⁴ 8.3g 10s* 9.1v 10s 9.1v³ Oct 28] rather leggy gelding: fairly useful performer on turf, fair on all-weather: won seller at Southwell (left P. D. Evans) in January, and handicap in June and seller (sold from A. Bailey 16,000 gns) in September, both at Ayr: stays 1½m: acts on all-weather, heavy and good to firm going: sometimes tongue tied: usually waited with. *P. Monteith*

HAWKSMOOR (IRE) 4 b.c. In The Wings 128 – Moon Cactus 118 (Kris 135) [2006 **–**
–: p12g Dec 13] tall colt: no form: tongue tied. *L. A. Dace*

HAWRIDGE KING 4 b.g. Erhaab (USA) 127 – Sadaka (USA) 77 (Kingmambo **76**
(USA) 125) [2006 74: 10.2g³ 10.2d³ 12g² 11.8d³ 12.6m² 12s Sep 22] quite good-topped gelding: fair maiden handicapper: stays 12.6f: acts on polytrack, firm and soft ground: visored last 2 starts: often held up: consistent: fair hurdler, successful in October. *W. S. Kittow*

HAWRIDGE PRINCE 6 b.g. Polar Falcon (USA) 126 – Zahwa 72 (Cadeaux **120**
Genereux 131) [2006 93: 12g 12g 11.6g⁵ 16g* 16d* 16d* Oct 14]
    The Devon stable of Rod Millman, put on the map in the past two seasons by the exploits of Sergeant Cecil, now houses a second candidate for the Cup races after the emergence in the autumn of Hawridge Prince. Sergeant Cecil may be much

David Wilson Homes Jockey Club Cup, Newmarket—Hawridge Prince, much improved since being stepped up in trip, easily completes a hat-trick; Bulwark hangs on to second from Balkan Knight

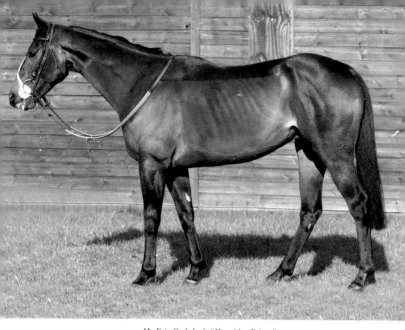

Mr Eric Gadsden's "Hawridge Prince"

better known but there is nothing between him and his stable-companion on form. Six-year-old Hawridge Prince progressed into a very smart stayer in the latest season, his first for the Millman stable to which he was transferred at the end of 2005 after the retirement of Millman's neighbour Gerald Cottrell. Hawridge Prince was developing along the right lines for Cottrell—winning two handicaps and finishing second in listed company as a four-year-old—but was forced to miss most of 2005 because of a paddock accident in which he injured his withers. Appearing for the first time for Millman after an absence of eleven months, Hawridge Prince finished in mid-division in a mile-and-a-half handicap at the Newmarket Craven meeting, giving the impression he would be better for the run. In the event, it was over three months before he was seen again and he showed little in another mile-and-a-half handicap at Ascot.

A better run when fifth in a listed event at Windsor (the race in which he had finished second two years earlier) was the signal for a new chapter in Hawridge Prince's career. Stepped up to two miles for the first time and starting at 20/1 off a BHB mark of 95, he put up a smart performance to win a handicap under 10-0 at Nottingham by five lengths in September and followed up nine days later with another five-length win, this time in the listed SIS Fenwolf Stakes over the same distance. Hawridge Prince couldn't have been more impressive at Ascot, improving on the bridle early in the straight and quickly settling the issue, value for even more than the winning margin over Frank Sonata. Striking while the iron was hot, connections saddled Hawridge Prince for the David Wilson Homes Jockey Club Cup on Champions Day at Newmarket. Sergeant Cecil had won the Prix du Cadran —a strong counter-attraction to the Jockey Club Cup—and Hawridge Prince completed a notable autumn double for the stable. The opposition was weaker than that faced by Sergeant Cecil at Longchamp but Hawridge Prince, who started 6/5 favourite in a field of seven, won smoothly, forging clear, despite hanging right, to win by six lengths from the Fenwolf fourth Bulwark. Hawridge Prince will face sterner tests in the next season but looks sure to give a good account of himself in top staying company.

Hawridge Prince (b.g. 2000)	Polar Falcon (USA) (b or br 1987)	Nureyev (b 1977)	Northern Dancer
			Special
		Marie d'Argonne (ch 1981)	Jefferson
			Mohair
	Zahwa (ch 1992)	Cadeaux Genereux (ch 1985)	Young Generation
			Smarten Up
		Peace Girl (b 1985)	Dominion
			Olderfleet

The big, lengthy Hawridge Prince is hardly stoutly bred, though his sire, the sprinter-miler Polar Falcon has been less of an influence for speed at stud than his own racing record would suggest, the average distance of races won by his progeny at three and above being nine furlongs. Hawridge Prince's dam Zahwa, a daughter of the useful Irish two-year-old sprinter Peace Girl, was only a fair maiden in Britain but she won at seven furlongs and a mile as a four-year-old in Germany after being exported. She is by Cadeaux Genereux, whose progeny have won at an average distance of just over seven furlongs. Zahwa is the dam of three winners, the others foaled either side of Hawridge Prince. Hawridge Prince's year-older half-brother, Hero's Journey (by Halling), was a smart miler at his best, while Hawridge Prince's year-younger half-brother, Psychiatrist (by Dr Devious), is a useful performer at around a mile. Hawridge Prince, who was gelded before he reached the racecourse, gives the impression he will stay beyond two miles (the Gold Cup at Royal Ascot is said to be on his agenda) and he acts on good to firm and good to soft going. *B. R. Millman*

HAWRIDGE SENSATION 4 ch.g. Polish Precedent (USA) 131 – Looks Sensational (USA) (Majestic Light (USA)) [2006 64: 7.1m 8.3f 8m 8.1f 7.6m 8.1m⁶ 8m p8.6g⁶ Sep 11] big, workmanlike gelding: modest performer: stays 1m, bred to be suited by further: acts on good to firm ground: visored penultimate outing (refused to race): tongue tied 3 of last 4 outings: ungenuine. *W. S. Kittow*   **59 §**

HAWRIDGE STAR (IRE) 4 b.g. Alzao (USA) 117 – Serenity 98 (Selkirk (USA) 129) [2006 83: 10.9g⁵ p12g 10.2d⁴ 11.6f 13.1m³ 16.2d⁵ Sep 16] close-coupled gelding: fair maiden handicapper: stays 13f: acts on soft and good to firm ground: tried visored: none too consistent: won over hurdles in November. *W. S. Kittow*   **78**

HAYDEN GRACE 3 ch.f. In The Wings 128 – Original Spin (IRE) 91 (Machiavellian (USA) 123) [2006 9.2f³ 10f⁴ Jul 11] 28,000Y: second foal: dam, 1¼m/1½m winner, half-sister to smart 1¼m performers Time Away and Time Ahead and granddaughter of Time Charter: fair form in frame in maidens at Hamilton and Pontefract: slowly away on debut: sold 10,000 gns in November. *M. Johnston*   **66**

HAYDOCK EXPRESS (IRE) 2 gr.g. (Feb 13) Keltos (FR) 132 – Blusienka (IRE) 102 (Blues Traveller (IRE) 119) [2006 p6g⁶ Dec 26] first foal: dam 2-y-o 1m winner: 25/1, looked green when sixth of 7 to Hollywood George in maiden at Wolverhampton, slowly away. *Peter Grayson*   **52**

HAYLEY'S FLOWER (IRE) 2 b.f. (May 3) Night Shift (USA) – Plastiqueuse (USA) (Quest For Fame 127) [2006 6s p7g p7.1g Nov 17] €3,500F: sturdy filly: fourth foal: half-sister to French 11f winner Anafield (by Anabaa): dam French 10.7f and 1½m winner: well held in maidens. *J. C. Fox*   **–**

HAYYANI (IRE) 4 ch.g. Almutawakel 126 – Just Rainbow (FR) (Rainbow Quest (USA) 134) [2006 86: p6g p7g* p7.1g p7g⁴ p8g p10g 7.1f⁶ 10g 11m 10f p10g 11g p7g⁴ Oct 5] close-coupled gelding: fairly useful performer on all-weather, fair on turf: won handicap at Lingfield in January: effective at 7f, barely stays 1¼m: acts on polytrack, best efforts on turf on good going: effective tongue tied or not: tried blinkered, including last 4 starts: free-going sort: sold 50,000 gns, sent to Saudi Arabia. *K. McAuliffe*   **76 a84**

HAZELHURST (IRE) 3 b.f. Night Shift (USA) – Iktidar 80 (Green Desert (USA) 127) [2006 67: 7f* 6.9g 8d Aug 18] strong, sturdy filly: has a quick action: fair performer: won handicap at Catterick in June: stays 7f: acts on firm and good to soft going: found little final start. *J. Howard Johnson*   **74**

HAZELNUT 3 b.f. Selkirk (USA) 129 – Cashew 80 (Sharrood (USA) 124) [2006 –p: 8.3d 8.3f p10g³ 10g* Oct 13] leggy filly: half-sister to several winners, most at least use-   **68**

ful, including smart 1m (including at 2 yrs)/1¼m winner Macadamia (by Classic Cliche) and 5-y-o Azarole: dam 1m winner: fair performer, lightly raced: won 3-runner handicap at Newmarket in October: stays 1¼m: acts on polytrack and good to soft going. *J. R. Fanshawe*

HAZEYMM (IRE) 3 b.c. Marju (IRE) 127 – Shimna 62 (Mr Prospector (USA)) [2006 **110** 98: 10g³ 11.5m² 10.5m 10m³ 12m⁴ Aug 1] lengthy, quite attractive colt: smart performer: won minor event at Newbury in April: good efforts after, including when head second to Linda's Lad in Derby Trial Stakes at Lingfield and 4¼ lengths fourth to Sixties Icon in BGC Stakes (Gordon) at Goodwood: stays 1½m: raced only on good/good to firm going: very reluctant at stall at Chantilly third outing: has made running: joined D. Selvaratnam in UAE. *M. R. Channon*

HAZIUM (IRE) 3 b.f. In The Wings 128 – Safe Care (IRE) (Caerleon (USA) 132) **65** [2006 –: p8g⁵ p10g p8g 8m 10m* p10g May 23] second foal: dam, unraced half-sister to smart sprinter Lugana Beach, out of half-sister to Mtoto: fair performer: won handicap at Navan in April: ran at Lingfield on 4 other occasions, well held final outing: stays 1¼m: acts on good to firm ground. *Patrick Morris, Ireland*

HAZZARD COUNTY (USA) 2 ch.c. (Apr 22) Grand Slam (USA) 120 – Sweet Lexy **80** May (USA) (Danzig (USA)) [2006 7m³ 7.1m³ 7m² 6d³ Oct 18] 45,000 2-y-o: leggy, quite attractive colt: fourth foal: half-brother to 3 winners in USA: dam unraced out of half-sister to top-class miler Northjet: fairly useful maiden: placed all starts: free-going type, should prove best up to 7f. *D. M. Simcock*

HEADLAND (USA) 8 b. or br.g. Distant View (USA) 126 – Fijar Echo (USA) (In Fijar **–** (USA) 121) [2006 47, a67: f8g p6g f6g p6g⁴ p7.1g³ f6g p6g 8g 8.5m f6g Nov 28] well- **a46** made gelding: poor performer: has form around 1m, better at shorter: acts on all-weather, soft and good to firm going: wears blinkers: tongue tied twice: sometimes slowly away. *D. W. Chapman*

HEADS TURN (IRE) 3 ch.f. Grand Lodge (USA) 125 – Belle Origine (USA) (Exclusive Native (USA)) [2006 –: 5.9m 7.2f⁵ 5.9m 11.1g 9.2d Sep 25] rather leggy filly: little form: blinkered final start. *E. J. Alston*

HEAD TO HEAD (IRE) 2 gr.g. (Mar 20) Mull of Kintyre (USA) 114 – Shoka (FR) 86 **44** (Kaldoun (FR) 122) [2006 p6g p6g f5g p5.1g³ Dec 29] poor maiden: gelded after second start: tried blinkered. *Peter Grayson*

HEALTH SPA 3 b.f. King's Theatre (IRE) 128 – Thermal Spring 77 (Zafonic (USA) **–** 130) [2006 –: p12g 9.7d Apr 11] neat filly: little form: visored in 2006. *B. R. Johnson*

HEART AND HAND (IRE) 2 b.f. (Apr 10) Bertolini (USA) 125 – Alchi (USA) 112 **46** (Alleged (USA) 138) [2006 6m 6g⁵ 7m p7.1g Dec 21] half-sister to several winners, including 3-y-o Supreme Charter and 9.4f to 13f winner Coolbythepool (by Bijou d'Inde), both fairly useful: dam French 2-y-o 1m winner and third in Prix Marcel Boussac: form only in seller second start (blinkered): left B. Meehan and off 6 months before final outing. *M. G. Quinlan*

HEARTBEAT 5 b.m. Pursuit of Love 124 – Lyrical Bid (USA) 77 (Lyphard (USA) **–** 132) [2006 48d: p10g Jan 14] good-bodied mare: maiden: well held only outing in 2006: tried visored/blinkered/tongue tied. *I. A. Wood*

HEARTCRUSHER (IRE) 4 ch.f. Alhaarth (IRE) 126 – Windini (Windjammer **61** (USA)) [2006 72: p9.5g 7g 10g⁴ 8.2m Jul 29] modest performer: stays 1¼m: acts on all-weather and heavy ground. *G. A. Swinbank*

HEARTHSTEAD DANCER (USA) 3 b. or br.f. Royal Academy (USA) 130 – **71** Amity (USA) (Afleet (CAN)) [2006 77p: 8d 10.5g⁴ Apr 29] leggy, workmanlike filly: has a rather round action: fair performer: stays 10.5f: acts on soft and good to firm ground: withdrawn, unruly at stall on intended final outing in May: joined N. Nevin in Ireland, 13,500 gns in July. *M. Johnston*

HEARTHSTEAD MAISON (IRE) 2 b.c. (May 16) Peintre Celebre (USA) 137 – **89 p** Pieds de Plume (FR) (Seattle Slew (USA)) [2006 8.1m* 8s⁵ Oct 7] fifth foal: half-brother to useful 1m (at 2 yrs)/1¼m winner Rave Reviews and 3-y-o Fermion (both by Sadler's Wells): dam, second at 1m in France on only start, half-sister to high-class French 1¼m performer Groom Dancer: impressive winner of maiden at Chepstow (beat Aaim To Prosper by 2½ lengths) in September: 7/2, better than result when well-held fifth behind Caldra in Autumn Stakes at Ascot, weakening after pressing on some way out (reportedly returned slightly lame): will be suited by 1¼m/1½m: should make a useful 3-y-o, and one to follow. *M. Johnston*

HEARTHSTEAD WINGS 4 b.g. In The Wings 128 – Inishdalla (IRE) 103 (Green **109 d**
Desert (USA) 127) [2006 108: 12m* 16m³ 13.9f 13.9d 12d 12s⁵ 11.6d Nov 4] rangy
gelding: useful performer: gelded, won minor event at Ripon (by 2 lengths from Palomar)
in April: creditable third to Cover Up in Sagaro Stakes at Lingfield next time: below form
after: effective at 1½m to easy 2m: acts on firm and soft going: edgy sort, tends to sweat:
tried blinkered (raced freely), visored nowadays: races prominently: joined P. Hobbs.
M. Johnston

HEART OF CORNWALL (IRE) 2 ch.c. (Feb 19) Singspiel (IRE) 133 – Kerenza **57 p**
(Seattle Dancer (USA) 119) [2006 8.2d Nov 1] lengthy, good-topped colt: sixth foal:
half-brother to smart French 1¼m to 1½m winner Jomana (by Darshaan) and fairly useful
2003 2-y-o 1m winner Massomah (by Seeking The Gold): dam, French 11f winner,
half-sister to high-class 2-y-o 6f/7f performer Local Suitor, Prix Jean Prat winner Local
Talent and to dam of outstanding miler Mark of Esteem: 11/1, needed experience when
seventh in maiden at Nottingham: should do better. Saeed bin Suroor

HEART OF GLASS (IRE) 2 ch.f. (Feb 14) Peintre Celebre (USA) 137 – Sallanches **–**
(USA) (Gone West (USA)) [2006 8.2d Nov 1] €58,000Y: rangy filly: fourth foal: half-
sister to 3 winners, including 3-y-o Leningrad: dam, French 9.5f winner, half-sister to
Arlington Million winner Mill Native: very green in maiden at Nottingham. M. L. W. Bell

HEART OF SVETLANA (IRE) 3 b. or br.f. Linamix (FR) 127 – Julius (IRE) 96 **91**
(Persian Bold 123) [2006 76: 10d⁴ 11v² 10g 13.1s* 12d 14d³ Nov 3] first foal: dam 1¼m/
1½m winner: fairly useful performer: successful in maiden at the Curragh at 2 yrs:
improved in 2006, leaving Ms F. Crowley in Ireland prior to winning handicap at Ayr in
September: good third in similar event at Musselburgh final start: stays 1¾m: raced
only on good going or softer (acts on heavy): gave trouble at stall penultimate outing.
M. Johnston

HEART'S CRY (JPN) 5 b.h. Sunday Silence (USA) – Irish Dance (JPN) (Tony **127**
Bin 134) [2006 127: 12m* 12m³ 12f Nov 26]
        Japanese-trained challengers in Europe are no longer looked on largely
for their curiosity value. Since the Group 1 victories of Seeking The Pearl and Taiki
Shuttle in France in 1998, there has been a steady stream of credible Japanese challengers for some of the top races. Agnes World won the Prix de l'Abbaye in 1999
and the July Cup in 2000 and El Condor Pasa won the Grand Prix de Saint-Cloud
and was runner-up in the 1999 Arc, since when Air Thule, Lohengrin, Telegnosis
and Zenno Rob Roy have all been placed in Group 1s in France or Britain. The
respective performances of Deep Impact and Heart's Cry in the latest Arc and King
George VI and Queen Elizabeth Stakes provided further evidence that the best
Japanese horses are able to hold their own in top company in Europe.
        Heart's Cry inflicted the first defeat on Japanese triple crown winner Deep
Impact in the Arima Kinen at Nakayama at the end of 2005. Though he finished
second in the previous year's Japanese Derby, Heart's Cry did not win at Group 1
level until pulling off his shock victory in the Arima Kinen, the first race in which
Deep Impact met horses outside his own age group. The Arima Kinen, Japan's end-
of-year, open-aged championship, was Heart's Cry's only victory as a four-year-
old, though he showed high-class form when finishing a close second in two other
Group 1s, the Takarazuka Kinen at Hanshin and the Japan Cup at Tokyo. The 2004
Japan Cup winner Zenno Rob Roy, just pipped in the International at York by Electrocutionist on his trip to Europe in 2005, was third in the two races, the Japan Cup
being won by British-trained Alkaased. Heart's Cry was lodged with Alkaased's
trainer Luca Cumani during his stay for the King George VI and Queen Elizabeth
Stakes, having been returned to Japan after the Dubai Sheema Classic at Nad Al
Sheba in March. Boosted significantly in prize money, the Sheema Classic
Sponsored by Nakheel overtook the Japan Cup as the world's most valuable event
over a mile and a half on turf, with a first prize of £1,714,286. Heart's Cry's stable-
companion Utopia got the Japanese off to a fine start on Dubai World Cup night by
winning the Godolphin Mile and Heart's Cry completed the double when making
all in the Sheema Classic, pushed out firmly to beat Collier Hill by four and a
quarter lengths, with ex-Irish Falstaff a length and a quarter further away in third,
ahead of Ouija Board (who started favourite) and Alexander Goldrun, the two
last-named held up and never able to reach the principals in a race in which it turned
out to be an advantage to lie handy. Heart's Cry was the second Japanese-trained
winner of the Sheema Classic, following Stay Gold in 2001.

Dubai Sheema Classic Sponsored By Nakheel, Nad Al Sheba
—the Japanese-trained Heart's Cry makes all in the joint-richest turf race ever run; he is clear of,
from right to left, Collier Hill, Falstaff and Ouija Board

Heart's Cry was not seen out between Nad Al Sheba and Ascot, an absence of four months which was apparently planned. Heart's Cry's trainer explained that the horse had been very immature as a three-year-old and, even at five, needed to be given several weeks to recover after his races. According to his trainer, Heart's Cry lost a lot of weight on the trip over for Ascot and things did not go so smoothly in his preparation as they had in Dubai—'Dubai was almost like being in Japan with all the horses together but, in the UK, Heart's Cry was by himself. When I arrived, he came up to me crying and upset which is very unlike him, though he ate well and was calm in his trackwork which allowed us to get him into what I would call "good condition", but not his best.' Connections said after the King George that they had briefly thought about scratching Heart's Cry. Heart's Cry had been ridden by French jockey Christophe Lemaire for the first time in the Japan Cup, in which Heart's Cry had been brought with a strong run in the straight. Lemaire rode him closer to the pace against Deep Impact in the Arima Kinen and sent him on in the Sheema Classic when none of his rivals seemed to want to make it. The change of tactics suited Heart's Cry but, with Cherry Mix acting as a pacemaker for Dubai World Cup winner Electrocutionist, he was ridden with more restraint at Ascot. Settled in third, Heart's Cry was actually reined back at around halfway and was in the last two in the small field before making ground smoothly rounding the home turn. Heart's Cry looked the likely winner after challenging strongly early in the final straight and hitting the front over a furlong out. In the end, he had to be content with third as he tired, changing his legs but finding no extra, going down by half a length and the same to Hurricane Run and Electrocutionist.

Heart's Cry's rider reported that the horse had 'blown up', though there had been no suggestion from paddock inspection that he had been produced anything but fully fit and raring to go. Heart's Cry's performance should give further confidence to Japanese owners and trainers, who receive significant incentives, including a bonus matching prize money won, from the Japan Racing Association to run their horses on the international stage. Hopefully, there will be a more regular flow of Japanese runners for Britain's major open-aged races. Heart's Cry was only the fourth Japanese challenger for the King George, following two that were housed with John Winter while in Britain, an early Japanese globe-trotter Speed Symboli, fifth to Park Top in 1969, and Sirius Symboli, eighth to Petoski in 1985. Air Shakur came fifth to Montjeu in 2000. Sirius Symboli and Air Shakur came over as three-year-olds, Sirius Symboli after winning the Japanese Derby and Air Shakur after finishing second in that race following victory in the Japanese Two Thousand Guineas. Whereas Speed Symboli and Sirius Symboli were sent off at 25/1 and 100/1 respectively in the King George, Air Shakur started at 10/1 and Heart's Cry at 3/1 second favourite behind odds-on Hurricane Run. Heart's Cry will not be returning to Britain. After being given another long break, he finished down the field in November behind Deep Impact in the Japan Cup and was retired after it was discovered that he had been affected by 'a whistling problem'.

```
                                                      ┌ Halo              ┌ Hail To Reason
                              ┌ Sunday Silence (USA) │  (b or br 1969)   │ Cosmah
                              │  (b or br 1986)      └ Wishing Well      └ Understanding
Heart's Cry (JPN)            │                         (b 1975)         ┌ Mountain Flower
(b.h. 2001)                  │                       ┌ Tony Bin         ┌ Kampala
                              │  Irish Dance (JPN)   │  (b 1983)        └ Severn Bridge
                              └  (b 1990)            └ Buper Dance      ┌ Lyphard
                                                        (b 1983)        └ My Bupers
```

Japanese breeding is rooted in European and American bloodstock—the country was once famed as a dumping ground for failed stallions—and some of the names in the extended pedigree of Heart's Cry will immediately be familiar to readers. His sire Sunday Silence won the Breeders' Cup Classic and two legs of the American Triple Crown and was champion sire in Japan in 2006 for the twelfth successive year (he is also sire of Deep Impact). Sunday Silence is now dead but the Shadai Stallion Station, where he stood and where Heart's Cry will be taking up stud duties in 2007, reportedly had fourteen of his sons on its roster in 2006, an indication of the enormous impact Sunday Silence has had in Japan. Heart's Cry's dam Irish Dance, who has bred two other Japanese winners to Sunday Silence, was a Group 3 winner in Japan, successful at up to a mile and a quarter. Irish Dance was at her best at four and five, the ages at which her sire the Prix de l'Arc de Triomphe winner Tony Bin reached his peak before embarking on a successful career at stud in Japan. Irish Dance is out of the unraced Lyphard filly Buper Dance, imported into Japan in 1989 and probably best known for being a three-parts sister to the one-time world-record-priced yearling Snaafi Dancer (10,200,000 dollars) who was retired to stud unraced, only to prove a failure as a stallion too. Buper Dance was also a sister to the very smart middle-distance performer Lyphard's Special and a half-sister to the champion American sprinter My Juliet who won twenty-four of her thirty-six starts and retired with earnings of 548,859 dollars, a far cry from the 1,581 dollars amassed by Heart's Cry's great grandam My Bupers in thirteen starts. My Juliet's Group 1-winning daughter Stella Madrid became the dam of the smart racemare in Japan, Diamond Biko. The tall, good-topped Heart's Cry, a substantial, imposing type, was best at around a mile and a half, and raced only on ground firmer than good. *K. Hashiguchi, Japan*

HEART SPRINGS 6 b.m. Parthian Springs 114 – Metannee 63 (The Brianstan 128) **55** [2006 68: p16g 16.2m Aug 28] leggy mare: handicapper: just modest form both starts in 2006: stays 2¼m: acts on firm and good to soft going: held up. *Dr J. R. J. Naylor*

HEATHCOTE 4 b.g. Unfuwain (USA) 131 – Chere Amie (USA) 75 (Mr Prospector **69** (USA)) [2006 77: 20s 14g Jun 1] leggy, plain gelding: fair performer: should stay 1¾m: acts on good to firm and good to soft going: wore cheekpieces final start: fairly useful form over hurdles. *G. L. Moore*

HEATHER MOOR (USA) 3 b.f. Diesis 133 – High Walden (USA) 111 (El Gran **80** Senor (USA) 136) [2006 79p: 8.2m³ 7.5g⁴ 8f* 9.7f⁵ Jul 27] smallish, well-made filly: fairly useful performer: won maiden at Brighton in July: good fifth in handicap at Folkestone final start: stayed 9.7f: acted on polytrack and firm ground: raced freely second start: sold 400,000 gns in November, and visits Araafa. *Sir Michael Stoute*

HEATHERS GIRL 7 ch.m. Superlative 118 – Kristis Girl 76 (Ballacashtal (CAN)) **57** [2006 p13.9g f11g* p9.5g⁴ p10g May 15] modest performer: won banded race at Southwell in April: stays 1½m: acts on all-weather: well held only outing in blinkers. *R. Dickin*

HEATHYARDS JOY 5 ch.m. Komaite (USA) – Heathyards Lady (USA) 76 (Mining **36** (USA)) [2006 47, a54: f8g⁴ p9.5g³ p8.6g⁴ p9.5g³ 10f⁵ Jun 20] smallish mare: modest **a51** maiden on all-weather: poor on turf: stays 10.2f: acts on all-weather and firm going: has worn cheekpieces: carried head awkwardly final start. *R. Hollinshead*

HEATHYARDS PRIDE 6 b.g. Polar Prince (IRE) 117 – Heathyards Lady (USA) 76 **–** (Mining (USA)) [2006 72, a85+: p12g⁶ f12g⁴ p12.2g p16g⁴ p12.2g p12.2m* f11g² f12g⁵ **a87** p12.2g³ Dec 26] fairly useful handicapper on all-weather, fair when last ran on turf in 2005: won at Wolverhampton in October: effective at 11f to easy 2m: acts on all-weather and firm ground: held up (has tended to idle): consistent. *R. Hollinshead*

HEAT OF THE NIGHT 4 b.f. Lear Fan (USA) 130 – Hot Thong (BRZ) (Jarraar **98**
(USA) 78) [2006 91: p8g⁶ 8g⁶ 7d³ 8g* 8d Nov 5] strong, quite attractive filly: useful performer: won listed race at Bremen by 2 lengths from Tech Engine: behind
in Kolner Herbst-Stuten-Meile at Cologne final start: has won at 9.5f, best form at 7f/1m:
acts on polytrack, good to firm and good to soft going. *P. W. Chapple-Hyam*

HEAVEN KNOWS 3 ch.c. Halling (USA) 133 – Rambling Rose 111 (Cadeaux Gene- **97 p**
reux 131) [2006 82p: 8s* 9m² 10.3m* Aug 25] strong, close-coupled colt: useful form:
impressive winner of handicaps at Thirsk in May and Chester (by 1½ lengths from Bin
Rahy, quickening once in clear) in August: good neck second to Count Trevisio in
similar event at Sandown in between: will stay 1½m: acts on polytrack, soft and good to
firm going: changed hands privately after final outing: smart performer in the making.
W. J. Haggas

HEAVEN SENT 3 ch.f. Pivotal 124 – Heavenly Ray (USA) 97 (Rahy (USA) 115) **92**
[2006 76p: 8.3m* 8s⁵ 7.2g⁶ 7m* 7f³ Aug 3] quite good-topped filly: fairly useful performer: won maiden at Windsor in April and handicap at Newmarket in July: good third
in handicap at Goodwood final start: stays 1m: acts on firm going. *Sir Michael Stoute*

HEAVEN'S GATES 2 ch.c. (Feb 11) Most Welcome 131 – Arcady 69 (Slip Anchor **52**
136) [2006 f8g f8g p8.6g Dec 27] modest form final start in maidens. *K. A. Ryan*

HEAVENS WALK 5 ch.h. Compton Place 125 – Ghost Dancing (Lion Cavern (USA) **82**
117) [2006 62: 5.1m 5f⁵ 5.3m³ 5m* p5g* 5.2f³ 5g 5m* p5g² p5.1g² p5g³ p5g² p5g⁴
Dec 16] strong horse: fairly useful handicapper: won at Lingfield and Kempton in July
and Goodwood in August: effective at 5f/6f: acts on polytrack and good to firm going:
blinkered final outing in 2005: usually tongue tied: held up: consistent. *P. J. Makin*

HEAVY SEAS 3 b.g. Foxhound (USA) 103 – Brookhead Lady 73 (Petong 126) [2006 **–**
7f 9v May 21] well held in maidens: gelded after final start. *P. D. Niven*

HEBENUS 7 b.g. Hamas (IRE) 125§ – Stinging Nettle 90 (Sharpen Up 127) [2006 34: **–**
5d 6v Oct 9] lengthy gelding: poor performer: well held in 2006: tried blinkered: often
races prominently. *T. A. K. Cuthbert*

HEIDI HI 2 b.f. (Mar 24) High Estate 127 – Alwal (Pharly (FR) 130) [2006 6d 6g⁶ 5d **49**
Sep 5] 800Y: closely related to fairly useful 1¼m to 2m winner Quedex (by Deploy) and
half-sister to 2 winners in Italy: dam won in Holland, including Dutch Oaks: poor form.
J. R. Turner

HEIGHT OF ESTEEM 3 b.g. Mark of Esteem (IRE) 137 – Biscay 67 (Unfuwain **54**
(USA) 131) [2006 8.5f 7.1m 7m 6v p5.1g⁶ p6g f6g Nov 2] modest maiden: should be
suited by 6f+: best effort on polytrack: wore cheekpieces last 3 starts: refused to enter
stall on intended debut, reportedly had breathing problem second outing. *M. Mullineaux*

HEIGHT OF FURY (IRE) 3 b.c. Sadler's Wells (USA) 132 – Height of Fantasy **80**
(IRE) 101 (Shirley Heights 130) [2006 74p: 8m 9.9g⁵ 12m⁶ 9.9m² 10s² 12v* Oct 31]
close-coupled colt: has a short action: fairly useful performer: runner-up in handicaps
before best effort to win maiden at Catterick in October: stays 1½m: acts on heavy and
good to firm going. *J. L. Dunlop*

HEIGHT OF SPIRITS 4 b.g. Unfuwain (USA) 131 – Kimono (IRE) (Machiavellian **56**
(USA) 123) [2006 52, a60: p10g p8g³ p8g* p8g p8g⁵ p8g³ p8g 8d p8g³ p10g p8g p10g **a69 d**
8m² 9m p11g p9.5g p10g p8g⁶ Dec 15] fair performer on all-weather, modest on turf:
won maiden at Lingfield in January: well below form last 4 starts, in cheekpieces/blinkers
last 3: effective at 1m/1¼m: acts on polytrack and good to firm ground: has carried head
awkwardly. *T. D. McCarthy*

HEIGHTS OF GOLAN 2 br.c. (May 27) Golan (IRE) 129 – Nemesia 111 (Mill Reef **80**
(USA) 141) [2006 8s⁶ p8g² p8g⁵ Nov 8] 10,500Y: half-brother to several winners, includ-
ing fairly useful 1m (at 2 yrs)/1¼m winner In Love (by Unfuwain) and 1½m winner
Rafiya (by Halling): dam, 1¼m and 13.5f winner, closely related to smart 1¼m performer
Elegant Air: easily best effort in maidens (fairly useful form) when runner-up at Ling-
field: will be suited by 1¼m/1½m. *I. A. Wood*

HELEN WOOD 3 b.f. Lahib (USA) 129 – Last Ambition (IRE) 29 (Cadeaux Genereux **52**
131) [2006 p8g 10g p10g p7g⁵ 7m p10g p12.2m 7f 10s* Oct 2] fifth foal: half-sister
to 1m/9.7f winner Hawkley (by Arctic Tern) and 1m winner Accomplish (by Desert
Story): dam, maiden, seemed best at 5f/6f: modest performer: won seller at Windsor (sold
12,000 gns, joined D. Pipe) in October: stays 1¼m: acts on polytrack and soft going.
M. D. I. Usher

HELIOSTATIC (IRE) 3 ch.c. Galileo (IRE) 134 – Affianced (IRE) 109 (Erins Isle **115** 121) [2006 85p: 8s² 10d 8v⁶ 10m* 12g 10g* 10m⁴ 8d⁵ 10m⁶ 10s Sep 30] first foal: dam, Irish 7f (at 2 yrs) and 1¼m winner who stayed 1¾m, half-sister to Irish Derby runner-up Sholokhov: smart performer: won listed race at the Curragh (by length from Cougar Bay) in June and Meld Stakes at Leopardstown (beat Lord Admiral 2 lengths) in July: pulled hard when creditable seventh to Dylan Thomas in Irish Derby at the Curragh in between: blinkered, well below form in listed race at Fairyhouse final outing: best at 1¼m: acts on good to firm ground: tongue tied on reappearance: has been accompanied to start by lead horse: makes running/races prominently. *J. S. Bolger, Ireland*

HELLBENT 7 b.g. Selkirk (USA) 129 – Loure (USA) 66 (Lyphard (USA) 132) [2006 **54** 59: p5.1g f5g f5g⁶ f5g Mar 14] modest performer: best efforts at 5f/6f: acts on all-weather and good to firm going: tried blinkered: best held up. *M. Appleby*

HELLO DEAUVILLE (FR) 3 ch.f. Alhaarth (IRE) 126 – Pulpeuse (IRE) (Pursuit of **–** Love 124) [2006 8.1m⁵ 8.1m 8.1g 6d⁶ p6g Dec 13] £1,100 2-y-o: first foal: dam, French 7.5f/1m winner, half-sister to smart 7f performer Thrilling Day: little form. *J. Akehurst*

HELLO MAN (IRE) 3 b.g. Princely Heir (IRE) 111 – Mignon (Midyan (USA) 124) **84** [2006 63: 9m 7f 7g² 7m 8.5m 7m⁵ 6g p6m* p6g² p6g⁵ p7g p6g² p6g* Dec 28] €7,000Y: fourth foal: half-brother to Irish 6f winner The Gollymocky (by Mujadil): dam unraced: fairly useful performer: won maiden in October and handicap in December, both at Wolverhampton: effective at 6f/7f: acts on polytrack, raced only on good going or firmer on turf: blinkered once at 2 yrs: signs of waywardness. *E. Tyrrell, Ireland*

HELLO MOLLY 5 b.m. Young Ern 120 – Treasurebound 63 (Beldale Flutter (USA) **–** 130) [2006 p6g p7g p7g 8d Apr 11] half-sister to useful but unruly 5f/6f (latter at 2 yrs) winner Batchworth Belle (by Interrex) and 5f winner Batchworth Bound (by Balla-cashtal): dam third at 6f at 4 yrs: no form. *E. A. Wheeler*

HELLO ROBERTO 5 b.m. Up And At 'em 109 – Hello Hobson's (IRE) 67 (Fayruz **78** 116) [2006 50: p5.1g⁴ p5.1g³ p5.1g³ p5.1g* f5g⁶ f6g* p5.1g⁴ p5.1g³ p6g⁴ 5.7d³ 5s 5.3m² 5g* p5.1g³ 5.7f² 5m⁴ 5g* 5m 6f⁶ 5f 5.1f⁵ 5g 5.3d Sep 25] quite good-topped mare: fair performer: won 5 times in first half of year, in banded races at Wolverhampton and South-well (2), and handicaps at Thirsk and Salisbury: effective at 5f/6f: acts on all-weather, firm and good to soft going: tried visored/blinkered, wears cheekpieces: usually ridden prominently nowadays. *R. A. Harris*

HELLO TIGER 5 b.g. Terimon 124 – Blue Peru (IRE) 48 (Perugino (USA) 84) [2006 **–** p12g f7g f8g May 9] of no account. *J. A. Supple*

HELLVELYN 2 gr.c. (Apr 7) Ishiguru (USA) 114 – Cumbrian Melody 83 (Petong 126) **108** [2006 5d⁵ 6d* 6m* 6m² 6d⁴ Sep 29] 32,000F, 100,000Y: rangy colt: half-brother to several winners, including useful 5f winner (including at 2 yrs) Golden Bounty (by Bahamian Bounty) and 6f (at 2 yrs) to 9.4f winner Cumbrian Princess (by Mtoto): dam 2-y-o 5f winner: useful performer: won maiden at Leicester in April, minor event at Pontefract in May and 21-runner Coventry Stakes at Royal Ascot (beat Major Cadeaux by ¾ length) in June: ran well after when 1¾ lengths second of 7 to Holy Roman Emperor

Coventry Stakes, Royal Ascot—Hellvelyn and Major Cadeaux fight out the finish to the first race at Britain's showcase Flat meeting following its return to a redeveloped Ascot

H. E. Sheikh Rashid bin Mohammed's "Hellvelyn"

in Phoenix Stakes at the Curragh and 4½ lengths fourth of 6 to Dutch Art in Middle Park Stakes (briefly squeezed) at Newmarket: will probably prove best at 5f/6f: yet to race on extremes of going. *B. Smart*

HEMISPEAR 2 ch.f. (Mar 26) Lear Spear (USA) 124 – Milladella (FR) (Nureyev (USA) 131) [2006 6f p6g p8g⁵ p8g⁶ 8.2g³ 8.1d⁶ p8.6m⁴ p10g³ Nov 29] workmanlike filly: second foal: dam French maiden (stayed 9f): fair maiden: shaped as if stamina stretched over 1¼m final start. *Miss J. R. Tooth*   **68**

HENCHMAN 3 b.g. Anabaa (USA) 130 – Gay Heroine 105 (Caerleon (USA) 132) [2006 70: 9.7m 8.2s⁶ p7.1g p10g⁴ 9.9m³ 10.2m p10g Oct 15] good-topped gelding: fair maiden handicapper: stays 1¼m: acts on polytrack and good to firm going: blinkered/in cheekpieces last 4 starts. *Lady Herries*   **67 a63**

HENRY BERNSTEIN (USA) 2 b. or br.c. (Apr 26) Bernstein (USA) 115 – Hidle (USA) (Unbridled (USA) 128) [2006 7g Oct 12] $85,000Y: well-made colt: fifth foal: half-brother to 3 winners abroad, including UAE 8.5f winner Pride of Baghdad (by Mr Prospector): dam unraced: 20/1, green and faded into mid-field in maiden at Newmarket won by Tredegar: likely to improve. *H. R. A. Cecil*   **64 p**

HENRY HALL (IRE) 10 b.h. Common Grounds 118 – Sovereign Grace (IRE) 101 (Standaan (FR) 118) [2006 82: 5d 5m³ 5.2g 5f⁶ 5f⁵ 5g² 5m 5m³ 5.1g* 5m⁴ 5m⁶ 5.1m 5f* 5g Sep 30] leggy horse: has a round action: fair handicapper nowadays: won at Nottingham in August and Redcar in September: best at 5f: acts on firm and soft going: visored (well beaten) once. *N. Tinkler*   **78**

HENRY HOLMES 3 b.g. Josr Algarhoud (IRE) 118 – Henrietta Holmes (IRE) 61 (Persian Bold 123) [2006 54: p10g⁴ p8g⁵ p10g p10g Jul 19] modest maiden: stays 1¼m: raced only on polytrack. *Mrs L. Richards*   **64**

HENRY THE SEVENTH 2 b.c. (Feb 22) Royal Applause 124 – Bombalarina (IRE) **67**
(Barathea (IRE) 127) [2006 6m p7g² p7.1g p7.1g³ p7.1g³ p8.6g⁶ Dec 23] 22,000Y: third
foal: half-brother to 4-y-o Prince Vettori and winner abroad by Dansili: dam unraced: fair
maiden: placed at Lingfield and in 2 nurseries (visored first time, wandered second) at
Wolverhampton: will stay 1m. *J. W. Hills*

HENRY TUN 8 b.g. Chaddleworth (IRE) 103 – B Grade 59 (Lucky Wednesday 124) **– §**
[2006 47§, a64§: f5g* p5.1g* p5.1g* f5g³ p5.1g p5.1g* p5.1g⁵ p5.1g p5.1g p5.1m f5g **a68 §**
p5.1g f5g Dec 28] tall gelding: fair performer: won 4 times between January and April, at
Southwell (seller) and Wolverhampton (2 sellers and a handicap): races mostly at 5f: acts
on all-weather and firm going: wears headgear: tried tongue tied (not since 2002): races
prominently: ungenuine. *J. Balding*

HENSTING HOUSE 3 b.g. Slip Anchor 136 – Pallas Athene (Jupiter Island 126) **–**
[2006 10m 10m 10.2m Oct 8] compact gelding: well beaten in maidens. *Dr J. R. J. Naylor*

HEPHAESTUS 2 b.g. (Mar 16) Piccolo 121 – Fragrant Cloud 37 (Zilzal (USA) 137) **75**
[2006 f5g* 6m 5.2g 5.1f⁵ 7m⁶ 6.1g⁶ p6g³ 5.1f³ 5g⁵ 6f⁵ p6g⁵ 5.2d³ p6g p6g⁵ p7.1g p5.1g⁴
Dec 6] 17,000Y: close-coupled gelding: first foal: dam, maiden who stayed 1½m, half-
sister to very smart 6f to 1m performer Young Ern: fair performer: won maiden in March
(off 3 months/gelded after) and nursery in October, both at Lingfield: left M. Channon
14,000 gns after thirteenth start: best at 5f/6f: acts on polytrack, firm and good to soft
going. *A. J. Chamberlain*

HERB PARIS (FR) 2 ch.f. (Mar 12) Halling (USA) 133 – Yaya (USA) (Rahy (USA) **72**
115) [2006 6m² p6g³ p7g⁴ p6g Nov 7] leggy filly: first foal: dam, French 1¼m winner
who stayed 12.5f, from excellent family of Swain: fair maiden: in frame first 3 starts:
should prove suited by 1¼m/1½m. *M. P. Tregoning*

HERE COMES BUSTER (IRE) 2 b.c. (May 15) Alhaarth (IRE) 126 – Blew Her **76**
Top (USA) (Blushing John (USA) 120) [2006 7.1m 8g⁶ 10.2m² 10.1d⁵ Oct 18] leggy colt:
fifth foal: brother to useful French/US performer up to 1¼m Arabic Song and half-brother
to fairly useful 2005 2-y-o 6f winner Musical High (by Mozart): dam unraced half-sister
to US Grade 1 9f/1¼m winner Life At The Top: fair maiden: second to Opera Crown at
Bath: stays 1¼m: acts on good to firm going: sold 18,000 gns, sent to USA. *R. Hannon*

HEREDITARY 4 ch.g. Hernando (FR) 127 – Eversince (USA) (Foolish Pleasure **–**
(USA)) [2006 58: p12g p16g Nov 6] maiden: well held on Flat in 2006 (in cheekpieces
final start): won over hurdles in December. *Mrs L. C. Jewell*

HEREFORD BOY 2 ch.g. (Apr 24) Tomba 119 – Grown At Rowan 75 (Gabitat 119) **68**
[2006 5d 6d p6g⁴ 5.1d² p5.1g³ p5g² p5g³ f5g* Dec 21] lengthy gelding: half-brother to
moody 7f winner Tworforten (by Robellino) and Irish 1¼m winner Wild Zing (by Jupiter
Island): dam 7f winner: fair performer: creditable efforts 2 starts prior to winning minor
event at Southwell in December by neck from Zadalla: should prove best at 5f: acts on
all-weather and good to soft ground. *D. K. Ivory*

HERE'S BLUE CHIP (IRE) 2 ch.c. (Mar 22) Barathea (IRE) 127 – Blasted Heath **–**
105 (Thatching 131) [2006 p8.6g Nov 28] last in maiden at Wolverhampton. *P. W. D'Arcy*

HERIOT 5 b.g. Hamas (IRE) 125§ – Sure Victory (IRE) 75 (Stalker 121) [2006 10.2m **54**
12.1f 16.2f Jul 28] modest maiden: stays 1¼m: acts on good to firm going: tried blink-
ered/visored. *S. C. Burrough*

HERNANDO ROYAL 3 b.c. Hernando (FR) 127 – Louis' Queen (IRE) 102 (Tragic **83**
Role (USA)) [2006 10v² p12g³ f11g* 12s⁵ 14g⁵ Sep 28] good-topped colt: fifth foal:
half-brother to 1999 2-y-o 6f winner Princess Louise (by Efisio) and winner around 1m
in Hong Kong by Lycius: dam 5f (at 2 yrs) to 1m winner: fairly useful performer: won
maiden at Southwell in July: good fifth in handicap at Newmarket final start: stays 1¾m:
acts on fibresand and heavy going: has looked no easy ride. *H. Morrison*

HERNANDO'S BOY 5 b.g. Hernando (FR) 127 – Leave At Dawn (Slip Anchor 136) **67**
[2006 82: 16v² 14m³ May 5] rather lightly-made, workmanlike gelding: handicapper,
just fair form in 2006: stays 2m: acts on soft and good to firm going: waited with.
K. G. Reveley

HERNINSKI 3 b.f. Hernando (FR) 127 – Empress Dagmar (Selkirk (USA) 129) [2006 **–**
63: 12f 10.1m 9.9m f11g Dec 28] close-coupled filly: maiden: no form in 2006.
M. C. Chapman

HEROES 2 b.g. (Apr 21) Diktat 126 – Wars (IRE) 60 (Green Desert (USA) 127) [2006 **88**
6m³ 6d* 7s⁵ Oct 21] 30,000Y: good-topped gelding: fourth foal: brother to fairly useful
2004 Irish 2-y-o 7f winner Redrightreturning and half-brother to 3-y-o Usk Poppy: dam,

maiden who stayed 7f, sister to very smart 7f to 9f performer Gabr: fairly useful form: won maiden at Windsor in October: 16/1, further progress when 7¾ lengths fifth of 10 to Dijeer in Horris Hill Stakes at Newbury (gelded after): stays 7f: nervy sort. *G. A. Huffer*

HERONS KISS (IRE) 2 b.f. (May 2) Heron Island (IRE) 116 – Kissimmee Bay (IRE) 54 (Brief Truce (USA) 126) [2006 6v 7s Aug 18] third foal: dam sprint maiden: tailed off in sellers. *B. S. Rothwell*   –

HEROTOZERO (IRE) 2 b.g. (Apr 4) Mull of Kintyre (USA) 114 – Free To Trade (IRE) (Royal Academy (USA) 130) [2006 7g 7.5g⁴ p6m² p6g² Nov 6] second foal: half-brother to Irish 1m winner Head And Shoulders (by Ashkalani): dam unraced: fairly useful maiden: best efforts when twice runner-up at Wolverhampton: may prove best at 5f/6f. *G. O'Leary, Ireland*   **80**

HERO WORSHIP (IRE) 3 b.c. Kalanisi (IRE) 132 – Shesasmartlady (IRE) (Dolphin Street (FR) 125) [2006 10v* 11.8g* 11.9f² Jun 10] 75,000F: rather leggy, quite attractive colt: second foal: half-brother to winner in USA by Royal Applause: dam Irish maiden half-sister to useful Irish performer up to 1m Dashing Colours: useful form: won maiden at Pontefract and 4-runner handicap at Leicester (by length from Soapy Danger), both in April: good 1¾ lengths second to same rival in handicap at Haydock final outing: stays easy 1½m: acts on any going. *M. A. Jarvis*   **98**

HERRING (IRE) 3 b.c. Orpen (USA) 116 – Moorfield Daisy (IRE) (Waajib 121) [2006 72: p8g* p8g⁴ 8.1g p10g³ 12m⁶ 10d p10g Sep 6] sturdy, lengthy colt: fairly useful handicapper: won maiden at Lingfield in April: good efforts when in frame after: stays 1½m: acts on polytrack and good to firm going: visored (below form) last 2 outings. *D. J. Coakley*   **80**

HE'S A DECOY (IRE) 2 b.c. (Apr 24) In The Wings 128 – Allegheny River (USA) (Lear Fan (USA) 130) [2006 7g* 6f* 7m² 7d 7m⁴ 7d Oct 14] €40,000Y: rather leggy colt: half-brother to several winners, including very smart 6f winner (including at 2 yrs) Danetime and useful Irish performer up to 7f Dane River (both by Danehill): dam Irish 7f winner: useful performer: won maiden at Leopardstown in May and listed race at Cork in June: improvement after when ½-length second of 7 to Halicarnassus in Superlative Stakes at Newmarket and 3 lengths fourth of 9 to Holy Roman Emperor in Prix Jean-Luc Lagardere at Longchamp (never nearer): eighth of 15 in Dewhurst Stakes at Newmarket final start: will be suited by 1m: acts on firm going, below form both tries on softer than good. *D. Wachman, Ireland*   **109**

HE'S A DIAMOND 4 ch.g. Vettori (IRE) 119 – Azira 45 (Arazi (USA) 135) [2006 58: p6g⁵ Feb 1] leggy gelding: fair performer: effective at 6f/7f: acts on polytrack and good to firm going. *T. G. Mills*   **71**

HESAGURU (IRE) 2 ch.g. (Feb 25) Ishiguru (USA) 114 – Lady Kinvarrah (IRE) 79 (Brief Truce (USA) 126) [2006 6m 6s 6m 8m Sep 21] close-coupled gelding: well beaten in maidens. *J. R. Norton*   –

HE'S A HUMBUG (IRE) 2 b.c. (Jan 9) Tagula (IRE) 116 – Acidanthera 81 (Alzao (USA) 117) [2006 6m* 6d⁵ 6m³ Sep 19] €22,000Y, 32,000 2-y-o: rangy, good sort: fourth foal: brother to Spanish 1m/1¼m winner Pacific Star: dam 7.5f winner: fairly useful form: impressive winning debut in maiden at Thirsk in July by 3½ lengths: didn't progress as anticipated, fifth of 6 behind Conquest in Gimcrack Stakes at York (favourite) and third to Traffic Guard in minor event at Newmarket: likely to stay 7f/1m. *K. A. Ryan*   **86**

HE'S A ROCKET (IRE) 5 b.g. Indian Rocket 115 – Dellua (IRE) 69 (Suave Dancer (USA) 136) [2006 60, a70: p5.1g p5.1g⁶ p5.1g p5.1g⁶ p5g f5g⁴ p5.1g² p5.1g² 5g 5f 5.7f p5.1g 5m p5g⁵ f5g⁴ Dec 27] close-coupled gelding: just modest at best on all-weather in 2006 (well behind on turf): best at 5f: acts on all-weather, firm and soft ground: usually wears headgear. *K. R. Burke*   **a62 d**

HE'S A STAR 4 ch.g. Mark of Esteem (IRE) 137 – Sahara Belle (USA) (Sanglamore (USA) 126) [2006 63: f14g* f14g² f16g³ f14g* f12s² f12g 20s p13.9g² 10m p12.2f* p12g Sep 10] sturdy gelding: fair performer on all-weather, well beaten on turf in 2006: won handicaps at Southwell in January and February and, having left Gay Kelleway £10,000 after eighth outing, seller at Wolverhampton (sold from P. D. Evans £4,200 gns) in August: effective at 1½m to 2m: acts on all-weather, firm and soft going: has run poorly on cheekpieces, failed to settle in blinkers. *B. D. Leavy*   **78**

HE'S MINE TOO 2 b.c. (Mar 17) Indian Ridge 123 – Screen Idol (IRE) 86 (Sadler's Wells (USA) 132) [2006 7m Sep 5] leggy, quite good-topped colt: fourth foal: brother to fairly useful Irish 6f winner Tough Chic and half-brother to 3-y-o Call My Number: dam,   **67 p**

Irish 2-y-o 7f winner, half-sister to useful Irish sprinter Catch A Glimpse: 15/2, seventh to Celtic Step in maiden at Leicester: open to improvement. *J. D. Bethell*

HESSIAN (IRE) 2 b.f. (Mar 26) Barathea (IRE) 127 – Red Letter 85 (Sri Pekan (USA) 117) [2006 5m May 13] 26,000Y: sturdy filly: second foal: dam 2-y-o 6f winner, out of half-sister to Irish 1000 Guineas winner Matiya: last in maiden at Newmarket. *M. L. W. Bell*   –

HESTER BROOK (IRE) 2 b.f. (Feb 10) Soviet Star (USA) 128 – Keen To Please 60 (Keen 116) [2006 6.1g 5.1f³ 5m² 6f³ 5.2f⁴ 7m² 6f Sep 18] €4,000Y: fourth foal: dam 2-y-o 5f winner out of half-sister to dam of Rock of Gibraltar: modest maiden: stays 7f: acts on firm going. *J. G. M. O'Shea*   59

HEUREUX (USA) 3 b.c. Stravinsky (USA) 133 – Storm West (USA) (Gone West (USA)) [2006 80: 10m⁴ 8d⁴ 8g⁶ 7f⁴ 7.6m⁴ 8d 7.1s Sep 24] good-topped colt: fairly useful handicapper: creditable efforts after reappearance until pulled up penultimate outing (said to have breathing problem): visored, ran poorly final appearance: stays 1m: acts on firm and good to soft going: blinkered fourth start. *J. Howard Johnson*   82

HEVERSHAM (IRE) 5 b.g. Octagonal (NZ) 126 – Saint Ann (USA) 66 (Geiger Counter (USA)) [2006 –: f8g f12g⁵ f12g Feb 5] quite good-topped gelding: no form on Flat since 2004: tried in cheekpieces. *J. Hetherton*   –

HEWARAAT (IRE) 4 b.g. Fasliyev (USA) 120 – Maraatib (IRE) 93 (Green Desert (USA) 127) [2006 74: 7d Apr 21] good sort: fair performer: best efforts at 6f: acted on good to firm and good to soft going: dead. *G. A. Swinbank*   68

HEY PRESTO 6 b.g. Piccolo 121 – Upping The Tempo (Dunbeath (USA) 127) [2006 79: p7g p8g p8g 7m p8g 7.6f 7g Oct 13] strong, good-topped gelding: usually takes the eye: handicapper: well held in 2006: tried blinkered/in cheekpieces. *R. Rowe*   –

HEYWOOD 2 b.g. (Apr 2) Tobougg (IRE) 125 – Owdbetts (IRE) 69 (High Estate 127) [2006 p7g 7.2d⁵ 7f³ p7g* 7m⁶ 7.1g*⁷ 7m* 8m⁶ p7.1g² p7g Oct 21] 72,000F: strong, sturdy gelding: fifth foal: half-brother to 3 winners, notably 8-y-o Rohio, and 3-y-o Rochdale: dam 7f (including at 2 yrs) and 1¼m winner: fairly useful performer: won maiden at Lingfield in July and nurseries at Sandown in August and Lingfield in September: looked unlucky when second in nursery at Wolverhampton: final run best excused (slowly away/hampered, gelded after): should stay 1m: acts on polytrack and firm going: tends to wander. *M. R. Channon*   91

HEZAAM (USA) 5 b.g. Red Ransom (USA) – Ashraakat (USA) 105 (Danzig (USA)) [2006 78: f8g f12g 12.4m⁶ 16.1d 12m* 12m* 12f Jul 5] quite attractive gelding: fair handicapper nowadays: left C. Fairhurst after reappearance: won twice at Ripon (former success in selling handicap) in June: stays 1½m: acts on soft and good to firm going: tried blinkered: carried head awkwardly on third outing. *Mrs A. Duffield*   65

H HARRISON (IRE) 6 b.g. Eagle Eyed (USA) 111 – Penrose (IRE) 75 (Wolfhound (USA) 126) [2006 88, a51: p7.1g⁶ p6g⁶ p6g* p6g* p7g 7.1g 7m 7m⁴ 6f³ 7g⁴ 7.1f³ᵈ 5f 7f 7.1m⁵ 7.6m 6f⁵ 6d³ 6m² 7.2v⁶ p6g Oct 17] smallish gelding: just fair handicapper in 2006: won twice at Lingfield within 3 days, in March and April: effective at 6f/7f: acts on polytrack, firm and good to soft going: tried in cheekpieces/blinkers: usually races prominently. *I. W. McInnes*   75

HIALEAH 5 ch.g. Bal Harbour 113 – Tommys Dream (Le Bavard (FR) 125) [2006 15.8m⁵ 12d Oct 8] maiden over jumps: well held both starts on Flat: tried blinkered. *Robert Gray*   –

HIAMOVI (IRE) 4 b.g. Monashee Mountain (USA) 115 – Dunfern (Wolver Hollow 126) [2006 –, a63: p6g f5g⁶ f5g p5.1g Feb 20] just poor form in 2006, reportedly lame final outing: best at 5f/6f: probably better on polytrack than fibresand, little form on turf: wears headgear. *R. M. H. Cowell*   – a46

HIATS 4 b.g. Lujain (USA) 119 – Naulakha (Bustino 136) [2006 –: f7g 5s 5d 12.4s p8.6g⁶ p7.1g⁴ f6g Dec 12] leggy gelding: modest maiden: left C. Teague after reappearance: stays 8.6f: acts on polytrack: wore cheekpieces last 2 starts. *J. O'Reilly*   56

HIAWATHA (IRE) 7 b.g. Danehill (USA) 126 – Hi Bettina 96 (Henbit (USA) 130) [2006 62: p8.6g p9.5g⁵ p10g⁴ p9.5g⁴ p10g⁴ p10g⁶ p10g³ Dec 22] modest performer nowadays: stays 1½m: acts on all-weather, firm and soft ground: tried blinkered/in cheekpieces. *A. M. Hales*   57

HI CALYPSO (IRE) 2 b.f. (Feb 11) In The Wings 128 – Threefold (USA) 99 (Gulch (USA)) [2006 7g 7d*⁵ 8d Oct 28] big, lengthy filly: first foal: dam, 1m winner who stayed 1¼m, out of half-sister to Prix Saint-Alary winner Treble and to dam of high-class sprin-   80 p ter Tamarisk: fairly useful form: won maiden at Leicester (still green, beat Beautiful Reward by neck) in October: 7/1, well-held seventh behind Passage of Time in listed race at Newmarket: will be suited by 1¼m/1½m: type to improve at 3 yrs. *Sir Michael Stoute*

HICCUPS 6 b.g. Polar Prince (IRE) 117 – Simmie's Special 75 (Precocious 126) [2006 **89** 84: 6m⁴ 7d² 6g 6g 6g 6m 7g* 7.1m⁵ 7.1m* 7.2d 6d 7s⁴ 7v* Oct 31] tall, quite good-topped gelding: fairly useful handicapper: left D. Nicholls, won at Thirsk in August, Warwick in September and Catterick (best effort, beat Bold Marc by neck) in October: stays 7f: acts on any turf going: has worn visor/cheekpieces: has been difficult at stall: sometimes slowly away/carries head awkwardly: usually waited with: none too reliable. *M. Dods*

HI DANCER 3 b.g. Medicean 128 – Sea Music (Inchinor 119) [2006 49: f8g* f8g⁴ 8s⁶ **61** 11.1f² 10g⁶ Aug 21] useful-looking gelding: modest handicapper: won at Southwell in January: stays 11f: acts on fibresand and firm ground: sometimes slowly away. *P. C. Haslam*

HIDDEN ACE (IRE) 2 b.f. (Apr 26) Iron Mask (USA) 117 – Kingdom Pearl 57 (Stat- **57** oblest 120) [2006 f5g⁴ p6f⁵ 6s 5m p7.1g Sep 16] leggy filly: sixth foal: half-sister to 6-y-o Unicorn Reward and winner in Belgium by Woodborough: dam 1½m winner: modest maiden: will stay 1m+: blinkered. *M. W. Easterby*

HIDDEN DRAGON (USA) 7 b.g. Danzig (USA) – Summer Home (USA) (Easy **92** Goer (USA)) [2006 97, a112: 7.5m³ a7f 6.5m⁵ 6m 6m 6m 6m⁴ 6m 6s 6m p7g Dec 3] big, **a–** lengthy gelding: just fairly useful handicapper in 2006: pulled up amiss final start: effective at 5f to easy 7f: acts on all-weather, firm and soft going: tried in headgear: tends to hang. *J. Pearce*

HIDDENSEE (USA) 4 b.g. Cozzene (USA) – Zarani Sidi Anna (USA) 113 (Danzig **93 §** (USA)) [2006 101: p16g⁶ p16g⁶ 18.7m 14m⁶ 16.2f 15m* p13.9g⁵ Jul 1] strong, lengthy gelding: just fairly useful handicapper in 2006: awarded race at Warwick in June: should be suited by 2m+: acts on polytrack, good to firm and good to soft going: blinkered/visored last 2 starts: temperamental, and one to treat with caution: sold 38,000 gns later in July. *M. Johnston*

HIGH ACTION (USA) 6 ch.g. Theatrical 128 – Secret Imperatrice (USA) (Secre- **114** tariat (USA)) [2006 105+: 13.3s⁵ 20m⁴ 16f 15.9d Aug 22] strong, close-coupled gelding: usually impresses in appearance: smart performer: seemingly better than ever when 7¼ lengths fourth to Yeats in Gold Cup at Royal Ascot: well held in Goodwood Cup and in Lonsdale Cup at York after: stays 2½m: acts on polytrack and firm going: has been tongue tied: usually races prominently. *Ian Williams*

HIGH AMBITION 3 b.g. High Estate 127 – So Ambitious (Teenoso (USA) 135) **62** [2006 p12.2g⁴ Dec 28] modest form in bumpers: 6½ lengths fourth of 6 to demoted Four-square Flyer in maiden at Wolverhampton. *P. W. D'Arcy*

HIGH ARCTIC 4 b.g. Pivotal 124 – Ladykirk 78 (Slip Anchor 136) [2006 77?: p8.6g **65** Jan 5] tall, leggy gelding: fair maiden, better on turf than all-weather: stays 1¼m: acts on polytrack and good to soft ground: often slowly away. *A. Bailey*

HIGHBAND 3 b.f. Band On The Run 102 – Barkston Singer 79§ (Runnett 125) [2006 **–** –: 8m⁶ 10.2m Sep 25] well held in maidens. *M. Madgwick*

HIGH BOUNCE (USA) 6 ch.g. Trempolino (USA) 135 – Top Hope 115 (High Top **–** 131) [2006 p13g Sep 29] no sign of ability. *R. J. Hodges*

HIGH BRAY (GER) 5 b.g. Zieten (USA) 118 – Homing Instinct (Arctic Tern (USA) **89** 126) [2006 96: 8m 7d⁴ 7m 7d Sep 30] tall, useful-looking gelding: fairly useful handi-capper: gelded, well below form in 2006 other than when creditable fourth at Newmarket: best form at 7f: acts on firm and good to soft ground. *D. R. C. Elsworth*

HIGH BULLEN 2 ch.f. (Feb 16) Inchinor 119 – Rock Face 77 (Ballad Rock 122) [2006 **53** 5.1d p7g 7.1m⁵ Jul 13] 20,000Y: half-sister to 2 winners, including fairly useful 7f (at 2 yrs) to 1¼m winner Sheer Face (by Midyan): dam 1¼m to 1¾m winner: modest form in maidens: likely to benefit from 1m/1¼m. *M. Meade*

HIGH CLASS PROBLEM (IRE) 3 b.c. Mozart (IRE) 131 – Sarah-Clare 67 (Reach **73** 122) [2006 67: 8.3g⁶ 8m⁴ 7f² 8.1f 8f* p8.6f⁴ 10m Sep 8] tall, leggy colt: fair handicapper: made all at Brighton in August: likely to prove at least as effective at 7f as 1m: acts on polytrack and firm ground: blinkered (found little) fourth start. *P. F. I. Cole*

HIGH COMMAND 3 b.c. Galileo (IRE) 134 – Final Shot 91 (Dalsaan 125) [2006 85: **103** 10d* 10s³ 9s 10m⁴ 9.9f p11g³ 10.1m* 10d⁴ Sep 23] medium-sized, good-topped colt: useful handicapper: won at Leicester in April (by neck from Soapy Danger) and Yar-mouth (beat Folio by 2½ lengths) in September: creditable 2½ lengths fourth to Rampallion at Newmarket final start: will stay 1½m: acts on polytrack, firm and soft going: tongue tied fourth outing: has carried head awkwardly. *E. A. L. Dunlop*

HIGH COUNTRY (IRE) 6 b.g. Danehill (USA) 126 – Dance Date (IRE) (Sadler's **57** Wells (USA) 132) [2006 62: p13.9g⁶ Mar 6] good-topped gelding: modest maiden handicapper: stays 2m: acts on polytrack and good to firm going, probably on soft: tried blinkered: fair hurdler, successful in August. *M. D. Hammond*

HIGH CURRAGH 3 b.g. Pursuit of Love 124 – Pretty Poppy 67 (Song 132) [2006 86: **96** 6g 6m² 6m³ 6m 7f² 6g Aug 19] strong, lengthy gelding: fluent mover: useful handicapper: good placed efforts at Ripon, York (1¾ lengths third to Prince Tamino in William Hill Trophy) and Goodwood (neck second to Dream Theme): stays easy 7f: acts on firm and good to soft going, ran poorly on soft: races up with pace. *K. A. Ryan*

HIGH DYKE 4 b.g. Mujahid (USA) 125 – Gold Linnet 69 (Nashwan (USA) 135) [2006 **§§** 85§: p7.1g 8₅ Mar 25] quite good-topped gelding: fairly useful performer at 3 yrs: one to avoid nowadays, having refused to race last 3 starts. *K. A. Ryan*

HIGHEST REGARD 4 b.g. Mark of Esteem (IRE) 137 – Free As A Bird 62 (Robel- **72** lino (USA) 127) [2006 83: p7g p8.6g p10g 10.1f* 12m⁶ 12m 10.1s Oct 10] just fair handicapper in 2006: left P. Gilligan 2,000 gns, won at Newcastle in July: stays 1¼m: acts on polytrack and firm ground: tongue tied last 2 outings. *N. P. McCormack*

HIGH FIVE SOCIETY 2 b.c. (Apr 12) Compton Admiral 121 – Sarah Madeline 48 **66** (Pelder (IRE) 125) [2006 p5.1g 7g² f7g p8.6m Oct 31] 2,000Y: third foal: dam ran once: fair maiden: clearly best effort when second at Newcastle, only turf start: should stay at least 1m. *S. R. Bowring*

HIGH FREQUENCY (IRE) 5 ch.g. Grand Lodge (USA) 125 – Freak Out (FR) (Ber- **60** ing 136) [2006 60: f12g⁶ f12g⁶ f12g² p12.2g⁶ f16g² p16.5g f14g⁶ f16g³ f12g² p16.5g f12g 14m⁵ f14g 16g* 16f² p16.5g³ 16g 15.8m⁴ f14g Nov 2] tall gelding: modest performer: won apprentice handicap at Musselburgh in May: claimed from T. D. Barron £6,000 after next start: stays 2m: acts on all-weather and firm going: often wears headgear: none too genuine. *A. Crook*

HIGH HEEL SNEAKERS 3 b.f. Dansili 127 – Sundae Girl (USA) 75 (Green Dancer **111** (USA) 132) [2006 99: 9.3d³ 10.4d⁵ 10g³ 12m⁴ p13g* Oct 26] tall filly: has a quick action: smart performer: off 4 months, won listed race at Lingfield in October by head from Taranto: creditable efforts when in frame at Longchamp (third to Danzon in Prix Vanteaux) and Royal Ascot (1½ lengths fourth to Mont Etoile in Ribblesdale Stakes) first/ fourth starts: not sure to stay beyond 13f: acts on polytrack, yet to race on extremes of going on turf. *P. F. I. Cole*

HIGH HOPE (FR) 8 ch.g. Lomitas 129 – Highness Lady (GER) (Cagliostro (GER)) **74 d** [2006 p12g⁴ p12g⁶ p16g p12.2g² p16g³ p16g 12m Aug 27] leggy gelding: missed 2005 and just fair performer in 2006 (on downgrade): effective at 1½m to 15f: acts on polytrack and soft going: tried blinkered/in cheekpieces, in former last 5 starts. *G. L. Moore*

HIGH (IRE) 4 b.g. Desert Story (IRE) 115 – Sesame Heights (IRE) 63 (High Estate **59** 127) [2006 55: f8g⁶ f12g f12g³ p12.2g* p16.5g p12.2g⁶ p12g³ May 15] modest performer, lightly raced: won banded race at Wolverhampton in March: stays 1½m: acts on all-weather, well held only outing on turf: blinkered (ran well) final outing. *W. J. Musson*

HIGHLAND BELLE 3 b.f. Robellino (USA) 127 – Scottish Spice 92 (Selkirk (USA) **59** 129) [2006 6f 8g Jun 2] quite good-topped filly: first foal: dam 7f (at 2 yrs)/1m winner: better effort (modest form) in maidens when eighth to Tasjeel at Bath final outing: stays 1m: visored both starts: withdrawn after unruly stall intended debut at 2 yrs: sold 3,000 gns in October. *A. M. Balding*

HIGHLAND BLAZE (USA) 3 ch.c. Unbridled's Song (USA) 125 – Green Lady **86** (IRE) 104 (Green Desert (USA) 127) [2006 66p: 7g² 8s* 8s Sep 22] leggy, quite good-topped colt: fairly useful performer: won maiden at Newmarket in August by 1¾ lengths from Sculastic: ran poorly on handicap debut next time: stays 1m: raced only on good and soft going: joined S. Seemar in UAE. *Saeed bin Suroor*

HIGHLAND CASCADE 4 ch.f. Tipsy Creek (USA) 115 – Highland Hannah (IRE) **78** (Persian Heights 129) [2006 87: 6d 6m⁶ 6m⁵ 6m⁶ 6.1f⁴ 7f³ 6f³ 6m³ 5.7m 6.1m 7g p7g³ **a72** p7g p7.1g p6s Dec 15] good-topped filly: just fair performer in 2006: probably stays 7f: acts on polytrack, firm and good to soft going: tried blinkered/in cheekpieces: has tended to hang. *J. M. P. Eustace*

HIGHLAND HARVEST 2 b.c. (Jan 25) Averti (IRE) 117 – Bee One (IRE) 81§ (Cat- **75** rail (USA) 123) [2006 6g⁶ 6m 8.2d³ p7g³ p7g³ Dec 20] close-coupled colt: first foal: dam, maiden (best form at 6f), became one to avoid: fair maiden: creditable efforts when third at Nottingham (to Regal Flush) and Lingfield (twice, again failed to settle when behind Danehillsundance on second occasion) last 3 starts: stays 1m: acts on polytrack and good to soft ground: hangs left. *D. R. C. Elsworth*

HIGHLAND LEGACY 2 ch.c. (Feb 20) Selkirk (USA) 129 – Generous Lady 98 **63 p** (Generous (IRE) 139) [2006 8.3d 8.2s⁴ Oct 25] 78,000Y: angular colt: fifth living foal: half-brother to very smart 7f (at 2 yrs) to 1½m winner (also runner-up in St Leger) High Accolade (by Mark of Esteem) and 1½m winner Summer Wine (by Desert King): dam Irish 1½m/1¾m winner: better run in maidens when fourth to Sahrati at Nottingham: bred to be well suited by 1¼m/1½m: should improve further. *M. L. W. Bell*

HIGHLAND SONG (IRE) 3 ch.g. Fayruz 116 – Rose 'n Reason (IRE) (Reasonable **73** (FR) 119) [2006 63: p6g⁴ 5d³ 5g³ 5m² 5g⁵ 5m 5g³ 5g 5f 5m* 5g 5m³ 5v⁴ 6s 5d p6g Nov 23] well-made gelding: fair handicapper: won at Ayr in August: effective at 5f/6f: acts on polytrack, soft and good to firm going: tried in cheekpieces (below form): tends to edge left. *R. F. Fisher*

HIGHLAND WARRIOR 7 b.g. Makbul 104 – Highland Rowena 59 (Royben 125) **93** [2006 88: 5d² 5f* 5m 5m 5f⁵ 6f 5s 6d 5g 5s 5d Nov 3] big, leggy gelding: fairly useful handicapper: won at Musselburgh in May by length from Harry Up: below form after fifth start: best at 5f/6f: acts on any turf going: in cheekpieces last 2 outings: usually slowly away/held up. *J. S. Goldie*

HIGHLINER 4 b.c. Robellino (USA) 127 – Bocas Rose 106 (Jalmood (USA) 126) **–** [2006 65: p9.5g Jan 9] close-coupled colt: maiden: well held only outing in 2006. *Mrs L. Williamson*

HIGH LITE 2 ch.f. (Apr 28) Observatory (USA) 131 – Shall We Run 59 (Hotfoot 126) **54 p** [2006 6d 6d⁶ 5.1d Nov 1] 52,000Y: good-topped filly: half-sister to several winners, including 5f/6f (Gimcrack Stakes at 2 yrs) winner Bannister (by Inchinor) and useful 1999 2-y-o 5f/6f winner Roo (by Rudimentary): dam lightly-raced half-sister to very smart but temperamental sprinter Dead Certain: some promise in maidens: raced on good to soft ground: type to progress. *M. L. W. Bell*

HIGH MEADOW GIRL 3 b.f. Pursuit of Love 124 – Immaculate (Mark of Esteem **–** (IRE) 137) [2006 65: 8d 6m 7g Sep 27] workmanlike filly: maiden: no form in 2006. *J. D. Bethell*

HIGH 'N DRY (IRE) 2 ch.f. (Feb 23) Halling (USA) 133 – Sisal (IRE) 84 (Danehill **72** (USA) 126) [2006 p7g p7g² Nov 11] 28,000Y: first foal: dam, 2-y-o 6f winner, out of half-sister to Alderbrook: fair form in maidens: second to Sell Out at Kempton: will stay 1m. *C. A. Cyzer*

HIGH OCTAVE (IRE) 3 b.c. Piccolo 121 – Flight Sequence 88 (Polar Falcon (USA) **71** 126) [2006 72: 7.1g 7m p7g² 7f² 7m⁶ 8f³ 8m² 7m⁵ 8m⁶ p10g p10g Nov 1] workmanlike colt: fair maiden handicapper: should stay 1¼m: acts on polytrack and firm going, probably on good to soft: tried blinkered (ran poorly). *B. G. Powell*

HIGH POINT (IRE) 8 b.g. Ela-Mana-Mou 132 – Top Lady (IRE) 83 (Shirley Heights **83** 130) [2006 85: p16g p16g² p16.5g⁵ p16g p16g⁵ p16g³ 18.7m 18m² 20m p16g* 16.2d 18d p16g* Nov 29] lengthy, leggy gelding: fairly useful handicapper: won at Kempton in August and November: effective at 1½m to 2¼m: acts on polytrack, soft and good to firm going: tried visored: none too consistent. *G. P. Enright*

HIGH REACH 6 b.g. Royal Applause 124 – Lady of Limerick (IRE) (Thatching 131) **93** [2006 65: 5g³ 6m 7m 6m 6f⁵ 5m³ 6f 6m 5g⁴ p6g p6g Oct 5] strong, compact gelding: fairly useful handicapper: below form last 2 starts, in cheekpieces final one: best at 5f/6f: acts on polytrack, firm and soft going: sold 3,500 gns. *W. R. Muir*

HIGH RIDGE 7 ch.g. Indian Ridge 123 – Change For A Buck (USA) 83 (Time For A **84** Change (USA)) [2006 84, a75: 6f* 6d p6g* 6m⁶ 6m p6g 6m⁴ 6f 6m² 6f 6g⁵ 6m³ 5.7m³ 6m p6g³ Oct 6] big, lengthy gelding: fairly useful handicapper: won at Folkestone and Lingfield, both in May: creditable efforts when in frame after: probably best around 6f: acts on polytrack, firm and soft going: wears cheekpieces: usually waited with: tough. *J. M. Bradley*

HIGH SEASONS 3 b.g. Fantastic Light (USA) 134 – El Hakma 94 (Shareef Dancer **72** (USA) 135) [2006 71: 10.2g* 11.6m⁵ 11.6d⁵ 10f² p12g⁵ p10g Dec 20] close-coupled gelding: fair handicapper: gelded, won at Bath in May: barely stays 11.6f: acts on firm and good to soft going, probably on polytrack: blinkered final outing: raced freely third start. *B. R. Millman*

HIGH STYLE 2 b.c. (Mar 16) Desert Style (IRE) 121 – Gracious Gift 96 (Cadeaux **86** Genereux 131) [2006 5d 6m³ 5m⁶ 6f⁴ p6g² p6g* 6s² 6m p6g² p6g Oct 21] neat colt: fourth foal: half-brother to 2004 2-y-o 5f winner Godsend (by Royal Applause), later successful in USA, and 5-y-o Instinct: dam, 6f/7f winner, half-sister to smart performer up to 7f Sharp Prod: fairly useful performer: won nursery at Kempton in August by 3½ lengths: placed another 4 times, second to Resplendent Alpha in minor event at Lingfield penultimate start: may prove best kept to 5f/6f: acts on polytrack, firm and soft going: sold 30,000 gns. *R. Hannon*

HIGH SWAINSTON 5 ch.g. The West (USA) 107 – Reamzafonic 46 (Grand Lodge **55** (USA) 125) [2006 58: f6g⁴ p6g⁶ f8g³ f8g² f8g⁴ f8g³ f8g 8m³ 9.3m 7.1d Aug 2] angular, quite good-topped gelding: modest maiden: stays 1m: acts on fibresand and good to firm ground: tried blinkered/visored. *R. Craggs*

HIGH TREASON (USA) 4 ch.g. Diesis 133 – Fabula Dancer (USA) (Northern **86** Dancer) [2006 63: 11.5m* p12g⁷ 11.6m⁵ 11m* 10g³ 11.5m* 11s* Oct 10] tall gelding: fairly useful handicapper: much improved in 2006, winning at Yarmouth in April and September and Newbury (apprentice event) in June and October: effective at 11f, should stay 2m: acts on polytrack, firm and soft going. *W. J. Musson*

HIGH TRIBUTE 2 ch.c. (Mar 17) Mark of Esteem (IRE) 137 – Area Girl 76 (Jareer **68** (USA) 115) [2006 p6g³ p7g⁵ p8.6g⁶ Dec 29] half-brother to several winners, including useful 6f (at 2 yrs)/7f winner Flying Officer (by Efisio) and 3-y-o Outlook: dam 2-y-o 5f winner: best effort in maidens when 1½ lengths fifth to Danehillsundance at Lingfield: not knocked about at Wolverhampton next time. *Sir Mark Prescott*

HIGH VOLTAGE 5 ch.g. Wolfhound (USA) 126 – Real Emotion (USA) (El Prado **74** (IRE) 119) [2006 94d: 6g 6f⁴ 6m 6g² 7.1s⁵ 6s 6.1d Oct 4] good-topped gelding: just fair handicapper in 2006: effective at 5f, barely stays 7f: acts on firm and soft going: usually tongue tied: races up with pace: tends to carry head high: sold 3,500 gns. *K. R. Burke*

HIGHWAY TO GLORY (IRE) 3 b.f. Cape Cross (IRE) 129 – Anita Via (IRE) **102** (Anita's Prince 126) [2006 92: 8d³ 8g² 8d 7d³ 7d² p8g Oct 26] €44,000Y: leggy, lengthy filly: fifth foal: half-sister to 2 winners, including 4-y-o Pride of Nation: dam unraced: useful performer: left A. & G. Botti in Italy after reappearance: good placed efforts in listed races at York (2½ lengths third to Silver Touch) and Ascot (1¾ lengths second to Makderah) fourth/fifth starts: ran poorly in similar event at Lingfield final outing: may prove best up to 1m: raced only on good going or softer on turf. *M. Botti*

HIGH WINDOW (IRE) 6 b.g. King's Theatre (IRE) 128 – Kayradja (IRE) (Last **–** Tycoon 131) [2006 44?: f11g⁴ Jan 1] little form on Flat. *G. P. Kelly*

HILLBILLY CAT (USA) 3 ch.g. Running Stag (USA) 124 – Flashy Cat (USA) **a67** (Mountain Cat (USA)) [2006 59: f6g f8g³ f7g² f8g⁴ 5.9g f6g* f6g* p6g³ p6g p6m p7g p6g f6g Dec 5] fair performer: won claimer and handicap, both at Southwell, within 4 days in May and June: claimed from T. D. Barron after next start: will probably prove best short of 1m: acts on fibresand, raced only on good/good to soft going on turf. *R. Ingram*

HILL BILLY ROCK (IRE) 3 b.g. Halling (USA) 133 – Polska (USA) 103 (Danzig **77 p** (USA)) [2006 7g⁶ 7.5f f11g⁵ 9d 12.4d* 12.1m⁴ Sep 13] 9,000 2-y-o: sixth foal: brother to useful 2004 2-y-o 7f winner Queen of Poland and half-brother to useful 2003 2-y-o 7f winner White Hawk (by Silver Hawk) and fairly useful 2001 2-y-o 5f/6f winner Grizel (by Lion Cavern): dam, 2-y-o 6f winner, closely related to useful 5f performer Millstream: fair form: won handicap at Newcastle in August: finished strongly when fourth in similar event at Beverley final outing: likely to stay 1¾m: acts on good to firm and good to soft going: open to further improvement. *G. A. Swinbank*

HILLFIELD FLYER (IRE) 6 b.m. Flying Spur (AUS) – Paul's Lass (IRE) (Al Hareb **46** (USA) 123) [2006 53: f8g p9.5g* p13.9g p9.5g May 5] poor performer nowadays: won maiden claimer at Wolverhampton in March: stays 9.5f: acts on polytrack, soft and good to firm going: tried blinkered/in cheekpieces. *Samuel Murphy, Ireland*

HILLHALL (IRE) 4 ch.g. Desert Prince (IRE) 130 – Factice (USA) 78 (Known Fact **55** (USA) 135) [2006 57: p9.5g² p9.5g³ p12g 10m 12.3g 10.3m⁵ 10f 10m Jul 29] modest maiden: stays 1½m: acts on polytrack, raced only on good ground or firmer on turf: tried blinkered. *W. M. Brisbourne*

HILL OF ALMHUIM (IRE) 3 b.g. City On A Hill (USA) 114 – Kitty Kildare (USA) **73 d** 68 (Seattle Dancer (USA) 119) [2006 77: p8g⁴ 8d⁵ 8.3g 10v⁵ 10m³ 10.3f³ 10.1d 9.2g³ 11g 9.1v⁴ 11.5d² f6g p7.1g⁶ p8g⁵ p6g Dec 18] quite good-topped gelding: fair performer: well below form after sixth outing, claimed from. K. Burke eleventh: barely stays 10.3f: acts on polytrack, firm and good to soft going: usually wears headgear. *Peter Grayson*

totescoop6 Stakes (Handicap), Sandown—further improvement from Hinterland,
who gradually asserts his superiority over the previous year's winner Ace of Hearts (striped sleeves)

HILL OF CLARE (IRE) 4 br. or b.f. Daylami (IRE) 138 – Sarah-Clare 67 (Reach 122) [2006 47: 8m p10g³ 8.1f p13.9g Nov 27] modest maiden, lightly raced: left P. Webber 4,500 gns after third start: stays 1¼m: acts on polytrack: tried tongue tied. *G. H. Jones*   **54**

HILL OF HOWTH (IRE) 3 b.c. Danehill Dancer (IRE) 117 – Elton Grove (IRE) (Astronef 116) [2006 80: p8.6g Jan 16] fairly useful maiden in 2005: well held only outing in 2006: tried blinkered. *K. A. Ryan*   **–**

HILL OF LUJAIN 2 b.c. (Apr 27) Lujain (USA) 119 – Cinder Hills 72 (Deploy 131) [2006 5d² 5d* 5d⁵ 5g⁴ May 29] 5,200Y: quite good-topped colt: second foal: dam 1¼m/1½m and hurdles winner: fair performer: won maiden at Hamilton in May: ran creditably in 2 minor events later in month, but not seen after. *M. W. Easterby*   **70**

HILLSIDE SMOKI (IRE) 2 b.f. (Mar 23) Soviet Star (USA) 128 – Najeyba 80 (Indian Ridge 123) [2006 6m Sep 21] €10,000Y: third foal: dam 6f winner: tailed off in maiden. *A. Berry*   **–**

HILLS OF ARAN 4 b.c. Sadler's Wells (USA) 132 – Danefair 109 (Danehill (USA) 126) [2006 101: 10g 11.7f 12m 17.1d 12s Oct 21] strong, well-made colt: fairly useful at 2 yrs, acted as pacemaker in Irish 2000 Guineas only outing at 3 yrs: left A. O'Brien in Ireland, well held in handicaps under 2 starts: blinkered last 2 starts. *W. K. Goldsworthy*   **–**

HILL SPIRIT 3 b.c. Polish Precedent (USA) 131 – Homing Instinct (Arctic Tern (USA) 126) [2006 79: 8m⁵ 8m³ 7m* 8g 8m³ 7s² 7g p7g Sep 29] tall, close-coupled colt: fairly useful performer: won maiden at Yarmouth in May and handicap at Salisbury in August: ran well next time: bred to stay beyond 1m: acts on soft and good to firm going, probably on polytrack: sold 45,000 gns, sent to Saudi Arabia. *D. R. C. Elsworth*   **90**

HILLS PLACE 2 b.c. (Jan 29) Primo Valentino (IRE) 116 – Moxby (Efisio 120) [2006 5m⁶ 5g⁵ 5d Sep 29] 14,000F, 16,000G, 20,000 2-y-o: strong colt: second foal: half-brother to 4-y-o Bow Wave: dam unraced sister to useful 7f performer Abbey's Gal: modest form in maidens, promising better when never-nearer fifth at Pontefract: will be suited by 6f/7f: should yet progress. *J. R. Best*   **52 p**

HILLTIME (IRE) 6 b.g. Danetime (IRE) 121 – Ceannanas (IRE) 77 (Magical Wonder (USA) 125) [2006 61: p12.2g⁶ 10f⁴ 10m³ Aug 9] modest handicapper: left J. J. Quinn after reappearance: stays 1½m: acts on polytrack, firm and good to soft ground: visored once earlier in career. *J. S. Wainwright*   **61**

HILLTOP DESTINY 3 b.c. Sure Blade (USA) 130 – Saferjel (Elmaamul (USA) 125) [2006 66: p9.5m 8.2v⁴ p12.2g* f12g* Dec 14] tall, unfurnished colt: fairly useful performer: much improved last 2 starts, winning handicaps at Wolverhampton and Southwell, making all both times: stays 1½m: acts on all-weather, raced only on good or softer going on turf. *V. Smith*   **85**

HILLTOP FANTASY 5 b.m. Danzig Connection (USA) – Hilltop 45 (Absalom 128) [2006 52: p9.5g p7.1g 7s 5.1g⁶ 5.3m 5.3m 6m f7m³ f8g⁵ p7g⁴ p8g³ p8g Dec 18] strong mare: modest maiden: barely stays 1m: acts on all-weather, best turf effort on good going: tried visored. *V. Smith*   **52**

HILVERSUM 4 ch.f. Polar Falcon (USA) 126 – Silky Heights (IRE) 67 (Head For   –
Heights 125) [2006 –p: p9.5g p12.2g p9.5g 7g May 29] lightly-raced maiden: no solid
form: tried in cheekpieces. *Miss J. A. Camacho*

HIMBA 3 b.g. Vettori (IRE) 119 – Be My Wish 80 (Be My Chief (USA) 122) [2006 10m   **64**
10d 10m 12m⁴ 14g² 16g 14.1d Sep 27] big, rangy gelding: modest maiden: stays 1¾m:
best effort on good going. *Mrs A. J. Perrett*

HINTERLAND (IRE) 4 b. or br.c. Danzig (USA) – Electric Society (IRE) 107 (Law   **111**
Society (USA) 130) [2006 104+: 8.5g* 8m⁴ 8.1m* 7m 10.5m⁵ 9d Sep 30] tall colt: smart
performer, lightly raced: won handicaps at Epsom (by 1½ lengths from Skidrow) in
June and Sandown (beat Ace of Hearts 1¼ lengths in totescoop6 Stakes) in July: best
effort after, though still below form, when fifth to Mulqat in Rose of Lancaster Stakes at
Haydock: should stay 1¼m: acts on good to firm and good to soft going: has given trouble
at stall: joined Godolphin. *M. A. Jarvis*

HINT OF SPRING 2 b.f. (Feb 12) Seeking The Gold (USA) – Cherokee Rose (IRE)   –
122 (Dancing Brave (USA) 140) [2006 p7.1g Nov 14] half-sister to 2 winners, including
smart 1m/11f winner Bowman (by Irish River): dam 6f (Haydock Park Sprint Cup)/7f
winner: 7/2, possibly amiss when well held in maiden at Wolverhampton, eased. *Saeed
bin Suroor*

HINTON ADMIRAL 2 b.c. (Apr 14) Spectrum (IRE) 126 – Shawanni 105 (Shareef   **100**
Dancer (USA) 135) [2006 6g* 7m⁶ 6g* 6s² p6g* Oct 21] rather leggy, good-topped
colt: half-brother to several winners, including useful 1¼m (at 2 yrs and in UAE) to 2m
(Queen's Vase) winner Shanty Star (by Hector Protector) and 3-y-o Lucky Token: dam,
2-y-o 7f winner, out of Rockfel Stakes winner Negligent: useful form: won maiden in
June and nursery in September, both at Hamilton, and listed race at Lingfield in October,
in last-named making most to beat Resplendent Alpha by 1¼ lengths: will probably stay
1m: acts on polytrack and good to firm going, not discredited on soft in listed event at
York (6 lengths second to Baby Strange) fourth start. *M. Johnston*

HI PERRY 4 b.c. Meqdaam (USA) – Hi Rock 55 (Hard Fought 125) [2006 8.2g Sep 26]   –
compact colt: tailed off only outing. *M. Wellings*

HIPPODROME CORNER 2 br.f. (Apr 15) Mujahid (USA) 125 – Raffelina (USA)   –
(Carson City (USA)) [2006 6s Oct 10] half-sister to 3 winners, including 1m winner Cello
(by Pivotal) and 5f (including at 2 yrs)/6f winner Prima Stella (by Primo Dominie): dam
unraced: behind in maiden at Newbury. *R. Hannon*

HIPPODROME (IRE) 4 b.g. Montjeu (IRE) 137 – Moon Diamond (Unfuwain (USA)   –
131) [2006 105: 10m 12m a10f 11.6g 16d Sep 24] good-bodied gelding: useful at 3 yrs:
left A. O'Brien in Ireland 110,000 gns after final 3-y-o outing (gelded): well held in 2006,
leaving H. Brown in UAE after third outing: stays 1½m: unraced on extremes of going on
turf: tried visored/blinkered: sent to Germany. *R. Simpson*

HIPPOLYTE (USA) 3 b.f. Monarchos (USA) 129 – Liberty School (USA) (Pine Bluff   **49**
(USA)) [2006 p8.6g 8.2m 8d⁶ 7m f8g² Oct 12] $10,000Y, 28,000 2-y-o: lengthy filly:
third foal: half-sister to winner in USA by Pulpit: dam 6f (at 2 yrs)/7f winner in USA:
poor maiden: stays 1m: acts on fibresand. *J. G. Given*

HIRVINE (FR) 8 ch.g. Snurge 130 – Guadanella (FR) (Guadanini (FR) 125) [2006   **52**
17.1d⁴ Oct 2] big, strong gelding: modest maiden on Flat: will stay beyond 17f: acts on
soft and good to firm going: tried blinkered: fairly useful hurdler/chaser. *D. McCain Jnr*

HIS HONOUR (IRE) 3 ch.g. Grand Lodge (USA) 125 – Knight's Baroness 116 (Rain-   **77**
bow Quest (USA) 134) [2006 8m⁵ 10d⁴ p12g² Sep 18] useful-looking gelding: has a
quick action: half-brother to several winners, including very smart 1¼m/1½m winner
Riyadian (by Polish Precedent) and useful 1m (at 2 yrs) and 1½m winner Wales (by
Caerleon): dam won Irish Oaks: fair maiden: stays 1½m: sold 33,000 gns. *R. Charlton*

HIS MASTER'S VOICE (IRE) 3 ch.c. Distant Music (USA) 126 – Glen of Imaal   **80**
(IRE) (Common Grounds 118) [2006 p6g³ p6g⁵ p6g² p7g³ p7g p8.6g 7m⁵ p7g* p6g⁴
7s⁴ 7m p7g 6g p6g Dec 20] €18,000Y: rather leggy colt: fourth living foal: half-brother
to 5-y-o Lakeside Guy and 2000 2-y-o 6f seller winner Somers Heath (by Definite
Article): dam, Irish maiden, sister to smart 2000 2-y-o Bad As I Wanna Be: fairly useful
handicapper: won at Lingfield in July: stays 7f: acts on polytrack and soft going.
D. W. P. Arbuthnot

HISTORIC APPEAL (USA) 3 b.g. Diesis 133 – Karasavina (IRE) (Sadler's Wells   **69**
(USA) 132) [2006 79: 9v² 12.1d⁶ 10.2s⁶ 9.8s⁶ 11.9g Sep 22] good-topped gelding: fair
maiden: should stay 1¼m: raced only on good going or softer (folded tamely)
third outing: not straightforward: sold 7,000 gns. *M. R. Channon*

HISTORY BOY 2 b.g. (Jan 23) Dr Fong (USA) 128 – Goldie 80 (Celtic Swing 138) [2006 7g⁴ 7g³ p7g⁴ p7.1g⁴ p8.6g* p8g⁴ Dec 16] leggy, quite attractive gelding: first foal: dam 5.7f (at 2 yrs) and 7f winner: fairly useful performer: won maiden at Wolverhampton in November: in frame all other starts, including third in listed event at Krefeld: stays 8.6f: raced on polytrack/good going: quirky, no easy ride. *D. J. Coakley* **84**

HISTORY PRIZE (IRE) 3 b.g. Celtic Swing 138 – Menominee (Soviet Star (USA) 128) [2006 p8.6g⁶ p9.5g Dec 11] poor form in seller (slowly away, claimed from D. Wintle £6,000) and maiden at Wolverhampton. *A. G. Newcombe* **48**

HITS ONLY CASH 4 b.g. Inchinor 119 – Persian Blue 64 (Persian Bold 123) [2006 74: p6g⁴ p6g² 6g p7.1g³ 5.1s 6d² p6g p7.1g 5d 6s 6d p7.1m⁴ Nov 8] close-coupled gelding: fairly useful handicapper: well worth another try over 1m: acts on polytrack and heavy ground: tried blinkered. *J. Pearce* **74 a80**

HITS ONLY HEAVEN (IRE) 4 ch.g. Bold Fact (USA) 116 – Algonquin Park (High Line 125) [2006 92: p8g³ p8.6g³ p6g 7f p7g p8g* p8g⁶ 6g² p8g⁶ 7m p7g⁵ f6g Dec 21] good-topped gelding: fairly useful handicapper: left J. Pearce after second start: won at Kempton in June: effective at 6f to 8.6f: acts on polytrack, best efforts on turf on good going: has worn blinkers: has run well when sweating: free-going sort. *D. Nicholls* **91**

HITS ONLY JUDE (IRE) 3 gr.g. Bold Fact (USA) 116 – Grey Goddess 117 (Gods-walk (USA) 130) [2006 82: p7g⁵ 6d 5m 5d⁵ p5.1g 6g p7.1m⁵ 7d p7.1g⁵ Nov 1] sturdy, close-coupled gelding: fair maiden handicapper nowadays: probably stays easy 7f: acts on polytrack, soft and good to firm going: blinkered (pulled hard) on debut. *J. Pearce* **71**

HITS ONLY LIFE (USA) 3 b.g. Lemon Drop Kid (USA) 131 – Southern Day (USA) (Dixieland Band (USA)) [2006 –: p6g f8g f8g* 8m 10d² 10g² 8.2s f11g Jun 3] modest performer: won banded race at Southwell in March: stays 1¼m: acts on fibresand and good to soft ground: none too resolute. *J. Pearce* **60**

HIT'S ONLY MONEY (IRE) 6 br.g. Hamas (IRE) 125§ – Toordillon (IRE) 69 (Contract Law (USA) 108) [2006 75: p7.1g f6g p7.1g³ 7d p7.1g 5.1f 6m 7g⁶ 7.1m 8m Sep 20] workmanlike gelding: usually beats well: just modest performer nowadays: left P. Blockley after reappearance, claimed from J. Pearce after fourth outing: should stay 1m: acts on polytrack and good to firm going: tried tongue tied/in cheekpieces: sold 1,000 gns. *R. A. Harris* **63**

HITS ONLY VIC (USA) 2 b. or br.c. (Apr 10) Lemon Drop Kid (USA) 131 – Royal Family (USA) (Private Terms (USA)) [2006 6m 6g 6m 7m f6g Nov 14] workmanlike colt: little form: bred to stay 1m. *J. Pearce* **–**

HIT THE ROAD (IRE) 2 gr.g. (Mar 18) Carrowkeel (IRE) 106 – Order of Success (USA) (With Approval (CAN)) [2006 9s p7g Nov 25] well beaten in minor event at Ballinrobe and maiden at Kempton. *Michael McElhone, Ireland* **–**

HOCINAIL (FR) 2 ch.c. (Apr 28) Majorien 118 – Flamme (FR) (Shining Steel 123) [2006 7f⁵ 7f⁶ 8.1m Sep 1] mid-field in maidens: will stay 1¼m. *P. Winkworth* **50**

HOGAN'S HEROES 3 b.g. Alhaarth (IRE) 126 – Icicle 104 (Polar Falcon (USA) 126) [2006 –: p5g 7f³ p8g⁵ 8m³ 8d 8f Jul 28] quite good-topped gelding: modest maiden: stays 1m: acts on firm going. *G. A. Butler* **63**

HOGMANEIGH (IRE) 3 b.g. Namid 128 – Magical Peace (IRE) 80 (Magical Wonder (USA) 125) [2006 86p: 6g 6.1s* 6s³ 5g* 5.4g³ 6d 6s Oct 7] strong, close-coupled gelding: progressed into a useful handicapper in 2006, winning at Nottingham in May and Sandown (by 1¼ lengths from Gimasha) in August: creditable 3½ lengths third to Fantasy Believer in Portland at York next time: ran as if amiss last 2 starts: effective at 5f/6f: raced only on good going or softer on turf (acts on soft). *S. C. Williams* **108**

HOH BLA DAA 3 b.g. Cape Cross (IRE) 129 – Monte Calvo 85 (Shirley Heights 130) [2006 71: 10g p12g³ 14.1m⁴ May 12] workmanlike gelding: fair maiden: likely to prove best short of 1¾m: raced only on good ground or firmer on turf: sold 17,000 gns in July. *S. Kirk* **68**

HOH BLEU DEE 5 b.g. Desert Style (IRE) 121 – Ermine (IRE) 86 (Cadeaux Genereux 131) [2006 64: p9.5g p10g p8.6g⁶ p9.5g Mar 20] smallish, well-made gelding: just poor performer in 2006: stays easy 1¼m: acts on polytrack, good to firm and good to soft going: tried blinkered/in cheekpieces. *T. Keddy* **49**

HOH HOH HOH 4 ch.g. Piccolo 121 – Nesting 47 (Thatching 131) [2006 92: 5g 5m 5m 5g⁶ 5m⁵ 5f⁴ 6d* 5.1m⁶ p6g Nov 1] good-topped gelding: useful performer: left A. Balding £5,500 after third start: easily best effort of 2006 when winning handicap at **98**

Salisbury in September by short head from Greek Renaissance: reportedly finished lame final start: effective at 5f/6f: acts on firm and good to soft going. *R. J. Price*

HOHLETHELONELY 2 ch.c. (Feb 21) Medicean 128 – Now And Forever (IRE) **86 p**
(Kris 135) [2006 8.3d² 8d* Nov 3] fifth living foal: half-brother to useful 1999 2-y-o 7f winner (stayed 1½m) Everlasting Love (by Pursuit of Love) and 1¼m winner Hoh My Darling (by Dansili): dam unraced half-sister to smart stayer Witness Box out of close relative to Dahlia: fairly useful form: confirmed debut promise when winning maiden at Musselburgh by 3 lengths from Salaasa, niggled most of way: will be suited by 1¼m/ 1½m: should go on progressing. *M. L. W. Bell*

HOH ME HOH YOU (IRE) 2 ch.g. (Apr 11) Redback 116 – Eastern Aura (IRE) 49 **56**
(Ahonoora 122) [2006 7.1m 7.1m 6m p6g Dec 22] modest form in maidens: gelded after third start. *S. Kirk*

HOH MIKE (IRE) 2 ch.c. (Apr 25) Intikhab (USA) 135 – Magical Peace (IRE) 80 **105**
(Magical Wonder (USA) 125) [2006 5m² 5m* 5d² 5m² 6m 5g³ 6g⁶ 5d² Oct 7] 55,000Y:
strong, lengthy colt: fourth foal: half-brother to fairly useful 2004 2-y-o 5f/6f winner Dario Gee Gee (by Bold Fact) and 3-y-o Hogmaneigh: dam Irish 6f winner, out of sister to dam of Vinnie Roe: useful performer: won 2 minor events at Windsor in May with plenty in hand: ran well after when placed in pattern company, beaten 1¾ lengths each time, second of 11 to Dutch Art in Norfolk Stakes at Royal Ascot (met trouble), third of 9 to Wi Dud in Flying Childers Stakes at York, and second of 10 to Alzerra in Cornwallis Stakes at Ascot: should stay 6f (below-form favourite both starts at trip): yet to race on extremes of ground. *M. L. W. Bell*

HOH WOTANITE 3 ch.c. Stravinsky (USA) 133 – West One 67 (Gone West (USA)) **–**
[2006 62: p5g² 5.1m p6g² p6g² p7g* p7.1m² 7.1m p7g p7.1g³ f8g Dec 23] fair handi- **a77**
capper on all-weather: won at Lingfield in July (left A. Balding £19,000): creditable efforts when placed after: stays 7f: acts on polytrack, raced only on good/good to firm ground on turf. *R. Hollinshead*

HOLBECK GHYLL (IRE) 4 ch.g. Titus Livius (FR) 115 – Crimada (IRE) (Mukad- **89**
damah (USA) 125) [2006 79: p5g⁵ 5g 5.7g⁵ 5f* 5m 5m³ 6g⁵ 5.2m⁵ Sep 12] rather leggy, good-topped gelding: fairly useful handicapper: won at Goodwood in August by 2½ lengths from Smokin Beau: creditable effort after only when third at Sandown: winner at 5.7f, but may prove best at bare 5f: raced only on polytrack and good ground or firmer on turf (acts on firm): sometimes slowly away: headstrong. *A. M. Balding*

HOLDIN FOLDIN (IRE) 2 ch.g. (Apr 18) Fayruz 116 – Escudo (IRE) 79 (Indian **99**
Ridge 123) [2006 5m* 5m 6m* p5g* 6s² 5d⁶ 5d² 5d⁶ 8f Nov 24] €16,000Y: sturdy gelding: half-brother to fairly useful 2005 2-y-o 5f winner Past Tender (by Indian Dane-hill): dam 2-y-o 5f winner who stayed 1m: useful performer: successful in small fields in maiden at Musselburgh in June and minor events at Newcastle in July and Lingfield in August: best effort when 1¼ lengths second to Alzerra in listed race at Ayr seventh start: left K. Burke before final outing: will prove best at 5f/6f (well held at 1m): acts on poly-track, soft and good to firm going: usually forces pace. *C. Dollase, USA*

HOLDING HANDS (IRE) 5 b.m. Turtle Island (IRE) 123 – Sakanda (IRE) (Vayrann
133) [2006 –: f11g Mar 28] no sign of ability: tried in cheekpieces. *Patrick Morris, Ireland*

HOLIDAY COCKTAIL 4 b.g. Mister Baileys 123 – Bermuda Lily 78 (Dunbeath **76**
(USA) 127) [2006 74: p7.1g² p7.1g² p10g p10g³ 8.3m³ p8.6g 10.5g p8.6m⁴ Oct 14] quite good-topped gelding: fair performer: left S. Williams after sixth start: stays easy 1¼m: acts on polytrack, firm and soft going: tongue tied (ran creditably) final outing: joined J. Quinn. *Miss J. Feilden*

HOLLIE DELLAMORE 4 b.f. Fumo di Londra (IRE) 108 – Acebo Lyons (IRE) 73
(Waajib 121) [2006 p6g 8.1m p7g 7g Aug 3] leggy filly: first foal: dam 1¼m and 1¾m winner: no form: tried visored. *A. P. Jarvis*

HOLLOW JO 6 b.g. Most Welcome 131 – Sir Hollow (USA) (Sir Ivor (USA) 135) **a80**
[2006 65: p6g* p7.1g³ p8g* p7g⁵ p8g³ p7g⁴ p7g p8g³ 6g p7g³ p7g³ p8g p7g² p7g⁵ p6g*
p6g³ Dec 22] strong, lengthy gelding: fairly useful handicapper: won at Lingfield in January/February, and Kempton and Lingfield in December: effective at 6f to easy 1m: acts on all-weather, firm and good to soft going (ran poorly only turf start of 2006): tried tongue tied. *J. R. Jenkins*

HOLLOW RIDGE 2 b.f. (May 8) Beat Hollow 126 – Bolas 118 (Unfuwain (USA) **91 p**
131) [2006 7s* 7s² Oct 21] rather leggy filly: ninth foal: half-sister to fairly useful 1¾m/2m winner Twice (by Rainbow Quest): dam, won Irish Oaks, out of half-sister to Gold

Cup winner Longboat: won 17-runner maiden at Newbury (beat Mr Napper Tandy by head) in October, despite greenness: improved form back there later in month when ½-length second to Party in listed race, again pulling hard but rallying for finish: bred to be suited by 1¼m/1½m: should make a useful 3-y-o. *B. W. Hills*

HOLLY SPRINGS 4 b.f. Efisio 120 – Anotheranniversary 95 (Emarati (USA) 74) **56**
[2006 64: p5.1g⁴ p6g p5.1g Feb 6] sturdy filly: modest maiden: stays 6.5f: acts on poly-track and firm going: in blinkers/cheekpieces of late: temperament under suspicion. *Mrs C. A. Dunnett*

HOLLYWOOD GEORGE 2 b.c. (Feb 24) Royal Applause 124 – Aunt Tate (Tate **75 +**
Gallery (USA) 117) [2006 p6g³ p6s³ p6g* Dec 26] 50,000Y: half-brother to several winners, including useful 7f winner Doctorate (by Dr Fong), later successful in USA, and useful performer up to 1½m in Bahrain/UAE Lodge Keeper (by Grand Lodge), 7f winner at 2 yrs: dam ran twice: fair form: won maiden at Wolverhampton in minor event there earlier in month: best effort when third to Beauchamp Viceroy in minor event there earlier in month: will stay at least 7f. *W. J. Haggas*

HOLLYWOOD HENRY (IRE) 6 b.g. Bahhare (USA) 122 – Takeshi (IRE) 67 (Cad- **–**
eaux Genereux 131) [2006 52: f11g Jan 24] well-made gelding: modest performer: stayed 1m: acted on polytrack, firm and soft going: often wore headgear: dead. *P. A. Blockley*

HOLY ROMAN EMPEROR (IRE) 2 b.c. (Mar 28) Danehill (USA) 126 – L'On **125**
Vite (USA) (Secretariat (USA)) [2006 6m* 6m 6g* 6m* 7g² 7m* 7d² Oct 14]
    For a horse with so many races behind him, and one that has achieved such a high level of form, Holy Roman Emperor still has some rough edges to him. He ended his first season with seven races under his belt, but, even in his most impor-tant victory, a clear-cut success in the Prix Jean-Luc Lagardere on his penultimate start, he still showed signs of greenness or perhaps quirkiness. Although running well again in defeat, he carved a less than straightforward path too in his final outing in the Dewhurst, when all but turning round previous running with the champion two-year-old Teofilo. It will be fascinating to see which way Holy Roman Emperor goes at three. If he does ever put it all together, he will take some beating in the top three-year-old races at a mile, Teofilo or no Teofilo.
    Holy Roman Emperor and Teofilo went their separate ways in the early part of the season, with Holy Roman Emperor campaigned exclusively at six furlongs. After a comfortable success in a maiden at Leopardstown on his debut in June, Holy Roman Emperor came unstuck on his first outing in pattern company in the Coventry Stakes at Royal Ascot, where he started joint favourite with the winner

Anheuser-Busch Adventure Parks Railway Stakes, the Curragh—
Holy Roman Emperor wears down Drayton to give Aidan O'Brien his eighth win in this event in ten years

Independent Waterford Wedgwood Phoenix Stakes, the Curragh—this time it's eight wins from the last nine runnings, as Holy Roman Emperor turns the tables on Coventry Stakes winner Hellvelyn

Hellvelyn in a field of twenty-one but could manage only fifteenth, drifting right the moment he was put under pressure. Holy Roman Emperor was a better horse by the time he met Hellvelyn again in the Phoenix Stakes at the Curragh in August. In between, he gained his first success in pattern company turned out twelve days after Ascot in the Group 2 Anheuser-Busch Adventure Parks Railway Stakes at the Curragh in early-July, winning by three quarters of a length from the useful Drayton, covered up and leading in the final fifty yards. With the penny seemingly dropping, Holy Roman Emperor again started joint favourite with Hellvelyn when stepped up to Group 1 company for the Independent Waterford Wedgwood Phoenix Stakes on the same course the following month, the pair going off at 13/8 after Holy Roman Emperor drifted from even money. Seven weeks on from Ascot, Holy Roman Emperor turned the tables convincingly, ridden in similar style to his previous start and nudging through a gap to go clear in the final furlong, merely pushed out to beat Hellvelyn by a length and three quarters with Miss Beatrix third. He was an eighth winner of the Phoenix Stakes in nine years for his stable.

Holy Roman Emperor was made ante-post favourite for the Two Thousand Guineas at as short as 6/1 with some bookmakers after the Phoenix Stakes, but he was replaced at the head of the betting for Newmarket after his defeat by Teofilo in the National Stakes at the Curragh in September. Holy Roman Emperor was a hot favourite for the National Stakes, going off at 9/4-on with Teofilo at 2/1, but Holy Roman Emperor was seemingly put in his place, giving chase from over a furlong out and making no impression until near the finish, beaten a length and a quarter, the pair four and a half lengths clear. O'Brien was keen to praise the winner afterwards. 'Teofilo is a special horse,' he said, adding 'Our fellow has plenty of pace and would have no problem dropping back in distance. He needs a really strongly-run race.' O'Brien also pointed out 'He's a hard horse to keep weight off and that type of animal can usually take plenty of racing.'

True to his thinking, O'Brien continued to adopt an attacking policy with Holy Roman Emperor, who was turned out two weeks after the Curragh in the Prix Jean-Luc Lagardère (Grand Critérium) over seven furlongs at Longchamp on Arc day. O'Brien has made almost as much of a habit of winning France's leading two-

Prix Jean-Luc Lagardere (Grand Criterium), Longchamp—just a seventh success for O'Brien in this particular race; Holy Roman Emperor, despite wandering markedly, draws clear of Battle Paint, Vital Equine, He's A Decoy (second right), Fleeting Shadow (rail) and Visionario (right)

year-old race as he has the Phoenix Stakes and Holy Roman Emperor gave him his seventh Jean-Luc Lagardere in ten years, his third on the trot following Oratorio and Horatio Nelson. Holy Roman Emperor started only second favourite, going off at 18/10 coupled with his stable companion Trinity College, behind home-trained Visionario, who was unbeaten in three starts including the Prix la Rochette, but made short work of his rivals on the good to firm ground, getting the strongly-run race his trainer wanted and bursting between horses to go clear in the final furlong. Oddly, for a horse of his experience, Holy Roman Emperor hung right then left then right again with the race won, snaking his way to the finish and pricking his ears, but he had enough in hand to beat the previously unbeaten Battle Paint by two lengths, with the Champagne Stakes winner Vital Equine three quarters of a length further away in third and Visionario only sixth.

All but one of Aidan O'Brien's five Jean-Luc Lagardere winners, since the race was reduced to seven furlongs in 2001, have gone on to contest the Dewhurst over the same trip at Newmarket, though only 2001 winner Rock of Gibraltar has completed the double. Holy Roman Emperor followed Oratorio and Horatio Nelson in finishing second, but he ran a fine race, his best of the season, narrowing the gap on Teofilo from the National Stakes. In a strong field of fifteen, Teofilo and Holy Roman Emperor dominated the betting, Teofilo starting favourite at 11/8 with Holy Roman Emperor at 3/1. Holy Roman Emperor had sidestepped a clash with Dutch Art in the Prix Morny in August due to soft ground and conditions threatened to blunt Holy Roman Emperor's speed at Newmarket. Clearly none the worse for his busy schedule, he travelled strongly early on, but was reined back and found himself in rear at halfway. With the field bunching to the stand rail, his rider was forced to attempt a daring route up the inside and Holy Roman Emperor ran into a pocket as he showed a fine turn of foot to make up several lengths on the leaders. Switched right in the Dip, Holy Roman Emperor nosed ahead of Teofilo for a few strides, but, as the favourite battled back, edged left under pressure from Michael Kinane, deputising for the suspended Kieren Fallon, being denied by a head. Teofilo and Holy Roman Emperor finished two and a half lengths ahead of Strategic Prince and, if anything, looked even more superior to the field than the bare result given the decisiveness and speed with which they came away late on. Holy Roman Emperor was a top-priced 9/2 for the Guineas afterwards.

		Danzig	Northern Dancer
	Danehill (USA)	(b 1977)	Pas de Nom
	(b 1986)	Razyana	His Majesty
Holy Roman Emperor (IRE)		(b 1981)	Spring Adieu
(b.c. Mar 28, 2004)		Secretariat	Bold Ruler
	L'On Vite (USA)	(ch 1970)	Somethingroyal
	(b 1986)	Fanfreluche	Northern Dancer
		(b 1967)	Ciboulette

On pedigree, Holy Roman Emperor should be well suited by the chance to tackle at least a mile. From the final crop of sprinter/miler Danehill, also responsible in 2006 for the stable's Royal Lodge winner Admiralofthefleet, Holy Roman Emperor is a brother to the Australian performer Milanova, runner-up in the ten-furlong Australasian Oaks. He is a half-brother to several other winners, including the useful Scandinavian performer at up to a mile Heart of Oak (by Woodman). Their dam, the unraced L'On Vite, is a daughter of the legendary broodmare Fanfreluche, herself Canadian Horse of the Year and dam of numerous winners, including dual Canadian Horse of the Year L'Enjoleur and prolific stakes winner La Voyageuse, also a Canadian champion. In many years, Holy Roman Emperor would have done enough as a two-year-old to be a champion himself in his first season, and he should win more good races at three. A smallish, round-barrelled colt, the type to carry plenty of weight, he lacks the size of his old rival Teofilo, but he is a powerhouse on looks, and there's little reason to think he won't train on, given the way he progressed as a two-year-old. Incidentally, he was foaled later than Teofilo, so he might even make the greater progress physically. Seemingly held up for a turn of foot, he has raced mainly on good ground or firmer and connections were reportedly close to withdrawing him under the good to soft conditions at Newmarket. *A. P. O'Brien, Ireland*

HOME AFFAIRS 4 b.c. Dansili 127 – Orford Ness 107 (Selkirk (USA) 129) [2006 **119** 115: 8.3m* 8.5m³ Jun 3] strong, close-coupled, quite attractive colt: good walker: smart performer: won listed event at Windsor in May by 2½ lengths from Momtic: unlucky ¾-length third to Nayyir in Diomed Stakes at Epsom next time, pocketed much of final 1f: reportedly found to be lame after final workout prior to Queen Anne Stakes at Royal Ascot later in June: stays 8.5f: acts on good to firm and good to soft going: has raced freely: stays in training. *Sir Michael Stoute*

HOMEBRED STAR 5 ch.g. Safawan 118 – Celtic Chimes (Celtic Cone 116) [2006 **54** 55: p7g p9.5g⁴ p9.5g p9.5g³ p10g p10g p12g p10g Dec 13] modest performer: stays 9.5f: acts on polytrack: sometimes wears cheekpieces: sometimes slowly away. *G. P. Enright*

HOMECROFT BOY 2 ch.g. (Apr 16) Kyllachy 129 – Quiz Time 90 (Efisio 120) **–** [2006 6f 7g 7.1m Aug 28] good-bodied gelding: little form in maidens, unseated leaving paddock final start (gelded after). *J. A. Osborne*

HOMES BY WOODFORD 2 ch.g. (Apr 24) Tumbleweed Ridge 117 – Partenza **71** (USA) (Red Ransom (USA)) [2006 5d 5g 5m 6m f5g⁶ 5m⁴ 6v 6v f7g³* p6g⁴ p7g p7.1g* f6g p7.1g* Dec 27] 3,500F, 5,500Y: big, good-topped gelding: fifth foal: half-brother to 5-y-o Imperium and 2005 2-y-o 5f winner Red Emerald (by Makbul): dam unraced: fair performer: won claimer at Southwell (left M. Easterby £4,000) in November and nursery at Wolverhampton in December: stays 7f: acts on all-weather and good to firm going: tried blinkered. *R. A. Harris*

HOME SWEET HOME (IRE) 3 b.f. Danehill (USA) 126 – Jungle Moon (IRE) **95** (Sadler's Wells (USA) 132) [2006 6g³ 6m* 6m* 6g 6m² 6d² 7m⁵ 8g 7d⁴ p8g Oct 26] €6,000 2-y-o: plain filly: second foal: dam, lightly-raced Irish maiden, closely related to smart 6f winner Zarani Sidi Anna: useful performer: won maiden at Ripon in June and handicap at Windsor (beat Lipizza by 2½ lengths) in July: good efforts when in frame after in handicap at Windsor and listed races at Pontefract (to Indian Maiden) and Ascot (behind Makderah): best at 6f/7f: acts on good to firm and good to soft going, well held on polytrack: wore cheekpieces last 2 outings: sold 110,000 gns. *P. D. Evans*

HOMETOMAMMY 4 b.g. Diktat 126 – Catania (USA) (Aloma's Ruler (USA)) [2006 **–** –: p8g p9.5g⁶ p12g p10g p12g p13.9g Dec 31] lightly-raced maiden: no solid form. *P. W. Hiatt*

HONDURAS (SWI) 5 gr.g. Daylami (IRE) 138 – High Mare (FR) (Highest Honor **97** (FR) 124) [2006 12f 16d p12g⁴ p10g Dec 8] tall, quite good-topped gelding: useful performer: won twice at Ovrevoll in 2004 when also second in Norsk Derby on same course: left A. Lund in Norway, best efforts in 2006 when seventh of 8 in listed race at Goodwood on reappearance and fourth in handicap at Lingfield: should stay beyond 1½m: acts on polytrack and firm ground: tried blinkered: looked none too keen second start. *G. L. Moore*

HONEST DANGER 2 b.c. (Jan 29) Dansili 127 – Allegresse (IRE) 76 (Alzao (USA) **77** 117) [2006 5m⁵ 5g* 5d⁴ 7d Sep 24] 7,500Y, 8,000 2-y-o: small, compact colt: second foal: dam, disappointing maiden, best efforts at 7f/1m: fair performer: won maiden at Folkestone in August: should have stayed 1m: dead. *J. R. Best*

HONEST INJUN 5 b.h. Efisio 120 – Sioux 76 (Kris 135) [2006 p8.6g p8.6g f7g Feb **–** 16] sturdy horse: fair performer: unraced on Flat at 4 yrs: well beaten in 2005: tried tongue tied. *A. G. Juckes*

HONEY FLAME 3 b.f. Fumo di Londra (IRE) 108 – Dulzie 56 (Safawan 118) [2006 –
47: p6g p8g Feb 7] no form since debut at 2 yrs. *A. P. Jarvis*

HONEY RYDER 4 b.f. Compton Place 125 – Urania 66 (Most Welcome 131) [2006 **79**
92: p6g⁶ p6g May 25] leggy filly: fluent mover: fair performer nowadays: likely to prove
best up to easy 7f: acts on polytrack and firm going: sold 40,000 gns in November. *Stef
Liddiard*

HONEY'S GIFT 7 b.m. Terimon 124 – Honeycroft (Crofter (USA) 124) [2006 p16g –
Feb 28] rather leggy mare: shows knee action: poor maiden handicapper: stays 1½m
when conditions aren't testing: acts on heavy and good to firm going: tried in cheekpieces: sometimes slowly away. *G. G. Margarson*

HONOR ME (IRE) 3 b.f. Beckett (IRE) 116 – Christmas Kiss 82 (Taufan (USA) 119) **53**
[2006 –: 6d 7g⁴ 6.1f 8f⁶ 5.9g 7.1m Aug 17] modest maiden: stays 1m: acts on firm going:
tried visored. *J. J. Quinn*

HOOFBEATS TOUR 4 b.g. Vettori (IRE) 119 – Sprite 71 (Fairy King (USA)) [2006 –
f8g f11g f8g f11g⁶ Dec 9] no form. *Miss J. Feilden*

HOOPLAH 3 b.f. Pivotal 124 – La Piaf (FR) (Fabulous Dancer (USA) 124) [2006 8.3d **57**
Jun 26] eighth foal: half-sister to several winners, including 7f/1m winner Gilded Dancer
(by Bishop of Cashel) and 6-y-o Merlin's Dancer, both useful: dam, French 2-y-o 7.5f
winner (later winner in USA), half-sister to very smart US 9f/1¼m performer Golden
Apples (by Pivotal): 8/1, 6½ lengths ninth of 12 to Our Putra in maiden at Windsor,
slowly away: visits Medicean. *J. H. M. Gosden*

HO PANG YAU 8 b. or br.g. Pivotal 124 – La Cabrilla 89 (Carwhite 127) [2006 7.2m⁴ **56**
7.2g 7.1d Oct 8] close-coupled gelding: modest performer: unraced on Flat in 2004/5:
stays 1m: acts on firm and good to soft ground: tried blinkered/in cheekpieces.
J. S. Goldie

HOPEFUL ISABELLA (IRE) 2 ch.f. (Feb 11) Grand Lodge (USA) 125 – Hopeful **– p**
Sign (Warning 136) [2006 7.1m 6d 6m Sep 22] €32,000Y: big filly: on weak side at 2 yrs:
fourth foal: half-sister to useful 7f (at 2 yrs)/1m winner Londonnetdotcom (by Night
Shift): dam, ran once, closely related to very smart 7f/1m winner Greensmith and half-
sister to dam of St Leger winner Toulon: towards rear in maidens in September: will be
suited by at least 1m: sort to flourish in 3-y-o handicaps. *Sir Mark Prescott*

HOPEFUL PURCHASE (IRE) 3 ch.g. Grand Lodge (USA) 125 – Funoon (IRE) 74 **102**
(Kris 135) [2006 88p: 8.1g⁴ 10g* 10m 9.9f Aug 3] sturdy, good-bodied gelding: useful
performer: landed odds in maiden at Redcar in May: best effort when 4 lengths seventh to
Snoqualmie Boy in listed race at Royal Ascot next time: gelded after final start: likely to
prove best at 1m/1¼m: acts on soft and good to firm ground. *W. J. Haggas*

HOPE'N'CHARITY (USA) 2 b.f. (Feb 12) Smart Strike (CAN) 121 – Celestic **93**
(USA) (Sky Classic (CAN)) [2006 6f* 6f* 6m⁴ 6m 7m⁴ 6d⁶ Sep 16] smallish, leggy,
close-coupled filly: first foal: dam unraced half-sister to smart performer up to 1¼m
Mysteries, from useful family of very smart sprinter Agnes World: fairly useful performer: won
maiden at Leicester in June and listed race at Newmarket (beat Satulagi by length) in
July: ran creditably in pattern events next 3 starts, in frame in Cherry Hinton Stakes at
Newmarket and Prestige Stakes at Goodwood (3 lengths fourth of 10 to Sesmen): stays
7f: raced on going firmer than good until final outing (below form). *C. G. Cox*

HOPE ROAD 2 ch.g. (Apr 9) Sakhee (USA) 136 – Bibliotheque (USA) 79 (Woodman **70 p**
(USA) 126) [2006 7d Oct 10] fifth foal: half-brother to 6-y-o McQueen and 5-y-o True:
dam, 1m winner, out of half-sister to very smart 6f to 1m performer Lycius: 20/1, seventh
to Mount Hadley in maiden at Leicester, not knocked about (gelded after): should do
better. *J. R. Fanshawe*

HOPE'S ETERNAL 3 ro.c. Highest Honor (FR) 124 – Tennessee Moon 73 (Darshaan –
133) [2006 –: 10d 11.5m p12g Jun 29] stocky colt: no form: tried blinkered. *J. L. Dunlop*

HOPE YOUR SAFE 2 b.f. (Apr 6) Tobougg (IRE) 125 – Sunday Night (GER) 51 **58**
(Bakharoff (USA) 130) [2006 6d p6g³ p6g⁵ Dec 2] fourth foal: dam placed up to 1m in
Germany: modest form in maidens with third at Lingfield and fifth at Kempton: should
stay 7f: acts on polytrack. *J. R. Best*

HORA 2 b.f. (Mar 28) Hernando (FR) 127 – Applecross 117 (Glint of Gold 128) [2006 **– p**
p7g p7.1g f7g Nov 14] half-sister to several winners, notably stayer Invermark (by
Machiavellian) and 1½m/1¾m performer Craigsteel (by Suave Dancer), both very smart:
dam, 1¼m to 13.3f winner, second in Park Hill Stakes: green in maidens on all-weather:
sure to improve at 1½m+ at 3 yrs. *Sir Mark Prescott*

HORATIO NELSON (IRE) 3 b.c. Danehill (USA) 126 – Imagine (IRE) 119 (Sad- **110**
ler's Wells (USA) 132) [2006 123+: 8m 12m Jun 3] small, strong, well-made colt: good
walker: very smart 2-y-o in 2005, winning Prix Jean-Luc Lagardere at Longchamp and
second in Dewhurst Stakes at Newmarket: tapped for speed when pace quickened when 7
lengths eighth to stable-companion George Washington in 2000 Guineas on latter course
on reappearance (reportedly suffered with bruised foot subsequently): in around sixth
place when suffering multiple injuries to near-fore under 2f out in Derby at Epsom in June
(put down after dislocating fetlock joint and fracturing cannon bone and sesamoid bone):
was bred to be suited by 1¼m+: acted on good to soft going: was genuine. *A. P. O'Brien,
Ireland*

HORNPIPE 4 b.g. Danehill (USA) 126 – Dance Sequence (USA) 105 (Mr Prospector **75 d**
(USA)) [2006 98: p6g 5g 5m⁶ 5.3f⁶ 5.7m p5.1s p5.1g⁴ Dec 23] close-coupled gelding:
useful handicapper in 2005 for Sir Michael Stoute (sold 22,000 gns and gelded): on
downgrade in 2006: raced at 5f/6f: acts on good to firm ground: tried in cheekpieces.
M. S. Saunders

HORSLEY WIZ 2 b.g. (Apr 5) Wizard King 122 – Breezy Palms (Tragic Role (USA)) **69**
[2006 8.1m⁴ 8.1g a7.5g a7.5g² Dec 14] tall gelding: better effort in maidens for
E. McMahon when fourth at Chepstow on debut: sold 2,600 gns after next start, second in
claimer at Deauville final outing: stays 7.5f: blinkered last 2 starts. *N. Minner, Belgium*

HOSIVA (GER) 3 b.f. Silvano (GER) 126 – Hosianna (GER) (Surumu (GER)) [2006 **–**
p12g⁵ 7.5m⁶ 7.5m⁶ Oct 1] €28,000Y: half-sister to several winners in Germany, notably
smart 7f/1m performer Horeion Directa (by Big Shuffle) and useful stayer Horatius (by
Lagunas): dam German 1m to 1½m winner: showed only newcomers race at Milan at 2 yrs: well
held in minor events in 2006 (including at Kempton on reappearance, only outing in
Britain), leaving M. Quinlan before final start. *A. Macchi, Italy*

HOSTAGE 2 b.f. (Feb 14) Dr Fong (USA) 128 – Catatonic (Zafonic (USA) 130) [2006 **71 p**
p8.6g⁴ f7g* Dec 14] 10,000Y: first foal: dam unraced half-sister to smart performer up
to 1¼m Brave Act: much improved from debut when winning at Southwell in December
by 1¼ lengths from Vadinka, still very green: should stay 1m: will progress further.
M. L. W. Bell

HOT AGNES 3 b.f. Agnes World (USA) 123 – Hot Tin Roof (IRE) 112 (Thatching 131) **63**
[2006 8m p6g⁵ f6g⁴ 6d² p8g⁴ 8g⁶ p7g⁴ p8.6g⁴ p7g Dec 30] 8,000 2-y-o: first foal: dam 6f/
7f winner: modest maiden: may prove best up to 7f: acts on all-weather and good to soft
ground: tongue tied last 4 starts. *H. J. Collingridge*

HOT BABY (IRE) 3 gr.f. Linamix (FR) 127 – House In Wood (FR) (Woodman (USA)) **–**
126) [2006 –: 10.2m Sep 25] close-coupled filly: well held in maidens: dead. *M. L. W. Bell*

HOT CHERRY 2 b.f. (May 8) Bertolini (USA) 125 – Cribella (USA) 71 (Robellino **–**
(USA) 127) [2006 6g 6g⁵ 7.1m Aug 28] 23,000Y: strong filly: third living foal: half-sister
to 4-y-o Ruby Wine: dam 1½m winner: little show in maidens. *J. M. P. Eustace*

HOTCHPOTCH (USA) 3 b.g. Dayjur (USA) 137 – Anagram (USA) (Farma Way **66**
(USA)) [2006 49: f5g 6f* 7.1m⁵ 7s⁵ 6m² 7f⁵ p7g³ p6g⁵ p8g p7g⁴ p7g* Dec 30] good-
bodied gelding: fair performer: won maiden at Folkestone in August and handicap at
Lingfield in December: stays 7f: acts on polytrack and firm going: visored/in cheekpieces
last 2 starts. *J. R. Best*

HOTEL DU CAP 3 br.c. Grand Lodge (USA) 125 – Miss Riviera Golf 106 (Hernando **93**
(FR) 127) [2006 73p: 10m² p12g* 12.5d⁶ Oct 18] big, good-topped colt: has scope: fairly
useful performer: won maiden at Kempton in September by 9 lengths: ran well when 7½
lengths sixth to Morna in listed race at Deauville next time: stays 1½m: acts on polytrack,
good to firm and good to soft ground. *G. Wragg*

HOTHAM 3 b.g. Komaite (USA) – Malcesine (IRE) 46 (Auction Ring (USA) 123) **73**
[2006 73: 7g 5m 5f* 5f⁴ 6m³ 5d p5.1g³ p6g⁵ 6s Oct 24] lengthy, quite attractive gelding:
fair performer: won maiden at Beverley in July: may prove best kept to 5f/6f: acts on
polytrack, firm and good to soft going: races prominently. *N. Wilson*

HOT SHOT HAMISH (IRE) 2 b.c. (Feb 21) Desert Prince (IRE) 130 – Barbuda **–**
(Rainbow Quest (USA) 134) [2006 7g p7g Oct 26] smallish, quite attractive colt: has a
free, round action: well held in maidens. *B. J. Meehan*

HOUSE ARREST 2 ch.f. (Mar 23) Auction House (USA) 120 – Mentro (IRE) 65 **52 §**
(Entrepreneur 123) [2006 6.1g p6g⁶ 7f³ p7.1g² 6f² 7f² 5.1f² 5.2g² 5g³ 5m⁵ 5d⁵ p7g p6g³
Dec 16] 1,500Y: compact filly: first foal: dam, lightly-raced maiden (third at 1¼m), out
of half-sister to very smart 1¼m/1½m winner Sudden Love: modest maiden: second in 5

sellers in summer, left I. Wood £6,000 eighth start: effective at 5f to 7f: acts on polytrack and firm going: tried in headgear: temperamental. *A. J. McCabe*

HOUSE MAIDEN (IRE) 2 b.f. (Feb 16) Rudimentary (USA) 118 – Dahoar 66 (Charnwood Forest (IRE) 125) [2006 6m^4 p7g^3 Oct 17] €16,000Y: first foal: dam, 12.5f winner in Germany, half-sister to smart performer up to 1½m Housemaster (by Rudimentary): promise in frame in maidens at Folkestone and Lingfield, nearest finish both times: will be suited by 1m: can do better. *D. M. Simcock*   **68 p**

HOUSE MARTIN 4 b.f. Spectrum (IRE) 126 – Guignol (IRE) 80 (Anita's Prince 126) [2006 77d: p8g^4 f8g p10g p9.5g p8.6g 10.1g^2 10.1f^4 f12m Oct 31] good-topped filly: modest maiden nowadays: stays 1¼m: acts on polytrack and good to firm going: tried in headgear: has raced freely. *C. R. Dore*   **59**

HOUT BAY 9 ch.g. Komaite (USA) – Maiden Pool 85 (Sharpen Up 127) [2006 59: 5m 6g^4 6d 6d 5g 5s 5g 6v f5m^5 f6g f5g^5 f6g^5 f7g Dec 21] big, lengthy gelding: modest performer: left R. Fahey after fifth start: best at 5f/easy 6f: acts on all-weather, firm and good to soft going: usually blinkered/in cheekpieces: waited in (sometimes slowly away). *D. W. Chapman*   **50**

HOWARDS CALL 3 b.g. Easycall 115 – Bouchra (IRE) 75 (Inchinor 119) [2006 45: p5.1g Nov 20] poor maiden: well held in banded race only outing in 2006: blinkered last 2 starts: has hung left: has given trouble at stall. *W. G. Harrison*   **–**

HOWARDS DREAM (IRE) 8 b.g. King's Theatre (IRE) 128 – Keiko 76 (Generous (IRE) 139) [2006 –: 16g 10d Sep 16] little form since 2003. *D. A. Nolan*   **–**

HOWARDS PRINCE 3 gr.g. Bertolini (USA) 125 – Grey Princess (IRE) 92 (Common Grounds 118) [2006 73: 5d^6 5m^5 5g^4 5m^4 5d^4 5m p5.1g Sep 11] close-coupled gelding: modest performer: probably best at 5f: acts on firm and good to soft going: tried blinkered, usually wears cheekpieces: none too consistent. *I. Semple*   **63**

HOWARDS PRINCESS 4 gr.f. Lujain (USA) 119 – Grey Princess (IRE) 92 (Common Grounds 118) [2006 79: 6v^5 6g^3 6m^2 5m 6g^2 5m 5g p5.1g* 5s^5 f6g f6g^2 f6g p6g Dec 22] sparely-made filly: fair performer: below best after third start, including when winning claimer at Wolverhampton (left I. Semple) in October: effective at 5f/6f: acts on all-weather, soft and good to firm going: usually wears headgear. *J. Hetherton*   **74 d**

HOWARDS ROCKET 5 ch.g. Opening Verse (USA) 126 – Houston Heiress (USA) (Houston (USA)) [2006 p12.2g^6 Nov 14] lightly-raced maiden: missed 2005: modest form only outing in 2006: stays easy 12.2f: acts on polytrack. *J. S. Goldie*   **50**

HOWARDS TIPPLE 2 b.c. (Apr 4) Diktat 126 – Grey Princess (IRE) 92 (Common Grounds 118) [2006 5m^6 6d^3 6g^3 5f^3 6v p7.1g^6 p6m Nov 9] 24,000F: third foal: half-brother to 3-y-o Howards Prince and 4-y-o Howards Princess: dam 2-y-o 5f/6f winner: fair maiden: third 3 times: best at 5f/6f: acts on firm and good to soft going: visored (found little) final start. *I. Semple*   **75**

HOWLE HILL (IRE) 6 b.g. Ali-Royal (IRE) 127 – Grandeur And Grace (USA) 75 (Septieme Ciel (USA) 123) [2006 110: p10g Jan 14] leggy gelding: smart performer at best: ran as if amiss sole outing on Flat in 2006 (won over fences in May and October): stays easy 13.3f: acts on polytrack, firm and soft ground: tried visored: tends to sweat: usually held up. *A. King*   **–**

HOW'S SHE CUTTIN' (IRE) 3 ch.f. Shinko Forest (IRE) – Magic Annemarie (IRE) 75 (Dancing Dissident (USA) 119) [2006 p6g^4 7m 5s* 5s^2 5d* 5v^2 5d* Nov 3] good-topped filly: fourth foal: dam, Irish 5f/6f winner, granddaughter of Cheveley Park Stakes winner Magic Flute: fair and progressive form: won maiden at Ripon (made all) in August and banded race in October and handicap in November, both at Musselburgh: best efforts at 5f: acts on heavy ground. *T. D. Barron*   **73 +**

HOWS THAT 4 ch.f. Vettori (IRE) 119 – Royalty (IRE) (Fairy King (USA)) [2006 58: f7g^4 f7g f7g f8g f7g 6m^3 8m 8d* 7.1d^4 9.1v Oct 28] angular filly: modest performer: won claimer at Newcastle in August: stays 1m: acts on all-weather, good to firm and good to soft going: effective with/without cheekpieces. *K. R. Burke*   **50 a–**

HUCKING HEAT (IRE) 2 b.g. (Feb 8) Desert Sun 120 – Vltava (IRE) 73 (Sri Pekan (USA) 117) [2006 p6g 5m 6f^4 Aug 10] €9,000F, 21,000Y: second foal: half-brother to Italian 5f/6f winner by Mull of Kintyre: dam Irish maiden who stayed 7f: fair maiden: much improved when fourth at College Scholar at Folkestone, then gelded: will probably stay 7f/1m. *J. R. Best*   **66**

HUCKING HILL (IRE) 2 ch.g. (Mar 14) City On A Hill (USA) 114 – Con Dancer (Shareef Dancer (USA) 135) [2006 p5g^4 p5g^2 5.2m^2 p5g* 5g^4 5.1m^6 5g p6g^6 6f^3 p6g^6 **78**

p6g p8g p6g⁶ p6g³ p6g* p6g* p7g⁴ Dec 20] 15,000Y: strong, useful-looking gelding: type to carry condition: fourth foal: dam placed in Belgium: fair performer: won maiden in April and 2 nurseries in November, all at Kempton: best at 5f/6f: acts on polytrack and good to firm going: blinkered last 5 starts. *J. R. Best*

HUCKING HOPE (IRE) 2 b.f. (Feb 21) Desert Style (IRE) 121 – Amarapura (FR) (Common Grounds 118) [2006 5m⁴ p5.1g* 5f p5g⁴ p5g² p5g 5.2d⁴ p5.1m⁴ Nov 8] €9,000Y: small, lengthy filly: first foal: dam, lightly-raced French maiden (runner-up at 11f/1¼m), out of half-sister to US Grade 1 9f/1¼m winner Greinton: fair performer: won maiden at Wolverhampton in June: made frame 4 of 5 nurseries: raced at 5f, bred for much further: acts on polytrack and good to soft ground. *J. R. Best* — **69**

HUCKING HOT 2 b.f. (Mar 13) Desert Prince (IRE) 130 – True Love (Robellino (USA) 127) [2006 p5.1g² 5f⁶ 5g³ 7.5f* 8f* 8f⁵ a8.5f⁴ Dec 17] 4,500Y: well-made filly: fourth foal: dam unraced half-sister to useful 2-y-o sprinter Hellvelyn: useful performer: third of 11 to Roxan in listed race at Beverley prior to winning maiden there (despite stumbling) in June: left J. Best and off 4 months, won non-graded stakes at Santa Anita in October (only outing for J. Lloyd): good efforts after, particularly when 4 lengths fourth to Romance Is Diane in Hollywood Starlet final outing: stays 8.5f: acts on firm going and Cushion Track. *P. Gallagher, USA* — **102**

HUE 5 ch.g. Peintre Celebre (USA) 137 – Quandary (USA) 104 (Blushing Groom (FR) 131) [2006 75: p12.2g⁵ p13.9g⁵ 13.8d 16d² 16s* May 24] leggy gelding: fairly useful performer: won handicap at Goodwood in May: stays 2m on all-weather, soft and good to firm going: tried in cheekpieces, blinkered final 2 starts: not a straightforward ride. *B. Ellison* — **83**

HUGGLE 3 b.g. Groom Dancer (USA) 128 – Perle de Sagesse 66 (Namaqualand (USA)) [2006 63: 8g p12g 12v Oct 31] tall gelding: maiden: well held in 2006: tried visored. *P. S. McEntee* — **–**

HUGS DESTINY (IRE) 5 b.g. Victory Note (USA) 120 – Embracing 91 (Reference Point 139) [2006 63, a67: 12m⁵ 14.1m 15.8g⁵ 17.2m⁴ 12m* 14.1g³ 14.1d 14m³ 14g⁵ 15.8m Sep 16] sturdy gelding: fair handicapper: won apprentice event at Catterick in July: stays 1¾m (seemingly not 2m): acts on polytrack, good to firm and good to soft going: tried blinkered/tongue tied: usually races prominently. *M. A. Barnes* — **65**

HULA BALLEW 6 ch.m. Weldnaas (USA) 112 – Ballon 63 (Persian Bold 123) [2006 71: 6v 7d³ 8m* 8.3m³ 8g* 8m* 7.2g⁵ 7.9g³ 7.9m⁴ 8m³ 8m³ 8g⁴ 8v⁴ 8d³ Sep 15] smallish mare: fairly useful handicapper: won at Pontefract in May and Thirsk (twice) in June: stays 9f: acts on any turf going: used to wear cheekpieces: reliable. *M. Dods* — **83**

HUMBLE GIFT 3 ch.f. Cadeaux Genereux 131 – West Humble 93 (Pharly (FR) 130) [2006 –: p7g Jun 7] better effort in maidens (poor form) when eighth at Kempton only outing in 2006. *Mrs L. J. Mongan* — **45**

HUMBLE OPINION 4 br.g. Singspiel (IRE) 133 – For More (FR) (Sanglamore (USA) 126) [2006 93: 10g 8.5g 8.1f* 8.1m 10g³ 9.9m Aug 1] useful-looking gelding: useful handicapper: won at Haydock in June by 1¼ lengths from Tyzack: stays easy 1¼m: raced only on polytrack and good going or firmer on turf. *B. J. Meehan* — **95**

HUMILITY 5 b.m. Polar Falcon (USA) 126 – Rich In Love (IRE) 95 (Alzao (USA) 117) [2006 60: p7g p7.1g⁶ p8g* p8g p6g⁴ p8g⁶ p7g³ p8g p6g p8g³ p7g⁵ p7g³ p7g Dec 8] fair performer: won handicap at Lingfield in April: effective at 6f to easy 1m: acts on polytrack. *C. A. Cyzer* — **66**

HUMUNGOUS (IRE) 3 ch.g. Giant's Causeway (USA) 132 – Doula (USA) (Gone West (USA)) [2006 100: p7g 8.3m³ 10f² 9.9f⁵ 8f² 10m Sep 16] tall, rather leggy gelding: useful performer: best effort when 2½ lengths second to Dark Islander in handicap at Bath fifth start: not discredited in John Smith's Stakes (Handicap) at Newbury final outing: gelded after: stays 1¼m: acts on polytrack, firm and good to soft going: consistent. *C. R. Egerton* — **105**

HUNTERS' GLEN (USA) 3 b.c. Bahri (USA) 125 – Hedera (USA) 90 (Woodman (USA) 126) [2006 8g² 9.9m* p12.2f³ 10.4s⁴ Oct 7] quite good-topped colt: fourth foal: half-brother to 1½m winner Heisse (by Darshaan) and French performer up to 11.5f Ivy League (by Doyoun), both useful: dam, 2-y-o 7f winner (stayed 1m), out of Ribblesdale runner-up Ivrea: useful form: won maiden at Beverley in August by 11 lengths: good efforts after, 5½ lengths fourth to Ofaraby in minor event at York: stays 1½m: acts on polytrack, soft and good to firm going: tongue tied all starts: joined D. Watson in UAE. *Saeed bin Suroor* — **98**

HUNTING CALL 2 b.c. (Mar 13) Foxhound (USA) 103 – Margaret's Gift 101 (Bevel- **73 d** ed (USA)) [2006 6g 7d 7.1m⁴ 7g³ 7s 6v⁶ p6m f6g³ Nov 15] 8,500Y: strong colt: half-brother to 3 winners, including fairly useful 2000 2-y-o 5f winner Game N Gifted (by Mind Games), later 7f to 8.5f winner in Italy: dam 5f (at 2 yrs) and 6f winner who stayed 7f: fair maiden: below form last 4 starts: stays 7f: acts on good to firm ground: usually blinkered: sent to Sweden. *K. A. Ryan*

HUNTING HAZE 3 b.g. Foxhound (USA) 103 – Second Affair (IRE) 85 (Pursuit of **65** Love 124) [2006 64: 9m 9.9f⁴ 12m³ 9.9m⁴ 12.4d Aug 28] fair maiden: stays 1½m: acts on firm ground: sold 23,000 gns. *Miss S. E. Hall*

HUNTING LODGE (IRE) 5 ch.g. Grand Lodge (USA) 125 – Vijaya (USA) (Lear **–** Fan (USA) 130) [2006 90: p16g Jul 5] strong gelding: fairly useful performer: blinkered, well held sole Flat start in 2006 (won twice over hurdles in June): tried visored. *H. J. Manners*

HUNTING PARTY (IRE) 3 ch.c. Grand Lodge (USA) 125 – Delilah (IRE) 114 **75** (Bluebird (USA) 125) [2006 71: p8.6g³ 10m 10f⁴ 10m6 10m Jul 12] tall, good-topped colt: has a fluent, quick action: fair maiden: bred to stay beyond 1¼m but is a free-going sort: acts on polytrack and firm ground: tongue tied last 3 starts: seems quirky: sold 12,500 gns. *B. W. Hills*

HUNTING TOWER 2 b.c. (Jan 30) Sadler's Wells (USA) 132 – Fictitious 100 (Mach- **82 +** iavellian (USA) 123) [2006 6m³ 7.1g³ 8d* Oct 19] leggy colt: first foal: dam, 1¼m winner (later Grade 3 8.5f winner in USA), sister to smart performer up to 13f Phantom Gold: progressive form in maidens (break between runs), third to Big Robert at Sandown before readily winning at Brighton final start: will be suited by 1¼m/1½m. *R. Hannon*

HURLINGHAM 2 b.c. (Jan 16) Halling (USA) 133 – Society (IRE) 73 (Barathea **79** (IRE) 127) [2006 7.1m³ 7.1m² 7d⁴ Oct 10] €150,000Y: tall, rather leggy, quite attractive colt: first foal: dam, 1¼m winner, half-sister to smart French 1m/9f performer Lone Bid: fair form in frame in maidens, off 3 months after second start (runner-up to Nur Tau at Sandown): will stay 1m/1¼m. *M. Johnston*

HURRICANE CAT (USA) 3 b.c. Storm Cat (USA) – Sky Beauty (USA) 129 (Blush- **111** ing Groom (FR) 131) [2006 106p: 7d³ 8v 10.5m 8m⁵ 7.5v³ Oct 1] sturdy, angular colt: smart performer: won Horris Hill Stakes at Newbury at 2 yrs: ran respectably first 2 starts in 2006 (seventh in Irish 2000 Guineas on second occasion): best efforts last 2 outings when 2¾ lengths fifth to Mustameet in International Stakes at the Curragh and 1¼ lengths third to Noelani in Concorde Stakes at Tipperary: stayed 1m (well held at 10.5f in Prix du Jockey Club): acted on heavy and good to firm going: to stand at Haras de la Haie Neuve, France, fee €3,000. *A. P. O'Brien, Ireland*

HURRICANE COAST 7 b.g. Hurricane Sky (AUS) – Tread Carefully 51 (Sharpo **81 d** 132) [2006 87: p8.6g⁴ f7g p6g⁵ p9.5g* p8.6g⁵ p8.6g p8.6g 6m 8.1d³ 7m⁵ 8f⁴ 7f p8.6g⁶ p8g p8g p7g⁶ Dec 10] tall gelding: fairly useful performer: won claimer at Wolverhampton in January, below form subsequently: left K. McAuliffe after ninth start, C. Dore after eleventh: stays easy 9.5f: acts on all-weather, firm and soft going: tried tongue tied, wears headgear: edgy sort: carries head awkwardly/tends to hang. *Ms J. S. Doyle*

HURRICANE DENNIS 2 ch.g. (Feb 15) Silver Wizard (USA) 117 – Thatcher's Era **–** (IRE) 57 (Never So Bold 135) [2006 6g 7m Jun 15] no sign of ability. *D. K. Ivory*

HURRICANE FLYER 2 b.c. (Mar 18) Royal Applause 124 – Cyclone Flyer 67 **75** (College Chapel 122) [2006 5g² 5d² 5.1d² Oct 4] small, sturdy colt: fourth foal: half-brother to 2 winners, including useful 5f (at 2 yrs)/6f winner Autumn Pearl (by Orpen): dam, 5f winner, half-sister to very smart sprinter Bolshoi: fairly useful maiden: second all starts, beaten ½ length by Now Look Out at Nottingham final one: will prove best kept to 5f: raced on good/good to soft going: sold 24,000 gns, sent to Denmark. *E. J. O'Neill*

HURRICANE RUN (IRE) 4 b.c. Montjeu (IRE) 137 – Hold On (GER) (Surumu **130** (GER)) [2006 134: 10.5v* 12d² 12m* 12m² 12m³ 10d³ 12f Nov 4]
And that was that! There was something unsatisfactory about Hurricane Run's four-year-old campaign. It wasn't just that his form tailed off and his enthusiasm seemed to wane after he had added to his Group 1 tally in the first half of the season, but also that, even when he was in good form, the opportunity never came along to enable him to show himself in the best light. Small fields followed Hurricane Run round all season, especially in the first half of the year. Having shown himself well suited by a truly-run mile and a half when beating fourteen rivals in clear-cut fashion in the Prix de l'Arc de Triomphe at Longchamp on his final outing

as a three-year-old, Hurricane Run met a total of only twelve opponents in his first three races as a four-year-old, each of which came in a Group 1 event. He won two of them, the Tattersalls Gold Cup at the Curragh and the King George VI and Queen Elizabeth Diamond Stakes, on its return to Ascot, but never quite showed himself the same horse he had been as a three-year-old, let alone improving on his Arc form as had looked possible after Longchamp.

That Hurricane Run should scare off all but two opponents in the Tattersalls Gold Cup run on heavy ground in early-May was hardly surprising, but that he should face only a handful of rivals in the King George in July was of greater concern. The smallest turnout for the race since the same number lined up in 1970 highlighted the lack of three-year-old representation which has begun to threaten the race's status as the traditional mid-season clash of the generations at a mile and a half. For the second time in five years, no three-year-old, colt or filly, appeared in the latest renewal. The two previous runnings boasted only one three-year-old apiece. Kris Kin in 2001 was the last Derby winner to tackle the King George and only two of those successful at Epsom in the last seven years have done so, compared to nine in the eleven previous editions. Only one Oaks winner has contested the last nineteen renewals of the King George and it is twenty years since both the Derby and Oaks winner took part.

In the essay on St Leger winner Scorpion, *Racehorses of 2005* raised the possibility of the King George succeeding the St Leger and being promoted as the third leg of the triple crown to help entice three-year-olds back to the race. No horse has won the traditional triple crown of Two Thousand Guineas, Derby and St Leger since Nijinsky in 1970 (Oh So Sharp won the fillies' equivalent in 1985) and Nashwan, the last horse in a position to attempt it after winning the first two legs, bypassed the 1989 St Leger in favour of an Arc trial, having already won the King George. The idea that the highest status attainable by a thoroughbred on the British turf is that of a triple crown winner seems to have become outmoded in its traditional form (though there is talk of Teofilo being aimed at it). Staging the triple crown in another form—the Derby, Irish Derby and King George would also work —must be well worth exploring. Competition for the presence of the top three-year-olds at Ascot has increased with the changes made to the Grand Prix de Paris in 2005 when its distance was moved up to a mile and a half and the race brought much closer to the King George. The move has been to the detriment of Ascot's

Tattersalls Gold Cup, the Curragh—only three runners for Ireland's first Group 1 of the season for older horses; Hurricane Run makes all to land the odds from Alexander Goldrun and Lord Admiral

showpiece, Scorpion winning at Longchamp in 2005 and Rail Link in 2006, both before being put away for an autumn campaign.

Mile-and-a-half racing in general in Europe is in need of the sort of boost that could be provided by a triple crown involving the King George. Since the King George was inaugurated in 1951, the International at York and the Irish Champion Stakes have sprung up as mile-and-a-quarter events, while the Prince of Wales's Stakes and the Tattersalls Gold Cup in Ireland have acquired Group 1 status at the distance. In all, there are eight Group 1 events open to older horses at around a mile and a quarter run in Britain, Ireland and France. There are only four such events at a mile and a half, the Coronation Cup, the Grand Prix de Saint-Cloud, the King George and the Arc, yet in most years more of the season's best performances are put up at a mile and a half than at any other single distance, which makes the imbalance between the number of big mile-and-a-half races and big mile-and-a-quarter races all the more surprising.

There are twenty-one Group 1 events open to older horses at up to a mile and a quarter each year in Britain, Ireland and France and only eight at a mile and a half plus. Given the number of horses contesting the top middle-distance events in 2006—none of the six Group 1 races open to three-year-olds and upwards of both sexes at a mile and a quarter to a mile and a half in Britain and Ireland attracted double-figure fields—it is perhaps not the best time to be arguing for increasing the number at a mile and a half. Past editions of *Racehorses* also floated the possibility of the St Leger becoming an all-aged mile-and-a-half event, though the race was going through a leaner period at the time than it is now. As far as the King George is concerned, a boost in prize money wouldn't go amiss either. The race was worth £425,850 to the winner in 2006, while the Arc was worth £766,980 and the Breeders' Cup Turf £852,632. The Dubai Sheema Classic, which succeeded the Japan Cup as the world's most valuable event over a mile and a half in the latest season, was worth £1,714,286 to the winner. Before leaving the subject, given the lack of runners generally in some minor pattern races over middle distances, it is perhaps high time to consider making some of them into limited handicaps, which would be more competitive than the current weight-for-age events, as well as providing a fairer alternative to the fixed penalty system in use in them. By the same token, some of the existing leading handicaps could be upgraded to pattern status, as they have been in National Hunt racing.

Hurricane Run began the year as the top rated in the World Thoroughbred Racehorse Rankings. He could justifiably be called the best racehorse in the world judged on the figures, which put him on 130. Among those likely to rival him in 2006, his stable-companion Shirocco was next best, rated 5 lb inferior, with the Japanese triple crown winner Deep Impact 6 lb behind, David Junior 7 lb, Heart's Cry, another trained in Japan, 8 lb, and Electrocutionist 9 lb. Successful on his only start as a two-year-old, Hurricane Run had earned his superiority over the rest of the world by winning on five of his six outings at three, suffering his only defeat when a strong-finishing second in the Prix du Jockey Club over ten and a half furlongs. He had gained compensation in the Irish Derby at the Curragh before capping his campaign in the Arc in which he beat the Gold Cup winner Westerner convincingly by two lengths with the previous year's winner Bago in third, putting up an above-average winning performance for the race.

Hurricane Run's reappearance in the Tattersalls Gold Cup at the Curragh did little to alter the impression that he was the one they would all have to beat in 2006. Starting at 4/1-on, he dismissed his only serious rival, the high-class mare Alexander Goldrun, by seven lengths, making all in a change of tactics from those used for most of his three-year-old season. The field of three was the joint-smallest seen in a European Group 1 event since the pattern began in 1971. Hurricane Run was 5/1-on to beat five rivals in the Grand Prix de Saint-Cloud a month after the Curragh, but came unstuck, suffering only the second defeat of his career. The opposition was stronger than the betting suggested and he still put up the best performance at the weights, going down by a head to the mare Pride, conceding her 3 lb, with the Prix d'Ispahan winner Laverock two lengths away in third, Hurricane Run collared close home after leading early in the straight. Following Egyptband, Aquarelliste, Sulamani and another Arc winner Bago, Hurricane Run was the fifth odds-on shot beaten in the race in the last six renewals.

The chance to tackle a more galloping track in the King George VI and Queen Elizabeth Diamond Stakes seemed sure to suit Hurricane Run and he started favourite for the seventh consecutive time at Ascot, going off at 6/5-on in a field of six. The King George was the last to carry 'Diamond' in its title, De Beers deciding not to renew its support after an illustrious thirty-five-year association with the race. Among the three-year-olds that would have bolstered the line-up, Derby winner Sir Percy was sidelined after Epsom, while the absence of Irish Derby winner Dylan Thomas and dual Oaks winner Alexandrova, or any other Ballydoyle runner, could be explained by Coolmore's ownership of Hurricane Run. With no representative of the classic crop in the field, the race relied on its international flavour, which has become an increasing part of its appeal with runners in recent seasons from America, South Africa and Hong Kong. Heart's Cry was the second Japanese-trained runner to contest the King George in seven years and was a far stronger contender than Air Shakur in 2000, going off second favourite at 3/1. Heart's Cry had inflicted the only defeat on his compatriot Deep Impact in the Arima Kinen at Nakayama in December, but hadn't been seen since gaining further Group 1 success in the Dubai Sheema Classic at Nad Al Sheba in March. Electrocutionist, a game winner of the Dubai World Cup at the same meeting, had shown his well-being at Royal Ascot, finishing a good second to Ouija Board in the Prince of Wales's Stakes. After an injury scare on the morning of the race, Electrocutionist was at 4/1 with Hardwicke Stakes winner Maraahel at 14/1 and Enforcer, third in the Hardwicke, at 50/1 along with Electrocutionist's stable-companion Cherry Mix.

Idiosyncrasies had been part of Hurricane Run's make-up as a three-year-old when he had shown a tendency to run in snatches and hang before unleashing his sharp turn of foot, and he looked no less quirky from the outset at four, giving considerable trouble to post at the Curragh and racing with little fluency at Saint-Cloud. Not to be caught out in a small field under the good to firm conditions at Ascot, Christophe Soumillon, deputising for the suspended Kieren Fallon, who had been on board since Hurricane Run changed ownership before the Irish Derby, kept his mount closest to Godolphin's pacemaker Cherry Mix from the outset. In what developed into a cat-and-mouse affair, run at a steady early pace, Hurricane Run became boxed in on the rail as first Electrocutionist and then Heart's Cry improved their position on his outside approaching the straight. Not that Hurricane Run could have gone any faster had he had more room. Characteristically, he was under pressure with three furlongs to run. To his credit, he responded to sustained driving, and, finding a gap one off the rail as the pacemaker weakened, he found his way through well inside the final furlong, winning by half a length from Electrocutionist, who rallied to beat Heart's Cry by the same distance for second, with Enforcer a length and three quarters further away in fourth. It was a pulsating finish, though some of the plaudits which appeared in print were typically exaggerated. The King

King George VI and Queen Elizabeth Diamond Stakes, Ascot—a thrilling finish to the final running of Britain's premier open-aged middle-distance event under De Beers sponsorship; Hurricane Run finds plenty to get the better of Electrocutionist, Heart's Cry (striped cap), Enforcer (rail), Maraahel (right) and Cherry Mix

George has provided many fine finishes since the legendary set-to between Grundy and Bustino in 1975: Golan and Nayef in 2002; Galileo and Fantastic Light in 2001; Lammtarra and Pentire in 1995; and Belmez and Old Vic in 1990 to name other recent examples.

Hurricane Run's victory at Ascot put him in illustrious company. He was only the seventh horse to win both the Arc de Triomphe and the King George. Ribot, who won the Arc twice, Ballymoss, Mill Reef, Dancing Brave and Lammtarra completed the double in the same season, while, like his son, Hurricane Run's sire Montjeu won the King George the season after he had won the Arc. Following Montjeu in 2000, Hurricane Run was only the second French-trained winner of the King George since Pawneese in 1976. He was a first success in the race for his trainer Andre Fabre, who expressed concerns over running one of his horses in mid-summer, traditionally used as a break for top middle-distance horses trained in France. Hurricane Run was a first major win in Britain for Belgian-born stable-jockey Christophe Soumillon. Hurricane Run's rider received a six-day ban for excessive use of the whip at Ascot, having hit his mount around twenty times in the straight, including down the shoulder. Soumillon also raised a few eyebrows with his victory celebration shortly after the winning post in which he gestured to his posterior before sticking his tongue out at the stands, presumably in response to those in the media who had questioned his tactical awareness on British tracks beforehand (including earlier in the month on Ouija Board in the Eclipse).

Some in the crowd might, with every justification, have claimed not to be offended by Soumillon's antics as they hadn't seen them. After the opening of its £200m grandstand earlier in the year, Ascot received fierce criticism from regular racegoers unable to obtain a clear view of racing from the ground-level steps on the stand and the lawns, or from overcrowded higher vantage points. Following Newmarket, which opened its Millennium Grandstand in 2000, Ascot is the second major British racecourse to have come in for criticism for seemingly giving a lower priority in its redevelopment to viewing facilities than to bars, restaurants and private boxes, a strategy that works against the traditional racegoer. In October, patrons of the Royal Enclosure at Ascot were sent a letter of apology from the Duke of Devonshire, chairman of the board of trustees at Ascot, which had a list of items to attend to after the official opening—to general acclaim at the time—of the revamped course at the Royal meeting in June. A £10m 'makeover' was announced late in the year which will include an added 2,000-seater stand for the Royal meeting in the Silver Ring, an extension to the Royal Enclosure beyond its controversial siting on the fourth floor of the new stand to include facilities on the site of the old paddock, and a re-grading of the lawns in front of the new stand to improve the view of the track.

Ascot was the last time Hurricane Run was seen in the winner's enclosure anywhere, and it is possible the race he had in the King George left its mark on him. He ran four times afterwards, running his two best subsequent races on his next two starts, both back in France at Longchamp under Kieren Fallon. Again odds on in a small field, he lost little caste in defeat in the five-runner Prix Foy, a traditional Arc trial, in September, going down by a neck to his stable-companion Shirocco in a sprint finish after running in snatches early on. As he had been at Saint-Cloud, Hurricane Run was provided with a pacemaker in the Prix Foy, but, somewhat surprisingly, he was left to his own devices in the Arc three weeks later. In the face of fanatical support for the odds-on Japanese-trained Deep Impact, Hurricane Run started second favourite at 4/1 in a field of eight. With the possibility of a muddling pace, there was some talk of him making the running, but in the event he was settled in. Like his sire had in his bid for a second Arc six years earlier, he managed only fourth, but he ran better than the bare result suggests, the luck he had sticking to the inside a year earlier deserting him. Carried back by a weakening rival on the home turn, Hurricane Run was forced to switch left as the runners bunched up the straight, and lost momentum in the process, running on well with too much to do as his rider accepted things, beaten just over three lengths by the close-finishers Rail Link and Pride, two and a half lengths for third by Deep Impact, who was subsequently disqualified for failing a dope test.

One consolation for connections at Longchamp was that Hurricane Run didn't have a hard race in the Arc, and he was turned out again in the Champion

Stakes at Newmarket two weeks later. Dropped back to a mile and a quarter, this time he did make the running, though asked to set only a steady pace by Michael Kinane, partnering him for the first time. Hurricane Run could manage only third, beaten a head for second by Rob Roy, three lengths behind the winner Pride. Hurricane Run seemed not to be applying himself at Newmarket and he again looked less than willing when turned out in the Breeders' Cup Turf three weeks later, this time re-united with Christophe Soumillon. The sharp track at Churchill Downs seemed not to suit him, but he hung left when ridden along in the straight, never threatening as he came home sixth of eleven, beaten five and a half lengths behind the winner Red Rocks, running by far his worst race of the season, despite starting favourite once more.

		Sadler's Wells	Northern Dancer
	Montjeu (IRE)	(b 1981)	Fairy Bridge
	(b 1996)	Floripedes	Top Ville
Hurricane Run (IRE)		(b 1985)	Toute Cy
(b.c. 2002)		Surumu	Literat
	Hold On (GER)	(ch 1974)	Surama
	(ch 1991)	Hone	Sharpen Up
		(ch 1974)	Lucy

Montjeu ran in the same seven races as Hurricane Run as a four-year-old, but went one better than his son, winning the first three including the Grand Prix de Saint-Cloud. Successful in the Prix du Jockey Club and the Irish Derby as a three-year-old, Montjeu won nine pattern races in all compared to Hurricane Run's six and was a top-class performer at three and four, putting up a second outstanding effort when toying with his rivals in one of the most one-sided King Georges ever run. Like Hurricane Run, Montjeu's form tailed off a little after Ascot, and, aside from the Arc, he was beaten in the Champion Stakes before finishing only seventh in the Breeders' Cup Turf, also at Churchill Downs. Connections will be hoping Hurricane Run can mirror Montjeu at stud. Montjeu made a sensational start as a stallion, his first crop also including Derby winner Motivator and St Leger winner Scorpion. Not surprisingly, his second crop paled by comparison, the best of his progeny being the very smart Papal Bull, but Montjeu's third crop has produced the Racing Post Trophy winner Authorized, who seems sure to keep his sire's name in the limelight in 2007. Like Montjeu, Hurricane Run is bred more for stamina than speed. His grandam Hone has bred numerous winners including the smart German middle-distance performer Hondo Mondo. His dam Hold On proved effective at middle distances, winning at up to eleven furlongs, and bred three winners before Hurricane Run. The pick of them was Hibiscus (by Law Society), a smart performer in Germany at a mile and a quarter and a mile and a half. Another of Hold On's produce, Farazdaq (by Linamix), was a useful winner in France at up to fifteen and a half furlongs. Her three-year-old filly High Fidelity (by Peintre Celebre) won over a mile and a half in a newcomers race from three starts in France in the latest season.

Montjeu's career at stud hasn't been held back by the quirks he showed on the racecourse, and Hurricane Run's should not be either. A rangy, good sort, if anything he was a better-looking version of his sire, if not quite his sire's equal on the course. A good mover with a long stride, and a top-class performer at his best, he stayed a mile and a half well and acted on heavy and good to firm ground. He almost invariably took the eye with his well-being and was often full of himself in the preliminaries. He will stand at Coolmore, County Tipperary, at a fee of €30,000. *A. Fabre, France*

HURRICANE SPIRIT (IRE) 2 b.c. (Mar 29) Invincible Spirit (IRE) 121 – Gale Warning (IRE) (Last Tycoon 131) [2006 5m⁶ p5g* p6g* p6g* p7g* Dec 20] 3,800F, €18,000Y: big, good-topped colt: half-brother to 3 winners, including useful 1½m/1¾m winner Takwin (by Alzao) and fairly useful Irish 1995 2-y-o 7f/8.5f winner Common Spirit (by Common Grounds): dam French 2-y-o 6f winner: useful form, progressing well: off 5 months after debut, and won all subsequent starts, namely maiden, minor event and nursery (by 3½ lengths from Teasing) at Lingfield and minor event at Kempton (simple task): probably stays 7f: acts on polytrack: smart prospect. *J. R. Best* **103 p**

HURRICANE THOMAS (IRE) 2 b.g. (Feb 29) Celtic Swing 138 – Viola Royale (IRE) 90 (Royal Academy (USA) 130) [2006 8g 8.2s³ p8g² 8d⁴ Nov 3] €45,000Y: big, good-topped gelding: fourth foal: brother to 6-y-o St Andrews and 4-y-o Celticello: dam **78**

Irish 2-y-o 6f/7f winner: fair maiden: placed at Nottingham and Lingfield (second to Guiseppe Verdi): will stay 1¼m: acts on polytrack and soft going: gelded after final start. *M. Johnston*

HURRY UP HELEN (IRE) 3 b.f. In The Wings 128 – Imitation (Darshaan 133) **72** [2006 60: 11.9g 14.1g 11.1f⁵ 14m 11.5f³ 11.1m² 11.1g² 10.1m* 10.2f⁴ 10m* 10d* 11.6d Oct 9] rangy filly: fair handicapper: won at Yarmouth in August and Brighton (2) in September: effective at 1¼m/11f: acts on firm and good to soft going. *Mrs L. Stubbs*

HUW THE NEWS 7 b.g. Primo Dominie 121 – Martha Stevens (USA) 102 (Super – Concorde (USA) 128) [2006 –: 8.1g 11.1g Jul 5] no sign of ability. *S. C. Burrough*

HUXLEY (IRE) 7 b.g. Danehill Dancer (IRE) 117 – Biddy Mulligan (Ballad Rock 122) **51** [2006 70d: f7g f7g p9.5g 8.1g⁶ 9d⁴ f8g p8g Dec 18] leggy gelding: modest performer nowadays: stays 1¼m: acts on firm and soft going: tried blinkered: usually tongue tied: sometimes slowly away. *D. J. Wintle*

HYDE PARK FLIGHT (IRE) 2 b.c. (Mar 17) Tendulkar (USA) 114 – Quaver – (USA) 74 (The Minstrel (CAN) 135) [2006 p8g⁵ p8.6s⁶ p8.6g Dec 29] little form in maidens, all in Britain. *John A. Quinn, Ireland*

HYPERALERT (USA) 3 ch.c. Rahy (USA) 115 – Annaba (IRE) 120 (In The Wings **86 +** 128) [2006 11f² 12g³ Jul 6] third foal: half-brother to Irish 1½m winner Auditor (by Polish Precedent): dam, 1¼m to 12.5f (Prix de Royallieu) winner, closely related to smart performer up to 1¼m Andean and half-sister to smart stayer Pozarica: similar form when placed in maidens at Redcar (neck second to Eta Draconis, going 3 lengths clear 2f out but idling as jockey eased off and collared on line (rider banned for 28 days)) and Newbury (1¾ lengths third to Ermine Sea): stays 1½m: acts on firm ground: sold 44,000 gns, joined M. Al Muhairi in UAE. *M. Johnston*

HYPNOSIS 3 b.f. Mind Games 121 – Salacious (Sallust 134) [2006 67: 6g 5m⁴ 5g³ 5g² **79** 5g* 5m² 5f² 5m² 5f³ 5m² 5s³ 5g² Sep 30] leggy filly: fair handicapper: won apprentice event at Catterick in June: best at 5f: acts on firm and soft going: tough and consistent. *D. W. Barker*

HYPNOTIC 4 ch.g. Lomitas 129 – Hypnotize 103 (Machiavellian (USA) 123) [2006 **88** 80: 8g p10g 8g 8f 7.6m⁵ 6f 6.9f* 8g 7.2v* 7.1s⁵ Sep 24] leggy gelding: fairly useful handicapper: won at Carlisle in August and Ayr (beat Zhitomir by 6 lengths, best effort since 2 yrs) in September: stays 1m: acts on polytrack and any turf going: tongue tied 5 of last 6 starts, also visored last 2. *D. Nicholls*

HYPOCRISY 3 b.f. Bertolini (USA) 125 – Glensara (Petoski 135) [2006 p6g* p6g* **85** p6g⁴ 6d⁴ 6g³ 7m p6g p6g³ Dec 9] 5,000Y: good-topped filly: third foal: closely related to 7f winner Skukusa (by Emarati) and half-sister to 7-y-o Chateau Nicol: dam unraced: fairly useful performer: won maiden in January (100/1) and handicap in March, both at Wolverhampton: left S. Williams 11,000 gns, good third in handicap there final start: should stay 7f: acts on polytrack: has raced freely. *D. Carroll*

HYPOTENEUSE (IRE) 2 b.f. (Apr 8) Sadler's Wells (USA) 132 – Phantom Gold 119 **72 p** (Machiavellian (USA) 123) [2006 7d Oct 28] leggy, lengthy filly: sister to Oaks runner-up Flight of Fancy (7f winner at 2 yrs) and 3-y-o Well Hidden, and half-sister to 2 winners, including fairly useful 1½m winner Daring Aim (by Daylami): dam, 1m (at 2 yrs) to 13.3f (Geoffrey Freer Stakes) winner, also won Ribblesdale Stakes: 12/1, prominent long way when seventh of 20 to Measured Tempo in maiden at Newmarket: bound to progress at 1¼m/1½m at 3 yrs. *Sir Michael Stoute*

HYTHE BAY 2 b.f. (Jan 31) Auction House (USA) 120 – Ellway Queen (USA) 71 **77** (Bahri (USA) 125) [2006 5f⁴ p6g³ 6m* 5m p6g⁴ 7g 7m p6g Oct 11] 13,000Y: tall, good sort: first foal: dam 1m winner: fair performer: won maiden at Folkestone in June: best run after (sometimes highly tried) when fourth in nursery at Lingfield fifth start: should stay 7f/1m: acts on polytrack and firm going: suspect temperament. *R. T. Phillips*

I

IAMBACK 6 b.m. Perugino (USA) 84 – Smouldering (IRE) (Caerleon (USA) 132) **54** [2006 58: 12s³ p12g 12d⁴ p13.9g⁶ p16g⁶ f14g³ 11.9m p12.2g³ p16g² f12g³ 11.5f 16f 16g p16g³ 16g f12m² f11g f14g⁴ p12g⁶ f12g Dec 12] leggy mare: modest performer: stays 2m: acts on all-weather, firm and soft going: has worn cheekpieces/blinkers: tongue tied: none too genuine. *Miss D. A. McHale*

IAMTHEONE (IRE) 2 b.g. (Feb 2) Soviet Star (USA) 128 – Just Aloof (IRE) (Entrepreneur 123) [2006 7f p8g Oct 23] last in maidens. *Bob Jones* –

IANNIS (IRE) 3 b.c. Danehill Dancer (IRE) 117 – Suave Lady (FR) (Suave Dancer (USA) 136) [2006 76p: 7d p7g³ p7g* Oct 23] fair performer, lightly raced: won maiden at Lingfield in October by neck from Cordelia: should stay 1m: acts on polytrack and good to firm ground. *J. Noseda* 79

IBERIAN LIGHT (USA) 3 b.g. Fantastic Light (USA) 134 – Spain Lane (USA) 115 (Seeking The Gold (USA)) [2006 p8g p7g p8g p8g 10m² 12.1m³ p9.5g 11.9m² 10f³ p12g 11.9f³ Jul 4] modest maiden handicapper: stays 1½m: acts on firm going: tried in headgear: sold 13,000 gns. *N. A. Callaghan* 61

IBERUS (GER) 8 b.g. Monsun (GER) 124 – Iberica (GER) (Green Dancer (USA) 132) [2006 62: p8.6g³ p10g p9.5g 10f⁵ Jul 3] leggy, angular gelding: modest handicapper: effective at 1m to 1½m: acts on polytrack and any turf going: tried in headgear: has found little· sold 1,800 gns. *S. Gollings* 62

ICANNSHIFT (IRE) 6 b.g. Night Shift (USA) – Cannikin (IRE) 82 (Lahib (USA) 129) [2006 59: p10g 12d⁶ 11.9m p12g³ 10m³ 10m 12f* 12f² 11.9f⁴ 11.9f⁵ 12d² 10.9m 11.9m Sep 19] small, good-bodied gelding: modest handicapper: won at Folkestone in June: effective at 1¼m/1½m: acts on polytrack, firm and soft going: tried visored: races prominently. *T. M. Jones* 59

ICE AND FIRE 7 b.g. Cadeaux Genereux 131 – Tanz (IRE) 79 (Sadler's Wells (USA) 132) [2006 55: f14g³ f12g⁶ f11g⁵ f16g⁶ p13.9g* p13.9g f14g⁴ p16.5g⁴ p13.9g⁵ f14g⁴ p12.2g⁴ p16.5g* p16.5f f14g* p13.9g⁶ p16.5g³ Dec 2] quite good-topped gelding: modest performer: won banded race in March and handicap in July, both at Wolverhampton, and banded race at Southwell in November: stays 16.5f: acts on all-weather, good to firm and good to soft ground: usually wears headgear: tends to edge right. *J. T. Stimpson* 61

ICE BOX (IRE) 2 ch.f. (Mar 5) Pivotal 124 – Thaisy (USA) (Tabasco Cat (USA) 126) [2006 7.2d 7g 6d⁴ p6g⁴ Dec 26] sturdy filly: second foal: dam, French maiden, half-sister to high-class 1½m performer Fruits of Love: modest maiden: should stay 1m. *M. Johnston* 63

ICECAP 6 b.m. Polar Falcon (USA) 126 – Warning Light (High Top 131) [2006 61: 10.9s p8.6g p8.6g 10g p7g⁵ 7m⁴ 7m⁶ 8f⁵ Jun 20] lengthy mare: modest performer: effective at 7f to easy 1¼m: acts on all-weather and firm ground: tried in cheekpieces: often slowly away: has raced freely. *W. G. M. Turner* 51

ICED DIAMOND (IRE) 7 b.g. Petardia 113 – Prime Site (IRE) (Burslem 123) [2006 59, a70: p7.1g² p7.1g² p7g p7.1g p7g³ 7m p7.1g* 7m⁴ p7.1g⁴ 7m* 7.2g⁴ p7.1g⁶ 7.6m³ 7f 7g 6.9f⁵ Aug 15] good-topped gelding: fair handicapper on all-weather, modest on turf: won at Wolverhampton in April and Brighton in June: has form at 1m, but raced mainly around 7f: acts on all-weather and firm going: tried in headgear and tongue tie: sometimes slowly away/wanders: held up. *W. M. Brisbourne* 64 a69

ICED TANGO 2 ch.g. (May 15) Verglas (IRE) 118 – Tangolania (FR) (Ashkalani (IRE) 128) [2006 6g p6g 6g Aug 2] well held in maidens: bred to stay 1m+. *F. Jordan* –

ICEMAN 4 b.c. Polar Falcon (USA) 126 – Virtuous 92 (Exit To Nowhere (USA) 122) [2006 115: 8.2g⁴ 7g 8d Sep 30] strong, good-bodied colt: had a quick, fluent action: smart performer at best (won Coventry Stakes at 2 yrs): seemingly best run in 2006 (useful form) when seventh to Sleeping Indian in listed race at Newbury: last of 8 in Joel Stakes at Newmarket final start: stayed 1m: unraced on heavy going, acted on any other turf: held up: to stand at Cheveley Park Stud, Newmarket, fee £5,000, Oct 1st terms, special live foal. *J. H. M. Gosden* 109

ICEMAN GEORGE 2 b.g. (Feb 18) Beat Hollow 126 – Diebiedale 58 (Dominion 123) [2006 7d Oct 28] close-coupled gelding: in rear in maiden at Newmarket. *D. Morris* –

ICE MOUNTAIN 2 br.g. (Mar 25) Kyllachy 129 – Sulitelma (USA) 63 (The Minstrel (CAN) 135) [2006 5g 5m² 5f* 5.2g 5g 5m² 6g Sep 30] 8,500Y, 9,000Y: deep-girthed gelding: half-brother to several winners, including fairly useful Irish 5f winner Neeze (by Cadeaux Genereux) and 5-y-o Tromp: dam, 5f winner (ran only at 2 yrs), out of half-sister to Petoski: fairly useful performer: won maiden at Beverley in July by 5 lengths, making all: sound effort after only when second to Handsome Falcon in minor event at same track: best at 5f: acts on firm going: gelded after final start. *B. Smart* 88

ICENI PRINCESS 2 b.f. (Apr 8) Victory Note (USA) 120 – Swing Job 58 (Ezzoud (IRE) 126) [2006 p8g Dec 20] second foal: dam maiden who stayed 1½m: 66/1, last in maiden at Kempton. *P. Howling* –

ICENI WARRIOR 4 b.g. Lake Coniston (IRE) 131 – Swing Job 58 (Ezzoud (IRE) **47**
126) [2006 –: p8g p8.6g³ p8.6g p9.5g⁴ p12g⁵ p10g⁴ Dec 18] poor maiden: stays 1½m:
acts on polytrack: tried blinkered. *P. Howling*

ICE PLANET 5 b.g. Polar Falcon (USA) 126 – Preference (Efisio 120) [2006 98: 6d⁴ **99**
6m² 6s⁵ 6m³ 6f⁵ 6f² 6g⁴ 6s³ 7.2d⁶ Sep 16] useful-looking gelding: useful handicapper:
mainly creditable efforts in 2006, including when length third to Excusez Moi in Great
St Wilfrid Stakes (successful in 2005 renewal) at Ripon on penultimate start: best form
around 6f: unraced on heavy going, acts on any other: has been bandaged fore joints:
tough and reliable. *D. Nicholls*

IDARAH (USA) 3 gr. or ro.c. Aljabr (USA) 125 – Fatina 98 (Nashwan (USA) 135) **97**
[2006 76: 10.5g* 10d² 12m 11.9g 11m 12s 10s³ Oct 18] lengthy, useful-looking colt:
useful performer: won handicap at Haydock in April: several creditable efforts after,
including when placed at Newmarket and Nottingham: barely stays 1½m: acts on soft and
good to firm going: sold 85,000 gns. *W. J. Haggas*

IDEALISTIC (IRE) 5 b.m. Unfuwain (USA) 131 – L'Ideale (USA) (Alysheba (USA)) **102**
[2006 100: 12s⁵ 10.9f⁵ 12m⁴ 9.9m 12.3m⁵ 12s p13g Oct 26] strong, lengthy, angular
mare: useful performer: good fourth to Fermion in listed event at Newbury: respectable
efforts next 2 starts but well below form last 2: should stay 1¾m: acts on firm going,
seemingly not on soft: once refused to enter stall. *L. M. Cumani*

IDEALLY (IRE) 2 ch.g. (Apr 13) Mark of Esteem (IRE) 137 – Ideal Lady (IRE) **78**
(Seattle Slew (USA)) [2006 p7g⁴ 7g⁴ Sep 15] strong gelding: fourth foal: half-brother to
3 winners, including 3-y-o Bouboulina and 4-y-o All That And More: dam unraced out of
smart half-sister to very smart 1m to 1½m performer Hatoof: fourth to Water Mill in
minor event at Kempton and to Proponent in maiden at Newbury (hinted at temperament,
gelded after): will stay 1m. *B. W. Hills*

IDLE POWER (IRE) 8 b. or br.g. Common Grounds 118 – Idle Fancy 79 (Mujtahid **103**
(USA) 118) [2006 97, a91: 6v⁵ 6g* p6g² 6m p6g⁴ 6d² 6m⁴ 6m 6g² 6m⁵ 6f² 6g* 6g 5d p6g **a93**
Nov 1] close-coupled gelding: useful handicapper on turf, fairly useful on all-weather:
won at Folkestone in April and Windsor (beat Kostar a head) in August: also ran well
when runner-up at Newmarket (beaten length by Greenslades), Epsom (¾ length behind
Steel Blue) and Goodwood (beaten 1½ lengths by Fantasy Believer): well below form
last 3 starts: effective at 6f/7f: acts on polytrack, firm and good to soft going: tried blink-
ered/in cheekpieces prior to 2006: races prominently. *J. R. Boyle*

IFATFIRST (IRE) 3 b.g. Grand Lodge (USA) 125 – Gaily Grecian (IRE) (Ela-Mana- **62**
Mou 132) [2006 p8g p8.6g p7g p13.9g⁶ p10g⁶ p12g* Dec 22] modest performer: won
handicap at Lingfield in December: should stay 1½m (failed to stay 1¾m): raced only on
polytrack: blinkered fourth/fifth outings: looked tricky ride second start. *M. P. Tregoning*

IFFRAAJ 5 b.h. Zafonic (USA) 130 – Pastorale 91 (Nureyev (USA) 131) [2006 **127**
123: 6m 6m² 7m* 7g⁴ Sep 9]
    St Leger day started grimly for the Godolphin team, with the death from a
heart attack of flagbearer Electrocutionist casting a shadow over proceedings at
York. The victory of Iffraaj in the GNER Park Stakes provided Godolphin with a
little compensation. Iffraaj had won the race the previous season, at its usual home
of Doncaster, and he didn't have to be at his best to land the odds in the latest
edition, getting up late to beat Somnus by three quarters of a length. This was the

Betfair Cup (Lennox), Goodwood—Iffraaj shows high-class form in defying his penalty in fine style;
Jedburgh (blinkers) and Assertive (stripes) fill the minor placings

Godolphin's "Iffraaj"

second of two pattern successes for Iffraaj in the latest season, and victory opened up an array of opportunities, with the Sprint Cup at Haydock and Breeders' Cup Mile at Churchill Downs mooted objectives. Iffraaj would have been an interesting contender at Churchill Downs where the sharpness of the course looked likely to suit him because of doubts about his proving fully effective at a mile on a conventional, galloping European track. Iffraaj was bred to get the trip but, unfortunately, the limits of his stamina remained untested as the Park Stakes turned out to be the final outing of his career. He reportedly failed to sparkle in his work after York and was put away at the end of September before suffering a slight injury and being retired the following month.

Many of Godolphin's horses were running below their best when Iffraaj reappeared in the Golden Jubilee Stakes at Royal Ascot and, given those circumstances, there was a fair bit of encouragement in his finishing seventh of eighteen, around four lengths behind the winner Les Arcs. Iffraaj wasn't subjected to an overly hard time by Frankie Dettori and came on a great deal when turned out three weeks later in the July Cup at Newmarket. As usual, he took the eye in the paddock and put up easily his best performance in four outings at Group 1 level, unlucky not to reel in Les Arcs. Travelling strongly, Iffraaj was caught behind a couple of the early leaders at a crucial stage, as the winner struck for home, but he finished to great effect to be beaten only a head, entitled to be rated as a narrow winner.

Next on the agenda for Iffraaj, in what turned out to be a fine second half of the season for Godolphin generally, was the Betfair Cup, registered as the Lennox, at Goodwood, where he put up comfortably the best performance seen in the race since it was relocated from its old home at Newcastle where it was run as the Beeswing before 2000. Given that Iffraaj had also been entered for the Sussex Stakes, it was relevant that the form of his Betfair Cup win was rated on a par with that of Court Masterpiece in winning the Group 1 event over a furlong further the following day. A well-backed 6/4 favourite at Goodwood, Iffraaj was penalised for his success in the previous year's Park Stakes and had to concede between 4 lb and 10 lb to the remainder of the ten-strong field. Iffraaj beat Jedburgh comfortably by four lengths after being always well placed and asserting two furlongs out. Some of those behind found trouble in running but Iffraaj was nonetheless a most impressive winner.

		Zafonic (USA)	Gone West	Mr Prospector
Iffraaj		(b 1990)	(b 1984)	Secrettame
(b.h. 2001)			Zaizafon	The Minstrel
			(ch 1982)	Mofida
		Pastorale	Nureyev	Northern Dancer
		(ch 1988)	(b 1977)	Special
			Park Appeal	Ahonoora
			(br 1982)	Balidaress

Iffraaj's pedigree was covered in depth in *Racehorses of 2005*. However, it is worth repeating that he hails from an excellent family, his dam being a half-sister to Lockinge winner Cape Cross and a close relative to the dam of another Darley stallion Diktat, out of Park Appeal, who herself won the Cheveley Park Stakes. It also bears reiterating that the game Iffraaj is a big, strong, attractive horse, who rarely failed to take the eye in the paddock. For all that it would have been intriguing to see how Iffraaj fared over a mile, it seems more than likely that he would have proved best at six or seven furlongs. He acted on firm ground, and all his best efforts came on good going or firmer. He will stand at Kildangan Stud in Ireland in 2007 under the Darley banner, at a fee of €12,000. *Saeed bin Suroor*

IF PARADISE 5 b.h. Compton Place 125 – Sunley Stars (Sallust 134) [2006 108: p6g **103** p5g⁶ 5.1s³ 5.2m⁶ 5g 5s³ 5s 6m 5m 6m 5s⁴ 5f³ 5g² 5.1m Oct 8] sturdy, useful-looking horse: useful handicapper: in-and-out form in 2006, though ran well at Newbury (sixth to Green Manalishi) and Goodwood (third to The Lord) fourth/sixth outings: below form after: best at 5f: acts on soft and firm ground: races prominently: blinkered sixth/seventh outings: none too genuine: sold 31,000 gns. *R. Hannon*

IFTIKHAR (USA) 7 b.g. Storm Cat (USA) – Muhbubh (USA) 108 (Blushing Groom **63** (FR) 131) [2006 59: p12.2g³ Jan 9] big, strong gelding: modest handicapper: effective at 8.6f to 1½m: acts on polytrack and firm ground: blinkered (raced freely) once in 2004. *W. M. Brisbourne*

IGNITION 4 ch.f. Rock City 120 – Fire Sprite 83 (Mummy's Game 120) [2006 72: **65** 8.3m 9d⁴ 8f⁶ 8d p8.6g⁶ p8.6g⁵ f8g p9.5g⁶ p9.5g⁶ Dec 29] leggy, close-coupled filly: fair handicapper: races freely, and probably best around 1m: acts on polytrack, firm and good to soft going: effective with or without cheekpieces: races prominently. *W. M. Brisbourne*

I HAVE DREAMED (IRE) 4 b.g. Montjeu (IRE) 137 – Diamond Field (USA) 71 (Mr **91** Prospector (USA)) [2006 80p: p12g⁶ p12g³ 10m* 10m 10g p12g Sep 18] tall gelding: fairly useful handicapper: won at Sandown in July: below form after: stays 1½m: acts on polytrack and good to firm going: has been gelded. *T. G. Mills*

IHURU 4 b.g. Atraf 116 – E Sharp (USA) 49 (Diesis 133) [2006 p12g⁴ p10g f12g⁴ Mar 8] **57** well held in bumper/juvenile hurdles: modest maiden: stays 1½m: wore cheekpieces/blinkers last 2 starts. *J. G. Portman*

IL CASTAGNO (IRE) 3 ch.g. Night Shift (USA) – Cartesian 78 (Shirley Heights 130) **79** [2006 78: p7.1g 8m² 8g⁵ 7g³ 7m 7m⁵ Jul 12] sturdy gelding: fair performer: below form last 2 starts: stays 1m: acts on good to firm and good to soft going, probably on soft: ran as though amiss on reappearance: usually makes running: gelded after final start. *B. Smart*

IL DIVO 3 b.g. Tipsy Creek (USA) 115 – Be My Hattie (Be My Chief (USA) 122) [2006 **–** –: 10d May 15] good-bodied gelding: tailed off all starts: tried visored. *C. Grant*

ILE MICHEL 9 b.g. Machiavellian (USA) 123 – Circe's Isle (Be My Guest (USA) **61** 126) [2006 73: p8g 10.2m p10g Dec 3] good-topped gelding: modest performer nowadays: stays easy 1¼m: acts on polytrack and firm ground (possibly not on softer than good): sometimes carries head high/hangs left. *Lady Herries*

I'LL DO IT TODAY 5 b.g. Mtoto 134 – Knayton Lass 94 (Presidium 124) [2006 59: **66** p16.5g⁴ p13.9g³ p16.5g⁶ p13.9g* 12m⁶ 14m p12.2g⁵ Sep 16] fair handicapper: won apprentice event at Wolverhampton in March: stays 1¾m: acts on polytrack and good to firm ground: awkward under pressure, and found little final start. *J. M. Jefferson*

ILLUMINISE (IRE) 3 ch.f. Grand Lodge (USA) 125 – Brief Escapade (IRE) 95 **109**
(Brief Truce (USA) 126) [2006 70p: 7g* 8d⁵ 8m⁶ 8.1m⁶ 7f⁶ 6.5f⁵ 8f* 9g⁴ Nov 5] leggy,
quite good-topped filly: useful performer: won maiden at Newmarket in April: good sixth
to Red Evie in Oak Tree Stakes at Goodwood on fifth start, then left E. Dunlop: further
improvement when winning non-graded handicap at Santa Anita in October by ¾ length
from Diplomat Lady: stays 1m (below form in Grade 3 event at 9f): acts on firm going.
N. D. Drysdale, USA

ILLUSTRIOUS BLUE 3 b. or br.c. Dansili 127 – Gipsy Moth 99 (Efisio 120) [2006 **109**
82: 7g* 7s³ p8g³ p10g⁵ 8g* 8m* 8s⁶ 7g* 9m* 9d 10s² Oct 7] strong, close-coupled colt:
has a rather round action: useful performer: won maiden at Goodwood in May and,
having left J. Osborne, handicaps at Newbury in July and Goodwood (3) in August/
September: much better than bare result (nearest finish) when ninth of 33 to Formal
Decree in Cambridgeshire (Handicap) at Newmarket penultimate start, then ran well
when equal-neck second to Book of Music in handicap at Ascot. stays 1¼m: acts on
polytrack and firm going, probably on soft: held up. *W. J. Knight*

IL PALIO (IRE) 2 b.c. (Mar 14) Invincible Spirit (IRE) 121 – Abundance 62 (Cadeaux **89**
Genereux 131) [2006 p5g* 5g 5g⁵ 5.1s* 5m p5g* p5g 5.5m* Aug 28] 5,000Y: medium-
sized, strong, sturdy colt: fifth foal: half-brother to 5-y-o Efistorm and 2002 2-y-o 7f
winner Xcess Baggage (by Air Express): dam, maiden, stayed 1m: fairly useful performer: won maiden at Kempton in March, minor event at Bath in May, and nurseries at
Lingfield in July and Warwick (beat Aahayson by 1¼ lengths, despite hanging throughout) in August: raced around 5f: acts on polytrack, soft and good to firm going: quirky:
sold 11,000 gns, sent to Bahrain. *B. R. Millman*

ILZA 3 b.f. Zilzal (USA) 137 – Chimere (FR) (Soviet Lad (USA)) [2006 10m 6m⁵ 10f 9v **64**
p12.2g³ p10g⁶ p7.1g Dec 28] 2,500Y: fifth foal: half-sister to French 4.5f (at 2 yrs) and 7f
winner Tambour Battant (by Tagula): dam French 2-y-o 1m winner: modest maiden:
stays easy 1½m: acts on polytrack. *E. Tyrrell, Ireland*

I'M IN LOVE (USA) 3 b. or br.f. Zafonic (USA) 130 – Bank On Her (USA) 76 (Rahy **88**
(USA) 115) [2006 82: 7g 8.2g 8m 7d 7m³ p7g* 7g p7g Oct 21] tall, quite good-topped
filly: fairly useful handicapper: improved to win at Lingfield in September: stays 1m: acts
on polytrack and good to firm going: in cheekpieces last 3 starts: sold 100,000 gns, sent
to USA. *M. A. Magnusson*

IMMACULATE RED 3 ch.g. Woodborough (USA) 112 – Primula Bairn 77 (Bairn **60**
(USA) 126) [2006 73: 5.1s⁶ 5g⁶ 6.1d 6m f6g⁵ 6g 6m 6d f7g Oct 12] compact gelding:
modest maiden: should be suited by 7f: acts on fibresand and soft going: tried blinkered.
R. Bastiman

IM OVA ERE DAD (IRE) 3 b.g. Second Empire (IRE) 124 – Eurolink Profile 74 **63**
(Prince Sabo 123) [2006 6g 6m⁶ 6m f8g* 10.1m f8g⁴ f8g⁵ Dec 14] workmanlike gelding:
modest handicapper: won at Southwell in July: stays easy 1m, seemingly not 1¼m: acts
on fibresand, raced only on good/good to firm going on turf. *D. E. Cantillon*

IMPECCABLE GUEST (IRE) 3 b.f. Orpen (USA) 116 – Perfect Guest (What A **60**
Guest 119) [2006 57: p8.6g⁶ 8s⁴ 14.1g³ f11g 11.1d⁶ 13.8s³ f12g² Nov 21] leggy filly:
modest maiden on Flat: stays 1¾m: acts on all-weather, firm and soft going: fell fourth
outing: won over hurdles in November/December. *P. C. Haslam*

IMPELLER (IRE) 7 ch.g. Polish Precedent (USA) 131 – Almaaseh (IRE) 63 (Danc- **103**
ing Brave (USA) 140) [2006 105: p8.6g³ p8.6g⁵ p10g 10.1g² 10m 10.1g 8m 9.9g⁵ 10.1g*
10.4f 10m⁴ 9.9m p10g* 9.9m⁵ 9.9m⁶ Sep 20] tall gelding: useful performer: won minor
event at Epsom (by ½ length from True Cause) in July and claimer at Lingfield (beat
Obrigado by 1¾ lengths) in September: also ran well last 2 starts, when fifth to Pictavia
in Select Stakes and sixth to Imperial Stride in listed event, both at Goodwood: effective
at 1m/1¼m: acts on polytrack, firm and good to soft going: blinkered (well below form)
once: carries head high: travels strongly, and usually waited with: sold 40,000 gns.
W. R. Muir

IMPERIAL BEACH (USA) 2 b.g. (Feb 21) Coronado's Quest (USA) 130 – Millie's **62**
Trick (USA) (Phone Trick (USA)) [2006 5m 6m Jun 29] leggy, unfurnished gelding:
weak as 2-y-o: modest form in maidens. *T. D. Barron*

IMPERIAL DRAGON (USA) 6 b.g. Meadowlake (USA) – South Cove (Forli **–**
(ARG)) [2006 –: p16g Feb 22] good-topped gelding: very lightly-raced maiden, no form
since 3 yrs: tried blinkered. *W. A. O'Gorman*

IMPERIAL ECHO (USA) 5 b.g. Labeeb 124 – Regal Baby (USA) (Northern Baby **90**
(CAN) 127) [2006 88: 6g 7.1m² 7m* 7m* 7m 7f⁶ 7.6m 7g Aug 19] leggy, quite good-

topped gelding: fairly useful handicapper: won at York in June and Newcastle in July: stays 7f: acts on firm and soft ground: tried blinkered/visored: sometimes slowly away. *T. D. Barron*

IMPERIAL GAIN (USA) 3 ch.g. High Yield (USA) 121 – Empress Jackie (USA) **82** (Mount Hagen (FR) 127) [2006 76p: p6g⁴ 6.1g⁶ 6m³ 7m² p7g⁵ 7m* 7f⁶ 8.3g 7.1m³ 7s Oct 10] useful-looking gelding: has scope: fairly useful performer: won handicap at Lingfield in July: hampered 2f out at Newbury final start: should stay 1m: acts on polytrack, firm and good to soft going: usually wears cheekpieces/visor nowadays: possibly none too genuine: sold 12,500 gns. *W. R. Swinburn*

IMPERIAL GLORY 5 b.g. Imperial Ballet (IRE) 110 – Sally Gardens 60 (Alzao **–** (USA) 117) [2006 p7g p5g Dec 10] well held both starts. *Mrs P. Townsley*

IMPERIAL HARRY 3 b.c. Alhaarth (IRE) 126 – Serpentara 75 (Kris 135) [2006 61p: **70** p7g⁴ 8.1d³ 8m⁴ 7f⁴ 9m⁶ p10g Nov 11] tall colt: fair maiden: in frame first 4 starts in 2006: stays 1m: acts on polytrack and firm going. *M. R. Channon*

IMPERIAL ICE (SAF) 4 ch.f. Western Winter (USA) 116 – Imperial Conquest (SAF) **98** (Royal Chalice (SAF)) [2006 7.5m a7f 8m⁴ a8f² a9f* a7.5g 7d Sep 24] strong, good-bodied South African-bred filly: useful performer: successful twice in native country in 2005, and in listed UAE Oaks at Nad Al Sheba (by length from Quality Special) in March: left H. Brown, well held in listed races at Deauville (for D. Lowther) and Ascot: stays 9f: acts on dirt, probably on good to firm going. *R. Simpson*

IMPERIALISTIC (IRE) 5 b.m. Imperial Ballet (IRE) 110 – Shefoog 90 (Kefaah **99** (USA) 124) [2006 85: f8g 8s 7g* 8.3d* 8m⁴ 8m³ 7.2g⁴ 8.3f³ Jun 29] leggy, close-coupled mare: useful performer: won handicaps at Catterick and Leicester in May: stayed 1m: acted on fibresand, heavy and good to firm going, probably on firm: tried in cheekpieces/visor: had carried head awkwardly: sometimes hung: very slowly away final outing: reportedly in foal to Lucky Story. *K. R. Burke*

IMPERIAL LUCKY (IRE) 3 b.f. Desert Story (IRE) 115 – Irina (IRE) 91 (Polar **63** Falcon (USA) 126) [2006 59: p7.1g² 7f 8m⁴ 8.1d² p7.1g⁴ 8.1f p8g³ p7.1g³ p7.1g² p7g **a80** Dec 10] workmanlike filly: fairly useful performer on all-weather, modest on turf: left M. Wallace after sixth start: stays 1m: acts on polytrack, firm and good to soft going: reliable. *D. K. Ivory*

IMPERIAL ROCKET (USA) 9 b. or br.g. Northern Flagship (USA) 96 – Starsa- **–** whirl (USA) (Star de Naskra (USA)) [2006 10.2m Jun 28] good-topped gelding: well held only outing on Flat since 2002: tried blinkered/tongue tied. *W. K. Goldsworthy*

IMPERIAL RULE (IRE) 4 b.g. Second Empire (IRE) 124 – Alikhlas 81 (Lahib **65** (USA) 129) [2006 76: p7.1g⁶ Mar 25] useful-looking gelding: fair performer: below form only start in 2006, carrying head awkwardly: best form at 6f: raced on polytrack and good/good to firm going. *W. J. Knight*

IMPERIAL STAR (IRE) 3 br.c. Fantastic Light (USA) 134 – Out West (USA) 103 **104** (Gone West (USA)) [2006 8s⁵ 10f* 10f* 10f⁵ Jul 20] 20,000Y: good-bodied colt: fourth foal: half-brother to 2 winners, notably Derby winner Motivator (by Montjeu), also 1m (Racing Post Trophy) winner at 2 yrs: dam, 7.5f (at 2 yrs)/1m winner, out of half-sister to US Grade 1 9f winner Wavering Monarch: useful performer: won maiden in June (easily by 5 lengths) and handicap in July (beat Salute Him by 1¼ lengths), both at Windsor: long odds on, returned with back injury when well held in minor event at Leicester final start: stays 1¼m: acts on firm going: stays in training. *J. H. M. Gosden*

IMPERIAL STRIDE 5 b.h. Indian Ridge 123 – Place de L'Opera 98 (Sadler's Wells **108** (USA) 132) [2006 127: 9.9m* 10s Nov 4] tall, good-bodied, attractive horse: developed into a high-class performer in 2005, winning last 4 starts: reportedly underwent ankle surgery in February: didn't need to be anywhere near best to win listed race at Goodwood in September on reappearance by short head from Kahlua Kiss: missed Caulfield Cup in October reportedly due to injury to off-fore: well below best when eighth to Desert War in Mackinnon Stakes at Flemington final outing (reportedly struck into): stays 1½m: acts on good to firm going. *Saeed bin Suroor*

IMPERIAL STYLE (IRE) 2 b.g. (Apr 10) Imperial Ballet (IRE) 110 – Marinka **–** (Pivotal 124) [2006 p6g 5m f5g f6g p7g Nov 29] no form. *D. Shaw*

IMPERIAL SWORD 3 b.g. Danehill Dancer (IRE) 117 – Hajat 64 (Mujtahid (USA) **92** 118) [2006 74: 5d² 6f⁴ 6d* 7.1s² 6g² 6m 6f 6g Aug 23] close-coupled, useful-looking, dipped-backed gelding: has a quick action: fairly useful handicapper: won at Hamilton in May: good efforts when runner-up at Haydock next 2 starts: stays 7f: acts on soft ground:

blinkered last 3 outings at 2 yrs: temperament under suspicion (once unseated/bolted to post). *T. D. Barron*

IMPERIOLI 4 b.g. Fraam 114 – Jussoli (Don 128) [2006 –: 11.1m Jun 14] quite good- –
topped gelding: no form. *P. A. Blockley*

IMPERIUM 5 b.g. Imperial Ballet (IRE) 110 – Partenza (USA) (Red Ransom (USA)) **68**
[2006 66§: f6g² f6g⁵ f6g p6g p6g* p6g⁶ p6g 6m⁴ 7m 5.3m 6m 5.3m* 5.3m² 5.3m³
p6g* p7g² p6g* p6g² Dec 15] leggy gelding: fair performer: won seller at Wolverhampton in March, handicap at Brighton in June, banded race at Kempton (first outing since
leaving Stef Liddiard) in October and handicap at Lingfield (dead-heated) in November:
effective at 5f to easy 7f: acts on all-weather, firm and soft going: wears headgear: tried
tongue tied: has looked ungenuine at times. *Jean-Rene Auvray*

IMPERO 8 b.g. Emperor Jones (USA) 119 – Fight Right (FR) (Crystal Glitters (USA) –
127) [2006 f12g Apr 3] maiden, lightly raced on Flat nowadays: tried visored/in cheek-
pieces/tongue tied. *G. F. Bridgwater*

IMPETIOUS 2 b.f. (Mar 11) Inchinor 119 – Kauri (USA) 63 (Woodman (USA) 126) **91**
[2006 7g⁴ 7m³ 8m* 8g⁴ 7g³ 8m 7d Oct 14] 18,000Y: lengthy, workmanlike filly: second
foal: dam 11f winner: fairly useful performer: won maiden at Bellewstown in August:
good third to Arch Swing in C. L. Weld Park Stakes at the Curragh and eighth to Finsceal
Beo in Prix Marcel Boussac at Longchamp (probably flattered) fifth/sixth starts: well
held final outing in Rockfel Stakes at Newmarket: stays 1m: acts on good to firm going.
E. Tyrrell, Ireland

IMPOSTOR (IRE) 3 b.g. In The Wings 128 – Princess Caraboo (IRE) (Alzao (USA) **81**
117) [2006 45: 10g⁵ 10g⁴ 11s⁵ 14g⁵ 16.2m⁶ 14.1d Sep 27] sturdy gelding: fairly useful
maiden handicapper: barely stays 1¾m: acts on soft going: visored final outing:
sold 16,000 gns, joined N. Twiston-Davies. *J. R. Fanshawe*

IMPRESS 3 ch.g. Fantastic Light (USA) 134 – Kissogram 120 (Caerleon (USA) 132) –
[2006 f12g⁶ Apr 7] 5/1, well beaten in maiden at Southwell, travelling with little fluency:
joined D. McCain Jnr 4,500 gns in May and gelded. *M. Johnston*

IMPRIMIS TAGULA (IRE) 2 b.c. (Feb 15) Tagula (IRE) 116 – Strelitzia (IRE) **65**
(Bluebird (USA) 125) [2006 5f 5.1g⁶ 5.1m⁵ p7.1g⁴ p7.1g² Dec 9] €8,500F, 35,000Y: big,
strong colt: first foal: dam no form in Ireland: fair maiden: stays 7f: acts on polytrack.
A. Bailey

IMPROMPTU 2 b.c. (Feb 28) Mujadil (USA) 119 – Pie In The Sky (Bishop of Cashel **80**
122) [2006 5f² 5m² f5g⁵ 6g⁴ 6m² Sep 22] 20,000Y: smallish, useful-looking colt: second
foal: dam unraced half-sister to smart performer up to 9f Umistim: fairly useful maiden:
runner-up 3 occasions, in nursery at Haydock final one: likely to stay 7f: acts on firm
going, well beaten on fibresand. *R. M. Beckett*

IMPULSIVE MADAM 3 b.f. Diktat 126 – Decorous (IRE) (Runnett 125) [2006 41: –
9.9d p10g Nov 27] maiden: well held in 2006. *S. Kirk*

I'M RIGHT (USA) 2 b.f. (Mar 12) Rahy (USA) 115 – Sheer Reason (USA) 110 **82**
(Danzig (USA)) [2006 p7g* p8g⁵ p7g² Nov 9] fourth foal: half-sister to 3-y-o Faith And
Reason and a winner in Spain by Cozzene: dam, French 2-y-o 6f winner, out of half-sister
to dam of Fantastic Light (by Rahy): fairly useful form: won maiden at Lingfield in
September: bit better efforts in nurseries there, head second to Salient: will stay 1¼m.
M. P. Tregoning

I'M SO LUCKY 4 b.g. Zilzal (USA) 137 – City of Angels (Woodman (USA) 126) **107**
[2006 104: 10m⁵ 12.1d⁴ 10m* 10.4f 9.9m 10.5m 8s 9m Sep 9] tall gelding: useful
handicapper: won listed Wolferton Handicap at Royal Ascot (by 1¼ lengths from Wild
Savannah, dictating pace) in June: failed to match that form after, well below it at Goodwood final start: effective at 1¼m/1½m: acts on any other: on heavy going, acts on any other:
often makes running: hurdling with R. Brookhouse. *M. Johnston*

IM SPARTACUS 4 b.g. Namaqualand (USA) – Captivating (IRE) 63 (Wolfhound **81**
(USA) 126) [2006 108: 14m⁶ 10f⁵ 10m 10.4d 10.5s⁴ 10.5g Sep 22] leggy gelding: reportedly became seriously ill after final 3-y-o outing: just fairly useful performer in 2006,
making little impact: probably stays 10.5f: acts on all-weather, soft and good to firm
going: has worn cheekpieces/blinkers, better without: joined Evan Williams, won over
hurdles in December. *D. W. Barker*

IMTALKINGGIBBERISH 5 b.g. Pursuit of Love 124 – Royal Orchid (IRE) 74 **60**
(Shalford (IRE) 124§) [2006 63, a67: f6s p7g p6g⁵ p8g 7f p5.1g p6g Nov 6] big, close-

coupled gelding: modest handicapper: left J. Jenkins after fifth outing: best at 5f/6f: acts on all-weather and firm going: wore cheekpieces final start: none too genuine. *V. Smith*

IN A FIT 5 b.m. Intikhab (USA) 135 – Millfit (USA) 62 (Blushing Groom (FR) 131) **45** [2006 45: p8g⁵ f7g p8g Feb 13] poor maiden: stayed 1m: raced only on all-weather: dead. *P. Howling*

INAMINUTE (IRE) 3 ch.f. Spectrum (IRE) 126 – Phantom Ring 62 (Magic Ring **80** (IRE) 115) [2006 57: f7g⁵ f7g* f8g² p7.1g* f8g⁵ f6g p7.1g* p6g⁴ 7d* 6.9m* p7.1g⁵ 7m² 7m* 7m p7g 7d⁴ Oct 28] workmanlike filly: fairly useful performer: left R. Harris after reappearance: progressed well after, winning seller at Southwell in January, claimer and seller at Wolverhampton in February/April, and handicaps at Newmarket in May, Carlisle in June and Yarmouth in August: best at 7f: acts on all-weather, good to firm and good to soft going. *K. R. Burke*

INASUS (GER) 2 ch.c. (Mar 23) Kornado 120 – Instinctive Dancer (USA) (Spend A **58 p** Buck (USA)) [2006 7.5m⁴ Aug 16] half-brother to several winners in Germany, including 6f winner Instinctive Girl and 7f/7.5f winner Indiana Man (both by Big Shuffle): dam 7f and 9f winner in Germany: 9/2, green when well-beaten fourth to Mesbaah in maiden at Beverley: should progress. *M. Johnston*

INCA SOLDIER (FR) 3 br.g. Intikhab (USA) 135 – Chrysalu 102 (Distant Relative – 128) [2006 71p: p6g 5g⁵ 6g 6.1m Jun 25] sturdy gelding: fair maiden at 2 yrs: gelded, well held in 2006: stays 7f: acts on polytrack. *R. C. Guest*

INCH BY INCH 7 b.m. Inchinor 119 – Maid Welcome 81 (Mummy's Pet 125) [2006 **80** 83: 5.7f⁴ 7g⁵ 6f⁴ 6g* 6f p7g p6g³ p6g p7.1g⁶ Dec 31] smallish mare: fairly useful handicapper: won at Lingfield in August: probably best at 5f/6f: acts on all-weather and firm going: usually blinkered (not final start). *P. J. Makin*

INCHDHUAIG (IRE) 3 ch.g. Inchinor 119 – Be Thankfull (IRE) 98 (Linamix (FR) **56** 127) [2006 58: 8m⁵ 8.5g 8.3g 8.3m 6.1f⁵ 10m³ Sep 11] lightly-made gelding: modest maiden: stays 1¼m: acts on fibresand and good to firm going. *P. C. Haslam*

INCHDURA 8 ch.g. Inchinor 119 – Sunshine Coast 86 (Posse (USA) 130) [2006 48: – f8g Jan 1] quite attractive gelding: poor performer nowadays: well held only outing in 2006: tried tongue tied/in cheekpieces. *N. Tinkler*

INCH FORWARD 2 b.f. (Feb 6) Inchinor 119 – Lets Be Fair 94 (Efisio 120) [2006 5m – 6g 6g Jun 5] 3,200Y: leggy filly: fourth foal: half-sister to winning sprinters Beauvrai (by Bahamian Bounty) and Head of State (by Primo Dominie): dam 2-y-o 5f winner: looks of no account. *D. W. Barker*

INCH HIGH 8 ch.g. Inchinor 119 – Harrken Heights (IRE) (Belmez (USA) 131) [2006 **59** 48: 8.3d⁶ 8v* 8d³ 7.2g⁵ 10d³ 10f³ 10m⁵ 9.1m⁶ 7.2g 9.2d 9d Oct 8] modest performer: won handicap at Ayr in May: stays 1¼m: acts on polytrack and any turf going: tried visored/in cheekpieces. *J. S. Goldie*

INCHIGEELAGH (IRE) 2 ch.f. (Feb 2) Inchinor 119 – Thank One's Stars (Alzao **54** (USA) 117) [2006 6g⁶ p6g 6.1m⁶ Sep 15] neat filly: closely related to fairly useful 1997 2-y-o 5f winner Thanksgiving (by Indian Ridge) and half-sister to several winners, including useful 1m/1¼m winner Be Thankfull (by Linamix): dam unraced: modest form in maidens. *H. Morrison*

INCHINATA (IRE) 2 b.f. (Mar 7) Inchinor 119 – Caviare (Cadeaux Genereux 131) **– p** [2006 7d Oct 28] 12,000F, 32,000Y: lengthy filly: first foal: dam unraced half-sister to useful French performer up to 1½m Leros: 33/1, needed experience in maiden at Newmarket: should do better. *B. W. Hills*

INCHLAGGAN (IRE) 2 ch.c. (Mar 18) Inchinor 119 – Lakatoi 82 (Saddlers' Hall **66 p** (IRE) 126) [2006 7d 7g⁶ Oct 12] workmanlike colt: first foal: dam, maiden who stayed 1¾m, out of Oaks winner Bireme: mid-field in maidens at Newmarket, staying on: will be suited by 1¼m/1½m: should progress. *B. W. Hills*

INCHLOCH 4 ch.g. Inchinor 119 – Lake Pleasant (IRE) 90 (Elegant Air 119) [2006 **92** 85: 10g* 10.1g⁴ 10g* 12d⁶ 10s 10s Oct 21] leggy gelding: fairly useful performer: won handicaps at Nottingham in June and Newbury in July: stays 1½m: acts on soft and good to firm ground: looks hard ride. *B. G. Powell*

INCH LODGE 4 ch.c. Grand Lodge (USA) 125 – Legaya 94 (Shirley Heights 130) **86** [2006 8d 10m² p10g⁴ 10.1f⁵ 8m p12.2g* p10g p12.2g* p12g⁵ p12.2s* Dec 13] good-topped colt: fairly useful performer: unraced in 2005 and left Sir Michael Stoute: won handicaps in September, November and December, all at Wolverhampton: stays 1½m: acts on polytrack and firm going: often races prominently. *Miss D. Mountain*

INCHLOSS (IRE) 5 b.g. Imperial Ballet (IRE) 110 – Earth Charter 60 (Slip Anchor   –
136) [2006 81d: f8g⁶ 10m f8g f8g Jul 7] smallish, sturdy gelding: fairly useful handicapper at 4 yrs: no form in 2006. *C. N. Kellett*

INCHMAHOME 3 b.f. Galileo (IRE) 134 – Inchmurrin 114 (Lomond (USA) 128)   **61**
[2006 8.2m⁶ 8s⁶ May 27] smallish, leggy filly: half-sister to several winners, including
7f/1m performer Inchinor (by Ahonoora) and 1999 2-y-o 7f winner (later stayed 1½m)
Inchlonaig (by Nashwan), both smart: dam 5f (at 2 yrs) and 1m winner: better effort in
maidens (sweating both times) when sixth to Muzher at Newmarket second start: will
stay 1¼m. *G. Wragg*

INCHMARLOW (IRE) 3 b.g. Cape Cross (IRE) 129 – Glenstal Priory 53 (Glenstal   **54**
(USA) 118) [2006 58: 10.5m 5.9m⁵ 6m 6.9f⁵ 10d f7g p6g Nov 14] good-topped gelding: modest maiden: stays 6f: acts on good to firm and good to soft going, unraced on
extremes: slowly away third outing. *T. H. Caldwell*

INCHNACARDOCH (IRE) 2 b.c. (Mar 1) Marju (IRE) 127 – Inchoate (Machia-   **73**
vellian (USA) 125) [2006 8.1g⁵ 8g³ Oct 17] 42,000F, 75,000Y: first foal: dam unraced
half-sister to smart 7f/1m performer Inchinor: fair form in maidens, third to Grey Rover
at Bath: sent to Oman. *A. King*

INCHNADAMPH 6 b.g. Inchinor 119 – Pelf (USA) 79 (Al Nasr (FR) 126) [2006 92:   **93**
12g p16g 16.1d 18d² Oct 14] tall, workmanlike gelding: fairly useful handicapper: easily
best effort in 2006 when length second to Detroit City in Cesarewitch (placed for second
successive year) at Newmarket: stays 2¼m: acts on firm and soft going: tongue tied.
T. J. Fitzgerald

INCIDENTALLY (IRE) 3 ch.c. Inchinor 119 – Top Sauce (Hector Protector (USA)   **86**
124) [2006 75: 8m³ 8m² 8s² 8m* 10m⁵ 8g 9m 11g 9.9d³ 12g² Oct 13] good-bodied colt:
fairly useful performer: won maiden at Goodwood in June: creditable efforts in claimers
last 2 starts, blinkered first occasion: blinkered/visored since: acts on soft and good to firm going:
finished lame seventh start: sold 30,000 gns. *R. Hannon*

INCONY 2 b.f. (Apr 4) Daggers Drawn (USA) 114 – Illustre Inconnue (USA) (Septieme   **54**
Ciel (USA) 123) [2006 6d p6g⁴ p7.1g Nov 14] half-sister to 3 winners abroad: dam,
French 7.5f and 1m winner, half-sister to very smart French/US 1½m performer Talloires:
modest form in maidens: stays 7f. *W. R. Swinburn*

INCURSION 5 b.g. Inchinor 119 – Morgannwg (IRE) 86 (Simply Great (FR) 122)   **82**
[2006 86: 12m³ 13d 12g⁵ 16m² 20m 16f⁵ 13.8m³ 11.7m² 12d² 15.8d* 17.5d Sep 15]
sturdy gelding: fairly useful handicapper: won at Catterick in September: suffered fatal
heart attack at Ayr: stayed 2m: acted on soft and good to firm going. *D. Nicholls*

INDEBTED 4 b.f. Royal Applause 124 – Briggsmaid 70 (Elegant Air 119) [2006 82:   –
f8g p9.5g 8g a8.7g⁵ Aug 13] fairly useful performer at best: no form in 2006, sold from
P. D’Arcy 4,500 gns after second start. *Madeleine Smith, Sweden*

INDIAN BALLET 3 ch.f. Indian Ridge 123 – Bolshaya 74 (Cadeaux Genereux 131)   **68**
[2006 –p: 5m⁵ p6g⁴ 5f⁶ Jul 8] good-topped filly: fair maiden: effective at 6f: acts on polytrack and good to firm going. *M. A. Jarvis*

INDIAN BAZAAR (IRE) 10 ch.g. Indian Ridge 123 – Bazaar Promise 58 (Native   **– §**
Bazaar 122) [2006 56§: 5.1f 5.7f Aug 8] big, good-topped gelding: modest performer:
well held in 2006: tried in blinkers/cheekpieces: usually races prominently: unreliable.
R. A. Harris

INDIAN CHASE 9 b.g. Terimon 124 – Icy Gunner (Gunner B 126) [2006 50, a60:   **64 d**
p16g f16g* f14g⁵ f16g⁵ 17.2s p16g p13.9g p16.5g p16.5f f16g f16g p16g Dec 18] leggy
gelding: modest performer: won banded race at Southwell in March: below form after:
stays 2¼m: acts on all-weather and soft going: tried visored: sometimes races freely.
Dr J. R. J. Naylor

INDIAN DAWN (IRE) 3 b.c. Indian Lodge (IRE) 127 – Degree of Charm (IRE) 65   –
(Alzao (USA) 117) [2006 55: 8.1m 10.2m 10d Oct 4] close-coupled colt: little form since
debut at 2 yrs. *T. H. Caldwell*

INDIAN EDGE 5 ch.g. Indian Rocket 115 – Beveled Edge 60 (Beveled (USA)) [2006   **80**
59, a56: p8.6g p7.1g⁵ p8.6g² f7g p9.5g* p9.5g² p8g* 8.1d* 8d* 8s* 8.1d⁶ p8g⁶ p8g 10d   **a70**
7s² 8.2s⁴ p8.6g p8.6g Nov 17] good-topped gelding: fairly useful on turf, fair on all-
weather: won banded race at Wolverhampton in March, and handicaps at Kempton in
April, and Chepstow and Bath (2) in May: below form after: effective at 7f to 9.5f: acts
on polytrack and soft going: formerly tricky ride: races up with pace nowadays: has
carried head high. *B. Palling*

INDIAN GEM 5 ch.m. Bijou d'Inde 127 – Cayla (Tumble Wind) [2006 53: p7.1g p7.1g **45** f6g p5.1g⁶ 6m p6g p7.1g⁵ 7m⁴ 8f⁶ 6m Jul 15] poor maiden: stays 7f: acts on polytrack and good to firm ground. *A. J. Chamberlain*

INDIAN GIRL 3 b.f. Erhaab (USA) 127 – Natchez Trace 52 (Commanche Run 133) **59** [2006 10f 10.2g⁵ 10.9m 10m 16.2m 15.8m⁶ 17.2g Oct 17] £700Y: half-sister to 3 winners, including 9-y-o Connect and 1½m winner Be True (by Robellino): dam maiden who should have proved suited by further than 1m: modest maiden: appears to stay 2m: raced on good going or firmer. *M. R. Channon*

INDIAN INK (IRE) 2 ch.f. (Mar 19) Indian Ridge 123 – Maid of Killeen (IRE) 97 **110** (Darshaan 133) [2006 6m 6m* 6m⁴ 6s² 6.5s* 6d* Sep 29]

Richard Hannon's record as a trainer of two-year-olds, particularly in pattern events over five and six furlongs, is exceptional, and not that many races in the category in Britain pass by without his having at least one runner. In the latest season, he saddled contenders for fourteen of the eighteen races, adding one to his tally of twenty-one Group 2 and Group 3 prizes garnered just in the period 1990 to 2005. Oddly, though, despite a victory in the Phoenix Stakes with Pips Pride in 1992, and Lyric Fantasy's success in the all-aged Nunthorpe Stakes the same year, neither of the two juvenile Group 1s over sprint distances in Britain, the Cheveley Park Stakes and Middle Park Stakes, had been won by a Hannon-trained horse in the same time span—or before for that matter, in a career spanning more than thirty years. The closest he had come was second place in the Middle Park with Rock City in 1989 and with Pips Pride, and in the Cheveley Park with Lyric Fantasy, swiftly followed by Risky in 1993. Now, at last, one of the gaps has been filled, thanks to Indian Ink's victory in the Cheveley Park in September. In the sense that the withdrawal of Sander Camillo because of the rain-softened going removed the certain favourite and probable winner, Indian Ink can be regarded as a shade fortunate, but she is a grand filly who hardly put a foot wrong through the season.

The Cheveley Park Stakes, sponsored by Sky Bet, attracted eleven runners but was only an average renewal. Most of the contenders had form in pattern races, headed by the joint-favourites Magic America, runner-up in the Prix Morny, and Indian Ink. The others included Beauty Is Truth, Dhanyata and Scarlet Runner, successful respectively in the Prix d'Arenberg, Sirenia Stakes and Princess Margaret Stakes, and Silca Chiave, a close second in the Moyglare Stud Stakes. Indian Ink had not hit the target in two attempts in pattern company but she had run creditably to be fourth in the Princess Margaret at Ascot when waited with and not having the run of the race, and half a length second to Silk Blossom, ahead of Scarlet Runner, in the Lowther Stakes at York. In the latter, Indian Ink was on her toes, made the running, as she had when successful in a maiden race at Newbury in June, and looked the likely winner when kicking clear two furlongs out only to be caught near the finish. She had also earned £136,570 when outclassing twenty-one opponents in the Watership Down Stud Sales Race at Ascot a week before the Cheveley Park. To give an indication of the lack of depth in that race, half the field started at 50/1 or longer and the eighth horse home was beaten more than fifteen lengths. This should

Watership Down Stud Sales Race, Ascot—clear form choice Indian Ink has no trouble in justifying favouritism in this very valuable event for two-year-old fillies; Siamese Cat is runner-up

Sky Bet Cheveley Park Stakes, Newmarket—Indian Ink is thriving and takes this Group 1 just a week after her Ascot success, edging ahead of Dhanyata (No.3) late on; Silca Chiave (No.9) and La Presse are next to finish

not be taken as a criticism of Indian Ink, who justified favouritism in great style by three lengths from Siamese Cat after being ridden less forcefully than at York and quickening ahead on the bit two furlongs out. There was never likely to be any quickening ahead on the bit in the Cheveley Park, and Indian Ink had to show all her battling qualities to gain the day. Once again ridden with more restraint than in the Lowther Stakes, though still showing plenty of speed, she was asked for her effort once Dhanyata made her move in the Dip. Indian Ink responded well, making ground steadily under pressure and catching the leader close home for a neck victory. Silca Chiave was a length and a quarter away third.

Indian Ink (IRE) (ch.f. Mar 19, 2004)	Indian Ridge (ch 1985)	Ahonoora (ch 1975)	Lorenzaccio
			Helen Nichols
		Hillbrow (ch 1975)	Swing Easy
			Golden City
	Maid of Killeen (IRE) (b 1996)	Darshaan (br 1981)	Shirley Heights
			Delsy
		Sovereign Touch (b 1989)	Pennine Walk
			Sovereign Dona

Three weeks after the Cheveley Park Stakes, Indian Ink's sire Indian Ridge died of a heart attack at the Irish National Stud. A very smart sprinter whose principal victory came in the King's Stand Stakes, he has been represented by winners of top races at five furlongs to a mile and a half. However, Relaxed Gesture's victory over the latter trip in the 2005 Canadian International, and National Stakes winner Definite Article's short-head second in the Irish Derby, were exceptions to the norm. In general, Indian Ridge's runners have excelled at up to a mile, with Compton Place (July Cup), Namid (Prix de l'Abbaye), Domedriver and Ridgewood Pearl (both successful in the Breeders' Cup Mile) the pick. Indian Ink, Indian Ridge's first two-year-old Group 1 winner, looks to be one of that ilk, though the distaff side of her pedigree holds its share of stamina. Indian Ink's dam Maid of Killeen scored at nine furlongs in Ireland as a two-year-old and finished second in a listed race over a mile and a half at three. Indian Ink is her fourth foal and second winner following the fairly useful Unavailable (by Alzao) who notched two races as a two-year-old and stayed a mile and a quarter. Maid of Killeen was sold for 650,000 guineas at the Newmarket December Sales in foal to Azamour and reportedly visits Galileo. Her dam Sovereign Touch was an unraced half-sister to Prix de la Foret runner-up Royal Touch, very smart middle-distance stayer Foresee, who finished third in the Irish Derby and Irish St Leger, and to a winner over a mile and three quarters by Darshaan. Indian Ink fetched 25,000 guineas as a yearling at New-

Mr Raymond Tooth's "Indian Ink"

market. Her success proved a bonus for the breeder, who received 180,000 guineas for Indian Ink's brother at the same venue a few days after the Cheveley Park. All things considered, although pace has been her preponderant racing characteristic so far, Indian Ink should stay a mile. She is not a tearaway and can be settled, as she showed at Ascot in particular, which should help her prospects in the One Thousand Guineas. Hannon's tendency to give his Guineas contenders a trial run is also likely to benefit punters by helping to clarify matters. Assuming she does stay, Indian Ink, a tough and genuine individual who acts on soft and good to firm going, will still need to improve to trouble Finsceal Beo and Sander Camillo. However, given her looks—she is a big, good-topped filly—Indian Ink should train on and, as she has progressed throughout her career, she certainly cannot be discounted. *R. Hannon*

INDIAN KATE 3 b.f. Komaite (USA) – Indian Nectar 68 (Indian Ridge 123) [2006 –: f6g Nov 15] no form. *R. Brotherton* — —

INDIAN LADY (IRE) 3 b.f. Namid 128 – Lady Eberspacher (IRE) 68 (Royal Abjar (USA) 121) [2006 63: 5.1g² 5m 5m 5.7g p6g 6g 6d⁶ 5.1m⁵ 6d² 6d Oct 3] fair performer: raced only at 5f/6f: acts on firm and good to soft going: wears headgear nowadays: has twice hung left. *Mrs A. L. M. King* **70**

INDIAN MAIDEN (IRE) 6 br.m. Indian Ridge 123 – Jinsiyah (USA) 98 (House-buster (USA)) [2006 114: p6g³ 5.5v² 6g 5.1g* 7m⁶ 6.1s² 5d⁶ 6f⁶ 6g* 6.1m³ 6m 6d* 6s* 6.1m⁴ 6g⁴ 7m 6g³ 6d Oct 28] tall, rather leggy mare: smart performer: enjoyed another **115**

508

Prix de Meautry Lucien Barriere, Deauville—a British-trained 1,2 as Indian Maiden, gaining the fifteenth win of her career, beats the blinkered Eisteddfod, with Ratio (rail) third

fine season, winning listed races at Bath (by neck from Dhekraa) in May, Leopardstown (by short head from Beauty Bright) in July and Pontefract (by 3½ lengths from Home Sweet Home) in August, and Prix de Meautry Lucien Barriere at Deauville (by length from Eisteddfod) later in August: best effort after when respectable third to Firenze in listed event at Newmarket: best at 5f/6f: acts on all-weather, has form on any turf going but all wins on good or softer: usually held up: tough, and a credit to connections. *M. S. Saunders*

INDIAN PRIDE 4 b.f. Groom Dancer (USA) 128 – Royal Patron 78 (Royal Academy (USA) 130) [2006 8.3d 9.7f⁴ 10.2g⁶ Jul 10] first foal: dam 1¾m winner out of Gold Cup winner Indian Queen: modest maiden: reportedly finished lame final start: should be suited by 1½m+: acts on firm ground: slowly away on debut. *D. J. Coakley*   **59**

INDIAN SABRE (IRE) 3 ch.c. Indian Ridge 123 – Kyka (USA) (Blushing John (USA) 120) [2006 7m 6f f6g* p6g⁵ p7g Sep 5] €37,000Y, 50,000 2-y-o: fifth foal: half-brother to several winners, including fairly useful 1¼m winner Theatre Time (by Theatrical) and Irish 1½m and 2m winner Always The Groom (by Darshaan): dam unraced half-sister to Poule d'Essai des Pouliches winner Madeleine's Dream: fair performer: won maiden at Southwell in July: should stay 7f: acts on all-weather. *J. Noseda*   **73**

INDIAN'S FEATHER (IRE) 5 ch.m. Indian Ridge 123 – Mashmoum 85 (Lycius (USA) 124) [2006 98: 8g 7d⁵ 8s 8.1g 7s Oct 10] 60,000Y: strong, compact ex-Irish mare: third foal: half-sister to Irish 2002 2-y-o 7f winner Zamunda (by Spectrum) and winner in Italy by Charnwood Forest: dam 7f winner: useful performer in 2005 (won handicap at Tralee and good fifth in listed race at Naas): left M. Grassick in Ireland 40,000 gns, well below form in 2006: effective at 7f/1m: acts on soft and good to firm going: usually blinkered. *N. Tinkler*   **79**

INDIAN SKY (IRE) 4 b.g. Indian Lodge (IRE) 127 – Bolero (Rainbow Quest (USA) 134) [2006 –: 8.1m Aug 10] reportedly fractured a shin bone in 2004: no solid form: has shown signs of temperament. *B. R. Millman*   **–**

INDIAN SONG (IRE) 2 b.f. (Jan 15) Indian Rocket 115 – Canoe Cove (IRE) 55 (Grand Lodge (USA) 125) [2006 5g 5g⁴ 5.1g⁴ 5.2g 5m⁴ 6.1g⁵ 5.1m⁶ p6g 5.3m² Sep 19] €10,000Y: sturdy filly: first foal: dam, sprint maiden (headstrong), ran only at 2 yrs: fair maiden at best: second in seller final start (blinkered): best at 5f: acts on good to firm going, probably polytrack: sold 3,000 gns. *R. F. Johnson Houghton*   **67 d**

INDIAN SPARK 12 ch.g. Indian Ridge 123 – Annes Gift (Ballymoss 136) [2006 71: 6g* 6v⁴ 6m 6m Jun 30] close-coupled gelding: poor mover (reportedly fractured off-fore joint earlier in career): fair handicapper: won at Ayr in May: effective at 5f, seems to stay 7f: acts on any going: often gets behind. *J. S. Goldie*   **73**

INDIAN STEPPES (FR) 7 b.m. Indian Ridge 123 – Ukraine Venture 96 (Slip Anchor 136) [2006 93: p7g⁴ 8m⁴ 8g* 8.2g⁵ 7m p8g² 8.1v² 8d⁶ 6g 8d Oct 28] strong, good-bodied mare: useful performer: left Mrs L. Featherstone after reappearance: won handicap at Ascot (by length from Kelucia) in May: creditable second in listed race at Haydock seventh outing: below form after: stays 1m: acts on dirt, all-weather, soft and good to firm going: tried in cheekpieces: has run well when sweating. *P. S. McEntee* **100**

INDIAN SUNDANCE (IRE) 3 b.g. Namid 128 – Can't Afford It (IRE) 44 (Glow (USA)) [2006 –: 5d 6.1d⁶ Oct 13] heavy-topped gelding: little form. *R. A. Fahey* **–**

INDIAN TRAIL 6 ch.g. Indian Ridge 123 – Take Heart 84 (Electric 126) [2006 104: p6g⁶ 7g 6m⁵ 6m⁶ 6m* 6g⁶ 7m 5.4g 6s Oct 7] big, strong gelding: smart handicapper: showed himself better than ever when winning at Newcastle (by 2 lengths from Woodcote) in July: well below form after: has won at 7f, probably best at 5f/6f: acts on firm and soft going: patiently ridden. *D. Nicholls* **112**

INDIAN WIZARD (IRE) 3 b.g. Indian Ridge 123 – Ragtime Rumble (USA) (Dixieland Band (USA)) [2006 71: p8g* p8g f7g Jan 26] tall gelding: fair performer: won seller at Lingfield in January (very slowly away): stays 1m: acts on polytrack, firm and good to soft going: has joined D. Rees. *P. Howling* **64**

INDIA RUN (IRE) 3 b.c. Hernando (FR) 127 – Sirdhana 79 (Selkirk (USA) 129) [2006 68p: 10m 12m Aug 5] well-made colt: fair maiden: well beaten in 2006: bred to be suited by 1½m+: raced on good/good to firm ground: sold 9,000 gns. *J. L. Dunlop* **–**

INDICATION 3 b.f. Sadler's Wells (USA) 132 – Insinuate (USA) 99 (Mr Prospector (USA)) [2006 7g² 8.1g² 10d p9.5g* p10g⁶ Nov 9] close-coupled, quite good-topped, attractive filly: third foal: half-sister to 4-y-o Stronghold: dam, 1m winner, out of Prix du Moulin winner and Oaks runner-up All At Sea: fair performer: won maiden at Wolverhampton in October: stayed 1¼m: acted on polytrack, raced only on good/good to soft going on turf: tongue tied last 2 starts: stud. *J. H. M. Gosden* **76**

INDIGO DANCER 3 b.g. Groom Dancer (USA) 128 – Violet (IRE) 77 (Mukaddamah (USA) 125) [2006 –: p8.6g* 10f⁵ p12g p11g p8.6g⁴ p9.5g Dec 4] strong, well-made gelding: modest performer: won banded race at Wolverhampton in April: effective at 8.6f to 11f: acts on polytrack and firm going: tried tongue tied, blinkered last 2 starts. *C. F. Wall* **50**

INDIGO NIGHTS (IRE) 3 b.f. Danehill Dancer (IRE) 117 – Bent Al Fala (IRE) 59 (Green Desert (USA) 127) [2006 89: 5g³ Apr 22] good-topped filly: fairly useful performer: sustained hairline fracture of pelvis after final 2-y-o start: creditable third in handicap at Thirsk only outing in 2006: was speedy, and best at 5f: unraced on extremes of going: dead. *Mrs A. Duffield* **85**

INDIGO ROSE (IRE) 2 b.f. (Feb 16) Cadeaux Genereux 131 – Colourfast (IRE) 88 (Spectrum (IRE) 126) [2006 7d p8g⁶ Oct 20] 240,000Y: long-backed, workmanlike filly: first foal: dam, Irish 1m winner, half-sister to dam of Shirocco: better effort in maidens when never-nearer sixth to Sunlight at Lingfield: should do better still. *J. H. M. Gosden* **64 p**

INDIGO SKY (IRE) 5 gr.h. Adieu Au Roi (IRE) 116§ – Urban Sky (FR) (Groom Dancer (USA) 128) [2006 54, a66: p8g p8g p8g⁴ p10g p10g³ p10g⁵ Apr 5] modest performer: stays 1¼m: acts on polytrack, firm and good to soft ground: sometimes blinkered. *B. G. Powell* **– a55**

INDONESIA 4 ch.g. Lomitas 129 – Idraak (Kris 135) [2006 72: 13.9s 14.1g³ 13.9m³ 16.1m* 16.1d⁴ Aug 28] strong, useful-looking gelding: fairly useful handicapper: upped in trip, first success when winning at Newcastle in August: creditable fourth there only subsequent start: acts on good to firm and good to soft ground. *T. D. Walford* **81**

IN DUBAI (USA) 3 ch.f. Giant's Causeway (USA) 132 – Bahr 119 (Generous (IRE) 139) [2006 91: 10g p10g⁴ Jul 14] leggy filly: fairly useful performer at 2 yrs: well held in handicaps in 2006: should stay 1¼m: acts on soft and good to firm going: joined D. Selvaratnam in UAE. *M. P. Tregoning* **–**

INDUSTRIAL STAR (IRE) 5 ch.g. Singspiel (IRE) 133 – Faribole (IRE) 106 (Esprit du Nord (USA) 126) [2006 66: 12s⁵ 15.8g⁴* 15.8m² 18f Jul 29] lengthy gelding: fair performer, lightly raced: won handicap at Catterick in June: stays 2m: acts on good to firm ground: tends to hang left. *M. D. Hammond* **73**

INESCAPABLE (USA) 5 b.g. Cape Town (USA) 125 – Danyross (IRE) 99 (Danehill (USA) 126) [2006 47: f7g p7.1g f7g f8g p8g p7.1g* p7g⁶ p7g p8g⁶ 7.6g Aug 12] modest performer: won banded race at Wolverhampton in May: stays 7f: acts on all-weather, best turf efforts on good going: has been gelded. *A. W. Carroll* **– a50**

IN FASHION 3 b.f. Bertolini (USA) 125 – Dress Design (IRE) 84 (Brief Truce (USA) **54** 126) [2006 –: 7s f5g² 5.1d⁴ 6f² 5.7g 5.1g 5.7f Jun 17] modest maiden: seems to stay 6f: acts on fibresand and firm ground: blinkered final start. *R. J. Hodges*

INFLAGRANTEDELICTO (USA) 2 ch.c. (Apr 15) Gentlemen (ARG) 136 – Imp- **63** rudent Love (USA) (Foolish Pleasure (USA)) [2006 p7.1g p8.6m f7g³ f8g³ f8g³ f8g⁴ f8g³ Dec 27] $8,000Y, resold 15,000Y: half-brother to numerous winners, notably very smart US performer up to 1¼m Momentum (by Nureyev), earlier 1m/9f winner in Britain: dam 1m to 11f winner in USA: modest maiden: claimed from M. Johnston third start: in frame after in maidens and nursery at Southwell: will be suited by 1¼m+: raced on all-weather: usually soon off bridle. *D. W. Chapman*

INFLAGRANTI 2 b.f. (Mar 18) Inchinor 119 – Another Fantasy (IRE) 103 (Danehill **67** (USA) 126) [2006 f5g 6m 5g* 6g 7f 5g 6.1d Oct 4] 3,500F, 16,500Y: small, sturdy filly: fourth foal: dam, 5f/6f winner at 2 yrs who probably stayed 1¼m (became disappointing), out of sister to Italian Group 1 1¼m winner Stufida (grandam of Pivotal): fair performer: won maiden at Beverley in August, easily best effort: should stay 6f/7f. *J. G. Portman*

INFLIGHT (IRE) 2 b.f. (Apr 18) Intikhab (USA) 135 – Red Eagle (IRE) 62 (Eagle **73** Eyed (USA) 111) [2006 5g 6f⁴ 5.3f² p5g² 5m⁵ 5.3f* p5g* 5g 5.1f 5.2d Oct 18] €4,000F, €12,000Y: lengthy filly: second foal: dam 5f winner, including at 2 yrs: fair performer: won nurseries at Brighton and Kempton in August: lost form after: best at 5f: acts on polytrack and firm going: sold 8,000 gns. *R. M. Beckett*

IN FULL CRY 3 ch.g. Grand Lodge (USA) 125 – Red Roses Story (FR) 118 (Pink **90** (FR) 123) [2006 87p: 9m⁶ 10.1m² 10m⁴ 10m³ 8.1m 10.2f 10.4s p12g Oct 23] lengthy, good-topped colt: fairly useful handicapper: best efforts when in frame: should stay 1½m (dam won Prix Royal-Oak): acts on good to firm ground: has hung left: sold 14,500 gns, then gelded. *M. Johnston*

INGLEBY ARCH (USA) 3 b.g. Arch (USA) 127 – Inca Dove (USA) (Mr Prospector **101** (USA)) [2006 86: 6g* 6m* 6m 6m⁵ 6m 6g⁴ 6g⁴ 7m 6d 6s Oct 7] strong, well-made geld- ing: useful performer: won handicap at Newmarket (beat Angus Newz by 3 lengths) in April and minor event at Hamilton (by short head from Obe Brave) in May: mostly at least respectable efforts after: gelded following final start: probably best around 6f: acts on good to firm and good to soft going: tried visored/blinkered: has a high head carriage. *T. D. Barron*

INGLEBY FLAME (IRE) 2 ch.g. (Apr 10) Redback 116 – Boobala (IRE) 78 (Gene- **69** ral Monash (USA) 107) [2006 7f⁴ 7f³ 7.1d³ 7.1m⁶ a6d Dec 17] €10,000F, 7,000Y: first foal: dam 2-y-o 5f winner: fair maiden: third at Catterick (minor event) and Musselburgh: sold from T. D. Barron 5,200 gns before final start: likely to stay 1m. *M. Kahn, Sweden*

INGLEBY HILL (IRE) 2 b.g. (Feb 18) Averti (IRE) 117 – Living Daylights (IRE) 73 **–** (Night Shift (USA)) [2006 5.1d⁶ 5.1s 7.1d Nov 3] good-topped gelding: little form in maidens. *T. D. Barron*

INGLEBY IMAGE 2 gr.f. (Feb 5) Averti (IRE) 117 – Miss Mirror 77 (Magic Mirror **80** 105) [2006 5v* 5.2g⁵ 5g 5m³ 5d³ 6d⁶ 5s Oct 14] 8,500Y: leggy filly: sister to 4-y-o San Deng and half-sister to several winners, including useful Swedish performers Magic Fact (6.5f/1½m winner, by Factual) and Tragic Love (1m/1¼m winner, by Tragic Role): dam 1m winner: fairly useful performer: won maiden at Musselburgh in March: best efforts when third in nursery there and minor event at Ripon (blinkered) in August: should stay at least 6f: acts on heavy and good to firm going: has looked nervy sort: sold 13,000 gns. *T. D. Barron*

INGLEBY PRINCESS 2 br.f. (Mar 2) Bold Edge 123 – Bob's Princess 69 (Bob's **78** Return (IRE) 123) [2006 5g* 7.1f* 7m⁴ 6m* 6g² 7d⁶ Oct 3] 7,000Y: leggy filly: fourth foal: half-sister to 3-y-o Bob's Your Uncle: dam 2-y-o 7f winner who stayed 1½m: fair performer: won maiden at Newcastle in May, minor event at Musselburgh in June and nursery at Hamilton in August: will stay 1m: raced on good or firmer going until final start (below form). *T. D. Barron*

INGLETON 4 b.g. Komaite (USA) – Dash Cascade (Absalom 128) [2006 85: 6g⁵ 6d⁵ **83** 5g⁴ p7g⁴ p6g* Jun 28] strong gelding: fairly useful handicapper: won at Kempton in June: gelded after: barely stayed 7f: acted on polytrack and soft going: tried in cheekpieces: dead. *G. L. Moore*

INGRATITUDE (IRE) 3 ch.g. Inchinor 119 – Merci (IRE) (Cadeaux Genereux 131) **98** [2006 74: 7.1g 8.3g* 8.2d² 8g 8.1g³ Sep 22] compact gelding: useful handicapper: much improved when winning at Windsor in May by short head from Plum Pudding: gelded, respectable third at Haydock final start: stays 1m: raced only on good/good to soft going: tried visored: has hung left: sold 48,000 gns, joined N. Henderson. *R. M. Beckett*

INHERIT (IRE) 4 b.g. Princely Heir (IRE) 111 – Flora Wood (IRE) 77 (Bob Back — (USA) 124) [2006 60, a–: 6m 7f Jun 24] modest maiden at 3 yrs: well held in 2006: tongue tied final start. *B. S. Rothwell*

IN HOPE 3 b.f. Most Welcome 131 – Frankie Fair (IRE) 73 (Red Sunset 120) [2006 57: **45** p6g⁶ p7g⁴ p6g p5g⁵ p8g⁵ p7.1g⁴ p7g² p7g⁴ p6g³ p6g⁴ p8.6g 10s⁶ Oct 2] quite attractive filly: poor maiden: left Andrew Reid after second outing and Ernst Oertel prior to final one: will prove best short of 1m: acts on polytrack. *D. K. Ivory*

INIMICAL 2 b.f. (Apr 4) Daggers Drawn (USA) 114 – Mara River 86 (Efisio 120) **54** [2006 p6g 7.1d 7d⁵ Oct 3] 8,500Y: sturdy filly: sixth foal: half-sister to 5-y-o Border Music and 2004 2-y-o 5f winner Marajuana (by Robellino): dam 6f to 1m winner: modest form in maidens: may prove best at 5f/6f. *W. S. Kittow*

INKA DANCER (IRE) 4 ch.f. Intikhab (USA) 135 – Grannys Reluctance (IRE) 63 **67** (Anita's Prince 126) [2006 57: 7.1d³ 7.1m³ 6f² 6d⁶ 5m 5d 6.1g⁴ 6m² p6g³ p6m² p6g **a64** Dec 2] small filly: fair handicapper on turf, modest on all-weather: won at Nottingham in September: effective at 5f to 7f: acts on polytrack, firm and good to soft going: has hung right. *B. Palling*

INKJET (IRE) 2 b.f. (Apr 26) Beckett (IRE) 116 – Aussie Aisle (IRE) (Godswalk — (USA) 130) [2006 5g⁵ p5.1g Jun 22] smallish filly: fifth foal: half-sister to 5f seller winner Ma Vielle Pouque (by Fayruz) and winner in Denmark by Petardia: dam Irish 1¼m winner: well held both starts. *Ms Deborah J. Evans*

INMARYSFOOTSTEPS 2 b.f. (Apr 12) Sugarfoot 118 – Mary Jane 77 (Tina's Pet — 121) [2006 5d May 15] 900Y: first foal: dam 5f (including at 2 yrs)/6f winner: last in maiden at Redcar. *N. Tinkler*

INMOM (IRE) 5 b.m. Barathea (IRE) 127 – Zakuska 96 (Zafonic (USA) 130) [2006 — f12g f8g⁶ p9.5g p8.6g Dec 18] good-topped mare: maiden: well held in 2006: tried tongue tied. *S. R. Bowring*

INNER VOICE (USA) 3 gr. or ro.c. Cozzene (USA) – Miss Henderson Co (USA) — (Silver Hawk (USA) 123) [2006 p9.5g⁶ Jun 10] 7/1, well held in maiden at Wolverhampton: sold 7,000 gns in July. *Sir Michael Stoute*

INN FOR THE DANCER 4 b.g. Groom Dancer (USA) 128 – Lady Joyce (FR) (Gal- — etto (FR) 118) [2006 57: p9.5g 10.2d Apr 25] workmanlike gelding: maiden: well held in 2006: tried in cheekpieces. *J. C. Fox*

INNOCENT AIR 3 ch.f. Galileo (IRE) 134 – Minskip (USA) 64 (The Minstrel (CAN) **110** 135) [2006 106p: 10d⁵ 11.9g⁵ 8.1g⁴ 10g* Oct 12] well-made filly: smart performer: below form first 3 starts in 2006 (found little first 2 occasions) before career-best effort when winning listed race at Newmarket (by 1¼ lengths from Anna Pavlova, sweating beforehand and failed to take the eye) in October: should have stayed 1½m: had worn crossed noseband/been attended by 2 handlers/blanketed for stall entry: tended to flash tail (did nothing wrong at Newmarket): raced prominently: stud. *J. H. M. Gosden*

INNPURSUIT 4 b.g. Inchinor 119 – Quest For The Best (Rainbow Quest (USA) 134) **?** [2006 69: p10g 9.3g³ 9.8d² 10m³ 9g⁴ 8d² 8.5g² 8g* 8g⁴ a9.8g* Nov 11] strong, close-coupled gelding: fair performer: sold from J. Eustace 2,000 gns after reappearance (blinkered): won handicaps at Cologne in October and Dortmund in November: stays 1¼m: acts on all-weather and good to soft ground. *N. Sauer, Germany*

IN ON THE ACT (IRE) 3 b.f. In The Wings 128 – Mosquera (GER) 108 (Acatenango **67** (GER) 127) [2006 p10g 11.5m 10d 10m⁵ 8m p8g 16.4m p10g Oct 15] 30,000Y: well-made filly: second foal: half-sister to fairly useful Irish 6f winner Bonanza (by Danehill): dam German 6.5f (at 2 yrs) to 9f winner: fair maiden: stays 1¼m: acts on good to firm ground: blinkered/visored last 2 outings. *Jamie Poulton*

INQUISITRESS 2 b.f. (Feb 7) Hernando (FR) 127 – Caribbean Star 81 (Soviet Star **71** (USA) 128) [2006 7m⁵ 8.3m 7g⁶ p8g⁶ p8.6m p8g* p7g³ p8g* p8g³ Dec 20] 9,000F: small, workmanlike filly: fifth foal: half-sister to 7-y-o Caribbean Coral: dam, 7f winner, half-sister to smart miler Caribbean Monarch: fair performer: won seller at Lingfield (left J. Eustace) in November and nursery at Kempton in December: stays 1m: acts on polytrack and good to firm ground. *J. J. Bridger*

IN RHUBARB 4 ch.g. Piccolo 121 – Versami (USA) (Riverman (USA) 131) [2006 44: –
8v f12g p11g f8g Dec 29] quite good-topped gelding: maiden: well held in 2006 (left
D. Nicholls after reappearance): tried tongue tied. *P. Howling*

INSCRIBED (IRE) 3 b.f. Fasliyev (USA) 120 – Fay (IRE) 64 (Polish Precedent (USA) **54**
131) [2006 p7.1g p8.6g Dec 18] €140,000F, 6,000 3-y-o: second foal: dam, ran 3 times
(should have been suited by 1½m+), closely related to useful 1m/1¼m performer Sundari: mid-field in maidens at Wolverhampton. *G. A. Huffer*

INSIDE STORY (IRE) 4 b.g. Rossini (USA) 118 – Sliding (Formidable (USA) 125) **74**
[2006 87: 7g 7g 10.1d 7f⁴ p8.6g* 8.1f* 8.9f 8.5s⁵ 8.5m 9.8d* 10s 10f* p9.5g³ p12g³ Dec
8] fair performer nowadays: won handicaps at Wolverhampton and Haydock in July,
seller at Ripon in August, and claimer at Leicester (claimed from M. Easterby £10,000)
in September: stays 1½m: acts on polytrack, firm and good to soft ground: blinkered
nowadays: slowly away first 2 outings. *G. P. Kelly*

INSIDE STRAIGHT (IRE) 2 b.c. (Mar 3) Raise A Grand (IRE) 114 – Starisa (IRE) –
(College Chapel 122) [2006 6g p7g 6d Oct 9] well held in maidens: sold 2,500 gns, sent
to Sweden. *R. Hannon*

INSIGNIA (IRE) 4 b.g. Royal Applause 124 – Amathea (FR) (Exit To Nowhere (USA) **a53**
122) [2006 60, a57: p9.5g⁴ p8.6g p10g p8.6g p8.6g⁴ p8.6g f8g⁴ Dec 12] modest maiden:
stays 9.5f: raced only on polytrack and good/good to firm ground: usually wears cheekpieces nowadays. *W. M. Brisbourne*

IN SOME STYLE (IRE) 3 ch.f. Grand Lodge (USA) 125 – Lovisa (USA) 55 (Gone –
West (USA)) [2006 –: 8.1s 8f 8m Jun 18] close-coupled filly: little form: tried visored/in
cheekpieces. *R. A. Harris*

INSPAINAGAIN (USA) 2 ch.c. (Feb 23) Miswaki (USA) 124 – Counter Cat (USA) **67**
(Hennessy (USA) 122) [2006 5m⁶ 5m² Aug 31] $4,000F, $4,000Y: second foal: half-
brother to winner in USA by Louis Quatorze: dam unraced: improved from debut (green)
when second to Durova in maiden at Redcar: will stay 6f/7f. *T. D. Barron*

INSPIRINA (IRE) 2 b.c. (Feb 21) Invincible Spirit 121 – La Stellina (IRE) 100 **73**
(Marju (IRE) 127) [2006 6f⁵ 6.1g³ 6g³ Aug 26] 16,000Y, 58,000 2-y-o: good-topped colt:
type to carry condition: first foal: dam Irish 5f (including at 2 yrs)/6f winner: fair maiden:
third to El Bosque in minor event at Windsor final start: should prove best at 5f/6f.
T. R. George

INSTINCT 5 b.g. Zafonic (USA) 130 – Gracious Gift 96 (Cadeaux Genereux 131) **42**
[2006 –: 5m 5.9m 5d⁵ 5m p5g⁶ f6g Dec 28] poor performer nowadays: barely stays 1m.
M. D. Hammond

INSTRUCTOR 5 ch.g. Groom Dancer (USA) 128 – Doctor's Glory (USA) 91 (Elma- **88**
amul (USA) 125) [2006 90: 10v 8g 10.5g⁴ 10d 8.9m³ 10f⁴ 10.1m 10.3m* 11.8m³ 12g 8.9s
Oct 7] good-topped gelding: easy mover: fairly useful handicapper: won at Chester in
July: stays 1½m: acts on all-weather and good to firm ground, no form on softer than
good: sometimes makes running. *R. A. Fahey*

INSUBORDINATE 5 ch.g. Subordination (USA) 120 – Manila Selection (USA) **66**
(Manila (USA)) [2006 59: 7.1v² 7g⁵ 7.1m³ 7d 7.1g⁵ 6g 8.3m⁵ 10g² 10d 9.2m* 8.3g⁵
9.2m⁵ 9.2m 9.2g⁴ 10s 9.2d Sep 25] leggy gelding: fair performer: won handicap at
Hamilton in July: stays 1¼m: acts on fibresand and any turf going: tried in cheekpieces in
2003: held up: usually slowly away, sometimes markedly so. *J. S. Goldie*

INTAVAC BOY 5 ch.g. Emperor Fountain 112 – Altaia (FR) 90 (Sicyos (USA) 126) **67**
[2006 63: 12.4g 12.4m³ 12.4d 12m² 10m² 12m² 12.1f* 12g Aug 7] sparely-made gelding:
fair handicapper: won at Beverley in July: effective at 1¼m to 12.4f: acts on polytrack,
firm and good to soft going: hung left on fourth outing: has joined R. Fahey.
C. W. Thornton

INTAVAC GIRL 3 b.f. Sinndar (IRE) 134 – Messila Rose (Darshaan 133) [2006 –: 9.8g –
12s 12f Jul 3] no form. *C. W. Thornton*

INTEGRATION 6 b.g. Piccolo 121 – Discrimination 72 (Efisio 120) [2006 53: f11g **50**
f11g f11g Dec 29] smallish, quite attractive gelding: modest maiden: sold from L. McAteer in
Ireland 5,200 gns after final 5-y-o start: stays 13f: acts on polytrack, firm and soft going:
usually races prominently. *Ronald Thompson*

INTENDED 4 b.f. Singspiel (IRE) 133 – Introducing 78 (Mtoto 134) [2006 64: p9.5g⁶ **–**
Jan 23] maiden: well held only outing in 2006: tongue tied since reappearance in 2005,
visored (well beaten) final 3-y-o start. *A. M. Balding*

INTENSIFIER (IRE) 2 b.c. (Mar 24) Sinndar (IRE) 134 – Licorne 93 (Sadler's Wells –
(USA) 132) [2006 f8g Dec 9] 20/1, slowly away in maiden at Southwell. *P. A. Blockley*

INTEREST (USA) 2 ch.g. (May 12) Banker's Gold (USA) 116 – Princess Kris 82 – p
(Kris 135) [2006 5.9g 6s 7.5m Sep 13] attractive gelding: not knocked about in maidens:
should do better. *T. D. Barron*

INTERSKY HIGH (USA) 4 b. or br.f. Royal Anthem (USA) 135 – Worood (USA) –
(Vaguely Noble 140) [2006 12g 10d Sep 14] $4,000Y: tall, leggy, good-topped filly:
closely related to French winner up to 15.5f winner Sixty And Steele (by Theatrical) and
half-sister to several winners: dam French 1m to 1½m winner: third only start in bumpers
for G. A. Swinbank: well held in 2 maidens: sold 9,500 gns. *K. A. Ryan*

INTERSKY MUSIC (USA) 3 b.g. Victory Gallop (CAN) 130 – Resounding Grace 58 p
(USA) (Thunder Gulch (USA) 129) [2006 8.3g⁶ Oct 16] $22,000Y: first foal: dam,
lightly raced in France/USA, half-sister to smart performer up to 1¼m Flat Spin: 25/1 and
green, sixth to Sound of Nature in maiden at Windsor: sold 18,000 gns, joined J. O'Neill.
P. W. Chapple-Hyam

INTERSKY SPORTS (USA) 2 gr.g. (Mar 19) Chester House (USA) 123 – Nightlong 65
(Night Shift (USA)) [2006 f6g² 6f⁴ 6m⁴ 7f⁴ p7.1f⁵ 8d p8.6g⁶ p7.1g⁵ f7g* Dec 19]
$20,000Y: half-brother to several winners in North America, including Canadian Grade 3
6f winner Quick Blue (by Cure The Blues): dam 6f winner in US (including at 2 yrs): fair
performer: won nursery at Southwell in December: stays 7f: acts on all-weather and firm
going: tried blinkered, better form in cheekpieces: has looked difficult ride. *K. A. Ryan*

INTERSTICE 9 b.g. Never So Bold 135 – Mainmast 63 (Bustino 136) [2006 f12g Jan –
3] handicapper: unraced on Flat in 2005, well held only start in 2006: tried in cheekpieces.
M. J. Gingell

INTER VISION (USA) 6 b.g. Cryptoclearance (USA) – Fateful (USA) 90 (Topsider 100
(USA)) [2006 95: 6v 7g 6g 6s⁴ 6m⁴ 7m* 7f⁴ 6s 5s² Oct 14] tall gelding: useful handicapper: won at Chester (by head from Areyoutalkingtome) in August: good ½-length
second to Dhaular Dhar at Catterick final start: effective from 5f to easy 7f: acts on polytrack, firm and soft ground: wore cheekpieces (ran creditably) once in 2004: usually held
up: tough. *A. Dickman*

IN THE FASHION (IRE) 3 b.f. In The Wings 128 – Tropical Lass (IRE) 67 (Ballad 88
Rock 122) [2006 87: 7m 10g Jun 7] close-coupled filly: fairly useful performer: not discredited in Fred Darling Stakes at Newbury (ninth to Nasheej) and listed race at Fontainebleau (made running): bred to be suited by 1m+: raced only on good/good to firm going:
sold 27,000 gns in November. *J. Noseda*

IN THE FOUNTAIN (IRE) 3 b.f. Mozart (IRE) 131 – Riviere du Diable (USA) (Irish 43
River (FR) 131) [2006 52d, a36: p6g p7.1g p7.1g⁴ p12.2g Jun 10] close-coupled filly: has
a markedly round action: poor maiden: left C. Dwyer 3,500 gns prior to final outing: stays
7f: acts on polytrack, best turf effort on good ground: has worn headgear. *R. A. Harris*

INTIQUILLA (IRE) 2 b.f. (Feb 10) Galileo (IRE) 134 – Orinoco (IRE) 53 (Darshaan 57
133) [2006 8.2s⁶ 8.2d Nov 1] good-topped filly: second foal: half-sister to 3-y-o Bran-
dama: dam, ran once in Ireland, half-sister to Irish Oaks winner Winona: green, mid-field
in maidens at Nottingham. *Mrs A. J. Perrett*

INTO ACTION 2 b.c. (Mar 26) Sendawar (IRE) 129 – Syrian Dancer (IRE) (Groom 75
Dancer (USA) 128) [2006 7m 8.1m⁴ p8.6g p10g² Nov 29] quite good-topped colt: first
foal: dam, placed at 1m in France at 2 yrs, out of half-sister to very smart sprinter/miler
Rock City: fair maiden: fourth to Mutadarrej at Chepstow: stumbled third start: best effort
at 1m on good to firm ground. *R. Hannon*

INTO THE BREEZE (IRE) 6 b.g. Alzao (USA) 117 – Catalane (USA) (Septieme 91
Ciel (USA) 123) [2006 86+: p7g⁸ 7m 7g² 7.6g 7m Sep 9] good-bodied gelding: fairly
useful handicapper: lightly raced in recent years: won at Kempton in April: probably best
at 7f: acts on polytrack, good to firm and good to soft going: joined M. Roberts. *J. W. Hills*

INTO THE DARK 5 ch.g. Rainbow Quest (USA) 134 – Land of Dreams 115 (Cadeaux 118
Genereux 131) [2006 112: 10m⁵ 12d² 10d* Oct 27] rather leggy, lengthy gelding: smart
performer: gelded before reappearance: just about back to best when winning listed race
at Newmarket in October by 6 lengths from Ofaraby: unlikely to stay beyond 1½m: acts
on soft and good to firm going: tongue tied: usually visored, not last 2 outings: often
makes running: has raced freely/found little. *Saeed bin Suroor*

INTO THE SHADOWS 6 ch.m. Safawan 118 – Shadows of Silver 89 (Carwhite 127) 98
[2006 91: 12v* 14.1s⁶ 14g 10.4s³ Oct 6] quite good-topped mare: useful performer: won
minor event at Southwell in March by 7 lengths from Shalapour: seemingly very good

sixth to Frank Sonata in listed race at Nottingham: not discredited in handicap final start: stays 1¾m: acts on heavy and good to firm going: held up: useful hurdler. *K. G. Reveley*

INTOXICATING 4 b.g. Mujahid (USA) 125 – Salalah 62 (Lion Cavern (USA) 117) [2006 105: p7g 6m 7.1m Jun 17] big, strong gelding: useful performer at 3 yrs: lightly raced and just fairly useful form in 2006, looking ungenuine: probably best at 6f: acts on firm and good to soft going: one to treat with caution: sold 26,000 gns, joined Anthony Mullins, Ireland. *R. F. Johnson Houghton* **90 §**

INTREPID JACK 4 b.c. Compton Place 125 – Maria Theresa (Primo Dominie 121) [2006 110: 6s^6 6m 7m^2 6m 7d 7g p6g^2 5.1m* p5g^2 p5.1g^5 Oct 29] lengthy colt: useful handicapper: won at Bath in October by length from Judd Street: at least creditable efforts when runner-up in 2006, 2 lengths behind Mine in Bunbury Cup at Newmarket and beaten 1½ lengths by Texas Gold at Lingfield third/penultimate outings: effective at 5f to 7f: acts on polytrack, soft and good to firm going: tried visored. *H. Morrison* **109**

INTRICATE WEB (IRE) 10 b.g. Warning 136 – In Anticipation (IRE) 93 (Sadler's Wells (USA) 132) [2006 80, a–: 10.5s May 26] sturdy, angular gelding: fairly useful performer in 2005: well held only outing in 2006: tried in headgear earlier in career: tends to race lazily. *E. J. Alston* **–**

INTRIGUED 4 gr.f. Darshaan 133 – Last Second (IRE) 121 (Alzao (USA) 117) [2006 11.9s^3 12m^3 11g^6 Aug 20] strong, rangy filly: useful performer: reportedly fractured pelvis in February 2005 and missed whole season: back to best when 2¾ lengths third to Fermion in listed race at Newbury second start: creditable sixth to Wurfscheibe in Group 3 at Bremen final outing: stays 1½m: acts on good to firm going. *Sir Mark Prescott* **105**

INTRIGUING GLIMPSE 5 b. or br.m. Piccolo 121 – Running Glimpse (IRE) 84 (Runnett 125) [2006 94: p5g^6 5m^6 p5g 5m 5.3f* 5m* 5m^5 6f^6 Jul 14] strong, deep-girthed mare: useful performer: better than ever in 2006, winning handicaps at Brighton and Salisbury (beat Our Fugitive by 1½ lengths) in June: good sixth to La Chunga in Summer Stakes at York final outing: stayed easy 6f: acted on polytrack, firm and soft going: was waited with: was tough and reliable: in foal to Avonbridge. *Miss B. Sanders* **100**

INVASIAN (IRE) 5 ch.g. Desert Prince (IRE) 130 – Jarrayan 64 (Machiavellian (USA) 123) [2006 –: 10m 10.4d 10.1m^3 10d* 8.9s Oct 7] close-coupled, quite attractive gelding: fairly useful handicapper nowadays, quite lightly raced: won at Nottingham in October by neck from Charlie Tokyo: stays 1¼m: acts on good to firm and good to soft ground (below form on soft). *B. J. McMath* **93**

INVASOR (ARG) 4 br.c. Candy Stripes (USA) 115 – Quendom (ARG) (Interprete (ARG)) [2006 a9g^4 a9.5f* a10f* a9f* a10f* Nov 4] top-class performer: unbeaten in 5 races in Uruguay in 2005, including 3 Grade 1s, namely Polla de Potrillos (2000 Guineas), Gran Premio Jockey Club and Gran Premio Nacional (Derby), all at Maronas: won all 4 starts in Grade 1 company in US in 2006 (when voted Horse Of The Year at Eclipse Awards), Pimlico Special at Pimlico (by 1¼ lengths from Wanderin Boy) in May, Suburban Handicap at Belmont (beat Wild Desert 4¼ lengths) in July, Whitney Handicap at Saratoga (by a nose from Sun King, battling on tenaciously) in August and Breeders' Cup Classic - Powered By Dodge at Churchill Downs (first race for 3 months, beat Bernardini by a length, edging left, but staying on well to lead inside final 1f) in November: suffered only defeat when 7 lengths fourth to Discreet Cat in UAE Derby at Nad Al Sheba in March: effective at 9f to 12.5f: acts in muddy conditions: genuine. *K. P. McLaughlin, USA* **133**

INVENTION (USA) 3 b.g. Lear Fan (USA) 130 – Carya (USA) (Northern Dancer) [2006 8g^6 10d* 10m 10m^5 9m Sep 16] angular, quite attractive gelding: has a moderate, quick action: brother to very smart 7f (at 2 yrs) to 1¼m winner Ryafan and useful 2002 2-y-o 7f winner who stayed 1½m Calibre, closely related to smart performer up to 1½m Epicentre (by Kris S) and half-brother to 2 winners: dam ran 3 times in France: fairly useful performer: won maiden at Newmarket in May: creditable fifth to Windsor Knot in minor event at Newmarket prior to tailed off in similar contest at Newbury (visored): will stay 1½m: acts on good to firm and good to soft going: sold 32,000 gns, then gelded. *J. H. M. Gosden* **91**

INVERARAY 3 ch.f. Selkirk (USA) 129 – Khalafiya 104 (Darshaan 133) [2006 9.5s^6 12s p12g p8.6g p8.6g^5 p10g p10g p8.6g Dec 29] half-sister to 3 winners, notably high-class 1¼m/1½m performer Predappio (by Polish Precedent), 7f winner at 2 yrs: dam Irish 1m and 1½m winner: modest maiden: left H-A. Pantall in France 5,000 gns after second outing: stays 1¼m: acts on polytrack. *P. S. Felgate* **55**

INVERTED 2 b.g. (Apr 9) Averti (IRE) 117 – Indian Silk (IRE) 74 (Dolphin Street (FR) 125) [2006 5d p6g f5g^5 f5g^4 Dec 27] poor maiden. *Mrs A. Duffield* **49**

Tattersalls Ireland Sale Stakes, the Curragh—
a valuable sales race which continues to be dominated by British-trained runners;
they provide the first four home, though only Invincible Force, Southandwest (left) and Bazroy are pictured

INVINCIBLE FORCE (IRE) 2 b.g. (Mar 16) Invincible Spirit (IRE) 121 – Highly **102** Respected (IRE) 57 (High Estate 127) [2006 5s² 5f² 5m* 5.1m* 5.1f⁴ 6.1m* 6g* 6g² 6d² 5d Oct 7] 19,000F, €10,500Y: fifth foal: half-brother to several winners, including 2004 2-y-o 7f winner King of Blues (by Bluebird) and Irish 2005 2-y-o 6f winner High Reservation (by Indian Danehill): dam, maiden who should have stayed at least 1m, closely related to smart Irish 1¼m performer Make No Mistake: useful performer: won maiden at Warwick, minor event and nursery at Chester, and 24-runner Tattersalls Ireland Sale Stakes at the Curragh between June/August: good second twice in September, to Brave Tin Soldier in listed event at the Curragh and to Iron Lips in Prix Eclipse at Chantilly: not well drawn and reportedly cut mouth final start (Cornwallis Stakes): effective at 5f/6f: yet to race on heavy going, probably acts on any other: often front runner: tough. *Ms Deborah J. Evans*

INWAAN (IRE) 3 b.g. King's Best (USA) 132 – Balaabel (USA) 83 (Sadler's Wells **72** (USA) 132) [2006 6v⁵ 9.5g⁴ 11g⁴ 8d 6d 8.3s Oct 2] half-brother to several winners, including fairly useful French 1m winner Maksad (by Machiavellian) and useful 2000 2-y-o 7f (Rockfel Stakes) winner Sayedah (by Darshaan): dam, 1m winner, half-sister to US Grade 2 7f winner Kayrawan: fair maiden in France: sold from J. Hammond 10,000 gns and gelded, well held in handicap at Windsor (tongue tied) final outing: effective at 6f, seems to stay 11f: acts on heavy going: tried blinkered. *P. R. Webber*

IOLANTHE 2 ch.f. (May 8) Vettori (IRE) 119 – Shakalaka Baby (Nashwan (USA) 135) – [2006 6d 7g Oct 12] 32,000Y: medium-sized, workmanlike filly: first foal: dam unraced half-sister to smart French sprinter Titus Livius: no show in maidens. *B. J. Meehan*

IONIAN SPRING (IRE) 11 b.g. Ela-Mana-Mou 132 – Well Head (IRE) (Sadler's **88** Wells (USA) 132) [2006 92: 10g⁵ 10.2d* 11.6f⁴ 10.3m³ 10.1f² f11g* Dec 19] sturdy gelding: has reportedly suffered from broken blood vessels: fairly useful performer: won claimers at Chepstow (left C. Cox £15,000) in May and Southwell in December: best around 1¼m: acts on all-weather and any turf going: still a free-going sort, and held up: tends to edge left. *D. Carroll*

IOWEYOU 2 ch.f. (Jan 23) Noverre (USA) 125 – Cuore di Aliante (Alhijaz 122) [2006 **60** p5g⁵ 6m⁴ 7.5f⁴ 6s Aug 26] 15,000Y: rather leggy filly: first foal: dam, Italian 2-y-o 5f winner, half-sister to high-class 7f/1m performer Le Vie dei Colori: modest maiden: should stay 7f/1m. *J. S. Moore*

I PREDICT A RIOT (IRE) 2 b.g. (Mar 3) Danehill Dancer (IRE) 117 – Manon's **68** Song (IRE) (Sadler's Wells (USA) 132) [2006 8s 7d Oct 28] 50,000Y: big, lengthy gelding: has plenty of scope: first foal: dam unraced out of half-sister to Irish 2000 Guineas winner Northern Treasure: better run in maidens when seventh to Go On Be A Tiger at Newbury on debut: gelded after second start. *J. W. Hills*

IRELAND DANCER (IRE) 2 ch.g. (Mar 26) Trans Island 119 – Come Dancing 48 **75** (Suave Dancer (USA) 136) [2006 6m⁵ 6m⁵ 7f Sep 5] €3,000F: sixth foal: half-brother to

5f winner Icenaslice and winner up to 7f Uhuru Dawn (both by Fayruz): dam disappointing maiden who should have stayed at least 7f: fair form in maidens only on debut: gelded after final start. *W. R. Muir*

IRISH BALLAD 4 b.g. Singspiel (IRE) 133 – Auenlust (GER) (Surumu (GER)) [2006 **66** 64: p12g 12f 16.4f³ 14.1m p16.5f² 15.8m p13.9m* Oct 2] neat gelding: fair handicapper: won at Wolverhampton in October: stays 16.5f: acts on polytrack and firm going: usually tongue tied: inconsistent: sold 14,000 gns. *W. R. Swinburn*

IRISH DANCER 2 b.f. (Jan 29) Danehill Dancer (IRE) 117 – Gaelic Swan (IRE) 80 **64 p** (Nashwan (USA) 135) [2006 7m 7g⁴ Aug 18] leggy filly: first foal: dam, lightly-raced maiden (runner-up at 1½m), sister to smart 1¼m/1½m winner Mary Stuart, and half-sister to smart middle-distance stayer Bonny Scot and the dam of Golan: better than bare result in maidens, again dropped out when fourth to Farley Star at Folkestone: sure to improve, particularly at 1¼m/1½m. *J. L. Dunlop*

IRISH POET (IRE) 2 b.c. (Apr 11) Trans Island 119 – Abecedarian (USA) 72 (Bara- **57** thea (IRE) 127) [2006 8.1m 9s⁵ Sep 24] modest form second start in maidens: sold 3,500 gns, sent to Sweden. *E. J. O'Neill*

IRISH RELATIVE (IRE) 2 b.g. (Apr 2) Indian Lodge (IRE) 127 – The Good Life **– p** (IRE) (Rainbow Quest (USA) 134) [2006 6m Aug 9] fourth foal: half-brother to useful French 7.5f winner Double Vie (by Tagula): dam, French 12.5f winner, out of smart French miler Once In My Life: 16/1, green in maiden at Newcastle: should progress at 1m+. *T. D. Barron*

IRISH WELLS (FR) 3 b.c. Poliglote 121 – Sign of The Vine (FR) (Kendor (FR) 122) **122** [2006 9s* 10.5s³ 10g³ 10.5m⁶ 12d* 12.5s* 12m⁵ Oct 1] big, lengthy colt: fourth foal: half-brother to 2 winners, including smart French 1m (including at 2 yrs) to 11f winner Sign of The Wolf (by Loup Solitaire): dam ran twice in France: very smart performer: won minor event at Marseilles-Borely in February, listed race at Vichy in July and Grand Prix de Deauville Lucien Barriere (beat Groom Tesse 2½ lengths) in August: creditable sixth to Darsi in Prix du Jockey Club at Chantilly fourth start and ran well when 5½ lengths sixth of 8 (promoted to fifth) to Rail Link in Prix de l'Arc de Triomphe at Long-champ (sweated up, led till 2f out) final start: stays 12.5f: acts on soft and good to firm ground: has worn earplugs. *F. Rohaut, France*

IRISH WHISPERS (IRE) 3 b.g. Marju (IRE) 127 – Muneera (USA) 67 (Green Dan- **67** cer (USA) 132) [2006 65: 11m⁵ 12f² p10g 13.1m⁴ Aug 25] lengthy gelding: fair maiden handicapper: stays 13f: acts on polytrack and firm going. *B. G. Powell*

Grand Prix de Deauville Lucien Barriere, Deauville—smart three-year-old Irish Wells sees off the older horses, headed by Italian challenger Groom Tesse (grey)

IRISH WOLF (FR) 6 b.h. Loup Solitaire (USA) 117 – Erins Run (USA) (Irish River **83**
(FR) 131) [2006 17.2s² 20m 16.4m* Sep 11] workmanlike horse: third foal: dam French
1¼m winner: fairly useful handicapper: left E. Danel in France after final outing in 2005:
won at Folkestone in September: should stay beyond 17f: acts on soft and good to firm
ground: effective blinkered/in cheekpieces or not: smart hurdler, successful in August
and October. *P. Bowen*

IRON DANCER (IRE) 2 b.c. (Apr 20) Iron Mask (USA) 117 – Sin Lucha (USA) **–**
(Northfields (USA)) [2006 7g p6f 8.1m p6m Oct 2] close-coupled colt: little form.
P. A. Blockley

IRON FIST (IRE) 2 b.c. (Feb 3) Desert Style (IRE) 121 – Ricadonna (Kris 135) [2006 **97 ?**
7f⁶ 7.1m* 7.5s* Aug 27] €38,000Y: strong, lengthy colt: second foal: closely related to
Italian winner around 7f (including at 2 yrs) by Bachir: dam unraced out of sister to 1000
Guineas/Oaks winner Midway Lady, herself dam of Oaks winner Eswarah: seemingly
useful performer: won maiden at Warwick (took plenty of driving) in July and listed race
at Deauville in August, in latter apparent great improvement to beat Lac Majeur by
length, making all and only one of the 6 runners to come stand side in straight (almost
collided with rail): will stay 1m: seems quirky: sent to Hong Kong. *E. J. O'Neill*

IRON PEARL 2 b.f. (Apr 6) Iron Mask (USA) 117 – Fast Tempo (IRE) 74 (Statoblest **66**
120) [2006 6f 6.5d p6g³ p6g* Dec 22] 4,200F, €14,500Y: third foal: half-sister to 6-y-o
Quicks The Word: dam, 2-y-o 5f winner, half-sister to useful performer up to 1½m Mara-
linga: fair performer: tongue tied when well held in maidens in Ireland for G. Lyons first
2 starts: won similar event at Lingfield in December by 2½ lengths from Tilapia: should
stay 7f: acts on polytrack. *Jane Chapple-Hyam*

IRONY (IRE) 7 gr.g. Mujadil (USA) 119 – Cidaris (IRE) (Persian Bold 123) [2006 96: **96**
7.1d³ p7g³ p7g* 7m 7.1f* 8m 7.1g⁵ 7.6g² Aug 26] good-topped gelding: useful handicapper: won at Kempton in June and Chepstow in July: good second to Ordnance Row at
Chester final outing: stays 1m: acts on polytrack, firm and good to soft going: effective
with/without cheekpieces: tried tongue tied in 2002: normally front runner. *A. M. Balding*

IRRIDESCENCE (SAF) 5 b.m. Caesour (USA) 110 – Meretricious (SAF) (Dancing **119**
Champ (USA)) [2006 8.9d* 10m* 8g⁵ 10m⁴ Oct 1] tall, leggy mare: smart performer:
winner of 6 races in South Africa, including South African Classic at Turffontein and
Woolavington 2200 at Greyville (both Group 1 events) in 2005: successful in listed race
at Nad Al Sheba (by 1¼ lengths from Satwa Queen) in February and Audemars Piguet
Queen Elizabeth II Cup at Sha Tin (held on by head from Best Gift, Ouija Board close
third) in April: left M. de Kock and off over 4 months, below best at Longchamp in Prix
du Moulin (fifth to Librettist) and Prix de l'Opera (fourth to Mandesha) last 2 starts: stays
11f: acts on soft and good to firm going: has got on edge in preliminaries (withdrawn after
injuring herself in parade ring at Nad Al Sheba prior to Dubai Duty Free second intended
start, mounted on course before final outing): usually front runner: has rejoined M. de
Kock in UAE. *J. E. Hammond, France*

IS 3 br.f. Diktat 126 – Blackpool Belle 70 (The Brianstan 128) [2006 –: p7.1g f6g 8m **43**
10.1f³ 10.1f⁶ 8m⁶ 12.1m 12.1m⁴ 13.9g⁶ Nov 25] close-coupled filly: poor maiden: stays
1¼m: acts on firm going, probably on good to soft. *Rae Guest*

ISA'AF (IRE) 7 b.g. Darshaan 133 – Shauna's Honey (IRE) 88 (Danehill (USA) 126) **79**
[2006 76: p13g f12g* p12.2g p13g² p13.9g³ f16g* 12v* 13.8d p16g 16.2g² 20s 14g 14.1g
15d 12s p13.9m⁵ f16g p13.9g⁵ f14g³ Dec 9] neat gelding: fair performer: won handicaps
at Southwell in January (apprentices) and March, and Pontefract (apprentices) in April:
effective at 1½m, barely stays 2¼m: acts on all-weather, heavy and good to firm going:
tough. *P. W. Hiatt*

ISABELLA BAY 6 b.m. Meqdaam (USA) – Orchard Bay 47 (Formidable (USA) 125) **–**
[2006 –: p8.6g f7g Dec 9] tall, workmanlike mare: no sign of ability: tried in cheekpieces.
M. Wellings

ISABELLA ROSSINI 4 b. or br.f. Rossini (USA) 118 – Misty Rain 61 (Polar Falcon **–**
(USA) 126) [2006 63d: p13g p10g Feb 22] maiden: well held in 2006: tried in headgear/
tongue tied. *A. M. Hales*

ISABELLA'S BEST (IRE) 2 ch.f. (Jan 28) King's Best (USA) 132 – Spanish Quest **53**
(Rainbow Quest (USA) 134) [2006 7f⁷ 7g⁵ 10.1d Oct 18] 16,000Y: first foal: dam, unraced
half-sister to 8-y-o Spanish Don, out of Irish Oaks winner Wemyss Bight:
modest maiden: should stay 1m/1¼m. *E. J. O'Neill*

ISHARRAM (IRE) 3 ch. or b.f. Muhtarram (USA) 125 – Ishaam 76 (Selkirk (USA) **–**
129) [2006 36: 6m 8.3m⁶ 8.1m Aug 10] stocky filly: has a round action: maiden: no form
in 2006: tried blinkered. *A. Berry*

ISHETOO 2 b.g. (Feb 20) Ishiguru (USA) 114 – Ticcatoo (IRE) 60 (Dolphin Street (FR) **58** 125) [2006 6f⁵ 6m⁶ 7f⁵ 7g Sep 27] modest maiden: best efforts at 6f: acts on firm going. *A. Dickman*

ISHI ADIVA 2 b.f. (Mar 4) Ishiguru (USA) 114 – Nightingale Song 66 (Tina's Pet 121) **85** [2006 5m⁴ 5m² 5.2g² 6s 5.1g* Oct 17] 10,000Y: strong filly: third foal: half-sister to fairly useful 2005 2-y-o 6f winner Lindus Atenor (by Fraam): dam 5f/6f (at 2 yrs) winner: fairly useful performer: won maiden at Bath: best form when twice runner-up in July, beaten length by Elhamri in 23-runner Super Sprint at Newbury third start: effective at 5f/6f: acts on good to firm going. *T. G. Dascombe*

ISHIBEE (IRE) 2 b.f. (Feb 28) Ishiguru (USA) 114 – Beauty (IRE) 74 (Alzao (USA) **63** 117) [2006 5m⁵ 5g³ 5f⁶ 5f⁴ p6g³ 5m³ 5m³ p6g* 5m⁵ 6d³ 5m 6d p6g⁵ p7.1m⁶ f6g⁶ Nov 14] 10,000Y: sturdy filly: second foal: dam, maiden who stayed 1¼m, out of half-sister to high-class 1m/1¼m performer Bijou d'Inde: modest performer: won seller at Lingfield in August: barely stays 7f: acts on polytrack, firm and good to soft going: usually wears cheekpieces: durable. *Mrs A. Duffield*

ISHIMAGIC 2 ch.f. (Apr 5) Ishiguru (USA) 114 – Triple Tricks (IRE) 70 (Royal **52** Academy (USA) 130) [2006 6d 7s 7d 6d p8g⁴ p7g⁴ p8g⁶ Dec 18] 2,200F: workmanlike filly: seventh foal: closely related to smart US Grade 2 8.5f winner Foxysox (by Foxhound) and half-sister to 3 winners, including 7-y-o Mythical Charm: dam maiden who stayed 1m: maiden, modest form on occasions. *J. J. Bridger*

ISHISMART 2 ch.f. (May 1) Ishiguru (USA) 114 – Smartie Lee 66 (Dominion 123) **–** [2006 p7g p6g p7.1g Nov 18] strong filly: half-sister to 3 winners, notably 8-y-o Lygeton Lad: dam, 7f (at 2 yrs) to 1½m winner who stayed 2m, also winning hurdler: well beaten in maidens in September. *R. Hollinshead*

ISIDORE BONHEUR (IRE) 5 b.g. Mtoto 134 – Way O'Gold (USA) (Slew O' Gold **93** (USA)) [2006 93: 7g⁶ p8g⁵ 8f 8f* 10f² 12g⁶ 10s Aug 26] big, strong, close-coupled gelding: fluent mover: fairly useful handicapper: won at Redcar in June: creditable efforts next 2 starts: effective at 1m, barely stays 1½m: acts on firm and good to soft going: tried blinkered/tongue tied: races freely: difficult ride. *G. A. Swinbank*

ISITLOVEYOURAFTER (IRE) 4 b.f. Orpen (USA) 116 – Pericolo (IRE) 92 (Kris **–** 135) [2006 47: f11g Jan 24] poor maiden: tried blinkered. *G. L. Moore*

IS IT ME (USA) 3 ch.c. Sky Classic (CAN) – Thea (GER) (Surumu (GER)) [2006 67: **79** p8.6g 10.9g 10.3g⁵ 10.9m² 11.7m² 12m⁴ 12f* Jul 19] sturdy colt: fair performer: won handicap at Catterick in July: stays 1½m: acts on polytrack and firm going: usually makes running: fairly useful juvenile hurdler. *P. A. Blockley*

IS IT TIME (IRE) 2 b.f. (Jan 24) Danetime (IRE) 121 – Ishaam 76 (Selkirk (USA) **49** 129) [2006 7g Aug 25] 3,700F, 4,800Y: workmanlike filly: second foal: dam 1m winner: poor form in maidens at Salisbury (poor to post debut). *Mrs P. N. Dutfield*

ISLAND GREEN (USA) 3 b.g. Cozzene (USA) – Legend of Spring 99 (Night Shift **54** (USA)) [2006 p6g p7g f5g 7m p8g* p8.6g² Dec 4] modest performer: won banded race at Kempton in October: stays 8.6f: acts on polytrack. *B. J. Curley*

ISLAND MYTH (IRE) 3 ch.g. Inchinor 119 – Jersey Lillie (IRE) (Hector Protector **90** (USA) 124) [2006 83: 10m⁴ 11s⁴ 12g 12g⁵ 12.1m* 11m² Sep 20] big, lengthy gelding: fairly useful performer: won maiden at Chepstow in September: good second to Robustian in handicap at Goodwood final outing: stays 1½m: acts on polytrack, soft and good to firm going: blinkered last 3 starts: sold 57,000 gns. *M. P. Tregoning*

ISLAND ODYSSEY 3 b.f. Dansili 127 – Tetravella (IRE) (Groom Dancer (USA) 128) **93** [2006 72: 11.6m* 11.6d³ 9.9g* p12g* 12f³ p12g 12d Oct 27] sturdy filly: fairly useful handicapper: improved in 2006, winning at Windsor in April, Salisbury in June and Kempton (beat Whatizzit by ½ length) in September: below form last 2 starts: stays 1½m: acts on polytrack and firm ground, probably on good to soft: often makes running. *E. A. L. Dunlop*

ISLAND PRINCE (IRE) 3 b.g. Mull of Kintyre (USA) 114 – Green Flower (USA) 56 **56** (Fappiano (USA)) [2006 73: 5m 6s 6d p7g Nov 1] strong, workmanlike gelding: just modest handicapper in 2006: probably stayed easy 7f: acted on any turf going: tried in cheekpieces: dead. *Mrs A. Duffield*

ISLAND RAPTURE 6 b.m. Royal Applause 124 – Gersey (Generous (IRE) 139) **–** [2006 72, a83: p8g p10g p10g³ p8g⁴ p7.1g² p7g⁵ p8g⁴ Jun 7] quite attractive mare: just **a77** fair handicapper in 2006: effective at 7f to easy 1¼m: acts on polytrack, firm and soft going: tried in cheekpieces: effective ridden prominently or held up. *J. A. R. Toller*

ISN'T IT GRAND (IRE) 2 b.f. (Mar 27) Raise A Grand (IRE) 114 – Fiona March (GER) (Big Shuffle (USA) 122) [2006 p7.1g Dec 31] first foal: dam German 7f winner: 50/1, well held in maiden at Wolverhampton. *Miss V. Haigh*   –

ISOBEL ROSE (IRE) 2 b.f. (Apr 21) Royal Applause 124 – Total Love 102 (Cadeaux Genereux 131) [2006 5g³ 5g³ 5.1g² 6f⁴ 5.1m³ 5m³ 6d p6g³ p6g² p6g⁶ Dec 6] quite good-topped filly: has a quick action: second foal: dam 2-y-o 6f winner who stayed 1m: fair maiden: placed 7 times: raced at 5f/6f: acts on polytrack and firm ground: visored (well held but stiff task) seventh start: has wandered: ungenuine. *E. A. L. Dunlop*   **73 §**

ISOLA MADRE 2 b.f. (Jan 24) Rainbow Quest (USA) 134 – High Standard 83 (Kris 135) [2006 8.1m 7s⁶ 8.2d⁵ p9.5g* Nov 18] leggy filly: sister to smart 1½m winner Al Moulatham, closely related to useful 1½m winner Clever Clogs (by Nashwan) and half-sister to fairly useful 7f (at 2 yrs) to 1½m winner Summer Song (by Green Desert): dam, 2-y-o 1m winner who stayed 1½m, out of close relative to Nureyev and half-sister to dam of Sadler's Wells: fair performer: won nursery at Wolverhampton in November by short head (looked to have more in hand): will stay at least 1½m: acts on polytrack: sold 14,000 gns. *M. Johnston*   **70**

ISPHAHAN 3 b.c. Diktat 126 – Waltzing Star (IRE) (Danehill (USA) 126) [2006 76: p7g p8g² p10g⁶ 8m³ 8.1g⁶ 8g⁴ 7g Jul 6] lengthy colt: fairly useful handicapper: creditable efforts when in frame: barely stays 1¼m: acts on polytrack and firm ground: visored last 4 starts: front runner. *A. M. Balding*   **80**

ITALIAN GIRL 2 b.f. (Feb 29) Danehill Dancer (IRE) 117 – Little Italy (IRE) 103 (Common Grounds 118) [2006 6g* 7m⁵ 7d⁴ Sep 30] 34,000Y: rangy filly: has scope: second foal: half-sister to French 1¼m winner Cristal Rose (by Montjeu): dam, 6f to 1½m winner, half-sister to smart stayer Romantic Affair: fairly useful form: won maiden at Ascot in July: kept better company after, fifth to Sesmen in Prestige Stakes at Goodwood and fourth to Selinka in listed event at Newmarket, still seeming green: will stay 1m. *A. P. Jarvis*   **91**

ITALIAN MIST (FR) 7 b.g. Forzando 122 – Digamist Girl (IRE) (Digamist (USA) 110) [2006 –, a68: p5g f7g 5f 5.3m⁶ 5.3m Jun 27] just poor performer nowadays: tried blinkered/in cheekpieces. *R. M. H. Cowell*   **42**

ITALIAN ROMANCE 3 b.g. Medicean 128 – Polish Romance (USA) 83 (Danzig (USA)) [2006 –: p8.6g⁵ p8g⁴ 8.1g p9.5g² p9.5g⁴ p12.2g³ Dec 22] strong, heavy-topped gelding: fairly useful maiden: left M. Bell 20,000 gns after third start, then gelded: stays 9.5f: acts on polytrack. *J. W. Unett*   **82**

ITALIAN STALLION (IRE) 2 b.c. (Mar 16) Grand Lodge (USA) 125 – Belle Alle-mande (CAN) (Royal Academy (USA) 130) [2006 7m 7m 8d² 8.1v⁵ 8g⁴ 8.3d² 8.3g² Oct 16] 52,000F, 67,000Y: strong, close-coupled colt: first foal: dam, French 11f winner, closely related to very smart performer up to 1½m in Germany/USA Que Belle: fair maiden: runner-up 3 times, twice in nurseries at Windsor: will be suited by 1¼m/1½m: acts on good to firm and good to soft going: sold 40,000 gns, sent to Austria. *R. Hannon*   **79**

ITALIC 4 ch.f. Medicean 128 – Ink Pot (USA) 73 (Green Dancer (USA) 132) [2006 63: 12m³ 11.6m⁶ 11m² 11.6m⁴ 8g Dec 30] tall, leggy filly: fair maiden: sold from Mrs A. Perrett 20,000 gns before final outing: stays 11.6f: acts on good to firm going, probably on good to soft: found little in blinkers third/fourth starts. *R. B. Priscott, New Zealand*   **77**

ITALSTAR (IRE) 2 ch.f. (Mar 2) Galileo (IRE) 134 – Jorghinia (FR) (Seattle Slew (USA)) [2006 p8g p8g p8g Dec 20] 60,000Y: third foal: half-sister to winner in USA by Charismatic: dam, maiden in France/USA, out of sister to US Grade 1 9f/1¼m winner Jade Hunter: behind in maidens, all within 3 weeks: sort to do better in middle-distance handicaps. *H. Morrison*   **– p**

ITCANBEDONE AGAIN (IRE) 7 b.g. Sri Pekan (USA) 117 – Maradata (IRE) 68 (Shardari 134) [2006 46: p9.5g* p9.5g* p9.5g⁴ p8.6g³ p9.5g 10.1m 10m 10g Aug 30] tall, good-topped gelding: unimpressive mover: fair performer: won banded race in January and handicap in February, both at Wolverhampton: probably best around 1¼m: acts on polytrack and any turf going. *Ian Williams*   **65**

ITCHYCOO PARK (IRE) 2 b.c. (Jan 31) Rossini (USA) 118 – Queen Molly 53 (Emarati (USA) 74) [2006 7.1m⁵ 7m Sep 13] lengthy, workmanlike colt: better effort in maidens when never-nearer fifth at Warwick: hung left next start: sold 7,500 gns. *E. J. O'Neill*   **62**

IT MUST BE SPEECH 5 b.g. Advise (FR) – Maiden Speech (Pitskelly 122) [2006 –, a54: f8g³ f8g⁶ f8g² p10g² p9.5g⁶ f8g⁶ f8g Mar 21] good-bodied gelding: modest maiden: stays 1½m: acts on all-weather: often visored. *S. L. Keightley*   **58**

IT'S A DREAM (FR) 3 b.g. Kaldounevees (FR) 118 – Bahia Mar (USA) (Arctic Tern **83**
(USA) 126) [2006 82p: 8g 10.5g 11.6s Oct 2] useful-looking gelding: fairly useful
performer: off 5 months, best effort when tenth in handicap at Haydock second outing:
stays 10.5f (didn't settle at 11.6f final outing, gelded after): acts on polytrack, best effort
on turf on good going: slowly away on reappearance. *D. R. C. Elsworth*

ITSAWINDUP 2 b.c. (Mar 23) Elnadim (USA) 128 – Topwinder (USA) (Topsider **–**
(USA)) [2006 p7g p7g Dec 3] well held in maidens: hung on debut. *W. J. Knight*

IT'S BASIL 3 b.g. Foxhound (USA) 103 – Marabela (IRE) 79 (Shernazar 131) [2006 **–**
56: p10g p10g 10m 11.5m p12g² p10g 12f 11.6m 8f Aug 15] modest maiden: stays 1½m: **a56**
acts on polytrack (little form on turf): blinkered of late. *R. M. Flower*

IT'S GONE 3 b.g. City On A Hill (USA) 114 – Shafaq (USA) 90 (Dayjur (USA) 137) **–**
[2006 6g 7f⁶ 8d p7.1m Nov 21] compact gelding: little form in maidens. *J. G. Given*

ITS MOON (IRE) 2 b.f. (Feb 11) Tobougg (IRE) 125 – Shallat (IRE) 59 (Pennekamp **71**
(USA) 130) [2006 6m 5m⁴ 7g³ Aug 26] smallish, workmanlike filly: second foal: dam,
ran 3 times (seemingly best effort at 1½m), half-sister to 1000 Guineas third Hathrah
and smart performers abroad up to 1½m Ivan Luis and Zero Problemo: fair maiden:
much improved when third to Ravi River at Chester: will stay 1m+: sold 14,000 gns.
M. R. Channon

IT'S NO PROBLEM (IRE) 2 b.f. (Mar 8) Averti (IRE) 117 – Polar Rock 66 (Polar **60**
Falcon (USA) 126) [2006 p5g⁵ 5s 5.7m⁶ 7g⁵ 7f⁵ 6m p6g Sep 10] first foal: dam, maiden
who stayed 1m, sister to 6-y-o Cold Turkey: modest maiden: stays 7f: acts on firm
ground, probably soft. *Jean-Rene Auvray*

IT'S RUMOURED 6 ch.g. Fleetwood (IRE) 107 – Etourdie (USA) (Arctic Tern **–**
(USA) 126) [2006 p16g Nov 28] maiden: blinkered, well beaten only Flat outing since
2003. *Jean-Rene Auvray*

IT'S TWILIGHT TIME 3 b.f. Royal Applause 124 – Mainly Sunset (Red Sunset **–**
120) [2006 –: 6m 7g Jun 28] rather leggy filly: little form in maidens: troublesome at start
on debut and reappearance. *R. Hannon*

IT'S UNBELIEVABLE (USA) 3 b. or br.g. Stravinsky (USA) 133 – Churn Dat **77**
Butter (USA) (Unbridled (USA) 128) [2006 75p: 8m* 8.5f⁴ 8.5g⁶ 8.1m⁵ 8m⁶ 8.5m⁴
p9.5m Oct 9] lengthy gelding: fair performer: won maiden at Ripon in June: claimed from
B. Meehan £6,000 after fourth start: stays 8.5f: acts on firm ground. *P. T. Midgley*

IVANA ILLYICH (IRE) 4 ch.f. Tipsy Creek (USA) 115 – Tolstoya (Northfields **–**
(USA)) [2006 49, a–: 9.9f⁶ 10m 16.2g Aug 17] close-coupled filly: maiden: no form in
2006: often blinkered/in cheekpieces. *J. S. Wainwright*

IVAN DENISOVICH (IRE) 3 b.c. Danehill (USA) 126 – Hollywood Wildcat (USA) **115**
125 (Kris S (USA)) [2006 110: 8g 8g 8m³ 8d 10f² 8g* 8d 10f³ Nov 26] close-coupled,
quite attractive colt: smart performer: won listed race at the Curragh in September by

Laing O'Rourke Solonaway Stakes, the Curragh—a drop in class for Ivan Denisovich
who gets his head in front in a photo finish with Latino Magic (far side) and Dunelight (No.6)

neck from Latino Magic: also ran well when placed in 2006, 3¾ lengths third to Araafa in St James's Palace Stakes at Royal Ascot, and behind Showing Up in both Secretariat Stakes at Arlington (1½ lengths second) and Hollywood Derby (3¾ lengths third): stayed 1¼m: acted on firm and good to soft going (in rear on dirt at 2 yrs): visored last 2 outings (ran as though amiss in Queen Elizabeth II Stakes at Ascot on first occasion): to stand at Coolmore Stud, Co Tipperary, Ireland, fee €9,000. *A. P. O'Brien, Ireland*

IVANS RIDE (IRE) 3 b.g. Night Shift (USA) – Ride Bold (USA) (J O Tobin (USA) 130) [2006 62: 8.5m p8.6g Nov 18] close-coupled gelding: modest maiden at 2 yrs: well held in 2006. *J. J. Quinn* —

IVORBELLA (IRE) 4 gr.f. Daylami (IRE) 138 – Ivorela (IRE) 61 (Ela-Mana-Mou 132) [2006 –: p9.5g³ p9.5g p10g⁵ May 15] €45,000Y: first foal: dam, Irish maiden who stayed 1¾m, from family of Irish Derby winner Grey Swallow (by Daylami): modest maiden: trained in Ireland at 3 yrs by Ms C. Hutchinson: stays 9.5f: acts on polytrack: tongue tied last 4 outings. *M. Botti* 55

IVORY GALA (FR) 3 b.f. Galileo (IRE) 134 – Rubies From Burma (USA) 104 (Forty Niner (USA)) [2006 10d⁵ 11.8m* 12m 12m² Sep 19] quite good-topped filly: second foal: dam, Irish 5f/6f winner, half-sister to smart miler Culture Vulture: useful and progressive form: won maiden at Leicester in June: best effort when neck second to Princesse Dansante in listed race at Saint-Cloud: stays 1½m: acts on good to firm going. *B. J. Meehan* 101

IVORY LACE 5 b.m. Atraf 116 – Miriam 59 (Forzando 122) [2006 82, a75: p7g p8g p6g² p7g² 6f⁶ 7f* 7m⁶ 7m* 7f³ 6f³ 6f* 6m⁶ p7g³ p6g⁶ p7g p6g Dec 3] rather leggy mare: fairly useful handicapper: won 3 times at Brighton in summer: effective at 5f to easy 7f: acts on polytrack and firm going, probably on good to soft: tried in blinkers/cheekpieces: effective held up or ridden prominently: reliable. *S. Woodman* 89

IVORYS SONG 2 b.f. (Mar 1) Averti (IRE) 117 – Katy Ivory (IRE) 68 (Night Shift (USA)) [2006 p5g f5g⁵ Apr 7] third foal: half-sister to Italian 6f/7f winner Gloria Day (by Pivotal): dam maiden who stayed 1m: poor form. *D. K. Ivory* 45

IVY CREEK (USA) 3 b.c. Gulch (USA) – Ivy Leaf (IRE) 76 (Nureyev (USA) 131) [2006 8.1s* 8.1g* 10.3d² 10m⁶ Jun 22] $40,000F, 85,000Y: tall, leggy, quite attractive colt: fifth foal: half-brother to several winners, notably 7-y-o Distinction: dam, Irish maiden who stayed 1½m, half-sister to Oaks d'Italia winner Ivyanna: smart performer: won maiden at Warwick and minor event at Sandown (by head from Tell) in April: further progress when neck second to Art Deco in Dee Stakes at Chester: respectable sixth to Snoqualmie Boy in listed race at Royal Ascot final outing: suffered back trouble after: will stay 1½m: acts on soft going, probably on good to firm: tends to take strong hold, and has worn dropped noseband: stays in training. *G. Wragg* 110

I WISH 8 ch.m. Beveled (USA) – Ballystate 71 (Ballacashtal (CAN)) [2006 69: p7.1g⁵ p6g p7g p6g p7.1g 5.1m p6g f7g² f6g p7g f7g f7g Dec 21] tall, leggy mare: modest performer: effective at 5.5f to 1m: acts on all-weather, firm and soft ground: tried in cheekpieces: headstrong, and has dropped away tamely. *Miss J. R. Tooth* 64 d

IWUNDER (IRE) 4 b.f. King's Best (USA) 132 – Sweetest Thing (IRE) 99 (Prince Rupert (FR) 121) [2006 73: 7m⁵ May 31] big, angular filly: fair maiden: bred to stay 1¼m: acts on firm and good to soft going. *Rae Guest* 73

IZABELA HANNAH 2 ch.f. (Apr 28) Kyllachy 129 – Papita (IRE) 77 (Law Society (USA) 130) [2006 6g 5.7m² 5.1g² Oct 17] fourth foal: half-sister to 3 fairly useful sprinters, including 3-y-o Charlie Delta: dam 2-y-o 6f winner who stayed 1¼m: fair form in maidens, twice second at Bath: should stay 6f. *R. M. Beckett* 72 +

IZA COMING (IRE) 2 b.f. (Mar 19) Fasliyev (USA) 120 – Boiling River (USA) (Dayjur (USA) 137) [2006 p6g³ p6g³ p6g³ Dec 8] €14,000Y: fourth foal: half-sister to winner in Greece by Marju: dam, maiden in USA, out of sister to very smart sprinter Dowsing: modest form in maidens: will stay 7f. *M. G. Quinlan* 59

IZADORE (IRE) 3 b.f. In The Wings 128 – Groom Order (Groom Dancer (USA) 128) [2006 10m 12.1d⁴ 10m³ p12g⁴ 11.7m⁶ p9.5g³ p9.5g⁵ Dec 11] unfurnished filly: seventh foal: closely related to useful Irish 7f and 1m (latter at 2 yrs) winner Barring Order (by Barathea) and half-sister to 2 winners, including smart Irish 6f (at 2 yrs) to 1m winner Beckett (by Fairy King): dam unraced daughter of half-sister to 2000 Guineas winner Entrepreneur: fair maiden: stays easy 1½m: acts on polytrack and good to firm going: blinkered final outing: signs of temperament. *E. A. L. Dunlop* 76

J

JAAD 3 b.c. Elnadim (USA) 128 – Off The Blocks 55 (Salse (USA) 128) [2006 82p: 8d³ **83** 7.1g³ 7.5g 8.1m² 8d³ 6d p7g a8f Dec 21] big, good-bodied colt: did well physically since 2 yrs: fairly useful handicapper: at least respectable efforts when placed in 2006: left M. Johnston 21,000 gns, below form last 3 starts: effective at 7f/1m: acts on good to firm and good to soft ground. *C. Wroe, UAE*

JAADY (USA) 2 b.g. (May 1) Coronado's Quest (USA) 130 – Aljawza (USA) 86 **77 p** (Riverman (USA) 131) [2006 p8g⁴ Oct 23] brother to smart 2002 2-y-o 7f/1m winner Al Jadeed and half-brother to several winners, including fairly useful 6f (at 2 yrs) and 1m (in UAE) winner Ishtihar (by Woodman): dam, Irish 2-y-o 6f winner, half-sister to Cheveley Park winner Gay Gallanta and very smart Irish 1¼m performer Sportsworld: 3/1 favourite, eye-catching fourth to Pairumani Princess in maiden at Lingfield, slowly away and finishing well while considerably handled: will improve and win races. *J. H. M. Gosden*

JAASOOS (IRE) 2 ch.c. (Apr 11) Noverre (USA) 125 – Nymphs Echo (IRE) (Muj- **87** tahid (USA) 118) [2006 7d³ 7m* 7d Sep 24] €160,000Y: leggy, useful-looking colt: half-brother to 3 winners in Ireland, including useful 1m/1¼m winner Sonorous (by Ashkalani): dam unraced: fairly useful form: won maiden at Yarmouth (made all, by 3 lengths) in September: only mid-field in nursery at Ascot later in month, but closer before squeezed out: will stay 1m. *M. A. Jarvis*

JAASSEY 3 b.g. Josr Algarhoud (IRE) 118 – Saaryeh 79 (Royal Academy (USA) 130) **66** [2006 58: 8s⁵ 9m⁴ 7.5f² 6.9m 9f 7.5g* 8f 8g 8.2s p12.2g f8g Nov 20] close-coupled geld- **a–** ing: fair performer: won claimer at Beverley in August: claimed from T. Walford £10,000 after next start: will stay 1¼m: acts on firm and good to soft going. *A. Crook*

JABBARA (IRE) 3 b.f. Kingmambo (USA) 125 – Isle de France (USA) 115 (Nureyev **65** (USA) 131) [2006 10.4d⁶ 8m 7m⁶ 9.7f 8.3m 10m 8m⁵ 6m⁶ 7f f6g* p7.1g⁶ p5.1g⁵ Dec 31] €65,000Y: quite good-topped filly: third foal: sister to fairly useful 1¼m winner Baie des Flamands: dam, French 6f (at 2 yrs) to 12.5f (Prix Minerve) winner, later Grade 3 9f winner in USA: fair performer: won maiden at Southwell (by 6 lengths) in November: has form at 1¼m, but may prove best around 6f: acts on all-weather and firm going: blinkered last 3 starts. *C. E. Brittain*

JABRAAN (USA) 4 b.g. Aljabr (USA) 125 – Miss Zafonic (FR) 98 (Zafonic (USA) **45** 130) [2006 61: f6g 8m 7.2g 7m⁵ 7m⁵ f6m p8.6g⁶ p8.6g Dec 11] good-bodied, angular gelding: good mover: only poor maiden in 2006: stays easy 8.6f: acts on polytrack and good to firm going: tried blinkered. *D. W. Chapman*

JACK ABSOLUTE (IRE) 3 gr.g. Fantastic Light (USA) 134 – Crepe Ginger (IRE) **65** 67 (Sadler's Wells (USA) 132) [2006 10g 11g 10g 14.1g 14m Jun 16] 130,000Y: tall, useful-looking gelding: fourth foal: half-brother to fairly useful 1¼m winner Poise (by Rainbow Quest) and 1½m seller winner Gin 'n' Fonic (by Zafonic): dam, ran 3 times in Ireland, half-sister to dam of Daylami and Dalakhani: fair maiden: seems to stay 1¾m: sold 18,000 gns, joined John Joseph Murphy in Ireland. *B. J. Meehan*

JACK DAWSON (IRE) 9 b.g. Persian Bold 123 – Dream of Jenny 73 (Caerleon **83** (USA) 132) [2006 83: 11.9f 14.1m* 16.2m⁴ 13.4f p16g Oct 20] neat gelding: fairly useful handicapper, lightly raced in recent years: reportedly fractured a cannon bone in 2005: won at Yarmouth in August: effective at 1½m to easy 2m: acts on polytrack, seems best on good going or firmer on turf: held up. *John Berry*

JACK DURRANCE (IRE) 6 b.g. Polish Precedent (USA) 131 – Atlantic Desire **38** (IRE) 100 (Ela-Mana-Mou 132) [2006 40: p9.5g⁶ p13.9g⁶ Jun 2] small, strong gelding: poor performer nowadays: tried visored. *G. A. Ham*

JACKIE FRANCIS (IRE) 3 b.g. Fasliyev (USA) 120 – Appalachia (IRE) 92 (Imp- **44** erial Frontier (USA) 112) [2006 45: f6g p5.1g 5.1g 5f⁴ 5m 5.7m p5g Oct 29] poor maiden: left P. Howling after second start: tried tongue tied. *R. Brotherton*

JACKIE KIELY 5 ch.g. Vettori (IRE) 119 – Fudge (Polar Falcon (USA) 126) [2006 **79** 69, a59: f14g² f12g f12g* f14g* f12g* f14g⁶ f14g⁴ f12g³ 11.5m f12g² 14.1m 11.5m 10.2m³ 10f² 10.2d 11.9m⁵ 10.1g* 10m³ 10.2m* 10g² 11.9g f12g* Dec 27] leggy gelding: fair performer: won 2 banded races and handicap at Southwell in winter and, having left P. Howling after eleventh start, handicaps at Epsom (apprentices) in August, Chepstow (first start since leaving Stef Liddiard) in September and Southwell in December: effective at 1¼m, probably stays 2m: acts on all-weather, firm and soft going: tongue tied nowadays. *R. Brotherton*

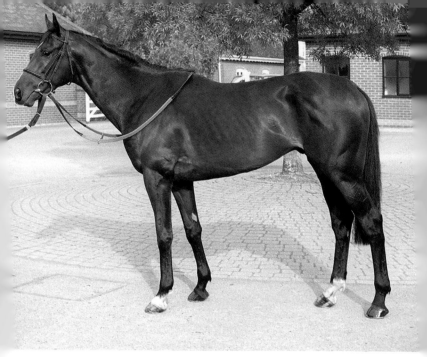

Sheikh Ahmed Al Maktoum's "Jadalee"

JACK JUNIOR (USA) 2 b. or br.c. (Feb 5) Songandaprayer (USA) 118 – Ra Hydee **103**
(USA) (Rahy (USA) 115) [2006 7.1d⁴ 7d⁶ Sep 29] $52,000F, $180,000 2-y-o: tall, attractive colt: third foal: half-brother to winner in USA by Devil's Bag: dam 8.5f winner in
USA: needed experience in maiden at Warwick, then useful form when 3½ lengths sixth
of 10 to Thousand Words in Somerville Tattersall Stakes at Newmarket (reared leaving
stall and soon niggled): will stay 1m. *B. J. Meehan*

JACK OF TRUMPS (IRE) 6 b.g. King's Theatre (IRE) 128 – Queen Caroline (USA) **92**
67 (Chief's Crown (USA)) [2006 95: 11.7d⁵ 12.3d² p10g⁵ 9.9m 12d 10.1m⁵ Sep 13]
strong gelding: just fairly useful handicapper in 2006, best effort when creditable second
at Chester: free-going sort, but should stay beyond 1½m: acts on polytrack, firm and soft
going: usually wears crossed noseband: sometimes finds little: gelded after final start.
G. Wragg

JACK OLIVER 2 ch.g. (Mar 24) Compton Place 125 – Glascoed (Adbass (USA) 102) **75**
[2006 6m 6m* 5.5m² p6g³ Sep 27] 24,000Y: tall, unfurnished gelding: third foal: dam
unraced: fair form: reportedly lost action debut: won maiden at Windsor in August: more
progress when placed in nurseries at Warwick and Lingfield: will prove best at 5f/6f:
raced on polytrack and good to firm going. *B. J. Meehan*

JACK RACKHAM 2 ch.c. (Apr 6) Kyllachy 129 – Hill Welcome 52 (Most Welcome **82**
131) [2006 5d³ 5m² 5m² 6d⁴ May 19] strong, sturdy colt: type to carry condition: third
foal: half-brother to 2004 2-y-o 5f winner Mary Read (by Bahamian Bounty) and 3-y-o
winner Tiana, both useful: dam, maiden who stayed 7f, half-sister to Middle Park winner
Stalker: fairly useful maiden: runner-up at Pontefract and Hamilton (beaten ½ length by
Mood Music): should stay 6f (too free final start). *B. Smart*

524

JACK ROLFE 4 b.g. Polish Precedent (USA) 131 – Haboobti (Habitat 134) [2006 59+: **70** p12g* Jan 3] fair performer: won maiden at Lingfield in January: stays 1½m: acts on polytrack. *G. L. Moore*

JACKS DELIGHT 6 b.g. Bettergeton 97 – Impromptu Melody (IRE) (Mac's Imp **46** (USA) 116) [2006 40, a56: f7g Jan 19] poor maiden: stays 1m: acts on all-weather, raced only on ground firmer than good on turf: tried visored. *C. N. Kellett*

JACK SULLIVAN (USA) 5 ch.g. Belong To Me (USA) – Provisions (USA) (Devil's **119** Bag (USA)) [2006 119: a9f* a8g³ Mar 25] strong, good-topped gelding: smart performer: won Sakhee Sheikh Maktoum bin Rashid Al Maktoum Challenge (Round 2) at Nad Al Sheba (for second successive year) in February by length from Blatant: fair third to Utopia in Godolphin Mile there final start (reportedly suffered minor setback week before): reported in May to be suffering from a tendon injury: stays 9f, not quite 1¼m: acts on dirt/polytrack, and good to soft going: blinkered (raced freely) fifth 3-y-o outing: usually tongue tied. *G. A. Butler*

JACOBIN (USA) 5 b.g. Tamayaz (CAN) 121 – Simply Follow Me (USA) (Green **–** Dancer (USA) 132) [2006 f8g Feb 16] no form, including over hurdles. *M. Scudamore*

JADALEE (IRE) 3 b.c. Desert Prince (IRE) 130 – Lionne (Darshaan 133) [2006 89p: **115** 10m⁵ 13m² 12m² 14g* 13.9g⁶ Sep 9] tall, leggy colt: progressed into a smart performer, winning listed race at Goodwood in August by a neck from Barolo: good efforts when second in similar event at Newmarket (length behind Youmzain) and BGC Stakes (Gordon) at Goodwood (beaten 1¾ lengths by Sixties Icon), and when 4¾ lengths sixth to Sixties Icon in St Leger at York (reportedly wrenched near-hind): resolute galloper, will be suited by 2m+: raced only on good ground or firmer: sweating/edgy last 2 starts: joined I. Mohammed in UAE. *M. P. Tregoning*

JADAN (IRE) 5 b.g. Imperial Ballet (IRE) 110 – Sports Post Lady (IRE) 72 (M Double **63** M (USA)) [2006 81: 5d 5.9g 5s 5f 5m 5.1g 5m⁵ 5g Jul 8] sturdy gelding: just modest handicapper in 2006: best at 5f: acts on good to firm and good to soft ground, probably on soft: tried in cheekpieces. *E. J. Alston*

JADEERON 7 b.g. Green Desert (USA) 127 – Rain And Shine (FR) 78 (Rainbow Quest **64** (USA) 134) [2006 66d: p13.9g⁵ p12.2g² p13g⁶ p13g⁵ p12.2g³ p12.2g⁶ p13.9g p13.9g 14.8m 11.5f 16f² 14.1d⁵ p16g* 16g p16.5m⁴ p16g⁴ f11m* p16g³ f11g p12.2g² Nov 18] useful-looking gelding: modest performer: won handicap at Lingfield in August and banded race at Southwell in October: effective at 11f to 2m: acts on all-weather, firm and good to soft going: wears headgear: tried tongue tied. *Miss D. A. McHale*

JADE'S BALLET 2 ch.f. (Jun 1) Ballet Master (USA) 92 – Another Jade 79 (Beveled **–** (USA)) [2006 p6g 6d p5.1g⁴ p6g⁵ p6g Dec 16] sixth foal: dam 5f (at 2 yrs)/6f winner: little form. *E. A. Wheeler*

JAFARU 2 b.g. (Feb 6) Silver Hawk (USA) 123 – Rafha 123 (Kris 135) [2006 7m p8g **–** 7.1m Sep 4] stocky gelding: well held in maidens: gelded after. *G. A. Butler*

JAHIA (NZ) 7 br.m. Jahafil 114 – Lana (NZ) (Tristrams Heritage (NZ)) [2006 56: f5g **53** p6g* 5f 5f⁶ 5f 5g 5m 6d⁶ p5g* p5g p6g Dec 30] very long-backed mare: modest per- **a61** former, better on all-weather than turf: won banded events at Wolverhampton in May and Kempton in October: has form at 1m, races mainly at 5f/6f: acts on polytrack, firm and good to soft going: tried in cheekpieces: often front runner. *P. T. Midgley*

JAISH (USA) 3 b. or br.f. Seeking The Gold (USA) – Khazayin (USA) 74 (Bahri (USA) **102** 125) [2006 92: 9.9g⁵ 10d⁴ 10g² 9.9m⁴ 10g Oct 12] close-coupled filly: useful performer: best effort in listed races in 2006 when 1½ lengths second to Princess Nada at Newbury, making running: stayed 1¼m: acted on soft and good to firm going: raced freely: wasn't entirely straightforward: visits Cape Cross. *J. L. Dunlop*

JAKARMI 5 b.g. Merdon Melody 98 – Lady Ploy 42 (Deploy 131) [2006 71: p9.5g⁵ **76** f8g² p9.5g² p9.5g³ p8.6g* p8.6g² 10.2d³ p8.6g³ 10.2d* 10g 10.2g p8.6g 10g 10d p8.6g Oct 29] smallish, heavy-topped gelding: fair handicapper: won at Wolverhampton in March and Bath in April: reportedly finished lame final outing: stays 1¼m: acts on all-weather and soft going: front runner. *B. Palling*

JAKEINI (IRE) 3 b.c. Rossini (USA) 118 – Talita Kumi (IRE) (High Estate 127) [2006 **80** 65: p6g⁵ 5g* 5g⁴ 5m* 5m⁵ 5g² 5m⁵ 5g Aug 21] strong colt: fairly useful performer: won maiden at Catterick in May and handicap at Haydock in June: well below form final start: should prove as effective at 6f as 5f: acts on polytrack, heavy and good to firm going: in cheekpieces last 2 starts. *E. S. McMahon*

JAKE THE SNAKE (IRE) 5 ch.g. Intikhab (USA) 135 – Tilbrook (IRE) 78 (Don't **73**
Forget Me 127) [2006 10m^d May 12] fair form: missed 2004/05 (reportedly suffered
from leg trouble): failed dope test and disqualified after finishing eighth in handicap at
Nottingham only outing in 2006: gelded after: stays 1¼m: raced only on polytrack and
good to firm going. *G. A. Huffer*

JALAMID (IRE) 4 b.g. Danehill (USA) 126 – Vignelaure (IRE) 74 (Royal Academy **98**
(USA) 130) [2006 109: 8m 7.5d 7m 7g 7.1m^6 8g 7d Sep 30] big, strong gelding: useful
handicapper: below best in 2006, leaving J. Gosden 23,000 gns after fifth outing: ran
as if amiss final start: stays 1m: unraced on extremes of going: tongue tied: held up.
G. C. Bravery

JALIL (USA) 2 b. or br.c. (Feb 15) Storm Cat (USA) – Tranquility Lake (USA) 120 **78 p**
(Rahy (USA) 115) [2006 8g^6 Oct 13] $9,700,000Y (at the time third highest-priced year-
ling ever sold at public auction): big, strapping colt: type to carry plenty of condition:
second foal: brother to US Grade 2 9f winner After Market: dam US Grade 1 9f/1¼m
winner: 6/4-on, 3¼ lengths sixth of 13 to Sam Lord in maiden at Newmarket, rallying
after outpaced: will stay 1¼m: will do better. *Saeed bin Suroor*

JALISSA 4 b.f. Mister Baileys 123 – Julia Domna (Dominion 123) [2006 83: 7.1d 8s^4 **71**
May 25] tall filly: fairly useful performer at 3 yrs, just fair form at best in 2006: stays 1m:
acts on good to soft ground: sold 45,000 gns in November. *R. M. Beckett*

JALOUHAR 6 b.g. Victory Note (USA) 120 – Orient Way (IRE) 61 (Danehill (USA) **59**
126) [2006 59: f6g^2 f6g^5 p6g^2 p6g^6 p7.1g^4 p6g* p6g^3 p7g p7.1g May 8] compact gelding:
modest performer: won claimer at Wolverhampton (claimed from B. Baugh) in February:
stayed 7f: acted on all-weather and good to firm going: sometimes wore visor/cheek-
pieces: dead. *J. R. Best*

JAMAAHIR (USA) 3 b.c. Bahri (USA) 125 – Elrehaan 96 (Sadler's Wells (USA) 132) **65**
[2006 64p: 8m 7g^6 May 6] rather leggy, useful-looking colt: has a round action: fair maid-
en: bred to stay 1¼m: acts on soft going: withdrawn after unruly at stall intended debut at
2 yrs: has raced freely/carried head awkwardly: sold 5,000 gns in August. *J. L. Dunlop*

JAMAAR 4 ch.g. Nashwan (USA) 135 – Kissogram 120 (Caerleon (USA) 132) [2006 **71**
60: p12.2g p16.5g^2 16g Apr 25] workmanlike gelding: fair maiden: stays 2m: acts on
polytrack: tried tongue tied. *C. N. Kellett*

JAMAICAN FLIGHT (USA) 13 b.h. Sunshine Forever (USA) – Kalamona (USA) **50**
(Hawaii) [2006 –: f16g f16g^5 f16g^6 18v^6 Apr 14] leggy horse: modest performer: stays
21f: acts on fibresand and any turf going: tried visored: front runner. *Mrs S. Lamyman*

JAMAICAN (UAE) 4 ch.g. Timber Country (USA) 124 – Notting Hill (Lammtarra **–**
(USA) 134) [2006 57, a63: p12g May 15] modest performer: finished lame only outing in
2006. *M. J. McGrath*

JAMES CAIRD (IRE) 6 ch.g. Catrail (USA) 123 – Polish Saga 59 (Polish Patriot **96**
(USA) 128) [2006 99: 8m^3 10.4f p10g p9.5g Dec 30] tall, leggy gelding: useful handicapper: creditable equal-third to Dansili Dancer at Goodwood, easily best effort in 2006:
stays 1¼m: acts on firm and good to soft going, probably polytrack: blinkered once at
3 yrs: held up. *M. H. Tompkins*

JAMES STREET (IRE) 3 b.g. Fruits of Love (USA) 127 – Humble Mission (Shack **80**
(USA) 118) [2006 65: 10m p7g* 6m^5 7m^5 8d^2 p10g^6 p8g^4 p8g^6 p7g^2 p7g Dec 10] quite
good-topped gelding: fairly useful handicapper: won at Lingfield in August: creditable
efforts when in frame after: best form at 7f/1m: acts on polytrack, firm and good to soft
ground: blinkered/in cheekpieces last 4 starts. *J. R. Best*

JAMIESON GOLD (IRE) 3 b.g. Desert Style (IRE) 121 – Princess of Zurich (IRE) **98**
(Law Society (USA) 130) [2006 89: 8m 7.1m^4 8g^4 7g* 7.6g 7d Sep 30] useful-looking
gelding: useful handicapper: gelded prior to reappearance: best effort when winning at
Newbury in August by head from Polar Magic: ran as though amiss last 2 starts: should
prove as effective at 1m as 7f: acts on soft and good to firm going. *B. W. Hills*

JANAAH 3 b.f. In The Wings 128 – Blodwen (USA) 52 (Mister Baileys 123) [2006 10g
11.5m p12g Sep 18] 24,000Y: good-topped filly: first foal: maiden who probably
stayed 1½m, out of Cheveley Park Stakes and 1000 Guineas winner Ma Biche: little form
in maidens: sold 2,500 gns. *C. E. Brittain*

JANE OF ARC (FR) 2 ch.f. (Feb 7) Trempolino (USA) 135 – Aerleon Jane 89 (Caer- **75**
leon (USA) 132) [2006 6g 7m* 7.1g^2 7d Sep 8] €8,000F: good-bodied filly: fourth foal:
half-sister to 3-y-o Broken Spur and winner in USA by Distant View: dam 7f and (in
USA) 1m winner: fair form: won maiden at Thirsk in June: more improvement when

second to Sans Reward in minor event at Warwick: off 2 months, well held in nursery (softer ground): will stay 1m. *T. D. Easterby*

JANUARY 3 gr.c. Daylami (IRE) 138 – Noushkey 118 (Polish Precedent (USA) 131) **69** [2006 10m⁵ Jun 23] lengthy, good-topped colt: third foal: half-brother to 10.5f winner Anaamil (by Darshaan): dam, 7f (at 2 yrs) and 1½m (Lancashire Oaks) winner and second in Oaks, half-sister to very smart stayer San Sebastian: favourite, 8 lengths fifth to Rhinebird in maiden at Newmarket, tending to carry head awkwardly: joined D. Selvaratnam in UAE. *Saeed bin Suroor*

JARDINES BAZAAR 2 b.g. (Feb 23) Halling (USA) 133 – Alumisiyah (USA) 93 **50** (Danzig (USA)) [2006 7d³ 9m 6g Sep 27] tall, leggy gelding: maiden: form (modest) only when third at Newcastle on debut. *T. D. Easterby*

JARVO 5 b.g. Pursuit of Love 124 – Pinkie Rose (FR) (Kenmare (FR) 125) [2006 59: **54** p9.5g⁴ p10g p10g² Dec 13] sturdy gelding: modest maiden: best around 1¼m: acts on polytrack, firm and soft going: tried tongue tied/blinkered. *I. W. McInnes*

JASMINE PEARL (IRE) 5 b.m. King of Kings (IRE) 125 – Tumbleweed Pearl 96 **41** (Aragon 118) [2006 52, a42: p6g 6m p5g 5f Jun 12] workmanlike mare: just poor performer in 2006: effective at 5f to easy 7f: unraced on heavy going, acts on any other turf and all-weather. *T. M. Jones*

JAUFRETTE 3 b.f. Kayf Tara 130 – Jucinda 58 (Midyan (USA) 124) [2006 11.7m **–** 10.2m Sep 25] brown filly: half-sister to fairly useful 6f (at 2 yrs)/1m winner Gems Bond (by Magic Ring): dam, 15.4f winner, sister to Goodwood Cup winner Tioman Island: well held in maidens at Bath, reluctant to enter stall latter occasion. *Dr J. R. J. Naylor*

JAWAAB (IRE) 2 ch.g. (Mar 20) King's Best (USA) 132 – Canis Star (Wolfhound **78** (USA) 126) [2006 6m⁴ 7g 7d⁴ 7.1g² 8m⁴ 8d⁶ 8d² Oct 19] 130,000Y: second foal: dam unraced half-sister to smart milers Guest Artiste and Inchmurrin, latter dam of smart 7f/ 1m performer Inchinor: fair maiden: in frame 5 times, twice in nurseries: stays 1m: acts on good to firm and good to soft going: sold 46,000 gns, and gelded. *E. A. L. Dunlop*

JAYANJAY 7 b.g. Piccolo 121 – Morica 88 (Moorestyle 137) [2006 100, a88+: 5g³ p6g⁶ **95** 5m 6m 6g 6m⁵ 5g 5d³ p6g p6g p6g³ p6g p5g p6g² p5g p6g p6g⁶ Dec 19] close-coupled **a83** gelding: useful handicapper on turf, fairly useful on all-weather: only 3 placings in 2006, best effort when third to Bond City at Epsom in August (left Miss B. Sanders after next start): effective at 5f to easy 7f: acts on polytrack, firm and soft going: blinkered/ visored earlier in career: held up: none too reliable. *P. Mitchell*

JAYER GILLES 6 br.g. Busy Flight 122 – Jadidh 64 (Touching Wood (USA) 127) **62** [2006 73: 14.1m 16.2m³ 16.4m² 17.2m⁶ 16v Oct 25] leggy gelding: fluent mover: just modest maiden handicapper in 2006: stays 2¼m: acts on polytrack, firm and good to soft going. *Dr J. R. J. Naylor*

JAY GEE'S CHOICE 6 b.g. Barathea (IRE) 127 – Llia 94 (Shirley Heights 130) **–** [2006 –: p8g p8g Jul 12] sturdy, well-made gelding: no form since 2004. *B. G. Powell*

JAY JAY OKOCHA 3 gr.g. Wizard King 122 – Schatzi 54§ (Chilibang 120) [2006 **–** p9.5g p6g Mar 6] last in maiden/seller. *James Moffatt*

JAYZEE (IRE) 2 b.f. (Mar 6) Iron Mask (USA) 117 – Golden Concorde (Super Concorde (USA) 128) [2006 7g 7.5f 7m 6.5d³ p7.1s f7g Dec 14] €13,000F, £15,000Y: half-sister to 3 winners in Italy: dam Italian 5f to 7f winner, including at 2 yrs: little form. *P. D. Deegan, Ireland*

JAZRAWY 4 b.g. Dansili 127 – Dalila di Mare (IRE) (Bob Back (USA) 124) [2006 69: **64** p8g p13g 11.5m p10g p8g 10m 11.8f² 14.1g² 15.8d 11.9m p12g 11.8d³ 16v⁴ p13.9g f11g³ f14g⁵ f11g* p12g* Dec 20] short-backed, deep-girthed gelding: modest performer: claimed from Gay Kelleway seventh start: won claimer at Southwell and handicap at Kempton in December: stays 1¾m: acts on all-weather, firm and good to soft going: tried tongue tied: races prominently. *P. W. Hiatt*

JAZZANOVA 2 b.g. (Apr 26) Fasliyev (USA) 120 – Stonegrave 57 (Selkirk (USA) **–** 129) [2006 5m 6s⁶ 6s 6s f8g f7g Nov 20] neat gelding: little form: trained by G. Kelly fifth start only, returned to former trainer: tried blinkered. *M. W. Easterby*

JAZZ AT THE SANDS (USA) 3 ch.g. Forest Wildcat (USA) 120 – Dahlia's Krissy **50** (USA) (Kris S (USA)) [2006 47: f6g p6g⁶ f8g p6g f5g⁴ f5g⁴ p6g⁵ p5.1g⁵ p8g p6g Dec 20] workmanlike gelding: modest maiden: stays 6f: acts on all-weather and soft ground: tried visored/blinkered: looks hard ride. *D. Shaw*

JAZZ FESTIVAL (USA) 2 b.g. (Mar 2) Jambalaya Jazz (USA) 111 – Violets Are –
Blue (USA) (Full Pocket (USA)) [2006 7s f8g Nov 2] well held in maidens: sold 1,800
gns. *T. D. Barron*

JEANMAIRE (IRE) 3 b.f. Dansili 127 – Lovely Lyca 76 (Night Shift (USA)) [2006   **95**
89: 6f⁶ 7g⁶ 8m 7m² 6g 6d⁵ Oct 27] small, leggy filly: useful performer: best effort when
second to Heaven Sent in handicap at Newmarket: likely to prove best short of 1m: only
win on good to soft going, but has raced mainly on good ground or firmer. *H. Morrison*

JEBEL ALI (IRE) 3 b.g. Fruits of Love (USA) 127 – Assertive Lass (USA) (Assert   **83**
134) [2006 59: p10g² p10g² p10g p10g* p10g⁶ 11.6g⁵ 9.9m 11.5m² 10g p10g⁶ 8d⁵
Oct 27] tall gelding: fairly useful handicapper: won at Lingfield in March: mostly at least
respectable efforts after: stays 11.5f: acts on polytrack and good to firm ground: tried in
cheekpieces/visor. *B. Gubby*

JEDBURGH 5 b.h. Selkirk (USA) 129 – Conspiracy 98 (Rudimentary (USA) 118)   **116**
[2006 114: 7.1g³ 7m* 7m⁶ 7m* 7m² 7g 7d 7d Oct 14] strong, compact horse: smart
performer: won minor event at Leicester (by neck from Philharmonic) in June and
3-runner Emirates Airline Minstrel Stakes at the Curragh (by neck from Noelani) in July:
best effort after when creditable 4 lengths second to Iffraaj in Betfair Cup at Goodwood:
best at 7f: acts on good to firm going: blinkered. *J. L. Dunlop*

JEEPSTAR 6 b.g. Muhtarram (USA) 125 – Jungle Rose 90 (Shirley Heights 130) [2006   **82**
95: 12g 16d 14.1g 12m⁵ 13.4f² p12g² Dec 2] leggy, lightly-made gelding: just fairly
useful handicapper: effective at 1½m to 2m: acts on polytrack, firm and soft
ground: front runner. *S. C. Williams*

JEER (IRE) 2 ch.c. (Feb 28) Selkirk (USA) 129 – Purring (USA) 79 (Mountain Cat   **78 p**
(USA)) [2006 p8g 8v² Sep 2] 38,000Y: first foal: dam, lightly-raced 7f winner, half-sister
to French winner up to 1m Ronda and winner up to 2m Silver Gilt, both smart: much
better effort in maidens when 1¼ lengths second to Hadahoo at Thirsk: will stay 1¼m:
likely to progress further. *E. A. L. Dunlop*

JELLYTOT (USA) 3 b.f. Minardi (USA) 119 – Dounine (Kaldoun (FR) 122) [2006   **68**
63: 5d 6g 8.2d² 7g* 7f 6.9m* 8m³ 7d p7.1g 7.1d⁴ Oct 13] neat filly: fair performer: won
maiden at Catterick in June and handicap at Carlisle in July: stays 1m: acts on good to
firm and good to soft going: carried head awkwardly fifth start. *K. A. Ryan*

JEMBER RED 3 b.f. Polish Precedent (USA) 131 – Arabellajill 97 (Aragon 118) [2006   –
–: p7.1m f11g⁵ Dec 14] lengthy filly: no form in maidens. *B. Smart*

JEMIMA GODFREY 2 b.f. (Feb 16) Ishiguru (USA) 114 – Quantum Lady 79 (Muja-   –
dil (USA) 119) [2006 p7.1g Dec 8] 6,000Y: first foal: dam 2-y-o 5f/6f winner: tongue
tied, last in maiden at Wolverhampton. *J. Pearce*

JENISE (IRE) 3 b.f. Orpen (USA) 116 – Griqualand (Connaught 130) [2006 64p: 7m   **51**
p8.6g⁶ 7s f7g p7.1m⁵ f7g p7.1g⁵ Dec 21] modest maiden: raced mainly at 7f: acts on
polytrack. *Mark Campion*

JENKINS LANE (IRE) 4 b.g. Revoque (IRE) 122 – Suzy Street (IRE) 71 (Dancing   –
Dissident (USA) 119) [2006 83: 8m 10s p8.6g Nov 25] fairly useful performer at best:
no form in 2006: stays 7f: acts on good to firm going: wore cheekpieces final outing.
J. J. Lambe, Ireland

JENNA STANNIS 4 ch.f. Wolfhound (USA) 126 – Darling Splodge (Elegant Air 119)   –
[2006 68d: 12m 9.3m 10f 7.1f Jun 26] workmanlike filly: fair maiden at 3 yrs: little form
in 2006: tried visored/tongue tied. *W. Storey*

JENNVERSE 4 b.f. Opening Verse (USA) 126 – Jennelle 97 (Nomination 125) [2006   **57**
62: p6g p7.1g p7g⁶ p6g⁶ p7g f6g p7g p6g⁴ p6g* p7g 6f p5g⁵ p7g 6g³ p6g* p7g⁴ f6g
p6g⁵ p6g⁶ p7g³ p7g Dec 30] modest performer: won banded races at Kempton in May
and October: effective at 6f, should stay 1m: acts on polytrack and good to soft going.
D. K. Ivory

JENNYFROMTHEBLOCK (IRE) 5 b.m. General Monash (USA) 107 – Notorious   –
(Auction Ring (USA) 123) [2006 –: f7g Jan 24] no form: tried in cheekpieces. *Samuel
Murphy, Ireland*

JENNY GEDDES (IRE) 2 b.f. (Apr 30) Intikhab (USA) 135 – Etiquette 66 (Law   **55 p**
Society (USA) 130) [2006 5g 5d⁵ 6m 6d Oct 2] €24,000F, 15,000Y: good-topped filly:
half-sister to 3 winners in France, including useful 6f (at 2 yrs) and 1m winner Uninhibited (by Lahib): dam, maiden, best at 1½m: more encouragement than bare result in
maidens: well held in nursery: will be suited by 1m+: should still do better. *R. A. Fahey*

Mrs Elizabeth Moran's "Jeremy"

JENNY SOBA 3 b.f. Observatory (USA) 131 – Majalis 79 (Mujadil (USA) 119) [2006 **66**
56: 6v 8d⁶ 9.3m 8f² 8f² 8m³ 8d⁶ 8.5m³ p9.5g Nov 2] lengthy filly: fair maiden: stays 8.5f:
acts on firm and good to soft going. *R. M. Whitaker*

JEREMY (USA) 3 b.c. Danehill Dancer (IRE) 117 – Glint In Her Eye (USA) 76 (Arazi **114**
(USA) 135) [2006 98: 7g² 7s* 7m* 7m⁶ 7d² 7d Oct 14] good-bodied colt: has scope: has
a short, choppy action: smart performer: much improved, winning listed race at Newmarket (by neck from Wake Up Maggie) in May and Jersey Stakes at Royal Ascot (beat
Asset 2 lengths) in June: creditable ½-length second to Welsh Emperor in Hungerford
Stakes at Newbury prior to badly hampered in Challenge Stakes at Newmarket final
outing: likely to stay 1m: acts on soft and good to firm going: has hung right, markedly so
in Betfair Cup at Goodwood fourth start (below form). *Sir Michael Stoute*

JESSICA WIGMO 3 b.f. Bahamian Bounty 116 – Queen of Shannon (IRE) 76 (Nor- **49**
dico (USA)) [2006 59: p7g p6g p6g 8.1m 8.1f 5m⁶ 5.7m³ 6s Oct 2] poor maiden: should
prove best at 5f/6f: acts on polytrack and good to firm going. *A. W. Carroll*

JE SUIS BELLE 4 ch.f. Efisio 120 – Blossom (Warning 136) [2006 71: p12.2g Jan 20] **–**
quite attractive filly: fair performer at 3 yrs (wore cheekpieces final start): blinkered, well
held in selling handicap only outing in 2006. *Miss Gay Kelleway*

JETE (IRE) 2 b.g. (Feb 14) Imperial Ballet (IRE) 110 – Jet Lock (USA) (Crafty Pros- **60**
pector (USA)) [2006 p6m 6g 5.1d⁵ Oct 18] leggy, workmanlike gelding: modest form
second start in maidens: visored. *D. Shaw*

JEU D'ESPRIT (IRE) 3 b.f. Montjeu (IRE) 137 – Cielo Vodkamartini (USA) (Con- **64**
quistador Cielo (USA)) [2006 8.1g p13g p9.5g³ p9.5g Nov 16] 43,000Y: second foal:

dam, 8.3f winner in USA, out of half-sister to high-class 1m/1¼m performer Lahib: modest maiden: may prove best around 1m: acts on polytrack. *J. G. Given*

JEUDI 3 b.g. Montjeu (IRE) 137 – Portorosa (USA) (Irish River (FR) 131) [2006 p8g p7.1g f8g Jan 17] no form in maidens: withdrawn (unruly paddock) intended debut: dead. *Sir Mark Prescott*

JEUNE LOUP 4 b.g. Loup Sauvage (USA) 125 – Secret Waters 100 (Pharly (FR) 130) [2006 –: f11g p7.1g Jul 3] rather leggy gelding: fair maiden at 2 yrs: well held all 3 starts since. *P. C. Haslam*

JEWAAR (USA) 3 ch.f. Diesis 133 – Ringshaan (FR) (Darshaan 133) [2006 9.9g³ **84** 10m⁴ 8m² 10m³ 8m² 8.1g* Aug 26] $450,000Y: workmanlike filly: fourth foal: half-sister to fairly useful 2003 2-y-o 1m winner Rinjani (by Gone West) and a winner in USA by Mr Prospector: dam, French 9f winner on only start, half-sister to very smart French/ US 1m/9f performer Special Ring: fairly useful performer: best effort when winning maiden at Sandown in August: stays 1¼m: raced only on good/good to firm going: wayward first 2 starts. *M. A. Jarvis*

JEWEL IN THE SAND (IRE) 4 b.f. Bluebird (USA) 125 – Dancing Drop 103 **97** (Green Desert (USA) 127) [2006 107: 5.1g 6g* 6f Jul 14] strong, sturdy filly: had a quick action: useful performer, lightly raced: easily best effort in 2006 when winning minor event at Newmarket in June by neck from Gloved Hand: best at 5f/6f: raced only on good going or firmer (appeared not to let herself down on firm ground final outing): stud. *R. Hannon*

JEWELLED DAGGER (IRE) 2 b.g. (Feb 26) Daggers Drawn (USA) 114 – Cappa- – doce (IRE) (General Monash (USA) 107) [2006 p8.6g p8.6g p7.1g Dec 28] no form: tried visored. *I. Semple*

JEWEL OF INDIA 7 ch.g. Bijou d'Inde 127 – Low Hill (Rousillon (USA) 133) [2006 **59** p8g⁶ p8g p9.5g 8.1g 8.5g* 8.5m f8g Nov 20] leggy, sparely-made gelding: missed 2005 and only modest form on return: won amateur handicap at Beverley in August: stays easy 1¼m: acts on all-weather and soft going, probably on good to firm: sometimes wears blinkers/cheekpieces. *Mrs A. L. M. King*

JIDAAR (IRE) 3 b.g. Grand Lodge (USA) 125 – Banaadir (USA) 50 (Diesis 133) **85** [2006 –: 9m* p12g p12.2g Nov 18] fairly useful performer, lightly raced: won maiden at Musselburgh in May, hanging left: left M. Johnston 35,000 gns in July, resold 16,000 gns in August, and gelded: well beaten in handicaps on polytrack on return: stays 9f: acts on good to firm going. *P. W. Hiatt*

JIDIYA (IRE) 7 b.g. Lahib (USA) 129 – Yaqatha (IRE) (Sadler's Wells (USA) 132) – [2006 73: 9.9g 17.1d 12.4s Oct 10] big, workmanlike gelding: fair handicapper: well held in 2006, leaving S. Gollings after reappearance: wore cheekpieces in 2005: often makes running. *Mrs H. O. Graham*

JIGGY SPRIGGY (IRE) 3 b.f. King Charlemagne (USA) 120 – Amneris (IRE) 73 – (Alzao (USA) 117) [2006 8.1s 7.1g 8s Aug 26] €14,500Y: smallish filly: second foal: half-sister to 2004 2-y-o 5f and 7f winner Lisa Mona Lisa (by Desert Style): dam, maiden, likely to have stayed 1¾m: well beaten in maidens. *V. Smith*

JIHAAZ (IRE) 3 ch.g. Elnadim (USA) 128 – Gazar (Kris 135) [2006 70: 7.1g⁴ 8.2m² **86** 8.1d* 8g 8.1g 8d³ Oct 2] good-topped gelding: fairly useful performer: won maiden at Chepstow in June: gelded after final outing: stays 1m: acts on good to firm and good to soft going: sent to UAE. *B. W. Hills*

JILL DAWSON (IRE) 3 b.f. Mull of Kintyre (USA) 114 – Dream of Jenny 73 (Caer- **66** leon (USA) 126) [2006 –: 6g 8s 8m* 8g² 9.3f Jul 21] angular filly: fair handicapper: won apprentice event at Salisbury (stumbled leaving stall) in June: should be suited by 1¼m+: acts on good to firm going: tends to edge left. *John Berry*

JILLY WHY (IRE) 5 b.m. Mujadil (USA) 119 – Ruwy 77 (Soviet Star (USA) 128) **72** [2006 80, a65: p8g⁴ p8.6g p7.1g⁶ 5s 6g⁶ 5f⁴ f5g³ p5.1g⁶ Dec 7] workmanlike mare: just **a63** fair handicapper on turf, modest on all-weather in 2006: effective at 5f, and seems to stay easy 1m: acts on all-weather, firm and good to soft going: visored (ran creditably) sixth outing: races up with pace: inconsistent. *Ms Deborah J. Evans*

JIMBOBALOU 2 b.c. (Apr 27) Mujahid (USA) 125 – Barsham 94 (Be My Guest – (USA) 126) [2006 6g Oct 12] big colt: backward, well beaten in maiden at Newmarket. *T. T. Clement*

JIMINOR MACK 3 bl.f. Little Jim – Copper Trader 53 (Faustus (USA) 118) [2006 **53** 8.3d 8g 9d⁵ 10m 10d⁴ f11g Dec 28] half-sister to 1¼m winner Mary Culi (by Liboi) and 15f to 21f winner Established (by Not In Doubt): dam third at 1¼m: modest maiden: should be suited by 1½m: acts on good to soft going: blinkered final outing. *W. J. H. Ratcliffe*

JIMMY THE GUESSER 3 ch.g. Piccolo 121 – Brush Away (Ahonoora 122) [2006 85: 5.1s* 5g⁵ 6m⁵ 5g p7g² 7.1m² 7m⁵ 7.5f⁴ 6m⁴ 7d² 7s³ 6d p7g⁶ p7g⁴ p6g⁴ p8.6g⁴ f6g² Dec 21] tall gelding: fairly useful handicapper, better on all-weather than turf: won at Bath in April: in frame 10 times after: effective at stiff 5f to 8.6f: acts on all-weather, firm and soft going: effective blinkered or not, wore cheekpieces twelfth outing (poorly drawn): consistent. *N. P. Littmoden*   **86 a94**

JINKSONTHEHOUSE 5 b.m. Whittingham (IRE) 104 – Aldwick Colonnade 62 (Kind of Hush 118) [2006 –. 5.7d 5.1d⁶ 5f 5f⁶ 5m 5.1g 5.1f⁶ 5.7f 8m Aug 19] close-coupled mare: modest performer at best: effective at 5f/easy 6f. *M. D. I. Usher*   **52**

JOB DONE 2 b.f. (Mar 20) Elmaamul (USA) 125 – Emma Amour 67 (Emarati (USA) 74) [2006 5g 5d⁵ May 29] 1,600Y: leggy, close-coupled filly: third foal: dam, maiden, stayed 6f: well held in claimers. *M. W. Easterby*   **–**

JOBURG GOLD (USA) 2 b. or br.c. (Mar 24) Johannesburg (USA) 127 – Churn Dat Butter (USA) (Unbridled (USA) 128) [2006 6s 5f Oct 9] tall, good-topped colt: well held in maidens at Newbury (raced freely, left B. Hills after) and Woodbine (blinkered) 4½ months later. *R. Baker, Canada*   **–**

JO'BURG (USA) 2 b.c. (Feb 5) Johannesburg (USA) 127 – La Martina 100 (Atraf 116) [2006 6s² 6m⁵ 6f* 7m p7g³ Oct 21] 200,000EUR, 215,000Y: smallish, strong, good-bodied colt: first foal: dam 7f/1m performer (successful in Italy/USA): useful performer: won maiden at Windsor in July: best form when 2½ lengths fifth of 21 to Hellvelyn in Coventry Stakes at Royal Ascot and third to Market Day in nursery at Lingfield: will stay 1m: acts on polytrack, firm and soft going. *Mrs A. J. Perrett*   **100**

JOCHESKI (IRE) 2 b.c. (Mar 31) Mull of Kintyre (USA) 114 – Ludovica (Bustino 136) [2006 p8.6m⁴ p8g⁴ Dec 1] half-brother to several winners, including useful 7.5f (at 2 yrs) to 1½m winner Weet-A-Minute (by Nabeel Dancer): dam unraced: modest form when fourth in maidens on polytrack. *M. J. Wallace*   **64**

JOCKSER (IRE) 5 b.g. Desert Story (IRE) 115 – Pupa Fiorini (ITY) (Indian Ridge 123) [2006 –: 16d² Sep 26] ex-Irish gelding: fair performer, lightly raced: creditable second in handicap at Goodwood only Flat run in 2006: stays 2m: acts on heavy ground: fairly useful hurdler. *J. W. Mullins*   **73**

JODRELL BANK (IRE) 3 ch.f. Observatory (USA) 131 – Aravonian 82 (Night Shift (USA)) [2006 45: 6g² 6g⁶ 6s Oct 2] first foal: dam 1m winner: rather leggy filly: modest maiden: left F. Ennis in Ireland after 2 yrs: bred to be suited by at least 7f: best effort on good going. *W. Jarvis*   **63**

JOE DRAPER 4 ch.g. Forzando 122 – Shanghai Lil 57 (Petong 126) [2006 p7.1m Oct 31] tailed off only start in bumpers and well held in maiden on Flat debut. *P. D. Evans*   **–**

JOE JO STAR 4 b.g. Piccolo 121 – Zagreb Flyer (Old Vic 136) [2006 55: p7.1g p7.1g² p8.6g* p9.5g³ p10g f8g p8.6g p9.5g p8.6g Dec 21] compact gelding: modest performer: left P. Blockley after reappearance: won banded race at Wolverhampton in February: below form after next outing: stays 11.7f: acts on polytrack and firm ground: has worn cheekpieces, including when successful. *B. P. J. Baugh*   **61 d**

JOELLA'S LAD 2 gr.g. (Feb 22) Bertolini (USA) 125 – Coffee To Go (Environment Friend 128) [2006 5m 5g⁶ f6g 8.1g f8g Dec 21] workmanlike gelding: no form in maidens: tried in cheekpieces. *Ms Deborah J. Evans*   **–**

JOHANNESBURG CAT (USA) 2 b.f. (Apr 1) Johannesburg (USA) 127 – High Society (IRE) 97 (Key of Luck (USA) 126) [2006 6g* 6.5s⁴ 6d p6g⁶ p7.1g⁴ f8g⁶ p7.1g Dec 9] 23,000 2-y-o: first foal: dam 5f (in Ireland at 2 yrs) to 6.5f (in USA) winner: fairly useful form when trained by A. Trybuhl in Germany first 3 starts, including win in maiden at Hamburg and fourth in listed race at Cologne: little impact in minor events/nursery on all-weather in Britain: should stay 7f/1m: acts on soft ground. *N. P. Littmoden*   **88 d**

JOHANNESBURG JACK (IRE) 2 b.c. (Mar 16) Johannesburg (USA) 127 – Out of Egypt (USA) (Red Ransom (USA)) [2006 5m 6m* 6m p7g² 7g³ 8g⁶ 7d Sep 19] 77,000EUR: strong, quite attractive colt: fluent mover: second foal: dam, ran once in USA, sister to smart performer up to 1½m in Britain/USA Wandering Star: fairly useful performer: won maiden at Brighton in May: better form next 3 starts, mid-field in Coventry Stakes at Royal Ascot then placed in minor events at Lingfield and Ascot: should stay 1m: acts on polytrack and good to firm going: sent to USA. *H. Morrison*   **90**

JOHANNES (IRE) 3 b.c. Mozart (IRE) 131 – Blue Sirocco (Bluebird (USA) 125) **101**
[2006 99p: 7g⁴ p7g 6m³ 6m 6f⁴ 5g Sep 23] good-topped colt: useful performer: best effort
when 5½ lengths fourth to Misu Bond in listed Free Handicap at Newmarket on reappearance: stays 7f: acts on good to firm going: tongue tied (ran as if amiss) final outing.
D. Nicholls

JOHANNIAN 8 b.g. Hernando (FR) 127 – Photo Call 73 (Chief Singer 131) [2006 8m⁵ **66**
8.1m⁶ 8.1m 8.2s Oct 18] quite good-topped gelding: unimpressive mover: fair handicapper nowadays: missed 2005: easily best effort in 2006 on reappearance: effective at
1m/1¼m: acts on firm and soft ground: tried tongue tied. *J. M. Bradley*

JOHN BRATBY (USA) 4 b. or br.c. Royal Academy (USA) 130 – Side Saddle (IRE) **53**
108 (Saddlers' Hall (IRE) 126) [2006 53p: p6g⁴ 6m Jul 29] thrice-raced maiden: modest
form: bred to stay 1m+: tongue tied on reappearance. *P. J. Makin*

JOHN CHARLES (IRE) 4 b.g. Fraam 114 – Norwegian Queen (IRE) (Affirmed **74**
(USA)) [2006 69p: p8.6g* p8.6g p8.6g 11g 10m Jul 24] fair performer: won maiden at
Wolverhampton in February: well held in handicaps after, leaving D. Elsworth following
third start: should stay 1¼m: acts on polytrack: gelded, and won over hurdles in October.
B. De Haan

JOHN CLAUDE (IRE) 3 b.g. Night Shift (USA) – Koukla Mou (Keen 116) [2006 68: **52**
f5g⁵ p5.1g f5g f6g Nov 28] strong, close-coupled gelding: only modest at best nowadays:
may prove best at 5f: acts on firm and good to soft ground, probably on fibresand: tried
blinkered/visored/tongue tied. *Ronald Thompson*

JOHN FORBES 4 b.g. High Estate 127 – Mavourneen (USA) (Dynaformer (USA)) **76**
[2006 75: p12.2g p12.2g 16v* 14g⁶ 13d⁶ 16.2g⁶ 14.1g 18m³ 16.1m Jul 13] strong gelding:
fair handicapper: won at Musselburgh in March: seems to stay 2¼m: acts on polytrack,
heavy and good to firm ground: tried blinkered. *B. Ellison*

JOHN KEATS 3 b.g. Bertolini (USA) 125 – Nightingale (Night Shift (USA)) [2006 82: **83 §**
7g 6m² 6d⁵ 7.2d⁵ 6g 5m 7d 7.1s 6s³ 7s 6s⁶ Oct 24] sturdy, lengthy gelding: fairly useful
handicapper: effective at 6f/7f: acts on soft and good to firm going: tried blinkered/in
cheekpieces: unsatisfactory temperament. *I. Semple*

JOHNNIE BLACK (IRE) 4 b.g. Fayruz 116 – Cunning Kate (IRE) 65 (Roi Danzig **–**
(USA)) [2006 7d p7g Oct 29] ran 20 times in Spain, winning minor event at Dos Hermanas early in 2005: well held in Britain in 2006 (tongue tied, reportedly finished lame latter
start): effective at 5f to 7f: acts on sand, best turf effort on good going. *E. J. Creighton*

JOHNNY ALLJAYS (IRE) 5 b.g. Victory Note (USA) 120 – It's Academic 73 **–**
(Royal Academy (USA) 130) [2006 –, a56: p16.5f⁴ f16g Oct 12] big gelding: only poor **a49**
in 2006 (pulled up final start): stays 2m: acts on all-weather, had form on firm going
earlier in career: tried in blinkers/cheekpieces at 3 yrs. *S. Lycett*

JOHNNY ALPHA (IRE) 3 b.g. Namid 128 – Green's Maud Earl (Night Shift (USA)) **–**
[2006 77: 6g Aug 18] strong, close-coupled gelding: type to carry condition: has a quick
action: fair form on debut at 2 yrs: has reportedly returned lame 2 starts, including in
handicap on only outing in 2006: should prove best at 5f/6f: acts on good to soft ground.
P. W. Chapple-Hyam

JOHNNY JUMPUP (IRE) 4 ch.g. Pivotal 124 – Clarice Orsini (Common Grounds **101**
118) [2006 108: 7s 9m 8.5g 8g 8g Oct 13] close-coupled gelding: useful handicapper:
form in 2006 only when eighth to Star of Light at Newmarket second outing: barely stays
9f: acts on soft going, probably on good to firm: sold 19,000 gns. *R. M. Beckett*

JOHN O'GROATS (IRE) 8 b.g. Distinctly North (USA) 115 – Bannons Dream (IRE) **42**
(Thatching 131) [2006 –: 5m 5s 5d 7.1d³ Oct 8] tall, close-coupled, good-topped geld-
ing: poor nowadays: effective at 5f/6f: acts on firm and soft going: tried in headgear.
W. G. Harrison

JOHN STANLEY (IRE) 2 b.g. (Mar 20) Imperial Ballet (IRE) 110 – Pivotable 75 **59**
(Pivotal 124) [2006 6m 5m⁵ 5g f5g Nov 10] workmanlike gelding: modest maiden: bred
for sprinting. *D. Carroll*

JOHNSTON'S DIAMOND (IRE) 8 b.g. Tagula (IRE) 116 – Toshair Flyer 88 **88**
(Ballad Rock 122) [2006 92, a81: 6v 6d⁵ f6g 6s* 5s⁶ 6m 6g 5.1g⁶ 6s⁵ 6d 6d p5.1g⁵ p6g⁵ **a69**
p6g p6g p6g Dec 2] big, workmanlike gelding: fairly useful on turf, fair on all-weather:
won handicap at Thirsk in May: best at 5f/6f: acts on all-weather, firm and soft going:
tried in blinkers/cheekpieces/tongue tie: carries head awkwardly: races prominently.
E. J. Alston

JOHN TERRY (IRE) 3 b.g. Grand Lodge (USA) 125 – Kardashina (FR) (Darshaan **94** 133) [2006 79p: 10g² 9m⁴ 12g³ 10s Oct 18] big, good sort: fairly useful performer: in frame in handicaps at Sandown (2) and Salisbury: stays 1½m: acts on good to firm and good to soft going: gelded after final start. *Mrs A. J. Perrett*

JOINT EXPECTATIONS (IRE) 2 b.g. (Jan 7) Indian Rocket 115 – Jenny Spinner **–** (IRE) 58 (Bluebird (USA) 125) [2006 5m 5d⁶ 6.1m 6m p6g p6g Dec 4] workmanlike gelding: little form in maidens: tried visored. *Mrs C. A. Dunnett*

JOJESSE 2 ch.g. (Mar 30) Compton Place 125 – Jodeeka 97 (Fraam 114) [2006 5s **52** 5.2m⁶ 5g 5f⁴ Jul 25] workmanlike gelding: first foal: dam 5f winner: modest form in maidens: likely to prove best at 5f: joined G. A. Swinbank. *S. Parr*

JOKING JOHN 3 b.g. Compton Admiral 121 – Bo' Babbity 75 (Strong Gale 116) **41** [2006 –: p6g* p6g f6g⁵ 6.1d 7m⁴ 7.1g⁴ 8.3m⁵ f7g Nov 21] quite attractive gelding: poor performer: won banded race at Wolverhampton in March: stays 7f: acts on all-weather and good to firm ground. *C. W. Fairhurst*

JOLIE (IRE) 4 b.f. Orpen (USA) 116 – Arabian Dream (IRE) (Royal Academy (USA) **–** 130) [2006 70: 7.1g May 1] good-topped filly: well held all 3 outings since winning handicap in 2005: tends to be slowly away, markedly so only run in 2006. *R. Dickin*

JOLIZERO 5 br.g. Danzero (AUS) – Jolis Absent 57 (Primo Dominie 121) [2006 12d **67** 14.1d³ 16g² 20s p16.5g⁴ 16.1s 15d⁴ Oct 13] big, good-bodied gelding: fair handicapper: stays 2m, seemingly not 2½m: acts on polytrack and any turf going: sold 6,500 gns. *John Berry*

JOMELAMIN 4 gr.f. Silver Patriarch (IRE) 125 – Jomel Amou (IRE) (Ela-Mana-Mou **–** 132) [2006 p9.5g p8g p8g Feb 15] sixth foal: half-sister to 5f (at 2 yrs) and 1m winner Cautious Joe and 2003 2-y-o 7f winner Machiventa (both by First Trump): dam Irish 1¼m/1½m winner: well beaten in claimers/seller. *R. J. Hodges*

JOMUS 5 b.g. Soviet Star (USA) 128 – Oatey 68 (Master Willie 129) [2006 55, a68: **– §** p8g⁴ p10g³ p10g⁶ p12g p10g² p10g³ p12g p10g⁴ p10g⁵ p8g² p8g² p8g⁴ p8g² p8g³ p8g³ **a67 §** Dec 16] close-coupled, quite good-topped gelding: fair handicapper: stays 1¼m: acts on all-weather and good to firm going: wears blinkers/cheekpieces: sometimes slowly away: patiently ridden: finds little. *L. Montague Hall*

JONNY EBENEEZER 7 b.g. Hurricane Sky (AUS) – Leap of Faith (IRE) 65 (North- **92 d** iam (USA)) [2006 111, a–: 6m³ 6s 6d 7m 6g p7g p7g 10g Aug 24] tall gelding: smart performer at best: very much on downgrade, and well held after third in minor event at Haydock on reappearance: effective at 5f to 7f: acts on all-weather, soft and good to firm going: often wears headgear. *M. Wellings*

JOOLS 8 b.g. Cadeaux Genereux 131 – Madame Crecy (USA) (Al Nasr (FR) 126) [2006 **72 d** 85, a69: p7g⁶ p7.1g p8g 8m 8.3g² 8.3f⁵ 8.3f⁶ 8.3m⁴ p8.6g⁶ 10.1g⁶ 8f p7g⁴ p7g⁵ Dec 30] **a64 d** rather leggy gelding: on downgrade, and just fair handicapper on turf, modest on all-weather in 2006: effective at 7f to 1¼m: acts on all-weather, firm and soft going: visored once (at 3 yrs): reportedly bled penultimate start. *D. K. Ivory*

JORDANS ELECT 6 ch.g. Fleetwood (IRE) 107 – Cal Norma's Lady (IRE) 87 **77** (Lyphard's Special (USA) 122) [2006 84: 7.1g⁶ 8.3d³ 9.2m² 10d³ 8.3f⁶ 8.3m⁶ 9.1g⁴ 10d 10m* 10m 8g 7s p8.6g Oct 29] tall, rather leggy, useful-looking gelding: fair handicapper: won at Ayr in July: left P. Monteith, ran poorly last 4 starts: effective at 1m/1¼m: acts on firm and good to soft ground: visored 4 of last 5 starts: often races up with pace: none too consistent. *T. J. Pitt*

JORDAN'S LIGHT (USA) 3 gr. or ro.g. Aljabr (USA) 125 – Western Friend (USA) **81** (Gone West (USA)) [2006 66: 8g* 7.2v⁶ 8m⁶ 8.5m p7g⁴ f8g²* p8.6g² p10g* p8g f8g⁴ Dec 27] tall gelding: fairly useful handicapper: won at Musselburgh in May, and South-well and Kempton in November: stays 1¼m: acts on all-weather and good to firm going: visored last 6 starts: suspended for 40 days after jockey failed to obtain best possible position third start. *T. J. Pitt*

JORDANS SPARK 5 ch.g. Opening Verse (USA) 126 – Ribot's Pearl (Indian Ridge **62** 123) [2006 57: 8v 8d⁶ 8.3m 8.3m⁵ 8m* 9.1m* 10.1s² 10s³ 11.1d 9.1v Oct 28] workman-like gelding: modest handicapper: won at Ayr in July and August: stays 1¼m: acts on firm and soft going: has worn headgear. *P. Monteith*

JORD (IRE) 2 b.f. (Feb 28) Trans Island 119 – Arcevia (IRE) 85 (Archway (IRE) 115) **75** [2006 5g⁴ 5f² 6m p7.1m² 7s f6g* 7.1g⁵ p6g⁴ f7g² Dec 19] 5,500Y: leggy, plain filly: fourth foal: half-sister to 5-y-o Chickado: dam 11f winner: fair performer: claimed from M. Channon debut, then from C. Dwyer next race, and left J. Osborne after third start:

won nursery at Southwell in November: good second in similar event there final outing: stays 7f: best efforts on all-weather. *A. J. McCabe*

JOSARTY 3 b.c. Josr Algarhoud (IRE) 118 – Search Party 78 (Rainbow Quest (USA) **58** 134) [2006 6d⁵ 6m³ 6d 6f 6m⁶ 6.9m⁵ 6g 6m⁵ f8g Nov 2] leggy colt: modest maiden: stays 7f: acts on good to firm and good to soft ground. *J. J. Quinn*

JOSE BOVE 4 ch.g. So Factual (USA) 120 – Dark Sirona 55 (Pitskelly 122) [2006 **–** p12.2g p7g⁶ p8g 8.3g p9.5g Nov 10] no sign of ability. *R. Dickin*

JOSEPH HENRY 4 b.g. Mujadil (USA) 119 – Iris May 87 (Brief Truce (USA) 126) **95** [2006 100: 6m 7g 6m 8.5g⁵ 8g⁴ 8m* 8m⁵ 9m⁴ 8g⁶ Oct 13] well-made gelding: useful handicapper: won at Ayr in July: good fifth at Goodwood next start: stays 1m: acts on firm and soft going: ran poorly in blinkers final 3-y-o outing: has run well when sweating: sold 45,000 gns. *M. Johnston*

JOSEPHINE MALINES 2 b.f. (May 3) Inchinor 119 – Alrisha (IRE) 90 (Persian **–** Bold 123) [2006 7d Oct 28] rather leggy filly: first foal: dam winner around 1¾m: 25/1, prominent to halfway only in maiden at Newmarket. *C. G. Cox*

JOSEPH LOCKE (IRE) 2 b.c. (Mar 13) Indian Rocket 115 – Faypool (IRE) (Fayruz **65** 116) [2006 5v⁴ 5d² 5m³ f5g 5g⁶ 5g⁵ 5g* 6d 5.1d⁴ Nov 1] €18,000Y: leggy colt: half-brother to several winners, including 2001 2-y-o 7f winner Mr Blue Sky (by Blues Traveller) and 2004 2-y-o 5f winner Dane's Castle (by Danetime): dam, maiden in Switzerland, half-sister to smart sprinter Croft Pool: fair performer: didn't need to match best (placed in maidens) to win seller at Musselburgh in August: should stay 6f: raced mostly on good or softer ground: in cheekpieces last 4 starts: tends to hang left: sold 5,000 gns. *M. Dods*

JOSH 4 b.g. Josr Algarhoud (IRE) 118 – Charlie Girl 70 (Puissance 110) [2006 102: **95** p6g⁶ 8s 7g 6s 6g⁶ 6s 7.6g⁴ 7f p7.1g Dec 6] tall, quite good-topped gelding: has a quick, unimpressive action: useful handicapper: won twice so good as at 2/3 yrs in 2006, easily best efforts first and third starts: stays easy 1m: acts on polytrack, soft and good to firm going: tried in cheekpieces. *K. A. Ryan*

JOSHUA'S GOLD (IRE) 5 b.g. Sesaro (USA) 81 – Lady of The Night (IRE) 54 **76** (Night Shift (USA)) [2006 69: p7.1g⁵ 8.1g⁵ 7.1m² 7d 7.1g³ p7.1g³ p7.1g* 7m⁴ 7.1f² 8m² 8.1m² p8.6g⁴ 8.3f p8.6m⁶ Oct 14] sturdy, close-coupled gelding: fair handicapper: won at Wolverhampton in June: effective at 7f to easy 8.6f: acts on polytrack, firm and good to soft going: usually visored. *D. Carroll*

JOSH YOU ARE 3 b.g. Josr Algarhoud (IRE) 118 – Cibenze 74 (Owington 123) [2006 **56** –: 10d⁵ 11.5d³ f8g f14g p11g* Dec 12] tall gelding: modest performer: left M. Wallace after second outing: won maiden claimer at Kempton in December: stays 11.5f: acts on polytrack and good to soft going. *D. E. Cantillon*

JOSIE MARCUS (USA) 3 ch.f. Gone West (USA) – Sheila's Revenge (USA) (Lord **83** Avie (USA)) [2006 7m 7f* 7m⁶ p8g 7g 8.5g Dec 20] well-made filly: fifth foal: sister to winner in USA and closely related/half-sister to 2 other winners there: dam US 6f to 9f winner: fairly useful performer: best effort when winning maiden at York in July: left J. Noseda before final outing: should stay 1m: acts on firm going. *R. B. Spatz, USA*

JOSR'S BANK 2 b.f. (Apr 25) Josr Algarhoud (IRE) 118 – Piggy Bank 71 (Emarati **–** (USA) 74) [2006 f5g 5g 6s Aug 28] deep-girthed filly: third foal: dam 5f (at 2 yrs)/6f winner: no form. *M. W. Easterby*

JOSR'S MAGIC (IRE) 2 b.g. (Jan 21) Josr Algarhoud (IRE) 118 – Just The Trick **75** (USA) 48 (Phone Trick (USA)) [2006 5d³ 5m³ 5g⁴ 5f⁵ 7m² 5m* 6d⁵ 6m 6d Oct 2] €15,000Y: strong, compact gelding: type to carry condition: good mover: first foal: dam 5f seller winner: fair performer: won maiden at Carlisle in August: below form in nurseries afterwards: effective at 5f to 7f: acts on good to firm going: blinkered/visored second half of season. *Mrs A. Duffield*

JOST VAN DYKE 2 b.g. (Mar 28) Foxhound (USA) 103 – Interregnum (Interrex **66 d** (CAN)) [2006 5.5d 6m⁵ 6f* 6.1m³ 5g³ 5.1f 6d² p7.1m⁴ f6g f6g⁵ p6g⁴ p6g⁴ Dec 16] close-coupled gelding: third foal: dam, of no account, half-sister to useful miler Lilli Claire: fair performer: won seller at Yarmouth in July: below form last 5 starts, claimed from B. R. Millman eighth: probably stays 7f: acts on polytrack, firm and good to soft going: in cheekpieces (below form) once. *J. R. Boyle*

JOUSTING 2 b.g. (Jan 26) Josr Algarhoud (IRE) 118 – Sweet Wilhelmina 87 (Indian **–** Ridge 123) [2006 p7.1g⁶ Dec 28] well held in maiden at Wolverhampton. *V. Smith*

JOY AND PAIN 5 b.g. Pursuit of Love 124 – Ice Chocolate (USA) 77 (Icecapade **75**
(USA)) [2006 66, a76: p7g⁶ p6g⁴ p7g p7g⁴ p6g² p7g⁵ p7.1g 6.1m* 7g* 7f* 6m⁴ 7f 6.1d
6.1d³ 6.1s p7g Nov 8] good-bodied gelding: fair handicapper: left J. Boyle after sixth
start: won at Nottingham (apprentices) in May, and Yarmouth and Lingfield in June: left
M. Attwater after twelfth outing: best at 6f/7f: acts on polytrack, firm and good to soft
ground: often wears headgear nowadays. *R. A. Harris*

JOYEAUX 4 b.f. Mark of Esteem (IRE) 137 – Divine Secret (Hernando (FR) 127) **75**
[2006 75: p6g* p6g⁶ p7.1g 7d 6d 7g p6g* p7.1g³ p7g⁵ p7.1f⁴ 6g⁵ 6d⁵ 5d² 6d⁴ 5d⁴ p6g³
p7.1g⁶ Dec 1] leggy filly: fair handicapper: won at Wolverhampton in January (final start
for S. Keightley) and June: stays 7f: acts on polytrack and soft ground: visored of late.
J. Hetherton

JOYFUL TEARS (IRE) 2 ch.f. (Jan 28) Barathea (IRE) 127 – Perils of Joy (IRE) 83 **75 p**
(Rainbow Quest (USA) 134) [2006 7g p7g⁵ 7d⁴ Oct 3] €75,000F, 150,000Y: good-topped
filly: seventh foal: sister to useful Irish/US 7f/1m winner Hymn of Love and half-sister to
3 winners: dam Irish 1m winner: progressive form in maidens, fourth to Hi Calypso at
Leicester (not knocked about): will stay 1m: should do better still. *E. A. L. Dunlop*

JOY IN THE GUILD (IRE) 3 b.f. Mull of Kintyre (USA) 114 – About Face (Midyan **60**
(USA) 124) [2006 –: p8.6g⁴ p8g⁵ 8m⁵ 10.9g* 12f* 12.1m⁴ 13.1m⁵ p12.2g Sep 11] modest
performer: won seller at Warwick and handicap at Folkestone, both in July: stays 1½m:
acts on firm ground: tried visored. *W. S. Kittow*

J R STEVENSON (USA) 10 ch.g. Lyphard (USA) 132 – While It Lasts (USA) 78 **–**
(Foolish Pleasure (USA)) [2006 60, a67: f12g p12.2g⁴ p12.2g p10g Feb 21] strong, close- **a53**
coupled gelding: has a quick action: modest performer: stays 1½m: acts on polytrack, soft
and good to firm going: tried visored (not since 2001)/in cheekpieces (in 2005): probably
best held up: sometimes finds little. *E. R. Oertel*

JUAN BOL (IRE) 2 b.g. (Feb 23) Fayruz 116 – Butterfly Morning (IRE) 49 (Distinctly **74**
North (USA) 115) [2006 5.2m⁵ 5p⁵* 6.1d⁶ p6g Jul 20] 2,000Y: first foal: dam Irish
maiden: fair performer: won maiden at Kempton in May, easily best effort: should stay
6f: acts on polytrack: sold 1,600 gns, sent to Sweden. *V. Smith*

JUBILEE DREAM 4 b.g. Bluebird (USA) 125 – Last Dream (IRE) 80 (Alzao (USA) **54**
117) [2006 70: p10g p16g 11.9m⁶ 7m 10m May 31] modest maiden: should stay 1½m:
acts on good to firm going: tried blinkered/tongue tied. *Mrs L. J. Mongan*

JUBILEE STREET (IRE) 7 b.g. Dr Devious (IRE) 127 – My Firebird (Rudimentary **91**
(USA) 118) [2006 85: 8g³ 8.1g* 7.2g⁴ 8f⁴ 8.5f³ 8f⁴ 8m⁴ 8m* 8g Sep 30] big gelding:
fairly useful handicapper: won at Haydock in April and Pontefract (hung markedly right)
in July: effective at 7f/1m: acts on firm and good to soft going: tried visored in 2003:
sometimes slowly away: consistent. *Mrs A. Duffield*

JUCEBABE 3 b.f. Zilzal (USA) 137 – Jucea 77 (Bluebird (USA) 125) [2006 65: 6.1d **68**
5.1g* 5m 5f⁵ 5.1g 5.1f² 5m³ 5d³ 5g³ 5.1m* 5m 5.5d Sep 16] fair performer: won claimer
at Bath in June and handicap there in August: raced only at 5f/6f: acts on firm and good to
soft going: has twice worn cheekpieces, including for latter win. *J. L. Spearing*

JUDD STREET 4 b.g. Compton Place 125 – Pudding Lane (IRE) 64 (College Chapel **104**
122) [2006 92: 6g* 5.1f² 5m³ 6m 6m 5g 6f⁶ 5.1m² p5g³ p5.1g² p6g Nov 11] sturdy,
close-coupled gelding: useful handicapper: won by ½ length from Tanforan at Windsor in
May: several at least creditable efforts after, notably when second to King Orchisios at
Wolverhampton penultimate start: winner at 6f, best at 5f: acts on polytrack and firm
going: tongue tied sixth outing: reliable. *R. F. Johnson Houghton*

JUDGE NEPTUNE 2 b.g. (Mar 28) Ocean of Wisdom (USA) 106 – Princess Louise **61**
86 (Efisio 120) [2006 7.2d⁴ 6s⁴ 7s Oct 10] good-bodied gelding: modest form in maidens,
all on going softer than good: will stay 1m. *J. S. Goldie*

JUDGE 'N JURY 2 ch.g. (Apr 23) Pivotal 124 – Cyclone Connie 98 (Dr Devious (IRE) **–**
127) [2006 6g p7g Oct 26] stocky gelding: well held in maidens: gelded after. *C. A. Cyzer*

JUDGE (USA) 3 b.c. Giant's Causeway (USA) 132 – Autumn Leaf (USA) (Gone West **92**
(USA)) [2006 94p: 9g Apr 20] big, strong colt: fairly useful performer, lightly raced: not
discredited when seventh to Atlantic Waves in listed Feilden Stakes at Newmarket only
outing in 2006: will stay 1¼m. *B. J. Meehan*

JUDRAAN 3 b.c. Alhaarth (IRE) 126 – Sakha 109 (Wolfhound (USA) 126) [2006 87: **–**
7.1m 8g Jun 28] rather leggy, attractive colt: good mover: fairly useful winner at 2 yrs:
tongue tied, below form in handicaps in 2006: sold 3,500 gns in July. *M. A. Jarvis*

JUICY FRUITS 3 b.f. King's Best (USA) 132 – Fruit Punch (IRE) 73 (Barathea (IRE) **67**
127) [2006 8.3d p10g⁵ 10m Jul 24] first foal: dam, French 1½m winner, out of half-sister
to Riverman: fair form in maidens: sold 3,000 gns in November. *E. A. L. Dunlop*

JULATTEN (IRE) 2 b.f. (Feb 24) Alhaarth (USA) 126 – Istibshar (USA) 78 (Mr Prospector (USA)) [2006 6m p6g f5g Jul 31] €27,000F, 16,000Y: sturdy filly: sister to fairly
useful 1¼m and 2m winner/high-class hurdler Iktitaf and 1m winner Uncle Bulgaria,
closely related to fairly useful 7f (in UAE) and 1½m winner Mostabshir (by Unfuwain)
and half-sister to 2 winners: dam 6f winner: no show in maidens over 5f/6f (will stay
much further). *G. A. Swinbank*

JULILLA 2 b.f. (Mar 1) Tobougg (IRE) 125 – Kiss Me Again (IRE) 80 (Cyrano de   **–**
Bergerac 120) [2006 5.2f⁵ 6g 7g Sep 27] 4,000F, 5,700Y: second foal: dam 6f (at 2 yrs) to
7f (in Germany) winner: well held in maidens. *G. G. Margarson*

JUMANJI (IRE) 3 b.f. Imperial Ballet (IRE) 110 – Toshair Flyer 88 (Ballad Rock 122) **48**
[2006 53: p9.5g p7.1g p8.6g⁵ 8m 7g p7.1m⁴ f7g p8g f6g p7.1g Dec 9] smallish filly: poor
maiden: stays 8.6f: acts on polytrack: visored/blinkered last 3 starts. *M. J. Attwater*

JUMBAJUKIBA 3 b.c. Barathea (IRE) 127 – Danseuse du Soir (IRE) 121 (Thatching **92**
131) [2006 92: 8s³ 8m⁶ 10m Jul 13] big, strong, angular colt: fairly useful handicapper,
lightly raced: creditable efforts first 2 starts in 2006, including sixth to Sir Gerard in
Britannia Stakes at Royal Ascot: ran as if amiss subsequent start: should be suited by
1¼m: acts on soft and good to firm going: sold 18,000 gns in October. *Mrs A. J. Perrett*

JUMEIRAH SCARER 5 b.g. Tagula (IRE) 116 – Mountain Harvest (FR) 64§ **66**
(Shirley Heights 130) [2006 67: 8f⁶ 12g² 16g⁵ 17.1d 14.1m 15.8d⁶ Oct 3] fair maiden
handicapper: barely stays 2m: acts on polytrack and firm going: sold 16,000 gns, joined
D. Marnane in Ireland. *K. A. Ryan*

JUMP SHIP 3 ch.f. Night Shift (USA) – Flagship 84 (Rainbow Quest (USA) 134) [2006 **74**
10g p12.2g* p13.9m Oct 9] well-made filly: fourth foal: half-sister to 4-y-o Cordage: dam,
1¼m winner, out of Oaks winner Bireme: fair performer: won maiden at Lingfield in
September by 1¾ lengths from Stumped: ran as if amiss in handicap at Wolverhampton
subsequent outing: should stay 1¾m: acts on polytrack. *M. P. Tregoning*

JUNCEA 2 b.f. (Feb 1) Elnadim (USA) 128 – Strelitzia (SAF) (Fort Wood (USA) 117) **76**
[2006 6g 6g p6g² p6g³ p6g* Oct 28] well-made filly: second foal: half-sister to 3-y-o
Orange Dancer: dam 1¼m winner in South Africa: fair performer: twice plagued prior to
winning maiden at Wolverhampton by 5 lengths, making all: raced at 6f. *H. Morrison*

JUNEBUG SYMPHONY (IRE) 4 b.f. Indian Lodge (IRE) 127 – Ladies View (IRE) **–**
64 (Turtle Island (IRE) 123) [2006 62, a–: p8.6g p7g Dec 18] maiden: well held in 2006:
tried in cheekpieces. *V. Smith*

JUN FAN (USA) 4 br.g. Artax (USA) 126 – Ringside Lady (NZ) (Clay Hero (AUS)) **63 §**
[2006 61: f6g p8.6g 5f³ 6m 5.5d⁶ 5g² 5m⁶ 5f³ 5m p5.1g Dec 31] big, good-bodied gelding: modest maiden: best at 5f: acts on polytrack and firm ground: tried in cheekpieces/
blinkers, tongue tied final outing: has looked quirky: inconsistent. *B. Ellison*

JUNIOR 3 ch.g. Singspiel (IRE) 133 – For More (FR) (Sanglamore (USA) 126) [2006 **85 +**
11.7m⁵ 11m³ p10g p12.2g* Oct 29] second foal: brother to 4-y-o Humble Opinion: dam,
French 9f to 12.5f winner, also successful over hurdles: fairly useful form: won handicap
at Wolverhampton (gambled on) in October: stays 12.2f: acts on polytrack: refused to
enter stall on intended debut. *B. J. Meehan*

JUNIPER GIRL (IRE) 3 b.f. Revoque (IRE) 122 – Shajara (FR) (Kendor (FR) 122) **103 +**
[2006 76p: 9.7s² 10d³ 12.1d² 12d* 12v² 12g² 11.9s² 16g* 18s* Oct 7] big, lengthy filly:
improved into a useful handicapper, winning at Pontefract in April, Nottingham in September and York (beat Tees Components 6 lengths) in October: stays 2¼m: acts on heavy
and good to firm going: hung right sixth outing: ridden by 7-lb claimer Luke Morris last 6
starts: reliable. *M. L. W. Bell*

JUNKANOO 10 ch.g. Generous (IRE) 139 – Lupescu 102 (Dixieland Band (USA)) **–**
[2006 63: 13.8s Oct 14] strong, good-topped gelding: lightly-raced handicapper: pulled
up only outing on Flat in 2006: won over hurdles in November. *K. G. Reveley*

JUPITERS MOON (IRE) 3 b.c. Galileo (IRE) 134 – Dance Treat (USA) 115 (Nure- **62**
yev (USA) 131) [2006 11.7m 12.1m⁶ p12g Sep 18] 80,000Y: sturdy, compact colt: fourth
foal: half-brother to 3 winners, including fairly useful 1¼m winner Jubilee Treat (by
Seeking The Gold): dam, won La Coupe (1¼m) and Prix de Flore (10.5f), out of half-

sister to Derby winner Golden Fleece: form in maidens only when sixth to Island Myth at Chepstow: should stay 1¾m: sold 5,500 gns. *R. Charlton*

JUROR (USA) 3 gr.c. Royal Academy (USA) 130 – Paper Princess (USA) (Flying Paster (USA)) [2006 90p: p7.1g* p8g⁵ Oct 15] fairly useful performer, lightly raced: won maiden at Wolverhampton in April by ¾ length from Captain Xaar: off 5½ months, best effort when 1½ lengths fifth to Zato in handicap at Lingfield final start, despite meeting trouble: stays 1m: raced only on polytrack and good to firm ground: sold 55,000 gns, joined I. Mohammed in UAE: open to further improvement. *Sir Michael Stoute*   **94 p**

JUST A FLASH (IRE) 2 b.g. (Apr 18) Redback 116 – Just Deserts 66 (Alhijaz 122) [2006 p6g Oct 17] well held in maiden at Lingfield. *B. R. Johnson*   **–**

JUST A FLUKE (IRE) 5 b.g. Darshaan 133 – Star Profile (IRE) 100 (Sadler's Wells (USA) 132) [2006 65§: p10g p10g May 3] strong, lengthy gelding: fair performer at best: well held in 2006: tried visored: usually tongue tied: has hung markedly: ungenuine. *M. R. Bosley*   **– §**

JUSTALORD 8 b.g. King's Signet (USA) 110 – Just Lady 72 (Emarati (USA) 74) [2006 89: 5s Oct 14] lengthy gelding: fairly useful handicapper in 2005: ended that season out of form, and well held only outing in 2006: wears cheekpieces/blinkers: races up with pace/carries head high. *A. Crook*   **–**

JUST BEWARE 4 b.f. Makbul 104 – Bewails (IRE) 53 (Caerleon (USA) 132) [2006 56d: 13.1s⁵ 16.4f Jul 13] maiden: on the downgrade: wore cheekpieces last 5 outings. *Miss Z. C. Davison*   **–**

JUST BOND (IRE) 4 b.g. Namid 128 – Give Warning (IRE) (Warning 136) [2006 62: p7.1g⁵ 7.5f⁴ 8d p7.1m³ p8.6g³ p8.6g³ p9.5g* p9.5g* p9.5g² Dec 28] sturdy gelding: fairly useful performer: left B. Smart after third outing: won handicaps at Wolverhampton in November and December: good second in similar event there final start: stays easy 9.5f: acts on polytrack, firm and good to soft ground: free-going sort. *G. R. Oldroyd*   **88**

JUST BONNIE 4 b.c. Lujain (USA) 119 – Fairy Flight (IRE) 86 (Fairy King (USA)) [2006 41: 5.1s 7g 6m Jun 21] little form: tried in cheekpieces/blinkers: has carried head high. *J. M. Bradley*   **–**

JUSTCALLMEHANDSOME 4 ch.g. Handsome Ridge 121 – Pearl Dawn (IRE) 91 (Jareer (USA) 115) [2006 –: f8g⁴ f8g f7g* f7g² f7g f7g p10g* p10g 10.2g 10m³ p8g 8.1m³ f11g² p10g p9.5g⁵ Nov 20] modest performer: won maiden claimer at Southwell in January and banded race at Kempton in April: stays 1¼m: acts on all-weather and good to firm ground: effective visored or not: sometimes makes running. *D. J. S. ffrench Davis*   **58**

JUST CHRISSIE 2 b.f. (Apr 6) Classic Cliche (IRE) 128 – Marsh Marigold 65 (Tina's Pet 121) [2006 5g⁶ Apr 29] first foal: dam, 6f (at 2 yrs) and 1¼m winner, also successful over hurdles: last in maiden at Haydock. *G. Fierro*   **–**

JUST DASHING 7 b.g. Arrasas (USA) 100 – Smitten 72 (Run The Gantlet (USA)) [2006 –: f12g Jan 31] compact gelding: of little account. *J. E. Long*   **–**

JUST DEVINE (IRE) 3 b.f. Montjeu (IRE) 137 – Shirley Blue (IRE) (Shirley Heights 130) [2006 10g³ 10g⁶ 10d 8.1f 8.3g Aug 21] 21,000Y: close-coupled filly: unfurnished at present: fifth foal: half-sister to 6-y-o Crathorne: dam, ran 3 times in France, half-sister to dam of Poule d'Essai des Pouliches winner Torrestrella: regressive maiden: bred to be suited by 1½m: withdrawn after injuring rider in paddock prior to intended debut at 2 yrs: reportedly bled third outing: raced freely second/third starts. *B. Palling*   **69 d**

JUST DOWN THE ROAD (IRE) 3 b.f. Night Shift (USA) – Avigail (USA) (Miswaki (USA) 124) [2006 71: p6g p5g p6g 6.1d 6.1s⁴ 6f* 6f⁶ 5f 6g* 6m 5.1f Jul 27] leggy filly: fair handicapper: won at Lingfield and Salisbury (hung left) in June: stays 7f: acts on firm ground: races up with pace. *R. A. Harris*   **69**

JUST DUST 2 b.g. (Mar 15) Makbul 104 – Dusty Bankes 59 (Greensmith 121) [2006 5.1d 5d 5m* 6.1m⁴ 6f* 7m* 7f* 7m² 7m³ 6s 6m² 7f* 6g Oct 13] smallish, workmanlike gelding: first foal: dam 2-y-o 5f/6f winner: fairly useful performer: won seller at Catterick in April, claimers at Brighton and Newcastle (left W. Turner £10,000) in July and nurseries at Goodwood in August and Ascot (beat Artimino by head) in September: effective at 6f/7f: acts on firm and good to soft going: effective with or without cheekpieces: races prominently: tough. *D. R. C. Elsworth*   **87**

JUSTENJOY YOURSELF 4 b.f. Tipsy Creek (USA) 115 – Habibi 50 (Alhijaz 122) [2006 49: p6g p6g³ p5g May 8] poor performer: effective at 5f/6f: acts on polytrack, firm and soft ground. *R. W. Price*   **44**

JUST FLY 6 b.g. Efisio 120 – Chrysalis 66 (Soviet Star (USA) 128) [2006 81, a85: p10g⁶ p10g⁵ p9.5g² p10g⁴ p12g p8g p8.6g p10g⁵ p8.6m p10g⁵ p9.5g⁶ Dec 11] sturdy gelding: just fair handicapper in 2006: stays easy 1¼m: acts on all-weather and good to firm going: often visored of late. *Dr J. R. J. Naylor*   **– a79**

JUST INTERSKY (USA) 3 gr.c. Distant View (USA) 126 – Hexane (FR) 108 (Kendor (FR) 122) [2006 75p: 8g³ 8g 7.1s⁶ p9.5m f8g Dec 27] fairly useful handicapper: below form after reappearance, leaving G. A. Swinbank following second start: stays 1m: best effort on good going: sometimes races freely. *K. A. Ryan*   **86 d**

JUST JAMES 7 b.g. Spectrum (IRE) 126 – Fairy Flight (IRE) 86 (Fairy King (USA)) [2006 108§: 5s 6m 6m 7m 6g⁴ 6m 7m 6g² p7.1g Sep 30] strong, compact gelding: useful performer nowadays, best effort in 2006 when fourth to Somnus in minor event at Haydock: beaten in claimers last 2 starts: effective at 6f/7f: acts on firm and soft going: has worn bandages: temperamental (virtually refused to race second outing). *D. Nicholls*   **97 §**

JUST JASMIN 3 b.f. Wizard King 122 – Rose Hill 73 (Sabrehill (USA) 120) [2006 7.1m 11.7m f8g Oct 12] leggy filly: first foal: dam 2-y-o 7f winner: no sign of ability. *P. D. Evans*   **–**

JUST JOEY 2 b.f. (Mar 22) Averti (IRE) 117 – Fly South (Polar Falcon (USA) 126) [2006 5g* 5g² 6m 5.1f⁵ 5m* 5d² Aug 31] 5,200Y: sturdy filly: fifth foal: closely related to 5-y-o Whitgift Rock: dam unraced: fairly useful performer: won maiden at Warwick in April and nursery at Haydock in August: good second to Danum Dancer in nursery at Beverley final start: best at 5f: acts on good to firm and good to soft going. *J. R. Weymes*   **87**

JUST LILLE (IRE) 3 b.f. Mull of Kintyre (USA) 114 – Tamasriya (IRE) (Doyoun 124) [2006 7f⁵ 8.5f⁴ 6f⁶ 7.2f* 8.1m* 8g³ 8d 8d Sep 14] €16,000Y: fifth foal: half-sister to 7-y-o Ulysees: dam French 9.5f winner: reportedly split a pastern in 2005: fairly useful performer: won handicaps at Ayr and Haydock (wandered) in July: should stay 9f: acts on firm going. *Mrs A. Duffield*   **82**

JUST LOGIC (IRE) 3 b. or br.c. Desert Prince (IRE) 130 – Tiavanita (USA) (J O Tobin (USA) 130) [2006 p8g² p8g² p8.6g⁴ 8.3g p8g³ Sep 27] €70,000Y: brother to fairly useful 2003 2-y-o 7f winner Park Accord and half-brother to several winners, notably 2000 Guineas winner Island Sands (by Turtle Island), 6f winner at 2 yrs: dam French maiden half-sister to very smart middle-distance performer Corrupt: fairly useful maiden: best efforts when close second at Lingfield first 2 starts, eased prematurely on second occasion: stays 1m: acts on polytrack: has made running: sold 16,000 gns. *J. Noseda*   **80**

JUST LOVELY 2 ch.f. (Mar 24) Inchinor 119 – Just Ice 90 (Polar Falcon (USA) 126) [2006 6g 6.1m Sep 15] lengthy filly: half-sister to useful sprinter Jezebel (by Owington), 5f/6f winner in Italy at 2 yrs, and German 9f to 1½m winner Franchetto (by Pursuit of Love): dam, 5f/6f winner, ran only at 2 yrs: well beaten in maidens: blinkered/tongue tied second start. *M. P. Tregoning*   **–**

JUST MATTY 3 b.g. Bertolini (USA) 125 – Frisson (Slip Anchor 136) [2006 8.1s May 29] 28/1, well beaten in maiden at Chepstow, slowly away and hanging left. *J. G. M. O'Shea*   **–**

JUST OBSERVING 3 ch.g. Observatory (USA) 131 – Just Speculation (IRE) 86 (Ahonoora 122) [2006 79: p8.6g² 9.7f* 9.8m⁵ p10g Jun 29] sturdy gelding: fair performer: landed odds in maiden at Folkestone in May easily: stays 9.8f: acts on polytrack, firm and good to soft going: visored (well beaten) final outing: has looked tricky ride: sold 23,000 gns, joined P. Haslam. *E. A. L. Dunlop*   **79**

JUST OSCAR (GER) 2 b.g. (Mar 25) Surako (GER) 114 – Jade Chequer 71 (Green Desert (USA) 127) [2006 6m 6m p6g³ 7m⁴ Aug 6] 6,500Y: fourth foal: brother to German 2003 2-y-o 7.5f winner Jurako and half-brother to German 2005 2-y-o 7f winner Jade Rheinberg (by Platini): dam, third at 5f (at 2 yrs) from 2 starts, out of half-sister to Ouija Board: fair maiden: creditable fourth to Gweebarra at Chester: stays 7f. *W. M. Brisbourne*   **65**

JUST TALLULAH 3 b.f. Tomba 119 – Tallulah Belle 92 (Crowning Honors (CAN)) [2006 –: p6g⁵ p5g 7m 6g⁶ p7g Jun 15] workmanlike filly: modest maiden: should stay 7f. *N. P. Littmoden*   **58**

JUST TILLY 3 b.f. Josr Algarhoud (IRE) 118 – Illana Bay (USA) (Manila (USA)) [2006 p8g⁵ p8g p8g 8.2d⁶ 10m⁶ p12.2g p8g⁴ p8.6g Dec 4] fourth foal: dam unraced: poor maiden: left P. Chamings after sixth outing. *L. Montague Hall*   **48**

JUST TWO NUMBERS 2 b.c. (Jan 21) Bahamian Bounty 116 – Khadino (Relkino 131) [2006 7d Sep 29] heavy-topped colt: 22/1 and burly, behind in maiden at Newmarket. *W. Jarvis*   **–**

JUST WAZ (USA) 4 ch.g. Woodman (USA) 126 – Just Tops (USA) (Topsider (USA)) **58**
[2006 67: 12v⁵ 9.9d 13.8g⁶ 12g⁶ 12g 16g⁶ 12.1g 16d³ 15.8m Sep 16] quite good-topped
gelding: modest handicapper: barely stays 2m: acts on soft going: tried in cheekpieces.
R. M. Whitaker

JUSTY (USA) 2 b. or br.c. (Apr 16) Danehill (USA) 126 – Saintly Speech (USA) 103 **79**
(Southern Halo (USA)) [2006 6m⁴ May 31] €620,000Y: third foal: brother to 3-y-o
Pure Illusion: dam won both starts (at 6f, ran only at 2 yrs), including Princess Margaret
Stakes: 9/2, fourth of 6 to Danebury Hill in minor event at Yarmouth: sent to USA.
M. L. W. Bell

JUVENESCENT (USA) 2 b.f. (Apr 15) Elusive Quality (USA) – June Moon (IRE) **57**
(Sadler's Wells (USA) 132) [2006 7f 6s⁵ 7.5m 6d p7.1g⁶ Dec 9] 30,000Y: tall filly: has a
markedly round action: closely related to several winners, including smart milers Dupont
and Pacino (both by Zafonic) and half-sister to several winners: dam unraced out of 1000
Guineas runner-up and smart sprinter Kerrera: modest maiden: may prove best at 5f/6f:
best effort on soft going. *R. D. E. Woodhouse*

JUWWI 12 ch.g. Mujtahid (USA) 118 – Nouvelle Star (AUS) (Luskin Star (AUS)) **41 §**
[2006 49§, a43§: f6g f5g p5.1g Jan 27] robust gelding: poor performer: best at 5f/6f: acts
on all-weather and any turf going: tried in cheekpieces: usually slowly away/gets behind:
unreliable. *J. M. Bradley*

JUZILLA (IRE) 2 b.f. (Feb 8) Marju (IRE) 127 – Mizillablack (IRE) 95 (Eagle Eyed **57 p**
(USA) 111) [2006 p7g Sep 18] €50,000Y: unfurnished filly: first foal: dam 2-y-o 5f
winner: 20/1 and backward, mid-field in maiden at Kempton: should progress.
W. R. Swinburn

K

KABEER 8 ch.g. Unfuwain (USA) 131 – Ta Rib (USA) 116 (Mr Prospector (USA)) **–**
[2006 73, a84: p8g p8.6g p8g² p7g 8g 8m 7g p8g p8g² f8g² p8g* p8g² Dec 30] big, **a89**
lengthy gelding: fairly useful handicapper on all-weather, no form on turf in 2006: left
Mrs L. Featherstone after third start, P. McEntee after seventh: won at Lingfield in December: barely stays 1¼m: acts on all-weather and firm going: tried in cheekpieces: tongue
tied: front runner. *A. J. McCabe*

KABIS AMIGOS 4 ch.g. Nashwan (USA) 135 – River Saint (USA) 73§ (Irish River **69**
(FR) 131) [2006 80: 7d 8m 8d 8m⁵ 7.1d 7m* 8m⁵ 7m² Aug 31] tall, leggy gelding: fair
handicapper: won at Catterick in August: likely to prove best up to 1m: acts on good to
firm and good to soft going: sometimes tongue tied: races prominently. *D. Nicholls*

KAFUU (IRE) 2 b.c. (Jan 22) Danehill Dancer (IRE) 117 – Nausicaa (USA) (Diesis **84 P**
133) [2006 6s* Oct 6] 115,000F, 220,000Y: tall, quite good-topped colt: has a quick
action: first foal: dam, French 2-y-o 7f/1m winner, later 1m winner in USA: 5/2, made
most impressive debut in maiden at York (beat Run Free by 2½ lengths), confidently
ridden and having plenty in hand: will stay 7f/1m: exciting prospect, sure to go on to
better things. *J. Noseda*

KAHARA 2 b.f. (Apr 6) Sadler's Wells (USA) 132 – Kithanga (IRE) 117 (Darshaan **70 p**
133) [2006 8.2m⁶ 8.2s³ Oct 18] lengthy, useful-looking filly: sixth foal: sister to high-
class 7f (at 2 yrs) to 1¾m (St Leger) winner Milan and 3-y-o Kibara, and half-sister to
smart performer up to 1¾m Go For Gold (by Machiavellian), 7f winner in Ireland at 2 yrs:
dam, won St Simon Stakes and third in Irish St Leger, out of half-sister to dam of Kahyasi:
promise in maidens at Nottingham, probably still green (ran in snatches) when third to
Metaphoric: will be well suited by 1½m+: should do better. *L. M. Cumani*

KAHLUA BEAR 4 b.g. Mister Baileys 123 – Crystal Magic 92 (Mazilier (USA) 107) **66**
[2006 49, a63: p6g⁵ p6g² 5m 6m⁴ 6f* 6g p6g p6m⁶ 6d Sep 25] quite good-topped gelding: **a59**
fair on turf, modest on all-weather: won maiden at Brighton in July: effective at 6f to 8.6f:
acts on polytrack and firm ground: wears headgear. *Miss K. B. Boutflower*

KAHLUA KISS 3 b.f. Mister Baileys 123 – Ring Queen (USA) (Fairy King (USA)) **103**
[2006 74: p7g⁶ 9.9m p10g³ 10m* 10m³ 10m* 10.4f* 9.9m³ 10g⁶ 10.4g³ 9.9m² p8g Oct
26] close-coupled, workmanlike filly: useful performer: won handicaps at Newbury (2)
and York in June/July, beating Mistress Twister by 5 lengths at York for last success: good
efforts when 1¾ lengths third to Rohaani in handicap on same course 3 outings later and

unlucky short-head second to Imperial Stride in listed race at Goodwood: stays 10.4f: acts on polytrack and firm going. *W. R. Muir*

KAI KURI (IRE) 5 br.m. Carroll House 132 – Lucy's Light (IRE) (Miner's Lamp 114)   –
[2006 p13g f12g Nov 20] second foal: dam unraced: fair form when placed in bumpers: well beaten in maidens on all-weather. *P. W. Hiatt*

KAILASHA (IRE) 2 br.f. (Mar 30) Kalanisi (IRE) 132 – Snow Peak (Arazi (USA)   **57 p**
135) [2006 7d Oct 28] 21,000F: tall, close-coupled filly: second foal: half-sister to 3-y-o Asset: dam, French 7.5f/1m winner, out of half-sister to William Hill Futurity winner Al Hareb: 25/1, green and not knocked about in mid-field in maiden at Newmarket won by Measured Tempo: will stay 1m/1¼m: will do better. *C. F. Wall*

KALAAM 4 b.g. Silver Patriarch (IRE) 125 – Phil's Folly 42 (Glasgow Central 91)   –
[2006 –: p12g Jan 3] tailed off in maidens. *G. P. Enright*

KALA DANCER 3 b.g. Kalanisi (IRE) 132 – Silly Mid-On (Midyan (USA) 124) [2006   **66**
9.9g[5] 11m[5] Sep 10] 5,000Y: fourth foal: dam once-raced half-sister to smart 1¼m to 2m winner Sarangani: fair form in maidens at Salisbury (green, not knocked about) and Goodwood (slowly away): will be suited by 1½m+. *Lady Herries*

KALADAR (IRE) 2 b.g. (Mar 22) Kalanisi (IRE) 132 – Desert Order (IRE) (Desert   **56**
King (IRE) 129) [2006 5m[5] 5d[2] p7.1g[4] 7.5g 8d 7m[5] p7.1g Sep 16] good-topped gelding: modest maiden: should stay 1m: acts on polytrack, good to firm and good to soft ground: tried in cheekpieces. *K. A. Ryan*

KALADIN 3 b.g. Kalanisi (IRE) 132 – Minstrel's Gift 92 (The Minstrel (CAN) 135)   **56**
[2006 59: 11.6g 11.9m Jun 15] workmanlike gelding: modest maiden: stayed 11.6f: acted on good to soft ground: dead. *G. L. Moore*

KALAFORTE (SAF) 4 b.f. Fort Wood (USA) 117 – Kal Sufi (SAF) (Al Mufti (USA)   **89**
112) [2006 8m[5] 8.9d a9f[4] 7.5g 9g 7d 10s Oct 10] lengthy filly: fairly useful performer: trained by H. Brown in South Africa at 3 yrs and for first 3 starts in 2006, winning maiden at Clairwood in 2005: best effort when fourth to Imperial Ice in listed UAE Oaks at Nad Al Sheba third outing: well held last 4 starts, leaving D. Lowther in France after fifth outing: stays 9f: acts on dirt: tried blinkered. *R. Simpson*

KALAMBARI (IRE) 7 b.g. Kahyasi 130 – Kalamba (IRE) (Green Dancer (USA) 132)   **§§**
[2006 12g[6] 11.9f Aug 15] leggy, useful-looking gelding: fairly useful performer: first Flat start since 2002 (fairly useful hurdler, refused to race 4 of last 6 outings), when sixth in handicap at Epsom in April: refused to race subsequent outing: stays 15f: acts on soft and good to firm going: often blinkered in 2002: held up: a thorough jade: banned from racing at Disciplinary Panel Enquiry in October. *S. Dow*

KALANDARA (IRE) 3 b.f. Rainbow Quest (USA) 134 – Kalamba (IRE) (Green   **72**
Dancer (USA) 132) [2006 p10g[6] 12g 10.3m[2] 11.7m[4] Sep 4] seventh foal: half-sister to several winners, including top-class 1¼m (Champion Stakes)/1½m (Breeders' Cup Turf) winner Kalanisi (by Doyoun) and very smart 1m/1¼m winner Kalaman (by Desert Prince): dam third at 9f (at 2 yrs) and 1¼m in France: fair maiden: bred to stay 1½m: acts on good to firm going: ran as if amiss second outing/tended to wander final start. *Sir Michael Stoute*

KALANI STAR (IRE) 6 b.g. Ashkalani (IRE) 128 – Bellissi (IRE) 77 (Bluebird   **48**
(USA) 125) [2006 64: f7s f8g 8.5d[6] 7g p8.6g[3] 8m[4] 10m[5] 7.5f 8f 7.5f 10f 10m[5] 8m Aug 9] rather leggy gelding: poor performer: stays 8.6f: acts on all-weather, firm and soft going: usually wears headgear/cheekpieces: often tongue tied: has looked a tricky ride/found little. *I. W. McInnes*

KALANKARI (IRE) 3 b. or br.c. Kalanisi (IRE) 132 – Stately Princess 70 (Robellino   **102**
(USA) 127) [2006 77: p8g* p8g[2] p8g* 8.1s[3] 8m 10m 7m[2] p8g[4] Sep 2] leggy, quite good-topped colt: useful performer: won maiden at Lingfield in March and handicap at Kempton (by 5 lengths) in May: good efforts when in frame after, in Silver Bowl (Handicap) at Haydock (third to Anna Pavlova), minor event at Goodwood (head second to Minority Report) and valuable handicap at Kempton (fourth to Killena Boy): effective at 7f/1m: acts on polytrack, firm and soft going: races prominently. *A. M. Balding*

KALANTERA (IRE) 3 b.g. Kalanisi (IRE) 132 – Tintera (IRE) (King's Theatre (IRE)   **67**
128) [2006 –: p8g[4] p10g 14m 13.8m[3] 16d Sep 26] workmanlike gelding: fair maiden: left A. Balding after fourth outing: stays 13.8f: acts on good to firm ground: tried visored/blinkered. *C. L. Popham*

KALASAM 2 ch.c. (May 30) Noverre (USA) 125 – Spring Sixpence 60 (Dowsing   **79**
(USA) 124) [2006 7d 7.1m[3] 8m[3] 6d Sep 29] 25,000Y: smallish colt: half-brother to 3

winners, including smart 5f/6f winner Torosay Spring and fairly useful 1m/1¼m winner Spring Jim (both by First Trump): dam 7f and 1½m winner: fair maiden: third at Warwick and Goodwood: stiff task in sales race final start: will stay 1¼m: acts on good to firm ground. *W. R. Muir*

KALATIME (IRE) 3 b. or br.f. Kalanisi (IRE) 132 – Dream Time 75 (Rainbow Quest (USA) 134) [2006 65: 10m p10g³ 10d⁶ 11.6d³ p10g⁴ 11.5m⁶ 9.9m³ p8.6g⁶ 10s² Oct 2] rangy filly: fair maiden: stays 11.6f: acts on polytrack, good to firm and good to soft going: joined M. Harris. *A. M. Balding* **74**

KALAWOUN (FR) 4 b.g. Highest Honor (FR) 124 – Kalajana (USA) 111 (Green Dancer (USA) 132) [2006 p13.9g Jun 2] fair form when winning handicap at Maisons-Laffitte final outing in 2005, then left A. de Royer Dupre in France: last in claimer at Wolverhampton on British Flat debut: stays 10.5f: probably acts on heavy going. *Ferdy Murphy* **–**

KALGOORLIE (USA) 2 br.c. (Feb 28) Gone West (USA) – Fair Kris (USA) (Kris S (USA)) [2006 6s⁵ 6m⁴ 7m* 7m Aug 12] tall, close-coupled colt: fifth foal: closely related to winner in USA by Crafty Prospector and half-brother to 2 winners there: dam 8.5f/9f US winner: useful performer: won maiden at Newmarket (odds on, beat Safe Investment by short head) in July: ran in pattern events either side, much better effort when 2¼ lengths fourth of 21 to Hellvelyn in Coventry Stakes at Royal Ascot: will stay 1m: raced on good to firm going after debut: sent to UAE. *J. Noseda* **99**

KALISHKA (IRE) 5 b.g. Fasliyev (USA) 120 – Andromaque (USA) 111 (Woodman (USA) 126) [2006 62: f8g f11g⁶ f11g Apr 4] leggy, angular gelding: modest maiden: stays 11f: acts on good to firm and good to soft going, probably on fibresand: tried blinkered: sometimes tongue tied. *R. Allan* **50**

KALLISTA'S PRIDE 6 b.m. Puissance 110 – Clan Scotia 47 (Clantime 101) [2006 77, a68+: p7.1g⁶ p5.1g⁶ p6g* p6g⁶ p7g p6g p7g⁶ p7g² p8g p6g p7g⁶ 5f⁵ 6d 6f⁴ 5.7m 5d⁴ 7g Aug 26] fair handicapper: won at Lingfield in January: stays easy 7f: acts on polytrack, firm and good to soft ground: tried visored: reared in stall and took no part once at 5 yrs. *J. R. Best* **70**

KALUANA COURT 10 b.m. Batshoof 122 – Fairfields Cone (Celtic Cone 116) [2006 63: 15s⁵ 15.8d 16.2g p16.5g⁵ 14.1g 14.1g p16g Aug 30] good-topped mare: modest handicapper: well below form after reappearance, leaving R. J. Price following second start: stays 17f: acts on good to firm and good to soft going: usually held up. *A. W. Carroll* **59 d**

KALUSH 5 b.g. Makbul 104 – The Lady Vanishes (Robin Des Pins (USA) 119) [2006 36: f8g f8g 8f 9.9s 15.8m 14.1d 12d f14g⁴ f16g⁶ f16g Dec 28] tall, leggy gelding: maiden: no form in 2006: left N. Tinkler after second start, J. Hetherton after fifth: pulled up final outing: tried tongue tied/visored/blinkered. *Miss A. Stokell* **–**

KAMANDA LAUGH 5 ch.g. Most Welcome 131 – Kamada (USA) (Blushing Groom (FR) 131) [2006 103: p7.1g² 8s 8m⁶ 7m 7g 10m³ 10.4d⁵ 9m 9d f8g⁶ Dec 2] strong gelding: useful performer: in-and-out form in 2006, running well when second to Border Music in minor event at Wolverhampton and third to Road To Love in handicap at Ascot: stays easy 1¼m: acts on polytrack, good to firm and good to soft going: races prominently: ran as if amiss second/fifth outings. *K. A. Ryan* **102**

KAMARI GOLD 3 b.g. Cloudings (IRE) 112 – Manse Key Gold 65 (Vaigly Great 127) [2006 –: p6g 10.5m 8.1s Sep 7] close-coupled gelding: little sign of ability. *M. Mullineaux* **–**

KAMARINSKAYA (USA) 3 b.f. Storm Cat (USA) – Mr P'S Princess (USA) (Mr Prospector (USA)) [2006 93: 7s* 8g 8v May 28] big, raw-boned filly: fifth foal: half-sister to 3 winners, notably very smart Irish 1999 2-y-o 5f/6f winner (including Phoenix Stakes and Prix Morny) Fasliyev (by Nureyev): dam unraced half-sister to very smart US Grade 1 9f winner Menifee, also runner-up in Kentucky Derby and Preakness Stakes: useful performer: won Dimitrova 1000 Guineas Trial Stakes at Leopardstown in April by 2 lengths from Beauty Bright, making running: well held after in Poule d'Essai des Pouliches at Longchamp and Irish 1000 Guineas at the Curragh: stays 7f: acts on soft going: veered left third 2-y-o outing: sold $2.2m in November. *A. P. O'Brien, Ireland* **105**

KAMES PARK (IRE) 4 b.g. Desert Sun 120 – Persian Sally (IRE) (Persian Bold 123) [2006 88: 10.5g 10.3m 10d⁶ 14m* 13.1g³ 16g f12g Dec 2] lengthy, good-bodied gelding: useful handicapper: won at Musselburgh in June by ¾ length from McEldowney: stays 1¾m: acts on soft and good to firm going: tried blinkered (looked wayward)/in cheekpieces: sweating/looked none too keen penultimate outing. *I. Semple* **96**

*totesport.com September Stakes, Kempton—a first pattern-race victory for Kandidate,
who partially obscures Crosspeace (star on cap) and Self Defense*

KANDIDATE 4 b.c. Kabool 119 – Valleyrose (IRE) (Royal Academy (USA) 130) **119**
[2006 115: 7.5m* 7.5m⁶ a7f 8g 8m p8g* p10g* 8s⁵ 8m⁶ 10m* 12f⁶ 10g³ p12g* 12d⁶
Sep 24] strong, good-topped colt: has a quick action: smart performer: impresses in
appearance: better than ever in 2006, winning handicap at Nad Al Sheba in January, listed
race at Lingfield (dead-heated with Vanderlin) in March, Coral Rosebery Handicap at
Kempton (top weight, beat Rohaani a length) in April, listed race at Sandown (by 2½
lengths from Windsor Knot) in July and totesport.com September Stakes at Kempton
(beat Crosspeace by 1¼ lengths): stays easy 1½m: acts on polytrack/dirt and firm going,
below form on softer than good: tried blinkered in 2005: tongue tied after third start.
C. E. Brittain

KANONKOP 2 b.f. (Feb 3) Observatory (USA) 131 – Camcorder (Nashwan (USA) **56**
135) [2006 7d p7g p8g Oct 20] compact filly: third foal: half-sister to 3-y-o Penryn and
minor winner in USA by Dehere: dam unraced half-sister to smart French/US 1m to 1¼m
winner Kirkwall: modest form in maidens. *Miss J. R. Gibney*

KANPAI (IRE) 4 br.g. Trans Island 119 – David's Star (Welsh Saint 126) [2006 59: **69**
17.2m³ 16m* Sep 10] angular gelding: fair performer: won NH jockeys handicap at
Goodwood in September: stays 17f: visored last 2 starts: has shown signs of temperament: useful hurdler, successful 7 times in 2006. *J. G. M. O'Shea*

KANSAS GOLD 3 b.g. Alhaarth (IRE) 126 – Star Tulip 99 (Night Shift (USA)) [2006 **73**
p6g 6m³ 6f² 6.1m² 6m* 6m⁶ 6m⁶ Aug 27] 32,000F: well-made gelding: fifth foal: half-
brother to several winners, including 5-y-o Choristar and 8-y-o Texas Gold: dam 6f
winner, including at 2 yrs: fair performer: won maiden at Salisbury in July: raced only at
6f: acts on firm going: slowly away on debut, has raced prominently otherwise: gelded
after final outing. *W. R. Muir*

KAPAROLO (USA) 7 ch.g. El Prado (IRE) 119 – Parliament House (USA) (General **–**
Assembly (USA)) [2006 14.1d f14g Jul 11] strong gelding: one-time fairly useful handicapper: lightly raced and no form after 2003. *John A. Harris*

KAPELLMEISTER (IRE) 3 b.g. Mozart (IRE) 131 – March Hare 60 (Groom **88**
Dancer (USA) 128) [2006 76p: p7.1g⁶ p7.1g 8.1m 9.9g⁶ 11.7g 11.6m* 11.8f* 11.6f²
Jul 31] sturdy gelding: fairly useful performer: won seller at Windsor (left C. Egerton)
and 4-runner handicap at Leicester in July: stays 1½m: acts on polytrack and firm ground:
wore cheekpieces last 6 starts: sometimes looks no easy ride. *M. S. Saunders*

KAPIOLANI (USA) 3 ch.f. Mr Greeley (USA) 122 – Iolani 59 (Alzao (USA) 117) **–**
[2006 8m p8g 10m May 13] $20,000Y: sturdy filly: half-sister to 1¼m winner Tannoor

(by Miswaki) and 2 winners in USA by Fly Till Dawn: dam, maiden, stayed 11f: well held in maidens: slowly away first 2 outings. *J. M. P. Eustace*

KAPTAIN KATE 2 ch.f. (Mar 14) First Trump 118 – Done And Dusted (IRE) 75 (Up – §
And At 'em 109) [2006 5d 6g 5.1d⁶ 6f⁵ Jul 4] second foal: dam 6f/7f winner (latter including at 2 yrs): no form, and looks wayward (jinked/unseated debut). *R. Brotherton*

KARASHINO (IRE) 4 ch.f. Shinko Forest (IRE) – Karisal (IRE) 80 (Persian Bold –
123) [2006 66, a–: p6g⁴ p7.1g⁶ f6g 8d May 16] tall filly: only modest performer in 2006: **a60**
left R. Fahey after second outing: best efforts at 6f: acts on polytrack and soft going: in cheekpieces/blinkers of late. *Mrs L. Williamson*

KARATHAENA (IRE) 6 b.m. Barathea (IRE) 127 – Dabtara (IRE) 88 (Kahyasi 130) –
[2006 55: 12v⁶ Oct 31] good-bodied mare: maiden: well held only outing in 2006: tried visored: possibly none too genuine. *M. E. Sowersby*

KARAYEL (IRE) 2 b.c. (Feb 1) Fasliyev (USA) 120 – Madamaa (IRE) 88 (Alzao **94**
(USA) 117) [2006 5.1d² 5f* 5m³ p6g* 6g² 7d Sep 19] €22,000Y: compact colt: second foal: half-brother to 3-y-o Methusaleh: dam, Irish 1¼m winner, out of half-sister to very smart miler Alflora: fairly useful performer: won maiden at Folkestone in May and minor event at Kempton in June: more improvement final start (after 3-month break) when seventh of 28 to Miss Beatrix in very valuable sales race at the Curragh: stays 7f: acts on polytrack, firm and good to soft going. *R. Hannon*

KAREEB (FR) 9 b.g. Green Desert (USA) 127 – Braari (USA) 97 (Gulch (USA)) **61**
[2006 79: 8d p8g 7f 7m⁶ 8m 7g⁵ 7m p8g³ p8g⁴ p8.6g⁴ p8.6g Dec 27] smallish, robust gelding: just modest handicapper in 2006: left W. Musson 4,000 gns after seventh start: stays 8.6f: acts on polytrack, firm and soft going: tried blinkered, in cheekpieces 3 of last 4 starts: held up, and reportedly needs tender handling to produce best nowadays. *Miss J. Feilden*

Mr A. J. Richards' "Kandidate"

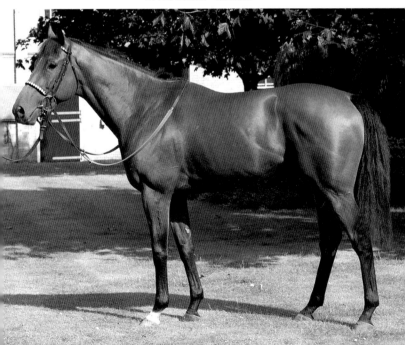

KARIJINI (IRE) 3 b.f. Anabaa (USA) 130 – Legaya 94 (Shirley Heights 130) [2006 –
p8g⁶ Mar 23] third live foal: half-sister to 4-y-o Inch Lodge and smart 7f (at 2 yrs) to 11f
winner Legal Approach (by Zafonic): dam Irish 1½m winner out of Oaks winner Jet Ski
Lady: well held in maiden at Lingfield: sold 4,000 gns in July. *E. A. L. Dunlop*

KARLANI (IRE) 3 br.g. Fantastic Light (USA) 134 – Karliyka (IRE) (Last Tycoon **81**
131) [2006 73p: 12d³ 12s 12g² 14g³ 11.9g Sep 22] lengthy gelding: fairly useful maiden
handicapper: good second to Bauer at Newbury third start: left Sir Michael Stoute 24,000
gns, ran poorly final outing: stays 1½m: acts on heavy ground: visored (below form)
second start: temperament under suspicion. *G. A. Swinbank*

KARLOVY 3 b.f. Halling (USA) 133 – Marienbad (FR) (Darshaan 133) [2006 10d **78**
11.8m² Jun 5] 170,000Y: strong filly: half-sister to several winners, notably high-
class 1½m (including Arc)/1¾m winner Marienbard (by Caerleon): dam, French 1m
winner (including at 2 yrs), out of half-sister to very smart winner up to 1m Sakuro Reiko:
better effort when 2 lengths second to Ivory Gala in maiden at Leicester: stays 11.8f.
M. A. Jarvis

KARLU (GER) 4 ch.g. Big Shuffle (USA) 122 – Krim (GER) (Lagunas) [2006 87: **80**
11.7d 11.5g 15m⁴ p16g 14g 11.9g³ Oct 13] lengthy gelding: fairly useful handicapper:
stays 1½m: acts on polytrack and soft ground: not straightforward: sold 28,000 gns.
Pat Eddery

KARMA LLAMA (IRE) 2 b.f. (Mar 3) Intikhab (USA) 135 – Ustka 60 (Lomond **70**
(USA) 128) [2006 7.1f³ 7.2d³ 7f³ 6d⁵ Aug 12] 12,000F, 21,000Y: sister to useful performer up to 1m Kunda, 6f winner at 2 yrs, and half-sister to several winners, including
smart 1¼m to 15f winner Travelmate (by Persian Bold) and 3-y-o King's Head: dam, 7f
winner, closely related to smart middle-distance stayer Braashee: fair maiden: inadequate
test in nursery final start: will be suited by 1m+. *B. Smart*

KARMEST 2 ch.f. (Feb 17) Best of The Bests (IRE) 122 – Karmafair (IRE) (Always **54**
Fair (USA) 121) [2006 8.1g⁶ Sep 23] strong, lengthy filly: first foal: dam, lightly-raced
maiden, out of half-sister to smart French 1¼m performer Karmiska: 33/1 and green
when sixth in maiden at Haydock. *E. S. McMahon*

KAROO BLUE (IRE) 2 b.c. (Apr 7) Cape Cross (IRE) 129 – Red Conquest 55 **83**
(Lycius (USA) 124) [2006 7.1m⁵ 6m³ 7.1m² 7f* 7s Oct 21] strong, useful-looking colt:
second foal: dam, maiden who probably stayed 1¼m, closely related to very smart 1m/
1¼m performer Crimplene: fairly useful form: won maiden at Redcar in September:
highly tried, seventh of 10 to Dijeerr in Horris Hill Stakes at Newbury: will stay 1m: acts
on firm and soft ground. *C. E. Brittain*

KARRRNAK 4 b.g. Hernando (FR) 127 – Maiden Aunt (IRE) 60§ (Distant Relative 128) **46**
[2006 –: p12.2g p16.5g p13g p10g⁴ p10g 11.6g⁵ 12.3m p12.2m⁵ 10.1m Sep 13] compact
gelding: poor maiden: probably stays 1½m: acts on polytrack and good to firm going:
tried blinkered/in cheekpieces/tongue tied. *Miss J. Feilden*

KARSHAAN (FR) 3 b.g. Kahyasi 130 – Mon Petitnamour (IRE) 38 (Darshaan 133) **72**
[2006 69: 11.6g 16g³ p16g⁵ 16d⁵ 15d Oct 13] neat gelding: fair maiden handicapper:
stays 2m: acts on good to soft going. *P. Winkworth*

KARTIKEYA (USA) 3 b. or br.f. War Chant (USA) 126 – Egoli (USA) 93 (Seeking **?**
The Gold (USA)) [2006 –p: 7m a8g² a8g a5g² a7g⁴ Dec 17] not knocked about in 2 maidens for J. Fanshawe: sold 3,000 gns after reappearance, second twice at Gran Canaria in
autumn: stays 1m. *J. Ojeda, Spain*

KASARAMI (IRE) 3 b.g. Bluebird (USA) 125 – Masakira (IRE) 58 (Royal Academy **–**
(USA) 130) [2006 –: 9m 8.3g 8.3m Jul 4] useful-looking gelding: little form: often slowly
away. *J. S. Goldie*

KASEEMA (USA) 2 b. or br.f. (Feb 25) Storm Cat (USA) – Onaga (USA) (Mr Pros- **88 p**
pector (USA)) [2006 6m* 7d Oct 14] $1,100,000Y: big, lengthy filly: closely related
to 7f winner Aragorn (by Giant's Causeway), subsequently high-class winner up to 9f
in USA, and half-sister to 2 winners abroad: dam, US maiden, sister to dam of very
smart performer up to 7f One Cool Cat: odds on, overcame greenness to win maiden at
Yarmouth in September: 12/1, another promising run when 9 lengths seventh of 14 to
Finsceal Beo in Rockfel Stakes at Newmarket, edgy in preliminaries and free in race
(held up): will stay 1m: should make a useful 3-y-o. *Sir Michael Stoute*

KASHMIR LADY (FR) 2 ch.f. (Apr 1) Rock of Gibraltar (IRE) 133 – Persian Walk **72**
(FR) (Persian Bold 123) [2006 7g⁶ 7d⁵ Oct 27] 42,000F: rangy filly: sixth foal: half-
sister to 5-y-o Prince of Thebes and UAE 11f winner/smart hurdler Royal Shakespeare
(by King's Theatre): dam, won both starts at 1½m in France, out of half-sister to Prix

Vermeille winner Walensee (dam of Westerner): fair form in maidens, fifth at Leicester and Newmarket, despite pulling hard: headstrong, possibly won't stay so far as breeding suggests. *H. Candy*

KASHTANKA (IRE) 4 ch.g. Ashkalani (IRE) 128 – Spark (IRE) 79 (Flash of Steel 120) [2006 –: f5g⁵ f5g⁶ f6g⁵ f6g f6g³ f7g⁴ 6g 5d 6f⁵ Aug 10] strong gelding: poor maiden: stays 7f: acts on fibresand, firm and good to soft ground: wears blinkers/cheekpieces. *J. Balding*   **44**

KASSIOPEIA (IRE) 3 b.f. Galileo (IRE) 134 – Brush Strokes (Cadeaux Genereux 131) [2006 79p: 11.9g* 11.5m⁵ 12g 16m 14f 14g⁴ p13g Oct 26] sturdy, close-coupled filly: useful performer: won maiden at Haydock in April: improved when 11 lengths seventh to Alexandrova in Oaks at Epsom third outing: below form after: should stay at least 1¾m: best effort on good going. *M. R. Channon*   **103**

KASSUTA 2 b.f. (Apr 19) Kyllachy 129 – Happy Omen (Warning 136) [2006 p6g p6g² Sep 29] 2,500Y: compact filly: third foal: dam, ran once, half-sister to Middle Park winner First Trump: fair form: better run in maidens (burly for debut) when second to Count Ceprano at Lingfield. *S. C. Williams*   **72**

KASTAN 2 ch.g. (Feb 16) Auction House (USA) 120 – Cashiki (IRE) 69 (Case Law 113) [2006 p6g Jun 26] 10/1, well held in maiden at Wolverhampton. *B. Palling*   **–**

KASTHARI (IRE) 7 gr.g. Vettori (IRE) 119 – Karliyka (IRE) (Last Tycoon 131) [2006 115: 15.9d 18d⁴ 16d Oct 14] tall, lengthy gelding: smart performer, lightly raced nowadays: creditable 4¾ lengths fourth to Sergeant Cecil in Doncaster Cup (dead-heated in 2004 and third in 2005) at York: last in Lonsdale Cup at York and Jockey Club Cup at Newmarket other starts in 2006: stays 2¼m: has won on soft going, best efforts on good/good to firm: has edged left: possibly temperamental nowadays. *J. Howard Johnson*   **112**

KASTORIA (IRE) 5 ch.m. Selkirk (USA) 129 – Kassana (IRE) 110 (Shernazar 131) [2006 116: 13m* 13.9s⁴ 14g* 12d* 14g* 12s 12m² Dec 10]   **124**

For the owner of a well-bred filly in training who has reached the age of four without making a single appearance on a racecourse, there must be a temptation to call it a day and pack her off to stud. That the Aga Khan resisted doing so with Kastoria, who apparently had shown plenty of ability at home, turned out to be a very rewarding decision. During the last two seasons Kastoria has won six races, notably the Irish St Leger, developing into a very smart performer, her progress all the more remarkable given the troubles she'd had as a three-year-old. Too big and backward to race at two, Kastoria developed a problem with an infected sinus at three, which led to a tooth becoming infected. Kastoria had to undergo surgery to remove the tooth and clear her sinuses, which meant drilling a hole in her head. The operation proved totally successful, though the hole, beneath her right eye, is still very much in evidence. Incidentally, the outstanding American performer Ghostzapper underwent a similar operation in 2005 and not long afterwards returned to run out an impressive winner at Belmont.

Kastoria, the winner of a maiden at Limerick and the Galtres Stakes at York in her first season, had three more successes to her name by the time she lined up for the Irish St Leger in September. They came in listed events at Navan and Leopardstown, and in the Group 3 At The Races Curragh Cup, Kastoria beating Collier Hill by a head at the Curragh on her third start. The Irish Field St Leger was run over the same course and distance as the Curragh Cup, and Kastoria faced seven rivals. For the first time there were no three-year-olds involved, and there wasn't much strength in depth among the older brigade. Yeats, impressive winner of the Gold Cup at Royal Ascot and the Goodwood Cup on his two previous starts, was at long odds on to give Aidan O'Brien victory in the only classic run in Britain and Ireland to have eluded him. Kastoria was second favourite at 6/1, half the odds of one of the four British-trained runners, Percussionist, who was next in the betting and the only other runner at shorter than 20/1. Percussionist made the running, but only until around six furlongs out where Yeats took it up, Kastoria still in close touch. Turning into the straight Yeats was under pressure with Kastoria travelling well just behind him, and the pair began to pull right away from the remainder shortly after, Kastoria also coming under pressure but finding plenty to wear down Yeats inside the final furlong and win by half a length. The Whistling Teal, a close second to Collier Hill twelve months earlier, took third place this time, but was ten lengths adrift. It was a third Irish St Leger victory for Kastoria's trainer John Oxx,

Irish Field St Leger, the Curragh—Kastoria (blaze) improves again and upsets the odds laid on Yeats

who won the race in the late-'eighties with the fillies Eurobird and Petite Ile. Yeats hadn't been quite at his best but it was still a cracking effort from Kastoria, making her first appearance in a Group 1 contest. Both of her subsequent races were at that level, and both took place abroad. Before the Irish St Leger, Kastoria had finished out of the first two just once, when a well-beaten fourth behind Percussionist in the Yorkshire Cup in May on the first occasion she raced on very soft ground. Her only other disappointing performance came on the second occasion she encountered soft, in the Canadian International at Woodbine in October, for which she started favourite, Kastoria managing only eighth behind Collier Hill. On good to firm going on her final outing, in the Hong Kong Vase at Sha Tin, Kastoria was unlucky not to turn the tables on Collier Hill, just failing to peg him back after suffering worst when the field bunched on the home turn, knocked back to last and still having only two behind her a furlong out. There was talk of Kastoria being kept in training for a little while in 2007—the Sheema Classic being the target—but the idea was shelved, and she is to visit Gone West.

Kastoria (IRE) (ch.m. 2001)	Selkirk (USA) (ch 1988)	Sharpen Up (ch 1969)	Atan
			Rocchetta
		Annie Edge (ch 1980)	Nebbiolo
			Friendly Court
	Kassana (IRE) (ch 1994)	Shernazar (b 1981)	Busted
			Sharmeen
		Kassiyda (b 1986)	Mill Reef
			Kadissya

Kastoria, who raced in a tongue tie, is the third foal of the Prix Minerve winner Kassana, who is out of a half-sister to the Aga Khan's dual Derby winner Kahyasi. Kassana is also responsible for the useful Irish nine-furlong winner Kassna (by Ashkalani), the fairly useful Irish mile-and-a-half winner Kassabat (by

H.H. Aga Khan's "Kastoria"

Entrepreneur) and Kasnani (by Indian Ridge), the last-named successful in a couple of two-mile events over hurdles in Ireland. Kastoria, a big, strong, good-bodied mare with a quick action, stayed a mile and three quarters well and acted on good to firm and good to soft going. She proved a thoroughly genuine and reliable sort. *J. Oxx, Ireland*

KASUMI 3 ch.f. Inchinor 119 – Raindrop 59 (Primo Dominie 121) [2006 p8g^2 f8g^4 p7g^4 **84** p7.1g 8.2g^3 8f 6.9m^2 7d^2 7g* 7.1m* 8s 7s p7g^3 p8g^3 Nov 5] second foal: dam ran 4 times (best effort at 7f): fairly useful handicapper: won at Salisbury (apprentices) in August and Sandown in September: good third at Lingfield final outing: stays 1m: acts on polytrack, good to firm and good to soft going: hung right seventh start. *H. Morrison*

KAT ACT TWO 2 gr. or br.f. (Feb 13) Act One 124 – Trempkate (USA) (Trempolino **65** (USA) 135) [2006 6m p7g^4 p6g Jun 28] 46,000F: fourth foal: half-sister to 3 winners, notably smart US Grade 2 1m/9f winner Katdogawn (by Bahhare), 5.7f winner in Britain at 2 yrs: dam, French 2-y-o 9f winner, half-sister to 5-y-o King Jock: fair maiden: best effort when fourth to Easy Lover at Kempton: will be suited by 1m. *J. A. Osborne*

KATCHIT (IRE) 3 b.g. Kalanisi (IRE) 132 – Miracle (Ezzoud (IRE) 126) [2006 74: **90** p8g^2 p9.5g^3 p8.6g^4 p10g^2 10m^4 p12g^2 10.2s^2 12.1s^5 9.9m^5 9.9g* p10g^2 p10g^6 Sep 2] leggy gelding: fairly useful handicapper: won at Salisbury in June (final start for M. Channon): good second at Kempton next time: stays easy 1½m: acts on polytrack, soft and good to firm ground: consistent: useful juvenile hurdler. *A. King*

KATEJACKIERA (IRE) 3 b.f. Rossini (USA) 118 – The Merry Widow (IRE) 44 **–** (Brief Truce (USA) 126) [2006 –: 11g 10.9g Jul 7] good-bodied filly: little form. *W. M. Brisbourne*

KATHLEEN KENNET 6 b.m. Turtle Island (IRE) 123 – Evaporate 51 (Insan (USA) **63**
119) [2006 10d 10g⁵ 9.9g 10.2m p10g p12.2g 8.2d² p8g² p8g³ p7g⁶ Dec 30] second foal:
half-sister to 8-y-o Charlie Kennet: dam 1½m winner: modest maiden: should stay 1½m:
acts on polytrack and good to soft going: signs of waywardness. *Mrs H. Sweeting*

KATHRYN JANEWAY (IRE) 4 b.f. In The Wings 128 – Freak Out (FR) (Bering **71**
136) [2006 69: 10.2d³ 11.7d³ 11.9m 10m⁴ Jun 10] good-topped filly: fair maiden handicapper: stays 11.7f: acts on good to firm and good to soft ground: very slowly away
penultimate outing. *W. R. Muir*

KATIE BOO (IRE) 4 br.f. Namid 128 – Misty Peak (IRE) 83 (Sri Pekan (USA) 117) **–**
[2006 73: 6g 6v p6g p6g Nov 18] lengthy filly: well held in 2006: withdrawn (lame at
start) intended second outing. *A. Berry*

KATIE KILLANE 4 ch.f. Komaite (USA) – Efficacy 62 (Efisio 120) [2006 39: f5g f5g **52**
f6g f6g f5g⁶ f5g⁴ p5.1g f5g³ p5.1g⁵ p5.1g² p5g³ p5g* p5g⁵ 5m p5.1g p5g⁴ Dec 6] modest
performer: won banded race at Kempton in May: best at 5f: acts on all-weather: tried in
cheekpieces, often visored. *M. Wellings*

KATIE KINGFISHER 2 b.f. (May 1) Fraam 114 – Sonic Sapphire 67 (Royal **48**
Academy (USA) 130) [2006 6g⁶ 6d p6g Dec 22] 6,500F, 11,500Y: fifth foal: half-sister to
2 winners, including 3-y-o Queen of Fire: dam, ran once, out of sister to Middle Park
winner/2000 Guineas runner-up Lycius: poor form in maidens. *R. M. Beckett*

KATIE LAWSON (IRE) 3 b.f. Xaar 132 – Idle Chat (USA) 93 (Assert 134) [2006 –: **70**
p9.5g⁶ p7.1g³ f8g* f7g f8g⁶ p7.1g* 8m Aug 25] fair handicapper: won at Southwell
(maiden event) in February and Wolverhampton in July: best form at 7f/1m: acts on
all-weather: visored. *D. Haydn Jones*

KATIES TUITOR 3 b.g. Kayf Tara 130 – Penny Gold (IRE) (Millfontaine 114) [2006 **77**
74: p10g⁵ 11.6m p12g 12g Sep 6] fair handicapper: ran as if amiss last 2 Flat starts over 4
months apart: twice successful over hurdles after: should stay 1½m: acts on polytrack.
B. W. Duke

KATIYPOUR (IRE) 9 ch.g. Be My Guest (USA) 126 – Katiyfa (Auction Ring (USA) **94**
123) [2006 97: p6g³ p6g⁵ p7g⁴ p7g⁵ p7g⁵ p7g⁶ p7g⁶ 7g⁶ 8.5g² 7m 8f² p7g² p6g³ 7d
Sep 23] quite attractive gelding: fairly useful performer: creditable efforts when in frame
in handicaps in 2006, leaving Miss B. Sanders after eleventh outing: finds 6f a minimum,
stays easy 1½m: acts on all-weather, firm and good to soft going: has been visored: sometimes races freely/carries head high. *P. Mitchell*

KATSUMOTO (IRE) 3 ch.g. Muhtarram (USA) 125 – Self Assured (IRE) 97 (Ahonoora 122) [2006 –: 10g 12.1g 12.1m⁶ 7.9g 8m Aug 10] big, workmanlike gelding: little
form: tried in cheekpieces. *N. P. Littmoden*

KATY CARR 2 b.f. (Mar 29) Machiavellian (USA) 123 – Khalafiya 104 (Darshaan **70**
133) [2006 p8.6g² p8.6g⁶ Nov 11] 26,000 2-y-o: half-sister to 3 winners, including high-
class 1¼m/1½m performer Predappio (by Polish Precedent), 7f winner at 2 yrs: dam Irish
1m and 1½m winner: encouraging second to Gull Wing in maiden at Wolverhampton:
odds on, possibly amiss there subsequent start. *M. J. Wallace*

KAVACHI (IRE) 3 b.g. Cadeaux Genereux 131 – Answered Prayer (Green Desert **74**
(USA) 127) [2006 73: 8d 10f³ 10.3g 11.6d 10f⁶ 8m* 9m⁵ 10g² 7g⁶ 8d 10d Nov 1]
workmanlike gelding: fair handicapper: left E. Dunlop 11,000 gns, won at Goodwood in
August: stays 1¼m: acts on firm and good to soft going. *G. L. Moore*

KAVERI (USA) 3 br.f. War Chant (USA) 126 – Valid Bonnet (USA) (Valid Appeal **88**
(USA)) [2006 84: p8g² 8m² 8m p7g* 8f³ 8f 8.2m⁶ 7d⁴ 7m 7m 6g⁵ 6d³ p6g Nov 1] leggy
filly: fairly useful handicapper: won at Lingfield in May: blinkered, ran creditably final
start: needs good test at 6f, and stays 1m: acts on polytrack and firm going. *C. E. Brittain*

KAVI (IRE) 6 ch.g. Perugino (USA) 84 – Premier Leap (IRE) 56 (Salmon Leap (USA) **65**
131) [2006 60, a79: p12.2g Feb 11] small, strong gelding: well held only outing in 2006:
tried blinkered. *Simon Earle*

KAYAH 2 b.f. (Feb 15) Kahyasi 130 – Kristina 92 (Kris 135) [2006 8.2g* Sep 26] neat **78 p**
filly: third foal: dam, 2-y-o 1m winner who stayed 1¾m, out of half-sister to smart French
sprinter Divine Danse and very smart sprinter/miler Pursuit of Love: 11/2, green but
readily won maiden at Nottingham, galloping on strongly to beat Wateera by 1½ lengths:
will be suited by 1¼m/1½m: should progress. *R. M. Beckett*

KAYF ARAMIS 4 b.g. Kayf Tara 130 – Ara (Birthright) [2006 56: 17.2s* 21.6d² 20s* **81**
18m⁵ p16g 17.1d⁵ 16.1d⁵ 16.2m² 16m² 16.2d² 18s⁵ 18s² 16d² Oct 27] plain gelding: fairly
useful handicapper: much improved in 2006, winning at Bath in April and York in May:

largely creditable efforts after: stays 21f: acts on soft and good to firm ground: in cheek-pieces of late: finished weakly eleventh outing. *J. L. Spearing*

KAY GEE BE (IRE) 2 b.c. (Feb 20) Fasliyev (USA) 120 – Pursuit of Truth (USA) 69 **80**
(Irish River (FR) 131) [2006 6v³ 6m² 7g* Aug 14] 20,000Y: quite good-topped colt: closely related/half-brother to several winners, including 1999 2-y-o 1m winner who stayed 10.5f First Truth and 6f (at 2 yrs) to 15f winner Spring Pursuit (both fairly useful, by Rudimentary): dam, 2-y-o 7f winner on only start, out of half-sister to Sun Princess and Saddlers' Hall: fairly useful form in maidens, placed at Ayr and Newmarket (second to Charlie Farnsbarns) prior to winning at Thirsk: will be suited by 1m: yet to race on firm going, acts on any other. *D. J. Daly*

KAYLIANNI 3 b.f. Kalanisi (IRE) 132 – Vivianna (Indian Ridge 123) [2006 84: 11.4m⁴ **101**
12g 10g* 12m 11g 10s⁵ 12s Oct 7] leggy, lengthy filly: useful performer: best effort when 13 lengths eighth to Alexandrova in Oaks at Epsom prior to winning maiden at Newbury in June: just respectable efforts at best after: reportedly finished lame when well held in listed race at Ascot final outing: stays 1½m: acts on good to firm going. *M. R. Channon*

KAYMICH PERFECTO 6 b.g. Sheikh Albadou 128 – Manhattan Diamond 54 **83**
(Primo Dominie 121) [2006 85, a63: 7g 8d⁴ 8g 8f* 8f* 8m 8m 8d⁴ 8g⁴ 8d Sep 14] close-coupled gelding: fairly useful handicapper: won at Redcar in June and Pontefract in July: effective at 1m/9f: acts on all-weather, firm and good to soft going: tried in blinkers/cheekpieces. *R. M. Whitaker*

KAY TWO (IRE) 4 ch.g. Monashee Mountain (USA) 115 – Tricky 66 (Song 132) **92**
[2006 105: a6f 6v 5d 6d⁶ 5m 5.1m⁶ 5m 5m 5g 5.1m 6m⁵ 5s* 5s* Oct 16] neat gelding: useful performer: left Ms F. Crowley in Ireland after fourth outing: won handicaps at York and Pontefract (by length from Rainbow Rising) in October: best at 5f/6f: probably acts on any going: blinkered (below form) final 3-y-o outing. *R. J. Price*

KEAGLES (ITY) 3 b.f. Indian Danehill (IRE) 124 – Athens Belle (IRE) 101 (Groom **–**
Dancer (USA) 128) [2006 p7.1m p9.5g Nov 24] €40,000Y: sister to 1½m winner League of Nations and half-sister to fairly useful 7f/1m winner Shalimar (by Indian Ridge): dam, 7f (at 2 yrs) and 1¼m winner, half-sister to very smart performer up to 1¾m Gamut: well held in maidens at Wolverhampton. *J. E. Long*

KEELINGS DONABATE 3 b.g. Desert Style (IRE) 121 – Sideloader Special 66 **70**
(Song 132) [2006 42: p6g⁴ p6g⁴ Mar 15] fair maiden: not sure to stay beyond 6f: raced only on polytrack. *K. R. Burke*

KEEL (IRE) 3 b.g. Carrowkeel (IRE) 106 – First Degree 50 (Sabrehill (USA) 120) **88**
[2006 72: p7.1g²* p7.1g⁴ p8.6g³ p10g⁴ p12g f8g⁴ 10f* 12g Sep 16] fairly useful performer, **a80**
better on turf than all-weather: won maiden at Wolverhampton in January and handicap at Nottingham in July: sold from J. Osborne 38,000 gns, well below form in similar event at the Curragh final outing: stays 1¼m: acts on all-weather, firm and good to soft ground. *Anthony Mullins, Ireland*

KEEP A WELCOME 3 ch.g. Most Welcome 131 – Celtic Chimes (Celtic Cone 116) **–**
[2006 8.2v p7.1m Nov 8] well beaten in maidens. *S. Parr*

KEEP BACCKINHIT (IRE) 4 b.f. Raise A Grand (IRE) 114 – Taispeain (IRE) 86 **67**
(Petorius 117) [2006 –: 7m² 8f² 7m³ 7f 8.5g⁶ 7f⁴ p8g 8m⁵ 7d⁴ Sep 25] fair performer: stays 1m: acts on firm and good to soft going: blinkered last 2 starts. *G. L. Moore*

KEEPERS KNIGHT (IRE) 5 b.g. Sri Pekan (USA) 117 – Keepers Dawn (IRE) 103 **–**
(Alzao (USA) 117) [2006 65, a61: p16.5g 15.8d 14g Aug 31] rangy gelding: well beaten in handicaps in 2006, gelded after second start: tried in blinkers/tongue tie/cheekpieces: no easy ride. *Karen McLintock*

KEEP YOUR DISTANCE 2 b.g. (Mar 9) Distant Music (USA) 126 – Queen G **67**
(USA) 57 (Matty G (USA) 119) [2006 6m⁵ 7f 7.1d² 8g⁴ 8s⁶ p9.5g⁵ p8.6g⁴ p8.6g² f7g³ p7.1g⁶ Dec 27] first foal: dam, 11f winner, out of half-sister to dam of top-class miler Observatory: fair maiden: in frame in nurseries in November/December (wore cheekpieces): best up to 8.6f: acts on all-weather and good to soft going: tried tongue tied. *K. R. Burke*

KEIDAS (FR) 2 b.f. (Mar 27) Lomitas 129 – Kahina (GER) (Warning 136) [2006 6g **74**
6.1m² p7g³ p8.6m⁶ Oct 31] 23,000F, 42,000Y: sturdy, close-coupled filly: third live foal: half-sister to fairly useful Irish 2003 2-y-o 6f/7f winner Kanisfluh (by Pivotal): dam German 6.5f/7f winner out of useful German sprinter: fair maiden: placed at Nottingham (looked unlucky) and Kempton: barely stays 8.6f. *C. F. Wall*

KEISHA KAYLEIGH (IRE) 3 b.f. Almutawakel 126 – Awtaar (USA) 67 (Lyphard **67**
(USA) 132) [2006 9v 9.8m⁶ 9.9g* 10d² 10.3g 8m⁴ 9.9f⁶ 10.1m² 8.5m⁵ 10f³ 11g² p9.5g²
p9.5g p12.2g⁴ Dec 27] €10,000Y: leggy filly: half-sister to several winners, including
fairly useful 1½m/1¾m winner Sharp Stepper (by Selkirk): dam, disappointing maiden,
out of half-sister to 1000 Guineas winner Fairy Footsteps and St Leger winner Light
Cavalry: fair performer: won seller at Beverley in May: stays easy 1½m: acts on polytrack, good to firm and good to soft going: in headgear last 6 starts. *B. Ellison*

KELLYS DOUBLE GOLD (IRE) 3 ch.f. Spinning World (USA) 130 – Delighting **–**
(USA) (Boundary (USA) 117) [2006 10.1g May 1] 1,000F, 2,700Y, 500 3-y-o: first foal:
dam third at 1m in France: well held in maiden at Newcastle. *Mrs H. O. Graham*

KELLYS DREAM (IRE) 3 br.f. Bertolini (USA) 125 – Fullfilling (IRE) (Red Ran- **65**
som (USA)) [2006 p5g⁵ p6g² p5g p6g 6f⁴ 5.1g⁶ p5.1g 6g Aug 16] €2,500F, €10,000Y:
third foal: half-sister to Irish 2004 2-y-o 7f winner John Ells (by Vettori), later 1m winner
in Hong Kong: dam unraced out of close relation to Oaks winner Intrepidity: fair maiden:
stays 6f: acts on polytrack and firm going: sold 2,500 gns. *M. Quinn*

KELTIC RAINBOW (IRE) 5 b.m. Spectrum (IRE) 126 – Secrets of Honour (Belmez **41**
(USA) 131) [2006 54: f14g f14g⁶ f14g⁵ p13.9g p12.2g Nov 24] leggy mare: just poor
performer in 2006: stays 1¾m: acts on all-weather and good to soft going: wears visor/
cheekpieces. *D. Haydn Jones*

KELUCIA (IRE) 5 ch.m. Grand Lodge (USA) 125 – Karachi (SPA) (Zino 127) [2006 **97**
92: p8g 8g² 8.1f⁴ 8g² 8f* 8g⁵ 8f 8d⁵ p8g Oct 15] lengthy mare: useful handicapper: won
at Newmarket in July by length from Bosset: at least respectable efforts when fifth at
Newbury and Ascot after: should stay 1¼m: acts on firm going: edgy sort, sometimes
early to post/slowly away/flashes tail: often held up. *R. M. Beckett*

KEMPSEY 4 ch.g. Wolfhound (USA) 126 – Mockingbird 64 (Sharpo 132) [2006 70: **81**
p6g⁶ p6g p5g³ p5g p5g³ p5g 5g 5g⁶ 5m⁶ 6g⁴ 5s⁴ 5g³ 6f 6f p5g⁶ p5g⁵ p6g Dec 22]
good-bodied gelding: fairly useful performer: best at 5f/6f: acts on polytrack, firm and
soft ground: wears headgear: often races prominently. *J. J. Bridger*

KENDOR DINE (FR) 4 gr.g. Kendor (FR) 122 – Michellisa 70 (Indian Ridge 123) **116**
[2006 110: 10v* 10g⁴ 8d² 9.3d 10g³ Jul 29] sixth foal: half-brother to French 1m/1¼m
winner Highest Ridge (by Highest Honor): dam, 7f winner, out of sister to Park Hill
Stakes winner Quay Line: smart performer: successful in 2005 in Prix La Force at Longchamp: improved in 2006, winning Prix Exbury at Saint-Cloud in March by 5 lengths
from Special Kaldoun: creditable efforts after when 2½ lengths second to Krataios in
Prix du Muguet at Saint-Cloud and (first start after leaving Y. de Nicolay in France) 2¾
lengths third to Heliostatic in Meld Stakes at Leopardstown: stays 1¼m: acts on heavy
and good to firm going: often front runner: won over hurdles in December. *E. Griffin,
Ireland*

KENMORE 4 b.g. Compton Place 125 – Watheeqah (USA) 60 (Topsider (USA)) [2006 **96**
103: 6m 6m 5m 6g⁵ 7m 5s² 6g 7d⁵ 7g Oct 13] strong, good sort: has a quick action: useful
handicapper: creditable neck second to Cape Royal at Haydock, best effort in 2006:
effective at 5f to 7f: acts on soft going: tends to sweat/get on edge. *D. Nicholls*

KENNINGTON 6 ch.g. Compton Place 125 – Mim 39 (Midyan (USA) 124) [2006 80: **78**
f6g⁴ p6g⁴ p6g p6g f5g⁵ 6d 5.1s³ 5.2g p6g 6.1m³ 5f f6g⁵ 5.1g⁵ 6m² 5.2m* 5m⁵ p6g⁴ p6g
6.1d 6.1d p5.1g Nov 11] small, sturdy gelding: just fair performer in 2006: won handicap
at Yarmouth in August: effective at 5f to easy 7f: acts on all-weather and any turf going:
tried visored, blinkered nowadays: races prominently. *Mrs C. A. Dunnett*

KEN'S GIRL 2 ch.f. (Apr 27) Ishiguru (USA) 114 – There's Two (IRE) 85 (Ashkalani **70**
(IRE) 128) [2006 5m 5.1m⁵ 5m² p6m⁶ Oct 2] second foal: half-sister to 3-y-o My
Reflection: dam, 6f winner (ran only at 2 yrs), out of half-sister to very smart 1¼m/1½m
performer Sudden Love: fair maiden: second to Blue Echo at Sandown: should stay 6f.
W. S. Kittow

KENSINGTON (IRE) 5 b.g. Cape Cross (IRE) 129 – March Star (IRE) 109 (Mac's **71**
Imp (USA) 116) [2006 68: p6g* p7.1g⁴ p7g p7.1g⁴ p7.1g⁴ p7g 6m 6g f7g² f7g Nov 28]
leggy gelding: fair performer: won handicap at Wolverhampton in January: effective at 5f
to easy 7f: acts on all-weather, firm and good to soft ground: usually blinkered/in cheekpieces. *P. D. Evans*

KENTAVR'S DREAM 3 b.f. Robellino (USA) 127 – Very Good (Noalto 120) [2006 **–**
–: p6g 8s 7f p8.6g Oct 8] small, leggy filly: little sign of ability. *P. Howling*

KENTUCKIAN 4 b.g. Kylian (USA) – Snowline (Bay Express 132) [2006 10d 14.1d **43**
10.2m 10.9f f12g 10g 10g 9.9g² 10g Sep 14] poor maiden: stays 1¼m. *P. W. Hiatt*

KENTUCKY BOY (IRE) 2 b.c. (Mar 20) Distant Music (USA) 126 – Delta Town (USA) (Sanglamore (USA) 126) [2006 7g 7s 7v Oct 31] little form in maidens: bred to stay 1m/1¼m. *Jedd O'Keeffe* –

KENTUCKY BULLET (USA) 10 b.g. Housebuster (USA) – Exactly So (Caro 133) [2006 –, a62: f11g⁵ p9.5g f11g f11g² f11g f11g⁴ f12m⁵ f12g* f11g³ Dec 28] leggy, angular gelding: modest on all-weather, little recent form on turf: won banded race at Southwell in December: stays 1½m: acts on all-weather, good to firm and good to soft ground: tried blinkered/in cheekpieces/tongue tied: none too trustworthy. *A. G. Newcombe* **a58**

KENTUCKY DYNAMITE (USA) 3 ch.c. Kingmambo (USA) 125 – Chelsey Flower (USA) 116 (His Majesty (USA)) [2006 10g* 11d⁵ 8m* 8d² 8g⁶ Sep 3] $250,000Y: fourth foal: half-brother to 7f (at 2 yrs) and 1m (in France) winner Indy Rose (by A P Indy) and a winner in USA by Storm Cat: dam US Grade 1 1¼m winner: smart performer: won minor events at Saint-Cloud at 2 yrs and on reappearance in April, and Prix Paul de Moussac at Chantilly (by head from Kendargent) in June: good ½-length second to Stormy River in Prix Jean Prat at Chantilly next time, leading briefly inside final 1f: below-form sixth to Librettist in Prix du Moulin de Longchamp final start: has won at 1¼m, best efforts at 1m: acts on good to firm and good to soft going. *A. de Royer Dupre, France* **118**

KENTUCKY WARBLER (IRE) 3 b.f. Spinning World (USA) 130 – Dollar Bird (IRE) 103 (Kris 135) [2006 9s⁴ 12.1m⁴ f11g³ p10g⁶ 12.1g* 14.1d p12.2g Oct 29] rangy filly: has scope: second foal: half-sister to useful 9.7f winner Higher Love (by Sadler's Wells): dam, 2-y-o 1m winner who stayed 1¾m, half-sister to smart French middle-distance stayer Legend Maker, herself dam of 1000 Guineas winner Virginia Waters: fair performer: won handicap at Hamilton in August: ran as if amiss next time and well beaten final start: stays 1½m: probably acts on soft ground: sold 64,000 gns. *H. Morrison* **77**

KEON (IRE) 4 b.g. Rossini (USA) 118 – Lonely Brook (USA) (El Gran Senor (USA) 136) [2006 66: 10m 8f p8.6m³ p8.6g³ f7g* p7g p8.6g* f7g p8.6g³ p8.6g⁵ p7.1g Dec 28] rather leggy gelding: just modest performer in 2006: won banded races at Southwell in October and Wolverhampton in November: stays 9f: acts on all-weather and soft ground, probably on good to firm. *R. Hollinshead* **63**

KERASHAN (IRE) 4 b.g. Sinndar (IRE) 134 – Kerataka (IRE) 103 (Doyoun 124) [2006 107: 12d 12f 14m 12d⁴ Aug 20] smallish, rather lightly-made gelding: useful handicapper: well held at Nad Al Sheba on reappearance (only outing for I. Mohammed): best effort in 2006 when tenth to Soulacroix at Goodwood third start: stays 1½m: acts on polytrack and good to soft going: tongue tied final outing: has worn crossed noseband: joined A. Al Raihe in UAE. *Saeed bin Suroor* **100**

KERESFORTH 4 b.g. Mind Games 121 – Bullion 85 (Sabrehill (USA) 120) [2006 –, a63d: f5g⁶ f5g⁵ 6m p5g 7m 6f 8f Jul 4] rather leggy gelding: just poor performer in 2006: usually wears headgear: untrustworthy. *Mrs L. C. Jewell* **37 §**

KERNEL DOWERY (USA) 6 b.g. Sri Pekan (USA) 117 – Lady Dowery (USA) (Manila (USA)) [2006 60: 12.6g³ 11.9f⁶ p10g⁶ 10.1g 10.9m Sep 4] leggy, quite good-topped gelding: modest handicapper: stays 1½m: acts on polytrack, firm and good to soft going: often wears cheekpieces: usually races prominently: somewhat wayward. *W. R. Swinburn* **57**

KERRIEMUIR LASS (IRE) 3 b.f. Celtic Swing 138 – Shabby Chic (USA) 114 (Red Ransom (USA)) [2006 59P: 10d² 10.2m² 11.8m³ 10m² 11.5m² 11.7m* 10.5g² 12d Oct 27] strong, sturdy filly: fairly useful performer: won maiden at Bath in September: good short-head second to Dayrose in handicap at Haydock next time: stays 1½m: unraced on extremes of going: usually races prominently. *M. A. Jarvis* **91**

KERRY'S BLADE (IRE) 4 ch.g. Daggers Drawn (USA) 114 – Treasure (IRE) 72 (Treasure Kay 114) [2006 58, a–: f14g f14g⁵ Jan 31] tall, leggy gelding: maiden: well held in 2006: tried blinkered/in cheekpieces. *P. C. Haslam* –

KERRY'S DREAM 2 ch.f. (Apr 13) Tobougg (IRE) 125 – Jetbeeah (IRE) 95 (Lomond (USA) 128) [2006 5d* 5s⁴ 5g⁵ 5.1f³ 5g 6s 5d Sep 15] 21,000Y: big, lengthy, good-topped filly: half-sister to several winners, including 1997 2-y-o 6f winner Dazilyn Lady (by Zilzal) and 3-y-o Simondiun, both useful: dam 1m winner: fairly useful performer: won maiden at Ripon in April: gradual progress next 3 starts, third to Not For Me in minor event at Chester, but below form after: best at 5f: acts on firm and soft ground. *T. D. Easterby* **84**

KERSWELL 2 b.f. (Feb 7) Komaite (USA) – Polgwynne 48 (Forzando 122) [2006 p6g 6m⁴ p7g 6g 6.1g Sep 15] 2,500Y: good-bodied filly: sixth foal: dam 7f winner: modest maiden: may prove best at 5f/6f. *B. R. Millman* **64**

KESHYA 5 b.m. Mtoto 134 – Liberatrice (FR) (Assert 134) [2006 78§: p9.5g³ p9.5g **74 §**
p13.9g² 14.8m p12.2g⁶ p12.2g⁴ 15m p12.2g p12.2m⁵ Nov 8] leggy mare: fair performer:
stays 1¾m: acts on all-weather and good to soft going: has refused to race, and not to be
trusted. *N. P. Littmoden*

KESTREL CROSS (IRE) 4 b.g. Cape Cross (IRE) 129 – Lady Rachel (IRE) 75 **100**
(Priolo (USA) 127) [2006 105: a9f 10m⁵ 10m 8m³ 10d Feb 24] first foal: dam 1¼m/1½m
winner: useful handicapper: won 4 races in Ireland for K. Prendergast, including Irish
Cambridgeshire at the Curragh in 2005: creditable efforts at Nad Al Sheba on second and
fourth starts in 2006, 2 lengths third to Royal Prince in latter: stays 1¼m: acts on firm and
good to soft going, well held only outing on dirt: blinkered once in 2005 (well below
form): has joined Declan Gillespie, Ireland. *V. Smith*

KEW GREEN (USA) 8 b. or br.g. Brocco (USA) 124 – Jump With Joy (USA) (Link- **116**
age (USA)) [2006 113: p10g⁵ p8.6g p10g² 9g² 10.3f³ 10m 10g 10d⁶ p10g Nov 18] rangy
gelding: smart performer: creditable second in listed event at Kempton (½ length behind
Simple Exchange) and Earl of Sefton Stakes at Newmarket (beaten 1¼ lengths by
Notnowcato): below form after: stays 10.5f: acts on polytrack, firm and soft going: tried
tongue tied: sometimes races freely. *P. R. Webber*

KEW THE MUSIC 6 b.g. Botanic (USA) – Harmonia (Glint of Gold 128) [2006 74: **65**
p8g⁶ p7.1g⁵ 7s⁴ p7g³ 7m⁴ 7.5f 6f 7.1d⁶ 8m⁶ 7.2s Sep 28] lengthy gelding: fair handi- **a70**
capper: stays 1m: acts on polytrack and good to firm ground: sometimes visored: often
starts slowly/gets behind: none too reliable. *M. R. Channon*

KEYAKI (IRE) 5 b.m. Shinko Forest (IRE) – Woodie Dancer (USA) (Green Dancer **83**
(USA) 132) [2006 83: 6f⁴ 7f 7d 7m p7g* p6g* p6g Oct 28] leggy mare: fairly useful
handicapper: won twice at Lingfield in October: stays 7f: acts on polytrack and firm
ground, probably on soft. *C. F. Wall*

KEYALZAO (IRE) 4 b.f. Alzao (USA) 117 – Key Partner (Law Society (USA) 130) **–**
[2006 37: 8f p12.2g⁵ 8m 10.1m⁵ 12f 10.1f 8g Aug 14] small filly: maiden: no form in
2006: tried in headgear. *A. Crook*

KEY IN 5 ch.m. Unfuwain (USA) 131 – Fleet Key (Afleet (CAN)) [2006 54d: p16.5g **–**
Jan 23] lengthy mare: lightly-raced maiden: well held only outing in 2006: tried in cheek-
pieces/blinkers. *I. W. McInnes*

KEY OF MAGIC (IRE) 3 b.g. Key of Luck (USA) 126 – Desirous of Peace (For- **–**
zando 122) [2006 –: p6g f7g Jan 12] no form: tried blinkered. *J. Hetherton*

KEY PARTNERS (IRE) 5 b.g. Key of Luck (USA) 126 – Teacher Preacher (IRE) 37 **70**
(Taufan (USA) 119) [2006 67: p9.5s p12.2g² Dec 27] quite good-topped gelding: fair
handicapper: stays 1½m: acts on polytrack, best turf form on ground softer than good:
tried tongue tied. *B. D. Leavy*

KEY TIME (IRE) 4 b.g. Darshaan 133 – Kasota (IRE) 72 (Alzao (USA) 117) [2006 **98**
68p: 16f⁴ 16.2m² 15.8m* 16.2f* 17.2f² 21m* 16.2m² 18d Oct 14] useful form: vastly
improved in 2006, winning 5 of his 8 starts, namely handicaps at Redcar in June, Catterick, Beverley and Carlisle in July, and Goodwood (beat Theatre by neck in quite valuable
event) in August: creditable ¾-length second of 7 to Som Tala (pair clear) in similar event
at Beverley next time: not disgraced when eleventh in Cesarewitch at Newmarket final

*Invesco Perpetual Goodwood Stakes (Handicap), Goodwood—fifth win of the season for Key Time;
Theatre runs him close, ahead of Master Cobbler (cheekpieces) and McEldowney (right)*

start: stays 21f: acts on firm and soft going: effective held up or racing prominently: has carried head awkwardly/hung: joined J. Howard Johnson, won over hurdles in December. *Sir Mark Prescott*

KHADIJA 5 ch.m. Kadastrof (FR) 86 – Dark Sirona 55 (Pitskelly 122) [2006 p12.2g **51** p12.2g p12.2g Apr 13] second foal: dam 1½m winner who stayed 2m: modest form on first of 3 starts in maidens. *R. Dickin*

KHALIDIA (USA) 5 b.g. Boundary (USA) 117 – Maniches Slew (USA) (Slew O' **65** Gold (USA)) [2006 –: 6g p6g p7g 6g Aug 24] strong, good-bodied gelding: fair handicapper, lightly raced: stays 6f: acts on polytrack and good to firm going: tongue tied last 2 outings. *M. A. Magnusson*

KHANJAR (USA) 6 ch.g. Kris S (USA) – Alyssum (USA) (Storm Cat (USA)) [2006 **82 d** 84: f14g³ f12g⁶ f12g² p13g f12g 12.1m² 11.5g⁵ 12.4m 11.9g 11.8f³ 12m³ 12s⁶ 12.1m 10s p12.2g² p12g Dec 16] sturdy, attractive gelding: fairly useful performer, on downgrade: claimed from K. Burke £6,000 prior to final start: stays 1½m: acts on all-weather/dirt and firm going: sometimes visored/in cheekpieces: has found little. *J. Pearce*

KHETAAB (IRE) 4 b.g. Alhaarth (IRE) 126 – Liberi Versi (IRE) (Last Tycoon 131) **57** [2006 69: p9.5g 7d f7g 7g⁴ 6f⁵ 7.6m 8.1f⁶ 10.9d 9s p8.6g² p7.1g² Dec 4] quite good-topped gelding: just modest maiden in 2006: left D. Weld in Ireland 9,000 gns prior to reappearance: stays 1m: acts on polytrack, firm and good to soft going: tried in cheekpieces/blinkers. *E. J. Alston*

KHUN JOHN (IRE) 3 b.g. Marju (IRE) 127 – Kathy Caerleon (IRE) (Caerleon (USA) **89 +** 132) [2006 p8g⁴ p8.6g* p10g* p10g* Nov 11] €26,000F: fourth foal: half-brother to 5f winner in Italy (including at 2 yrs) by Fayruz: dam unraced half-sister to Chester Vase winner High Baroque: fairly useful form: won maiden at Wolverhampton and handicaps at Lingfield and Kempton (by neck from Birkside) in October/November: stays easy 1¼m: raced only on polytrack. *B. J. Meehan*

KHYBERIE 3 b.f. Kahyasi 130 – Reading Habit (USA) (Half A Year (USA) 130) [2006 **52** p8g⁴ 8.2v⁵ Oct 25] 12,000Y: leggy filly: second foal: half-sister to fairly useful 2004 2-y-o 7f winner Read Federica (by Fusaichi Pegasus): dam 5f (at 2 yrs) to 6f (minor stakes) winner in USA: modest form in maidens. *G. Wragg*

KHYBER KIM 4 b.g. Mujahid (USA) 125 – Jungle Rose 90 (Shirley Heights 130) **116** [2006 107p: 10g³ 10m² 11.6g² 12d⁴ Sep 29] tall, lengthy gelding: made up into a smart performer in 2006 and placed in listed race at Newbury (third of 4 to Tam Lin), minor event at Newmarket (½-length second to Windsor Knot) and listed race at Windsor (best effort, beaten head by Crocodile Dundee): well below form final outing: stays 11.6f: acts on good to firm and good to soft going: has raced freely: joined H. Henderson. *H. Candy*

KHYBER KNIGHT (IRE) 3 b.f. Night Shift (USA) – Peshawar (Persian Bold 123) **56** [2006 –: 9.9g 8f 8f³ 8m⁴ 8f⁴ 8.1f³ 8.5m 8m 8m 10.2m³ 10m Sep 19] leggy filly: modest maiden: stays 1¼m: acts on firm going. *Jane Southcombe*

KIAMA 4 b.f. Dansili 127 – Catriona 75 (Bustino 136) [2006 72: f14g 15.4m 11.1m⁴ **60** 12m 12f⁵ 14.1d Aug 21] well-made filly: just modest maiden handicapper in 2006: stays 2m: acts on polytrack, heavy and good to firm ground. *M. Johnston*

KIA ORA 3 b.g. College Chapel 122 – Anastasia Venture 70 (Lion Cavern (USA) 117) **–** [2006 p8g 8.3g Oct 16] well held in maidens: in cheekpieces final outing. *J. Akehurst*

KIBARA 3 b.f. Sadler's Wells (USA) 132 – Kithanga (IRE) 117 (Darshaan 133) [2006 **88** 9.8m³ 10.9m² 11.5m* 11.6m² 12g 12d Oct 27] sturdy filly: fifth foal: sister to high-class 7f (at 2 yrs) to 1¾m (St Leger) winner Milan and half-sister to smart performer up to 1¾m Go For Gold (by Machiavellian), 7f winner in Ireland at 2 yrs: dam, won St Simon Stakes and third in Irish St Leger, out of half-sister to dam of Kahyasi: fairly useful performer: won maiden at Lingfield in July: good second in handicap at Windsor next time, but well below form in similar events last 2 starts: should be suited by 1¾m: acts on good to firm going. *L. M. Cumani*

KICKAHEAD (USA) 4 b.g. Danzig (USA) – Krissante (USA) (Kris 135) [2006 p8.6g **65** 8d⁵ 10g⁴ Jun 7] sturdy gelding: fair maiden handicapper: left Mme C. Head-Maarek €12,000 after final 3-y-o outing: barely stays 1¼m: acts on good to firm and good to soft going. *Ian Williams*

KICK AND PRANCE 3 ch.g. Groom Dancer (USA) 128 – Unerring (Unfuwain **61** (USA) 131) [2006 63: 8.2s p8g 11.7g p12.2g² 11.9d* Oct 19] lengthy gelding: modest handicapper: won at Brighton (apprentices) in October: gelded after: stays 1½m: acts on polytrack and good to soft going: tongue tied last 4 starts. *J. A. Geake*

KID MAMBO (USA) 2 b.c. (Apr 14) Lemon Drop Kid (USA) 131 – Spring Pitch **102 +**
(USA) (Storm Cat (USA)) [2006 p7g⁴ 7m⁵ 8.1d* 8s² Oct 7] 115,000 2-y-o: good-topped,
quite attractive colt: fourth foal: half-brother to winner in Japan by Danzig: dam, ran
twice in USA, half-sister to high-class miler Selkirk: useful form: won maiden at Sandown by 3½ lengths in September: much improved when 5 lengths second of 8 to Caldra
in Autumn Stakes at Ascot, responding well to pressure (suited by stamina test): likely to
stay 1½m. *T. G. Mills*

KILBURN 2 b.c. (Jan 16) Grand Lodge (USA) 125 – Lady Lahar 106 (Fraam 114) [2006 **93**
6m³ 6g 7m* 8d⁵ Sep 16] 52,000Y: strong, stocky colt: type to carry condition: second
foal: dam 6f (at 2 yrs) to 1m winner: fairly useful form: won maiden at Goodwood in
August by ½ length from Mariotto, across from wide draw to make all: only fifth in
nursery at Ayr (softer ground): should stay 1m. *C. G. Cox*

KILCUSNIN QUEEN (IRE) 2 ch.f. (Apr 22) Indian Rocket 115 – Pip'n Judy (IRE) **68**
76 (Pips Pride 117) [2006 5m⁵ 5d³ 6m 5.1d² p6g⁶ p6g⁴ p6g⁶ Dec 8] good-bodied filly:
second foal: half-sister to 2005 Irish 2-y-o 5f winner Oceans Pip (by Blue Ocean): dam,
Irish 6.5f winner, out of half-sister to high-class sprinter Hallgate: fair maiden: raced
mainly in Britain, in frame 3 starts, nursery final one: effective at 5f/6f: acts on polytrack,
good to firm and good to soft going. *Adrian Sexton, Ireland*

KILDARE SUN (IRE) 4 b.g. Desert Sun 120 – Megan's Dream (IRE) 56 (Fayruz 116) **87**
[2006 –: 8d 9m⁴ 10d p9.5m* p8.6g³ p9.5g* p9.5g* p9.5g p9.5g² Dec 30] lightly-raced
gelding: fairly useful performer: left Ms F. Crowley in Ireland after only 3-y-o outing
(debut): won 3 handicaps at Wolverhampton in October/November: stays 9.5f: acts on
polytrack. *J. Mackie*

KILGARY (USA) 3 ch.f. Pleasant Tap (USA) – Fitzy (USA) (A P Indy (USA) 131) **70**
[2006 7.1m⁵ p8.6g³ p7.1m p10g² p12.2g* Dec 28] $240,000F: second foal: dam unraced
half-sister to smart US Grade 1 9f winner Tap To Music (by Pleasant Tap): fair performer:
awarded maiden at Wolverhampton (forced to switch) in December: stays 1½m: acts on
polytrack. *J. Noseda*

KILIMANDSCHARO (USA) 4 b.g. Rahy (USA) 115 – Landaria (FR) (Sadler's **72**
Wells (USA) 132) [2006 10d² 10d³ 8.3f p9.5g* Dec 21] ran only 4 times in Germany for
P. Schiergen, including when placed in minor event at Frankfurt and maiden at Baden-
Baden in 2006: second start in Britain (6 months after first, for Miss Victoria Roberts),
improved to win handicap at Wolverhampton in December: should stay 1½m: acts on
polytrack and good to soft going. *P. J. McBride*

KILLENA BOY (IRE) 4 b.g. Imperial Ballet (IRE) 110 – Habaza (IRE) 68 (Shernazar **91**
131) [2006 90: p7g³ p8g 8m 8.1g* p8g* 8g p8g⁶ Oct 15] good-bodied gelding: fairly
useful handicapper: won at Sandown in August and Kempton (beat Ans Bach by neck in
valuable event) in September: has won at 1¼m, probably best around 1m nowadays: acts
on polytrack, soft and good to firm going. *W. Jarvis*

KILLER HEELS 2 b.f. (Mar 6) Kirkwall 118 – High Habit 79 (Slip Anchor 136) [2006 **51**
p7g 7f⁶ 7g 10g Sep 26] good-bodied filly: half-sister to 3 winners, including 6f winner
Alegria (by Night Shift) and 5-y-o Brother Cadfael: dam, second at 11.5f, half-sister to
smart sprinter Blue Siren: modest form. *S. Kirk*

KILLING JOKE 6 b.g. Double Trigger (IRE) 123 – Fleeting Vision (IRE) 79 (Vision **–**
(USA)) [2006 8s p13.9g⁴ Nov 25] lengthy gelding: fairly useful handicapper at 3 yrs:
little form since, leaving J. Given 4,000 gns after final 4-y-o outing. *J. J. Lambe, Ireland*

KILLYBEGS (IRE) 3 b.c. Orpen (USA) 116 – Belsay 68 (Belmez (USA) 131) [2006 **120**
105: 8g* 8m 8m⁴ 8g 8m² 8d⁴ 7d² Oct 14] sturdy, good-topped colt: has a quick action:
very smart performer: won Unicorn Asset Management Craven Stakes at Newmarket (by
3½ lengths from Metropolitan Man) in April: eleventh in 2000 Guineas on same course
next time: good efforts last 3 starts, short-head second to Caradak in Celebration Mile at
Goodwood, 4½ lengths fourth to George Washington in Queen Elizabeth II Stakes at
Ascot and length second to Sleeping Indian in Challenge Stakes at Newmarket: should
stay 1¼m: acts on good to firm and good to soft going: has run well when sweating:
joined Godolphin. *B. W. Hills*

KILMEENA MAGIC 4 b.f. Fumo di Londra (IRE) 108 – Kilmeena Lady (Inca Chief **52**
(USA)) [2006 p7g 8d 8.1g 10m 7g 8.3m⁵ 7f⁴ 8d p8g⁵ p7g⁶ p11g⁴ p12g⁴ p10g³ p10g⁵
p10g² p11g³ Dec 22] first foal: dam of little account: modest maiden: stays easy 1½m:
acts on polytrack: tried in cheekpieces. *J. C. Fox*

KILVICKEON (IRE) 2 b.g. (Apr 21) Daggers Drawn (USA) 114 – Queen of Sweden **46**
(IRE) (Solid Illusion (USA) 117) [2006 p6g p7.1g p6g p5.1g p5.1g² p6g⁴ p7.1g³ Dec 27]
poor maiden: tried blinkered. *Peter Grayson*

KILWORTH (IRE) 3 gr.c. Kalanisi (IRE) 132 – Perugia (IRE) 94 (Perugino (USA) **105**
84) [2006 105: a8f⁶ a9f⁵ p8.6g* 10d³ Oct 27] lengthy, good sort: good walker: useful
performer: trained by N. Callaghan in 2005 and by I. Mohammed in UAE first 2 starts at
3 yrs: off 7 months, won minor event at Wolverhampton in October by 1½ lengths from
Party Boss: good 6 lengths third behind Into The Dark in listed race at Newmarket final
outing: stays easy 1¼m: acts on polytrack, good to firm and good to soft going. *Saeed bin
Suroor*

KIMONO KISS (USA) 2 ch.f. (Mar 8) Seeking The Gold (USA) – Geisha Girl 99 **53 p**
(Nashwan (USA) 135) [2006 p7g Oct 26] $80,000Y: fourth foal: closely related to winner
in USA by Mr Prospector: dam, Irish 2-y-o 7f winner who stayed 1¾m, half-sister to
high-class middle-distance stayer Zindabad: 16/1, needed experience (slowly away) and
some promise in maiden at Lingfield: open to improvement. *M. P. Tregoning*

KIMONO MY HOUSE 2 ch.f. (Apr 22) Dr Fong (USA) 128 – Roselyn 66 (Efisio **54**
120) [2006 7s p7g p8.6m Nov 21] 14,000Y: second foal: dam, maiden who stayed 7f,
sister to smart winner up to 1¼m Riberac: modest maiden. *J. G. Given*

KIMPTON CARER 2 b.g. (Mar 25) Groom Dancer (USA) 128 – So True 116 (So **–**
Blessed 130) [2006 p8g⁵ p8.6g Dec 27] well held in minor event and maiden: once
refused at stalls. *J. A. Geake*

KIMS ROSE (IRE) 3 b.f. Desert Prince (IRE) 130 – Pinta (IRE) (Ahonoora 122) **46**
[2006 7.1g 7f⁶ 8m Jul 30] €38,000Y: sister to 2 winners, including 4-y-o Rain Stops Play,
and half-sister to 3 winners: dam 5f to 7.5f winner in Ireland/Italy, including at 2 yrs: poor
form in maidens. *R. A. Harris*

KINCAID 3 ch.g. Dr Fong (USA) 128 – Peacock Alley (IRE) 98 (Salse (USA) 128) **–**
[2006 –: 7m Sep 16] no form. *D. W. Thompson*

Mr John C. Grant & Mr D. M. James's "Killybegs"

KINDALLACHAN 3 b.f. Magic Ring (IRE) 115 – Moore Stylish 65 (Moorestyle 137) **52**
[2006 7m 8.1m⁶ p8g p5g² p6g p5.1g⁴ Dec 4] quite good-topped filly: sister to 1m winner
Magic Flo and half-sister to 2 winners, including fairly useful 5f to 7f winner Mr Stylish
(by Mazilier): dam, middle-distance maiden, winning hurdler: modest maiden: seems
best at 5f: acts on polytrack. *G. C. Bravery*

KINDLELIGHT BLUE (IRE) 2 gr.c. (Feb 29) Golan (IRE) 129 – Kalimar (IRE) **70**
(Bigstone (IRE) 126) [2006 5m⁵ 7m 6m⁴ Jul 30] €15,000Y, 20,000 2-y-o: tall, leggy colt:
second foal: dam, ran once in France, half-sister to dam of smart stayer Kasthari: fair
form in maidens at Carlisle and Newmarket: stiff task in Chesham Stakes in between: will
benefit from 1m+. *N. P. Littmoden*

KINDLELIGHT DEBUT 6 b.m. Groom Dancer (USA) 128 – Dancing Debut 83 **92**
(Polar Falcon (USA) 126) [2006 78: p7.1g* p9.5g* p7.1g* p8g² p9.5g³ p7g* p7.1g³ **a105**
p10g² p8g⁶ p8g p8g p7.1g* 7m 7.6m⁵ 7d⁶ 8.3g² 7.6g⁵ 7m⁴ 8d p7g⁶ p8g³ p10g⁴ p10g⁴ p8g³
p7g⁴ p9.5g⁴ Dec 31] smallish mare: useful on all-weather, fairly useful on turf: much
improved in 2006, winning handicaps at Wolverhampton (3, first one apprentices) in
January, Lingfield in March and Wolverhampton in July: several other good efforts late
in season, including when in frame in listed races twenty-first and twenty-second (fourth
to Nayyir at Lingfield) outings: effective at 7f to easy 1¼m: acts on polytrack and firm
going: tried in cheekpieces: tough. *N. P. Littmoden*

KINDLING 4 br.f. Dr Fong (USA) 128 – Isle of Flame (Shirley Heights 130) [2006 105: **99**
15.5d 16d 15d Oct 9] small, angular filly: useful performer: best effort in 2006 when
seventh to Hawridge Prince in listed race at Ascot second start: well held at Longchamp
and Chantilly other outings: stays 2m: acts on soft and good to firm going: tried blinkered.
M. Johnston

KIND OF FIZZY 2 b.f. (May 16) Efisio 120 – Kind of Light 83 (Primo Dominie 121) **54**
[2006 6d 6d Oct 27] €8,200F, €18,000Y: neat filly: fourth foal: half-sister to 7f winner
Menai Straights (by Alhaarth) and winner in Norway by Persian Bold: dam 6f and (at
2 yrs) 7f winner: modest form in maidens. *Rae Guest*

KINETA (USA) 3 b.f. Miswaki (USA) 124 – Kibitzing (USA) (Wild Again (USA)) **61**
[2006 69: 8m 8.1d⁵ 7.1m⁴ p6g³ 6ug Aug 16] close-coupled filly: just modest maiden in
2006: should stay 7f: acts on polytrack, good to firm and good to soft going. *W. R. Muir*

KINETIC POWER (IRE) 3 gr.g. Alhaarth (IRE) 126 – Nichodoula 65 (Doulab **52**
(USA) 115) [2006 –p: p8g p10g 10m p10g May 23] modest maiden: stays 1¼m: raced
only on polytrack and good to firm going. *D. R. C. Elsworth*

KING AFTER 4 b.g. Bahamian Bounty 116 – Child Star (FR) 58 (Bellypha 130) [2006 **64**
70: 8.3f p8g p6m 8g p8.6g⁶ p9.5s p8.6g p7g² Dec 30] leggy gelding: just modest handicapper in 2006: barely stays easy 1¼m: acts on polytrack, good to firm and good to soft
ground. *J. R. Best*

KING CHARLES 2 b.g. (Apr 22) King's Best (USA) 132 – Charlecote (IRE) (Caer- **94 p**
leon (USA) 132) [2006 7.1m 6d 5f⁵ 6f 7f* p7g* 8m* Sep 19] 26,000Y: strong, close-
coupled gelding: second foal: dam unraced out of sister to Barathea and Gossamer: fairly
useful form: much improved to complete hat-trick in nurseries in September, at Lingfield
(2) and Newmarket (beat subsequent listed winner Zafonical Storm by short head): will
probably stay 1¼m: acts on polytrack and firm going, promise on good to soft: should
progress further. *E. A. L. Dunlop*

KING CUGAT KID (USA) 3 b. or br.c. King Cugat (USA) 122 – Let's Dance (USA) **–**
(Thorn Dance (USA) 107) [2006 –: 5.7m p10g 10.2m p16g p16.5m Nov 21] smallish
colt: little form. *Simon Earle*

KINGDOM OF DREAMS (IRE) 4 b.g. Sadler's Wells (USA) 132 – Regal Portrait **78**
(IRE) 57 (Royal Academy (USA) 130) [2006 89: 8.1f⁶ 8m p8g Aug 2] close-coupled,
attractive gelding: just fair handicapper in 2006: will prove best short of 1½m: yet to
race on heavy going, probably acts on any other: often tongue tied: sold 10,000 gns, then
gelded. *J. Noseda*

KING EGBERT (FR) 5 b.g. Fasliyev (USA) 120 – Exocet (USA) (Deposit Ticket **65**
(USA)) [2006 54: p5.1g⁵ p5.1g p5g² p5g* 6.1m 5m⁴ 5.1g* 5.1f⁴ 5g² 5.1g⁵ 5.1m⁶ 5.1m⁴
5m Sep 20] lengthy, good-bodied gelding: fair performer: won banded race at Kempton
in May and handicap at Bath in July: effective at 5f/6f: acts on polytrack and firm going:
tried blinkered/tongue tied: sometimes slowly away. *A. W. Carroll*

KING FAZ (IRE) 3 b.g. Fasliyev (USA) 120 – White Satin (IRE) 83 (Fairy King **–**
(USA)) [2006 63: 7m 6g 8.1m Aug 10] maiden: little form in 2006, leaving P. Haslam
after second outing: tried tongue tied: edgy sort/tends to hang. *P. A. Blockley*

KING FOREVER 4 b.g. King's Best (USA) 132 – Elude (Slip Anchor 136) [2006 77: **61 d**
f7g³ p9.5g f7g⁴ f8g⁴ 6f 15.8m³ p12.2m⁶ p13g Sep 29] strong, close-coupled gelding:
maiden, just modest form at best in 2006: free-going sort, should prove best short of
15.8f: acts on all-weather, good to firm and good to soft going: tried visored: has worn
crossed noseband: none too reliable. *D. E. Cantillon*

KING GABRIEL (IRE) 4 b.g. Desert King (IRE) 129 – Broken Spirit (IRE) (Slip **61**
Anchor 136) [2006 56: p9.5s⁵ p9.5g⁴ Dec 29] tall gelding: modest maiden: should be well
suited by 1½m+: acts on soft ground, probably on polytrack: tried tongue tied. *Andrew
Turnell*

KING GEORGES (FR) 8 b.g. Kadalko (FR) – Djoumi (FR) (Brezzo (FR) 113) [2006 **–**
p13.9g Jun 2] lightly raced on Flat in France in 2001, winning 1¼m/11f events at Durtal
and Vichy: well held only outing on Flat since (won over hurdles in between). *J. C. Tuck*

KING HARSON 7 b.g. Greensmith 121 – Safari Park 43 (Absalom 128) [2006 96§: 7g **87 §**
7g⁶ 7m 7g 7.1m* 7m⁴ 7.1s* p7.1m 7s³ 7v Oct 31] close-coupled, good-bodied gelding:
just fairly useful handicapper: won at Musselburgh in August and September (dead-
heated with Muzuzah): races mainly at 7f nowadays: acts on any going: has been
blinkered, often visored in past: usually races prominently: unreliable. *J. D. Bethell*

KING HENRIK (USA) 4 b.g. King of Kings (IRE) 125 – Ma Biche (USA) 125 (Key **–**
To The Kingdom (USA)) [2006 –: 6g 6f 8d Aug 2] close-coupled gelding: no form since
2 yrs: tried in cheekpieces: somewhat temperamental. *A. Crook*

KING JOCK (USA) 5 b.h. Ghazi (USA) – Glen Kate 118 (Glenstal (USA) 118) [2006 **117**
112: 7.5m* 7.5m⁵ 8g⁴ 8m⁵ 8m⁴ 8d* 7g⁴ 7d³ 8m* 7g* Dec 24] leggy, quite good-topped
horse: smart performer: won handicap at Nad Al Sheba in January and, having left
E. Charpy in UAE after fourth start, Desmond Stakes at Leopardstown (by ¾ length from
Arch Rebel) in August and listed races at Abu Dhabi in December (both from National
Captain, by a neck on first occasion and ¾ length on second one): good 2¾ lengths
third to Stronghold in Supreme Stakes at Goodwood eighth start: effective at 7f/1m: acts
on any going: held up. *R. J. Osborne, Ireland*

KING JOSHUA (IRE) 2 b.c. (Apr 11) King's Best (USA) 132 – Lady Joshua (IRE) **86**
88 (Royal Academy (USA) 130) [2006 6m 7g³ 7d⁵ p6g⁵ 8d⁵ Oct 19] 70,000Y: rather
leggy, quite attractive colt: half-brother to several winners, including smart 6f (at 2 yrs) to
9f (including in USA) winner Privy Seal (by Cape Cross) and fairly useful 1½m/1¾m
winner Lord Joshua (by King's Theatre): dam, maiden who stayed 1½m, closely related
to very smart performer up to 1¾m Sapience: fairly useful maiden: best effort when close
third behind One To Follow and Big Robert at Ascot: should stay 1m: tongue tied once
(ran creditably): sold 45,000 gns. *G. A. Butler*

KING KASYAPA (IRE) 4 b.c. Darshaan 133 – Ezana (Ela-Mana-Mou 132) [2006 **68**
10.2m⁶ 12.1d⁵ 12g³ Jul 13] 170,000Y, 600,000Y: brother to smart Irish 7f (at 2 yrs) to
1½m winner Ebaziya (dam of 3 Group 1 winners, including Gold Cup winner Enzeli) and
half-brother to 3 winners, including fairly useful Irish 1½m winner Erzadjan (by
Kahyasi): dam French 11.5f winner: maiden: useful form at 2 yrs for A. Fabre in France:
missed 2005 (sold 11,500 gns): just fair form in 2006: should prove suited by 1½m+: acts
on good to soft going, probably on good to firm. *P. Bowen*

KINGKOHLER (IRE) 7 b.g. King's Theatre (IRE) 128 – Legit (IRE) (Runnett 125) **–**
[2006 80: p12.2g Jan 30] lightly raced on Flat, fairly useful at best: well held only outing
in 2006: has carried head awkwardly. *K. A. Morgan*

KING MARJU (IRE) 4 b.g. Marju (IRE) 127 – Katoushka (IRE) (Hamas (IRE) 125§) **89**
[2006 105: 7.5m 6.5m 7.5d³ p7g³ 7m 7.1m⁵ 7.2d⁵ p7g p7g⁶ f6g p7.1g Dec 31] lengthy, **a97**
good-topped gelding: useful handicapper on all-weather, fairly useful on turf: good run
in 2006 only when third to Something at Lingfield fourth start: best form at 7f: acts on
polytrack, soft and good to firm going: often visored: free-going sort. *K. R. Burke*

KING MARRAKECH (IRE) 4 b.g. King's Best (USA) 132 – Tenue d'Amour (FR) **–**
(Pursuit of Love 124) [2006 –, a54: f6g⁶ f5g f6g p6g f7s p6g p6g⁵ 7f a11g 5g a4.8g a10.5g **a43**
Nov 18] just poor performer in 2006: left B. Baugh after seventh start: best at 5f/6f: acts
on fibresand: wears headgear nowadays. *R. Verheye, Belgium*

KING NICHOLAS (USA) 7 b.g. Nicholas (USA) 111 – Lifetime Honour (USA) **44**
(Kingmambo (USA) 125) [2006 –, a72: f8g⁴ f8g 9g 10m 7.9m f8g Oct 12] good-topped
gelding: just poor performer in 2006: effective at 6f to 9.5f: acts on all-weather and heavy
going: wears headgear: tongue tied. *J. Parkes*

KING NOV (ARG) 4 bl.c. Romanov (IRE) 119 – Queen Wonder (ARG) (Southern **103**
Halo (USA)) [2006 a8g⁴ a6g⁵ 5.8g⁶ 5.8g⁶ 6g² 8g⁶ a6g 5.8s³ 5.8g a6.8g³ a6.8g² a6g* p7g

Nov 18] won twice in Argentina early in 2005, including Group 3 event at San Isidro: useful performer in Scandinavia in 2006, winning minor event at Taby in October by neck from Hide And Seek: well held in handicap at Lingfield (tongue tied) final outing: best around 5f/6f: acts on dirt. *B. Bo, Sweden*

KING OF ARGOS (IRE) 3 b.g. Sadler's Wells (USA) 132 – Wannabe Grand (IRE) 116 **94**
(Danehill (USA) 126) [2006 77p: 11g 10d² 10.2m* p9.5g⁵ p8.6g² p9.5g² Dec 9] close-coupled, good-topped gelding: fairly useful performer: won maiden at Chepstow in June (gelded after): better form in handicaps at Wolverhampton after, particularly when neck second to Daring Affair final start (visored): stays 1¼m: acts on polytrack, good to firm and good to soft ground. *E. A. L. Dunlop*

KING OF CHARM (IRE) 3 ch.g. King Charlemagne (USA) 120 – Pumpona (USA) **63**
(Sharpen Up 127) [2006 5m³ 6f 5f⁵ p6g p6g p7g Dec 19] modest maiden: bred to stay 6f: tried blinkered. *G. L. Moore*

KING OF CHAV'S (IRE) 3 ch.g. Beckett (IRE) 116 – La Paola (IRE) 68 (Common **–**
Grounds 118) [2006 –: 10d 7f 7.2v 11.5f 10m Jul 24] leggy gelding: little form. *A. Bailey*

KING OF DIAMONDS 5 b.g. Mtoto 134 – Capricious Lass (Corvaro (USA) 124) **–**
[2006 79: 8m 6g 7g p8g Sep 3] leggy gelding: handicapper: well below form in 2006: tried in cheekpieces. *J. R. Best*

KING OF KNIGHT (IRE) 5 gr.g. Orpen (USA) 116 – Peace Melody (IRE) 69 **67**
(Classic Music (USA)) [2006 74: p12g p10g³ p10g⁶ p10g² p13g p10g⁴ p9.5g⁵ 11.5m p9.5g p10g⁴ p8g² Dec 10] quite good-topped gelding: fair handicapper: best at 1¼m/ 1½m: acts on polytrack, good to firm and good to soft ground: tried visored/tongue tied: sometimes slowly away. *G. Prodromou*

KING OF MAGIC 2 b.g. (Mar 29) King O' The Mana (IRE) 112 – Mountain Magic **45**
58 (Magic Ring (IRE) 115) [2006 8.3g 8.2s Oct 25] angular gelding: poor form in sellers. *W. G. M. Turner*

KING OF MEZE (IRE) 5 b.g. Croco Rouge (IRE) 126 – Cossack Princess (IRE) 72 **57**
(Lomond (USA) 128) [2006 66: 6v p7.1g³ p8g² 8m 7.2g 12f⁴ 10m Jul 29] just modest maiden in 2006: stays 1m: acts on polytrack and firm ground: tried tongue tied: in cheekpieces of late: usually makes running. *J. S. Wainwright*

KING OF MUSIC (USA) 5 ch.g. Jade Hunter (USA) – Hail Roberta (USA) (Roberto **68**
(USA) 131) [2006 71: p8.6g* p12.2g p8g⁶ p8g⁴ p10g⁶ p8.6g⁴ f7g 9.7d 8m Apr 27] rather leggy, angular gelding: fair handicapper: won at Wolverhampton in January: stays easy 1½m: acts on all-weather and good to firm ground: often visored in 2006. *G. Prodromou*

KING OF RHYTHM (IRE) 3 b.g. Imperial Ballet (IRE) 110 – Sharadja (IRE) (Doy- **67**
oun 124) [2006 10v⁵ 11g⁴ 10.5m 10.5v 8.5m² Sep 19] €32,000Y: sturdy, workmanlike gelding: second foal: half-brother to 5-y-o She's Our Lass: dam unraced granddaughter of Prix Vermeille winner Sharaya: fair maiden: likely to prove best up to 1m: acts on heavy and good to firm going. *D. Carroll*

KING OF SCOTS 5 ch.g. Halling (USA) 133 – Ink Pot (USA) 73 (Green Dancer **–**
(USA) 132) [2006 f12g f8g p12.2g Apr 28] no form. *R. J. Price*

KING OF SWORDS (IRE) 2 b.c. (Mar 14) Desert Prince (IRE) 130 – Okey Dorey **93**
(IRE) 96 (Lake Coniston (IRE) 131) [2006 5v 5v² 5f* 6.3m⁶ 5m 6m 6d Oct 15] close-coupled colt: first foal: dam, Irish 1m winner, stayed 1¼m: fairly useful performer: won maiden at Navan ran June: good 3 lengths second to Drayton in listed race at the Curragh time before and ran respectably in Anglesey Stakes at the Curragh (sixth to Regional Counsel) and Molecomb Stakes at Goodwood (eighth of 13 to Enticing, hampered 2f out) next 2 starts: below form in nursery at Naas final outing: should stay 6f: acts on any turf going. *C. Collins, Ireland*

KING OF THE BEERS (USA) 2 gr. or ro.c. (Mar 31) Silver Deputy (CAN) – Pracer **58**
(USA) (Lyphard (USA) 132) [2006 7m 7.6f p8.6g p9.5g p8.6g Dec 27] close-coupled colt: modest maiden: stays 9.5f: tried in cheekpieces. *R. A. Harris*

KING OF THE MOORS (USA) 3 b.g. King of Kings (IRE) 125 – Araza (USA) **91 d**
(Arazi (USA) 135) [2006 70: 7.1g* 8m³ 7g³ 8m 8g 8g 8d 7.1s Sep 24] close-coupled gelding: fairly useful performer: won maiden at Musselburgh in April: good third in handicaps there and Epsom next 2 starts, but below form in similar events after: stays 1m: acts on good to firm going. *T. D. Barron*

KING OF TRICKS 2 b.g. (Feb 28) First Trump 118 – Antithesis (IRE) 75 (Fairy King **55**
(USA)) [2006 5m 6m 5.1f⁵ 5g 5g³ 5d⁵ 5.1d Nov 1] compact gelding: modest maiden: raced mainly at 5f: tried in visor. *M. D. I. Usher*

KING ORCHISIOS (IRE) 3 ch.c. Tagula (IRE) 116 – Wildflower 84 (Namaqualand **108**
(USA)) [2006 93p: 7g³ 5s⁵ 6s 6m 5m² 6g* 6g⁵ 5.4g 6d p5g p5.1g* Oct 29] strong, lengthy
colt: reportedly sustained stress fracture of hind joint and off over 10 months after debut
at 2 yrs: improved into a useful handicapper: won at Haydock (beat Burning Incense by
short head) in July and Wolverhampton (by length from Judd Street) in October: best at
5f/6f: acts on polytrack and good to firm going: races prominently: in cheekpieces/blink-
ers of late. *K. A. Ryan*

KING'S ACCOUNT (USA) 4 ch.g. King of Kings (IRE) 125 – Fighting Countess **–**
(USA) (Ringside) [2006 p9.5g p8.6g Nov 16] well-made, good sort: fairly useful
performer at 2 yrs: left M. Johnston 2,800 gns, gelded and off over 2 years, well beaten in
handicaps in 2006. *S. Gollings*

KING'S APOSTLE (IRE) 2 b.c. (Feb 6) King's Best (USA) 132 – Politesse (USA) **80**
(Barathea (IRE) 127) [2006 6m⁶ 7m² 7f² Sep 20] well-made colt: first foal: dam unraced
daughter of Cheveley Park Stakes winner Embassy: fairly useful form in maidens, second
at Chester and Redcar (beaten head by Karoo Blue): will stay 1m. *W. J. Haggas*

KINGS ART (IRE) 2 b.g. (Feb 7) King's Best (USA) 132 – Descant (USA) (Nureyev **64**
(USA) 131) [2006 6m 7g 6.1m⁵ p7.1m Oct 2] useful-looking gelding: has a fluent
action: modest maiden: tried in tongue tie: sold 4,000 gns, joined W. M. Brisbourne,
gelded. *B. W. Hills*

KING'S ATTITUDE 2 b.c. (Mar 24) King's Theatre (IRE) 128 – Sarah's Dream (IRE) **–**
(Lion Cavern (USA) 117) [2006 7m Aug 11] 66/1 and poorly to post, well held in maiden
at Newmarket. *B. J. Meehan*

KING'S BASTION (IRE) 2 b.g. (Feb 17) Royal Applause 124 – Aunty Mary 82 **87**
(Common Grounds 118) [2006 5g⁴ 5m* 6g⁵ 5.1f³ 6f² 6m 6m 6s Oct 6] 72,000Y: quite
good-topped gelding: first foal: dam, 2-y-o 5f winner, half-sister to high-class miler
Attraction: fairly useful performer: won maiden at Lingfield in May: good second in
nursery there: below form last 3 starts: effective at 5f/6f: acts on firm going. *M. L. W. Bell*

KING'S CAPRICE 5 ch.g. Pursuit of Love 124 – Palace Street (USA) 103 (Secreto **112**
(USA) 128) [2006 97: p7g 7g* 7g 7.1m³ 6m³ 7g⁴ 6.1f* 7m 7g 7m* 7d³ 7g* Oct 13] rather
leggy gelding: has a round action: smart handicapper: had a good season, winning at
Newmarket in April, Chepstow in July, Goodwood (beat Bayeux by neck) in September
and Newmarket (by neck from Woodcote Place) in October: effective at 6f/7f: acts on
polytrack, firm and soft going: tongue tied: has been mounted on track: races prominently, sometimes freely. *J. A. Geake*

KING'S CAUSEWAY (USA) 2 b. or br.c. (Mar 19) Giant's Causeway (USA) 132 – **76**
Dealer's Dream (USA) (A P Indy (USA) 131) [2006 7f⁴ 7.5d³ 7d³ 7m⁵ p8g Oct 6] 80,000
2-y-o: medium-sized colt: first foal: dam, lightly-raced US maiden, half-sister to US
Grade 1 1m to 1¼m winner Clear Mandate: fair maiden: in frame first 3 starts, and better
than bare result final one in nursery (hampered/eased): should stay 1m: acts on firm and
good to soft going: sold 32,000 gns, sent to USA. *W. J. Haggas*

KINGS CAVALIER (USA) 3 b.g. Stormin Fever (USA) 116 – Port of Silver (USA) **58 d**
(Silver Hawk (USA) 123) [2006 77: p7g p6g² p5g 6d 5g 7m 5.9m 6m 7.5f 7.5f⁶ 8f 8m⁵
p6g p6g Dec 6] just modest maiden at best in 2006: claimed from S. Dow £6,000 after
second outing: best efforts at 5f/6f: acts on polytrack and firm ground: tried blinkered,
usually visored: has taken strong hold: reportedly bled ninth start. *I. W. McInnes*

KING'S CHARTER (USA) 3 b.g. Red Ransom (USA) – Extry (USA) (Broad Brush **51**
(USA)) [2006 –: p8g³ 10m 7m Jun 17] tall gelding: modest performer: stays 1m: acts on
polytrack: visored final outing: has shown signs of temperament. *S. Dow*

KINGS COLLEGE BOY 6 b.g. College Chapel 122 – The Kings Daughter 79 **84**
(Indian King (USA) 128) [2006 78: 5g 5.1s 5s⁶ 5m⁴ 5m² 5f* 5m³ 5f² 5m⁴ 5m* 5f⁴ 5.4f²
5f³ 5m² 5f⁵ 5m 5.1g³ 5.1m⁵ 5m⁴ 5m⁵ 5s⁶ Oct 6] strong, well-made gelding: fairly useful
handicapper: won at Beverley in June and Hamilton in July: held form well after: best
at 5f/6f: acts on firm and soft going: usually blinkered/visored: waited with: tough and
consistent. *R. A. Fahey*

KING'S COLLEGE (USA) 3 b.c. Stravinsky (USA) 133 – Talent Quest (IRE) (Rain- **–**
bow Quest (USA) 134) [2006 p6g p8g p10g 9.7s 10m 11.5m 13.1m 16.2m 10.2m Sep 7]
little form, leaving G. L. Moore after sixth outing: bred to stay 1m+: wore headgear last 7
starts. *P. D. Evans*

KINGS CONFESSION (IRE) 3 b.g. Danetime (IRE) 121 – Night Rhapsody (IRE) **67**
81 (Mujtahid (USA) 118) [2006 7m p8.6g² Jun 26] €14,000Y: first foal: dam Irish 1m

winner: badly in need of experience on debut: much better effort in maidens when 3 lengths second to Empire Dancer at Wolverhampton, nearest at finish. *D. Carroll*

KING'S CREST 8 b.g. Deploy 131 – Classic Beauty (IRE) 65 (Fairy King (USA)) **63** [2006 p12.2g² 11g f12g⁶ 9.9g² 12g² 10d May 30] medium-sized gelding: modest per- **a56** former: unraced on Flat in 2004/5: was effective at 1¼m to 13f: acted on polytrack, firm and good to soft going: won over hurdles in July: dead. *J. J. Quinn*

KINGSCROSS 8 ch.g. King's Signet (USA) 110 – Calamanco 71 (Clantime 101) [2006 **88** 89: 6g⁵ 6g 6d² 5.7g⁴ 7g 6.1f 6g³ 6m 7g 6s⁶ 6m⁴ 6d⁵ p6g⁵ p6g p7.1g⁶ p6g³ Dec 20] strong, **a85** good-bodied gelding: fairly useful handicapper: several creditable efforts in 2006, includ- ing when in frame: stays 7f, raced mainly at 6f: acts on polytrack, soft and good to firm going: held up. *M. Blanshard*

KING'S ENVOY (USA) 7 b.g. Royal Academy (USA) 130 – Island of Silver (USA) **–** 107 (Forty Niner (USA)) [2006 –: f16g* f14g⁶ 16m⁶ Jul 10] tall gelding: modest perform- **a54** er on Flat nowadays: first success when winning banded race at Southwell in February: stays 2m: acts on fibresand and good to firm ground: tried visored/in cheekpieces. *Mrs J. C. McGregor*

KING'S FABLE (USA) 3 b.g. Lear Fan (USA) 130 – Fairy Fable (IRE) 95 (Fairy **60** King (USA)) [2006 57: p9.5g³ p9.5g⁴ 12d⁵ 12.6g 12f 13g² 12f 11.5m 14.1g 12d* 12d Nov 3] modest handicapper: won at Catterick in September: stays 13f: acts on polytrack and heavy going: has sometimes looked none too keen: none too consistent. *M. Johnston*

KING'S GAIT 4 b.g. Mujahid (USA) 125 – Miller's Gait 74§ (Mill Reef (USA) 141) **103** [2006 102: 6v³ 5d² 6m 5s⁵ 6g 6s Aug 19] leggy, quite good-topped gelding: useful handi- capper: good efforts at Southwell (third to Philharmonic) and Beverley (short-head second to Trinculo) first 2 starts: below form after, slowly away final outing: stays 6f: best form on good ground or softer: usually blinkered nowadays. *T. D. Easterby*

KINGSGATE PRINCE (IRE) 3 b.g. Desert Sun 120 – Princess Mood (GER) (Muh- **110** tarram (USA) 125) [2006 69: p6g⁶ p7g* p6g⁴ p7g* p8g⁴ p8g² 6m² 6d⁵ 7g³ 7m³ 6m⁵ Dec 23] big, strong gelding: smart performer: vastly improved in 2006, winning maiden in January, 2 handicaps in February, listed race (beat Saabiq by 1¼ lengths) in March (all at Lingfield) and listed race at Newbury (led close home when beating Assertive ½ length) in May: good 2¼ lengths third to Jeremy in Jersey Stakes at Royal Ascot on penultimate start: left J. Best, off 6 months and renamed Sunny King, below form final outing: effective at 6f to easy 1m: acts on polytrack, good to firm and good to soft going: sometimes races freely, and usually held up. *J. Moore, Hong Kong*

KING'S HEAD (IRE) 3 b.c. King's Best (USA) 132 – Ustka 60 (Lomond (USA) 128) **103** [2006 87: 8.1g* 10.1m⁴ 10.4m³ 10m⁴ 12m³ p12.2f⁴ Aug 30] useful-looking colt: useful handicapper: much improved in 2006, dead-heating with Yarqus at Sandown in April: good efforts next 4 starts including when third to Reem Three at York and Strategic Mount in cantorspreadfair.com Stakes at Goodwood: well below form at Wolverhampton on all-weather debut final start: stays 1½m: acts on good to firm going: in cheekpieces last 2 outings: sold 130,000 gns. *M. A. Jarvis*

KINGS HEIR (IRE) 3 b.g. Princely Heir (IRE) 111 – Unimpeachable (IRE) 65 (Nam- **76 d** aqualand (USA)) [2006 78: 8.3m 8.1d 7f² 7f 7m⁵ 6g⁵ 7m p6g p9.5g p6s f5g³ Dec 27] leggy, quite attractive gelding: fair performer: left R. Beckett 4,000 gns and gelded after seventh start: ended year out of form, tried in claimer/seller: stays 8.3f: acts on firm and good to soft going: blinkered 4 of last 5 starts. *Peter Grayson*

KINGSHOLM 4 ch.g. Selkirk (USA) 129 – Putuna 98 (Generous (IRE) 139) [2006 84: **93** 8.1m 10g⁶ 8s⁵ p8g⁶ p8.6g⁴ p8g⁵ 8d* 8m* 10g² 10d Nov 4] leggy gelding: has a quick action: fairly useful handicapper: won at Goodwood in September and Bath in October, and good second at Windsor later in October: stays 1¼m: acts on polytrack, good to firm and good to soft ground: free-going sort: joined J. O'Neill. *A. M. Balding*

KING'S JESTER (IRE) 4 b.g. King's Best (USA) 132 – Scent of Success (USA) 84 **69 ?** (Quiet American (USA)) [2006 7d 5d 5.8m 5.8f 10g 9.1v⁴ 8s p8.6g Nov 23] ex-French gelding: fairly useful performer for R. Pritchard-Gordon at 3 yrs, winning minor event at Longchamp: just fair form at best in 2006: left A. Martin after fifth start: stays 1¼m: acts on heavy going. *J. J. Lambe, Ireland*

KINGSMAITE 5 b.g. Komaite (USA) – Antonias Melody 86 (Rambo Dancer (CAN) **–** 107) [2006 63, a92: f6g⁶ f6g⁵ f8s 6.1m 7.5f 5f f6g⁴ p7.1g p8.6m⁵ f8g³ f8g* p9.5g⁶ Dec 18] **a86 d** workmanlike gelding: fairly useful handicapper on all-weather; no form on turf in 2006: not at best after second outing, though won at Southwell in December: effective at 6f to

1m: acts on all-weather, probably on firm ground: tried visored, usually blinkered nowadays: tongue tied last 5 starts: none too consistent. *S. R. Bowring*

KING'S MAJESTY (IRE) 4 b.c. King's Best (USA) 132 – Tiavanita (USA) (J O Tobin (USA) 130) [2006 102: 8s Mar 25] close-coupled, well-made colt: lightly-raced handicapper, useful at 3 yrs: fair form when seventh of 30 to Blythe Knight in Lincoln at Redcar only outing in 2006: stays 1m: acts on polytrack and good to soft ground: sold 13,000 gns in October. *Sir Michael Stoute* **78**

KINGSMEAD (USA) 2 b.c. (Apr 4) Kingmambo (USA) 125 – Astor Place (USA) (Deputy Minister (CAN)) [2006 7m 8m² 8g Sep 14] close-coupled colt: second at Yarmouth, easily best effort in maidens: stays 1m. *Miss J. Feilden* **58**

KING'S MELODY 3 b.g. King Charlemagne (USA) 120 – Anabaa's Music (Anabaa (USA) 130) [2006 p7.1g p7.1g p7.1g 7.1s 10g 10.2g p8g⁶ May 15] modest maiden at best: tried blinkered. *B. R. Millman* **49 d**

KINGS POINT (IRE) 5 b.h. Fasliyev (USA) 120 – Rahika Rose 91 (Unfuwain (USA) 131) [2006 110: 9g⁴ 8.1m³ 8s⁶ 8.5m⁶ 8m 8f² 8g³ 8.9g 8d⁶ Sep 30] strong, compact horse: unimpressive mover: smart performer: good efforts in 2006 at Sandown (third to Rob Roy in Sandown Mile), York (length second to Momtic in minor event) and Salisbury (third to Belenus in Sovereign Stakes): best around 1m: acts on firm and soft ground: blinkered once, sometimes wears cheekpieces. *R. A. Fahey* **112**

KINGS QUAY 4 b.c. Montjeu (IRE) 137 – Glen Rosie (IRE) 102 (Mujtahid (USA) 118) [2006 109: 8s 8m 8f³ 10.1g⁴ 10m 8.1m 8f Aug 4] quite attractive colt: has a quick action: useful handicapper: creditable efforts when in frame at Thirsk (1¼ lengths third to Minority Report) and Epsom (2 lengths fourth to Chancellor in Rose Bowl): below form last 3 starts: best at 1m/1¼m: acts on firm and good to soft going: sometimes takes good hold: fairly useful hurdler, winner in August and September. *J. J. Quinn* **105**

KING'S RANSOM 3 b.g. Daylami (IRE) 138 – Luana 101 (Shaadi (USA) 126) [2006 70: 7g⁴ p7g 8.5g p9.5g p12.2s Dec 14] fair maiden: left A. Balding after third outing: headstrong sort, best form at 7f: acts on polytrack: blinkered last 2 starts, pulled up latterly (reportedly had breathing problem). *W. R. Muir* **73**

KING'S REGIMENT (IRE) 2 b.c. (Mar 29) King's Best (USA) 132 – Gardenia (IRE) (Sadler's Wells (USA) 132) [2006 7m p7.1f Aug 30] modest form second start in maidens (made running): sold 9,000 gns. *M. A. Jarvis* **60**

KING'S REVENGE 3 br.g. Wizard King 122 – Retaliator 80 (Rudimentary (USA) 118) [2006 76: 7.1g⁶ p8.6g* 10v⁴ 12g⁶ 10f⁵ 9.9g 8.3g* 8d⁶ 8.9s Oct 7] good-topped gelding: fairly useful performer: won maiden at Wolverhampton in May and handicap at Hamilton in September: well below form last 2 starts: barely stays 1½m: acts on polytrack, best effort on turf on good ground: blinkered 5 of last 6 starts: soon off bridle second/third outings, stumbled leaving stall on fourth: sold 17,500 gns, joined A. King. *T. D. Easterby* **86**

KINGS SHILLINGS 2 br.g. (Apr 21) Superior Premium 122 – The Kings Daughter 79 (Indian King (USA) 128) [2006 5g 6m 8.2s f6g⁴ f7g⁶ Dec 14] close-coupled gelding: modest maiden: bred for sprinting: blinkered last 3 starts. *D. Carroll* **50**

KING'S SPEAR (IRE) 3 b.c. Lear Spear (USA) 124 – First Veil 94 (Primo Dominie 121) [2006 8g 7.1m⁶ 8.1m² p9.5m p8.6g² Nov 3] well-made colt: half-brother to winner in Greece by Lake Coniston: dam, 6f/7f winner, sister to Middle Park winner First Trump: fair maiden: stays 8.6f: acts on polytrack and good to firm going: ran as if amiss fourth start. *P. W. Chapple-Hyam* **68**

KINGS SQUARE 6 b.g. Bal Harbour 113 – Prime Property (IRE) 60 (Tirol 127) [2006 16g⁶ Jul 3] strong, workmanlike gelding: no sign of ability on Flat: unreliable winning hurdler. *M. W. Easterby* **–**

KING'S THOUGHT 7 b.h. King's Theatre (IRE) 128 – Lora's Guest 99 (Be My Guest (USA) 126) [2006 100: 8v p10g p10g³ p10g⁴ p10g⁶ 12d Aug 28] angular, good-topped horse: fairly useful handicapper nowadays: best at 1m/1¼m: acts on polytrack and any turf going: wore cheekpieces once at 6 yrs: front runner. *S. Gollings* **82**

KINGS TOPIC (USA) 6 ch.g. Kingmambo (USA) 125 – Topicount (USA) (Private Account (USA)) [2006 67: p9.5g⁶ p8.6g⁵ Apr 28] deep-bodied gelding: fair performer, lightly raced: stays 1¼m: acts on polytrack, little form on turf. *A. B. Haynes* **65**

KING ZAFEEN (IRE) 4 b.c. Lend A Hand 124 – Groom Dancing (Groom Dancer (USA) 128) [2006 58: 10g² p7g p9.5g May 5] neat colt: has a quick action: modest maiden: will prove best around 1m: acts on fibresand and good to firm ground: blinkered final start: tongue tied twice at 2 yrs. *M. W. Easterby* **60**

Gran Criterium, Milan—an ordinary renewal of Italy's top 2-y-o race is dominated by the visitors, with Kirklees (star on cap) and Strobilus fighting it out ahead of Chinese Whisper (right)

KINRANDE (IRE) 4 b.g. Sri Pekan (USA) 117 – Pipers Pool (IRE) 94 (Mtoto 134) **92**
[2006 95: 12m 12m⁴ Jul 14] strong, close-coupled gelding: useful handicapper in
2005: much better effort (fairly useful form) in 2006 when fourth at Newmarket: stays
1½m: raced only on polytrack and good/good to firm ground: usually makes running.
P. J. Makin

KINSMAN (IRE) 9 b.g. Distant Relative 128 – Besito 79 (Wassl 125) [2006 46, a61: **–**
p10g p10g⁴ p10g p8g⁶ p10g p8g p10g³ p10g⁶ Dec 13] leggy, useful-looking gelding: **a52**
modest performer on all-weather, poor on turf: effective at 7f to easy 1¼m: acts on all-
weather, firm and soft going: has worn headgear: tried tongue tied: often slowly away:
sometimes carries head high/hangs: held up. *T. D. McCarthy*

KINSYA 3 ch.g. Mister Baileys 123 – Kimono (IRE) (Machiavellian (USA) 123) [2006 **96**
75: 8d* 8s³ 8.5f⁴ 8g* 8d⁴ 8d 8.9s* Oct 7] strong, close-coupled gelding: useful handicapper: won at Ripon in April, Newmarket in August and York (by neck from Bold Act)
in October: stays 9f: acts on soft going, possibly unsuited by firmer than good: none too
genuine (has hung/carried head awkwardly), but looked more straightforward at York.
M. H. Tompkins

KINTBURY CROSS 4 b.g. Kylian (USA) – Cebwob 85 (Rock City 120) [2006 84: **71**
f8g² Feb 14] leggy gelding: maiden: just fair form when second at Southwell only outing
in 2006: stays 11.6f: acts on firm and good to soft going, probably on fibresand: held up.
P. D. Cundell

KINVARA LASS (IRE) 3 b.f. Singspiel (IRE) 133 – Risarshana (FR) (Darshaan 133) **73**
[2006 8.1g 8m³ p10g³ 10m⁶ p10g⁴ p12.2g Aug 31] quite good-topped filly: third foal:
half-sister to useful 1½m winner Selebela (by Grand Lodge): dam ran once in France: fair
maiden: broke down and unseated rider 4f out at Wolverhampton final start: stayed 1¼m:
acted on polytrack and good to firm going: dead. *L. M. Cumani*

KIRIN 4 b.c. Selkirk (USA) 129 – Amaryllis (IRE) 71 (Sadler's Wells (USA) 132) [2006 **–**
74, a71?: f8g Jan 1] sturdy colt: maiden: well held only outing in 2006: tongue tied last 2
starts. *D. E. Cantillon*

KIRKBY'S BELLE (IRE) 3 b.f. Namid 128 – Saltwood 74 (Mujtahid (USA) 118) **–**
[2006 –: 5g Aug 21] workmanlike filly: no form. *G. A. Swinbank*

KIRKBY'S TREASURE 8 gr.g. Mind Games 121 – Gem of Gold 52 (Jellaby 124) **69**
[2006 84: 8v⁵ 7g 7.1g 7.9m Jul 8] tall, leggy gelding: has a round action: just fair handicapper in 2006: effective at 6f to 1m: acts on fibresand, firm and soft ground: tried in
blinkers/cheekpieces: sometimes slowly away/wanders: held up. *A. Berry*

KIRKHAMMERTON (IRE) 4 ch.g. Grand Lodge (USA) 125 – Nawara 75 (Welsh – Pageant 132) [2006 –, a62: p12.2g⁵ f11g⁴ p9.5g p12.2g p12.2g⁵ f8g* f8g² f8g⁶ 10m 7.1d **a63** f11g* p13.9g Oct 30] sturdy gelding: modest performer on all-weather, little form on turf: won banded races at Southwell in May and, having left M. Polglase after eighth start, October: effective at 1m, probably stays easy 1¾m: acts on all-weather: blinkered/visored nowadays: reportedly finished lame final start. *A. J. McCabe*

KIRKLEES (IRE) 2 b.c. (Feb 15) Jade Robbery (USA) 121 – Moyesii (USA) (Diesis **107** 133) [2006 7m² 7f* 7m³ 7g⁴ 8d³ 8g* Oct 15] big, strong colt: second foal: dam, French 9f winner, half-sister to smart miler Bowman (later 11f winner in UAE) out of Haydock Sprint Cup winner Cherokee Rose: useful performer: won maiden at Catterick in July and 11-runner Gran Criterium at Milan (rallied to beat Strobilus by short head) in October: in frame in other pattern events in between, 2¼ lengths third of 10 to Strategic Prince in Vintage Stakes at Goodwood, 2½ lengths fourth of 8 to Vital Equine in Champagne Stakes at York, and 4½ lengths third of 7 to Admiralofthefleet in Royal Lodge Stakes at Ascot: stays 1m: acts on firm and good to soft going: usually front runner: joined Godolphin. *M. Johnston*

KIRK MICHAEL 2 b.c. (Mar 29) Selkirk (USA) 129 – Pervenche (Latest Model 115) **87** [2006 7m⁴ 7d² Sep 29] leggy, useful-looking colt: closely related to 11-y-o Gorse and 4-y-o Puya: dam unplaced in Britain/USA: fairly useful form in maidens, fourth to Dijeerr at Leicester and second to Supersonic Dave at Newmarket: may prove best up to 7f. *H. Candy*

KIRKSTALL LANE 3 b.g. Selkirk (USA) 129 – L'Animee (Green Tune (USA) 125) **46** [2006 –: 10d 12.1s 10m³ 10.9g 11.6m⁶ Jul 17] tall gelding: poor maiden: probably stays 11.6f: acts on good to firm ground: blinkered last 3 starts: sold 7,000 gns. *R. Hannon*

Sheikh Mohammed's "Kirklees"

KIRKSTONE (IRE) 5 b.g. Alzao (USA) 117 – Night Mirage (USA) 80 (Silver Hawk **72** (USA) 123) [2006 p10g² p8.6g² p10g² p12.2g* p12g Feb 21] big, good-topped gelding: fair performer: missed 2004/5: won maiden at Wolverhampton in February: stays 1½m: acts on polytrack and good to firm going: sent to USA. *J. A. Osborne*

KIRSTYS LAD 4 b.g. Lake Coniston (IRE) 131 – Killick 69 (Slip Anchor 136) [2006 **51** –: p7.1g⁴ f7g p6g⁶ 7.6m⁶ 7.6m p12.2m f16g f12m Oct 31] modest maiden: stays 1½m: acts on polytrack and good to firm going: tried blinkered. *M. Mullineaux*

KISS CHASE (IRE) 2 b.c. (May 18) Val Royal (FR) 127 – Zurarah (Siberian Express – (USA) 125) [2006 p7g p8g Nov 8] well beaten in maidens. *P. Mitchell*

KISSI KISSI 3 b.f. Paris House 123 – Miss Whittingham (IRE) 68 (Fayruz 116) [2006 **43** –: p8.6g² p8.6g 8.2m p8.6g³ 8.1m⁵ f8g 8.5f⁶ 8.2g p6m⁵ f7g f6g f7g p6g* Nov 28] **a57** tall, close-coupled filly: modest performer on all-weather, poor on turf: won maiden at Wolverhampton in February: stays 8.6f: acts on polytrack: tried visored (including when successful)/tongue tied. *M. J. Attwater*

KISSIMEE 3 br.f. Whittingham (IRE) 104 – Shalyah (IRE) 65 (Shalford (IRE) 124§) – [2006 –: p6g p7g Feb 28] no form: tried tongue tied. *N. P. Littmoden*

KISS THE RAIN 6 b.m. Forzando 122 – Devils Dirge 68 (Song 132) [2006 55: p5.1g **48** p6g p7.1g 5.7f Jun 17] small mare: poor performer nowadays: best at 5f/6f: acts on all-weather, firm and soft ground: visored/blinkered. *R. Brotherton*

KISWAHILI 4 ch.f. Selkirk (USA) 129 – Kiliniski 119 (Niniski (USA) 125) [2006 100: **105** 12.5s 14m* 12f⁶ 13.9f⁵ 14g* 13.4g⁴ 12g³ p16g⁴ Nov 11] big, lengthy filly: useful performer: won minor event at Leopardstown (very easily) in June and listed race at Munich (by ¾ length from Amoroso) in July: ran well when fourth to New Guinea in listed handicap at Chester sixth start: stays 2m: acts on firm and soft going (well below form on all-weather debut final outing): tried blinkered: tends to race freely: often reluctant at stall (refused to enter once at 3 yrs, subsequently wore blanket). *Sir Mark Prescott*

KITABAAT (IRE) 3 ch.f. Halling (USA) 133 – Nabadhaat (USA) 72 (Mr Prospector **66** (USA)) [2006 10g⁶ 12g Aug 7] tall, angular filly: second foal: half-sister to 4-y-o Tarabut: dam, maiden who should have stayed at least 1¼m, out of Yorkshire Oaks winner Roseate Tern: better effort in maidens when 6¾ lengths sixth to Kaylianni at Newbury on debut: well below form at Ripon next time. *E. A. L. Dunlop*

KITCHEN SINK (IRE) 4 ch.g. Bold Fact (USA) 116 – Voodoo Rocket 56 (Lycius **66** (USA) 124) [2006 65, a61: p6g³ p6g³ p6g 6d 6m⁴ 5.1g² 5.7m² 6.1m p6g² Dec 20] good-bodied gelding: fair maiden handicapper: best at 5f/6f: acts on polytrack, good to firm and good to soft going: tried blinkered: none too resolute. *P. J. Makin*

KLASSEN (USA) 3 br.c. Pine Bluff (USA) – One Great Lady (USA) (Fappiano **60** (USA)) [2006 10m 9.9g 10g Aug 7] leggy colt: modest form in maidens. *A. King*

KNAPTON HILL 2 b.f. (Mar 20) Zamindar (USA) 116 – Torgau (IRE) 109 (Zieten **60** (USA) 118) [2006 6m 6m⁶ 6.1d f6g⁵ Dec 23] €30,000Y: quite good-topped filly: third foal: dam 2-y-o 5f/6f (Cherry Hinton Stakes) winner: modest maiden: left H. Morrison 10,000 gns after third outing. *R. Hollinshead*

KNEAD THE DOUGH 5 b.g. Wolfhound (USA) 126 – Ridgewood Ruby (IRE) 77 **58** (Indian Ridge 123) [2006 45, a53: 10.2f 5.7m 5.2f³ 6m² 6d² 6m³ 5.7m 6s p6g⁶ Oct 23] smallish, strong gelding: modest maiden: best form at 5f/6f: acts on all-weather, firm and good to soft going: tried in cheekpieces/visor/tongue tie. *A. E. Price*

KNICKERLESS (IRE) 3 b.f. Fayruz 116 – June Lady (Junius (USA) 124) [2006 48: – 5.9m 8.3m 7.5f 7g⁵ 7d Aug 25] leggy filly: maiden: little form in 2006: stays 7f: acts on firm going: sold 800 gns, sent to Italy. *N. P. Littmoden*

KNICKYKNACKIENOO 5 b.g. Bin Ajwaad (IRE) 119 – Ring Fence 74 (Polar – Falcon (USA) 126) [2006 59: f7g May 31] big, plain gelding: handicapper: well held only outing in 2006. *T. T. Clement*

KNIGHT VALLIANT 3 bl.g. Dansili 127 – Aristocratique 71 (Cadeaux Genereux **64** 131) [2006 59p: 9.8m 10.1m³ 10.1m² 12g Sep 5] close-coupled filly: modest performer: should stay 1½m: acts on good to firm ground. *J. Howard Johnson*

KNOCK BRIDGE (IRE) 4 b.f. Rossini (USA) 118 – Touraneena (Robellino (USA) **60** 127) [2006 79, a–: f8g p8.6g 10f⁵ 8.3m⁴ Aug 5] leggy filly: modest performer nowadays: **a–** left P. D. Evans after reappearance: stays 1¼m: acts on soft and good to firm going: tried in cheekpieces: sometimes slowly away. *D. Carroll*

KNOT IN WOOD (IRE) 4 b.g. Shinko Forest (IRE) – Notley Park 71 (Wolfhound 107 (USA) 126) [2006 82: 5s⁴ 6f³ 6m³ 6m² 6f* 6f⁴ 6g³ 6d* 6d⁵ 6g² 6s² Oct 7] sturdy gelding: useful handicapper: progressed very well in 2006, winning at Haydock in July and York in August: very good efforts when runner-up last 2 starts, beaten short head by Stanley Goodspeed at Haydock and neck by Rising Shadow in valuable event at York: effective at 6f/7f, well worth another try over 5f: acts on firm and soft going: effective held up or making running: tough and reliable. *R. A. Fahey*

KNOTTED 3 b.f. Xaar 132 – Ash Glade (Nashwan (USA) 135) [2006 9.9g⁶ May 18] 62 sixth foal: half-sister to 7-y-o Magic Glade and a winner in Greece by Inchinor: dam unraced close relative of very smart 1¼m/1½m performer Ulundi and half-sister to 1000 Guineas winner Wince, herself dam of Yorkshire Oaks winner Quiff: 8/1, 8¼ lengths sixth to Oh Glory Be in maiden at Salisbury. *R. Charlton*

KODIAC 5 b.h. Danehill (USA) 126 – Rafha 123 (Kris 135) [2006 107: 6.5m² 6.5m* 112 6.5g⁶ 8m 6g³ 6g² 6.5g⁴ 6s 5m Oct 1] small, sturdy horse: smart performer: trained by E. Charpy in UAE first 4 outings in 2006, including when winning handicap at Nad Al Sheba in February by ½ length from Royal Storm: returned to former trainer, good efforts after when neck second to Fayr Jag in Hackwood Stakes at Newbury and 3 lengths fourth to Marchand d'Or in Prix Maurice de Gheest at Deauville: well below form in Sprint Cup at Haydock and Prix de l'Abbaye at Longchamp (missed break, always trailing) last 2 outings: was best around 6f: acted on good to firm going, well held on softer than good: usually blinkered: tended to edge right: to stand at Tally-Ho Stud, Co Westmeath, Ireland, fee €5,000. *J. L. Dunlop*

KOFFIEFONTEIN (USA) 2 ch.f. (Feb 20) Diesis 133 – Kimberley Mine (SAF) – (Fort Wood (USA) 117) [2006 6.1f 6g Aug 7] strong filly: first foal: dam 5f (at 2 yrs) to 9f winner in South Africa: behind in maidens, not fully wound up. *L. M. Cumani*

KOKILA 3 b.f. Indian Danehill (IRE) 124 – Poetry In Motion (IRE) 76 (Ballad Rock 63 122) [2006 53p: p6g p8.6g² p8.6g⁶ 11g f8g⁶ p12.2m 17.2g Oct 17] lengthy filly: modest maiden: left W. Haggas after fifth start: stays 8.6f: blinkered fifth start. *M. H. Tompkins*

KOLHAPUR (IRE) 3 ch.c. Barathea (IRE) 127 – Koniya (IRE) (Doyoun 124) [2006 – 61p: 10.2g 8.2s May 20] maiden: well held in handicaps in 2006: blinkered final start. *J. L. Dunlop*

KOMPETE 2 b.f. (Mar 31) Komaite (USA) – Competa (Hernando (FR) 127) [2006 91 5.2m³ 6g 5.1d* 6d⁴ p6m³ Nov 8] 2,500Y: good-topped filly: second foal: sister to 3-y-o Punjabi: dam unraced: fairly useful form: off 5 months after debut: won maiden at Nottingham in October: much improved when fourth to Blue Echo in listed race at Newmarket: will stay 7f: acts on good to soft going, below best on polytrack final start. *V. Smith*

KOMREYEV STAR 4 b.g. Komaite (USA) – L'Ancressaan 67 (Dalsaan 125) [2006 60 60: p9.5g 8.1s p13.9g 8.3d 10g 10g 9d* 9.1v² p8g f8g⁶ Dec 12] sturdy gelding: modest **a45** performer: won banded event at Musselburgh in October: stays 9.5f: acts on all-weather (below best on it in 2006) and any turf going (best efforts on softer than good): in cheek-pieces last time. *M. Mullineaux*

KONDAKOVA (IRE) 2 b.f. (Jan 31) Soviet Star (USA) 128 – Solar Star (USA) 93 **77 p** (Lear Fan (USA) 130) [2006 6m³ p6m* Oct 2] good-topped filly: closely related to fairly useful 2001 2-y-o 1m winner Star Cross (by Ashkalani) who stayed 15f, and half-sister to several winners, including useful French 1999 2-y-o 7f winner Bintalreef (by Diesis): dam, 2-y-o 6f winner, half-sister to smart US 6f/7f performer Gold Land: fair form: confirmed Yarmouth promise (third to Kaseema) by winning maiden at Wolverhampton, despite again drifting left: will be suited by 1m: type to go on progressing. *M. L. W. Bell*

KON TIKI 2 b.f. (Feb 25) Red Ransom (USA) – First Fleet (USA) 106 (Woodman 69 (USA) 126) [2006 6g 7m⁵ p7g⁶ p8.6m³ Oct 31] sturdy, good-topped filly: second foal: dam, French 1m/1¼m winner (including at 2 yrs), out of close relative to high-class middle-distance performer Assatis: fair maiden: third in nursery at Wolverhampton final start: will stay 1¼m. *M. Johnston*

KOOL ACCLAIM 5 b.m. Royal Applause 124 – Carrie Kool 69 (Prince Sabo 123) 61 [2006 6m 6m 5.5g 5.2f 6m⁶ Aug 9] workmanlike mare: modest performer nowadays: missed 2005: stays 6f: raced on good ground or firmer. *S. C. Williams*

KOOL OVATION 4 b.g. Royal Applause 124 – Carrie Kool 69 (Prince Sabo 123) 85 [2006 79: 6d 6m 5.9m² 6f² 6f³ 7m² 7d 6m⁵ Aug 31] tall gelding: fairly useful handicapper: runner-up 3 times in 2006: stays 7f: acts on firm going. *A. Dickman*

KORIKANCHA (IRE) 3 b.f. Fasliyev (USA) 120 – Amravati (IRE) 88 (Project Manager 111) [2006 72: f8g³ p8g 8.1m Aug 10] rather leggy filly: left J. Noseda 3,200 gns after second start: stays 1m: acts on all-weather, soft and good to firm ground: ungenuine. *Miss Z. C. Davison*   **71 §**

KOROLIEVA (IRE) 3 b.f. Xaar 132 – Dark Hyacinth (IRE) 65 (Darshaan 133) [2006 70: 8d p8.6m p8.6g f7g Dec 9] leggy filly: fair performer at 2 yrs: well held in handicaps in 2006: tried blinkered. *K. A. Ryan*   **–**

KORTY 2 b.g. (May 3) Averti (IRE) 117 – Promissory (Caerleon (USA) 132) [2006 5m Jun 16] close-coupled gelding: burly and green in maiden at York (gelded after). *W. J. Musson*   **–**

KOSSIES MATE 7 b.m. Cosmonaut – Pola Star (IRE) (Un Desperado (FR) 125) [2006 16.2f Jul 28] first foal: dam unraced: no form in bumpers/poor form over hurdles: well beaten in claimer at Chepstow on Flat debut. *P. W. Hiatt*   **–**

KOSTAR 5 ch.g. Komaite (USA) – Black And Amber 45 (Weldnaas (USA) 112) [2006 101: p6g² 7m* 6m 7m⁶ 7m⁴ 6g² 6d Sep 16] useful handicapper: won valuable event at Lingfield (beat Munaddam ¾ length) in May: also ran very well when head second to Idle Power at Windsor penultimate start: stays 7f: acts on polytrack, firm and good to soft ground: withdrawn after unruly in stall once, and sometimes slowly away: has been early to post. *C. G. Cox*   **104**

KOVA HALL (IRE) 4 ch.g. Halling (USA) 133 – My Micheline (Lion Cavern (USA) 117) [2006 90: 10g² 10m 9.9g Jun 28] compact gelding: fairly useful handicapper: won at Tipperary in 2005 (when trained by D. Weld in Ireland): fit from hurdling, good neck second at Nottingham on reappearance: below form after: stays 1¼m: acts on good to firm going: tried blinkered: sold 9,000 gns in October, joined M. Harris. *B. G. Powell*   **94**

KRAKATAU (FR) 2 b.c. (Mar 5) Noverre (USA) 125 – Tomanivi (Caerleon (USA) 132) [2006 p7g⁵ p6g³ Dec 23] modest form in maiden at Kempton and minor event (third of 4) at Wolverhampton. *D. J. Wintle*   **55**

KRASIVI'S BOY (USA) 4 b. or br.g. Swain (IRE) 134 – Krasivi (USA) (Nijinsky (CAN) 138) [2006 64: 11.9m p16g⁵ f11g Dec 28] modest maiden: stays 2m: acts on polytrack, soft and good to firm going: blinkered 5 of last 6 starts. *G. L. Moore*   **56**

KRATAIOS (FR) 6 b.h. Sabrehill (USA) 120 – Loxandra 76 (Last Tycoon 131) [2006 109: 8s* 8v⁵ 8d* 9.3d³ 8m⁶ 8g⁴ Oct 29] big, heavy-topped horse: very smart performer: won 4 races in 2005, including listed race at Marseilles-Borely: better than ever in 2006, winning listed race at Saint-Cloud in March and Prix du Muguet there (by 2½ lengths from Kendor Dine) in May: ran well when ¾-length third to Laverock in Prix d'Ispahan at Longchamp next time: respectable effort after 4-month break when fourth to Passager in Prix Perth at Saint-Cloud final start: effective at 1m/1¼m: acts on heavy and good to firm ground: races prominently. *C. Laffon-Parias, France*   **121**

KRIKKET 2 ch.f. (May 8) Sinndar (IRE) 134 – Star of The Course (USA) 95 (Theatrical 128) [2006 p7g p7g 6.1g Sep 26] smallish filly: fourth foal: closely related to 1¼m and (in Spain) 11f winner Grand Course (by Grand Lodge) and half-sister to winner in Italy by Indian Ridge: dam 1½m winner: modest form in maidens: caught the eye third start when seventh of 15 at Nottingham, finishing well from rear not knocked about (trainer fined £5,000, jockey suspended for 28 days and horse banned for 40 days): bred to be suited by 1¼m/1½m: open to improvement, and should do well in handicaps. *W. J. Haggas*   **55 p**

KRIS SPRING 4 b.f. Kris S (USA) – Crown of Spring (USA) (Chief's Crown (USA)) [2006 –: p7g p6g p7.1g f6g⁵ May 16] tall, rather leggy filly: no form: in cheekpieces/visored last 2 starts. *R. M. H. Cowell*   **–**

KRISTALCHEN 4 b.f. Singspiel (IRE) 133 – Crystal Flite (IRE) 76 (Darshaan 133) [2006 –: 7d 9.2f 8m 12f* 12m⁵ 15.8m Aug 8] lightly-made filly: poor performer: won claimer at Catterick in July: stays 1½m: probably acts on any ground on turf. *D. W. Thompson*   **43**

KRISTENSEN 7 ch.g. Kris S (USA) – Papaha (FR) 103 (Green Desert (USA) 127) [2006 88: f12s 16v⁶ 14g³ 21.6d⁵ 18.7m 15m² 16f³ 21m 14m² 14m* 14g⁵ Aug 31] smallish, sturdy gelding: fairly useful handicapper: won apprentice event at Musselburgh in August: effective at 1¾m to 21f: acts on all-weather, firm and soft going: usually wears cheekpieces/visor: held up: unreliable: sold 4,200 gns. *Karen McLintock*   **81 §**

KRISTIANSAND 6 b.g. Halling (USA) 133 – Zonda 100 (Fabulous Dancer (USA) 124) [2006 –: 10g 12g⁶ 12m⁴ 15m⁵ 13m² 15m 12.4s 9.1v⁶ Oct 28] tall gelding: modest handicapper nowadays: stays 15f: acts on any turf going. *P. Monteith*   **59**

totesport 0800 221 221 Stakes (Handicap), Lingfield—Kostar shows the best finishing speed
stepped up in trip; Munaddam (striped cap), Romany Nights (blinkers)
and Coleorton Dancer (left) also make the frame

KRISTINOR (FR) 4 ch.g. Inchinor 119 – Kristina 92 (Kris 135) [2006 68: f11g 8f² ?
May 1] big, lengthy gelding: modest maiden: changed hands £3,000 after reappearance:
second in handicap at L'Ancresse (Guernsey) final start: stays 1m: acts on polytrack and
good to firm going: tried in headgear: edgy sort, and refused to enter stall once at 3 yrs.
G. L. Moore

KRISTOFFERSEN 6 ch.g. Kris 135 – Towaahi (IRE) (Caerleon (USA) 132) [2006 66
p12.2g⁴ 14.1g 12g⁶ Jul 13] smallish, well-made gelding: fairly useful at 3 yrs: reportedly
fractured knee and hock in fall over hurdles in 2004: unraced on Flat at 5 yrs: fair at
best in 2006: stays 1½m: acts on polytrack, raced only on good ground or firmer on turf:
blinkered final 4-y-o start: tends to carry head high: won over fences later in July. *Ian
Williams*

KRUGERRAND (USA) 7 ch.g. Gulch (USA) – Nasers Pride (USA) (Al Nasr (FR) 94
126) [2006 100: p8g 10g 8.5g 8.9m³ 8m 10m² 10.5m 10g 10s* 10.4s⁵ 10s 10d Nov 4]
big, lengthy gelding: fairly useful handicapper nowadays: won at Ayr in September: stays
1¼m: acts on firm and soft going: tongue tied once at 2 yrs: held up: none too genuine.
W. J. Musson

KUDBEME 4 b.f. Forzando 122 – Umbrian Gold (IRE) 83 (Perugino (USA) 84) [2006 69
75: 7d 7.5f 8g 7m 7.5m⁵ Sep 19] smallish, strong, sturdy filly: fair performer: stays 1m:
acts on good to firm and good to soft going: blinkered (raced too freely) on reappearance: often slowly away: has tended to hang left. *N. Bycroft*

KUKA 5 b.g. Polar Prince (IRE) 117 – Crissem (IRE) 70 (Thatching 131) [2006 –: f12g –
Feb 5] big, rangy gelding: little form since debut at 2 yrs. *R. Hollinshead*

KUMAKAWA 8 ch.g. Dancing Spree (USA) – Maria Cappuccini 70 (Siberian Express – §
(USA) 125) [2006 –§, a54§: p8.6g f7g⁴ f8g f8g⁵ f8g* f8g Feb 26] tall gelding: modest on a54 §
all-weather, bad on turf: won apprentice handicap at Southwell (seventh course success)
in February: stays 9.4f: acts on fibresand: tried in headgear: difficult ride: unreliable.
D. K. Ivory

KUNTE KINTEH 2 b.g. (Jan 30) Indian Lodge (IRE) 127 – Summer Siren (FR) (Saint **67 p** Cyrien (FR) 128) [2006 5m⁴ 7m⁶ 6d Sep 14] 27,000Y: third foal (a twin): brother to 4-y-o Native American: dam, ran once in France, half-sister to smart French/US 1m to 1¼m performer Val des Bois: modest form in maidens, off 3 months before second start (shaped well), gelded after final one: will be suited by 1m/1¼m: should make a better 3-y-o. *D. Nicholls*

KURKOVA (IRE) 4 b.f. Fasliyev (USA) 120 – Bellissi (IRE) 77 (Bluebird (USA) 125) **48** [2006 66?: 6m 5f 5f p5g Dec 6] poor sprint maiden: tried blinkered/tongue tied. *John A. Quinn, Ireland*

KURUMDA 2 b.g. (Mar 19) Montjeu (IRE) 137 – Susun Kelapa (USA) 94 (St Jovite – (USA) 135) [2006 p7g Nov 11] 75,000F, 400,000Y: brother to fairly useful Irish 7f winner Monsusu and half-brother to 1m seller winner Non Ultra (by Peintre Celebre): dam, Irish 1m (at 2 yrs)/9f winner, out of half-sister to dam of Green Tune and Pas de Reponse: 4/1, well beaten in maiden at Kempton: gelded after. *C. R. Egerton*

KUSSHARRO 5 ch.g. Case Law 113 – Risking 88 (Risk Me (FR) 127) [2006 p9.5g p8g – p5.1g p7g 8f Jun 20] well-made gelding: little form: tried tongue tied: reportedly bled final outing. *Mrs L. J. Young*

KUSTER 10 b.g. Indian Ridge 123 – Ustka 60 (Lomond (USA) 128) [2006 80: 10m⁶ **84** 11.7m Aug 21] good-bodied gelding: unimpressive mover: fairly useful nowadays: reportedly finished lame final outing: stays 1½m: acts on firm and soft going: usually blinkered: hung left on reappearance: usually held up. *L. M. Cumani*

KUT (IRE) 3 b.c. Royal Applause 124 – Amber Tide (IRE) 75 (Pursuit of Love 124) **71** [2006 60p: p7.1g³ p7.1g⁴ Jan 30] fair maiden: stays 7f: acts on polytrack. *J. Noseda*

KYATHOS (GER) 5 br.g. Dashing Blade 117 – Kajaana (Esclavo (FR)) [2006 a8.5g* **?** p13.9g⁶ Nov 27] won minor event at Dusseldorf and handicap at Neuss in 2005 and handicap (dead-heated) at Dortmund (final outing on Flat for P. Schiergen in Germany) in January): well beaten over hurdles and in amateur event on Flat subsequently: stays 8.5f: acts on dirt and good to soft going. *M. F. Harris*

KYLE (IRE) 2 ch.g. (Jan 27) Kyllachy 129 – Staylily (IRE) (Grand Lodge (USA) 125) **79** [2006 5.1g³ 5.1m³ 6d² 6g² 6d² 6g² Nov 13] 41,000Y: lengthy gelding: first foal: dam unraced out of half-sister to Coronation Cup winner Be My Native: fair maiden: placed all starts: gelded after: will prove best kept to 5f/6f: acts on polytrack, untried on extremes of going on turf: once in cheekpieces: no battler. *R. Hannon*

KYLE OF LOCHALSH 6 gr.g. Vettori (IRE) 119 – Shaieef (IRE) 66 (Shareef Dancer **61** (USA) 135) [2006 55: p9.5g 12m³ 12f* 12g³ 12m⁶ 11.1g² 11.1m³ 12.1m* p13.9g⁵ 12d⁶ p12.2g Nov 18] leggy gelding: modest handicapper: won at Musselburgh in June and Hamilton in August: barely stays easy 1¾m: acts on polytrack, firm and good to soft ground: tried in cheekpieces/blinkers: held up. *J. S. Goldie*

KYLES PRINCE (IRE) 4 b.g. In The Wings 128 – Comprehension (USA) 87§ **86** (Diesis 133) [2006 82+: 11.6g 12g 11s⁵ p12g* p12g Nov 5] big, strong gelding: fairly useful performer: improved to win handicap at Lingfield in October: should stay 1¾m: acts on polytrack and soft ground. *P. J. Makin*

KYLKENNY 11 b.g. Kylian (USA) – Fashion Flow (Balidar 133) [2006 93: f12g² p12g **75** f12g* f12s* 10g 10.2d⁵ 10f 11m⁵ 9.9s⁵ 10g³ 11.1d⁵ 10g³ 12s⁶ p12g p10g f12g⁴ p10g **a94** Dec 20] angular, workmanlike gelding: fairly useful on all-weather, fair on turf: won claimer at Southwell (left H. Morrison £14,000) in February and handicap there in March (only outing for D. Carroll): left P. Cundell and rejoined former trainer after ninth start: effective at 1¼m/1½m: acts on fibresand, firm and soft going: usually tongue tied: free-going sort: sometimes wanders. *H. Morrison*

KYLLACHY STORM 2 b.c. (Mar 27) Kyllachy 129 – Social Storm (USA) (Future **67** Storm (USA)) [2006 5.1g 7g 5.7m⁵ p7.1g⁶ p5.1g⁶ Nov 25] 27,000Y, 35,000 2-y-o: compact colt: second foal: dam, US 7f/8.5f winner (including at 2 yrs), out of sister to Park Hill Stakes winner Quay Line: fair maiden: mid-field in nurseries: should prove best at 5f/6f: acts on good to firm going, probably polytrack: blinkered final start. *R. J. Hodges*

KYLOE BELLE (USA) 2 b.f. (May 4) Elusive Quality – Besha (USA) (Turko- **60** man (USA)) [2006 6g 6d 6d Oct 18] $65,000Y: strong filly: half-sister to winner in USA by Miswaki: dam, ran twice in USA, half-sister to US 2-y-o Grade 1 8.5f winner Script Ohio: modest form in maidens. *Mrs A. J. Perrett*

KYOTO CITY 2 b.f. (Apr 18) Vettori (IRE) 119 – Cominna (Dominion 123) [2006 – p5.1g 5f p5.1g 5d f6m⁵ f6g f6g p6g⁵ p6g⁶ Dec 11] 1,000 2-y-o: half-sister to several winners, including fairly useful 7.5f to 1¼m winner Forty Forte (by Pursuit of Love): dam unraced sister to very smart sprinter Primo Dominie: little form. *D. W. Chapman*

KYOTO SUMMIT 3 ch.c. Lomitas 129 – Alligram (USA) 61 (Alysheba (USA)) **94** [2006 83: 10d* 12g⁴ 9.9f p12g³ Sep 18] leggy colt: fairly useful performer: won maiden at Nottingham (by 5 lengths) in April: creditable third in handicap at Kempton final start: stays 1½m: acts on polytrack and good to soft going: sold 50,000 gns. *L. M. Cumani*

KYRENIA GIRL (IRE) 2 b.f. (Mar 20) King Charlemagne (USA) 120 – Cherry Hills **52** (IRE) (Anabaa (USA) 130) [2006 5m⁶ Jul 8] €11,000F, 8,500Y: first foal: dam, ran once, half-sister to 1m/1¼m performer Mubeen: 25/1 and green, 7½ lengths sixth in maiden at Carlisle. *T. D. Easterby*

KYRHENA 2 b.f. (Feb 5) Desert Prince (IRE) 130 – Kyle Rhea 104 (In The Wings 128) **–** [2006 7.1d p8.6m p9.5g Dec 7] £9,200Y: fifth foal: half-sister to useful winner around 1m in Britain/USA Kirtle and 1m winner Sewmore Character (both by Hector Protector): dam 1¼m/11.4f winner: well beaten in maidens. *C. W. Thornton*

KYSHANTY 2 b.c. (Apr 20) Kyllachy 129 – War Shanty 66 (Warrshan (USA) 117) **77** [2006 6m 6.1g* 6m* p5g⁶ 6.1m² 7.1g 6s Oct 6] 10,500Y: good-topped colt: fifth foal: half-brother to 5-y-o All Quiet and 1½m winner Busaco (by Mister Baileys): dam lightly-raced half-sister to very smart sprinter Bold Edge: fair performer: won maiden at Chepstow and minor event at Salisbury in July: ran well only once in nurseries after: best at 6f: acts on good to firm going, probably polytrack: sold 18,000 gns, sent to Czech Republic. *R. Hannon*

L

LABELLED WITH LOVE 6 ch.g. Zilzal (USA) 137 – Dream Baby (Master Willie **64** 129) [2006 64, a59: p8g³ p8g p7g⁵ p6g⁵ p7g* p7g² p7.1g³ p6g⁵ p8g⁶ p6g⁵ Dec 5] tall gelding: modest performer: won claimer at Lingfield in May: effective at 6f to easy 1¼m: acts on all-weather, good to firm and good to soft going: usually tongue tied: often slowly away/races freely. *J. R. Boyle*

LA BOMBA VELOCE 3 b.f. Tomba 119 – Charleigh Keary 55 (Sulaafah (USA) 119) **–** [2006 –: p6g Jan 4] little form: blinkered last 2 starts. *Mrs L. Williamson*

LACEWORK 2 ch.f. (Mar 28) Pivotal 124 – Entwine 92 (Primo Dominie 121) [2006 **79 p** p8g² p7.1g* Dec 1] third foal: sister to 4-y-o Cyclical and 3-y-o Envision: dam, 2-y-o 5f winner, half-sister to smart sprinter Feet So Fast (by Pivotal): confirmed debut promise when winning 9-runner maiden at Wolverhampton by neck from Fidelia, still looking green and hanging right: slowly away on debut: capable of better still. *Sir Michael Stoute*

LA CHESNERAIE 2 b.f. (Mar 17) Groom Dancer (USA) 128 – Oomph 83 (Shareef **48** Dancer (USA) 135) [2006 7.1d f7g p9.5g⁶ Dec 9] second foal: closely related to 3-y-o Very Agreeable: dam, 7f winner, half-sister to smart 7f/1m performer Swiss Law: poor maiden: tongue tied. *P. C. Haslam*

LA CHUNGA (USA) 3 br.f. More Than Ready (USA) 120 – Gypsy Monarch (USA) **109** (Wavering Monarch (USA)) [2006 109: 8s 5m 6f* 6.5g 6d Sep 24] strong, sturdy filly: useful performer: back to best when winning Summer Stakes at York by 1¼ lengths from Donna Blini, soon under pressure but getting up final 1f) in July: below form in Prix Maurice de Gheest at Deauville next time: visored, respectable seventh to Red Clubs in Diadem Stakes at Ascot final start: likely to prove best at 5f/6f (stamina stretched in 1000 Guineas at Newmarket on reappearance): acts on firm going: has worn crossed noseband: sold 485,000 gns. *J. Noseda*

LA COLLINE (GER) 3 ch.f. Ocean of Wisdom (USA) 106 – La Laja (GER) (Be My **76 p** Guest (USA) 126) [2006 6d² 6.1d* f6g* f6g* f6g* Dec 23] 10,500F: compact filly: third foal: half-sister to Italian 7.5f to 1¼m winner Los Vascos (by Efisio) and German 6f to 7.7f winner La Rosa (by Perugino): dam 7.5f to 8.5f winner in Germany: fair form, winning maiden at Warwick in October and handicaps at Southwell in November (2) and December: will stay 7f: open to further improvement. *W. J. Haggas*

LA COMMARA (IRE) 4 ch.f. Dr Devious (IRE) 127 – Siva (FR) (Bellypha 130) **70 d** [2006 70: 8v 8.7d 8.5s 11d³ 11v⁴ 12g 13d 8v 10v⁶ f11g Nov 14] half-sister to several winners, including 6f to 9f winner May Queen Megan (by Petorius): dam French 1m to 11f winner: fair maiden handicapper: below form after fifth outing: stays 11f: acts on heavy going: blinkered last 2 outings. *D. Loughnane, Ireland*

Audi Stakes (King George), Goodwood—
La Cucaracha quickens past the pacesetting Desert Lord (blinkers); Pivotal Flame (cheekpieces) is third

LA CUCARACHA 5 b.m. Piccolo 121 – Peggy Spencer 77 (Formidable (USA) 125) **119**
[2006 119: 5m 6m 5f* Aug 3] good-topped mare: smart performer: won 4 races at 4 yrs, notably Nunthorpe Stakes at York: ninth in King's Stand Stakes at Royal Ascot (in need of outing) and eleventh in July Cup at Newmarket (raced on unfavoured side) prior to readily justifying favouritism by ¾ length from Desert Lord in Audi Stakes (King George) at Goodwood in August: missed Nunthorpe Stakes at York later in month reportedly due to a pulled ligament: effective at 5f/6f: acts on good to firm going, seemingly not on soft: has been bandaged hind joints: travels strongly, and has a good turn of foot: sold 525,000 gns in November, sent to USA. *B. W. Hills*

LA CUVEE 2 b.f. (May 12) Mark of Esteem (IRE) 137 – Premiere Cuvee 109 (Formid- **–**
able (USA) 125) [2006 6d p5.1g p5g Nov 9] half-sister to several winners, including Italian 1m winner She Bat (by Batshoof) and 7f/1m winner Cask (by Be My Chief), both useful: dam sprinter: little show in maidens. *R. M. Beckett*

LADAS LAD 2 ch.g. (May 14) Efisio 120 – Ordained 66 (Mtoto 134) [2006 5.1d⁵ 6f⁴ **–**
7m Jul 26] little form in sellers: tried in cheekpieces. *W. G. M. Turner*

LADDIES POKER (USA) 2 gr.c. (May 1) Stravinsky (USA) 133 – Lady In Waiting **100**
(USA) (Woodman (USA) 126) [2006 7d p7g⁴ 7d⁵ Sep 19] €110,000Y: sixth foal: brother to useful Irish 2003 2-y-o 6f winner Acciacatura and half-brother to 2 winners in USA, including Grade 3 8.5f winner Kid Grindstone (by Grindstone): dam, US 8.5f/9f winner, out of champion US older mare Princess Rooney: modest form in 2 maidens: 100/1, much improved and useful form when 2½ lengths fifth of 28 to Miss Beatrix in very valuable sales race at the Curragh: will stay 1m: slow starter: sold 60,000 gns, sent to USA. *J. Noseda*

LADIES BEST 2 b.c. (May 1) King's Best (USA) 132 – Lady of The Lake 104 (Caer- **99 p**
leon (USA) 132) [2006 7g 8d* 8g* Oct 12] 60,000Y: angular, good-bodied colt: has a quick action: fifth foal: half-brother to useful 1m (at 2 yrs) and 2m winner Coventina (by Daylami) and 1½m winner Largo (by Selkirk): dam, 2m/17f winner, out of smart performer up to 9f Llyn Gwynant: useful form: progressed fast after debut, winning maiden at Salisbury in September and nursery at Newmarket in October, in latter beating Buccellati by length (value extra), coming through from well back: sure to be suited by 1¼m/1½m: smart prospect. *Sir Michael Stoute*

LADIES KNIGHT 6 b.g. Among Men (USA) 124 – Lady Silk 67 (Prince Sabo 123) **–**
[2006 –, a59: p5.1g⁶ p6g⁶ p8g p8.6g f7s f5g Mar 14] leggy, angular gelding: modest per- **a56**
former: effective at 5f/6f: acts on all-weather: tried visored: often slowly away. *D. Shaw*

LADY ALGARHOUD (FR) 4 b.f. Josr Algarhoud (IRE) 118 – Lady of Limerick **66**
(IRE) (Thatching 131) [2006 57+, a70: f6g⁶ 5.1m* 5.1m⁵ p5.1g 5.2m⁶ p5.1f 6g Aug 12] fair performer: hampered final 1f and awarded race after finishing second in handicap at Nottingham in May: claimed from D. Ivory £6,000 fifth start: stays 6f: acts on all-weather, good to firm and good to soft going. *M. Appleby*

LADY ALIZE (USA) 2 b.f. (Apr 11) Indian Charlie (USA) 126 – Marina Duff **83**
(Caerleon (USA) 132) [2006 7m³ 7d⁶ 6s² 7s⁵ 8d⁵ p7.1g³ Nov 18] $45,000Y, 160,000 2-y-o: leggy, close-coupled filly: half-sister to several winners, including useful Italian/US performer up to 1½m Sopran Mariduff (by Persian Bold): dam Italian 6f and 1m (including Group 3 event at 2 yrs) winner: fairly useful form: best runs at Newbury third/fourth starts (behind Party both times), second in maiden then fifth in listed race: should stay 1m: acts on soft going: tongue tied. *R. A. Kvisla*

LADY ALTHEA 3 ch.f. Danzig Connection (USA) – Lady Keyser 68 (Le Johnstan –
123) [2006 10s Oct 18] half-sister to 6f winner (including at 2 yrs) Lady-Bo-K (by
Komaite) and winner in Italy by Superlative: dam 5f winner, including at 2 yrs: 100/1,
tailed off in maiden at Nottingham. *Mrs C. A. Dunnett*

LADY AMBITIOUS 3 ch.f. Pivotal 124 – Ambitious 98 (Ardkinglass 114) [2006 p7g⁵   **43**
p7g 7d p11g p9.5g p8g Nov 27] 22,000Y: leggy filly: first foal: dam 5f/6f winner: poor
maiden. *D. K. Ivory*

LADY BAHIA (IRE) 5 b.m. Orpen (USA) 116 – Do The Right Thing 71 (Busted 134)   **79**
[2006 f5g p5g⁶ p6g p5g f5g⁵ f5p² p5g* p5.1g p5.1g p5g⁶ p5g³ p5.1g⁶ 5.1g 5f* 5m 5m*
6m 5.1m⁴ 5s p5g p5g p5.1g³ p5.1m² p5.1g p5.1s p5.1g Dec 23] big, good-topped mare:
has a short, unimpressive action: fair handicapper: won at Lingfield in March, Musselburgh in June and Hamilton in August: best at 5f: acts on all-weather and firm going:
tried in cheekpieces, usually blinkered: often slowly away, sometimes markedly so: has
wandered/flashed tail. *Peter Grayson*

LADY BECKS (IRE) 3 b.f. Mull of Kintyre (USA) 114 – Alca Egeria (ITY) (Shareef   **55 d**
Dancer (USA) 135) [2006 p6g⁶ p7g⁶ 6g 6.1f 8.1m 10s Oct 2] €9,000F, €15,500Y: close-
coupled filly: second foal: dam unraced: modest form only on debut, leaving R. Harris
after fifth start: wore cheekpieces last 2 outings. *C. Roberts*

LADY BEST (IRE) 2 b.f. (Feb 14) Best of The Bests (IRE) 122 – Star of Cayman   **51 ?**
(IRE) (Unfuwain (USA) 131) [2006 7.5m² 7g 8.5g 8m Sep 21] €18,000Y: good-bodied
filly: first foal: dam unraced sister to Irish Oaks winner Bolas: seemingly modest form
only on debut: tried blinkered. *J. R. Weymes*

LADY CARTUCCIA 2 b.f. (Mar 2) Fasliyev (USA) 120 – Cartuccia (IRE) (Doyoun   –
124) [2006 p7.1g⁵ Dec 31] 7,500Y: fifth foal: half-sister to 6.5f (at 2 yrs) to 10.5f winner
in Holland/Germany by Abou Zouz: dam unraced half-sister to Derby/Irish Derby second
City Honours: 7/1 and very green, beaten 11 lengths in maiden at Wolverhampton, very
slowly away and not knocked about: bred to stay 1m. *J. J. Quinn*

LADY CHASTITY 2 b.f. (Feb 12) Iron Mask (USA) 117 – Carati 86 (Selkirk (USA)   **65 d**
129) [2006 5.1m⁴ 7.1g⁵ 6m⁶ p7.1m f5g p6s p8.6g Dec 31] sparely-made filly: half-sister
to 3-y-o Sea Salt: dam 2-y-o 6f winner: fair maiden at best: well below form after second
start: stays 7f. *Mrs L. J. Young*

LADY CREE (IRE) 3 b.f. Medicean 128 – Nightitude 93 (Night Shift (USA)) [2006   **62**
76: p8g 7m⁶ 7.1m 8.3m⁵ 8f 8m⁶ 10.2m⁶ 10.2f 10d 11.9d Oct 19] strong, close-coupled
filly: just modest performer at 3 yrs: stays 1m: acts on good to firm going: blinkered/in
cheekpieces nowadays: reportedly swallowed tongue on reappearance (tongue tied next
time): sold 22,000 gns. *W. R. Muir*

LADY DAVALI 2 b.f. (Apr 21) Defacto (USA) – Tangalooma 56 (Hotfoot 126) [2006   –
6f 7.5f⁶ 6f⁶ Jul 6] 1,500Y: half-sister to several winners, including 5f/6f winner Time To
Tango (by Timeless Times) and 2000 2-y-o 1m winner Tupgill Tango (by Presidium):
dam, maiden on Flat who stayed 1½m, winner over hurdles: no form, in seller final start
(blinkered) *S. Parr*

LADY DIKTAT 4 b.f. Diktat 126 – Scared (Royal Academy (USA) 130) [2006 81:   –
11.8d 12g Apr 25] lengthy filly: fairly useful maiden at best: well held both starts in 2006.
Mrs A. J. Hamilton-Fairley

LADY DISDAIN 3 b.f. Foxhound (USA) 103 – Much Ado 66 (Mujtahid (USA) 118)   **82**
[2006 67: 8g 8s 8.1f³ 10.4m⁴ 9.8g 9.8s* 9.8s* 11m⁵ 10.5g⁶ 10d 10s Oct 18] lengthy, good-
topped filly: fairly useful handicapper: much improved to win twice within 10 days at
Ripon in August (latter by 8 lengths): below form last 3 starts: stays 10.4f: acts on firm
and soft going: sent to USA. *G. M. Moore*

LADY DUXYANA 3 b.f. Most Welcome 131 – Duxyana (IRE) (Cyrano de Bergerac   **45**
120) [2006 p6g 6g 7s 8.2g 7m 7g p7.1g 8.3m⁶ 8.5m 8m⁴ p9.5g 7f³ 10s³ Oct 2] 17,000Y:
leggy, close-coupled filly: sister to useful 2001 2-y-o 5f winner Kelsey Rose (stayed easy
1m) and half-sister to 2 winning sprinters by Petong: dam unraced: poor maiden: stays
1m: acts on firm ground: visored last 3 starts: sometimes slowly away. *M. D. I. Usher*

LADY EDGE (IRE) 4 ch.f. Bold Edge 123 – Lady Sheriff 90 (Taufan (USA) 119)   **63**
[2006 64: 7.1g⁶ 7m⁶ 8.1f⁶ 6f 6g 6.9g 8.1m* 10.9d Oct 13] quite good-topped filly: modest
performer: won maiden at Warwick in September: stays 1m: acts on good to firm ground:
tried visored. *A. W. Carroll*

LADY EVI 3 ch.f. Lord of Men 116 – Clued Up 63§ (Beveled (USA)) [2006 –: p10g   –
f7g⁶ f8g 11g Apr 25] leggy filly: little form. *D. K. Ivory*

LADY FIRECRACKER (IRE) 2 b.f. (Apr 18) Almutawakel 126 – Dazzling Fire **59 p**
(IRE) 78 (Bluebird (USA) 125) [2006 5g 6g p6g Oct 5] €11,000Y: half-sister to 6f winner
Mohawk (by Indian Ridge), later successful in Scandinavia, and 1m winner Dazzling Rio
(by Ashkalani): dam 1½m winner: mid-field in maidens, not knocked about: will benefit
from at least 1m: type to do better. *J. R. Best*

LADY GALADRIEL (USA) 3 ch.f. Woodman (USA) 126 – Dramatically (USA) **54**
(Theatrical 128) [2006 8.3d 10g 8.3d 10s Oct 18] 48,000Y: sparely-made filly: first foal:
dam unraced sister to Irish Derby winner Zagreb: modest maiden: should be suited by
1¼m+: mulish at stall third start (said to have been in season): sold 7,000 gns, sent to
Qatar. *J. M. P. Eustace*

LADY GEORGETTE (IRE) 3 b.f. Fasliyev (USA) 120 – Georgia Venture 98 **66**
(Shirley Heights 130) [2006 p7g p10g 8d⁴ 8d 7f 7m⁴ 11.5f³ 12g⁶ 12g³ 10m² p13.9g⁵ **a61**
p12g³ p12g³ Dec 22] lengthy filly: second foal: half-sister to fairly useful 7f winner
Lady Georgina (by Linamix): dam, 1¾m/2m winner, out of half-sister to Kentucky Derby
winner Cannonade: fair maiden on turf, modest on all-weather: stays 1½m: acts on
polytrack and firm going, probably on good to soft. *E. J. O'Neill*

LADY GRACE (IRE) 2 b.f. (Apr 13) Orpen (USA) 116 – Lady Taufan (IRE) (Taufan **91**
(USA) 119) [2006 p6g⁵ p7g* p7.1g⁵ p8g* 8d⁴ Oct 28] 34,000F, 110,000Y: strong, lengthy
filly: sister to useful 2003 2-y-o 6f/7f (Prestige Stakes) winner Gracefully and 4-y-o
Visionist, and half-sister to 2 winners: dam, Irish maiden, stayed 9f: fairly useful form:
won maiden at Kempton in September and nursery at Lingfield (beat Aaim To Prosper
by 1¼ lengths) in October: respectable fourth to Passage of Time in listed event at
Newmarket final start: free-going sort, and likely to prove best up to 1m: raced on polytrack and good to soft ground. *W. J. Haggas*

LADY GREGORY (IRE) 4 b.f. In The Wings 128 – Athlumney Lady 98 (Lycius **77**
(USA) 124) [2006 74: p12.2g* 16g Jul 22] fair performer, lightly raced: won maiden at
Wolverhampton in February (left E. O'Neill after): stays 1½m: acts on polytrack and
good to firm ground. *N. Meade, Ireland*

LADY GREY BEAR 2 gr.f. (Apr 5) Tobougg (IRE) 125 – Southern Psychic (USA) **–**
(Alwasmi (USA) 115) [2006 6s 7.5m Sep 13] 8,000F, 13,000Y: tall filly: half-sister to
several winners, including smart 6f (at 2 yrs) to 1m winner Rumpold (by Mister Baileys),
7-y-o Wing Commander, and 4-y-o Trew Style: dam sprint winner in USA: last in maidens: dead. *R. A. Fahey*

LADY HOPEFUL (IRE) 4 b.f. Lend A Hand 124 – Treble Term 66 (Lion Cavern **54**
(USA) 117) [2006 59: p6g⁶ p5.1g* p6g⁵ p5.1g p5g p5.1g⁴ p6g⁶ p6g⁶ 5m 5g* 5.2m **a60**
p5.1g p5g p5.1g² p5g³ p6g p5.1g Dec 31] good-topped filly: modest performer: won
handicaps at Wolverhampton in January and Folkestone in August: effective at 5f to easy
7f: acts on all-weather, firm and good to soft ground: wears headgear. *Peter Grayson*

LADY KINTYRE 2 b.f. (Apr 7) Mull of Kintyre (USA) 114 – Lady Sheriff 90 (Taufan **–**
(USA) 119) [2006 6.1d p6g p5.1g Nov 10] big, strong filly: sixth foal: half-sister to
4-y-o Lady Edge: dam 5f winner, including at 2 yrs: no form: pulled up lame final outing.
A. W. Carroll

LADY KORRIANDA 5 ch.m. Dr Fong (USA) 128 – Prima Verde 81 (Leading Coun- **47**
sel (USA) 122) [2006 p8g⁴ p12g Dec 20] maiden: missed 2005: poor form in handicaps
in 2006: stays 1m. *B. R. Johnson*

LADY LAFITTE (USA) 2 b.f. (May 2) Stravinsky (USA) 133 – Ready For Action **73 p**
(USA) (Riverman (USA) 131) [2006 6m⁶ 7.1m⁴ 7g⁶ 7d Sep 29] 60,000Y: good-topped
filly: sister to 3-y-o Miss Highjinks and half-sister to several winners, including 7f/1m
winner Major Force (by Woodman) and 1½m/1¾m winner Quality Team (by Diesis),
both smart in Ireland: dam Irish 1¼m winner out of half-sister to Lyphard: fair maiden:
better than bare result last 2 starts, going strongly long way: type to improve at 5f/6f.
B. W. Hills

LADY LILY (IRE) 2 ch.f. (Jan 2) Desert Sun 120 – Sheila Blige 83 (Zamindar (USA) **90**
116) [2006 6d⁶ 6f² 6d⁴ 5.2g 5d* 6f* p6g³ Oct 21] €38,000Y: sturdy filly: first foal: dam,
2-y-o 5f winner, half-sister to smart performer up to 1½m Naked Welcome: fairly useful
performer: won maiden at Catterick and nursery at Leicester in September: further
progress when third to Hinton Admiral in listed race at Lingfield: free-going type, will
prove kept to 5f/6f: acts on polytrack, firm and good to soft going. *H. R. A. Cecil*

LADY LIVIUS (IRE) 3 b.f. Titus Livius (FR) 115 – Refined (IRE) 95 (Statoblest 120) **98**
[2006 90: 6s 6m* 7m 6g² 6m⁶ 6d 6g Sep 28] close-coupled, quite good-topped filly:
useful performer: much improved to win minor event at Newbury (by 1¼ lengths from

Murfreesboro) in June: good second to Dark Missile in handicap at Ascot after: below form last 3 starts, though poorly drawn final one: stays 6f: acts on good to firm going. *R. Hannon*

LADY LOCHINVER (IRE) 3 ch.f. Raise A Grand (IRE) 114 – Opening Day (Day Is Done 115) [2006 57: 8.2m 9.3m³ 8d³ 9.8s⁴ 11.1d Sep 25] quite good-topped filly: modest maiden handicapper: probably stays 9f: acts on soft going. *M. D. Hammond* **54**

LADY LONDRA 4 b.f. Fumo di Londra (IRE) 108 – Lady Phyl 67 (Northiam (USA)) [2006 62: p6g p8g f6g Jan 26] modest performer: stays 6f: acts on polytrack. *D. K. Ivory* **54**

LADY LUCAS (IRE) 3 b.f. Night Shift (USA) – Broadfield Lass (IRE) (Le Bavard (FR) 125) [2006 a8.3s p6g p8.6g Dec 9] second foal: dam unraced: well held in maidens. *E. J. Creighton*

LADY LUCINDA 5 b.m. Muhtarram (USA) 125 – Lady Phyl 67 (Northiam (USA)) [2006 –: 10d f14g p13.9g Nov 6] big, leggy mare: no sign of ability. *J. R. Holt* **–**

LADY LUISA (IRE) 4 b.f. Lujain (USA) 119 – Lady of Dreams (Prince Rupert (FR) 121) [2006 –: 6f 7f 7.1g 13.8m⁶ 7f Jul 28] close-coupled filly: no longer of any account: tried in cheekpieces/blinkers, tongue tied last 5 starts. *Miss A. Stokell* **–**

LADY MISHA 4 b.f. Mister Baileys 123 – Hakone (IRE) 78 (Alzao (USA) 117) [2006 68: p16.5g³ f16g⁶ 16.1m⁴ Jun 29] close-coupled filly: fair handicapper: stays easy 2m: acts on polytrack, soft and firm ground. *Jedd O'Keeffe* **66**

LADY ORPEN (IRE) 3 b.f. Orpen (USA) 116 – Annahala (IRE) (Ridgewood Ben 113) [2006 80: p6g* 5v* 6d⁶ 6d* 5.1g³ 6.3g 6d⁵ 5s Sep 1] sturdy, lengthy filly: first foal: dam well beaten in Ireland both starts: useful performer: won maiden at Lingfield in February, minor event at Tipperary in April and handicap at Naas in May: creditable third to Glenviews Youngone in handicap at Nottingham next time: best form at 5f/6f: acted on polytrack, heavy and good to firm going: dead. *Patrick Morris, Ireland* **100**

LADY PALMA NOVA 3 b.f. Danehill Dancer (IRE) 117 – Sangra (USA) 69 (El Gran Senor (USA) 136) [2006 54: f6g f7g p7.1g⁶ p8.6g f5g 5f Jun 14] workmanlike filly: poor maiden at 3 yrs: left M. Easterby after fourth outing: stays 7f: acts on all-weather and heavy ground: tried blinkered. *G. P. Kelly* **42**

LADY PEKAN 7 b.m. Sri Pekan (USA) 117 – Cloudberry 88 (Night Shift (USA)) [2006 61: f5g f5g p5.1g f5g p5.1g f5g Feb 26] smallish, strong mare: poor performer: best at 5f: acts on all-weather, firm and soft ground: often wears headgear (has looked ungenuine): front runner. *P. Howling* **49**

LADY PICKPOCKET 2 b.f. (May 3) Benny The Dip (USA) 127 – Circe 73 (Main Reef 126) [2006 7.5m 7g Sep 30] 2,000Y: close-coupled filly: half-sister to several winners, including 9f to 1½m winner My Learned Friend (by Broken Hearted) and 1¼m winner Vamp (by Dracula), both fairly useful: dam, 1m winner who stayed 1¼m, half-sister to smart 6f to 1m winner Atavus: well held in maidens. *M. H. Tompkins* **–**

LADY PILOT 4 b.f. Dansili 127 – Mighty Flyer (IRE) (Mujtahid (USA) 118) [2006 56, a74: p10g⁴ p10g⁶ p12g⁵ p16g³ p16g³ p16.5g* p16g⁵ 12d p12g p16g⁵ p13.9g p13.9m p12g⁶ p10g⁴ p11g p10g³ p10g p12g p10g³ Dec 22] workmanlike filly: fair performer: won handicap at Wolverhampton in March (hung left): left Dr J. Naylor after eleventh start: stays easy 2m: acts on polytrack and good to firm going: sometimes wears headgear. *Ms J. S. Doyle* **– a69**

LADY PREDOMINANT 5 b.m. Primo Dominie 121 – Enlisted (IRE) 83 (Sadler's Wells (USA) 132) [2006 –: f8g f7g Jan 2] sturdy mare: no longer of any account: tried visored/blinkered/tongue tied. *Robert Gray* **–**

LADY ROCKSAM 2 b.f. (Mar 1) Samraan (USA) 117 – Whittle Rock 91 (Rock City 120) [2006 6m Sep 11] 2,200F: sparely-made filly: sixth foal: half-sister to Italian 7f winner by Averti: dam 5f (at 2 yrs) to 7f winner: broke down in maiden at Redcar. *G. M. Moore* **–**

LADY ROMANOV (IRE) 3 br.f. Xaar 132 – Mixremember (FR) (Linamix (FR) 127) [2006 67: 8.5g p10g³ f12g* Jul 1] tall filly: fair performer: improved to win handicap at Lingfield in July: stays 1½m: acts on all-weather. *M. H. Tompkins* **79**

LADY SAFFRON (IRE) 2 b.f. (Jan 30) Distant Music (USA) 126 – Classic Ring (IRE) 50 (Auction Ring (USA) 123) [2006 5.1f³ 6f 6g Aug 30] 14,500Y: big, useful-looking filly: half-sister to several winners, including 9-y-o Seven No Trumps and 7-y-o Waterside: dam 2-y-o 7f seller winner who stayed 1m: well beaten in maidens. *J. Balding* **–**

LADY SHIRLEY HUNT 2 ch.f. (Feb 29) Zaha (CAN) 106 – Kathy Fair (IRE) 46 – (Nicholas Bill 125) [2006 7.1m p8.6g Sep 16] tall, good-topped filly: sixth foal: half-sister to ungenuine 5f (at 2 yrs) and 7f winner Quite Remarkable (by Danzig Connection): dam headstrong maiden who stayed 1¼m: no show in maidens. *A. D. Smith*

LADY'S LAW 3 b.f. Diktat 126 – Snugfit Annie 49 (Midyan (USA) 124) [2006 7f⁶ **40** 8d⁴ 10d Sep 14] half-sister to 5f to 7f (including at 2 yrs) winner Enchanted (by Magic Ring) and 4-y-o Golden Asha, both useful: dam third in 6f seller at 2 yrs: poor maiden. *G. G. Margarson*

LADY SMOCK 2 ch.f. (Mar 14) Elmaamul (USA) 125 – Funky 69 (Classic Music (USA)) [2006 p8.6m⁵ Sep 2] first foal: dam, maiden who stayed 1m, winning hurdler: tailed off in minor event at Wolverhampton. *J. R. Holt*

LADY SONGBIRD (IRE) 3 b.f. Selkirk (USA) 129 – Firecrest (IRE) 107 (Darshaan **72** 133) [2006 8.3f 10m⁶ Jul 29] €80,000Y: rather leggy filly: second foal: half-sister to fairly useful 12.4f winner Grey Plover (by Alzao): dam, 1½m winner, half-sister to smart stayer Anak Pekan: better effort in maidens when sixth to Early Evening at Nottingham: will be suited by 1½m. *W. R. Swinburn*

LADY STARDUST 3 b.f. Spinning World (USA) 130 – Carambola (IRE) 100 **90 p** (Danehill (USA) 126) [2006 7g* (Aug 18) 55,000Y: good-topped filly: has scope: second foal: dam, Irish 1m winner, half-sister to Irish 1000 Guineas winner Matiya: 8/1 and green, won maiden at Newbury in August by 2½ lengths from Indication, leading 1f out under hands and heels before hanging right: bred to stay 1m: open to improvement. *J. R. Fanshawe*

LADY STRATAGEM 7 gr.m. Mark of Esteem (IRE) 137 – Grey Angel (Kenmare – (FR) 125) [2006 45: f12g Apr 27] sturdy mare: maiden: well held only outing in 2006: tried blinkered. *E. W. Tuer*

LADY SUESANNE (IRE) 4 b.f. Cape Cross (IRE) 129 – Lady At War (Warning 136) – [2006 54, a63: f8g* f7g f7g⁶ f8g² f8g* f8g⁴ f7g Feb 16] strong filly: fair performer: won **a66** seller (claimed from N. Wilson £6,000) and handicap (by 5 lengths) in January, both at Southwell: stays 1m: acts on all-weather, good to firm and good to soft ground: usually blinkered/visored. *M. J. Attwater*

LADY SUFFRAGETTE (IRE) 3 b.f. Mull of Kintyre (USA) 114 – Miss Senate **51** (IRE) (Alzao (USA) 117) [2006 7m 10.1m 10d⁴ p12g³ Oct 23] €6,000Y: workmanlike filly: third foal: half-sister to winner in Greece by Bluebird: dam unraced sister to smart performer up to 1½m Suplizi: modest maiden: stays 1½m: acts on polytrack and good to soft ground: reportedly pulled muscles second start. *John Berry*

LADY SYNTHIA 3 b.f. Mull of Kintyre (USA) 114 – Yo-Cando (IRE) 64 (Cyrano de – Bergerac 120) [2006 66: 8.3d 5.1m 7.1m Sep 1] fair maiden at 2 yrs: last in handicaps in 2006: visored final start at 2 yrs. *B. Palling*

LADY TAVERNER 5 b.m. Marju (IRE) 127 – Prompting 76 (Primo Dominie 121) **67** [2006 63: p10g⁵ p10g p12.2g² 9.7d² p12.2g³ 13.1s⁴ 11.5m⁶ p12g⁶ 10.9d p12.2m² p12.2g Dec 9] leggy mare: fair handicapper: stays 1¾m: acts on polytrack, good to firm and good to soft ground: often slowly away, and usually patiently ridden. *J. E. Long*

LADY TILLY 9 b.m. Puissance 110 – Lady of Itatiba (BEL) (King of Macedon 126) – [2006 8.3f⁵ Jun 29] workmanlike mare: no longer of any account: tried tongue tied/blinkered. *W. G. Harrison*

LADY TOYAH (IRE) 2 ch.f. (Apr 9) Titus Livius (FR) 115 – Secur Pac (FR) (Halling – (USA) 133) [2006 6m 6m p5.1g f6m Oct 31] 800Y: sparely-made filly: second foal: dam unraced: little form. *Mrs L. Williamson*

LADY TRAILL 2 b.f. (Mar 29) Barathea (IRE) 127 – Halska (Unfuwain (USA) 131) **63** [2006 p8g⁶ p8g Nov 5] 120,000Y: third foal: half-sister to 4-y-o Smooth Jazz: dam un-raced close relation to Old Vic out of sister to 2000 Guineas winner High Top: outpaced in maidens at Lingfield, modest form on debut. *B. W. Hills*

LADY VEE (IRE) 4 b.f. Rossini (USA) 118 – Dama de Noche (Rusticaro (FR) 124) **41** [2006 48, a56: p6g Jan 23] leggy filly: poor handicapper: stays 6f: acts on polytrack: wore cheekpieces sole 4-y-o outing. *P. D. Niven*

LADY WARNING 2 b.f. (Apr 9) Averti (IRE) 117 – Lady Smith (Greensmith 121) – [2006 p5g⁵ p6g Dec 16] first foal: dam unraced sister to US Grade 3 9f winner Lord Smith and half-sister to useful sprinter The Lord (by Averti): well held in maiden and seller. *W. G. M. Turner*

LADY ZANZARA (USA) 3 ch.f. Lion Cavern (USA) 117 – Pace (USA) (Indian **56**
Ridge 123) [2006 65: p5g p5g p7g² p8g 7m p6g⁵ Jul 12] lengthy filly: modest maiden:
stays easy 7f: acts on polytrack and firm going: withdrawn after getting loose second
intended start at 2 yrs: sometimes restless in stall/slowly away. *J. W. Hills*

LA ESPERANZA 2 b.f. (Apr 30) Mind Games 121 – Chantilly Myth 81 (Sri Pekan **53**
(USA) 117) [2006 5m³ 5f² 6g 5m Sep 11] 2,800Y: smallish, leggy filly: second foal: half-
sister to 3-y-o Chalentina: dam 6f (at 2 yrs)/7f winner: modest maiden: placed in minor
event and seller: form at 5f: sold 800 gns. *T. D. Barron*

LA ESTRELLA (USA) 3 b.c. Theatrical 128 – Princess Ellen 114 (Tirol 127) [2006 **90 +**
10d 10g⁵ 10s⁶ p12g p9.5g* p12.2s² Dec 13] $100,000Y: lengthy, useful-looking colt: first
foal: dam, 2-y-o 6f/7f winner and runner-up in 1000 Guineas, later 1m winner in USA:
fairly useful performer: won maiden at Wolverhampton in November: good second in
handicap on same course: stays 1½m: acts on polytrack. *J. G. Given*

LA FANCIULLA 3 b.f. Robellino (USA) 127 – Molly Brown 95 (Rudimentary (USA) **68**
118) [2006 69: 6s⁴ p7.1g 7g* 6.1s⁵ 7m³ 7m² 6g 7g⁶ Aug 3] sturdy filly: fair performer:
won claimer at Salisbury in May: stays 7f, not 1m: acts on firm and good to soft going:
sold 52,000 gns in November. *R. Hannon*

LAFI (IRE) 7 ch.g. Indian Ridge 123 – Petal Girl 96 (Caerleon (USA) 132) [2006 113: **111**
6g⁴ 5g⁴ 5m 5g⁵ 5.4g 5m³ 5d 5s Oct 14] good-topped gelding: smart performer: best effort
in 2006 when third to Philharmonic in minor event at Beverley in September: broke leg
at Catterick in October: was best at 5f/6f: acted on firm and good to soft going: dead.
D. Nicholls

LAFONTAINE BLEU 2 b.f. (Apr 29) Piccolo 121 – Russell Creek 80 (Sandy Creek **66**
123) [2006 5f 5m³ 6s* 6d² 6s Oct 6] 9,500Y: good-topped filly: half-sister to several
winners, including 2003 2-y-o 6f winner Among Dreams (by Among Men): dam 1m
winner: fair performer: won maiden at Ripon in August: second to Algol in nursery there
next time: will be suited by 7f: acts on soft and good to firm going. *R. A. Fahey*

LA GESSA 4 gr.f. Largesse 112 – En Grisaille 53 (Mystiko (USA) 124) [2006 62: p9.5g **69**
p9.5g 11.5m⁴ 11.5m³ 12.6m* Jun 25] fair performer: won handicap at Warwick in June:
stays 12.6f: acts on good to firm ground. *John Berry*

LAGGAN BAY (IRE) 6 b.g. Alzao (USA) 117 – Green Lucia 116 (Green Dancer **74**
(USA) 132) [2006 16.1d³ 11.7m p16g 17.2m⁴ 17.1d² 18d 16v Oct 25] small gelding:
fluent mover: fair handicapper: unraced on Flat in 2005: barely stays 17f: acts on polytrack, firm and soft going: tried visored, blinkered nowadays: usually held up. *J. S. Moore*

LAGO D'ORTA (IRE) 6 ch.g. Bahhare (USA) 122 – Maelalong (IRE) 77 (Maelstrom **79**
Lake 118) [2006 –: 8f 7.9g 7f⁶ Jul 14] close-coupled, quite good-topped gelding: fair performer nowadays: stays 9.3f: acts on firm going: tongue tied twice at 5 yrs: often slowly
away. *D. Nicholls*

LAGOON ROYALE 2 b.c. (Apr 16) Lugana Beach 116 – Lutine Royal 46 (Formid- **–**
able (USA) 125) [2006 6g Aug 14] well beaten in maiden at Windsor. *B. W. Duke*

LA GRANDE ZOA (IRE) 3 b.f. Fantastic Light (USA) 134 – Majestic Sister (IRE) **50**
(Last Tycoon 131) [2006 10.2m 10d 12v Oct 31] €75,000Y, resold €50,000Y, €16,000
3-y-o: third foal: half-sister to winner in Greece by Pennekamp: dam unraced sister to
high-class 1¼m/1½m performer Ezzoud and half-sister to high-class miler Distant Relative: modest form in maidens. *R. M. Beckett*

LAGUNA REEF 2 b.g. (Mar 12) Lugana Beach 116 – Trina's Pet 65 (Efisio 120) [2006 **–**
5m May 4] 14/1, soon off bridle in maiden at Redcar: sold 3,000 gns in November.
T. D. Easterby

LAHEEN (IRE) 3 b.f. Bluebird (USA) 125 – Ashirah (USA) (Housebuster (USA)) **60**
[2006 p8g⁵ p7.1g⁵ p7g 8.5g 10d 8d⁴ 12.4s⁶ p9.5g Nov 2] €88,000Y: angular filly: second
foal: sister to fairly useful Irish 2002 2-y-o 5f winner New Design: dam unraced half-
sister to smart US performer up to 1½m Mustanfar, out of close relative to Unfuwain and
half-sister to Nashwan and Nayef: modest maiden: stays 1m: acts on polytrack: blinkered
final start. *M. H. Tompkins*

LAHOB 6 ch.g. First Trump 118 – Mystical Song 68 (Mystiko (USA) 124) [2006 46: **–**
f11g f14s⁵ Mar 7] small, strong gelding: maiden: well held in 2006: tried tongue tied/in
cheekpieces/blinkers: usually races up with pace. *P. Howling*

LAISH YA HAJAR (IRE) 2 ch.g. (Mar 21) Grand Lodge (USA) 125 – Ya Hajar 106 **75**
(Lycius (USA) 124) [2006 7.1m⁴ p8g³ Aug 12] big, heavy-topped gelding: first foal: dam,
6f and 7f (Prix du Calvados) winner at 2 yrs, half-sister to very smart miler Zafeen: in

frame in maidens at Sandown (fourth to Nur Tau) and Lingfield (stretched by trip): subsequently gelded. *M. R. Channon*

LAITH (IRE) 3 b.g. Royal Applause 124 – Dania (GER) (Night Shift (USA)) [2006 84: **71 d**
5.2m 5.3f⁶ p6g 7f 7.1d 6m 6m 6d⁶ 7.1m 6f f6g Dec 23] big, strong, attractive gelding: has
a quick action: regressive handicapper: left B. Hills 18,000 gns after third start: best
efforts at 5f: acts on firm going: tried blinkered. *Miss V. Haigh*

LAKE ANDRE (IRE) 5 b.g. Lake Coniston (IRE) 131 – Shadow Casting 72 (Warning **87 d**
136) [2006 98: p6g p7g 8g 7.2g 6s 7g Jun 13] useful handicapper in 2005: on the downgrade: acts on fibresand, probably on any turf going, goes well on ground softer
than good: blinkered (well held) once. *K. A. Ryan*

LAKE CHINI (IRE) 4 b.g. Raise A Grand (IRE) 114 – Where's The Money 87 (Loch- **85**
nager 132) [2006 80: p7g p6g² p7g⁵ p7.1g³ 6g² 6g³ 6d⁴ May 19] strong, good sort: has a
round action: fairly useful handicapper at least: creditable efforts all starts in 2006: stays
easy 7f: acts on polytrack and soft ground: wears cheekpieces/blinkers nowadays:
consistent: sold 7,500 gns in October. *M. A. Jarvis*

LAKE GARDA 5 b.g. Komaite (USA) – Malcesine (IRE) 46 (Auction Ring (USA) **84**
123) [2006 83d: 6g² 6m² 5f⁶ 6m³ 6g 6m⁴ 6s³ p6g Sep 16] good-topped gelding: fairly
useful handicapper: creditable efforts when in frame in 2006: effective at 5f/6f: acts on
soft and good to firm going (well held on all-weather debut final start): tried tongue tied
(well below form), blinkered 4 of last 5 outings: usually races prominently. *K. A. Ryan*

LAKE IMPERIAL (IRE) 5 b.g. Imperial Ballet (IRE) 110 – Lakes of Killarney (IRE) **54**
(Ahonoora 122) [2006 10g 10.2m 11m Jun 27] big, good-topped gelding: modest maiden:
very lightly raced on Flat: has been slowly away. *Mrs H. Dalton*

LAKE 'O' GOLD 7 ch.m. Karinga Bay 116 – Ginka 57 (Petoski 135) [2006 21.6d Apr **–**
24] workmanlike mare: modest maiden handicapper at 4 yrs: lightly raced and little form
since. *D. W. Thompson*

LAKE POET (IRE) 3 ch.c. Galileo (IRE) 134 – Lyric 58 (Lycius (USA) 124) [2006 **98**
86: p7g² p8g³ 7g p8g⁵ 10.1m² 10d* 10.1m³ 12m⁴ 10m 12f⁴ 12d 10s² 10d⁵ f11g⁵ **a83**
p12.2s Dec 13] leggy, close-coupled colt: useful handicapper on turf, fairly useful on
all-weather: won at Newmarket (on toes) in May, showing good attitude: stays 1½m: acts
on polytrack, firm and soft going: consistent. *C. E. Brittain*

LAKE PONTCHARTRAIN (IRE) 2 b.f. (Mar 3) Invincible Spirit (IRE) 121 – **69**
Sunny Slope 77 (Mujtahid (USA) 118) [2006 6m 5.7f⁵ 5.1m⁵ 6f⁶ p7.1m⁶ p6g³ p7.1m*
p8.6g² p8g* Nov 24] €16,000Y: sturdy filly: third foal: dam Irish 1m/9f winner: fair performer: won nurseries at Wolverhampton and Kempton in November: stays 8.6f: acts on
polytrack and firm going: tricky ride, seemingly best delivered late. *S. Kirk*

LAKE SHABLA (USA) 3 b.f. Silver Hawk (USA) 123 – Miss Zafonic (FR) 98 (Zaf- **90**
onic (USA) 130) [2006 p8g* 10.4d⁴ 10g² 10.5g 10s⁵ p10g² p9.5g Nov 25] big, good-
topped filly: fourth foal: half-sister to winner in USA by Dehere: dam, 6f (at 2 yrs) and 7f
winner, half-sister to smart sprinter Central City: fairly useful performer: won maiden at
Lingfield in February: good efforts when in frame after in Musidora Stakes at York and
handicaps at Sandown and Lingfield: stays 1¼m: acts on polytrack and good to soft
going: sold 48,000 gns, sent to USA. *E. A. L. Dunlop*

LAKESIDE GUY (IRE) 5 b.g. Revoque (IRE) 122 – Glen of Imaal (IRE) (Common **52**
Grounds 118) [2006 57: f5g f5g f6g p7.1g⁴ f7g p8.6g p9.5g p7.1g⁵ p8.6g Feb 20] modest
performer: stays 8.6f: acts on all-weather and firm going: tried visored/blinkered,
sometimes tongue tied (including last 6 starts). *M. Appleby*

LAKE SUPRIMA (IRE) 3 b.f. Primo Valentino (IRE) 116 – Sulaka (Owington 123) **–**
[2006 51: f7g 6g 5g Aug 21] modest maiden at 2 yrs: well held in 2006. *R. M. Whitaker*

LAKE TOYA (USA) 4 b.f. Darshaan 133 – Shinko Hermes (IRE) (Sadler's Wells **109**
(USA) 132) [2006 110: p13g³ 10d* Nov 4] strong, good-topped filly: fourth foal: half-
sister to 3 winners, including useful 1m winner Glen Innes (by Selkirk): dam, ran once in
Japan, sister to Oaks winner Imagine and half-sister to Generous: smart performer: won
maiden at Argentan at 2 yrs, and minor event at Longchamp and listed event at Toulouse
in 2005: left A. Fabre in France and off 12 months, creditable 2 lengths third to High Heel
Sneakers in listed race at Lingfield: won similar event at Windsor (heavily bandaged, by
¾ length from Mango Mischief) in November: stays 13f: acts on polytrack, raced only on
good going or softer on turf (acts on heavy). *Saeed bin Suroor*

LAKE WAKATIPU 4 b.f. Lake Coniston (IRE) 131 – Lady Broker 54 (Petorius 117) **67**
[2006 59: p12.2g³ p16.5g³ p12.2g³ p12.2g p13.9g⁶ p9.5g⁶ p13.9g⁶ p16.5g* p13.9g²

p13.9g³ 14.1s⁶ 14m⁶ 12.3g* 12f³ 13f* 15.9m⁵ 15.8d 12s⁴ Oct 21] lengthy filly: fair performer: won banded race at Wolverhampton in April, and ladies handicaps at Chester and Hamilton in June: effective at 1½m to 2m: acts on all-weather and any turf going. *M. Mullineaux*

LAKSHMI (IRE) 2 b.f. (Mar 24) Efisio 120 – Effie (Royal Academy (USA) 130) [2006 6m⁴ p6g* Jul 12] 10,000Y: good-bodied filly: second foal: dam unraced half-sister to useful milers Jay Gee's Choice and Kootenay: fairly useful form: promise at Newbury (fourth to Indian Ink), then won maiden at Lingfield by 3½ lengths from Smokey Oakey: likely to stay 1m: should make a useful 3-y-o. *M. R. Channon* **87 p**

LALINA (GER) 3 ch.f. Trempolino (USA) 135 – Lanciana (IRE) (Acatcnango (GER) 127) [2006 12g³ 9.3g² a9.5g² 10.8g* 11d p10g p8.6m p13.9g Nov 17] first foal: dam, won around 1¼m in France/Germany, out of half-sister to dam of Deutsches Derby winners Lando and Laroche: placed first 3 starts before winning maiden at Gotha in August: left M. Hofer in Germany, well beaten in handicaps in Britain: stays 1½m. *Jane Chapple-Hyam* **?**

LA MARMOTTE (IRE) 2 b.f. (Feb 12) Mujadil (USA) 119 – Zilayah (USA) 79 (Zilzal (USA) 137) [2006 5.1m 5v² 5.7f p6g³ f7g⁴ 7m* 7.1g³ p6g⁶ 6d⁴ p7.1m p7g³ p7g⁶ Nov 25] 10,000Y: compact filly: seventh foal: half-sister to fairly useful French 1m/9f winner Billowing Sail (by Bering): dam, 2-y-o 7f winner, half-sister to smart French stayer Molesnes and to dam of very smart French sprinter Cherokee Rose: fair performer: won seller at Newmarket in August: stays 7f: acts on all-weather, heavy and good to firm ground: signs of temperament, and none too reliable. *J. W. Hills* **65**

LA MATANZA 3 b.f. Hunting Lion (IRE) 115 – Lawless Bridget 62 (Alnasr Alwasheek 117) [2006 7m³ 8.2g⁶ 7f 7m⁵ 7.1d³ 7d⁶ 6g* Sep 17] 7,200Y: quite attractive filly: third foal: half-sister to 4-y-o Melalchrist: dam, maiden, best effort at 6f at 2 yrs: fair performer: won maiden at Redcar in May and handicap at Hamilton in September: unlikely to stay beyond 7f (raced freely at 1m): acts on good to firm and good to soft ground. *T. D. Barron* **79**

LAMBENCY (IRE) 3 b.f. Daylami (IRE) 138 – Triomphale (USA) (Nureyev (USA) 131) [2006 –: 8m 8g 8m 9m⁵ 11.5f 10.1d³ 6g⁶ 5v Oct 9] quite good-topped filly: modest maiden: left J. Given after sixth start: stays easy 1¼m, effective at much shorter: acts on polytrack and good to firm going. *J. S. Goldie* **61**

LA MOTTA (IRE) 6 b.g. Sesaro (USA) 81 – Cheviot Indian (IRE) 71 (Indian Ridge 123) [2006 64: 5s 5m³ 5f² 5f* 5f³ 5f* 5f³ 5m⁵ 6g⁵ 5s* 5g 6v p6g p6g⁴ p5.1g Dec 2] fair handicapper: all 3 wins in June, at Down Royal in June and September and Bellewstown in between: best form at 5f: acts on polytrack/sand and any turf going: tried in cheekpieces, usually blinkered/tongue tied nowadays. *A. McGuinness, Ireland* **76**

LA MOTTIE 3 ch.f. King's Best (USA) 132 – Bareilly (USA) (Lyphard (USA) 132) [2006 95: 8.3g* 8m² 8.1m* 8.1g³ 9g⁶ 9f 8f² Dec 9] leggy, close-coupled filly: useful performer: won handicap at Windsor (by 2½ lengths from Queen's Best) in June: good efforts after in listed handicap at Royal Ascot (head second to Red Evie), Garden City Breeders' Cup at Belmont (4¼ lengths sixth to Magnificent Song, final outing for J. Noseda) and non-graded stakes at Hollywood (2¼ lengths second to Captive Melody): stays 9f: acts on firm going: refused to enter stall once at 2 yrs. *B. D. A. Cecil, USA* **106**

LA MUSIQUE 4 b.g. Merdon Melody 98 – Daleside Ladybird 66 (Tolomeo 127) [2006 48: p6g p8g p9.5g f7g² p7.1g f8g³ f7g* f7g³ f7g⁵ f8g Jun 3] workmanlike gelding: modest performer: won banded race at Southwell in April: barely stays 1m: acts on fibresand, lightly raced and no form on turf. *P. J. McBride* **– a54**

LANCASTER'S QUEST 2 ch.c. (Apr 2) Auction House (USA) 120 – Gabibti (IRE) 82 (Dara Monarch 128) [2006 5g 6m⁵ Jun 10] mid-field in maidens in early-June. *R. Ingram* **58**

LAND AHOY 2 b.c. (Jan 31) Observatory (USA) 131 – Night Haven 99 (Night Shift (USA)) [2006 5g⁶ 6g³ 5.1g 5g Aug 25] 20,000Y: sturdy colt: second foal: half-brother to 3-y-o Secret Night: dam 5f (at 2 yrs) to 6f winner: fair maiden: third to Sans Reward at Salisbury: creditable seventh in nursery (stiff mark) final start: effective at 5f/6f: raced on good ground. *D. W. P. Arbuthnot* **77**

LANDELA 4 ch.f. Alhaarth (IRE) 126 – Imbabala (Zafonic (USA) 130) [2006 p7g⁴ p8g⁴ Mar 18] €52,000 3-y-o: second foal: half-sister to smart French 1¼m winner who stayed 1½m (dam by Kahyasi): dam, French 1m winner, half-sister to smart French performer up to 1¾m Short Pause: better effort in maidens at Lingfield when fourth to Tommy Toogood second start: will stay 1¼m. *M. A. Jarvis* **64**

Addleshaw Goddard Stakes (Esher), Sandown—
outsider of five Land 'n Stars (left) accounts for Sergeant Cecil and the virtually-obscured Winged d'Argent

LAND 'N STARS 6 b.g. Mtoto 134 – Uncharted Waters 68 (Celestial Storm (USA) **113** 132) [2006 109: 12m 12m* 12d⁵ 12m⁵ 14m⁵ 16.4m* 16f⁶ 12g 16g⁵ 12g Dec 20] leggy, close-coupled gelding: smart performer: won handicap at Nad Al Sheba (by ½ length from Go For Gold) in February and listed race at Sandown (best effort when beating Sergeant Cecil by neck) in July: not discredited after when sixth to Yeats in Goodwood Cup and fifth to Delta Blues in Melbourne Cup at Flemington: effective at 1½m to 2½m: acts on polytrack, firm and soft going, well beaten on heavy. *Jamie Poulton*

LAND OF LIGHT 3 ch.g. Fantastic Light (USA) 134 – Russian Snows (IRE) 113 **69** (Sadler's Wells (USA) 132) [2006 –: 14m² p12g⁴ Aug 30] good-topped gelding: has a quick action: fair form in maidens in 2006: may prove better at 1½m than 1¾m: acts on good to firm ground. *G. L. Moore*

LAND'S END (IRE) 2 b.c. (May 11) Danehill Dancer (IRE) 117 – Statistic (USA) (Mr **– p** Prospector (USA)) [2006 6g Oct 12] €40,000Y, 200,000 2-y-o: rangy, good-topped colt: eighth foal: half-brother to 3 winners, including fairly useful 2002 Irish 2-y-o 8.5f winner King's Mountain (by King of Kings): dam, 7f winner in USA, out of close relative of Nureyev and half-sister to dam of Sadler's Wells: 7/2, very green when behind in maiden won by Truly Royal at Newmarket: should be capable of better. *J. Noseda*

LAND SUN'S LEGACY (IRE) 5 b.g. Red Sunset 120 – Almost A Lady (IRE) 70 **–** (Entitled 126) [2006 –: 8.5g Aug 17] compact gelding: modest maiden at 2 yrs, no form since: wears headgear nowadays. *J. S. Wainwright*

LANDUCCI 5 b.g. Averti (IRE) 117 – Divina Luna 96 (Dowsing (USA) 124) [2006 91: **90** p8g p8g⁶ 7.1m⁵ p6g⁶ 7f⁵ 8f 7m p8g* p7g⁴ 8d² p7g* p7g³ p7g⁴ p8g⁶ p7.1g Dec 6] big, close-coupled gelding: fairly useful handicapper: won twice at Kempton (first occasion apprentices) in September: effective at 7f/1m: acts on polytrack, firm and soft going: tried tongue tied: sometimes edges left. *J. W. Hills*

LA NEIGE 2 b.c. (Apr 4) Royal Applause 124 – Mint Royale (IRE) 44 (Cadeaux Gene- **97 §** reux 131) [2006 5.1d* 6g² 6m⁶ 6m⁴ 5m⁴ 5.2g 6f⁴ 6s⁴ p6g² 7.1d³ 6d p6g Oct 21] 35,000Y: leggy, quite attractive colt: second foal: half-brother to 3-y-o Ten Shun: dam maiden sister to Prix Morny/Middle Park Stakes winner Bahamian Bounty: useful performer: won maiden at Nottingham in April: inconsistent after, though ran well when sixth to Hellvelyn in Coventry Stakes at Royal Ascot, fourth to Hamoody in Richmond Stakes at Goodwood, and second to Dhanyata in Sirenia Stakes at Kempton third, seventh and ninth starts: should stay 7f: acts on polytrack, good to firm and good to soft going: often troublesome at stall (once reared/unseated): ungenuine: sold 46,000 gns, sent to USA. *M. R. Channon*

LANFREDO 3 b.g. Fraam 114 – Lana Turrel (USA) (Trempolino (USA) 135) [2006 **57** p8g p8g⁶ p8g 10m 10d p10g 12.1m⁵ 9.9d 10d² 11.8d² f11g⁶ p16.5m⁵ p13.9g⁶ f11g²

578

Dec 14] modest maiden: claimed from D. Arbuthnot tenth start: barely stays 2m: acts on all-weather and good to soft ground: usually in cheekpieces/blinkers. *Miss M. E. Rowland*

LANGFORD 6 ch.g. Compton Place 125 – Sharpening 72 (Sharpo 132) [2006 105: 9m³ 8m 8m⁵ 8.1m 8f 10s⁴ p8.6m⁶ f8g p10g⁵ p9.5g³ Dec 31] well-made gelding: useful handicapper: best efforts in 2006 at Newmarket (third behind Star of Light) and Newcastle (fifth to Flipando) first/third starts: effective at 1m, barely stays 11f: acts on poly-track and firm going: effective making running or held up: sometimes starts slowly: often finds little. *M. H. Tompkins* — **105**

LANG SHINING (IRE) 2 ch.c. (Apr 30) Dr Fong (USA) 128 – Dragnet (IRE) 72 (Rainbow Quest (USA) 134) [2006 7g³ Oct 12] leggy, angular colt: first foal: dam, 1¼m winner, sister to Irish 2000 Guineas/Champion Stakes winner Spectrum and half-sister to dam of high-class 1¼m/1½m performer Petrushka: 11/2 and green in paddock/to post, encouraging third of 15 to Perfect Star in maiden at Newmarket, clear of rest: will be suited by 1m/1¼m: certain to improve and should win races. *Sir Michael Stoute* — **84 p**

LANSDOWN 2 b.f. (Feb 21) Lomitas 129 – Reamzafonic 46 (Grand Lodge (USA) 125) [2006 5g 6.1s³ 7f² 6m 7f² 7.5f² 7m⁴ Jul 18] 11,000F, 7,000Y: lengthy, unfurnished filly: fourth foal: half-sister to 4-y-o Wester Lodge: dam, maiden, should have been suited by 1m: modest maiden: runner-up in sellers, claimed from M. Meade £6,000 third start, left R. Gray after sixth: will stay 1m: acts on firm going: tried in cheekpieces. *B. Ellison* — **51**

LA NUAGE 2 gr.f. (Apr 13) Tobougg (IRE) 125 – Cole Slaw (Absalom 128) [2006 7s Oct 10] 4,500F, 30,000Y: eighth foal: half-sister to 3 winners, including 1998 2-y-o 5f winner Ivory's Promise and 1999 2-y-o 6f winner Coley (both by Pursuit of Love): dam unraced: last in maiden at Newcastle. *T. J. Etherington* — **–**

LAPHONIC (USA) 3 b.g. Labeeb 124 – Speechless (USA) (Hawkin's Special (USA)) [2006 57: 7.1m 5m⁴ 5m⁶ 6f 5m* Jul 15] big, lengthy gelding: modest performer: tongue tied, won maiden at Hamilton in July: effective at 5f to 7f: acts on soft and good to firm ground. *T. J. Etherington* — **58**

LAPINA (IRE) 2 ch.f. (Jan 26) Fath (USA) 116 – Alpina (USA) 69 (El Prado (IRE) 119) [2006 6m p7g⁴ p7g Oct 6] 15,000Y: fourth foal: half-sister to 1¼m/10.5f winner in Spain by Trans Island: dam lightly-raced half-sister to dam of Rodrigo de Triano: modest form in maidens, soon off bridle. *Pat Eddery* — **50**

LAP OF HONOUR (IRE) 2 b.g. (Apr 30) Danehill Dancer (IRE) 117 – Kingsridge (IRE) 89 (King's Theatre (IRE) 128) [2006 6m 6g⁴ 6m⁵ 6s p8g Nov 13] strong, well-made gelding: has a powerful, rather rounded action: second foal: dam, Irish 9f winner, half-sister to smart sprinter Pharaoh's Delight (grandam of 3-y-o Red Rocks): fair maiden: no impact both starts in nurseries: should stay 1m: gelded after final start. *N. A. Callaghan* — **71**

LAP OF THE GODS 2 b.g. (Apr 6) Fleetwood (IRE) 107 – Casarabonela (Magic Ring (IRE) 115) [2006 p8g Dec 19] tailed off in maiden at Lingfield. *Miss Z. C. Davison* — **–**

LA PRESSE (USA) 2 b.f. (Apr 20) Gone West (USA) – Journalist (IRE) 102 (Night Shift (USA)) [2006 6m² 6d* 6d³ 6d⁴ 6d² Oct 27] compact filly: second foal: half-sister to 4-y-o Paper Talk: dam, 2-y-o 6f winner, half-sister to useful sprinter Sheer Viking: useful performer: won maiden at York (beat Brave Tin Soldier by length) in August: best effort when 1¾ lengths fourth of 11 to Indian Ink in Cheveley Park Stakes at Newmarket, making running: beaten at short odds either side of that run, third in Firth of Clyde Stakes at Ayr and second (short-headed by Blue Echo) in listed event at Newmarket: should prove best at 5f/6f: yet to race on extremes of going: sent to UAE. *B. W. Hills* — **105**

LAQATAAT (IRE) 3 b.f. Alhaarth (IRE) 126 – Jawlaat (USA) 91 (Dayjur (USA) 137) [2006 75: 7s 7f 7m 10m Aug 6] big, lengthy filly: fair maiden at 2 yrs: well held in handicaps in 2006: tongue tied last 2 outings. *J. L. Dunlop* — **–**

LA QUINTA (IRE) 2 ch.f. (Mar 2) Indian Ridge 123 – Peneia (USA) (Nureyev (USA) 131) [2006 p6g⁶ 6f⁵ 5m⁴ p5g p5g³ p6g³ p6g Dec 8] 150,000Y: third foal: half-sister to fairly useful Irish winners Nurenberg (9f/1¼m, by Giant's Causeway) and Addicted (1m, by Machiavellian): dam, fairly useful French maiden who stayed 1m, out of sister to Coronation Stakes winner Chimes of Freedom: fair maiden: likely to stay 1m: acts on polytrack and firm ground. *B. J. Meehan* — **67**

LARAD (IRE) 5 br.g. Desert Sun 120 – Glenstal Priory 53 (Glenstal (USA) 118) [2006 62: p9.5g⁶ p10g² p13.9g² 13.9g² p16.5g³ p12g² p10g p12g⁶ 12.3g 10.2m p12g p12g Dec 6] good-bodied gelding: modest performer: effective at 9.5f, barely at 2m: acts on all-weather, soft and good to firm ground: tried in cheekpieces, wears blinkers: usually held up: tough. *J. S. Moore* — **58**

LARGS 6 ch.m. Sheikh Albadou 128 – Madam Zando 51 (Forzando 122) [2006 54: f5g⁶ **a46**
f5g 5.5g 5.2f Jul 25] good-bodied mare: poor performer: stays easy 7f: acts on firesand,
firm and probably soft going: in cheekpieces/blinkers nowadays. *J. Balding*

LARKWING (IRE) 5 b.h. Ela-Mana-Mou 132 – The Dawn Trader (USA) 70 (Naskra **108**
(USA)) [2006 108: 14.1s⁴ 16m⁴ May 3] leggy, close-coupled horse: useful performer:
creditable efforts both starts in 2006, fourth to Frank Sonata in listed event at Nottingham
and Cover Up in Sagaro Stakes at Lingfield: stays 18.7f: acts on soft and good to firm
going: visored (found little) third outing at 4 yrs: has shown signs of temperament: sold
40,000 gns in October. *G. Wragg*

LARKY'S LOB 7 b.g. Lugana Beach 116 – Eucharis 41 (Tickled Pink 114) [2006 52, –
a69d: f5g⁴ p5.1g f6g⁵ p6g³ f5g* f6g* f6g³ Dec 23] leggy, plain gelding: fair performer: **a73**
better on all-weather than turf: won handicaps at Southwell in November and December: effective at 5f to 7f: acts on all-weather, good to firm and good to soft ground: tried
in headgear: usually a front runner. *J. O'Reilly*

LA ROCA (IRE) 2 b.f. (Mar 21) Rock of Gibraltar (IRE) 133 – Zanella (IRE) 87 **87**
(Nordico (USA)) [2006 5g⁶ 6s³ 6g* 6m 8g⁵ 7d Sep 30] €70,000Y: smallish, sturdy filly:
closely related to 1½m winner Monsal Dale (by Desert King) and half-sister to several
winners, including fairly useful 1½m/1¾m winner Zalimar (by Montjeu): dam Irish 2-y-o
1m winner who stayed 1¼m: fairly useful performer: won maiden at Windsor in June: ran
creditably in face of stiff tasks after, in Albany Stakes, listed race and nursery (top weight,
tongue tied): will stay 1¼m. *R. M. Beckett*

LAS BEATAS 3 b.f. Green Desert (USA) 127 – Dora Carrington (IRE) 106 (Sri Pekan **74**
(USA) 117) [2006 7d² May 12] small, sturdy filly: first foal: dam, 2-y-o 6f winner (including Cherry Hinton Stakes), half-sister to Middle Park winner Primo Valentino: 10/1
and green, length second of 5 to Tawaajud in maiden at Chester: suffered injury after.
W. R. Swinburn

LASCELLES 2 b.c. (Apr 24) Halling (USA) 133 – Poppy's Song 76 (Owington 123) **76 p**
[2006 p6g p7.1g³ Dec 31] 42,000 2-y-o: second foal: dam, 5f winner, half-sister to high-
class 5f performer Kyllachy: off 7 months, better effort in maidens when 1½ lengths third
to All of Me at Wolverhampton: likely to do better still. *J. A. Osborne*

LA SPEZIA (IRE) 2 b.f. (Mar 31) Danehill Dancer (IRE) 117 – Genoa 96 (Zafonic **75**
(USA) 130) [2006 7d⁴ 7.5g² 7.5m² 7g⁴ Sep 30] leggy, quite good-topped filly: fifth foal:
half-sister to useful 1m winner Brindisi (by Dr Fong) and fairly useful 7f winner Fellow
Ship (by Elmaamul): dam possibly temperamental 11.5f winner: fair maiden: in frame all
starts, twice runner-up at Beverley: will stay 1¼m. *M. L. W. Bell*

LASSER LIGHT (IRE) 6 b.g. Inchinor 119 – Light Ray (Rainbow Quest (USA) 134) –
[2006 p12.2g Apr 25] tall gelding: little form: tried blinkered. *D. G. Bridgwater*

LAST CHAPTER (IRE) 4 b.g. Desert Story (IRE) 115 – Dutosky 80 (Doulab (USA) **48**
115) [2006 –: f8g p10g p10g³ 10m³ Jun 11] strong gelding: poor maiden: stays 1¼m: acts
on polytrack: tried blinkered. *Mrs J. L. Le Brocq, Jersey*

LAST DOG STANDING (IRE) 2 b.g. (Mar 2) King Charlemagne (USA) 120 – Rite –
of Spring 86 (Niniski (USA) 125) [2006 6g 7m 8.1m 6.1g 8.3g Oct 16] tall, close-coupled
gelding: well beaten in varied events: once blinkered. *B. G. Powell*

LAST FLIGHT (IRE) 2 b.f. (Mar 11) In The Wings 128 – Fantastic Fantasy (IRE) 85 **58 p**
(Lahib (USA) 129) [2006 8.3m 8.2g 8.3d⁴ Oct 10] tall, close-coupled filly: second foal:
dam, 1¼m to 1¾m winner, half-sister to useful performers Lucky Guest (at 1m/1¼m) and
Fantasy Hill (stayer): modest form in maidens, fourth to Glen Nevis at Leicester: should
improve at 1¼m/1½m, and type to make mark in handicaps. *J. L. Dunlop*

LASTING IMAGE 4 br.f. Zilzal (USA) 137 – Minsden's Image 78 (Dancer's Image –
(USA)) [2006 –: 12f Jun 12] close-coupled filly: no form. *S. C. Williams*

LASTING LOVE 3 ch.f. Primo Valentino (IRE) 116 – Miss Beverley (Beveled (USA)) **42**
[2006 59: p6g⁵ p6g p5.1g⁶ p7.1g f6g³ f7g⁵ p6g Apr 24] unfurnished filly: poor maiden:
stays 6f: acts on all-weather: usually races prominently: blinkered last 3 starts: reportedly
bled final start at 2 yrs. *C. R. Dore*

LAST PIONEER (IRE) 4 b.g. New Frontier (IRE) 110 – Toordillon (IRE) 69 (Con- **65**
tract Law (USA) 108) [2006 67: 12d⁶ 16d Aug 29] strong gelding: fair maiden: stays
1½m: acts on soft going: often carries head high. *R. Ford*

LAST SOVEREIGN 2 b.c. (Mar 15) Pivotal 124 – Zayala (Royal Applause 124) **68 p**
[2006 p7g⁴ p6g⁶ Dec 2] 80,000Y: first foal: dam unraced half-sister to smart performer up

to 1m Fizzed: fair form in maidens at Kempton, soon plenty to do when sixth of 9 to Estimator, not knocked about: remains open to improvement. *R. Charlton*

LAST WARRIOR 3 ch.c. Rainbow Quest (USA) 134 – Sena Desert 89 (Green Desert **84** (USA) 127) [2006 11.6f⁴ 12d Aug 12] second foal: half-brother to fairly useful 7f winner Sydney Star (by Machiavellian): dam, 1¼m winner, half-sister to very smart 1¼m performer Best of The Bests: much better effort in maidens when fourth to Peppertree at Windsor on debut: well held at Newmarket next time: sold 13,000 gns. *J. H. M. Gosden*

LATANAZUL 2 b.f. (Apr 13) Sakhee (USA) 136 – Karamah 78 (Unfuwain (USA) 131) **87** [2006 7d 8.2m² 7d² Oct 3] unfurnished filly: first foal: dam, ran 3 times (best efforts at 6f), out of half-sister to 1000 Guineas winner Shadayid: fairly useful form in maidens, second at Nottingham (beaten ½ length by Treat) and Leicester: will stay at least 1¼m. *J. L. Dunlop*

LATE ARRIVAL 9 b.g. Emperor Jones (USA) 119 – Try Vickers (USA) 72 (Fuzz- **–** buster (USA)) [2006 50: p16.5g Jan 6] tall gelding: modest performer nowadays: reportedly finished lame only start in 2006: usually blinkered/visored: none too genuine. *M. D. Hammond*

LATE NIGHT LOVE 3 b.f. Bluebird (USA) 125 – Syringa 61 (Lure (USA) 131) **?** [2006 –: f8g 6g⁴ 7.5s* 7.5f⁴ Jun 10] little sign of ability on all-weather in Britain (sold from K. Burke 1,000 gns after reappearance): won maiden at Copenhagen in May: stays 7.5f: acts on soft ground: tried blinkered. *Ms K. Stenefeldt, Sweden*

LATERAL 3 b.c. Singspiel (IRE) 133 – Ligona (Aragon 118) [2006 103p: 9s³ 10d³ 8g* **123** 8s* 8v³ 8g* Sep 23] very smart performer: won all 3 starts at 2 yrs, notably 4-runner Gran Criterium at Milan: plenty of improvement in 2006, winning Jaxx-Pokal at Hamburg (by 4 lengths from Willingly) in July, Oppenheim Pramerica Meile at Cologne (by neck from same rival) in August and Grosse Europa-Meile at Cologne (by 6 lengths from Vega's Lord) in September: unsuited by run of race when only third to Notability in Oettingen-Rennen at Baden-Baden penultimate start: best at 1m: acts on soft ground. *P. Schiergen, Germany*

LATIF (USA) 5 b.g. Red Ransom (USA) – Awaamir 102 (Green Desert (USA) 127) **81** [2006 77d, a45: p8.6g* p8.6g⁵ f8g² p9.5g² f8g* f8g² p9.5g* p8.6g³ p12g⁴ p12g* p13.9g⁶ 9.9d³ p8.6g* 10g³ 8.1m² 10.5s⁶ 7.9g Jun 28] strong, good-topped gelding: fairly useful performer: successful in 2006 in banded races at Wolverhampton and Southwell (2), and handicaps at Wolverhampton (2) and Lingfield between January and April: effective at 1m to easy 1½m: acts on all-weather, firm and good to soft going (well beaten both starts on soft): tried blinkered/tongue tied. *Ms Deborah J. Evans*

LATIN EXPRESS (IRE) 4 b.g. Marju (IRE) 127 – Sea Port (Averof 123) [2006 54: **–** p12g Jan 28] workmanlike gelding: maiden: well held only outing in 2006: tried blink-ered (well beaten)/tongue tied: has found little. *W. R. Muir*

LATINO MAGIC (IRE) 6 ch.h. Lion Cavern (USA) 117 – Tansy 75 (Shareef Dancer **114** (USA) 135) [2006 115: 8.9m³ 8g 8.9m 8m⁶ 10g⁴ 8.5d⁴ 8d⁴ 8m⁴ 8.5f² 8g² 7.5v⁴ 8.5s⁵ Oct 14] smart performer: creditable 1½ lengths third to Linngari in Dubai Al Rashidiya on reappearance, easily best of first 3 starts at Nad Al Sheba: similar form afterwards only when fourth to Quinmaster in valuable handicap at Galway sixth start and neck second to Ivan Denisovich in listed race at the Curragh tenth outing: effective at 1m/1¼m: acts on firm and good to soft ground: tried tongue tied: has wandered: sold €240,000. *R. J. Osborne, Ireland*

LAUDER 2 ch.f. (Jan 26) First Trump 118 – Madam Zando 51 (Forzando 122) [2006 **47** f8g⁶ f7g Dec 14] fifth foal: half-sister to 5-y-o Uig and 6-y-o Largs: dam maiden who stayed 7f: mid-field in maidens at Southwell. *J. Balding*

LAUGH 'N CRY 5 b.m. In The Wings 128 – The Kings Daughter 79 (Indian King **63** (USA) 128) [2006 74: p8g 8.3g 8.3g p8g 8m p7g p7g⁶ p10g p10g⁵ Dec 4] good-topped mare: modest maiden nowadays: stays 1¼m: acts on polytrack and good to firm going: blinkered last 3 starts. *C. A. Cyzer*

LAUNCH IT LILY 2 br.f. (Feb 29) Kyllachy 129 – Bermuda Lily 78 (Dunbeath (USA) **61** 127) [2006 5.7m 6.1d³ Oct 13] close-coupled filly: closely related to 8-y-o Native Title and half-sister to several winners, including useful 1m/1¼m winner Sir Talbot (by Ardross): dam 2-y-o 5f winner: better effort in maidens when third at Warwick (80/1, dictated pace). *W. G. M. Turner*

LAURA'S BEST (IRE) 2 b.f. (Apr 15) Green Desert (USA) 127 – Lassie's Gold **75 p** (USA) (Seeking The Gold (USA)) [2006 p6g² 6d Oct 27] close-coupled filly: fifth foal: half-sister to Irish 1m winner Who Could Tell (by Thunder Gulch) and winner in USA by

Sea Salute: dam unraced close relation to top-class US performer up to 1½m Lemon Drop Kid: promising 5 lengths second to Rainbow Promises in maiden at Lingfield: seemed amiss in listed race at Newmarket 3 weeks later: should yet do better. *W. J. Haggas*

LAUREL DAWN 8 gr.g. Paris House 123 – Madrina 70 (Waajib 121) [2006 47: f5g – f5g⁵ f6g f5g* p6g⁴ f5g² f5g p6g 5f 5m f5g Dec 29] leggy, plain gelding: modest performer nowadays: won banded race at Southwell in April: left C. Kellett before final start: effective at 5f/6f: acts on all-weather, firm and good to soft going: tried in cheekpieces, often blinkered. *Miss A. Stokell* **a54**

LAURELDEAN EXPRESS 2 ch.f. (Feb 20) Inchinor 119 – Triple Sharp 80 (Selkirk **90** (USA) 129) [2006 p6g³ p7g² 7f³ p8.6m³ 8d² 9d⁶ Nov 18] 23,000F, €40,000Y: workmanlike filly: second foal: half-sister to winner in Spain by Vettori: dam 1¼m and hurdles winner: fairly useful maiden: placed 5 times, including ¾-length second of 6 to Literato in listed race at Toulouse fifth start, possibly flattered (dictated): stays 1m: acts on polytrack, firm and good to soft going: once withdrawn after unseating paddock: sent to USA. *E. J. O'Neill*

LAURELS LADY 2 b.f. (Mar 9) Timeless Times (USA) 99 – Superstream (Super- – power 113) [2006 5f 5f 5m Jul 24] sixth foal: sister to untrustworthy but fairly useful 5f/ 6f (including at 2 yrs) winner Tommy Smith and half-sister to 2 winners, including 5-y-o Baron Rhodes: dam unraced: more signs of temperament than ability. *I. W. McInnes*

LAUREN LOUISE 4 b.f. Tagula (IRE) 116 – Movie Star (IRE) (Barathea (IRE) 127) **53** [2006 55: p6g⁴ p6g⁵ p6g* p6g⁵ p6g May 15] leggy, good-topped filly: modest performer: won claimer at Lingfield in February: should stay 1m: acts on polytrack and good to firm ground: tried visored, tongue tied at 2 yrs. *T. T. Clement*

LAURENTINA 2 b.f. (Mar 3) Cadeaux Genereux 131 – Trois Heures Apres (Soviet **87** Star (USA) 128) [2006 6g⁴ p6g* 7d* 8d³ Oct 28] 27,000Y, 44,000 2-y-o: good-bodied filly: half-sister to 3 winners, including fairly useful 1¼m winner Feaat (by Unfuwain) and useful French 1m to 1¼m winner Rising Talent (by Bering): dam unraced half-sister to Oaks third Mezzogiorno: fairly useful form: won maiden at Kempton in September and nursery at Catterick in October: good 5¼ lengths third to Passage of Time in listed event at Newmarket: stays 1m: raced on polytrack and good going or softer. *B. J. Meehan*

LAURO 6 b.m. Mukaddamah (USA) 125 – Lapu-Lapu 62 (Prince Sabo 123) [2006 78d: **72** p9.5g⁶ 9g³ 9.2g⁴ 9.3g* 10.1d⁶ p9.5m p9.5m Oct 14] strong mare: fair handicapper: won **a66** at Carlisle in August: stays easy 1¼m: acts on all-weather, firm and soft going: wore cheekpieces final start: held up. *Miss J. A. Camacho*

LAUROLLIE 4 b.f. Makbul 104 – Madonna Da Rossi 53 (Mtoto 134) [2006 59: 12.6m **50** 12.1g 10f f11g⁶ f12m³ p13.9g⁶ p12g⁶ p12.2g⁶ f12g⁴ Dec 29] modest performer: left Dr J. Naylor after third start: stays 1½m: acts on all-weather and firm going. *B. P. J. Baugh*

LAVA MAN (USA) 5 b. or br.g. Slew City Slew (USA) – Li'l Ms. Leonard (USA) **130** (Nostalgia's Star (USA)) [2006 124: a9f* a10f* 9f* 10f* a10f* a10f* a9f* a10f Nov 4] top-class performer: reportedly split a frog when well held in Japan Cup Dirt at Tokyo on final outing in 2005: unbeaten in first 7 races in 2006, very valuable event at Santa Anita in January, Santa Anita Handicap in March, valuable event in April, Charles Whittingham Memorial Handicap in June and Hollywood Gold Cup (for second successive year, gave Ace Blue 10 lb and beat him a nose) in July, all 3 at Hollywood, Pacific Classic at Del Mar (by 2½ lengths from Good Reward, quickening away from front 3f out) in August and Grade 2 Goodwood Breeders' Cup Handicap at Santa Anita in October: best effort when giving weight away all round in last-named race, beating Brother Derek by 2¼ lengths, clear on home turn: second favourite, below form when seventh to Invasor in Breeders' Cup Classic at Churchill Downs final outing, weakening before home turn: stays 1¼m: effective on dirt and on firm going on turf: wears blinkers: races prominently: game and genuine, but has a poor record outside California. *D. F. O'Neill, USA*

LA VECCHIA SCUOLA (IRE) 2 b.f. (Mar 21) Mull of Kintyre (USA) 114 – Force **66** Divine (FR) (L'Emigrant (USA) 129) [2006 5m 5f² 5g⁶ 5f 6d⁶ Oct 3] €14,000F, €14,000Y: fourth foal: half-sister to unreliable 2004 2-y-o 6f winner Selkirk Storm (by Trans Island): dam French 6f (at 2 yrs) to 1¼m winner: fair maiden: short-head second to Vale of Belvoir at Catterick: didn't go on, off 3 months before final start (stamina stretched): best at 5f. *D. Nicholls*

LAVENHAM (IRE) 3 b.f. Kalanisi (IRE) 132 – Antigonel (IRE) 59 (Fairy King **79** (USA)) [2006 74: 7m* 7s³ 7f 7m 7m⁴ 8.1d³ Sep 13] rather leggy filly: fair performer: won maiden at Lingfield in May: not discredited when in frame in handicaps after: stays 1m: acts on soft and good to firm going: effective making running or held up. *R. Hannon*

Prix d'Ispahan, Longchamp—a close finish between Laverock (second left),
Manduro (No.10) and Krataios (rail); Ganay winner Corre Caminos (No.7) is only fifth

LAVEROCK (IRE) 4 b.c. Octagonal (NZ) 126 – Sky Song (IRE) (Sadler's Wells **123**
(USA) 132) [2006 118: 10m 9.3d* 12d³ 10g² 10.4d⁵ 12g* Oct 15]

All Group 1s are equal, but some are more equal than others. The improved
Laverock showed very smart form to run out a narrow winner of both the Prix
d'Ispahan and the Gran Premio del Jockey Club Italiano. However, the same level
of form wasn't good enough in the Grand Prix de Saint-Cloud, in which Laverock
came up against Pride and Hurricane Run and—on his sole appearance in Britain—
he managed only fifth in anything but a vintage renewal of the International at York,
just one of the seven runners starting at longer odds.

Laverock seemed exposed at three as a horse good enough to contest
Group 1 races but not good enough to win them. He was third past the post in the
Criterium de Saint-Cloud at two and in the Prix du Jockey Club (demoted to sixth
after his jockey barged his way through). His record at three also included unplaced
efforts in the Poule d'Essai des Poulains and the Grand Prix de Paris, and he did not
win above Group 3 level until the latest season when he was raced exclusively in
Group 1 company. Laverock's six races were spread around five countries and
yielded the two victories. Laverock started at odds of over 25/1 in the Prix d'Ispahan in May, following a below-par effort in the Queen Elizabeth II Cup in Hong
Kong on his reappearance. Waited with as usual at Longchamp, he came through to

Gran Premio del Jockey Club Italiano, Milan—Laverock (second left) is carrying different colours
as he gains his second Group 1 win; this time it's Fair Nashwan (right) who runs him close,
with the grey Cherry Mix taking third

lead inside the final furlong and held off the strong-finishing Manduro by a short neck, with Laverock's shorter-priced stable-companion Krataios half a length away third in a field of eleven in which the odds-on Corre Caminos, winner of the Prix Ganay, pulled too hard for his own good and managed only fifth. Having previously raced in the colours of Gainsborough Stud, Laverock was having his first start in Sheikh Mohammed's livery when running in the Gran Premio del Jockey Club Italiano at Milan in October, a race with more strength in depth than many Italian Group 1s. Coupled with the Godolphin-owned Cherry Mix, Laverock led a furlong out and held on to beat Fair Nashwan by a head. Cherry Mix, who went on to win the Premio Roma at Rome the following month, was a further length and a half back in third.

Despite his d'Ispahan win, Laverock had again been afforded little respect by French punters when running in the Grand Prix de Saint-Cloud. The outsider in the six-strong field, Laverock ran on well to be nearest at the finish in third, another good effort for all that he was unable to get closer than two lengths to Pride and Hurricane Run, who fought out the finish. Laverock did not reproduce his best form when runner-up to Lord of England in a poorly-contested and slowly-run Grosser Dallmayr-Preis, a Group 1 run at Munich, nor did he in the International at York where perhaps he should not be judged too harshly, left with far too much to do in a race which developed into something of a sprint, finishing around four lengths fifth to Notnowcato.

		Zabeel	Sir Tristram
	Octagonal (NZ)	(b 1986)	Lady Giselle
	(br 1992)	Eight Carat	Pieces of Eight
Laverock (IRE)		(bl 1975)	Klairessa
(b.c. 2002)		Sadler's Wells	Northern Dancer
	Sky Song (IRE)	(b 1981)	Fairy Bridge
	(b 1997)	Criquette	Shirley Heights
		(b 1990)	Ghislaine

Sired by the champion Australian racehorse Octagonal, also responsible for the Australasian champion Lonhro, Laverock is the first foal out of the French maiden Sky Song who stayed a mile and a half. Sky Song (also responsible for the useful French two-year-old mile winner Right Note, by Daylami) was out of Criquette, a half-sister to the top-class miler Markofdistinction. Criquette won at seven furlongs as a two-year-old, showing useful form when running away with the listed Radley Stakes at Newbury, but she refused to enter the stalls on both her intended starts at three, before later winning at nine furlongs in the UAE. The tall, rather leggy, attractive Laverock, who has joined Ismael Mohammed in the UAE, stays a mile and a half and acts on soft and good to firm going. He has worn a tongue tie, and is usually held up. *C. Laffon-Parias, France*

LA VIA FERRATA (IRE) 3 ch.c. Mark of Esteem (IRE) 137 – Verify (IRE) (Polish Precedent (USA) 131) [2006 51: p10g* f11g* 11.6g⁴ 11.9m³ p12g² p12.2g* 14g⁴ 14.1d⁴ 17.2g⁴ p13.9g Nov 6] fair performer: won handicaps at Lingfield in January and Southwell in February, and claimer at Wolverhampton (looked none too keen, left P. Cole £20,000) in July: fell at Wolverhampton final outing: stayed 1¾m: acted on all-weather, good to firm and good to soft going: held up: dead. *A. G. Newcombe*   **68**

LA VIOLA 4 b.f. Fraam 114 – Arasong 76 (Aragon 118) [2006 65: p8.6g 7.9m² p8.6g² p8.6g 8.3m² p8.6g 9m⁶ p8.6g p8.6g⁴ 8d Oct 18] quite good-topped filly: modest form at best in 2006: stays 8.6f: acts on polytrack and firm going: wears headgear. *K. R. Burke*   **64 d**

LAWAAHEB (IRE) 5 b.g. Alhaarth (IRE) 126 – Ajayib (USA) 84 (Riverman (USA) 131) [2006 62: p16g p12g³ p8.6g⁵ Mar 3] rangy gelding: modest performer: stays 1½m: acts on polytrack, raced only on good ground or firmer on turf: usually wears headgear. *B. R. Johnson*   **58**

LAW MAKER 6 b.g. Case Law 113 – Bo' Babbity 75 (Strong Gale 116) [2006 68, a81: p5g² p6g p5g* f5g p5.1g⁶ p6g² p5g p6g 5.1s p5g 5f 5.1g 5m⁵ 5s Sep 14] good-topped gelding: fairly useful handicapper on all-weather, fair on turf: won at Lingfield in January: effective at 5f/easy 6f: acts on polytrack (seemingly not on fibresand), firm and good to soft going: blinkered/visored: races up with pace. *A. Bailey*   **71 a86**

LAW OF THE LAND (IRE) 2 b.g. (Apr 10) Trans Island 119 – Bella's Dream (IRE) (Case Law 113) [2006 6s 7f² 7f⁵ 7.6f³ 7d 7f p7.1m³ p9.5m⁵ p8g Nov 8] tall, close-coupled   **65**

gelding: fair maiden: placed on 3 occasions, including in nursery: stays 9.5f: acts on poly-track and firm going: gelded after final start. *W. R. Muir*

LAWOOD (IRE) 6 gr.g. Charnwood Forest (IRE) 125 – La Susiane (Persepolis (FR) – 127) [2006 14.1s 11.7d 8.3f 10.9m 12.1g f16g⁴ Dec 12] good-topped gelding: has a quick action: fairly useful performer at 4 yrs for K. Ryan: unraced on Flat in 2005: no show in 2006, leaving L. Grassick after fifth start: tried in cheekpieces/blinkered, visored last 5 starts. *M. Scudamore*

LAWYERS CHOICE 2 b.f. (Apr 18) Namid 128 – Finger of Light 89 (Green Desert 69 (USA) 127) [2006 6.1d p7g⁴ p7.1g⁴ Dec 1] good-topped filly: seventh foal: half-sister to 3 winners, including 2002 2-y-o 7f winner The Local (by Selkirk) and fairly useful Italian 5f (at 2 yrs) to 7f winner Far Hope (by Barathea): dam 2-y-o 6f winner out of Lowther winner Circus Ring: fair form when fourth in maidens at Lingfield and Wolverhampton. *Pat Eddery*

LAWYER TO WORLD 2 gr.c. (Feb 8) Marju (IRE) 127 – Legal Steps (IRE) (Law 66 Society (USA) 130) [2006 6m⁶ p8g⁴ p7g⁶ 7d⁵ p8.6g p7g² p7g⁶ Dec 19] 125,000Y: useful-looking colt: brother to smart 6f (including at 2 yrs) winner Stormont and half-brother to several winners, including fairly useful 1m winner Stilett (by Tirol): dam Irish 12.5f winner: fair maiden: runner-up in nursery at Kempton: barely stays 8.6f: acts on polytrack and good to soft going. *N. A. Callaghan*

LAYAZAAL (IRE) 3 b.c. Mujadil (USA) 119 – Law Review (IRE) 63 (Case Law 113) 100 [2006 93: 7g⁵ 7s² 9s* 8m 9.9g 10d⁵ 10s Oct 21] close-coupled, quite good-topped colt: useful handicapper: won at Goodwood in May by a head from Multakka: also ran well when neck second to Levera and fifth to Rampallion, both at Newmarket, second/penultimate outings: stays 1¼m: acts on soft going: joined M. Al Muhairi in UAE. *J. L. Dunlop*

LAYED BACK ROCKY 4 ch.g. Lake Coniston (IRE) 131 – Madam Taylor 81 (Free 58 State 125) [2006 62: p6g p9.5g p12.2g f8m p8.6g³ p8.6g³ p7.1g⁶ Dec 21] workmanlike gelding: modest maiden: stays 8.6f: acts on all-weather and heavy going: tried in cheek-pieces: reportedly bled third start. *M. Mullineaux*

LAY THE CASH (USA) 2 ch.g. (Mar 25) Include (USA) 121 – Shanade (USA) (Sen- 66 timental Slew (USA)) [2006 7f⁵ 7g 6g 8d p7g p6g* p7.1g⁶ Nov 18] $50,000: heavy-topped gelding: fourth foal: half-brother to 3 winners in USA: dam US 2-y-o 4.5f winner: fair performer: won nursery at Kempton in November: best form at 6f/7f on polytrack: blinkered last 2 starts (forced pace): gelded after. *J. S. Moore*

LAZY DARREN 2 b.g. (Apr 14) Largesse 112 – Palmstead Belle (IRE) 79 (Wolfhound 80 p (USA) 126) [2006 7d p8.6g* Dec 27] 1,700Y: tall, useful-looking gelding: third foal: brother to 3-y-o Bel Cantor: dam 2-y-o 5f winner: left M. Wigham after debut: well-backed favourite, won maiden at Wolverhampton nearly 3 months later by 3½ lengths from Lord Oroko, going away: looks capable of better still. *R. Hannon*

LAZZAZ 8 b.g. Muhtarram (USA) 125 – Astern (USA) 67 (Polish Navy (USA)) [2006 – 62: p12.2g May 8] modest handicapper: effective at 1½m to easy 2m: acts on all-weather and any turf going: tried blinkered/in cheekpieces: races up with pace. *P. W. Hiatt*

LAZZOOM (IRE) 3 b.g. Zilzal (USA) 137 – Bring On The Choir 87 (Chief Singer – 131) [2006 55: 8m 9m 7.9m 8f 9s Sep 24] modest performer at 2 yrs: no show in 2006: tried in cheekpieces/tongue tied. *Miss Tracy Waggott*

LEAH'S PRIDE 5 b.m. Atraf 116 – First Play 59 (Primo Dominie 121) [2006 59: p6g³ 57 f5g⁵ p5.1g² p5g⁵ p6g p5.1g⁵ Apr 24] modest performer: left P. Howling after fifth start: best at 5f/6f: acts on polytrack (unraced on turf): tried tongue tied: races prominently. *Miss D. A. McHale*

LEAMINGTON LAD (IRE) 3 gr.c. Beckett (IRE) 116 – Nicea (IRE) 90 (Dominion 67 123) [2006 50: 7.1s* 7.5d⁵ 8.1g* 7d 8.2m 10m⁴ 10.2m⁴ 10d⁵ 11.6d³ Oct 9] leggy, close-coupled colt: fair handicapper: won at Warwick in April and May: stays 11.6f: acts on soft and good to firm going. *J. A. Geake*

LE CHIFFRE (IRE) 4 br.g. Celtic Swing 138 – Implicit View 63 (Persian Bold 123) 77 [2006 86: 7.9m⁴ 7g⁵ 7.5f p7.1g* 7.1f* 7m⁴ 7.1f⁶ 7.6d p7.1g f6g* f5g Dec 5] tall gelding: fair performer: won apprentice claimer at Wolverhampton and handicap at Haydock, both in July, and claimer at Southwell (left R. Harris) in November: effective at 6f to 1m: acts on all-weather and firm going: in cheekpieces/blinkered nowadays *K. R. Burke*

LE COLOMBIER (IRE) 3 ch.c. Alhaarth (IRE) 126 – Wide Range (IRE) (Spectrum 85 (IRE) 126) [2006 87p: p8.6g² 8d⁴ p9.5g* 12g p10g 12g Aug 19] leggy, quite attractive colt: fairly useful performer: won maiden at Wolverhampton in June: likely to prove best around 1¼m (well held at 1½m): acts on polytrack and good to firm going: sold 18,000 gns. *J. W. Hills*

LE CORVEE (IRE) 4 b.g. Rossini (USA) 118 – Elupa (IRE) 98 (Mtoto 134) [2006 95: 12g 12.3d May 12] well-made gelding: fairly useful handicapper: better effort in 2006 on reappearance: stays 1½m: acts on polytrack and firm ground: joined A. Carroll and gelded. *A. King* **88**

LEFONIC 4 ch.c. Zafonic (USA) 130 – La Adrada (Arazi (USA) 135) [2006 –: p12.2g⁵ 14.1d p13.9g* 16f⁶ p16g* 14.1f 16f⁴ p16g p13.9m⁵ Oct 2] good-topped colt: fair performer on all-weather, modest on turf: won claimers at Wolverhampton and Lingfield in June: stays easy 2m: acts on polytrack and firm going. *G. C. H. Chung* **60 a74**

LEFT HAND DRIVE 3 b.g. Erhaab (USA) 127 – Eyelet (IRE) (Satco (FR) 114) [2006 –: f11g² 9.7s 12.6g p12g Jun 29] modest maiden: gelded prior to reappearance: should stay at least 1½m: acts on fibresand: often tongue tied: won juvenile hurdles in August/October. *B. W. Duke* **59**

LEFT NOSTRIL (IRE) 3 b.f. Beckett (IRE) 116 – Baywood (Emarati (USA) 74) [2006 47: p5.1g p6g p6g 6m⁴ 6.1d³ f6g² p6g p5g² Dec 10] leggy filly: poor maiden: will prove best at 5f/6f: acts on all-weather, good to firm and good to soft going: tried blinkered. *P. S. McEntee* **48**

LEGACY (JPN) 6 b.g. Carnegie (IRE) 129 – Idraak (Kris 135) [2006 54: p8.6g* f8g p10g⁵ p9.5g⁴ p8.6g p10g p9.5g³ p8.6g 10f⁴ p10g p8g Nov 6] sturdy gelding: modest performer: won banded race at Wolverhampton in January: stays 1¼m: acts on polytrack and firm ground: blinkered/visored last 5 starts. *P. D. Evans* **60**

LEGAL CALL 3 b.g. Easycall 115 – Legal Sound 85 (Legal Eagle 126) [2006 57: p6g 5.1m 8f 8m⁴ 8.1m⁶ 7.1g 8.1m Aug 10] poor maiden: stays 1m: acts on good to firm ground: tried in cheekpieces/visored. *M. Appleby* **45**

LEGAL DRAM 5 ch.g. Case Law 113 – Moonshine Malt (Superlative 118) [2006 60: f8g f8g 7.5f* 7.2m 7.9m⁶ 8g Aug 14] modest performer: won selling handicap at Beverley in July: should stay 1¼m: acts on polytrack and firm ground. *M. Dods* **57**

LEGAL LOVER (IRE) 4 b.g. Woodborough (USA) 112 – Victoria's Secret (IRE) 70 (Law Society (USA) 130) [2006 60: f8g⁴ f8g⁴ f8g* 8.5d⁵ f8g² f8g⁴ f8g 8m* 8g⁵ 8d² f8g* f8g f8g² f8g² Dec 27] sturdy gelding: fair performer: won banded races at Southwell in April and November and seller at Bath in September: stays 8.6f: acts on all-weather, good to firm and good to soft going: front runner. *R. Hollinshead* **70**

LEGALLY FAST (USA) 4 b.g. Deputy Minister (CAN) – Earthly Angel (USA) (Crafty Prospector (USA)) [2006 67: 15m Jun 24] tall gelding: fair performer at 3 yrs: well held only start on Flat in 2006: stays 1¾m: acts on good to firm ground: blinkered final 3-y-o outing: joined P. Bowen, won over hurdles in November. *S. C. Burrough* **–**

LEGAL SET (IRE) 10 gr.g. Second Set (IRE) 127 – Tiffany's Case (IRE) 65 (Thatching 131) [2006 70, a61: p6g p5.1g p5.1g f6g 5d p5g⁵ p5g p7g 5d p5.1m f14g Dec 5] rather leggy, close-coupled gelding: modest performer nowadays: effective at 5f, seems to stay 1m: acts on all-weather and any turf going: tried in cheekpieces, usually blinkered/tongue tied. *Miss A. Stokell* **54**

LEGEND HOUSE (FR) 2 b.f. (Apr 10) Grand Lodge (USA) 125 – Legaya 94 (Shirley Heights 130) [2006 8.2g p8.6g⁵ f8g* Nov 20] sturdy filly: fourth living foal: sister to 4-y-o Inch Lodge and half-sister to smart 7f (at 2 yrs) to 11f winner Legal Approach (by Zafonic): dam Irish 1½m winner out of Oaks winner Jet Ski Lady: progressive form, won minor event at Southwell: will prove suited by 1¼m/1½m: better still to come. *M. Johnston* **70 p**

LEGEND OF DANCE 4 b.f. Dansili 127 – Hard Task 82 (Formidable (USA) 125) [2006 34: f14g p12.2g p12.2g Feb 13] poor maiden: seemingly stays 1½m: acts on polytrack. *J. L. Spearing* **–**

LEGERETE (USA) 2 b.f. (Feb 2) Rahy (USA) 115 – Sea Hill (USA) (Seattle Slew (USA)) [2006 6.5g³ 8g* 8m³ Oct 1] good-topped filly: sixth foal: half-sister to several winners abroad, including useful French 1¼m winner Underwater (by Theatrical) who stayed 1½m: dam, French 9f winner, half-sister to high-class French 1¼m performer Groom Dancer: very ready winner of minor event at Longchamp in September: somewhat on edge, improved again when 5¼ lengths third to Finsceal Beo in Prix Marcel Boussac there following month, weaving through late: bred to be suited by 1¼m: sure to improve further. *A. Fabre, France* **107 p**

LEIGHTON BUZZARD 4 b.g. Cyrano de Bergerac 120 – Winsome Wooster 71 **71**
(Primo Dominie 121) [2006 64: 7.5f 7d 7.9m* 8.3f⁵ 8f² 9f 10g² 9.7f⁵ p9.5g p9.5s Dec 13] **a56**
compact gelding: fair handicapper on turf, modest on all-weather: won apprentice event
at Carlisle in June: left Mrs A. Duffield after sixth start: stays 1¼m: acts on firm and good
to soft going, below form on polytrack: usually held up. *N. B. King*

LE MASQUE 2 b.g. (Mar 24) Iron Mask (USA) 117 – Red Millennium (IRE) 102 **66**
(Tagula (IRE) 116) [2006 5g 6g 5m⁵ 6d⁶ p6g f6g² p6g² Dec 26] 40,000Y: neat, quite
attractive gelding: first foal: dam 5f winner, including at 2 yrs: fair maiden: gelded, good
short-head second to Hollywood George at Wolverhampton final start: stays 6f: acts on
all-weather and good to firm going. *B. Smart*

LE MIRACLE (GER) 5 b.g. Monsun (GER) 124 – L'Heure Bleue (IRE) (Kendor **117**
(FR) 122) [2006 12v 15d 15.5m* 14g* 14.5d* 15g* 15s³ 15.5m* 20m³ Oct 1] tall, leggy
gelding: third foal: half-brother to 2 winners by Platini, including useful German 9f/1¼m
winner Lomicelli (by Platini): dam German 7f/1m winner: smart performer: much improved in 2006, winning claimers at Saint-Cloud in May and Longchamp in June, minor
event at Clairefontaine and listed race at Chantilly (by 6 lengths) in July and Prix Gladiateur Royal Thalasso Barriere at Longchamp (beat Salutino by 5 lengths, held up before
bursting clear impressively) in September: creditable 1¼ lengths third to Sergeant Cecil
in Prix du Cadran at Longchamp final start, making most: stays 2½m: acts on good to
firm and good to soft going: has worn blinkers/earplugs: has been mulish at start.
W. Baltromei, Germany

LEMON DROP LAD (USA) 3 ch.g. Lemon Drop Kid (USA) 131 – April Starlight **80**
(USA) 94 (Storm Bird (CAN) 134) [2006 70p: p8g⁴ 9.2d* 12s Sep 30] well-made gelding: fairly useful performer: won maiden at Hamilton in May: sold from Sir Michael
Stoute 33,000 gns and gelded, tailed off in handicap at Fairyhouse final start: should stay
beyond 9f. *T. J. Arnold, Ireland*

LEMON SILK (IRE) 2 ch.g. (Mar 11) Barathea (IRE) 127 – Bois de Citron (USA) 88 **81**
(Woodman (USA) 126) [2006 6f⁵ 5m⁵ 6g³ 7.5g* 8d 8s² 7s Oct 14] 27,000Y: close-
coupled gelding: second foal: half-brother to winner in Greece by Shinko Forest: dam,
2-y-o 5f winner, out of smart performer up to 1m Lemon Souffle: fairly useful performer:
won nursery at Beverley in August: best run when short-head second to Foxxy in nursery
at Ayr following month: stays 1m: acts on soft ground. *T. P. Tate*

LENARD FRANK (IRE) 2 b.g. (Mar 10) Daggers Drawn (USA) 114 – Princess Sofie **41**
84 (Efisio 120) [2006 5g p5.1g 6.1s⁶ 5f⁴ 6f 5.1d⁴ 6f 5m 5.1m Aug 20] poor maiden:
usually visored. *M. D. I. Usher*

LENINGRAD (IRE) 3 gr.c. Montjeu (IRE) 137 – Sallanches (USA) (Gone West **102**
(USA)) [2006 p10g* 10.4s⁴ 10m 8m 8m² 8.1m³ 8g⁶ Sep 28] €82,000F, €520,000Y:
close-coupled colt: third foal: closely related to 7f winner Royal Robe (by King of Kings),
later successful in USA, and half-brother to winner in Hong Kong by Belong To Me:
dam, French 9.5f winner, half-sister to Arlington Million winner Mill Native: useful
performer: won maiden at Lingfield in April: with tasks next 2 starts: good efforts in
handicaps at Newmarket (1½ lengths second to Bosset) and Haydock (¾-length third to
Charlie Cool) fifth/sixth appearances: looked none too keen final outing: free-going sort,
but stays 1¼m: acts on polytrack and good to firm going: probably none too genuine: sold
190,000 gns, sent to Saudi Arabia. *M. L. W. Bell*

LENNEL 8 b.g. Presidium 124 – Ladykirk 78 (Slip Anchor 136) [2006 63, a78: 10.1f **59 §**
16m⁴ 14.1f 15m⁴ 15m⁵ 14m⁶ 17.5d³ f16g² p16.5m Oct 14] leggy, close-coupled gelding: **a52 §**
modest handicapper: stays 17.5f: acts on all-weather and any turf going: usually wears
headgear: ungenuine (has been reluctant to race). *A. Bailey*

LENNOXTOWN (IRE) 3 ch.g. Selkirk (USA) 129 – Pump (USA) (Forli (ARG)) **64**
[2006 –p: 8m 8.5f⁶ 8m p10g⁴ p8g p9.5g⁵ p10g⁶ p12g p12g² p12g⁶ Dec 22] good-topped
gelding: modest maiden handicapper: left M. Jarvis 800 gns after third start: stays 1½m:
acts on polytrack and firm ground: tried in blinkers/cheekpieces. *J. Ryan*

LENOIR (GER) 3 b.g. Lujain (USA) 119 – Luna de Miel (Shareef Dancer (USA) 135) **67**
[2006 66: p10g³ p8g p10g² p8g p10g⁴ 8.2s 8.5g 10.2f 10m 9.9m* 10g⁶ 10m⁵ p10g³ **a74**
Oct 20] leggy, close-coupled gelding: fair handicapper, better on all-weather than turf:
won at Goodwood in August: stays 1¼m: acts on polytrack, good to firm and good to soft
going: tried in cheekpieces, visored nowadays: has looked no easy ride: sold 12,500 gns,
joined C. Von Der Recke, Germany. *V. Smith*

LENWADE 5 gr.m. Environment Friend 128 – Branitska (Mummy's Pet 125) [2006 54: **49**
p10g p9.5g 11.9m⁴ 10g⁶ 10m 12f³ 12f⁶ 16.4f 11.5f⁴ 16f³ 16g⁴ 14.1m² 16g p16g Oct 23]

leggy mare: poor performer: effective at 1¼m to 2m: acts on firm and good to soft going: tried in headgear: has run in snatches: usually waited with. *G. G. Margarson*

LEOBALLERO 6 ch.g. Lion Cavern (USA) 117 – Ball Gown 98 (Jalmood (USA) 126) **80**
[2006 87: p8g⁴ 8m⁴ 8.3g⁶ Aug 14] tall gelding: fairly useful handicapper: effective at 7f/
1m: acts on polytrack and good to firm going: tongue tied: wore cheekpieces final outing
in 2005: held up: sometimes carries head high. *D. J. Daly*

LEO MCGARRY (IRE) 3 ch.g. Fantastic Light (USA) 134 – Lilissa (IRE) (Doyoun **68**
124) [2006 –p: p7g 8.1g 12.1f⁴ 12f⁶ 16.2m* 16g* 16.1m⁴ 17.1d⁴ 16.1g² 17.2g⁵ p16.5g
Dec 29] fair handicapper: won at Beverley in July and Nottingham in August: left
S. Williams 31,000 gns before final start: stays 17f: acts on good to firm and good to soft
ground: tends to wander. *N. B. King*

LEONARD CHARLES 2 b.g. (Feb 26) Best of The Bests (IRE) 122 – Iris May 87 **77**
(Brief Truce (USA) 126) [2006 p7.1g* p7.1g³ Dec 30] fourth foal: half-brother to 4-y-o
Joseph Henry and 2005 5f winner Royal Engineer (by Royal Applause): dam, 5f
winner (including at 2 yrs), half-sister to smart sprinter Cathedral: won maiden at Wolverhampton in December by ¾ length from Bold Indian, starting slowly and wandering
markedly: still green, good ½-length third of 6 in nursery there (tended to hang): likely to
stay 1m. *Sir Mark Prescott*

LEONARDS GIRL (IRE) 3 b.f. Beckett (IRE) 116 – Persian Light (IRE) 52 (Persian **–**
Heights 129) [2006 55: f6g Jun 3] €7,000F, €11,000Y: closely related to fairly useful 7f/
1m winner Inch Island (by Turtle Island) and half-sister to several winners: dam Irish
maiden best at 6f to 1m: modest maiden when trained by P. Casey at 2 yrs: tailed off in
handicap at Southwell only start in 2006: raced on good to firm. *P. M. Mooney, Ireland*

LEONIDE 2 b.g. (Mar 14) Noverre (USA) 125 – Marionetta (USA) 63 (Nijinsky (CAN) **80**
138) [2006 7m 7m 6m² 6m³ 6m* Sep 22] 34,000Y: lengthy, angular gelding: has a quick
action: half-brother to several winners in Italy: dam second at 1½m: fairly useful performer: won nursery at Haydock (beat Impromptu by head) final start: should stay 7f/1m:
raced on good to firm going: sold 50,000 gns, sent to USA. *B. J. Meehan*

LEON KNIGHTS 2 b.c. (Feb 25) Inchinor 119 – Valnerina (IRE) (Caerleon (USA) **70**
132) [2006 7.1m p7g³ Oct 20] 52,000Y: strong, lengthy colt: third foal: dam, unraced
half-sister to high-class Irish performer up to 1¼m Entitled and National Stakes winner
El Prado, out of Irish 1000 Guineas winner Lady Capulet: fair form in maidens at Warwick and Lingfield (third to Escape Route): will stay 1m. *G. A. Butler*

LEOPARD KING (USA) 2 b.c. (Feb 24) Kingmambo (USA) 125 – Hidden Cat **86**
(USA) (Storm Cat (USA)) [2006 6m² 6m* 6m³ p7.1g Oct 8] $400,000Y: sturdy, close-
coupled colt: second foal: closely related to winner in USA by Fusaichi Pegasus: dam,
US 7f to 9f winner, half-sister to very smart 1m/9f performer Century City: fairly useful
form: second to Ready For Spring at Newmarket, then won maiden at Yarmouth later in
August: better run in nurseries when third to Captain Marvelous at Newbury: well held in
visor final start: should stay 7f/1m: sold 19,000 gns. *Sir Michael Stoute*

LEOPOLDINE 3 br.f. Desert Prince (IRE) 130 – Beaming 93 (Mtoto 134) [2006 72: **98**
p6g² 5g* 5m* 5m⁴ 6f 5f⁴ 6g³ 6g⁵ Oct 12] strong, lengthy filly: useful performer: won maiden
at Lingfield (by 8 lengths) in June: good efforts last 3 starts, including when third to Cape
in handicap and 3 lengths fifth to Firenze in listed race, both at Newmarket: effective
at 6f, but speedy and may prove best at 5f: acts on polytrack and good to firm going.
H. Morrison

LEO'S LUCKYMAN (USA) 7 b. or br.g. Woodman (USA) 126 – Leo's Lucky Lady **–**
(USA) (Seattle Slew (USA)) [2006 110: 10.4d Aug 23] big, strong, lengthy, attractive
gelding: smart performer at best: modest form over hurdles (for R. Brookhouse) prior to
well held only Flat outing in 2006: tried blinkered/tongue tied at 3 yrs: often makes
running. *M. Johnston*

LEPRECHAUN'S GOLD (IRE) 2 ch.c. (Apr 24) Spectrum (IRE) 126 – Ashirah **64**
(USA) (Housebuster (USA)) [2006 f7g² p7.1g p7.1g Dec 22] 8 lengths second to stable-
companion Autograph Hunter in maiden at Southwell: soundly beaten in similar events
on polytrack after. *M. Johnston*

LEPRECHAUN'S MAITE 4 b.g. Komaite (USA) – Leprechaun Lady 57 (Royal **40**
Blend 117) [2006 –: 8.3g Aug 23] twice-raced maiden on Flat, poor form only outing in
2006. *B. N. Pollock*

LEPTIS MAGNA 2 ch.g. (Mar 30) Danehill Dancer (IRE) 117 – Dark Eyed Lady **69**
(IRE) 82 (Exhibitioner 111) [2006 6m⁵ 7.1m 6m⁴ Sep 21] 52,000Y: half-brother to several winners, including 2002 2-y-o 6f winner Vision of Dreams (by Efisio) and 2000 2-y-o

5f winner Oh So Dusty (by Piccolo), both fairly useful: dam 5f/6f winner, including at 2 yrs: fair form in maidens: should stay 7f: sold 24,000 gns, and gelded. *W. J. Knight*

LERIDA 4 ch.g. Groom Dancer (USA) 128 – Catalonia (IRE) 76 (Catrail (USA) 123) – [2006 –: 9.2d Sep 25] close-coupled gelding: winning hurdler: well beaten in maidens/claimer on Flat. *Miss Lucinda V. Russell*

LES ARCS (USA) 6 br.g. Arch (USA) 127 – La Sarto (USA) (Cormorant (USA)) **126** [2006 104: p6g* p5g* p5g* 6s* 6g² 5d 5m 6m* 6m* 6f Oct 1]

The story of Les Arcs makes him almost a suitable case for treatment by a romantic novelist or, even better, one specialising in the picaresque in the vein of Henry Fielding. The plot certainly has enough swings, roundabouts and false turns to satisfy anyone in search of a good yarn. First, picture the main character in a setting where extravagant amounts of cash change hands—the sales ring at Keeneland. For the record, the latest September sale there grossed almost four hundred million dollars, a figure higher than the gross domestic product of more than twenty countries across the globe. The date for our story, however, is September 13th 2001 and Les Arcs' prospects enjoy a distinct upswing when he is knocked down to John Ferguson for 140,000 dollars on behalf of Sheikh Mohammed and is sent into training with John Gosden. Everything goes reasonably well once he reaches the racecourse as a three-year-old, with a second and a win in maidens over a mile and a quarter at Bath and Ripon on his first two appearances. However, he then finishes tailed-off last in a minor event on his only other start and clearly has no pretensions to being a stakes performer. Predictably, therefore, he is one of a large batch that his owner culls at the end of the year and he heads for pastures new after being bought by Richard Guest for 32,000 guineas at the Newmarket Autumn Sales. In 2004 Les Arcs manages to win a minor event over a mile at Hamilton and gain three placings, but shows nothing tried over a mile and a half and—the nadir—is beaten almost seventy lengths in a maiden hurdle at Cartmel. The year ends with victory in a handicap over almost nine furlongs on the all-weather at Wolverhampton but he is rated only 85 in *Racehorses of 2004*, with the comment noting him as 'effective at 7f to 1¼m: none too consistent'.

As a five-year-old Les Arcs has to work hard for his corn as Guest runs him twelve times, ten of his races, significantly, over six or seven furlongs, resulting in victories in handicaps at Musselburgh and Chester and five places. However, in both his races at six Les Arcs is nearest at the finish, once after being slowly away—he is also withdrawn having been unruly at the start on one occasion—so despite being a free-running individual he doesn't have the profile of a specialist sprinter when leaving Guest and joining Tim Pitt early in the winter, soon after the trainer has received his licence. A change promptly proves much better than a rest, because, raced exclusively at five and six furlongs, Les Arcs proceeds to mop up five races in a row from mid-December to the end of March. The improvement, given his advanced age, is remarkable, but there is even better to come as Les Arcs establishes himself one of the best sprinters in training by winning two of the most prestigious six-furlong events in the calendar, the Golden Jubilee Stakes and July Cup. Some horse, some journey, and the final chapter in this cracking tale, which

Golden Jubilee Stakes, Royal Ascot—Les Arcs gives jockey John Egan a second 33/1 winner of the week as they hold off fast-finishing 50/1-shot Balthazaar's Gift (rail), with the favourite Takeover Target (dark noseband) third just ahead of Ashdown Express

*Darley July Cup, Newmarket—Les Arcs wins his second Group 1,
strongly pressed by unlucky Iffraaj (fourth left), Ashdown Express (second left),
Amadeus Wolf (light noseband), Moss Vale (right), Quito (blinkers) and Takeover Target (dark noseband)*

pays a huge compliment to his young trainer, has not yet been written because Les Arcs is a gelding and stays in training.

Les Arcs' successes came in handicaps at Lingfield in December, Wolverhampton in early-January and Lingfield in February and in a minor event at Lingfield again in March. He showed plenty of speed, and in the last two defeated Fyodor by half a length, coming out the better horse at the weights both times. With the last of these victories coming after voting had finished, Fyodor was a clear winner of the All-Weather Horse of the Season award by readers of the *Racing Post*, but it was even odder that the runner-up was Graze On, whose form was at least a stone below that shown by fourth-placed Les Arcs. Similarly, Les Arcs did not make the line-up for the Racehorse Owners Association all-weather award at the end of the year even though his form on the surface was better than that of two of the four horses short-listed, Kingsgate Prince and Young Mick. Young Mick, whose form on the all-weather was more than a stone below that of Les Arcs, won the vote. The answer to this eccentricity presumably is that any elections connected with thoroughbreds—and often those connected with people—tend to have their own imperatives, which sometimes ignore strict merit.

Five days after the result of the vote by *Racing Post* readers was announced, Les Arcs reverted to turf and showed further improvement in the williamhill.co.uk Cammidge Trophy at Redcar. This was a tougher assignment up against such established sprinters as the market leaders Pivotal Flame and Quito but the result was the same, Les Arcs travelling strongly all the way and holding on resolutely by three quarters of a length from Quito, with Reverence, also showing improvement on his reappearance, third. Three defeats followed, in two of which Les Arcs ran creditably. He lost only by a short head to Paradise Isle in the listed Abernant Stakes at Newmarket and was less than two lengths behind the Australian-trained winner Takeover Target when eleventh in the King's Stand Stakes at Royal Ascot. In between, Les Arcs lost his action after halfway and finished only eighth in the Temple Stakes at Sandown. And so to the Golden Jubilee Stakes four days after the King's Stand. Six of the runners in the King's Stand turned out again including Takeover Target, who was favourite ahead of Godolphin's very smart five-year-old Iffraaj making his seasonal reappearance, a second Australian challenger Glamour Puss, Middle Park Stakes winner Amadeus Wolf reverting to sprinting, and Gift Horse, successful in the 2005 Stewards' Cup but with only one race behind him at five. Les Arcs was at 33/1, with nearly half the eighteen runners starting at those odds or longer. Regrettably for a championship event, the run of the race played a crucial part, the first six home all racing on the stand side. Les Arcs, drawn four, was in the perfect position and took advantage, making headway from two furlongs out, bursting through to take the measure of Takeover Target at the furlong pole and holding on gamely by a neck from Balthazaar's Gift, who finished with a tremendous rattle, having been dropped out from stall fourteen. Takeover Target came third, two lengths further back, while Iffraaj in seventh ran as if he needed the race. This was not the first time a horse who had failed over jumps had won a Group 1 sprint—My Best Valentine, successful in the Prix de l'Abbaye in 1998 after being placed over hurdles, is another recent example.

Far from all the field in the Golden Jubilee Stakes showed their true form, but any doubts some might have felt about Les Arcs' standing since the leading sprinters were dispelled in the Darley July Cup nearly three weeks later. The July Cup is the jewel in the crown of the Newmarket July meeting and, to keep it ahead of the Golden Jubilee Stakes, the race received a hefty increase in prize money of forty-four per cent to £360,000. The announcement, in March, came soon after one revealing that the meeting was being re-branded as the Newmarket July Festival. The latter decision had a touch of keeping up with the Joneses because in the last few years the word 'festival' has been bolted on to a number of meetings. As well as 'The' Festival at Cheltenham, we now have the Guineas Festival, also at Newmarket, the Epsom Festival built around the Derby, the St Leger Festival, the Glorious Goodwood Festival, the Ascot Festival of British Racing (now transmogrified into the Mile Championships), the May and Ebor Festivals at York, the Northumberland Plate Festival, the Ayr Gold Cup Festival, the Brighton Festival, the Eastern Festival at Yarmouth and, winning first prize in the numbers game, the May, July and August Festivals at Chester. Frankly this is laughable. Epsom around Derby Day, with the fair and all the accompanying entertainment, was always a genuine festival if one takes the word to mean 'a day or period of time set aside for feasting and celebration.' But that hardly applies to all those listed above. On the other hand, if one uses an alternative definition—'an organized series of acts and performances (usually in one place)'—the term could fairly be applied to every race meeting in the calendar. Maybe it will be applied, saving us all confusion.

The latest July Cup attracted as strong a field as was assembled all year for a sprint, though that should not be taken to suggest it was outstanding by the race's superb standards. Nine of the fifteen runners had contested the Golden Jubilee, including two that had won pattern races in the interim, Fayr Jag and Pivotal Flame. Takeover Target was favourite again from Iffraaj, 2005 Nunthorpe Stakes winner La Cucaracha and Australian-trained Falkirk, fourth in the King's Stand. Les Arcs started 10/1 co-fifth favourite with Amadeus Wolf, fifth in the Golden Jubilee, and another three-year-old, Red Clubs, who had won the Greenham Stakes and finished sixth in the Jersey Stakes. Les Arcs, who gave a bit of trouble at the stalls, again received the rub of the green with his starting position, since the first four were all drawn twelve or higher—he was fifteen—and he also had the run of the race compared with the runner-up Iffraaj. Held up in the middle of the field, Les Arcs got a perfect run through to hit the front in the final furlong while Iffraaj was hemmed in. Running on strongly, Les Arcs had sufficient in reserve to hold on by a head with Ashdown Express three quarters of a length back in third, followed by Amadeus Wolf, Moss Vale, Quito and Takeover Target, who was drawn one. Accepting that Iffraaj was unlucky, this was still another high-class effort by the winner, on a par with the form of his win in the Golden Jubilee Stakes. British racegoers did not see Les Arcs again. The Sprint Cup at Haydock was mentioned as a possible target but he was aimed instead at the Sprinters Stakes at Nakayama at the start of October, the next but one leg of the Global Sprint Challenge (for which the King's Stand and Golden Jubilee are the British legs). Ridden by Eric Saint-Martin because the Japanese authorities refused to let his usual jockey John Egan take the mount on account of problems he had in Hong Kong dating back to 2002, Les Arcs was never dangerous in finishing seventh behind his old rival Takeover Target. He was promptly put away with the intention of doubling up again in the Golden Jubilee Stakes and July Cup in the next season.

Starting Les Arcs off over a mile and more was an understandable policy given his breeding. The sire Arch did not race much, his career encompassing only seven races of which he won five. Although he did not see more action, he was undoubtedly high class, putting up a cracking display to beat the previous year's Belmont Stakes winner Touch Gold in a Grade 3 at Keeneland at a stone worse terms than weight-for-age, having won the Grade 1 Super Derby over a mile and a quarter—the longest trip he tried—decisively by three lengths. He did not do himself justice in the Breeders' Cup Classic, finishing sore. Arch was retired to Claiborne at a fee of 20,000 dollars but he attracted only small books by modern standards, had little impact with his first runners and his services were soon available for 5,000 dollars. At the price he fetched as a yearling, Les Arcs was well above the average for Arch's progeny for his stud career as a whole, but that is set

Mr Willie McKay's "Les Arcs"

		Arch (USA) (b 1995)	Kris S (b 1977)	Roberto Sharp Queen
Les Arcs (USA) (br.g. 2000)			Aurora (b 1988)	Danzig Althea
	La Sarto (USA) (b 1990)	Cormorant (b 1974)	His Majesty Song Sparrow
			Dame Sybil (b 1978)	Elocutionist Anne Campbell

to change as Arch's fee has risen from 15,000 dollars to 25,000 dollars for 2007, largely because he is now responsible for five Group or Grade 1 scorers in all. These also include the leading American three-year-old fillies Pine Island and Arravale. Prior to her death in the Breeders' Cup Distaff, for which she started second favourite, the former had shown herself the best of her age on dirt with victories in the Alabama Stakes and Gazelle Stakes. Arravale proved a cut above on turf, landing the E. P. Taylor Stakes and Del Mar Oaks and being voted Horse of The Year in Canada. A mile or more suited both fillies but not, intriguingly, Arch's dual champion South African sprinter Overarching or Montgomery's Arch. The latter, the first horse to bring his sire to notice in Britain, won the Richmond Stakes and finished third in the Dewhurst in 2004. It is not exactly speed all the way with Les Arcs' dam La Sarto either, though her pedigree is far from stamina laden. A minor winner of four races at six and seven furlongs, she has produced two other winners, the better of them the 2001 colt White Mountain Boy (by Meadowlake), successful in two minor stakes races as a juvenile. By a middle-distance horse in Cormorant, La Sarto was a sister to sprint stakes winner Princess Sybil and half-sister to dual Grade 2 winner Alannan, who stayed a mile. The most notable mare in the bottom line of the pedigree is the third dam Anne Campbell, once Broodmare of the Year in the States. She foaled seven winners from ten starters, notably a couple of high-class performers at up to a mile and a quarter in Desert Wine, who won three Grade 1 races, and Menifee, who won two, both of them also runner-up in the Kentucky Derby and Preakness Stakes. Anne Campbell is also grandam of champion 1999 juvenile Fasliyev. La Sarto's two-year-old is a filly by Menifee, representing intriguing inbreeding to Anne Campbell; she fetched 35,000 dollars at Keeneland as a yearling. Les Arcs, a tall, quite good-topped gelding who acts on polytrack, soft and good to firm going, is both tough and genuine though he has his idiosyncrasies, given that he has now caused some difficulty at the start three times and needed to pass a stalls test at Southwell part way through the season. He usually wore blinkers, a visor or cheekpieces when trained by Guest, and has been tongue tied, bandaged in front and worn a crossed noseband. *T. J. Pitt*

LES FAZZANI (IRE) 2 b.f. (Feb 19) Intikhab (USA) 135 – Massada 106 (Most **83 p** Welcome 131) [2006 p8g* Dec 4] €20,000F, 55,000Y: fourth foal: half-sister to 2 winners in Germany by Big Shuffle, including useful winner up to 7.5f Miss Lips: dam, German 2-y-o 7f/1m winner who stayed 1¼m: 6/1, impressive debut when winning maiden at Lingfield by 1½ lengths from Miss Saafend Plaza, good headway from rear 3f out and quickening to lead inside final ½f: useful filly in making. *M. J. Wallace*

LE SINGE NOIR 2 b.g. (May 12) Averti (IRE) 117 – Prends Ca (IRE) 98 (Reprimand **75** 122) [2006 7f p6m³ p6g² Oct 17] 2,500Y: sixth foal: half-brother to winner in USA by Danehill: dam 6f (including at 2 yrs) to 7.5f winner: fair form in maidens, second to Genuine Call at Lingfield: should be as good at 7f as 6f. *D. M. Simcock*

LESLINGTAYLOR (IRE) 4 b.g. Orpen (USA) 116 – Rite of Spring 86 (Niniski **86** (USA) 125) [2006 77: 12.4d 13.8g 12m³ 10.1m³ 12f 12.1m⁴ 11.8g* 11.9s* 12m 12s* 15d³ Oct 13] good-topped gelding: fairly useful handicapper: won at Leicester in August, Haydock (by 8 lengths) in September and York (apprentices) in October: effective at 1¼m to 1¾m: acts on soft and good to firm going. *J. J. Quinn*

LE SOLEIL (GER) 5 b.g. Monsun (GER) 124 – La Blue (GER) 119 (Bluebird (USA) **64** 125) [2006 61: f14g 9.7d* 10g 10m 10.9d Oct 13] tall, good-topped gelding: modest performer: won handicap at Folkestone in April: has form at 2m, but likely to prove best at 1¼m/1½m: acts on all-weather, good to soft and good to firm going. *B. J. Curley*

LESTER LEAPS IN (USA) 3 b. or br.c. Red Ransom (USA) – Rose Aurora (USA) **74** (Majestic Light (USA)) [2006 61: 8.2d³ 10.2g⁶ p10g³ 10.2f* 10f 10f² p10g² 10g p10g² **a78** Oct 11] strong colt: fair handicapper: won at Bath in June: stays 10.2f: acts on polytrack, firm and good to soft going: sold 42,000 gns. *R. Hannon*

LETHAL 3 ch.g. Nashwan (USA) 135 – Ipanema Beach 67 (Lion Cavern (USA) 117) **85** [2006 p8g 7.1m⁴ 7f³ p6g* Dec 19] good-topped gelding: first foal: dam 1m/8.5f winner: fairly useful form: left E. Oertel/off 3 months, much improved to win handicap at Lingfield in December: speedy, will probably be best up to 7f: raced only on polytrack and going firmer than good. *D. K. Ivory*

LETHAM ISLAND (IRE) 2 b.f. (Feb 10) Trans Island 119 – Common Cause 87 **74** (Polish Patriot (USA) 128) [2006 7.1d⁴ f7g² p8.6m² f8g* Dec 2] 10,500Y: third foal: half-sister to 3-y-o winner Wovoka: dam, 11.5f/1½m winner, out of half-sister to smart French/US performer up to 1¼m Kirkwall: fair performer: won maiden at Southwell in December: good close second to Stravita in similar event at Wolverhampton time before: acts on all-weather. *M. Johnston*

LET IT BE 5 ch.m. Entrepreneur 123 – Noble Dane (IRE) 79 (Danehill (USA) 126) **69** [2006 73: 12.4g 12.4d 14.1g⁴ 14m⁵ 14.1f* 16f⁴ 14m⁵ 14m³ 14.1m⁵ 14.1m 15.8m* 13.9s Oct 7] lengthy mare: fair handicapper: won at Redcar in June and Catterick in September: effective at 1½m to 2m: unraced on heavy going, acts on any other turf. *K. G. Reveley*

LETS BE LUCKY (IRE) 4 b.g. Desert King (IRE) 129 – Mo Pheata (Petorius 117) **–** [2006 10d f8g p8.6g 10m Jul 29] close-coupled gelding: no form. *F. Jordan*

LET'S FACE IT (IRE) 2 b.g. (Feb 29) Iron Mask (USA) 117 – Jay And-A (IRE) 98 **–** (Elbio 125) [2006 p6g p5.1g Sep 11] well beaten both starts: dead. *Peter Grayson*

LETS GET CRACKING (FR) 2 b. or gr.c. (Mar 15) Anabaa Blue 122 – Queenhood **76** (FR) (Linamix (FR) 127) [2006 7g⁶ 8.3g³ 8s⁵ p9.5m* 8s Nov 25] €16,000Y, €42,000 2-y-o: rather leggy, useful-looking colt: second foal: dam French 1½m winner: fair form:

won maiden at Wolverhampton in October: well held in listed race at Saint-Cloud final start: will stay 1½m: acts on polytrack and soft going. *K. A. Ryan*

LET SLIP 4 b.f. Second Empire (IRE) 124 – Loose Talk 68 (Thatching 131) [2006 68: **87** p10g* 10g 9d3 p10g2 p10g* 9.8s6 p10g4 Sep 6] lengthy, good-topped filly: fairly useful handicapper, better on all-weather than turf: won at Kempton in April and Lingfield in July: stays easy 1¼m: acts on polytrack, good to firm and good to soft going: sold 32,000 gns, sent to Saudi Arabia. *W. Jarvis*

LETS ROLL 5 b.g. Tamure (IRE) 125 – Miss Petronella (Petoski 135) [2006 97: 12g6 **98** 16m5 12d2 12d3 13.1g2 11.9g 14m3 13.9d 14v5 13.1d* 13d5 18d 14d4 Nov 3] leggy, close-coupled gelding: useful handicapper: won at Ayr in September (also successful in corresponding event 12 months earlier) by 3 lengths from Crow Wood: stays 14.8f, not 2¼m: acts on heavy and good to firm going: races prominently: tough and consistent. *C. W. Thornton*

LETS TRY AGAIN (IRE) 9 b.g. Barathea (IRE) 127 – Intricacy 65 (Formidable **57** (USA) 125) [2006 17.2s 14.1m5 17.2f5 12.1g p13.9g 12.1f6 p16.5f Aug 14] smallish, sturdy gelding: maiden: unraced on Flat in 2004/5: just modest at best on return: stays 1¾m: acts on good to firm and good to soft going: tried visored. *R. A. Farrant*

LEVEL PAR (IRE) 6 ch.g. Cadeaux Genereux 131 – Howaida (IRE) 85 (Night Shift **46** (USA)) [2006 57: p9.5g4 p9.5g p10g p9.5g Mar 29] ex-Irish gelding: poor maiden: stays 9.5f: acts on polytrack: blinkered once: tongue tied nowadays: found little final outing. *J. A. Supple*

LEVERA 3 b.c. Groom Dancer (USA) 128 – Prancing 98 (Prince Sabo 123) [2006 88: **107** 7g* 7s* 7d* 7m Jun 21] close-coupled colt: improved into a useful performer, winning handicaps at Newmarket in April and May and listed handicap at York (beat Antica easily by 5 lengths) later in May: 5/1, found to be lame after tailed-off last in Jersey Stakes at Royal Ascot final outing: stays 7f: yet to race on heavy going, probably acts on any other: usually makes running. *A. King*

LEVIN (IRE) 3 b.g. Fantastic Light (USA) 134 – Knight's Place (IRE) 72 (Hamas **52** (IRE) 125§) [2006 8d 7m 7m6 8.1s May 29] leggy gelding: modest maiden: should stay 1m: acts on good to firm going: withdrawn (fractious in stall) final intended outing in July: sold 800 gns in October. *J. L. Dunlop*

LEWIS ISLAND (IRE) 7 b.g. Turtle Island (IRE) 123 – Phyllode (Pharly (FR) 130) **73** [2006 70: p13g4 p16g 11.7d* 16s May 24] angular, lengthy gelding: fair handicapper: won at Bath in May: effective at 11.7f to easy 2m: acts on polytrack, soft and good to firm ground: tried tongue tied: sometimes slowly away: free-going sort: none too reliable. *G. L. Moore*

LEWIS LLOYD (IRE) 3 b.g. Indian Lodge (IRE) 127 – Sandy Fitzgerald (IRE) (Last **59** Tycoon 131) [2006 46: p8.6g 9.7s 10g 9.8m5 10d6 p8.6g4 8.1m 8m 12f 9.3m* 10m 9.9m Sep 19] strong gelding: modest performer: won claimer at Carlisle in August: stays 9.3f: acts on polytrack and good to firm ground: tried blinkered/tongue tied. *I. A. Wood*

LEYAALY 7 ch.m. Night Shift (USA) – Lower The Tone (IRE) 74 (Phone Trick (USA)) **–** [2006 –: f11g5 f11g Feb 12] poor performer: no form since 2004: tried tongue tied/in cheekpieces. *Miss Z. C. Davison*

LIABILITY 4 b.f. Bluebird (USA) 125 – Madaniyya (USA) 96 (Shahrastani **–** (USA) 135) [2006 44: f8g Feb 12] big, leggy filly: poor maiden: stays 7f. *Miss S. E. Hall*

LIAKOURA (GER) 4 b.g. Royal Academy (USA) 130 – Lady Member (FR) (Saint **89** Estephe (FR) 123) [2006 95: 10g 10g 8.1f 8.1m5 8d p8g5 Oct 11] rather leggy, quite attractive gelding: fairly useful handicapper: below form after reappearance: stays 1¼m: acts on good to soft going: effective in cheekpieces or not: tried blinkered/tongue tied: joined N. Gifford. *Mrs A. J. Perrett*

LIAMELISS 4 ch.f. Dr Fong (USA) 128 – Ivory Palm (USA) 93 (Sir Ivor (USA) 135) **–** [2006 55: 12f 11.5f 16f 11.9f Aug 9] maiden handicapper: well held in 2006: tried visored. *M. A. Allen*

LIBERATE 3 ch.g. Lomitas 129 – Eversince (USA) (Foolish Pleasure (USA)) [2006 **93** –p: 12.1m4 12.1g* f11g2 11.1f* 14.1m2 13.9f2 p16g* 11.5m* 14m3 Jul 27] rangy gelding: fairly useful handicapper: won at Beverley in May, Hamilton in June and Lingfield (2) in July, beating Jebel Ali easily by 3½ lengths final occasion: stays easy 2m: acts on all-weather and firm going: hung left third start: sold privately, joined P. Hobbs, and useful winner over hurdles. *Sir Mark Prescott*

LIBERATION SQUARE 3 ch.g. Compton Place 125 – Class Wan 74 (Safawan 118) –
[2006 –: 5m 5f Jun 26] no form: tried in cheekpieces. *J. S. Goldie*

LIBERMAN (IRE) 8 b.g. Standiford (USA) – Hail To You (USA) (Kirtling 129) [2006 –
18d³ p16.5g Oct 8] fairly useful hurdler: fair performer on Flat, lightly raced: won maiden
at Tramore for T. Mullins in 2004: well held on return to Flat. *R. Curtis*

LIBERTY RUN (IRE) 4 ch.g. Grand Lodge (USA) 125 – Bathe In Light (USA) 72 **77**
(Sunshine Forever (USA)) [2006 66: 10.2g 11.6m 11.9m* 12d p11g⁵ p13g Dec 22]
neat gelding: fair handicapper: won at Brighton in September: stays 1½m: acts on polytrack, good to firm and good to soft ground: tried tongue tied/visored· inconsistent.
Mrs A. J. Hamilton-Fairley

LIBERTY SEEKER (FR) 7 ch.g. Machiavellian (USA) 123 – Samara (IRE) 108 **76**
(Polish Patriot (USA) 128) [2006 69: 15.8d* 15.8g³ 14m⁴ Jun 10] angular gelding: fair
handicapper: won at Catterick in April: stays 15.8f: acts on soft and good to firm going:
tried in cheekpieces: sold 18,000 gns in July. *G. A. Swinbank*

LIBOR (IRE) 3 b.c. Lend A Hand 124 – America Lontana (FR) (King's Theatre (IRE) **88**
128) [2006 6g³ 5.1g² 6m² 5.7g* 6m⁵ p6g² 6m² 5m² Sep 12] €15,000F, 27,000Y: heavy-
bodied colt: type to carry condition: first foal: dam Italian 5f winner: fairly useful performer: won handicap at Bath in July: effective at 5f/6f: consistent. *L. M. Cumani*

LIBRE 6 b.g. Bahamian Bounty 116 – Premier Blues (FR) 35 (Law Society (USA) 130) **71**
[2006 86: p10g p9.5g⁶ p7g p8g² p8.6g² p8.6g⁴ 8.2s⁴ 10g 10d⁴ 8.2g³ 10g 8.2f³ 10d 8d **a77**
Oct 19] leggy gelding: fair performer: trained by A. Reid first 2 starts in 2006, by Ernst
Oertel next 2: stays easy 1¼m: acts on polytrack and any turf going: tried in blinkers/
cheekpieces/tongue tie earlier in career: waited with. *F. Jordan*

LIBRETTIST (USA) 4 b.c. Danzig (USA) – Mysterial (USA) (Alleged (USA) **124**
138) [2006 8.2g* 8.3m* 8m* 8s* 8g* 8d⁶ 8f Nov 4]
    The ups and downs of Godolphin's season bore a striking resemblance to a
game of snakes and ladders. After eye-catching successes by Electrocutionist in
the Dubai World Cup and Discreet Cat in the UAE Derby at the end of March,
Saeed bin Suroor had saddled only twelve runners and one winner in Europe by
May 27th, reportedly because just about all the horses were under the weather for
some undiagnosed reason. The stable had only one runner in Britain in the week or
so after the end of the York May meeting and then shut down completely for ten
days until resuming at the end of the first week in June. There were no victories
at Royal Ascot but a spate of successes came from July onwards and, despite the
disappointing start, Godolphin went on to regain the owners' championship in
Britain from Hamdan Al Maktoum, its horses earning £1,513,116 (more than the
previous year) in first-three prize money. That said, the fifty-plus three-year-olds in
Europe managed only one listed victory between them. The twenty juveniles to
face the starter—unlike in previous years, the whole band had wintered in Newmarket—notched a mere six races, none of those a stakes event; some carried on
running on the all-weather until near the end of November. The final tally from well
over a hundred horses that ran for Godolphin from a string of over two hundred in
Europe was five Group 1 races, four Group 2s and seven Group 3s, some way below
the norm. None of the Group 1s was in Britain, the first time this has happened
since Godolphin started in 1994.
    Most of the horses brought in to strengthen Godolphin's challenge for the
top races fell way below expectations. Among the transfers, Plea Bargain did not
run, Goodricke was very disappointing, Proclamation was below his best in two
outings and Astronomia (from Australia) was below her best in three. Among the
purchases made in 2005, Shawanda, Opera Cape, Palace Episode, Royal Proposal
(who broke her leg on the way to post at Leicester in October on her planned
reappearance), Silca's Sister, The Geezer, Valixir and Winged Cupid failed to make
any impact, or even run. Utopia, bought in March after winning the Godolphin Mile
at Nad Al Sheba, wasn't seen out again. While Imperial Stride notched a listed race,
he did not reproduce his fine form of the year before. There were also injuries at one
stage or another to Imperial Stride, Librettist and Proclamation, while the death of
Electrocutionist early in September removed Godolphin's principal hope in the
major end-of-season middle-distance events.

By comparison, the smaller Godolphin contingent in America made a significant impact, with Ashkal Way winning two Grade 2 races and the Grade 1 Citation Handicap, and Discreet Cat (another purchase in 2005) picking up the Grade 2 Jerome Handicap and Grade 1 Cigar Mile. Add the achievements of the Maktoum-owned Bernadini, Henny Hughes, Jazil and Invasor and America offered something approaching an annus mirabilis for Dubai's ruling family. Godolphin's ambitions are global and its worldwide performance in 2006 of 101 wins from 330 races (a strike rate of 30.6% the highest in its history) perhaps paints a different picture to that portrayed by some in the British media. The total of Group/Grade 1 wins was down to eight but total prize money was up to 11m dollars (around £6m). Looking ahead in Europe, the lack of form from the two-year-olds suggests they will have to make quick progress if the classics aren't to come too soon for most in training with Godolphin, while, apart from Cherry Mix, there is no certainty of a top-flight middle-distance performer unless, possibly Hala Bek, or new purchases Best Name, Killybegs and Ramonti turn up trumps, or the very promising Desert Authority and Counterpunch make further progress, which is quite possible. With a tally of thirty-seven Group 1 or Grade 1 victories in the last four years, compared with sixty from 1999 to 2002, Godolphin's second century in that category looks as if it may take a fair while longer to compile than the first. This despite the operation's number of runners being significantly higher nowadays than formerly—they have had four hundred and sixty-seven runners in Britain in the last three years compared to three hundred and eighty in the previous seven.

On a more positive note, the three horses which provided the Group 1 wins in Europe in the latest season all came from private purchases, two of whom, Cherry Mix and Caradak, were from other stables. The third had been with Godolphin from the start. He is Librettist, whose splendid campaign admittedly tailed off but not before he showed himself one of the best older milers with wins in the Prix Jacques le Marois and Prix du Moulin. A clear case of patience—something Sheikh Mohammed seems to have in abundance—paying off handsomely given the absence of Librettist from the track for the whole of his three-year-old season. He had been a promising two-year-old, winning his first two starts before taking on the best in the Dewhurst Stakes, in which he finished four lengths fifth to Shamardal. The niggling ankle problem Librettist experienced in his classic season gave no trouble another year on and he didn't take long making up for lost time. Librettist was the first runner for Godolphin after its shut down. He reappeared in an eight-runner minor event at Nottingham early in June when he made the running and quickened clear to beat Alfie Flits by two lengths. He followed up in the totepool Midsummer Stakes at Windsor, landing the odds from Prince of Light with the minimum of fuss after being held up, and then moved into pattern company in the Prix Messidor at Maisons-Laffitte towards the end of July. After making the running, Librettist stretched his rivals from two furlongs out and defeated Helios Quercus by a length with Manduro third. Those two took him on again the

Prix du Haras de Fresnay-le-Buffard Jacques le Marois, Deauville—a first Group 1 win of the season in Europe for Godolphin as Librettist just holds on from Manduro (No.6), Peeress and the grey Stormy River

Prix du Moulin de Longchamp, Longchamp—Frankie Dettori displays masterly waiting-in-front tactics on Librettist; Stormy River (grey), Manduro (right) and Aussie Rules are in pursuit

following month in a much tougher test, the Prix du Haras de Fresnay-le-Buffard Jacques le Marois at Deauville. Librettist's seven other opponents included the favourite Stormy River, runner-up in the St James's Palace Stakes and winner of the Prix Jean Prat, Group 1 winners Ad Valorem and Peeress, and Ramonti, successful in the Premio Emilio Turati. Librettist won, but it was harder work as he was settled just off the pace, quickened ahead over a furlong out and battled on, edging left under the whip, to hold Manduro by a neck, with Peeress a head away third.

The going at Deauville, as so often, was soft—Librettist also acted on good to firm—and it was good when he lined up for the Prix du Moulin de Longchamp three weeks later. Effective front running on a horse with an obvious chance is a more difficult art to perfect than effective pacemaking on a runner which is perceived to have no prospects of success. The tactic requires skilful judgement of pace, especially for a horse possessing more stamina than acceleration, and precise judgement of the moment to try and quicken in order to gain a decisive advantage if the mount has a turn of foot. There have been several masters in the last few decades, with Lester Piggott and Steve Cauthen probably the pick. Kerrin McEvoy gave an exemplary show on Rule of Law in the 2004 St Leger, and Frankie Dettori has done so on a number of occasions, none better than on Librettist in the Moulin. The field was not top class, less noteworthy in fact than at Deauville. Manduro and Stormy River tried their luck again and new rivals included Poule d'Essai des Poulains winner Aussie Rules, Prix Jean Prat runner-up Kentucky Dynamite and ex-South African mare Irridescence, successful in the Queen Elizabeth II Cup in Hong Kong but having her first outing for more than four months. Dettori dictated a steady pace before extracting a fine turn of foot out of Librettist two furlongs out. The colt answered the call splendidly, and gained an advantage which stood him in good stead to the finish, where the pursuing pack, outwitted by Dettori's move and outpaced, was still unable to mount a decisive challenge. Stormy River was second, beaten half a length, with Manduro the same distance further back. A classic ride.

It was the first time the double in France's two top all-aged mile races had been achieved since Spinning World in 1997, and there were some interesting comments by connections of the first two after the race. Dettori said: 'He won the Jacques le Marois and now the Moulin, so he must be a champion miler.' Even bolder, Stormy River's trainer Nicolas Clement stated: 'The colt has shown he is the best three-year-old miler in Europe.' Not quite, since, on the subject of being champion, even at that stage Court Masterpiece's victory in the Sussex Stakes and Ad Valorem's in the Queen Anne Stakes gave them the edge on Librettist, while Stormy River's form did not match that of the colt who beat him at Royal Ascot, Araafa, let alone George Washington judged on his Two Thousand Guineas win. The obvious targets for Librettist if he was to stay at a mile—he never raced over further—were the Queen Elizabeth II Stakes and the Breeders' Cup Mile. He contested both but garnered no more glory. At Ascot he did not reproduce his best in coming home sixth of eight to George Washington. There were mitigating circumstances, since he finished lame and did not get the run of the race, taking a very wide course partly because of the tactics of the rider of the winner's stable-companion Ivan Denisovich and also being bumped by that colt in the straight. Even at his best, though, Librettist would have been no certainty to finish in the first three at Ascot. Librettist flopped in the Breeders' Cup Mile at Churchill Downs, where it was perhaps significant that Dettori preferred to ride Echo of Light. Librettist broke a bit slowly and did not show his customary turn of foot, finishing tenth to Miesque's Approval. At his best, he should have been in the shake-up in a substandard renewal.

Librettist (USA) (b.c. 2002)	Danzig (USA) (b 1977)	Northern Dancer (b 1961)	Nearctic
			Natalma
		Pas de Nom (b or br 1968)	Admiral's Voyage
			Petitioner
	Mysterial (USA) (b or br 1994)	Alleged (b 1974)	Hoist The Flag
			Princess Pout
		Mysteries (b 1986)	Seattle Slew
			Phydilla

Librettist, a well-made colt with a fluent, round action, has been retired to stand alongside his half-brother Dubai Destination at Dalham Hall Stud at a fee of £10,000. His pedigree was analysed in *Racehorses of 2004* but it bears a recap. His sire, the deceased Danzig, had two other major winners in Europe during the season, Ad Valorem and Soapy Danger, the latter distinctly untypical in being fully effective at two miles. Librettist and Ad Valorem, each best at a mile, are much more the norm for a Danzig and Librettist comes from a speedy distaff family too. The dam Mysterial raced twice without success. She has had two other winners,

Godolphin's "Librettist"

notably Dubai Destination (by Kingmambo), mentioned above, who landed the Champagne Stakes at two and the Queen Anne Stakes at four. Mysterial's three-year-old filly Slovakia (also by Danzig) made the frame twice in the Provinces from three starts at a mile in France, while the two-year-old colt Amarna, by the same sire, has yet to race. The grandam Mysteries similarly failed to win but she did finish third in the Musidora Stakes and her progeny also include top sprinter Agnes World and very smart Japanese sprinter-miler Hishi Akebono. *Saeed bin Suroor*

LIFE (IRE) 2 b.c. (Feb 24) Sadler's Wells (USA) 132 – Inchyre 102 (Shirley Heights **87 p** 130) [2006 8g² 8.3d⁵ Oct 10] 260,000Y: medium-sized, quite attractive colt: has a quick action: fourth foal: brother to useful 1¼m/1½m winner Inchiri and half-brother to useful 9.5f to 11f winner Whirly Bird (by Nashwan): dam, 1m winner who stayed 1½m, half-sister to smart performer up to 1m Inchinor: promising 5 lengths second of 15 to Asperity in maiden at Newmarket: odds on, only fifth at Leicester under 2 weeks later: will be suited by 1¼m/1½m: remains useful prospect. *J. Noseda*

LIFE IS ROSIE (IRE) 4 ch.f. Rossini (USA) 118 – Rachcara (IRE) (Kefaah (USA) **–** 124) [2006 –: p6g Feb 1] well beaten in maidens: very slowly away only outing in 2006. *D. K. Ivory*

LIFE PEER 3 b.g. Mark of Esteem (IRE) 137 – Sadaka (USA) 77 (Kingmambo (USA) **63** 125) [2006 57: p10g⁵ 10.9g 11.6g p10g⁶ p12g⁴ p12g⁵ Dec 1] useful-looking gelding: had a fluent action: modest maiden: stayed 1½m: acted on polytrack: wore cheekpieces penultimate start: reportedly finished lame final outing: dead. *J. G. Portman*

LIFE'S A WHIRL 4 b.f. Machiavellian (USA) 123 – Spinning Top 105 (Alzao (USA) **61** 117) [2006 77: 8m p7g 8m 7m 7f⁴ 7f⁴ 7f³ 8f* 7f 8m 7m p8.6m Nov 9] close-coupled filly: modest handicapper: won at Yarmouth in July: should stay 1¼m: acts on firm going: in cheekpieces after third start: none too consistent. *Mrs C. A. Dunnett*

LIFTED WAY 7 b.g. In The Wings 128 – Stack Rock 111 (Ballad Rock 122) [2006 83: **60** 8m p8g p8g p6g Aug 31] lengthy gelding: one-time fairly useful handicapper: only modest in 2006: effective at 7f (given a test) to 1¼m: acts on polytrack, good to firm and good to soft going: blinkered final 6-y-o outing: usually races up with pace: inconsistent. *P. R. Chamings*

LIGHT DREAMS 3 b.f. Fantastic Light (USA) 134 – Dreamawhile 85 (Known Fact **70** (USA) 135) [2006 10.2g 10m 12.1d 11.5m 8m² 8m³ 7g⁵ p7.1m⁵ Nov 8] quite good-topped, close-coupled filly: seventh living foal: half-sister to several winners, notably sprinters Vision of Night and Struggler (both by Night Shift) and German 1½m performer Baroon (by Rainbow Quest), all smart: dam, 7f winner, half-sister to Derby Italiano winner My Top: fair maiden: best efforts at 1m: acts on good to firm going: visored 4 starts prior to final one when looking none too keen early. *W. J. Knight*

LIGHTED SMILE (FR) 3 b.f. Emperor Jones (USA) 119 – Light The Sky (FR) (Per- **?** sepolis (FR) 127) [2006 10d 8.8v² 9.3d³ 7.8d³ 11g⁴ 11g³ 7.8d 7.8g³ 10g* 8.1m 7m 10.1m Sep 13] neat filly: half-sister to 3 winners, including 6f (at 2 yrs in France) to 9f (in UAE) winner Luminoso (by Machiavellian): dam, French maiden, stayed 1m: won claimer at Salon de Provence in June for J. Piccone in France: no form in Britain last 3 starts. *C. J. Gray*

LIGHT MOZART 3 b.f. Mozart (IRE) 131 – Footlight Fantasy (USA) 68 (Nureyev **71** (USA) 131) [2006 59: p6g⁵ 6f² 6.1d³ p5g² 5.3m² 5m p6g⁶ p6g Oct 15] fair maiden handicapper: effective at 5f/6f: acts on polytrack and firm ground. *C. E. Brittain*

LIGHTNING FLASH 4 br.c. Docksider (USA) 124 – Threatening 95 (Warning 136) **110** [2006 94p: p8g* 7s² Aug 24] good-topped, attractive colt: smart performer: unraced at 2 yrs: won maiden at Lingfield sole 3-y-o start and minor event there in July (absent due to knee problems in between), showing excellent turn of foot and winning going away both times: further improvement only subsequent outing, when length second to Quito (pair clear) in listed event at York (on edge beforehand): stays 1m: raced on polytrack and soft going: has worn blanket for stall entry: sold 20,000 gns in October. *J. R. Fanshawe*

LIGHTNING QUEEN (USA) 2 b.f. (May 6) Thunder Gulch (USA) 129 – Fairy **56** Dancer (USA) 94 (Nijinsky (CAN) 138) [2006 7.1m 8m 8g Oct 17] $70,000Y: rather leggy, quite attractive filly: half-sister to several winners, including smart 1m (at 2 yrs) to 1½m winner Monsajem and fairly useful 1m winner Lothlorien (both by Woodman): dam, twice-raced 6f winner, closely related to Sadler's Wells: modest form in maidens: likely to benefit from 1¼m/1½m. *B. W. Hills*

LIGHTNING STRIKE (GER) 3 ch.g. Danehill Dancer (IRE) 117 – La Capilla **99**
(Machiavellian (USA) 123) [2006 p9.5g⁶ p10g² p12g* p12g* 11.6g² 11.6d⁴ 16m⁵ 16g* 14.1m
16g⁵ 16d² 18d Oct 14] €55,000Y, 52,000 2-y-o: big, good-topped gelding: third foal:
half-brother to winners in Germany by Night Shift and Linamix: dam winner around 1m
in Germany: useful performer: won maiden and handicap in March, both at Lingfield,
and handicap at Ascot (by 1¼ lengths from Nordwind) in July: also ran well at Ascot in
Queen's Vase (fifth of 11 to Soapy Danger) sixth start and in handicap (flashed tail when
3 lengths second to Theatre) penultimate outing: still close up, hampered over 1f out
when twelfth in Cesarewitch at Newmarket final appearance: should stay beyond 2m:
acts on polytrack, good to firm and good to soft going: shied and unseated at flip start
eighth outing: sold 200,000 gns, joined Venetia Williams, and gelded. *T. G. Mills*

LIGHT OF DAY (IRE) 3 b.f. Mutamam 123 – Top of The Morning 56 (Keen 116) **50**
[2006 –: p7g⁵ p10g p6g² Apr 24] strong filly: modest maiden: left Miss D. Weeden after
second outing: should stay 7f: acts on polytrack. *J. R. Best*

LIGHT SENTENCE 3 b.g. Fantastic Light (USA) 134 – Almela (IRE) (Akarad (FR) **64**
130) [2006 7m 7f⁶ 8d⁵ 12d⁴ 11g* Sep 30] modest performer: won seller at Redcar in
September: stays 1½m: acts on firm and good to soft going. *G. A. Swinbank*

LIGHT SHIFT (USA) 2 b.f. (Mar 22) Kingmambo (USA) 125 – Lingerie (Shirley **93**
Heights 130) [2006 6g² 7m³ 8m* Sep 19] close-coupled filly: sister to winner in USA,
closely related to 1¼m winner Mahasi (by Woodman) and half-sister to several winners,
including high-class 8.5f to 10.5f winner Shiva and very smart French 10.5f and 1½m
winner Limnos (both by Hector Protector): dam, French maiden, out of top-class middle-
distance filly Northern Trick: fairly useful form: raced at Newmarket, twice placed prior
to winning maiden (beat Sunlight by ½ length): will stay 1¼m. *H. R. A. Cecil*

LIGHTS OF VEGAS 2 b.c. (Mar 16) Traditionally (USA) 117 – Catch The Lights 86 **71**
(Deploy 131) [2006 6m³ 7g Aug 19] strong, sturdy colt: sixth foal: half-brother to 4-y-o
Montjeu Baby: dam, 7f/1m winner, half-sister to smart performer up to 1m King's Iron-
bridge: fair form in maidens at Newbury: third to Astronomer Royal on debut: should
stay 1m. *B. J. Meehan*

LIGHTS OUT (DEN) 6 ch.g. Kateb (IRE) 68 – Skee The Feen (Viking (USA)) [2006 **?**
102: p16g 10.2d⁶ 8.8g² 8g⁶ Jun 18] Danish-bred gelding: useful performer at best: well
held for C. Horgan first 2 starts: third in handicap at Ovrevoll next time, better effort on
Flat afterwards (later won over hurdles): has won up to 1¾m, best recent efforts at 1¼m:
acts on dirt and soft ground, probably on polytrack: tried blinkered, has had tongue tied.
R. Haugen, Norway

LIGNE D'EAU 5 ch.g. Cadeaux Genereux 131 – Miss Waterline 77 (Rock City 120) **43**
[2006 63: f6g⁶ p7.1g f8g Dec 14] sturdy, close-coupled gelding: poor performer nowadays: effective at 6f/7f: acts on polytrack, good to firm and good to soft going: wears
visor/blinkers. *P. D. Evans*

LIHUSN AL HAZ (USA) 3 br.f. King Cugat (USA) 122 – Chaste (USA) (Cozzene **–**
(USA)) [2006 –: 10g f11g⁶ f12m Oct 31] smallish filly: little form: tried in cheekpieces.
C. E. Brittain

LII NAJMA 3 b.f. Medicean 128 – Opari (IRE) (Night Shift (USA)) [2006 60: 5f³ p8g* **78**
7m⁶ p7.1g⁶ 7f* p8g⁴ 7d⁵ p6g p7.1g⁴ f8g³ p7g⁶ p7.1s Dec 14] fair handicapper: won at **a70**
Kempton in May and Yarmouth in July: best at 7f/1m: acts on all-weather and firm going.
C. E. Brittain

LIKE TO GOLF (USA) 2 b. or br.g. (Mar 30) Bianconi (USA) 123 – Like To Shimmy **55**
(USA) (Shimatoree (USA)) [2006 7d 7f 8m Sep 19] strong, good-topped gelding: mid-
field in maidens, then gelded. *Mrs A. J. Perrett*

LILAC MOON (GER) 2 b.f. (Feb 23) Dr Fong (USA) 128 – Luna de Miel (Shareef **–**
Dancer (USA) 135) [2006 6m Sep 11] 10,000F, €31,000Y: good-bodied filly: second
foal: half-sister to 3-y-o Lenoir: dam placed up to 1¼m in Germany: backward and well
held in maiden. *Mrs A. Duffield*

LILAC STAR 3 ch.f. Observatory (USA) 131 – La Sorrela (IRE) (Cadeaux Genereux **72**
131) [2006 7m 8.2m³ 7g² 8.3m p7.1m⁴ p10g² Dec 2] strong, well-made filly: half-sister **a57**
to 2 winners, notably 7-y-o Colisay: dam unraced half-sister to smart sprinter Central
City: fair maiden on turf, modest on all-weather: seems to stay easy 1¼m. *Pat Eddery*

LILAKIYA (IRE) 3 b.f. Dr Fong (USA) 128 – Lidakiya (IRE) 105 (Kahyasi 130) **60**
[2006 10g 10f 12g⁶ 12d 10v p12.2g* 12v Dec 10] €26,000 2-y-o: second foal: half-sister

to 4-y-o Linngari: dam, 1¼m/1½m winner, half-sister to smart Irish 1m/1¼m winner Livadiya: modest performer: won maiden at Wolverhampton in November: stays easy 1½m: acts on polytrack and heavy going: tried in cheekpieces. *James Leavy, Ireland*

LILLEBROR (GER) 8 b.g. Top Waltz (FR) 119 – Lady Soliciti (GER) (Solicitor (FR) 121) [2006 65: f14g⁴ Jul 11] small gelding: lightly-raced handicapper: poor form only outing in 2006: stays 1¾m: acts on heavy and good to firm going: tried visored/in cheekpieces. *B. J. Curley* **46**

LILLIE LOU 3 b.f. Tomba 119 – Tread Carefully 51 (Sharpo 132) [2006 6g 8m Jun 6] rather leggy filly: half-sister to 7-y-o Hurricane Coast: dam, maiden who stayed 1m, half-sister to high-class stayer and Champion Hurdle winner Royal Gait: well held in maidens: sold 1,500 gns. *T. D. Easterby* **–**

LILLYELLA (IRE) 3 ch.f. Raise A Grand (IRE) 114 – Somers Heath (IRE) 58 (Definite Article 121) [2006 53: p8g⁶ Feb 7] mid-field in maiden and seller at Lingfield over 3 months apart. *M. J. Wallace* **42**

LILLY HAWK (IRE) 5 b.m. Shernazar 131 – Bloomfield (IRE) (Alzao (USA) 117) [2006 –: p7.1g Jan 21] little form, including in blinkers at Wolverhampton on British debut. *Adrian Sexton, Ireland* **–**

LILY ELSIE (IRE) 3 b.f. Danehill (USA) 126 – Toroca (USA) 112 (Nureyev (USA) 131) [2006 63p: 8g 7m³ 9f* 8m² 9m³ 7m⁶ 9.5d 9m Aug 27] lengthy, good-topped filly: first foal: dam Irish 6f (at 2 yrs) and 1m winner: fairly useful performer: won handicap at Tipperary in July: mostly creditable efforts after, including third in handicap at Goodwood: stays 9.5f: acts on firm and good to soft ground: sent to USA. *A. P. O'Brien, Ireland* **87**

LILY ON A HILL 3 b.f. City On A Hill (USA) 114 – Gulfstream Park (Barathea (IRE) 127) [2006 –: f7g⁶ f7g f6g Feb 7] no form. *B. Smart* **–**

LIMBO KING 2 b.c. (Apr 30) Barathea (IRE) 127 – Ermine (IRE) 86 (Cadeaux Genereux 131) [2006 7s³ 7d Oct 28] 65,000Y: medium-sized, quite attractive colt: third foal: half-brother to 5-y-o Hoh Bleu Dee and 4-y-o Carnivore: dam, 1m winner, half-sister to very smart 1¼m/1½m winner Border Arrow: fair form in maidens at Newbury (third to Mythical Red) and Newmarket: will be suited by 1m+. *J. W. Hills* **73**

LIMIT DOWN (IRE) 5 b.g. Desert Story (IRE) 115 – Princess Raisa (Indian King (USA) 128) [2006 p7.1g⁵ p7g⁵ 7m³ 6m⁴ 8d p7g² p7g⁴ Dec 13] poor maiden: stays 7f: acts on polytrack and good to firm ground: tried visored. *John Berry* **48**

LIMITED MAGICIAN 5 b.m. Wizard King 122 – Pretty Scarce (Handsome Sailor 125) [2006 35: f6g⁶ p5.1g* 5f p5g Jul 26] workmanlike mare: modest performer: won claimer at Wolverhampton in April: raced only at 5f/6f: acts on polytrack: visored 4 of last 5 starts: inconsistent. *C. Smith* **–**
a51

LIMONIA (GER) 4 b.f. Perugino (USA) 84 – Limoges (GER) (Konigsstuhl (GER)) [2006 62: f5g⁵ f6g p8g 5.3m⁵ p7g 6m⁶ 6f 6g* 6f² 6g* p6g p6m⁵ 6.1g⁴ 6d⁶ 5d Oct 3] rather leggy filly: fair performer: left D. Ivory after second start: won 2 claimers at Hamilton in July and handicap at Folkestone in August: stays easy 7f: acts on all-weather and firm going: tried blinkered: usually races prominently. *N. P. Littmoden* **64**

LINAS SELECTION 3 ch.c. Selkirk (USA) 129 – Lines of Beauty (USA) (Line In The Sand (USA)) [2006 76: 10g² 10g* 12m* 13.9f* 12m³ Aug 1] workmanlike colt, still unfurnished at present: smart performer: rapid improvement to win handicaps at Sandown in April, Royal Ascot (beat Enjoy The Moment by 3½ lengths in King George V Stakes) in June and York (by a length from Balkan Knight in listed event) in July: **114**

King George V Stakes (Handicap), Royal Ascot—Linas Selection is firmly in control as Enjoy The Moment (blaze) stays on well to take second; Bandama (rail) finishes third and Lake Poet (spots on sleeves) fourth

Mrs R. J. Jacobs' "Linas Selection"

creditable 2¼ lengths third to Sixties Icon in BGC Stakes (Gordon) at Goodwood final outing, leading 2f out and briefly unbalanced: stays 1¾m: acts on firm going. *M. Johnston*

LINCOLNEUROCRUISER 4 b.g. Spectrum (IRE) 126 – Rush Hour (IRE) (Night **82** Shift (USA)) [2006 83: f6g³ f7g⁶ p7.1g² f6g p7.1g* p7.1g⁵ p8.6g⁴ p7.1g² p8.6g f8s⁵ p7.1g² p7.1g⁴ p8g p7.1g⁶ 6d 7d⁴ 8d p7.1g 7m⁵ 8m⁴ 8m⁴ 7f* f7g² 7.1f³ 7m* 7m⁴ Aug 9] good-topped gelding: fairly useful handicapper: won at Wolverhampton in January and Newmarket (apprentices) and Ascot (ladies) in July: stays 8.6f: acts on all-weather, firm and soft going: tried in cheekpieces/visor (last on both occasions): often claimer ridden. *Mrs N. Macauley*

LINDA GREEN 5 b.m. Victory Note (USA) 120 – Edge of Darkness 62 (Vaigly Great **78** 127) [2006 73: 7s 5.7d² 5.7s⁵ 6.1d 7m 6m* 6f⁶ 6.1f³ 6f⁴ 6m⁴ 6f² 6g⁴ 6f 5.7f 6s 6d⁴ p6g² 6g* p6g⁵ p6g* p6g p6g⁶ Dec 20] rather leggy mare: fair handicapper: won at Windsor in July and October, and Kempton in November: best at 6f: acts on all-weather and any turf going: held up: tough. *M. R. Channon*

LINDA'S COLIN (IRE) 4 b.g. Xaar 132 – Capable Kate (IRE) (Alzao (USA) 117) **79** [2006 65: p7.1g 7g⁵ 8.2g 9.7f⁵ 8.1f⁴ 7m* 7f³ 7.6d² 7g 7.5m p7g⁶ p7.1g p10g³ Dec 20] lengthy gelding: fair handicapper: won at Newbury (apprentices) in July: effective at 7f to 9.7f: acts on polytrack, firm and good to soft going: tried in cheekpieces. *R. A. Harris*

LINDA'S LAD 3 b.c. Sadler's Wells (USA) 132 – Colza (USA) 89 (Alleged (USA) **116** 138) [2006 111: 10.5g⁴ 11.5m* 12m 10m³ Jul 23] rangy colt: smart performer: successful in Criterium de Saint-Cloud at 2 yrs: came on from reappearance to win 4-finisher totesport.com Derby Trial at Lingfield in May all out by a head from Hazeymm: below form after in Derby at Epsom (ninth to Sir Percy, thoroughly mulish before going to post

602

totesport.com Derby Trial Stakes, Lingfield—Linda's Lad is all out to get the better of Hazeymm (right), the pair clear of Baan (striped cap) and Before You Go

and taken down very quietly) and Prix Eugene Adam at Maisons-Laffitte (losing touch before running on for third behind Flashing Numbers): should stay 1½m: acts on soft and good to firm ground: none too straightforward, and has hung left, including at Epsom. *A. Fabre, France*

LINDBERGH 4 b.g. Bold Edge 123 – Halland Park Girl (IRE) 106 (Primo Dominie 121) [2006 94, a–: p5g² p6g⁴ p5g³ p5g 5g⁶ 5m Jun 18] lengthy, good-topped gelding: fairly useful handicapper: best form at 5f: acts on polytrack, good to firm and good to soft going: blinkered penultimate outing: sold 5,500 gns. *R. Hannon* — **92**

LINDENBURGH WAY (IRE) 3 b.c. Red Ransom (USA) – Strange Destiny 94 (Mujadil (USA) 119) [2006 84p: 7s³ f8g⁴ 7m Aug 5] close-coupled, quite attractive colt: fairly useful maiden: should have stayed 1m: acted on soft going: had been bandaged in front: dead. *B. J. Meehan* — **88**

LINDEN LIME 4 ch.f. Double Trigger (IRE) 123 – Linden Grace (USA) 88 (Mister Baileys 123) [2006 70: p10g⁵ p13g 15.4m² p16g⁴* 15d⁵ 17.1m p16g⁵ p16g⁴ 14m* 14.1g 16m³ 13.4f* p12g³ p13g⁵ p13g⁶ p16g⁴ Dec 15] quite good-topped filly: fair handicapper: won at Kempton in May, Haydock in August and Chester in September: stays 2m: acts on polytrack, firm and good to soft going. *Jamie Poulton* — **76**

LINDEN'S LADY 6 b.m. Compton Place 125 – Jubilee Place (IRE) 76 (Prince Sabo 123) [2006 61: 7.1g⁵ 7.2d² 7f⁵ 7.9m 7.1g 8m⁶ 7.2m 7.1m⁵ Aug 24] leggy mare: modest handicapper: below form after second start: stays 1m: acts on firm and good to soft going: usually wears headgear. *J. R. Weymes* — **64 d**

LINDHOVEN (USA) 2 gr.c. (May 3) Monarchos (USA) 129 – Bevel (USA) (Mr Prospector (USA)) [2006 8.3d Oct 10] ninth living foal: half-brother to 3 winners, including fairly useful 1½m winner Heavenly Bay (by Rahy) and 1¼m winner Payola (by Red Ransom): dam, French 1m winner, out of close relation to Ajdal: 100/1, faded into eighth in maiden at Leicester, and not knocked about: open to improvement. *C. E. Brittain* — **57 p**

LINDY LOU 2 b.f. (Feb 7) Hernando (FR) 127 – Daylight Dreams 77 (Indian Ridge 123) [2006 p7g 7d Oct 28] close-coupled filly: fourth foal: half-sister to 1m winner Dixie Dancing (by Greensmith) and 4-y-o Ten Cents: dam 2-y-o 5f winner who probably stayed 1m: behind in maidens. *C. A. Cyzer* — **–**

LINKSLADE LAD 2 b.g. (Apr 2) Mujahid (USA) 125 – Goodwood Lass (IRE) 71 (Alzao (USA) 117) [2006 6m 7f⁶ 5.1g 5.7f 6m² 7f 5.5m 6d⁵ Sep 25] compact gelding: modest and irresolute maiden: should stay 7f: usually in blinkers/cheekpieces: often reluctant, once refused to race. *W. R. Muir* — **64 §**

LINLITHGOW (IRE) 2 gr. or br.c. (Jan 21) Linamix (FR) 127 – Diarshana (GER) (Darshaan 133) [2006 8.2d p7g p8g Dec 10] 12,000F, 31,000Y: angular colt: first foal: dam unraced half-sister to smart French performer up to 12.5f Diamond Tango out of smart French performer up to 1½m Diamond Dance: form in maidens only when seventh at Nottingham on debut: will benefit from 1¼m/1½m. *J. L. Dunlop* — **56**

LINNGARI (IRE) 4 ch.c. Indian Ridge 123 – Lidakiya (IRE) 105 (Kahyasi 130) [2006 120: 8.9m* 8g* 8.9m 6.5g⁶ 6d* 7m² 6d⁴ 8m⁵ Dec 10] rather leggy, quite attractive colt: very smart performer: successful in Dubal Al Rashidiya (by ½ length from Greys Inn) and Al Rostamani Al Fahidi Fort (beat Lord Admiral 2¼ lengths) at Nad Al Sheba in February: off over 4 months and joined D. Lowther in France for next 3 outings only: won — **120**

603

bestwetten.de Goldene Peitsche at Baden-Baden in August by ¾ length from Donatello and ran well when dead-heating for second (beaten short neck) behind Caradak in Prix de la Foret at Longchamp and when length fourth to New Girlfriend in Prix de Seine-et-Oise at Maisons-Laffitte: creditable 2 lengths fifth to The Duke in Hong Kong Mile at Sha Tin final start: effective at 6f to 9f: acts on polytrack, firm and good to soft going. *H. Brown, South Africa*

LINNING WINE (IRE) 10 b.g. Scenic 128 – Zallaka (IRE) (Shardari 134) [2006 –§, a95§: p8.6g⁴ p8g* p9.5g p10g⁶ p8.6g p8.6g p10g⁵ Jul 22] lengthy gelding: useful in 2005, just fair in 2006: won claimer at Lingfield in February: below form after, reportedly lame final outing: effective at 7f to 1¼m: acts on polytrack, good to firm and good to soft going: in cheekpieces/blinkers last 6 starts: held up, and sometimes finds little: one to treat with caution. *P. A. Blockley* — § a74 §

LINTON DANCER (IRE) 3 b.f. Mujadil (USA) 119 – Daisy Grey 46 (Nordance (USA)) [2006 52: 10g⁶ 8g³ 9.3m³ 10f⁵ 8f⁵ 10m⁶ 11.1m 9.8s p7.1m³ f7g⁶ p8.6g⁴ f16g⁶ Dec 28] modest maiden: stays easy 1¼m: acts on polytrack and firm going: tried tongue tied. *J. R. Weymes* 60

LION SANDS 2 b.c. (Apr 25) Montjeu (IRE) 137 – Puce 112 (Darshaan 133) [2006 7d³ 8g⁴ Sep 14] 300,000Y: neat, attractive colt: sixth foal: closely related to smart 1¼m (at 2 yrs)/11f winner Pukka (by Sadler's Wells) and smart 1¼m/1½m winner Pongee (by Barathea) and half-brother to 2 winners, including 4-y-o Garhoud: dam, 1¼m/1½m winner who stayed 14.6f, closely related to dam of 3-y-o Alexandrova: promise in maidens at Newmarket (third to Moudez) and Yarmouth (odds on): will be suited by 1¼m/1½m: should make a useful 3-y-o, and sure to win races. *L. M. Cumani* 80 p

LION'S DOMANE 9 b.g. Lion Cavern (USA) 117 – Vilany 87 (Never So Bold 135) [2006 –§: 8.3m Jun 14] strong, workmanlike gelding: little Flat form since 2003: wayward. *K. W. Hogg, Isle of Man* — §

LIPIZZA (IRE) 3 b.f. Spinning World (USA) 130 – Lipica (IRE) 99 (Night Shift (USA)) [2006 77: 6m 6m² 5m⁶ 6g 6g² 7d⁶ Aug 18] strong filly: fairly useful handicapper: best efforts at 5f/6f: acts on polytrack, heavy and good to firm going. *N. A. Callaghan* 81

LIPOCCO 2 br.g. (Apr 17) Piccolo 121 – Magical Dancer (IRE) 53 (Magical Wonder (USA) 125) [2006 5.1g² 5.1g³ 5.1f² 6f* 6s⁶ 6m Sep 16] 14,000F, 13,000Y: lengthy, good-topped gelding: fifth foal: brother to fairly useful 2003 2-y-o 7f winner Scotch N' Dry: dam, 1m winner, half-sister to smart sprinter Don't Worry Me: fairly useful performer: won nursery at Leicester in July: held form well otherwise, sixth to Doctor Brown in sales race at York fifth start, gelded after final one: effective at 5f/6f: acts on firm and soft going. *R. M. Beckett* 87

LIQUID LOVER (IRE) 4 b.g. Night Shift (USA) – New Tycoon (IRE) (Last Tycoon 131) [2006 53: f12g³ f11g² f12g p11g⁴ f11g⁴ p12.2g⁴ f11g⁶ p12.2g p12g f12g⁵ f12g Dec 29] sturdy gelding: modest maiden: stays 1½m: acts on all-weather: tried in cheekpieces/blinkers: tends to be slowly away. *W. M. Brisbourne* 59

LISATHEDADDY 4 br.f. Darnay 117 – Erith's Chill Wind 61 (Be My Chief (USA) 122) [2006 p7g⁴ p8g⁴ p7g³ p10g* 10m 8.3g p10g³ p10g* p12g² p11g² p12g⁴ Dec 1] first foal: dam 1¼m winner: fairly useful handicapper: won at Lingfield in May and October (apprentices): stays 1½m: acts on polytrack. *B. G. Powell* 86

LISFANNON 3 ch.f. Bahamian Bounty 116 – Amazed 58 (Clantime 101) [2006 68: 6v⁴ 7.5d⁴ 8m⁶ 7g 7m⁶ Jul 1] angular filly: fair maiden, lightly raced: below form after second outing: stays 7.5f: acts on heavy ground: sold 36,000 gns later in July. *B. W. Hills* 68

LI SHIH CHEN 3 ch.g. Dr Fong (USA) 128 – Mad Annie (USA) (Anabaa (USA) 130) [2006 61: p6g p7g* p7g p8g³ 7f Jul 14] neat gelding: fair performer: won maiden at Lingfield in March: stays 7f: acts on polytrack. *A. P. Jarvis* 75

LISKAVEEN BEAUTY 3 gr.f. Danehill Dancer (IRE) 117 – Smooth Princess (IRE) 63 (Roi Danzig (USA)) [2006 6d⁵ 6g 6m f8g Dec 29] strong, lengthy filly: fourth foal: sister to fairly useful 1m winner Fancy Foxtrot: dam 2-y-o 7f seller winner: poor maiden. *T. J. Fitzgerald* 48

LISSELAN DANCER (USA) 2 b.f. (Mar 19) Outflanker (USA) 83 – Sambacarioca (USA) (Irish Tower (USA)) [2006 7g Aug 23] half-sister to several minor winners in USA: dam US Grade 3 8.5f winner: 33/1 and green, well held in maiden at Leicester: sold 1,800 gns. *Mrs A. J. Perrett* —

LIT ET MIXE (FR) 3 gr.g. Linamix (FR) 127 – Lit (IRE) (Danehill (USA) 126) [2006 10s⁶ 10g* 11s⁴ p8g p12g Dec 2] €125,000Y: third foal: dam 7f/1m winner: fair performer: ran only 3 times in France for J-C. Rouget, clearly best effort when winning 68

maiden at Auch in March: off 8 months, well held in handicaps at Kempton last 2 starts. *Noel T. Chance*

LITTLE BISCUIT (IRE) 4 br.f. Indian Lodge (IRE) 127 – Arjan (IRE) 88 (Paris House 123) [2006 44: f5g f5g Jan 19] small, sturdy filly: only poor nowadays and well held in 2006. *K. R. Burke* –

LITTLE BOB 5 ch.g. Zilzal (USA) 137 – Hunters of Brora (IRE) 102 (Sharpo 132) [2006 80: 8.2s 9.8v 10.5s 9.1v³ 9.1v 10d⁶ Nov 1] good-topped gelding: fair handicapper: stays 1¼m: acts on any turf going: blinkered. *J. D. Bethell* 66

LITTLE BRITAIN (USA) 3 b.g. Stravinsky (USA) 133 – I Don't Know (USA) (Restivo (USA)) [2006 53: 7g 9m 12.4d 7m³ 8g Nov 10] modest maiden: stays 7f: acts on good to firm going: tried blinkered: sold 3,000 gns. *J. Howard Johnson* 62

LITTLE CARMELA 2 gr.f. (Jan 20) Beat Hollow 126 – Carmela Owen (Owington 123) [2006 6d 6d Nov 4] third foal: half-sister to 4-y-o Zowington and 3-y-o Finsbury: dam unraced: well held in maidens. *S. C. Williams* –

LITTLEDODAYNO (IRE) 3 b.f. Mujadil (USA) 119 – Perfect Welcome (Taufan (USA) 119) [2006 78: p6g p7g⁶ 6d p7g 7m 6g 8.1f⁶ 5.9m³ 6m* 6m* 6.1g² 6f³ Sep 20] smallish, leggy, close-coupled filly: fair handicapper: left J. Noseda after reappearance: won at Lingfield in August and Folkestone in September: best form at 6f: acts on polytrack and firm going: warm and got loose in parade ring fifth outing. *M. Wigham* 79

LITTLE EDWARD 8 gr.g. King's Signet (USA) 110 – Cedar Lady (Telsmoss 91) [2006 80d: 5f* 5m p6g 5g³ p5g² p5g* p5g* p5g* p6g⁵ Dec 1] angular gelding: useful handicapper: won at Sandown in July and Lingfield (twice) and Kempton (beat Pamir a head) in November: best at 5f/6f: acts on polytrack, firm and good to soft going: tried in cheekpieces. *R. J. Hodges* 95

LITTLE ESKIMO 2 b.c. (Apr 24) Johannesburg (USA) 127 – Karla June (Unfuwain (USA) 131) [2006 6d⁴ f7g³ p7.1g* Dec 1] 120,000F: strong, lengthy colt: first foal: dam, 1m winner in USA, sister to useful stayer Sweetness Herself, herself dam of smart stayer Jagger: fair form: won 5-runner maiden at Wolverhampton by length from Dr McFab: should do better still, particularly at 1m+. *B. Smart* 69 p

LITTLE EYECATCHER (IRE) 3 b.g. Beckett (IRE) 116 – Black Jack Girl (IRE) (Ridgewood Ben 113) [2006 54: 10.1d 14.1g May 29] lengthy gelding: modest form in 2-y-o maidens: no form in 2006. *T. D. Easterby* –

LITTLE GANNET 5 ro.m. Bien Bien (USA) 125 – Lady Kalliste (Another Realm 118) [2006 51: p10g p12g Mar 6] lightly-raced maiden: well held in 2006. *T. D. McCarthy* –

LITTLE HOTPOTCH 2 b.f. (Apr 11) Erhaab (USA) 127 – Berzoud 69 (Ezzoud (IRE) 126) [2006 p5g⁵ 5v⁴ 7m f7g Oct 12] smallish, good-bodied filly: second foal: dam 9f to 11.5f winner: little form. *J. R. Jenkins* –

LITTLE IRIS 2 ch.f. (Feb 16) Inchinor 119 – Galanthus (USA) 59 (Rahy (USA) 115) [2006 6g 7.1m 6.1g Sep 26] quite good-topped filly: first foal: dam, 1½m winner, out of useful performer up to 1½m Tiger Flower: never on terms nor knocked about in maidens, all over 6f/7f (bred to be suited by middle distances): type to improve at 3 yrs. *L. M. Cumani* 50 p

LITTLE JIMBOB 5 b.g. Desert Story (IRE) 115 – Artistic Licence (High Top 131) [2006 92: p9.5g³ p10g 9.8v 10.5g⁵ 9.8m² 9.9f⁵ 8m² f8g⁵ Dec 14] close-coupled gelding: fairly useful handicapper on turf, fair on all-weather: barely stays 9.8f: acts on polytrack, firm and good to soft going: races prominently. *R. A. Fahey* 85 a77

LITTLE LILY MORGAN 3 gr.f. Kayf Tara 130 – Cool Grey 49 (Absalom 128) [2006 8d 9.8g 9v⁶ May 21] compact filly: fourth foal: dam in frame in 7f sellers at 2 yrs: well held in maidens: very slowly away on debut. *R. Bastiman* –

LITTLEMADGEBOB 2 b.f. (Mar 13) Primo Valentino (IRE) 116 – Midnight Orchid (IRE) 74 (Petardia 113) [2006 6m 7d 6g f6m Oct 31] 3,000Y: second foal: dam, unreliable 2-y-o 6f winner, out of half-sister to 2000 Guineas winner To-Agori-Mou: well beaten in maidens. *J. R. Norton* –

LITTLE MISS DAISY 3 br.f. Zilzal (USA) 137 – Jimgareen (IRE) 66 (Lahib (USA) 129) [2006 71: 8.2s 7m May 12] leggy filly: fair maiden at 2 yrs: well held in handicaps in 2006: stayed 7f: acted on good to firm going, probably on soft: dead. *A. B. Haynes* –

LITTLE MISS GRACIE 4 gr.f. Efisio 120 – Circled (USA) 83 (Cozzene (USA)) [2006 105: 8g⁴ 8v⁴ 8.3f² 8g 8m 8s Aug 28] tall, leggy filly: useful performer: best efforts 98

in 2006 when respectable fourth in listed race at Goodwood and Ridgewood Pearl Stakes at the Curragh first 2 starts: ran poorly last 3 outings (upset in stall and dropped away tamely final one): stays 1m: has won on firm going, best efforts on good or softer (acts on heavy): blinkered fourth outing: usually races prominently. *A. B. Haynes*

LITTLE MISS TARA (IRE) 2 b.f. (Mar 29) Namid 128 – Circled (USA) 83 (Cozzene (USA)) [2006 6g 7g⁵ 7f² 7.1d² 7d⁵ Sep 27] leggy filly: half-sister to several winners, including 4-y-o Little Miss Gracie: dam 2-y-o 7f winner who stayed 1½m: fair maiden: second at Folkestone and Warwick: stays 7f: acts on firm and good to soft going. *A. B. Haynes* **75**

LITTLE MISS VERITY 3 b.f. Danzig Connection (USA) – Little White Lies 78 (Runnett 125) [2006 8.3m 7g 8.1m³ p7g p6g p8g p10g Dec 13] half-sister to 1m winners Singers Image (by Chief Singer) and Diliza (by Dilum): dam maiden who stayed 1m: little form. *J. A. Geake* **–**

LITTLE MISS WIZZY 2 b.f. (Mar 11) Bertolini (USA) 125 – Magical Veil 73 (Majestic Light (USA)) [2006 6.1g³ p7g⁵ 7f² 7f* 7m⁴ 8d² Aug 25] 6,000Y: good-topped filly: closely related to winner in Greece by Emperor Jones and half-sister to several winners, including 5-y-o Mr Lambros: dam 11.6f winner: fair performer: won nursery at Yarmouth in July: ran well after in similar events at Newmarket: stays 1m: acts on firm and good to soft going: sent to USA. *M. L. W. Bell* **69**

LITTLE RICHARD (IRE) 7 b.g. Alhaarth (IRE) 126 – Intricacy 65 (Formidable (USA) 125) [2006 60: p13.9g* p12.2g* p16.5g³ p13.9g⁵ p16.5g³ p16.5g⁶ p12.2g p12.2m⁴ p12.2g⁶ p12g⁶ p13.9g* p12.2g² p13.9g* Dec 31] small, workmanlike gelding: fair performer: won banded race and handicap in January and 2 handicaps in December, all at Wolverhampton: effective at 1½m to 16.5f: acts on all-weather and good to firm going: wears headgear. *M. Wellings* **71**

LITTLE RIDGE (IRE) 5 b.g. Charnwood Forest (IRE) 125 – Princess Natalie 78 (Rudimentary (USA) 118) [2006 –, a85: f5g f5g⁴ f5s⁶ p5g 5.1s Apr 11] close-coupled, quite attractive gelding: on downgrade and just fair handicapper in 2006: best at 5f: acts on all-weather, soft and good to firm ground: visored (well held) final outing: sometimes slowly away. *H. Morrison* **73 d**

LITTLE RUTLAND 2 ch.g. (Mar 21) Mark of Esteem (IRE) 137 – Prickly Poppy 72 (Lear Fan (USA) 130) [2006 p7g p8.6g p9.5g⁶ Nov 16] modest form in maidens on polytrack. *E. J. O'Neill* **55**

LITTLESTAR (FR) 5 b.g. Robellino (USA) 127 – Green Charter 77 (Green Desert (USA) 127) [2006 f14g Jul 11] sturdy gelding: maiden unraced in 2005 and well held only outing in 2006: tried blinkered. *B. D. Leavy* **–**

LITTLE TASK 8 b.g. Environment Friend 128 – Lucky Thing (Green Desert (USA) 127) [2006 38: 12f Jun 22] smallish, close-coupled gelding: poor performer: well beaten on only Flat outing in 2006: tried blinkered (not since 2001): won over hurdles in August. *J. S. Wainwright* **–**

LITTLE TINY TOM 2 b.g. (Feb 8) Tobougg (IRE) 125 – Villa Del Sol 86 (Tagula (IRE) 116) [2006 p6g p6g 7m⁶ 7g 7s³ 10g 7.1d 8.2s f7g⁵ Nov 14] sturdy gelding: poor maiden: best efforts at 7f on going softer than good: usually in blinkers/cheekpieces. *C. N. Kellett* **44**

LITTLE TOMMY FELLA 2 b.c. (Feb 14) Diktat 126 – Francia 59 (Legend of France (USA) 124) [2006 5.1s⁵ 5g 8.2s a7.5g⁶ a9.5g Dec 19] strong colt: sixth foal: half-brother to 8.5f and 1¼m winner Gracia (by Linamix) and 9f/1¼m winner Suave Performer (by Suave Dancer): dam 7f (at 2 yrs) and 1½m winner: sold from S. Williams 6,500 gns after third start: best effort when seventh in minor event on all-weather at Deauville final start: will stay 1¼m. *Mme G. Rarick, France* **67**

LITTLETON ALDOR (IRE) 6 b.g. Pennekamp (USA) 130 – Belle Etoile (FR) (Lead On Time (USA) 123) [2006 p7.1g 7m p10g 10.2m p8.6g Sep 11] poor maiden: should stay 1½m: acts on polytrack. *W. G. M. Turner* **46**

LITTLETON TELCHAR (USA) 6 ch.g. Atticus (USA) 121 – Miss Waikiki (USA) (Miswaki (USA) 124) [2006 75: 8d⁵ 8g⁴ 7m* 7f² 7f⁵ 7.5f³ 7m 7d p7g* p8g⁶ p7g⁵ Dec 15] quite good-topped gelding: fairly useful handicapper: won at Roscommon in June and (having left H. O'Driscoll in Ireland after seventh start) Kempton in November: effective at 7f to 1¼m: acts on polytrack and firm going. *S. W. Hall* **89**
a82

LITTLETON ZEPHIR (USA) 7 b.m. Sandpit (BRZ) 129 – Miss Gorgeous (IRE) 76 (Damister (USA) 123) [2006 57, a74: p7g p8g p8g Feb 15] sturdy mare: fair handicapper **–**

at 6 yrs: well held in 2006: wore headgear earlier in career: tongue tied final start. *Mrs P. Townsley*

LITTLETOWN BRIDGE (USA) 4 b.f. Stormin Fever (USA) 116 – Fire The **91** Deputy (USA) (Deputy Minister (CAN)) [2006 8.9d⁵ 12m⁶ 12m Aug 6] $35,000Y, $70,000 2-y-o: fifth foal: half-sister to 3 winners in USA: dam unraced half-sister to dam of top-class sprinter Stravinsky: useful performer at best: won minor event and second in UAE Oaks at Nad Al Sheba in 2005 (rated 98): below form on turf in 2006 (left D. Watson in UAE after reappearance), including in Britain last 2 starts: should stay 1½m: acts on dirt: sometimes tongue tied: sent to USA. *C. Wroe, UAE*

LITTLE TRINKET 3 b.f. Magic Ring (IRE) 115 – Leen 68 (Distant Relative 128) – [2006 –: 6d⁶ 6v 6m Sep 12] no form in maidens. *Mrs C. A. Dunnett*

LITTLE WISHES 3 b.f. Most Welcome 131 – Zac's Desire (Swing Easy (USA) 126) – [2006 8.2g 10d Oct 4] neat filly: third foal: dam unraced: well held in maidens at Nottingham. *S. Parr*

LIVALEX 2 b.f. (Apr 8) Zamindar (USA) 116 – Evie Hone (IRE) 69 (Royal Academy **50** (USA) 130) [2006 7f⁵ Jul 28] 5,000Y: fourth foal: half-sister to 5-y-o Arran Scout: dam, lightly-raced maiden (virtually refused to race final outing), half-sister to US Grade 2 1m/ 9f winner Uncharted Haven: 17/2, fifth to Carwell in maiden at Thirsk. *M. Dods*

LIVE AND DANGEROUS 5 b.m. Mark of Esteem (IRE) 137 – Mazaya (IRE) 105 – (Sadler's Wells (USA) 132) [2006 54: p6g Jan 23] lightly-raced maiden: well held only outing in 2006. *D. Carroll*

LIVERTI 3 b.f. Averti (IRE) 117 – Light of Aragon 41 (Aragon 118) [2006 –: p7.1m f6g – Dec 5] no sign of ability. *D. Carroll*

LIVING ON A PRAYER 3 b.f. Josr Algarhoud (IRE) 118 – Denton Lady 49 (Inch- **a56** inor 119) [2006 p7.1g p8g⁶ p8g* p8.6g 9.7s p8.6g⁶ 8m May 11] third foal: dam maiden (probably best around 1m): modest performer: won maiden at Lingfield in February: stays 1m: acts on polytrack. *J. Pearce*

LIVVIES LADY (IRE) 4 b.f. Opening Verse (USA) 126 – Indian Wardance (ITY) – (Indian Ridge 123) [2006 –: f8g Jan 3] no sign of ability. *D. K. Ivory*

LIZARAZU (GER) 7 b.g. Second Set (IRE) 127 – Lilly (GER) (Motley (USA) 123) **82** [2006 82: 8d⁶ 9.7f 7.1d* 8.2d 7s 7.1f 8.1m⁴ 7.1f⁵ 7g 7m⁴ 7m⁶ 8d⁴ 6.1d² 6.1d p7g p7.1g **a–** Dec 22] close-coupled gelding: fairly useful handicapper: won at Warwick in May: effective at 6f, had form at 1¼m earlier in career: acts on polytrack, firm and soft going: tried blinkered, usually wears cheekpieces. *R. A. Harris*

LIZZIE ROCKET 6 gr.m. Paris House 123 – Jane's Affair (Alleging (USA) 120) – [2006 47, a55: f5g f5g f5g 5f 5f Jun 22] modest winner at 5 yrs: well held in 2006: blinkered/visored. *J. O'Reilly*

LLAMADAS 4 b.g. Josr Algarhoud (IRE) 118 – Primulette 82 (Mummy's Pet 125) **87** [2006 82: p10g p13g* f12s⁵ p16g* p16g p16g³ 12s⁶ 14g p16g⁵ Nov 29] rather leggy, close-coupled gelding: fairly useful handicapper: won at Lingfield in February and Kempton in March: stays easy 2m: acts on all-weather, best turf efforts on good ground or softer: has worn headgear: sometimes looks difficult ride: inconsistent. *C. Roberts*

LOADED GUN 6 ch.g. Highest Honor (FR) 124 – Woodwardia (USA) 93 (El Gran **50** Senor (USA) 136) [2006 55: 12g 9.3m 12.4m⁴ 12m 16.1s⁵ Sep 4] leggy gelding: modest performer: effective at 8.6f to 1½m: acts on polytrack, soft and good to firm going. *W. Storey*

LOADERFUN (IRE) 4 br.g. Danehill Dancer (IRE) 117 – Sideloader Special 66 **80 d** (Song 132) [2006 98: 5d 7.2g 6s 6g⁵ 6m 6m p7.1g 7.5g 6v p8.6g f8g Nov 20] sturdy gelding: useful at 3 yrs: very much on downgrade, and form in 2006 only on fourth start: stays 6f: acts on soft and good to firm going: tried blinkered/tongue tied. *N. Wilson*

LOBENGULA (IRE) 4 b.g. Spectrum (IRE) 126 – Playwaki (USA) (Miswaki (USA) **70** 124) [2006 65: p7.1g p8.6g 10.5f⁴ 10g³ 10.3m² 10.1s p9.5g⁴ p8g⁴ p8g p10g p9.5g² p8.6g³ **a67** Dec 27] fair handicapper: stays 10.5f: acts on polytrack, soft and firm ground: in cheekpieces (ran poorly) once: races up with pace. *I. W. McInnes*

LOCAL FANCY 3 b.f. Bahamian Bounty 116 – Local Abbey (IRE) (Primo Dominie **85** 121) [2006 78: 7m 7s⁵ 7.1s³ p8g 7d³ 7d³ 7s Oct 10] angular, sparely-made filly: fairly useful handicapper: stays 7f: acts on soft and good to firm ground. *J. M. P. Eustace*

LOCAL POET 5 b.g. Robellino (USA) 127 – Laugharne (Known Fact (USA) 135) **82 d** [2006 79: f7g* f6g⁵ p7.1g* 7v 6v 7.2d 6g p7.1g 7.1m Aug 3] sturdy gelding: fairly useful handicapper on all-weather, fair on turf: won at Southwell in January and Wolverhampton in March: below form after: stays 7f: acts on all-weather, good to firm and good to soft going: tried in cheekpieces, tongue tied/blinkered nowadays. *I. Semple*

LOCAL SPIRIT (USA) 3 ch.f. Lion Cavern (USA) 117 – Crimson Conquest (USA) 85 (Diesis 133) [2006 66: 15g3 7g3 p7g3 p10g* 11.9g2 10.1f2 12m 8.1g 9.9m Sep 20] neat filly: useful performer: won maiden at Lingfield in July: good second next 2 starts, beaten 3 lengths by Allegretto in Lancashire Oaks at Haydock and 2½ lengths by Reunite in listed race at Yarmouth: ran poorly last 2 starts: stays 1½m: acts on polytrack and firm going: temperamental. *C. E. Brittain* **101 §**

LOCH AWE 3 b.f. Inchinor 119 – Lochbelle 70 (Robellino (USA) 127) [2006 64: 9.8g 10d5 11.5m 14g6 16g Aug 4] big, close-coupled filly: modest maiden: seems to stay 1¼m: acts on good to soft going. *J. G. Given* **50**

LOCH CLUTHA (IRE) 2 b.f. (Feb 3) Averti (IRE) 117 – Loch Fyne 70 (Ardkinglass 114) [2006 5m5 5g 5g 5f6 5m3 6g2 6f6 6m5 7m Sep 5] 6,000Y: workmanlike filly: third foal: sister to 2004 2-y-o 5f seller winner Theatre of Dreams: dam, sprint maiden, half-sister to useful sprinter Lennox Lewis: poor maiden: placed in sellers: best at 5f/6f: acts on firm going: tried in cheekpieces. *K. R. Burke* **49**

LOCH TAY 2 b.g. (Apr 23) Cape Cross (IRE) 129 – Taysala (IRE) (Akarad (FR) 130) [2006 7m3 7d4 p7g5 8g Oct 12] 44,000F, 30,000Y, 45,000 2-y-o: quite attractive gelding: seventh foal: half-brother to 3 winners, including 8-y-o Tiyoun and 3-y-o Night Groove: dam unraced: fair maiden: no progress after debut (third to Safe Investment at Newmarket): should be suited by 1m. *M. L. W. Bell* **78**

LOCH VERDI 3 b.f. Green Desert (USA) 127 – Lochsong 129 (Song 132) [2006 75p: 6d3 5.1g* 5g2 5f* 5f3 5d5 Aug 23] strong, lengthy filly: useful handicapper: won at Bath and Hamilton in June: good third to Terentia at Goodwood after: raced at 5f/6f: acts on firm and good to soft going: carried head a little awkwardly on reappearance/hung left final outing: makes running. *A. M. Balding* **95**

LOCKSTOCK (IRE) 8 b.g. Inchinor 119 – Risalah (Marju (IRE) 127) [2006 78, a72: f8g f8g p9.5g p10g f8g 10.2d 8d 8s3 8.1d5 8.3g3 p9.5g5 8m 8.1m3 8.1m* 8d 8d p9.5g6 f7g Dec 12] quite good-topped gelding: fair handicapper on turf, just modest on all-weather in 2006: won at Chepstow in September: stays easy 9.5f: acts on all-weather, heavy and good to firm going: usually wears blinkers/cheekpieces: races prominently: none too consistent. *M. S. Saunders* **69 a57**

LOCOMBE HILL (IRE) 10 b.g. Barathea (IRE) 127 – Roberts Pride 62 (Roberto (USA) 131) [2006 77, a66: p8.6g Jan 6] very big, rather dipped-backed gelding: fair performer at 9 yrs: well held only outing in 2006: tried visored: takes good hold, and usually races prominently. *N. Wilson* **–**

LODGICIAN (IRE) 4 b.c. Grand Lodge (USA) 125 – Dundel (IRE) 82 (Machiavellian (USA) 123) [2006 61: 14.1f4 17.2m* 17.2f2 18f2 16.1m 15.8d Sep 5] useful-looking colt: has a quick action: fair handicapper: won maiden event at Carlisle in July: stays 2¼m: acts on firm and good to soft going: won over hurdles later in September. *J. J. Quinn* **72**

LOGGER RHYTHM (USA) 6 b.g. Woodman (USA) 126 – Formidable Dancer (USA) (Danzig (USA)) [2006 –: f16g6 f14g2 f16g2 f16g3 f16g4 f16g Oct 12] compact gelding: modest maiden: left R. Dickin after fifth outing: stays 2m: acts on fibresand: tried visored/blinkered/tongue tied. *Dr R. J. Naylor* **52**

LOGSDAIL 6 b.g. Polish Precedent (USA) 131 – Logic 94 (Slip Anchor 136) [2006 89, a83: p7g 6d 5g 5m 8m p8g3 p8g* p8g3 8d2 7g 7.1s2 10d5 8d p10g2 10d Nov 1] good-topped gelding: fair handicapper: won at Kempton in July: stays easy 1¼m: acts on polytrack, good to firm and soft going, probably on soft: usually wears cheekpieces. *G. L. Moore* **78**

L'OISEAU DE FEU (USA) 2 b.g. (Jan 16) Stravinsky (USA) 133 – Off You Go (USA) (Seattle Slew (USA)) [2006 6f 6f3 6g3 Sep 14] good-topped gelding: first foal: dam, French maiden, half-sister to smart winner up to 9f Divine Task out of half-sister to very smart 1m to 1½m performer Hatoof: fair form in maidens: third at Folkestone and Yarmouth: raced at 6f on good ground or firmer. *E. A. L. Dunlop* **78**

LOITOKITOK 4 b.g. Piccolo 121 – Bonita Bee 50 (King of Spain 121) [2006 –: 12f Jun 12] sturdy, close-coupled gelding: no form. *P. D. Cundell* **–**

LOL DRAPER 3 ch.f. Forzando 122 – Shanghai Lil 57 (Petong 126) [2006 8d 7.1g 10.2g p7.1g May 15] third foal: dam 6f to 1½m winner: little form: tried visored. *P. D. Evans* **–**

LOLITA (GER) 3 b.f. Lavirco (GER) 125 – Little Movie Star 81 (Risk Me (FR) 127) **111**
[2006 8s* 8v* 8m 8d Jul 30] €6,000 2-y-o: rather sparely-made filly: second foal: half-
sister to useful German 6.5f/7f winner Lamargue (by Mujahid): dam, 2-y-o 5f winner, out
of half-sister to very smart German performer up to 1½m Kornado: smart performer:
successful at Dusseldorf in maiden at 2 yrs and listed race and pferdewetten.de Stuten-
preis (German 1000 Guineas, by 2 lengths from Almerita, pair clear, making all) in April:
sold privately, in rear in Coronation Stakes at Royal Ascot and Prix d'Astarte at Deauville: stays 1m: acts on heavy going: joined P. Biancone in USA. *A. Lowe, Germany*

LOLLA'S SPIRIT (IRE) 3 b.f. Montjeu (IRE) 137 – Glenarff (USA) (Irish River **68**
(FR) 131) [2006 55?: 9.9m 12f³ 16g 11.1g⁴ p12.2g* p12g³ p12g² p12g Nov 11] tall filly:
fair performer: won maiden at Hamilton in August and handicap at Wolverhampton in
September: stays 1½m: acts on polytrack and firm going: consistent: sold 25,000 gns.
M. L. W. Bell

LONDOLOZI (USA) 2 b. or br.f. (May 22) Forest Wildcat (USA) 120 – Dearly 107 **69**
(Rahy (USA) 115) [2006 p6g⁴ p7g³ p6g⁶ f7g⁶ Dec 19] second foal: closely related to
3-y-o True Cause: dam Irish 7f (at 2 yrs) to 1¼m (Blandford Stakes) winner: fair maiden:
best effort when third to Malaath at Lingfield: stays 7f: acts on polytrack. *M. A. Jarvis*

LONDON EXPRESS (IRE) 3 b.c. King Charlemagne (USA) 120 – Robin (Slip **100**
Anchor 136) [2006 89p: 10v* 12m² 11g⁴ 10.1m 12m⁵ 10m² 12m⁴ 12d* Aug 22] lightly-
made colt: useful handicapper: won at Pontefract in April and York (beat Stretton by
head, edging left after jockey had dropped whip) in August: several good efforts in
between, including when fifth to stable-companion Linas Selection in King George V
Stakes at Ascot: will stay 1¾m: acts on heavy and good to firm going: usually races prominently: tough and consistent: sent to Hong Kong. *M. Johnston*

LONE PLAINSMAN 5 b.g. Royal Applause 124 – Suprematie (FR) (Gay Mecene **91**
(USA) 128) [2006 86: 5d 5d⁵ 5f 5g⁶ 5f* 5m² 5.1g² 5d* Sep 19] fairly useful handicapper:
won at Tipperary in July and the Curragh in September: creditable second at Chester
penultimate start: best at 5f: acts on firm and good to soft going: tried blinkered.
P. F. O'Donnell, Ireland

LONGHILL TIGER 3 b.c. Tiger Hill (IRE) 127 – Lauren (GER) (Lightning (FR) **83**
129) [2006 10f² 11.5m⁶ 10d⁵ Oct 4] strong colt: half-brother to several winners in
Germany, including listed winners Lisieux (at 1m, by Sternkonig) and Laurel (at 11f, by
Goofalik): dam German 1m (including at 2 yrs) and 11f winner: best effort in maidens
when second to Virtuosity at Pontefract: stays 1¼m: acts on firm going. *G. G. Margarson*

LONGING FOR CINDY (USA) 4 ch.f. Belong To Me (USA) – I C Cindy (USA) **49**
(Gallapiat (USA) 119) [2006 58: f12g p9.5g⁶ p10g p10g 17.2m Jul 8] lengthy filly: poor
maiden: stays 9.7f: acts on polytrack and good to firm ground: sometimes wears headgear. *W. M. Brisbourne*

LONGQUAN (IRE) 2 b.g. (Mar 23) Invincible Spirit (IRE) 121 – Pipers Pool (IRE) 94 **92**
(Mtoto 134) [2006 5m⁴ 5g² 5.7g³ 6m² 6m* 6g Sep 30] €35,000Y: strong, close-coupled
gelding: half-brother to several winners, including French/US 1m/9f winner Miss Chryss
(by Indian Ridge) and 4-y-o Kinrande, both useful: dam, maiden who stayed 1¼m, closely related to smart middle-distance stayer Pipsted: fairly useful performer: in frame 4
times prior to winning maiden at Haydock by 4 lengths in September: 9/1, mid-field in
24-runner Two-Year-Old Trophy at Redcar final start (gelded after): will prove best kept
to 5f/6f: acts on good/good to firm going. *P. J. Makin*

LONG WEEKEND (IRE) 8 b.g. Flying Spur (AUS) – Friday Night (USA) (Trempo- **–**
lino (USA) 135) [2006 54, a61: p6g Jan 23] sturdy, angular gelding: modest performer:
reportedly bled when well held only outing in 2006: often wears headgear: sometimes
slowly away: none too consistent. *D. Shaw*

LONGY THE LASH 3 b.g. Contract Law (USA) 108 – Hello Hobson's (IRE) 67 (Fay- **–**
ruz 116) [2006 5f 5.9g 8.1m Aug 10] sturdy gelding: no sign of ability. *K. G. Reveley*

LOOK AGAIN 5 ch.g. Zilzal (USA) 137 – Last Look (Rainbow Quest (USA) 134) **98**
[2006 98: 8.1m⁶ 9m² 10.4d² 10.1g² Jun 2] rather leggy gelding: useful handicapper: good
efforts when close second last 3 starts, behind Star of Light at Newmarket (unlucky), Blue
Spinnaker at York and Chancellor at Epsom: free-going sort, seems best around 1¼m:
acts on good to firm and good to soft going. *R. A. Fahey*

LOOK AT THE STARS (IRE) 4 b.g. Bachir (IRE) 118 – Pizzazz 47 (Unfuwain **60**
(USA) 131) [2006 54d: p8.6g⁴ p9.5g⁴ f11g³ p9.5g p9.5g⁵ p9.5g p9.5g Mar 20] neat gelding: modest performer: stays 9.5f: acts on polytrack, raced on good/good to firm ground
on turf: tried visored/tongue tied, often blinkered. *R. Hollinshead*

LOOKER 3 b.f. Barathea (IRE) 127 – Last Look (Rainbow Quest (USA) 134) [2006 75: **71**
10.2s³ 9.9m 9.9g 9.9d* 10d Oct 10] leggy filly: fair performer: won claimer at Salisbury
(left R. Beckett) in September: stays 1¼m: acts on soft going: races prominently: sometimes finds little. *J. Gallagher*

LOOK HERE'S MAY 4 b.f. Revoque (IRE) 122 – Where's Carol 67 (Anfield 117) –
[2006 –: 6d f8g 7.1m⁵ 7.1g 6f 5d Aug 31] tall filly: little sign of ability. *R. Hollinshead*

LOOKING GREAT (USA) 4 b.g. Gulch (USA) – Shoofha (IRE) 70 (Bluebird (USA) –
125) [2006 40: p16g May 8] poor maiden: well held only Flat outing in 2006: tried blinkered. *R. F. Johnson Houghton*

LOOK NO MORE 5 ch.g. First Trump 118 – Jadebelle 66 (Beldale Flutter (USA) –
130) [2006 f11g Mar 14] maiden: tailed off in banded race only run on Flat since 2003.
W. G. M. Turner

LOOK OF EAGLES 4 b.f. Fraam 114 – Dreamtime Quest (Blakeney 126) [2006 66, **a71**
a78: p7g p6g⁶ p7g f6g⁵ p6g⁵ p7g f8g³ Dec 27] fair handicapper: likely to prove best up to
7f: acts on all-weather and firm going: blinkered (well held) on reappearance. *P. F. I. Cole*

LOOKS COULD KILL (USA) 4 b. or br.g. Red Ransom (USA) – Mingling Glances **85 §**
(USA) 106 (Woodman (USA) 126) [2006 91: 7.2g 6m 7g³ 6m 6f⁵ 7m 7d⁶ 7m 7.1s 6d Sep
15] good-topped gelding: fairly useful handicapper: effective at 5f to 1m: acts on polytrack, soft and good to firm going: tried in blinkers/cheekpieces, usually tongue tied in
2005: sometimes sweats: often slowly away: held up: tends to find little. *E. J. Alston*

LOOKS THE BUSINESS (IRE) 5 b.g. Marju (IRE) 127 – Business Centre (IRE) 58 **69**
(Digamist (USA) 110) [2006 71: 11m² 11.5f* 11.6f³ 11.6g³ 9.7f Sep 18] workmanlike
gelding: fair performer: won apprentice handicap at Yarmouth in July: stays 1½m: acts
on polytrack and firm going: often wore cheekpieces at 4 yrs: tongue tied in 2003/4.
W. G. M. Turner

LOOK WHO'S DANCING 2 ch.f. (May 1) Observatory (USA) 131 – Dust Dancer **69**
116 (Suave Dancer (USA) 136) [2006 6m 7m⁶ 7d⁵ 8m 7d Oct 3] quite good-topped filly:
half-sister to 3 winners, including smart 7f (at 2 yrs) to 9f (in USA) winner Spotlight (by
Dr Fong) and useful 2001 2-y-o 7f winner Dusty Answer (by Zafonic): dam, 7f to 1½m
winner (including 1¼m Prix de la Nonette), half-sister to very smart performer up to 1½m
Zimzalabim: fair maiden: little impact in nurseries: should stay at least 1m: sold 41,000
gns. *J. L. Dunlop*

LOOSE CANON 2 b.f. (Mar 13) Josr Algarhoud (IRE) 118 – Trust In Paula (USA) 54 –
(Arazi (USA) 135) [2006 7f 6m p7g Sep 5] first foal: dam untrustworthy 1½m winner: no
form in maidens. *Mrs C. A. Dunnett*

LOPINOT (IRE) 3 br.g. Pursuit of Love 124 – La Suquet 72 (Puissance 110) [2006 **80**
66?: 8g p8g² p8g² Dec 16] robust gelding: fairly useful maiden: left B. Meehan after reappearance: good second at Kempton last 2 starts, in handicap latterly: stays 1m: acts on
polytrack. *P. J. Makin*

LORD ADMIRAL (USA) 5 b.h. El Prado (IRE) 119 – Lady Ilsley (USA) (Trem- **115**
polino (USA) 135) [2006 114: 8g² 8.9m² 8d³ 10.5v³ 8m³ 7m² 10g² 10m³ 9f² Nov 3]
rather leggy, close-coupled, quite attractive horse: smart performer: placed all 10 starts in
2006, including in Group 2 events won by Linngari and Touch of Land at Nad Al Sheba
first 2 outings, Ballycorus Stakes at Leopardstown (1½ lengths second to An Tadh) sixth
start and Meld Stakes at same course (didn't look to be putting it all in after struck by
winner's whip when 2 lengths second to Heliostatic) next time: ran well last 2 outings
when 1½ lengths third to Aragorn in Grade 2 Oak Tree Breeders' Cup Mile at Santa Anita
and 1½ lengths second to Bayeux in Grade 3 River City Handicap at Churchill Downs
(blinkered): has form up to 13f, best efforts at 1m to 1¼m: acts on firm and good to soft
going: has worn crossed noseband: consistent but hard to win with. *Charles O'Brien,
Ireland*

LORD ADONIS (IRE) 3 b.g. Galileo (IRE) 134 – Flaming June (USA) 69 (Storm –
Bird (CAN) 134) [2006 –: f12g⁵ 11.9g 14.1d 9.1v Oct 9] good-bodied gelding: little
form: left M. Attwater after third start: tried tongue tied: fair form in juvenile hurdles.
K. J. Burke

LORD BLUE BOY 2 gr.g. (Apr 29) Atraf 116 – Flair Lady 55 (Chilibang 120) [2006 **51**
5g⁶ 5g⁵ 5m³ 5f 5.3m p5.1g Sep 30] tall, lengthy gelding: modest maiden, raced mainly in
sellers: tried blinkered. *W. G. M. Turner*

LORD CHAMBERLAIN 13 b.g. Be My Chief (USA) 122 – Metaphysique (FR) **68**
(Law Society (USA) 130) [2006 65, a73: p7.1g³ p7.1g⁴ p9.5g³ p9.5g p7.1g* p8.6g² p8g⁴ **a74**

8.1g 7m* 8.1f³ p8g⁶ 8.1g 7f 8m 8.1m Aug 10] big gelding: fair performer: won handicaps at Wolverhampton in April and Brighton in May: effective at 7f to easy 9.5f: acts on all-weather and any turf going: blinkered: sometimes slowly away: usually held up: tough. *J. M. Bradley*

LORD CHARLES 2 b.g. (Mar 30) Atraf 116 – Just Run (IRE) 45 (Runnett 125) [2006 **86** p5g* 5g² 5.1m⁴ 5d² 6m⁶ 5m 5s p6g Oct 11] big, lengthy gelding: half-brother to several winners, including 1995 2-y-o 5f winner Just Lady (by Emarati) and 6f (at 2 yrs) to 1m winner Lady Mo (by Young Ern): dam ran twice: fairly useful performer: won maiden at Lingfield in April: best efforts when runner-up in minor events at Newmarket and Windsor second/fourth starts: mostly well held after: best at 5f: acts on polytrack and good to soft going: sold 20,000 gns. *W. G. M. Turner*

LORD CONYERS (IRE) 7 b.m. Inzar (USA) 112 – Primelta 55 (Primo Dominie 121) – [2006 57d: p7.1g p6g 7m f7g Dec 9] leggy mare: modest at best: no form in 2006: tried in headgear. *G. Woodward*

LORD DU SUD (FR) 5 gr.h. Linamix (FR) 127 – Marseillaise (FR) (Esprit du Nord **116** (USA) 126) [2006 116: 12.5s* 15.5v* 15.5d² 15s* 15.5g⁴ Oct 22] leggy, angular horse: fifth foal: half-brother to several winners in France, including useful 1m (at 2 yrs) to 13f winner Escuchasme (by Green Tune): dam French 5f (at 2 yrs) to 1¼m winner: smart performer: won Prix Hocquart at Longchamp in 2004 and listed races at Nantes and Toulouse late in 2005: in good form again in 2006, winning listed races at Cagnes-sur-Mer in February and Saint-Cloud in April and Darley Prix Kergorlay at Deauville (made all again, easily beating Policy Maker 5 lengths) in August: creditable efforts at Longchamp other starts when 2½ lengths second to Petite Speciale in Prix de Barbeville and 2 lengths fourth to Montare in Prix Royal-Oak: should stay beyond 2m: acts on heavy going: has worn cheekpieces: usually makes running. *J-C. Rouget, France*

LORD LAHAR 7 b.g. Fraam 114 – Brigadiers Bird (IRE) (Mujadil (USA) 119) [2006 **45** 56: f8g⁶ Jan 24] poor performer: stays 13f: acts on polytrack, firm and good to soft going: often wears cheekpieces. *M. A. Buckley*

LORD LAING (USA) 3 br.g. Chester House (USA) 123 – Johanna Keene (USA) **64** (Raise A Cup (USA)) [2006 64p: p10g 8m 10m p12g⁴ Dec 16] modest maiden handicapper: stays 1½m: acts on polytrack, well held both turf starts. *H. J. Collingridge*

LORD LINKS (IRE) 5 ch.g. Daggers Drawn (USA) 114 – Lady From Limerick (IRE) **57** 61 (Rainbows For Life (CAN)) [2006 91: f8g f8g⁶ f7g p6g p6g Apr 1] strong, workman-like gelding: modest handicapper nowadays: stays 9f: acts on soft and good to firm going: tried blinkered (raced freely). *D. J. Daly*

LORD MAYFAIR (USA) 4 b. or br.g. Silic (FR) 125 – Spring Wedding (USA) **65** (Prized (USA)) [2006 50: 6g f6g³ 5.9g 5.1g⁴ 5.3m⁵ 5f⁵ 5f 6f* 7m Jul 12] quite good-topped gelding: fair performer: won maiden at Catterick in July: was best at 5f/6f: acted on firm and good to soft going: blinkered at 4 yrs: dead. *Miss A. Stokell*

LORD MAYOR 5 b.g. Machiavellian (USA) 123 – Misleading Lady (Warning 136) **96 d** [2006 106: p8g 9.8d⁵ 10.1g 8f 7m 7g p10g 5g⁴ 6m 6d 8d 9g Sep 12] quite good-topped gelding: useful performer: on downgrade and well below best most outings in 2006: reportedly finished lame final start (claimed £6,000 after): stays 1¼m: acts on polytrack, firm and soft going: wore cheekpieces final outing. *R. M. H. Cowell*

LORD OF ADVENTURE (IRE) 4 b.g. Inzar (USA) 112 – Highly Fashionable – (IRE) 68 (Polish Precedent (USA) 131) [2006 66d: p16g Feb 28] maiden: well held only Flat outing in 2006: tried in headgear. *Mrs L. C. Jewell*

LORD OF BEAUTY (FR) 6 ch.g. Medaaly 114 – Arctic Beauty (USA) (Arctic Tern – (USA) 126) [2006 p9.5g p12.2g⁶ Nov 18] useful performer up to 1½m in France for H-A. Pantall at 2/3 yrs: well beaten both Flat outings in Britain: fairly useful over hurdles, winner in December. *Noel T. Chance*

LORD OF DREAMS (IRE) 4 ch.c. Barathea (IRE) 127 – The Multiyorker (IRE) 72 **73** (Digamist (USA) 110) [2006 73: p7.1g⁶ p8.6g⁵ f8g p9.5g* p9.5g* 10.2d 8d p8.6g p8.6g 8.1m p8.6g p9.5m⁵ p10g p12.2g Nov 6] strong colt: fair handicapper: won at Wolverhampton in March and April: stays easy 1¼m: acts on polytrack and soft going, seemingly not on firmer than good: tried in cheekpieces. *D. W. P. Arbuthnot*

LORD OF ENGLAND (GER) 3 ch.c. Dashing Blade 117 – Loveria (Los Santos **119** (FR)) [2006 98: 8.5s² 8g³ 8.8m* 10g* Jul 30] half-brother to several winners in Germany, including useful stayer Loriango (by Acatenango): dam, German 2-y-o 6.5f winner, half-sister to Deutsches Derby winner Lagunas and very smart German miler Lirung: smart performer: successful at 2 yrs in newcomers race and listed event at Milan: improved in

2006, 1¼ lengths third to Royal Power in Mehl-Mulhens-Rennen at Cologne before winning Grosser Preis der Wirtschaft at Dortmund (by 3½ lengths from Lazio) in June and Grosser Dallmayr-Preis at Munich (slowly-run race, by length from Laverock) in July: stayed 1¼m: acted on soft and good to firm ground: retired after suffering tendon injury, and to stand at Gestut Etzean, Germany, fee €3,000. *M. Hofer, Germany*

LORD OF METHLEY 7 gr.g. Zilzal (USA) 137 – Paradise Waters 73 (Celestial Storm (USA) 132) [2006 p12.2f⁶ Aug 14] leggy, good-topped gelding: modest performer in 2004: unraced on Flat at 6 yrs: tongue tied, showed little only Flat outing in 2006: usually wears headgear. *S. Lycett* —

LORD OF THE EAST 7 b.g. Emarati (USA) 74 – Fairy Free (Rousillon (USA) 133) [2006 97, a74: p7.1g 7g 7m³ 7.1m 7.2g 7m² 7g⁶ 7m 7.2m p7.1f² 7m 7.6g Aug 26] lengthy gelding: fairly useful handicapper, better on turf than all-weather: unseated rider to post, pulled up after repeatedly bucking on ninth start: stays 7.2f: acts on polytrack, firm and soft going: tried tongue tied/blinkered/in cheekpieces (not since 2003): usually makes running: inconsistent: temperamental. *I. W. McInnes* **89 §** **a81 §**

LORD OROKO 2 ch.g. (Apr 15) Lord of Men 116 – Wannaplantatree 72 (Niniski (USA) 125) [2006 8.1d⁴ f8g⁴ p9.5g² p8.6g² Dec 27] rather leggy, quite attractive gelding: fourth foal: half-brother to 3 winners, including fairly useful 11f/1½m winner Aker Wood (by Bin Ajwaad) and 1¾m winner/smart hurdler Blazing Bailey (by Mister Baileys): dam 1¾m/2m winner: fair form in maidens: second twice at Wolverhampton: will be suited by 1½m. *K. A. Ryan* **72**

LORD ORPHEUS 2 b.g. (Apr 2) Auction House (USA) 120 – Lady of The Realm (Prince Daniel (USA)) [2006 7d 6s 6m Sep 10] tall, close-coupled, useful-looking gelding: no show in maidens (gelded after). *B. W. Hills* —

LORD RAFFLES 4 b.g. Zafonic (USA) 130 – Dawna 106 (Polish Precedent (USA) 131) [2006 p9.5g p12g p12g³ Mar 6] modest maiden: stays easy 1½m: raced only on polytrack: tried visored. *P. R. Webber* **58**

LORDSHIP (IRE) 2 b.g. (Mar 17) King's Best (USA) 132 – Rahika Rose 91 (Unfuwain (USA) 131) [2006 6.1m p7g 8m Sep 9] modest form in maidens: sold 8,000 gns. *M. A. Jarvis* **59**

LORDSWOOD (IRE) 2 b.c. (Feb 1) Mark of Esteem (IRE) 137 – Dinwood (Charnwood Forest (IRE) 125) [2006 6g 6m p7g* p7g³ Dec 4] rangy colt: first foal: dam unraced out of half-sister to winners up to 7f So Factual (very smart performer) and Bold Fact (smart): fair form: won claimer at Lingfield in November: creditable third in nursery there: stays 7f. *A. M. Balding* **67**

LORD THEO 2 b.g. (Mar 23) Averti (IRE) 117 – Love You Too 88 (Be My Chief (USA) 122) [2006 5f p6g³ 6m* Jul 17] first foal: dam, 6f (including at 2 yrs)/7f winner who became temperamental: fairly useful form in maidens: third to Not For Me at Wolverhampton prior to winning at Windsor in July: likely to stay 7f. *D. K. Ivory* **84**

LORENA WOOD (USA) 2 ch.f. (Jan 28) Woodman (USA) 126 – Vilikaia (USA) 125 (Nureyev (USA) 131) [2006 5d⁴ 5.1g³ 6d⁴ Sep 26] $90,000Y: strong, well-made filly: sister to 7-y-o Compton Dragon, closely related to useful 7f (including at 2 yrs)/1m (in UAE) winner Vilayet (by Machiavellian) and half-sister to several winners: dam, effective from 5f to 1m: fairly useful form: off 3 months, won maiden at Goodwood by head from Gentle Guru: will probably stay 7f/1m: sent to USA. *B. J. Meehan* **81**

LORIINAE 3 b.f. Generous (IRE) 139 – Courtain (USA) (Diesis 133) [2006 9.7f³ 9.9g 10m⁵ May 31] third foal: half-sister to winner in Russia by Mark of Esteem: dam unraced out of half-sister to very smart performer around 7f Condrillac: poor form in maidens/seller: has been slowly away. *T. G. Mills* **45**

LORIKEET 7 b.g. Rainbow Quest (USA) 134 – Destiny Dance (USA) 100 (Nijinsky (CAN) 138) [2006 74: p10g p12g p12g Nov 13] ex-Irish gelding: fair handicapper: won at Fairyhouse in 2004: left M. Halford and off nearly 14 months, well held in 2006: stays 2m: acts on firm ground: tried in cheekpieces/blinkers. *Noel T. Chance* —

LOS CABOS (IRE) 3 b.g. Mozart (IRE) 131 – Limelighting (USA) 107 (Alleged (USA) 138) [2006 79: p10g⁶ 14.1f² 14m⁶ 14.1d⁴ p16g⁵ Sep 2] close-coupled, attractive gelding: fairly useful handicapper: best effort when second at Nottingham: stays 1¾m (possibly not 2m): acts on firm and good to soft ground, probably polytrack: sold 62,000 gns, then gelded. *J. H. M. Gosden* **88**

LOS CRISTIANOS 2 b.f. (May 2) Atraf 116 – Portite Sophie 54 (Doulab (USA) 115) [2006 p7.1g Nov 2] fourth foal: dam 8.5f to 11f winner: last in maiden at Wolverhampton. *M. Brittain* —

LOST ALL ALONE 2 b.c. (May 19) Bertolini (USA) 125 – Wandering Stranger 69 – (Petong 126) [2006 p5g p6g p5.1g⁴ Dec 29] 13,500Y: half-brother to 3 winners, including 7f/1m winner Leofric and 1¼m winner Stepastray (both by Alhijaz): dam 6f winner: little form. *D. M. Simcock*

LOST INHERITANCE 2 b.f. (Mar 28) Bertolini (USA) 125 – Jewel (IRE) 64 (Cyr- 44 ano de Bergerac 120) [2006 5g 6f 5g 6d 5d⁵ 6s 5g⁶ Sep 14] 8,000Y: smallish filly: fifth foal: dam, sprint maiden, half-sister to smart 1996 2-y-o 5f/6.5f winner Deadly Dudley: poor maiden. *P. T. Midgley*

LOST IN WONDER (USA) 2 b.f. (Jan 25) Galileo (IRE) 134 – Arutua (USA) (River- 82 p man (USA) 131) [2006 7m 7.5g* 8d Sep 23] good-bodied filly: closely related to use- ful Irish 7f (at 2 yrs) and 1½m winner Juliette (by Sadler's Wells), and half-sister to useful Irish 6f (at 2 yrs) and 1m winner Plato (by Lure) and fairly useful 6f (including at 2 yrs) winner Farha (by Nureyev): dam unraced out of top-class middle-distance mare All Along: fairly useful form: won maiden at Beverley in August: stiff task, last of 8 in Fillies' Mile at Ascot: will be suited by 1¼m/1½m: still looks capable of better. *Sir Michael Stoute*

LOST SOLDIER THREE (IRE) 5 b.g. Barathea (IRE) 127 – Donya 74 (Mill Reef 114 (USA) 141) [2006 115: 12m³ 13.9f³ 13.4g⁵ 16d³ Sep 24] close-coupled gelding: smart performer: creditable efforts when third to Linas Selection in listed handicap at York, fifth to New Guinea in handicap at Chester, and third to easy winner Hawridge Prince in listed event at Ascot last 3 starts: stays 2m: acts on firm and soft going: tried visored: sweated when well below form third 4-y-o outing: usually waited with: sold 75,000 gns, joined D. Nicholls. *L. M. Cumani*

LOTTIE 5 b.m. Robellino (USA) 127 – Montserrat 81 (Aragon 118) [2006 47: 6g⁵ 8.5m 48 7m² 8f f7m⁴ f7g Nov 2] smallish mare: poor maiden: stays 8.5f: acts on fibresand and good to firm going: tried in cheekpieces. *G. Woodward*

LOUGH ARROW (IRE) 3 b.g. Carrowkeel (IRE) 106 – State of Dream (IRE) (Car- – melite House (USA) 118) [2006 –: f7g f6g p5.1g p6g Nov 28] good-bodied gelding: no sign of ability. *P. S. Felgate*

LOUGH BOW (IRE) 8 b.g. Nicolotte 118 – Gale Force Seven (Strong Gale 116) 45 [2006 f14g f11g Jan 24] quite good-topped gelding: modest performer in 2002: lightly raced and little form since: stays 1½m: acts on soft and good to firm going: visored/blinkered nowadays. *M. W. Easterby*

LOUIE LOUIE (IRE) 3 b.c. King Charlemagne (USA) 120 – Rose of Mooncoin 91 (IRE) 99 (Brief Truce (USA) 126) [2006 88: 6g⁴ 8m⁶ 8s 7.1m* 8m⁶ 7m³ 7m³ 7.1m 8.1m⁶ p7g⁵ Oct 21] lengthy, good-topped colt: has a fluent action: fairly useful handicapper: won at Sandown in June: twice good third at Newmarket after: effective at 6f to 1m: acts on polytrack and firm going, seems unsuited by soft: found little fifth start: sold 60,000 gns, then won in Qatar in December. *N. A. Callaghan*

LOUISE DUPIN (IRE) 3 b.f. King of Kings (IRE) 125 – Soubrette (USA) (Opening 56 Verse (USA) 126) [2006 8.2m p7g 7.1m⁶ 8.2m 9.9m 10.2m p9.5g⁵ 11.5d Oct 18] €30,000Y: strong filly: second foal: half-sister to French 2004 2-y-o 1m winner Aldo L'Argentin (by Anabaa): dam unraced out of US Grade 2 9f winner Dame Mysterieuse: modest maiden: stays 1¼m (seemingly not 11.5f): acts on polytrack and good to firm going. *R. M. Beckett*

LOUISIADE (IRE) 5 b.g. Tagula (IRE) 116 – Titchwell Lass 57 (Lead On Time (USA) 57 123) [2006 72: p6g⁶ p7g⁴ p7g p8.6g⁶ 7g 6m⁴ 6d f8g² f7g³ p7g⁵ f8g² Dec 28] strong, a71 lengthy gelding: fair on all-weather, modest on turf: effective at 6f to 1m: acts on all-weather and firm ground: tried in blinkers/cheekpieces: none too consistent. *K. A. Ryan*

LOULWA (IRE) 2 b.f. (Apr 15) Montjeu (IRE) 137 – Refined (IRE) 95 (Statoblest 120) 82 p [2006 p7g² Oct 21] 370,000Y: fourth foal: half-sister to smart 6f (at 2 yrs)/7f winner Galeota and 2003 2-y-o 5f winner Vermillionn (both by Mujadil), and 3-y-o Lady Livius: dam, 2-y-o 5f winner, half-sister to smart 7f/1m performer Pipe Major: 5/1, shaped well when 2½ lengths second to Cast In Gold in maiden at Lingfield, slowly away but run- ning on strongly for hand riding: will be suited by 1m: sure to improve and win races. *J. Noseda*

LOUPHOLE 4 ch.g. Loup Sauvage (USA) 125 – Goodwood Lass (IRE) 71 (Alzao 77 (USA) 117) [2006 85: p7.1g⁴ p6g² p6g p6g 5.5d³ 6g³ 6f³ 5.7m* 6g² 6f* p6g² Dec 19] close-coupled gelding: fair handicapper: won at Bath in June and Leicester in July: has form at easy 1m, better at shorter: acts on polytrack and firm going: reliable. *P. J. Makin*

LOUP SIFFLET (IRE) 4 b.g. Loup Sauvage (USA) 125 – Bee-Bee-Gee (IRE) (Lake – Coniston (IRE) 131) [2006 53: p10g 8.2s May 20] modest maiden at 3 yrs: well held in 2006. *R. A. Fahey*

LOURDES (IRE) 3 b.f. Spectrum (IRE) 126 – Loure (USA) 66 (Lyphard (USA) 132) – [2006 f11g Jul 7] half-sister to several winners, notably smart 7f (at 2 yrs) to 1¼m winner Entice (by Selkirk): dam, ran 3 times, half-sister to Royal Lodge winner Royal Kingdom and to dam of high-class Japanese 1m/1¼m performer Agnes Digital: 8/1, well beaten in maiden at Southwell, not knocked about. *J. R. Fanshawe*

LOUVE HEUREUSE (IRE) 5 ch.m. Peintre Celebre (USA) 137 – Louve Sereine **54** (FR) 70 (Sadler's Wells (USA) 132) [2006 62: f8g 10.2g³ 8f 10.9f 9.7f p10g p10g p10g³ f11g⁶ Dec 28] modest performer: claimed from J. Boyle after second start: stays 11f: acts on all-weather and any turf going. *B. G. Powell*

LOVE ACADEMY 11 b.g. Royal Academy (USA) 130 – Quiet Week-End 99 (Town **44** And Country 124) [2006 f7g p8g 7.6g f14g p7g p8g Dec 15] leggy, good-topped gelding: one-time fairly useful handicapper, raced in Ireland in 1999 to 2002: missed next 3 years: ran only in Britain in 2006, showing poor form: stays 1½m: acts on all-weather, firm and soft going: sometimes blinkered. *Luke Comer, Ireland*

LOVE ALWAYS 4 b.f. Piccolo 121 – Lady Isabell 62 (Rambo Dancer (CAN) 107) **81** [2006 78: 11.7d 10m⁵ 12m* 11.6f 14m 11.9f⁴ 11.8g² 11.7f³ 12m 14.1d³ Sep 27] tall, attractive filly: fairly useful handicapper: won at Salisbury in June: barely stays 1¾m: acts on firm and good to soft going. *S. Dow*

LOVE AND AFFECTION 3 b.g. Groom Dancer (USA) 128 – Fox Star (IRE) 61 – (Foxhound (USA) 103) [2006 p9.5g p9.5g p10g⁶ Dec 2] well held in maidens: said to have had breathing problem second outing: tongue tied next time. *P. S. McEntee*

LOVE ANGEL (USA) 4 b. or br.g. Woodman (USA) 126 – Omnia (USA) 85 (Green **68** Dancer (USA) 132) [2006 80: p12g 10.9g 11g 10.2d⁶ 12g 14m p16g 14m 11.6g⁴ 11m⁵ Aug 19] good-topped gelding: fair performer nowadays: stays 11.5f: acts on any going: tried blinkered/visored: won over hurdles in September/November. *J. J. Bridger*

LOVE BEAUTY (USA) 4 b.g. Seeking The Gold (USA) – Heavenly Rhythm (USA) **?** (Septieme Ciel (USA) 123) [2006 77: 15d a9.8g⁶ a11.5g³ a12.5g a16g⁵ Dec 31] big, leggy gelding: has a quick action: fair maiden at best: below form in 2006, leaving M. Harris after reappearance: stays 1½m: acts on firm and soft going: has looked none too keen: blinkered on reappearance. *C. Von Der Recke, Germany*

LOVE BROTHERS 2 b.g. (Mar 3) Lomitas 129 – Morning Queen (GER) (Konigs- **76** stuhl (GER)) [2006 7g 7.1m 7m⁶ 8.1v³ 8g 10g* 8.3d Oct 9] 32,000Y: rangy gelding: seventh foal: half-brother to 1m (in France at 2 yrs) to 11.5f (in Switzerland) winner Moonrise (by Grand Lodge): dam, German 1m winner, sister to very smart German 1½m performer Monsun: fair performer: won nursery at Nottingham in September: will stay 1½m: acts on heavy and good to firm going: gelded after final start. *M. R. Channon*

LOVE DUBAI (USA) 2 b. or br.c. (Feb 10) E Dubai (USA) 124 – Omnia (USA) 85 **94** (Green Dancer (USA) 132) [2006 6d³ 6s² 7.1d⁴ 6s p7.1g p8.6g* p9.5s* Dec 14] $47,000F: close-coupled, useful-looking colt: closely related to 2 winners, including 4-y-o Love Angel and half-brother to 2 winners in USA: dam, 7f winner, half-sister to smart performer up to 1m Firm Pledge: fairly useful performer: third to La Presse in maiden at York on debut: back near that form when winning nurseries at Wolverhampton in November and December, racing lazily in latter: stays 9.5f: acts on polytrack, raced on going softer than good on turf. *M. Johnston*

LOVE IN MAY (IRE) 2 ch.f. (Feb 3) City On A Hill (USA) 114 – May Hinton 82 **78** (Main Reef 126) [2006 p5g* 5g 7.5f⁴ 6f⁴ p6s* p7.1g² p7.1g⁴ Dec 29] €3,000Y: strong, useful-looking filly: half-sister to 3 winners, including fairly useful 1994 2-y-o 5f winner Hinton Rock (by Ballad Rock), later successful in Belgium, and 1m winner Hint of Victory (by Ron's Victory): dam 2-y-o 6f winner: fair performer: won minor event at Lingfield in March and nursery at Wolverhampton in December: best at 5f/6f: acts on polytrack. *J. S. Moore*

LOVELACE 2 b.c. (Feb 10) Royal Applause 124 – Loveleaves 93 (Polar Falcon (USA) **80** 126) [2006 5d* Apr 21] 16,000F, 76,000Y: tall colt: has scope: first foal: dam, lightly-raced 1m winner, out of half-sister to useful 2-y-o sprinters Maid For Walking and Maid For The Hills: 11/2, overcame inexperience (hung markedly left) to win minor event at Thirsk in April: looked sure to improve. *M. Johnston*

LOVELY HIDENKA (USA) 3 b.f. Fusaichi Pegasus (USA) 130 – Eliza (USA) 118 **58** (Mt Livermore (USA)) [2006 47: f8g² 10m 11.5m Jun 7] quite good-topped filly: modest maiden: should stay 1½m: acts on fibresand: sold 100,000 gns in July, sent to USA. *C. E. Brittain*

LOVE ON SIGHT 2 b.f. (Mar 23) Beat Hollow 126 – Greek Dream (USA) 79 (Distant **93** View (USA) 126) [2006 6m³ 6m⁶ 7d⁶ Aug 13] 13,000Y: deep-girthed filly: second foal: dam, 7f winner, out of very smart performer up to 13.5f Wandesta: fairly useful form: clearly best effort when 2¾ lengths sixth of 10 to Scarlet Runner in Princess Margaret Stakes at Ascot: odds-on defeat back in maiden final start: should stay 1m. *A. P. Jarvis*

LOVE ON THE ROCKS 2 b.c. (Feb 21) Hernando (FR) 127 – Indian Love Bird **68** (Efisio 120) [2006 7m 8.1v² 10d Oct 21] leggy, workmanlike colt: first foal: dam unraced sister to smart 6f/7f performer Tomba and half-sister to Prix du Jockey Club winner Holding Court (by Hernando): fair maiden: second to Striving Storm at Haydock: probably stays 1¼m: sold 8,000 gns, sent to Holland. *K. A. Ryan*

LOVE OR MONEY 3 b.f. In The Wings 128 – Lafite 100 (Robellino (USA) 127) **–** [2006 p10g Jul 5] second foal: dam, 1m/1¼m winner, half-sister to very smart 1¼m/ 1½m performer Imperial Dancer: 16/1 and green, not knocked about in rear in maiden at Kempton. *W. J. Haggas*

LOVE RIDOT (IRE) 3 b.f. Fruits of Love (USA) 127 – Ridotto (Salse (USA) 128) **80** [2006 6m³ 5.8f⁴ 6d p10g⁴ Dec 30] second foal: half-brother to useful 2004 2-y-o 5f winner Salsa Brava (by Almutawakel): dam lightly raced in France: fairly useful maiden: easily best effort at the Curragh on debut: left D. O'Gorman in Ireland before final start: will be suited by 1½m. *M. Johnston*

LOVERS KISS 2 b.f. (Mar 31) Night Shift (USA) – Evening Promise 108 (Aragon **52** 118) [2006 5m 5g 5s³ 6f⁵ 5g⁶ f5g⁴ 6v 6s⁴ p9.5g f6g* f7g⁴ p6s f6g Dec 23] 10,000Y: good-topped filly: third foal: dam, 2-y-o 6f winner, later won up to 1m in USA (including Grade 3 6.5f events): modest performer: won claimer at Southwell in November: stays 7f: acts on fibresand and soft going: sometimes wears blinkers, including at Southwell: none too consistent. *N. Wilson*

LOVES BIDDING 2 b.c. (Mar 31) Auction House (USA) 120 – Charlottevalentina **73** (IRE) 80 (Perugino (USA) 84) [2006 p5g⁴ 5.1g 6m⁵ 5.1g⁴ 5m 5.2f* 5m Aug 11] small, close-coupled colt: second foal: dam 2-y-o 6f winner: fair performer: won maiden at Yarmouth in July: sometimes highly tried, including when fifth of 6 to Sadeek in listed race at Epsom third start: may prove best at 5f: acts on firm going. *R. Ingram*

LOVE'S DESIGN (IRE) 9 b. or br.g. Pursuit of Love 124 – Cephista 61 (Shirley **54** Heights 130) [2006 42: p8g p7g 8f² 10m⁶ 8f Jul 9] modest performer: best at 7f to 8.5f: **a–** acts on all-weather, firm and good going: often wears headgear: often finds little. *Miss J. Feilden*

LOVES TRAVELLING (IRE) 6 b.g. Blues Traveller (IRE) 119 – Fast Love (IRE) **70** (Second Set (IRE) 127) [2006 80: 12m 9.9g 15.8g Jun 2] rather leggy gelding: fair handicapper nowadays: stays 1½m: acts on polytrack, firm and good to soft going: tried tongue tied: held up. *N. Wilson*

LOVE THIRTY 4 b.f. Mister Baileys 123 – Polished Up 51 (Polish Precedent (USA) **91 d** 131) [2006 93: 8g 8g 7d p8g Sep 18] leggy filly: fairly useful performer at best: well held after reappearance: stays at least 7f: acts on good to firm and good to soft ground: sold 29,000 gns. *M. R. Channon*

LOVE YOU ALWAYS (USA) 6 ch.g. Woodman (USA) 126 – Encorenous (USA) **63** (Diesis 133) [2006 63: p13.9g p10g f8g 12d 10m⁵ 10g⁴ 12.6m³ 10g 10.1m 9m² 12s p13.9g p10g p8g⁶ Dec 10] lengthy gelding: modest performer nowadays: brought down eleventh outing: stays 12.6f: acts on good to firm going: tongue tied nowadays: has shown signs of temperament. *Miss J. Feilden*

LOVINGLY 3 b.f. Grand Lodge (USA) 125 – Easy To Love (USA) 86 (Diesis 133) **–** [2006 –p: p10g Jul 5] useful-looking filly: well beaten in maidens. *W. Jarvis*

LOW CLOUD 6 b.g. Danehill (USA) 126 – Raincloud (Rainbow Quest (USA) 134) **70** [2006 74: p9.5g⁵ 9.8m Jun 21] useful-looking gelding: fair handicapper: stays 1¼m: acts on polytrack, firm and good to soft going: often visored/in cheekpieces. *J. J. Quinn*

LOWE GO 6 b.g. First Trump 118 – Hotel California (IRE) 58 (Last Tycoon 131) [2006 **–** 17.2s Apr 11] sparely-made gelding: maiden: well held only outing on Flat since 2003: tried in cheekpieces. *Miss J. S. Davis*

LOWESTOFT PLAYBOY 4 ch.g. Pivotal 124 – Red Typhoon 75 (Belfort (FR) 89) **72** [2006 67: p8g² p8g² p7g⁴ p10g* p8.6g² p10g⁵ Mar 2] leggy gelding: fair handicapper:

won at Lingfield in February: stays easy 1¼m: acts on polytrack and good to firm going. *J. Jay*

LOWICZ 4 b.f. Polish Precedent (USA) 131 – Eldina (Distant Relative 128) [2006 41: 8.3m Jul 14] poor maiden: well held only outing on Flat in 2006. *D. Carroll* —

LOYAL FRIEND (IRE) 3 ch.g. Docksider (USA) 124 – Spartan Girl (IRE) 91 (Ela-Mana-Mou 132) [2006 p7g Mar 17] 16/1, tailed off in maiden at Lingfield, slowly away. *Niall Moran, Ireland* —

LOYAL ROYAL (IRE) 3 b.c. King Charlemagne (USA) 120 – Supportive (IRE) (Nashamaa 113) [2006 89: 7g⁵ 6f* 6d⁴ 6s 6m⁶ 7g 6m⁵ Sep 3] tall colt: useful performer: won maiden at Salisbury (by 6 lengths, hanging and flashing tail) in May: good fourth to Kingsgate Prince in listed race at Newbury next time: likely to prove best at 5f/6f: acts on firm and good to soft going: free-going sort. *D. R. C. Elsworth* **98**

LOYAL TYCOON (IRE) 8 br.g. Royal Abjar (USA) 121 – Rosy Lydgate 53 (Last Tycoon 131) [2006 91: 6g⁶ p5.1g⁶ p6g Dec 20] robust, close-coupled gelding: just fair handicapper in 2006: effective at 6f/7f: acts on all-weather, firm and soft going: tried visored/blinkered: effective held up or making running. *D. K. Ivory* **77**

LOYALTY LODGE (IRE) 4 ch.g. Grand Lodge (USA) 125 – Gaily Grecian (IRE) (Ela-Mana-Mou 132) [2006 –: 7.1f Jun 26] good-topped gelding: has a quick action: lightly-raced maiden: no form since 2 yrs. *M. W. Easterby* —

LUAS LINE (IRE) 4 b.f. Danehill (USA) 126 – Streetcar (IRE) 69 (In The Wings 128) [2006 114: 8m⁴ 8m⁵ 8f³ Jul 1] neat filly: smart performer: ran well when 1¼ lengths fourth to Mustameet in listed race at Leopardstown on reappearance: not discredited after in Windsor Forest Stakes at Royal Ascot (4¾ lengths fifth to Soviet Song) and Grade 3 Cashcall Invitational at Hollywood (2¼ lengths third to Dance In The Mood): best around 1m/9f: acts on firm and good to soft going: has worn crossed noseband. *D. Wachman, Ireland* **115**

LUBERON 3 b.c. Fantastic Light (USA) 134 – Luxurious (USA) (Lyphard (USA) 132) [2006 94: p8g⁵ 10g⁴ 11.6m* 12f* 12m⁵ 12d⁴ 13.4g Aug 26] angular colt: useful performer: won handicaps at Windsor (beat Pevensey 3 lengths) and York (by 2 lengths from Gringo) in July: creditable efforts after when fifth to Sixties Icon in BGC Stakes (Gordon) at Goodwood and seventh to New Guinea in handicap at Chester: stays 13.4f: acts on firm going: usually makes running. *M. Johnston* **109**

LUCAYAN DANCER 6 b.g. Zieten (USA) 118 – Tittle Tattle (IRE) 80 (Soviet Lad (USA)) [2006 85: 7v² 10.1m 7g 11.1m² 9.8v⁶ 10.5g 10.3g* 11.5g² 12d³ 9.9m⁵ 9m* 9.9g 11m⁶ Sep 6] close-coupled gelding: has a markedly round action: fairly useful handicapper: won at Chester in June and Goodwood (apprentice event, beat Diktatorial by short head) in August: stays 1½m: acts on any going: tried in cheekpieces/blinkers at 3 yrs: has flashed tail: has run well when sweating: usually held up. *D. Nicholls* **91**

LUCAYOS 3 ch.g. Bahamian Bounty 116 – Indian Flag (IRE) 39 (Indian Ridge 123) [2006 67, a64: f5g⁴ p6g² f5g* p6g⁶ 5.1g² 5.3f 5.3m* 5m³ 6m⁵ 6d³ 5g⁵ 5f p5.1g p5.1s³ p5.1g⁶ p6g² Dec 28] sturdy gelding: fairly useful handicapper: won at Southwell (hung right) in April and Brighton in June: best at 5f/6f: acts on all-weather, firm and good to firm going: usually blinkered nowadays: often slowly away (all but refused to race twelfth outing, gelded after): one to treat with caution. *Mrs H. Sweeting* **81 §**

LUCEFER (IRE) 8 b.g. Lycius (USA) 124 – Maharani (USA) (Red Ransom (USA)) [2006 52: p12.2g 10m 11.6m Jul 24] leggy gelding: modest performer: well held in 2006: tried blinkered, often tongue tied at 5 yrs: sometimes carries head high. *G. C. H. Chung* —

LUCIDITY LIGHT (IRE) 3 ch.f. Dr Fong (USA) 128 – Moonlight (IRE) 69 (Night Shift (USA)) [2006 63: p8.6g 6.9m 12g Aug 14] workmanlike filly: modest maiden at 2 yrs: well held in handicaps in 2006. *J. D. Bethell* —

LUCIDUS 4 b.g. Danzero (AUS) – Lady In Colour (IRE) 71 (Cadeaux Genereux 131) [2006 –: 8m² p9.5g 10.5g Sep 22] tall, angular gelding: fair maiden: stayed 9.5f: acted on polytrack and good to firm going: dead. *W. J. Haggas* **68**

LUCIFEROUS (USA) 4 ch.f. Devil's Bag (USA) – Vital Laser (USA) (Seeking The Gold (USA)) [2006 54: p7g p10g p7g³ p8.6g p8.6g⁶ 10m 10.2f Jun 17] plain filly: modest maiden: will prove best short of 1m: acts on polytrack and firm going: visored last 5 starts. *P. G. Murphy* **52**

LUCIUS VERRUS (USA) 6 b.g. Danzig (USA) – Magic of Life (USA) 118 (Seattle Slew (USA)) [2006 –, a64: p6g p7.1g* p8.6g⁴ f7g² f8g⁵ f7g p7g p7.1g p8.6g p7g p6g p8g⁴ p7.1g⁶ f7g³ f8g⁶ f8g⁴ Dec 28] fair performer: won handicap at Wolverhampton in **– a67**

January: below form after fifth start: stays 8.6f: acts on all-weather, lightly raced and no recent form on turf: tried blinkered, visored nowadays: sometimes slowly away. *D. Shaw*

LUCK IN RUNNING (USA) 3 b. or br.g. Running Stag (USA) 124 – Mystery Number (USA) (Secret Hello (USA)) [2006 9v⁶ 9.8m⁴ 12.1d⁶ 11.1d⁴ p8.6g² p8g 8.9f Jul 27] $23,000Y, 48,000 2-y-o: big, strong gelding: second foal: half-brother to winner in USA by Lucky Lionel: dam 5f to 6.5f winner in USA: fair maiden: best effort at 8.6f on polytrack: gelded after final start. *M. Johnston* — **75**

LUCKNAM (IRE) 2 b.f. (Apr 18) Namid 128 – Lady Rushmore (IRE) 75 (Fairy King (USA)) [2006 5.1s⁵ 7.1g⁶ 5m Jul 17] 7,000Y: sixth foal: half-sister to 3-y-o Rapsgate and winner in Hong Kong by Marju: dam, Irish maiden, stayed 1½m: little form. *M. Meade* — **–**

LUCKSIN (IRE) 3 b.g. Key of Luck (USA) 126 – Swallowcliffe 83 (Caerleon (USA) 132) [2006 80: 6d² 5m² 5g³ 7g² 6f² 7.1m³ 7f² 5m* 6m⁶ Aug 9] sturdy gelding: fair performer: placed all starts in 2006 prior to winning maiden at Leicester in July: stayed 7f: acted on firm and good to soft going: dead. *N. Tinkler* — **74**

LUCK WILL COME (IRE) 2 b.f. (Mar 11) Desert Style (IRE) 121 – Petite Maxine 70 (Sharpo 132) [2006 p7g² p7g Nov 11] €72,000Y, 50,000 2-y-o: sister to useful 2005 2-y-o 7f winner Under My Thumb and half-sister to 3 winners, including fairly useful 5f (including at 2 yrs)/6f winner Pipadash (by Pips Pride): dam maiden who stayed 7f: much better run in maidens when second to Malaath at Lingfield. *M. J. Wallace* — **70**

LUCKY BAMBLUE (IRE) 3 b.g. Key of Luck (USA) 126 – Bamboo (IRE) (Thatching 131) [2006 –: 11g May 30] no form. *P. C. Haslam* — **–**

LUCKY BEE (IRE) 2 b.f. (Apr 22) Indian Danehill (IRE) 124 – All Laughter (Vision (USA)) [2006 5m³ 5g* 5.1f⁵ 6d Oct 2] €13,000Y: close-coupled filly: sister to a winner in Greece, closely related to 7-y-o Flying Spirit and half-sister to 2 winners, including Irish 9.5f winner Gabby Hayes (by Tirol): dam placed at 7f/1m in Ireland at 2 yrs: fair form: won maiden at Beverley in August, not extended: better than bare result in nursery at Chester next time: should stay at least 6f: acts on firm going, below form on soft final start (hung right). *G. A. Swinbank* — **78**

LUCKY EMERALD (IRE) 4 b.f. Lend A Hand 124 – Anita's Love (IRE) 53 (Anita's Prince 126) [2006 53: p6g p7.1g 7g Jun 13] poor performer nowadays: well held in 2006: tried tongue tied. *B. Palling* — **–**

LUCKY FIND (IRE) 3 b.f. Key of Luck (USA) 126 – Recherchee (Rainbow Quest (USA) 134) [2006 13.8m³ Sep 16] 6,000 3-y-o: half-sister to several winners, including useful 5f (at 2 yrs) to 1m (in France) winner Recondite (by Polish Patriot): dam unraced: 14/1 and green, 3½ lengths third to Tuscany Rose in seller at Catterick. *M. Mullineaux* — **50**

LUCKY LARGO (IRE) 6 b. or br.g. Key of Luck (USA) 126 – Lingering Melody (IRE) 59 (Nordico (USA)) [2006 –§: p8.6g 9.2m 9.2d 8.3m 12f Jun 26] leggy gelding: no longer of any account: usually wears headgear. *D. A. Nolan* — **– §**

LUCKY LARK 3 b.g. Key of Luck (USA) 126 – Meadow Pipit (CAN) 113 (Meadowlake (USA)) [2006 p8.6g* 10s 10v 10.9m³ 11.9f* 12.1f³ 10s 11g 10f⁹ 11v* 11v 11g³ Dec 10] fifth foal: brother to useful 7f winner (including at 2 yrs) Lucky Pipit and half-brother to 2 winners, including 4-y-o Desert Commander: dam 7f to 1¼m winner: fairly useful performer: won maiden at Wolverhampton in March and handicaps at Brighton (by 7 lengths) in July and (after being sold from M. Johnston 21,000 gns following sixth start) Madrid in November: should stay 1¾m: acts on any ground: hung left on debut: carried head high on third start, gelded afterwards. *F. Rodriguez, Spain* — **85**

LUCKY LEO 6 b.g. Muhtarram (USA) 125 – Wrong Bride (Reprimand 122) [2006 81, a–: 11.6m 12.6m² 11.9g² 11m⁵ Jul 21] lengthy gelding: fairly useful handicapper: stays 12.6f: acts on firm and soft going, well held on all-weather: usually held up: reportedly finished lame final start. *Ian Williams* — **81 a–**

LUCKY LIL 4 ch.f. Cadeaux Genereux 131 – Amalia (IRE) 111 (Danehill (USA) 126) [2006 –: 7g 7.2d³ p7.1g 7m f8g Oct 12] sturdy filly: modest maiden: should stay 1m: acts on good to soft ground. *R. M. Whitaker* — **53 a–**

LUCKYLOVER 3 b.c. Key of Luck (USA) 126 – Hang Fire (Marju (IRE) 127) [2006 66: 8.1s⁵ 8.2m* 8m 8m p8g 8m⁴ 8g³ p10g⁴ Dec 20] quite good-topped colt: fair performer: won handicap at Nottingham in May: changed hands 15,500 gns before final outing (tongue tied): stays 1¼m: acts on polytrack, soft and good to firm going. *M. G. Quinlan* — **74**

LUCKY LUCIONI (IRE) 3 b.g. Key of Luck (USA) 126 – Fanny Blankers (IRE) (Persian Heights 129) [2006 83: p10g 5f p7g³ p5.1g a8.8g* a8.7g² 8g³ a8g² Oct 19] fairly useful performer at 2 yrs, winning maiden at Limerick: well below that form in 2006, — **?**

leaving K. Prendergast after reappearance and G. Butler after fourth start: won handicap at Ovrevoll in August: stays 8.8f: acts on polytrack/dirt, soft and good to firm ground. *L. Jarven, Sweden*

LUCKY TERN 3 b.g. Sooty Tern 79 – Miss Money Spider (IRE) 65 (Statoblest 120) [2006 8.2g p8.6g 6.1d Oct 13] small gelding: well beaten in maidens. *J. M. Bradley* –

LUCKY TOKEN (IRE) 3 gr.f. Key of Luck (USA) 126 – Shawanni 105 (Shareef Dancer (USA) 135) [2006 66p: p7g² p8.6g* 8s⁴ 8m² p10g³ Jul 12] close-coupled filly: fair performer: landed odds in maiden at Wolverhampton in March: creditable efforts in frame in handicaps after: dam 2-y-o 1m winner in USA: 33/1 and backward, mid-field in maiden at Newmarket won by Measured Tempo: type to do better. *M. R. Channon* **77**

LUCKY UNO 10 b.g. Rock City 120 – Free Skip 68 (Free State 125) [2006 –§: f8g Jan 31] big gelding: of no account nowadays: tried blinkered. *C. Smith* **– §**

LUCY BABE 3 ch.f. Groom Dancer (USA) 128 – La Puce Volante (Grand Lodge (USA) 125) [2006 10d 8.3m 9.7f⁵ 10.9g⁶ 11.5f 11.5d p11g Dec 22] third foal: dam unraced: poor maiden: stays 10.9f: jinked left and unseated rider at start on debut. *G. Prodromou* **40**

LUCY REBECCA 2 b.f. (Mar 22) Diktat 126 – Crown Water (USA) (Chief's Crown (USA)) [2006 7d Oct 28] 15,000F, 55,000Y: big, strong filly: half-sister to several winners abroad: dam 2-y-o 1m winner in USA: 33/1 and backward, mid-field in maiden at Newmarket won by Measured Tempo: type to do better. *M. R. Channon* **61 p**

LUCYS LADY 3 b.f. Primo Valentino (IRE) 116 – Sandblaster 55 (Most Welcome 131) [2006 57: p6g p5.1g p6g 6d⁵ 6m 8.3d² 8.3d² 7m 8.3m 7m Sep 12] smallish filly: modest performer: barely stays 8.3f: acts on polytrack, good to firm and good to soft going: tried in cheekpieces: none too consistent. *K. R. Burke* **54**

LUDOVICO 3 b.c. Zilzal (USA) 137 – Devastating 70 (Bluebird (USA) 125) [2006 78: p7.1g³ f7g* p7g* p8g 7s p8g p7g p7g* Dec 4] tall colt: useful performer: won handicaps at Southwell in March and Kempton in April, and claimer at Lingfield (blinkered) in December: should stay 1m: acts on all-weather and good to firm ground: often races prominently. *K. A. Ryan* **93**

LUFERTON LANE (IRE) 9 b.m. Ela-Mana-Mou 132 – Saddle 'er Up (IRE) (Sadler's Wells (USA) 132) [2006 12m 16.2g⁶ p13.9g Nov 6] poor performer: missed 2004/5: no form on return. *R. F. Marvin* **–**

LUIS MELENDEZ (USA) 4 ch.g. Horse Chestnut (SAF) 119 – Egoli (USA) 93 (Seeking The Gold (USA)) [2006 68d: p8g⁵ p8g³ p8g 10.2g 10m³ 9g⁵ 10.1f* p8.6g* 10m* 10d p8.6g* Sep 30] strong, good-topped gelding: fairly useful performer: back to near best for new trainer in 2006, winning claimers at Yarmouth and Wolverhampton in July, ladies handicap at Newbury in August, and handicap at Wolverhampton in September: stays 1¼m: acts on polytrack and firm going: tried blinkered/tongue tied: races prominently: stumbled and unseated rider at start fourth outing: sold 17,500 gns, sent to Spain. *T. G. Dascombe* **82**

LUJAIN ROSE 4 b.f. Lujain (USA) 119 – Rose Chime (IRE) 58 (Tirol 127) [2006 53: f12g Jan 19] unfurnished filly: maiden: well held only outing in 2003: tried visored. *N. M. Babbage* **–**

LUKE AFTER ME (IRE) 6 b.g. Victory Note (USA) 120 – Summit Talk (Head For Heights 125) [2006 55§: 7d 7m 7g 6.9f Aug 15] lengthy gelding: ungenuine maiden: well held in 2006: tried in cheekpieces. *Miss Tracy Waggott* **– §**

LULOAH 3 b.f. Mujahid (USA) 125 – Bangles 83 (Chilibang 120) [2006 67: p5g² p6g* p6g f5g³ p6g⁴ f6g⁴ p6g p5.1g⁵ f5g p6g f5g p5.1g p6g p6g Dec 20] modest performer: won apprentice claimer at Lingfield in January: best at 5f/easy 6f: acts on all-weather and good to firm ground: tried in blinkers/cheekpieces: front runner. *P. S. McEntee* **63 d**

LUNA LANDING 3 ch.g. Allied Forces (USA) 123 – Macca Luna (IRE) 78 (Kahyasi 130) [2006 81: 8m³ 8.5f³ 10f⁶ 10m* 10g³ 10m⁴ 12d* 12s 14d Nov 3] close-coupled, good-topped gelding: fairly useful performer: won handicaps at Pontefract in July and Catterick in October: stays 1½m: acts on good to firm and good to soft going: pulled hard sixth outing. *Jedd O'Keeffe* **84**

LUNAR EXIT (IRE) 5 gr.g. Exit To Nowhere (USA) 122 – Moon Magic 62 (Polish Precedent (USA) 131) [2006 p16g⁵ p16g Apr 26] good-bodied gelding: fairly useful performer: unraced on Flat in 2005: much better effort in 2006 on reappearance: probably **87**

stays easy 2m: acts on polytrack and good to firm ground: blinkered/in cheekpieces last 3 starts: tends to hang left: has looked none too keen. *Lady Herries*

LUNAR EXPRESS (USA) 3 b.f. Giant's Causeway (USA) 132 – June Moon (IRE) **88** (Sadler's Wells (USA) 132) [2006 83p: p7g² 8.3g⁶ 7m² p8g³ 8g 7m Aug 27] close-coupled filly: fairly useful handicapper: good efforts when placed in 2006: stays 1m: acts on polytrack, raced only on good/good to firm going on turf. *W. J. Haggas*

LUNAR LANDSCAPE (USA) 3 ch.c. Giant's Causeway (USA) 132 – Melikah **74** (IRE) 116 (Lammtarra (USA) 134) [2006 p10g⁵ 11.9g³ Oct 13] second foal: half-brother to fairly useful 1¼m/11f winner Villarrica (by Selkirk): dam, 1¼m winner and placed in Oaks/Irish Oaks, half-sister to Galileo and Black Sam Bellamy out of Arc winner Urban Sea, herself close relation to King's Best: similar form in maidens at Kempton and Brighton: reared as stall opened on debut: joined S. Seemar in UAE. *Saeed bin Suroor*

LUNAR PROMISE (IRE) 4 b.g. Mujadil (USA) 119 – Lunadine (FR) (Bering 136) **73** [2006 81: p9.5g⁵ Dec 2] big gelding: fair handicapper: not disgraced only outing in 2006: stays 1¼m: acts on polytrack and good to firm going. *Ian Williams*

LUNAR RIVER (FR) 3 b.f. Muhtathir 126 – Moon Gorge 78 (Pursuit of Love 124) **73** [2006 60: 10d⁵ p10g² p10g³ 12m² 10g³ 10d⁶ 10.2m* Oct 8] big filly: fair performer: won maiden at Bath (by 5 lengths) in October: stays 1½m: acts on polytrack and good to firm going: tongue tied after debut: tried visored: sold 38,000 gns. *E. A. L. Dunlop*

LUNAR SOVEREIGN (USA) 7 b. or br.g. Cobra King (USA) 122 – January Moon **76 ?** (CAN) (Apalachee (USA) 137) [2006 p10g⁶ Sep 3] lengthy, attractive gelding: very smart performer at best: unraced on Flat in 2005, visored when only sixth in claimer sole start on Flat in 2006: blinkered once in 2002: tongue tied: sold £850. *D. E. Pipe*

LUNA TACUMANA (IRE) 6 b.m. Bahhare (USA) 122 – Orange And Blue 50 **80** (Prince Sabo 123) [2006 73: p7.1g⁵ p8g³ p8g* p8.6g Feb 11] fairly useful handicapper on all-weather, fair on turf: best effort when winning at Lingfield in February: raced mainly at 7f/1m: acts on polytrack and firm going: formerly tongue tied, blinkered last 2 starts in 2005. *J. J. Lambe, Ireland*

LUNCES LAD (IRE) 2 gr.g. (Jan 29) Xaar 132 – Bridelina (FR) (Linamix (FR) 127) **85** [2006 7m 7d* 7d6 7d p7g⁴ Oct 15] 27,000F, 34,000Y: lengthy, good-topped gelding: fourth foal: half-brother to useful Irish 2005 2-y-o 6.5f winner De Roberto (by Barathea) and winner in Switzerland by Tiger Hill: dam French 1m/1¼m winner: fairly useful performer: won maiden at Newbury in August, easily best effort: will stay 1m: acts on good to soft going: gelded after final start. *M. R. Channon*

LUSCIVIOUS 2 ch.g. (Feb 28) Kyllachy 129 – Lloc 79 (Absalom 128) [2006 5m⁶ 5.1m **99** f6g⁵ 6.1g 6m⁵ 5d* 5s* Oct 14] 8,000F, 14,000Y: workmanlike gelding: sixth foal: half-brother to fairly useful 5f (at 2 yrs) to 1m winner Aimee's Delight (by Robellino): dam, 5f winner (including at 2 yrs), half-sister to July Cup winner Compton Place: useful performer: left M. Polglase after third start: much improved when winning maiden and minor event at Catterick in October, latter by 3 lengths from Spoof Master: best at 5f: acts on soft going: blinkered last 3 starts. *A. J. McCabe*

LUSOLLY 2 br.c. (Feb 20) Lujain (USA) 119 – Speak 63 (Barathea (IRE) 127) [2006 **68** 7m⁴ 7.1m³ 7g 6s⁶ Oct 16] 10,000Y: first foal: dam, maiden who stayed 7f (ran only at 2 yrs), half-sister to useful German performer up to 9f Sharp Domino: fair maiden: best run when third to Iron Fist at Warwick: stays 7f. *M. G. Quinlan*

LYGETON LAD 8 b.g. Shaamit (IRE) 127 – Smartie Lee 66 (Dominion 123) [2006 73, **–** a104: p7g⁵ p10g p7g⁶ p8g 8m p8g⁶ Jul 19] tall gelding: useful on all-weather, fair on **a100** turf: has won 9 times at Lingfield: creditable close fifth to Bonus in handicap there on reappearance: below form after: effective at 7f, barely stays easy 1¼m: better form on polytrack than fibresand (well beaten on dirt), and acts on good to firm and good to soft going: tried in cheekpieces, usually tongue tied: sometimes slowly away: reportedly bled fourth outing, very reluctant to post on fifth. *Miss Gay Kelleway*

LYNDALEE (IRE) 3 b.f. Fasliyev (USA) 120 – Itsibitsi (IRE) (Brief Truce (USA) **78** 126) [2006 72: 5m⁴ 5g⁵ 5m 5f² 5m⁶ 5g 7s 5s 5s* 6v⁶ 5d p5.1g p6g p5.1g Dec 23] **a70** tall, good sort: fair handicapper: left T. Easterby after fifth outing: won at Cork in October: left T. Hogan in Ireland after thirteenth start: stays 6f: acts on any turf going: sometimes wears cheekpieces: inconsistent. *P. D. Evans*

LYNFORD LADY 3 b.f. Zaha (CAN) 106 – Little Miss Rocker 65 (Rock Hopper 124) **60** [2006 49: p12.2g³ 12.1d 11g 10.2m p9.5g Sep 30] workmanlike filly: modest maiden: left P. D'Arcy after third start: stays 1½m: acts on polytrack: blinkered final outing. *D. J. S. ffrench Davis*

LYRICAL BLUES (IRE) 3 ch.g. Namid 128 – Latest (IRE) (Bob Back (USA) 124) – [2006 81: p7g 6.1g 7.1m⁶ 7g Aug 2] workmanlike gelding: fairly useful performer at 2 yrs: well beaten in 2006, racing too freely first 2 starts. *B. R. Millman*

LYRICAL GIRL (USA) 5 b.m. Orpen (USA) 116 – Lyric Theatre (USA) (Seeking – The Gold (USA)) [2006 p9.5g f8g Apr 7] sturdy mare: modest performer at 3 yrs: missed 2005: well held in 2006. *H. J. Manners*

LYRICAL SOUND (IRE) 3 ch.f. Distant Music (USA) 126 – Unscathed (Warning **85** 136) [2006 76: 8.5g 7f* 7m 7m² 8m⁵ 8.3g⁵ 8s⁴ Sep 22] smallish, sparely-made filly: fairly useful performer: won handicap at Leicester in June: in-and-out form after: stays 8.3f: acts on firm and soft going: possibly not straightforward: sold 10,000 gns, resold 19,000 gns, sent to USA. *B. W. Hills*

LYRIC DANCES (FR) 4 ch.f. Sendawar (IRE) 129 – Romanche (FR) (Galetto (FR) – 118) [2006 49, a45: f12g Jan 3] poor maiden: tongue tied last 2 starts. *J. Jay*

LYSANDER'S QUEST (IRE) 8 br.g. King's Theatre (IRE) 128 – Haramayda (FR) **57** (Doyoun 124) [2006 59: p16.5g⁴ p13g⁴ p16.5g p12g² p13.9g³ p16g⁴ p12g 12f⁶ 12f 16.4f² 16f* p16.5f 16.4m⁵ 16d p16g² p16g² p16g³ p16g² Dec 18] tall gelding: modest performer: won handicap at Yarmouth in July: stays 17f: acts on polytrack, firm and good to soft going: infrequently wears headgear: waited with: consistent. *R. Ingram*

LYSANDRA (IRE) 4 b.f. Danehill (USA) 126 – Oriane 109 (Nashwan (USA) 135) **81** [2006 88: 10m⁶ 12d 9.9f 9.9f² 10.1m 10.1g⁴ 10.5m² 10.4f⁴ 7.9f⁵ 10m* 10g* 10.5g 12s Oct 6] small, deep-girthed filly: fairly useful handicapper: won apprentice events at Leicester and Pontefract in September: stays 1¼m: acts on firm and good to soft ground: sometimes slowly away: usually held up. *N. Tinkler*

M

MA'AM (USA) 4 ch.f. Royal Anthem (USA) 135 – Hide The Bride (USA) (Runaway **82** Groom (CAN)) [2006 93d: 12s⁵ p8g* 10.4s⁵ 10m 10g 10g p9.5g Dec 11] big filly: fairly useful performer: won handicap at Kempton in April: flattered in Middleton Stakes at York next time, well held in handicaps after: stays 1¼m: acts on polytrack, good to firm and good to soft going, seemingly on soft: tried in cheekpieces/blinkers: sometimes slowly away: has shown signs of temperament. *I. A. Wood*

MAAREES 5 b.m. Groom Dancer (USA) 128 – Shemaleyah 84 (Lomond (USA) 128) – [2006 –: p12g Jan 3] well held both starts on Flat: blinkered in latter. *G. P. Enright*

MAAYAFUSHI 3 ch.f. Fraam 114 – Pastelle 52 (Tate Gallery (USA) 117) [2006 49: 5m – 6.1m 6m 5g Aug 7] close-coupled filly: has a round action: maiden: well held since debut at 2 yrs. *M. D. Hammond*

MABADI (USA) 3 b.f. Sahm (USA) 112 – Barakat 93 (Bustino 136) [2006 –: 10g³ **87** 10.3m* 10.5g³ 11.8d⁶ Oct 3] tall filly: fairly useful performer: won maiden at Chester in July: good third in handicap at Haydock next time: barely stays 10.5f: acts on good to firm going: hung under pressure on reappearance: sold 20,000 gns, sent to USA. *B. W. Hills*

MABELLA (IRE) 4 b.f. Brave Act 119 – Wee Merkin (IRE) (Thatching 131) [2006 – 45: 10.2m 8.1g 10.2f Jul 27] maiden: no form in 2006: tried tongue tied/in cheekpieces. *B. J. Llewellyn*

MACADEMY ROYAL (USA) 3 b.g. Royal Academy (USA) 130 – Garden Folly **68** (USA) (Pine Bluff (USA)) [2006 74p: p6g² 6.1m May 3] quite good-topped gelding: fair maiden: mulish at start (dismounted and led behind stall) final outing (reportedly returned with sore shins): stays 6f: acts on polytrack: sold 7,000 gns in October. *H. Morrison*

MACARONI GIN (IRE) 2 b.g. (Mar 12) Grand Slam (USA) 120 – Polyandry (IRE) **69** 99 (Pennekamp (USA) 130) [2006 7d 7f⁵ 8g² Sep 27] $85,000Y, 150,000 2-y-o: first foal: dam 6f (at 2 yrs in France) to 9f (in USA) winner: best effort in maidens when second at Newcastle: gelded after: stays 1m. *J. Howard Johnson*

MACARONI GOLD (IRE) 6 b.g. Rock Hopper 124 – Strike It Rich (FR) 88 (Rhein- – gold 137) [2006 71, a80: f12g* f14g⁶ Jan 29] fairly useful on all-weather, fair on turf: **a80** won seller at Southwell (by 6 lengths) in January: effective at 1½m to 2½m: acts on all-weather, soft and good to firm going: effective blinkered/visored or not: has flashed tail/carried head awkwardly/found little: has joined E. Williams. *D. J. Daly*

MACARTHUR 2 b.c. (Mar 16) Montjeu (IRE) 137 – Out West (USA) 103 (Gone West **95 P** (USA)) [2006 8v* Oct 25] fifth foal: brother to Derby winner Motivator, also 1m (Racing Post Trophy) winner at 2 yrs, and half-brother to 2 winners, including useful 1¼m winner Imperial Star (by Fantastic Light): dam, 7.5f (at 2 yrs)/1m winner, out of half-sister to US Grade 1 9f winner Wavering Monarch: 7/4 favourite, won 17-runner maiden at Navan by 3 lengths from Copper Bell (pair long way clear), leading 2f out and staying on: will be suited by 1¼m/1½m: likely to prove capable of good deal better. *A. P. O'Brien, Ireland*

MACEDON 3 b.g. Dansili 127 – Hypnotize 103 (Machiavellian (USA) 123) [2006 69: **89** 7f* 7f* 7s⁵ 8.1m⁵ Sep 8] big, strong gelding: fairly useful performer: won maiden at Folkestone in July and handicap at Lingfield (took strong hold) in August: stays 1m: acts on firm and soft going. *J. S. Moore*

MAC GILLE EOIN 2 b.c. (Apr 18) Bertolini (USA) 125 – Peruvian Jade 76 (Petong **79 +** 126) [2006 5.1d⁶ p5g⁴ 5.7m 5m p5g⁵ 5.7m* 6m⁶ 6.1g⁴ p5g² p6g⁵ p6g* Nov 7] second foal: dam 2-y-o 6f winner: fair performer: won maiden at Bath in August and nursery at Wolverhampton in November: effective at 5f/6f: acts on polytrack and good to firm going. *J. Gallagher*

MAC HAN (IRE) 7 ch.g. Pennekamp (USA) 130 – Ryazana (IRE) 81 (Fairy King **57** (USA)) [2006 64: p16g⁶ 12m Jun 12] modest handicapper: stays easy 2m: acts on polytrack and any turf going: tried in blinkers/cheekpieces. *E. Tyrrell, Ireland*

MACHHAPUCHHARE 3 ch.g. Most Welcome 131 – Spring Flyer (IRE) 66 (Waajib **–** 121) [2006 –: 10d⁵ f11g⁵ 9.9m 12m 10m f8g² Oct 12] modest maiden: stays 11f: acts on **a57** fibresand, little form on turf: wore cheekpieces final start: has raced freely/been slowly away. *W. M. Brisbourne*

MACHINATE (USA) 4 b. or br.g. Machiavellian (USA) 123 – Dancing Sea (USA) 80 **–** (Storm Cat (USA)) [2006 65: 10.1m 10m Jun 16] fair performer at 3 yrs: well held in 2006: tongue tied final start. *W. M. Brisbourne*

MACHINIST (IRE) 6 br.g. Machiavellian (USA) 123 – Athene (IRE) 83 (Rousillon **98** (USA) 133) [2006 99: p6g⁵ 6d 6m 6m² 5m* 6s 6m² 6g Sep 23] good-topped gelding: useful handicapper: won 23-runner Hong Kong Jockey Club Sprint at Ascot in July by short head from One More Round: also ran well when runner-up at Hamilton and Goodwood: effective at 5f/6f: acts on polytrack, firm and good to firm going: sometimes slowly away. *D. Nicholls*

MACHO DANCER (IRE) 3 ch.f. Desert Prince (IRE) 130 – Mynador (USA) 90 **53** (Forty Niner (USA)) [2006 73: p8g p7g³ f7g⁵ 7d⁴ p12.2g³ 10.9m⁵ 10.3m³ p12.2g⁴ 11.9f⁶ 10.3m⁶ 10.1d⁵ Aug 28] half-sister to Irish 2001 2-y-o 6f winner Munda Nai (by Spinning World) and Irish 9f winner Door of Knowledge (by Theatrical): dam 6f (in Ireland at 2 yrs) and 9f (in USA) winner: modest performer: left C. Collins in Ireland after final 2-y-o outing and R. Beckett after third start in 2006: stays 1½m: acts on polytrack, unraced on extremes of going on turf: tried in cheekpieces. *K. J. Burke*

Hong Kong Jockey Club Sprint (Handicap), Ascot—Machinist has a short head to spare over One More Round (No.9) who is a neck in front of Golden Dixie (hooped cap); Fydor (No.6) is fourth

MAC LOVE 5 b.g. Cape Cross (IRE) 129 – My Lass 91 (Elmaamul (USA) 125) [2006 **109** 117: 7.1g^2 7m^3 7f^2 7m^3 7m 7d^4 7g^5 7g Sep 15] strong, compact gelding: smart performer at best: just useful form in 2006, best efforts when third to Jedburgh in minor event at Leicester and head second to Suggestive in Criterion Stakes at Newmarket second/third starts: stays 1m, raced only at 7f in 2006: acts on polytrack and firm going, possibly not on softer ground: free-going sort (often wears crossed noseband): held up: has joined J. Noseda. *R. Charlton*

MACORVILLE (USA) 3 b.g. Diesis 133 – Desert Jewel (USA) (Caerleon (USA) **99** 132) [2006 75: 9.8m^2 10.4d^4 9v* 11g^4 9.8d* 10.5s* 13d* 12s Oct 7] leggy, workmanlike gelding: has a markedly round action: useful performer: improved in 2006, winning maiden at Ripon in May, and handicaps at Ripon in August and Haydock and Hamilton (beat Cool Customer by a neck) in September: below form in handicap at Ascot final start: stays 13f: best form on good or softer going (acts on heavy): races prominently. *G. M. Moore*

MACS ALL HEART (IRE) 3 ch.f. Alhaarth (IRE) 126 – Top of The Form (IRE) 79 **36** (Masterclass (USA) 116) [2006 45: f7g 5.7g^4 6m Jun 5] small filly: poor maiden: best form at 5f/6f: acts on all-weather and firm going: tried tongue tied. *A. B. Coogan*

MACS RANSOM (USA) 3 b.f. Red Ransom (USA) – Gaye's Express (USA) (Time- **52** less Native (USA)) [2006 57: 7d 8m 8f^3 8f^3 8.3m^3 12g^6 Aug 18] leggy, lengthy filly: modest maiden: claimed from N. Callaghan after fifth outing: stays 1m (not 1¼m): acts on firm ground: raced freely second start, carried head high and looked none too keen third one. *S. C. Williams*

MAD 5 br.m. Pursuit of Love 124 – Emily-Mou (IRE) 80 (Cadeaux Genereux 131) [2006 **–** –, a61: p8g^6 p8g^3 p8g^5 p10g^6 p8g Jun 7] tall mare: modest performer: stays 1¼m: acts on **a57** polytrack, well below form all 3 turf outings: has joined P. Hobbs. *E. R. Oertel*

MADAAREK (USA) 2 b.c. (May 9) Kingmambo (USA) 126 – Hachiyah (IRE) 91 **76** (Generous (IRE) 139) [2006 8g 7d Oct 28] strong, medium-sized colt: fifth foal: closely related to 3-y-o Adraaj and half-brother to 2 winners, including useful 6f (at 2 yrs) and 1m winner Nasij (by Elusive Quality): dam, 1¼m winner, closely related to useful performer up to 1½m Mutawwaj: better effort in maidens at Newmarket when seventh to Sam Lord on debut. *E. A. L. Dunlop*

MADAARES (USA) 3 ch.c. Rahy (USA) 115 – Tajannub (USA) 104 (Dixieland Band **84** (USA)) [2006 74p: 6d^5 8.5f^2 8g^3 8.5f^2 7f Jul 5] good-topped colt: fairly useful maiden: likely to stay 1¼m: acts on firm going: sold 26,000 gns later in July. *M. Johnston*

MADAME CONSTANZE (IRE) 3 b.f. Mozart (IRE) 131 – Darbela (IRE) 102 **52** (Doyoun 124) [2006 62: p7g 8m 8g 7f^6 12d 11.5m p13g^6 f12m Oct 31] tall, leggy, useful- **a47** looking filly: modest maiden on turf, poor on all-weather: stays easy 13f: acts on polytrack, good to firm and good to soft going: free-going sort. *Miss Gay Kelleway*

MADAME DIKTATIT 3 b.f. Diktat 126 – Madame Jones (IRE) 79 (Lycius (USA) **–** 124) [2006 7.9m 8.3m 8.1m Aug 10] 10,500Y: leggy filly: first foal: dam 6f to 9.4f winner: little sign of ability. *Ms Deborah J. Evans*

MADAME GUILLOTINE 4 b.f. Sure Blade (USA) 130 – Delicious 51 (Dominion **44** 123) [2006 41: f6g^3 f6g f6g f7g^5 f7g 6f 6g Jul 22] poor maiden: stays 7f: acts on fibresand and firm ground: tried in cheekpieces/blinkered. *P. T. Midgley*

MADAME MEDUSA (IRE) 3 b.f. Mozart (IRE) 131 – Belize Tropical (IRE) (Bailla- **77** mont (USA) 124) [2006 74: 7g^6 8m 7m^2 7m^2 6f^3 7f^2 6g* 6d^5 6g 6d^4 p5g Nov 5] angular filly: fair performer: won maiden at Yarmouth in August: flattered in listed race at Newmarket ninth outing: effective at 5f to 7f: acts on polytrack, firm and good to soft ground: visored/blinkered last 7 starts: hasn't always looked easiest of rides: sold 25,000 gns. *J. A. R. Toller*

MADAM GAFFER 2 ch.f. (Apr 22) Tobougg (IRE) 125 – True Precision 84 (Presid- **69** ium 124) [2006 p6g^4 p7g^5 p6f^3 6.1g 6d p7.1m* p7.1m^3 p7.1g^3 Nov 24] 16,500Y: sturdy filly: half-sister to several winners, notably 6-y-o Pivotal Point: dam 6f to 7f winner: fair performer: won seller at Wolverhampton in October: placed in nurseries there last 2 starts: effective at 6f/7f: best form on polytrack: sold 18,000 gns. *B. J. Meehan*

MADAM MAC (IRE) 3 b.f. Royal Applause 124 – Wild Woman (Polar Falcon (USA) **45** 126) [2006 –: p7g 8d f7g^3 8.1m^3 10.1f p12.2m Sep 2] quite attractive filly: poor maiden: stays 1m: acts on fibresand and good to firm ground: blinkered final start. *B. J. Meehan*

MADAM MOSCHATA 3 b.f. Muhtarram (USA) 125 – Casaque Rose (USA) (Lord **–** Avie (USA)) [2006 62?: 7m 6g 7g 6f 5m 6m 7m Sep 16] neat filly: maiden: seemingly modest form second outing at 2 yrs: well held in 2006. *D. W. Barker*

MADAM PATTI 3 b.f. Monashee Mountain (USA) 115 – Thabeh 57 (Shareef Dancer **46** (USA) 135) [2006 52: 7.1f 5.1m 7.1m f6g⁵ f6g p8.6g p8.6g Dec 4] leggy filly: poor maiden. *B. Palling*

MAD CAREW (USA) 7 ch.g. Rahy (USA) 115 – Poppy Carew (IRE) 110 (Danehill **83** (USA) 126) [2006 85: p12.2g³ p10g² p12g³ Feb 7] sturdy gelding: fairly useful performer: was effective at 1m to easy 13f: acted on all-weather, firm and soft going: often wore headgear: sometimes hung/carried head awkwardly: held up: dead. *J. R. Boyle*

MADDOX (POL) 4 b.g. Upper Heights (GER) 107 – Muddy's Girl (SWE) (Muddy **48** Blues) [2006 51: p8g⁶ Feb 6] poor performer nowadays: stays 1m: acts on polytrack: tried blinkered. *Mrs P. Townsley*

MADEMOISELLE 4 b.f. Efisio 120 – Shall We Dance 83 (Rambo Dancer (CAN) **60** 107) [2006 60: f7g³ f8g⁴ 10m 11.9d Oct 19] lengthy filly: modest handicapper: left B. Hills after second start: may prove best up to 1m: acts on fibresand and soft going. *R. Curtis*

MADGE 4 b.f. Marju (IRE) 127 – Aymara 85 (Darshaan 133) [2006 61d: f8g Jul 11] – useful-looking, rather unfurnished filly: regressive maiden: blinkered/visored last 6 starts. *W. Storey*

MADHAVI 4 gr.f. Diktat 126 – Grey Galava 64 (Generous (IRE) 139) [2006 76§: p10g⁵ **74 §** p9.5g* p8g⁶ p10g⁴ p10g p10g 11.7d⁴ 11.7f* 11.9m² 11.6m* 12m² 12m 12g p9.5g Nov 11] compact filly: fair handicapper: won at Wolverhampton in January, Bath in June and Windsor in July: left R. Hannon before final start: stays 1½m: acts on polytrack, firm and good to soft going: tried in headgear: sometimes finds little: ungenuine. *B. S. Rothwell*

MADIBA 7 b.g. Emperor Jones (USA) 119 – Priluki 65 (Lycius (USA) 124) [2006 64, **58** a80d: p16.5g⁴ f16g³ f14g³ 16g p16g³ 16.1d* 18m⁴ p16g p16.5g* p16g⁵ 16.1m⁵ 16d⁶ **a70** p16g 18d p16g f16g⁴ Dec 19] leggy, useful-looking gelding: fair handicapper on all-weather, modest on turf: won at Newcastle in May and Wolverhampton (apprentices) in July: stays 2¼m: acts on all-weather, firm and soft going: formerly visored/blinkered. *P. Howling*

MADISON AVENUE (GER) 9 b.g. Mondrian (GER) 125 – Madly Noble (GER) – (Irish River (FR) 131) [2006 47: p16g Oct 23] lightly-raced maiden on Flat: tried blinkered. *T. M. Jones*

MAD MARTY WILDCARD 4 ch.g. Komaite (USA) – Done And Dusted (IRE) 75 – (Up And At 'em 109) [2006 47: p7.1g f6g f7g Mar 28] close-coupled gelding: poor maiden: tried tongue tied/blinkered. *R. Brotherton*

MAD MAURICE 5 ch.g. Grand Lodge (USA) 125 – Amarella (FR) (Balleroy (USA) **56** 115) [2006 55: f8g* f12g 10.1g p9.5g Nov 27] sturdy gelding: modest performer: won banded race at Southwell (well backed) in January: suffered fatal fall at Wolverhampton in November: stayed 1¼m: acted on fibresand and good to soft going: tried in cheekpieces/blinkers. *B. J. Curley*

MAD PROFESSOR (IRE) 3 b.g. Mull of Kintyre (USA) 114 – Fancy Theory (USA) – (Quest For Fame 127) [2006 65: 8.3g 10m May 31] quite good-topped gelding: maiden: well held in 2006: often blinkered: tried tongue tied. *D. J. S. ffrench Davis*

MADRASEE 8 b.m. Beveled (USA) – Pendona 72 (Blue Cashmere 129) [2006 60, a69: **60** p6g p5.1g p6g⁶ p5g² p5g⁴ p6g⁶ p6g p5.1g p5g p6g p6g⁵ 5.7f⁴ 5.3m 5.5g² Aug 28] leggy mare: modest performer: left P. Murphy after twelfth outing: effective at 5f/6f: acts on polytrack, firm and soft going. *N. E. Berry*

MADRIGALE 2 b.f. (Mar 12) Averti (IRE) 117 – Shy Minstrel (USA) (The Minstrel **61** (CAN) 135) [2006 5.1f³ 6d⁵ Sep 26] half-sister to several winners, including useful French 7.5f/1m winner Green Minstrel (by Green Tune) and 4-y-o Croon: dam 5f and (at 2 yrs) 6f winner in USA: modest form in maidens, not knocked about: likely to stay 7f/1m. *G. L. Moore*

MADROOS 3 ch.c. Medicean 128 – Soolaimon (IRE) 71 (Shareef Dancer (USA) 135) **88** [2006 73p: 11s* p12g³ 12g⁶ 12g³ 14g⁵ Sep 23] good-topped colt: fairly useful handicapper: won at Goodwood in May: stays 1¾m: acts on polytrack and good ground: waited with: consistent: sold 60,000 gns, joined J. Culloty in Ireland. *J. L. Dunlop*

MAE CIGAN (FR) 3 gr.g. Medaaly 114 – Concert (Polar Falcon (USA) 126) [2006 50: **76** p9.5g² p8.6g⁴ 9.7s³ p9.5g 10.2s* 10.3g p10g 10.5m⁴ 10g 10.5v* 11.9g³ 10d Oct 4] fair handicapper: won at Bath in May and Haydock in September: stays 1½m: acts on polytrack, heavy and good to firm going: tried visored at 2 yrs. *M. Blanshard*

MAEVE (IRE) 2 b.f. (Feb 22) Tomba 119 – Boozy 111 (Absalom 128) [2006 p7.1g p6g **53** p8g Dec 10] half-sister to several winners, including 6-y-o Pintle and fairly useful 5f/6f winner Double Brew (by Primo Dominie): dam best at 5f: best effort in maidens when seemingly modest form on debut. *E. J. Creighton*

MAFEKING (UAE) 2 b.c. (May 2) Jade Robbery (USA) 121 – Melisendra (FR) **80** (Highest Honor (FR) 124) [2006 p8g p8g* p10g³ Nov 25] 5,000 2-y-o: brother to 3-y-o Three Thieves and half-brother to 2002 2-y-o 7f/1m winner Roskilde (by Danehill) and 10.3f winner Murray (by Darshaan), both useful: dam useful French 5.5f (at 2 yrs) to 1m winner: fairly useful form: won maiden at Kempton in November: third to Montalembert in minor event at Lingfield: stays 1¼m: raced on polytrack. *M. R. Hoad*

MAGADAR (USA) 3 b.f. Magadar (USA) 119 – Slow Jazz (USA) 106 (Chief's Crown **76** (USA)) [2006 78: 7.1m 6s p8g Nov 22] tall, leggy filly: fair handicapper, lightly raced: reportedly suffered stress fracture and off 10 months before reappearance (not discredited): well held after: stays at least 6f: acts on polytrack, soft and good to firm going: edgy sort: sold 20,000 gns. *C. E. Brittain*

MAGDALENE 2 ch.f. (Feb 12) Act One 124 – Three Terns (USA) (Arctic Tern (USA) **63** 126) [2006 8.2m 8.2d⁶ Nov 1] 25,000Y: tall, good-topped filly: half-sister to several winners, including smart French performer up to 1¼m Thames (by Fabulous Dancer), 4-y-o Three Wrens, and fairly useful 5f (at 2 yrs) to 1¾m winner Swift (by Sharpo): dam, French 9f winner, out of Arc winner Three Troikas: mid-field in maidens at Nottingham: will stay 1¼m. *Rae Guest*

MAGENA GOLD 2 b.g. (Feb 8) Bertolini (USA) 125 – Linens Girl (Thowra (FR)) **?** [2006 p7g p7.1f p6g a8g* Dec 17] modest form in maidens for R. Charlton only on debut: sold 1,700 gns, won minor event at Gran Canaria in December: stays 1m: raced only on polytrack/sand. *S. Hernandez, Spain*

MAGENIKEN (USA) 2 ch.g. (Mar 8) Giant's Causeway (USA) 132 – Freshwater **– §** Pearl (IRE) 90 (Alzao (USA) 117) [2006 7m Aug 8] 10/1, showed temperament in maiden at Catterick, refusing to race after 1f: gelded after. *J. Howard Johnson*

MAGGIES FARM (USA) 3 ch.f. Forest Wildcat (USA) 120 – Moss (USA) (Wood- **78** man (USA) 126) [2006 85: 10.4d 10.1m 9.1v p8g⁵ p9.5g Nov 25] smallish, leggy, angular filly: just fair handicapper in 2006: barely stays 9.5f: acts on polytrack, good to firm and good to soft ground: sold 50,000 gns. *M. Johnston*

MAGICAL MIMI 5 b.m. Magic Ring (IRE) 115 – Naval Dispatch (Slip Anchor 136) **–** [2006 58d: p6g* p6g⁶ p6g p6g 6m Jun 5] modest performer: won seller at Wolverhamp- **a63** ton in March: effective at 6f to 1m: acts on polytrack and firm going: tried blinkered: tongue tied. *K. G. Wingrove*

MAGICAL MUSIC 3 b.f. Fraam 114 – Magical Flute 75 (Piccolo 121) [2006 50, a63: **62** p8.6g* p8g⁶ p8.6g² p9.5g p8.6g* 8m 8.3m⁶ 8m p8g³ p8.6f p8.6g³ p8g⁴ p9.5g* **a96** p9.5g* p9.5g* Dec 28] strong filly: improved into a useful handicapper on all-weather, winning at Wolverhampton in March, April and December (3, beat Just Bond by neck on third occasion): stays 9.5f: acts on all-weather, just modest form on turf. *J. Pearce*

MAGICALMYSTERYTOUR (IRE) 3 b.c. Sadler's Wells (USA) 132 – Jude 53 **93** (Darshaan 133) [2006 10d² 10v² 12m* 10g⁶ 12m 12s Oct 8] strong, good-bodied colt: fifth foal: brother to Irish 1000 Guineas winner Yesterday, also 7f and 9f winner at 2 yrs, and 2001 Moyglare Stud Stakes winner Quarter Moon, both second in Oaks: dam lightly-raced sister to dam of Alborada/Albanova and half-sister to very smart 1¼m performer Last Second (dam of Poule d'Essai des Poulains winner Aussie Rules): fairly useful performer: landed odds in maiden at Leopardstown in June: better form in handicaps at the Curragh and Goodwood (ninth to Strategic Mount, hanging right) next 2 starts: stays 1½m: acts on heavy and good to firm going. *A. P. O'Brien, Ireland*

MAGICAL WORLD 3 b.f. Agnes World (USA) 123 – Otaru (IRE) (Indian Ridge **–** 123) [2006 –: 6.1f 6g Aug 4] smallish, lengthy filly: no form. *J. M. Bradley*

MAGIC AMERICA (USA) 2 b.f. (Apr 4) High Yield (USA) 121 – Shoofha (IRE) 70 **112** (Bluebird (USA) 125) [2006 5g* 5g⁶ 5.5m³ 6s² 6d⁶ 7d* Oct 28] rangy filly: third foal: dam lightly-raced sister to smart middle-distance stayer Delilah: smart performer: won newcomers race at Longchamp in May and Prix Miesque at Maisons-Laffitte (not hard pressed to beat Nuqoosh 1½ lengths) in October: placed in between in Prix Robert Papin at Maisons-Laffitte and Prix Morny at Deauville, in latter beaten length by Dutch Art (Excellent Art third): better than bare result (sixth to Indian Ink) in Cheveley Park Stakes at Newmarket, never much room: will stay 1m: acts on soft and good to firm going: blinkered first 3 starts. *Mme C. Head-Maarek, France*

MAGIC AMIGO 5 ch.g. Zilzal (USA) 137 – Emaline (FR) 105 (Empery (USA) 128) **79**
[2006 81: 11.5m⁶ 11.5m³ 10s 11.8m⁶ 14.1m⁵ p10g p12g³ Dec 16] tall, leggy gelding: fair **a67**
handicapper, better on turf than all-weather: stays 1½m: acts on all-weather, heavy and
good to firm ground. *J. R. Jenkins*

MAGIC AMOUR 8 ch.g. Sanglamore (USA) 126 – Rakli 84 (Warning 136) [2006 65: **71**
f7g³ p6g* f7g* p5.1g³ f7g² f6g⁴ p7.1g* p6g⁴ f7g Feb 23] strong, lengthy gelding: fair
performer: won banded races at Wolverhampton and Southwell in January and seller
at Wolverhampton in February: effective at 5f to 1m: acts on all-weather and firm going:
blinkered/visored: usually races up with pace. *P. A. Blockley*

MAGIC CHARM 8 b.m. Magic Ring (IRE) 115 – Loch Clair (IRE) 53 (Lomond **37**
(USA) 128) [2006 –: p9.5g May 5] angular mare: poor performer: little form after 2004:
tried visored/blinkered/tongue tied: no easy ride. *K. G. Wingrove*

MAGIC ECHO 2 b.f. (Apr 26) Wizard King 122 – Sunday News'n'echo (USA) 78 **76**
(Trempolino (USA) 135) [2006 7s* 8s⁶ Oct 21] close-coupled, compact filly: sister to
5-y-o Queen's Echo: dam, 1¼m/1½m winner, also successful over hurdles: fair form:
won maiden at Newcastle in October: sixth in nursery at Newbury 11 days later: will stay
1¼m. *M. Dods*

MAGIC GLADE 7 b.g. Magic Ring (IRE) 115 – Ash Glade (Nashwan (USA) 135) **91**
[2006 96: f5g⁶ f5g⁶ f5g⁶ p5g 5.1s 5g⁶ 5.1g* 5g 5.1m p5.1g³ Dec 27] compact gelding:
fairly useful handicapper: won at Chester in June: left R. Brotherton after ninth start: best
at 5f: acts on all-weather, firm and soft going: tried in cheekpieces/blinkers: has bled,
including fifth outing: races prominently. *T. G. Dascombe*

MAGIC MERLIN 5 b.g. Magic Ring (IRE) 115 – St James's Antigua (IRE) 79 (Law **–**
Society (USA) 130) [2006 82+: p8.6g Jan 21] fairly useful handicapper at best, lightly
raced: well held only Flat outing in 2006. *W. R. Swinburn*

MAGIC MOTH 3 b.c. Mtoto 134 – Majoune (FR) 105 (Take Risks (FR) 116) [2006 **73**
p12.2g* Feb 13] second foal: brother to fairly useful 1¼m to 14.4f winner Marias Magic:
dam, French 1m (at 2 yrs) to 11f (Prix Corrida) winner, half-sister to smart French filly up
to 1½m Mousse Glacee (by Mtoto): 15/8 and very green, won maiden at Wolverhampton
in February by length from Opera Comica, making all but running in snatches and hanging on bends: seemed sure to improve. *M. Johnston*

MAGIC MOUNTAIN (IRE) 2 b.c. (Mar 17) Dr Fong (USA) 128 – Hard Task 82 **82**
(Formidable (USA) 125) [2006 6g⁴ 6m 6m* Jul 29] €40,000F, 34,000Y: half-brother to
several winners, notably useful 1m/9f winner Gryffindor (by Marju): dam, 1½m winner,
half-sister to smart middle-distance stayer Midnight Legend: fairly useful form: tongue
tied, won maiden at Salisbury by 2 lengths from St Philip: found little second start: will
stay at least 1m. *R. Hannon*

MAGIC PEAK (IRE) 3 b.f. Danehill (USA) 126 – Magic Cove (USA) 108 (King- **78**
mambo (USA) 125) [2006 72p: 8.1g² 8.3d* 8.2g 8f⁴ 8.3g Aug 7] lengthy, good-topped
filly: fair performer: won maiden at Windsor in May: will stay 1¼m: acts on firm and
good to soft ground. *Sir Michael Stoute*

MAGIC RED 6 ch.g. Magic Ring (IRE) 115 – Jacquelina (USA) 66 (Private Account **–**
(USA)) [2006 –, a55: f16g⁵ p16.5g Jan 23] big, rather leggy gelding: has a round action:
modest performer: well beaten in banded races in 2006: tried in headgear/tongue tie:
usually races prominently, sometimes in snatches. *J. Ryan*

MAGIC RUSH 4 b.g. Almaty (IRE) 113§ – Magic Legs 54 (Reprimand 122) [2006 **88**
p7g³ p8g² 7m³ p7.1f* 6s⁵ 7d⁶ p7g p7.1g³ p8g Dec 30] first foal: dam ran once: fairly
useful performer: won handicap at Wolverhampton in August: best form at 6f/7f: acts on
polytrack and soft going: front runner. *Mrs Norma Pook*

MAGIC STING 5 ch.g. Magic Ring (IRE) 115 – Ground Game 95 (Gildoran 123) **90**
[2006 90: 10v 10.9g 10g 10f⁶ 10.1g* 10.1g² 9.9m⁴ 9.8g³ 10.1d⁶ 9.2g² Sep 17] smallish,
workmanlike gelding: fairly useful handicapper: won at Epsom in July: stays 11f: acts on
heavy and good to firm going: free-going sort, usually races up with pace. *M. L. W. Bell*

MAGIC WARRIOR 6 b.g. Magic Ring (IRE) 115 – Clarista (USA) 67 (Riva Ridge **68**
(USA)) [2006 53, a65: p8g⁶ 9.7d p8.6g² p8.6g* p9.5g² 8m⁴ 8.3f* p10g³ 8.3f⁴ p8g* 10g **a76**
8.1m⁵ p8.6m p8g* p8.6g p8g⁴ p8g* Dec 16] fair performer, better on all-weather than
turf: won banded race at Wolverhampton in May, and handicaps at Leicester in June and
Kempton in August, November and December: stays easy 1¼m: acts on polytrack and
firm ground: said to have bled fifteenth outing. *J. C. Fox*

MAGNUM OPUS (IRE) 4 b.g. Sadler's Wells (USA) 132 – Summer Breeze 101 – (Rainbow Quest (USA) 134) [2006 10.3m 14.1d⁵ 12.1m⁵ 12m 11.9g Sep 22] sturdy gelding: fairly useful maiden at best: left A. Fabre 85,000 gns after final start in 2005, well below form in Britain: stays 15f: acts on good to soft ground: tried visored. *T. J. Pitt*

MAGUIRE (GER) 5 ro.g. Medaaly 114 – Mayada (USA) (The Minstrel (CAN) 135) – [2006 –: 10.9d Sep 16] lightly raced and no form in Britain: tried visored. *M. F. Harris*

MAHMJRA 4 b.g. Josr Algarhoud (IRE) 118 – Jamrat Samya (IRE) 79 (Sadler's Wells (USA) 132) [2006 73: 16g p12g p16.5g Dec 29] big, strong gelding: fair performer at best: well held in handicaps in 2006: effective with/without visor: usually makes running. *C. N. Allen*

MAHRAJAAN (USA) 3 b. or br.c. Machiavellian (USA) 123 – Karen S (USA) (Kris S (USA)) [2006 80p: 8m³ 7m³ 7.1m* 7.6f p7g Sep 6] tall, leggy colt: fairly useful performer: won maiden at Warwick in June: should be suited by 1¼m: acts on good to firm and good to soft going: sold 6,000 gns. *J. H. M. Gosden* — **81**

MAIDEN INVESTOR 3 b.f. Orpen (USA) 116 – Actress 73 (Known Fact (USA) 135) [2006 6g Aug 26] 12,000Y: lengthy filly: half-sister to several winners, including 4-y-o Algharb and 5-y-o Constable Burton: dam 7f winner: 33/1 and backward, 6¼ lengths seventh to Woodsley House in maiden at Goodwood, never dangerous. *Stef Liddiard* — **54**

MAIDFORD (IRE) 3 ch.f. Singspiel (IRE) 133 – Milde (USA) (Desert Wine (USA)) [2006 –: 9.7d p7.1g⁴ p8g* 8m⁶ 8f* 8.1d³ p10g* 10.3m 13.1m⁶ Aug 25] leggy performer: won banded race at Kempton in May and handicaps at Bath in June and Lingfield in July: stays 1¼m: acts on polytrack, firm and good to soft ground: consistent. *M. Meade* — **57 a63**

MAID IN ENGLAND 3 b.f. Mujadil (USA) 119 – Lalique (IRE) (Lahib (USA) 129) [2006 43: 7m* 8.1g 8m Sep 4] leggy filly: poor performer: left M. Tregoning after winning seller at Leicester in June: no form after: raced only at 7f/1m: acts on good to firm going: tongue tied final 2-y-o outing. *G. A. Ham* — **46**

MAID OF ALE (IRE) 2 b.f. (Apr 10) Barathea (IRE) 127 – Borders Belle (IRE) 96 (Pursuit of Love 124) [2006 5d 6m⁶ 6g 7m⁴ 7.1d 6.5s Sep 22] 40,000Y: first foal: dam 1m (at 2 yrs) and 1½m winner: modest maiden: stays 7f: best efforts on good to firm going: once blinkered: has worn crossed noseband. *B. J. Meehan* — **61**

MAID TO BELIEVE 2 b.f. (Mar 30) Galileo (IRE) 134 – Maid For The Hills 101 (Indian Ridge 123) [2006 8m 8.3d* 8d Oct 28] leggy, close-coupled, quite attractive filly: sixth foal: closely related to useful 7f (at 2 yrs)/1¼m winner Maid To Perfection (by Sadler's Wells) who stayed 1½m, and half-sister to 3 winners, including useful performer up to 1½m Artistic Lad (by Peintre Celebre): dam 2-y-o 6f winner: fair form: won maiden at Leicester in October: stiff task, well held in listed race at Newmarket (sweating): will be suited by 1¼m/1½m. *J. L. Dunlop* — **73**

MAIL EXPRESS (IRE) 3 b.f. Cape Cross (IRE) 129 – Mystic Tempo (USA) 76 (El Gran Senor (USA) 136) [2006 6f⁶ 7f³ 6f* Aug 5] 130,000F: lengthy filly: sixth foal: half-sister to 3 winners, notably high-class 7f/1m performer Le Vie dei Colori (by Efisio): dam 6f winner (including at 2 yrs): fairly useful form: won maiden at Lingfield in August by 4 lengths from Discotheque, still green: will stay 1m: capable of better still. *L. M. Cumani* — **82 p**

MAISON DIEU 3 br. or b.g. King Charlemagne (USA) 120 – Shining Desert (IRE) 82 (Green Desert (USA) 127) [2006 50: 6d 6g* 6g² 6f² 5g 6f 6m⁵ 6g Sep 17] useful-looking gelding: fair performer: won apprentice seller at Ripon (left J. Howard Johnson) in May: raced mainly at 6f: acts on firm going: tried in cheekpieces. *E. J. Alston* — **68**

MAJAALES (USA) 3 b.g. Diesis 133 – Roseate Tern 123 (Blakeney 126) [2006 10m⁵ 9.9g* 11m⁶ Aug 5] well-made gelding: brother to useful 7f (at 2 yrs) and 1¼m winner Esloob and half-brother to useful 1¼m winner Siyadah (by Mr Prospector) and fairly useful 1997 2-y-o 7f winner who stayed 1½m Fakhr (by Riverman): dam, won Yorkshire Oaks and placed in Oaks/St Leger, half-sister to high-class performer up to 1¾m Ibn Bey: fairly useful form: won maiden at Salisbury in June: still bit green, good sixth to Numeric in handicap at Goodwood final outing: will stay 1½m: acts on good to firm going: open to further improvement. *M. P. Tregoning* — **90 p**

MAJEHAR 4 b.g. Marju (IRE) 127 – Joonayh 81 (Warning 136) [2006 53: p8g³ p10g² f8g³ p9.5g² p10g p9.5g⁵ 10.2m 9d⁵ p10g* p10g³ p8g* p8.6g⁴ Dec 27] modest performer, better on all-weather than turf: won banded races at Kempton in October and December: stays easy 1¼m: acts on all-weather, good to firm and good to soft going. *A. G. Newcombe* — **50 a61**

MAJESTAS (IRE) 2 b.c. (Apr 21) Val Royal (FR) 127 – Pantera Piceno (IRE) (College **71**
Chapel 122) [2006 6.1g 7m 7.1m⁴ 8.3g⁵ 8m Oct 8] 27,000Y: smallish, rather leggy colt:
second foal: dam Italian 7f winner: fair maiden: stays 1m: raced on good going or firmer.
J. G. M. O'Shea

MAJESTICAL (IRE) 4 b.g. Fayruz 116 – Haraabah (USA) 99 (Topsider (USA)) **59**
[2006 67: p6g p6g² p6g* p7g⁴ p6g⁵ p5g p6g 5.2g 5.7f 5.3m 5f p6g p6g p6g Dec 30] **a73**
tall gelding: fair handicapper on all-weather, modest on turf: won at Wolverhampton in
January: effective at 5f to easy 7f: acts on polytrack and firm going: wears cheekpieces/
blinkers: has hung right/carried head high. *J. M. Bradley*

MAJESTIC CHEER 2 b.g. (Feb 12) Royal Applause 124 – Muwasim (USA) (Mead- **75**
owlake (USA)) [2006 p7g⁶ 6m 7s⁶ p7.1g* Nov 3] quite good-topped gelding: fourth foal:
half-brother to 6-y-o Black Falcon: dam unraced: fair form: improved to win maiden at
Wolverhampton: gelded after: stays 7f: acts on polytrack. *M. R. Channon*

MAJESTIC CHIEF 2 b.c. (Apr 2) Xaar 132 – Grand Splendour 79 (Shirley Heights **–**
130) [2006 7s 8.2s Oct 25] good-topped colt: no show in maidens. *K. A. Ryan*

MAJESTIC HALO 3 b.f. Royal Applause 124 – Circle of Light 102 (Anshan 119) **76**
[2006 8d² 8m³ 10m² p10g² 8v p9.5g⁵ p10g* Nov 13] leggy filly: first foal: dam 2-y-o 1m
winner who stayed 1¼m: fair performer: won maiden at Lingfield in November: stays
1¼m: acts on polytrack, good to firm and good to soft going: sold 22,000 gns, sent to
Qatar. *E. A. L. Dunlop*

MAJESTIC MISSILE (IRE) 5 b.h. Royal Applause 124 – Tshusick 81 (Dancing **117**
Brave (USA) 140) [2006 118: 5m 5m 5m² 5f 5m* 5m Oct 1] tall, quite good-topped
horse: smart performer: won Molecomb Stakes at Goodwood and Cornwallis Stakes at
Ascot at 2 yrs: best effort in 2006 when winning Prix du Petit Couvert Casino Barriere de
Dinard at Longchamp in September by a length from Peace Offering: never in contention
after tardy start when seventh to Desert Lord in Prix de l'Abbaye on same course final

Flying Tiger Partnership I's "Majestic Missile"

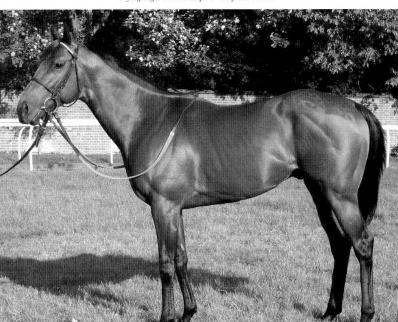

outing: largely disappointing in Britain earlier in 2006 (visored second start), including when ¾-length second to Donna Blini in minor event at Newmarket in July, meeting trouble: free-going sort, best at 5f: acted on firm going: had been bandaged hind joints/ taken steadily to post: usually tongue tied at 4 and 5 yrs: had worn crossed noseband: to stand at Ballyhane Stud, Co Carlow, Ireland, fee €5,000. *W. J. Haggas*

MAJESTIC ROI (USA) 2 ch.f. (Apr 13) Street Cry (IRE) 130 – L'Extra Honor (USA) (Hero's Honor (USA)) [2006 6s 6f* Jun 8] 25,000Y: quite good-topped filly: half-sister to several winners, including 3-y-o Ransom Strip and useful performer up to 14.6f Hiddnah (by Affirmed), 7f winner at 2 yrs: dam, French 1½m winner (including listed race), half-sister to very smart 1¼m winner Montelimar: better for debut (too free), won maiden at Hamilton by ½ length from Adaptation, still green: bred to stay at least 1m: looks useful prospect. *M. R. Channon* **86 p**

MAJIK 7 ch.g. Pivotal 124 – Revoke (USA) 70 (Riverman (USA) 131) [2006 64, a80: f6g² f6g f6g² f6g⁵ 5d f6g f6g⁴ f6g³ f6g* f6g³ f6g² Dec 5] close-coupled gelding: just fair performer on all-weather in 2006 (well held only outing on turf): left D. ffrench Davis after third start, P. Blockley after eighth: best at 5f/6f: acts on all-weather, heavy and good to firm going: tried tongue tied/visored, usually wears cheekpieces. *P. T. Midgley* **– a72**

MAJOLICA 2 br.f. (Feb 27) Lujain (USA) 119 – Marjorie's Memory (IRE) 76 (Fairy King (USA)) [2006 6g Jun 30] 26,000Y: close-coupled filly: sister to useful 2005 2-y-o 6f winner Mixed Blessing and half-sister to 3 winners by Petong, including 8.5f to 1¼m winner Pay The Silver: dam 5f winner, including at 2 yrs: well held in maiden at Newmarket (moved poorly to post). *N. P. Littmoden*

MAJOR BLADE (GER) 8 b.g. Dashing Blade 117 – Misniniski (Niniski (USA) 125) [2006 8.1g p9.5g* p10g² p13.9g 12.1m Aug 10] one-time fairly useful performer in Germany, modest nowadays: won apprentice handicap at Wolverhampton in May: probably stays 1¼m: acts on polytrack and good to soft going. *Mrs H. Dalton* **55**

MAJOR CADEAUX 2 ch.c. (Mar 1) Cadeaux Genereux 131 – Maine Lobster (USA) 71 (Woodman (USA) 126) [2006 6s* 6m² Jun 20] 37,000F, €65,000Y: strong, lengthy colt: second foal: dam, maiden who stayed 1¼m, out of US Grade 1 2-y-o 8.5f winner Capades: useful form: good impression in winning maiden at Newbury in May by 1¼ lengths from Jo'burg (Champlain third, Conquest fifth): not fluent to post but improvement when ¾-length second of 21 to Hellvelyn in Coventry Stakes at Royal Ascot, always prominent (jarred up after): likely to stay 7f/1m. *R. Hannon* **104**

MAJOR LEAGUE (USA) 4 b.g. Magic Cat (USA) – Quick Grey (USA) (El Prado (IRE) 119) [2006 p7g p8g May 1] big, strong gelding: successful 3 times in USA (trained by P. Murphy), including in allowance race at Lone Star Park in 2005: well held in handicaps for current stable: stays 8.5f: acts on dirt and firm going. *K. Bishop* **–**

MAJOR MAGPIE (IRE) 4 b.g. Rossini (USA) 118 – Picnic Basket (Pharly (FR) 130) [2006 72: 8d⁶ 8d* 8m⁶ 8g 8.9m 8f 8d² 10f² 8m³ 8g⁶ 8d* 8.9s Oct 7] close-coupled gelding: fairly useful handicapper: easily best efforts when winning at Pontefract in April and September: stays 1¼m: acts on firm and good to soft going: held up. *M. Dods* **83**

MAJORS CAST (IRE) 5 b.h. Victory Note (USA) 120 – Ziffany 68 (Taufan (USA) 119) [2006 123: 7.1m* 8s² May 20] good-topped horse: very smart performer: much improved in 2005, winning 3 handicaps at Nad Al Sheba: landed odds in 3-runner listed race at Haydock in May comfortably by 1½ lengths from Philharmonic: good 1¾ lengths second to Peeress in Lockinge Stakes at Newbury 2 weeks later, that rival getting first run: was effective at 7f/1m: acted on polytrack, firm and soft going: had good turn of foot: was tough and reliable: put down in June after fracturing off-fore on gallops. *J. Noseda* **123**

MAJOR SPECULATION (IRE) 6 b.g. Spectrum (IRE) 126 – Pacific Grove 89 (Persian Bold 123) [2006 54: f8g Jan 19] smallish, sturdy gelding: modest performer at 5 yrs: well held only outing in 2006. *J. M. Bradley* **–**

MAJOR THIRD (IRE) 2 b.c. (Feb 3) Daggers Drawn (USA) 114 – Red Rosie (USA) 83 (Red Ransom (USA)) [2006 5d⁶ 5m* 5g 5g⁶ 5m 6d Sep 29] 13,000Y: lengthy colt: first foal: dam, 1¼m winner, half-sister to US Grade 3 8.5f winner Gentleman Beau: fair performer: won maiden at Redcar in May: good eleventh of 28 to Caldra in sales race at Newmarket final start: effective at 5f/6f: acts on good to firm and good to soft going: sold 5,000 gns, sent to Spain. *T. D. Easterby* **70**

MAJOUNES SONG 2 gr.f. (Apr 13) Singspiel (IRE) 133 – Majoune (FR) 105 (Take Risks (FR) 116) [2006 6m³ 6m³ 7f* 7.1m⁶ Jul 27] strong, good-bodied filly: third foal: half-sister to fairly useful 1¼m to 14.4f winner Maria's Magic and 3-y-o Magic Moth (both by Mtoto): dam, French 1m (at 2 yrs) to 11f (Prix Corrida) winner, half-sister to **86**

smart French filly up to 1½m Mousse Glacee: fairly useful form: won maiden at Yarmouth in July by 3½ lengths from Millestan, making all: only sixth of 7 behind Sudoor in listed event at Sandown final start: will stay 1½m: raced on ground firmer than good: carries head awkwardly. *M. Johnston*

MAJURO (IRE) 2 b.c. (Apr 29) Danetime (IRE) 121 – First Fling (IRE) 63 (Last **97** Tycoon 131) [2006 7g 7f* 7g² p8.6m* p8g³ 7d* Oct 10] 16,000Y: good-topped colt: half-brother to 6-y-o Escayola and to 3 winners abroad: dam, 1½m seller winner, half-sister to smart French middle-distance fillies Premier Amour and Fleur d'Oranger: useful performer: won maiden at Folkestone in August and minor events at Wolverhampton in September and Leicester in October: ran well when placed in 2 other minor events, third to Rallying Cry at Kempton fifth start: will stay 1¼m: acts on polytrack, firm and good to soft going. *M. R. Channon*

MAKABUL 3 b.g. Makbul 104 – Victoria Sioux 54 (Ron's Victory (USA) 129) [2006 **84** 92: 6f 5d⁶ 5g⁴ 6d 6m⁶ 5g Aug 30] rather leggy, lengthy gelding: fairly useful handicapper: best effort at 3 yrs on third outing: should stay 6f: acts on good to soft ground. *B. R. Millman*

MAKAI 3 ch.g. Cayman Kai (IRE) 114 – Young Sue 76 (Local Suitor (USA) 128) [2006 **66** 71, a65: 9.8g f8g* 8.2m⁶ 7.5f⁵ 8.1g p8.6g⁶ 9.3m³ 7.1m 9g⁵ 10d 10d* p13g³ p12g Nov 13] **a73** rather leggy gelding: fair handicapper: won at Southwell in May and Brighton (selling event, left M. Johnston) in October: stays 1¼m: acts on fibresand, firm and soft going: blinkered last 4 starts. *J. J. Bridger*

MAKARIM (IRE) 10 ch.g. Generous (IRE) 139 – Emmaline (USA) (Affirmed **57 §** (USA)) [2006 55§: p16.5g⁵ p16.5g⁵ f14g²* f16g³ f14g² f14g f14g⁴ f14g³ p13.9g f14g² f16g⁵ f14g p16g f14g Dec 29] tall gelding: modest performer: won banded race at Southwell in January: effective at 1½m to 16.5f: acts on all-weather and firm ground: tried blinkered/visored, wears cheekpieces: tends to wander: ungenuine. *M. R. Bosley*

MAKDERAH (IRE) 3 b.f. Danehill (USA) 126 – Wijdan (USA) 101 (Mr Prospector **111** (USA)) [2006 76p: 8m* 10d³ 8m³ 7f² 7d* 7d Oct 14] very big, lengthy filly: on weak side at 3 yrs: impresses in appearance: has a powerful action: smart performer: won maiden at Newbury in April and listed race at Ascot (beat Highway To Glory 1¾ lengths) in September: placed in between, best effort when ½-length second to Red Evie in Oak Tree Stakes at Goodwood: best effort at 7f: acts on good to firm and good to soft going: blinkered (well held in Challenge Stakes) final outing: weak finisher: joined K. McLaughlin in USA. *M. P. Tregoning*

MAKE HASTE (IRE) 2 b.c. (Mar 28) Sadler's Wells (USA) 132 – Mosaique Bleue **66 p** (Shirley Heights 130) [2006 8s Oct 10] 240,000Y: big, good-bodied colt: brother to smart 1¼m to 1½m winner Subtle Power and Irish 13f winner Mosaique Beauty, closely related to 9f and 11f winner Poker School (by Night Shift), and half-brother to 2 winners, including useful 1m winner Arhaaff (by Danehill): dam unraced half-sister to Prix Saint-Alary winner Muncie and Prix Royal-Oak winner Mersey: 12/1, slowly away and green when eighth behind Go On Be A Tiger in maiden at Newbury: has plenty of scope, and sure to improve at 3 yrs. *R. Charlton*

MAKE IT HAPPEN NOW 4 b. or br.f. Octagonal (NZ) 126 – Whittle Woods Girl **–** 80 (Emarati (USA) 74) [2006 43: p6g 5.7m 5.3g Oct 13] no form in 2006, leaving S. Keightley after reappearance. *P. A. Blockley*

MAKE ME AN OFFER (IRE) 2 b.c. (Apr 16) Fasliyev (USA) 120 – Rafif (USA) 68 **75** (Riverman (USA) 131) [2006 5.2m³ 6s 5.7g⁴ 5.1g Jun 13] €55,000Y: neat colt: closely related to useful Italian 1¼m winner Pressing (by Soviet Star), and half-brother to 8-y-o Rajam and fairly useful 1¾m winner Kadir (by Unfuwain): dam, 1¼m winner, out of close relative to Ribblesdale winner Thawakib, herself dam of Sakhee: fair maiden: likely to stay 1m: sold 6,500 gns in October, sent to Spain. *B. W. Hills*

MAKE MY DREAM 3 b.g. My Best Valentine 122 – Sandkatoon (IRE) (Archway **62** (IRE) 115) [2006 59: 6m³ p7g 6f² 6f 6.1m 6m p6g p6g² p6g⁵ Dec 20] close-coupled gelding: modest maiden: stays easy 7f: acts on polytrack and firm going: blinkered (ran to form) final start. *J. Gallagher*

MAKE MY HAY 7 b.g. Bluegrass Prince (IRE) 110 – Shashi (IRE) 79 (Shaadi (USA) **–** 126) [2006 52: p13.9g f14g Nov 21] leggy, sparely-made gelding: modest performer at best: well held in 2006: blinkered: held up. *J. Gallagher*

MAKER'S MARK (IRE) 2 b.g. (Apr 23) Invincible Spirit (IRE) 121 – Certain Imp- **85** ression (USA) (Forli (ARG)) [2006 6m³ 6m² 6g² 5.7m* 5.1m Oct 8] €15,000F, 19,000Y: half-brother to 3 winners, including 6f winners Impressive Flight (useful, by Flying Spur) and Moyanna (ungenuine, by Sri Pekan), both later successful in USA: dam unraced: fairly useful form in maiden: second at Newbury (behind Astronomer Royal) and Salisbury prior to winning at Bath in September: favourite, well held in nursery final start (gelded after): should prove best at 5f/6f: raced on good/good to firm going. *H. Candy*

MAKEUSABUCK 2 ch.f. (Jan 19) Foxhound (USA) 103 – Just A Gem (Superlative 118) [2006 5d 5d 6v 7s 7.1m Aug 24] fifth foal: half-sister to 7f/1m winner Flash Ram (by Mind Games): dam unraced: no form. *A. Berry* –

MAKE US FLUSH 4 b.f. Mind Games 121 – Pearls (Mon Tresor 113) [2006 61d, a–: 7d 6g 6.9g 8f Sep 20] leggy filly: no form in 2006. *A. Berry* –

MAKFLY 3 b.g. Makbul 104 – Flying Flip 67 (Rolfe (USA) 77) [2006 87: 6.1f 6s³ 7d 8d⁴ 7d p7.1m p12.2g Dec 6] workmanlike gelding: fairly useful performer: upped in trip and well below form after second start: stays 6f: acts on heavy ground: tried in cheekpieces. *R. Hollinshead* **90 d**

MAKING MOVES 3 b.f. Afternoon Deelites (USA) 122 – Simona (CHI) (Dancing Groom (USA)) [2006 59: p7.1g Apr 22] lightly-raced maiden: well held in seller only outing in 2006. *Miss J. A. Camacho* –

MAKING MUSIC 3 b.f. Makbul 104 – Crofters Ceilidh 101 (Scottish Reel 123) [2006 70: 6d 6f 5g² 6g³ 5m³ 6m³ 6m⁶ 6f⁶ 5g⁶ 6s 6s⁵ Oct 24] lengthy, good-topped filly: fair handicapper: effective at 5f/6f: acts on firm going: blinkered (badly drawn) once at 2 yrs: effective with/without cheekpieces: sometimes wanders. *T. D. Easterby* **72**

MAKSHOOF (IRE) 2 b.g. (Feb 22) Kyllachy 129 – Tres Sage (Reprimand 122) [2006 5f² 6m³ 6s* 5.1m Oct 8] 100,000 2-y-o: good-topped gelding: has a fluent action: fifth foal: closely related to 7f winner Siouxsie Sioux (by Pivotal) and half-brother to Spanish 1¼m/1½m winner by Royal Applause: dam, French 1m winner, closely related to smart performer up to 1m Aragon: fairly useful form: third to Chataway at Goodwood, then won maiden at Haydock (made all, hung left) in September: disappointing in nursery (subsequently gelded): will probably stay 7f: acts on good and soft ground. *M. A. Jarvis* **84**

MAKTAVISH 7 b.g. Makbul 104 – La Belle Vie 73 (Indian King (USA) 128) [2006 84: f5g* f5g p5.1g⁴ f5g* p5.1g 5m 5.1g 5s p5.1m p5.1g p5.1g⁵ p5.1s⁵ Dec 14] close-coupled gelding: fairly useful performer: won claimers in January (apprentices) and March (left I. Semple), both at Southwell: claimed from D. Carroll fifth start, and below form after: best at 5f: acts on all-weather and any going (all 6 turf wins on good or softer): usually blinkered: has run well when sweating: tends to hang right: speedy front runner. *R. Brotherton* – **a87**

MAKTU 4 ch.g. Bien Bien (USA) 125 – Shalateeno 80 (Teenoso (USA) 135) [2006 –: 10.9d p12.2m⁶ p16.5m Nov 21] modest maiden, lightly raced: stays easy 1½m: acts on polytrack and soft going. *P. G. Murphy* **53**

MAKTUB (ITY) 7 b.h. Love The Groom (USA) 123 – Carmen The Best (IRE) (Waajib 121) [2006 –: 12d May 27] close-coupled, good-topped horse: smart performer in 2004 (reportedly strained some muscles behind saddle final start): tailed off both starts since: has worn tongue tie: sold 16,000 gns in October. *E. R. Oertel* –

MALAAQ 2 b.f. (Mar 31) Green Desert (USA) 127 – Izwah (USA) 97 (Bahri (USA) 125) [2006 6m³ 6m⁴ 5f³ 6f² 6m² p5g⁶ 5.2d* Oct 18] small filly: first foal: dam, 2-y-o 5f winner, granddaughter of Salsabil: fair performer: in frame all turf starts, on final one winning nursery at Yarmouth: likely to prove best kept to 5f/6f: acts on firm and good to soft going: tends to hang left. *M. A. Jarvis* **75**

MALAATH (IRE) 2 b.f. (Feb 13) Green Desert (USA) 127 – Mouwadh (USA) 64 (Nureyev (USA) 131) [2006 p7g⁷* Oct 21] first foal: dam, ran twice, out of half-sister to 1000 Guineas winner Harayir: 5/4, smooth winning debut in maiden at Lingfield, quickening through from rear to beat Luck Will Come by ½ length (value extra): not sure to stay beyond 7f: useful prospect. *Saeed bin Suroor* **78 p**

MALACARA 2 b.c. (Feb 10) Rock of Gibraltar (IRE) 133 – Treacle (USA) (Seeking The Gold (USA)) [2006 7.5f* 8s⁴ 8s Oct 21] 200,000Y: leggy colt: second foal: dam, ran twice in France, closely related to smart 1¼m winner Flame Valley out of sister to Prix de la Salamandre winner Common Grounds and half-sister to dam of Derby winner Kris Kin: fairly useful form: won maiden at Tipperary in June: off 3 months, highly tried in Beresford Stakes at the Curragh (12 lengths fourth to Eagle Mountain) and Racing Post Trophy at Newbury (beat only one home): will stay 1¼m. *A. P. O'Brien, Ireland* **86**

MALAHIDE EXPRESS (IRE) 6 gr.g. Compton Place 125 – Gracious Gretclo 54 (Common Grounds 118) [2006 62, a44: p6g⁴ p6g⁶ Jan 5] angular gelding: modest perfor- **57**

mer: stays easy 6f: acts on all-weather, firm and good to soft ground: tried in cheekpieces/
tongue tie, often blinkered earlier in career: often pulls hard/hangs: has found little.
E. J. Alston

MALAKIYA (IRE) 3 b.g. Sadler's Wells (USA) 132 – State Crystal (IRE) 114 (High **80**
Estate 127) [2006 66p: 7.1g 11.7g³ 9.9m³ 11m⁴ 13.1m⁶ 17.2g* Oct 17] fairly useful
handicapper: won at Bath in October: stays 17f: acts on good to firm going: has wandered
and looked none too straightforward: sold 42,000 gns, joined J. O'Neill. *G. A. Butler*

MALAPROPISM 6 ch.g. Compton Place 125 – Mrs Malaprop 83 (Night Shift (USA)) **93**
[2006 96: p5g 5g⁶ 5d 6d 5m 5m* 5m⁴ 5f² 5g² 5.3f⁴ 5m⁵ 5f* 5.2f² 5f⁴ 5f² 5f 5.2m⁵ 5d
5.1m 5.1f 5s Oct 16] well-made gelding: fairly useful handicapper: won at Sandown in
June and York in July: good second at Newcastle fifteenth start: best at 5f/easy 6f: acts on
dirt, firm and soft going: sometimes rears in stall: tends to hang/carry head awkwardly:
usually races prominently: tough. *M. R. Channon*

MALCHEEK (IRE) 4 br.g. Lend A Hand 124 – Russland (GER) (Surumu (GER)) **94**
[2006 87: 7g² 7f* 7.6d 7m³ 7m 7f 6d 7.1m⁵ 7f p7.1m* p7g Oct 26] tall, lengthy gelding:
fairly useful handicapper: won at Thirsk in May and Wolverhampton in October: best
form at 7f: acts on polytrack and firm ground: reportedly bled third outing: sometimes
edges right/races freely: usually races up with pace. *T. D. Easterby*

MALECH (IRE) 3 b.g. Bahhare (USA) 122 – Choral Sundown 81 (Night Shift (USA)) **74**
[2006 66: 8m* 8m 8m² 8.2f⁴ 10m⁵ 8d 8m³ 8m 8m Sep 25] lengthy gelding: fair handicapper:
won at Yarmouth in March: stays 8.3f, possibly not 1¼m: acts on firm going, below form
both starts on good to soft: swerved right at start second outing: sold 11,000 gns, joined
K. Reveley. *M. L. W. Bell*

MALELANE (IRE) 3 b.f. Prince Sabo 123 – Indigo 86 (Primo Dominie 121) [2006 –: **48**
6.1g 5f³ 6g 5d² 5g Aug 21] lengthy filly: poor maiden: raced only at 5f/6f: acts on good to
soft going: reared leaving stall final outing. *A. Dickman*

MALIBU (IRE) 5 b.g. Second Empire (IRE) 124 – Tootle (Main Reef 126) [2006 75: **68 d**
p12g p13g p12g p12g⁵ 10g p12.2g p10g⁴ p10g⁵ p12g⁵ p13.9g² p16g⁴ p13.9g Dec 31]
tall, good-topped gelding: fair performer, on downgrade: left S. Dow after fourth outing,
S. R. Bowring after sixth: stays easy 1¾m: acts on polytrack and good to firm ground:
tried in headgear. *M. Appleby*

MALINSA BLUE (IRE) 4 b.f. Desert Style (IRE) 121 – Talina's Law (IRE) 83 (Law **69**
Society (USA) 130) [2006 86: 8m⁵ 6.9g 8.2f 7.5m⁵ 6m 6d Sep 14] workmanlike filly: just
fair performer in 2006: stays 1m: acts on firm going: sometimes blinkered (including last
3 starts). *S. Parr*

MALTESE FALCON 6 b.g. Mark of Esteem (IRE) 137 – Crime Ofthecentury 80 **109**
(Pharly (FR) 130) [2006 110: 5m 5f 5.1g 5m⁶ 5g 5m 5.1m⁴ p5g⁴ p6g p6g* p6g* p6g⁵
Dec 16] strong, good-topped gelding: smart performer: reverted to front-running tactics
and returned to form to win handicaps at Lingfield in November and December, latter by
neck from Woodnook: effective at 5f/6f: acts on polytrack, good to firm and good to soft
going: usually tongue tied, tried blinkered: reportedly lost shoe second/third outings:
none too consistent. *P. F. I. Cole*

MALT OR MASH (USA) 2 gr.c. (Feb 11) Black Minnaloushe (USA) 123 – Southern **80**
Tradition (USA) (Family Doctor (USA)) [2006 7f⁶ 7.1d³ 8g² Oct 10] 38,000Y: big,
lengthy colt: unfurnished at 2 yrs: fifth living foal: half-brother to 3 minor winners in
USA: dam US Grade 3 winner at 8.5f/9f: progressive form in maidens, third at Warwick
and Newbury (beaten 5¼ lengths by Sunshine Kid): stays 1m. *R. Hannon*

MALUTI 5 ch.g. Piccolo 121 – Persian Blue 64 (Persian Bold 123) [2006 54: p5g 5.9m **–**
Jun 19] small, close-coupled gelding: modest performer at best: well held in 2006:
blinkered final outing. *Rae Guest*

MALYANA 2 b.f. (Feb 24) Mtoto 134 – Pass The Peace 116 (Alzao (USA) 117) [2006 **79**
7d⁶ p7g² 8.1g² 8g* Oct 13] strong, good-bodied filly: type to carry condition: sister to
smart 7f (at 2 yrs) to 1¼m winner Tarfshi and half-sister to several winners, including
1997 Cheveley Park Stakes winner Embassy (by Cadeaux Genereux): dam won Cheveley
Park Stakes and second in Poule d'Essai des Pouliches: fair form in maidens, twice
runner-up before winning at Brighton (edged left again): will stay 1¼m: makes running.
M. A. Jarvis

MAMALINI 2 b.f. (Mar 1) Bertolini (USA) 125 – Mamalama 50 (Nishapour (FR) 125) **51**
[2006 5s 6m⁵ p6g 5.1m Sep 4] 1,600Y: third foal: closely related to 2 winners abroad
by Foxhound: dam, staying maiden on Flat, winning hurdler: poor form: trained by
J. Gallagher on debut. *P. D. Cundell*

MAMBAZO 4 b.g. Dansili 127 – Kalindi 102 (Efisio 120) [2006 53, a62: p6g^2 p6g^6 **a85** p5.1g* p5.1g^5 p5.1g^3 p5g* p5g^4 6m 5.1m p5g^5 p6g^5 5.2m p6g^2 p6g^2 p7g p6g^5 p6g p6g Dec 28] stocky gelding: fairly useful handicapper on all-weather: won at Wolverhampton (amateurs) in January, Lingfield in March and Wolverhampton in September: effective at 5f/6f: acts on all-weather, had form on good to firm going earlier in career: tried blinkered: sometimes starts slowly: held up. *S. C. Williams*

MAMBOMOON 2 b.c. (May 13) Zaha (CAN) 106 – Moontime (FR) (Habitat 134) – [2006 6m 5.9g 6s Oct 24] well held in maidens (tongue tied once): bred to stay 1m. *T. D. Easterby*

MAMBONOW (USA) 3 b.c. Kingmambo (USA) 125 – Easy Now (USA) (Danzig **67** (USA)) [2006 7s 8m^4 7m^6 7.1m^3 p7g^5 Oct 15] close-coupled, useful-looking colt: eighth foal: closely related to winner in USA by Mr Prospector and half-brother to 2 winners: dam, US Grade 1 9f winner, half-sister to Belmont Stakes winner Easy Goer: fair maiden: stays 1m: acts on soft and good to firm going: visored (below form) final outing: sold 22,000 gns, sent to Saudi Arabia. *J. Noseda*

MAMBO SPIRIT (IRE) 2 b.g. (Apr 8) Invincible Spirit (IRE) 121 – Mambodorga **84** (USA) (Kingmambo (USA) 125) [2006 5m 5g^4 5g^2 6d 5.5m* 5.1f* 5.1m Oct 8] €22,000F, 15,000Y, 17,000 2-y-o: tall, good-topped gelding: second foal: dam, French maiden: half-sister to useful French 1m winners Direcvil and Spring Star: fairly useful performer: won nurseries at Warwick and Chester in September: not clear run final start (gelded after): should prove best at 5f/6f: acts on firm going. *J. G. Given*

MAMBO SUN 3 b.g. Superior Premium 122 – The Manx Touch (IRE) 70 (Petardia **71** 113) [2006 63, a71: f11g^4 p7g^4 p8.6g^3 p9.5g^3 10.9g^2 9.9f^2 12.1g 11.7f^5 8.5f^2 9.3f^2 Jul 21] leggy gelding: fair handicapper: stays easy 11f: acts on all-weather and firm going: effective with or without blinkers/cheekpieces: winning juvenile hurdler. *P. A. Blockley*

MAMELA (GER) 5 b.m. Protektor (GER) 120 – My Rita (IRE) (Brief Truce (USA) **104** 126) [2006 105: 9s^6 8m^2 10.1f^6 7d^6 8d^3 p8g^4 Oct 26] workmanlike mare: first foal: dam German 2-y-o 7f winner: useful performer: won listed race at Mulheim and Premio Dormello at Milan at 2 yrs, and listed race at Deauville at 3 yrs: left A. Lowe in Germany after only outing in 2005: best effort in 2006 when 1¼ lengths third to Wagtail in listed handicap at Ascot, veering right 2f out and hampering more than half the field: stays 1m: acts on polytrack, soft and good to firm going: sold 72,000 gns. *L. M. Cumani*

MAMICHOR 3 br.g. Mamalik (USA) 115 – Ichor 52 (Primo Dominie 121) [2006 68: **50** 6g 8.5g p8.6g p6g 6m p10g 10.1f^5 Jul 24] modest maiden: stays 1¼m: acts on polytrack, firm and good to soft ground: tried blinkered: tended to hang left final outing. *J. R. Boyle*

MAMONTA 3 b.f. Fantastic Light (USA) 134 – Mamoura (IRE) 97 (Lomond (USA) **63** 128) [2006 11.5m 10.2m^6 10.2g p12g^5 Dec 22] 45,000Y: half-sister to several winners, notably smart Irish 1½m winner (including Prix de Royallieu) winner Mouramara (by Kahyasi): dam Irish 1¼m/1½m winner: modest maiden: sold from D. Simcock 25,000 gns before final start: stays 1½m. *M. J. Wallace*

MAMORA REEF 2 b.f. (Feb 9) Primo Valentino (IRE) 116 – Aubrieta (USA) 73 **72 d** (Dayjur (USA) 137) [2006 6m 5g^3 5m^6 p6g^5 p5.1g^6 Sep 11] 5,200Y: sturdy, workmanlike filly: first foal: dam 6f/7f winner: maiden: third at Carlisle in June: well below that form after: sold 3,000 gns, sent to Sweden. *J. R. Weymes*

MANAAL (USA) 2 b.f. (Mar 31) Bahri (USA) 125 – Muwakleh 115 (Machiavellian **88 p** (USA) 123) [2006 7d* Oct 19] second foal: dam, won both starts at 1m in UAE (including UAE 1000 Guineas) and second in 1000 Guineas, sister to Dubai World Cup winner Almutawakel out of useful half-sister to White Muzzle: odds on, won maiden at Brighton unextended by 2½ lengths from Benllech: will be suited by 1m: certain to improve. *Sir Michael Stoute*

MANBALA (FR) 3 gr.f. Linamix (FR) 127 – Do The Mambo (USA) (Kingmambo – (USA) 125) [2006 97: 8v 10d Nov 4] rather leggy filly: useful performer at 2 yrs: well beaten in listed races 7 months apart in 2006, looking no easy ride (also reluctant to post/enter stall) latter outing: should stay 1¼m: raced only on good or softer going: sold 80,000 gns. *J. L. Dunlop*

MANCHURIAN 2 b.c. (Mar 25) Singspiel (IRE) 133 – Royal Passion 78 (Ahonoora **92** 122) [2006 6m^3 p7.1f^6 8s^6 Oct 7] quite good-topped colt: half-brother to several winners, including smart 6f to 1¼m winner Attache (by Wolfhound) and smart 5f (including at 2 yrs)/6f winner Tadeo (by Primo Dominie): dam, fairly useful from: won maiden at Wolverhampton (beat Thunder Storm Cat by 3 lengths) in August: well held in Autumn Stakes at Ascot 2 months later: should stay 1m/1¼m. *M. J. Wallace*

MANDARIN DANCER (IRE) 3 gr.f. King Charlemagne (USA) 120 – Shamneez – (IRE) 75 (Pharly (FR) 130) [2006 –: 8.3d 7g 11.1f Jun 8] little form: tried in cheekpieces. *Miss L. A. Perratt*

MANDARIN GRAND (IRE) 3 b.f. Raise A Grand (IRE) 114 – Playa Del Sol (IRE) 36 (Alzao (USA) 117) [2006 –: 8.3d 7g⁴ 7.9m 8m 8f 6m⁶ 7.1d 7.2m 7.1m Aug 17] poor maiden: stays 1m: in cheekpieces after reappearance. *Miss L. A. Perratt*

MANDARIN LADY 3 ch.f. Timeless Times (USA) 99 – Lapu-Lapu 62 (Prince Sabo 60 123) [2006 p6g 6g⁴ 6m 6g⁴ 6s⁶ Sep 4] lengthy filly: second foal: half-sister to 6-y-o Lauro: dam, 1m/1¼m winner, became one to avoid: modest maiden: will be suited by 7f: unruly at start and withdrawn intended second outing. *Miss J. A. Camacho*

MANDARIN ROCKET (IRE) 3 ch.c. Titus Livius (FR) 115   Two Thousand (IRE) 59 (Polish Patriot (USA) 128) [2006 50p: 6m² 5d⁶ 8f⁶ 7.1g⁶ 9m Jul 10] modest maiden: best form at 6f: acts on good to firm going. *Miss L. A. Perratt*

MANDARIN SPIRIT (IRE) 6 b.g. Primo Dominie 121 – Lithe Spirit (IRE) 74 86 (Dancing Dissident (USA) 119 [2006 79: p7g p7.1g* p7g p7.1g 7g p7.1g⁵ 7m p6g⁵ 6m² 5.7m⁶ p7g p6g⁶ p6g⁴ p7.1g⁶ p6g* p6g³ p7.1g* p7.1g² Dec 31] compact gelding: fairly useful handicapper: won at Wolverhampton in March, Kempton in November and Wolverhampton in December: effective at 5.7f to 7.1f: acts on all-weather, firm and good to soft going: usually blinkered, wore cheekpieces sixth/seventh starts: effective front running or waited with: reluctant to race and tailed off fourth outing. *G. C. H. Chung*

MANDATUM 5 b.g. Mtoto 134 – Reamur 68 (Top Ville 129) [2006 91: p12g² p12g⁵ 88 14m 11.9m² 11.7f² Sep 9] rather leggy, lengthy gelding: fairly useful handicapper: should stay 2m: acts on polytrack, firm and soft ground: often makes running: sold 55,000 gns, joined J. O'Neill. *L. M. Cumani*

MANDESHA (FR) 3 b.f. Desert Style (IRE) 121 – Mandalara (IRE) (Lahib (USA) 124 129) [2006 10d 10.5d* 11.5m* 9g*ᵈⁱˢ 8d* 12m* 10m* Oct 1]
Versatility in a top modern thoroughbred is harder to find than it was half a century or more ago, when stayers were not stigmatised and the influence in Europe of essentially speedy American-bred stallions was virtually non-existent. The chances of finding another Sun Chariot, let alone a Tristan, are very slim. The former headed the Free Handicap after winning the Queen Mary Stakes and Middle Park Stakes, started her three-year-old campaign over six furlongs and then won the One Thousand Guineas, Oaks and St Leger. Tristan won the July Cup and Gold Cup in the 1880s. Still, in an era of almost dull specialisation, it is pleasing to record the achievements of Mandesha, who did not race at two but developed apace into the best three-year-old of her sex in Europe, winning Group 1 events over a mile, a mile and a half and a mile and a quarter in the space of two months. Admittedly, that did

Prix d'Astarte, Deauville—Mandesha eclipses some of the principals from the Poule d'Essai des Pouliches;
Impressionnante (left) is second, ahead of Tie Black (No.6);
In Clover (rail) beats Price Tag (second left) for fourth

Prix Vermeille Lucien Barriere, Longchamp—in a steadily-run race, Mandesha has far too much finishing speed for her rivals; Montare is runner-up, ahead of Royal Highness (No.1)

not quite match Meld, successful in the One Thousand Guineas, Oaks, Coronation Stakes and St Leger in 1955, or Petite Etoile, who was switched around in distance in 1959 but kept on coming up trumps, recording victories in the One Thousand Guineas, Oaks, Sussex Stakes, Yorkshire Oaks and Champion Stakes. Besides Mandesha, Triptych and Kazzia are other fillies in recent history to go up, then down, in distance in the course of winning Group 1 races in the same season.

Mandesha's career before her three big victories—in the Prix d'Astarte at Deauville and the Prix Vermeille and Prix de l'Opera at Longchamp—takes little describing. She was only seventh in a newcomers race at Longchamp at the end of April, then won a maiden event at Saint-Cloud a month later before narrowly justifying favouritism from Flow Chart in the Prix Urban Sea at Le Lion-d'Angers in the Provinces in the middle of June. This listed race was run two days after the Prix de Diane, so Mandesha needed to progress pretty swiftly if she was to make her presence felt among the best of her sex. The first sign that she might achieve this came on her next start in the Prix Chloe at Maisons-Laffitte just over a fortnight later. Her winning run came to an end there, but only through the intervention of the stewards, Mandesha being clearly best on the day when beating Sexy Lady by a length and a half, showing a good turn of foot in a race which developed into a sprint. However, Mandesha had edged left and caused interference so, under the more stringent French rules, was disqualified.

Mandesha did not need to show vast improvement on her Prix Chloe form to go close in the Prix d'Astarte at the end of July. Elevated to Group 1 status in 2004, this race has not yet consistently matched the others over a mile which were similarly boosted, namely the Falmouth Stakes, Sun Chariot Stakes and Matron Stakes. The latest renewal of the d'Astarte was not exactly vintage, with no runners from Britain, Rajeem having been pulled out because of an infected heel. Mandesha started favourite opposed by nine, notably the first three in a substandard Poule d'Essai des Pouliches, Tie Black, Price Tag and Impressionnante. Reportedly fitted with a special bit to prevent her hanging, Mandesha improved to dispute the lead over a furlong out, soon took it up and stayed on well to defeat Impressionnante by half a length, with Tie Black beaten a total of two lengths in third. Given the difference in distance between the two races, tackling the Prix Vermeille Lucien Barriere six weeks later was a bold move. Mandesha looked in superb shape but, in a field of eleven, she did not start favourite, that honour, if such it be, going to the four-year-old Freedonia, winner of the Prix de Pomone from a field including three other Vermeille runners, Montare, Royal Highness and the lone British hope, Time On. Fermion, a listed winner at Newbury, provided an Irish challenger while Wurf-scheibe, successful in Group 3 events on her last two starts, came from Germany. Again, not a vintage renewal but Mandesha could hardly have been more impressive. Held up in touch behind a steady pace, she did not need to be put under strong pressure when asked to go past Montare and Royal Highness halfway up the straight and she quickened smoothly clear to win by a length and a half from the former. Freedonia did not get a clear run and should have finished second instead of fourth, though she would not have troubled the winner, who gave her trainer Alain de Royer Dupre his fifth victory in the race.

634

Success in the Prix Vermeille encouraged bookmakers to introduce Mandesha into betting for the Prix de l'Arc de Triomphe at between 8/1 and 12/1, but she would have had to be supplemented for that race at a cost of €60,000. Her owner decided to wait until 2007 for a crack at the Arc, Mandesha being trained instead for the Prix de l'Opera Casino Barriere d'Enghien Les Bains on Arc day, in which she faced her toughest opponent so far in Alexandrova, reverting to a mile and a quarter after destroying her opponents over a mile and a half in the Oaks, Irish Oaks and Yorkshire Oaks. Alexandrova started a shade of odds on with Mandesha at 6/5, followed by Irridescence (Queen Elizabeth II Cup), Dionisia (Oaks d'Italia), Satwa Queen (Prix Jean Romanet) and the outsider of the party Nannina (Coronation Stakes). The field was the smallest since the Opera was made a Group 1 in 2000 but, in quality, it was well up to scratch. Mandesha put up her best performance so far to win. Held up on the inside as Irridescence led, she began to make ground once Satwa Queen took over in front early in the straight. Sticking to the rail, Mandesha was bumped by Satwa Queen but Soumillon persevered, Mandesha got room and her turn of foot proved decisive as she burst through to win by three quarters of a length. Alexandrova, staying on after taking time to reach top pace, was two and a half lengths away third. In all probability, Alexandrova needs further, or at least needs to be ridden closer to the pace over this trip, but victory still put Mandesha at the top of the class. The chance of adding to her laurels in the Hong Kong Cup in December was scotched when Mandesha failed to shine in her work in November. She had had a long season and had been going in her coat on Arc day.

Mandesha was not bred by the Aga Khan but by his daughter Princess Zahra Aga Khan. However, one of the principles of their studs is the use of a wide range of sires, including some which can hardly be called fashionable. Mandesha's sire Desert Style, also responsible for an Aga Khan-bred Group 1 winner in Caradak, stood at €10,000 in the latest season, less than his fee when covering Mandesha's dam Mandalara, which was €12,750. While Desert Style has done reasonably well, with smart milers Bachir and Cape Town and Deutsches Derby winner Next Desert also among his principal winners, he is not right out of the top drawer as a sire. He showed very smart form over six and seven furlongs at two and three, including when winning the Phoenix Sprint and finishing a close second in the Hong Kong International Bowl. Next Desert was from a stout female line and Mandesha's stamina is also down to the influence of Mandalara, who won her only race at nine and a half furlongs and has had no other runners. Her only previous foal, the unraced four-year-old filly Mandaraka, was picked up for what has proved a snip of €2,000 at Goffs in June 2005, while Mandalara fetched only €16,000 when culled in 2004, in foal to the relatively obscure Numerous. The mare proved rather more popular at the same venue—Deauville's December Sale—two months after Mandesha's Prix de l'Opera victory, being sold for €1.7 million in foal to Dinyeper, Turkish Horse of the Year in 2003. Mandalara's dam Madiriya was suited by middle distances, winning the Galtres Stakes, and is dam of a dual Grade 1 scorer at around a mile and a quarter in Manndar. Further back, this is a very speedy family, with

Prix de l'Opera Casino Barriere d'Enghien Les Bains, Longchamp—in the smallest field since the race was upgraded to Group 1 in 2000, Mandesha (rail) is given a daring ride between the rail and runner-up Satwa Queen; Oaks winner Alexandrova (No.5) is only third, ahead of Irridescence (rail) and Nannina

Princess Zahra Aga Khan's "Mandesha"

such as Palariva, Rivaz and Mumtaz Mahal, but that is of purely academic interest. Rivaz is in the eighth generation, and as Phil Bull pointed out in his notes on Dante in *Best Horses of 1944*, the importance of a mare in that position in a pedigree, as an element of ancestry, is 1/16,384th of the importance of the subject horse's sire and dam.

Mandesha (FR) (b.f. 2003)	Desert Style (IRE) (b 1992)	Green Desert (b 1983)	Danzig / Foreign Courier
		Organza (b 1985)	High Top / Canton Silk
	Mandalara (IRE) (ch 1997)	Lahib (b 1988)	Riverman / Lady Cutass
		Madiriya (ch 1997)	Diesis / Majanada

Both Sun Chariot and Tristan, mentioned above, were temperamental, with the filly impersonating a mule more than once and Tristan reportedly ending up killing himself by hitting his head against a wall in a fit of temper. Happily, Mandesha is of equable temperament and she should continue to be a force to reckon with. At the moment, thoughts of an Arc triumph may be somewhat optimistic, but, as a strong, stocky filly who impresses in appearance, she has the scope to improve physically, and, after all, has raced only seven times. Whatever her fate against the colts, Mandesha should be hard to beat in any fillies' and mares' race she contests at up to a mile and a half. She has a fine turn of foot (usually held up) and acts on good to firm and good to soft going. *A. de Royer Dupre, France*

MANDINKA 6 b.g. Distinctly North (USA) 115 – Primo Panache (Primo Dominie 121) –
[2006 –, a73: f11g Feb 7] big, good-topped gelding: fair on all-weather, little form on
turf: well held only outing in 2006. *J. F. Coupland*

MANDRAGOLA 2 b.c. (Apr 27) Machiavellian (USA) 123 – Viz (USA) (Kris S –
(USA)) [2006 7d Aug 25] half-brother to several winners, notably smart 1½m performer
(Oaks third) Relish The Thought (by Sadler's Wells), 7f winner at 2 yrs, and useful 7f (at
2 yrs)/1m winner Secret Charm (by Green Desert): dam, US 2-y-o 1m winner and third in
Grade 1 1m event, out of half-sister to Breeders' Cup Juvenile winner Brocco: 33/1, no
show in maiden at Newmarket. *B. W. Hills*

MANDRIANO (ITY) 2 b.g. (Mar 18) Averti (IRE) 117 – My Penny (USA) (Gulch 52
(USA)) [2006 7.2d 6g 7s 6s⁵ f5g³ p5.1g Nov 16] maiden: form only when third at Southwell (first of 2 starts in cheekpieces): should stay 6f/7f: gelded. *D. W. Barker*

MANDURAH (IRE) 2 b.g. (Jan 15) Tagula (IRE) 116 – Fearfully Grand (Grand Lodge 53
(USA) 125) [2006 5.1m 6m³ 7.1d⁶ Aug 2] strong, sturdy gelding: modest maiden: third to
Algol at Catterick: gelded after final start: should stay 7f. *D. Nicholls*

MANDURO (GER) 4 br.c. Monsun (GER) 124 – Mandellicht (IRE) (Be My Guest 123
(USA) 126) [2006 118: 10g* 10.5d³ 9.3d² 10m³ 8m³ 8s² 8g³ 9.8m² Sep 30] good-bodied
colt: very smart performer: trained by P. Schiergen in Germany prior to reappearance:
won Prix d'Harcourt at Longchamp in April by ½ length from Corre Caminos, getting
first run on runner-up: placed in pattern races all subsequent starts, running well when
short-neck second to Laverock in Prix d'Ispahan on same course, 1¼ lengths third to
Ouija Board in Prince of Wales's Stakes at Royal Ascot, and staying-on neck second to
Librettist in Prix Jacques le Marois at Deauville and to Soldier Hollow (who got first run
on him) in Prix Dollar at Longchamp: found steady pace against him when third to
Librettist in Prix du Moulin de Longchamp penultimate start: needs good test at 1m, and
stays 1¼m well: acts on soft and good to firm going: on toes at Royal Ascot: held up.
A. Fabre, France

MANDY'S MAESTRO (USA) 2 br.c. (Feb 22) Brahms (USA) 118 – Belle Masque 62
(USA) (Devil's Bag (USA)) [2006 6m 6f⁵ 6s³ 6g Sep 30] compact colt: modest maiden:
stiff task in Two-Year-Old Trophy at Redcar final start: raced at 6f. *R. M. Whitaker*

MANEKI NEKO (IRE) 4 b.g. Rudimentary (USA) 118 – Ardbess (Balla Cove 119) 82
[2006 73: 13.8d* 12g⁵ 13.9s 16m⁴ 12f 13.8m⁵ Aug 8] close-coupled gelding: fairly
useful handicapper: won at Catterick in April and Thirsk in June: stays 13.8f: acts on firm
and good to soft going: blinkered (below form) final 2-y-o start: tends to wander/hang,
and lacks resolution. *E. W. Tuer*

MANGANO 2 b.g. (Mar 1) Mujadil (USA) 119 – Secret Dance (Sadler's Wells (USA) –
132) [2006 6m⁵ 5d 5.1d f5g⁶ p6g⁵ Dec 6] sturdy gelding: little form. *A. Berry*

MANGO MISCHIEF (IRE) 5 ch.m. Desert King (IRE) 129 – Eurolink Mischief 84 107
(Be My Chief (USA) 122) [2006 110: 9s³ 10.4s² 10.9f² 10s⁶ 11g 10g⁴ 10d² 12.5s⁴
Nov 22] tall, leggy mare: useful performer: good placed efforts in 2006 in Dahlia Stakes
at Newmarket (close third to Violet Park) and Middleton Stakes at York (3 lengths second
to Strawberry Dale) first 2 starts, and in listed event at Windsor (¾-length second to Lake
Toya) penultimate outing: also ran well when beaten short head by Atlantic Air in Prix
Gontaut-Biron at Deauville (made virtually all, but disqualified having come off a true
line) fourth appearance: stays 1¼m: acts on soft and good to firm going: has hung right.
J. L. Dunlop

MANGO MUSIC 3 ch.f. Distant Music (USA) 126 – Eurolink Sundance 85 (Night 90
Shift (USA)) [2006 6s* 6d⁶ 7s⁶ 6d² 6g² 6d 6g⁵ 6f* 6m 5m* 6g 6g⁴ Oct 12] angular filly:
first foal: dam, 6f winner (including at 2 yrs), half-sister to smart winners up to 1¼m
Bonecrusher and Mango Mischief: fairly useful performer: won maiden at Folkestone in
March, and handicaps at Brighton in August and Sandown in September: flattered when
1½ lengths fourth to Firenze in listed race at Newmarket (well ridden up with pace) final
outing: effective at 5f/6f: acts on firm and soft going. *M. R. Channon*

MANHASSET INDIAN (USA) 2 b.c. (Feb 24) Johannesburg (USA) 127 – Half A 80 p
Scent (USA) (Judge Smells (USA)) [2006 6g³ 5s⁶ Sep 1] $35,000Y, 160,000 2-y-o: half-
brother to 3 winners abroad: dam, 7f/1m winner in USA, half-sister to US Grade 2 winner
at around 1m Top Secret: encouraging 6½ lengths third to Sakhee's Secret in maiden at
Windsor, racing alone long way and briefly clear: possibly unsuited by soft ground when
well-beaten favourite at Haydock 2 weeks later: sent to USA: still likely to do better.
J. Noseda

MANHATTAN JACK 5 ch.g. Forzando 122 – Manhattan Diamond 54 (Primo Domi-   –
nie 121) [2006 67: 12d⁵ f11m Oct 31] quite good-topped gelding: fair maiden at best: well
below form in 2006: tried blinkered. *G. A. Swinbank*

MANIC 4 br.f. Polar Falcon (USA) 126 – Gentle Irony 65 (Mazilier (USA) 107) [2006   57
65, a67: p6g² Feb 1] fair performer in 2005: modest form in claimer only outing in 2006:
effective at 6f/7f: acts on polytrack, heavy and good to firm ground. *E. R. Oertel*

MANIPULATE 3 b.c. Machiavellian (USA) 123 – Balalaika 108 (Sadler's Wells   85 p
(USA) 132) [2006 10m 8m³ 8.3g² Aug 21] good-topped colt: fifth foal: half-brother to
very smart 7f to 1¼m winner Alkaadhem (by Green Desert) and useful 1m/1¼m winner
Lookalike (by Rainbow Quest): dam, 9f winner who stayed 1½m, sister to high-class
1¼m performer Stagecraft: improved significantly with each run in maidens, 1¼ lengths
second to Star Crowned at Windsor final outing, tending to hang: should be suited by
return to 1¼m: likely to do better still. *L. M. Cumani*

MANKANJA (IRE) 2 b.f. (Apr 3) Orpen (USA) 116 – Whispered Melody 68 (Primo   76 p
Dominie 121) [2006 p7.1g² p6g f7g* Dec 23] €3,000F, 6,000Y: sixth foal: half-sister to
fairly useful 7f (at 2 yrs) to 10.5f winner Prayers For Rain (by Darshaan): dam, 1m
winner, half-sister to smart 9f/1¼m winner Supreme Sound and useful stayer Top Cees:
fair form: trained by D. Daly on debut: improved to win maiden at Southwell in December by ¾ length from Musical Beat, forced to switch: should stay 1m: open to further
improvement. *W. Jarvis*

MANNELLO 3 b.f. Mamalik (USA) 115 – Isle of Sodor 63 (Cyrano de Bergerac 120)   62
[2006 –: 6.1d⁶ 6.1s² 6.1m⁵ 6g² 6.1m Sep 1] leggy filly: modest maiden: stays 6f, should
be as effective at 5f: acts on soft and good to firm going. *B. Palling*

MANNIKKO (IRE) 3 gr.g. Green Desert 127 – Cassandra Go (IRE) 119   82
(Indian Ridge 123) [2006 65p: 5.1s² 5.1g* 6m³ 5g⁵ 5.2f³ 6g Aug 18] big, strong gelding:
fairly useful handicapper: won at Bath in May: effective at 5f/6f: acts on soft and good to
firm ground: sometimes looks none too keen. *G. Wragg*

MAN OF FORTUNE (IRE) 2 b.g. (Feb 26) Trans Island 119 – Missfortuna 71   –
(Priolo (USA) 127) [2006 7d 8.5g Aug 27] well beaten in maidens. *D. Shaw*

MAN OF VISION (USA) 2 b.c. (Mar 3) Kingmambo (USA) 125 – Nalani (IRE)   74 p
(Sadler's Wells (USA) 132) [2006 p8g³ Dec 19] first foal: dam, French 1½m/13f winner,
closely related to smart 1¼m/1½m winner Altamura and half-sister to smart French 1½m
and 15f winner Affidavit: 7/2, prominent throughout when third to Grande Caiman in
maiden at Lingfield: will be suited by 1¼m/1½m: should do better. *M. R. Channon*

MANOUCHE 3 b.g. Highest Honor (FR) 124 – Green Charter 77 (Green Desert (USA)   70
127) [2006 77d: p9.5g³ p9.5g² 9v* p9.5g² 8s 9.8m Jun 6] sturdy, close-coupled gelding:
fair performer: won maiden at Musselburgh in March: stays 9.5f: acts on polytrack and
any turf going: tried blinkered, usually in cheekpieces nowadays: has hung. *K. A. Ryan*

MANSIYA 4 ch.f. Vettori (IRE) 119 – Bay Shade (USA) 90 (Sharpen Up 127) [2006 63:   64
p9.5g³ p10g p7g 6.1m f7g Jun 3] smallish, leggy filly: modest maiden handicapper: no
form after reappearance: blinkered final start: sold 31,000 gns in July. *C. E. Brittain*

MANSTON (IRE) 3 ch.g. Indian Ridge 123 – Bye Bold Aileen (IRE) (Warning 136)   102
[2006 106: 7g⁵ p7g⁶ 6d 7m p7g³ Oct 21] leggy gelding: useful performer: reportedly
returned home sick after final 2-y-o start: off 4 months and gelded, back to near best
when 2¾ lengths third to Mostashaar in minor event at Lingfield: stays easy 7f: acts on
polytrack, soft and good to firm going: usually front runner (seemed to take little interest
when held up penultimate start): sold 60,000 gns, sent to Saudi Arabia. *B. J. Meehan*

MANTLE 4 b.f. Loup Sauvage (USA) 125 – Kyle Rhea 104 (In The Wings 128) [2006   73
61p: p9.5g² p12g³ p12.2m² 12s p13.9g Nov 16] good-bodied filly: fair maiden: clear and
looked sure to win when breaking down in straight at Wolverhampton final outing: stays
1½m: acts on polytrack. *J. R. Fanshawe*

MANTOLINI 3 b.g. Bertolini (USA) 125 – Leading Princess (IRE) 55 (Double   –
Schwartz 128) [2006 p8g 8.2m p8g p6g Nov 27] tall gelding: little form: tried blinkered.
Pat Eddery

MANY VOLUMES (USA) 2 b.c. (Apr 18) Chester House (USA) 123 – Reams of   93
Verse (USA) 124 (Nureyev (USA) 131) [2006 7m³ 7d⁶ Aug 25] close-coupled, quite
attractive colt: on weak side at 2 yrs: fourth foal: closely related to useful 2003 2-y-o 7f
winner Ithaca (by Distant View) and fairly useful 2001 2-y-o 6f winner Western Verse (by
Gone West) and half-brother to French 9f winner General Knowledge (by Diesis): dam,
won Fillies' Mile and Oaks, half-sister to high-class 1¼m performer Elmaamul: shaped

well when close third to Kalgoorlie in maiden at Newmarket, going freely up with pace: odds on, only sixth behind Moudez there next start, finding little in softer conditions: will stay 1m/1¼m. *H. R. A. Cecil*

MARAAGEL (USA) 3 b.c. Danzig (USA) – Hasnaael Reef (USA) (Seattle Slew (USA)) [2006 67p: 6m Sep 12] blanketed for stall entry (upset at start), much better effort in maidens at Yarmouth 13 months apart when fourth on debut, edging left: again odds on, found nothing only outing in 2006: has left Godolphin. *Saeed bin Suroor* –

MARAAHEL (IRE) 5 b.h. Alzao (USA) 117 – Nasanice (IRE) 97 (Nashwan (USA) 135) [2006 126: a10g⁶ 12g³ 10.3f* 12m* 12m⁵ 10.4d² 10d⁶ 12m⁵ Dec 10] **126**

Maraahel visited most of the same venues as in 2005 and was unable to throw off a reputation for a lack of generosity at times. That said, on balance, in some ways his record was slightly improved on the previous campaign. For a start, he went one better than twelve months earlier when adding a win in the Hardwicke Stakes at Royal Ascot to a second consecutive success in the Huxley Stakes at Chester. Maraahel also improved a place on his effort the previous year in the International Stakes at York in August, putting up his best performance of the season and showing high-class form in going down by a short head to stablemate Notnowcato.

After again beginning his season at Nad Al Sheba in March, failing to take to the dirt in the Dubai World Cup, Maraahel reappeared in Britain in the John Porter Stakes at Newbury the following month, finishing a close third to Mubtaker. His Newbury effort was good enough to justify his starting at 11/4-on in the Group 3 Jardine Lloyd Thompson Huxley Stakes at Chester in May, and he duly landed the odds comfortably by three lengths from Counsel's Opinion in a field of only four. Maraahel was only third best in the market among his stable's three representatives in a strong renewal of the Hardwicke, going off at 9/2 behind the favourite Mountain High and Hard Top in a field of eight. In a race run at a steady early gallop, the speed Maraahel had shown at shorter trips stood him in good stead returned to a mile and a half, but, all the same, he did well as the race went, having

Jardine Lloyd Thompson Huxley Stakes, Chester—
Maraahel is successful for the second year running; Counsel's Opinion is runner-up

Hardwicke Stakes, Royal Ascot—
Maraahel (No.7) puts his best foot forward to beat stable-companion Mountain High;
Enforcer (No.5) finishes well to take third, ahead of Day Flight and Hard Top

to wait as Mountain High made his move and then cutting him down to win by a head, with Enforcer a length and half away third. Maraahel was returned to Group 1 company for his last four races of the season. He seemed not to apply himself when a modest fifth of six in the King George VI and Queen Elizabeth Stakes back at Ascot in July and also when a disappointing sixth in the Champion Stakes at Newmarket on his final outing in Britain in October, but he was on his best behaviour in the International at York in between. Only fifth favourite of seven at 9/1, Maraahel looked unlucky, having three lengths to make up on the winner as the race turned into a sprint and going down only on the nod, coming the closest he has to a Group 1 success. He rounded off his campaign with a fair sixth in the Hong Kong Vase at Sha Tin, having been third in the Hong Kong Cup the previous year.

		Lyphard	Northern Dancer
	Alzao (USA)	(b 1969)	Goofed
	(b 1980)	Lady Rebecca	Sir Ivor
Maraahel (IRE)		(b 1971)	Pocahontas
(b.h. 2001)		Nashwan	Blushing Groom
	Nasanice (IRE)	(ch 1986)	Height of Fashion
	(b 1995)	Mathaayl	Shadeed
		(br 1989)	Manal

There is little new to say about Maraahel's pedigree. His half-brother Mostashaar (by Intikhab) again showed useful form in 2006, when another half-brother Mustamad (by Anabaa) showed fair form in three maiden races and Safwa (by Green Desert), a two-year-old half-sister, was unraced, all of them for Sir Michael Stoute. Maraahel seems likely to be busy again in 2007. Whatever else, he has proved a sound and resilient sort. A quite good-topped horse, he again thrived physically on racing in 2006, taking the eye in condition to the end in Europe, his tendency to sweat on occasions seeming to have become a thing of the past. A fluent mover with a round action, Maraahel acts on firm and good to soft ground. Visored in 2006 except at Newbury, he is effective at a mile and a quarter and a mile and a half, and is versatile so far as riding tactics are concerned. *Sir Michael Stoute*

MARAAKEZ 3 b.g. Kalanisi (IRE) 132 – Questabelle (Rainbow Quest (USA) 134) **72** [2006 11m⁴ 10s Oct 18] 90,000Y: first foal: dam lightly-raced half-sister to high-class 1¼m performer Stagecraft: easily better effort in maidens when 5½ lengths fourth to Counterpunch at Goodwood: sold 5,000 gns. *J. H. M. Gosden*

MARACA (IRE) 2 b.c. (Mar 6) Danehill Dancer (IRE) 117 – Marasem 86 (Cadeaux **82 p** Genereux 131) [2006 7d p8.6g* Nov 7] €60,000F, 105,000Y: sturdy colt: second foal: half-brother to fairly useful 7f winner Faleh (by Silver Hawk): dam, 7f winner from 2 starts, half-sister to Rockfel Stakes winner Sayedah: much improved from debut to win maiden at Wolverhampton by 3 lengths from Arctic Wings: stays 8.6f: should do better still. *J. H. M. Gosden*

MARACHI BAND (USA) 3 b.f. Dixieland Band (USA) – Khamsin (USA) (Mr Prospector (USA)) [2006 56: f8g² p7g³ f11g p10g* 12.1d* p10g² 9.9f³ 11.4m⁵ 12s 11.5m³ 11.9g Jul 8] close-coupled filly: fair performer: left E. Dunlop after reappearance: successful in handicaps at Lingfield and Beverley in April: flattered in listed races at Chester and Le Lion d'Angers eighth/tenth starts: very stiff task, said to have finished lame in Lancashire Oaks at Haydock final outing: effective at 1¼m/1½m: acts on all-weather, firm and good to soft going. usually blinkered: sold 130,000 gns in November, sent to USA. *E. J. O'Neill*   **75 +**

MARAJAA (IRE) 4 b.g. Green Desert (USA) 127 – Ghyraan (IRE) 106 (Cadeaux Genereux 131) [2006 p7g 7m⁶ 7m p7.1m 7d p7g* p7g² Dec 3] good-topped gelding: first foal: dam French 1¼m winner: useful handicapper: won at Compiegne and Maisons-Laffitte in 2005 when trained by F. Head in France: won at Kempton in November by 1¾ lengths from Cape Greko: good short-head second to Areyoutalkingtome at Lingfield subsequent outing: effective at 6f to 1m: acts on polytrack and heavy ground, probably on good to firm. *W. J. Musson*   **101**

MARAJEL (IRE) 3 b.c. Marju (IRE) 127 – Idilic Calm (IRE) 78 (Indian Ridge 123) [2006 8g 7m⁴ 6v* 7d 6d Oct 9] €10,000F, €26,000Y, resold 44,000Y: medium-sized, good-topped colt: third foal: half-brother to smart 5f (in Ireland at 2 yrs) to 7f (in North America) winner Steel Light (by Stravinsky): dam, Irish 7f winner, out of half-sister to dam of Refuse To Bend and Media Puzzle: fair performer: best effort when winning maiden at Thirsk in September: stays 7f: acts on heavy and good to firm going: sold 6,000 gns. *P. W. Chapple-Hyam*   **79**

MARASEEL (USA) 3 br.f. Machiavellian (USA) 123 – Cymbala (FR) (Assert 134) [2006 14.1m⁴ Aug 31] $180,000F, $100,000Y: fifth foal: closely related to fairly useful 1m (at 2 yrs)/1½m winner Editor In Chief (by Kingmambo) and half-sister to 7f winner Stay Close (by Belong To Me): dam 5.5f (in France) to 1½m (US Grade 3 event) winner: 50/1, always behind in minor event at Salisbury: not bred to stay 1¾m. *C. E. Brittain*   **–**

MARAVAL 3 b.g. Mark of Esteem (IRE) 137 – Mayaro Bay 108 (Robellino (USA) 127) [2006 55: 10m p12g Jul 1] tall, sturdy gelding: maiden: well held in 2006: tried visored. *M. Wellings*   **–**

MARBAA (IRE) 3 b.c. Peintre Celebre (USA) 137 – Bahareeya (USA) (Riverman (USA) 131) [2006 8m⁴ p7g⁵ 8.1d⁵ p8g⁴ p8g p8g p10g⁶ p10g² Dec 30] smallish colt: first foal: dam unraced sister to high-class miler Bahri and half-sister to very smart performer up to 1¼m Bahhare: fair maiden: left E. Dunlop 10,000 gns after third start: stays 1¼m: acts on polytrack and good to firm ground: often slowly away. *S. Dow*   **75**

MARCELLO 3 b.c. Diktat 126 – Girl From Ipanema 106 (Salse (USA) 128) [2006 p8.6g p8g² p8g⁵ 10.9g 8.3g p10g p8.6m 8m 7d⁶ Oct 10] 45,000Y: lengthy colt: sixth foal: half-brother to 3 winners, including useful 1m/1¼m winner Wondrous Joy (by Machiavellian) and 1m (at 2 yrs)/1¼m winner Mr Tambourine Man (by Rainbow Quest): dam 7f (at 2 yrs)/1m winner: fair maiden: well below form last 5 starts: stays 1m: acts on polytrack: tried blinkered/tongue tied: sold 5,800 gns, sent to Belgium. *P. F. I. Cole*   **65**

MARCHAND D'OR (FR) 3 gr.g. Marchand de Sable (USA) 117 – Fedora (FR) (Kendor (FR) 122) [2006 7d⁴ 7v² 7g* 7d* 6g⁶ 6.5g* 7m Sep 30]   **121**
    The success of Marchand d'Or, who made his racecourse debut in a claimer, in the Prix Maurice de Gheest at Deauville in August may have come as something of a surprise on two other counts. Firstly, the progress made as a three-year-old had seemingly come to a halt when Marchand d'Or was well held on his previous outing. Secondly, it had taken nine years for his trainer Freddie Head, from one of racing's great dynasties, to achieve his first Group 1 success since switching from riding. The race was also notable for the Head family in that it resulted in Freddie's sister, Criquette, describing Olivier Peslier's ride on fifth-placed Quiet Royal as 'a stinker' and 'disgraceful'. The episode resulted in Criquette Head-Maarek and Peslier splitting, with the Wertheimer brothers standing by the jockey and removing nine horses from her care. New tactics were tried in the Maurice de Gheest on Marchand d'Or, who was held up and improved markedly on his previous form to win a shade comfortably by two lengths from Satri, with Amadeus Wolf doing best of a strong British-trained contingent to finish third.

Prix Maurice de Gheest, Deauville—Marchand d'Or gives Freddie Head his first Group 1 winner as a trainer; runner-up is Satri (far left), then come Amadeus Wolf (noseband) and Kodiac (No.5); the ride given to fifth-placed Quiet Royal (blaze, third right) leads to a split between Head's sister, Criquette Head-Maarek, and owners the Wertheimers

After running out a convincing winner of a minor event at Compiegne on his return in March, Marchand d'Or, who had had only the one start at two (not claimed), came up against Stormy River in the Prix Djebel at Maisons-Laffitte. In testing conditions Marchand d'Or was no match for Stormy River, but still ran encouragingly in second, and went on to land a listed event in May and a Group 3 in June, both at Longchamp, making all on each occasion. He didn't need to improve to win the Prix du Pont-Neuf by a length and a half from Mednaya, but stepped up on that form in the Prix de la Porte Maillot, dictating despite a wide draw and, with nothing able to land a blow, beating a field composed almost entirely of older horses in good style. It was then, however, that, dropping back from seven to six, Marchand d'Or recorded his first disappointing effort of the campaign, in the Prix de Ris-Orangis at Maisons-Laffitte, where he was a well-held favourite after racing too freely. Following victory at 13/1 in the Prix Maurice de Gheest, Marchand d'Or started second favourite behind Stormy River for the Prix de la Foret back at Longchamp, where a reproduction of the waiting tactics that had seemed to serve him well at Deauville proved to be against him in a steadily-run event, the field finishing bunched, with Marchand d'Or not discredited in coming under two lengths seventh, closest at the finish.

Marchand d'Or (FR) (gr.g. 2003)	Marchand de Sable (USA) (b 1990)	Theatrical (b 1982)	Nureyev
			Tree of Knowledge
		Mercantile (b 1983)	Kenmare
			Mercuriale
	Fedora (FR) (gr 1998)	Kendor (gr 1986)	Kenmare
			Belle Mecene
		Far But Near (b 1989)	Far North
			Kesar Queen

From the seventh crop of his sire Marchand de Sable, Marchand d'Or can justifiably be considered the best of his sire's progeny. Marchand de Sable won the Criterium de Saint-Cloud over a mile and a quarter as a juvenile, but, despite being a consistent and genuine type, failed to win again until the age of five when successful twice at up to thirteen furlongs in the Provinces. Marchand d'Or's dam Fedora, whose first foal he is, was only lightly raced in France and failed to reach a place. Her grandsire Kenmare, incidentally, who was twice leading sire in France, is also the maternal grandsire of Marchand de Sable. Marchand d'Or's grandam Far But Near was a minor winner but his great grandam Kesar Queen won the Coronation Stakes and finished third in the One Thousand Guineas, and was out of a half-sister to Irish Derby and King George winner Meadow Court. Front-running Kesar Queen was trained by Scobie Breasley, the four-times champion jockey famed for his well-timed late runs who died at the age of 92 in December. Despite the stamina influences in his pedigree, Marchand d'Or is likely to prove best at six and seven furlongs. He acts on heavy ground. *F. Head, France*

MARCH GOLD (IRE) 3 ch.f. Rich Man's Gold (USA) – Dog Wood (SAF) (Fort **54** Wood (USA) 117) [2006 p8g 9.7d⁵ 10g 7g 10d Jun 26] second foal: half-sister to winner in South Africa by Al Mufti: dam Group 1 winner in South Africa at 9f/1¼m: modest maiden: below form after second start: stays 9.7f: flashed tail final outing. *H. Morrison*

MARCHING SONG 4 b.g. Royal Applause 124 – Marl 94 (Lycius (USA) 124) [2006 **104** 102: p7g⁵ 7g² 7m 7m³ 7m³ 8g⁵ 7m 7d Sep 23] good-topped gelding: useful performer: creditable efforts in 2006 when placed in Victoria Cup at Ascot (second to Partners In Jazz), Bunbury Cup at Newmarket (third to Mine) and totesport International at Ascot (third to Dabbers Ridge), and when fifth to Belenus in Sovereign Stakes at Salisbury: stays 1m: acts on polytrack and good to firm going: sold 65,000 gns, joined S. Seemar in UAE. *R. Hannon*

MARC OF BRILLIANCE (USA) 3 ch.g. Sunday Silence (USA) – Rahcak (IRE) 80 **–** (Generous (IRE) 139) [2006 78: 11.9g⁴ Oct 13] lengthy, quite attractive gelding: fair maiden for Saeed bin Suroor at 2 yrs: won over hurdles in September, but well held at Brighton on Flat return: stays 1¼m: acts on firm ground: visored/blinkered last 3 starts at 2 yrs: has looked none too keen. *G. L. Moore*

MARCOSDREAM (IRE) 5 ch.m. Lord of Appeal 109 – Lady Taleca (IRE) 49 (Exhi- **48** bitioner 111) [2006 10s⁴ 12s 14s p9.5g Nov 28] poor maiden: should stay further than 1¼m. *Jarlath P. Fahey, Ireland*

MARCUS ANDRONICUS (USA) 3 b.c. Danehill (USA) 126 – Fiji 125 (Rainbow **117** Quest (USA) 134) [2006 102: 7m² 8g² 8m⁴ 6m Jul 14] small, strong, attractive colt: smart performer: in frame in Greenham Stakes at Newbury (1¾ lengths second to Red Clubs), Poule d'Essai des Poulains at Longchamp (best effort, ½-length second to stable-companion Aussie Rules) and St James's Palace Stakes at Royal Ascot (4½ lengths fourth to Araafa): dropped in trip, soon outpaced in July Cup at Newmarket final outing: stays 1m: acts on soft and good to firm ground: reportedly had muscle problem behind after final 2-y-o outing. *A. P. O'Brien, Ireland*

MARDI 2 b.g. (Jan 26) Montjeu (IRE) 137 – Portorosa (USA) (Irish River (FR) 131) **73 p** [2006 8s⁵ p7.1g³ f8g* Dec 9] rather finely-made, quite attractive gelding: second foal: dam, French 9.5f winner, out of 10.5f Prix Cleopatre winner Garendare: fair form: improved to win maiden at Southwell in December by neck from Algarade: gelded after: will stay 1¼m: acts on all-weather and soft ground: will do better still. *W. J. Haggas*

MARGARET'S DREAM (IRE) 5 b.m. Muhtarram (USA) 125 – Acidanthera 81 **56** (Alzao (USA) 117) [2006 52: f8g p8g p8g p7.1g² p7.1g³ p7g p7g 7g³ 7.2g 7.2m 7.6g³ **a47** Aug 12] modest maiden on turf, poor on all-weather: stays 1m: acts on polytrack, firm and soft going: tried in cheekpieces. *D. Carroll*

MARGARETS WISH 6 gr.m. Cloudings (IRE) 112 – Gentle Gain 58 (Final Straw **–** 127) [2006 –: p16.5g p12.2g Feb 10] lightly raced and no form since 2004: tried blinkered. *T. Wall*

MARIA ANTONIA (IRE) 3 ch.f. King's Best (USA) 132 – Annieirwin (IRE) 94 **64** (Perugino (USA) 84) [2006 8.1g 6d p9.5g⁵ 10.2m 10d* 12s* 11.9d f12g* f11g⁵ Dec 9] €35,000Y: second foal: dam Irish 1m/9f winner: modest performer: left M. Wallace after third start: won seller at apprentice claimer at Catterick in October and seller at Southwell in November: stays 1½m: acts on fibresand and soft ground. *P. A. Blockley*

MARIA LUISA (IRE) 4 b.f. King's Best (USA) 132 – Miss Amy R (USA) (Deputy **87** Minister (CAN)) [2006 90: 8m⁴ 8d⁶ 8g 10g⁴ 10m² 12g Aug 18] angular filly: fourth foal: half-sister to French/Belgian winner up to 1¾m Matabele (by Highest Honor): dam, 1m/ 8.5f winner in USA, half-sister to dam of smart sprinter Cassandra Go and Irish 2000 Guineas runner-up Verglas: fairly useful performer: won maiden at Cork and handicap at Navan in 2005 when trained by K. Prendergast: creditable efforts in handicaps in 2006 when in frame: below form at Ascot third start: stays 1¼m: acts on heavy and good to firm ground. *D. Myerscough, Ireland*

MARIA MARIA (IRE) 5 ch.m. Among Men (USA) 124 – Yiayia's Girl (Smackover – 107) [2006 –: f11g Feb 5] no form. *Mrs N. Macauley*

MARIAVERDI 2 b.f. (Mar 25) Diktat 126 – Belinda 64 (Mizoram (USA) 105) [2006 **51** p7g p6g⁴ Dec 5] first foal: dam 1m to 14.8f winner: modest form in maidens at Lingfield and Kempton: should be suited by 1m+: slowly away on debut. *B. J. Meehan*

MA RIDGE 2 ch.c. (May 12) Tumbleweed Ridge 117 – Ma Barnicle (IRE) 76 (Al Hareb – (USA) 123) [2006 5f 7g 6m Sep 10] well beaten in maidens. *T. D. McCarthy*

MARIKHAR (IRE) 4 b.g. Alzao (USA) 117 – Marilaya (IRE) 96 (Shernazar 131) **82** [2006 56: 7.5v⁶ 10d⁴ 8.2d* 12v⁶ 16d⁶ 12s 12g 16g 13d p16.5g² Dec 9] fourth foal: half-brother to fairly useful Irish 1½m winner Maralan (by Priolo): dam 9f/10.5f winner: fairly useful performer: sold from J. Oxx €34,000 after only start at 3 yrs: won maiden at Limerick in May: creditable second in handicap at Wolverhampton final start: stays 16.5f: acts on polytrack and good to soft ground. *Seamus Fahey, Ireland*

MARINA GAMBA (IRE) 3 b.f. Galileo (IRE) 134 – Appreciatively (USA) (Affirm- **52** ed (USA)) [2006 9.8m 8.3f Jul 31] 150,000Y: tall, angular filly: fifth foal: half-sister to winner in USA by Tabasco Cat: dam, US maiden, sister to very smart performer up to 1¼m Zoman: modest form in maidens at Ripon and Windsor: sold 8,000 gns in Novem- ber. *E. A. L. Dunlop*

MARINE PARADE 2 b.c. (Apr 4) Royal Applause 124 – Ipanema Beach 67 (Lion **75** Cavern (USA) 117) [2006 6s⁶ 6s⁶ 6.1g⁴ 6f⁴ 6g⁵ 6d p7g² Nov 13] 38,000F, 47,000Y: lengthy, angular colt: second foal: half-brother to 3-y-o Lethal: dam 1m/8.5f winner: fair maiden: good second in claimer final start: stays 7f: acts on polytrack, firm and soft going: suspect temperament: sold 13,500 gns, sent to Denmark. *R. Hannon*

MARIOTTO (USA) 2 b.c. (Mar 17) Swain (IRE) 134 – Shamaat Hayaaty (IRE) **96 p** (Sadler's Wells (USA) 132) [2006 7m² 8.1g* Aug 17] good-topped colt: second foal: dam, useful French 11.5f winner, sister to top-class 1½m performer Doyen and Oaks winner Moonshell: useful form: confirmed Goodwood promise (second to Kilburn) when impressive winner of maiden at Sandown by 7 lengths from Teslin, pushed out: will be suited by 1½m: joined Godolphin: looks smart performer in making. *M. Johnston*

MARIST MADAME 2 ch.f. (Mar 2) Tomba 119 – Linda's Schoolgirl (IRE) (Grand **44** Lodge (USA) 125) [2006 6m 6p7.1g³ p6g⁵ 7m Sep 5] strong filly: second foal: dam unraced: poor form, raced in sellers: stays 7f. *D. K. Ivory*

MARJU'S GOLD 2 b.c. (May 5) Marju (IRE) 127 – Dubious (Darshaan 133) [2006 **52** p8.6g Dec 27] 16/1 and green, slow-starting eighth in maiden at Wolverhampton. *E. J. O'Neill*

MARKER 6 ch.g. Pivotal 124 – Palace Street (USA) 103 (Secreto (USA) 128) [2006 **80 d** 80d: 7s⁵ 6m⁵ 6g 6m 6g⁵ 6g 6.1d⁵ p7g p7g Nov 25] sturdy, close-coupled gelding: fairly useful handicapper: below form after second outing: stays 7f: acts on firm and soft going: tried visored. *J. A. Geake*

MARKESTINO 3 b.g. Mark of Esteem (IRE) 137 – Mademoiselle Chloe 106 (Night **56** Shift (USA)) [2006 –: f7g* f7g² 8.3g 8.5f³ 10m 5.9m⁶ 6g³ 6s Sep 4] strong, well-made gelding: modest performer: won banded race at Southwell in May and handicap at Carlisle in August: effective at 5.9f, seems to stay 8.5f: acts on fibresand and firm ground: tried tongue tied. *T. D. Easterby*

MARKET DAY 2 b.f. (Feb 2) Tobougg (IRE) 125 – Makhsusah (IRE) (Darshaan 133) **105** [2006 6.1g⁶ 7g² p6g* p6g* 6m⁴ 7d⁵ 6.5s p7g* a7f Nov 19] 22,000Y: smallish, strong filly: has a quick action: first foal: dam unraced out of half-sister to very smart 1¼m/ 1½m performer Mutamam and smart sprinter Lafi: useful performer: won maiden at Wolverhampton in July and nurseries at Lingfield in July and November, last one a well-contested event by head from Count Ceprano: sold from L. Cumani 100,000 gns, well held in non-graded stakes at Hollywood final outing: stays 7f: acts on polytrack and good to firm going, below form on softer than good. *E. Harty, USA*

MARKET FORCES 2 b.f. (Apr 10) Lomitas 129 – Quota 102 (Rainbow Quest (USA) **75 p** 134) [2006 p8g⁴ Nov 5] fifth living foal: half-sister to 3 winners, including useful 2001 2-y-o 7f winner Protectress (by Hector Protector) who stayed 1¼m and French 1½m winner Share Option (by Polish Precedent): dam, 1¼m winner, sister to Racing Post Trophy winner/St Leger second Armiger: 5/2 and green, 1¾ lengths fourth of 12 to Happy Go Lily in maiden at Lingfield, slowly away and pushed along with bit to do over 3f out before finishing well: will be suited by at least 1¼m: sure to do better. *H. R. A. Cecil*

MARKET WATCHER (USA) 5 b.g. Boundary (USA) 117 – Trading (USA) (A P **73** Indy (USA) 131) [2006 77: 12s⁵ 12s² 17.8d³ p16.5m* p16.5g* Dec 2] fairly useful winner in 2004: lost way subsequently and left J. Bolger after final 4-y-o start: fair form when easily winning handicaps at Wolverhampton in November and December: stays 16.5f: acts on polytrack, soft and good to firm going: tried blinkered, tongue tied last 5 starts. *Seamus Fahey, Ireland*

MARKINGTON 3 b.g. Medicean 128 – Nemesia 111 (Mill Reef (USA) 141) [2006 66: p9.5g2 9s4 p9.5g4 10.3f5 9.8m3 12f3 10f2 11f* 10.3m5 12.1m Sep 13] close-coupled gelding: fairly useful performer: won 4-runner handicap at Redcar in July: stays 11f: acts on polytrack, firm and soft going: tried blinkered: patiently ridden: sold 25,000 gns, joined P. Bethell. *J. D. Bethell* — **81**

MARKO JADEO (IRE) 8 b.g. Eagle Eyed (USA) 111 – Fleeting Quest (Rainbow Quest (USA) 134) [2006 86: p7g2 p6g p7g2 p7g* p7g4 p7g* p6g6 p7g 6g 7m3 7g3 p6g p5g p7g2 p6s5 p6g* p7.1g3 p7.1g4 Dec 26] workmanlike gelding: fairly useful performer: won claimer and handicap at Lingfield in February and, having been claimed from S. Dow, amateur handicap at Wolverhampton in December: effective at 6f to easy 1m: acts on sand, polytrack, firm and good to soft ground: tried in cheekpieces: held up (regularly starts slowly). *R. A. Harris* — **82 a90**

MARKOVITCH 3 b.c. Mark of Esteem (IRE) 137 – Perdicula (IRE) (Persian Heights 129) [2006 7p5: 10g* 10s3 10m4 10.5m 10d6 10d6 Oct 27] rangy colt: has scope: useful performer: won maiden at Newmarket (beat Degas Art ¾ length) in April: mostly creditable efforts after, including when third to Red Rocks in listed race at Newmarket, fourth to Flashing Numbers in Prix Eugene Adam at Maisons-Laffitte and sixth behind Best Name in Prix du Prince d'Orange at Longchamp and Into The Dark in listed race at Newmarket: stays 1¼m: acts on soft and good to firm going: ran as if amiss fourth outing. *P. W. Chapple-Hyam* — **102**

MARKUSHA 8 b.g. Alhijaz 122 – Shafir (IRE) 68 (Shaadi (USA) 126) [2006 44: p8g p10g Feb 13] leggy gelding: mostly well held since 2003. *Jamie Poulton* — –

MARLION (FR) 4 gr.g. Linamix (FR) 127 – Marzipan (IRE) 74 (Green Desert (USA) 127) [2006 10m May 13] unfurnished gelding: poor form in bumpers: well held only outing on Flat. *B. R. Johnson* — –

MARLYN RIDGE 2 b.g. (Apr 9) Tumbleweed Ridge 117 – Kayartis 57 (Kaytu 112) [2006 5f 7f p6g6 6d Sep 29] little form. *D. K. Ivory* — –

MARMAIDA (IRE) 2 b.f. (Apr 6) Danetime (IRE) 121 – Marathon Maid 82 (Kalaglow 132) [2006 6g* 6.1m2 6f 5.2f3 6g5 6g6 6d Sep 29] 17,000Y: leggy filly: fourth foal: dam 5f (at 2 yrs) to 1m winner: fair performer: won maiden at Yarmouth in June: twice placed in minor events: effective at 6f, may prove best at 5f: acts on firm going: tends to wander: sold 14,000 gns, sent to USA. *W. J. Knight* — **79**

MARMOOQ 3 ch.g. Cadeaux Genereux 131 – Portelet 91 (Night Shift (USA)) [2006 69p: 7.1g2 8g 7.2d* 7f3 8f5 7g2 p6m* p7.1m* p7.1g6 p7g Oct 11] tall, leggy gelding: fairly useful performer on turf, fair on all-weather: won maiden at Ayr in June and, having left M. Johnston after sixth start, claimer at Wolverhampton (left S. Williams) in September: stays 7f: acts on polytrack, firm and good to soft going: sometimes races freely. *A. M. Hales* — **82 a69**

MARMOTA (IRE) 3 b.c. King's Best (USA) 132 – Reloy (USA) 119 (Liloy (FR) 124) [2006 p12.2g* 12d p12.2g p12.2g5 Jul 3] angular colt: half-brother to several winners, including 1994 2-y-o 5f/6f winner Loyalize (by Nureyev) and Irish 1¼m winner Relish (by Sadler's Wells), both useful: dam won 10.5f Prix de Royaumont and US Grade 1 9f/1¼m events: 9/2 and unseated rider to post, made all in maiden at Wolverhampton in March: well below that form in handicaps after, looking awkward and wandering final outing: sold 6,000 gns later in July. *M. Johnston* — **71**

MAROMITO (IRE) 9 b.g. Up And At 'em 109 – Amtico (Bairn (USA) 126) [2006 60: 6v f5g3 p5.1g4 p5.1g3 p5g3 p5g May 23] well-made gelding: modest performer: best at 5f: acts on all-weather, firm and good to soft going: tried blinkered at 6 yrs: has hung left: often front-runner. *R. Bastiman* — **50**

MAROUSSIES WINGS (IRE) 3 b.f. In The Wings 128 – Maroussie (FR) 115 (Saumarez 132) [2006 86: 10m2 10.4d3 12m3 12.5d* 13.9d4 Sep 8] good-topped filly: smart performer: much improved when third to Short Skirt in Musidora Stakes at York (beaten 3¾ lengths) and to Mont Etoile in Ribblesdale Stakes at Royal Ascot (beaten a length): won Prix Minerve - Shadwell at Deauville in August by ½ length from Mary Louhana, making most: creditable 2¼ lengths fourth to Rising Cross in Park Hill Stakes at York final outing: stays 1¾m: acts on heavy and good to firm going. *P. C. Haslam* — **111**

MAROZI (USA) 2 ch.c. (Jan 31) Forest Wildcat (USA) 120 – Chitka (USA) (Jade **81 p** Hunter (USA)) [2006 6d² Oct 27] $90,000F, $250,000Y: well-made colt: third foal: closely related to winner in USA by Forestry: dam, US 5.5f to 1m winner (including 6f minor stakes), out of half-sister to US Grade 2 8.5f winner Jade Flush: 9/2, encouraging 2 lengths second to Miss Lucifer in maiden at Newmarket, racing alone (by rider's design) until hanging towards pack: will go on and win races. *M. A. Jarvis*

MARQUEE (IRE) 2 b.c. (Mar 3) Mark of Esteem (IRE) 137 – Queen's Ransom (IRE) **54** 70 (Last Tycoon 131) [2006 6m⁵ 7d Oct 10] tall colt: better effort in maidens when fifth at Southwell. *P. A. Blockley*

MARRIAGE VALUE (IRE) 3 b.f. Marju (IRE) 127 – Braari (USA) 97 (Gulch **72** (USA)) [2006 85: 7v³ 7g 7s 5g p6g 6d Oct 3] rather leggy, close-coupled filly: fairly useful performer at 2 yrs: only fair at best in 2003: may prove best short of 7f: acts on heavy going: tried blinkered: sold 25,000 gns. *J. A. Osborne*

MARRIAJ (USA) 2 b. or br.c. (Apr 9) Giant's Causeway (USA) 132 – Be My Sweet- **80 +** heart (USA) (No Robbery) [2006 7s³ 8.2s² Oct 25] $140,000Y, 35,000 2-y-o: leggy colt: closely related to smart performer up to 1¼m in USA/UAE Inamorato (by Tale of The Cat) and half-brother to numerous winners in USA: dam US maiden: placed in maidens: much better effort when head second to Sahrati (pair clear) at Nottingham: will stay 1¼m: raced on soft going. *B. Smart*

MARRON FLORE 3 ch.f. Compton Place 125 – Flore Fair (Polar Falcon (USA) 126) **46** [2006 –: p6g p6g p6g⁵ p5g⁵ p5g f5g⁴ p6g⁶ f7g⁴ f6g⁶ Dec 28] poor maiden: effective at 5f to 7f: raced only on all-weather: wore cheekpieces last 4 starts, tongue tied last 2. *A. J. Lidderdale*

MARRONNIER (IRE) 3 ch.g. Vettori (IRE) 119 – Reservation (IRE) 78 (Common **–** Grounds 118) [2006 68: 10s⁶ 12d Apr 24] big, leggy gelding: fair maiden at 2 yrs: well held in handicaps in 2006. *T. D. Easterby*

MARRYL 2 b.g. (Apr 13) Warningford 119 – Nordico Princess 71 (Nordico (USA)) **–** [2006 5d 5m 6g p7.1g 7m Jul 26] quite good-topped gelding: no form: tried blinkered. *M. W. Easterby*

MARSAD (IRE) 12 ch.g. Fayruz 116 – Broad Haven (IRE) (Be My Guest (USA) 126) **52** [2006 72: p6g p7.1g p7g Feb 8] lengthy, good-topped gelding: modest handicapper nowa- days: effective at 6f/easy 7f: acts on polytrack and any turf going: has run creditably when sweating: waited with. *J. Akehurst*

MARSHALLSPARK (IRE) 7 b.g. Fayruz 116 – Lindas Delight 54 (Batshoof 122) **59** [2006 75, a65: p6g p6g f6g 5d p6g² p6g³ May 8] sturdy, lengthy gelding: modest perfor- mer: effective at stiff 5f to 7f: acts on all-weather, firm and good to soft going: wears headgear. *R. A. Fahey*

MARSHMAN (IRE) 7 ch.g. College Chapel 122 – Gold Fly (IRE) (Be My Guest **98 d** (USA) 126) [2006 98: 7s⁶ 7m² 7m 7m 7m 7.2d 7g 7d p7g Nov 8] good-topped gelding: useful handicapper: creditable second to Imperial Echo at York: below form otherwise in 2006: stays 7f: acts on polytrack, firm and soft going: blinkered (below form) once in 2004: usually held up. *M. H. Tompkins*

MARTHARUM 3 ch.f. Muhtarram (USA) 125 – Needwood Truffle (IRE) 76 (Brief **44** Truce (USA) 126) [2006 50: 5f f5g 5f 5g⁴ 5g⁶ 5s Sep 4] poor maiden: raced only at 5f: acts on good to soft ground: tried in cheekpieces. *J. J. Quinn*

MARTIAN MYSTERY 3 ch.f. Bluegrass Prince (IRE) 110 – Martian Melody 62 (En- **–** chantment 115) [2006 –: 6m 6m Aug 5] tall filly: no form. *M. Madgwick*

MARVIN GARDENS 3 b.g. Largesse 112 – En Grisaille 53 (Mystiko (USA) 124) **48** [2006 –: 6s⁶ 10d f8g 8m³ 7m 6d Oct 2] poor maiden: stays 1m. *P. S. McEntee*

MARVO 2 b.c. (Mar 14) Bahamian Bounty 116 – Mega (IRE) 66 (Petardia 113) [2006 **82 p** 6m 7s* Oct 10] 12,000Y: first foal: dam maiden who should have stayed 1½m: fairly useful form: better for debut, won maiden at Newcastle by 3 lengths from Akiyama: will stay 1m: likely to progress further. *M. H. Tompkins*

MARY ANASTATIA (USA) 4 ch.f. Lion Cavern (USA) 117 – Vannozza 58 (Kris 135) [2006 56: p8g Jan 11] half-sister to 3 winners, including 5f/6f winner Steval (by Efisio): dam twice-raced daughter of high-class performer up to 1m Vilikaia: lightly- raced maiden, modest form at best: well held at Lingfield on British debut: raced only at 7f/1m. *E. Tyrrell, Ireland*

MARY DELANEY (USA) 3 b.f. Hennessy (USA) 122 – Crafty Emerald (USA) **70 +**
(Crafty Prospector (USA)) [2006 67p: p7g* 5.7d 6.1g² p6f⁴ p7f* a8f p6f* Dec 15] fair
performer: successful in maiden at Lingfield in April: left M. Wallace after third outing:
won allowance races at Keeneland in October and Turfway Park in December: out of
depth penultimate start: stays 7f: acts on polytrack. *E. Kenneally, USA*

MARY GRAY 4 gr.f. Mujahid (USA) 125 – Ancestry (Persepolis (FR) 127) [2006 69: **59 d**
p13.9g⁵ 14.1s 14.1d 14m³ p12.2g 12m 13d² 12f⁶ 16g⁵ Jul 3] tall, quite good-topped filly:
modest handicapper: on downgrade: stays 1¾m: acts on polytrack and firm ground: tried
blinkered/visored. *M. Johnston*

MASAI MOON 2 b.c. (Jan 25) Lujain (USA) 119 – Easy To Imagine (USA) (Cozzene **79**
(USA)) [2006 6g 6f⁴ 6m⁵ 6g³ 6s² 7d⁴ 6s² Oct 6] 8,000Y: rather leggy colt: first foal: dam
unraced sister to useful stayer Hiddensee out of smart performer up to 1m Zarani Sidi
Anna: fair maiden: in frame 5 times, including 3 nurseries, ¾-length second to Algol at
York final start: effective at 6f/7f: acts on soft and firm going. *B. R. Millman*

MASEEM 3 ch.c. Generous (IRE) 139 – Entail (USA) 97 (Riverman (USA) 131) [2006 **60 ?**
p10g 10f⁴ Jul 21] 4,000Y: second foal: half-brother to 4-y-o Entailment: dam 7f/1m
winner: seemingly better effort in maidens when 7 lengths last of 4 to Dawera at Pontefract. *Rae Guest*

MASHAAHED 3 b.c. In The Wings 128 – Patacake Patacake (USA) 67 (Bahri (USA) **112**
125) [2006 100p: 10g³ 12.3f³ 10g* 10m⁵ 10d* 12d³ 9d⁴ Oct 14] lengthy, quite attractive
colt: has a quick, rather unimpressive action: smart performer: won maiden at Sandown
(hung right) in June and listed race at Ayr (beat Ouninpohja by 6 lengths) in September:
also ran well when 1¾ lengths third to Papal Bull in Chester Vase and 2½ lengths third to
Degas Art in listed event at Newmarket on second/sixth starts: only fourth to Stage Gift
in Darley Stakes at Newmarket final outing: barely stays 1½m: acts on firm and good to
soft going. *B. W. Hills*

MASHAAIR (IRE) 3 ch.c. King's Best (USA) 132 – Al Bahathri (USA) 123 (Blushing **82 d**
Groom (FR) 131) [2006 78p: 7s³ 7f³ 7.1m² 8s⁵ p8g Sep 27] attractive, quite good-topped
colt: good mover: fairly useful maiden: below form after reappearance: should be suited
by 1m: acts on soft going: has pulled hard/carried head high/found little: best treated with
caution: sold 15,000 gns. *B. W. Hills*

MASKARAID 2 b.g. (Jan 25) Iron Mask (USA) 117 – Radiant Sky (IRE) 62 (Spectrum **–**
(IRE) 126) [2006 6m p7.1g 6d Sep 29] no form. *B. R. Millman*

MASLAK (IRE) 2 b.g. (Mar 27) In The Wings 128 – Jeed (IRE) 86 (Mujtahid (USA) **86**
118) [2006 7m⁵ 8.2d⁵ p8g² Sep 1] good-bodied gelding: third foal: half-brother to 3-y-o
Nidhaal: dam, 2-y-o 6f winner who stayed 7f, out of half-sister to Prix du Jockey Club
winners Assert and Bikala: fairly useful maiden: fifth behind Kalgoorlie at Newmarket
and Sesmen at Nottingham (minor event), and second to Monzante at Kempton (gelded
after): stays 1m. *E. A. L. Dunlop*

MASON ETTE 2 br.f. (Feb 15) Grand Lodge (USA) 125 – Karlaska (Lashkari 128) **78**
[2006 6m³ 6m² 6m² Aug 10] 9,000Y: quite good-topped filly: sixth foal: half-sister to
winners in Italy by Linamix and Halling: dam useful French 1½m winner: fair form in
maiden: second to English Ballet at Windsor and Fishforcompliments at Haydock: will
stay at least 1m: raced on good to firm going. *C. G. Cox*

Doonside Cup Stakes (Sponsored By Easy-Breaks.com), Ayr—
Mashaahed stretches clear of Ouninpohja and Profit's Reality

MASSARO PAPE (IRE) 4 b.c. Intikhab (USA) 135 – Megeve (IRE) (Ahonoora 122)　**85**
[2006 p7g* 7m³ May 13] half-brother to several winners in Italy: dam Italian 6f (at 2 yrs)
to 1m winner: won maiden at Kempton in April on debut: better form when third in ladies
handicap at Lingfield: dead. *L. M. Cumani*

MASSENZIO (IRE) 2 b.c. (Feb 7) Green Desert (USA) 127 – Monnavanna (IRE) 109　**72**
(Machiavellian (USA) 123) [2006 6m⁵ 6m⁴ p7.1f⁶ 7m³ 6g⁶ a5.5g* Nov 2] 170,000Y:
sturdy colt: has a quick action: first foal: dam, 6f to 1m winner, half-sister to smart 1m/
1¼m performer Monturani: fair performer: sold from J. Gosden 28,000 gns before winning maiden at Ovrevoll in November: stays 7f: acts on dirt and good to firm ground.
R. Haugen, Norway

MASSEY 10 br.g. Machiavellian (USA) 123 – Massaraat (USA) (Nureyev (USA) 131)　**–**
[2006 –, a72d: f6g⁵ f6g p6g f6g⁴ f6g f7g f6g f8g f6g* Dec 28] big gelding: useful　**a57**
performer in prime on all-weather (little recent form on turf), just modest nowadays: won
banded race at Southwell in December: best at 6f/7f: acts on all-weather: occasionally
visored (not since 2004): sometimes front runner. *C. R. Dore*

MASSIF CENTRALE 5 ch.g. Selkirk (USA) 129 – Madame Dubois 121 (Legend of　**101**
France (USA) 124) [2006 104: 12s 12s⁴ 12m 14.8d 14.1g Sep 14] big, lengthy gelding:
useful handicapper: has reportedly had respiratory operation: creditable fourth to Gavroche at Goodwood but well below form otherwise in 2006: stays 1½m: acts on soft and
good to firm going: tongue tied. *D. R. C. Elsworth*

MASSIVE (IRE) 2 b.c. (Mar 3) Marju (IRE) 127 – Khatela (IRE) 91 (Shernazar 131)　**103**
[2006 7m 7.2g* 8s² 10d² 9g² 10g Nov 12] €40,000F, €80,000Y: well-made colt: third
living foal: half-brother to French winner around 1¼m Jimbeck (by Night Shift): dam
Irish 1m/9f winner: useful performer: won maiden at Ayr in August: close second in next
3 races, minor events at Ayr and Leicester and Prix de Conde (beaten nose by Midnight
Beauty) at Longchamp: well below form in Criterium de Saint-Cloud final start, eased:
stays 1¼m: raced on good going or softer after well held on debut. *M. R. Channon*

MASTA PLASTA (IRE) 3 b.c. Mujadil (USA) 119 – Silver Arrow (USA) 67 (Sha-　**103**
deed (USA) 135) [2006 107: 6m⁵ 5f 6.1m⁵ 6s⁶ 5.4g Sep 9] good-topped colt: useful
performer: creditable efforts in 2006 only when ninth in handicap at Ayr and 3 lengths
fifth to The Kiddykid in listed race at Chester second/third outings: well held in Portland
(Handicap) at York final outing: will prove best kept to 5f/easy 6f: acts on good to firm
going: has worn crossed noseband. *J. Howard Johnson*

MASTER BEN (IRE) 3 b.g. Carrowkeel (IRE) 106 – Java Jive 63 (Hotfoot 126) [2006　**–**
56?: p8.6g f8g⁶ 11g f7g May 9] useful-looking gelding: maiden: well held at 3 yrs: tried
blinkered/tongue tied. *S. R. Bowring*

MASTER COBBLER (IRE) 4 b.g. Alhaarth (IRE) 126 – Lady Joshua (IRE) 88　**86**
(Royal Academy (USA) 130) [2006 84: 14.1s⁴ 14g 14.1g* 21m³ Aug 2] tall, lengthy,
quite good-topped gelding: fairly useful handicapper: won at Salisbury in June, carrying
head to one side: stays 21f: acts on firm and soft going: wears cheekpieces: edgy sort.
J. Akehurst

MASTER GOLFER (USA) 2 br.g. (Apr 22) Mr Greeley (USA) 122 – Princess Leia　**–**
(USA) (Skywalker (USA)) [2006 6g 7m 6f Jul 31] heavy-topped gelding: behind in
maidens in July: gelded, then sold 1,500 gns. *B. W. Hills*

MASTER MAHOGANY 5 b.g. Bandmaster (USA) 97 – Impropriety (Law Society　**84**
(USA) 130) [2006 87: 8m⁴ p8.6g⁵ p7.1m³ p8.6g Nov 16] fairly useful handicapper:
effective at 1m/1¼m: acts on polytrack and any turf going: consistent. *R. J. Hodges*

MASTER MALARKEY 3 b.g. Tipsy Creek (USA) 115 – Girl Next Door 58 (Local　**44**
Suitor (USA) 128) [2006 –: 7m 8d 6m⁶ p5g⁴ f6g 5.3m⁴ 6m 5f⁵ 5.1g 6d⁵ p6m Oct 9] workmanlike gelding: poor maiden: best at 5f/6f: acts on polytrack and good to firm going:
blinkered nowadays. *Mrs C. A. Dunnett*

MASTER MARK 3 b.g. Mark of Esteem (IRE) 137 – Sur Le Fil (IRE) (Funambule　**52**
(USA) 118) [2006 55: 10g 8.2d 10m May 12] tall, close-coupled gelding: modest maiden:
seems to stay easy 1¼m: looked none too keen final outing. *P. D. Evans*

MASTER'N COMMANDER 4 ch.g. Zafonic (USA) 130 – Magical Retreat (USA)　**71**
115 (Sir Ivor (USA) 135) [2006 73: p10g⁵ p12g³ p16.5g p10g³ p12g³ p12g p10g⁵ 10m
p10g² Jun 17] tall gelding: fair maiden: free-going sort, but should stay 1¾m (seemed not
to stay 2m): acts on polytrack and good to firm ground. *C. A. Cyzer*

MASTER NIMBUS 6 b.g. Cloudings (IRE) 112 – Miss Charlie 59 (Pharly (FR) 130)　**56**
[2006 53: 10.9f⁶ 10.1f² 14.1d* Aug 12] strong, angular gelding: modest handicapper:

won at Redcar in August: stays 1¾m, at least with emphasis on speed: acts on firm and good to soft going: inconsistent: fair hurdler. *J. J. Quinn*

MASTER OF DESTINY (IRE) 2 ch.g. (Jan 16) Compton Place 125 – Memo **52** (Groom Dancer (USA) 128) [2006 5m⁶ 7.1m p7g⁶ Sep 27] good-topped gelding: modest form in maidens. *H. J. Collingridge*

MASTEROFTHECOURT (USA) 3 ch.g. Horse Chestnut (SAF) 119 – Great Ver- **84** dict (AUS) (Christmas Tree (AUS)) [2006 8m 10m* 10g⁵ 11.6m Jul 17] sturdy gelding: type to carry condition: third foal: half-brother to very smart South African 1¼m/1½m performer Greys Inn (by Zabeel): dam 5.5f to 7f winner in Australia: fairly useful performer: won maiden at Windsor in May: good fifth in handicap at Sandown next time: gelded after final start: stays 1¼m. *H. Morrison*

MASTER OF THE RACE 4 ch.g. Selkirk (USA) 129 – Dust Dancer 116 (Suave **89** Dancer (USA) 136) [2006 82: 8.1d² 8.9m p10g 10g p9.5g⁴ Dec 30] strong, close-coupled gelding: fairly useful maiden: left Sir Michael Stoute 24,000 gns prior to final outing: should stay 1½m: acts on good to firm and good to soft going, probably on polytrack: appeared reluctant to go by on final outing at 3 yrs. *T. G. Dascombe*

MASTER PEGASUS 3 b.g. Lujain (USA) 119 – Seeking Utopia 76 (Wolfhound **91** (USA) 126) [2006 71: 7s* 8m 8.1m⁶ 8.3g³ Aug 26] big, lengthy gelding: fairly useful performer: won maiden at Newbury in May: creditable third in handicap at Windsor after: stays 1m: acts on soft and good to firm ground: edged left latter 2-y-o start: consistent. *C. F. Wall*

MASTER PIP 4 b.g. Wizard King 122 – Tachelle (IRE) (Elbio 125) [2006 12f⁶ 8.3g **–** Aug 14] no form in maidens: has refused to enter stall. *T. H. Caldwell*

MASTERSHIP (IRE) 2 ch.c. (Feb 18) Best of The Bests (IRE) 122 – Shady Point **86** (IRE) 76 (Unfuwain (USA) 131) [2006 6m⁵ p7g⁵ p8g 8.5g 8f* 8s² p8.6g² p8.6g* Dec 23] good-topped colt: third foal: dam, 1m winner, out of Sun Chariot winner/Irish 1000 Guineas runner-up Warning Shadows: fairly useful performer: won nurseries at Redcar in September and Wolverhampton (never off bridle) in December: stays 8.6f: acts on polytrack, firm and soft going: blinkered 4 of last 5 starts: not straightforward ride. *C. E. Brittain*

MASTER THEO (USA) 5 b.g. Southern Halo (USA) – Lilian Bayliss (IRE) 100 **–** (Sadler's Wells (USA) 132) [2006 77, a93: p8.6g⁵ Jan 6] small, sturdy gelding: fairly **a80** useful on all-weather, fair on turf: respectable effort only outing in 2006: stays 9.5f: acts on polytrack, good to firm and good to soft ground: wears cheekpieces: tried tongue tied: sold 20,000 gns. *Mrs Lucinda Featherstone*

MASTER WILLIAM 2 b.g. (May 10) Hello Mister 106 – Grecian Melody (Heroic **–** Air 96) [2006 5.1s Oct 25] strong gelding: last in maiden at Nottingham. *W. G. M. Turner*

MATARAM (USA) 3 b.g. Matty G (USA) 119 – Kalinka (USA) (Mr Prospector **–** (USA)) [2006 57: p7g* p7g² 7m p8g* 8d p8.6g³ Dec 19] tall, leggy, long-backed **a84** gelding: fairly useful handicapper: won at Lingfield in June and Kempton in September: also ran well last 2 starts: stays 8.6f: acts on polytrack, only modest form (at 2 yrs) on turf: edgy before pulling too hard third outing. *W. Jarvis*

MATERIALIZE (USA) 3 b.f. Chester House (USA) 123 – A La Mode (USA) 77 **74** (Known Fact (USA) 135) [2006 70p: 11.5m³ 11.5m 10.9m³ 8d⁵ 9.9g 10d Oct 10] angular filly: fair maiden: left P. McBride after second start: stays 11.5f, seems effective at much shorter: tried in cheekpieces: found little third outing. *H. R. A. Cecil*

MATERIAL WITNESS (IRE) 9 b.g. Barathea (IRE) 127 – Dial Dream (Gay Mec- **93** ene (USA) 128) [2006 97, a91: 7s² p7g⁵ 7m 7.1f² 7m 7.1g 7g⁴ 7d p7.1g Oct 29] angular **a81** gelding: fairly useful performer, better on turf than all-weather: effective at 6f/7f: acts on polytrack, firm and soft going: tried in headgear: carries head high: front runner. *W. R. Muir*

MATHOOR 3 ch.c. Fantastic Light (USA) 134 – Madame Dubois 121 (Legend of **58** France (USA) 124) [2006 8m May 13] 230,000Y: sturdy colt: half-brother to several winners, including smart 6f (at 2 yrs) to 1m (Irish 2000 Guineas) winner Indian Haven (by Indian Ridge) and to dam of 3-y-o Hala Bek and 5-y-o Imperial Stride: dam 9f to 14.6f (Park Hill Stakes) winner: 12/1 and green, 10 lengths ninth to Supaseus in maiden at Newmarket, starting slowly and squeezed out as he faded: sold 17,000 gns in July, sent to Italy. *Sir Michael Stoute*

MATINEE IDOL 3 ch.f. In The Wings 128 – Bibliotheque (USA) 79 (Woodman **62 d** (USA) 126) [2006 10m⁵ 11.7m⁵ 10m³ 10.1m⁶ 14.1g 18d⁴ p13.9g f16g Dec 28] fourth foal: closely related to 6-y-o McQueen and 5-y-o True: dam, 1m winner, out of half-sister to very smart 6f to 1m performer Lycius: modest maiden: mostly well below form after third start, leaving H. Candy after fourth one: should stay 1¾m: slowly away on debut/third outing. *Mrs S. Lamyman*

MATSUNOSUKE 4 b.g. Magic Ring (IRE) 115 – Lon Isa 80 (Grey Desire 115) [2006 **88** 79: 5m⁴ 5f* 5g 5.2g 5m 5m* 5f³ 5.4f⁶ 5m 5m² 5g 5m² Sep 8] workmanlike gelding: fairly useful handicapper: won at Thirsk in May and Newmarket in July: effective at 5f/6f: acts on firm and good to soft going: clipped heels and unseated rider ninth outing. *A. B. Coogan*

MATTEROFACT (IRE) 3 b.f. Bold Fact (USA) 116 – Willow Dale (IRE) 89 (Dane- **70** hill (USA) 126) [2006 77: 6m 5.7g 5f⁶ 6g⁶ 5.7g 5.1f³ 5m 5.1m⁵ 5.7f⁶ Sep 9] strong filly: fair handicapper: raced only at 5f/6f: acts on firm going: sold 5,800 gns. *Mrs P. N. Dutfield*

MATTY TUN 7 b.g. Lugana Beach 116 – B Grade 59 (Lucky Wednesday 124) [2006 **79** 89: 5m 5.2d⁴ 5d 5d⁵ 5g 5s Oct 16] strong gelding: handicapper: just fair form at best in 2006: best at 5f: acts on fibresand and any turf going: tongue tied once at 3 yrs: sometimes slowly away: tends to carry head awkwardly/idle. *J. Balding*

MATUZA (IRE) 3 ch.c. Cadeaux Genereux 131 – Aoife (IRE) 83 (Thatching 131) **88** [2006 85p: 6g 5g³ 5f² p6g⁴ 6m³ 5f6g* f5g³ p6g⁵ f5g⁴ Dec 5] big, strong colt: fairly useful handicapper: won at Lingfield in November: mostly creditable efforts otherwise: effective at 5f/6f: acts on all-weather and firm going: blinkered (hung and well beaten) sixth outing: sometimes carries head high. *W. R. Muir*

MAUD'S CAT (IRE) 3 b.f. Black Minnaloushe (USA) 123 – Tree House (USA) **62** (Woodman (USA) 126) [2006 p10g⁶ 9d² 8.1m⁴ 10.5v f8g⁶ p10g Dec 19] €19,000F: first foal: dam, 1m winner in USA, half-sister to smart performer up to 9f Susurration out of high-class Italian/French performer up to 1½m Grease: modest maiden: headstrong, should be best short of 1¼m: acts on good to firm and good to soft going: has given trouble at stall (once refused). *A. P. Jarvis*

MAUNBY REVELLER 4 b.g. Benny The Dip (USA) 127 – Aunt Tate (Tate Gallery **54** (USA) 117) [2006 50: f16g⁴ f16g⁵ f16g Mar 21] modest maiden: stays 2m: acts on fibresand, good to firm and good to soft ground: tried in cheekpieces/visor/tongue tie. *P. C. Haslam*

MAWAZEEN (IRE) 5 b.m. Unfuwain (USA) 131 – Atnab (USA) 64 (Riverman **71 d** (USA) 131) [2006 9.9g⁴ 9.9g⁵ 12m 12g Aug 17] workmanlike mare: second foal: dam 1½m winner: fair maiden at best, lightly raced: left F. Head in France and off 20 months before 2006: should stay 1½m: acts on soft going: blinkered in 2004. *N. I. M. Rossiter*

MAXEMULL 3 b.f. Mull of Kintyre (USA) 114 – Silver Gyre (IRE) 65 (Silver Hawk **–** (USA) 123) [2006 f8g p9.5g p6g f8g Mar 8] second foal: dam, 17f winner, half-sister to dam of smart performer up to 1½m Housemaster: well beaten in maidens/banded race. *D. J. Wintle*

MAXIMIX 3 gr.g. Linamix (FR) 127 – Time Will Show (FR) (Exit To Nowhere (USA) **72** 122) [2006 –: p7g⁵ p8g 10f 11.6d⁶ 10.1m p12g* Oct 17] useful-looking gelding: fair performer: won handicap at Lingfield in October: stays 1½m: acts on polytrack and good to soft going: got worked up in paddock/injured rider intended debut: sold 28,000 gns, joined G. L. Moore. *B. W. Hills*

MAXIM'S (ARG) 5 b.h. Lode (USA) – Mari's Ballerina (USA) (Mari's Book (USA)) **90** [2006 p5g Jul 15] won twice in Argentina in 2004 and (exported to Sweden after reappearance) 2 handicaps at Jagersro in 2005: tongue tied, fairly useful form when ninth in handicap at Lingfield on British debut: effective at 5f/6f: best form on dirt: tried blinkered. *R. A. Kvisla*

MAXOLINI 3 ch.g. Bertolini (USA) 125 – Evening Falls 82 (Beveled (USA)) [2006 –: **–** 6g Apr 25] quite good-topped gelding: behind in maidens. *J. J. Quinn*

MAX SCAL (IRE) 5 b.g. Danehill Dancer (IRE) 117 – Slightly Latin (Ahonoora 122) **82** [2006 83: p8.6g 8v* 7s 8d a7g⁴ 7s 5s 7v⁵ Oct 29] leggy, shallow-girthed gelding: fairly useful performer: won handicap at Thurles in March: well below form subsequently, leaving P. Rothwell after fourth outing: stays 1m: acts on heavy going, below form on sand/polytrack: wore cheekpieces/blinkers last 3 starts. *J. F. O'Shea, Ireland*

MAYADEEN (IRE) 4 b.g. King's Best (USA) 132 – Inaaq 109 (Lammtarra (USA) **77 d** 134) [2006 88: 7.9m⁵ 8.3m⁵ 12m 8.1m 10s Oct 16] good-topped gelding: handicapper: regressive form in 2006: needs further than 1m (should stay 1½m): acts on firm going: tried in cheekpieces/visor. *J. G. M. O'Shea*

MAYA'S PRINCE 4 b.g. Easycall 115 – Delciana (IRE) 61 (Danehill (USA) 126) **47**
[2006 7s p8g p7g 8m p10g p8.6g p5.1g⁶ Jul 17] poor maiden: should be suited by 1m+:
form only on polytrack: refused to enter stall intended fifth outing. *M. D. I. Usher*

MAYBACH 5 gr.h. Machiavellian (USA) 123 – Capote Line (USA) (Capote (USA)) **109**
[2006 113: 9.5s⁴ a8.7g⁴ 9.8g⁶ 9.8m² 8m³ a8g* a8g* a12g² a10g² p10g Nov 18] fair form
in 2 starts for J. Noseda at 2 yrs: useful performer in Scandinavia nowadays: winner of 7
races there, including handicap in August and listed race (by length from Salt Track) in
September, both if Taby: below form in listed race at Lingfield final start: effective at 1m
to 1½m: acts on dirt. *B. Bo, Sweden*

MAYDEN DAWN 3 ch.f. Silver Wizard (USA) 117 – Delight of Dawn 74 (Never So **53**
Bold 135) [2006 57: 11.5m p10g 8m 8m 6d p6g Nov 28] modest maiden: best form at 1m:
acts on polytrack: visored last 2 starts. *Miss E. C. Lavelle*

MAYDEN DREAM 4 b.f. Silver Wizard (USA) 117 – I Have A Dream (SWE) (Mango **–**
Express 106) [2006 p7g Feb 4] fourth foal: dam unraced: 66/1, well beaten in maiden at
Lingfield. *D. K. Ivory*

MAYIRENEYRBEL 2 ch.f. (Apr 24) Auction House (USA) 120 – Travel Secret **58**
(Blakeney 126) [2006 7g 7.1m⁵ p8g⁵ p10g Nov 29] 3,000F: fifth foal: half-sister to Italian
7f to 1¼m winner by Presidium: dam unraced: modest maiden: should stay 1m: acts on
good to firm ground. *R. Ingram*

MAYLEA GOLD (IRE) 3 b.g. Fasliyev (USA) 120 – Clipping 76 (Kris 135) [2006 5f **41**
5m 7m 8g 6.1f Jul 8] lengthy, well-made gelding: poor maiden. *Miss J. Feilden*

MAYNOOTH PRINCE (IRE) 4 b.g. Spectrum (IRE) 126 – Muffle 70 (Sadler's **–**
Wells (USA) 132) [2006 58: f8g Nov 2] sturdy gelding: modest maiden at best: well
beaten only outing in 2006. *A. Dickman*

MAYONGA (IRE) 3 ch.f. Dr Fong (USA) 128 – Mayara (IRE) 85 (Ashkalani (IRE) **104**
128) [2006 80: p7g* p8g* a7.5g² Nov 23] first foal: dam, lightly-raced Irish 1m winner,
out of half-sister to smart French middle-distance winners Madaiyn and Malakim: useful
form: trained by H. Rogers in Ireland at 2 yrs: much improved in 2006, winning maiden
and listed event (beat Emily Bronte by length, quickening readily to assert close home) at
Lingfield in October: creditable 2 lengths second to Goetot in listed race at Deauville
final start: should stay 1¼m: acts on polytrack, raced only on good going or firmer on
turf. *Sir Mark Prescott*

MAYOR OF LONDON (USA) 2 b.c. (Apr 23) Carson City (USA) – Lustre (USA) **78**
90 (Halo (USA)) [2006 6.1g⁴ 7d* 8d 8m p8g Oct 20] strong, good-topped colt: brother to
useful 7f (at 2 yrs) and 1m (in UAE) winner Dublin, closely related to winner in Saudi
Arabia by Mr Prospector, and half-brother to 3 winners, including smart French 1½m
winner Dream Play (by In The Wings) and smart 1¼m/1½m performer Valley of Gold
(by Shirley Heights): dam 2-y-o 6f winner who stayed 9f: fair performer: won maiden at
Newcastle in August: well held in nurseries: should stay 1m: acts on good to soft going:
sold 22,000 gns, sent to Denmark. *M. Johnston*

MAYSARAH (IRE) 2 b.f. (Mar 15) Green Desert (USA) 127 – Royale (IRE) 102 **72**
(Royal Academy (USA) 130) [2006 p7g² 7d Sep 19] €175,000Y: rather leggy, lengthy
filly: fourth foal: sister to 1m winner in Hong Kong and half-sister to 1¼m winner Love
Appeal (by Singspiel): dam Irish 7f/1m winner: 1¼ lengths second to Emulate in minor
event at Kempton (didn't settle): down field in valuable 27-runner sales race at the Curragh: likely to prove best up to 7f. *G. A. Butler*

MAYSOOR 3 ch.c. Selkirk (USA) 129 – Just Dreams 85 (Salse (USA) 128) [2006 –p: **74**
11.9g⁶ 12s⁴ May 20] lightly-raced maiden: fourth to Alfie Flits at Thirsk final outing: will
be suited by 1¾m+: slowly away on reappearance: sold 15,000 gns in July. *M. Johnston*

MAYSTOCK 6 ch.m. Magic Ring (IRE) 115 – Stockline (Capricorn Line 111) [2006 **81**
74, a87: p16g p16g 15d* 12g² 12.1s⁴ 14m⁴ 14.1g³ 14.8m² 12m³ 14.1g⁴ 16.2d 17.2m* **a85**
p16g² p16g⁵ Nov 11] sturdy mare: fairly useful performer: won handicaps at Warwick in
May and Bath in September: effective at 1½m to 17f: acts on polytrack, and on firm and
good to soft going: has worn visor/cheekpieces/tongue tie: formerly none too genuine.
B. G. Powell

MAYYAS 6 b.g. Robellino (USA) 127 – Amidst 86 (Midyan (USA) 124) [2006 p12.2g⁴ **55**
f11g² Dec 29] tongue tied, modest form both starts on Flat: will be suited by 1¾m+.
C. C. Bealby

MAZINDAR (USA) 4 b. or br.g. Zamindar (USA) 116 – Fantastic Bloom (VEN) (Imp- **–**
erial Ballet (IRE) 110) [2006 –, a58d: p8.6g p7.1g May 2] modest maiden at best: well
held in 2006. *P. T. Midgley*

MAZIN LADY 2 b.f. (Apr 20) Kyllachy 129 – Amazing Bay 100 (Mazilier (USA) 107) **67**
[2006 5.9g⁶ 5g⁵ 5m⁴ 5m² 5.5m⁴ 5m² 5d² p5.1g² p5.1m² Nov 8] 25,000Y: leggy, quite
good-topped filly: sixth foal: half-sister to several winners, including useful Italian 7f/1m
(including at 2 yrs) winner Scartozz (by Barathea): dam 2-y-o 5f/6f winner: fair maiden:
second 5 times, 3 in nurseries: best at 5f: acts on polytrack, good to firm and good to soft
going. *Miss J. A. Camacho*

MAZORAN (FR) 2 ch.g. (Apr 20) Majorien 118 – Isgala (FR) (Galetto (FR) 118) **–**
[2006 7.1m 6.1m Sep 15] workmanlike gelding: well beaten in maidens. *D. G. Bridgwater*

MCCORMACK (IRE) 4 b.g. Desert Story (IRE) 115 – La Loba (IRE) 73 (Treasure **55**
Kay 114) [2006 –: f7s 8.5f 12.1d⁵ 9g 10.9f 10f 9.2m Jul 14] close-coupled gelding:
modest maiden: best efforts around 9f. *M. D. Hammond*

MCELDOWNEY 4 b.g. Zafonic (USA) 130 – Ayodhya (IRE) (Astronef 116) [2006 **97**
82: 12v⁴ 13.8d 12m² f11g* 12.4d 13.8g* 12g* 14m⁴ 14m² 20m⁵ p16g 16g⁵ 21m⁴ 16g²
16.1d⁶ 14v⁴ 14.1g⁵ 18s Oct 7] useful-looking gelding: useful handicapper: won at Southwell and Catterick in May and Catterick in June: stays 21f: acts on fibresand and any turf
going: blinkered (below form) once at 2 yrs: lazy sort. *M. Johnston*

MCNAIROBI 3 b.f. Josr Algarhoud (IRE) 118 – Bonita Bee 50 (King of Spain 121) **87**
[2006 7m⁶ p7g² 8.3f⁶ p8g* p8g* p8g* p8g 8.1d⁴ p8g Sep 30] tall filly: sixth foal: half-
sister to fairly useful 2002 2-y-o 7f/1m winner Lady McNair (by Sheikh Albadou) and
winner in Italy by Petong: dam, maiden, best at 6f: fairly useful performer: won maiden
at Lingfield in July and handicaps at Kempton and Lingfield in August: stays 1m: acts on
polytrack and good to soft ground, probably on firm. *P. D. Cundell*

MCQUEEN (IRE) 6 ch.g. Barathea (IRE) 127 – Bibliotheque (USA) 79 (Woodman **–**
(USA) 126) [2006 68: p9.5g p16.5g Jul 13] lengthy gelding: fair handicapper in 2005:
well beaten on Flat in 2006, leaving Mrs H. Dalton after reappearance: tried visored:
modest hurdler, won in July. *B. D. Leavy*

ME 3 b.f. Green Desert (USA) 127 – Myself 110 (Nashwan (USA) 135) [2006 69: 7g 6m **62**
5.1f⁵ Jul 27] smallish, sturdy, lengthy filly: has a fluent action: lightly-raced maiden: only
modest at best in 2006: effective at 5f/6f: raced only on good ground or firmer: tried
tongue tied. *P. W. Chapple-Hyam*

MEADOW FLOSS 3 b.f. Cyrano de Bergerac 120 – Pea Green 98 (Try My Best **59**
(USA) 130) [2006 p7g 7f³ Jun 30] sister to 2003 2-y-o 5f/6f winner Skyharbor and
half-sister to several winners, including useful 1m to 1½m winner The Green Grey (by
Environment Friend): dam 2-y-o 5f winner who probably stayed 1m: much better effort
in maidens when 3¾ lengths third to Baleegh at Folkestone (saddle reportedly slipped):
will stay 1m: slowly away on debut. *S. Kirk*

MEADOW MISCHIEF (FR) 3 ch.c. Halling (USA) 133 – Moonlight Saunter (USA) **92**
85 (Woodman (USA) 126) [2006 74: p8.6g⁵ p12g² p12g² f12g* 14.1m² 14.1m³ 14.1f³
14g* 14.8d³ 13.4f Sep 23] angular, good-topped colt: fairly useful performer: won
maiden at Southwell in April and handicap at Sandown in August: stays 1¾m: acts on all-
weather and good to firm going: often blinkered, including for both wins: seems quirky:
sold 115,000 gns, sent to Saudi Arabia. *E. A. L. Dunlop*

MEADOW SOPRANO (IRE) 4 b.f. Imperial Ballet (IRE) 110 – Good Aim (IRE) **53**
(Priolo (USA) 127) [2006 47: 8m 7f 9.9g² 8s⁵ Oct 26] €1,600Y: third foal: half-sister to
7f winner Gilly's General (by General Monash): dam unraced: modest maiden handicapper: good second at Beverley penultimate outing: stays 1¼m: acts on soft going: tried in
cheekpieces/blinkers/tongue tie. *M. P. Sunderland, Ireland*

ME AND MINE (USA) 2 b.g. (Jan 3) Belong To Me (USA) – Iron Miss (USA) (Fit To **58**
Fight (USA)) [2006 5.1d⁶ 5m² 5g⁴ 5m² Jul 12] modest maiden: runner-up in sellers: raced
at 5f: dead. *T. D. Barron*

MEANTIME (USA) 3 b.g. Point Given (USA) 134 – Interim 117 (Sadler's Wells **64**
(USA) 132) [2006 73: 11.5m⁵ 11.5m f8g 11.6d 14.1m⁶ 10d Oct 4] close-coupled, deep-
girthed gelding: modest maiden: stays 11.5f: acts on good to firm and good to soft going:
tried blinkered/visored: probably not straightforward. *G. Prodromou*

MEASURED RESPONSE 4 ch.g. Inchinor 119 – Seal Indigo (IRE) 93 (Glenstal **74 d**
(USA) 118) [2006 74: p10g³ p9.5g p10g 10.2d 8.1d⁴ 7.1m⁶ 7m 7.1m⁶ p8g Nov 1] lengthy
gelding: fair maiden: below form after second start: stays 1¼m: acts on polytrack and soft
ground. *J. G. M. O'Shea*

MEASURED TEMPO 2 b.f. (Mar 25) Sadler's Wells (USA) 132 – Allez Les **100 P**
Trois (USA) 114 (Riverman (USA) 131) [2006 7d* Oct 28]

Although by way of a change they were wintered in Britain, only a fraction of Godolphin's two-year-olds were seen on the racecourse in 2006. After a slow start to the season all round, Godolphin ran only two juveniles before the start of October and only twenty by the end of the year, a tiny figure compared to the ninety-one representatives it had in 2004 and seventy-three in 2005, the first two years that the juveniles were trained on a bigger scale. All five of Godolphin's two-year-old winners came in maiden company, but among them were at least three who gave the impression they could have made their mark in better company had their season started earlier. Truly Royal was most impressive on his only start at Newmarket, while Eastern Anthem, the first foal of One Thousand Guineas and Oaks winner Kazzia, and Measured Tempo were also most decisive winners of their only start. Measured Tempo lined up in the bet365.com EBF Maiden Fillies' Stakes over seven furlongs at Newmarket in October. In a field of twenty, most of them newcomers, Siamese Cat was a warm favourite at 6/4 after showing useful form when second to Indian Ink in a sales race at Ascot on her previous start. The imposing-looking Measured Tempo, big and good-topped, was virtually the only runner backed against her, going off at 4/1. Measured Tempo came out comfortably on top. A bit slowly into her stride, she began to improve smoothly as Siamese Cat went to the front approaching the Dip and went past her rival readily, drawing away up the hill, despite edging right through greenness. Measured Tempo won by three lengths from the favourite, with Eternal Path, another well-bred newcomer, taking third. Her rider was impressed. 'We've found one,' declared Dettori afterwards.

		Northern Dancer	Nearctic
	Sadler's Wells (USA)	(b 1961)	Natalma
	(b 1981)	Fairy Bridge	Bold Reason
Measured Tempo		(b 1975)	Special
(b.f. Mar 25, 2004)		Riverman	Never Bend
	Allez Les Trois (USA)	(b 1969)	River Lady
	(ch 1991)	Allegretta	Lombard
		(ch 1978)	Anatevka

Measured Tempo could hardly be better bred. By Sadler's Wells, sire of five Oaks winners among his many achievements, she is a half-sister to four winners, notably the very smart French middle-distance colt Anabaa Blue (by Anabaa), successful in the Prix du Jockey Club over a mile and a half. Reunite (by Kingmambo),

bet365.com EBF Maiden Fillies Stakes, Newmarket—Measured Tempo makes a big impression

another of the offspring of Measured Tempo's dam, Allez Les Trois, progressed into a smart three-year-old for Godolphin at up to a mile and a half in 2006, winning twice over a mile and a quarter, including in listed company. Allez Les Trois, a smart winner up to ten and a half furlongs in France (including the Prix de Flore), where she went well in soft ground, is a daughter of the excellent broodmare Allegretta, dam also of the Arc winner Urban Sea and the Two Thousand Guineas winner King's Best. The family tradition has continued from there. Urban Sea is the dam of the Sadler's Wells brothers Galileo and Black Sam Bellamy, and also of Melikah and (also by Sadler's Wells) All Too Beautiful, both of whom were unraced as two-year-olds but went on to be placed in the Oaks, Melikah in the colours of Godolphin for whom she was also second in the Irish Oaks. Also part of the success story is Turbaine, a half-sister to Urban Sea and the dam of the smart three-year-old Tusculum, fifth in the latest St Leger and yet another good horse by Sadler's Wells from this family. Given the stamina in her pedigree, it is most encouraging that Measured Tempo showed useful form over as short as seven furlongs on her debut. She is unlikely to have the speed for the One Thousand Guineas, but will be a most interesting contender for an Oaks trial in the spring. Indeed, her odds, at the time of writing, of 25/1 for the Oaks itself could well look generous come June. *Saeed bin Suroor*

MEATHOP (IRE) 2 b.g. (May 2) Imperial Ballet (IRE) 110 – Jacobina 71 (Magic Ring (IRE) 115) [2006 6s p8.6g p6g Dec 6] well held in maidens. *R. F. Fisher* —

MECCA'S MATE 5 gr.m. Paris House 123 – Clancassie (Clantime 101) [2006 108: 6d 5d³ 6m³ 5m 6m⁶ 5s 5g 5g⁵ 6d 6g⁶ 6s⁵ 5g* 5s⁴ Oct 14] leggy, lengthy mare: smart performer: good third to Reverence in Temple Stakes at Sandown and Yomalo in Ballyogan Stakes at Leopardstown on second/third starts: won handicap at Newmarket in October by short head from Bond City, confidently ridden: creditable fourth to Dhaular Dhar in similar event at Catterick final outing: best at 5f/6f: acts on polytrack, soft and good to firm going: tried in cheekpieces: usually held up: tough and genuine. *D. W. Barker* **110**

MEDALLA (FR) 6 gr.h. Medaaly 114 – Sharp Cracker (IRE) 80 (Hamas (IRE) 125§) [2006 9.3g p12.2g Aug 31] workmanlike horse: lightly-raced maiden: well beaten in 2006. *M. Brittain* —

MEDDLE 3 b.f. Diktat 126 – Ingerence (FR) (Akarad (FR) 130) [2006 –: p6g p8g 10f 14.1g p7g Oct 29] workmanlike filly: little form: tried tongue tied. *J. Jay* —

MEDFAE (KSA) 3 b.c. Florida's Son (ARG) – Maureen's Hope (USA) (Northern Baby (CAN) 127) [2006 p8g 8.3d⁵ p10g* Jul 22] second foal: dam 1m to 11f (minor stakes) winner in USA: fair form: won seller at Lingfield in July: stays easy 1¼m: acts on polytrack and good to soft going: sent to Saudi Arabia. *C. F. Wall* **71**

MEDIA PUZZLE (USA) 9 ch.g. Theatrical 128 – Market Slide (USA) 94 (Gulch (USA)) [2006 10s⁵ 14g* 20m Jun 22] big, strong, lengthy gelding: was a fluent mover: smart performer: successful in Melbourne Cup in 2002: reportedly fractured pelvis at 3 yrs and suffered with leg problems after (missed 2003, when reportedly fired on both tendons, and also 2005): won listed race at Leopardstown in May by length from Good Surprise: broke sesamoid bones in near-fore and pulled up before line in Gold Cup at Royal Ascot final outing: was effective at 1½m to 2m: acted on any going: often blinkered: dead. *D. K. Weld, Ireland* **113**

MEDICI CODE 2 ch.c. (Apr 7) Medicean 128 – Fiveofive (IRE) 61 (Fairy King (USA)) [2006 7g p7g⁵ 7.1d Sep 16] 21,000F, 12,000 2-y-o: half-brother to several winners, including 7-y-o My Only Sunshine and 1m/9.6f winner Lilli Marlane (by Sri Pekan), both fairly useful: dam 5f (at 2 yrs) and 1m winner: modest form in maidens: will stay at least 1m. *H. Morrison* **59**

MEDICINE PATH 2 b.c. (Feb 12) Danehill Dancer (IRE) 117 – Indian Mystery (IRE) 69 (Indian Ridge 123) [2006 7f* 7m⁵ 8d² 8s³ Oct 21] 34,000Y: good-topped, attractive colt: first foal: dam Irish 5f winner: smart performer: won maiden at York in July: kept pattern company after, improvement when 2½ lengths second of 7 to Admiralofthefleet in Royal Lodge Stakes at Ascot and 3¼ lengths third of 14 to Authorized in Racing Post Trophy at Newbury, tricky ride both times: stays 1m: acts on firm and soft ground: seemingly lazy. *E. J. O'Neill* **110**

MEDIEVAL MAIDEN 3 gr.f. Zaha (CAN) 106 – Brillante (FR) 118 (Green Dancer (USA) 132) [2006 8g² 8.3g p9.5g Aug 31] 7,000Y: lengthy, quite good-topped filly: half-sister to several winners, including fairly useful 9f/1¼m winner Intensity (by Bigstone) **78**

and 13f to 17f winner Arc Bright (by Trempolino): dam French 1m (at 2 yrs) and 11f winner: easily best effort when short-headed in claimer at Newmarket: should stay 1¼m. *W. J. Musson*

MEDITATION 4 ch.f. Inchinor 119 – Trojan Desert 97 (Troy 137) [2006 67: p8g⁴ p7g² **88** p7g* p7g² 7m² 7.1g⁴ 7m⁶ 7g³ 7g 7m³ 7m* 7.1f* 7.6f⁶ 7.1m* 7m* 6g⁶ 7g⁴ 7m 7g p8g Dec 19] workmanlike filly: fairly useful handicapper: won at Lingfield in March, Newbury and Warwick in June, and Warwick and Salisbury in July: effective at 6f/7f: acts on polytrack, firm and good to soft going: tried cheekpieces at 3 yrs: front runner: reportedly finished lame final outing. *A. Wood*

MEDLEY 2 ch.f. (Feb 26) Danehill Dancer (IRE) 117 – Marl 94 (Lycius (USA) 124) **95** [2006 6g² 6m⁴ 6m* Jul 14] good-topped filly: has scope: half-sister to several winners, including smart 7f to 8.5f winner Green Line (by Green Desert) and 4-y-o Marching Song: dam 2-y-o 5f winner who stayed 6f: useful form: never-nearer fourth of 18 to Sander Camillo in Albany Stakes at Royal Ascot before landing odds in maiden at Newmarket: jarred up after: likely to stay 7f/1m. *R. Hannon*

MEDNAYA (IRE) 3 b.f. Anabaa (USA) 130 – Sopran Dandy (IRE) (Doyoun 124) **107** [2006 105: 8s³ 8d 7g² 7m 6d* 6s⁵ 7g⁵ Sep 6] lengthy, useful-looking filly: third foal: half-sister to winner in Italy by Fasliyev: dam Italian 2-y-o 7f/7.5f winner: useful performer: on toes/pulled hard when well held in Jersey Stakes at Royal Ascot fourth start: back to best when winning minor event at Deauville in August and ran well when 2¾ lengths fifth to Indian Maiden in Prix de Meautry there later in month: effective at 6f to 1m: acts on soft going: has worn crossed noseband. *R. Gibson, France*

MEDORA LEIGH (USA) 4 ch.f. Swain (USA) 134 – Gaily Tiara (USA) (Caerleon **–** (USA) 132) [2006 63: p12g p13.9g 11.5g⁶ Aug 20] modest maiden at 3 yrs: well held in 2006: covered by Red Ransom, sold from J. Toller 4,200 gns after second start: stays 1½m. *J.-C. Rouget, France*

MEELUP (IRE) 6 ch.g. Night Shift (USA) – Centella (IRE) (Thatching 131) [2006 74: **65** p8g p8g 10.2d 10.2d p10g 9m⁶ 10m⁴ p10g⁶ 10.9m² 11.9f² 11.6f⁵ 11.9f 10m⁵ 11.5m p12g Sep 29] sturdy, deep-girthed gelding: unimpressive mover: fair handicapper: stays 11.9f: acts on polytrack, firm and soft going: tried blinkered, usually wears cheekpieces. *P. G. Murphy*

MEERLUST 2 ch.f. (Mar 27) Compton Place 125 – Le Pin 59 (Persian Bold 123) [2006 **–** 5.7m 6g p7.1m Oct 9] medium-sized filly: fourth foal: half-sister to 2003 2-y-o 6f winner La Landonne (by Fraam): dam, maiden bred to stay 1½m, half-sister to very smart 1m/1¼m performer Handsome Ridge: little form: visored/blinkered after debut. *E. F. Vaughan*

MEETING OF MINDS 2 b.f. (Apr 7) Mind Games 121 – Turn Back 73 (Pivotal 124) **50** [2006 p6s⁶ p6g⁵ Dec 22] 14,000Y: first foal: dam 9f winner: mid-division in maidens on polytrack. *W. Jarvis*

ME FEIN 2 gr.g. (Feb 18) Desert Prince (IRE) 130 – Attachment (USA) (Trempolino **–** (USA) 135) [2006 7.1m 7m 6g Oct 12] lengthy, good-bodied gelding: behind in maidens. *B. J. Curley*

MEGALALA (IRE) 5 b.g. Petardia 113 – Avionne 59 (Derrylin 115) [2006 –: p8g p8g **60** p7g⁴ p7g p10g 8m 10m⁶ 10m⁴ 11m 7m 7.6m 7f⁴ 7d* Sep 25] lengthy gelding: modest performer: won claimer at Brighton final start: stays 1m: acts on polytrack, good to firm and good to soft going: tried in cheekpieces. *J. J. Bridger*

MEGALO MANIAC 3 b.g. Efisio 120 – Sharanella (Shareef Dancer (USA) 135) **51** [2006 9v 7.1g 8.5f 5.9m 10f 8f 5.9m² 5m² 5m² 5g⁴ Aug 21] modest maiden: left K. Reveley after sixth start: stays 6f: acts on good to firm going. *R. A. Fahey*

MEGATON 5 ch.g. Nashwan (USA) 135 – Pan Galactic (USA) 105 (Lear Fan (USA) **75** 130) [2006 15.4m⁵ Apr 25] fairly useful performer when trained in France by M. Zilber in 2004, winning 9f maiden at Le Croise-Laroche: fair form in handicap at Folkestone on Flat return: stays 10.5f: acts on soft ground, probably on good to firm: fairly useful hurdler, winner 4 times in 2006. *P. Bowen*

MEGAVEGAS 3 b.f. Erhaab (USA) 127 – Jade Pet 90 (Petong 126) [2006 8g 8g² a8g **38** 5f 6v 6d⁶ p6m 6.1d⁴ f7g p7.1m Nov 21] 12,500Y: leggy, close-coupled filly: seventh foal: half-sister to 3 winners, including 9-y-o Hail The Chief: dam 5f winner: poor maiden: left S. Santella in Italy after third start: stays 1m. *P. T. Midgley*

MEIKLE BARFIL 4 b.g. Compton Place 125 – Oare Sparrow 75 (Night Shift (USA)) **69** [2006 83, a71: 6g 6m 5m 5f 5.1g 5.1g 5m⁵ 5m* 5.1m 5.5d p5.1m Oct 9] strong, good-bodied gelding: fair handicapper: won at Salisbury in August: best at 5f: acts on polytrack, good to firm and good to soft ground: in cheekpieces last 6 starts. *J. M. Bradley*

MEIKLE BEOCH 4 b.f. Magic Ring (IRE) 115 – Portvasco 90 (Sharpo 132) [2006 –: – p16.5g Jul 28] no sign of ability. *Mrs H. Sweeting*

MELAAYA (USA) 3 b.f. Aljabr (USA) 125 – Saint Emilia (PER) (Saint Ballado – (CAN)) [2006 93: 7d³ 7m Jul 12] unfurnished filly: fairly useful performer, lightly raced: well held in 2006: sold 24,000 gns in August. *M. Johnston*

MELALCHRIST 4 b.g. Almaty (IRE) 113§ – Lawless Bridget 62 (Alnasr Alwasheek **87 d** 117) [2006 87: 5d⁵ 6g 5g 6g⁶ p6g⁶ p6g Oct 28] compact gelding: fairly useful handicapper: well below form after reappearance: effective at 5f/6f: acts on good to firm and good to soft going (won on heavy at 2 yrs): tried in cheekpieces: sometimes races freely. *J. J. Quinn*

MELANDRE 4 b.f. Lujain (USA) 119 – Talighta (USA) 62 (Barathea (IRE) 127) [2006 – 74: p6g Dec 9] close-coupled filly: fair handicapper at 3 yrs: well beaten only outing in 2006: usually races prominently. *M. Brittain*

MELEE 4 ch.f. Cadeaux Genereux 131 – Nashmeel (USA) 121 (Blushing Groom (FR) **61** 131) [2006 –: p8g² p8.6g³ p8.6g⁴ a8f* a8.5s 8f² Jun 28] modest performer: left J. Jay after third outing: won maiden at Beulah Park in April by 24 lengths: will stay 1¼m: acts on dirt and firm going: tongue tied only run at 2 yrs. *J. Corrigan, USA*

MELMOTT 6 ch.g. Piccolo 121 – Time For Tea (IRE) 73 (Imperial Frontier (USA) – 112) [2006 p12g 8.5g 6f May 7] good-topped gelding: little form: tried blinkered. *R. Ingram*

MELODIAN 11 b.h. Grey Desire 115 – Mere Melody 88 (Dunphy 124) [2006 55: 12v **60** 10d 12g 10.1d³ 10.1s³ 12.4s Oct 10] leggy horse: modest handicapper: stays 1½m: acts on any turf going: wears blinkers nowadays, visored once. *M. Brittain*

MELOGRANO (IRE) 6 ch.g. Hector Protector (USA) 124 – Just A Treat (IRE) 47 **35** (Glenstal (USA) 118) [2006 59: f11g⁴ p12.2g Mar 20] only poor form in 2006: stays 1½m: acts on all-weather and heavy ground: none too consistent. *Mark Campion*

MELPOMENE 3 ch.f. Peintre Celebre (USA) 137 – Lady Joyce (FR) (Galetto (FR) **90** 118) [2006 –: 12s² 9.2d² f12g* p13g* Dec 22] fairly useful form, lightly raced: won maiden at Southwell (by 8 lengths) in November and handicap at Lingfield in December: will stay 1¾m: acts on all-weather and soft ground. *M. Johnston*

MELROSE AVENUE (USA) 4 b.c. Kris S (USA) – Sham Street (USA) (Sham – (USA)) [2006 111: 12f Aug 4] big, leggy, close-coupled colt: not the best of walkers: smart performer at 3 yrs for M. Johnston: on toes and sweating, dropped away tamely when last in listed race at Goodwood only outing in 2006 (found to have bled): stays 2m: acts on soft and good to firm going: usually makes running: looks less than straightforward: sold 27,000 gns in October. *Saeed bin Suroor*

MEL'S MOMENT (USA) 4 b.g. Storm Creek (USA) – One Moment In Time (USA) – § (Magesterial (USA) 116) [2006 57§: p12.2g 12.6m p7.1g 7f Jul 25] good-topped gelding: ungenuine maiden: no form in 2006: tried blinkered. *R. J. Price*

MELVINO 4 b.g. Josr Algarhoud (IRE) 118 – Safe Secret 50 (Seclude (USA)) [2006 74, **69** a66: 12g 12.4g⁶ 12.4d 11.5m 10m 12m⁵ 12f⁵ 12f² 12g² 12m³ 12.1s³ 12.1m³ 12.1g 14m⁵ 11.5m⁴ 11.9m⁴ 12s⁶ 12d p12.2g⁶ p10g² p12.2g* p12g⁵ p12.2g* Dec 27] rather leggy gelding: fair handicapper: won twice at Wolverhampton in December: stays 1½m: acts on all-weather, firm and soft going: tried visored/in cheekpieces: sometimes slowly away: consistent, though quirky. *T. D. Barron*

MEMPHIS BELLE 3 gr.f. Linamix (FR) 127 – Clipper 95 (Salse (USA) 128) [2006 –: **61** 10m 10d f11g f11g³ Dec 19] compact filly: modest maiden: left Mrs H. Sweeting, improved when third in claimer final start: stays 11f: acts on fibresand: has flashed tail. *G. A. Swinbank*

MEMPHIS MAN 3 b.g. Bertolini (USA) 125 – Something Blue (Petong 126) [2006 **79** 85: p6g⁵ f7g⁵ p7g³ 7.5f⁶ 7m f6g 8.2m 5g* 5m⁵ 6g² 6m³ 5g⁵ p6g p6g p6s⁶ f7g Dec 21] leggy, close-coupled gelding: fair performer: left G. Bravery prior to winning handicap at Sandown in August: claimed from Miss V. Haigh thirteenth start: effective at 5f to 7f: acts on all-weather, best efforts on turf on good/good to firm going: in cheekpieces (ran respectably) once: joined W. M. Brisbourne. *D. G. Bridgwater*

MEMPHIS MARIE 2 b.f. (Feb 2) Desert Sun 120 – Spirito Libro (USA) 89 (Lear Fan – (USA) 130) [2006 7d Aug 12] 40,000Y: workmanlike filly: fifth foal: half-sister to smart

6f winner Prince Aaron (by Marju): dam 5f (at 2 yrs) to 1¼m winner: 50/1 and backward, behind in maiden at Newmarket. *C. N. Allen*

ME NO PUPPET 2 b.f. (Apr 30) Mtoto 134 – Puppet Play (IRE) 82 (Broken Hearted – 124) [2006 p7.1g Oct 30] first foal: dam 6f to 1m winner: well held in maiden at Wolverhampton. *E. J. Alston*

MEOHMY 3 b.f. Marju (IRE) 127 – Meshhed (USA) 102 (Gulch (USA)) [2006 –p: 8.1g **57** 10d 11.5m⁶ 12.1f 12f f8g 11.6m Jul 17] lengthy, unfurnished filly: modest maiden: tried visored. *M. R. Channon*

MEPHISTOS KICK 5 b.g. Kingmambo (USA) 125 – Mempari (IRE) 102 (Fairy King **46** (USA)) [2006 49: p7g Feb 20] poor maiden: seems to stay 7f. *Jean-Rene Auvray*

MERCARI 4 ch.f. Bahamian Bounty 116 – Aonach Mor (Anabaa (USA) 130) [2006 **55**: 9.2m⁵ 8v May 25] modest performer: well held in 2006: tried in cheekpieces. *Mrs J. C. McGregor*

MERCHANT BANKES 3 b.c. Observatory (USA) 131 – Lady Bankes (IRE) 69 **71** (Alzao (USA) 117) [2006 70: p10g⁴ p12.2g⁵ 12g³ 8.1s⁴ 9.9g 8f⁶ p8g p12.2m⁶ Oct 2] workmanlike colt: fair maiden: stays 1½m: acts on polytrack, soft and good to firm ground: reared leaving stall sixth outing: has looked no easy ride. *W. G. M. Turner*

MERDIFF 7 b.g. Machiavellian (USA) 123 – Balwa (USA) 101 (Danzig (USA)) [2006 **46** –, a76: p7.1g p7.1g³ p7.1g p6g⁶ p6g p6g p8.6g* p8.6g p8.6g p8.6g³ p7.1g p7.1g² 7m⁶ **a64** p8.6g⁴ p7.1g p7.1g p8.6g³ p8.6g⁵ p8.6g Dec 27] big gelding: modest on all-weather, poor on turf: won seller at Wolverhampton in March: stays 8.6f: acts on all-weather and firm ground: tongue tied (won) once at 4 yrs: none too consistent. *W. M. Brisbourne*

MERIDIAN GREY (USA) 2 gr.c. (Feb 15) More Than Ready (USA) 120 – Love **62** Rhythm (CAN) (Seeking The Gold (USA)) [2006 7m 7.2d Jul 9] better run in maidens when seventh at Thirsk on debut (faded). *K. A. Ryan*

MERLIN'S DANCER 6 b.g. Magic Ring (IRE) 115 – La Piaf (FR) (Fabulous Dancer **106** (USA) 124) [2006 101: p5g⁴ 5f⁴ 5.1f* 5m 5m⁴ 6m 5m 6m 5.4g Sep 9] good-bodied gelding: unimpressive mover: useful handicapper: won at Chester in May by ¾ length from Judd Street: good handicap to Handsome Cross in quite valuable event at Musselburgh 2 outings later, but well below form last 4 starts: effective at 6f, better still at 5f: acts on polytrack, firm and good to soft ground: blinkered (below form) once: often makes running. *D. Nicholls*

MERLINS DREAMS 3 b.c. Dansili 127 – Red Leggings 84 (Shareef Dancer (USA) **–** 135) [2006 8.2v Oct 25] stocky colt: 100/1, last in maiden at Nottingham. *S. Parr*

MERLINS PROFIT 6 b.g. Wizard King 122 – Quick Profit 78 (Formidable (USA) **69** 125) [2006 66: p8.6g⁴ p7.1g* p8.6g⁴ 7m 8m 9m² 8d² 9s² Sep 26] fair performer on turf, **a64** modest on all-weather: won banded race at Wolverhampton in April: left G. A. Swinbank after fourth start: effective at 7f to 1¼m: acts on polytrack, firm and soft going: tried blinkered. *T. G. McCourt, Ireland*

MERLINS QUEST 2 b.c. (Apr 22) Wizard King 122 – Wonderland (IRE) 55 (Dolphin **60** Street (FR) 125) [2006 5g 5.1g⁶ 5.7g 7f 5.5m 5.1f⁵ 6d² 5.1d Nov 1] strong, lengthy colt: modest maiden: second in nursery at Catterick: effective at 5f/6f: acts on firm and good to soft going. *J. M. Bradley*

MERMAID'S CRY 4 b.f. Danzero (AUS) – Little Tramp (Trempolino (USA) 135) **–** [2006 f6g May 16] sturdy filly: maiden: no form since 2-y-o debut. *R. Brotherton*

MERRYMADCAP (IRE) 4 b.g. Lujain (USA) 119 – Carina Clare (Slip Anchor 136) **83** [2006 68: p9.5g* p9.5g* p8.6g* p8g 8d³ p8g³ 8d² 8s² 8.3f p8g 8.1m⁴ 8.3g⁵ 8d³ 8.1s⁶ p8g⁴ p8.6m⁵ p8.6g³ Oct 30] leggy gelding: fairly useful handicapper: won at Wolverhampton in February (twice) and March: effective at 1m to 9.5f: acts on polytrack, firm and soft ground: tried blinkered: patiently ridden, and has tended to idle: reliable. *M. Blanshard*

MERRYMAKER 6 b.g. Machiavellian (USA) 123 – Wild Pavane (Dancing Brave **81** (USA) 140) [2006 83: 12.3d³ 13.8g⁵ 12m³ 12m⁶ 13.1g 15.9m* 18f 12.3m⁶ 15.9g⁴ 15.9m⁴ 13.4f Sep 23] angular gelding: fairly useful handicapper: won at Chester in July: stays easy 2m: acts on polytrack, firm and soft going: tried visored/blinkered: held up: joined N. Richards, won over hurdles in December. *W. M. Brisbourne*

MERRY MOON (IRE) 2 b.f. (Mar 28) Night Shift (USA) – Adaja (Cadeaux Gene- **58** reux 131) [2006 6.1g² 6g 6g* p6g⁶ 7.5g 6d 6v Oct 9] €17,000Y: workmanlike filly: first foal: dam unraced half-sister to Racing Post Trophy/Dante Stakes winner Dilshaan:

modest performer: won seller at Haydock in July: best form at 6f: acts on polytrack and good to soft going. *M. Dods*

MERRYVALE MAN 9 b.g. Rudimentary (USA) 118 – Salu 65 (Ardross 134) [2006 – 48: f16g Feb 5] leggy gelding: poor performer: well held on Flat after 8-y-o reappearance: tried blinkered/in cheekpieces: won over hurdles in May. *Miss Kariana Key*

MERSEY SOUND (IRE) 8 b.g. Ela-Mana-Mou 132 – Coral Sound (IRE) 67 (Glow **88** (USA)) [2006 72: 13.3m³ 16.2m³ 16.1m* 14.8m* 21m 16.1d² 13.3g p16g6 16d Oct 27] good-topped gelding: fairly useful handicapper: won twice at Newmarket in July: should stay 2¼m: acts on polytrack, firm and good to soft going: visored once: usually held up. *D. R. C. Elsworth*

MERU CAMP (IRE) 2 ch.g. (Mar 22) Loup Sauvage (USA) 125 – Morgan Le Fay 70 **61** (Magic Ring (IRE) 115) [2006 5d² 5m 5.1g4 6f² 6f³ 6m 8g Sep 14] sturdy gelding: modest maiden: placed in claimer/sellers: effective at 5f/6f, well beaten at 1m final start (blinkered): acts on firm and good to soft going: gelded after final start. *P. Winkworth*

MERVEILLES 3 b.g. Vettori (IRE) 119 – Finlaggan 83 (Be My Chief (USA) 122) **89** [2006 90: 10.1m³ 10.1m 12f4 10m4 Jul 8] quite good-topped, useful-looking gelding: fairly useful handicapper, lightly raced: stays 1½m: raced only on good going or firmer: blinkered (ran creditably) final outing: sold 32,000 gns, joined Mrs J. Harrington in Ireland. *J. H. M. Gosden*

MESBAAH (IRE) 2 b.g. (Mar 30) Noverre (USA) 125 – Deyaajeer (USA) 64 (Dayjur **93** (USA) 137) [2006 7f4 7g6 7.5m* 8m5 Sep 9] strong, lengthy gelding: type to carry condition: half-brother to 5-y-o Barathea Dreams and useful 7f (including at 2 yrs) to 9f (in UAE) winner Al Mohallab (by Marju): dam, ran once, half-sister to Nashwan, Unfuwain and Nayef: fairly useful form: improvement in cheekpieces last 2 starts, winning maiden at Beverley (made all by 6 lengths) in August, then fifth to Caldra in listed event at Goodwood (gelded after): stays 1m: raced on good going or firmer. *M. A. Jarvis*

MESCALERA (GER) 5 b.m. Alkalde (GER) – Miskinissa (GER) (Esclavo (FR)) **49** [2006 42: p8.6g6 p7.1g² p7g p7g p7g4 Jun 15] poor maiden: stays 8.5f: acts on polytrack, good to firm and good to soft going: tried blinkered. *B. G. Powell*

MESMERIC (IRE) 8 b.g. Sadler's Wells (USA) 132 – Mesmerize (Mill Reef (USA) – 141) [2006 89: p16g Feb 15] good-topped gelding: fairly useful handicapper in 2005: well held only outing in 2006: effective blinkered/visored or not: sometimes carries head awkwardly: often held up: has had breathing problems. *B. G. Powell*

MESSIAH GARVEY 2 b.c. (Feb 27) Lear Fan (USA) 130 – Maid of Camelot 102 **77** (Caerleon (USA) 132) [2006 7m4 7.1m5 8.5g 7g4 p7g* Dec 15] 40,000Y: sturdy colt: fourth foal: dam 1¼m winner: fair form: won maiden at Kempton in December, making all: free-going type, but should stay 1m. *M. R. Channon*

METAL GURU 2 ch.f. (Mar 29) Ishiguru (USA) 114 – Gemtastic 70 (Tagula (IRE) **65** 116) [2006 5d5 5.7m4 Sep 25] first foal: dam 5f (at 2 yrs)/6f winner: better effort in maidens when fourth to Maker's Mark at Bath. *R. Hollinshead*

METAPHORIC (IRE) 2 b.c. (Apr 23) Montjeu (IRE) 137 – Virgin Hawk (USA) **85 P** (Silver Hawk (USA) 123) [2006 8.2s* Oct 18] €145,000Y: good-topped, attractive colt: sixth foal: half-brother to 3 winners, including fairly useful 1¼m winner Meadaaf (by Swain) and Irish 7f winner Java Lady (by Mt Livermore): dam, lightly-raced US maiden, out of half-sister to top-class 1½m performer Cacoethes: 10/1, deal of promise in winning maiden at Nottingham (beat Toccata by neck), picking up well from poor position then idling markedly in front: will be suited by 1¼m/1½m: exciting prospect, sure to go on to much better things. *M. L. W. Bell*

METHAALY (IRE) 3 b.g. Red Ransom (USA) – Santorini (USA) (Spinning World **76** (USA) 130) [2006 6g* 6s6 Oct 10] 95,000Y: compact gelding: first foal: dam unraced half-sister to St Leger winner Mutafaweq and smart performer to 1¼m Dimitrova: fair form: won maiden at Haydock in June by short head from Rogue, starting slowly and needing every yard: below form in handicap at Newcastle on subsequent outing: bred to be suited by further than 6f: sold 5,000 gns, joined Jane Chapple-Hyam. *W. J. Haggas*

METHODICAL 4 b.f. Lujain (USA) 119 – Simple Logic 73 (Aragon 118) [2006 56: – p12.2g Jan 28] close-coupled filly: maiden on Flat, won over hurdles in January, but well held only Flat outing in 2006. *B. G. Powell*

METHUSALEH (IRE) 3 b.g. Mutamam 123 – Madamaa (IRE) 88 (Alzao (USA) **80** 117) [2006 73: 9s 8d³ 8m* 8m5 10m5 8.2m4 8f6 p7.1g6 p8.6g Dec 21] sturdy gelding:

fairly useful handicapper: won at Redcar in May: left T. Easterby 9,000 gns after seventh start: stays 1¼m: acts on firm and good to soft going: held up. *D. Shaw*

METROPOLITAN CHIEF 2 b.c. (Apr 29) Compton Place 125 – Miss Up N Go – (Gorytus (USA) 132) [2006 6m 7g Oct 12] tall colt, unfurnished at 2 yrs: well held in maidens at Newmarket. *D. M. Simcock*

METROPOLITAN MAN 3 ch.c. Dr Fong (USA) 128 – Preceder (Polish Precedent 109 (USA) 131) [2006 101: 8g² 8d² 8m⁵ 8.3g* 8m² 8.9g⁴ Sep 9] close-coupled colt: useful performer: landed odds in 3-runner minor event at Hamilton in July by 2½ lengths from Desert Realm: ran well otherwise in 2006 when 3½ lengths second to Killybegs in Craven Stakes at Newmarket on reappearance, 6 lengths fifth to Araafa in St James's Palace Stakes at Royal Ascot and ¾-length second to Prince of Light in listed event at Goodwood: stays 1m: acts on good to firm going: has been attended by 2 handlers in paddock: sweating (ran respectably) final outing. *D. M. Simcock*

MEXICAN BOB 3 b.g. Atraf 116 – Eskimo Nel (IRE) 75 (Shy Groom (USA)) [2006 71 p8.6g⁶ 8.1m⁴ 8.1d⁶ 8.2f⁵ 10f³ 10d² 9.9m⁶ Aug 27] strong, good-bodied gelding: type to carry condition: fourth living foal: brother to 6-y-o Mexican Pete: dam, 1¼m/1½m winner, also useful hurdler: fair maiden handicapper: stays 1¼m: acts on firm and good to soft going. *Mrs H. Dalton*

MEXICAN PETE 6 b.g. Atraf 116 – Eskimo Nel (IRE) 75 (Shy Groom (USA)) [2006 82 87: 12g 11.9m³ 12.6m* 12m Jul 14] close-coupled gelding: fairly useful handicapper: won amateur event at Warwick in July: stays 12.6f: acts on polytrack, firm and good to soft going. *A. W. Carroll*

MEXICAN (USA) 7 b.g. Pine Bluff (USA) – Cuando Quiere (USA) (Affirmed (USA)) – § [2006 55: f8g Mar 21] quite attractive gelding: maiden: well held only Flat outing in 2006: usually wears headgear: tried tongue tied: modest/ungenuine chaser. *M. D. Hammond*

MEZEREON 6 b.m. Alzao (USA) 117 – Blown-Over 41 (Ron's Victory (USA) 129) – [2006 p9.5g Feb 20] quite good-topped mare: missed 2005: well held only Flat outing in 2006: successful over hurdles in March. *D. Carroll*

MEZUZAH 6 b.g. Barathea (IRE) 127 – Mezzogiorno 108 (Unfuwain (USA) 131) 91 § [2006 82§: 8s* 8g 8.1g 8.1s⁶ 8m 7f² 8m⁵ 7m⁶ 8.1s 7.1s* 8g 8.2s* 8v³ Oct 28] lengthy gelding: fairly useful handicapper: won at Redcar in March, Musselburgh (dead-heated) in September and Nottingham in October: barely stays 1¼m: acts on any going: tried tongue tied/blinkered: tends to carry head high: usually races prominently: unreliable. *M. W. Easterby*

MEZZO 3 b.f. Singspiel (IRE) 133 – Real Time (Polish Precedent (USA) 131) [2006 – p10g Jun 21] third foal: dam unraced half-sister to smart stayer Boreas: 12/1, well held in maiden at Kempton: sold 3,500 gns in October, sent to Qatar. *L. M. Cumani*

MIACARLA 3 b.f. Forzando 122 – Zarzi (IRE) (Suave Dancer (USA) 136) [2006 –: f6g 44 6m³ 5d⁶ Aug 31] workmanlike filly: poor maiden, lightly raced. *A. Berry*

MIAMI TALLYCE (IRE) 3 b.f. (Apr 4) Montjeu (IRE) 137 – Altishaan (Darshaan 55 133) [2006 p7g p8.6m p8g⁴ Dec 20] third foal: half-sister to 2003 2-y-o 6f winner Easily Averted (by Averti): dam unraced out of useful half-sister to disqualified Oaks winner Aliysa: modest form in maidens on polytrack: will benefit from 1¼m/1½m. *E. J. O'Neill*

MIA (POL) 5 b.m. Llandaff (USA) – Mykos-Dream (SWI) (Mykonos) [2006 p10g p8g Feb 20] won 4 times up to 9f in Poland prior to 2006: blinkered, well held in banded race/seller at Lingfield. *Mrs P. Townsley*

MIA'S BOY 2 b.c. (Mar 1) Pivotal 124 – Bint Zamayem (IRE) 95 (Rainbow Quest 73 p (USA) 134) [2006 7m⁶ Sep 19] 90,000 2-y-o: half-brother to 3 winners, including useful Irish 6f (at 2 yrs)/7f winner Sweet Deimos (by Green Desert) and fairly useful 2004 2-y-o 1m winner Rumbalara (by Intikhab): dam, 1¼m winner, half-sister to smart French miler Rouquette: 6/4 favourite but lethargic, sixth to Adagio in maiden at Newmarket: should do better. *P. W. Chapple-Hyam*

MICHABO (IRE) 5 b.g. Robellino (USA) 127 – Mole Creek 91 (Unfuwain (USA) 97 131) [2006 93: p16g 14.1f² 14g² 20m 14m 13.3g⁶ Aug 18] strong, good sort: useful handicapper: better than ever when runner-up at Salisbury and Sandown (beaten head by Salute): below form last 3 outings: stays 1¾m, not 2½m: acts on firm and soft going: free-going sort, usually makes running: sold 16,000 gns, joined P. Bowen. *H. Morrison*

MICHAELS DREAM (IRE) 7 b.g. Spectrum (IRE) 126 – Stormswept (USA) 74 – § (Storm Bird (CAN) 134) [2006 55: p16.5g 13m 14.1d 14.1m Aug 31] smallish gelding:

unreliable performer: little form on Flat in 2006 but won over hurdles: usually in headgear. *N. Wilson*

MICHAELS PRIDE (IRE) 4 b.f. Distant View (USA) 126 – Ruacana Falls (USA) 86 **65** (Storm Bird (CAN) 134) [2006 78: 10m⁵ 9.2m Jul 4] rather leggy filly: fair performer: well below best in 2006: will stay 1½m: acts on any turf going. *M. Johnston*

MICK IS BACK 2 b.g. (Feb 28) Diktat 126 – Classy Cleo (IRE) 102 (Mujadil (USA) **53** 119) [2006 6m⁴ 7m⁶ 6m Aug 11] small gelding: modest maiden: probably stays 7f. *P. D. Evans*

MICKLEBERRY (IRE) 2 b.f. (Apr 14) Desert Style (IRE) 121 – Miss Indigo 62 **66** (Indian Ridge 123) [2006 f6g⁶ 6m⁴ 5m⁵ 5g⁵ Aug 1] 8,200Y: leggy, lengthy filly: second foal: dam maiden half-sister to useful performer up to 1½m Musetta: fair maiden: fourth to Pretty Majestic at Pontefract: will stay 7f/1m (found 5f inadequate last 2 starts). *J. D. Bethell*

MICKLEDO 4 b.g. Perryston View 114 – Ever So Lonely 63 (Headin' Up) [2006 38: **–** p5.1g p6g May 5] leggy gelding: maiden: no form in 2006: often wears blinkers/visor. *A. Bailey*

MICKY MAC (IRE) 2 b.g. (Feb 4) Lend A Hand 124 – Gazette It Tonight 63 (Merdon **–** Melody 98) [2006 5d 5m 6m⁴ 7m Aug 8] smallish, lengthy gelding: little form: tried in blinkers. *I. W. McInnes*

MIDAS WAY 6 ch.g. Halling (USA) 133 – Arietta's Way (IRE) 71 (Darshaan 133) **105** [2006 110: 16d⁶ 16d⁶ 11.6d⁵ Nov 4] leggy, close-coupled gelding: smart performer at 5 yrs: only useful in 2006, best effort when sixth to Hawridge Prince in listed event at Ascot on reappearance: stays 2m: acts on firm and soft going: visored (below form) final 5-y-o start. *P. R. Chamings*

MIDDLE EASTERN 4 b.g. Mujahid (USA) 125 – Swissmatic 54 (Petong 126) [2006 **65** 53, a72: f8g⁶ f6g 7f p7.1g 5.7m 5m³ 5g 6d⁴ p6m³ p6g³ f7g⁵ Nov 28] big, leggy gelding: fair handicapper: stays 7f: acts on all-weather, good to firm and good to soft going: tried in cheekpieces (including last 2 starts)/blinkered. *P. A. Blockley*

MIDDLEHAM (IRE) 2 ch.c. (Mar 8) Best of The Bests (IRE) 122 – Taalluf (USA) 82 **98** (Hansel (USA)) [2006 6m⁵ 5g* 5g 7m³ 7g² 8m⁶ Sep 9] 22,000F: strong, useful-looking colt: fourth foal: half-brother to 3-y-o Sun Catcher and winner around 7f/1m in Italy by Desert Style: dam placed at 5f/6f at 2 yrs: useful performer: won maiden at Carlisle in May: improved form when placed in listed events at Royal Ascot (third to Champlain) and Leopardstown (1¾ lengths second to Teofilo): possibly amiss final start: should stay 1m: raced on good/good to firm going. *M. Johnston*

MIDDLEMARCH (IRE) 6 ch.g. Grand Lodge (USA) 125 – Blanche Dubois (Nash- **81** wan (USA) 135) [2006 94d: 8s 8.3f² 9.1g² 9.2m⁵ 9.3g² 8d⁵ 8g³ 8.3g* 8.3g³ 8g⁶ p7.1g² p8.6g* p8.6g⁶ Nov 16] tall, angular gelding: fairly useful handicapper: won at Hamilton in August and Wolverhampton in October: stays 1¼m: acts on polytrack, firm and good to soft going: often wears headgear (has won without). *J. S. Goldie*

MIDDLETHORPE 9 b.g. Noble Patriarch 115 – Prime Property (IRE) 60 (Tirol 127) **66** [2006 12v² 14.1s 12g p12g 10s⁶ May 20] rather sparely-made gelding: poor mover: fair handicapper: unraced on Flat in 2005: below form after reappearance: effective at 1½m/1¾m: acts on heavy and good to firm going, below form on firm/all-weather: blinkered: very slowly away final outing: tends to wander. *M. W. Easterby*

MIDDLETON GREY 8 gr.g. Ashkalani (IRE) 128 – Petula 103 (Petong 126) [2006 **77** 86, a90: p6g p7g p7.1g p6g 7g 6g 6g⁴ 5.7f 7d* 7g⁴ p7g Nov 24] leggy gelding: fairly **a89** useful handicapper on all-weather, just fair on turf in 2006: won apprentice event at Leicester in October: effective at 6f to 8.5f: acts on all-weather, good to firm and good to soft going: wears headgear: sometimes slowly away: often held up. *A. G. Newcombe*

MIDGE'S GIRL (IRE) 3 b.f. Indian Lodge (IRE) 127 – Blue Sky Lady (IRE) (Blue- **49** bird (USA) 125) [2006 46: p6g f6g f7g² f6g⁵ f7g* 6m⁴ 8d 7.1d Oct 8] poor performer: won banded race at Southwell in March: stays 7f: acts on fibresand and good to firm going: visored 5 of last 6 starts: often starts slowly: sold 1,200 gns, sent to Denmark. *Mrs A. Duffield*

MIDMAAR (IRE) 5 b.g. Cape Cross (IRE) 129 – Khazinat El Dar (USA) 78 (Slew O' **62** Gold (USA)) [2006 52: f7g⁵ p7.1g³ p7.1g⁴ p6g² p5g p6g p6g* p6g⁶ p6g* p7g² Dec 30] modest performer: won banded races at Kempton in November and December: stays 7f: acts on all-weather: usually wears headgear. *M. Wigham*

MIDNIGHT CREEK 8 b.g. Tragic Role (USA) – Greek Night Out (IRE) 54 (Ela-Mana-Mou 132) [2006 48, a60: f16g f14g Apr 7] leggy gelding: no form in 2006: tried tongue tied/in cheekpieces/blinkered: carries head awkwardly, and none too genuine. *A. Sadik* –

MIDNIGHT DIAMOND (IRE) 3 b.c. Alzao (USA) 117 – Derena (FR) (Crystal Palace (FR) 132) [2006 10.1d⁶ 9.8m p8.6g Jul 11] close-coupled colt: little form in maidens. *Mrs L. Williamson* –

MIDNIGHT LACE 4 ch.f. Tomba 119 – Royal Passion 78 (Ahonoora 122) [2006 74: p9.5g p8g² f8g² p8g p7.1g⁶ May 15] lengthy filly: modest performer: stays 8.6f: acts on all-weather, good to firm and good to soft ground. *J. R. Boyle* **63**

MIDNIGHT MOONLIGHT 3 ro.f. Bahamian Bounty 116 – Magnolia 52 (Petong 126) [2006 10g p10g² 9f⁴ 8.5f⁶ Dec 18] 26,000Y: lengthy filly: fourth foal: sister to 1m winner One Upmanship: dam, ran twice, sister to useful sprinter Petula and half-sister to smart 7f winner Naahy (by Bahamian Bounty): second in maiden at Lingfield in July, much the better effort in Britain: sold from C. Wall 15,000 gns and off 4 months, beaten 4½ lengths in similar events at Hollywood after: stays 1¼m: acts on polytrack: blinkered final outing. *S. Shulman, USA* **70**

MIDNIGHT PEARL (USA) 3 br.f. Woodman (USA) 126 – Elegant Ridge (IRE) 102 (Indian Ridge 123) [2006 59: 5f 5f Jul 23] neat filly: lightly-raced maiden: modest at 2 yrs, no form in 2006. *J. Howard Johnson* –

MIDNIGHT SKY 2 b.f. (Feb 19) Desert Prince (IRE) 130 – Midnight Shift (IRE) 73 (Night Shift (USA)) [2006 p6g⁶ Nov 24] half-sister to several winners, including 5f/6f winners Out After Dark (smart) and Move It (useful) (both by Cadeaux Genereux): dam, 6f winner, half-sister to very smart sprinter Owington: 10/1, 7¼ lengths sixth of 9 to Bussel in maiden at Kempton, fading after taking strong hold: likely to prove best at 5f/6f: should do better. *Rae Guest* **52 p**

MIDNIGHT TRAVELLER 3 b.c. Daylami (IRE) 138 – Swift Dispersal 87 (Shareef Dancer (USA) 135) [2006 78: 7m² 8d³ 9.9m² 10m⁶ 10m² 10d⁵ Oct 9] leggy, attractive colt: fairly useful maiden handicapper: bred to stay 1½m, but has raced freely: acts on soft and good to firm going: sold 40,000 gns, joined T. Cooper in Ireland. *L. M. Cumani* **85**

MID OCEAN 2 ch.f. (Apr 9) Sakhee (USA) 136 – Wavy Up (IRE) (Brustolon 117) [2006 7d p7g 8.2d Nov 1] 50,000Y: well-made filly: fourth foal: half-sister to 4-y-o Ti Adora and 3-y-o Cousteau: dam, French 8.5f winner, half-sister to smart performer up to 1m Wavy Run: modest form: saddle slipped final start: will stay 1¼m+. *P. W. D'Arcy* **61**

MIDSHIPMAN 8 b.h. Executive Man 119 – Midler (Comedy Star (USA) 121) [2006 67, a74: p8.6g² p9.5g p9.5g p8.6g 10.9s p8g⁴ p9.5g 8d p12g 10.9d 8d Oct 18] good-topped horse: fair performer: left A. Carroll following seventh outing: little form after: effective 1m (given test) to 1½m: acts on all-weather and soft going: tried in blinkers, usually visored/tongue tied nowadays: waited with. *T. Keddy* **71 d**

MID VALLEY 3 ch.c. Zilzal (USA) 137 – Isabella d'Este (IRE) 65 (Irish River (FR) 131) [2006 –: p6g f7g* f8g³ 9.7m⁵ 8g 8f⁶ 7f 7m³ 7f f7g p8g⁶ p7.1g² p8g⁶ Dec 6] modest performer: won banded race at Southwell in February: effective at 7f to 9.7f: acts on all-weather and firm going: wears cheekpieces/visored nowadays. *J. R. Jenkins* **56**

MIGHTY 3 ch.c. Pivotal 124 – Miswaki Belle (USA) 73 (Miswaki (USA) 124) [2006 8d³ 8m³ Jun 17] strong, good-bodied colt: has scope: sixth foal: brother to useful 1m to 10.5f (Prix Penelope) winner Humouresque and half-brother to smart 5f/6f winner Danehurst (by Danehill): dam, second at 7f on only start, closely related to smart performer up to 1m Dazzle: similar form when third in maidens at Newmarket and York (still green): sold 8,500 gns in October, joined Jane Chapple-Hyam. *Sir Michael Stoute* **68**

MIGHTY DANCER (IRE) 3 b.g. Danehill Dancer (IRE) 117 – K S Sunshine (USA) 43 (Sunshine Forever (USA)) [2006 61: p8.6g² p8g² 10d 9.7m² p10g 8.3d 10.2f³ p12.2g 10.1f⁴ 11.9f* p12.2g⁵ Sep 11] sturdy gelding: fair performer: won claimer at Brighton in August: stays 1½m: acts on all-weather and firm going. *S. Kirk* **65**

MIGHTY DUEL 3 b.g. Daggers Drawn (USA) 114 – Runs In The Family 69 (Distant Relative 128) [2006 –: 7g 8.2m 7f⁵ 9f f8g f16g Dec 28] good-bodied gelding: little form: tried tongue tied/in cheekpieces. *J. R. Norton* –

MIGHTY KITCHENER (USA) 3 br.g. Mighty (USA) 118 – Libeccio (NZ) (Danzatore (CAN) 120) [2006 67: f8g p9.5g⁴ p12g⁵ f11g 12m p12g⁴ p12.2g³ Dec 28] fair maiden: stays 1½m: acts on all-weather: none too consistent. *P. Howling* **68**

MIGHTY MISSOURI (IRE) 2 b.g. (Jan 30) Danehill (USA) 126 – Pietra Dura 96 **66** (Cadeaux Genereux 131) [2006 6m 6m⁶ 6m Aug 4] 90,000Y: sturdy, angular gelding: first foal: dam, Irish 2-y-o 7f winner who stayed 9.5f, out of Moyglare Stud Stakes winner Bianca Nera: fair form last 2 starts in maidens: gelded after. *W. R. Swinburn*

MIGHTY MOON 3 gr.g. Daylami (IRE) 138 – Moon Magic 62 (Polish Precedent **90** (USA) 131) [2006 69?: 10m 14m 10g* 14m² 11.5m³ 13.8v* p12g⁶ f12g² p12.2s⁵ Dec 15] small, leggy gelding: improved into a fairly useful handicapper, proving more straight-forward with experience: won amateur event at Newmarket in July and, having been sold from Lady Herries (16,000 gns) after fifth start, at Catterick (by 27 lengths) in October: stays 1¾m: acts on fibresand, heavy and good to firm going: blinkered/tongue tied nowadays. *J. O'Reilly*

MIGHTY OBSERVER (IRE) 3 b.g. Observatory (USA) 131 – Staff Approved 94 **53** (Teenoso (USA) 135) [2006 –: f8g⁶ 11.5m⁵ 10m Jul 8] modest maiden, lightly raced: probably stays 1m: has hinted at temperament (bolted to post/withdrawn once at 2 yrs). *M. H. Tompkins*

MIGHTY SPLASH 3 b.f. Cape Cross (IRE) 129 – Serotina (IRE) 73 (Mtoto 134) **66** [2006 –p: 11.5f 11.9m* p9.5g Nov 6] strong filly: fair performer, lightly raced: easily best effort when winning 4-runner handicap at Brighton (raced freely, carried head high) in August: stays 1½m: acts on good to firm ground. *R. Charlton*

MIGRATION 10 b.g. Rainbow Quest (USA) 134 – Armeria (USA) 79 (Northern Dan- **67** cer) [2006 44: 12g* 11.5m 14.1s 12d⁴ 10m Jun 16] tall gelding: fair handicapper: won apprentice event at Southwell in April: stays 1½m: acts on soft and good to firm going: tried in cheekpieces. *Mrs S. Lamyman*

MIKAO (IRE) 5 b.g. Tagula (IRE) 116 – Oumaladia (IRE) 84 (Waajib 121) [2006 93: **99** 12g* 18.7m 16.1m 16g⁶ 12g³ 12d 14.1g³ 12d* 12g Oct 12] rather leggy, useful-looking gelding: useful handicapper: won at Newmarket in April (beat Nawamees by short head) and September (beat Ti Adora by ¾ length): effective at 1½m to 2m, possibly not 18.7f: acts on polytrack, soft and good to firm going. *M. H. Tompkins*

MIKA'S FABLE (FR) 3 ch.f. Muhtathir 126 – Baie Des Anges (Pas de Seul 133) **–** [2006 10m 10.9d 8.2v Oct 25] €14,000F, €38,000 2-y-o: workmanlike filly: half-sister to 3 winners abroad, including French 1m (at 2 yrs) to 12.5f winner Lost Bay (by Lost World): dam won in Belgium: well beaten in maidens, leaving M. Meade after second start: slowly away first 2 outings, racing freely second occasion. *Miss Tor Sturgis*

MIKES MATE 5 b.g. Komaite (USA) – Pitcairn Princess (Capricorn Line 111) [2006 **–** –: f11g May 16] rather unfurnished gelding: of little account. *C. J. Teague*

MIKEY (IRE) 3 b.g. Danetime (IRE) 121 – Sharp Hint 60 (Sharpo 132) [2006 8v 6s 8v **73** f5g p7.1g³ Dec 9] third foal: dam maiden (best at 5f): fair maiden: improved form when third to Barney McGrew at Wolverhampton final outing: worth a try back at 6f: acts on polytrack: tongue tied last 2 starts. *Edgar Byrne, Ireland*

MIKIMOTO (IRE) 4 b.f. Enrique 121 – Etiquette 66 (Law Society (USA) 130) [2006 **53** –: 6f 8f p12g³ p13.9g⁵ p10g⁵ f11g³ Dec 29] €11,000Y: half-sister to 3 winners in France, including useful 6f (at 2 yrs) and 1m winner Uninhibited (by Lahib): dam, maiden, best at 1½m: modest maiden: left H. Rogers in Ireland after second start: stays 1¾m: acts on all-weather, raced on good or firmer going on turf. *S. C. Williams*

MILITARY CROSS 3 b.g. Cape Cross (IRE) 129 – Tipsy 95 (Kris 135) [2006 94: **102** 7s 10.1m² 8m 10m⁵ 8g³ 8.1m³ Aug 12] close-coupled, quite attractive gelding: useful handicapper: several creditable efforts in 2006, including 1¼ lengths second to Stage Gift at Epsom (hung left) and third to Audience at Haydock final outing: stays 1¼m: acts on good to firm going, below form on softer than good: sold 45,000 gns in November. *W. J. Haggas*

MILK AND SULTANA 6 b.m. Millkom 124 – Premier Princess 45 (Hard Fought 125) **62** [2006 56: p10g⁴ p12.2g p10g p9.5g* p10g* p10g* p9.5g³ p10g* 11.7f⁵ 10.2f 10.9m³ 10m² p10g 10.2f⁵ p10g⁴ 10d p10g* p12g⁶ p11g⁴ p9.5g² p10g² p10g Dec 10] modest performer: won sellers at Wolverhampton and Lingfield in February, and banded race at Kempton in October: stays easy 1½m: acts on all-weather and firm going, probably good to soft. *G. A. Ham*

MILKY BAR KID (IRE) 3 ch.c. Night Shift (USA) – Baileys Cream 79 (Mister **?** Baileys 123) [2006 –: p5g⁶ 7g⁴ 6g 6g⁶ 6d 5v⁶ 6g Oct 3] strong colt: maiden: sold from C. Wall 6,000 gns after reappearance: best placing when fourth at Cologne next time: stays 7f: tried tongue tied/blinkered: has looked wayward. *N. Sauer, Germany*

MILLACHY 2 b.f. (Feb 5) Kyllachy 129 – Millazure (USA) 71 (Dayjur (USA) 137) **65 p**
[2006 5.1m² Sep 4] 10,500F: sixth foal: half-sister to 7-y-o Millennium Hall and a winner
in Italy by Mozart: dam, ran 4 times (should have stayed beyond 7f), out of top-class
miler Milligram: 4/1, neck second to Foxy Games in maiden at Bath, racing wide and
finishing well: will do better. *B. W. Hills*

MILLAGROS (IRE) 6 b.m. Pennekamp (USA) 130 – Grey Galava 64 (Generous **76**
(IRE) 139) [2006 79: p12.2g* p12.2g 12d 16d⁴ p13.9g Nov 14] lengthy, good-bodied
mare: fair handicapper: won at Wolverhampton in January: stays 13f: acts on polytrack,
firm and soft going: tried in visor/cheekpieces: has hung left: signs of temperament.
I. Semple

MILLA'S ROCKET (IRE) 2 b.f. (Jan 17) Galileo (IRE) 134 – Tenable (Polish **53**
Precedent (USA) 131) [2006 8m p8.6g Oct 29] 25,000Y: sturdy filly: second foal: dam
unraced half-sister to 5-y-o Day Flight: modest form in maidens: will benefit from 1½m:
joined K. Ryan. *D. J. Daly*

MILLBROOK STAR (IRE) 3 b.g. Orpen (USA) 116 – Lady Bodmin (IRE) (Law **46**
Society (USA) 130) [2006 –: f8g 11g f8g⁶ 7g f6g 8.2f 8f³ 7m 8d p6m f7g f8g Dec 29]
lengthy gelding: poor and inconsistent maiden: stays 1m: acts on fibresand and firm
ground: tried visored, often blinkered nowadays. *M. C. Chapman*

MILL BY THE STREAM 4 b.g. Lujain (USA) 119 – Lonesome 60 (Night Shift **57**
(USA)) [2006 57: f6g³ p6g⁵ 5g 6m 5.9m 6f⁵ 7.5f³ 6m f6g³ 7d p6g p7.1m Sep 2] close-
coupled gelding: modest performer: left P. Midgley after ninth start: effective at 6f to 1m:
acts on all-weather and firm going: tried in cheekpieces/visored. *R. Brotherton*

MILL END CHATEAU 4 ch.g. Paris House 123 – Mill End Quest 65 (King's Signet **50**
(USA) 110) [2006 –: f6g⁶ p6g p5g⁶ f5g Nov 21] leggy, lengthy gelding: modest maiden,
lightly raced: best effort at 5f on polytrack: tongue tied last 2 starts. *D. K. Ivory*

MILL END (IRE) 4 br.g. Trans Island 119 – Tumble (Mtoto 134) [2006 p8.6g 8.1m⁵ **64**
8.2g p7.1m⁴ p9.5g Nov 28] big, strong gelding: modest maiden: may prove best short of
1m: acts on polytrack and good to firm going. *R. M. H. Cowell*

MILLENNIUM FORCE 8 b.g. Bin Ajwaad (IRE) 119 – Jumairah Sun (IRE) 98 **99 d**
(Scenic 128) [2006 112: 7.5m 7.5m³ 7.5d 6v 7g 7m 7g 7f 7.6m 7g 7g² 7d⁴ p7.1m³ Oct 9]
tall, lengthy gelding: smart handicapper at best: useful form when third in handicap at
Nad Al Sheba second start, only fairly useful at best after: effective at 6.5f to 1m: acts on
polytrack and any going on turf: has run creditably in visor: usually held up: sometimes
wanders: none too reliable: sold 20,000 gns. *M. R. Channon*

MILLENNIUM HALL 7 b.g. Saddlers' Hall (IRE) 126 – Millazure (USA) 71 (Day- **64**
jur (USA) 137) [2006 73: 13f 13d³ 13f 13g⁶ 14.1g 12.1m 12.1g Aug 23] leggy gelding:
had a quick action: modest handicapper: all 4 wins at Hamilton: stayed 13f: acted on any
going: tried in cheekpieces at 4 yrs: usually waited with: won over hurdles in September:
dead. *Miss Lucinda V. Russell*

MILLESTAN (IRE) 2 b.f. (Feb 2) Invincible Spirit (IRE) 121 – Atnab (USA) 64 **87**
(Riverman (USA) 131) [2006 6f 7f² 8.3m* 7d⁵ 8d Oct 28] compact filly: fifth foal: half-
sister to useful French 9.5f (at 2 yrs) to 15f winner Grey Mystique (by Linamix): dam,
1½m winner, out of half-sister to 1000 Guineas winner Fairy Footsteps and St Leger
winner Light Cavalry: fairly useful form: won maiden at Leicester in September: better
effort after in listed races at Newmarket when fifth to Selinka: stays 8.3f: acts on firm and
good to soft going. *H. R. A. Cecil*

MILLFIELD (IRE) 3 br.g. Elnadim (USA) 128 – Eschasse (USA) (Zilzal (USA) 137) **79 d**
[2006 79: 6m 6m⁵ 6f⁶ 7d 7.5g 5s 5g Sep 30] tall, close-coupled gelding: fair performer:
ran creditably in 2006 only in handicap at Thirsk on second start: stays easy 7f: acts on
good to firm going: blinkered (very slowly away) final outing. *J. Howard Johnson*

MILLFIELDS DREAMS 7 b.g. Dreams End 93 – Millfields Lady 75 (Sayf El Arab **70**
(USA) 127) [2006 5f* 6m⁵ 6.1d² 5f³ p5.1g² 6f² 6f² 5m 6g p6g 6g⁴ 6d⁴ p7g⁶ f6g⁶ p6g*
p6g⁴ Dec 30] tall gelding: fair handicapper: won at Folkestone in June and Kempton in
December: likely to prove best at 5f/6f: acts on polytrack, firm and good to soft going:
sometimes wears cheekpieces. *M. G. Quinlan*

MILLIEGAIT 2 b.f. (Apr 22) Tobougg (IRE) 125 – Miller's Gait 74§ (Mill Reef (USA) **81**
141) [2006 6s⁴ 5.9g⁶ 7.5m 7g* Sep 27] 11,000Y: tall, unfurnished filly: half-sister to
several winners, including smart 11f to 2m winner Bold Gait (by Persian Bold) and 4-y-o
King's Gait: dam, ungenuine middle-distance maiden, half-sister to top-class hurdler/
stayer Royal Gait: fairly useful form: won maiden at Newcastle, making all: should stay
1m. *T. D. Easterby*

MILLINSKY (USA) 5 ch.m. Stravinsky (USA) 133 – Millyant 114 (Primo Dominie   **85**
121) [2006 80: 5m² 5g² 5f⁴ 5m 5f³ 5m² 5.2m² p5g³ p5.1g⁵ p5.1g⁴ Dec 27] sturdy mare:
fairly useful handicapper: best at 5f: acts on polytrack and firm going: tried blinkered
(looked none too genuine): has been slowly away: held up. *Rae Guest*

MILLION ALL DAY (IRE) 3 gr.f. Daylami (IRE) 138 – Madame Nureyev (USA)   **57**
(Nureyev (USA) 131) [2006 10: 8.2g 11.5m³ p10g³ p12.2g Jul 3] sturdy filly: modest
maiden: should stay 1½m: acts on polytrack and good to firm going. *W. R. Muir*

MILLION PERCENT 7 b.g. Ashkalani (IRE) 128 – Royal Jade 82 (Last Tycoon 131)   **72**
[2006 83: p6g p6g* p6g p6g 6m³ p7.1g* 6m² 6d² p7g* p6g² p6g⁶ 6d 6d 5.2m p6g²   **a76**
p6m⁴ 7.1m² p7.1g⁵ p8g² p8.6g p7g* p7g² p8g⁴ Dec 16] small, strong gelding: fair
performer: won sellers at Wolverhampton in February and May, claimer at Lingfield in
June (claimed from K. Burke after next start) and handicap at Kempton in November:
effective at 6f to 1m: acts on polytrack, firm and soft going: tried in headgear earlier in
career. *C. R. Dore*

MILLISECOND 2 b.f. (Apr 28) Royal Applause 124 – Milligram 130 (Mill Reef   **77**
(USA) 141) [2006 7m³ 7d³ p7g⁵ Oct 26] lengthy filly: half-sister to several winners,
including 3-y-o Millistar and useful 1m to 11.5f (in France) winner Millafonic (by
Zafonic): dam won Coronation Stakes and Queen Elizabeth II Stakes, daughter of 1000
Guineas winner One In A Million: fair form in maidens, best run on debut at Salisbury
(third to Puggy): likely to be as effective at 6f as 7f. *M. A. Jarvis*

MILLISTAR 3 b.f. Galileo (IRE) 134 – Milligram 130 (Mill Reef (USA) 141) [2006   **88**
10d⁴ 10m⁴ p10g* 9m 10d* Aug 19] unfurnished filly: half-sister to 3 winners, including
fairly useful 1¼m winner Millennium Dash (by Nashwan) and useful 1m to 11.5f (in
France) winner Millafonic (by Zafonic): dam won Coronation Stakes and Queen Elizabeth II Stakes, daughter of 1000 Guineas winner One In A Million: fairly useful
performer: won maiden at Kempton in July and handicap at Newbury (beat Prince Ary by
¾ length) in August: bred to stay 1½m: acts on polytrack, good to firm and good to soft
going: carried head awkwardly second start. *M. A. Jarvis*

MILLKOM ELEGANCE 7 b.m. Millkom 124 – Premier Princess 45 (Hard Fought   **–**
125) [2006 –, a51: p12.2g May 8] small, quite good-topped mare: modest performer: well
beaten only outing in 2006: usually blinkered/visored. *G. A. Ham*

MILLSINI 2 b.f. (Jan 30) Rossini (USA) 118 – Millyant 114 (Primo Dominie 121)   **– p**
[2006 5.1g⁶ Oct 17] closely related to fairly useful 5f/6f winner Juantorena (by Miswaki)
and half-sister to 2 winners, including useful 6f winner Millybaa (by Anabaa): dam, 5f
performer, half-sister to very smart sprinter Prince Sabo: 20/1, considerately handled
when sixth in maiden at Bath: should do better. *Rae Guest*

MILLSY 4 b.f. Pursuit of Love 124 – Jucea 77 (Bluebird (USA) 125) [2006 63: 5.9g   **–**
5.3m 5g 6s Oct 2] well-made filly: maiden: little form in 2006. *J. L. Spearing*

MILLVILLE 6 ch.g. Millkom 124 – Miss Top Ville (FR) (Top Ville 129) [2006 101:   **115**
12d* 11.6m³ 12d 12d⁵ p12g* p10g⁶ p12.2s² Dec 15] tall, leggy gelding: smart performer:
better than ever at 6 yrs, and won handicaps at York in May and Lingfield (beat Hasayar
by 5 lengths) in October: good neck second to Sweet Indulgence in similar event at Wolverhampton final start: stays 1¾m: acts on polytrack, firm and soft going: has been
bandaged hind joints: held up: consistent. *M. A. Jarvis*

MILLWOOD LAD (IRE) 3 ch.g. Most Welcome 131 – Triple Concerto (Grand   **–**
Lodge (USA) 125) [2006 7g 10.1d 9v May 21] tailed off in maidens: visored final outing:
looks wayward. *B. S. Rothwell*

MILLY BEAT 2 b.f. (Apr 14) Beat All (USA) 120 – Keep Ikis 66 (Anshan 119) [2006   **–**
5g 5f Apr 27] 4,000F, 1,000Y: first foal: dam 2m/17f winner: no show in seller and claimer (unseated to post) in spring. *C. Grant*

MILLYJEAN 2 ch.f. (Mar 23) Whittingham (IRE) 104 – Taken Aback (IRE) (Robel-   **52**
lino (USA) 127) [2006 6d p6g⁴ Dec 22] sturdy filly: first foal: dam ran twice: better effort
in maidens when fourth of 7 to Galaxy Stars at Kempton. *John Berry*

MILSON'S POINT (IRE) 2 b.g. (May 15) Fasliyev (USA) 120 – Hilbys Brite Flite   **76**
(USA) (Cormorant (USA)) [2006 6s 6d 7.2v³ p8.6g³ p7.1g* p6g* Dec 23] €17,000Y,
22,000 2-y-o: sixth foal: half-brother to winners in USA by Irish Open (2) and Relaunch:
dam US Grade 3 8.5f winner: fair performer: won nursery and minor event (made all) at
Wolverhampton in December: has form at 8.6f, may prove best up to 7f: acts on polytrack
and heavy ground. *I. Semple*

MILTONS CHOICE 3 b.g. Diktat 126 – Starosta (Soviet Star (USA) 128) [2006 55: **65**
5.1s* 5.7d 6.1d 7m 5.9m Jun 5] workmanlike gelding: fair handicapper: won at Nottingham in April: well held after: best at 5f/6f: acts on soft and good to firm going.
J. M. Bradley

MILTON'S KEEN 3 gr.g. Largesse 112 – Not A Word (Batshoof 122) [2006 61: 7d **61**
p7g 6g 6m 6s² Oct 2] leggy, quite attractive gelding: modest maiden: bred to be suited by
1m+: acts on heavy going. *P. S. McEntee*

MILTON STAR (IRE) 7 ch.g. Mukaddamah (USA) 125 – Bajan Girl (IRE) (Pips **70**
Pride 117) [2006 p12.2g p13.9m 12.4s³ Oct 10] ex-Irish gelding: fair handicapper, lightly
raced nowadays: stays 1½m: raced mainly on ground softer than good: blinkered last 5
starts at 2 yrs. *John A. Harris*

MIMI MOUSE 4 br.f. Diktat 126 – Shifty Mouse 44 (Night Shift (USA)) [2006 98: 5s³ **91**
5m 5m 5.4f⁴ 5m 5.1m³ 5.1f⁶ Sep 23] smallish, close-coupled filly: fairly useful handicapper: best form at 5f: acts on firm and soft ground: sometimes on toes/early to post:
tends to hang right: reportedly bled third start. *T. D. Easterby*

MIMISEL 2 ch.f. (Mar 21) Selkirk (USA) 129 – Milly-M (Cadeaux Genereux 131) **84**
[2006 6g³ 6g³ 6m⁴ 6m² 7s* 6d Oct 27] 62,000F: leggy, close-coupled, sparely-made filly:
second foal: half-sister to 3-y-o Conrad: dam unraced daughter of smart 5f performer
Millyant: fairly useful performer: in frame first 4 starts, including in listed race at Salisbury (fourth to Vital Statistics), prior to winning weak maiden at Newcastle in October by
3 lengths: stays 7f: acts on soft and good to firm going. *Rae Guest*

MIMITEH (USA) 3 ch.f. Maria's Mon (USA) 121 – Green Minstrel (FR) 106 (Green **77**
Tune (USA) 125) [2006 76: 7.1d⁴ 6f* 7m⁴ 6f⁴ 6f⁴ 6d Sep 27] fair performer: won
handicap at Brighton in June: effective at 6f/7f: acts on firm and good to soft ground.
R. M. Beckett

MINA 4 ch.f. Selkirk (USA) 129 – Midnight Shift (IRE) 73 (Night Shift (USA)) [2006 **73**
66: 6m² 6.1m⁵ 7.2d⁴ 6d² p7g⁵ p6g* p6g³ f6g² p6g p6g⁴ f6g Dec 23] tall filly: fair handicapper: won at Kempton in November: stays easy 7f, raced mainly at 6f: acts on all-weather, good to firm and good to soft going. *Rae Guest*

MINA A SALEM 4 b.g. Singspiel (IRE) 133 – Amber Fizz (USA) (Effervescing **83**
(USA)) [2006 86: p8.6g p10g* 10g 7.6d³ 8.1d 7m⁴ p8g² 7.6d⁵ p8g p8g* p8g⁴ Dec 30] **a101**
leggy, workmanlike gelding: reportedly partially sighted in left eye: useful handicapper
on all-weather, fairly useful on turf: won at Lingfield in March and December (by ½
length from Tamagin): good fourth to Happy As Larry there final start: effective at 7f to
1¼m: acts on polytrack, firm and good to soft going: often makes running. *C. E. Brittain*

MINAASH (USA) 2 b.c. (Feb 1) Dixie Union (USA) 121 – Metanoia (USA) (Seeking **84**
The Gold (USA)) [2006 p6g² 6m⁴ 5m* 5.1f⁶ 5m⁶ Aug 24] $40,000F, $110,000Y:
workmanlike colt: third living foal: dam, 7f/7.5f winner in USA, half-sister to smart
performer up to 1¼m Placerville: fairly useful performer: twice shaped well before
winning maiden at Lingfield in July: ran poorly both starts after: effective at 5f/6f: raced
on polytrack and going firmer than good. *J. Noseda*

MIND ALERT 5 b.g. Mind Games 121 – Bombay Sapphire (Be My Chief (USA) 122) **–**
[2006 –, a66: f6g f6g⁴ p6g² p5.1g³ f6g p6g* p6g⁶ p6g p6g⁶ 5.9g p5.1g p6g⁵ p6g² f6g p6g **a65**
p6g⁶ p6s p6g⁵ f6g² p7g³ Dec 30] good-topped gelding: fair handicapper: won at Lingfield
in February: trained thirteenth/fourteenth starts only by S. R. Bowring: acts on
all-weather, good to firm and good to soft ground: wears headgear: held up. *D. Shaw*

MIND OUT (USA) 3 b.g. Minardi (USA) 119 – Tapped Twice (USA) (Pleasant Tap **62**
(USA)) [2006 f8g⁵ p9.5g f7g² p6g² f7g² Apr 27] modest maiden: left J. Osborne after
third start: stayed 7f: acted on fibresand: visored final start: dead. *J. T. Stimpson*

MIND THAT FOX 4 b.g. Mind Games 121 – Foxie Lady 77 (Wolfhound (USA) 126) **–**
[2006 –: p7g p5.1g p5.1g f5g p5.1g p8.6g p6g Dec 2] no solid form. *T. Wall*

MIND THE STYLE 2 b.g. (Mar 12) Mind Games 121 – Sioux Lady (Petong 126) **78**
[2006 5d² 5.3m* 5.1m³ 5s⁵ 5.1m⁵ 6d⁴ 5.3f³ 5m Sep 19] 1,600Y: good-bodied gelding:
fourth foal: dam unraced: fair performer on balance: won maiden at Brighton in April:
possibly flattered when third in minor event at Chester and nursery at Brighton (last): best
at 5f: acts on firm and good to soft going: once tongue tied. *W. G. M. Turner*

MINE BEHIND 6 b.g. Sheikh Albadou 128 – Arapi (IRE) 89 (Arazi (USA) 135) [2006 **93**
96: 5.1f⁴ 6m 6m⁴ 6m 6.1f³ 7m 6f Aug 4] lengthy gelding: fairly useful handicapper: ran
creditably in 2006 only when in frame: effective at 5f (given a test) to 7f: acts on polytrack, firm and soft going: tried in cheekpieces. *J. R. Best*

665

MINE (IRE) 8 b.h. Primo Dominie 121 – Ellebanna 69 (Tina's Pet 121) [2006 114: **117**
8s 8m 7g 8m 7m* 7m 7.1s² 7d Sep 23]

    The essay on Baltic King alluded to the changed circumstances that have
brought about a compression of the weights in the traditional big handicaps in
recent years. Baltic King's Wokingham had a weight range of just 15 lb and it was a
similar story in the Ladbrokes Bunbury Cup at Newmarket in which another veteran entire, the eight-year-old Mine, put up a fine performance to win under top
weight. Mine has now won five major handicaps—including three Bunbury Cups
—but most of his rivals in the latest Bunbury Cup were weighted up to the hilt,
like him. The lightly-raced four-year-old Zidane, who started favourite, and the
Britannia Stakes runner-up Easy Air, were the only three-year-old in
the nineteen-runner line-up that could be viewed as progressive sorts. The field had
a weight range of 18 lb and was made up mainly of exposed handicappers who had
been running in similar events. Four, including Mine, had run in the Royal Hunt
Cup, three in the Wokingham and two in the Buckingham Palace at Royal Ascot.
The stand-side runners ended up dominating the Bunbury Cup, those drawn in
single figures (including Easy Air) having it all to do, while others (including
Zidane) met trouble in running, which reduced the race's competitiveness further.
Mine, who had been first home among the disadvantaged far-side group when
eighth in the Royal Hunt Cup, was in the right place at Newmarket and quickened
virtually from last to first to win convincingly by two lengths from the Wokingham
tenth Intrepid Jack and the Buckingham Palace eighth Marching Song (earlier
runner-up in the Victoria Cup).

    Mine has been running with credit in valuable handicaps since his four-
year-old days, when he won his first Bunbury Cup, awarded the race outright after
dead-heating with the Wokingham winner Capricho whose rider weighed in 9 lb
light. Mine progressed into a smart handicapper as a five-year-old, with his best
effort again coming in the Bunbury Cup in which he was just pipped by Patavellian,
storming home after having a lot of ground to make up. Mine completed an Ascot
big-handicap double as a six-year-old, taking the Victoria Cup and the Royal Hunt
Cup, and, since then, his BHB handicap mark has varied only between 102 and 108
(the mark off which he ran when down the field in the totesport.com Stakes at
Ascot in September in the latest season). Mine's victory in the Royal Hunt Cup
resulted in his BHB mark going too high as a six-year-old for the Bunbury Cup (a
0-105 handicap), but he has taken the last two editions—his only victories in the
last two years—off BHB marks of 104 and 102, prevailing in a finish of short heads
as a seven-year-old. Mine usually needs a race or two to come to himself and con-

*Ladbrokes Bunbury Cup (Handicap), Newmarket—top weight Mine wins the race for the second year
running and the third time in all; Intrepid Jack is second, Marching Song third and Swinbrook fourth*

Mr M. J. Dawson's "Mine"

nections will be hoping the handicapper drops him enough to allow him to take in the Bunbury Cup for a fifth time. Mine is well up to winning in listed and minor pattern company and he ran his best race in the latest season, apart from at Newmarket, when going down by a neck to Quito in a strong listed event at Haydock in September. That race showed that, although Mine's style of racing lends itself to strongly-run races and big fields, he can cope well enough with tactical affairs, something that had been called into question by some of his previous efforts in listed and pattern company. Conditions at Haydock were soft and Mine is proven on all going except heavy.

		Dominion		Derring-Do
	Primo Dominie	(b 1972)		Picture Palace
	(b 1982)	Swan Ann		My Swanee
Mine (IRE)		(ch 1971)		Anna Barry
(b.h. 1998)		Tina's Pet		Mummy's Pet
	Ellebanna	(b 1978)		Merry Weather
	(b 1988)	Mainly Dry		The Brianstan
		(gr or ro 1980)		Sunny Spell

Mine, a tall, useful-looking horse, is by the sprinter Primo Dominie out of the sprint-bred five-furlong winner Ellebanna, a half-sister to King's Stand winner Bolshoi. The best of Ellebanna's other progeny, who include the fair winning three-year-old Ours (by Mark of Esteem), who barely stays a mile, is King Midas (by Bluebird), a useful winner at around seven furlongs in Britain and the UAE.

Mine, who wears a visor, has not run at sprint distances since his four-year-old days and is effective at seven furlongs to a mile. He is waited with, and travels strongly. *J. D. Bethell*

MINERAL RIGHTS (USA) 2 ch.g. (Apr 24) Gulch (USA) – Long Vacation (IRE) **69 p** (Thatching 131) [2006 7.2d 7g p8.6g⁶ p7.1g⁵ p8.6g⁵ Nov 28] $25,000Y, 11,000 2-y-o: big, rangy gelding: third foal: dam, 5f/6f winner in Japan, out of half-sister to Irish Derby winner Law Society: fair maiden: often shaped better than bare result: should prove best short of 8.6f: type to improve yet. *I. Semple*

MINERAL STAR (IRE) 4 b.g. Monashee Mountain (USA) 115 – Summit Talk (Head **82** For Heights 125) [2006 92: p8g 7m 10m 7.9g 7g 8d Sep 14] tall, leggy, angular gelding: fairly useful handicapper: not at best in 2006: stays 1m: acts on soft and good to firm ground. *M. H. Tompkins*

MINE THE BALANCE (IRE) 3 b.g. Desert Style (IRE) 121 – Dia (IRE) (Astronef **62** 116) [2006 45: p7g p5g² p6g p5g⁵ p6g³ p7g² p8g 7m⁶ p7g p8g p6g³ p6g* Dec 20] leggy gelding: modest handicapper: won at Lingfield in December: stays 7f: acts on polytrack: blinkered last 3 starts. *J. R. Best*

MING VASE 4 b.g. Vettori (IRE) 119 – Minstrel's Dance (CAN) (Pleasant Colony **54** (USA)) [2006 62: f8g⁴ f8g f8g⁵ p12.2g f8g f8g² 8d p8.6g⁶ f8g⁵ f8g⁶ 7g⁶ f8g 8.2f⁶ 10m* 11s⁶ 10.1d⁶ 9.8d³ 10m⁵ f11g Oct 12] strong gelding: modest performer: won selling handicap at Nottingham in July, hanging once in front: stays 11f: acts on all-weather, firm and good to soft going: tried in visor/cheekpieces. *P. T. Midgley*

MINIMUM BID 5 b.m. First Trump 118 – La Noisette (Rock Hopper 124) [2006 82: **67** 6g⁵ 6f 6g Aug 4] just fair handicapper in 2006, form only on reappearance: effective at 5f to easy 7f: acts on polytrack, raced only on good ground or firmer on turf: often blinkered/visored: sold 2,000 gns. *B. Smart*

MINIMUM FUSS (IRE) 2 b.f. (Mar 18) Second Empire (IRE) 124 – Jamis (IRE) (Be **60** My Guest (USA) 126) [2006 5v f5g⁴ 5g⁶ 6v⁶ 6g² 7f³ 6m f5g* 7m⁴ 5d⁴ 5m 6f³ 6d 5.2d f5g³ Dec 5] 1,000Y: tall filly: second foal: dam unraced out of half-sister to very smart 1¼m performer Batshoof: modest performer: won seller at Southwell in July (final start for M. Easterby): inconsistent after, twice placed in nurseries: best at 5f/6f: acts on fibresand, firm and good to soft going: often blinkered: suspect temperament. *M. C. Chapman*

MINISTER OF STATE 3 ch.c. Machiavellian (USA) 123 – Mystic Goddess (USA) **91** 94 (Storm Bird (CAN) 134) [2006 8g² 8m³ 8.2m* 8f* 8m⁴ 8.1m Sep 8] medium-sized, robust colt: type to carry condition: has a short, quick action: seventh foal: brother to high-class 1m (Lockinge)/1¼m (Eclipse) winner Medicean and half-brother to useful 1m winner Moon Goddess (by Rainbow Quest): dam, 2-y-o 6f/7f winner who stayed 1m, half-sister to Gran Criterium winner Sanam: fairly useful performer: won maiden at Nottingham in June and handicap at Thirsk in July: will be suited by 1¼m: folded tamely in cheekpieces final outing: front runner: sold 90,000 gns, sent to Bahrain. *M. A. Jarvis*

MINIVET 11 b.g. Midyan (USA) 124 – Bronzewing 103 (Beldale Flutter (USA) 130) **42** [2006 –: 15.8d 14m⁶ 16g Jul 3] workmanlike gelding: poor handicapper nowadays: tried blinkered: often slowly away. *R. Allan*

MINNIE MAGICIAN 2 b.f. (May 6) Wizard King 122 – Moving Princess 71 (Prince **43** Sabo 123) [2006 5g 5m³ 5d⁴ 6v 6g 5m⁴ 5m Aug 3] small filly: fourth foal: half-sister to 4-y-o Sabo Prince and 5f to 6.5f winner in Italy by Mind Games: dam maiden who stayed 1¼m: poor maiden: raced at 5f/6f. *C. Grant*

MINNIE MILL 2 b.f. (Feb 8) Mind Games 121 – Sometime Never (IRE) (College **60** Chapel 122) [2006 p6s p6g³ Dec 26] third foal: half-sister to Italian 7.5f to 1¼m winner by Opening Verse: dam unraced: better run in maidens at Wolverhampton when close third to Hollywood George. *B. P. J. Baugh*

MINNIS BAY (CAN) 2 b.g. (May 15) Royal Academy (USA) 130 – Aly's Daylite **83** (USA) (Dayjur (USA) 137) [2006 6m⁵ p7.1g² p7g⁴ Oct 17] $40,000Y: leggy gelding: half-brother to several minor winners in USA: dam unraced half-sister to dam of Fillies' Mile winner Teggiano: fairly useful maiden: neck second to Dream Lodge at Wolverhampton: not run of final race: gelded after: will stay 1m. *E. F. Vaughan*

MINNOW 2 b.f. (Apr 26) Averti (IRE) 117 – Tharwa (IRE) 63 (Last Tycoon 131) [2006 **76 p** 7f⁶ 5g⁶ 6s p5.1g⁴ p5.1g* Dec 2] 9,500Y: big, lengthy filly: half-sister to 3 winners, including 5-y-o Enchantment and 9-y-o Nisr: dam, 5f (at 2 yrs)/6f winner, half-sister to dam of very smart 7f to 9f winner Bin Rosie: fair form: progressed to win nurseries at

Kempton and Wolverhampton (by 2 lengths, value more) in December: best at 5f: acts on polytrack: has scope, and should do better still. *S. C. Williams*

MINORITY REPORT 6 b.g. Rainbow Quest (USA) 134 – Queen Sceptre (IRE) 97 **104** (Fairy King (USA)) [2006 94+: 8f* 8m 7m* 7g³ 7d 7g Oct 13] stocky gelding, type to carry condition: useful performer: won quite valuable handicap at Thirsk (by length from Flipando) in May and minor event at Goodwood (beat Kalankari a head) in August: easily best other effort when creditable third to Illustrious Blue in handicap at Goodwood: effective at 7f/1m: acts on firm and good to soft going. *L. M. Cumani*

MINOS (IRE) 2 ch.c. (Feb 29) Grand Lodge (USA) 125 – Miniver (IRE) (Mujtahid **90** (USA) 118) [2006 7g⁵ 7g² 8m* 7d 8g² Oct 13] €46,000F, €90,000Y: good-bodied colt: fluent mover: fifth foal: brother to 4-y-o Chateau and half-brother to 6-y-o Night Warrior and useful Irish 1¼m/1½m winner Mon Michel (by Montjeu): dam, ran once in Ireland at 2 yrs, half-sister to high-class performer up to 1½m Legal Case and to dam of Oaks winner Love Divine/grandam of St Leger winner Sixties Icon: fairly useful performer: won maiden at Goodwood in September: 6 lengths second of 4 to Proponent in minor event at Newmarket final start: will stay 1¼m. *R. Hannon*

MINT 3 b.f. Bahamian Bounty 116 – Tick Tack (Primo Dominie 121) [2006 72: 6m³ 5m **77** 5m⁶ 6m 6d 5f 5g Sep 27] smallish filly: fair handicapper: best effort in 2006 on reappearance: stays 6f: acts on good to firm going: hung markedly left once at 2 yrs: none too consistent. *D. W. Barker*

MINTHARE (IRE) 3 br.g. Bahhare (USA) 122 – Mintaka (IRE) (Fairy King (USA)) **69** [2006 54: 11.9s² 11.1d² 12.1m³ 12.1g⁵ 12.4d⁶ 15.8d Sep 5] lengthy gelding: fair maiden: stays 12.4f: best efforts on good ground or softer: wore cheekpieces last 3 starts: modest form in 2 juvenile hurdles, then sold 8,000 gns. *C. Grant*

MINT STATE 2 b.g. (Mar 11) Zilzal (USA) 137 – Pure (Slip Anchor 136) [2006 5d⁵ **69** 6g⁵ 7f 7m 7d⁶ 8g Oct 13] 24,000Y: good-topped gelding: has a quick action: sixth foal: half-brother to 3 winners, including 1¼m/1½m winner Clueless (by Royal Applause) and 3-y-o Champions Gallery, both useful: dam unraced sister to Oaks/St Leger winner User Friendly: fair maiden: gelded before final start (found little): should stay 1m: edgy sort, tends to sweat/race freely. *D. R. C. Elsworth*

MI ODDS 10 b.g. Sure Blade (USA) 130 – Vado Via 56 (Ardross 134) [2006 –, a90d: **–** f14g f11g f12g² f14g f11g p12.2g f11g f11g Dec 19] tall gelding: generally on downgrade **a75 d** and just fair form at best in 2006: effective at 8.5f to 1½m: acts on all-weather, had form on good to firm going earlier in career: tried in cheekpieces/visor. *Mrs N. Macauley*

MIRACLE BABY 4 b.f. Atraf 116 – Musica 82 (Primo Dominie 121) [2006 39: p8.6g **–** 5.7m p10g p12g Dec 1] strong filly: maiden: well held in 2006. *A. J. Chamberlain*

MIRACLE RIDGE (IRE) 11 ch.g. Indian Ridge 123 – Highly Delighted (USA) (Ver- **78** batim (USA)) [2006 48: f6g⁴ f5g* f5g 6g³ 6d* 5.8m* 6g* 5m⁶ 6m³ 6g² 5s a5g* 5g⁵ 6g* 5s 6v Oct 22] fair performer: won banded race at Southwell in January and handicaps at Cork and Navan in April, Ballinrobe in May, and Laytown and Listowel in September: effective at 5f to 7f: acts on all-weather/sand and any turf going: tried tongue tied: usually wears blinkers (didn't at Laytown). *A. McGuinness, Ireland*

MIRAGE PRINCE (IRE) 4 ch.g. Desert Prince (IRE) 130 – Belle Bijou 61 (Midyan **53** (USA) 124) [2006 –: p7.1g 8.1g 12.4m 11.7d 10.5m 6.1m Jun 16] rather leggy gelding: modest maiden handicapper nowadays: tongue tied final 3-y-o outing. *D. Shaw*

MIRASOL PRINCESS 5 ch.m. Ali-Royal (IRE) 127 – Yanomami (USA) 71 (Slew **59** O' Gold (USA)) [2006 74, a62: p6g⁵ f5g³ p6g p6g p6g² p6g p6g* 5.7f⁶ p5.1g⁵ 6f⁶ p5g⁴ 6g* 6g⁶ Aug 12] smallish mare: modest performer: won claimer at Lingfield in June and handicap at Windsor in August: stays 6f: acts on all-weather and firm going: tried in cheekpieces/blinkered. *D. K. Ivory*

MIRIN 2 b.f. (Feb 1) Generous (IRE) 139 – Musetta (IRE) 107 (Cadeaux Genereux 131) **70 p** [2006 6.1d p8g⁴ Dec 16] unfurnished filly: half-sister to 3 winners, including 13f winner Meissen (by Amfortas) and 1¼m winner Mineko (by Nashwan): dam, 7f (at 2 yrs) and 1¼m winner, fourth in Oaks: needed debut then staying-on fourth to Colchium in maiden at Kempton: will improve further at 1¼m/1½m. *G. Wragg*

MIRJAN (IRE) 10 b.g. Tenby 125 – Mirana (IRE) (Ela-Mana-Mou 132) [2006 98: **102** 12d⁵ 16.2f⁴ 16.1m 16g³ 16.1d* 18d 14d Nov 3] strong, sturdy gelding: useful handicapper, lightly raced on Flat: won at Newcastle in August by 1¼ lengths from Numero Due: creditable tenth in Cesarewitch at Newmarket next time: stays 2¼m: acts on firm and soft going: effective blinkered or not. *L. Lungo*

MIRKO 2 b.c. (Jan 24) Dansili 127 – Marithea (IRE) (Barathea (IRE) 127) [2006 p8g — Oct 23] 25/1, pulled too hard in maiden at Lingfield. *Pat Eddery*

MIRTH 3 b.f. Alhaarth (IRE) 126 – Justine Au Jardin (USA) (Black Tie Affair 128) — [2006 71: p10g 12.1d Apr 19] maiden, ran only 4 times: well held in 2006: dead. *R. Hannon*

MIRTHFUL (USA) 2 b.f. (May 11) Miswaki (USA) 124 – Musicanti (USA) (Nijinsky **75 p** (CAN) 138) [2006 7g Sep 15] useful-looking filly: seventh foal: closely related to 2 winners by Distant View, notably high-class 7f (at 2 yrs, including Dewhurst Stakes) to 9f winner Distant Music, and half-sister to 1¼m winner New Orchid (by Quest For Fame): dam French 14.5f winner: 16/1, encouraging seventh of 13 to Darrfonah in minor event at Newbury, looking to be learning all the time, not knocked about: will do better. *B. W. Hills*

MISAINE (IRE) 2 b.g. (May 9) Fasliyev (USA) 120 – Rose Paille (FR) (General **59** Holme (USA) 128) [2006 5g p6g 5s 5m⁶ Sep 13] strong, lengthy gelding: modest maiden: shapes as if 5f should suit best. *T. J. Etherington*

MISARO (GER) 5 b.g. Acambaro (GER) 118 – Misniniski (Niniski (USA) 125) [2006 **84** 75: f6g³ f6g p6g³ 6m⁶ 5.3m⁶ 6f 5.7g p6g⁵ 5f* 5.3f² 5f⁴ 5.7m 5.7m 5.3d p5.1g p5.1g p5g⁶ **a75** p5.1g Dec 23] leggy gelding: fairly useful handicapper on turf, fair on all-weather: left P. D. Evans and rejoined former trainer after reappearance: won at Folkestone (apprentices) and Brighton in April, and Lingfield in June: effective at 5f/6f: acts on all-weather, firm and soft going: has won in visor, blinkered nowadays: usually races prominently. *R. A. Harris*

MISBEHAVIOUR 7 b.g. Tragic Role (USA) – Exotic Forest 66 (Dominion 123) [2006 **50** 39: p12g⁴ f16g³ Dec 12] leggy gelding: modest maiden, lightly raced on Flat nowadays: tried in cheekpieces/visor: half fair hurdler. *G. L. Moore*

MIS CHICAF (IRE) 5 b.m. Prince Sabo 123 – Champagne Season (USA) 54 (Vaguely — Noble 140) [2006 73: 6.1m 5.1s 5f 5m 6g 5f 6f 7.1m Aug 24] strong, workmanlike mare: useful mare at 3 yrs: very much on downgrade since and little form in 2006: tongue tied: races prominently. *Robert Gray*

MISKINA 5 b.m. Mark of Esteem (IRE) 137 – Najmat Alshemaal (IRE) 98 (Dancing — Brave (USA) 140) [2006 54, a67: f6g p7.1g⁵ p7.1g⁴ p7.1g p7g⁶ p7g² p7g⁴ p7.1g⁶ 6.1f **a65** p7g² p6g³ 7.1d p7.1m p6m p7.1g⁵ Nov 25] rather leggy mare: fair on all-weather, modest at best on turf: effective at 6f/7f: acts on polytrack, good to firm and good to soft going: tried tongue tied: sold 10,000 gns. *W. M. Brisbourne*

MISPHIRE 3 b.f. Mister Baileys 123 – Bombay Sapphire (Be My Chief (USA) 122) **87** [2006 84: 7m 6g 7m⁴ 6g² 6v⁵ Oct 28] big, good-topped filly: fairly useful handicapper: left T. Easterby after second start: stays 7f: acts on good to firm and good to soft going. *M. Dods*

MISS A BARGAIN (IRE) 3 ch.f. Bahamian Bounty 116 – Miss Clarinet (Pharly (FR) **47** 130) [2006 44: p6g⁴ p7.1g p6g Mar 6] poor maiden: best effort at 6f: raced on polytrack. *K. R. Burke*

MISS APRICOT 3 ch.f. Indian Ridge 123 – Mora (IRE) 100 (Second Set (IRE) 127) **48** [2006 p7.1m⁶ p6g⁴ Dec 6] 38,000F, 30,000Y: third foal: half-sister to 5-y-o Orchestration: dam, Irish 7f/1m winner, half-sister to useful dam of smart sprinter Eastern Purple: better effort in maidens at Wolverhampton on second start. *J. D. Bethell*

MISSATACAMA (IRE) 4 b.f. Desert Style (IRE) 121 – Delta Town (USA) (Sangla- **?** more (USA) 126) [2006 86: p10g 8f 8.5f* 9f⁵ 8.5f⁴ 8f⁴ Dec 3] rather leggy filly: fairly useful performer at 3 yrs: below form first outing in 2006, then sold from D. Daly 12,000 gns: won claimer at Hollywood in May: stays 1¼m: acts on polytrack, firm and soft going. *S. Shulman, USA*

MISS AUTUMNAL (IRE) 2 b.f. (Feb 17) Night Shift (USA) – Autumnal (IRE) 104 **64** (Indian Ridge 123) [2006 5m p6g⁵ 5.1g p5.1g Nov 2] first foal: dam 5f (at 2 yrs)/6f winner: modest maiden: best effort only start at 6f: blinkered after debut. *N. A. Callaghan*

MISS BEAR (IRE) 4 b.f. Orpen (USA) 116 – The Poachers Lady (IRE) (Salmon Leap — (USA) 131) [2006 52: f12g f11g Jan 11] good-bodied filly: modest winner in 2005: well held in 2006: tried blinkered. *B. Smart*

MISS BEATRIX (IRE) 2 b.f. (Mar 5) Danehill Dancer (IRE) 117 – Miss Beabea **106** (IRE) 105 (Catrail (USA) 123) [2006 5v² 5f³ 7m* 7g 6g² 6m³ 7m* 7d* Sep 19]
Which was the highest-earning two-year-old in Europe? Was it the best of the bunch, Teofilo, or the other dual Group 1 winners, Holy Roman Emperor and Dutch Art? Respectively they amassed £346,876, £407,711 and £275,027, which

are pretty fair totals, but the presence of massive prize-money funds for races connected with yearling auctions meant none of the trio could muster even half of what the top earner collected for her owner. The horse in question is Miss Beatrix, a grand filly, tough, and genuine, but one the best part of a stone behind the leaders of her sex Finsceal Beo and Sander Camillo. Her tally of £817,868 was principally the result, not of her victory in the Group 1 Moyglare Stud Stakes, worth £114,694, but the Goffs Million, a new race and the richest for juveniles anywhere in the northern hemisphere, with £665,541 going to the winner. The Breeders' Cup Juvenile had first prize money of £568,421; the world leader is the Golden Slipper Stakes in Australia, which was worth around £780,000 to the latest winner, Miss Finland. For the record, Silk Blossom, successful in the fillies-only Goffs sales race worth £330,405, was the third-highest earner among the two-year-olds in Europe. Miss Beatrix's win effectively guaranteed her sire Danehill Dancer the title of champion sire of juveniles. This, and the filly's position at the top of the earnings table distort the various statistics, but that hardly matters because there are better criteria than earnings by which to judge racehorses and stallions, Timeform ratings and medians for example. That said, the earnings tables for owners, trainers and sires certainly get plenty of exposure, though they do not have anything like the same status as, for example, the Order of Merit table for golfers in Europe, based entirely on earnings, rather than official rankings or tournament victories.

Sales races essentially are an advertising medium for auction houses, though they are funded mainly by fees paid by vendors of the selected yearlings at the time of the promoted sale, and by race entry and acceptance fees paid by the purchasers. They offer the prospect of a boost to trade at the sales connected with the races, but they are not to be decried on that account as there are also advantages for the racing public. Admittedly, the inevitable presence of runners of proven modest ability, aiming at a pot of gold, is an inevitable consequence—eight of the twenty-eight runners in the Goffs Million started at 50/1 or longer, and only eight of the twenty-seven runners in the Goffs Fillies Five Hundred were winners. But with large fields almost guaranteed and usually making for an open market among the above-average contenders, the advantages of sales and auction races outweigh the disadvantages. Sales races, going back to the Cartier Million in the late-'eighties, have occasionally come under fire for supposedly posing a threat to the established pattern system by providing a more remunerative and attractive alternative. Such a view has always been questionable, and there is no evidence that the latest Goffs sales races adversely affected the quality of Group 2 and Group 3 races run in the same period. As it happens, the sales races in both Britain and Ireland contained a good number of runners who had done well, or went on to do well, in

Moyglare Stud Stakes, the Curragh—Miss Beatrix (No.7) pips Silca Chiave; third-placed Supposition is largely obscured by the winner

Shelbourne Hotel Goffs Million, the Curragh—Miss Beatrix wins Europe's richest two-year-old race; runner-up Regime is first home on the near side, while Drumfire (fourth left) pips Emerald Hill (noseband) for third, ahead of the grey Laddies Poker, with Finsceal Beo second home on the near side

pattern company. Besides Miss Beatrix, there were two fillies among the runners in the various sales and auction races who landed a Group 1 race, Finsceal Beo and Indian Ink, plus pattern winners Silk Blossom, Caldra and Drumfire, subsequent Group 1 runner-up Charlie Farnsbarns, and Group 2 runner-up Doctor Brown.

For most of the season the idea of a Group 1 victory had looked wishful thinking for Miss Beatrix since she had tried her luck, and been found wanting, in listed races at the Curragh and Leopardstown before the end of July. Much her better effort was in the Silver Flash Stakes on the latter course where she was beaten a length and a quarter by Chanting after being outpaced. As a result, when Miss Beatrix lined up for the Phoenix Stakes at the Curragh in mid-August on her next start she had a record of just one win from five starts, in a ten-runner maiden at Leopardstown in June when easily landing the odds from Evening Rushour. She started at 50/1 for the Phoenix Stakes but belied those odds, staying on well down the centre of the course, after being held up, to finish two and a quarter lengths third behind Holy Roman Emperor, only half a length adrift of Hellvelyn and a head in front of her shorter-priced stable-companion Brazilian Bride. The runner-up and fourth had already won pattern races and this was clearly an improved performance by Miss Beatrix, though it did little to persuade punters of her improvement judged on her starting at 14/1 in the twelve-runner Moyglare Stud Stakes on the same course a fortnight later. Perhaps the fact that her trainer apparently had reservations about the seven-furlong trip, despite Miss Beatrix's victory having come over that distance, put people off. Either way, the favourite was the wide-margin Galway maiden winner Supposition. Next came British challenger Simply Perfect, beaten under a length when third in the Princess Margaret Stakes, Brazilian Bride again, Debutante Stakes third Alexander Tango, the winner of that race Gaudeamus, and another raider Silca Chiave, successful in a maiden race at Newbury. It was the last-named who gave Miss Beatrix most to do. Settled towards the back as Diamond Necklace, Gaudeamus and Supposition set a strong pace, Miss Beatrix came with a steady but relentless run to lead in the dying strides, collaring Silca Chiave, who had taken it up from Alexander Tango a hundred yards out. The margin was a short head with Supposition, who had been a bit short of room at one point, a length further away.

Miss Beatrix clearly stayed seven furlongs and was clearly on the upgrade, so there was every incentive to strike while the iron was hot three weeks later in the Shelbourne Hotel Goffs Million over the same course and distance. The race conditions allow fillies to run in the Million but not colts in the Fillies Five Hundred on the same card. So much for even-handedness. In the first running of the two Goffs races the number of fillies in the Million certainly had an effect on the quality of the Five Hundred. Five fillies contested the Million including not only Miss Beatrix but also Finsceal Beo and two promising maiden race winners, Fly Free and Four Sins. In a race in which thirteen of the twenty-eight runners were trained in Britain, including Solario Stakes winner Drumfire and Beverley maiden winner Regime, the fillies dominated the betting. Fly Free was favourite ahead of Miss Beatrix and Four Sins, with Cork listed winner He's A Decoy and Drumfire next followed by Finsceal Beo. Regrettably, the draw played a part in the outcome as the runners split into two groups in line for home with the high numbers dominating—seven of the first nine to finish drawn nineteen or higher. Miss Beatrix, drawn twenty-nine (there was one withdrawal), chased the leaders on the far side, led a furlong out and ran on well to beat Regime on the stand side by a length and a quarter with Drumfire third and Finsceal Beo, also on the 'wrong' side, sixth. Finsceal Beo was not in the form she later showed but this was still a useful performance by the winner, whose victory possessed a touch of irony. Although she went though the ring at Goffs as a yearling for €180,000, she was not sold in any meaningful sense of the term since she was knocked down to Kevin Prendergast, who has trained for her breeder Bill Durkan for a number of years. Miss Beatrix races in Durkan's colours.

Miss Beatrix (IRE) (b.f. Mar 5, 2004)	Danehill Dancer (IRE) (b 1993)	Danehill (b 1986)	Danzig Razyana
		Mira Adonde (b or br 1986)	Sharpen Up Lettre d'Amour
	Miss Beabea (IRE) (ch 1999)	Catrail (b 1990)	Storm Cat Tough As Nails
		Lady Ellen (b 1987)	Horage Hillbrow

Danehill Dancer has been carving out a successful career at Coolmore, as indicated by the number of mares he covers—one hundred and sixty-nine in 2005, followed by one hundred and eighty-four—and by his rising fee, which has gone from €75,000 to €115,000 for the 2007 season after starting out at just IR 4,000 guineas. As a horse who was suited by six and seven furlongs at both two and three, it is no surprise that the majority of his progeny, led by Choisir, Indesatchel,

Mr William Durkan's "Miss Beatrix"

Monsieur Bond, Speciosa and Where Or When, have shown more speed than stamina. Most of that quintet stayed a mile but, judged on the distaff side of her pedigree, Miss Beatrix, who acts on good to firm and good to soft going, is no certainty to be fully effective at that trip. Encouragingly, though, the way she races, and the fact that she was by no means coming to the end of her tether over seven furlongs, suggest she may well find a mile within her compass. It is speed virtually all through with the dam Miss Beabea, whose first produce she is (the second is a filly foal by Montjeu). By a sprinter in Catrail, Miss Beabea was tough, running nineteen times in two seasons, and capable of useful form at five and six furlongs. She won the listed Blenheim Stakes as a juvenile, when also a five-length runner-up to Johannesburg in the Phoenix Stakes and a close fourth in the Moyglare, and went on to be second in the Ballyogan Stakes at three. Miss Beabea is a half-sister to two other tough and speedy performers, Ellens Lad and Ellens Academy, who annexed twenty of their one hundred and sixty-nine starts between them. The grandam Lady Ellen picked up three races at seven furlongs and a mile and was a half-sister to the very smart sprinter and good sire Indian Ridge. Miss Beatrix, who was not seen out again after the Goffs Million, will doubtless have a go at the classics over a mile but, unless she makes significant improvement, which does not look certain, it is hard to see her coming up trumps at Newmarket or the Curragh. *K. Prendergast, Ireland*

MISS BRUSH 3 b.f. Foxhound (USA) 103 – Tattinger 85 (Prince Sabo 123) [2006 72: 6f 5m⁶ Jun 10] useful-looking filly: just modest performer at 3 yrs: should stay 6f: acts on polytrack and good to soft going. *J. R. Fanshawe* **60**

MISS CAPRICORN 2 b.f. (Jan 5) Forzando 122 – Miss Flirtatious 75 (Piccolo 121) [2006 5.1m⁶ 5g Aug 5] 20,000Y, 30,000 2-y-o: good-bodied filly: first foal: dam 5f/6f winner: last in maidens. *K. A. Ryan* **–**

MISS CHAMPAGNE (IRE) 3 b.f. Tagula (IRE) 116 – Champagne Lady (IRE) 65 (Turtle Island (IRE) 123) [2006 53: p7g⁵ p8.6g⁴ p6g p8g⁴ p7.1g² p7g* 7m 6d⁶ p7.1g² Apr 22] modest performer: won handicap at Lingfield in February: stays easy 8.6f: acts on polytrack. *M. Quinn* **54**

MISS CHARISMATIC 2 br.f. (Mar 30) Kalanisi (IRE) 132 – Mild Deception (IRE) (Glow (USA)) [2006 p8.6g Oct 29] 9,000Y: seventh foal: half-sister to several winners, including 6f to 1m (in Germany) winner Gresatre (by Absalom): dam unraced half-sister to Irish Oaks winner Margarula: 50/1, well held in maiden at Wolverhampton. *E. Tyrrell, Ireland* **–**

MISS CUE 4 b.f. Polish Precedent (USA) 131 – Sharp Girl (FR) 114 (Sharpman) [2006 –: p10g Apr 7] no sign of ability: tried visored. *J. Pearce* **–**

MISS DAAWE 2 b.f. (Mar 2) Daawe (USA) 103 – Feiticeira (USA) 79 (Deposit Ticket (USA)) [2006 6m 6.1d Oct 4] smallish, good-bodied filly: fourth foal: half-sister to winner in Hungary by Wolfhound: dam ran 3 times (second at 1m on debut): no show either start. *S. Parr* **–**

MISS DAGGER (IRE) 3 b.f. Daggers Drawn (USA) 114 – Royal Rumpus (Prince Tenderfoot (USA) 126) [2006 –: p7g⁴ p7g* p7g p6g⁵ p7g Apr 7] tall, leggy, plain filly: modest performer: won handicap at Lingfield in March: stays easy 7f: acts on polytrack: injured rider and withdrawn at start prior to intended debut: refused to race third/final outings: covered by Desert Sun, sold 7,000 gns, and sent to Saudi Arabia. *J. R. Best* **64 §**

MISSDEVINA (IRE) 3 b.f. Namid 128 – Vintage Escape (IRE) 84 (Cyrano de Bergerac 120) [2006 71: 7.5g p7g 7.1m⁵ Jul 13] lengthy filly: no form since debut at 2 yrs. *M. G. Quinlan* **–**

MISS DIXIE 3 b.f. Bertolini (USA) 125 – Dixie Favor (USA) 82 (Dixieland Band (USA)) [2006 66: 5.1g 5g 6f 5d Aug 31] leggy filly: maiden: no form in 2006, leaving Miss J. Camacho after third start: signs of temperament. *T. D. Easterby* **–**

MISS DONOVAN 3 b.f. Royal Applause 124 – Cumbrian Melody 83 (Petong 126) [2006 76: 6d 6m* 6d⁴ 5v³ 6g Oct 12] 28,000F: angular filly: half-sister to several winners, including useful 5f winner (including at 2 yrs) Golden Bounty (by Bahamian Bounty): dam 2-y-o 5f and 6f winner: useful performer: won maiden at Cork in August: very good 3 lengths third to Peace Offering in listed race at Tipperary after: only tenth in similar event at Newmarket final outing: likely to prove best at 5f/6f: winner on good to firm ground, best effort on heavy. *Declan Gillespie, Ireland* **100**

MISS DOUBLE DAISY 3 ch.f. Compton Place 125 – Stealthy 73 (Kind of Hush 118) **41**
[2006 p6g⁵ p6g Nov 28] 2,200Y: half-sister to 3 winners, including fairly useful 1999
2-y-o 6f winner Stealthy Times (by Timeless Times) and 6f winner Skiddaw Wolf (by
Wolfhound): dam 1m winner: better effort in maidens at Wolverhampton on debut (poor
form). *B. Smart*

MISSED A BEAT 4 b.f. Mister Baileys 123 – Lonely Heart 101 (Midyan (USA) 124) **83**
[2006 81: p7g 7m 8m⁵ 8.1g² 8.2f* 8m⁵ 8.5g⁴ 8f p8g 8m⁴ Sep 13] close-coupled filly:
fairly useful handicapper: won at Nottingham in July: stays 8.5f: acts on polytrack, firm
and soft going: sweating (ran poorly) once at 3 yrs. *M. Blanshard*

MISSED TURN 4 b.f. Mind Games 121 – Miss Beverley (Beveled (USA)) [2006 52: **?**
p8g p8g 8m⁴ a8.8g³ 8m 8m⁶ 8m 7.5d⁶ 6.5m⁶ Dec 2] good-topped filly: modest performer:
sold from J. Eustace 800 gns after second start. *D. Vitti, Italy*

MISS FANCY PANTS 2 gr.f. (Mar 10) Act One 124 – Sweetness Herself 106 (Unfu- **63**
wain (USA) 131) [2006 p9.5m⁴ p9.5g² p9.5g³ Dec 7] 21,000Y: fourth foal: half-sister to
3-y-o Noble Minstrel and smart 1¼m to 1¾m winner Jagger (by Linamix): dam 1½m to
16.5f winner: green, in frame in maidens at Wolverhampton, odds on when second (hung
badly right): will stay 1½m+. *M. Johnston*

MISS GLORY BE 8 b.m. Glory of Dancer 121 – Miss Blondie (USA) (Stop The Music **–**
(USA)) [2006 59: f8g⁴ f7g p8.6g⁵ p9.5g² p8.6g³ p10g p9.5g* p10g³ p10g 10m 11.5f⁶ **a62**
Jul 24] modest performer: won banded race at Wolverhampton in April: effective at 1m
to 11f: acts on all-weather, firm and good to soft going: tried visored (tailed off), wears
cheekpieces: reportedly bled sixth and final outings: sometimes carries head awkwardly.
E. R. Oertel

MISS HAVISHAM (IRE) 2 b.f. (Feb 14) Josr Algarhoud (IRE) 118 – Agony Aunt 81 **–**
(Formidable (USA) 125) [2006 7.5d 7d 6m⁴ 6m⁶ Sep 21] 5,000Y: big, strong filly: half-
sister to several winners, including smart winner around 6f (including at 2 yrs), including
in UAE, Doctor Hilary (by Mujahid) and 5-y-o Only If I Laugh: dam 1¼m winner: little
form. *J. R. Weymes*

MISS HIGHJINKS (USA) 3 ch.f. Stravinsky (USA) 133 – Ready For Action (USA) **92**
(Riverman (USA) 131) [2006 73p: p8g* 7.5d p8g 10.2d p8g³ Nov 28] strong filly: fairly
useful performer: won maiden at Lingfield (by 7 lengths) in January: good third in handicap there final start: stays 1m, seemingly not 1¼m: acts on polytrack. *E. J. O'Neill*

MISS HOLLY 7 b.m. Makbul 104 – Seraphim (FR) 48 (Lashkari 128) [2006 12.1d 10g **63**
12d 12s f12g* Dec 29] lightly raced on Flat nowadays: just modest form when winning
banded race at Southwell (heavily backed) in December: should stay beyond 1½m: acts
on fibresand, good to firm and good to soft ground. *D. Carroll*

MISS HOOLIE 2 b.f. (May 18) Danehill Dancer (IRE) 117 – Silky Dawn (IRE) 100 **– p**
(Night Shift (USA)) [2006 6g Oct 16] 37,000F: second foal: half-sister to 3-y-o Cat-
bang: dam 1m winner: 20/1, needed experience in maiden at Windsor: likely to improve.
W. R. Swinburn

MISSIE BAILEYS 4 ch.f. Mister Baileys 123 – Jilly Woo 60 (Environment Friend **66**
128) [2006 60: p12.2g p10g* p12g p13g⁴ p10g⁵ 12f³ 11.5m p16g p12g² p12g p12g
p12g³ p12.2m³ p12.2g* p10g p12.2g⁵ Dec 9] close-coupled filly: fair handicapper: won
at Lingfield in February and Wolverhampton in November: effective at 1¼m, barely at
easy 1¾m: acts on polytrack, firm and good to soft going: tried in cheekpieces. *Mrs
L. J. Mongan*

MISS IMPERIOUS 3 b.f. Imperial Ballet (IRE) 110 – Birthday Belle 70 (Lycius **50**
(USA) 124) [2006 p6g p6g 7m⁶ 8s⁶ p8.6g f8g³ f8g⁴ Dec 29] 5,000Y: quite good-topped
filly: first foal: dam German 6.5f/7.5f winner: modest maiden: stays 1m: acts on fibresand, soft and good to firm ground: clipped heels/unseated second outing. *B. Smart*

MISS INCH 4 b.f. Inchinor 119 – Twitcher's Delight (Polar Falcon (USA) 126) [2006 **61**
65: p9.5g p8.6g³ p8g Mar 6] rather leggy filly: modest maiden: should stay 1¼m: acts on
polytrack and good to soft ground: fell leaving stall on reappearance: sold 3,500 gns in
July. *G. Wragg*

MISSIN MARGOT 4 b.f. Fraam 114 – Abstone Queen 66 (Presidium 124) [2006 51: **–**
f6g⁵ f7g p7.1g Feb 6] good-topped filly: little form in 2006: visored last 3 outings: tail
flasher. *P. D. Evans*

MISSION AFFIRMED (USA) 5 ch.g. Stravinsky (USA) 133 – Affirmed Legacy **–**
(USA) (Affirmed (USA)) [2006 72, a78: f7g³ f8g f7g³ p9.5g³ p6g³ p8.6g⁵ p7.1g p7.1g² **a78 d**
7m p6g⁴ p7.1g f6g Nov 14] good-bodied gelding: fair performer: on downgrade: claimed

from T. Tate £6,000 after third start: left R. Harris, refused to race and unseated rider at Southwell final one: effective at 7f to easy 9.5f: acts on all-weather, best turf efforts on good ground: usually wears headgear. *Peter Grayson*

MISS IPPOLITA 2 b.f. (Feb 11) Diktat 126 – Isabella d'Este (IRE) 65 (Irish River 73 (FR) 131) [2006 5s⁴ 6d⁵ p6g⁵ 6s 6.1g* Sep 26] tall, lengthy filly: unfurnished at 2 yrs: second foal: half-sister to 3-y-o Mid Valley: dam maiden who should have stayed 1½m: fair form: won maiden at Nottingham by ½ length, getting first run on Party: out of depth in Lowther Stakes time since: likely to stay 7f/1m: acts on polytrack, raced on good going or softer on turf. *J. R. Jenkins*

MISSISIPI STAR (IRE) 3 b.f. Mujahid (USA) 125 – Kicka (Shirley Heights 130) 98 [2006 8g³ 8.2m* 10g 10.1m³ 10d² 9m³ 12m⁶ Sep 9] €7,000Y: strong, lengthy filly: third foal: dam, maiden in Italy, out of close relation to Derby runner-up Glacial Storm: useful performer: won maiden at Nottingham in May: ran well when second in handicap at Leopardstown and 2 lengths third to Blessyourpinksox in listed race at the Curragh fifth/ sixth starts: stays 1¼m: acts on good to firm and good to soft going: sold 220,000 gns, joined I. Mohammed in UAE. *E. Tyrrell, Ireland*

MISS JENNY (IRE) 2 b.f. (Jan 21) Desert Prince (IRE) 130 – Please Believe Me 93 83 (Try My Best (USA) 130) [2006 5m⁶ 6g² 6s⁶ p6g* 7d p7g⁶ Oct 21] compact filly: type to carry condition: half-sister to several winners, 3 by Indian Ridge, including useful 5f (at 2 yrs)/6f winners Autumnal and Mazepa: dam 2-y-o 5f winner: fairly useful performer: won maiden at Lingfield in September: better run in nurseries after when sixth to Market Day there: highly tried in Lowther Stakes third start (8/1, sixth of 7): should prove best at 5f/6f: acts on polytrack and soft going. *B. J. Meehan*

MISS KITTY 2 br.f. (Mar 3) Monsieur Cat (USA) – Upstream 79 (Prince Sabo 123) – [2006 f5g Nov 10] 18,000 2-y-o: first foal: dam, 5f winner, half-sister to smart 2003 2-y-o 6f/7f winner Peak To Creek: 28/1 behind in maiden at Southwell. *T. D. Easterby*

MISS KOOL KAT (USA) 2 b. or br.f. (Mar 3) Exploit (USA) 117 – Pristine (USA) 66 (Gone West (USA)) [2006 p5g⁴ 5d⁴ 5.1m 5.1f 5.1g⁶ Oct 17] $15,000F, 17,000Y: close-coupled filly: second foal: half-sister to winner in USA by Saint Ballado: dam, useful 6.5f winner (including at 2 yrs) in USA, out of half-sister to outstanding broodmare Fall Aspen: fair maiden: last only start in nursery: raced at 5f: best effort on good to soft going: sold 11,000 gns. *K. A. Ryan*

MISS LACEY (IRE) 3 b.f. Diktat 126 – Launch Time (USA) (Relaunch (USA)) [2006 – –: f8g Feb 7] little form. *J. A. Osborne*

MISS LEMON (IRE) 3 b.f. Tagula (IRE) 116 – Sesame Heights (IRE) 63 (High Estate – 127) [2006 –: 7f 6g May 27] strong filly: little sign of ability. *J. Hetherton*

MISS LOPEZ (IRE) 3 br.f. Key of Luck (USA) 126 – Legit (IRE) (Runnett 125) [2006 67 61p: p7.1g⁵ p6g³ f6g* 6g p6g 6.9m 7.1m 6m³ 6g³ Sep 17] fair performer: won maiden at Southwell (wandered) in March: bred to be suited by 7f+: acts on all-weather and good to firm ground: has raced freely: sold 22,000 gns. *K. R. Burke*

MISS LUCIFER (FR) 2 b.f. (Mar 11) Noverre (USA) 125 – Devil's Imp (IRE) 84 86 p (Cadeaux Genereux 131) [2006 6s³ 6d* Oct 27] strong, compact filly: fourth foal: half-sister to 2 winners, including fairly useful 6f (at 2 yrs)/7f winner Desert Imp (by Green Desert): dam, 6f and (private sweepstakes at 2 yrs) 7f winner, half-sister to smart 1½m winners Amfortas and Legend Maker (latter dam of 1000 Guineas winner Virginia Waters): shaped well in maidens, close third to Party at Newbury (ran green in front) before winning readily at Newmarket by 2 lengths from Marozi, making all (flashed tail): likely to stay 7f: useful prospect. *B. W. Hills*

MISS MADAME (IRE) 5 b.m. Cape Cross (IRE) 129 – Cosmic Countess (IRE) 74 54 (Lahib (USA) 129) [2006 69: p8g p8g p10g 8m⁶ 7m⁵ 8m 6f 7f³ 7m Aug 22] modest a57 performer nowadays: best at 7f/1m: acts on all-weather and firm ground: sometimes races prominently. *T. G. Mills*

MISS MARLENE 3 ch.f. Shahrastani (USA) 135 – Harlequin Walk (IRE) 57 (Pennine – Walk 120) [2006 p10g p8g Jul 22] third foal: half-sister to 1½m winner Earlsfield Raider (by Double Trigger): dam, 1m to 1½m winner, also successful over hurdles: well beaten in maiden at Kempton and claimer at Lingfield. *B. G. Powell*

MISS MARVELLOUS (USA) 2 ch.f. (Apr 16) Diesis 133 – Sue Warner (USA) – p (Forli (ARG)) [2006 p7g Sep 5] $150,000Y: half-sister to several winners, including useful French 1m (at 2 yrs) and 8.5f winner Lady Ilsley (by Trempolino) and to dam of Breeders' Cup Juvenile winner Action This Day: dam unraced half-sister to very smart performer up to 7f Beaudelaire: 10/1, travelled well fair way when tenth in maiden at Lingfield: will benefit from experience. *J. R. Fanshawe*

MISS MCGUIRE 3 b.f. Averti (IRE) 117 – Friend For Life 64 (Lahib (USA) 129) [2006 8g² 8m* 7m⁶ᵈ 9m Aug 2] tall, quite attractive filly: third foal: sister to fairly useful 6f (at 2 yrs) to 8.5f winner Amica and 7f winner Averami: dam, fourth at 1m, out of useful half-sister to Shirley Heights: fair form: didn't need to repeat debut form to win maiden at Brighton in June: stays 1m: acts on good to firm ground: has raced freely. *G. L. Moore* **72**

MISS MEGGY 4 b.f. Pivotal 124 – Selkirk Rose (IRE) 74 (Pips Pride 117) [2006 86: p7.1g 7d* 7.2g³ 7.1m⁶ p7.1g Jul 20] leggy filly: fairly useful handicapper: better on all-weather than turf: reportedly covered by Dansili in May: won at Redcar later in month: best at 6f/7f: acts on polytrack, soft and good to firm going: tried visored, wears blinkers/cheekpieces nowadays. *Miss J. A. Camacho* **89 a74**

MISS MONICA (IRE) 5 ch.m. Grand Lodge (USA) 125 – Bea's Ruby (IRE) 86 (Fairy King (USA)) [2006 54: p8.6g f8g p10g p9.5g⁵ p9.5g⁴ 10g² 10d⁴ 10m 10f* 10f³ 10m² 10f 10f⁴ 10.1d⁴ 10m⁴ 10g 10.9m³ Sep 4] rather sparely-made mare: modest performer: won claimer at Brighton in June: stays 11f: acts on polytrack, firm and good to soft going. *P. W. Hiatt* **54**

MISS MUJAHID TIMES 3 b.f. Mujahid (USA) 125 – Stealthy Times 80 (Timeless Times (USA) 99) [2006 47: f5g 5.9g⁶ f6g³ f5g* 5g 5g* 6s 5d⁶ 5v Oct 31] modest performer: won handicaps at Southwell in July and Leicester in August: best efforts at 5f: acts on fibresand, best turf efforts on good going: blinkered after reappearance. *A. D. Brown* **59**

MISS ODD SOX 3 ch.f. Primo Valentino (IRE) 116 – Dam Certain (IRE) 61 (Damister (USA) 123) [2006 p6g p7g⁶ p9.5g⁴ p10g Apr 8] modest maiden: stays 9.5f: raced only on polytrack. *R. Ingram* **62**

MISS OTIS 2 b.f. (Apr 17) Danetime (IRE) 121 – Nesting 47 (Thatching 131) [2006 5d* 5g 5f⁴ Jul 2] 28,000Y: well-made filly: good walker: third foal: half-sister to 4-y-o Hoh Hoh Hoh: dam, ran 3 times, half-sister to dam of 2-y-o Wi Dud: fair form: won maiden at Windsor in May: ran creditably after in listed/minor events: speedy, raced at 5f: sold 19,000 gns in November. *P. Winkworth* **78**

MISSOULA (IRE) 3 b.f. Kalanisi (IRE) 132 – Medway (IRE) 60 (Shernazar 131) [2006 78p: 10m³ May 3] leggy, useful-looking filly: fair performer: shaped well when 3½ lengths third in handicap at Pontefract only start in 2006: will be suited by 1½m: acts on good to firm going. *M. H. Tompkins* **79**

MISSOURI (USA) 3 b.g. Gulch (USA) – Coco (USA) 105 (Storm Bird (CAN) 134) [2006 –: 5g 6d 10g⁵ 12d f12m⁴ p13.9g f11g f11g* Dec 29] rather leggy gelding: modest performer: improved form to win maiden claimer at Southwell in December, hanging left: stays 1½m: acts on fibresand. *G. M. Moore* **60**

MISS PATRICIA 4 b.f. Mister Baileys 123 – Zoena 67 (Emarati (USA) 74) [2006 85: p7g* Mar 22] leggy filly: fair performer: won maiden at Lingfield in March: effective at 7f/1m: acts on polytrack, firm and good to soft going: tried in cheekpieces/visor. *J. G. Portman* **75**

MISS PEBBLES (IRE) 6 ch.m. Lake Coniston (IRE) 131 – Sea of Stone (USA) 71 (Sanglamore (USA) 126) [2006 80: 10s Oct 16] sturdy mare: fairly useful handicapper at 5 yrs: well held only Flat start in 2006: often visored, and has run well in cheekpieces. *R. Dickin* **–**

MISS PERCY 2 b.f. (Mar 25) Mark of Esteem (IRE) 137 – Anabaa's Music (Anabaa (USA) 130) [2006 6g 6s³ 6m Sep 22] 13,500Y: second foal: dam unraced: modest form in maidens, third at Newcastle: will benefit from 1m: should progress. *R. A. Fahey* **64 p**

MISSPERON (IRE) 4 b.f. Orpen (USA) 116 – Secret Hideaway (USA) (Key To The Mint (USA)) [2006 77d: p5.1g p6g f6g* f7g f6s 6f 5m 6.9g³ 6d² 6d Aug 18] lengthy filly: fair handicapper: won at Southwell in February: stays 7f: acts on fibresand and any turf going: usually in cheekpieces/blinkered: hung right penultimate start. *K. A. Ryan* **66**

MISS PHUKET 2 b. or br.f. (Feb 17) Hernando (FR) 127 – Miss Amanpuri 92 (Alzao (USA) 117) [2006 6m 7.1m⁶ 7g⁵ Sep 30] leggy filly: third foal: half-sister to 2003 2-y-o 6f winner Miss Langkawi (by Daylami): dam 2-y-o 7f winner who stayed 1¼m: fair form in maidens: dead. *G. Wragg* **73**

MISS PORCIA 5 ch.m. Inchinor 119 – Krista 73 (Kris 135) [2006 50: p5.1g p6g⁶ p7.1g 6m² 7.1f⁶ 6f⁶ 6g⁶ p7g⁴ p9.5g⁶ p8.6g* p7.1g p8.6g Dec 27] tall, lengthy mare: modest performer: left S. Keightley 4,500 gns after third start: won banded race at Wolverhampton **61**

in November: stays 9.5f: acts on polytrack and any turf going: tried tongue tied/visored.
P. A. Blockley

MISS PROVENCE 3 b.f. Hernando (FR) 127 – Miss Beaulieu 106 (Northfields **88**
(USA)) [2006 8d 10s⁴ p9.5g* 12.5s⁶ Nov 22] good-bodied filly: sister to 7f (at 2 yrs)/
1¼m winner Miss Corniche and 1m winner Miss Riviera Golf, both useful, closely related to 2 winners by Niniski, including 1¼m/12.5f winner Riviera Magic, and half-sister to
several winners: dam 6f (at 2 yrs) and 1¼m winner: fairly useful and progressive form:
won maiden at Wolverhampton in November: good sixth in listed event at Saint-Cloud
final start: stays 1½m: acts on polytrack and soft ground. *G. Wragg*

MISS PROVVIDENCE (IRE) 4 b.f. Grand Lodge (USA) 125 – My Southern Love **98**
(ITY) (Southern Arrow (USA)) [2006 95: 10g* 10.4d⁵ 10m³ 10m 12d Aug 22] useful-
looking filly: useful handicapper: won at Windsor (badly impeded 3f out) in May: easily
best effort after when creditable third at Pontefract: stays 1½m: acts on polytrack and
good to firm going: sold 58,000 gns, sent to Bahrain. *W. R. Swinburn*

MISS PUFFLE 2 b.f. (Apr 28) Superior Premium 122 – Selkirk Rose (IRE) 74 (Pips **–**
Pride 117) [2006 6m⁴ 6.1m Sep 15] 5,000Y: workmanlike filly: second living foal: half-
sister to 4-y-o Miss Meggy: dam 5f (at 2 yrs)/6f winner: tailed off both starts. *S. Parr*

MISS REDACTIVE 3 b.f. Whittingham (IRE) 104 – Gold And Blue (IRE) (Bluebird **46**
(USA) 125) [2006 65: 7.1g⁶ 6f 6g 6m⁶ 7g 7m 6m 9g Sep 12] close-coupled filly:
poor maiden: stays 7f: raced on good going or firmer: slowly away fourth outing.
M. D. I. Usher

MISS RUBY 4 ch.f. Tagula (IRE) 116 – Ruby Heights 63 (Shirley Heights 130) [2006 **40**
6.1g 7m p8.6g 10.1g 6.1d⁴ Oct 13] strong, heavy-bodied filly: fifth foal: half-sister to
winner in Poland by Robellino: dam 1¼m winner: poor maiden. *Rae Guest*

MISS SAAFEND PLAZA (IRE) 2 b.f. (Apr 5) Danetime (IRE) 121 – Coup de **83**
Coeur (IRE) (Kahyasi 130) [2006 6d 7.1m² 7m⁶ 7m³ 7g⁴ 7m² 7m³ 7d p7.1g⁴ p7g² p8g²
p8g² Dec 16] lengthy, good-topped filly: first foal: dam unraced
half-sister to smart French middle-distance performers Premier Amour and Fleur d'Oranger: fairly useful maiden: made frame 9 times, many in nurseries: stays 1m: acts on
polytrack and good to firm going: blinkered final start. *R. Hannon*

MISS SALLY (IRE) 4 b.f. Danetime (IRE) 121 – Evictress (IRE) 70 (Sharp Victor **115**
(USA) 114) [2006 118: 6d* 6v³ 6m⁴ 6m⁶ 6s 6s⁴ Oct 8] good-bodied filly: smart performer: won listed race at Cork (by ½ length from Senor Benny) in May: creditable 3 lengths
third to Moss Vale in Greenlands Stakes at the Curragh next time: below form last 3 starts,
markedly so in Sprint Cup at Haydock penultimate one: stays 7.5f: acts on any turf going:
tongue tied third to fifth starts. *M. Halford, Ireland*

MISS SHONTAINE 4 b.f. Fumo di Londra (IRE) 108 – Stockline (Capricorn Line **–**
111) [2006 40: f7g Feb 12] poor maiden: well held only outing on Flat in 2006.
B. G. Powell

MISS SILVER SPURS 2 gr.f. (Apr 27) Mujahid (USA) 125 – Wakeful Night (FR) **–**
(Linamix (FR) 127) [2006 7.1m p7g 8.3m p8g Sep 18] close-coupled filly: fourth foal:
half-sister to a winner in Greece by Compton Place: dam second at 10.5f in France: well
beaten in maidens. *M. D. I. Usher*

MISS SUDBROOK (IRE) 4 ch.f. Daggers Drawn (USA) 114 – Missed Opportunity **–**
(IRE) (Exhibitioner 111) [2006 7.1m 6g 6d p9.5g⁶ p7.1g p7g p11g Dec 22] maiden:
missed 2005: no form in 2006: tried visored/tongue tied. *A. W. Carroll*

MISS SURE BOND (IRE) 3 ch.f. Danehill Dancer (IRE) 117 – Desert Rose (Green **67**
Desert (USA) 127) [2006 68: 6g 7g⁴ 6s⁵ 6d Oct 18] tall, lengthy filly: fair maiden: barely
stays 7f: acts on good to firm going: often blinkered. *B. Smart*

MISS TABOO (IRE) 2 b.f. (Feb 20) Tobougg (IRE) 125 – Miss Croisette 69 (Her- **–**
nando (FR) 127) [2006 7d 7.5m f8g Nov 10] smallish filly: first foal: dam maiden who
stayed 1½m: no form. *Miss V. Haigh*

MISS THAILAND 3 b.f. Grand Lodge (USA) 125 – Miss Amanpuri 92 (Alzao (USA) **68**
117) [2006 86p: 8.2m⁶ 7g⁴ 7m² 10d Oct 4] leggy, close-coupled filly: just fair maiden at
3 yrs: should stay 1¼m: acts on good to firm going: sold 3,000 gns. *G. Wragg*

MISS TRINIDAD (USA) 3 b.f. Kingmambo (USA) 125 – Miznah (IRE) 102 **81**
(Sadler's Wells (USA) 132) [2006 10d⁶ 12.1m³ 10m² 12g⁵ 10m² 10s Oct 10] good-topped
filly: has a fluent action: half-sister to several winners, notably high-class middle-
distance stayer Zindabad (by Shirley Heights) and useful 1¼m/11.6f winner Navado (by
Rainbow Quest): dam, Irish 2-y-o 6f winner, closely related to dam of US champion turf

mare Flawlessly: fairly useful maiden: placed 3 times: stayed 1½m: acts on good to firm ground: tended to wander fourth outing: sent to USA. *B. J. Meehan*

MISS WEDGE   3 b.f. Fraam 114 – Tough Nell (IRE) 61 (Archway (IRE) 115) [2006 69: 9.7s 8.5g⁴ 8.3g³ p8g⁵ p7g⁵ Jun 14] tall, angular filly: modest maiden nowadays: stays 8.5f: acts on polytrack and firm ground: visored final start: races prominently: signs of temperament. *T. G. Mills*   **64**

MISTER ALWAYS   2 b.g. (Mar 23) Titus Livius (FR) 115 – Pieta (IRE) 52 (Perugino (USA) 84) [2006 p6f 6m p6g⁵ Dec 16] poor maiden: left C. Dore before final start (hung, wore cheekpieces/tongue strap). *Ms J. S. Doyle*   **48**

MISTER ARJAY (USA)   6 b.g. Mister Baileys 123 – Crystal Stepper (USA) (Fred Astaire (USA)) [2006 72: 12.4d 12m 17.1m³ 16f³ 16.1m* 16.2f² 17.2f³ 18f⁴ 16.1m² 17.1d* 15.8d² 17.1d³ 18s⁵ 16d Nov 3] smallish, good-bodied gelding: fair handicapper: won at Newcastle in June and Pontefract (by 6 lengths) in August: stays 2¼m: acts on firm and soft going: tried blinkered: has hung right: much more consistent nowadays. *B. Ellison*   **73**

MISTER AZIZ (IRE)   4 b.g. Mister Baileys 123 – Aziz Presenting (IRE) 86 (Charnwood Forest (IRE) 125) [2006 51: p7g p7g³ f6g⁵ f7g³ f7g⁴ f6g³ p6g⁴ p6g Apr 5] smallish, close-coupled gelding: modest maiden: stays 7f: acts on all-weather, good to firm and good to soft ground: wears headgear nowadays. *J. R. Jenkins*   **51**

MISTER BECKS (IRE)   3 b.g. Beckett (IRE) 116 – Cappuchino (IRE) 59 (Roi Danzig (USA)) [2006 –: f8g⁶ 7v⁶ f5g³ 5g 6g f6g* f6g⁴ 5f f6g 6.1f 8d Oct 2] strong gelding: poor performer: won banded race at Southwell in May: stays 6f: acts on fibresand: tried blinkered. *M. C. Chapman*   **49**

MISTER BELL   4 gr.g. Lujain (USA) 119 – Zaragossa 80 (Paris House 123) [2006 f6g p5.1g Mar 29] maiden: missed 2005: well held both outings in 2006: wore cheekpieces final start. *J. G. M. O'Shea*   **–**

MISTER BENEDICTINE   3 b.g. Mister Baileys 123 – Cultural Role 95 (Night Shift (USA)) [2006 84: 8m 9.9f⁵ 7g² 7f⁶ 7.1m⁶ 7m³ 6g⁶ p7g⁵ 7m Sep 16] sturdy, quite attractive gelding: fairly useful handicapper: should stay 1m: acts on polytrack and firm going: sometimes races freely: joined B. Duke 15,000 gns, won juvenile hurdle in November. *W. R. Muir*   **82**

MISTER BENJI   7 b.g. Catrail (USA) 123 – Katy-Q (IRE) 58 (Taufan (USA) 119) [2006 –, a64: f8g⁵ f8g² f7g³ p8.6g³ p8.6g* p8.6g⁶ f7g p8.6g⁴ p8.6g p8.6g f7g³ 8.3f p8.6g p8.6g⁴ Dec 23] quite good-topped gelding: fair handicapper: won at Wolverhampton in February: stays 8.6f: acts on all-weather, little recent form on turf: has worn headgear. *B. P. J. Baugh*   **– a71**

MISTERBIANCO (IRE)   3 b.g. Danehill Dancer (IRE) 117 – Price of Passion 83 (Dolphin Street (FR) 125) [2006 56p: 7g p8g 8g 7.1g Jul 5] good-topped gelding: maiden: well held in 2006: blinkered final start: usually slowly away. *B. J. Meehan*   **–**

MISTER COMPLETELY (IRE)   5 b.g. Princely Heir (IRE) 111 – Blue Goose (Belmez (USA) 131) [2006 56: p16.5g⁴ f11g³ p16g* p16.5g* p16.5g³ p16g⁵ 14.1m* 11.9g p16.5g p12g⁶ 11s p12g p13.9g p12g⁶ p16g* Dec 18] sturdy gelding: fair performer: won seller at Lingfield (left J. Best) and banded race at Wolverhampton, both in January, handicap at Nottingham in May, and (having left Miss S. West after ninth start) banded race at Kempton in December: stays 16.5f: acts on all-weather and firm going. *Ms J. S. Doyle*   **65**

MISTER CRICKET (IRE)   2 b.c. (May 9) Tendulkar (USA) 114 – Fire Reply (IRE) (Royal Academy (USA) 130) [2006 5g 6v 7f⁴ 7f Jun 24] leggy colt: of no account. *M. E. Sowersby*   **–**

MISTER ELEGANT   4 b.c. Fraam 114 – Risky Valentine 68 (Risk Me (FR) 127) [2006 60: p7.1g³ f7g* p7.1g³ f7s³ p8g 7m 7.1m p7.1g* p7g* 7g² 7.1m p7.1m⁵ f7g p7.1s⁴ p7.1g Dec 22] fair handicapper: won at Southwell in January, Wolverhampton (seller) in June and Kempton (apprentices) in July: best up to 1m: acts on all-weather, good to firm and good to soft going: tried blinkered: none too consistent. *J. L. Spearing*   **66**

MISTER FIZZBOMB (IRE)   3 b.g. Lend A Hand 124 – Crocus (IRE) 70 (Mister Baileys 123) [2006 –: 9.8m 9.9g² 11g² 12.1f* 12f⁴ Jul 3] smallish, sturdy gelding: modest performer: won handicap at Beverley in June: stays 1½m: acts on firm going: blinkered/visored last 4 starts: withdrawn after giving trouble at start prior to intended final Flat outing. *J. S. Wainwright*   **63**

679

MISTER INCREDIBLE 3 b.c. Wizard King 122 – Judiam 74 (Primo Dominic 121)   **–**
[2006 67: f6g* f5g³ p6g p6g f6g⁴ f5g² p5.1g³ 5s 5.3g p6m p6g p7.1g⁶ Dec 28] lengthy, **a68**
unfurnished colt: fair handicapper on all-weather: won at Southwell in January: left
C. Dwyer after seventh start: probably stays 7f: acts on all-weather (and on heavy and
good to firm ground when last showed form on turf at 2 yrs): usually wears headgear.
V. Smith

MISTER JINGLES 3 ch.g. Desert Story (IRE) 115 – Fairy Free (Rousillon (USA)   **50**
133) [2006 8d 6g p6g⁵ 5.9m 6g f6m² f6g⁶ Nov 15] lengthy, workmanlike gelding: modest
maiden: stays 6f: acts on all-weather. *R. M. Whitaker*

MISTER JUNGLE (FR) 4 b.g. Saint Cyrien (FR) 128 – Fabuleuse Histoire (FR)   **–**
(Fabulous Dancer (USA) 124) [2006 12s Aug 18] fair form in bumpers: well beaten in
maiden at Catterick: successful over hurdles in October. *Mrs S. C. Bradburne*

MISTER LUCKY (FR) 2 b.c. (Feb 20) Key of Luck (USA) 126 – Ma Paloma (FR)   **67**
(Highest Honor (FR) 124) [2006 6m 6g⁴ 7m⁴ 7m Sep 16] €60,000F, 100,000Y: third foal:
half-brother to smart 9f (at 2 yrs) to 10.5f (Prix Noailles) winner Ruwi (by Unfuwain) and
12.5f winner Bloke (by Vettori), both in France: dam French 8.5f/10.5f winner: fair
maiden: well beaten in nursery: will stay 1m/1¼m: tried in visor: sold 2,000 gns, sent to
Spain. *Sir Michael Stoute*

MISTER MAQ 3 b.g. Namaqualand (USA) – Nordico Princess 71 (Nordico (USA))   **65**
[2006 61?: 8g⁵ 10d⁴ 8.5g 7.9m⁴ 10m⁵ 8f* 9.3m² 8.1g⁴ 10d p8.6g p12.2g f11g⁶ f11g **a53**
Dec 9] leggy gelding: fair performer on turf, modest on all-weather: won selling handicap
at Thirsk in July: left M. Dods after ninth start: stays 1¼m: acts on firm and good to soft
going: wears cheekpieces/blinkers. *A. Crook*

MISTER MARMADUKE 5 b.g. Marju (IRE) 127 – Lalique (IRE) (Lahib (USA)   **41 §**
129) [2006 67§, a80d: 5d 6d 5g 5m 5f 6f 5m Jul 10] poor performer nowadays: tried
tongue tied, often wears cheekpieces: temperamental. *D. A. Nolan*

MISTER MINTY (IRE) 4 b.g. Fasliyev (USA) 120 – Sorb Apple (IRE) 79 (Kris 135)   **–**
[2006 –: 8d May 13] very big, plain gelding: no form. *J. O'Reilly*

MISTER PETE (IRE) 3 b.g. Piccolo 121 – Whistfilly 49 (First Trump 118) [2006 8d   **–**
Apr 20] compact gelding: 50/1 and backward, well held in maiden at Ripon: sold 700 gns
in August. *D. W. Barker*

MISTER REGENT 5 b.g. Mind Games 121 – River of Fortune (IRE) 68 (Lahib (USA)   **–**
129) [2006 –: p6g f7g⁵ Mar 28] tall, angular gelding: maiden: little form since 2004: has
worn blinkers/cheekpieces. *W. M. Brisbourne*

MISTER RIGHT (IRE) 5 ch.g. Barathea (IRE) 127 – Broken Spirit (IRE) (Slip Anc-   **84**
hor 136) [2006 80: p12g⁶ 14g 11g³ p12g⁴ 13.3m* 20m⁶ 14m³ 14m³ 11.7m Aug 20]
lengthy, plain gelding: fairly useful handicapper: won at Newbury in June: stays at least
1¾m (seemingly not 2½m): acts on polytrack and firm going: consistent. *D. J. S. ffrench
Davis*

MIST OPPORTUNITY (IRE) 4 b.g. Danetime (IRE) 121 – Lady of The Mist (IRE)   **–**
46 (Digamist (USA) 110) [2006 f14g Jan 31] tall gelding: little sign of ability: tongue
tied/visored only Flat start in 2006. *P. C. Haslam*

MISTRAL SKY 7 b.g. Hurricane Sky (AUS) – Dusk In Daytona 64 (Beveled (USA))   **73**
[2006 77, a85: p7.1g p7.1g p7.1g⁴ p7.1g⁴ p7.1g⁵ p7.1g³ p7g⁶ 7m³ p6g⁴ 7.1m p7.1g² 7.1f
7f⁴ p7.1f p7.1g⁵ p6g* Dec 30] angular gelding: fair performer: won claimer at Lingfield
in December: best at 6f/7f: acts on polytrack (well beaten both outings on fibresand), firm
and good to soft going: wears headgear: tends to wander. *Stef Liddiard*

MISTRESS TWISTER 5 b.m. Pivotal 124 – Foreign Mistress (Darshaan 133) [2006   **83**
80: 8.3m* 8.9m 10m* 8.3m* 10.4f² 9.2m⁶ 10g⁵ 10m Sep 16] leggy, unfurnished mare:
fairly useful handicapper: won at Hamilton in May, Pontefract in June and Hamilton in
July: stays 1¼m: acts on firm and soft going: held up. *T. D. Barron*

MISTY PRINCESS 4 gr.f. Paris House 123 – Miss Whittingham (IRE) 68 (Fayruz   **48**
116) [2006 38, a52: f5g³ f5g⁴ p6g p6g² f6g* f6g⁴ p6g* p6g 5f⁵ 6m Jul 26] tall, leggy **a58**
filly: modest performer on all-weather, poor on turf: won banded races at Southwell and
Wolverhampton in April: stays 6f: acts on all-weather, firm and soft going: tried visored/
blinkered: edgy sort: sometimes carries head high, hung right final outing. *M. J. Attwater*

MISU BOND (IRE) 3 b.c. Danehill Dancer (IRE) 117 – Hawala (IRE) 97 (Warning   **114**
136) [2006 108: 7g³* 8m⁵ 7m³ Jun 14] strong, good-topped colt: smart performer: won
listed banshaehousestables.com European Free Handicap at Newmarket (by neck from
Jeremy) in April: good 5¼ lengths fifth to George Washington in 2000 Guineas at New-

Mr R. C. Bond's "Misu Bond"

market next time: disappointing third of 4 to An Tadh in Ballycorus Stakes at Leopardstown only other outing in 2006: suffered pulled muscle in his back and a tendon injury after: stays 1m, likely to prove at least as effective at shorter: acts on soft and good to firm going. *B. Smart*

MISWADAH (IRE) 3 b.f. Machiavellian (USA) 123 – Khulan (USA) 103 (Bahri (USA) 125) [2006 7m 7g⁶ p9.5g f7g p6g⁵ Dec 15] medium-sized filly: first foal: dam, 2-y-o 6f winner, out of close relative to high-class sprinter Elnadim and half-sister to Irish 1000 Guineas winner Mehthaaf: modest maiden: left E. Dunlop 26,000 gns after second start: best effort in handicap final one (visored): stays 7f: acts on polytrack and good to firm ground. *Kevin Francis O'Donnell, Ireland* **62**

MITANNI (USA) 3 b.g. Lear Fan (USA) 130 – Maria Dolores (USA) (Prized (USA)) [2006 73p: 8.2m⁵ 8.3g³ p7g⁴ Oct 23] workmanlike gelding: fair maiden: stays 8.3f: acts on polytrack and firm ground. *Mrs A. J. Perrett* **71**

MITCHELLAND 4 b.f. Namaqualand (USA) – Precious Girl 76 (Precious Metal 106) [2006 63: p8.6g Feb 3] leggy, close-coupled filly: modest performer: last only start in 2006: tried visored. *E. J. Alston* **–**

MIXING 4 gr.g. Linamix (FR) 127 – Tuning 114 (Rainbow Quest (USA) 134) [2006 71: 10d⁶ 11g 10.5s⁴ p10g 11g⁴ 10.1g⁵ 9g 10.9d⁶ 8.2d Nov 1] close-coupled gelding: fair performer: on downgrade: likely to prove best at 1¼m/1½m: acts on soft ground: reluctant to race fourth start. *W. Jarvis* **67 d**

MIZZLE (USA) 2 ch.f. (Apr 8) Rahy (USA) 115 – Loving Claim (USA) 110 (Hansel (USA)) [2006 7f³ p7g⁶ Jul 19] fifth foal: half-sister to 1¼m winner First Celebration (by Cadeaux Genereux): dam, French 2-y-o 1m winner (including Prix Marcel Boussac) who stayed 1¼m, half-sister to July Stakes winner City On A Hill: fair form in maidens at Yarmouth and Kempton in July: has left Godolphin. *Saeed bin Suroor* **69**

MIZZ TEE (IRE) 4 b.f. Orpen (USA) 116 – D D's Jakette (USA) (Deputy Minister **82**
(CAN)) [2006 95: p10g⁶ p9.5g Jan 27] strong, lengthy filly: fluent mover: fairly useful
handicapper: much better effort in 2006 on reappearance: stays easy 1¼m: acts on polytrack, soft and good to firm going: mounted on course and reluctant to post on 3-y-o
reappearance: sold 22,000 gns in July. *T. D. Easterby*

MKUZI 7 ch.g. Halling (USA) 133 – African Peace (USA) (Roberto (USA) 131) [2006 **115**
111: 14g³ 14g³ 14g² 14m Aug 26] strong, close-coupled gelding: has a round action:
smart performer: better than ever when around 1½ lengths third to Media Puzzle in listed
race at Leopardstown and to Kastoria in Curragh Cup first 2 starts: creditable 3 lengths
second to Foreign Affairs in listed race at Leopardstown, but well held in similar event at
the Curragh final outing: stays 1¾m: acts on firm and good to soft going, possibly not on
soft: blinkered once at 4 yrs. *J. Oxx, Ireland*

MOAYED 7 b.g. Selkirk (USA) 129 – Song of Years (IRE) 89 (Shareef Dancer (USA) **86**
135) [2006 102, a107: f8g³ p6g* p7g⁶ p5g⁵ f6g p7g² p8.6g p7g⁶ p8g⁴ p7g⁶ 6m 7m 6d **a105**
7.1m 7m Jun 22] workmanlike gelding: useful on all-weather, fairly useful on turf: won
minor event at Lingfield (by 1½ lengths from Secret Night) in January: also ran well in
handicaps on same course fourth/sixth starts and in listed event there on ninth: little
impact in handicaps back on turf last 5 starts: winner at 9f, best form at shorter nowadays
(effective at 6f): acts on all-weather and any turf going: wears blinkers, often tongue tied:
best held up, and tends to miss break. *N. P. Littmoden*

MOBAASHER (USA) 3 ch.c. Rahy (USA) 115 – Balistroika (USA) (Nijinsky (CAN) **91**
138) [2006 10g³ 10.3f² 11f³ 12.3m² 11.7m³ 10d* 11.8d⁵ Oct 3] $825,000Y: big, good-
bodied colt: brother to smart 7f (at 2 yrs) to 1½m winner Perfectperformance, closely
related to winner in USA by Mt Livermore, and half-brother to several winners, including
very smart 6f (at 2 yrs) to 1¼m winner (including 1000 Guineas) Russian Rhythm (by
Kingmambo): dam unraced half-sister to Cheveley Park winners Park Appeal and Desirable and Irish Oaks winner Alydaress: fairly useful performer: won maiden at Pontefract
in September, tending to hang: best efforts in handicaps on fourth (runner-up at Chester)
and final outings: stays 1½m: acts on firm and good to soft ground: tried visored: signs of
waywardness: sold 55,000 gns, joined C. Mann. *Sir Michael Stoute*

MOBANE FLYER 6 b.g. Groom Dancer (USA) 128 – Enchant 92 (Lion Cavern **57**
(USA) 117) [2006 73: 10.1d* 9g p12.2g 8.5m 10m 12s Oct 14] modest performer nowadays: won claimer at Newcastle in May: stays 10.3f: acts on any turf going. *R. A. Fahey*

MOBSIR 3 b.c. Mozart (IRE) 131 – Pretty Sharp 64 (Interrex (CAN)) [2006 80: 7m* **92**
7s⁶ 7m² p8g⁴ Sep 30] smallish, well-made colt: fairly useful performer: won maiden at
Lingfield in May: good fourth in handicap at Kempton final start: barely stays easy 1m,
likely to prove best at shorter: acts on polytrack and good to firm going: sent to UAE.
E. A. L. Dunlop

MOCAIRDE (USA) 3 ch.f. Royal Academy (USA) 130 – White Wisteria (Ahonoora –
122) [2006 53p: 7f 8m⁵ Jul 21] 180,000Y: half-sister to 3 winners, including useful 1997
2-y-o 5f/6f winner Bodyguard (by Zafonic) and useful Italian performer up to 7.5f White
Gulch (by Gulch): dam unraced half-sister to dam of Irish 2000 Guineas winner Bachelor
Duke: modest form in maiden at Gowran only 2-y-o outing, leaving D. Weld after: well
held in similar events in Britain. *J. R. Best*

MOCHA JAVA 3 b.c. Bertolini (USA) 125 – Coffee Cream 87 (Common Grounds 118) **76**
[2006 68: 8.2s⁴ 7.1d⁵ 7g⁴ 8.3d⁶ 7.1g* 7f² 7d* 7.1m 6.1d p8.6g p7g Dec 8] good-topped **a–**
colt: fair performer: won seller at Chepstow in July and, having left P. Cole after next
start, handicap at Yarmouth in August: stays 8.3f: acts on firm and soft going (and on
polytrack at 2 yrs). *Mrs L. J. Mongan*

MO CHROI 3 ch.f. Observatory (USA) 131 – Away To Me (Exit To Nowhere (USA) –
122) [2006 –: p8.6g Jan 16] compact, close-coupled filly: no form. *C. G. Cox*

MODAFFAA 6 b.g. Darshaan 133 – Irish Valley (USA) (Irish River (FR) 131) [2006 –: **88**
p12.2g³ p16.5g⁴ p12g⁵ 11.7d³ 13.9s³ p12g⁴ 12m⁴ Jun 18] leggy gelding: fairly useful
handicapper: creditable efforts most starts in 2006: stays 1¾m: acts on polytrack, soft and
good to firm ground: slowly away penultimate outing. *P. R. Webber*

MODDLIJ (IRE) 2 b.g. (Mar 8) Cape Cross (IRE) 129 – Moet (IRE) 72 (Mac's Imp –
(USA) 116) [2006 6g Jul 6] behind in maiden at Newbury: sold 2,500 gns and gelded.
M. R. Channon

MODEEROCH (IRE) 3 gr.f. Mozart (IRE) 131 – Majinskaya (FR) 110 (Marignan **112**
(USA) 117) [2006 102: 8d² 6m⁵ 7m³ 8m³ 6g 7.5g* 8g⁴ 7.5v⁵ 7d* Nov 5] strong filly:
smart performer: won listed races at Tipperary (by short head from Cheyenne Star) in

August and Leopardstown (best effort, by 2½ lengths from Ugo Fire) in November: needs further than 6f and stays 1m: acts on good to firm and good to soft ground: blinkered second start, tongue tied last 2 outings. *J. S. Bolger, Ireland*

MOFARIJ 2 ch.c. (Feb 17) Bering 136 – Pastorale 91 (Nureyev (USA) 131) [2006 7d² Oct 28] well-made colt: half-brother to several winners, including 5-y-o Iffraaj and useful 1998 2-y-o 7f winner Kareymah (both by Zafonic) and useful 1m winner Jathaabeh (by Nashwan): dam, 7f winner from 3 starts, half-sister to Cape Cross and closely related to dam of Diktat: 7/2, promising 1¾ lengths second of 19 to Spanish Moon in maiden at Newmarket, not well drawn (took time to tuck in) but travelling impressively long way: will improve and win races. *Saeed bin Suroor* **92 p**

MOFFIED (IRE) 6 b.g. Nashwan (USA) 135 – Del Deya (IRE) 117 (Caerleon (USA) 132) [2006 f11g Feb 5] well held in bumpers/over jumps, and in maiden claimer at Southwell. *J. Barclay* **–**

MOGOK RUBY 2 gr.c. (Apr 15) Bertolini (USA) 125 – Days of Grace 79 (Wolfhound (USA) 126) [2006 p5g³ 5g 5m⁶ 5m³ p6g³ p5g³ 5.5m 5g* p6g⁵ Sep 27] first foal: dam 5f (including at 2 yrs)/6f winner: fair performer: won nursery at Sandown in September: probably best at 5f: acts on polytrack and good to firm going. *L. Montague Hall* **72**

MOHAWK STAR (IRE) 5 ch.g. Indian Ridge 123 – Searching Star 63 (Rainbow Quest (USA) 134) [2006 –: 8.3f p8g⁴ p8g⁴ 8d⁴ 7m 8d f8g⁵ Dec 9] fair handicapper: best form around 1m: acts on polytrack and heavy going, below form on firmer than good: sometimes blinkered: has shown signs of waywardness. *I. A. Wood* **78**

MOHEEBB (IRE) 2 b.g. (Apr 1) Machiavellian (USA) 123 – Rockerlong 112 (Deploy 131) [2006 7m Jul 21] heavy-bodied gelding: 9/1, behind in maiden at Newbury: sold 11,000 gns, gelded, joined D. Chapman. *M. P. Tregoning* **–**

MOHTARRES (USA) 3 b.c. Kingmambo (USA) 125 – Adored Slew (USA) (Seattle Slew (USA)) [2006 56p: 10d 9.9g⁴ 12d Jul 31] good-topped, attractive colt: fair maiden: sold from M. Jarvis 38,000 gns after second start: stays 1½m: raced only on good/good to soft going. *A. J. Martin, Ireland* **75**

MOI AUSSI (USA) 3 ch.f. Mt Livermore (USA) – Acquiesce (Generous (IRE) 139) [2006 87: p8g³ p8.6g² 10.8s p10g⁵ p8g⁵ p8g 8.1s⁴ 8d⁵ f8g Nov 10] fairly useful performer: below form in handicaps last 2 starts: stays 8.6f: acts on all-weather and heavy going: usually blinkered, visored final outing: no easy ride. *Sir Mark Prescott* **88**

MOIST 2 b.f. (Feb 1) Mark of Esteem (IRE) 137 – Native Ring (FR) (Bering 136) [2006 6d 6f 7m⁶ p7.1g³ 7.5f⁴ 7f 7.1m Aug 24] small filly: third foal: dam French 10.5f winner: poor maiden: raced mainly in sellers: left N. Callaghan after sixth start: will stay 1m. *Jedd O'Keeffe* **45**

MOLEM 4 b.g. Green Desert (USA) 127 – Injaad (Machiavellian (USA) 123) [2006 76: p8g* 8m² p8g² p10g 8.5g⁴ 10m⁶ 8.1m⁵ p8g* p8g⁶ Oct 23] neat gelding: fair handicapper: won at Lingfield in April and October: best efforts at 1m, barely stays 1¼m: acts on polytrack, unraced on firm going, acts on any other turf: tongue tied: in cheekpieces/visored nowadays: sold 13,000 gns. *Lady Herries* **78**

MOLLYANKO 2 gr.f. (Apr 24) Komaite (USA) – Molly Malone 60 (Formidable (USA) 125) [2006 6g⁴ 6.1s* 6g p7.1g⁶ 8.2s p7.1g Oct 30] close-coupled filly: first foal: dam, maiden who stayed 1m, half-sister to sprinter 7f/1m performer A Touch of Frost: modest performer: kept to sellers, winning at Chepstow in May: stays 1m: tried blinkered: ungenuine. *W. G. M. Turner* **50 §**

MOLLY PITCHER (IRE) 2 ch.f. (Feb 27) Halling (USA) 133 – American Queen (FR) (Fairy King (USA)) [2006 7m p8.6g p8.6m Nov 21] €110,000Y: lengthy filly: fourth foal: dam, French maiden, closely related to very smart French middle-distance performer Antheus: modest form in maidens, absent 4 months after debut. *M. A. Jarvis* **59**

MOLLYPUTTHEKETELON (USA) 5 b.m. Rainbow Quest (USA) 134 – Nemea (USA) 97 (The Minstrel (CAN) 135) [2006 78, a73: p12.2g p12g 8g 6m 6m⁴ 7m⁵ 7.5m⁵ 9.5d² Aug 16] well-made mare: fair maiden handicapper: left M. Wallace after second start: best at 7.5f to 1¼m: acts on polytrack, firm and good to soft going: has worn headgear, including last 7 starts. *T. Hogan, Ireland* **67 a–**

MOLLY'S SECRET 8 b.m. Minshaanshu Amad (USA) 91§ – Secret Miss 55 (Beveled (USA)) [2006 55: f12g⁵ p12.2g⁶ 11v³ p12.2g⁴ f12g p12.2g³ f12g⁶ f12g p12.2g² p12.2f⁴ Aug 14] workmanlike mare: modest performer: stays 1¾m: acts on all-weather and good to firm going: tried blinkered, wears cheekpieces: takes good hold: sometimes carries head awkwardly. *Miss S. J. Wilton* **51**

MOLOTOV 6 b.g. Efisio 120 – Mindomica 63 (Dominion 123) [2006 63: 5d⁶ p5g **46** Oct 29] just poor form in 2006: tried blinkered/in cheekpieces: has refused to go to post: races up with pace. *M. Dods*

MOLTO DURO (IRE) 2 b.f. (Apr 22) Tagula (IRE) 116 – Dieci Anno (IRE) 72 (Clas- **41** sic Music (USA)) [2006 5g 6g 5d 6s 5.1d⁶ f5g⁴ f6g⁶ f5g⁵ Dec 27] strong filly: sixth foal: half-sister to fairly useful 2001 2-y-o 5f winner Anima Mundi (by Namaqualand), later successful in USA: dam Irish 5f winner: poor maiden: blinkered last 5 starts. *N. Wilson*

MOMTIC (IRE) 5 ch.h. Shinko Forest (IRE) – Uffizi (IRE) (Royal Academy (USA) **114** 130) [2006 114: 8.1m 8.3m² 8.5m⁴ 10m 8.1m³ 8f* 8m⁵ 8g⁴ 8f⁶ p8.6g Oct 8] well-made horse: smart performer: won minor event at York (by length from Kings Point) in July: also ran well in Diomed Stakes at Epsom (fourth to Nayyir) and handicap at Sandown (1¾ lengths third to Hinterland) third/fifth starts: well below form in minor event at Wolverhampton (all-weather debut) final outing: best at 1m/9f: acts on firm and good to soft going: sometimes races freely: reliable: sold 210,000 gns, joined S. Seemar in UAE. *W. Jarvis*

MONACHELLO (USA) 2 b.g. (Feb 6) Lemon Drop Kid (USA) 131 – Antoniette **80** (USA) (Nicholas (USA) 111) [2006 7.1m* 7g⁶ p8g Oct 20] $50,000Y: rangy gelding: third foal: brother to French 6f to 1m winner Jano and half-brother to winner in USA by Gulch: dam, 6f to 8.5f (Grade 3 event) winner in USA, out of half-sister to high-class performer up to 1m Mukaddamah: fairly useful form: won maiden at Warwick (hung left/ jumped path) in June: sixth in well-contested minor event won by Thousand Words at Newbury, but well held in nursery (after 3-month break) final start: gelded after: should stay 1m. *Mrs A. J. Perrett*

MONACO PRINCE (IRE) 3 ch.g. King Charlemagne (USA) 120 – Maytpleasethe- **66** court (IRE) 86 (Persian Heights 129) [2006 6m⁶ Jul 1] 12/1, good speed when sixth to Falmassim in maiden at Windsor (injured a knee). *G. A. Huffer*

MONASHEE BRAVE (IRE) 3 b.g. Monashee Mountain (USA) 115 – Miss Butter- **80** field (Cure The Blues (USA)) [2006 61p: 5g³ 5m³ 5d* 5.1f⁵ Sep 23] tall, attractive geld- ing: fairly useful performer: justified favouritism in maiden at Beverley (by 7 lengths) in August: raced only at 5f: acts on firm and good to soft going: carried head high on reappearance. *J. J. Quinn*

MONASHEE EXPRESS (IRE) 4 ch.g. Monashee Mountain (USA) 115 – Curie **–** Express (IRE) 65 (Fayruz 116) [2006 56: p8.6g 8.1m Aug 10] modest maiden at 3 yrs, well held in 2006. *G. H. Yardley*

MONASHEE GREY (IRE) 3 b.g. Monashee Mountain (USA) 115 – Ex-Imager **40** (Exhibitioner 111) [2006 –: 12g 16.2m⁴ 16g Aug 4] stocky gelding: poor maiden: will stay beyond 2m: raced only on good/good to firm going: joined P. Bowen. *R. A. Fahey*

MONASHEE PRINCE (IRE) 4 ch.g. Monashee Mountain (USA) 115 – Lodema **72** (IRE) (Lycius (USA) 124) [2006 79, a72: p10g² p8g p8g³ p7g³ p8g p6g³ 6g² 6g 6m³ 5m p6g p7g³ p10g⁵ Dec 19] tall, leggy gelding: fair handicapper: effective at 6f, seemingly at easy 1¼m: acts on polytrack, good to firm and good to soft going: visored (ran creditably) once: races prominently: consistent. *J. R. Best*

MONASHEE RIVER (IRE) 3 b.f. Monashee Mountain (USA) 115 – Dixie Jazz 51 **58** (Mtoto 134) [2006 8.2v⁶ p7.1m³ p8.6g³ p12g p9.5g p9.5g Dec 21] €5,000Y: tall filly: third foal: half-sister to useful 6f (at 2 yrs) and 10.5f winner Jazz Scene (by Danehill Dancer): dam maiden who should have stayed 1¼m: modest maiden: stays 8.6f: acts on polytrack. *Miss V. Haigh*

MONASH LAD (IRE) 4 ch.g. General Monash (USA) 107 – Story Time (IRE) (Man- **71** sooj 118) [2006 76: p8.6g p10g 8.2s 10d 10m⁴ 9m 9.7f⁶ 9.3m³ 12.4m⁶ 11.9f* 11.6m* 11.8d Aug 13] rather leggy gelding: fair performer: won apprentice handicap at Brighton and seller at Windsor (sold from M. Tompkins 11,500 gns) in July: stays 1½m: yet to race on heavy ground, acts on any other turf: blinkered fifth/sixth starts. *Mrs K. Waldron*

MONDA 4 b.f. Danzig Connection (USA) – Fairey Firefly 64 (Hallgate 127) [2006 57: **48** 6g⁵ Jun 24] workmanlike filly: modest performer at best: stays 7f: acts on polytrack: refused to enter stall once. *Miss J. A. Camacho*

MONET'S LADY (IRE) 2 gr.f. (Apr 11) Daylami (IRE) 138 – Wide Range (IRE) **–** (Spectrum (IRE) 126) [2006 6m⁶ 6m Aug 9] €32,000F, €60,000Y: angular filly: second foal: dam, second at 1m in France, half-sister to St Leger second Air Marshall: no impact in maidens: will be suited by 1m/1¼m. *R. A. Fahey*

MONETS MASTERPIECE (USA) 3 b.c. Quiet American (USA) – Math (USA) **78 §**
(Devil's Bag (USA)) [2006 78: p12g³ 11.9m³ 10m⁴ 11m p12g² p13g² Dec 22] lengthy,
good-topped colt: fair maiden: left Mrs A. Perrett after third start: stays 13f: raced only
on polytrack and good/good to firm going: tried blinkered/tongue tied: ungenuine.
G. L. Moore

MONEYFORCREDIT (IRE) 6 b.g. Charente River (IRE) 67 – Bridesglen (Paddy's **–**
Stream 80) [2006 p12.2g Dec 2] modest form in bumpers in 2005: 66/1, well held in
maiden at Wolverhampton. *Jarlath P. Fahey, Ireland*

MONEY FOR FUN 2 b.f. (Mar 17) Whittingham (IRE) 104 – Urban Dancer (IRE) 89 **62**
(Generous (IRE) 139) [2006 6g⁶ p6g⁴ 5.1g³ p5.1g³ f5g⁴ p5.1g⁵ p6g Dec 11] 2,000Y,
€11,000 2-y-o: fourth foal: half-sister to German 7.5f winner Perfect Dancer (by Pyramus): dam Irish 1m winner: modest maiden: blinkered, broke leg at Wolverhampton in
December: stayed 6f: acted on polytrack: dead. *J. S. Moore*

MONEY HILLS 4 b.g. Vettori (IRE) 119 – Starfida (Soviet Star (USA) 128) [2006 44: **–**
f11g Apr 4] maiden: well held only outing in 2006. *Mrs C. A. Dunnett*

MONEY MATE (IRE) 3 ch.g. Titus Livius (FR) 115 – Xania 32 (Mujtahid (USA) **63**
118) [2006 77d: f6g⁵ f6g² f6g f5g⁴ p6g 5d⁶ 8d 5f* f5g⁵ 5f 5f³ 5.9g⁵ 5g Aug 23] modest
handicapper: left C. Teague, won at Redcar in June: stayed 6f: acted on fibresand and any
turf going: tried in cheekpieces: dead. *J. O'Reilly*

MONKEY GLAS (IRE) 2 b.c. (Mar 12) Mull of Kintyre (USA) 114 – Maura's Pet **78**
(IRE) 58 (Prince of Birds (USA) 121) [2006 p5g³ 6g⁵ 6f* 6f³ 7m* 7m p7.1g³ Oct 8]
€9,000F, €26,000Y: strong, lengthy colt: third foal: brother to 2005 2-y-o 7f seller winner
Cumbrae: dam, Irish maiden, stayed 9f: fair performer: won maiden at Redcar in June and
nursery at Newcastle (looked to idle) in August: good third to Ghost Dancer in nursery at
Wolverhampton final start (hung left): free-going type, but likely to stay 1m: acts on polytrack and firm ground. *K. R. Burke*

MONKEY MADGE 4 br.f. Cape Cross (IRE) 129 – Runelia (Runnett 125) [2006 61: **61 d**
f7g⁴ f7g² f7g f8g f7g⁴ f8g f7g⁴ f7g Dec 28] leggy filly: modest maiden: well below form
after second outing: stays 7f: acts on all-weather, raced only on good/good to soft ground
on turf. *B. Smart*

MONKSHILL 2 b.f. (Mar 6) Fraam 114 – Fatah Flare (USA) 121 (Alydar (USA)) **–**
[2006 8g 8.2s Oct 25] 11,000Y: neat filly: half-sister to several winners, including 6-y-o
Compton Eclipse: dam 6f (at 2 yrs) and 10.5f (Musidora Stakes) winner: in rear in
maiden/seller. *Miss Tor Sturgis*

MONKSTOWN ROAD 4 b.g. Makbul 104 – Carolside 108 (Music Maestro 119) **64 d**
[2006 75§: p8.6g f8g p10g⁶ f12g 11.5m 10m 8.3d 10d p12.2g Dec 23] good-topped
gelding: modest performer: on downgrade: left E. McMahon 1,500 gns and gelded after
reappearance: stays 7f: wears headgear: unreliable. *C. N. Kellett*

MONMOUTHSHIRE 3 b.g. Singspiel (IRE) 133 – Croeso Cariad 107 (Most Wel- **63 ?**
come 131) [2006 11.5m⁶ 10g⁶ 10d 8f 10.1m⁶ p9.5g p9.5g Nov 6] good-topped gelding:
modest maiden: seemingly best effort on second start: stumbled and nearly unseated rider
penultimate outing: stays 1¼m: visored last 3 starts: sold £3,100. *M. L. W. Bell*

MONOLITH 8 b.g. Bigstone (IRE) 126 – Ancara 109 (Dancing Brave (USA) 140) **89**
[2006 83: 20s³ 18m* 14g 18d Oct 14] smallish gelding: fairly useful handicapper, lightly
raced on Flat nowadays: won at Pontefract in June: well beaten in Cesarewitch final start:
stays 2½m: acts on good to firm and heavy ground: fairly useful hurdler, successful in
October. *L. Lungo*

MON PETITE AMOUR 3 b.f. Efisio 120 – Food of Love 109 (Music Boy 124) [2006 **58**
–: p5g p5g p7g p7g⁴ p8.6g⁵ p6g 7m* p7g² 7m⁵ p8g⁴ 7d⁴ f7g³ p7.1g⁴ f7g p7g* p7g Dec 30]
modest performer: won seller at Brighton in May and banded event at Kempton in December: stays 8.6f: acts on all-weather, good to firm and good to soft going: tried visored,
usually wears cheekpieces: withdrawn once (unruly at start). *D. W. P. Arbuthnot*

MONSIEUR DUMAS (IRE) 2 b.c. (Apr 23) Iron Mask (USA) 117 – Serenity 98 **68**
(Selkirk (USA) 129) [2006 5.9g 7g³ 9m³ 10g p8.6g⁵ Oct 28] €26,000Y: workmanlike
colt: fourth foal: half-brother to useful 6f to 8.5f winner Camille Pissarro (by Red Ransom): dam 2-y-o 6f winner: fair maiden: stays 1¼m: acts on polytrack, probably good to
firm going. *T. P. Tate*

MONSIGNOR FRED 4 b.g. Fraam 114 – Monsoon 66 (Royal Palace 131) [2006 10d **70**
9m⁵ 10.2g 8.3f Sep 18] tall, leggy gelding: fair maiden: stays 9f: acts on good to firm
ground. *H. Candy*

MONSOON WEDDING 2 b.f. (Feb 24) Monsun (GER) 124 – Hyabella 111 (Shirley **75**
Heights 130) [2006 8.2m 8.1g³ Sep 23] half-sister to several winners, including useful
2001 2-y-o 6f winner Hothaifah (by Green Desert) and fairly useful 1m/1¼m winner
High Reserve (by Dr Fong): dam, 1m winner, half-sister to high-class 1¼m performer
Stagecraft: better run in maidens when third to Tarteel at Haydock, possibly still green
(wandered). *M. Johnston*

MONTAGE (IRE) 4 b.g. Montjeu (IRE) 137 – Ocean View (USA) 109 (Gone West **57**
(USA)) [2006 –: 10m⁵ p12g⁵ p12g 12g p13.9g* p16.5g² p16g⁶ 14.1g 16m p13.9m² **a68**
p16.5m² p13.9g Nov 17] good-topped gelding: fair handicapper on all-weather, modest
on turf: won at Wolverhampton in July: fell final outing: stayed 2m: acted on polytrack
and good to firm going: wore cheekpieces last 3 starts: dead. *J. Akehurst*

MONTALEMBERT (USA) 2 b. or br.c. (Feb 11) Kalanisi (IRE) 132 – Garendare **86**
105 (Vacarme (USA) 121) [2006 6s 7m 6g 7.5m* 7g⁴ p10g* Nov 25] $12,000F, 8,500Y:
lengthy, good-topped colt: half-brother to fairly useful French 9.5f winner Portorosa and
a winner in USA (both by Irish River): dam, French 10.5f (Prix Cleopatre) winner who
later won in USA, half-sister to smart 1¼m performer Port Vila: fairly useful performer:
won maiden at Beverley in September and minor event at Lingfield in November: often
highly tried otherwise, fourth to Rolling Home in listed race at Mulheim fifth start: stays
1¼m: acts on polytrack and good to firm going. *J. S. Moore*

MONTANA 6 b.g. Puissance 110 – Mistral's Dancer (Shareef Dancer (USA) 135) [2006 **48 §**
65: 6m 6d⁵ 6g 5f 7m 6g⁴ 5s⁵ Aug 19] tall gelding: poor maiden nowadays: stays 6f: acts
on heavy and good to firm ground: ungenuine. *C. W. Fairhurst*

MONTANAH JET 4 b.g. Montjoy (USA) 122 – Nashwanah 57 (Nashwan (USA) 135) **–**
[2006 p7g f8g 11v⁵ Mar 24] no sign of ability: tried tongue tied/blinkered. *C. N. Kellett*

MONTANA SKY (IRE) 3 b.c. Peintre Celebre (USA) 137 – Catch The Lights 86 **–**
(Deploy 131) [2006 10m 12.1d 11.7m⁶ 13.1m 9.9d 16v p16g Nov 8] signs of a little
ability, leaving S. Kirk after second start. *R. A. Harris*

MONTARA (IRE) 7 b.g. Perugino (USA) 84 – Tatra (Niniski (USA) 125) [2006 61: **55**
7.1v 11.9g 10g 10.5f³ 9m 11.1m Aug 5] modest handicapper: stays 11f: acts on polytrack
and firm ground: usually wears headgear: tried tongue tied at 3 yrs. *B. Potts, Ireland*

MONTARE (IRE) 4 b.f. Montjeu (IRE) 137 – Contare 108 (Shirley Heights 130) **116**
[2006 110: 10.5d⁵ 15.5d² 14m² 12.5g² 12m² 12.5m* 15.5g* Oct 22]
She has shown her form during the spring and summer when not wearing
headgear, but the arrival of autumn and the re-fitting of cheekpieces has coincided
in the last two seasons with Montare's transformation from bridesmaid into bride.
In 2005 she won her last three starts, including the Prix du Conseil de Paris; and in
2006 she won her last two, gaining her first success at Group 1 level on her final
one, in the Prix Royal-Oak.
Montare was runner-up in four races in succession before getting off the
mark in the latest season, three of those at Longchamp where she was beaten a nose
by Shamdala in the Prix Vicomtesse Vigier, and a length and a half by Bellamy Cay
in the Prix Maurice de Nieuil and by Mandesha in the Prix Vermeille. On the other
occasion Montare went down by two lengths to Freedonia in the Prix de Pomone at
Deauville. Re-fitted with cheekpieces in the Vermeille (she had worn a sheepskin
noseband on her three previous starts), Montare was similarly equipped on her
two subsequent appearances, both of which were also at Longchamp. In the Prix de
Royallieu Hotel Hermitage Barriere de La Baule, all eight runners bar Montare and
Irish challenger Chelsea Rose were three-year-olds, and they included Rising Cross
and Short Skirt, second and third in the Oaks at Epsom, and Lahudood, winner of a
listed event at Longchamp on her previous outing. Montare was sent off favourite,
and just managed to justify the support, even though a little below top form. Held
up as usual, she was ridden along firmly on the home turn but ran on well to collar
Lahudood near the line and win by a head. Rising Cross, who finished fifth,
reopposed Montare in the Prix Royal-Oak on terms 7 lb better. Rising Cross was
the only three-year-old in a field which also featured Sergeant Cecil and Shamdala,
first and second respectively in the Prix du Cadran earlier in October, and Lord
du Sud, winner of the Prix Kergorlay on his previous outing. It was another former
rival, Bellamy Cay, who got closest to Montare. A short neck separated the pair at
the line, Montare quickening to lead inside the final furlong after being checked
twice by the runner-up when beginning her effort, and there was a length back to

Prix Royal-Oak, Longchamp—Montare (No.9) puts her tongue out at the opposition as she pips Bellamy Cay; Sergeant Cecil (No.2) comes late for third, ahead of the grey Lord du Sud

Sergeant Cecil in third. Montare, typically, looked ungainly in the closing stages, her tongue out as she carried her head awkwardly and also flashing her tail, though it has to be said she lacked nothing in resolution. Montare has finished out of the frame only twice in seventeen appearances—on her debut and over an inadequate trip in the Prix Ganay on her reappearance in 2006—and she also scores highly when it comes to consistency of performance. It is good news that she is to stay in training, and it is to be hoped that racegoers outside France will have an opportunity to see her in action. 'She's the best filly I've ever trained,' is what Jonathan Pease said of Montare after the Royal-Oak, a race he also won with Turgeon in 1991.

Montare (IRE) (b.f. 2002)	Montjeu (IRE) (b 1996)	Sadler's Wells (b 1981)	Northern Dancer / Fairy Bridge
		Floripedes (b 1985)	Top Ville / Toute Cy
	Contare (b 1993)	Shirley Heights (b 1975)	Mill Reef / Hardiemma
		Balenare (b 1986)	Pharly / Flashy

Montare, like Turgeon, runs in the colours of George Strawbridge, who also bred her. From the first crop of Montjeu, whose leading progeny have tended to display the odd quirk (though it has not stopped them from excelling), Montare is the fifth foal of Contare, a useful winner (including of two listed races) at seven to nine furlongs in France. Contare is responsible for four other winners, all in France, including a close relation of Montare's named Salutare, a filly by Sadler's Wells who was a useful winner at a mile and a half to fifteen furlongs. Contare's three-year-old Gabier (by Galileo) was an eleven-furlong winner in the Provinces in the latest season. Montare's grandam Balenare raced in France and the States and was successful three times; while her great grandam Flashy, from an excellent family, won the Strensall Stakes at York and is also the great grandam of the very smart Wizard King. Montare, a tall, leggy individual, needs at least a mile and a half and stays an extended fifteen furlongs. Raced under less testing conditions since winning on soft ground at two, Montare has shown herself fully effective on both good to firm and good to soft. *J. E. Pease, France*

MONTCHARA (IRE) 3 b.g. Montjeu (IRE) 137 – Mochara (Last Fandango 125) [2006 –p: 9.9d⁴ 10d Oct 9] modest form in maidens: stays 1¼m: acts on good to soft ground. *G. Wragg* **60**

MONTE ALTO (IRE) 2 b.c. (Feb 14) Danehill Dancer (IRE) 117 – Peruvian Witch (IRE) (Perugino (USA) 84) [2006 7m³ 7d³ Oct 10] 92,000Y: sturdy colt: first foal: dam unraced out of half-sister to very smart 1m/1¼m performer Great Dane: promise when **83 p**

third in maidens at Yarmouth and Leicester, at latter behind Mount Hadley and Cabinet: will stay 1m: type to improve as 3-y-o. *L. M. Cumani*

MONTE CARRIO 3 ch.g. Observatory (USA) 131 – Kundalini (USA) (El Gran Senor (USA) 136) [2006 –: p12g f11g Dec 29] well-made gelding: no sign of ability: tried blinkered. *C. Drew* –

MONTECRISTO 13 br.g. Warning 136 – Sutosky 78 (Great Nephew 126) [2006 –: p12g 11.9d p16.5g⁴ Dec 2] leggy, close-coupled gelding: fair performer in 2004: lightly raced since and only poor nowadays. *Rae Guest* **48**

MONTE CRISTO (FR) 8 ch.g. Bigstone (IRE) 126 – El Quahirah (FR) (Cadoudal (FR) 124) [2006 77: p16.5g p16g⁴ p16g⁵ p16g* p16g² 17.2s⁵ p16g⁵ p16g May 1] fair performer: won apprentice handicap at Lingfield in March: reportedly struck into final start: stays 16.5f: acts on all-weather: visored nowadays: sold 13,500 gns. *Mrs L. C. Taylor* **78**

MONTE MAJOR (GER) 3 ch.g. Trempolino (USA) 135 – Monbijou (GER) (Dashing Blade 117) [2006 –: p10g² p12g p16g⁵ p13.9g² Nov 16] strong, lengthy, good sort: poor maiden: stays 1½m: acts on polytrack: visored final outing. *D. J. Daly* **48**

MONTE MAJOR (IRE) 5 b.g. Docksider (USA) 124 – Danalia (IRE) 78 (Danehill (USA) 126) [2006 43: p5.1g p5.1g* p5.1g f5g p5g³ p5.1g 5.1m 5m⁴ 5g³ 6.1m p6g p6g³ p6g⁴ p5.1g³ Dec 31] modest handicapper: won at Wolverhampton in February: effective at 5f to 7f: acts on all-weather, good to firm and good to soft going: visored. *D. Shaw* **59**

MONTE MAYOR BOY 4 b.g. First Trump 118 – Risalah (Marju (IRE) 127) [2006 76: f8g⁵ p8g⁴ p9.5g⁶ p8.6g p8.6g f8g⁵ 8d 8.1d 8f p12.2g⁶ f8g Jul 31] fair handicapper: generally below form in 2006: will probably prove best short of 9.5f: acts on all-weather: usually wears headgear: has twice reared in stall and unseated rider, including on fourth outing in 2006. *D. Haydn Jones* **74 d**

MONTE MAYOR JUNIOR 3 b.g. Mull of Kintyre (USA) 114 – Monte Mayor Golf (IRE) 80 (Case Law 113) [2006 60: f8g³ f8g* p8.6g 10.9g f8g³ f8g⁶ 10g⁵ 10.2m p9.5g p12.2g Dec 9] good-bodied gelding: modest handicapper: won maiden event at Southwell in February (veered left in front): stays easy 1¼m: acts on fibresand: in cheekpieces/visored nowadays. *D. Haydn Jones* **60**

MONTEMAYORPRINCESS (IRE) 2 b.f. (Apr 25) Fath (USA) 116 – Blonde Goddess (IRE) (Godswalk (USA) 130) [2006 5.1d 5g 5.1d² 5.7f⁴ 6f⁶ f7g⁶ p7.1g Oct 30] sixth foal: half-sister to 3 winners, including 1½m winner Ocean Drive (by Dolphin Street) and Irish 1m winner Packie Tam (by Tipsy Creek): dam Irish 7f and 1m winner: modest maiden: should stay 7f: acts on fibresand, firm and good to soft going. *D. Haydn Jones* **59**

MONT ETOILE (IRE) 3 b.f. Montjeu (IRE) 137 – Troyes 81 (Troy 137) [2006 80: 11.5m* 11.4m² 12m* 12m⁴ 13.9g Sep 9] sturdy filly: smart performer: won maiden at Yarmouth in April and Ribblesdale Stakes at Royal Ascot (beat Scottish Stage by a neck after not clearest of runs) in June: creditable 5¼ lengths fourth to Alexandrova in Irish Oaks at the Curragh next time: below form when 9 lengths eighth to Sixties Icon in St Leger at York final start (got warm beforehand): should be suited by 1¾m: acts on good to firm going: has been bandaged: stays in training. *W. J. Haggas* **112**

Ribblesdale Stakes, Royal Ascot—Mont Etoile comes from last to first up the inside to get the better of Scottish Stage (No.9); Maroussies Wings is third

MONTEVIDEO 6 b.g. Sadler's Wells (USA) 132 – Montessori (Akarad (FR) 130) – [2006 11.6m 12m Jul 15] strong, lengthy gelding: fairly useful winner at 3 yrs for J. Oxx (sold €120,000): unraced on Flat in 2004/5: well beaten on return: stays 2m: acts on firm going: won over hurdles in September. *Jonjo O'Neill*

MONTGOMERY'S ARCH (USA) 4 b. or br.c. Arch (USA) 127 – Inny River **111** (USA) (Seattle Slew (USA)) [2006 106: 6.5m 6m* 6.5m Mar 9] tall, quite good-topped colt: smart performer: won handicap at Nad Al Sheba (by ¾ length from Bygone Days) in February: below form in similar event three final start: effective at 6f, should stay 1m: acts on soft and good to firm going: visored last 2 starts: sent to USA. *J. Noseda*

MONTILLIA (IRE) 4 b.f. Monashee Mountain (USA) 115 – Steel Tap (IRE) (Flash **58** of Steel 120) [2006 58: p6g p5.1g⁶ 5f² 5f² 5m³ p5.1g p5.1g p5.1g Dec 8] modest handicapper: left C. Wall 5,000 gns after fifth start: front runner, best at 5f: acts on polytrack and firm going. *J. W. Unett*

MONTJEU BABY (IRE) 4 b.f. Montjeu (IRE) 137 – Catch The Lights 86 (Deploy **70** 131) [2006 70: p10g 10.2g 10.2m⁵ 10g² Aug 23] fair handicapper: left S. Kirk after third start: stays 1¼m: acts on polytrack, firm and soft going: tried blinkered. *B. J. Meehan*

MONTJEU MAN 3 b.c. Montjeu (IRE) 137 – Camp Fire (IRE) 81 (Lahib (USA) 129) **83** [2006 83p: 8d³ p9.5g² 10m 12.1m⁴ Sep 7] fairly useful maiden: stayed 9.5f: acted on polytrack, good to firm and good to soft going: dead. *E. A. L. Dunlop*

MONTJEU'S MELODY (IRE) 2 b.f. (Feb 26) Montjeu (IRE) 137 – Pride of Place **– p** (IRE) 71 (Caerleon (USA) 132) [2006 7d Aug 13] €73,000Y: fourth foal: dam, ran twice at 2 yrs, half-sister to Oaks winner Unite: 16/1, ninth in maiden at Redcar, prominent until running green (hung left): should progress. *E. J. O'Neill*

MONTOSARI 7 ch.g. Persian Bold 123 – Sartigila 67 (Efisio 120) [2006 –, a71: p13g² **63** p16g⁴ p16g* p16g⁴ p16g p16g⁵ 12.1f³ 14.1f* 12.3m p16g p13g⁶ p16g* Nov 28] fair **a75** handicapper on all-weather, modest on turf: won at Lingfield in April, Carlisle (amateurs) in August and Lingfield in November: effective at 1½m to easy 2m: acts on all-weather and firm going. *P. Mitchell*

MON TOUR 2 b.g. (Mar 30) Montjeu (IRE) 137 – Flamingo Queen (GER) 105 (Sur- **–** umu (GER)) [2006 8s Oct 10] useful-looking gelding: 66/1, last in maiden at Newbury. *I. A. Wood*

MONTPELLIER (IRE) 3 b.g. Montjeu (IRE) 137 – Ring of Esteem (Mark of Esteem **89** (IRE) 137) [2006 10m³ 10m³ 10m³ 10m 8.3f² 9.2d* p9.5g⁶ Oct 28] 65,000F, 130,000Y: big, rangy gelding: first foal: dam unraced half-sister to smart German 1½m performer Catella out of half-sister to Diamond Shoal and Glint of Gold: fairly useful performer: straightforward task in maiden at Hamilton in September: good sixth on handicap/all-weather debut at Wolverhampton final start: stays 1¼m: acts on polytrack, good to firm and good to soft ground: hasn't always impressed with attitude. *E. A. L. Dunlop*

MONTRACHET BELLE 4 ch.f. Kadeed (IRE) – Swiss Hat (Hatim (USA) 121) **–** [2006 –: 7m f11g Jul 7] workmanlike filly: no form: tried tongue tied. *R. Johnson*

MONTROSE MAN 2 ch.g. (Mar 23) Foxhound (USA) 103 – Don't Jump (IRE) 71 **56 p** (Entitled 126) [2006 7s Oct 10] 12,500F, 28,000Y: workmanlike gelding: sixth foal: half-brother to fairly useful winner 2004 2-y-o 6f winner The Pheasant Flyer (by Prince Sabo) and 2003 2-y-o 7f winner Head Boy (by Forzando): dam 1m winner: 7/1, mid-field in maiden at Newbury won by Hollow Ridge: should do better. *B. J. Meehan*

MONTZANDO 3 b.g. Forzando 122 – Clashfern (Smackover 107) [2006 79: 5.7d 6g **60** 8.1s 7g 5f³ 5.1f* 5m⁵ 5g⁶ 5.7f⁵ 5.7m Sep 25] good-topped gelding: modest performer nowadays: won handicap at Bath in July: best efforts at 5f: acts on firm going: often wears headgear. *B. R. Millman*

MONZANTE (USA) 2 gr. or ro.g. (Apr 28) Maria's Mon (USA) 121 – Danzante **110 p** (USA) 107 (Danzig (USA)) [2006 7m³ p8g* p8g² Sep 30] unfurnished gelding: half-brother to several winners, including useful French 1996 2-y-o 7f winner Alpha Plus (by Mr Prospector) and 1m winner Roman Villa (by Chester House): dam, won up to 8.5f in France/USA, half-sister to Breeders' Cup Classic winner Skywalker: smart form: won maiden at Kempton in September by 2½ lengths from Maslak with something in hand: further improvement when head second to Rallying Cry in minor event there, still somewhat green: will stay 1¼m: should go on and make mark in stronger company. *R. Charlton*

MOOD MUSIC 2 b.c. (Apr 1) Kyllachy 129 – Something Blue (Petong 126) [2006 **99** 5.1d² 5m* 5g² 5m⁶ 6f⁶ 5g³ 5d³ 5d² Oct 9] 34,000Y: smallish, quite good-topped colt:

sixth foal: half-brother to 3 winners, including 6-y-o Steel Blue and 3-y-o Memphis Man: dam, ran 3 times, half-sister to dam of smart sprinters Astonished and Bishops Court: useful performer: won maiden at Hamilton in May: ran creditably when twice tried in pattern company (sixth in Norfolk and Richmond Stakes) and placed all 5 starts in listed races, neck second to Beta at Chantilly final one: best at 5f: acts on firm and good to soft going: sold 55,000 gns. *E. J. O'Neill*

MOODY GOOSE 2 b.f. (Feb 27) Beat Hollow 126 – Brecon Beacons (IRE) 71 (Shirley Heights 130) [2006 p5g p7.1g⁵ Jun 30] 3,000Y: half-sister to 3 winners abroad: dam maiden best at 2 yrs (should have stayed at least 1¼m): well held in claimer/seller. *M. Meade* —

MOODY TUNES 3 b.g. Merdon Melody 98 – Lady-Love 70 (Pursuit of Love 124) [2006 71: 7.1s 8m* 8s* 7.2v* 7.1s² 8g⁴ 8g 7s Oct 24] lengthy, good-topped gelding: fairly useful handicapper: won at Newcastle (dead-heat), Thirsk and Ayr (by 5 lengths) in May: stays 1m: acts on heavy and good to firm ground: blinkered final 2-y-o outing: usually travels strongly. *K. R. Burke* **87**

MOOHIMM (IRE) 3 b.c. Sadler's Wells (USA) 132 – Lurina (IRE) 111 (Lure (USA) 131) [2006 –: 11g⁵ 10g⁴ p10g⁴ 9.8d⁶ Aug 29] fairly maiden: stays 11f: acts on polytrack and good to soft going: has hung left/carried head awkwardly: joined D. Selvaratnam in UAE. *M. P. Tregoning* **77**

MOOKERR (IRE) 3 b.g. Mtoto 134 – Seyooll (IRE) 78 (Danehill (USA) 126) [2006 8g p10g⁶ Aug 12] lengthy gelding: modest form in maidens at Newmarket (blinkered) and Lingfield (carried head high): should stay 1½m: joined D. Selvaratnam in UAE. *M. P. Tregoning* **58**

MOON BIRD 4 b.f. Primo Dominie 121 – Time For Tea (IRE) 73 (Imperial Frontier (USA) 112) [2006 71: p6g p7g p7g p7g* p7.1g p7g 6f p6m 8m p7g⁶ p7g* p7g² p6g⁴ Dec 30] fair performer: won handicap in June and claimer in December, both at Lingfield: stays 7f: acts on polytrack, lightly raced on turf. *C. A. Cyzer* **a68**

MOONDANCER (GER) 7 br.g. General Assembly (USA) – Miskinissa (GER) (Esclavo (FR)) [2006 57: p10g f8g Jan 31] modest form in 2005, well held in 2006: has reportedly bled twice, including final start. *B. G. Powell* —

MOONDINE (IRE) 2 b.f. (Apr 16) Princely Heir (IRE) 111 – Second Dream (IRE) (Second Set (IRE) 127) [2006 7.5m 6s Oct 16] €3,000Y: third foal: dam ran once in Ireland: well beaten in maidens. *B. S. Rothwell* —

MOONE CROSS (IRE) 3 b.f. Cape Cross (IRE) 129 – Cannikin (IRE) 82 (Lahib (USA) 129) [2006 84: 7v⁵ 6d⁴ 6d 6m⁶ 6.3g 6m⁴ 6.1m⁴ 6.1m⁶ 6d Sep 19] €25,000F, €65,000Y: fourth living foal: half-sister to 6-y-o Icannshift and Italian 7f (at 2 yrs) to 11f winner Gioell (by In The Wings), both fairly useful: dam, Irish 2-y-o 6f winner, half-sister to useful Irish performer up to 1½m Tout A Coup: useful performer: won maiden at Cork in April and minor event at Naas in July: good 1¾ lengths fourth to The Kiddykid in listed race at Chester next time: below form after: seems best at 6f: acts on good to firm and good to soft going: often front runner/races prominently. *Mrs J. Harrington, Ireland* **102**

MOON EMPEROR 9 b.g. Emperor Jones (USA) 119 – Sir Hollow (USA) (Sir Ivor (USA) 135) [2006 77d: f14g⁴ f16g* p16.5g* p16g⁵ p16g p16g³ f16g⁴ p16g 15.4m p16g⁴ 16g p16.5m p16g⁶ Nov 8] tall, close-coupled gelding: fairly useful handicapper on all-weather: won at Southwell and Wolverhampton in January: below form after sixth start: stays 2m: acts on all-weather, firm and soft going: usually wears headgear: sometimes looks none too keen: held up. *J. R. Jenkins* **82 d**

MOON EMPRESS (FR) 3 gr.f. Rainbow Quest (USA) 134 – Diamoona (FR) (Last Tycoon 131) [2006 p10g 8.3f 10g³ f12g⁶ p10g³ Dec 30] €150,000Y: first foal: dam, French 1m winner, half-sister to smart French middle-distance performers Diamond Mix and Diamond Dance: fair maiden: shaped well when third at Lingfield final start: should be suited by 1½m: acts on polytrack and firm going: remains capable of better. *W. R. Muir* **72 p**

MOON FOREST (IRE) 4 br.g. Woodborough (USA) 112 – Ma Bella Luna 76 (Jalmood (USA) 126) [2006 68: 7d 7.1d 7m³ 7f 6.1m⁵ 5m 6g 7.1m* 7m³ 6g² 6d 7g³ p8g p7.1g² p6m Nov 21] good-topped gelding: modest performer nowadays: won handicap at Chepstow in September: stays 7f: acts on polytrack, soft and good to firm going: wears cheekpieces nowadays: usually races up with pace. *J. M. Bradley* **64**

MOONHAWK 3 b.g. Montjeu (IRE) 137 – Enclave (USA) (Woodman (USA) 126) [2006 78: 11.9g⁵ 12s⁴ 10g² 11.5m⁵ Aug 7] strong gelding: fair maiden: will prove best short of 1½m: best efforts on good going: gelded after final start. *J. Howard Johnson* **75**

MOONLIGHT APPLAUSE 2 b.f. (Mar 5) Royal Applause 124 – Antonia's Choice **46** 73 (Music Boy 124) [2006 5s⁴ 6.1g Jun 1] 28,000Y: fourth foal: half-sister to fairly useful 2002 2-y-o 5f winner Ivania (by First Trump): dam 2-y-o 5f winner: poor form in maidens. *T. D. Easterby*

MOONLIGHT FANTASY (IRE) 3 b.g. Night Shift (USA) – County Girl (IRE) **58** (Prince Rupert (FR) 121) [2006 52: f6g 7f⁴ 7f 7g 6m 7m⁵ 9.8m* 10m³ 10.1m* 10g⁴ 12d Sep 5] sturdy gelding: modest performer: won seller at Ripon in July and apprentice handicap at Newcastle in August: stays 1¼m: acts on firm ground: tried in cheekpieces: has hung left/raced freely: usually ridden prominently. *N. Tinkler*

MOONLIGHT (GER) 3 b.f. Kornado 120 – Miskinissa (GER) (Esclavo (FR)) [2006 **39** –: p7g p8.6g 10d⁶ p12.2g Jun 22] tall filly: poor maiden. *Dr J. R. J. Naylor*

MOONLIGHT MAN 5 ch.g. Night Shift (USA) – Fleeting Rainbow 65 (Rainbow **–** Quest (USA) 134) [2006 105: p7g 7g Apr 19] good-topped gelding: useful handicapper at 4 yrs: well held in 2006: tried blinkered: gelded after final outing. *R. Hannon*

MOONLIGHT MUSIC (IRE) 3 ch.f. Rossini (USA) 118 – Jarmar Moon (Unfuwain **70** (USA) 131) [2006 76: 10.1d² 8g³ 10g⁵ p10g³ 11.5m⁴ 10f 12.4s² Oct 10] leggy filly: fair maiden: stays 1½m, at least when emphasis is on speed: acts on polytrack, soft and good to firm going. *E. J. O'Neill*

MOONLIGHT SAFARI (IRE) 3 b.f. Desert Prince (IRE) 130 – Moon Masquerade **–** (IRE) 69 (Darshaan 133) [2006 10d f12g Nov 20] 5,000Y: fourth foal: half-sister to fairly useful 11f winner Masked (by Soviet Star): dam maiden who stayed 1¾m: well beaten in maidens. *P. Winkworth*

MOONLIT SKIES 3 b.c. Singspiel (IRE) 133 – Truly Special 116 (Caerleon (USA) **85** 132) [2006 9.9d* 10s Oct 18] good-topped colt: closely related to fairly useful 11f winner True Glory (by In The Wings) and half-brother to several winners, including very smart stayer Wareed (by Sadler's Wells): dam French 1m (at 2 yrs) and 10.5f winner: fairly useful form: won maiden at Goodwood in September by 1¾ lengths from Muntada: well held in handicap at Nottingham next time: stayed 1¼m: dead. *Saeed bin Suroor*

MOON MELODY (GER) 3 b.g. Montjeu (IRE) 137 – Midnight Fever (IRE) (Sure **57** Blade (USA) 130) [2006 11g 10.1g 10.9d⁵ 8.2g Jun 1] rather lightly-made gelding: modest maiden: joined M. Sowersby and gelded. *M. L. W. Bell*

MOON ON A SPOON 3 b.f. Dansili 127 – Tinashaan (IRE) 100 (Darshaan 133) [2006 **86** 70p: p8g 9.8m* 10m⁴ 9.8d² p12g² 10g Oct 16] rather leggy filly: fairly useful handicapper: won at Ripon (easily) in June: effective at 1½m: acts on polytrack, and good to firm and good to soft going: sold 36,000 gns. *J. R. Fanshawe*

MOONSHADOW 3 ch.f. Diesis 133 – La Sky (IRE) 107 (Law Society (USA) 130) **75** [2006 11.5m³ 11.8m³ 12.1m² p12g 16g 12v⁴ p12g⁶ Nov 9] leggy, lengthy filly: sister to 2 winners, notably very smart 1¼m/1½m (Oaks) winner Love Divine (now dam of St Leger winner Sixties Icon), and half-sister to 3 winners, including useful 1½m winner Floreeda (by Linamix): dam, 1¼m winner (probably stayed 1¾m), closely related to Champion Stakes winner Legal Case: fair maiden: should stay 1¾m (didn't stay 2m): acts on good to firm going. *H. R. A. Cecil*

MOONSHINE BEACH 8 b.g. Lugana Beach 116 – Monongelia 98 (Welsh Pageant **–** 132) [2006 86: 18m 17.1m Jun 12] leggy, lengthy gelding: fairly useful handicapper at best: well beaten in 2006: tried in cheekpieces, visored final outing at 7 yrs: races prominently. *P. W. Hiatt*

MOONSHINE BILL 7 ch.g. Master Willie 129 – Monongelia 98 (Welsh Pageant 132) **52** [2006 57: 10g 12.1m* 10g Sep 14] lengthy, workmanlike gelding: modest performer: won claimer at Chepstow in September: stays 1½m: acts on polytrack, soft and good to firm ground: often races prominently. *P. W. Hiatt*

MOONSHINE CREEK 4 b.g. Pyramus (USA) 78 – Monongelia 98 (Welsh Pageant **58** 132) [2006 10g 14.1d 10.2m Jun 3] leggy gelding: form only on debut. *P. W. Hiatt*

MOON SHOT 10 gr.g. Pistolet Bleu (IRE) 133 – La Luna (USA) (Lyphard (USA) 132) **70** [2006 77d: p13.9g² p13.9g² f12g² f12g² f14g⁴ f12g³ p12g p12.2g Dec 18] good-bodied gelding: fair performer: won banded race at Southwell (hung right) in January: stays 1¾m: acts on all-weather, firm and good to soft going: blinkered once: has been tongue tied: no battler. *A. G. Juckes*

MOONSTREAKER 3 b.g. Foxhound (USA) 103 – Ling Lane (Slip Anchor 136) **71** [2006 66: 7m⁵ 7g⁴ 6f⁵ 8.1f 7.5m p7.1m f8g³ f8g* Dec 21] tall, leggy gelding: fair handicapper: won at Southwell in December: stays 1m: acts on fibresand and good to firm going. *R. M. Whitaker*

MOON UNIT (IRE) 5 b.m. Intikhab (USA) 135 – Chapka (IRE) 68 (Green Desert **119**
(USA) 127) [2006 114: 5d* 6d⁴ 6v² 5m² Jun 5] smart performer: won listed race at Naas
(by length from Dandy Man) in April: good length second to Moss Vale in Greenlands
Stakes at the Curragh third start: just respectable 1½ lengths second to Osterhase in listed
race at Naas final outing: effective at 5f/6f: has form on firm going, probably best on
good or softer (acts on heavy): wore cheekpieces final starts at 2/3 yrs: tried tongue tied:
reportedly in foal to Rock of Gibraltar. *H. Rogers, Ireland*

MOON VALLEY 3 ch.f. Halling (USA) 133 – Crescent Moon (Mr Prospector (USA)) **79**
[2006 8m³ 8.1g³ 10.2m² Sep 25] second foal: dam, placed up to 10.5f in France, out of
Oaks and Irish Derby winner Balanchine: fair maiden: placed all starts: probably stays
1¼m: sold 20,000 gns. *M. P. Tregoning*

MOONWALKING 2 b.c. (Mar 21) Danehill Dancer (IRE) 117 – Macca Luna (IRE) 78 **78**
(Kahyasi 130) [2006 6m 6g* 6m⁵ 7m² 7.5g 8d⁶ 8g Oct 12] good-topped colt: fourth foal:
half-brother to 3-y-o Luna Landing and 5-y-o General Flumpa: dam 1m (at 2 yrs) and
1½m winner: fair performer: won maiden at Ayr in June: best run in nurseries when
second at Newcastle: likely to stay 1¼m/1½m: acts on good to firm and good to soft
going. *Jedd O'Keeffe*

MOORHOUSE LAD 3 b.g. Bertolini (USA) 125 – Record Time 69 (Clantime 101) **92**
[2006 77: 5g 5m* 6m⁴ 5f⁴ 5m* 5.1f⁵ 5g⁶ p6g⁶ f5g² Dec 5] neat gelding: fairly useful
performer: won maiden at Newcastle in May and handicap at Newmarket in June: good
second at Southwell final start: will prove best at 5f/6f: acts on all-weather and firm
ground: often races prominently: joined B. Smart and gelded. *G. Woodward*

MOORLANDER (USA) 2 ch.g. (Mar 19) Cozzene (USA) – Forest Key (USA) **74**
(Green Forest (USA) 134) [2006 6m⁶ 7.1m³ 8g Oct 17] $340,000F, $190,000Y: lengthy,
good-bodied gelding: brother to 3 winners abroad, notably very smart US Grade 1 9f
winner Gaviola, and half-brother to winner in USA by Woodman: dam 1m/8.5f winner in
USA: fair maiden: third to Slate at Warwick: should be suited by 1m: gelded after final
start. *Mrs A. J. Perrett*

MOORS MYTH 5 b.g. Anabaa (USA) 130 – West Devon (USA) (Gone West (USA)) **56**
[2006 73: p8g p8g f7s p8.6g Dec 27] big, good-topped gelding: just modest form in 2006:
left B. Hills after third start: barely stays 1m: acts on firm going: takes strong hold/races
prominently: has looked awkward ride. *B. G. Powell*

MORAADI 3 b.f. Lujain (USA) 119 – Saleyma 73 (Mtoto 134) [2006 –: f5g f6g f7g⁶ **–**
f8g⁶ f5g f5g f7g⁴ 7g Jun 2] tall, good-topped filly: poor maiden: wears cheekpieces/ **a30**
blinkers nowadays. *D. W. Chapman*

MORAL CODE (IRE) 2 ch.c. (May 14) Danehill Dancer (IRE) 117 – Scruple (IRE) **63 p**
(Catrail (USA) 123) [2006 p9.5g⁶ Dec 7] €82,000Y: third foal: half-brother to 3-y-o
Critic: dam unraced half-sister to smart 6f/7f performer Hot Tin Roof: 5/2 favourite from
8/1, very green when sixth of 10 to Encircled in maiden at Wolverhampton: will prove
capable of better. *E. J. O'Neill*

MORAL FIBRE (IRE) 2 b.c. (Feb 5) Green Desert (USA) 127 – Mellow Park (IRE) **65 ?**
114 (In The Wings 128) [2006 6g 7s⁵ p8.6g Nov 7] first foal: dam, 1¼m/1½m (Lancashire
Oaks) winner, sister to very smart performer up to 2m winner Central Park and half-sister
to useful dam of Dubai World Cup winner Moon Ballad: seemingly fair form final start.
M. Johnston

MORGAN LEWIS (IRE) 5 b.g. Orpen (USA) 116 – Party Piece (Thatch (USA) 136) **66**
[2006 75: 7.1d 8s p7g p8g 7g³ 8.2d Nov 1] fair handicapper: stays 7f: acts on soft and
good to firm going: tried visored, usually wears cheekpieces: often waited with.
J. A. Geake

MORGHIM (IRE) 3 b.c. Machiavellian (USA) 123 – Saleela (USA) 85 (Nureyev **101**
(USA) 131) [2006 92p: 9g⁶ 10m³ 12m⁶ 13m⁵ 10m³ a9f* a10f Dec 22] leggy, lengthy,
quite attractive colt: useful performer: creditable efforts most starts in 2006, including
when third at Newmarket in listed race (4½ lengths behind Mulaqat) and minor event
(beaten 6½ lengths by Windsor Knot): left J. Dunlop, won minor event at Jebel Ali in
December by 2¼ lengths from Anani: below form in listed race there final start: probably
stays 1½m: acts on dirt, good to firm and good to soft going: blinkered last 3 outings.
E. Charpy, UAE

MORINQUA (IRE) 2 b.f. (Feb 27) Cadeaux Genereux 131 – Victoria Regia (IRE) 90 **82**
(Lomond (USA) 128) [2006 6.1g p6g 5d* 7d 5s Oct 14] €11,200Y: leggy filly: fourth
foal: half-sister to useful 5f (at 2 yrs)/6f winner Topkamp (by Pennekamp): dam 6f (at
2 yrs) to 1m (in USA) winner: fairly useful performer: won maiden at Ripon (made all) in
August, easily best effort: best at 5f: acts on good to soft going. *K. A. Ryan*

MORMEATMIC 3 b.g. Orpen (USA) 116 – Mimining 83 (Tower Walk 130) [2006 66: **80**
5v⁴ 5d* 6g 5g* 5d* 5m 5g* 5f⁶ 5m 5d Nov 3] good-topped gelding: fairly useful handicapper: won at Catterick in April, Carlisle in May and twice at Ayr in June: best form at
5f: acts on good to soft going, below form on good to firm/firm. *M. W. Easterby*

MORNING FAREWELL 2 br.c. (Apr 18) Daylami (IRE) 138 – Got To Go 99 **74**
(Shareef Dancer (USA) 135) [2006 7m 7m⁵ 8g Oct 13] 48,000Y: unfurnished colt: second
foal: half-brother to 3-y-o Piano Player: dam, 2-y-o 6f winner who stayed 1¼m, out of
sister to very smart Japanese miler Zenno El Cid: fair form in maidens at Newmarket.
P. W. Chapple-Hyam

MORNING SONG (IRE) 2 b.f. (Mar 15) Fath (USA) 116 – John's Ballad (IRE) **–**
(Ballad Rock 122) [2006 5m 6d p6g Sep 1] €24,000F, 34,000Y: sturdy filly: half-sister to
several winners, including smart 5f to 7f winner (latter including at 2 yrs) Peruvian Chief
(by Foxhound) and fairly useful 2003 2-y-o 1m winner Cusco (later winner in USA, by
Titus Livius): dam unraced: well held in maidens. *N. P. Littmoden*

MORRISTOWN MUSIC (IRE) 2 b.f. (Feb 26) Distant Music (USA) 126 – Tonga- **71**
bezi (IRE) 75 (Shernazar 131) [2006 5m² 6s² 5s⁶ Oct 14] close-coupled filly: seventh
foal: half-sister to 3 winners, including 10-y-o Beyond The Clouds and 7-y-o Catch The
Cat: dam Irish 2-y-o 7f winner: fair maiden: second at Beverley and Ayr: should prove
best at 5f/6f. *J. S. Wainwright*

MORSE (IRE) 5 b.g. Shinko Forest (IRE) – Auriga 73 (Belmez (USA) 131) [2006 91: **86**
p6g² p7g 6.1d p6g⁵ p6g p6g* Dec 20] close-coupled gelding: fairly useful handicapper:
won at Kempton in December: effective at 6f to 1m: acts on polytrack, soft and good to
firm going: races prominently. *J. A. Osborne*

MORTARBOARD 3 gr.c. Daylami (IRE) 138 – Miss University (USA) (Beau Genius **75**
(CAN)) [2006 78: 10.2m³ 11.7g⁶ Jul 10] tall colt: fair maiden: creditable efforts both
starts in 2006: stays 11.6f: acts on good to firm and good to soft ground: sold 9,000 gns in
October. *E. J. O'Neill*

MOSHARREF (IRE) 3 b.g. Alhaarth (IRE) 126 – Murjana (IRE) 80 (Pleasant Colony **99 p**
(USA)) [2006 8g² p8g³ 8d* 8.1m* 10d Sep 29] sturdy, lengthy, attractive gelding: good
walker: has a fluent, quick action: first foal: dam, 1¼m winner, out of US Grade 2 2-y-o
6f winner Golden Reef: useful performer: won maiden at Pontefract in August and
handicap at Sandown (by 1¼ lengths from South Cape) in September: free-going sort, not
sure to stay beyond 1m: acts on good to firm and good to soft going: tongue tied final
outing (gelded after): probably capable of better still. *B. W. Hills*

MOSQUERA'S ROCK (IRE) 2 ch.f. (Apr 26) Rock of Gibraltar (IRE) 133 – Mos- **–**
quera (GER) 108 (Acatenango (GER) 127) [2006 7s Oct 10] €80,000Y: third foal: closely
related to fairly useful Irish 6f winner Bonanza (by Danehill): dam German 6.5f (at 2 yrs)
to 9f winner: 6/1, needed experience (soon off bridle) in maiden at Newcastle: sold 7,500
gns. *M. Johnston*

MOSSMANN GORGE 4 b.g. Lujain (USA) 119 – North Pine (Import 127) [2006 75, **72**
a60: f12g³ f12g p12.2g⁵ p12.2g⁶ p12.2g f12g* f11s* f12g⁴ f11g⁵ 12g 11.7d⁵ 10s² 12.1d² **a68**
10.2m³ 10m³ 11m f11g p12.2g f11g² f11g⁴ Dec 19] quite good-topped gelding: fair performer: won sellers at Southwell in February and March: stays 1½m: acts on all-weather,
soft and good to firm going: wears headgear: held up: tricky ride, and often finds little.
M. Wellings

MOSS VALE (IRE) 5 b.h. Shinko Forest (IRE) – Wolf Cleugh (IRE) 65 (Last **126**
Tycoon 131) [2006 117: 5m 6d 6v* 5m* 5m 6m⁵ 6m* 5s 5m³ 6s⁵ Oct 22]
        It is a vagary of the pattern-race system that some of the best performances
each season are put up in Group 2 and Group 3 contests, rather than in the Group 1
events which are generally recognised as being the pinnacle. A variety of weight
conditions, in the form of allowances and penalties, can give some runners in lesser
pattern events stiffer tasks than they might face in Group 1 contests run at level
weights. Moss Vale did not win any of the most prestigious prizes in 2006, but the
form he showed in winning three times at minor pattern level was high class, more
or less the equal of any shown in the sprinting ranks all season.
        British racegoers didn't see the best of Moss Vale as a five-year-old, his
improvement in danger of passing unnoticed at home, but he was a better horse all
round than in 2005, when he gained his only win in a dead heat for a listed event at
Goodwood. Bought out of Barry Hills's stable for 260,000 guineas at the Newmarket Autumn Sales, Moss Vale made into an imposing specimen for his new

Prix du Gros-Chene Mitsubishi Motors, Chantilly—Moss Vale produces a fine burst of speed; Benbaun (visor) takes second, ahead of Tax Free (third left), Balthazaar's Gift (noseband), Pivotal Flame (cheekpieces) and Pivotal Point (third right), the first six all trained in Britain

yard, as many do in his trainer's care, and it took him only three runs to start to show improvement. Once he did find his form, he held it well in the main, gaining successive wins in Ireland and France before Royal Ascot and then making a successful return to Ireland in August. Usually held up for his old yard, Moss Vale showed a new versatility as regards tactics in 2006. In a race started by tape because of the very heavy ground, he was smartly away in the Group 3 Weatherbys Ireland Greenlands Stakes at the Curragh in late-May, and was clear from halfway, beating the home-trained Moon Unit easing down by a length. With his stable-companion Tax Free one of those disputing the lead, Moss Vale reverted to being more patiently ridden in the twelve-runner Group 2 Prix du Gros-Chene Mitsubishi Motors at Chantilly in June, and proved no less impressive back at five furlongs on very different ground, quickening through late on to beat Benbaun by two lengths, a decisive margin in a five-furlong event under firmish conditions, with Tax Free half a length further away.

Moss Vale had escaped a penalty at Chantilly—he still gave weight to those unplaced in a pattern race since July 1st 2005 who received an allowance—but he was forced to carry one in minor pattern company for the rest of the season. Things didn't go his way when favourite for the King's Stand Stakes at Royal Ascot, where he finished eighth of twenty-eight, beaten little over a length after a slow start. He again didn't have the rub of the green when fifth of fifteen in the July Cup at Newmarket, racing away from the main action, but he then underlined his merit in the Group 3 Patrick P. O'Leary Memorial Phoenix Sprint Stakes at the Curragh next time out. Penalised 5 lb for victory at Chantilly, Moss Vale was a convincing winner, making a decisive move at halfway and holding Red Clubs by a length and three quarters with Pivotal Point, third in the King's Stand, a length and a half further away. Moss Vale had two more outings in Group 1 company after the Curragh. He repeatedly met trouble when second favourite in the Nunthorpe Stakes at York later in August, eventually eased right up and finishing last, but he showed much more like his form in the Prix de l'Abbaye at Longchamp on his final European start, going down only by a neck and a short neck to Desert Lord and Reverence when third of fourteen. Moss Vale was some way below his best on his only subsequent outing in the Grade 2 Nearctic Stakes at Woodbine in Canada, finishing a modest fifth of twelve after starting second favourite.

Moss Vale (IRE) (b.h. 2001)	Shinko Forest (IRE) (b 1993)	Green Desert (b 1983)	Danzig
			Foreign Courier
		Park Express (br 1983)	Ahonoora
			Matcher
	Wolf Cleugh (IRE) (b 1993)	Last Tycoon (b 1983)	Try My Best
			Mill Princess
		Santa Roseanna (br 1979)	Caracol
			Santa Vittoria

Moss Vale, a big, strong, lengthy horse, is presumably destined to find a job as a sire of sprinters when his racing days are over. By Shinko Forest, a sprinting son of Green Desert, a fine sire of sires of sprinters, Moss Vale is comfortably the

Patrick P. O'Leary Memorial Phoenix Sprint Stakes, the Curragh—
third overseas success of the season for Moss Vale in another race dominated by British-trained runners;
Red Clubs is second ahead of Pivotal Point, The Trader (blinkers) and Fayr Jag

best produce from his sire's first four crops, which have also included the smart performers Close To You, Momtic and Presto Shinko. Moss Vale is the third foal of his dam, the lightly-raced maiden Wolf Cleugh, and is a half-brother to the fairly useful mile and a quarter winner Street Life (by Dolphin Street), as well as Natural Force (by King's Best), a fairly useful mile winner as a two-year-old. Wolf Cleugh is a half-sister to the smart six-furlong winner King's College. The quick-actioned Moss Vale is effective at five and six furlongs and acts on heavy and good to firm ground. If everything falls into place on the right day, he certainly has the ability to win one of the top prizes in 2007. *D. Nicholls*

MOSTAKBEL (USA) 7 b. or br.g. Saint Ballado (CAN) – Shamlegh (USA) (Flying **60** Paster (USA)) [2006 –: f11g³ p12.2g² Feb 17] fair form in bumpers: modest maiden: stays 1½m: raced only on all-weather: visored last 2 starts. *M. D. I. Usher*

MOSTANAD 4 b.g. Alhaarth (IRE) 126 – Jeed (IRE) 86 (Mujtahid (USA) 118) [2006 **64** 64: p6g 5.1s³ 6f² 6.1m 5f⁴ 6g 6g² 6.1m 5.1m p6g p6g⁴ p6g Dec 6] lengthy gelding: modest **a48** maiden: stays 6f: acts on firm and soft going, only poor form on polytrack: tried blinkered. *J. M. Bradley*

MOSTAQELEH (USA) 3 ch.f. Rahy (USA) 115 – Istiqlal (USA) (Diesis 133) [2006 **108** 93p: 7g⁵ 8m² 8m Jun 23] well-made filly: had a short, quick action: useful performer: very good 1½ lengths second to Impressionnante in Prix de Sandringham at Chantilly in June, challenging over 1f out and running on despite flashing tail repeatedly under whip: in rear in Coronation Stakes at Royal Ascot final outing: stayed 1m: raced only on good/good to firm going: visits El Prado. *J. L. Dunlop*

MOSTARSIL (USA) 8 ch.g. Kingmambo (USA) 125 – Naazeq 80 (Nashwan (USA) **79** 135) [2006 69: p13g p16.5g⁵ p12g³ p12g p12g* 17.2f* 11.9m* 12g* Jul 6] workmanlike gelding: fair handicapper: completed 4-timer at Lingfield, Bath, Brighton and Epsom in June/July: stays 17f, effective at 1½m: acts on polytrack, firm and soft going: tried blinkered/visored, usually wears cheekpieces: usually races prominently. *G. L. Moore*

MOSTASHAAR (FR) 4 b.c. Intikhab (USA) 135 – Nasanice (IRE) 97 (Nashwan (USA) 135) [2006 113p: 7.6m⁴ 8g⁴ 7s 7.1m² 9m⁵ p7g* Oct 21] good-topped colt: fluent mover: just useful performer in 2006: won minor event at Lingfield (all-weather debut, by neck from Council Member) in October: also ran creditably when fourth to Stronghold in listed race at Lingfield and 1¾ lengths second to Sesare in minor event at Warwick reappearance/fourth outing: effective at 7f/1m, seemingly not 9f: acts on polytrack, good to firm and good to soft going: joined D. Watson in UAE. *Sir Michael Stoute*   **108**

MOST DEFINITELY (IRE) 6 b.g. Definite Article 121 – Unbidden Melody (USA) (Chieftain) [2006 98: 16m⁶ 12d 14m⁵ 13.1g⁶ 16.1m 12f 12d 13.8m⁶ 12d² 12d 16.2d³ p13g 16d⁶ f14g² f12g Dec 2] good-bodied gelding: fairly useful handicapper: left T. Easterby after tenth start: effective at 1½m to 17f: acts on fibresand, firm and good to soft going: tried blinkered/in cheekpieces: held up: tends to finish weakly. *R. M. Stronge*   **90**

MOTAFARRED (IRE) 4 ch.g. Machiavellian (USA) 123 – Thurayya (Nashwan (USA) 135) [2006 94: 12m⁶ 13.9s 10.5g⁶ 20m 13m 12f⁶ 9.8g Aug 7] leggy, workmanlike gelding: fairly useful performer: won minor event at Galway in 2005, leaving D. Weld in Ireland and gelded after final start: solid form in 2006 only when sixth in handicap at Haydock third start: stays 1½m: raced only on good ground or firmer: tried tongue tied. *M. D. Hammond*   **81 d**

MOTARAQEB 3 b.g. Grand Lodge (USA) 125 – Pink Cristal 113 (Dilum (USA) 115) [2006 8g⁵ 8d* 8s² 8m 8g 8g⁴ 8g Oct 13] 160,000Y: rangy, good sort: second foal: half-brother to smart 7f (at 2 yrs) to 1½m (US Grade 2) winner Always First (by Barathea): dam 7f/1m winner: fairly useful performer: won maiden at Thirsk in May: gelded, good fourth in handicap at Newmarket penultimate start: will be suited by 1¼m+: acts on soft going: tongue tied below form) fourth/fifth starts: possibly not straightforward: sold 22,000 gns, joined J. Carr in Ireland. *Sir Michael Stoute*   **93**

MOTIVE (FR) 5 ch.g. Machiavellian (USA) 123 – Mistle Song 112 (Nashwan (USA) 135) [2006 104: 12m³ 10.4f Jul 15] lengthy, good-topped gelding: useful performer: respectable third of 6 to Hearthstead Wings in minor event at Ripon on reappearance: well below form in John Smith's Cup at York only other start in 2006: stays 1½m: acts on good to firm going. *J. Howard Johnson*   **99**

MOTU (IRE) 5 b.g. Desert Style (IRE) 121 – Pink Cashmere (IRE) (Polar Falcon (USA) 126) [2006 59§, a65§: p7.1g 7m 8.5d³ 7.5f 8m³ 8m⁶ 7f 7.5f⁵ 8.3f 7.5f⁴ 8f⁶ 7.2m* 7.1d³ 7m² 7.2g* 7.1m² 7.1m³ 7.5m Sep 19] good-topped gelding: fair handicapper: won at Ayr in July/August: stays 1m: acts on polytrack, firm and good to soft going: tried blinkered, visored nowadays: hung markedly left sixth outing. *I. W. McInnes*   **69**

MOUCHOIR 3 b.g. Bahamian Bounty 116 – Mouchez Le Nez (IRE) 41 (Cyrano de Bergerac 120) [2006 76: 5g⁵ 5m p7.1g 6m Aug 30] close-coupled gelding: just modest handicapper in 2006: may prove best at 5f: acts on firm and good to soft going: blinkered: sold 4,500 gns. *P. J. Makin*   **64**

MOUDEZ (IRE) 2 b.c. (Feb 5) Xaar 132 – Summer Dreams (IRE) 79 (Sadler's Wells (USA) 132) [2006 7d* 8s³ 8.5d Nov 25] 22,000F, €87,000J: second foal: dam, Irish maiden who stayed 1¾m, half-sister to Deutsches Derby winner All My Dreams: useful form: won maiden at Newmarket (beat Strobilus by 2 lengths) in August: 8 lengths third to Caldra in Autumn Stakes at Ascot next time, held up: left D. Simcock, well held in non-graded Laurel Futurity final outing: will stay at least 1¼m: raced on going softer than good. *W. I. Mott, USA*   **95**

MOUNTAIN CALL (IRE) 2 b.c. (May 14) Monashee Mountain (USA) 115 – Amazonian (CAN) (Geiger Counter (USA)) [2006 7m p8.6m Oct 31] sturdy, good-bodied colt: no show in maidens, in blinkers second start: sold £400 in December. *Mrs A. J. Perrett*   **–**

MOUNTAIN CAT (IRE) 2 b.g. (Apr 15) Red Ransom (USA) – Timewee (USA) (Romanov (IRE) 119) [2006 6d 6d Oct 27] stocky gelding: backward when mid-field in maidens at Windsor and Newmarket: gelded after. *W. J. Musson*   **53**

MOUNTAIN HIGH (IRE) 4 b.c. Danehill (USA) 126 – Hellenic 125 (Darshaan 133) [2006 107: 10m* 9.9s² 12m² 12m² Jul 13]   **124**

'Money doesn't talk, it swears . . .!' Mountain High's backers have had good reason to curse the phoney influence of money at times in the last two seasons, but the latest campaign at least demonstrated that the claims made about Mountain High's ability have been genuine for the most part. Favourite six times in seven

Stanscasino.co.uk Conditions Stakes, Newmarket—Mountain High makes a fine start to the season; Boule d'Or pips Blythe Knight (rail) for second

subsequent starts since finishing third in a division of the Wood Ditton Stakes at Newmarket on his debut, Mountain High has managed to justify the support only twice, though he showed very smart form in 2006 before his season was cut short in July.

Mountain High started favourite each time he ran as a four-year-old. He began back at Newmarket in May by justifying odds of 11/10 most impressively in a minor event on Two Thousand Guineas day, beating Boule d'Or eased down by five lengths. Mountain High seemed suited by the good to firm ground, so soft going looked a plausible reason for his failure to land the odds in a listed race at Goodwood the following month, though, in going down by three lengths to Blue Monday, he edged left under pressure. Mountain High ran very well back on firmish ground and stepped up to pattern company on his last two starts. Favourite for the second year running at Royal Ascot, he improved on his fourth in the King Edward VII Stakes when beaten only a head by his high-class stable-companion Maraahel in a field of eight for the Hardwicke Stakes. Mountain High saw the trip out well under the conditions racing at a mile and a half for the first time in twelve months, showing no lack of tenacity as he battled back inside the last furlong after leading briefly over a furlong out. Mountain High again showed no shortage of resolution when beaten—at odds on—in the Princess of Wales's Stakes at Newmarket on his final outing, going down only by three quarters of a length to the three-year-old Soapy Danger, with Hardwicke third Enforcer again a place behind him, the same distance further away.

			Danzig (b 1977)	Northern Dancer
	Danehill (USA)			Pas de Nom
	(b 1986)	Razyana (b 1981)	His Majesty
Mountain High (IRE)				Spring Adieu
(b.c. 2002)		Darshaan (br 1981)	Shirley Heights
	Hellenic			Delsy
	(b 1987)	Grecian Sea (ch 1978)	Homeric
			Sea Venture

Mountain High is not the only member of his family on whom backers have had their fingers burned. His half-brother Greek Well (by Sadler's Wells) was as low as 7/1 for the Derby in January only to meet with a setback; he was sent off at 10/1 on the first of three runs in maidens when eventually making his debut at Windsor in June. Other matings between Sadler's Wells and Hellenic have been much more productive. They have included the very smart pair Islington, twice winner of the Yorkshire Oaks as well as being successful in the Breeders' Cup Filly & Mare Turf as a four-year-old, and Greek Dance, a Group 1 winner at a mile and a

697

quarter in the Grosser Dallmayr-Preis as a five-year-old when he was also runner-up in the Irish Champion Stakes. As well as the Brigadier Gerard Stakes winner New Morning and Gold Cup third Election Day, Sadler's Wells is also responsible for Hellenic's latest produce of racing age, Praxiteles, unraced as a two-year-old for Sir Michael Stoute in 2006. Hellenic, who also won the Yorkshire Oaks as well as finishing second in the St Leger, raced only on good and good to soft going, whereas Mountain High has shown his best form on good to firm ground, though it was good to soft when he won a maiden as a three-year-old. A good-topped, attractive colt, he tends to take the eye in appearance, though he was sweating in the paddock on his final outing when he also swished his tail on the way to post. Mountain High is effective at a mile and a quarter and a mile and a half. *Sir Michael Stoute*

MOUNTAIN (IRE) 3 b.g. Montjeu (IRE) 137 – Skidmore Girl (USA) (Vaguely Noble 140) [2006 91p: 10m⁴ 10d² 12m 12g⁶ 12m 13.9g 10s* 12s² Oct 21] €30,000Y: big, good-topped gelding: half-brother to 3 winners in Italy: dam, maiden in USA, out of high-class sprinter/miler Sanedtki: smart performer: landed odds in listed race at Fairyhouse (beat Cool Touch 1¾ lengths) in September: creditable efforts in better company in Derrinstown Stud Derby Trial at Leopardstown (1½ lengths second to stable-companion Dylan Thomas), Derby at Epsom (eighth to Sir Percy, not ideally suited by track), Irish Derby at the Curragh (sixth to Dylan Thomas), Grand Prix de Paris at Longchamp (seventh to Rail Link), St Leger at York (seventh to Sixties Icon) and St Simon Stakes at Newbury (2 lengths second to Short Skirt): probably stays 1¾m: acts on soft and good to firm going: consistent: gelded, and joined J. O'Neill. *A. P. O'Brien, Ireland* **114**

MOUNTAIN PASS (USA) 4 b.g. Stravinsky (USA) 133 – Ribbony (USA) (Dayjur (USA) 137) [2006 75: p5g* p5.1g 5g 5m 6g p6g⁴ p6g⁶ p6g⁵ p7.1g⁴ 5.2f⁴ 6f⁴ 6g 7m* 7m* 7d³ p7g p6g⁴ p7g² f8g⁵ p7.1g³ p7g p6g⁵ Dec 30] fair performer: trained by C. O'Brien in Ireland at 3 yrs: won maiden at Lingfield in February, seller at Brighton in August and handicap at Yarmouth in September: claimed from M. Wallace after twentieth start: effective at 5f to 1m: acts on polytrack, firm and soft going: usually wears headgear: tried tongue tied. *S. Dow* **65 a74 d**

MOUNT BENGER 6 ch.g. Selkirk (USA) 129 – Vice Vixen (CAN) (Vice Regent (CAN)) [2006 –: p16.5g Mar 15] tall gelding: lightly raced and well beaten on Flat since 2004: often wears visor/cheekpieces nowadays. *Mrs A. J. Hamilton-Fairley* **–**

MOUNT GEORGE (IRE) 8 b. or br.g. Greensmith 121 – Baylands Sunshine (IRE) (Classic Secret (USA) 91) [2006 11.9f Aug 9] poor handicapper: won 3 races when trained in Ireland by N. Meade: refused to race on British Flat debut (has also refused to race over hurdles): stays 13f: acts on firm going: wears cheekpieces/tongue tie, tried in blinkers. *Evan Williams* **– §**

MOUNT HADLEY (USA) 2 b.c. (May 6) Elusive Quality (USA) – Fly To The Moon (USA) 90 (Blushing Groom (FR) 131) [2006 7d 7d* Oct 10] tall, good-topped colt: half-brother to 3 winners, including useful 1996 2-y-o 5f winner Moonshine Girl (by Shadeed) and fairly useful UAE 5f to 1m winner Tala Ya (by Storm Bird): dam, 1m winner (later successful in USA), sister to smart 1987 2-y-o sprinter Digamist: better for debut, won maiden at Leicester by 1¼ lengths (value more) from Cabinet: will stay 1m: joined I. Mohammed in UAE. *E. A. L. Dunlop* **92**

MOUNT HERMON (IRE) 2 b.c. (Feb 29) Golan (IRE) 129 – Machudi (Bluebird (USA) 125) [2006 7g³ 7f² 6d Sep 29] 28,000Y: big, strong, heavy-bodied colt: third foal: half-brother to 2004 2-y-o 5f winner Rightprice Premier (by Cape Cross): dam, maiden, stayed 7f: fair form: shaped well when placed in maidens at Salisbury and Lingfield (second to Farleigh House): not knocked about once held in big-field sales race at Newmarket: stays 7f: sort to thrive and win races at 3 yrs. *H. Morrison* **79 p**

MOUNT KILIMANJARO (IRE) 3 b.c. Sadler's Wells (USA) 132 – Hill of Snow 80 (Reference Point 139) [2006 11g⁶ 12.1s* 16m Jun 23] strong, lengthy colt: sixth foal: brother to smart Derby Trial winner Kong and half-brother to 3 winners, including Irish 7f (Moyglare Stud Stakes)/1m winner (stayed 1¼m) Preseli (by Caerleon) and 1000 Guineas second Snowfire (by Machiavellian), 7f winner at 2 yrs, both smart: dam Irish 1¼m winner: useful form: won maiden at Chepstow (by 7 lengths) in May: further improvement when 5¾ lengths eighth to Soapy Danger in Queen's Vase at Royal Ascot final start: probably stays 2m: acts on soft and good to firm ground: whinnied in preliminaries on debut: open to further progress. *J. L. Dunlop* **96 p**

MOUNT NELSON 2 b.c. (Apr 7) Rock of Gibraltar (IRE) 133 – Independence **114 p**
116 (Selkirk (USA) 129) [2006 7s² 7v* 8g* Oct 29]

The betting on the sixth Criterium International suggested strongly that it would go the way of its first five runnings and be won by a home-trained runner, by one in particular. The hot favourite Spirit One was considered the top two-year-old in France following a runaway victory in the Prix des Chenes, a race which the four previous winners of the International had taken on the way to Saint-Cloud. Sent off at odds on to maintain the trend, Spirit One was beaten by Mount Nelson, one of two Aidan O'Brien representatives, the other Yellowstone, who added further gloss to the result for Ballydoyle by taking third.

Mount Nelson and Yellowstone were two of the least experienced in the first double-figure field for the Criterium International, one in which French-trained runners were outnumbered, with a challenger from Germany and three from Britain also in the line-up. Both Mount Nelson and Yellowstone had run twice and won a maiden, Mount Nelson on his second start just a week before the Criterium. That was on heavy ground at the Curragh, Mount Nelson already looking a colt well out of the ordinary in trouncing his twenty-eight rivals, six lengths his winning margin after taking up the running well over two furlongs out. With Kieren Fallon in Australia to ride Yeats in the Melbourne Cup, Seamus Heffernan was on board Mount Nelson once again at Saint-Cloud, where he adopted more patient tactics than at the Curragh as Spirit One set a good pace. The runners fanned out after rounding the home turn, Mount Nelson coming under pressure soon after but responding to take a narrow advantage inside the final furlong and hold on by a head as Spirit One rallied. Yellowstone, who came from further back than his stablemate, was a length and a half behind the pair. The winner's time was slightly quicker than that recorded by the three-year-old Passager, who was carrying 3 lb less, when winning the Group 3 Prix Perth on the same card. 'He's a lovely horse who will be even better next year, when he should stay further,' is what O'Brien had to say about Mount Nelson immediately after the race, going on to mention that he had the Two Thousand Guineas or, probably more likely, the Poule d'Essai des Poulains in mind for the colt. Mount Nelson is certainly open to more improvement, enough, probably, to make him a credible contender for whichever of the afore-mentioned races he is eventually aimed at. How much further he will stay is less clear-cut.

		Rock of Gibraltar (IRE) (b 1999)	Danehill (b 1986)	Danzig
Mount Nelson (b.c. Apr 7, 2004)				Razyana
			Offshore Boom (ch 1985)	Be My Guest
				Push A Button
		Independence (b 1998)	Selkirk (ch 1988)	Sharpen Up
				Annie Edge
			Yukon Hope (b 1993)	Forty Niner
				Sahara Forest

A quick look at Mount Nelson's pedigree gives little encouragement for thinking that he will stay much beyond a mile. He is by a miler out of a mare,

Criterium International, Saint-Cloud—in a driving finish,
Mount Nelson holds the rallying Spirit One (noseband); Yellowstone (No.8) finishes strongly for third

Independence, who was raced only at seven furlongs and a mile. There is stamina in Independence's family, though, with her grandam Sahara Forest an unraced half-sister to Reference Point, and it would not be a surprise if Mount Nelson were to prove effective over as far as a mile and a quarter. Independence, following a couple of runs at two, progressed very well at three and won four races, showing smart form when successful in the Matron Stakes at the Curragh and the Sun Chariot Stakes at Newmarket on her last two starts. Mount Nelson, a 320,000-guinea year-ling, is Independence's second foal. Her first, the three-year-old filly Off Message (by In The Wings), showed fairly useful form in the latest season, putting up her best performance when winning over nine and a half furlongs on her debut. Incidentally, Rock of Gibraltar, whose first crop also includes Yellowstone and O'Brien's Beresford Stakes winner Eagle Mountain, has been leased to Japan for the next covering season. *A. P. O'Brien, Ireland*

MOUNT PARNASSUS 2 b. or br.c. (Feb 12) Rock of Gibraltar (IRE) 133 – Qui Liz **86** (USA) (Benny The Dip (USA) 127) [2006 7g 7d⁶ 7d Oct 14] 110,000Y: close-coupled, quite good-topped colt: first foal: dam unraced half-sister to William Hill Futurity winner Bakharoff and smart miler Emperor Jones: fairly useful form: mid-field in maidens at the Curragh and Newmarket: helped force pace in Dewhurst Stakes final start. *A. P. O'Brien, Ireland*

MOUNT ROYALE (IRE) 8 ch.g. Wolfhound (USA) 126 – Mahabba (USA) 74 (Elo- **–** cutionist (USA)) [2006 47, a64: f7g f7g³ f7g² f7g⁴ f7g² f7g* p7.1g² f7g³ f6g³ p7.1g⁶ **a60** a6g⁵ a5g² a6.5g* f7g⁶ 6g 5s⁴ Nov 12] close-coupled gelding: has knee action: modest on all-weather, poor on turf: won banded race at Southwell in March and (having left N. Tinkler after tenth outing) minor event at Mijas in August: best at 6f/7f: acts on all-weather/sand, firm and soft going: tried blinkered, usually visored: has been tongue tied: has found little. *J. L. Eyre, Spain*

MOUNT SINAI 3 b.g. Green Desert (USA) 127 – Apache Song (USA) (Dynaformer **70 d** (USA)) [2006 p8g 8d 8m⁶ 8g p7g 6g 6m⁵ p6g Sep 27] second living foal: closely related to French 1¼m to 11.5f winner Apache Legend (by Perugino): dam French 9f winner: fair maiden: didn't progress after debut: bred to be best at 1m: acts on polytrack. *W. J. Knight*

MOUNT USHER 4 br.g. Polar Falcon (USA) 126 – Division Bell (Warning 136) [2006 **80** 63: 7.5f* 8m⁵ 7g⁶ 9.9f⁴ 10.1m* 9.9f² 9.8d⁵ 9.9g⁴ p12.2f⁶ Aug 30] lengthy gelding: fairly useful handicapper: won at Beverley in April and Newcastle in June: effective at 7.5f to 1½m: acts on polytrack, firm and good to soft ground. *G. A. Swinbank*

MO (USA) 2 br.c. (Jan 23) Cherokee Run (USA) 122 – Mambo Mate (USA) (King- **75** mambo (USA) 125) [2006 6g⁶ 7d⁴ 7s 5.1g⁴ p7g³ p6g² p5.1g⁵ Dec 22] 46,000 2-y-o: rather leggy, close-coupled colt: second foal: dam, lightly-raced US maiden, half-sister to US Grade 1 1½m winner Fairy Garden: fair maiden: in frame 4 starts: stays 7f: acts on polytrack and good to soft going: tongue tied: has looked awkward. *R. A. Kvisla*

MOUSEEN (IRE) 3 ch.g. Alhaarth (IRE) 126 – Marah 93 (Machiavellian (USA) 123) **65** [2006 81: 7d 6v 6m 8g 7m 7.5m* 8m f7g⁶ p8.6g Dec 21] just fair handicapper at 3 yrs, best effort when winning at Tipperary in August: left P. Henley in Ireland after next start: stays 7.5f: acts on soft and good to firm going, probably on fibresand: in cheekpieces in Britain. *R. A. Harris*

MOVE ON (IRE) 3 b.f. Night Shift (USA) – Beaufort Lady (IRE) 74 (Alhaarth (IRE) **–** 126) [2006 –: 10d 9.8m 9m 8d Aug 28] little form: tried tongue tied. *B. Ellison*

MOVES GOODENOUGH 3 ch.g. Woodborough (USA) 112 – Rekindled Flame **73** (IRE) (Kings Lake (USA) 133) [2006 7m³ 8g⁴ 8.1d 10.2m³ p9.5g³ p8g Nov 22] compact gelding: half-brother to 3 winners, including 10-y-o Goodenough Mover: dam unraced: fair maiden: stays 9.5f: acts on polytrack and good to firm ground. *Andrew Turnell*

MOVETHEGOALPOSTS 2 ch.c. (Mar 27) Dr Fong (USA) 128 – Rohita (IRE) 94 **74 d** (Waajib 121) [2006 6f 6.1g 6g* 6m³ 6s 6d p6g Nov 1] 30,000Y: good-bodied colt: brother to useful 6f/7f winner (including at 2 yrs) Mahmoom and half-brother to 2 winners, including 5f (at 2 yrs) and 7f winner Kalindi (by Efisio): dam, 2-y-o 5f/6f winner, bred to stay 1m: fair performer: won maiden at Hamilton in July: well below form after (signs of temperament, twice blinkered): raced at 6f: sold 2,800 gns. *M. Johnston*

MOVIE KING (IRE) 7 ch.g. Catrail (USA) 123 – Marilyn (IRE) 72 (Kings Lake **–** (USA) 133) [2006 –, a65: f8g Jan 1] workmanlike gelding: fair performer in 2005: reportedly suffered breathing problem when well held only outing in 2006: tried visored/in cheekpieces, tongue tied last 4 starts: races up with pace. *S. R. Bowring*

MOVING STORY 3 b.g. Desert Story (IRE) 115 – Arianna Aldini (Habitat 134) [2006 10.1d 9.8m p8.6g Jun 26] strong gelding: well held in maidens at Newcastle (slowly away), Ripon and Wolverhampton. *T. J. Fitzgerald*   –

MOVING TARGET (IRE) 7 ch.g. Karaar 74 – Lucky Noire 73 (Aragon 118) [2006 7f Sep 5] 33/1, well held in maiden at Lingfield (reportedly had a breathing problem) on debut. *Luke Comer, Ireland*   –

MOWAZANA (IRE) 3 ch.f. Galileo (IRE) 134 – Taqreem (IRE) 73 (Nashwan (USA) 135) [2006 10m³ 10.2m² 10.2g* Oct 17] seventh foal: closely related to 1¼m winner Haadef (by Sadler's Wells) and half-sister to 7f winner (stayed 1¼m) Ma-Arif (by Alzao) and 2004 2-y-o 6f winner Shohrah (by Giant's Causeway), all useful: dam, middle-distance maiden, half-sister to Ibn Bey and Roseate Tern: fair form: similar efforts in maidens, winning at Bath in October by 4 lengths from Wonderful One: should stay 1½m: raced only on good/good to firm going. *M. P. Tregoning*   **74**

MOYNE PLEASURE (IRE) 8 b.g. Exit To Nowhere (USA) 122 – Ilanga (IRE) 92 (Common Grounds 118) [2006 –: f16g Dec 12] small, sparely-made gelding: no form in 2 runs on Flat since 2004, but modest winning hurdler in 2006: used to wear cheekpieces: sometimes looks none too keen (refused to race once). *R. Johnson*   –

MOYOKO (IRE) 3 b.f. Mozart (IRE) 131 – Kayoko (IRE) 74 (Shalford (IRE) 124§) [2006 52: 8m⁶ p10g 7g² 7g⁴ 8g² 9.5g³ p8g* p9.5g⁶ Dec 21] close-coupled filly: modest handicapper: won at Kempton in December: stays 9.5f: acts on polytrack, probably on firm ground. *M. Blanshard*   **64**

MOZAKHRAF (USA) 4 b.g. Miswaki (USA) 124 – Anakid (USA) (Danzig (USA)) [2006 73: p7.1g 5f⁴ 6.1m 6m 5.9m⁴ 6m 8m⁴ p7.1g³ p7.1m³ f7g² f7g* p7g Dec 10] good-topped gelding: fair performer: won handicap at Southwell in December: best form at 7f: acts on all-weather and firm going: wore cheekpieces (ran respectably) fifth start: has found little. *K. A. Ryan*   **73**

MOZAYADA (USA) 2 ch.f. (Apr 25) Street Cry (IRE) 130 – Fatina 98 (Nashwan (USA) 135) [2006 7f 7g⁵ 7.5m⁴ Sep 13] big, strong filly: fourth foal: half-sister to 3 winners, including 3-y-o Idarah and fairly useful 1½m winner Elraawy (by Red Ransom): dam, 2-y-o 1m winner, sister to smart performer up to 2½m Shaya: modest form in maidens: bred to stay 1m+, but shows plenty of speed. *M. Johnston*   **60**

MOZIE CAT (IRE) 3 b.f. Mozart (IRE) 131 – Golden Cat (USA) 102 (Storm Cat (USA)) [2006 7g 8m 6g⁴ p8.6g* p8.6g Dec 22] 10,000F: good-topped filly: fourth foal: closely related to useful 2003 2-y-o 5f winner Celtic Cat (by Danehill), later successful in Hong Kong: dam Irish 1m winner (stayed 1¼m) out of Irish St Leger winner Eurobird: fair performer: left D. Daly after second start: off 4 months, easily best effort when winning handicap at Wolverhampton (still looked green) in December: stays 8.6f: acts on polytrack: gave trouble (reared and unseated rider) before final outing. *John Berry*   **72**

MR AITCH (IRE) 4 b.g. Soviet Star (USA) 128 – Welsh Mist 102 (Damister (USA) 123) [2006 78: 12.3d 10.5g 10.3g⁴ 11.8m* 10.5m⁵ 12.3m* 11.9m³ 12d Aug 28] big, good-topped gelding: fairly useful handicapper: improved in 2006, winning at Leicester in June and Chester in August: stays 1½m: acts on polytrack and firm going (seemingly not on good to soft): tongue tied last 3 starts. *R. T. Phillips*   **83**

MR AVIATOR (USA) 2 b. or br.c. (Mar 10) Lear Fan (USA) 130 – In Bloom (USA) (Clever Trick (USA)) [2006 p7g p8g* Dec 10] 75,000 2-y-o: seventh foal: half-brother to winners in USA by Wavering Monarch and Ascot Knight: dam US maiden: heavily backed, much better effort in maidens at Kempton (fairly useful form) when winning 9-runner event in good style by 2 lengths from Risque Heights, soon disputing and asserting under hands and heels from 2f out: likely to stay 1¼m: should continue to progress. *R. Hannon*   **80 p**

MR BELVEDERE 5 b.g. Royal Applause 124 – Alarming Motown (Warning 136) [2006 41§, a54§: p8.6g³ p8g³ p8g* 10.2g p8g⁶ May 23] sturdy gelding: modest performer: won banded race at Lingfield in February: stays easy 1½m: acts on polytrack, firm and good to soft ground: tried in headgear: has hung left: unreliable. *A. J. Lidderdale*   **– §**
a56 §

MR BILBO BAGGINS 3 ch.g. Magic Ring (IRE) 115 – I'll Try 71 (Try My Best (USA) 130) [2006 –: 10g 9.9g 16.1g Sep 27] no form. *J. S. Moore*   –

MR CELLOPHANE 3 ch.g. Pursuit of Love 124 – Fresh Fruit Daily 92 (Reprimand 122) [2006 57: 6g⁶ 6m⁶ 7m³ 7d² 6f² 6m² 7d⁴ 6m² 6m* 7f² 6d³ p6g² p5.1g* p5.1m³ Nov 21] tall, lengthy gelding: fairly useful performer: won maiden at Yarmouth in September and handicap at Wolverhampton in November: effective at 5f to 7f: acts on polytrack, firm and good to soft going. *J. R. Jenkins*   **85**

MR CHAD 3 b.c. Mujahid (USA) 125 – Robanna 60 (Robellino (USA) 127) [2006 p8g³ Jul 19] second foal: half-brother to 4-y-o Aastral Magic: dam, maiden who stayed 1¾m, half-sister to Jersey Stakes winner Lots of Magic: 10/1, length third to McNairobi in maiden at Lingfield, soon pushed along in wide position but keeping on well: sold only 1,000 gns in October. *E. J. O'Neill*   **82**

MR CHEERS 3 b.g. Bertolini (USA) 125 – Plie 75 (Superlative 118) [2006 59d: p6g f8g⁶ p7.1g* p7g* p7g⁶ f7g p8g 8.2d 8m p6g Nov 20] smallish, close-coupled gelding: modest performer: won claimers at Wolverhampton (claimed from Miss J. Camacho) in February and Lingfield (for C. Dwyer, awarded race after finishing second to African Concerto) in March: trained next 5 starts by R. Harris: stays 7f: acts on polytrack and soft going: blinkered/in cheekpieces at 3 yrs. *C. A. Dwyer*   **–/a63**

MR CHOCOLATE DROP (IRE) 2 b.g. (Feb 15) Danetime (IRE) 121 – Forest Blade (IRE) (Charnwood Forest (IRE) 125) [2006 p7.1g 7.1m f8g f8g⁵ Dec 21] well beaten in maidens. *M. J. Attwater*   **–**

MR CRYSTAL (FR) 2 ch.c. (May 5) Trempolino (USA) 135 – Iyrbila (FR) (Lashkari 128) [2006 p8.6g f7g Dec 14] well held in maidens. *M. D. Hammond*   **–**

MR DIP 6 b.g. Reprimand 122 – Scottish Lady (Dunbeath (USA) 127) [2006 54d: p16g Jun 29] leggy gelding: poor performer: stays 1¾m: acts on polytrack, soft and good to firm ground: sometimes slowly away/finds little. *L. A. Dace*   **–**

MR ED (IRE) 8 ch.g. In The Wings 128 – Center Moriches (IRE) 74 (Magical Wonder (USA) 125) [2006 92: 16.2d 12d 18d Oct 14] tall, angular gelding: fairly useful handi-capper at best: no form in 2006: tried blinkered, wears cheekpieces nowadays: sometimes slowly away/wanders: held up. *P. Bowen*   **–**

MR EXCEL (IRE) 3 b.g. Orpen (USA) 116 – Collected (IRE) (Taufan (USA) 119) [2006 71: f12g* p16g³ Nov 29] good-topped gelding: fairly useful handicapper, lightly raced: won at Southwell in November: creditable third at Kempton next time: barely stays easy 2m: acts on all-weather. *J. A. Osborne*   **86**

MR FAST (ARG) 9 ch.g. Numerous (USA) – Speediness (ARG) (Etienne Gerard 118) [2006 f14g Mar 1] Argentinian-bred gelding: winner in native country (last ran there in 2002), including when dead-heating in Grade 2 9f event: since successful in Spain, including in minor event at Mijas and handicap at Dos Hermanas in 2005: well held in handicap at Southwell on British debut: stays 1¾m: acts on sand: sold £900 in June. *J. Gallagher*   **–**

MR FLOODLIGHT (IRE) 3 b.g. Bertolini (USA) 125 – French River (Bering 136) [2006 78: p8g* p7g⁴ Jan 14] good-topped gelding: fairly useful performer: won handicap at Lingfield in January: stays easy 1m: acts on polytrack, good to firm and good to soft going: sent to Hong Kong. *R. Hannon*   **83**

MR FORTHRIGHT 2 b.c. (Apr 4) Fraam 114 – Form At Last (Formidable (USA) 125) [2006 6m 5.1f⁶ 6d⁶ 8.1d Oct 13] big, lengthy colt: modest maiden: should stay 7f/1m. *J. M. Bradley*   **55**

MR GARSTON 3 b.g. Mull of Kintyre (USA) 114 – Ninfa of Cisterna (Polish Patriot (USA) 128) [2006 82p: p6g⁵ Nov 1] fairly useful form: off 15 months and having only second outing, encouraging return when fifth to Saviours Spirit in handicap at Kempton: likely to prove best at 5f/6f: raced only on good to firm going and polytrack. *M. P. Tregoning*   **92**

MR JACK DANIELLS (IRE) 5 b.g. Mujadil (USA) 119 – Neat Shilling (IRE) (Bob Back (USA) 124) [2006 97: 12m 8m 10m 10g 10d⁶ p12.2s Dec 13] big gelding: fairly useful handicapper: respectable efforts at best in 2006, including at Wolverhampton: stays 1½m: acts on polytrack, soft and good to firm ground: tried blinkered. *Anthony Mullins, Ireland*   **92**

MR JAWBREAKER (IRE) 7 b.g. Sadler's Wells (USA) 132 – Abury (IRE) 104 (Law Society (USA) 130) [2006 p12.2g p12.2g Feb 6] fair form in bumpers but has looked temperamental over hurdles: seemingly modest form on Flat debut: tailed off only other start. *J. T. Stimpson*   **59**

MR KAYOS 4 b.g. Kayf Tara 130 – Highland Heights (IRE) (Lomond (USA) 128) –
[2006 –: f14g p13.9g⁴ Nov 16] little sign of ability. *Mrs G. S. Rees*

MR KLICK (IRE) 2 b.g. (Mar 6) Tendulkar (USA) 114 – Lake Poopo (IRE) 79 79
(Persian Heights 129) [2006 5g 5d⁶ 5f* 5d³ 6g 5f⁵ 5g³ 5m⁶ 5d⁵ 5m⁴ 6s Oct 6] €40,000F,
9,000Y: tall gelding: sixth foal: half-brother to winners abroad by Be My Guest and
Up And At 'em: dam 13f/15f winner: fair performer: won claimer at Beverley (left
M. Wallace £8,000) in April: ran well several times after, including fifth to Numerieus in
listed race at Deauville ninth start, but below form last 2 (having been gelded): best efforts
at 5f: acts on firm and good to soft going: not straightforward. *N. Wilson*

MR LAMBROS 5 ch.g. Pivotal 124 – Magical Veil 73 (Majestic Light (USA)) [2006 –
89, a95: p7.1g p7g* p7g² p7g* 7m 7d p7g p7g⁵ Nov 18] good-topped gelding: useful a105
performer on all-weather: much improved in 2006, winning handicap in February (by 4
lengths from Spring Goddess) and minor event in April (by 6 lengths from Chief Exec),
both at Lingfield: well beaten both outings on turf at 5 yrs: effective at 6f/7f: acts on polytrack and firm ground: races prominently. *A. M. Balding*

MR LOIRE 2 b.g. (Apr 26) Bertolini (USA) 125 – Miss Sancerre 95 (Last Tycoon 131) 75
[2006 5.1f³ 5.7m² p5.1g³ 7d p6g* p6g³ p6s³ Dec 15] 22,000Y: sixth foal: half-brother to
3 winners, including 2004 2-y-o 7f winner Miss L'Augeval (later successful at 1m in
USA) and 1m winner Mr Mistral (both fairly useful and by Zilzal): dam 2-y-o 7f winner:
fair form: won maiden at Kempton in November: third in nurseries at Wolverhampton:
should stay 7f: acts on polytrack and firm going. *R. Charlton*

MR MAJESTIC 4 b.g. Vettori (IRE) 119 – Alacrity 62 (Alzao (USA) 117) [2006 68: 71
11g⁴ 12.4g⁵ 14.1g⁵ 16m* 16f² 14.1f⁵ 18f Jul 29] big, workmanlike gelding: fair handicapper: won at Ripon in June: stays 2m: acts on firm going, well held both outings on
softer than good: tried in cheekpieces. *R. M. Whitaker*

MR MARUCCI (USA) 4 b.g. Miner's Mark (USA) 120 – Appealing Style (USA) 46
(Valid Appeal (USA)) [2006 –: p8.6g p8.6g p8.6g 7g May 1] tall, leggy gelding: poor
maiden: stays 8.6f: blinkered last 3 outings. *B. Ellison*

MR MAXIM 4 ch.g. Lake Coniston (IRE) 131 – White Hare 56 (Indian Ridge 123) 59
[2006 65: 13f⁵ 13.9m⁶ 12.1f³ 12m⁵ 16.2g² Aug 17] workmanlike gelding: modest maiden
on balance: stays 2m: acts on firm going: visored last 3 starts. *R. M. Whitaker*

MR MINI SCULE 2 b.g. (Mar 17) Piccolo 121 – Courtisane (Persepolis (FR) 127) 56
[2006 5.1d p5.1g⁵ 5.2g⁵ 5m⁵ 7f³ 7m 6m³ 5.3m⁴ p5.1g p6m Nov 8] modest maiden:
made frame only in sellers: stays 7f: acts on polytrack and firm going: tried in blinkers.
A. B. Haynes

MR NAPPER TANDY 2 ch.c. (Mar 19) Bahamian Bounty 116 – Starfleet 66 (Inch- 84 p
inor 119) [2006 7s² 7d* Oct 28] 22,000F, 60,000Y: useful-looking colt: second foal:
half-brother to 3-y-o Wind Star: dam, maiden who may have proved best around 1m,
half-sister to useful performers Pool Music (stayed 8.5f) and Russian Music (stayed
1¼m): fairly useful form: gained compensation for unlucky debut at Newbury (baulked
and beaten head by Hollow Ridge) when winning 19-runner maiden at Newmarket by
½ length from Walking Talking, making most: likely to stay 1m: capable of better.
M. R. Channon

MR REIN (IRE) 4 b.g. Indian Danehill (IRE) 124 – Lady's Vision (IRE) 93 (Vision –
(USA)) [2006 64: f14g p9.5g Mar 15] modest maiden: gelded, well beaten in 2006
(tongue tied last time). *J. Parkes*

MR RIGSBY 3 gr.g. Forzando 122 – Rain Splash 74 (Petong 126) [2006 70: p6g 69
p6g³ p7.1g² p7.1g⁴ p7g p6g p8.6g p7.1g a8g* a8g* Nov 5] fair performer: sold from
P. Howling 2,500 gns after eighth start: won minor events at Gran Canaria in October/
November: stays 1m: raced only on polytrack/sand: none too consistent in Britain.
B. Rama, Spain

MR ROONEY (IRE) 3 b.c. Mujadil (USA) 119 – Desert Bride (USA) (Key To The 78
Kingdom (USA)) [2006 84: 6m⁶ 6m p8g 7.1d⁵ 6s Aug 28] strong colt: fairly useful performer at 2 yrs: below form after reappearance: best at 5f/6f: acts on firm and soft going:
often leads: sold 3,500 gns. *M. Johnston*

MR SANDICLIFFE 3 b.c. Mujahid (USA) 125 – Crinkle (IRE) (Distant Relative 128) 93 §
[2006 95: 6g² 6.1m* 7s⁶ 6m* 6m 6m 7m Jul 29] big colt: fairly useful performer: won
maiden at Nottingham in May and handicap at Ripon in June: left B. Hills 47,000 gns

after sixth start: stays 6f: acts on good to firm ground: often wears cheekpieces, blinkered final start: often looks none too keen: sent to USA. *C. N. Allen*

MRS CROSSY (IRE) 2 b.f. (Mar 14) Alhaarth (IRE) 126 – God Speed (IRE) 74 (Be My Guest (USA) 126) [2006 p5g⁵ 5g 5.3m⁴ p5g* p5.1g⁵ p5g* 6f² p7g 6m⁵ 6.1m⁴ 5g 5.5m p5g p5.1g p5.1g Nov 16] €15,000Y: leggy filly: sixth foal: half-sister to fairly useful Irish 2000 2-y-o 6f winner Ceann Amhain Eile (by Lake Coniston): dam, Irish 6f winner, half-sister to smart Irish 5f to 7f performer Social Harmony: modest performer at best: won claimer at Kempton in May and seller at Lingfield in June: claimed from R. Hannon £6,000 seventh start: below form after: effective at 5f/6f, on polytrack and firm going. *A. W. Carroll* — **59 d**

MRS MOONEY (IRE) 3 b.f. Vettori (IRE) 119 – Mrs Moonlight (Ajdal (USA) 130) [2006 –: 10s p13.9g Nov 20] closely related to winner in Japan by Machiavellian and half-sister to smart 7f (at 2 yrs)/1m winner Soviet Flash (by Warning) and 4-y-o Play Me: dam unraced half-sister to Jupiter Island and Precocious: no form: left C. Collins in Ireland after first start at 3 yrs. *E. J. O'Neill* — **–**

MRS PHILIP 7 b.m. Puissance 110 – Lightning Legacy (USA) 78 (Super Concorde (USA) 128) [2006 –: 12.1f Jul 28] winning hurdler: lightly-raced maiden on Flat. *P. J. Hobbs* — **–**

MR SPLIFFY (IRE) 7 b.g. Fayruz 116 – Johns Conquerer (IRE) 74 (Conquering Hero (USA) 116) [2006 54§: f6g f6g f5g⁴ f5g Apr 4] close-coupled gelding: unimpressive mover: poor performer: best at 5f: acts on all-weather, firm and good to soft going: often wears headgear: has bolted/been early to post: usually races prominently: irresolute. *M. C. Chapman* — **48 §**

MRS QUINCE 4 b.f. Mark of Esteem (IRE) 137 – T G'S Girl 57 (Selkirk (USA) 129) [2006 7m⁴ 7m 7m⁴ Sep 16] £10,000Y, 500 2-y-o: workmanlike filly: first foal: dam maiden who should have stayed 7f: poor form in maidens. *F. Watson* — **46**

MRS SOLESE (IRE) 3 b.f. Imperial Ballet (IRE) 110 – Sugar (Hernando (FR) 127) [2006 p8g 10d p10g⁵ 10.2m⁵ Oct 8] €7,000Y: leggy, close-coupled filly: second foal: dam unraced daughter of smart performer up to 10.5f Ahohoney: modest maiden: stays 1¼m: acts on polytrack and good to soft ground: very slowly away on debut. *J. R. Boyle* — **63**

MR STROWGER 5 b.g. Dancing Spree (USA) – Matoaka 72 (Be My Chief (USA) 122) [2006 44: p10g f11g⁵ p12.2f⁵ Aug 14] poor performer: left J. Fox and gelded after second start: stays easy 13f: acts on all-weather, raced only on good ground or softer on turf: wore cheekpieces final start. *S. Curran* — **44**

MR VELOCITY (IRE) 6 b.g. Tagula (IRE) 116 – Miss Rusty (IRE) (Mukaddamah (USA) 125) [2006 80: p8g Apr 8] compact, quite attractive gelding: fairly useful handicapper at best: well beaten only start in 2006. *E. F. Vaughan* — **–**

MR WALL STREET 2 b.g. (Mar 17) Efisio 120 – La Suquet 72 (Puissance 110) [2006 5d 6f³ p7.1g 6s p9.5m p6g Nov 14] good-topped gelding: modest maiden: below form after second start: stays 6f: tried in cheekpieces/blinkers: hard ride. *Mrs L. Williamson* — **58 d**

MR WHIZZ 9 ch.g. Manhal – Panienka (POL) 70 (Dom Racine (FR) 121) [2006 56, a40: f12g⁴ Jan 31] lengthy gelding: poor performer: stays 1¾m: acts on fibresand and any turf going: tried tongue tied: usually wears headgear. *A. P. Jones* — **–**

MR WISEGUY 3 b.c. Groom Dancer (USA) 128 – Tassagh Bridge (IRE) (Double Schwartz 128) [2006 8d 10m p10g⁴ p10g 10g 10.2m 12d p16g⁵ 15.8s⁶ p13.9g³ Nov 6] leggy, close-coupled colt: fourth foal: dam bad maiden: fair maiden handicapper: stays easy 2m: acts on polytrack and good to firm ground. *G. C. Bravery* — **65**

MR WOLF 5 b.g. Wolfhound (USA) 126 – Madam Millie 99 (Milford 119) [2006 97: 6g 6d 5f 6f* 6m 6f 5f* 6m* 6.1m 6s⁵ 5g⁶ 5g 5m⁶ p5g Oct 21] tall, leggy gelding: useful performer: improved in 2006, winning handicaps at Catterick in June and Pontefract (2, beating Carribbean Coral by 2 lengths in latter) in July: creditable sixth to Philharmonic in minor event at Beverley penultimate outing: best at 5f/6f: acts on firm and soft going (below form on all-weather debut final outing): usually wears cheekpieces: tends to hang left: races up with pace. *D. W. Barker* — **102**

MR WONG (IRE) 10 br.g. Be My Native (USA) 122 – Adare Boreen (Boreen (FR) 123) [2006 –: f12g² Apr 3] fairly useful performer for Mrs J. Harrington in Ireland: modest form at best in Britain: stayed 1½m: acted on fibresand and firm ground: wore cheekpieces final start in 2004: dead. *M. Sheppard* — **64**

MS POLLY GARTER 4 b.f. Petong 126 – Utopia (Primo Dominie 121) [2006 –: 6.1m –
5.7f 6m 5.1f Jul 27] little form since debut at 2 yrs: wore cheekpieces final start.
J. M. Bradley

MS RAINBOW RUNNER 3 b.f. Josr Algarhoud (IRE) 118 – Silk Law (IRE) 80 –
(Barathea (IRE) 127) [2006 64: p7g² p8g³ p8g⁶ p8g⁶ p8g⁵ p10g⁵ p7g⁶ p10g 10m 8m **a60**
Aug 19] smallish, strong filly: modest performer: stays 1¼m: acts on polytrack and (in
2005) good to firm ground: blinkered (raced freely) once at 2 yrs: has hung: pulled up
(reportedly lame) on hurdling debut. *P. Butler*

MS VICTORIA (IRE) 2 b.f. (Jan 26) Fasliyev (USA) 120 – Musical Refrain (IRE) **79**
(Dancing Dissident (USA) 119) [2006 5g⁵ 6g³ Aug 21] big, leggy filly: third foal: dam
unraced half-sister to very smart 6f/7f performer Monsieur Bond: fair form in maidens: fifth to Enticing at Salisbury and third behind Alovera and Blue Echo at Windsor.
B. J. Meehan

MT DESERT 4 b.g. Rainbow Quest (USA) 134 – Chief Bee 89 (Chief's Crown (USA)) **73 §**
[2006 80§: 15d May 13] strong, lengthy gelding: just fair form only Flat outing in 2006:
stays 13f: acts on good to soft going: visored/blinkered last 2 starts at 3 yrs: one to treat
with caution: won over hurdles in July: sold 10,000 gns in October. *C. J. Mann*

MTILLY 5 br.m. Mtoto 134 – Corn Lily 78 (Aragon 118) [2006 9.9g Aug 31] lengthy –
mare: very lightly-raced maiden. *K. G. Reveley*

MUARA 4 ch.f. Wolfhound (USA) 126 – Darussalam 78 (Tina's Pet 121) [2006 61: f5g **64**
f6g⁶ 5v⁴ 6m⁶ 5f 5f* 6f³ 5m 5g f6g⁶ f5g² p5g* p6g Dec 22] smallish, strong filly: modest
performer: won handicap at Beverley in June and banded race Kempton in November:
effective at 5f/6f: acts on all-weather and any turf going: often leads: reportedly finished
lame eighth start. *D. W. Barker*

MUBAASHIR (IRE) 2 ch.c. (Mar 25) Noverre (USA) 125 – Birdsong (IRE) 73 **97**
(Dolphin Street (FR) 125) [2006 p5g* 5.1m* 6m⁴ 6m 6m 6g p7g⁴ Oct 21] 60,000Y: rather
leggy, quite good-topped colt: impresses in appearance: fluent mover with a round action:
second foal: half-brother to fairly useful French 1m winner Filimeala (by Pennekamp):
dam, lightly-raced 6f winner, half-sister to dam of Luso, Needle Gun, Cloud Castle and
Warrsan: useful performer: won maiden at Kempton and minor event at Chester in May:
best form when seventh to Hellvelyn in Coventry Stakes at Royal Ascot and fourth to
Market Day in nursery at Lingfield fourth/final starts: stays 7f: acts on polytrack and good
to firm going. *E. A. L. Dunlop*

MUBTAKER (USA) 9 ch.h. Silver Hawk (USA) 123 – Gazayil (USA) 80 (Irish River **122**
(FR) 131) [2006 120: 12g* 13.4d⁵ 16.4s⁶ May 29] strong, lengthy horse: unimpressive
mover: had numerous training troubles, but was a top-class performer at his best, winning
13 races (7 of them pattern events, including 3 successive runnings of Geoffrey Freer
Stakes), also second in Prix de l'Arc de Triomphe in 2003: still very smart in later years,
and gained sixth success at Newbury when winning Dubai Tennis Championships Stakes
(John Porter) there in April, beating Munsef by a neck: eased as if amiss in Ormonde
Stakes at Chester next time, and seemed not to stay in Henry II Stakes at Sandown final
outing: was effective at 1¼m to 1¾m: acted on any going: was genuine: put down in late-
June after reportedly sustaining multiple fractures to off-hind on gallops. *M. P. Tregoning*

*Dubai Tennis Championships Stakes (John Porter), Newbury—a sixth course success for ill-fated Mubtaker
(rail), as he beats Munsef; Maraahel (striped cap) completes a 1,2,3 for owner Hamdan Al Maktoum*

totesport Ebor (Handicap), York—in one of the shocks of the season, Mudawin (nearest camera) finishes strongly to head Glistening (No.7) and Young Mick (centre); top weight Geordieland is fourth

MUCHO LOCO (IRE) 3 ch.g. Tagula (IRE) 116 – Mousseux (IRE) (Jareer (USA) 115) [2006 62: f7g 7g² 8.1s² 7g⁶ 8.3f⁴ 7g² 8.1m 8.1g⁶ 7d⁵ 8m 7d³ f7m² Oct 31] lengthy gelding: fair maiden: stays 8.3f: acts on fibresand, firm and soft going: wore cheekpieces second outing, blinkered after. *J. G. Portman* — **65**

MUCKLE 3 gr.f. Muhtarram (USA) 125 – Crackle 85 (Anshan 119) [2006 54p: p7g p10g⁵ 11.5m p12g f8g Jul 11] modest maiden: stays 1¼m: acts on polytrack. *S. C. Williams* — **58**

MUDAWIN (IRE) 5 b.g. Intikhab (USA) 135 – Fida (IRE) (Persian Heights 129) [2006 12v³ 9.8d⁶ 10g p12g* 14m³ 14m* 16g 13.9d* 13.9d³ 16s p16g² Nov 11] big, lengthy, good-topped gelding: has a round action: useful performer: trained by M. Tregoning in 2004: missed 2005: successful in handicaps at Kempton (reared up and unseated rider in stall beforehand) in May, Sandown (beat Rio de Janeiro by short head) in July and York (100/1, back to best when beating Glistening and Young Mick in very close finish to Ebor, hanging left) in August: good 1½ lengths second to Odiham in listed event at Kempton final start: stays easy 2m: acts on polytrack, good to firm and good to soft going: reportedly finished lame seventh outing. *Jane Chapple-Hyam* — **102**

MUD MONKEY 2 ch.c. (Feb 24) Muhtarram (USA) 125 – Tenderfoot 61 (Be My Chief (USA) 122) [2006 8m p8g⁵ 8d p9.5g² Nov 7] 6,000Y, 15,000 2-y-o: tall colt: first foal: dam 1¾m winner: fair maiden: second in nursery at Wolverhampton: will stay 1½m. *B. G. Powell* — **71**

MUFFETT'S DREAM 2 b.f. (Apr 1) Fraam 114 – Loveless Carla (Pursuit of Love 124) [2006 7g 8g p8g Nov 5] 9,000Y: second foal: dam, unraced, out of close relative to US Grade 1 9f winner Jovial: modest form in maidens. *J. A. Geake* — **60**

MUGEBA 5 b.m. Primo Dominie 121 – Ella Lamees 61 (Statoblest 120) [2006 69: 7g⁶ 6m 6m 7m 7m* 7m⁴ 6g⁵ 6d³ 6d⁵ Oct 18] workmanlike mare: fair handicapper: won at Yarmouth (all wins there) in August: effective at 6f/7f: acts on polytrack and any turf going: tried blinkered/visored: usually tongue tied. *Miss Gay Kelleway* — **68**

MUHANNAK (IRE) 2 b.c. (Mar 14) Chester House (USA) 123 – Opera 84 (Forzando 122) [2006 7.6f Aug 5] 8/1 and green, behind in maiden at Lingfield. *G. A. Butler* — **–**

MUJAHAZ (IRE) 2 b.c. (Apr 13) Act One 124 – Sayedati Eljamilah (USA) 64 (Mr Prospector (USA)) [2006 7g 8m 8d⁶ 8d³ Oct 19] strong, useful-looking colt: third foal: half-brother to fairly useful 2004 2-y-o 6f winner Motarassed, later successful in Spain, and 3-y-o Nudrah (both by Green Desert): dam, ran twice, half-sister to Derby winner Erhaab: fair form in maidens: again outpaced when third to Hunting Tower at Brighton: type to do better in 3-y-o handicaps over 1¼m/1½m. *J. L. Dunlop* — **68 p**

MUJAMEAD 2 b.c. (May 5) Mujahid (USA) 125 – Island Mead 86 (Pharly (FR) 130) **51**
[2006 f7g⁴ f5g⁵ p7.1g Dec 28] best effort in maidens (all in December) when fourth to
Hostage at Southwell (hung left) on debut. *P. C. Haslam*

MUJARAD (USA) 6 b.g. King of Kings (IRE) 125 – Happy Result (USA) (Diesis 133) **–**
[2006 –: p8.6g f8g Jun 3] well-made gelding: has a quick action: fairly useful performer
for J. Gosden in 2003: lightly raced and no form since: tried visored/blinkered/tongue
tied. *P. M. Mooney, Ireland*

MUJART 2 b.f. (Mar 27) Mujahid (USA) 125 – Artifact 73 (So Factual (USA) 120) **58**
[2006 p7.1g p6g 6.1m 6.1g⁶ 6.1d⁵ 5.1d³ p6m³ p5.1g² p5.1g⁴ Dec 11] close-coupled filly:
first foal: dam 6f to 8.5f winner: modest maiden: effective at 5f/6f: acts on polytrack and
good to soft going. *J. A. Pickering*

MUJAZAF 4 b.g. Grand Lodge (USA) 125 – Decision Maid (USA) 105 (Diesis 133) **54**
[2006 66: p16g³ p13g p13g³ p12.2g p12g² p8.6g p12g Jun 24] smallish, quite good-
topped gelding: maiden: just modest form in 2006: claimed from Miss S. West £6,000
after fifth start: should have stayed 2m: acted on polytrack and firm going: tried visored/
in cheekpieces: dead. *D. Burchell*

MUJEAK (IRE) 3 b.g. Mujadil (USA) 119 – Break For Peace (IRE) 65 (Brief Truce **70**
(USA) 126) [2006 70: 6d⁵ 6m 6.1g⁶ 5s³ 6g 6.1d⁵ p6g Nov 7] leggy, quite attractive gelding:
fair maiden: best form at 5f: acts on good to firm and good to soft going: wore cheekpieces final start: has been early to post. *J. J. Quinn*

MUJELLE 3 b.g. Mujahid (USA) 125 – Jennelle 97 (Nomination 125) [2006 67: 7m 7d **63 d**
f6g 8m p7g f8g⁵ 10.1g⁶ 8m p8.6g Sep 11] smallish gelding: modest performer: below
form after third outing: effective at 6f/7f: acts on all-weather and good to firm going: tried
in cheekpieces/blinkers. *D. K. Ivory*

MUJIMAC (IRE) 4 b.g. Mujadil (USA) 119 – Cross Dall (IRE) 58§ (Blues Traveller **52**
(IRE) 119) [2006 56: p9.5g f11g f12g p10g Feb 13] modest maiden: stays 1½m: acts on
polytrack, probably on good to firm ground: tried tongue tied/visored/in cheekpieces.
P. A. Blockley

MUJMA 2 b. or gr.c. (Mar 11) Indian Ridge 123 – Farfala (FR) 106 (Linamix (FR) 127) **66**
[2006 7d p7g⁶ Oct 26] 210,000Y: third foal: half-brother to 3-y-o Under The Rainbow
and 2004 2-y-o 1m winner Speightstown (by Grand Lodge), later successful at 1½m in
Spain: dam, French 10.5f and 1½m winner, sister to very smart French middle-distance
performer Fragrant Mix: mid-field in maidens at Leicester and Lingfield. *Sir Michael
Stoute*

MUJOBLIGED (IRE) 3 b.c. Mujadil (USA) 119 – Festival of Light (High Top 131) **–**
[2006 –: p9.5g 8m p8.6g Nov 20] little form, including at Wolverhampton: tried tongue
tied. *Seamus G. O'Donnell, Ireland*

MUJOOD 3 b.g. Mujahid (USA) 125 – Waqood (USA) 75 (Riverman (USA) 131) [2006 **91**
81: p8g 9.9f⁴ 10.1m⁵ p8g² 8.1m p8g³ p6g⁵ 8g⁴ 8.5g² 8f⁴ 7g* 7.5g⁵ p8g⁶ p7g³ 6d* 6d⁶
Oct 27] quite good-topped gelding: fairly useful performer: won handicaps at Folkestone in August and Brighton in October: effective at 6f to 1¼m: acts on polytrack, firm
and good to soft ground: has worn cheekpieces/blinkers (in latter last 2 starts): usually
races prominently: not straightforward. *R. F. Johnson Houghton*

MUKAABER 3 ch.c. Pivotal 124 – Placement (Kris 135) [2006 8m 10.2g May 2] tall **–**
colt: well held in maidens in July: sold 17,500 gns in July. *M. P. Tregoning*

MUKTASB (USA) 5 b.g. Bahri (USA) 125 – Maghaarb 104 (Machiavellian (USA) **52**
123) [2006 49, a63: f5g⁵ p6g f6g f5g³ p5.1g² f5g⁴ p5.1g² p5g p5.1g* p5.1g⁵ 5m 5g **a63**
p5g² p5g p5g² p5.1g² p5.1g⁴ Dec 31] good-topped gelding: has a quick action: modest
performer, better on all-weather than turf: won banded race at Wolverhampton in April:
effective at 5f, should stay 7f: acts on all-weather and good to firm going: wears headgear:
sometimes slowly away: held up. *D. Shaw*

MULAAZEM 3 b.g. King's Best (USA) 132 – Harayir (USA) 119 (Gulch (USA)) **82 +**
[2006 65p: 8.1m² 10.5m* Aug 10] medium-sized, quite attractive gelding: fairly useful
form in maidens: second to Desert Authority at Sandown on reappearance, then won
at Haydock in August: should stay 1½m: sold 20,000 gns in October, and gelded.
M. P. Tregoning

MULAQAT 3 b.c. Singspiel (IRE) 133 – Atamana (IRE) 82 (Lahib (USA) 129) [2006 **120**
96: 8g⁶ 10m* 8.5m 10m⁴ 10m⁵ 10g⁴ 10.5m* 10g⁵ Aug 26] smallish, strong colt: smart
performer: won listed race at Newmarket (by 2½ lengths from Purple Moon) in May and
Petros Rose of Lancaster Stakes at Haydock (beat Notable Guest 1¾ lengths) in August:
below-form fifth to Tam Lin in Winter Hill Stakes at Windsor final start (not for first time

Sheikh Ahmed Al Maktoum's "Mulaqat"

finding little): will stay 1½m: unraced on extremes of going: blinkered last 2 starts: wears crossed noseband: none too consistent: joined D. Selvaratnam in UAE. *M. P. Tregoning*

MULBERRY LAD (IRE) 4 b.g. Entrepreneur 123 – Taisho (IRE) 96 (Namaqualand **54** (USA)) [2006 60: f6g p5.1g⁴ p6g⁴ f7g⁴ p6g* p6g p6g⁴ p6g⁵ f8g⁴ f6g⁴ p7g 6m⁵ p7.1g* 6g **a64** 7m 6m 8.1f f7g f7g p6g* p6g p6g* f6g p7g⁵ p6g³ p7g⁶ Dec 30] modest performer: won claimer at Lingfield in February, banded race at Wolverhampton in May, handicap at Lingfield in November and banded race at Kempton in December: effective at 6f to 1m: acts on all-weather and firm going: tried tongue tied/blinkered. *P. W. Hiatt*

MULLADY PENELOPE 3 b.f. Mull of Kintyre (USA) 114 – Gracious Imp (USA) **60** (Imp Society (USA)) [2006 52: 6d⁵ 5f⁶ 5f² 5.3f* 6.1f⁶ 5f 5g 5.1f⁶ Aug 8] good-topped filly: modest handicapper: won at Brighton in July: best at 5f: acts on firm and good to soft going: sold 1,400 gns, sent to Denmark. *Mrs A. Duffield*

MULLIGAN'S GOLD (IRE) 3 b.g. Fasliyev (USA) 120 – Magic Lady (IRE) (Big- **72** stone (IRE) 126) [2006 66: 6d* 6g² 5s 5g³ 5m⁵ 5g⁴ 6m² 6f⁶ 6d⁴ 6s 6g Sep 17] lengthy gelding: fair performer: won maiden at Catterick in April: raced only at 5f/6f: acts on good to firm and good to soft ground: gelded after final start. *T. D. Easterby*

MULLIGAN'S PRIDE (IRE) 5 b.g. Kahyasi 130 – Babs Mulligan (IRE) (Le Bavard **63** (FR) 125) [2006 16f* 16.1m⁶ 16.2f⁶ 17.2f⁴ 16.1m⁶ 16.2g³ 16d Aug 29] strong, good-bodied gelding: fair performer: won claimer at Redcar in June on Flat debut: stays 2m: acts on firm going: tried blinkered: sold 5,000 gns. *G. A. Swinbank*

MULL OF DUBAI 3 b.g. Mull of Kintyre (USA) 114 – Enlisted (IRE) 83 (Sadler's **78** Wells (USA) 132) [2006 69: 6.1d⁴ 6g⁶ 8.1s³ 7g⁵ 9.9m² 11.7g* 11.6m³ 11.5m⁴ 11.9m² 12.1m* 14g 11.6d* 11.9g⁴ Oct 13] fair handicapper: won at Bath in July, Beverley in September and Windsor in October: stays 1½m: acts on good to firm and good to soft going: blinkered final 2-y-o start: has shown signs of temperament. *J. S. Moore*

MULLZIMA (IRE) 3 b.f. Mull of Kintyre (USA) 114 – Habaza (IRE) 68 (Shernazar – 131) [2006 48: 10g Apr 10] tall, lightly-made filly: poor maiden: well held sole outing in 2006: stays 1m: acts on polytrack and good to firm going. *P. D. Evans*

MULTAHAB 7 b. or br.g. Zafonic (USA) 130 – Alumisiyah (USA) 93 (Danzig (USA)) 72 [2006 62, a52: p7g 5.3m* 5.3f⁵ 5.2f 5m* 5.3m* 5.2m p6g Oct 15] smallish gelding: fair handicapper: won at Brighton in June, and Catterick and Brighton in August: effective at 5f/6f: acts on all-weather and firm ground: tried blinkered/in cheekpieces: tongue tied nowadays. *Miss D. A. McHale*

MULTAKKA (IRE) 3 b.c. Alhaarth (IRE) 126 – Elfaslah (IRE) 107 (Green Desert 90 (USA) 127) [2006 90: 8d³ p7g³ 9s² 8m² 8m 7f⁴ Aug 3] strong, rangy, attractive colt: keen walker: fairly useful maiden: best efforts in 2006 when in frame in handicaps second, third and final (blinkered) starts: should stay 1¼m: yet to race on heavy going, acts on any other turf and polytrack. *M. P. Tregoning*

MULTIDIMENSIONAL (IRE) 3 b.c. Danehill (USA) 126 – Sacred Song (USA) 115 p 116 (Diesis 133) [2006 8m* 8m* 8m 10s* Aug 19] smallish, well-made colt: first foal: dam, 6f (at 2 yrs) to 1½m (Princess Royal/Lancashire Oaks) winner, half-sister to smart Canadian performer up to 1½m Strut The Stage: smart form: won maiden at Newmarket in June, handicap there in July (wandered) and Prix Guillaume d'Ornano - Haras d'Etreham at Deauville in August: seemed to relish much softer conditions when beating Boris de Deauville ¾ length in last-named, though not for first time hung right: last in listed race at Goodwood other start: stays 1¼m: acts on soft and good to firm ground: should progress again at 4 yrs. *H. R. A. Cecil*

MULTITUDE (IRE) 2 b.g. (Apr 24) Mull of Kintyre (USA) 114 – Sea Modena (IRE) 65 (Mac's Imp (USA) 116) [2006 5d 6m³ 5.1d³ 6s⁴ Oct 16] sturdy gelding: fair maiden: third at Pontefract and Nottingham: gelded after final start: may prove best at 5f/6f. *T. D. Easterby*

Niarchos Family's "Multidimensional"

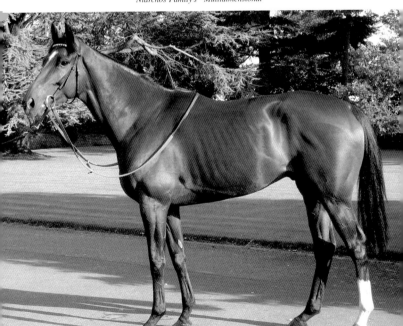

MULVANY (IRE) 2 b.c. (Feb 28) Mull of Kintyre (USA) 114 – Flamanda 67 (Niniski **60** (USA) 125) [2006 6g 7m 6m⁴ 6.1m⁶ 7m⁶ p7.1m⁶ Oct 9] close-coupled, good-quartered colt: has a quick action: modest maiden: stays 7f: blinkered from third start: sold 8,000 gns, sent to Belgium. *B. J. Meehan*

MUMAATHEL (IRE) 3 b.g. Alhaarth (IRE) 126 – Alhufoof (USA) 100 (Dayjur **84** (USA) 137) [2006 7.1g³ 7g² p7g² 7.1m 7.1m³ p7g² Oct 15] rather leggy gelding: second foal: dam, 2-y-o 6f winner (stayed 7f), half-sister to dam of 1000 Guineas winner Lahan: reportedly suffered from sore shins at 2 yrs: fairly useful maiden: placed 5 of 6 starts, below form only outing in handicap other occasion: will stay 1m: raced only on polytrack and good/good to firm going: edged right third start: sold 39,000 gns. *M. P. Tregoning*

MUMBLESWERVE (IRE) 2 b.c. (May 10) City On A Hill (USA) 114 – Dolcezza **67** (FR) (Lichine (USA) 117) [2006 7d p7g Dec 20] 36,000Y: lengthy colt: half-brother to several winners, including useful 2001 2-y-o 7f winner who stayed 1¼m Martin House (by Mujadil): dam unraced close relation to smart French performer up to 10.5f Caprarola: no threat in maidens but fair form second start. *W. Jarvis*

MUM'S MEMORIES 2 ch.g. (Mar 12) Zaha (CAN) 106 – Trevorsninepoints 71 **50** (Jester 119) [2006 5d 6m 6g Jun 1] good-topped gelding: modest form only on debut: gelded after final start. *Jedd O'Keeffe*

MUNAA (IRE) 3 b.f. Alhaarth (IRE) 126 – Beseeching (IRE) 50 (Hamas (IRE) 125§) **79** [2006 71: 10m⁴ 8.1g 8.3d* 8g⁴ 8.3g² 8d Oct 2] close-coupled filly: fair performer: won handicap at Leicester in August: stays 8.3f: acts on heavy and good to firm going: sold 12,000 gns. *K. R. Burke*

MUNADDAM (USA) 4 ch.g. Aljabr (USA) 125 – Etizaaz (USA) 117 (Diesis 133) **109** [2006 91: 7m² 7g 7m 6m 6d 6f* Sep 18] sturdy gelding: improved into a useful handicapper, winning at Folkestone in September by ¾ length from Diane's Choice: gelded after: best earlier efforts when second to Kostar in valuable event at Lingfield and when ninth to Borderlescott in Stewards' Cup at Goodwood (shaped well) fourth start: effective at 6f/7f: acts on firm going. *E. A. L. Dunlop*

MUNCASTER CASTLE (IRE) 2 b.g. (Apr 24) Johannesburg (USA) 127 – Eubee **54** (FR) (Common Grounds 118) [2006 5g⁵ 7.2g⁵ 5.9g⁵ 7.1m² 6v 8s⁶ Oct 16] lengthy gelding: modest maiden: second in seller: stays 1m: acts on soft and good to firm going: gelded after final start. *R. F. Fisher*

MUNDO'S MAGIC 2 b.g. (Apr 7) Foxhound (USA) 103 – Amber's Bluff 80 (Mind **76** Games 121) [2006 5g 6m 6f* 6m⁵ 6s 6d⁵ Sep 15] 10,000Y: big, close-coupled gelding: first foal: dam 6f winner: fair performer: gelded prior to winning maiden at Pontefract in July: no impact in nurseries: should prove best at 5f/6f: acts on firm going. *D. W. Barker*

MUNGO JERRY (GER) 5 b.g. Tannenkonig (IRE) 111 – Mostly Sure (IRE) (Sure – Blade (USA) 130) [2006 80d: p13.9g f14g Jul 11] tall gelding: on downgrade in 2005 and well held in 2006: tried tongue tied. *B. N. Pollock*

MUNSEF 4 b.g. Zafonic (USA) 130 – Mazaya (IRE) 105 (Sadler's Wells (USA) 132) **119** [2006 116: 12g² 12s² 12m 13.3d³ 12d² 12s⁵ Oct 21] strong, close-coupled gelding: smart performer: improved again in 2006, best efforts when placed in John Porter Stakes at Newbury (neck second to Mubtaker), Jockey Club Stakes at Newmarket (3½ lengths second to Shirocco) and Geoffrey Freer Stakes at Newbury (close third to Admiral's Cruise): ran in snatches when well below form final outing: gelded after: likely to stay 1¾m: acts on soft and good to firm going: held up: stays in training. *J. L. Dunlop*

MUNSTER MOUNTAIN (IRE) 2 ch.c. (Feb 22) Monashee Mountain (USA) 115 – **58** The Voice (ITY) (Catrail (USA) 123) [2006 7.5f⁵ 6.1g 7.1m 7.1d p7.1m f7g Nov 20] strong colt: modest maiden: will stay 1m: tried in cheekpieces. *P. A. Blockley*

MUNTADA 3 b.f. King's Best (USA) 132 – Inaaq 109 (Lammtarra (USA) 134) [2006 **76** p8g 9s³ 9m² 8.1m³ 9.9g⁵ 9.9d² p10g⁴ Nov 13] well-made filly: second foal: sister to 4-y-o Mayadeen: dam, 1¼m winner who stayed 1½m, half-sister to Dubai World Cup winner Almutawakel and 1000 Guineas runner-up Muwakleh: fair maiden: in frame 5 of 7 starts: stays 1¼m: acts on soft and good to firm ground: races prominently: awkward leaving stall final outing. *M. P. Tregoning*

MUNTAMI (IRE) 5 gr.g. Daylami (IRE) 138 – Bashashah (IRE) 83 (Kris 135) [2006 – 78: f14g⁵ 14m⁴ a7g Sep 5] fairly useful performer at best: no form in 2006 (left J. Harris after reappearance): stays 1¼m: acts on heavy going: tried blinkered/visored. *S. Donohoe, Ireland*

MUQARRAR (IRE) 7 ch.g. Alhaarth (IRE) 126 – Narjis (USA) 87 (Blushing Groom – (FR) 131) [2006 59: f12g Jan 19] workmanlike gelding: modest performer in 2005, well

held only outing in 2006: tried in blinkers/eyeshields, tongue tied/visored nowadays.
T. J. Fitzgerald

MUQTADI (IRE) 8 b.g. Marju (IRE) 127 – Kadwah (USA) 80 (Mr Prospector (USA)) – §
[2006 48§: p12g Oct 23] leggy gelding: unreliable performer, well held only outing in
2006. *Mrs Barbara Waring*

MURBEK (IRE) 2 b.c. (Apr 20) Dansili 127 – Flagship 84 (Rainbow Quest (USA) 88
134) [2006 7.1m² 7d⁴ Sep 29] 26,000Y, 78,000 2-y-o: useful-looking colt: unfurnished at
2 yrs: fifth foal: half-brother to 4-y-o Cordage and 3-y-o Jump Ship: dam, 1¼m winner,
out of Oaks winner Bireme: fairly useful form in maidens at Sandown (second to Overturn) and Newmarket (free to post/hung left in finish): will be suited by 1m/1¼m.
M. A. Jarvis

MURDOCH 2 b.c. (Apr 2) Mutamarkiz (IRE) 77 – Miss Pharly (Pharly (FR) 130) [2006 77
8g² Oct 17] first foal: dam unraced: 50/1, ¾-length second to Grey Rover in maiden at
Bath, prominent throughout. *E. S. McMahon*

MUREE QUEEN 2 b.f. (Mar 11) Diktat 126 – Bright Future (FR) (Akarad (FR) 130) 49
[2006 7.1s³ 7.5m³ 7g⁶ Sep 27] 7,000Y: leggy filly: fourth foal: half-sister to 2 winners
abroad, including useful German performer up to 10.5f Blue Baloo (by Turtle Island):
dam race once in France: poor form in maidens: will stay 1m+. *R. Hollinshead*

MURFREESBORO 3 b.c. Bahamian Bounty 116 – Merry Rous 66 (Rousillon (USA) 99
133) [2006 98p: 6d 6m² 6m 5g Sep 28] useful-looking colt: good walker: useful performer: creditable effort in 2006 only when 1¼ lengths second to Lady Livius in minor
event at Newbury second start: will probably prove best at 5f/6f: acts on good to firm
going: visored final start: sold 30,000 gns in October, resold 20,000 gns in November.
J. H. M. Gosden

MURRIETA 4 ch.f. Docksider (USA) 124 – Lafleur (IRE) 75 (Grand Lodge (USA) 55
125) [2006 57: 10.2g⁴ p12.2g³ 11.9g⁵ 13.1s 11.9m⁶ May 31] modest maiden: stays easy
1½m: acts on polytrack and soft ground: blinkered/visored in 2006. *Miss J. R. Gibney*

MURRIN (IRE) 2 b. or br.g. (Mar 20) Trans Island 119 – Flimmering (Dancing Brave 74
(USA) 140) [2006 7.1g⁶ 8m⁵ 7g⁸* p7g⁵ 7g⁴ Nov 9] €15,000Y, 26,000 2-y-o: close-
coupled gelding: half-brother to 3 winners abroad, including French 1¼m/11f winner
Peak of Joy (by Anshan): dam unraced out of Musidora winner Fatah Flare: fair performer: won maiden at Lingfield in September: free-going type, best short of 1m: gelded
after final start. *T. G. Mills*

MURRISK 2 ch.g. (Apr 21) Groom Dancer (USA) 128 – Food of Love 109 (Music Boy 74
124) [2006 p7g⁵ p8.6g⁴ p7.1g² Nov 18] 4,000F, €23,000Y: closely related to 7-y-o Tough
Love and half-brother to 3 winners, including 3-y-o Mon Petite Amour: dam 5f performer: fair maiden: twice in frame at Wolverhampton: stays 8.6f: raced on polytrack:
tongue tied debut. *E. Tyrrell, Ireland*

MURRUMBIDGEE (IRE) 3 gr.g. Bluebird (USA) 125 – Blanche Neige (USA) (Lit 70
de Justice (USA) 125) [2006 62: p8g⁵ p8g⁴ 8.1g² 10m⁶ p8g⁶ 8f 8m² 8g* 8.2f⁶ 8g⁵ 8f³
8m 9m³ 8d⁶ 8d Oct 27] good-topped gelding: fair handicapper: won apprentice event at
Salisbury in June: stays 1¼m: acts on polytrack and firm ground: tried visored: none too
genuine. *J. W. Hills*

MURTS MAGIC (IRE) 3 ch.c. Rossini (USA) 118 – Clover Tina (IRE) (Coquelin –
(USA) 121) [2006 –: p10g p10g Mar 27] no form: dead. *M. J. McGrath*

MUSADIF (USA) 8 ch.g. Shadeed (USA) 135 – Tadwin 109 (Never So Bold 135) 105
[2006 111: 5m 6m 5d Aug 28] useful performer: one of top sprinters in Scandinavia since
2003: won listed race at Taby on reappearance in 2005 and placed in race for third year
running when beaten neck by Pipoldchap in Taby Open Sprint Championship final start:
best effort in Britain in 2006 when eighth to Pivotal Point in Sprint Stakes at Sandown on
reappearance: best up to 7f: acts on good to firm ground: tongue tied in 2006. *R. A. Kvisla*

MUSANGO 3 b.g. Night Shift (USA) – Imbabala (Zafonic (USA) 130) [2006 p8g⁶ 66
p12g⁵ p10g⁵ Dec 30] 6,000 3-y-o: third foal: half-brother to smart French 1¼m winner
who stayed 1½m Kalabar (by Kahyasi): dam, French 1m winner, half-sister to smart
French performer up to 1¾m Short Pause: fair form in maidens at Kempton (2) and
Lingfield. *B. R. Johnson*

MUSARDIERE 4 b.f. Montjeu (IRE) 137 – Majestic Image 86 (Niniski (USA) 125) 72 d
[2006 74: 8.7d 9.5g 12s⁶ 13g 11v 8.5g 10g 10.9d f11m⁴ p12g Dec 6] leggy, close-coupled
filly: fair maiden, on downgrade: left T. Hogan in Ireland after sixth start in 2006: stays
1½m: acts on soft ground: tried tongue tied/in cheekpieces. *J. Balding*

MUSCA (IRE) 2 b.g. (Feb 18) Tendulkar (USA) 114 – Canary Bird (IRE) 59 (Catrail **88 p**
(USA) 123) [2006 7.2g² 7s* Oct 14] 50,000Y: fourth foal: half-brother to useful 2004
2-y-o 1m winner in Ireland/Canada Fearless Flyer (by Brave Act) and 3-y-o Stonehaugh:
dam, lightly raced in Ireland, half-sister to useful Irish performer up to 1½m Tout A Coup:
fairly useful form: confirmed promise of debut (4 months earlier) when winning maiden
at Catterick by 6 lengths from Princess Palatine, making all: will stay 1m: should progress
further. *J. Howard Johnson*

MUSCARI 4 ch.f. Indian Ridge 123 – Desert Serenade (USA) (Green Desert (USA) **68**
127) [2006 p8g 10m⁶ 10f f12g 10m 7g³ 9d⁶ p7.1m³ 8g* 8m⁴ p8.6m p7g² p6g⁴ p6g²
Dec 22] 800 3-y-o: fifth foal: half-sister to German 6f/7f winner Oasis Song (by Selkirk)
and fairly useful French 1m (at 2 yrs) to 13f winner Major Performance (by Celtic
Swing): dam, ran twice, sister to high-class sprinter Sheikh Albadou: fair handicapper:
won at Pontefract in September: claimed from A. Jarvis twelfth start: effective at 6f to
1m: acts on polytrack and firm going. *S. Woodman*

MUSETTE (IRE) 3 b.f. Mujadil (USA) 119 – Repique (USA) 88 (Sharpen Up 127) **43**
[2006 44: p7g f6g⁶ 5f⁶ 6m⁶ 5m⁴ 5s 6d Sep 5] leggy filly: poor maiden: left E. Cox after
second start: stays 6f: acts on good to firm ground: tried in cheekpieces. *R. E. Barr*

MUSHEED (IRE) 2 b.c. (Mar 7) King's Best (USA) 132 – Khulan (USA) 103 (Bahri **–**
(USA) 125) [2006 7m Sep 19] lengthy, good-topped colt: second foal: dam, 2-y-o 6f
winner, out of close relative to high-class sprinter Elnadim and half-sister to Irish 1000
Guineas winner Mehthaaf: 33/1, reportedly had breathing problem when behind in
maiden at Newmarket: sold 3,000 gns, sent to Qatar. *E. A. L. Dunlop*

MUSICAL AFFAIR 2 b.f. (Apr 12) Alflora (IRE) 120 – Song For Jess (IRE) (Accor- **52**
dion) [2006 6.1m p6g² 7.1m 7.1d 5.1d Nov 1] lengthy filly: second foal: dam poor
winning hurdler: modest maiden: should stay at least 1m. *F. Jordan*

MUSICAL AWARD (IRE) 2 b.c. (May 6) Tobougg (IRE) 125 – Emy's Girl (USA) **69**
(Prospect Bay (CAN) 117) [2006 7m 7m 8.5g⁵ 10g 6d 8g Oct 13] 34,000Y: leggy, useful-
looking colt: second foal: half-brother to a winner in Greece by Stravinsky: dam maiden
in USA: fair maiden: stays 8.5f: sold 8,000 gns. *M. G. Quinlan*

MUSICAL BEAT 2 ch.f. (Mar 9) Beat Hollow 126 – Warbler 110 (Warning 136) [2006 **75 +**
p7.1g³ p8g³ f7g² Dec 23] 15,000 2-y-o: sixth foal: half-sister to 1m winner Reed Minder
(by Zamindar) and 1¼m winner Trill (by Highest Honor), both useful in France, and
fairly useful Irish 1¼m winner Voliere (by Zafonic): dam French 10.5f/11.5f winner who
stayed 15f well: placed in all-weather maidens: second to Mankanja at Southwell: will be
suited by 1¼m/1½m. *Miss V. Haigh*

MUSICAL CHIMES 3 b.f. Josr Algarhoud (IRE) 118 – Sally Slade 80 (Dowsing **45**
(USA) 124) [2006 p8g 9.7d p6g 7f p7g⁵ p10g p8g⁶ 6.1d p7.1g Nov 20] good-bodied
filly: fifth foal: half-sister to several winners, including 5-y-o Port 'N Starboard: dam 5f
winner, including at 2 yrs: poor maiden: left C. Cyzer after seventh start: stays 7f: acts on
polytrack. *W. M. Brisbourne*

MUSICAL CITY 3 ch.f. City On A Hill (USA) 114 – Royal Musical 39 (Royal Abjar **35**
(USA) 121) [2006 44: p6g f7g⁶ f7g Feb 9] poor maiden: best form at 6f: tried in cheekpieces. *B. Smart*

MUSICAL ECHO 3 b.f. Distant Music (USA) 126 – Distant Music (Darshaan 133) **73**
[2006 64: 8.3d p7g⁵ p7g⁴ p8g⁴ p10g* 9f⁵ Nov 12] good-topped filly: fair performer: won
handicap at Kempton in August: left G. Chung after: will stay 1½m: acts on polytrack and
firm going. *T. H. West, USA*

MUSICAL GIANT (USA) 3 ch.g. Giant's Causeway (USA) 132 – Music House **–**
(USA) (Sadler's Wells (USA) 132) [2006 8m⁵ 9.2f⁶ 10.1m⁶ Jul 18] strong, lengthy
gelding: well held in maidens. *J. Howard Johnson*

MUSICAL GIFT 6 ch.g. Cadeaux Genereux 131 – Kazoo 108 (Shareef Dancer (USA) **–**
135) [2006 50, a64: f8g² p8.6g f7g⁴ p8.6g p8.6g* f8g² p8g f8g 10d p9.5g p8g⁵ f8g p7g³ **a57**
Dec 18] sturdy gelding: modest performer: won banded event at Wolverhampton in April:
stays easy 1¼m: acts on all-weather: wears cheekpieces/visor. *P. A. Blockley*

MUSICAL GUEST (IRE) 3 b.g. Mozart (IRE) 131 – Hoh Dear (IRE) 106 (Sri Pekan **–**
(USA) 117) [2006 83: p7g⁶ 7.1g 6.1d Oct 4] close-coupled, quite attractive gelding:
has a quick action: fairly useful performer at 2 yrs: no form in 2006: tried visored.
G. G. Margarson

MUSICAL LAND (IRE) 2 ch.c. (Apr 27) Distant Music (USA) 126 – Esquiline **76**
(USA) (Gone West (USA)) [2006 7.1f⁴ 7.2d⁴ 7.5d 8g² 9s² 8d⁶ Nov 3] close-coupled colt:
sixth foal: half-brother to 3 winners, including useful 6f to 1m winner Wixoe Express (by

Anabaa), later successful in USA, and 3-y-o Aspen Falls: dam, maiden, out of half-sister to Arlington Million winner Mill Native: fair maiden: runner-up at Musselburgh (2): stays 9f: acts on soft and firm ground: difficult ride. *J. R. Weymes*

MUSICAL MAGIC 3 b.f. Mozart (IRE) 131 – Kirk 79 (Selkirk (USA) 129) [2006 7g **65** 8m⁴ 10f 10.1f⁴ 10f³ 11.1g³ p13.9m Oct 9] unfurnished filly: third foal: half-sister to useful 1¼m (including at 2 yrs) winner Natalie Jane (by Giant's Causeway) and winner in Greece by Fasliyev: dam, 1m winner (would have been suited by 1¼m), closely related to smart performer up to 1¼m Carmelite House: fair maiden: stays 1¼m: raced only on good ground or firmer on turf: visored final start: sold 20,000 gns. *J. Noseda*

MUSICAL MIRAGE (USA) 2 b.f. (Mar 2) Royal Anthem (USA) 135 – Fantasy 80 **83** (Cadeaux Genereux 131) [2006 5m 7d* 7g⁴ 8g Sep 9] 9,500Y: unfurnished filly: third foal: dam lightly-raced sister to smart performer up to 1m Stetchworth Prince and half-sister to smart 7f/1m winner Smirk: fairly useful form: won maiden at Redcar in August by 4 lengths: stiff task in May Hill Stakes at York (seventh of 9 behind Simply Perfect) final start: races freely, but probably stays 1m. *G. A. Swinbank*

MUSICAL ROMANCE (IRE) 3 b.f. Mozart (IRE) 131 – Dear Girl (IRE) 105 (Fairy **76** King (USA)) [2006 67: p7.1g⁵ p7.1g p5g 5.1g³ 5m* 5m⁴ 5m 5f* 5.7g⁴ 5m⁶ 5.1f² 5m⁵ Sep 9] sturdy filly: fair handicapper: won at Goodwood in June and Windsor in July: best at 5f/6f: acts on polytrack and firm going: blinkered of late: often slowly away. *B. J. Meehan*

MUSICAL SCRIPT (USA) 3 b.g. Stravinsky (USA) 133 – Cyrillic (USA) 106 (Irish **72** River (FR) 131) [2006 p7g⁵ 7s² 8d³ 7d 7g 6m³ 6f³ 6d 6g 5.3g² p6m* p6g² Nov 8] 15,500 2-y-o: sturdy gelding: third foal: half-brother to 5-y-o Slavonic: dam, 1m to 1½m winner in France/USA, out of smart French/US performer up to 1¼m Polemic: fair performer: won handicap at Wolverhampton in October: free-going sort, and will prove best at 5f/6f: acts on polytrack, firm and soft going. *Mrs A. J. Hamilton-Fairley*

MUSICANNA 5 b.m. Cape Cross (IRE) 129 – Upend 120 (Main Reef 126) [2006 110: **114** 9s 8.5g² 8m³ 8d⁴ 9d Oct 14] leggy, good-topped mare: smart performer, lightly raced (has reportedly had knee problems): easily best efforts in 2006 when ½-length second to Echelon in Princess Elizabeth Stakes at Epsom (hung markedly left) and 1½ lengths third (improved form) to Rajeem in steadily-run Falmouth Stakes at Newmarket: stays 1m: acts on soft and good to firm going: tongue tied: sold 320,000 gns. *J. R. Fanshawe*

MUSIC BY MOZART 3 b.c. Mozart (IRE) 131 – Dayville (USA) 86 (Dayjur (USA) **80** 137) [2006 7⁴p: 6g⁴ 7g³ 6g p6g Jul 19] neat colt: fairly useful maiden: best efforts first 2 starts in 2006: stays 7f: raced only on polytrack and good ground: has been bandaged behind: has looked rather wayward: sold 8,000 gns, sent to Germany. *P. W. Chapple-Hyam*

MUSIC CELEBRE (IRE) 6 b.g. Peintre Celebre (USA) 137 – Marwell 133 (Habitat **81** 134) [2006 81: 7m² 8m 8m 8.5d 9.5s⁵ p9.5g⁵ Dec 28] fairly useful handicapper: won at Leopardstown in 2005: creditable second at Roscommon on reappearance, but below form after, leaving D. Weld in Ireland 9,000 gns before final outing: stays 1m: acts on firm and soft ground: usually blinkered, in cheekpieces final start. *S. Curran*

MUSICMAESTROPLEASE (IRE) 3 b.c. Rossini (USA) 118 – Who Told Vicky **70** (IRE) 50 (Anita's Prince 126) [2006 60: f6g⁵ p6g⁴ 7m* 7f² 8m 8.1f⁴ 7.9m² 7f² 8g⁶ 8.1m⁵ 8.1d p7g p8.6g² Nov 7] sturdy, close-coupled colt: fair performer: won handicap at Yarmouth in March: very stiff task and flattered in steadily-run minor event at Lingfield penultimate start: stays easy 8.6f: acts on all-weather and firm going. *S. Parr*

MUSIC NOTE (IRE) 3 b.c. Indian Ridge 123 – Samara Middle East (FR) 87 (Marju **90** (IRE) 127) [2006 81: 8s* 8g 10s Aug 26] leggy, attractive colt: fairly useful performer: best effort when winning handicap at Newmarket in May by 2½ lengths from Motaraqeb: well below form after: stays 1m: acts on firm and soft going: sold 9,000 gns. *M. R. Channon*

MUSIC TEACHER 4 ch.f. Piccolo 121 – Duena (Grand Lodge (USA) 125) [2006 **53** 62: p6g p5.1g f5g p5.1g⁶ Apr 24] angular filly: modest performer: stays easy 6f: acts on polytrack and good to firm ground. *N. A. Callaghan*

MUSIOTAL 5 ch.g. Pivotal 124 – Bemuse 89 (Forzando 122) [2006 59: p8.6g⁶ f6g⁶ **57** f7g⁵ p7.1g³ p8g⁶ p8.6g³ p8.6g⁵ p8.6g³ p7.1g⁴ 8.3m p8g⁴ Jul 22] lengthy, useful-looking gelding: modest performer: stays easy 8.6f: acts on all-weather, soft and good to firm ground: usually visored/in cheekpieces. *P. A. Blockley*

MUSTAJED 5 b.g. Alhaarth (IRE) 126 – Jasarah (IRE) 70 (Green Desert (USA) 127) **91** [2006 92: 10g³ May 1] sturdy gelding: fairly useful handicapper: creditable third at Windsor on sole start in 2006: barely stays 1½m: acts on good to firm and good to soft ground: visored once: consistent. *B. R. Millman*

*United Arab Emirates Racing And Equestrian Federation Royal Whip Stakes, the Curragh—
Mustameet completes a four-timer, beating Chelsea Rose, Soar With Eagles (No.4) and Heliostatic*

MUSTAKHLAS (USA) 5 ch.g. Diesis 133 – Katiba (USA) 99 (Gulch (USA)) [2006 **59**
59: p12.2g p12.2g⁵ p12.2g* p12.2g p12.2g 12.3g 12f 12.6g p13.9g⁵ p13.9g⁴ Dec 31]
rangy gelding: modest performer: won banded race at Wolverhampton in March: probably stays easy 1¾m: acts on polytrack: tried in cheekpieces. *B. P. J. Baugh*

MUSTAMAD 3 b.g. Anabaa (USA) 130 – Nasanice (IRE) 97 (Nashwan (USA) 135) **74**
[2006 10m⁶ 10.9d² 9.8m⁶ Jun 7] big, strong, lengthy gelding: fourth foal: half-brother to
3 winners, including 5-y-o Maraahel and 3-y-o Mostashaar: dam Irish 9f winner: best
effort in maidens when 3 lengths second to Barodine at Warwick on second outing:
gelded after final outing: will stay 1½m: sold 17,000 gns. *Sir Michael Stoute*

MUSTAMEET (USA) 5 b.h. Sahm (USA) 112 – Hamasah (USA) 83 (Irish River (FR) **123**
131) [2006 116: 7s² 8m* 8d⁴ 8m* 8g* 8m* 10m* 10m⁴ 8m Dec 10] very smart performer:
improved again in 2006, winning listed races at Leopardstown in April and June, similar
event at the Curragh (by 4 lengths from Arch Rebel) in July, ladbrokes.com International
Stakes (by head from Ace) later in July and United Arab Emirates Racing and Equestrian
Federation Royal Whip Stakes (by 3 lengths from Chelsea Rose) in August, last 2 also at
the Curragh: respectable fourth to Dylan Thomas in Irish Champion Stakes at Leopardstown before well held in Hong Kong Mile at Sha Tin: stays 1¼m: acts on heavy and
good to firm going: reportedly lost 2 teeth when banging head in stall on reappearance:
sometimes edges right: held up: stays in training. *K. Prendergast, Ireland*

MUSTAMMER 3 b.g. Fasliyev (USA) 120 – Alazima (USA) 64 (Riverman (USA) **51**
131) [2006 p8g 10d 8s⁶ p7g f6g p6g p6g p6g p5.1g⁵ p6s² p6g⁵ Dec 18] sturdy, close-coupled
gelding: modest maiden: left M. Tregoning after second start, S. R. Bowring after third:
best effort at 6f on polytrack: sometimes visored. *D. Shaw*

MUSTANG ALI (IRE) 5 ch.g. Ali-Royal (IRE) 127 – Classic Queen (IRE) (Classic **62**
Secret (USA) 91) [2006 59: p10g p16.5g² p13g p16.5g⁵ 16.4f* 14.1g Aug 25] workmanlike gelding: modest performer: won handicap at Folkestone in July: stays 16.5f: acts on
polytrack, firm and good to soft going: tried blinkered. *Dr J. R. J. Naylor*

MUSTANG LIL 5 b.m. Mark of Esteem (IRE) 137 – Quivira 81 (Rainbow Quest **–**
(USA) 134) [2006 50: 6f May 16] very lightly-raced maiden: little form. *Ms J. S. Doyle*

MUST BE KEEN 7 b.g. Emperor Jones (USA) 119 – As Mustard (Keen 116) [2006 **57**
f11g 10d p7g⁶ p8g p8g 8m p8.6m p10g⁴ p8g Oct 29] modest maiden: probably stays
1¼m: acts on polytrack and good to soft going: tried tongue tied/in cheekpieces.
E. R. Oertel

MUTADARREJ (IRE) 2 ch.c. (Apr 11) Fantastic Light (USA) 134 – Najayeb (USA) **91 p**
(Silver Hawk (USA) 123) [2006 7m 8.1m* Aug 28] leggy, sparely-made colt: first foal:

dam unraced sister to Prix de l'Arc de Triomphe winner Sakhee: much improved from debut (nervy in paddock) when winning maiden at Chepstow by neck from Teslin: will be suited by 1¼m/1½m: useful prospect. *J. L. Dunlop*

MUTAJARRED 2 ch.g. (Feb 16) Alhaarth (IRE) 126 – Bedara 93 (Barathea (IRE) 127) **73 P** [2006 6d⁴ Oct 27] 75,000Y: big, strong gelding: third foal: half-brother to fairly useful 2004 2-y-o 1m winner Mozafin (by Zafonic), later successful in Austria, and 3-y-o Arm Candy: dam, 10.5f winner, out of useful French stayer Cutting Reef: 16/1, very promising fourth to Miss Lucifer in maiden at Newmarket, green and soon behind but finishing strongly, not knocked about: gelded after: will be suited by 1m+: sure to improve considerably, and one to follow. *W. J. Haggas*

MUTAKARRIM 9 ch.g. Mujtahid (USA) 118 – Alyakkh (IRE) 78 (Sadler's Wells **112** (USA) 132) [2006 106: 12d⁶ 12v* 14g Jul 1] good-topped gelding: smart performer: back to very best when winning quite valuable handicap at the Curragh in May by 3 lengths from Princess Nala: well-held last of 7 behind Kastoria in Curragh Cup only subsequent Flat outing: stays 1¾m: acts on any going: usually blinkered, though not last 2 starts: normally reliable: fairly useful hurdler/chaser. *D. K. Weld, Ireland*

MUTAMAASEK (USA) 4 b. or br.g. Swain (IRE) 134 – Tamgeed (USA) 66 (Wood- **71** man (USA) 126) [2006 66: 10g 11.6m 11.6f⁶ 12m⁶ p12g p12g² Sep 29] smallish, strong gelding: fair maiden: stays easy 1½m: acts on polytrack, firm and good to soft going: sometimes tongue tied: tried visored/in cheekpieces. *Lady Herries*

MUTAMARED (USA) 6 ch.g. Nureyev (USA) 131 – Alydariel (USA) (Alydar **115** (USA)) [2006 99: p6g* 6m* 5m 6m 6m² p6g* Sep 30] lengthy gelding: smart handi- capper: further improvement in 2006, winning at Lingfield in April, Newmarket in May and Kempton (best effort, beat Intrepid Jack by ¾ length) in September: also good neck

Errigal Racing's "Mutamared"

second of 27 to Borderlescott in Stewards' Cup at Goodwood: best form at 6f: acts on dirt, polytrack, good to firm and good to soft going: tried tongue tied at 3 yrs. *K. A. Ryan*

MUTAMARRES 3 b.g. Green Desert (USA) 127 – Injaad (Machiavellian (USA) 123) **99**
[2006 86: p8g p7g 6m* 6m² 6f 6g² 5d Aug 28] good-topped gelding: has a quick action: useful handicapper: won at Ripon in June: good second in valuable events at Newmarket won by Dark Missile (beaten a head) and Burning Incense (went down by 1¼ lengths): has won at 7f, but likely to prove best at 5f/6f: acts on firm and soft going: visored last 5 starts: races prominently: joined D. Watson in UAE. *Sir Michael Stoute*

MUTANASEB (USA) 2 b.c. (May 14) Mr Greeley (USA) 122 – Rose Rhapsody **87 p**
(USA) (Pleasant Colony (USA)) [2006 6g⁵ 7d³ Oct 28] $40,000F, 135,000 2-y-o: tall colt: seventh foal: brother to 2 winners in USA and half-brother to 2 winners abroad by Louis Quatorze: dam placed in USA: shaped well in maidens at Newmarket won by Truly Royal and Spanish Moon, beaten 2½ lengths into third (of 19) on second occasion: sort to improve and do well as 3-y-o. *M. A. Jarvis*

MUTARED (IRE) 8 b.g. Marju (IRE) 127 – Shahaada (USA) 57 (Private Account **52**
(USA)) [2006 58: f8g⁵ p10g p8.6g Feb 20] lengthy gelding: modest performer now-adays: stays 1m: acts on all-weather, firm and good to soft going: tried in headgear. *N. P. Littmoden*

MUTAWAFFER 5 b.g. Marju (IRE) 127 – Absaar (USA) 76 (Alleged (USA) 138) **97**
[2006 107d: 6s⁴ 7g⁵ 8.1m² 8f⁵ 10m² 10.4d 10.4g⁵ 10.4s⁴ Oct 6] strong, well-made geld-ing: useful handicapper: several creditable efforts, including when 2¼ lengths fifth to Rohaani at York seventh outing: stays 1¼m: acts on soft and good to firm going: tongue tied second outing. *R. A. Fahey*

MUTAWAJID (IRE) 3 b.c. Zafonic (USA) 130 – Zeiting (IRE) 105 (Zieten (USA) **95**
118) [2006 105: 6d⁵ 7g⁶ 6m⁵ Jun 27] big, strong, lengthy colt: useful performer: respect-able fifth to Kingsgate Prince in listed event at Newbury on reappearance, but well below form in similar race at Epsom (jockey reported colt didn't handle race) and minor event at Newbury after: should stay 7f: acts on good to firm going: reportedly had palate problem fourth start at 2 yrs, tongue tied next 2 outings: sold 9,000 gns, sent to Spain. *R. Hannon*

MUTAWAQED (IRE) 8 ch.g. Zafonic (USA) 130 – Waqood (USA) 75 (Riverman **79**
(USA) 131) [2006 85: 6d 5g Jun 1] heavy-bodied gelding: useful handicapper in 2004: lightly raced since and just fair form on reappearance, much better effort in 2006: best at 5f/6f: acts on all-weather, firm and soft going: tried visored/blinkered: wears tongue tie: usually bandaged: best held up (tends to idle). *M. A. Magnusson*

MUTAYAM 6 b.g. Compton Place 125 – Final Shot 91 (Dalsaan 125) [2006 47: 5m 5f –
5m 5m 5m Aug 3] modest winner at best: little form in 2006. *D. A. Nolan*

MUTOON (IRE) 2 b.f. (Apr 21) Erhaab (USA) 127 – Nafhaat (USA) 91 (Roberto **52**
(USA) 131) [2006 p8g Oct 20] sister to winner in South Africa and half-sister to numer-ous winners, including smart 1¼m to 14.6f (Park Hill Stakes) winner Ranin (by Unfu-wain): dam 1½m winner: 10/1, mid-field in maiden at Lingfield: sold 35,000 gns, joined S. Williams. *E. A. L. Dunlop*

MUTUAL FRIEND (USA) 2 b.c. (Mar 14) Aljabr (USA) 125 – Dubai Visit (USA) **71 p**
101 (Quiet American (USA)) [2006 7d Oct 28] tall colt: second foal: dam, 1m winner (including at 2 yrs in USA), half-sister to very smart performer around 1m China Visit (by Red Ransom) out of close relative to 2000 Guineas winner King of Kings: 66/1, better than position (ninth of 19) in maiden at Newmarket won by Mr Napper Tandy, good headway before inexperience told: will improve. *E. A. L. Dunlop*

MUZHER (IRE) 3 ch.g. Indian Ridge 123 – Almurooj 54 (Zafonic (USA) 130) [2006 **98**
87: 7g⁴ 8s* p8g 7s* 7d⁴ 7g³ Oct 13] strong gelding: useful performer: won maiden in May and handicap in August, both at Newmarket: best effort when third to King's Caprice in handicap there final start (gelded after): stays 1m: acts on soft and good to firm going: below form in cheekpieces fifth start: has looked none too keen/carried head high: joined S. Seemar in UAE. *B. W. Hills*

MY AMALIE (IRE) 3 b.f. Galileo (IRE) 134 – Princess Amalie (USA) (Rahy (USA) **92**
115) [2006 85: p7g* 7m 7m 8d⁴ 8.1m 8p 8g Sep 30] leggy, useful-looking filly: fairly useful performer: won maiden at Lingfield in April: good efforts when eighth in Fred Darling Stakes at Newbury and seventh in Chartwell Fillies' Stakes at Lingfield next 2 starts: should be suited by 1m+: acts on polytrack, unraced on extremes of going on turf: slowly away fifth outing. *C. E. Brittain*

MY ARCH 4 b.g. Silver Patriarch (IRE) 125 – My Desire 88 (Grey Desire 115) [2006 **88**
9.2d³ 9.8m⁴ 8m³ 9.8g² 8d² 9.9g* 12d Sep 30] good-bodied gelding: half-brother to 5-y-o
My Paris and 1½m to 2m winner My Line (by Perpendicular): dam suited by thorough
test of stamina (also winning hurdler): fairly useful performer: won maiden at Beverley in
August by ¾ length from Piety: should stay 1½m: acts on good to soft going. *K. A. Ryan*

MY BEAUTAFUL 2 ch.f. (Mar 25) Classic Cliche (IRE) 128 – Ginger Rogers 71 (Gil- **49 p**
doran 123) [2006 p8.6s³ Dec 13] second foal: dam 1¾m to 17f winner: 33/1, staying-on
third to Benny The Bat in maiden at Wolverhampton: stoutly bred: should progress.
Miss J. S. Davis

MY BEST SECRET 7 ch.g. Secret Appeal – Mohibbah (USA) 86 (Conquistador Cielo **–**
(USA)) [2006 8m Jul 10] modest form in bumpers: showed nothing in seller sole Flat
outing. *L. Lungo*

MY BOO 4 b.f. Sri Pekan (USA) 117 – Malwiya (USA) (Shahrastani (USA) 135) [2006 **46**
49: p12.2g p13g p12.2g 15.8g 12f p16g Jun 29] poor performer: stays 1½m: acts on
polytrack and good to firm going: wears cheekpieces/blinkers nowadays: tongue tied.
T. Keddy

MYCENEAN PRINCE (USA) 3 b.g. Swain (IRE) 134 – Nijinsky's Beauty (USA) **49**
(Nijinsky (CAN) 138) [2006 –: 8d 8g 7.1m 10m 9d⁶ f8m f8g⁵ Dec 12] strong, compact
gelding: poor maiden: stays 9f: tried visored. *R. C. Guest*

MY DROP (IRE) 2 b.c. (Apr 10) Danetime (IRE) 121 – Notluckytochange (IRE) 91 **52 p**
(King of Clubs 124) [2006 p6g⁴ Dec 22] €5,800Y: fifth foal: dam Irish 5f to 7f winner:
10/1, 3¾ lengths fourth to Iron Pearl in maiden at Lingfield, keeping on after slow start:
will do better. *E. J. O'Neill*

MYFRENCHCONNECTION (IRE) 2 b.g. (Apr 17) Tendulkar (USA) 114 – Pap- **63**
inette (IRE) (Maelstrom Lake 118) [2006 7d 7.5m⁴ 7g⁶ Sep 27] strong gelding: modest
maiden: stays 7.5f. *P. T. Midgley*

MY GACHO (IRE) 4 b.g. Shinko Forest (IRE) – Floralia 81 (Auction Ring (USA) **93**
123) [2006 82: f7g 6g* 6m 6m* 6f² 6m⁴ 6m⁶ 6f⁵ 6f³ Sep 18] good-topped gelding: fairly
useful handicapper: won at Haydock and Thirsk in June: good efforts after when second
to Folga at Redcar and third to Munaddam at Folkestone fifth/final starts: best at 6f: acts
on all-weather and firm ground: visored/blinkered nowadays: races prominently: reared
as stall opened third outing (lost all chance): withdrawn after breaking out of stall intended ninth start. *T. D. Barron*

MY GIRL PEARL (IRE) 6 b.m. Sri Pekan (USA) 117 – Desert Bloom (FR) (Last **58**
Tycoon 131) [2006 59: p7.1g 7m 6m 7g² 7.1m⁵ 6f³ 6m 5.5g³ 6m 6f 6f⁶ 6m⁶ 6g⁵ p6g⁵
p7.1g Nov 20] angular mare: modest performer: stays 7f: acts on all-weather and firm
going: tried blinkered: none too consistent. *M. S. Saunders*

MY JEANIE (IRE) 2 ch.f. (Mar 18) King Charlemagne (USA) 120 – Home Comforts **46 +**
(Most Welcome 131) [2006 6m p8g p7g³ p8g² Dec 18] €3,000Y: sixth foal: half-sister to
winners in Italy by Orpen and Victory Note: dam, ran twice in Ireland, half-sister to smart
winner up to 10.5f Glowing With Pride: poor maiden on balance: stays 1m. *J. C. Fox*

MYKEYTA 3 b.f. Key of Luck (USA) 126 – Mylania 70 (Midyan (USA) 124) [2006 –: **42**
f8g² f8g⁴ f8g⁴ p10g⁶ Apr 5] poor maiden: stays 1m: acts on fibresand. *J. G. Given*

MY LEARNED FRIEND (IRE) 2 b.c. (Apr 11) Marju (IRE) 127 – Stately Princess **86**
70 (Robellino (USA) 127) [2006 7m 7m⁵ 7m* 7d³ Sep 24] 15,500F, 33,000Y: close-
coupled, useful-looking colt: fifth foal: half-brother to 5-y-o Cottingham and 3-y-o
Kalankari: dam 5f (at 2 yrs) and 6f winner: fairly useful performer: won minor event at
Lingfield in August by short head from Safe Investment: third to Just Dust in nursery at
Ascot: will stay 1m. *A. M. Balding*

MY LEGAL EAGLE (IRE) 12 b.g. Law Society (USA) 130 – Majestic Nurse 80 **62**
(On Your Mark 125) [2006 74, a50: 15s³ 14.1d⁴ 14.1m 12.1d³ 14m⁴ 14d⁵ Oct 8] small- **a–**
ish gelding: modest performer nowadays: effective at 1½m to 17f: acts on fibresand,
heavy and good to firm going: occasionally blinkered earlier in career: usually held up.
E. G. Bevan

MY LOVELY LADY (IRE) 3 b.f. Cape Cross (IRE) 129 – Lace Flower (Old Vic **73**
136) [2006 69: 8m² 10m⁴ 10v⁴ 8.2g⁴ 8f* 8f³ 8.1f² 8m⁶ 8f 8f Aug 9] lightly-made filly:
fair performer: won handicap at Brighton in June: best form at 1m: acts on firm going:
often hangs/flashes tail: sold 3,000 gns, sent to Bahrain. *M. L. W. Bell*

MY LOVELY LESLEY (USA) 2 ch.f. (Feb 22) Hennessy (USA) 122 – My Cherie **86**
(USA) (Woodman (USA) 126) [2006 5g p6g* 6f³ 8f⁵ a6f⁵ Oct 15] $95,000Y, $170,000

2-y-o: smallish, sturdy filly: has a quick action: half-sister to several winners abroad: dam, 2-y-o 8.5f winner in USA, half-sister to high-class 6f to 9f performer Green Line Express: fairly useful performer: won maiden at Lingfield in June: good 1¼ lengths third to Hope'n'Charity in listed race at Newmarket (hung left) next time, then left B. Meehan: off nearly 3 months, below form in allowance race and non-graded stakes for new trainer: should stay 7f: acts on firm going. *P. Pugh, USA*

MY LOVE THOMAS (IRE) 2 b.f. (Mar 2) Cadeaux Genereux 131 – Flanders (IRE) 110 (Common Grounds 118) [2006 p6g* Nov 13] 155,000Y: third foal: half-sister to useful French/US 7f/1m (including at 2 yrs) winner Louvain (by Sinndar) and German 7f winner Farbenspiel (by Desert Prince): dam 5f winner (including at 2 yrs): 11/4, won 5-runner maiden at Lingfield by short head from Kyle, green, carried across course and hit in face by runner-up's rider's whip but getting on top close home: sure to do better. *E. A. L. Dunlop* — **77 p**

MY MAITE MICKEY 2 b.g. (May 21) Komaite (USA) – Mrs Plum 72 (Emarati (USA) 74) [2006 5g 5d f6m Oct 31] unfurnished gelding: well held in maidens. *R. C. Guest* — **–**

MY MICHELLE 5 b.m. Ali-Royal (IRE) 127 – April Magic (Magic Ring (IRE) 115) **60** [2006 65: 8.1d p7g⁴ 7g⁵ 7.1m⁵ 8.1m Sep 1] leggy, quite good-topped mare: modest handicapper: stays 1m: acts on good to firm and good to soft going. *B. Palling*

MY MIRASOL 2 ch.f. (Feb 5) Primo Valentino (IRE) 116 – Distinctly Blu (IRE) 70 **72** (Distinctly North (USA) 115) [2006 5v² 5d² 5d³ 6m 6g f8g⁵ f8g⁴ p8.6g* Dec 18] 20,000Y: lengthy filly: third foal: half-sister to 4-y-o Distinctly Game: dam 5f winner: fair performer: won claimer at Wolverhampton final start: stays 8.6f: acts on all-weather and heavy going: in cheekpieces last 3 starts. *K. A. Ryan*

MY MONNA 2 b.f. (Mar 31) Josr Algarhoud (IRE) 118 – Albarsha 75 (Mtoto 134) **–** [2006 7m p8g Dec 20] third foal: half-sister to fairly useful 2004 2-y-o 7f winner Donyana (by Mark of Esteem): dam, ran twice (second at 1½m), half-sister to 1000 Guineas winner Ameerat: well held in maidens, off 6 months/left M. Channon in between. *Miss S. West*

MYND 6 b.g. Atraf 116 – Prim Lass 65 (Reprimand 122) [2006 69, a62: f5g 6v² 5d³ 5.1m **73** 6g³ 5s 5.1d* p5.1m p5.1m⁵ Nov 8] workmanlike gelding: fair performer on turf, modest **a55** on all-weather: won claimer at Chepstow in May (left R. Whitaker after): effective at 5f/ 6f: acts on all-weather and heavy going: tried in cheekpieces/visored: sometimes slowly away. *B. Palling*

MY OBSESSION (IRE) 4 b.g. Spectrum (IRE) 126 – Little Love (Warrshan (USA) **68 d** 117) [2006 68: 7s⁴ 7g 8d 7m 10s Oct 16] fair performer: won maiden at Folkestone in March: well below form after: will probably stay 1m: acts on soft ground. *John Berry*

MY ONLY SUNSHINE 7 b.g. First Trump 118 – Fiveofive (IRE) 61 (Fairy King **63** (USA)) [2006 78: 5g 6d⁶ 6.1d³ 6d 6.1s Oct 25] dipped-backed gelding: modest handicapper nowadays: effective at 6f/7f: acts on good to firm and good to soft ground: visored (ran poorly) once at 6 yrs: sometimes carries head high/wanders. *M. J. Wallace*

MY PARIS 5 b.g. Paris House 123 – My Desire 88 (Grey Desire 115) [2006 110: p8.6g **110** 8s 7.1m³ 9m⁵ 8.2g³ 8.1m 8f 8d 9d Sep 30] leggy, lengthy gelding: smart performer: best effort in 2006 when creditable fifth to Star of Light in quite valuable handicap at Newmarket fourth start: stays 1¼m: acts on soft and good to firm going, lightly raced on all-weather: tried in cheekpieces (below form): races prominently: genuine. *K. A. Ryan*

MY PENSION (IRE) 5 b.g. Orpen (USA) 116 – Woodenitbenice (USA) (Nasty And **–** Bold (USA)) [2006 –, a78: p9.5g⁴ p10g p8.6g⁶ p10g⁴ p9.5g p8.6g p8.6g Dec 18] lengthy, **a70** rather sparely-made gelding: fair handicapper: effective at 1m/easy 1¼m: acts on polytrack and any turf ground: inconsistent. *P. Howling*

MY PETRA 3 b.f. Midnight Legend 118 – Lac Marmot (FR) (Marju (IRE) 127) [2006 **86** 75p: 10.5m³ 11.6d² p10g⁶ 12.1d² 11.6m* 12g³ 12f² 11.6s⁵ Oct 2] leggy, close-coupled filly: fairly useful handicapper: won at Windsor in August: stays 1½m: acts on firm and good to soft ground: fairly useful winner over hurdles. *A. King*

MY PRINCESS (IRE) 4 b.f. Danehill Dancer (IRE) 117 – Shanoora (IRE) 53 (Don't **87** Forget Me 127) [2006 88: 8m⁴ 8.3m⁶ 8d⁶ 7f 8m⁶ 8.5g³ 8m² 8f⁴ 7f⁵ 8m³ 8d* p12g⁶ Oct 23] close-coupled filly: fairly useful handicapper: best effort when winning apprentice event at Brighton in September by neck from Landucci: stays 8.5f: acts on firm and good to soft going: tried blinkered: often races freely: sold 32,000 gns, sent to Saudi Arabia. *N. A. Callaghan*

MY PUTRA (USA) 4 b. or br.g. Silver Hawk (USA) 123 – Petite Triomphe (USA) **60**
(Wild Again (USA)) [2006 69: p12.2g⁵ 10g 12d May 28] quite good-topped gelding:
has a round action: lightly-raced maiden: just modest form in 2006, gelded after final
start (blinkered): will probably prove best short of 1½m: acts on good to firm ground.
P. F. I. Cole

MY RASCAL (IRE) 4 b.g. Imperial Ballet (IRE) 110 – Derena (FR) (Crystal Palace **51**
(FR) 132) [2006 63: 5.1m 6m 5f 5m Aug 8] big, strong gelding: modest handicapper: best
effort at 6f on good ground: visored on 3-y-o return, wore cheekpieces/blinkers last 6
starts. *J. Balding*

MY REFLECTION 3 b.g. Cape Cross (IRE) 129 – There's Two (IRE) 85 (Ashkalani **–**
(IRE) 128) [2006 –: p6g* f5g⁵ p7.1g⁵ p6g² f7g p6g⁵ f6g p6g p5 1g⁶ 5m a8g Oct 15] **a50**
lengthy gelding: modest performer: won banded event at Wolverhampton in January: sold
from D. Shaw 1,500 gns prior to final start: best form at 6f: acts on polytrack: tried visored. *F. Ramirez, Spain*

MYRTLE BAY (IRE) 3 bl.g. Pennekamp (USA) 130 – Moneypenny (GER) (Neshad **62**
(USA) 108) [2006 75: 9.8m⁵ 12s 11.6g 11.1m⁴ 14g 11.1m³ 16.2m³ 16g 13.8m² Sep 16]
useful-looking gelding: fair maiden at best: stays 2m: acts on polytrack and good to
firm going: tried in visor/cheekpieces: sometimes races freely, and looks no easy ride.
K. R. Burke

MY SARA 2 b.f. (Apr 28) Mujahid (USA) 125 – Ancestry (Persepolis (FR) 127) [2006 **55**
6g p6g p6g⁴ p7.1g⁵ Dec 30] €18,000Y: sister to 4-y-o Mary Gray and half-sister to several
winners, including useful 5f/6f winner Night Flight (by Night Shift) and fairly useful 6f
(at 2 yrs) to 1¼m winner Devilry (by Faustus): dam unraced: modest maiden: best effort
when fourth to Not For Me at Wolverhampton: left D. Daly and off 6 months, little impact
in nursery there final outing. *R. A. Fahey*

MY SECRETS 2 b.c. (Mar 18) Fantastic Light (USA) 134 – St Radegund 85 (Green **85**
Desert (USA) 127) [2006 6g 6f³ 7.2v⁵ p8g* p8.6g* Nov 23] 34,000Y: sturdy colt: half-
brother to 7f/1m (latter at 2 yrs) winner Chubbes (by Kris) and 4-y-o Halla San: dam, 7f
winner from 2 starts, out of 1000 Guineas and Sussex Stakes winner On The House:
fairly useful form: won nurseries at Kempton and Wolverhampton in November: will stay
1¼m/1½m: acts on polytrack, probably firm ground. *M. Johnston*

MY SILVER MONARCH (IRE) 2 b.f. (Mar 12) Bertolini (USA) 125 – April View **–**
(USA) (Distant View (USA) 126) [2006 p6g Oct 5] €5,000Y: first foal: dam ran twice:
well beaten in maiden. *H. S. Howe*

MYSTERIOSA 4 b.f. Mujahid (USA) 125 – Mrs Gray 61 (Red Sunset 120) [2006 52: **–**
p9.5g Dec 21] lightly-raced maiden: well held only outing in 2006: difficult ride.
B. R. Millman

MYSTERY OCEAN 2 b.f. (May 4) Dr Fong (USA) 128 – Tiriana (Common Grounds **86**
118) [2006 5.1m* 6f 6g² 6d Oct 27] leggy, lengthy filly: fifth foal: half-sister to 3 winners,
including smart 6f (at 2 yrs)/7f winner Penkenna Princess (by Pivotal) and 5-y-o Salut
Saint Cloud: dam third at 1m in France: fairly useful performer: won maiden at Bath
in August: improvement when unlucky short-head second to Cheap Street in nursery at
Newmarket (stirred up beforehand): no impression in listed race there final start: will be
suited by 1m. *R. M. Beckett*

MYSTERY PIPS 6 b.m. Bin Ajwaad (IRE) 119 – Le Shuttle 49 (Presidium 124) [2006 **71**
63, a51: f5g f5g⁴ f5g* f5g² f5g⁶ 5.2m* p5.1g* p5.1g² 5f 5f⁴ 5m⁵ 5d 5d 5d p5.1m⁴ p5.1g
p5.1g³ Nov 18] fair performer: won banded event at Southwell in March and handicaps at
Yarmouth in May and Wolverhampton in June: best at bare 5f: acts on all-weather, firm
and good to soft going: wears blinkers/visor: races up with pace. *N. Tinkler*

MYSTERY RIVER (USA) 2 ch.f. (Apr 5) Dr Fong (USA) 128 – Bacinella (USA) (El **78**
Gran Senor (USA) 136) [2006 6g 7m⁶ 8.3s³ p8g³ Oct 20] 120,000Y: good-bodied filly:
sixth foal: sister to smart 7f and (including at 2 yrs in USA) 1m winner Fong's Thong and
half-sister to 2 winners, including fairly useful 2004 2-y-o 5f winner Golden Anthem (by
Lion Cavern): dam unraced close relative to smart 1½m winner Xtra: fair maiden: third at
Windsor and Lingfield: stays 8.3f. *B. J. Meehan*

MYSTERY WORLD 2 b.g. (May 11) Agnes World (USA) 123 – Dahshah 77 (Mujta- **61**
hid (USA) 118) [2006 5d 5g⁵ 5.5d⁴ 5g⁶ 7f Sep 5] quite good-topped gelding: modest
maiden: off 3 months/gelded before final start (trip too far in nursery): should prove best
at 5f: sold 1,500 gns. *M. Johnston*

MYSTIC 2 ch.f. (Mar 15) Bahamian Bounty 116 – Sweet Myrtle (USA) (Mutakddim (USA) 112) [2006 5g 5g Jul 22] workmanlike filly: first foal: dam unraced half-sister to very smart 6f/7f winner Soldier's Tale: well held in maidens. *D. W. Barker* —

MYSTICAL AYR (IRE) 4 br.f. Namid 128 – Scanno's Choice (IRE) 54 (Pennine Walk 120) [2006 5g 5g Jul 22] [...] capper: stays 1¾m: acts on heavy going: tried in cheekpieces first start. *Miss L. A. Perratt* **65**

MYSTICAL MOON 2 b.g. (Apr 21) Medicean 128 – Moon Carnival 94 (Be My Guest (USA) 126) [2006 8g 8m⁶ 8d⁵ Sep 27] quite good-topped gelding: half-brother to 3 winners, including 1998 2-y-o 7f winner Distant Moon (by Distant Relative) and 7f (at 2 yrs) to 2m winner Carousing (by Selkirk), both fairly useful: dam, won around 1½m, half-sister to St Leger winner Moon Madness and Coronation Cup winner Sheriff's Star: fair form in maidens, green and not knocked about: will benefit from 1¼m/1½m: should progress, and do well in handicaps. *Lady Herries* **69 p**

MYSTIC DANCER 2 ch.c. (May 1) Machiavellian (USA) 123 – Mystic Goddess (USA) 94 (Storm Bird (CAN) 134) [2006 7d⁵ p7g² Oct 20] tall, attractive colt: has a fluent, round action: brother to high-class 1m/1¼m winner Medicean and 3-y-o Minister of State and half-brother to useful 1m winner Moon Goddess (by Rainbow Quest): dam, 2-y-o 6f/7f winner (stayed 1m), half-sister to Gran Criterium winner Sanam: shaped encouragingly in maidens at Newmarket and Lingfield (odds on, second to Escape Route): will be suited by 1m/1¼m: has plenty of scope, and sure to do better at 3 yrs. *Sir Michael Stoute* **79 p**

MYSTIC FOREST 7 b.g. Charnwood Forest (IRE) 125 – Mystic Beauty (IRE) (Alzao (USA) 117) [2006 –: f16g Jan 17] leggy gelding: handicapper: lightly raced and no form since 2003: has worn blinkers/visor. *Miss J. A. Camacho* —

MYSTIC MAN (FR) 8 b.g. Cadeaux Genereux 131 – Shawanni 105 (Shareef Dancer (USA) 135) [2006 86: p7.1g⁸ p9.5g² p8g* p7g² p8g p7.1g³ p7.1g* p8g 8m 8g 8.1g 7g⁵ 7g⁵ 7.5g 7m 7d p7.1g p7g⁶ p7.1g⁶ Dec 26] strong, angular gelding: fairly useful performer: won claimers at Wolverhampton and Lingfield (left K. Ryan £12,000) in January, and handicap at Wolverhampton in March: below form after: stays 1m: acts on all-weather, soft and good to firm going: often blinkered: tried tongue tied early in career: held up, tends to race freely: struck into ninth outing. *I. W. McInnes* **89 d**

MYSTIC PROMISE (IRE) 5 gr.g. Among Men (USA) 124 – Ivory's Promise 74 (Pursuit of Love 124) [2006 –: p12g Jan 3] leggy, lengthy gelding: no form since 2004: tried in headgear/tongue tie. *Mrs N. Macauley* —

MYSTIC QUEEN (IRE) 3 b.f. Woodborough (USA) 112 – Speed Queen (IRE) 52 (Goldmark (USA) 113) [2006 –: p9.5g f7g⁵ f6g² p6g⁴ p6g⁵ f5g² 5g p5.1g p6g³ f6g⁴ f7g p6g Dec 5] tall filly: modest maiden: stays 6f: acts on all-weather. *A. P. Jarvis* **a60**

MYSTIC ROLL 3 br.g. Medicean 128 – Pain Perdu (IRE) (Waajib 121) [2006 75: 8.3m 8m 7f 7d 8.3g p12.2g p10g⁴ Dec 3] quite good-topped gelding: fair maiden: left B. Meehan after third start: stays 1m: acts on good to firm ground: tried blinkered. *Jane Chapple-Hyam* **65**

MYSTIC STORM 3 b.g. Medicean 128 – Mrs Nash 66 (Night Shift (USA)) [2006 –: p7g 8d² p10g* 9.9m³ 10m 11m 8d Aug 20] big, good-bodied gelding: fair performer: won handicap at Lingfield in May: stays 1¼m, probably not 11f: acts on polytrack, good to firm and good to soft going: tongue tied at 2 yrs. *Lady Herries* **77**

MYSTIFIED (IRE) 3 b.g. Raise A Grand (IRE) 114 – Sunrise (IRE) 58 (Sri Pekan (USA) 117) [2006 63: p8.6g* p8g p9.5g 8g 8m p12.2g⁵ p12.2g⁵ 14d² 15.8s p13.9g Nov 17] useful-looking gelding: fair performer: won handicap at Wolverhampton in February: seemingly effective at 8.6f to 1¾m: acts on polytrack, good to firm and good to soft ground: tried in cheekpieces, usually blinkered. *R. F. Fisher* **62**

MY SUPER BIRD (USA) 2 b.g. (Jan 23) Gulch (USA) – Tadwiga 104 (Fairy King (USA)) [2006 6m⁴ 8.3d⁶ 8d⁶ Oct 19] $50,000: fifth foal: half-brother to 2 winners in USA, including Grade 3 9.5f winner Rock Lobster (by Mt Livermore): dam 6f (at 2 yrs) and 1m winner: fair maiden: stays 8.3f. *M. Johnston* **66**

MYTASS 3 b.g. Averti (IRE) 117 – Emerald Dream (IRE) 47 (Vision (USA)) [2006 48: f7g p7.1g 11g 10d 8.3m p8.6g 7m 8.3m Jul 26] close-coupled gelding: poor maiden: stays 8.6f: acts on all-weather and good to firm ground: blinkered nowadays (tried earlier in cheekpieces/visor). *J. A. Pickering* **42 d**

MYTHICAL CHARM 7 b.m. Charnwood Forest (IRE) 125 – Triple Tricks (IRE) 70 (Royal Academy (USA) 130) [2006 69, a64: p8g⁶ 7.6f³ 8.3m³ 8.3m 8.1m 7g 8.1m² 7g 8d⁵ p7g⁵ p8g² p8g* p8g⁶ p8g* p8g Dec 16] good-topped mare: fair performer: won banded races at Kempton in November and December: effective at 7f to easy 1¼m: acts on all-weather, firm and soft ground: tongue tied: patiently ridden. *J. J. Bridger*

MYTHICAL KID (USA) 2 b. or br.c. (Apr 21) Lemon Drop Kid (USA) 131 – **111 p** Myth To Reality (FR) (Sadler's Wells (USA) 132) [2006 7s* 7s² Oct 21]

Training two-year-olds for the top races has seemed less of a priority for Sir Michael Stoute than might be expected of a man who has been champion trainer nine times. Although he won the Dewhurst with Ajdal in 1986, high-profile juvenile wins have been thin on the ground for Stoute more recently, at least among the colts. Stoute won only a handful of two-year-old pattern events of any description for colts in the whole of the 'nineties and his last success at Group 1 level in the new decade came with Dilshaan in the Racing Post Trophy at Doncaster in 2000. All the more reason then to take notice when Stoute has a juvenile colt showing as much promise as Mythical Kid so early in its career, something which did not escape the attention of Godolphin, who will train him in 2007. Mythical Kid achieved smart form in only two starts within the space of twelve days in October, both over seven furlongs at Newbury. Up against fifteen rivals, he started joint favourite for the second division of a maiden on his debut and ran out a convincing winner, held up before showing himself too strong for market rival Contentious, winning by three lengths. If anything, Mythical Kid looked as though in need of the race that day and he showed much improved form when stepped up in class for the Group 3 Stan James Horris Hill Stakes later in the month. Clear favourite this time in a field of ten, he looked sure to follow up when quickening smartly to lead inside the final furlong, only to idle in front under a sympathetic ride, caught on the post by the more experienced Dijeerr, the pair four lengths clear.

Mythical Kid (USA) (b. or br.c. Apr 21, 2004)	Lemon Drop Kid (USA) (b 1996)	Kingmambo (b 1990)	Mr Prospector Miesque
		Charming Lassie (b 1987)	Seattle Slew Lassie Dear
	Myth To Reality (FR) (b 1986)	Sadler's Wells (b 1981)	Northern Dancer Fairy Bridge
		Millieme (b 1977)	Mill Reef Hardiemma

Mythical Kid was bought for 1,400,000 dollars as a yearling at the Keeneland September Sale. His purchase represented a fine return on the 125,000 dollars paid by his breeders, Cumbrian businessman Gary Middlebrook and his wife, for his in-foal dam Myth To Reality when she was culled from the Niarchos family studs early in 2003. The Mt Livermore foal in question, subsequently named Anse Victorin, was still unraced as a three-year-old in 2006, but Myth To Reality's produce before her sale have since added untold value to the family. Whipper (by Miesque's Son) proved a high-class performer over three seasons in France, successful at five and a half furlongs to a mile, notably in the Prix Morny at two, the Prix Jacques le Marois at three and the Prix Maurice de Gheest at four, while Divine Proportions (by Miesque Son's brother Kingmambo) won nine of her ten races, including the Prix Marcel Boussac at two and the Poule d'Essai des Pouliches and the Prix de Diane at three. Mythical Kid is closely related to both Whipper and Divine Proportions, his sire Lemon Drop Kid being a son of Kingmambo. Lemon Drop Kid, who won seven Grade 1 events, including the Belmont Stakes and the Woodward Stakes, has produced his best performers in the States, where Lemons Forever won the Kentucky Oaks over nine furlongs on dirt in 2006 and Cosmonaut was a Grade 3 winner over a mile and a quarter in soft ground on turf. Mythical Kid, who is also a half-brother to the useful stayer Assos (by Alleged) and closely related to the mile and a half winner Mambo Jambo (another by Kingmambo), dam of the Yorkshire Oaks runner-up Ocean Silk, should be well suited by a mile and further at three, and odds of 33/1 for the Two Thousand Guineas could well underestimate his chance if he gets the go-ahead after the Godolphin trials in the spring. A good-topped colt, still green second time when a little coltish in the preliminaries, Mythical Kid looks sure to progress. He has raced only on soft ground. *Sir Michael Stoute*

MYTHICAL KING (IRE) 9 b.g. Fairy King (USA) – Whatcombe (USA) 88 (Alleged (USA) 138) [2006 61: 15s⁶ Apr 4] deep-girthed gelding: modest handicapper: stays 2¼m: acts on firm and good to soft going. *R. Lee* **59**

MYTHOLOGICAL (USA) 9 b.g. El Gran Senor (USA) 136 – Finance Charge – (USA) (Pretense) [2006 p12g Jun 7] well held sole outing in 2006 (first start since 2001). *Luke Comer, Ireland*

MYTHS AND VERSES 3 b.f. Primo Valentino (IRE) 116 – Romantic Myth 105 **65** (Mind Games 121) [2006 63: 5.1d⁶ 6.1g⁵ 7.1g³ 8.1g³ 8.1m³ 5.9g 7.1m⁵ 8v⁶ 8s p8g³ p7.1g⁴ p8.6g² Dec 23] good-bodied filly: has a short, unimpressive action: fair maiden: left T. Easterby after second start: stays 8.6f: acts on polytrack and any turf going: tried in cheekpieces: has raced freely. *K. A. Ryan*

MY TIGER LILLY 2 ch.f. (Feb 9) Tobougg (IRE) 125 – Ashantiana 64 (Ashkalani **56** (IRE) 128) [2006 6m p6g⁶ 6m³ 7m⁶ 6f³ Sep 18] first foal: dam, maiden who stayed 1¼m, half-sister to smart performer up to 9f Missile: modest maiden: third at Windsor and Folkestone (nursery): best form at 6f: acts on polytrack and firm going. *W. J. Knight*

MYTORI 4 ch.f. Vettori (IRE) 119 – Markievicz (IRE) 73 (Doyoun 124) [2006 –: p9.5g – Jan 30] little form. *D. Shaw*

MY TRIP (IRE) 4 b. or br.g. Midhish 109 – Crissy (IRE) 65 (Entitled 126) [2006 p10g **50** 7d May 13] modest maiden: missed 2005, well held in handicaps in 2006: tried tongue tied/blinkered. *Kieran P. Cotter, Ireland*

MYTTON'S DREAM 4 b.f. Diktat 126 – Courtisane (Persepolis (FR) 127) [2006 57: **46** p9.5g p7.1g f7g p7.1g⁵ p8.6g p7.1g p6g⁶ May 5] leggy filly: poor performer: barely stays 1m: acts on all-weather and good to soft ground: tried blinkered. *R. Brotherton*

MYTTON'S PRIDE 3 b.g. Tagula (IRE) 116 – Pictina (Petong 126) [2006 69: 5d 5g³ **66 d** 5.3f⁴ 5s 5d 5.1g p5.1g⁴ 5f⁶ 5m Aug 12] leggy gelding: has a quick action: fair handicapper: below form after third outing: will prove best kept to 5f: acts on polytrack, firm and good to soft going: tried in cheekpieces, blinkered final start. *A. Bailey*

MY TWO GIRLS (IRE) 2 b.f. (Apr 16) Danetime (IRE) 121 – Sanctuary Line (IRE) **61** (Lake Coniston (IRE) 131) [2006 5g⁶ 5f⁵ 5g 5m Sep 11] €4,200Y, resold 4,500Y: close-coupled filly: second foal: dam unraced half-sister to smart sprinter Lugana Beach: modest maiden: reportedly lost action on nursery debut: raced at 5f. *P. T. Midgley*

MY VALERINA (IRE) 2 b.f. (Mar 19) Danehill Dancer (IRE) 117 – Witching Hour **71** (IRE) 88 (Alzao (USA) 117) [2006 5g² 6s⁵ 5g² 5m² 5m* 6m³ 5m* 5g⁴ 6d⁶ 6g⁴ 7s⁶ Oct 14] 10,000Y: smallish, well-made filly: sixth foal: half-sister to 3 winners, including useful 2004 2-y-o 1m winner Night Hour (by Entrepreneur) and 9f winner Unafraid (by Unfuwain): dam, 2-y-o 6f winner who stayed 1m, half-sister to very smart 1m/1¼m performer Great Dane: fair performer: won minor event at Carlisle in June and nursery at Haydock in July: made frame further 7 times: should stay 7f: acts on soft and good to firm going: edgy sort (tends to sweat): races lazily but is reliable: sold 30,000 gns, sent to Kazakhstan. *Mrs A. Duffield*

N

NAAYLA (IRE) 2 br.f. (Feb 16) Invincible Spirit (IRE) 121 – Pink Cashmere (IRE) **85** (Polar Falcon (USA) 126) [2006 6f⁵ 6m² f6g* 6m 5g⁵ 6.1g⁴ 6.5s p5g³ 5.1m Oct 8] 75,000Y: robust filly: closely related to 5-y-o Motu and half-sister to 3 winners, including 2004 2-y-o 5f winner Pike Bishop (by Namid) and German 2001 2-y-o 6f winner Medina (by Pennekamp), both useful: dam unraced half-sister to very smart sprinter Owington: fairly useful form: second to Indian Ink at Newbury before winning maiden at Southwell in July: ran creditably in nurseries (twice highly tried otherwise), in blinkers last 2 starts: may prove best at 5f: acts on all-weather and good to firm going. *B. J. Meehan*

NABIR (FR) 6 gr.g. Linamix (FR) 127 – Nabagha (FR) (Fabulous Dancer (USA) 124) **65** [2006 74: p9.5g 10.1m 7.9m Jun 5] fair handicapper, better on all-weather than turf: stays 11f: acts on fibresand and soft going: tongue tied last 2 starts, also in cheekpieces final one: won over fences in September/October. *P. D. Niven*

NABRA 2 b.f. (Feb 24) Kyllachy 129 – Muja Farewell 94 (Mujtahid (USA) 118) [2006 **65** 6g³ 6d p7g Oct 26] 105,000Y: first foal: dam 5f winner (including at 2 yrs): fair maiden: clearly best run when third at Yarmouth: should prove suited to 5f/6f. *J. H. M. Gosden*

NADAWAT (USA) 2 b.f. (Mar 27) Kingmambo (USA) 125 – Tashawak (IRE) 118 **80** (Night Shift (USA) 118) [2006 6m 7d³ 6m² 7g³ Sep 30] close-coupled, rather leggy filly: first foal: dam, 6f (at 2 yrs) and 1m (Falmouth Stakes) winner, closely related to very smart 1½m performer Acropolis and Ribblesdale Stakes winner Fairy Queen: fairly useful maiden: placed all starts after debut, third to Ransom Captive at Redcar final one: will probably stay 1m. *J. L. Dunlop*

NAEMI (GER) 4 b.f. Tannenkonig (IRE) 111 – Noanah (GER) (Konigsstuhl (GER)) – [2006 –: f11g⁶ Jan 1] little sign of ability in bumper/maidens. *S. L. Keightley*

NAHAAR (IRE) 3 b.g. Royal Applause 124 – Elhida (IRE) 99 (Mujtahid (USA) 118) **61** [2006 73: 7m 6f⁴ Jun 9] lengthy gelding: fair maiden, lightly raced: effective at 6f: acts on firm ground: in cheekpieces final start: sold 5,000 gns. *M. P. Tregoning*

NAHLASS 3 ch.f. Bluegrass Prince (IRE) 110 – Nahla (Wassl 125) [2006 p8g 10.2m **58** 10.5g p10g Dec 30] lengthy, plain filly: third foal: dam, ran once on Flat, useful bumper winner: modest maiden: best effort final start. *Ms J. S. Doyle*

NAIGANI (USA) 2 ch.c. (Apr 10) Storm Cat (USA) – Fiji 125 (Rainbow Quest (USA) **81** 134) [2006 7.5f² 7.5m⁴ 7d⁴ 6m² 5g³ 6s³ 7d 5v² Oct 23] $200,000Y: close-coupled colt: third foal: half-brother to 3-y-o Marcus Andronicus: dam 1m (at 2 yrs) to 1¼m (including US Grade 1 event) winner: fairly useful maiden: in frame 7 of 8 starts (200/1 and helped force pace in Dewhurst Stakes at Newmarket other one): effective at 5f to 7.5f: acts on any going. *A. P. O'Brien, Ireland*

NAINI TAL 3 ch.f. Inchinor 119 – Royal Patron 78 (Royal Academy (USA) 130) [2006 **73** 8.2m 9.9g 10m⁶ 14m⁴ p12g⁵ 10.5g Sep 22] lightly-made filly: second foal: dam 1¾m winner out of Gold Cup winner Indian Queen: fair maiden: best effort at 1½m: acts on polytrack, raced only on good/good to firm going on turf: flashes tail under pressure: sold £3,500. *D. R. C. Elsworth*

NAKHEEL 3 b.c. Sadler's Wells (USA) 132 – Matiya (IRE) 116 (Alzao (USA) 117) **107** [2006 108p: 8.9g⁵ 9.9m⁵ 10d⁵ Oct 27] good-bodied colt: useful performer: won both 2-y-o starts: as low as 10/1 for 2000 Guineas in mid-April, but found to be suffering from a pelvic problem following week: below form on belated return in September, but back to near best when close fifth to Imperial Stride in listed race at Goodwood next time: respectable fifth behind Into The Dark in similar event at Newmarket final start: stays 1¼m: acts on good to firm and good to soft going: stirred up beforehand on reappearance. *M. Johnston*

NAKWA (IRE) 8 b.g. Namaqualand (USA) – Cajo (IRE) (Tirol 127) [2006 61: p13.9g⁶ **55** p8.6g 12.4m 13f p12.2g⁶ 12f³ 12g⁴ 11.1g³ 15m² 11.1m⁴ 14m⁶ 14g f11g f12m Oct 31] tall gelding: modest performer: stays 15f: acts on fibresand, soft and good to firm going: has reportedly broken blood vessels. *E. J. Alston*

NAMARIAN (IRE) 2 b.f. (Mar 30) Namid 128 – Zalamera 45 (Rambo Dancer (CAN) **58** 107) [2006 6m⁵ 6.1f⁶ 5g⁶ 7m Sep 16] €19,000Y: big, leggy filly: half-sister to 3 winners, including 1m winner Just Woody (by Charnwood Forest): dam, poor maiden, half-sister to dam of very smart Irish middle-distance performer Definite Article: modest maiden: should stay 7f. *T. D. Easterby*

NAMIBIAN PINK (IRE) 2 b.f. (Apr 30) Cape Cross (IRE) 129 – Sky Pink (Warning **55** 136) [2006 p8g³ Dec 20] €15,000F, 12,500Y: fourth foal: half-sister to 2003 Italian 2-y-o 7f winner by Mukaddamah: dam unraced: 25/1, late headway when third (beaten 8 lengths) in maiden at Kempton. *R. M. Beckett*

NAMID REPROBATE (IRE) 3 br.g. Namid 128 – Morning Surprise 58 (Tragic **89** Role (USA)) [2006 84: p8g² p8g⁴ p7g* 7.1s³ 7f 7.1m 7s⁶ 8g 7g Oct 13] compact gelding: fairly useful handicapper: won at Kempton in May: stays easy 1m: acts on polytrack and soft going: blinkered (below form) penultimate start: gelded after final outing. *P. F. I. Cole*

NAMIR (IRE) 4 b.g. Namid 128 – Danalia (IRE) 78 (Danehill (USA) 126) [2006 90d: **74** p5g⁵ p5.1g p5g³ p5.1g p6g p5.1g p5g⁵ 5.1m⁵ 5m* 5m⁴ 5m 6.1f⁵ 5m² 5m⁴ 5d 5.5d⁵ 5m* 5g 5.3g 6.1d Oct 18] strong, good-topped gelding: fair handicapper: won at Pontefract in June (left Stef Liddiard later in month), selling event at Nottingham in July and, having left S. R. Bowring after fifteenth start, Pontefract in September: best at 5f/easy 6f: acts on polytrack, firm and soft going: tried in cheekpieces, usually wears visor: tongue tied nowadays. *D. Shaw*

NAMOOS (USA) 3 b. or br.f. Sahm (USA) 112 – Shuhrah (USA) 101 (Danzig (USA)) **74** [2006 67: 6.1m³ 7s⁶ 7g 7g⁶ Aug 18] sturdy, close-coupled filly: fair maiden: should stay 7f: acts on good to firm going: blinkered final start: sent to France. *J. L. Dunlop*

NAMROC (IRE) 5 b.g. Indian Ridge 123 – Hesperia (Slip Anchor 136) [2006 92: **91** 10.1m² 8g² 7m 10d 7m⁴ 8m Jul 12] strong, lengthy gelding: fairly useful handicapper:

good efforts in 2006 when second: stays 1¼m: acts on firm and good to soft going, well held on heavy: tried in cheekpieces/blinkers: sold 20,000 gns. *N. A. Callaghan*

NAMROUD (USA) 7 b.g. Irish River (FR) 131 – Top Line (FR) (Top Ville 129) [2006 **92** 93, a81: 8g* 8g 8m² 7.6g 8d 8s 8d p9.5g Oct 29] tall gelding: fairly useful handicapper: won at Ayr in June: good second at Pontefract following month: effective at 7f/1m: acts on heavy and good to firm going, probably on polytrack: tried in cheekpieces/blinkers. *R. A. Fahey*

NAMU 3 b.f. Mujahid (USA) 125 – Sheraton Heights 52 (Deploy 131) [2006 76: 6.1g⁴ **76** 6m⁴ 6.1m* 5.7g⁶ 6f* 6.1m³ 6f⁶ 6m³ 6d* p6g⁵ p6g Oct 6] smallish filly: fair performer: won maiden at Warwick and apprentice handicap at Folkestone in July and handicap at Pontefract in September: stays 7f: acts on polytrack and any turf going: races prominently. *B. W. Hills*

NANDO'S DREAM 3 ch.f. Hernando (FR) 127 – Dream Quest 102 (Rainbow Quest **82** (USA) 134) [2006 p10g³ p12g³ p12.2m* p12.2m² p13g* Nov 25] second foal: dam, 1¼m winner who stayed 1½m, sister to smart German 1½m performer Baroon and half-sister to smart sprinters Struggler and Vision of Night: fairly useful form: won maiden at Wolverhampton in October and handicap at Lingfield (idled) in November: stays 13f: raced only on polytrack. *J. Noseda*

NAN JAN 4 b.f. Komaite (USA) – Dam Certain (IRE) 61 (Damister (USA) 123) [2006 – 61, a80: p7.1g⁵ p7g f7g 8d f7g⁵ p8g 8.3g Aug 26] compact filly: modest performer: stays **a63** 7f: acts on all-weather, raced mainly on good/good to firm ground on turf: usually tongue tied: tried blinkered. *R. Ingram*

NANNINA 3 b.f. Medicean 128 – Hill Hopper (IRE) 106 (Danehill (USA) 126) **119** [2006 114: 8s 8m* 8m² 9.9m³ 8m⁴ 10m⁵ Oct 1]

Cheveley Park Stud continued its splendid run in the latest season, finishing in the top four in the list of leading owners in Britain for the third year in four. Not for the first time, its 'red, white sash, royal blue cap' was carried with particular distinction by the fillies and mares, among them the Group 1 winners Nannina and Peeress, and the pattern and listed winners Echelon, Allegretto, Portal and Dance Partner. Add to these the Prix de Diane winner Confidential Lady and Red Bloom, who won the Blandford Stakes at the Curragh for the second year running, and the Cheveley Park broodmare band can look forward to a batch of exciting recruits in due course, though nearly all of those mentioned will be in training again in 2007. Most of those that race for Cheveley Park are homebreds—Allegretto was the only yearling purchase among the fillies mentioned—and well over half of the stud's one hundred and twenty mares are covered nowadays by the Cheveley Park stallions, four of which, Pivotal, Medicean, Carnival Dancer and Iceman, also raced in the Cheveley Park colours. The American influence is a feature of the operation (four of the seven stallions for 2007, following an injury to Starcraft, are by American-bred sires), though none of the stud's mares are based in North America, a reflection perhaps of the wealth of good stallions with American backgrounds now available in Europe. For example, Cheveley Park's flagship stallion the sprinter Pivotal, the sire of Peeress among others and the highest-priced sire standing in Britain, is a grandson of Nureyev, who spent nearly all his stud career in the States, while Cozzene, the sire of Pivotal's dam, was also American based. The sire of Cheveley Park's other British Group 1-winning female in the latest season, Nannina, is Medicean, second in the Cheveley Park stallion pecking order, and both his sire and dam have the USA suffix. Confidential Lady's dam Confidante, the Lowther winner Dance Sequence and the Cheveley Park winner Gay Gallanta are among the stud's broodmares which were purchased as yearlings in America.

Both Peeress and Nannina began the latest season as Group 1 winners, having won the Sun Chariot and the Fillies' Mile respectively in 2005. Nannina contested four pattern races as a two-year-old, also winning the Prestige Stakes at Goodwood before getting the better of Alexandrova by a short head in a cracking race for the Fillies' Mile, run at Newmarket with Ascot closed for rebuilding. The form of the Fillies' Mile looked strong at the time, independently confirmed by the fast timefigures for the first two, and it was underlined in the spring, with third-placed Nasheej winning the Fred Darling at Newbury, sixth-placed Salut d'Amour coming third in the Nell Gwyn at Newmarket and fourth-placed High Heel Sneakers (second to Nasheej in the May Hill at two) showing further improvement to finish a close third in one of the recognised Prix de Diane trials, the Prix Vanteaux at Longchamp. There was a cold start to the spring and Nannina herself was reported in mid-April by her trainer (who had completed a winter move from Manton to Newmarket) to be 'backward in her coat and yet to do any serious work.' She lined up for the One Thousand Guineas, like ten of the thirteen runners, without a preparatory race but looked forward enough in the paddock. Starting joint third favourite, Nannina beat only one home, seemingly unable to cope with the prevailing soft ground, and wisely not subjected to a hard race once that became clear.

Back on a sound surface at Royal Ascot, Nannina made amends in a strong renewal of the Coronation Stakes which attracted four fillies who had passed the post first in a classic at the trip, One Thousand Guineas winner Speciosa, Irish One Thousand Guineas winner Nightime, German Guineas winner Lolita and Price Tag, who had been demoted in the Poule d'Essai des Pouliches (another runner, Vague, had won the Dubai version, which has listed status). The classics at Newmarket, the Curragh and Dusseldorf had taken place on soft or heavy going and two-year-old form proved the best guide to the Coronation Stakes. Alexandrova had played her part in further advertising the Fillies' Mile form by winning the Oaks by six lengths, with Speciosa fourth, and Nannina, looking in superb shape, put up a performance at Ascot that was a step up on her two-year-old form. In touch all the way, she ran on strongly after being ridden clear inside the two-furlong marker. Flashy Wings was another to bounce back from a poor effort in the One Thousand Guineas and, in finishing runner-up to Nannina, beaten two lengths, she more or less repeated the pick of her two-year-old form (won the Queen Mary and the Lowther). Nasheej was three quarters of a length further back in third, just ahead of the Irish Guineas fourth Race For The Stars, 150/1-shot Rajeem and the Newmarket Guineas fourth Silca's Sister. Vague came seventh, Price Tag eighth, Speciosa ninth, Lolita eleventh and Nightime last of the fifteen. Nannina's victory wasn't the only one for her owners at Royal Ascot where another homebred Cesare won the Royal Hunt Cup, these performances and prominent efforts from Echelon (runner-up in the Windsor Forest Stakes) and Peeress (fourth in the Queen Anne) helping to make Cheveley Park both the leading owner and leading breeder at the meeting. Nannina's sire Medicean was also successful with Dutch Art in the Norfolk Stakes.

There was talk of Nannina's taking on the colts in the Sussex Stakes but, in the end, the Nassau Stakes was chosen as her Goodwood target in early-August. By that time, however, Nannina's reputation had taken something of a knock. Rajeem turned the tables on her in a muddling race for the Falmouth Stakes at Newmarket in July but, potentially more damaging, there had been a leak to the media that Nannina had failed a post-race dope test at Royal Ascot and was facing disqualification. 'Royal Ascot dope shock' ran the headlines, just the sort of publicity Nannina's connections, and the sport in general, could have done without. The positive test was never officially confirmed by the Horseracing Regulatory Authority but Nannina's trainer revealed it had shown up traces of a prohibited substance derived from 'a routine treatment used on hundreds of horses all the time.' Nannina had been on precisely the same treatment, following strict veterinary guidelines, before

Coronation Stakes, Royal Ascot—Nannina records a clear-cut success;
Flashy Wings (striped sleeves) is second, ahead of Nasheej (light sleeves), Race For The Stars (No.10),
Rajeem (striped cap) and Silca's Sister

Cheveley Park Stud's "Nannina"

the Falmouth and had tested negative. Astonishingly, connections were not told of the Ascot test result until after the Falmouth, and then had to wait until mid-September for news that Nannina's 'B' sample had been returned as negative and no inquiry would take place into her Coronation Stakes victory. The lengthy time lapses and the discrepancy between the 'A' and 'B' test results, something which has happened before (including with 2005 Cheltenham Festival winner King Harald), rightly prompted the HRA to commission an independent review into its analysis procedures. An unacceptably extended period elapsed before Nannina's 'B' sample was finally examined, the sample being flown at first to Hong Kong where officials at a specially-appointed laboratory would not provide access to a scientific witness representing Nannina's connections. Continuing the saga, none of which was of Cheveley Park's making, the sample then had to be transported to France so that a Cheveley Park witness could be present during analysis. There was a suggestion that the 'B' sample might have deteriorated over time, or possibly become contaminated, the last possibility raising the question of whether a contaminated 'B' sample should be returned as a negative. The HRA had not published the findings of the independent review at the time of writing.

Concerns that the Royal Ascot dope test might have raised a question mark in some quarters over Nannina's performance had already been allayed by a repetition of her Coronation Stakes form in the Nassau at Goodwood. She finished a good two lengths third to the five-year-olds Ouija Board and Alexander Goldrun, decisively beating the rest, including Race For The Stars and Nasheej. Nannina might have finished closer at Goodwood had she not had to be switched to make her challenge as the two leaders struck for home. She looked the best of the three-year-old fillies at a mile to a mile and a quarter at the time, but failed to match either her Coronation Stakes or her Nassau Stakes effort on either of her outings in the autumn. She managed only fourth behind the most progressive three-year-old Red Evie, who had won in handicap company at the Royal meeting, when favourite for the Matron Stakes over a mile at Leopardstown where Flashy Wings also finished ahead of her. Two other three-year-olds, the winner Mandesha and third-placed Alexandrova, beat Nannina at a mile and a quarter in the Prix de l'Opera, in which she finished fifth of six.

		Machiavellian	Mr Prospector
	Medicean	(b 1987)	Coup de Folie
	(ch 1997)	Mystic Goddess	Storm Bird
Nannina		(ch 1990)	Rose Goddess
(b.f. 2003)		Danehill	Danzig
	Hill Hopper (IRE)	(b 1986)	Razyana
	(b 1991)	Sea Harrier	Grundy
		(ch 1979)	Anchor

The sturdy, attractive Nannina, a strong-galloping sort with a round action, is a daughter of the useful six- to seven-furlong winner Hill Hopper who also raced in the Cheveley Park colours after being purchased by the stud at the yearling sales. Hill Hopper was from a family that enjoyed plenty of success in the post-war era until its reputation faded from the mid-'eighties onwards, only to be revived by the achievements of Nannina and Norse Dancer, the last-named high class on his day. Norse Dancer and Hill Hopper both have the distinguished broodmare Felucca as their fifth dam. Felucca bred three winners of the Park Hill Stakes who all made their mark at stud, one of them, Kyak, producing Ripeck, the dam of Oaks winner Bireme, Coronation Cup winner Buoy, the smart sprinter Fluke and, among others, the Nell Gwyn winner Anchor who is the grandam of Hill Hopper and the great grandam of Nannina. Hill Hopper's dam Sea Harrier, a twice-raced twin, was a half-sister to the Doncaster Cup winner Sea Anchor and produced the useful Water Boatman who won the Adelaide Cup over two miles after being exported to Australia. Hill Hopper's illustrious antecedents were not enough to keep her at Cheveley Park after an unexceptional start to her career as a broodmare which nonetheless yielded four winners from as many foals prior to Nannina. She was dispatched to the December Sales when Nannina was a foal and fetched 67,000 guineas, carrying to Kyllachy. The colt foal, now named Fawri and unraced as a juvenile, made 300,000 guineas as a yearling, a fortnight after Nannina won the Fillies' Mile. Nannina is effective at a mile to a mile and a quarter and acts on good to firm going, running well below form on her only outing on soft. She stays in training. *J. H. M. Gosden*

NANNY STATE (IRE) 2 b.f. (Jan 31) Averti (IRE) 117 – Roxy (Rock City 120) [2006 **50** 5g 5f⁵ Jul 5] 5,000Y: fourth living foal: half-sister to 7f winner (including at 2 yrs) Night Kiss (by Night Shift): dam unraced half-sister to Irish 1000 Guineas runner-up Goodnight Kiss: mid-division in maidens: will be suited by 6f/7f. *P. C. Haslam*

NANOSECOND (USA) 3 ch.g. Kingmambo (USA) 125 – Easy 'n Gold (USA) (Slew **61** O' Gold (USA)) [2006 10m 10m Sep 5] well-made gelding: modest form when ninth to Aryaamm in maiden at Leicester on second outing: sold 4,500 gns. *J. H. M. Gosden*

NANTON (USA) 4 gr. or ro.g. Spinning World (USA) 130 – Grab The Green (USA) **92** (Cozzene (USA)) [2006 89: 8.5g⁵ p8.6g 8m⁴ 8.3g⁶ 8.3g² 8.1m³ 8f* 8g* 8g p9.5g Nov 2] leggy, quite good-topped gelding: fairly useful performer: won claimer (claimed from P. Cole £23,000) and handicap (best effort) at Redcar in September: stays 1¼m: acts on polytrack, firm and good to soft going: held up. *N. Wilson*

NANTYGLO 3 b.f. Mark of Esteem (IRE) 137 – Bright Halo (IRE) (Bigstone (IRE) **101** 126) [2006 97: 8g* 8.5g 8m 6f Jul 14] leggy, lengthy filly: useful performer: won listed race at Goodwood in May by 1¼ lengths from Sweet Treat: below that form after, in Princess Elizabeth Stakes at Epsom, Coronation Stakes at Royal Ascot and Summer Stakes at York: takes strong hold, and should prove as effective back at 7f as 1m: acts on good to firm going: has worn crossed noseband: carries tail awkwardly. *M. L. W. Bell*

NAPAPIJRI (FR) 4 gr.f. Highest Honor (FR) 124 – Les Marettes (FR) (Baillamont — (USA) 124) [2006 –: f8g p9.5g Mar 6] good-topped filly: has a quick action: no form since 2 yrs: tried visored. *W. G. M. Turner*

NAPOLEON DYNAMITE (IRE) 2 b.c. (Apr 25) Danetime (IRE) 121 – Anita's **70** Contessa (IRE) 68 (Anita's Prince 126) [2006 5s 6m⁶ p6g⁴ 6d p6g² p6m² p6g² Nov 25] €36,000Y: fourth foal: half-brother to 7-y-o A One and 2002 2-y-o 5f winner Among Friends (by Among Men): dam 6f/7f winner: fair maiden: runner-up last 3 starts (one in nursery): likely to stay 7f: acts on polytrack and good to firm going. *J. W. Hills*

NAPOLETANO (GER) 5 b.h. Soviet Star (USA) 128 – Noble House (GER) (Siberian **62** Express (USA) 125) [2006 7s⁶ 7s⁵ 7.5d⁶ 9v 8.8f* p8g p8g p7g Dec 8] ex-German horse: half-brother to several winners in Germany, including useful performer around 1m Night Devil (by Nebos): dam German 7f (at 2 yrs) and 1m winner: useful performer at 3 yrs for A. Trybuhl, winning minor event at Longchamp and placed in 2 listed races: missed 2005 and nowhere near so good in 2006, though won handicap at Halle in September final start for A. Wohler: little impact in handicaps in Britain: stays 8.8f: acts on firm and soft ground: blinkered last 2 starts in Germany. *S. Dow*

NARRJOO (USA) 2 ch.c. (Feb 1) Elusive Quality (USA) – Edhkerini 70 (Lammtarra **87** (USA) 134) [2006 6m* 6m⁶ 5m 6.1g³ 6g Sep 17] strong, good-bodied colt: first foal: dam, third at 1½m only start, half-sister to Nassau Stakes winner Zahrat Dubai: fairly useful performer: won maiden at Hamilton in June: better form after when sixth of 9 to Strategic Prince in July Stakes (pulled hard) at Newmarket and ninth of 13 to Enticing in Molecomb Stakes at Goodwood: well beaten in nursery final start: bred to stay 1m, but shapes like a sprinter: raced on good/good to firm going: joined D. Selvaratnam in UAE. *M. R. Channon*

NARVIK (IRE) 3 ch.c. Galileo (IRE) 134 – Arctic Hunt (IRE) (Bering 136) [2006 98p: **101** 10d⁶ Nov 4] tall, attractive colt: useful form: having only second race when sixth to Folio in handicap at Windsor, making running: will stay 1½m. *Saeed bin Suroor*

NASHAAB (USA) 9 b.g. Zafonic (USA) 130 – Tajannub (USA) 104 (Dixieland Band **75 §** (USA)) [2006 97: 7.6d 8m 8.9m 10.3m⁴ 8.1g* 10.3m⁵ 8m⁵ 8.1m 8.1m² p8.6m 8d Oct 18] small, quite attractive gelding: fair performer: won claimer at Chepstow in July: stays 10.3f: acts on all-weather, firm and soft going: usually blinkered/visored: starts slowly and often gets behind. *P. D. Evans*

NASHEEJ (USA) 3 b.f. Swain (IRE) 134 – El Nafis (USA) 73 (Kingmambo (USA) **112** 125) [2006 103: 7m* 8s³ 8v 8m³ 8m⁵ 9.9m Aug 5] good-topped filly: smart performer: won Dubai Duty Free Stakes (Fred Darling) at Newbury in April by short head from Cantabria: good efforts after when third in 1000 Guineas at Newmarket (beaten 3½ lengths by Speciosa) and Coronation Stakes at Royal Ascot (2¾ lengths behind Nannina) and fifth to Rajeem in Falmouth Stakes at Newmarket: below form in Nassau Stakes at Goodwood final start: stays 1m: acts on soft and good to firm going, well below form in Irish 1000 Guineas on heavy: sometimes gets warm beforehand: reliable: sent to USA. *R. Hannon*

NASHHARRY (IRE) 2 b.f. (Apr 8) Ishiguru (USA) 114 – Abbey Park (USA) 71 **61** (Known Fact (USA) 135) [2006 6g p7g⁴ 6d³ Sep 25] €10,000F, €20,000Y: first foal: dam, maiden who stayed 7f, form only at 2 yrs: modest form in maidens: should prove best up to 7f. *R. Hannon*

NASSAR (IRE) 3 b.c. Danehill (USA) 126 – Regent Gold (USA) (Seeking The Gold **65** (USA)) [2006 8m 8m⁶ 7m 8.3d 10.1f 10f⁴ 10.1f 11.1g⁵ 10.1m⁶ p12.2g⁶ f7g Oct 12] compact colt: second living foal: dam 6.5f/7f winner in USA: fair maiden: stays 1¼m: acts on firm going: tried visored/in cheekpieces: has looked wayward. *G. Prodromou*

NASSMAAN (IRE) 2 b.c. (Mar 16) Alhaarth (IRE) 126 – Just In Love (FR) (Highest **79** Honor (FR) 124) [2006 8g 8.2d p7g³ Nov 11] 30,000F, 58,000Y: medium-sized colt: first foal: dam unraced sister to useful French middle-distance performer Justful: fair form: much improved when second (hung, demoted to third) to Russki in maiden at Kempton: will stay 1m: acts on polytrack: has been attended by 2 handlers in paddock. *P. W. Chapple-Hyam*

NATACHA ROSTOW 3 b.f. Pursuit of Love 124 – Piroshka (Soviet Star (USA) 128) **46** [2006 8.2m p8g p7g Oct 15] 2,700F: fourth foal: good-bodied filly: half-sister to 4-y-o Red Rudy and winner up to 11f in Italy by Case Law: dam unraced: poor maiden: left L. Cumani after second start. *C. A. Dwyer*

NATIONAL EXPRESS (IRE) 4 b.g. Nashwan (USA) 135 – National Portrait (IRE) — (Royal Academy (USA) 130) [2006 75: p8.6g Mar 3] fair maiden: well held only start in 2006: stays 7.5f: acts on firm going. *D. Marnane, Ireland*

NATION STATE 5 b.g. Sadler's Wells (USA) 132 – Native Justice (USA) 115 (Alleged   –
(USA) 138) [2006 63: 16d Oct 27] fairly useful maiden in France: well held only start on
Flat in 2006: stays 15f: acts on soft ground: tried in cheekpieces: fairly useful hurdler.
G. L. Moore

NATIVE AMERICAN 4 b.g. Indian Lodge (IRE) 127 – Summer Siren (FR) (Saint   **61**
Cyrien (FR) 128) [2006 73: 9.7f 10d 11.5m p12g 12f 10m^6 10.1g^6 10g^6 10.2m^2 10.9d
Oct 13] quite attractive gelding: modest handicapper nowadays: stays 1¼m: acts on soft
and good to firm going: races prominently. *T. D. McCarthy*

NATIVE TIPTOES 3 b.f. Arkadian Hero (USA) 123 – Waltham Skylark 40 (Puis-   –
sance 110) [2006 58: p6g p5g p7g f6g Mar 21] close-coupled filly: little form: tried in
cheekpieces: sold £1,500. *Miss Gay Kelleway*

NATIVE TITLE 8 b.g. Pivotal 124 – Bermuda Lily 78 (Dunbeath (USA) 127) [2006   **87**
96: f6g f5g^2 p6g^3 p5g* p5g* 5g^4 5d Apr 16] big, close-coupled gelding: has had breathing
operation: fairly useful performer: won claimer at Lingfield in February and handicap at
Kempton in March: best at 5f/6f: acts on all-weather, firm and soft going: tried blinkered:
held up, travels strongly. *D. Nicholls*

NATURAL FORCE (IRE) 3 b.c. King's Best (USA) 132 – Wolf Cleugh (IRE) 65   –
(Last Tycoon 131) [2006 95: 8f 10s Oct 18] smallish, quite attractive colt: fairly useful
performer at 2 yrs: well held in 2006: sold 16,000 gns later in October. *Saeed bin Suroor*

NAUGHTY BY NATURE 3 b.g. Machiavellian (USA) 123 – Rumpipumpy 80 (Shir-   **70 §**
ley Heights 130) [2006 77: 10g^5 7.1s^6 May 29] good-topped gelding: fair maiden: last
both starts in 2006, though not discredited first occasion: seems to stay 1¼m: has looked
none too keen and is one to treat with caution: sold 18,000 gns in July, joined P. Nolan in
Ireland. *Sir Michael Stoute*

NAUGHTY GIRL (IRE) 6 b.m. Dr Devious (IRE) 127 – Mary Magdalene 78 (Night   **50 §**
Shift (USA)) [2006 59§, a35§: f8g f8g^6 f7g^6 f8g^2 f8g Mar 16] smallish, sturdy mare:
modest performer, better on turf than all-weather: stays 1m: acts on polytrack, good to
firm and good to soft going: has been visored/tongue tied: tried blinkered: ungenuine.
John A. Harris

NAUGHTY THOUGHTS (IRE) 2 b.f. (Apr 24) Grand Lodge (USA) 125 – Gentle   **69**
Thoughts 73 (Darshaan 133) [2006 6m^3 6g 6.5s^6 8v^3 Oct 9] fourth foal: closely related to
3-y-o Picacho and half-sister to 4-y-o Blue Bajan: dam, Irish maiden (should have been
suited by 1¼m+), half-sister to smart stayer Anak Pekan: fair maiden: third at Haydock
and Ayr: will stay 1¼m/1½m. *K. A. Ryan*

NAUTICAL 8 gr.g. Lion Cavern (USA) 117 – Russian Royal (USA) 108 (Nureyev   **88**
(USA) 131) [2006 84: p8g p8.6g^5 p7.1g^2 p7.1g^3 p6g^4 8s 6g* 6m^3 6g^2 6d^3 6f^2 p6g^4 p6g^2 **a81**
5f 6g^3 6d 7g Sep 30] good-topped gelding: fairly useful handicapper, better on turf
than all-weather: won at Windsor in April: winner up to 1¼m, but probably best around
6f (finds bare 5f bit too sharp): acts on dirt, polytrack, firm and good to soft going: tried in
headgear: used to wear tongue tie (not since 2003): usually held up. *A. W. Carroll*

NAUTICO 3 ch.f. Compton Place 125 – Sabre Lady 82 (Sabrehill (USA) 120) [2006 42:   **46**
6m 6f 5m 5f^5 6m 5g 7.1m 5g^2 7m Sep 16] poor maiden: best at 5f/6f: acts on firm going:
tried blinkered. *Miss L. A. Perratt*

NAVAJO SQUAW (IRE) 2 b.f. Noverre (USA) 125 – Molomo 104 (Barathea (IRE)
127) see ONIDA (IRE)

NAVAJO WARRIOR (IRE) 3 b.g. Namid 128 – Nassma (IRE) 95 (Sadler's Wells   –
(USA) 132) [2006 –: f8g 12f 16.2m Jul 24] good-bodied gelding: no form: dead.
T. D. Easterby

NAVAL ATTACHE 4 b.g. Slip Anchor 136 – Cayla (Tumble Wind) [2006 58: p9.5g^5 **62**
p8g^3 p8g^3 p8.6g^2 6.9f^3 6g Aug 4] modest maiden: trained by B. Johnson second to fourth
outings (claimed £6,000 and returned to former trainer): stays 9.5f: acts on polytrack and
firm going: sold 3,200 gns in November. *P. A. Blockley*

NAVAL HERO (IRE) 3 b.g. Arkadian Hero (USA) 123 – Isla Negra (IRE) (Last Ty-   –
coon 131) [2006 10.5m 9v^4 11.9m 16g 16.2m Aug 28] little form. *Mrs L. Williamson*

NAVIGATION (IRE) 4 ch.g. Bahamian Bounty 116 – Bridge Pool 74 (First Trump   **63 d**
118) [2006 71: 5m 5m 6m 7m 6m p8.6g Nov 10] lengthy gelding: on downgrade and just
modest handicapper nowadays: effective at 5f/6f: acts on polytrack, firm and soft going:
tried tongue tied (looked ungenuine). *T. J. Etherington*

Vodafone Diomed Stakes, Epsom—
in a tight finish, Nayyir (blaze) squeezes through to beat Boule d'Or (striped sleeves);
Home Affairs (third left) switches too late and is unlucky, but catches Momtic (rail) for third

NAWAADI 3 b.g. Intikhab (USA) 135 – Elhilmeya (IRE) 94 (Unfuwain (USA) 131) **85**
[2006 81: 8m⁶ p8g² 10s³ Oct 18] good-bodied gelding: type to carry condition: fairly
useful maiden: stays 1¼m: acts on polytrack and soft going: sold 32,000 gns, joined
P. Hobbs. *M. P. Tregoning*

NAWAMEES (IRE) 8 b.g. Darshaan 133 – Truly Generous (IRE) 104 (Generous (IRE) **97**
139) [2006 97: p13g³ p16g⁴ 12g² 12s² 12m⁴ 14m⁶ 12g p11g⁵ p12g⁴ p13g² Oct 15] close-
coupled gelding: useful handicapper: good second at Newmarket and Goodwood third/
fourth starts: stays 2m: acts on polytrack, soft and good to firm going: tried blinkered, usually wears cheekpieces. *G. L. Moore*

NAWAQEES 3 b.c. Danehill (USA) 126 – Elrafa Ah (USA) 105 (Storm Cat (USA)) **65**
[2006 77: 8.1d⁵ May 9] quite good-topped colt: fair performer: stays 1m: acts on soft
going. *J. L. Dunlop*

NAWAYEA 3 b.f. Lujain (USA) 119 – Shallat (IRE) 59 (Pennekamp (USA) 130) [2006 **47**
70: 8m⁴ p5g³ Dec 10] just poor maiden in 2006: should stay 1m. *C. N. Allen*

NAWOW 6 b.g. Blushing Flame (USA) 109 – Fair Test 95 (Fair Season 120) [2006 73, **73**
a80: p12g p13g p16g² p16g⁵ p16.5g 13.3m⁴ p16g⁵ 11.9g² p12g* Dec 20] tall, good- **a77**
topped gelding: fair handicapper: won at Lingfield in December: stays easy 2m: acts on
all-weather, good to firm and soft going: tends to hang. *P. D. Cundell*

NAYYIR 8 ch.g. Indian Ridge 123 – Pearl Kite (USA) 106§ (Silver Hawk (USA) 123) **116**
[2006 120: p8.6g* p10g³ p10g⁴ 8.5m* 7f⁴ 7m⁴ 8f 8.9g⁶ 8d p10g* Nov 18] strong, lengthy,
angular gelding: has a round action: smart performer nowadays: won minor event at Wolverhampton in February, Vodafone Diomed Stakes at Epsom (by neck from Boule d'Or)
in June and listed race at Lingfield (blinkered, by short head from Blue Bajan) in
November: shaped better than results (not clear run) when fourth in Criterion Stakes at
Newmarket (1¼ lengths behind Suggestive) and Betfair Cup (Lennox) at Goodwood (4¼
lengths behind Iffraaj) fifth/sixth outings: effective at 7f to easy 1¼m: acts on polytrack,
firm and soft going: has worn crossed noseband: held up. *G. A. Butler*

NAZAAHA (USA) 4 gr.f. Elnadim (USA) 128 – Taatof (IRE) (Lahib (USA) 129) **49**
[2006 66: p7.1g⁶ p6g 5.7d⁵ 6g⁶ 6.1m⁶ 5f Jun 23] tall filly: just poor maiden in 2006: stays
7f: acts on polytrack and firm going: tried in cheekpieces. *A. G. Newcombe*

NDOLA 7 b.g. Emperor Jones (USA) 119 – Lykoa (Shirley Heights 130) [2006 56: p10g **56**
p9.5g p12g* p10g6 p12g f12g⁴ Nov 21] rather leggy, quite good-topped gelding: modest
performer: won banded race at Kempton in May: stays 1½m: acts on all-weather, best turf
effort on good going: tried blinkered/visored. *B. J. Curley*

NEAR DOCK (GER) 5 b.h. Docksider (USA) 124 – Night Year (IRE) (Jareer (USA) **109**
115) [2006 114: a8f 8.9m 8g⁵ 8m³ p10g³ 10d³ 10.3f⁴ May 11] smart performer for
P. Schiergen in Germany in 2005, second twice in pattern races at Baden-Baden: useful

in 2006, mostly creditable efforts, including when third in handicap at Nad Al Sheba (to Seihali, then left V. Smith), listed race at Kempton (beaten 1¼ lengths by Simple Exchange) and Mooresbridge Stakes at the Curragh (behind Alayan): was effective at 1m to 1¼m: acted on polytrack, good to firm and good to soft going, well held only outing on dirt: to stand at Bridge Stud, Co Waterford, Ireland, fee €750. *K. R. Burke*

NEARDOWN BEAUTY (IRE) 3 br.f. Bahhare (USA) 122 – Habla Me (IRE) (Fairy **93**
King (USA)) [2006 67: 7m² 7m⁶ 7d³ 7f* p7g⁴ 7.1m⁶ 8f⁵ p7g³ 7m² 7m⁴ 7m² 7g³ p7g² 7s³ p8g² p8g* p8g² Nov 25] leggy filly: fairly useful handicapper: won at Lingfield in June and November: creditable second at Kempton final start: stays 1m: acts on polytrack, firm and soft going: tongue tied at 2 yrs: tried in cheekpieces: held up: tends to carry head high but is consistent. *I. A. Wood*

NEARDOWN QUEEN 3 b.f. Lugana Beach 116 – Polgwynne 48 (Forzando 122) **50**
[2006 p7g⁴ 5.7g 6f 5.3f² p5.1g 5.7f a6d Dec 17] 5,200Y: fifth foal: dam 7f winner: modest maiden: sold from I. Wood 900 gns before final start: stays easy 7f: acts on polytrack and firm ground. *Pia Westman, Sweden*

NEAT 'N TIDY 2 b.f. (Apr 12) Josr Algarhoud (IRE) 118 – Raspberry Sauce 65 (Nini- **–**
ski (USA) 125) [2006 5.1m⁶ p7.1f 6m 5.7m Sep 25] fourth foal: half-sister to 5-y-o Boot 'N Toot: dam 1m to 11.6f winner: little form in maidens: sold 3,000 gns. *C. A. Cyzer*

NEBDI (IRE) 5 b.g. Fayruz 116 – Miss Nutwood (IRE) 77 (Prince Rupert (FR) 121) **62**
[2006 75: 6m 6m p9.5g p7.1g⁶ f6g² p6s⁴ Dec 15] one-time fairly useful winner: modest in 2006, left W. Browne in Ireland after second start: stays 7f: acts on all-weather and good to firm going: tried blinkered, often in cheekpieces. *E. J. Alston*

NEBRASKA CITY 5 b.g. Piccolo 121 – Scarlet Veil 75 (Tyrnavos 129) [2006 50: **–**
p9.5g f7g 7d 7m 7.2m Aug 12] compact gelding: maiden: no form in 2006: tried in head-gear/tongue tie. *D. W. Thompson*

NEBRASKA LADY (IRE) 4 b.f. Lujain (USA) 119 – Montana Lady (IRE) 83 (Be **84**
My Guest (USA) 126) [2006 87: 7.2g p7.1g³ 7m 7d⁶ Aug 20] €8,500Y: first foal: dam Irish 7f winner: fairly useful performer: left P. Martin in Ireland prior to reappearance: stays 7f: acts on polytrack and good to soft going, possibly not on good to firm: reportedly in foal to Bahamian Bounty. *E. J. O'Neill*

NED LUDD (IRE) 3 b.g. Montjeu (IRE) 137 – Zanella (IRE) 87 (Nordico (USA)) **83**
[2006 84: 10f⁶ 10.1m² 11m 10g Oct 16] leggy, close-coupled gelding: bred to stay beyond 1¼m: raced only on good going or firmer: sold 9,000 gns, joined J. Portman: fairly useful winner over hurdles. *R. Hannon*

NEE LEMON LEFT 4 b.f. Puissance 110 – Via Dolorosa (Chaddleworth (IRE) 103) **–**
[2006 –: 10.3m Aug 25] little form since 2004. *M. Mullineaux*

NEFSKI ALEXANDER (USA) 3 b.c. Minardi (USA) 119 – Reluctant Guest (USA) **77**
(Hostage (USA)) [2006 64: 7g p8g 10m⁶ 10d⁴ 9.7f* 10m 10.1m³ 10m 9.9d Sep 27] good-bodied colt: fair performer: won maiden at Folkestone in June: stays 1¼m: acts on firm and good to soft going: tried blinkered: sold 9,000 gns, sent to Saudi Arabia. *P. F. I. Cole*

NEIDEEN (IRE) 4 ch.f. Elnadim (USA) 128 – Mynador (USA) 90 (Forty Niner **–**
(USA)) [2006 68: 7f Jun 6] lengthy filly: maiden: well below form only start in 2006. *J. Akehurst*

NEIL'S LEGACY (IRE) 4 br.f. Second Empire (IRE) 124 – Eliade (IRE) 82 (Flash of **58**
Steel 120) [2006 57: 10d⁵ 8.3m³ 11.1m⁶ 9.2g² 10.1s 9.2g* Sep 17] leggy filly: modest performer: won claimer at Hamilton in September: stays 1½m: acts on all-weather, heavy and good to firm going: has carried head high. *Miss L. A. Perratt*

NELL GWYN (IRE) 2 b.f. (Jan 20) Danehill (USA) 126 – Offshore Boom 96 (Be My **85**
Guest (USA) 126) [2006 7m 8g* 7g 8m Oct 1] strong, well-made filly: sister to top-class 5f (at 2 yrs) to 1m winner Rock of Gibraltar and useful 2002 Irish 2-y-o 6f winner Great Pyramid, and half-sister to several winners, including Irish 1m to 1¼m winner Eloquent Way (by Dowsing): dam, Irish 2-y-o 6f winner, out of half-sister to Riverman: fairly useful form: won maiden at Tralee in August: stiff tasks after, well held in C. L. Weld Park Stakes (hampered) at the Curragh and Prix Marcel Boussac at Longchamp: stays 1m. *A. P. O'Brien, Ireland*

NELLIE 2 b.f. (Apr 9) Lake Coniston (IRE) 131 – Boomerang Blade 100 (Sure Blade **–**
(USA) 130) [2006 5.1d Nov 1] rangy filly: third foal: dam 6f winner (including at 2 yrs): tailed off in maiden. *R. M. Whitaker*

NELLIE GWYN 4 b.f. King's Best (USA) 132 – On Tiptoes 107 (Shareef Dancer – (USA) 135) [2006 6m 6d 5f 5f 5d a6.5g Dec 23] little form: left J. Given 32,000 gns after fourth outing. *H-A. Pantall, France*

NELLIE SOPRANO (IRE) 2 br.f. (Apr 22) Key of Luck (USA) 126 – Danalia (IRE) **60** 78 (Danehill (USA) 126) [2006 6g 7.5m³ 8.2g⁵ a8g³ Dec 17] €18,000F, 16,500Y: neat filly: half-sister to several winners, including 4-y-o Namir and 2002 2-y-o 5f/6f winner Margaret's Fancy (by Ali-Royal): dam Irish 2-y-o 5f winner: modest maiden: sold from K. Burke 4,000 gns before final start: will prove best up to 1m. *J. Guerra, Spain*

NELL TUPP 3 b.g. Killer Instinct 111 – Eternal Triangle (USA) 76 (Barachois (CAN)) – [2006 56?: 6d 6v f6g Dec 27] medium-sized, well-made gelding: maiden: no form in 2006: tried in cheekpieces. *G. Woodward*

NELSON (POL) 4 ch.g. Fourth of June (USA) 82 – Neustria (POL) (Who Knows 114) – [2006 –: p13g Feb 6] no form in Britain: tried blinkered/tongue tied: dead. *Jean-Rene Auvray*

NELSONS COLUMN (IRE) 3 b.g. Benny The Dip (USA) 127 – Sahara Rose (Green **93** Desert (USA) 127) [2006 74: 10d⁶ 10m 8m² 8.3m³ 8.5f* 9.8d* 9.8g* 9.9g 9.9g⁵ 11.8d⁴ Oct 3] strong gelding: fairly useful handicapper: reportedly has no left eye: won at Beverley and Ripon in July and Ripon in August: stays 11.8f: acts on firm and good to soft going: has carried head awkwardly: races prominently. *G. M. Moore*

NELSON VETTORI 2 ch.c. (Mar 20) Vettori (IRE) 119 – Eskimo Nel (IRE) 75 (Shy – Groom (USA)) [2006 6g Aug 25] behind in maiden over 6f (bred for 1¼m+). *R. M. Beckett*

NEON 2 b.f. (Mar 12) Fantastic Light (USA) 134 – River Saint (USA) 73§ (Irish River **69** (FR) 131) [2006 7.5g 8.2m Sep 15] quite attractive filly: fourth foal: half-sister to 4-y-o Kabis Amigos: dam, unreliable maiden who should have stayed 1m, half-sister to champion US filly Serena's Song (up to 9f), herself dam of Coronation Stakes winner Sophisticat: more encouraging run in maidens (very green debut) when seventh to Treat at Nottingham: sold 20,000 gns. *J. R. Fanshawe*

NEON BLUE 5 b. or br.g. Atraf 116 – Desert Lynx (IRE) 79 (Green Desert (USA) 127) **80** [2006 80: 7m 7g 7.2m² 7f* 7m³ 7m⁶ 7.2v f7g p8.6g Nov 17] smallish, compact gelding: fairly useful performer: won claimer at York in July: stays 7f: acts on firm and soft going: often visored/in cheekpieces. *R. M. Whitaker*

NEPHETRITI WAY (IRE) 5 b.m. Docksider (USA) 124 – Velvet Appeal (IRE) 101 **75** (Petorius 117) [2006 82: p7g 7.1m⁵ 7m⁵ 6f 6.1m 7.1m⁶ Sep 12] rather leggy, quite good-topped mare: fair handicapper: best at 6f/7f: acts on polytrack and good to firm going: hung right final outing: sent to Greece. *P. R. Chamings*

NEPOS 2 b.g. (Apr 3) Piccolo 121 – Blushing Victoria 74 (Weldnaas (USA) 112) [2006 **64** 5m 5.7f² p6f⁶ 5.5m 5.1f⁶ p7.1m Oct 2] sturdy gelding: modest maiden: left J. Osborne after fifth start: should prove best at 5f/6f: acts on polytrack and firm going. *A. J. McCabe*

NEPRO (IRE) 4 b.g. Orpen (USA) 116 – My Gray (FR) (Danehill (USA) 126) [2006 ?: **75** a5g* f5g² f6g⁴ p5g⁵ Feb 25] fair performer: won minor event at Mijas in January: creditable efforts in handicaps at Southwell (2) and Lingfield last 3 starts: stays 1m: acts on all-weather/sand, firm and good to soft going: tried visored, tongue tied in 2006. *E. J. Creighton*

NEPTUNE 10 b.g. Dolphin Street (FR) 125 – Seal Indigo (IRE) 93 (Glenstal (USA) – 118) [2006 –, a50: p13.9g p10g⁵ f12g 12d May 28] leggy gelding: handicapper: no form in 2006: tried in cheekpieces: sometimes looks difficult ride. *J. C. Fox*

NERONE (GER) 5 ro.g. Sternkoenig (IRE) 122 – Nordwahl (GER) (Waajib 121) – [2006 –: 13d May 7] well held on Flat in Britain, but fair winner over hurdles. *P. Monteith*

NERO'S RETURN (IRE) 5 b.g. Mujadil (USA) 119 – Snappy Dresser (Nishapour **89** (FR) 125) [2006 100: 8s 8v 8g⁶ 10g⁶ 10.4d 8.1s⁴ 10.1g 8m⁵ 12d² 11.8m² 12g⁵ 12d* 12m⁵ Sep 16] rather leggy gelding: fairly useful handicapper: won amateur event at Epsom in August: stays 1½m: acts on any turf going: tried blinkered: often sweats. *M. Johnston*

NESHLA 3 ch.f. Singspiel (IRE) 133 – Nordica 99 (Northfields (USA)) [2006 f11g³ **– p** p10g Dec 30] 55,000Y: half-sister to several winners, including 6f/1m winner Marika (by Marju) and Fred Darling winner/Oaks fourth Sueboog (by Darshaan, subsequently dam of very smart Best of The Bests), both useful: dam 6f and 1m winner: green in maidens at Southwell (considerately handled) and Lingfield: should do better. *C. E. Brittain*

NESNO (USA) 3 ch.c. Royal Academy (USA) 130 – Cognac Lady (USA) (Olympio **81**
(USA)) [2006 77: p10g 11g² 10m³ 10f* 9.8g 11m Sep 6] big, lengthy colt: fairly useful
performer: blinkered, awarded handicap at Pontefract in July: stays 11f: acts on polytrack
and firm going. *J. D. Bethell*

NESSEN DORMA (IRE) 5 b.g. Entrepreneur 123 – Goldilocks (IRE) (Caerleon **85**
(USA) 132) [2006 94: 13.8d⁶ 12.3d 12d⁵ 12m² 11.5g Jun 28] lengthy gelding: fairly useful handicapper: stays 2m: acts on all-weather, firm and soft going: tried in cheekpieces,
often visored nowadays: races prominently: tends to run in snatches. *J. G. Given*

NETWORKER 3 ch.g. Danzig Connection (USA) – Trevorsninepoints 71 (Jester 119) **74**
[2006 –: 6d⁶ 5m 5f 5f⁵ 5d⁶ p6.8g³ p7.1g* p7.1g⁴ Dec 28] workmanlike gelding: fair performer: left K. Reveley, upped in trip, improved form last 3 starts, winning maiden at
Wolverhampton in December: stays 8.6f: acts on polytrack. *P. J. McBride*

NEUTRINO 4 b.g. Mtoto 134 – Fair Seas 72 (General Assembly (USA)) [2006 80: **81**
11.9g 11.9m⁴ 12.1g² p13.9f⁶ 13.9s Oct 7] rather leggy, good-topped gelding: fairly useful
handicapper: stays 1½m: acts on firm and soft ground: tried visored: carried head awkwardly second start. *P. C. Haslam*

NEVADA DESERT (IRE) 6 b.g. Desert King (USA) 129 – Kayanga (Green Desert **81**
(USA) 127) [2006 88: 8.1g 8g 10.5s⁵ 8.3f* 8.9m 8.5f⁴ 8.5s² 8m 8.3g² 8.1s* 8d² 8g p9.5g⁴ **a91**
f8g* f8g³ Dec 2] useful-looking gelding: fairly useful handicapper, better on all-weather
than turf: won at Hamilton in June, Haydock in September and Southwell in November:
effective at 7f to 11f: unraced on heavy ground, acts on any other turf and all-weather:
tried in cheekpieces: tends to carry head high: consistent. *R. M. Whitaker*

NEVER CROSS (IRE) 2 b.f. (Apr 17) Cape Cross (IRE) 129 – Itsy Bitsy Betsy (USA) **–**
(Beau Genius (CAN)) [2006 8v Oct 9] 21,000Y: fourth foal: dam US 6f winner: tailed off
in maiden at Ayr. *B. Storey*

NEVERLETME GO (IRE) 4 b.f. Green Desert (USA) 127 – Cassandra Go (IRE) **–**
119 (Indian Ridge 123) [2006 91: 5.1s 5.1g May 2] strong filly: fairly useful performer at
best: stiff tasks and well held in 2006. *G. Wragg*

NEVERONAMONDAY (IRE) 2 br.f. (Mar 26) Night Shift (USA) – Appalachia **–**
(IRE) 92 (Imperial Frontier (USA) 112) [2006 5f⁵ 5m Aug 31] €8,000Y: third foal: dam
Irish 2-y-o 5f winner: last in maidens. *A. Berry*

NEVER SAY DEYA 3 b.f. Dansili 127 – Dream On Deya (IRE) (Dolphin Street (FR) **55**
125) [2006 55: p8.6g 10f 8m⁴ 8.3d³ 8f² 8m 7d² 8s 8g p8g⁴ f8g Nov 15] tall, leggy filly:
modest maiden: stays 1m: acts on polytrack, firm and soft going. *M. R. Channon*

NEVER WILL 5 b.g. Cadeaux Genereux 131 – Answered Prayer (Green Desert (USA) **81 d**
127) [2006 95: 7f⁶ 8.9s 9.5g f8g p9.5g⁶ Dec 2] strong, lengthy gelding: just fairly useful
handicapper at best in 2006: left E. Griffin in Ireland 5,000 gns after reappearance: stays
easy 9.5f: acts on good to firm and good to soft ground: tried tongue tied, wore cheekpieces final start. *K. A. Ryan*

NEVER WITHOUT ME 6 ch.g. Mark of Esteem (IRE) 137 – Festival Sister (Belmez **74**
(USA) 131) [2006 69: 5.1m³ 5g⁶ 5.2g² 5m⁵ 5f* 5f 5f⁴ 6m 5.2m 5m⁶ Sep 13] tall gelding:
fair handicapper: won at Ripon in June: effective at 5f/6f: acts on fibresand, firm and
good to soft going: tried visored/blinkered. *J. F. Coupland*

NEVINSTOWN (IRE) 6 b.g. Lahib (USA) 129 – Moon Tango (IRE) 81 (Last Tycoon **55**
131) [2006 64, a58: f7g 7.2m⁵ 6s⁴ 8d Oct 8] modest performer: stays 7f: acts on fibresand
and good to firm going: tried visored/blinkered/tongue tied. *C. Grant*

NEW BEGINNING (IRE) 2 b.c. (Jan 31) Keltos (FR) 132 – Goldthroat (IRE) 79 **82**
(Zafonic (USA) 130) [2006 7d 7m⁴ 10d⁶ 8s⁵ p9.5g* p9.5s Dec 14] 20,000 2-y-o: good-
topped colt: first foal: dam Irish 2-y-o 7f winner, out of half-sister to smart 1m winner
Killer Instinct: fairly useful form: won maiden at Wolverhampton (hung right) in November: good fifth to Sweet Lilly in listed race at Pontefract previous start: stays 1¼m:
acts on polytrack, soft and good to firm ground. *Mrs S. Lamyman*

NEW BLOOD (IRE) 3 b.g. Beckett (IRE) 116 – Utmost (IRE) 30 (Most Welcome **–**
131) [2006 –: 7m 6f 7m Jun 29] of no account. *J. M. Bradley*

NEWCASTLES OWEN (IRE) 3 b.g. Elnadim (USA) 128 – Brittas Blues (IRE) 52 **34**
(Blues Traveller (IRE) 119) [2006 –: 6.9f 9d 5g Aug 21] poor maiden. *R. Johnson*

NEWCORP LAD 6 b.g. Komaite (USA) – Gleam of Gold (Crested Lark 78) [2006 63: **62**
p8.6g p8.6g² 8.5m 12d p9.5g p9.5g Dec 21] strong gelding: modest handicapper: stays
8.6f: acts on polytrack and any turf going: tried in visor/cheekpieces. *Mrs G. S. Rees*

NEW DESTINY (IRE) 2 b.c. (Mar 11) Xaar 132 – Order of The Day (USA) (Dayjur – (USA) 137) [2006 5m May 12] broke leg on debut at Hamilton. *J. Howard Johnson*

NEW DIAMOND 7 ch.g. Bijou d'Inde 127 – Nannie Annie 60 (Persian Bold 123) – [2006 12.1f Jul 28] fair performer at best: unraced on Flat in 2004/5: well held only start at 7 yrs: tried blinkered. *Mrs P. Ford*

NEW ENGLAND 4 ch.g. Bachir (IRE) 118 – West Escape 95 (Gone West (USA)) **72 §** [2006 64: p8.6g² p8.6g² p8.6g² p8.6g* p8.6g² p8.6g³ p8.6g 9g 10.5s 10.3m* p9.5m⁶ p9.5m⁴ p8.6g⁵ Oct 29] fair handicapper: won at Wolverhampton in February and Chester in September: stays 10.3f: acts on polytrack and good to firm going: loses ground at start (virtually refused to race eighth outing): one to treat with caution. *W. M. Brisbourne*

NEW GUINEA 3 b.g. Fantastic Light (USA) 134 – Isle of Spice (USA) 74 (Diesis 133) **110 p** [2006 –p: 10m⁵ 10.5m² 10g² 12m³ f11g* 11m² 12d* 13.4g* Aug 26] sturdy, compact gelding: smart form: much improved, winning maiden at Southwell (by 17 lengths) in July and handicaps at Pontefract (beat Most Definitely by 3 lengths) and Chester (by 2 lengths from Sunday Symphony) in August: gelded after: stays 13.4f: acts on firbresand, good to firm and good to soft going: joined Godolphin: capable of better still. *M. A. Jarvis*

NEWKEYLETS 3 b.f. Diktat 126 – Jay Gee Ell 78 (Vaigly Great 127) [2006 52: 5g **63** 5m² 5d⁵ 5m³ 6g 5m⁵ 6m² 5m⁵ 6g² 5s² 5d³ 5s⁴ 5v⁵ 5d p6g³ p6g⁴ p7.1g³ Dec 21] modest maiden: placed 8 times, many in handicaps: best at 5f/6f: acts on polytrack, soft and good to firm ground: in cheekpieces/blinkers nowadays: once withdrawn (unruly at start): quirky. *I. Semple*

NEW LIGHT 2 ch.f. (Feb 15) Generous (IRE) 139 – May Light 62 (Midyan (USA) **56** 124) [2006 8d Sep 27] half-sister to 5-y-o Bygone Days and fairly useful 1998 2-y-o 1m winner Trio (by Cyrano de Bergerac): dam maiden who stayed 7f: 33/1, raced freely when eighth in maiden at Salisbury. *R. F. Johnson Houghton*

NEWNHAM (IRE) 5 ch.g. Theatrical 128 – Brief Escapade (IRE) 95 (Brief Truce **81** (USA) 124) [2006 80, a70: p12.2g² p10g* p12.2g* p9.5g* p12.2g* p12g⁶ p10g p12g p12.2m⁴ p13g⁵ f12g⁵ Nov 15] lengthy gelding: fairly useful performer: completed 4-timer in January/February, in maiden at Lingfield and 3 handicaps at Wolverhampton: stays 13f: acts on all-weather, good to firm and good to soft going: tried visored/in cheek-pieces. *J. R. Boyle*

NEW OPTIONS 9 b.g. Formidable (USA) 125 – No Comebacks 70 (Last Tycoon 131) – [2006 56, a63: p5.1g f5g p5.1g² p5.1g³ p6g p5g 5f 5m 5.1g 5g p5.1m p5.1g⁶ p5.1g² **a66** p5.1g⁴ p5g² p5g² p5.1g Dec 31] strong gelding: fair on all-weather, no form on turf in 2006: effective at 5f to easy 7f: acts on all-weather/dirt, firm and soft going: tried in cheekpieces, blinkered nowadays: tends to carry head high/finish weakly. *Peter Grayson*

NEWPORT BOY (IRE) 3 b.g. Montjeu (IRE) 137 – Dream Chaser 92 (Record Token **67** 128) [2006 –: p10g* 11.8d⁴ p12g 12.1m⁵ 10g³ 10d p13.9m p12.2g Nov 18] rather leggy, **a62** attractive gelding: fair maiden on turf, modest on all-weather: left S. Kirk after third start: should stay 1½m+: acts on polytrack and good to firm ground: wore cheekpieces final outing: has hung left: races prominently. *R. A. Harris*

NEWPORT LASS (IRE) 2 b.f. (Jan 29) Mull of Kintyre (USA) 114 – Mari-Ela (IRE) **52** 60 (River Falls 113) [2006 p6g⁴ 6d 6m Sep 16] 12,000Y: fourth foal: closely related to fairly useful 5f/6f winner Chimali (by Foxhound) and half-sister to 4-y-o Colonel Bilko: dam 7f seller winner: modest form in maidens: will be at least as effective at 5f as 6f. *K. R. Burke*

NEW PROPOSAL (IRE) 4 b.g. Orpen (USA) 116 – Woodenitbenice (USA) (Nasty – And Bold (USA)) [2006 55: p6g May 3] lengthy gelding: maiden: well held only start in 2006 (said to have finished lame). *A. P. Jarvis*

NEW SEEKER 6 b.g. Green Desert (USA) 127 – Ahbab (IRE) 81 (Ajdal (USA) 130) **115** [2006 115: 7g⁵ 8s 7.1g² 7f³ 7m 7g* 7s Oct 29] tall, good sort: impresses in appearance: smart performer: left C. Cox after fifth start: won listed race at Redcar in September by 2½ lengths from Suggestive: best effort earlier in season when ½-length second to Quito in similar event at Haydock: stays 1m: acts on good to firm and good to soft ground, well below form on soft (including in Premio Chiusura at Milan final outing): effective with or without blinkers: tried visored: front runner: tough and genuine. *P. F. I. Cole*

NEWS OF THE DAY (IRE) 2 ch.f. (May 14) Diesis 133 – Etoile Ascendante (USA) **61** (Arctic Tern (USA) 126) [2006 7d⁶ 6s⁴ p7g⁶ p8g Nov 24] 6,000Y: tall filly: fourth foal: half-sister to winner in USA by Fantastic Fellow: dam, placed in France, half-sister to Breeders' Cup Classic/Dubai World Cup winner Pleasantly Perfect: modest maiden: should stay 1m/1¼m: acts on soft ground. *M. Johnston*

NEWSROUND 4 ch.g. Cadeaux Genereux 131 – Ring The Relatives 75 (Bering 136) **56**
[2006 –: f5g f7g 6g f7g f5g⁴ p6g⁵ 5m 7.2g² 6d³ f7g Nov 21] well-made gelding: modest
performer: stays 7f: acts on fibresand, unraced on extremes of going on turf: usually
wears blinkers/cheekpieces: often slowly away. *D. W. Chapman*

NEW YORK OSCAR (IRE) 2 b.g. (Feb 4) Tobougg (IRE) 125 – Special Dissident **68**
(Dancing Dissident (USA) 119) [2006 p6g² p5g⁵ f5g* f5g² Dec 27] €21,000Y: half-
brother to 2003 2-y-o 7f winner Spin King (by Intikhab) and winner up to 8.5f in Italy by
Spectrum: dam, 5f/6f winner in Italy, half-sister to smart 1996 2-y-o 6f winner (also
second in Dewhurst) Musical Pursuit: fair form: claimed from N. Callaghan on debut:
won maiden at Southwell in December: should prove best at 5f/6f: raced on all-weather:
awkward first 2 starts: joined A. Hales. *A. J. McCabe*

NEXT FLIGHT (IRE) 7 b.g. Woodborough (USA) 112 – Sans Ceriph (IRE) 75 (That- **–**
ching 131) [2006 60: f14g⁵ 15.8d 14d⁶ Oct 8] good-bodied gelding: no form in 2006: well
beaten only try in visor. *R. E. Barr*

NEXT NESS (IRE) 3 b.g. Indian Lodge (IRE) 127 – Fauna (IRE) 65 (Taufan (USA) **58**
119) [2006 54: p7g⁴ p7.1g³ p8.6g p7.1g 7.2v 7g⁶ 6f 7.1f Jun 26] modest performer: won
claimer at Catterick in June: said to have finished lame final outing: stayed 7f: acted on
polytrack and any turf going: dead. *R. F. Fisher*

NEXT TIME AROUND (IRE) 4 b. or br.g. Namid 128 – In Due Course (USA) (A P **80**
Indy (USA) 131) [2006 5.1s 5s May 27] good-topped gelding: unimpressive mover:
fairly useful performer: missed 2005 and not at best in 2006: should stay 6f: acts on firm
and good to soft ground: has looked ungenuine: sold 5,500 gns. *Mrs L. Stubbs*

NICADA (IRE) 2 ch.c. (Mar 31) Titus Livius (FR) 115 – Rhapsani (IRE) 24 (Persian **73**
Bold 123) [2006 5f p5.1g⁴ 6s⁵ 5.3f³ 6m⁴ p5g⁵ 7f⁴ f7g⁵ 6g p7.1m* p8.6m p7.1g f8g³ f8g*
f7g⁴ Dec 19] €4,500Y, resold 5,000Y: workmanlike colt: first foal: dam showed little in
Ireland: fair performer: claimed from M. Easterby second start: won nurseries at Wolverhampton in October and Southwell in December: probably stays 8.6f: acts on all-weather
and firm ground: sometimes wears cheekpieces. *Miss Gay Kelleway*

NICE ONE 2 b.f. (Mar 18) Almaty (IRE) 113§ – Roecliffe (Totem (USA) 118) [2006 **–**
f5g 6g 6s Aug 28] first foal: dam unraced: well beaten in sellers. *J. R. Turner*

NICE TO KNOW (FR) 2 ch.f. (Mar 8) Machiavellian (USA) 123 – Entice (FR) 111 **66 p**
(Selkirk (USA) 129) [2006 7m⁵ Sep 13] big, leggy filly: fifth foal: half-sister to 2 winners
abroad by Anabaa, including fairly useful 2002 French 2-y-o 5.5f winner Energetic Star:
dam 7f (at 2 yrs) to 1¼m winner: 40/1 and backward, staying-on fifth to Jaasoos in
maiden at Yarmouth: should progress, particularly at 1m/1¼m. *E. A. L. Dunlop*

NICE TUNE 4 b.f. Diktat 126 – Military Tune (Nashwan (USA) 135) [2006 83: **99**
p7.1g* p7g⁴ p10g* p10g² p8g³ 10.3m² p10g⁴ p10g² 9m* 9.9m⁶ Aug 19] angular, good-
topped filly: useful handicapper: won at Wolverhampton in February, Lingfield in March
and Goodwood (beat Princess Cocoa by length) in August: stays 1¼m: acts on polytrack
and any turf going: consistent. *C. E. Brittain*

NICOMEDIA (IRE) 2 br.f. (Mar 5) Key of Luck (USA) 126 – Ladylishandra (IRE) 82 **76**
(Mujadil (USA) 119) [2006 7m⁵ 7m⁵ p6g⁴ 7d p7g³ Dec 20] €77,000Y: strong, compact
filly: second foal: dam Irish 2-y-o 6f winner: fair maiden: third to Basaata at Lingfield,
rallying: will stay 1m: acts on polytrack and good to firm going. *R. Hannon*

NICOZETTO (FR) 6 b.g. Nicolotte 118 – Arcizette (FR) (Sarhoob (USA) 124) [2006 **59**
51: f8g⁵ f11g* f11g³ 10f 12f⁵ Jul 5] modest performer, better on all-weather than turf:
won banded race at Southwell in April: stays 1½m: acts on fibresand and firm going: tried
in cheekpieces/blinkers: slowly away fourth outing. *N. Wilson*

NIDHAAL (IRE) 3 ch.f. Observatory (USA) 131 – Jeed (IRE) 86 (Mujtahid (USA) **101**
118) [2006 107: 6f² 6f 7f 5g² 6g Oct 12] smallish, strong, lengthy filly: useful performer:
said to have suffered a fracture final start at 2 yrs: creditable second in 2006 in listed
races at Haydock (1¼ lengths behind Paradise Isle) and Hamilton (beaten ½ length by
Angus Newz): stayed 6f: raced only on good going or firmer: free-going sort: visits Oasis
Dream. *E. A. L. Dunlop*

NIGELLA 3 b.f. Band On The Run 102 – Yabint El Sham 83 (Sizzling Melody 117) **90**
[2006 92: 5.1g 5.1f⁴ May 11] strong, good-bodied filly: fairly useful performer: raced
mainly at 5f: acts on polytrack and firm going. *E. S. McMahon*

NIGHT CRESCENDO (USA) 3 br. or b.g. Diesis 133 – Night Fax (USA) (Known **102**
Fact (USA) 135) [2006 87: 8m* 9s³ May 25] tall, useful-looking gelding: useful form:
further improvement in 2006, winning handicap at Newbury in April by a neck from

Acheekyone: creditable third to Layazaal in similar event at Goodwood only subsequent outing: gelded after: should stay 1¼m: acts on soft and good to firm ground. *Mrs A. J. Perrett*

NIGHT CRU 3 b.g. Night Shift (USA) – Jouet 71 (Reprimand 122) [2006 68: 8.3g 8m³ 10f⁶ 8.3f* 8g* p8.6f⁵ 8s Sep 22] strong, compact gelding: fair handicapper: won at Windsor and Newmarket, both in July: stays 8.6f: acts on polytrack, firm and good to soft going. *C. F. Wall* — **78**

NIGHT CRUISE (IRE) 3 b.g. Docksider (USA) 124 – Addaya (IRE) (Persian Bold 123) [2006 p12g* p12.2s² Dec 14] sixth foal: half-brother to several winners, including smart 7f (including at 2 yrs)/1m winner Priors Lodge (by Grand Lodge) and useful 7f/8.5f winner Penny Cross (by Efisio): dam ran once: fairly useful form: won maiden at Kempton by 3½ lengths in November: good second to Pagano in handicap at Wolverhampton following month: should improve further. *J. A. Osborne* — **80 p**

NIGHT EXPLOSION (IRE) 8 ch.g. Night Shift (USA) – Voodoo Rocket 56 (Lycius (USA) 124) [2006 43: p10g⁶ Jan 7] poor performer: stays 1¼m: acts on sand/polytrack: tried blinkered/tongue tied. *D. J. S. ffrench Davis* — **44**

NIGHT FALCON 2 b.f. (Mar 17) Act One 124 – Original Spin (IRE) 91 (Machiavellian (USA) 123) [2006 s p8.6g Oct 29] 30,000Y: angular, useful-looking filly: third foal: dam, 1¼m/1½m winner, half-sister to smart 1¼m performers Time Away and Time Ahead and granddaughter of Time Charter: burly and behind in maidens. *H. Morrison* — **–**

NIGHT GROOVE (IRE) 3 b.g. Night Shift (USA) – Taysala (IRE) (Akarad (FR) 130) [2006 61: p10g² p8.6g⁶ p10g f12g³ 10g² 10g² 10m p8.6g⁵ Dec 30] sturdy gelding: modest performer: best form at 1¼m: acts on polytrack (probably on fibresand), yet to race on extremes of going on turf: tried in blinkers/cheekpieces. *N. P. Littmoden* — **63**

NIGHTIME (IRE) 3 ch.f. Galileo (IRE) 134 – Caumshinaun (IRE) 114 (Indian Ridge 123) [2006 89p: 8.7d* 8v* 8m Jun 23] — **113**

Contrary to what the betting might have suggested, the home-trained runners came very much to the fore in the Boylesports Irish One Thousand Guineas at the Curragh in May. They filled the first five placings, with 12/1-shot Nightime, trained close to the racecourse by Dermot Weld, followed across the line, eventually, by Ardbrae Lady (50/1), Queen Cleopatra (11/1), Race For The Stars (7/1) and Abigail Pett (14/1). The 5/2 favourite Confidential Lady, runner-up in the One Thousand Guineas at Newmarket on her previous outing and one of four British challengers, was sixth, failing by a long way to show her form. That applied to most of the fifteen-strong field. Plenty were floundering by halfway in the very testing conditions, though not Nightime who seemed to revel in them. Not far behind the pacesetting Confidential Lady at that stage, Nightime made steady progress from thereon, took the lead after two furlongs out and stayed on strongly to draw six lengths clear. No filly in the previous sixty years had won the Irish One Thousand by such a wide margin. Despite that, it is difficult to rate Nightime's performance all that highly, in what was a below average renewal of the race. The runner-up, Ardbrae Lady, for instance, had looked exposed as no more than useful after ten appearances—her sole win during that time gained in a maiden at Gowran at two—and defeats in all eight of her races, most of them listed events, after the Guineas did nothing to alter that view.

Nevertheless, to win a classic as impressively as Nightime is still a notable achievement, and to do so as the least experienced in the field reflects greater credit still. The Irish One Thousand was only Nightime's third race. She had come seventh of eight in the Group 3 C. L. Weld Park Stakes at the Curragh in October, 2005, on her debut and didn't need to run up to that form to land the odds in a ten-runner maiden at Cork in April on her reappearance, both races taking place on good to soft going. Nightime encountered very different conditions on her only outing after the Irish One Thousand, in the Coronation Stakes at Royal Ascot. The ground was good to firm there, and Nightime proved a totally different proposition on it, unable to hold her prominent position once in line for home and weakening quickly after catching a bit of a bump. Eased once her chance had gone, Nightime trailed home last of fifteen behind Nannina, and was found to have pulled a muscle. The Blandford Stakes at the Curragh in September was mentioned as a possible race for Nightime's return, but her trainer reportedly wasn't entirely happy with her

Boylesports Irish 1000 Guineas, the Curragh—
Nightime revels in the heavy ground as she records a six-length win over Ardbrae Lady;
Queen Cleopatra beats her stable-companion Race For The Stars (dark colours) for third

and the following month it was announced that she would be retired for the season. 'But she'll be back and will make a lovely four-year-old,' said Weld.

Nightime (IRE) (ch.f. 2003)	Galileo (IRE) (b 1998)	Sadler's Wells (b 1981)	Northern Dancer
			Fairy Bridge
		Urban Sea (ch 1989)	Miswaki
			Allegretta
	Caumshinaun (IRE) (ch 1997)	Indian Ridge (ch 1985)	Ahonoora
			Hillbrow
		Ridge Pool (ch 1991)	Bluebird
			Casting Couch

Nightime was Weld's third Irish One Thousand Guineas winner, Prince's Polly having provided him with his first in 1982 and Trusted Partner his second six years later. It was a first success in the race for Nightime's rider Pat Smullen, whose wife Frances Crowley had saddled Saoire to win it twelve months earlier, becoming the first female licence-holder to be credited officially with a win in an Irish classic. Nightime is owned by Weld's mother Marguerite and was also bred by her, as was Weld's 2004 Irish Derby winner Grey Swallow. Mrs Weld usually sells her yearlings and apparently her son wanted her to send Nightime to the sales, but she thought the filly could be 'a bit special' and decided to keep her. Nightime's four-year-old half-sister Mermaid Island (by Mujadil) had been sold as a yearling, for 100,000 guineas, though she went into training with Weld, for whom she won over a mile at two and showed useful form at around nine furlongs at three. Mermaid Island made a couple of appearances in the sales ring in 2006. In February she

Mrs C. L. Weld's "Nightime"

fetched €110,000 but, having been covered by Nightime's sire Galileo and had her half-sister win the Irish One Thousand in the meantime, it took a bid of 290,000 guineas to secure Mermaid Island five months later, a sum which broke the record for a broodmare at the Tattersalls July Sales. The half-sisters are the first two foals of Caumshinaun, a mare also owned and trained by the Welds. Caumshinaun, a sister to the useful sprinter Candleriggs, won five races at six furlongs to a mile at three and four, getting off the mark when first tried in blinkers and equipped with them on all her subsequent starts. She put up her best performance on her final appearance, showing smart form to win a mile listed event at Cork by three lengths. Caumshinaun's dam Ridge Pool and grandam Casting Couch both won over six furlongs in Ireland as two-year-olds. Nightime, leggy, lightly-made and plain, wouldn't win any prizes in a show-ring, but she is a smart performer on the race-course, as she demonstrated in the Irish One Thousand. The further Nightime went the better she looked that day, and she will definitely stay a mile and a quarter. *D. K. Weld, Ireland*

NIGHT IN (IRE) 3 b.g. Night Shift (USA) – Sherannda (USA) (Trempolino (USA) 135) [2006 75: 5g 6.1f 5g⁶ 6.1g³ 5m 6f³ 6m 7d 8v 6s Oct 10] tall, good-topped gelding: fair handicapper: stays 6f: acts on firm going: usually tongue tied: none too consistent. *N. Tinkler* **75**

NIGHTINSHINING (IRE) 2 ch.c. (Jan 8) Night Shift (USA) – Malthouse Mistress (IRE) (Peintre Celebre (USA) 137) [2006 7g p7g² 7d* 7.1g⁶ Aug 26] €16,000F, 24,000Y: strong, sturdy colt: first foal: dam unraced out of sister to Prix Marcel Boussac winner **90**

Juvenia: fairly useful form: won maiden at Leicester in August: good 3½ lengths sixth of 8 to Drumfire in Solario Stakes at Sandown (hung left): will stay 1m. *A. King*

NIGHT MARKET 8 ch.g. Inchinor 119 – Night Transaction 59 (Tina's Pet 121) [2006 – §
f7g Jan 3] strong gelding: modest but unreliable winner in 2004: missed 2005, and well held only outing at 8 yrs: tried blinkered/in cheekpieces. *Ronald Thompson*

NIGHT PRAYERS (IRE) 4 ch.g. Night Shift (USA) – Eleanor Antoinette (IRE) –
(Double Schwartz 128) [2006 7v 6g⁶ p8.6g Jul 28] fairly useful performer in Ireland at
2 yrs for J. Hayden: little form in 2006: left D. Nicholls after reappearance. *B. Smart*

NIGHT PROSPECTOR 6 b.g. Night Shift (USA) – Pride of My Heart 74 (Lion **92**
Cavern (USA) 117) [2006 100, a91: p6g p5g 5g 5s² 5m 5g 5f³ 6g⁶ 5d⁴ 6m 6m 6d⁴ p5.1m³
p6g* f6g* p5.1g* f5g⁶ f6g Dec 21] close-coupled, good-topped gelding: fairly useful
handicapper: claimed from G. L. Moore, then won at Wolverhampton (2) and Southwell
in November/December: best at 5f/6f: acts on all-weather, firm and good to soft going:
tried blinkered, often in cheekpieces: tends to wander: none too consistent. *R. A. Harris*

NIGHT RAINBOW (IRE) 3 ch.f. Night Shift (USA) – Teresita (Rainbow Quest **60**
(USA) 134) [2006 60: p8g p8g⁶ 6m⁴ 6.1f³ 6f 5g p6g Aug 31] close-coupled filly: modest
maiden: left A. Lidderdale after reappearance: stays 6f: acts on polytrack and firm going.
C. Tinkler

NIGHT REVELLER (IRE) 3 b.f. Night Shift (USA) – Tir-An-Oir (IRE) (Law –
Society (USA) 130) [2006 –: f6g f7g f8g 6d 7g 15.8m 8m 7.5g p6m 11.5d p6g⁶ Dec 6]
small, strong filly: little form. *M. C. Chapman*

NIGHT ROCKET (IRE) 3 b.f. (Jan 19) Night Shift (USA) – Exorcet (FR) 78 (Selkirk **71 p**
(USA) 129) [2006 p6g³ Nov 24] second foal: sister to 3-y-o Dark Missile: dam, 6f winner,
out of smart sprinter Stack Rock: 14/1, very green when 5 lengths third of 9 to Bussel in
maiden at Kempton, running on strongly once getting hang of things: likely to stay 7f:
sure to improve. *A. M. Balding*

NIGHTSPOT 5 ch.g. Night Shift (USA) – Rash Gift 78 (Cadeaux Genereux 131) [2006 **80**
89: 10.1g 10m 10.2d⁶ 10f⁵ 8.1m⁵ 10m Aug 5] tall, quite attractive gelding: fairly useful
handicapper: stays 1½m: acts on polytrack and soft ground, probably on firm: tried vis-
ored/in cheekpieces. *B. R. Millman*

NIGHT STORM 5 b.m. Night Shift (USA) – Monte Calvo 85 (Shirley Heights 130) **81**
[2006 71, a74: p10g⁴ p10g⁵ p8g⁶ p8g² p10g 9m* 8f* 8m⁴ 8.1m² 9m 8f⁵ 9g⁶ 8.5d⁵ p8g⁶ **a75**
8.3f p8g⁶ p8g p8g p8g⁵ Dec 4] smallish, workmanlike mare: fairly useful handicapper
on turf, fair on all-weather: won at Goodwood and Bath in June: stays easy 1¼m: acts on
polytrack and firm ground: has worn tongue tie, visored once (ran poorly): has worn
crossed noseband: usually slowly away nowadays. *S. Dow*

NIGHTSTRIKE (IRE) 3 b.f. Night Shift (USA) – Come Together 68 (Mtoto 134) **68**
[2006 6.1g 7g⁶ p6g³ f6g⁴ 6m⁶ 7.1m* 7g⁵ 7m 6d Oct 3] 9,000F, 23,000Y: third foal: half-
sister to 4-y-o Chairman Rick: dam 11f winner: fair performer: won maiden at Chepstow
in August: stays 7f: acts on polytrack and good to firm ground: sold 4,000 gns. *H. Candy*

NIGHT WARRIOR (IRE) 6 b.g. Alhaarth (IRE) 126 – Miniver (IRE) (Mujtahid –
(USA) 118) [2006 47, a63: f12g⁴ p12.2g* p10g p12g f14g p8.6g Jun 9] modest per- **a62**
former: won handicap at Wolverhampton in January: stays 1½m: acts on all-weather and
firm going: often wears headgear: has found little: held up: sold 10,000 gns in July.
N. P. Littmoden

NIGHT WOLF (IRE) 6 gr.g. Indian Ridge 123 – Nicer (IRE) 113 (Pennine Walk 120) **55 §**
[2006 64§: p8g⁴ p8g⁶ p7g p7g Dec 19] modest handicapper: stays 1m: acts on polytrack
and firm going: inconsistent. *Jamie Poulton*

NIHAL (IRE) 3 b.f. Singspiel (IRE) 133 – Katie McLain (USA) 85 (Java Gold (USA)) **94**
[2006 86: 10m² 10.1m 10.1m 10.3f⁵ 12f* 12m 9.9g 12d Sep 30] good-bodied filly: good
walker: fairly useful handicapper: won 4-runner event at York in July: stays 1½m: raced
mainly on ground firmer than good (acts on firm): sweating (well below form) third
outing: has been bandaged hind joints. *M. Johnston*

NIHIL PETERE (IRE) 2 b.f. (Apr 20) Xaar 132 – Forest Berries (IRE) (Thatching –
131) [2006 5f⁶ 7.1m 7f 7g 7.5g 7m Sep 15] 7,000Y: good-topped filly: half-sister to several
winners, including 4-y-o Vancouver Gold: dam unraced: little form. *P. T. Midgley*

NIKKI BEA (IRE) 3 ch.f. Titus Livius (FR) 115 – Strong Feeling (USA) (Devil's Bag **63**
(USA)) [2006 54p: p8g² 8.3m p10g⁴ p10g² 9.9m p8g* 10d 10f⁴ p10g p8g p10g Dec 16]
£900Y: leggy filly: modest handicapper: won at Lingfield in June: effective at 1m/1¼m:
acts on polytrack and firm going. *Jamie Poulton*

NILSATISOPTIMUM (USA) 3 ch.c. Gilded Time (USA) – Fluid Emotion (USA) **59 d**
(Rhythm (USA)) [2006 63: p7g⁶ p7.1g 7f p7.1g p6g 5f 5.9g⁶ 6m 5g³ 5g 7.1d p6g⁴ f6m
f7g p7.1m Nov 8] sparely-made colt: modest maiden: below form after reappearance:
stays 7f: acts on polytrack, good to firm and good to soft going: tried tongue tied/in cheek-
pieces/blinkered. *M. Mullineaux*

NIMBLE STAR 3 b.f. Foxhound (USA) 103 – Deerlet 64 (Darshaan 133) [2006 32: f5g **37**
7m 7g² 8.2m 6.9m Jun 19] poor maiden: stays 7f: tried blinkered. *C. W. Fairhurst*

NIMELLO (USA) 10 b.g. Kingmambo (USA) 125 – Zakota (IRE) (Polish Precedent **– §**
(USA) 131) [2006 65§, a78§: p9.5g p9.5g⁵ p9.5g⁴ p8.6g⁴ p8.6g p9.5g f8g⁴ p9.5g Dec 29] **a70 §**
smallish, well-made gelding: fair performer: best at 1m/9f: acts on all-weather, best turf
efforts on softer than good: tried blinkered: held up: temperamental. *A. G. Newcombe*

NIMRANA FORT 3 b.g. Indian Ridge 123 – Ninotchka (USA) 110 (Nijinsky (CAN) **60**
138) [2006 71: 10g 10v 10s p8.6g Oct 30] leggy, dipped-backed gelding: just modest
maiden in 2006, leaving I. Semple after second outing: should stay 1m: best effort on
good going. *G. A. Swinbank*

NIMRA (USA) 3 gr. or ro.f. Cozzene (USA) – Purity (USA) (Fappiano (USA)) [2006 **85**
12f² 11.5m⁶ 12.1m² 11.6f³ 12d² p12g² p13g Sep 29] $180,000Y: good-topped filly: sister
to US winners Call An Audible (Grade 2-placed) and Chaste (Grade 3-placed), and half-
sister to 3 winners abroad: dam 6f/7f winner in USA: fairly useful maiden: placed 5 times:
stays 1½m: acts on polytrack, firm and good to soft going. *G. A. Butler*

NINA BLINI 2 b.f. (Feb 23) Bertolini (USA) 125 – Film Buff 60 (Midyan (USA) 124) **90**
[2006 5m⁶ 5g* 5m³ 6m 5.2g 6m 5m⁵ p6s² Dec 14] 21,000Y: strong, good-bodied filly:
fourth foal: half-sister to winner in USA by Robellino: dam maiden who stayed 1¾m:
fairly useful performer: won maiden at Warwick in May: third of 15 to Gilded in Queen
Mary Stakes at Royal Ascot next time: ran creditably in nurseries (stiff mark) and minor
event last 3 starts: effective at 5f/6f, bred to stay further: acts on polytrack and good to
firm going. *B. J. Meehan*

NINA FONTENAIL (FR) 5 gr.m. Kaldounevees (FR) 118 – Ninon Fontenail (FR) **66**
(Turgeon (USA) 123) [2006 66: p10g³ 10.2d² 11.7d⁶ 12.6m⁵ 11.6m p10g³ 12.1m² Aug
10] leggy, close-coupled mare: fair handicapper: stays 12.6f, probably 1¾m: acts on
polytrack, firm and good to soft going: consistent. *B. R. Millman*

NINETAILS (IRE) 3 b.f. Rainbow Quest (USA) 134 – Minerva (IRE) (Caerleon **67**
(USA) 132) [2006 p10g 12g⁵ Jul 28] close-coupled filly: second foal: half-sister to US
8.5f/1¼m winner Key of Solomon (by Machiavellian): dam, unraced, closely related to
US Grade 2 11f winner Sword Dance out of half-sister to smart Irish miler Fatherland:
fair form in maidens at Kempton and Newmarket: stays 1½m. *E. J. O'Neill*

NINTH HOUSE (USA) 4 b.c. Chester House (USA) 123 – Ninette (USA) 101 **93**
(Alleged (USA) 138) [2006 82: 8m p8g* 8d p8g p10g⁴ p8g p7.1g* p7g p8g p9.5g⁶ Dec 9]
good-topped colt: fairly useful performer: won handicap at Kempton in August and
claimer at Wolverhampton (claimed from D. Daly £14,000) in September: stays 1¼m:
acts on polytrack and firm going: tongue tied since debut: said to have had breathing
problems fifth/sixth starts. *N. P. Littmoden*

NIQAAB 2 ch.f. (Feb 11) Alhaarth (IRE) 126 – Shanty 94 (Selkirk (USA) 129) [2006 **70 p**
7m p7g⁵ Oct 11] 110,000Y: lengthy, useful-looking filly: second foal: dam, 1m winner
(from 2 starts at 2 yrs), half-sister to useful 5f to 7f winner Nightbird from family of
2000 Guineas winner Footstepsinthesand: more promise than bare result in maidens at
Newbury (hampered) and Lingfield (soon lot to do) 4 months apart: will stay 1m: capable
of better. *B. W. Hills*

NISR 9 b.g. Grand Lodge (USA) 125 – Tharwa (IRE) 63 (Last Tycoon 131) [2006 72, **–**
a55: p9.5g* f8g⁴ p8g* p8g² p12g Feb 20] lengthy gelding: modest performer: won **a63**
apprentice banded race at Wolverhampton in January and seller at Lingfield in February:
effective at 6f to easy 1¼m: acts on polytrack, firm and good to soft going: tried blinkered, tongue tied of late: not one to trust implicitly. *Miss Gay Kelleway*

NISTAKI (USA) 5 ch.g. Miswaki (USA) 124 – Brandywine Belle (USA) (Trempolino **72**
(USA) 135) [2006 80: p6g p5g⁶ p6g p6g 6d⁵ 6.1m 5m⁵ 6f⁵ p6m p7g p6g² p6g Dec 9]
strong, compact gelding: fair performer: best at 6f/7f: acts on polytrack, soft and
good to firm going: reportedly bled on 4-y-o reappearance. *D. Shaw*

NITEOWL LAD (IRE) 4 ch.g. Tagula (IRE) 116 – Mareha (IRE) 95 (Cadeaux Gene- **77**
reux 131) [2006 84: 6m 5m 5.5m⁶ 5m⁶ 5.1g Aug 4] lengthy gelding: fair handicapper:
best at 5f: acts on firm going: tongue tied last 3 starts. *J. Balding*

NIZA D'ALM (FR) 5 b. or br.m. Passing Sale (FR) 125 – Bekaa II (FR) (Djarvis (FR)) – [2006 p10g Jun 21] non-thoroughbred mare: well beaten in bumpers/maiden: sold 1,000 gns in August. *Miss Suzy Smith*

NOAH JAMEEL 4 ch.c. Mark of Esteem (IRE) 137 – Subtle One (IRE) (Polish Patriot – (USA) 128) [2006 68: 9.9d Sep 27] fair maiden at best, very lightly raced: well held in claimer only start at 4 yrs. *A. G. Newcombe*

NOBBLER 4 br.g. Classic Cliche (IRE) 128 – Nicely (IRE) 94 (Bustino 136) [2006 66: – 14.1s 11.9m Apr 30] leggy gelding: fluent mover: maiden handicapper: well held in 2006: tried visored. *N. A. Callaghan*

NOBELIX (IRE) 4 gr.g. Linamix (FR) 127 – Nataliana 103 (Surumu (GER)) [2006 81: **90** p12g3 p12g3 14m* 14m 12d Sep 30] compact gelding: fairly useful handicapper: won at Haydock in July by 7 lengths: stays 1¾m: acts on polytrack, firm and good to soft going: won twice over hurdles in November. *J. R. Fanshawe*

NOBELMANN (GER) 7 ch.g. Lomitas 129 – Ninova (GER) (Esclavo (FR)) [2006 –: **53** p12g4 p12.2g3 p10g5 p10g May 15] modest performer: stayed 1½m: acted on polytrack and soft going: dead. *A. W. Carroll*

NOBILISSIMA (IRE) 2 b.f. (Feb 7) Orpen (USA) 116 – Shadow Smile (IRE) 74 (Slip **71** Anchor 136) [2006 6m6 5m* 5g5 5.1m6 Oct 8] fourth living foal: half-sister to fairly useful 8.6f winner Watchmyeyes (by Bold Fact), later successful abroad: dam placed twice at 1¼m in Ireland from 3 starts: fair performer: won maiden at Lingfield in July: ran respectably in nurseries after: likely to stay 7f/1m. *J. L. Spearing*

NOBLE CALLING (FR) 9 b.g. Caller I D (USA) – Specificity (USA) 103 (Alleged – (USA) 138) [2006 –: 10m 9.7f p16g Oct 23] angular gelding: no form since 2004: sometimes blinkered/visored. *R. J. Hodges*

NOBLE EDGE 3 ch.g. Bold Edge 123 – Noble Soul 67 (Sayf El Arab (USA) 127) **68 d** [2006 60: p8.6g3 f7g2 f7g5 f8g3 f11s2 f11g5 12d2 11g6 12m2 12.1g6 12.1s4 14m 12.4d 9.9m Sep 19] sturdy gelding: fair performer: claimed from P. Blockley £6,000 after second start: well below form last 4 starts: stays 1½m: acts on all-weather, good to firm and good to soft going: tried in blinkers, effective in cheekpieces or not. *Robert Gray*

NOBLE GENT (IRE) 3 b.c. Danehill (USA) 126 – Blanche Dubois (Nashwan (USA) **102** 135) [2006 84: 10m2 10m2 10m* 9.9g3 10.3f Sep 23] improved into a useful handicapper, winning at Newmarket in August by length from Crime Scene: creditable 2½ lengths third to Champions Gallery at Beverley next time: below form at Chester final outing, again tending to edge left: stays 1¼m: acts on good to firm and good to soft going: joined E. Charpy in UAE. *Saeed bin Suroor*

NOBLE LOCKS (IRE) 8 ch.g. Night Shift (USA) – Imperial Graf (USA) (Blushing – John (USA) 120) [2006 –: p6g Nov 20] smallish gelding: well held both starts since 2004: tried blinkered/visored/tongue tied. *J. W. Unett*

NOBLE MIND 5 b.g. Mind Games 121 – Lady Annabel 54 (Alhijaz 122) [2006 65: **55** f12g5 p9.5g5 f11g4 p12g4 p12g p16.5g p13.9g May 2] leggy gelding: modest maiden: stays 1½m: acts on polytrack: wears visor/cheekpieces nowadays. *P. G. Murphy*

NOBLE MINSTREL 3 ch.g. Fantastic Light (USA) 134 – Sweetness Herself 106 **68** (Unfuwain (USA) 131) [2006 65p: p6g 8.2g p12.2g* p12.2g5 Dec 6] lengthy gelding: fair performer: upped in trip, won handicap at Wolverhampton in November: will stay 1¾m: acts on polytrack: tongue tied last 3 starts. *S. C. Williams*

NOBLE MOUNT 5 b.g. Muhtarram (USA) 125 – Our Poppet (IRE) 58 (Warning 136) **52** [2006 62: p6g p6g6 p7.1g p5.1g 6f2 p6g p6g6 p6g6 Dec 13] modest performer: effective at 5f, should stay 7f: acts on all-weather and firm ground: usually wears cheekpieces. *A. B. Haynes*

NOBLE NOVA 3 br.f. Fraam 114 – Noble Destiny 89 (Dancing Brave (USA) 140) **69** [2006 60: 8m6 8.1g3 8m 7.2v4 8.1s 7.5f 8d* 8.3m* 8f* 8.3g3 8m4 p8g 8m 7g Sep 27] useful-looking filly: fair handicapper: won at Ayr (2) and Hamilton (in between) within space of 9 days in July: likely to prove best up to 1m: acts on any turf going: sold 12,000 gns. *M. R. Channon*

NOBLE TIGER (IRE) 5 b.m. Tiger Hill (IRE) 127 – Noble Conquest (USA) (Vaguely – Noble 140) [2006 9g Jul 3] half-sister to 2 winners, including 1¼m winner Kind Sir (by Generous): dam French 1m winner: no sign of ability in bumpers/novice hurdle and a claimer. *Mrs S. C. Bradburne*

NO COMMISSION (IRE) 4 b.g. General Monash (USA) 107 – Price of Passion 83 **– §**
(Dolphin Street (FR) 125) [2006 60, a66: 10m p13.9g Nov 27] sturdy gelding: well held
both outings on Flat in 2006: tried in cheekpieces/blinkers: has edged left: reluctant, and
one to leave alone. *R. F. Fisher*

NODDIES WAY 3 b.c. Nomadic Way (USA) 104 – Sharway Lady 50 (Shareef Dancer **67**
(USA) 135) [2006 12m 11.5m^5 14m^3 16g^6 13.1m p13g^3 p16g^4 p16g Nov 8] leggy colt:
second foal: dam, 1m seller winner, also won over hurdles: fair maiden: stays easy 2m:
acts on polytrack and good to firm going: blinkered final start: unruly in stall and withdrawn intended second outing. *J. F. Panvert*

NODDLEDODDLE (IRE) 2 b.f. (Feb 6) Daggers Drawn (USA) 114 – En Retard **53**
(IRE) 97 (Petardia 113) [2006 6g p7g p8g^3 p8g^4 p7.1g^5 Dec 28] €6,000F, 1,600 2-y-o:
big, useful-looking filly: third foal: half-sister to 5-y-o George The Best: dam Irish 5f/6f
winner: modest maiden: best effort at Wolverhampton final start: tongue tied. *J. Ryan*

NOD'S STAR 5 ch.m. Starborough 126 – Barsham 94 (Be My Guest (USA) 126) [2006 **47**
43: p12g^4 Dec 13] close-coupled mare: poor maiden: stays 1¾m: acts on polytrack and
good to soft going: tongue tied last 2 starts. *Mrs L. C. Jewell*

NOELANI (IRE) 4 b.f. Indian Ridge 123 – Dawnsio (IRE) 102 (Tate Gallery (USA) **114**
117) [2006 113: 6d 6m^2 6m 7m^2 7.5g 6g^2 7.5v* Oct 1] smallish, workmanlike filly: smart
performer: won Coolmore Stud Home of Champions Concorde Stakes at Tipperary (by
neck from Ugo Fire) in October: runner-up earlier in Ballyogan Stakes at Leopardstown
(beaten ½ length by Yomalo), Minstrel Stakes at the Curragh (went down by neck to
Jedburgh) and Renaissance Stakes (1¼ lengths behind Beauty Bright) at the Curragh:
mid-division in Golden Jubilee Stakes at Royal Ascot third start: stays 7.5f: acts on heavy
and good to firm going: has been blanketed for stall entry: races prominently. *J. Oxx,
Ireland*

Lady Clague's "Noelani"

NO GROUSE 6 b.g. Pursuit of Love 124 – Lady Joyce (FR) (Galetto (FR) 118) [2006 **70** 76: 7g⁵ 6g⁴ 6m⁵ 6m³ 7g 6.9f p7.1g⁴ 6f p7.1g p7.1m⁵ p7g⁴ p7g⁴ Dec 8] strong, round- **a63** barrelled gelding: fair handicapper: effective at 6f to 7.5f: acts on all-weather, good to firm and good to soft going: tried in cheekpieces: held up. *E. J. Alston*

NO INKLING (IRE) 3 b.f. Xaar 132 – No Tippling (IRE) 72 (Unblest 117) [2006 53?: **–** f5g⁴ p6g f5g⁴ 5g 7.5g 7f 10d f7g⁴ f6g⁴ Dec 28] plain filly: poor maiden: stays 7f: acts on **a37** fibresand: tried visored/in cheekpieces. *John A. Harris*

NOISY SILENCE (IRE) 2 b.c. (May 12) Giant's Causeway (USA) 132 – Golightly **79** (USA) (Take Me Out (USA)) [2006 8g⁴ 7d⁶ Oct 28] 42,000Y: big, leggy, close-coupled colt: second foal: dam, 6f/7f winner in USA, out of sister to champion US filly/excellent broodmare Personal Ensign: fair form in maidens at Newmarket, sixth of 19 to Spanish Moon: stays 1m. *P. W. Chapple-Hyam*

NOMOREBLONDES 2 ch.f. (May 6) Ishiguru (USA) 114 – Statuette 57 (Statoblest **54** 120) [2006 5m 5m⁶ Jul 10] 3,000Y: fourth foal: dam, 5f seller winner, ran only at 2 yrs: mid-field in maidens at Ripon. *P. T. Midgley*

NONA 3 ch.f. Halling (USA) 133 – Zarma (FR) (Machiavellian (USA) 123) [2006 60: **–** p12.2g 11.1g Aug 23] quite good-topped filly: modest maiden at 2 yrs: well held in 2006, unseated rider and loose beforehand on first occasion. *Jedd O'Keeffe*

NON COMPLIANT 2 b.c. (Mar 15) Lujain (USA) 119 – Flourish (Selkirk (USA) 129) **88** [2006 6m² p6g² p7.1f⁴ 6m⁶ p6g* p6g⁴ Oct 23] 25,000Y: leggy colt: fourth foal: half- brother to 2003 2-y-o 5f/6f winner Baltic Wave (by Polish Precedent) and 3-y-o Rondo: dam unraced half-sister to useful 1¼m performer Forthwith: fairly useful performer: won maiden at Wolverhampton by 5 lengths in September: best at 5f/6f: raced on polytrack/ good to firm going. *J. W. Hills*

NOOJOOM (IRE) 2 ch.f. (Mar 27) Machiavellian (USA) 123 – Abeyr 106 (Unfuwain **75 p** (USA) 131) [2006 7g⁶ Sep 15] big, lengthy filly: closely related to useful 7f winner Raheibb (by Lion Cavern) and half-sister to several winners, including useful 7f winner (including at 2 yrs) Makfool (by Spectrum): dam 7f/1m winner: 33/1 and green, sixth to Darrfonah in minor event at Newbury, isolated from main action: should progress. *M. P. Tregoning*

NOORAIN 4 ch.f. Kabool 119 – Abeyr 106 (Unfuwain (USA) 131) [2006 56: p8.6g **46** f7g² p8g 8.3m⁴ 8f⁴ p7.1g³ f8g 7d p10g p8g Dec 6] strong filly: modest on all-weather, **a54** poor on turf: left Stef Liddiard £400 after eighth start: stays 9.5f: acts on all-weather and good to firm ground: usually tongue tied. *A. M. Hales*

NOORA (IRE) 5 ch.m. Bahhare (USA) 122 – Esteraad (IRE) 90 (Cadeaux Genereux **86** 131) [2006 84: p10g⁶ 10m² 10m⁵ 10m² 9.7g 10s Oct 10] good-topped mare: fairly useful handicapper: stays 1¼m: acts on polytrack, firm and good to soft going: blinkered/ visored nowadays: has started slowly/looked reluctant. *C. G. Cox*

NOPLEAZINU 6 ch.m. Sure Blade (USA) 130 – Vado Via 56 (Ardross 134) [2006 –: **–** f11g Feb 5] no form: tried tongue tied. *Mrs N. S. Evans*

NORAKIT 3 b.f. Mull of Kintyre (USA) 114 – Thailand (Lycius (USA) 124) [2006 7g **59** 8.1m⁵ 8.3f 8f³ Aug 10] rangy filly: first foal: dam, little form, out of half-sister to 1000 Guineas winner Sayyedati: modest form at best in maidens. *M. R. Channon*

NORCROFT 4 b.g. Fasliyev (USA) 120 – Norcroft Joy 82§ (Rock Hopper 124) [2006 **81** 79: p7.1g⁵ p6g p6g p7.1g⁶ 6m³ p6g* 6m 6m p6g⁶ p6g p6g 5m 6d⁴ 6m* 6g p6g p6g⁵ p6g 6.1d p6g Nov 3] leggy, good-topped gelding: fairly useful handicapper: won at Wolverhampton in April, Kempton (apprentices) in July and Yarmouth in August: effec- tive at 6f to 1m: acts on all-weather, firm and good to soft ground: tried blinkered, usually wears cheekpieces. *Mrs C. A. Dunnett*

NORDIC AFFAIR 2 b.c. (Mar 19) Halling (USA) 133 – Affair of State (IRE) 99 (Tate **85** Gallery (USA) 117) [2006 7m 7s p7g* p8g² Dec 16] 50,000Y: sturdy colt: half-brother to several winners, including 2004 2-y-o 5f/7f winner Bibury Flyer and 1¼m/1½m winner Mojalid (both useful, by Zafonic): dam 2-y-o 5f/6f winner: fairly useful form: won maid- en at Lingfield in December: further improvement when second to Sweeney in minor event there: stays 1m: acts on polytrack. *D. R. C. Elsworth*

NORDIC LIGHT (USA) 2 b. or br.g. (Apr 4) Belong To Me (USA) – Midriff (USA) **65** (Naevus (USA)) [2006 5m 6m Aug 10] $45,000Y: smallish, strong gelding: second foal: half-brother to winner in USA by Open Forum: dam 6f winner in USA: no threat in maid- ens (well backed), fair form at York on debut: gelded after final start. *P. W. Chapple-Hyam*

NORDWIND (IRE) 5 b.g. Acatenango (GER) 127 – Narola (GER) (Nebos (GER) **91**
129) [2006 96: 12g 12d 12g* 11.9g 16g² Jul 28] tall, quite attractive gelding: fairly useful
handicapper nowadays: won at Thirsk (by head from Sualda) in June: good second at
Ascot final start: stays 2m: acts on polytrack and firm going. *W. R. Swinburn*

NO RECOLLECTION (IRE) 3 b.g. Mozart (IRE) 131 – Good Standing (USA) **71** **93**
(Distant View (USA) 126) [2006 58: p10g² p10g⁵ 10.2m³ Sep 7] fair maiden: trained by
D. Wachman in Ireland at 2 yrs: stayed easy 1¼m: acted on polytrack: in cheekpieces/
visor in 2006: joined W. Goldsworthy: dead. *M. J. Wallace*

NORISAN 2 ch.c. (Apr 3) Inchinor 119 – Dream On Deya (IRE) (Dolphin Street (FR) **97**
125) [2006 6m 7m* p7g* 7m³ 7.1g⁴ 8m³ 8s Oct 7] 20,000F, 57,000Y: lengthy colt: fourth
foal: half-brother to 1m (including at 2 yrs) winner Dream Tonic (by Zafonic) and 2003
2-y-o 7f winner Wavertree Dream (by Dushyantor): dam, tailed off only start, half-sister
to smart sprinter Proud Native: useful performer: won maiden at Newmarket (dead-
heated with Halicarnassus) in June and minor event at Lingfield in July: ran well when in
frame in listed events and Solario Stakes (1½ lengths fourth of 8 to Drumfire) at Sandown: stays 1m: raced on polytrack and good going or firmer until final start (well
beaten). *R. Hannon*

NORMAN BECKETT 3 b.g. Beckett (IRE) 116 – Classic Coral (USA) (Seattle **75**
Dancer (USA) 119) [2006 71: p10g⁴ p9.5g p8g⁴ 9.7s⁶ 10v* 10.4m 12.3m² 13m⁶ 10.3m⁶
10.5v⁶ 9.2g⁴ 9.1v* Oct 9] rather leggy, close-coupled gelding: fair performer: left
M. Channon after fourth start: won handicap at Ayr (by 7 lengths) in May and claimer
there in October: stays 1½m: acts on any going: tried in cheekpieces, blinkered/visored
last 2 starts. *I. Semple*

NORMAN NORMAN 4 b.g. Double Trigger (IRE) 123 – Nour El Sahar (USA) (Sag- **–**
ace (FR) 135) [2006 53: p12.2g May 5] modest maiden at 3 yrs: well held only outing in
2006. *W. S. Kittow*

NORMAN THE GREAT 2 b.c. (Apr 19) Night Shift (USA) – Encore du Cristal **51**
(USA) 82 (Quiet American (USA)) [2006 p8.6g p8g Nov 8] modest form in maidens.
Jane Chapple-Hyam

NORMAN TRADITION 2 ch.f. (Feb 16) Traditionally (USA) 117 – Normandy **–**
(CHI) (Great Regent (CAN)) [2006 p7g Sep 6] second foal: closely related to fairly useful
2005 2-y-o 7f/1m winner Santiago Star (by Hussonet): dam unraced: in rear in maiden at
Kempton. *A. M. Balding*

NORSE DANCER (IRE) 6 b.h. Halling (USA) 133 – River Patrol 96 (Rousillon **102 §**
(USA) 133) [2006 127§: 12m 10m 12g 11g⁴ 8d Sep 30] big, rangy, good sort: had a quick
action: high-class performer on his day: won 4 races, including Earl of Sefton Stakes at
Newmarket in 2005: in frame in 10 Group 1 events, including 2000 Guineas at Newmarket and Derby at Epsom at 3 yrs, and King George VI and Queen Elizabeth Stakes at
Newbury at 4 yrs: just useful form in 2006, best effort when 7¾ lengths fourth to Blue
Monday in Arc Trial at Newbury: was effective at 1m to 1½m: acted on good to firm and
good to soft going, below form on firm and soft: tried visored/blinkered (better without):
had sweated up: waited with: temperamental: to stand at Littleton Stud, Hampshire, fee
£4,000. *D. R. C. Elsworth*

NORTHERN BOY (USA) 3 ch.g. Lure (USA) 131 – Catala (USA) (Northern Park **88**
(USA) 107) [2006 75: 8.1s² 8m* 8f⁶ 7.5f 8.1s 8.3g⁴ 9.1v⁵ Oct 9] quite good-topped
gelding: fairly useful performer: landed odds in maiden at Musselburgh in June: below
form in handicaps after: gelded following final start: stays 1m: acts on good and good to
firm going: often races prominently. *T. D. Barron*

NORTHERN CANDY 2 ch.g. (Mar 18) Sugarfoot 118 – Thalya (Crofthall 110) [2006 **–**
5d 5d Oct 8] well beaten in maidens. *A. Dickman*

NORTHERN CHORUS (IRE) 3 ch.g. Distant Music (USA) 126 – Nationalart- **77**
gallery (IRE) (Tate Gallery (USA) 117) [2006 61: 5d³ 6g 5g² 6f² 5m² 5m⁴ 6m 5f* 5d⁵
Aug 28] fair handicapper: won at Redcar in July: stays 6f: acts on firm and good to soft
ground: visored last 4 starts (hasn't looked straightforward): sold 2,500 gns in October.
A. Dickman

NORTHERN DARE (IRE) 2 b.g. (May 6) Fath (USA) 116 – Farmers Swing (IRE) **–**
(River Falls 113) [2006 7g Sep 27] 100/1, mid-division in maiden at Newcastle (gelded
after). *D. Nicholls*

NORTHERN DESERT (IRE) 7 b.g. Desert Style (IRE) 121 – Rosie's Guest (IRE) **–**
(Be My Guest (USA) 126) [2006 72, a89: p8g* p8g³ p8g* p8g⁵ p7.1g⁵ p8g⁵ p10g 8.1m **a95**
p7g p8g p8g p7g p8g Dec 30] lengthy, quite good-topped gelding: useful handicapper

on all-weather: won at Lingfield in January (for second consecutive year) and February: stays 1m: acts on polytrack, firm and soft going: held up. *P. W. Hiatt*

NORTHERN DUNE (IRE) 2 b.c. (Mar 2) Dilshaan 119 – Zoudie 79 (Ezzoud (IRE) 126) [2006 p6g Dec 22] 7/1, behind in maiden at Lingfield, looking hard ride. *B. J. Curley*

NORTHERN EMPIRE (IRE) 3 ch.g. Namid 128 – Bumble (Rainbow Quest (USA) 134) [2006 103: 6m⁴ 6m⁴ Jun 27] strong, good-topped gelding: useful performer at 2 yrs, reportedly sustaining minor injury after final start: below best in listed/minor events in 2006: gelded after: may prove best kept to 5f/6f: raced only on good going or firmer. *B. J. Meehan*   **84**

NORTHERNER (IRE) 3 b.c. Mark of Esteem (IRE) 137 – Ensorceleuse (FR) (Fabulous Dancer (USA) 124) [2006 46: f11g⁶ f12g⁶ 12d² 12m³ May 3] tall colt: modest maiden: stays 1½m: acts on fibresand and good to soft ground: makes running. *J. R. Norton*   **63**

NORTHERN FLING 2 b.g. (Mar 11) Mujadil (USA) 119 – Donna Anna (Be My Chief (USA) 122) [2006 5.1m 5.1g* 5.1m⁴ p5g³ 6m* 6g Aug 26] 10,000F, €33,000Y: quite good-topped gelding: first foal: dam, no form, sister to smart 1m/1¼m performer Donna Viola and half-sister to dam of July Cup winner Frizzante: fairly useful performer: won maiden at Chester in June and nursery at Goodwood in August: faded into ninth in sales race at the Curragh final start (gelded after): will prove best kept to 5f/6f: raced on polytrack and good going or firmer: has reportedly suffered sore shins: tricky ride at times. *D. Nicholls*   **87**

NORTHERN JEM 2 b.c. (Mar 20) Mark of Esteem (IRE) 137 – Top Jem 85 (Damister (USA) 123) [2006 6m³ 7d⁶ Oct 7] fourth foal: half-brother to useful 9f to 1½m winner Polar Jem (by Polar Falcon): dam, 9f/1¼m winner, half-sister to smart performer up to 1½m Polar Red: fairly useful form: third in maiden at Yarmouh and sixth (behind Charlie Farnsbarns) in minor event at Ascot: will be suited by 1m/1¼m. *G. G. Margarson*   **86**

NORTHERN PROMISE (IRE) 3 b.g. Brief Truce (USA) 126 – Sudden Hope (FR) (Darshaan 133) [2006 9.8m 11g 9.8d 13.8m 10d Oct 3] leggy, dipped-backed gelding: no form: tried blinkered. *J. Parkes*   **–**

NORTHERN SPLENDOUR (USA) 4 ch.c. Giant's Causeway (USA) 132 – Ribbonwood (USA) 100 (Diesis 133) [2006 10.4s² 10d Oct 27] strong, good-bodied colt: useful performer: off over 2 years, good ¾-length second to Ofaraby in minor event at York in October: well below form in listed race at Newmarket only other start in 2006: stays 1¼m: acts on soft going: joined S. Seemar in UAE. *Saeed bin Suroor*   **104**

NORTHERN SVENGALI (IRE) 10 b.g. Distinctly North (USA) 115 – Trilby's Dream (IRE) (Mansooj 118) [2006 –: 5g 5g 5f 6f 6m 5m⁶ Aug 3] small, sturdy gelding: little form since 2004: tried blinkered/in cheekpieces/tongue tied. *D. A. Nolan*

NORTH FLEET 3 b.g. Bertolini (USA) 125 – Rhiann (Anshan 119) [2006 –: 7.1g 6g⁵ 5.3f 6f 6g 6d 6d* 8g p7g p6m Nov 21] good-topped gelding: modest performer: won maiden at Windsor in October: stays 6f: acts on good to soft ground. *J. M. Bradley*   **64**

NORTH LANDING (IRE) 6 b.g. Storm Bird (CAN) 134 – Tirol Hope (IRE) 100 (Tirol 127) [2006 16m Jul 10] leggy, quite good-topped gelding: maiden on Flat, no form in 3 runs since 2003: tried in cheekpieces: winning hurdler. *R. C. Guest*   **–**

NORTH LODGE (GER) 6 b.g. Grand Lodge (USA) 125 – Nona (GER) (Cortez §) [2006 p16g 11g 12m Aug 8] quite good-topped gelding: useful performer when trained by M. Hofer in Germany, winning maiden at Krefeld and listed race at Hanover at 3 yrs and minor event at Frankfurt in 2004: down field in handicaps in 2006: left A. King 7,600 gns after second start: stays 11f. *J. F. O'Shea, Ireland*   **–**

NORTHSIDE LODGE (IRE) 8 b.g. Grand Lodge (USA) 125 – Alongside 58 (Slip Anchor 136) [2006 75, a81: p12g p10g p10g 10.1m 10m 10m⁵ p10g² 10g⁶ p12g⁴ p10g² Oct 20] good-topped gelding: fair handicapper on all-weather, modest on turf: effective at 1¼m (all 9 wins)/1½m: acts on polytrack and firm going: below form on softer than good: won in blinkers in 2001, often wears cheekpieces nowadays: tried tongue tied. *W. R. Swinburn*   **59 a74**

NORTH WALK (IRE) 3 b.g. Monashee Mountain (USA) 115 – Celtic Link (IRE) 66 (Toca Madera 111) [2006 84: 6d 8g 8s² 8f 7.6f⁴ 8.2m³ 7s p7g 7s f8g⁶ p8g p8.6g² Dec 21] good-topped gelding: fairly useful handicapper: creditable efforts when placed in 2006: stays 8.6f: acts on polytrack, firm and soft going: wore cheekpieces final start: edgy on second outing. *K. A. Ryan*   **86**

NORTON (IRE) 9 ch.g. Barathea (IRE) 127 – Primrose Valley 99 (Mill Reef (USA) 141) [2006 101: 8m 8.1s⁵ 8g 8m⁵ 8m 8.3g⁴ p8g² 8m p8g⁵ Dec 2] strong, useful-looking   **92**

gelding: fairly useful handicapper nowadays: only placing in 2006 when creditable second to Cross The Line at Kempton: effective at 1m to 10.4f: acts on polytrack, firm and soft going: tried visored (found little): often makes running. *T. G. Mills*

NORWEGIAN 5 b.g. Halling (USA) 133 – Chicarica (USA) 112 (The Minstrel (CAN) 135) [2006 51, a56: 10g 10.5m 10d p9.5g p8.6g p9.5g* Dec 4] good-topped gelding: modest performer: won banded race at Wolverhampton in December: stays 1¼m: acts on all-weather and good to firm ground: usually wears headgear. *Ian Williams* — **a54**

NOR'WESTER 4 br.g. Inchinor 119 – Princess Nawaal (USA) 86 (Seattle Slew (USA)) [2006 77p: p7g p8.6g Jul 1] lengthy gelding: fair maiden: no impact in handicaps at Kempton (hampered) and Wolverhampton in 2006: bred to be suited by further than 1m: acts on good to firm going. *J. R. Fanshawe* — **67**

NOSFERATU (IRE) 3 b.c. In The Wings 128 – Gothic Dream (IRE) 113 (Nashwan (USA) 135) [2006 85p: 10g³ 10d* Oct 9] strong colt, lightly raced: fairly useful form in maidens: won at Windsor in October by 1¼ lengths from Conservation: will be suited by 1½m+: raced only on good/good to soft going: open to further improvement. *Mrs A. J. Perrett* — **84 p**

NO SUPPER (IRE) 2 ch.c. (Mar 15) Inchinor 119 – Be Thankful (IRE) 98 (Linamix (FR) 127) [2006 p8.6g⁵ Dec 27] 30,000Y: second foal: dam 1m/1¼m winner: 4/1, 10½ lengths fifth to Lazy Darren in maiden at Wolverhampton: should prove suited by 1¼m. *M. G. Quinlan* — **56**

NOTA BENE 4 b.g. Zafonic (USA) 130 – Dodo (IRE) 90 (Alzao (USA) 117) [2006 116: 5.2m 5m May 6] strong gelding: smart performer at 3 yrs: better effort in 2006 (useful form) when twelfth to Dandy Man in Palace House Stakes at Newmarket on final outing (tongue tied): subsequently gelded: should prove just as effective at 5f as 6f: acts on soft and good to firm going: reportedly bled final 3-y-o start. *D. R. C. Elsworth* — **102**

NOTABILITY (IRE) 4 b.c. King's Best (USA) 132 – Noble Rose (IRE) 113 (Caerleon (USA) 132) [2006 107: 7g⁶ 7m p8g³ 8g² 8v* 8m⁴ 8g² Oct 14] leggy, quite good-topped colt: smart performer: improved in 2006, placed in Summer Mile at Lingfield (3¾ lengths third to Echo of Light) and Sovereign Stakes at Salisbury (1¼ lengths second to Belenus) prior to winning Darley Oettingen-Rennen at Baden-Baden (by 1½ lengths from Azarole) in August: ran creditably when 3 lengths fourth to Echo of Light in Prix Daniel Wildenstein at Longchamp and 2½ lengths second to Ramonti in Premio Vittorio di Capua at Milan after: bred to stay beyond 1m: acts on polytrack, good to firm and heavy going: races prominently: genuine: has joined Godolphin. *M. A. Jarvis* — **116**

NOTABLE GUEST (USA) 5 b.h. Kingmambo (USA) 125 – Yenda 116 (Dancing Brave (USA) 140) [2006 120: 10g² 10.5m 10.5m² p12g⁶ Sep 2] strong, good-bodied horse: has a quick action: very smart performer: good efforts when length second to Day Flight in Gordon Richards Stakes at Sandown and 1¾ lengths second to Mulaqat in Rose of Lancaster Stakes at Haydock: well below form in September Stakes at Kempton (all-weather debut, last of 6) final start: best at 1¼m/1½m, seemingly on good or firmer ground: has been mulish at stall, and has flashed tail: joined R. Frankel in USA. *Sir Michael Stoute* — **120**

NOTA LIBERATA 2 b.g. (Mar 30) Spinning World (USA) 130 – Kyda (USA) 78 (Gulch (USA)) [2006 6g 5g² 5g⁵ 5m 6f⁵ 7m⁴ 8d⁶ 7m² 7m³ 6d² 6s 7s² 7v² Oct 31] 10,000Y: leggy gelding: first foal: dam, 11f winner, out of smart French/US winner up to 1½m Trampoli: fair maiden: runner-up 5 times, including 3 nurseries: should stay 1m: acts on heavy and good to firm going: gelded after final start. *G. M. Moore* — **72**

NOT ANOTHER CAT (USA) 2 ch.c. (Mar 16) Hennessy (USA) 122 – Isle Be Loving You (USA) (Stuka (USA) 116) [2006 p7.1f⁵ p7.1g³ Oct 30] $160,000Y: second foal: dam won 8.5f minor stakes in USA: fair form in maidens at Wolverhampton, good speed: will prove best up to 7f. *K. R. Burke* — **75**

NOT FOR ME (IRE) 2 b.c. (Jan 26) Mull of Kintyre (USA) 114 – Floral Hall (IRE) (Tagula (IRE) 116) [2006 5.1m p6g² p6g* 5.1f* 5.5m⁵ 5d* 5g Sep 8] 8,000L, 12,000Y: strong, sturdy colt: has a quick action: second foal: dam unraced: useful performer: won maiden at Wolverhampton in June, minor event at Chester in July and listed race at York (beat Fanlight Fanny by 1¾ lengths) in August: not discredited both starts in pattern company (Prix Robert Papin and Flying Childers Stakes): winner at 6f, best form at 5f: acts on polytrack, firm and good to soft going: usually forces pace: sold 80,000 gns, joined S. Seemar in UAE. *T. J. Pitt* — **105**

NOTHING IS FOREVER (IRE) 2 b.g. (Apr 14) Daylami (IRE) 138 – Bequeath (USA) (Lyphard (USA) 132) [2006 8.1g⁴ p8g⁵ 10.1d Oct 18] €30,000Y, 80,000 2-y-o: — **70**

brother to German 7.5f to 1½m winner Commemoration Day and half-brother to several winners, notably very smart 7f/1m winner Decorated Hero (by Warning): dam French 9f winner: fair maiden: best effort on debut: wandered second start, seemed amiss final one (then gelded): should stay 1¼m. *Mrs A. J. Perrett*

NO TIME (IRE) 6 b.h. Danetime (IRE) 121 – Muckross Park 41 (Nomination 125) **67** [2006 77, a92: p5g p5g 5g p5g⁵ 5m p5g⁴ 5.9g p5g 5.1g⁴ 6m³ 7g p6g p5g* p5.1s Dec 14] **a82** smallish, good-topped horse: fairly useful handicapper on all-weather, fair on turf: left M. Polglase after eighth start, J. Osborne after twelfth: won handicap at Kempton in December: effective at 5f/6f: acts on dirt/polytrack (seemingly not on fibresand): firm and good to soft going: tried in cheekpieces: sometimes flashes tail. *A. J. McCabe*

NOTNOWCATO 4 ch.c. Inchinor 119 – Rambling Rose 111 (Cadeaux Generoux **126** 131) [2006 114p: 9g* 10d* 10m⁵ 10m² 10.4d* 10d Oct 14]

As regular readers of *Racehorses* will have appreciated, it was just a matter of time before Ryan Moore became champion Flat jockey, though few could have predicted that the unassuming twenty-three-year-old would have things so much his own way in taking his first title in 2006. The subsequent records of those who have achieved so much at a similarly tender age suggests that he will be at the top of the tree for years to come. Fred Archer was just sixteen when winning the first of his thirteen consecutive titles in 1874. In the twentieth century, Sir Gordon Richards became champion in his first full season as a jockey, in 1925, at the age of twenty-one. He went on to win the title on another twenty-five occasions. Pat Eddery is the youngest to have won the championship since Richards, just twenty-two when winning the first of eleven titles. Frankie Dettori was twenty-three, and around nine months older than Moore, when taking the title for the first time in 1994. In the States, the remarkable Steve Cauthen became the leading jockey by the number of race wins (487) in 1977 when aged seventeen, in that year picking up two Eclipse awards as outstanding apprentice jockey and outstanding jockey. In the following year he rode Affirmed to become the youngest jockey to win the Triple Crown. Interestingly, 2006 saw a rise to prominence in North America even more meteoric than that of Moore. The French-born Julien Leparoux, who started race-riding only in August 2005, has already taken the title of leading rider by number of wins (403) in the United States. He excels particularly on polytrack, the surface now being introduced on several North American tracks. Moore himself rode his one hundred and fiftieth winner of the latest season the day before his twenty-third birthday, and four weeks before that had won his first Group 1 on Notnowcato in the Juddmonte International Stakes at York for champion trainer Sir Michael Stoute, the British ban incurred by Kieren Fallon, resulting in the subsequent use by Ballydoyle of Michael Kinane, and the injury-proneness of Robert Winston, accelerating Moore's increasing links with Stoute. The success in the International displayed perfectly the qualities of both trainer and rider, Notnowcato benefiting from Stoute's patient approach as he completed the graduation from handicap company to Group 1, beating stablemate Maraahel by a short head. Moore struck for home some way out, getting first run on Maraahel, and Notnowcato held

Juddmonte International Stakes, York—a first Group 1 success for champion jockey-designate Ryan Moore as Notnowcato (left) pips stable-companion Maraahel in a ding-dong finish; Blue Monday (second right) takes third, ahead of the favourite Dylan Thomas (right)

Anthony & David de Rothschild's "Notnowcato"

on under a strong ride. For all that Notnowcato might have been considered a slightly fortunate winner, the form of the race proved solid, with Dylan Thomas (below his best at York), Blue Monday and Laverock all winners next time.

At the end of the 2005 season, the smart Notnowcato impressed as the type to progress further, and, after being scratched from the season's first big handicap the Lincoln because he couldn't be made ready in time, he showed marked improvement on his reappearance to win the Weatherbys Earl of Sefton Stakes at Newmarket, his first venture into pattern company. Under a confident ride from Michael Kinane, Notnowcato won going away by a length and a quarter from Kew Green. Notnowcato didn't need to reproduce that form to justify favouritism in a below-average renewal of the betfair.com Brigadier Gerard Stakes at Sandown six weeks later. He again looked a high-class prospect, winning the steadily-run six-runner event by a length and a quarter from Boule d'Or, asserting over a furlong from home, and again appearing to have something to spare.

Notnowcato next ran in the Prince of Wales's Stakes at Royal Ascot, where he performed creditably in a muddling race to finish two lengths fifth of seven to Ouija Board. Notnowcato had shown himself to be an edgy sort before, and on this occasion he got particularly worked up in the preliminaries, exhibiting coltish behaviour and whinnying. Notnowcato went on to produce a similar level of form in the Eclipse at Sandown, where he was much more settled in the preliminaries having been fitted with a severe halter. Soon well positioned behind the winner's pacemaker, Notnowcato was hemmed in as that horse weakened, unable to get into the clear until David Junior had quickened, but he stayed on well thereafter, finishing a length and a half second, Notnowcato reportedly suffering a puncture wound on his near-fore joint. In the International, Notnowcato's regular jockey Kinane was aboard hot favourite Dylan Thomas, an impressive winner of the Irish

Derby on his previous outing. Ryan Moore kept the mount on Notnowcato in the Champion Stakes at Newmarket, where the colt was once again edgy and had also gone in his coat, this possibly a race too many as he trailed home last of eight behind Pride.

	Inchinor (ch 1990)	Ahonoora (ch 1975)	Lorenzaccio
			Helen Nicholls
		Inchmurrin (b 1985)	Lomond
Notnowcato (ch.c. 2002)			On Show
	Rambling Rose (ch 1995)	Cadeaux Genereux (ch 1985)	Young Generation
			Smarten Up
		Blush Rambler (ch 1988)	Blushing Groom
			Nikitina

The strong, lengthy Notnowcato, who has a quick action, is the third foal of Rambling Rose—not her second as stated in *Racehorses of 2004*—a smart and genuine performer who was placed in the Cheshire Oaks, Ribblesdale Stakes, Lancashire Oaks and Prix de Pomone prior to winning the Galtres Stakes at York, also for Sir Michael Stoute. Notnowcato's year-younger half-brother Heaven Knows (by Halling), a useful winner at six furlongs (as a two-year-old) to a mile and a quarter, was an impressive winner of handicaps at Thirsk and Chester in the latest season and, as with Notnowcato, looks the type to progress further, especially with a stiffer test of stamina. Notnowcato's two-year-old half-sister, Maigold Lass (by Mark of Esteem), is also in training with Sir Michael Stoute. Interestingly their grandam, Blush Rambler, shares her name with another former Stoute inmate, the American-bred 1992 Grand Criterium runner-up and sire of 2000 Prix du Jockey Club runner-up Lord Flasheart. Trained by John Oxx, the Irish-bred Blush Rambler won a mile and a half maiden at Sligo from her four starts. As well as Rambling Rose, she has produced useful performers Magnifico and Ponderon, as well as progressive three-year-old Dayrose, also trained by Stoute. Notnowcato sometimes has two handlers and has also had his fore joints bandaged. He acts on firm and good to soft going, and is effective at a mile and at a mile and a quarter. Notnowcato was the biggest earner of 2006 for the Stoute stable—his 1,2,3 prize money of £439,457 put him fourth in the British list—and he will be in training as a five-year-old when he is likely to be targeted again at the major mile and a quarter races. *Sir Michael Stoute*

NOT TO KNOW 2 b.g. (Mar 11) Mujahid (USA) 125 – Little Tramp (Trempolino (USA) 135) [2006 p7.1g⁴ p7.1s³ Dec 13] 8,000Y: fifth foal: half-brother to 5f winner Red China (by Inchinor) and Italian 6f and 1m (latter at 2 yrs) winner Fault Line (by Groom Dancer): dam unraced out of smart winner up to 1m Chipaya: better effort in maidens at Wolverhampton when ¾-length third to Putra Laju: slowly away both outings. *John A. Quinn, Ireland* — **68**

NOT TOO TAXING 2 b.g. (Mar 22) Forzando 122 – Areish (IRE) 66 (Keen 116) [2006 p7g³ p6g³ Dec 22] 18,000Y: second foal: dam 1m to 1½m winner: fair form when placed in maidens at Kempton, good late headway when third to Galaxy Stars in latter: will stay 1m. *R. Hannon* — **67**

NOU CAMP 2 ch.c. (Mar 12) Compton Place 125 – Real Popcorn (IRE) 52 (Jareer (USA) 115) [2006 6m p5g⁴ 6g 5g² p6g p6g⁴ p6g² p6g² p5g³ Dec 16] well-made colt: modest maiden: second in 3 nurseries (in blinkers first occasion): effective at 5f/6f: acts on polytrack: races freely: none too keen. *N. A. Callaghan* — **59**

NOUL (USA) 7 ch.g. Miswaki (USA) 124 – Water Course (USA) (Irish River (FR) 131) [2006 –, a63: f8g p7.1g⁶ f8g⁴ Mar 8] sturdy gelding: poor performer: barely stays 9.4f: acts on fibresand, soft and good to firm ground: usually wears blinkers/cheekpieces: waited with. *J. S. Moore* — **47**

NOVA TOR (IRE) 4 b.f. Trans Island 119 – Nordic Living (IRE) 53 (Nordico (USA)) [2006 69: p6g³ p5.1g² p5.1g³ p5.1g p6g⁴ p6g p6g⁴ p5.1g⁶ 6g May 8] small, strong, close-coupled filly: modest performer: effective at 5f/easy 6f: acts on all-weather, firm and good to soft going: tried in cheekpieces, usually blinkered: usually races up with pace: reportedly lost action sixth start. *Peter Grayson* — **61**

NOVELLARA 3 b.f. Sadler's Wells (USA) 132 – Modena (USA) (Roberto (USA) 131) [2006 9.9g* 12m 14f 14g* Sep 28] tall, angular filly: sister to useful 11.5f and 1¾m winner Modesta, closely related to 2 winners, including 7f (at 2 yrs) to 1½m (Oaks) winner — **107**

Reams of Verse (by Nureyev), and half-sister to several winners, notably high-class 1¼m performer Elmaamul (by Diesis): dam unraced: useful performer, lightly raced: won maiden at Salisbury (by 1½ lengths from Dayrose) in May and listed event at Newmarket (beat Zurbaran by short head) in September: creditable eighth to Mont Etoile in Ribblesdale Stakes at Royal Ascot second start: stayed 1¾m: raced only on good going or firmer: stud. *H. R. A. Cecil*

NOVERFANCY (IRE) 2 b.f. (Jan 31) Noverre (USA) 125 – Fair McLain (IRE) 76 **51** (Fairy King (USA)) [2006 7m⁵ p7.1g⁶ 8.2s⁴ a10.5g⁶ Nov 24] 7,500Y: compact filly: second foal: dam Irish 7f winner: modest maiden: fourth in seller at Nottingham (tongue tied), then left M. Botti: stays 8.2f. *F. Sheridan, Italy*

NOVISTA (IRE) 2 b.g. (Feb 19) Anabaa Blue 122 – Bistranova (USA) (Torrential **73** (USA) 117) [2006 6g² 7m⁴ 7.1m Aug 28] 20,000Y: strong, close-coupled gelding: first foal: dam French maiden half-sister to smart French/US performer up to 8.5f Borodislew: fair maiden: signs of temperament after second at Goodwood on debut: gelded after final start: should stay 1m. *M. H. Tompkins*

NOW LOOK OUT 2 gr.c. (Feb 11) Bahamian Bounty 116 – Where's Carol 67 (Anfield **77 p** 117) [2006 5.1d⁸ 6d⁶ Nov 4] strong, close-coupled colt: good walker: half-brother to 3 winners, including 6f/7f winners Now Look Here (smart, by Reprimand) and Look Here's Carol (useful, by Safawan): dam 2-y-o 6f winner: fair form: won maiden at Nottingham (beat Hurricane Flyer by ½ length) in October: raced freely when sixth in nursery at Windsor: likely to prove best at 5f/6f: will still do better. *E. S. McMahon*

NO WORRIES YET (IRE) 2 b.f. (Mar 12) Orpen (USA) 116 – Charming Victoria **69** (IRE) (Mujadil (USA) 119) [2006 5.1d* 5g² 5m 5g³ 5.1f⁴ 6m⁵ Sep 22] €1,000F, €4,500: angular filly: second foal: dam Italian 5f and 7f winner (including at 2 yrs): fair performer: won seller at Bath in April: in frame in 3 minor events: best at 5f: acts on firm and good to soft going. *J. L. Spearing*

NOW TELL ME THIS 3 b.g. Mister Baileys 123 – Inimitable 66 (Polish Precedent **47** (USA) 131) [2006 12g 12.1d⁴ 9.2d⁶ 11.1m Jun 14] well held in maidens/claimer: tried visored/blinkered. *I. Semple*

NUDRAH 3 b.f. Green Desert (USA) 127 – Sayedati Eljamilah (USA) 64 (Mr **67** Prospector (USA)) [2006 77: 6m⁶ 7m Jun 10] small filly: fair performer: below form both starts in 2006, though plenty to do and not knocked about on reappearance: should stay 7f/1m: acts on good to firm ground: sold 19,000 gns in July, sent to Kuwait. *J. L. Dunlop*

NUFOUDH (IRE) 2 b.g. (Jan 28) Key of Luck (USA) 126 – Limpopo 49 (Green Desert **66 d** (USA) 127) [2006 5m⁴ 5.1d⁴ 5f⁶ 7m⁶ Aug 31] €130,000Y: half-brother to several winners, including very smart sprinter Pipalong (by Pips Pride) and useful 2003 2-y-o 5f winner China Eyes (by Fasliyev): dam maiden half-sister to smart French performer up to 1½m Alost: fair form only on debut: gelded before final run (pulled hard). *M. Johnston*

NUIT SOMBRE (IRE) 6 b.g. Night Shift (USA) – Belair Princess (USA) (Mr Pros- **80** pector (USA)) [2006 87: p8g³ p8g⁶ 10.2d² 8m* 10.3m 10f⁶ Jul 31] good-topped gelding: **a68** fairly useful on turf, fair on all-weather: won claimer (apprentices) at Brighton in June: effective at 1m to 10.5f: acts on polytrack, firm and good to soft going: sometimes wears headgear: usually makes running, and has finished weakly. *J. G. M. O'Shea*

NUMERICAL (IRE) 2 ch.g. (Mar 6) Numerous (USA) – Conspiracy 98 (Rudimen- **56** tary (USA) 118) [2006 6m 7g 7m 7m⁶ Aug 10] robust gelding: modest form in maidens, in blinkers final start (gelded after): will probably stay 1m. *J. L. Dunlop*

NUMERIC (GER) 3 br.g. Singspiel (IRE) 133 – Narola (GER) (Nebos (GER) 129) **98** [2006 73p: 8m⁴ 10.3f* 10s⁴ 12m 11.9g³ 11m* 13.9s⁵ 10.3f⁶ 12g Oct 12] well-made gelding: useful performer: won maiden at Chester (made all) in May and handicap at Goodwood (by neck from New Guinea) in August: shaped better than bare result next 2 starts, but below form final outing: stays 1½m, seemingly not 1¾m: acts on firm and soft going: blinkered last 5 outings: sold 130,000 gns, sent to Saudi Arabia. *J. H. M. Gosden*

NUMERO DUE 4 b.g. Sinndar (IRE) 134 – Kindle (Selkirk (USA) 129) [2006 88: **97** 13.8d³ 16m² 16d* 16.2f 20m 16.1d² 15.9m* 16.2d⁶ Sep 16] compact gelding: useful handicapper: improved in 2006, winning at Thirsk in May and Chester (made most) and Warwick (tended to go in snatches and hung left when beating Kayf Aramis 1¼ lengths) in September: stays 2m: acts on firm and good to soft going: not straightforward ride. *G. M. Moore*

NUMIDAS (POL) 4 bl.c. Duke Valentino 86 – Numata (POL) (Freedom's Choice **–** (USA) 97) [2006 p6g 8.1g May 1] won 5f maiden in Poland at 2 yrs: no form in 2 runs in Britain. *Mrs A. L. M. King*

NUR TAU (IRE) 2 b.g. (Apr 2) Peintre Celebre (USA) 137 – Litchfield Hills (USA) **80**
(Relaunch (USA)) [2006 6m 7.1m* 7m 8g Aug 25] 46,000Y: quite attractive gelding:
third living foal: half-brother to 5-y-o Clearing Sky: dam 1m/8.5f winner in USA: fairly
useful form: won maiden at Sandown in July: stiff task in Vintage Stakes at Goodwood
(didn't settle) next start: well beaten in nursery final one (then gelded): should stay at
least 1m. *M. P. Tregoning*

NUSOOR (IRE) 3 b.g. Fasliyev (USA) 120 – Zulfaa (USA) 97 (Bahri (USA) 125) **79**
[2006 6d* 6g³ p7g 6m 7s⁴ p6g p5.1m Nov 21] sturdy gelding: first foal: dam 7.6f (at
2 yrs) to 1¼m winner: fair performer: won maiden at Thirsk in May, overcoming greenness: gelded after second start: left W. Haggas 22,000 gns after fifth outing: headstrong,
and should be best at 5f/6f: blinkered (found little) final outing: reportedly lame third
start: has run well when sweating. *Peter Grayson*

NUT (IRE) 3 b.f. Fasliyev (USA) 120 – La Rosetta (IRE) 88 (Alzao (USA) 117) [2006 **52**
65: p7.1g⁴ p7g Feb 1] workmanlike filly: just modest maiden in 2006: should stay 7f: acts
on good to soft ground. *J. W. Hills*

NUTLEY QUEEN (IRE) 7 b.m. Eagle Eyed (USA) 111 – Secret Hideaway (USA) **42**
(Key To The Mint (USA)) [2006 50: p12.2g⁶ p12.2g 10.2f Jul 27] poor maiden: stays
1½m: acts on polytrack, good to firm and good to soft going: tried in blinkers/cheek-
pieces/tongue tie. *M. Appleby*

NYARHINI 3 b.f. Fantastic Light (USA) 134 – Nuryana 107 (Nureyev (USA) 131) **103**
[2006 80p: p8g³ 9.9g³ Jun 21] smallish, leggy filly: good walker: useful performer:
good efforts in 2006 when third in listed races at Kempton (not right in coat and still green
when 2¼ lengths behind Dont Dili Dali) and Goodwood (beaten 3 lengths by dead-
heaters Rising Cross and Soft Centre): ran poorly in listed handicap at Royal Ascot final
start: stayed easy 1¼m: acted on polytrack: stud. *G. Wragg*

O

OAKBRIDGE (IRE) 4 b.g. Indian Ridge 123 – Chauncy Lane (IRE) 90 (Sadler's **57**
Wells (USA) 132) [2006 78d: p6g p7.1g⁵ Dec 4] tall, lengthy gelding: modest performer
nowadays: gelded after reappearance: bred to stay 7f+: acts on good to firm ground: looks
temperamental. *D. J. Wintle*

OAKLEY ABSOLUTE 4 ch.g. Bluegrass Prince (IRE) 110 – Susie Oakley VII (Dam- **66**
sire Unregistered) [2006 72: p8g* p8g⁵ 10g 8.5g⁴ 10d 8.3g 9m 9.9g 10g⁵ 10m 10.2m⁴ **a73**
10.2f 8m³ 10.2m p10g Oct 26] strong, lengthy gelding: fair handicapper: won at Lingfield
in March: effective at 1m to 11f: acts on polytrack, firm and good to soft going: tried
visored/in cheekpieces: gelded since final outing. *R. Hannon*

OAKLEY HEFFERT (IRE) 2 b.c. (Apr 4) Titus Livius (FR) 115 – Daftiyna (IRE) **81**
74 (Darshaan 133) [2006 6g⁵ 7d 7f⁴ 7d⁶ 8.3g* p8g³ Nov 13] €60,000Y: eighth foal: half-
brother to 3 winners, including 1m/1¼m winner Golden Island (by Selkirk) and 3-y-o
Gandor, both useful: dam, placed up to 9f in Ireland, out of very smart sprinter Dafayna,
herself half-sister to 2000 Guineas winner Doyoun: fairly useful performer: won nursery
at Windsor in October: good third in similar event at Lingfield: stays 8.3f: acts on polytrack and firm going. *R. Hannon*

OASIS FLOWER 3 b.f. Green Desert (USA) 127 – Carpet of Leaves (USA) (Green **53**
Forest (USA) 134) [2006 8.2m 8.5f⁵ 10f⁶ Jul 11] fifth foal: dam, ran twice in France,
half-sister to smart French performers Glorify (up to 15f) and Doree (sprinting 2-y-o) and
to dams of Ryafan and Tillerman: modest form in maidens: visored final start: slowly
away all 3 outings. *J. R. Fanshawe*

OASIS SUN (IRE) 3 ch.f. Desert Sun 120 – Albaiyda (IRE) (Brief Truce (USA) 126) **53**
[2006 –p: p10g p7g³ 8m 8m p8g Dec 15] modest maiden: should stay 1½m: acts on
polytrack. *J. R. Best*

OBE BOLD (IRE) 5 b.m. Orpen (USA) 116 – Capable Kate (IRE) (Alzao (USA) 117) **65 d**
[2006 63d, a53d: p5.1g² p5.1g³ p6g² p5.1g f6g⁶ p6g* 6m* 6g 5m 6d 6g 6m² 7.1d 6g⁵ 6g
6m 5f f6g f6g Dec 5] small, lengthy mare: fair performer: made all in amateur handicaps
at Wolverhampton in April and Hamilton in May: below form after: effective at 5f/6f:
acts on all-weather, firm and good to soft going: tried tongue tied/in headgear: sometimes
starts slowly/hangs right. *A. Berry*

OBE BRAVE 3 b.g. Agnes World (USA) 123 – Pass The Rose (IRE) (Thatching 131)   **107**
[2006 88P: 7g² 6m* 6m² 6s⁴ 7f 7g 6m² 6d 6s Oct 7] strong gelding: has a quick action:
useful performer: won handicap at Ripon (by short head from High Curragh) in April:
several other creditable efforts, including when short-head second to Ingleby Arch in
minor event at Hamilton and to Gimasha in handicap at Lingfield after: stays 7f: acts on
soft and good to firm going: has hung right. *M. R. Channon*

OBE GOLD 4 b.g. Namaqualand (USA) – Gagajulu 75 (Al Hareb (USA) 123) [2006   **110**
107: 6.5m* 6.5m⁶ 6m³ 6d* 6.5m⁶ 6s p6g⁵ 6m 6m⁴ 6.1f 6f 6m 6g⁴ 6s⁶ 6d Sep 16]
tall, useful-looking gelding: smart handicapper: won at Nad Al Sheba in January and
February: several creditable efforts after, including at Windsor (fourth behind One More
Round) and Goodwood (Stewards' Cup, eighth to Borderlescott) ninth/twelfth starts:
effective at 6f/7f: acts on soft and good to firm going: tried blinkered, effective visored or
not. *M. R. Channon*

OBE ONE 6 b.g. Puissance 110 – Plum Bold 83 (Be My Guest (USA) 126) [2006 70:   **61**
6v⁴ 7.1m⁶ 5m 5.9m 6m² 7m² 6m 5s Sep 14] leggy gelding: modest handicapper: best at
6f/7f nowadays: acts on any turf going: tried blinkered/in cheekpieces: usually held up:
sold 3,800 gns. *D. Nicholls*

OBERGURGL (IRE) 3 b.g. Titus Livius (FR) 115 – Lorella (IRE) 62 (Fayruz 116)   **50**
[2006 51: 5g⁶ 5g⁵ p5.1g Jun 26] good-bodied gelding: modest maiden handicapper:
should prove best at 5f/6f: acts on polytrack. *Mrs A. Duffield*

OBERON'S PRIZE 4 b.g. King's Theatre (IRE) 128 – Taj Victory 68 (Final Straw   –
127) [2006 –: p12.2g f12g May 9] no form: wore cheekpieces (pulled up) final start.
V. Smith

OBE ROYAL 2 b.g. (Apr 10) Wizard King 122 – Gagajulu 75 (Al Hareb (USA) 123)   **75 d**
[2006 7f⁵ 5m⁶ 5g 8.1v³ 7m 8.3d Oct 9] close-coupled gelding: brother to 2 fairly useful
winners, including 5f (at 2 yrs)/6f winner Under My Spell, and half-brother to 4-y-o Obe
Gold and 3-y-o Ardbrae Lady: dam 2-y-o 5f winner: fair maiden: well held both starts in
nurseries: stays 1m: acts on any turf going: gelded after final start. *M. R. Channon*

OBEZYANA (USA) 4 ch.g. Rahy (USA) 115 – Polish Treaty (USA) (Danzig (USA))   **88**
[2006 91: p10g⁶ p8g Oct 15] quite good-topped gelding: fairly useful handicapper: ran
just twice in 2006, at Lingfield in January (not disgraced, reportedly finished lame) and
October (shaped better than bare result): should stay 1¼m: acts on polytrack, unraced on
extremes of going on turf: tried tongue tied/blinkered: sold 20,000 gns. *G. A. Huffer*

OBRIGADO (USA) 6 b.g. Bahri (USA) 125 – Glorious Diamond (USA) (His Majesty   **102 §**
(USA)) [2006 88§: p8.6g⁵ p8g² p8g⁶ p10g* p10g⁵ p10g³ 12m p10g² 10m² 10m⁴ p10g²
p12g⁵ p8g Oct 15] big, leggy gelding: useful performer: improved in 2006 and won handicap at Kempton by 5 lengths from Nice Tune) in April: good third to Fairmile in similar
event on same course: left W. Haggas £35,000 prior to below form last 2 starts: stays
1¼m: acts on polytrack, firm and good to soft going: visored once: tends to sweat:
free-going sort, held up: ungenuine. *Miss K. M. George*

OBSCENE 3 b.g. Key of Luck (USA) 126 – Scene (IRE) 87 (Scenic 128) [2006 63: 10s   **53**
6d p7g 7.1m 8s p7.1g Dec 21] leggy, good-topped gelding: modest maiden: left
M. Polglase after fifth start: seems to stay 1m: acts on polytrack. *A. J. McCabe*

OBSERVATORY STAR (IRE) 3 br.g. Observatory (USA) 131 – Pink Sovietstaia   **74**
(FR) (Soviet Star (USA) 128) [2006 73: 6s 6m 7.5f 7.6f 6g 6f⁶ 6d³ 6s* Oct 24] fair
performer: won handicap at Catterick in October: acts on firm and soft
going: blinkered last 2 outings: slowly away fourth outing. *T. D. Easterby*

OBSTREPEROUS WAY 4 ch.g. Dr Fong (USA) 128 – Fleet Key (Afleet (CAN))   –
[2006 59d: 9.8m f14g⁶ Dec 29] lightly-raced maiden: showed nothing in 2006: tried
blinkered/in cheekpieces. *Miss Tracy Waggott*

OBSTRUCTIVE 2 ch.g. (Mar 2) Zilzal (USA) 137 – Emily-Mou (IRE) 80 (Cadeaux   **80**
Genereux 131) [2006 p7g⁴ p6g² p7g Sep 27] half-brother to 1¾m seller winner Dangerous Deploy (by Deploy) and 5-y-o Mad: dam 1¼m winner: fairly useful form: clearly
best run when second to Miss Jenny at Lingfield, only start at 6f: left Ernst Oertel prior to
final start: raced on polytrack. *D. K. Ivory*

OCEANA GOLD 2 ch.g. (Mar 12) Primo Valentino (IRE) 116 – Silken Dalliance 91   **73**
(Rambo Dancer (CAN) 107) [2006 6g⁵ 7.5m* 8.3d Oct 9] strong, close-coupled gelding:
fourth foal: half-brother to 3-y-o Snake Skin: dam 6f and 1m winner: fair form: won
maiden at Beverley in September: favourite, only mid-field in nursery at Windsor: gelded
after: should stay 1m: once refused at stall. *A. M. Balding*

OCEAN AVENUE (IRE) 7 b.g. Dolphin Street (FR) 125 – Trinity Hall 67 (Hallgate **84** 127) [2006 75: 11g² p12g 12g³ 11.6f² 13.3g 11g Sep 15] strong gelding: fairly useful handicapper: creditable efforts when placed in 2006: effective at 11f to 14.4f: acts on firm going: front runner. *C. A. Horgan*

OCEAN BLAZE 2 b.f. (Feb 23) Polar Prince (IRE) 117 – La Belle Vie 73 (Indian King **71** (USA) 128) [2006 6m 6g⁵ 6.1g 5.1g³ Oct 17] strong, lengthy filly: half-sister to several winning sprinters, including 7-y-o Maktavish and 3-y-o Phantom Whisper: dam 6f/7f winner: fair maiden: should prove best at 5f/6f: hung badly third start. *B. R. Millman*

OCEANCOOKIE (IRE) 4 b.f. Dashing Blade 117 – Sankaty Light (USA) 55 **81** (Summer Squall (USA)) [2006 71: 7.1g* 7m⁵ Jun 23] big, unfurnished filly: fairly useful handicapper: won at Warwick in May: effective at 7f/1m: acts on good to firm ground: tongue tied last 2 starts: often slowly away: sold 4,000 gns in October. *A. M. Balding*

OCEANICO DOT COM (IRE) 4 br.f. Hernando (FR) 127 – Karen Blixen (Kris **–** 135) [2006 75: p5.1g p5.1g p5.1g 5v 5.1s 5f 5m 5d 5s Sep 28] small, sturdy filly: well held in 2006: tried tongue tied/in cheekpieces: races prominently. *A. Berry*

OCEAN KING (USA) 5 ch.g. Sky Classic (CAN) – From Sea To Sea (CAN) (Gre- **61** gorian (USA) 124) [2006 69: p16.5g⁶ f14s⁴ 12f Sep 6] modest performer nowadays: left W. M. Brisbourne after reappearance, M. Quinlan after second start: stays 1¾m: acts on dirt and polytrack: tongue tied final start. *M. G. Holden, Ireland*

OCEAN OF CHAMPAGNE 2 ch.f. (Mar 4) Arkadian Hero (USA) 123 – Cham- **59** pagne Grandy 84 (Vaigly Great 127) [2006 6g⁵ 6g⁵ 6f 6v² Oct 9] 2,600Y: good-topped filly: half-sister to 2-y-o 5f winners Ninety Degrees (in 1999, by Piccolo) and Intersky Champagne (in 2001, by Emperor Jones), latter also 6f winner in Hong Kong: dam 5f to 7f winner: modest maiden: off 3 months, second in nursery at Ayr (visored): raced at 6f: acts on heavy ground. *A. Dickman*

OCEAN OF DREAMS (FR) 3 b.g. Ocean of Wisdom (USA) 106 – Tifosa (USA) **78** (Hickman Creek (USA)) [2006 83: p7g 6m p6g 7m 6f Jul 27] strong, stocky gelding: fairly useful performer at 2 yrs: well below form after reappearance in 2006: bred to stay 7f, but not short of speed: acts on all-weather: pulled up fourth outing: gelded after final start. *J. D. Bethell*

OCEAN OF STORMS (IRE) 11 b. or br.g. Arazi (USA) 135 – Moon Cactus 118 **73 §** (Kris 135) [2006 69§: 14.1f⁴ 16s 16d 14.1m³ 21m 14.1g Aug 17] workmanlike gelding: fair performer: stays 15f: acts on dirt, firm and soft going: tried tongue tied/in cheek-pieces: often slowly away (has refused/virtually refused to race on several occasions, including 3 times in 2006): has been banned from racing. *N. I. M. Rossiter*

OCEAN PRIDE (IRE) 3 b.g. Lend A Hand 124 – Irish Understudy (ITY) (In The **86** Wings 128) [2006 89: 10d⁵ p8g 8m 8.1d⁴ 8.2d⁴ 7m* 7.1m 7g 8.1m 7d p6g p12g* p12.2s⁵ p13g⁵ Dec 22] strong, neat gelding: fairly useful performer: won handicap at Folkestone in June and claimer at Lingfield (left R. Hannon £10,000) in December: barely stays 13f: acts on polytrack, heavy and good to firm going: sometimes blinkered. *D. E. Pipe*

OCEAN ROCK 5 b.g. Perugino (USA) 84 – Polistatic 53 (Free State 125) [2006 61: **62** p12.2g⁶ p12.2g p12g⁵ p13.9g⁴ p12g* p11g⁶ p12g* p12.2g⁴ Dec 23] strong, workmanlike gelding: modest performer: won banded races at Kempton in October and December: effective at 11f to 2m: acts on polytrack, little form on turf. *C. A. Horgan*

OCEANS APART 3 ch.f. Desert Prince (IRE) 130 – Ffestiniog (IRE) 96 (Efisio 120) **90** [2006 90: 7.1m 7m⁴ 7.1m⁵ 7f 7m⁶ 8.1d² Sep 13] good-topped filly: has scope: good mover: fairly useful performer: mostly creditable efforts at 3 yrs: stays 1m: acts on firm and good to soft going: effective in blinkers or not: sent to USA. *P. F. I. Cole*

OCEAN SUNRISE (IRE) 3 b.f. Danehill (USA) 126 – Wind Silence (USA) (A P **–** Indy (USA) 131) [2006 66: 7.2d 8m Jul 10] strong, lengthy filly: fair maiden at 2 yrs: last both starts in 2006: sold 15,000 gns in November. *M. Johnston*

OCEAN TIDE 9 b.g. Deploy 131 – Dancing Tide (Pharly (FR) 130) [2006 71: 18v³ **69** 21.6d⁶ Apr 24] angular gelding: fair handicapper: stays 2¼m: acts on any going: visored/ blinkered: races prominently. *R. Ford*

OCEAN VALENTINE 3 gr.g. King Charlemagne (USA) 120 – Dolly Bevan 53 **43** (Another Realm 118) [2006 63: p7g⁶ 6g 8.2s May 20] just poor maiden in 2006: stays 7f: acts on good to firm ground. *B. R. Millman*

OCHIL HILLS DANCER (IRE) 4 b.f. Bluebird (USA) 125 – Classic Dilemma **–** (Sandhurst Prince 128) [2006 30: 7f 7.1d 6g 7m⁶ 5d Sep 25] angular filly: no longer of any account: sometimes wears headgear: tried tongue tied. *A. Crook*

OCHRE BAY 3 b.c. Polar Prince (IRE) 117 – Cloudy Reef 57 (Cragador 110) [2006 80, **82** a75: 6d 5m 6.1g 6m f7g⁵ p7.1g⁴ p7.1g* Dec 22] good-bodied colt: fairly useful handicapper: in cheekpieces, won at Wolverhampton in December: stays 7f: acts on all-weather. *R. Hollinshead*

OCKUMS RAZOR (IRE) 3 b.g. Mozart (IRE) 131 – Merlannah (IRE) (Shy Groom **78** (USA)) [2006 65: p7.1g³ f6g² p6g* f5g p7.1g* f7g p10g⁶ p7g p7g p6g⁵ p7.1g p6g⁶ 7m p7g 7m* p6g² p6g⁴ Oct 17] compact gelding: fair performer: won claimer at Wolverhampton in January (claimed from N. Callaghan £12,000), handicap there in February and, having left M. Polglase after tenth start, seller at Yarmouth in September: stays 7f: acts on all-weather and good to firm going: sold 9,000 gns. *C. A. Dwyer*

OCTOBER BEN 3 b.f. Killer Instinct 111 – Birmania (IRE) (Rainbow Quest (USA) **72** 134) [2006 53: p8g 7s 8.2g² 8m p8g* p10g p8g² p8g³ 8.3g p8g² p8g³ Sep 10] tall, leggy, close-coupled filly: fair handicapper: won apprentice event at Kempton in June: should stay 1¼m: acts on polytrack: often slowly away: held up. *M. D. I. Usher*

OCTOBER MIST (IRE) 12 gr.g. Roselier (FR) – Bonny Joe (Derring Rose 97) [2006 –: 12v 15.8g Jun 2] strong gelding: fair hurdler nowadays: lightly raced and well held on Flat since 2004. *K. G. Reveley*

OCTOBER SUN 3 b.c. Dansili 127 – Autumn Pride (USA) (Lear Fan (USA) 130) **29** [2006 –: p9.5g⁶ f7g⁴ f7g⁵ f8g p12.2g Jun 10] bad maiden: tried in cheekpieces/blinkers. *Miss D. Mountain*

ODDSMAKER (IRE) 5 b.g. Barathea (IRE) 127 – Archipova (IRE) (Ela-Mana-Mou **78** 132) [2006 81d: 7g 7.2d 10.5g⁴ 10.5m² 13.9m 12m³ 9.1g³ 16.1m² 10.5f³ 14m* 21m 11.9m* 11.9f 11.9s² 11.9g² 14g Sep 23] angular gelding: fair handicapper: won at Haydock in July and August: effective at 1½m to 2m: acts on firm and soft going: tried in headgear: tongue tied: can be headstrong, often front runner: sometimes hangs. *M. A. Barnes*

ODESSA STAR (USA) 3 gr.f. Stravinsky (USA) 133 – Cryptocari (USA) (Crypto- **78** clearance (USA)) [2006 47: p8.6g* 8f³ 8.1d⁶ 8g p10g* 10m⁶ p12.2g p10g p11g p10g p9.5g* Dec 26] third foal: sister to winner in USA: dam, 1m/9f winner in USA, half-sister to US Grade 1 9f/1½m winner Itsallgreektome: fair performer: showed little at 2 yrs for D. Weld in Ireland: won claimer at Wolverhampton (left J. Fanshawe £10,000) in June and handicaps at Kempton in July and Wolverhampton in December: stays 1¼m: acts on polytrack and firm ground. *J. G. Portman*

ODIHAM 5 b.g. Deploy 131 – Hug Me 96 (Shareef Dancer (USA) 135) [2006 102: 16d³ **102** 16.1m p16g* 13.9d 12d 18d p16g* 15.5s Nov 25] tall, leggy gelding: useful performer: in-and-out form in 2006: won listed race at Kempton by 1½ lengths from Mudawin) in November: also ran well in handicaps at Ascot (third to Toldo) and Lingfield (fourth to Finalmente): stays 2¼m: acts on polytrack, firm and soft going: sometimes visored/blinkered: has been bandaged hind joints: found little third outing. *H. Morrison*

ODIN DAWN 2 b.c. (Feb 3) Desert Style (IRE) 121 – Desert Dawn 108 (Belfort (FR) **82** 89) [2006 6m⁴ 7g⁵ 6m* Sep 21] 32,000Y: leggy colt: half-brother to several winners, including 4-y-o Folga: dam 5f performer: fairly useful form in maidens, winning at Pontefract: should have stayed 1m: dead. *R. Hannon*

O'DWYER (IRE) 2 ch.g. (May 3) Namid 128 – Leopardess (IRE) 79 (Ela-Mana-Mou **68 d** 132) [2006 5d⁶ 6d³ 6d⁵ 5m⁵ 5f⁴ 6.5d⁶ 5d 5.1d 5.1s p7.1g p6g² f5g Dec 27] €8,000Y: close-coupled, workmanlike gelding: half-brother to 3 winners, including useful 2001 2-y-o 1m winner Snow Leopard (by Highest Honour) and fairly useful Irish 1¼m winner Madamaa (by Alzao): dam, 1¼m winner, half-sister to very smart miler Alflora: fair maiden in Ireland, leaving K. Condon after sixth start: well below form in Britain: stays 6f: acts on polytrack and good to soft going: wore cheekpieces last 2 starts. *A. D. Brown*

OEDIPUSS (IRE) 2 b.c. (Apr 16) Mujadil (USA) 119 – Evrobi (IRE) 84 (Grand Lodge **–** (USA) 125) [2006 6.1m 7m⁴ 6m 10d⁴ 7d³ Oct 10] sturdy colt: little form. *K. J. Burke*

OEUF A LA NEIGE 6 b.g. Danehill (USA) 126 – Reine de Neige 96 (Kris 135) [2006 **59** 64: p6g p6g p6g p7g 6g 5m⁵ 6g* 6s 5d² 5s 5d 5s 6v Oct 9] leggy gelding: modest handicapper: left G. Chung after fifth start: won at Ayr in August: effective at 5f to 1m: acts on polytrack, good to firm and good to soft going: tried blinkered: sometimes slowly away: none too consistent. *Miss L. A. Perratt*

OFARABY 6 b.g. Sheikh Albadou 128 – Maristax 74 (Reprimand 122) [2006 108: **107** 10.1g 10.3m⁴ 10g 10.4d 10m 9d 10.4s* 10d² 10d³ Nov 4] leggy gelding: useful performer: won minor event at York (by ¾ length from Northern Splendour) in October: good efforts both starts after, 6 lengths second to Into The Dark in listed race at Newmarket and very close third to Folio in handicap at Windsor: best at 1¼m: acts on all-weather, heavy and good to firm going: has been bandaged: held up: sometimes wanders. *M. A. Jarvis*

OFF HIRE 10 b.g. Clantime 101 – Lady Pennington 51 (Blue Cashmere 129) [2006 45: f5g⁶ f6g f5g⁶ f6g⁵ f6g⁵ May 9] leggy, angular gelding: poor performer: effective at 5f/6f: acts on fibresand and any turf going: tried blinkered, visored otherwise: usually races prominently. *C. Smith* **46**

OFF MESSAGE (IRE) 3 b.f. In The Wings 128 – Independence 116 (Selkirk (USA) 129) [2006 p9.5g* 11.4m p12g³ 10m⁵ Jun 27] big, lengthy, good-topped filly: first foal: dam 7f/1m winner (including Sun Chariot Stakes): fairly useful performer: won maiden at Wolverhampton (readily by a neck from Soapy Danger) in February: just respectable efforts at best after in listed race at Chester, minor event at Kempton (blinkered) and handicap at Newbury: stays 1¼m: acts on polytrack. *E. A. L. Dunlop* **84**

OFF THE RECORD 2 b.c. (Mar 4) Desert Style 121 – Record Time 69 (Clantime 101) [2006 5.1d⁴ f5g* Nov 13] compact colt: third foal: half-brother to 4-y-o Pro Tempore and 3-y-o Moorhouse Lad: dam 5f winner: better for debut, won maiden at Southwell by 4 lengths (value more): should go on progressing. *J. G. Given* **70 p**

OGEE 3 ch.g. Generous (IRE) 139 – Aethra (USA) 89 (Trempolino (USA) 135) [2006 71p: 10.2d³ 11.6m* 11.6d* 16m Jun 23] well-made gelding: useful performer: upped in trip, improved to win 2 handicaps at Windsor in May: should stay 1¾m (always behind in Queen's Vase at Royal Ascot at 2m): acts on polytrack, good to firm and good to soft going. *Sir Michael Stoute* **100**

OHANA 3 b.g. Mark of Esteem (IRE) 137 – Subya 107 (Night Shift (USA)) [2006 72: p10g⁶ f8g* p8g⁴ p8.6g⁵ f7g p7g² f7g 8.3g p9.5m 8d p9.5g⁶ p10g p9.5g⁶ Nov 27] strong, close-coupled gelding: fair performer: won claimer at Southwell (claimed from N. Callaghan £12,000) in January: below form after sixth outing, leaving N. Littmoden after seventh one: stays easy 9.5f: acts on all-weather: often wears cheekpieces/blinkers: reportedly bled sixth start: one to be wary of. *Miss Gay Kelleway* **75 d**

OH BOY (IRE) 6 b.g. Tagula (IRE) 116 – Pretty Sally (IRE) 51 (Polish Patriot (USA) 128) [2006 68: 8m⁴ 8m⁵ 7m³ 7f⁵ Jun 9] good-bodied gelding: modest handicapper: stayed 1m: acted on firm going: tried blinkered/tongue tied: had looked ungenuine: dead. *J. M. Bradley* **59**

OH DANNY BOY 5 b.g. Cadeaux Genereux 131 – Final Shot 91 (Dalsaan 125) [2006 69: 8m p8g p8.6g⁵ 10.1m⁴ 10g* 10g 10m Sep 15] sturdy gelding: fair performer: won handicap at Newmarket in August: stays 1¼m: acts on polytrack and good to firm ground: sold 4,000 gns, joined M. Chapman. *Jane Chapple-Hyam* **66**

OH DARA (USA) 4 b.f. Aljabr (USA) 125 – Sabaah Elfull 75 (Kris 135) [2006 69: f5s p6g Mar 25] strong filly: fairly useful performer at best: well held in 2006. *M. J. Attwater* **–**

OH GLORY BE (USA) 3 b.f. Dixieland Band (USA) – Long View (USA) (Damascus (USA)) [2006 53: 9.9g* 9.9m 12g* 12m Aug 2] lengthy filly: fairly useful performer: won maiden at Salisbury in May and handicap there in June: tailed off at Goodwood final start: stays 1½m: best efforts on good going. *R. Hannon* **90**

OH GOLLY GOSH 5 ch.g. Exit To Nowhere (USA) 122 – Guerre de Troie (Risk Me (FR) 127) [2006 p8.6g 8.5g Aug 17] workmanlike gelding: fair at 3 yrs: missed 2005: well held in 2006, very slowly away final outing: usually wears cheekpieces/visor. *N. P. Littmoden* **–**

OH GRACIOUS ME (IRE) 2 b.c. (Apr 17) Traditionally (USA) 117 – Classic Jenny (IRE) 69 (Green Desert (USA) 127) [2006 6m⁶ 7s Oct 14] well held in maidens 3 months apart (reportedly had mucus on larynx second start). *P. A. Blockley* **–**

OH SO SAUCY 2 b.f. (Mar 30) Imperial Ballet (IRE) 110 – Almasi (IRE) 96 (Petorius 117) [2006 6d 6m⁵ 5g³ 6f Sep 18] second foal: dam 6f winner (including at 2 yrs): modest maiden: poorly drawn on nursery debut: better at 6f than 5f. *C. F. Wall* **58**

OI VAY JOE (IRE) 2 b.c. (Apr 12) Namid 128 – Nuit Des Temps (Sadler's Wells (USA) 132) [2006 5g³ 6d* 6m² 6d 6m² 7d Sep 24] €17,000F, 20,000Y: strong, heavy-topped colt: eighth foal: half-brother to useful Irish 7f/7.5f winner (including at 2 yrs) Mrs Evans (by College Chapel) and 1½m winner San Marco (by Brief Truce): dam ran once in Ireland: fairly useful performer: won maiden at Windsor in June: better form when second in nurseries at Goodwood and Newbury (beaten ½ length by Captain Marvelous): should stay 7f: acts on good to firm going, gained win on good to soft but below form both subsequent starts on it. *W. Jarvis* **84**

OKIKOKI 2 b.g. (Mar 14) Ishiguru (USA) 114 – Crofters Ceilidh 101 (Scottish Reel **77**
123) [2006 6f 6d² 5m⁴ 6.1f* p6g 6d 6m⁴ 6g Oct 13] 13,500F, 17,000Y: quite good-topped
gelding: sixth foal: half-brother to useful 2003 2-y-o 5f/6f winner Cop Hill Lad (by Atraf)
and 2005 2-y-o 5f winner Making Music (by Makbul): dam, 5f winner (including at
2 yrs), half-sister to smart sprinter Lord Kintyre: fair performer: won maiden at Chepstow
in July: ran creditably in nurseries last 2 starts (blinkered, gelded after): should prove best
kept to 5f/6f: acts on firm and good to soft going. *W. R. Muir*

OK PAL 6 b.g. Primo Dominie 121 – Sheila's Secret (IRE) 97 (Bluebird (USA) 125) **–**
[2006 89, a102: f5g* Jan 26] lengthy gelding: useful on all-weather, fairly useful on turf: **a104**
best effort when winning handicap at Southwell (by length from Dancing Mystery) in
January: injured after: was effective at 5f/6f: acted on all-weather and good to soft going:
tried blinkered: raced prominently: retired. *T. G. Mills*

OKTIS MORILIOUS (IRE) 5 b.g. Octagonal (NZ) 126 – Nottash (IRE) 74 (Royal **–**
Academy (USA) 130) [2006 48: f12g Jan 10] sparely-made gelding: poor performer:
stays 2m: acts on polytrack, firm and good to soft ground. *A. W. Carroll*

OLD BAILEY (USA) 6 gr.g. Lit de Justice (USA) 125 – Olden Lek (USA) (Cozzene **54**
(USA)) [2006 –, a75d: f7g⁶ f8g³ f7g⁵ p7g Feb 13] good-topped gelding: modest performer on balance: best at 6f/7f: acts on fibresand and any turf going: usually wears
headgear: tried tongue tied: has looked none too keen. *G. L. Moore*

OLDENWAY 7 b.g. Most Welcome 131 – Sickle Moon (Shirley Heights 130) [2006 85, **80**
a74: f14g* p12.2g³ p13g f14g³ 12g⁶ 12g* 12g³ 11.5g* 11.1m³ 12.1f⁴ 12.4m³ 13m⁵ 11.8f⁴
Jul 20] lengthy gelding: fairly useful performer: won handicap at Southwell in January,
and claimers at Catterick in May and Yarmouth in June: stays 1¾m: acts on all-weather
and any turf going: reportedly bled once at 6 yrs. *R. A. Fahey*

OLD GOLDEN GREY 9 gr.g. Thethingaboutitis (USA) 106 – Modina April (New **–**
Member 119) [2006 11.9g⁵ Oct 13] no sign of ability in bumpers/over hurdles, and in
maiden on Flat debut. *M. Wellings*

Mr W. J. Gredley's "Olympian Odyssey"

OLDJOESAID 2 b.g. (Apr 10) Royal Applause 124 – Border Minstral (IRE) 69 (Sri **97** Pekan (USA) 117) [2006 6.1f 6g² 5m* 5s* Oct 2] 40,000Y: first foal: dam 2-y-o 6f winner: useful form: developed well, winning maiden at Sandown in September and nursery at Windsor (impressive, by 3½ lengths from Fairfield Princess) in October: will prove best at 5f/6f. *H. Candy*

OLD ROMNEY 2 br.c. (Jan 26) Halling (USA) 133 – Zaeema 93 (Zafonic (USA) 130) **92** [2006 7m⁴ 7.1m* 8.3m* 7d⁶ Aug 22] tall, lengthy colt: on weak side at 2 yrs: first foal: dam, 7f winner at 2 yrs only start, out of Sun Chariot Stakes winner Talented: fairly useful form: won maiden at Sandown in July and minor event at Hamilton (idled) in August: 9/2, outpaced when sixth of 7 to Big Timer in Acomb Stakes at York: will stay at least 1¼m: acts on good to firm going. *M. Johnston*

OLD TIME DANCING 3 b.f. Danehill Dancer (IRE) 117 – Rare Old Times (IRE) 72 **45** (Inzar (USA) 112) [2006 56: p7g Jan 4] maiden: poor form only outing in 2006: best effort at 6f on good to soft going. *M. J. Wallace*

OLGARENA (IRE) 2 b.f. (Feb 7) Xaar 132 – Copine (Selkirk (USA) 129) [2006 7f⁶ **–** 7.5g 6m Sep 11] 24,000Y: close-coupled filly: first foal: dam lightly-raced French maiden: well held in maidens, early speed. *T. D. Easterby*

OLIMPO (FR) 5 ch.g. Starborough 126 – Emily Allan (IRE) (Shirley Heights 130) **83** [2006 10m⁴ 10.2d* 11.6m* 11.6f⁵ 10m⁵ 10m 12.6m⁶ Aug 28] raced 3 times over 1¼m on Flat in French Provinces at 3 yrs for F. Rohaut: fairly useful form when winning handicaps at Chepstow in May and Windsor in June: stays 11.6f: acts on firm and good to soft ground: joined N. Williams. *B. R. Millman*

OLIVAIR (IRE) 3 b.f. Daggers Drawn (USA) 114 – Exhibit Air (IRE) 77 (Exhibitioner **–** 111) [2006 49: 10f 7f Jun 24] close-coupled filly: maiden: well held in 2006. *M. E. Sowersby*

OLIVINO (GER) 5 ch.g. Second Set (IRE) 127 – Osdemona (GER) (Solarstern (FR)) **63** [2006 65: p16.5g³ p12.2g p16g p16g² p12g⁶ 12.1g⁵ Jul 5] German-bred gelding: modest form in Britain: claimed from S. Dow £5,000 after fifth start: stays easy 16.5f: acts on polytrack, best form on good going or firmer on turf: none too consistent: won over hurdles in August. *B. J. Llewellyn*

OLLIE GEORGE (IRE) 3 ch.g. Fruits of Love (USA) 127 – The Iron Lady (IRE) **85** (Polish Patriot (USA) 128) [2006 69: 8.1s 8.3d⁵ 8m³ 9.9g² 11g* 12f² 12m² 11.7f* 11.7m Aug 20] good-topped gelding: fairly useful handicapper: won at Newbury (apprentices) in July and Bath in August: stays 1½m: acts on polytrack, firm and good to soft going: visored 6 of last 7 starts (not at Newbury): awkward leaving stall on third outing: looked none too keen first 2 appearances, but did nothing wrong after: gelded following final outing. *A. M. Balding*

OLYMPIAN ODYSSEY 3 b.c. Sadler's Wells (USA) 132 – Field of Hope (IRE) 119 **120** (Selkirk (USA) 129) [2006 94: 9g² 8m³ 10.5m 8.9g³ 8d⁵ 10d⁴ Oct 14] rather leggy, close-coupled colt: very smart performer: unlucky second to Atlantic Waves in listed race at Newmarket on reappearance, and further progress when 4 lengths third to George Washington in 2000 Guineas there next time: disappointing in Prix du Jockey Club at Chantilly third start: reported in mid-June to have suffered fracture above off-fore knee: returned to form when 4¾ lengths fourth to Pride in Champion Stakes at Newmarket final start: free-going sort, at least as good at 1m as 1¼m: acts on soft and good to firm going: sold privately, and joined I. Mohammed in UAE. *B. W. Hills*

OMAN GULF (USA) 5 b.g. Diesis 133 – Dabaweyaa 118 (Shareef Dancer (USA) **–** 135) [2006 89d: 12.4g 10m 12.4s p12.2g Nov 24] good-bodied gelding: fairly useful performer at best: no form in 2006. *M. D. Hammond*

OMMADAWN (IRE) 2 b.f. (Feb 16) Montjeu (IRE) 137 – Bonheur (IRE) 93 (Royal **72 p** Academy (USA) 130) [2006 7.1d⁴ Sep 16] 33,000F, €160,000Y, 100,000 2-y-o: second foal: half-sister to French 2005 2-y-o 9.5f winner Happy Lodge (by Grand Lodge): dam, Irish 6f winner, out of US Grade 1 1¼m winner Queen To Conquer: easy to back (12/1), fair form when fourth to Elusive Flash in maiden at Warwick: will improve. *J. R. Fanshawe*

OMMRAAN (IRE) 2 ch.c. (Mar 21) King's Best (USA) 132 – Auntie Maureen (IRE) **83 p** 73 (Roi Danzig (USA)) [2006 8m* Sep 21] 175,000Y: seventh foal: half-brother to 3 winners, including Irish 2000 2-y-o 6f winner Coney Kitty (by Lycius), later Grade 3 9f winner in USA, and 2m winner Intrum Morshaan (by Darshaan), both useful: dam Irish 9f/1¼m winner: odds on, winning debut in maiden at Pontefract (beat Alpes Maritimes by neck), good hold and forced wide but responding well in finish: will stay 1¼m: useful prospect. *M. A. Jarvis*

ON AIR (USA) 3 gr. or ro.f. Cozzene (USA) – Cumulate (USA) 69 (Gone West (USA)) **71 d**
[2006 74: 10g 9.9f⁴ 14.1m 10m⁴ 11.7g 8m⁴ p8.6m Sep 2] rather leggy, lengthy filly: fair maiden: below form after second outing, leaving M. Johnston 7,500 gns after fifth one: stays 1¼m: acts on firm going. *E. J. O'Neill*

ONATOPP (IRE) 2 b.f. (Apr 1) Soviet Star (USA) 128 – Blueprint (USA) (Shadeed **67**
(USA) 135) [2006 7f⁵ 6m 7s² 6s² p7.1g Nov 2] 12,000F, 27,000Y: strong, good-bodied filly: fluent mover: fourth foal: half-sister to useful French 11f winner Toujours Amour (by Croco Rouge): dam unraced: fair maiden: second at Newcastle and Catterick: will stay 1m: acts on firm and soft going. *T. D. Easterby*

ONCE IN A BLUEMOON (IRE) 3 ch.f. Beckett (IRE) 116 – Ma Bella Luna 76 **–**
(Jalmood (USA) 126) [2006 –: 5f May 4] of no account. *A. Berry*

ONE ALONE 5 b.m. Atraf 116 – Songsheet 74 (Dominion 123) [2006 p12g p12.2g **49**
p12g⁵ May 8] poor maiden: missed 2005: stays 1½m: form only on polytrack: visored/blinkered last 5 starts. *Jean-Rene Auvray*

ONE AND GONE (IRE) 2 b.g. (Mar 12) Machiavellian (USA) 123 – Bright Smile **63 p**
(IRE) 83 (Caerleon (USA) 132) [2006 7.5m⁴ 8g 7s⁵ Oct 10] 18,000Y, 27,000 2-y-o: sturdy gelding: first foal: dam, 1¼m winner, closely related to dam of St Leger winner Rule of Law: more promise than bare result in maidens, staying on: will be suited by 1¼m: capable of better. *R. A. Fahey*

ONE AND ONLY (GER) 5 ch.m. Kornado 120 – On My Guest (IRE) (Be My Guest **–**
(USA) 126) [2006 p9.5g 15.8m Aug 8] won 9.7f maiden on sand at Honzrath in 2005: left C. Von Der Recke in Germany, tailed off in banded race/seller (visored) in Britain. *D. W. Thompson*

ONE GOOD THING (USA) 4 b.g. Touch Gold (USA) 127 – Once To Often (USA) **–**
(Raise A Native) [2006 8d Sep 27] quite attractive gelding: little form since 2004: gelded after only start at 4 yrs. *C. Wroe, UAE*

ONEIRO WAY (IRE) 4 b.g. King's Best (USA) 132 – Koumiss (Unfuwain (USA) **57**
131) [2006 68: p6g p6g² 6m³ 6.1d 7m Jun 15] leggy gelding: fair maiden on all-weather, **a75**
modest on turf: effective at 6f, should stay 1m: acts on polytrack and good to firm ground. *P. R. Chamings*

ONE LAST TIME 6 b.g. Primo Dominie 121 – Leap of Faith (IRE) 65 (Northiam **45**
(USA)) [2006 50: 5.3m 7m Jun 17] good-topped gelding: has a quick action: poor former nowadays: ran as though amiss final start: stays 1m: acts on polytrack and good to firm ground: tried blinkered. *Miss B. Sanders*

ONE MORE ROUND (USA) 8 b.g. Ghazi (USA) – Life of The Party (USA) (Plea- **111 §**
sant Colony (USA)) [2006 111§: f8g p8.6g⁶ p8.6g p5g³ p5.1g⁵ p6g p5g³ p5g³ p6g 5.2m 6m 7g 6m* 5m² 6m 5.4g 6d p6g⁴ Dec 16] rather leggy gelding: smart performer: won handicap at Windsor in July by head from The Kiddykid: also ran well when placed in minor event at Lingfield (1¼ lengths third to Les Arcs) and valuable handicap at Ascot (short-head second of 23 to Machinist) seventh/fourteeth starts: effective 8.5f, races mainly at 5f/6f nowadays: acts on dirt, polytrack, firm and good to soft going: tried in cheekpieces, blinkered nowadays: sometimes slowly away: held up: temperamental. *N. P. Littmoden*

ONE MORE THAN TEN 3 b.g. Piccolo 121 – Julietta Mia (USA) 72 (Woodman **51**
(USA) 126) [2006 6m p6g p6g⁵ 5g 5d Aug 31] modest maiden: raced only at 5f/6f: acts on polytrack: tried blinkered: sold 1,700 gns, sent to Denmark. *T. D. Easterby*

ONENIGHTINLISBON (IRE) 2 br.f. (Apr 9) Bold Fact (USA) 116 – Mickey **86**
Towbar (IRE) 41 (Mujadil (USA) 119) [2006 5g⁴ 5g⁴ 5g 6m⁵ 6m⁵ 5m* 5m* 6d⁴ 5d³ p6g⁶ p6m² p6g² p6g⁴ p8g³ Dec 16] short-backed filly: third living foal: dam Irish maiden (ran only at 2 yrs): fairly useful performer: won claimer at Beverley (left P. Midgley £15,000) in July and nursery at Musselburgh in August: ran well when twice runner-up in November, in minor event (behind Prime Defender) and nursery: likely to prove best at 5f/6f: acts on polytrack, good to firm and good to soft going. *K. R. Burke*

ONE NIGHT IN PARIS (IRE) 3 b. or br.f. Danetime (IRE) 121 – Forget Paris (IRE) **75**
(Broken Hearted 124) [2006 67: 6g p6m² p7.1m* p9.5g⁴ p9.5g² Dec 1] sturdy filly: fair performer: won maiden at Wolverhampton in October: stays 9.5f: acts on polytrack and good to soft going. *M. J. Wallace*

ONE PUTRA (IRE) 4 b.c. Indian Ridge 123 – Triomphale (USA) (Nureyev (USA) **112** 131) [2006 108: 6g⁶ 6m* 6m* 6m 5m 6m 6s⁵ 5.4g² 5.5d² 5g⁶ Oct 15] strong colt: smart performer: better then ever in 2006, winning minor event at Haydock (by 1¼ lengths from Peace Offering) in May and listed race at Windsor (beat Presto Shinko by head) in June: creditable efforts when runner-up in Portland Handicap at York (3 lengths behind Fantasy Believer) and listed race at Chantilly (beaten 2 lengths by Strike Up The Band): effective at 5f/6f: acts on soft and good to firm ground: effective tongue tied or not: has worn crossed noseband: races prominently. *M. A. Jarvis*

ONE TO FOLLOW 2 b.g. (Mar 18) Mtoto 134 – Becalmed (Dilum (USA) 115) [2006 **87 +** 7g* 10d Oct 28] lengthy gelding: second foal: half-brother to winner in Serbia by Mark of Esteem: dam unraced: fairly useful form: won maiden at Ascot (beat Big Robert by neck) in July: off 3 months, only seventh to Empire Day in listed race at Newmarket, stamina possibly stretched (still second over 1f out): gelded after. *C. G. Cox*

ONE TO WIN (IRE) 4 b.f. Cape Cross (IRE) 129 – Safe Exit (FR) (Exit To Nowhere **80** (USA) 122) [2006 96: 8m Feb 16] tall, unfurnished filly: useful performer: well held in handicap at Nad Al Sheba only outing in 2006: should stay 1½m: acts on polytrack and firm going: sold 40,000 gns in July. *J. Noseda*

ONE TRICK PONY 3 ch.g. Timeless Times (USA) 99 – Lavernock Lady (Don't **–** Forget Me 127) [2006 64: 5d 6g May 1] good-topped gelding: modest performer at 2 yrs: well held both starts in 2006, visored in latter: often wore cheekpieces at 2 yrs. *Karen McLintock*

ON EVERY STREET 5 b.g. Singspiel (IRE) 133 – Nekhbet 74 (Artaius (USA) 129) **53** [2006 –: f8g f11g³ 10.1m 12s Aug 18] close-coupled gelding: modest performer nowadays: stays 11f: acts on fibresand and firm going: has been visored/tongue tied, tried blinkered. *R. Bastiman*

ONE WAY TICKET 6 ch.h. Pursuit of Love 124 – Prima Cominna 86 (Unfuwain **88** (USA) 131) [2006 93, a–: 5.3f³ 5m 5.3f* 5.5m 5m⁶ 5f 5.1g 5m 5.2m 5s f5g p6g² p5g² **a64** p5.1g³ p6g⁴ Dec 20] lengthy, workmanlike horse: fairly useful handicapper on turf, modest on all-weather: won at Brighton in July: best form at 5f: acts on polytrack, firm and soft going: wears cheekpieces: usually makes running: carries head high: none too consistent. *J. M. Bradley*

ONE WHITE SOCK 2 b.f. (Mar 31) Compton Admiral 121 – Night Gypsy 74 (Mind **49** Games 121) [2006 5.1m⁶ 6.1m⁴ p6g p7g p6g⁵ p6g⁶ Dec 22] 1,700Y: neat filly: second foal: half-sister to 3-y-o Safari Mischief: dam, 5f winner, ran only at 2 yrs: poor maiden: visored/blinkered last 3 starts: has looked none too keen. *J. L. Spearing*

ONIDA (IRE) 2 b.f. (Feb 16) Noverre (USA) 125 – Molomo 104 (Barathea (IRE) 127) **89** [2006 6g⁵ 7.1m⁴ 7d² 7d 7d* 7d 8f Nov 25] €100,000Y: smallish, good-bodied filly: second foal: dam, Irish 1½m winner, sister to useful Irish winner up to 1¾m Pepperwood: fairly useful performer: won maiden at Leicester in October readily by 1¼ lengths from Latanazul, making all: also ran well when 2 lengths fourth behind Sudoor in listed race at Sandown: well held in Rockfel Stakes at Newmarket sixth outing, then left C. Cox 85,000 gns and name changed from Navajo Squaw: tenth of 12 to Valbenny in Grade 3 Miesque Stakes at Hollywood final start: bred to stay 1m+: acts on good to soft going. *Carla Gaines, USA*

ONLINE INVESTOR 7 b.g. Puissance 110 – Anytime Baby 56 (Bairn (USA) 126) **– §** [2006 64§: f5g⁵ Jan 17] leggy, quite good-topped gelding: untrustworthy performer: well held only outing in 2006: tried in headgear: often slowly away: carries head awkwardly. *C. Smith*

ONLY A GRAND 2 b.f. (Mar 14) Cloudings (IRE) 112 – Magic Orb 81 (Primo Domi- **63** nie 121) [2006 p5.1g 6v⁶ 6m 7m² 7.5g 5m⁴ 5d* 5.2d⁵ 6v⁴ Oct 28] 1,000Y, 1,400 2-y-o: strong filly: fourth living foal: dam 5f winner (including at 2 yrs): modest performer: won maiden at Musselburgh in October: effective at 5f to 7f: acts on good to firm and good to soft going: usually blinkered. *R. Bastiman*

ONLY A SPLASH 2 b.g. (Mar 26) Primo Valentino (IRE) 116 – Water Well 96 (Sad- **53 §** ler's Wells (USA) 132) [2006 f6g⁶ 6m⁵ p6f 7s² 7m⁵ 7m p7.1g 8.2s⁶ f6m p9.5g Nov 18] sparely-made gelding: modest and ungenuine maiden: probably stays 8.2f: acts on soft ground. *D. W. Chapman*

ONLYBAYINVILLAGE (IRE) 3 b.g. Monashee Mountain (USA) 115 – Hierarchy **–** 91 (Sabrehill (USA) 120) [2006 6m 8.3g³ Jul 20] well held in minor events at Hamilton, very slowly away on debut. *A. Berry*

ONLY FOR SUE 7 ch.g. Pivotal 124 – Barbary Court (Grundy 137) [2006 14.1d   **47**
p13.9g 12.1d⁶ May 30] rather leggy, angular gelding: missed 2005: only poor form in
2006: probably stays 1¾m: acts on fibresand and soft going: sometimes blinkered/in
cheekpieces: fairly useful winner over hurdles in November/December. *W. S. Kittow*

ONLY HOPE 2 b.f. (Jan 31) Marju (IRE) 127 – Sellette (IRE) 88 (Selkirk (USA) 129)   **65**
[2006 6.1g 6f⁵ 8g³ 7f⁵ p7.1g⁴ 7d 8g³ 8d p8g p9.5g⁵ p8.6g Nov 27] 23,000Y: big, work-   **a53**
manlike filly: fourth foal: sister to 2004 2-y-o 6f winner Corniche Dancer: dam, 1m
winner who stayed 1¼m, half-sister to useful Irish 7f/1m performer Dashing Colours: fair
maiden on turf, modest on all-weather: claimed from M. Channon £6,000 fifth start: well
beaten in nurseries: stays 1m: wore headgear last 6 outings. *E. R. Oertel*

ONLY IF I LAUGH 5 ch.g. Piccolo 121 – Agony Aunt 81 (Formidable (USA) 125)   **64**
[2006 63§: f7g* f7g³ f8g p7.1g* f7g² 7m⁵ 7f² 7m⁶ p7.1g⁵ 7.6g² 7.1m² p6m* 7m p7g f6g
Nov 14] big, strong gelding: modest performer nowadays: won banded races at Southwell in January and Wolverhampton in March, and handicap at Wolverhampton (left
M. Attwater after) in September: stays 7.6f: acts on all-weather, firm and good to soft
going: has worn headgear. *R. A. Harris*

ONLYTIME WILL TELL 8 ch.g. Efisio 120 – Prejudice 83 (Young Generation 129)   **75**
[2006 84: p7.1g p7.1g³ p7.1g p7.1g⁶ 7d³ 7g* 7g² 6d 6d* 7.1g² 7g 7.2v Oct 9] lengthy
gelding: just fair performer in 2006: won seller at Southwell in April and claimer at Redcar in May: best at 6f/7f: acts on all-weather and any turf going: tried visored: sometimes
wanders: waited with. *D. Nicholls*

ONLY WORDS (USA) 9 ch.g. Shuailaan (USA) 122 – Conversation Piece (USA)   **–**
(Seeking The Gold (USA)) [2006 9.9f Jul 18] sturdy gelding: maiden: well held only Flat
outing since 2004: tried tongue tied. *A. J. Lockwood*

ON THE GO 2 b.f. (Jan 26) Tobougg (IRE) 125 – Altaweelah (IRE) 104 (Fairy King   **62**
(USA)) [2006 7m 7g Aug 18] sturdy filly: fourth foal: half-sister to fairly useful 2003
2-y-o 7f winner who stayed 8.5f Qasirah (by Machiavellian): dam, 10.5f/1½m winner,
out of half-sister to Rothman's International winner French Glory: better effort (modest
form) in maidens on debut (hung left): sold 3,500 gns, sent to Iran. *M. A. Jarvis*

ON THE MAP 2 b.f. (Mar 22) Agnes World (USA) 123 – Noor El Houdah (IRE) 61   **64**
(Fayruz 116) [2006 p8g p8g⁶ Nov 5] 36,000Y: half-sister to several winners, including
useful 5f/6f (latter including at 2 yrs) winner J M W Turner (by Forzando) and 4-y-o California Laws: dam 5f (at 2 yrs) to 7f winner: seemingly better run in maidens at Lingfield
when never-nearer sixth. *A. P. Jarvis*

ON THE TRAIL 9 ch.g. Catrail (USA) 123 – From The Rooftops (IRE) (Thatching   **39**
131) [2006 54: f5g³ f5g² f5g f5g p5.1g f5g p6g p5.1g p5g 5d 5m 5m⁵ 5m⁴ f6g p5.1g   **a50**
f5g⁵ f5g⁵ Dec 29] strong gelding: modest on all-weather, only poor on turf in 2006: best
at 5f/6f: acts on all-weather, firm and good to soft going: has been blinkered/tongue tied,
usually wears cheekpieces: sometimes slowly away: races up with pace: none too consistent. *D. W. Chapman*

ON WATCH 2 b.f. (Apr 20) Josr Algarhoud (IRE) 118 – Sole Control (Jupiter Island   **–**
126) [2006 8.2m Sep 15] close-coupled filly: third foal: dam lightly raced on Flat/over
hurdles: backward and behind in maiden at Nottingham. *H. Candy*

ONYERGO (IRE) 4 b.g. Polish Precedent (USA) 131 – Trick (IRE) 76 (Shirley   **68**
Heights 130) [2006 68: 12.4m 12m³ 14.1g⁴ 14m* 14g² 15.8m 15.8d² 13.8s² 12s² 16d⁵
Nov 3] sturdy gelding: fair handicapper: won at Musselburgh in August: effective at 1½m
to 2m: acts on firm and soft going: tried in cheekpieces/blinkers. *J. R. Weymes*

OOH AAH CAMARA (IRE) 3 b.f. Danehill Dancer (IRE) 117 – Simla Bibi 69   **93**
(Indian Ridge 123) [2006 96d: p7g p8g 6m 5m³ 6.1f* 6.1s³ 6g 7.1m³ 6f⁶ 5.1m³ 6.1m
6.1m⁵ Sep 9] useful-looking filly: has scope: fairly useful performer: won handicap at
Chester in May: seemingly very good efforts in listed races there tenth and final outings,
¾-length third to Tournedos on first occasion (though probably flattered): may prove best
at 5f/6f: acts on firm and soft going: tried blinkered/visored/tongue tied. *T. J. Pitt*

OPAL NOIR 2 b.g. (Mar 17) Lujain (USA) 119 – Wrong Bride (Reprimand 122) [2006   **86**
5d* 5g⁵ 5f³ 6d 6s⁶ Oct 6] close-coupled gelding: fifth foal: half-brother to 6-y-o Lucky
Leo: dam, ran once, half-sister to useful sprinter Funfair Wane: fairly useful performer:
won maiden at Redcar in May: best effort when third to Siren's Gift in minor event
at Beverley: will stay 7f: acts on firm going, probably soft: gelded after final start.
J. Howard Johnson

OPAL'S HELMSMAN (USA) 7 b.g. Helmsman (USA) 121 – Opal's Notebook – (USA) (Notebook (USA)) [2006 12g Apr 16] maiden: little form: tried visored. *W. S. Coltherd*

OPAL WARRIOR 3 b.f. Orpen (USA) 116 – Indian Wardance (ITY) (Indian Ridge 59 123) [2006 63: p6g⁴ p6g p6g p8.6g Dec 29] modest performer: left P. D'Arcy 4,000 gns after reappearance: may prove best at 6f: acts on all-weather. *Jane Southcombe*

OPEN ARMS 10 ch.g. Most Welcome 131 – Amber Fizz (USA) (Effervescing (USA)) 55 [2006 p12g p12g⁶ Feb 20] strong gelding: fair handicapper in 2002, just modest form only outing since: effective at 1¼m to easy 2m: acts on polytrack, good to firm and good to soft going: blinkered (well held) once. *Mrs A. L. M. King*

OPENIDE 5 b.g. Key of Luck (USA) 126 – Eyelet (IRE) (Satco (FR) 114) [2006 16m 70 14.1d³ 10d 17.1m⁴ 18m⁴ 16.2g⁵ 15.9m⁶ 18f Jul 29] sturdy, close-coupled gelding: fair maiden on Flat: probably stays 17f: acts on good to firm going: fairly useful hurdler/chaser, winner 3 times in 2006. *B. W. Duke*

OPENING LINE 4 ch.g. Opening Verse (USA) 126 – Denton Lady 49 (Inchinor 119) – [2006 f6g p7.1g Jan 13] last in maidens. *E. R. Oertel*

OPEN LOOP (IRE) 4 b.g. Danehill (USA) 126 – Last Exit 91 (Dominion 123) [2006 67 7.5v 5m 7.5f⁵ 7.5f⁴ 7g 8m⁶ 9d 7f⁴ 7s 8v p8.6g⁶ p9.5g⁶ Dec 9] €2,500 3-y-o: half-brother to several winners, including useful Irish 1m (at 2 yrs)/1¼m winner Apparatchik (by Selkirk): dam, 2-y-o 6f winner, out of Fillies' Mile winner Nepula: fair maiden: caught eye when sixth in handicap at Wolverhampton final start, not knocked about unduly: stays 9.5f: acts on polytrack and firm going: blinkered/tongue tied last 3 starts. *Edgar Byrne, Ireland*

OPERA BELLE 4 b.f. Dr Fong (USA) 128 – Opera Lover (IRE) 97 (Sadler's Wells 58 d (USA) 132) [2006 77d: p10g⁶ p12.2g f8g p10g 11.9m⁶ f8g⁵ 7f⁶ 8d⁶ Aug 21] sturdy filly: maiden: just modest form at best in 2006: left A. Jarvis after third outing: stays 1¼m: acts on polytrack, good to firm and good to soft ground: tried visored/blinkered: tongue tied last 3 starts. *Miss Gay Kelleway*

OPERA CAPE 3 b.c. Barathea (IRE) 127 – Optaria 83 (Song 132) [2006 117: 8m – May 6] close-coupled colt: smart performer at 2 yrs: left S. Kirk tongue tied, eased as if amiss when last in 2000 Guineas at Newmarket only outing in 2006: suffered ankle problem after: should stay 1m: acts on good to firm and good to soft going: on edge before (ran well) final 2-y-o start: often races freely. *Saeed bin Suroor*

OPERA COMICA 3 b.f. Dr Fong (USA) 128 – Comic (IRE) 87 (Be My Chief (USA) 66 122) [2006 76: p10g³ p10g p12.2g² p12.2g² p12g⁵ p12g Sep 29] sturdy filly: fair maiden: stays easy 1½m: acts on polytrack and good to soft ground: tried visored. *J. H. M. Gosden*

OPERA CROWN (IRE) 2 b.g. (Feb 13) Grand Lodge (USA) 125 – Silly Goose (IRE) 84 77 (Sadler's Wells (USA) 132) [2006 7g² 10.2m* 8g 8s Oct 21] 80,000F, 45,000Y: good-bodied gelding: second foal: dam 1½m winner: fairly useful performer: second to Proponent at Newbury, then won maiden at Bath later in September: better effort in nurseries when eighth at Newmarket: found little in blinkers final start (gelded after): will stay 1½m: acts on good to firm going. *P. F. I. Cole*

OPERA KNIGHT 6 ch.g. In The Wings 128 – Sans Escale (USA) (Diesis 133) [2006 54 58: p9.5g* f7g p10g⁴ p9.5g⁵ p9.5g p9.5g⁵ p12g² p12g⁴ p10g* 10.2f 12.1m⁵ 10.9m⁴ p12g Oct 23] good-bodied gelding: modest performer: won banded races at Wolverhampton in January and Kempton in May: stays 1½m: acts on polytrack and good to firm ground: tried blinkered: held up: once refused to race at 5 yrs. *A. W. Carroll*

OPERA MUSIC 2 b.c. (Apr 25) Kirkwall 118 – Optaria 83 (Song 132) [2006 6m² 7g* 94 7s⁴ Oct 21] sturdy colt: closely related to fairly useful 7f to 8.5f winner Highland Shot (by Selkirk) and half-brother to several winners, including 7f (at 2 yrs) to 2m winner Grey Shot (by Sharrood), 5f winner Night Shot (by Night Shift), and 3-y-o Opera Cape, all 3 smart: dam sprinter: fairly useful form: won maiden at Newbury in September: further progress when 5¼ lengths fourth of 10 to Dijeerr in Horris Hill Stakes there, making running (again drifted left): stays 7f. *S. Kirk*

OPERA WRITER (IRE) 3 b.g. Rossini (USA) 118 – Miss Flite (IRE) (Law Society 74 (USA) 130) [2006 71: 5m⁵ 6d⁶ 6g⁴ 7m⁴ p7.1g⁵ f8g* p8g* p8g 8.1g⁵ p8.6f p8.6g p12.2g² f12g² f12g² Dec 23] strong, compact gelding: fair performer: won claimers at Southwell (left T. Easterby £10,000) and Lingfield in July: left J. Boyle £6,000 after eleventh start: stays 1½m: acts on all-weather and good to firm going: tried visored. *R. Hollinshead*

OPO

OPORTO (UAE) 3 b.f. Jade Robbery (USA) 121 – Potentille (IRE) 88 (Caerleon (USA) 132) [2006 54p: 10g p9.5g³ p8.6g* 11.6g 8f 13d p8.6m Oct 14] close-coupled filly: fair performer on all-weather, little form on turf in 2006: won handicap at Wolverhampton in May: left M. Jarvis after fifth outing: should stay at least 1¼m: acts on polytrack. *D. M. Fogarty, Ireland* **– a73**

OPTICAL ILLUSION (USA) 2 b.c. (May 2) Theatrical 128 – Paradise River (USA) (Irish River (FR) 131) [2006 7d Oct 10] $200,000Y: fifth foal: half-brother to several winners, notably 4-y-o David Junior: dam, maiden in USA, sister to top-class US performer up to 1¼m Paradise Creek and half-sister to very smart US Grade 1 winners Forbidden Apple (1m/1¼m) and Wild Event (9f): 11/2, eighth to Mount Hadley in maiden at Leicester, not knocked about: will do better. *E. A. L. Dunlop* **69 p**

OPTICAL SECLUSION (IRE) 3 b.g. Second Empire (IRE) 124 – Theda 61 (Mummy's Pet 125) [2006 63: 5.9m³ 5m⁵ 6f 5m⁵ 5.9g p6m⁵ p7.1m Nov 8] useful-looking gelding: modest maiden: may prove best at 5f/6f: acts on good to firm and good to soft going: tried tongue tied, blinkered 3 of last 4 starts: none too genuine. *T. J. Etherington* **61**

OPTIMUM (IRE) 4 b.g. King's Best (USA) 132 – Colour Dance (Rainbow Quest (USA) 134) [2006 67: 12g 10.2m p10g f14g* 17.1d p12.2g f14g⁶ f16g⁵ p16.5g Dec 29] close-coupled gelding: fair handicapper on all-weather, little form on turf in 2006: made all at Southwell in July: below form after: stays 1¾m: acts on all-weather: visored final start: races up with pace. *J. T. Stimpson* **69**

OPTIMUS (USA) 4 ch.g. Elnadim (USA) 128 – Ajfan (USA) 112 (Woodman (USA) 126) [2006 6g 7m⁶ 8.3f² 8m* 8m⁴ 8m p8g³ 9.9d⁴ 10g⁵ p12g³ p9.5m Nov 9] sturdy gelding: fairly useful performer: won handicap at Newmarket in June: left G. Butler after eighth outing: stays 1½m: acts on polytrack and firm going: tried tongue tied: usually held up. *B. G. Powell* **86**

OPUS MAGNUS (IRE) 3 b.g. Mozart (IRE) 131 – Bold As Love (Lomond (USA) 128) [2006 5f p8g p7g⁶ Oct 15] modest form in maidens: very slowly away on debut: gelded after final start. *P. J. Makin* **62**

ORANGE 2 ch.f. (Feb 29) Giant's Causeway (USA) 132 – Shopping For Love (USA) (Not For Love (USA)) [2006 7d Aug 12] 105,000Y: angular filly: first foal: dam 6f (at 2 yrs) to 9f (minor stakes) winner in USA: 8/1, behind in maiden at Newmarket won by Passage of Time: should improve. *W. J. Haggas* **54 p**

ORANGE BLUE (GER) 4 b.c. Laroche (GER) 123 – Onanga (GER) (Acatenango (GER) 127) [2006 97: f11g⁵ a11.5g² 11g² 9g⁶ 8d* 8g³ 8d² 8d³ 10s Nov 19] fifth foal: half-brother to 3 winners in Germany: dam, 8.5f and 9.5f winner, closely related to 6-y-o Orange Touch: one-time useful performer: trained by C. Von Der Recke first 4 starts only in 2006 (fifth in maiden at Southwell on reappearance): rejoined former trainer, won maiden at Frankfurt in August: stays 11f: acts on good to soft ground. *P. Remmert, Germany* **74**

ORANGE DANCER (IRE) 3 b.f. Danehill Dancer (IRE) 117 – Strelitzia (SAF) (Fort Wood (USA) 117) [2006 72: p7.1g⁴ 6.1s* 6f⁵ 6m⁵ p6g⁴ Jul 26] sturdy filly: fair handicapper: won at Chepstow in May: should stay 7f: acts on polytrack, firm and soft going: sent to South Africa. *H. Morrison* **77**

ORANGE LADY (IRE) 2 b.f. (Mar 15) Montjeu (IRE) 137 – Young Affair (IRE) (Mukaddamah (USA) 125) [2006 7d Oct 3] 38,000F, 100,000Y: smallish filly: fourth foal: half-sister to useful 1m/9f winner Day Fort (by Tagula) and fairly useful Irish 2005 2-y-o 5f winner Northern Flight (by Fasliyev): dam unraced: no show in maiden at Leicester: sold 2,000 gns. *M. L. W. Bell* **–**

ORANGE LILY 2 b.f. (Apr 16) Royal Applause 124 – Tarsa 81 (Ballad Rock 122) [2006 6m⁵ Aug 27] half-sister to several winners, including useful Irish 6f/7f winners Churchill (by Kylian), later successful at 1m in USA, and Antrim Coast (by Mujtahid): dam, 6f winner, later successful in Italy: needed experience in maiden at Yarmouth: should progress. *M. A. Jarvis* **– p**

ORANGE PEKOE (USA) 2 b.c. (Feb 12) Miswaki (USA) 124 – Rascal Lass (USA) (Ack Ack (USA)) [2006 p7g⁵ 6f⁵ 7m⁵ p7g 7g³ Nov 7] $15,000Y, 50,000 2-y-o: half-brother to several minor winners in USA: dam US Grade 1 8.5f winner: fair maiden: seemingly best efforts in minor events at Lingfield and (having left P. Mitchell) Maisons-Laffitte third/final starts: stays 7f. *M. Delzangles, France* **71**

ORANGES AND LEMONS (FR) 3 b.f. Zafonic (USA) 130 – Tarte Aux Pommes (USA) (Local Talent (USA) 122) [2006 55?: p8g p7.1g Dec 27] angular, workmanlike filly: no form since debut at 2 yrs: off 18 months prior to reappearance. *C. E. Brittain* **–**

ORANGE STRAVINSKY 3 b.g. Stravinsky (USA) 133 – Orange Sunset (IRE) 99 **62** (Roanoke (USA)) [2006 72: 8g 10v 12.1m⁴ 11.1g p9.5g Sep 30] good-topped, useful-looking gelding: just modest maiden in 2006: stays 1½m: acts on good to firm ground: tailed off in cheekpieces final start. *P. C. Haslam*

ORANGE TOUCH (GER) 6 b.g. Lando (GER) 128 – Orange Bowl (General **104** Assembly (USA)) [2006 101: 12m⁴ 12f⁴ 14g⁵ 12g 11.6d p16g⁶ Nov 11] well-made gelding: one-time smart listed winner: just useful performer nowadays: creditable fourth in minor event won by Balkan Knight and listed race won by Crosspeace, both at Goodwood: below form after: stays 1¾m: acts on firm and soft going. *Mrs A. J. Perrett*

ORANGINO 8 b.g. Primo Dominie 121 – Sweet Jaffa 73§ (Never So Bold 135) [2006 **–** 45§: 13m Aug 3] maiden: tried blinkered: none too reliable. *J. S. Haldane*

ORANMORE CASTLE (IRE) 4 b.g. Giant's Causeway (USA) 132 – Twice The **87** Ease 46 (Green Desert (USA) 127) [2006 88: 6g 6d⁶ 6m³ 6m² 6m 5f* 5f 5d³ 5s Oct 16] good-topped gelding: has a quick action: fairly useful handicapper: won at Beverley in July: left B. Hills 25,000 gns, creditable efforts last 3 starts: probably best at 6f/testing 5f: acts on firm and soft going: often tongue tied. *D. Nicholls*

ORCADIAN 5 b.g. Kirkwall 118 – Rosy Outlook (USA) 79 (Trempolino (USA) 135) **115** § [2006 109: 10g 13.4d² 13.9s³ 12d⁶ 12s³ 11.6d² p12g Nov 18] well-made gelding: fluent mover: smart performer: best efforts in 2006 when placed in Ormonde Stakes at Chester (remarkable performance, all but pulling himself up 4f out, then going clear off home turn only to be caught close home and beaten ½ length by The Whistling Teal) and St Simon Stakes at Newbury (off nearly 5 months, 2¼ lengths third to Short Skirt) second/fifth starts: much better effort after when respectable second to Alfie Flits in listed race at Windsor: stays 1¾m: acts on heavy and good to firm going: usually makes running: temperamental and untrustworthy. *J. M. P. Eustace*

ORCHARD HOUSE (FR) 3 b.g. Medaaly 114 – Louisa May (IRE) (Royal Abjar **45** (USA) 121) [2006 8d 8.1m 10.2m⁶ p8g p11g⁵ f14g³ Dec 29] poor maiden: stays 11f: acts on polytrack: tried blinkered. *J. Jay*

ORCHARD SUPREME 3 ch.c. Titus Livius (FR) 115 – Bogus Penny (IRE) 80 **88** (Pennekamp (USA) 130) [2006 75: p7g³ p7g² p8g* p7g⁵ p7g⁸ 8.3g 7.1m⁴ 7f 7g⁶ p8g³ **a109** p7g⁶ p7g² p8g* p7g⁵ p8g* Dec 22] good-topped colt: useful handicapper on all-weather, fairly useful on turf: much improved, winning at Lingfield in February, March and May, Kempton in November and Lingfield again (beat Secret Night by ¾ length) in December: stays 1m: acts on polytrack, soft and good to firm going: visored once at 2 yrs: held up: reliable on polytrack. *R. Hannon*

ORCHESTRATION (IRE) 5 ch.g. Stravinsky (USA) 133 – Mora (IRE) 100 (Second **46** Set (IRE) 127) [2006 36, a65: f5g⁵ f6g³ f6g⁴ f5g f5g² 6m f6g² p5.1g³ 5f p6g p6g f6g f5m⁴ **a63** f6g³ f5g p6g⁵ f6g⁶ p6g f5g² f5g* Dec 29] compact gelding: modest on all-weather, poor on turf: won banded race at Southwell in December: best at 5f/6f: acts on all-weather and firm going: tried blinkered/in cheekpieces, usually visored. *M. J. Attwater*

ORCHESTRATOR (IRE) 2 b.g. (May 19) Docksider (USA) 124 – Summerhill **– p** (Habitat 134) [2006 p7g Dec 15] 30,000Y: half-brother to several winners, including fairly useful 7f (at 2 yrs)/1m winner Mana-Mou-Bay and useful 7f and 1¼m winner Evaluator (both by Ela-Mana-Mou): dam Irish 6f winner: 10/1, shaped better than result suggests when 10½ lengths seventh to Messiah Garvey in maiden at Kempton, disputing second well over 1f out until fading as if in need of run: will improve. *T. G. Mills*

ORDNANCE ROW 3 b.c. Mark of Esteem (IRE) 137 – Language of Love 63 (Rock **100** City 120) [2006 94p: 8g 8m 7m⁵ 7.6g* Aug 26] close-coupled colt: useful handicapper: second outing in 2 days, won at Chester in August by length from Irony: should be suited by 1m: possibly best on good going or softer (acts on heavy). *R. Hannon*

ORENAY (USA) 4 ch.g. Grand Slam (USA) 120 – Moonfire 76 (Sadler's Wells (USA) **44** 132) [2006 73d: p10g Jan 7] maiden: just poor form only outing in 2006: stays 8.7f: acts on heavy going: tried tongue tied/visored. *M. J. Wallace*

ORIENTAL DANCE 2 b.f. (Feb 26) Fantastic Light (USA) 134 – Oriental Fashion **–** (IRE) 110 (Marju (IRE) 127) [2006 p7g Oct 26] fourth foal: half-sister to 3 winners, including 3-y-o Green Coast and useful 2003 2-y-o 6f/7f winner Oriental Warrior (by Alhaarth): dam, 1m winner (including at 2 yrs), out of close relation to Nayef and half-sister to Nashwan and Unfuwain: 9/2, well held in maiden at Lingfield: joined J. Hyde in UAE. *Saeed bin Suroor*

ORIENTOR 8 b.h. Inchinor 119 – Orient 106 (Bay Express 132) [2006 116: p6g 6s⁶ **114** 5.2m⁴ 5s² 5d⁴ 5m 5f³ 5m 5s 5g² 6d Sep 16] close-coupled horse: smart performer: best effort in 2006 when length third to Fantasy Explorer in quite valuable handicap at Ayr seventh start: creditable efforts in listed race at York (¾-length second to Celtic Mill) and Ayr Gold Cup (ninth behind Fonthill Road) last 2 outings: effective at 5f (given test)/6f: acts on firm and soft going: usually gets behind. *J. S. Goldie*

OROTUND 2 b.g. (May 1) Orpen (USA) 116 – Soyalang (FR) (Alydeed (CAN) 120) – [2006 6g 7.5m 5d Oct 3] big gelding: well held in maidens. *T. D. Easterby*

ORPENDONNA (IRE) 4 b.f. Orpen (USA) 116 – Tetradonna (IRE) 102 (Teenoso 70 (USA) 135) [2006 68: p8.6g* p9.5g⁵ p7.1g Mar 15] strong, lengthy filly: fair performer: won maiden at Wolverhampton in January: stays 8.6f: acts on all-weather and good to firm ground: in cheekpieces of late. *K. A. Ryan*

ORPENLINA (IRE) 3 b.f. Orpen (USA) 116 – Westlife (IRE) 32 (Mind Games 121) 57 [2006 5g 5.1g 5s* 5d 5s Sep 28] €14,500Y: lengthy filly: first foal: dam lightly-raced half-sister to useful sprinter Pepperoni: form (modest) only when winning maiden at Ripon in August: may be best kept to 5f: acts on soft going: sold 800 gns. *R. A. Fahey*

ORPEN PRINCE (IRE) 2 b.g. (Apr 12) Orpen (USA) 116 – She's The Tops 83 (Sher- 81 d nazar 131) [2006 6v² 6.1m 5.9g² 7m* 7m p7.1g Oct 8] £25,000F, €26,000Y: good-bodied, workmanlike gelding: half-brother to 3 winners, including smart 7f (at 2 yrs) to 1¼m winner Lady Upstage (by Alzao) and 17f winner The Blues Academy (by Royal Academy): dam 1½m winner: fairly useful performer: gelded, won nursery at Chester in August: ran poorly after, in cheekpieces final start: will stay 1m: acts on heavy and good to firm ground: sold 11,000 gns. *K. A. Ryan*

ORPEN QUEST (IRE) 4 b.g. Orpen (USA) 116 – Pursuit of Truth (USA) 69 (Irish 69 River (FR) 131) [2006 55: p9.5g⁶ f11g⁶ p7g 8.2s² 8f 7.1m* 10f³ p8.6g* 8.2m 8m 8.1m Sep 1] fair performer: won maiden at Warwick and handicap at Wolverhampton, both in July: probably stays 1¼m: acts on all-weather, soft and good to firm going: tried in cheekpieces, visored of late. *M. J. Attwater*

ORPEN'S ASTAIRE (IRE) 3 b.g. Orpen (USA) 116 – Rhythm And Style (USA) 53 61 (Keen 116) [2006 –: 8d⁶ 8m 7m 8g Sep 14] strong gelding: modest maiden: stays 1m: best effort on good going. *Jedd O'Keeffe*

ORPEN WIDE (IRE) 4 b.g. Orpen (USA) 116 – Melba (IRE) 62 (Namaqualand 89 (USA)) [2006 77: f6g 8g³ f8g f5g 8d 8m 7.5f* 10.1f 10g⁴ 7.5m² 8g* f8g* Dec 27] strong gelding: fairly useful handicapper: won at Beverley in June, Newcastle in September and Southwell in December: stays 1m: acts on all-weather and any turf going: effective with/without blinkers: tried tongue tied: tough: fairly useful hurdler, won 5 times in 2006. *M. C. Chapman*

ORPHAN (IRE) 4 b.g. Orpen (USA) 116 – Ballinlee (IRE) (Skyliner 117) [2006 85: 79 6m 6f 6d⁵ 7f 5s 6.1d Oct 18] big, good-topped gelding: just fair handicapper in 2006: best at 6f: acts on soft and good to firm going. *K. R. Burke*

ORPHINA (IRE) 3 b.f. Orpen (USA) 116 – Keralba (USA) (Sheikh Albadou 128) 61 [2006 63: 8.3g 8.1s⁵ 8.3m p7g 8.3f 8.1f 7f 8g p8g⁶ p10g p10g³ Dec 13] neat filly: modest maiden: left P. Eddery 7,000 gns after eighth start: stays 1m: acts on polytrack, soft and good to firm going: tried visored/blinkered/tongue tied: sometimes looks no easy ride. *B. G. Powell*

ORPHIR (IRE) 3 b.g. Orpen (USA) 116 – Silver Moon (Environment Friend 128) – [2006 f12g f12g Dec 9] well held in maidens at Southwell. *Mrs N. Macauley*

ORPSIE BOY (IRE) 3 b.g. Orpen (USA) 116 – Nordicolini (IRE) 64 (Nordico (USA)) 94 [2006 83: 6.1f² 6s 6m⁴ 6m⁶ 8m³ 6m⁵ 7f 6g 6s Aug 26] big, useful-looking gelding: fairly useful handicapper: very good 2 lengths fourth to Prince Tamino in William Hill Trophy at York: should stay 7f: acts on polytrack and firm ground: has been tongue tied/ blinkered: gelded after final outing. *N. P. Littmoden*

ORVIETAN (IRE) 3 b.c. Sadler's Wells (USA) 132 – Fiamma (IRE) 97 (Irish River 71 (FR) 131) [2006 –: p12g* f12g² p10g⁴ 10.9g⁶ p10g⁵ 10d May 15] angular, good-topped colt: fair performer: won maiden at Lingfield in February: stays 1½m: acts on all-weather: tried visored/blinkered: signs of temperament: sold 14,000 gns, joined N. Nevin in Ireland. *M. Johnston*

OSCARSHALL (IRE) 2 ch.g. (Apr 29) Halling (USA) 133 – Mafaatin (IRE) (Royal 63 Academy (USA) 130) [2006 6m 7m 8s p8.6m Oct 31] leggy gelding: modest maiden: last in nursery: likely to stay 1¼m: gelded after final start. *M. H. Tompkins*

OSCAR SNOWMAN 3 b.g. Selkirk (USA) 129 – Chilly Start (IRE) (Caerleon (USA) 62 + 132) [2006 81p: 8.3g⁴ Oct 16] fair maiden: off almost 16 months after debut, in need of run only outing since: gelded after: should be suited by 1m/1¼m: raced on good/good to firm going. *M. P. Tregoning*

OSCILLATOR 3 b.g. Pivotal 124 – Craigmill 85 (Slip Anchor 136) [2006 74p: p9.5g* **79** 10m 10d⁴ p12g⁵ Sep 6] strong gelding: fair performer, lightly raced: won maiden at Wolverhampton in April: should stay 1½m: acts on polytrack and soft going: sold 42,000 gns, and gelded. *G. A. Butler*

OSIRIS WAY 4 ch.g. Indian Ridge 123 – Heady (Rousillon (USA) 133) [2006 p8.6g **45** 8.3g Oct 16] poor form in maidens 3 months apart, gelded in between. *P. R. Chamings*

OSOLOMIO (IRE) 3 b.g. Singspiel (IRE) 133 – Inanna 105 (Persian Bold 123) [2006 **70** –: p8.6g 10.1g 10f² 9.9m⁴ 12f² 12m² 14m² 14.1d⁴ p12.2g² p12.2g* Nov 6] good-bodied gelding: fair performer: left J. Given after eighth start: won handicap at Wolverhampton in November: stays 1¾m: acts on polytrack and firm going. *G. A. Swinbank*

OSTEOPATHIC REMEDY (IRE) 2 ch.g. (Mar 20) Inchinor 119 – Dolce Vita **86 p** (IRE) 85 (Ela-Mana-Mou 132) [2006 6d* 6s⁴ Oct 6] 27,000F, €32,000Y, 8,000 2-y-o: sparely-made gelding: first foal: dam Irish 1¼m winner: fairly useful form: won maiden at Ayr (40/1, beat Doric Charm by neck) in September: similar form when fourth to Algol in nursery at York, nearest finish: will stay 1m: remains open to improvement. *M. Dods*

OSTERHASE (IRE) 7 b.g. Flying Spur (AUS) – Ostrusa (AUT) (Rustan (HUN)) **120** [2006 117: 5d 5m* 5g³ 5m* 6m* 5v² 6s Oct 8]

The very smart Irish sprinter Osterhase was as good as ever in 2006. At the age of seven he won three times—adding to nine previous successes—including when putting up another excellent weight-carrying performance in the Ladbrokes Rockingham Handicap at the Curragh in July, a race he first won as a five-year-old when carrying 10-1. Osterhase carried even more weight in the latest renewal, humping 10-3 and showing all his usual battling qualities when beating Leitra by a head. Wearing blinkers as usual, Osterhase typically rallied in tremendous fashion when headed approaching the final furlong to get back up on the line, in the process

Ladbrokes Rockingham Handicap, the Curragh—
under 10-3, the blinkered Osterhase just beats Leitra in this valuable event

producing the best effort by any horse in a handicap in Ireland all season. Though he had shown smart form previously, Osterhase first came to prominence in the summer of 2004 when his first win in the Rockingham was preceded by consecutive successes in listed events at the Curragh, in the second of those showing plenty of his trademark speed to break the twenty-five-year-old track record for five furlongs. Osterhase ran in pattern company for the rest of that campaign, his best performance coming when a good length-and-three-quarters fourth to Var in the Prix de l'Abbaye at Longchamp. Osterhase was a bit below his best as a six-year-old but he still won twice, most notably when narrowly gaining his first, and so far only, pattern success in the Phoenix Sprint Stakes at the Curragh, winning by a short head from Balmont. Osterhase's two other wins during his most recent campaign both came in listed events. After reportedly finishing lame on his reappearance, Osterhase bounced right back to his best to win an eleven-runner event at Naas in June by a length and a half from the smart Moon Unit, but, having finished a highly creditable third to Dandy Man in a listed event at the Curragh next time out, he had to battle much harder for his second listed win in July only eight days on from his Rockingham success. He showed plenty of grit to beat the progressive Borderlescott by a head in a five-runner event at Fairyhouse, conceding that rival 5 lb, once again rallying very gamely after looking beaten a furlong out. Ruled out of an intended bid for the Flying Five Stakes at the Curragh in August after scoping poorly, Osterhase was not discredited next time on heavy ground when a length second to Peace Offering in a listed race at the Curragh in October, but he can be forgiven a below-par effort on his final start when he almost certainly failed to stay the testing six furlongs.

Osterhase (IRE) (b.g. 1999)	Flying Spur (AUS) (b 1992)	Danehill (b 1986)	Danzig
			Rayzana
		Rolls (ch 1984)	Mr Prospector
			Grand Luxe
	Ostrusa (AUT) (b 1989)	Rustan (b 1968)	Imperial
			Rhapsodie
		Ostara (b 1975)	Segnes
			Odessa

There can be few horses in training with so cosmopolitan a background as Osterhase. Foaled in Ireland and owned by the Austrian businessman Michael Rosenfeld, Osterhase is by the Australian-registered sire Flying Spur out of the Austrian mare Ostrusa who is herself by the Hungarian sire Rustan. Flying Spur stood in Ireland from 1997 to 1999 before being returned to Australia, with his best runner in Europe—apart from Osterhase—being the very smart sprinter Steenberg. Ostrusa won seven races in Austria (her own dam and grandam also won there) and has bred three other winners, including Riolo (by Priolo), a seven-furlong winner at Brighton in the latest season. Osterhase is a sprinter purely and simply who has shown all his very best form on good or firmer going, though as he showed on his penultimate start he is no slouch on heavy, at least over five furlongs. He has yet to race in Britain, but as a very speedy front runner—and provided time does not catch up with him as an eight-year-old—the very game and genuine Osterhase would be an ideal type for the King George Stakes at Goodwood. *J. E. Mulhern, Ireland*

OSTFANNI (IRE) 6 b.m. Spectrum (IRE) 126 – Ostwahl (IRE) 97 (Waajib 121) [2006 **72** 63: 15.8g⁵ 16g* 16m* 18f⁶ Jul 29] compact mare: fair handicapper: won twice at Musselburgh in July, in amateur event on first occasion: stays 2m: acts on firm going, probably on good to soft: fairly useful hurdler. *M. Todhunter*

OTAKI (IRE) 2 gr.f. (May 1) King's Best (USA) 132 – On Call 103 (Alleged (USA) **– p** 138) [2006 p7g Dec 15] fifth foal: half-sister to several winners, including 1¼m (in USA) to 15f winner One Off (by Barathea) and 9f to 1½m winner Oblique (by Giant's Causeway), both useful: dam 1½m to 2m winner: 16/1, not knocked about after fading in maiden at Kempton: sort to do better. *Sir Mark Prescott*

O'TARA (IRE) 3 b.c. Danehill (USA) 126 – Utr (USA) (Mr Prospector (USA)) [2006 **84** 79p: 8d³ 9.2d² 8m² 8m* 10.3m³ 8.1g Sep 22] lengthy, angular colt: fairly useful performer: won maiden at Pontefract in August: creditable third on handicap debut next time: stays easy 10.3f: acts on good to firm and good to soft going. *M. H. Tompkins*

OTELCALIFORNI (USA) 3 b.f. Gulch (USA) – Ive Gota Bad Liver (USA) (Mt **80** Livermore (USA)) [2006 54p: 8.3m² 9m² 9.2f* 10m⁵ Jul 30] fairly useful performer: won maiden at Hamilton in June: stays 9f: acts on firm going: unruly at start (below form) final outing: sold 85,000 gns in November. *J. Noseda*

OTIS B DRIFTWOOD 3 b.g. Tipsy Creek (USA) 115 – Gi La High 68 (Rich Charlie 117) [2006 64: p6g⁵ p5.1g³ p5g⁶ p5.1g⁴ f5g³ p5.1g 5m² p6g 5.7g³ 5.1g⁶ p6g p5g p5g p5.1g⁶ Dec 8] well-grown gelding: modest performer: gradually regressed, leaving M. Quinn after eleventh start: likely to prove best at 5f/easy 6f: acts on all-weather, best turf effort on good going: wears headgear. *Miss J. R. Tooth*　**62 d**

OTRANTO (USA) 4 ch.c. Rahy (USA) 115 – Tethkar 75 (Machiavellian (USA) 123) [2006 a9f a11f³ a11f² a11f³ a8f 10.2d 10f² 10f* 12f³ 10.1g⁴ Aug 3] second foal: brother to a winner in Saudi Arabia: dam maiden who should have stayed beyond 1m: won maiden at Jebel Ali at 3 yrs: fair handicapper in 2006, leaving A. Al Raihe in UAE after fifth start: won at Ayr in July: stays 1½m: acts on dirt and firm going: usually tongue tied: rejoined former trainer in UAE. *M. Johnston*　**72**

OUIJA BOARD 5 b.m. Cape Cross (IRE) 129 – Selection Board 75 (Welsh Pageant 132) [2006 121: 12m⁴ 10m³ 12g² 10m* 10m⁵ 9.9m* 10m² 11f* 12f³ Nov 26]　**125**

　　In terms of merit, there have been better middle-distance fillies and mares than Ouija Board trained in Britain, even in relatively recent times, but the sterling exploits of this experienced international performer, particularly in the latest season, contributed greatly to the contemporary racing scene and earned her unique status among the leading British-trained fillies and mares of the modern era. There was never an air of invincibility about Ouija Board—she was beaten in more races than she won—but career prize money earned in three trips to America, two to Hong Kong, two to Japan and one to Dubai (not to mention two to Ireland and one to France) helped to boost her earnings to over £3.5m, easily a record for a filly or mare trained in Britain. The figure that will be quoted in most record books is £3,510,682, though exact figures are always open to question because of currency movements, and the figures depend on conversion rates used for overseas prize money. Had Ouija Board been able to meet her engagement in the Hong Kong Vase in December—her intended swansong—second place would have been enough to take her earnings past those of Japan Cup and Dubai World Cup winner Singspiel, whose total is usually quoted as £3,671,039, while victory would have left her just short of the British and European record holder Fantastic Light who earned £4,207,030 (including £279,720 when officially trained in Dubai for a second in the Sheema Classic). Like Singspiel and Fantastic Light, Ouija Board won Group/Grade 1 races in four different countries, her seven career victories in that category coming in Britain (Oaks, Prince of Wales's Stakes, Nassau Stakes), Ireland (Irish Oaks), America (Breeders' Cup Filly & Mare Turf, twice) and Hong Kong (Hong Kong Vase). She had half her races on foreign soil, failing to make the frame only once in eleven Group/Grade 1 events overseas, when fifth in the Japan Cup as a four-year-old. As well as winning the Racehorse Owners' Association's Horse of The Year award in the latest season, Ouija Board also ran away with the Eclipse Award for best female turf horse in North America, the second time she has won the award.

Prince of Wales's Stakes, Royal Ascot—Ouija Board shows the best turn of foot to see off Electrocutionist and Manduro (rail); David Junior (No.3) and Notnowcato come next

Vodafone Nassau Stakes, Goodwood—in a sustained duel, Ouija Board (white cap) pulls out extra to deny Alexander Goldrun; Nannina is third, ahead of Chelsea Rose

Between putting up the best performance in the Oaks since User Friendly and being returned two years later to Epsom for the Coronation Cup, Ouija Board was seen out only twice in Britain. After her injury-hit four-year-old campaign was crowned by victory in the richly-endowed Hong Kong Vase, Ouija Board was on her travels again in the spring. She was left with far too much to do under Kieren Fallon, never able to reach the principals in the home straight, when fourth in the Dubai Sheema Classic at Nad Al Sheba in March, though Fallon claimed a pre-race fireworks display affected her performance. 'We're not kidding ourselves, life will be very tough for her in Europe where the older division looks very strong,' her trainer said after Nad Al Sheba, reflecting the relatively easier pickings abroad for a high-class horse that can keep travelling. Dunlop indicated that the Queen Elizabeth II Cup at Sha Tin and the Singapore Airlines International Cup were possibly Ouija Board's next targets. With Fallon replaced by Frankie Dettori, the strong-finishing Ouija Board went down in a photo to the South African-trained mare Irridescence and Best Gift in the Queen Elizabeth II Cup, a tardy start contributing to her being left with plenty to do again, though not so much as in the Sheema Classic. Ouija Board's performance over a mile and a quarter at Sha Tin, particularly her magnificent finishing effort, seemed to lead to a change of heart about gearing her five-year-old campaign around an international programme. Her connections had complained about the lack of opportunities for top-class fillies and mares in Europe at a mile and a half, her four Group/Grade 1 wins at three and four having come at or around that distance (she won the Breeders' Cup Filly & Mare Turf over eleven furlongs but was beaten, staying on relentlessly, when attempting a repeat in the 2005 edition over a furlong shorter).

British racegoers saw Ouija Board in action four times in the summer, three times over a mile and a quarter, including at Royal Ascot and Glorious Goodwood where her reputation was enhanced by two victories, the first in the Prince of Wales's Stakes over the colts, including Dubai World Cup winner Electrocutionist and Dubai Duty Free winner David Junior, and the second after a sustained duel with another globe-trotting mare, Irish-trained Alexander Goldrun, in the Nassau Stakes, a stirring contest which, with the Derby, was one of the strongest candidates for race of the season. Ouija Board's summer campaign began at Epsom where her presence (ridden again by Dettori) and that of French-trained Breeders' Cup Turf winner Shirocco made the Coronation Cup anything but a supporting act on the day to the Oaks. Ouija Board looked in wonderful shape but went down by a length and three quarters in a tactical affair to the odds-on Shirocco. David Junior and Electrocutionist dominated the betting on the Prince of Wales's Stakes for which Ouija Board was 8/1 third choice in a field of seven. Neither Fallon, Dettori nor Jamie Spencer—the first three choices—was available and the mount went instead to Olivier Peslier. To general surprise, Ouija Board justified her owner's decision to take on the big guns instead of going for the less valuable Hardwicke Stakes, run over a mile and a half three days later. The steady tempo set by Dettori on Electrocutionist resulted in the Prince of Wales's turning into a less than satisfactory examination of all the attributes of the runners. Ouija Board coped well with the test of speed, sweeping into the lead inside the final furlong after Peslier had to switch her off the rail to get a run. Half a length was the winning margin over Electrocutionist, with one of the French-trained challengers Manduro a further three quarters of a length away third. David Junior came fourth in a bunched finish. The Prince of Wales's was a defining race for Ouija Board's owners. Lord Derby continued to the bitter end to wear the 'lucky' clothes for all Ouija Board's races that he had worn since her victory in the Pretty Polly as a three-year-old (though he could wear only the tie at Royal Ascot because of the dress code). The latest Royal meeting, however, saw Lady Derby in a different outfit—a change disapproved of by her more superstitious husband—and the clothes she had worn for the Pretty Polly were not seen again in any of Ouija Board's later races. Lady Derby had argued that if the Queen had taken the trouble to build a new stand, she would have to wear a new outfit!

Ouija Board, David Junior and the close Prince of Wales's fifth Notnowcato met again in the Eclipse at Sandown two and a half weeks later when Ouija Board had another new jockey, Christophe Soumillon, who became the eighth to ride her after the beleaguered Fallon (contracted to ride Aussie Rules for Ballydoyle if free), the suspended Dettori and Spencer (David Junior), as well as Peslier (riding at Deauville), were ruled out. Ouija Board's eagerly-anticipated appearance at Sandown, where she started favourite, turned into an anti-climax when she got little or no chance to repeat her Prince of Wales's performance, hemmed in for most of the home straight and unable to get clear until too late. Ouija Board managed only fifth behind David Junior and Notnowcato, returning stiff and sore, with cuts on three legs, after being bumped a number of times as Soumillon tried unsuccessfully to extricate her. With her Eclipse experience ruling out a possible tilt at the King George VI and Queen Elizabeth Stakes (for which she would have had to be supplemented), Ouija Board made her final appearance on home soil in the Vodafone Nassau Stakes in early-August. In a memorable encounter, Ouija Board and the previous year's winner Alexander Goldrun were separated at the line by a short head after being locked together for much of the last three furlongs, putting up the

Emirates Airline Breeders' Cup Filly & Mare Turf, Churchill Downs—
a second success in the race in three years for Ouija Board, who quickens away from Film Maker;
fourth-placed Wait A While and sixth-placed My Typhoon (rail) are the others in the picture

best performance in the race since it was upgraded to Group 1 status in 1999. Ouija Board was given a tremendous reception when Dettori took her on an impromptu parade in front of the stands before returning to the winner's enclosure where both she and Alexander Goldrun—a winner of five Group/Grade 1s in four different countries—were given a rousing 'three cheers' in a show of popularity and appreciation seldom seen after a major Flat race. Some reports of the race, by the way, claimed that Ouija Board and Alexander Goldrun 'left the others toiling'. For the record, the Coronation Stakes winner Nannina (who might have finished a little closer still but for having to be steered wide) was two lengths away in third, doing best of the three-year-olds, with the in-and-out four-year-old Chelsea Rose, who was allowed to dictate a fairly sedate pace until past halfway, a further two and a half back in fourth.

Ouija Board's fourth season on the racecourse was easily her busiest and she revealed a particularly strong constitution that had not been evident in her three- and four-year-old days. A 'farewell tour' involving America, for the Breeders' Cup Filly & Mare Turf, and the Far East, for the Japan Cup and the Hong Kong Vase, had always been the aim, and it was preceded by a challenge for Ireland's most important, all-aged championship event the Irish Champion Stakes in September. Alexander Goldrun opposed Ouija Board again but victory went to the classic generation with Irish Derby winner Dylan Thomas rallying gamely to lead again near the line after Ouija Board had been sent into the lead over a furlong out by Spencer, who became the fifth different jockey to partner her as a five-year-old. Running up to her best, Ouija Board went down by a neck, finishing ahead of third-placed Alexander Goldrun, who didn't show her Nassau form, for the third time in as many meetings. There was talk of Ouija Board's having a final outing

Lord Derby's "Ouija Board"

in Europe in the Prix de l'Opera and then, after that was ruled out by the prospect of soft ground (it was good to firm on the day) at Longchamp, of her making an appearance in the Champion Stakes. Rain put paid to that plan too and Ouija Board had a break of eight weeks—much the longest between any of her races as a five-year-old—which contributed to her enjoying a smoother preparation than the previous year for the Breeders' Cup meeting, which was staged at Churchill Downs, Kentucky, in early-November.

Heavy rain also arrived at Churchill Downs, but the weather relented in time and the ground dried out. The turf course was firm as Ouija Board became only the second horse to regain a Breeders' Cup title, following the Michael Dickinson-trained gelding Da Hoss who won the Breeders' Cup Mile for a second time in 1998, also at Churchill Downs, having had only one outing (the month before) in the two years since his first win in the race. Ouija Board wasn't the only runner in the Breeders' Cup Filly & Mare Turf making a third appearance in the race. The reliable Film Maker had been runner-up to Ouija Board in Texas at Lone Star Park (where a race has been named in Ouija Board's honour), and third behind Inter-continental and Ouija Board at Belmont, New York. Ouija Board, who started favourite, and Film Maker filled the first two places again, Dettori bringing Ouija Board from mid-division to lead over a furlong out and win by two and a quarter lengths. Honey Ryder, who had beaten Film Maker in the Flower Bowl Invitational at Belmont the previous month, was a neck away in third, with Wait A While, the best turf filly in North America, a below-form fourth, ahead of the Prix de l'Opera runner-up Satwa Queen, one of two French-trained challengers. Although Ouija Board was reportedly struck into at Churchill Downs, the injury was not serious enough to jeopardise her participation for the Japan Cup at Tokyo at the end of November. Ouija Board improved two places on her performance in 2005, losing no caste in defeat when going down by two lengths and half a length to the home-trained pair Deep Impact and Dream Passport, beaten around the same distance by the winner as she had been by British-trained Alkaased twelve months earlier. Ouija Board was a warm favourite to repeat her success in the Hong Kong Vase at Sha Tin, but she suffered a recurrence of an old splint injury, stiffness being found in a foreleg after her final piece of work, and was ruled out of the race the day before. She has been retired and visits Kingmambo.

Even before the latest season, there was never much to choose between Ouija Board's form at a mile and a quarter and her form at a mile and a half, and there were certainly no grounds, judged on her pedigree, to support the seemingly widely-held view expressed before the Prince of Wales's Stakes that she was better suited by the longer trip. She is by the miler Cape Cross, who was not himself bred to stay any further, being by Green Desert out of the Cheveley Park winner Park Appeal. On the distaff side, Ouija Board's dam, the twice-raced Selection Board, was by the top-class miler Welsh Pageant, who stayed a mile and a quarter, and a sister to another notable miler in Teleprompter, who won the Queen Elizabeth II Stakes. Teleprompter also won the Arlington Million over a mile and a quarter, at which distance he was a creditable third in the Eclipse. A half-sister, however, the useful miler Rosia Bay, produced—admittedly to matings with Derby winners Mill Reef and Blakeney—an Irish St Leger winner in Ibn Bey and a winner of the Yorkshire Oaks in Roseate Tern who was also placed in the St Leger.

Ouija Board (b.m. 2001)	Cape Cross (IRE) (b 1994)	Green Desert (b 1983)	Danzig
			Foreign Courier
		Park Appeal (br 1982)	Ahonoora
			Balidaress
	Selection Board (b 1982)	Welsh Pageant (b 1966)	Tudor Melody
			Picture Light
		Ouija (b 1971)	Silly Season
			Samanda

The story of how Ouija Board's family was introduced into the Stanley House studs by the present Earl of Derby's uncle was recounted in *Racehorses of 2004* in which the essay on Ouija Board also outlines the long association with the sport of the Earl's ancestors, stretching back to the 12th Earl who gave his name to Flat racing's most famous race and also founded the Oaks, named after the country house he leased in Surrey. The pick of the six winners produced by the now-deceased Selection Board before Ouija Board was Star Selection (by Rainbow Quest), useful at up to a mile and a half on the Flat and a winner both over hurdles and fences. Among the small band of broodmares Ouija Board will be joining at Stanley House is her useful half-sister Cruinn A Bhord (by Inchinor) who foaled a filly by Cape Cross the year Ouija Board won the Oaks; that filly raised £350,000 at an NSPCC charity function in the latest season, leased from Lord Derby by the successful bidder until the end of her three-year-old season. She will be trained by Ed Dunlop who will become a public trainer in the next season after twelve years employed by Gainsborough, the racing arm of Maktoum Al Maktoum, eldest of the four brothers, who died in January. Dunlop will not have Ouija Board but his other stable star Court Masterpiece, who initiated a notable big-race double at Goodwood in the Sussex Stakes, stays in training. The tall, leggy Ouija Board, who was not the best of walkers in the latter part of her career, acted on firm and good to soft going and was tough, game and reliable. She was a credit to her sporting connections, whose decision to keep her in training for two further seasons beyond her classic year provided the racing public with so much pleasure. The phrase 'we won't see the like again' is overused but it seems apt for Ouija Board whose global achievements, coupled with resilience and consistency over three seasons, will take some matching by future generations of British fillies and racemares. *E. A. L. Dunlop*

OULAN BATOR (FR) 6 b.g. Astair (FR) 121 – Scarieuse (FR) (Crackao (FR)) [2006 64: 10m 9.2g⁶ 15.8d⁵ 15.8m Sep 16] workmanlike gelding: modest handicapper at 5 yrs: no form in 2006: tried blinkered. *R. A. Fahey* —

OUNINPOHJA (IRE) 5 b.g. Imperial Ballet (IRE) 110 – Daziyra (IRE) (Doyoun 124) [2006 112+: 12.1d² 14m² 12f² 11.9g² 12g² 11.6g³ 10d² Sep 16] good-topped gelding: smart performer: runner-up 6 times in 2006, good efforts in Old Newton Cup (Handicap) at Haydock (length behind Consular) and minor event at Newmarket (beaten 2½ lengths by Guadalajara) fourth/fifth starts (left G. A. Swinbank after): much better subsequent run when creditable third to Crocodile Dundee in listed race at Windsor: stays 1½m: acts on firm and soft going: visored last 2 starts: consistent but ungenuine: joined P. Nicholls, won over hurdles in November. *I. Semple* **116 §**

OUR ARCHIE 2 b.c. (Apr 23) Kyllachy 129 – Oriel Girl 65 (Beveled (USA)) [2006 6.1g p6g Jul 13] last in maidens. *M. J. Attwater* —

OUR BLESSING (IRE) 2 b.c. (Apr 4) Lujain (USA) 119 – Berenice (ITY) (Marouble 116) [2006 p5g⁴ 6.1m 7g⁴ 6g 6s* p7.1g⁵ p6g² p7g⁵ Dec 19] 13,000Y: tall, close-coupled colt: half-brother to 3 winners, including useful Irish 6f winner (including at 2 yrs) Berenica (by College Chapel) and 6-y-o Gaelic Princess: dam unraced: fair performer: won maiden at Pontefract in October: second in nursery at Kempton: barely stays 7f: acts on polytrack and soft going. *A. P. Jarvis* **78**

OUR CHELSEA BLUE (USA) 8 ch.m. Distant View (USA) 126 – Eastern Connection (USA) (Danzig Connection (USA)) [2006 f5g f5g p5.1g Apr 25] modest performer at 6 yrs: missed 2005: no form in 2006: tried tongue tied. *J. R. Jenkins* —

OUR CHOICE (IRE) 4 b.g. Indian Danehill (IRE) 124 – Spring Daffodil 97 (Pharly (FR) 130) [2006 78: p13.9g⁴ p16.5g³ p16g⁶ 13.8d 12.4g⁴ 12d³ 11.5m² 13.3m 12m 14.1f p16.5m Oct 14] tall, good-topped gelding: fair handicapper: stays 2m: acts on polytrack, firm and good to soft going: sold 12,000 gns. *N. P. Littmoden* **75**

OUR FAYE 3 b.f. College Chapel 122 – Tamara 83 (Marju (IRE) 127) [2006 p8.6g³ p8g⁴ 8.3g* 8.1d⁶ 7g p8.6m³ p10g Oct 26] third foal: dam 2-y-o 5f winner: fair performer: won maiden at Leicester in August: stays 1¼m: acts on polytrack and good to soft going: reared at start (below form) fifth outing. *S. Kirk* **74**

OUR FUGITIVE (IRE) 4 gr.g. Titus Livius (FR) 115 – Mystical Jumbo (Mystiko (USA) 124) [2006 84: 5s² 5m² 5d⁴ 5.1f 5s Oct 6] leggy gelding: fairly useful handicapper: at least respectable efforts first 3 starts, but well below form last 2: effective at 5f/6f: acts on soft and good to firm going: races up with pace. *A. W. Carroll* **85**

OUR GEORGIA 3 b.f. Mind Games 121 – Our Krissie 65 (Kris 135) [2006 f5g p6g⁶ Dec 7] 800Y: first foal: dam staying maiden: last in maidens. *T. D. Barron* —

OUR GLENARD 7 b.g. Royal Applause 124 – Loucoum (FR) 93 (Iron Duke (FR) 122) [2006 50§: p12g p12g 11.9f* p16g p12g⁴ p12g² Dec 13] smallish, sturdy gelding: modest performer: won selling handicap at Brighton in August: stays 13f: acts on all-weather and firm going: tried tongue tied: sometimes slowly away: untrustworthy. *J. E. Long* **50 §**

OUR HERBIE 2 b.g. (Apr 16) Tobougg (IRE) 125 – Trevillari (USA) (Riverman **83**
(USA) 131) [2006 6f p7.1g² 7m⁵ 8g⁶ p7g⁵ 7d* 8g p7.1g⁴ p8g⁶ Nov 13] 28,000Y: half-
brother to several winners, including smart French/US performer up to 1m Tsigane and
3-y-o Armada (both by Anabaa): dam, French maiden sister to Prix Saint-Alary winner
Treble, out of half-sister to Triptych: fairly useful performer: won nursery at Lingfield in
September: should stay 1m: acts on polytrack and good to soft ground: gelded after final
start. *J. W. Hills*

OUR KES (IRE) 4 gr.f. Revoque (IRE) 122 – Gracious Gretclo 54 (Common Grounds **–**
118) [2006 –, a80: 8f a6.5f p9.5g p9.5g³ p9.5g⁶ p9.5g⁵ Dec 22] strong, lengthy filly: fair **a75**
performer nowadays: successful for current trainer at 2/3 yrs: left Cathal Lynch in USA
after second start in 2006: stays 9.5f: acts on polytrack/dirt, probably on good to firm
going: tried blinkered. *P. Howling*

OUR LITTLE SECRET (IRE) 4 ch.f. Rossini (USA) 118 – Sports Post Lady (IRE) **76**
72 (M Double M (USA)) [2006 62: 5d* 5g* 5f³ 5f 5m⁵ 5s³ 5s² 5g³ p5.1g Oct 14] leggy
filly: fair performer: won at Ripon (apprentices) in April and Catterick in May: raced only
at 5f: acts on polytrack, firm and soft going: tried in cheekpieces: front runner. *A. Berry*

OUR MARY (IRE) 3 b.f. Mujadil (USA) 119 – Desert Gem 87 (Green Desert (USA) **55**
127) [2006 62: 6m 6f³ 7f g f6g 6f 5.9g⁴ 6m² 7.1m⁶ 8s 7d Oct 10] strong, lengthy filly:
modest maiden handicapper: should stay 7f: acts on fibresand and firm going: tongue tied
last 4 outings. *Robert Gray*

OUR MONA (USA) 2 b.f. (Apr 16) Diesis 133 – Buckeye Gal (USA) (Good Counsel **–**
(USA)) [2006 5.1m Aug 25] $65,000Y: closely related to 5.5f (in France at 2 yrs) and 8.5f
(in USA) winner Filha Do Ar (by Trempolino) and half-sister to several winners, notably very smart French/US performer up to 1½m River Bay (by Irish River): dam stakes
winner up to 9f in USA: 5/1, last in maiden at Bath: sold 41,000 gns. *M. R. Channon*

OUR MONOGRAM 10 b.g. Deploy 131 – Darling Splodge (Elegant Air 119) [2006 **82**
77: p16g 18m* 18m² 16.1m² 21m 16.2m 17.2m Sep 25] big, strong gelding: fairly
useful handicapper: won at Chepstow in June: stays 19f: acts on firm and good to soft
going (well held only outing on all-weather): front runner/races prominently: game.
R. M. Beckett

OUR PUTRA 3 b.g. King's Best (USA) 132 – Prima Volta 80 (Primo Dominie 121) **89**
[2006 6d³ 8.3d* p8g² p8g 8.3g 8.1g Sep 22] 52,000Y: fifth foal: half-brother to useful 5f
(at 2 yrs) to 1m winner Bouncing Bowdler (by Mujadil): dam 6f (at 2 yrs) and 9f winner:
fairly useful performer: won maiden at Windsor in June: good second in handicap at
Kempton next time: well below form last 2 outings (reportedly had irregular heartbeat
first occasion): stays 8.3f: acts on polytrack and good to soft going: often tongue tied.
M. A. Jarvis

OUR RUBY 2 b.f. (Mar 18) Diktat 126 – Almost Amber (USA) 88 (Mt Livermore **77**
(USA)) [2006 5g⁶ 6d 7g 6g* Aug 30] 14,000Y: fourth foal: sister to fairly useful 2004
2-y-o 6f winner Little Dalham, later 7f winner in South Africa: dam, 2-y-o 5f winner,
became temperamental: fair form: improvement to win maiden at Leicester: will prove
best up to 7f. *P. W. Chapple-Hyam*

OUR SERENDIPITY 3 ch.f. Presidium 124 – Berl's Gift 44 (Prince Sabo 123) [2006 **–**
58: 8m 8d 7f 7.9m 8.1m Aug 10] tall filly: maiden: no form in 2006. *K. G. Reveley*

OUR SHEILA 3 ch.f. Bahamian Bounty 116 – Shifting Mist 76 (Night Shift (USA)) **82**
[2006 75: 7m³ 6d² 6g* 6f* 6f* 5.9m⁶ 6m Jul 24] leggy filly: fairly useful performer: won
maiden at Catterick in May, and handicaps there and Redcar in June, and Carlisle in
July: refused to go to post and led down, well below form final outing (hung throughout): should prove best at 5f/6f: acts on firm and good to soft going: sold 48,000 gns in
November. *B. Smart*

OURS (IRE) 3 b.g. Mark of Esteem (IRE) 137 – Ellebanna 69 (Tina's Pet 121) [2006 **68**
68: 6.1d 7f² 7m⁶ 7.2f³ 7.9g³ 8g p8.6g⁴ p7.1m² p7.1m* Nov 21] strong, close-coupled
gelding: fair performer: won maiden at Wolverhampton in November: barely stays 1m:
acts on polytrack and firm going: in cheekpieces (hinted at temperament) fourth start,
blinkered last 2. *J. D. Bethell*

OUR SUSIE (IRE) 2 b.f. (Jan 29) Bold Fact (USA) 116 – Paris Model (IRE) (Thatch- **60**
ing 131) [2006 5s⁵ 5g³ p5.1g³ p5g⁶ May 8] €3,000Y: neat filly: sixth foal: half-sister to 2
winners, including 7-y-o French Mannequin: dam Irish 5f winner: modest maiden: twice
placed in early season: raced at 5f: dead. *M. D. I. Usher*

OUR TEDDY (IRE) 6 ch.g. Grand Lodge (USA) 125 – Lady Windley (Baillamont **91**
(USA) 124) [2006 84: 10m 10f⁵ 9.9f* 12m* 12d⁶ 12m* 11.7m 11.7f⁴ 12m Sep 16] sturdy,

lengthy gelding: fairly useful handicapper: won at Beverley and Salisbury in July and Newmarket in August: stays 1½m: acts on polytrack, firm and good to soft going: tried in headgear. *P. A. Blockley*

OUR TOY SOLDIER 2 b.g. (Mar 19) Forzando 122 – The Wild Widow 84 (Saddlers' **62 §** Hall (IRE) 126) [2006 5v⁶ 5d³ 5g f6g 6f² 5m Jul 10] quite good-topped gelding: modest maiden: placed at Beverley and Hamilton (flashed tail): effective at 5f/6f: acts on firm and good to soft going: temperamental. *B. Smart*

OUT AFTER DARK 5 b.g. Cadeaux Genereux 131 – Midnight Shift (IRE) 73 (Night **110** Shift (USA)) [2006 112: 6g 5g³ 5d 6m 6m 6d⁶ 6s³ Oct 7] strong, useful-looking gelding: has a quick action: smart performer: creditable efforts in minor event at Beverley (third to Corridor Creeper), and in handicaps at Ayr (sixth behind Fonthill Road in Ayr Gold Cup) and York (third to Rising Shadow in valuable event): effective at 5f to 6.5f: acts on firm and soft going: in cheekpieces/blinkers nowadays: sometimes looks ungainly. *C. G. Cox*

OUTER HEBRIDES 5 b.g. Efisio 120 – Reuval 102 (Sharpen Up 127) [2006 89: **76** p7.1g p7g² p7g⁶ p8.6g⁶ p8g⁶ 8s p7g³ p7g² p8g³ p7g 7m⁵ p7g² p8g⁵ p8g 6g³ 7g⁴ p7g² 8d³ **a90** p7g⁶ p7g⁶ p7g³ Dec 4] sturdy gelding: has a round action: fairly useful performer, better on all-weather than turf: creditable efforts when runner-up in handicaps in 2006: left Stef Liddiard after fifteenth start, J. Boyle (returned to former trainer) before final one: stays easy 8.6f: acts on all-weather, firm and good to soft going: usually visored/tongue tied, effective when not: tried in cheekpieces. *Stef Liddiard*

OUT FOR A STROLL 7 b.g. Zamindar (USA) 116 – The Jotter 99 (Night Shift **71** (USA)) [2006 79: p8g p7.1g p8.6g⁶ p7.1g 7m p8g⁵ 8d p7.1g 7m 8f* p8g⁴ 7.6m* 8.1f³ 8.5d⁴ p8g⁶ p9.5g Dec 2] sturdy, deep-girthed gelding: fair handicapper: won at Brighton and Chester (apprentices) in July: best at 7f/1m: acts on polytrack, firm and good to soft going: tough. *S. C. Williams*

OUTLOOK 3 ch.c. Observatory (USA) 131 – Area Girl 76 (Jareer (USA) 115) [2006 **82** 72, a82: f7g⁴ p7g⁵ p10g p8.6g* f7g³ p8.6g* 7v Nov 5] close-coupled colt: fairly useful performer: won claimer at Wolverhampton in February and handicap there in March: left N. Littmoden before final start: stays 8.6f: acts on all-weather, raced only on good/ good to soft going on turf: blinkered: not entirely straightforward. *J. L. Eyre, Spain*

OUT OF INDIA 4 b.f. Marju (IRE) 127 – Tide of Fortune (Soviet Star (USA) 128) **78** [2006 78: f8g² f7g p7.1g 7d 6.9f⁵ Jul 21] leggy filly: fair handicapper: stays 8.6f: acts on all-weather and firm going. *B. Smart*

OUT OF THIS WAY 3 b.c. Spectrum (IRE) 126 – Pirouette 114 (Sadler's Wells (USA) **61** 132) [2006 p9.5g p9.5g⁵ p9.5g⁵ f11g p12.2g Dec 18] modest maiden: stays 9.5f: acts on polytrack: tried tongue tied. *I. A. Wood*

OUT OF TOWN 2 ch.g. (Feb 13) Namid 128 – Superstore (USA) (Blushing Groom **–** (FR) 131) [2006 f8g Dec 2] 50/1, showed nothing in maiden at Southwell. *Ronald Thompson*

OUTRAGEOUS FLIRT (IRE) 4 b.f. Indian Lodge (IRE) 127 – Sofia Aurora (USA) **58** (Chief Honcho (USA)) [2006 59: f7g⁵ 6m* 7.1f⁶ 7m 6m 7.2m⁴ 6g⁶ 6.9m 6s² 7m³ 10.5g³ Dec 17] sturdy filly: modest handicapper: won at Hamilton (amateurs) in June: sold from A. Dickman 5,000 gns before final start: effective at 6f to 10.5f: acts on polytrack, firm and soft going. *T. Betegon, Spain*

OVERDRAWN (IRE) 5 b.g. Daggers Drawn (USA) 114 – In Denial (IRE) (Mael- **53** strom Lake 118) [2006 64: p7g f12g p10g⁶ Nov 27] leggy, quite good-topped gelding: modest performer nowadays: seems to stay 9.8f: acts on all-weather, good to firm and good to soft going: often blinkered, tongue tied last 3 outings. *A. J. McCabe*

OVER ICE 3 b.f. Mister Baileys 123 – Oublier L'Ennui (FR) 79 (Bellman (FR) 123) **70** [2006 7.1g⁴ 8g⁶ p10g 8.1m⁵ 10.2m³ Sep 25] 1,800Y: close-coupled filly: half-sister to several winners, including fairly useful 6f winner (including at 2 yrs) Shudder (by Distant Relative): dam, maiden on Flat who probably stayed 1½m, winning hurdler/chaser: fair maiden: stays 1¼m: acts on good to firm going. *Miss K. M. George*

OVERJOY WAY 4 b.f. Cadeaux Genereux 131 – May Light 62 (Midyan (USA) 124) **58** [2006 67: p8g p8g⁴ p10g⁵ 8.1s⁴ May 29] tall filly: just modest maiden in 2006: stays easy 1¼m: acts on polytrack and good to soft going: blinkered last 3 starts: sent to Greece. *P. R. Chamings*

OVERLOOK 3 b.f. Generous (IRE) 139 – Spurned (USA) 91 (Robellino (USA) 127) **60** [2006 59: p12g⁴ 11.6f 14m 16.2m³ 13.1m Sep 4] big, close-coupled filly: modest maiden:

stays 2m: probably acts on firm and good to soft going: visored last 2 starts: sold 70,000 gns. *A. M. Balding*

OVERLORD WAY (GR) 4 br.g. Tony Galvin (GR) – Fortunate Way (GR) (Wadood (USA) 97) [2006 85: p7g p8g p8g⁶ p12.2f² p12g Sep 27] fairly useful handicapper: gelded, good second at Wolverhampton penultimate outing: stays 1½m: raced only on polytrack: returned to Greece. *P. R. Chamings* **84**

OVERRULE (USA) 2 b.c. (Feb 17) Diesis 133 – Her Own Way (USA) 87 (Danzig (USA)) [2006 8g Sep 27] $60,000F, $190,000Y: first foal: dam, lightly-raced maiden, closely related to useful Irish performer up to 1m Sheffield: 5/2 but very green (always behind) in maiden at Newcastle: should do better. *J. Noseda* **– p**

OVERSTAYED (IRE) 3 ch.g. Titus Livius (FR) 115 – Look Nonchalant (IRE) 61 (Fayruz 116) [2006 89: 5g⁴ 6d⁶ May 17] strong, close-coupled gelding: fairly useful performer: better effort in handicaps in 2006 when fourth at Thirsk: best form at 5f: acts on heavy and good to firm going. *P. A. Blockley* **91**

OVERSTRAND (IRE) 7 b.g. In The Wings 128 – Vaison La Romaine 100 (Arctic Tern (USA) 126) [2006 69: 20s² 18m³ 18m⁶ 16.2f Jul 8] lengthy gelding: fair handicapper on Flat: stays 2½m: acts on polytrack, firm and soft going: blinkered final start at 6 yrs: sold 10,000 gns in October, joined Dr R. D. P. Newland: useful hurdler, winner in November/December. *Robert Gray* **68**

OVER TIPSY 4 b.g. Tipsy Creek (USA) 115 – Over Keen 58 (Keen 116) [2006 7.6g 10.2m⁶ 9g Sep 12] poor maiden. *R. Hannon* **40**

OVER TO YOU BERT 7 b.g. Overbury (IRE) 116 – Silvers Era 72 (Balidar 133) [2006 45: p8g Nov 6] poor performer: well held only outing in 2006: tried in cheekpieces/visor at 4 yrs. *R. J. Hodges* **–**

OVERTURN (IRE) 2 b.c. (Apr 22) Barathea (IRE) 127 – Kristal Bridge 75 (Kris 135) [2006 7m⁵ 7.1m* 8s⁴ Oct 7] fifth foal: closely related to fairly useful 11.6f/1¾m winner Palamedes (by Sadler's Wells) and half-brother to 4-y-o Arbella: dam, maiden best around 1¼m, out of Nassau Stakes and Yorkshire Oaks winner Connaught Bridge: useful form: much improved from debut (green) when winning maiden at Sandown in August by 3 lengths from Murbek: 8/1 and tongue tied, took time to settle then found little (testing conditions) when 15 lengths fourth of 8 to Caldra in Autumn Stakes at Ascot: should be suited by 1m/1¼m. *W. R. Swinburn* **96**

OVERWING (IRE) 3 b.f. Fasliyev (USA) 120 – Sierva (GER) (Darshaan 133) [2006 73: p5g⁵ 5m⁴ 5.3m⁴ 5m⁴ 5m³ 5g⁴ 6f⁶ 5.1f* 5d² 6d* 6d p5g⁵ p5g⁴ Nov 5] leggy filly: fairly useful handicapper: left R. Hannon after reappearance: won at Bath and Epsom in August: good efforts last 2 starts: effective at 5f/6f: acts on polytrack, firm and good to soft going: sometimes makes running: signs of temperament. *R. M. H. Cowell* **84**

OWED 4 b.g. Lujain (USA) 119 – Nightingale (Night Shift (USA)) [2006 –, a71: f6g* f8g f6g⁴ f6g f6g f6g p7.1g Mar 25] good-topped gelding: fairly useful on all-weather: won handicap at Southwell in January: well below form last 4 starts, leaving Robert Gray before final one: effective at 6f/7f: acts on all-weather, lightly raced on turf (modest at 2 yrs): tongue tied: hung left/swished tail for last 3 wins. *B. Ellison* **a81 d**

OWNERS BISCUITS 3 gr.f. Diktat 126 – Delta Tempo (IRE) (Bluebird (USA) 125) [2006 49: 9.8d 10.2m p12g f8m⁵ p8g* Nov 6] leggy filly: modest performer: won banded race at Kempton in November: stays easy 1m: acts on polytrack: blinkered last 2 starts: sold 3,500 gns, sent to Sweden. *M. Johnston* **63**

P

PAB SPECIAL (IRE) 3 b.g. City On A Hill (USA) 114 – Tinos Island (IRE) (Alzao (USA) 117) [2006 73: p7.1g² p8g⁴ p8g³ p7g⁶ 7m⁵ 7.2d⁶ 7.1g³ 8.1f⁴ 8d⁴ 8s* 8m⁵ 9.1v⁶ p8.6g² Oct 29] good-topped gelding: fair performer: reportedly cracked withers and off 6 months after second outing at 2 yrs: won maiden at Ripon in August: stays 8.6f: acts on polytrack, firm and soft going: visored (reportedly finished lame) fourth outing: consistent. *K. R. Burke* **78**

PACEMAN (USA) 2 b.c. (Feb 26) Diesis 133 – Innes (USA) (A P Indy (USA) 131) [2006 6g⁵ 7d⁴ 8g* 8g Oct 12] lengthy, quite good-topped colt: third foal: half-brother to useful French 7.5f (at 2 yrs)/1m winner Melanosporum (by Royal Anthem): dam unraced **82**

daughter of smart Irish/US 1m/1¼m performer Kostroma: fairly useful performer: won maiden at Yarmouth in September: mid-field in well-contested nursery at Newmarket: stays 1m: raced on good/good to soft going. *R. Hannon*

PACE SHOT (IRE) 4 b.g. Montjeu (IRE) 137 – Pacific Grove 89 (Persian Bold 123) **61**
[2006 83: p12g⁶ Feb 15] good-bodied gelding: lightly-raced maiden on Flat, modest form only outing in 2006: barely stays 1½m: acts on polytrack: useful hurdler. *G. L. Moore*

PACE TELECOM FLYER (IRE) 2 b.c. (Apr 13) Fath (USA) 116 – Contravene **56**
(IRE) 64 (Contract Law (USA) 108) [2006 5.7g 7m⁵ 7d 8.1m 7.6f⁶ 8g Oct 13] modest maiden: stays 1m: acts on firm going: sold 2,500 gns, sent to Germany. *J. W. Hills*

PACHELLO (IRE) 4 b.g. Priolo (USA) 127 – Most Charming (FR) (Darshaan 133) **79**
[2006 p6g 6s 5m 7g 6g⁴ 6f 6f 5m 6m Sep 19] fair-topped gelding: fair performer: won minor event at Maisons-Laffitte in 2005 (left A. Fabre after final 3-y-o start): form in Britain only when fourth in handicap at Epsom: had form at 1m, likely to be best at 5f/6f: acts on good to firm going: tried tongue tied. *J. M. Bradley*

PACIFIC PRIDE 3 b.g. Compton Place 125 – Only Yours 113 (Aragon 118) [2006 **105**
108: 6m³ 7s⁵ 7m 6d² 7m⁴ 6d⁶ 6s Oct 7] big, strong gelding: useful performer: best effort in 2006 when neck second to Knot In Wood in handicap at York fourth start: below form after: speedy, and likely to prove best at 5f/6f: acts on good to firm and good to soft going: blinkered fourth/fifth starts, visored sixth outing: sold 100,000 gns, and gelded.
J. Howard Johnson

PACKERS HILL (IRE) 2 b.c. (Apr 9) Mull of Kintyre (USA) 114 – Head For The **70**
Stars (IRE) (Head For Heights 125) [2006 5.9g 6m 8.5g⁴ 7.5m² 7g Sep 27] 5,000F: good-topped colt: eighth foal: half-brother to 3 winners, including Irish 8.5f/9f winner In Other Words (by Lake Coniston): dam of little account: fair maiden: brought down second start: stays 8.5f. *G. A. Swinbank*

PACOLET (IRE) 7 b.g. Revoque (IRE) 122 – Elupa (IRE) 98 (Mtoto 134) [2006 77: **81**
14g² 16g* 16m³ 20m 16d 16g⁶ 16s Oct 8] strong gelding: fairly useful handicapper: won at Clonmel in May: stays 2m (seemed not to stay 2½m in Ascot Stakes): acts on good to firm going. *P. J. Flynn, Ireland*

PACTOLOS WAY 3 b.g. Docksider (USA) 124 – Arietta's Way (IRE) 71 (Darshaan **75**
133) [2006 63: p8.6g p8g f8g⁵ p10g⁶ p10g⁵ p10g² p9.5g* p10g Oct 6] close-coupled gelding: fair performer: won maiden at Wolverhampton in August: stays easy 1¼m: acts on polytrack. *P. R. Chamings*

PADDY MOON 3 b.g. Lujain (USA) 119 – Tara Moon (Pivotal 124) [2006 58: 8.2d **44**
8.2m 7.2v f8g⁵ Jul 11] tall gelding: poor maiden: seems to stay 1m: acts on fibresand and soft ground. *J. G. Given*

PADDY'S PLACE 3 b.f. Compton Place 125 – Lamarita 92§ (Emarati (USA) **–**
74) [2006 50: p7g 7f May 4] maiden: well held in 2006. *M. Blanshard*

PADDY'S TERN 4 b.g. Fraam 114 – Great Tern 59 (Simply Great (FR) 122) [2006 **–**
61: f12g 17.2f Jun 11] leggy gelding: modest maiden at 3 yrs: well held in 2006.
N. M. Babbage

PADDYWACK (IRE) 9 b.g. Bigstone (IRE) 126 – Millie's Return (IRE) 71 (Ballad **71**
Rock 122) [2006 65: 5.9m⁶ 5f* 7.1g⁵ 6m² 5f* 5f² 5d* 6g 5m⁶ 5g⁵ 6m 6m 5m² 5m 5d⁴ 5g⁶ p5.1m* 6.1s Oct 25] small gelding: fair handicapper: won at Beverley in June (apprentices), July and August and Wolverhampton in October: effective at 5f/6f: acts on all-weather and any turf going: blinkered: often slowly away. *D. W. Chapman*

PADRE NOSTRO (IRE) 7 ch.g. Grand Lodge (USA) 125 – Meglio Che Posso (IRE) **65**
93 (Try My Best (USA) 130) [2006 65: f12g* f14g f11g³ f12g⁴ f14g 10s 11.8d 12.1g* 10m² 10m 12.1m 11.8g 10m⁶ 12d⁶ 13.8s f14g⁴ f14g f11g* Dec 28] sturdy ex-Irish gelding: fair performer: won handicaps at Southwell in January and Chepstow in July and banded race at Southwell in December: stays 13f: acts on fibresand, firm and good to soft going. *J. R. Holt*

PAGAN CREST 3 ch.g. Indian Ridge 123 – Maria Theresa (Primo Dominie 121) [2006 **79**
65: 8.3g⁵ 8.2g 8m⁴ 10f² 10m* 10.1m⁵ 10m* 9m Aug 27] quite good-topped gelding: good walker: has a moderate, quick action: fair handicapper: won at Goodwood and Leicester in June and Sandown in August: stays 1¼m: acts on firm going: blinkered (raced too freely) sixth start: tricky ride (tends to hang left). *Mrs A. J. Perrett*

PAGAN GAME (IRE) 4 b.f. Montjeu (USA) 137 – Pagan Rhythm (USA) (Joanie's **–**
Chief (USA)) [2006 p12.2g Mar 3] €75,000Y: fifth foal: closely related to French 6f (at 2 yrs)/7f winner Salut L'Artiste (by Theatre Critic) and half-sister to winner in USA by

Southern Halo: dam won in USA: well held in maidens at Lyon-Parilly (for J. Hammond in 2005) and Wolverhampton. *D. Marnane, Ireland*

PAGAN ISLAND 3 b.c. Polish Precedent (USA) 131 – Dodo (IRE) 90 (Alzao (USA) – 117) [2006 8.3g 8.1m 8.2m Sep 15] sturdy, lengthy colt: well held in maidens. *J. A. R. Toller*

PAGANO (IRE) 3 b.g. Night Shift (USA) – Frippet (IRE) 87 (Ela-Mana-Mou 132) **79** [2006 8.3f⁵ 8.3g p8.6g⁴ p10g⁶ p12g* p12.2s* Dec 14] €26,000Y: second foal: dam, 11f winner, out of half-sister to St Leger winner Snurge: fair performer: upped in trip, won handicaps at Kempton and Wolverhampton (tended to hang left) in December: stays 1½m: acts on polytrack. *W. R. Swinburn*

PAGAN PRINCE 9 br.g. Primo Dominie 121 – Mory Kante (USA) (Icecapade (USA)) [2006 f8g p10g Jan 25] leggy gelding: fairly useful performer at best: trained by P. Haley in Spain in 2005, winning twice at Mijas: well held in handicaps in 2006: stays 1½m: acts on fibresand/sand, firm and soft going: usually waited with. *J. Gallagher*

PAGAN RULES (IRE) 2 b.g. (Feb 18) Desert Prince (IRE) 130 – Fernanda 95 (Be My **64** Chief (USA) 122) [2006 6g⁶ 7g 7m 8m Sep 4] modest maiden: well held in nursery (gelded after): should stay 1m. *Mrs A. J. Perrett*

PAGAN STARPRINCESS 2 b.f. (Apr 4) Robertico 111 – Pagan Star (Carlitin 50) **61 p** [2006 7m⁴ Aug 8] second reported foal: dam unraced: 66/1, strong-finishing fourth to Coconut Queen in maiden at Catterick: open to improvement. *G. M. Moore*

PAGAN SWORD 4 ch.g. Selkirk (USA) 129 – Vanessa Bell (IRE) (Lahib (USA) 129) **95** [2006 103: 10g 12m 9.9m⁶ 10.5m⁵ 10g Aug 26] tall, well-made gelding: useful handicapper: best efforts in 2006 when sixth to Crosspeace at Goodwood and fifth to Dansili Dancer at Haydock: should stay 1½m: acts on polytrack, firm and good to soft going: twice visored, including when successful: tricky ride. *Mrs A. J. Perrett*

PAIN IN THE NECK (IRE) 3 br.g. Orpen (USA) 116 – Ravishing (IRE) 88 (Big- **61** stone (IRE) 126) [2006 p7g p7.1m³ p6g⁵ Nov 28] modest form in maidens: should be as effective at 6f as 7f. *M. J. Wallace*

PAINT FOR PLEASURE (IRE) 2 ch.g. (Jan 30) Namid 128 – Kyra Crown (IRE) **59** (Astronef 116) [2006 6m⁶ Jun 9] €16,000F, €28,000Y: big, useful-looking gelding: half-brother to several winners, including fairly useful 5f winner (including at 2 yrs) Sir Ernest (by Daggers Drawn) and French 10.5f winner Croga Crown (by Mukaddamah): dam French 7-y-o 7.5f winner: 10/1, needed experience when sixth to Alzerra in maiden at Haydock (reportedly returned lame). *P. W. Chapple-Hyam*

PAINT THE LILY (IRE) 5 b.m. Barathea (IRE) 127 – Chocolate Box 70 (Most Wel- **–** come 131) [2006 48d: 10g 13f 16m Jul 10] maiden: no form in 2006: tried visored/in cheekpieces. *F. Watson*

PAIRUMANI PRINCESS (IRE) 2 b.f. (Apr 20) Pairumani Star (IRE) 110 – Persian **75 p** Fantasy 94 (Persian Bold 123) [2006 7.6f⁶ 8.2g⁴ p8g* Oct 23] close-coupled filly: half-sister to 3 winners, including smart 1m to 11.5f winner Persian Lightning (by Sri Pekan) and useful 1¾m/2m winner Height of Fantasy (by Shirley Heights): dam 1½m winner who stayed 2m: progressive form in maidens, won at Lingfield despite barely adequate test: capable of better still at 1¼m+. *E. A. L. Dunlop*

PAIRUMANI'S GIRL (IRE) 3 b.f. Pairumani Star (IRE) 110 – Persian Fantasia **–** (Alzao (USA) 117) [2006 77: 8.1d 8.2g Jun 7] smallish, rather leggy filly: fair maiden at 2 yrs: well held in handicaps in 2006: bred to be suited by 1¼m/1½m. *J. L. Dunlop*

PAJADA 2 b.f. (Apr 15) Bertolini (USA) 125 – Last Ambition (IRE) 29 (Cadeaux Gene- **–** reux 131) [2006 6s p7g p7g Nov 25] sixth foal: half-sister to 3 winners, including 1m/9.7f winner Hawkley (by Arctic Tern) and 3-y-o Helen Wood: dam, maiden, seemed best at 5f/6f: well held in maidens. *M. D. I. Usher*

PALACE EPISODE (USA) 3 br.c. Machiavellian (USA) 123 – Palace Weekend **–** (USA) (Seattle Dancer (USA) 119) [2006 115: 10.4s⁶ May 18] rather leggy, close-coupled colt: has a quick action: smart winner for K. Ryan at 2 yrs, including in Racing Post Trophy at Doncaster: tailed-off last behind Septimus in Dante Stakes at York (all but pulled up) only outing in 2006: reportedly weak and lost some condition after: should stay 1¼m: acts on soft going, winner on good to firm: flashed tail under whip last 2 starts in 2005, but is game. *Saeed bin Suroor*

PALACE WALK (FR) 4 b.g. Sinndar (IRE) 134 – Page Bleue (Sadler's Wells (USA) **65** 132) [2006 –: 12f² 12.6m⁴ 12f Jun 30] quite good-topped gelding: fair maiden on Flat: should stay 1¾m: acts on firm going: races prominently: fair hurdler/winning chaser. *B. G. Powell*

PALAIS POLAIRE 4 ch.f. Polar Falcon (USA) 126 – Palace Street (USA) 103 **61**
(Secreto (USA) 128) [2006 –: p6g⁵ 7m⁴ 6.1d 7m⁴ 7g³ 8.3g⁴ f6g³ f7g Dec 2] rather leggy
filly: modest maiden: stays 7f: acts on all-weather, good to firm and good to soft ground.
J. A. Geake

PALAMOUN 2 b.c. (Apr 2) Mtoto 134 – Princess Minnie (Mistertopogigo (IRE) 118 **86**
[2006 8g 8g³ 7g² Oct 12] 32,000Y: strong, close-coupled colt: third foal: dam unraced
half-sister to very smart 1m/1¼m performer Supreme Leader out of half-sister to dam of
Pebbles: fairly useful form when placed in maidens at Newmarket, third to Asperity and
second to Perfect Star: travels strongly, will prove best up to 1m: refused to enter stall
intended debut. *B. W. Hills*

PALATINATE (FR) 4 br.g. Desert Prince (IRE) 130 – Dead Certain 123§ (Absalom –
128) [2006 –: 10f 8.3f 7f 8.1m Aug 11] strong, sturdy gelding: good walker: fairly useful
performer at 2 yrs: lightly raced and well held since: tried tongue tied/visored. *C. G. Cox*

PALM DESERT (IRE) 3 b.g. Spectrum (IRE) 126 – Dixieline City (USA) (Dixieland –
Band (USA)) [2006 p7.1g p9.5g Jan 27] well held in maidens at Wolverhampton.
M. H. Tompkins

PALMETTO POINT 2 ch.c. (May 19) Bahamian Bounty 116 – Forum 86 (Lion –
Cavern (USA) 117) [2006 7s p7g⁶ p7g Oct 26] strong colt: green (slowly away) and no
threat in maidens, all in October. *H. Morrison*

PALMIRO 2 ch.g. (Feb 12) Medicean 128 – Tolyatti (Green Desert (USA) 127) [2006 –
p7g p7g Sep 6] well held in maidens (gelded in between). *W. J. Haggas*

PALMISTRY 3 br.g. Lend A Hand 124 – Divina Mia 66 (Dowsing (USA) 124) [2006 **59**
6d 6.1d³ Oct 13] lengthy gelding: much better effort in maidens when 3¼ lengths third to
Efisio Princess at Warwick: sold 9,000 gns. *A. M. Balding*

PALOMAR (USA) 4 b. or br.g. Chester House (USA) 123 – Ball Gown (USA) (Silver **110**
Hawk (USA) 123) [2006 105: 12m² 12m² 16d 12m³ 13.9f⁴ 10.4d⁴ 10m 12d Sep 24]
$160,000Y: tall, good-topped gelding: third foal: half-brother to 1½m winner Hayhaat
(by Irish River) and a winner in USA by Diesis: dam related to top-class
1982 2-y-o 7f winner Gorytus: smart performer: won newcomers race at Maisons-Laffitte
in 2005 for P. Bary in France (sold 320,000 gns and gelded): further improvement in 2006
(in frame in 5 of 8 starts), particularly good efforts when 3 lengths second to Admiral's
Cruise in minor event at Newmarket and ½-length third to Young Mick in Duke of Edinburgh Stakes (Handicap) at Ascot, second/fourth outings: has form at 2m, best efforts
around 1½m: acts on heavy and good to firm going: below form in cheekpieces last 2
starts: has worn earplugs: consistent: has joined N. Richards. *R. Charlton*

PALO VERDE 2 b.c. (Apr 20) Green Desert (USA) 127 – Aquaba (USA) (Damascus **86**
(USA)) [2006 6f³ 5m² 5g* 6.1g² 6d 6m⁴ 6s p6g* Oct 23] close-coupled colt: brother to 7f
winner Auvergne, closely related to 3 winners, including 5f winner (including at 2 yrs)
Millstream (by Dayjur) and 1995 2-y-o 6f winner Polska (by Danzig), both useful, and
half-brother to 2 winners: dam, 7f (including at 2 yrs) to 9f winner in USA, including
Grade 3 8.5f event: fairly useful performer: won maiden at Thirsk in August and minor
event at Lingfield (beat Espartano by ¾ length) in October: twice in frame in nurseries in
between: likely to stay 7f: acts on polytrack and firm going, below form on softer than
good: sold 18,000 gns. *M. Johnston*

PAMIR (IRE) 4 b.g. Namid 128 – Mijouter (IRE) (Coquelin (USA) 121) [2006 86: f6g **81**
p7g p8g p7.1g p7g 6g f7g⁶ 6.1d³ p6g 6d* 6.1s³ p5g² p6g⁵ p5g Dec 5] good-topped
gelding: fairly useful handicapper: won at Windsor in October: effective at 5f to 7f: acts
on polytrack and heavy going: tried in cheekpieces, blinkered nowadays: has carried head
high: effective held up or making running. *P. R. Chamings*

PAMPAMEE 4 b.f. Meqdaam (USA) – Running Row (FR) (Pampabird 124) [2006 –
p12.2g f11g Jan 29] half-sister to several winners: dam French 1m winner: well beaten in
maiden and seller. *M. Wellings*

PANFIELD BELLE (IRE) 5 b.m. Danetime (IRE) 121 – Make Hay (Nomination –
125) [2006 9g 5m Jul 26] lightly raced and no form. *R. Allan*

PANGO 7 ch.g. Bluegrass Prince (IRE) 110 – Riverine (Risk Me (FR) 127) [2006 107: **98**
7.5m⁴ 8m Feb 2] useful handicapper: much better effort at Nad Al Sheba in 2006 when
respectable 5 lengths fourth to Kandidate: eased as if amiss next time: probably best at 7f/
1m nowadays: acts on all-weather, firm and soft going: usually held up: formerly consistent. *H. Morrison*

PANGO'S LEGACY 2 ch.c. (Jan 26) Bertolini (USA) 125 – Sans Egale (FR) (Lash- **71**
kari 128) [2006 6f⁶ 6g² 6.1f⁵ 5g³ p6g 6d Oct 9] 22,000 2-y-o: fourth foal: dam, maiden

who stayed 1½m, half-sister to smart 1¼m performer Maidment: fair maiden: third to Abunai in nursery at Newmarket: will stay 1m: acts on firm going. *H. Morrison*

PANIC STATIONS 3 ch.f. Singspiel (IRE) 133 – Fiddle-Dee-Dee (IRE) (Mujtahid (USA) 118) [2006 p7g 8.2m⁵ 7m 7g² p8g⁴ p7.1g² p7g 8.2m² 8d⁴ p8.6m² p8g³ p8.6g* Nov 7] 42,000Y: fourth foal: sister to winner up to 11.5f in Belgium and half-sister to fairly useful 5f and (at 2 yrs) 6f winner Fiddle Me Blue (by Bluebird): dam unraced: fair performer: won handicap at Wolverhampton in November: will stay 1¼m: acts on polytrack, good to firm and good to soft going: consistent. *M. L. W. Bell* **77**

PANSHIR (FR) 5 ch.g. Unfuwain (USA) 131 – Jalcamin (IRE) (Jalmood (USA) 126) [2006 71d: f7g⁵ p6g 11.5m 8m⁵ 10.1m 8f⁶ 7f⁶ 7f 8m² 8d* 8m³ Aug 27] tall, leggy gelding: modest handicapper: left Julian Poulton after second start: won at Yarmouth in August: stays 1m: acts on good to firm and good to soft going: often races freely: usually waited with. *Mrs C. A. Dunnett* **62**

PANTOMIME PRINCE 3 b.g. Royal Applause 124 – Floppie (FR) (Law Society (USA) 130) [2006 71: p7.1g³ p8g 6f 6f⁶ p6g p8.6g Nov 25] maiden: just modest at best in 2006: left R. Hannon after reappearance: should stay 1m: acts on good to firm going, probably on polytrack: wore cheekpieces 3 of last 4 starts. *C. A. Dwyer* **52**

PAPAL BULL 3 b.c. Montjeu (IRE) 137 – Mialuna (Zafonic (USA) 130) [2006 87p: 10g* 12.3f* 12m 12m* 12d 12m⁵ Sep 10] **120**

    A four-way photo to the Derby could so easily have involved five horses. Hala Bek might be remembered best as the unlucky horse of the race after swerving away his chance inside the final furlong, but 11/1-shot Papal Bull had a hard-luck tale of his own, and would probably have bustled up the principals with a clear run. Papal Bull's problems were not so much of his own making as Hala Bek's. Dropped out in rear by Robert Winston, having his first ride in the race, Papal Bull had taken hold of his bridle and was making eye-catching headway when stopped in his tracks towards the rail over two furlongs out, eased off after pursuit became hopeless, finishing tenth of eighteen, over eight lengths behind the winner.

    Papal Bull was supplemented for the Derby at a cost of £75,000 after getting the better of the subsequent Derby second Dragon Dancer in the MBNA Europe

King Edward VII Stakes, Royal Ascot—Papal Bull (noseband) gains quick compensation for poor luck in running in the Derby and takes the notable scalps of Red Rocks and Sixties Icon

Bank Chester Vase in May. Papal Bull was sent off a warm favourite after a ready success from Linas Selection in a handicap at Newmarket on his reappearance and, in a field of five at Chester, he looked a smart colt in the making, holding on by three quarters of a length. Papal Bull showed his quirks at Chester, starting slowly and then going in snatches before diving left as he hit the front inside the final furlong, but he did nothing untoward in adding to his tally in the King Edward VII Stakes at Royal Ascot on his first start after Epsom. One consolation of Papal Bull's performance at Epsom was that he didn't have a hard race and he was full of himself beforehand at Ascot. With prize money for the King Edward raised considerably in 2006, the race was particularly valuable for a Group 2, and Papal Bull more than recouped the cost of supplementing him for Epsom, starting favourite at 5/4 and getting the better of Red Rocks after a couple of slaps in the finish, holding on by a neck, with Sixties Icon, seventh at Epsom, two and a half lengths away third. Papal Bull was given a break afterwards, but he was below his best on his return, running poorly in the Great Voltigeur Stakes at York in August and coming only a respectable fifth of six in the Prix Niel at Longchamp the following month, beaten five and a quarter lengths by the winner Rail Link.

Papal Bull (b.c. 2003)	Montjeu (IRE) (b 1996)	Sadler's Wells (b 1981)	Northern Dancer
			Fairy Bridge
		Floripedes (b 1985)	Top Ville
			Toute City
	Mialuna (b 1997)	Zafonic (b 1990)	Gone West
			Zaizafon
		Mamaluna (ch 1986)	Roberto
			Kadesh

Mrs J. Magnier, Mr D. Smith & Mr M. Tabor's "Papal Bull"

Papal Bull, who made 20,000 guineas as a foal and 100,000 guineas as a yearling, is the best representative of the second crop of his sire Montjeu. It would have been amazing if Montjeu's second crop had come close to rivalling his exceptional first crop, which included Arc winner Hurricane Run, Derby winner Motivator and Scorpion, winner of the St Leger. All the same, the second crop did produce two other Royal Ascot winners in Mont Etoile, successful in the Ribblesdale Stakes, and Snoqualmie Boy, successful in a listed event at the meeting, as well as Mountain, another with smart form over middle distances. Papal Bull's dam Mialuna remained a maiden in Italy (and her only foal before Papal Bull, Octaluna, by Octagonal, failed to win in three starts in the French Provinces), but she was out of Mamaluna, a smart three-year-old, who won the Nassau Stakes for Guy Harwood after finishing fourth in the Oaks (promoted to third on Aliysa's disqualification). Mamaluna's best progeny was the smart Italian sprinter St Paul House, a prolific winner at Rome, where his successes included successive victories in the Premio Tudini and the Premio Umbria as a six- and seven-year-old. Papal Bull is unlikely to be around for so long, but he will be back in action as a four-year-old, when he should hold his own in pattern races, though penalties will make him none too easy to place successfully. A good-bodied sort, who should stay a mile and three quarters, he acts on firm ground and ran poorly on his one outing on good to soft. He has shown his quirks, including a high head carriage, but has proved generally reliable, winning four of his nine starts, his first victory coming in a seven-furlong maiden at Leicester as a two-year-old. *Sir Michael Stoute*

PAPARAAZI (IRE) 4 b.g. Victory Note (USA) 120 – Raazi 46 (My Generation 111) **79** [2006 79: p12g p10g6 10.3m6 8.9f2 9.2m2 9.9g6 10.5s3 9.2d2 9.5p5 p10g5 Dec 20] **a70** lengthy gelding: fair handicapper: barely stays 10.5f: acts on all-weather, firm and soft going: tried visored. *R. A. Fahey*

PAPEETE (GER) 5 b.m. Alzao (USA) 117 – Prairie Vela (Persian Bold 123) [2006 76: **72** p16g6 13.3m6 14m3 p12g6 12g 14m p16g4 14.1g p16g6 Sep 1] leggy, close-coupled mare: fair handicapper: stays easy 2m: acts on polytrack, firm and soft going: tried blinkered: found little final start: joined Mrs N. Smith. *Miss B. Sanders*

PAPER DOLL 4 ch.f. Mister Baileys 123 – Grand Coronet 66 (Grand Lodge (USA) **53** 125) [2006 56: f7g6 f7g3 p8g f8g p7.1g6 p8.8g6 g9.5g6 May 2] modest maiden: should stay 1¼m: raced only on all-weather: wears cheekpieces/blinkers. *B. P. J. Baugh*

PAPER MAITE 5 b.m. Komaite (USA) – Cliburnel News (IRE) 76 (Horage 124) [2006 **–** p6g f5g f8g f11g Dec 29] second foal: dam 6f (at 2 yrs) to 2m winner: no form. *S. R. Bowring*

PAPER TALK (USA) 4 gr.c. Unbridled's Song (USA) 125 – Journalist (IRE) 102 **104** (Night Shift (USA)) [2006 99: 7g 7g5 7m 7g* 8f 7d* 7d Sep 23] tall, useful-looking colt: has a quick action: useful handicapper: won at Newbury (by ½ length from Grizedale) in July and Newmarket (beat Compton's Eleven by short head) in August: effective at 7f/ 1m: acts on firm and good to soft going: reluctant to enter stall once at 3 yrs: joined I. Mohammed in UAE. *B. W. Hills*

PAPPAS IMAGE 2 b.g. (Apr 13) Arkadian Hero (USA) 123 – Fair Attempt (IRE) (Try **54** My Best (USA) 130) [2006 p7g p6g3 p5.1g4 Dec 22] modest form in maidens, blinkered when in frame at Wolverhampton. *A. J. McCabe*

PAPPAS RUBY (USA) 3 b.f. Red Ransom (USA) – Pappa Reale 104 (Indian Ridge **52** 123) [2006 –: 9m6 7.2v3 9m 8f 10m Jul 24] leggy, quite attractive filly: modest maiden: form only in handicap on second start: tried in cheekpieces. *J. S. Goldie*

PAPRADON 2 b.g. (Mar 12) Tobougg (IRE) 125 – Salvezza (IRE) 97 (Superpower 113) **–** [2006 6d p6g5 p6g6 Nov 22] little form in maidens. *J. R. Best*

PARADISE EXPECTED 3 ch.f. North Briton 67 – Phenomenon (Unfuwain (USA) **69** 131) [2006 51p: p8g* 10m p8g Oct 23] tall, unfurnished filly: fair performer, lightly raced: best effort when winning maiden at Lingfield in January: should stay 1¼m: acts on polytrack: sold 4,000 gns, joined C. Grant. *P. W. Chapple-Hyam*

PARADISE FLIGHT (IRE) 5 ch.m. In The Wings 128 – Aloft (IRE) (Ela-Mana- **70** Mou 132) [2006 76: 12d 16m3 18m 16.2f5 21m Aug 2] leggy mare: fair handicapper: stays 2½m: acts on polytrack, soft and firm going: has worn cheekpieces, blinkered nowadays. *K. A. Ryan*

Timeform Silver Salver (Cecil Frail), Haydock—
Paradise Isle shows herself to be better than ever at the age of five; Nidhaal is second

PARADISE ISLE 5 b.m. Bahamian Bounty 116 – Merry Rous 66 (Rousillon (USA) **112**
133) [2006 108: 6g* 5m 6f* 6f³ 6.1m 6m⁴ Sep 9] leggy, rather sparely-made mare: smart
performer: won listed races at Newmarket (by short head from Les Arcs) in April and
Haydock (best effort, beat Nidhaal by 1¼ lengths) in June: creditable fourth of 5 to Tax
Free in similar event at Goodwood final outing: best efforts at 6f: acts on firm and good to
soft going: tends to carry head high/swish tail, but races genuinely enough: ridden up with
pace nowadays. *C. F. Wall*

PARADISE STREET (IRE) 3 b.f. Machiavellian (USA) 123 – Tani (USA) (Theat- **69**
rical 128) [2006 –p: 10g 8m Jun 30] good-topped filly: fair maiden, lightly raced: should
stay 1½m. *J. R. Fanshawe*

PARADISE VALLEY 6 b.g. Groom Dancer (USA) 128 – Rose de Reve (IRE) (Per- **–**
sian Heights 129) [2006 –, a52: p13.9g Jan 4] good-bodied gelding: modest performer:
stays easy 1¾m: acts on all-weather and firm ground: tried visored/in cheekpieces:
tongue tied: possibly temperamental. *Stef Liddiard*

PARADISE WALK 2 b.f. (Feb 16) Sakhee (USA) 136 – Enclave (USA) (Woodman **68**
(USA) 126) [2006 7m 7s⁶ Oct 10] small, close-coupled filly: third foal: dam, ran twice in
France, half-sister to smart performer up to 1¼m Comfy: fair form in maidens at
Salisbury and Newbury (sixth to Hollow Ridge): will stay 1m. *R. Charlton*

PARAGUAY (USA) 3 b.c. Pivotal 124 – Grisonnante (FR) (Kaldoun (FR) 122) [2006 **86**
8g⁵ 8s³ 10m 9.9f 8g* 8.5f² 8.5g* 8m² 7m 8.1m 8g f8g⁴ p7g p8g⁵ p9.5g Dec 31] $80,000Y,
$200,000 2-y-o: smallish, rather leggy colt: eighth foal: half-brother to 3 winners abroad,
notably Breeders' Cup Filly & Mare Turf winner Starine (by Mendocino): dam French
maiden: fairly useful performer: left A. Fabre in France after debut: won claimer at Newmarket (left M. Channon) in June and handicap at Epsom in July: stays 8.5f: acts on
all-weather, firm and soft going: held up. *Miss V. Haigh*

PARA SIEMPRE 2 b.f. (Mar 5) Mujahid (USA) 125 – Miriam 59 (Forzando 122) **81 +**
[2006 6s⁶ 6d⁵ p6m⁵ p6g² f6g* Dec 23] 24,000Y: strong filly: closely related to 2 winners
by Emarati, including 8-y-o Viewforth, and half-sister to 3 winners, including 5-y-o Ivory
Lace: dam 5f winner, including at 2 yrs: fairly useful form: blinkered, much improved
when winning nursery at Southwell by 7 lengths: should stay 7f: acts on fibresand.
B. Smart

PARAZONE 3 b.c. Superior Premium 122 – Instinction (Never So Bold 135) [2006 59: **49**
p6g⁶ Jan 6] maiden: just poor form only outing in 2006: stays 7f: acts on polytrack: sold
4,000 gns, sent to Saudi Arabia. *E. J. O'Neill*

PARCHMENT (IRE) 4 ch.g. Singspiel (IRE) 133 – Hannalou (FR) 70 (Shareef **66**
Dancer (USA) 135) [2006 55: 7.5f 8d 10f³ 7.5f⁶ 9.9f² 9f² 9.9s⁴ 12m² 12.1m* 14.1m³
15.8m³ 15.8d Oct 3] smallish gelding: fair handicapper: won at Beverley in August: stays
1½m: acts on firm going: blinkered last 5 starts. *A. J. Lockwood*

PAR EXCELLENCE 3 gr.f. Wizard King 122 – Great Intent (Aragon 118) [2006 56: **55**
p5g p6g² p6g⁶ p7g 5.1g 6.1d f6g May 31] leggy filly: modest performer: stays 6f:
acts on polytrack, good to firm and good to soft going: usually tongue tied in 2005.
W. G. M. Turner

The Equema Partnership's "Paradise Isle"

PARIS BELL 4 gr.g. Paris House 123 – Warning Bell 88 (Bustino 136) [2006 86: 7d 6g* 6g³ 6s³ 6v⁶ 6f 6m 6f⁵ 6g 6d 6m* 6d³ 7s⁶ Oct 24] rather leggy gelding: fairly useful handicapper: won at Redcar in April and Southwell in September: stays 7f: acts on any turf going: tends to race freely: sometimes slowly away. *T. D. Easterby* — **86**

PARISETTE 4 b.f. Dansili 127 – Moulin Rouge 77 (Shareef Dancer (USA) 135) [2006 78: 8d p8.6g Oct 30] strong, good-topped filly: fair performer at 3 yrs: tongue tied, well beaten in handicaps in 2006: visored (raced too freely) final 3-y-o start. *A. J. Lidderdale* — **–**

PARIS HEIGHTS 4 gr.g. Paris House 123 – Petra Nova 51 (First Trump 118) [2006 59: 7.5f 8.5g 7g 8.5m 7.2g² Aug 21] quite good-topped gelding: modest performer: stays 1m: acts on firm and soft ground: tried visored/in cheekpieces. *R. M. Whitaker* — **60**

PARISIAN DREAM 2 b.c. (Apr 19) Sakhee (USA) 136 – Boojum 101 (Mujtahid (USA) 118) [2006 6s Sep 1] 30,000Y: fifth foal: half-brother to fairly useful 2001 2-y-o 6f winner Esenin (by Danehill): dam 2-y-o 6f/7f winner: 6/1, better than result (seventh to Makshoof) in maiden at Haydock, very slowly away: will progress. *B. W. Hills* — **56 p**

PARISIAN PLAYBOY 6 gr.g. Paris House 123 – Exordium (Exorbitant 81) [2006 59: f8g p9.5g⁶ p9.5g f8g 10m f8g Nov 21] tall gelding: poor performer: tried tongue tied/blinkered. *A. D. Brown* — **45**

PARISI PRINCESS 5 ch.m. Shaddad (USA) 75 – Crambella (IRE) 30 (Red Sunset 120) [2006 –, a43: 7.6f 7m⁵ 7g 7f⁵ 8m Aug 20] poor maiden: tried visored. *D. L. Williams* — **38**

PARIS POWER 3 b.g. Superpower 113 – Gables Turner (Paris House 123) [2006 –: p7g⁵ f8g² p7.1g p7.1g f7g³ f8g Mar 8] rather leggy gelding: poor maiden: stays 1m: acts on all-weather: visored/blinkered. *D. Morris* — **43**

PARK ESTEEM (IRE) 3 b.f. Singspiel (IRE) 133 – Park Special (Relkino 131) [2006 10s³ p12g² 12m Jun 22] quite good-topped filly: closely related to very smart 6f (at 2 yrs) — **99**

to 1½m winner Central Park, who stayed 2m, and smart 1¼m/1½m (Lancashire Oaks) winner Mellow Park (both by In The Wings) and half-sister to several winners, including useful 6f (at 2 yrs, including Lowther Stakes) and 1¼m winner Velvet Moon (by Shaadi), herself dam of Moon Ballad: dam Irish 1¼m winner: useful form: placed in listed race at Newmarket (green, 6 lengths third to Riyalma) and minor event at Kempton (1¾ lengths second to impressive winner Alessandria) before creditable ninth to Mont Etoile in Ribblesdale Stakes at Royal Ascot, racing up with pace: stays 1½m: bandaged hind coronets final outing: sold 580,000 gns in November. *J. Noseda*

PARK LANE PRINCESS (IRE) 3 ch.f. King of Kings (IRE) 125 – Heated Debate **59** (USA) 72 (Woodman (USA) 126) [2006 57: 8m 10d p12.2g³ 11.9f³ 12g² 12.4d³ 10d² Oct 4] modest maiden: effective at 1¼m to 12.4f: acts on polytrack, good to firm and good to soft ground: found little fourth outing: joined D. Pipe, and won over hurdles in November. *D. M. Simcock*

PARK'S GIRL 2 b.f. (Jan 27) Averti (IRE) 117 – Halland Park Girl (IRE) 106 (Primo **71** Dominie 121) [2006 6m⁶ p6g³ 6f³ Jul 29] 17,000Y: workmanlike filly: third foal: half-sister to 4-y-o Lindbergh and 2005 2-y-o 7f winner Hallandale (both by Bold Edge): dam 5f (at 2 yrs)/6f winner: fair form: third in maidens at Wolverhampton and York (beaten length by Valdan) in July: should prove best at 5f/6f. *P. C. Haslam*

PARKSIDE PURSUIT 8 b.g. Pursuit of Love 124 – Ivory Bride 86 (Domynsky 110) **77** [2006 74: 5.5d 5g 5m* 5m⁶ 5.1g 5f² 5f⁴ 5.1f 5.1g 6g⁴ 5.7m³ 6.1m 5.7f 6g 6m Sep 19] lengthy, dipped-backed gelding: fair handicapper: won at Warwick in June: best at 5f/6f: has won on good to soft going, ideally suited by good or firmer nowadays (acts on firm): best held up. *J. M. Bradley*

PARK STAR 6 b.m. Gothenberg (IRE) 117 – Miriam 59 (Forzando 122) [2006 50, a57: **–** f6g³ p6g⁵ p6g⁵ p6g³ p6g⁵ f6g⁶ Feb 14] leggy, good-topped mare: modest performer: stays **a56** easy 7f: acts on all-weather and heavy going: tried visored early in career. *D. Shaw*

PARKVIEW LOVE (USA) 5 b. or b.g. Mister Baileys 123 – Jerre Jo Glanville **70** (USA) (Skywalker (USA)) [2006 66, a75: p9.5g* p8.6g⁴ f8s p8g⁴ 8d³ p7.1g* 8.2g⁶ p10g⁶ **a78** p8g p7.1g f8g p8g⁵ p9.5g p7.1g Dec 22] leggy, good-topped gelding: fair handicapper nowadays: won at Wolverhampton in February and April: effective at 7f to 11f: acts on all-weather, firm and good to soft going: wears headgear: usually races prominently: sometimes looks none too keen. *D. Shaw*

PARNASSIAN 6 ch.g. Sabrehill (USA) 120 – Delphic Way 63 (Warning 136) [2006 85: **80** p8g 10.9g 10g 8d 8d⁵ 8m 8.1d 8.3s* 8.2s⁵ 10d Nov 1] angular, sparely-made gelding: fairly useful handicapper: won at Windsor in October: effective at 7f to 1¼m: acts on any turf going, but goes particularly well on good or softer: has carried head awkwardly (including for win): waited with. *J. A. Geake*

PARTHENOPE 3 gr.f. Namid 128 – Twosixtythreewest (FR) 69 (Kris 135) [2006 6m **43** 7g 6m Jul 29] 3,500F: tall, leggy filly: half-sister to German 7f winner Twosixty Four (by Beldale Flutter): dam 1m winner: poor form in maidens: has hung/started slowly. *J. A. Geake*

PARTICIPATION 3 b.g. Dansili 127 – Andaleeb (USA) 104 (Lyphard (USA) 132) **83** [2006 88: p8g 10m³ 10s 9.9m 8g³ 10m* p8g³ Jul 14] good-topped gelding: fairly useful performer: won claimer at Leicester in July: stays 1¼m: usually wears headgear: sometimes tongue tied: joined A. Jones. *M. J. Wallace*

PARTICLE (IRE) 3 ch.g. Selkirk (USA) 129 – Bernique (USA) (Affirmed (USA)) **92** [2006 10.9m² 12f⁴ 10d³ p13g* p13g⁴ 16d Oct 27] half-brother to several winners, including 6.5f (at 2 yrs) to 13.5f winner Bernimixa and 7.5f to 15.5f winner Miraculous (both smart in France, by Linamix): dam minor 1m US stakes winner: fairly useful form: won maiden at Lingfield in September by 3½ lengths from Dream Shared: good fourth in handicap there next time: ran as if amiss final outing: stays 13f: acts on polytrack: ran in snatches on debut. *M. Johnston*

PARTNERS IN JAZZ (USA) 5 ro.g. Jambalaya Jazz (USA) 111 – Just About **109** Enough (USA) (Danzig (USA)) [2006 106: 7g 7g* May 27] tall gelding: useful handicapper: won totesport Victoria Cup at Ascot (beat Marching Song by 1¼ lengths) in May: best at 6f (given bit of a test)/7f: acts on soft and good to firm going: starts slowly on occasions: genuine. *T. D. Barron*

PART TIMER (IRE) 2 b.c. (Feb 19) Mujadil (USA) 119 – Dame Laura (IRE) 100 **84** (Royal Academy (USA) 130) [2006 6m⁵ 5f* 6g³ 6m³ 7m⁴ 6m² 6m⁵ 6s p7g 8f Dec 30] 18,000Y: well-made colt: fourth foal: half-brother to 7f and 8.5f winner Sennen Cove (by Bering): dam, 5f (at 2 yrs)/6f winner, out of smart French 1¼m winner Aunty: fairly useful performer: won maiden at Haydock in June: generally creditable efforts in minor events/nurseries next 5 starts: left M. Channon before final outing: stays 7f: acts on firm going. *J. Metz, USA*

PARTY BELLE 3 b.f. Silver Patriarch (IRE) 125 – Third Party 63 (Terimon 124) **67** [2006 61: p8g^2 p7.1g^2 Feb 24] fair maiden: effective at 7f to 9.5f: acts on polytrack. *C. E. Brittain*

PARTY BEST 2 b. or gr.f. (Mar 7) Best of The Bests (IRE) 122 – Third Party 63 **58** (Terimon 124) [2006 5f^6 p7g^5 p7g Dec 3] half-sister to 4-y-o Party Boss and 7f winner Party Turn (by Pivotal): dam, 6f winner, half-sister to smart sprinter Passion For Life: modest form in maidens. *C. E. Brittain*

PARTY BOSS 4 gr.c. Silver Patriarch (IRE) 125 – Third Party 63 (Terimon 124) [2006 **100** 103, a113: a8f 7.5m a7s 7g p8.6g^2 p7g p7g p8.6m^3 Nov 21] tall, close-coupled colt: smart performer on all-weather, useful on turf at 3 yrs: easily best effort in 2006 (well held on turf) when 1½ lengths second to Kilworth in minor event at Wolverhampton, dictating: effective at 7f, and seems to stay easy 11.5f: acts on all-weather, probably on firm ground: tongue tied second/third starts: races prominently. *C. E. Brittain*

PARTY BOY (IRE) 4 b.g. Indian Rocket 115 – Bajan Girl (IRE) (Pips Pride 117) **36** [2006 –: 6g 7f 10.2m f12g^5 Nov 10] poor maiden, including in Britain: usually tongue tied, in cheekpieces/blinkered last 3 starts. *Edgar Byrne, Ireland*

PARTY (IRE) 2 ch.f. (Feb 12) Cadeaux Genereux 131 – Forty Belles (USA) (Forty **92** Niner (USA)) [2006 p7g^3 6g^6 6m^2 7f^4 6.1g^2 6s* 7s* Oct 21] 55,000Y: strong, lengthy filly: fifth foal: sister to fairly useful 2002 2-y-o 7f winner Jummana: dam French maiden half-sister to smart French performer up to 1½m Bayourida: fairly useful performer: improved in autumn, winning maiden and listed race at Newbury in October, in latter beating Hollow Ridge by ½ length: likely to stay 1m: acts on firm and soft going, probably polytrack. *R. Hannon*

PARTY PALACE 2 b.f. (Mar 8) Auction House (USA) 120 – Lady-Love 70 (Pursuit **54** of Love 124) [2006 5g 5.5d 5.7f^3 6m* 6f 7m p6g p8.6g^3 p9.5g^4 p8.6g^3 p8.6g^4 Dec 31] 16,000Y: small, sparely-made filly: second foal: half-sister to 3-y-o Moody Tunes: dam 2-y-o 5f winner who stayed 7f: modest performer: won seller at York in June: should stay beyond 8.6f: acts on polytrack and firm going. *J. A. Osborne*

PARTY PRINCESS (IRE) 5 b.m. Orpen (USA) 116 – Summer Queen 80 (Robellino **– §** (USA) 127) [2006 64§: p6g^5 p6g p5.1g p6g p6g Feb 13] strong mare: poor performer: **a45 §** stays 6f: acts on polytrack and good to firm ground: tried in headgear: unreliable. *S. Parr*

PAS DE TROIS 2 b.g. (Apr 17) Victory Note (USA) 120 – Maziere 45 (Mazilier (USA) **48** 107) [2006 5g 6m^4 7.1m p6g 6d^6 7m 8g^5 7d p9.5g 7g^4 Nov 14] neat gelding: poor maiden: claimed from F. J. Houghton £4,000 fifth start: should stay 1m: tried blinkered. *J. Pearce*

PASO DOBLE 8 b.g. Dancing Spree (USA) – Delta Tempo (IRE) (Bluebird (USA) **46** 125) [2006 54, a75: f8g f6g^6 f7g^6 p9.5g p7g p8g^4 p10g^3 p12.2g p7.1g^5 f8g^3 p8.6g^2 **a66** p8.6g^6 p10g 8m^6 f8g^2 f8g^6 f8g^2 p8g^4 f7g^5 f8g* Dec 28] fair on all-weather, poor on turf: left B. R. Millman after seventeenth start: won banded race at Southwell in December: effective at 7f to 11f: acts on all-weather and firm going: sometimes wears headgear: held up: has looked none too keen. *D. K. Ivory*

PASSAGE OF TIME 2 b.f. (Jan 22) Dansili 127 – Clepsydra 78 (Sadler's Wells **113 p** (USA) 132) [2006 7f^5 7d* 8d* 10g* Nov 12]

Henry Cecil has achieved nearly all there is to achieve in the sport. He has been champion trainer on ten occasions, the last time in 1993 when just pipping Richard Hannon on first prize money (since 1994 the title has been decided by total prize money). Cecil has saddled twenty-three domestic classic winners and has won each of the five classics at least twice. His last classic success was with Love Divine in the millennium season in the Oaks, a race he has won seven times, but that success came after a year in which the trainer seemed beset by personal problems, and the Warren Place string was struck by a virus which caused respiratory problems. The stable had a second Group 1 winner that season when Derby third Beat Hollow followed his Epsom effort with victory in the Grand Prix de Paris. Even in a lean year—by its own high standards at the time—the Cecil stable still sent out forty-seven individual winners of sixty-one races in Britain, for prize money earnings of over £1m, finishing ninth in the table. Also among Cecil's winners in 2000 was the Sadler's Wells filly Clepsydra, out of a half-sister to the

Criterium de Saint-Cloud, Saint-Cloud—a first Group 1 win since 2000 for Henry Cecil as the progressive Passage of Time gets the better of Soldier of Fortune (right); Empire Day (left) is third with Spirit One fourth

versatile All At Sea, the last-named winner of the Prix du Moulin and runner-up in both the International at York and in the Oaks for Cecil. Clepsydra ran only as a three-year-old, winning a maiden over a mile and a half at Epsom, after hanging in behind the leader for much of the straight. She was only a fair performer but looks like making much more of a name for herself at stud, her third foal Passage of Time providing Henry Cecil with his first Group 1 winner since Beat Hollow when winning the Criterium de Saint-Cloud in November.

Passage of Time wasn't the first Group 1 winner sent out from Warren Place since Beat Hollow. As Cecil's string has been reduced—his number of winners and prize money has fallen significantly in recent years—parts of the Warren Place complex have been rented out to other trainers and one of them, Jonathan Jay, sent out the winner of the Prix Cambaceres, France's top three-year-old hurdle, in 2005, which rather surprisingly earned Tidal Fury the title of Jumps Horse of The Year in France. Cecil himself is not one to dwell on his own past glories. 'I am not great at reminiscing, it's not what I've done but what I am going to do that counts,' he says. Cecil has had to fend off rumours of retirement as his fortunes have declined, but Passage of Time, a most progressive filly with clear classic potential, should dampen speculation for the time being. The fortunes of the Cecil string—set to increase from fifty-five in 2006 to around eighty—showed something of a general upturn in the latest season when the number of horses running for the stable in Britain rose from thirty-six the previous year to forty-five, the number of individual winners from ten to nineteen and the number of races won from twelve to twenty-five. Total first three prize money was up from £82,312 to £186,445, though the stable still languished at eighty-fourth in the table. More significant was another pattern success in France, when Prix Guillaume d'Ornano winner Multidimensional provided his trainer with his first victory in a pattern race of any kind since Burning Sun won the Prix Eugene Adam in 2002. Neither of those wins, incidentally, had been enough for Cecil to raise the traditional standard at Warren Place, a flag depicting a family heirloom, the Horn of Leys, said to have been given to one

786

of Cecil's ancestors by Robert The Bruce (the horn itself is displayed in the Great Hall at the ancestral home Crathes Castle near Banchory). The standard was, however, hoisted for Passage of Time's victory in the Criterium de Saint-Cloud, as it had been for Love Divine and Beat Hollow in 2000 and for Cecil-trained Group 1 winners before that, in a training career stretching back to 1969 when he started off with the Newmarket string of his stepfather Sir Cecil Boyd-Rochfort (champion five times) before taking over at Warren Place in 1977—the year after he became champion for the first time—on the retirement of his father-in-law Sir Noel Murless, who was champion trainer nine times and won nineteen domestic classics.

Many of the British-based owner-breeders who traditionally sustained Warren Place in its heyday have either died or reduced the scale of their operations, but Juddmonte has continued to supply horses for Cecil. The Khalid Abdulla-owned Sound of Nature, an Irish Two Thousand Guineas entry, was thought to be the stable's main hope at the start of the season but he was kept off the course until the autumn when he landed the odds in a maiden at Windsor on the second of only two starts. Passage of Time, also owned by Abdulla, was a well-backed favourite on her debut at Yarmouth in July but never got into what looked just an ordinary maiden. Clearly sharper for the experience, she made amends in a similar event at Newmarket the following month, battling back to justify favouritism by a head from Fretwork. Stepped up in both class and distance in the listed EBF bet365.com Montrose Fillies' Stakes over a mile, back at Newmarket in October, Passage of Time improved again, producing a useful performance to win by five lengths from Sues Surprise. Even so, it came as something of a surprise to see her pulled out a fortnight later for the Criterium de Saint-Cloud, for which she was a supplementary entry. Passage of Time took another step up in class and distance in her stride—the Criterium is over a mile and a quarter—and her victory put the French owners' title beyond doubt for her owner whose Irish-trained maiden winner Consul General had also been supplemented with a similar aim.

Conditions were nothing like so soft as they can be at Saint-Cloud in November which, coupled with the Criterium International runner-up and favourite Spirit One setting a good pace, resulted in Passage of Time recording the fastest time for the race since Darshaan in 1983. Patiently ridden early on, Passage of Time moved up just behind the leaders early in the straight and quickened in good style, after her jockey had to wait for a gap, to get the better of the Ballydoyle challenger Soldier of Fortune by three quarters of a length, with a further three lengths to the Zetland Stakes winner Empire Day completing an overseas-trained one, two, three. Spirit One was fourth, the second Ballydoyle runner Red Rock Canyon fifth, German challenger Meridia sixth and Consul General seventh in the field of thirteen, the largest since the race was promoted to Group 1 in 1987. Goldamix, the last filly to win the Criterium de Saint-Cloud in 1999, went on to reach a place in the Prix de Diane, while Escaline, the last filly before Goldamix to win the Criterium (in 1982), won the Diane. Passage of Time looked a smart prospect for 2007 when winning the Montrose, but she showed a level of form in the Criterium de Saint-Cloud that now makes her a must for any classic short-list. She is due to reappear in the Musidora Stakes at York, a race used as a stepping stone to Epsom by three of the Cecil-trained Oaks winners, Diminuendo, Snow Bride (who got the Oaks on the disqualification of Aliysa) and Reams of Verse, all of whom won at York. Whether Passage of Time is sent to Epsom, or to Chantilly for the Prix de Diane, she looks very much the type to blossom in the next summer—much as her trainer's famous roses have continued to do every year.

Passage of Time (b.f. Jan 22, 2004)	Dansili (b 1996)	Danehill (b 1986)	Danzig
			Razyana
		Hasili (b 1991)	Kahyasi
			Kerali
	Clepsydra (b 1997)	Sadler's Wells (b 1981)	Northern Dancer
			Fairy Bridge
		Quandary (b 1991)	Blushing Groom
			Lost Virtue

The tall, useful-looking Passage of Time has plenty of scope and should train on well. She is home bred, by the young Juddmonte stallion Dansili who has had three crops of racing age and was also represented in the latest season, among others, by the Prix de l'Arc de Triomphe winner Rail Link, another Juddmonte homebred, in whose essay more can be found. Dansili had two other pattern winners among his latest crop of juveniles, Strategic Prince (July Stakes and Vintage Stakes) and Thousand Words (Somerville Tattersall Stakes). Passage of Time's dam Clepsydra, who is also the dam of the useful mile and a quarter winner Sandglass (by Zafonic), carried the Abdulla colours, as did Dansili, and as did Passage of Time's grandam Quandary, with whom Cecil persevered to win three times (she was also disqualified once for her jockey's irresponsible riding) at nine furlongs to a mile and a quarter as a four-year-old, one of her successes by six lengths in the listed James Seymour Stakes at Newmarket. As well as being a half-sister to All At Sea, Quandary was a half-sister to numerous other winners in Britain and abroad, including the Free Handicap winner Over The Ocean. Passage of Time's great grandam, the unraced Lost Virtue, was out of a half-sister to America's Horse of The Year in 1967, Damascus. Passage of Time stays a mile and a quarter well and looks to have good prospects of staying a mile and a half, though All At Sea's defeat by User Friendly in the Oaks (twenty lengths clear of the third) raised question marks over her stamina in some quarters and she was brought back to shorter distances. Passage of Time has won on good and good to soft going; the going was firm when she was beaten on her debut though it would be unwise to draw conclusions from that. *H. R. A. Cecil*

PASSAGER (FR) 3 b.g. Anabaa (USA) 130 – Passionnee (USA) 90 (Woodman (USA) 126) [2006 8v³ 8g² 7.5s* 8m* 9.3g² 8g* Oct 29] sixth foal: brother to 6.5f (in USA)/7.5f (at 2 yrs in France) winner Parfumeur and half-brother to several winners, including smart French performer up to 1¼m Premier Pas (by Sillery), 7f winner at 2 yrs: dam French 1m/1¼m winner: smart performer: won maiden at Saint-Cloud at 2 yrs, minor events at Maisons-Laffitte in May and Chantilly in June (off 4 months afterwards) and Prix Perth at Saint-Cloud (beat Gwenseb ½ length) in October: best at 1m: acts on soft and good to firm ground. *Mme C. Head-Maarek, France* **117**

PASSARELLE (USA) 2 b.f. (Mar 24) In The Wings 128 – Kitza (IRE) 113 (Danehill (USA) 126) [2006 8.2d⁴ Nov 1] good-topped filly: fourth foal: half-sister to smart 7f (at 2 yrs) and 1m winner Fort Dignity (by Seeking The Gold) and fairly useful French 1m winner Ascension Island (by Rahy): dam, Irish 6f (at 2 yrs) and 1m winner (later won in USA), half-sister to smart sprinter Marouble: 22/1, 9¼ lengths fourth to Sagredo in maiden at Nottingham, steadily warming to task: sold 125,000 gns: should do better. *R. M. Beckett* **61 p**

PASS GO 5 b.g. Kris 135 – Celt Song (IRE) (Unfuwain (USA) 131) [2006 p6g a7g⁵ 10s Sep 13] modest maiden: well held at Wolverhampton on reappearance: stays 7f: acts on polytrack/sand, little form on turf: tried tongue tied/blinkered/visored. *J. J. Lambe, Ireland* **59**

PASSIFIED 2 ch.f. (Jan 30) Compton Place 125 – Passiflora 75 (Night Shift (USA)) [2006 6m* 6d⁴ 7d 8f⁶ Nov 25] 28,000Y: strong, good-bodied filly: type to carry condition: fourth foal: half-sister to fairly useful 2002 2-y-o 6f winner Bond Royale (by Piccolo) and 4-y-o Zomerlust: dam, 2-y-o 6f winner, half-sister to very smart 6f/7f performer Harmonic Way, out of half-sister to In The Groove: fairly useful form: won maiden at Pontefract in September: improvement after, 6 lengths fourth of 28 to Caldra in sales race and eighth to Finsceal Beo in Rockfel Stakes, both at Newmarket (then left D. Elsworth 125,000 gns) and sixth to Valbenny in Grade 3 Miesque Stakes at Hollywood: stays 1m: acts on firm and good to soft going. *J. M. Cassidy, USA* **89**

PASSING HOUR (USA) 2 b.f. (Mar 4) Red Ransom (USA) – Timely 104 (Kings Lake (USA) 133) [2006 6g⁵ Jul 28] sturdy filly: sister to 1999 2-y-o 5f winner (including Queen Mary) winner Shining Hour and 6f (in USA) and 1m winner (at 2 yrs) Titian Time, both useful, and closely related/half-sister to several winners: dam 1m winner: 11/2, needed experience when fifth to Italian Girl in maiden at Ascot. *G. A. Butler* **76**

PASSIONATELY ROYAL 4 b.g. Royal Applause 124 – Passionelle 56 (Nashwan (USA) 135) [2006 70: 7m 8f Jul 21] strong, close-coupled gelding: fair handicapper at 3 yrs: well held in 2006. *R. A. Fahey* **–**

PASSION FRUIT 5 b.m. Pursuit of Love 124 – Reine de Thebes (FR) 67 (Darshaan 133) [2006 79: 7d⁵ 8g 7.5f⁴ 6.9g* p7.1g⁵ 7.1m 8v 7m² 6d⁴ 7g* 6g⁶ 7d Oct 28] close-coupled, good-topped mare: fairly useful performer: won handicaps at Carlisle in **89**

June and Newcastle in September: good sixth to Firenze in listed event at Newmarket penultimate start: stays 7f: acts on soft and good to firm going: sometimes wears blinkers (only on second start in 2006). *C. W. Fairhurst*

PASS THE PORT 5 ch.g. Docksider (USA) 124 – One of The Family 73 (Alzao (USA) 117) [2006 86: p12g f12g* p12.2g⁶ p12g⁶ 12s p12.2m⁵ p12.2g⁴ p12.2g² p12g³ p12.2s³ p13g⁶ Dec 22] leggy gelding: fairly useful handicapper: won at Southwell in January: creditable placed efforts after: stays 1¾m: acts on all-weather and soft going: visored (looked none too keen) once. *D. Haydn Jones*   **86**

PASTEL ROSE (USA) 2 b.f. (Feb 26) Diesis 133 – Seba 95 (Alzao (USA) 117) [2006 8.2g Sep 26] small filly: first foal: dam, 6f (at 2 yrs) to 8.5f (in USA) winner, half-sister to very smart French sprinter Do The Honours: soon detached in maiden at Nottingham: sold 21,000 gns. *M. R. Channon*   **–**

PATAVELLIAN (IRE) 8 b.g. Machiavellian (USA) 123 – Alessia 91 (Caerleon (USA) 132) [2006 115: 5m⁶ May 6] tall, useful-looking gelding: smart performer: creditable sixth to Dandy Man in Palace House Stakes at Newmarket in 2006, ending up with bit to do: reportedly suffered recurrence of joint problem after: best at 5f/6f: acts on firm and soft going: usually blinkered nowadays: has worn crossed noseband/been bandaged in front: has run well when sweating: usually races prominently: stays in training. *R. Charlton*   **115**

PATAVIAN (IRE) 2 b.g. (Mar 31) Titus Livius (FR) 115 – Five of Wands 71 (Caerleon (USA) 132) [2006 7g⁶ 8.1m⁵ Sep 7] €60,000Y: rather leggy gelding: second foal: half-brother to Italian 2004 2-y-o 8.5f winner Lujana Boy (by Lujain): dam staying maiden out of half-sister to dam of Vintage Crop: mid-field in maidens, better run when sixth to Prince Forever at Newbury: sold 4,000 gns, joined I. Semple. *M. R. Channon*   **72**

PATAVIUM (IRE) 3 b.g. Titus Livius (FR) 115 – Arcevia (IRE) 85 (Archway (IRE) 115) [2006 74: 11g⁵ 14.1m 14.1m⁶ p8.6g⁵ 7f 13.8v⁴ Oct 31] good-topped gelding: just modest maiden in 2006: left E. O'Neill after fifth start: should prove best up to 1m: acts on good to firm going, probably on polytrack: races prominently: has looked temperamental. *E. W. Tuer*   **58**

PATAVIUM PRINCE (IRE) 3 ch.g. Titus Livius (FR) 115 – Hoyland Common (IRE) (Common Grounds 118) [2006 66: p7g⁴ p6g⁴ p5g⁴ 7m 6g* 7f³ 6f³ 5m² 6d⁴ 5m⁴ 6m⁵ 7m⁴ 6f⁷ 7g⁴ 7f⁴ 6g² 6d⁵ 6m 6d 6g⁴ p5.1g⁵ p7.1g Nov 7] compact gelding: fair handicapper: won at Salisbury in May: effective at 5f to 7f: acts on polytrack, firm and good to soft going: held up. *J. R. Best*   **75 a70**

PATH TO GLORY 2 b.c. (Mar 25) Makbul 104 – Just Glory (Glory of Dancer 121) [2006 7.1d⁵ 8.1d⁵ 6d p6g 5g³ p6g⁵ Dec 22] sturdy, workmanlike colt: modest maiden: effective at 5f/6f: wore cheekpieces last 2 starts. *Miss Z. C. Davison*   **51**

PATITIRI (USA) 3 ch.f. Rahy (USA) 115 – Dharma (USA) (Zilzal (USA) 137) [2006 –: 6f 7f Jul 13] well held in 3 maidens. *M. G. Quinlan*   **–**

PATRIXPRIAL 5 gr.g. Linamix (FR) 127 – Magnificent Star (USA) 122 (Silver Hawk (USA) 123) [2006 71+: 14.1s³ 16g Apr 22] well-made gelding: fair handicapper on Flat: should stay 2m: acts on soft going: blinkered last 2 starts. *M. H. Tompkins*   **76**

PATTERNMAKER (IRE) 4 b. or br.g. Elnadim (USA) 128 – Attasliyah (IRE) (Marju (IRE) 127) [2006 76: p5g p7.1g f6g³ p6g* p7g p6g p6g⁶ 5.5d p6m p5.1m p6g p6g⁶ p6g⁴ Dec 18] fair performer: left W. Jarvis prior to winning claimer at Lingfield in February: best at 5f/6f: acts on polytrack (probably on fibresand), soft and good to firm going: tried blinkered/visored. *A. M. Hales*   **66**

PAT WILL (IRE) 2 b.f. (Apr 28) Danetime (IRE) 121 – Northern Tara (IRE) 84 (Fayruz 116) [2006 5.1m 5d 5f⁴ 5.1g³ 6f 5m* 5.1f p7.1g p6g⁶ Dec 28] leggy filly: second foal: dam 5f winner (ran only at 2 yrs): modest performer: won seller at Leicester in July: best at 5f: acts on firm going. *P. D. Evans*   **60**

PATXARAN (IRE) 4 b.f. Revoque (IRE) 122 – Stargard (Polish Precedent (USA) 131) [2006 80: 11.9m² 15.8m⁵ Jul 12] strong, lengthy filly: fairly useful handicapper: stays 1½m: acts on firm going, probably on soft: tongue tied in 2006: sometimes hangs. *P. C. Haslam*   **84**

PAULINE'S PRINCE 4 b.c. Polar Prince (IRE) 117 – Etma Rose (IRE) (Fairy King (USA)) [2006 62: p7.1g f8g* f7g p8.6g* p8.6g p8.6g 8.1s⁶ 8m 8.1f 8.2m⁴ 8s 10.9m 8g⁴ p9.5m Oct 2] leggy colt: fair handicapper, better on all-weather than turf: won at Southwell (apprentices) and Wolverhampton in March: stays 8.6f: acts on all-weather, firm and soft going: tried blinkered/in cheekpieces/tongue tied. *R. Hollinshead*   **66 a76**

PAUVIC (IRE) 3 b.g. Fayruz 116 – Turntable (IRE) 59 (Dolphin Street (FR) 125) [2006 **76**
57: p5.1g⁶ p6g* p6g* p5g² p6g* p5g² 6d⁵ Apr 20] workmanlike gelding: fair handicapper: won at Wolverhampton in January and Lingfield (2) in February: raced only at 5f/
6f: acts on all-weather and good to soft going: visored last 6 outings: races prominently.
Mrs A. Duffield

PAVLOVIA 2 b.f. (Mar 15) Diktat 126 – Waseyla (IRE) 71 (Sri Pekan (USA) 117) [2006 **69**
5g⁵ 6g⁶ f5g² Jul 31] 20,000F: lengthy filly: first foal: dam 1¼m winner: fair form in
maidens, 4 lengths second to Stevie Gee at Southwell: suffered a fracture after: likely to
stay 7f/1m. *T. D. Easterby*

PAWAN (IRE) 6 ch.g. Cadeaux Genereux 131 – Born To Glamour (Ajdal (USA) 130) **84**
[2006 84: f5g⁵ p7.1g⁴ f5g⁴ f5g⁴ f6g⁵ f7g⁵ f6g⁶ p6g p6g 6g⁵ 7g 5g 9.7m⁴ 8.2g⁶ 5m **a90**
6.1m² 5f⁵ 5f² 5.5m⁴ 5.4f⁵ 7f 5m* 5.2d⁵ 5g 5m⁵ 6d⁴ 6d f5g f5g³ Dec 5] lengthy, angular
gelding: fairly useful performer on balance of form (often flatters in face of stiff tasks):
won handicap at Beverley in August: effective at 5f to 9f: acts on all-weather and any turf
going: tried in cheekpieces, blinkered nowadays: usually races prominently, though often
slowly away: trainer ridden: tough. *Miss A. Stokell*

PAWN BROKER 9 ch.g. Selkirk (USA) 129 – Dime Bag 87 (High Line 125) [2006 –: **–**
15m Jun 24] rather leggy gelding: one-time smart performer: left D. Elsworth after 7 yrs,
well held since: tried blinkered. *Miss J. R. Tooth*

PAWN IN LIFE (IRE) 8 b.g. Midhish 109 – Lady-Mumtaz (Martin John) [2006 –, **–**
a70d: f8g f8g f8g⁵ f7g² f7g² f7g* f8g³ f8g⁵ f8g⁵ f7g⁶ f8g³ 7.1g⁵ f7g³ f7g* p8g f7g p9.5g **a67 d**
f8g f7g f7g⁵ f7g Dec 12] lengthy gelding: fair performer: won handicaps at Southwell
in February and May: well below form subsequently, leaving M. Polglase after sixteenth
outing: stays easy 1m: acts on all-weather: usually wears headgear: sometimes slowly
away. *M. J. Attwater*

PAX 9 ch.g. Brief Truce (USA) 126 – Child's Play (USA) (Sharpen Up 127) [2006 79: 7d **–**
Apr 12] tall gelding: fairly useful performer at best: reportedly bled final start at 8 yrs and
on return: often blinkered in 2001. *D. Nicholls*

PAY ATTENTION 5 b.m. Revoque (IRE) 122 – Catch Me 75 (Rudimentary (USA) **66**
118) [2006 14.1g⁶ May 29] quite good-topped mare: fair performer: creditable effort only
outing on Flat since 2004: stays 1¾m: unraced on heavy going, acts on any other turf:
fairly useful hurdler/chaser, winner over fences in December. *T. D. Easterby*

Abergwaun Stakes, Tipperary—Peace Offering puts up a career-best effort to beat Osterhase

PAYMASTER GENERAL (IRE) 2 b.g. (Feb 20) Desert Style (IRE) 121 – Khawafi   **65**
86 (Kris 135) [2006 6s³ 6g⁵ 6d⁵ Jun 26] €10,500Y: lengthy gelding: has scope: third foal:
dam, 1¼m winner, half-sister to 6-y-o Tolpuddle: fair form in maidens in May/June: will
stay 1m. *M. D. I. Usher*

PAY ON (IRE) 3 ch.g. Danehill Dancer (IRE) 117 – Richly Deserved (IRE) (Kings   **61**
Lake (USA) 133) [2006 –: 7d 10m p12.2g 10.1f⁴ Jul 18] workmanlike gelding: modest
maiden: seems to stay 1¼m: visored last 2 starts: gelded after. *W. Jarvis*

PAYS D'AMOUR (IRE) 9 b.g. Pursuit of Love 124 – Lady of The Land 75 (Wollow   **– §**
132) [2006 43§: p6g 7d 6m May 11] strong gelding: well held in 2006: tried tongue tied/
in cheekpieces: often slowly away: ungenuine. *D. A. Nolan*

PAY TIME 7 ch.m. Timeless Times (USA) 99 – Payvashooz 78 (Ballacashtal (CAN))   **72**
[2006 44: 7f² 7.1g* 7m* 6.9f² 6f 8s 7m* Aug 31] dipped-backed mare: fair handicapper:
won at Musselburgh and Catterick in July and Redcar (apprentices) in August: stays 7f:
acts on fibresand and firm going: tried tongue tied: reared in stall/took no part once in
2005: races prominently. *R. E. Barr*

PEACE EMBLEM (IRE) 5 b.m. Bahhare (USA) 122 – Beseeching (IRE) 50 (Hamas   **–**
(IRE) 125§) [2006 53: p9.5g Jan 4] modest performer: well held only outing in 2006:
tried in blinkers/tongue tie, wears cheekpieces nowadays. *J. W. Unett*

PEACE LILY 4 b.f. Dansili 127 – Shall We Run 59 (Hotfoot 126) [2006 66: 7.1g² 7d²   **69**
8m 7m 7m* 7.1m p7g 7m Jul 29] tall, useful-looking filly: fair handicapper: won at Salisbury in June: poor efforts after: effective at 6f/7f: acts on good to firm and good to soft
ground: tried tongue tied/in cheekpieces. *R. F. Johnson Houghton*

PEACE OFFERING (IRE) 6 b.g. Victory Note (USA) 120 – Amnesty Bay 63 (That-   **113**
ching 131) [2006 101: p5g⁴ p6g³ 5d⁴ 6m² 5.1f 5m 5m² 6m 5m* 5f⁴ 5m⁶ 6m 5.1g* 5d
5m² 5v* 6s Oct 22] good-topped gelding: smart performer: improved in 2006, winning
Gosforth Park Cup (Handicap) at Newcastle (by 1¼ lengths from Grigorovitch) in June,
minor event at Nottingham (beat Fictional by 1¾ lengths) in August and listed race at
Tipperary (by length from Osterhase) in October: also ran well when length second to
Majestic Missile in Prix du Petit Couvert at Longchamp on fifteenth start: last in Grade 2
Nearctic Stakes at Woodbine final outing: best at 5f: acts on polytrack and any turf going:
tried in blinkers/cheekpieces early in career: front runner. *D. Nicholls*

PEACHY PEAR 3 b.f. Mark of Esteem (IRE) 137 – Sea Quest (IRE) (Rainbow Quest   **–**
(USA) 134) [2006 11.7m 12.1m 12.1m Sep 17] 4,200Y: fourth foal: half-sister to 4-y-o
Captain General: dam, ran twice in France, half-sister to Yorkshire Oaks winner/St Leger
second Hellenic: no sign of ability. *Mrs L. J. Young*

PEAK PARK (USA) 6 b. or br.g. Dynaformer (USA) – Play Po (USA) (Play On   **–**
(USA)) [2006 62, a79: f16g² p16.5g 20s f14g⁶ May 31] strong, close-coupled gelding: **a74**
fair handicapper: well beaten after reappearance: stays 2m: acts on all-weather, had form
on firm ground earlier in career: has been visored. *P. L. Gilligan*

PEAK SEASONS (IRE) 3 ch.g. Raise A Grand (IRE) 114 – Teresian Girl (IRE) 52   **61**
(Glenstal (USA) 118) [2006 66: p6g p7g 10m 8s p8.6g⁵ p12g⁵ 10.9m⁴ p10.1g 10.1f* 9.9m
12d 8g 8d Oct 2] leggy gelding: modest performer: won seller at Yarmouth (left W. de
Best-Turner) in July: well beaten after: stays 1¼m: acts on firm and soft going: blinkered
last 5 starts: races prominently. *M. C. Chapman*

PEARL FARM 5 b.m. Foxhound (USA) 103 – Trinity Hall 67 (Hallgate 127) [2006 61:   **57**
p7g 7.6m⁴ p7g³ Aug 11] modest maiden: should stay 1m: acts on polytrack, good to firm
and good to soft going: tried tongue tied. *C. A. Horgan*

PEARL FISHER (IRE) 5 ch.m. Foxhound (USA) 103 – Naivity (IRE) 72 (Auction   **54**
Ring (USA) 123) [2006 –: p7.1g p8.6g⁶ f11g 16g Apr 25] strong mare: modest maiden:
tried visored. *D. Carroll*

PEARL (IRE) 2 b.f. (Apr 22) Daylami (IRE) 138 – Briery (IRE) 66 (Salse (USA) 128)   **67 p**
[2006 p7.1g⁵ Nov 14] second foal: sister to 3-y-o Fregate Island: dam, 7f winner, granddaughter of Cheveley Park winner Woodstream: 20/1, 6¾ lengths fifth to Whazzis in
maiden at Wolverhampton, starting slowly and running green in rear before getting going
at finish, not knocked about: will stay 1m: sure to improve. *W. J. Haggas*

PEARL ISLAND (USA) 5 b.g. Kingmambo (USA) 125 – Mother of Pearl (IRE) 113   **–**
(Sadler's Wells (USA) 132) [2006 –: f7g² f8g* f8g f8g f8g³ Apr 10] sturdy gelding: mod-   **a61**
est performer: won maiden claimer at Southwell in January: stays 1m: acts on fibresand:
often blinkered. *D. J. Wintle*

London Paddy Power Gold Cup (Handicap), Newbury—
a third successive win for Pearly King; Salute The General (right) is a good second ahead of
High Command (hooped sleeves) and Numeric (rail)

PEARL OF ESTEEM 3 ch.f. Mark of Esteem (IRE) 137 – Ribot's Pearl (Indian Ridge 123) [2006 9.7d⁵ 10m 10.2m⁶ p10g Nov 1] leggy filly: third foal: half-sister to 5-y-o Jordans Spark: dam 7f/1m winner in Italy: modest maiden. *J. Pearce* **56**

PEARL OYSTER 4 ch.g. Spectrum (IRE) 126 – Upper Strata 109 (Shirley Heights 130) [2006 f11g p12.2g p12.2g Feb 17] no form, leaving A. Fabre 800 gns and off 14 months before 2006 reappearance. *D. J. Wintle*

PEARL'S GIRL 3 gr.f. King's Best (USA) 132 – Karsiyaka (IRE) (Kahyasi 130) [2006 77p: 7m⁴ 8m⁴ 7f² 8m* 8v⁶ Sep 2] lengthy filly: fairly useful performer: won maiden at Ascot in July: fair sixth in handicap at Thirsk final outing: stays 1m: acts on firm and soft going. *W. J. Haggas* **80**

PEARLS OF WISDOM 2 b.f. (Feb 24) Kyllachy 129 – Placement (Kris 135) [2006 6d Oct 18] 210,000Y: fifth foal: half-sister to useful 5f (at 2 yrs) and 7f winner Presto Vento (by Air Express): dam unraced close relative of smart French sprinter Pole Position: easy to back (8/1), slowly away and not knocked about in maiden at Yarmouth: will improve. *J. H. M. Gosden* **– p**

PEARLY KING (USA) 3 br.c. Kingmambo (USA) 125 – Mother of Pearl (IRE) 113 (Sadler's Wells (USA) 132) [2006 –p: 8m* 10m* 10s* 12m 9.9f³ 9.9g² 10m⁶ 9d Sep 30] tall colt: useful performer: won maiden at Yarmouth in April and handicaps at Redcar and Newbury (quite valuable event, beat Salute The General by ½ length) in May: good efforts in handicaps next 4 starts, length second to Champions Gallery at Beverley and sixth to Pinpoint in John Smith's Stakes at Newbury: tongue tied and sweating badly, well held in Cambridgeshire at Newmarket final outing: may prove best around 1¼m: acts on firm and soft going: joined I. Mohammed in UAE. *Sir Michael Stoute* **106**

PEARLY POLL 3 ch.f. Prince Sabo 123 – Bit of A Tart (Distant Relative 128) [2006 75: 7s 6g 6m⁵ 5.7g 6.1g 6d Oct 9] quite good-topped filly: fair handicapper: form in 2006 only when fifth at Windsor: should stay 7f: acts on heavy and good to firm ground: wore cheekpieces final outing: sold £2,400. *R. M. Beckett* **70**

PEARLY WEY 3 b.g. Lujain (USA) 119 – Dunkellin (USA) (Irish River (FR) 131) [2006 6g* 6f² 6g² 6m 6m 7f 7d⁴ 6m⁶ Sep 10] 12,000F, 34,000Y: close-coupled gelding: half-brother to several winners, including smart 1m/1¼m performer Green Card (by Green Dancer) and 15f winner Irish Sea (by Zilzal): dam, winning sprinter in USA, half-sister to Criterium des Pouliches winner Oak Hill: useful performer: won maiden at Newmarket in April: good second after in handicaps at Salisbury and Ascot (beaten ½ length by Trafalgar Bay): races freely, and should be as effective at 5f as 6f: acts on firm going: twice slowly away, markedly so sixth outing. *C. G. Cox* **99**

PEARSON GLEN (IRE) 7 ch.g. Dolphin Street (FR) 125 – Glendora (Glenstal (USA) 118) [2006 60: p12.2g May 5] good-topped gelding: modest performer: well held only Flat outing in 2006: tried visored/in cheekpieces/tongue tied. *James Moffatt* **–**

PEAS 'N BEANS (IRE) 3 ch.g. Medicean 128 – No Sugar Baby (FR) (Crystal Glitters (USA) 127) [2006 –: 14.1g 11.5m³ 10.9m⁶ 12f⁴ 10.1m 14.1g⁴ 12d⁶ 11.1d² p12g p13.9g² p13.9g p13.9g f14g⁴ Dec 29] leggy gelding: modest maiden handicapper: left M. Bell after eighth start: stays 1¾m: acts on polytrack, firm and good to soft going. *T. Keddy* **62**

PEDLAR OF LUCK 3 ch.c. Zaha (CAN) 106 – Victoriet 54 (Hamas (IRE) 125§) [2006 –: p6g p6g Jan 29] well held in 3 maidens. *A. G. Newcombe* **–**

PEE JAY'S DREAM   4 ch.g. Vettori (IRE) 119 – Langtry Lady 91 (Pas de Seul 133)   **66**
[2006 66: 15.8d² 14.1d⁶ p13.9g⁵ f12g⁴ 12d* 12.4s² 13.8s⁴ 13.8v³ Oct 31] sturdy gelding:
fair handicapper: won at Pontefract in October: effective at 1½m to 2m: acts on all-
weather, heavy and good to firm going: tried blinkered: won over hurdles in December.
M. W. Easterby

PEEPHOLE   3 ch.g. Pursuit of Love 124 – Goodwood Lass (IRE) 71 (Alzao (USA)   **68**
117) [2006 60, a56: p7g p7.1g⁶ p8g³ f8g⁶ 8.2d* 8.3f 8.3g⁴ 10.3m 11.5d Oct 18] good-   **a54**
bodied gelding: fair performer: won selling handicap at Nottingham (left P. Makin)
in May: below form after: stays 1¼m: acts on polytrack and good to soft going: usually
visored nowadays, blinkered final start: sold 1,500 gns. *A. Bailey*

PEERESS   5 ch.m. Pivotal 124 – Noble One 107 (Primo Dominie 121) [2006 118:   **124**
8s* 8m⁴ 8m⁴ 8s³ 8m² Sep 9]

    Almost as impressive as Sir Michael Stoute's record in the Lockinge Stakes
is that of David and Patricia Thompson, owners of the Cheveley Park Stud. Prior
to the 2006 season Stoute had won the race six times, with Scottish Reel in 1986,
Safawan in 1990, Soviet Line in 1995 and 1996, Medicean in 2001 and Russian
Rhythm in 2004, Soviet Line the only one in which the Thompsons weren't
involved. However, they were associated with one winner who wasn't trained by
Stoute, namely Polar Falcon who, in 1991, provided French-based John Hammond
with his first success on British soil. Back then the Lockinge was a Group 2, but it
was upgraded four years later and is now firmly established as a Group 1 contest,
the first of the season in Britain for horses above the age of three.

    Stoute was responsible for two of the nine who lined up for the latest Judd-
monte Lockinge Stakes at Newbury in May. His four-year-old colt Rob Roy had
already shown his well-being by winning the betfred.com Mile at Sandown the
previous month, whereas Peeress, running in the colours of the Cheveley Park Stud
and ridden by Kieren Fallon, who had also won on Medicean and Russian Rhythm,
was making her seasonal reappearance. Also returning to action was Soviet Song,
who had finished third to Peeress in the previous season's Windsor Forest Stakes
before reversing the placings in the Falmouth Stakes. Soviet Song already had five
Group 1 wins under her belt, including one against the colts in the 2004 Sussex
Stakes. Peeress on the other hand had just the one, that having come when up
against her own sex in the 2005 Sun Chariot Stakes. The betting on what looked
just an ordinary renewal was tight, with Soviet Song just shading favouritism ahead
of Peeress, Rob Roy and Majors Cast, the last-named an easy winner of a listed race
at Haydock on his reappearance. Conditions were testing, but that wasn't a problem
for Peeress who had won on soft ground on her first appearance at four and on good

*Juddmonte Lockinge Stakes, Newbury—Peeress vindicates connections' decision to keep her in training;
the ill-fated Majors Cast (rail) is second ahead of Court Masterpiece,
Soviet Song (black cap) and Kandidate*

to soft in the Sun Chariot, and she travelled well, held up in rear, as New Seeker dictated the pace. After making up her ground smoothly, Peeress quickened when asked for her effort and took up the running over a furlong out, soon enough for one who has a tendency to idle in front. She showed no signs of stopping on this occasion, however, keeping on very well and always holding Majors Cast, who pulled clear of the remainder but was a length and three quarters behind at the line. As in each of the two previous seasons, Peeress had shown further improvement. Her form didn't match up to that of recent Lockinge winners such as Keltos, Hawk Wing and Rakti, but it bettered that shown in the same race by her connections' previous winners. Peeress failed to run up to that level in four subsequent appearances, coming closest to it on the only other occasion she encountered soft ground. That was in the Prix Jacques le Marois at Deauville in which she finished third behind Librettist and Manduro, beaten a neck and a head. Peeress does go particularly well in the mud, but she has plenty of sound efforts to her name on ground firmer than good, with her first two wins both gained on firm. The going was good to firm for Peeress' three other starts in 2006, and she wouldn't have been far below her best in the first of those, when fourth to Ad Valorem in the Queen Anne Stakes at Royal Ascot, but for being hampered inside the last furlong. Peeress occupied the same position behind Rajeem in the slowly-run Falmouth Stakes next time, and on her final appearance she went down only by a short head to Red Evie in the Matron Stakes at Leopardstown, finishing strongly.

Peeress (ch.m. 2001)	Pivotal (ch 1993)	Polar Falcon (b or br 1987)	Nureyev Marie d'Argonne
		Fearless Revival (ch 1987)	Cozzene Stufida
	Noble One (ch 1996)	Primo Dominie (b 1982)	Dominion Swan Ann
		Noble Destiny (b 1988)	Dancing Brave Tender Loving Care

Peeress, who was bred by Cheveley Park Stud, is the first foal of the useful Noble One who won the first two of her five starts. Both wins were gained over five furlongs, in a maiden at Catterick at two and in a minor event at Newmarket at three. Noble One is a half-sister to several winners, including the fairly useful Maiden Castle, successful at a mile and a quarter, and Sunsu Desura, a useful winner at ten to twelve furlongs in Italy. Their dam Noble Destiny won a seven-furlong maiden at Leicester on her sole appearance as a juvenile, but disappointed on her only two subsequent starts. The next dam Tender Loving Care was also a winner at seven furlongs as a two-year-old, and she went on to finish runner-up to Midway Lady in the May Hill Stakes. Noble One's second foal, Carte Royale (by Loup Sauvage), was a fairly useful winner at five furlongs as a two-year-old; her third, the ill-fated Eastern Empress (by Mujadil), finished third in a two-year-old maiden on her final start. Peeress, a strong, rangy mare who is best at a mile, shows a quick action, and she is usually bandaged on her hind joints. It's worth mentioning that she shaped well on her only start away from turf, when fourth in a listed event at Lingfield on her final appearance as a three-year-old. She remains in training. *Sir Michael Stoute*

PEGASUS DANCER (FR) 2 b.g. (Apr 30) Danehill Dancer (IRE) 117 – Maruru **76** (IRE) (Fairy King (USA)) [2006 5d* 6m³ 6s Oct 6] €17,000Y, 27,000 2-y-o: quite good-topped gelding: half-brother to winners in Italy by Slip Anchor and Sikeston: dam Italian 5f winner including at 2 yrs: fair form: won maiden at Pontefract in August (bolted to post): progress when third of 4 to Bazroy in minor event at Southwell: well beaten in nursery: should prove best at 5f/6f: edgy sort. *K. A. Ryan*

PEGASUS PRINCE (USA) 2 b.g. (Feb 26) Fusaichi Pegasus (USA) 130 – Avian **–** Eden (USA) (Storm Bird (CAN) 134) [2006 7d 7f⁶ Sep 20] well held in maidens. *Miss J. A. Camacho*

PEGGYS FIRST 4 b.g. Wolfhound (USA) 126 – Peggys Rose (IRE) 65 (Shalford **–** (IRE) 124§) [2006 p5g⁵ f6g⁶ p6g² 6m p8.6g p6g⁵ p6g³ p8g 6m p6g p5g f6g³ Dec 28] **a55** modest maiden: effective at 6f to 1m: acts on all-weather: tried in cheekpieces/blinkered. *D. E. Cantillon*

PEGGYS FLOWER 2 b.f. (Mar 31) Arkadian Hero (USA) 123 – Peggys Rose (IRE) 65 (Shalford (IRE) 124§) [2006 p5g³ 5f 5f² 6f* 6f² p5g 5.2f² 6f⁵ 5.2g⁵ 5.3m Sep 19] third foal: dam 6f seller winner: fair performer: won seller at Windsor in June: effective at 5f/ 6f: acts on polytrack and firm going: tried in cheekpieces: irresolute. *N. A. Callaghan*   **65 §**

PEGGY'S PEARL 2 ch.f. (Apr 23) Ishiguru (USA) 114 – Sweet Compliance 71 (Safawan 118) [2006 6m p5g 6m p5.1g* a6.8g³ Dec 3] third foal: dam 2-y-o 7f winner: poor form: cheekpieces, won seller at Wolverhampton in August (final start for J. S. Moore): third in minor event at Taby: stays 6.8f. *C. Bjorling, Sweden*   **46**

PEINTRE'S WONDER (IRE) 2 b.f. (Apr 15) Peintre Celebre (USA) 137 – Ring The Relatives 75 (Bering 136) [2006 8.3m 8v² Oct 9] workmanlike filly: third foal: half-sister to 4-y-o Newsround: dam, second at 1¼m (ran twice), out of smart half-sister to very smart 1¼m performer One So Wonderful: better effort in maidens (green on debut) when 8 lengths second to Fashion Statement at Ayr: will stay 1¼m/1½m: sold 32,000 gns. *E. J. O'Neill*   **70**

PELHAM CRESCENT (IRE) 3 ch.g. Giant's Causeway (USA) 132 – Sweet Times 60 (Riverman (USA) 131) [2006 77: p7g⁶ 8.1g 9.9m Aug 16] close-coupled gelding: fair performer: left R. Hannon after reappearance: well held in handicaps last 2 starts: stays easy 1m: acts on polytrack, good to firm and good to soft ground: tried blinkered (ran well). *B. Palling*   **70**

PELICAN HILL (IRE) 3 b.g. Black Minnaloushe (USA) 123 – Perusha (USA) (Southern Halo (USA)) [2006 8m 8.1s May 26] sturdy gelding: tailed off in maidens. *T. H. Caldwell*   **–**

PELICAN KEY (IRE) 2 b.f. (Feb 7) Mujadil (USA) 119 – Guana Bay (Cadeaux Genereux 131) [2006 5f* 6m 5.2g⁵ p6g Oct 21] €130,000Y: rather leggy, useful-looking filly: fourth live foal: half-sister to 2-y-o 5f winner in Italy by Orpen: dam unraced close relative of very smart sprinter Prince Sabo: fairly useful performer: won minor event at Windsor in July: tailed off (reportedly distressed) in Princess Margaret Stakes at Ascot later in month: better run in listed races when fifth to Abbey Road at Newbury: will prove best kept to 5f/6f: acts on firm going. *D. M. Simcock*   **80**

PELLEAS 2 b.g. (May 7) Mark of Esteem (IRE) 137 – Questabelle (Rainbow Quest (USA) 134) [2006 8g Oct 17] 30,000Y: second foal: dam, ran twice, half-sister to high-class 1¼m performer Stagecraft: 40/1, behind in maiden at Bath: gelded after. *R. Charlton*   **–**

PENALTY CLAUSE (IRE) 6 b.g. Namaqualand (USA) – Lady Be Lucky (IRE) 57 (Taufan (USA) 119) [2006 –: 17.2m f16g Oct 12] leggy gelding: maiden: lightly raced and no form on Flat after 2004: tried blinkered/tongue tied/in cheekpieces: won over fences in September. *P. Howling*   **–**

PENANG CINTA 3 b.g. Halling (USA) 133 – Penang Pearl (FR) 106 (Bering 136) [2006 –: p7.1g* f8g 10m³ 8m 8m² 10f⁵ p10g p8g p8.6g³ Dec 11] smallish gelding: modest performer: won handicap at Wolverhampton in January: left G. Butler after seventh start: stays 1¼m: acts on polytrack and good to firm going: tried blinkered: carried head awkwardly sixth outing: quirky. *A. J. Chamberlain*   **64**

PENDING (IRE) 5 b.g. Pennekamp (USA) 130 – Dolcezza (FR) (Lichine (USA) 117) [2006 67, a62: f8g p9.5g² p8.6g⁶ p9.5g² f7s⁴ f8g³ p8.6g⁵ f6g p8.6g p8.6g f7g May 9] tall, lengthy gelding: fair performer, regressive in 2006: left R. Fahey after fourth outing, trained by R. Harris tenth start only: stays 9.5f: acts on all-weather, firm and soft going: tried blinkered, usually wears cheekpieces: tends to race freely/find little, and is one to treat with caution. *J. R. Boyle*   **– § a69 d**

PENEL (IRE) 5 b.g. Orpen (USA) 116 – Jayess Elle 55 (Sabrehill (USA) 120) [2006 58: f7g⁵ f7g f8g⁴ f7g⁵ f7g* f8g f7g² f7g f6g* f6g⁵ f7g f7g* May 31] smallish gelding: modest performer: won banded races at Southwell in February and April, and handicap there in May: effective at 6f to 1¼m: acts on all-weather and good to soft going: wears headgear. *P. T. Midgley*   **58**

PENFECTION (IRE) 3 b.f. Orpen (USA) 116 – Pharfetched 84 (Phardante (FR) 123) [2006 8s⁴ 9m³ 10m⁴ 10.1m⁵ 8m⁴ 9.7g² p8g⁵ 8.3d³ 10m³ Nov 5] €5,000Y: half-sister to winner in Japan by Foxhound: dam Irish 1¼m to 2m hurdles winner: fairly useful performer: won maiden at Rome in March on debut: trained by M. Botti in Britain fourth to eighth starts only (ran creditably all 3 outings in handicaps): returned to former yard, good 4¼ lengths third to Mount Eliza in listed race at Rome final outing: stays 1¼m: acts on polytrack, soft and good to firm going: tried tongue tied: sometimes finds little. *A. & G. Botti, Italy*   **94**

795

PENMARA 3 b.f. Mtoto 134 – Pendulum 82 (Pursuit of Love 124) [2006 62: 12.1g 10m   **59**
10d 10.1f³ 9.7f 10.1f³ 10.1m⁴ Aug 9] good-bodied filly: modest maiden: bred to stay
1½m: acts on firm going: awkward leaving stall/raced freely third start. *M. H. Tompkins*

PENNY FROM HEAVEN (IRE) 2 b.f. (Mar 4) Machiavellian (USA) 123 – Flying   **75**
Kiss (IRE) (Sadler's Wells (USA) 132) [2006 p8.6g⁶ p8g³ Nov 5] fourth foal: half-sister
to fairly useful 2004 2-y-o 6f winner Sun Kissed (by Sunday Silence): dam, ran twice in
France, sister to Racing Post Trophy winner Commander Collins, and closely related to
Breeders' Cup Sprint winner Lit de Justice and Derby third Colonel Collins: fair form in
maidens (on polytrack), third to Happy Go Lily at Lingfield. *E. A. L. Dunlop*

PENNY GLITTERS 3 br.f. Benny The Dip (USA) 127 – Lucy Glitters (USA) 60   **63**
(Cryptoclearance (USA)) [2006 63: 7m⁴ 7g 7.1m 9.8m 6.9m² 7.5f 8f⁵ 7.6m 6m p7g   **a56**
p7g p6g p7.1g* p7.1g p8g Dec 6] smallish filly: modest performer: won banded event at
Wolverhampton in November: stays 7f: acts on polytrack, raced only on good going or
firmer on turf: tried blinkered. *S. Parr*

PENNY POST (IRE) 2 b.f. (May 2) Green Desert (USA) 127 – Blue Note (FR) 122   **93 p**
(Habitat 134) [2006 p7g p6g* p6g* Nov 22] closely related to several at least useful
winners, including 5f (at 2 yrs, when also successful in Cheveley Park Stakes) to 7f
winner Blue Duster and 5f (at 2 yrs) to 1m winner Zieten (both smart, by Danzig), and
half-sister to 2 winners: dam French 5f to 7f winner: fairly useful form: improved fast
after debut, winning maiden at Wolverhampton and nursery at Kempton in November, in
latter still green but beating Boreal Applause by 1¼ lengths with something in hand: will
prove best up to 7f: raced on polytrack: should go on progressing. *M. Johnston*

PENNY RICH (IRE) 12 br.g. Little Bighorn 106 – Musical Puss (Orchestra 118)   **63 d**
[2006 81: 12s⁶ 12g 12d 16g 16g 14s⁶ p12g Nov 11] only modest handicapper at best in
2006: stays 2m: all 7 wins on going softer than good (acts on heavy): wears tongue tie.
T. Hogan, Ireland

PENNYROCK (IRE) 2 b.c. (Apr 19) Rock of Gibraltar (IRE) 133 – Inforapenny 111   **62**
(Deploy 131) [2006 7.5f³ 7.5m³ 7d Aug 28] close-coupled colt: third foal: dam, 1¼m
winner and third in Irish Oaks, half-sister to very smart performer up to 1½m Mons:
modest maiden: third to Champery (minor event) and Mesbaah (beaten 14 lengths), both
at Beverley: will stay 1¼m. *K. A. Ryan*

PENNY THOUGHTS 3 b.f. Prince Sabo 123 – United Passion 74 (Emarati (USA) 74)   **38**
[2006 61: p5.1g⁴ p5.1g Apr 22] good-topped filly: maiden: just poor form since debut at
2 yrs. *E. S. McMahon*

PENNY WHISPER (IRE) 3 b.f. Orpen (USA) 116 – Ionian Secret 56 (Mystiko   **–**
(USA) 124) [2006 71: 8.2s 7.1d 6g 7.2s f6g Oct 12] leggy, quite good-topped filly: fair
performer at 2 yrs: well held in 2006. *I. W. McInnes*

PENRYN 3 ch.g. Selkirk (USA) 129 – Camcorder (Nashwan (USA) 135) [2006 8s   **75**
8.2m* 12g⁴ Oct 13] 62,000Y: leggy, quite good-topped gelding: second foal: half-brother
to winner in USA by Dehere: dam unraced half-sister to smart French/US 1m/1¼m
performer Kirkwall (by Selkirk): fair form: won maiden at Nottingham in September: ran
creditably in claimer at Newmarket final start, though again hung: seems to stay 1½m:
slowly away first 2 outings. *D. R. C. Elsworth*

PENSATA 3 b.f. Compton Place 125 – Artistic Merit (Alhaarth (IRE) 126) [2006 –: 5m   **–**
5f⁶ 5d 6m⁶ 5m 6d 5s 5v Oct 9] little form: tried blinkered. *Miss L. A. Perratt*

PENTATONIC 3 b.f. Giant's Causeway (USA) 132 – Fascinating Rhythm 85 (Slip   **86 p**
Anchor 136) [2006 8.1g⁵ 11m² 10.2m* Sep 25] third foal: dam, 2-y-o 1m winner out of
Fillies' Mile runner-up Pick of The Pops: fair form in maidens, second to Counterpunch
at Goodwood prior to winning at Bath in September comfortably by 2½ lengths from
Moon Valley: should prove as effective at 1m as 1¼m: slowly away on debut: capable of
better still. *L. M. Cumani*

PENTECOST 7 ch.g. Tagula (IRE) 116 – Boughtbyphone 62 (Warning 136) [2006 108:   **109**
7.5m³ 8m* 8.9m 8m⁵ 8.1m 8g⁶ 8d⁶ Sep 23] sturdy gelding: useful handicapper: won at
Nad Al Sheba (from Spirit of France, leading on line) in February, best effort in 2006:
mostly at least respectable efforts after: stays 9f: yet to race on heavy going, acts on any
other turf: tried visored, not since 2003: has worn dropped noseband, and is usually held
up/pulls hard. *A. M. Balding*

PENWAY 5 b.g. Groom Dancer (USA) 128 – Imani 83 (Danehill (USA) 126) [2006 59:   **–**
p8g f12g f7g f8g f6g Feb 7] maiden: no form in 2006: tried tongue tied, blinkered nowadays. *A. Sadik*

PENWELL HILL (USA) 7 b.g. Distant View (USA) 126 – Avie's Jill (USA) (Lord
Avie (USA)) [2006 54, a85: f6g⁶ f7g p12.2g f8g³ f8g f7g f7s p9.5g f8g² Dec 14] quite
good-topped gelding: just fair form at best in 2006: left M. Attwater after seventh start,
J. Williams after eighth: stays 8.6f: acts on fibresand and firm going, no form on polytrack: sometimes blinkered/visored: front runner. *Miss M. E. Rowland* –
a70 d

PENZO (IRE) 3 gr.g. Shinko Forest (IRE) – Thatchabella (IRE) (Thatching 131) [2006
7g⁴ 6d² 8m² 8v Sep 14] 15,000Y: fourth foal: half-brother to winner in Hong Kong by
Alzao: dam unraced out of close relation to smart Irish 1991 2-y-o El Prado and half-sister
to high-class 1¼m performer Entitled: fair maiden: runner-up at Pontefract (edged right)
and Musselburgh: stays 1m: said to have lost action final outing. *J. Howard Johnson* 73

PEOPLETON BROOK 4 b.c. Compton Place 125 – Merch Rhyd-Y-Grug (Sabrehill
(USA) 120) [2006 88: 5d 5g* 5m* 5s 5m 5f 5f⁶ 5.1m 5s p5g⁵ Nov 11] leggy colt: useful
handicapper: won at Goodwood and Lingfield in May: below form after: best at 5f: acts
on firm and soft ground: blinkered (ran too freely) once at 2 yrs: races up with pace.
J. M. Bradley 97

PEP IN HER STEP (IRE) 3 b.f. Cape Cross (IRE) 129 – Monzitta (GER) (Monsun
(GER) 124) [2006 67: p8g⁴ 7d 6m 7d Jul 31] €19,000Y, second foal: dam German 9.5f
winner: fair maiden: ran creditably in 2006 only in handicap at Lingfield on reappearance: stays 1m: acts on polytrack and firm ground: tried blinkered. *E. Tyrrell, Ireland* 67

PEPPERMINT GREEN 2 b.f. (Apr 25) Green Desert (USA) 127 – One So Wonderful 121 (Nashwan (USA) 135) [2006 7d 7g Sep 15] strong filly: fourth live foal:
half-sister to winner in USA by Machiavellian: dam 7f (at 2 yrs) to 1¼m (Juddmonte
International) winner: not fully wound up for maiden at Newmarket and minor event at
Newbury (eighth to Darrfonah): sure to improve as 3-y-o. *L. M. Cumani* 73 p

PEPPER ROAD 7 ch.g. Elmaamul (USA) 125 – Floral Spark 69 (Forzando 122) [2006
58: f8g⁶ p7.1g⁴ 8m 8.5g 7.1m 8f Sep 20] poor performer: effective at 7f/1m: acts on
polytrack, firm and good to soft going: tried in cheekpieces (below form): often early to
post: withdrawn at start (broke through stall) intended third outing. *R. Bastiman* 47

PEPPERTREE 3 b.f. Fantastic Light (USA) 134 – Delauncy (Machiavellian (USA)
123) [2006 8.2m⁶ 11.6f* 12m³ 12s Oct 7] €50,000Y: leggy, quite attractive filly: second
foal: half-sister to smart 1¼m winner who stayed 13.4f Delsarte (by Theatrical): dam,
useful French 2-y-o 1m winner who stayed 1¼m, daughter of Park Hill winner Casey:
useful form: won maiden at Windsor in July: good third to Rayhani in handicap at Ascot
next time: well held in listed race on soft ground at Ascot final outing: should stay 1¾m:
acts on firm going. *J. R. Fanshawe* 95

PEPPERTREE LANE (IRE) 3 ch.c. Peintre Celebre (USA) 137 – Salonrolle (IRE)
103 (Tirol 127) [2006 83: 8d* 8s* 8.1s⁵ 8m 11.9g 12s* 14v* 12d³ 12s* 11.6d Nov 4]
rather leggy, quite attractive colt: good walker: had a fine season, developing into a smart
performer: won maiden at Ripon in April and handicaps at York in May, Ripon in August,
Haydock (beat Quizzene by ¾ length in betfredpoker.com Old Borough Cup) in Septem-

betfredpoker.com Old Borough Cup Stakes (Handicap), Haydock—the fourth of Peppertree Lane's wins;
next come the grey Quizzene, Solent (rail) and McEldowney

ladbrokes.com Stakes (Handicap), Ascot—Peppertree Lane continues his fine season, winning comfortably from St Savarin, Alessano (blinkers) and Purple Moon

ber and Ascot (beat St Savarin by 1¼ lengths in ladbrokes.com Stakes) in October: well held in November Handicap at Windsor final outing: will probably stay 2m: has form on good to firm going, but all wins on softer than good (acts on heavy): races prominently: tends to wander and carry head awkwardly, but is game. *M. Johnston*

PEPPIN'S GOLD (IRE) 2 b.f. (Apr 4) King Charlemagne (USA) 120 – Miss Senate (IRE) (Alzao (USA) 117) [2006 p5g 5g² 5g p6g 7m 6m⁵ p7.1g 7.1d² p7.1g⁵ f6g⁴ Nov 10] €5,000Y: lightly-made filly: fourth foal: half-sister to winner in Greece by Bluebird: dam unraced sister to smart performer up to 1½m Suplizi: modest maiden: below form after fourth outing: stays 7f: acts on polytrack and good to soft ground: tongue tied final start. *B. R. Millman* **63 d**

PERCUSSIONIST (IRE) 5 b.g. Sadler's Wells (USA) 132 – Magnificient Style (USA) 107 (Silver Hawk (USA) 123) [2006 118: 13.9s* 14g Sep 16] **121**

Percussionist made a successful debut over fences a little more than two years after finishing fourth in the Derby, which gives some indication of the twists and turns his career has taken since he won a three-year-old maiden at Newmarket, shortly after the death of his then on owner Robert Sangster. Now racing in another set of well-known colours, those of Andrea and Graham Wylie who paid 340,000 guineas for him at the Doncaster November Sales in 2004, Percussionist looks to have a fairly bright future as a chaser. Yet he is still very smart on the Flat, as he demonstrated when winning the Emirates Airline Yorkshire Cup at York in May, and it seems almost certain that he will continue in the role for which he was purchased, that of a dual-purpose performer.

Percussionist had put himself very much in the Derby picture with a remarkable performance on his next outing after Newmarket, winning the Derby Trial at Lingfield by ten lengths despite cocking his jaw and hanging markedly right. He acquitted himself well at Epsom, staying on strongly to be beaten less

Emirates Airline Yorkshire Cup, York—
Percussionist shows he's as good as ever on the Flat with a three-length success from Sergeant Cecil

than two lengths by North Light, but proved rather disappointing after, not always looking genuine and tried in blinkers on his final outing that season. Transferred from John Gosden to Howard Johnson following his sale, Percussionist was then gelded and ran twice on the Flat for his new stable in 2005, finishing a neck second to Franklins Gardens in the Yorkshire Cup and down the field in the Gold Cup. The Yorkshire Cup was the race chosen for the return to Flat racing after Percussionist had won twice from four starts over hurdles in the winter. He faced six opponents in what looked an up-to-standard renewal, only one of them at longer odds than Percussionist, who started at 9/1. The ground at York was very testing, as it had been twelve months earlier, and suited Percussionist ideally. Racing with more zest than he had often done earlier in his career, Percussionist took the lead under pressure over two furlongs out and found plenty to pull three lengths clear of Sergeant Cecil, the remainder well strung out behind. With connections unwilling to race Percussionist on ground firmer than good—he has been well below form on all three starts under such conditions since the Derby—it was September before he was seen in action again. That was in the Irish St Leger at the Curragh, for which he looked the strongest of the four British contenders. He failed by a long way to do himself justice, the race being won by Kastoria, who was only fourth in the Yorkshire Cup. As far as the Flat was concerned that was it for Percussionist in 2006. In October he won a maiden chase at Wetherby by nineteen lengths, and the following month he finished second in a novice chase at Ayr.

		Northern Dancer (b 1961)	Nearctic
	Sadler's Wells (USA) (b 1981)		Natalma
		Fairy Bridge (b 1975)	Bold Reason
Percussionist (IRE) (b.g. 2001)			Special
		Silver Hawk (b 1979)	Roberto
	Magnificient Style (USA) (b 1993)		Gris Vitesse
		Mia Karina (b 1983)	Icecapade
			Basin

Percussionist's dam, the Musidora Stakes winner Magnificient Style, has a one hundred per cent record with her foals. Percussionist was preceded by a minor stakes winner in the States by Storm Cat and by the smart filly Echoes In Eternity (by Spinning World), winner of the Sun Chariot and Park Hill Stakes: and since Percussionist Magnificient Style has been responsible for another smart filly in Playful Act, a sister to Percussionist who won the May Hill Stakes, Fillies' Mile and Lancashire Oaks, and by the fairly useful nine-furlong winner Distinctive Look (by Danehill) and Petara Bay (by Peintre Celebre), successful in a two-year-old maiden over a mile at Haydock in September. Percussionist, a tall, close-coupled gelding with a powerful round action, stays two miles. The ground was against him the only time he was tried over further, in the Gold Cup. An edgy sort who tends to sweat, Percussionist wears a crossed noseband and has worn earplugs. He reportedly had a breathing problem on the two occasions he was beaten over hurdles. *J. Howard Johnson*

PERCY DOUGLAS 6 b.g. Elmaamul (USA) 125 – Qualitair Dream 80 (Dreams To Reality (USA) 113) [2006 67§, a51§: f5g f5g p5.1g⁴ f5g⁴ p5.1g p5.1g f5g⁶ f5g² f5g* f5g³ p5.1g* f5g⁵ f5g² 5d p5g 5g 5f 5f 5m² 5f 5f 5m p5.1g f5g Dec 28] good-topped gelding: modest performer: won banded races at Southwell and Wolverhampton in March: effective at 5f/6f: acts on all-weather, firm and soft ground: wears headgear: usually tongue tied: has bled: usually races prominently: inconsistent. *Miss A. Stokell* **62 §**

PERCY'S PEARL (USA) 4 ch.g. Rainbow Quest (USA) 134 – Ridgewood Pearl 125 (Indian Ridge 123) [2006 87: 8.1d⁴ 8.3f⁵ Jul 2] tall, useful-looking gelding: lightly-raced handicapper: just fair form in 2006: should stay at least 1¼m. *D. R. C. Elsworth* **78**

PEREGRINE FALCON 2 b.c. (Mar 7) In The Wings 128 – Island Race 93 (Common Grounds 118) [2006 p8.6g⁴ p8.6g* p10g⁵ Nov 25] 160,000Y: fifth foal: brother to 6-y-o Soldier Hollow and half-brother to 4-y-o Day Walker (by Dr Devious): dam 6f winner: fair form: confirmed débbefore promise when winning maiden at Wolverhampton by 1¾ lengths from Cavalry Twill: favourite, eased as if amiss in minor event at Lingfield week later: should stay at least 1¼m. *M. Johnston* **77**

PEREZ (IRE) 4 b.g. Mujadil (USA) 119 – Kahla (Green Desert (USA) 127) [2006 72: p8g³ p8.6g³ p8g⁶ p8.6g² 10g p8.6g* 8g 9.8d p8.6g 9.2g⁶ 10.5g Sep 22] good-bodied geld- **–** **a76**

ing: fair performer: won seller at Wolverhampton (left Pat Eddery) in June: well below form after: should stay 1¼m: acts on polytrack and good to firm going: tried blinkered, often visored: has hung left. *W. Storey*

PERFECT COURTESY (IRE) 2 ch.g. (Feb 21) Danehill Dancer (IRE) 117 – Kate **74** Maher (IRE) (Rainbow Quest (USA) 134) [2006 7m 7.1m³ p8g 8d⁵ Aug 25] lengthy, workmanlike gelding: first foal: dam, ran twice, out of Italian Oaks winner/Irish Oaks dead-heater Melodist: fair maiden: third to Old Romney at Sandown: gelded after final start: should stay 1m: blinkered (forcefully ridden) once. *P. W. Chapple-Hyam*

PERFECT COVER (IRE) 3 b.f. Royal Applause 124 – See You Later 98 (Emarati **48** (USA) 74) [2006 6m⁵ p6g 6m Sep 12] 75,000Y: second foal: half-sister to fairly useful 2004 2-y-o 5f winner Annatalia (by Pivotal): dam 5f winner (including at 2 yrs): poor form in maidens. *J. A. R. Toller*

PERFECTIONIST 4 b.f. In The Wings 128 – Lady Donatella 57 (Last Tycoon 131) **56** [2006 54: 12.1f 10.1f p12.2g⁵ f12g 12m⁵ 14.1d⁵ 14.1m⁴ p12.2m 10.1m Sep 13] workmanlike maiden: modest maiden: stays 1½m: acts on good to firm going: sometimes wears headgear. *Mrs C. A. Dunnett*

PERFECT ORDER (USA) 3 br. or b.f. Red Ransom (USA) – Ideal Index (USA) **55** (Copelan (USA)) [2006 62d: p7g f8g² f8g f12g 8m⁴ 7.1s 7f⁶ p10g 8.5m 8f³ 8d f8g³ p8.6g p10g Nov 27] modest maiden: stays 1m: acts on all-weather, firm and soft going: usually wears cheekpieces: often slowly away: sold 7,000 gns. *N. A. Callaghan*

PERFECTPERFORMANCE (USA) 4 ch.c. Rahy (USA) 115 – Balistroika (USA) **107 +** (Nijinsky (CAN) 138) [2006 –: 12d* Aug 18] strong, good-bodied colt: type to carry condition: has fluent, quick action: smart performer at best: successful in Royal Lodge Stakes at Ascot at 2 yrs: reportedly fractured left ilial wing only outing in 2005: injured a suspensory when winning minor event at Newmarket (by ¾ length from Camrose, pair clear) only outing in 2006: stays 1½m: acts on firm and good to soft going: sometimes wears blanket for stall entry: tends to edge right. *Saeed bin Suroor*

PERFECT PRACTICE 2 ch.f. (Feb 4) Medicean 128 – Giusina Mia (USA) (Diesis **54** 133) [2006 p7g⁶ p7g Dec 20] 16,000 2-y-o: first foal: dam 1¼m winner in Italy: modest form in maidens at Lingfield. *J. A. R. Toller*

PERFECT PUNCH 7 b.g. Reprimand 122 – Aliuska (IRE) 70 (Fijar Tango (FR) 127) **60** [2006 –: 11g 14.1d 13.9m 14.1f Jun 24] modest handicapper: stays 1¾m: acts on polytrack and good to firm going. *K. G. Reveley*

PERFECT REFLECTION 2 b.f. (Apr 4) Josr Algarhoud (IRE) 118 – Surrealist **–** (ITY) (Night Shift (USA)) [2006 5m 6f⁴ 6m Jul 24] half-sister to 3 winners, including fairly useful 5f/6f (including at 2 yrs) winner Mitsuki (by Puissance) and 3-y-o Crafty Fox: dam unraced: last in maidens. *A. Berry*

PERFECT REWARD 2 b.c. (Jan 24) Cadeaux Genereux 131 – Maid To Perfection **62** 102 (Sadler's Wells (USA) 132) [2006 7.1m 7s 8.2s⁵ Oct 25] close-coupled colt: modest form in maidens: likely to prove best up to 1m. *Mrs A. J. Perrett*

PERFECT SOLUTION (IRE) 4 ch.f. Entrepreneur 123 – Pearl Barley (IRE) 79 **62** (Polish Precedent (USA) 131) [2006 67: p6g 6g p8g Jun 28] sturdy filly: modest handicapper: should stay 1m: acts on good to soft going, probably on polytrack and good to firm. *J. A. R. Toller*

PERFECT STAR 2 b.f. (Apr 12) Act One 124 – Granted (FR) 100 (Cadeaux Genereux **84 p** 131) [2006 7f² 7g* Oct 12] 25,000Y: rather leggy filly: third foal: half-sister to 3-y-o Barodine: dam 1m winner who stayed 9f: confirmed debut promise (second to Cumin) when winning maiden at Newmarket 2 months later by length from Palamoun, making all: will be suited by 1m: useful prospect. *C. G. Cox*

PERFECT STORY (IRE) 4 b.f. Desert Story (IRE) 115 – Shore Lark (USA) (Storm **93** Bird (CAN) 134) [2006 89: p7g⁶ p7g³ p6g⁴ 6g⁴ p7g⁵ p6g* p6g Dec 16] good-topped filly: fairly useful handicapper: won at Lingfield in December: effective at 6f to 1m: acts on polytrack, firm and good to soft ground: reliable. *J. A. R. Toller*

PERFECT STYLE (IRE) 2 b.f. (Apr 3) Desert Style (IRE) 121 – Seymour (IRE) 78 **50** (Eagle Eyed (USA) 111) [2006 6f 6g 5m⁶ p6f⁵ Aug 14] 25,000Y: smallish filly: second foal: half-sister to 3-y-o Charles Darwin: dam, maiden best at 5f at 2 yrs, closely related to very smart 6f/7f performer Mount Abu: modest maiden: raced at 5f/6f: sold 5,500 gns. *M. Blanshard*

PERFECT TREASURE (IRE) 3 ch.f. Night Shift (USA) – Pitrizza (IRE) (Machia- **77** vellian (USA) 123) [2006 70: p6g⁵ 6f* 5.3m³ 6g 6f² p7g p7.1g p6g⁵ Dec 19] sturdy **a66**

filly: fair performer, better on turf than all-weather: won maiden at Brighton (carried head bit awkwardly) in May: stays 6f: acts on polytrack and firm going: tried tongue tied. *J. A. R. Toller*

PERFIDIOUS (USA) 8 b.g. Lear Fan (USA) 130 – Perfolia (USA) 104 (Nodouble (USA)) [2006 74: p12g p12g Jun 6] sturdy gelding: fair handicapper in 2005, well held in 2006: tried visored, blinkered nowadays: sometimes slowly away: often leads, and tends to race moodily when unable to do so. *J. R. Boyle* —

PERIANTH (IRE) 4 ch.g. Bluebird (USA) 125 – Meandering Rose (USA) (Irish River (FR) 131) [2006 –, a45: f8g Jan 1] lengthy gelding: poor maiden: well held only outing in 2006: has run creditably in blinkers. *J. G. M. O'Shea* —

PERILORE (IRE) 2 b.f. (Mar 26) Traditionally (USA) 117 – Titania (Fairy King (USA)) [2006 5d 5g 7.1d⁵ 8m⁴ 7.1m 6v 6s Oct 24] €5,000Y: fifth foal: half-sister to 3 winners, including 3-y-o Charles Parnell: dam unraced: no form: tried blinkered: sold 2,000 gns. *A. Berry*

PERLACHY 2 b.g. (Mar 30) Kyllachy 129 – Perfect Dream 72 (Emperor Jones (USA) 119) [2006 5d⁵ 6v⁴ 5m³ 6f² 5f³ 5f² 6f⁴ 5g³ 6d⁶ f5g⁶ p6g⁵ Dec 26] 24,000Y: quite good-topped, close-coupled gelding: first foal: dam lightly-raced Irish middle-distance maiden: fair maiden: placed 5 times: sold from T. Easterby 15,000 gns after ninth start, and gelded: effective at 5f/6f: best form on good going or firmer. *Mrs N. Macauley* — 76

PERMANENT WAY (IRE) 3 b.c. Fantastic Light (USA) 134 – Itab (USA) 71 (Dayjur (USA) 137) [2006 p9.5g⁶ p10g³ p12g²* 10g p12g* Jun 14] €110,000Y: third foal: dam, 7f winner, half-sister to Poule d'Essai des Pouliches winner Ta Rib: fairly useful form: won maiden at Lingfield (very easily by 7 lengths) in February and handicap at Kempton in June: stays 1½m: acts on polytrack: reportedly returned very sore after penultimate outing. *B. J. Meehan* — 94

PERNOMENTE (IRE) 2 b.g. (Apr 29) Orpen (USA) 116 – Tread Softly (IRE) 70 (Roi Danzig (USA)) [2006 p5g³ p5g² 5.1d⁵ 5d⁴ 5f 5f³ 5m 5.1f² p5g⁵ 5.1g* a6d² Nov 7] €12,000Y: fourth foal: half-brother to 2003 2-y-o 5f winner Silent Revenge (by Daggers Drawn) and Swedish 2005 2-y-o 8.7f winner Soft Pearl (by Titus Livius): dam 2-y-o 6f winner: fair performer: won maiden at Bath (dictated) in October: sold from J. S. Moore 16,000 gns before final outing: stays 6f: acts on polytrack/dirt and firm going: tongue tied after fourth start (has reportedly had breathing problem). *Y. Durant, Sweden* — 79

PERSIAN CARPET 4 b.f. Desert Style (IRE) 121 – Kuwah (IRE) 77 (Be My Guest (USA) 126) [2006 62: p12.2g Apr 29] workmanlike filly: modest maiden: well held only outing in 2006: usually races prominently. *B. I. Case* —

PERSIAN CONQUEROR (IRE) 3 b.g. Sinndar (IRE) 134 – Persian Fantasy 94 (Persian Bold 123) [2006 –p: 10d⁵ 14.1g 16g⁴ 16.2m⁴ Aug 28] smallish gelding: poor maiden: should stay 2m: acts on good to soft going. *J. L. Dunlop* — 49

PERSIAN EXPRESS (USA) 3 b.f. Bahri (USA) 125 – Istikbal (USA) (Kingmambo (USA) 125) [2006 72: 10m³ 12g 10m⁴ 8m⁵ p8.6f²* p8g⁴ p8g* p8g* Nov 5] tall filly: useful handicapper on all-weather, fair on turf: won at Wolverhampton in August, Kempton in September and Lingfield (beat Neardown Beauty convincingly by ¾ length) in November: stays 1¼m: acts on polytrack and firm going. *B. W. Hills* — 76 a97

PERSIAN FOX (IRE) 2 b.g. (Apr 29) King Charlemagne (USA) 120 – Persian Mistress (IRE) (Persian Bold 123) [2006 5g 5.5d 7f² 8m* 8d 8m 6m Sep 19] 15,000Y: leggy gelding: half-brother to Irish 6.5f winner Pip 'n Judy (by Pips Pride) and 4-y-o Belly Dancer: dam unraced half-sister to high-class sprinter Hallgate: fair performer: won maiden at Yarmouth in August: little impact in nurseries (once in cheekpieces), then gelded: stays 1m: acts on firm going. *G. A. Huffer* — 73

PERSIAN PERIL 2 br.g. (May 3) Erhaab (USA) 127 – Brush Away (Ahonoora 122) [2006 5m⁴ 6.1m⁴ 6g² f6g² 7.1d* Aug 2] 11,000Y: half-brother to numerous winners, including useful 1997 2-y-o 6f winner Bintang (by Soviet Star) and 3-y-o Jimmy The Guesser: dam unraced: fair form in maidens, second at Ayr and Southwell (behind Naayla) before landing odds at Musselburgh: stays 7f. *G. A. Swinbank* — 77

PERSIAN WARRIOR (IRE) 3 b.g. Desert Prince (IRE) 130 – Viscaria (IRE) 97 (Barathea (IRE) 127) [2006 10m 10g p12g 10m Sep 19] well held in maidens/handicap: tried in cheekpieces. *W. R. Swinburn* —

PERSONA (IRE) 4 b.f. Night Shift (USA) – Alonsa (IRE) 69 (Trempolino (USA) 135) [2006 65: p12g 9.7f 10.9d² 12s⁵ p10g Nov 15] unfurnished filly: fair maiden handi- — 68 capper: stays 11f: acts on good to soft going: reportedly had breathing problem on reappearance. *B. J. McMath*

PERSONAL COLUMN 2 ch.g. (Apr 1) Pursuit of Love 124 – Tromond 94 (Lomond **76 p** (USA) 128) [2006 p8g³ p10g* Nov 29] 10,000F, 48,000Y: eighth foal: brother to useful 1m winner (including at 2 yrs) Embraced and half-brother to several winners, including very smart 1m (at 2 yrs) to 1½m winner Nowhere To Exit (by Exit To Nowhere) and 5-y-o Cesare: dam, 9f winner who stayed 1½m, half-sister to 3-y-o Mont Etoile: landed odds in maiden at Kempton by 1¼ lengths from Into Action, still green and getting on top only late on: will be suited by 1½m: will do better still. *T. G. Mills*

PERSONIFY 4 ch.g. Zafonic (USA) 130 – Dignify (IRE) 105 (Rainbow Quest (USA) **81** 134) [2006 8d 10m 8.3f 8m* 8.1f² 9g² 8.1m* 8m Oct 8] rather leggy gelding: fairly useful handicapper: missed 2005: won at Bath in June and Sandown in September: barely stays 9f: acts on firm going: visored and tongue tied final outing in 2004, in cheekpieces last 6 starts. *C. G. Cox*

PERTEMPS GREEN 3 b.g. Green Desert (USA) 127 – Pure Misk 55 (Rainbow Quest **69** (USA) 134) [2006 61: 7m⁵ 7g Aug 17] leggy, close-coupled gelding: lightly-raced maiden: best effort when fifth at Newmarket on reappearance: will stay 1m: raced on good/good to firm going. *Stef Liddiard*

PERTEMPS HEROINE 3 b.f. Arkadian Hero (USA) 123 – Watheeqah (USA) 60 **48** (Topsider (USA)) [2006 55: p7g 7g p6m⁶ p8g p8.6g Dec 4] strong, heavy-topped filly: poor maiden: left A. Smith prior to final start. *A. G. Newcombe*

PERTEMPS NETWORKS 2 b.g. (Apr 13) Golden Snake (USA) 127 – Society Girl **57** 73 (Shavian 125) [2006 6m p6g 6m p6f Aug 14] tall, workmanlike gelding: modest maiden: bred for 1m+, but free-going type. *M. W. Easterby*

PERUVIAN PRINCESS 7 gr.m. Missed Flight 123 – Misty View 73 (Absalom 128) **–** [2006 f12g Mar 8] no form. *J. T. Stimpson*

PERUVIAN PRINCE (USA) 4 b.g. Silver Hawk (USA) 123 – Inca Dove (USA) (Mr **89** Prospector (USA)) [2006 83: 8m³ 8m 10m² 9.7m³ 12m⁶ p9.5m² f8g³ p9.5g* p9.5s* p8.6g* p9.5g² Dec 22] strong, well-made gelding: fairly useful handicapper: left J. Toller 26,000 gns after sixth start: won 3 times at Wolverhampton in December: stays 1¼m: acts on polytrack and good to firm going: tried visored. *R. A. Fahey*

PERUVIAN STYLE (IRE) 5 b.g. Desert Style (IRE) 121 – Lady's Vision (IRE) 93 **66** (Vision (USA)) [2006 60, a78: p7g 6m⁴ 7.1d 7d 7.1m⁴ 6f² p6g⁶ 5.7f* 6m² 5g 6.1m⁴ **a58** 5.7f² 6g3 6d p5.1m⁶ p5.1m Nov 8] strong gelding: fair performer on turf, modest on all-weather: won claimer at Bath in August: best at 5f to easy 7f: acts on polytrack and firm ground, below form on ground softer than good: tried blinkered: has raced freely. *J. M. Bradley*

PESCATORIO (USA) 3 b.c. Storm Cat (USA) – Morning Devotion (USA) 102 **76** (Affirmed (USA)) [2006 7g 8.2d² 8g 7.5f 12g⁴ 12d Jul 31] strong colt: brother to useful Irish 2002 2-y-o 7f winner Some Kind of Tiger, closely related to 2 winners by Storm Bird, notably top-class Oaks/Irish Derby winner Balanchine (also 7f winner at 2 yrs), and half-brother to 3 winners, including smart 7f to 1½m winner Romanov (by Nureyev): dam, 2-y-o 6f winner, stayed 1½m: as low as 20/1 for 2000 Guineas during winter: fair form in maidens: green and not knocked about at Newmarket on debut: in frame at Limerick and the Curragh (apprentice minor event) after: stays 1½m: acts on good to soft going: blinkered (well held) final outing: sent to USA. *A. P. O'Brien, Ireland*

PETANA 6 br.m. Petong 126 – Duxyana (IRE) (Cyrano de Bergerac 120) [2006 51§: **42** p5.1g⁶ p5.1g p5.1g p6g p5.1g⁶ p5g May 15] compact mare: poor performer: effective at 5f/6f: acts on polytrack, firm and good to soft ground: usually wears blinkers/cheekpieces: tends to get behind early on. *Peter Grayson*

PETARA BAY (IRE) 2 b.c. (May 4) Peintre Celebre (USA) 137 – Magnificient Style **89 p** (USA) 107 (Silver Hawk (USA) 123) [2006 8.1m 8.1g* 8s Oct 21] 340,000Y: big colt: sixth foal: closely related to smart 1m (Sun Chariot Stakes) to 14.6f (Park Hill Stakes) winner Echoes In Eternity (by Spinning World) and half-brother to several winners, notably smart 7f (at 2 yrs) to 1½m (Lancashire Oaks) winner Playful Act and 5-y-o Percussionist: dam won Musidora Stakes: fairly useful form: much improved from debut when winning maiden at Haydock in September by 2½ lengths from Ajhar: stiff task when tenth of 14 to Authorized in Racing Post Trophy at Newbury: will be suited by 1¼m/1½m: type to progress more at 3 yrs. *T. G. Mills*

PETER ISLAND (FR) 3 b.g. Dansili 127 – Catania (USA) (Aloma's Ruler (USA)) **85** [2006 77: p7g p6g⁵ p6g⁴ p7.1g p6g* 6f² 6.1f⁴ 6d 6m⁵ p6g⁴ 5.5m⁵ 5f⁵ 6.1m² 6m³ p6g* p6g[6] p6g Sep 18] smallish, strong gelding: fairly useful handicapper: won at Kempton in April and August: stays 7f: acts on polytrack and firm going: has been blinkered, visored last 6 starts: usually races prominently. *J. Gallagher*

PETERS DELITE 4 b.g. Makbul 104 – Steadfast Elite (IRE) 58 (Glenstal (USA) 118) **56** [2006 74: 7.1g 7.5f 7.5f 9.9f[5] 10.5f 8.2m[6] 6.9m[5] 8m[5] 8.6m[6] 10m[4] 10f Sep 20] quite good-topped gelding: modest maiden: best form at 6f/7f: acts on firm and soft going: tried in cheekpieces. *R. A. Fahey*

PETER'S IMP (IRE) 11 b.g. Imp Society (USA) - Catherine Clare 58 (Sallust 134) **–** [2006 55: 13f 13m 14.1f Aug 15] good-bodied gelding: well held on Flat in 2006 (won over hurdles in August): tried blinkered/visored earlier in career: usually held up. *A. Berry*

PETITE BOULANGERE (IRE) 3 b.f. Namid 128 – Preponderance (IRE) 85 (Cyr- **–** ano de Bergerac 120) [2006 7g p6g p5.1g Oct 14] 40,000Y: seventh foal: half-sister to 3 winners, including smart sprinter Guinea Hunter (by Pips Pride): dam Irish 2-y-o 5f winner: well held in maidens. *S. Kirk*

PETITE MAC 6 b.m. Timeless Times (USA) 99 – Petite Elite 47 (Anfield 117) [2006 **74** 63: 7m[3] 5g* 6m[6] 5.9m[5] 6.9g[2] 6f 7g 6d[3] 6d* 6d 6f[2] 5g[4] Sep 27] small mare: fair handi- capper, better on turf than all-weather: won at Carlisle in May and Newcastle in August: effective at 5f to 7f: acts on fibresand, firm and good to soft going: tried blinkered/in cheekpieces: ridden by 7-lb claimer Suzzanne France. *N. Bycroft*

PETITE PARAMOUR (IRE) 5 b.m. Malmsey (USA) 110 – Fleet Petite (IRE) 87 **68 +** (Posen (USA)) [2006 87d: p9.5g[3] p10g[2] a8.3g* a12g 10.6d[5] 7.8d[4] 10.5g* 7.6d[2] 10.5g[5] a8.8g* a10.5g[3] a6.5g* 11g* 8g 15v 11g[6] Dec 3] fair performer: left Gay Kelleway after second outing and rejoined former stable: won minor events at Mijas in February, Marseilles-Borely in May and Mijas in June, handicap at Mijas in July, and €22,000 event at San Sebastian in August: effective at 6.5f, has form up to 1¾m: acts on polytrack/sand and good to soft ground: tried tongue tied: tough. *Ms J. Bidgood, Spain*

PETITO (IRE) 3 b.g. Imperial Ballet (IRE) 110 – Fallacy (Selkirk (USA) 129) [2006 **65** 10g[6] 10g[5] 10m May 15] strong gelding: easily best effort in maidens when fifth to Sixties Icon at Windsor. *Ian Williams*

PETRICHAN (IRE) 3 b.g. Medicean 128 – Numancia (IRE) (Alzao (USA) 117) **71** [2006 39: f8g* f8g* p8.6g[5] p8.6g[3] 8.5g p12.2g Jul 3] quite good-topped gelding: fair performer: won banded race and handicap, both at Southwell in January: stays 8.6f: acts on all-weather: blinkered third start at 2 yrs, wore cheekpieces last 5 outings: races prominently: sold 3,800 gns, joined S. Clark. *K. A. Ryan*

PETROGLYPH 2 ch.c. (Feb 17) Indian Ridge 123 – Madame Dubois 121 (Legend of **68 p** France (USA) 124) [2006 8.2d[3] Nov 1] 220,000Y: very tall colt: brother to smart 6f (at 2 yrs) to 1m (Irish 2000 Guineas) winner Indian Haven, and half-brother to several winners, including dam of 5-y-o Imperial Stride and 3-y-o Hala Bek: dam 9f to 14.6f (Park Hill Stakes) winner: 11/8, 8 lengths third to Sagredo in maiden at Nottingham, looking green and ungainly: should improve. *Saeed bin Suroor*

PETROSIAN 2 b.g. (Mar 29) Sakhee (USA) 136 – Arabis 88 (Arazi (USA) 135) [2006 **63 §** 7.5m[4] 8m[3] 10.1d[6] p8.6m Oct 31] modest maiden: should stay 1¼m/1½m: temperamental (gelded after final outing). *M. Johnston*

PETROSS 3 b.g. Efisio 120 – Zoena 67 (Emarati (USA) 74) [2006 7.2d[6] 6m 7.9g[6] 6g **65** 8v[2] 8s[2] 7.2v[3] Oct 9] modest performer: won maiden at Mijas at 2 yrs when trained in Spain by P. Haley: good efforts in handicaps in Britain last 3 starts: stayed 1m: acted on sand and heavy going: dead. *R. M. Whitaker*

PETROVICH (USA) 3 ch.c. Giant's Causeway (USA) 132 – Pharma (USA) 118 **111 p** (Theatrical 128) [2006 8g* 10m[2] Jun 22] 150,000 2-y-o: good-topped colt: has scope: fifth foal: half-brother to French 1½m winner Pharma West (by Gone West): dam US Grade 1 9f winner out of high-class sprinter Committed: landed odds comfortably in newcomers event at Newmarket in April: improved considerably when ½-length second to Snoqualmie Boy in listed race at Royal Ascot, still looking green and closing fast (rated as winner): reportedly suffered a setback following month: should still improve, and make an impact in pattern races. *J. Noseda*

PETRULA 7 ch.g. Tagula (IRE) 116 – Bouffant (High Top 131) [2006 73: 12.3d 12d **66** May 28] good-bodied gelding: fair handicapper: lightly raced nowadays: best form around 1¼m: acts on firm and soft going: usually wears headgear: races up with pace: sometimes finishes weakly. *K. A. Ryan*

totesport 0800 221 221 Stakes (Handicap), Ascot—a valuable win for the small stable of Mark Buckley as Pevensey (noseband) beats Group Captain and Peppertree Lane (left)

PEVENSEY (IRE) 4 b.g. Danehill (USA) 126 – Champaka (IRE) (Caerleon (USA) **98** 132) [2006 94: p10g 8m 10g⁴ 10g 10.5g 11.6m² 12f³ 11.8m* 10m⁴ 12g⁴ 10.1m⁴ 12d* 12s⁶ p12g⁵ Oct 21] compact gelding: useful handicapper: won at Leicester in July and Ascot (beat Group Captain by neck in valuable event) in September: stays 1½m: acts on firm and good to soft going, probably on polytrack: tried blinkered early in career: usually held up: reliable: joined J. J. Quinn, won over hurdles in December. *M. A. Buckley*

PHANTOM WHISPER 3 b.g. Makbul 104 – La Belle Vie 73 (Indian King (USA) **94** 128) [2006 90: p6g³ p5g⁶ 6.1s² 5g* 5f 6m 6g³ 6d Sep 22] workmanlike gelding: fairly useful handicapper: won at Windsor in June by 1½ lengths from Loch Verdi: raced only at 5f/6f: acts on polytrack and soft ground: tried blinkered in 2005: hung right twice at 2 yrs. *B. R. Millman*

PHARAOH PRINCE 5 b.g. Desert Prince (IRE) 130 – Kinlochewe 102 (Old Vic 136) **58** [2006 63: p12.2g p9.5g⁵ p12g p9.5g² p10g⁶ p9.5g p12.2g³ p10g⁶ Dec 22] modest performer: stays 1½m: acts on polytrack, firm and good to soft ground: tried tongue tied, sometimes blinkered/visored. *G. Prodromou*

PHAROAH'S GOLD (IRE) 8 b.g. Namaqualand (USA) – Queen Nefertiti (IRE) 61 **–** (Fairy King (USA)) [2006 –, a56: f8g f8g f12g Feb 5] smallish, strong gelding: no form in 2006: left D. Burchell after reappearance: often wears headgear. *Mrs N. S. Evans*

PHEBE 3 b.f. Sadler's Wells (USA) 132 – Puce 112 (Darshaan 133) [2006 10m⁴ 12g⁶ **70** Aug 7] smallish, sturdy filly: fifth foal: sister to smart 1¼m (at 2 yrs)/11f winner Pukka, closely related to smart 1¼m/1½m winner Pongee (by Barathea) and half-sister to 2 winners: dam, 1¼m/1½m winner who stayed 14.6f, half-sister to dam of 3-y-o Alexandrova: fair form in maidens at Windsor and Ripon (favourite, mulish leaving paddock): bred to stay 1½m: sold 155,000 gns in November. *L. M. Cumani*

PHECKLESS 7 ch.g. Be My Guest (USA) 126 – Phlirty (Pharly (FR) 130) [2006 61: **48** p6g⁵ p7.1g p8.6g p7g³ p7g p7.1g⁵ p7.1g 8m May 16] poor performer nowadays: tends to race freely, but stays easy 1m: acts on polytrack, soft and good to firm going: has been slowly away: held up. *J. M. Bradley*

PHILANDERING 2 b.c. (Mar 3) Robellino (USA) 127 – Just My Hobby (Kris 135) **–** [2006 7s p7g Oct 20] good-bodied colt: well held in maidens: tongue tied debut: sold 2,500 gns, sent to Spain. *R. F. Johnson Houghton*

PHILANTHROPY 2 ch.c. (Apr 20) Generous (IRE) 139 – Clerio 108 (Soviet Star **96** (USA) 128) [2006 7d 9m* 10d* 10d Oct 28] lengthy colt: sixth foal: half-brother to 3 winners, including 8.5f winner Theorist (by Machiavellian) and 4-y-o Cleveland: dam, French 1m/1¼m winner, half-sister to Ribblesdale winner/Oaks second Bahr (by Generous): useful form: won maiden at Goodwood in September and 4-runner minor event at Leicester (beat Massive by head) in October: ran as if amiss on debut, and did so again final start in listed race at Newmarket: will stay 1½m. *M. Johnston*

PHILHARMONIC 5 b.g. Victory Note (USA) 120 – Lambast 70 (Relkino 131) [2006 **115** 106: 6v* 7g² 7.1m² 6d 7m² 6m² 6m⁴ 6s 5m* 5g 5g Oct 12] strong, lengthy gelding: smart performer: won handicap at Southwell in March and minor event at Beverley (beat Strike Up The Band by neck) in September: also ran well when runner-up, in listed races won by Etlaala at Leicester and Salisbury, and in listed event at Haydock (behind Majors Cast)

804

and minor event at Leicester (behind Jedburgh) in between: stays 7f: acts on any turf going: waited with: genuine. *R. A. Fahey*

PHILLS PEARL 3 gr.f. Piccolo 121 – Cole Slaw (Absalom 128) [2006 –: p7g 9.9g May 18] 3,200Y, 800 2-y-o: half-sister to 3 winners, including 1998 2-y-o 5f winner Ivory's Promise and 1999 2-y-o 6f winner Coley (both by Pursuit of Love): dam unraced: well held in maidens, trained by Miss D. Weeden on reappearance (tongue tied) only. *D. Burchell*

PHINERINE 3 ch.g. Bahamian Bounty 116 - Golden Panda 77 (Music Boy 124) [2006 **71** 61: p5g⁴ p6g⁵ p6g³ f6g⁵ p5.1g² p5g⁵ p5.1g³ 5.7d⁶ 6f⁶ 5.7g* 5.1d⁵ p5.1g 5f 5d⁵ f6g p5.1g p6s³ p6g p5.1g⁶ Dec 31] fair performer: won claimer at Bath in May (hung left in front): below form after: effective at 5f/6f: acts on polytrack and good to firm going: usually blinkered: also hung right once at 2 yrs: reared leaving stall on eighth outing: none too consistent. *R. A. Harris*

PHLAUNT 4 b.f. Faustus (USA) 118 – Phlirty (Pharly (FR) 130) [2006 51: 6g⁴ 7d **54** 10.2m⁴ f12m⁶ p11g Nov 6] small filly: modest maiden: stays easy 1½m: acts on fibresand and good to firm going, probably on polytrack: blinkered final start. *R. F. Johnson Houghton*

PHLUKE 5 b.g. Most Welcome 131 – Phlirty (Pharly (FR) 130) [2006 80: p8g 7g* 7.1d⁵ **97** 8.3f³ 7m² 7g* p8g⁴ 7.5m* 7.1g⁴ 7.1m 7f⁶ p7g 7g 7d⁶ p7g Nov 24] good-bodied gelding: useful handicapper: won at Southwell in April, Epsom and Beverley in July and Chester (best effort, beat Dhaular Dhar a neck) in September: below form after: best at 7f/1m: acts on all-weather, firm and good to soft going: races up with pace. *R. F. Johnson Houghton*

PHOEBE WOODSTOCK (IRE) 4 ch.f. Grand Lodge (USA) 125 – Why So Silent **74** (Mill Reef (USA) 141) [2006 70: 8d 10m 12g 10m⁵ 14.1f³ p16g 12m⁴ 16.4m Sep 11] leggy, quite good-topped filly: fair maiden handicapper: seems to stay 1¾m: acts on firm ground: tried in cheekpieces. *W. R. Swinburn*

PHOENIX EYE 5 b.h. Tragic Role (USA) – Eye Sight 67 (Roscoe Blake 120) [2006 **56** 59: p9.5g⁴ p9.5g⁴ 11.1m⁵ 10.5m p10g Nov 27] close-coupled horse: modest performer: effective at 9.5f, seems to stay easy 2m: acts on polytrack and good to firm going. *M. Mullineaux*

PHOENIX HILL (IRE) 4 b.g. Montjeu (IRE) 137 – Cielo Vodkamartini (USA) (Con- **65** quistador Cielo (USA)) [2006 73: p13.9m p13.9g⁴ Oct 30] fair maiden, lightly raced: trained by J. Oxx in Ireland at 3 yrs: probably stays 1¾m: acts on good to soft going, probably on polytrack. *D. R. Gandolfo*

PHOENIX NIGHTS (IRE) 6 b.g. General Monash (USA) 107 – Beauty Appeal – (USA) (Shadeed (USA) 135) [2006 11.1g 8d 10.1d Aug 18] smallish, workmanlike gelding: little form since 2003 (missed 2005). *A. Berry*

PHOENIX REACH (IRE) 6 b.h. Alhaarth (IRE) 126 – Carroll's Canyon (IRE) – (Hatim (USA) 121) [2006 124: 10f 11g Sep 15] good-topped horse: very smart performer at best: suffered various setbacks (had 3 screws inserted in near-fore fetlock at 2 yrs and underwent further surgery early in 2004), but won 3 Group/Grade 1 races, namely Canadian International at Woodbine in 2003, Hong Kong Vase at Sha Tin in 2004 and Dubai Sheema Classic at Nad Al Sheba in 2005: reportedly struck into on near-fore and subsequently suffered hairline fracture to off-fore pastern on gallops, missing second half of 2005: well below form in Arlington Million and Arc Trial at Newbury (pulled hard) only outings in 2006: needed good test at 1¼m, and stayed 1¾m: acted on firm and good to soft going: effective blinkered/visored or not: bled third 4-y-o start: held up: genuine: to stand at National Stud, Newmarket, fee £3,500. *A. M. Balding*

PHOENIX TOWER (USA) 2 b.c. (Apr 8) Chester House (USA) 123 – Bionic 105 **85 p** (Zafonic (USA)) [2006 p7.1g* Oct 30] fourth foal: half-brother to 2004 2-y-o 6f winner Krynica (by Danzig) and winner in USA by Deputy Minister: dam, 2-y-o 7f winner on only start, half-sister to 5-y-o Day Flight: 5/1, winning debut in maiden at Wolverhampton by 1½ lengths from Calabash Cove, swerving left once in front (put another runner through rail): should progress. *H. R. A. Cecil*

PHONE IN 3 b.g. Sinndar (IRE) 134 – Patria (USA) 76 (Mr Prospector (USA)) [2006 **74** 58p: p10g⁴ p12g² p12.2g² p12.2g⁴ p12.2g² 11.8f² 12g 13.1m² 13.1m⁴ p13.9m⁶ p16g⁵ p12.2g p12g Dec 8] big, good-bodied gelding: fair maiden: left Sir Mark Prescott after fourth outing: stays 13f: acts on polytrack and firm going: blinkered last 3 starts. *R. Brotherton*

PHYSICAL (IRE) 4 b.g. Efisio 120 – St Clair (Distant Relative 128) [2006 67: p7g **52** p6g p8g³ p8g p7g⁴ p8g² p8g* p8g⁵ p8g³ p8g 8.1g May 1] good-bodied gelding: fair **a67** on all-weather, modest on turf: won handicap at Lingfield in March: free-going sort, but stayed easy 1m: acted on polytrack: tried blinkered/tongue tied, wore cheekpieces latterly: dead. *Mrs A. J. Perrett*

PIANOFORTE (USA) 4 b.g. Grand Slam (USA) 120 – Far Too Loud (CAN) (No Louder (CAN)) [2006 77: p8g f7g 12g 10s 7.9m 9.2m 8m* 8.1f² 8f Jul 21] strong, close-coupled gelding: fair handicapper: won at Ripon in July: stays 1m, not 1¼m: acts on all-weather and firm ground: has been visored (including for win in 2005)/blinkered. *E. J. Alston* **74**

PIANO KEY 2 ch.f. (Feb 27) Distant Music (USA) 126 – Ivorine (USA) (Blushing Groom (FR) 131) [2006 p7g Oct 26] half-sister to several winners, including 4-y-o All Ivory: dam, French 11f winner, out of Poule d'Essai des Pouliches and Arc winner Ivanjica: very green in maiden at Lingfield: sold 7,000 gns. *R. Charlton* **–**

PIANO MAN 4 b.g. Atraf 116 – Pinup 44 (Risk Me (FR) 127) [2006 68: p10g⁶ 8m Jul 29] smallish, sturdy gelding: maiden: just modest form in 2006: probably stays 1¼m: acts on polytrack, good to firm and good to soft going: tried blinkered. *J. C. Fox* **57**

PIANO PLAYER (IRE) 3 b.g. Mozart (IRE) 131 – Got To Go 99 (Shareef Dancer (USA) 135) [2006 p7.1g⁴ p7g* p8g* 8m⁴ 9.9m⁶ p8g* 8m² 8f p8g³ Aug 23] 46,000F, 90,000Y: first foal: dam, 2-y-o 6f winner who stayed 1¼m, out of sister to very smart Japanese miler Zenno El Cid: fairly useful performer: won maiden in March, handicap in April and claimer in July, all at Lingfield: stays 1m (raced freely at 1¼m): acts on polytrack, raced only on going firmer than good on turf: joined R. Phillips. *J. A. Osborne* **80**

PICACHO (IRE) 3 b.f. Sinndar (IRE) 134 – Gentle Thoughts 73 (Darshaan 133) [2006 –: 12.1s³ 14m⁵ 16g* 17.2g Oct 17] quite good-topped filly: fair performer: won maiden handicap at Goodwood in August: stays 2m: acts on soft ground: sold 25,000 gns. *J. L. Dunlop* **74**

PICADOR 3 b.g. Pivotal 124 – Candescent (Machiavellian (USA) 123) [2006 –p: p9.5g² p10g* p10g⁵ Dec 8] fair form: much improved in handicaps on belated return, winning at Lingfield in December: stays 1½m: form only on polytrack. *Sir Mark Prescott* **64**

PICCLED 8 b.g. Piccolo 121 – Creme de Menthe (IRE) (Green Desert (USA) 127) [2006 83§, a91§: p5g p5.1g Apr 10] good-topped gelding: one-time useful performer: has become very temperamental, refusing to race on 4 occasions, including on reappearance: banned from racing. *E. J. Alston* **§§**

PICCLEYES 5 b.g. Piccolo 121 – Dark Eyed Lady (IRE) 82 (Exhibitioner 111) [2006 61d: f5g p5.1g³ p6g⁵ p6g⁵ f6g* 6m⁶ 6d 5g p5.1g Jun 2] modest handicapper: won at Southwell in April: best at 5f/6f: acts on all-weather, good to firm and good to soft going: usually blinkered. *M. J. Polglase* **64**

PICCOLENA BOY 2 b.c. (Mar 5) Piccolo 121 – Bella Helena (Balidar (133)) [2006 5.7g 5.7m⁴ 5.1g² 5.2f³ 5.7m⁵ 5m p5g Sep 30] half-brother to 3 winners, including fairly useful 5f (including at 2 yrs) winner Bevelena (by Beveled) and 2005 2-y-o 5f winner Bloodstocktv (by Lujain): dam Italian sprint winner (tailed off only British outing): fair maiden: placed at Bath and Yarmouth: last in 2 nurseries: best at 5f: acts on firm going: sold 3,000 gns. *P. Winkworth* **69**

PICCOLINI 2 b.f. (May 17) Bertolini (USA) 125 – Piccolo Cativo 67 (Komaite (USA)) [2006 p5.1g 5m 6g⁶ Jul 20] second foal: dam 5f (including at 2 yrs) to 7.8f winner: well beaten in maidens (blinkered debut). *Mrs G. S. Rees* **–**

PICCOLO DIAMANTE (USA) 2 b. or br.c. (May 6) Three Wonders (USA) – Bafooz (USA) 48 (Clever Trick (USA)) [2006 p5.1g⁶ p6m Nov 9] better run in maidens at Wolverhampton when sixth. *T. J. Pitt* **59**

PICCOLOMINI 4 b.g. Diktat 126 – La Dama Bonita (USA) 87 (El Gran Senor (USA) 136) [2006 80d: 17.1m 10f 12m 12m Aug 8] good-bodied gelding: regressive maiden, well held in 2006: tried blinkered. *E. W. Tuer* **–**

PICCOLO PREZZO 2 ch.f. (Mar 8) Piccolo 121 – Bon Marche 89 (Definite Article 121) [2006 p5g f5g³ 5.1m 6m p5g 6m⁵ p6g Jul 12] leggy filly: first foal: dam 7f winner (including at 2 yrs) who stayed 1m: poor and ungenuine maiden: left Stef Liddiard after third start: has refused to enter stalls. *I. A. Wood* **47 §**

PICCOLO PRINCE 5 ch.g. Piccolo 121 – Aegean Flame 86 (Anshan 119) [2006 70, a62: f6g⁶ p6g p6g p7.1g⁵ f6g² 6v* 6m⁵ 6g 6m⁵ 6d⁴ 6g⁶ 6v f6g² f6g² p6g⁵ p6g Dec 18] strong, stocky gelding: modest handicapper: won at Pontefract in April: left E. Alston £6,500 after fifteenth start: effective at 5f/6f: acts on fibresand and any turf going: tried in cheekpieces. *P. A. Blockley* **64**

PICCOSTAR 3 b.f. Piccolo 121 – Anneliina 80 (Cadeaux Genereux 131) [2006 66, a72: p6g³ p5.1g⁶ 6f⁶ 5.3m² 6m² 6f* 6g⁴ 6m p6g 6m p6g p6g⁶ p6g Nov 23] quite good- **75**

topped filly: fair handicapper: won at Brighton in June: stays 6f: acts on polytrack and firm ground. *A. B. Haynes*

PICK A NICE NAME 4 ch.f. Polar Falcon (USA) 126 – Opuntia (Rousillon (USA) 133) [2006 6d* 6g 6m² 6f⁶ Jul 16] 8,000Y: strong, lengthy filly: half-sister to several winners, including 6f winner (including at 2 yrs) Boomerang Blade (by Sure Blade) and 6f/7f winner Point of Dispute (by Cyrano de Bergerac), both useful: dam unraced: fair performer: won maiden at Redcar in May: should stay 7f: acts on good to firm and good to soft going: has looked awkward ride/flashed tail. *R. M. Whitaker* **75**

PICKERING 2 br.c. (Apr 3) Prince Sabo 123 – On The Wagon (Then Again 126) [2006 6d p7.1g⁴ p6g Nov 6] sturdy colt: third foal: dam unraced: seemingly best effort (fair form) in maidens when fourth at Wolverhampton (hung right): stays 7f. *E. J. Alston* **67**

PICKLED AGAIN 2 br.f. (Mar 18) Piccolo 121 – Queen of Tides (IRE) 62 (Soviet Star (USA) 128) [2006 6g Aug 7] fourth foal: dam, maiden, best effort at 7f on debut at 2 yrs: no show in maiden at Windsor. *S. Dow* **–**

PICK OF THE CROP 5 ch.g. Fraam 114 – Fresh Fruit Daily 92 (Reprimand 122) [2006 46: p9.5g Mar 20] tall gelding: poor nowadays: well held only outing in 2006: tried visored/tongue tied. *J. R. Jenkins* **–**

PICKWICK MISS (USA) 3 b.f. Repriced (USA) – Sihasapa (USA) (Diesis 133) [2006 p7g p8.6g 8.2g 10d³ 11.5d Oct 18] fourth living foal: half-sister to 3 winners in USA: dam unraced out of half-sister to very smart 1¼m performer Knifebox: modest maiden: stays 1¼m: acts on good to soft going: sold 2,000 gns, sent to Qatar. *D. M. Simcock* **53**

PICOT DE SAY 4 b.g. Largesse 112 – Facsimile 67 (Superlative 118) [2006 65: p12g 12.6g Jul 7] unfurnished gelding: modest performer: stays 11.5f: acts on soft ground: won 3 times over hurdles in 2006. *C. Roberts* **52**

PICTAVIA (IRE) 4 ch.f. Sinndar (IRE) 134 – Insijaam (USA) 112 (Secretariat (USA)) [2006 114: 10.1m* 12m³ 9.9m* 9.9m* 10s⁵ Oct 22] compact filly: smart performer: left J. Bolger after 3 yrs: at least as good as ever in 2006, winning listed races at Newcastle in June and Salisbury (beat Summer's Eve by 4 lengths) in August, and Select Racing UK On Sky 432 Stakes at Goodwood (beat Crosspeace by neck, rallying having made running) in September: below-form fifth to Floriot in Premio Lydia Tesio at Rome final outing: stays 1½m: acts on firm going, below form on softer than good: sometimes tongue tied/blinkered at 3 yrs: often makes running: game. *Saeed bin Suroor* **115**

PICTURE FRAME 2 ch.g. (Apr 14) Fraam 114 – Floral Spark 69 (Forzando 122) [2006 5g³ 5f³ 5d² 5g³ 5g* 6d Aug 29] 2,600Y, resold 6,000Y: well-made gelding: half-brother to several winners, including 7.5f to 1¼m (8.5f at 2 yrs) winner Wilemmgeo (by Emarati) and 7-y-o Pepper Road: dam 5f winner: fair performer: won maiden claimer at Haydock (left N. Tinkler £12,000) in June: should be suited by 7f/1m. *J. T. Stimpson* **69**

PICTURE SHOW (USA) 3 b.f. Swain (IRE) 134 – Impetuous Image (USA) (Mr Prospector (USA)) [2006 58: p8g² p10g 6f⁵ p7g 8f 10.1f 8m p9.5g³ p8g Nov 11] compact filly: fair maiden: stays 9.5f: acts on polytrack and firm ground: blinkered final start. *C. E. Brittain* **67**

PIC UP STICKS 7 gr.g. Piccolo 121 – Between The Sticks 83 (Pharly (FR) 130) [2006 97: 6g² 6d 6m 5m⁵ p8g⁶ 6g 5m* 5m* 6d 6m³ 5f p6g 5.1m p6g⁴ Nov 11] tall gelding: useful handicapper: won at Sandown (by neck from Royal Challenge) and Newmarket (beat Woodnook a head) in July: effective at 5f to 6.5f: acts on firm and good to soft going, probably on polytrack: tried in cheekpieces: sold 11,000 gns. *B. G. Powell* **96**

PIDDIES PRIDE (IRE) 4 b.f. Indian Lodge (IRE) 127 – Fairybird (FR) 70 (Pampabird 124) [2006 75, a55: 7m 6d⁶ 6.1m 6f* 6f⁵ 6m⁴ 6.1g⁵ f6g Oct 12] smallish, lengthy filly: fair performer: won seller in July and handicap in August, both at Folkestone: stays 7f: acts on polytrack, firm and soft going: wears cheekpieces/visor. *Miss Gay Kelleway* **65 a–**

PIETER BRUEGHEL (USA) 7 b.g. Citidancer (USA) – Smart Tally (USA) (Smarten (USA)) [2006 101: 6v⁴ p6g⁶ 6m⁵ 6s 7g 6m³ 5m 6s⁴ 6g 6g⁵ p6g³ Nov 16] big, good-topped gelding: useful handicapper: in-and-out form in 2006, one of best efforts when fourth to Excusez Moi in Great St Wilfrid Stakes at Ripon eighth outing: races mainly around 6f, stays easy 7f: acts on polytrack and any turf going: has been tongue tied: makes running/races up with pace. *D. Nicholls* **99 a89**

PIETERSEN (IRE) 2 ch.g. (Apr 20) Redback 116 – Faye 79 (Monsanto (FR) 121) [2006 5g⁶ 6m 7s⁴ 6v³ f6g f6g⁵ p7.1g Dec 7] compact, good-quartered gelding: has a quick action: modest maiden: probably stays 7f: acts on polytrack and heavy going: usually blinkered. *T. D. Barron* **59**

PIETY (IRE) 3 b.f. Danehill (USA) 126 – Quest of Passion (FR) (Saumarez 132) [2006 **95**
76p: 10f² 10.9m⁵ 9.9g² 10m* 10d 12d* 14d² 12.5s Nov 22] leggy, lengthy filly: useful
performer: won maiden at Sandown in September and handicap at Newmarket (beat
Wannabe Posh by 3½ lengths) in October: ran well next time, but well held in listed race
at Saint-Cloud final outing: stays 1¾m: acts on firm and good to soft going: sold 90,000
gns. *M. Johnston*

PIGEON FLIGHT 2 ch.g. (Mar 10) Compton Admiral 121 – Fervent Fan (IRE) 65 **68**
(Soviet Lad (USA)) [2006 8.1d 8.2s³ Oct 25] strong, workmanlike gelding: fourth foal:
dam 2-y-o 6f winner: better run in maidens when third to Sahrati at Nottingham (raced
freely). *M. L. W. Bell*

PIGEON ISLAND 3 gr.g. Daylami (IRE) 138 – Morina (USA) (Lyphard (USA) 132) **75**
[2006 77p: 10g³ 10m⁶ 10g 8m 7.1m⁶ 8m p9.5m Oct 9] quite attractive gelding: fair maid-
en: stays 1¼m: raced only on polytrack and good/good to firm going: joined N. Twiston-
Davies. *H. Candy*

PIKABOO 3 ch.f. Pivotal 124 – Gleam of Light (IRE) 81 (Danehill (USA) 126) [2006 **62**
8.3g⁶ p7g f6g⁴ Dec 27] 41,000F, 85,000Y: half-sister to several winners, including useful
2000 2-y-o 7f winner Opening Ceremony (by Quest For Fame): dam, 7.5f winner, out of half-sister to
2000 Guineas winner Don't Forget Me: modest maiden, best effort on debut: left
J. Gosden 20,000 gns after second start: stays 8.3f. *S. C. Williams*

PILLARS OF WISDOM 4 ch.c. Desert Prince (IRE) 130 – Eurolink Mischief 84 (Be **84**
My Chief (USA) 122) [2006 87: 8d 7m 7f⁶ 7f² 8f p8g³ p7g Sep 30] tall, good-topped colt:
fairly useful handicapper: free-going sort, best at 7f/1m: acts on polytrack, firm and good
to soft ground: tried visored at 3 yrs, tongue tied last 5 starts: flashed tail fourth outing:
front runner: sold 10,000 gns. *J. L. Dunlop*

PINAFORE 4 ch.f. Fleetwood (IRE) 107 – Shi Shi (Alnasr Alwasheek 117) [2006 62: **42**
6f 6f Aug 5] poor maiden nowadays: stays 7f: acts on polytrack and good to soft going: in
cheekpieces last 3 starts at 3 yrs. *P. Winkworth*

PINCHBECK 7 b.g. Petong 126 – Veuve Hoornaert (IRE) 88 (Standaan (FR) 118) **83**
[2006 90: f6g* f6g³ f6g⁴ p7g 6g⁶ 6d p6g p6s⁴ Dec 15] strong, good sort: fairly useful **a89**
handicapper, better on all-weather: won at Southwell in January: best at 6f: acts on all-
weather, good to firm and good to soft ground: effective blinkered or not, usually wears
cheekpieces nowadays. *M. A. Jarvis*

PINCH OF SALT (IRE) 3 b.g. Hussonet (USA) – Granita (CHI) (Roy (USA)) [2006 **81**
81+: 8.1g⁶ 8d² 10s⁶ 11.9f⁶ 12.1m⁶ Sep 13] big, lengthy gelding: fairly useful maiden:
likely to prove best short of 1½m: acts on soft and good to firm ground: usually tongue
tied: gelded after final start. *A. M. Balding*

PINDAR (GER) 2 b.g. (May 9) Tertullian (USA) 115 – Pierette (GER) (Local Suitor **–**
(USA) 128) [2006 p8.6g Dec 29] 50/1, slowly away in maiden at Wolverhampton.
B. J. Curley

PINEAPPLE POLL 2 b.f. (Mar 9) Josr Algarhoud (IRE) 118 – Petrovna (IRE) 78 **–**
(Petardia 113) [2006 p6g 6g p6g Jul 12] good-topped filly: third foal: half-sister to 7f
winner Mitzi Caspar (by Kirkwall) and 3-y-o Brunelleschi: dam 2-y-o 5f winner: no
form. *P. L. Gilligan*

PINE CONE (IRE) 4 ch.f. Dr Fong (USA) 128 – Pine Needle 89 (Kris 135) [2006 85: **99**
12g 10m* 10.9f⁴ 10.1f⁴ 14f 12s Oct 7] useful performer: won handicap at Newbury in
June by length from Noora: good 1¼ lengths fourth of 6 to Power Girl in listed event at
Warwick third start: should stay 1½m: acts on firm and good to soft going: withdrawn
after unruly in stall intended second outing: sold 40,000 gns. *A. King*

PINKABOUT (IRE) 2 br.f. (Mar 11) Desert Style (IRE) 121 – Dinka Raja (USA) **85**
(Woodman (USA) 126) [2006 p6g* 6m Jul 29] €250,000Y: leggy, lengthy filly: fourth
foal: half-sister to useful 2003 2-y-o 6f winner (including Lowther/Cheveley Park Stakes)
Carry On Katie (by Fasliyev) and winner in USA by Peintre Celebre: dam, French 1m
winner from 2 starts, out of half-sister to very smart fillies up to 1¼m Grise Mine and
Kostroma: fairly useful form: impressive winner of maiden at Kempton (quickened to
beat Bright Moon by 2½ lengths) in July: 15/2, reportedly lost action in Princess Margaret
Stakes at Ascot 2 weeks later: likely to stay 1m. *J. H. M. Gosden*

PINK BAY 4 b.f. Forzando 122 – Singer On The Roof 62 (Chief Singer 131) [2006 76: **57**
p7g 7g 7.1m 7m⁴ 6f⁴ 7.1f³ 6m⁵ 7.1m 8m⁶ Sep 20] leggy filly: modest handicapper: barely
stays 1m: acts on polytrack and firm going: sometimes visored/blinkered. *W. S. Kittow*

PINK NOTES 2 ch.c. (Apr 22) Bandmaster (USA) 97 – Pink Petal (Northern Game) **–**
[2006 7.1d Sep 16] well beaten in maiden at Warwick. *R. J. Hodges*

PINK PYJAMAS 3 ch.f. Compton Place 125 – Pagan Princess 54 (Mujtahid (USA) –
118) [2006 –: p6g 6f 5.3f Jul 9] little sign of ability: tried visored. *J. A. R. Toller*

PINK SALMON 2 ch.f. (Mar 5) Dr Fong (USA) 128 – West Humble 93 (Pharly (FR) –
130) [2006 p8g Nov 5] fifth foal: half-sister to 3 winners, including fairly useful 5f (at
2 yrs) to 7f winner Flying Fulmar (by Bahamian Bounty): dam 7f winner: last in maiden
at Lingfield, slowly away. *Mrs L. J. Mongan*

PINKY 3 ro.f. Bluebird (USA) 125 – Lost Dream (Niniski (USA) 125) [2006 9.7f Jun 12] –
fifth foal: dam ran twice: 40/1, slowly away when tailed off in maiden at Folkestone.
B. J. McMath

PINPOINT (IRE) 4 b.g. Pivotal 124 – Alessia (GER) (Warning 136) [2006 105: 7g⁴   **106**
8m⁶ 10m⁶ 9d³ 10d Nov 4] tall gelding: useful handicapper, quite lightly raced: won John
Smith's Stakes at Newbury in September by ¾ length from Charlie Cool: creditable 5
lengths third of 33 to Formal Decree in Cambridgeshire at Newmarket next time: stays
1¼m: acts on good to firm and good to soft going: consistent. *W. R. Swinburn*

PINSON (IRE) 4 b.c. Halling (USA) 133 – Tadorne (FR) (Inchinor 119) [2006 119: 8d²   **116**
9d Oct 14] strong, medium-sized colt: left J-C. Rouget in France after 3 yrs: close to best
when 1¼ lengths second to Satchem in Joel Stakes at Newmarket in September, though
none too keen under pressure: ran as though all wasn't well when tailed off in Darley
Stakes there (ducked right when pulled out to challenge) only subsequent outing: stays
1¼m: acts on soft and good to firm going: has left Godolphin. *Saeed bin Suroor*

PINTLE 6 b.m. Pivotal 124 – Boozy 111 (Absalom 128) [2006 90: 7.6m⁶ 7m² 8.1f   **96**
8.1m* 8.3f² 7m 8m 7m p8g Oct 26] good-topped mare: useful handicapper: won at
Warwick in June: well below form last 4 starts, said to have bled on first occasion: stays
1m: raced on good ground or firmer on turf: usually races up with pace. *J. L. Spearing*

PIPER GENERAL (IRE) 4 br.g. General Monash (USA) 107 – Pipewell (IRE) 84   **71**
(Lake Coniston (IRE) 131) [2006 81: f14g p13.9g Mar 6] fairly useful at 3 yrs: only fair
form in 2006: stays 1¼m: acts on all-weather: tried tongue tied. *J. Mackie*

PIPER LILY 4 b.f. Piccolo 121 – Polly Golightly 84 (Weldnaas (USA) 112) [2006 62:   **43**
p5.1g⁵ 6m Jun 23] small filly: only poor form in 2006: likely to prove best at 5f/easy 6f:
acts on good to firm and good to soft going, probably on polytrack: often blinkered/in
cheekpieces earlier in career. *M. Blanshard*

PIPER'S SONG (IRE) 3 gr.g. Distant Music (USA) 126 – Dane's Lane (IRE) (Dane-   **73**
hill (USA) 126) [2006 8g 8.1d⁴ p8g⁶ 7.1m* 8.3s⁵ Oct 2] €38,000F, 7,000Y: seventh foal:
half-brother to 3 winners, including 7f/1m winner (including at 2 yrs) Hoh Steamer, later
successful in USA, and 9f winner Peruvia, both fairly useful by Perugino: dam unraced:
fair performer: won handicap at Sandown in September, still green: stays easy 1m: acts
on good to firm going, probably on polytrack: sometimes slowly away. *H. Candy*

PIPPA'S DANCER (IRE) 4 b.f. Desert Style (IRE) 121 – Soreze (IRE) 102 (Gallic   **86**
League 119) [2006 76: p7g p6g* p6g² 6m⁵ 6f* 6.1m* 5d Jul 9] leggy, good-topped filly:
fairly useful handicapper: won at Kempton in May and Leicester and Warwick in June:
effective at 5f/6f: acts on polytrack and firm ground: has been early to post/raced freely.
W. R. Muir

---

*John Smith's Stakes (Handicap), Newbury—this valuable Cambridgeshire trial
goes to Pinpoint (hooped cap); Charlie Cool (striped sleeves), Formal Decree (noseband),
Dansili Dancer (second right) and Great Plains (rail) are next*

PIPS ASSERTIVE WAY 5 ch.m. Nomadic Way (USA) 104 – Return To Brighton 51 – (Then Again 126) [2006 –: p12.2g p12.2g Jan 21] no form on Flat: won novice selling hurdle in July. *A. W. Carroll*

PIP'S BABY 3 ch.g. Groom Dancer (USA) 128 – Captivating (IRE) 63 (Wolfhound (USA) 126) [2006 69: 11.6d p10g p10g p9.5g Oct 29] lengthy gelding: fair performer at 2 yrs: no form in 2006. *S. Kirk*

PIPSSALIO (SPA) 9 b.g. Pips Pride 117 – Tesalia (SPA) (Finissimo (SPA)) [2006 20s – May 18] workmanlike gelding: poor performer, well held only outing on Flat in 2006: sometimes blinkered/tongue tied: fair hurdler. *Jamie Poulton*

PIQUET 8 br.m. Mind Games 121 – Petonellajill 73 (Petong 126) [2006 49, a58: p10g **43** p10g p10g⁵ p10g⁶ 12s p10g⁶ 10.2g⁵ p10g p7g⁶ p8g 9m p8g p10g⁶ p12g p10g p10g³ p10g⁵ **a52** Dec 22] modest performer on all-weather, poor on turf: effective at 1m to 1½m: acts on polytrack and firm going: wore cheekpieces final outing. *J. J. Bridger*

PIRES 2 br.g. (Jan 31) Generous (IRE) 139 – Kaydee Queen (IRE) (Bob's Return (IRE) **93** 123) [2006 6m² 6f³ 7m⁴ 7f² 7f* 7m² 7g⁵ Aug 18] big, rangy gelding: second foal: dam unraced: fairly useful performer: won maiden at Redcar in July: also ran well in listed races at Ascot in June (fourth to Champlain) and late-July (second to Satulagi): bred to stay very well: acts on firm going: long-striding sort, below form on sharp tracks. *M. R. Channon*

PIRNER'S BRIG 2 b.c. (Apr 10) Warningford 119 – Loch Maree 65 (Primo Dominie **64** 121) [2006 5f p5.1g 5g³ f7g 5m p6g* f6g² Dec 23] workmanlike colt: modest performer: much improved when making all in seller at Wolverhampton in December: stays 6f: acts on all-weather. *M. W. Easterby*

PIROUETTING 3 b.f. Pivotal 124 – Jitterbug (IRE) (Marju (IRE) 127) [2006 78: 7g³ **81** 7s⁴ 7g² 7.1m² 8.1m³ 8.1m* 10m³ 10g p10g Nov 9] big filly: fairly useful performer: won maiden at Sandown in August: stays 1¼m: acts on soft and good to firm going, probably on polytrack: held up last 3 starts. *B. W. Hills*

PISTOL DAWN 3 b.f. Primo Valentino (IRE) 116 – Pearls (Mon Tresor 113) [2006 60: **69** 12s⁴ 10s 9.8s 7m Sep 16] 14,000Y: fifth foal: half-sister to 3 winners, including fairly useful 2001 2-y-o 6f winner Perle d'Azur (by Mind Games) and 4-y-o Make Us Flush: dam unraced: fair maiden: well below form after reappearance (left J. Murphy in Ireland after second start): stays 1½m: acts on soft going. *J. J. Quinn*

PITBULL 3 b.g. Makbul 104 – Piccolo Cativo 67 (Komaite (USA)) [2006 65: 8.1f 6m⁵ **65** 6.9m 7.6f² 8.1m p7.1m⁶ Sep 2] smallish, good-bodied gelding: fair maiden: stays 7.6f: acts on polytrack and firm going. *Mrs G. S. Rees*

PITCH UP (IRE) 4 b.g. Cape Cross (IRE) 129 – Uhud (IRE) (Mujtahid (USA) 118) **78** [2006 85: 6g 5m⁴ 6f a6g⁴ a6g⁵ Dec 3] angular gelding: useful handicapper on all-weather, fair on turf: fourth at Lingfield second start, easily best effort in Britain in 2006: sold from T. Mills 7,000 gns, won at Jagersro in October: effective at 5f/6f: acts on polytrack/dirt, probably acts on firm and good to soft going on turf: tried blinkered/in cheekpieces: usually races up with pace. *Jacqueline Henriksson, Sweden*

PITITANA (IRE) 3 b.f. Xaar 132 – Jet Cat (IRE) (Catrail (USA) 123) [2006 p6g³ p5g² **78** 6g³ 5f* 6m⁵ 5m 5g⁶ Aug 7] €23,000F, €70,000Y: good-bodied filly: did well physically: type to carry condition: first foal: dam unraced: fair performer: landed odds in maiden at Folkestone in May: stays 6f: sold 8,000 gns. *R. Hannon*

PITSI KAHTOH 4 b.f. Petoski 135 – Pletchow 58 (Adonijah 126) [2006 42: p12.2g⁶ **44** p9.5g⁶ f11g 11.8d⁶ 12m⁵ 10m 11.5f 12.6g 11.8f⁶ Jul 20] poor maiden: should stay 1¾m: acts on good to soft going: wore cheekpieces final start. *P. W. Hiatt*

PITTON JUSTICE 4 ch.c. Compton Place 125 – Blind Justice (Mystiko (USA) 124) – [2006 p5g Feb 22] 50/1, well held in claimer at Lingfield. *W. G. M. Turner*

PITTSBURGH 4 ch.g. Nashwan (USA) 135 – Oatey 68 (Master Willie 129) [2006 64: **67** 8.1d p10g⁵ 11.6m⁴ 12g⁶ 11m Jun 27] strong gelding: fair maiden handicapper: stays 11.6f: acts on good to firm going: tongue tied in 2005: sold 13,000 gns in July. *A. M. Balding*

PIVOTAL FLAME 4 b.c. Pivotal 124 – Reddening 82 (Blushing Flame (USA) 109) **118** [2006 108: 6s⁴ 6g⁴ 5m² 5m⁵ 6m³ 5m 5f³ 5s³ 5.2m⁴ 5m Oct 1] strong, good-topped colt: usually looks well: made up into a smart performer in 2006, best efforts when 1¼ lengths second to Dandy Man in Palace House Stakes at Newmarket and 2 lengths third to Reverence in Nunthorpe Stakes at York third/eighth starts: has form at 6f/7f, but is speedy and best at 5f: acts on soft and good to firm going: tried in blinkers/visor, usually in cheekpieces nowadays: often wanders under pressure: usually races prominently. *E. S. McMahon*

Laurent-Perrier Champagne Sprint Stakes, Sandown—Pivotal Point gains his first win in nearly two years as he beats Benbaun (left) and The Trader (striped sleeves)

PIVOTALIA (IRE) 2 b.f. (Apr 5) Pivotal 124 – Viscaria (IRE) 97 (Barathea (IRE) 127) [2006 p7g p7g4 Nov 11] €60,000Y: third foal: dam, Irish 7.8f (at 2 yrs)/1¼m winner, half-sister to smart performers Hathrah (at 1m) and Ivan Luis (up to 1½m): more promising run in maidens when fourth to Sell Out at Kempton: will go on improving, particularly at 1m. *W. R. Swinburn*   **63 p**

PIVOTAL POINT 6 b.g. Pivotal 124 – True Precision 84 (Presidium 124) [2006 –: 5m 5m6 5m3 6m 5m* 6m 6m3 Aug 13] big, strong, close-coupled gelding: has a quick, fluent action: very smart performer at 4 yrs, well held both starts at 5 yrs: almost as good as ever in 2006, and won Laurent-Perrier Champagne Sprint Stakes at Sandown (by ½ length from Benbaun) in July: also ran well when ½-length third of 28 to Takeover Target in King's Stand Stakes at Royal Ascot third start: respectable efforts last 2 outings, when eighth to Les Arcs in July Cup at Newmarket and third to Moss Vale in Phoenix Sprint Stakes at the Curragh: effective at 5f/6f: acts on firm going, below form only outing on softer than good: usually races up with pace. *P. J. Makin*   **119**

PIVOTAL'S PRINCESS (IRE) 4 ch.f. Pivotal 124 – Art Princess (IRE) (Fairy King (USA)) [2006 103: 5.1f 5s 5m2 5g2 5.4g 5g3 5g3 Sep 28] small, sturdy filly: useful performer: good efforts in listed races when head second to Baltic King at Beverley and length third to Fantasy Believer at Newmarket fourth/final starts: stays easy 6f: yet to race on heavy ground, acts on any other turf. *E. S. McMahon*   **106**

PIX 3 b.f. Bertolini (USA) 125 – Fair Kai (IRE) (Fayruz 116) [2006 51: p7g p6g4 Jan 11] sparely-made filly: poor maiden: stays 1¼m: acts on polytrack, firm and good to soft ground: tried blinkered. *S. Kirk*   **39**

PIXIE RING 2 b.f. (Feb 3) Pivotal 124 – Ard Na Sighe (IRE) (Kenmare (FR) 125) [2006 p6s* p6g* Dec 30] fifth foal: half-sister to useful Irish 6f winner Dr Dignity (by Dr Devious) and winner in Italy by Danehill: dam unraced half-sister to top-class sprinter Marwell, herself dam of very smart miler Marling: fairly useful form: won maiden (by length from Darling Belinda) and 3-runner minor event (by head from Shustraya, tending to hang before rallying) at Wolverhampton in December: capable of better. *Sir Mark Prescott*   **85 p**

PLAIN CHAMPAGNE (IRE) 4 b.f. Victory Note (USA) 120 – Paddys Cocktail (IRE) (Tremblant 112) [2006 –: 12m p12g6 p10g4 11.9m* 10m2 12m6 12.1g2 11.9f 12m 11.9m 11.9d p16g Oct 23] modest performer: won handicap at Brighton in May: stays 1½m: acts on polytrack and good to firm going: free-going sort. *Dr J. R. J. Naylor*   **62**

PLANE PAINTER (IRE) 2 b.g. (May 6) Orpen (USA) 116 – Flight Sequence 88 (Polar Falcon (USA) 126) [2006 7.1m3 7m* p7g Oct 21] €65,000Y: second foal: dam 1¼m winner: fairly useful form: encouraging third to Overturn at Sandown, then made all in maiden at Chester in September: well held on nursery/all-weather debut at Lingfield: will stay 1m. *M. Johnston*   **83**

PLANTERS PUNCH (IRE) 5 br.g. Cape Cross (IRE) 129 – Jamaican Punch (IRE) **66** (Shareef Dancer (USA) 135) [2006 66: 10.1f⁴ 10m⁴ 10g² 14.1m⁵ 11.1d⁴ 15.8d Oct 3] strong, useful-looking gelding: fair handicapper: barely stays 15.8f: acts on firm and good to soft ground: tried visored: sometimes slowly away. *G. M. Moore*

PLATEAU 7 b.g. Zamindar (USA) 116 – Painted Desert 89 (Green Desert (USA) 127) **91 d** [2006 93: p6g³ 6v 6m⁵ 5g⁶ 5f⁴ 5g⁵ 5m 5.1m² 5m 5m⁵ 6f 5.1g 5g⁵ p5g p6g p6g p7.1g* Dec 27] good-bodied gelding: fairly useful handicapper: not at best after reappearance (left D. Nicholls £12,000 after thirteenth start), though won at Wolverhampton in December: effective at 5f to easy 7f: acts on polytrack, firm and good to soft going: sometimes early to post/finds little. *C. R. Dore*

PLATINUM CHARMER (IRE) 6 b.g. Kahyasi 130 – Mystic Charm (Nashwan **71 d** (USA) 135) [2006 71: 12v⁶ 11g² 12g² 12m⁴ 9.9g⁶ 10.2g 12f⁶ 12f 14.1f² 14.1f³ 13m⁶ 12d 12s⁴ 12d⁴ Nov 3] compact gelding: fair handicapper: below form after third start: stays 1¾m: acts on all-weather, firm and good to soft going: usually wears cheekpieces, tried visored: has wandered: waited with. *K. R. Burke*

PLATINUM HOUND (IRE) 3 b.f. Vettori (IRE) 119 – Dog Rose (SAF) (Fort Wood **59** (USA) 117) [2006 –: 8.2m 9.9g May 18] unfurnished filly: modest form in maidens: stays 1¼m. *H. Morrison*

PLAUSABELLE 5 b.m. Royal Applause 124 – Sipsi Fach 100 (Prince Sabo 123) **–** [2006 67, a77: p8.6m p8.6g⁶ p9.5s p8.6g⁴ Dec 30] lengthy mare: fair performer: stays **a65** 9.5f: acts on polytrack, firm and soft ground: tried blinkered. *G. G. Margarson*

PLAYING GAMES 2 b.c. (Apr 10) Mind Games 121 – Contradictory 48 (Reprimand **–** 122) [2006 5g⁶ 6m Jun 16] tall, leggy colt: well held both starts: dead. *M. W. Easterby*

PLAY MASTER (IRE) 5 b.g. Second Empire (IRE) 124 – Madam Waajib (IRE) **72** (Waajib 121) [2006 61: p9.5g² p9.5g p8.6g³ p9.5g* f7g p10g⁵ Apr 7] tall, rather leggy, useful-looking gelding: fair performer: won claimer at Wolverhampton (claimed from B. Smart £8,000) in March: stays 9.5f: acts on all-weather and soft going: tried visored: has raced freely/idled: has joined C. Roberts. *R. A. Harris*

PLAY ME 4 b.f. Nashwan (USA) 135 – Mrs Moonlight (Ajdal (USA) 130) [2006 93?: **102** 10.9f³ 11.9g⁴ 9.9m³ p12g⁵ Sep 2] useful-looking filly: useful performer, lightly raced: good efforts in listed race at Warwick (third to Power Girl), listed handicap at Goodwood (third to Portal) and September Stakes at Kempton (fifth to Kandidate): stays 1½m: acts on polytrack, firm and soft going: sent to New Zealand. *P. W. Chapple-Hyam*

PLAY STRAIGHT 2 ch.f. (Apr 11) Piccolo 121 – Align 69 (Petong 126) [2006 p7g⁵ **69** p6g p7.1g* Dec 28] 8,500Y: third foal: half-sister to 4-y-o Arnie de Burgh: dam, 1m winner, half-sister to useful 1¼m performer Arriving: fair form: improved to win maiden at Wolverhampton in December by neck from Doubtful Sound: will be suited by 1m. *R. M. Beckett*

PLAY THE BALL (USA) 4 ch.g. Boundary (USA) 117 – Copper Play (USA) (Fast **78** Play (USA)) [2006 80: p7.1g p7.1g⁴ 8m p8g⁴ p7g 8d 8s p7.1g Nov 23] fair handicapper: sold from G. Butler 6,000 gns after fifth outing: stays 1m: acts on polytrack: tried blinkered/in cheekpieces: none too consistent. *J. J. Lambe, Ireland*

PLAYTOTHEAUDIENCE 3 b.g. Royal Applause 124 – Flyfisher (USA) (Riverman **–** (USA) 131) [2006 90: 7.1m 8g 8.1m 8m 10g Sep 30] tall, useful-looking gelding: fairly useful performer at 2 yrs: little impact in handicaps in 2006. *R. A. Fahey*

PLAY UP POMPEY 4 b.g. Dansili 127 – Search For Love (FR) (Groom Dancer **62** (USA) 128) [2006 61: 9.7d p10g⁵ p10g 10m 9m 11m⁶ 12g 10.1g p16g p8g p11g p12g p10g* p10g⁴ p10g⁵ Dec 22] angular gelding: modest performer: won maiden at Kempton in December: stays 1½m: acts on polytrack, firm and good to soft going. *J. J. Bridger*

PLEASANT 5 b.m. Topanoora 118 – Devon Peasant 74 (Deploy 131) [2006 66: p12g **–** Apr 23] quite good-topped mare: fair handicapper at best, lightly raced: well held only start in 2006: often held up. *D. P. Keane*

PLEASING 3 b.f. Dr Fong (USA) 128 – Trounce (Barathea (IRE) 127) [2006 69: 8.3g* **80 +** 8.2s⁴ p7g⁶ 8.3g⁴ 8.1m 8d³ 8d* 10d Nov 4] smallish, useful-looking filly: fairly useful performer: won handicaps at Leicester in April and Newmarket (apprentices) in October: flattered when seventh to Lake Toya in slowly-run listed race at Windsor final start: seems to stay 1¼m: acts on polytrack and soft going: sold 15,000 gns. *J. L. Dunlop*

PLEASING GIFT 3 b.f. Largesse 112 – Pleasure Dome 77 (Most Welcome 131) [2006 **58** 7.1m 8.1m p8g⁶ 8g p8.6g⁵ p12.2g Nov 24] leggy filly: first foal: dam, 1m winner, half-sister to 3-y-o Angus Newz: modest maiden: stays 8.6f: acts on polytrack and good to firm ground: tried blinkered. *J. M. P. Eustace*

PLEASURE PURSUIT 2 b.g. (May 17) Pursuit of Love 124 – Glen Falls (Comманche Run 133) [2006 6d 6d Nov 4] big gelding: last in maidens: gelded after second start. *B. W. Hills* –

PLEMONT BAY 3 b.g. Robellino (USA) 127 – Jezyah (USA) 80 (Chief's Crown (USA)) [2006 p8g⁵ p8.6g⁶ p7g 11.5m⁵ p12g³ 14g⁴ 12m* 12g⁴ 12.4d⁴ Aug 28] sixth foal: half-brother to useful French 6f/7f winner Royal Guard (by Hector Protector): dam 2-y-o 7f winner: fair performer: won handicap at Newmarket in August by 5 lengths: stays 12.4f: acts on polytrack, good to firm and good to soft going: visored last 3 starts: sold 28,000 gns. *M. L. W. Bell* 71

PLENTY CRIED WOLF 4 b.g. Wolfhound (USA) 126 – Plentitude (FR) (Ela-Mana-Mou 132) [2006 72: f11g⁶ 11.5m p12.2g³ p12.2g 14m⁴ 12.1d 10.9d⁴ 12s Oct 24] workmanlike gelding: fair performer: stays 1¾m: acts on polytrack, soft and good to firm going: often races prominently. *R. A. Fahey* 69

PLOUGH MAITE 3 b.g. Komaite (USA) – Plough Hill (North Briton 67) [2006 44: 12.1g 10.1m 14.1d⁶ 13.8m⁵ 11.8d Oct 10] workmanlike gelding: poor maiden: stays 13.8f: acts on polytrack and good to firm ground: tried blinkered/in cheekpieces: swerved right leaving stall on debut: withdrawn after refusing to enter stall intended final outing at 2 yrs, and troublesome at start second outing in 2006. *D. E. Cantillon* 48

PLUM BLOSSOM 3 br.f. Beat All (USA) 120 – Plum Bold 83 (Be My Guest (USA) 126) [2006 42: p5.1g Jun 10] poor maiden. *S. A. Brookshaw* –

PLUM PUDDING (IRE) 3 b.g. Elnadim (USA) 128 – Karayb (IRE) 93 (Last Tycoon 131) [2006 77: p8g² 8.3g² 8m* 8m 8m² 9m 8g* 7d⁶ 8g 8d Oct 28] strong, good-topped gelding: impresses in appearance: useful handicapper: won at Newmarket in May and September (beat Rain Stops Play by ¾ length): below form there last 3 starts: gelded after: will probably prove best up to 1m: acts on polytrack and good to firm going (below form all 3 starts on ground softer than good): usually races prominently. *R. Hannon* 104

PLUSH 3 ch.c. Medicean 128 – Glorious (Nashwan (USA) 135) [2006 p7.1g f8g² f8g³ p10g 12m Aug 4] modest maiden: left Sir Mark Prescott 7,000 gns after fourth start: bred to stay 1¼m. *A. J. Martin, Ireland* 64

POCHARD 3 br.f. Inchinor 119 – Pomorie (IRE) 67§ (Be My Guest (USA) 126) [2006 10f⁶ 10f² p10g³ 11.5m p13g⁴ Sep 29] 1,200Y: seventh foal: half-sister to 3 winners, including 5-y-o Habitual Dancer and 4-y-o Swords: dam, 1¼m winner (also successful over hurdles), became untrustworthy: fair maiden: stays 1¼m: acts on polytrack, probably on firm ground. *J. M. P. Eustace* 69

POCKET TOO 3 b.g. Fleetwood (IRE) 107 – Pocket Venus (IRE) (King's Theatre (IRE) 128) [2006 66?: p10g p12g 11.6m 11s p13.9g³ Dec 31] close-coupled gelding: winning hurdler: fair maiden on Flat: left J-R. Auvray after third outing: tried blinkered/in cheekpieces. *M. Salaman* 66

POCKETWOOD 4 b.g. Fleetwood (IRE) 107 – Pocket Venus (IRE) (King's Theatre (IRE) 128) [2006 86: 16d p16.5g⁴ Nov 6] well-made gelding: fairly useful handicapper at 3 yrs: well held in 2006. *Jean-Rene Auvray* –

POETICAL (IRE) 5 ch.m. Croco Rouge (IRE) 126 – Abyat (USA) (Shadeed (USA) 135) [2006 100d: 7m 9.5d⁶ Aug 16] good-topped mare: useful performer at best: won maiden at the Curragh in 2004 (only success): sold from M. Grassick 50,000 gns after final start at 4 yrs: seventh in handicap at Newmarket on reappearance: much better effort when sixth to Race For The Stars in Denny Cordell Fillies Stakes at Gowran: seems to stay 1¼m: acts on any ground: tried blinkered: sold 110,000 gns. *D. J. Daly* 92

POIROT 4 b.g. Montjeu (IRE) 137 – Opari (IRE) (Night Shift (USA)) [2006 56?: f8g 12s Aug 18] strong, good sort: little solid form: tried blinkered. *J. Howard Johnson* –

POISIEDON (IRE) 2 b.c. (Mar 6) King's Best (USA) 132 – Lizanne (USA) (Theatrical 128) [2006 p7.1g³ p7.1g⁵ Dec 22] 30,000Y, 55,000 2-y-o: third foal: dam unraced half-sister to US Grade 1 8.5f (at 2 yrs) to 1½m winner Hawkster and smart French 1½m performer Silver Lane: better effort in maidens at Wolverhampton when third to Leonard Charles: again raced very freely next time. *L. McAteer, Ireland* 61

POKER PLAYER (IRE) 4 ch.g. Raise A Grand (IRE) 114 – Look Nonchalant (IRE) 61 (Fayruz 116) [2006 84: f6g⁴ f6g p7g p7g p6g⁶ p5g 6g 7g² 7m 7f 7m⁵ 7f Jul 31] tall gelding: has a short, unimpressive action: fair performer: stays 1m: acts on all-weather, good to firm and good to soft ground: sometimes blinkered, including for sole success: races prominently. *G. C. Bravery* 78

POLAR BEN 7 b.g. Polar Falcon (USA) 126 – Woodbeck 90 (Terimon 124) [2006 117: 7g⁴ 7s* 8m³ 7.1s⁴ 7g⁴ 7d⁴ 7d⁶ 8d⁵ Oct 28] rather leggy, useful-looking gelding: smart 117 performer: won minor event at Goodwood (by 2 lengths from Turnkey) in May: good efforts in similar event at Newmarket (third to Belenus) and listed race at Newbury (fourth to Sleeping Indian) third/fifth outings: best at 7f/1m: acts on soft and good to firm going: held up, and can look difficult ride. *J. R. Fanshawe*

POLAR FORCE 6 ch.g. Polar Falcon (USA) 126 – Irish Light (USA) 91 (Irish River (FR) 131) [2006 81: p5g⁶ p6g³ p6g 6m 5m p6m p6g 6d⁶ p5.1g² p6g⁵ p6m* p5.1g p6g Dec 28] neat gelding: only fair handicapper nowadays: won at Wolverhampton in November: stays 6f: acts on polytrack, soft and good to firm going: sometimes slowly away. *Mrs C. A. Dunnett* **74**

POLAR HAZE 9 ch.g. Polar Falcon (USA) 126 – Sky Music 85 (Absalom 128) [2006 50§: f6g f6g⁵ f6g⁶ f6g f6g Feb 26] lengthy, good-quartered gelding: poor performer nowadays: best at 6f: acts on all-weather, firm and soft ground: usually wears headgear. *J. Pearce* **44**

POLAR MAGIC 5 ch.g. Polar Falcon (USA) 126 – Enchant 92 (Lion Cavern (USA) 117) [2006 100: 7s* 7m⁴ 7m⁶ 7g² 7d⁴ Sep 23] lengthy gelding: useful handicapper: won at Goodwood (by 3½ lengths from Material Witness) in May: also ran well after, notably when head second to Jamieson Gold at Newbury and fourth to All Ivory in valuable event at Ascot last 2 starts: stays 1m: acts on polytrack, soft and good to firm going: edged right first 2 outings: held up: sold 120,000 gns, sent to UAE. *J. R. Fanshawe* **109**

POLESWORTH 4 b.f. Wizard King 122 – Nicholas Mistress 56 (Beveled (USA)) [2006 –, a50: f6g⁶ f7g Feb 5] poor performer on all-weather: best at 7f: acts on fibresand, no form on turf: often blinkered: sometimes slowly away. *C. N. Kellett* **41**

POLIAMA 4 b.f. Polish Precedent (USA) 131 – Amal (Top Ville 129) [2006 –: 10.2m 8.3g Oct 16] well held in maidens. *Evan Williams* **–**

POLICY MAKER (IRE) 6 b.h. Sadler's Wells (USA) 132 – Palmeraie (USA) (Lear Fan (USA) 130) [2006 119: 12g³ 12d⁴ 12m* 12d⁴ 15s² 15.5m⁵ 12g Oct 15] tall, rather leggy horse: smart performer: won 4 pattern races during career, including Grand Prix de Chantilly Mitsubishi Motors in June (for second time) by 2 lengths from Salutino: creditable 4¼ lengths fourth to Pride in Grand Prix de Saint-Cloud, carrying head awkwardly, but just respectable 5 lengths second behind Lord du Sud in Prix Kergorlay after: was best around 1½m: acted on firm and soft going: had worn ear plugs/hood/blinkers: held up: to stand at Haras du Pin, France. *E. Lellouche, France* **119**

POLISHED GEM (IRE) 3 b.f. Danehill (USA) 126 – Trusted Partner (USA) 114 (Affirmed (USA)) [2006 89: 7d⁴ 8m 7d⁴ Sep 12] leggy, close-coupled filly: sister to very smart Irish 7f (at 2 yrs)/1m winner Dress To Thrill, later Grade 1 9f winner in USA, closely related to 6f winner Foolish Thought (by Green Desert) and half-sister to several winners, including useful Irish 1½m winner Blend of Pace (by Sadler's Wells): dam won Irish 1000 Guineas: fairly useful form at 2 yrs, winning maiden at Leopardstown: well held in 2006, making little impression when badly hampered 2f out in listed handicap at Royal Ascot on second outing: should stay 1m: acts on heavy going: blinkered final start. *D. K. Weld, Ireland* **–**

POLISH EFFIGY 3 b.g. Bertolini (USA) 125 – Corn Dolly (IRE) 60 (Thatching 131) [2006 –: p8.6g⁶ Feb 18] little form: blinkered only outing in 2006. *B. W. Duke* **–**

POLISH EMPEROR (USA) 6 ch.g. Polish Precedent (USA) 131 – Empress Jackie (USA) (Mount Hagen (FR) 127) [2006 95, a101: 5g 5.3f⁵ 5m 5.2f⁶ 6m⁶ 5.2d² 5.1g 5m 6.1g 6d² 5d f5g p5.1g Dec 27] lengthy gelding: fairly useful handicapper: below form after sixth outing, left W. Swinburn 20,000 gns after tenth: best at 5f/6f: acts on all-weather, firm and soft going: often wears headgear: races prominently: sometimes hangs, and looked none too keen on reappearance: untrustworthy. *D. W. Barker* **89 d**

POLISH INDEX 4 b.g. Polish Precedent (USA) 131 – Glossary (Reference Point 139) [2006 55: 9.7d 8m* 8d 7m⁵ p8g 7g⁴ 6.1m⁰¹ 6.1g Sep 26] leggy, angular gelding: fair handicapper: improved and won at Yarmouth in April and Warwick in August: effective at 6f to 1m: acts on good to firm going: wears cheekpieces: has hung right. *J. R. Jenkins* **76**

POLISH POWER (GER) 6 b.h. Halling (USA) 133 – Polish Queen (Polish Precedent (USA) 131) [2006 68d: f12g⁵ p12.2g⁵ f12g² p12g* f14g² p13g* p10g* p12g* p12g⁴ 12m² 12.4d* 12m³ 12m p12g⁴ p12g p12g* p13g⁴ Dec 22] tall horse: fairly useful handicapper: successful 6 times in 2006, at Lingfield (4), Kempton and Newcastle: stays easy 1¾m: acts on all-weather, soft and good to firm going: tried blinkered/in cheekpieces: has run well when sweating. *J. S. Moore* **87**

POLISH PROSPECT (IRE) 2 ch.f. (Mar 13) Elnadim (USA) 128 – Always True (USA) 67 (Geiger Counter (USA)) [2006 8g Oct 17] €3,000Y: fourth foal: half-sister to 3-y-o Blues In The Night and French 11f winner Touch And Dream (by Bering): dam Irish 2-y-o 7.8f winner: well beaten in maiden at Bath. *H. S. Howe* **–**

POLISH RED 2 b.c. (Feb 12) Polish Precedent (USA) 131 – Norcroft Joy 82§ (Rock **75** Hopper 124) [2006 7d⁵ 8.1m⁶ 8g⁵ Sep 14] good-topped colt: second foal: half-brother to 4-y-o Norcroft: dam 1½m/1¾m winner: fair form in maidens, staying on: will be suited by 1¼m/1½m. *G. G. Margarson*

POLISH STAR 2 b.g. (Mar 26) Polish Precedent (USA) 131 – Apennina (USA) (Gulch **–** (USA)) [2006 7g Sep 15] 20,000Y: big, strong gelding: third foal: half-brother to 3-y-o Dictatrix and to 6f winner in Sweden, both by Diktat: dam unraced half-sister to smart sprinter Blue Goblin: needed experience (soon detached) in maiden at Newbury won by Proponent: sold 10,000 gns. *R. Hannon*

POLISH WELCOME 3 ch.f. Polish Precedent (USA) 131 – Three White Sox 73 **56** (Most Welcome 131) [2006 –: 7g 8.1g 10f p10pg⁴ 11.5f⁴ 12f⁶ 10f⁵ 9.9g⁴ 9.9m Sep 19] lightly-made filly: modest maiden handicapper: should stay 1½m: acts on polytrack and firm going. *S. C. Williams*

POLISH WORLD (USA) 2 b.c. (Mar 4) Danzig (USA) – Welcometotheworld (USA) **52 p** (Woodman (USA) 126) [2006 7s p7g⁶ Oct 20] $550,000Y: medium-sized, stocky colt: second foal: dam 1m winner in USA, half-sister to Prix Morny winner Orpen: mid-field in maidens at Newbury and Lingfield, not knocked about: capable of better. *E. A. L. Dunlop*

POLITE REPLY (USA) 3 gr.f. With Approval (CAN) – Tsar's Pride (Sadler's Wells **57** (USA) 132) [2006 p8.6g⁵ May 8] 6,000 3-y-o: third foal: half-sister to 4-y-o Exhibit One and 1m winner in Spain by Distant View: dam, useful French 1¼m winner, out of half-sister to Zafonic: 25/1, 2¾ lengths fifth of 9 to King's Revenge in maiden at Wolverhampton, travelling smoothly for long way. *D. M. Simcock*

POLITKOVSKAYA 3 ch.f. Medicean 128 – Soluce 98 (Junius (USA) 124) [2006 –: **–** 8.2v Oct 25] leggy filly: no sign of ability. *T. H. Caldwell*

POLLIWILLINE (IRE) 3 b.f. Mull of Kintyre (USA) 114 – Zelah (IRE) 91 (Alzao **83** (USA) 117) [2006 80: 8.3m* 7d⁴ 8g 7m³ 7m⁶ 8m³ 10.2f 7d 6g Oct 16] good-bodied filly: fairly useful handicapper: won at Windsor in April: stays 8.3f: acts on good to firm and good to soft going: sold 15,000 gns, sent to Sweden. *R. Hannon*

POLLY JONES (USA) 2 b.f. (May 15) Lear Fan (USA) 130 – Polly's Link (USA) **48** (Phone Trick (USA)) [2006 6m 6g 8.1d p8g p6g* p6g⁶ Dec 16] $19,000F, $13,500Y, 27,000 2-y-o: workmanlike filly: fourth foal: half-sister to winner in South Africa by Royal Academy: dam, French 1m winner, half-sister to smart French middle-distance performer Solid Illusion: poor performer: left B. Powell after second start: won seller at Lingfield in December: should stay 1m: acts on polytrack. *G. L. Moore*

POLLY ROCKET 2 ch.f. (Mar 22) Tendulkar (USA) 114 – Celts Dawn (Celtic Swing **–** 138) [2006 p6g Dec 11] second foal: dam, little form, half-sister to smart 5f performer Repertory: slowly away and detached when brought down in seller at Wolverhampton. *P. D. Niven*

POLONIUS 5 b.g. Great Dane (IRE) 122 – Bridge Pool 74 (First Trump 118) [2006 p8g **87** p7g p10g Mar 4] fairly useful performer: little impact in handicaps in 2006, though not discredited first 2 starts: probably stays 1m: acts on good to firm ground, probably on polytrack. *P. R. Webber*

POLYGONAL (FR) 6 b.g. Octagonal (NZ) 126 – Sectarine (FR) (Maelstrom Lake **100** 118) [2006 102: p12g* p10g³ p10g³ p12g³ p10g 8s 10.1g 12m⁴ 11.9g Jul 8] quite good-topped gelding: useful handicapper: won at Lingfield (by neck from Rehearsal) in January: good efforts when third to Sri Diamond there and fourth to Young Mick in Duke of Edinburgh Stakes at Royal Ascot third/seventh outings: effective at 1¼m/1½m: acts on polytrack, firm and good to soft going: tried blinkered, better form without: has been bandaged behind. *E. R. Oertel*

POLYQUEST (IRE) 2 b.f. (May 10) Poliglote 121 – Seren Quest 90 (Rainbow Quest **52** (USA) 134) [2006 8.1m p8g p9.5g⁵ Nov 16] closely related to smart 1¼m to 11.6f winner Saddler's Quest (by Saddlers' Hall) and half-sister to 3 winners, including useful 1m (at 2 yrs) to 12.5f winner Seren Hill (by Sabrehill): dam 1¼m winner: modest form in maidens: will benefit from 1½m. *P. F. I. Cole*

POMFRET LAD 8 b.g. Cyrano de Bergerac 120 – Lucky Flinders 77 (Free State 125) **81** [2006 88: 5d⁶ 5m* 6g⁶ 5s 6f 6f* 6m 6g⁴ 5f 5d 8d⁵ Aug 28] good-topped gelding: fairly useful performer: won handicap in April and claimer in June, both at Ripon: effective at 5f to 7f: acts on firm and soft going: tried blinkered/visored: none too reliable. *J. J. Quinn*

POMMES FRITES 3 b.f. Bertolini (USA) 125 – Picolette 56 (Piccolo 121) [2006 80: **78** 8.3g p8g⁶ p7.1f p8.6f 8.1d² 8d p8.6g p8g p7g p7.1g² Nov 27] close-coupled filly: fair performer: stays 1m: acts on polytrack, good to firm and good to soft going: sold 4,500 gns. *W. R. Muir*

PONIARD (IRE) 2 b.g. (Mar 26) Daggers Drawn (USA) 114 – It's Academic 73 **64 §** (Royal Academy (USA) 130) [2006 5g 5g⁵ 5d 6g⁴ 5m 6s³ 6s Sep 28] small, good-bodied gelding: modest maiden: in frame in sellers: raced at 5f/6f: often shapes as if amiss: unreliable. *D. W. Barker*

PONTEFRACT GLORY 3 b.g. Lujain (USA) 119 – Final Glory (Midyan (USA) **45** 124) [2006 45: 7f 8d 7g 6m⁵ 7m² 7.9m⁵ 6m 7d⁶ 6g⁶ 7f⁴ Sep 18] close-coupled gelding: poor maiden: stays 1m: acts on firm ground: wears cheekpieces/blinkers nowadays. *M. Dods*

PONTE VECCHIO (IRE) 2 b.g. (Mar 24) Trans Island 119 – Gino Lady (IRE) 79 **–** (Perugino (USA) 84) [2006 p8g 7d p6g⁴ p8g⁴ Dec 8] tall, close-coupled gelding: little form: edgy sort. *J. R. Boyle*

PONT NEUF (IRE) 6 b.m. Revoque (IRE) 122 – Petite Maxine 70 (Sharpo 132) [2006 **–** 73d: 12v 11g 12s Oct 14] angular mare: fair performer at best: well held in 2006: usually tongue tied: held up. *A. Crook*

PONT WOOD 2 b.c. (Apr 30) Iron Mask (USA) 117 – Bajan Rose 89 (Dashing Blade **63** 117) [2006 p6g³ p6g⁵ Dec 8] better effort (modest form) in maidens at Wolverhampton when 3 lengths third of 5 to Danapali, racing freely. *M. Blanshard*

PONTY CARLO (IRE) 3 b.g. Mujadil (USA) 119 – Distant Shore (IRE) 71 (Jareer **39** (USA) 115) [2006 49: 5s⁶ 5d 6d Sep 5] good-topped gelding: poor maiden: tried tongue tied: sold 1,800 gns, sent to Denmark. *T. D. Easterby*

PONTY ROSSA (IRE) 2 ch.f. (Feb 25) Distant Music (USA) 126 – Danish Gem **89** (Danehill (USA) 126) [2006 6g² 5g* p6g* 6m* 6d 6d⁵ Sep 16] €7,500F, €15,000Y: sturdy, lengthy filly: first foal: dam French 9f winner: fairly useful form: won maiden at Carlisle in June, minor event at Wolverhampton in July and nursery at Newmarket (beat Gremlin by ¾ length) in August: good 2½ lengths fifth of 7 to Princess Iris in Firth of Clyde Stakes at Ayr, no clear run: likely to stay 7f/1m: acts on polytrack, good to firm and good to soft going. *T. D. Easterby*

POOR NELLY 2 ch.f. (Apr 27) King's Best (USA) 132 – Kootenay (IRE) 109 (Selkirk **–** (USA) 129) [2006 6f 6.1f 6f⁶ p7g Oct 11] compact filly: first foal: dam 7f (at 2 yrs)/1m winner: well held in maidens. *J. L. Dunlop*

POP MUSIC (IRE) 3 b.g. Tagula (IRE) 116 – Easy Pop (IRE) (Shernazar 131) [2006 **70** p7.1g³ p8.6g³ p8.6g³ p8g⁵ 8m⁶ f7g⁴ p8.6g 8.2g⁶ p8.6m p8.6g⁶ p9.5g* p9.5g³ p8.6g² Dec 29] €70,000Y, 4,000 2-y-o: brother to useful 2004 2-y-o 6f to 1m winner Merchant and half-brother to 3 winners, including 6f and 1½m winner Ile Facile (by Turtle Island): dam unraced: fair performer: won handicap at Wolverhampton in November: will stay 1¼m: acts on polytrack: tried blinkered, wears cheekpieces last 3 starts. *Miss J. Feilden*

POPOLO (IRE) 2 b.f. (Apr 14) Fasliyev (USA) 120 – Delisha (Salse (USA) 128) [2006 **66** 5m 6m³ 5.1m³ 6s⁵ 6f⁴ Sep 18] €50,000Y: rather leggy, lengthy filly: sixth foal: half-sister to 3 winners, notably 3y-o Al Qasi: dam, German 1m winner, half-sister to very smart Hong Kong miler Olympic Express: fair maiden: made frame 3 times, in nursery final start (never nearer): will stay 7f/1m: acts on firm going. *M. L. W. Bell*

POPPYS FOOTPRINT (IRE) 5 ch.m. Titus Livius (FR) 115 – Mica Male (ITY) **72** (Law Society (USA) 130) [2006 88, a75: p9.5g p8.6g³ p8.6g² p10g p7.1g 7.5m Jul 24] leggy, workmanlike mare: fair handicapper: stays 9.5f: acts on polytrack, unraced on extremes of going on turf: often wears cheekpieces/blinkers: has carried head high: sold 20,000 gns in November. *K. A. Ryan*

PORCELAIN (IRE) 2 ch.f. (Feb 25) Peintre Celebre (USA) 137 – Clunie 84 (Inchinor **82** 119) [2006 7f⁴ 7.6f* 8d Oct 28] good-topped filly: fourth foal: half-sister to 1m winner Poker (by Hector Protector), later successful in Denmark, and fairly useful 2004 2-y-o 6f winner Propellor (by Pivotal): dam 6f winner, including at 2 yrs: fairly useful form: won maiden at Chester (held Shake On It by short head) in September: weakened and eased in listed race at Newmarket (softer conditions): should stay 1m: acts on firm going. *A. Dickman*

PORJENSKI 2 ch.f. (Apr 6) Piccolo 121 – Stygian (USA) 73 (Irish River (FR) 131) **46** [2006 p7.1g⁵ p6g³ p5.1g⁶ 5.3m p6m Nov 8] 1,400F, £600Y: sixth foal: half-sister to 8-y-o Ambersong and 5-y-o Friends Hope: dam 5f/6f winner (ran only at 2 yrs): poor maiden, raced in sellers. *A. B. Haynes*

PORTACARRON (IRE) 4 b.f. Rossini (USA) 118 – Night Patrol (IRE) (Night Shift **63** (USA)) [2006 69: p8.6g 8d 6.1m 8f³ 8m Jul 26] rather leggy, close-coupled filly: modest performer: down field in handicaps in Britain 2 of first 3 starts in 2006: tailed off when saddle slipped and unseated rider final start: stays 1m: acts on firm and good to soft ground: blinkered on reappearance, in cheekpieces after (also tongue tied final start): sold 1,500 gns in October. *E. Tyrrell, Ireland*

PORTAL 3 b.f. Hernando (FR) 127 – White Palace 80 (Shirley Heights 130) [2006 85p: **105** 9.9m* 10m³ 9.9m* 10g⁵ Oct 12] rather leggy filly: useful form: successful on 3 of 5 starts, including handicaps at Goodwood in June and August (beat Grain of Truth by head in listed event): backward in coat, respectable fifth to Innocent Air in listed race at Newmarket final start, not getting run of race: stays 1¼m: raced only on good/good to firm ground: held up. *J. R. Fanshawe*

PORTERS (USA) 3 b. or br.g. Minardi (USA) 119 – Time For The Show (USA) **97** (Academy Award (USA)) [2006 85: p8g* p7g² p7g 8m 10m² 10m⁵ 9.9f 8d⁵ Oct 2] leggy, useful-looking gelding: useful handicapper: won at Kempton in March, hanging left: good second after on same course and at Newmarket (beaten 1¼ lengths by Formal Decree): below form otherwise (gelded after sixth start): stays 1¼m: acts on polytrack and good to firm going: tongue tied once at 2 yrs: tried in cheekpieces. *R. Hannon*

PORTLAND 3 b.c. Zafonic (USA) 130 – Bayswater 76 (Caerleon (USA) 132) [2006 –: **88** 7.1g* Apr 17] strong colt: fairly useful form: much better effort in maidens when winning at Warwick (by ½ length from Street Warrior) only outing in 2006: should stay 1m: sold 15,500 gns in July. *B. W. Hills*

PORT LUANDA (IRE) 2 ch.g. (May 11) Docksider (USA) 124 – Lady Angola (USA) **–** 83 (Lord At War (ARG)) [2006 p6g p7g Jul 26] behind in maidens. *R. M. Flower*

PORT MACQUAIRIE (IRE) 2 b.g. (Mar 28) Val Royal (FR) 127 – Hishmah 79 **52** (Nashwan (USA) 135) [2006 p8.6g p8.6s⁴ Dec 13] better effort (modest form) in maidens at Wolverhampton when fourth of 6 to Benny The Bat. *R. M. Beckett*

PORTMEIRION 5 b.m. Polish Precedent (USA) 131 – India Atlanta (Ahonoora 122) **96** [2006 72: 6.1m p6g³ p6g* 6d 6.1m² 5g⁶ 5d⁶ Oct 22] leggy mare: useful performer: won handicap at Lingfield in July: far better form in listed races at Chester (second to Ripples Maid), Hamilton and Baden-Baden last 3 outings: effective at 5f/6f: acts on polytrack, good to firm and good to soft going. *S. C. Williams*

PORT 'N STARBOARD 5 ch.g. Polar Falcon (USA) 126 – Sally Slade 80 (Dowsing **75** (USA) 124) [2006 68: p10g* p10g² p10g³ p10g p10g p9.5g² p10g* p9.5g⁴ p10g p10g⁴ Dec 16] fair performer: won maiden at Lingfield in January and handicap at Kempton in April: stays 1¼m: acts on polytrack: tried visored. *C. A. Cyzer*

PORTRAYAL (USA) 4 b.f. Saint Ballado (CAN) – True Glory (IRE) 84 (In The Wings **101 +** 128) [2006 114p: 10.4s³ May 18] big, lengthy filly: smart performer at best, lightly raced: just useful form when 5½ lengths third to Strawberry Dale in Middleton Stakes at York only start in 2006: should stay 1½m: acts on soft and good to firm going: has worn crossed noseband: left Godolphin, and sent to USA. *Saeed bin Suroor*

POSEIDON'S SECRET (IRE) 3 b.c. Night Shift (USA) – Chita Rivera 61 (Chief **68** Singer 131) [2006 8g p12g³ Nov 24] 26,000Y: big, strong, useful-looking colt: has a round action: fifth foal: half-brother to useful but untrustworthy performer up to 1½m Sunstone (by Caerleon): dam, staying maiden, half-sister to Oaks winner Lady Carla: better effort in maidens when third at Kempton, though looked difficult ride: stays 1½m: very green on debut. *Pat Eddery*

POSSESSED 3 b.f. Desert Prince (IRE) 130 – Obsessive (USA) 102 (Seeking The Gold **73** (USA)) [2006 74: p10g p8g⁴ p7g p8g 8m 8m³ 8.3f 7m p8g⁶ p10g⁶ p8g² Sep 10] leggy, close-coupled filly: fair handicapper: stays 8.6f (seemingly not 1¼m): raced only on polytrack and ground firmer than good: tried visored: carried head high/hung left second start. *T. D. McCarthy*

POSTAGE STAMPE 3 b.f. Singspiel (IRE) 133 – Jaljuli 107 (Jalmood (USA) 126) **95** [2006 80p: p10g* 10.1f p10g p12g⁵ Nov 18] useful performer: won handicap at Lingfield in June by 4 lengths from Distinctive Look: below form after in listed race at Yarmouth and handicaps at Lingfield: should stay 1½m: acts on polytrack and good to firm going. *D. M. Simcock*

POSTAGE (USA) 3 b. or br.g. Chester House (USA) 123 – Nimble Mind (USA) 103 **62** (Lyphard (USA) 132) [2006 p7.1g p8g⁶ p7.1g³ 7.2v p7g Jun 15] modest maiden: stays 7f: acts on polytrack: in cheekpieces last 3 starts: gelded after. *K. A. Morgan*

POSTGRADUATE (IRE) 4 b.g. Almutawakel 126 – Institutrice (IRE) 87 (College **96** Chapel 122) [2006 99: 8s p8g 8m 7g Jul 6] tall, good-topped gelding: useful handicapper nowadays: stays 1m: acts on polytrack, soft and good to firm going: visored last 2 starts, brought down final one. *W. J. Knight*

POSTMASTER 4 b.g. Dansili 127 – Post Modern (USA) (Nureyev (USA) 131) [2006 **60**
68d: p10g p12g⁵ p12g p16g 10.2d p8g⁵ 7m 7.1m³ 8.5g 7f 7.6m⁵ 10m⁶ 8d p8.6m⁴
Sep 2] good-bodied gelding: just modest maiden nowadays: stays 1½m: acts on polytrack
and good to firm going: tried in cheekpieces: has worn tongue tie: none too consistent.
R. Ingram

POSTSPROFIT (IRE) 2 b.c. (Mar 28) Marju (IRE) 127 – Housekeeper (IRE) 97 **69**
(Common Grounds 118) [2006 7g⁶ 8d p7.1g⁶ Nov 3] 58,000F, 100,000Y: good-topped
colt: has a round action: second foal: dam, 7f (at 2 yrs)/1m winner (later 5f to 1m winner
in USA), half-sister to smart performer up to 1¼m Polar Prince: fair form: hinted at better
when sixth in maidens at Newmarket and Wolverhampton: too free in cheekpieces in
between: should stay 1m. *N. A. Callaghan*

POTENTIALE (IRE) 2 ch.g. (Apr 28) Singspiel (IRE) 133 – No Frills (IRE) 62 (Dar- **55**
shaan 133) [2006 7g p7g p7g Nov 11] sturdy gelding: modest form in maidens: will be
suited by 1m/1¼m: gelded after final outing. *J. W. Hills*

POTHOS WAY (GR) 3 ch.g. Wadood (USA) 97 – Evropi's Way (Sanglamore (USA) **65**
126) [2006 p8.6g⁶ p10g* p10g⁴ 10.2m p10g Oct 15] fair performer: won maiden at Lingfield in August: not sure to stay much beyond 1¼m: acts on polytrack. *P. R. Chamings*

POUND SIGN 3 ch.g. Singspiel (IRE) 133 – Profit Alert (IRE) 97 (Alzao (USA) 117) **84**
[2006 85: p10g* p10g Apr 21] fairly useful form: readily won maiden at Lingfield (idled/
hung right) in March: not suited by run of race but wasn't discredited on handicap debut
at Kempton next time: suffered knee problems after, and also gelded: stays 1¼m: acts on
polytrack. *M. L. W. Bell*

POUTU (FR) 3 b.f. Acteur Francais (USA) 118 – Sanctus Lady (IRE) (High Estate 127) **–**
[2006 –: 10g 7.5g Aug 31] leggy filly: of little account. *A. Berry*

POWER ALERT 2 b.g. (Feb 13) Averti (IRE) 117 – Crystal Power (USA) (Pleasant **47**
Colony (USA)) [2006 6.1m⁶ 7s p6g p8.6g⁵ p8.6g⁵ Dec 31] close-coupled gelding: poor
maiden. *B. R. Millman*

POWER AND DEMAND 9 b.g. Formidable (USA) 125 – Mazurkanova 63 (Song **–**
132) [2006 9.9f Jul 18] maiden: lightly raced and no form on Flat since 2001: tried
blinkered/tongue tied. *C. W. Thornton*

POWER ASSISTED 3 ch.f. Observatory (USA) 131 – Caribbean Star 81 (Soviet Star **74**
(USA) 128) [2006 71: p7g³ p7g p7g Feb 21] fair maiden: stays easy 7f: acts on polytrack
and firm going: sold 5,200 gns in July, sent to Germany. *C. F. Wall*

POWER BALLAD 2 ch.f. (Mar 2) Titus Livius (FR) 115 – Sea Music (Inchinor 119) **67**
[2006 7f⁴ Jul 27] second foal: closely related to 3-y-o Hi Dancer: dam unraced out of
half-sister to smart performers up to 1½m White Heart and Kind Regards: pulled hard/
hung left when fourth to Zefooha in maiden at Folkestone. *W. J. Knight*

POWER BROKER 3 b.c. Mark of Esteem (IRE) 137 – Galatrix 72 (Be My Guest **–**
(USA) 126) [2006 76: p8g 8.3d⁶ May 29] tall, rather leggy colt: has a quick unimpressive
action: fair maiden at 2 yrs: well held in 2006: tongue tied final start. *P. F. I. Cole*

POWER GIRL (GER) 4 b.f. Dashing Blade 117 – Picara (GER) (Prince Ippi (GER)) **107**
[2006 10.9f* 12m⁶ 14f⁶ 12s⁵ 12s Sep 22] big, good-bodied filly: half-sister to 3 winners
in Germany, including 1¼m/10.5f winner Pastorale (by Goofalik): dam, German 11f and
hurdles winner, sister to Deutsches Derby winner Philipo: useful performer: trained by
P. Rau in Germany at 3 yrs: successful British début in listed race at Warwick (beat
Mango Mischief by short head) in June: good efforts in similar events at Newmarket
(sixth to Quenched) and York (fifth to Anna Pavlova) second/fourth starts: dropped away
tamely final outing: stays 1¾m: acts on firm and soft going. *P. F. I. Cole*

POWER GLORY 4 b.g. Namaqualand (USA) – Belamcanda (Belmez (USA) 131) **–**
[2006 58: f11g⁴ 10g f11g Oct 12] good-topped gelding: modest winner at 3 yrs: little form
in 2006, leaving R. Fahey after reappearance. *M. J. Gingell*

POWER OF FUTURE (GER) 3 ch.f. Definite Article 121 – Pik Konigin (GER) **89**
(Konigsstuhl (GER)) [2006 67p: 12.1d* 14d⁵ 12g⁶ 14.1d³ 16.2d 12d⁵ p13.9m* Nov 9]
tall, leggy filly: fairly useful performer: won maiden at Hamilton in May and handicap
at Wolverhampton in November: stays 1¾m: acts on polytrack and good to soft going.
H. R. A. Cecil

POWER POLITICS (USA) 3 b.c. Seeking The Gold (USA) – Stormy Pick (USA) **95**
112 (Storm Creek (USA)) [2006 92p: 7m³ 8d⁶ p7g Oct 26] good-bodied, attractive colt:
useful performer: sustained ligament injury after final start at 2 yrs: creditable third to

Blades Girl in handicap at Southwell on reappearance: well below form both starts after: stays 7f: acts on good to firm going: joined M. Al Muhairi in UAE. *Saeed bin Suroor*

POWER STRIKE (USA) 5 b.g. Coronado's Quest (USA) 130 – Galega (Sure Blade (USA) 130) [2006 64, a52: p13.9g 12g Apr 16] well-made gelding: maiden: well held in 2006: blinkered second outing at 4 yrs. *Mrs L. B. Normile* –

POYLE JOSH 6 b.g. Danzig Connection (USA) – Poyle Jezebelle 58 (Sharpo 132) [2006 f6g p8.6g Nov 25] maiden: modest form at 2 yrs: off over 4 years, showed nothing on return: tried blinkered/in cheekpieces: ungenuine. *H. J. Manners* – §

POYLE KIERA 2 b.f. (Apr 14) Diktat 126 – Poyle Amber 55 (Sharrood (USA) 124) [2006 7f⁵ 7m⁵ p8g⁶ 8.1m⁴ p8.6m⁶ Oct 31] seventh foal: half-sister to 6f winner Railroader (by Piccolo), later successful in USA, and 6f (at 2 yrs) to 1½m winner Wilton (by Sharpo), both fairly useful: dam, sprint maiden, half-sister to smart sprinter Poyle George: modest maiden: stays 8.6f: no easy ride. *M. Blanshard* 56

POYLE RUBY 2 b.f. (Apr 18) Josr Algarhoud (IRE) 118 – Poyle Jezebelle 58 (Sharpo 132) [2006 p8g Dec 18] fourth foal: dam, 6f winner, sister to smart sprinter Poyle George: eighth of 9 in maiden at Kempton. *M. Blanshard* –

PRACTICALLYPERFECT (IRE) 2 b.f. (Feb 8) King Charlemagne (USA) 120 – Morningsurprice (USA) (Future Storm (USA)) [2006 5m 7.5m* 8m³ Oct 8] €17,000Y: compact filly: third living foal: half-sister to fairly useful 2003 2-y-o 7f winner Withor-withoutyou (by Danehill): dam unraced half-sister to dam of Oaks/Irish Derby winner Balanchine: fair form: off 4 months/left M. Johnston after debut: won maiden at Beverley in September: third to Golden Balls in minor event at Bath: barely stays 1m. *H. R. A. Cecil* 78

PRAGMATICA 5 b.m. Inchinor 119 – Isabella Gonzaga 75 (Rock Hopper 124) [2006 60, a61d: p9.5g 8f 8m Aug 9] poor maiden nowadays: stays 8.6f: acts on all-weather and good to firm going: often wears cheekpieces: races prominently. *R. M. H. Cowell* – a42

PRAIRIE SUN (GER) 5 b.m. Law Society (USA) 130 – Prairie Flame (IRE) 85 (Marju (IRE) 127) [2006 78, a?: 13.8d 21.6d 15.8g* 16.2g* 16.1d⁴ 17.1m² Jun 12] quite good-topped mare: fairly useful handicapper on turf: won at Catterick and Beverley in May: good neck second at Pontefract final start: stays 17f: acts on good to firm and good to soft ground: tried visored/in cheekpieces at 3 yrs: tough and reliable. *Mrs A. Duffield* 81 a–

PRECAUTIONARY 3 b.f. Green Desert (USA) 127 – Well Warned 104 (Warning 136) [2006 73: p7g p8.6g p6g⁵ p7g 7f 7m⁴ 5.7m 7m p5.1g Oct 14] compact filly: modest maiden: stays 7f: acts on polytrack and good to firm going: blinkered final start. *Miss J. Feilden* 51

PRECIOUS DANCER 3 b.c. Sinndar (IRE) 134 – Crodelle (IRE) (Formidable (USA) 125) [2006 56: 8d 10m* 11.6m⁴ May 15] fair performer: won handicap at Brighton in April: ran well next time: will be suited by 1½m: acts on good to firm ground: sold 3,500 gns in October. *W. R. Muir* 69

PRECIOUS LUCY (FR) 7 gr.m. Kadrou (FR) 126 – Teardrops Fall (FR) (Law Society (USA) 130) [2006 10.9m Jun 25] third foal: half-sister to 2 winners in France by The Wonder, including 9f to 12.5f winner Wonderfall: dam placed up to 1½m in France: well beaten both starts on Flat in France at 3 yrs for R. Hobson: tailed off on Flat return: poor hurdler nowadays. *G. F. Bridgwater* –

PRECIOUS MYSTERY (IRE) 6 ch.m. Titus Livius (FR) 115 – Ascoli (Skyliner 117) [2006 74, a67: 15s* 17.2s⁴ 15d Oct 13] tall, angular mare: fair handicapper: won at Warwick in April: stays 15f: acts on polytrack, soft and good to firm going: visored last 3 starts. *A. King* 76 a–

PRECOCIOUS STAR (IRE) 2 ch.f. (Mar 16) Bold Fact (USA) 116 – Flames (Blush-ing Flame (USA) 109) [2006 5d⁵ 6m* 6m* 7.1m² 7d⁴ Aug 12] strong, workmanlike filly: second foal: dam unraced half-sister to 6-y-o Kindlelight Debut: fairly useful performer: off 2½ months after debut (sore shins): won maiden at Pontefract in June and minor event at Haydock in July: better form when length second to Sudoor in listed race at Sandown and 4¾ lengths fourth of 6 to English Ballet in Sweet Solera Stakes at Newmarket: stays 7f: yet to encounter extremes of going. *K. R. Burke* 91

PREMIER CRU 3 b.g. King's Best (USA) 132 – No Rehearsal (FR) (Baillamont (USA) 124) [2006 56: 6.1d 7g p7g p10g Nov 27] modest maiden at 2 yrs: little form in 2006. *Andrew Turnell* –

PREMIER DANE (IRE) 4 b.g. Indian Danehill (IRE) 124 – Crystal Blue (IRE) (Bluebird (USA) 125) [2006 101: 8.9m⁶ 12f⁴ 10.5m Aug 12] neat gelding: useful perfor-mer (including over hurdles): trained by K. Prendergast in Ireland on Flat at 2/3 yrs: best 96 effort in 2006 when fourth in handicap at York: stays 1½m: all wins on good to firm/firm going, though has form on heavy. *N. G. Richards*

PREMIER ESCALON 2 ch.g. (May 14) Alflora (IRE) 120 – Premiere Foulee (FR) – 45 (Sillery (USA) 122) [2006 7.1d Sep 16] tailed off in maiden. *F. Jordan*

PREMIER FANTASY 4 b.g. Pivotal 124 – Hemaca (Distinctly North (USA) 115) 88 [2006 74+: 7m* 7.1f p6g⁶ p6g* p6g³ p6g² p6g³ Nov 24] quite good-topped gelding: fairly useful handicapper: won at Brighton in June and, having left W. Haggas, Wolverhampton in November: stays easy 7f: acts on polytrack and good to firm going: tried tongue tied: has been slowly away: sent to Hong Kong. *T. J. Pitt*

PREMIO LOCO (USA) 2 ch.c. (Apr 7) Prized (USA) – Crazee Mental 107 (Magic 58 p Ring (IRE) 115) [2006 p7.1g Oct 30] 19,000Y: second foal: brother to 4-y-o Ramsgill: dam 2-y-o 6f winner who stayed 1m: 66/1, green and not knocked about in maiden at Wolverhampton: should improve. *C. F. Wall*

PRESENT 2 ch.f. (Feb 16) Generous (IRE) 139 – Miss Picol (Exit To Nowhere (USA) 49 122) [2006 7m 7g 8g Sep 14] good-topped filly: third foal: dam French 10.5f and hurdles winner: poor form in maidens. *D. Morris*

PRESENTLY BLESSED (IRE) 3 ch.f. Inchinor 119 – Present Imperfect 61 (Cade- – aux Genereux 131) [2006 55: 7.5f 8f p12.2g Dec 27] €70,000Y: fifth foal: half-sister to useful 2002 2-y-o 6f winner who stayed 7f Hector's Girl (by Hector Protector): dam twice-raced half-sister to very smart performer up to 7f College Chapel: modest maiden at 2 yrs: little form at 3 yrs, leaving D. Marnane in Ireland before final outing. *K. A. Ryan*

PRESKANI 4 b.g. Sri Pekan (USA) 117 – Lamarita 92§ (Emarati (USA) 74) [2006 67: a65 f8g⁶ f8g f7g³ f7g f7s² f7g⁴ f7g⁵ p7.1g p8.6g 7d p8g f8g³ f8g⁵ f8m² f7g* f7g³ f6g² f7g f8g Dec 14] fair performer on all-weather, little form on turf: won banded race at Southwell in November: stays 1m: acts on fibresand, seemingly less effective on polytrack: tried visored/usually in cheekpieces: has hung right. *Mrs N. Macauley*

PRESQUE PERDRE 2 ch.g. (Apr 14) Desert Prince (IRE) 130 – Kindle (Selkirk – (USA) 129) [2006 6g 7s Oct 14] behind in maidens: will be suited by 1m+. *K. G. Reveley*

PRESS EXPRESS (IRE) 4 ch.g. Entrepreneur 123 – Nawaji (USA) 45 (Trempolino 82 d (USA) 135) [2006 84: 10m² 10d 10f⁵ 10m 10g⁶ 9.7m 10g 10d Nov 1] strong gelding: fairly useful handicapper: largely below form in 2006, leaving M. Bell 22,000 gns after seventh start: should prove as effective at 1m as 1¼m: acts on good to firm and good to soft going: visored seventh start: edgy, free-going sort. *R. A. Fahey*

PRESS THE BUTTON (GER) 3 b.g. Dansili 127 – Play Around (IRE) 105 (Niniski 92 (USA) 125) [2006 p7g 8s⁵ 8m³ 8.3d p7g⁴ 8m² 8.5g* 8g² p7g⁴ Sep 6] 20,000Y, 10,000 2-y-o: workmanlike gelding: half-brother to 3 winners, including useful French 9f winner Priere (by Machiavellian) and Irish 1m winner Port Natal (by Selkirk): dam, French 1¼m/1½m winner, closely related to smart French performer up to 12.5f Playact: fairly useful performer: won handicap at Epsom in August: good second in similar event at Newmarket next time: free-going sort, but should stay 1¼m: acts on polytrack and good to firm going. *J. R. Boyle*

PRESSURE PUTT 3 ch.g. Tipsy Creek (USA) 115 – Carnbrea Belle (IRE) 76 (Kefaah 91 (USA) 124) [2006 77: 7m* 8m* 6m⁶ Dec 20] strong, sturdy gelding: fairly useful handi-capper: improved in 2006, winning at Brighton in April and Musselburgh in June: left W. Haggas, off 6½ months and renamed Brilliant Treasure, below form final start: stays 1m: acts on polytrack, heavy and good to firm going. *A. T. Millard, Hong Kong*

PRESTO SHINKO (IRE) 5 b. or br.g. Shinko Forest (IRE) – Swift Chorus (Music 119 Boy 124) [2006 114: p6g² 6g 6m² 6m⁴ 6g* 6.5g 6d 6g⁶ 6d² Nov 4] tall gelding: smart performer: won Prix de Ris-Orangis at Maisons-Laffitte (by neck from demoted Tycoon's Hill) in July: in cheekpieces, improved form when head second of 10 to Rising Shadow in listed race at Windsor final outing: best at 6f: acts on polytrack and any turf going: sweating (below best) second start: waited with. *R. Hannon*

PRESUMPTIVE 6 b.g. Danehill (USA) 126 – Demure (Machiavellian (USA) 97 123) [2006 99: p7g² Apr 1] leggy, useful-looking gelding: useful handicapper, lightly raced: good 2½ lengths second to Visionist at Kempton only start in 2006: effective at 6f to 1m: acts on polytrack, good to firm and good to soft going: blinkered (seemed to take little interest) once at 4 yrs: held up: none too reliable. *R. Charlton*

PRET A PORTER (UAE) 2 b. or br.f. (Jan 26) Jade Robbery (USA) 121 – Velour 94 73 (Mtoto 134) [2006 6m 7d⁴ 7.5g⁶ 7d p8.6g p9.5g² p8.6g⁴ Dec 23] fifth foal: closely related to French 2002 2-y-o 1m winner Verneau (by Lion Cavern): dam, 2-y-o 7f winner, half-sister to smart 7f winner Beraysim: fair performer: left M. Channon 12,500 gns after fourth start: won claimer at Wolverhampton in December: stays 9.5f: acts on polytrack and good to soft going: blinkered last 2 starts. *P. D. Evans*

PRETTILINI 3 ch.f. Bertolini (USA) 125 – Pretiosa (IRE) 47 (Royal Abjar (USA) 121) **70** [2006 68: p6g f6g* p6g³ p7.1g* f6g* f7g⁶ p7.1g p7.1g 7.1f 7m⁴ p7.1m 6.1g p7.1g⁶ f6g⁴ p7.1g f7g² p7.1g Dec 28] smallish, workmanlike filly: fair performer: won handicap at Southwell in January and claimers at Wolverhampton and Southwell (claimed from A. Carroll) in February: left P. Howling after seventh outing, Stef Liddiard after tenth: stays 7f: acts on all-weather and good to firm going. *R. Brotherton*

PRETTY GAME 2 b.g. (Mar 8) Mind Games 121 – Catwalk Girl 53 (Skyliner 117) **–** [2006 5.9g 7d Aug 18] well held in maidens. *K. A. Ryan*

PRETTY MAJESTIC (IRE) 2 b.f. (Apr 4) Invincible Spirit (IRE) 121 – Cheeky **92** Weeky (Cadeaux Genereux 131) [2006 5f² 6g⁴ 6m* 6m³ 6.1m* 6.5s Sep 22] 13,000F, 28,000Y: good-topped filly: fifth foal: half-sister to 3 winners, including 2005 2-y-o 6f winner Tent (by Distant Music) and 1¼m winner Cellarmaster (by Alhaarth): dam, French maiden who stayed 1½m, out of close relative of smart 1990 2-y-o sprinter Mujadil and half-sister to high-class 1½m performer Fruits of Love: fairly useful form: won maiden at Pontefract in June and minor event at Chester in August: ran well in between when third (after trouble) to Ponty Rossa in nursery at Newmarket: should prove best at 5f/6f: raced on good going or firmer until final start (below form in valuable sales event). *M. R. Channon*

PRETTY MISS 2 b.f. (Apr 20) Averti (IRE) 117 – Pretty Poppy 67 (Song 132) [2006 **76** 5m 5.1m² 5g² 5m Sep 11] small filly: half-sister to several at least useful sprinters, notably high-class 5f performer Kyllachy (by Pivotal): dam 2-y-o 5f winner who stayed 7.6f: fair maiden: runner-up at Chepstow and Beverley: better than bare result in nursery (contributed to strong pace): will prove best kept to 5f. *H. Candy*

Major A. M. Everett's "Presto Shinko"

PRETTY SELMA 2 b.f. (Apr 18) Diktat 126 – Brave Vanessa (USA) 62 (Private – Account (USA)) [2006 p6g⁶ f5g⁵ p6g Dec 8] ninth foal: half-sister to 1¼m winner Simiola (by Shaamit): dam, 6f winner who stayed 1m, sister to US Grade 2 winner around 1m Topicount: little form: tried in cheekpieces. *R. M. H. Cowell*

PRETTY SISTER 3 ch.f. Groom Dancer (USA) 128 – Remarkable 53 (Wolfhound 57 (USA) 126) [2006 p7.1g³ p7.1g p9.5g⁶ a8g* a8d⁵ Nov 7] first foal: dam, maiden who seemed to stay 1½m, half-sister to Middle Park winner First Trump: modest form in maidens at Wolverhampton only on debut: sold from W. Haggas 5,000 gns and off nearly 7 months, won amateur handicap at Taby in September: stays 1m: yet to race on turf. *Helena Gartner, Sweden*

PRETTY STAR (GER) 6 b.g. Lando (GER) 128 – Pretty Ballerina (Sadler's Wells 89 (USA) 132) [2006 12s⁴ 16s 14m⁴ Jun 23] tall gelding: useful performer at best: unraced on Flat in 2005, fairly useful form in handicaps in 2006: stays 1½m (stamina stretched at 2m): acts on good to soft going: blinkered when trained in Germany early in career: useful hurdler and fairly useful chaser (won in December). *A. King*

PRICELESS MELODY (USA) 2 b. or br.c. (Mar 29) Orientate (USA) 127 – Regatta 44 Queen (USA) (Danzig Connection (USA)) [2006 6f 7g 6g p7g⁵ p7g Nov 29] strong, good-bodied colt: poor form, including in nurseries (blinkered): probably stays 7f. *Mrs A. J. Perrett*

PRICEOFLOVE (IRE) 3 ch.f. Inchinor 119 – Piaf 62 (Pursuit of Love 124) [2006 72: 72 7m³ 7v⁴ 8v p7.1g⁴ Dec 9] €45,000Y: first foal: dam, maiden who stayed 1¼m, half-sister to useful performers Nightbird (sprinter) and Night Air (up to 8.6f): fair maiden: left N. Meade in Ireland prior to final start: stays 7f: acts on firm ground: tried tongue tied. *P. J. Makin*

PRICE TAG 3 b.f. Dansili 127 – Tarocchi (USA) (Affirmed (USA)) [2006 8g³ 8g³ 8m 115 8d⁵ 7g* 7m 8f* Nov 26] good-topped, angular filly: has a round action: second foal: half-sister to French 11f winner Latchkey (by Unfuwain): dam, French 10.5f winner, half-sister to smart French/US performer up to 1½m Privity: smart performer: won minor event at Deauville at 2 yrs: first past post in Poule d'Essai des Pouliches at Longchamp in May (beat Tie Black by 1½ lengths but demoted to third after edging right and causing interference), Prix du Pin on same course (by length from Gwenseb) in September and Matriarch Stakes at Hollywood (first start after leaving P. Bary in France, by ½ length from Three Degrees, quickening to lead close home) in November: below form otherwise, including in Coronation Stakes at Royal Ascot third start: should stay 9f: acts on firm going: held up. *R. J. Frankel, USA*

PRIDE (FR) 6 b.m. Peintre Celebre (USA) 137 – Specificity (USA) 103 (Alleged 128 (USA) 138) [2006 124: 10.5d⁴ 10.5d* 12d* 12m³ 12m² 10d* 10m* Dec 10]

Rudyard Kipling's claim that 'the female of the species is more deadly than the male' does not usually apply to the world of horse racing. There is evidence that the standard sex allowance of 3 lb that fillies and mares receive from the colts is around 3 lb to 5 lb less than they deserve. The top fillies have, however, always been able to enjoy a highly successful time at two and three in Europe without taking on the colts, though, until recent years, the racing programme has offered limited opportunities for them against their own sex after the age of three. It was no surprise that it used to be common practice to retire top fillies after the age of three on this side of the Atlantic. The early signs are that the significantly upgraded programme for older fillies and mares, initiated in 2004 and following the long-standing example of North America, seems to be encouraging the connections of more fillies of pattern class to keep them in training at four, and even beyond. There are signs too that, with more older fillies and mares around, the so-called 'weaker sex' may well be experiencing an upturn in its fortunes in open-aged competition against the colts. The older fillies and mares Peeress (Lockinge), Ouija Board (Prince of Wales's Stakes), Pride (Grand Prix de Saint-Cloud and Champion), Kastoria (Irish St Leger), Shamdala (Gran Premio di Milano) and Montare (Prix Royal-Oak) all won Group 1s in the major European countries in the latest season against colts, an achievement which has generally been the exception over the years.

The game and consistent Pride may not be a Triptych—the ultra-tough French-trained filly of the 'eighties—but, in a year which also featured two other redoubtable middle-distance racemares in Ouija Board and Irish-trained Alexander Goldrun, Pride stood out. Triptych's amazing record included five Group 1 wins as a five-year-old in open-aged competition against the colts (she won nine Group 1s

Grand Prix de Saint-Cloud, Saint-Cloud—Pride (second left) catches the long odds-on Hurricane Run; Laverock (left) and Policy Maker (noseband) also make the frame

in all). Pride's two Group 1 successes in open championship events in the latest season would have been three but for just being foiled by the three-year-old colt Rail Link in the Prix de l'Arc de Triomphe. Pride came from last turning for home at Longchamp in the unusually small field and some thought her unlucky because she had to be switched as Rail Link and third-placed Deep Impact came together. However, the move cost her hardly any momentum and she was being held at the finish where she was still a neck behind. It was Pride's third successive appearance in the Arc, her record in the race mirroring the progress made during her career. A slow starter, raced only once at two and three times as a three-year-old (including winning at Newbury for Gerard Butler), Pride developed into a smart performer at four in France, winning twice in pattern company, finishing an unlucky third in the Prix Vermeille (opened for the first time to four-year-old fillies that season) and coming fifth in the Grand Prix de Saint-Cloud and thirteenth in the Arc (a race in which Ouija Board was third on the only occasion the pair met). Pride improved further at five, adding two more pattern events, the second of them the Prix Foy, before a creditable seventh to Hurricane Run in the Arc, followed by narrow defeats in two more open Group 1s, the Champion Stakes at Newmarket and the Hong Kong Cup at Sha Tin, running on strongly late on in both and looking a little unfortunate, the winners getting first run.

Pride was nearly retired at the end of her five-year-old campaign but she reportedly returned from Hong Kong to France in late-December in such good form that connections decided to give her one more season. It soon began to pay off, Pride picking up the winning thread on her second start, in the Prix Corrida at Saint-Cloud, a pattern event restricted to four-year-old fillies and mares which was promoted to Group 2 in 2004. Pride then gained the first Group 1 success of her career when upsetting the odds laid on Hurricane Run in the Grand Prix de Saint-Cloud in June. Pride produced her usual strong finish, after being held up, to collar Hurricane Run near the line and win by a head, with Laverock two lengths further away in third in the field of six. It was only the second defeat of Hurricane

Emirates Airline Champion Stakes, Newmarket—Pride is a clear-cut winner just thirteen days after a fine effort in the Arc; Rob Roy (dark colours) takes second off Hurricane Run (striped cap), with Olympian Odyssey (striped sleeves) fourth

Cathay Pacific Hong Kong Cup, Sha Tin—Pride goes one better than the previous year and crowns a marvellous season; the Japanese three-year-old Admire Moon is a strong-finishing second, with 2005 winner Vengeance of Rain third

Run's career and the general view seemed to be that Pride, the first filly or mare to win the Grand Prix de Saint-Cloud since User Friendly in 1993, had caught him on an off-day. However, Pride again had Hurricane Run behind her in the Arc, after the pair had filled the places behind Shirocco in the Prix Foy, a 'trial' in which none of the protagonists was unduly knocked about, Pride quickening well and all but catching the first two.

Pride and Hurricane Run met for a fourth time in the season—and the fifth in all—less than two weeks after the Arc over two furlongs shorter in the Emirates Airline Champion Stakes, a race in which fillies and mares have a surprisingly good record (Pride's win was the twenty-second by a female in the last fifty years). Despite the relatively short period between the two races, defeat at Longchamp has proved no bar to success at Newmarket, though fewer Arc runners have gone on to the Champion in recent years than used to do so. Montjeu was beaten at odds on by Kalanisi after being a beaten favourite, finishing fourth, in the Arc in 2000, but Pilsudski and the filly In The Groove won the Champion in the 'nineties after prominent showings in the Arc, as did Legal Case and Triptych (twice, each time after coming third at Longchamp) in the 'eighties. Pride went one better than in 2005, stalking the International winner Notnowcato and Derby winner Sir Percy when they pressed on over three furlongs out after Hurricane Run had set only a modest pace. All eight runners were more or less in line over a furlong out but Pride already looked the winner and stretched clear to win by three lengths and a head from Rob Roy and Hurricane Run, Sir Percy and Notnowcato dropping back to finish seventh and eighth.

Pride brought her career to a close when also gaining consolation for defeat the previous year in the Cathay Pacific Hong Kong Cup in December. She wasn't seen out between Newmarket and Sha Tin and, though not reproducing her Champion Stakes form, still turned the tables on 2005 winner Vengeance of Rain. Quickening to lead in the final furlong, Pride just held off the strong-finishing Japanese-trained three-year-old Admire Moon, winning by a short head, with Vengeance of Rain a length and three quarters away in third. Of the other European challengers (all of them fillies or mares), Satwa Queen finished sixth, three places ahead of 2004 winner Alexander Goldrun (also behind Pride in the Champion and the Hong Kong Cup in 2005), with Musical Way tenth. European-trained fillies and mares, incidentally, have now won both the Hong Kong Cup and the Hong Kong Vase (over a mile and a half) twice in the last four years, French-trained Vallee Enchantee having won the last-named in 2003, followed in 2005 by Ouija Board, who was withdrawn on the eve of the latest edition—intended to be her swansong —with stiffness in a foreleg.

Pride (FR) (b.m. 2000)	Peintre Celebre (USA) (ch 1994)	Nureyev (b 1977)	Northern Dancer Special
		Peinture Bleue (ch 1987)	Alydar Petroleuse
	Specificity (USA) (b 1988)	Alleged (b 1974)	Hoist The Flag Princess Pout
		Mandera (b 1970)	Vaguely Noble Foolish One

The leggy, quite good-topped Pride was trained by John Hammond for her only outing as a two-year-old in France, but the following spring she suffered a setback, which proved troublesome and apparently difficult to diagnose at first. Her Swedish-born owner-breeder transferred her temporarily to England so that ex-Swedish trainer Aage Paus, working as an osteopath near Lambourn, could treat her. Pride ended up running three times at the back end for Gerard Butler, seeming to step up considerably on the form of her Newbury maiden win when seventh, facing a stiff test, in a listed event at Doncaster on her final start. It had always been the owner's intention to have Pride returned to France—'because the programme is better there for fillies'—and Alain de Royer Dupre had charge of her at four, five and six. Pride's sire Peintre Celebre, also the sire of Vallee Enchantee among others, won the Prix du Jockey Club and was an outstanding winner of the Arc. Pride's dam

N P Bloodstock's "Pride"

Specificity, who was bought by Pride's owner in the mid-'nineties, is a half-sister to the Derby runner-up Touching Wood who went on to complete the Anglo-Irish St Leger double, in the final year before the Irish version was opened to horses above the age of three. Specificity was also a stayer, but she didn't make her race-course debut until towards the end of her three-year-old days when she won an apprentice event over a mile and a half at Catterick. She was second in the Cesarewitch at four which she followed by winning a listed event over two miles, also at Newmarket. Specificity, who has bred seven winners to date in Britain and abroad, including Specifically the dam of One Thousand Guineas winner Speciosa, was out of the Princess Royal Stakes winner Mandera and her grandam, the unraced Foolish One, was a half-sister to Bold Ruler, an outstanding racehorse who was champion sire in North America eight times in the 'sixties. Pride was effective at a mile and a quarter to a mile and a half, acted on soft and good to firm going, and had a good turn of foot. She is said to be starting her career as a broodmare with a visit to Shirocco's sire Monsun. *A. de Royer Dupre, France*

PRIDE OF JOY 3 ch.f. Pursuit of Love 124 – Ivory's Joy 109 (Tina's Pet 121) [2006 –: p5g³ p6g⁴ 5.1g p5g³ p5.1g⁵ p5g Jul 5] smallish filly: fair maiden: free-going sort, best at 5f: acts on polytrack: wandered/flashed tail fourth start. *D. K. Ivory* — **73**

PRIDE OF KINLOCH 6 ch.m. Dr Devious (IRE) 127 – Stormswept (USA) 74 (Storm Bird (CAN) 134) [2006 65§, a–§: p6g 8v⁵ 7.2g² 6d⁵ 7.2m 7m⁵ 7s Aug 18] strong mare: modest performer on all-weather: little form on dirt: effective at 6f to 1m: acts on, good to firm and good to soft going: wears cheekpieces nowadays: sometimes slowly away: one to treat with caution. *N. Wilson* — **54 §** **a– §**

PRIDE OF NATION (IRE) 4 b.c. Danehill Dancer (IRE) 117 – Anita Via (IRE) (Anita's Prince 126) [2006 81p: 8d* 8.1s* 8m 8s³ Aug 24] tall, quite attractive colt: useful performer: much improved in 2006, winning handicaps at Bath (easily by 5 lengths) in April and Haydock (by 2 lengths from Goodbye Mr Bond) in May: below form in Royal Hunt Cup at Royal Ascot (raced on unfavoured side): back to best final start when third to Smart Enough at York: stays 1m, will prove as effective at 7f: acts on soft and good to firm ground. *L. M. Cumani* — **106**

PRIMA LUNA 2 b.f. (Jan 30) Primo Valentino (IRE) 116 – Ash Moon (IRE) 92 (General Monash (USA) 107) [2006 p6g p7.1g⁶ p7.1m 7.1d Oct 13] angular filly: first foal: dam 2-y-o 5f/6f winner who stayed 1½m: poor maiden. *K. R. Burke* — **48**

PRIMA MARKOVA 3 b.f. Mark of Esteem (IRE) 137 – Ball Gown 98 (Jalmood (USA) 126) [2006 –: 8.2m p10g 7m 8.1m p5.9g 10f p7g f7g Dec 12] close-coupled, sparely-made filly: well held all starts: tried blinkered/tongue tied. *J. Jay* — **–**

PRIMA PATRONA 6 b.m. Hector Protector (USA) 124 – Ballet Rambert 69 (Rambo Dancer (CAN) 107) [2006 p9.5g Feb 10] small mare: modest maiden at 2 yrs: tailed off only start since. *Mrs H. Sweeting* — **–**

PRIMARILY 4 b.g. Mind Games 121 – Prim N Proper (Tragic Role (USA)) [2006 70, a–: 6d³ 5d³ 5d⁵ 6f³ 6f 8.3m³ 6.9f 6v³ 6m 7m⁶ 6v p6g³ p5.1g³ p5g⁵ Dec 13] leggy, quite good-topped gelding: fair maiden: left A. Berry after eleventh start: effective at 6f/7f: acts on polytrack and any turf going: effective in cheekpieces/visored or not. *Peter Grayson* — **67**

PRIMARY (USA) 3 b.c. Giant's Causeway (USA) 132 – Prospective (USA) (Mr Prospector (USA)) [2006 95p: 10m* 12.3f⁵ 10m* 10f³ 9.9m⁴ Sep 10] big, strong colt: has scope: smart performer: won Betfred Classic Trial at Sandown (by neck from The Last Drop, dictating pace) in April and listed race at Milan (by 2½ lengths from Fa A Mezz, patiently ridden) in June: below par when third to Showing Up in Secretariat Stakes at Arlington penultimate start, then good 2 lengths fourth to Pictavia in Select Stakes at Goodwood: stays 1¼m (found stamina stretched in 1½m Chester Vase): acts on good to firm and good to soft going: sent to USA. *W. J. Haggas* — **116**

PRIME CONTENDER 4 b.g. Efisio 120 – Gecko Rouge (Rousillon (USA) 133) [2006 81: p12g³ 16g 11g⁴ 14s⁶ 10.3g² 10.1g³ 11.9g p11g* p12g* Dec 2] tall, quite good-topped gelding: fairly useful performer: left B. Hills after sixth start: blinkered, won handicaps at Kempton in November and December: stays easy 1½m: acts on polytrack and soft going, probably on firm. *G. L. Moore* — **81**

PRIME DEFENDER 2 ch.c. (Mar 30) Bertolini (USA) 125 – Arian Da 81 (Superlative 118) [2006 6g² 5m* 6s³ 7d p6m* Nov 8] 14,000Y: strong, good-bodied colt: good walker: has a round action: fourth foal: dam 2-y-o 5f winner: useful performer: won maiden at Sandown in July and minor event at Wolverhampton (made all, course record) in November: best run when third of 19 in St Leger Yearling Stakes at York in August, losing momentum when checked by winner Doctor Brown: stamina stretched when — **108**

eleventh of 15 in Dewhurst Stakes at Newmarket: best at 5f/6f: acts on polytrack, soft and good to firm going. *B. W. Hills*

PRIMED UP (IRE) 4 b.g. Rainbow Quest (USA) 134 – Cape Mist (USA) (Lure (USA) 131) [2006 60: p8g 10m* 10m 10f p10g 11.7m⁵ 10.2m Sep 7] tall gelding: modest performer: won seller at Brighton in May: below form subsequently, leaving G. L. Moore after fourth start: stays 11.6f: acts on good to firm ground, poor efforts all 3 runs on polytrack: often blinkered. *R. M. Beckett* **58 d**

PRIME NUMBER (IRE) 4 gr.g. King's Best (USA) 132 – Majinskaya (FR) 110 (Marignan (USA) 117) [2006 96: 8m 10m⁶ 10g⁶ Aug 4] sturdy gelding: just fairly useful handicapper in 2006: stays 9f: acts on firm and good to soft going: tried tongue tied: none too consistent: has joined J. Akehurst. *G. A. Butler* **85**

PRIME POWERED (IRE) 5 b.g. Barathea (IRE) 127 – Caribbean Quest 90 (Rainbow Quest (USA) 134) [2006 77§: p13g 11g⁵ 10d* 10d* p12g* p10g Aug 9] close-coupled gelding: has a round action: fairly useful handicapper: completed hat-trick at Newbury and Newmarket (amateurs) in May, and Kempton in June: left G. L. Moore after fifth start: stays 1½m: acts on polytrack, good to firm and good to soft ground: sometimes wears cheekpieces/blinkers: sometimes reluctant to race/hangs left. *R. M. Beckett* **83**

PRIME RECREATION 9 b.g. Primo Dominie 121 – Night Transaction 59 (Tina's Pet 121) [2006 70d: f5g⁵ p5.1g² p5g* p5.1g p5.1g 5.2m p5.1g⁶ p5g⁶ p5g p5g⁵ Dec 18] strong, rangy gelding: modest nowadays: won banded race at Kempton in April: best at 5f: acts on all-weather, heavy and good to firm going: tried in cheekpieces: sometimes slowly away/finds little/hangs right: probably best when able to lead: unreliable. *P. S. Felgate* **– §**
a61 §

Highclere Thoroughbred Racing XXVI's "Primary"

PRIMESHADE PROMISE 5 ch.m. Opening Verse (USA) 126 – Bonnie Lassie 74 **65** (Efisio 120) [2006 67: p10g 10.2d p8.6g² 8s 8.1d⁴ p9.5g p8.6g⁴ 8.1g⁶ 8m 8.1m* 7m 8m 8.2s p8g Nov 11] lengthy, angular mare: fair handicapper: won at Chepstow (carried head high) in September: stays 8.6f: acts on polytrack, soft and good to firm ground: tried in cheekpieces. *J. M. Bradley*

PRIMITIVE ACADEMY 4 b.c. Primitive Rising (USA) 113 – Royal Fontaine (IRE) **70** 84 (Royal Academy (USA) 130) [2006 10.9m³ 12f⁶ p12g⁵ p13g⁴ 15d p10g⁶ p9.5g Dec 2] tall colt: second foal: dam 1¼m winner: poor form in 2 bumpers for Heather Dalton: fair maiden on Flat: may prove best short of 1½m: acts on polytrack and good to firm going. *H. R. A. Cecil*

PRIMO GOLD 3 b.g. Primo Valentino (IRE) 116 – Bullion 85 (Sabrehill (USA) 120) **72** [2006 61: p8g³ 8s⁴ p8g² p8.6m² Oct 14] fair handicapper: won at Kempton in September: stays 8.6f: acts on all-weather (below best both starts on turf): tried tongue tied/in cheekpieces: sold 14,500 gns. *W. R. Swinburn*

PRIMONDO (IRE) 4 b.g. Montjeu (IRE) 137 – Tagiki (IRE) (Doyoun 124) [2006 66p: **71** 14.1m 14m² p16g³ 16g³ 16.2m* 16d⁴ p16g Nov 28] smallish gelding: fair handicapper: won at Warwick (hung right) in August: left J. Fanshawe 16,000 gns after sixth start: will stay beyond 2m: acts on polytrack, good to firm and good to soft going: visored last 2 starts on turf: often held up: has tended to wander. *A. W. Carroll*

PRIMO WAY 5 b.g. Primo Dominie 121 – Waypoint 95 (Cadeaux Genereux 131) [2006 **87** 99: 7g 7g⁴ 7.1m 8d* 8m 8.1s³ 8d 8.1g 7v p9.5m f6g p8.6g⁵ p9.5g³ p7.1g² Dec 26] tall **a78** gelding: fairly useful performer on turf, fair on all-weather nowadays: won handicap at Ayr in July: stays 9.5f: acts on polytrack, soft and good to firm going: often wears head-gear: sometimes slowly away. *I. Semple*

PRIMROSE QUEEN 3 b.f. Lear Fan (USA) 130 – Primrose Place (USA) (Dayjur – (USA) 137) [2006 8m Jun 18] second foal: dam, French 2-y-o 7.5f winner, out of very smart 1m/9f performer in France/USA Fitzwilliam Place: 40/1, eleventh of 13 in maiden at Salisbury, taking good hold after slow start and not knocked about: reportedly injured, and sold only 1,500 gns in November. *D. R. C. Elsworth*

PRIMUS INTER PARES (IRE) 5 b.g. Sadler's Wells (USA) 132 – Life At The – Top 107 (Habitat 134) [2006 100: 8s 8v Apr 4] smallish, close-coupled gelding: useful handicapper at best: well beaten in 2006: tried visored: suspect temperament: sold 30,000 gns and joined N. Williams. *D. Nicholls*

PRINCEABLE LADY (IRE) 4 b.f. Desert Prince (IRE) 130 – Saucy Maid (IRE) 69 – (Sure Blade (USA) 130) [2006 52: p9.5g p9.5g Feb 20] rather unfurnished filly: modest performer: well held in 2006. *J. A. Pickering*

PRINCE ARY 3 b.g. Desert Prince (IRE) 130 – Aryaf (CAN) (Vice Regent (CAN)) **89** [2006 72: p8g³ 10g²* 10d² 8s³ 10d⁴ 10g³ Oct 16] well-made gelding: fairly useful per-former: off over 4 months, won maiden at Windsor in August: good efforts in frame in handicaps after: stays 1¼m: acts on soft going, probably on polytrack: blinkered final 2-y-o outing: joined D. Pipe, and won over hurdles in December. *B. W. Hills*

PRINCE CHARLEMAGNE (IRE) 3 br.g. King Charlemagne (USA) 120 – **89** Ciubanga (IRE) (Arazi (USA) 135) [2006 53: p7g³ p8g* p10g²* p10g* p10g²* 10.2d⁴ 10s 11g* 12m p9.5g⁶ Dec 30] quite good-topped gelding: fairly useful handicapper: much improved in 2006, winning 4 times at Lingfield (first one apprentices) in January/Feb-ruary and at Redcar in May: gelded and off 6 months before final outing: stays 1½m: acts on polytrack, good to firm and good to soft going: consistent. *N. P. Littmoden*

PRINCE CYRANO 7 b.g. Cyrano de Bergerac 120 – Odilese 82 (Mummy's Pet 125) **83 §** [2006 81§: 6g 6g p6g* 6m⁵ 6g 6f 5d⁵ p6g p6g⁶ 6.1d p6g Nov 11] quite good-topped geld-ing: fairly useful handicapper: won at Wolverhampton in June: best at 5f/6f: acts on poly-track, firm and soft going: tried blinkered: temperamental: sold 4,200 gns. *W. J. Musson*

PRINCE DARIUS 3 br.g. Efisio 120 – Celt Song (IRE) (Unfuwain (USA) 131) [2006 **57** –: p8g⁵ p10g Feb 8] tall, leggy gelding: modest maiden: gelded after only outing at 2 yrs: best effort at 1m on polytrack: sold 7,500 gns, joined P. W. Sweden. *P. W. Chapple-Hyam*

PRINCE DAYJUR (USA) 7 b. or br.g. Dayjur (USA) 137 – Distinct Beauty (USA) **82** (Phone Trick (USA)) [2006 83§: p7.1g⁶ p7.1m p7.1g² p7g* p7.1g* p7.1g² p7.1g⁴ Dec 23] close-coupled, quite attractive gelding: fairly useful performer: won claimer at Lingfield and handicap at Wolverhampton, both in October: stays 7f: acts on all-weather and good to firm ground: tried visored: none too reliable. *J. Pearce*

PRINCE DUVAL (IRE) 3 b.g. Desert Prince (IRE) 130 – Ladylishandra (IRE) 82 **54** (Mujadil (USA) 119) [2006 57: 7g⁶ 7f 8d⁶ 7g⁶ 7m⁴ Sep 11] close-coupled gelding: modest maiden: stays 7f: acts on firm and good to soft going: wore cheekpieces final 2-y-o outing. *D. Carroll*

PRINCE EGOR (IRE) 3 b.g. Imperial Ballet (IRE) 110 – Harifana (FR) (Kahyasi **69** 130) [2006 8d⁵ 8g² 10.1d⁵ 8.1f Jun 10] €19,000F, €28,000Y: quite good-topped gelding: fourth foal: brother to 10.5f/11f winner in Spain: dam French 13f winner: fair maiden: should be suited by 1¼m+: slowly away first 2 outings. *M. Dods*

PRINCE EVELITH (GER) 3 b.g. Dashing Blade 117 – Peace Time (GER) (Surumu **82 p** (GER)) [2006 71: 9m 8.2m* 8m* 8.1g³ 8.5m* Sep 19] workmanlike gelding: fairly useful handicapper: won at Nottingham in June, Newcastle in July and Beverley (beat King of Rhythm by length) in September: will stay 1¼m: acts on soft and good to firm going: should continue to improve. *G. A. Swinbank*

PRINCE FLORI (GER) 3 b.c. Lando (GER) 128 – Princess Liberte (GER) (Nebos **119** (GER) 129) [2006 10s* 10g* 12g⁴ 12g 12g* Sep 3] half-brother to 3 winners in Germany, including 11f/13¼m winner Prince Nico (by Lagunas): dam German 8.5f to 11f winner: smart performer: successful at Frankfurt in maiden in April and Fruhjahrspreis (by head from Sommertag) in May: fourth to Rail Link in Prix du Lys at Longchamp and ninth to Schiaparelli in Deutsches Derby at Hamburg before much improved form when beating Oriental Tiger by 3 lengths in Grosser Volkswagen Preis von Baden at Baden-Baden in September, leading 2f out: stays 1½m: acts on soft going. *S. Smrczek, Germany*

PRINCE FOREVER (IRE) 2 b.c. (Feb 29) Giant's Causeway (USA) 132 – Routi- **96 p** lante (IRE) 96 (Rousillon (USA) 133) [2006 7g* 7g Sep 9] 180,000Y: strong, good sort: has scope: half-brother to several winners, including useful 1997 2-y-o 7f winner Amabel (by Silver Hawk) and fairly useful 2000 2-y-o 8.5f winner Changing Scene (by Theat- rical): dam, 6f (at 2 yrs) to 9f (in USA) winner, probably ungenuine: excellent impression when winning maiden at Newbury (beat Thabaat by 1¼ lengths) in August: 9/2, pulled too hard when last of 8 in Champagne Stakes at York following month: remains a good prospect. *M. A. Jarvis*

PRINCE GOLAN (IRE) 2 b.c. (Mar 31) Golan (IRE) 129 – Mohican Princess (Shir- **95** ley Heights 130) [2006 6g⁴ 6v* 6m 7.1g 8s Oct 21] 55,000Y: good-topped colt: third foal: half-brother to 4-y-o Satchem: dam, ran once, out of smart 1¼m performer Mohican Girl, herself half-sister to Yorkshire Oaks winners Untold and Sally Brown: useful performer: won maiden at Ripon in May: much improved when 3¾ lengths ninth of 21 to Hellvelyn in Coventry Stakes at Royal Ascot next time: ran as if amiss in other pattern events last 2 starts, off 2 months each time: should be suited by 1m/1¼m: acts on heavy and good to firm going. *K. A. Ryan*

PRINCELY ROYAL 2 b.g. (May 9) Prince Sabo 123 – Premium Princess 78 (Distant **62** Relative 128) [2006 5g⁴ 5m p5g 5s⁴ 5.1d⁶ p7g 6f⁵ 5.1m Oct 8] well-grown gelding: modest and inconsistent maiden: best efforts at 5f: acts on soft ground. *J. J. Bridger*

PRINCELY TED (IRE) 5 b.g. Princely Heir (IRE) 111 – Just Out (IRE) (Bluebird **55** (USA) 125) [2006 a9s⁵ a8.3s³ a8.3g* 8d p9.5m 10d⁵ p12.2m p9.5g Nov 27] ran in Spain for current trainer, winning 5 times, including handicap at Mijas in March: modest form in handicaps in Britain after: probably stays easy 1½m: acts on sand: tried visored: tongue tied. *E. J. Creighton*

PRINCELY VALE (IRE) 4 b.g. Princely Heir (IRE) 111 – Lomalou (IRE) (Lightning **62** Dealer 103) [2006 72: 7f 6g 5.3m 6.1f⁵ 6f² 7d³ 5.7m Sep 25] leggy gelding: just modest performer in 2006: effective at 6f/easy 7f nowadays: acts on polytrack, firm and soft ground: usually wears headgear: hung left third start. *W. G. M. Turner*

PRINCE MARJU (IRE) 3 b.g. Marju (IRE) 127 – Playwaki (USA) (Miswaki (USA) **–** 124) [2006 p8.6g p9.5g 7.1g 8.3g 6.1m⁵ Jul 2] sturdy gelding: no form in maidens/ handicap. *P. A. Blockley*

PRINCE NAMID 4 b.g. Namid 128 – Fen Princess (IRE) 72 (Trojan Fen 118) [2006 **101** 86: 5d 5g* 5s⁵ 5s* 6m² 6m³ 5g 6d 5d⁶ 5s⁵ p6g Nov 1] quite good-topped gelding: useful performer: progressed further in 2006, winning handicaps at Beverley and Haydock (by ½ length from Stoneacre Lad) in May: good efforts in similar events at Epsom (neck second to Beaver Patrol) and York (2 lengths third to Don Pele) next 2 starts: stays 6f: acts on any turf going (below form on polytrack): sometimes starts slowly. *Mrs A. Duffield*

PRINCE NOEL 2 b.g. (Apr 22) Dr Fong (USA) 128 – Baileys On Line 60 (Shareef **56** Dancer (USA) 135) [2006 6m 6g⁴ 7g 7s Oct 14] modest maiden: will be suited by 1¼m+. *N. Wilson*

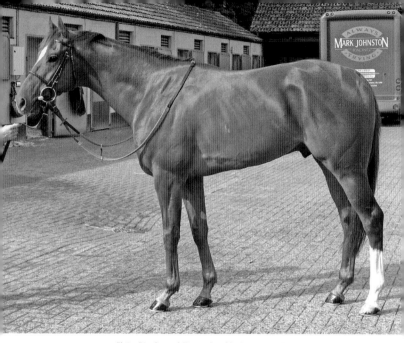

Claire Riordan and Kieran Coughlan's "Prince of Light"

PRINCE OF BLUES (IRE) 8 b.g. Prince of Birds (USA) 121 – Reshift 94 (Night Shift (USA)) [2006 59: 5.1m Jul 1] good-topped, useful-looking gelding: poor mover: modest performer: probably best at 5f/6f: acts on all-weather, firm and soft going: usually wears blinkers/cheekpieces: none too reliable. *M. Mullineaux* **–**

PRINCE OF CHARM (USA) 2 ch.c. (Jan 28) Mizzen Mast (USA) 121 – Pretty Clear (USA) 89 (Mr Prospector (USA)) [2006 p6g⁶ 7.1m 6d³ 7.1g p6g 8d⁵ 8s p8g⁴ p8g² p7g* Nov 29] 15,000 2-y-o: neat colt: first foal: dam, 6f winner, sister to high-class miler Distant View: fair performer: won nursery at Kempton in November: stays 1m: acts on polytrack and good to soft going: wore blinkers/cheekpieces last 4 outings. *P. Mitchell* **74**

PRINCE OF DELPHI 3 b.c. Royal Applause 124 – Princess Athena 119 (Ahonoora 122) [2006 5m² 6m⁴ Jun 10] brother to smart 5f/6f (Diadem Stakes) winner Acclamation and half-brother to several winners, including useful 6f/7f winner Waypoint (by Cadeaux Genereux): dam 5f winner, including Queen Mary Stakes: fair form in maidens. *H. Candy* **67**

PRINCE OF ELEGANCE 2 b.c. (Mar 14) Cape Cross (IRE) 129 – Elegant Lady 89 (Selkirk (USA) 129) [2006 p6g⁵ 6m* 7m³ 7m⁶ Jul 29] 45,000Y: good-topped colt: third foal: dam, 6f winner, closely related to useful German 6f to 1m performer Sharp Domino: fairly useful performer: won maiden at Goodwood in June: better effort in listed races when strong-finishing third to Dazed And Amazed at Newbury: should stay 7f/1m. *Mrs A. J. Perrett* **92**

PRINCE OF GOLD 6 b.g. Polar Prince (IRE) 117 – Gold Belt (IRE) 61 (Bellypha 130) [2006 67, a69: f7g⁴ f8g² p8.6g f8g³ p7.1g⁶ f7s p7.1g³ f7g⁶ p7g⁶ 8.1g 8.5m f7g³ f7g² f6g³ f7g⁶ f7g Dec 28] good-topped gelding: just modest performer in 2006: gelded after tenth outing (seemed reluctant to race next time): effective at 5f to 9.5f: acts on all-weather, firm and good to soft going: often wears headgear: sometimes slowly away: usually waited with. *R. Hollinshead* **51 a60**

PRINCE OF LIGHT (IRE) 3 ch.c. Fantastic Light (USA) 134 – Miss Queen (USA) **112**
(Miswaki (USA) 124) [2006 106: 8.3m² 7m* 7m 8m* 8g 7g⁶ 7g Sep 30] good-topped,
quite attractive colt: has a quick action: smart performer: reportedly suffered from foot
problems prior to reappearance in July: good 1¼ lengths second to Librettist in listed race
at Windsor prior to making all in minor event at Chester (by 1¼ lengths from Vanderlin)
later in month and listed race at Goodwood (beat Metropolitan Man by ¾ length) in
August: creditable 2 lengths sixth to Sleeping Indian in listed race at Newbury, best
subsequent effort: stays 1m: winner on good to soft going, best form on good/good to
firm. *M. Johnston*

PRINCE OF LOVE (IRE) 3 b.c. Fruits of Love (USA) 127 – Teodora (IRE) 93 (Fairy **73**
King (USA)) [2006 75p: 10g 10d 8d f11g² f11g⁴ f12g² Dec 14] fair handicapper: stays
1½m: acts on fibresand, good to firm and good to soft going. *Jedd O'Keeffe*

PRINCE OF MEDINA 3 ch.g. Fraam 114 – Medina de Rioseco 70 (Puissance 110) **63**
[2006 –: 9.9m p16g² 16.4m³ p16g Oct 11] rangy gelding: fair maiden on all-weather, **a69**
modest on turf: will stay beyond 2m: acts on polytrack and good to firm going. *J. R. Best*

PRINCE OF THEBES (IRE) 5 b.g. Desert Prince (IRE) 130 – Persian Walk (FR) **104**
(Persian Bold 123) [2006 100: p7g 7g² 7g³ 8m 7m 8f³ 8g* 7m³ 7d 7d Oct 20] good-topped
gelding: useful performer: won handicap at Ascot in August by short head from Tucker:
good efforts when third in similar events at Ascot (1½ lengths behind Partners In Jazz
in Victoria Cup) and Goodwood (2, beaten 1½ lengths by Spectait in totesport Mile, then
length behind King's Caprice): effective at 7f/1m: acts on firm going: fractious in paddock fourth/fifth starts: usually races prominently. *J. Akehurst*

PRINCE OF THE MAY 4 ch.g. Bluegrass Prince (IRE) 110 – Maytime 55 (Pivotal **59**
124) [2006 63: 8.1g⁴ 10s 8f⁶ 8m⁴ 10.1g⁴ Aug 16] modest maiden handicapper: stays 1m:
acts on firm going: hung right final outing. *H. Morrison*

Sony Shergar Cup Mile (Handicap), Ascot—
Prince of Thebes (Seb Sanders) battles to a short-head victory over Tucker (Hayley Turner),
giving GB and Ireland a total of 158 points to the Rest of The World's 95 in the Shergar Cup

PRINCE PICASSO 3 b.g. Lomitas 129 – Auspicious 103 (Shirley Heights 130) [2006 **88**
–p: 8m* 8d⁵ 10f* 9.3f* 9.7f³ 11m Sep 6] lengthy gelding: fairly useful handicapper: much
improved in 2006, winning at Yarmouth in May, then Brighton and Carlisle in July: below
form final outing: stays 1¼m: acts on firm going (well below par on good to soft): races
prominently: sold 18,000 gns, joined E. McNamara in Ireland. *Sir Mark Prescott*

PRINCE RICHARD 3 b.g. Diktat 126 – Princess Latifa 63 (Wolfhound (USA) 126) **–**
[2006 –: 8d 9.8m 12.1g Aug 1] maiden: little form: tried in cheekpieces. *B. Smart*

PRINCE ROSSI (IRE) 2 b.c. (Mar 25) Royal Applause 124 – Miss Rossi (Artaius **79**
(USA) 129) [2006 6v² 6m* 6m 6d 7m⁶ 7m Sep 16] 20,000Y: neat colt: has a quick action:
half-brother to several winners, including useful sprinters Dancing Music (by Music
Boy), Heather Bank (by Nordance) and Rosselli (by Puissance): dam unraced: fair performer: won maiden at Ripon in June: stiff task in listed race next start, then little impact in
nurseries: should prove best at 5f/6f: acts on heavy and good to firm going. *J. D. Bethell*

PRINCE SABAAH (IRE) 2 b.c. (Mar 15) Spectrum (IRE) 126 – Princess Sabaah **82**
(IRE) 90 (Desert King (IRE) 129) [2006 8.1m³ 9m³ 10d² Oct 2] big, lengthy colt: first
foal: dam 6f winner (ran only at 2 yrs): fairly useful form: placed all starts, second to
Eglevski at Pontefract: will stay 1½m: tongue tied after debut. *R. Hannon*

PRINCE SAMOS (IRE) 4 b.c. Mujadil (USA) 119 – Sabaniya (FR) (Lashkari 128) **96**
[2006 95: p8g 8.3g⁵ 10g* 10.5g² 9m 10g⁵ Jun 1] neat colt: useful handicapper: won at
Newbury in April by neck from River Alhaarth: creditable efforts at Haydock and Nottingham (blinkered) next/final starts: stays 10.6f: acts on polytrack, soft and good to firm
going: sold 32,000 gns in October. *R. Hannon*

PRINCESS ARWEN 4 b.f. Magic Ring (IRE) 115 – Absolutelystunning 63 (Aragon **43**
118) [2006 51: f7g f7g p6g f6g p6g⁶ p7g p6g f6g p6g Dec 6] close-coupled filly: only
poor performer in 2006: stays 7f: acts on fibresand: tried in cheekpieces. *Mrs Barbara
Waring*

PRINCESS CLEO 3 ch.f. Mark of Esteem (IRE) 137 – Classy Cleo (IRE) 102 (Muj- **75**
adil (USA) 119) [2006 81: 6m 6v⁴ 6f 5g⁵ 6d⁴ 5m Sep 21] sturdy filly: just fair handicapper
in 2006: should prove best kept to 5f/6f: acts on fibresand, good to firm and good to soft
going: tends to wander. *T. D. Easterby*

PRINCESS COCOA (IRE) 3 b.f. Desert Sun 120 – Daily Double (FR) (Unfuwain **81**
(USA) 131) [2006 42: 7m⁶ 9.8g⁴ 12.1g³ 10.3g* 9.9f² 12m² 9.9m* 9m² Aug 2] sturdy
filly: fairly useful handicapper: progressive form in 2006, winning at Chester in June and
Beverley in July: creditable second to Nice Tune at Goodwood final outing: effective at
9f to 1½m: acts on firm going. *R. A. Fahey*

PRINCESS DANAH (IRE) 3 b.f. Danehill (USA) 126 – Thaidah (CAN) 105 (Vice **67**
Regent (CAN) [2006 8.3d⁶ 8m 7.1g⁶ p10g 9.7f² 10.2f p9.5g* p10g⁶ Oct 15] €90,000Y:
half-sister to several winners, including smart 1m winner Kismah (by Machiavellian):
dam, 5f (at 2 yrs) to 7f winner, half-sister to top-class American filly Glorious Song (dam
of Singspiel) and champion US 1983 2-y-o Devil's Bag: fair performer: won handicap at
Wolverhampton in September: stays 9.7f: acts on polytrack and firm going: tongue tied
last 4 starts, in cheekpieces last 2: reportedly struck into fourth outing: sold 80,000 gns,
sent to USA. *W. R. Swinburn*

PRINCESS ELLIS 2 ch.f. (Mar 4) Compton Place 125 – Star Cast (IRE) 82 (In The **64**
Wings 128) [2006 5m 5m² 5g 5g⁴ 5.1f³ 5s⁵ Oct 14] second foal: closely related to
3-y-o That's Blue Chip: dam 1½m winner: modest maiden: placed at Carlisle and Chester
(nursery): raced at 5f. *E. J. Alston*

PRINCESS GALADRIEL 5 b.m. Magic Ring (IRE) 115 – Prim Lass 65 (Reprimand **–**
122) [2006 70: 8d 7g 7f Jun 6] rather leggy mare: fair handicapper in 2005: no form in
2006: tried in cheekpieces/blinkers: temperament under suspicion. *J. M. P. Eustace*

PRINCESS GEORGINA 2 b.f. (Apr 11) Royal Applause 124 – Degree 81 (Warning **78**
136) [2006 6.1m³ 6f 5g³ 5.2f* 5.5g Sep 6] sturdy filly: sister to 2003 2-y-o 6f winner
Auditorium and 5f (at 2 yrs) to 1m winner Mister Cosmi, both smart: dam 1m winner: fair
performer: won maiden at Yarmouth in July: stiff task second/final starts (apparently best
efforts), in listed race at Newmarket and Prix d'Arenberg (seventh of 8 to Beauty Is Truth)
at Chantilly: will prove best at 5f/6f: acts on firm going. *S. C. Williams*

PRINCESS ILEANA (IRE) 2 b.f. (Mar 21) Uhud (IRE) 121 – Uhud (IRE) **68**
(Mujtahid (USA) 118) [2006 5g² p5.1g³ 5f² 5f² 5d³ 5.1f Sep 23] €16,000Y: fifth foal:
half-sister to 4-y-o Pitch Up and winner in Italy by Distinctly North: dam unraced: fair
maiden: placed all starts before tried in nursery final one: withdrawn in October when
upset in stall (multiple injuries): raced at 5f: acts on polytrack and firm going. *K. R. Burke*

PRINCESS IRIS (IRE) 2 ch.f. (Feb 16) Desert Prince (IRE) 130 – Athlumney Lady **99**
98 (Lycius (USA) 124) [2006 5.1g* 5m 7m⁶ 6d* Sep 16] small, strong filly: second foal:
half-sister to 4-y-o Lady Gregory: dam Irish 2-y-o 7f (Killavullan Stakes)/1m winner:
useful form: won maiden at Nottingham in June and The Sportsman Newspaper Firth of
Clyde Stakes at Ayr in September, in latter beating Roxan by 1¼ lengths: probably best at
5f/6f (stamina waned in 7f Prestige Stakes): acts on good to firm and good to soft going:
sent to USA. *E. J. O'Neill*

PRINCESS KAI (IRE) 5 b.m. Cayman Kai (IRE) 114 – City Princess 62§ (Rock City **50**
120) [2006 52: p5g p6g 7m⁵ 5.3m² 5.3m⁶ 7m 7m p5g p6g⁶ Dec 30] modest performer:
stays easy 7f: acts on polytrack, firm and good to soft ground: has worn blinkers/cheek-
pieces: sometimes slowly away/wanders. *R. Ingram*

PRINCESS LAVINIA 3 ch.f. Fraam 114 – Affaire de Coeur 55 (Imperial Fling (USA) **72**
116) [2006 55p: 7g 7d³ 8g 8d 7.1d⁵ p8g Nov 29] useful-looking filly: fair maiden: should
stay at least 1¼m: acts on good to soft going: probably temperamental. *G. Wragg*

PRINCESS NADA 3 b.f. Barathea (IRE) 127 – Zomaradah 118 (Deploy 131) [2006 **108**
79: 8.2m* 10g* 11.9g³ 9.9m² 10g⁶ 10d⁶ Nov 4] big, strong, well-made filly: has a markedly round action: useful performer: much improved for new trainer in 2006: won maiden
at Nottingham in May and listed race at Newbury (by 1½ lengths from Jaish) in June:
good 2½ lengths sixth to Lake Toya in similar event at Windsor final outing: stays 1¼m
(below best when third in Lancashire Oaks at 1½m): acts on good to firm and good to soft
going. *L. M. Cumani*

PRINCESS OF AENEAS (IRE) 3 b.f. Beckett (IRE) 116 – Romangoddess (IRE) **61**
(Rhoman Rule (USA)) [2006 63: 8m⁵ 8.3m⁶ 9d 10g³ p12.2g 9s 12d* Oct 8] close-coupled
filly: modest performer: won maiden claimer at Musselburgh (claimed to join D. McCain
Jnr) in October: stays 1½m: acts on good to firm and good to soft ground: in cheekpieces
last 3 starts: sometimes slowly away. *I. Semple*

PRINCESS PALATINE (IRE) 2 b.f. (Apr 7) Iron Mask (USA) 117 – Kitty Kildare **74**
(USA) 68 (Seattle Dancer (USA) 119) [2006 6g³ 6g⁴ 8.1g⁴ 7s² Oct 14] 11,500Y: fourth
foal: half-sister to 3 winners, including fairly useful 6f/7f winner (including at 2 yrs)
Countykat and 9.4f winner Woodboro Kat (both by Woodborough): dam, Irish maiden
who stayed 7f, out of sister to smart 7f/1m performer Arjuzah, herself dam of high-class
sprinter Malhub: fair maiden: in frame all starts: should prove best up to 1m: raced on
good ground or softer. *K. R. Burke*

PRINCESS RIOJA 6 b.m. Man Among Men (IRE) – Miss Gruntled (Arctic Lord 114) **–**
[2006 f8g p8.6g Apr 29] ex-Spanish mare: 1m winner at Mijas for M. Lambert in 2003:
unraced at 5 yrs: last both starts in Britain. *J. M. Bradley*

PRINCESS SOCIETY (IRE) 3 b.f. Desert Prince (IRE) 130 – Ballet Society (FR) **65**
(Sadler's Wells (USA) 132) [2006 67p: p7g² p8.6g³ f12g 12d Apr 12] rather leggy,
lengthy filly: fair maiden: should be suited by 1¼m+: acts on polytrack, best effort on turf
on good going: sold 9,000 gns in July. *E. A. L. Dunlop*

PRINCESS TAISE (USA) 2 gr.f. (Apr 24) Cozzene (USA) – Cumulate (USA) 69 **100**
(Gone West (USA)) [2006 7m* 7d² 7m 8m Oct 1] big, strong, angular filly: fourth foal:
half-sister to French 10.5f/1½m winner Graphic Design (by Swain) and winner in USA
by Broad Brush: dam twice-raced half-sister to US Grade 2 9f winner Composer: useful
form: won maiden at Newmarket (hung left) in July: improvement when length second of
6 to English Ballet in Sweet Solera Stakes there month later: lost her way after, last in
Prestige Stakes at Goodwood (stirred up in paddock) and Prix Marcel Boussac at
Longchamp: will stay 1¼m/1½m. *M. Johnston*

PRINCESS TAYLOR 2 ch.f. (Mar 4) Singspiel (IRE) 133 – Tapas En Bal (FR) (Mille **70**
Balles (FR) 124) [2006 7m⁶ 7g³ 7g⁴ p8.6m⁴ Nov 21] leggy filly: second foal: dam,
French 7f/1m winner (including at 2 yrs), half-sister to very smart performer up to 2m
Give The Slip: fair maiden: stays 8.6f: in cheekpieces/tongue tie final start. *M. Botti*

PRINCESS TOTO 3 b.f. Mtoto 134 – Flower Princess (Slip Anchor 136) [2006 9.8g **55**
10f³ 11g f11g Dec 29] 2,000Y: sparely-made filly: half-sister to several winners, including 1996 2-y-o 7f winner Beryllium and 1½m winner Benjamin Frank (both fairly useful,
by Tragic Role): dam unraced: modest maiden: stays 1¼m: acts on firm ground: visored
final start. *P. C. Haslam*

PRINCESS VALERINA 2 ch.f. (Apr 23) Beat Hollow 126 – Heart So Blue (Dilum **94 p**
(USA) 115) [2006 6d² 6d* Oct 27] sturdy, attractive filly: third foal: half-sister to 3-y-o
Bonnie Prince Blue: dam unraced half-sister to useful performer up to 1½m Prince of My
Heart: confirmed debut promise when winning maiden at Newmarket (beat Shmookh by

2½ lengths), making all and eased down: bred to stay 1m+, but clearly not short of speed: will make a useful 3-y-o. *B. W. Hills*

PRINCESS ZADA 2 ch.f. (Mar 15) Best of The Bests (IRE) 122 – Barnacla (IRE) 83 **64** (Bluebird (USA) 125) [2006 6m 6f 5.7f⁶ 7.1m 6.1d³ Oct 4] leggy filly: fourth foal: half-sister to 3-y-o Suesam: dam 6f winner: modest maiden: best run when third to Doric Charm in minor event at Nottingham, only start on going softer than good to firm: should stay 7f: twice lost her action. *B. R. Millman*

PRINCE TAMINO 3 b.g. Mozart (IRE) 131 – Premiere Dance (IRE) (Loup Solitaire **115** (USA) 117) [2006 83: p5g² 5.1g⁴ 5f* 6m* 6m³ 5g² Sep 28] good-topped gelding: smart performer: much improved in 2006, winning handicaps at Windsor and York (beat Tawaassol by 1½ lengths in William Hill Trophy) within a week in June: very good efforts at Newmarket after, close third to Dark Missile in totesport.com Stakes (Handicap) and short-head second to Fantasy Believer in listed race: best at 5f/6f: acts on polytrack and firm going: has worn crossed noseband: joined I. Mohammed in UAE. *H. Morrison*

PRINCETON (IRE) 2 ch.c. (May 7) Maria's Mon (USA) 121 – Enrich (USA) 103 **85** (Dynaformer (USA)) [2006 7g⁴ p7.1g* 7g⁴ 7m⁴ 8.3m² 8m² 8d² 8s⁵ Sep 28] close-coupled colt: second foal: brother to 2005 2-y-o 7f winner Blue Grouse: dam, Irish 2-y-o 6f winner, half-sister to UAE 1000 Guineas winner Infinite Spirit (by Maria's Mon): fairly useful performer: won minor event at Wolverhampton in July: held form well after, runner-up 3 times, until final start on soft ground: stays 1m: acts on polytrack, good to firm and good to soft going: sold 32,000 gns, sent to USA. *M. R. Channon*

PRINCE TUM TUM (USA) 6 b.g. Capote (USA) – La Grande Epoque (USA) 120 **92** (Lyphard (USA) 132) [2006 104d, a110d: p6g⁴ p7g 7g 7.1m⁴ 6g² p6g 7g 6m 7m 6f 6g p6g p6g³ p6g p6g p7.1m* p7g⁴ p6g² p8g⁶ Dec 22] lengthy gelding: just fairly useful handicapper in 2006: left D. Barker after twelfth start: won at Wolverhampton and Kempton in November: creditable efforts both outings after: has won at 9f, but best efforts at 6f to 1m: acts on polytrack, firm and good to soft going: has been blinkered/visored/tongue tied: sometimes reluctant to post: formerly none too reliable. *D. Shaw*

PRINCE VALENTINE 5 b.g. My Best Valentine 122 – Affaire de Coeur 55 (Imperial **63** Fling (USA) 116) [2006 56: f12g p10g⁶ p10g⁴ p10g⁶ 10m² 10f² 10m² 8f* 8f² 8f* 8m 7g Oct 13] modest performer: won seller in June and handicap in August, both at Brighton: effective at 1m to easy 1½m: acts on polytrack and any turf going: tried tongue tied, blinkered/in cheekpieces nowadays: consistent. *G. L. Moore*

PRINCE VECTOR 4 b.g. Vettori (IRE) 119 – The In-Laws (IRE) 90 (Be My Guest **91** (USA) 126) [2006 89: 11.7d² p12g³ 14.1g⁶ 13.3g Aug 18] tall gelding: fairly useful handicapper: at least creditable efforts first 3 starts: stays 1¾m: acts on polytrack, firm and good to soft going: visored final outing. *A. King*

PRINCE VETTORI 4 b.g. Vettori (IRE) 119 – Bombalarina (IRE) (Barathea (IRE) **–** 127) [2006 –, a69: p8.6g⁴ f8g⁵ p10g² Dec 30] angular gelding: fair performer: stays 1¼m: **a69** acts on all-weather, little form on turf. *D. J. Coakley*

William Hill Trophy (Handicap), York—the most prestigious three-year-old sprint handicap of the season is won by the progressive Prince Tamino; behind are Tawaassol (striped cap), High Curragh (right) and Orpsie Boy (left); this was the principal race on Timeform Charity Day which raised £221,037, taking the total in 36 years to over £4m

Thurloe Finsbury II's "Prince Tamino"

PRINCE ZAFONIC 3 ch.c. Zafonic (USA) 130 – Kite Mark 58 (Mark of Esteem **69** (IRE) 137) [2006 69p: 7g 8m 8.1m 16d Nov 3] big, strong colt: fair maiden: left W. Jarvis and off 4½ months prior to final outing: will stay 1¼m: acts on soft and good to firm going. *M. W. Easterby*

PRINCIPAL WITNESS (IRE) 5 b.g. Definite Article 121 – Double Eight (IRE) 77 **75** (Common Grounds 118) [2006 77, a71: p13g* p12g² p13g p12.2g² p13.9g May 15] strong, useful-looking gelding: fair performer: won handicap at Lingfield in January: claimed from T. Dascombe £14,000 penultimate start: barely stays 1¾m: acts on polytrack, soft and good to firm ground: free-going sort. *Evan Williams*

PRINQUET (USA) 3 ch.f. Marquetry (USA) 121 – Princess Kris 82 (Kris 135) [2006 **–** –: 6g⁶ 9m Aug 31] close-coupled, useful-looking filly: little form in maidens: sold 40,000 gns in November. *C. E. Brittain*

PRINS WILLEM (IRE) 7 b.g. Alzao (USA) 117 – American Garden (USA) (Alleged **95** (USA) 138) [2006 p16g* 20m p16g* p16g⁵ Jul 15] sturdy gelding: useful handicapper: won at Lingfield (by 1¼ lengths from Nawow) in February and Kempton (by head from Velvet Heights) in July: stays easy 2m: acts on polytrack, good to firm and good to soft going: has been visored/tongue tied: usually waited with. *J. R. Fanshawe*

PRINTSMITH (IRE) 9 br.m. Petardia 113 – Black And Blaze (Taufan (USA) 119) **– §** [2006 51§: f8g p9.5g May 2] leggy mare: modest performer in 2005: well held in 2006: tried in cheekpieces/visor: inconsistent. *J. R. Norton*

PRIORINA (IRE) 4 b.f. Priolo (USA) 127 – Strina (IRE) (Indian Ridge 123) [2006 58: **56** p8.6g f7g* f8g⁶ p7g⁶ p7g f8g⁴ f7g⁶ f8g⁶ 8.1g 8.2f² 7f 8m⁵ f7g² Oct 12] modest performer: won seller at Southwell in February: stays 8.3f: acts on all-weather and firm ground: wears visor/cheekpieces. *D. Haydn Jones*

PRIORS DALE 6 b.g. Lahib (USA) 129 – Mathaayl (USA) 79 (Shadeed (USA) 135) – [2006 p12g Sep 10] leggy, good-topped gelding: fair maiden in 2004, well held only outing on Flat since (won twice over fences in November): tried tongue tied. *Miss E. C. Lavelle*

PRIORS HILL (IRE) 3 b.c. Danehill (USA) 126 – Lailati (USA) 66 (Mr Prospector **104** (USA)) [2006 97: 10d² 10.4s⁶ 14d Nov 3] good-topped, attractive colt: has scope: has a fluent action: useful handicapper: good neck second to Rampallion at Newmarket on belated reappearance: well below form after: should stay 1½m: acts on good to firm and good to soft going: tongue tied in 2006: joined E. Charpy in UAE. *Saeed bin Suroor*

PRIORY BAY (USA) 2 b.c. (May 10) Lear Fan (USA) 130 – Isla Del Rey (USA) 103 **74** (Nureyev (USA) 131) [2006 7m⁶ 7f⁶ p7g² 8.2s Oct 18] medium-sized, quite attractive colt: half-brother to several winners, including smart 1m/9f (including in USA) winner L'Oiseau d'Argent (by Silver Hawk) and 3-y-o Eilean Ban: dam 6f (in UAE)/7f (including at 2 yrs in Ireland) winner: fair maiden: runner-up at Lingfield: should stay 1m: acts on polytrack and good to firm going: sold 25,000 gns, sent to Czech Republic. *E. A. L. Dunlop*

PRIVATE BENJAMIN 6 gr.g. Ridgewood Ben 113 – Jilly Woo 60 (Environment – Friend 128) [2006 60: p12g Jan 25] angular gelding: has a round action: modest performer in 2005, well held only outing on Flat in 2006: tried blinkered: sometimes looks hard ride: none too consistent. *M. R. Hoad*

PRIVATE BUSINESS (USA) 3 gr. or ro.c. Cozzene (USA) – Privity (USA) 114 **106** (Private Account (USA)) [2006 101: 10m⁴ 16m 13m⁴ 13.4g 8g³ Oct 13] quite attractive colt: useful performer: just respectable efforts in pattern/listed races first 3 starts: best effort when 1¾ lengths third to Rain Stops Play in handicap at Newmarket final outing: effective at 1m, barely stays 13.4f: unraced on extremes of going: wore cheekpieces/blinkers third/fourth starts: sold 250,000 gns, sent to Saudi Arabia. *B. W. Hills*

PRIVATE PEACHEY (IRE) 2 b.g. (Mar 2) Shinko Forest (IRE) – Adamas (IRE) 75 **56** (Fairy King (USA)) [2006 5.1d 5.1g⁴ p7g 7m Aug 16] leggy gelding: modest maiden: best effort at 5f. *B. R. Millman*

PRIVATE REASON (USA) 2 b.c. (May 30) Red Ransom (USA) – Sultry Lass (USA) **75** (Private Account (USA)) [2006 7g 8.1d⁴ 8g⁵ Oct 17] €30,000Y, 70,000 2-y-o: strong, sturdy colt: half-brother to several minor winners in USA: dam, minor winner in USA, half-sister to Musidora winner Cassis (by Red Ransom): fair form: fourth in maiden won by Kid Mambo at Sandown: stays 1m. *R. Hannon*

PRIX MASQUE (IRE) 2 b.c. (Mar 15) Iron Mask (USA) 117 – Prima Marta (Primo **56** Dominie 121) [2006 6m 6g⁴ Jun 21] strong, close-coupled colt: has quick action: better run in maidens when seventh behind Alzerra at Haydock: joined S. Seemar in UAE. *B. Smart*

PROCLAMATION (IRE) 4 gr.c. King's Best (USA) 132 – Shamarra (FR) (Zayyani **120** 119) [2006 130: 8m³ 8d⁵ Sep 23] big, lengthy colt: top-class performer for J. Noseda at 3 yrs, winning Sussex Stakes at Goodwood: just very smart form in 2006, better effort when 1¾ lengths third to Ad Valorem in Queen Anne Stakes at Royal Ascot: well-held fifth behind George Washington in Queen Elizabeth II Stakes at Ascot final start (subsequently found to be lame): best form at 7f/1m: acted on soft going: had worn crossed noseband: sometimes hung right/carried head awkwardly: was held up, and had a fine turn of foot: to stand at Overbury Stud, Gloucestershire, fee £4,000. *Saeed bin Suroor*

PROCRASTINATE (IRE) 4 ch.g. Rossini (USA) 118 – May Hinton 82 (Main Reef – 126) [2006 48: 14m 12d Oct 8] quite good-topped gelding: maiden: well held in 2006: tried in blinkers/cheekpieces. *R. F. Fisher*

PROFESSOR TWINKLE 2 ch.c. (Feb 4) Dr Fong (USA) 128 – Shining High 90 **72** (Shirley Heights 130) [2006 7.1g 8.1d 8.3s⁵ Oct 2] compact colt: sixth foal: half-brother to 3 winners, including fairly useful 1m winners Bright Green (by Green Desert) and Flying Adored (by Polar Falcon): dam, 2m winner, half-sister to useful miler Polar Boy: fair form in maidens, staying on: will be suited by 1¼m/1½m. *W. J. Knight*

PROFITABLE 3 b.f. Daylami (IRE) 138 – Manuetti (IRE) 86 (Sadler's Wells (USA) **78** 132) [2006 70p: 12m⁵ 9m² p12g⁴ 14g p16g Oct 20] leggy filly: fair performer: won maiden at Kempton in September: stays 1½m: acts on polytrack, raced only on good/good to firm going on turf. *B. W. Hills*

PROFIT'S REALITY (IRE) 4 br.g. Key of Luck (USA) 126 – Teacher Preacher **108** (IRE) 37 (Taufan (USA) 119) [2006 101: p10g 9.8d* 10.1g⁴ 12.1d³ 12d³ 10.1g 10d³ 12d⁵ 12d Sep 29] big gelding: useful performer: won minor event at Ripon in April by short head from Blue Monday: creditable third behind Akarem in listed handicap at Hamilton and listed race at Ascot fourth/fifth starts, and when fifth to Young Mick in Cumberland Lodge Stakes at Ascot: stays 1½m: acts on good to firm and good to soft ground: tongue tied first 3 starts in 2006: hung right seventh outing. *P. A. Blockley*

PROJECT SUNSHINE (GER) 3 b. or br.g. Xaar 132 – Prada (GER) (Lagunas) – [2006 10m 10.9d[6] p12g p10g Aug 2] well held in maidens/handicap. *J. A. Osborne*

PRONTO VENDE (IRE) 3 b.g. Fasliyev (USA) 120 – Hilbys Brite Flite (USA) (Cormorant (USA)) [2006 p7g p6g f6g Jul 11] little form in maidens. *G. A. Butler* –

PROPER ARTICLE (IRE) 4 b.g. Definite Article 121 – Feather 'n Lace (IRE) 73 **73** (Green Desert (USA) 127) [2006 70+: 11s[6] 16m 12s[2] 12g[6] 12d f16g Dec 19] fair handicapper: good second at Sligo in August: left D. Weld in Ireland 20,000 gns, below form at Southwell final start: acts on soft and good to firm ground: blinkered last 6 outings, tongue tied on latest. *Miss J. E. Foster*

PROPER (IRE) 2 b.g. (Mar 24) Rossini (USA) 118 – Pardoned (IRE) 74 (Mujadil **70** (USA) 119) [2006 6s 6g[3] 6m* 5.1f[4] 5.2g 6.1m[6] Aug 6] €10,000F, 4,500Y: leggy, lightly-made gelding: third foal: dam, Irish maiden (placed at 6f/7f at 2 yrs), half-sister to useful miler Resplendent One: fair performer: won maiden at Goodwood in June: should prove best at 5f/6f: acts on firm and soft going: gelded after final start. *M. R. Channon*

PROPHET PREACHER (IRE) 3 b.f. Imperial Ballet (IRE) 110 – Teacher Preacher **55 d** (IRE) 37 (Taufan (USA) 119) [2006 8d 8.2m 9.8g f11g 11.1f f11g[6] p12.2g[3] 16.2m f12g Dec 9] 4,000Y, 8,000 2-y-o: good-topped filly: fourth foal: half-sister to 4-y-o Profit's Reality and 5-y-o Key Partners: dam Irish 7f winner: modest maiden: tried visored. *M. Wellings*

PROPINQUITY 4 b.g. Primo Dominie 121 – Lydia Maria 70 (Dancing Brave (USA) – 140) [2006 98: 8.2g Jun 7] robust gelding: useful performer at best: well held only outing in 2006: sold 3,000 gns in October. *W. R. Swinburn*

PROPONENT (IRE) 2 b.c. (Mar 2) Peintre Celebre (USA) 137 – Pont Audemer **100 P** (USA) 108 (Chief's Crown (USA)) [2006 7g* 8g* Oct 13]

Since saddling Quest For Fame to win the 1990 Derby, Roger Charlton has had just one runner in the race, Mystic Knight, a 14/1-shot who finished sixth of twenty behind Shaamit in 1996. The yard seems to have another colt with classic potential in Proponent who looks well worth his place in one of the early-season Derby trials. Proponent has yet to run in pattern company but was unbeaten in two starts as a two-year-old, starting favourite both times, and is bred to come into his own as a three-year-old over middle distances.

Given his stable, which tends not to rush its staying-bred two-year-olds, it was significant that Proponent was a well-backed 2/1 favourite when making his debut in the second division of an ordinary maiden at Newbury in September. Proponent had no problem justifying the support, soon on top when shaken up and winning smoothly by two lengths from Opera Crown who won next time out. Interestingly, after the race, Charlton inferred that Proponent was still in need of the experience, claiming that his contender in the first division of the same event, Fifty Cents, would have won Proponent's race as he was the sharper of the pair. Four weeks later, Proponent was sent off at 7/2-on against three rivals in the Racing

EBF Dubai Tennis Championships Maiden Stakes, Newbury—
Proponent creates a big impression on his debut; Opera Crown and Atraas (striped cap) chase him home

South Africa Houghton Conditions Stakes at Newmarket. Proponent travelled freely under restraint and was wisely given his head a fair way out, keeping on strongly and beating his only serious challenger Minos by six lengths. The form is not easy to evaluate, though the useful winning timefigure went some way to supporting the view that the exciting Proponent will make his mark at a higher grade.

		Nureyev (b 1977)	Northern Dancer
	Peintre Celebre (USA) (ch 1994)		Special
		Peinture Bleue (ch 1987)	Alydar
Proponent (IRE)			Petroliuse
(b.c. Mar 2, 2004)		Chief's Crown (b 1982)	Danzig
	Pont Audemer (USA) (b 1992)		Six Crowns
		Peruvienne (b 1980)	Luthier
			Perlita

The tall, close-coupled Proponent made 51,000 guineas as a foal, and 160,000 guineas as a yearling. Like most of Peintre Celebre's offspring, Proponent will almost certainly be seen to best advantage when tackling a mile and a quarter or more, and a mile and a half should be well within his compass. The seventh foal of the useful French dual listed winner at around a mile and a half Pont Audemer, Proponent is a half-brother to the useful French winner Pont d'Or (by Exit To Nowhere), successful at up to ten and a half furlongs. Pont Audemer is out of a half-sister to the high-class French middle-distance performer Persepolis who was himself one of the favourites for the Derby when fourth in 1982. Proponent made an excellent impression as a two-year-old and remains open to considerable improvement. He looks an attractive ante-post bet for the Derby at his winter odds of 33/1. *R. Charlton*

PROPOSAL 2 b.f. (Mar 30) Tobougg (IRE) 125 – Patiala (IRE) (Nashwan (USA) 135) **52**
[2006 p7g 7.5m⁵ 8.2g Sep 26] sturdy filly: fifth foal: half-sister to unreliable 9f winner Finmar (by Efisio): dam no sign of ability: modest form second start in maidens: likely to stay 1¼m. *C. E. Brittain*

PROPRIOCEPTION (IRE) 4 ch.f. Danehill Dancer (IRE) 117 – Pepper And Salt **62**
(IRE) (Double Schwartz 128) [2006 59: 10.2d⁴ 12.1f p16.5g⁵ p16.5g⁶ Dec 2] leggy filly: modest maiden handicapper: should stay 1½m: acts on good to firm and good to soft ground: winning hurdler. *W. K. Goldsworthy*

PROSPECT COURT 4 ch.g. Pivotal 124 – Scierpan (USA) 86 (Sharpen Up 127) **64**
[2006 66: 5f 7.2g 7.1g³ 6d² 6m⁶ 6m⁵ 6m 7.1m 6s* Sep 4] close-coupled gelding: modest handicapper: won at Newcastle in July (apprentices) and September: best at 6f: acts on soft and good to firm going, probably on polytrack: below form when blinkered. *A. C. Whillans*

PROSPECT PLACE 2 b.c. (Feb 5) Compton Place 125 – Encore My Love 68 (Royal **86**
Applause 124) [2006 5d* 5g 6g⁵ 6d 6s* Sep 7] 26,000Y: small, workmanlike colt: first foal: dam, second at 6f at 2 yrs on only start, half-sister to Racing Post Trophy winner Be My Chief: fairly useful performer: won maiden at Beverley in April and nursery at Haydock in September: effective at 5f/6f: raced on good going or softer. *M. Dods*

PROTECTIVE 5 ch.g. Hector Protector (USA) 124 – You Make Me Real (USA) (Give **–**
Me Strength (USA)) [2006 –: 14g 13d May 7] quite good-topped gelding: fairly useful at 3 yrs, but very lightly raced and no form on Flat since: tried blinkered. *J. G. Given*

PRO TEMPORE 4 b.f. Fraam 114 – Record Time 69 (Clantime 101) [2006 61: p6g **55**
p5.1g 5.1m 5.5d p6g 5f⁴ 6f⁵ 5.1g⁶ 5f⁵ 5.1f 5.1f 5.3m 7.1m f6m Oct 31] sturdy filly: modest performer: probably best at 5f: acts on polytrack and firm going: tried visored. *David Pinder*

PROTOCOL (IRE) 12 b.g. Taufan (USA) 119 – Ukraine's Affair (USA) (The Mins- **–**
trel (CAN) 135) [2006 13.8f⁴ 16.2g⁵ Aug 17] rather leggy gelding: little form in recent years: tried visored/in cheekpieces: usually tongue tied. *Mrs S. Lamyman*

PROUD 2 b.f. (Mar 26) Kyllachy 129 – Precious 65 (Danehill (USA) 126) [2006 5.1g **71**
6.1f³ 6.1m³ 5m⁵ 5g Aug 19] close-coupled filly: second foal: dam, ran twice, out of half-sister to high-class miler Barathea: fair maiden: twice third at Nottingham: better at 6f than 5f: acts on firm going: sold 4,000 gns. *M. L. W. Bell*

PROUD KILLER 3 b.g. Killer Instinct 111 – Thewaari (USA) 68 (Eskimo (USA)) **73**
[2006 60: 6s³ 6.1d* 7m p7g Jul 19] big, rather leggy, useful-looking gelding: fair performer: won maiden at Chepstow in May: should stay 7f: acts on soft going. *J. R. Jenkins*

PROUD RULER (IRE) 6 b.h. Spectrum (IRE) 126 – La Pellegrina (IRE) 73 (Be My **51**
Guest (USA) 126) [2006 p10g⁵ Dec 6] modest maiden: off nearly 3½ years, visored and
tongue tied, best effort when fifth of 12 to Shaheer in banded event at Kempton: stays
1¼m. *Niall Moran, Ireland*

PROUD SCHOLAR (USA) 4 br. or b.f. Royal Academy (USA) 130 – Proud Fact **58**
(USA) 108 (Known Fact (USA) 135) [2006 60?: 9.7f 11.6f p10g⁶ p12.2s Dec 13] leggy
filly: modest maiden nowadays: probably stays 1¼m: tried tongue tied/in cheekpieces.
R. A. Kvisla

PROUD WESTERN (USA) 8 b.g. Gone West (USA) – Proud Lou (USA) (Proud **53**
Clarion) [2006 50: 7.1m⁵ p7g⁴ 8m⁴ 6m⁴ 5f⁶ 7.1f Jun 26] good-topped gelding: modest
performer: effective at 5f to 1m: acts on all-weather and soft going, probably on firm:
tried in blinkers/cheekpieces, usually tongue tied: none too reliable. *B. Ellison*

PROVIDENCE FARM 2 b.c. (Mar 27) Best of The Bests (IRE) 122 – Aneen Alka- **53**
manja (Last Tycoon 131) [2006 5d 5m 6m⁴ 7f³ 7m⁶ 7m⁴ 7g 8m³ Aug 17] lengthy colt:
modest maiden: stayed 7f: acted on firm going: tried blinkered: dead. *M. W. Easterby*

PROVOST 2 ch.c. (Mar 1) Danehill Dancer (IRE) 117 – Dixielake (IRE) 84 (Lake **66 p**
Coniston (IRE) 131) [2006 8g⁵ Sep 27] 72,000Y: third foal: closely related to useful Irish
5f/6f winner Chief Crazy Horse (by Dansili) and half-brother to 6f winner Dixieanna (by
Night Shift): dam 1m winner: evens favourite, 2 lengths fifth to Centenary in maiden at
Newcastle: will do better. *M. Johnston*

PROWESS (IRE) 3 ch.f. Peintre Celebre (USA) 137 – Yawl 112 (Rainbow Quest **103**
(USA) 134) [2006 76: 11.4m³ 12g 12m* 11.9g² 12m 12m 10.5d Nov 6] close-coupled,
attractive filly: useful performer: ninth in Oaks at Epsom prior to winning maiden at York
in June: good ½-length second to Futun in handicap at Haydock next time: below form
afterwards, leaving B. Hills before final start: stays 1½m: unraced on extremes of going:
usually races prominently. *R. Gibson, France*

PSEUDONYM (IRE) 4 ch.g. Daylami (IRE) 138 – Stage Struck (IRE) 83 (Sadler's **76**
Wells (USA) 132) [2006 65, a74: 15m*ᵈⁱˢ Jun 24] lengthy gelding: has reportedly had **a–**
wind operation: fair performer: first past post in handicap at Warwick in June (disqualified after failing dope test): successful twice over hurdles earlier in year: should stay 2m:
acts on polytrack and good to firm going. *M. F. Harris*

PSYCHIATRIST 5 ch.g. Dr Devious (IRE) 127 – Zahwa 72 (Cadeaux Genereux 131) **90**
[2006 96, a101: p8.6g³ p10g p8g p9.5g Dec 31] tall, angular gelding: just fairly useful
performer in 2006: left R. Hannon after reappearance: barely stays 9f: acts on polytrack,
good to firm and good to soft going: blinkered final start: often races prominently. *Miss
J. R. Tooth*

PSYCHIC STAR 3 b.f. Diktat 126 – Southern Psychic (USA) (Alwasmi (USA) 115) **87**
[2006 87: 8m 10f⁵ 9.7g⁴ p11g 11g 11.6s⁶ Oct 2] leggy filly: fairly useful handicapper:
creditable effort in 2006 only when fourth at Folkestone: below form final outing: barely
stays 9.7f: acts on good to firm going: none too resolute: sold 8,000 gns, joined Miss
L. Russell. *W. R. Swinburn*

PSYCHO CAT 3 b.g. Hunting Lion (IRE) 115 – Canadian Capers 70 (Ballacashtal **65 §**
(CAN)) [2006 74, a68: f7g³ f6g³ f7g² 6d² 6g 8.3m⁶ Jul 26] fair performer: effective at 6f
to 8.6f: acts on all-weather, good to firm and good to soft going: in cheekpieces/blinkers
in 2006: quirky, and is a tricky ride: fortunate winner over hurdles in August, then sold
£7,400. *P. A. Blockley*

PTARMIGAN RIDGE 10 b.h. Sea Raven (IRE) 75 – Panayr (Faraway Times (USA) **86 §**
123) [2006 86§: 5f⁵ 5s 5m³ 5m⁴ 5g² 5f 5f 5m³ 5g³ 5s 5d* 5.1f² 6v 5d⁵ Nov 3] quite good-
topped horse: fairly useful handicapper: won at Ayr in September: probably best at 5f:
acts on any going: effective ridden prominently or held up: unreliable. *Miss L. A. Perratt*

PUBLIC FORUM 4 b.c. Rainbow Quest (USA) 134 – Valentine Girl 109 (Alzao **104**
(USA) 117) [2006 101: 8.1m* 10m 10.4f 13.9d 10s⁵ Oct 21] smallish, well-made colt:
useful handicapper, lightly raced: best effort when winning at Sandown in April by neck
from Hail The Chief: effective at 1m, winner at 11f: acts on heavy and good to firm going:
sold 32,000 gns, joined D. Watson in UAE. *Sir Michael Stoute*

PUERTO RICO (IRE) 3 b.c. Sadler's Wells (USA) 132 – Commanche Belle 74 **113**
(Shirley Heights 130) [2006 92p: 12s³ 10v* 12g 12m 12d³ Aug 22] tall, rather leggy,
useful-looking colt: smart performer: won Airlie Stud Gallinule Stakes at the Curragh in
May by 4 lengths from Mon Michel: well held in Irish Derby there and Grand Prix de
Paris at Longchamp next 2 starts: warm beforehand, good 3¼ lengths third to Youmzain

in Great Voltigeur Stakes at York final outing: stays 1½m: acts on heavy going: has worn crossed noseband: sent to Hong Kong. *A. P. O'Brien, Ireland*

PUGGY (IRE) 2 b.f. (Mar 14) Mark of Esteem (IRE) 137 – Jakarta (IRE) 79 (Machia- **95** vellian (USA) 123) [2006 7m⁵ 7d² 7d³ Oct 14] €16,000Y, 75,000 2-y-o: workmanlike filly: first foal: dam, 7f winner, half-sister to 5-y-o Blue Monday: useful form: won maiden at Salisbury in August: much better form when short-head second to Selinka in listed race and 6½ lengths third to Finsceal Beo in Rockfel Stakes, both at Newmarket: will stay 1m: tongue tied. *R. A. Kvisla*

PUGILIST 4 b.g. Fraam 114 – Travel Mystery 99 (Godswalk (USA) 130) [2006 89: **79** 10.4s p9.5m Nov 9] fairly useful in 2005: well held both starts in 2006: usually makes running. *B. J. Meehan*

PUISSANT PRINCESS (IRE) 2 b. or br.f. (May 24) Rock of Gibraltar (IRE) 133 – **52 p** Toroca (USA) 112 (Nureyev (USA) 131) [2006 8.2g Sep 26] €140,000Y: useful-looking filly: second foal: closely related to 3-y-o Lily Elsie: dam Irish 6f (at 2 yrs) and 1m winner: prominent long way when seventh to Shorthand in maiden at Nottingham: sure to improve. *E. J. O'Neill*

PUKKA TIQUE 3 b.g. Groom Dancer (USA) 128 – Surf Bird (Shareef Dancer (USA) **71** 135) [2006 71: 12d⁵ 11.8g⁴ p12.2g⁶ 16.1g 13.9s p12g Oct 17] good-topped gelding: fair maiden handicapper: seems to stay easy 1½m: acts on good to soft going, probably on good to firm: blinkered final outing. *R. Hollinshead*

PUNJABI 3 b.g. Komaite (USA) – Competa (Hernando (FR) 127) [2006 59: 8.2d 8m* **86** 8.2g* p8g⁴ 8g* 8.3m⁶ 8.5m p8.6g p8g³ Oct 11] strong gelding: fairly useful handicapper: improved to win at Newcastle in May, and Nottingham and Ayr in June: unlucky third at Lingfield final outing: stays 9.5f: acts on polytrack and good to firm ground: sold 42,000 gns. *Mrs G. S. Rees*

PUNTA GALERA (IRE) 3 br.g. Zafonic (USA) 130 – Kobalt Sea (FR) (Akarad (FR) **93** 130) [2006 93: 9s⁶ 10.1m p10g³ 10.3m⁴ p11g 10m* 10.3f 10s 10d p12g³ p10g⁶ Nov 25] big, strong, close-coupled gelding: fairly useful handicapper: won at Sandown in September: barely stays 1½m: acts on polytrack, good to firm and good to soft going: tried blinkered (well held): gelded after final outing. *R. Hannon*

PURE FICTION 3 b.f. Zilzal (USA) 137 – Once Upon A Time 77 (Teenoso (USA) **72** 135) [2006 78: 7.1g⁵ p7g May 25] fair performer: should stay at least 1m: acts on good to firm going: raced freely on reappearance: sold 22,000 gns. *R. Hannon*

PURE ILLUSION (IRE) 3 b.f. Danehill (USA) 126 – Saintly Speech (USA) 103 **91** (Southern Halo (USA)) [2006 95: 8.3d* p8g⁶ Oct 26] tall, rather leggy, attractive filly: has scope: fairly useful performer: left J. Gosden and off 13 months, won 3-runner minor event at Leicester in October: creditable sixth to Mayonga in listed race at Lingfield final start: stays 1m: acts on polytrack, good to firm and good to soft going: left Godolphin, and sent to USA. *Saeed bin Suroor*

PURE IMAGINATION (IRE) 5 ch.g. Royal Academy (USA) 130 – Ivory Bride 86 **79** (Domynsky 110) [2006 89: 6g 6g⁶ 7.2g⁶ 6d 7.1m⁵ 7.1m⁴ p8.6g⁵ 7.1f³ 7m 7f³ 7m⁵ 7m⁶ p6g p7.1g⁵ 7g 8.2s* p8.6g⁶ 10d Nov 1] workmanlike gelding: just fair performer in 2006: won apprentice handicap at Nottingham in October: effective at 6f to 8.6f: acts on poly-track, firm and soft going: sometimes blinkered, including on last 4 starts. *J. M. Bradley*

PURE VELVET (IRE) 2 b.f. (Apr 2) Mull of Kintyre (USA) 114 – Velvet Slipper 50 **– p** (Muhtafal (USA)) [2006 7f Sep 15] second foal: dam, maiden who stayed 7f, half-sister to dam of 6-y-o New Seeker out of half-sister to 1000 Guineas winner Fairy Footsteps and St Leger winner Light Cavalry: 66/1, considerably handled in maiden at Lingfield: should progress. *S. Kirk*

PURPLE DANCER (FR) 4 b.g. Daylami (IRE) 138 – Stage Manner 104 (In The **58** Wings 128) [2006 64: 10m 12m⁶ 10m 10g Sep 14] smallish gelding: modest maiden handicapper: left G. A. Swinbank after third outing: should stay 1½m: acts on firm and good to soft going. *J. P. L. Ewart*

PURPLE MOON (IRE) 3 ch.g. Galileo (IRE) 134 – Vanishing Prairie (USA) 93 **103** (Alysheba (USA)) [2006 8m* 10m² 10m 12d 10.3f³ 12s⁴ Oct 7] €550,000Y: good-topped gelding: good walker and a fluent mover: closely related to smart French 1¼m/10.5f winner La Sylphide (by Barathea) and half-brother to several winners, including high-class 1m to 1¼m winner Vespone (by Llandaff): dam, Irish 1¼m and 1½m winner, half-sister to very smart French performers Vetheuil (miler) and Verveine (up to 1½m): useful performer: won maiden at Newbury in April: on edge, good 2½ lengths second to Mula-qat in listed race at Newmarket next time: creditable efforts in frame in handicaps at

Chester and Ascot (3¼ lengths fourth to Peppertree Lane in quite valuable event) last 2 starts: stays 1½m: acts on firm and soft going: sold 440,000 gns (a record for an untried jumping prospect), joined N. Richards, and gelded. *Sir Michael Stoute*

PURPLE SANDS (IRE) 2 b.g. (Apr 27) Desert Prince (IRE) 130 – Violet Spring (IRE) 32 (Exactly Sharp (USA) 121) [2006 p7.1g⁶ 6m 6g p6g 6g Oct 16] modest maiden: raced mainly at 6f. *B. J. Meehan* **55**

PURUS (IRE) 4 b.g. Night Shift (USA) – Pariana (USA) (Bering 136) [2006 p7g p7g 5g⁵ p6g⁵ 7m p7g* 6g⁵ p8g p6g p7g p7g p7g⁴ p7.1g³ Dec 9] close-coupled gelding: fairly useful handicapper: left P. Schiergen in Germany after final 3-y-o outing: won at Kempton in June: stays 1m: acts on polytrack and soft going: tongue tied on reappearance: often races prominently. *P. Mitchell* **90**

PUSEY STREET LADY 2 b.f. (Mar 29) Averti (IRE) 117 – Pusey Street Girl 87 (Gildoran 123) [2006 5f⁵ Jun 19] 1,000Y: fourth foal: half-sister to 3 winners, including useful 5f winner Mornin Reserves (by Atraf) and 4-y-o Quality Street: dam 7f winner: 40/1, fifth in maiden at Warwick, hanging right. *J. Gallagher* **56**

PUSKAS (IRE) 3 b.g. King's Best (USA) 132 – Chiquita Linda (IRE) (Mujadil (USA) 119) [2006 93: 6d³ 6g 6f⁵ 6.1s⁶ 6g May 27] strong gelding: fairly useful performer: best efforts in minor event at Leicester (third to Angus Newz) and handicap at Salisbury (fifth to Bentong): will probably stay 7f: acts on firm and good to soft going: sold 11,000 gns in October. *M. R. Channon* **94**

PUTERI SAS (IRE) 3 b.f. Fasliyev (USA) 120 – Puteri Wentworth 88 (Sadler's Wells (USA) 132) [2006 83: 9.7d 10g 8.2m May 3] tall, lengthy filly: maiden: fairly useful form only 2-y-o outing: well held in 2006. *P. F. I. Cole* **–**

PUT IT ON THE CARD 2 ch.r. (Mar 25) Bertolini (USA) 125 – Madame Jones (IRE) 79 (Lycius (USA) 124) [2006 p5.1g 6m⁵ 6m² 6g p7.1g⁶ p6m² f6g⁵ p6g Dec 11] close-coupled rig: modest maiden: second in sellers: best form at 6f: acts on polytrack and good to firm going: usually in headgear. *P. D. Evans* **59**

PUTRA KUANTAN 6 b.g. Grand Lodge (USA) 125 – Fade (Persepolis (FR) 127) [2006 94: 8m² 10.1g⁶ 8.1f Jun 10] angular, quite attractive gelding: useful handicapper: creditable efforts at Newmarket (beaten head by Fajr) and Epsom (sixth to Chancellor in quite valuable event): possibly amiss final outing: stays 1¼m: best efforts on good ground or firmer (acts on firm): tried in cheekpieces: usually races prominently. *M. A. Jarvis* **99**

PUTRA LAJU (IRE) 2 b.c. (May 6) Trans Island 119 – El Corazon (IRE) (Mujadil (USA) 119) [2006 p6g p7g⁵ p7.1g⁵ p7.1g³ p7.1s* Dec 13] 22,000Y: third foal: dam Scandinavian 5f (at 2 yrs) to 1½m (including Swedish Oaks) winner: fair performer: won maiden at Wolverhampton: will stay 1m: raced only on polytrack. *J. W. Hills* **72**

PUTRA SAS (IRE) 5 b.h. Sri Pekan (USA) 117 – Puteri Wentworth 88 (Sadler's Wells (USA) 132) [2006 99: p8.6g* Jan 6] strong, lengthy horse: useful performer at best, lightly raced: won minor event at Wolverhampton in January by head from Trifti, only outing in 2006: was effective at 8.6f to 1½m: acted on polytrack, firm and good to soft ground: retired. *P. F. I. Cole* **92**

PUTRA SQUARE 2 b.c. (Jan 26) Cadeaux Genereux 131 – Razzle (IRE) 68 (Green Desert (USA) 127) [2006 7m² 7d⁴ 7g³ 8s⁴ Oct 10] 95,000Y: big, good-topped colt: first foal: dam, maiden who stayed 1¼m, sister to very smart 6f/7f performer Desert Style: fairly useful maiden: in frame all starts, including 6 lengths fourth of 7 to Big Timer in Acomb Stakes at York in August: should stay 1m. *P. F. I. Cole* **87**

PUYA 4 b.f. Kris 135 – Pervenche (Latest Model 115) [2006 85: 7d⁵ 7.1d p7g³ p8g 7.1f⁴ 8m² 7d* 7m⁶ Aug 31] tall, rangy filly: fairly useful handicapper: won at Newmarket (by 1¾ lengths from Arm Candy) in August, hanging left: better at 7f than 1m: acts on polytrack, soft and good to firm ground. *H. Candy* **88**

PYRAMID 4 ch.g. Pivotal 124 – Mary Cornwallis 87 (Primo Dominie 121) [2006 52: p7g 5.1m 5g p6g p6g p8.6g 7d p8g p5g Oct 29] modest maiden: left P. Gilligan 2,000 gns after sixth outing: stays 1m: acts on polytrack and good to firm going: tried blinkered/in cheekpieces/tongue tied. *A. J. Lidderdale* **53**

Q

QAASI (USA) 4 ch.g. Rahy (USA) 115 – Recording (USA) (Danzig (USA)) [2006 79: 8.1g 10m 9.8m 8.9m 7.5f 6g p9.5g³ p12.2m* p12.2g p12.2g⁴ p9.5g Dec 29] lengthy **71 a65**

gelding: fair handicapper: left Mrs K. Walton after sixth outing: won at Wolverhampton in November: stays easy 1½m: acts on polytrack and good to firm going: tried blinkered. *M. Brittain*

QADAR (IRE) 4 b.g. Xaar 132 – Iktidar 80 (Green Desert (USA) 127) [2006 96: p10g **109** f6g f6g⁵ p5.1g² p5g* p7.1g⁴ p5g p5g* p6g³ 5.2m 5.1f⁶ 5.4g p6g p5g⁵ p5.1g p6g³ p7g³ p6g³ p6g² Dec 16] strong, good sort: useful performer: won handicaps at Lingfield in February and March, latter by 1¼ lengths from Fromsong: several at least creditable efforts after: effective at 5f to 7f: acts on polytrack (probably on fibresand) and firm going: has been tongue tied: said to have breathing problem twelfth start: held up. *N. P. Littmoden*

QIK DIP (IRE) 3 b.g. Desert Style (IRE) 121 – Noble Clare (IRE) (The Noble Player **62** (USA) 126) [2006 –: 10m⁴ 10.2m p9.5g⁴ p9.5g⁵ p8.6g p11g Dec 22] good-topped gelding: modest maiden: stays 1¼m: acts on polytrack and good to firm ground: once refused to enter stall. *P. D. Evans*

QOBTAAN (USA) 7 b.g. Capote (USA) – Queen's Gallery (USA) 98 (Forty Niner **–** (USA)) [2006 –, a70: f8g p8g p9.5g p7.1g p8.6g p8.6g⁶ p8.6g May 2] big, strong gelding: **a47** only poor performer in 2006: stays 8.6f: acts on all-weather: sometimes wears headgear: tried tongue tied. *M. R. Bosley*

QUADROPHENIA 3 b.f. College Chapel 122 – Truly Madly Deeply (Most Welcome **60** 131) [2006 63: 5.1d⁵ 5m³ 5.9g⁴ 5.9m 6m 5g 5g⁴ 7.2s 6d f5m Oct 31] smallish filly: modest performer: stays 6f: acts on good to firm going. *J. G. Given*

QUADRUPA (GER) 4 ch.f. Big Shuffle (USA) 122 – Queen's Diamond (GER) (Kon-**90** igsstuhl (GER)) [2006 106: p8g 8s 6.8g* 7d⁴ 8.5g* 8g² 8v³ 8d⁴ Oct 29] sparely-made filly: third foal: sister to German 7.5f/8.5f winner Quadrata and half-sister to German 10.5f winner Quirino (by Lagunas): dam German maiden: useful performer at 3 yrs, winning listed race at Dusseldorf and second in Henkel-Rennen on same course: just fairly useful performer in 2006: well beaten in listed race at Kempton (said to have finished lame) on reappearance: won minor events at Saarbrucken in August and Krefeld in September: stays 8.5f: acts on heavy ground. *C. Von Der Recke, Germany*

QUAICH 3 b.f. Danehill (USA) 126 – Quecha (IRE) 45 (Indian Ridge 123) [2006 7m* **79** 9.7g⁵ Aug 18] useful-looking filly: first foal: dam, lightly-raced headstrong maiden, out of smart French sprinter Spain Lane, herself close relation to US Grade 1 9f/1¼m winner Marquetry: fair form: won maiden at Thirsk in August: odds on, only fifth in handicap at Folkestone after: has left Godolphin. *Saeed bin Suroor*

QUAKER BOY 3 b.g. Agnes World (USA) 123 – La Brise (IRE) (Llandaff (USA)) **60** [2006 66: 5.1s 7f 7.1m⁴ 5.9g² 5.9m 7m⁴ Jun 29] good-topped gelding: just modest maiden handicapper in 2006: stays 7f: acts on firm going: tried in cheekpieces. *M. Dods*

QUALIFY 3 b.g. Mark of Esteem (IRE) 137 – Raneen Alwatar 80 (Sadler's Wells **–** (USA) 132) [2006 78: 9.9f⁶ 12v⁶ May 21] strong, close-coupled gelding: fair performer: ran as if amiss final outing: stays 1¼m: acts on soft going, probably on polytrack: sold 16,000 gns, joined Miss S. West. *M. R. Channon*

QUALITAIR WINGS 7 b.g. Colonel Collins (USA) 122 – Semperflorens (Don 128) **74** [2006 71: 9.9d 10m 9.2m⁶ 8d 9.2m² 10.1g⁵ 10m⁴ 10g² 10m³ 10g⁶ 10g⁵ 10g⁵ 9.2d⁵ 12d p12g p8.6g² p9.5g* p9.5g⁵ p9.5g⁴ Dec 9] lengthy, quite good-topped gelding: fair handicapper: won at Wolverhampton in November: stays 1¼m: acts on polytrack, firm and soft going: tried in cheekpieces/blinkers: sometimes starts slowly/wanders: held up. *J. Hetherton*

QUALITY STREET 4 ch.f. Fraam 114 – Pusey Street Girl 87 (Gildoran 123) [2006 **86** 80: 5g⁵ 5.3f² 5f⁵ 5m³ 5f⁶ 5f 6m⁴ 5g 5s p5g³ p5g p6g³ p5g p6g³ Dec 19] lengthy, rather **a77** leggy filly: fairly useful performer on turf, fair on all-weather: will prove best at 5f: acts on polytrack and firm going: in cheekpieces last 5 starts: edgy type, tends to sweat: withdrawn after unruly stall intended second outing: front runner. *P. Butler*

QUANTICA (IRE) 7 b.g. Sri Pekan (USA) 117 – Touche-A-Tout (IRE) (Royal Acad-**54** emy (USA) 130) [2006 62: 6g² 5g 6f 6f 6m 7.2m³ 6d 6m⁵ 7.2s Sep 28] very tall, work-manlike gelding: modest performer: effective at 5f to 7f: acts on fibresand, heavy and good to firm going: tried tongue tied. *N. Tinkler*

QUANTUM (IRE) 3 b.f. Alhaarth (IRE) 126 – Frappe (IRE) 93 (Inchinor 119) [2006 **89** 65: 7m⁴ 9.7f³ 10m⁴ 11m³ 14g² 12d³ Oct 27] useful-looking filly: fairly useful handi-capper: won at Newmarket in July: creditable placed efforts last 3 starts: stays 1¾m: acts on firm and good to soft going: visored/blinkered last 2 outings: not straightforward: sold 140,000 gns. *J. H. M. Gosden*

QUANTUM LEAP 9 b.g. Efisio 120 – Prejudice 83 (Young Generation 129) [2006 82: 79
p7g⁵ p7g³ p8g⁶ p8g p7g* p7g⁴ p7g⁴ p7g* p7g p7g 7g² 8.1m 8.5d p7g p7g⁵ p7g⁶ p7g³
p7g Dec 10] quite good-topped gelding: fair handicapper: won at Lingfield in March and
Kempton in May: probably best at 7f, winner at 1¼m: acts on polytrack, good to firm and
good to soft going: usually visored: waited with. *S. Dow*

QUASIMODO (IRE) 4 b.g. Night Shift (USA) – Daziyra (IRE) (Doyoun 124) [2006 –
73: 8.3g 8.1m May 6] fair handicapper at 3 yrs: well held on Flat in 2006 (won over
hurdles in January): blinkered/visored of late. *A. W. Carroll*

QUEBECOIS 3 b.g. Zaha (CAN) 106 – Fanciful (FR) (Gay Mecene (USA) 128) [2006 –
–: 11.7m Aug 25] no sign of ability. *P. D. Evans*

QUEEN CLEOPATRA (IRE) 3 b.f. Kingmambo (USA) 125 – Sequoyah (IRE) 113 112
(Sadler's Wells (USA) 132) [2006 94: 7s² 8g⁴ 8d* 8v³ 10.5m³ 10g⁵ Jul 1] rangy filly:
smart performer: won Derrinstown Stud 1000 Guineas Trial at Leopardstown in May by
¾ length from Modeeroch: 7½ lengths third to Nightime in Irish 1000 Guineas at the
Curragh before very good 1½ lengths third to Confidential Lady in Prix de Diane at
Chantilly next time: well held in Pretty Polly Stakes at the Curragh final outing: stayed
10.5f: acted on heavy and good to firm going: reportedly visits George Washington.
A. P. O'Brien, Ireland

QUEEN COBRA (IRE) 3 b.f. Indian Rocket 115 – Miss Sabre (Sabrehill (USA) 120) 80
[2006 80: 5d³ 5g³ 5d⁴ 5g² 5d⁶ p6g 5s Oct 6] fairly useful handicapper: below form last 3
starts: speedy, best form at 5f: acts on fibresand and soft ground: tried visored: sometimes
hangs left: sold 8,000 gns. *H. Morrison*

QUEEN ISABELLA 3 gr.f. El Prado (IRE) 119 – Ausherra (USA) 106 (Diesis 133) 68
[2006 10g 10d⁵ 10m Jun 23] 100,000Y: big, strong filly: half-sister to several winners,
including smart 1m (at 2 yrs) to 2¼m winner Yorkshire (by Generous) and 4-y-o Red
Admiral: dam, 6f (at 2 yrs) and 11.5f (Lingfield Oaks Trial) winner, sister to Oaks winner
Ramruma: fair maiden, best effort on second start: signs of waywardness. *J. R. Fanshawe*

QUEEN JEAN 3 ch.f. Pivotal 124 – Composition 82 (Wolfhound (USA) 126) [2006 73
47: 8d* 8.2g 8.3g 8d⁵ 9m Jul 10] leggy filly: fair handicapper: won at Redcar in May:
stays 1m: acts on good to soft going: below form in blinkers/cheekpieces. *J. G. Given*

QUEEN MEABH (IRE) 6 ch.m. Eagle Eyed (USA) 111 – Wide Outside (IRE) 50 –
(Don't Forget Me 127) [2006 f8g Mar 28] no form. *P. J. Rothwell, Ireland*

QUEEN NOVERRE (IRE) 2 b.f. (May 13) Noverre (USA) 125 – Tafrah (IRE) 71 83
(Sadler's Wells (USA) 132) [2006 p6g² 6m³ 7g³ 7d p7g⁶ Oct 11] €41,000F, €40,000Y,
50,000 2-y-o: leggy, quite attractive filly: half-sister to 3 winners, including smart 7f (at
2 yrs) to 1½m winner Falak (by Diesis) and 3-y-o Acheekyone: dam, 1¼m winner, sister
to Prix du Cadran winner Chief Contender: fairly useful maiden: best efforts first 2 starts:
should stay 7f/1m: acts on polytrack and good to firm going. *E. J. O'Neill*

QUEEN OF DIAMONDS (IRE) 3 b.f. Fruits of Love (USA) 127 – Royal Jubilee 53
(IRE) 81 (King's Theatre (IRE) 128) [2006 51: p10g 12.1d 14.1m 16.2m 10d⁴ p12g
f11g³ Nov 2] tall, sturdy filly: modest maiden: stays 1½m: acts on heavy going. *Mrs
P. N. Dutfield*

QUEEN OF FIRE 3 b.f. Dr Fong (USA) 128 – Sonic Sapphire 67 (Royal Academy 82
(USA) 130) [2006 93: 8s³ 10g 7m 8g p10g Nov 9] quite lightly-made filly: fairly useful
performer: in-and-out form in 2006, leaving M. Channon after third outing: probably
stays easy 1¼m: acts on good to firm going: visored/sweated (well below form) third
start: sold 75,000 gns. *D. R. C. Elsworth*

QUEEN OF FOOLS (IRE) 2 b.f. (Mar 26) Xaar 132 – Foolish Fun (Fools Holme –
(USA)) [2006 6m 6g 7d p9.5g Nov 7] €11,000Y, 40,000 2-y-o: rather leggy filly: eighth
foal: half-sister to 3 winners, including useful Irish 1998 2-y-o 6f winner Hunan (by
College Chapel) and Irish 5f/6f winner Vijay (by Eagle Eyed): dam Irish maiden: little
form. *R. Hannon*

QUEEN OF FRANCE (USA) 2 b.f. (Jan 13) Danehill (USA) 126 – Hidden Storm 85 p
(USA) (Storm Cat (USA)) [2006 8d² 7d Oct 14] $1,450,000Y: strong, good-topped filly:
good walker: second foal: half-sister to US 2004 2-y-o 6.5f winner Fusaichi Samurai (by
Fusaichi Pegasus): dam unraced half-sister to US Grade 3 8.5f/9f winner Jazz Club: fairly
useful form: second in maiden at Cork: 16/1, showed inexperience when tenth of 14
behind Finsceal Beo in Rockfel Stakes at Newmarket 2 weeks later: should still do better.
D. Wachman, Ireland

QUEEN OF ICENI 4 b.f. Erhaab (USA) 127 – Princess Genista 108 (Ile de Bourbon **80**
(USA) 133) [2006 81: 16g⁴ 12g³ 13.3m 9.9g⁵ Jun 29] leggy, workmanlike filly: fairly
useful handicapper: likely to prove suited by 2m+: acts on soft going: often visored.
J. L. Dunlop

QUEEN OF NARNIA 2 b.f. (May 11) Hunting Lion (IRE) 115 – Fading (Pharly (FR) **67**
130) [2006 5s³ 5g⁵ 5f⁴ 5f 5f* 6d⁴ 5.5m 5m⁵ 5m⁴ 6f⁵ p5g 5s⁶ 5.2d p5.1g³ p6g p6g⁵ p5.1g⁶
Dec 1] smallish, good-bodied filly: sister to 3-y-o Garlogs and half-sister to 3 winners by
Fraam, including useful 5f (at 2 yrs) to 8.5f winner Dayglow Dancer: dam unraced: fair
performer: won seller at Folkestone in June: placed only once in 11 nurseries: probably
best at 5f: acts on polytrack, firm and soft going. *M. R. Channon*

QUEEN OF NIGHT 6 b.m. Piccolo 121 – Cardinal Press (Sharrood (USA) 124) [2006 **52 §**
64§, a69§: p5.1g 5m 5f Jun 26] tall mare: just modest handicapper in 2006: best at 5f/6f:
acts on all-weather, soft and good to firm going: often starts slowly, and has twice refused
to race: unreliable. *D. W. Chapman*

QUEEN OF SONG 4 b.f. Singspiel (IRE) 133 – Fascination Waltz 83 (Shy Groom **–**
(USA)) [2006 11.9m 11.6f p10g Aug 13] fifth foal: dam 6f winner: no form in maidens.
G. L. Moore

QUEEN'S BEST 3 b.f. King's Best (USA) 132 – Cloud Castle 119 (In The Wings 128) **95**
[2006 94p: 8.3g² 8s* 8s Oct 6] smallish, close-coupled filly: useful performer, lightly
raced: won handicap at Ascot in September by 1¾ lengths from Don Pietro, showing
good turn of foot: gone in coat and edgy when running poorly in similar event at York
final start: should stay 1¼m: raced only on good ground or softer. *Sir Michael Stoute*

QUEENS BOUNTY 3 b.f. Bahamian Bounty 116 – Queen Shirley (IRE) (Fairy King **–**
(USA)) [2006 48: 5m Apr 26] workmanlike filly: poor maiden: best at 5f: acts on good to
firm ground: once withdrawn (upset stall). *B. Ellison*

QUEEN'S COMPOSER (IRE) 3 b.g. Mozart (IRE) 131 – Queen Leonor (IRE) 72 **82**
(Caerleon (USA) 132) [2006 73: p8.6g 8s⁴ 8d 7f* 8.1m³ 7.2m³ 8m Aug 5] rangy gelding:
fairly useful handicapper: won at Redcar in June: effective at 7f/1m: acts on all-weather
and on any turf going: gelded after final start. *B. Smart*

QUEENS DESTINY 3 b.f. First Trump 118 – Eventuality 77 (Petoski 135) [2006 10d **– p**
Oct 9] second foal: dam 6f/7f winner: 100/1, late headway after slow start when eighth of
15 to Nosferatu in maiden at Windsor: should do better. *P. W. Hiatt*

QUEEN'S ECHO 5 b.m. Wizard King 122 – Sunday News'n'echo (USA) 78 (Trem- **62**
polino (USA) 135) [2006 74: 7g 8g⁴ 8d⁵ 8d⁵ p8.6g 8g⁶ 7.2s³ 7.2v⁴ Oct 28] modest
handicapper: stays 1m: acts on heavy going: tried tongue tied: none too reliable. *M. Dods*

QUEEN'S FORTUNE (IRE) 2 b.f. (Apr 10) Iron Mask (USA) 117 – No Shame 56 **–**
(Formidable (USA) 125) [2006 6m Jul 21] 4,000Y: fifth foal: half-sister to 2001 2-y-o 6f
winner Bright Spangle (by General Monash): dam maiden who stayed 7f: last in maiden
at Newbury: dead. *M. R. Channon*

QUEENSGATE 2 b.f. (Apr 29) Compton Place 125 – Ring Queen (USA) (Fairy King **60**
(USA)) [2006 5m 5.7g 5f⁴ 5m 7m 5g⁶ 5.5m 5.1f² 6f² p5g⁴ p6g Nov 1] good-bodied filly:
fourth foal: half-sister to 2004 2-y-o 1m winner Mister Genepi (by Mister Baileys) and
3-y-o Kaluka Kiss: dam unraced close relation to very smart 1m/9f winner in France/
USA Special Ring: modest maiden: twice runner-up in nurseries: effective at 5f/6f: acts
on polytrack and firm going. *M. Blanshard*

QUEEN'S LODGE (IRE) 6 ch.m. Grand Lodge (USA) 125 – Manilia (FR) (Kris **–**
135) [2006 93: 6v May 25] deep-girthed mare: lightly raced: fairly useful performer at 5
yrs: well held sole outing in 2006: tried in cheekpieces. *J. S. Wainwright*

QUEEN'S PUDDING (IRE) 3 b.f. Royal Applause 124 – Gooseberry Pie 63 (Green **74**
Desert (USA) 127) [2006 84P: 7m 7d Aug 18] good-bodied filly: lightly raced: impressive winner of maiden at Nottingham at 2 yrs: disappointing in handicaps both starts in
2006: should stay at least 7f. *J. R. Fanshawe*

QUEENS QUAY 2 b.f. (Feb 1) Grand Lodge (USA) 125 – Nirvana 82 (Marju (IRE) **–**
127) [2006 7g Sep 15] 105,000Y: close-coupled filly: first foal: dam, 11.7f winner, half-
sister to very smart middle-distance performers Kingfisher Mill and Wellbeing: no show
in minor event at Newbury. *R. Hannon*

QUEENS RHAPSODY 6 gr.g. Baryshnikov (AUS) – Digamist Girl (IRE) (Digamist **75 d**
(USA) 110) [2006 83: p7g p7g f6g⁶ p7.1g p7.1g 6g 7.6m Jul 15] tall gelding: handi-

capper: just fair form at best in 2006: stays easy 1m: acts on all-weather and heavy ground: tried visored/in cheekpieces: held up. *A. Bailey*

QUEENSTOWN (IRE) 5 b.g. Desert Style (IRE) 121 – Fanciful (IRE) (Mujtahid (USA) 118) [2006 –, a64: f8g p8g f8g Nov 14] long-backed gelding: modest winner in 2005: well held in 2006: often wears blinkers/cheekpieces. *J. E. Long* —

QUEEN TARA 4 b.f. Kayf Tara 130 – Lucy Tufty 44 (Vin St Benet 109) [2006 –: p8.6g 11.8d 12g p10g May 8] smallish filly: no form. *Mrs C. A. Dunnett* —

QUEL ANGE (FR) 4 b.c. Tel Quel 125 – Corrossol (FR) (Kaldounevees (FR) 118) [2006 8.1s⁵ 10.2m⁵ 8.2m 10.2d² 8.1f 11.5m Aug 11] ran 3 times in France at 2/3 yrs (for E. Libaud): fair maiden in Britain in 2006: stays 1¼m: acts on good to soft going. *R. J. Hodges* — 78

QUENCHED 3 br.f. Dansili 127 – Love The Rain (Rainbow Quest (USA) 134) [2006 9s² 10m* 12m⁶ 12m* 12.5g⁶ 13.9d⁵ 12s Sep 22] tall, leggy, useful-looking filly: third foal: dam, French 11f winner, sister to smart performer up to 1½m Bonash (dam of 5-y-o Day Flight) and half-sister to dam of Prix de Diane winner Nebraska Tornado: smart performer: won maiden at Lingfield in June and listed race at Newmarket (hemmed in, picked up well to beat Cresta Gold ½ length) in July: best effort when 2½ lengths fifth to Rising Cross in Park Hill Stakes at York sixth start: stayed 1¾m: acted on good to firm and good to soft going (well held on soft final outing): stud. *J. H. M. Gosden* — 111

QUESTION (USA) 3 ch.f. Coronado's Quest (USA) 130 – Royal Shyness 104 (Royal Academy (USA) 130) [2006 6m⁵ 6m 6m Jul 29] $45,000Y: second foal: half-sister to 4-y-o Shy Glance: dam, 2-y-o 6f winner, later 5.5f/6.5f winner in USA: modest form in maidens only on debut. *J. M. Bradley* — 56

QUESTIVE 3 b.g. Rainbow Quest (USA) 134 – Hawait Al Barr 100 (Green Desert (USA) 127) [2006 58p: p8g⁴ p8g⁵ p10g⁶ p10g⁴ 9.7s* Mar 28] fair performer: improved on turf/handicap debut to win at Folkestone in March by 1¼ lengths from Juniper Girl: will stay 1½m: acts on polytrack and soft going: tongue tied: sold only 6,000 gns in July. *E. A. L. Dunlop* — 79

QUEST ON AIR 7 b.g. Star Quest 79 – Stormy Heights 62 (Golden Heights 82) [2006 50: p13.9g Mar 27] modest performer at best, well held only outing on Flat in 2006: wore cheekpieces/visor last 7 starts. *J. R. Jenkins* —

QUEUE UP 4 b.g. Royal Applause 124 – Faraway Lass 94 (Distant Relative 128) [2006 65, a59: f11g p10g f8g f8g⁶ p9.5g⁴ f8g⁴ p12.2g⁴ p9.5g⁴ 10.2f⁶ 8f Aug 10] lengthy gelding: poor maiden nowadays: seems to stay 1½m: acts on all-weather and good to firm ground: tried in cheekpieces. *A. G. Newcombe* — 38 / a47

QUICKSHARP (IRE) 3 b.rg. Imperial Ballet (IRE) 110 – Jack-N-Jilly (IRE) 43 (Anita's Prince 126) [2006 71: 7d 7d⁴ 7m 10.5f² 10g⁴ 10m 7.5g³ 8g² 8.5g⁵ 7v p10g Oct 11] €7,000Y: fifth foal: half-brother to 2001 2-y-o 5f and 7f winner Strandiam (by Darnay): dam, placed in 5f/6f sellers, ran only at 2 yrs: fair maiden handicapper: best effort at 1m on good going. *D. Loughnane, Ireland* — 78

QUICKS THE WORD 6 b.g. Sri Pekan (USA) 117 – Fast Tempo (IRE) 74 (Statoblest 120) [2006 7g 6m³ 6m⁵ 7m⁵ 7.2m² Jul 24] rather leggy gelding: modest handicapper: effective at 6f to 1m: acts on heavy and good to firm going: sometimes blinkered (not in 2006): inconsistent. *T. A. K. Cuthbert* — 54

QUIDDITY (IRE) 2 ch.f. (Feb 27) Diesis 133 – The Strand (Gone West (USA)) [2006 p6g³ 7m² 8.2m⁵ Sep 15] 35,000Y: good-topped filly: second foal: dam unraced sister to smart US 6f/7f performer Gold Land out of half-sister to very smart miler Soviet Line: fair form in maidens: fifth to Treat at Nottingham: stays 1m: sold 32,000 gns, sent to USA. *E. J. O'Neill* — 73

QUIET READING (USA) 9 b.g. Northern Flagship (USA) 96 – Forlis Key (USA) (Forli (ARG)) [2006 68: f8g² f8g⁶ f8g⁶ f8g⁶ 7g f8g² f8g⁴ f8g f8g⁶ f8g⁶ Dec 28] big, lengthy gelding: modest handicapper: won at Southwell in January: has form at 15f, best at 7f to 8.5f: acts on fibresand and any turf going: wears headgear: held up: often a weak finisher. *M. R. Bosley* — 64

QUIET TIMES (IRE) 7 ch.g. Dolphin Street (FR) 125 – Super Times (Sayf El Arab (USA) 127) [2006 –, a102: f5g p6g f6g p6g p6g² p6s* Dec 15] strong gelding: useful handicapper on all-weather, fair form when last ran on turf in 2004: off over 9 months, back to form in December, winning at Wolverhampton by 2 lengths from Buy On The Red, making all: best at 5f/6f: acts on all-weather, heavy and good to firm going: — / a95 wears headgear: often slowly away, refused to race (for a second time) on reappearance. *K. A. Ryan*

QUINCANNON (USA) 5 b.g. Kayrawan (USA) 91 – Sulalat 82§ (Hamas (IRE) 125§) **45**
[2006 56, a67: p7.1g⁴ f8g Mar 16] lengthy, good-topped gelding: fair on all-weather, modest on turf at best, just poor form in 2006: should stay 1m: acts on all-weather and good to firm going: has been blinkered: sold 3,200 gns, sent to Israel. *W. M. Brisbourne*

QUINCE (IRE) 3 b.g. Fruits of Love (USA) 127 – Where's Charlotte 53 (Sure Blade **92**
(USA) 130) [2006 83: 10g⁶ 10.4d² 10d⁵ 10m² 10.5g⁶ 10d⁶ 10s p12.2g* p12.2s⁴ p12.2g²
Dec 26] strong, close-coupled gelding: fairly useful handicapper: won at Wolverhampton in November: stays easy 1½m: acts on polytrack, good to firm and good to soft going: tried in cheekpieces, usually visored: usually held up: quirky. *J. Pearce*

QUINTIN 3 ch.f. Spinning World (USA) 130 – Quadri (Polish Precedent (USA) 131) **45**
[2006 –: 9v 11.9m 9.9f⁵ 7m 7.1m 7m⁵ f7g Nov 2] leggy filly: poor maiden: stays 7f.
T. D. Easterby

QUINTRELL 3 b.f. Royal Applause 124 – Peryllys 67 (Warning 136) [2006 7m⁴ 7s² **92**
8f² 8m⁵ 7g 7f* 8d³ 7s* Oct 10] rather leggy filly: half-sister to several winners, including useful 6f/7f winner Penelewey (by Groom Dancer) and 5-y-o Fossgate: dam maiden who stayed 1¼m: fairly useful performer: won maiden at Lingfield in September and handicap at Newbury (beat Indian Edge by 5 lengths, despite tending to wander): stays 1m: acts on firm and soft going: reportedly in season fifth start. *H. Candy*

QUITO (IRE) 9 b.r. Machiavellian (USA) 123 – Qirmazi (USA) 113 (Riverman (USA) **121**
131) [2006 119: p6g² 6s² 6g 7g³ 6d² 7.1g* 6m 6m⁶ 7m 7s* 5g 6s² 7.1s* 7g 7d 6g 7d 8d⁶
Oct 28] tall, leggy rig: very smart performer: better than ever in 2006, winning listed races at Haydock (by ½ length from New Seeker) in June, York (by length from Lightning Flash) in August and Haydock (twentieth career victory when beating Mine by a neck, pair clear) in September: several other good efforts, including second in listed race at Redcar (to Les Arcs), Duke of York Stakes at York (beaten ½ length by Steenberg) and Sprint Cup at Haydock (neck behind Reverence, finishing strongly): out of form at back end of season: needs testing conditions at 6f nowadays, and stays 7f: acts on all-weather, soft and good to firm going: best in blinkers: has been bandaged fore joints/worn crossed noseband/been on toes: tried tongue tied earlier in career: sometimes slowly away: held up, and best in well-run race: saddle slipped eleventh start: usually very tough and reliable. *D. W. Chapman*

Cervoglass Fortune Stakes, Haydock—veterans Quito and Mine (far side) fight out the finish

QUIZZENE (USA) 4 gr.g. Cozzene (USA) – Company Binness (USA) (Seattle **93** Dancer (USA) 119) [2006 90: 12g⁵ 12.3d⁶ 14s² 14g 12d 14v² 14g 18d Oct 14] big, good-topped gelding: fairly useful handicapper: best efforts in 2006 when runner-up at Newmarket (beaten length by Finalmente) and Haydock (valuable event, beaten ¾ length by Peppertree Lane): should stay 2m: acts on heavy going: blinkered sixth/seventh starts: temperament under suspicion: has joined A. King. *M. Johnston*

QUIZZICAL QUESTION (IRE) 4 ch.f. Bob Back (USA) 124 – Quality of Life **81** (Auction Ring (USA) 123) [2006 82p: p10g 11.7g⁴ May 2] fairly useful performer, lightly raced: better effort in 2006 when 2 lengths fourth to Desert Island Disc in handicap at Bath, still green and best work late on: will be suited by 1½m+: sold 80,000 gns in November. *L. M. Cumani*

QUOTE UNQUOTE 3 ch.f. Allied Forces (USA) 123 – Quiz Time 90 (Efisio 120) **50** [2006 72, a67: f6g 5f 5f 6d 7f⁵ p6g f6m³ f5g f7g Dec 12] smallish filly: modest maiden: left J. Parkes prior to final outing: stays 6f: acts on all-weather and good to firm going. *M. Brittain*

QUSOOR (IRE) 3 b.f. Fasliyev (USA) 120 – Winsa (USA) 80 (Riverman (USA) 131) **83** [2006 87: 6g 5f 6f⁴ 6m⁶ 6m Aug 19] quite attractive filly: fairly useful performer: raced only at 5f/6f, bred to stay further: acts on firm and good to soft going: covered by Oasis Dream (to Southern Hemisphere time), and sent to South Africa. *J. L. Dunlop*

R

RABATASH (USA) 2 b. or br.c. (Feb 27) Johannesburg (USA) 127 – Attasliyah (IRE) **104** (Marju (IRE) 127) [2006 5f² 5m 5f* 6m⁶ 6m* Aug 27] $280,000F, $385,000Y: good-topped, attractive colt: second foal: half-brother to 4-y-o Patternmaker: dam unraced half-sister to useful performer up to 7f Al Ihsas: useful performer: still green when seventh of 18 to Elhamri in listed Windsor Castle Stakes at Royal Ascot second start: progressed well after, winning maiden at Tipperary in July and Go And Go Round Tower Stakes at the Curragh (beat Chivalrous by 3 lengths) in August: sixth to Holy Roman Emperor in Phoenix Stakes at the Curragh in between: effective at 5f/6f: raced on going firmer than good. *D. Wachman, Ireland*

RABBIT FIGHTER (IRE) 2 ch.c. (Feb 11) Observatory (USA) 131 – Furnish 87 **91** (Green Desert (USA) 127) [2006 7m⁶ 6m² 7.1g⁵ 7m³ Sep 6] €11,000F, 39,000 2-y-o: close-coupled, workmanlike colt: fourth foal: dam, 5f winner who stayed 7f, out of half-sister to Derby winner Quest For Fame: fairly useful maiden: clearly best effort when 3¼ lengths fifth of 8 to Drumfire in Solario Stakes at Sandown: free-going sort, not sure to stay much beyond 7f: raced on good/good to firm going. *P. A. Blockley*

RABSHIH (IRE) 2 b.f. (Feb 6) Green Desert (USA) 127 – Kylemore (IRE) (Sadler's **62** Wells (USA) 132) [2006 6m⁴ 6.1m Sep 15] 200,000Y: compact filly: third foal: dam, ran twice in Ireland, sister to Racing Post Trophy winner Aristotle and Canadian International winner Ballingarry and half-sister to high-class 1m/9f performer Starborough: mid-field in maidens at Yarmouth (fourth to Winged Flight) and Nottingham (carried head high). *Sir Michael Stoute*

RACCOON (IRE) 6 b.g. Raphane (USA) 102 – Kunucu (IRE) 94 (Bluebird (USA) **76 §** 125) [2006 76: 5f³ 5g⁴ 5m 6f³ 5m⁵ 5g⁶ 5m³ 6f³ 5f 5m 5g 5s⁶ Sep 14] strong, good-quartered gelding: just fair handicapper nowadays: left T. D. Barron after sixth start in 2006: effective at 5f/6f: acts on firm going: sometimes visored: tried tongue tied: tends to edge right: races up with pace: ungenuine. *D. W. Chapman*

RACE FOR THE STARS (USA) 3 b.f. Fusaichi Pegasus (USA) 130 – La Lorgnette **113** (CAN) (Val de L'Orne (FR) 133) [2006 108p: 8s 8v⁴ 8m⁴ 9.9m⁶ 9.5d* 8m⁵ 10d Sep 19] tall, close-coupled filly: smart performer: didn't have to be at best to win Denny Cordell EBF Fillies Stakes at Gowran in August by ½ length from Blessyourpinksox: best efforts when 2¾ lengths fourth to Nannina in Coronation Stakes at Royal Ascot and 1½ lengths fifth to Red Evie in Matron Stakes at Leopardstown third/sixth starts: has won at 9.5f, best form at 1m: acts on good to firm and good to soft going: has worn crossed noseband: sent to USA. *A. P. O'Brien, Ireland*

RACER FOREVER (USA) 3 b.g. Rahy (USA) 115 – Ras Shaikh (USA) 105 (Sheikh **106** Albadou 128) [2006 99: 6d⁶ 7g* 7m 6.1m⁶ Aug 6] attractive, well-made gelding: useful performer: improved effort when winning listed race at Epsom in June by 3 lengths from Bouboulina: easily better effort after when creditable sixth to The Kiddykid in similar event at Chester final start (gelded after): stays 7f: yet to race on extremes of going. *J. H. M. Gosden*

RACING STRIPES (IRE) 2 ch.g. (Apr 21) Night Shift (USA) – Swan Lake (IRE) 65 **75** (Waajib 121) [2006 5s² 5f³ 5f* 5.1f³ 5m p6g 6d Nov 4] 5,700F, 5,500Y, resold 6,500Y: big, lengthy gelding, unfurnished at 2 yrs: fourth foal: dam sprint maiden: fair performer: won maiden at Windsor in June: stiff task in Molecomb Stakes at Goodwood fifth start, well held in nurseries last 2 (left A. Haynes in between): best at 5f: acts on firm going: has twice hung badly right. *Miss E. C. Lavelle*

RACING TIMES 2 b.g. (May 6) Danetime (IRE) 121 – Cartesian 78 (Shirley Heights **78** 130) [2006 6m⁵ 7g⁴ p8g⁴ p7.1g⁵ p7g³ Dec 19] 27,000Y: rangy gelding: fourth foal: half-brother to 3 winners, including 3-y-o Il Castagno: dam, maiden who stayed 1½m, half-sister to very smart 6f/7f performer Danger Over: fair maiden: creditable effort in nursery final start: may prove best up to 7f: acts on polytrack and good to firm going: edgy sort. *B. J. Meehan*

RADA (IRE) 3 b.f. Danehill (USA) 126 – Old Domesday Book 93 (High Top 131) **52** [2006 7m 8.2m 10g 11.5m Jun 15] 65,000F, €480,000Y: small, heavy-topped filly: sister to 5.5f to 1m winner in Sweden, closely related to 2 winners by Green Desert, including very smart Owington, and half-sister to several winners, including 5-y-o Fiddlers Ford: dam 10.4f winner: modest form at best in maidens/handicap. *R. Hannon*

RADIANT BRIDE 6 ch.m. Groom Dancer (USA) 128 – Radiancy (IRE) 77 (Mujtahid – **§** (USA) 118) [2006 –§: p16.5g f14g f14g Jan 31] lightly raced and no form since 2004: sometimes wears cheekpieces/blinkers: ungenuine. *P. A. Blockley*

RADIATOR ROONEY (IRE) 3 br.g. Elnadim (USA) 128 – Queen of The May **73** (IRE) 80 (Nicolotte 118) [2006 72: f6g² p6g² f6g p5g* p5g⁶ p6g² 5v 5.8m³ 5s 6m⁶ 6f⁶ 5f 6f⁴ 5f 5m Aug 6] fair gelding: won maiden at Lingfield in February: effective at 5f/6f: acts on all-weather and firm ground: usually blinkered (has run well without), below form both starts in cheekpieces. *Patrick Morris, Ireland*

RADICAL ATTRACTION (USA) 3 b. or br.f. Silver Hawk (USA) 123 – Running **44** Flame (IND) (Steinbeck (USA) 119) [2006 –: p8g p10g Mar 18] poor form in maidens at Lingfield: covered by Desert Style, sold €17,000 in November. *R. Hannon*

RADICAL VIEWS 2 ch.c. (Jan 22) Machiavellian (USA) 123 – Nawaiet (USA) (Zil- **72** zal (USA) 137) [2006 6g 7.1m⁶ 7.1d² Sep 16] strong, compact colt: seventh foal: brother to 3 winners, including very smart 7f (at 2 yrs)/1m winner No Excuse Needed and useful 2004 2-y-o 5f winner Skywards: dam, French 6f winner, half-sister to high-class French middle-distance filly Fitnah out of very smart sprinter Greenland Park: progressive form in maidens, 5 lengths second to Don't Panic at Warwick: will probably stay 1m. *B. W. Hills*

RADIUS 3 b.g. Lujain (USA) 119 – Georgianna (IRE) (Petardia 113) [2006 78: p6g p6g **57** 5.7d 7g³ 7g⁶ Jun 13] maiden: fairly useful at 2 yrs: just modest form in 2006: stays 7f: tried visored, tongue tied last 3 starts: sold 8,500 gns. *H. Morrison*

RADLETT LADY 5 ch.m. Wolfhound (USA) 126 – Royal Dream 81 (Ardkinglass **49** 114) [2006 53: f6g p6g f6g³ f6g Feb 26] leggy mare: poor performer: stays 6f: acts on all-weather and good to soft ground: in cheekpieces final 2 starts. *D. K. Ivory*

RAETIHI 5 b.m. Wizard King 122 – Foreno (Formidable (USA) 125) [2006 32: p5.1g – Jan 5] poor maiden. *P. S. Felgate*

RAFELITE 4 b.f. Fraam 114 – Megan's Flight 74 (Welsh Pageant 132) [2006 65: p12g **67** 13.1s² 13d 12.6g Jul 7] quite good-topped filly: fair maiden: will stay 1¾m: acts on soft going: sold 6,000 gns in November. *Lady Herries*

RAFFAAS 2 b.g. (Apr 21) Green Desert (USA) 127 – Felawnah (USA) 111 (Mr Pros- **71** pector (USA)) [2006 7g³ 7m⁶ 7m 7d Sep 29] tall, good-topped gelding: brother to 3-y-o Shelhom, closely related to smart but untrustworthy 7f/1m winner Aramram (by Danzig), and half-brother to 3 winners, including 9f/1¼m winner Felona (by Caerleon): dam 1¼m winner and fourth in 1000 Guineas: third in maiden at Salisbury on debut, but disappointing after (blinkered final start, then gelded): should stay 1m. *M. P. Tregoning*

RAFFERTY (IRE) 7 ch.g. Lion Cavern (USA) 117 – Badawi (USA) 103 (Diesis 133) – [2006 83, a97: p7.1g² f6g⁴ f7g⁴ 7v⁵ f7g² Dec 21] angular gelding: fairly useful handi- **a94 d** capper: creditable efforts in 2006 on first/third starts, well below form after: best form up to 8.5f: acts on all-weather, firm and soft going: tried blinkered/visored: has been early to post: usually races prominently. *T. D. Barron*

RAFFIENE (IRE) 3 ch.f. Spectrum (IRE) 126 – Alcove (USA) (Valdez (USA)) [2006 –
p12g⁶ 10m p9.5g Jul 1] half-sister to several winners, including useful French 1½m
winner Wild Arms (by Pistolet Bleu): dam, ran once in France, half-sister to Breeders'
Cup Classic winner Arcangues: little form in maidens. *E. J. O'Neill*

RAFFISH 4 ch.g. Atraf 116 – Valadon 72 (High Line 125) [2006 72: 10g Jun 15] close-
coupled gelding: fair performer at best: well held sole Flat outing in 2006. *M. Scudamore*

RAGAD 3 b.c. Alhaarth (IRE) 126 – Waafiah 57 (Anabaa (USA) 130) [2006 6.1d p6g⁵ **74 +**
p6g² f6g* Dec 27] sturdy colt: first foal: dam, second at 7f on only start, daughter of Prix
Morny winner First Waltz: fair form: improved to win maiden at Southwell (by 5 lengths)
in December: needs to settle to stay 7f: slowly away on debut. *W. Jarvis*

RAGASAH 8 b.m. Glory of Dancer 121 – Slight Risk 72 (Risk Me (FR) 127) [2006 42, –
a54: p7.1g p8g Apr 8] sparely-made mare: no form in 2006, pulled up (reportedly lame)
final outing: usually wears cheekpieces. *E. R. Oertel*

RAGLAN COPENHAGEN 2 b.g. (Feb 12) Lahib (USA) 129 – Peperonata (IRE) 91 –
(Cyrano de Bergerac 120) [2006 7.1g Aug 25] strong, deep-girthed gelding: backward,
last in maiden at Sandown: gelded after. *B. R. Millman*

RAG TAG (IRE) 3 b.g. Tagula (IRE) 116 – Lovat Spring (USA) (Storm Bird (CAN) **82**
134) [2006 85: 5g 5g 5f³ 5.2f 5.7f Aug 8] strong gelding: fairly useful performer: creditable effort in 2006 only when third in handicap at Haydock: raced mainly at 5f: acts on
firm going: tongue tied. *A. M. Balding*

RAHIYAH (USA) 2 ch.f. (Jan 21) Rahy (USA) 115 – Meiosis (USA) 98 (Danzig **105 p**
(USA)) [2006 6m² 6m* 7d² Oct 14] strong, lengthy, attractive filly: has scope: second
foal: sister to useful 2005 2-y-o 5f/6f winner League Champion: dam, 7f winner, out of
high-class sprinter/miler Golden Opinion: unlucky second on debut, then easily won
maiden back at Goodwood later in August: useful form when 3 lengths second of 14 to
Finsceal Beo in Rockfel Stakes at Newmarket, clear of rest: will stay 1m: sure to go on
and win good races in 2007. *J. Noseda*

RAHY'S CROWN (USA) 3 b.c. Rahy (USA) 115 – Inca Princess (USA) (Big Spruce **75**
(USA)) [2006 62: p10g⁴ 10.9g* 11.6g⁶ 14.1m⁴ p12g* 11.7f² 11.9f Aug 15] tall colt: has
scope: fair handicapper: won at Warwick in April and Lingfield in June: left R. Hannon
25,000 gns after: stays 1½m: acts on polytrack and firm going. *G. L. Moore*

RAIL LINK 3 b.c. Dansili 127 – Docklands (USA) (Theatrical 128) [2006 10.5d **132**
10.5s² 10.5d* 12g* 12m* 12m* 12m* Oct 1]

Europe's richest race, the Prix de l'Arc de Triomphe Lucien Barriere,
attracted the three horses almost universally acknowledged at the time as the best
on turf in the northern hemisphere. The star Japanese four-year-old Deep Impact,
the Arc and King George winner Hurricane Run and the Breeders' Cup Turf and
Coronation Cup winner Shirocco topped both the Timeform ratings and the most
recently-published list of the world's top performers from the International Federation of Horseracing Authorities. Here were all the ingredients—or so it seemed
reading the media build-up—for a magical event that was set to reveal a true
champion and be the defining race of the season. Andre Fabre, trainer of both
Hurricane Run and Shirocco, offered a more down-to-earth assessment beforehand.
Fabre has now been champion trainer in France for twenty seasons in a row but he
rarely communicates with the French racing public through the French media, once
memorably saying: 'When I go racing, it is to work. I don't have the time to say
hello, I let my horses do the talking.' Fabre did give an interview on Arc day to
BBC television which was covering the event for British viewers. 'Is this one of the
best Arcs you have seen?' Fabre's answer wasn't the one that most viewers, or the
interviewer come to that, were probably expecting. 'Obviously not,' he began. 'We
are missing all the good three-year-olds, missing the Derby winner, the French
Derby winner and missing all the top classic fillies among the three-year-olds. It is
very interesting because of the presence of Deep Impact, but I am sorry to say it is
not the best Arc we have ever seen. Obviously not.'

Fabre has a string of around two hundred and trains for an elite group of
owners, including Sheikh Mohammed, Khalid Abdulla, the Wertheimer brothers,
Edouard de Rothschild, Coolmore and German banker Baron Georg Von Ullman,
the last two-named represented by four-year-old Hurricane Run and five-year-
old Shirocco respectively. Although circumspect about his Arc runners in public,

Fabre reportedly privately predicted before the 'day of Arc trials' at Longchamp in September that he would saddle the first three home in the latest edition, in which his third runner was the three-year-old Rail Link, carrying the colours of Khalid Abdulla. Fabre was seeking his seventh victory in the Arc, five of his six previous successes having come with three-year-olds. The Arc and Europe's other great test of the top middle-distance horses, the King George VI and Queen Elizabeth Stakes, are designed to bring together the best from different generations and different countries. When Fabre won the 1992 Arc—a race not shown live in Britain, incidentally—with the four-year-old Subotica, the nine three-year-olds in the eighteen-runner line-up had won between them the Derby, Irish Derby, Prix du Jockey Club, King George VI and Queen Elizabeth Stakes, Oaks, Irish Oaks, Yorkshire Oaks, St Leger, Prix de Diane and Prix Vermeille. It could not be said of the latest Arc, for example, that it attracted a field with anything like the strength in depth of a typical renewal. There were too many good horses missing, as Fabre said, among them Sir Percy, Dylan Thomas, Youmzain, Alexandrova and Mandesha, all prominent members of the current classic crop whose presence would have added significantly to the occasion.

Derby winner Sir Percy missed the Arc through injury, while Irish Derby winner Dylan Thomas (in similar ownership to Hurricane Run) was not among the final declarations and the fillies Alexandrova (Oaks, Irish Oaks and Yorkshire Oaks) and Mandesha (Prix Vermeille) ran instead in the Prix de l'Opera on the same day, the last three all among the twelve left in the Arc earlier in the week. Eight went to post on the day, two fewer than in Sinndar's year and the smallest field since 1941, eight years before the Arc was elevated to worldwide prominence by a sharp rise in value. The six-year-old mare Pride, conqueror of Hurricane Run in the Grand Prix de Saint-Cloud, joined 'the big three' to complete a very strong quartet of older horses. The representatives of the classic generation were Rail Link, the supplemented St Leger winner Sixties Icon, who was the only British-trained challenger, and the rank outsiders Best Name and Irish Wells, who had won the Prix du Prince d'Orange and the Grand Prix de Deauville respectively since finishing second and sixth in a blanket finish to a substandard Prix du Jockey Club. In a pari-mutuel market distorted by a massive on-course plunge by the thousands of Japanese visitors, Deep Impact, a sporting icon in his own country, started at 2/1-on for the Arc, with Hurricane Run at 4/1 and Shirocco at 41/10, Sixties Icon at 17/1, Pride at 22/1 and Rail Link at nearly 24/1.

The five previous Fabre-trained Arc winners who had been successful as three-year-olds included three who had contested the Prix du Jockey Club, Peintre Celebre, who won at Chantilly, and Trempolino and Hurricane Run who were narrowly beaten (Hurricane Run went on to win the Irish Derby). Rail Link had more in common with Fabre's other three-year-old Arc winners, the later-develop-

Juddmonte Grand Prix de Paris, Longchamp—
Rail Link provides Khalid Abdulla with a fourth winner on the day;
Red Rocks (rail) is second ahead of Sudan (noseband), Grand Couturier (right) and Art Deco (No.6)

Prix Niel Casino Barriere d'Enghien Les Bains, Longchamp—one of five winners on the day for Christophe Soumillon as Rail Link books his place in the Arc by beating Youmzain (left), who had bypassed the St Leger for this; Sudan (No.4) takes third off Dragon Dancer

ing types Carnegie and Sagamix, neither of whom ran as two-year-olds and neither of whom contested the classics, the progressive Carnegie having his first outing in a Group 1 when winning the Arc, and Sagamix being put away over the summer 'because of his immaturity' after winning two minor events in April. Rail Link had anything but an ideal introduction to racing, reportedly striking into a rival before unseating his rider in a newcomers race won by Sudan at Saint-Cloud in April. He was beaten on his second start at Chantilly by Lauro, who went on to finish seventh in the Deutsches Derby, but was then unbeaten in four more races before the Arc, winning a maiden at Saint-Cloud in May comfortably, the Prix du Lys at Longchamp in June easily from Sudan and then the Grand Prix de Paris, back at Longchamp in July. It was the second running of the Grand Prix de Paris over a mile and a half, but British-trained Art Deco's fourth and Numide's strong-finishing fifth in the Prix du Jockey Club was the best form achieved by any of those who had previously contested a Group 1. In the event, the first four places were filled by runners making their Group 1 debuts, Rail Link showing further improvement, quickening to lead entering the final furlong and winning by two lengths and a head from the King Edward VII Stakes runner-up Red Rocks and Sudan. Rail Link's victory crowned a most successful evening for the sponsors of the Grand Prix de Paris, Juddmonte, Rail Link's owner winning four races on the card.

In common with Andre Fabre's previous three-year-old Arc winners, Rail Link contested the Prix Niel on the 'day of Arc trials'. Trempolino, Carnegie, Sagamix and Hurricane Run were all successful, while Peintre Celebre all but got home, showing tremendous acceleration in a muddling five-runner contest in which his rider found himself boxed in until it was too late. There were no such alarms for Rail Link who started at 2/1-on and booked his place in the Arc line-up with a rather workmanlike half-length victory—staying on as opposed to quickening—over the Great Voltigeur winner Youmzain; Sudan filled third again, two lengths further behind, ahead of Dragon Dancer and Papal Bull. The clash of Rail Link's stablemates in the Prix Foy—Shirocco beating Hurricane Run with Pride a close third —attracted more attention than the Prix Niel on the day, as did Mandesha's winning performance in the Prix Vermeille. All three trial winners were among five on the card ridden by Christophe Soumillon. He would have been retained to ride Mandesha had she been allowed to take her chance in the Arc, and his preference for Shirocco resulted in the mount on Rail Link going to Stephane Pasquier, who had ridden Shirocco when he was fourth in the previous year's Arc. Pasquier was fifth in the French jockeys' table at the time and riding regularly for Fabre who described him as 'a star of the future'. Fabre's summary of Rail Link's prospects, in his BBC interview, was that, of his trio, he was 'the one with the most improvement in him, a very good contender . . . not a spectacular type but he has a very good record.'

Prix de l'Arc de Triomphe Lucien Barriere, Longchamp—a seventh Arc success for Andre Fabre as Rail Link holds off Pride; the Japanese-trained Deep Impact is third past the post, having come in for fanatical support on the pari-mutuel

Fears that the latest Arc might degenerate into a crawl, because of the small field, proved groundless. Irish Wells did the donkey work, cutting out a pace that was respectable and largely even, though a little removed from the tempo at which the Arc is usually run. The riding tactics on Deep Impact, who came from well behind in his races in Japan, were changed in the Arc and he travelled really well in close touch with the leader, looking early in the straight as though he was about to stretch away, but then finding less than expected when asked to quicken. Rail Link took over halfway up the straight and ran on strongly, gamely holding off the strong-finishing Pride by a neck, with Deep Impact (who subsequently failed a dope test and was disqualified) half a length away third. Hurricane Run passed the post fourth, a further two and a half lengths back, never looking like repeating his victory of twelve months previously after being trapped on the rail at a vital stage off the home turn, losing momentum when his rider was forced to switch. Sixties Icon, running a lacklustre race, and Shirocco, folding tamely in the straight, were both disappointing, filling the last two places. The official time announced for the winner, 2m 31.7sec, was considerably at variance with the hand-held time of 2m 26.38sec taken by Timeform's racecourse representative and with those taken from television pictures. Timeform's time for Rail Link was less than two seconds outside Peintre Celebre's record and had been bettered only four times in twenty years (also by Bago, Sinndar and Trempolino, the record holder before Peintre Celebre). The 'official' time for the latest Arc was amended to 2m 26.3sec two days later, the chief executive of France Galop, Louis Romanet, saying that the racecourse was 'not sure what happened . . . maybe it was because we have never had so much radio and video equipment in use for the Arc before, we wonder if it affected the technology.' More likely, however, the timekeeping settings had not been changed after the Prix Jean-Luc Lagardere, the race before the Arc, which finishes at a different winning post. The extra five seconds was commensurate with Rail Link's being timed over just short of half a furlong further than the Arc distance. Rail Link, incidentally, continued the excellent run in the Arc of three-year-old colts, who have won eleven of the last thirteen runnings. Rail Link was also the eighth Prix Niel winner to go on to success in the Arc in the same period, while two Niel runners-up Peintre Celebre and Bago have also won in that time.

Rail Link's success in the Arc came twenty years after Dancing Brave, the best Arc winner of the modern era, produced an electrifying burst to beat a magnificent field in record time, carrying the same colours, which were also worn by Rainbow Quest who was awarded the 1985 Arc on a disqualification. Both Rainbow Quest and Dancing Brave were purchased for their owner at the American yearling sales, Rainbow Quest for 950,000 dollars, making him the second-highest-priced yearling at that year's Kentucky Summer Sale, and Dancing Brave for 200,000 dollars. Rail Link is entirely home bred, both his sire and dam bred by Juddmonte Farms—the former by the British arm and the latter in Kentucky—and raced in the Abdulla colours. Rail Link's sire, the high-class miler Dansili, who was trained by Fabre, was never successful in a Group 1 race but was certainly good enough to have been so and should have won the Breeders' Cup Mile as a four-year-old, beaten a neck and a nose after encountering all sorts of trouble. Dansili's sire, Danehill (sold for £4m at the end of his racing career), and his dam, Hasili, both raced for Abdulla, Hasili being a descandant of Cheveley Park winner Sookera who was purchased for the Juddmonte studs from Robert Sangster. The reputations of both the Danzig stallion Danehill and Hasili have grown considerably since Dansili was racing and starting out at stud (he stood his first two seasons at £8,000). Danehill's two posthumous sires' championships in Britain and Ireland in 2005 and 2006 have added considerably to interest in his successful sons at stud (Dansili's fee in 2007 is up from £12,500 to £30,000), while Hasili, a useful racemare in the French Provinces, successful at up to eight and a half furlongs at two, is now one of the world's most celebrated broodmares. Dansili was her first foal and her next four have all become Group/Grade 1 winners, namely Dansili's sisters Banks Hill and Intercontinental, his brother Cacique (who joins him at Banstead Manor Stud in 2007) and his three-parts sister Heat Haze (by another Danzig stallion, Green Desert).

Rail Link's dam Docklands didn't appear on a racecourse until she was three but, after being beaten when favourite for a back end maiden at Newcastle on her only start in Britain, she was sent to race in the French Provinces at four, when successful on five of her ten starts, winning at up to a mile and a quarter. Docklands began her career as a broodmare with a visit to Danehill, producing the fairly useful veteran staying handicapper (won at a mile in his younger days) and useful hurdler Silvertown who was still going strongly at the age of eleven in the latest season when he won twice over a mile and three quarters at Musselburgh. Docklands did even better when sent to another sire from the Danzig 'dynasty' Grand Lodge, like Dansili a grandson of Danzig, producing Chelsea Manor, a smart mile and a quarter winner successful in La Coupe de Maisons-Laffitte and third in the Prix Ganay and Prix d'Ispahan. Docklands had two other useful winners in France before Rail Link, the mile- and mile-and-a-quarter winner Minds Locked (by Zamindar), and another by Grand Lodge, Shipping Lane, successful in a minor event at Deauville at a mile and a quarter.

Docklands is a daughter of Dockage, a listed winner in France over nine furlongs who is also the dam of the smart winner at up to nine furlongs, Wharf, who won the July Stakes in the Abdulla colours, and of Colza, dam of Criterium de Saint-Cloud and Lingfield Derby Trial winner Linda's Lad. The family came into the Juddmonte studs when unraced Golden Alibi, who went on to have a chequered career as a broodmare, producing only half a dozen foals, came into Abdulla's possession as a six-year-old. The attraction at the time of Golden Alibi, who had fetched 1.1m dollars as a yearling, was that she was out of Charming Alibi, the dam of Dahlia (Golden Alibi was by the Derby winner Empery, a son of Dahlia's sire Vaguely Noble). Dahlia was one of the best racemares of the post-war era, eleven of her fifteen victories in a long career coming at Group/Grade 1 level, including two in the King George VI and Queen Elizabeth Stakes and four in America, headed by success in the Washington D.C. International. Dahlia also went on to be an outstanding broodmare, producing eight winners from eleven runners, four of the winners at Grade 1 level, Dahar, Rivlia, Delegant and Dahlia's Dreamer, and two at Group/Grade 2, Wajd (dam of St Leger winner Nedawi) and Llandaff. Dahlia's Dreamer was a daughter of Theatrical, the sire of Docklands; Rivlia, who won three Grade 1s and, like Dahar, had only limited success as a stallion in Japan, was by Riverman, sire of Dockage.

Mr K. Abdulla's "Rail Link"

Rail Link (b.c. 2003)	Dansili (b 1996)	Danehill (b 1977)	Danzig
			Razyana
		Hasili (b 1991)	Kahyasi
			Kerali
	Docklands (USA) (b 1989)	Theatrical (b 1982)	Nureyev
			Tree of Knowledge
		Dockage (b 1984)	Riverman
			Golden Alibi

Rail Link was not seen out after winning the Prix de l'Arc de Triomphe, connections announcing immediately afterwards that he was to be campaigned as a four-year-old, though he will first have to recover fully after suffering a bone chip for which he was treated at Newmarket during the winter. The 2005 Arc winner Hurricane Run went on to add the King George VI and Queen Elizabeth Stakes at four but the earlier three-year-old Arc winners trained by Fabre who stayed in training enjoyed mixed fortunes. Peintre Celebre suffered a career-ending injury without reaching the track and Sagamix was seen out only twice at four before being sold to Godolphin, for whom he failed to win in three starts as a five-year-old and was then retired to stud. Carnegie fared better, winning the Grand Prix de Saint-Cloud and coming a good third in the Breeders' Cup Turf, though he ran below form in the King George and the Arc, his main objectives, before being sold to stand in Japan. It will be interesting to see how Rail Link fares. Like Carnegie and Sagamix, he made great strides as a three-year-old after being thought short of the experience and maturity needed to challenge for the Prix du Jockey Club. Rail

Link soon made up for lost time, becoming the only horse to win four pattern races in Europe in the latest season. He improved with every outing and was a better winner of the Arc than either Carnegie or Sagamix. Judged on his Arc form, Rail Link was the best middle-distance three-year-old in Europe in the latest season and he should prove a formidable opponent in the big races for the best of the up-and-coming classic generation. British racegoers have yet to see him and will be hoping he follows in the footsteps of Hurricane Run and puts in an appearance at Ascot in July. A big, strong, angular colt, he stays a mile and a half well and acts on good to firm ground (he won his maiden on good to soft). *A. Fabre, France*

RAIN AND SHADE 2 ch.c. (May 15) Rainbow Quest (USA) 134 – Coretta (IRE) 118 **52** (Caerleon (USA) 132) [2006 p8.6g⁶ Dec 27] fourth foal: brother to 3-y-o Call Me George and half-brother to 2 winners by Seeking The Gold, including useful 1¼m/1½m (including in USA) winner Shared Dreams: dam, 1¼m/1½m winner (including Grade 2 in USA), out of half-sister to high-class miler Barathea: sixth in maiden at Wolverhampton, green and never a threat: will be suited by 1¼m+. *M. Johnston*

RAINBOW BAY 3 b.g. Komaite (USA) – Bollin Victoria 51 (Jalmood (USA) 126) **77** [2006 68: 6g⁴ 5g* 6d⁶ 6m 6g 6m⁴ 6m⁴ 5g 6s⁶ 6g 6s p5.1m Nov 8] smallish, close-coupled gelding: fair handicapper: won at Ayr in May: likely to stay 7f: acts on good to firm going: in headgear last 7 starts. *R. A. Fahey*

RAINBOW FOX 2 b.g. (Mar 5) Foxhound (USA) 103 – Bollin Victoria 51 (Jalmood **79** (USA) 126) [2006 5.1g 5g² 5m* p6g⁴ 6.1m² 6d⁴ 6s³ 6d 7m⁴ Sep 6] smallish, good-topped gelding: half-brother to several winners, including useful 2003 2-y-o 5f winner Axis (by Pivotal) and 3-y-o Rainbow Bay: dam, ran only at 2 yrs, third at 7f: fair performer: won maiden at Musselburgh in July: in frame 4 of 5 starts in nurseries, gelded after final one: stays 7f: acts on polytrack, soft and good to firm going. *R. A. Fahey*

RAINBOW MIRAGE (IRE) 2 b.c. (Mar 31) Spectrum (IRE) 126 – Embers of Fame **98** (IRE) (Sadler's Wells (USA) 132) [2006 6g⁵ 6.1m* 6g* 6s³ 6g² 6s Oct 7] €2,200F: strong colt: third foal: dam, ran twice in Ireland, closely related to smart Irish miler Free To Speak: useful performer: won maiden at Chepstow and minor event at Salisbury in June: kept listed company after, improvement when second of 24 to Danum Dancer in Two-Year-Old Trophy at Redcar: will be suited by 7f/1m: acts on soft and good to firm going. *E. S. McMahon*

RAINBOW PRINCE 3 b.g. Desert Prince (IRE) 130 – Eve 81 (Rainbow Quest (USA) **50** 134) [2006 7v 8d 8.5f 7g 7m 5.9m 5g⁵ 5s⁶ Sep 4] strong, workmanlike gelding: modest maiden: seems to stay 7f: acts on soft and good to firm going. *A. Dickman*

RAINBOW PROMISES (USA) 2 b. or br.f. (Apr 29) Came Home (USA) 122 – **99 P** To Be A Lover (USA) (The Minstrel (CAN) 135) [2006 p6g* Oct 5]

Statistics show Brian Meehan to be one of the more patient trainers with two-year-olds. The two best horses that he has trained showed little at first, David Junior beaten in a maiden at Thirsk and Red Rocks ending his first season without a win from three attempts. Of Meehan's juveniles that ended the latest season with a Timeform rating over 100—Charlie Farnsbarns, Dhanyata, Bicoastal, Jack Junior and Doctor Brown—only the last-named made a successful debut. The readiness of a newcomer is generally reflected in the betting, with increasing accuracy in these days of exchanges, and support for a representative from a traditionally patient yard is all the more significant. Doctor Brown's reputation preceded him and he started 7/4 favourite at Leicester.

Rainbow Promises was odds on for her first race, a twelve-runner maiden for fillies at Lingfield in October. She made a big impression, proving in a different class to her rivals and lowering the juvenile course record. Partnered by Frankie Dettori, the busiest and most successful of a host of riders used by the stable in 2006, Rainbow Promises needed only to be shaken up to sprint away in the straight, winning very easily by five lengths. Runner-up Laura's Best was stepped up to listed company at Newmarket later in October but failed to do herself justice, eased down as if amiss.

Rainbow Promises's pedigree may be unfamiliar to British readers, but her family is full of winners. She is from the first crop of Came Home, a son of Gone West out of Grade 1-placed Nice Assay. Came Home's only defeats in two seasons' racing in America came at the Breeders' Cup (Juvenile and Classic) and in the

Kentucky Derby. Among his nine wins, all on dirt, were three Grade 1 events, including the seven-furlong Hopeful Stakes at Saratoga as a two-year-old and the Pacific Classic at Del Mar over ten furlongs. Pick of his first crop in America is the smart Grade 2 Futurity Stakes runner-up C P West. Rainbow Promises, bought for 95,000 guineas at the Newmarket Breeze Up Sale, after going through unsold at Keeneland as a yearling, is the sixth foal of her dam To Be A Lover, who was successful up to nine furlongs in Italy and a half-sister to useful performers Chadayed and Stoneleigh, the former in Germany at up to eleven furlongs and the latter a Grade 3 winner over an extended mile in the States. Grandam Chaudennay won the Cheshire Oaks and is a half-sister to Derby runner-up Glacial Storm. As well as Rainbow Promises, To Be A Lover has produced two minor winners in America and one in Hong Kong.

	Rainbow Promises (USA) (b. or br.f. Apr 29, 2004)	Came Home (USA) (b or br 1999)	Gone West (b 1984)	Mr Prospector
				Secrettame
			Nice Assay (b or br 1988)	Clever Trick
				In Full View
		To Be A Lover (USA) (b or br 1991)	The Minstrel (ch 1974)	Northern Dancer
				Fleur
			Chaudennay (b or br 1984)	Assert
				Hortensia

Rainbow Promises did not run again after Lingfield, with the Guineas said to be a possibility for her. A classic is a far cry from a polytrack maiden, but there were few more impressive debuts in the whole of 2006, and Rainbow Promises' breeding shows she will be well suited by a mile. Whether or not she gets to Newmarket (she is generally third favourite at 14/1 in most lists for the Guineas), Rainbow Promises looks all set to make a name for herself at three. *B. J. Meehan*

RAINBOW RISING (IRE) 4 b. or br.g. Desert King (IRE) 129 – Fantastic Bid (USA) **93** (Auction Ring (USA) 123) [2006 93: 7g⁵ 6g² 6s 6d 5s² Oct 16] close-coupled, good-topped gelding: fairly useful handicapper: creditable efforts in 2006 when runner-up at Ripon (short head behind Rising Shadow) and Pontefract (beaten length by Kay Two): raced mainly at 5f/6f: acts on soft ground: has been early to post. *J. Howard Johnson*

RAINBOW'S CLASSIC 3 b.g. Muhtarram (USA) 125 – Legend of Aragon 67 (Ara- **70** gon 118) [2006 71: 8d 9v⁴ 8.2m⁵ 8m 8g 9.8s⁵ 8.5m⁵ Sep 19] strong gelding: fair maiden: barely stays testing 9f: acts on any going: tried in blinkers/cheekpieces: sold 5,400 gns. *K. A. Ryan*

RAINBOW'S EDGE 3 b.f. Rainbow Quest (USA) 134 – Film Script 105 (Unfuwain **85** (USA) 131) [2006 11.9g³ 11.9s* 16g³ Sep 26] lengthy filly: second foal: dam 1¼m/1½m winner who stayed 14.6f: fairly useful form: won maiden at Haydock in May by 8 lengths from Minthare: off 4 months, good 1¼ lengths third to Juniper Girl on handicap debut at Nottingham final start, shaping as if possibly in need of run: seems to stay 2m: acts on soft going: lightly raced. *R. Charlton*

RAINBOWS GUEST (IRE) 3 ch.f. Indian Lodge (IRE) 127 – Maura's Guest (IRE) **75** (Be My Guest (USA) 126) [2006 73: p7.1m p8g f8g⁶ Dec 23] strong filly: fair performer: should stay 1m: acts on fibresand: visored last 4 starts. *A. M. Balding*

RAINBOW TREASURE (IRE) 4 ch.f. Rainbow Quest (USA) 134 – Gaily Royal **–** (IRE) (Royal Academy (USA) 130) [2006 –: p9.5g Apr 24] leggy filly: no solid form. *R. M. Beckett*

RAINBOW ZEST 3 b.c. Rainbow Quest (USA) 134 – Original (Caerleon (USA) 132) **79** [2006 11.9m⁶ 10m⁵ 8s³ 8.1s⁵ Sep 7] 25,000Y: good-topped colt: not a good walker: second foal: half-brother to 4-y-o Aunt Julia: dam unraced half-sister to smart 1½m winner Xtra: fair maiden: best effort when third at Newmarket: bred to be suited by further than 1m: acts on soft ground. *P. W. Chapple-Hyam*

RAINCOAT 2 b.c. (Feb 16) Barathea (IRE) 127 – Love The Rain (Rainbow Quest **91 p** (USA) 134) [2006 7.1m* Jun 16] rangy colt: fourth foal: half-brother to 3-y-o Quenched: dam, French 11f winner, sister to smart performer up to 1½m Bonash (dam of 5-y-o Day Flight) and half-sister to dam of Prix de Diane winner Nebraska Tornado: 10/3, won maiden at Sandown in good style by 2½ lengths from Miss Saafend Plaza: missed rest of season due to sickness, but remains useful prospect. *J. H. M. Gosden*

RAIN HOLLY (IRE) 4 b.f. Indian Rocket 115 – Holly Bird (Runnett 125) [2006 57: **–** f8g Jan 3] modest maiden in Ireland at 3 yrs: no show in Britain: stays 7f: acts on good to firm going. *R. A. Harris*

RAIN STOPS PLAY (IRE) 4 b.g. Desert Prince (IRE) 130 – Pinta (IRE) (Ahonoora 122) [2006 84§: 7v 7d 8d 8d* 8.2g* 8.1f 8g 8m 8m 8.5d* 8.3g 8g² 8g* 8d³ f8g Nov 10] **97 §**
leggy, useful-looking gelding: useful handicapper: won at Newmarket in May, Nottingham in June, Epsom in August and Newmarket (best effort, beat Salinja by ¾ length) in October: stays 9f: acts on firm and soft going: visored (below form) ninth start in 2006: front runner: sometimes hangs/carries head awkwardly: unreliable. *M. Quinn*

RAISE THE GOBLET (IRE) 2 b.g. (Apr 16) Almutawakel 126 – Saninka (IRE) 82 (Doyoun 124) [2006 7g 6d p6g⁵ Nov 25] workmanlike gelding: modest form on first of 3 **60**
starts in maidens: will stay at least 1m. *W. J. Haggas*

RAISE THE HEIGHTS (IRE) 3 b.g. Orpen (USA) 116 – Blue Heights (IRE) (Persian Heights 129) [2006 60: p8g p10g⁶ 10d¹* 11.6g 11.8d p10g⁵ p12g p12g Nov 11] **67**
fair handicapper: won at Nottingham in April: stays 1¼m: raced only on polytrack and good/good to soft ground. *C. Tinkler*

RAJAALL 3 b.c. Royal Applause 124 – Gorgeous Dancer (IRE) (Nordico (USA)) [2006 76: 11.6g³ 11.6g⁵ 14m⁶ p12.2g² 11m⁶ 11.7f⁶ a6f Dec 22] neat colt: fairly useful **82**
maiden: left M. Channon before final outing: stays 1½m: acts on polytrack and good to firm going: visored (folded tamely) penultimate start: has raced freely. *D. J. Selvaratnam, UAE*

RAJAM 8 b.g. Sadler's Wells (USA) 132 – Rafif (USA) 68 (Riverman (USA) 131) [2006 –: 12.4d 12g 12m⁶ 13g 12m 12.1m 14.1m 15.8d⁶ 13.8s⁶ Oct 14] sturdy gelding: **63 d**
modest performer on Flat nowadays (fair hurdler): effective at 1½m/1¾m: acts on firm and soft going: tried tongue tied/in headgear. *G. A. Harker*

RAJAYOGA 5 ch.g. Kris 135 – Optimistic 90 (Reprimand 122) [2006 62: 16f⁵ 16.1m p13.9g⁴ p16g⁶ p16.5g⁴ Dec 29] modest maiden: stays 2m: acts on polytrack, firm and **53**
good to soft going. *M. H. Tompkins*

RAJEEF ASHOG 2 ch.c. (May 27) Dr Fong (USA) 128 – Dakhla Oasis (IRE) 107 (Night Shift (USA)) [2006 6g 7m⁶ 6m⁵ 7d⁶ Oct 19] sturdy colt: second foal: half-brother **67**
to German 1m winner Double Fantasy (by Indian Ridge): dam, German 7.5f (at 2 yrs) to 9f winner, sister to smart French sprinter Dyhim Diamond: fair maiden: never-nearer sixth in nursery at Brighton: will be suited by 1m: sold 31,000 gns, sent to Austria. *L. M. Cumani*

RAJEEM 3 b.f. Diktat 126 – Magic Sister 63 (Cadeaux Genereux 131) [2006 98: **116**
p8g 9g⁵ 8v 8m⁵ 8m* Jul 12]
    Clive Brittain has long enjoyed a reputation for producing shock results in major events, and in the latest season Rajeem provided him with another such long-priced winner, landing the UAE Equestrian And Racing Federation Falmouth Stakes at Newmarket in July at 50/1. It was Brittain's longest-priced winner of a Group 1 event, eclipsing his first classic winner Julio Mariner's 28/1 success in the 1978 St Leger. Brittain caused his biggest upset in all pattern events with the 66/1 victory of Amfortas in the King Edward VII Stakes at Royal Ascot in 1996, the horse having come tenth in a maiden at Newbury on his previous start. Other shocks include Abuzz (40/1, 1987 Hungerford Stakes), Top of The World (33/1, 1991 Henry II Stakes), Cool Jazz (33/1, 1995 Diadem Stakes under American jockey Corey Nakatani), Cloud Castle (33/1, 1998 Nell Gwyn Stakes), Radetzky (25/1, 1978 Queen Anne Stakes) and Mr Martini (25/1, 1995 Diomed Stakes). Surprisingly, considering Brittain's record, his five British classic winners since Julio Mariner have all been at odds of 8/1 or shorter, though Terimon finished second in the Derby in 1989 at 500/1 and Game Plan occupied the same position in the Oaks the following year at 50/1. Crimplene was the longer priced of Brittain's two classic successes in Ireland, starting at 16/1 when winning the One Thousand Guineas there in 2000.
    Brittain was asked after the Falmouth Stakes if he had been worried about tackling Group 1 company with a filly who had finished out of the frame on all four of her starts earlier in the season. 'I've never been frightened of anything in my life,' was his reply, which sums up his approach to the placing of some of his horses. Some of the aforementioned winners probably wouldn't have run had they been with another trainer: easier options would have been sought. Rajeem's previous outing had been in the Coronation Stakes at Royal Ascot, where, starting at 150/1, she had shown improved form in fifth behind Nannina, Flashy Wings and Nasheej. Just under four lengths behind the winner, Rajeem was arguably a little unlucky not

UAE Equestrian And Racing Federation Falmouth Stakes, Newmarket—
Rajeem causes an upset by beating Nannina (right), Musicanna (fourth left) and Peeress (third left)

to have finished closer as she weaved through in the closing stages towards the far rail. Rajeem faced a stiff task in the Falmouth, coming up against Nannina and Nasheej again, as well as two of the best older mares in Soviet Song, winner of the race in the two previous years, and Peeress, successful in the Lockinge Stakes at Newbury on her reappearance before finishing fourth after being hampered in the Queen Anne. The Falmouth was run at a slow pace, which told against Soviet Song and Peeress given the tactics employed on them, though neither seemed at their best on the day anyway. Rajeem was ridden in contrasting style to Royal Ascot, very much having the run of things in front under Kerrin McEvoy, being headed only briefly by Nasheej, who eventually weakened into fifth. Nannina came second, three quarters of a length behind Rajeem, sensibly kept close up to the pace, though still unsuited by the test of speed. Musicanna was third, Peeress fourth and Soviet Song sixth of the seven runners.

Rajeem had shown useful form as a two-year-old, winning the last two of her five races, a maiden at Nottingham and the listed Montrose Fillies' Stakes at Newmarket, the latter at 25/1. Only eighth on her reappearance at Kempton in the Masaka Stakes, run on polytrack for the first time, Rajeem performed with more credit in the Feilden Stakes at Newmarket, beaten under a length when fifth of eight to Atlantic Waves. She was then sent to Dusseldorf for the German version of the One Thousand Guineas, but reportedly lost a lot of weight as a result of a bad journey and was well below her best. Rajeem wasn't seen out again after the Falmouth, a heel infection in her off-fore forcing her out of the Prix d'Astarte at Deauville at the end of July on the eve of the race. Despite being declared in August 'almost certain' to go for the Sun Chariot the following month, she missed that as well. She will not be in training at four, having been retired to the paddocks, her career as a broodmare starting with a visit to Bernardini.

		Warning	Known Fact
	Diktat	(b 1985)	Slightly Dangerous
	(br 1995)	Arvola	Sadler's Wells
Rajeem		(b or br 1990)	Park Appeal
(b.f. 2003)		Cadeaux Genereux	Young Generation
	Magic Sister	(ch 1985)	Smarten Up
	(ch 1997)	Gunner's Belle	Gunner B
		(ch 1980)	Crimson Belle

Rajeem's sire Diktat was a high-class performer, at his peak as a four-year-old when he won the Prix Maurice de Gheest and the Sprint Cup at Haydock. Rajeem is from his second crop, which also contains the Musidora and St Simon Stakes winner Short Skirt, the Cambridgeshire winner Formal Decree, Dixie Belle, 50/1 winner of Newbury's World Trophy, as well as the useful performers Terentia and Yarqus, the last-named a stable-companion of Rajeem. Diktat's two-year-olds were less successful, though they included the promising Short Skirt, a full sister to Short Skirt. Rajeem, a 27,000-guinea yearling, is the second foal out of Magic Sister, who ran six times and came closest to winning when third in a maiden over

Mr Saeed Manana's "Rajeem"

seven furlongs at Thirsk as a three-year-old before reportedly breaking her pelvis. She was sold for 145,000 guineas at the December Sales in the latest season. Her first foal, Sister Golightly (by Mtoto), was in training with John Gosden, but never raced and was sold, covered by Redback, for 50,000 guineas on the same day as her dam. Magic Sister was barren to Mtoto in 2004 and had a filly by Cape Cross in 2005. Her colt foal by Lucky Story in 2006 died, and she was then covered by Kyllachy. Rajeem's grandam, Gunner's Belle, won three times at seven furlongs to a mile and a quarter, and produced the Prix Morny winner Hoh Magic, a full sister to Magic Sister. Gunner's Belle is a half-sister to the very smart, front-running, mile and a quarter performer Crimson Beau, winner of the Prince of Wales's Stakes in 1979. Their dam, Crimson Belle, won three times, all over seven furlongs, and produced seven other winners. Diktat has produced winners over a wide range of distances so far, and Rajeem might well have been worth a try at a mile and a quarter, having already proved herself at nine furlongs in the Feilden, albeit in a race that wasn't truly run. An angular, useful-looking filly, Rajeem acted on soft and good to firm going. *C. E. Brittain*

RAKATA (USA) 4 b.f. Quiet American (USA) – Haleakala (IRE) 99 (Kris 135) [2006 **83** 77: 8m⁶ 7.1g³ 7g⁴ 8.3d⁴ 10m⁵ 8.3m³ p8g 8.1m* 8.3g* 8.3f⁴ p8g* Oct 11] fairly useful handicapper: won at Chepstow and Windsor in August, and Lingfield in October: stays easy 1¼m: acts on polytrack, soft and good to firm going: tried tongue tied: free-going sort. *P. F. I. Cole*

RALLYING CRY (USA) 2 b. or br.c. (Apr 8) War Chant (USA) 126 – Turning Wheel **110** (USA) 108 (Seeking The Gold (USA)) [2006 7f* 7m⁴ p8g* 7d⁶ 8g⁵ Oct 29] $90,000Y: rangy, quite good-topped colt: half-brother to useful 2001 2-y-o 6f winner Carinae (by Nureyev) and fairly useful French 7.5f/1m winner Imago Mundi (by Spinning World): dam, 1¼m/11f winner in Britain/France, closely related to smart miler Ajfan and half-sister to smart performer up to 14.6f Minds Music: smart performer: won maiden at Newmarket in July and minor event at Kempton (beat Monzante by head) in September: ran in pattern races other starts, on last two 4 lengths sixth of 15 to Teofilo in Dewhurst Stakes at Newmarket and 2½ lengths fifth of 10 to Mount Nelson in Criterium International at Saint-Cloud: stays 1m: acts on polytrack, firm and good to soft going: sent to UAE. *J. H. M. Gosden*

RAMBLING LIGHT 2 b.c. (Mar 29) Fantastic Light (USA) 134 – Rambler 74 **69 p** (Selkirk (USA) 129) [2006 8g Oct 13] smallish, well-made, attractive colt: first foal: dam, 7f winner, half-sister to smart performers Cassandra Go (best at 5f) and Verglas (Irish 2000 Guineas runner-up): 100/1 and backward, tenth behind Sam Lord in maiden at Newmarket: will do better for experience. *A. M. Balding*

RAMBLING SOCKS 3 ch.f. Rambling Bear 115 – Cledeschamps 46 (Doc Marten **42** 104) [2006 60: 7d p6g⁴ f8g f5g f6g f5g Dec 28] leggy filly: just poor maiden in 2006: should prove best at 5f/6f: acts on all-weather: blinkered/in cheekpieces nowadays. *S. R. Bowring*

RAMBO BLUE 6 b.g. Elmaamul (USA) 125 – Copper Trader 53 (Faustus (USA) 118) **–** [2006 –: f8g f11g Feb 7] maiden: very lightly raced and no form since 2004. *G. J. Smith*

RAMBO HONOURS (IRE) 2 b.g. Martino Alonso (IRE) 113§ – Rousseline (USA) **67 d** (Silver Hawk (USA) 123) [2006 6m² 7.6f p8.6g⁵ p8g⁵ Dec 2] €12,000Y: first foal: dam unraced half-sister to Derby/Irish Derby runner-up City Honours: maiden: easily best effort when runner-up at Salisbury on debut: left R. Beckett/off 3 months after second start: should stay 1¼m/1½m. *K. A. Ryan*

RAMONTI (FR) 4 b.c. Martino Alonso (IRE) 113§ – Fosca (USA) (El Gran Senor **122** (USA) 136) [2006 112: 8d* 9g² 8m* 8m* 8s 8s² 8g* 8m* 8m³ Dec 10] third foal: half-brother to winners in Italy by Glen Jordan and Tibullo: dam ran twice in Italy: very smart performer: won 3 races at 3 yrs, notably Premio Parioli at Rome: off over 10 months, in excellent form in 2006, winning minor event in April, listed race in April, Premio Emilio Turati (by 2½ lengths from Ryono) in June and Premio Vittorio di Capua (by 2½ lengths from Notability) in October, all at Milan, and Premio Ribot at Rome (beat Mullins Bay in good style by 5 lengths) in November: creditable 1½ lengths third to The Duke in Hong Kong Mile at Sha Tin final start: best at 1m (though beaten only a head in Derby Italiano at 1½m in 2005): acts on good to firm and good to soft ground: has had tongue tied: makes running: consistent (only time out of first 3 when seventh in Prix Jacques le Marois at Deauville fifth start): joined Godolphin. *A. & G. Botti, Italy*

RAMPAGE 5 ch.m. Pivotal 124 – Noor El Houdah (IRE) 61 (Fayruz 116) [2006 88p: **80** f7g Feb 9] fairly useful performer, lightly raced: respectable effort in handicap at Southwell (slowly away) sole outing in 2006: stays 7f: acts on all-weather: sold 27,000 gns in November. *W. J. Haggas*

RAMPALLION 3 b.c. Daylami (IRE) 138 – Minute Waltz (Sadler's Wells (USA) 132) **106 p** [2006 87P: 10d* 10d² Nov 4] big, good-topped colt: useful form: won handicap at Newmarket by neck from Priors Hill on belated reappearance in September: good short-head second to Folio in similar event at Windsor next time: should stay 1½m: raced only on good to soft ground: lightly raced, and should do better again at 4 yrs. *Saeed bin Suroor*

RAMSGILL (USA) 4 b.g. Prized (USA) – Crazee Mental 107 (Magic Ring (IRE) 115) **72** [2006 75: p10g⁴ p10g p12.2g⁵ f12g⁶ p10g³ p10g² p12.2g* 10g³ 12.6m⁴ 10g 12s³ 12.3m* **a79** Aug 25] leggy gelding: fair performer: claimed from N. Littmoden £9,000 sixth start: won amateur handicaps at Wolverhampton (by 5 lengths) in May and Chester in August: stays 1½m: acts on polytrack and firm going (bit below best on soft): tried blinkered: sold 9,000 gns. *J. Pearce*

RANAVALONA 2 br.f. (May 28) Diktat 126 – Syrian Queen 82 (Slip Anchor 136) **54** [2006 5f⁵ 6m 6d⁶ p6s Dec 13] 22,000Y: sixth foal: half-sister to 3 winners, including 9f winner Sham Sharif (by Be My Chief) and French 15f winner Sargon (by Oscar): dam 1½m winner: modest form in maidens second/third starts. *A. M. Balding*

RANCHO CUCAMONGA (IRE) 4 ch.f. Raphane (USA) 102 – Kunucu (IRE) 94 **66** (Bluebird (USA) 125) [2006 83: 5v 5d 6.1m 6g⁶ p7g 6g² 6m⁶ 6m* 6g² 6m⁶ f6g 6m⁵ 6m* 6g³ p6m 6m⁴ 6.1g 6g³ p7.1g³ Dec 28] strong, good-topped filly: fair handicapper: won apprentice events at Hamilton in July and August: best at 6f: acts on all-weather, firm and soft going: visored/blinkered: sometimes slowly away: held up. *T. D. Barron*

RANDALL'S DIANA (IRE) 3 b.f. Monashee Mountain (USA) 115 – Altiyna 109 **63** (Troy 137) [2006 8v 7.5v³ 7.5s⁵ 7v 10m 10m 10s f8g Nov 15] half-sister to 3 winners, including Irish 1½m winner Altishar (by Darshaan): dam, 2-y-o 7f winner and third in

Park Hill Stakes, half-sister to disqualified Oaks winner Aliysa: modest maiden: should stay 1m: acts on heavy ground. *D. Loughnane, Ireland*

RANDOM CALL (USA) 3 b.f. War Chant (USA) 126 – Lignify (ARG) (Confidential Talk (USA)) [2006 74p: 10g Jun 15] big, good-topped filly: fair form: won maiden at Yarmouth only start at 2 yrs: still looked awkward when last of 9 in listed race at Newbury sole outing in 2006: should be suited by 1m+: sold 15,000 gns in November. *Sir Michael Stoute* **79**

RANGALI BELLE 2 b.f. (Feb 6) Diktat 126 – Dalaauna 62 (Cadeaux Genereux 131) [2006 7g⁵ Sep 15] 24,000Y: workmanlike filly: second foal: dam, sprint maiden, sister to Prix Morny winner Hoh Magic and to dam of 3-y-o Rajeem: 25/1 and backward, 6 lengths fifth to Proponent in maiden at Newbury: open to improvement. *C. A. Horgan* **68 p**

RANN NA CILLE (IRE) 2 b.f. (Jan 24) Agnes World (USA) 123 – Omanah (USA) (Kayrawan (USA) 91) [2006 6.5d 8d⁴ 8.5g 7s 6v p8g⁴ f7g⁴ Dec 23] first foal: dam ran twice in USA: maiden: trained by D. O'Sullivan in Ireland first 5 starts: best effort when fourth in maiden at Lingfield next time: stays 1m: acts on polytrack, raced on good going or softer on turf. *K. A. Ryan* **67**

RANSOM CAPTIVE (USA) 2 b.f. (Feb 22) Red Ransom (USA) – Cap Rouge (USA) (Summer Squall (USA)) [2006 7g* 7s⁴ Oct 21] $125,000Y: big, strong, close-coupled filly: fifth foal: half-sister to several winners, including fairly useful UAE 1m winner Dildaar (by Woodman): dam, US maiden, half-sister to US Grade 2 9f winner Islefaxyou: fairly useful form: won maiden at Redcar in September: still green when fourth to Party in listed race at Newbury, rallying: will be suited by 1m: sort to do better at 3 yrs. *M. A. Magnusson* **85 p**

RANSOM STRIP (USA) 3 b.g. Red Ransom (USA) – L'Extra Honor (USA) (Hero's Honor (USA)) [2006 p6g⁶ p8.6g* p8.6g 10g³ 10v 10.1m 10.1f³ 10m⁵ 13.9s p12.2g⁶ Oct 29] 15,000Y: brother to winner in USA and half-brother to 3 winners, including useful performer up to 14.6f Hiddnah (by Affirmed), 7f winner at 2 yrs: dam, French 1½m winner (including listed race), half-sister to very smart 1¼m winner Montelimar: fair performer: won maiden at Wolverhampton in February: left M. Johnston after eighth start: should stay 1½m: acts on polytrack and firm ground. *M. Brittain* **71**

RAPID CITY 3 b.g. Dansili 127 – West Dakota (USA) (Gone West (USA)) [2006 6g 8.3g² 7d⁶ p8.6g* p10g* Dec 16] second foal: half-brother to 4-y-o Great Plains: dam French 1m winner: ran 3 times in France: left Mme C. Head-Maarek 17,000 gns, fairly useful form when winning maiden at Wolverhampton and handicap at Lingfield, both in December, beating Happy As Larry by a head in latter, edging left: stays 1¼m: acts on polytrack: capable of better still. *Miss J. Feilden* **87 p**

RAPID FLOW 4 b.g. Fasliyev (USA) 120 – Fleet River (USA) 93 (Riverman (USA) 131) [2006 –: p5.1g p6g⁴ p6g 6m 8.2s⁵ 8m 6m Aug 11] lengthy, workmanlike gelding: has a quick action: poor maiden: left W. M. Brisbourne after reappearance, J. Unett after third outing and P. D. Evans after sixth: should stay 7f. *J. W. Unett* **47**

RAPSCALLION (GER) 7 b.g. Robellino (USA) 127 – Rosy Outlook (USA) 79 (Trempolino (USA) 135) [2006 p9.5g³ p10g 12g Aug 19] leggy gelding: useful performer at best: has run only 3 times on Flat since 2003, best effort when third in claimer at Wolverhampton: seems to stay 1¼m: acts on polytrack, best turf form on good or softer going: tried in blinkers. *Mrs H. Dalton* **82**

RAPSGATE (IRE) 3 b.f. Mozart (IRE) 131 – Lady Rushmore (IRE) 75 (Fairy King (USA)) [2006 78, a68: p5g⁶ p6g⁵ p5g³ p5g⁴ 5.1d* 6d 6d⁴ 6g⁶ 6f² p6g Jul 12] tall, good-topped filly: fair handicapper: won at Nottingham in April: stays 6f: acts on polytrack, firm and good to soft going: blinkered after reappearance. *R. Hannon* **74**

RAQUEL WHITE 2 b.f. (May 14) Robellino (USA) 127 – Spinella (Teenoso (USA) 135) [2006 6d⁶ 7.1d⁴ p8.6g⁴ p7.1g⁶ f8g p7.1g³ Dec 22] 2,500Y: workmanlike filly: second foal: half-sister to winner in Greece by Inchinor: dam unraced: modest maiden: claimed from S. Kirk £8,000 second start: little impact in 2 nurseries: stays 8.6f: acts on polytrack. *P. D. Evans* **57**

RARATOMBA 3 b.c. Tomba 119 – Bit On The Side (IRE) 87 (Vision (USA)) [2006 7.1m 12.1m Sep 7] well beaten in maidens. *P. D. Evans* **–**

RARE BREED 3 b.g. Foxhound (USA) 103 – Rare Indigo 80 (Timeless Times (USA) 99) [2006 75: 5g⁵ 5m 5f 5g Aug 14] good-topped gelding: fairly useful performer: reportedly had chip removed from knee after win at 2 yrs (off almost a year): made successful return in handicap at Redcar in May: speedy, raced only at 5f: acts on good to soft going, probably on firm. *Mrs L. Stubbs* **85**

RARE COINCIDENCE 5 ch.g. Atraf 116 – Green Seed (IRE) 78 (Lead On Time **66** (USA) 123) [2006 70: f12g p12.2g³ p16.5g² p12.2g³ 16v⁵ 15.8d³ 12g⁵ 13f⁴ 13d* 12g⁵ p16.5g 14.1g* 15m² 14m⁵ p13.9m 18s 16d Nov 3] quite good-topped gelding: fair handicapper: won apprentice events at Hamilton in June and Carlisle in August: stays 2m: acts on all-weather, firm and soft ground: wears cheekpieces: tongue tied once: front runner: won over hurdles in April and September. *R. F. Fisher*

RARE CROSS (IRE) 4 b.f. Cape Cross (IRE) 129 – Hebrides (Gone West (USA)) **87** [2006 90: 5g⁴ p5g p5g p5g Dec 10] sturdy filly: fairly useful handicapper, lightly raced: ran creditably on reappearance (only start for Miss B. Sanders), below form after: head-strong, best at 5f: acts on heavy going, probably on firm. *P. Mitchell*

RASAMAN (IRE) 2 b.g. (Jan 27) Namid 128 – Rasana 74 (Royal Academy (USA) **73** 130) [2006 6m 6g⁴ Oct 12] 51,000F, 72,000Y: sturdy gelding: first foal: dam, Italian/ Irish maiden, half-sister to top-class 1m/1¼m performer Rakti: fair form in maidens at Newbury and Newmarket (fourth to Truly Royal): gelded after: shapes like a sprinter. *M. A. Jarvis*

RASHIDA 4 b.f. King's Best (USA) 132 – Nimble Lady (AUS) (Fairy King (USA)) **73 d** [2006 73: p12.2g p9.5g 8.1d p8.6m p9.5g⁶ Nov 6] rangy filly: fair handicapper: stays 8.6f: acts on polytrack and good to firm going: tried in cheekpieces/visor/tongue tie. *M. Appleby*

RASID (USA) 8 b.g. Bahri (USA) 125 – Makadir (USA) (Woodman (USA) 126) [2006 **48** 71: p12.2g⁶ p10g p10g p12g⁵ p12g⁶ Mar 22] rangy gelding: poor performer nowadays: stays easy 1½m: acts on polytrack, heavy and good to firm ground: tried visored/blinkered: signs of temperament. *C. A. Dwyer*

RASLAN 3 b.g. Lomitas 129 – Rosia (IRE) (Mr Prospector (USA)) [2006 –: p12g² 10v⁶ **89** p12.2g⁴ p12g⁴ 16.2m⁵ 16.2g* Jul 7] lengthy gelding: has a round action: not best of movers in slower paces: fairly useful performer: trained by Saeed bin Suroor only start at 2 yrs: upped in trip, further improvement when winning 2 handicaps at Warwick within 6 days in July, beating Trials 'n Tribs by 2½ lengths on second occasion: stays 2m: acts on polytrack and good to firm ground: sold 45,000 gns, gelded and joined D. Pipe: won over hurdles in December. *M. Johnston*

RATHNAIT 2 b.f. (Mar 27) Weet-A-Minute (IRE) 106 – Dahlidya 74 (Midyan (USA) **–** 124) [2006 p7.1g Jul 28] first foal: dam 5f/6f winner: last in seller. *M. J. Attwater*

RATIO 8 ch.g. Pivotal 124 – Owdbetts (IRE) 69 (High Estate 127) [2006 114: 5g 5d³ 6s³ **114** 6d⁵ 5.5d⁴ Oct 5] angular, good-topped gelding: carries plenty of condition: smart performer: good efforts in 2006 when third in listed race (beaten ½ length by Biniou) and Prix de Meautry (1¼ lengths behind Indian Maiden), both at Deauville in August: respectable efforts last 2 starts, blinkered when fifth to Red Clubs in Diadem Stakes at Ascot on first occasion: best up to 6.5f: acts on firm and soft going: effective blinkered/ visored or not: has been tongue tied: reportedly had fibrillating heart final 5-y-o start: held up *J. E. Hammond, France*

RATIONALE (IRE) 3 b.g. Singspiel (IRE) 133 – Logic 94 (Slip Anchor 136) [2006 **93** p7g⁵ 7s⁵ 6g⁵ 8.2m³ 8.3m* 10d* 11.7m* 14.1g* 12s Oct 7] 17,000Y: tall, lengthy gelding: fourth living foal: half-brother to 2004 2-y-o 6f winner Ecologically Right (later successful up to 1¼m abroad, by Entrepreneur) and 6-y-o Logsdail: dam, maiden ran only at 2 yrs (bred to stay 1¼m), half-sister to useful 1½m winner Port Helene: fairly useful form: shaped well most starts prior to winning handicaps at Leicester in July and August, Bath later in August and Yarmouth (beat Duty by ½ length) in September: raced wide in similar event at Ascot final start: stays 1¾m: acts on good to firm and good to soft ground. *S. C. Williams*

RATZIA (IRE) 3 b.f. Sinndar (IRE) 134 – Imelda (USA) (Manila (USA)) [2006 8.2v **63** p9.5g⁵ Nov 24] €85,000F, 28,000Y: neat filly: fourth foal: half-sister to 2001 2-y-o 6f winner Rapadash (by Boundary), successful in USA, and 6-y-o Todlea: dam, ran once, half-sister to very smart French miler Shaanxi: much better effort in maidens (modest form) when fifth at Wolverhampton: will stay 1¼m: sold 27,000 gns, joined J. Eustace. *C. E. Brittain*

RAUCOUS (GER) 3 b.g. Zinaad 114 – Roseola (GER) (Acatenango (GER) 127) **89 p** [2006 77p: 10f² 12g* Aug 7] tall, leggy gelding: fairly useful form: still green, improved form when winning maiden at Ripon in August by neck from Behlaya: stays 1½m: lightly raced, and should progress again at 4 yrs. *T. P. Tate*

RAUL SAHARA 4 br.g. Makbul 104 – Sheraton Heights 52 (Deploy 131) [2006 59: **–** p9.5g 11.8f 8.1m p9.5f Aug 14] maiden: no form in 2006 (left P. Blockley after reappearance): stays easy 9.5f: acts on polytrack, good to firm and good to soft ground. *J. W. Unett*

RAVARINO (USA) 2 ch.f. (Mar 16) Unbridled's Song (USA) 125 – Sous Entendu (USA) (Shadeed (USA) 135) [2006 7.1m Sep 4] good-topped filly: half-sister to 3 winners, including smart 7f (at 2 yrs)/1m winner Slip Stream (by Irish River) and useful French 1m to 10.5f winner Banafsajee (by Pleasant Colony): dam, French 8.5f winner, half-sister to dam of high-class 1¼m/1½m performer Storming Home: 13/2, caught eye when seventh to Swift Image in maiden at Warwick, soon lot to do and finishing well, not knocked about: type to improve considerably, and sure to win races. *Sir Michael Stoute* **57 P**

RAVEN (IRE) 4 b.f. Alzao (USA) 117 – Eman's Joy 68 (Lion Cavern (USA) 117) [2006 –: p6g f8g Mar 8] rather leggy filly: no form since 2 yrs. *Mark Campion* **–**

RAVENNA 2 ch.f. (Apr 14) Compton Place 125 – Cultural Role 95 (Night Shift (USA)) [2006 p6g³ Dec 22] 32,000Y: fifth foal: half-sister to several winners, including 3-y-o Mister Benedictine and 5-y-o Dont Call Me Derek: dam Irish 2-y-o 7f winner: 7/2, 2¾ lengths third to Iron Pearl in maiden at Lingfield, slowly away: should do better. *M. P. Tregoning* **50 p**

RAVEN RASCAL 2 b.f. (Apr 23) Zaha (CAN) 106 – Eccentric Dancer 47 (Rambo Dancer (CAN) 107) [2006 6g p6g 5m Jun 21] half-sister to 2 winners, including 8-y-o College Queen: dam maiden who stayed 9.4f: well beaten in maidens. *J. F. Coupland* **–**

RAVINIA (USA) 2 ch.f. (Mar 5) Rahy (USA) 115 – Reverie (USA) (Nijinsky (CAN) 138) [2006 6m p7.1g* Nov 18] strong filly: seventh foal: sister to 2 winners in USA and half-sister to winner there by American Chance: dam ran twice in USA: better for debut, readily won maiden at Wolverhampton 2 months later: sold 50,000 gns later in November: should go on progressing. *B. J. Meehan* **72 p**

RAVI RIVER (IRE) 2 ch.c. (Feb 10) Barathea (IRE) 127 – Echo River (USA) 101 (Irish River (FR) 131) [2006 7g³ 7g* 7m³ Sep 9] strong, good-bodied colt: first foal: dam, 2-y-o 6f/7f winner, out of half-sister to dam of high-class 1¼m/1½m performer Storming Home: fairly useful form: confirmed debut promise when winning maiden at Chester later in August by ½ length from Minos: 11/10, wide throughout when third to Grand Prix in nursery there: will stay 1m. *B. W. Hills* **91 +**

RAVISH 3 b.f. Efisio 120 – Looks Sensational (USA) (Majestic Light (USA)) [2006 58: 8.3d³ 8m 8d 6g p5.1g 5.7m Sep 25] leggy filly: modest maiden: stays 1m: tongue tied in 2006, also blinkered last 3 starts: virtually refused to race final outing, and is one to treat with caution: sold 18,000 gns. *W. J. Haggas* **53 §**

RAWAABET (IRE) 4 b.g. Bahhare (USA) 122 – Haddeyah (USA) 68 (Dayjur (USA) 137) [2006 75: p10g 10.9g p8g f8g 8.3g 8.3f Jun 19] good-topped gelding: fair performer: stays 8.3f: acts on fibresand, good to firm and good to soft going. *P. W. Hiatt* **65**

RAWDON (IRE) 5 b.g. Singspiel (IRE) 133 – Rebecca Sharp 122 (Machiavellian (USA) 123) [2006 98: 12g 10d 10.5g 10g6 10f6 10m³ 10s 10.5s² 10.5g 10d Oct 4] tall, good-topped gelding: just fairly useful handicapper in 2006: should stay 1½m: acts on polytrack, soft and good to firm going, below form on heavy: usually visored. *M. L. W. Bell* **85**

RAYHANI (USA) 3 b.g. Theatrical 128 – Bahr Alsalaam (USA) (Riverman (USA) 131) [2006 86p: 10g p12g² 12m* 13.3g5 14g Aug 31] big, strong, attractive gelding: useful handicapper: best effort when winning at Ascot in July by head from Ollie George: seemed not to stay longer trip after, racing too freely in blinkers on second occasion (gelded after): stays 1½m: acts on good to firm going, well held only start on softer than good. *M. P. Tregoning* **99**

RAYMOND'S PRIDE 6 b.g. Mind Games 121 – Northern Sal 59 (Aragon 118) [2006 92, a73: 6g4 6g 6s² 6v³ 5.1m³ 6m 6d 5s 6v Oct 28] tall gelding: fairly useful handicapper on turf, fair when last ran on all-weather in 2005: effective at 5f to easy 7f: acts on all-weather and heavy going: tried in cheekpieces: blinkered: often races prominently: sometimes finds little. *K. A. Ryan* **87**

RAZA CAB (IRE) 4 b.g. Intikhab (USA) 135 – Laraissa (Machiavellian (USA) 123) [2006 71: p7g* p7.1g² p7.1g p8g* p8g* p7g 8.3f p8g Jun 28] heavy-topped gelding: fairly useful performer: won handicap at Lingfield in January, and claimer there and handicap at Kempton in March: stays 1m: acts on polytrack, good to firm and good to soft going: blinkered once (raced freely) at 3 yrs. *Miss K. M. George* **– a85**

RAZED 3 b.g. King's Best (USA) 132 – Key Academy 103 (Royal Academy (USA) 130) [2006 77: p9.5g 9.8m 10f 12d6 p10g f8g Dec 27] big, leggy gelding: fair winner at 2 yrs: just modest handicapper in 2006, leaving M. Johnston 8,500 gns after fifth start: should stay 1¼m: acts on good to firm going. *P. L. Gilligan* **59**

RAZZANO (IRE) 2 b.f. (Apr 29) Fasliyev (USA) 120 – Shewillifshewants (IRE) **63 ?** (Alzao (USA) 117) [2006 5d⁴ 5m⁶ 7m⁵ 6m⁶ p7.1s⁵ p8.6g⁴ Dec 27] sixth foal: half-sister to 3-y-o Billy Bling and 4-y-o Formidable Will: dam unraced half-sister to Arc fourth Acropolis and smart performers Fairy Queen (stayed 12.5f) and Tashawak (miler): modest maiden: sold from G. Lyons in Ireland €11,500 after fourth start: stays 8.6f. *P. D. Evans*

REACHING OUT (IRE) 4 b.g. Desert Prince (IRE) 130 – Alwiyda (USA) (Trem- **71** polino (USA) 135) [2006 81: 10d⁴ 9.9f 10g p8g 10g 9.3f p8g 8m p10g* p9.5g² Dec 29] smallish, close-coupled gelding: just fair performer in 2006: left N. Henderson after reappearance: won handicap at Lingfield in December: effective at 1m to 11f: acts on polytrack, firm and soft going: blinkered last 3 starts: sometimes slowly away: sometimes races freely. *N. P. Littmoden*

READYFORONE 2 b.g. (Mar 31) Mutamarkiz (IRE) 77 – Blackpool Mamma's 73 **59 d** (Merdon Melody 98) [2006 f5g⁵ 5g⁵ p5.1g 6.1s² 6m 8.3g Oct 16] modest maiden: best effort in seller second outing: blinkered after debut: signs of temperament. *P. D. Evans*

READY FOR SPRING (USA) 2 b.c. (Mar 12) More Than Ready (USA) 120 – **97** Maybe In May (USA) (Miswaki (USA) 124) [2006 6m* 7d³ p6g⁴ 7f* Sep 18] tall, quite attractive colt, unfurnished at 2 yrs: has a quick action: fourth foal: brother to US 8.5f winner Just As Ready and half-brother to winner in USA by Mecke: dam ran twice in USA: useful performer: won maiden at Newmarket in August and minor event at Leic-ester in September: better form in between, 2½ lengths third of 7 to Big Timer in Acomb Stakes at York and 4¼ lengths fourth of 9 to Dhanyata in Sirenia Stakes at Kempton: will stay 1m: acts on polytrack, firm and good to soft going (unraced on softer): sold 230,000 gns, joined D. Hayes in Australia. *J. Noseda*

READY TEDDY GO 4 b.g. Danzig Connection (USA) – Mariette 35 (Blushing Scribe **41** (USA) 107) [2006 46: f8g p10g p13.9g p12.2g⁵ 11.9m p16g May 8] poor maiden: stays 1¼m: acts on polytrack: tried in cheekpieces/visor. *J. Ryan*

REAL CHIEF (IRE) 8 b.g. Caerleon (USA) 132 – Greek Air (IRE) 107 (Ela-Mana- **–** Mou 132) [2006 p12.2g⁶ p12.2g⁴ p12.2g f16g⁶ 14.1m May 3] modest maiden: probably **a59** stays 1½m: blinkered fourth outing. *Miss M. E. Rowland*

REALISM (FR) 6 b.g. Machiavellian (USA) 123 – Kissing Cousin (IRE) 116 (Danehill **104** (USA) 126) [2006 107: 10m 10m 12m⁵ 10d² 8s p10g Apr 15] strong, good-bodied geld-ing: useful handicapper: best effort in 2006 when 1¼ lengths second to Anani at Nad Al Sheba fourth start: stays 10.4f: acts on fibresand, good to firm and good to soft going: has run well when sweating: tongue tied (well held) fifth start. *R. A. Fahey*

REALITY TIME (IRE) 3 b.f. Daggers Drawn (USA) 114 – Vitality 98 (Young Gene- **43** ration 129) [2006 67: p6g p7g⁶ p6g⁶ 6.1f 7.1g⁴ 6f 7m Aug 22] just poor maiden at 3 yrs: left I. Osborne after fourth start: should stay 7f: acts on polytrack and firm ground: tried blinkered. *W. J. Knight*

REALY NAUGHTY (IRE) 2 b.c. (Apr 27) Night Shift (USA) – Naughty Reputation **67 ?** (IRE) 31 (Shalford (IRE) 124§) [2006 p7g⁶ p7.1g⁴ Dec 31] €5,000F: first foal: dam lightly-raced Irish maiden: seemingly fair form but never dangerous in maidens at Lingfield and Wolverhampton. *B. G. Powell*

REBALLO (IRE) 3 b.c. King's Best (USA) 132 – Lyrical Dance (USA) (Lear Fan **69** (USA) 130) [2006 p7g² Apr 23] fifth foal: half-brother to fairly useful Irish 6f winner Lightwood Lady (by Anabaa) and a winner in USA by Diesis: dam, 8.5f winner in USA, half-sister to Pennekamp, Black Minnaloushe and Nasr El Arab: favourite, promising 1½ lengths second to Massaro Pape in maiden at Kempton, very green following slow start, short of room 2f out and not knocked about: not seen out again. *J. R. Fanshawe*

REBEL DUKE (IRE) 2 ch.c. (Apr 21) Namid 128 – Edwina (IRE) 63 (Caerleon **76** (USA) 132) [2006 5f³ 6m⁴ p5.1g* Dec 29] tall colt: closely related to fairly useful 7f/1m winner (including in Ireland) Your The Lady (by Indian Ridge) and half-brother to 3 winners, including smart 7f (at 2 yrs) and 1m (in UAE) winner Seihali (by Alzao): dam maiden (should have stayed beyond 6f): fair form in maidens, winning at Wolverhampton by 4 lengths from Wibbadune, making all: should prove best at 5f/6f. *M. G. Quinlan*

REBELLING (IRE) 3 ch.g. Peintre Celebre (USA) 137 – El Divino (IRE) (Halling **69 §** (USA) 133) [2006 68: 10.9g 12s³ 14.1g 11.7g 17.2m Sep 25] leggy gelding: fair maiden: left F. J. Houghton prior to final outing: stays 1½m: acts on soft ground: tried blinkered: temperamental. *M. F. Harris*

REBELLION 3 b.c. Mozart (IRE) 131 – Last Resort 116 (Lahib (USA) 129) [2006 78: **81** p7g² p7g* p7g* p7g⁵ 7.5f³ 7.5g Dec 30] lengthy colt: fairly useful performer: won maiden in February and handicap in March, both at Lingfield: left M. Johnston 30,000 gns and off course 8 months before final start: stays 1m: acts on polytrack and any turf going: front runner. *H. G. Motion, USA*

REBELLIOUS SPIRIT 3 b.g. Mark of Esteem (IRE) 137 – Robellino Miss (USA) **74** (Robellino (USA) 127) [2006 77: p6g² p6g⁴ f5g⁵ p6g 8.2d² 8.2m³ 9.8g³ 8d⁶ 8.3m f8g³ Dec 23] tall, quite good-topped gelding: fair maiden: claimed from J. Given £3,000 after fourth outing: likely to prove best up to 1m: acts on all-weather, good to firm and good to soft going. *P. W. Hiatt*

REBEL PEARL (IRE) 2 b.f. (Mar 25) Barathea (IRE) 127 – Rebel Clan (IRE) **69 +** (Tagula (IRE) 116) [2006 p9.5m p7.1g⁵ Nov 17] first foal: dam unraced half-sister to smart Irish sprinter Capricciosa: better effort in Wolverhampton maidens when never-nearer fifth to Giant Slalom. *M. G. Quinlan*

RECALCITRANT 3 b.g. Josr Algarhoud (IRE) 118 – Lady Isabell 62 (Rambo Dancer **61** (CAN) 107) [2006 64: 11.6m p12g p12g⁴ p12g⁶ p12g⁶ p12g² Dec 22] modest maiden handicapper: stays easy 1½m: acts on polytrack and good to firm going: once refused to enter stall. *S. Dow*

RECORD BREAKER (IRE) 2 b.c. (Feb 26) In The Wings 128 – Overruled (IRE) 91 **81 p** (Last Tycoon 131) [2006 7g⁴ Jul 28] €83,000F, 110,000 2-y-o: tall colt: has scope: sixth foal: closely related to smart Irish 7f (at 2 yrs) to 1½m (Irish Oaks) winner Vintage Tipple (by Entrepreneur) and half-brother to useful 2000 2-y-o 7f/1m winner Spettro (by Spectrum, later successful up to 1½m in Italy): dam, 1m (at 2 yrs)/1¼m winner who stayed 1¾m, half-sister to smart performer up to 1½m Overbury out of sister to dam of Vintage Crop: 9/4, shaped well when over 2 lengths fourth in maiden at Ascot won by One To Follow (Big Robert second), travelling best long way: useful prospect, likely to win races. *M. Johnston*

RECRUIT 2 b.g. (Mar 8) Mujahid (USA) 125 – Georgianna (IRE) (Petardia 113) [2006 **73** p6g 6m⁶ 7g³ 8g⁴ p8g⁴ p8g Oct 6] 14,500F, 32,000Y: close-coupled, useful-looking gelding: second foal: dam unraced out of half-sister to smart 1¼m performer Elegant Air: fair maiden: in frame 3 times, including behind Sweet Lilly in nursery at Salisbury fourth outing: stays 1m: none too keen in blinkers final start: sold 4,000 gns. *R. Hannon*

RECTANGLE BLUE 4 b.g. Atraf 116 – Golden Decoy 73 (Decoy Boy 129) [2006 –: **–** f7g Feb 7] little sign of ability. *M. D. Hammond*

RECTANGLE (IRE) 6 ch.g. Fayruz 116 – Moona (USA) 73 (Lear Fan (USA) 130) **57 d** [2006 67: 6m 5f 6g 5m 5m 5d Aug 20] strong gelding: on downgrade and just modest form in 2006: stays 6f: acts on good to firm and good to soft going: tried tongue tied. *M. D. Hammond*

RED 2 ch.f. (Mar 6) Fraam 114 – Great Tern 59 (Simply Great (FR) 122) [2006 5.1m 6g **68** 5.1f⁵ 8m² 10g⁶ p9.5g³ Nov 7] leggy filly: fourth foal: dam 1¾m winner: fair maiden: placed 2 of 3 runs in nurseries: will stay 1½m: acts on polytrack and good to firm going. *R. M. Beckett*

RED ADMIRAL (USA) 4 b.g. Red Ransom (USA) – Ausherra (USA) 106 (Diesis **100** 133) [2006 100: 12m³ 13d 10s² 11.6d Nov 4] tall, close-coupled gelding: useful handicapper, lightly raced: creditable efforts in 2006 when placed at Southwell and Newbury, 2 lengths second to Best Prospect in latter: stays 1½m (raced too freely at 1¾m): acts on soft and good to firm going: visored first 3 starts at 3 yrs: often makes running: none too genuine. *Saeed bin Suroor*

RED APACHE (IRE) 4 b.g. Namid 128 – Special Dissident (Dancing Dissident **–** (USA) 119) [2006 –: 5.2g 7g Aug 17] leggy gelding: no form. *H. J. Collingridge*

RED BIRR (IRE) 5 b.g. Bahhare (USA) 122 – Cappella (IRE) 75 (College Chapel 122) **83** [2006 80: p9.5g² p10g² p10g² 10.9g⁶ p10g⁵ p10g² p10g⁴ Nov 28] leggy, quite good-topped gelding: fairly useful handicapper: stays 1¼m: acts on polytrack, good to firm and good to soft going. *P. R. Webber*

RED BLOODED WOMAN (USA) 2 b.f. (Mar 8) Red Ransom (USA) – Maskaya **71 p** (IRE) 92 (Machiavellian (USA) 123) [2006 6m⁵ Sep 13] 270,000Y: smallish, sturdy filly: first foal: dam, Irish 2-y-o 5f winner, half-sister to 3-y-o Modeeroch: 15/2 and burly, 3¼ lengths fifth to Kaseema in maiden at Yarmouth, rallying: should do better. *E. A. L. Dunlop*

Irish National Stud Blandford Stakes, the Curragh—Red Bloom wins for the second successive year, beating Sina Cova and Paris Winds (stars on cap)

RED BLOOM 5 b.m. Selkirk (USA) 129 – Red Camellia 116 (Polar Falcon (USA) 126) **117**
[2006 117: 10.4s⁴ 10g³ 10s³ 10d* 10s⁶ Oct 22] tall, rather leggy mare: had a quick, rather choppy action: smart performer: as good as ever in 2006, third in Pretty Polly Stakes at the Curragh (2¼ lengths behind Alexander Goldrun) and Prix Jean Romanet at Deauville (beaten 2½ lengths by Satwa Queen) before winning Irish National Stud Blandford Stakes at the Curragh in September for second year running, beating Sina Cova by 1¾ lengths: below form in E. P. Taylor Stakes at Woodbine final start: stayed 1¼m: acted on firm going, probably on soft: tended to take strong hold: had carried head awkwardly: visits Sadler's Wells. *Sir Michael Stoute*

RED CAPE (FR) 3 b.g. Cape Cross (IRE) 129 – Muirfield (FR) (Crystal Glitters (USA) **99**
127) [2006 88: 7g 7m* 8g 6m 7d⁵ 8.1g⁵ 7m⁴ p7g p7g⁴ Oct 21] big, rangy colt: useful performer: won handicap at Newmarket in June, well ridden in tactical affair: left N. Callaghan after fourth start: good 2¾ lengths fourth to Mostashaar in minor event at Lingfield final outing: stays 1m: acts on polytrack and good to firm going: upset in stall on reappearance: sometimes edges left. *Jane Chapple-Hyam*

RED CHAIRMAN 4 b. or br.g. Red Ransom (USA) – Chine 100 (Inchinor 119) [2006 **66 d**
80d: 12g 8.3m 10.1m⁵ 10.1m⁶ 7m 6d⁵ 7d⁶ 11.1g⁴ 5s⁴ 10m 8f⁵ Sep 20] good-topped, close-coupled gelding: fair maiden: regressive form in 2006: effective at 6f to 1¼m: acts on polytrack, good to firm and good to soft going: tried in headgear/tongue tied: slowly away fifth outing: pulled hard first/third starts: unreliable. *R. Johnson*

REDCLIFF (GER) 2 ch.g. (Mar 7) Lomitas 129 – Rhode Island (GER) (Waajib 121) **75**
[2006 7.6f 7f* 7m⁶ 6v 6d Nov 4] €35,000Y: workmanlike gelding: has been fired: brother to German 7f (at 2 yrs) and 9.5f winner Ramius and half-brother to 3 winners in Germany:

dam German 6.5f (at 2 yrs) and 1m winner: fair performer: won maiden at Brighton in August: left Mrs A. Perrett 14,500 gns after third start, then well beaten in 2 nurseries: will stay 1m: acts on firm going. *M. W. Easterby*

RED CLUBS (IRE) 3 br.c. Red Ransom (USA) – Two Clubs 111 (First Trump **119** 118) [2006 114: 7m* 8m 7m⁶ 6m 6m² 5s⁵ 6s⁵ 6d* 5m Oct 1]

With the leading Guineas candidates again largely restricted to stretching their legs at home or in racecourse gallops, the trials in the latest season did not look so strong at the time as in some years. As a result, the BHB undertook a review of the classic trials, which confirmed that the number of horses making their seasonal debut in the Newmarket classics has increased significantly in recent years, and is now approaching half. The review concluded, however, that the main trials were still producing satisfactory field sizes and meeting the relevant rating parameters for their pattern grouping. Barry Hills is one leading trainer who believes in warming up his potential Guineas horses in the traditional trials. He campaigned to keep the listed Thirsk Classic Trial, a race last held in 2003, which was run as the Timeform Race Card Stakes in 1979 when the Hills-trained Tap On Wood won from Abbeydale, the former going on to win the Two Thousand Guineas while the latter was runner-up in the One Thousand. The other Two Thousand Guineas winner saddled by Hills, Haafhd, won the Craven Stakes on his reappearance, a race Hills won again in the latest season with Killybegs. The stable also won another traditionally important Two Thousand Guineas trial, the Lane's End Greenham Stakes at Newbury, with Red Clubs, while its third runner in the Two Thousand Guineas, Olympian Odyssey, would have won the Feilden Stakes with a clear run. The stable's One Thousand Guineas representative Spinning Queen finished second in the Nell Gwyn. The odds of the Hills classic runners illustrate how significantly the performances were viewed at the time. Killybegs scored with authority in the Craven but started at 16/1 in the Guineas, Red Clubs was a 25/1-shot and Olympian Odyssey at 33/1, the last-named doing easily the best of the three on the day, coming third to George Washington. Spinning Queen was a 50/1-shot in the One Thousand Guineas, in which she came sixth behind the Nell Gwyn winner Speciosa, who started at 10/1.

Red Clubs was a speedy two-year-old, kept busy and winning the Coventry and finishing runner-up in the Gimcrack and the Middle Park, but he seemed to find his stamina stretched in the Dewhurst and a tilt at the Guineas might have been regarded as sending him on a fool's errand. Little is lost, however, in tackling the Guineas with a three-year-old who might well turn out to be a sprinter. There is virtually no early-season programme for three-year-old sprinters and the first Group 1 sprint of the year—the all-aged Golden Jubilee—is not until Royal Ascot.

John Guest Diadem Stakes, Ascot—
Red Clubs (second right) shows himself to be better than ever despite veering markedly left;
Baltic King (left), Fayr Jag (halved sleeves) and Assertive (behind winner) are in pursuit

The Greenham wasn't strongly contested and Red Clubs quickened well to beat Marcus Andronicus by a length and three quarters in a race that turned into a test of speed after a muddling pace. Red Clubs was prominent for a long way in the Guineas but didn't stay, dropping out to finish twelfth of fourteen. His performance apparently failed to convince connections fully that he was purely a sprinter and he ran in the Group 3 Jersey Stakes for three-year-olds over seven at Royal Ascot, rather than in the Golden Jubilee or the other big, open-aged sprint the King's Stand. There was more of a premium on stamina in the Jersey than there had been in the Greenham and Red Clubs left the firm impression that he didn't get the trip, though still running creditably to finish sixth, carrying a Group 2 penalty. Red Clubs spent the rest of the campaign in the big sprints. His chance in the July Cup was ruined by a low draw, the main action towards the stand side, his rider wisely not persevering once he saw the way the race was developing. Red Clubs was then runner-up in the Phoenix Sprint Stakes at the Curragh, where he was the only one to present any sort of challenge to Moss Vale. Next for Red Clubs came a creditable fifth in the Nunthorpe, before he failed to last out the six furlongs of the Sprint Cup on very soft going at Haydock, leading or disputing the lead with the winner Reverence for a long way. Red Clubs received due reward for his labours when winning an up-to-standard renewal of the John Guest Diadem Stakes at Ascot in September, when the margin of his victory over Baltic King, a length and a quarter, would have been doubled had he not veered sharply left, possibly shying at a shadow cast by the stand. There was only a week between the Diadem and the Prix de l'Abbaye at Longchamp, where Red Clubs ran below form, already beaten when forced to be checked two furlongs out. He was ruled out of the Hong Kong Sprint in December after arriving at Sha Tin with a high temperature.

			Hail To Reason
	Red Ransom (USA) (b 1987)	Roberto (b 1969)	Bramalea
		Arabia (b 1977)	Damascus
Red Clubs (IRE) (br.c. 2003)			Christmas Wind
		First Trump (ch 1991)	Primo Dominie
	Two Clubs (br 1996)		Valika
		Miss Cindy (br 1975)	Masingh
			Iridium

Red Clubs is a small, strong, well-made colt—a real powerhouse—with a sharp, fluent action. Red Ransom, the sire of Red Clubs, had only a brief racing career because of injury, winning at five and six furlongs as a two-year-old. He was not bred on sprinting lines, however, and the average distance of races won by his offspring at three and above in Europe is around nine furlongs—he is the sire of three Group 1 winners at a mile and a half, Electrocutionist, Casual Look and Ekraar. Two Clubs, the dam of Red Clubs, was a sprinter from a sprinting background, being a half-sister to Gipsy Fiddler, who won the Windsor Castle Stakes at two, out of Miss Cindy, a fair handicapper on the balance of her form who ran until she was six, winning at five to seven furlongs. Miss Cindy was a sister to Haydock Sprint Cup and Stewards' Cup winner Petong. Red Clubs, who has won at an easy seven, has shown his best form at shorter distances. He acts on soft and good to firm going. *B. W. Hills*

RED CONTACT (USA) 5 b.g. Sahm (USA) 112 – Basma (USA) 104 (Grey Dawn II 132) [2006 75, a91: f8g p10g⁴ 8s p10g⁴ p8g 8.1f p7.1m² f8g* p9.5g Dec 9] leggy gelding: fairly useful handicapper: left Mrs L. Featherstone after second start, J. R. Best after sixth: won at Southwell (by 5 lengths) in November: stays easy 1¼m: acts on all-weather: tried blinkered, usually wears cheekpieces: tongue tied once at 4 yrs. *A. Dickman* — a91

RED CORONET 2 br.f. (Mar 19) Singspiel (IRE) 133 – Red Tiara (USA) 60 (Mr Prospector (USA)) [2006 p7g⁵ p8.6m⁶ Nov 21] fourth foal: half-sister to 1m winner Argent (by Barathea) and 3-y-o Red Diadem: dam, disappointing maiden, closely related to very smart Japanese sprinter Meiner Love out of 1000 Guineas runner-up Heart of Joy: better effort (modest form) in maidens when fifth to Sell Out at Kempton: should be suited by 1m+: sold 8,000 gns. *W. J. Haggas* — 62

RED COUNTESS 3 b.f. Pivotal 124 – Red Empress 88 (Nashwan (USA) 135) [2006 10g³ 10g⁴ p8.6g² 10d Nov 1] big filly: second foal: dam, 1½m winner, closely related to — 78 smart 1¼m/1½m performer Happy Valentine out of smart sister to Salsabil: regressed after showing fair form in maiden at Newbury on debut: will stay 1½m. *Mrs A. J. Perrett*

RED CURRENT 2 b.f. (May 8) Soviet Star (USA) 128 – Fleet Amour (USA) (Afleet (CAN)) [2006 7.1m³ p7.1g Nov 2] leggy, close-coupled, quite attractive filly: seventh foal: half-sister to 3 winners, including 7f winner Affaire Royale (by Royal Academy) and 7.5f/1¼m winner Fleet of Light (by Spectrum), both fairly useful: dam, ran 4 times in USA, closely related to US Grade 1 1m winner Quiet American: better run in maidens when third to Swift Image at Warwick: not knocked about at Wolverhampton 2 months later: will be suited by 1m. *J. R. Fanshawe*   **72**

RED DIADEM 3 b.f. Pivotal 124 – Red Tiara (USA) 60 (Mr Prospector (USA)) [2006 67p: p7g² f8g⁴ 6f 6g 9f² 9f⁵ 8.5f* 8f Dec 26] tall, leggy filly: fair form in Britain: sold from W. Haggas 28,000 gns after fourth outing: won maiden at Hollywood in November: stays 9f: acts on polytrack and firm going. *B. D. A. Cecil, USA*   **?**

RED EVIE (IRE) 3 b.f. Intikhab (USA) 135 – Malafemmena (IRE) 96 (Nordico (USA)) [2006 51p: 7m* 8m* 7s* 7d* 8m* 7f* 8m* 8d⁵ Sep 30]   **117**

Every season has its share of horses who show dramatic improvement, though few match the latest one in the number who hit the bullseye in a Group 1 event. Among the older brigade, Les Arcs, Reverence and Desert Lord all made at least 20 lb improvement and the pick of the classic generation in this respect, Red Evie, did even better. Rated 51p after finishing ninth of seventeen at 100/1 in a maiden at Newmarket in September as a two-year-old, she ran to 80 when convincingly landing a similar event at Yarmouth at the end of March as fourth favourite in a field of twelve. Six races, and over five months, later she won at the highest level with a game success in the Matron Stakes at Leopardstown. All credit to Red Evie for her achievements, and to her trainer for campaigning her so skilfully.

Red Evie's progress was certainly rapid, and the handicapper was unable to keep tabs on her after that initial victory at Yarmouth. She won fillies' handicaps at Yarmouth again in April and Newbury in mid-May before landing the odds in facile fashion from Star Cluster in a four-runner minor event at Leicester at the end of the month. The style of her victories was similar as she showed a bright turn of

Coolmore Fusaichi Pegasus Matron Stakes, Leopardstown—Red Evie holds on from the strong-finishing Peeress to gain her seventh win in a row; Flashy Wings (No.5) is another to finish well in third, with Nannina fourth and Race For The Stars (far side) fifth

Mr Terry Neill's "Red Evie"

foot after being held up, idling in front at Newbury and being eased. The listed
Sandringham Handicap for three-year-old fillies at Royal Ascot provided a sterner
test, partly because Red Evie did not have the run of the race. Indeed, in a contest
with nineteen runners she looked out of it when still stuck in the mid-division
halfway up the straight, after being held up towards the back from the off. Desperate needs led to desperate measures as Jamie Spencer switched her right and
barged through over a furlong out, earning a four-day suspension as a result. Red
Evie responded in style, accelerating smartly to catch La Mottie and beat her by a
head, with Makderah third. Evidently Red Evie was up to winning in pattern
company and there was talk of her going for the Falmouth Stakes or the Brownstown Stakes. Perhaps the fact that she had had five races in less than three months
encouraged a change of plan, because Red Evie wasn't seen out again until the
start of August in the Oak Tree Stakes at Goodwood. Dropping back to seven
furlongs, Red Evie started favourite in a field of nine which also included
Makderah, Brownstown Stakes winner Spinning Queen, Fred Darling Stakes
runner-up Cantabria and Short Dance, wide-margin winner of a listed event at York
in May. Waited with in last place, Red Evie still had plenty to do two furlongs out
but, once switched outside, she produced a tremendous run to catch Makderah fifty
yards out and win going away by half a length.

    Red Evie clearly deserved a shot at a Group 1 and the Coolmore Fusaichi
Pegasus Matron Stakes at Leopardstown just over a month later offered the chance.
Since its elevation to the top level in 2004—it had been Group 3 until 2002—this

870

race has been won exclusively by fillies trained in Britain, through Soviet Song and Attraction. The Matron had been a happy hunting ground for trainers based in Britain before that too, with five victories between 1996 and 2003. The British challenge this time in a field of eight was typically powerful, headed by Lockinge Stakes winner Peeress, the first two in the Coronation Stakes, Nannina and Flashy Wings, and Red Evie. The pick of a weak home defence looked to be Race For The Stars, fourth in the Coronation Stakes before winning a Group 3 event at Gowran. Nannina started favourite with Red Evie only fourth choice. The elevation in company made no difference to the tactics used on Red Evie by Spencer, who gets on well with the filly and was back on board after missing Goodwood through suspension. As Race For The Stars made the running, Red Evie was held up at the back before making smooth headway to lead a furlong out. Peeress, also held up, was unable to go with her but, as Red Evie ran on with verve to the line, Peeress and Flashy Wings produced last-ditch challenges, which made for a cracking finish in which Red Evie held on by the skin of her teeth from Peeress, with Flashy Wings beaten three quarters of a length into third, just ahead of Nannina. The result had rather a muddling look to it, but it represented further improvement from Red Evie, who started second favourite for the Sun Chariot Stakes at Newmarket on her final start. The run is best forgotten, however, as she was beaten a distance into last of five behind Spinning Queen, never travelling well at any stage and probably over the top after a long campaign.

		Intikhab (USA)	Red Ransom	Roberto
Red Evie (IRE)		(b 1994)	(b 1987)	Bramalea
(b.f. 2003)			Crafty Example	Crafty Prospector
			(b 1987)	Real Crafty Lady
		Malafemmena (IRE)	Nordico	Northern Dancer
		(b 1992)	(b 1981)	Kennelot
			Martinova	Martinmas
			(b 1978)	Pavlova

Red Evie, a big, lengthy filly who was never likely to be highly tried at two, acts on firm and soft going and has been bandaged on her hind joints. After being entered in the December Sales she was withdrawn and stays in training with a race on Dubai World Cup day a possible early target. Though effective at seven furlongs and a mile, she may be worth trying at a mile and a quarter. She has not been stopping at the end of her races, and the waiting tactics employed on her would give her every chance of getting the trip. Equally, however, there is more speed than stamina and the plentiful opportunities for older fillies and mares at a mile in the pattern system nowadays mean there may be no necessity to look beyond that distance. Red Evie's sire Intikhab was suited by a mile, showing the best form by any horse in training over any trip as a four-year-old in 1998 when landing the Queen Anne Stakes at Royal Ascot. However, he ran only once more before retirement to Derrinstown Stud for the 2000 covering season. Even through rose-tinted spectacles, his career there cannot be described as a great success, with only one other Group 1 winner on the scoresheet in the shape of Paita, who collected the Criterium de Saint-Cloud in 2004. Intikhab is still covering books of around a hundred mares but the Maktoums are not giving him much patronage, with just two mares from Sheikh Hamdan's Shadwell Stud visiting the stallion in the latest covering season. His fee has dropped from IR12,000 guineas when he retired to €8,000. The dam of Red Evie, Malafemmena, was a useful two-year-old for John Dunlop, winning a listed event over six furlongs at Milan and proving effective at up to a mile. Red Evie cost €50,000 as a foal at Goffs and 58,000 guineas as a yearling at Tattersalls and is her fourth foal and second winner following the Affirmed colt Affirmed Admiral, successful twice in the States. The main claim to fame on the racetrack of the grandam Martinova was a third in the Irish One Thousand Guineas—she also won the Athasi Stakes—and she did pretty well as a broodmare too. The pick of her eight winners was the smart French sprinter Export Price but, in complete contrast, she also foaled top American steeplechaser Ninepins, successful in the Colonial Cup. There is stamina one generation further back, Pavlova being a minor winner over a mile and a half and a half-sister to Gold Cup winner Random Shot. Pavlova's seven other winning offspring included very smart mile-to mile-and-a-quarter colt Lucky Wednesday, winner of the Prince of Wales's Stakes. *M. L. W. Bell*

REDEYE SPECIAL 4 b.f. Efisio 120 – Red May (IRE) 70 (Persian Bold 123) [2006 **70**
78p: p7g* p8g³ 8.1d 8m³ p8g² p8g² p8g³ 10g³ Aug 30] fair handicapper: won at Lingfield in April: barely stays 1¼m: acts on polytrack and good to firm going: consistent.
M. L. W. Bell

RED FAMA 2 ch.g. (May 6) Fraam 114 – Carol Again 48 (Kind of Hush 118) [2006 7s –
Oct 10] in rear in maiden at Newcastle. *N. Bycroft*

RED FINESSE 4 b.f. Soviet Star (USA) 128 – Jouet 71 (Reprimand 122) [2006 64: p6g **56**
f7g⁴ p8g Jan 29] good-topped filly: modest maiden: may prove best short of 7f: sold 2,200
gns, sent to Germany. *M. A. Jarvis*

RED FLARE (IRE) 2 b.g. (Jan 25) Redback 116 – Cwm Deri (IRE) (Alzao (USA) **54**
117) [2006 5.1g⁶ 6v 6m Jun 9] well-made gelding: modest form on first of 3 outings in
maidens. *M. R. Channon*

REDFLO 2 b.f. (Feb 10) Redback 116 – Button Hole Flower (IRE) (Fairy King (USA)) –
[2006 p5g⁶ p5g⁶ Dec 16] 800F: fifth foal: half-sister to 2002 2-y-o 7f winner in Italy by
Millkom: dam, Italian 5f (including at 2 yrs)/6f winner, out of half-sister to Racing Post
Trophy winner Be My Chief: sixth in maidens at Kempton. *Ms J. S. Doyle*

RED FOREST (IRE) 7 b.g. Charnwood Forest (IRE) 125 – High Atlas 65 (Shirley **66**
Heights 130) [2006 75d: f14g⁵ 14m³ 14.1f³ 14.1m 14m² 11.8g³ Aug 30] medium-sized
gelding: fair handicapper: stays 2m: acts on all-weather, soft and firm going: tongue tied:
free-going sort: none too consistent. *J. Mackie*

RED GALA 3 b.c. Sinndar (IRE) 134 – Red Camellia 116 (Polar Falcon (USA) 126) **90**
[2006 10m⁵ p12g² 10d² 11.9g* Oct 13] good-bodied colt: fourth foal: half-brother to
5-y-o Red Bloom: dam, 2-y-o 6f/7f (Prestige Stakes) winner who was third in Poule
d'Essai des Pouliches, out of half-sister to Ibn Bey and Roseate Tern: fairly useful
performer: best effort when winning maiden at Brighton in October by 9 lengths from
Flame Creek, off bridle 4f out and pulling clear despite carrying head bit awkwardly:
probably better at 1½m than shorter: acts on polytrack and good to soft going: has worn
crossed noseband. *Sir Michael Stoute*

RED HOT JAZZ (IRE) 2 b. or br.f. (Mar 30) Danetime (IRE) 121 – That's Jazz 67 **53**
(Cool Jazz 116) [2006 5g 6m⁵ 6m⁵ 5g Sep 13] 3,000Y: first foal: dam 6f winner: modest
maiden: should prove best at 5f/6f. *Mrs P. N. Dutfield*

REDI (ITY) 5 b.g. Danehill Dancer (IRE) 117 – Rossella (Shareef Dancer (USA) 135) –
[2006 –: p12g Mar 23] tall, angular gelding: has a quick action: lightly raced and no form
on Flat since 2004: tongue tied last 3 starts. *A. M. Balding*

RED IRIS (IRE) 3 ch.f. Soviet Star (USA) 128 – Last Rolo (Mark of Esteem (IRE) –
137) [2006 –: 7m 8.3d May 7] sturdy, close-coupled filly: little form. *G. A. Swinbank*

RED LANCER 4 b.g. Deploy 131 – Miss Bussell 65 (Sabrehill (USA) 120) [2006 **102 d**
108: 10.1g⁵ 11.9g 13.9d 14v 10m⁵ 10s⁶ 12s 12g Oct 12] small, stocky gelding: useful
handicapper: good fifth to Chancellor in Rose Bowl (Handicap) at Epsom on reappearance: below form after: stays 13f: acts on all-weather, soft and good to firm going: has got
on edge beforehand: tends to edge left: sold 30,000 gns. *R. A. Fahey*

RED LANTERN 5 ch.g. Young Ern 120 – Croft Sally (Crofthall 110) [2006 46: 8.2s 8f **47**
7f 8.2g⁶ p8.6g p8.6g p8.6g Nov 18] sturdy gelding: poor maiden: stays 9.5f: acts on polytrack and good to firm going: tried in cheekpieces, visored/tongue tied last 2 starts.
M. J. Attwater

REDOUBLE 10 b.g. First Trump 118 – Sunflower Seed 70 (Mummy's Pet 125) [2006 –
f12g Apr 3] good-topped gelding: well held only outing on Flat since 2003. *N. B. King*

RED PETAL 2 ch.f. (Apr 28) Medicean 128 – Red Garland (Selkirk (USA) 129) [2006 **67**
p8.6s³ p8.6g³ Dec 27] first foal: dam unraced sister to 5-y-o Red Bloom: fair form when
third in maidens at Wolverhampton, still green (hung left) in race won by Lazy Darren:
should stay 1¼m. *Sir Mark Prescott*

RED PRIDE (IRE) 3 b.g. Fasliyev (USA) 120 – True Love (Robellino (USA) 127) –
[2006 56: 8m p8.6g p7g f11g Nov 2] well-made gelding: modest maiden at 2 yrs: well
held in 2006. *Miss J. Feilden*

RED RACKETEER (USA) 4 b.c. Red Ransom (USA) – Furajet (USA) 101 (The **104**
Minstrel (CAN) 135) [2006 100: p10g⁶ 12g² 10.4d May 17] well-made colt: useful handicapper: good efforts when sixth to Kandidate at Kempton and length second to Vengeance
at Epsom (made running) first 2 starts: well below form final outing: stays 1½m, at least
as effective at 1¼m: acts on polytrack, raced on good going or softer on turf: sold 18,000
gns in October, joined A. Al Raihe in UAE. *E. A. L. Dunlop*

RED RAPTOR 5 ch.g. Polar Falcon (USA) 126 – Star Precision 103 (Shavian 125) **57**
[2006 7s^6 7m 8.1s p8.6g^6 Dec 27] little form in bumpers/hurdles: modest maiden: will be
suited by 1m+: tongue tied. *J. A. Geake*

RED RIVER REBEL 8 b.g. Inchinor 119 – Bidweaya (USA) 45 (Lear Fan (USA) **58**
130) [2006 62, a52: p13.9g^4 12.4m 12f 12.1f^4 12.1s^2 12.1m^6 11.8g^6 f16g^2 f14g^2 f14g* **a61**
f16g^2 f14g* Dec 29] tall, leggy gelding: modest performer: won banded races at Southwell in November and December (by 10 lengths): stays 2m: acts on all-weather, soft and
firm going: tried visored. *J. R. Norton*

RED RIVER ROCK (IRE) 4 b.g. Spectrum (IRE) 126 – Ann's Annie (IRE) 78 **56**
(Alzao (USA) 117) [2006 –: 10.1m 8d 9d f11g^5 f11m^2 f14g^2 p13.9g Dec 4] modest
maiden: stays 1¾m: acts on all-weather, best effort on turf on good going: blinkered last
4 starts. *T. J. Fitzgerald*

RED ROCK CANYON (IRE) 2 b.c. (May 8) Rock of Gibraltar (IRE) 133 – Imagine **105**
(IRE) 119 (Sadler's Wells (USA) 132) [2006 7m^2 7m^3 7s^2 8s 10g^5 Nov 12] well-made
colt: second foal: closely related to 3-y-o Horatio Nelson: dam, Irish 1000 Guineas and
Oaks winner (also successful at 7f at 2 yrs), half-sister to Generous: useful form: placed
in maidens (odds on), including at Goodwood: highly tried last 2 starts in Racing Post
Trophy at Newbury and Criterium de Saint-Cloud, in latter much improved when 4½
lengths fifth of 13 to Passage of Time: stays 1¼m. *A. P. O'Brien, Ireland*

RED ROCKS (IRE) 3 b.c. Galileo (IRE) 134 – Pharmacist (IRE) 108 (Machia- **124**
vellian (USA) 123) [2006 96: 10m* 10s* 12m^2 12m^2 12d^2 13.9g^3 12f* Nov 4]
    Brian Meehan could hardly have made a better start at Manton. His string
won seventy-four races in Britain (the highest achieved by the trainer in his career
to date), accruing £1,365,779 in first three prize money (also a personal best).
Meehan's domestic achievements consolidated his position in the top ten in the
trainers' table, a position he reached for the first time, since taking out a licence in
1992, in his final season at Lambourn in 2005. But that was only half the story—or,
more accurately, a third of it, so far as prize money goes. Meehan was also the
leading British-based trainer in terms of foreign earnings, David Junior and Red
Rocks picking up the two most valuable races won by a British stable overseas in
the latest season. Those respective victories, in the Dubai Duty Free at Nad Al
Sheba and the John Deere Breeders' Cup Turf at Churchill Downs, accounted for
the lion's share of the £2,777,688 won by the Meehan stable abroad.
    Meehan will not have David Junior, whose victory in the Coral-Eclipse was
the biggest for the stable in Britain in the latest season, but Red Rocks stays in
training with his first aim to follow in the footsteps of David Junior on Dubai World
Cup night, when he will run in either the Duty Free or the Sheema Classic, the
last-named over a mile and a half on turf looking much the more likely option,
judged on his performance at Churchill Downs. The richest day's racing in North
America became even richer in 2006, total prize money raised from fourteen
million dollars to twenty million dollars for the eight Breeders' Cup races (which,
from 2007, will be eleven, including a new Breeders' Cup Juvenile Turf). The aim
of the 'Breeders' Cup World Championships' (the word 'Thoroughbred' was
dropped in 2006), according to its organisers, is to 'enhance the Breeders' Cup as
the pre-eminent racing brand . . . to take the event to the next level.' There are
certainly signs that, rather belatedly, the Breeders' Cup has now become acutely
aware of the challenge presented, in particular, by the Dubai World Cup programme
which now stages not only the world's most valuable race on dirt, the World Cup
itself, but also the world's two most valuable races on turf, the Duty Free and the
Sheema Classic, both of which were more valuable than the richest race on the
Breeders' Cup card, the Breeders' Cup Classic, despite the rise in value of the
Classic. Those four races, incidentally, were the most valuable in the world in 2006,
a list compiled by the International Racing Bureau placing Europe's richest race,
the Prix de l'Arc de Triomphe, in eleventh place and the Derby, the most valuable
race in Britain by some way, in fifteenth. The first prize won by Red Rocks in the
Breeders' Cup Turf, the second most valuable of the Breeders' Cup races and ninth
on the world list, was around half of that collected by David Junior in the Dubai
Duty Free.
    The Breeders' Cup Turf is an event in which the Europeans have done
particularly well, and, as a group, they now lead the North Americans twelve and a

John Deere Breeders' Cup Turf, Churchill Downs—
another victory in the race for the Europeans as Red Rocks gives Frankie Dettori
his second success on the day; the 2004 winner Better Talk Now (bandages) is runner-up this time

half to ten and a half (including the dead heat in 2003) since 1984 when the Breeders' Cup was inaugurated. Red Rocks was one of only three European challengers in the latest edition and he started at longer odds than the others, the King George VI and Queen Elizabeth Stakes winner Hurricane Run (who was favourite) and the 2005 Grand Prix de Paris and St Leger winner Scorpion (second to Hurricane Run in the 2005 Irish Derby), who had shaped well on his return in a listed event at the Curragh after being off for a year because of injury. Red Rocks had come second in the latest renewal of the Grand Prix de Paris and third in the latest edition of the St Leger, among a series of smart efforts in a campaign in which he had shown himself a genuine and reliable performer, and a straightforward type, often making the running. He did not, in all honesty, look an obvious candidate for a championship event like the Breeders' Cup Turf. The owner of Red Rocks had, however, been keen on an American turf campaign earlier in the year, the Virginia Derby in July being mentioned at one time. Red Rocks had not won a pattern race, his previous victories at three coming on his first two starts, in a maiden at Windsor (he had shown useful form in maidens at two, placed twice in three starts) and the listed Shadwell Estates Fairway Stakes at Newmarket, both of which he won impressively. The closest Red Rocks came to winning in four outings in pattern company before the Breeders' Cup was when beaten a neck by Papal Bull in the King Edward VII Stakes at Royal Ascot (on his last start before being beaten two lengths by Rail Link in the Grand Prix de Paris) and then when going down by a head to Youmzain, looking the winner for much of the last two furlongs until collared close home, in the Great Voltigeur at York. Red Rocks started second favourite behind Sixties Icon for the St Leger (from which Youmzain was a notable absentee) and he gave the impression that the distance stretched his stamina, patiently ridden but not finding so much as seemed likely and finishing third to Sixties Icon.

Frankie Dettori rode Red Rocks in four of his first six races as a three-year-old (though not in the St Leger in which he partnered the winner) and he took the mount again in the Breeders' Cup Turf, for which Red Rocks, on lasix for the first time, started at 108/10. As well as Hurricane Run and Scorpion, three of the home defenders in the field of eleven also started at odds shorter than Red Rocks, the Joe Hirsch Turf Classic winner English Channel, and the first two in the Man o' War Stakes, ex-French Cacique and the consistent Go Deputy, the latter narrowly beaten since by Collier Hill in the Canadian International. Also in the line-up was the 2004 Breeders' Cup Turf winner Better Talk Now. Dettori, and Ramon Dominguez on Better Talk Now, judged things to perfection, both ignoring the overly strong pace set by the outsiders Icy Atlantic and Rush Bay, and challenging from well back in the straight. Red Rocks took the lead a furlong out and was ridden out to hold the challenge of Better Talk Now by half a length, with English Channel a further two and a quarter lengths away third. Scorpion came fifth and Hurricane Run, suffering his fourth defeat since the King George, sixth. Dettori had earlier ridden Ouija Board to her second success in the Breeders' Cup Filly & Mare Turf, becoming the first European-based rider to win two Breeders' Cup races on the same day and going some way to silencing his American critics who still refer to his much-criticised ride on Swain in the 1998 Breeders' Cup Classic, one having warned before the latest Breeders' Cup 'Heads up on the outside rail, Frankie's in town.' Dettori outrode most of the locals in the Turf, after a copybook ride in the Filly & Mare, so it is to be hoped he receives a fairer press in future. Both Red Rocks and Ouija Board made the short-list for an Eclipse Award in their respective divisions, the awards determined by a ballot of one hundred and fifty-seven members of the National Turf Writers Association, seventy-nine employees of *Daily Racing Form* and seventy-seven representatives of the National Thoroughbred Racing Association. Ouija Board ran away with the award for the female turf horse of the year, adding to her award in 2004, following Banks Hill in 2001 and Islington in 2003, who also landed it after winning the Filly & Mare Turf, while Pebbles, Daylami,

Mr J. Paul Reddam's "Red Rocks"

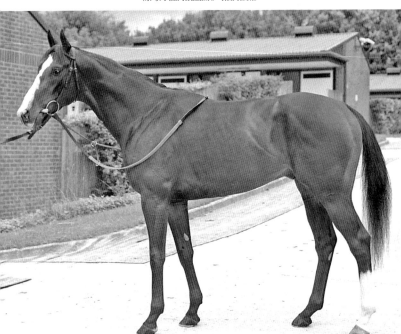

RED

Kalanisi, Fantastic Light and High Chaparral (twice) were European-trained Breeders' Cup Turf winners who had previously been honoured. The trend in recent years of honouring European winners of the two races with Eclipse Awards had been broken when Shirocco was overlooked in 2005, the award as the year's best male turf performer going to Leroidesanimaux who won eight in a row before finishing second in the Breeders' Cup Mile. Red Rocks finished fourth in the voting for male turf horse behind Breeders' Cup Mile winner Miesque's Approval, the Arlington Million winner The Tin Man and English Channel.

Red Rocks (IRE) (b.c. 2003)	Galileo (IRE) (b 1998)	Sadler's Wells (b 1981)	Northern Dancer Fairy Bridge
		Urban Sea (ch 1989)	Miswaki Allegretta
	Pharmacist (IRE) (b 1996)	Machiavellian (b 1987)	Mr Prospector Coup de Folie
		Pharaoh's Delight (b 1987)	Fairy King Ridge The Times

The rather leggy, attractive Red Rocks, who has a quick, fluent action, provided his sire Galileo with a fourth Group/Grade 1 winner of the year, following Nightime (Irish One Thousand Guineas), Sixties Icon (St Leger) and champion two-year-old Teofilo (National Stakes and Dewhurst Stakes). The essay on Teofilo contains more details about Galileo's first two crops and his promotion to Europe's stallion elite. Galileo is the most likely source of Red Rocks's stamina since his dam Pharmacist and his grandam Pharaoh's Delight were both sprinters. Pharmacist won a listed race over six furlongs at Leopardstown as a two-year-old, while Pharaoh's Delight won the Group 1 Phoenix Stakes at the same age and made her mark in top company at three when placed in races such as the Nunthorpe, the Haydock Sprint Cup and the Prix de l'Abbaye. Pharaoh's Delight is by Fairy King, a full brother to Galileo's sire Sadler's Wells, out of a five-furlong nursery winner Ridge The Times. Fairy King and Sadler's Wells were stablemates at Ballydoyle but Fairy King was beset by training difficulties and ran only once. He did, however, make a name for himself as a stallion, taking more after his three-parts brother Nureyev than after Sadler's Wells, and becoming noted as an influence for speed, the average distance of races won by his offspring at three and above being around a mile. The pedigree of Red Rocks provides another notable instance of inbreeding, with Mr Prospector, the paternal grandsire of Pharmacist, also appearing a generation further back in Galileo's pedigree as the sire of his maternal grandsire Miswaki (Northern Dancer and Fairy Bridge also appear twice in the first four generations of Red Rocks' pedigree, featuring in the fourth as the sire and dam of Fairy King). With both Northern Dancer and Mr Prospector among the most dominant stallions in world breeding in the modern era, finding suitable mares for Red Rocks when he is retired to stud will provide something of a challenge. Red Rocks is the third foal produced by Pharmacist, whose first was the smart Medicinal (by Linamix) who won over seven as a two-year-old and then in listed company as a three-year-old over a mile and a quarter at Leopardstown before being sent to France where he was successful at the same trip. Pharmacist was also represented on the racecourse in the latest season by her second foal, the fairly useful Caheerloch (by Sinndar), successful in a handicap over nine and a half furlongs at Gowran in July, and her fourth, Blue Coral (by Grand Lodge), who won a maiden over eight and a half at Galway in August. Pharmacist, barren to Rock of Gibraltar in 2005, produced a full sister to Medicinal in the latest season. Red Rocks, who has worn a crossed noseband, is probably best at around a mile and a half, and he acts on firm and soft going. Though he was sweating and edgy on his final two-year-old start, he is thoroughly reliable. *B. J. Meehan*

RED ROMEO 5 ch.g. Case Law 113 – Enchanting Eve 67 (Risk Me (FR) 127) [2006 **90** 90: p7g 7.1m³ 6f⁴ 7g⁶ 6m 8d³ 7.1m² Sep 4] tall gelding: fairly useful handicapper: creditable efforts in 2006 when placed: needs good test at 6f nowadays, stays 1m: acts on polytrack, good to firm and good to soft going: tried in blinkers (raced freely): often races prominently. *G. A. Swinbank*

RED RUDY 4 ch.g. Pivotal 124 – Piroshka (Soviet Star (USA) 128) [2006 71: p7g² **77** 9.7d³ p8g² 7g² 7.1m* 8.1d⁵ p8.6g Nov 23] tall, close-coupled gelding: fair handicapper:

won at Chepstow in August: barely stays 9.7f: acts on polytrack, firm and good to soft going: consistent. *A. W. Carroll*

RED RUTH LADY 4 ch.f. Karinga Bay 116 – Equilibrium 67 (Statoblest 120) [2006 f7g p6g p9.5g May 5] sixth foal: half-sister to 1¼m winner State of Balance (by Mizoram): dam 2-y-o 6f winner: no form. *D. L. Williams* —

RED SAIL 5 ch.m. Dr Fong (USA) 128 – Manhattan Sunset (USA) 76 (El Gran Senor (USA) 136) [2006 70, a64: p10g⁴ p10g³ p10g³ p10g* 11.9m 9.7f³ 11.5f 10m³ p9.5g p10g⁵ Dec 10] angular mare: modest handicapper nowadays: first success when winning at Lingfield in May: stays 1½m: acts on polytrack and firm going: blinkered. *Dr J. D. Scargill* **62**

RED SANS 4 b.g. Rainbow Quest (USA) 134 – Sarah Georgina 79 (Persian Bold 123) [2006 71: p10g Jan 14] fair maiden at best, lightly raced: respectable effort only start in 2006: should stay 1½m: raced only on polytrack: sold 1,000 gns in March, sent to Sweden. *P. Mitchell* **63**

RED SOMERSET (USA) 3 b.c. Red Ransom (USA) – Bielska (USA) (Deposit Ticket (USA)) [2006 8g³ p8g* 8s⁴ 10s⁵ 9m⁶ 10d Sep 29] €320,000Y: strong, good-bodied colt: first foal: dam, French 2-y-o 1m winner, half-sister to smart performer up to 1½m Wandering Star (by Red Ransom): fairly useful performer: confirmed debut promise when winning maiden at Kempton in May: tailed off in handicap final outing (kicked at start and withdrawn penultimate intended start): may prove best short of 1¼m: acts on polytrack and good to firm ground. *R. Hannon* **94**

RED SOVEREIGN 5 b.m. Danzig Connection (USA) – Ruby Princess (IRE) 70 (Mac's Imp (USA) 116) [2006 81§, a69§: p6g f5g⁶ p5.1g* p5.1g³ 5.3m² 5.7d p5.1g 5d³ 6.1g Sep 15] leggy mare: fair on turf, modest on all-weather: won banded race at Wolverhampton in March: best at 5f/6f: acts on polytrack, firm and good to soft going: tried blinkered: usually races prominently: unreliable. *D. G. Bridgwater* **70 §**
a62 §

RED SPELL (IRE) 5 ch.g. Soviet Star (USA) 128 – A-To-Z (IRE) 101 (Ahonoora 122) [2006 97, a106: p7g² p10g² p10g² 8m³ 8.1m⁴ a8.7g² 7s⁴ 8m² 8m 8g 8f⁵ 8g 9m 9m⁴ 9d p7g⁶ p8g² p7g² Dec 22] good-topped gelding: smart performer on all-weather, useful on turf: in frame 12 times in 2006, including when 1½ lengths second to Arturius in handicap and fourth to Sri Diamond in Winter Derby, both at Lingfield, second/fourth outings: creditable head second to Vortex in minor events there last 2 starts: effective at 7f to easy 1¼m: acts on polytrack, soft and good to firm going: tried blinkered/in cheekpieces. *R. Hannon* **102**
a111

RED SPINEL 2 ch.f. (Jan 30) Fantastic Light (USA) 134 – Golden Digger (USA) 66 (Mr Prospector (USA)) [2006 p7g Sep 18] well-made filly: half-sister to several winners, including smart 7f (at 2 yrs) to 1½m winner Naheef (by Marju) and useful 6f (at 2 yrs)/7f winner Golden Sahara (by Green Desert): dam, maiden who failed to progress from only 2-y-o start, sister to dam of Irish Oaks/Nassau Stakes winner Lailani and half-sister to very smart pair Always Fair and Faithful Son: tongue tied and backward, well held in maiden at Kempton: sold 30,000 gns. *E. A. L. Dunlop* —

REDSPIN (IRE) 6 ch.g. Spectrum (IRE) 126 – Trendy Indian (IRE) 71 (Indian Ridge 123) [2006 65d: 17.2f² 14.1f 16.4f⁶ 14.1f⁶ 16f⁶ Jul 31] leggy gelding: poor handicapper nowadays: effective at 1¾m to 2½m: acts on polytrack and firm going: tried in visor/cheekpieces: sometimes hangs: none too reliable. *J. S. Moore* **43**

RED SUN 9 b.g. Foxhound (USA) 103 – Superetta 65 (Superlative 118) [2006 69: p16.5g* p16.5g f16g⁵ 15.9m Jul 15] smallish gelding: fair handicapper: won amateur event at Wolverhampton in January: stays 17f: acts on all-weather, good to firm and good to soft going: often makes running: tongue tied: won over hurdles in September (claimed £6,000). *J. Mackie* **66**

RED TSARINA 3 b.f. Russian Red 72 – Tudor Bay Lady (Faustus (USA) 118) [2006 –: p9.5g f8g Feb 7] close-coupled filly: no sign of ability. *V. Smith* —

RED VIXEN (IRE) 3 b.f. Agnes World (USA) 123 – West Escape 95 (Gone West (USA)) [2006 51: p6g p6g⁶ 7m p6g* p5.1g² p6g³ 5m⁴ 6g 6m⁶ 7f³ p7g 7.2s 7d p6g p8.6g f6g⁵ Dec 28] smallish filly: modest performer: won banded event at Wolverhampton in April: stays 7f: acts on polytrack and firm ground, well beaten on soft: blinkered final outing: held up. *C. N. Allen* **57**

REDWOOD ROCKS (IRE) 5 b.g. Blush Rambler (USA) 119 – Crisp And Cool (USA) (Ogygian (USA)) [2006 79: p8.6g p7.1g p8.6g⁶ 7.1g 7.9m 7.9m 8.3m² 7.5m⁴ 7d³ p7.1g* p7.1g f6g Dec 23] rather leggy gelding: fluent mover: fair handicapper: won at **75**

Wolverhampton in November: stays 1m: acts on polytrack, firm and good to soft going: tried blinkered: headstrong front runner. *B. Smart*

REDWOOD STAR 6 b.m. Piccolo 121 – Thewaari (USA) 68 (Eskimo (USA)) [2006 **68** 75: 5.1s 5.3m⁴ Apr 30] fair handicapper: best around 5f: acts on firm and good to soft going: tried tongue tied/blinkered: refused to enter stall and withdrawn in June. *P. L. Gilligan*

REEBAL 2 b.c. (Mar 7) Danehill (USA) 126 – Applaud (USA) 105 (Rahy (USA) 115) **86** [2006 6.1g⁶ 6m⁶ 6m⁵ 5d* 5s³ 6g 6d⁴ Nov 4] 60,000Y, 75,000 2-y-o: smallish, good-topped colt: sixth foal: half-brother to 2 winners abroad, including French 9f to 10.5f winner Framboise (by Diesis): dam 2-y-o 5f/6f (Cherry Hinton Stakes) winner: fairly useful performer: won minor event at Ripon in August: made frame twice (at Windsor) from 3 starts in nurseries: will prove best kept to 5f/6f: acts on soft going: blinkered after second outing. *B. J. Meehan*

REEFSCAPE 5 gr.h. Linamix (FR) 127 – Coraline (Sadler's Wells (USA) 132) [2006 **118** 118: 15.5v⁴ 15.5d³ 15.5d³ 20m² 16f 15s⁵ 20m⁴ Oct 1] rather leggy, good-topped horse: smart performer: creditable third at Longchamp in Prix de Barbeville (to Petite Speciale) and Prix Vicomtesse Vigier (1½ lengths behind Shamdala) before good 4 lengths second to Yeats in Gold Cup at Royal Ascot: failed to impress with attitude in Goodwood Cup and poor effort in Prix Kergorlay at Deauville next 2 outings: fared better when 2¾ lengths fourth to Sergeant Cecil in Prix du Cadran (won race in 2005) at Longchamp final start, going in snatches before staying on: stayed 2½m: acted on soft and good to firm going: ideally suited by being ridden prominently: to stand at Glebe House Stud, Co Down, Northern Ireland, fee £1,500. *A. Fabre, France*

REELING N' ROCKING (IRE) 3 b.f. Mr Greeley (USA) 122 – Mystic Lure 70 **77 +** (Green Desert (USA) 127) [2006 7g 7s 8.1g 8m³ p7g* p7g³ p7g* Nov 25] 140,000Y: big, lengthy filly: sixth foal: half-sister to useful 6f winner (including at 2 yrs) Entrap (by Phone Trick) and maiden in Japan by Rubiano: dam, maiden who stayed 7f, half-sister to top-class French/US 1m/9f winner Thrill Show: fair performer: won maiden at Lingfield in October and handicap at Kempton in November: should stay 9f: acts on polytrack and good to firm going. *B. W. Hills*

REEM AL FALLAH (IRE) 2 br.f. (May 16) Cape Cross (IRE) 129 – Hanna Dome **68** (IRE) 67 (Salt Dome (USA)) [2006 5f³ 5f⁴ 5.7f² 6s⁴ 8g³ 7m⁴ 6s Oct 16] 14,500Y: sixth foal: half-sister to Italian 7.5f (at 2 yrs) to 1¼m winner Hasta La Victoria (by Turtle Island): dam Irish maiden half-sister to smart French performer up to 7f Harifa: fair maiden: in frame first 6 starts: stays 1m: acts on firm going: has looked none too keen: sold 7,000 gns. *M. R. Channon*

REEM THREE 3 b.f. Mark of Esteem (IRE) 137 – Jumaireyah 91 (Fairy King (USA)) **103** [2006 65p: p8.6g* 10.4d* 10.4m* 10.1m² 12m 10d Nov 4] strong, good-bodied filly: useful performer: won maiden at Wolverhampton in April and handicaps at York in May and June: good 1¼ lengths second to Pictavia in listed race at Newcastle fourth start: not discredited when mid-field in handicap won by Folio at Windsor final outing: will need to settle better to stay beyond 1¼m: acts on polytrack, good to firm and good to soft going: sent to USA. *L. M. Cumani*

REFLECTING (IRE) 3 gr.f. Daylami (IRE) 138 – Church Light 88 (Caerleon (USA) **69** 132) [2006 77p: 8.2m⁴ 8.1m³ 10d p10g 8.1m⁶ p8g 8m Sep 12] rather leggy, close-coupled filly: fair maiden: stays easy 1¼m: acts on polytrack and good to firm going: clipped heels and unseated rider sixth outing. *J. W. Hills*

REFLECTIVE GLORY (IRE) 2 ch.f. (Apr 19) City On A Hill (USA) 114 – **60** Sheznice (IRE) 58 (Try My Best (USA) 130) [2006 5d⁶ 5g⁶ 5f⁴ 6m⁴ 7f⁴ f6g p7.1g Nov 24] good-topped filly: half-sister to several winners, including 6f winner Woody Bathwick (by Woodborough), later successful up to 1m abroad, and 2m winner Matthias Mystique (by Sharrood): dam ran twice: modest maiden: well beaten in nurseries (on all-weather): should stay 7f/1m: acts on firm and good to soft going. *J. J. Quinn*

REFORM ACT (USA) 3 b.f. Lemon Drop Kid (USA) 131 – Solar Colony (USA) **112** (Pleasant Colony (USA)) [2006 86: 10g* 10m³ 11.3m⁴ 12m* 12s⁴ 12g³ Nov 4] $130,000Y: leggy, useful-looking filly: fourth foal: half-sister to 2 winners by A P Indy, including 1¼m winner Lunar Colony: dam, US 8.5f and 9f winner, sister to Breeders' Cup Juvenile Fillies winner Pleasant Stage: improved into a smart performer: won maiden at Navan at 2 yrs, handicap at Leopardstown in May and listed race at Cork (beat Sina Cova by a length) in August: good 1½ lengths third to Safari Queen in Grade 2 Long Island Handicap at Aqueduct final outing: stamina seemed stretched under testing conditions when only fourth to Acts of Grace in Princess Royal Stakes at Ascot on penultimate start: stays 1½m: acts on good to firm going. *D. K. Weld, Ireland*

REGAL CONNECTION (USA) 3 b.f. Deputy Commander (USA) 124 – Clever Empress (Crafty Prospector (USA)) [2006 76: 12s⁵ 10m 10.4m⁶ 10f⁴ 10m⁴ 11.5m* 11.9m³ 10.5s⁵ 11.6d Oct 9] tall, leggy filly: fair performer: won handicap at Carlisle in August, racing alone in straight: stays 11.5f: acts on good to firm and good to soft going: blinkered last 5 starts: races prominently: found little/hung right seventh outing: sold 55,000 gns, sent to Saudi Arabia. *M. Johnston* **75**

REGAL CURTSY 2 b.f. (Mar 1) Royal Applause 124 – Giant Nipper (Nashwan (USA) 135) [2006 p8g 6s p6g⁴ Nov 24] smallish filly: fifth foal: sister to 5-y-o Take A Bow and half-sister to 3 winners, including 3-y-o Woodcote Place: dam ran once: maiden: seemingly best run when seventh to Party at Newbury (only start on turf). *P. R. Chamings* **67**

REGAL DREAM (IRE) 4 b.c. Namid 128 – Lovely Me (IRE) 70 (Vision (USA)) [2006 82, a76: p7g⁵ p7g 7m³ 7m⁴ 7m⁵ 6f 6m⁴ 7m 7m⁵ p7.1g⁶ 7d Sep 25] fair handicapper: stays 7f: acts on polytrack and firm going: tried tongue tied/visored: has been slowly away: usually held up: sold 15,000 gns. *J. W. Hills* **75**

REGAL FANTASY (IRE) 6 b.m. King's Theatre (IRE) 128 – Threesome (USA) 79 (Seattle Dancer (USA) 119) [2006 –: 13d⁵ Jun 21] poor performer: stays 2m: acts on firm going, seemingly on good to soft. *P. A. Blockley* **42**

REGAL FLUSH 2 b.c. (Mar 17) Sakhee (USA) 136 – Ruthless Rose (USA) (Conquistador Cielo (USA)) [2006 7m⁴ 7.1g² 8.2d* Nov 1] strong, close-coupled colt: half-brother to several winners, including smart 2000 2-y-o 6f (including Cheveley Park Stakes) winner Regal Rose (by Danehill) and 3-y-o Regal Velvet: dam twice-raced half-sister to high-class miler Shaadi: fairly useful form in maidens, in frame at Newbury and Sandown (second to Big Robert) prior to winning at Nottingham by 4 lengths from Dawn Sky: will stay 1¼m: will do better. *Sir Michael Stoute* **83 p**

REGAL LASS 3 b.f. Royal Applause 124 – Faraway Lass 94 (Distant Relative 128) [2006 –: 7m f7g Oct 12] little form. *J. G. Given* **–**

REGAL OVATION 2 b.g. (Apr 2) Royal Applause 124 – Briggsmaid 70 (Elegant Air 119) [2006 5.1g 6g 6m³ 7m⁶ 7m 8g 7f⁶ 10g² Sep 26] sturdy gelding: modest maiden: second in nursery final start (gelded after): stays 1¼m: raced on good going or firmer. *W. R. Muir* **60**

REGAL QUEST (IRE) 2 b.f. (Mar 9) Marju (IRE) 127 – Princess Sceptre (Cadeaux Genereux 131) [2006 6m⁶ 7f p7g* 7d⁵ Sep 30] 27,000F: good-bodied filly: third foal: half-sister to 5-y-o Soviet Sceptre: dam lightly-raced half-sister to useful performer up to 1½m Humourless: fairly useful form: won maiden at Kempton by 4 lengths in September: again raced freely when sixth to Blithe in nursery at Newmarket: should stay 1m. *S. Kirk* **83**

REGAL RAIDER (IRE) 3 b.g. King's Best (USA) 132 – Alegranza (IRE) 106 (Lake Coniston (IRE) 131) [2006 7g 7f⁴ 8m p7.1g* p7.1g p7.1g³ Dec 31] €160,000F, 11,000 2-y-o: leggy gelding: first foal: dam, Irish 5f winner, out of half-sister to very smart 6f/7f performer Mount Abu: fairly useful performer: won handicap at Wolverhampton in December: stays 7f: acts on polytrack. *I. Semple* **84**

REGAL RIBAND 2 b.f. (Jan 9) Fantastic Light (USA) 134 – Regal Rose 110 (Danehill (USA) 126) [2006 p7.1s⁴ p7.1g* p7.1g³ Dec 28] second foal: half-sister to 3-y-o Regal Royale: dam, 2-y-o 6f winner (including Cheveley Park Stakes), out of half-sister to high-class miler Shaadi: green on debut, and improved to win maiden at Wolverhampton (by 5 lengths from Conny Nobel, eased) in December: odds on, carried head awkwardly when last of 3 in minor event there: will stay 1m. *Sir Mark Prescott* **79**

REGAL ROYALE 3 b.g. Medicean 128 – Regal Rose 110 (Danehill (USA) 126) [2006 93p: 7g 8m² 10.1m 8m⁵ 8m 8m⁵ p7g⁶ p7g p10g Nov 25] well-made gelding: useful performer: good efforts at Newmarket (1½ lengths second to Dunelight), Ascot (fifth behind Sir Gerard in Britannia Stakes) and Lingfield second/fourth/seventh outings: left Sir Michael Stoute 21,000 gns, well held last 2 starts: bred to stay 1¼m: acts on polytrack, raced only on good/good to firm going on turf: tried visored (found little): seems none too genuine. *Peter Grayson* **98**

REGAL SETTING (IRE) 5 br.g. King's Theatre (IRE) 128 – Cartier Bijoux 96 (Ahonoora 122) [2006 82: 14m Jun 3] quite good-topped gelding: useful performer at 3 yrs: lightly raced on Flat since, and tailed off only outing in 2006. *J. Howard Johnson*

REGAL SUNSET (IRE) 3 b.g. Desert Prince (IRE) 130 – Sunsetter (USA) 94 (Diesis **73** 133) [2006 p8g⁶ p9.5g⁴ 8.3d⁴ p8g p6g 7.1d Oct 13] €60,000Y: close-coupled, good-topped gelding: first foal: dam ninth in Cheveley Park Stakes and sixth in Nell Gwyn Stakes, only starts: fair maiden: stays 9.5f: acts on polytrack and good to soft going: visored/in cheekpieces last 2 starts: sold 9,000 gns, joined D. Cantillon. *W. R. Swinburn*

REGAL VELVET 3 b.f. Halling (USA) 133 – Ruthless Rose (USA) (Conquistador **81** Cielo (USA)) [2006 72p: 8.3f³ 8m⁶ 8.1m² 10.2m* 10g Oct 12] rather leggy filly: fairly useful performer: won maiden at Bath in September: stiff task and well held in listed race at Newmarket next time: stays 1¼m: raced only on good going or firmer. *J. H. M. Gosden*

REGENCY RED (IRE) 8 ch.g. Dolphin Street (FR) 125 – Future Romance (Distant **64** Relative 128) [2006 56, a60: p9.5g² p12.2g* p12.2g⁶ p12.2g⁵ f12g⁵ 12f² 11.5f² 13m³ 14.1f³ 11.9m² 13.4f⁵ p13.9g⁴ p12.2g⁴ p12.2g² p12.2g³ p12.2s* p12.2g⁶ Dec 23] lengthy gelding: modest performer: won handicaps at Wolverhampton in January (seller) and December: effective at 9.5f to 2m: acts on all-weather and firm going: sometimes carries head awkwardly/finds little, but is reliable. *W. M. Brisbourne*

REGENT'S PARK 3 b.f. Green Desert (USA) 127 – New Assembly (IRE) 99 **83** (Machiavellian (USA) 123) [2006 7m⁵ 8.2m⁴ p10g³ 11.7g⁴ 10m² 9.7d² 10g* Sep 12] useful-looking filly: third foal: dam, 9f (in USA) to 1½m winner, sister to very smart 1m/ 1¼m performer Right Approach: fairly useful performer: in frame 5 starts prior to winning handicap at Lingfield in September: stays 11.6f: acts on polytrack, good to firm and good to soft ground: races prominently. *R. Charlton*

REGENT'S SECRET (USA) 6 br.g. Cryptoclearance (USA) – Misty Regent (CAN) **89** (Vice Regent (CAN)) [2006 87: 7.1g 7.1m⁵ 10d 8.3m³ 7.9g* 7.9m² 10m⁶ 8.1m⁶ 8.3g 8.3g² p9.5g⁵ p9.5m³ p9.5g⁴ Nov 25] leggy, useful-looking gelding: fairly useful handicapper: won at Carlisle in June: stays 1¼m: acts on polytrack, firm and soft going (well beaten on heavy): tried visored/in cheekpieces: waited with: consistent. *J. S. Goldie*

REGGAE RHYTHM (IRE) 12 b.g. Be My Native (USA) 122 – Invery Lady 65 **83** (Sharpen Up 127) [2006 72: p16g* p16g³ p16g² 16s May 24] strong gelding: fairly useful performer: won handicap at Lingfield in January: barely stays 2¼m: acts on polytrack and soft going. *A. J. Lidderdale*

REGIME (IRE) 2 b.c. (Apr 10) Golan (IRE) 129 – Juno Madonna (IRE) (Sadler's **106** Wells (USA) 132) [2006 8d⁴ 8.5g* 7d² 8s Oct 21] 17,000F, €120,000Y: close-coupled colt: sixth foal: half-brother to 3 winners, including 3-y-o Salut d'Amour and Irish 1½m and 17f winner Coquette Rouge (by Croco Rouge): dam, ran twice in France, closely related to useful sprinters Title Roll and Northern Express: useful form: won maiden at Beverley in August: further marked progress when 1¼ lengths second of 28 to Miss Beatrix in very valuable sales race at the Curragh, clear on his side (from Finsceal Beo): 15/2, nervy beforehand when only seventh of 14 to Authorized in Racing Post Trophy at Newbury, beaten when bumped wider still over 1f out: will probably stay 1¼m/1½m: raced on good going or softer. *M. L. W. Bell*

REGIONAL COUNSEL 2 b.c. (Mar 10) Medicean 128 – Regency Rose (Danehill **99** (USA) 126) [2006 6m² 7m* 6.3m* 7g⁵ Aug 26] 45,000F, 80,000Y: first foal: dam un-raced sister to Cheveley Park Stakes winner Regal Rose: useful performer: won maiden at Limerick in June and 7-runner Dubai Duty Free Anglesey Stakes at the Curragh (beat Sadeek by neck) in July: around 6 lengths fifth of 7 to Teofilo in Futurity Stakes at the Curragh: likely to stay 1m: raced on good/good to firm ground. *K. Prendergast, Ireland*

REHEARSAL 5 b.g. Singspiel (IRE) 133 – Daralaka (IRE) (The Minstrel (CAN) 135) **102** [2006 102: p12g² p12g⁴ 12.1d⁴ 12m⁶ 12f⁶ 16g⁴ 13.1d⁵ Sep 16] lengthy, good-topped gelding: useful handicapper: several at least creditable efforts in 2006, including at Lingfield first 2 starts and Royal Ascot (sixth to Young Mick in Duke of Edinburgh Stakes) on fourth: blinkered, well below form final outing: probably stays 2m: acts on polytrack, firm and good to soft going: free-going sort. *L. Lungo*

REHEARSED (IRE) 3 ch.f. In The Wings 128 – Emilia Romagna (GER) (Acatenango **79** (GER) 127) [2006 67: 11.6g⁴ 14.1g⁵ 14m 14.1m* 14.1g³ 14.1g² 16g p16.5m* p13.9g* Nov 2] strong filly: fair handicapper: won at Salisbury in July and Wolverhampton in October and November: stays 2m: acts on polytrack, unraced on extremes of going on turf. *H. Morrison*

REINSTATED (IRE) 3 b.f. Galileo (IRE) 134 – Miletrian (IRE) 113 (Marju (IRE) **80** 127) [2006 –: 7s 10g³ 11.7m³ 12g⁴ 14g³ p12g³ 16g² p16.5g⁶ p16.5g² f12g⁵ Nov 20] angular filly: fairly useful maiden: stays 2m: acts on polytrack and good to firm ground: has run well when sweating. *B. W. Hills*

RELKIDA 2 b.f. (Mar 14) Bertolini (USA) 125 – Roofer (IRE) 80 (Barathea (IRE) 127) **76**
[2006 5d³ 6g³ 5m* 5.1f² 5.1f² 7m 5g⁴ 6m⁵ Sep 7] lengthy filly: has scope: first foal: dam,
maiden who stayed 9f, half-sister to smart 7f/1m winner Brunel: fair performer: won
maiden at Windsor in July: largely creditable efforts otherwise: should stay 7f/1m: acts
on firm and good to soft going: often slowly away. *M. R. Channon*

RELOAD (IRE) 3 b.c. Minardi (USA) 119 – Rapid Action (USA) (Quest For Fame **66**
127) [2006 p8g⁴ p8g Sep 27] 46,000Y: first foal: dam unraced half-sister to smart 1998
2-y-o 7f winner Auction House: better efforts in maidens when fourth at Kempton on
debut: pulled hard early, then off bridle before halfway next time. *J. Noseda*

RELOCATION (IRE) 5 b.g. Grand Lodge (USA) 125 – Olean (Sadler's Wells (USA) **–**
132) [2006 60: p16.5g Mar 3] fair form only 2-y-o outing: modest form at best since: left
P. Prendergast in Ireland, well beaten in handicap at Wolverhampton only start in Britain:
probably stays 1¾m: acts on firm going. *J. J. Lambe, Ireland*

RELUCTANT SUITOR 4 b.g. Singspiel (IRE) 133 – Belle Esprit (Warning 136) **79**
[2006 76: 14g* 14m² 13.9s⁵ 13m³ 12f² 14g³ 10d⁶ 13.4f⁴ 13.1s² 16d² Nov 3] close-
coupled gelding: fair handicapper: won at Musselburgh in April: stays 2m: acts on firm
and soft ground: wore cheekpieces last 2 starts: races freely. *J. S. Goldie*

REMARK (IRE) 2 b.g. (Feb 19) Machiavellian (USA) 123 – Remuria (USA) 93 **50**
(Theatrical 128) [2006 5.5g⁴ 8s⁵ 5.1d⁵ 6d Nov 4] unfurnished gelding: third foal: dam,
Irish 1¼m winner, out of smart French/US performer up to around 1¼m Reloy: flattered
in minor events for A. Fabre in France first 2 starts (sold 5,500 gns, and gelded): modest
form on first of 2 outings in maidens in Britain (tongue tied). *M. W. Easterby*

REMBRANDT QUALITY (USA) 3 b.c. Elusive Quality (USA) – My Sister Sarah **67**
(USA) (Dr Geo Adams (USA)) [2006 77: 7.1m 7m 6f⁵ 8m² 7m² 7.5m Sep 19] rangy colt:
fair maiden: left Mrs A. Perrett 17,000 gns after second outing: likely to stay 1¼m: acts
on polytrack, good to firm and good to soft going: blinkered last 2 starts: sold 13,000 gns.
N. A. Callaghan

REMEMBER RAMON (USA) 3 ch.g. Diesis 133 – Future Act (USA) 94 (Known **95**
Fact (USA) 135) [2006 77: 12g* 11.6g* 12.3m⁶ 12g⁵ 16d⁴ Oct 27] good-topped gelding:
useful performer: won maiden at Musselburgh in April and handicap at Windsor in
May: bit slipped through mouth and virtually pulled up next time: gelded after fourth
start: creditable fourth in handicap at Newmarket final outing: barely stays 2m: unraced
on extremes of going on turf: joined P. Hobbs. *M. J. Wallace*

REMINISCENT (IRE) 7 b.g. Kahyasi 130 – Eliza Orzeszkowa (IRE) 69 (Polish **–**
Patriot (USA) 128) [2006 63, a66: p12.2g⁵ f14g p13.9g* p12.2g⁴ p12.2g 13f⁶ 13.9m **a65**
p12.2g Dec 23] rather leggy gelding: fair handicapper on all-weather, modest at best (no
form in 2006) on turf: won at Wolverhampton (amateurs) in March: stays 2m: acts on
all-weather and firm going: usually wears headgear: often slowly away. *B. P. J. Baugh*

REM TIME (IRE) 6 b.m. Fraam 114 – Any Dream (IRE) 81 (Shernazar 131) [2006 **55**
57: 7f⁵ p9.5f³ 8d Aug 21] modest performer: stays 10.5f: acts on polytrack, good to soft
and good to firm ground. *John Berry*

RENDEROC (USA) 3 ch.g. Mt Livermore (USA) – Rewarding (USA) (Storm Bird **84**
(CAN) 134) [2006 83: a7f a8f 8s⁵ 8.3m⁵ 8m 7.5f⁶ 8g 8m⁴ p7g Oct 11] workmanlike
gelding: fairly useful performer: stays 1m: acts on polytrack and firm going, well held on
dirt: in cheekpieces last 4 starts: sweating (finished last) at Ascot seventh outing: sold
15,000 gns. *J. S. Moore*

RENEE LARD (IRE) 3 ch.f. Titus Livius (FR) 115 – Miss Body (IRE) (Hamas (IRE) **–**
125§) [2006 –: 8.3f⁶ 13.8m Sep 16] little form. *A. Berry*

RENEGADE (IRE) 5 b.g. Fasliyev (USA) 120 – Arcade (Rousillon (USA) 133) [2006 **64**
65, a60: p5g 6m³ p8g 6d 7m* 6g 6f⁶ 7m⁴ 7g⁴ 6g p6g p8g Dec 10] modest performer: won **a–**
seller at Brighton in June: stays 1m: acts on polytrack, soft and good to firm going: often
in cheekpieces/blinkers: races prominently. *Mrs L. J. Mongan*

RESCUE (USA) 2 b.c. (Feb 2) Red Ransom (USA) – Distinct Beauty (USA) (Phone **–**
Trick (USA)) [2006 6s May 27] good-bodied colt: 9/1: needed experience when seventh
in maiden at Newmarket won by Tariq. *M. R. Channon*

RESIGNATION (IRE) 2 b.c. (Mar 15) Invincible Spirit (IRE) 121 – Madrina 70 **99**
(Waajib 121) [2006 5g⁶ 5.1f* 5m 5.2g 5d⁴ 6m² 6d² p6g⁴ Oct 21] €44,000F, 20,000Y: tall;
close-coupled colt: sixth foal: half-brother to 3 winners, including 8-y-o Laurel Dawn
and 6-y-o Telepathic: dam, 6f winner, out of half-sister to very smart sprinter Bolshoi:
useful performer: won minor event at Bath in June: ran well most other starts, including

when second in similar races at Newmarket and Salisbury (short-headed by Dubai Builder) in September: best form at 6f: acts on polytrack, firm and good to soft going: sold 150,000 gns, sent to Hong Kong. *R. Hannon*

RESONANCE 5 b.m. Slip Anchor 136 – Music In My Life (IRE) 59 (Law Society (USA) 130) [2006 15.9m 14.1d Sep 27] useful-looking mare: maiden: well held both starts on Flat since 2004: blinkered final start: often slowly away. *S. Lycett* —

RESONATE (IRE) 8 b.h. Erins Isle 121 – Petronelli (USA) (Sir Ivor (USA) 135) [2006 87, a78: p10g⁵ 10g 7.9g 10m² 11.7m⁶ 10.1d* 11m⁴ 12d⁶ 10s⁶ 11.6d² p12g³ Dec 2] useful-looking horse: fairly useful handicapper on turf, fair on all-weather: won at Epsom in August: needs further than 1m nowadays, and stays 1½m: acts on polytrack, firm and soft going: held up: consistent. *A. G. Newcombe* **89 a79**

RESPECT MY WISHES 2 b.f. (Jan 17) Dansili 127 – Snow Shoes 84 (Sri Pekan (USA) 117) [2006 6d 5m p6g p8g Dec 18] 2,500Y: first foal: dam 6f winner (including at 2 yrs): last in maidens. *R. Ingram* —

RESPLENDENT ACE (IRE) 2 b.c. (May 4) Trans Island 119 – Persian Polly 99 (Persian Bold 123) [2006 p7g² Dec 3] €57,000Y: brother to 4-y-o Something and half-brother to several winners, including top-class 6f (including July Cup) winner Lake Coniston (by Bluebird) and useful performer up to 1¼m Treble Eight (by Kings Lake): dam Irish 2-y-o 7f winner: 6/1, encouraging short-head second to Nordic Affair in maiden at Lingfield, slowly away but finishing best of all: sure to improve, and should win a similar event. *P. Howling* **88 p**

RESPLENDENT ALPHA 2 ch.c. (Feb 11) Best of The Bests (IRE) 122 – Sunley Scent 85 (Wolfhound (USA) 126) [2006 p5g* 6g² 6m⁴ p6g* p6g² Oct 21] 31,000Y, 38,000 2-y-o: rather leggy colt: first foal: dam, 6f/7f winner, out of half-sister to dam of high-class miler Sonic Lady: useful form: won maiden in August (for T. Mills) and minor event (beat High Style by 1½ lengths) in October, both at Lingfield: strong-finishing second to Hinton Admiral in listed race there final start: will be suited by 7f/1m. *P. Howling* **97**

RESPLENDENT GLORY (IRE) 4 ch.c. Namid 128 – Aoife (IRE) 83 (Thatching 131) [2006 115: 5d 5m Jun 20] tall, leggy colt: smart performer: unraced at 2 yrs: won 6 of 7 starts in 2005, including Sprint Stakes at Sandown: suffered knee injury after: well held in Temple Stakes at Sandown (dismounted after line) and King's Stand Stakes at Royal Ascot (sweating, hung throughout) in 2006: raced only at 5f/6f: acted on polytrack, good to firm and good to soft going: raced up with pace: to stand at Benson Stud, Colchester, Essex, fee £2,000, Oct 1st terms. *T. G. Mills* —

RESPLENDENT NOVA 4 b.g. Pivotal 124 – Santiburi Girl 77 (Casteddu 111) [2006 72, a89: 7s³ 7d⁶ 6m² 6m p8.6m 7g* 7d² p7g² p7g² Nov 24] sturdy gelding: fairly useful performer: left T. Mills after fourth start: won handicap at Brighton in October: good efforts all 3 subsequent outings: effective at 6f to 1m: acts on polytrack, soft and good to firm going: tried visored (ran poorly): sometimes makes running. *P. Howling* **90**

RESPLENDENT PRINCE 4 ch.g. Primo Dominie 121 – Last Result (Northern Park (USA) 107) [2006 60, a73: f7g* f7g⁵ p7g f7g⁵ f7g p8.6g 7g p7.1g⁴ p7.1g f8g* p7.1g² p7.1g Jul 11] leggy, lengthy gelding: fair on all-weather, modest on turf: won seller at Southwell in January and, having been claimed from T. Mills £6,000 after fourth start, similar event there in June: stays 1m: acts on all-weather, best turf effort on good to firm ground: visored: sometimes races freely: sold 6,500 gns. *P. Howling* **a71**

RESSOURCE (FR) 7 b.g. Broadway Flyer (USA) 121 – Rayonne (Sadler's Wells (USA) 132) [2006 41: p16.5g Jan 6] poor maiden, lightly raced: probably stays 2m: acts on polytrack: blinkered last 4 starts. *G. L. Moore* —

RESTLESS SOUL 2 b.f. (Mar 1) Singspiel (IRE) 133 – Seasonal Splendour (IRE) 95 (Prince Rupert (FR) 121) [2006 p8g Nov 15] half-sister to 3 winners, including smart 1¾m winner When In Rome (by Saddlers' Hall) and useful 1¼m/1½m winner Strength 'n Honour (by Hernando): dam 1½m and hurdles winner who stayed 2m: 20/1 and green, always towards rear in maiden at Kempton (fractious in stall). *C. A. Cyzer* —

RETALIATE 2 br.f. (Jan 15) Wizard King 122 – Retaliator 80 (Rudimentary (USA) 118) [2006 5.1g⁵ 5g⁵ 5.2f³ 5.7f 6d* 7m 6d* 6g³ 6v² Oct 31] 3,200Y: strong, workmanlike filly: third foal: sister to 3-y-o King's Revenge and half-sister to 2003 2-y-o 6f winner Melody King (by Merdon Melody): dam 6f (including at 2 yrs)/7f winner: fair performer: won claimers at Yarmouth in August and Lingfield in September: placed in nurseries after, better run when third to Cheap Street at Newmarket: should prove best at 5f/6f: acts on good to soft going: forces pace. *M. Quinn* **75**

RETIREMENT 7 b.g. Zilzal (USA) 137 – Adeptation (USA) (Exceller (USA) 129) –
[2006 71d: 8.1d p10g Sep 27] leggy, good-topped gelding: unimpressive mover: on
downgrade and well held both outings in 2006: tried in cheekpieces. *R. M. Stronge*

RETURN IN STYLE (IRE) 5 b.g. Desert Style (IRE) 121 – Silver Echo (Caerleon 53
(USA) 132) [2006 p8g 8d 10f³ p10g Jun 24] lightly-raced maiden: fairly useful form in
2004: well held both outings at 4 yrs, then left J. de Roualle in France: only placing in
2006 (probably flattered on reappearance) when third in claimer at Brighton: stays 1¼m:
acts on good to soft ground, probably on polytrack: tried blinkered/in cheekpieces.
J. W. Hills

REUNITE (IRE) 3 ch.f. Kingmambo (USA) 125   Allez Les Trois (USA) 114 (River- 111
man (USA) 131) [2006 79p: 10m* 12m⁵ 10.1f* 12m² 10g² Aug 26] useful-looking filly:
progressed into a smart performer in 2006, winning handicap at Nottingham in June and
listed race at Yarmouth (beat Local Spirit easily by 2½ lengths) in July: good second in
listed event at Newbury (1¼ lengths behind Fermion) and Winter Hill Stakes at Windsor
(beaten ½ length by Tam Lin) last 2 starts: suffered minor setback after: stays 1½m: acts
on any going. *Saeed bin Suroor*

REVE LUNAIRE (USA) 3 b.c. Hennessy (USA) 122 – My Dream Castles (USA) 104
(Woodman (USA) 126) [2006 7d³ 7m⁴ 8s⁴ 8g² a9.5g* Jul 30] medium-sized, lengthy colt:
first foal: dam, 8.5f winner in USA, out of close relative to July Cup winner Agnes World
and half-sister to dam of Dubai Destination and Librettist: useful performer: won newcomers race at Maisons-Laffitte only start at 2 yrs and 4-runner listed race at Deauville
(beat Pointilliste a nose) in July: mostly creditable efforts previously, including when 3¼
lengths fourth of 5 to Red Clubs in Greenham Stakes at Newbury second outing: stays
9.5f: acts on all-weather at Deauville and good to firm going, probably on soft: sold
€150,000 in September. *A. Fabre, France*

Godolphin's "Reunite"

REVERENCE   5 ch.g. Mark of Esteem (IRE) 137 – Imperial Bailiwick (IRE) 104   **127**
(Imperial Frontier (USA) 112) [2006 106p: 6s³ 5.1s* 5m⁴ 5d* 5m 5m⁵ 5s* 6s* 5m²
Oct 1]

    A fractured pelvis can be a grave injury for a thoroughbred and usually
results in fatality if the horse is going full tilt at the time and the break leads to
internal bleeding. Stress fractures of the pelvis in training, which are much less
likely to lead to death and often allow the victim to return to action, are pretty small
in number judged on a thesis presented to London University in 2005. One of the
findings of this thesis, based on a study for up to two years of more than a thousand
horses in the care of thirteen trainers, including Luca Cumani, Simon Dow, John
Gosden, Mark Johnston, Jeremy Noseda and Marcus Tregoning, was that twenty of
the subjects suffered pelvic stress fractures. Assuming this figure of less than two
per cent is applicable to the whole population of horses in training, the influence
during the last few seasons of horses who have suffered this injury and recovered
is noteworthy. Media Puzzle fractured his pelvis in 2000 before going on to win
the Melbourne Cup two years later, while the smart sprinter Bishops Court, who
cracked his pelvis in 2001, bounced back to win two listed races the following year.
The 2005 Prix Royal-Oak winner Alcazar had no fewer than three fractures of his
pelvis. A year on, the stallion Intikhab, who broke his pelvis on his only start as a
five-year-old in 1999, was responsible for Matron Stakes winner Red Evie. And
then there is Reverence, who offers almost as striking an example as Alcazar.
Initially in training with Mark Johnston, he broke his pelvis as a juvenile, then
repeated the dose at three with William Haggas. Working on the theory that being
trained on uphill gallops doesn't work for some young horses who may be
vulnerable to injury because still growing, or those who have had pelvic fractures,
Reverence's owners moved him to Eric Alston, whose training is done on flatter
terrain. Reverence, who had been gelded as a three-year-old, reached the track for
the first time at the age of four but such are the strides he has made in his first two
seasons that he is now the best specialist sprinter trained in Europe. Even his
owners, it seems, must briefly have regarded Reverence as a lost cause, entering
him at the sales as a three-year-old before withdrawing him (they had bought him
back for 97,000 guineas as a yearling). Let's hope Reverence remains sound and in
good heart and stays in the top flight for at least another season, maybe more.

    Reverence did not win on his debut in May 2005 and was off the course for
three months afterwards, but he soon made up for lost time on his return, winning
a maiden at Ripon and three handicaps from four more appearances and his Timeform
rating rose from 75 to 106p. His only defeats came on his two outings at six furlongs
and all his races were run on good going or softer, a reflection of his trainer's
understandable caution. The final success at Doncaster, where Reverence won in
great style by three and a half lengths from King's Gait, indicated he was well worth
his place in better company and he didn't take long confirming the point when
reappearing. Beaten by fitter horses when third to Les Arcs in the Cammidge
Trophy at Redcar in March, when he also showed he was fully effective at six
furlongs, Reverence easily landed the odds from Bahamian Pirate in a minor event
at Nottingham and was beaten only a length into fourth behind Dandy Man on his

VC Bet Nunthorpe Stakes, York—
Reverence makes further improvement on his first outing in Group 1 company;
Amadeus Wolf (noseband) is second ahead of Pivotal Flame, The Trader (right) and Red Clubs (No.15)

Betfred Sprint Cup, Haydock—Reverence completes the Nunthorpe/Sprint Cup double last achieved by Dayjur in 1990; Quito runs a fine race to be second with Amadeus Wolf (rail) again making the frame ahead of Somnus (far right), Red Clubs and Excusez Moi

first outing in pattern company in the Palace House Stakes at Newmarket in May. Reverence finished strongly in the latter, his first outing on ground faster than good, giving the impression more testing conditions would probably suit him over five furlongs. The going was good to soft for the betfair.com Temple Stakes at Sandown at the end of May and Reverence, who started favourite, showed his best form to that point by storming three lengths clear over a furlong out and winning by a length and a quarter from The Trader after tending to lose concentration and coming under the whip in the last fifty yards.

The firmish going was not in Reverence's favour in the King's Stand Stakes at Royal Ascot or the Sprint Stakes at Sandown on his next two starts. Nor did he have the run of the race in either, being buffeted and squeezed when sixteenth to Takeover Target in the King's Stand and having to race widest of all when fifth behind Pivotal Point at Sandown. Reverence's form in the latter, in which he gave weight away all round, was on a par with the Temple Stakes. With the going at York turned soft by heavy rain overnight before the VC Bet Nunthorpe Stakes towards the end of August, conditions were ideal for Reverence. Notable absentees from the field of fourteen included Les Arcs and Takeover Target and, in truth, it was not a vintage line-up except in terms of the age of the runners—there were two seven-year-olds, two eight year-olds and a nine-year-old. However, there were only two Group 1 winners, Amadeus Wolf, who had yet to get off the mark as a three-year-old, and Fayr Jag. Reverence started joint third favourite with Amadeus Wolf behind the in-form three-year-old Dandy Man and Moss Vale, who had been successful in three pattern races during the season. The only other runner at odds shorter than 14/1 was the two-year-old Enticing, who had won the Molecomb Stakes. In a race where few of the runners were able to get involved, the first three home were in the firing line throughout, Reverence being one of them. Bursting clear entering the final furlong, he passed the post with two lengths to spare over

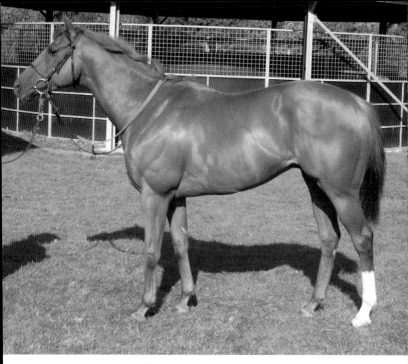

Mr & Mrs G. Middlebrook's "Reverence"

Amadeus Wolf with Pivotal Flame a close third, followed by veteran The Trader and Greenham Stakes winner Red Clubs. Reverence's task was made easier by the fact that Dandy Man, Enticing and Moss Vale were below form and the last three to finish, but it was still a high-class performance from Reverence, one which placed him at the top of the tree among the season's sprinters.

The Yorkshire-Lancashire Group 1 sprint double of Nunthorpe Stakes and Sprint Cup at Haydock has not been landed that often in the same season. Even though the two races come fairly close together, with a gap of nine days between the latest renewals, plenty of Nunthorpe winners have tried to do the double. Reverence added his name to a roll of honour containing only three names, Habibti, Ajdal and Dayjur, though Sheikh Albadou and Nuclear Debate won the two races in different seasons. Sheikh Albadou was second at Haydock the year he won the Nunthorpe and Nuclear Debate was second in the Nunthorpe before his win at Haydock. To the extent that the ground was soft for the Betfred-sponsored race, forcing the withdrawal of certain favourite Iffraaj, the elements favoured Reverence and he headed the market against ten rivals. These included four he had beaten at York, notably Amadeus Wolf, plus the Sprint Cup's standing dish Somnus, Golden Jubilee Stakes runner-up Balthazaar's Gift, tough-as-teak Quito, and Excusez Moi, successful in the Great St Wilfrid Handicap under 9-4. Given a canny ride by Kevin Darley, Reverence was soon handy, kicked two lengths clear a furlong out and, despite tiring noticeably near the finish, held on by a neck from Quito with Amadeus Wolf, who faltered in the middle of the race, staying on strongly in third. The time was one of the slowest in the race's history and the form was not quite on a par with the Nunthorpe, though it was still very smart. Back on good to firm going again in the Prix de l'Abbaye de Longchamp in October, Reverence still started favourite. Unable to get near the front in the early stages before keeping on in fine style from halfway, the post came just too soon as Reverence went down by a neck to Desert Lord with Moss Vale a close third. This was the second time Reverence's trainer had saddled a runner-up in the Abbaye—the six-year-old mare Stack Rock was second to Lochsong in 1993. Perhaps Reverence will go one better in 2007.

		Mark of Esteem (IRE) (b 1993)	Darshaan (br 1981)	Shirley Heights
				Delsy
Reverence			Homage (b 1989)	Ajdal
(ch.g. 2001)				Home Love
		Imperial Bailiwick (IRE) (b 1991)	Imperial Frontier (ch 1984)	Lyphard
				Hartebeest
			Syndikos (b 1973)	Nashua
				Court Action

Reverence's speed appears to come principally from his dam since he is the only pattern winner over five furlongs by Mark of Esteem. Not that Mark of Esteem has had an abundant supply of pattern winners over any distance, with a strike rate of only five per cent. Ironically, after the achievements of Sir Percy and Reverence had given him his best year, his stud career is now in abeyance while declining fertility is investigated. Reverence's dam Imperial Bailiwick was certainly speedy, showing useful form when winning three of her ten races as a two-year-old including the Flying Childers. A small filly, she trained on well enough to finish third in the Prix du Petit Couvert. Imperial Bailiwick has been covered by a wide variety of stallions, including Efisio, Generous, Rainbow Quest and Oasis Dream in Europe and Woodman and Wild Again in the States. The Efisio colt Luciano Brioschi won at five to seven furlongs in Italy and, despite being by Generous, the three-year-old filly Fortress seems best at six furlongs, over which trip she landed a handicap at Carlisle in August. Imperial Bailiwick's colt by Wild Again, the smart Helm Bank, showed more stamina than his siblings after picking up the listed Chesham Stakes as a juvenile, winning over a mile and staying a mile and a quarter. The foal by Oasis Dream produced in April looks a safe bet to be a sprinter. The grandam Syndikos and third dam Court Action were both raced in America without success, though the former was placed six times. Court Action was a half-sister to high-class colt Stupendous, but, until Imperial Bailiwick turned up, recent stakes performers were few and far between in the family. Considering the size, or lack of size, of Imperial Bailiwick, Reverence's imposing appearance is an eye-opener. He is a typical sprinter, strong and heavy-bodied, and invariably takes the eye in the preliminaries. Reverence is also as game, genuine and consistent as they come, a thoroughly admirable individual in every respect and a credit to his owners and his trainer. *E. J. Alston*

REVEUR 3 b.f. Rossini (USA) 118 – Without Warning (IRE) (Warning 136) [2006 68: p9.5g* p8.6g⁵ 10.5g² 12.3m⁵ 8.2s p12.2g 10.3g p9.5g p8.6g Dec 30] angular filly: fair handicapper: won at Wolverhampton in January: stays 10.5f: acts on polytrack, raced mainly on good/good to firm ground on turf. *M. Mullineaux*   **69**

REVIEN (IRE) 4 b.g. Rossini (USA) 118 – Kazimiera (IRE) 77 (Polish Patriot (USA) 128) [2006 67, a65: p6g p5.1g p7.1g p7.1g 6m 6m⁶ 6m 5m 6m Aug 11] well-made gelding: modest performer on all-weather, poor on turf nowadays: stays 7f, but likely to prove best at 5f/6f: acts on polytrack, raced only on good/good to firm going on turf: tried blinkered: usually tracks pace: has looked difficult ride. *Miss J. R. Tooth*   **46 a56**

REVISIONIST (IRE) 2 b.g. (Feb 3) Indian Danehill 124 – Lady of Dreams (IRE) 84 (Prince Rupert (FR) 121) [2006 6g 7g 7m⁶ 7m 10g⁴ 8s³ p8.6g Nov 3] 33,000Y: big, strong gelding: half-brother to several winners, including 3-y-o Shogun Prince and 6-y-o Trance: dam, 1¼m winner, out of half-sister to very smart miler Pennine Walk: fair maiden: twice in frame in nurseries: stays 1¼m: acts on soft and good to firm going: gelded after final start. *R. Hannon*   **67**

REVIVING (IRE) 3 b.g. Fasliyev (USA) 120 – Hartstown House (IRE) 83 (Primo Dominie 121) [2006 77: p6g 7s 8.3m 5.3m 6.1f Jul 8] close-coupled gelding: fair maiden at 2 yrs: little form in 2006: pulled hard second/third outings. *R. F. Johnson Houghton*   **–**

REVOLVE 6 b.g. Pivotal 124 – Alpine Time (IRE) 85 (Tirol 127) [2006 57: p10g* **63** p10g* p10g² p10g⁴ p10g⁶ p12g⁴ p11g⁵ p10g⁴ p10g² p10g* p10g* Dec 22] modest performer: won banded races at Lingfield in February, Kempton in May, and Lingfield and Kempton in December: effective at 1¼m to 13f: acts on polytrack, good to firm and good to soft ground: usually blinkered/in cheekpieces: bled final 5-y-o start. *Mrs L. J. Mongan*

REVOLVING WORLD (IRE) 3 b.c. Spinning World (USA) 130 – Mannakea **55** (USA) (Fairy King (USA)) [2006 –: 10.1g 9v 9m 12.4d p12g f12g Dec 29] modest maiden: tried blinkered/in cheekpieces: tongue tied last 2 starts. *T. J. Fitzgerald*

REYADI (IRE) 6 b.g. Peintre Celebre (USA) 137 – Valley of Hope (USA) (Riverman **–** (USA) 131) [2006 7s Oct 14] good-bodied gelding: lightly raced: fairly useful form at 3 yrs: well held only outing since. *T. D. Easterby*

REZEEZ (USA) 2 b. or br.c. (Mar 6) Seeking The Gold (USA) – Mehthaaf (USA) **– p** 121 (Nureyev (USA) 131) [2006 7.1m Sep 4] small colt: half-brother to several winners, including 1¼m winners Najah (smart, by Nashwan) and Tanaghum (useful, by Darshaan), latter stayed 1½m: dam, 6f (at 2 yrs) to 1m (Irish 1000 Guineas) winner, closely related to July Cup winner Elnadim from family of Dubai Millennium (by Seeking The Gold): 16/1, hampered after 2f and not knocked about in maiden at Warwick: capable of better. *W. J. Haggas*

REZZAGO (USA) 6 b.g. Night Shift (USA) – Western Friend (USA) (Gone West **85** (USA)) [2006 88: p6g³ p6g⁵ p6g 6m⁴ p7g² 7f⁵ p6g⁴ p7g⁵ p7.1m⁴ p7.1g³ p7g⁵ p7g⁵ Nov 29] good-topped gelding: fairly useful handicapper: best at 6f/7f: acts on polytrack and firm going: waited with: consistent. *W. R. Swinburn*

RHAAM 2 b.c. (Apr 4) Fantastic Light (USA) 134 – Elhilmeya (IRE) 94 (Unfuwain **80 p** (USA) 131) [2006 7d⁴ Sep 29] fourth foal: half-brother to 4-y-o Alfie Flits: dam won at 10.5f from 2 starts: 12/1, promising 5½ lengths fourth to Supersonic Dave in maiden at Newmarket: sure to improve as stamina is tested more (will stay 1½m). *B. W. Hills*

RHETORICAL 5 b.g. Unfuwain (USA) 131 – Miswaki Belle (USA) 73 (Miswaki **–** (USA) 124) [2006 –: p13g p16g 11.9m Apr 30] tall gelding: of little account nowadays: tried in headgear/tongue tied. *P. Butler*

RHINEBIRD 3 b.g. Lomitas 129 – Twitcher's Delight (Polar Falcon (USA) 126) [2006 **89** 67: 10m 10m* 9.9g p11g Sep 1] rather leggy gelding: fairly useful performer: won maiden at Newmarket in June: stays 1¼m: acts on good to firm going: held up: sold 20,000 gns. *J. R. Fanshawe*

RHUEPUNZEL 2 b.f. (Mar 2) Elnadim (USA) 128 – Fairy Story (IRE) 80 (Persian **62 p** Bold 123) [2006 6.1g⁴ Sep 26] closely related to 7f/1m winner (including at 2 yrs) Welenska (by Danzig Connection) and 6f (at 2 yrs) to 1m winner Zietory (by Zieten), both useful: dam, 7f winner (including at 2 yrs), out of half-sister to dam of Derby winner Shaamit: 7/1, fourth to Miss Ippolita in maiden at Nottingham: should progress. *P. F. I. Cole*

RHYMING SLANG (USA) 2 b. or br.c. (Feb 27) Street Cry (IRE) 130 – Purr Plea- **63 p** sure (USA) (El Gran Senor (USA) 136) [2006 6d⁵ Oct 9] $90,000Y: third foal: half-brother to a winner in USA by Mt Livermore: dam 6f to 9f (including at 8.5f at 2 yrs) winner in USA: 9/2, green before late headway into fifth in maiden at Windsor: will improve. *J. Noseda*

RIBH 3 b.f. Zafonic (USA) 130 – Torgau (IRE) 109 (Zieten (USA) 118) [2006 92: 6v **81** 6m⁴ p7g⁴ p7g³ p8.6g p7g Nov 29] quite good-topped filly: fairly useful maiden: had knee chip removed in 2005 and reported in late-May to be suffering from a stress fracture: returned in September: well below form last 3 starts: stays 7f: acts on polytrack, best effort on turf on good going: tried blinkered: flashed tail second outing. *C. E. Brittain*

RICHARDS CLAIRE (IRE) 5 b.m. Darazari (IRE) 123 – Loquacious (IRE) 79 **–** (Distinctly North (USA) 115) [2006 57: 16f p10g Dec 18] first foal: dam Irish 1½m/ hurdles winner: placed in bumpers: lightly-raced maiden on Flat: left C. Murphy in Ireland prior to final start (tongue tied). *D. P. Keane*

RICHELIEU 4 b.c. Machiavellian (USA) 123 – Darling Flame (USA) 101 (Capote **69** (USA)) [2006 5.8f³ 5f² 6s⁶ 7.2v 6v 7s p6g Nov 23] 12,000 3-y-o: fourth foal: closely related to 2003 2-y-o 6f winner Catherine Howard (by Kingmambo) and half-brother to smart French 7f winner Bezrin (by Danzig) and fairly useful Irish 7.5f winner Flamelet (by Theatrical): dam, 6f (at 2 yrs)/7f winner, half-sister to smart 7f/1m performer Heart

Lake: fair maiden: creditable seventh in handicap at Wolverhampton final start: stays 6f: acts on polytrack and firm ground. *J. J. Lambe, Ireland*

RICHIE BOY 5 b.g. Dr Fong (USA) 128 – Alathezal (USA) (Zilzal (USA) 137) [2006 –: 12g 10s May 20] smallish, leggy gelding: fair performer in 2004: lightly raced and well held since: tried in cheekpieces: gelded after final outing. *Jennie Candlish* —

RICHTEE (IRE) 5 ch.m. Desert Sun 120 – Santarene (IRE) 46 (Scenic 128) [2006 80: 9.9g 12g 12m* 11.8m 12f³ 12f 14.1f 10.5s 9.9m 12d Oct 2] strong mare: fair handicapper: won amateur event at York in June, easily best effort in 2006: stays easy 13f: acts on firm and soft going: tried in cheekpieces. *R. A. Fahey* **76 d**

RIDGEWAY CROSS (IRE) 3 gr.f. Cape Cross (IRE) 129 – Karatisa (IRE) 93 (Nishapour (FR) 125) [2006 62: p7g 8f Jul 9] tall, leggy filly: modest maiden at 2 yrs: well held in 2006: sometimes slowly away. *E. R. Oertel* —

RIFAAT 3 ch.g. Nashwan (USA) 135 – Swame (USA) (Jade Hunter (USA)) [2006 10d May 19] big, lengthy gelding: 28/1 and better for race, well held in maiden at Newbury: withdrawn (unruly stall) in June. *C. A. Horgan* **58**

RIFF RAFF 3 b.f. Daylami (IRE) 138 – Rafiya 89 (Halling (USA) 133) [2006 10m⁵ 11.5m⁵ 11.8m⁶ 14m⁴ 12m 14m* 15.9g⁵ p16g⁴ Sep 2] 37,000Y: small, quite attractive filly: first foal: dam, 1½m winner, daughter of smart 1¼m and 13.5f winner Nemesia: fair performer: won maiden at Lingfield in August: stays 2m: acts on good to firm ground: has started slowly/run in snatches: sold 18,000 gns. *W. Jarvis* **78**

RIFLEMAN (IRE) 6 ch.g. Starborough 126 – En Garde (USA) 82 (Irish River (FR) 131) [2006 7d p9.5m Oct 14] compact gelding: fairly useful handicapper in 2003: lightly raced and little form on Flat since (won over fences in April): tried visored/in cheekpieces/tongue tied. *B. Ellison* —

RIGAT 3 b.g. Dansili 127 – Fudge (Polar Falcon (USA) 126) [2006 7m 5f⁴ 7f* 8m 7s⁵ Oct 14] 26,000F, 32,000Y: tall, good-topped gelding: fourth foal: half-brother to 4-y-o Gloved Hand and 5-y-o Jackie Kiely: dam unraced half-sister to dam of Irish Derby second Definite Article: fair performer: won maiden at Thirsk in July: stays 1m: acts on firm ground. *T. D. Barron* **72**

RIGHT ANSWER 4 b.f. Lujain (USA) 119 – Quiz Show 82 (Primo Dominie 121) [2006 94: 5d 5.1g 5.1f May 11] tall, attractive filly: fairly useful performer at 3 yrs: well held in 2006. *T. D. Easterby* —

RIGHT OPTION (IRE) 2 b.g. (Mar 9) Daylami (IRE) 138 – Option (IRE) 52 (Red Ransom (USA)) [2006 p5g⁵ 6s 7.1m 8m⁵ p7.1g³ p8.6g p8.6g² p9.5g³ p8.6g³ f8g⁴ p9.5g² Dec 9] smallish, close-coupled gelding: modest maiden: left A. Jarvis after fifth start: placed in nurseries/claimer at Wolverhampton after: stays 9.5f: acts on polytrack, probably soft ground: tried in cheekpieces/blinkers: sometimes slowly away. *J. R. Weymes* **64**

RIGHT TED (IRE) 3 b.f. Mujadil (USA) 119 – Islandagore (IRE) 97 (Indian Ridge 123) [2006 76: 7s 8.1m⁴ 8.3d⁵ 8.3m* 8.1f⁵ 8.2m 8.1m 8.1m p7.1g 8.2s p9.5g² p8.6g p9.5g⁴ p9.5s Dec 15] smallish, compact filly: fair performer: won claimer at Windsor (claimed from R. Hannon £16,000) in July: below form after next start: probably stays 9.5f: acts on polytrack and firm ground. *T. Wall* **78 d**

RIGHT TO PLAY (USA) 3 b. or br.c. Kingmambo (USA) 125 – Possibly Perfect (USA) 122 (Northern Baby (CAN) 127) [2006 p10g 10s⁶ Oct 18] $950,000Y: big, good-topped colt: fourth living foal: closely related to 3 winners, including US 8.5f (at 2 yrs) and 9f (Grade 3 event) winner Promontory Gold (by Gone West) and fairly useful 2001 2-y-o 7f winner Dubai Status (by Seeking The Gold): dam, champion turf mare in USA, multiple Grade 1 winner at 9f/1¼m: 7/2 from 14/1, better effort in maidens when seventh to Woolfall Blue at Kempton on debut: sweating and on edge, failed to confirm that promise when below form at Nottingham. *J. H. M. Gosden* **71**

RIGUEZ DANCER 2 b.g. (Apr 27) Dansili 127 – Tricoteuse (Kris 135) [2006 f8g⁶ Dec 9] 16,000Y, 28,000 2-y-o: first foal: dam unraced out of half-sister to very smart middle-distance performers Kingfisher Mill and Wellbeing: 20/1, sixth to Mardi in maiden at Southwell, soon off bridle: should stay 1¼m+: open to improvement. *P. C. Haslam* **56 p**

RIKOCHET 2 ch.c. (Apr 5) Generous (IRE) 139 – Narva (Nashwan (USA) 135) [2006 7m 7.1m 7.1m 10g p8.6m Oct 31] big, good-topped colt: has a fluent action: sixth foal: half-brother to useful 1m (including in USA) winner Pretence (by Danehill): dam unraced half-sister to high-class winner up to 1½m Predappio: fair maiden: well beaten in nurseries: should stay 1¼m/1½m: sold 12,000 gns. *Mrs A. J. Perrett* **70**

RILEY BOYS (IRE) 5 ch.g. Most Welcome 131 – Scarlett Holly 81 (Red Sunset 120) **93**
[2006 89: 7g 8.2d 9.9f* 9.9f* 7.9g² 8.5f² 10m⁴ 9.9g Aug 17] close-coupled gelding: fairly
useful handicapper: has a very good record at Beverley (4 wins and 6 placings from 11
starts), 2 of those wins gained in June: badly hampered there final start: stays 1¼m: acts
on fibresand and any turf going: tried in cheekpieces/visor. *J. G. Given*

RILEYS DREAM 7 b.m. Rudimentary (USA) 118 – Dorazine 77 (Kalaglow 132) **– §**
[2006 49§: 5.1g Jul 10] poor performer: effective at 5f to 7f: acts on firm and soft ground:
usually wears cheekpieces: tried tongue tied: unreliable. *C. J. Price*

RINGAROOMA 4 b.f. Erhaab (USA) 127 – Tatouma (USA) 79 (The Minstrel (CAN) **50**
135) [2006 57: p8.6g⁶ p10g* p9.5g p10g⁴ p8g⁵ p10g p12g 10m⁴ 10f⁵ Jun 9] quite good- **a59**
topped filly: modest performer: won banded race at Lingfield in February: stays easy
1¼m: acts on polytrack, good to soft and good to firm ground: sometimes tongue tied:
often slowly away: free-going sort: sold 30,000 gns in November. *C. N. Allen*

RINGSIDER (IRE) 5 ch.g. Docksider (USA) 124 – Red Comes Up (USA) (Blushing **–**
Groom (FR) 131) [2006 98: p12.2g p10g 10g 12d Jul 22] close-coupled gelding: useful
handicapper at best: last all starts in 2006: tried in cheekpieces/tongue tied: sometimes
slowly away. *G. A. Butler*

RINTY (NZ) 4 ch.g. Istidaad (USA) 114 – Nearco Gold (NZ) (Virginia Privateer **55**
(USA)) [2006 7s 8g p9.5g p8g⁶ Dec 5] lightly-raced maiden: modest form, including in
New Zealand first 2 starts. *C. G. Cox*

RIODAN (IRE) 4 ch.f. Desert King (IRE) 129 – Spirit of The Nile (FR) 72 (Generous **82**
(IRE) 139) [2006 12s² 11.1d* 16m³ 16.2m⁴ 17.5d⁶ Sep 15] €2,000F, 4,200Y: second foal:
half-sister to fairly useful Irish 2m winner Man On The Nile (by Snurge): dam 13f winner
who stayed 2m: won bumper in May: fairly useful on Flat: won maiden at Hamilton in
June: better form in handicaps after: stays 17f: acts on soft and good to firm going.
J. J. Quinn

RIO DE JANEIRO (IRE) 5 b.g. Sadler's Wells (USA) 132 – Alleged Devotion **78**
(USA) (Alleged (USA) 138) [2006 76: p12g⁴ p12g⁵ 14m² Jul 7] sturdy gelding: fair
handicapper: won over hurdles prior to short-head second at Sandown in July: suited by
1¾m: acts on polytrack, firm and good to soft going: has wandered. *Miss E. C. Lavelle*

RIOLO (IRE) 4 ch.g. Priolo (USA) 127 – Ostrusa (AUT) (Rustan (HUN)) [2006 p7g⁶ **65**
p7g p7g 6f⁴ 7f 6.1m⁴ 8m 6.1m³ 6f 6m⁶ 7m* 7m⁵ 6d Sep 25] tall, workmanlike gelding:
well held in bumper: fair performer: won handicap at Brighton in August: stays 7f: acts
on firm going: blinkered/in cheekpieces nowadays: not an easy ride. *K. F. Clutterbuck*

RIO RIVA 4 b.g. Pivotal 124 – Dixie Favor (USA) 82 (Dixieland Band (USA)) [2006 **103**
97: 8g⁸ 8.9m 8m⁶ 8s* 8d⁴ 8g² 8d² Oct 28] tall gelding: useful handicapper: progressed
again in 2006, winning at Redcar in April (gelded afterwards) and Ripon (by ½ length
from Granston) in August: good second at Redcar (beaten ¾ length by Nanton, slowly
away) and Newmarket (beaten 3 lengths by Arm Candy) last 2 starts: should stay 1¼m:
acts on polytrack, soft and good to firm ground: got very warm before below-par second
outing, on toes at Ripon: held up. *Miss J. A. Camacho*

RIOTOUS APPLAUSE 3 b.f. Royal Applause 124 – Wiener Wald (USA) (Woodman **100 p**
(USA) 126) [2006 95: 6m* Sep 12] leggy, attractive filly: progressive form:
off over 11 months and easy to back, won minor event at Yarmouth (by 2 lengths from
Vortex) in September, only outing in 2006: raced only at 6f: acts on good to firm going:
has had expert for stall entry: open to further improvement. *J. R. Fanshawe*

RIOTOUS ASSEMBLY 3 b.g. Dansili 127 – Pretty Pollyanna (General Assembly **–**
(USA)) [2006 55: 8.2m Jun 16] big, good-bodied gelding: modest form only on debut at
2 yrs. *B. Smart*

RIOTOUS (IRE) 2 b.g. (Feb 7) Royal Applause 124 – Takarna (IRE) 70 (Mark of **69**
Esteem (IRE) 137) [2006 5m⁴ 5m² 5m² 5.1f³ 5m⁵ Aug 17] 33,000F, 14,000Y: smallish,
sturdy gelding: first foal: dam, ran 3 times in Ireland, half-sister to smart performers up to
1½m Takarian and Takali: fair maiden: raced at 5f on going firmer than good. *A. Dickman*

RIPPING 2 b.f. (Apr 23) Green Desert (USA) 127 – Zooming (IRE) (Indian Ridge 123) **71**
[2006 5m⁴ 5m 5g³ 6m³ 6m Sep 19] smallish, sturdy filly: fourth foal: sister to Irish 2005
2-y-o 6f winner Gripping and 5-y-o Holbox: dam, French maiden, half-sister to smart
French sprinter Zipping out of half-sister to top-class sprinter/miler Last Tycoon: fair
maiden: left R. Hannon before final outing: best at 5f: sold €85,000. *P. Bary, France*

RIPPLES MAID 3 b.f. Dansili 127 – Rivers Rhapsody 104 (Dominion 123) [2006 54: **106** p5g* 5.7d* 6d* 5.1g⁵ 6m⁶ 6m⁴ 6g⁵ 6d³ 6.1m* 6d⁴ 6g² Oct 12] sturdy filly: smart performer: won maiden at Lingfield in April, handicaps at Bath in April and Newmarket in May and listed race at Chester (by 1½ lengths from Portmeirion) in September: excellent neck second to Firenze in listed event at Newmarket final start: stays 6f: acts on polytrack, good to firm and good to soft ground: slipped badly as stall opened fifth outing. *J. A. Geake*

RIPPLING RIVER 2 b.c. (Apr 11) Foxhound (USA) 103 – Mylania 70 (Midyan **76** (USA) 124) [2006 5g² p5g² 5.3m² 5.1d Oct 18] 14,000Y: rather leggy, quite attractive colt: third foal: dam maiden who stayed 1m: fair maiden: runner-up first 3 starts, then absent 6 months: raced around 5f: acts on polytrack and good to firm going: sold 8,500 gns. *W. Jarvis*

RIQUEWIHR 6 ch.m. Compton Place 125 – Juvenilia (IRE) 55 (Masterclass (USA) **82** 116) [2006 73, a68: p7.1g p6g² p7g* p6g³ p7g* p7g³ 7d⁴ 6.1m² 6d² 5.7d⁶ p6g 6f² 6.9g⁴ 6f² 6m³ 6m⁴ 5m 5g⁴ 6d² 6d² 6d⁵ Oct 3] quite good-topped mare: fairly useful handicapper: claimed from P. Howling £6,000 after second start: won at Lingfield in February and March: mainly creditable efforts after: effective at 6f/7f: acts on polytrack and any turf going: wears cheekpieces nowadays: consistent. *J. S. Wainwright*

RISING CROSS 3 bl.f. Cape Cross (IRE) 129 – Woodrising 64 (Nomination 125) **115** [2006 95: p7g³ p8g⁶ p8g⁵ 9.9g* 12g² 11m 12m³ 9.5f 13.9d* 12.5m⁵ 15.5g⁵ Oct 22] Does size matter? The small, sparely-made Rising Cross, who stands only 14.3 hands, turned her pony-sized stature to advantage when squeezing through a reducing narrow gap in a bunched field to lead well inside the final furlong and land her first pattern win in the Irish Thoroughbred Marketing Park Hill Stakes at York in September. The success for this tough and genuine filly was richly deserved, her victory by three quarters of a length and a length and a quarter from two other three-year-olds, Anna Pavlova and Allegretto, matching the form she had shown when producing good placed efforts behind the impressive Alexandrova in the Oaks and the Irish Oaks. Rising Cross was having her ninth outing of the season in the Park Hill and started the outsider of seven, at 16/1, punters probably feeling that the fighting policy pursued with her was probably taking its toll. She had trailed in last the time before when sent to the States for the Beverly D Stakes for her first tilt at older fillies, though she faced a stiff task at Arlington where she was also dropped back a fair bit in trip.

Rising Cross's size made her original owner, the punter and TV pundit Dave Nevison, think that she must have been delivered by mistake—'on her way to the local riding school'—when she arrived at her trainer's yard as a yearling with the rest of a consignment purchased at Goffs. She had made 10,500 guineas as a foal, and agent David Minton got her for €20,000 as a yearling, recommending her to Nevison and trainer John Best as a 'cheapy who looks like she could go a bit.' 'She was tiny—and scrawny to boot—and could barely see out of her box,' said Nevison, 'and, after more and more syndicates rejected her, I thought the guys who eventually bought into her must have had a few too many at the pub!' Rising Cross exceeded all expectations at two, winning three of her eleven starts and running

Irish Thoroughbred Marketing Park Hill Stakes, York—Rising Cross (third left) responds willingly to beat Anna Pavlova (left), Allegretto (second right) and Maroussies Wings (stars on sleeves)

well in pattern company, including when second to Nannina in the Prestige Stakes at Newmarket. 'We had had our day in the sun and it was time to be sensible,' said Nevison, explaining the decision to send Rising Cross to the sales. As luck would have it, she failed to reach her relatively modest reserve and the syndicate persevered with her at three, deciding on a policy of 'running her in races that looked like cutting up, with the aim of collecting enough place money to cover costs until the December Sales.' Rising Cross picked up place money on one of her first three outings, in a listed event at Lingfield on polytrack in March, and only one of the six runners in the 32Red.com Lupe Stakes at Goodwood in May started at longer odds. That runner, 25/1-shot Soft Centre, dead-heated with 8/1-shot Rising Cross, who was joined on the line in a race in which the only Oaks entry, the Marcel Boussac third Deveron, who started favourite, trailed in last. Rising Cross was supplemented for the Oaks at the five-day stage, at a cost of £20,000. Rising Cross's stature was accentuated at Epsom by the fact that she was ridden by George Baker who had won on her at Goodwood—the smallest filly in the race partnered by the tallest jockey. The pair momentarily looked in danger of parting company at Epsom when Rising Cross stumbled a furlong out, but she kept on gamely to finish runner-up to Alexandrova, beaten six lengths but, nevertheless, recording a near-smart effort, clearly suited by being stepped up to a mile and a half. Rising Cross was bought after Epsom by Gary Tanaka, who has enjoyed much success by purchasing proven performers. He also bought the subsequent Italian Derby winner and Irish Derby runner-up Gentlewave in the latest season, though Rising Cross fared less well when sent to Italy for her first outing in the Tanaka colours in the Oaks d'Italia. She managed no better than mid-division but proved her running all wrong when a good third to Alexandrova and Scottish Stage in the Irish Oaks next time. Rising Cross proved her toughness after winning the Park Hill by running well in two races at Longchamp, when fifth (under a 7-lb Group 2 penalty) in the Prix de Royallieu and in the Prix Royal-Oak, running at least as well as ever over the longest trip she has tackled so far behind Montare in the latter.

			Danzig
	Cape Cross (IRE)	Green Desert	Foreign Courier
	(b 1994)	(b 1983)	Ahonoora
Rising Cross		Park Appeal	Balidaress
(bl.f. 2003)		(br 1982)	Dominion
	Woodrising	Nomination	Rivers Maid
	(b 1992)	(b 1983)	Bustino
		Bodham	Cley
		(b 1978)	

Rising Cross is by Cape Cross, the sire of Ouija Board, out of the mile and a quarter winner Woodrising who also won a selling hurdle at Hexham when in foal to Inchinor. That foal failed to win but Rising Cross's older half-brothers Skiddaw Jones (by Emperor Jones) and Willhego (by Pivotal) were both successful, the last-named showing fairly useful form when successful twice at Lingfield, at a mile and a quarter and a mile and a half, in the latest season. Rising Cross's trainer had Woodrising's two-year-old Woodygo (by Tobougg) in his care, but he did not reach the racecourse; the yearling full brother to Woodygo, now named Howdigo, fetched €55,000 at the Goffs Million Sale in September and has also joined Best. Woodrising was bred by the Budgett family, her dam Bodham, who bred several winners, being successful at a mile and a half and thirteen furlongs, and her grandam Cley, a winner at a mile and a half, being a half-sister to Arthur Budgett's two Derby winners Blakeney and Morston. The tough and genuine Rising Cross is reportedly set for a Cup campaign as a four-year-old. She acts on polytrack, good to firm and good to soft going. *J. R. Best*

RISING SHADOW (IRE) 5 b.g. Efisio 120 – Jouet 71 (Reprimand 122) [2006 99: 6d **113** 6m 6s² 6v² 6m 6.3g 6.1f⁶ 6g* 6s 6d⁴ 6d³ 6g⁴ 6s* 6d* Nov 4] close-coupled gelding: developed into a smart performer in 2006 and won handicaps at Ripon in August and York (beat Knot In Wood by neck in Coral Sprint Trophy) in October and listed event at Windsor (by head from Presto Shinko) in November, leading close home each time: stays 7f: acts on heavy and good to firm going: has started slowly: consistent. *T. D. Barron*

RISKA KING 6 b.g. Forzando 122 – Artistic Licence (High Top 131) [2006 77d, a–: **60** p7.1g f8g p8.6g 7g⁴ p8.6g Jul 11] smallish, good-bodied gelding: modest performer **a46**

nowadays, better on turf than all-weather: stays 8.6f: acts on polytrack, heavy and good to firm ground: tried in headgear. *P. A. Blockley*

RISK CHALLENGE (USA) 4 ch.g. Mt Livermore (USA) – Substance (USA) (Diesis 133) [2006 p7.1g p12.2g⁵ Dec 22] fairly useful bumper winner: well held in maidens at Wolverhampton. *C. J. Price* —

RISK FREE 9 ch.g. Risk Me (FR) 127 – Princess Lily 65 (Blakeney 126) [2006 –, a62: p8.6g* p9.5g⁴ p9.5g p9.5g p9.5g³ p8.6g³ p8.6g* p9.5m p9.5g³ p9.5g⁵ p8.6m Nov 9] lengthy gelding: fair performer: won seller in January and claimer in February, both at Wolverhampton: stays easy 1¼m: acts on all-weather, firm and good to soft going: wears blinkers/visor: usually tongue tied. *P. D. Evans* **a66**

RISK RUNNER (IRE) 3 b.g. Mull of Kintyre (USA) 114 – Fizzygig 71 (Efisio 120) [2006 74: 11.6m 10.2s⁴ 11.6g² 12g⁵ 11.6f 10g² 10d Oct 9] rather leggy gelding: fairly useful handicapper: good efforts when second at Windsor and Nottingham: stays 11.6f: acts on heavy and good to firm going (below form on firm): usually visored: none too consistent: fair form in juvenile hurdles, successful in December. *A. King* **86**

RISQUE HEIGHTS 2 b.g. (Jan 14) Mark of Esteem (IRE) 137 – Risque Lady 109 (Kenmare (FR) 125) [2006 7d 7.1d² p8g² p8.6g³ Dec 29] 35,000Y: medium-sized gelding: third foal: brother to 3-y-o Chris Corsa: dam, 5f (at 2 yrs)/1m winner, half-sister to smart sprinter To The Roof: fair maiden: second at Musselburgh (left with plenty to do, hung right) and Kempton: stays 1m: blinkered last 2 starts: doesn't look straightforward. *G. A. Butler* **72**

RITSI 3 b.g. Marju (IRE) 127 – Anna Comnena (IRE) 71 (Shareef Dancer (USA) 135) [2006 65: 11.6m³ 12m⁶ 11.6g 14m³ 16.2g³ p16g 14.1g³ Aug 25] good-topped gelding: fair maiden handicapper: stays 2m: acts on good to firm going (well below form only outing on polytrack): tongue tied last 5 starts: looks none too keen: sold 5,000 gns. *Mrs A. J. Perrett* **77**

RIVER CHAARTH (IRE) 4 b.c. Alhaarth (IRE) 126 – Sudden Interest (FR) (Highest Honor (FR) 124) [2006 88: 10g² 12.3d⁴ 12d² 16.1m² 13.9d⁵ 14v Sep 2] smallish, close-coupled colt: useful performer: cracked cannon bone only start in 2005: second in handicaps in 2006 at Newbury, Newmarket and Newcastle (best effort when beaten neck by Toldo in Northumberland Plate, finishing strongly): shaped better than bare result when fifth to Mudawin in Ebor (Handicap) at York: reportedly finished lame final start: stays 2m: acts on good to firm and good to soft going: tried visored: carried head awkwardly second outing. *P. W. Chapple-Hyam* **103**

Coral Sprint Trophy, York—a smart performance by Rising Shadow,
who leads close home to win from Knot In Wood (left), Out After Dark (cheekpieces),
River Falcon (hidden by runner-up) and the grey Mecca's Mate

RIVER BEAU (IRE) 3 ch.f. Galileo (IRE) 134 – Dafariyna (IRE) 71 (Nashwan (USA) **47**
135) [2006 –: 8v 8.2s p12g⁶ p11g p10g Nov 27] first foal: dam Irish maiden (second at
1m/9f), out of Cork And Orrery winner Dafayna, herself half-sister to 2000 Guineas
winner Doyoun: poor maiden: left M. Halford in Ireland after second start: stays 1½m:
acts on polytrack. *E. J. O'Neill*

RIVER BISCUIT (USA) 4 ch.g. Diesis 133 – Elle Est Revenue (IRE) 91 (Night Shift **–**
(USA)) [2006 64: p7g 8s 11.5m Apr 17] strong, close-coupled gelding: fair winner at
2 yrs: lightly raced since, and no form in 2006: tried blinkered. *M. J. Polglase*

RIVER BRAVO (IRE) 3 b.c. Indian Ridge 123 – Sheer Spirit (IRE) 86 (Caerleon **100**
(USA) 132) [2006 94p: 7.1s* 6m Jun 17] good-bodied colt: useful performer: won
3-runner handicap at Haydock (by 1½ lengths from Imperial Sword) in May: unsuited by
test of speed when well below form in William Hill Trophy (Handicap) at York next time:
bred to stay at least 1m: acts on soft going. *P. W. Chapple-Hyam*

RIVER CITY (IRE) 9 b.g. Norwich 118 – Shuil Na Lee (IRE) (Phardante (FR) 123) **71**
[2006 p12.2g³ 10.2m⁴ p9.5g 14.8m⁶ p12.2g⁶ Dec 6] rangy gelding: fairly useful hurdler/
smart chaser: fair maiden: best effort at Chepstow second start: should be suited by at
least 1½m: acts on good to firm ground. *Noel T. Chance*

RIVER CLUB 2 ch.g. (Mar 3) Kyllachy 129 – Amused 78 (Prince Sabo 123) [2006 5.1s **–**
Oct 25] sturdy gelding: backward and behind in maiden at Nottingham. *A. Dickman*

RIVER CROSSING 3 b.f. Zafonic (USA) 130 – Vax Star 96 (Petong 126) [2006 79: **–**
7m May 10] fair winner on debut at 2 yrs: last all starts since: mulish behind stall only
outing in 2006: sold 20,000 gns in July. *T. D. Easterby*

RIVER DEUCE 2 b.c. (Feb 25) Zaha (CAN) 106 – Light Hand 80 (Star Appeal 133) **71**
[2006 7d 8g f8g² Nov 2] close-coupled, workmanlike colt: half-brother to fairly useful 1998 2-y-o 5f/7f winner Light Fingered (by Soviet Lad): dam 1¼m winner: fair
maiden: well held on turf (Newmarket) before second at Southwell (50/1): stays 1m.
M. H. Tompkins

RIVER FALCON 6 b.g. Pivotal 124 – Pearly River 72 (Elegant Air 119) [2006 102: **101**
6g² 6d⁶ 6d 5g⁴ 6s⁴ p5.1g Oct 29] useful-looking gelding: useful performer: creditable
efforts when 2½ lengths second to Welsh Emperor in minor event at Thirsk and fourth to
Rising Shadow in handicap at York reappearance/penultimate outings: effective at 5f/6f:
acts on polytrack, firm and soft ground. *J. S. Goldie*

RIVER GYPSY 5 b.g. In The Wings 128 – River Erne (USA) (Irish River (FR) 131) **58**
[2006 73, a60: p12g⁴ p12g⁴ p12.2g p12g⁴ p12g³ 10.2d⁵ p16g p10g⁴ 11.6m 11.6f 9.9m⁴ 8.1m⁶ Sep 12] **a68**
fair maiden on all-weather, modest on turf in 2006: should stay 1¾m: acts on polytrack,
soft and good to firm ground. *D. R. C. Elsworth*

RIVERHILL (IRE) 3 b.g. Mull of Kintyre (USA) 114 – Thrill Seeker (IRE) (Treasure **56**
Kay 114) [2006 –p: 9v² 11.1d³ 7m 6.9m⁶ 9.9g⁵ 10.5g 9.1v⁴ f7g Nov 10] well-made
gelding: modest maiden: stays 11f: acts on heavy and good to firm ground: gelded after
final start. *J. Howard Johnson*

RIVER KINTYRE 3 b.c. Mull of Kintyre (USA) 114 – Our Pleasure (IRE) (Lake **80**
Coniston (IRE) 131) [2006 80: 7g 6m⁶ 6g 7.1m³ 8m 7m 7.1d² Oct 13] tall, useful-looking
colt: fairly useful performer: stays 7f: acts on good to firm and good to soft ground: has
looked none too straightforward: sold 11,000 gns. *B. W. Hills*

RIVER KIROV (IRE) 3 b.c. Soviet Star (USA) 128 – Night Shifter (IRE) 74 (Night **87**
Shift (USA)) [2006 7m² 7.1g⁵ 6g* 6g⁴ 6.1m* 5g⁴ 6m⁶ Sep 6] 11,500Y, 46,000 2-y-o:
strong colt: first foal: dam 2-y-o 5f winner: fairly useful performer: won maiden at Redcar
in May and handicap at Nottingham (tongue tied) in July: creditable efforts both starts
after: effective at 6f, should stay 1m: raced only on good/good to firm going: sold 9,000
gns. *P. W. Chapple-Hyam*

RIVER LOGIC (IRE) 3 b.g. Fasliyev (USA) 120 – Grey Again 63 (Unfuwain (USA) **65**
131) [2006 56: 7f⁵ 7g 7.9m* 9.9f³ 8f³ 10m* 11.1m* 10m⁴ 10g² 10.2m⁶ 10.3m 10m
Sep 21] quite good-topped gelding: fair performer: won seller at Carlisle (sold from
J. Howard Johnson) in July and handicaps at Ayr in July and Hamilton in August: stays
11f: raced only on good ground or firmer: fair hurdler, successful in November and
December. *A. D. Brown*

RIVER MIST IMAGE (USA) 4 ch.f. Swain (IRE) 134 – Cat's Image (CAN) (Storm **–**
Cat (USA)) [2006 67: p12.2g 10m 10.1f⁶ 7d Oct 18] sturdy filly: fair maiden at 3 yrs: well
held in 2006: visored/tongue tied last 2 outings: has carried head awkwardly: sold 10,500
gns. *J. R. Fanshawe*

RIVER OF BABYLON 5 b.m. Marju (IRE) 127 – Isle of Flame (Shirley Heights 130) **73** [2006 88: 8g 7m 8.1m⁵ Jul 2] lengthy mare: fairly useful performer at best: just fair form in 2006: was effective at 7f/1m: acted on polytrack, firm and soft going: sometimes raced freely: dead. *M. L. W. Bell*

RIVER OF DIAMONDS 5 b.g. Muhtarram (USA) 125 – City Gambler 74 (Rock City **–** 120) [2006 55d: f11g Jan 29] modest performer at best: well held only outing in 2006: tried blinkered. *R. A. Harris*

RIVER PRINCE 2 br.g. (Apr 6) Riverwise (USA) – Princess Penny 46§ (King's Signet **55** (USA) 110) [2006 5.1d⁴ 5.3m⁵ Apr 30] modest form in maidens in April: gave trouble in preliminaries. *W. G. M. Turner*

RIVER ROSIE (IRE) 2 b.f. (Apr 12) Bertolini (USA) 125 – Young Rosein 74 (Distant **52** Relative 128) [2006 5g p5g p7g 5.1g* 5f⁶ 5g Aug 26] €11,000Y: small, close-coupled filly: second foal: half-sister to 3-y-o Alistair John: dam, 7f/1m winner, half-sister to useful sprinter Proud Boast: modest performer: won seller at Bath in July: best at 5f/6f. *J. G. Portman*

RIVER ROYALE 4 b.g. Royal Applause 124 – Trundley Wood 66 (Wassl 125) [2006 **95** 97: 7g 8m 8m Jun 21] well-made gelding: fluent mover: useful performer: easily best effort in 2006 when creditable seventh in handicap at Newmarket on reappearance: stayed 7f: acted on good to firm and good to soft going: dead. *P. W. Chapple-Hyam*

RIVERSIDE DANCER (USA) 2 ch.f. (Apr 28) Stravinsky (USA) 133 – Odori **85** (USA) (The Minstrel (CAN) 135) [2006 p5g⁴ 5m* 6m 5.2g 5g 6s 6.5s p5.1m³ Nov 8] $40,000F, 24,000Y: tall, rather leggy filly: has a powerful, round action: eighth foal: sister to fairly useful 2003 2-y-o 6f winner Savitsky and half-sister to several winners, including fairly useful 1998 2-y-o 6f winner Georgette (by Geiger Counter): dam lightly raced in USA: fairly useful performer: won maiden at Ripon in April: ran well next 2 starts only, seventh in Albany Stakes at Royal Ascot and Super Sprint at Newbury: effective at 5f/6f: acts on good to firm going, probably polytrack: wore cheekpieces/blinkers last 2 outings: sometimes slowly away. *K. A. Ryan*

RIVER TARRANT 2 b.f. (Apr 5) Compton Place 125 – Altizaf 66 (Zafonic (USA) **63 §** 130) [2006 6m⁵ 6.1m⁶ 5m⁶ 7d⁶ p5.1g Nov 2] 2,000F: leggy, quite good-topped filly: fourth foal: half-sister to 4-y-o Trim Image: dam, ran twice around 1¼m, out of half-sister to disqualified Oaks winner Aliysa: modest maiden: best efforts at 5f/6f: temperamental (reluctant to race final start): sold 2,800 gns. *P. W. Chapple-Hyam*

RIVER THAMES 3 b.c. Efisio 120 – Dashing Water 87 (Dashing Blade 117) [2006 **85** 93: 6g 6d 6g 5g⁶ p6g 6d Oct 19] sturdy, useful-looking colt: fairly useful performer: will prove best at 5f/6f: acts on polytrack, soft and good to firm going: sold 40,000 gns. *J. A. R. Toller*

RIVER TIBER 3 b.c. Danehill (USA) 126 – Heavenly Whisper (IRE) 105 (Halling **90** (USA) 133) [2006 85p: 8s* 8v 8m⁴ 8d Sep 23] 580,000Y: good-topped colt: first foal: dam, 1m winner (including at 2 yrs) who stayed 1¼m, out of half-sister to very smart performer up to 1m Rock City: fairly useful performer on balance: landed odds in maiden at Gowran in May: acted as pacemaker last 2 starts, flattered when 2¾ lengths fourth to Caradak in Celebration Mile at Goodwood on first occasion: stays 1m: acts on soft and good to firm going: joined Declan Gillespie in Ireland. *A. P. O'Brien, Ireland*

RIVERWELD 4 ch.g. Weldnaas (USA) 112 – Riverain 65 (Bustino 136) [2006 10g **–** p11g Nov 6] sparely-made gelding: modest maiden in 2004: well held only outing on Flat since. *J. R. Holt*

RIVETTING 3 b.g. Vettori (IRE) 119 – Frog 84 (Akarad (FR) 130) [2006 –p: 10g⁵ **53 p** 14.1g⁶ 14.1m³ Jun 15] big, good-topped gelding: modest maiden: will stay 2m: acts on good to firm going: unseated rider to post on debut: should do better when stamina tested fully. *Sir Mark Prescott*

RIVIERA RED (IRE) 6 b.g. Rainbow Quest (USA) 134 – Banquise (IRE) (Last **44** Tycoon 131) [2006 57: p10g p7g p8g May 15] just poor performer in 2006: should stay beyond 1m: acts on polytrack: visored last 4 starts. *L. Montague Hall*

RIYALMA (IRE) 3 b.f. Selkirk (USA) 129 – Riyafa (IRE) 112 (Kahyasi 130) [2006 **107** 85p: 10s* 12g Jun 22] strong, good sort: useful form: won listed Pretty Polly Stakes at Newmarket (beat Bunood 2½ lengths) in May: 9/2 joint second favourite, but still not right in coat and laid back in paddock, last of 10 behind Alexandrova in Oaks at Epsom next time, squeezed for room after 2f out and rolling around camber before being eased: should have stayed 1½m: acted on soft ground: dead. *Sir Michael Stoute*

ladbrokes.com Stakes (Handicap), Goodwood—
Road To Love defies a 5-lb penalty in style from Desert Realm and Pearly King

ROAD HOME 3 ch.g. Grand Lodge (USA) 125 – Lady In Waiting 113 (Kylian (USA)) **77**
[2006 10m³ 10m⁶ Jul 12] 130,000Y: tall, close-coupled gelding: second foal: dam, 5f (at
2 yrs) to 10.4f winner, closely related to smart stayer Savannah Bay: better effort in
maidens when 4¼ lengths third to Rhinebird at Newmarket on debut: respectable sixth
there next time, finding little: gelded after: bred to stay 1½m+. *G. Wragg*

ROAD TO LOVE (IRE) 3 ch.g. Fruits of Love (USA) 127 – Alpine Flair (IRE) (Tirol **118**
127) [2006 87: 10.1m⁶ 10m² 12m 10m* 10m 10m* 9.9f* 10.5m⁶ 10.1d³ 9.9m³ 8d³
Sep 30] strong, close-coupled gelding: smart performer: much improved in 2006, winning handicaps at Sandown and Ascot (by 7 lengths from London Express) in July, and
Goodwood (by 5 lengths from Desert Realm) in August: below form next 2 starts, then
third in Select Stakes at Goodwood (beaten 2 necks by Pictavia) and Joel Stakes at
Newmarket (trip a minimum, behind Satchem): best around 1¼m: acts on firm going,
winner on good to soft: front runner. *M. Johnston*

ROAD TO MANDALAY (IRE) 3 b.c. Galileo (IRE) 134 – Child Prodigy (IRE) 87 **112 ?**
(Ballad Rock 122) [2006 13m* 16m⁴ 14g 12d⁴ Aug 20] 280,000F, 420,000Y: smallish.
close-coupled colt: fourth foal: half-brother to 3 winners, including fairly useful 2002
2-y-o 8.5f winner Menuhin (by Royal Academy), later successful in USA, and 1m winner
Du Pre (by Singspiel): dam, 6f (at 2 yrs) and 1m (in USA) winner, half-sister to very
smart performer up to 1½m Kutub: smart form: won minor event at Navan in June: 3½
lengths fourth to Soapy Danger in Queen's Vase at Royal Ascot next time: seemingly
much better effort in listed races at Leopardstown after when 4 lengths fourth of 5 to
Kastoria final start, though again looked awkward under pressure: stays 2m: acts on good
to firm and good to soft going: hung and flashed tail (reportedly lost action) third outing:
sent to Norway. *A. P. O'Brien, Ireland*

ROAD TO RECOVERY 2 b.g. (Feb 7) Mujahid (USA) 125 – Legend of Aragon 67 **66**
(Aragon 118) [2006 5m⁵ 5m⁵ 6.1g 5.1f⁵ Sep 9] 19,000F, 23,000Y: leggy gelding: sixth
foal: brother to fairly useful 2004 2-y-o 6f winner Mafaheem and half-brother to UAE
1¼m winner by Robellino: dam 2-y-o 5f winner who stayed 1m: fair maiden: favourite,
fifth in nursery at Bath (visored): should stay at least 6f. *A. M. Balding*

ROBBIE CAN CAN 7 b.g. Robellino (USA) 127 – Can Can Lady 82 (Anshan 119) **65**
[2006 71: f12g² p13g² f12g p13g 12d² 14.1d² 14.1m 11.8d 12.1f* 12.1f⁵ 15d p12g⁶
Nov 11] leggy, useful-looking gelding: fair handicapper: won apprentice event at Chepstow in July: effective at 11f to 2¼m: acts on all-weather, firm and soft going: sometimes
carries head high/drifts left: held up: won over hurdles in October. *A. W. Carroll*

ROBBIE SCOTT 2 b.g. (Feb 23) Robellino (USA) 127 – Milly of The Vally 93 **68 p**
(Caerleon (USA) 132) [2006 p8.6f⁵ 8.3g⁴ 9s³ Sep 24] 30,000Y: fourth foal: half-brother
to 3 winners, including very smart performer up to 1¾m Scott's View (by Selkirk) and
3-y-o Doctor Scott: dam, 1½m winner, half-sister to smart stayer Bosham Mill: fair form
in maidens: gelded after final start: will benefit from 1½m+: likely to do better in
handicaps as 3-y-o. *M. Johnston*

ROBBIE WILL 5 b.g. Robellino (USA) 127 – Life's Too Short (IRE) 49 (Astronef **–**
116) [2006 54: f14g⁵ f14g⁶ f16g Mar 8] quite good-topped gelding: maiden: no form in
2006. *F. Jordan*

ROBBO 12 b.g. Robellino (USA) 127 – Basha (USA) (Chief's Crown (USA)) [2006 60: **59**
18v⁴ Apr 4] small gelding: modest performer, very lightly raced on Flat nowadays: stays
2¼m: acts on fibresand and heavy ground: tried blinkered: hard ride. *K. G. Reveley*

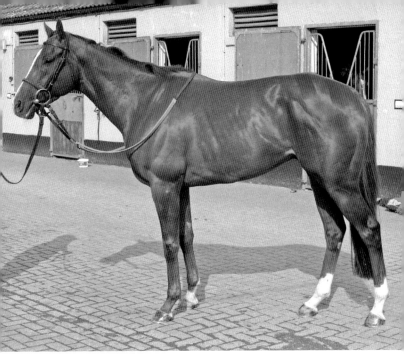

Mr Grant Mercer's "Road To Love"

ROBEMA 3 b.f. Cadeaux Genereux 131 – Germane 100 (Distant Relative 128) [2006 **88**
7.5g² 7.5f* 8.1g* Jul 7] 9,500Y: seventh foal: sister to useful 1m winner Granted and
4-y-o Eminence Gift and half-sister to 5-y-o Ganymede: dam, 2-y-o 7f (Rockfel Stakes)
winner, out of half-sister to very smart performer up to 11f Running Stag: fairly useful
form: won maiden at Beverley (by 5 lengths) in June and handicap at Haydock (still bit
green, beat Gelder ½ length) in July: met with setback after: raced only on good and firm
going. *J. J. Quinn*

ROBERT THE BRAVE 2 b.c. (Mar 10) Primo Valentino (IRE) 116 – Sandicliffe **69**
(USA) 66 (Imp Society (USA)) [2006 p8.6g³ 7s p8.6g² p8.6g⁴ Nov 23] 5,000Y: third foal:
closely related to winner in Greece by Primo Dominie and half-brother to winner in Japan
by Compton Place: dam 7f/1m winner: fair maiden: in frame all starts at Wolverhampton:
will be suited by 1¼m: acts on polytrack, well held only outing on turf. *A. J. McCabe*

ROBESON 4 br.g. Primo Dominie 121 – Montserrat 81 (Aragon 118) [2006 71: 9.9g **48**
10f⁵ 12d⁴ Oct 8] strong, close-coupled gelding: maiden: just poor form in 2006: stays
1¼m: acts on polytrack and good to firm going: bolted to post on reappearance at 3 yrs:
headstrong type, often makes running. *D. M. Simcock*

ROBIN SHARP 8 ch.h. First Trump 118 – Mo Stopher 47 (Sharpo 132) [2006 44d: **–**
p7g p8g p8g Dec 13] strong horse: little form in 2006: tried visored/tongue tied, wears
cheekpieces. *J. Akehurst*

ROBINZAL 4 b.g. Zilzal (USA) 137 – Sulitelma (USA) 63 (The Minstrel (CAN) 135) **73**
[2006 78: 8.3s³ Oct 2] tall, close-coupled gelding: fair performer: creditable third in
handicap at Windsor only Flat outing in 2006: should stay 1¼m: acts on soft and good to
firm ground: tried tongue tied: won over hurdles in August. *C. J. Mann*

betfred.com Mile, Sandown—Rob Roy justifies favouritism,
beating Babodana (black cap), Kings Point (rail) and Democratic Deficit (right)

ROB ROY (USA) 4 b. or br.c. Lear Fan (USA) 130 – Camanoe (USA) 63 (Gone West **122** (USA)) [2006 120: 8.1m* 8s⁶ 8m³ 8m⁶ 10d² 8f⁵ 8.5f⁵ Nov 24] big, rangy, good sort: very smart performer: pin-fired after damaging shin in 2000 Guineas at 3 yrs: won betfred.com Mile at Sandown in April by a length from Babodana: also ran well when placed in Sussex Stakes at Goodwood (2½ lengths third to Court Masterpiece) and Champion Stakes at Newmarket (3 lengths second to Pride): 3½ lengths fifth to Miesque's Approval in Breeders' Cup Mile at Churchill Downs on penultimate start, staying on strongly after bit slowly away: left Sir Michael Stoute, bit below form when fifth to Ashkal Way in Citation Handicap at Hollywood final outing: effective at 1m/1¼m: acts on good to firm and good to soft going, probably on firm: held up: suspect temperament. *N. D. Drysdale, USA*

ROBUSTIAN 3 b.g. Robellino (USA) 127 – Pontressina (USA) (St Jovite (USA) 135) **88** [2006 77: 8.3m³ 8.1g² 8g² 9.9f³ 10f⁴ 11.6m² 12f² 10g 10.2f⁵ 11m* p12g Oct 21] leggy, workmanlike gelding: fairly useful handicapper: won at Goodwood in September: stays 11.6f: acts on firm going: consistent. *R. F. Johnson Houghton*

ROCAMADOUR 4 b.c. Celtic Swing 138 – Watch Me (IRE) 106 (Green Desert (USA) **110** 127) [2006 116: 9g⁶ 10m⁴ 8s 8f³ 8m⁴ 10d 10m⁴ 9d Sep 30] good-topped colt: has a quick action: smart performer: not quite so good in 2006 as in 2005: best effort when fourth to Distant Way in Premio Presidente della Repubblica at Rome second start: effective at 1m to 10.5f: acts on firm and soft going: visored last 2 outings: races prominently. *M. R. Channon*

ROCA REDONDA (IRE) 2 b.f. (Feb 23) Fasliyev (USA) 120 – Devil's Crown **62** (USA) (Chief's Crown (USA)) [2006 7g⁵ 6m⁶ Sep 13] lengthy, good-topped filly: sixth foal: half-sister to 3 winners abroad: dam, maiden in USA, out of sister to Glint of Gold and Diamond Shoal: mid-field in maidens at Folkestone and Yarmouth (sixth to Kaseema): joined M. Wallace. *D. J. Daly*

ROCHDALE 3 ch.g. Bertolini (USA) 125 – Owdbetts (IRE) 69 (High Estate 127) **100** [2006 77: 6d⁴ 5m* 5g 5m³ 6g 6m* 6m⁶ p7g² Oct 6] lengthy, well-made gelding: improved into a useful handicapper, winning at Newmarket in May and Haydock (beat Charles Darwin by 1½ lengths) in July: good head second to Ceremonial Jade at Lingfield final start: stays 7f: acts on polytrack, good to firm and good to soft going: joined A. Al Raihe in UAE. *M. A. Jarvis*

ROCHESIS 3 b.f. Mujahid (USA) 125 – Northern Bird 86 (Interrex (CAN)) [2006 72: **65 +** 6f⁵ Jul 31] fair form: off over 9 months, creditable fifth in handicap at Windsor only start in 2006: will stay 7f: acts on firm going. *Miss K. B. Boutflower*

ROCK ANTHEM (IRE) 2 ch.c. (Apr 4) Rock of Gibraltar (IRE) 133 – Regal Portrait **78** (IRE) 57 (Royal Academy (USA) 130) [2006 7d 7g⁴ 8g Oct 13] 100,000Y: close-coupled colt: seventh foal: half-brother to 3 winners, including 7f (at 2 yrs) and 8.5f (in USA) winner Atarama (stayed 1½m, by Sadler's Wells) and Italian sprinter King's Ivory (by Lake Coniston), both useful: dam lightly-raced half-sister to King's Theatre and High Estate: fair form in maidens: fourth to Opera Music at Newbury: should prove best short of 1m. *J. L. Dunlop*

ROCKATORRI 3 b.f. Vettori (IRE) 119 – Lady Rockstar 90 (Rock Hopper 124) [2006 **43**
10d 9s 10m 12f 10.1m⁵ 10.1g⁴ 16.2m⁵ 13.8m⁶ 12.1m³ 10d 11.5d⁶ Oct 18] close-coupled
filly: second foal: dam 1m to 1¼m winner: poor maiden: left M. Channon after third outing: stays 1½m: acts on good to firm going: wears headgear nowadays. *G. G. Margarson*

ROCKBURST 4 b.f. Xaar 132 – Topwinder (USA) (Topsider (USA)) [2006 71d: 6f⁵ **62**
7m 8m⁵ Jun 25] quite good-topped filly: modest performer nowadays: best at 6f: acts on
good to firm ground: tried visored: races prominently. *K. R. Burke*

ROCK CONCERT 8 b.m. Bishop of Cashel 122 – Summer Pageant 81 (Chief's
Crown (USA)) [2006 –, a63d: p9.5g f11g f8g Feb 26] deep-girthed mare: fair performer
at best: no form in 2006: occasionally visored. *I. W. McInnes*

ROCK DIVA (IRE) 2 ch.f. (Mar 13) Rock of Gibraltar (IRE) 133 – Merlannah (IRE)
(Shy Groom (USA)) [2006 p7.1g Nov 14] €37,000Y: closely related to 3-y-o Ockums
Razor and half-sister to 3 winners, including smart 5f winner (including at 2 yrs) Kier
Park (by Foxhound): dam, Irish maiden, half-sister to high-class sprinter Anita's Prince:
66/1, well held in maiden at Wolverhampton. *P. C. Haslam*

ROCKER 2 b.g. (Feb 25) Rock of Gibraltar (IRE) 133 – Jessica's Dream (IRE) 114 **70**
(Desert Style (IRE) 121) [2006 6m 5m³ 6m³ 5d⁴ p5g* Dec 16] 60,000Y: first foal: dam,
5f/6f winner (including at 2 yrs), half-sister to 5-y-o Majors Cast: fair performer: in frame
3 starts (left P. Chapple-Hyam and gelded after final one) prior to winning maiden at
Kempton by head from Telltime: effective at 5f/6f. *B. R. Johnson*

ROCKET FORCE (USA) 6 ch.g. Spinning World (USA) 130 – Pat Us (USA) **80**
(Caucasus (USA) 127) [2006 80: 12g⁴ 12.4d² 12d² 12g³ 13.1g p12.2g Jul 20] well-made
gelding: fairly useful performer: creditable efforts in frame first 4 starts in 2006: stays
13.9f: acts on good to firm and good to soft ground: tried visored. *N. Wilson*

ROCKET (IRE) 5 ch.g. Cadeaux Genereux 131 – Prends Ca (IRE) 98 (Reprimand **–**
122) [2006 –: p9.5g 8m 8.3g Oct 16] of no account nowadays. *H. J. Manners*

ROCK FEVER (IRE) 4 ch.f. Desert Sun 120 – Icefern 88 (Moorestyle 137) [2006 46, **50**
a52: p5.1g p6g p5.1g p5.1g p5.1g* p5g p5g May 23] tall filly: modest performer: won
banded race at Wolverhampton in May: effective at 5f/6f: acts on polytrack and good to
firm going: visored/blinkered. *Peter Grayson*

ROCKFONIC 2 br.c. (Feb 10) Rock of Gibraltar (IRE) 133 – Procession 72 (Zafonic **49**
(USA) 130) [2006 7.1d⁴ 7.2g⁶ 8.3g 7g Sep 27] poor maiden: bred to stay 1m, but free-
going sort: tried blinkered: sold 4,000 gns, sent to Sweden. *J. R. Weymes*

ROCK HAVEN (IRE) 4 b.g. Danehill Dancer (IRE) 117 – Mahabba (USA) 74 (Elocu- **56**
tionist (USA)) [2006 67: p8.6g p9.5g 10m⁶ 11s* 10g 10f⁵ Sep 20] workmanlike gelding:
modest performer nowadays: won seller at Redcar in August: stays 11f: acts on soft and
good to firm going: tried in cheekpieces. *J. Mackie*

ROCK 'N' ROLLER (FR) 2 b. or br.c. (May 3) Sagacity (FR) 125 – Diamond Dance **75**
(FR) 112 (Dancehall (USA) 127) [2006 7g 8d⁴ Sep 27] €62,000Y: tall colt: half-brother
to 2 winners in France, notably smart 10.5f/12.5f (Prix de Pomone) winner Diamond
Tango (by Acatenango): dam, French 1¼m and 10.5f (Prix Penelope) winner, half-sister
to smart French winner up to 10.5f Diamond Mix: fair form in maidens: staying-on fourth
to Ladies Best at Salisbury: will be suited by 1¼m/1½m. *W. R. Muir*

ROCK OF CLOONAVERY (IRE) 3 b.g. Desert Prince (IRE) 130 – Mackla 109 **55**
(Caerleon (USA) 132) [2006 70: p8g p7g p8.6g⁴ p8g⁶ 8.2d 8.2d⁴ 8.3d 8m Jun 15] modest
maiden nowadays: stays 8.6f: acts on polytrack and soft ground: blinkered final start.
S. C. Williams

ROCKPILER 4 b.g. Halling (USA) 133 – Emma Peel 113 (Emarati (USA) 74) [2006 **–**
49: 11f 12f 16.1m 14.1m Aug 31] smallish, close-coupled gelding: maiden: no form in
2006. *D. W. Thompson*

ROCKY REPPIN 6 b.g. Rock City 120 – Tino Reppin 46 (Neltino 97) [2006 56§: f7g **52 §**
f8g f7g³ f8g³ f7g² p8.6g f7g⁶ f8g f7g f8g⁶ f8g⁶ Dec 29] leggy, close-coupled gelding:
modest performer: effective at 7f/1m: acts on fibresand and good to firm ground: wears
headgear: unreliable. *J. Balding*

ROCLETTE (USA) 2 ch.f. (Jan 30) Rock of Gibraltar (IRE) 133 – Rose Bourbon **76**
(USA) (Woodman (USA) 126) [2006 6f⁶ 7m⁴ 6m 6m³ Aug 27] $250,000Y: workmanlike
filly: sixth foal: half-sister to 3 winners, including useful 2002 2-y-o 7f winner who stayed 1¼m Bourbonnais (by Singspiel) and Irish 1m winner Georgina (by Polish Precedent):
dam, useful French maiden who should have stayed 1m, half-sister to Poule d'Essai des

Pouliches winner Baiser Vole: fair maiden: fourth to Sudoor at Newbury: fell (after saddle slipped) next start, and none too keen final one: will stay 1m. *B. W. Hills*

RODEO 3 ch.g. Pivotal 124 – Flossy 107 (Efisio 120) [2006 83p: 8m² 8g⁶ 8s⁴ Aug 26]   **83**
tall, useful-looking gelding: has a moderate, round action: fairly useful maiden: well below form last 2 starts: gelded after: will stay 1¼m: acts on soft and good to firm going. *B. W. Hills*

ROGERS LODGER 2 b.g. (May 18) Cyrano de Bergerac 120 – Bertrade 75 (Home-   **–**
boy 114) [2006 6d Nov 4] well beaten in maiden at Windsor. *J. Akehurst*

ROGUE 4 b.f. Royal Applause 124 – Mystique (Mystiko (USA) 124) [2006 56p: 6f 6g²   **74**
6m³ 6m² 6m⁴ 5.7m Sep 4] strong filly: fair maiden: likely to stay 7f: raced on good ground or firmer on turf. *Jane Southcombe*

ROHAANI (USA) 4 ch.c. High Yield (USA) 121 – Strawberry's Charm (USA) (Straw-   **109**
berry Road (AUS) 128) [2006 108: p10g² 10g 8f 8s 10.4g* 9d Sep 30] big, strong colt: useful performer: won handicap at York (by length from Topatoo) in September: also ran well when length second to Kandidate in Rosebery Handicap at Kempton (reared leaving stall and tended to wander): stays 1¼m: acts on polytrack, good to firm and good to soft going: has shown reluctance to enter stall (refusing twice): joined D. Watson in UAE. *Sir Michael Stoute*

ROHERYN (IRE) 2 b.g. (Apr 25) Efisio 120 – Special One 66 (Aragon 118) [2006 5g*   **77**
5.1f³ 6s p5.1m⁶ Nov 8] 13,500Y, 16,000 2-y-o: neat gelding: has a quick action: sixth foal: half-brother to 3 winners by Whittingham, including useful 5f winners Inya Lake (including Molecomb Stakes at 2 yrs) and Old Blue Eyes (at 2 yrs in 2001): dam, 2-y-o 5f winner, best at 6f: fair form: won maiden at Pontefract in September: only good run in nurseries when equal-third at Chester: should prove best at 5f/6f: acts on firm going. *John A. Quinn, Ireland*

ROKO 4 b.g. Komaite (USA) – Robert's Daughter (Robellino (USA) 127) [2006 –§,   **– §**
a38§: f6g⁵ f6g f5g⁶ p6g f6g⁴ f8g 6m p5.1g 7d f6g Dec 28] plain gelding: poor performer: **a47 §**
stays 6f: acts on all-weather, little recent form on turf: usually wears headgear: tongue tied last 6 starts: temperamental. *S. R. Bowring*

ROKOCOKO (IRE) 4 b.g. Fasliyev (USA) 120 – Early Memory (USA) 83 (Devil's   **63**
Bag (USA)) [2006 75: 5f 5d⁶ 5s a5g Sep 5] modest maiden: best effort at Naas final 3-y-o start: better than result when sixth in handicap at Pontefract second outing, not unduly knocked about: raced mainly at 5f/6f: acts on firm and good to soft going: blinkered 3 of last 5 starts: tongue tied. *John A. Quinn, Ireland*

ROLLERBIRD 4 b.f. Sinndar (IRE) 134 – Speedybird (IRE) 71 (Danehill (USA) 126)   **59**
[2006 69: 11v 6s⁶ 7v p9.5g Nov 11] modest maiden, lightly raced: well held in cheek-pieces at Wolverhampton final start: stays 1m: acts on polytrack and soft ground. *T. Hogan, Ireland*

ROLONS ADVICE 5 ch.g. Weldnaas (USA) 112 – Clova (Move Off 112) [2006 p9.5g   **–**
p12.2g Nov 14] well held in maidens at Wolverhampton. *V. Smith*

ROL'OVER BEETHOVEN (FR) 3 b.c. Mozart (IRE) 131 – Don't Worry Me (IRE)   **90**
113 (Dancing Dissident (USA) 119) [2006 88: 7m² 8g⁶ 6f³ 6m² 6f⁴ 6m* 6m² 7f Aug 3] tall colt: fairly useful performer: won handicap at Fairyhouse in July: got no room and finished full of running in similar event at Goodwood final start: stays 7.5f: acts on firm and good to soft ground. *A. P. O'Brien, Ireland*

ROMAN BOY (ARG) 7 ch.g. Roy (USA) – Roman Red (USA) (Blushing Groom   **60**
(FR) 131) [2006 f6g⁶ f8g Dec 21] fair performer at best: little show in Hong Kong in 2004 for C. Shum, and unraced in 2005: modest form both starts on return to Britain: stays 1m: acts on good to firm and good to soft ground: races freely. *Stef Liddiard*

ROMAN EMPIRE 6 b.g. Efisio 120 – Gena Ivor (USA) (Sir Ivor (USA) 135) [2006   **65**
65: f6g p6g³ f7g* f6g f7g³ p7.1g² p6g² f7g³ p9.5g⁵ f7g⁵ Apr 27] lengthy, good-bodied gelding: fair performer: won handicap at Southwell in January: left K. Ryan after seventh outing: seems to stay easy 9.5f (all wins at 6f/7f): acts on all-weather and soft going: wears visor/blinkers nowadays: has looked hard ride. *P. A. Blockley*

ROMAN HISTORY (IRE) 3 b.g. Titus Livius (FR) 115 – Tetradonna (IRE) 102   **60**
(Teenoso (USA) 135) [2006 60§: f7g 8.5d 7g⁵ 9.3m⁶ 7.9m² 9f 8d⁶ 7.2m* 6.9f⁶ 7.5g⁴ 10m* Sep 11] sturdy gelding: modest performer: left Robert Gray after reappearance: won claimer at Ayr in August and selling handicap at Redcar in September: stays 1¼m: acts on good to firm going: often wears cheekpieces: none too consistent, and has shown temperament. *Miss Tracy Waggott*

ROMAN MAZE 6 ch.g. Lycius (USA) 124 – Maze Garden (USA) (Riverman (USA) **94**
131) [2006 104: p6g³ 7.1g⁴ 7.6d⁴ 7g 6f⁶ 7m³ 7.6m³ 7m 7.6g 6d 7f p7.1m Oct 9] good-
bodied gelding: just fairly useful handicapper nowadays: needs good test at 6f, and stays
7.6f: acts on all-weather, firm and good to soft going: usually held up. *W. M. Brisbourne*

ROMANOVA (IRE) 4 b.f. Grand Lodge (USA) 125 – Millitrix 82 (Doyoun 124) **56**
[2006 –: p10g p8g 12m⁶ 11.7d 13.3m 10m 9.7f 11.7m 9g Sep 12] tall, leggy filly:
modest maiden: probably stays 1½m: acts on good to firm going: blinkered last 4 starts.
Dr J. R. J. Naylor

ROMANOV DYNASTY (IRE) 2 gr. or br.c. (Apr 15) Green Desert (USA) 127 – **79**
Russian Rebel (Machiavellian (USA) 123) [2006 6m² 7m 6m 7.1m⁴ 7d 8g 7v 6g⁴ Dec 24]
€40,000Y, 58,000 2-y-o: rather leggy, close-coupled colt: fourth foal: dam unraced sister
to useful French miler Queen Catherine: fair maiden: best effort on debut when second in
minor event at Newmarket: sold from R. Hannon 30,000 gns after sixth start: should stay
1m: acts on good to firm going: tried in cheekpieces. *F. Rodriguez, Spain*

ROMAN QUEST 3 b.g. Lujain (USA) 119 – Roma 61 (Second Set (IRE) 127) [2006 **79**
60p: p7g⁵ 6g* p6g⁴ 6.1d 6g* 6g³ 7m⁴ 6m Sep 20] tall, good-topped gelding: has scope:
fair handicapper: won at Folkestone in April and Goodwood in June: should prove as
effective at 7f as 6f: may prove best on good ground or firmer: fractious in stall on debut.
H. Morrison

ROMAN QUINTET (IRE) 6 ch.g. Titus Livius (FR) 115 – Quintellina 83 (Robellino **82**
(USA) 127) [2006 81: p6g⁴ p7g 6g⁶ 6g³ 6d p6g² 6m p6g⁴ p7g p6g Oct 17] fairly
useful performer: effective at 6f to easy 1m: acts on all-weather, firm and good to
soft going: tried tongue tied/in headgear: free-going sort: quirky and has found little.
D. W. P. Arbuthnot

ROMANY NIGHTS (IRE) 6 b.g. Night Shift (USA) – Gipsy Moth 99 (Efisio 120) **94**
[2006 88, a73: 6g 6g* 7m³ 6d 7m² 6m⁴ 6g 6m² 6f Sep 18] strong gelding: fairly useful **a–**
handicapper on turf, fair when last ran on all-weather in 2005: won at Goodwood in May:
creditable efforts when placed after: effective at 6f/7f: acts on all-weather, firm and good
to soft going: tried visored, blinkered nowadays. *Miss Gay Kelleway*

ROME (IRE) 7 br.g. Singspiel (IRE) 133 – Ela Romara 124 (Ela-Mana-Mou 132) **–**
[2006 64: p13g Feb 1] fair handicapper at 5 yrs: little form on Flat since, well held only
outing in 2006: often wears cheekpieces/blinkers: has looked none too keen. *G. P. Enright*

ROMIL STAR (GER) 9 b.g. Chief's Crown (USA) – Romelia (USA) (Woodman **57**
(USA) 126) [2006 53§, a81§: f16g⁴ f14g⁶ f12g² f11g² f12g⁴ f12g³ f12g² f14g³ f14s² **a73 d**
f12g⁵ f12g* 15.8d f12g² 12g⁴ f14g⁴ 13.8f³ 16f⁵ f12g² f14g³ f12g⁶ f12g³ p16.5g⁵
p13.9g f12g⁵ Dec 29] strong, workmanlike gelding: fair performer on all-weather (on
downgrade), modest on turf: won amateur claimer at Southwell (eighth course success)
in April: left K. Burke after eighteenth start, M. Attwater after twentieth: stays 1¾m: acts
on all-weather and any turf going: usually wears headgear. *M. Wellings*

RONALDO 3 b.g. Tomba 119 – Satiric (IRE) (Doyoun 124) [2006 8.1s 8d 7.1g⁵ 8.1g **–**
8m 7.6g 11.9m⁴ 10.2m p10g Sep 5] strong gelding: little form: left W. Muir £900 and
gelded after fifth start: blinkered/visored last 2 starts. *A. M. Hales*

RONALDSAY 2 gr.f. (Apr 13) Kirkwall 118 – Crackling 57 (Electric 126) [2006 p6g⁶ **80**
7f² 7g² 7d* Sep 8] 34,000Y: leggy, workmanlike filly: half-sister to several winners,
including fairly useful 5.7f (at 2 yrs) to 1¼m winner Crackle (by Anshan) and 3-y-o Fen
Guest: dam 9f and 1½m winner who stayed 2m: fairly useful form: runner-up in maidens
at Folkestone (hung markedly left second time) before winning nursery at York: will be
suited by 1m/1¼m. *R. Hannon*

RONANNIS 2 b.c. (May 4) Efisio 120 – Blown-Over 41 (Ron's Victory (USA) 129) **–**
[2006 6m 6m⁶ 6.1m Sep 15] good-bodied colt: well held in maidens. *J. Jay*

RONDO 3 b.g. Piccolo 121 – Flourish (Selkirk (USA) 129) [2006 64: 6d* 6m 5g 5g⁶ 6m **75 d**
6m 6.1m 6m 6g⁴ 7f⁶ 8s 6v Oct 9] tall, good-topped gelding: fair performer: won maiden
at Thirsk in April: didn't progress in handicaps after: stays 6f: acts on firm and good to
soft going: blinkered (ran poorly) final start. *T. D. Barron*

RON IN ERNEST 2 ch.g. (Mar 11) Medicean 128 – Viewfinder (USA) (Boundary **61**
(USA) 117) [2006 6g⁶ 7g 6m³ 7m 6m Sep 16] lengthy gelding: modest maiden: third to
Simply Perfect at Lingfield: well beaten in nurseries: should stay 1m: gelded after final
outing. *J. A. Geake*

RONNIE FROM DONNY (IRE) 6 b.g. Eagle Eyed (USA) 111 – New Rochelle **–**
(IRE) 65 (Lafontaine (USA) 117) [2006 51d: f5g 7f f5g Dec 27] sturdy, useful-looking

gelding: one-time fairly useful performer: no form in 2006: tried in cheekpieces/tongue tie/visor. *C. J. Teague*

RONNIE HOWE 2 b.g. (Mar 10) Hunting Lion (IRE) 115 – Arasong 76 (Aragon 118) **72** [2006 6m 5m² 5m⁴ 5f⁴ 6m 5d³ 5d³ Oct 3] sturdy gelding: half-brother to 7f winner (including at 2 yrs) Annie's Song (by Farfelu) and 4-y-o La Viola: dam 5f winner, including at 2 yrs: fair maiden: in frame 5 times: best at 5f: acts on firm and good to soft going. *M. Dods*

RONNIES LAD 4 b.g. Lake Coniston (IRE) 131 – Lycius Touch 50 (Lycius (USA) **40** 124) [2006 59d: 8.3m⁶ 10f 12.4m 9f 8.5m f7g f8g p8.6g⁵ Dec 21] poor performer nowadays: stays 1¼m: acts on polytrack and firm going: tried in cheekpieces/visor. *J. R. Norton*

RONSARD (IRE) 4 b.g. Spectrum (IRE) 126 – Touche-A-Tout (IRE) (Royal Academy **71 d** (USA) 130) [2006 74: p10g p9.5g p8.6g p8.6g 10.2d p7.1g⁶ 8.2m 7d⁵ 10g⁵ 10.2m p10g³ p12.2m Nov 8] leggy gelding: fair handicapper, on downgrade: left Heather Dalton after fifth outing, T. Pitt after tenth and P. D. Evans after eleventh: needs further than 7f, and stays easy 1¼m: acts on polytrack and soft going (below form on firmer than good): tried blinkered/visored. *J. C. Tuck*

ROODOLPH 2 ch.g. (Feb 2) Primo Valentino (IRE) 116 – Roo 97 (Rudimentary (USA) **84 p** 118) [2006 7f* Sep 18] big, lengthy gelding: second foal: half-brother to useful 5f (at 2 yrs) and 7f winner Roodeye (by Inchinor): dam 2-y-o 5f/6f winner: 25/1, winning debut in maiden at Folkestone, merely pushed out to beat Sir Liam by 2½ lengths: withdrawn (broke through stall) month later: potentially useful. *R. F. Johnson Houghton*

ROOFTOP PROTEST (IRE) 9 b.g. Thatching 131 – Seattle Siren (USA) 101 **78** (Seattle Slew (USA)) [2006 88: 12s 14g⁵ 16g 16m⁴ 16g 17m 16d⁶ 16s³ 16d 16g Sep 19] tall gelding: fair handicapper nowadays: creditable fifth at Musselburgh second start: stays 17f: acts on any going: tried blinkered, usually wears cheekpieces: tongue tied. *T. Hogan, Ireland*

ROONAH (FR) 3 b.f. Xaar 132 – Caer Mecene (FR) (Caerwent 123) [2006 63d: f7g **–** p7.1g 7m 6d 12v Oct 31] modest maiden at 2 yrs: no show in 2006: tried blinkered/visored. *Karen McLintock*

ROSALIE 3 ch.f. Fantastic Light (USA) 134 – Tularosa (In The Wings 128) [2006 11m **–** p10g Jul 12] fourth living foal: half-sister to fairly useful 1¼m/1½m winner Ambrosine (by Nashwan) and 5-y-o Camrose: dam, French 11f winner, half-sister to Most Welcome: modest maiden for R. Gibson in France at 2 yrs: well beaten in handicaps in Britain. *C. F. Wall*

ROSAPENNA (IRE) 4 b.f. Spectrum (IRE) 126 – Blaine (USA) (Lyphard's Wish (FR) **83** 124) [2006 84: 6m⁶ 6m³ 6m* 6m 6f* Jul 31] workmanlike filly: fairly useful handicapper: won at Yarmouth in June and Windsor in July: stays 7f: acts on polytrack, firm and good to soft going: carries head awkwardly: sometimes finds little: reportedly in foal to Dansili. *C. F. Wall*

ROSBAY (IRE) 2 b.c. (Jan 26) Desert Prince (IRE) 130 – Dark Rosaleen (IRE) **87** (Darshaan 133) [2006 6g⁶ 6v⁴ 6m⁵ 7f* 7f² 8d* 8d⁴ 7s Oct 14] 12,000Y: lengthy colt: first foal: dam unraced: fairly useful performer: won maiden at Thirsk in July and nursery at Newcastle in August: seemed amiss final start: will stay 1¼m: acts on any ground. *T. D. Easterby*

ROSCOMMON 3 br.g. Fraam 114 – Gaelic Air 65 (Ballad Rock 122) [2006 74p: 8m **–** 8m⁵ 10m 7.2g Aug 21] rather leggy gelding: fair winner only start at 2 yrs: well held in handicaps in 2006, looking temperamental on reappearance: tried visored. *I. Semple*

ROSE AMBER 5 ch.m. Double Trigger (IRE) 123 – Sun Follower (Relkino 131) [2006 **–** –: p8g p10g Jan 14] no sign of ability. *J. J. Bridger*

ROSE BIEN 4 b. or br.f. Bien Bien (USA) 125 – Madame Bovary 82 (Ile de Bourbon **70** (USA) 133) [2006 62: p13g p12.2g 11.5m⁵ p16.5g² p13.9g* p13.9g⁴ 12f* 16.2f* 14.1f* 18f⁵ 17.1d² 16.2m⁵ 16g² p13.9m Oct 9] sparely-made filly: fair performer: successful in banded race at Wolverhampton in May, and handicaps at Folkestone in June and Beverley and Redcar (apprentices) in July: stays 17f: acts on polytrack, firm and good to soft going: usually wears cheekpieces, blinkered final outing. *P. J. McBride*

ROSE BRIAR (IRE) 3 b.f. Grand Lodge (USA) 125 – My Branch 111 (Distant Rela- **60** tive 128) [2006 7g 8.2m⁵ 7s 8.3m p10g Aug 2] strong filly: good mover: fifth foal: half-sister to several winners, including very smart 6f (including at 2 yrs) and 7f winner Tante Rose (by Barathea) and useful 2003 2-y-o 6f/7f winner Bay Tree (by Daylami):

dam, 5f (at 2 yrs) to 7f winner, also third in Irish 1000 Guineas: modest form in maidens: well held in handicaps last 2 starts. *R. Charlton*

ROSECLIFF 4 b.g. Montjeu (IRE) 137 – Dance Clear (IRE) 99 (Marju (IRE) 127) –
[2006 81: 12s Oct 6] good-topped gelding: fairly useful performer at best: well held only Flat start in 2006: tried visored: fairly useful hurdler. *Mrs H. Dalton*

ROSE COURT 2 b.f. (May 13) Celtic Swing 138 – Smart Spirit (IRE) 71 (Persian Bold –
123) [2006 5d 6f 6g 7m 6d 7g Sep 30] tall, rather leggy filly: third foal: dam, 1¼m winner, also winning hurdler: little form: sold 1,200 gns, sent to Iran. *K. G. Reveley*

ROSE GERMANY 2 ch.f. (Apr 15) Inchinor 119 – Hoist (IRE) 75 (Bluebird (USA) 59
125) [2006 7m 7.1d 6s Oct 10] 22,000Y: half-sister to several winners, including useful Italian 5f (at 2 yrs) to 1m winner Golden Polar (by Polar Falcon): dam, 6f winner, half-sister to smart stayer Capal Garmon: modest form in maidens: sold 2,500 gns, sent to Spain. *M. R. Channon*

ROSEIN 4 b.f. Komaite (USA) – Red Rosein 97 (Red Sunset 120) [2006 72: f7g* p6g 69
6m⁶ p7.1g² f6g² p7.1f⁵ p6g p6g* 6.1g⁵ p6g* p6g⁴ p6g⁴ Nov 16] big, heavy-topped filly: a86
fairly useful handicapper on all-weather, fair on turf: won at Southwell in June and Wolverhampton in September and October: will prove best at 6f/7f: acts on all-weather, soft and good to firm going: sometimes slowly away. *Mrs G. S. Rees*

ROSE LADY (IRE) 3 ch.f. King of Kings (IRE) 125 – Shamisen 86 (Diesis 133) [2006 71 d
8.2m² 7s 8m p7.1m Sep 2] 30,000Y: strong, lengthy filly: seventh foal: half-sister to 3 winners, including smart 6f (at 2 yrs)/7f winner Membership (by Belong To Me) and useful 5f to 7f winner Lone Piper (by Warning): dam, 2-y-o 7f winner, sister to smart miler Enharmonic: fair maiden: little impact after debut: stays 8.2f: acts on good to firm ground: sold 18,000 gns in November. *M. R. Channon*

ROSEMARKIE 2 br.f. (Apr 2) Diktat 126 – Sparkling Isle 66 (Inchinor 119) [2006 p8g –
Nov 15] third foal: half-sister to useful 6f (at 2 yrs) to 1m winner in France/Spain Trip To The Moon (by Fasliyev): dam, maiden, form only at 6f/7f at 2 yrs: last in maiden at Kempton, slowly away. *J. L. Spearing*

ROSE MUWASIM 3 ch.f. In The Wings 128 – Muwasim (USA) (Meadowlake (USA)) 71
[2006 57p: p8g² p7g² p8g⁵ 9.8g⁶ 10d f6g p7.1g⁵ p8.6g² Dec 30] small filly: fair maiden: left E. Dunlop after fifth start: probably stays 1¼m: acts on polytrack: tried blinkered: doesn't impress with attitude. *M. J. Attwater*

ROSE OF INCHINOR 3 b.f. Inchinor 119 – Rosa Canina 91 (Bustino 136) [2006 73: 70
8.1g p7.1g 7g³ 7.5g 6s Oct 10] leggy filly: fair maiden: claimed from M. Tregoning £8,000 after fourth start: bred to be suited by at least 1m: form only on good ground. *R. E. Barr*

ROSE OF PETRA (IRE) 2 b.f. (Feb 29) Golan (IRE) 129 – Desert Beauty (IRE) 103 88
(Green Desert (USA) 127) [2006 7d 8.3m² 7m* p8g⁴ Oct 20] angular, useful-looking filly: fourth foal: half-sister to 2 winners abroad by Machiavellian: dam, 7f/1m winner, half-sister to very smart performers Greek Dance (at 1¼m) and Islington (1¼m/1½m) and 4-y-o Mountain High: fairly useful form: won maiden at Brighton by 4 lengths in September: fourth to Lady Grace in competitive nursery at Lingfield: will stay 1¼m. *Sir Michael Stoute*

ROSE THISTLE (UAE) 4 b.f. Timber Country (USA) 124 – Ines Bloom (IRE) 52
(Sadler's Wells (USA) 132) [2006 –: p12.2g p7.1g p9.5g 6m 8m Aug 23] eighth foal: dam, 9f winner in Japan at 2 yrs, half-sister to very smart performer up to 1½m Flame of Tara, herself dam of Salsabil and Marju: fair form in maiden at Fairyhouse only 2-y-o outing: modest at best since, leaving J. Oxx after final 3-y-o start and J. A. Quinn after running at Wolverhampton first 3 outings in 2006: tried tongue tied/visored. *Seamus Fahey, Ireland*

ROSHANAK (IRE) 2 b.f. (Feb 19) Spinning World (USA) 130 – Desert Bloom (IRE) 91 p
(Pilsudski (IRE) 134) [2006 6m 6d* Aug 2] strong, compact filly: first foal: dam unraced out of half-sister to very smart middle-distance performers Greek Dance, Islington and Mountain High: much improved from debut (hung) when winning maiden at Leicester by ½ length from Russian Rosie, idling: will be suited by 1m: should make a useful 3-y-o. *B. J. Meehan*

ROSIE CROSS (IRE) 2 b.f. (Feb 15) Cape Cross (IRE) 129 – Professional Mom 64
(USA) (Spinning World (USA) 130) [2006 p6g⁴ 6m⁶ p7g 6g p7.1m Oct 2] 5,000F: first foal: dam unraced out of half-sister to dam of Peintre Celebre: modest maiden: should stay 1m+: best efforts on polytrack. *R. F. Johnson Houghton*

ROSIELLA 4 b.f. Tagula (IRE) 116 – Queen of Silk (IRE) 93 (Brief Truce (USA) 126) **45**
[2006 53: p5.1g p7g p6g 10m⁴ 9.9g 8f⁶ 11.6m 16.2f⁶ Jul 28] leggy filly: poor performer
nowadays: left M. Blanshard after third outing: best at 5f/6f: acts on polytrack and good
to firm going, probably on soft: tried blinkered: tongue tied last 5 outings: sold 1,000 gns,
sent to Sweden. *M. Appleby*

ROSIE'S GLORY (USA) 2 b. or br.f. (Apr 4) More Than Ready (USA) 120 – Cukee **79**
(USA) (Langfuhr (CAN) 124) [2006 7d 8m³ 8m⁶ Oct 8] $90,000Y, $215,000 2-y-o:
well-made filly: first foal: dam unraced: easily best effort (fair form) when third to
Empire Day in maiden at Newmarket: stays 1m. *B. J. Meehan*

ROSIE'S RESULT 6 ch.g. Case Law 113 – Precious Girl 76 (Precious Metal 106) **52 §**
[2006 55§: p5.1g 5g⁶ 5f³ 5f 5d⁶ 5m² 5m⁶ 5m* Aug 17] sparely-made gelding: modest
performer: second start in 24 hrs, won handicap at Musselburgh in August: best at 5f: acts
on firm and good to soft going: tried visored/in cheekpieces: unreliable. *M. Todhunter*

ROSINKA (IRE) 3 b.f. Soviet Star (USA) 128 – Last Drama (IRE) (Last Tycoon 131) **72 +**
[2006 96p: 7m⁴ 8.1g p8.5f* Oct 28] tall filly: fairly useful form at 2 yrs: sustained injury
after, and well below form first 2 starts on belated return in 2006: left J. Dunlop, won
allowance race at Keeneland in October: stays 8.5f: acts on polytrack and soft going:
upset in stall and withdrawn on intended reappearance. *H. G. Motion, USA*

ROSITA MIA (IRE) 3 ch.f. Dr Fong (USA) 128 – Intercede (Pursuit of Love 124) **60**
[2006 62: 6f⁶ 6g³ 6f 6m⁶ Jun 21] close-coupled filly: modest maiden: should stay 7f: acts
on good to soft going. *D. W. Barker*

ROSSIN GOLD (IRE) 4 b.g. Rossini (USA) 118 – Sacred Heart (IRE) 45 (Catrail **55**
(USA) 123) [2006 57: 9.2m³ 16.1s² Sep 4] modest performer: stays 2m: acts on polytrack,
firm and soft ground: blinkered at 2 yrs: has shown signs of waywardness: fair hurdler,
successful in May and October. *P. Monteith*

ROSS IS BOSS 4 gr.g. Paris House 123 – Billie Grey 72 (Chilibang 120) [2006 –: f6g **–**
f6g Dec 29] tall gelding: no form. *C. J. Teague*

ROSS MOOR 4 b.g. Dansili 127 – Snipe Hall 93 (Crofthall 110) [2006 68: p13g* **74 +**
Dec 22] big, strong, close-coupled gelding: fair performer: sold from Mrs A. Perrett
15,000 gns and gelded, improved to win maiden at Lingfield (all-weather debut) only
start in 2006: stays 13f: acts on polytrack, raced only on good/good to firm ground on
turf: tried blinkered. *N. P. Littmoden*

ROSTHWAITE (IRE) 3 b.f. Desert Style (IRE) 121 – Thirlmere (Cadeaux Genereux **–**
131) [2006 73: f7g⁵ 10s 8d 7f 7s 7m f7g Dec 2] deep-girthed filly: fair performer at 2 yrs:
well below form in 2006: blinkered final start: hung left throughout once at 2 yrs. *Ronald Thompson*

ROTATION (IRE) 2 b.g. (Mar 25) Galileo (IRE) 134 – Termania (IRE) (Shirley **–**
Heights 130) [2006 6m 6.1m 6d Oct 9] sturdy gelding: behind in maidens: gelded after
final outing. *J. W. Hills*

ROTHESAY DANCER 3 b.f. Lujain (USA) 119 – Rhinefield Beauty (IRE) 52 (Shal- **73**
ford (IRE) 124§) [2006 73: 5d 5m 5d³ 5m 5f⁵ 5f³ 5m² 5f* 5f² 5m⁴ 5m 5s 5d 5g 5s 5d
p5.1g² p5.1g Nov 27] leggy filly: has a quick action: fair handicapper: won at Ayr in July:
speedy, and will prove best at 5f: acts on polytrack, firm and good to soft going: wears
cheekpieces nowadays. *J. S. Goldie*

ROTUMA (IRE) 7 b.g. Tagula (IRE) 116 – Cross Question (USA) 84 (Alleged (USA) **63**
138) [2006 76d, a62: p9.5g 9.9d 10.1m² 10s³ 10.1m⁵ 10.1g⁴ 10g 10m² 10.1d* **a–**
9.9m⁶ 10.9d Oct 13] smallish, useful-looking gelding: modest performer nowadays: won
handicap at Newcastle in August: best around 1¼m: acts on polytrack and any turf going:
blinkered: has worn tongue tie: tends to carry head awkwardly. *M. Dods*

ROUEN (IRE) 2 b.c. (Mar 8) Noverre (USA) 125 – Sheezalady (Zafonic (USA) 130) **82**
[2006 5s² 5g⁴ 6g² 5.1g May 17] 15,000F: good-topped colt: third foal: dam unraced:
fairly useful maiden: second at Redcar (minor event) and Ripon: broke down badly at
Bath: should have stayed 1m. *M. R. Channon*

ROUGE ET NOIR 8 b.g. Hernando (FR) 127 – Bayrouge (IRE) (Gorytus (USA) 132) **57 §**
[2006 61: 12g 16f³ 16g 16m³ 15m 14g 14d Oct 8] lengthy gelding: modest performer:
claimed from K. Reveley £10,000 after second start: stays 17.2f: acts on polytrack and
firm going: sometimes tongue tied: has high head carriage: ungenuine. *P. Monteith*

ROWANBERRY 4 b.f. Bishop of Cashel 122 – Raintree Venture (Good Times (ITY)) **50**
[2006 54: p5.1g³ p6g² p6g² 5f⁶ 6.1m 5d³ 5.2f p5.1g² p6g Dec 13] modest performer: **a59**

effective at 5f/6f, should stay 7f: acts on polytrack, firm and good to soft going: sometimes slowly away. *R. M. H. Cowell*

ROWAN LODGE (IRE) 4 ch.g. Indian Lodge (IRE) 127 – Tirol Hope (IRE) 100 **79**
(Tirol 127) [2006 84: 8.1m³ p8g⁴ p8g 10d³ 11.9s⁵ 10d 10g³ 8.3s⁶ 10.1s 8d* 8.2s Oct 25]
sturdy gelding: fair performer: won claimer at Yarmouth (hung left) in October: stays
1¼m: acts on heavy and good to firm going, probably on polytrack: tried blinkered,
visored last 2 starts: free-going sort. *M. H. Tompkins*

ROWAN PURSUIT 5 b.m. Pursuit of Love 124 – Golden Seattle (IRE) (Seattle **–**
Dancer (USA) 119 [2006 53, a63: p8g³ p8g⁴ p8g⁵ p7g p7g p8g⁵ Apr 3] small mare: **a56**
modest performer: stays 1¼m: acts on polytrack and firm ground: blinkered: has carried
head awkwardly: held up. *J. Akehurst*

ROWAN RIVER 2 b.f. (Mar 13) Invincible Spirit (IRE) 121 – Lemon Tree (USA) **62**
(Zilzal (USA) 137) [2006 5m⁶ 7g⁵ 7.1d Sep 16] third foal: dam 2-y-o 7f winner in Italy:
modest form in maidens: looks quirky. *M. H. Tompkins*

ROWAN VENTURE 2 b.g. (Feb 18) Vettori (IRE) 119 – Golden Seattle (IRE) (Seattle **65**
Dancer (USA) 119) [2006 6g p7g p7g 6s⁵ 6d p7.1m 8.3g⁶ Oct 16] third foal: half-
brother to 4-y-o Rowan Warning and 5-y-o Rowan Pursuit: dam Italian 2-y-o 5f/6f
winner: maiden: fifth to Makshoof at Haydock: poor form otherwise: usually blinkered.
M. H. Tompkins

ROWAN WARNING 4 b.g. Diktat 126 – Golden Seattle (IRE) (Seattle Dancer (USA) **67**
119) [2006 71: p7.1g⁴ p8.6g⁴ p8g⁵ p7.1g² 7g 7f³ 7m 8.3m 7d p8g² p8g* Dec 15]
close-coupled, quite good-topped gelding: fair handicapper: won at Kempton in December: stays 8.6f: acts on polytrack and firm ground: tried visored/in cheekpieces.
J. R. Boyle

ROWE PARK 3 b.g. Dancing Spree (USA) – Magic Legs 54 (Reprimand 122) [2006 **77 +**
11.6f p8g 7f⁶ p6g p5g* p5g* p5.1g* Dec 31] £1,200 2-y-o: second foal: half-brother to
4-y-o Magic Rush: dam ran once: fair performer: won maiden at Lingfield in November
and handicaps there and Wolverhampton in December: best efforts at 5f: acts on polytrack: races prominently. *Mrs L. C. Jewell*

ROXAN (IRE) 2 b.f. (Feb 12) Rock of Gibraltar (IRE) 133 – Gamra (IRE) 73 (Green **93**
Desert (USA) 127) [2006 5g* 5m 6d² Sep 16] 78,000F, 160,000Y: tall, quite good-topped
filly: first foal: dam, 1m winner, sister to smart 6.5f (in USA) to 1m winner Distant Oasis
and half-sister to very smart performers Reprimand (miler) and Wiorno (stayed 1½m):
fairly useful form: impressive winning debut in listed event at Beverley in May: 6/4,
reportedly lame when well held in Queen Mary Stakes at Royal Ascot: off 3 months, good
1¼ lengths second of 7 to Princess Iris in Firth of Clyde Stakes at Ayr: will probably stay
1m: has been heavily bandaged. *K. A. Ryan*

ROXY SINGER 2 b.f. (Mar 24) Erhaab (USA) 127 – Rainy Day Song 61 (Persian Bold **–**
123) [2006 6m p7g p7.1g 7m Aug 11] leggy, close-coupled filly: sixth foal: half-sister
to 3 winners, including 1m/1¼m winner Broughton Spirit (by Bishop of Cashel): dam
lightly-raced maiden: little form. *W. J. Musson*

ROYA 3 b.c. Daylami (IRE) 138 – Aegean Dream (IRE) 97 (Royal Academy (USA) 130) **72**
[2006 68: 10.2s⁵ 11m 11.7g⁵ 11.5m⁴ 8.1g² 10.2m Sep 1] lightly-made colt: fair maiden:
will stay 1½m: acts on soft and good to firm going: sold 13,500 gns. *R. Hannon*

ROYAL AGREEMENT 3 b.g. Royal Applause 124 – Another Fantasy (IRE) 103 **57**
(Danehill (USA) 126) [2006 56: 7f 8f³ 8.1m 7f Jul 4] modest maiden: stays 1m: acts on
firm going. *B. G. Powell*

ROYAL ALCHEMIST 4 b.f. Kingsinger (IRE) 94 – Pure Gold 88 (Dilum (USA) 115) **107**
[2006 107: p8g* 9s² 8v³ 8m³ 10m p8g 9d Sep 30] good-topped filly: useful performer:
won listed race at Kempton (by ½ length from Violet Park) in April: creditable efforts in
pattern races next 3 starts, including when 3¾ lengths third to Soviet Song in Windsor
Forest Stakes at Ascot fourth outing: left M. Usher, acted as pacemaker in Eclipse Stakes
at Sandown fifth outing: well below form in Cambridgeshire (Handicap) at Newmarket
final start: stays 1¼m: acts on polytrack, heavy and good to firm going: sometimes hangs:
sent to UAE. *B. J. Meehan*

ROYAL AMNESTY 3 b.c. Desert Prince (IRE) 130 – Regal Peace 94 (Known Fact **–**
(USA) 135) [2006 53: p8.6g* p8.6g* p8.6g* p9.5g* p10g* 10s p8g* p10g 8m p8g⁶ p10g⁴ p10g³ **a87**
p12g⁴ p12g⁵ p9.5g³ Dec 28] close-coupled colt: fairly useful on all-weather, winning
seller and 2 handicaps at Wolverhampton in March/April and handicaps at Kempton in
May and June: good efforts when in frame after: stays easy 1½m: acts on polytrack, no
form on turf in 2006: tried blinkered: patiently ridden. *G. C. H. Chung*

ROYAL AND REGAL (IRE) 2 b.c. (Mar 24) Sadler's Wells (USA) 132 – Smart 'n   **97 P**
Noble (USA) (Smarten (USA)) [2006 8d² 8g* Oct 29] €380,000Y: fifth foal: half-brother
to smart 2000 2-y-o 6f/7f winner who stayed 2m Celtic Silence (by Celtic Swing): dam
won 12 races in USA, including Grade 2 7f event: created good impression in both races,
finishing strongly, having been niggled along some way out, when 2½ lengths second to
Bernando in newcomers race at Chantilly, then winning maiden at Saint-Cloud later in
month by 2 lengths from Prince Fasliyev, leading 1f out and eased slightly near finish:
will be suited by 1¼m+: well regarded, and likely to go on to much better things at 3 yrs.
A. Fabre, France

ROYAL APPROACH 5 b.m. Royal Applause 124 – Passionelle 56 (Nashwan (USA)   **–**
135) [2006 11g f8g⁴ f11g Nov 2] rather leggy mare: maiden: off over 2 years, well held in
2006. *J. R. Norton*

ROYAL AUDITON 5 ch.m. First Trump 118 – Loriner's Lass 80 (Saddlers' Hall (IRE)   **–**
126) [2006 70: p12.2g 14m 13.1s⁶ May 22] fair maiden at 4 yrs: well held in 2006.
T. T. Clement

ROYAL AXMINSTER 11 b.g. Alzao (USA) 117 – Number One Spot 71 (Reference   **52**
Point 139) [2006 48, a60: p12.2g p12g f11g* f14g⁴ f12g⁴ 11.7f³ f12g Jul 31] useful-   **a60**
looking gelding: modest performer: won banded event at Southwell in March: stays
1½m: acts on all-weather, firm and good to soft going: tried blinkered/in cheekpieces:
makes running/races prominently. *Mrs P. N. Dutfield*

ROYAL BANDIT 3 b.c. King Charlemagne (USA) 120 – Cutpurse Moll 76 (Green   **69 d**
Desert (USA) 127) [2006 p6g² p5g⁴ p6g⁶ 6m⁴ 6m 7f Sep 18] 21,000Y: lengthy colt:
half-brother to several winners, including 7-y-o Colonel Cotton and fairly useful 7f (at
2 yrs) and 1½m winner Lola Sapola (by Benny The Dip): dam 7f winner: fair form in
maiden at Kempton on debut: regressed after: should stay 7f: acts on polytrack: blinkered
final start: sold 4,000 gns. *N. A. Callaghan*

ROYAL BOROUGH 3 ch.g. Compton Place 125 – Norpella 95 (Northfields (USA))   **52**
[2006 6g 7f Sep 5] good-topped gelding: modest form in maidens only on debut: sold
3,500 gns. *R. M. Beckett*

ROYAL CHALLENGE 5 b.g. Royal Applause 124 – Anotheranniversary 95 (Ema-   **92**
rati (USA) 74) [2006 86: 6g 6d³ 6g⁵ 6v⁵ 6m* 6m 5m² 5.4f* Jul 27] well-made gelding:
fairly useful handicapper: won at Windsor (by 1¼ lengths from Border Music) in June
and York (by short head from Kings College Boy) in July: effective at 5f to easy 7f: acts
on firm and good to soft going, possibly not on soft/heavy: waited with: slowly away
sixth outing. *M. H. Tompkins*

ROYAL CHOIR 2 ch.f. (Mar 9) King's Best (USA) 132 – Harmonic Sound (IRE)   **76**
(Grand Lodge (USA) 125) [2006 p7g⁴ Oct 26] 35,000Y: second foal: dam unraced half-
sister to 4-y-o Army of Angels (by King's Best): 50/1, always prominent when around
2½ lengths fourth to Dalvina in maiden at Lingfield. *C. E. Brittain*

ROYAL CITADEL (IRE) 3 b.f. City On A Hill (USA) 114 – Royal Baldini (USA)   **75 d**
(Green Dancer (USA) 132) [2006 73: 6.1m² 7d⁴ 7g 5.7g 8.3m 7.1m 7f p6m Oct 9] rather
leggy, close-coupled filly: fair maiden: regressed during year: stays 7f: acts on good to
firm and good to soft going: in headgear last 7 starts: sold 2,500 gns. *C. G. Cox*

ROYAL COMPOSER (IRE) 3 b.g. Mozart (IRE) 131 – Susun Kelapa (USA) 94 (St   **72**
Jovite (USA) 135) [2006 67: 6d⁶ 7m² 7.5g⁴ 8.1f⁵ 8.5f³ 7.5f 8m 8.5m Sep 19] lengthy,
good-topped gelding: has a quick action: fair maiden: stays 8.5f: acts on firm going: tried
visored (on edge): temperament under suspicion. *T. D. Easterby*

ROYAL CRESCENT (IRE) 3 b.f. Spectrum (IRE) 126 – Marling (IRE) 124 (Lom-   **43**
ond (USA) 128) [2006 p5.1g⁶ f6g Jan 26] half-sister to several winners, including smart
6f/1m winner Mugharreb and fairly useful 7f/1m winner Pilgrim's Way (both by Gone
West): dam won Cheveley Park and Sussex Stakes: better effort in maidens when sixth on
debut: well held next time: should be suited by 7f+. *Sir Mark Prescott*

ROYAL CURTSY 3 b.f. Pivotal 124 – Fen Princess (IRE) 72 (Trojan Fen 118) [2006   **70**
52p: p9.5g² Jun 10] tall filly: on weak side at 2 yrs: fair maiden: upped in trip, much
improved when 1¼ lengths second to Sarwin on handicap debut at Wolverhampton only
start in 2006: should stay 1½m: sold 3,500 gns in November. *Sir Mark Prescott*

ROYAL DIGNITARY (USA) 6 b. or br.g. Saint Ballado (CAN) – Star Actress (USA)   **95**
(Star de Naskra (USA)) [2006 85: 7v 7g 8m* 7.6d 7.1m* 7m⁶ 7f³ 7m 8d⁶ 8g* 7.2d
Sep 16] useful-looking gelding: useful handicapper: won at Musselburgh in May, June
(despite swerving right away from whip) and August, best effort of 2006 when beating

Coalpark by 1¼ lengths on last occasion: best at 7f/1m: acts on dirt and firm going: sometimes wears blinkers/visor: front runner. *D. Nicholls*

ROYAL EMBRACE 3 b.g. Bertolini (USA) 125 – Tight Spin (High Top 131) [2006 **61** 54: p9.5g p9.5g[6] p7.1g[2] p7.1g[2] p8.6g p7.1g[4] p7.1g[4] Dec 21] strong, compact gelding: modest maiden: stays 9.5f: acts on all-weather and heavy going: visored nowadays. *D. Shaw*

ROYAL ENVOY (IRE) 3 b.g. Royal Applause 124 – Seven Notes (Zafonic (USA) **82** 130) [2006 77p: 8m[2] 7f* 7g 7m 6d Oct 19] strong, lengthy gelding: fairly useful performer: landed odds in maiden at Thirsk in May: below form after: likely to prove best short of 1m: acts on firm and good to soft going: sold 11,000 gns, and gelded. *B. W. Hills*

ROYAL FANTASY (IRE) 3 b. or br.f. King's Best (USA) 132 – Dreams 88 (Rainbow **75** Quest (USA) 134) [2006 59p: 8.1g[5] 8m[2] Jun 18] leggy, useful-looking filly: progressive form in maidens, second at Salisbury final start: likely to stay 1¼m: acts on good to firm ground. *J. R. Fanshawe*

ROYAL FLYNN 4 b.g. Royal Applause 124 – Shamriyna (IRE) (Darshaan 133) [2006 **70** 78d: 12m[6] 12.4d[5] 11.8d[4] 12g 10.1m[3] 10d[2] 9.9m[4] 10g 10g[3] 10.1s[4] 10.9d* 10.1s 10.9d* 10d[4] Nov 1] rather leggy, close-coupled gelding: fair handicapper: won at Warwick in September and October: stays 1½m: acts on soft and good to firm going: below form in cheekpieces seventh/eighth starts: usually patiently ridden. *M. Dods*

ROYAL GLEN (IRE) 8 b.m. Royal Abjar (USA) 121 – Sea Glen (IRE) (Glenstal **–** (USA) 118) [2006 –: 12g 14m 8m Jul 25] rather leggy mare: maiden on Flat: modest hurdler, winner in June. *W. S. Coltherd*

ROYAL GUEST 2 b.g. (Feb 12) Royal Applause 124 – Bajan Blue 59 (Lycius (USA) **55** 124) [2006 6m p7.1g Oct 30] quite attractive gelding: mid-field in maidens, not knocked about: gelded after second start. *M. R. Channon*

ROYAL INDULGENCE 6 b.g. Royal Applause 124 – Silent Indulgence (USA) **63** (Woodman (USA) 126) [2006 p8.6g[4] p10g[6] 8f 7.9m[3] 8f* 9.2m 8f[4] 8.2m[3] 9.3g 9.1m[4] 9g* 10.3m[3] 10m[6] 9.2d Sep 25] sturdy gelding: modest handicapper: won at Carlisle in June and Newbury (apprentices) in August: stays 10.3f: acts on polytrack and firm ground: tried in cheekpieces/blinkers: starts slowly. *W. M. Brisbourne*

ROYAL ISLAND (IRE) 4 b.c. Trans Island 119 – Royal House (FR) 104 (Royal **106** Academy (USA) 130) [2006 106: p10g[3] a10g[4] p8.6g 8s[2] p10g 9m 8.5g 8g 8s 9d Sep 30] sturdy colt: has a round action: useful performer: good efforts when third to Tiger Tiger in handicap at Lingfield and ¾-length second of 30 to Blythe Knight in Lincoln (Handicap) at Redcar: stays 1¼m: acts on polytrack, heavy and good to firm ground: sold 60,000 gns. *M. Johnston*

ROYAL JET 4 b.g. Royal Applause 124 – Red Bouquet (Reference Point 139) [2006 **96** 92: 11.9g 12f[5] 12g[2] 12m p11g[2] p12g[2] p12g[3] p12g[3] Oct 21] leggy gelding: useful handicapper: good placed efforts, including when third to Millville at Lingfield final outing: will stay 1¾m: acts on polytrack, firm and good to soft going: tried visored. *M. R. Channon*

ROYAL LASS 3 b.f. Fraam 114 – Sabotini 62 (Prince Sabo 123) [2006 –: p6g[6] f7g **–** Feb 26] little sign of ability. *Rae Guest*

ROYAL LUSTRE 5 b.g. Deputy Minister (CAN) – Snow Bride (USA) 121 (Blushing **56** Groom (FR) 131) [2006 54: f12g f14g f12g p9.5g[2] May 5] good-topped gelding: modest maiden: stays 1½m: acts on all-weather and good to firm ground: tried in cheekpieces. *Robert Gray*

ROYAL MASTER 4 b.g. Royal Applause 124 – High Sevens 90 (Master Willie 129) **64** [2006 65: 9.9d 9g 10m[2] Sep 21] modest maiden handicapper: pulled hard and saddle slipped on reappearance: stays 1¼m: acts on polytrack and firm ground: tried visored/in cheekpieces: winning hurdler. *P. C. Haslam*

ROYAL MELBOURNE (IRE) 6 ch.g. Among Men (USA) 124 – Calachuchi 74 **65** (Martinmas 128) [2006 71, a59: p13.9g 12.4g 12.1d[2] 15.8d[5] 12s Oct 24] lengthy, work- **a46** manlike gelding: fair handicapper on turf, poor on all-weather: stays 1¾m: acts on polytrack and soft going: not straightforward. *Miss J. A. Camacho*

ROYAL MILLENNIUM (IRE) 8 b.g. Royal Academy (USA) 130 – Galatrix 72 (Be **–** My Guest (USA) 126) [2006 110: 6g 6d 6m Jul 1] lengthy, angular gelding: unimpressive mover: very smart performer at best: well held in 2006: has run well when sweating: held up (tends to idle). *M. R. Channon*

ROYAL MOON (USA) 3 ch.g. Royal Academy (USA) 130 – Wedding Gift (FR) 108 **58 d**
(Always Fair (USA) 121) [2006 53: f6g⁶ p9.5g⁴ 12d p7.1g⁵ 8.3d⁶ May 7] modest maiden
at best: stays 9.5f: best effort on polytrack. *T. D. Barron*

ROYAL OATH (USA) 3 b.c. Kingmambo (USA) 125 – Sherkiya (IRE) (Goldneyev **100**
(USA) 114) [2006 7s 8.1m* p8g² 8g⁵ p7g Oct 26] strong, good-bodied colt: has a
quick action: fourth foal: half-brother to French 1m (at 2 yrs)/1¼m winner Choc Ice (by
Kahyasi) and Irish/French 1m to 10.5f winner Quinmaster (by Linamix), both smart: dam
unraced out of sister to Shergar: useful performer: won maiden at Haydock in June and
handicap at Lingfield (beat Mina A Salem by 3 lengths) in July: not discredited after:
likely to stay 1¼m: acts on polytrack and good to firm going: tongue tied after debut: has
worn crossed noseband/American halter/had 2 handlers. *J. H. M. Gosden*

ROYAL OBSESSION (IRE) 2 b.f. (May 1) Val Royal (FR) 127 – Britique (USA) **–**
(Critique (USA) 126) [2006 5.1g 6d Nov 4] €17,000F, €20,000Y: half-sister to several
winners in Italy: dam 5.5f (at 2 yrs) and 1m winner in Italy: no show in maidens.
J. G. M. O'Shea

ROYAL ORISSA 4 b.g. Royal Applause 124 – Ling Lane (Slip Anchor 136) [2006 93: **72 d**
p6g 6g 6g 6d 5.7g 6g 6f p6g Nov 23] leggy gelding: fair handicapper: well below form
last 4 starts: best at 6f: acts on firm and soft ground: sometimes tongue tied: wore
cheekpieces (ran creditably) fourth outing. *D. Haydn Jones*

ROYAL PARDON 4 b.f. Royal Applause 124 – Miss Mercy (IRE) 62 (Law Society **61**
(USA) 130) [2006 58: 8d 8.3d⁵ 8.3m² 8d³ 7g 6m 8m 9.2m⁵ 7.2m 6.9g² 6.9m³ 7.9f Aug 15]
sturdy filly: modest maiden handicapper: stays 9f: acts on good to firm and good to soft
going: wears headgear nowadays. *R. C. Guest*

ROYAL POWER (IRE) 3 b.c. Xaar 132 – Magic Touch (Fairy King (USA)) [2006 **108**
96: p8g² 8g² 8g* 8m 8d 7d⁵ 7g Sep 15] tall colt: good sort: useful performer: won
Mehl-Mulhens-Rennen at Cologne (by head from Aspectus) in May: also ran well in
Premio Parioli at Rome (1¼ lengths second to Rattle And Hum), St James's Palace Stakes
at Royal Ascot (seventh to Araafa) and Hungerford Stakes at Newbury (3¼ lengths fifth
to Welsh Emperor) second, fourth and sixth outings: well below form in listed race at
Newbury final start: will probably stay 1¼m: acts on polytrack, good to firm and good to
soft going. *M. R. Channon*

*Mehl-Mulhens-Rennen - German 2000 Guineas, Cologne—the Mick Channon-trained Royal Power
goes one better than in the Italian version; Aspectus (right), Lord of England (white cap)
and Chief Commander (left), another trained in Britain, are next*

ROYAL PREMIER (IRE) 3 b.c. King's Theatre (IRE) 128 – Mystic Shadow (IRE) **65**
80 (Mtoto 134) [2006 69: 10.9g 10m 11.8d⁶ 10.2m* 10.9d p9.5g p12g p12.2s² Dec 13]
quite good-topped colt: fair handicapper: won at Chepstow in September: stays 1½m:
acts on polytrack, soft and good to firm going: visored last 7 starts. *H. J. Collingridge*

ROYAL RATIONALE (IRE) 2 b.g. (Mar 13) Desert Prince (IRE) 130 – Logic 94 **79**
(Slip Anchor 136) [2006 6s⁵ 7m p6g⁶ p7.1g² Oct 30] strong, good-bodied gelding: fifth
living foal: half-brother to 3 winners, including 6-y-o Logsdail and 3-y-o Rationale: dam,
maiden ran only at 2 yrs (bred to stay 1¼m), half-sister to useful 1½m winner Port
Helene: fair maiden: second to Wait For The Light at Wolverhampton: gelded after: will
be suited by 1m. *W. J. Haggas*

ROYAL RESERVATION 3 b.c. Royal Applause 124 – Wig Wam (IRE) (Indian **87**
Ridge 123) [2006 84p: p10g* 10g p8g p8g p10g Oct 20] lengthy colt: fairly useful handicapper: won at Lingfield in February: below form after: stays 1¼m: acts on polytrack:
sold 16,500 gns. *P. W. Chapple-Hyam*

ROYAL SAILOR (IRE) 4 b.g. Bahhare (USA) 122 – Old Tradition (IRE) 76 (Royal **–**
Academy (USA) 130) [2006 60, a52: p12.2g 8f 8f 7.6m 7f 8m 8d p10g f11g⁴ Dec 29] tall **a53**
gelding: modest maiden: stays 11f: acts on polytrack and firm ground: tried blinkered.
J. Ryan

ROYAL SENGA 3 b.f. Agnes World (USA) 123 – Katyushka (IRE) 73 (Soviet Star **67**
(USA) 128) [2006 p6g 6m⁴ 6m⁴ 5.7m⁵ Sep 4] third foal: half-sister to 5-y-o Future Deal:
dam, 7f winner, out of smart 5f performer Welsh Note: fair maiden: stays 6f: raced only
on polytrack and good to firm going. *C. A. Horgan*

ROYAL SONG 3 b.c. Royal Applause 124 – La Caprice (USA) 84 (Housebuster **34**
(USA)) [2006 –: p6g f7g⁶ 8g 7.5g Aug 31] poor maiden: stays 7f. *D. Shaw*

ROYAL SPELL 4 b.f. Wizard King 122 – Manadel (Governor General 116) [2006 **–**
p9.5g Feb 3] first foal: dam of little account: 100/1, tailed off in maiden at Wolverhampton. *M. Appleby*

ROYAL STORM (IRE) 7 b.h. Royal Applause 124 – Wakayi 87 (Persian Bold 123) **107**
[2006 107: 6.5m² 6m² 6d⁴ 6g⁵ 7.6m 6m 6m Jun 24] tall, lengthy horse: useful performer:
ran well when runner-up in 2 handicaps at Nad Al Sheba: best effort after when creditable
fifth to Paradise Isle in listed race at Newmarket: effective at 6f/7f: acts on polytrack, firm
and soft going: usually races up with pace/makes running. *Mrs A. J. Perrett*

ROYAL SUPREMACY (IRE) 5 ch.m. Desert Prince (IRE) 130 – Saucy Maid (IRE) **40**
69 (Sure Blade (USA) 130) [2006 5f 5.5g 5.1g 5.1f 5.3m Aug 22] poor maiden nowadays:
tried tongue tied. *J. M. Bradley*

ROYAL TAVIRA GIRL (IRE) 3 b.f. Orpen (USA) 116 – Just Like Annie (IRE) 65 **62**
(Mujadil (USA) 119) [2006 51p: p7g³ 6s⁵ 6m⁵ p8g 7m² 7.1m² 8.5m² 7f⁵ 8.3d p9.5g
Sep 30] modest maiden handicapper: stays 8.5f: acts on polytrack and firm ground (below
form both outings on softer than good). *M. G. Quinlan*

ROYAL TENDER (IRE) 2 gr.f. (Apr 7) Woods of Windsor (USA) – Tender Guest **–**
(IRE) (Be My Guest (USA) 126) [2006 p8g p9.5g Dec 7] fifth foal: half-sister to 3-y-o
Tender The Great: dam well beaten in Ireland: well held in maidens. *V. Smith*

ROYAL TIARA (UAE) 2 br.f. (Jan 24) Machiavellian (USA) 123 – Crown of Light **– p**
112 (Mtoto 134) [2006 p7g Oct 21] fourth foal: half-sister to 6-y-o Balkan Knight and
5-y-o Augustine: dam, 7f (at 2 yrs) and 11.5f winner, also third in Oaks: 5/1, needed
experience in maiden at Lingfield: open to improvement. *Saeed bin Suroor*

ROYALTIES 4 b.f. Mujahid (USA) 125 – Rock Face 77 (Ballad Rock 122) [2006 –: **–**
f11g p12.2m Oct 2] no sign of ability. *M. A. Allen*

ROYLE DANCER 3 b.g. Makbul 104 – Foxtrot Pie 77 (Shernazar 131) [2006 63: **67**
9.9m 8m⁴ 8.1d³ p9.5g p8.6g f11g p8.6g⁵ Dec 29] strong, close-coupled gelding: fair
maiden: below form last 4 starts, amiss and pulled up on first occasion: stays 1m: acts on
polytrack, firm and good to soft going. *R. Hollinshead*

RUBBER DUCK (IRE) 2 b.f. (Apr 29) Daggers Drawn (USA) 114 – Dhuhook (USA) **–**
96 (Dixieland Band (USA)) [2006 p6g p6g p5g p5.1g p5.1g⁶ Dec 29] €3,700F, €4,600Y:
second foal: half-sister to Swedish winner up to 1m by Muhtarram: dam 9f winner: no
form: tried blinkered. *Peter Grayson*

RUBBER (IRE) 3 b.f. Namid 128 – Bold Fashion (FR) (Nashwan (USA) 135) [2006 **66**
88: p6g³ 6g³ p6f³ a5.5f a5.5f⁶ Dec 5] rangy filly: fairly useful maiden at 2 yrs: just fair
form in 2006, leaving R. Hannon after reappearance: may prove best at 5f/6f: best effort
on good to firm going. *J. Good, USA*

RUBENSTAR (IRE) 3 b.g. Soviet Star (USA) 128 – Ansariya (USA) 83 (Shahrastani (USA) 135) [2006 83: 7g p7g⁶ 7.5g³ 8.1m² 8g⁵ 8m⁵ 8g 8s⁶ 8m⁵ p7g* Oct 21] strong gelding: fairly useful handicapper: won apprentice event at Lingfield in October: stays 1m: acts on polytrack, soft and good to firm going: has raced freely: usually held up: consistent. *M. H. Tompkins*   **85**

RUBILINI 2 ch.f. (Feb 28) Bertolini (USA) 125 – Aunt Ruby (USA) 67 (Rubiano (USA)) [2006 6m 7f⁴ Jul 9] unfurnished filly: second foal: half-sister to 3-y-o South Cape: dam 7f seller winner: better effort in maidens when seventh to Indian Ink at Newbury. *M. R. Channon*   **58**

RUBY LEGEND 8 b.g. Perpendicular 119 – Singing High 87 (Julio Mariner 127) [2006 59: 10.1d 7.9m⁶ 9.3m 10f² 10d⁴ 10.5f* 10.1f⁵ 10.5m⁶ 10.1d 10.1s⁵ 10m* 10m³ 10s Oct 16] leggy gelding: fair handicapper: won at Haydock in July and Nottingham in September: ran as though amiss final outing: stays 10.5f: acts on firm and soft going: usually wears blinkers/cheekpieces: reared and unseated rider at start ninth outing. *K. G. Reveley*   **67**

RUBY MUJA 4 b.f. Mujahid (USA) 125 – Ruby Julie (Clantime 101) [2006 49: p6g 5v Apr 13] quite good-topped filly: poor performer: well beaten in 2006, in claimer at Wolverhampton on reappearance: best at 5f: acts on polytrack and good to soft ground: tried visored. *T. G. McCourt, Ireland*   **–**

RUBY RUBBLE 3 b.f. Distant Music (USA) 126 – Topwinder (USA) (Topsider (USA)) [2006 52: 6.9m⁶ 8d 8f Jul 28] maiden: just poor form in 2006: best effort at 6f: acts on good to firm ground: once withdrawn (unruly in preliminaries) at 2 yrs: slowly away second outing. *K. R. Burke*   **42**

RUBY'S DREAM 4 b.f. Tipsy Creek (USA) 115 – Sure Flyer (IRE) (Sure Blade (USA) 130) [2006 64: p5.1g p5g 6.1m 5.7d 5m³ 5m* 5.5g² 6f 7.1f 6m 6.1m Sep 1] workmanlike filly: modest handicapper, better on turf than all-weather: won ladies event at Leicester in June: stays 6f: acts on any turf going: wears blinkers/cheekpieces. *J. M. Bradley*   **62 a53**

RUBY SUNRISE (IRE) 4 ch.f. Polish Precedent (USA) 131 – Kinlochewe 102 (Old Vic 136) [2006 57: p8.6g p7.1g p8.6g p8.6g f7m p9.5g p10g p9.5g p9.5g⁶ p8.6g Dec 21] leggy filly: poor mover: modest maiden: stays 9.5f: acts on polytrack: blinkered last 2 starts. *B. P. J. Baugh*   **50**

RUBY WINE 4 b.f. Kayf Tara 130 – Cribella (USA) 71 (Robellino (USA) 127) [2006 107: 10.1f³ 12m⁵ 12s Aug 24] big, close-coupled filly: useful performer: shaped as if retaining all of her ability when fifth to Fermion in listed race at Newbury second start: broke down next time: should stay 1¾m: acts on good to firm going. *J. M. P. Eustace*   **101**

RUDAKI 4 ch.g. Opening Verse (USA) 126 – Persian Fountain (IRE) 67 (Persian Heights 129) [2006 57: 10g 8f 10f⁴ 10f⁶ 9f 10m³ 9d⁴ 8.5m⁶ 9.8d⁶ 10m Sep 11] close-coupled gelding: modest performer: stays 1¼m: acts on polytrack, firm and good to soft going: wore cheekpieces fifth outing. *M. E. Sowersby*   **58**

RUDI'S PET (IRE) 12 ch.g. Don't Forget Me 127 – Pink Fondant (Northfields (USA)) [2006 86: 5g⁴ 5f 5g⁵ p5.1g⁴ 5m* 5f³ 5m³ Jul 26] strong gelding: fair performer nowadays: made all in handicap at Musselburgh in July (for second successive year): best at 5f: acts on firm and soft going: effective blinkered/visored or not: usually races prominently. *D. Nicholls*   **79**

RUDRY DRAGON (IRE) 2 b.c. (Feb 5) Princely Heir (IRE) 111 – Jazz Up (Cadeaux Genereux 131) [2006 6m⁶ 7d p7.1g Oct 8] has a quick action: second foal: half-brother to useful Irish 6.5f to 8.5f (including at 2 yrs) winner Jazz Princess (by Bahhare): dam unraced: fair form first 2 sarts in maidens: twice slowly away. *P. A. Blockley*   **75**

RUDRY WORLD (IRE) 3 ch.g. Spinning World (USA) 130 – Fancy Boots (IRE) 62 (Salt Dome (USA)) [2006 p7.1g p9.5g f8g⁴ p8.6g Mar 6] modest maiden: stays 1m: acts on all-weather. *P. A. Blockley*   **51**

RUE SOLEIL 2 ch.f. (Apr 12) Zaha (CAN) 106 – Maria Cappuccini 70 (Siberian Express (USA) 125) [2006 5g 5m 7f 6d⁴ 5g³ 5.5m 6g⁶ 6d⁴ 6s³ f6m Oct 31] 1,800Y: unfurnished filly: half-sister to 3 winners, including 8-y-o Kumakawa and 7f winner Agent (by Anshan): dam 5f winner who stayed 7f: modest maiden: best at 5f/6f: acts on soft ground. *J. R. Weymes*   **63**

RUFFIE (IRE) 3 b.f. Medicean 128 – Darling Lover (USA) 56 (Dare And Go (USA) 125) [2006 65: p8.6g² p8.6g³ f8g³ p10g 10.1g p8.6g⁵ f8g² f8g Dec 9] fair on all-weather, modest (at 2 yrs) on turf: stays 8.6f: acts on all-weather and good to firm going: tried visored (ran poorly). *Miss Gay Kelleway*   **– a72**

RULE FOR EVER 4 br.g. Diktat 126 – Tous Les Jours (USA) 70 (Dayjur (USA) 137) **71 §**
[2006 79: 14g 13d 16d 16g⁵ 18m 16.1m⁵ 17.2f⁵ 16m Aug 5] big, lengthy gelding: fair handicapper: stays 17.5f: acts on soft and good to firm going: tried blinkered/visored/tongue tied: moody and one to treat with caution. *M. Johnston*

RULE OF LIFE 2 br.c. (Mar 11) Dansili 127 – Prophecy (IRE) 109 (Warning 136) **80**
[2006 6m 6d³ p7g² Nov 11] strong, sturdy colt: has a round action: eighth foal: half-brother to 3 winners, including useful 6f winner Arabesque (by Zafonic), now dam of smart 6f/7f performer Camacho: dam, 2-y-o 5f/6f (including Cheveley Park Stakes) winner who stayed 1m, out of Lancashire Oaks winner Andaleeb: fairly useful form: off 3 months after debut: placed in maidens at Newmarket (third to Miss Lucifer) and Kempton (odds on): stays 7f. *B. W. Hills*

RULING REEF 4 b.f. Diktat 126 – Horseshoe Reef 88 (Mill Reef (USA) 141) [2006 **55**
59: 10.2d⁴ 14.1m p10g 10.2f 11.5f⁵ 10m⁴ 10.1g² 10.2m³ 10.2f Sep 9] close-coupled filly: **a–**
modest handicapper on turf: effective at 1¼m, probably stays 1¾m: acts on firm and soft going, poor form on polytrack: tended to run in snatches fifth start. *M. D. I. Usher*

RUMAN (IRE) 4 b.g. Fayruz 116 – Starway To Heaven (ITY) (Nordance (USA)) [2006 **67**
65: f6g² p6g* f6g f6g⁶ p6g Jun 30] lengthy gelding: fair handicapper: won at Wolverhampton in January: should stay 7f: acts on all-weather and good to soft ground. *M. J. Attwater*

RUMBLED 2 b.f. (Feb 23) Halling (USA) 133 – Tatanka (IRE) (Lear Fan (USA) 130) **62**
[2006 6g 7m 6.1g³ 7d Oct 19] 28,000F: second foal: dam unraced out of half-sister to Coronation Cup winner Be My Native: modest maiden: third at Nottingham: will stay 1m. *J. A. Geake*

RUMPLESTILTSKIN (IRE) 3 b.f. Danehill (USA) 126 – Monevassia (USA) (Mr **–**
Prospector (USA)) [2006 116: 8s May 7] small, quite attractive filly: smart performer: the best 2-y-o filly in Europe in 2005, winning 5 times, including Moyglare Stud Stakes at the Curragh and Prix Marcel Boussac at Longchamp: 3/1 favourite, but not right in coat, no impression when 11 lengths seventh to Speciosa in 1000 Guineas at Newmarket only outing in 2006: reported in mid-May to have injured a ligament close to her pelvis: stays 1m: raced only on good ground or firmer at 2 yrs: carries head awkwardly. *A. P. O'Brien, Ireland*

RUMSFELD (ITY) 3 b.c. Martino Alonso (IRE) 113§ – Radura (Brook 125) [2006 **104**
10g² 12g 9.9f 10s⁴ a8g* 8s* 8m³ Nov 5] tall, leggy colt: half-brother to 3 winners in Italy: dam Italian 5f (at 2 yrs) to 1¼m winner: useful performer: won minor events at Merano and Milan (2) at 2 yrs for A. & G. Botti: best efforts in Britain in 2006 when second in minor event at Newbury (walked to post) and fourth in handicap at Newmarket: successful at Rome in minor event (final start for M. Botti) in September and listed race (by head from Silex) in October: ran well when staying-on 7 lengths third to Ramonti in Premio Ribot at Rome final start: stays 1¼m: acts on dirt, soft and good to firm ground: has worn tongue tie: started awkwardly third outing. *A. & G. Botti, Italy*

RUNAWAY RUBY 12 ch.m. Respect 95 – Chrislim VII (Damsire Unregistered) [2006 **–**
–: 6m Apr 27] strong, workmanlike mare: no sign of ability. *B. J. McMath*

RUN FOR EDE'S 2 b.f. (Feb 16) Peintre Celebre (USA) 137 – Raincloud (Rainbow **66 p**
Quest (USA) 134) [2006 7.1d⁵ Sep 16] 22,000Y: fourth foal: half-sister to 6-y-o Low Cloud and French 2005 2-y-o 6f winner Overshadow (by Desert Prince), both fairly useful: dam, French 1½m winner, sister to smart Ebor winner Tuning: 33/1, fifth to Elusive Flash in maiden at Warwick: should improve. *R. M. Beckett*

RUN FREE 2 b.g. (Mar 14) Agnes World (USA) 123 – Ellie Ardensky 100 (Slip Anchor **77**
136) [2006 6m 6s² 7s⁴ Oct 14] 11,500Y, 28,000 2-y-o: good-bodied gelding: half-brother to smart 1m and 14.6f winner Pole Star (by Polar Falcon) and 2004 2-y-o 1m winner Emile Zola (by Singspiel): dam 9f/1¼m winner: fair form: second to Kafuu in maiden at York: should stay 7f/1m: gelded after final start. *N. Wilson*

RUSE 3 b.f. Diktat 126 – Reuval 102 (Sharpen Up 127) [2006 51p: 7m⁴ 8.2g⁴ p8g⁵ **66**
10.2m² p12g p13g⁵ Dec 22] fair maiden: probably stays 1¼m: acts on good to firm ground: probably not straightforward. *J. R. Fanshawe*

RUSKIN 3 ch.g. Bluebird (USA) 125 – Scenic Venture (IRE) (Desert King (IRE) 129) **–**
[2006 8.1m Sep 4] robust gelding: tongue tied, started very slowly when tailed off in maiden at Warwick. *K. McAuliffe*

RUSKY DUSKY (USA) 4 b.g. Stravinsky (USA) 133 – Celtic Shade (Lomond (USA) **– §**
128) [2006 p7g 7.1m Jun 16] strong, good-quartered gelding: fair maiden at 2 yrs: unraced in 2005: gelded, well held both starts in 2006: tried visored/blinkered: ungenuine. *R. Hannon*

RUSSALKA 5 b.m. Opening Verse (USA) 126 – Philarmonique (FR) (Trempolino – §
(USA) 135) [2006 46§: 10d May 26] workmanlike mare: unreliable maiden: tried in
cheekpieces/visor. *M. Wigham*

RUSSIAN CAFE (IRE) 5 b.m. Stravinsky (USA) 133 – Bistro (USA) (Strawberry –
Road (AUS) 128) [2006 –: f8g Apr 10] tall, leggy mare: no form since 2004: tongue tied.
N. Tinkler

RUSSIAN CONSORT (IRE) 4 ch.g. Groom Dancer (USA) 128 – Ukraine Venture **88**
96 (Slip Anchor 136) [2006 8.2m 9.9g⁴ 10m⁵ Jul 30] lengthy gelding: fairly useful performer nowadays: unraced in 2005 (reportedly injured a tendon): creditable efforts in
handicaps last 2 starts: may prove best short of 1¼m: acts on polytrack, best effort on turf
on good going: slowly away/raced freely on reappearance. *A. King*

RUSSIAN DREAM (IRE) 3 b.g. Xaar 132 – Summer Dreams (IRE) 79 (Sadler's **75**
Wells (USA) 132) [2006 p8g⁶ 10g 10f p12.2g³ p12.2g p12.2g p13.9g⁴ p13.9g f12g³
Dec 21] 19,000F, €85,000Y: first foal: dam, Irish maiden who stayed 1¾m, half-sister to
Deutsches Derby winner All My Dreams: fair maiden: stays 1¾m: acts on all-weather:
held up. *W. R. Swinburn*

RUSSIAN GIFT (IRE) 2 b.f. (Feb 7) Soviet Star (USA) 128 – Birthday Present **68**
(Cadeaux Genereux 131) [2006 6g⁴ 6g⁵ 5.1m⁴ Aug 25] 3,000F: first foal: dam unraced
half-sister to smart sprinter Border Subject: steady improvement in maidens, fair form at
Bath final outing: should prove best kept to 5f/6f. *C. G. Cox*

RUSSIAN MIST (IRE) 3 gr.g. Xaar 132 – Cape Mist (USA) (Lure (USA) 131) [2006 **69**
p8g⁴ p9.5g⁵ 7.1g 9.8g p12.2g Jun 2] €28,000F: tall gelding: second foal: half-brother to
4-y-o Primed Up: dam unraced: fair maiden: stays 9.4f: acts on polytrack. *M. J. Wallace*

RUSSIAN ROCKET (IRE) 4 b.g. Indian Rocket 115 – Soviet Girl (IRE) (Soviet Star **85**
(USA) 128) [2006 –: p5g f5s⁵ 5m 5.2m⁶ 5.1s⁴ 5.2g⁵ 6g² 6.1m* 6m p6g* 5m⁵ 6s p6g p6g⁴
p6g Dec 28] small, leggy maiden: fairly useful performer: won handicaps at Nottingham
in June and Lingfield in July: flattered in minor event at Newmarket eleventh start, good
fourth in handicap at Kempton penultimate outing: stays 6f: acts on polytrack (probably
on fibresand), firm and soft going. *Mrs C. A. Dunnett*

RUSSIAN ROSIE (IRE) 2 b.f. (Mar 15) Traditionally (USA) 117 – Pink Sovietstaia **90**
(FR) (Soviet Star (USA) 128) [2006 6m⁴ 6d² 6g* 6m³ 6.5s Sep 22] 12,500F, 8,000Y: tall,
unfurnished filly: third living foal: half-sister to fairly useful 2003 2-y-o 6f/7f winner
Russian Ruby (by Vettori) and 3-y-o Observatory Star: dam awarded 9f event in France:
fairly useful form: won maiden at Newbury by 3½ lengths in August: third to Vital
Statistics in listed race at Salisbury: will stay 7f: acts on good to firm and good to soft
going, below form on soft (valuable sales event) final start. *J. G. Portman*

RUSSIAN SERVANA (IRE) 4 b.f. Rossini (USA) 118 – Ring of Light (Auction Ring –
(USA) 123) [2006 f6g May 16] modest maiden at 2 yrs: missed 2005: well beaten only
outing in 2006. *J. Pearce*

RUSSIAN SILK 2 b.f. (Mar 29) Fasliyev (USA) 120 – Queen of Silk (IRE) 93 (Brief **76**
Truce (USA) 126) [2006 5m* 5m³ 5.2d Oct 18] fourth foal: half-sister to 6-y-o Brief
Goodbye and 4-y-o Rosiella: dam, Irish 1m winner who stayed 9f, half-sister to smart
Irish 7f/1m performer Tarry Flynn: fair form: won maiden at Carlisle in June: better effort
after 3-month break when third to Handsome Falcon in minor event at Beverley: will stay
6f/7f. *Jedd O'Keeffe*

RUSSIAN SYMPHONY (USA) 5 ch.g. Stravinsky (USA) 133 – Backwoods Teac- **83**
her (USA) (Woodman (USA) 126) [2006 95, a100: p6g 6m 6g Jul 28] just fairly useful
form at best in 2006: best at 6f/7f: acts on polytrack and firm going: usually blinkered,
wore cheekpieces final outing: tends to race freely. *C. R. Egerton*

RUSSKI (IRE) 2 b.c. (Jan 26) Fasliyev (USA) 120 – Rose of Mooncoin (IRE) 99 (Brief **88 p**
Truce (USA) 126) [2006 p7g p7g* Nov 11] 25,000F, 50,000Y: third foal: half-brother to
3-y-o Louie Louie: dam 2-y-o 6f winner: better for debut (slowly away), won maiden at
Kempton by 3 lengths from demoted Nassmaan, making all: should continue to progress.
Mrs A. J. Perrett

RUST EN VREDE 7 b.g. Royal Applause 124 – Souveniers (Relko 136) [2006 –: 8.5g –
Aug 17] tall gelding: fair winner in 2004: lightly raced and well beaten on Flat since: tried
visored: won over hurdles in August. *J. J. Quinn*

RUSTIC GOLD 2 ch.c. (May 16) Tobougg (IRE) 125 – Suave Shot (Suave Dancer –
(USA) 136) [2006 p7g p7g p7g Dec 20] signs of ability in polytrack maidens. *J. R. Best*

RUTHLES PHILLY 2 b.f. (Mar 18) Primo Valentino (IRE) 116 – Compton Amber 78 **58** (Puissance 110) [2006 5g 6m 6f 5d⁶ 6m⁶ Sep 11] 14,000Y: leggy filly: fourth foal: half-sister to 3-y-o Amber Glory: dam, temperamental maiden (placed at 5f to 7f at 2 yrs), half-sister to useful sprinter Golden Nun: modest maiden: should prove best at 5f/6f. *D. W. Barker*

RYAN'S FUTURE (IRE) 6 b.h. Danetime (IRE) 121 – Era 70 (Dalsaan 125) [2006 **95** 88: 10d* Jun 1] leggy, useful-looking horse: useful handicapper: career-best effort when winning at Ayr (by 2 lengths from Trouble Mountain) on sole start in 2006: suffered ligament injury afterwards: stays 1¼m: acts on polytrack, heavy and good to firm going: often slowly away. *Miss L. A. Perratt*

RYDAL MOUNT (IRE) 3 b.f. Cape Cross (IRE) 129 – Pooka 65 (Dominion 123) **80** [2006 7m³ 7s* 7m 6m 6m⁵ 7m 6g Oct 16] 46,000Y: smallish, sturdy, angular filly: has a quick action: half-sister to several winners, including smart German performer up to 1m Chagall (by Fraam) and 4-y-o Dove Cottage: dam placed at 5f at 2 yrs: fairly useful performer: confirmed debut promise when winning maiden at Goodwood in May: shows plenty of speed and may prove best up to 7f: acts on soft and good to firm ground. *W. S. Kittow*

RYDAL (USA) 5 ch.g. Gilded Time (USA) – Tennis Partner (USA) (Northern Dancer) **?** [2006 88, a94: f5g 5.5f 8f⁶ 8.5g⁴ Oct 25] good-topped gelding: fairly useful performer: well below form at Southwell on reappearance, then left E. Alston: effective at stiff 5f to 8.5f: acts on all-weather, firm and good to soft going: often wears headgear/tongue tie: reportedly bled once at 4 yrs. *D. L. Romans, USA*

RYEDALE OVATION (IRE) 3 b.g. Royal Applause 124 – Passe Passe (USA) 78 **92 d** (Lear Fan (USA) 130) [2006 81p: 6d³ 6m³ 6.1s⁴ 6g 6g 6g⁴ 7d³ 8m⁵ Aug 31] big, useful-looking gelding: fairly useful handicapper: below form after reappearance: probably stays 1m: acts on good to firm and good to soft ground: wore cheekpieces (raced freely) fifth start. *T. D. Easterby*

RYEDANE (IRE) 4 b.g. Danetime (IRE) 121 – Miss Valediction (IRE) (Petardia 113) **77** [2006 84: f5g p5.1g 5d 5f 5g⁶ 6g 6m 5f* 5m* 5f 5m³ 5f⁶ 5g 5s 5f⁴ 5g⁴ 5d⁵ Nov 3] tall, leggy gelding: fair handicapper nowadays: won at Catterick and Newcastle in July: effective at 5f/6f: acts on polytrack (has won 3 times at Wolverhampton), firm and good to soft going. *T. D. Easterby*

RYHOPE CHIEF (IRE) 3 b.g. Indian Danehill (IRE) 124 – Rachel Pringle (IRE) **–** (Doulab (USA) 115) [2006 –: p10g 10g Apr 10] little form on Flat. *M. F. Harris*

RYTHM N RHYME (IRE) 7 ch.g. Danehill Dancer (IRE) 117 – Valley Heigh (IRE) **–** (Head For Heights 125) [2006 f11g p12.2g p12.2g⁵ f8g p9.5g p12.2g f12g⁵ May 9] showed little in bumpers/over hurdles in Ireland in 2003 for Mrs M. Murphy: little sign of ability on Flat: tried in cheekpieces. *John A. Harris*

S

SAABIQ (USA) 3 br.f. Grand Slam (USA) 120 – Lucky Lineage (USA) (Storm Cat **95** (USA)) [2006 96: p7g² 7g⁶ 10s⁴ 8.5g 8m p5g⁴ 6f p6g Sep 30] big, close-coupled filly: useful performer: in frame in listed races at Lingfield (second to Kingsgate Prince) and Newmarket, and handicap at Lingfield: effective at 5f, seems to stay 1¼m: acts on polytrack, soft and good to firm going: tried in cheekpieces. *C. E. Brittain*

SAAMEQ (IRE) 5 b.g. Bahhare (USA) 122 – Tajawuz 82 (Kris 135) [2006 60: p12.2g **61** p13.9g⁴ p16.5g 12.4m p12.2g* Dec 18] strong gelding: modest performer: won seller at Wolverhampton in December: stays 1½m: acts on polytrack and good to firm going: wore cheekpieces sixth/seventh 4-y-o starts. *D. W. Thompson*

SAARATT 2 ch.f. (Feb 25) Mark of Esteem (IRE) 137 – Cambara 97 (Dancing Brave **60 p** (USA) 140) [2006 p7g⁶ Nov 11] half-sister to several winners, including smart 7f (at 2 yrs)/1m winner Samhari (by Indian Ridge), 6-y-o Habshan and 3-y-o Dubai On: dam, 1m winner, half-sister to smart middle-distance performers Pluralisme, Classic Tale and Singletta: 20/1, 5½ lengths sixth to Sell Out in maiden at Kempton, slowly away and keeping on well out wide: will stay 1m: should improve. *M. P. Tregoning*

SABAH 3 ch.f. Nashwan (USA) 135 – Massorah (FR) 108 (Habitat 134) [2006 8.3g⁴ **91** 10f² 8.3f* 8m³ Aug 20] 14,500F, 39,000Y: closely related to 3 winners, including fairly useful 1999 2-y-o 7f winner Miss Orah (later successful in USA) and 1¼m winner La

Yolam (both by Unfuwain), and half-sister to several winners, notably 7-y-o Vanderlin: dam French sprinter: fairly useful form: won maiden at Windsor in July: good third to Three Wrens in listed race at Bath final start: effective at 8.3f, not sure to stay beyond 1¼m: acts on firm ground: withdrawn after damaging stall gate prior to intended debut at 2 yrs. *A. M. Balding*

SABBIOSA (IRE) 4 b.f. Desert Prince (IRE) 130 – Alla Marcia (IRE) 64 (Marju (IRE) 127) [2006 67: 12s² 14.1s⁶ 11.7d² 12.1s* p12g Jun 28] quite good-topped filly: has shown traces of stringhalt: fairly useful handicapper: won at Chepstow in May: stays 1½m: acts on soft going: sold 5,000 gns in November. *J. L. Dunlop* **80**

SABO PRINCE 4 ch.g. Atraf 116 – Moving Princess 71 (Prince Sabo 123) [2006 56: p7.1g p7.1g⁴ f8g p6g Apr 12] good-bodied gelding: modest performer: stays 7f: acts on polytrack and good to firm going: tried blinkered, usually wears cheekpieces: reportedly bled final start. *J. M. Bradley* **50**

SABRINA BROWN 5 br.m. Polar Falcon (USA) 126 – So True 116 (So Blessed 130) [2006 85²: 7d 6g 6d⁵ 6s 6d 6d 6.1s Oct 25] good-topped mare: fair handicapper: has form at 1m, but best efforts over 6f/7f: acts on polytrack and soft going: tongue tied: flashes tail. *J. A. Geake* **69**

SACRANUN 4 ch.c. Pivotal 124 – Spanish Craft (IRE) 50 (Jareer (USA) 115) [2006 90: 10m 10.5g³ p12g Oct 21] sturdy, close-coupled colt: fairly useful handicapper: reportedly split a pastern after final start at 3 yrs: easily best effort in 2006 when creditable equal-third at Haydock: should prove at least as effective at 1½m as 1¼m: acts on soft and good to firm going: visored last 2 starts: sold 21,000 gns, sent to Bahrain. *L. M. Cumani* **90**

SACRE COEUR 2 b.f. (Mar 10) Compton Place 125 – Take Heart 84 (Electric 126) [2006 5m⁵ 6m* Aug 2] 57,000Y: useful-looking filly: closely related to 6-y-o Indian Trail and half-sister to 3 winners, including useful 1¼m winner Lonely Heart (by Midyan): dam 7f to 1¼m winner: much improved from debut when winning maiden at Goodwood by neck from Rahiyah, impressing with speed: likely to prove a sprinter: has scope, and should progress further. *J. L. Dunlop* **90 p**

SADDLER'S QUEST 9 b.g. Saddlers' Hall (IRE) 126 – Seren Quest 90 (Rainbow Quest (USA) 134) [2006 38: p12.2g p16.5g Dec 29] rather leggy gelding: poor performer nowadays: tried in cheekpieces: has been very slowly away. *B. P. J. Baugh* **–**

SADEEK 2 ch.c. (Mar 3) Kyllachy 129 – Miss Mercy (IRE) 62 (Law Society (USA) 130) [2006 6s* 6m* 6m 6.3m² 6s 7d Sep 29] 40,000Y: strong, lengthy colt: easy walker: has a quick action: half-brother to several winners, including useful 2001 2-y-o 5f winner Pachara (by Mind Games), later successful in USA, and 3-y-o Balik Pearls: dam 2-y-o 6f winner: useful performer: won maiden at York in May and listed race at Epsom in June: better form next 2 starts, eighth of 21 to Hellvelyn in Coventry Stakes at Royal Ascot and neck second to Regional Counsel in Anglesey Stakes at the Curragh: below form last 2 races (worked up beforehand): will prove best at 5f/6f: acts on soft and good to firm going: sold 110,000 gns. *K. A. Ryan* **98**

SADLER'S HILL (IRE) 2 b.g. (Apr 16) Sadler's Wells (USA) 132 – Dedicated Lady (IRE) 101 (Pennine Walk 120) [2006 8.1d 8m p7g Oct 11] no show in maidens: gelded and joined M. McGrath. *N. A. Callaghan* **–**

SAD TIMES (IRE) 2 b.f. (Feb 27) Tendulkar (USA) 114 – Mrs Kanning 61 (Distant View (USA) 126) [2006 p5g⁶ p5g⁶ 5s² 5.1d⁴ 5m 6v⁵ 7m* 7f³ 7f p7.1g* Jul 28] €3,000F, 800Y: workmanlike filly: first foal: dam ran 4 times: modest performer: raced mostly in sellers, winning at Yarmouth in June and Wolverhampton in July: stays 7f: acts on polytrack, soft and firm going: best form in cheekpieces, but also in them when once refused to race: ungenuine. *W. G. M. Turner* **57 §**

SAFAAH 3 b.g. Almushtarak (IRE) 122 – Lawn Order 51 (Efisio 120) [2006 –: p10g f5g f6g p10g Apr 5] little sign of ability. *G. Prodromou* **–**

SAFARI 3 b.f. Namaqualand (USA) – Breakfast Creek 63 (Hallgate 127) [2006 –: 7s² p8.6g 5.7g⁵ 5.1g Jun 2] poor maiden. *R. J. Hodges* **44**

SAFARI MISCHIEF 3 b.g. Primo Valentino (IRE) 116 – Night Gypsy 74 (Mind Games 121) [2006 65: 5f* 5.7g³ 5m 5g² 5.1m² 5m* 5.3d⁶ Sep 25] fair performer: won maiden at Folkestone in June and handicap at Goodwood in September: may prove best at 5f: acts on firm going, probably on heavy: makes running. *P. Winkworth* **77**

SAFARI SUNDOWNER (IRE) 2 b.c. (Mar 16) Daggers Drawn (USA) 114 – Acadelli (IRE) 71 (Royal Academy (USA) 130) [2006 6m 6d 7m 6.1g Sep 15] €7,000F, €36,000Y: strong, useful-looking colt: third foal: half-brother to winner in Italy by **65**

Rossini: dam, Irish maiden, stayed 1m: maiden: seemingly best effort when ninth at Newmarket third start: well held in nursery. *P. Winkworth*

SAFARI SUNSET (IRE) 4 b.g. Fayruz 116 – Umlani (IRE) (Great Commotion (USA) 123) [2006 94: 6m 6m⁶ 6g p6g p7g⁴ p8g p7.1g Dec 1] strong, close-coupled gelding: fair handicapper nowadays: seems to stay easy 7f: acts on polytrack, firm and good to soft going: wore cheekpieces last 3 starts: sometimes gives trouble in preliminaries: races up with pace. *P. Winkworth* **78**

SAFE INVESTMENT (USA) 2 b.c. (Feb 16) Gone West (USA) – Fully Invested (USA) 99 (Irish River (FR) 131) [2006 7m² 7m* 7m² Aug 30] first foal: dam, 7f (at 2 yrs) and 8.5f (in USA) winner, out of useful sister to Irish Derby runner-up Deploy: fairly useful form: good start in maidens at Newmarket, second to Kalgoorlie prior to winning readily (though wandered in front) later in July: progress when short-head second to My Learned Friend in minor event at Lingfield: will stay 1m: raced on good to firm going: capable of better still. *J. H. M. Gosden* **94 p**

SAFE SHOT 7 b.g. Salse (USA) 128 – Optaria 83 (Song 132) [2006 47: f11g 12f 12g 12m Jul 10] maiden: no form in 2006: in headgear last 7 starts. *Mrs J. C. McGregor*

SAFQA 3 b.f. Singspiel (IRE) 133 – Shamah 96 (Unfuwain (USA) 131) [2006 81p: 10g² 8.2m² 8m* 8.2m² 9m² 10.2f³ 10.3f⁴ 10s³ Oct 10] medium-sized, lengthy filly: fairly useful performer: won maiden at York in June: at least respectable efforts in handicaps after: stays 1¼m: acts on firm and soft going: slowly away seventh outing. *B. W. Hills* **91**

SAFRANINE (IRE) 9 b.m. Dolphin Street (FR) 125 – Webbiana (African Sky 124) [2006 52: 5m f5g⁶ p5g³ 5g⁶ p5.1g 5m 5m³ 5.5g* 6.1f² 6f³ 6m⁵ 6f 6m⁶ 6d 5d⁴ 6.1m 7m⁶ 6f Sep 20] rather leggy mare: modest performer: won handicap at Warwick in July: effective at 5f/6f, probably stays 7f: acts on all-weather, yet to race on heavy ground, acts on any other turf going: effective with/without headgear: tried tongue tied: usually trainer ridden. *Miss A. Stokell* **63**

SAGASSA 2 b.f. (Mar 28) Largesse 112 – Sally's Trust (IRE) 51 (Classic Secret (USA) 91) [2006 5m 6g 6m 6d 7s⁴ p8g p7g⁴ Nov 25] half-sister to 8-y-o Beltane and winner in Sweden by Forzando: dam maiden who stayed 1m: little form in maidens/minor events. *W. de Best-Turner* **–**

SAGEMACCA (IRE) 4 ch.f. Danehill Dancer (IRE) 117 – Aubretia (USA) 84 (Hatchet Man (USA)) [2006 10f Jul 11] sister to 2 winners, including Irish 1½m/2m winner Hanorla, and half-sister to 3 winners, including 1m winner Charming Gift (by Petorius): dam 2-y-o 7f winner: tailed off in maiden at Pontefract. *J. J. Quinn* **–**

SAGREDO (USA) 2 b.g. (Mar 25) Diesis 133 – Eternity 77 (Suave Dancer (USA) 136) [2006 p7.1g⁴ 8.2s² 8.2d* p7.1g² Nov 6] tall, useful-looking gelding: fifth foal: half-brother to 1½m to 2m winner Etching (by Groom Dancer): dam, 11f/1½m winner, half-sister to Fillies' Mile winner Tessla: useful form: progressed well, winning maiden at Nottingham by 4 lengths (value more) in November: clear of rest when second to Tredegar in minor event at Wolverhampton final start: will be well suited by 1¼m/1½m: type to go on thriving at 3 yrs. *Sir Mark Prescott* **95 p**

SAHARA CRYSTAL 2 b.f. (Apr 3) Desert Prince (IRE) 130 – Laser Crystal (IRE) 67 (King's Theatre (IRE) 128) [2006 6.1f⁵ 6g 7m⁵ Sep 9] small filly: first foal: dam, maiden who should have stayed 1½m, out of May Hill Stakes winner Solar Crystal, herself half-sister to Fillies' Mile winner Crystal Music and smart middle-distance performers Dubai Success and Tchaikovsky: modest form in maidens: will stay at least 1m: sold 10,000 gns, sent to Kazakhstan. *H. Candy* **60**

SAHARA DAWN (IRE) 2 b.f. (Mar 22) Desert Sun 120 – Sharadja (IRE) (Doyoun 124) [2006 6.1g 6.1m⁴ 6m f7g Oct 12] €32,000Y: good-topped filly: third foal: half-sister to 5-y-o She's Our Lass: dam unraced granddaughter of Prix Vermeille winner Sharaya: modest maiden: best effort when fourth at Nottingham, only start in blinkers: will stay 1m. *C. G. Cox* **53**

SAHARA PRINCE (IRE) 6 b.g. Desert King (IRE) 129 – Chehana 78 (Posse (USA) 130) [2006 90d: p8g⁵ p7g p8g 7g p7g Dec 30] tall gelding: modest performer nowadays: best at 6f/7f: acts on firm and soft going, probably on polytrack: usually wears headgear. *K. A. Morgan* **– a57**

SAHARA SECRET (IRE) 3 b.f. Revoque (IRE) 122 – Buddy And Soda (IRE) 75 (Imperial Frontier (USA) 112) [2006 –: p8.6g f8g f8g Feb 7] no sign of ability: visored last 2 starts. *D. Shaw* **–**

SAHARA SILK (IRE) 5 b.m. Desert Style (IRE) 121 – Buddy And Soda (IRE) 75 **62** (Imperial Frontier (USA) 112) [2006 70: f6g p5.1g² p6g* f6g⁴ f5g p6g⁶ p6g³ p5.1g² **a83** p5.1g² p5g p6g² 5.7d p5.1g⁴ 5.5g 5g p6g³ p6g p5.1g* f6g⁴ p5.1g⁵ Dec 27] well-made mare: fairly useful handicapper on all-weather, modest on turf: won at Wolverhampton in January and December: effective at 5f/6f: acts on all-weather and firm ground, possibly unsuited by softer than good: visored: tends to edge left: usually races prominently: very slowly away twelfth outing. *D. Shaw*

SAHARA SPHINX (USA) 3 ch.c. Giant's Causeway (USA) 132 – Sculpture (USA) **76** (Deputy Minister (CAN)) [2006 10s⁴ 8.2v Oct 25] $400,000Y: strong colt: first foal: dam, lightly-raced US maiden, half-sister to Middle Park and Dewhurst runner-up Tomahawk: much better effort in maidens at Nottingham on debut: evens favourite, possibly found race coming too soon 7 days later: joined M. Al Muhairi in UAE. *Saeed bin Suroor*

SAHARA STYLE 3 b.g. Desert Style (IRE) 121 – Scapavia (FR) (Alzao (USA) 117) **57** [2006 54: f11g⁵ p8.6g p12.2g f11g⁶ 11g⁶ 12m 9.9g⁴ p12.2g 10.9g Jul 7] workmanlike gelding: modest maiden: stays 11f: acts on all-weather: usually wears headgear. *R. Hollinshead*

SAHARA SUN (IRE) 3 b.f. Desert Sun 120 – Perfect Rainbow (Rainbow Quest – (USA) 134) [2006 51: 10.2m p12g p11g Nov 6] no form since debut at 2 yrs. *A. King*

SAHEM (IRE) 9 b.g. Sadler's Wells (USA) 132 – Sumava (IRE) (Sure Blade (USA) **62** 130) [2006 –: 16m 13d 16f⁴ 16.2f Jul 8] well-made gelding: fairly useful handicapper in 2004: lightly raced and modest form since: effective at 1½m to 2¼m: acts on firm and good to soft going. *Robert Gray*

SAHF LONDON 3 b.g. Vettori (IRE) 119 – Lumiere d'Espoir (FR) 81 (Saumarez 132) **51** [2006 –: 10g f11g p12g⁴ Oct 23] modest maiden: stays 1½m: acts on polytrack. *G. L. Moore*

SAHRATI 2 ch.c. (Apr 24) In The Wings 128 – Shimna 62 (Mr Prospector (USA)) [2006 **81** 7f² 7m⁶ 7m 8.2s* f8g⁴ Dec 27] leggy colt: fourth living foal: half-brother to 3-y-o Hazeymm and 2004 2-y-o 7f winner Santa Fe (by Green Desert), both useful: dam, ran once in Ireland, half-sister to St Leger winner Shantou out of smart daughter of Oh So Sharp: fairly useful form: won maiden at Nottingham in October by head from Marriaj (pair clear): shaped as if amiss on nursery debut: will stay 1½m: yet to race on heavy going, acts on any other. *C. E. Brittain*

SAIF SAREEA 6 b.g. Atraf 116 – Slipperose 72 (Persepolis (FR) 127) [2006 72: 9.9d² **85** 12m* 12m* 12m⁵ Jun 17] sturdy gelding: fairly useful handicapper: unlucky on reappearance: won easily at Catterick in April and Musselburgh (by 6 lengths) in May, subsequently left R. Fahey 50,000 gns: stays easy 1½m: acts on good to firm and good to soft going, probably on heavy: blinkered once: usually patiently ridden, but made running for last 2 wins: free-going sort: fairly useful hurdler. *N. G. Richards*

SAILING DAYS 4 b.f. Kris 135 – Uncharted Waters 68 (Celestial Storm (USA) 132) – [2006 67: 10m Jun 4] tall filly: has scope: fair maiden at 3 yrs: pulled up amiss only start in 2006. *C. A. Cyzer*

SAILOR KING (IRE) 4 b.g. King's Best (USA) 132 – Manureva (USA) (Nureyev **87** (USA) 131) [2006 8d p6g p7g p6g f6g⁶ Dec 21] useful performer for A. Fabre in France: gelded, just fairly useful form in handicaps in Britain in 2006: stays 1m, at least as effective at shorter: acts on heavy and good to firm ground. *D. K. Ivory*

SAINARA (IRE) 2 b.f. (May 3) Fasliyev (USA) 120 – Reem Al Fala (Green Desert – (USA) 127) [2006 5s 5g 5.1m 5d⁶ 5.2g⁶ Jun 1] 9,500F, 3,500Y: big, good-topped filly: second foal: dam unraced half-sister to dam of 3-y-o Balthazaar's Gift: no form: tried in headgear. *J. M. Bradley*

SAINT ALEBE 7 b.g. Bishop of Cashel 122 – Soba Up 74 (Persian Heights 129) [2006 **94 +** 14.1g⁶ 16d⁵ 18d Oct 14] heavy-topped gelding: poor mover: made up into a useful handicapper in 2003 and won Tote Ebor at York final outing: missed 2004 and 2005: seemingly good effort when 6¾ lengths fifth to Hawridge Prince in listed event at Ascot: didn't get run of race when mid-field in Cesarewitch (Handicap) at Newmarket final start: should stay beyond 2m: acts on firm and soft going: has run well when sweating. *D. R. C. Elsworth*

SAINT BERNADETTE 3 b.f. Bertolini (USA) 125 – Primulette 82 (Mummy's Pet – 125) [2006 –: 6g Apr 25] no sign of ability. *P. T. Midgley*

SAINTLY PLACE 5 ch.g. Compton Place 125 – Always On A Sunday 101 (Star **45 §** Appeal 133) [2006 44§, a55§: p5g 6f⁴ 5g³ 5g Sep 13] poor performer nowadays: left

C. Smith after reappearance: effective at 5f to 7f: acts on fibresand and firm ground: has raced freely: tried blinkered/visored/tongue tied: unreliable. *A. W. Carroll*

SAINT NICK 3 b.g. Delta Dancer – Queen's Hat 72 (Cadeaux Genereux 131) [2006 –: p8g 6f Aug 5] no form: reportedly finished lame on reappearance. *J. J. Bridger* —

SAINT REMUS (IRE) 2 b.g. (Feb 3) Diktat 126 – Fur Will Fly 66 (Petong 126) [2006 p8.6f⁶ p6m Oct 2] well held in maidens: gelded after second outing. *Peter Grayson* —

SAITAMA 4 b.f. Pursuit of Love 124 – Sea Ballad (USA) (Bering 136) [2006 p13.9g Dec 8] ex-French filly: half-sister to 1m winner Kazana (by Salse) and winner in Holland by In The Wings: dam once-raced daughter of useful 1½m winner Ocean Ballad: fair performer: won claimer at Saint-Cloud in 2005: left Mme M. Bollack-Badel after final 3-y-o outing: well held on British debut: stays 1½m: often blinkered. *A. M. Hales* —

SAJAAYA (AUS) 3 b.f. Secret Savings (USA) – Million In Mind (AUS) (Snaadee (USA) 114) [2006 7s⁵ 8m 7f⁶ a5f⁶ a6f a6f Dec 22] born to Northern Hemisphere time: good sort: fourth foal: sister to Australian 5f/5.5f winner Secrets In Mind: dam Australian 5f winner: modest maiden: left Sir Michael Stoute after third outing: best effort on soft going: tried tongue tied. *A. Selvaratnam, UAE* 57

SAKABULA (USA) 3 b.f. King of Kings (IRE) 125 – Sianema 62 (Persian Bold 123) [2006 72: 8.3f 10m 8.1m Sep 7] compact filly: fair performer: should stay 1m: reportedly bled final start. *G. C. Bravery* 67

SAKE (IRE) 4 b.g. Shinko Forest (IRE) – Drosera (IRE) (Thatching 131) [2006 71: 7g³ 8.1m 7d* 8d² 7.5f* 7.9g 8f⁶ 8.2g² 7d⁵ 8g⁵ Aug 21] sturdy gelding: fairly useful handicapper: won at Newcastle in May and Beverley in June: effective at 7f/1m: acts on firm and good to soft ground: tried tongue tied: tends to race freely. *N. Tinkler* 80

SAKHEE'S SECRET 2 ch.c. (Mar 13) Sakhee (USA) 136 – Palace Street (USA) 103 (Secreto (USA) 128) [2006 6f³ 6g* 7d⁴ Oct 7] half-brother to several winners, including 5f to 7f winner Palace Affair and 5-y-o King's Caprice (both smart and by Pursuit of Love), and useful 6f to 1m winner Duke of Modena (by Salse): dam 6f/7f winner: excellent impression in maidens at Windsor, unlucky third to Jo'burg then won in August by 6 lengths from Oldjoesaid despite switched right across track in straight: odds on, only fourth to Charlie Farnsbarns in minor event at Ascot, taking strong hold and carried right before finding little: should stay 7f: should still make a smart 3-y-o. *H. Morrison* 104 p

SALAASA (USA) 2 ch.c. (Feb 10) Swain (IRE) 134 – Jawla 97 (Wolfhound (USA) 126) [2006 8g⁴ 8d² Nov 3] useful-looking colt, somewhat unfurnished at 2 yrs: first foal: dam, 7f/1m winner, half-sister to high-class miler Muhtathir: promise in maidens, fourth to Asperity at Newmarket and second to Hohlethelonely at Musselburgh (still green): will stay 1¼m: likely to prove capable of better. *M. Johnston* 79 p

SALAMANCA 4 ch.f. Pivotal 124 – Salanka (IRE) 68 (Persian Heights 129) [2006 103: p8g⁵ 8g³ 8g⁶ 10m 9.9m 9.9m 9m³ 10.1m⁵ 10m⁶ Sep 21] leggy, attractive filly: useful performer: generally creditable efforts in 2006, including when third in listed race (3¼ lengths behind Nantyglo) and handicap (1½ lengths behind Illustrious Blue), both at Goodwood: stays 1¼m: acts on good to firm and good to soft going: sometimes slowly away: held up nowadays: consistent. *S. Kirk* 100

SALAWAT 3 b.f. Tomba 119 – Galadriel (Fairy King (USA)) [2006 f7g 13.8m⁵ p12g Sep 5] 800Y: first foal: dam unraced half-sister to useful 7f winner Sandova: well held in maidens, leaving T. Clement after second start. *G. Prodromou* —

SALESIN 3 ch.c. Lomitas 129 – Elisita (ARG) (Ride The Rails (USA) 116) [2006 78p: 10.2g³ 10.2s* 11.9f³ 13.9s⁴ 14g Sep 23] angular, workmanlike colt: useful performer: won maiden at Bath (by 7 lengths) in May: creditable efforts in frame in handicaps at Haydock and York (Melrose) next 2 starts: stays 1¾m: acts on firm and soft going: sold 58,000 gns, joined J. O'Neill. *L. M. Cumani* 98

SALFORD MILL (IRE) 2 b.c. (Mar 27) Peintre Celebre (USA) 137 – Razana (IRE) 71 (Kahyasi 130) [2006 p8g² Dec 19] 45,000Y: half-brother to several winners, including smart 1¼m/1½m winner Ovambo (by Namaqualand) and useful 2001 2-y-o 6f/7f winner Tahitian Storm (by Catrail), later successful up to 9f in Hong Kong (under name of Gold Field): dam, winner up to 1½m, including in France, half-sister to dam of Prix de l'Opera winner Kinnaird: promising 2½ lengths second to Grande Caiman in maiden at Lingfield, running on strongly under hands and heels: will improve. *D. R. C. Elsworth* 80 p

SALIENT 2 b.c. (May 2) Fasliyev (USA) 120 – Savannah Belle 84 (Green Desert (USA) 127) [2006 7d⁵ 6m p7g* p7g* p7.1g³ p8g⁴ Nov 28] sturdy, good-bodied colt: third foal: half-brother to Italian 6.5f to 1m winner by Second Empire: dam, 2-y-o 5f winner, out of 85

Ribblesdale winner Third Watch: fairly useful performer: won maiden (100/1) in September and (having left W. Knight 57,000 gns) nursery in November, both at Lingfield: ran well when fourth (of 4) to Solid Rock in nursery there final start: likely to prove best up to 1m: acts on polytrack. *J. Akehurst*

SALINGER (USA) 4 b.g. Lear Fan (USA) 130 – Sharp Flick (USA) (Sharpen Up 127) **58** [2006 76: p10g p8g p8g⁶ 10m p7g p12g⁶ p12g⁵ p10g 6f⁵ 7m³ 9g⁴ Sep 12] leggy gelding: modest performer: stays easy 1¼m: acts on polytrack, good to firm and good to soft going: tried in cheekpieces/blinkered (including last 5 starts). *Mrs L. J. Mongan*

SALINJA (USA) 4 b.g. Boundary (USA) 117 – Lasha (USA) (Rahy (USA) 115) [2006 **103** 99: 8g 8g* 9.9m 10.4d 9m⁵ 9d 8g² 8d Oct 28] well-made gelding: useful handicapper: won at Newbury (by neck from Audience, edging right) in July: best other effort when good second to Rains Stops Play at Newmarket: stays 1¼m: acts on soft and good to firm going: blinkered last 2 starts: sent to USA. *Mrs A. J. Perrett*

SALISBURY PLAIN 5 b.h. Mark of Esteem (IRE) 137 – Wild Pavane (Dancing Brave **59** (USA) 140) [2006 –: p12g 11.7d May 17] smallish horse: lightly-raced handicapper: only modest nowadays. *N. I. M. Rossiter*

SALISBURY WORLD (IRE) 3 ch.g. Spinning World (USA) 130 – Dinka Raja **47 §** (USA) (Woodman (USA) 126) [2006 72p: p8g³ p8g p7g⁶ p8g⁵ 8.2m 6d 6m 7.5f⁵ 7.9m 8f 8m 7.5g 7f Sep 18] rather leggy gelding: just poor maiden in 2006, leaving D. Elsworth 4,500 gns after fourth outing: stays easy 1m: acts on polytrack and firm going: headstrong: has carried head awkwardly: often slowly away: one to treat with caution. *J. F. Coupland*

SALONGA (IRE) 3 b.f. Shinko Forest (IRE) – Alongside 58 (Slip Anchor 136) [2006 **65** 8m 10d p10g⁶ 12g p10g³ 10m 10.2m⁴ p8.6g* Nov 11] €7,000Y: tall, quite good-topped filly: seventh foal: half-sister to fairly useful 1½m winner Common Cause (by Polish Patriot) and 8-y-o Northside Lodge: dam, Irish 9f winner who probably stayed 2m, half-sister to smart French/US performer up to 1¼m Kirkwall: fair performer: won maiden at Wolverhampton in November: stays 1¼m: acts on polytrack and good to firm ground. *C. F. Wall*

SALON PRIVE 6 b.g. Green Desert (USA) 127 – Shot At Love (IRE) 79 (Last Tycoon **55** 131) [2006 69, a79: p5g⁴ p5.1g p5g⁴ 5.2f Jul 25] leggy gelding: fair performer on all- **a71** weather, modest on turf: effective at 5f to 7f: acts on polytrack, best effort on turf on good to soft ground: tried blinkered: races prominently: sold £900. *C. A. Cyzer*

SALOON (USA) 2 b.c. (Feb 5) Sadler's Wells (USA) 132 – Fire The Groom (USA) 115 **– p** (Blushing Groom (FR) 131) [2006 7d Aug 25] $400,000Y: brother to smart Irish 7.5f (at 2 yrs) and 1¼m winner Moscow Ballet and useful Irish 1¼m winner Sweet Firebird, closely related to 2 winners, notably top-class sprinter Stravinsky (by Nureyev), and half-brother to 2 winners: dam, 1m winner and later Grade 1 9.5f winner in USA, half-sister to high-class sprinter Dowsing: 7/1, very green when beating 2 in maiden at Newmarket: should do better for experience. *Sir Michael Stoute*

SALSA STEPS (USA) 2 ch.f. (Mar 16) Giant's Causeway (USA) 132 – Dance Design **80 p** (IRE) 119 (Sadler's Wells (USA) 132) [2006 6s⁴ p7g² Oct 26] useful-looking filly: fifth foal: half-sister to fairly useful 1½m winner Sindy (by A P Indy) and 11.5f/1½m winner Science Academy (by Silver Hawk): dam Irish 7f (at 2 yrs) to 1½m (Irish Oaks) winner: fairly useful form in maidens, fourth to Party at Newbury and second to Dalvina at Lingfield: will stay 1m/1¼m: should still improve. *H. Morrison*

SALTHILL (IRE) 3 ch.f. Fruits of Love (USA) 127 – Ambria (ITY) (Final Straw 127) **–** [2006 39: 10g 12.5s p9.5g⁶ p13.9g Dec 4] €5,000Y: sixth foal: half-sister to winner up to 1¼m in Italy by Perugino: dam Italian 6f winner: little form: left E. Tyrrell after reappearance: tried blinkered. *Jarlath P. Fahey, Ireland*

SALT MAN 3 b.c. Mtoto 134 – Romaneh (Lahib (USA) 129) [2006 82p: 9g 9m³ 9.9f **92** 10g Aug 26] big, strong, lengthy colt: fairly useful performer: good third in handicap at Sandown second start: poor efforts in similar events both starts after: should stay 1¼m: raced freely on reappearance: joined D. Selvaratnam in UAE. *M. P. Tregoning*

SALTO CHICO 2 b.g. (Mar 30) Fraam 114 – Miss Tango 61 (Batshoof 122) [2006 7.2g **53** 7.2d⁶ 7m 8f 8s Oct 16] modest maiden: will stay 1¼m: best efforts on going softer than good. *W. M. Brisbourne*

SALTRIO 8 b.g. Slip Anchor 136 – Hills' Presidium (Presidium 124) [2006 f12g **74** p12.2g² p13.9g* p12.2g³ Dec 6] tall, angular, attractive gelding: missed 2004/5 and just fair handicapper nowadays: won at Wolverhampton in November: stays 15.5f: acts on polytrack, soft and firm ground: held up: none too consistent. *W. M. Brisbourne*

SALUSCRAGGIE 4 b.f. Most Welcome 131 – Upper Caen (High Top 131) [2006 52: **60** 10d 10g³ 10g 14.1g 14.1d³ 11.8g 12.4s⁵ 13.8s* Oct 14] workmanlike filly: modest performer: gained first success in handicap at Catterick in October: stays 1¾m: acts on soft going: flashed tail last 2 starts: sold 5,800 gns. *K. G. Reveley*

SALUT D'AMOUR (IRE) 3 ch.f. Danehill Dancer (IRE) 117 – Juno Madonna (IRE) **99** (Sadler's Wells (USA) 132) [2006 99: 7g³ 8s² May 19] good-bodied filly: useful performer: creditable 1¾ lengths third to Speciosa in Nell Gwyn Stakes at Newmarket on reappearance: below form when 12 lengths second to Short Dance in listed race at York next time, almost unseating rider as she jinked leaving stall before hanging right: stays 7f: acts on good to firm and good to soft going: very reluctant at stall fifth 2-y-o outing: quirky, often soon off bridle: sent to USA. *J. Noseda*

SALUTE HIM (IRE) 3 b.g. Mull of Kintyre (USA) 114 – Living Legend (ITY) **98** (Archway (IRE) 115) [2006 88: 7v 8m⁶ 7s 10g* 10f² 10m 9.9f 10g* 10.3f² Sep 23] big, good-topped gelding: useful handicapper: won at Sandown in June and August, making running both times: good second to Stotsfold at Chester final start: stays 1¼m: acts on any going: races prominently: joined A. Martin in Ireland. *M. R. Channon*

SALUTE (IRE) 7 b.g. Muhtarram (USA) 125 – Alasib 93 (Siberian Express (USA) **89** 125) [2006 93, a88: p12g p16g p16g³ p16g 15d³ 16s⁵ 14g* 14m p16g⁵ 21m p12.2f³ **a82** 16.2d⁴ p16.5g² 16d p13.9g³ p16.5g* p16g* Dec 15] lengthy, quite attractive gelding: fairly useful handicapper, better form on turf: won at Sandown in June and Wolverhampton and Kempton in December: stays 16.5f: acts on all-weather, firm and soft going: tried in headgear: edgy sort, has carried head awkwardly. *P. G. Murphy*

SALUTE THE GENERAL 3 ch.c. Mark of Esteem (IRE) 137 – Oiselina (FR) (Lina- **91** mix (FR) 127) [2006 79: 10g² 10s² 10.1m 12m 11.9g⁶ Jul 8] tall, leggy colt: fairly useful handicapper: runner-up twice in 2006: stays 1½m: acts on all-weather, soft and good to firm going: often waited with: sold 75,000 gns in October. *W. R. Muir*

SALUTINO (GER) 4 ch.c. Monsun (GER) 124 – Saderlina (IRE) (Sadler's Wells **116** (USA) 132) [2006 117: 9.6g* 12d² 12m² 12g³ 15.5m² Sep 10] strong, good-bodied colt: smart performer: trained by A. Schutz in Germany prior to reappearance: won minor event at Longchamp in April: placed after in Prix d'Hedouville at Longchamp (beaten ¾ length by Bellamy Cay), Grand Prix de Chantilly (2 lengths second to Policy Maker), Deutschland-Preis at Dusseldorf (third to Donaldson, slowly-run race not suiting) and Prix Gladiateur at Longchamp (5 lengths second to Le Miracle), though not at best on last 2 occasions: should prove effective beyond 1½m: acts on soft and good to firm ground: has worn crossed noseband: consistent, but lacks turn of foot. *A. Fabre, France*

SALUT SAINT CLOUD 5 b.g. Primo Dominie 121 – Tiriana (Common Grounds **75** 118) [2006 58: p16.5g* f14g² p16g f16g* Dec 19] close-coupled gelding: fair handi- capper: won at Wolverhampton in March and Southwell in December: stays 2m: acts on all-weather, firm and soft going: has worn headgear, including cheekpieces in 2006. *G. L. Moore*

SALVESTRO 3 b.g. Medicean 128 – Katy Nowaitee 112 (Komaite (USA)) [2006 69: **67** 9.7m³ 10m⁶ 10.2f⁵ 10f³ p10g 8.5g⁵ 8f² 8m⁵ p8g 8m 8g Oct 13] smallish, useful-looking gelding: fair maiden handicapper: stays 10.2f: acts on polytrack and firm going: tried blinkered: often held up: sold 8,500 gns, and gelded. *Mrs A. J. Perrett*

SALVIA 3 ch.f. Pivotal 124 – Satin Bell 99 (Midyan (USA) 124) [2006 7m Apr 21] **–** good-topped filly: fifth foal: half-sister to 3 winners, including useful 6f (at 2 yrs) to 11f (in Hong Kong) winner Zabaglione (by Zilzal) and fairly useful 1m/9f winner Strawberry Leaf (by Unfuwain): dam 7f winner: 28/1 and green, well held in maiden at Newbury, slowly away (gave trouble at stall). *R. Charlton*

SALVIATI (USA) 9 b.g. Lahib (USA) 129 – Mother Courage 67 (Busted 134) [2006 **75 d** 87: p5g⁶ 5m 5g 5m⁵ 5f 5.2m 5m 6d 6m⁶ 5f 5m⁶ 5d 5m 5m⁶ 5d Oct 3] sturdy gelding: fair handicapper at best nowadays, on long losing run: best at 5f: acts on firm and good to soft ground: sometimes wears cheekpieces: often slowly away: held up. *J. M. Bradley*

SALYM (FR) 5 ch.g. Limnos (JPN) 124 – Tina's Crest (FR) (Ocean Falls 113) [2006 **56** 12v³ 14d³ 10g 12f⁴ 14m⁴ 14.1g Aug 25] fairly useful performer at best: won claimer at Clairefontaine in 2005: claimed (to B. Coutin in France €11,306 after third in similar event at Compiegne second start and ran in Channel Islands for T. Bougourd next 3 outings: well held on British debut: stays 12.5f: acts on soft going: often blinkered. *D. J. S. ffrench Davis*

SAMA DUBAI (AUS) 3 b.f. Secret Savings (USA) – Eajaab (Tragic Role (USA)) **82** [2006 7g* 8.3m⁶ a7.5f Nov 30] born to Northern Hemisphere time: third foal: dam unraced out of close relation to US Grade 1 9f winner Life's Hope: fairly useful form: won maiden at Salisbury in June: not discredited in handicap at Windsor, then left Sir Michael Stoute and off 4½ months: last in handicap at Nad Al Sheba final outing: should prove suited by 1m+. *A. Selvaratnam, UAE*

SAMAHIR (USA) 2 b.f. (Jan 29) Forest Wildcat (USA) 120 – Saabga (USA) 83 **71** (Woodman (USA) 126) [2006 5d⁵ May 22] sixth foal: half-sister to 3 winners, including fairly useful 7f (at 2 yrs) and 8.5f winner Jazmeer (by Sabrehill) and 1m/1¼m (in France) winner Sabbaag (by Mark of Esteem): dam, second at 7f at 2 yrs (only outing), half-sister to smart middle-distance performers Close Conflict and Newton's Law: withdrawn intended debut (upset stall): fifth in maiden at Windsor: underwent surgery after for hairline fracture of leg: sold 5,000 gns. *M. A. Jarvis*

SAMA (IRE) 2 gr.f. (Mar 17) Machiavellian (USA) 123 – Amellnaa (IRE) 86 (Sadler's **75 p** Wells (USA) 132) [2006 6m⁶ Aug 31] third foal: half-sister to 1¼m winner Amerigo Vespucci (by Zafonic): dam, 1¼m winner, sister to 10.5f Prix Cleopatre winner Allurement out of Irish Oaks winner Alydaress: 40/1, sixth behind Vital Statistics in listed race at Salisbury, soon off bridle: will be suited by 1m/1¼m: should progress. *C. E. Brittain*

SAMARINDA (USA) 3 ch.g. Rahy (USA) 115 – Munnaya (USA) 101 (Nijinsky **76** (CAN) 138) [2006 8s 10f p9.5g⁴ 8d⁵ p8g⁶ p10g* Dec 30] good-topped gelding: brother to useful French 1¼m/11f winner Yaya and half-brother to 2 winners, including useful French 7f (at 2 yrs)/1m winner Mystic Melody (by Seattle Slew): dam 11.5f winner: fair performer: left E. Dunlop 20,000 gns and gelded after third start: won maiden at Lingfield in December: should stay 1½m: acts on polytrack and firm ground. *Mrs P. Sly*

SAMDANIYA 2 b.f. (Mar 1) Machiavellian (USA) 123 – Cloud Castle 119 (In The **79** Wings 128) [2006 6m 7m p6g Sep 29] fifth foal: half-sister to smart French 1½m winner Reverie Solitaire (by Nashwan) and 3-y-o Queen's Best: dam, won Nell Gwyn Stakes and second in Prix Vermeille, half-sister to Luso, Warrsan and Needle Gun: fair form: highly tried in Prestige Stakes at Goodwood second start (ninth of 10 to Sesmen): will stay 1m+. *C. E. Brittain*

SAME OLD SCENE (IRE) 3 b.g. Orpen (USA) 116 – Saratoga Scene (USA) (Grey Dawn II 132) [2006 p6g Oct 6] 33/1, well held in seller at Lingfield, (reportedly had breathing problem). *J. R. Best*

SAM LORD 2 ch.g. (Apr 18) Observatory (USA) 131 – My Mariam 79 (Salse (USA) **86** 128) [2006 p7g⁵ 6m⁶ 8g* Oct 13] 35,000Y, 95,000 2-y-o: stocky, close-coupled gelding: half-brother to several winners, including useful Irish 1¼m winner Crookhaven (by Dansili) and fairly useful French 1½m winner In The Ribbons (by In The Wings): dam, 6f winner at 2 yrs, sister to Moyglare Stud Stakes winner Bianca Nera: fairly useful form: improved to win maiden at Newmarket (beat Diamond Tycoon by ¾ length), making most: gelded after: will probably stay 1¼m. *J. H. M. Gosden*

SAMORRA (IRE) 2 b.f. (Mar 27) In The Wings 128 – Walesiana (GER) (Star Appeal **74 p** 133) [2006 6s* May 26] well-made filly: half-sister to several winners, notably Musidora/Nassau Stakes winner Zahrat Dubai (by Unfuwain): dam German 6f (at 2 yrs) to 1m (Group 2) winner: 7/4, won maiden at Goodwood, rallying to beat Caldra by neck: will benefit from 1m: should improve. *M. P. Tregoning*

SAMSON QUEST 4 b.g. Cyrano de Bergerac 120 – Zenita (IRE) (Zieten (USA) 118) **69** [2006 65: p8g² p8g² p8g⁴ p8g⁵ p8g* p8.6g⁴ p9.5g f8g 8.1g p8.6g p8.6g⁴ p10g⁶ 8m Aug 19] sturdy gelding: fair performer: left N. Littmoden after reappearance: won seller at Lingfield in February: left A. Carroll after tenth start: stays easy 1¼m: acts on polytrack and good to firm going: usually wears headgear: often slowly away. *G. F. Bridgwater*

SAMSOUMA (IRE) 3 b.f. Marju (IRE) 127 – St Bride's Bay (Caerleon (USA) 132) **47** [2006 58: p7g f11g f7g 10f Jun 13] close-coupled filly: poor maiden: should stay 7f: best effort on good to firm going. *C. E. Brittain*

SAM'S SECRET 4 b.f. Josr Algarhoud (IRE) 118 – Twilight Time (Aragon 118) [2006 **73** 76: 7f⁴ 8.9f 7m 8m 7.5m 7v Oct 31] quite good-topped filly: fair performer: left S. Parr after fifth start: stays 7f: acts on polytrack and firm ground: tried visored/in cheekpieces: sometimes races freely: often slowly away. *G. A. Swinbank*

SAM THE SORCERER 5 b.g. Wizard King 122 – Awham (USA) (Lear Fan (USA) **–** 130) [2006 44: f7g 6m Jul 26] quite good-topped gelding: poor performer: tried visored/in cheekpieces. *J. R. Norton*

SAMUEL 2 ch.c. (Jan 17) Sakhee (USA) 136 – Dolores 111 (Danehill (USA) 126) [2006 **54** 7d Oct 28] lengthy colt: first foal: dam 1m winner: 40/1, shaped as if needing run when beating 3 in maiden at Newmarket. *J. L. Dunlop*

SAMUEL CHARLES 8 b.g. Green Desert (USA) 127 – Hejraan (USA) 73 (Alydar **89** (USA)) [2006 55, a78: p7.1g* f8g* f8g⁴ p7.1g² f8s p7g 7g p8g² p8g* p7.1g p8g* 8.2m* p8g⁵ p8.6g² 8m⁶ 8f⁶ 8.1m p7g⁵ p8g⁶ p7.1g⁵ Dec 31] tall gelding: fairly useful handi-capper: won at Wolverhampton (apprentices) and Southwell in January, and Lingfield, Kempton and Nottingham in June: stays 8.6f: acts on all-weather, firm and good to soft going: tried in visor/cheekpieces: sometimes slowly away: has awkward head carriage. *C. R. Dore*

SAMUEL JOHN PEPLOE (IRE) 4 b.g. Intikhab (USA) 135 – Sadalsud (IRE) **–** (Shaadi (USA) 126) [2006 –: p10g Jan 4] tall gelding: always behind in maidens 8 months apart. *G. L. Moore*

SAMURAI JACK (IRE) 3 b.g. Mark of Esteem (IRE) 137 – Kasota (IRE) 72 (Alzao **70** (USA) 117) [2006 72: p9.5g* p8.6g⁴ 12s⁶ 10f⁵ 11.7f 10m Aug 26] €20,000Y: sturdy gelding: third foal: closely related to 4-y-o Key Time: dam, 1¾m winner in Ireland, half-sister to Yorkshire Oaks winner Key Change (by Darshaan) from family of Kahyasi: fair performer: left J. Burns in Ireland, won maiden at Wolverhampton in March: should stay 1½m: acts on polytrack, firm and good to soft going: often tongue tied. *John A. Quinn, Ireland*

SAMURAI WAY 4 b.c. Darshaan 133 – Truly Special 116 (Caerleon (USA) 132) [2006 **79** 79: 9.9g³ 10d² 12s⁶ Oct 6] angular colt: fair maiden: creditable efforts first 2 starts in 2006: raced only on good ground or softer. *L. M. Cumani*

SAN ANTONIO 6 b.g. Efisio 120 – Winnebago 63 (Kris 135) [2006 98: p7g² p7g⁴ **84** 8v⁴ 6d⁶ 8.1s⁶ 8.3f 8.3g p7g Oct 6] strong, well-made gelding: has a round action: useful **a98** handicapper on all-weather, fairly useful on turf nowadays: best efforts in 2006 on first 2 starts: effective at 6f to 1m: acts on polytrack, heavy and good to firm going: usually blinkered: often races prominently: modest hurdler, successful in November. *Mrs P. Sly*

SA NAU 3 b.g. Generous (IRE) 139 – Trellis Bay 100 (Sadler's Wells (USA) 132) [2006 **67** p8g 8d p9.5g 11.6d 12f⁵ 14.1d 14.1g* 14.1m² 16.1g* Sep 27] 20,000 2-y-o: rather leggy, quite good-topped gelding: third foal: half-brother to 4-y-o Bellamy Cay: dam 1½m winner who stayed 2m: fair performer: won handicaps at Redcar in August and New-castle in September: stays 2m: acts on firm going, probably on good to soft. *T. Keddy*

SANBUCH 2 b.c. (Feb 19) Tobougg (IRE) 125 – Monte Calvo 85 (Shirley Heights 130) **83 p** [2006 6g p7g* Jun 28] 34,000Y: third foal: half-brother to 5-y-o Night Storm: dam 1¾m and 17f winner: fairly useful form: twice raced in June, still green when winning maiden at Kempton: will be suited by 1¼m+: should improve further. *L. M. Cumani*

SANCHI (IRE) 4 b.c. Darshaan 133 – Samara (IRE) 108 (Polish Patriot (USA) 128) **102** [2006 83: 11m* 10s⁵ 12g⁶ Oct 12] medium-sized, sturdy, attractive colt: useful handi-capper, lightly raced: best effort when winning at Southwell in September by 1¾ lengths from St Savarin: just respectable efforts at Ayr and Newmarket after: stays 1½m: acts on good to firm going, probably on soft: joined E. Charpy in UAE. *Saeed bin Suroor*

SANCTITY 3 ch.f. Pivotal 124 – Blessed Honour 77 (Ahonoora 122) [2006 59p: 7m⁵ **70** 8.2g p7.1g² p7g 9.9m* p9.5m² p10g³ Oct 15] sister to useful Italian 5f/6f winner Crucial, closely related to 2 winners by Polar Falcon, including 1999 2-y-o 6f/7f (Prestige Stakes) winner Icicle, and half-sister to 11f winner Invincible (by Slip Anchor): dam, 2-y-o 7f winner on only start, half-sister to smart performer up to 1¾m Sacrament: fair handi-capper: won at Beverley in August: visored, good efforts next 2 starts: stays 1¼m: acts on polytrack and good to firm going. *J. R. Fanshawe*

SAND AND STARS (IRE) 5 ch.m. Dr Devious (IRE) 127 – Charm The Stars (Roi **71** Danzig (USA)) [2006 87: 11.7g 14m 12m 11.6m³ 11.5m³ Jul 12] sturdy mare: fairly use-ful handicapper at best: just fair form in 2006: stayed 1¾m: acted on firm and good to soft going: tried blinkered at 2 yrs: had flashed tail: was inconsistent: dead. *M. H. Tompkins*

SAN DENG 4 gr.g. Averti (IRE) 117 – Miss Mirror 77 (Magic Mirror 105) [2006 71: **72** 11g⁶ 10.1m 12g² 12.1m³ 12m² 12m⁵ 12g 12d⁴ Oct 3] tall gelding: fair handicapper: stays 1½m: acts on polytrack, good to firm and good to soft going: raced freely seventh outing: possibly none too resolute, but is consistent. *M. D. Hammond*

SANDER CAMILLO (USA) 2 b.f. (Mar 8) Dixie Union (USA) 121 – Staraway **116 p** (USA) (Star de Naskra (USA)) [2006 6d⁴ 6m* 6m* Jul 12]
Sales of two-year-olds in training are becoming increasingly big business, particularly in the States, and some of the horses undoubtedly justify the expense. Of the thirteen juveniles who fetched a million dollars or more after 'breezing' before auctions in Florida, California and Kentucky in the first part of the year, six

Chippenham Lodge Stud Cherry Hinton Stakes, Newmarket—Sander Camillo is a cut above the opposition; Alzerra holds second, ahead of Gilded and Hope'n'Charity (partially hidden)

won and two landed Grade 3 events. Two-million-dollar purchase Belgravia hit the bullseye in the Hollywood Prevue Stakes in November and E Z Warrior, who cost 1.2m dollars, promised to become the best of Bob Baffert's invariably strong team of youngsters only to fall foul of sore shins after winning the Hollywood Juvenile Championship in July. However, the highest-priced horse of any age ever sold at auction, The Green Monkey, a sixteen-million-dollar buy by Demi O'Byrne for Coolmore at the Fasig-Tipton Calder sale in February, did not reach the track. He suffered a muscular injury in the summer and was packed off to Ashford Stud when it recurred, with a view to trying again in the new year. The main expectation when buying a horse that gallops so strikingly before a sale is to do well with him or her in the first season. The failure of The Green Monkey to reach the racecourse can hardly be viewed with equanimity by his connections. The same applies to the previous record-priced two-year-old, Ever Shifting, who cost Darley 5.2m dollars in 2005 but didn't make his debut until December as a three-year-old when ninth in a maiden event at Aqueduct. The careers of three cheaper buys at Calder exemplify what can happen when things go right. Tiz Wonderful, who cost 475,000 dollars, won his three starts culminating in the Grade 2 Kentucky Jockey Club Stakes in record time. Appealing Zophie, purchased for 150,000 dollars, landed the Grade 1 Spinaway Stakes and finished fourth in the Breeders' Cup Juvenile Fillies. And Sander Camillo, a 500,000-dollar buy, proved one of the best juvenile fillies in Europe.

The first indication that Sander Camillo possessed above-average ability came on her second appearance, in the eighteen-runner Albany Stakes at Royal Ascot for which she started favourite up against ten winners, including second favourite Bahama Mama, Silk Blossom and Scarlet Runner. Sander Camillo's reputation rather than her form was responsible for her heading the market. On her only previous start she had seemed to need the experience in a maiden race at Newmarket in May, running on under hands and heels once she got the hang of things to finish fourth to another Albany Stakes contender Bicoastal. Bicoastal and the rest had no answer to Sander Camillo at Ascot where she was always going strongly disputing the lead, quickened readily two furlongs out and was soon on top, running on strongly, despite drifting right, to account for Silk Blossom by a length and a half with Scarlet Runner third. The Albany Stakes has proved a worthwhile addition to the Royal meeting since its inauguration in 2002, attracting an average of sixteen fillies and requiring a useful performance from its winners, Duty Paid, Silca's Gift, Jewel In The Sand and La Chunga (a 270,000-dollar two-year-old purchase for Sander Camillo's owner).

Sander Camillo was clearly in the same mould and, like Jewel In The Sand, she headed next for the Chippenham Lodge Stud Cherry Hinton Stakes at Newmarket in July. Like her predecessor, she completed the double, only in much more

922

impressive style. All ten runners were winners but, despite the presence of unbeaten Gilded carrying a 3-lb penalty for winning the Queen Mary Stakes, Sander Camillo started a hot favourite at 11/8. Next in the betting came Alderney, four-length winner of a maiden at York, Silk Blossom, Gilded, Newmarket listed winner Hope'n'Charity and Alzerra, who had landed a maiden at Haydock. Close up and going well within herself from the outset as 100/1-shot Three Decades led, Sander Camillo was soon in command after being given the office a quarter of a mile out, none of her rivals, headed by Alzerra, finding anything in reply under pressure. By contrast, Sander Camillo continued to find more without coming under anything like full pressure, drawing clear and passing the post with five lengths to spare over Alzerra, with Gilded a neck away third. A breathtaking victory, one made colourful by the winner's rider Frankie Dettori sporting Italian flags painted on his cheeks in celebration of Italy's victory in the World Cup.

The Cherry Hinton Stakes has a good record and two recent champion fillies won it, Dazzle in 1996 and Attraction in 2003, while Sayyedati (1992), Wannabe Grand (1998) and Donna Blini (2005) each added the Cheveley Park Stakes to her tally. Sander Camillo's success was very reminiscent of Attraction's sparkling five-length victory and the similarity does not end there, since neither filly ran again as a two-year-old. Attraction suffered an injury but Sander Camillo remained fit, apart from having an unsatisfactory blood test result which caused her withdrawal from the Lowther Stakes won by Silk Blossom. However, Sander Camillo's connections bypassed the Moyglare Stud Stakes and she was taken out of the Prix Marcel Boussac six days beforehand and the Cheveley Park Stakes on the day. Mention was also made of the Breeders' Cup Juvenile Fillies—trainer Jeremy Noseda had won the Juvenile with Wilko in 2004—but that too went by without her. The reason given for withdrawing Sander Camillo from the Cheveley Park at Newmarket was the going, which had changed from good to firm earlier in the week to an official soft, though it was actually good to soft. Both Sander Camillo's

Sir Robert Ogden's "Sander Camillo"

wins have been on good to firm. Noseda, who also trained Wannabe Grand, is apparently convinced that Sander Camillo is incapable of running to her best on soft and he will presumably try to steer her away from such ground in her classic campaign. The policy may hamper her prospects if the ground for the classics over a mile in the spring is on the soft side, as it is more likely to be than for races in the summer. Time will tell, but there is no real racecourse evidence that Sander Camillo does not act on soft. It was good to soft for her debut when she shaped so promisingly. Good, fluent movers such as her are not always at home on soft going, though some definitely are. Provided she lines up for the One Thousand Guineas, Sander Camillo is likely to give Finsceal Beo plenty to think about, her form being only slightly behind that of the Prix Marcel Boussac winner, and, what's more, Sander Camillo can be expected to improve.

Sander Camillo (USA) (b.f. Mar 8, 2004)	Dixie Union (USA) (b 1997)	Dixieland Band (b 1980)	Northern Dancer Mississippi Mud
		She's Tops (b 1989)	Capote She's A Talent
	Staraway (USA) (b or br 1991)	Star de Naskra (b 1975)	Naskra Candle Star
		Iceaway (gr 1977)	Icecapade Gayway

Sander Camillo will stay a mile and possibly a shade further because, although having abundant speed, she is not headstrong, another way in which she resembles Attraction. Sander Camillo's sire Dixie Union was a very smart colt who won at up to nine furlongs on dirt, winning the Haskell Invitational Handicap over that trip and the Malibu Stakes over seven furlongs. Dixie Union has not yet sired a Group 1 or Grade 1 winner from three crops of racing age. Even so, he has made a reasonably promising start, though whether that justifies a jump in his fee from 30,000 dollars to 50,000 dollars is debatable. Sander Camillo's dam Staraway cost only 16,000 dollars as a yearling and proved a splendid buy. As tough as old boots, she raced for six seasons in Canada, winning twenty and finishing second in fifteen of her fifty-four starts from six furlongs to nine furlongs, including fourteen minor stakes events. Sander Camillo, who fetched 160,000 dollars as a yearling in Kentucky, is her third live foal; one of the others, Square Pants (by King of Kings), was successful over six furlongs in the States. Staraway's yearling filly by Malibu Moon failed to reach her reserve at 240,000 dollars at Keeneland in September. Staraway was the best of six winners out of her dam Iceaway, who notched two races including a minor stakes event at two. The next dam, Gayway, was stakes placed and a daughter of smart two-year-old Thataway, but this can hardly be called a tip-top family. Sander Camillo, a well-made filly, is already well on the way to putting that right. *J. Noseda*

SANDERS BOY 3 gr.g. Arkadian Hero (USA) 123 – Rising of The Moon (IRE) 82 **41** (Warning 136) [2006 41: p6g⁴ p7.1g p6g 6d p5.1g³ f6g⁶ f6g p5.1g p6s Dec 15] leggy gelding: poor maiden: should stay 7f: acts on all-weather. *J. R. Norton*

SANDGLASS 3 b.f. Zafonic (USA) 130 – Clepsydra 78 (Sadler's Wells (USA) 132) **101** [2006 80p: 10g* 10d⁶ 12s 10g Oct 12] big, leggy filly: useful performer: won maiden at Newbury in June: further improvement when 4¾ lengths sixth to Chaibia in Prix de Psyche at Deauville next time: raced freely/ran as if amiss in listed races at York and Newmarket last 2 starts: stayed 1¼m: raced only on good going or softer: stud. *Mrs A. J. Perrett*

SANDHILL DANCER 4 b.f. Perryston View 114 – Just Like You (Sandhurst Prince **–** 128) [2006 f11g f8g p8.6g Feb 24] third foal: dam well beaten: soundly beaten in sellers/claimer (blinkered). *S. Parr*

SAND IRON (IRE) 4 b.f. Desert Style (IRE) 121 – Mettlesome (Lomond (USA) 128) **58** [2006 66: f6g 8.1d p8g⁵ p8g⁴ p8.6g⁶ f8g p10g Dec 10] quite good-topped filly: modest performer: left S. Keightley after reappearance: stays 1m: acts on polytrack and good to soft going. *John Allen*

SAND REPEAL (IRE) 4 b.g. Revoque (IRE) 122 – Columbian Sand (IRE) (Salmon **77** Leap (USA) 131) [2006 74: f11g² f11g* p12.2g* f11g² p12.2g p12g f14g* 12g⁵ f11g² 14.1s f14g f14g f12g⁵ Dec 27] leggy gelding: fair performer: won maiden at Southwell and handicaps at Wolverhampton and Southwell in January/April: stays 1¾m: acts on all-weather and heavy ground: wore cheekpieces final start. *Miss J. Feilden*

SANDREY (IRE) 2 b.c. (Feb 27) Noverre (USA) 125 – Boudica (IRE) (Alhaarth (IRE) 126) [2006 7m⁴ 6m 6g* Oct 16] 36,000F, 60,000 2-y-o: useful-looking colt, unfurnished at 2 yrs: first foal: dam, no form, half-sister to several useful sprinters: fairly useful form: promise both starts before making all in maiden at Windsor: will prove best up to 7f. *P. W. Chapple-Hyam* **80**

SANDS CROONER (IRE) 3 b.c. Imperial Ballet (IRE) 110 – Kurfuffle (Bluebird (USA) 125) [2006 81, a71: p5.1g* p6g⁴ p6g³ p5g* p5g* 5g 5.1f p6g p5g p5.1g⁵ Dec 23] workmanlike colt: fairly useful performer: won maiden at Wolverhampton in January and handicaps at Lingfield in February and March: off 6 months after seventh outing (reportedly bruised a pedal bone): effective at 5f/6f: acts on all-weather, soft and good to firm going: visored nowadays: used to wear tongue tie: has hung. *D. Shaw* **– a80**

SANDS OF BARRA (IRE) 3 gr.g. Marju (IRE) 127 – Purple Risks (FR) 80 (Take Risks (FR) 116) [2006 74: p7g⁵ p7g⁴ 7m⁴ 7m* 8s 7m 7f 7f⁵ 7d 7m p7g p8g⁵ p7.1g p7g p7g p7.1g Dec 27] quite good-topped gelding: fairly useful performer on turf, fair on all-weather: won handicap at Yarmouth in May: left N. Callaghan 14,000 gns after twelfth start: effective at 7f/easy 1m: acts on polytrack, firm and good to soft going, below form on soft and heavy. *I. W. McInnes* **82 a73**

SAND SPRITE (IRE) 3 b.f. Green Desert (USA) 127 – Fleet Amour (USA) (Afleet (CAN)) [2006 –p: 8d 7.5f Jun 14] well-made filly: modest maiden: sold 10,500 gns in August. *Sir Michael Stoute* **51**

SANDTON CITY (IRE) 3 ch.c. Daggers Drawn (USA) 114 – Inter Madera (IRE) (Toca Madera 111) [2006 86: 10s³ 10.3d 10m² 10g⁵ 12m⁴ 12m 12d 10m Aug 27] well-made colt: good walker: sixth foal: brother to Irish 13f winner Tauranga and half-brother to 3 winners, including fairly useful 2002 2-y-o 5f/6f winner Sanbenito (by Elbio), later won at 7f in Hong Kong: dam unraced half-sister to smart Irish 1m/9f performer Scottish Memories: useful performer: won maiden at Galway at 2 yrs: mostly creditable efforts in 2006, though well held in Dee Stakes at Chester second start: stays 1½m: acts on soft and good to firm going. *Francis Ennis, Ireland* **98**

SANDWAKI (USA) 2 b.c. (Apr 6) Dixieland Band (USA) – Wakigoer (USA) (Miswaki (USA) 124) [2006 5g* 5d* 5g* 6s⁴ 7m Oct 1] smallish, close-coupled colt: lacks scope: fourth foal: half-brother to French 5f (at 2 yrs) to 9f (Prix Chloe) winner Acago and French 2005 2-y-o 7f winner Quiet Royal (both smart, by Royal Academy): dam, French 1m winner, half-sister to high-class US Grade 1 1¼m winner Dare And Go: useful performer: won minor event at Maisons-Laffitte in May, listed race at Longchamp in June and Prix du Bois at Maisons-Laffitte (made all again, pushed out to beat Boccassini 1½ lengths) in July: respectable fourth to Dutch Art in Prix Morny at Deauville: well below form in Prix Jean-Luc Lagardere at Longchamp final start: should stay 7f: acts on soft ground: sent to USA. *C. Laffon-Parias, France* **109**

SANDWITH 3 ch.g. Perryston View 114 – Bodfari Times 72 (Clantime 101) [2006 68, a60: 5d* 5g⁶ May 8] fair performer: won handicap at Musselburgh in April: probably best at 5f: acts on good to firm and good to soft ground: tried in cheekpieces. *I. Semple* **75**

SANDY'S LEGEND (USA) 4 ch.g. Tale of The Cat (USA) 113 – Avasand (USA) (Avatar (USA)) [2006 65: p12g⁶ p13g p16.5g⁴ p16.5g⁵ 16d Aug 29] leggy, useful-looking gelding: modest maiden: left Jamie Poulton after second start: stays 2m: acts on polytrack: tried visored/in cheekpieces: has looked hard ride. *Mrs L. Williamson* **63**

SANGFROID 2 gr.g. (Mar 26) With Approval (CAN) – Affaire d'Amour 100 (Hernando (FR) 127) [2006 p6g p8.6g 6d Sep 25] 50,000Y: first foal: dam, 15f/2m winner, sister to 8-y-o Foreign Affairs: behind in maidens (all within 2 weeks): gelded after: likely to prove different proposition over 1½m+ as 3-y-o. *Sir Mark Prescott* **– p**

SANGREAL 2 ch.f. (May 30) Medicean 128 – La Belle Dominique 76 (Dominion 123) [2006 6.1g 5.1s⁵ p6g⁵ f5g³ Dec 2] 9,500Y: neat filly: fourth foal: dam 5f winner: fair maiden: should stay 7f. *K. R. Burke* **66**

SAN HERNANDO 6 b.g. Hernando (FR) 127 – Sandrella (IRE) (Darshaan 133) [2006 67: 16s² 14.1g Jun 29] big, lengthy gelding: shows knee action: fair handicapper: lightly raced: stays 2m: acts on polytrack, firm and soft going: tried in cheekpieces/visor: sometimes slowly away/carries head high. *Miss E. C. Lavelle* **79**

SAN MARCO (IRE) 8 b.g. Brief Truce (USA) 126 – Nuit Des Temps (Sadler's Wells (USA) 132) [2006 f14g Apr 7] no form on Flat since 2003: usually blinkered/in cheekpieces. *M. Sheppard* **–**

SANSEL 3 b.f. Well Beloved 86 – Abbisluckystar (IRE) (Soughaan (USA) 111) [2006 – p12g 7m 11.9m 10.1m 16.1s Sep 4] first known foal: dam unraced: no form. *J. Ryan*

SANS REWARD (IRE) 2 b.f. (Mar 15) Barathea (IRE) 127 – Fritta Mista (IRE) (Lina- **99** mix (FR) 127) [2006 5.5d⁵ p5g² 6g* 7.1g* 7d⁵ 8g³ 8d Oct 17] 18,000Y: good-topped, quite attractive filly: first foal: dam, lightly raced in France/Ireland, out of half-sister to Yorkshire Oaks winner/excellent broodmare Hellenic: useful performer: won maiden at Salisbury in June and minor event at Warwick in July: better form after when fifth (met trouble) in Sweet Solera Stakes at Newmarket and third (2 lengths behind Simply Perfect) in May Hill Stakes at York: clearly not herself in France final outing: stays 1m: raced only on good/good to soft going on turf, and acts on polytrack: blinkered last 2 starts. *B. J. Meehan*

SANTANDO 6 b.g. Hernando (FR) 127 – Santarem (USA) 71 (El Gran Senor (USA) **57** 136) [2006 91d: p12.2g p13g p12g⁴ 11.5m p10g³ p12g² p10g⁵ p12g 10d⁵ p13.9m* p16g **a76** Oct 20] tall, useful-looking gelding: fair handicapper nowadays: won at Wolverhampton in October: stays 1¾m: acts on all-weather, had form on good to firm and good to soft going earlier in career: often wears headgear: has run well when sweating: lazy sort, often soon off bridle: sold 11,000 gns, joined P. Bowen. *C. E. Brittain*

SANT ELENA 3 ch.f. Efisio 120 – Argent du Bois (USA) (Silver Hawk (USA) 123) **88** [2006 84P: p7g³ 8m³ 8m p6g* p6g³ p7g² 6d p6g Nov 5] strong filly: fairly useful handi- capper: won handicap at Kempton in July: effective at 6f/7f, should stay 1m: acts on polytrack and good going. *G. Wragg*

SANTERA (IRE) 2 br.f. (Mar 14) Gold Away (IRE) 125 – Sainte Gig (FR) (Saint Cyr- – ien (FR) 128) [2006 p8.6g Nov 18] fourth foal: dam unraced half-sister to smart French/ US 1m/1¼m performer Val des Bois: soundly beaten in maiden at Wolverhampton. *Mrs A. Duffield*

SAPIENZA 3 ch.f. Singspiel (IRE) 133 – Kameez (IRE) 72 (Arazi (USA) 135) [2006 **71** 71: 9.7m⁴ Apr 25] well-made filly: fair maiden: would have stayed 1¼m+: acted on good to firm going: dead. *C. E. Brittain*

SAPPHIRE DREAM 4 b.f. Mind Games 121 – Bombay Sapphire (Be My Chief – (USA) 122) [2006 66, a49: p6g f5g⁵ f6g⁶ p6g f6g p6g May 5] close-coupled, quite good- **a46** topped filly: poor performer nowadays: effective at 5f/6f: acts on all-weather, heavy and good to firm ground: tried in headgear. *A. Bailey*

SAPPHIRE STORM (IRE) 3 b.f. Elnadim (USA) 128 – Blu Tu Miami (USA) **65** (Robin Des Pins (USA) 119) [2006 55: p7g⁴ p6g p8.6g 7g 5.9g⁴ 7g³ 6m* 6m 7.5f³ 7.1m* 7m* Sep 16] fair handicapper: left Miss D. McHale after third outing: won at Lingfield in June, Musselburgh in August and Catterick (edged right) in September: stays 7f: acts on polytrack, firm and good to soft going: tried in headgear/tongue tie for previous stable. *P. T. Midgley*

SARAH'S ART (IRE) 3 gr.g. City On A Hill (USA) 114 – Treasure Bleue (IRE) (Trea- **79** sure Kay 114) [2006 –: p6g⁵ 7s⁶ p5.1g² p5.1g* 5m* p5g³ 6f² 6m* 6f² 6d 5g² 6f p6g Dec 19] lengthy gelding: fair performer: won banded race at Wolverhampton and handicaps at Hamilton in May and Brighton in June: left N. Callaghan after eleventh outing: sold 16,000 gns and off 5 months before final start: effective at 5f/6f: acts on polytrack and firm going: blinkered nowadays: looked wayward second outing. *Miss D. A. McHale*

SARAH'S PRINCE (IRE) 3 b.g. Royal Applause 124 – Peaceful Sarah 82 (Sharpo **49** 132) [2006 56?: p5g 7g p6g² f5g⁴ f6g f7g⁵ p6g Oct 23] poor maiden: left P. Mooney in Ireland after 2 yrs: stays 7f: acts on all-weather. *D. K. Ivory*

SARA MANA MOU 3 b.f. Medicean 128 – Sarabah (IRE) 83 (Ela-Mana-Mou 132) **41** [2006 –: 10g f11g⁴ 16g 12g⁵ 14.1g Aug 24] big, strong filly: poor maiden. *J. G. Portman*

SARATOGA 3 b.c. Danehill (USA) 126 – Rockerlong 112 (Deploy 131) [2006 8m – May 13] good-bodied colt: has a short, scratchy action: 25/1 and very green in prelim- inaries, last of 11 in maiden at Newmarket, starting slowly: sold 5,000 gns, joined Miss D. Mountain. *Sir Michael Stoute*

SARDIS ROAD 2 ch.c. (May 2) Daggers Drawn (USA) 114 – Ave Atque Vale (FR) **66** (Most Welcome 131) [2006 5s 5.1d² a6g⁶ 8d⁴ 5.8g² 5.8g* a6d⁴ a8g³ Nov 19] first foal: dam French 1m winner: fair performer: claimed from W. Turner £6,000 sixth start: won maiden at Taby in September: stays 1m: acts on dirt and good to soft ground. *C. Bjorling, Sweden*

SARENNE 5 b.m. Desert Sun 120 – Fabulous Pet (Somethingfabulous (USA)) [2006 – f12g⁶ f11g f16g Mar 8] little sign of ability. *John Berry*

SARRAAF (IRE) 10 ch.g. Perugino (USA) 84 – Blue Vista (IRE) (Pennine Walk 120) **64**
[2006 70: p8.6g³ p7.1g⁴ 8.3m⁴ Jun 14] smallish, strong gelding: modest performer: effective at 7f to 1¼m: acts on all-weather and any turf going: tried in blinkers/visor. *I. Semple*

SARWIN (USA) 3 gr. or ro.g. Holy Bull (USA) 134 – Olive The Twist (USA) 94 (The- **60**
atrical 128) [2006 49: 10d 10m³ p9.5g* 10f⁶ 11.6d p10g⁵ p10g³ p12.2g² p10g⁵ Dec 20] **a70**
strong gelding: fair handicapper on all-weather, modest on turf: won at Wolverhampton in June: stays easy 1½m: acts on polytrack and good to firm ground: has looked no easy ride. *W. J. Musson*

SASETTI (IRE) 3 ch.f. Selkirk (USA) 129 – My Potters (USA) (Irish River (FR) 131) **64**
[2006 8m p8.6g⁶ 10m 12g⁴ 10m⁶ Sep 19] leggy, close-coupled filly: half-sister to several winners, including very smart 7f (at 2 yrs) and 1½m (Irish Oaks) winner Winona (by Alzao): dam, Irish 1m winner, half-sister to champion US sprinter My Juliet: fair maiden: probably stays 1½m: acts on good to firm going: sometimes tongue tied: sold 60,000 gns in November. *J. R. Fanshawe*

SASS CAFE (IRE) 2 gr.f. (Apr 2) Sendawar (IRE) 129 – Ashtarka (Dalsaan 125) [2006 **– p**
p7g Sep 10] 11,500F, €22,000Y: half-sister to 2 winners, notably high-class French miler Ashkalani (by Soviet Star): dam, French 1m winner, half-sister to Prix du Cadran winner Shafaraz: 6/1, prominent fair way when seventh to Lady Grace in maiden at Kempton: should do better. *T. J. Pitt*

SATCHEM (IRE) 4 br.c. Inchinor 119 – Mohican Princess (Shirley Heights 130) **119**
[2006 108: 8g* p8g² 7g³ 8d* 7d³ Oct 14] smallish colt: very smart performer: better than ever in 2006, winning listed race at Goodwood (by short head from Stronghold) in June and Countrywide Steel And Tubes Joel Stakes at Newmarket (beat Pinson 1¼ lengths) in September: also ran well when placed all other starts, length third to Sleeping Indian in Challenge Stakes at Newmarket final one: should stay beyond 1m: acts on polytrack, firm and good to soft ground: tongue tied: genuine. *Saeed bin Suroor*

Godolphin's "Satchem"

SATIN BRAID 2 b.f. (Jan 14) Diktat 126 – Beading 82 (Polish Precedent (USA) 131) **73**
[2006 7m⁵ 8m⁵ 8pg⁴ p7.1g⁵ Nov 2] well-made filly: second foal: half-sister to 3-y-o
Cindertrack: dam, 1m winner, half-sister to useful 1m winner Intrepidous: fair maiden:
stays 1m. *B. J. Meehan*

SATIN DOLL 3 b.f. Diktat 126 – Unconditional Love (IRE) 104 (Polish Patriot (USA) **68**
128) [2006 50: p8g⁵ 8m p10g p7g Jul 19] fair maiden: below form after reappearance:
stays 1m: acts on polytrack: tried in cheekpieces/blinkers. *M. P. Tregoning*

SATIN ROSE 4 b.f. Lujain (USA) 119 – Shamwari (USA) 63 (Shahrastani (USA) 135) **–**
[2006 56: p13g p13g Feb 8] modest at 3 yrs: no form in 2006. *K. J. Burke*

SATINTHESLIP (IRE) 5 b.m. Idris (IRE) 118 – Gauloise Bleue (USA) (Lyphard's **–**
Wish (FR) 124) [2006 10.2g p9.5g Oct 29] sister to winner in Turkey and half-sister to 2
winners by Treasure Kay, including fairly useful 1995 2-y-o 7f winner Fag End: dam
twice-raced maiden: poor form in bumpers: well beaten in maiden/claimer. *Mrs P. Ford*

SATISFACTION (IRE) 3 b.c. Dansili 127 – Presentation (IRE) 98 (Mujadil (USA) **–**
119) [2006 63: p9.5g 10.5m⁴ 7m Sep 13] sturdy, close-coupled colt: lightly-raced maiden
(reportedly injured a hind leg after only 2-y-o start): well held in 2006. *E. J. O'Neill*

SATULAGI (USA) 2 b.f. (Feb 29) Officer (USA) 120 – Shawgatny (USA) 83 (Danzig **98**
Connection (USA)) [2006 p5g³ 5.2m* 5d⁶ 6m⁵ 6f² 5.2g 7m* 7d³ 8d⁴ a8.5f Nov 4]
$70,000F: good-topped filly: half-sister to 3 winners, including fairly useful 2003 2-y-o
6f winner Mister Saif (by Miswaki) and 1m winner September Harvest (by Mujtahid):
dam, Irish 2-y-o 9f winner, sister to very smart 1m to 1¼m performer Star of Gdansk:
useful performer: won maiden at Yarmouth in April and listed event at Ascot in July: ran
well after when 2¾ lengths third of 6 to English Ballet in Sweet Solera Stakes at
Newmarket and 4¾ lengths fourth of 8 to Simply Perfect in Fillies' Mile at Ascot: always
behind (stumbled early) in Breeders' Cup Juvenile Fillies at Churchill Downs final start:
will stay 1¼m: acts on firm and good to soft going. *J. S. Moore*

SATWA QUEEN (FR) 4 ch.f. Muhtathir 126 – Tolga (USA) 75 (Irish River (FR) 131) **120**
[2006 113: 7.5m² 8.9d² 10s* 10m² 11f⁵ 10m⁶ Dec 10] leggy, close-coupled filly: half-
sister to several winners, including smart French 1m and 1¼m (Criterium de Saint-Cloud)
winner Spadoun (by Kaldoun) and useful French 1m/11f winner Fier Danseur (by
Fabulous Dancer): dam, maiden, best at 1m: very smart performer: won 3 times in 2005,
notably Prix Vanteaux at Longchamp and Prix de Psyche at Deauville: second on return
at Nad Al Sheba in handicap (beaten neck by Clinet) and listed race (beaten 1¼ lengths
by Irridescence): off 6 months, better than ever when winning Darley Prix Jean Romanet
at Deauville in August by 1½ lengths from Sweet Stream and when ¾-length second to

Darley Prix Jean Romanet, Deauville—Satwa Queen runs on strongly from Sweet Stream (striped cap),
who beats Red Bloom for second; In Clover (No.6) is fourth, ahead of Strawberry Dale

Mandesha in Prix de l'Opera at Longchamp: not entirely discredited last 2 starts when fifth to Ouija Board in Breeders' Cup Filly & Mare Turf at Churchill Downs and sixth to Pride in Hong Kong Cup at Sha Tin: stays 1¼m: acts on soft and good to firm ground. *J. de Roualle, France*

SATYRICON 2 b.c. (Apr 20) Dr Fong (USA) 128 – Belladera (IRE) 82 (Alzao (USA) 117) [2006 p7g⁶ p8g⁴ p8.6f⁴ Aug 30] 24,000Y: fifth foal: half-brother to fairly useful Irish 1½m to 2m winner Mrs Gillow (by Danzero) and a winner in Italy by Spinning World: dam 2-y-o 6f winner: best effort (fair form) in maidens on polytrack on debut. *M. Botti* — **72**

SAUCEPOT 4 ch.f. Bold Edge 123 – Apple Sauce 70 (Prince Sabo 123) [2006 52: 6m 5.1d May 30] sturdy filly: maiden: no form in 2006: tried in cheekpieces/blinkers. *Miss J. R. Tooth* — **–**

SAUCY 5 b.m. Muhtarram (USA) 125 – So Saucy 59 (Teenoso (USA) 135) [2006 63: p10g 8m p10g 9.7f⁶ p10g p10g³ p10g* Dec 13] modest performer: won banded race at Lingfield final start: stays 1½m: acts on polytrack: tried in blinkers in 2004: often races freely. *A. W. Carroll* — **56**

SAVANAGH FOREST (IRE) 2 b.f. (Mar 15) Shinko Forest (IRE) – Adieu Cherie (IRE) (Bustino 136) [2006 p6g 6d Oct 18] €17,000Y: sister to 3-y-o Goodbye Girl and half-sister to several winners, including 6f winner Lord Yasmin (by Lahib): dam unraced: in rear in maidens. *M. Quinn* — **–**

SAVANNAH 3 b.c. Sadler's Wells (USA) 132 – La Papagena (Habitat 134) [2006 –p: 10m* 12m⁶ 14m⁶ 12d 10d³ p7g⁶ Dec 22] smallish, attractive colt: brother to useful Irish 1m (at 2 yrs)/1½m winner Sorcerous and half-brother to several winners, notably high-class 1m/1¼m performer Grand Lodge (by Chief's Crown): dam unraced: useful performer: won maiden at Naas in July: easily best effort when sixth of 7 to Sixties Icon in BGC Stakes (Gordon) at Goodwood next time: left A. O'Brien 47,000 gns prior to final outing: stays 1½m: acts on good to firm ground: tried blinkered. *Luke Comer, Ireland* — **104 d**

SAVANNAH BAY 7 ch.g. In The Wings 128 – High Savannah 77 (Rousillon (USA) 133) [2006 p16g 16m 12m 20m 16.1m Jul 1] good-topped gelding: one-time smart performer: unraced on Flat in 2005 (won over fences for P. Hobbs): just fairly useful nowadays: stays 2½m: acts on firm going: tried blinkered/tongue tied: carries head awkwardly: usually waited with. *B. Ellison* — **93**

SAVANNAH PRIDE (IRE) 3 b.f. Namid 128 – Milady Lillie (IRE) 65 (Distinctly North (USA) 115) [2006 64d: p7g 7f 6g Aug 16] good-topped filly: modest performer at 2 yrs: no form in 2006: tried visored/tongue tied. *E. R. Oertel* — **–**

SAVERNAKE BLUE 3 b.g. Mtoto 134 – Mrs Malaprop 83 (Night Shift (USA)) [2006 86p: 7g 7.1g 6d 6f* 6m 6m 7m 6f 6s p6g p7g p6g Oct 8] tall, quite good-topped gelding: fairly useful handicapper on turf, fair on all-weather: won at Newmarket in July: below best after: stays 7f: acts on firm and good to soft ground: fly-jumped leaving stall fifth appearance/reared and unseated rider at start final outing: sold 7,000 gns. *M. R. Channon* — **83 a74**

SAVERNAKE BRAVE (IRE) 5 b.g. Charnwood Forest (IRE) 125 – Jordinda (IRE) 64 (Indian Ridge 123) [2006 48§, a60§: p9.5g 7g 8f Jul 18] compact gelding: modest but unreliable performer at best: no form in 2006: tried blinkered/visored. *Mrs H. Sweeting* — **– §**

SAVE THE SECRET (AUS) 3 b.c. Secret Savings (USA) – Nothing To Do (USA) (Nijinsky (CAN) 138) [2006 10m Jul 24] 6/1, in rear in maiden at Windsor, green and never going well: sent to UAE. *Sir Michael Stoute* — **–**

SAVILE'S DELIGHT (IRE) 7 b.g. Cadeaux Genereux 131 – Across The Ice (USA) (General Holme (USA) 128) [2006 83, a76: f6g³ p6g³ p5.1g p6g³ p5.1g p6g⁴ 5.7s 6g⁵ p6g Jun 22] fair handicapper: effective at 5f to 7f: acts on all-weather, heavy and good to firm going: often wears headgear: has worn tongue tie: front runner. *R. Brotherton* — **70**

SAVILLE ROAD 3 br.c. Mozart (IRE) 131 – In Full Cry (USA) (Seattle Slew (USA)) [2006 95: 7g* 7m 7m² 7s Aug 24] tall, leggy, close-coupled colt: useful performer: won minor event at Newmarket in April: good ½-length second of 4 to Caradak in similar race at Newbury (dictated), only other form in 2006: stays 7f: acts on good to firm going: has been on toes/free and early to post/worn crossed noseband: often races prominently. *D. J. Daly* — **102**

SAVIOUR SAND (IRE) 2 b.c. (Mar 31) Desert Sun 120 – Teacher Preacher (IRE) 37 (Taufan (USA) 119) [2006 p8g² p8g⁶ Dec 19] €20,000Y: fifth foal: half-brother to 4-y-o Profit's Reality and 5-y-o Key Partners: dam Irish 7f winner: much better effort in maidens at Lingfield when short-head second to Sweeney, making most and finding plenty. *D. R. C. Elsworth* — **76**

SAVIOURS SPIRIT 5 ch.g. Komaite (USA) – Greenway Lady (Prince Daniel (USA)) **81**
[2006 80: p6g³ p6g* p6g* p5g p6g* p6g² 6g p6g⁴ 6m 6d⁶ p6g* p6g⁵ p6g⁴ Dec 1] useful **a98**
handicapper on all-weather, fairly useful on turf: won at Lingfield in January, February
and March and at Kempton (best effort, beat Don Pele ¾ length) in November: effective
at 5f/6f: acts on all-weather, soft and good to firm going: often races prominently.
T. G. Mills

SAVOY CHAPEL 4 br.g. Xaar 132 – Royal Gift (Cadeaux Genereux 131) [2006 –, **–**
a75: p7.1g p7.1g⁵ p7.1g⁵ p8.6g f8g⁶ p9.5g p8g f8g f8g p8g² p8g⁴ Nov 6] lengthy gelding: **a54**
modest nowadays: trained by D. Carroll seventh/eighth starts only: stays 1m: acts on
all-weather, little form on turf: tried blinkered/visored/tongue tied. *A. W. Carroll*

SAWWAAH (IRE) 9 ch.g. Marju (IRE) 127 – Just A Mirage 76 (Green Desert (USA) **75 §**
127) [2006 91d: p8g⁶ 8.3g 7.1g² 7g 8m² 7.9m⁵ 7.1m⁶ 9.3m⁴ 7f* p7.1g⁵ 8m* 8d² 8m²
8.5m³ 9.2g 7.2v 9s⁴ Sep 24] big, useful-looking gelding: fair performer: won claimer at
Redcar in June and seller at Musselburgh in July: stays 9f: acts on firm and soft going:
usually wears headgear: usually held up, and no easy ride (often hangs/finds little, and
has carried head high): has joined S. Mason. *D. Nicholls*

SAXENBERG 2 b.f. (Feb 9) Foxhound (USA) 103 – Latour 79 (Sri Pekan (USA) 117) **54**
[2006 f5g 6f⁵ 7f p7g 8.3g Oct 16] second foal: dam, placed at 1m, half-sister to useful
sprinter Watch Me: modest maiden: best effort 7f on firm going. *Miss J. R. Gibney*

SAXON LIL (IRE) 4 b.f. Second Empire (IRE) 124 – Salva 73 (Grand Lodge (USA) **78**
125) [2006 63: 7d 7d p7g 7m⁶ 7m 7m² 7.5f⁶ 7.1m⁶ 7f 7g² 7.6d⁶ 7.5g⁴ 8.3f 7s Oct 10]
small filly: fair handicapper: won at Beverley in August: stays 7.6f: acts on polytrack,
firm and soft going: tried in cheekpieces: sold 5,000 gns. *J. L. Spearing*

SAXON SAINT 3 b.g. Josr Algarhoud (IRE) 118 – Antithesis (IRE) 75 (Fairy King **–**
(USA)) [2006 76: 5g p6g Jun 21] close-coupled gelding: has a quick action: fair performer at 2 yrs: well held in handicaps in 2006. *M. D. I. Usher*

SAXON STAR 3 b.g. Vettori (IRE) 119 – Thicket 87 (Wolfhound (USA) 126) **44**
[2006 53: p6g³ p6g p7.1g p5g p6g 7s⁵ f5g² f5g⁶ p6g 8m 10.1f 7g 6f 11.5d p8g f14g p12.2g
Nov 24] tall, leggy gelding: poor maiden: left M. Usher after thirteenth outing: stays 7f:
acts on all-weather and good firm ground: sometimes visored. *P. Howling*

SAY GREAT (IRE) 2 ch.c. (Jun 12) Beckett (IRE) 116 – Say Wonderful (IRE) 76 **–**
(Roi Danzig (USA)) [2006 7m Jul 12] big, workmanlike colt: well beaten in maiden at
Newmarket: dead. *V. Smith*

SCAMPERDALE 4 br.g. Compton Place 125 – Miss Up N Go (Gorytus (USA) 132) **67**
[2006 63: p9.5g⁵ p9.5g⁴ p8.6g p9.5g* p9.5g² 12.1g p8.6g³ p9.5f² p8.6g* Dec 29] good-
topped gelding: fair performer: left Miss K. George after reappearance: won maiden
claimer in May and handicap in December, both at Wolverhampton: stays 1¼m: raced
only on polytrack and good ground: tried in cheekpieces. *B. P. J. Baugh*

SCANDAL KEEPER (USA) 3 br.c. Danzig (USA) – Canny Miss (AUS) (Marscay **96**
(AUS)) [2006 86p: p7g Oct 26] good-bodied colt: useful performer, lightly raced: off
over 12 months, best effort when close seventh in handicap at Lingfield on only outing in
2006, travelling strongly for long way: stays easy 7f: has worn crossed noseband/been
bandaged in front: tongue tied: has left Godolphin. *Saeed bin Suroor*

SCANTLEBURY 2 b.g. (May 23) Mark of Esteem (IRE) 137 – Krameria 72 (Kris 135) **– p**
[2006 6m Sep 19] tall, close-coupled, good-topped gelding: half-brother to 3 winners,
including fairly useful 5f to 7f winner Palawan (by Polar Falcon): dam, 2-y-o 5f winner,
half-sister to Nunthorpe winner So Factual: 10/1, much too green in maiden at Newmarket: gelded after: will improve. *S. Kirk*

SCARAMOUSHCA 3 gr.g. Most Welcome 131 – Kinraddie (Wuzo (USA) 99) [2006 **–**
p13g⁶ Dec 22] fourth foal: half-brother to sprint winner in Scandinavia by Emarati: dam
won in Norway: 25/1, never on terms in maiden at Lingfield. *P. S. McEntee*

SCARFACE 9 ch.g. Hernando (FR) 127 – Scarlatine (IRE) 81 (Alzao (USA) 117) [2006 **–**
16.2f Jul 28] winner of 5 races in Germany/Holland for C. Von Der Recke: won over
hurdles prior to well beaten only Flat outing in 2006: has been blinkered. *J. L. Spearing*

SCARLET BABY 2 ch.g. (Feb 19) Elmaamul (USA) 125 – Eastern Ruby (Be My **–**
Chief (USA) 122) [2006 6m 7g⁵ Aug 24] big, leggy gelding: weak at 2 yrs: well beaten
both starts. *K. A. Ryan*

SCARLET FLYER (USA) 3 b.g. Gilded Time (USA) – Tennis Partner (USA) (North- **83**
ern Dancer) [2006 80: p8g 7g⁵ 7.1m⁴ 7g⁴ 7m² 6g⁴ 6f⁵ 5m³ 7m³ 7d Sep 26] good-topped
gelding: fairly useful handicapper: effective at 5f to 7f: raced mainly on good going or
firmer (acts on firm): tried blinkered/in cheekpieces. *G. L. Moore*

SCARLET IBIS 2 b.f. (Apr 12) Machiavellian (USA) 123 – Flagbird (USA) 119 (Nureyev (USA) 131) [2006 p7g⁵ p7.1g² Nov 14] sixth foal: closely related to 2 winners by Mr Prospector, including smart 1m (in UAE)/1¼m winner Marhoob, and half-sister to winner in USA by A P Indy: dam, 1m (including in France at 2 yrs)/1¼m winner, half-sister to US Grade 1 1m/8.5f winner Prospectors Delite (herself dam of high-class US performer Mineshaft) and very smart US Grade 1 1¼m winner Runup The Colors: fair form in maidens at Lingfield and Wolverhampton (second to Whazzis): will stay at least 1m: should do better. *Saeed bin Suroor* **74 p**

SCARLET KNIGHT 3 b.g. Lujain (USA) 119 – Gem 58 (Most Welcome 131) [2006 85: p6g² 6g⁶ 6f 7s⁵ 6g p10g⁵ 8m³ Aug 19] good-topped gelding: fairly useful handicapper: stays 1m: acts on polytrack, heavy and good to firm going: tried blinkered: no easy ride, and one to treat with caution. *P. Mitchell* **87 §**

SCARLET ROMANCE 4 ch.f. Pursuit of Love 124 – Scarlet Livery 63 (Saddlers' Hall (IRE) 126) [2006 f6g 9v f8g⁵ Apr 10] first foal: dam maiden who stayed 7f: tailed off both starts in bumpers: no form on Flat. *M. W. Easterby* **–**

SCARLET RUNNER 2 b.f. (Feb 2) Night Shift (USA) – Sweet Pea 94 (Persian Bold 123) [2006 6d 6f* 6m³ 6m* 6s⁵ 6d Sep 29] strong filly: third foal: half-sister to Irish 1½m winner Scent (by Groom Dancer): dam 1m winner: useful performer: won maiden at Windsor in June and Princess Margaret Stakes at Ascot (beat Vital Statistics by ½ length) in July: ran well in between when 2 lengths third of 18 to Sander Camillo in Albany Stakes at Royal Ascot: below form in Lowther/Cheveley Park Stakes last 2 starts: not sure to stay beyond 6f: possibly unsuited by ground softer than good. *J. L. Dunlop* **103**

SCARLETT HEART (IRE) 2 b.f. (Mar 17) Lujain (USA) 119 – Scarlett Ribbon 104 (Most Welcome 131) [2006 p6g⁵ p5.1g² Dec 11] first foal: dam 6f (at 2 yrs)/7f winner: modest form in maidens at Kempton and Wolverhampton (second to Bungie): will prove suited by further than 5f. *P. J. Makin* **55**

SCARRABUS (IRE) 5 b.g. Charnwood Forest (IRE) 125 – Errazuriz (IRE) 94 (Classic Music (USA)) [2006 59: 12g 12m 16.2g May 13] angular, good-topped gelding: modest maiden: stays 1½m: acts on polytrack and firm ground: usually held up. *A. Crook* **54**

SCAR TISSUE 2 ch.f. (Mar 17) Medicean 128 – Possessive Lady 62 (Dara Monarch 128) [2006 p8g³ Dec 8] 9,000Y: half-sister to 3 winners, including fairly useful 5f (at 2 yrs)/6f winner Protectorate (by Hector Protector), who stayed 1m, and 1½m winner Basher Jack (by Suave Dancer): dam, 1m winner, half-sister to Irish Oaks winner Possessive Dancer: 16/1 and upset in stall, 3½ lengths third to Summer Dancer in maiden at Kempton, green: should improve. *T. G. Dascombe* **55 p**

SCENE THREE 2 gr.f. (Feb 23) Act One 124 – Ferber's Follies (USA) (Saratoga Six (USA)) [2006 6m 7s Oct 10] 4,500Y: half-sister to 3 winners, including useful 6f (including at 2 yrs)/7f winner Injaaz (by Sheikh Albadou): dam 2-y-o 5.5f winner in USA: mid-field in maidens. *J. J. Quinn* **–**

SCENTED PRESENT 2 b.c. (Mar 18) Foxhound (USA) 103 – Its Another Gift 64 (Primo Dominie 121) [2006 5g⁴ 5m² 5f* 5m 5m 5m³ 5.1f* 5.2g 5m⁶ 6d⁴ p6g Oct 21] 26,000Y: stocky, good-quartered colt: third foal: half-brother to 4-y-o Gifted Gamble: dam sprint maiden: useful performer: won maiden at Lingfield in June and minor event at Chepstow in July: best effort when 3 lengths sixth of 13 to Enticing in Molecomb Stakes at Goodwood: best at 5f: acts on firm going: below form only try in blinkers: sold 9,000 gns. *B. J. Meehan* **95**

SCHERZO A LA RUSSE (USA) 3 b. or br.f. Stravinsky (USA) 133 – Zadracarta (CAN) 117 (Bold Ruckus (USA)) [2006 52: p6g p6g Feb 6] tall filly: modest maiden at 2 yrs: well held in 2006: was best at 5f: tried blinkered: dead. *A. G. Newcombe* **–**

SCHIAPARELLI (GER) 3 ch.c. Monsun (GER) 124 – Sacarina (Old Vic 136) [2006 11v* 11g* 11g* 12g² 12g* 12g⁶ 14g* Oct 1] seventh foal: brother to German 1½m performers Samum (high-class) and Salve Regina (smart) and half-brother to 2 winners in Germany: dam unraced: smart performer: won maiden at Cologne in April, handicap at Hanover in May, listed race on same course in June, BMW Deutsches Derby at Hamburg (best effort, beat Dickens ¾ length) in July and Grosser Preis von DSW21 - Deutsches St Leger at Dortmund (by 1½ lengths from N'Oubliez Jamais) in October: creditable ¾-length second of 7 to Donaldson in Deutschlandpreis at Dusseldorf fourth outing, disappointing sixth in Grosser Preis von Baden at Baden-Baden penultimate start: stays 1¾m: acts on heavy ground. *P. Schiergen, Germany* **116**

SCHINKEN OTTO (IRE) 5 ch.g. Shinko Forest (IRE) – Athassel Rose (IRE) (Reasonable (FR) 119) [2006 –: p9.5g⁴ f8g⁴ p9.5g p9.5g⁶ Feb 20] strong gelding: poor maiden: **47**

931

stays 9.5f: acts on all-weather: gelded after final start, then won 4 races over fences. *J. M. Jefferson*

SCHOONER (GER) 6 b.g. Slip Anchor 136 – Sweet Enough 79 (Caerleon (USA) **65** 132) [2006 14s 16.2g⁴ Jul 7] fair maiden: very lightly raced: stays 2m: acts on polytrack. *Lady Herries*

SCIATIN (IRE) 3 b.c. Alhaarth (IRE) 126 – Robalana (USA) (Wild Again (USA)) **–** [2006 93: 10s Oct 18] well-made colt: fairly useful performer, lightly raced: off 13 months, well held in handicap at Nottingham only outing in 2006: stays 1m: acts on good to firm and good to soft going: sold 32,000 gns. *L. M. Cumani*

SCONCED (USA) 11 ch.g. Affirmed (USA) – Quaff (USA) 115 (Raise A Cup (USA)) **52 §** [2006 16v⁴ 14m May 4] leggy gelding: modest handicapper: stays 19f: acts on fibre- sand and any turf going: usually visored/blinkered: tends to run in snatches: ungenuine. *R. C. Guest*

SCOOBY DUDE (IRE) 3 b.g. Tagula (IRE) 116 – Miraculous (IRE) (Marju (IRE) **88** 127) [2006 81: p6g 5g² 5g² 5.1f³ 5s³ 5s⁴ 5.1g⁶ 5.1f³ p5.1g⁴ p5.1g⁴ Dec 7] rather leggy, **a84** close-coupled gelding: fairly useful handicapper: speedy, and best at 5f: acts on poly- track, firm and soft going: consistent. *Ms Deborah J. Evans*

SCORCH 5 b.g. Mark of Esteem (IRE) 137 – Red Hot Dancer (USA) (Seattle Dancer **–** (USA) 119) [2006 p7g p7.1g p9.5g Dec 4] lightly-raced maiden: no form in 2006. *V. Smith*

SCORCHIO (IRE) 5 b.g. Desert Sun 120 – White-Wash 94 (Final Straw 127) [2006 **43** 53: f8m f12g f16g Dec 28] lightly raced and only poor nowadays: stays 11f: acts on polytrack and firm ground. *B. Smart*

SCORPION (IRE) 4 b.c. Montjeu (IRE) 137 – Ardmelody (Law Society (USA) 130) **111** [2006 126: 12s² 12f⁵ 12m Dec 10] tall, rangy colt: high-class performer at 3 yrs, winning Grand Prix de Paris at Longchamp and St Leger at Doncaster: shaped encouragingly after year's absence (reportedly fractured hind pastern) when length second to Frank Sonata in listed race at the Curragh, but showed no better than form afterwards when 5 lengths fifth to Red Rocks in Breeders' Cup Turf at Churchill Downs and 5½ lengths seventh to Collier Hill in Hong Kong Vase at Sha Tin: stays 14.6f: acts on soft and good to firm ground, winner on heavy: got worked up in paddock and taken steadily to post at Doncaster: has worn crossed noseband. *A. P. O'Brien, Ireland*

SCOTCH PANCAKE 3 ch.f. Selkirk (USA) 129 – Galette 94 (Caerleon (USA) 132) **74** [2006 89P: 10m p10g² p12g⁵ p10g Nov 28] tall, useful-looking filly: just fair maiden in 2006, second to Woolfall Blue (pulled hard) at Kempton: saddle slipped on reappearance. *D. R. C. Elsworth*

SCOTLAND THE BRAVE 6 ch.m. Zilzal (USA) 137 – Hunters of Brora (IRE) 102 **76** (Sharpo 132) [2006 76: 6.9g⁵ 8.5s⁴ 7d 7.5g 7.2s* 7.2v² 7.2v² Oct 28] leggy, lengthy mare: fair handicapper: won at Ayr in September: stays 1m: has form on any going, goes well on soft/heavy: wears cheekpieces/visor. *J. D. Bethell*

SCOTLAND YARD (UAE) 3 b.g. Jade Robbery (USA) 121 – Aqraba 69 (Polish **93** Precedent (USA) 131) [2006 p10g⁴ p8.6g⁴ p9.5g² 12f* 11.5g 12m* 12f³ Jul 27] quite good-topped gelding: fluent mover: second foal: dam, ran twice (runner-up at 1m), closely related to useful sprinter Millstream: fairly useful performer: won handicaps at Ripon in June and July (left M. Johnston 62,000 gns after): should be suited by 1¾m+: acts on polytrack and firm going: gelded after final outing. *D. E. Pipe*

SCOT LOVE (IRE) 3 b.c. Dansili 127 – Fashion 84 (Bin Ajwaad (IRE) 119) [2006 72: **90** p8g² p8g² p8g* 10.4d⁵ 8.3g⁵ p7g p8g Jul 5] good-bodied colt: fairly useful performer: won maiden at Kempton in May: below form in handicaps after: best form at 1m: acts on polytrack and good to soft ground: visored (folded tamely) final outing: sold 20,000 gns, joined T. O'Mara in Ireland. *J. Noseda*

SCOTT 5 gr.g. Polar Falcon (USA) 126 – Circled (USA) 83 (Cozzene (USA)) [2006 70: **–** p16.5g Feb 17] fair handicapper at best: reportedly lame final 4-y-o start: well held only run in 2006: stays easy 2m: acts on all-weather, firm and soft ground. *J. Jay*

SCOTTISH RIVER (USA) 7 b.g. Thunder Gulch (USA) 129 – Overbrook 95 (Storm **69 §** Cat (USA)) [2006 84, a80: p8.6g⁵ p10g p10g p9.5g p9.5g p10g⁴ p9.5g² p9.5g* p12.2g **a73 §** 10.2d 10m 8.3f 10m 11.6f 10m⁵ 11.6g 10g 10.5s² p12g 12s 11s⁶ p13.9g⁶ p12g⁶ f8g³ p9.5g² p9.5g p9.5s⁶ p8.6g Dec 29] strong gelding: fair handicapper: won at Wolver- hampton in April: effective at 1m to 1½m: acts on all-weather, firm and soft going: tried visored earlier in career: often slowly away, sometimes markedly so: held up: not one to trust. *M. D. I. Usher*

Swettenham Stud Fillies' Trial Stakes, Newbury—
Scottish Stage holds on narrowly from Guilia (No.5), with Makderah (rail) third

SCOTTISH SPIRIT (IRE) 2 b.c. (Feb 3) Invincible Spirit (IRE) 121 – Triphibious 69 (Zafonic (USA) 130) [2006 6s 6g Sep 27] tailed off in maidens. *J. S. Haldane* —

SCOTTISH STAGE (IRE) 3 ch.f. Selkirk (USA) 129 – Drama Class (IRE) 102 (Caerleon (USA) 132) [2006 102p: 10d* 12m² 12m² 14f⁵ 12s Sep 22] strong, lengthy filly: has scope: smart performer: landed odds in listed race at Newbury in May by head from Guilia: creditable second after in Ribblesdale Stakes at Royal Ascot (ran in snatches/bumped by winner, going down by a neck to Mont Etoile) and Irish Oaks at the Curragh (beaten 4 lengths by Alexandrova): ran as if amiss in Princess Royal Stakes at Ascot (reportedly lost action) final outing: stays 1½m, seemingly not 1¾m: acts on polytrack, good to firm and good to soft going. *Sir Michael Stoute* **112**

SCOTT'S MILL 4 ch.g. Unfuwain (USA) 131 – Mill On The Floss 117 (Mill Reef (USA) 141) [2006 52: f12g³ f14g p16.5g Apr 24] rangy gelding: lightly-raced maiden: no form since debut (at 3 yrs). *M. Johnston* —

SCOTTY'S FUTURE (IRE) 8 b.g. Namaqualand (USA) – Persian Empress (IRE) 51 (Persian Bold 123) [2006 75: p8.6g⁶ p9.5g⁵ p9.5g f8g⁶ p10g³ p9.5g³ p9.5g⁵ 11v⁴ 8.5d* 7g⁵ 8.3d⁴ 9.9g* 12f 10.3m 9.3g³ 7.9m⁴ 10g 10g⁶ 10s⁵ 9.2d 12s 12s³ 9.1v⁶ 12d f12g Nov 21] close-coupled, quite good-topped gelding: fair performer: won seller at Beverley in April and, having left D. Nicholls after tenth start, ladies handicap there in May: stays 1½m: acts on polytrack, firm and soft going: visored once: edgy sort: held up: sometimes reluctant to race: unreliable. *A. Berry* **68 §**

SCRATCH THE DOVE 9 ch.m. Henbit (USA) 130 – Coney Dove (Celtic Cone 116) [2006 18m 17.2m⁶ Jul 8] poor hurdler/chaser: very lightly raced on Flat nowadays and well held in 2006 (very slowly away latter start). *A. E. Price* —

SCREENPLAY 5 ch.g. In The Wings 128 – Erudite 114 (Generous (IRE) 139) [2006 75: p16g Feb 15] smallish, sturdy gelding: has a rather round action: fair performer: not discredited only Flat outing in 2006: stays 2½m: acts on polytrack, soft and good to firm going: wore cheekpieces (ran well) twice in 2004. *Miss S. West* **69**

SCREEN TEST 4 b.f. Danzero (AUS) – Audition 81 (Machiavellian (USA) 123) [2006 69: p13g⁶ p16.5g³ 15s² p13.9g 11.9m⁵ 17.2f 12.1g Jul 8] fair maiden handicapper on Flat (won over hurdles in April): stays easy 2m: acts on polytrack, soft and good to firm ground: blinkered (refused to race) final outing: has flashed tail: sold £3,300. *B. G. Powell* **67 §**

SCREWDRIVER 4 b.g. Entrepreneur 123 – Lust (Pursuit of Love 124) [2006 89: p7.1g³ p7g⁵ p7.1g p8.6g 8.5s Aug 1] stocky, strong-quartered gelding: fairly useful handicapper: stays 1m: acts on polytrack and good to firm going: usually wears cheekpieces/blinkers: has run well when sweating: none too consistent: sold 5,500 gns. *Miss J. R. Tooth* **81**

SCRIPTWRITER (IRE) 4 b.g. Sadler's Wells (USA) 132 – Dayanata (Shirley Heights 130) [2006 97: 10.4s* 11.6d Nov 4] smart performer, lightly raced: suffered minor ligament problem after 3 yrs (also gelded): further marked improvement to win handicap at York in October on reappearance by 1½ lengths from Topatoo (pair clear), despite wandering: in cheekpieces, well below form in similar event at Windsor only subsequent start: should be at least as effective at 1½m as 1¼m: acts on firm and soft going: quirky. *Saeed bin Suroor* **111**

SCROLL 3 b.g. Mark of Esteem (IRE) 137 – Bella Bellisimo (IRE) 84 (Alzao (USA) **61**
117) [2006 70: p8g⁴ p7g⁵ p8g² p8g³ p7g³ p7g³ p8g³ p8.6g⁵ p7g* p7g⁴ p8g⁶ p8g⁵ 8m **a77**
p8g p8g⁵ p8g p7.1s⁵ p7.1g⁵ Dec 28] angular, useful-looking gelding: fair performer on
all-weather, modest on turf: won maiden at Lingfield in March: stays 8.6f: raced only on
polytrack and good ground or firmer on turf: visored. *P. Howling*

SCRUMMAGE 3 b.c. Sinndar (IRE) 134 – Ghariba 112 (Final Straw 127) [2006 –p: **84**
10m 7g 7f* 7m* 7.1m² 7m³ 7.1m² p7g² Oct 21] well-made colt: fairly useful handicapper: won at Yarmouth and Epsom in July: should stay 1m: acts on polytrack and firm
going: visored last 6 starts: front runner: sold 52,000 gns, sent to USA. *Sir Michael Stoute*

SCRUNCH 5 b.m. Royal Applause 124 – Antonia's Folly 64 (Music Boy 124) [2006 6f **–**
Jun 17] good-bodied mare: lightly-raced maiden: tailed off in cheekpieces only outing in
2006: virtually unrideable once at 3 yrs. *Miss J. R. Tooth*

SCUBA (IRE) 4 b.g. Indian Danehill (IRE) 124 – March Star (IRE) 109 (Mac's Imp **75**
(USA) 116) [2006 66: f6g² p7.1g* f7g⁵ p6g² 7m p7.1g p6g* 6m p7.1g⁴ f6g* 6g* 6.1g 7.2v
f7g² p7g p7g⁶ p7.1g⁶ Dec 27] well-made gelding: fair handicapper: won at Wolverhampton in February and June, Southwell in July and Hamilton in August: stays 7f: acts on
all-weather, best effort on turf on good going (seemed ill at ease on heavy): visored/
blinkered nowadays: often races up with pace. *H. Morrison*

SCULASTIC 3 b.g. Galileo (IRE) 134 – Mutual Consent (IRE) 107 (Reference Point **82**
139) [2006 8s² 10d⁴ 10s² Oct 18] tall, quite good-topped gelding: fifth foal: half-brother
to 1¼m/1½m winner Prenup (by Diesis): dam French 1m (at 2 yrs) and 1¼m winner
who stayed 1½m: fairly useful form in maidens, second to Emirates Line (pair clear) at
Nottingham final start: will stay 1½m: sold 80,000 gns, joined J. Howard Johnson and
gelded. *L. M. Cumani*

SCURRA 7 b.g. Spectrum (IRE) 126 – Tamnia 106 (Green Desert (USA) 127) [2006 61: **56 d**
f16g² f16g 13f 14.1g p16.5f 16.1s⁴ 15.8s⁵ Oct 24] leggy gelding: fair performer in his
day: on downgrade: stays 2m: acts on fibresand and any turf going. *A. C. Whillans*

SCUTCH MILL (IRE) 4 ch.g. Alhaarth (IRE) 126 – Bumble (Rainbow Quest (USA) **73**
134) [2006 75: p10g p10g² 10f 9.9g⁶ 8m³ p8g 8d⁴ p9.5m p7.1g p10g p8g* p9.5s* Dec 13]
leggy gelding: fair handicapper: won at Kempton (apprentices) and Wolverhampton in
December: stays 1¼m: acts on polytrack and firm going: often tongue tied: has joined
P. Haslam. *Miss K. M. George*

SCUZME (IRE) 3 br.g. Xaar 132 – Decatur (Deploy 131) [2006 53: 7m⁴ 8.3d* 8.2d³ **58**
10m⁶ 17.2g p10g⁶ Dec 20] leggy gelding: modest performer: won seller at Hamilton in
May: left B. Ellison after third start, C. Gray after fourth one: should stay 1¼m: acts on
good to soft going, probably on good to firm: has been slowly away (markedly so fourth
outing). *Miss S. West*

SCYLLA CADEAUX (IRE) 3 ch.f. Cadeaux Genereux 131 – She's Classy (USA) **61**
(Boundary (USA) 117) [2006 8.3m⁶ 8.1s³ 7g⁵ 6.9g p6g⁴ Aug 23] €70,000Y: angular filly:
second foal: half-sister to winner in USA by Saint Ballado: dam, useful 2-y-o winner in
USA (placed in Grade 1s at 7f/8.5f), out of half-sister to Coronation Cup winner Be My
Native: modest maiden: stays 1m: acts on polytrack and soft ground: visored (ran credit-
ably) final outing: sold 11,000 gns. *Sir Michael Stoute*

SEABOW (USA) 3 b.c. Rainbow Quest (USA) 134 – Dream Bay (USA) (Mr Prospec- **91 p**
tor (USA)) [2006 87p: 8.2g² 10d* Oct 4] close-coupled colt: fairly useful form: shaped
well first 2 starts (a year apart), then impressive winner of maiden at Nottingham in October by 2½ lengths (eased) from Galactic Star: stays 1¼m: raced only on good/good to
soft going: tongue tied in 2006: capable of better still. *Saeed bin Suroor*

SEA COOKIE 2 b.f. (Apr 9) Largesse 112 – Maylan (IRE) 47 (Lashkari 128) [2006 6d **–**
p6g⁵ p8g³ Dec 3] first foal: dam maiden who probably stayed 1¼m: well held in maidens/
minor event. *W. de Best-Turner*

SEAFLOWER REEF (IRE) 2 b.f. (Mar 15) Robellino (USA) 127 – Sankaty Light **68**
(USA) 55 (Summer Squall (USA)) [2006 6g 5f⁵ p5.1g² p6g Aug 9] fourth foal: half-
sister to 3 winners, including 3-y-o Trans Sonic and 4-y-o Oceancookie: dam maiden
who should have stayed beyond 1m: fair maiden: second to Enticing in minor event at
Wolverhampton: will be suited by 1m. *A. M. Balding*

SEA FROLIC (IRE) 5 b.m. Shinko Forest (IRE) – Centre Travel (Godswalk (USA) **48**
130) [2006 54: f7g f7g 8g⁶ 8.2g⁵ 8s³ 7m f8g⁴ f8m f7g³ f8g p9.5g p8.6g³ f8g Dec 12]
rather leggy mare: only poor performer in 2006: stays 1¼m, all wins at 1m: acts on
all-weather, firm and good to soft going: tried blinkered/in cheekpieces, usually visored.
Jennie Candlish

SEA GRAIN (IRE) 3 b.g. Beckett (IRE) 116 – Tara View (IRE) (Wassl 125) [2006 66: **57**
7.1m 8d 12.1f 10m⁶ 12m⁴ Jul 30] good-topped gelding: modest maiden: stays 1½m: acts
on good to firm and good to soft going: tried tongue tied. *Robert Gray*

SEA HOLLY (IRE) 6 b.g. Barathea (IRE) 127 – Mountain Holly 69 (Shirley Heights **60**
130) [2006 10.1m 10g 10m⁵ 12s Oct 21] big gelding: has a round action: one-time fairly
useful performer: missed 2005, only modest on return: stays 13f: acts on all-weather, best
turf efforts on good ground: has started slowly, markedly so on reappearance: carries head
high. *G. G. Margarson*

SEA LAND (FR) 2 ch.c. (Mar 27) King's Best (USA) 132 – Green Bonnet (IRE) **79 p**
(Green Desert (USA) 127) [2006 p7g² Oct 26] 140,000Y: fifth foal: half-brother to 3
winners, including 3-y-o Edaara: dam, French maiden, sister to useful 7f/1m performer
Mauri Moon: 16/1, promising 3½ lengths second in maiden at Lingfield, briefly clear
with winner Cabinet before hanging right: should improve. *M. P. Tregoning*

SEALED BID 3 b.g. Zilzal (USA) 137 – Thea (USA) 95 (Marju (IRE) 127) [2006 45: **–**
f8g Feb 14] workmanlike gelding: poor maiden: twice slowly away. *M. W. Easterby*

SEALLARAIN 3 ch.f. Perryston View 114 – Bergliot 51 (Governor General 116) [2006 **–**
–: 5f 6m 9.1v Oct 9] little form. *A. Berry*

SEAL OF HOPE 3 b.g. Cape Cross (IRE) 129 – Heavenly Waters 64 (Celestial Storm **63**
(USA) 132) [2006 p7g 8m 9m⁶ 11.7g 16g Aug 26] modest maiden: easily best effort on
third start: should stay 1½m+: blinkered (looked none too keen) final outing: fractious in
stall second appearance. *M. P. Tregoning*

SEAL POINT (USA) 2 ch.c. (May 16) Point Given (USA) 134 – Maudie May (USA) **79**
(Gilded Time (USA)) [2006 8s⁵ 7d Oct 28] $65,000Y, 72,000 2-y-o: big, good-topped
colt: fourth foal: half-brother to useful 2004 2-y-o 5f winner Notjustaprettyface (by Red
Ransom): dam, 8.5f winner in USA, half-sister to smart 1994 2-y-o Sri Pekan: fair form
in maidens at Newbury (fifth to Sunshine Kid) and Newmarket. *C. Wroe, UAE*

SEAMUS SHINDIG 4 b.g. Aragon 118 – Sheesha (USA) (Shadeed (USA) 135) [2006 **88**
6d⁵ 6m⁶ p6g³ 6g⁴ 6m⁴ 5d⁵ 5m Sep 8] big, sturdy gelding: fairly useful handicapper:
likely to prove best at 6f/7f: acts on polytrack, firm and good to soft going: in cheekpieces
(said to have finished distressed) final outing. *H. Candy*

SEAN OG (IRE) 4 gr.g. Definite Article 121 – Miss Goodbody (Castle Keep 121) **64 d**
[2006 69: 12f 12m⁴ 13m⁶ 12f 17m⁶ 12d 12f 8.5d p16g f12g p10g Dec 18] modest maiden
at best in 2006: left R. Brabazon in Ireland and gelded after eighth start: stays 13f: acts
on good to firm going: tried in cheekpieces. *E. J. Creighton*

SEA OF CALM (USA) 3 b.f. Quiet American (USA) – Ocean Ridge (USA) 115 **60**
(Storm Bird (CAN) 134) [2006 74p: 8m⁵ 8.1g⁶ 7g p10g⁵ p12.2g p12.2g³ p12g⁴ Nov 25]
close-coupled filly: modest maiden: stays 1½m: acts on polytrack, raced only on good/
good to firm going on turf: has been slowly away/taken strong hold/looked none too keen:
sold 16,000 gns. *E. A. L. Dunlop*

SEA OF SERENITY (IRE) 3 b.f. Namid 128 – Serenity 98 (Selkirk (USA) 129) **–**
[2006 –: p6g p6g Feb 7] big, useful-looking filly: little form. *P. A. Blockley*

SEA SALT 3 b.g. Titus Livius (FR) 115 – Carati 86 (Selkirk (USA) 129) [2006 65: 5g² **82**
5f* 5s⁶ 6f 5d* 5d 5s 5d⁴ Nov 3] good-topped gelding: fairly useful performer: won
maiden at Musselburgh in May and handicap at Newcastle in August: best form at 5f: acts
on firm and good to soft ground, probably on soft. *T. D. Barron*

SEA SPRITE (IRE) 3 ch.g. Bahhare (USA) 122 – Khawater (USA) (Silver Hawk **–**
(USA) 123) [2006 p12.2g Jun 10] 14/1, tailed off in seller at Wolverhampton. *S. Kirk*

SEA STORM (IRE) 8 b.g. Dolphin Street (FR) 125 – Prime Interest (IRE) (Kings **–**
Lake (USA) 133) [2006 91, a84: 7.1g 8.1g 8g May 8] big, strong gelding: fairly useful
handicapper in 2005, well held in 2006: sometimes wears cheekpieces, blinkered once.
D. R. MacLeod

SEATON SNOOKS 2 b.g. (Jan 25) Diktat 126 – Buck's Fizz (Kris 135) [2006 6m 5s³ **65**
5m⁶ 6m⁵ 6d Aug 29] 10,000Y: angular gelding: second foal: dam unraced: fair maiden:
gelded after final start: likely to stay 7f/1m: acts on soft and good to firm going.
T. D. Easterby

SEATTLE ROBBER 4 b.g. Robellino (USA) 127 – Seattle Ribbon (USA) 70 (Seattle **70**
Dancer (USA) 119) [2006 67: p8.6g² p9.5g⁶ p8.6g⁶ p9.5g p12.2g⁶ p9.5g³ p9.5g³ p10g²
9.9g⁴ 10.2g² 12d⁵ 10f* 10f³ 11.9f 10.2f* 9.2m³ 10f Sep 20] smallish, strong gelding: fair
performer: trained by Mrs L. Featherstone for second run in 2006 only: won apprentice

handicap at Brighton in June and seller at Bath in July: probably stays 1½m: acts on polytrack, firm and good to soft going: not straightforward and wears headgear: consistent. *P. A. Blockley*

SEATTLE SPY (USA) 3 b. or br.g. Catienus (USA) 115 – Theyrplayinoursong (USA) – (Seattle Dancer (USA) 119) [2006 50: p9.5g Jan 5] modest maiden at 2 yrs: blinkered, well held in handicap only outing in 2006. *G. A. Huffer*

SEBAAQ (USA) 3 ch.g. Rahy (USA) 115 – Malibu Karen (USA) (Seeking The Gold – § (USA)) [2006 62§: 10m⁶ 7g 11s Aug 13] rangy gelding: temperamental maiden: left M. Tregoning after second start: tried in visor/blinkers/tongue tie. *M. E. Sowersby*

SECAM (POL) 7 gr.g. Alywar (USA) – Scytia (POL) (Euro Star) [2006 66: p7g⁴ p8g⁶ **60** p7g p7g⁶ p8g³ p8.6g p8g p8g⁵ p8g p7g Dec 19] modest performer: stays 1m: acts on polytrack, lightly raced on turf: tried in cheekpieces, blinkered nowadays. *Mrs P. Townsley*

SECOND CITY 3 ch.f. Mark of Esteem (IRE) 137 – Trefoil (FR) (Blakeney 126) [2006 – p8.6g p12.2g p12.2g Dec 2] 11,000F: closely related to useful 1½m winner Firecrest (by Darshaan) and half-sister to several winners, including smart 1¾m to 18.7f winner Anak Pekan (by In The Wings): dam French 10.5f to 1½m winner: no form in maidens. *E. J. Alston*

SECOND REEF 4 b.g. Second Empire (IRE) 124 – Vax Lady 98 (Millfontaine 114) **62** [2006 70: f6g p7.1g³ 7g f7g 8.1s p7.1g⁶ p6g 7.1f²⁴ 7.1g² 7m³ 7.2m 7m 8d⁴ p8.6g² 10f* p9.5g p12.2m p8.6g² p8.6g² p8.6g⁴ p9.5s² Dec 15] good-topped gelding: modest performer: won seller at Redcar in September: stays 1¼m: acts on all-weather, firm and good to soft going: tried blinkered/in cheekpieces: often races freely. *E. J. Alston*

SECOND WIND 11 ch.g. Kris 135 – Rimosa's Pet 109 (Petingo 135) [2006 §§: 6g §§ Jul 20] lengthy, workmanlike gelding: little form since 2002: sometimes refuses to race: one to leave alone. *D. A. Nolan*

SECRETARY GENERAL (IRE) 5 b.g. Fasliyev (USA) 120 – Katie McLain (USA) **87** 85 (Java Gold (USA)) [2006 92d: p10g⁵ 9.7f* 10d 10m* 10f⁴ 10.1g⁵ p12.2g⁶ p10g⁵ p10g⁵ p10g Sep 6] big, good-topped gelding: has a quick action: fairly useful handicapper: won at Folkestone in May and Lingfield in June: stays 1½m: acts on polytrack, firm and soft going: has worn blinkers/cheekpieces: has looked no easy ride: sold 13,000 gns. *P. F. I. Cole*

SECRET ASSASSIN (IRE) 3 b.g. Daggers Drawn (USA) 114 – Lypharden (IRE) **81** (Lyphard's Special (USA) 122) [2006 75: 7f⁵ 7.1m² 7f⁴ 7f* 7d² 7m³ 7.1m⁴ p7g⁶ Oct 5] smallish, lengthy gelding: fairly useful performer: won maiden at Catterick in July: stays 7f: acts on polytrack, firm and good to soft going: sometimes hangs: races up with pace. *W. R. Muir*

SECRET CAVERN (USA) 4 b.g. Lion Cavern (USA) 117 – River Dyna (USA) (Dyn- – aformer (USA)) [2006 48: p7g Oct 15] tall gelding: poor maiden: tried in cheekpieces. *Mrs Barbara Waring*

SECRET LIAISON 3 gr.g. Medicean 128 – Courting 108 (Pursuit of Love 124) [2006 **89** 73p: p8g 8g* 10v³ f8g⁵ 10f⁴ p8.6g⁵ 7.1d* 7f* 7d* 7.1m Sep 4] leggy gelding: improved into a fairly useful performer, winning maiden at Ayr in May and handicaps at Musselburgh, Brighton (jinked left) and Folkestone in August: effective at 7f to 1¼m: acts on polytrack and any turf going: usually races up with pace: has carried head a bit high. *Sir Mark Prescott*

SECRET MOMENT 4 b.g. Polar Prince (IRE) 117 – Inchtina 85 (Inchinor 119) [2006 **66** 10m⁶ 10.2m 9.9g p10g p9.5g Dec 9] big gelding: fair maiden: raced around 1¼m: best effort on good going. *C. G. Cox*

SECRET NIGHT 3 gr.f. Dansili 127 – Night Haven 99 (Night Shift (USA)) [2006 84: **88** p6g² p7g⁴ p8g⁴ p7g³ p7g⁵ 7.1m² 6m³ 6g⁵ 7g⁵ p7g³ p7g p8g² Dec 22] tall, useful-looking **a99** filly: useful on all-weather, fairly useful on turf: second three times in 2006, to Spinning Queen in listed race at Warwick and Orchard Supreme in handicap at Lingfield on last 2 occasions: stays easy 1m: acts on polytrack and good to firm going: has been slowly away: consistent. *J. A. R. Toller*

SECRET PACT (IRE) 4 br.g. Lend A Hand 124 – Schust Madame (IRE) 46 (Second – Set (IRE) 127) [2006 14g Jun 1] leggy, useful-looking gelding: fairly useful at 2 yrs, well held only outing on Flat since: races prominently: won over hurdles in November. *A. M. Hales*

SECRET TENDER (IRE) 3 ch.g. Beckett (IRE) 116 – Mystery Bid (Auction Ring **49** (USA) 123) [2006 60, a52: p8.6g f8g* 9.8m 10d 7.5g Aug 31] just modest performer in 2006: won selling handicap at Southwell in March: needs to settle to stay 1¼m: acts on fibresand: tried blinkered. *J. R. Weymes*

SECRET VISION (USA) 5 ch.m. Distant View (USA) 126 – Secret Angel (Halo (USA)) [2006 50, a58: f5g p5.1g⁵ p6g f5g⁴ 6m⁶ p5g* 6.1m p5.1g p6g p5g³ p5g p5g Dec 18] modest performer: won banded race at Kempton in May: stays 6f: acts on all-weather and firm going: effective with/without cheekpieces. *R. M. H. Cowell* — **a56**

SECRET WORLD (IRE) 3 ch.c. Spinning World (USA) 130 – Classic Park 115 (Robellino (USA) 127) [2006 8g* 7m⁵ Jun 21] €165,000Y: big, lengthy colt: fifth foal: half-brother to 4-y-o Walk In The Park and fairly useful Irish 6f/7f winner Mufradat (by Desert Prince): dam Irish 5f (at 2 yrs) to 1m (Irish 1000 Guineas) winner: useful form: won newcomers race at Newmarket in April impressively by 1¼ lengths from Mosharref, confidently ridden: subject of pre-race scare (reportedly travelled badly to course) but well-backed favourite and looked in fine shape when 3 lengths fifth to Jeremy in Jersey Stakes at Royal Ascot, missing break, meeting trouble and carrying head awkwardly: reportedly suffered a stress fracture after: will be suited by return to 1m. *J. Noseda* — **106**

SECURITY TIGER (IRE) 2 b.f. (Apr 10) Desert Prince (IRE) 130 – Nuit Chaud (USA) (Woodman (USA) 126) [2006 7m 7m 7.5d² 7g⁵ 7d 7.6f⁴ Sep 23] 20,000Y: leggy, sparely-made filly: sixth foal: half-sister to 3 winners, including useful 7f (at 2 yrs) and 1¼m winner Hallhoo (by Indian Ridge): dam maiden half-sister to dam of smart 6f/7f performer Danehill Dancer: fair maiden: will stay 1m: acts on good to firm and good to soft going: sold 12,000 gns. *M. R. Channon* — **70**

SEDGE (USA) 6 b.g. Lure (USA) 131 – First Flyer (USA) (Riverman (USA) 131) [2006 60: f7s⁵ f7g² 7.5f 8f³ 8m² 7f² 6.9m² 7m³ p7.1g² p8.6m Oct 14] fair handicapper: effective at 7f, probably at 9f: acts on all-weather, firm and good to soft ground: tried blinkered, usually wears cheekpieces. *P. T. Midgley* — **71**

SEDGWICK 4 b.g. Nashwan (USA) 135 – Imperial Bailiwick (IRE) 104 (Imperial Frontier (USA) 112) [2006 p7.1g⁶ Feb 10] half-brother to several winners, notably 5-y-o Reverence (by Mark of Esteem): dam 2-y-o 5f (including Flying Childers Stakes) winner: 100/1, some promise on belated debut when sixth to Violent Velocity in maiden at Wolverhampton, running green under pressure. *J. G. Given* — **59**

SEE IN THE DARK (IRE) 2 b.g. (Mar 18) Night Shift (USA) – Ms Mary C (IRE) 68 (Dolphin Street (FR) 125) [2006 5.2m² 5f² 5m² 5m 6f* 7m 6d 6m⁵ p6g⁵ Oct 11] €32,000F: useful-looking gelding: fluent mover: first foal: dam, Irish maiden, half-sister to Cheveley Park Stakes winner Seazun: fair performer: won nursery at Windsor in July: ran creditably most other starts: should stay 7f: acts on polytrack and firm going: sold 18,000 gns, sent to Bahrain. *B. J. Meehan* — **78**

SEEJAY 6 b.m. Bahamian Bounty 116 – Grand Splendour 79 (Shirley Heights 130) [2006 –, a53: 8.5g 7m 10g Sep 12] modest performer at best: well held in 2006: in cheekpieces last 2 starts. *B. R. Johnson* — **–**

SEEKING KALI (IRE) 3 br.f. Kalanisi (IRE) 132 – Sought Out (IRE) 119 (Rainbow Quest (USA) 134) [2006 10g p10g⁴ 10.2m⁵ Sep 25] well-made filly: half-sister to several winners, notably Derby winner North Light (by Danehill) and 9-y-o Cover Up: dam won Prix du Cadran: fair form in maidens last 2 starts, looking bit wayward in visor final one: worked up at stall before well held on debut. *Sir Michael Stoute* — **67**

SEEKING STRAIGHT (IRE) 3 b.g. Rainbow Quest (USA) 134 – Alignment (IRE) 98 (Alzao (USA) 117) [2006 10g Apr 18] leggy, useful-looking gelding: has a markedly round action: fourth foal: dam, headstrong maiden (fourth in Musidora Stakes), half-sister to smart performer up to 14.6f Bonny Scot and to dam of Golan, out of half-sister to Prix du Cadran winner Sought Out (herself dam of Derby winner North Light): 50/1, burly and green, never a threat in maiden at Newmarket (took good hold to post): sold 16,000 gns in July, joined Lucinda Russell and gelded. *Sir Michael Stoute* — **80**

SEEKING THE BUCK (USA) 2 b.c. (Mar 15) Seeking The Gold (USA) – Cuanto Es (USA) (Exbourne (USA) 125) [2006 7m Aug 11] close-coupled colt: behind in maiden at Newmarket (stirred up in paddock). *M. A. Magnusson* — **–**

SEESAWMILU (IRE) 3 b.g. Almutawakel 126 – Clos de Tart (IRE) (Indian Ridge 123) [2006 –: f6g p8.6g p6g* 5.9g 6m⁴ 6m⁴ 6g f6g Oct 12] sturdy gelding: modest performer: won handicap at Wolverhampton in May: stays 6f: acts on polytrack and good to firm going. *E. J. Alston* — **54**

SEGORIA (IRE) 4 b.f. Shinko Forest (IRE) – Moon Tango (IRE) 81 (Last Tycoon 131) [2006 62: p6g⁶ p6g* p6g³ p6g 6m⁴ 7g⁶ 7g³ 6m⁵ 6m* 6m* Jul 26] fairly useful handicapper: won at Wolverhampton in January and (having left A. Hales after fourth start) at Ballinrobe and Naas in July: effective at 6f/7f: acts on polytrack, soft and good to firm going: tried in cheekpieces/blinkers/tongue tie in 2005. *Edgar Byrne, Ireland* — **80**

SEHOYA (IRE) 4 b. or br.f. Second Empire (IRE) 124 – Blue Jazz (IRE) 70 (Bluebird **51** (USA) 125) [2006 60: 9.5g⁵ p9.5g p9.5g Nov 27] €4,000Y: second foal: dam Irish 9f winner: modest handicapper: stays 1¼m: acts on good to firm and good to soft going: tongue tied on reappearance: very slowly away second outing: joined R. C. Guest. *Eoin Doyle, Ireland*

SEKULA PATA (NZ) 7 b.g. Pompeii Court (USA) – Torquay (NZ) (Wharf (USA)) **76** [2006 10m a12f a10f 10d a7g 8g⁶ 8.5g 8m 8.1m 8d p10g³ p10g³ p12g Dec 1] former winner in South Africa (where Group 1-placed) and Mauritius: just fair form in handicaps in Britain last 8 starts in 2006: stays 1½m: acts on polytrack, soft and good to firm going: sometimes wears cheekpieces/blinkers (not last 5 outings): tried tongue tied. *C. Wroe, UAE*

SELDEMOSA 5 br.m. Selkirk (USA) 129 – Baldemosa (FR) (Lead On Time (USA) **55** 123) [2006 67: p9.5g 9d 10.2g 7.6g⁵ 8m⁶ 10.2m p8.6g⁶ p8g⁵ p8.6g Dec 27] big, workmanlike mare: modest performer: stays 9.5f: acts on all-weather, best effort on turf on good going. *M. S. Saunders*

SELECTIVE 7 b.g. Selkirk (USA) 129 – Portelet 91 (Night Shift (USA)) [2006 90: **79** p10g p8g p7.1g 7g² 8m 7s³ 8.3f⁴ 7.1f³ Jun 19] good-bodied gelding: fair handicapper nowadays: effective at 7f/1m: acts on polytrack, firm and soft going: in cheekpieces/visor, sometimes tongue tied: has run well when sweating: carries head awkwardly: waited with. *A. W. Carroll*

SELF DEFENSE 9 b.g. Warning 136 – Dansara (Dancing Brave (USA) 140) [2006 **115** 117: 12s⁴ 12d⁵ 12m⁶ 13.3d⁴ p12g³ Sep 2] good-topped gelding: smart performer: almost as good as ever in 2006, running creditably when in frame in Jockey Club Stakes at Newmarket (fourth to Shirocco), Geoffrey Freer Stakes at Newbury (fourth to Admiral's Cruise) and September Stakes at Kempton (2½ lengths third to Kandidate): best at 1½m/1¾m: acts on polytrack, heavy and good to firm going: smart hurdler at best, successful in October. *Miss E. C. Lavelle*

SELF DISCIPLINE 4 b.g. Dansili 127 – Cosh (USA) (A P Indy (USA) 131) [2006 –: **–** f8g Nov 14] no form. *Mrs L. B. Normile*

SELF RESPECT (USA) 4 b.g. Lear Fan (USA) 130 – Cap of Dignity (Shirley Heights **88** 130) [2006 90: 12d 14g 12m⁴ 12d⁵ Aug 22] big, rangy gelding: fairly useful handicapper: stays 1¾m: acts on polytrack, soft and good to firm going: effective with/without visor: wears crossed noseband: has looked difficult ride: fairly useful hurdler, successful in October. *A. King*

SELINKA 2 b.f. (Feb 28) Selkirk (USA) 129 – Lady Links 100 (Bahamian Bounty 116) **95** [2006 6g⁶ 6g³ 6.1m* 7d* Sep 30] leggy filly: first foal: dam 6f winner (including at 2 yrs): useful form: progressed well, winning maiden at Nottingham and listed Oh So Sharp Stakes at Newmarket in September, latter by short head from Puggy, sweeping through from last: likely to stay 1m. *R. Hannon*

SELKIRK LADY 3 ch.f. Selkirk (USA) 129 – Dubious (Darshaan 133) [2006 8.3d⁵ **69** p10g 10m p12.2g⁴ 12d⁴ Oct 2] 50,000Y: tall, close-coupled filly: first foal: dam, ran once in USA, closely related to high-class 1¼m performer Shady Heights: fair maiden: stays easy 1½m: acts on polytrack and good to soft going: raced too freely third outing. *W. R. Swinburn*

SELL OUT 2 gr.f. (May 4) Act One 124 – Nordica 99 (Northfields (USA)) [2006 7g **76 p** p7g* Nov 11] close-coupled filly: has a rounded action: half-sister to several winners, including 6f/1m winner Marika (by Marju) and Fred Darling winner/Oaks fourth Sueboog (by Darshaan, dam of very smart Best of The Bests), both useful: dam 6f/1m winner: much improved when winning maiden at Kempton, quickening well to beat High 'n Dry by 1¼ lengths: will be suited by 1m: likely to progress further. *G. Wragg*

SEMAHS HOLLY 2 b.f. (Mar 25) Beat All (USA) 120 – Semah's Dream 39 (Gunner **–** B 126) [2006 7f 6m 5d p9.5g Nov 7] third foal: dam maiden who probably stayed 7f: no form. *J. O'Reilly*

SEMENOVSKII 6 b.g. Fraam 114 – Country Spirit (Sayf El Arab (USA) 127) [2006 **72** 77: 5f⁶ 6g⁶ 5g⁶ 5.3d 5.3g p6g p6g Dec 15] strong gelding: fair handicapper: left Miss B. Sanders after third start: effective at 5f/6f: acts on polytrack, firm and good to soft going: tried visored/blinkered, often tongue tied of late: usually races prominently: none too reliable. *Mrs N. Smith*

SEMI DETACHED (IRE) 3 b.c. Distant Music (USA) 126 – Relankina (IRE) (Brok- **72** en Hearted 124) [2006 79: p8g⁶ 8s⁵ 8m 10m⁶ p9.5g⁵ Aug 31] tall, quite good-topped colt: fair maiden: stays 1m: acts on polytrack and soft ground: tried tongue tied. *J. R. Boyle*

SEMPER PARATUS (USA) 7 b.g. Foxhound (USA) 103 – Bletcha Lass (AUS) **49 §**
(Bletchingly (AUS)) [2006 55§: f8g³ f8g⁵ p10g May 15] close-coupled gelding: unimpressive mover: unreliable performer, only poor form in 2006: stays 1m: acts on
fibresand, firm and soft going: wears headgear. *V. Smith*

SENATORS ALIBI 8 b.g. Caerleon (USA) 132 – Salul (Soviet Star (USA) 128) [2006 **93**
99: 8v⁶ 7m 6.3g 6m³ 8.5m³ 7g 6.5d 8d 7v⁵ 8b⁶ 6v 8d Nov 5] strong gelding: fairly useful
handicapper: well held at Royal Ascot second start: stays 8.5f: acts on any going:
sometimes blinkered (not when successful): tried tongue tied. *T. J. O'Mara, Ireland*

SENDALI (FR) 2 b.c. (Mar 13) Daliapour (IRE) 122 – Lady Senk (FR) (Pink (FR) 123) **75**
[2006 7f⁵ 7g⁴ 8g⁶ Sep 27] €24,000Y, €50,000 2-y-o: close-coupled, useful-looking colt:
fifth foal: half brother to winners in France by Epervier Bleu (at 11.5f) and Cardoun
(10.5f/11f): dam French 1m and 10.5f winner: best effort (fair form) in maidens when
fourth of 5 to Ravi River at Chester: should prove suited by 1m+. *J. D. Bethell*

SENDINPOST 3 b.f. Dansili 127 – Colleville 97 (Pharly (FR) 130) [2006 60p: p5g **71**
11.6f* 12g⁵ 13.4f p13.9g⁴ p12g² Dec 8] sturdy filly: fair performer: upped significantly
in trip, won handicap at Windsor in July: likely to stay 2m: acts on polytrack and firm
ground: failed to settle fourth outing. *S. C. Williams*

SEND ME HOME (IRE) 4 b.g. Victory Note (USA) 120 – Purty Dancer (IRE) 71 **52**
(Foxhound (USA) 103) [2006 49: 8m* 8g 8s p8.6g³ p7.1g Dec 4] modest performer, **a56**
lightly raced: won handicap at Bellewstown in August: stays 8.6f: acts on polytrack and
good to firm going, probably on soft. *A. McGuinness, Ireland*

SENESCHAL 5 b.g. Polar Falcon (USA) 126 – Broughton Singer (IRE) 61 (Common **76**
Grounds 118) [2006 90, a78: p7g⁶ 7s⁶ p6g⁵ p6g² p6g*ᵈⁱˢ 7d⁵ 5.7s⁶ p6g 5g 5.7m p7g²
p6g⁴ p6g Jul 26] big, leggy gelding: fair handicapper: first past post at Kempton (failed
dope test and subsequently disqualified) in May: stays 7f: acts on polytrack, soft and
good to firm going: sometimes slowly away/edges left: wore cheekpieces once at 4 yrs.
A. B. Haynes

SENORA LENORAH 2 ch.f. (Apr 3) Tumbleweed Ridge 117 – Blue Diamond (First **–**
Trump 118) [2006 5d 7.2v⁶ 7.1d Nov 3] 1,200Y: third foal: half-sister to Italian 2003
2-y-o 7.5f winner Bohun (by Woodborough): dam little sign of ability: no form.
D. A. Nolan

SENOR BENNY (USA) 7 br.h. Benny The Dip (USA) 127 – Senora Tippy (USA) (El **112**
Gran Senor (USA) 136) [2006 107: 5v² 6v³ 6d* 5d⁵ 5d* 6d² 8v 5m 6g 5d⁶ 5v⁶ 6s² 6v³ 7d
Nov 5] lengthy horse: smart performer: won handicaps at Cork in April and the Curragh
in May: very good ½-length second to Miss Sally in listed event at Cork next time: not at
best afterwards, though placed in listed race and handicap at the Curragh in October: best
at 5f/6f: acts on sand, heavy and good to firm going: blinkered once. *M. McDonagh,
Ireland*

SENOR DALI (IRE) 3 ch.c. Peintre Celebre (USA) 137 – Far Fetched (IRE) 92 **109**
(Distant Relative 128) [2006 75: 10g⁴ 11g³ 10d* 10m 10m* 10v² 10d⁴ Sep 16] leggy,
close-coupled colt: useful performer: won maiden at Sandown (hung left) in May and
minor event at Ascot (beat Desert Realm easily) in July: good 1¾ lengths
second to Waleria in Furstenberg-Rennen at Baden-Baden before respectable fourth to
Best Name in Prix du Prince d'Orange at Longchamp final outing: barely stays 11f: acts
on heavy and good to firm going: became unbalanced first 2 outings in 2006: sold
privately, and joined I. Mohammed in UAE. *J. L. Dunlop*

SENOR EDUARDO 9 gr.g. Terimon 124 – Jasmin Path (Warpath 113) [2006 52, a58: **–**
p9.5g Apr 24] good-topped gelding: well held only run in 2006: often wears cheekpieces.
S. Gollings

SENOR MAC 3 b.g. Fraam 114 – Annie Hall (Saddlers' Hall (IRE) 126) [2006 8.5d **–**
Apr 19] strong, lengthy gelding: tailed off in seller at Beverley. *B. J. Meehan*

SENOR SET (GER) 5 b.g. Second Set (IRE) 127 – Shine Share (IRE) (El Gran Senor **66**
(USA) 136) [2006 61d: 16g³ 14.1m⁴ 15.8g² p13.9g* 14.8m⁴ 16m² p16g Jul 29] leggy
gelding: fair handicapper: won at Wolverhampton in May: stays 2m: acts on all-weather,
good to firm and good to soft going: tried in blinkers/cheekpieces. *J. Pearce*

SENSUOUS 3 b.f. Royal Applause 124 – Zafaaf 105 (Kris 135) [2006 81: 7.6m³ 6.1d² **67**
6f⁵ 6f 6g 7g² 7d⁴ Aug 25] lengthy, unfurnished filly: maiden: just fair form at 3 yrs: stayed
7f: best effort on good going: dead. *R. Hannon*

SENTIERO ROSSO (USA) 4 b.g. Intidab (USA) 115 – Kheyrah (USA) 100 (Dayjur **76**
(USA) 137) [2006 87: 5f 5g 6s 5g 6m 6m p6g⁵ 6m 7.1d* 7.1m³ 7s² 7.5g⁶ 7.2v 7s p7.1g

7v⁴ f7g⁴ f8g* f8g² f8g⁶ Dec 14] small, strong gelding: just fair handicapper in 2006: won at Musselburgh in August and Southwell in November: stays easy 1m: acts on all-weather and heavy going: has been blinkered/in cheekpieces, tongue tied of late: has looked reluctant. *B. Ellison*

SEPIA PRINT (IRE) 2 b.f. (Jan 26) Tagula (IRE) 116 – Photo Flash (IRE) 76 (Bahamian Bounty 116) [2006 6g 7f⁶ p6g² 7m Sep 5] leggy filly: first foal: dam, 1m winner, half-sister to smart miler Atlantis Prince (by Tagula): modest maiden: second in seller: should stay 7f/1m: has flashed tail. *W. J. Knight*   **53**

SEPTIMUS (IRE) 3 b.c. Sadler's Wells (USA) 132 – Caladira (IRE) 81 (Darshaan 133) [2006 109p: 10g 10.4s* 12m Jun 3]   **121**

Septimus missed his date with destiny, sidelined at the time when the St Leger was switched to York, reputedly the place where his namesake, one of the black emperors of Rome, met his death. Even as a two-year-old, he looked tailor-made for the race, and, judged on the form of his victory in the Dante Stakes on the course in May, Septimus would have given St Leger winner Sixties Icon most to do at York. Furthermore, he would probably have been closely involved in the finish of the Derby had he been himself on the day at Epsom. As it was, Septimus finished a remote twelfth, looking a fish out of water on the undulating course under firmish conditions, never in the race under Michael Kinane, and hanging left the moment his rider asked for any sort of effort. He returned home with a jarred shoulder, having started fourth favourite at 17/2, easy to back after Kieren Fallon opted for Horatio Nelson among Aidan O'Brien's quartet.

A 25/1-shot for the Derby in the winter, Septimus was promoted to second favourite for Epsom behind Visindar at as short as 9/2 straight after his runaway win under Fallon in the totesport Dante Stakes in May. On soft ground at York, he left the form of his reappearance, when seventh in the Prix La Force at Longchamp the previous month well behind him. Winner of a maiden at Leopardstown and the Beresford Stakes at the Curragh before finishing third when favourite for the Racing Post Trophy at Doncaster in three outings as a juvenile, Septimus was preferred to Doncaster winner Palace Episode in the Dante betting, starting favourite at 13/8 and turning the Dante into a one-horse race, taking over two furlongs out and forging clear to win by eight lengths. He had subsequent Irish Derby third Best Alibi in second, with Snoqualmie Boy, winner afterwards of a listed race at Royal Ascot, a further eleven lengths away, and Palace Episode tailed off last of six.

		Sadler's Wells (USA) (b 1981)	Northern Dancer (b 1961)	Nearctic Fairy Bridge
Septimus (IRE) (b.c. 2003)			Fairy Bridge (b 1975)	Bold Reason Special
		Caladira (IRE) (br 1991)	Darshaan (br 1981)	Shirley Heights Delsy
			Cape Race (b 1974)	Northern Dancer Sticky Case

By Sadler's Wells out of a Darshaan mare who was successful over a mile and a half in Ireland, Septimus should be suited by a mile and a half and would have had no trouble with the St Leger distance. He is easily the most noteworthy produce

totesport Dante Stakes, York—Septimus revels in the conditions; Best Alibi is second

of his dam Caladira, though his unraced close relative Escolhida (by Montjeu) changed hands for 200,000 guineas at the Newmarket Breeze Up Sale in April, having made €43,000 as a yearling. Septimus may well do more to enhance his dam's value in 2007. Rather leggy and still unfurnished at three, he should be more the finished article as a four-year-old and is still lightly raced. He should make up into the high-class performer he promised to be in the Dante. Unraced on extremes of ground, he gained his first win as a two-year-old on good to firm going, but seems to go particularly well on soft. *A. P. O'Brien, Ireland*

SERENE DANCER 3 b.f. Danehill Dancer (IRE) 117 – Bliss (IRE) 75 (Statoblest 120) **59**
[2006 7m 6f⁵ May 7] big, angular filly: third foal: half-sister to 6f (including at 2 yrs) winner Blofeld (by Royal Applause): dam 2-y-o 5f winner: much better effort in maidens when fifth at Salisbury: slowly away both outings. *Mrs P. N. Dutfield*

SERENE HIGHNESS (IRE) 2 b.f. (Feb 28) Highest Honor (FR) 124 – Dollysister **66**
(FR) (Alydar (USA)) [2006 7f³ 7g Aug 18] seventh foal: half-sister to 3 winners, including French 1¼m winner Composition (by Sillery) and winner in Japan by Red Ransom: dam, French 9f winner, half-sister to smart French performer up to 1½m Beau Sultan: better run in maidens when third to Darfour at Lingfield: raced in less-favoured group at Folkestone: will stay 1m. *J. L. Dunlop*

SERENGETI 2 b.c. (Feb 26) Singspiel (IRE) 133 – Tanzania (USA) (Darshaan 133) **80 p**
[2006 p8.6s* Dec 15] first foal: dam, unraced half-sister to useful 1¼m winner Roscius, out of Prix Saint-Alary winner Rosefinch, herself out of Oh So Sharp: won maiden at Wolverhampton by neck from Sister Maria, green and tending to drift left: will be well suited by 1¼m: should progress. *M. Johnston*

SEREVI (IRE) 3 b.c. Cape Cross (IRE) 129 – Winter Tern (USA) (Arctic Tern (USA) **77**
126) [2006 77: p6g³ p5g⁴ 7g⁶ a6g⁴ a8.5g* Dec 3] quite good-topped colt: fair performer: sold from J. Noseda 9,000 gns after third start: won maiden at Dortmund in December: stays 8.5f: acts on sand: signs of waywardness. *T. H. Hansen, Germany*

SERGEANT CECIL 7 ch.g. King's Signet (USA) 110 – Jadidh 64 (Touching **120**
Wood (USA) 127) [2006 118: 12g⁴ 13.9s² 20m⁵ 16.4m² 16f⁴ 15.9d* 18d* 20m* 15.5g³ Oct 22]
     Sergeant Cecil's popularity—if not his racing record—is starting to approach that of two other stayers of the past decade or so who caught the racing public's imagination, Double Trigger and Persian Punch. Double Trigger won twelve pattern races, including the Gold Cup and three editions each of the Goodwood Cup and the Doncaster Cup, while Persian Punch's thirteen pattern wins included three Henry II Stakes, three Jockey Club Cups, two Goodwood Cups and a Doncaster Cup. St Leger third Double Trigger's career in the Cup races began as a four-year-old, while Persian Punch was placed in the Goodwood Cup and Jockey Club Cup as a three-year-old. Sergeant Cecil has had to work his way up from the bottom, and didn't even win his first race until he was a four-year-old, going nine outings without a success at three. He improved into a tough, useful and consistent handicapper at five and, as a six-year-old, won three of the major staying handicaps, the Northumberland Plate, the Ebor and the Cesarewitch, completing a treble never achieved before in the same season. Sergeant Cecil also had his first outing in pattern company as a six-year-old, coming second to Millenary in the Doncaster Cup, form upon which he improved marginally when going on to win the Cesarewitch under 9-8.
     Sergeant Cecil's Cesarewitch performance effectively ended his career in handicaps but he had proved himself good enough for pattern and listed races. It wasn't plain sailing at first, however, as Sergeant Cecil took six more outings in such company to get off the mark. He made what seemed a most encouraging return over an inadequate trip when fourth in the John Porter and then completed his preparation for the Gold Cup with a creditable second behind Percussionist in the Yorkshire Cup. Sergeant Cecil's Cesarewitch performance suggested he would stay the Gold Cup trip but, on the day, he gave the opposite impression when fifth to runaway winner Yeats, one-paced in the closing stages after travelling strongly for a long way. After being beaten at odds on in a muddling listed event won by Land 'n Stars at Sandown in July, Sergeant Cecil improved one place on his Gold Cup effort, again behind Yeats, who was a wide-margin winner, in the Goodwood Cup.

GNER Doncaster Cup, York—Sergeant Cecil gains his second win of the year on the course, holding Alcazar; Baddam is third, ahead of the grey Kasthari

Sergeant Cecil met trouble early in the home straight at Goodwood and was best not judged too harshly on his performance, but memories of his splendid performances of 2005 were now in danger of fading. However, back at the scene of his Ebor victory (and of his second in the Yorkshire Cup), Sergeant Cecil belatedly registered a first pattern win in the Weatherbys Insurance Lonsdale Cup, which was switched to the round course at York for the first time. In the absence of Yeats, and of Reefscape and Distinction the placed horses in the Gold Cup, Sergeant Cecil started favourite for a run-of-the-mill renewal of the Lonsdale which he won by half a length from Franklins Gardens, being brought with a well-timed run by Frankie Dettori, partnering him for the first time when regular jockey Alan Munro was forced to stop riding after suffering a convulsion two days earlier. Munro is set to be out of race-riding for a year and was unable to partner Sergeant Cecil in either the Doncaster Cup or the Prix du Cadran, both of which Sergeant Cecil won with Dettori in the saddle.

The GNER Doncaster Cup was among the principal races at the St Leger meeting transferred to a two-day fixture at York while building work was going on at Doncaster. Carrying a 3-lb Group 2 penalty for his triumph in the Lonsdale, Sergeant Cecil marched on to his second pattern win, looking in control some way out but, in the end, winning by a length from the rallying Alcazar, crossing that horse after hitting the front over a furlong out, sooner than usual for him. Sergeant Cecil met a good field on Arc day in the Prix du Cadran Casino Les Princes Barriere de Cannes, including Reefscape (winner the previous year), the second and third

Prix du Cadran Casino Les Princes Barriere de Cannes, Longchamp—a Group 1 for Sergeant Cecil who leaves it late, completing a hat-trick, ahead of Shamdala and German-trained Le Miracle

Mr Terry Cooper's "Sergeant Cecil"

from the Doncaster Cup Alcazar and Baddam, the smart French stayer Shamdala and a much improved German challenger in Le Miracle. Underfoot conditions were similar at Longchamp to those which had prevailed in the Gold Cup and Sergeant Cecil, who started favourite, proved that he stays two and a half miles well, at least when conditions are not testing. The Cadran, the most important race in France for out-and-out stayers, was won by Westerner in the two years before Reefscape and it took another very smart performance from Sergeant Cecil to pull off victory in an event that neither Double Trigger (who ran in the race three times) nor Persian Punch (four appearances) managed in their long careers.

Sergeant Cecil was held up as usual but was still only third a furlong out, with three lengths still to make up. Dettori produced him to swoop on Shamdala and Le Miracle close home and score by three quarters of a length and half a length, eased approaching the line as his rider began to celebrate. Sergeant Cecil was given a memorable ovation by the large visiting British contingent as he made his way back to the unsaddling enclosure where Dettori performed his trademark flying dismount. Dettori's Group 1 wins at Longchamp include three Arcs but he said he had never received a more enthusiastic reception. 'Did you hear the roar out there? I've never known anything like it, it felt like the crowd were all pushing him on. What a horse. What a story.' Sergeant Cecil's trainer Rod Millman, saddling his first Group 1 winner, and Dettori both went out of their way in the post-race celebrations to mention Alan Munro who 'made the horse'. Victory in the Cadran took Dettori's record on Sergeant Cecil to three wins from three rides but he was unable to take the mount on Sergeant Cecil's final start, in the Prix Royal-Oak at Longchamp at the end of October when Ryan Moore took over—Dettori was riding in Italy for Godolphin. Sergeant Cecil finished a creditable third over a trip that is a minimum for him nowadays, staying on well to be beaten a short neck and a length by the home-trained pair Montare and Bellamy Cay.

Sergeant Cecil's humble beginnings—he was bought as a yearling by his owner for less than £1,000 'out of a field'—have added to his unusual story. According to the breeder who sold him, Don Hazzard, there was a contingency that he would get 'an extra £400' if Sergeant Cecil won two races. 'One day at Windsor after we had been beaten for the third or fourth time in a photo, Terry [Cooper] gave me the £400 anyway, writing out the cheque as we were leaving the racecourse.' Sergeant Cecil's dam Jadidh, a leggy, plain filly, was bought as a three-year-old on behalf of Hazzard for 2,800 guineas at the Newmarket Autumn Sales, a homebred cast off from the Maktoums after finishing second in a Yarmouth maiden on her only start for Alec Stewart. Jadidh remained a maiden on the Flat, but was successful over jumps, developing into a fair staying handicap hurdler at her best, though inconsistent and sometimes looking a difficult ride. Sergeant Cecil, who is by the sprinter King's Signet (whose dam won the Prix de l'Abbaye), is Jadidh's first foal and she was also represented on the racecourse in the latest season by the modest maiden staying handicapper Jayer Gilles (by Busy Flight), the only other foal Jadidh produced for her veteran breeder before he sold her on. Jadidh also had a three-year-old gelding by Kayf Tara, called Jau, and a two-year-old filly by Muhtarram, called Jambles, neither of which reached the racecourse in the latest season.

		Nureyev	Northern Dancer
	King's Signet (USA)	(b 1977)	Special
	(ch 1989)	Sigy	Habitat
Sergeant Cecil		(b 1976)	Satu
(ch.g. 1999)		Touching Wood	Roberto
	Jadidh	(b 1979)	Mandera
	(b 1988)	Petrol	Troy
		(b 1981)	Rambling Rose

Sergeant Cecil won the Racehorse Owners' Association's Horse of the Year award in 2005 (decided by a poll of ROA members and readers of the *Racing Post*). He made the short-list of six again in the latest season—when the award went to Ouija Board—and has become a firm favourite with racegoers. A workmanlike gelding in appearance, he stays two and a half miles and acts on firm and soft going. He sometimes races freely and carries his head awkwardly (ran poorly tried in cheekpieces in 2003) but is as tough and reliable as they come. He is usually held up to make best use of his good turn of foot. *B. R. Millman*

SERGEANT LEWIS 4 gr.g. Mind Games 121 – Silver Blessings (Statoblest 120) [2006 –, a71: p6g 6d p6g⁶ Jun 7] quite good-topped gelding: just modest performer in 2006: stays 7f: acts on all-weather, no form on turf: tried blinkered: tongue tied: sometimes slowly away. *R. M. Flower* — a60

SERGEANT SLIPPER 9 ch.g. Never So Bold 135 – Pretty Scarce (Handsome Sailor 125) [2006 53§, a50§: f5g f6g f6g³ f6g³ f6g³ 6m p7.1g f6g² f7g⁵ p7g May 23] workmanlike gelding: modest performer: best at 6f: acts on fibresand, heavy and good to firm going: tried blinkered, wears visor: usually slowly away, often markedly so: untrustworthy. *C. Smith* — 53 §

SERIEUX 7 b.g. Cadeaux Genereux 131 – Seranda (IRE) (Petoski 135) [2006 86§: p7g 7v⁴ p8g⁶ 7d³ p7g⁵ 7.6d⁵ 7.1m⁴ 7m² 7f⁵ 7m⁶ 8m⁴ 6m⁵ p7.1g Sep 30] strong, lengthy, useful-looking gelding: fairly useful performer: best at 7f/1m: acts on polytrack, soft and good to firm going: often in cheekpieces/visored nowadays: free-going sort: usually races prominently: ungenuine. *D. Nicholls* — 81 §

SERIOUSLY LUCKY (IRE) 2 b.g. (Mar 23) Key of Luck (USA) 126 – Serious Delight (Lomond (USA) 128) [2006 5m 6m⁶ 6f⁶ Jul 17] angular, quite good-topped gelding: no show in maidens: gelded after final start. *D. Nicholls* — –

SERRAMANNA 5 ch.m. Grand Lodge (USA) 125 – Spry 84 (Suave Dancer (USA) 136) [2006 64: p10g 11.7d 11.6m p12g³ 11m³ 11g 12.1f³ 11.5m³ p12g 12m³ 16m 12s⁵ 16d* 11s⁴ 11.9g⁵ 16v p13g² p12g² p12g p16g p12g³ Dec 20] leggy mare: fair handicapper: left Dr J. Naylor after seventh start: won at Goodwood in September: stays 2m: acts on polytrack, soft and good to firm ground: tried blinkered. *Ms J. S. Doyle* — 67

SERVILLIA (IRE) 3 b.f. Dansili 127 – Housekeeper (IRE) 97 (Common Grounds 118) [2006 71p: 8.3m 7m May 31] just modest form in maidens in 2006: stayed 1m: dead. *W. R. Swinburn* — 60

Scuderia Rencati's "Sesmen"

SESMEN 2 br. or gr.f. (Mar 10) Inchinor 119 – Poetry In Motion (IRE) 76 (Ballad Rock **106**
122) [2006 p7g* 8.2d* 7m* 8d⁶ Sep 23] 24,000F, 27,000Y: neat filly: fourth foal: dam, 5f
winner, out of smart performer up to 1m Nasseem: useful form: successful first 3 starts,
in maiden at Kempton, minor event at Nottingham and Normandie Stud Prestige Stakes
at Goodwood, in last-named idled when beating Bicoastal by neck: 3/1, raced too freely
in lead when only sixth of 8 in Fillies' Mile at Ascot: stays 1m: acts on polytrack, good to
firm and good to soft going. *M. Botti*

SESSILE (USA) 3 b. or br.f. Forestry (USA) 121 – Madam Lagonza (USA) (King- **61**
mambo (USA) 125) [2006 69p: 8m 8.3f p7g Aug 30] modest maiden: raced only at 7f/
1m: acts on polytrack: sent to USA. *J. H. M. Gosden*

SET ALIGHT 5 b.m. Forzando 122 – Me Spede (Valiyar 129) [2006 75: f8g³ p7.1g **59**
f7g* f7g p7g⁵ p7g f7g³ 7m⁶ 7g f7g f7g Nov 28] big mare: fair handicapper on all- **a74**
weather, modest on turf: won at Southwell in February: stays 1m: acts on all-weather (all
wins at Southwell) and good to firm going: wears visor/cheekpieces: looks hard ride.
Mrs C. A. Dunnett

SETEEM (USA) 2 ch.g. (Feb 22) Diesis 133 – Inscrutable Dancer (USA) (Green **74**
Dancer (USA) 132) [2006 8.1m 8.1d⁵ Sep 13] $75,000Y: fourth foal: dam US 8.5f/9f
winner: better effort in maidens when fifth to Kid Mambo at Sandown, hampered briefly:
sold 12,000 gns. and gelded. *M. P. Tregoning*

SET THE SCENE (IRE) 2 b.f. (Feb 12) Sadler's Wells (USA) 132 – Margarula (IRE) **74 p**
120 (Doyoun 124) [2006 p8g⁵ Nov 5] first foal: dam Irish 1m (at 2 yrs) to 1½m (Irish
Oaks) winner: 2¼ lengths fifth to Happy Go Lily in maiden at Lingfield, very slowly
away: will be suited by 1¼m+: sure to do better. *J. H. M. Gosden*

SETTLE (IRE) 7 b.g. Ali-Royal (IRE) 127 – Airport (Warpath 113) [2006 50: f12g p9.5g 9g 16m Jun 19] poor performer: trained first 2 outings only by W. M. Brisbourne before rejoining former stable: effective at 1m to 1½m: acts on polytrack, firm and soft ground: often blinkered/in cheekpieces: none too consistent. *M. Flannery, Ireland* —

SEULEMENT (USA) 4 ch.g. Rahy (USA) 115 – Only Seule (USA) (Lyphard (USA) 132) [2006 8.5g 8.1m 8g 7d⁵ 7.6g⁶ 7m⁴ 9d⁶ 8g⁵ Oct 13] rather leggy, lengthy gelding: useful performer: left C. Laffon-Parias in France after final 3-y-o outing: mostly credit-able efforts in handicaps in 2006: stays 1¼m: acts on soft and good to firm going: sold 55,000 gns, sent to Saudi Arabia. *L. M. Cumani* **98**

SEVEN NO TRUMPS 9 ch.g. Pips Pride 117 – Classic Ring (IRE) 50 (Auction Ring (USA) 123) [2006 88, a66: 5.1s⁵ 5m³ 5g⁵ 5.1s 5s 5m⁶ 5f³ 5d 5f⁶ 5.1f³ 5m 5.1m³ 5m⁴ f5m Oct 31] rangy, good-topped gelding: just fair performer in 2006: effective at 5f/6f: acts on polytrack and any turf going: blinkered once at 3 yrs, tried in cheekpieces: edgy sort: tends to carry head high. *J. M. Bradley* **66**

SEVEN SHIRT 5 b.g. Great Dane (IRE) 122 – Bride's Answer 81 (Anshan 119) [2006 –: f7g Jan 24] tall gelding: maiden: no form since 2004: tried blinkered/tongue tied: tends to carry head awkwardly. *E. G. Bevan* —

SEVEN STEPS (IRE) 2 b.f. (Mar 6) Best of The Bests (IRE) 122 – Seven Wonders (USA) (Rahy (USA) 115) [2006 7.1m⁶ p7g³ 6.5s p7g² 8.5f² Nov 19] 26,000F, 15,000Y: third foal: half-sister to 4-y-o Connotation and winner in Holland by Elnadim: dam unraced half-sister to smart US 1¼m performer Boatman out of half-sister to Irish 1000 Guineas winner Al Bahathri, herself dam of Haafhd: fair maiden: placed at Kempton, Lingfield and Hollywood: very stiff task third outing: will stay 1¼m: acts on polytrack and firm going. *J. W. Hills* **71**

SEW IN CHARACTER 2 ch.g. (Mar 24) Woodborough (USA) 112 – Elegant Rose 72 (Noalto 120) [2006 p7.1f 7.1d Sep 16] well held in maidens. *M. Blanshard* —

SEW'N'SO CHARACTER (IRE) 5 b.g. Imperial Ballet (IRE) 110 – Hope And Glory (USA) 87 (Well Decorated (USA)) [2006 99: p8g² 8s p8g⁶ 10.3m⁶ 8.1s⁴ 8.1f⁵ 8g* 8.1m⁴ 8m 8s⁴ 10.1m⁶ 10.4s p9.5g⁵ p9.5g⁵ Dec 30] good-topped gelding: useful handicapper: won at Salisbury (beat Kelucia ¾ length) in June: effective at 7.5f to 10.5f: acts on polytrack, soft and good to firm going: blinkered once: waited with: consistent. *M. Blanshard* **95**

SEYAADI 4 b.g. Intikhab (USA) 135 – Sioux Chef 78 (Be My Chief (USA) 122) [2006 80: 12d 10g May 29] strong, well-made gelding: has markedly round action: fairly useful performer at best: well held in 2006: tried visored. *Robert Gray* —

SFORZANDO 5 b.m. Robellino (USA) 127 – Mory Kante (USA) (Icecapade (USA)) [2006 76, a68+: p9.5g p9.5g⁵ 8d 8m 8d⁴ 9g² 10m³ 9.9f⁴ 10.1m⁵ 10.5m* 10d* 10g⁴ 10m 11.9g* 10g² 12s 11s Oct 10] well-made mare: fairly useful handicapper: won at Haydock and Nottingham in August, and Haydock in September: stays 1½m: acts on polytrack, good to firm and good to soft going: sometimes slowly away: often ridden by 7-lb claimer of late. *Mrs L. Stubbs* **81**

SGT PEPPER (IRE) 5 b.g. Fasliyev (USA) 120 – Amandine (IRE) (Darshaan 133) [2006 –: p7.1g p8g p12g Apr 2] compact gelding: no form on Flat since 2004. *P. L. Gilligan* —

SGT SCHULTZ (IRE) 3 b.g. In The Wings 128 – Ann's Annie (IRE) 78 (Alzao (USA) 117) [2006 68, a74: p7g⁶ p7.1g⁶ 7.1m³ 8m 8.2m² 8.3f³ 8.1f² 8f⁶ 10g³ p12.2g² p12.2g⁴ p13.9m³ Nov 9] lengthy gelding: fair maiden handicapper: may prove best short of 1¾m: acts on polytrack and firm going: sometimes slowly away. *J. S. Moore* **75 a78**

SHAABAN (IRE) 5 b.g. Woodman (USA) 126 – Ashbilya (USA) (Nureyev (USA) 131) [2006 71d: 8.1f p12.2g³ p8.6g Jul 11] good-bodied gelding: fair performer at best at 4 yrs: no form in 2006: tried blinkered, usually wears cheekpieces. *R. J. Price* —

SHABERNAK (IRE) 7 gr.g. Akarad (FR) 130 – Salinova (FR) (Linamix (FR) 127) [2006 114: 14.1s³ Apr 12] smallish, lengthy gelding: smart performer at best: respectable 5½ lengths third to Frank Sonata in listed race at Nottingham only outing in 2006: stays 2m: acts on firm and soft going: races prominently: sold 24,000 gns. *M. L. W. Bell* **109**

SHADE COZY (USA) 4 gr. or ro.g. Cozzene (USA) – Fire And Shade (USA) 91 (Shadeed (USA) 135) [2006 72+: p6g² 5.2m p6g p6g* p5.1g² p6g² Dec 1] well-made gelding: fairly useful handicapper: reportedly found to have stress fracture of pelvis and off 7 months after reappearance (gelded in interim): won at Wolverhampton in November: **86**

good second there and at Lingfield last 2 starts: effective at 5f/6f: acts on polytrack: has been tongue tied: reared leaving stall third outing. *A. M. Balding*

SHADED EDGE 2 b.g. (Mar 11) Bold Edge 123 – Twilight Mistress 84 (Bin Ajwaad (IRE) 119) [2006 p6g p6g Dec 22] poor form in maidens. *D. W. P. Arbuthnot* **49**

SHADOW ASPECT 3 b.c. Nashwan (USA) 135 – Hedonic (Gone West (USA)) [2006 10g 10v Oct 22] quite good-topped colt: modest form in maidens, leaving Sir Michael Stoute 12,000 gns and off nearly 6 months after debut. *Eoin Doyle, Ireland* **59**

SHADOW JUMPER (IRE) 5 b.g. Dayjur (USA) 137 – Specifically (USA) (Sky Classic (CAN)) [2006 68: f6g2 p6g* f6g* f6g4 f6g2 f6g5 f6s p5.1g f6g f6g May 2] ex-Irish gelding: fair performer: won seller at Wolverhampton and handicap at Southwell in January: claimed from M. Attwater £10,000 after next start: best at 5f/6f: acts on all-weather, firm and good to soft ground: tried tongue tied: usually wears headgear nowadays. *J. T. Stimpson* **71**

SHADY GREEN (IRE) 2 b.g. (Feb 24) Kalanisi (IRE) 132 – Albacora (IRE) 98 (Fairy King (USA)) [2006 10d 7.2v4 f7g Nov 14] close-coupled, good-topped gelding: fifth foal: half-brother to 3 winners, including 2005 2-y-o 1m winner Achill Bay (by Peintre Celebre) and 8.5f and 11.4f winner Hammiya (by Darshaan), both useful: dam, French 2-y-o 7.5f winner, closely related to smart French sprinter Pont Aven, herself dam of smart performers Josr Algarhoud (7f/1m) and Sainte Marine (5f): best effort (fair form) in maidens on debut for K. Ryan: sold 13,000 gns after: gelded after final outing. *M. W. Easterby* **69**

SHAHEER (IRE) 4 b.g. Shahrastani (USA) 135 – Atmospheric Blues (IRE) 91 (Double Schwartz 128) [2006 64, a56: f12g6 p9.5g3 f11g* p12.2g6 f11s 12m4 12.6m 11.6m5 10.2f2 11.9f2 11.7m f12g4 p13.9g p10g* p10g* p10g Dec 22] sturdy gelding: fluent mover: modest performer: won maiden claimer at Southwell (claimed from P. Howling) in February and banded races at Kempton in November and December: stays 1½m: acts on all-weather and firm ground: tried tongue tied, usually wears headgear nowadays. *J. Gallagher* **57**
a62

SHAHIN (USA) 3 b.c. Kingmambo (USA) 125 – String Quartet (IRE) 109 (Sadler's Wells (USA) 132) [2006 104p: 9.9m6 Sep 10] tall, quite attractive colt: useful performer: off nearly 11 months (reported in April to have suffered a leg injury), not discredited when last behind Pictavia in Select Stakes at Goodwood only outing in 2006: should stay 1¼m: raced only on good to firm/good to soft going. *M. P. Tregoning* **102**

SHAHMINA (IRE) 3 b.f. Danehill (USA) 126 – My Ballerina (USA) 94 (Sir Ivor (USA) 135) [2006 10m4 12d3 p12g3 p13g2 p12g4 Nov 9] big, good-topped filly: sister to 2 winners, including useful 2001 2-y-o 6f/1m winner Sundari who stayed 1¼m, and half-sister to several winners, including fairly useful 7f (at 2 yrs)/10.5f winner Starry Night (by Sheikh Albadou): dam 1¼m/1½m winner: fair maiden: stays 1½m: acts on polytrack, better effort on turf on good to firm going. *J. H. M. Gosden* **78**

SHAHM (IRE) 7 b.g. Marju (IRE) 127 – Istibshar (USA) 78 (Mr Prospector (USA)) [2006 p8g2 Nov 6] good-topped gelding: modest performer: off over 2½ years prior to creditable second in banded race at Kempton: stays 1m: acts on all-weather, good to firm and good to soft going: tried visored/blinkered/tongue tied: sometimes carries head high/ looks none too genuine. *B. J. Curley* **55**

SHAHZAN HOUSE (IRE) 7 b.g. Sri Pekan (USA) 117 – Nsx 74 (Roi Danzig (USA)) [2006 104: p12g p12g p12g6 10.1g 10m 10g p10g 9.7m 11.9g Sep 22] sturdy gelding: fluent mover: on downgrade and just fairly useful performer at best in 2006: claimed from Stef Liddiard £10,000 after third start: best around 1¼m: acts on soft and good to firm going: usually wears cheekpieces, once visored. *P. G. Murphy* **91 d**

SHAIKA 3 b.f. Almushtarak (IRE) 122 – Subtle Girl (Selkirk (USA) 129) [2006 f6g 7m 9.7d6 f8g 10d* p12.2g 11.5m 10.1f4 10.1m3 10d6 11.5d* f12m p11g p12g Dec 13] unfurnished filly: second foal: dam unraced: modest performer on turf, poor on all-weather: won sellers at Leicester in May and Yarmouth in October: stays 11.5f: acts on good to soft going, probably on good to firm: wore cheekpieces penultimate outing: sometimes slowly away. *G. Prodromou* **60**
a44

SHAKE ON IT 2 b.c. (Feb 18) Lomitas 129 – Decision Maid (USA) 105 (Diesis 133) [2006 6g 7.1m2 7.6f2 Sep 23] 2,000F, 12,000Y: leggy colt: second foal: dam, 2-y-o 7f winner, closely related to useful 7f/1m winner Miss Ivanhoe: fairly useful form in maidens: tongue tied, short-head second at Warwick and Chester: stays 7.6f. *R. F. Johnson Houghton* **80**

SHAKERATTLEANDROLL (IRE) 5 b.g. Dr Fong (USA) 128 – Speedybird (IRE) – 71 (Danehill (USA) 126) [2006 81: p12g p12g 15.4m 10s p12g 16m Sep 10] close-coupled gelding: fairly useful form at 4 yrs: no show in handicaps in 2006. *Mrs L. Richards*

SHAKE THE SPEAR (IRE) 3 b.g. Lear Spear (USA) 124 – Milladella (FR) (Nure- – yev (USA) 131) [2006 61: 12g Aug 7] strong gelding: modest maiden: gelded, tailed off only outing in 2006: should stay 1m: acts on polytrack. *Miss J. R. Tooth*

SHALAPOUR (IRE) 4 b.c. Darshaan 133 – Shalama (IRE) 91 (Kahyasi 130) [2006 **99** 116: 12v² Mar 24] smart performer at 3 yrs: left J. Oxx in Ireland, just useful form when 7 lengths second of 4 behind Into The Shadows in minor event at Southwell on return: stayed 1½m: acted on heavy and good to firm going: often tongue tied at 3 yrs: dead. *M. Johnston*

SHAMAYOUN (FR) 4 b.g. Kahyasi 130 – Shamanara (IRE) (Danehill (USA) 126) **90** [2006 20m³ Jun 20] compact gelding: fairly useful performer: won newcomers race at Evreux and minor event at Saint-Cloud in 2005: left A. de Royer Dupre in France after: in cheekpieces, good 5¼ lengths third of 29 to Baddam in Ascot Stakes (Handicap) at Royal Ascot only outing on Flat in Britain (had shown fairly useful form over hurdles): stayed 2½m: acted on soft and good to firm going: was quirky: dead. *C. R. Egerton*

SHAMBAR (IRE) 7 ro.g. Linamix (FR) 127 – Shamawna (IRE) (Darshaan 133) [2006 – 11.6d Nov 4] tall gelding: lightly-raced maiden: seemingly useful form final 5-y-o outing: showed nothing only outing on Flat since. *Miss E. C. Lavelle*

SHAMDALA (IRE) 4 b.f. Grand Lodge (USA) 125 – Shamadara (IRE) 114 (Kahyasi **115** 130) [2006 114: 15.5d⁴ 15.5d* 12m* 14m⁴ 12d⁶ 20m² 15.5g 12m³ Dec 10] sturdy filly: smart performer: won Prix Vicomtesse Vigier at Longchamp (by nose from Montare) in May and Gran Premio di Milano (by 1½ lengths from Groom Tesse) in June: creditable efforts afterwards when 2 lengths fourth to Bellamy Cay in Prix Maurice de Nieuil at Longchamp, ¾-length second to Sergeant Cecil in Prix du Cadran on same course and length third to Collier Hill in Hong Kong Vase at Sha Tin (not best of runs before keeping on well): likely to have made frame with clearer run when seventh to Montare in Prix Royal-Oak at Longchamp penultimate start: below form for second successive year in Yorkshire Oaks at York fifth outing: effective at 1½m to 2½m: acts on soft and good to firm going: early to post and mounted on track prior to Prix du Cadran: genuine. *A. de Royer Dupre, France*

SHAMHOOTA (USA) 2 b. or br.c. (Feb 4) Danzig (USA) – Lucky Rainbow (USA) **83 p** 75 (Rainbow Quest (USA) 134) [2006 6m³ 5.2d* Aug 21] $400,000Y: medium-sized, quite attractive colt: has a quick action: first foal: dam, 1¼m winner, out of half-sister to very smart French middle-distance performer Panoramic, and to dam of Giant's Causeway: promising third to Ready For Spring at Newmarket, then easily won 3-runner maiden at Yarmouth later in August: speedy, likely to prove best at 5f/6f: joined K. McLaughlin in USA: will make a useful 3-y-o. *Sir Michael Stoute*

SHAMI 7 ch.h. Rainbow Quest (USA) 134 – Bosra Sham (USA) 132 (Woodman (USA) **54** 126) [2006 –: p12.2g⁵ f12g f11g⁶ f8g³ p10g⁶ May 23] tall, lengthy horse: modest performer nowadays: effective at 1¼m/1½m: acts on polytrack and firm going, probably on soft: has been tongue tied/visored/blinkered. *D. W. Chapman*

SHAMILA 3 b.f. Green Desert (USA) 127 – Shamaiel (IRE) 113 (Lycius (USA) 124) **77** [2006 80p: p7g² 9.2m⁵ 9.9g³ 9.7f² p10g² p10g⁵ Jul 22] tall filly: has scope: just fair maiden in 2006: stays 1¼m: acts on polytrack, firm and soft going: blinkered (below form) second outing: sometimes slowly away/races freely: sent to Bahrain. *G. A. Butler*

SHAMROCK BAY 4 b.f. Celtic Swing 138 – Kabayil 75 (Dancing Brave (USA) 140) **73 d** [2006 77: 12g³ 11.9g³ 14.1s² 14.1g 11.8d⁵ 15.8m p13.9m 13.8s Oct 14] close-coupled filly: fair performer: claimed from L. Lungo £9,000 after reappearance: stays 1¾m: acts on soft and good to firm ground: tongue tied final outing: formerly headstrong: held up. *C. R. Dore*

SHAMROCK TEA 5 b.g. Imperial Ballet (IRE) 110 – Yellow Ribbon (IRE) 72 – (Hamas (IRE) 125§) [2006 –: f5g f8g Apr 4] no longer of any account: tried blinkered. *M. E. Sowersby*

SHAM RUBY 4 ch.f. Tagula (IRE) 116 – Bistro (USA) (Strawberry Road (AUS) 128) **34** [2006 –: p7g 6.1f 7m 6m Sep 12] poor maiden: tongue tied. *M. R. Bosley*

SHAMSALMAIDAN (IRE) 3 ch.f. Fantastic Light (USA) 134 – Maggi For Marg- **63** aret 97 (Shavian 125) [2006 67: 7m 10f 11.5f 11.7m⁵ 11.9m⁵ p13g⁵ 12d Oct 2] sturdy, quite attractive filly: just modest maiden in 2006: stays 1½m: acts on good to firm going: sold 5,000 gns. *C. E. Brittain*

SHAMWARI FIRE (IRE) 6 ch.g. Idris (IRE) 118 – Bobby's Dream 53 (Reference Point 139) [2006 55§, a–§: 10f⁴ 8f 7.5f 8f 8m⁵ 10.1f³ 8m⁶ 8m⁵ Aug 9] only poor performer in 2006: stays 1¼m: acts on firm and good to soft ground, little recent form on all-weather: tried visored, blinkered last 5 starts: unreliable. *I. W. McInnes* **42 §**

SHANAGOLDEN JUAN (IRE) 3 ch.g. King Charlemagne (USA) 120 – Ida Lupino (IRE) (Statoblest 120) [2006 p12g Aug 30] well beaten in maiden at Lingfield. *M. R. Bosley* **–**

SHANAWA (IRE) 2 b.f. (May 20) Cape Cross (IRE) 129 – Yulara (IRE) 99 (Night Shift (USA)) [2006 7m 7.5m⁶ Sep 13] €95,000Y: unfurnished filly: third living foal: half-sister to 7f seller winner Devious Ayers (by Dr Devious): dam 7f winner out of half-sister to Vintage Crop: modest form in maiden on debut: sold 7,000 gns, sent to Kazakhstan. *M. R. Channon* **61**

SHANDELIGHT (IRE) 2 b.f. (Apr 6) Dilshaan 119 – By Candlelight (IRE) 84 (Roi Danzig (USA)) [2006 7d 6g 6g⁶ Sep 27] 11,000Y: half-sister to 3 winners, including useful 2005 2-y-o 6f winner Romantic Evening (by Dr Fong) and fairly useful 5f to 7f winner Twilight Mistress (by Bin Ajwaad): dam 6f winner: little impact in maidens. *Mrs A. Duffield* **–**

SHANE (GER) 2 ch.f. (Mar 3) Kornado 120 – Semplice (IRE) (Common Grounds 118) [2006 6.5g* 8d* Oct 22] €49,000Y: sister to 5-y-o Shapira and half-sister to 3 winners, including useful French performer up to 10.5f Serpenta (by Protektor): dam German maiden: won maiden at Krefeld (by 4½ lengths) in September and 12-runner Preis der Winterkonigin at Baden-Baden (beat Touch My Soul 2½ lengths) in October: stays 1m: joined Godolphin: smart prospect. *A. Lowe, Germany* **106 p**

SHANGAZI (USA) 3 ch.f. Miswaki (USA) 124 – Gran Ole Flag (USA) (El Gran Senor (USA) 136) [2006 8g 7s⁴ 8m 10.3m 8d Oct 2] $20,000F, 31,000Y: workmanlike filly, unfurnished at 3 yrs: fourth foal: half-sister to winners in USA by West By West and Chief Seattle: dam ran 4 times in USA: modest maiden: best efforts first 2 starts. *B. W. Hills* **61**

SHANKLY BOND (IRE) 4 ch.g. Danehill Dancer (IRE) 117 – Fanellan 76 (Try My Best (USA) 130) [2006 82: p9.5g Jan 13] good-topped gelding: fairly useful performer at best: eased as if amiss only outing in 2006. *B. Smart* **–**

SHANK ON FOURTEEN (IRE) 5 b.g. Fayruz 116 – Hever Rosina 63 (Efisio 120) [2006 5d 5f 6f 5.9m 5m 5.1f 5f* 5m⁶ Aug 19] small, good-bodied gelding: missed 2004/05: just fair performer in 2006: won apprentice handicap at Thirsk in July: best at 5f: unraced on heavy going, acts on any other turf and fibresand. *K. R. Burke* **71**

SHANNON ARMS (USA) 5 b.g. Wolf Power (SAF) – Cresta's Best (USA) (Cresta Rider (USA) 124) [2006 76: f6g p7.1g f6g p8.6g* p8.6g² f7g p7.1g⁵ 6v 7m p7.1g p9.5g³ f8g 8.1f p8.6g⁵ p8.6g 7f p8.6g⁴ p8g⁵ p7.1g Dec 4] fair performer: won claimer at Wolverhampton in February: below form after next outing: claimed from K. Ryan fifth start, left P. Howling before twelfth: probably stays easy 9.5f: acts on polytrack and soft going: tried blinkered: sometimes in cheekpieces in 2006: makes running: not straightforward. *R. Brotherton* **74 d**

SHANNON HOUSE 3 ch.g. Inchinor 119 – Sulitelma (USA) 63 (The Minstrel (CAN) 135) [2006 63: p8g⁶ p8g 8m⁵ 7m⁶ 7m⁵ 6.1d⁵ 6f⁵ 6f⁵ p10g Jun 29] modest maiden: stays 1m: acts on polytrack and good to firm ground: tried in cheekpieces/visor. *M. J. McGrath* **62**

SHANTINA'S DREAM (USA) 2 b.f. (Apr 9) Smoke Glacken (USA) 120 – J'Aime Jeblis (USA) (Jeblar (USA)) [2006 6.1g⁵ 6g⁶ 5m Sep 12] $32,000Y, resold $35,000Y: half-sister to several winners in USA: dam US 6f winner, including at 2 yrs: modest form in maidens first 2 starts (stumbled badly debut): weakened quickly final one (reportedly lost tongue tie): once withdrawn (unruly stalls). *H. Morrison* **60**

SHAPE UP (IRE) 6 b.g. Octagonal (NZ) 126 – Bint Kaldoun (IRE) 82 (Kaldoun (FR) 122) [2006 85: 10v² 10.5g⁶ 10.5g 11m 12m⁴ 10g 12.4s f12g⁴ Nov 15] close-coupled, quite good-topped gelding: fairly useful handicapper: below form after reappearance: stays 1½m: acts on all-weather and any turf going: blinkered. *R. Craggs* **86 d**

SHAPIRA (GER) 5 ch.m. Kornado 120 – Semplice (IRE) (Common Grounds 118) [2006 117: 8m 8s⁵ 8g² Sep 3] strong, close-coupled mare: just fairly useful in 2006: well held in Windsor Forest Stakes at Royal Ascot on reappearance: better effort after when second in listed race at Baden-Baden: raced mainly at 1m: acts on good to soft going. *A. Lowe, Germany* **93**

SHARAAB (USA) 5 b. or br.g. Erhaab (USA) 127 – Ghashtah (USA) (Nijinsky (CAN) **52** 138) [2006 59: p12g 16g* p16g⁵ Oct 23] tall, rather leggy gelding: has a quick action: modest performer: won handicap at Thirsk in August: stays 2m: acts on polytrack, good to firm and good to soft going: effective tongue tied or not: none too reliable: won over fences in August. *D. E. Cantillon*

SHARAPOVA (IRE) 3 b.f. Elusive Quality (USA) – Naazeq 80 (Nashwan (USA) 135) **72** [2006 87: 7d* 8m 7d⁵ 8d Oct 15] tall, quite good-topped filly: sixth foal: half-sister to 3 winners, notably smart 7f to 9f (in USA) winner Tamweel (by Gulch): dam, 10.5f winner, sister to smart performer up to 2½m Shaya: just fair performer in 2006: won 24-runner maiden at the Curragh in May: well held in listed handicap at Royal Ascot next time: should stay 1m: acts on heavy going. *M. J. Grassick, Ireland*

SHARDDA 6 b.m. Barathea (IRE) 127 – Kronengold (USA) (Golden Act (USA)) [2006 **–** –: f8g May 9] tall mare: maiden: no recent form: tried tongue tied/visored. *F. Watson*

SHARDIA (IRE) 3 b.f. Marju (IRE) 127 – Shabarana (FR) (Nishapour (FR) 125) [2006 **58** 51: p7.1g⁶ p8.6g 10d³ 14.1m⁵ 12m 9.9g 10d³ 9.1v Oct 28] good-topped filly: modest maiden: stays 1¼m: acts on polytrack and good to soft going. *J. Jay*

SHARES (IRE) 6 b.g. Turtle Island (IRE) 123 – Glendora (Glenstal (USA) 118) [2006 **–** –: 12.4g May 1] good-bodied gelding: lightly-raced maiden on Flat: tried tongue tied/ blinkered: fair hurdler/chaser. *P. Monteith*

SHARE THE FEELING (IRE) 4 b.f. Desert King (IRE) 129 – Antapoura (IRE) 82 **68** (Bustino 136) [2006 12g⁵ 10v 12f⁴ 14m⁵ 13f 14s⁵ 16d⁴ 12f 14v p13.9g* p13.9g² p16.5g* Dec 29] fourth foal: half-sister to 3 winners, including fairly useful 2001 2-y-o 6f/7f winner Richest Vein (by Ali-Royal) and unreliable 5f (at 2 yrs) to 8.5f winner Rocinante (by Desert Story): dam Irish 1¾m/2m winner and useful staying hurdler: fair handi-capper: left S. Slevin in Ireland after ninth outing: won twice (first one apprentice event) at Wolverhampton in December: stays 2m: acts on polytrack and firm going, probably on soft. *J. W. Unett*

SHARIKI (USA) 3 br. or b.c. Spectrum (IRE) 126 – Zahrat Dubai 114 (Unfuwain **83** (USA) 131) [2006 83p: p10g⁵ Sep 2] quite good-topped colt: fairly useful performer, very lightly raced: tongue tied, creditable fifth to Stotsfold in handicap at Kempton only out-ing in 2006: stays 1¼m: raced on polytrack, good to firm and good to soft going: joined D. Selvaratnam in UAE. *Saeed bin Suroor*

SHARMY (IRE) 10 b.g. Caerleon (USA) 132 – Petticoat Lane (Ela-Mana-Mou 132) **–** [2006 12m 11.8d Aug 13] close-coupled, quite attractive gelding: useful performer at best: missed 2005: well held in 2006. *Ian Williams*

SHARPAZMAX (IRE) 2 b.c. (Apr 20) Daggers Drawn (USA) 114 – Amour Toujours **86 p** (IRE) (Law Society (USA) 130) [2006 6m⁵ p7g* p7g* p7g* Dec 19] €17,000F, 22,000Y: brother to Italian 8.5f to 11.5f winner and half-brother to several winners, including 8-y-o Caliban: dam placed at 2 yrs in France over 9f: fairly useful form: progressed well late in year (off 3½ months after debut), winning maiden and minor event in November, and nursery (by neck from Baylini) in December, all at Lingfield: will stay 1m: capable of better still. *P. J. Makin*

SHARP DRESSER (USA) 2 ch.f. (Mar 25) Diesis 133 – A La Mode (USA) 77 **80 p** (Known Fact (USA) 135) [2006 p7g² Oct 26] seventh foal: half-sister to fairly useful 7f winner More Modern (by Mt Livermore): dam, 9f winner in USA at 5 yrs, half-sister to Oaks winner Reams of Verse and Eclipse winner Elmaamul (by Diesis): not knocked about when 2½ lengths second to Baylini in maiden at Lingfield: will stay 1m+: sure to improve. *Mrs A. J. Perrett*

SHARP DUO (IRE) 3 ch.g. Daggers Drawn (USA) 114 – Fay's Song (IRE) 84 (Fayruz **–** 116) [2006 60: p8.6g 7.1m 8m 7d Oct 10] big, strong gelding: modest maiden at 2 yrs: little form in 2006. *M. S. Saunders*

SHARPE IMAGE (IRE) 3 b.f. Bluebird (USA) 125 – Silvretta (IRE) 73 (Tirol 127) **–** [2006 –p: 8.2m 7.5f 12f Jul 3] leggy filly: little form. *G. Woodward*

SHARP HAT 12 ch.g. Shavian 125 – Madam Trilby (Grundy 137) [2006 54, a50: f5g* **61** p5.1g p6g⁴ f5g⁵ p5g⁴ 5.9m 5f* 5f⁴ 6m³ 5m⁵ 5m 5m 5s³ 5d² f5m p5.1g⁵ p5g² f5g⁶ **a55** Dec 29] leggy, angular gelding: modest performer, better on turf than all-weather: won banded race at Southwell in April and handicap at Musselburgh in June: best at 5f/6f: acts on all-weather and any turf going: tried in cheekpieces/blinkers. *D. W. Chapman*

SHARPLAW AUTUMN (USA) 3 b.f. Red Ransom (USA) – Hawzah (Green Desert **83** (USA) 127) [2006 83p: 8.5f* 10m⁶ 8.3m² 8m³ 9m p10g Oct 20] leggy filly: fairly useful performer: won maiden at Beverley in April: should stay at least 1¼m: acts on firm going: visored (below form) final outing: sold 28,000 gns, sent to USA. *W. J. Haggas*

SHARP N FROSTY 4 b.g. Somayda (IRE) 98 – Wily Miss (Teenoso (USA) 135) **67** [2006 67: 11.8d 14m* 16m 14m Aug 11] good-bodied gelding: fair handicapper: won at Haydock in June: stays 1¾m: acts on good to firm and good to soft going: has hung left. *W. M. Brisbourne*

SHARP REPLY (USA) 4 b.g. Diesis 133 – Questonia 107 (Rainbow Quest (USA) **80** 134) [2006 87: 10.5g 10g 12m⁴ 11.5g 12d 10d⁶ 11m 14g⁶ 13.9s² Oct 7] lengthy gelding: fairly useful handicapper: stays 1¾m: acts on firm and soft going: has been visored: sold 20,000 gns, joined Mrs S. Bradburne, won on hurdling debut in December. *R. M. Whitaker*

SHARPSBURG (USA) 3 b.c. Giant's Causeway (USA) 132 – Sofitina (USA) (Alydar **89** (USA)) [2006 89p: 9.9g* Aug 25] tall, lengthy colt: left J. Gosden, won maiden at Salisbury by 2½ lengths from Accompanist on belated return in August: would have been suited to 1¼m+: looked a useful prospect, but was put down in October. *Saeed bin Suroor*

SHARP THRUST (IRE) 3 b.g. Daggers Drawn (USA) 114 – Oumaladia (IRE) 84 **–** (Waajib 121) [2006 75: p6g p8g Feb 8] fair maiden at 2 yrs: gelded, well held in 2006: stayed 6f: acted on polytrack and good to firm ground: dead. *A. P. Jarvis*

SHARP TUNE (USA) 4 ch.g. Diesis 133 – Moonflute (USA) 82 (The Minstrel (CAN) **–** 135) [2006 –: p8g Dec 15] no form. *J. D. Frost*

SHATIN LEADER 4 b.f. Atraf 116 – Star Dancer (Groom Dancer (USA) 128) [2006 **47 §** 50§: 5g 6f⁵ 5m 5f 6m⁴ 5d⁴ 5m⁶ 6g⁵ Jul 20] only poor performer in 2006: stays 6f: acts on firm going: usually wears cheekpieces: tends to hang right: ungenuine. *Miss L. A. Perratt*

SHAUNAS VISION (IRE) 7 b.m. Dolphin Street (FR) 125 – In Behind (IRE) 52 **78** (Entitled 126) [2006 74: p12g* 12s* p12g² p12g* 11.7g⁵ p12g⁵ p13.9g p12.2g² Jul 20] **a88** second foal: dam 1½m to 2m winner: fairly useful handicapper on all-weather, fair on turf: left M. Halford in Ireland, won handicaps at Lingfield (2) and Folkestone in March/April: stays 1½m: acts on polytrack, firm and soft going: tried in cheekpieces/blinkers/tongue tie. *D. K. Ivory*

SHAVA 6 b.g. Atraf 116 – Anita Marie (IRE) (Anita's Prince 126) [2006 p7g³ p7.1g p7g³ **57** p6g* Dec 13] modest performer: won banded race at Lingfield in December: stays 7f: acts on polytrack and good to firm going: tried blinkered/in cheekpieces/tongue tied. *H. J. Evans*

SHAVOULIN (USA) 2 b. or br.c. (Jan 16) Johannesburg (USA) 127 – Hello Josephine **79** (USA) (Take Me Out (USA)) [2006 6m 7s⁴ Oct 10] leggy colt: first foal: dam 6f winner in USA (including at 2 yrs): better run in maidens when fourth to Hollow Ridge at Newbury (edgy), forcing pace: likely to prove best up to 7f. *C. Wroe, UAE*

SHAWL 3 ch.f. Shahrastani (USA) 135 – Circlet 74 (Lion Cavern (USA) 117) [2006 **–** 9.7d 12m Apr 25] first foal: dam 1m winner: well held in maidens at Folkestone. *B. J. Meehan*

SHAYDREAMBELIEVER 3 ch.g. Daggers Drawn (USA) 114 – Aunt Sadie 71 **74** (Pursuit of Love 124) [2006 70: 10v⁶ 10m 10.3f² 11f³ 10.3m 9.8s 11.6d f12g Dec 23] big, strong, workmanlike gelding: fair handicapper: likely to prove best around 1m/1¼m: acts on firm and good to soft going, probably on soft: said to have bled final start. *R. A. Fahey*

SHEA'S ROUND 2 b.c. (Apr 3) Josr Algarhoud (IRE) 118 – Elms Schoolgirl 79 (Ema- **–** rati (USA) 74) [2006 p7g⁶ p8g Dec 19] well held in minor event/maiden. *G. L. Moore*

SHEBANG (IRE) 2 b.f. (Mar 22) Trans Island 119 – Mystery Hill (USA) 72 (Danehill **72** (USA) 126) [2006 7.6f² 7d² p7g⁴ 6d* 7d p6m⁴ Nov 8] 17,000Y: third foal: half-sister to Irish 5f/6f winner Lilly Be (by Titus Livius): dam 7f winner in UAE: fair performer: won maiden at Brighton in September: in frame all other starts bar only try in nursery: stays 7.6f: acts on polytrack, firm and good to soft going: sent to USA. *M. G. Quinlan*

SHEIKH SHAKEY 5 b.g. Muhtarram (USA) 125 – Princesse Zelda (FR) 45 (Defen- **–** sive Play (USA) 118) [2006 p12.2g 10g Apr 29] lengthy gelding: behind in maidens. *R. Hannon*

SHEKAN STAR 4 b.f. Sri Pekan (USA) 117 – Celestial Welcome 96 (Most Welcome **62** 131) [2006 57: p12g* 9.9f² 12.4m p12g 10d³ 13f* 13f⁵ 12.1f² 12m² 11.8d² 12.1g³ 12.1d⁶ 11.1d Sep 25] smallish, close-coupled filly: modest performer: won banded race at Kempton in April and handicap at Hamilton in June: stays 13f: acts on polytrack, firm and soft going: often slowly away: tough and consistent. *K. G. Reveley*

SHE KNOWS TOO MUCH 2 ch.f. (Mar 23) Tobougg (IRE) 125 – How Do I Know 91 (Petong 126) [2006 p7g Nov 11] second foal: half-sister to 3-y-o What Do You Know: dam 5f (at 2 yrs)/6f winner: last in maiden at Kempton. *G. A. Butler* —

SHELHOM 3 b.g. Green Desert (USA) 127 – Felawnah (USA) 111 (Mr Prospector (USA)) [2006 101p: p8.6g⁶ 10s Oct 21] quite good-topped gelding: fairly useful form: won maiden at Doncaster for M. Jarvis on sole start at 2 yrs: better effort in 2006 when eleventh to Best Prospect in handicap at Newbury: should stay at least 1m: joined D. Selvaratnam in UAE. *Saeed bin Suroor* **91**

SHEPHERDESS (USA) 2 ch.f. (May 16) Stravinsky (USA) 133 – Hushi (USA) (Riverman (USA) 131) [2006 p5g⁴ p6g p5.1g⁵ Nov 25] $62,000F: half-sister to several winners abroad: dam 5f (at 2 yrs) to 6.5f winner in USA, including minor stakes: modest form in maidens on polytrack. *D. M. Simcock* **55**

SHERAFEY (IRE) 2 br.f. (Mar 8) Celtic Swing 138 – Babolna (Generous (IRE) 139) [2006 6v p8.6g Nov 11] €50,000Y: fourth foal: half-sister to Italian winners Baby Pekan (up to 7f) and Squirren (up to 1½m), both by Sri Pekan: dam ran once: well beaten in maidens, tongue tied in second at Wolverhampton. *Edgar Byrne, Ireland* —

SHERGAEL (IRE) 5 b.g. Barathea (IRE) 127 – Shergress 62 (Siberian Express (USA) 125) [2006 55: p8g p6g Dec 22] maiden: no form in 2006: tried tongue tied/blinkered/in cheekpieces. *J. L. Spearing* —

SHERIFF'S DEPUTY 6 b.g. Atraf 116 – Forest Fantasy 61 (Rambo Dancer (CAN) 107) [2006 68: 10g 10.2m p8.6m p9.5g Nov 20] strong gelding: just modest performer in 2006: stays 10.5f: acts on all-weather, firm and good to soft ground: tried tongue tied/in cheekpieces. *C. N. Kellett* **53**

SHERIFF'S SILK 2 b.c. (Feb 21) Forzando 122 – Sylhall (Sharpo 132) [2006 7f f7g³ f8g⁵ f7g* f8g Dec 9] brother to 6-y-o Crimson Silk and fairly useful 2001 2-y-o 5f winner Dearest Daisy, and half-brother to 2 winners: dam unraced: modest performer: won seller at Southwell in November: stays 1m. *B. Smart* **63**

SHERIFF STAR 3 b.f. Killer Instinct 111 – Westcourt Ruby (Petong 126) [2006 7m 8d Oct 2] tall filly: third foal: dam lightly-raced half-sister to useful sprinter Proud Boast: always behind in maidens, fractious before latter start. *N. Tinkler* —

SHERJAWY (IRE) 2 b.c. (Mar 8) Diktat 126 – Arruhan (IRE) 87 (Mujtahid (USA) 118) [2006 6m⁶ 6m⁶ p7g 7d⁴ 6d Nov 4] stocky colt: modest maiden: left L. Cumani 5,000 gns before final start (well beaten in nursery): stays 7f. *Miss Z. C. Davison* **63**

SHERSHA (IRE) 7 b.m. Priolo (USA) 127 – Sheriya (USA) (Green Dancer (USA) 132) [2006 103: 7.5m 6.5m 8m³ 8g 8.9d⁴ 8v⁶ 8m³ 7m⁵ 8.5g⁴ 7m 7m⁶ Jul 8] strong, useful-looking mare: has a rather round action: useful performer: best efforts when length third to Adoration in handicap at Navan and 1¼ lengths fourth to Echelon in Princess Elizabeth Stakes at Epsom seventh/ninth outings: stays 9f: acts on firm and good to soft going: tried tongue tied in 2003: has worn crossed noseband: sold, covered by Bahamian Bounty, 75,000 gns in November, and sent to UAE. *Kevin F. O'Donnell, Ireland* **105**

SHE'S A SOFTIE (IRE) 2 b.f. (Apr 28) Invincible Spirit (IRE) 121 – New Tycoon (IRE) (Last Tycoon 131) [2006 6d Nov 4] 20,000 2-y-o: half-sister to fairly useful 2003 2-y-o 6f winner Matt Blanc (by Night Shift), later winner at 1m in USA, and to several winners in USA: dam, won at 8.5f in USA, half-sister to dam of St Leger winner Mutafaweq: well held in maiden at Windsor. *C. F. Wall* —

SHE'S DUNNETT 3 b.f. Diktat 126 – College Night (IRE) 54 (Night Shift (USA)) [2006 –: f7g 7m² 6d² p6g Nov 18] tall, leggy filly: modest maiden: off nearly 7 months, ran as if amiss final outing: stays 7f: acts on good to firm and good to soft going. *Mrs C. A. Dunnett* **60**

SHES MILLIE 2 b.f. (Mar 18) Auction House (USA) 120 – Wintzig 72 (Piccolo 121) [2006 5.1d 5.5d⁶ 6.1f 5f* 6m⁴ 7f 8g⁴ Sep 14] £1,000Y: unfurnished filly: second foal: half-sister to 3-y-o Shes Minnie: dam 1m winner at 2 yrs: modest performer: won seller at Leicester in July: stays 1m: acts on firm and good to soft going. *J. G. M. O'Shea* **51**

SHES MINNIE 3 b.f. Bertolini (USA) 125 – Wintzig 72 (Piccolo 121) [2006 67: 6v³ p6g⁴ 6m⁶ 5d² 5.1m² p6g 5f² 5f* 5m² 5g⁴ 5.1f 5s Oct 16] strong filly: fairly useful performer: won maiden at Kempton in April and handicap at Haydock in July: stays 6f: acts on polytrack and any turf going: below form in visor/cheekpieces. *J. G. M. O'Shea* **82**

SHE'S MY DREAM (IRE) 4 ch.f. General Monash (USA) 107 – She's My Love 80 (Most Welcome 131) [2006 –: p12.2g Jan 6] lightly-raced maiden: little form. *A. J. Lidderdale* —

SHE'S MY OUTSIDER 4 b.f. Docksider (USA) 124 – Solar Flare (IRE) (Danehill **82** (USA) 126) [2006 82: 10g⁴ 7f p6g² p6g* p7g 6g Oct 12] useful-looking filly: fairly useful performer: won handicap at Kempton in September: effective at 6f to 1m: acts on polytrack, good to firm and good to soft going: free-going sort. *I. A. Wood*

SHE'S OUR BEAUTY (IRE) 3 b.f. Imperial Ballet (IRE) 110 – Eleonora d'Arborea **58** 78 (Prince Sabo 123) [2006 69d: f6g⁵ 5m 5m p6g 5f 5d⁵ 5g³ 5m⁵ 5d 5d 5v f5g* p5.1g f5g Dec 28] just modest performer in 2006: left D. Nicholls after tenth outing: won banded race at Southwell in November: probably best at 5f: acts on fibresand and good to soft ground: visored nowadays: looked very reluctant on reappearance. *S. T. Mason*

SHE'S OUR LASS (IRE) 5 b.m. Orpen (USA) 116 – Sharadja (IRE) (Doyoun 124) **80** [2006 78, a68: 8d 8.9m² 8.1g* 8.1f⁴ 8.9f³ 8d* 8v² 8d⁴ 8.9s Oct 7] sturdy mare: fairly useful handicapper: won at Haydock in July and Newmarket in August: stays easy 1¼m: acts on fibresand (probably on polytrack) and any turf going: held up: reliable. *D. Carroll*

SHE'S SO PRETTY (IRE) 2 ch.f. (Feb 22) Grand Lodge (USA) 125 – Plymsole **65** (USA) 84 (Diesis 133) [2006 7m 7d 8.2m Sep 15] €170,000Y: angular, useful-looking filly: first foal: dam, 2-y-o 7.5f winner who stayed 1¼m, sister to very smart miler Docksider: mid-division in maidens: should be suited by 1¼m/1½m. *W. R. Swinburn*

SHESTHEBISCUIT 4 b.f. Diktat 126 – Selvi (Mummy's Pet 125) [2006 74d: f12g **64 ?** 9m⁵ 12g 9.5d⁶ 8g⁶ 11.9d 9s Oct 20] angular filly: modest maiden: left J. Parkes after reappearance: stays 9.5f: acts on good to firm and good to soft going: tried blinkered. *P. J. Flynn, Ireland*

SHEVCHENKO (IRE) 2 b. or br.c. (Feb 2) Rock of Gibraltar (IRE) 133 – Hula Angel **85 p** (USA) 111 (Woodman (USA) 126) [2006 7m³ 6d³ Oct 27] €250,000Y: good sort, with scope: third foal: half-brother to 3-y-o Sicilian: dam 7f (at 2 yrs, including Rockfel Stakes) and 1m (Irish 1000 Guineas) winner: shaped promisingly when third in maidens (favourite) at Newmarket, left with plenty to do on second occasion when beaten 2½ lengths by Princess Valerina: will improve, and should win races as a 3-y-o. *J. Noseda*

SHE WHISPERS (IRE) 3 b.f. Royal Applause 124 – Zariyba (IRE) (In The Wings **54** 128) [2006 61: p8.6g² p8.6g⁴ p7.1g⁶ p7g⁵ p6g³ p8.6g³ 7.1s⁵ p7.1g⁴ 7f 8d⁶ Oct 8] strong, sturdy filly: modest performer: left G. Chung after second start: effective at 6f to 8.6f: acts on polytrack, firm and soft going: held up. *W. M. Brisbourne*

SHE WHO DARES WINS 6 b.m. Atraf 116 – Mirani (IRE) 55 (Danehill (USA) 126) **–** [2006 52: f5g f6g May 16] smallish, workmanlike mare: maiden: no form in 2006. *L. R. James*

SHE WONT WAIT 2 b.f. (Mar 13) Piccolo 121 – Who Goes There 63 (Wolfhound **61 d** (USA) 126) [2006 p5g⁶ 5g⁴ 5.3m³ 5m⁴ 5m 5m⁵ p5g Jul 12] unfurnished filly: first foal: dam 7f winner who stayed 1m: modest maiden at best: raced around 5f. *T. M. Jones*

SHIBUMI 5 ch.m. Cigar 68 – Hurricane Rose (Windjammer (USA)) [2006 –: 10.2m p8g **–** p7.1g 9.7f Aug 10] tall mare: maiden: lightly raced and no form since 3 yrs. *P. A. Trueman*

SHIFTY 7 b.g. Night Shift (USA) – Crodelle (IRE) (Formidable (USA) 125) [2006 72, **67** a62: 8d⁵ 8m 8.2d⁵ 8.1s f8g² 7.9m 10g⁶ 8.1f f7g* f7g f8g³ f8g³ f8g⁵ f8g⁵ Dec 27] well-**a78** made gelding: has a round action: fair handicapper: won at Southwell in July: all wins at 7f/1m: acts on all-weather and any turf going: tried blinkered/visored: often claimer ridden. *D. Carroll*

SHIFTY NIGHT (IRE) 5 b.m. Night Shift (USA) – Bean Island (USA) (Afleet **–** (CAN)) [2006 62, a70: f6g² f6g⁴ f6g p6g⁴ f6s³ f6g² 6m f6g² 6m f6g 6.1s 6g⁵ Jun 30] **a68** workmanlike mare: fair performer: best at 6f/7f: acts on all-weather, soft and good to firm going: tried in cheekpieces, usually visored nowadays: none too consistent. *Mrs C. A. Dunnett*

SHIITAKE 3 b.f. Cayman Kai (IRE) 114 – Petticoat Rule (Stanford 121§) [2006 7m³ **65** 7m² 8s⁶ Sep 4] lengthy, angular filly: sixth foal: dam of little account over hurdles: fair form in maidens at Thirsk first 2 starts: said to have had breathing problem final outing: should be suited by 1m+. *Miss L. A. Perratt*

SHIMONI 2 b.f. (Mar 10) Mark of Esteem (IRE) 137 – Limuru (Salse (USA) 128) [2006 **75 p** 8m 10.1d* Oct 18] good-topped filly: second foal: dam unraced sister to very smart Italian/US performer up to 1½m Timboroa out of half-sister to very smart 7f/1m performer Efisio: very green on debut, then won maiden at Yarmouth (20/1, beat Cordwain by 1½ lengths) month later: likely to go on improving granted test of stamina. *W. J. Knight*

SHINE AND RISE (IRE) 2 b.c. (Apr 25) Marju (IRE) 127 – Ela Cassini (IRE) (Ela- **62 p** Mana-Mou 132) [2006 p7g Nov 11] €30,000Y, 65,000 2-y-o: third foal: dam unraced half-sister to very smart winner up to 1½m in Hong Kong Indigenous (by Marju): seventh to Russki in maiden at Kempton, not knocked about: should improve. *C. G. Cox*

SHINGLE STREET (IRE) 4 b.g. Bahhare (USA) 122 – Sandystones 60 (Selkirk (USA) 129) [2006 76: p13.9g⁴ 17.2s⁶ f12g 15d 18m 16.2g p13.9g p16g p16.5f p12.2m⁴ Sep 2] leggy gelding: regressive maiden: left Miss V. Williams after fifth start: likely to prove best up to 2m: acts on polytrack, soft and good to firm going: tried in headgear: sometimes looks none too genuine: modest hurdler, joined M. Harris after first of 2 wins in October. *I. A. Wood* **68 d**

SHINKO FEMME (IRE) 5 b.m. Shinko Forest (IRE) – Kilshanny 70 (Groom Dancer (USA) 128) [2006 48: 5.9g 6.9m Aug 7] tall mare: poor performer: stays 7.5f: acts on firm and soft ground: often slowly away, virtually refused to race once at 3 yrs: none too reliable. *J. O'Reilly* **38**

SHINKO (IRE) 3 b.f. Shinko Forest (IRE) – Sharp Circle (IRE) 83 (Sure Blade (USA) 130) [2006 62: p8.6g⁵ p7.1g⁵ 7m 7f³ 8m³ 8f⁵ 8.5m 6f⁴ 7f* 8m 6m Sep 19] quite good-topped filly: modest performer: won maiden handicap at Brighton in August: stays 1m: acts on polytrack and firm ground: tried in cheekpieces/blinkers. *Miss J. Feilden* **60**

SHIPMASTER 3 b.g. Slip Anchor 136 – Cover Look (SAF) (Fort Wood (USA) 117) [2006 71: 11.9g² 14.1d* 16m⁶ Jun 23] angular gelding: useful performer: landed odds in maiden at Nottingham in May: plenty of improvement when 4 lengths sixth to Soapy Danger in Queen's Vase at Royal Ascot only subsequent start: stays 2m: acts on good to firm and good to soft going. *A. King* **98**

SHIP MATE (IRE) 3 b.f. Docksider (USA) 124 – Universal Star 74 (Unfuwain (USA) 131) [2006 58: 10g⁴ p12g⁴ 9.2g 10m 9f Jul 14] €11,000Y: first foal: dam, ran 3 times (would have stayed beyond 1½m), half-sister to Oaks winner Lady Carla: fair maiden at best: well below form in Britain second/third starts: stays 1¼m: best effort on good going: free-going sort. *E. Tyrrell, Ireland* **70**

SHIRAZI 8 b.g. Mtoto 134 – Al Shadeedah (USA) 86 (Nureyev (USA) 131) [2006 p10g⁵ p12g Jan 25] strong gelding: twice-raced on Flat since 2003, better effort (fair form) when fifth in handicap at Lingfield: should stay 1½m: acts on polytrack, firm and soft ground: has been tongue tied: held up. *D. R. Gandolfo* **73**

SHIRLEY OAKS (IRE) 8 b.m. Sri Pekan (USA) 117 – Duly Elected (Persian Bold 123) [2006 56: f5g³ p6g p6g* p6g⁴ p7g f5g f5g³ p6g p7g Dec 19] small, sparely-made mare: modest performer: won claimer at Lingfield in February: best at 6f/7f: acts on all-weather, good to firm and good to soft going: has been blinkered/visored/tongue tied: sometimes slowly away. *Miss Z. C. Davison* **56**

SHIROCCO (GER) 5 b.h. Monsun (GER) 124 – So Sedulous (USA) 102 (The Minstrel (CAN) 135) [2006 128: 12s* 12g* 12m* 12m Oct 1] **129**

'How can I compare them? It is like comparing me with Naomi Campbell.' Andre Fabre's reluctance during the latest season to pronounce on the respective merits of the two top older horses in his stable, Shirocco and Hurricane Run, was natural, especially given that they were in different ownership. The question seemed less pressing after both were beaten behind their three-year-old stablemate Rail Link in the Prix de l'Arc de Triomphe, fourth past the post Hurricane Run forced to switch at a vital stage and never looking like repeating his victory of twelve months earlier, and Shirocco folding tamely in the straight to finish last of the eight runners. It was Shirocco's first defeat since his fourth in the same race the previous year when, after being transferred to Fabre only in late-summer, he finished just over four lengths behind the winner, his trainer, in hindsight, believing that he 'wasn't fit enough for an Arc.' The only other time Shirocco and Hurricane Run met was in the Prix Foy Gray d'Albion Barriere on the 'day of trials' at Long-champ three weeks before the latest Arc. Shirocco beat Hurricane Run by a neck, with Pride the same distance away third, in a race that developed into a sprint and was very much a 'trial', none of the protagonists unduly knocked about and the strong-finishing Pride all but getting up. Hurricane Run was soon out twice after the Arc, finishing third in the Champion Stakes and sixth in the Breeders' Cup Turf, the last-named a race Shirocco had won the year before. After veterinary checks failed to turn up any explanation for Shirocco's performance in the Arc, it was announced that he would probably be going for the Turf again, though he would have had to be supplemented. However, Shirocco, who had won Group/Grade 1 races in Germany,

Vodafone Coronation Cup, Epsom—Shirocco lands the odds, staying on too strongly for Ouija Board; Enforcer is third, ahead of Ace and Notable Guest

Italy, North America and Britain, was then purchased by Sheikh Mohammed as a stallion for Dalham Hall Stud at Newmarket and wasn't seen out after Longchamp.

Shirocco and Hurricane Run looked at one time as if they would meet in Britain's most prestigious, open-aged championship, the King George VI and Queen Elizabeth Stakes at Ascot in July. Shirocco's campaign in the first half of the season was geared around the British programme, his reappearance in the StanJamesUK.com Jockey Club Stakes at Newmarket in early-May providing an additional highlight on One Thousand Guineas day. Shirocco was still relatively lightly raced before the latest season, having run six times as a three-year-old (for Andreas Schutz in Germany), when the Deutsches Derby and the Gran Premio del Jockey Club were among his three wins, and only three times at four (all for Fabre, starting with a third after a lengthy lay-off in the Prix Foy). Shirocco had led home a European one, two, three, four in the Breeders' Cup Turf, winning from Ace, the unlucky Azamour and Bago. Shirocco's performance in the Jockey Club Stakes, readily going clear to beat Munsef very smoothly by three and a half lengths, suggested that he was probably better than ever and his presence in the line-up for the Vodafone Coronation Cup on Oaks day, along with another of the Breeders' Cup winners, the 2004 Oaks winner Ouija Board, created nearly as much interest as in the classic itself.

Shirocco started odds on at Epsom, as he had at Newmarket, and was always holding Ouija Board through the last two furlongs after being sent on and making the best of his way home from Tattenham Corner. With 66/1-shot Enforcer close behind Ouija Board in third, in what was initially a muddling, tactical affair, the form of the Coronation Cup could not be rated so highly as that shown by Shirocco in the Jockey Club Stakes. However, it was clear that Shirocco was going

Prix Foy Gray d'Albion Barriere, Longchamp—Shirocco maintains his unbeaten record for the season in this Arc trial, holding stable-companion Hurricane Run and Pride

to be a major contender for the King George, in which, as well as Hurricane Run, he looked set to meet the Dubai World Cup winner Electrocutionist and high-class Japanese challenger Heart's Cry. Shirocco had still to tackle going firmer than good in his career, conditions which often prevail at Ascot in July, but, when the announcement came in June that he would not, after all, be running in the King George, the reason given by the owner's racing manager was that the owner preferred to save Shirocco for the autumn, as 'the Arc is definitely the main aim and not many King George winners go on to win the Arc.' There seemed a presumption in the statement that Shirocco would have beaten Hurricane Run, Electrocutionist and Heart's Cry, the first three in the King George, but, if Shirocco's connections were indeed so confident, they must have regretted passing up the opportunity, given the way the rest of Shirocco's season turned out. His victory in the Prix Foy, by the way, arguably showed that he could handle good to firm going, though his performance under similar conditions in the Arc three weeks later was easily the worst since he had been stepped up to top company, as well as being the only time in his career that he finished out of the frame. The genuine Shirocco was probably ideally suited by good going or softer, and he acted on heavy. He was campaigned throughout his career at around a mile and a half.

Shirocco (GER) (b.h. 2001)	Monsun (GER) (br 1990)	Konigsstuhl (br 1976)	Dschingis Khan
			Konigskronung
		Mosella (b 1985)	Surumu
			Monasia
	So Sedulous (USA) (b 1991)	The Minstrel (ch 1974)	Northern Dancer
			Fleur
		Sedulous (b 1986)	Tap On Wood
			Pendulina

Baron G. Von Ullmann's "Shirocco"

The strong, good-bodied Shirocco, who has a powerful, rounded action, will be standing at a fee of £10,000 in 2007. Stallions who have the maximum sixty-two different names in their extended five-generation pedigree—like Shirocco—are becoming rarer in these days when sires such as Northern Dancer and Mr Prospector have so much influence. Finding suitable mates for Shirocco should, therefore, be straightforward, while the emergence of his own sire Monsun as a major force can only help further in giving Shirocco a good start. Monsun was a high-class middle-distance performer, one of the best horses of his era in Germany who was at his best when the mud was flying. He sired the winners of sixteen pattern races in Europe in the latest season, only two fewer than the leading sire in that category, Danehill. The totals of both Monsun and Danehill were achieved with eleven individual winners, two more than the total of any other stallion, including Sadler's Wells who was third behind Danehill and Monsun. Monsun, who stands in Germany, was champion sire in both Germany (for the fourth time), where one son Schiaparelli won the Deutsches Derby, and in Italy, where another Gentlewave won the Derby Italiano. Monsun also finished second to Rail Link's sire Dansili in the sires' list in France. Shirocco's dam So Sedulous, a useful and consistent miler who won twice for Geoff Wragg, has also made a name for herself at stud in Germany where her offspring include two smart brothers to Shirocco in Subiaco and Storm Trooper who were placed in the Deutsches Derby. Another useful brother, September Storm, started third favourite for the 2005 edition, only to slip and unseat his rider. So Sedulous has two other offspring by Monsun coming along, a two-year-old filly called So Squally and a yearling filly called Swish. Shirocco is not so stoutly bred as many top German horses, his grandam Sedulous, also a useful race-mare, being successful at five furlongs to a mile at two in Ireland, where she won the Killavullan Stakes (she was later successful in North America). Sedulous was a sister to another useful two-year-old in Tapolite and a half-sister to the unraced Disregard That, dam of the smart sprinter Miss Emma. *A. Fabre, France*

SHMOOKH (USA) 2 b.c. (May 4) Green Desert (USA) 127 – Elrafa Ah (USA) 105 **85** (Storm Cat (USA)) [2006 7f 6g³ 6d² Oct 27] sturdy, good-bodied colt: closely related to high-class 1998 2-y-o 6f/7f (Dewhurst Stakes) winner Mujahid (by Danzig) and 3-y-o Nawaqees, and half-brother to 7f winner Raajiya (by Gulch): dam 5f (at 2 yrs) and 6f winner who stayed 1m: progressive form in maidens at Newmarket, placed behind Truly Royal then Princess Valerina in autumn: will prove best up to 7f. *J. L. Dunlop*

SHOGUN PRINCE (IRE) 3 b.g. Shinko Forest (IRE) – Lady of Dreams (IRE) 84 **88** (Prince Rupert (FR) 121) [2006 88: 8.2d 7m 8.3d² 8g³ 10g³ 10d⁵ p10g⁶ p8g Sep 18] sturdy, compact gelding: fairly useful handicapper: reportedly split a pastern final 2-y-o outing: stays 1¼m: acts on polytrack and good to soft ground, trip too short only start on good to firm: tried visored: gelded after final outing. *A. King*

SHOLTO 8 b.g. Tragic Role (USA) – Rose Mill (Puissance 110) [2006 54: 5f 6m Jul 4] **45** close-coupled gelding: poor performer nowadays: best at 5f: acts on polytrack, firm and soft going: blinkered: tried tongue tied: often hangs: has bolted to post: reportedly bled final outing. *J. O'Reilly*

SHOOF (USA) 7 b.m. Dayjur (USA) 137 – Shemaq (USA) 98 (Blushing John (USA) **–** 120) [2006 f8g f11g Feb 5] fair maiden in 2002 for A. Stewart: well held both outings since (had a foal in 2004). *M. J. Gingell*

SHOPFITTER 3 b.c. Sugarfoot 118 – Madam Wurlitzer (Noble Patriarch 115) [2006 **49** 56d: p6g 6m 6d⁶ f5g³ f6g³ 6.1d⁶ f6g⁵ 6m Jun 17] good-bodied colt: poor maiden: stays 6f: acts on fibresand: blinkered/visored. *Mrs C. A. Dunnett*

SHORE THING (IRE) 3 b.c. Docksider (USA) 124 – Spicebird (IRE) 67 (Ela-Mana- **82** Mou 132) [2006 68p: 7m⁶ 8g 14.1m* 14g² 13.9f³ 14.1m³ 14.1g² 12m Sep 20] big, strong colt: fairly useful handicapper: won at Yarmouth in June: twice good second after: stays 1¾m: acts on firm going: sometimes finds little: sold 80,000 gns. *M. H. Tompkins*

SHORTBREAD 4 ch.g. Selkirk (USA) 129 – Breadcrumb 111 (Final Straw 127) [2006 **–** 69: 8.1d 10g 11g 11.6m 7d Aug 13] plain gelding: lightly-raced maiden, no form in 2006: tried in cheekpieces/tongue tied. *M. Salaman*

SHORT DANCE (USA) 3 b.f. Hennessy (USA) 122 – Clog Dance 103 (Pursuit of **105** Love 124) [2006 98: 7m³ 8s* 8v 7f⁴ 7g 7.5v⁶ Oct 1] big, strong filly: useful performer: won listed race at York in May by 12 lengths from Salut d'Amour, dictating pace: creditable 2½ lengths fourth to Red Evie in Oak Tree Stakes at Goodwood fourth start: below form in Park Stakes at York (on edge) and Concorde Stakes at Tipperary last 2 starts: stayed 1m: acted on firm and soft going: often raced prominently: stud. *B. W. Hills*

SHORTEST DAY 3 b.f. Zafonic (USA) 130 – Winter Solstice 104 (Unfuwain (USA) 131) [2006 92: 10m* 11.5m 8m⁴ 9.9m Aug 19] good-topped filly: good walker, easy mover: useful performer: won handicap at Pontefract in May: good 3 lengths fourth to Red Evie in listed handicap at Royal Ascot third start: ran poorly over 2 appearances (lost a shoe first occasion): stayed 1¼m: raced only on good/good to firm going: tongue tied last 2 outings: stud. *Sir Michael Stoute* **98**

SHORTHAND 2 b.f. (Apr 16) Diktat 126 – Much Too Risky 87 (Bustino 136) [2006 8.2g* 7d⁴ Oct 14] useful-looking filly: sister to 3-y-o Short Skirt, closely related to very smart 7f (at 2 yrs) to 1½m winner Little Rock (by Warning) and half-sister to several winners, notably smart 1m to 13.5f winner Whitewater Affair (by Machiavellian) and 5-y-o Cleaver: dam 2-y-o 7f/1m winner: smooth winning debut in maiden at Nottingham in September: 8/1, useful form when 6¾ lengths fourth of 14 to Finsceal Beo in Rockfel Stakes at Newmarket, rallying: will be suited by 1¼m/1½m: sure to go on to better things at 3 yrs. *Sir Michael Stoute* **95 p**

SHORT SKIRT 3 br.f. Diktat 126 – Much Too Risky 87 (Bustino 136) [2006 95p: 10.4d* 12g³ 12d² 12.5m⁶ 12s* Oct 21] tall, quite good-topped filly: has plenty of scope: smart performer: much improved in 2006, winning Tattersalls Musidora Stakes at York (by 1¼ lengths from Alexandrova, not clear run 2f out) in May and Stan James St Simon Stakes at Newbury (beat Mountain by 2 lengths, despite edging right/idling) in October: also ran well when 3½ lengths second to Alexandrova in Yorkshire Oaks at York third start: stays 1½m: acts on soft going (below form in Prix de Royallieu at Longchamp on good to firm): joint second favourite, on toes in paddock and fairly mulish before entering stall in Oaks at Epsom (7¼ lengths third to Alexandrova, running around on undulations): tends to look awkward under pressure: sold 1,400,000 gns in November, joined Godolphin. *Sir Michael Stoute* **117**

SHORT STUFF 2 b.g. (Apr 29) Atraf 116 – Cedar Lady (Telsmoss 91) [2006 p7.1g p8g⁶ p6g⁶ Dec 4] little form in sellers. *R. J. Hodges* **–**

SHOSHONI 3 ch.f. Indian Ridge 123 – Vituisa (Bering 136) [2006 7m 7m 6.1m⁴ 7.5g* a7.5g Oct 17] lengthy, good-bodied filly: second foal: sister to useful French 7.5f/1m winner Terra Verde: dam, French 11.5f winner, out of smart 1m/1¼m (Sun Chariot Stakes) winner La Confederation: well held in maidens in Britain first 3 starts: left M. Jarvis 10,000 gns, won amateurs event at Rome in September: will stay 1m. *G. Colella, Italy* **?**

SHOSOLOSA (IRE) 4 br.f. Dansili 127 – Hajat 64 (Mujtahid (USA) 118) [2006 10d f7g⁴ 8f³ 8f³ 8f 10m² 10g 9m 10.2m Oct 8] close-coupled filly: fair maiden handicapper: missed 2005: left B. Meehan after fourth outing: stays 1¼m: yet to race on heavy going, acts on any other turf and fibresand: tried in cheekpieces. *Mrs A. L. M. King* **65**

SHOTFIRE RIDGE 3 ch.g. Grand Lodge (USA) 125 – Darya (USA) (Gulch (USA)) [2006 8.2g* Sep 26] lengthy, angular gelding: third foal: half-brother to useful 6f (at 2 yrs) and 1¼m winner Brave Call (by Theatrical): dam unraced close relative to US Grade 1 1¼m winner Stuka: 28/1, won maiden at Nottingham in September by 1¼ lengths from Seabow, waited with before sweeping down outside and getting first run: sold 27,000 gns in October: open to improvement. *E. F. Vaughan* **80 p**

Tattersalls Musidora Stakes, York—Short Skirt (noseband) beats Alexandrova in a strong Oaks trial; Maroussies Wings is third, ahead of Lake Shabla

SHOTLEY DANCER 7 ch.m. Danehill Dancer (IRE) 117 – Hayhurst (Sandhurst Prince 128) [2006 55, a–: f12g⁴ Jan 3] leggy mare: fluent mover: modest performer at best on turf: effective at 1¼m to 2m: acts on firm and soft ground, poor form on fibresand: tried blinkered/in cheekpieces. *N. Bycroft*

– a46

SHOTLEY MAC 2 ch.g. (Mar 30) Abou Zouz (USA) 109 – Julie's Gift (Presidium 124) [2006 5m⁴ 5g 6g Aug 24] workmanlike gelding: maiden: fourth at Carlisle on debut, only form: gelded after final start. *N. Bycroft*

63

SHOT TO FAME (USA) 7 b.g. Quest For Fame 127 – Exocet (USA) (Deposit Ticket (USA)) [2006 107: 8s 8m 8f 7.6d² 7s⁵ 8.5g³ 8m 8m 8f 8s 8d 7f Sep 23] angular, lightly-made gelding: useful handicapper: best efforts in 2006 when placed at Chester (second to Dabbers Ridge) in May and Epsom (third to Hinterland, well ridden from front) in June: tongue tied, well held last 3 starts (also visored penultimate outing): best at 1m/9f: acts on any going: usually races prominently. *D. Nicholls*

98 d

SHOULDNTBETHERE (IRE) 2 ch.g. (Mar 14) Soviet Star (USA) 128 – Octomone (USA) 74 (Hennessy (USA) 122) [2006 7g 6.1m 8d f6m³ f8g* f8g² Nov 28] 1,000F, 4,000Y: good-topped gelding: first foal: dam, Irish maiden who stayed 1½m, out of half-sister to Irish 1000 Guineas winner Trusted Partner: fair performer: won claimer at Southwell in November: good second in nursery there: will stay 1¼m: acts on fibresand. *Mrs P. N. Dutfield*

69

SHOUT (IRE) 3 ch.f. Halling (USA) 133 – Spout 115 (Salse (USA) 128) [2006 10g⁴ 11.4m 10.2m³ 12v p12g* p12.2g⁵ Nov 18] strong, lengthy filly: fourth living foal: half-sister to fairly useful 11f winner Reservoir (by Green Desert) and useful winner around 1½m Sea Wall (by Giant's Causeway): dam 7f (at 2 yrs) to 1½m (Lancashire Oaks) winner who stayed 13.5f: fairly useful performer, lightly raced: won maiden at Lingfield in November: stays 1½m: acts on polytrack and good to firm going: sold 30,000 gns. *R. Charlton*

83

SHOW BUSINESS (IRE) 2 ch.g. (Feb 3) Distant Music (USA) 126 – Gertie Laurie (Lomond (USA) 128) [2006 p6g³ Dec 11] third of 6 finishers in seller at Wolverhampton. *Sir Mark Prescott*

–

SHOW HOUSE (USA) 2 b.f. (Jan 25) Chester House (USA) 123 – Galanty Show 76 (Danehill (USA) 126) [2006 6m⁶ 7g Aug 18] fourth foal: closely related to 5-y-o Chatshow: dam, 6f winner, out of half-sister to Cheveley Park winners Desirable and Park Appeal, Irish Oaks winner Alydaress and to dam of Russian Rhythm: better effort in maidens when sixth to Cheap Street at Windsor: sold 3,000 gns, sent to Spain. *Mrs A. J. Perrett*

57

SHOW ME THE LOLLY (FR) 6 b.m. Sri Pekan (USA) 117 – Sugar Lolly (USA) (Irish River (FR) 131) [2006 64: p9.5g p10g⁵ Dec 13] leggy mare: modest performer: stays 1¼m: acts on polytrack and good to firm going: tried visored. *P. J. McBride*

51

SHOW NO FEAR 5 b.g. Groom Dancer (USA) 128 – La Piaf (FR) (Fabulous Dancer (USA) 124) [2006 f14g⁶ 15.8d Sep 5] good-topped gelding: well held both starts on Flat since 2004: tried visored/tongue tied. *G. M. Moore*

–

SHOW THYME 3 ch.g. Compton Place 125 – Souaadah (USA) (General Holme (USA) 128) [2006 58: f8g Jan 26] lightly-raced maiden: tailed off only outing in 2006. *K. A. Ryan*

–

SHOWTIME ANNIE 5 b.m. Wizard King 122 – Rebel County (IRE) 97 (Maelstrom Lake 118) [2006 58: f11g Oct 12] good-bodied mare: modest performer in 2005, well held only outing in 2006: wears cheekpieces/blinkers. *A. Bailey*

–

SHOWTIME FAYE 4 b.f. Overbury (IRE) 116 – Rebel County (IRE) 97 (Maelstrom Lake 118) [2006 39: f11g p9.5g Mar 27] poor performer: tried visored. *A. Bailey*

–

SHOW TRIAL (IRE) 2 b.f. (Feb 1) Jade Robbery (USA) 121 – Court Lane (USA) 81 (Machiavellian (USA) 123) [2006 6.1f 6m 5.2d² 5m p7g³ 6g⁵ 7.1d* f6g⁶ p7g⁴ p6s³ p7.1g³ Dec 21] close-coupled filly: second reported foal: half-sister to smart 2003 2-y-o 5f winner Holborn (by Green Desert): dam, 6f (at 2 yrs) and 1m (in France) winner, out of Cherry Hinton winner Chicarica: modest performer: claimed from M. Channon £6,000 fourth outing: won maiden at Musselburgh in November: in frame in nurseries last 3 starts: stays 7f: acts on all-weather and good to soft going. *D. J. S. ffrench Davis*

61

SHOW WINNER 3 b.c. Mtoto 134 – Rose Show (Belmez (USA) 131) [2006 p9.5g⁶ 10m² 9.9d³ 10d³ 8.2v* Oct 25] good-topped colt: fifth foal: brother to smart 1¼m winner Prize Winner and half-brother to 4-y-o First Show: dam unraced: fairly useful performer:

81

won maiden at Nottingham in October: stays 1¼m: acts on heavy and good to firm going: veered left on debut. *J. Noseda*

SHREDDY SHRIMPSTER 2 ch.f. (Jan 29) Zilzal (USA) 137 – Empress Dagmar **57** (Selkirk (USA) 129) [2006 5.1g⁶ 5m³ 5.1d² p5g³ 6f⁵ 6f p5.1g Nov 2] unfurnished filly: second foal: dam unraced: modest maiden: claimed from M. Wallace £6,000 third start: raced at 5f/6f. *A. B. Haynes*

SHREWD DUDE 2 b. or br.c. (Apr 15) Val Royal (FR) 127 – Lily Dale (IRE) 78 **54** (Distinctly North (USA) 115) [2006 5.1d 6g p5g p7g⁵ Nov 29] €18,000Y, 20,000 2-y-o: workmanlike colt: first foal: dam, Irish 9f winner, out of Cheveley Park and Irish 1000 Guineas runner-up Millingdale Lillie: modest maiden: will be suited by 1m/1¼m. *C. Llewellyn*

SHRINE MOUNTAIN (USA) 4 b.g. Distorted Humor (USA) 117 – Fancy Ruler **60** (USA) (Half A Year (USA) 130) [2006 66d: p8.6g f7g⁵ f7g f8g² p10g f8g⁴ 8.5d f8g* f8g* **a72** 8.3m³ 8.3f⁴ 8m³ 10g 10.9d⁵ 8d p8.6m³ f8g⁵ f8g f7g* p7.1g Dec 28] good-topped gelding: fair performer on all-weather, modest on turf: won seller and banded race at Southwell in May, and seller there (left J. Holt) in December: stays 10.9f: acts on all-weather, good to firm and good to soft ground: has worn visor, including for all wins: tried tongue tied: free-going sort. *R. A. Harris*

SHRINK 5 b.m. Mind Games 121 – Miss Mercy (IRE) 62 (Law Society (USA) 130) **74** [2006 75: 5g³ 5f 5m⁶ Jul 4] rather leggy mare: fair handicapper: best at 5f: acts on poly-track, firm and good to soft ground: tried blinkered/tongue tied. *M. Dods*

SHROPSHIRELASS 3 b.f. Beat All (USA) 120 – Emma-Lyne 65 (Emarati (USA) 74) **55** [2006 52: p6m 10.2m 8g³ p10g Dec 4] modest maiden: seems to stay 1¼m: acts on polytrack and good to firm going. *Mrs Norma Pook*

SHUMOOKH (IRE) 3 b.g. Mujahid (USA) 125 – Midway Lady (USA) 126 (Alleged **108** (USA) 138) [2006 10f⁴ 8.2g* 8d* 8.3g² 8d* 8.2d⁵ Nov 1] close-coupled, rather lightly-made gelding: closely related to 3 winners by Green Desert, including smart 9f to 1½m (Princess Royal Stakes) winner Itnab and half-brother to several winners, notably Oaks winner Eswarah (by Unfuwain): dam won 1000 Guineas and Oaks: useful performer: made all in maiden at Nottingham and handicap at Pontefract, both in August, and handicap at Pontefract (further improvement when beating Collateral Damage by 6 lengths) in October: 6/4 on, well below form in minor event won by With Interest at Nottingham final outing: should stay 1¼m: raced only on good/good to soft ground after debut (hung left). *M. A. Jarvis*

SHUNKAWAKHAN (IRE) 3 b.g. Indian Danehill (IRE) 124 – Special Park (USA) **61** (Trempolino (USA) 135) [2006 69: p5g⁵ 5f³ p6g 6f p7g³ p8g⁶ 7m⁵ p6g⁶ p6g⁶ p6g² p6g⁴ p5g⁵ p6g Dec 22] quite good-topped gelding: modest maiden: stays 7f: acts on all-weather, firm and good to soft going: tried blinkered. *G. C. H. Chung*

SHUSTRAYA 2 b.f. (Feb 18) Dansili 127 – Nimble Fan (USA) (Lear Fan (USA) 130) **84** [2006 6g⁴ 6g⁴ 6g² p5g² p6g* p6g⁴ p6g² Dec 30] sturdy, close-coupled filly: first foal: dam, lightly-raced French maiden, out of sister to smart performer up to 10.4f Skimble, herself dam of very smart US 1¼m performer Skimming: fairly useful performer: gene-rally progressive, winning maiden at Lingfield in November and nursery at Wolverhamp-ton in December: will prove best at 5f/6f. *P. J. Makin*

SHY GLANCE (USA) 4 b.g. Red Ransom (USA) – Royal Shyness 104 (Royal Acad- **72 +** emy (USA) 130) [2006 –: 10g⁴ 7g⁵ 9.2m⁴ 9.3g⁵ 10.5m³ 12.1g⁶ p8.6g³ 9.2d p7.1g* Nov 3] good-topped gelding: fair handicapper: won at Wolverhampton final start: effective at 7f, barely stays 10.5f: acts on polytrack and good to firm going: reportedly had breathing problem third start, tongue tied next 3 outings. *G. A. Swinbank*

SIAKIRA 3 ch.f. Golden Snake (USA) 127 – Minette 55 (Bishop of Cashel 122) [2006 **72** 67: 8m 10d⁶ 12.1f² 11.5m⁵ p10g⁴ 12m⁶ 10.2m² 10d⁴ p10g Oct 11] sturdy filly: fair maid-en handicapper: stays easy 1½m: acts on polytrack, firm and soft going: sold 8,000 gns. *I. A. Wood*

SIAMESE CAT (IRE) 2 ch.f. (Mar 26) Rock of Gibraltar (IRE) 133 – Real Cat (USA) **99** (Storm Cat (USA)) [2006 6m³ 6.5s² 7d² Oct 28] 70,000Y: smallish, good-bodied filly: first foal: dam unraced half-sister to US Grade 3 6f winner Ifyoucouldseemenow: useful form: placed all 3 starts, in maidens at Newbury and Newmarket (behind Measured Tempo) either side of 3 lengths second of 22 to Indian Ink in sales race at Ascot: stays 7f. *B. J. Meehan*

SICILIAN (IRE) 3 b.g. Sadler's Wells (USA) 132 – Hula Angel (USA) 111 (Woodman **83** (USA) 126) [2006 71: 8.3g³ 8g 8.3d* p8g 8g Aug 19] strong, stocky gelding: fairly useful handicapper: made all at Windsor in June: well held after: stays 8.3f: acts on good to soft going: usually races prominently: sold 16,000 gns, joined P. O'Brady in Ireland. *B. W. Hills*

SIEGFRIEDS NIGHT (IRE) 5 ch.g. Night Shift (USA) – Shelbiana (USA) (Chief- **56** tain) [2006 –: 15.8d⁵ 20s 15.8g⁶ Jun 2] quite good-topped gelding: modest handicapper: probably stays 15.8f: acts on fibresand and firm ground, probably on good to soft: wore tongue strap last 2 starts: fair hurdler, won in June. *M. C. Chapman*

SIENA GOLD 4 br. or b.f. Key of Luck (USA) 126 – Corn Futures 78 (Nomination **74** 125) [2006 94: 5.1g 7.2g p7.1g 6d 6d Aug 28] sturdy filly: only fair performer in 2006: stays 6f: acts on heavy and good to firm going: tried blinkered. *J. G. Given*

SIENA STAR (IRE) 8 b.g. Brief Truce (USA) 126 – Gooseberry Pie 63 (Green Desert **70** (USA) 127) [2006 69: f12s 12g 10.1d⁴ 10m⁶ p12g⁴ 10m⁶ 10.9f* 10.9m 10.1m³ 10g⁶ 9.7f² p12.2g p10g⁴ p10g⁵ p10g² p10g² p10g⁵ p10g* p12.2g Dec 27] close-coupled gelding: has a quick action: just fair nowadays: left Robert Gray after reappearance and Miss Tracy Waggott after third start: won handicaps at Warwick in June and, having left Stef Liddiard after tenth outing and J. Boyle after fourteenth, Lingfield in December: stays easy 1½m: acts on polytrack, firm and soft going: tried blinkered: waited with. *Stef Liddiard*

SIENNA STORM (IRE) 3 b.g. Peintre Celebre (USA) 137 – Saint Ann (USA) 66 **101** (Geiger Counter (USA)) [2006 79: 10.1g³ 11g² 12m 12d 8.9g 14g⁶ Sep 28] angular, well-made gelding: useful performer: good 4 lengths second of 5 to easy winner Championship Point in listed Predominate Stakes at Goodwood in May, drifting right: not discredited when fourteenth behind Sir Percy in Derby at Epsom next time: well held last 3 starts: gelded after: stays at least 11f: blinkered third and fifth outings. *M. H. Tompkins*

SIERRA 5 ch.m. Dr Fong (USA) 128 – Warning Belle (Warning 136) [2006 65: f7g³ **62** f8g* f7g* f8g³ f7g⁵ Feb 16] workmanlike mare: modest performer: won 2 banded races at Southwell in January: effective at 7f, probably at 1¼m: acts on all-weather and firm going. *A. W. Carroll*

SIERRA VISTA 6 ch.m. Atraf 116 – Park Vista (Taufan (USA) 119) [2006 108: 5.1g⁴ **108** 5g² 5m⁴ 5m³ 5.1m 5f 6g 6.1m 5g 5g* 5g³ Oct 12] leggy mare: useful performer: won handicap at Haydock in September by 1½ lengths from If Paradise, making all: ran creditably otherwise in 2006 when making the frame, 2 lengths third to Mecca's Mate in similar event at Newmarket final outing: effective at 5f/6f: acts on polytrack, firm and soft going: tried in cheekpieces: makes running/races up with pace. *D. W. Barker*

SIESTA (IRE) 2 ch.f. (Apr 17) King Charlemagne (USA) 120 – Quiescent 88 (Primo **– p** Dominie 121) [2006 6m Sep 11] €7,000Y: third foal: half-sister to winner up to 9f in Scandinavia by Desert King: dam 2-y-o 5f winner: 8/1, needed experience when beating one in maiden at Folkestone: should do better. *J. R. Fanshawe*

SI FOO (USA) 2 ch.c. (Feb 23) Fusaichi Pegasus (USA) 130 – Ascension (IRE) 110 **79 p** (Night Shift (USA)) [2006 p6g² 6f* Jul 31] second foal: dam 6f (at 2 yrs) to 1m (Prix d'Astarte) winner: confirmed debut promise (second to Al Khaleej) when winning maiden at Windsor later in July, still rather green: will stay 7f/1m: capable of better. *A. M. Balding*

SIGISMUNDUS (IRE) 3 b.g. Mozart (IRE) 131 – Bella Vie (IRE) (Sadler's Wells **–** (USA) 132) [2006 69: p8g p7g² p6g⁶ p7.1g* p7g p6g 7s⁶ 7f p6g p6g⁶ 7d p7g Oct 11] fair **a72** performer: won handicap at Wolverhampton in January: below form after: stays 7f: acts on polytrack, no form on turf: tried in cheekpieces: sold 5,000 gns. *J. R. Boyle*

SIGNAL HILL 3 ch.g. Observatory (USA) 131 – Rose Des Andes (IRE) (Royal Aca- **74** demy (USA) 130) [2006 64: 8d² 8f⁴ 8f² p8.6f³ p8.6g² p9.5m Oct 9] fair maiden handicapper: stays 8.6f, pulled hard in blinkers at 9.5f: acts on polytrack, firm and good to soft ground: also tried visored: sold 31,000 gns. *W. J. Haggas*

SIGNATORY (USA) 4 b.c. Kris S (USA) – Escrow Agent (USA) (El Gran Senor **105** (USA) 136) [2006 97: 12d* 11.9g⁴ 13.9d Aug 23] big, rangy colt: has a fluent, round action: useful handicapper, lightly raced: impressive return to win at Newmarket (beat River Alhaarth 3 lengths) in May, dictating pace: fair fourth to Consular in Old Newton Cup at Haydock next time: well-backed favourite, ran as though amiss when last in Ebor at York final outing: should stay at least 1¾m: yet to race on extremes of going: has been bandaged hind joints: sold 90,000 gns, joined N. Meade in Ireland. *J. H. M. Gosden*

SIGN OF THE CROSS 2 b.c. (Mar 29) Mark of Esteem (IRE) 137 – Thea (USA) 95 **77 p** (Marju (IRE) 127) [2006 p8g² Nov 8] sixth foal: half-brother to 3 winners, including fairly useful 2001 2-y-o 1m winner Zone (by Zilzal) and useful winner around 1¼m Song of Songs (by Singspiel): dam 7f winner: head second to Mafeking in maiden at Kempton, looking green under pressure: sure to improve. *J. R. Fanshawe*

SIGNOR ALBERTINI (IRE) 3 b.g. Bertolini (USA) 125 – Snow Eagle (IRE) 57 – (Polar Falcon (USA) 126) [2006 –: 7g 9.8d Aug 29] little sign of ability. *P. C. Haslam*

SIGNOR PANETTIERE 5 b.g. Night Shift (USA) – Christmas Kiss 82 (Taufan ? (USA) 119) [2006 5.1m a5g³ Aug 5] well-made gelding: has reportedly had wind operation: fair performer for R. Hannon (left him during 2004): completed 4-timer at Mijas in 2005: well beaten in handicap at Chester on reappearance (tongue tied), then third of 4 in minor event at Mijas: headstrong and best at 5f: acts on sand and firm going: has looked hard ride: formerly untrustworthy. *R. J. Smith, Spain*

SIGNOR PELTRO 3 b.g. Bertolini (USA) 125 – Pewter Lass 56 (Dowsing (USA) 100 124) [2006 79: 6m³ 6s² p6g³ 7.1m* 7g⁶ Oct 13] strong, rangy gelding: developed into a useful handicapper: won at Sandown in August by head from Blades Girl: just respectable sixth to King's Caprice at Newmarket final outing: effective 6f/7f: acts on polytrack, soft and good to firm ground: edged left second start. *H. Candy*

SIGNOR WHIPPEE 3 ch.g. Observatory (USA) 131 – Revoltosa (IRE) (Catrail 64 § (USA) 123) [2006 48: f5g 5m⁶ 5.9g 5f⁵ p5.1g 5m² 5m 5d³ 6m 5s⁵ 5d⁴ 5s* 5v p5.1g Dec 31] smallish gelding: modest performer: won maiden at Newcastle in September: mostly well below that level otherwise: should stay 6f: acts on polytrack, soft and good to firm ground: usually blinkered: unreliable. *A. Berry*

SILAAH 2 b.c. (Mar 12) Mind Games 121 – Ocean Grove (IRE) 84 (Fairy King (USA)) 59 p [2006 6s Nov 19] good-topped colt: brother to fairly useful 2002 2-y-o 5f winner On The Brink and half-brother to 3 winners, including 5-y-o Blue Tomato and 5f (at 2 yrs) and 7f winner Sea Hunter (by Lend A Hand), both useful: dam 2-y-o 6f winner who stayed 1m: 9/1, green (very slowly away) and not knocked about in maiden at Newmarket: will improve. *E. A. L. Dunlop*

SILCA CHIAVE 2 ch.f. (Apr 26) Pivotal 124 – Silca-Cisa 93 (Hallgate 127) [2006 6g³ 106 6g* 7m² 6d³ Sep 29] useful-looking filly: half-sister to several winners, including 3-y-o Silca's Sister and 5f (at 2 yrs) to 9f winner Golden Silca (both by Inchinor), and 5-y-o Green Manalishi, all smart: dam 5f winner, including at 2 yrs: useful form: won maiden at Newbury in August: soon upgraded to Group 1s, much improved when short-head second of 12 to Miss Beatrix in Moyglare Stud Stakes at the Curragh and 1½ lengths third of 11 to Indian Ink in Cheveley Park Stakes (left with most to do of principals) at Newmarket: will stay 1m. *M. R. Channon*

SILCA KEY 2 ch.f. (Mar 25) Inchinor 119 – Baalbek 76 (Barathea (IRE) 127) [2006 77 7g³ 7d² p7g⁶ 7d³ 8g⁴ Oct 12] 72,000Y: lightly-made filly: third foal: half-sister to 4-y-o Cross The Line: dam, 1m winner, granddaughter of Irish 1000 Guineas winner Front Row: fair maiden: in frame 4 of 5 starts, in nurseries at Newmarket last 2: stays 1m: raced on good/good to soft going on turf. *M. R. Channon*

SILCA SOPRANO 2 br.f. (Mar 25) Kyllachy 129 – Broughton Singer (IRE) 61 72 (Common Grounds 118) [2006 5.2d² 6s⁶ 6f³ 6m⁶ 7g⁴ f7g* 8d⁴ 8m Sep 4] 42,000Y: quite good-topped filly: sixth foal: half-sister to 5-y-o Seneschal and 8.5f (at 2 yrs)/9.7f winner Keltic Bard (by Emperor Jones), both fairly useful: dam 9f winner: fair performer: won nursery at Southwell in July: stays 1m: acts on fibresand, firm and soft going: sold 15,000 gns, sent to Saudi Arabia. *M. R. Channon*

SILCA'S SISTER 3 ch.f. Inchinor 119 – Silca-Cisa 93 (Hallgate 127) [2006 112p: 8s⁴ 112 8m⁶ 8.5f² Nov 5] angular filly: smart performer: won Prix Morny at Deauville at 2 yrs, then sold privately out of M. Channon's stable: bit below that form first 2 starts in 2006, in 1000 Guineas at Newmarket (5 lengths fourth to Speciosa, taking strong hold) and Coronation Stakes at Royal Ascot (reportedly struck into when 3¾ lengths sixth to Nannina): off 4½ months, back to form when nose second to Sabellina in Grade 3 Cardinal Handicap at Churchill Downs final outing: stays 9f: acts on firm and good to soft going: races prominently. *Saeed bin Suroor*

SILENT APPLAUSE 3 b.c. Royal Applause 124 – Billie Blue 63 (Ballad Rock 122) 77 [2006 7.5f⁶ 7m² 7f³ p8g 8.3g³ 8s Sep 22] lengthy colt: half-brother to several winners, including smart 5f (at 2 yrs) and 7f winner Tumbleweed Ridge (by Indian Ridge) and useful 6f winner (including at 2 yrs) Tumbleweed Pearl (by Aragon): dam runner-up at 7f only outing: fair maiden: stays 1m: acts on firm going: tended to wander third outing. *Dr J. D. Scargill*

SILENT BEAUTY (IRE) 2 b.f. (May 10) Intikhab (USA) 135 – Precedence (IRE) 88 – (Polish Precedent (USA) 131) [2006 7s 6d Nov 4] €35,000F: fourth foal: half-sister to

4-y-o Wingman and 5-y-o Charlie Tango: dam, Irish maiden who stayed 9f, out of smart 1¼m performer Braiswick: no show in maidens. *S. C. Williams*

SILENT STORM 6 ch.g. Zafonic (USA) 130 – Nanda 83 (Nashwan (USA) 135) [2006 **79** 83: p6g* p8g p6g⁶ p7g⁶ 6g p6g p7.1g³ p7g 7f² 7m⁵ 7m² p8.6g Sep 30] sturdy gelding: **a82** fairly useful handicapper: won at Lingfield in January: free-going sort, likely to prove best short of 1m: acts on all-weather and firm going: tried visored at 4 yrs: usually races prominently. *C. A. Cyzer*

SILENT TIMES (IRE) 3 b. or br.c. Danehill Dancer (IRE) 117 – Recoleta (USA) **–** (Wild Again (USA)) [2006 108p: p9f 7d May 1] big, rangy colt: useful performer at 2 yrs, dead-heating in Champagne Stakes at Doncaster: in rear both starts in 2006, in Grade 2 Lane's End Stakes at Turfway Park and Tetrarch Stakes at the Curragh: raced mainly at 7f: raced only on dirt and good/good to soft going on turf: sold 220,000 gns in October, and to stand at Loughtown Stud, Co Kildare, Ireland, fee €4,000. *E. J. O'Neill*

SILENT WAVES (USA) 2 gr.c. (May 3) Cozzene (USA) – Michelle's Monarch **102** (USA) (Wavering Monarch (USA)) [2006 7.2g* 7.5m* 7m⁴ 8s³ Oct 8] $100,000Y: tall, good-topped colt: brother to 2 winners in USA, notably Breeders' Cup Juvenile Fillies runner-up Platinum Tiara, and half-brother to 3 winners there: dam 5.5f to 1m winner in USA: useful performer: won maiden at Ayr in June and minor event at Beverley (by 9 lengths) in July: better form in pattern company, 3 lengths fourth of 10 to Strategic Prince in Vintage Stakes (not clear run) at Goodwood and 7¾ lengths third of 7 to Eagle Mountain in Beresford Stakes at the Curragh: will probably stay 1¼m: acts on soft and good to firm going. *M. Johnston*

SILENT WILLOW (IRE) 5 ch.g. Gothenberg (IRE) 117 – Ardee Flo Jo (IRE) 60 **43** (Horage 124) [2006 –: 7g 7.1d⁶ 6g Aug 23] poor maiden: left Thomas O'Neill in Ireland after second start: stays 7f: acts on good to soft ground: tried in cheekpieces/blinkers. *D. Nicholls*

SILIDAN 3 b.g. Dansili 127 – In Love Again (IRE) 86 (Prince Rupert (FR) 121) [2006 **–** 92: 7.6d⁶ 8.5f⁵ 7m 7f Jul 29] compact gelding: fairly useful performer at 2 yrs: well below form in handicaps in 2006: headstrong, and usually makes running. *T. P. Tate*

SILK BLOSSOM (IRE) 2 ch.f. (Jan 26) Barathea (IRE) 127 – Lovely Blossom **107** (FR) (Spinning World (USA) 130) [2006 5g* 6m² 6m⁶ 6s* 7d* Sep 19]
    Silk Blossom might be viewed as being somewhat fortunate to have earned £330,405 after being promoted to first in the Shelbourne Hotel Goffs Fillies Five Hundred at the Curragh in September. After reportedly slipping over in the parade ring, 9/4 favourite Silk Blossom looked like getting a good run up the stand rail, before being badly hampered when the leader Wait Watcher, whose jockey switched her whip to the 'wrong' hand, crossed her about a hundred and fifty yards out. Silk Blossom was unable to quicken again, finishing a length and a quarter behind Wait Watcher. With a difference of around £240,000 between coming first and second, the stewards could be excused for taking time over their deliberations but, after a lengthy wait, it was announced that the placings had been reversed. Wait Watcher's trainer Paul Blockley understandably lodged an appeal but it was unsuccessful.

Jaguar Cars Lowther Stakes, York—Silk Blossom (spotted cap) storms home to catch Indian Ink;
Darrfonah (striped cap) is third, ahead of Siren's Gift and Scarlet Runner (rail)

Shelbourne Hotel Goffs Fillies Five Hundred, the Curragh—
Silk Blossom is awarded the race on the demotion of Wait Watcher, who crosses her late on;
Cliche (armlets) snatches third, ahead of In Safe Hands (stars on sleeves) and Theann (crossbelts)

The merits or otherwise of valuable sales races are discussed in detail in the essay on Miss Beatrix, but there was no disguising the fact that the inaugural running of the Fillies Five Hundred wasn't a strong contest considering the money on offer, with just eight of the twenty-seven runners having a race beforehand. Silk Blossom had won two, and it was the form of the most recent of these, the Lowther Stakes at York, that resulted in her being sent off favourite. Silk Blossom had three races before the Lowther, making an encouraging debut when winning a fillies maiden at Newmarket in April by a length and a quarter from Tarkamara and,

Mr E. D. Kessly's "Silk Blossom"

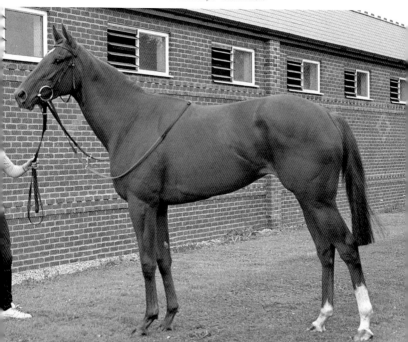

after a two-month absence, improving on that to finish a length and a half second to Sander Camillo in the Albany Stakes at Royal Ascot, taking time to quicken after being waited with. Even allowing for the patient tactics adopted on Silk Blossom were less suited to the way the Cherry Hinton Stakes unfolded, Silk Blossom none-theless disappointed in managing only sixth behind the same rival at Newmarket. In the absence of Sander Camillo, it was a weak renewal of the Lowther. Silk Blossom, who was on her toes in the paddock, encountered a soft surface for the first time at York where she again shaped as if further than six would suit her, showing plenty of resolution to beat Indian Ink, who had looked the likely winner for much of the final two furlongs, by half a length. Although the first prize for the Lowther was a fraction of that for the Fillies Five Hundred, Silk Blossom's performance is rated a stone ahead of that which she recorded at the Curragh.

Silk Blossom (IRE) (ch.f. Jan 26, 2004)	Barathea (IRE) (b 1990)	Sadler's Wells (b 1981)	Northern Dancer
			Fairy Bridge
		Brocade (b 1981)	Habitat
			Canton Silk
	Lovely Blossom (FR) (ch 1999)	Spinning World (ch 1993)	Nureyev
			Imperfect Circle
		Lomond Blossom (b 1985)	Lomond
			December Blossom

The rather leggy, close-coupled Silk Blossom, who cost €50,000 as a year-ling, is the first foal of Lovely Blossom, a half-sister to the smart performer at up to a mile Debbie's Warning. Lovely Blossom finished third over nine and a half furlongs in France on her only start. Grandam Lomond Blossom was a useful two-year-old, winning the Killavullan Stakes at Leopardstown, and she later stayed a mile and a half, her own dam being a half-sister to Le Moss and Levmoss. Silk Blossom's sire Barathea is widely considered the fastest of Sadler's Wells's Group 1-winning progeny, but just three of the one hundred and seventy-seven wins recorded by his progeny in Britain over the past four seasons have come at five furlongs, the most recent of these being Silk Blossom's debut success. Silk Blossom put up her best performance on soft ground, but also acts on good to firm. She is likely to prove better suited by seven furlongs than shorter and will get a mile. She is usually bandaged on her hind joints. *B. W. Hills*

SILKEN ACT (CAN) 3 b.f. Theatrical 128 – Silca Key Service 102 (Bering 136) [2006 78: 10f³ 9.9g³ p10g 11.7m³ 11.6d⁵ p9.5g Nov 11] leggy: fair maiden: stays 11.7f: acts on polytrack, firm and good to soft ground: blinkered last 2 starts. *Mrs A. J. Perrett* **73**

SILKEN DANCE (IRE) 3 b.g. Kalanisi (IRE) 132 – Lady Ela (IRE) (Ela-Mana-Mou 132) [2006 9.9g Jun 29] compact gelding: 50/1, well held in maiden at Salisbury. *G. L. Moore* **–**

SILKIE SMOOTH (IRE) 2 b.f. (Feb 2) Barathea (IRE) 127 – Whassup (FR) (Midyan (USA) 124) [2006 6s³ 6m³ 7m² 7d⁶ 7d 6d p6g³ Nov 6] 28,000F, 48,000Y: rangy filly: has a quick action: first foal: dam, French maiden who stayed 10.5f, out of May Hill Stakes winner Bright Crocus: fairly useful maiden: best efforts when placed at Newmarket and Chester (second to Gweebarra) in summer, only starts on going firmer than good: stays 7f. *B. W. Hills* **83**

SILK MERCHANT (IRE) 3 b.g. Distant Music (USA) 126 – Space Travel (Dancing Dissident (USA) 119) [2006 56: 6d 6g³ 7.2d⁵ 7.2f⁶ 7.2s Sep 28] angular, workmanlike gelding: modest maiden: stays 6f: best effort on good going: sold 2,200 gns. *J. Howard Johnson* **63**

SILK PURSE 3 b.f. Mujahid (USA) 125 – Cieladeed (USA) (Shadeed (USA) 135) [2006 8.3d p10g 10m 9.7f 11.7m Aug 25] third foal: closely related to 7f winner Sofisti-cation (by Dayjur): dam unraced: little form, leaving Rae Guest after second start: tried blinkered. *M. Madgwick* **–**

SILK TOPPER (IRE) 3 b.g. Spectrum (IRE) 126 – Dances With Dreams 109 (Be My Chief (USA) 122) [2006 7.5f 8.5f⁶ 8d³ 9d⁴ Aug 12] modest maiden: should stay 1¼m: acts on good to soft ground. *R. A. Fahey* **60**

SILLOTH SPIRIT 6 b.g. Atraf 116 – Gaelic Air 65 (Ballad Rock 122) [2006 –: f6g f8g Mar 14] workmanlike gelding: seems of little account. *Mrs A. M. Naughton* **–**

SILLY GILLY (IRE) 2 b.f. (Mar 8) Mull of Kintyre (USA) 114 – Richly Deserved **51**
(IRE) (Kings Lake (USA) 133) [2006 5m 6g 5.9g 5m⁵ 6s 6.1m 5g⁴ 5.1f 6s⁵ 5.1d⁵ f5g⁴
Dec 2] €4,500F, €3,000Y: unfurnished filly: half-sister to several winners, including 6f
(at 2 yrs) to 1¼m winner Kingsdon (by Brief Truce): dam unraced: modest maiden: raced
at 5f/6f: tried in cheekpieces. *A. Berry*

SILMI 2 gr.c. (Feb 11) Daylami (IRE) 138 – Intimaa (IRE) 104 (Caerleon (USA) 132) **81 p**
[2006 7d p7g² Nov 22] neat colt: second living foal: half-brother to 3-y-o Tawaafud: dam
2-y-o 6f winner who stayed 1m: better for debut, 3 lengths second to Boscobel in maiden
at Kempton, finishing strongly: should improve further. *E. A. L. Dunlop*

SILSONG (USA) 4 ch.f. Stephen Got Even (USA) 125 – Silver Trainor (USA) (Silver **–**
Hawk (USA) 123) [2006 63, a55: p9.5g⁴ f8g² f11g⁶ f12g² f8g* Mar 14] leggy filly: **a53**
modest performer, better on turf than all-weather: won maiden claimer at Southwell final
start: stays 1½m: acts on all-weather, good to firm and good to soft ground: blinkered/
visored: sold 42,000 gns in November. *Miss Gay Kelleway*

SILVAANI (USA) 8 gr.g. Dumaani (USA) 115 – Ruby Silver (USA) (Silver Hawk **48**
(USA) 123) [2006 p16g⁴ p16g⁵ Nov 28] workmanlike gelding: fair performer in 2002:
poor form both starts since (said to have finished lame final outing): stays 2m: acts on
all-weather, good to firm and good to soft going: tried visored/blinkered. *B. Forsey*

SILVABELLA (IRE) 3 gr.f. Monashee Mountain (USA) 115 – Siva (FR) (Bellypha **–**
130) [2006 –: p9.5g p8.6g 8.2m 8m 7.1g Jul 5] tall, close-coupled filly: little form: tried
visored/in cheekpieces. *D. Haydn Jones*

SILVANELLA (IRE) 3 b. or gr.f. Namid 128 – Mystical 77 (Mystiko (USA) 124) **55**
[2006 6g 6.1d⁵ 5.1s⁶ 5m⁶ 6.1m 6d p6m Oct 9] €7,000Y, resold 5,000Y: third foal: dam
5f/6f winner: maiden: form only when sixth at Folkestone fourth start. *M. S. Saunders*

SILVER APPRAISAL 2 gr.f. (Feb 12) Royal Applause 124 – Arinaga (Warning 136) **61**
[2006 6m⁶ 6f³ 7g 6.1g³ 6d p6g f6g Nov 10] 23,000F, 16,000Y: smallish filly: fifth
foal: half-sister to useful but untrustworthy 2001 2-y-o f7/7.5f winner Lascombes (by
Bluebird) and French 6f to (at 2 yrs) 1m winner Jamaicaine (by Emperor Jones): dam
Norwegian 2-y-o 1m winner: modest maiden: best run when third in nursery at Nottingham: stays 6f. *B. Smart*

SILVER BANK 3 b.f. Silver Patriarch (IRE) 125 – Piggy Bank 71 (Emarati (USA) 74) **–**
[2006 –: 11g 9.9g⁶ 9v³ 11g⁶ May 30] big, rather leggy filly: little form. *M. W. Easterby*

SILVER BLUE (IRE) 3 ch.g. Indian Lodge (IRE) 127 – Silver Echo (Caerleon (USA) **99 d**
132) [2006 96: 9g³ 8.1g⁴ 10m⁶ 10m 8g 10m 10g 8.1g 10d 10g 10s p10g⁵ Nov 28]
good-topped gelding: useful performer: creditable efforts 3 of first 4 outings in 2006,
including when close third to Atlantic Waves in listed race at Newmarket: stays 1¼m:
acts on polytrack and good to firm going, probably on soft: blinkered last 3 starts: has run
well when sweating. *R. Hannon*

SILVER BOLT (IRE) 2 gr.c. (Mar 25) Night Shift (USA) – Missie Madam (IRE) **–**
(Kenmare (FR) 125) [2006 5.2d³ p6g 6d Sep 29] no form: tried blinkered. *N. P. Littmoden*

SILVER CHARIOT 3 gr.g. Silver Patriarch (IRE) 125 – Asian Love (Petong 126) **76**
[2006 75p: p8g⁴ 10.2d 8.1g 10d⁶ Aug 19] good-bodied gelding: fair handicapper: below
form after reappearance: stays 1m (seemingly not 1¼m): acts on polytrack: free-going
sort: sold 7,500 gns. *B. W. Hills*

SILVER COURT 4 b.g. Silver Patriarch (IRE) 125 – Double Stake (USA) (Kokand **54**
(USA)) [2006 46: f8g 11.8d p8.6g 9.7f² p10g 10.1m 10.2m 8.3m 10m² 9.3g 10.1g⁵ 10.2m
Aug 28] modest maiden: left R. Harris after reappearance: stays 1¼m: acts on polytrack,
firm and good to soft going. *A. W. Carroll*

SILVER DANE (IRE) 4 b.g. Danetime (IRE) 121 – Silver Prairie (IRE) (Common **81**
Grounds 118) [2006 68, a62: p5g f5s 6m* 5d p5g* p5g 5m³ p5g⁶ 5.2g 6f⁶ 5.2f⁴ 5.2f*
5.1g⁶ 5.2m p6g p5g Oct 17] close-coupled gelding: fairly useful handicapper: won at Yarmouth in March, Kempton in April, and Yarmouth (ridden with more restraint than usual)
in July: effective at 5f/6f: acts on all-weather, firm and good to soft ground: visored: often
races prominently: none too consistent. *Mrs C. A. Dunnett*

SILVER DIP 3 gr.f. Gulch (USA) – Silver Bandana (USA) (Silver Buck (USA)) [2006 **90**
81: 7s 7g²* 7.1m 7m⁵ 7.1m 7m²* 7f⁶ 8g Oct 13] tall, rather leggy, good-topped filly: fairly
useful handicapper: won at Thirsk in June and Goodwood in August: should stay 1m: acts
on firm going. *B. W. Hills*

SILVER FLAME 2 ch.f. (Mar 18) Dr Fong (USA) 128 – Pastel 95 (Lion Cavern (USA) **55**
117) [2006 6d 6f 6m⁶ Jul 14] leggy, close-coupled filly: has a quick action: first foal: dam
2-y-o 5f winner: modest form in maidens: joined A. Carroll. *B. J. Meehan*

SILVERHAY 5 b.g. Inchinor 119 – Moon Spin 83 (Night Shift (USA)) [2006 78: 9.9d⁴ **82**
10m 8.1m⁴ 12.3d⁵ 12g⁴ 9.9f³ 10f³ 10f* 10.5m⁴ 9.9s 10g* 10g⁴ Sep 26] well-made
gelding: fairly useful handicapper: won ladies races at Pontefract in July and Redcar in
August: effective at 1¼m/1½m: acts on any going: wears cheekpieces nowadays: usually
races prominently: consistent: joined L. Corcoran. *T. D. Barron*

SILVER HOTSPUR 2 b.c. (Feb 14) Royal Applause 124 – Noble View (USA) 68 **70**
(Distant View (USA) 126) [2006 5s 5m³ 5m² 5f⁴ 5g p7g Dec 19] 50,000Y: neat colt:
first foal: dam, maiden who stayed 9f, half-sister to Poule d'Essai des Pouliches winner
Houseproud: fair maiden: placed at Sandown and Lingfield: left P. Chapple-Hyam prior
to final outing: raced mainly at 5f: acts on good to firm going: blinkered (well below
form) fourth start: has looked none too keen. *M. Wigham*

SILVER MITZVA (IRE) 2 b.f. (Mar 31) Almutawakel 126 – Ribblesdale 80 (North- **55**
ern Park (USA) 107) [2006 p8g⁵ Dec 16] third foal: sister to smart Italian/US winner up
to 9f Silver Cup: dam, unreliable 1¼m winner, stayed 11.6f: tongue tied, fifth in maiden
at Kempton. *M. Botti*

SILVER MONT (IRE) 3 b.g. Montjeu (IRE) 137 – Silvernus (Machiavellian (USA) **59**
123) [2006 54: 11.1f⁶ 8d 9m 16.2m 16g⁶ 14.1d⁶ 14.1g⁵ 12.4d 16.1g f8g* p10g f14g³
Nov 2] heavy-topped gelding: modest performer: left Mrs A. Duffield after eighth start:
won banded race at Southwell in October: stays 1¾m, effective at much shorter: acts on
fibresand, firm and good to soft going: visored/blinkered nowadays, tongue tied last 4
starts. *S. R. Bowring*

SILVER NUN 3 b.f. Mind Games 121 – Sapphire Mill (Petong 126) [2006 –: f6g² f7g³ **–**
f7g³ p6g⁴ 6g f6g 5.9g May 18] leggy, workmanlike filly: poor maiden: stays 7f: acts on **a42**
all-weather, no form on turf: blinkered (unruly to post and reluctant to race) second
outing, wore cheekpieces final outing: sometimes slowly away. *T. D. Easterby*

SILVER PIVOTAL (IRE) 2 br.f. (Feb 17) Pivotal 124 – Silver Colours (USA) 94 **73 p**
(Silver Hawk (USA) 123) [2006 7d⁵ Oct 28] 130,000Y: tall, close-coupled filly: third
foal: half-sister to 2004 2-y-o 7.5f winner Gold Queen (by Grand Lodge): dam, 2-y-o
1m winner, half-sister to Japanese Group 2 7f winner God of Chance: 40/1, prominent
long way when fifth to Measured Tempo in maiden at Newmarket: should progress.
G. A. Butler

SILVER PRELUDE 5 b.g. Prince Sabo 123 – Silver Blessings (Statoblest 120) [2006 **73**
p5g 6g 5m 5.2g 5g⁶ 5m Jul 17] good-bodied gelding: missed 2005: fair handicapper
nowadays: best at bare 5f: acts on firm going: usually races up with pace. *D. K. Ivory*

SILVER PROPHET (IRE) 7 gr.g. Idris (IRE) 118 – Silver Heart (Yankee Gold 115) **–**
[2006 70, a55: p12.2g⁵ May 5] rather leggy gelding: fair performer on turf in 2005: **a55**
modest on all-weather: best at 1¼m/1½m: acts on polytrack, soft and good to firm going:
tried visored/in cheekpieces/tongue tied: sometimes slowly away. *M. R. Bosley*

SILVER REIGN 5 gr.g. Prince Sabo 123 – Primo Donna Magna (Primo Dominie 121) **38**
[2006 38: p7g p6g p5g⁶ p6g 6m Apr 30] poor maiden: tried in headgear. *J. J. Bridger*

SILVER SAIL 3 gr.f. Daylami (IRE) 138 – Fiveofive (IRE) 61 (Fairy King (USA)) **44**
[2006 44: 6.9m 7.1g 8f³ 10g 8s⁴ 9.2d⁶ 8d⁵ Oct 2] compact filly: poor maiden: probably
stays 9f: acts on firm and good to soft going: in cheekpieces last 2 starts. *J. S. Wainwright*

SILVER TOUCH (IRE) 3 b.f. Dansili 127 – Sanpala (Sanglamore (USA) 126) [2006 **111**
7m* 8g 8.1m² 7d* 7m 7d⁵ Oct 14] €60,000Y: strong, good-bodied filly: third foal: dam,
ran once in France, half-sister to 7-y-o Vortex: smart performer: won maiden at Newbury
in April and listed race at York (by 1¼ lengths from Wake Up Maggie) in September: ran
creditably after in Prix de la Foret at Longchamp (ninth to Caradak) and Challenge Stakes
at Newmarket (fifth to Sleeping Indian): stays 1m: acts on good to firm and good to soft
going: reportedly pulled muscles behind in Poule d'Essai des Pouliches second outing.
M. R. Channon

SILVERTOWN 11 b.g. Danehill (USA) 126 – Docklands (USA) (Theatrical 128) **89**
[2006 81: 14m* 14m* 13.1g⁵ 13.8m 14g⁶ 16d Nov 3] lengthy gelding: fairly useful
handicapper: has reportedly had wind operation: won at Musselburgh in May and June:
stays 2m: acts on all-weather, firm and good to soft going: makes running: has tended to
flash tail: consistent. *L. Lungo*

SILVERTOWN SKY (IRE) 3 b.f. Lahib (USA) 129 – Miss Verity 74 (Factual (USA) **42**
108) [2006 p8.6g f6g⁵ 5.7g² f6g⁵ f7g⁵ Jun 3] first foal: dam 5f winner (ran only at 2 yrs):
poor maiden: stays 6f: acts on fibresand: sent to Iran. *P. L. Gilligan*

SILVER VISAGE (IRE) 4 b.g. Lujain (USA) 119 – About Face (Midyan (USA) 124) **58**
[2006 66, a62: f6g p6g p6g 7m 6m 6f 8f* 8.2f 8m 7m⁶ Aug 22] unfurnished gelding:
modest performer: won seller at Brighton in July: stays 1m: acts on all-weather and firm
going: tried blinkered, usually wears cheekpieces. *Miss J. Feilden*

SILVO (NZ) 7 gr.g. Lowell (USA) 114 – Silvadella (NZ) (Silver Prospector (USA)) **–**
[2006 p10g p12g 8m p10g May 15] won 1m maiden at Avondale in 2004 from 18 starts
on Flat in New Zealand: well held on Flat in Britain in 2006, though won selling hurdle in
May. *M. F. Harris*

SIMBA SUN (IRE) 2 b.g. (Feb 28) Intikhab (USA) 135 – Lions Den (IRE) 76 (Desert **90**
Style (IRE) 121) [2006 6.1m³ 7f* 6g 7d Sep 24] €22,000F, €21,000Y: unfurnished
gelding: second foal: half-brother to 2005 Irish 2-y-o 6f winner Damjanich (by Mull of
Kintyre): dam Irish 6.5f winner: fairly useful performer: won maiden at Lingfield (made
all, by 7 lengths) in June: below form after in sales race/nursery, then gelded: stays 7f:
acts on firm going. *R. M. Beckett*

SIMLET 11 b.g. Forzando 122 – Besito 79 (Wassl 125) [2006 43: f16g Feb 9] angular **–**
gelding: poor handicapper: well held only run in 2006: had flashed tail/wandered: often
blinkered/visored earlier in career: tongue tied last 2 starts: dead. *E. W. Tuer*

SIMNEL (IRE) 7 b.m. Turtle Island (IRE) 123 – Caca Milis (IRE) (Taufan (USA) 119) **–**
[2006 f8g f8g⁶ Mar 28] no sign of ability: tried visored: had a foal by Advise in 2005.
S. L. Keightley

SIMONDA 5 ch.m. Singspiel (IRE) 133 – Jetbeeah (IRE) 95 (Lomond (USA) 128) **91**
[2006 95: 11.7g² 16s 12m⁵ 12g 12d Oct 27] strong mare: fairly useful handicapper: ran
creditably in 2006 only on reappearance: barely stays 1¾m: acts on firm and soft going:
tried blinkered. *Mrs A. J. Perrett*

SIMONDIUN 3 b.g. Hernando (FR) 127 – Jetbeeah (IRE) 95 (Lomond (USA) 128) **97**
[2006 10d* 12g 11m 14.1d² Aug 15] good-topped gelding: half-brother to several winners, including useful 1997 2-y-o 6f winner Dazilyn Lady (by Zilzal) and 5-y-o Simonda:
dam 1m winner: useful performer: won maiden at Newbury in May by 6 lengths from
Valverde, taking while to find full stride: best effort when ½-length second to Zurbaran in
handicap at Nottingham final outing, tending to edge left: stays 1¾m: acts on good to soft
going: sold 105,000 gns, joined W. Haggas. *Mrs A. J. Perrett*

SIMPLE EXCHANGE (IRE) 5 b.h. Danehill (USA) 126 – Summer Trysting (USA) **112 d**
83 (Alleged (USA) 138) [2006 112: p10g* 10d⁵ 8m⁶ 14g³ 10g⁶ p10g Nov 18] good-
topped horse: smart performer: won listed race at Kempton in April by ½ length from
Kew Green, well ridden up with steady pace: below form after: best form up to 1¼m: acts
on polytrack and firm going: blinkered/visored last 2 starts: none too consistent: sold
72,000 gns. *D. K. Weld, Ireland*

SIMPLIFIED 3 b.f. Lend A Hand 124 – Houston Heiress (USA) (Houston (USA)) **55**
[2006 p8g⁵ p8g p7g⁴ p7g 7m 8.2d 8m⁵ 8m 10.9g² 10.1f³ 12.1g⁵ 10.1g³ 10.1m⁴ p10g p10g
p11g² Dec 22] sparely-made filly: third foal: half-sister to winner in Spain by Opening
Verse: dam maiden in Italy: modest maiden: left J. Pearce after thirteenth outing: stays
11f: acts on polytrack and good to firm going. *N. B. King*

SIMPLIFY 4 b.g. Fasliyev (USA) 120 – Simplicity 93 (Polish Precedent (USA) 131) **61 d**
[2006 75§: p7g p8g p8g 9.7d 7g⁶ 8.3f p8g⁶ 8.3f 10m 9.9m⁵ 8.1m⁴ Sep 12] sturdy, quite
attractive gelding: modest handicapper, on downgrade: stays 1m: acts on polytrack and
firm going: often wears headgear: unreliable. *T. M. Jones*

SIMPLY PERFECT 2 gr.f. (Jan 14) Danehill (USA) 126 – Hotelgenie Dot Com **110**
107 (Selkirk (USA) 129) [2006 5m² 5m² 6m* 6m³ 7m 8g* 8d* Sep 23]
    For those among them who credit the existence of Providence, racehorse
owners often appear in the guise of supreme tempters of the deity. For every
example of a grand naming which proves accurate or inspired—Dubai Millennium
is a classic instance—there are dozens, if not hundreds, which do not, leaving the
victims of this form of hubris open to ridicule. Since the 'sixties, horses who did not
exactly live up to their names include four of the five optimistically named
Brilliant. The British-bred version won four amateur races from thirty-three starts
and was never rated higher than 75, the German-bred won an ordinary handicap
then failed over hurdles, the French-bred won three of her nineteen outings and the

South-African-bred won a maiden, the only time he made the first three in eleven appearances. The American-bred Brilliant is rather better—without fully living up to his name—since he won the Grade 2 Jefferson Cup in June and the Grade 3 Kent Breeders' Cup in September. In the same vein, two juvenile fillies in particular showed sufficient ability to indicate that they might live up to their elevated names. Finsceal Beo (Living Legend in English) proved herself the best of her sex by winning the Prix Marcel Boussac and Rockfel Stakes, and Simply Perfect landed the Meon Valley Stud Fillies' Mile hot on the heels of the May Hill Stakes.

Simply Perfect made steady progress through her campaign, in all probability her development going hand-in-hand with her gaining the strength to match her substantial frame—she is a heavy-topped filly—as well as being stepped up gradually in trip. Exceptionally for a filly who won the two principal races for juvenile fillies over a mile in Britain, she started her career over five furlongs in early June. No Fillies' Mile winner since Culture Vulture in 1991 had run that early or been tried at five furlongs—three earlier winners, Icing (1975), Miss Pinkie (1976) and Nepula (1983), had made their debuts in May. Simply Perfect copied Culture Vulture by finishing second in the Queen Mary at Royal Ascot, where she gave the impression she needed further when staying on to be beaten a length by Gilded. She still looked green that day, despite having one run under her belt, catching a tartar in Dutch Art when runner-up in a maiden event at Windsor. An easy victory at 13/2-on in a maiden at Lingfield in July got Simply Perfect off the mark before two more defeats followed, in the Princess Margaret Stakes at Ascot, in which she stayed on strongly to be beaten three quarters of a length into third behind Scarlet Runner, and in the Moyglare Stud Stakes at the Curragh. In the latter, near the end of August, on her first outing over further than six furlongs, Simply Perfect started second favourite but was never able to land a blow after racing in mid-division and being a little short of room, coming home seventh of twelve to Miss Beatrix. Unsurprisingly, punters looked elsewhere for the market leaders in the nine-runner Keepmoat May Hill Stakes at York (transferred from Doncaster) a fortnight later, making penalised Sweet Solera Stakes winner English Ballet favourite followed by Sudoor, successful in a listed event at Sandown. Simply Perfect was third choice ahead of Sweet Solera fifth Sans Reward. Held up as Sans Reward dictated the pace, Simply Perfect made headway from three furlongs out and knuckled down to her task in good style to hit the front inside the last hundred yards, keeping on to beat English Ballet by a length and a quarter, with Sans Reward third.

The May Hill Stakes represented Simply Perfect's best form to that point, but not by much, and clearly she would need to progress to land the Meon Valley Stud Fillies' Mile at Ascot at the end of September. This race has a rich tradition, with four of the last twelve winners (Bosra Sham, Reams of Verse, Soviet Song and

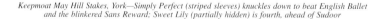

Keepmoat May Hill Stakes, York—Simply Perfect (striped sleeves) knuckles down to beat English Ballet and the blinkered Sans Reward; Sweet Lily (partially hidden) is fourth, ahead of Sudoor

Nannina) going on to win at least one Group 1 event and two of them (Red Bloom and Playful Act) scoring in Group 2 company. Unfortunately, coming as close as it does to the Prix Marcel Boussac, the Fillies' Mile doesn't attract French-trained challengers but there is no obvious solution given the way the European season is arranged, and the unwillingness of French-based trainers generally to tackle races in Britain or Ireland. The field for the latest renewal was not outstanding but it certainly looked competitive with English Ballet in the line-up again, this time at level weights, and two other pattern winners in Gaudeamus (Debutante Stakes) and Sesmen (Prestige Stakes). Satulagi and Alexander Tango had form in pattern races, having finished third in the Sweet Solera Stakes and fifth in the Moyglare Stud Stakes respectively, while promising maiden winners Treat and Lost In Wonder, the latter a rare modern Group 1 contender for the Queen, completed the field. English Ballet was favourite again in a close market, ahead of Simply Perfect and Sesmen. Simply Perfect was sweating and on her toes in the preliminaries and went to post early. After tracking the leaders while Sesmen set a strong gallop, she was ridden to challenge soon after turning for home and showed a good turn of foot to take it up over a furlong out. However—perhaps a slight cause for concern given the hint of temperament before the race—she wandered markedly in front and had to be driven out to beat Treat, whom she hampered by drifting right near the finish, by a length and a half, with English Ballet, who had to wait for a run, three quarters of a length away third. The form was up to scratch for the race, though still some way behind that of Finsceal Beo and Simply Perfect's stable-companion Sander Camillo.

		Danzig	Northern Dancer
Simply Perfect (gr.f. Jan 14, 2004)	Danehill (USA) (b 1986)	(b 1977)	Pas de Nom
		Razyana	His Majesty
		(b 1981)	Spring Adieu
	Hotelgenie Dot Com (gr 1998)	Selkirk	Sharpen Up
		(ch 1988)	Annie Edge
		Birch Creek	Carwhite
		(gr 1982)	Deed

Simply Perfect is well bred, though at 220,000 guineas, the price she fetched at the Newmarket October Sales, she was nowhere near the most expensive of the thirty-eight yearlings from her sire Danehill's final crop. Thirteen fetched more, headed by Queen of France who, after costing 1,450,000 dollars at Keeneland, came second in a maiden at Cork before finishing tenth in the Rockfel Stakes. The second foal out of Hotelgenie Dot Com, Simply Perfect was also much cheaper than her three-year-old sister One Moment In Time, a 520,000-guinea buy at the same venue but as yet unraced. The next foal, a colt by Royal Applause, also went

Meon Valley Stud Fillies' Mile, Ascot—Simply Perfect is the winner on merit from the hampered Treat

Mr D. Smith, Mr M. Tabor & Mrs J. Magnier's "Simply Perfect"

through the ring, for 120,000 guineas, and there is a colt foal by Sadler's Wells. The dam of Simply Perfect, Hotelgenie Dot Com, was a useful filly and at her best as a two-year-old, winning a minor event at Sandown and gaining places in the Moyglare Stud Stakes and Fillies' Mile; she beat only three of her twenty-nine rivals in three listed races at three. Hotelgenie Dot Com was a half-sister to Bianca Nera, successful in the Lowther Stakes and Moyglare Stud Stakes, out of the highly-tried maiden Birch Creek, who showed useful form in France and Italy, notably when third in the Group 3 Premio Royal Mares over a mile. Birch Creek was one of seven winners out of Deed, who scored over five furlongs as a juvenile. The best of them was useful sprinter Great Deeds, who numbered the Group 3 Ballyogan Stakes at five furlongs among her four victories. There is more stamina another generation back, Deed's dam Aurorabella being a sister to good stayer Double Bore, successful in the Goodwood Cup. For academic interest, the family traces to brilliant racemare Pretty Polly. Simply Perfect, a tough filly who acts on good to firm and good to soft going, is likely to fall between two stools in the classics in Britain and Ireland. Finsceal Beo and Sander Camillo should have too much speed for her over a mile, while Simply Perfect is far from certain to stay the Oaks trip. The French classics, including the Prix de Diane, may offer Simply Perfect the best chance of glory. *J. Noseda*

SIMPLY ST LUCIA 4 b.f. Charnwood Forest (IRE) 125 – Mubadara (IRE) 80 (Lahib (USA) 129) [2006 69, a74: f8g⁶ p12.2g f11g⁵ p16.5g f8g Jul 7] fair handicapper at 3 yrs, only modest on all-weather in 2006: stays 8.6f: acts on all-weather and good to soft ground: tried in cheekpieces: races prominently. *J. R. Weymes* **– a63**

SIMPLY THE GUEST (IRE) 7 b.g. Mujadil (USA) 119 – Ned's Contessa (IRE) 48 **54** (Persian Heights 129) [2006 –, a72: f11g f11g f11g f12g⁴ f11g⁶ f11g³ f11g³ f11g² Apr 10] lengthy, workmanlike gelding: modest performer: stays 1½m: acts on all-weather and firm going: often visored: tongue tied. *N. Tinkler*

SIMPSONS GAMBLE (IRE) 3 b.g. Tagula (IRE) 116 – Kiva (Indian Ridge 123) **60** [2006 –: 7f p6g 8.3g p7g⁵ p7g⁵ p8g⁴ Nov 24] strong gelding: modest maiden: stays easy 1m: acts on polytrack: ran out once at 2 yrs. *R. M. Flower*

SIMPSONS ROSS (IRE) 3 b.g. Imperial Ballet (IRE) 110 – Brunswick (Warning **64** 136) [2006 50: p6g⁶ p8g² p8g p8g p10g 7f² 7m⁵ 7f⁴ p8g⁵ p7g⁶ 7m 7f 7f p8g² p8g⁴ Nov 25] leggy gelding: modest maiden: stays 1m: acts on polytrack and firm going: tried blinkered. *R. M. Flower*

SINA COVA (IRE) 4 b.f. Barathea (IRE) 127 – Kumta (IRE) (Priolo (USA) 127) [2006 **116** 96: 8v 10s² 9.5s 10m³ 12f* 12m² 12d⁵ 10d² 8d* 10s Oct 30] rangy filly: half-sister to useful Irish 8.5f (at 2 yrs) to 1½m winner Blessyourpinksox (by Cadeaux Genereux) and fairly useful Irish 1¾m winner/smart staying hurdler Kadoun (by Doyoun): dam unraced half-sister to dams of Kahyasi and Yorkshire Oaks winner Key Change: smart performer: much improved in 2006, winning Kerry Group EBF Noblesse Stakes at Cork (beat Kushnarenkovo 4½ lengths) in June and listed race at Naas (beat Cheyenne Star 2½ lengths) in October: creditable second in between to Reform Act in listed race at Cork and to Red Bloom (beaten 1¾ lengths) in Blandford Stakes at the Curragh: below form in Yorkshire Oaks at York seventh outing and in listed race at Leopardstown final start: effective at 1m to 1½m: acts on firm and good to soft ground: has won in blinkers: reared and unseated leaving stall third outing. *Peter Casey, Ireland*

SINCERELY 4 b.f. Singspiel (IRE) 133 – Noble Form (Double Form 130) [2006 66, **74** a56: p7.1g 7m 7g² 8.1m 7m² 8m² p8g³ 8d p8g³ p7g* p8g⁴ p7g³ Dec 8] leggy filly: fair handicapper: won at Lingfield in November: stays 1m: acts on polytrack, good to firm and good to soft going: blinkered last 3 starts. *B. W. Hills*

SIN CITY 3 b.g. Sinndar (IRE) 134 – Turn of A Century 85 (Halling (USA) 133) [2006 **78** 79p: 12g⁵ 13.9f⁵ Jul 14] rather leggy, close-coupled gelding: has a quick action: fair handicapper, lightly raced: stays 1¾m: raced only on good ground or firmer. *R. A. Fahey*

SINDIRANA (IRE) 3 br.f. Kalanisi (IRE) 132 – Sinndiya (IRE) 84 (Pharly (FR) 130) **107** [2006 87p: 11.5m* 12m 12m⁵ 12m⁶ Aug 6] leggy filly: useful performer: won listed race at Lingfield in May by neck from Fusili: good efforts in listed races last 2 starts, fifth to Quenched at Newmarket (warm beforehand, best effort, beaten 2 lengths) and sixth to Fermion at Newbury: stays 1½m: acts on good to firm ground: eased as if amiss in Ribblesdale Stakes at Royal Ascot second outing. *Sir Michael Stoute*

SINGHALONGTASVEER 4 b.g. Namaqualand (USA) – Felinwen (White Mill 76) **50** [2006 55: 15.8g⁴ 15.8g 16d 16.1s⁶ Sep 4] compact gelding: modest maiden handicapper: stays easy 2m: acts on good to firm and good to soft going: often visored/in cheekpieces: tongue tied: won over hurdles in November. *W. Storey*

SINJAREE 8 b.g. Mark of Esteem (IRE) 137 – Forthwith 104 (Midyan (USA) 124) **–** [2006 –: f8g Mar 8] leggy gelding: modest performer at 6 yrs: no form since: tried in visor/cheekpieces. *Mrs S. Lamyman*

SINNER OR SAINT (IRE) 3 ch.g. Sinndar (IRE) 134 – Hillquest (Rainbow Quest **67** (USA) 134) [2006 72: 12.1d 8s 7.9m⁶ 8g³ 9m³ 9.8s 8v p8.6g f8g Nov 13] close-coupled gelding: fair maiden: should stay 1¼m: acts on good to firm going: races prominently: sold 3,000 gns. *T. D. Easterby*

SION HILL (IRE) 5 b.g. Desert Prince (IRE) 130 – Mobilia 67 (Last Tycoon 131) **51** [2006 55, a46: f8g³ 8.2m f7m⁶ f6g⁶ f6g² f5g⁶ f6g² f6g⁵ f7g f6g Dec 28] well-made gelding: modest maiden: left M. Chapman after reappearance: effective at 5f to 9.5f: acts on fibresand and good to firm going: often wears headgear: sometimes races freely. *Mrs N. Macauley*

SIRAJ 7 b.g. Piccolo 121 – Masuri Kabisa (USA) 48 (Ascot Knight (CAN) 130) [2006 **70** 74d: p6g⁶ p7g f6g p6g 6f⁴ 6m⁴ 6d 6f³ 6g⁵ p7g⁵ p6g* p6g* p6g* p6g⁴ p6g* Dec 15] good-bodied gelding: fair performer: won banded races at Wolverhampton and Kempton in November, and 2 handicaps at Kempton in December: best at 6f: acts on all-weather and any turf going: wears headgear: tried tongue tied. *J. Ryan*

SIR ARTHUR (IRE) 3 ch.g. Desert Prince (IRE) 130 – Park Express 123 (Ahonoora **83** 122) [2006 –: 9.2m³ 9v* 9.8m 9.9f* 10.1g 10g 10m⁶ Jul 30] big, lengthy gelding: fairly useful performer: won maiden at Ripon in May and handicap at Beverley in June: disappointing after, blinkered final start: stays 1¼m: acts on any going: races prominently. *M. Johnston*

SIR BOND (IRE) 5 ch.g. Desert Sun 120 – In Tranquility (IRE) (Shalford (IRE) 124§) **72**
[2006 69: f7g² p7.1g² p8.6g* f8g³ f7g 9.3g 8m p8.6g³ Dec 30] lengthy, heavy-bodied gelding: fair handicapper: won at Wolverhampton in April: left B. Smart before final outing: stays 8.6f: acts on all-weather, firm and soft ground: held up: sometimes slowly away: flashes tail. *G. R. Oldroyd*

SIRBRIT 3 b.g. Cadeaux Genereux 131 – Evening Promise 108 (Aragon 118) [2006 54: **44**
8.2d 9.9m 12f 10d 11.9d⁵ Oct 19] good-topped gelding: poor maiden handicapper: tried visored. *W. J. Musson*

SIRCE (IRE) 4 b.f. Josr Algarhoud (IRE) 118 – Trading Aces 71 (Be My Chief (USA) **111**
122) [2006 94: 11.5m³ p16g8* 16d⁴ 14m* 14f³ Aug 3] strong filly: smart performer: further marked improvement in 2006, winning handicap at Kempton (by 3½ lengths from The Nawab) in April and listed race at Musselburgh (by length from Ouninpohja) in June: very close third to Tartouche in Lillie Langtry Stakes at Goodwood final outing, finishing best of all (rated narrow winner): stays 2m: acts on polytrack, firm and soft going: visored: consistent: reported in September to have suffered slight leg injury. *D. J. Coakley*

SIR CHARLES 2 b.g. (Apr 28) Mujahid (USA) 125 – Chocolate (IRE) 77 (Brief Truce **71**
(USA) 126) [2006 5m 6m² 5.9g² Aug 3] leggy, angular gelding: second foal: dam maiden at 2 yrs in Britain (later 6f and 1m winner in France/Belgium): fair form in maidens, runner-up at Newcastle and Carlisle: will probably stay 7f/1m. *M. Dods*

SIR DESMOND 8 gr.g. Petong 126 – I'm Your Lady 77 (Risk Me (FR) 127) [2006 86: **87**
f6g³ f6g 6g 6g⁴ 6g* May 8] workmanlike gelding: fairly useful handicapper: won at Windsor (by head from Nautical) final outing: probably best at 6f: acts on all-weather and any turf going: blinkered once, wears cheekpieces: tends to edge left. *Rae Guest*

SIR DON (IRE) 7 b.g. Lake Coniston (IRE) 131 – New Sensitive (Wattlefield 117) **63**
[2006 53§: 6f 6.1m² 7m⁶ 6f5 6d² 6m p5.1g* p5.1g⁴ p6g Dec 22] sparely-made gelding: modest handicapper: won at Wolverhampton in November: effective at 5f/6f: acts on polytrack, firm and good to soft going: often wears headgear: found little sixth outing. *E. S. McMahon*

SIR DOUGLAS 3 ch.c. Desert Sun 120 – Daintree (IRE) 66 (Tirol 127) [2006 p6g* **80**
p6g⁶ p7g⁵ 7m 8d Oct 27] 24,000F, 24,000Y: strong colt: second foal: half-brother to smart performer abroad (best around 9f/1¼m) Billy Allen (by Night Shift), 7f winner in Britain at 2 yrs: dam, 1m winner, half-sister to 9-y-o The Tatling: fairly useful performer: won maiden at Wolverhampton in February: below that level in handicaps after, tending to hang: stays 6f: acts on polytrack. *J. A. Osborne*

SIR DUKE (IRE) 2 b.c. (Jan 28) Danehill (USA) 126 – Dimanche (IRE) (Sadler's **–**
Wells (USA) 132) [2006 8g Sep 28] strong, useful-looking colt: 33/1, last in maiden at Newmarket. *P. W. D'Arcy*

SIR EDWIN LANDSEER (USA) 6 gr.h. Lit de Justice (USA) 125 – Wildcat Blue **106**
(USA) (Cure The Blues (USA)) [2006 90: 6.5m⁵ 6m* a5g 6m 6m 5g⁵ p6g⁴ Sep 30] **a99**
good-quartered horse: useful handicapper: better on turf than all-weather: as good as ever when winning at Nad Al Sheba (beat Royal Storm by length) in February: best efforts after at Haydock and Kempton (fourth to Mutamared) in February: effective at 5f to 7f: acts on dirt, firm and good to soft going, probably on soft: tried blinkered/in a hood, usually wears cheekpieces: tends to get behind (often starts slowly). *C. Wroe, UAE*

SIREN'S GIFT 2 ch.f. (Mar 8) Cadeaux Genereux 131 – Blue Siren 113 (Bluebird **98**
(USA) 125) [2006 5m⁶ 5g² 5f* 5m⁴ 6s⁴ 5g⁴ Sep 8] quite good-topped filly: fifth foal: sister to useful 5f winner (including at 2 yrs) Speed Cop and half-sister to fairly useful 6f winner Indiana Blues (by Indian Ridge): dam, 5f (at 2 yrs) to 7f winner, first past post in Nunthorpe Stakes: useful performer: won minor event at Beverley in July: better form when fourth in pattern races, in Molecomb Stakes at Goodwood and Lowther Stakes (stamina stretched) and Flying Childers Stakes (3 lengths behind Wi Dud) at York: best at 5f: acts on firm going, probably on soft. *A. M. Balding*

SIR GERARD 3 b.c. Marju (IRE) 127 – Chapeau (Zafonic (USA) 130) [2006 86p: **114 p**
7.5f* 8.1s² 8m* 8f⁴ Aug 4]
Don't panic! By season's end, it seemed a storm in a teacup, but in Royal Ascot week, jockeys, trainers and the media alike appeared convinced about a strong draw bias on the straight course at the new Ascot. Hopes that the revamped track, with its new turf and drainage, would provide a 'level playing field' seemed

Britannia Stakes (Handicap), Royal Ascot—Sir Gerard gives Jamie Spencer his third James Fanshawe-trained winner of the week; Easy Air (rail) snatches second, ahead of Upper Hand (checked cap), Smart Enough and Regal Royale (left)

to be dashed as the lowly-drawn runners had an edge. Various explanations were put forward, including that some parts of the course might have been more heavily watered than others, which the clerk of the course denied, and that a ridge had been created towards the far rail by the different camber on the home turn. There was even speculation that one side of the very wide track might be shorter than the other, though official measurement of the straight mile reportedly put the difference in length between the two sides at 3mm!

Individual fixtures tend to be a breeding ground for misconceptions about the effect of the draw. Theories which take seed in the minds of riders over a limited number of races can have a powerful influence on events. After the result of the second race of the five-day fixture at Royal Ascot, the King's Stand Stakes, in which the stand-side group came out ahead of the far-side pack, the vast majority of runners came stand side for all but one of the remaining contests. In the five straight-course handicaps at the fixture, the most competitive races, lowly-drawn runners did continue to have the better of things, but this could be explained by the way races shaped, rather than by any 'permanent' draw bias. Once riders believed there was an advantage for lowly-drawn horses at Ascot, the stand rail became the focal point for races. As a result, the strongest pace tended to be set stand side, leaving higher-drawn horses adrift, and giving the advantage to those up with the gallop or those tracking the pace on the stand side. When the focal point changed, as is it did over a larger sample of races at subsequent fixtures, the supposed draw bias was shown to have been much exaggerated.

Oddly, one factor which sometimes tends to be underestimated in analysing the effect of the draw on the result of races is the ability of the horses. In three-year-old handicaps, for example, there can be a wide discrepency—at least in hindsight—between the chances of some of the runners at the weights. So quickly was Sir Gerard improving, for example, that he would probably have been hard to beat from almost any draw in the Britannia Handicap, run on the Thursday of the Royal fixture. Successful in a seven-furlong maiden on polytrack at Lingfield from two starts as a juvenile, he scrambled home on his handicap debut at Beverley in April, but improved considerably when an unlucky second to Anna Pavlova in a valuable handicap at Haydock the following month, going down by a neck after needing to be switched late on. Sir Gerard got a far from straightforward run at Ascot either, but won most decisively in the end, landing a gamble. Held up from stall two in a field of thirty, he had it all to do at halfway, but, switched right in the final furlong, flew home to beat Easy Air going away by two lengths. Raised 10 lb in the weights, Sir Gerard ran equally well in defeat on his only subsequent start, when a strong-finishing fourth of seventeen to Spectait in the totesport Mile at Goodwood in August, doing particularly well from stall one in a race dominated by highly-drawn runners, meeting trouble to boot.

Joint favourite for the Cambridgeshire before being ruled out by an infected corn, Sir Gerard is likely to stay a mile and a quarter. By Marju, sire of the same

Miss Rose-Anne Galligan's "Sir Gerard"

		Last Tycoon	Try My Best
Sir Gerard	Marju (IRE)	(b 1983)	Mill Princess
(b.c. 2003)	(br 1988)	Flame of Tara	Artaius
		(b 1980)	Welsh Flame
	Chapeau	Zafonic	Gone West
	(ch 1999)	(b 1990)	Zaizafon
		Barboukh	Night Shift
		(ch 1990)	Turban

stable's high-class miler Soviet Song, Sir Gerard is out of the once-raced Chapeau, a half-sister to the smart French mile and a quarter performer Barbola, whose dam the winning miler Barboukh is out of a half-sister to Old Vic, winner of the Prix du Jockey Club and the Irish Derby. A 20,000-guinea yearling, Sir Gerard made 56,000 guineas as a two-year-old at the Newmarket Breeze Up Sale and no doubt changed hands for a good deal more when sold to Sheikh Mohammed after his final run. A strong, lengthy colt, and a good walker, he acts on polytrack, firm and soft ground. Already smart, he looks sure to progress to pattern company for Ismael Mohammed in the UAE, and he may return to Europe with Godolphin depending on how he does at the Dubai Carnival. *J. R. Fanshawe*

SIR HAYDN 6 ch.g. Definite Article 121 – Snowscape (Niniski (USA) 125) [2006 73, a86: p10g* Jan 4] big, leggy gelding: fairly useful handicapper on all-weather, fair on turf: won at Lingfield in January on only outing in 2006: stays 11f: acts on all-weather, firm and soft ground: usually wears headgear: sometimes finds little. *J. R. Jenkins*

–

a83

SIR LAUGHALOT 6 b.g. Alzao (USA) 117 – Funny Hilarious (USA) 76 (Sir Ivor **63** (USA) 135) [2006 p10g⁶ p8g 12g Jul 13] strong gelding: maiden: missed 2005: only modest handicapper in 2006: stays 1m, probably not 1½m: acts on polytrack, good to firm and good to soft going. *Miss E. C. Lavelle*

SIR LIAM (USA) 2 b.c. (Mar 12) Monarchos (USA) 129 – Tears (USA) (Red Ransom **77** (USA)) [2006 p7g 7f² 8s Oct 10] $27,000Y: well-made colt: fifth foal: half-brother to 3 winners in USA: dam, maiden in USA, half-sister to dam of Breeders' Cup Classic winner Saint Liam: fair form when second to Roodolph in maiden at Folkestone: should stay 1m: acts on firm going, well beaten on soft. *P. Mitchell*

SIR LOIN 5 ch.g. Compton Place 125 – Charnwood Queen 61 (Cadeaux Genereux 131) **64** [2006 65: 5f⁵ 5f p5.1g³ 7.6m p5.1g* 5m 5.1g⁴ 5d* 5.1m⁴ 5m Sep 13] leggy gelding: fair handicapper: won at Wolverhampton (apprentices) in July and Pontefract in August: raced mainly at 5f (doesn't stay 7.6f): acts on polytrack, good to firm and good to soft going: has worn cheekpieces, usually visored nowadays: races prominently. *N. Tinkler*

SIR MIKEALE 3 b.c. Easycall 115 – Sleep Standing (IRE) (Standaan (FR) 118) [2006 **50** –: p5.1g p5g⁶ Feb 4] modest form in maidens. *G. Prodromou*

SIR MONTY (USA) 4 ch.g. Cat's Career (USA) – Lady of Meadowlane (USA) **89** (Pancho Jay (USA)) [2006 80: 12g* 14.1g 21m⁵ 16.1d* 16m³ 18d 16d Oct 27] leggy, workmanlike gelding: fairly useful handicapper: won at Salisbury in June and Newmarket (best effort, beat Mersey Sound ¾ length) in August: effective at 1½m, barely stays 21f: acts on firm and soft going: has run well when sweating. *Mrs A. J. Perrett*

SIR NOD 4 b.g. Tagula (IRE) 116 – Nordan Raider 81 (Domynsky 110) [2006 88: 6g⁵ **87** 6f³ 6m 6d 6m² 5m* 5s p6g² Nov 10] fairly useful handicapper: won at Beverley in September: good second at Wolverhampton final start: effective at 5f to 7f: acts on polytrack and firm going: races prominently. *Miss J. A. Camacho*

SIR ORPEN (IRE) 3 gr.g. Orpen (USA) 116 – Yalciyna 92 (Nishapour (FR) 125) **81** [2006 82: 7g* 8s⁵ 6s⁵ 7m⁵ 6f⁴ 7m⁴ 6f⁴ 6d³ 7d⁴ 6.1d 6.1d Oct 18] lengthy, good-topped gelding: has scope: fairly useful performer: won maiden at Catterick in May: below form last 3 starts: effective at 6f to 1m: acts on firm and soft going: tried blinkered. *T. D. Barron*

SIR PERCY 3 b.c. Mark of Esteem (IRE) 137 – Percy's Lass 120§ (Blakeney 126) **129** [2006 122+: 8m² 12m* 10d Oct 14]

The summer was officially one of the longest and hottest on record. In July, temperatures approached 100F. For the most part, however, the summer of sport simmered without coming to the boil. At Wimbledon, Roger Federer took a fourth consecutive men's singles title, losing only one set on the way, and in golf Tiger Woods, also the pre-eminent player of his day, had a stranglehold on the Open virtually throughout as he recorded his third victory in the tournament, taking irons off most of the tees. In cricket, after the excitement of regaining the Ashes the previous summer, England's 3-0 Test series win over Pakistan was overshadowed by controversy as Pakistan forfeited the final match in the series after allegations of ball-tampering. It was also World Cup year, but even that lost much of its interest at home with England's exit to Portugal on penalties at the quarter final stage in Germany. Late in the summer, home hopes were fulfilled in Ireland as Europe defeated the USA in a surprisingly one-sided Ryder Cup. The award for BBC Sports Personality of The Year went to Zara Phillips, winner of the individual gold medal for the three-day event at the World Equestrian Games in Germany in August. Not unusually, there was no horseracing personality on the short-list for the award, though racing was responsible for arguably the most exciting single event of the summer. Although not a vintage renewal on form, the 227th Derby will go down as the most action-packed in many years, the four-way photo for first telling only part of the story of a race touched by twists and misfortune, in terms of drama probably second only to the suffragette Derby of 1913 in the race's long history.

The death of militant suffragette Emily Davison after falling under the hooves of the King's horse Anmer just after Tattenham Corner lifts the 1913 Derby above all others in terms of its sensationalism, but the race was dramatic as a contest as well, the only one in the history of the Derby to see the winner disqualified. In his book *The History of the Derby Stakes* Roger Mortimer describes the 1913 Derby as 'the most sensational, the most tragic, and the most unsatisfactory in the history of the race.' Four horses passed the post virtually in a line, though the judge failed to identify Day Comet, shielded from his view on the inside but subsequently shown by photographic evidence to have finished in the frame, the judge placing Louvois third and Great Sport, who was on their heels, fourth. At a subsequent inquiry, acting on their own initiative, the stewards lodged an objection to the first-past-the-post Craganour, the 6/4 favourite, and promoted the runner-up, 100/1-shot Aboyeur, finding that 'Craganour, by not keeping a straight course, had at one point of the race seriously interfered with Shogun, Day Comet and Aboyeur, and had afterwards bumped and bored the latter so as to prevent him winning.' Interestingly, neither jockey nor owner of Aboyeur objected themselves. The judge was reportedly a key witness at the inquiry, as was Louvois' jockey, who had been replaced on Craganour after a narrow defeat in the Two Thousand Guineas in which he had been considered by many to have ridden an ill-judged race. In his account, admittedly second hand, Mortimer stated that Aboyeur, flinching from the whip in his rider's left hand, came away from the rails inside the final furlong and collided with Craganour, though he also added 'There can be little doubt that it was Reiff (Craganour's jockey) who had instigated the serious trouble in the straight.' Further intrigue was added by the suggestion that Craganour's owner, who had been associated with a trainer who had been warned off, was of 'stained character' which might have influenced the inquiry. By comparison with the 1913 renewal, the crowded finish to the latest Derby was as 'clean as a whistle', at least so far as the stewards were concerned.

The two races in 1913 and 2006 vie for the title of the closest Derby ever run. According to the information available, no winning distance was returned for the first Derby won by Diomed in 1780 and it was not until 1805 that winning distances in the Derby were recorded on a regular basis, terms such as 'easily' or 'very easily' in more common usage to add to the picture of the race. It was 1844 before the distance back to the third in the Derby was recorded. With the naked eye, the judge for the 1913 Derby gave the winning distances as a head and a neck, though, considering the Day Comet debacle, the distance back to the third was probably shorter. There have been other tight finishes involving more than two horses since. Fifinella won by a neck and a head in 1916, Ocean Swell by a neck and a short head when the race was run at Newmarket in 1944 and Nimbus by a head and the same in 1949 when the outcome was decided by photo for the first time. Sir Percy won by a short head, a head and a short head, and, taking the distance back to the fourth as a guide, there are grounds for calling the 2006 Derby the closest ever run, though it can't be stated with certainty.

Vodafone Derby Stakes, Epsom—catch us if you can!
Dylan Thomas and Dragon Dancer (noseband) go for home rounding Tattenham Corner;
Snoqualmie Boy and Championship Point (armlets) are the closest pursuers; Sir Percy (blaze) is partially
hidden behind Hala Bek; Linda's Lad (check cap) and Visindar (widest of all) are to his right

Vodafone Derby Stakes, Epsom—
Sir Percy squeezes through between Dylan Thomas and the rail as Dragon Dancer is still right there;
Philip Robinson does well to keep his partnership with Hala Bek (left) intact

But for the skill of his trainer and those who worked with him at Kingwood House, Sir Percy might not have been there at all on Derby Day. He returned 'a little bit sore' after his reappearance in the Two Thousand Guineas at Newmarket in May, reportedly having pulled a muscle in his back. A leading two-year-old, capping a four-race unbeaten campaign with a narrow win over Horatio Nelson in the Dewhurst at Newmarket, Sir Percy showed he had trained on well when a clear second of fourteen to George Washington in the Guineas. Considered by his trainer not to need a lot of work, Sir Percy went to Newmarket without a run, completing his preparation with a public workout in a gallop at Newbury. With connections convinced that he would stay beyond a mile, second favourite Sir Percy was ridden handily from the start at Newmarket but proved no match for a rival with a sharper turn of foot, staying on strongly after failing to handle the descent into the Dip particularly well and going down by two and a half lengths to the winner, a length and a half in front of third-placed Olympian Odyssey, with the subsequent Irish Two Thousand Guineas winner Araafa in fourth.

Sir Percy was briefly favourite for the Derby at 4/1 immediately after Newmarket, but lost his position as market leader to the French-trained Visindar. Once-raced as a two-year-old, Visindar maintained his unbeaten record with an impressive success on his second start at three in the Prix Greffulhe at Saint-Cloud nine days after Newmarket. The pick of the middle-distance trials in Britain looked to be the Dante Stakes at York, won impressively by one of Ballydoyle's Derby candidates Septimus. Sir Percy received intensive physiotherapy after Newmarket and was given the go-ahead for the Vodafone Derby after pleasing connections in a racecourse gallop on Lingfield's polytrack a week before Epsom. The ground at Epsom had been soft in the run up to the race, but, with drying conditions, it was good to firm on the day. In a field of eighteen including runners from France and Ireland, Visindar started a heavily-backed favourite at 2/1, the shortest-priced runner since Entrepreneur went off at odds on in 1997. Horatio Nelson, only eighth in the Guineas but the choice of Kieren Fallon ahead of Septimus among Aidan O'Brien's four runners, was next best at 11/2, with Sir Percy well backed at 6/1 and Septimus at 17/2. Visindar's stable-companion Linda's Lad, successful in the Lingfield Derby Trial and the mount of Frankie Dettori seeking a first Derby win (Godolphin was without a runner), was at 9/1 along with once-raced Hala Bek, with Chester Vase winner Papal Bull at 11/1.

The normal Derby Day tension was heightened when Horatio Nelson delayed the start by ten minutes while his soundness was checked at the stalls, the racecourse vet examining him and also consulting the colt's trainer who was at the start to supervise his runners. Once the race got under way, it was unusually slow to develop, though that only served to increase the drama at the finish as more runners than normal still had plenty of running left in them in the closing stages. Dylan Thomas, another Aidan O'Brien-trained runner, was the first to be sent for home, pressed by Dragon Dancer from the turn. Two furlongs out, the pair were briefly clear with Hala Bek and Visindar in closest pursuit, and Sir Percy, who had been held up, making ground relentlessly behind them. Half a furlong later, Horatio Nelson broke down fatally when chasing the leaders. Back with the main action, there was another twist inside the last furlong. As Hala Bek drew virtually upsides the leading pair, he swerved sharply right under the whip, almost unseating his rider. Sir Percy, who had been switched inside, continued his run on the rail, just getting up in the dying strides. Sir Percy was a first Derby winner for his trainer Marcus Tregoning, formerly assistant to three-times Derby winning trainer Dick Hern, and a first for jockey Martin Dwyer, successful in the Oaks in 2003 and able to take the ride only after recovering from an injury scare when damaging his ribs at Bath the evening before. Dwyer, who like all riders in the latest season had the option of being referred to in race cards by his full name instead of merely by his surname and his initials, has long been a master of the post-race quip for the media and was in customary good humour. Referring to his mount being tight for room in the early stages, he accused Frankie Dettori of 'wanting to ride my horse as well'. 'Perhaps he wanted to feel what it was like to be on a Derby winner!' he added mischievously.

The dramatic finish deflected attention somewhat from the unfortunate mishap which befell Horatio Nelson, the second horse to be killed in action in recent renewals of the Derby, following Coshocton's demise in 2002. The race had to share the spotlight on the sports pages of Britain's national newspapers with England's final warm-up game for the World Cup, which took place earlier the same afternoon. The Football Association had been pursuaded by the BBC and representatives of racing to bring forward the kick-off time of England's match with Jamaica, which England won 6-0, avoiding a direct clash with the Derby. Terrestrial television coverage of Derby Day on *Grandstand* was split, with the first four races on the card being shown on BBC2. The Derby remained on BBC1, though given only a twenty-minute build up. Fears that the Derby might be marginalised by the football proved largely groundless. The television audience for the coverage broke through the four-million barrier for the first time since the race returned to the BBC from Channel 4 in 2001, peaking at 4.1m for the race, 43% of the viewing audience, the highest market share since 1994. The scheduled off time of the Derby was 4.20. The idea of running the Derby in future as the last race on the seven-race card was dismissed by officials at a Press conference at Epsom in April, Epsom managing

Vodafone Derby Stakes, Epsom—a close four-horse finish rivalled only by the dramatic 1913 Derby; Sir Percy (right) is the narrow winner, ahead of Dragon Dancer (noseband), Dylan Thomas and the rallying Hala Bek (left)

director Stephen Wallis citing 'logistical' problems, though a tea-time Derby, suggested in *Racehorses of 2003*, would almost certainly be a step forward in further re-establishing the race with the television audience.

It is likely that a good proportion of the Derby Day audience from 2006 will watch the race again in 2007. Following Roberto in 1972, Secreto in 1984 and Benny The Dip in 1997, Sir Percy was only the fourth short-head winner of the Derby since the First World War. The 66/1-shot Dragon Dancer finished runner-up, a head in front of 25/1-chance Dylan Thomas with Hala Bek a short head further back. The first four were two lengths ahead of Visindar in fifth, but the overall form looked below par for the race. All the same, to label the Derby simply a substandard one would be doing it an injustice. It was a muddling contest. Dragon Dancer, who ended the season a maiden, was enterprisingly ridden on the day and almost certainly flattered relative to those who finished around him. Dylan Thomas did plenty for the form, going on to win the Irish Derby in clear-cut fashion before beating older horses in the Irish Champion Stakes, albeit ridden on each occasion with more restraint than at Epsom. Sir Percy was well below form on his only run after Epsom, but he did well to win the Derby, given the run of the race. It might be assumed that the Derby is run in a similar way each year, and to an extent, that is true. The size of the field, the anxiety of most riders to hold a good position at Tattenham Corner and the need for the most likely stayers to have their stamina brought into play helps see to it that the early pace is rarely pedestrian. All the same, there can be considerable variation in the way the Derby is run from year to year. In the last ten renewals, the slowest winning timefigure was recorded by Oath, who returned a figure equivalent to a timerating of 114. The fastest was Motivator's figure of 128 in 2005. Allowing that Motivator was the superior Derby winner, that is a big difference, equivalent to seven and a half lengths over a mile and a half on good ground. Sir Percy's timerating of 115 underlines the muddling pace at which the Derby was run and also helps to put his achievement in winning in context. Sir Percy was only eleventh into the straight, easily the worst-placed of those that figured in the finish, and he did well to make up the amount of ground he did. As we read it, the bare form of Sir Percy's Guineas effort is superior to the bare form he showed on Derby Day, enough to consider him a high-class colt.

Echoes of much earlier summers came back with Sir Percy's victory at Epsom. He was the first Derby winner since Generous in 1991 even to have run in the Two Thousand Guineas. There was a time when it was commonplace for the Two Thousand Guineas to prove the best trial for the Derby—in the 'seventies alone five Derby winners, Nijinsky, Mill Reef, Roberto, Grundy and The Minstrel, ran in the Guineas—but no Derby winner since Nashwan in 1989 has completed the double. Sir Percy was also unusual among modern Derby winners in his type of two-year-old career. He was the first Derby winner since Dr Devious in 1992 to have won the Dewhurst, and the first since the same horse to have been seen out as early as May at two, winning a maiden over six furlongs at Goodwood before taking a minor event over the same trip at Salisbury in June and the Vintage Stakes over seven at Goodwood in July. At one point during the summer, there was even talk of Sir Percy's becoming the first Derby winner since Reference Point in 1987 to tackle the St Leger. His trainer's initial reaction to success in the Derby was to aim Sir Percy at the Irish Derby. 'I'd prefer to keep him at a mile and a half for the moment,' he said immediately after Epsom. Two days later, there had been a change of mind. 'It may be sensible to win again over a trip short of a mile and a half, simply to give encouragement to those breeders who look for speed in a stallion,' Tregoning said, nominating the Eclipse as the likely target. All the talk came to nothing, at least so far as the rest of the summer was concerned. Later in June, it was announced that Sir Percy had returned 'stiff' and 'jarred up' from Epsom. Sir Percy came back into gentle exercise shortly afterwards, but in July a further delay in the timing of his next appearance was announced, ruling out the St Leger. 'Sir Percy is not in work and we are waiting until the autumn. The grass gallops are much too firm at present. It has been a fantastic summer, but the result is the ground is too quick,' said Tregoning.

Sir Percy's problems ruled out the possibility of his contesting a trial for the Prix de l'Arc de Triomphe, and he missed the Arc itself with 'a niggling shoulder muscle' in the week of the race. In a potentially strong field, Sir Percy was generally a 14/1-shot for Longchamp at the time, odds which arguably seemed on the generous side, provided all was well with him. Sir Percy was initially installed as 7/2 favourite for the Champion Stakes at Newmarket two weeks after Longchamp and went off second favourite behind Hurricane Run at 11/4 in a field of eight on the day. Sir Percy was the first Derby winner to tackle the Champion since Benny The Dip finished sixth in 1997. Sir Percy looked fit enough to do himself justice, but he ran a long way below form, shaping as though he would play a part until two furlongs out, but then quickly coming under pressure and fading to finish seventh, beaten seven and a half lengths by the winner Pride.

Sir Percy is to stay in training as a four-year-old when he looks set to make an early start to his campaign in Dubai in March, reportedly taking in the Jebel Hatta over nearly nine furlongs prior to the Dubai Sheema Classic over a mile and a half, both at Nad Al Sheba. In the last twenty-five years, Derby winners Teenoso, Slip Anchor, Quest For Fame, High-Rise, High Chaparral and North Light have remained in training at four. Among those, only Teenoso and High Chaparral added significantly to their reputations, Teenoso winning the King George and High Chaparral the Irish Champion Stakes over a mile and a quarter, as well as dead-heating to earn a second Breeders' Cup Turf.

No review of the 2006 Derby would be complete without mention of the fact that, for the first time in nearly half a century, no North American-bred runner took part in the race. The use of suffixes was introduced in the mid- to late-'sixties, as an alternative to the Roman numerals which used to be added to imported horses to differentiate them from domestic performers with the same name. Imports of American-breds to Europe in larger numbers prompted the change to suffixes when

Mr A. E. Pakenham's "Sir Percy"

the proliferation of Roman numerals began to cause confusion. At first, suffixes were added for individual horses when their names were recorded in Britain, but soon it became routine for crops of foals. Including The Minstrel, who, like Nijinsky, carried the Canadian suffix, a further fourteen North American-bred horses have won the Derby since Nijinsky did so in 1970, the most recent being Kris Kin in 2003. Following Motivator in 2005, Sir Percy was only the second Derby winner bred in Britain since Commander In Chief in 1993. His pedigree is virtually devoid of American influence close up, his dam Percy's Lass descending from Horama the legendary foundation mare of the Moller brothers' White Lodge Stud. Percy's Lass's dam Laughing Girl, a great granddaughter of Horama, is a half-sister to Irish One Thousand Guineas winner Favoletta and Oaks runner-up Furioso, dam of the Mollers' 1983 Derby winner Teenoso. Percy's Lass was part of the wholesale purchase by Sheikh Mohammed of the Moller bloodstock on the death of Eric Moller in 1989. She had been a big disappointment at stud, from seven foals producing only one winner, Blue Lion (by Lomond), successful over a mile and a mile and a quarter. Percy's Lass was weeded out of Darley Stud in 1998, sold for 28,000 guineas carrying the filly Love Token (by Mark of Esteem). Love Token showed useful form in winning at nine furlongs to eleven furlongs in Ireland and her conformation reportedly encouraged her breeder to return the dam to Mark of Esteem, to whom she produced Sir Percy's sister Lady Karr, a winner over a mile and a half, before being responsible for Sir Percy. Percy's Lass died three weeks after Sir Percy was foaled, though her stud record has also been improved since by her unraced daughter Lionne (by Darshaan), a close relative of Sir Percy, who has produced Jadalee, a smart three-year-old for Sir Percy's stable in 2006.

		Mark of Esteem (IRE)	Darshaan	Shirley Heights
Sir Percy		(b 1993)	(br 1981)	Delsy
(b.c. 2003)			Homage	Ajdal
			(b 1989)	Home Love
		Percy's Lass	Blakeney	Hethersett
		(b or br 1984)	(b 1966)	Windmill Girl
			Laughing Girl	Sassafras
			(b 1973)	Violetta III

A 20,000-guinea foal, knocked down to Sir Percy's trainer for only 16,000 guineas at the Tattersalls October Yearling Sales, Sir Percy is one of only six Derby winners in the last thirty years to be sold at public auction in Britain and Ireland. He was much the cheapest. Among the others, Generous made IR200,000 guineas, Dr Devious 56,000 guineas, Oath IR450,000 guineas, High Chaparral 270,000 guineas and Motivator 75,000 guineas, each of them as yearlings. The average yearling price for the progeny of Sir Percy's sire Mark of Esteem in 2004 was only 18,569 guineas. Mark of Esteem was retired to stud in 1997. Prior to Sir Percy, he had produced only one Group 1 winner, Ameerat, successful in the One Thousand Guineas. As a consequence, Mark of Esteem's fee at Darley Stud had fallen to £7,000 in 2006 but had been raised to £12,000 for 2007. However, a decline in his fertility has led to his being withdrawn from stud duties on veterinary advice, for the 2007 season at least. Ironically, Mark of Esteem was given a further boost in the latest season with the emergence of Reverence, the leading sprinter successful in the Nunthorpe Stakes and the Sprint Cup at Haydock. Mark of Esteem never raced beyond a mile, winning the Two Thousand Guineas (in a three-way photo) and showing himself one of the best milers of the last thirty years when beating Bosra Sham in a vintage Queen Elizabeth II Stakes. Mark of Esteem hasn't been a strong influence for stamina at stud, the average distance of races won by his three-year-olds being just short of nine furlongs. Percy's Lass, however, was well suited by middle distances. Unbeaten at two and restricted to two outings at three through injury, she was better than ever at four, winning the September Stakes and finishing a creditable fifth in the King George VI and Queen Elizabeth Stakes. Unfortunately, she blotted her copybook that season, becoming inconsistent and temperamental, showing a reluctance both to go to the start and to race. So far, the only sign of temperament with Sir Percy came when he gave a deal of trouble—he had to be blindfolded—before entering the stalls at Epsom, where he was on his toes before-hand. He is generally an exuberant sort and was on his toes before the Guineas, when he had two handlers, while he began to sweat before his final outing.

A genuine sort, effective at a mile and a mile and a half, at least when the emphasis is on speed, he acts on soft and good to firm ground and has yet to race on extremes. A winner of five of his seven starts, it hardly needs saying that he has already proved a rare bargain—no matter how he fares at four. *M. P. Tregoning*

SIR SANDICLIFFE (IRE) 2 b.g. (Apr 24) Distant Music 126 – Desert Rose **74** (Green Desert (USA) 127) [2006 6g³ 6m⁵ 7g⁴ Aug 23] 30,000Y: leggy gelding: fourth foal: dam, race once (at 2 yrs), half-sister to smart sprinter Feet So Fast and Lowther Stakes winner Soar: fair form in maidens, fourth to Cold Quest at Leicester (made running): stays 7f. *B. W. Hills*

SIR SANDROVITCH (IRE) 10 b.g. Polish Patriot (USA) 128 – Old Downie (Be My **56** Guest (USA) 126) [2006 70: f5g³ p5.1g⁴ p6g⁶ p6g f5g⁵ f6g⁵ f6g⁶ Mar 20] tall gelding: modest performer: left R. Fahey after third start: best at 5f: acts on all-weather, all 8 turf wins on good ground or firmer: wears headgear: sometimes slowly away. *R. W. Price*

SIR XAAR (IRE) 3 b. or br.c. Xaar 132 – Cradle Brief (IRE) (Brief Truce (USA) 126) **103** [2006 104: 8g 7d² 7f⁵ 7d 7.1m⁴ 7g Sep 15] good-topped colt: has a quick action: useful performer: good 3½ lengths second to Decado in Tetrarch Stakes at the Curragh second start: respectable efforts at best after: effective at 6f/7f: acts on good to firm and good to soft going. *B. Smart*

SISTER ETIENNE (IRE) 2 b.f. (Apr 7) Lend A Hand 124 – Final Favour (IRE) **68** (Unblest 117) [2006 p5.1g 5m³ 5g⁴ 5m⁴ 6d 5g⁴ 5m* p5.1m⁵ f5g² f5g* Dec 27] compact filly: first foal: dam unraced: fair performer: won selling nursery at Beverley in September and seller at Southwell in December: should stay 6f: acts on fibresand and good to firm going: races prominently. *T. D. Barron*

SISTER GEE (IRE) 4 b.f. Desert Story (IRE) 115 – My Gloria (IRE) (Saint Estephe **46** (FR) 123) [2006 46: 6g³ 6m f8g⁶ 7m p6g f7m⁵ Oct 31] sturdy filly: poor maiden: best at 6f: acts on fibresand and good to soft going. *R. Hollinshead*

SISTER MARIA (USA) 2 b. or br.f. (Apr 22) Kingmambo (USA) 125 – Fraulein 117 **75** (Acatenango (GER) 127) [2006 7d p8g³ p8.6s² Dec 15] first foal: dam 7f (at 2 yrs) to 1¼m (E. P. Taylor Stakes) winner: fair form in maidens: signs of waywardness. *E. A. L. Dunlop*

SITULA (IRE) 2 ch.f. (Apr 22) Pairumani Star (IRE) 110 – Suspiria (IRE) 87 (Glenstal **73** (USA) 118) [2006 7f⁴ 7g² p7.1g* p7.1g² p7g³ Dec 10] ex-Irish filly: half-sister to 1999 2-y-o 7f winner Gin Oclock (by Bin Ajwaad) and winner in Turkey by Anshan: dam, 5f winner in Italy at 2 yrs, half-sister to smart miler Ventiquattrofogli: fair performer: trained by G. Lyons in Ireland first 2 starts: won maiden at Wolverhampton in November: better run after when second in nursery there: will stay 1m. *H. J. L. Dunlop*

SIVIVATU (USA) 3 b.g. Stravinsky (USA) 133 – Belle Sultane (USA) (Seattle Slew **77** (USA)) [2006 83: 7g p10g⁶ 8f⁶ Jun 30] strong, attractive gelding: just fair performer at 3 yrs, leaving J. Noseda before final outing: should stay 7f. *Kathy Walsh, USA*

SIVOTA (IRE) 2 b.g. (Mar 29) Sakhee (USA) 136 – Mamara Reef 71 (Salse (USA) **77 p** 128) [2006 8g³ 7s³ 8.2d² Nov 1] €105,000F, 50,000Y: neat gelding: half-brother to several winners, notably Irish 1000 Guineas third Storm Dream (by Catrail), later Grade 3 8.5f winner in USA: dam, 1¾m/hurdles winner, half-sister to smart French 1½m performer Foundation Spirit: progressive form when placed in maidens, second to Sagredo at Nottingham: will improve further at 1¼m/1½m. *T. P. Tate*

SIWA 3 b.f. Green Desert (USA) 127 – Criquette 104 (Shirley Heights 130) [2006 65p: **72** p7.1g² p7.1g² p6g⁵ p7g p10g May 12] fair maiden: needs further than 6f and should be suited by 1m+: has wandered/found little: sent to Australia. *E. A. L. Dunlop*

SIX MILE BOTTOM (IRE) 2 b.f. (Mar 25) Mull of Kintyre (USA) 114 – Nizamiya **75** (Darshaan 133) [2006 5d⁶ 6g³ 6d⁴ 6d Aug 25] €6,000Y, resold 8,000Y: closely related to 3 winners, including Irish 7.5f winner Mountain Melody (by Monashee Mountain), and half-sister to 2 winners: dam, ran twice, half-sister to Cherry Hinton winner Nasseem: fair maiden: third in listed race at Hamburg in July: well held in sales race at Newmarket final start: stays 6f: usually blinkered. *Bruce Hellier, Germany*

SIX OF TRUMPS (IRE) 2 b.g. (Mar 17) Fasliyev (USA) 120 – Run To Jane (IRE) **–** (Doyoun 124) [2006 7g Jul 28] useful-looking gelding: green, last in maiden at Ascot: gelded after. *J. A. Osborne*

SIX SHOTS 2 b.c. (Mar 5) Josr Algarhoud (IRE) 118 – Captive Heart (Conquistador **67** Cielo (USA)) [2006 6s 7f 7g Aug 17] 3,500F, €34,000Y: good-bodied colt: half-brother to several winners, including fairly useful 6f winner (including at 2 yrs) Caught In The Dark (by Night Shift), later 7f winner in USA, and 15f winner Windfall (by Polish Precedent): dam, maiden who was suited by 7f, half-sister to Irish Oaks winner Knight's Baroness: mid-division at best in maidens, fair form at Salisbury (behind Streets Ahead) final start. *J. A. Osborne*

SIXTIES ICON 3 b.c. Galileo (IRE) 134 – Love Divine 120 (Diesis 133) [2006 **125** 10g⁶ 10g* 12m 12m³ 12m* 13.9g* 12m Oct 1]

When asked what he considers his finest achievement, Vincent O'Brien doesn't select any of the training feats with the long line of champions he sent out from Ballydoyle. 'I would feel most satisfaction in having done my bit for the Irish bloodstock industry,' is his reply. The expansion of the Coolmore stud empire was built on the successful strategy devised in the 'seventies by O'Brien, John Magnier and Robert Sangster of buying the best yearlings, with top pedigrees, at the Keeneland Sales, many of them sired by Northern Dancer who was set to become the height of fashion. The specific aim was to turn them into classic winners and then stand the successful ones at stud. Coolmore had no connection with O'Brien or Magnier and stood only two stallions in 1971, the year John Magnier purchased the high-class sprinter Green God from owner David Robinson for his family's Castle Hyde Stud. Magnier met Robert Sangster when Green God won the Sprint Cup at Haydock, a race sponsored at the time by Vernons, a pools company to which Sangster was heir.

Two years later, by which time Sangster had horses in training at Ballydoyle, O'Brien bought two-thirds of Coolmore and approached Magnier, soon to be his son-in-law, to manage it. The Coolmore and Castle Hyde studs were amalgamated and, with the backing of Sangster and other wealthy syndicate members, O'Brien and Magnier set about reversing the flow of top stallions and good mares to America. Among the first crop of yearlings bought in 1975 at Keeneland was the Northern Dancer colt The Minstrel, whose dam was a half-sister to Nijinsky (also by Northern Dancer) with whom O'Brien had won the triple crown in 1970 during a period when O'Brien's success with such as Sir Ivor and Nijinsky had helped to advertise the virtues of North American bloodlines. The Minstrel and the other Keeneland purchases were joined by Alleged, who was bought at a two-year-old in-training auction, and those two, syndicated for nine million dollars and sixteen million dollars respectively at the end of their racing careers, got the syndicates off to a flying start. American-bred Be My Guest (by Northern Dancer out of champion filly What A Treat), who was bought at Goffs for a European record price as a yearling, was a contemporary of The Minstrel and Alleged. He became Coolmore's first champion sire of Britain and Ireland.

By the end of the 'seventies, around three quarters of the O'Brien string at Ballydoyle were American-breds. The concept of 'buying to make stallions' continued to reap rich dividends, the expansion of Coolmore continuing apace thanks to the magnificent stud career enjoyed by Sadler's Wells who, though overshadowed as a racehorse by his contemporary El Gran Senor, pushed the Northern Dancer

BGC Stakes (Gordon), Goodwood—Sixties Icon advances his St Leger claims; Jadalee takes second from Linas Selection (stars on sleeves)

*Ladbrokes St Leger Stakes, York—in a race run at York for the first time since 1945,
Sixties Icon is a comfortable winner from The Last Drop; Red Rocks (left) takes third, ahead of Ask (No.1)*

influence to new heights, establishing himself as the greatest sire in European bloodstock history. Two sons of the ageing Sadler's Wells are now really making their mark as stallions at Coolmore, Montjeu and Galileo, the last-named equalling the feat achieved by his sire in the 2001 Oaks—the year Galileo won the Derby—by siring the first three home in a British classic. Sadler's Wells, who also achieved the feat in the 1999 Irish Derby, has essentially been an influence for stamina and has sired two St Leger winners, Milan and Brian Boru, in 2001 and 2003 (he has also had four runners-up and is grandsire of two more winners, Silver Patriarch and Scorpion). Galileo's first crop were three-year-olds in the latest season and he had his first British classic winner in the St Leger with Sixties Icon who led home a one, two, three for his sire who had five runners in the race, Sadler's Wells and Montjeu being responsible for another two runners each.

The success of Sixties Icon crowned a splendid season for Coolmore stallions in the British and Irish classics, with eight of the nine (not counting the all-aged Irish St Leger) being won by their offspring. Danehill had the Two Thousand Guineas and Irish Derby winners George Washington and Dylan Thomas; Sadler's Wells sired Alexandrova who completed the Anglo-Irish Oaks double; Danehill Dancer was represented by One Thousand Guineas winner Speciosa; Mull of Kintyre was the sire of Irish Two Thousand Guineas winner Araafa; and Galileo also had his first Irish classic winner with Nightime in the One Thousand Guineas. In the 'one that got away', Dragon Dancer (by Sadler's Wells) and Dylan Thomas finished second and third in one of the closest finishes in Derby history (Coolmore sires had won seven of the eight previous runnings). In all, nine of the twelve Group 1 races in Ireland were won by progeny of Coolmore stallions, while fourteen of the thirty-one in Britain were from the same source. At the same time, Group 1 winners with the USA suffix were in fairly short supply as things more or less came full circle and Vincent O'Brien's dream became reality, Irish-breds, particularly those based at Coolmore, dominating the British and Irish scene. The IRE suffix, by the way, was not applied to Irish-breds racing in Britain until Irish breeders asked for its use about twenty years after suffixes first began to be introduced for American-breds in the mid- to late-'sixties. At the request of the Irish Thoroughbred Breeders' Association, the latest volume of the General Stud Book, published in 2006, has been split on the basis of where each mare is normally domiciled. The Irish section is the larger, though some mares appear in both sections.

The Ladbrokes St Leger, the second most valuable of the British classics after the Derby, had a temporary home in the latest season, transferred to York (where it was also run in 1945) while reconstruction went on at Doncaster. The race was also run over a distance one hundred and forty-five yards shorter than at its traditional home at Town Moor, the York executive starting the Leger at the Ebor start rather than creating a new one, the race decided over one mile five furlongs and one hundred and ninety-seven yards. Critics would have been hard pressed to argue that the result would have been different if the St Leger had been run over its usual distance. Frankie Dettori, riding his hundredth winner of the season in Britain, described Sixties Icon as 'probably one of the easiest' of his eleven British classic winners, which was something of an understatement. Sixties Icon had promised from early in his career to be suited by the St Leger trip and, starting 11/8 favourite, he was ridden very confidently, travelling through the race really well and sprinting clear in the final furlong once shaken up to defy rumours—vehemently refuted as 'bullshit' by his trainer—that had circulated about his well-being leading up to the race.

Dettori had those in front covered from early in the straight and, two furlongs out, was looking behind to check on his main rival 4/1-shot Red Rocks who was the only other runner still on the bridle at that stage. Sixties Icon wasn't at all extended to win by two and a half lengths and a length from 50/1-shot The Last Drop and Red Rocks, who shaped as if the race stretched his stamina, failing to find so much as looked likely. The present incumbent at Ballydoyle, Aidan O'Brien (no relation to Vincent), had won the St Leger three times in the previous six years, his 2005 winner Scorpion also by a Coolmore stallion in Montjeu. His three representatives in the latest edition, Tusculum (by Sadler's Wells out of a half-sister to Galileo's dam), Mountain (by Montjeu) and Fire And Rain (by Galileo) finished fifth, seventh and tenth in the eleven-runner field. Galileo's fifth representative, Galient, who dictated the largely sound pace until the straight, filled last place. Galient had finished second to the progressive Soapy Danger in the Queen's Vase at Royal Ascot. Soapy Danger, who fractured a pastern when fifth in the Great Voltigeur, and the Voltigeur winner Youmzain were among a number of absentees whose presence would have given an ordinary St Leger field more strength in depth. Soapy Danger had been second favourite to Sixties Icon in the ante-post market the day before the Voltigeur, when Papal Bull, who was a disappointing favourite in the Voltigeur and didn't run in the Leger, was joint third favourite with the intended Ballydoyle number-one Septimus who also failed to make the Leger line-up.

The Great Voltigeur at York has probably been the most significant trial for the St Leger in recent years—Red Rocks and The Last Drop finished second and fourth in the latest edition—but Sixties Icon had finished his preparation in another race that is rivalling it as a pointer. Nedawi, who dead-heated in the Gordon Stakes, and Millenary had both gone on to complete the Gordon/St Leger double and Sixties Icon became the third to do so in nine years. The race, sponsored by BGC, illustrated the progress of Sixties Icon who, unraced at two, had got off the mark on his second start, despite showing greenness, in a maiden at Windsor in May, before finishing a staying-on seventh to Sir Percy in the Derby, beaten just over five lengths. Sixties Icon showed that he was learning all the time when improving again to finish third to Papal Bull and Red Rocks in the King Edward VII Stakes at Royal Ascot. Sixties Icon's first pattern win in the Gordon was achieved smoothly from Jadalee and Linas Selection. Sixties Icon showed a good turn of foot and Dettori was able to take things easily inside the final furlong, winning by a length and three quarters, a margin that could have been doubled at least.

Sixties Icon, who stays in training, ran once after the St Leger, when the only British-trained challenger for the eight-runner Prix de l'Arc de Triomphe, for which he had to be supplemented at a cost of €60,000. His owners didn't get much of a run for their money, Sixties Icon, who was sweating freely by post time, never showing with a chance and beating only the very disappointing Shirocco home, Dettori reporting that Sixties Icon pulled up feelingly. His trainer, Jeremy Noseda, for whom the St Leger was his first British classic (he also trained Irish Two Thousand Guineas winner Araafa), subsequently confirmed that Sixties Icon was 'not right after the Arc, though it is nothing serious.' In winning a classic, Sixties Icon, a 230,000-guinea yearling, followed in the footsteps of both his sire (about whom more can be found in the essay on Teofilo) and his dam. Sixties Icon is the second foal of Oaks winner Love Divine (who beat the Noseda-trained Kalypso Katie at Epsom in 2000). Love Divine's sire Diesis, who has had two other Oaks winners in Diminuendo and Ramruma, both of whom went on to finish second in the St Leger, enjoyed something of a red-letter day on St Leger day, as he is also the sire of the dam of Dylan Thomas, Ballydoyle's top middle-distance three-year-old who won the Irish Champion Stakes at the Curragh the same afternoon. Retired from stud duties in April, Diesis was put down in November after fracturing a hip.

Sixties Icon (b.c. 2003)	Galileo (IRE) (b 1998)	Sadler's Wells (b 1981)	Northern Dancer Fairy Bridge
		Urban Sea (ch 1989)	Miswaki Allegretta
	Love Divine (b 1997)	Diesis (ch 1980)	Sharpen Up Doubly Sure
		La Sky (b 1988)	Law Society Maryinsky

Love Divine's first foal Love Me Well (by Sadler's Wells) was second twice from just three starts in France. Sixties Icon is followed by a two-year-old filly by Grand Lodge (named Kissing and in training with Sir Mark Prescott), a yearling colt by Red Ransom and a colt foal by Cape Cross. Sixties Icon's second dam La Sky finished second in the Lancashire Oaks after winning her first two starts, a maiden at Newbury and a minor event at Nottingham, both at a mile and a quarter. She also finished a creditable third over a mile and three quarters in the March Stakes at Goodwood. La Sky is closely related to Champion Stakes winner Legal Case (by Law Society's sire Alleged) out of Maryinsky who won twice at up to nine furlongs in the States. Further back, in a branch of the celebrated Pretty Polly family, Sixties Icon's fifth dam Rich Relation was a sister to the 1951 Derby runner-up Sybil's Nephew and a half-sister to Sybil's Niece, the dam of champion sire Great Nephew. The same branch of the Pretty Polly family also produced dual King George VI and Queen Elizabeth Stakes winner Swain. Sixties Icon has the looks to match his pedigree, being a strong, well-made, attractive colt who was turned out in tremendous shape for the St Leger. Still relatively lightly raced, he should do well at four when a campaign in the staying events is said to be planned. Sixties Icon has worn a crossed noseband but settled very well in the St Leger. He has been raced only on good and good to firm going. *J. Noseda*

SKELLIGS ROCK (IRE) 6 b.g. Key of Luck (USA) 126 – Drew (IRE) (Double Schwartz 128) [2006 –: p12g⁶ p9.5g 10.9f 16.2f 11.9f⁴ Aug 9] poor maiden: stays 1½m: acts on firm and good to soft going. *A. W. Carroll*   **42**

SKEZAHRA 3 b.f. Zaha (CAN) 106 – Skedaddle 57 (Formidable (USA) 125) [2006 –: p8g⁶ Jan 3] strong, workmanlike filly: little form. *T. M. Jones*   **–**

SKHILLING SPIRIT 3 b.g. Most Welcome 131 – Calcavella 75 (Pursuit of Love 124) [2006 93: 6m⁵ 7s² 6s* 6g 6d 7d² 6s Oct 7] strong, close-coupled gelding: has a short, unimpressive action: useful performer: won listed race at Haydock in May by neck from Guto: creditable second to Army of Angels in handicap at Newmarket after: stays 7f: acts on firm and soft going: tried blinkered: signs of temperament, often looks reluctant and hangs. *T. D. Barron*   **101**

SKIDDAW FOX 2 ch.c. (May 25) Foxhound (USA) 103 – Stealthy Times 80 (Timeless Times (USA) 99) [2006 p6g Nov 14] last in maiden at Wolverhampton. *Mrs L. Williamson*   **–**

SKIDMARK 5 b.g. Pennekamp (USA) 130 – Flourishing (IRE) 85 (Trojan Fen 118) [2006 101d: p10g⁶ p9.5g⁶ p12.2g p10g Apr 2] lengthy, useful-looking gelding: just fairly useful handicapper in 2006: stays 1¼m: acts on polytrack, best efforts on turf on good ground: tried in cheekpieces, pulled too hard in blinkers final outing. *Miss J. R. Tooth*   **83**

SKI

SKIDROW 4 b.g. Bachir (IRE) 118 – Flourishing (IRE) 85 (Trojan Fen 118) [2006 101: **98**
8m 8m³ 8.1s³ 8.5g² 8f² 8g⁵ 8s 8.1g² 8s Oct 6] quite attractive gelding: useful handicapper:
mainly creditable efforts in 2006, short-head second to Abbey Cat at Haydock on penultimate start: should stay 1¼m: acts on any going: reliable: sold 60,000 gns, sent to Saudi
Arabia. *M. L. W. Bell*

SKI FOR LUCK (IRE) 2 br.g. (Feb 14) Key of Luck (USA) 126 – Ski For Me (IRE) **–**
88 (Barathea (IRE) 127) [2006 7m 8d⁵ 8m Sep 9] well held in maidens: gelded after.
J. L. Dunlop

SKI JUMP (USA) 6 gr.g. El Prado (IRE) 119 – Skiable (IRE) (Niniski (USA) 125) **87**
[2006 93: 11.5m 13.8d 13.9s 14m² 18m* p16g 21m 12d 16g³ 18s⁴ 18d⁴ Oct 14] good-
bodied gelding: fairly useful handicapper: won at York in June: creditable efforts last 3
starts, fourth in Cesarewitch at Newmarket final one: effective at 1½m to 2½m: acts on
firm and soft going, folded only outing on polytrack: wears headgear. *R. A. Fahey*

SKIN SURE THING 3 b.f. Zaha (CAN) 106 – Bay Bianca (IRE) (Law Society (USA) **39**
130) [2006 –: f8g p8.6g² p8.6g p8.6g⁵ p8g 11.6m 11.9f⁶ p12.2f Aug 14] poor maiden: left
A. Smith after fifth start: visored/in cheekpieces nowadays. *D. G. Bridgwater*

SKIP OF COLOUR 6 b.g. Rainbow Quest (USA) 134 – Minskip (USA) 64 (The **65**
Minstrel (CAN) 135) [2006 63d: p6g f6g* p6g Dec 18] fair performer: won seller at
Southwell in December: best at 5f/6f: acts on all-weather and good to soft going: tongue
tied last 2 starts. *P. A. Blockley*

SKIT 3 b.g. In The Wings 128 – Skew (Niniski (USA) 125) [2006 –: 10.3f 10.3m⁴ 14m **51**
16.2m* Aug 28] modest performer, lightly raced: won handicap at Chepstow in August:
stays 2m: raced only on firm/good to firm going. *W. M. Brisbourne*

SKODGER (IRE) 3 b.c. Nashwan (USA) 135 – Ghay (USA) 61 (Bahri (USA) 125) **–**
[2006 8d 8s Aug 28] tailed-off last in maidens: tongue tied (said to have had breathing
problem) final outing. *G. Woodward*

SKY AT NIGHT (IRE) 3 b.g. Beckett (IRE) 116 – Grade A Star (IRE) (Alzao (USA) **52**
117) [2006 51: p7g p8g 8.2d⁵ 11.6f⁶ p12g⁵ p10g⁵ 11.6m p10g 12g Aug 18] modest
maiden: seems to stay 1½m: acts on polytrack and firm ground: in headgear last 5 starts:
sometimes slowly away. *P. Mitchell*

SKY BEAM (USA) 2 b.f. (Mar 31) Kingmambo (USA) 125 – Weekend In Seattle **–**
(USA) (Seattle Slew (USA)) [2006 7m 8.1m 8.3d Oct 10] $250,000Y: tall, leggy, quite
good-topped filly: seventh foal: closely related to winner in USA by Seeking The Gold
and half-sister to winner there by Danzig: dam, 8.5f (including at 2 yrs)/9f winner in USA
and third in Grade 1 event, sister to Breeders' Cup Classic winner A P Indy: behind in
maidens. *J. L. Dunlop*

SKY CRUSADER 4 b.g. Mujahid (USA) 125 – Red Cloud (IRE) 61 (Taufan (USA) **91**
119) [2006 97: 8m 7.1m 8.5g 7.1m 7m 7g Jul 6] tall, leggy gelding: just fairly useful
handicapper in 2006: best at 7f/1m: acts on polytrack, firm and good to soft going:
visored (well held) final start: gelded and sold 12,000 gns. *R. Ingram*

SKYE BOAT SONG 3 b.c. Inchinor 119 – Nebulae (IRE) 82 (Unfuwain (USA) 131) **43**
[2006 –: f8g p10g p8.6g³ p8g May 15] poor maiden: stays 8.6f: acts on polytrack: tongue
tied last 2 outings, had breathing problem final one. *J. Jay*

SKYE BUT N BEN 2 b.g. (Mar 14) Auction House (USA) 120 – Island Colony (USA) **47**
(Pleasant Colony (USA)) [2006 5m⁶ 6m 7s 7.1d p8.6g⁶ Nov 27] lengthy, quite attractive
gelding: good walker: poor maiden: probably stays 8.6f. *T. D. Barron*

SKYELADY 3 b.f. Dansili 127 – Song of Skye 84 (Warning 136) [2006 92d: p8g 8d⁶ **83**
8v³ 8d 8.2s Oct 25] close-coupled, rather lightly-made filly: has a quick action: fairly useful handicapper: barely stays testing 1m: acts on heavy going. *Miss J. A. Camacho*

SKY HIGH GUY (IRE) 3 b.g. Galileo (IRE) 134 – Well Bought (IRE) 35 (Auction **76**
Ring (USA) 123) [2006 –: p10g² p8g³ p10g² p9.5g³ 10.2g 11.6m 11.6d⁵ 9.9g³ 8.5m⁴
12.4d² Aug 28] leggy gelding: fair maiden handicapper: stays 12.4f: acts on polytrack,
unraced on extremes of going on turf. *S. Kirk*

SKY QUEST (IRE) 8 b.g. Spectrum (IRE) 126 – Rose Vibert (Caerleon (USA) 132) **83**
[2006 91: 10g 10f⁵ 9.9f⁴ 11.8m⁵ p10g⁴ 12.6m⁵ 11.7f⁵ p8g Dec 16] smallish, quite good-
topped gelding: fairly useful handicapper: left W. Swinburn 3,000 gns prior to final
outing: effective at 1¼m/1½m: acts on polytrack, firm and good to soft going: usually
wears cheekpieces/tongue tie: suited by waiting tactics: has carried head awkwardly/
found little. *J. R. Boyle*

SKY WALK 3 b.g. Josr Algarhoud (IRE) 118 – Jamrat Samya (IRE) 79 (Sadler's Wells – (USA) 132) [2006 p10g p12g Sep 18] smallish, compact gelding: well held in maidens at Lingfield and Kempton. *Jamie Poulton*

SLALOM (IRE) 6 b.g. Royal Applause 124 – Skisette (Malinowski (USA) 123) [2006 – p13.9g Mar 31] well-made gelding: fair performer at 4 yrs, well held only outing on Flat since: has worn cheekpieces: often slowly away. *D. Burchell*

SLATE (IRE) 2 b.c. (Mar 13) Rock of Gibraltar (IRE) 133 – Sharp Catch (IRE) 98 **78 p** (Common Grounds 118) [2006 7.1m* 7d Sep 24] €190,000Y: rather leggy colt: third foal: half-brother to 6f winner Bohola Flyer (by Barathea) and 2004 Irish 2-y-o 7f winner Cappa Blanca (by Giant's Causeway), both fairly useful: dam, Irish 5f (at 2 yrs) and 1m winner, half-sister to smart sprinter Catch The Blues: fair form: won maiden at Warwick (beat Thabaat by length) in September: repeatedly hampered in nursery at Ascot: free-going type, likely to prove best up to 7f: remains likely to improve. *J. A. Osborne*

SLAVONIC LAKE 2 b.c. (Feb 19) Lake Coniston (IRE) 131 – Slavonic Dance **56** (Muhtarram (USA) 125) [2006 7f* 8m 8f 8s Oct 16] modest performer: won seller at Thirsk in July: well beaten in nurseries (blinkered final start): should stay 1m. *I. A. Wood*

SLAVONIC (USA) 5 ch.g. Royal Academy (USA) 130 – Cyrillic (USA) 106 (Irish – River (FR) 131) [2006 72: 7g 9g Jul 3] strong, close-coupled gelding: fair performer at 4 yrs, well held in 2006: tried blinkered/visored, usually wears cheekpieces: has looked difficult ride. *B. Storey*

SLEEPING INDIAN 5 b.h. Indian Ridge 123 – Las Flores (IRE) 102 (Sadler's **122** Wells (USA) 132) [2006 122: 7g* 7m 7d* 8f⁴ Nov 4]

The National Stud may at last have turned the corner, having recorded an operating surplus in 2005 for the first time in a decade. The popularity of Bahamian Bounty—who has had three-figure books in each of the past three seasons—is largely responsible for the change of fortune, the stud also cashing in by syndicating forty per cent of him. Bahamian Bounty's son Pastoral Pursuits, who won the 2005 July Cup, is also at the National Stud and had ninety-eight mares in his first season. The National Stud still has some way to go, however, to match the amazing success story—considering the relatively limited resources available—of its Irish counterpart. Stallions such as Ahonoora and his son Indian Ridge have proved goldmines for the Irish National Stud, where Invincible Spirit, like his predecessors not an obvious top stallion prospect at first glance, made an excellent start with his first runners in 2006. The death of Indian Ridge at the age of twenty-one, just a fortnight or so after the victory of his daughter Indian Ink in the Cheveley Park, must have been a blow. King's Stand winner Indian Ridge soon followed his very successful

VC Bet Challenge Stakes, Newmarket—Sleeping Indian goes one better than in 2005, beating the three-year-old Killybegs (No.14) and Satchem

sire to the Irish National Stud after starting his stud career in England in 1990. Irish One Thousand Guineas and Breeders' Cup Mile winner Ridgewood Pearl, Irish Derby runner-up Definite Article (sire of Vinnie Roe) and July Cup winner Compton Place (now a top twenty stallion) were among those foaled or conceived while Indian Ridge was standing in England. He added considerably to his tally of good winners after being moved to Ireland and now has several sons at stud in Europe, among them the Group/Grade 1 winners Namid (Prix de l'Abbaye), Domedriver (Breeders' Cup Mile) and Indian Haven (Irish Two Thousand Guineas), the last-named securing a place alongside his sire at the Irish National Stud and covering books of eighty-five and sixty-seven in his first two seasons.

The lightly-raced Sleeping Indian is the latest son of Indian Ridge to earn a place at stud. He will be at Tweenhills Farm in Gloucestershire in 2007, standing at a fee of £5,000. Sleeping Indian didn't win at Group 1 level but he was a very smart performer at seven furlongs and a mile and went one better than in 2005 in the Group 2 VCBet Challenge Stakes on Champions Day at Newmarket in October. The race showed off his strengths as he quickened readily to take the lead over two furlongs out and then pulled out more to hold the very smart pair, three-year-old Killybegs and four-year-old Satchem, by a length and a head, with a good-sized, representative field behind. Sleeping Indian also had Satchem back in third when beating Spinning Queen relatively smoothly by a neck in a blanket finish to the Dubai Duty Free Cup at Newbury on his belated reappearance in September. The race was a good one for a listed contest, though Sleeping Indian was a short-priced favourite, going unpenalised for his listed and Group 3 (Hungerford Stakes) wins the previous season. Sleeping Indian's two other outings in the latest season were in Group 1s. He was persistently denied room and unable to get in a blow in the Prix de la Foret at Longchamp on Arc weekend when eleventh of fourteen in a bunched finish. He didn't have much luck either when a strong-finishing fourth in the Breeders' Cup Mile at Churchill Downs, having to be switched round several horses to get a run a furlong and a half out, beaten a head and a neck behind the second and third, and doing best of the seven European-trained challengers. Sleeping Indian should have finished second to Miesque's Approval.

		Ahonoora (ch 1975)	Lorenzaccio
Sleeping Indian (b.h. 2001)	Indian Ridge (ch 1985)		Helen Nichols
		Hillbrow (ch 1975)	Swing Easy
			Golden City
	Las Flores (IRE) (b 1991)	Sadler's Wells (b 1981)	Northern Dancer
			Fairy Bridge
		Producer (br 1976)	Nashua
			Marion

The strong, good-topped Sleeping Indian is fairly typical of the progeny of his sire who was an influence for speed and built up a particularly strong record with his older horses. Sleeping Indian's dam the Sadler's Wells mare Las Flores was useful, placed in the Lingfield Oaks Trial and the Oaks d'Italia, and Sleeping Indian's grandam Producer won the Prix de la Foret and the Prix de l'Opera as well as finishing placed in the Prix de Diane and Irish Oaks. Las Flores, a half-sister to the very smart mile/mile and a quarter performer Bach, has bred five winners, the four others all at least fairly useful, among them the Golden Daffodil Stakes winner Felicity (by Selkirk) who showed her best form at around a mile and a quarter, and La Paz (by Nashwan) who won twice at around a mile and a half. Sleeping Indian was never tried beyond a mile. He acted on firm and good to soft going, probably also on soft, and was genuine. *J. H. M. Gosden*

SLEEPING STORM (IRE) 3 b.f. Danehill Dancer (IRE) 117 – Caribbean Escape **78** (Pivotal 124) [2006 85: p8g 6g 6m 5d 7.1m 8.3d⁴ 6g* 6m⁴ p6g⁵ 6g³ 6d⁴ 7m p7g Oct 21] lengthy, good-bodied filly: fair handicapper: won at Newbury in July: has form at 1m, but best at 6f: acts on polytrack and good to firm going, probably on good to soft: blinkered (last) on fourth outing. *B. J. Meehan*

SLING BACK (IRE) 5 b.m. Desert Style (IRE) 121 – Arabian Princess (Taufan (USA) **87** 119) [2006 72: p7.1g⁵ 6m⁵ 7f* 7g² 7g 7m* 6m⁵ 7m² 6g³ 6g a7g² 7m 7g Sep 15] fairly useful handicapper: won at Cork in June and the Curragh in July: good placed efforts after, including at Ascot ninth outing: best at 6f/7f: acts on all-weather/sand and firm going: tried visored/blinkered. *E. Tyrrell, Ireland*

SLIPASEARCHER (IRE) 2 b.f. (Apr 18) Danetime (IRE) 121 – Imperialist (IRE) 93 **76 d**
(Imperial Frontier (USA) 112) [2006 6.1m⁴ 5.7f* 5m⁵ 5f³ 6m 7.1m 7g⁴ 6m 6m p7g
p8.6g⁵ p7.1g⁴ p7g⁵ p6s⁴ p5.1g⁶ Dec 26] €16,000Y: unfurnished filly: third foal: dam
2-y-o 5f winner: fair performer: won maiden at Bath in June: mostly highly tried in
summer, sometimes flattered, including when fifth in Queen Mary Stakes on third start:
little impact in nurseries on all-weather (in headgear) later in year: best efforts at 5f/6f:
acts on firm going: free-going sort: ungenuine. *P. D. Evans*

SLIP DANCE (IRE) 4 br.f. Celtic Swing 138 – Hawala (IRE) 97 (Warning 136) [2006 **108**
103: 6.5m² 6.5m⁵ 6d⁶ 5m May 6] lengthy filly: useful performer: ran in handicaps at Nad
Al Sheba first 3 starts, very good short-head second to Compton's Eleven on reappearance: sweating and stiff task, well held in Palace House Stakes at Newmarket final outing:
winner at 8.7f, best form up to 6.5f: acts on firm and soft ground: tried blinkered: genuine:
sold 250,000 gns in November. *E. Tyrrell, Ireland*

SLIPPERFOOT 3 ch.f. Sugarfoot 118 – She's A Breeze 35 (Crofthall 110) [2006 54: **63**
5f² 5m⁴ 5m⁶ 5d 5g² 5s 5f 5d Oct 3] smallish filly: modest maiden: should stay 6f: acts on
firm going, well held on softer than good: tried visored/in cheekpieces. *J. J. Quinn*

SLIP STAR 3 b.f. Slip Anchor 136 – Shiny Kay 65 (Star Appeal 133) [2006 7m p8.6g **–**
Nov 11] quite good-topped filly: half-sister to several winners, including useful 1995
2-y-o 5f winner Home Shopping and useful winner up to 1m Kayo, both by Superpower:
dam 1½m winner: no show in maidens. *T. J. Etherington*

SLO MO SHUN 2 b.f. (May 19) Polish Precedent (USA) 131 – Malvadilla (IRE) 77 **45**
(Doyoun 124) [2006 6.1d 6d p8.6m Nov 21] tall filly, unfurnished at 2 yrs: fifth foal:
half-sister to fairly useful Irish 7f winner Blava (by Ashkalani): dam, Irish 9f winner,
granddaughter of sister to Mill Reef: mid-division at best in maidens: should stay 1m.
B. R. Millman

SMALL FORTUNE 2 b.f. (Mar 9) Anabaa (USA) 130 – New Assembly (IRE) 99 **74 p**
(Machiavellian (USA) 123) [2006 6m³ Jul 21] quite good-topped filly: second foal:
closely related to 3-y-o Regent's Park: dam, 9f (in USA) to 1½m winner, sister to very
smart 1m/1¼m performer Right Approach: 14/1, under 3 lengths third to Vital Statistics
in maiden at Newbury, finishing well despite looking green: will stay at least 1m: sure to
progress. *R. Charlton*

SMALL STAKES (IRE) 4 b.g. Pennekamp (USA) 130 – Poker Chip 106 (Bluebird **78**
(USA) 125) [2006 6g² 6g² 5.5d³ 6s⁴ p6g³ p6g* p6g* p6g⁵ Dec 16] strong gelding: fair
performer: missed 2005: won maiden at Wolverhampton in November and, having been
gelded, handicap at Lingfield in December: bred to stay 7f: acts on polytrack and good to
soft going: tongue tied in 2006: visored last 3 starts. *P. J. Makin*

SMALL TIME BLUES (IRE) 4 b.f. Danetime (IRE) 121 – Barinia (Corvaro (USA) **–**
124) [2006 –: f16g p13.9g Jan 13] little form: tried blinkered/tongue tied. *J. Parkes*

SMART ANGUS 2 gr.g. (Feb 23) Agnes World (USA) 123 – She's Smart 88 (Absalom **–**
128) [2006 6s 5m Sep 13] good-topped gelding: behind in maidens. *R. A. Fahey*

SMART ASS (IRE) 3 b.f. Shinko Forest (IRE) – Jayess Elle 55 (Sabrehill (USA) 120) **91**
[2006 44: f6g p6g⁴ p6g³ f7g* f7g* p8.6g² 8.3m 8g 7m 7m² 7g² 7.1d⁶ p7.1g⁶ p8g³ f8g*
f8g* f8g² Dec 27] leggy, quite good-topped filly: fairly useful performer: won seller in
February and handicaps in February and December (2), all at Southwell: good second to
Orpen Wide in handicap there final outing: stays 8.6f: acts on all-weather and firm going.
J. S. Moore

SMART BOY PRINCE (IRE) 5 b.g. Princely Heir (IRE) 111 – Miss Mulaz (FR) 114 **44**
(Luthier 126) [2006 –: f16g* f14g² f14g 16g⁴ Jul 3] workmanlike gelding: modest per- **a58**
former on all-weather, poor on turf: won banded race at Southwell in January: stays 2m:
acts on all-weather and good to firm ground: often makes running: fair hurdler. *C. Smith*

SMART CASSIE 3 ch.f. Allied Forces (USA) 123 – Katy-Q (IRE) 58 (Taufan (USA) **69 d**
119) [2006 77: 5.2m 5m 5m 5g⁶ 5f p5.1g 5g] close-coupled, useful-looking filly: fair
handicapper: well below form after reappearance: may prove best at 5f: acts on good to
firm going. *D. Shaw*

SMART CAT (IRE) 3 ch.f. Barathea (IRE) 127 – Lioness 74 (Lion Cavern (USA) 117) **55 p**
[2006 10d⁶ Sep 14] 22,000Y: second foal: half-sister to 4-y-o Wilford Maverick: dam,
maiden who stayed 9f, half-sister to smart French/US 7f to 1¼m performer Puppeteer:
33/1 and green, 10¾ lengths sixth to Mobaasher in maiden at Pontefract, behind at halfway: open to improvement. *A. P. Jarvis*

Addleshaw Goddard Stakes (Handicap), York—
Smart Enough continues his progress, making all to win with his ears pricked;
Bolodenka is second, ahead of the favourite Pride of Nation and Blythe Knight (hooped cap)

SMART ENOUGH 3 gr.c. Cadeaux Genereux 131 – Good Enough (FR) 109 (Mukad-damah (USA) 125) [2006 80p: 8m² 8s* 8m⁴ 8m* 8s* 9d⁵ Sep 30] tall, lengthy colt: has scope: smart performer, lightly raced: progressed well in 2006, winning maiden at Goodwood in May and handicaps at Newmarket (beat Plum Pudding by 1¾ lengths) in July and York (beat Bolodenka by 2½ lengths) in August: below-form fifth of 33 to Formal Decree in Cambridgeshire (Handicap) at Newmarket final outing: reported the following week to be suffering from an infection: will prove best at 7f/1m: acts on soft and good to firm going: exuberant type, who tends to sweat, and usually makes running. *M. A. Magnusson*   **113**

SMART GAL (IRE) 3 ch.f. Galileo (IRE) 134 – Spring Easy (IRE) (Alzao (USA) 117) [2006 74: 9.9f³ 14d 14m 13.1m Sep 4] leggy filly: fair maiden handicapper: seemingly amiss after reappearance (reported to have suffered breathing problem second outing): bred to be suited by 1½m+: acts on firm and good to soft going: tongue tied final outing: sold 5,000 gns in November, sent to Germany. *J. L. Dunlop*   **71**

SMART GOLDEN BOY (IRE) 3 ch.g. Raise A Grand (IRE) 114 – Stoneware (Big-stone (IRE) 126) [2006 52: p8g p10g p7g 7f p10g p11g p6g Dec 13] maiden: little form in 2006: tried in cheekpieces/visor. *Mrs L. C. Jewell*   **–**

SMART INSTINCT (USA) 2 ch.g. (Feb 4) Smart Strike (CAN) 121 – Smile N Molly (USA) (Dixieland Band (USA)) [2006 5m* 6s* 5d³ Aug 23] strong, lengthy gelding: has scope: sixth foal: closely related to 3 winners in USA, including 1999 2-y-o Grade 3 6f winner Dont Tell The Kids (by Carson City) and half-brother to winner there by After-noon Deelites: dam 8.5f winner in USA: useful form: won maiden at Pontefract in July and minor event at Ripon (beat Holdin Foldin by 2 lengths) in August: favourite, unsuited by test of speed when third to Not For Me in listed race at York, going on well at finish: will be suited by 7f. *R. A. Fahey*   **100**

SMART JOHN 6 b.g. Bin Ajwaad (IRE) 119 – Katy-Q (IRE) 58 (Taufan (USA) 119) [2006 77: 8d 12.6m 11.9s⁴ Sep 7] good-topped gelding: fair handicapper at 5 yrs: well held in 2006, looking ungenuine final start. *D. Shaw*   **–**

SMART TIGER (GER) 4 b.g. Tiger Hill (IRE) 127 – Smoke Signal (IRE) 72 (College Chapel 122) [2006 79: p9.5g⁵ p10g Mar 2] successful twice for A. Kleinkorres in Germany in 2005: fair form at best in 3 handicaps in Britain: stays 10.5f: raced only on   **73**

polytrack and good/good to soft going: wore cheekpieces (well held, looked wayward) final outing: has joined Evan Williams. *N. P. Littmoden*

SMASH N'GRAB (IRE) 2 ch.f. (Mar 6) Jade Robbery (USA) 121 – Sallwa (IRE) **63** (Entrepreneur 123) [2006 5.1m 6m* 6d Oct 3] €18,000Y: good-topped, quite attractive filly: first foal: dam French 9.5f/11.5f winner: off 4 months after debut: won maiden at Southwell in September: effort best excused (hampered) in nursery: likely to stay 1m. *K. A. Ryan*

SMEMI AN NADA 4 b.g. Selkirk (USA) 129 – One Way Street 119 (Habitat 134) **60** [2006 8d⁵ 7m Apr 25] modest form in maidens at Bath (slowly away) and Folkestone, only outings on Flat. *P. Bowen*

SMIDDY HILL 4 b.f. Factual (USA) 108 – Hello Hobson's (IRE) 67 (Fayruz 116) **79** [2006 82d: 5.2m² 5g⁴ 5.2f² 5m* 5d⁶ 5g* p5g⁶ p5.1g Nov 11] lengthy filly: fair handicapper: won at Musselburgh (2) in August: best at bare 5f: acts on polytrack and firm going: usually races up with pace: hung right third start. *R. Bastiman*

SMILE FOR US 3 b.g. Whittingham (IRE) 104 – Don't Smile 76 (Sizzling Melody **73** 117) [2006 –: p7g⁶ p7g p6g² p6g⁶ p6g² f6g² f5g⁵ 6m* 6.1d f6g⁶ 6m⁴ 7f⁶ 7m⁵ f6g Dec 23] fair handicapper: won at Yarmouth in April: will prove best at 5f/6f: tried in cheekpieces, blinkered nowadays: has looked none too keen/carried head awkwardly. *C. Drew*

SMIRFYS DIAMOND 2 b.g. (Apr 22) Mujahid (USA) 125 – Jade Pet 90 (Petong **83** 126) [2006 5g² 6m⁴ 5g* 6d⁴ Aug 25] 20,000Y: lengthy, workmanlike gelding: eighth foal: half-brother to 3 winners, including 9-y-o Hail The Chief: dam 5f winner: fairly useful form: won maiden at Thirsk in August: first home on stand side when fourth of 20 to Cheap Street in sales race at Newmarket: likely to have proved best at 5f/6f: tended to hang: dead. *D. Nicholls*

SMIRFYS GOLD (IRE) 2 ch.c. (Feb 17) Bad As I Wanna Be (IRE) 115 – Golden **58** Jorden (IRE) (Cadeaux Genereux 131) [2006 5.1f 6m 5.1d⁵ Oct 4] good-topped colt: modest form on last of 3 starts in maidens: should stay 6f/7f. *E. S. McMahon*

SMIRFYS NIGHT 7 b.g. Tina's Pet 121 – Nightmare Lady 29 (Celestial Storm (USA) **56** 132) [2006 56: 6m³ 6f 7m Aug 8] quite good-topped gelding: modest performer: stays 7f: acts on polytrack, firm and good to soft going. *E. S. McMahon*

SMIRFYS PARTY 8 ch.g. Clantime 101 – Party Scenes (Most Welcome 131) [2006 **53** 54: p6g p8.6g p6g⁶ p7.1g⁵ p7.1g 6m⁶ 5.7f⁶ 6f² 6m 6m Aug 12] rather leggy gelding: modest handicapper: best at 5f/6f: acts on all-weather, firm and good to soft going: usually wears headgear. *W. M. Brisbourne*

SMIRFY'S SILVER 2 b.g. (Mar 8) Desert Prince (IRE) 130 – Goodwood Blizzard 97 **62 d** (Inchinor 119) [2006 5d⁴ 5.1m⁵ 6m 6g p6g 5m Aug 11] strong, quite attractive gelding: modest maiden: below form after second start: will probably stay 1m. *W. M. Brisbourne*

SMIRFYS SYSTEMS 7 b.g. Safawan 118 – Saint Systems 68 (Uncle Pokey 116) **58** [2006 p6g 6g 6g 6m⁶ 5d Oct 3] close-coupled, workmanlike gelding: unraced in 2005, and just modest form in 2006: best at 6f: acts on firm and good to soft going, well held on soft: blinkered once at 5 yrs: free-going sort. *W. M. Brisbourne*

SMITH N ALLAN OILS 7 b.g. Bahamian Bounty 116 – Grand Splendour 79 (Shirley **–** Heights 130) [2006 61: f7g Jan 17] sparely-made gelding: modest handicapper: well held only outing in 2006: tried blinkered, has worn cheekpieces. *C. Smith*

SMOKE IT (IRE) 3 b.g. Carrowkeel (IRE) 106 – Deerussa (IRE) (Jareer (USA) 115) **–** [2006 9v 8.1s 10.3m⁵ 9.3m Aug 7] well held in maidens/claimer. *A. Berry*

SMOKEY BLUE 3 gr.g. Tomba 119 – Miss Goddess (IRE) 63 (Godswalk (USA) 130) **63** [2006 59p: p8g p9.5g⁵ 8.2s p8g p9.5g⁴ p12g Jul 1] modest maiden: stays 9.5f: acts on polytrack: visored last 2 starts. *M. J. Wallace*

SMOKEY OAKEY (IRE) 2 b.c. (Mar 25) Tendulkar (USA) 114 – Veronica (Persian **89** Bold 123) [2006 6d³ p6g² 6m³ 6g 8d* 8g p7g Oct 21] €4,500F, €13,500Y: smallish, strong colt: half-brother to several winners, including Irish 1½m winner El Bueno and 1¼m winner Canford (both useful, by Caerleon): dam winner around 1m in USA: fairly useful performer: won nursery at Ayr by 3½ lengths in September: respectable ninth in similar event at Newmarket next time: stays 1m: acts on polytrack, good to firm and good to soft going. *M. H. Tompkins*

SMOKIN BEAU 9 b.g. Cigar 68 – Beau Dada (IRE) 66 (Pine Circle (USA)) [2006 **93** 107d: 6g⁴ 5s⁵ 5.7g 5g 5.1m 5f² 6f³ 5f² 5m* 5s 5d 5g³ p5g⁴ p6g Dec 16] smallish, robust gelding: fairly useful handicapper: left N. Littmoden after fifth start: won at Musselburgh in August: left D. Nicholls and returned to former trainer, better effort after when creditable fourth at Kempton: effective at 5f/6f: acts on all-weather and any turf going: tried in headgear: usually races prominently: has bled. *N. P. Littmoden*

SMOKINCANON 4 ch.g. Fumo di Londra (IRE) 108 – Secret Miss 55 (Beveled (USA)) [2006 52+: p6g p7g p6g⁵ p6g³ p6g p6g p7g⁵ 7g⁴ 6f 6.1f³ 6f² 6f 5.7f Aug 8] modest performer: stays easy 7f: acts on polytrack, firm and soft going (some promise on fibresand). *W. G. M. Turner* **57**

SMOKING STAR 3 b.f. Observatory (USA) 131 – Gitane (FR) (Grand Lodge (USA) 125) [2006 56: 8f 8m 8m 8m 8m 10.2m 17.2m Sep 25] modest maiden. *N. I. M. Rossiter* **54**

SMOKIN JOE 5 b.g. Cigar 68 – Beau Dada (IRE) 66 (Pine Circle (USA)) [2006 –, a88: p7g³ p6g p6g p7g p8g⁴ p8g³ p8g p8g⁴ p7g⁴ p10g³ p10g Dec 20] small, quite attractive gelding: fairly useful handicapper: creditable efforts when in frame in 2006: effective at 6f to easy 1¼m: acts on all-weather, little form on turf: usually blinkered/visored: held up. *J. R. Best* **– a80**

SMOOCH 3 b.f. Inchinor 119 – Two Step 60 (Mujtahid (USA) 118) [2006 89: p6g f5g⁶ p5.1g 5.2m³ 5m⁶ 6d 6f⁶ 5f⁶ 5g⁶ Aug 26] small, round-barrelled filly: fairly useful handicapper on turf, little form on all-weather in 2006: well below form last 4 starts: should stay 6f: acts on polytrack (won on it in 2005), good to firm and good to soft going: tried in cheekpieces/visor: irresolute. *R. M. H. Cowell* **81 § a– §**

SMOOTHIE (IRE) 8 gr.g. Definite Article 121 – Limpopo 49 (Green Desert (USA) 127) [2006 59: p16.5g p13.9g⁴ p12.2g p12.2g⁶ 10.2d⁶ 14.1m³ 11.5m⁶ 12.1f Jul 28] close-coupled gelding: modest handicapper: stays 16.5f: acts on all-weather, firm and soft going: tried blinkered, sometimes wears cheekpieces: held up: none too consistent. *Ian Williams* **59**

Mr J. C. Smith's "Snoqualmie Boy"

SMOOTH JAZZ 4 b.g. Zafonic (USA) 130 – Halska (Unfuwain (USA) 131) [2006 72: **83**
10m³ 10.2g* 10.5g 10g⁴ 11.6f 12m p10g⁶ p10g 11v⁵ 11g Dec 3] big, good-topped geld- **a73**
ing: fairly useful handicapper on turf, fair on all-weather: won at Bath in June: sold from
R. Beckett 15,000 gns after eighth start: should stay 1½m: acts on polytrack, soft and
good to firm ground: visored (below form) once: inconsistent. *A. Sanchez, Spain*

SMOOTHLY DOES IT 5 b.g. Efisio 120 – Exotic Forest 66 (Dominion 123) [2006 **65**
72: 8s⁵ 8.1d p10g 10.2m Oct 8] leggy gelding: fair handicapper: stays 1¼m: acts on
polytrack and good to firm ground, but ideally suited by softer than good (acts on heavy):
won over hurdles for R. Fahey in December. *Mrs A. J. Bowlby*

SMUGGLERS BAY (IRE) 2 b.g. (Mar 21) Celtic Swing 138 – Princess Mood (GER) **67**
(Muhtarram (USA) 125) [2006 7m 7f³ 7d Aug 18] €5,000F, 16,000Y: shows plenty of
knee action: second foal: half-brother to 3-y-o Kingsgate Prince: dam German maiden:
fair form when third to Babieca in maiden at Newcastle: gelded after final start: will stay
1m. *T. D. Easterby*

SNAAFY (USA) 2 b.c. (Feb 16) Kingmambo (USA) 125 – Nafisah (IRE) 109 (Lahib **66 p**
(USA) 129) [2006 7d Aug 25] first foal: dam, 7f (at 2 yrs) to 1¼m winner, half-sister to
smart Irish 1½m winner Mutakarrim, out of half-sister to 2000 Guineas/Champion Stakes
winner Haafhd: 11/1, very green when eighth to Moudez in maiden at Newmarket: will
be suited by 1m/1¼m: sure to improve. *B. W. Hills*

SNAEFELL (IRE) 2 gr.g. (Apr 22) Danehill Dancer (IRE) 117 – Sovereign Grace **94**
(IRE) 101 (Standaan (FR) 118) [2006 5s² 5v⁵ 5m* 5m⁴ Jun 20] good-bodied gelding:
brother to useful Irish 6f winner (including at 2 yrs) Daganya and half-brother to several
winners, including 10-y-o Henry Hall: dam Irish 5f winner: fairly useful form: won
maiden at Down Royal in June: further progress when fourth of 18 to Elhamri in listed
race at Royal Ascot, finishing well: should prove best at 5f/6f: yet to race on firm going,
acts on any other: tongue tied after debut. *M. Halford, Ireland*

SNAKE'S HEAD 2 b.f. (Feb 27) Golden Snake (USA) 127 – Satin Bell 99 (Midyan **81**
(USA) 124) [2006 7m² 7f⁵ 8.1m⁵ Aug 28] rather leggy, attractive filly: sixth foal: half-
sister to 3 winners, including useful 6f (at 2 yrs) to 11f (in Hong Kong) winner Zabaglione
(by Zilzal) and 4-y-o Strawberry Leaf: dam 7f winner: fairly useful form when second to
Golden Balls at Salisbury on debut, best effort in maidens: should stay 1m. *J. L. Dunlop*

SNAKE SKIN 3 ch.f. Golden Snake (USA) 127 – Silken Dalliance 91 (Rambo Dancer **59**
(CAN) 107) [2006 59: p8g⁶ 10.2f⁶ 10d⁴ p10g⁴ 8f 10d³ p9.5g p9.5g Nov 27] leggy,
workmanlike filly: modest handicapper: stays 10.2f: acts on all-weather and any turf
going: has run poorly in blinkers/cheekpieces. *J. Gallagher*

SNARK (IRE) 3 b.g. Cape Cross (IRE) 129 – Agoer 61 (Hadeer 118) [2006 82p: 8.3m **82**
10m³ 12g⁵ 12m⁴ 10d p10g p10g⁴ Nov 11] lengthy gelding: fairly useful handicapper:
stays 1½m: acts on polytrack and good to firm going: tongue tied final outing. *P. J. Makin*

SNOQUALMIE BOY 3 b.c. Montjeu (IRE) 137 – Seattle Ribbon (USA) 70 (Seattle **111**
Dancer (USA) 119) [2006 81p: 11g³ 9.9f* 10.4s³ 12m 10m* 10m⁶ 8m 10.4d 9m³ 9d⁵
Oct 14] rangy, good-bodied, attractive colt: smart performer: won handicap at Salisbury
(hung left/idled) in May and listed race at Royal Ascot (much improved when beating
Petrovich by ½ length) in June: good 4¾ lengths sixth to David Junior in Eclipse Stakes
at Sandown next time: respectable efforts last 2 starts, including fifth to Stage Gift in
Darley Stakes at Newmarket: best form at 9f/1¼m (well held in Derby at 1½m): acts on
firm going, probably on good to soft: seems to get on toes. *D. R. C. Elsworth*

SNOW BALLERINA 2 b.f. (Mar 4) Sadler's Wells (USA) 132 – Snow Bride (USA) **61 p**
121 (Blushing Groom (FR) 131) [2006 7m Aug 31] sister to 3-y-o Abhisheka, closely
related to top-class 1½m (Derby, King George and Arc) winner Lammtarra (by Nijinsky),
also 7f winner at 2 yrs, and half-sister to several winners, including smart 1m/1¼m (latter
in UAE) winner Kammtarra (by Zilzal): dam, awarded Oaks, out of Yorkshire Oaks
winner Awaasif: 10/1, needed experience in maiden at Salisbury won by Puggy: will do
better. *E. A. L. Dunlop*

SNOWBERRY HILL (USA) 3 b.g. Woodman (USA) 126 – Class Skipper (USA) **59**
(Skip Trial (USA)) [2006 67: 8g 12v p10g p10g p13g⁶ Sep 29] workmanlike gelding:
modest maiden: left K. Ryan after fourth outing: probably stays 1¼m: acts on firm going:
tried blinkered/in cheekpieces. *P. Howling*

SNOW BUNTING 8 ch.g. Polar Falcon (USA) 126 – Marl 94 (Lycius (USA) 124) **69**
[2006 71, a62+: p7.1g 6m⁶ 7.2g* 5.9m 7f⁴ 7m 7.1m* 7m 7.1m p7.1m² p7.1s² p7.1g Dec
22] leggy gelding: fair handicapper: won at Ayr in June and Musselburgh in August:

effective at 6f/7f: acts on polytrack and firm going: suited by waiting tactics. *Jedd O'Keeffe*

SNOW CRYSTAL (IRE) 3 ch.f. Kingmambo (USA) 125 – Crystal Spray 75 (Beldale Flutter (USA) 130) [2006 87p: 8d Aug 20] big, close-coupled filly: fairly useful winner at 2 yrs for D. Loder: off nearly 14 months, raced freely, found little and carried head awkwardly in handicap at Pontefract on return: should stay at least 1m. *J. H. M. Gosden* —

SNOW DANCER (IRE) 2 b.f. (Feb 13) Desert Style (IRE) 121 – Bella Vie (IRE) (Sadler's Wells (USA) 132) [2006 6s³ 6s² 7v³ p7.1g⁶ p8.6g² p8.6g² Dec 29] €6,000Y: second foal: half-sister to 3-y-o Sigismundus: dam unraced close relative of useful Irish sprinter Immovable Option: fair maiden: placed 5 times: stays 8.6f: acts on polytrack, raced on soft/heavy going on turf. *A. Berry* **69**

SNOWED UNDER 5 gr.g. Most Welcome 131 – Snowy Mantle 54 (Siberian Express (USA) 125) [2006 83: 10.9g² p10g³ 10s 10f* 12m⁵ 10m⁴ 10d⁶ 9.8d 11g Sep 15] good-topped gelding: fairly useful handicapper: won at Leicester (successful 4 times there) in June: stays 1½m: acts on polytrack, firm and good to soft going. *J. D. Bethell* **88**

SNOWFLIGHT 2 b.c. (Mar 15) Danehill Dancer (IRE) 117 – Sadler's Song 54 (Saddlers' Hall (IRE) 126) [2006 6m⁴ 7.2m⁵ 7m³ Aug 6] third foal: dam maiden who stayed 1½m: fair form in maidens, 8¾ lengths third to Gweebarra at Chester: will stay 1m. *R. A. Fahey* **71**

SNOW SYMPHONY (IRE) 3 b.g. Distant Music (USA) 126 – Snowspin 75 (Carwhite 127) [2006 60: 8m² 8.5m⁵ 8f⁴ p7g 10.1m⁵ 7d⁴ 8d Oct 18] strong gelding: fair maiden: should stay 1¼m+: acts on firm going: blinkered (ran poorly) once at 2 yrs: sold 5,000 gns. *D. M. Simcock* **66**

SNOW WOLF 5 ch.g. Wolfhound (USA) 126 – Christmas Rose (Absalom 128) [2006 77, a67: 5g 5.1s 6f 5.3m 5.7f⁵ 6f⁵ 6f⁴ 6f⁶ 5.1m Aug 28] smallish, quite attractive gelding: modest performer: effective at 5f/6f: acts on polytrack, firm and soft going: sometimes wears cheekpieces. *J. M. Bradley* **59**

SNOWY DAY (FR) 3 b.g. Pennekamp (USA) 130 – Snow White (Polar Falcon (USA) 126) [2006 f7g³ f7g* p9.5g² Nov 28] €25,000Y: fourth foal: dam unraced half-sister to very smart US Grade 1 9f winner Jovial: fair form: won maiden at Southwell in April: off 7 months, further progress when length second to Tous Les Deux in handicap at Wolverhampton final outing: stays 9.5f: open to further improvement. *W. J. Haggas* **73 p**

SNUGFIT 2 b.f. (Mar 31) Agnes World (USA) 123 – Snugfit Annie 49 (Midyan (USA) 124) [2006 7d 7s Oct 10] tall filly: half-sister to useful 5f to 7f (including at 2 yrs) winner Enchanted (by Magic Ring) and 4-y-o Golden Asha: dam third in 6f seller at 2 yrs: last in maidens. *G. G. Margarson* —

SNUGFIT DUBARRY 6 ch.m. Ali-Royal (IRE) 127 – Spanish Serenade 76 (Nashwan (USA) 135) [2006 f8g f7g 9.9f Apr 27] leggy mare: modest winner in 2002: subsequently went to stud, well held in handicaps on return. *M. W. Easterby* —

SOAPY DANGER 3 b.c. Danzig (USA) – On A Soapbox (USA) 119 (Mi Cielo (USA)) [2006 p9.5g² p9.5g* 10d² 12.1d* 11.8g² 11.9f* 16m* 12m* 12d⁵ Aug 22] **120**

As they build their ladders to the stars, Mark Johnston's horses tend to climb rung by rung. Johnston doesn't believe in throwing them into races before they have proved themselves at the level below, a policy which has paid dividends over the years. It is commonplace to see Johnston's three-year-olds, in particular, set up a sequence on their way up, and, if the stable has lacked a runner that has

Queen's Vase, Royal Ascot—Soapy Danger makes a successful step up in class; Galient is second, ahead of Ermine Sea (No.2) and Road To Mandalay

Princess of Wales's wbx.com Stakes, Newmarket—Soapy Danger takes a step back to a mile and a half in his stride; Mountain High (right) is second, ahead of Enforcer (left) and Bandari

reached right to the top in the last couple of seasons, winners have continued to flow. Although he has yet to be champion trainer in terms of prize money, 2006 saw Johnston saddle more winners than any other trainer for the sixth time since first achieving the feat in 1996, his total of one hundred and fifty-eight winners including his thirteenth successive century. Soapy Danger made a handsome contribution to Johnston's total, typically coming through the ranks from humble beginnings, capping his campaign with two victories in pattern races—before injury intervened —as he showed himself one of the best three-year-olds.

Plagued by problems and unraced as a two-year-old, Soapy Danger gained his first victory as a three-year-old in a maiden at Wolverhampton in February on his second start. His next four outings came in handicaps and he recorded further victories at Beverley in April and Haydock in June. Soapy Danger put up a particularly useful performance when making all under top weight at Haydock and earned himself a step up in class at Royal Ascot, where he tackled the Queen's Vase in preference to the King George V Handicap. Stepped up to two miles, Soapy Danger more than justified the decision, starting third favourite at 4/1 and winning by a length and a quarter from favourite Galient, leading off the turn and holding on well to give the stable its fourth winner of the race in six years. The gallop in the Queen's Vase tested stamina less than it might have done and Soapy Danger was returned to a mile and a half when raised further in class for his next outing. He faced only three rivals in the Group 2 Princess of Wales's wbx.com Stakes at Newmarket's July meeting, but started at 5/1 behind the odds-on four-year-old Mountain High, runner-up in the Hardwicke at the Royal meeting. Dropped back in trip, Soapy Danger reverted to front running and put up a much improved and most genuine performance, seeing off his rivals at the foot of the hill and holding the favourite by three quarters of a length with Enforcer, another four-year-old, the same distance away in third. On the strength of his Newmarket win, Soapy Danger was among the five-day entries for the King George VI and Queen Elizabeth Stakes at Ascot later in the month. Instead, however, he was returned to his own age group for the Great Voltigeur Stakes at York in August, when he sustained a fracture to his near-fore pastern in finishing a below-par fifth.

Soapy Danger (b.c. 2003)	Danzig (USA) (b 1977)	Northern Dancer (b 1961)	Nearctic
			Natalma
		Pas de Nom (br 1968)	Admiral's Voyage
			Petitioner
	On A Soapbox (USA) (b 1996)	Mi Cielo (b 1990)	Conquistador Cielo
			My Inheritance
		Makin A Statement (br 1990)	Stage Door Johnny
			Halcyon Queen

Soapy Danger is a rare bird among the progeny of his sire Danzig in being a winner over two miles, let alone a pattern winner at the trip. The majority of Danzig's better performers have had far more speed than stamina and the average distance of races won by his three-year-olds is less than a mile. Soapy Danger was bought by his trainer for 270,000 dollars at Keeneland as a yearling, though he ended up racing in the colours of his breeders, Klaus Jacobs' Newsells Park Stud. The same connections were also represented by another smart and progressive staying three-year-old colt Linas Selection, he too successful at Royal Ascot, in the King George V Handicap. Newsells Park Stud is assembling an impressive band of broodmares, with a Timeform rating of at least 90 one of the criteria by which mares are selected for the stud. Two notable additions to the band at the end of the year were Speciosa's dam Specifically (also a half-sister to Pride) and High Chaparral's sister Helena Molony who were bought for 1.85m and 1.1m guineas respectively at the Tattersalls December Sales. On A Soapbox was a 1.25m-dollar purchase by Newsells Park at Keeneland in November 2002. She was a stayer by American standards, winning the Grade 1 Coaching Club American Oaks at Belmont over a mile and a half. Soapy Danger is her only foal so far, though she was in foal to Singspiel in 2006. The next two dams in the pedigree also won in the States, great grandam Halcyon Queen being out of a half-sister to Bold Lad and Successor, who were both champion two-year-olds in the USA in the 'sixties. A strong, good-bodied colt and a fluent mover, Soapy Danger had four screws inserted in his injured pastern after York, but should do well again at four if he makes a full recovery, something which must be on the cards as he is in good hands. A winner on good to soft going and polytrack, Soapy Danger's best form is on good to firm and firm ground and at a mile and a half, though he clearly stays two miles. He is effective patiently ridden or making the running. *M. Johnston*

SOAR WITH EAGLES (USA) 3 b.c. Kingmambo (USA) 125 – Bound (USA) **116** (Nijinsky (CAN) 138) [2006 8m 10m* 10m³ Aug 13] smallish, strong colt: poor walker: closely related/half-brother to several winners, including fairly useful Irish 7f winner Septimus Severus (by Seeking The Gold) and US 1m minor stakes winner Limit (by Cox's Ridge): dam, minor 1m stakes winner, closely related to Nureyev and half-sister to dam of Sadler's Wells: off nearly 3 months after debut (at Newbury), won maiden at the Curragh in July by length from Carnbridge: plenty more improvement when staying-on 4½ lengths third of 4 to Mustameet in Royal Whip Stakes there final outing, getting slightly detached before home turn and not knocked and ridden along at closing stages: should be suited by further than 1¼m: sold privately, and sent to USA. *A. P. O'Brien, Ireland*

SOBA FELLA 3 b.g. Puissance 110 – Cedar Jeneva 34 (Muhtarram (USA) 125) [2006 – 6d 6d 8m 12.1f Jun 27] big gelding: well beaten in maidens/claimer. *P. T. Midgley*

SOBA JONES 9 b.g. Emperor Jones (USA) 119 – Soba 127 (Most Secret 119) [2006 **71** 75: f6g* p6g f6g² f6g⁵ f6g* f6g* f6g⁴ f6g³ 5g⁴ f6g⁵ f6g⁵ Dec 23] tall gelding: fair performer: won claimer in January, handicap in February and claimer in March, all at Southwell: best at 5f/6f: acts on fibresand and any turf going: tried in blinkers/cheekpieces, not since 2004: races prominently. *J. Balding*

SOCIAL RHYTHM 2 b.f. (May 21) Beat All (USA) 120 – Highly Sociable 56 (Puis- **75 +** sance 110) [2006 p6f* p7.1g³ p6g³ p6g² p7.1g² Dec 30] third foal: dam, maiden, raced only at 6f/7f: fair performer: won maiden at Wolverhampton in August: off 3 months, placed in minor event/nurseries: should stay 1m: raced on polytrack. *H. J. Collingridge*

SOCIETY MUSIC (IRE) 4 b.f. Almutawakel 126 – Society Fair (FR) (Always Fair **77** (USA) 121) [2006 86: 8g 8.1g 8g 8.3d³ 7.2d³ 8g⁵ 7m 7.5g⁴ 8.1d Sep 16] leggy filly: fair handicapper: stays 1m: acts on any going: tried blinkered at 2 yrs, wore cheekpieces 4 of last 5 starts: tends to wander/race lazily. *M. Dods*

SO ELEGANT (IRE) 4 b.f. Bahhare (USA) 122 – Soignee (Night Shift (USA)) [2006 **59** 63: p12.2g p10g⁶ 17.2f p13.9g³ 12m⁴ 12m p16g Aug 30] good-bodied filly: modest handicapper: stays 1¾m: acts on polytrack, form only on good ground on turf. *J. Jay*

SOFFOOH (USA) 2 b.c. (Apr 8) Elusive Quality (USA) – United Kingdom (USA) 93 **57** (Danzig (USA)) [2006 6.1g 6m² 6f⁴ p7.1f 7.1d Oct 13] compact colt: modest maiden: claimed from M. Channon £6,000 third start: form at 6f on going firmer than good. *W. J. Musson*

SOFIA ROYALE 2 b.f. (Apr 16) Royal Applause 124 – Once In My Life (IRE) 114 **51** (Lomond (USA) 128) [2006 6d⁴ Nov 4] 10,000Y: half-sister to unreliable 1m winner Genius (by Lycius) and French 12.5f winner The Good Life (by Rainbow Quest): dam French 6.5f (at 2 yrs) and 1m (Prix de Sandringham) winner: 50/1, fourth (beaten 8 lengths) in maiden at Windsor. *B. Palling*

SOFINELLA (IRE) 3 gr.f. Titus Livius (FR) 115 – Mystical Jumbo (Mystiko (USA) **66**
124) [2006 72: 5d 5m 6g 5m⁴ 5m⁶ p5g p5.1g p5g Dec 3] leggy filly: fair handicapper:
best form at 5f: acts on polytrack and good to firm going: has given trouble at stall, once
withdrawn. *A. W. Carroll*

SOFT CENTRE 3 ch.f. Zafonic (USA) 130 – Foodbroker Fancy (IRE) 113 (Halling **109**
(USA) 133) [2006 76: 9.9g* 12s Sep 22] rather leggy, quite attractive filly: useful performer, lightly raced: much improved when dead-heating with Rising Cross in listed
Lupe Stakes at Goodwood in May, still green and poorly placed when tempo increased:
tailed off in Princess Royal Stakes at Ascot 4½ months later: stays 1¼m: won on good to
firm going at 2 yrs. *Mrs A. J. Perrett*

SOFT FOCUS (IRE) 4 b.f. Spectrum (IRE) 126 – Creme Caramel (USA) 88 (Sept- **–**
ieme Ciel (USA) 123) [2006 55, a58: p6g² f7g² p7.1g² p6g⁴ p6g⁴ f6g p6g⁵ Feb 21] leggy **a67**
filly: fair on all-weather, modest on turf: stayed 7f: acted on all-weather and good to firm
going: blinkered: dead. *J. A. Osborne*

SOFT MORNING 2 b.f. (Apr 28) Pivotal 124 – Summer Night 94 (Nashwan (USA) **75 p**
135) [2006 p7g⁶ p7.1g² Dec 31] fourth foal: half-sister to 3 winners, including smart
performer up to 14.6f Songerie (7f/1m winner at 2 yrs) and 3-y-o Souvenance (both by
Hernando): dam, 6f winner who ran twice, out of half-sister to Petoski: better effort in
maidens when short-head second to All of Me at Wolverhampton, still green and
wandering: will stay 1m: will improve further. *Sir Mark Prescott*

SOHO SQUARE 3 ch.g. Generous (IRE) 139 – Stardance (USA) (Rahy (USA) 115) **80**
[2006 75p: p10g* p12g³ 11.6g⁴ 14d 11.9g⁶ Jul 7] rather leggy gelding: fairly useful
performer: won maiden at Lingfield in February: failed to progress in handicaps after:
should stay 1¾m: acts on polytrack and soft going: tended to wander final 2-y-o start:
temperament under suspicion: sold 23,000 gns, joined L. Lungo and gelded. *M. Johnston*

SOHRAAB 2 b.c. (Mar 5) Erhaab (USA) 127 – Riverine (Risk Me (FR) 127) [2006 6f⁶ **69 p**
Jul 31] half-brother to 7-y-o Pango: dam, ran twice, out of half-sister to Yorkshire Oaks
winner/excellent broodmare Hellenic: 33/1, sixth in maiden at Windsor, learning all the
time: will improve, particularly over further (bred for 1¼m/1½m). *H. Morrison*

SOIZIC (NZ) 4 ch.f. Istidaad (USA) 114 – Nellie May (NZ) (Babarooom (USA)) [2006 **76**
7g² 7g³ 7d 8g p9.5g⁵ p9.5g Dec 2] won maiden at Te Rapa on first of 4 starts in New
Zealand in early-2006: off 8 months, much better effort (fair form) in handicaps at
Wolverhampton when fifth on British debut: stays 9.5f: acts on polytrack. *C. G. Cox*

SOKOKE 5 ch.g. Compton Place 125 – Sally Green (IRE) 79 (Common Grounds 118) **50**
[2006 –: 5f⁵ 5d⁶ 5d 5d Nov 3] workmanlike gelding: modest maiden: best at 5f: acts on
firm ground: tried tongue tied. *D. A. Nolan*

SOLARIAS QUEST 4 b.g. Pursuit of Love 124 – Persuasion 79 (Batshoof 122) [2006 **–**
84: p12.2s Dec 13] sturdy gelding: fairly useful handicapper at 3 yrs: well held only Flat
outing in 2006: should stay 1¾m: acts on heavy and good to firm going. *A. King*

SOLDIER FIELD 2 b.g. (Mar 1) Fantastic Light (USA) 134 – Khambani (IRE) 80 **–**
(Royal Academy (USA) 130) [2006 p8g Dec 1] 8,500Y: eighth foal: dam, Irish 6.5f
winner, half-sister to top-class middle-distance performer Celestial Storm and Ribblesdale winner Thawakib, herself dam of Sakhee: never dangerous in maiden at Lingfield.
A. M. Balding

SOLDIER HOLLOW 6 br.h. In The Wings 128 – Island Race 93 (Common Grounds **119**
118) [2006 121: 11s⁵ 10m² 8g² 10f³ 9.8m* 10m⁴ Nov 5] smart performer: tends to come
to hand in second half of year, good 2¼ lengths third to The Tin Man in slowly-run
Arlington Million before winning Prix Dollar Casino Barriere de Montreux at Longchamp in September by neck from Manduro, quickening ahead 2f out and getting first run
on runner-up: never able to land blow from rear when fourth to Cherry Mix in Premio
Roma at Rome final start (had won race 2 previous years): best around 1¼m/11f: acts on
firm and soft ground. *P. Schiergen, Germany*

SOLDIER OF FORTUNE (IRE) 2 b.c. (Feb 20) Galileo (IRE) 134 – Affianced **114 p**
(IRE) 109 (Erins Isle 121) [2006 8s² 8d* 10g² Nov 12]
'He was an idle little devil when we took the lead but this was only his third
race and he'll surely turn into a top-class three-year-old.' Kieren Fallon's comment
on Soldier of Fortune after partnering the colt to finish second to Passage of Time
in the Criterium de Saint-Cloud, out which turned out to be the jockey's final mount
before his six-month suspension for failing a drug test, may prove particularly
prophetic, taking into account the horse's profile. Having his third outing, just five

weeks after his racecourse debut, Soldier of Fortune stepped up significantly on the form he had shown in two maidens, taking closer order from halfway and improving to lead over a furlong out. He kept on well to finish three quarters of a length second to Passage of Time, the pair three lengths clear of the remainder. Soldier of Fortune shapes as though he'll prove best at beyond a mile and a quarter in the next season and, if Fallon's prediction is to be proven correct, it is likely to be in a Derby—33/1 in Epsom ante-post betting at the time of writing—or St Leger that he shows himself to be a top-class performer.

    Soldier of Fortune made his debut in a mile maiden at Gowran in October when a narrow runner-up to the Jim Bolger-trained La Conquistadora, after pulling clear with that rival. Bolger bred Soldier of Fortune, who used to share a paddock with Two Thousand Guineas and Derby favourite Teofilo. With Seamus Heffernan deputising for Fallon eleven days later, Soldier of Fortune showed the benefit of experience when justifying favouritism in a similar eighteen-runner event at Navan by a length and a quarter from Mores Wells.

Soldier of Fortune (IRE) (b.c. Feb 20, 2004)	Galileo (IRE) (b 1998)	Sadler's Wells (b 1981)	Northern Dancer
			Fairy Bridge
		Urban Sea (ch 1989)	Miswaki
			Allegretta
	Affianced (IRE) (b 1998)	Erins Isle (b 1978)	Busted
			Chemise
		La Meillure (ch 1985)	Lord Gayle
			Gradille

    Soldier of Fortune is the second foal of Affianced, a seven-furlong two-year-old winner who won at a mile and a quarter at three for Bolger when she showed form verging on smart in pattern and listed company, in the process showing she stayed a mile and three quarters. Soldier of Fortune is a brother to the three-year-old Heliostatic, a smart performer who also won at seven as a juvenile. Heliostatic was successful twice at a mile and a quarter in the latest season, but pulled hard when raced for the only time over a distance as far as a mile and a half in the Irish Derby. Soldier of Fortune's dam is a sister to the useful Irish mile- (at two) and mile-and-a-quarter winner Irish Summit, and a half-sister to several other winners, notably the Irish Derby and Eclipse runner-up Sholokhov. Soldier of Fortune has raced on good ground and softer on his three starts so far. Already smart, he seems sure to progress further. *A. P. O'Brien, Ireland*

SOLDIERS ROMANCE 3 b.g. Allied Forces (USA) 123 – Still In Love 75 (Emarati (USA) 74) [2006 p8.6g³ Mar 31] tall, good-topped gelding: 20/1 and green (reluctant at stall), 3 lengths equal-third to Lucky Token in maiden at Wolverhampton in March: got loose whilst blindfolded and ran into car at start next intended outing in April. *T. D. Easterby*   **54**

SOLE AGENT (IRE) 4 b.g. Trans Island 119 – Seattle Siren (USA) 101 (Seattle Slew (USA)) [2006 66: 12s Oct 21] fair maiden: blinkered, well held only Flat outing in 2006: won over hurdles in December. *G. L. Moore*   **–**

SOLENT (IRE) 4 b.g. Montjeu (IRE) 137 – Stylish (Anshan 119) [2006 96: 10g⁵ 12s* 12m 14m² p16g 14m⁴ 13.9d⁶ 14v³ 12d⁵ Sep 30] big, good-topped gelding: impresses in appearance: useful handicapper: won at Newbury in May by 3 lengths from Castle Howard: several creditable efforts after, including when second to Wunderwood at Goodwood and third to Peppertree Lane in Old Borough Cup at Haydock: stays 1¾m, should get 2m: acts on heavy and good to firm going: free-going sort: often early to post: has run well when sweating: gelded after final outing. *R. Hannon*   **105**

SOLICITUDE 3 ch.f. Bertolini (USA) 125 – Sibilant (Selkirk (USA) 129) [2006 75: 7m 7g p8.6g 8.1g p6g³ p6g² p7.1g f7g³ f8g³ Dec 21] modest performer on all-weather, little form on turf: stays 1m: acts on all-weather: wore cheekpieces final outing. *D. Haydn Jones*   **–** **a62**

SOLID ROCK (IRE) 2 b.c. (Apr 23) Rock of Gibraltar (IRE) 133 – Sheer Spirit (IRE) 86 (Caerleon (USA) 132) [2006 5m⁵ 7m⁴ p7.1g⁶ 6d* p6g⁴ p8g* p7g* Dec 4] 35,000Y: close-coupled colt: third foal: half-brother to 3-y-o River Bravo and 4-y-o Sovereign Spirit: dam, 1½m winner, half-sister to Derby winner Oath and high-class 1m/1¼m performer Pelder: useful performer: progressed really well, winning nurseries at Windsor and Lingfield (2) towards end of year: stays 1m: acts on polytrack, good to firm and good to soft going. *T. G. Mills*   **100**

SOLIPSIST (IRE) 5 ch.g. Grand Lodge (USA) 125 – Mijouter (IRE) (Coquelin (USA) **46**
121) [2006 –: p12.2g p12.2g f12g⁵ 12d Apr 11] poor maiden. *N. I. M. Rossiter*

SOLIS OBITUS 2 b.g. (Feb 28) Foxhound (USA) 103 – Tramonto 91 (Sri Pekan **–**
(USA) 117) [2006 6.1m Jun 3] tailed off in maiden. *B. R. Millman*

SOLO CITY 2 b.g. (Mar 4) Averti (IRE) 117 – Surakarta 67 (Bin Ajwaad (IRE) 119) **–**
[2006 8.3d 8g f8g Dec 2] no show in maidens. *P. A. Blockley*

SOLO FLIGHT 9 gr.g. Mtoto 134 – Silver Singer 65 (Pharly (FR) 130) [2006 98: **95**
11.7d⁴ 10d 12m 10g³ 10.1d 10.5g p12g³ p10g* p10g⁶ Dec 20] angular gelding: useful
handicapper: won at Lingfield (by ¾ length from Activo) in November: effective at 1¼m/
1½m: acts on polytrack, firm and good to soft going: sometimes finds little, and best
produced late. *H. Morrison*

SOLOMANS PROSPECT 3 b.c. Hazaaf (USA) 62 – Our Stella (Petong 126) [2006 **–**
p7g p9.5g 10.1m Aug 9] tailed off in maidens/claimer: visored on debut. *Miss
D. A. McHale*

SOLOMON'S MINE (USA) 7 b.g. Rahy (USA) 115 – Shes A Sheba (USA) (Aly- **–**
sheba (USA)) [2006 72: 21.6d Apr 24] strong gelding: poor mover: fair handicapper at 6
yrs: pulled up only outing in 2006: tried in blinkers early in career: races up with pace.
M. J. Polglase

SOLO STAR 3 ch.f. Observatory (USA) 131 – Aura of Grace (USA) 80 (Southern Halo **–**
(USA)) [2006 56: p8.6g f11s p8.6g Mar 15] workmanlike filly: modest on turf at 2 yrs:
stays 7.5f: acts on firm ground, well held on all-weather in 2006: tried blinkered: tends to
race freely/hang/carry head high: sold 1,600 gns, sent to Israel. *Miss J. A. Camacho*

SOL ROJO 4 b.g. Efisio 120 – Shining Cloud 73 (Indian Ridge 123) [2006 49, a64: **66**
f12g p9.5g³ p12.2g p9.5g³ p9.5g p9.5g³ p8.6g* p9.5g f12g³ 11.5m³ 9.8m³ 8m* 8.3g 8.1f **a80**
p8.6g* 8m 8.5g⁴ 10.5s* p13.9g² p8.6g* p13.9g³ Nov 27] fairly useful on all-weather,
fair on turf: won seller at Wolverhampton (left M. Attwater) in March and handicaps at
Yarmouth in May, Wolverhampton in June, Haydock in September and Wolverhampton
again in November: effective at 1m to 13.9f: acts on all-weather, soft and good to firm
going: usually wears headgear: often contests amateur events, including for last 3 wins.
J. Pearce

SOLVA 3 b.f. Singspiel (IRE) 133 – Annapurna (IRE) 101 (Brief Truce (USA) 126) **99**
[2006 76: 10m* 10m² 10m² 11.9g 9m⁶ 9.9m 10.2f* 10.1m⁴ Sep 13] lengthy filly: useful
performer: won handicaps at Nottingham in May and Bath in September: good 2½
lengths fourth to Dance Partner in listed event at Yarmouth final outing: stays 1¼m: acts
on firm going: sent to USA. *B. J. Meehan*

SOLWIND (USA) 2 b.f. (May 2) Johannesburg (USA) 127 – For Love (USA) (Sultry **59**
Song (USA)) [2006 5g⁵ 6m⁵ 7g p7.1m p6g Nov 25] 50,000 2-y-o: leggy filly: first foal:
dam, 8.5f winner in USA, half-sister to useful performer up to 1¼m Coqueteria: modest
maiden: likely to prove best at 5f/6f. *B. Smart*

SOME DIVA 3 ch.f. Dr Fong (USA) 128 – Dorothea Brooke (IRE) 80 (Dancing Brave **75**
(USA) 140) [2006 64p: 7m 6.1g⁶ 6.1f² 6g³ p7g⁵ p7g 7m⁴ 8g⁴ p9.5g* p9.5g³ Nov 16]
close-coupled filly: fair performer: won handicap at Wolverhampton in November, hanging left: stays 9.5f: acts on polytrack and firm going: in cheekpieces/visor last 3 starts.
W. R. Swinburn

SOMERSAULT 3 ch.f. Pivotal 124 – Rash (Pursuit of Love 124) [2006 9.9g 8m² 8g* **69**
9.8s⁴ p8g Sep 6] leggy, small-looking filly: fifth foal: closely related to fairly useful 1m
winners Loveleaves and (in USA) Contagious (both by Polar Falcon) and half-sister to 2
winners, including 4-y-o Guadaloup: dam unraced: fair performer: won maiden at Thirsk
in August, carrying head high: stays 1m: acts on good to firm ground. *Sir Michael Stoute*

SOMETHING EXCITING 4 ch.f. Halling (USA) 133 – Faraway Waters 102 (Pharly **100**
(FR) 130) [2006 114: 12g⁶ 12g³ 11.6g Aug 26] smallish, close-coupled filly: has a quick
action: smart performer at 3 yrs, second in Oaks at Epsom: just useful in 2006, best
effort when 9½ lengths third to Guadalajara in minor event at Newmarket: may prove
best at 1½m: acts on soft going: has hung right, and sometimes travels with little fluency.
D. R. C. Elsworth

SOMETHING (IRE) 4 b.g. Trans Island 119 – Persian Polly 99 (Persian Bold 123) **114**
[2006 96: p7g* p7g* 8.1m⁶ 6m May 6] big, lengthy gelding: smart performer, lightly
raced: won handicaps at Lingfield in February (by 3½ lengths from Moayed) and March
(beat Mr Lambros by 1¼ lengths): poorly drawn final outing: gelded after: stays 7f (raced

freely and below form in Mile at Sandown over further): acts on polytrack and good to firm going: takes strong hold. *T. G. Mills*

SOMETHING SIMPLE (IRE) 3 ch.g. Raise A Grand (IRE) 114 – Baccara (IRE) **67**
(Sri Pekan (USA) 117) [2006 63: 10s³ 12g 10s p13.9g⁵ Nov 27] fair maiden: left P. Henley in Ireland after third start: stays 1¼m: unraced on firm going, acts on any other turf. *R. Ford*

SOMNUS 6 b.g. Pivotal 124 – Midnight's Reward 84 (Night Shift (USA)) [2006 117: **115**
6d³ 7.1g⁵ 6g* 6.5g 7s⁴ 6s⁴ 7g² 6d⁶ 7d⁴ 8d⁴ Oct 28] good-topped gelding: high-class performer at best, winner of 3 Group 1s: smart nowadays: won minor event at Haydock in July by short head from Excusez Moi: also showed his form in Duke of York Stakes at York (third to Steenberg), Sprint Cup at Haydock (fourth to Reverence), Park Stakes at York (¾-length second to Iffraaj) and Challenge Stakes at Newmarket (fourth to Sleeping Indian) first/sixth/seventh/ninth starts: best at 6f/7f: acts on soft and good to firm going. *T. D. Easterby*

SOM TALA 3 ch.c. Fantastic Light (USA) 134 – One of The Family 73 (Alzao (USA) **97**
117) [2006 11.8d³ 11g⁴ 12f² 14d⁴ 14.1m* 13.9f⁴ 14m⁴ 16.2m* 18d* 18s⁶ Oct 7] 100,000Y: workmanlike colt: third foal: half-brother to 5-y-o Pass The Port: dam, maiden who stayed 9f, half-sister to Juddmonte International winner One So Wonderful and Dante winner Alnasr Alwasheek: useful performer: won handicaps at Salisbury in June and Beverley (by ¾ length from Key Time) in August, and minor event at Pontefract (beat Ebtikaar by ¾ length) in September: stays 2¼m: acts on firm and good to soft going: carried head awkwardly third outing/edged left fourth start. *M. R. Channon*

SONARA (IRE) 2 b.g. (Feb 9) Peintre Celebre (USA) 137 – Fay (IRE) 64 (Polish **60 p**
Precedent (USA) 131) [2006 7d 7.2d 8g Sep 28] €36,000Y: strong, good-bodied gelding: third foal: dam, ran 3 times (should have been suited by 1½m+), closely related to useful 1m/1¼m performer Sundari: shaped better than bare result in maidens, eighth to Asperity at Newmarket final start: gelded after: type to do better in middle-distance handicaps at 3 yrs. *M. H. Tompkins*

Phil Bull Trophy Conditions Stakes, Pontefract—
the three-year-old Som Tala upsets the favourite Ebtikaar over this marathon trip

SONAR SOUND (GER) 2 b.c. (Apr 6) Slickly (FR) 128 – Samothrace (IRE) (Arazi **79** (USA) 135) [2006 7.5d 8.2d⁴ 8.3g⁶ Sep 17] €22,000Y: big colt: second foal: dam unraced out of half-sister to Prix de l'Arc de Triomphe winner Sagace: easily best effort when fourth of 5 to Sesmen in minor event at Nottingham. *T. P. Tate*

SONDERBORG 5 b.m. Great Dane (IRE) 122 – Nordico Princess 71 (Nordico (USA)) **52** [2006 55: f8g* f8g 8.2m 8s p8.6g f7g⁵ f8g⁵ p8.6g⁶ p9.5g⁵ f8g* f8g Dec 28] workmanlike mare: modest performer: won banded races at Southwell in January (dead-heated) and December: best form at 7f/1m: acts on all-weather, firm and good to soft going: wears headgear. *J. Mackie*

SONG HUNTRESS 3 b.f. Foxhound (USA) 103 – Eastern Lyric 93 (Petong 126) **38** [2006 54: p6g 5.7g p6g 5.3f⁴ 6f 7.1d⁶ p8g Oct 29] just poor form in 2006, leaving D. Bridgwater after third start: tried blinkered/in cheekpieces. *A. G. Newcombe*

SONGMASTER (USA) 3 b.g. Singspiel (IRE) 133 – One Beautiful Lady (USA) **–** (Broad Brush (USA)) [2006 10m Jun 17] good-bodied gelding: tailed off in maiden at Sandown: subsequently gelded. *Mrs A. J. Perrett*

SONG OF PASSION (IRE) 3 b.f. Orpen (USA) 116 – Bint Al Balad (IRE) 63 (Aho- **100** noora 122) [2006 82p: 7.6d* 7g* 8m p7.1g⁴ 7m³ 8d⁴ Sep 23] sturdy, lengthy filly: useful performer: won handicaps at Chester in May and Epsom (by 3½ lengths from Mister Benedictine) in June: just respectable efforts last 3 starts: probably stays 1m: acts on polytrack and good to soft going. *R. Hannon*

SONG OF SILENCE (USA) 3 b.f. Unbridled's Song (USA) 125 – State Secret **–** (Green Desert (USA) 127) [2006 69: p8g* p10g² p8g* p8.6g⁴ p8g² 7m 7f Aug 3] leggy, **a97** workmanlike filly: useful performer: much improved in 2006, winning handicaps at Lingfield in January and February: very good 2 lengths second to Dont Dili Dali in listed race at Kempton fifth start: ran as if amiss last 2 outings: may prove best at 7f/1m: acts on all-weather: sent to USA. *E. A. L. Dunlop*

SONIC ANTHEM (USA) 4 b.g. Royal Anthem (USA) 135 – Whisperifyoudare **–** (USA) (Red Ransom (USA)) [2006 56: f11g* f12g⁵ p8.6g 8d Apr 21] tall, good-topped **a72** gelding: fair performer on all-weather, modest at best on turf: won apprentice maiden at Southwell in January by 16 lengths: free-going sort, but stays 11f: acts on fibresand and firm ground: has joined P. Haslam. *D. Nicholls*

SONNING STAR (IRE) 2 b.g. (Apr 24) Desert Prince (IRE) 130 – Fantazia 100 **–** (Zafonic (USA) 130) [2006 6m 7g Oct 12] strong, useful-looking gelding: well held in maidens at Newmarket (signs of temperament): gelded after. *D. R. C. Elsworth*

SONNTAG BLUE (IRE) 4 b.g. Bluebird (USA) 125 – Laura Margaret (Persian Bold **56** 123) [2006 57: p8g p9.5g p7g³ p7g 7m Apr 17] leggy gelding: modest handicapper: stays 8.6f: acts on all-weather and good to firm ground: effective blinkered or not, visored last 3 starts: has looked none too keen. *Miss J. Feilden*

SONNY MAC 3 b.c. Pivotal 124 – Sea Drift (FR) 72 (Warning 136) [2006 –p: 10m **74** 9.9g⁶ p10g⁵ 9.9m Aug 27] rather leggy, close-coupled colt: fair maiden: blinkered, ran as if amiss final outing: will prove just as effective at 1m as 1¼m: acts on polytrack, best turf effort on good going: tongue tied in 2006. *B. J. Meehan*

SONNY PARKIN 4 b.g. Spinning World (USA) 130 – No Miss Kris (USA) (Capote **87** (USA)) [2006 83: p10g 8m⁶ 8m³ 8m* 10m⁴ 12g⁶ 10s² p10g 10.1m Sep 13] tall, leggy **a75** gelding: fairly useful handicapper on turf, fair on all-weather: won at Newmarket in August: creditable efforts when in frame after: stays 1¼m: acts on polytrack, soft and good to firm ground: wears headgear: has looked none too keen: held up. *G. A. Huffer*

SONNY RED (IRE) 2 b.c. (Feb 15) Redback 116 – Magic Melody 62 (Petong 126) **100** [2006 5s* 5s* 5m⁴ Jun 22] €26,000F, 26,000Y: well-made colt: good walker: fifth foal: half-brother to 6f winner Molly Ellen (by Fayruz) and 2004 2-y-o 1m winner Raise A Tune (by Raise A Grand): dam, maiden best at 6f at 2 yrs, half-sister to 3 useful sprinters: useful form: won maiden at Newmarket and listed race at Goodwood (beat Chief Editor 3 lengths) in May: 9/2, 4¾ lengths fourth of 11 to Dutch Art in Norfolk Stakes at Royal Ascot (jarred up after): will probably prove best at 5f/6f. *R. Hannon*

SONO 9 b.g. Robellino (USA) 127 – Sweet Holland (USA) (Alydar (USA)) [2006 **57** p16.5g p16.5g p16.5g Mar 15] close-coupled gelding: missed 2005: just modest per- former in 2006: stays 2m: acts on soft and good to firm going: tried in cheekpieces. *P. D. Niven*

SON OF BATHWICK (IRE) 4 b.g. Dr Fong (USA) 128 – Bathwick Babe (IRE) 71 **–** (Sri Pekan (USA) 117) [2006 59d: p12g a8g⁵ Dec 3] leggy gelding: maiden: little form since debut at 3 yrs: left Mrs N. Pook after reappearance: tried visored/tongue tied. *J. Kelly, Sweden*

SON OF GREEK MYTH (USA) 5 b.g. Silver Hawk (USA) 123 – Greek Myth – (IRE) 58 (Sadler's Wells (USA) 132) [2006 75: p13g Feb 25] sturdy, quite attractive gelding: maiden on Flat: won over hurdles in September: tried blinkered. *G. L. Moore*

SON OF SAMSON (IRE) 5 b.g. Diesis 133 – Delilah (IRE) 114 (Bluebird (USA) – 125) [2006 p12.2g Feb 13] tailed off in bumper, and at Wolverhampton on Flat debut (tongue tied). *R. J. Price*

SON OF SOPHIE 4 b.g. Band On The Run 102 – Fair Enchantress 64 (Enchantment **38** 115) [2006 36: f8g f7g f12g⁵ f12g⁶ Mar 8] poor maiden: tried blinkered. *C. N. Kellett*

SON OF THUNDER (IRE) 5 ch.g. Dr Fong (USA) 128 – Sakura Queen (IRE) 52 **61** (Woodman (USA) 126) [2006 70: 11g 7.9m³ 7.9m⁶ 8m⁵ 8.1f 8m 7.9m⁵ 10.1d* 10s⁶ 11g³ 10.2m³ Oct 8] leggy, close-coupled gelding: just modest performer in 2006: won seller at Newcastle in August, hanging right: stays easy 11f: acts on firm and soft going: has worn headgear, including of late: sold 6,000 gns. *M. Dods*

SONOVISHI 2 b.g. (Feb 29) Ishiguru (USA) 114 – Kastaway 91 (Distant Relative 128) – [2006 p8g⁶ Aug 12] soon off bridle when sixth in maiden at Lingfield. *E. J. O'Neill*

SOPHIA GARDENS 2 ch.f. (Apr 27) Barathea (IRE) 127 – Lovely Lyca 76 (Night **72** Shift (USA)) [2006 6g⁵ 7.1m² 7d⁶ 8.3g⁶ Oct 16] 34,000Y: smallish, quite good-topped filly: sixth foal: half-sister to several winners, including 3-y-o Jeanmaire and 4-y-o Topiary Ted: dam, 1m and 1½m winner, out of half-sister to Old Vic: fair maiden: second to Swift Image at Warwick (dictated): should stay 1m. *D. W. P. Arbuthnot*

SOPHIE JAMES 3 b.f. Mujahid (USA) 125 – Night Trader (USA) (Melyno 130) – [2006 8.2m p6g p10g Aug 13] big filly: fifth foal: closely related to 2 winners by Emperor Jones, including fairly useful 7f/1m winner Night Empress and half-sister to useful 7f to 1¼m winner Jath (by Bishop of Cashel): dam lightly raced: little form in maidens. *M. G. Quinlan*

SOPHIE'JO 3 b.f. Agnes World (USA) 123 – Maureena (IRE) (Grand Lodge (USA) – 125) [2006 73: 8.2m⁶ 9.9g p10g p8.6m f8g⁵ f12g⁵ p11g⁶ Dec 22] strong, lengthy filly: has unimpressive round action: little form in 2006: left H. Cecil after third outing: stays 1m: acts on firm and good to soft going: tried visored/in cheekpieces. *Miss J. Feilden*

SOPHIE'S DREAM 2 b.g. (Feb 21) Averti (IRE) 117 – Sophielu 80 (Rudimentary **57** (USA) 118) [2006 5d⁵ 5m 5m p7.1m⁴ p7g p6s Dec 13] sturdy gelding: modest maiden: stays 7f: acts on polytrack and good to soft going: once refused to enter stall. *G. S. Given*

SORBIESHARRY (IRE) 7 gr.g. Sorbie Tower (IRE) 120 – Silver Moon (Environ- – ment Friend 128) [2006 60, a82: f8g p9.5g⁶ f8g p9.5g p8.6g⁶ p9.5g⁵ p9.5g p9.5g **a62 d** p10g p9.5g f8g³ p10g p12g f12g⁵ f11m⁶ f8g f12g⁴ Dec 12] leggy gelding: poor mover: just modest performer at best in 2006: effective at 1m to 1½m: acts on all-weather, raced only on good ground or firmer on turf: tried visored, effective in cheekpieces or not. *Mrs N. Macauley*

SORREL POINT 3 b.c. Bertolini (USA) 125 – Lightning Princess (Puissance 110) **62** [2006 –: p6g p6g⁴ 5f p7g 8.2g⁵ 7d³ Aug 21] modest maiden: stays 1m: acts on polytrack and good to soft going. *H. J. Collingridge*

SO SHY (IRE) 2 ch.f. (Apr 2) Fath (USA) 116 – Mytilene (IRE) 103 (Soviet Star (USA) **60** 128) [2006 5.1g⁴ 6g p5g Nov 9] €12,500F, 5,000Y: tall filly: half-sister to 3 winners, including 1¼m winner Coruscating (by Highest Honor): dam 2-y-o 7f winner: modest form in maiden on debut (for Stef Liddiard). *J. R. Boyle*

SO SOBER (IRE) 8 b.g. Common Grounds 118 – Femme Savante 89 (Glenstal (USA) **44** 118) [2006 43: p5.1g⁴ f5g p5.1g May 5] compact gelding: poor performer: effective at 5f/ 6f: acts on all-weather, firm and soft going: has reportedly bled. *D. Shaw*

SOSUEME NOW 2 ch.f. (Feb 20) Foxhound (USA) 103 – So Discreet (Tragic Role – (USA)) [2006 8.1m⁵ 10.2m⁵ p8.6g Oct 28] 6,500Y: first foal: dam unraced half-sister to smart 7f/1m performer Gothenberg: no impact in maidens. *A. B. Haynes*

SO SWEET (IRE) 2 b.f. (Feb 28) Cape Cross (IRE) 129 – Announcing Peace (Danehill **97** (USA) 126) [2006 7.1m⁶ 7m* 7m* 7d Sep 19] €92,000F, €180,000Y: smallish, quite attractive filly: fourth foal: sister to 4-y-o Crosspeace and half-sister to Italian 5f (at 2 yrs) and 7.5f winner by College Chapel: dam Irish maiden: useful form: won maiden at New-market and nursery at Redcar (impressive, beat Nota Liberata by 4 lengths) in August:

faded into mid-field in valuable 27-runner sales race at the Curragh final start: will be suited by 1m+. *M. R. Channon*

SOTANNA (IRE) 4 b.f. Stravinsky (USA) 133 – Festive Season (USA) (Lypheor 118) – [2006 7f⁴ p8.6m Sep 2] sister to fairly useful 6f (including at 2 yrs)/7f winner Dvinsky and half-sister to several winners, including 1995 2-y-o 1m winner D'Naan (by Royal Academy): dam, ran twice, half-sister to Prix Marcel Boussac winner Mary Linoa: modest form in maidens at 2 yrs for J. Oxx in Ireland: missed 2005: well beaten in 2006: sold 1,400 gns. *P. R. Webber*

SOTIK STAR (IRE) 3 b.c. Elnadim (USA) 128 – Crystal Springs (IRE) 79 (Kahyasi 92 130) [2006 75: 8g⁴ p8g* p8g* p8g Dec 19] strong colt: fairly useful performer: won maiden in September and handicap in November (by head from Bee Stinger), both at Lingfield: stays 1m: acts on polytrack, unraced on extremes of going on turf: tongue tied last 2 starts. *P. J. Makin*

SOTO 3 b.g. Averti (IRE) 117 – Belle of The Blues (IRE) (Blues Traveller (IRE) 119 83 [2006 87: 6d 6f 6d³ 7.2d² 6m 6m 6m³ 6f* 6m⁴ 6g⁴ Sep 17] small, leggy gelding: fairly useful handicapper: won at Newcastle in July: best form at 6f, stays 7f: acts on fibresand, firm and soft going: sometimes starts awkwardly: usually races prominently. *M. W. Easterby*

SOUBRIQUET (IRE) 3 b.g. Daylami (IRE) 138 – Green Lucia 116 (Green Dancer 76 d (USA) 132) [2006 10m⁴ 10d 9.9g p16g 14g p10g⁵ Sep 27] 26,000Y: close-coupled gelding: half-brother to numerous winners, including smart 1½m performer Luchiroverte (by Slip Anchor) and useful stayer Ravenswood (by Warning), 7f winner at 2 yrs: dam, placed in Irish and Yorkshire Oaks, half-sister to Old Vic: fair maiden: should be suited by 1½m+: acts on good to firm going: blinkered final outing: looked ungainly second start: sold £2,000. *T. G. Mills*

SOUFAH (IRE) 4 b.g. Desert Style (IRE) 121 – Entracte 109 (Henbit (USA) 130) 76 [2006 54+: 10d 10g² 10d² 12m² 12m² Jul 15] strong gelding: fair maiden: stays 1½m: acts on good to firm and good to soft going. *J. L. Dunlop*

SOUFFLEUR 3 b.c. In The Wings 128 – Salinova (FR) (Linamix (FR) 127) [2006 10d² 84 12m⁴ 14.1d* 14d* 14.8m⁴ Jul 30] tall, sturdy colt: has a moderate, quick action: fourth living foal: half-brother to 7-y-o Shabernak and fairly useful 1¾m winner Silver Sash (by Mark of Esteem): dam unraced sister to useful French 1½m winner Six Zero: fairly useful performer: won maiden at Nottingham and handicap at Sandown (coltish in preliminaries) in May: well below form in handicap at Newmarket final start: will stay 2m: acts on good to firm and good to soft going: sold 5,000 gns in October. *M. L. W. Bell*

SOULACROIX 5 b.g. Kylian (USA) – California Dreamin (Slip Anchor 136) [2006 110 100: 12m* 14m* 12.3m² 12d 12.5s⁶ Nov 4] sturdy gelding: smart performer: won handicaps at York (Queen Mother's Cup, by 2 lengths from Thyolo) in June and Goodwood (beat Wunderwood comfortably by 1¼ lengths) in August: ran creditably when ½-length second to Foxhaven in listed race at Chester and seventh to Pevensey in valuable handicap at Ascot: below form in Group 3 handicap at Flemington final outing: effective at 1½m to 2m: acts on good to firm and good to soft going: tends to carry head awkwardly. *L. M. Cumani*

Tatler Summer Season Stakes (Handicap), Goodwood—the whole field is in the picture near the finish of this mile and three quarter event; Soulacroix (star on face) bursts through to beat Wunderwood (checks), Lets Roll (spots), Solent (rail) and Swordsman (sash)

SOULARD (USA) 3 b.c. Arch (USA) 127 – Bourbon Blues (USA) (Seeking The Gold **76** (USA)) [2006 10m⁶ 10.5m⁴ 14.1d⁶ 11f² 11.5f³ 13.8m* Jul 12] $45,000Y: third foal: brother to winner in USA and half-brother to winner there by Seattle Slew: dam, 2-y-o 7f winner in USA, out of US Grade 2 2-y-o 1m winner Beal Street Blues: fair performer: made all in maiden at Catterick in July: stays 13.8f: acts on firm ground: visored last 2 starts: often races freely: sold 30,000 gns. *J. Noseda*

SOUL BLAZER (USA) 3 b.g. Honour And Glory (USA) 122 – See You (USA) **74** (Gulch (USA)) [2006 p7g⁴ p9.5g³ p9.5g³ p8g Dec 16] $100,000Y: fifth foal: half-brother to 3 winners, including useful performer up to 1½m Carte Sauvage (by Kris S), 7f winner at 2 yrs: dam, US 2-y-o 5f/6f winner, out of half-sister to US Grade 1 2-y-o 1m winner Eastern Echo: fair maiden: stays 9.5f. *A. M. Balding*

SOUL PROVIDER (IRE) 5 ch.m. Danehill Dancer (IRE) 117 – Wing And A Prayer **49** (IRE) 63 (Shalford (IRE) 124§) [2006 50: f6g p8g⁴ p8g Feb 13] leggy mare: only poor performer in 2006: effective at 5f to easy 1m: acts on all-weather, firm and good to soft ground: tried blinkered/in cheekpieces/tongue tied. *G. Prodromou*

SOUND AND VISION (IRE) 4 b.g. Fayruz 116 – Lyrical Vision (IRE) (Vision **58** (USA)) [2006 63, a60: f8g* Jan 3] leggy gelding: modest performer: won maiden claimer at Southwell (claimed by J. K. Price) in January: effective at 1m, probably stays 1½m: acts on fibresand, firm and soft going: wears headgear: tried tongue tied. *M. Dods*

SOUNDASAPOUND 2 b.f. (Mar 26) Pursuit of Love 124 – Blue Nile (IRE) 70 (Blue- **60 d** bird (USA) 125) [2006 5d 6m 6g 6m 7g 7m p8g Nov 24] 4,200Y: good-topped filly: eighth foal: half-sister to 3 winners, including 8-y-o Gone Too Far: dam 1¼m winner: little form except on second start: tried in blinkers/cheekpieces. *I. W. McInnes*

SOUND OF NATURE (USA) 3 b.c. Chester House (USA) 123 – Yashmak (USA) **78 p** 118 (Danzig (USA)) [2006 8.2g⁶ 8.3g* Oct 16] good-bodied colt: fifth foal: closely related to 1m winner Eyes Only (by Distant View): dam, (at 2 yrs) to 1½m (Ribblesdale Stakes) winner, half-sister to Warning, Commander In Chief and Deploy: fair form: much better effort in maidens when winning at Windsor in October by neck from Heat O'Arti- fice: will stay 1¼m/1½m: sweated badly on debut: will improve further. *H. R. A. Cecil*

SOUNDS SIMLA (IRE) 3 b.f. Indian Rocket 115 – Evocative (IRE) (Double Sch- **56 §** wartz 128) [2006 82§: p6g p6g⁵ p7g p8g p5g* p6g⁴ p5.1g p5.1g 6m⁴ 6f 6d 5s² 5.1m 5g⁶ 5m p5.1g⁶ p5.1g p6g f6g p6s f5g Dec 29] neat filly: just modest performer in 2006: won seller at Lingfield in February: left Rae Guest prior to eighth outing, J. Coupland after twelfth: seems best at 5f/6f: acts on polytrack, soft and good to firm going: usually blinkered/in cheekpieces of late: not straightforward. *R. A. Harris*

SOUND THAT ALARM 4 b.g. Groom Dancer (USA) 128 – Warning Star 104 (Warn- **42** ing 136) [2006 67d, a–: f6g p6g 8s 10.2m Jun 3] only poor performer in 2006: stays 6f: acts on heavy going: tried headgear/tongue tied. *P. D. Evans*

SOUTHANDWEST (IRE) 2 ch.g. (Feb 5) Titus Livius (FR) 115 – Cheviot Indian **93** (IRE) 71 (Indian Ridge 123) [2006 6.1m² 5.1f* 5m⁵ 5.1f* 6g² 5d Sep 15] €8,000F, €8,000Y: good-topped gelding: fourth foal: half-brother to 6-y-o La Motta: dam Irish maiden who stayed 7f: fairly useful performer: won maiden and minor event at Bath in summer: best effort when 2½ lengths second of 24 to Invincible Force in sales race at the Curragh fifth start: effective at 5f/6f: acts on firm going. *J. S. Moore*

SOUTHBOROUGH LAD 3 ch.g. Woodborough (USA) 112 – Caribbee Beach (IRE) **–** (Magical Strike (USA) 114) [2006 –: 7m Apr 6] sturdy gelding: no form. *Mrs C. A. Dunnett*

SOUTH CAPE 3 b.g. Cape Cross (IRE) 129 – Aunt Ruby (USA) 67 (Rubiano (USA)) **102** [2006 97: 7v* 8.1g 7d⁵ 8g 8m⁴ p8g³ 8m³ 8d 8.1m² 8d² 8g 7g Oct 13] small, leggy gelding: useful performer: won minor event at Southwell in March: good second in handicaps at Sandown (beaten 1¼ lengths by Mosharref) and Ascot (2 lengths behind Supaseus): below form last 2 starts: stays 1m: acts on polytrack, heavy and good to firm going: some- times races freely. *M. R. Channon*

SOUTHERN BAZAAR (USA) 5 ch.g. Southern Halo (USA) – Sunday Bazaar **–** (USA) (Nureyev (USA) 131) [2006 62: 12m Aug 8] good-bodied gelding: modest perfor- mer at 4 yrs: no show only outing in 2006: tried tongue tied/blinkered. *M. C. Chapman*

SOUTHERN SHORE (IRE) 4 ch.g. Erhaab (USA) 127 – Intisab 90 (Green Desert **–** (USA) 127) [2006 65: p13.9g Jan 13] fair performer at 3 yrs: tailed off in seller only Flat outing in 2006. *D. Burchell*

SOUTHERN TIDE (USA) 4 b.c. Southern Halo (USA) – My Own Lovely Lee –
(USA) (Bucksplasher (USA)) [2006 43, a55: p10g⁴ 10m 8m f8g p8g f8g⁶ p7g⁵ Dec 6] **a53 d**
compact colt: modest performer on all-weather (well below form after reappearance),
little recent form on turf: stays easy 1¼m: acts on polytrack: tried in cheekpieces/visor.
J. Pearce

SOUTHGATE LADY (IRE) 3 b.f. Night Shift (USA) – German Lady (Mon Tresor –
113) [2006 –: f8g Jan 11] no form: tried tongue tied. *N. P. Littmoden*

SOUTH HILL 3 b.f. Marju (IRE) 127 – Briggsmaid 70 (Elegant Air 119) [2006 –: –
10.2g 11.9m p9.5g Dec 4] neat filly: little form: reared in stall second outing (left
M. Blanshard after). *R. J. Price*

SOUTH O'THE BORDER 4 b.g. Wolfhound (USA) 126 – Abbey's Gal 100 (Efisio **84**
120) [2006 86: p10g³ 10g 9.7f³ 10s² 10m³ 10f 9g* 10d³ 9.9d² Sep 27] good-topped
gelding: fairly useful performer: won handicap at Sandown in August: best form at 9f/
1¼m: acts on polytrack, firm and soft ground: has run well when sweating: tends to hang:
races up with pace: consistent: sold 36,000 gns, joined Venctia Williams and won on
hurdling debut in December. *T. G. Mills*

SOUTHPORT STAR (IRE) 3 b.g. King's Best (USA) 132 – Danzig's Girl (USA) **83**
(Danzig (USA)) [2006 73: p7g p7g³ 8m³ 8m⁵ 7.1g* 7d p8.6g³ p7g p10g Oct 20] sturdy
gelding: fairly useful performer: won maiden at Warwick in July: good third in handicap
at Wolverhampton after: effective at 7f to 8.6f: acts on polytrack and good to firm ground:
no easy ride: sold 16,000 gns, sent to Bahrain. *J. R. Fanshawe*

SOUVENANCE 3 b.f. Hernando (FR) 127 – Summer Night 94 (Nashwan (USA) 135) **110**
[2006 97: 11g³ 11m³ 12m⁴ 12m³ 12d² 18d⁵ Sep 8] smart performer: mostly creditable
efforts in 2006, in frame in Schwarzgold-Rennen at Cologne (third to Quelle Amore),
Oaks d'Italia at Milan (third to Dionisia) and listed races at Longchamp (fourth to Village
Fete), Cork (third to Reform Act) and Ovrevoll (second to Miss The Boat): upped in trip,
appeared to run well when fifth to Sergeant Cecil in Doncaster Cup at York: stays 2¼m:
acts on good to firm and good to soft going: usually races prominently. *Sir Mark Prescott*

SOVEREIGN DREAMER (USA) 6 b.g. Kingmambo (USA) 125 – Spend A Dream –
(USA) (Spend A Buck (USA)) [2006 68: 10.2d p12g 11.6f Jun 12] tall gelding: one-
time fairly useful 1½m winner: last all starts in 2006: has been blinkered/tongue tied.
P. F. I. Cole

SOVEREIGN SPIRIT (IRE) 4 b.g. Desert Prince (IRE) 130 – Sheer Spirit (IRE) 86 **61**
(Caerleon (USA) 132) [2006 67: f12g* p13.9g* f14g⁴ p12.2g⁴ 16g p13.9g² p16.5m³ **a77**
p13.9g⁶ Dec 8] leggy gelding: fair handicapper on all-weather, modest on turf: won at
Southwell in January and Wolverhampton in February: barely stays 2m: acts on all-
weather, good to firm and good to soft going: usually tongue tied nowadays: sometimes
races freely. *W. R. Swinburn*

SOVEREIGN STATE (IRE) 9 b.g. Soviet Lad (USA) – Portree 82 (Slip Anchor 136) **58**
[2006 59, a51: 21.6d 12g 12f⁵ 14d Oct 8] small, well-made gelding: modest performer, **a–**
better on turf than all-weather: stays 1¾m: acts on polytrack, firm and good to soft going:
tried visored, usually wears cheekpieces. *D. W. Thompson*

SOVEREIGNTY (JPN) 4 b.g. King's Best (USA) 132 – Calando (USA) 110 (Storm **77**
Cat (USA)) [2006 79: 8g 7d 6f 5g⁴ p5.1g* 6f p7g⁴ p7g² p8g⁶ p7.1g* p8g⁴ p7g⁶ p7g³ p6g
p7g³ p7g⁵ p7.1s* p7.1g⁶ Dec 22] lengthy gelding: fair performer: won seller at Wolver-
hampton (sold from I. Semple 6,500 gns) in July and handicaps there in September and
December: stays 1m: acts on all-weather and good to firm going: visored (found little)
third start: tends to wander: none too genuine. *D. K. Ivory*

SOVIET JOY (IRE) 5 b. or br.g. Russian Revival (USA) 125 – Danny's Joy (IRE) 65 **50**
(Maelstrom Lake 118) [2006 –: 11v² 8.5d Apr 19] modest maiden: stays 11f: acts on
heavy going. *J. J. Quinn*

SOVIET LEGEND (IRE) 3 b.c. Soviet Star (USA) 128 – Another Legend (USA) **49**
(Lyphard's Wish (FR) 124) [2006 45, a52: p5.1g⁵ p6g 5m² 5m 6m 5f 5d 5f Sep 20] rather
leggy, lengthy colt: just poor handicapper in 2006: may prove best at 5f: acts on polytrack
and good to firm ground: blinkered/visored: tried tongue tied: signs of temperament: sold
2,200 gns, sent to Denmark. *T. J. Etherington*

SOVIET PALACE (IRE) 2 b.g. (Jan 26) Jade Robbery (USA) 121 – Daisy Hill **88**
(Indian Ridge 123) [2006 6m⁶ 6m* 7f 6d Aug 29] 16,000Y: big, good-topped gelding:
first foal: dam, French 1m winner, out of useful half-sister to Ribblesdale winner and

Oaks runner-up Bahr: fairly useful form: won maiden at Leicester in June: last both tries in nurseries, then gelded: free-going sort, likely to prove best short of 7f: acts on good to firm going. *K. A. Ryan*

SOVIET PROMISE (IRE) 3 b.f. Soviet Star (USA) 128 – Akarita (IRE) 92 (Akarad (FR) 130) [2006 –: 9.7f⁶ 7m 8.2f 10.1f⁵ Jul 25] tall, good-topped filly: little form: tried blinkered. *G. G. Margarson* —

SOVIET SCEPTRE (IRE) 5 ch.g. Soviet Star (USA) 128 – Princess Sceptre (Cadeaux Genereux 131) [2006 63, a50: p12g² p12g 10.9s⁴ p16.5g⁵ p12.2g⁶ May 8] lengthy gelding: modest performer: stays 1¾m: acts on polytrack, soft and good to firm going: has been tongue tied, including of late: modest hurdler, claimed by Evan Williams in July. *R. T. Phillips* **60**

SOVIET SONG (IRE) 6 b.m. Marju (IRE) 127 – Kalinka (IRE) 88 (Soviet Star (USA) 128) [2006 126: 8s⁴ 8m* 8m⁶ 8m² 8m⁵ 8d² Sep 30] sturdy, lengthy mare: high-class performer at her best, successful in 5 Group 1 events, including Sussex Stakes at Goodwood at 4 yrs: very smart form in 2006: won Windsor Forest Stakes at Royal Ascot in June comfortably by 2 lengths from Echelon: second after in Sussex Stakes at Goodwood (beaten 2 lengths by Court Masterpiece) and Sun Chariot Stakes at Newmarket (well below form when beaten 9 lengths by Spinning Queen): stayed 1m: acted on firm and soft going: often sweated up, was sometimes on toes/had 2 handlers (calmer than usual at Royal Ascot): used to take strong hold: was waited with: visits Montjeu. *J. R. Fanshawe* **120**

SOVIET SOUND (IRE) 2 ch.c. (Feb 18) Soviet Star (USA) 128 – Orange Grouse (IRE) 105 (Taufan (USA) 119) [2006 6m 6m 5g 6v⁵ Oct 9] good-bodied colt: modest form in maiden second start. *Jedd O'Keeffe* **51**

SOVIETTA (IRE) 5 b.m. Soviet Star (USA) 128 – La Riveraine (USA) 90 (Riverman (USA) 131) [2006 68, a–: 12s⁴ 12g³ 11.7d 13.1s² 11.8d* p12g Dec 16] just modest handicapper in 2006: won apprentice event at Leicester in May: stays 13f: acts on heavy and good to firm ground: often tongue tied in 2006. *A. G. Newcombe* **61 a–**

SOVIET THREAT (IRE) 5 ch.g. Soviet Star (USA) 128 – Veiled Threat (IRE) 105 (Be My Guest (USA) 126) [2006 71: p7.1g⁶ p7.1g⁶ 8.2d p7g Jun 6] just modest performer in 2006: stays 1m: acts on polytrack: wore cheekpieces final outing. *A. G. Juckes* **58**

SOWDREY 2 b.c. (Feb 15) In The Wings 128 – Baaderah (IRE) 102 (Cadeaux Genereux 131) [2006 7m⁵ Jul 21] leggy, attractive colt: seventh foal: closely related to a winner in Greece by Singspiel and half-brother to fairly useful 1m winner Badr Rainbow (by Rainbow Quest): dam 6f (including at 2 yrs) winner who stayed 1m: 33/1, fifth to Aqmaar in maiden at Newbury: should improve. *M. R. Channon* **77 p**

SOWERBY 4 b.g. Grey Desire 115 – Brief Star (IRE) 49 (Brief Truce (USA) 126) [2006 –: f5g Apr 4] quite good-topped gelding: lightly-raced maiden, poor nowadays: should stay 6f: tried blinkered. *M. Brittain* **46**

SOYLENT GREEN 2 b.f. (Mar 27) Primo Valentino (IRE) 116 – Slipperose 72 (Persepolis (FR) 127) [2006 6m 6s Oct 16] half-sister to 3 winners, including 11-y-o Yorkies Boy and 6-y-o Saif Sareea: dam 11.5f winner: well beaten in maidens. *S. Parr* —

SPACE COWBOY (IRE) 6 b.g. Anabaa (USA) 130 – Lady Moranbon (USA) (Trempolino (USA) 135) [2006 –: 12g Jul 6] very lightly raced on Flat, no form since 2003: fairly useful hurdler, winner in July. *G. L. Moore* —

SPACEMAN 3 b.c. In The Wings 128 – Souk (IRE) 98 (Ahonoora 122) [2006 50: 8m 10m 11.9m⁴ 11.5f⁶ 11.5f* 11.7f⁴ 11.5m⁶ p13.9m⁴ Oct 2] smallish, good-bodied colt: fair performer: won handicap at Yarmouth in July: stays 1¾m: acts on polytrack and firm going: visored 5 of last 6 outings: sold 38,000 gns. *L. M. Cumani* **66**

Windsor Forest Stakes, Royal Ascot—Soviet Song's final success is a convincing one; Echelon is second, ahead of Royal Alchemist and Zaya Zen (partially hidden)

Elite Racing Club's "Soviet Song"

SPAINNASH (IRE) 6 b.g. Nashwan (USA) 135 – Agreed (Green Desert (USA) 127) **82**
[2006 85: 7s⁶ 7d⁵ 7m⁴ 8.5m 12s p9.5g Nov 25] useful performer when trained in France
in 2003/04 by F. Rohaut, winning 3 times including handicap at Saint-Cloud: fairly useful
handicapper nowadays: left Mrs V. Keatley after fourth start: probably best at 7f/1m: acts
on soft and good to firm going: tried blinkered/in cheekpieces. *J. J. Lambe, Ireland*

SPANISH ACE 5 b.g. First Trump 118 – Spanish Heart 86 (King of Spain 121) [2006 **90 d**
88: 5g* 5m* 6m 5g² 5m 5m 5.2f⁶ 5f 5m 5m Sep 8] rather leggy, close-coupled gelding:
fairly useful handicapper: won at Warwick and Folkestone (broke course record) in April:
good second at Beverley fourth outing, but below form after: effective at 5f/6f: acts on
good to firm and good to soft going: often wore headgear in 2004/5: sometimes slowly
away: often races up with pace. *J. M. Bradley*

SPANISH AFFAIR 2 b.c. (Mar 20) Pursuit of Love 124 – Catalonia (IRE) 76 (Catrail **–**
(USA) 123) [2006 7s f8g Nov 2] behind in maidens. *Jedd O'Keeffe*

SPANISH AIR 2 b.f. (Mar 13) Muhtarram (USA) 125 – Spanish Heart 86 (King of **57**
Spain 121) [2006 6s p6g⁴ p7g⁶ p7.1g Jul 11] 8,000Y: close-coupled filly: half-sister to
several winners, including 5-y-o Spanish Ace and 7f/1m winner Bold King (by Anshan),
both useful: dam, effective at 7f to 9f, half-sister to smart sprinter Northern Goddess:
modest maiden: likely to stay 1m. *J. W. Hills*

SPANISH CONQUEST 2 b.g. (Mar 23) Hernando (FR) 127 – Sirena (GER) (Tejano **– p**
(USA)) [2006 p7g 7.2d p7g Sep 27] 57,000Y: tall, leggy, useful-looking gelding: third
foal: brother to 5-y-o Vinando: dam, German 1m to 9.5f winner, half-sister to high-class

German 1¼m/1½m performer Silvano and smart German 1½m performer Sabiango: no threat in maidens (all in September), then gelded: sort to flourish as 3-y-o at 1½m+. *Sir Mark Prescott*

SPANISH DON 8 b.g. Zafonic (USA) 130 – Spanish Wells (IRE) (Sadler's Wells (USA) 132) [2006 108: 9g 9m 8m 8s Aug 24] big, lengthy gelding: smart performer at best: well held in 2006: blinkered once: usually waited with. *D. R. C. Elsworth* —

SPANISH HARLEM (IRE) 2 br.c. (Feb 13) Danehill (USA) 126 – Sleepytime (IRE) 121 (Royal Academy (USA) 130) [2006 8d⁴ 7v* Oct 23] fourth foal: brother to 5-y-o Gentleman's Deal: dam, won 1000 Guineas (7f winner at 2 yrs), sister to high-class miler Ali-Royal and half-sister to very smart 1¼m/1½m performer Taipan: better effort in maidens when winning 23-runner event at the Curragh by ¾ length from stable-companion Archipenko, always prominent: will improve further. *A. P. O'Brien, Ireland* **98 p**

SPANISH HIDALGO (IRE) 2 b.c. (Apr 8) Night Shift (USA) – Spanish Lady (IRE) 61 (Bering 136) [2006 7.1m² 7m³ 7.6f* 8d* 8s Oct 7] fourth foal: half-brother to 4-y-o Spanish Ridge: dam, maiden who stayed 1½m, out of half-sister to Mtoto: fairly useful performer: won maiden at Lingfield and nursery at Newmarket (by 3 lengths) in August: weakened and eased in Autumn Stakes at Ascot final start: will probably stay 1½m: acts on firm and good to soft going. *J. L. Dunlop* **94**

SPANISH LACE 3 b.f. Hernando (FR) 127 – Kabayil 75 (Dancing Brave (USA) 140) [2006 71p: p9.5g* 11g⁵ 14g Jul 7] strong filly: fair performer: won maiden at Wolverhampton in January: should stay 1¼m+: acts on polytrack: joined N. Henderson. *Miss J. A. Camacho* **69**

SPANISH LAW 4 b.g. Zaha (CAN) 106 – Misty Moon (Polar Falcon (USA) 126) [2006 58: 7.5f 8d⁴ 8.3f² 7.2g⁶ 7.1f⁵ 8m 8g Aug 14] modest handicapper: eased as if amiss final outing: stays 1m: acts on firm and good to soft going: blinkered nowadays. *M. Dods* **58**

SPANISH MOON (USA) 2 b.c. (Apr 26) El Prado (IRE) 119 – Shining Bright 98 (Rainbow Quest (USA) 134) [2006 7d* Oct 28] tall, attractive colt: brother to smart 7f (at 2 yrs) and 1½m (Ribblesdale Stakes) winner Spanish Sun and half-brother to 3 winners, including fairly useful 1½m winner Eagle's Cross (by Trempolino): dam, French 1½m winner, half-sister to smart French middle-distance performers Apogee and Daring Miss: 6/1, won maiden at Newmarket (beat Mofarij by 1¾ lengths), green and niggled by halfway but going clear at finish: will be suited by 1¼m/1½m: smart prospect, sure to win more races. *Sir Michael Stoute* **97 p**

SPANISH MUSIC 4 b.f. Piccolo 121 – Raffelina (USA) (Carson City (USA)) [2006 63, a53: p6g⁵ p7g⁴ p8g p8.6g⁶ p6g⁴ p7g p6g³ p7g⁵ p7g May 15] close-coupled filly: modest maiden: stays 7f: acts on polytrack and firm ground: tried blinkered/tongue tied. *R. Ingram* **51**

SPANISH RAINBOW (IRE) 3 ch.f. Rainbow Quest (USA) 134 – Spanish Lady (IRE) 61 (Bering 136) [2006 69: 10g Apr 21] maiden: just modest form only outing in 2006: should be suited by 1½m+: raced only on good going. *J. L. Dunlop* **56**

SPANISH RIDGE (IRE) 4 b.g. Indian Ridge 123 – Spanish Lady (IRE) 61 (Bering 136) [2006 82: 16g 16d 14.1g 14.8m⁶ 14.8m 14m Aug 11] big, good-topped gelding: fairly useful handicapper at 3 yrs, well held in 2006: tongue tied final outing: said to have had breathing problem when pulled up fifth start: usually held up: ungenuine. *J. L. Dunlop* **– §**

SPANISH STAR 9 b.g. Hernando (FR) 127 – Desert Girl (Green Desert (USA) 127) [2006 –, a55: f11g f12g Feb 23] compact gelding: modest performer: well held in 2006: tried visored. *Mrs N. Macauley* —

SPANISH STORY 3 br.f. Vettori (IRE) 119 – Spanish Heart 86 (King of Spain 121) [2006 48: p7g⁵ 7m p8.6g 7g f8g Nov 2] close-coupled filly: poor maiden: left A. Balding after fourth outing: tried in cheekpieces. *J. G. Portman* **47**

SPARKBRIDGE (IRE) 3 b.g. Mull of Kintyre (USA) 114 – Persian Velvet (IRE) (Distinctly North (USA) 115) [2006 56: p7g 9v⁴ 8m 8g 10v 11.1f 8m 14d Oct 8] good-topped gelding: modest maiden: stays 9f: acts on heavy and good to firm going. *R. F. Fisher* **56**

SPARKLING EYES 2 b.f. (Mar 9) Lujain (USA) 119 – Lady Georgia 94 (Arazi (USA) 135) [2006 6g 5m⁴ 5m⁴ f6g⁵ 6m⁶ 5m* 5d² 5m⁶ 7s 6d³ p6g⁴ Nov 22] leggy filly: fourth foal: half-sister to winner in Greece by Bien Bien: dam 7.8f winner: fair performer: made all in maiden at Sandown in August: in frame another 5 starts (flattered in Queen Mary **77**

Stakes at Royal Ascot on third), in nurseries last 2: best at 5f/6f: acts on good to firm and good to soft going, probably polytrack. *C. E. Brittain*

SPARK UP 6 b.m. Lahib (USA) 129 – Catch The Flame (USA) (Storm Bird (CAN) 134) **64**
[2006 64: p9.5g⁴ p8.6g⁴ p7.1g* p7.1g⁴ p9.5g p8.6g⁶ p7.1g⁴ p7.1g³ p8.6g² p8.6g⁴
7m p8.6g³ p8.6g⁴ p8.6g* p8.6g³ p8.6g² Dec 30] smallish, quite attractive mare: modest handicapper: won at Wolverhampton in February and December: stays 8.6f: acts on all-weather, good to firm and good to soft going: wears headgear: sometimes slowly away. *J. W. Unett*

SPARKWELL 4 b.c. Dansili 127 – West Devon (USA) (Gone West (USA)) [2006 82: **76**
7m 6m 6m 6m p5.1m³ p6g⁶ p5.1g⁵ p5.1s* p6g p5.1g⁶ Dec 27] good-topped colt: just fair handicapper in 2006: left D. Barker after fourth outing: won at Wolverhampton in December: effective at 5f to 7f: raced only on polytrack and good/good to firm ground. *D. Shaw*

SPARKY VIXEN 2 b.f. (Mar 28) Mujahid (USA) 125 – Lucy Glitters (USA) 60 (Cryp- **–**
toclearance (USA)) [2006 6d 6s 8.2d Nov 1] 4,700Y: fourth foal: half-sister to 3-y-o Penny Glitters and winner in Italy around 1m by Unfuwain: dam, maiden, showed little after debut: no form in maidens. *S. Parr*

SPARTAN DANCE 2 ch.g. (Feb 24) Groom Dancer (USA) 128 – Delphic Way 63 **65**
(Warning 136) [2006 8.2s 8.2d⁵ f8g³ f8g³ Dec 2] useful-looking gelding: fourth foal: half-brother to 6-y-o Parnassian: dam, disappointing maiden, half-sister to smart 6f/7f performer Palace Affair: fair maiden: third in minor event (looked awkward) and nursery at Southwell: will stay 1¼m. *J. A. Geake*

SPARTAN ODYSSEY 5 b.g. Overbury (IRE) 116 – Spartan Native (Native Bazaar **–**
122) [2006 51: 15m f12g⁶ Nov 20] plain gelding: poor maiden on balance: stays 1½m. *A. Bailey*

SPASIBA 3 b.f. Pivotal 124 – Skimra 91 (Hernando (FR) 127) [2006 46: f8g⁵ p9.5g f7g **–**
Apr 4] poor maiden: left Sir Mark Prescott after reappearance: should be suited by 1m+: tried blinkered/visored. *Mrs L. Williamson*

SPEAGLE (IRE) 4 ch.c. Desert Sun 120 – Pohutakawa (FR) (Affirmed (USA)) [2006 **89**
68: 10f 10g* a7g* p9.5g p8.6g* p9.5g* f12g* Dec 21] fairly useful performer: won claimers at Sligo (left A. Mullins in Ireland after) in June and Laytown in September, seller at Wolverhampton (left A. McGuinness in Ireland after) in November and handicaps at Wolverhampton and Southwell (by 6 lengths, best effort) in December: stays 1½m: acts on all-weather and sand, best effort on turf on good going: often races prominently. *D. Carroll*

SPEAKERBOXXX 4 ch.g. Zafonic (USA) 130 – Trounce (Barathea (IRE) 127) [2006 **49**
62: p7.1g f7g Jan 17] tall gelding: poor performer: stays 7f: acts on all-weather: tried blinkered/tongue tied: sold 4,500 gns, sent to Saudi Arabia. *P. F. I. Cole*

SPEARIT (IRE) 3 ch.c. Lear Spear (USA) 124 – French Gift 99 (Cadeaux Genereux **81**
131) [2006 80: 5d 6d⁶ 6g⁴ 6d⁵ 6g 6g⁶ 6m* p6g² 6d² Aug 28] well-made colt: fairly useful handicapper: won at Newmarket in August: good second last 2 starts: should have been suited by 7f: acted on polytrack, good to firm and good to soft going: dead. *D. R. C. Elsworth*

SPEAR THISTLE 4 ch.g. Selkirk (USA) 129 – Ardisia (USA) 87 (Affirmed (USA)) **91**
[2006 95: p16g³ p16g 16d 12d³ 10s Oct 21] tall, close-coupled gelding: just fairly useful handicapper in 2006: form in 2006 only when third at Kempton and Newmarket: effective at 1½m to 2m: acts on polytrack, heavy and good to firm going: often races prominently. *Mrs N. Smith*

SPECIAL BALLOT (IRE) 5 br.m. Perugino (USA) 84 – Election Special 78 (Chief **49**
Singer 131) [2006 12.1d 5d 6d p8.6g p12.2g⁵ f14g Nov 21] sixth foal: sister to smart stayer First Ballot and fairly useful 7f winner La Speziana, and half-sister to fairly useful 1m and 1¼m winner Devolution (by Distinctly North): dam 2-y-o 6f winner who probably stayed 1¼m: modest form in bumpers: poor maiden on Flat: may prove best short of 1½m: acts on polytrack. *G. A. Swinbank*

SPECIAL DAY 2 b.f. (Mar 13) Fasliyev (USA) 120 – Mustique Dream 87 (Don't **79**
Forget Me 127) [2006 5m* Jun 16] 12,000F, €42,000Y: lengthy filly: third foal: closely related to 2003 2-y-o 7f winner in Italy by Stravinsky: dam 1m winner: 7/4, won maiden at Sandown, quickening once gap came to beat Gentleman Pirate by head: looked sure to improve, but suffered a pulled muscle behind. *B. W. Hills*

SPECIAL GOLD 4 b.g. Josr Algarhoud (IRE) 118 – Inya Lake 101 (Whittingham **76** (IRE) 104) [2006 76: 5f 5.1s 5f 6f³ 6m³ 6.1f² 6m 6m 5d³ 5g* p5.1g² p5.1g⁴ p6g⁶ p5g* p5g³ Dec 16] rather leggy gelding: fair performer: won handicaps at Newcastle in September and, having left T. Easterby 8,000 gns after next start, Lingfield in December: effective at 5f/6f: acts on polytrack, firm and soft ground: tried in cheekpieces, usually blinkered. *A. D. Brown*

SPECIAL LAD 4 b.g. Spectrum (IRE) 126 – Oh Hebe (IRE) 74 (Night Shift (USA)) **97** [2006 87: 6d p6g* p6g⁴ p6g² Oct 5] close-coupled, good-topped gelding: useful handicapper: won at Kempton in September by 1½ lengths from She's My Outsider: tongue tied, very good short-head second to Grand Show at Lingfield final outing: effective at 6f/ 7f: acts on polytrack and firm ground: sold 50,000 gns, sent to Bahrain. *P. F. I. Cole*

SPECIAL MOMENT (IRE) 3 b.f. Sadler's Wells (USA) 132 – Upper Circle (Shirley **72** Heights 130) [2006 65p: p12g⁶ 12.1d³ 12m⁵ p12.2g 10.5v³ 11.6d² p12.2g f14g³ Nov 20] compact filly: fair maiden handicapper: effective at 10.5f to 1¾m: acts on fibresand and heavy going: tried blinkered: sold 62,000 gns. *B. W. Hills*

SPECIAL PLACE 3 b.g. Compton Place 125 – Petarga 87 (Petong 126) [2006 7g p7g⁶ **72** p10g 7f⁵ p8g³ p7g⁵ p7g* Dec 19] sturdy gelding: first foal: dam 5f (including at 2 yrs)/6f winner: fair performer: improved form on handicap debut when winning at Lingfield in December: stays 1m: acts on polytrack. *J. A. R. Toller*

SPECIOSA (IRE) 3 b.f. Danehill Dancer (IRE) 117 – Specifically (USA) (Sky **115** Classic (CAN)) [2006 104: 7g* 8s* 12g⁴ 8m 7g⁶ Sep 9]

Even if the temperamental George Washington had eventually been persuaded to enter the winner's enclosure after the Two Thousand Guineas, he wouldn't have met a reception on the scale of that accorded to Speciosa twenty-four hours later. A classic winner from a smallish stable, she was given the most tumultuous welcome seen at Newmarket for many a year, perhaps matched in recent years only by that given to the redoubtable Persian Punch after he battled back to win his third Jockey Club Cup in 2003. Speciosa's victory in the Stan James One Thousand Guineas earned her trainer Pam Sly the distinction of becoming the first woman officially credited with training a classic winner in Britain. Mrs Sly, who described herself as 'only a Fenland farmer', received three cheers from those surrounding the winner's enclosure, the first time that had occurred on such a scale at Newmarket since Henry Cecil was similarly feted after Bosra Sham's emotional victory in the 1996 Champion Stakes. The Sly stable, more familiar to followers of jumping, housed only a dozen Flat horses in the latest season. Speciosa's rise from Doncaster Breeze Up purchase to classic winner provided one of the most heartwarming stories of the racing year and prompted her trainer to say: 'I hope this gives all the little people hope. Don't give up. You can do it.'

George Washington, the most expensive yearling of his year at 1,150,000 guineas and one of a host of blue-blooded classic hopes at Ballydoyle, was clear ante-post favourite for the Two Thousand Guineas from the moment he won the Railway Stakes at the Curragh on Irish Derby day on his third start as a two-year-old. Speciosa hadn't won a race of any sort by then and a fortnight after the Irish Derby managed only eighth in a run-of-the-mill maiden at Nottingham. Speciosa finally got off the mark on her fourth start, in a maiden at Beverley in August, before being stepped up to pattern company. After finishing a good third to Nasheej in the May Hill Stakes at Doncaster, Speciosa won the Rockfel Stakes at Newmarket in October. Speciosa may have had little else in common with George Washington but, like him, she was a quirky individual. Her trainer described her as 'a witch' as a two-year-old when she was on a magnesium supplement, said to be a calming influence. Staff had a job to groom her, or even to wipe her down with a cloth, and when *Timeform* sent a photographer to take a posed portrait for *Racehorses of 2005* Speciosa proved too difficult. It took forty-five minutes to persuade her to stand anything like properly and even the resultant shot wasn't deemed correct enough for publication. Although still far from straightforward as a three-year-old, Speciosa was more amenable, coming off the magnesium and, thankfully, behaving much better for our photographer!

Turning down at least two large offers for Speciosa in the winter, her three owners—the trainer, the trainer's son Michael and Tom Davies, a general practitioner (who each put in £10,000 to buy her as a yearling)—decided to 'live the dream', as they put it. Speciosa started off in the Shadwell Nell Gwyn Stakes at the Newmarket Craven meeting, conceding 3 lb to her eight rivals because of her win in the Rockfel. She was sent off at 9/1 joint-fifth best with Spinning Queen, behind the Fabre-trained favourite Sweet Travel, the Queen Mary and Cherry Hinton runner-up Salut d'Amour and a pair of Hamdan Al Maktoum fillies from the John Dunlop and Sir Michael Stoute stables. Speciosa earned her place in the One Thousand Guineas field with an all-the-way win, readily holding on by a length from Spinning Queen, with Salut d'Amour three quarters of a length away third and Sweet Travel only fourth. Speciosa showed her eccentricity, drifting left across the track when ridden in earnest and finishing alone against the stand rail. Speciosa and Spinning Queen were the only Nell Gwyn runners to go on to the Guineas. They started at 10/1 and 50/1 respectively in a field of thirteen, in which Nasheej, winner of the Fred Darling at Newbury and 16/1 for the Guineas, was the only other runner to have contested a 'trial'. Ballydoyle's principal challenger, the 3/1 favourite Rumplestiltskin (winner of the Moyglare and the Marcel Boussac), was tuned up in a racecourse gallop—along with George Washington—at the Curragh, while the second favourite Silca's Sister (plucked by Godolphin from the Channon stable after winning the Prix Morny) wintered in Dubai, and Flashy Wings (Queen Mary and Lowther) and Nannina (Fillies' Mile) were others sent straight to the Guineas. Southern parts of Britain had their coldest winter for nearly twenty years. Generally, it was the coldest March since 1996 and, for the first time in twenty years, temperatures in Britain in April never reached 20C. The wintry weather obviously had an effect on the preparation of some classic hopes, the bypassing of the traditional trials by most of the leading Guineas contenders prompting a review by the BHB, the findings of which are outlined in the essay on Red Clubs.

More than an inch of rain fell at Newmarket between the Two Thousand Guineas, run on good to firm ground on Saturday, and Sunday's One Thousand

Stan James 1000 Guineas Stakes, Newmarket—Speciosa leads throughout,
making Pam Sly the first woman officially to train a British classic winner; Confidential Lady is second,
ahead of Nasheej, Silca's Sister, Wake Up Maggie and Spinning Queen

Guineas, for which the going turned soft. It is rare for a Guineas to be run on soft or heavy going and some of the One Thousand Guineas contenders seemed unable to cope with the conditions. With the race turning into a much more severe test than usual, Speciosa, Nasheej and Spinning Queen probably reaped the benefit of having an outing beforehand, all finishing in the first six in a field of thirteen. The best two-year-old form—as represented by Rumplestiltskin, Flashy Wings and Nannina—proved a poor guide on the day, though Speciosa improved again and more or less matched the form achieved by the market leaders as two-year-olds. Speciosa achieved victory in what was becoming typical style, making all and again not unduly inconvenienced by hanging left when first coming under the whip, keeping on strongly once across to the rail. Confidential Lady, a first British classic runner for her trainer Sir Mark Prescott and subsequent winner of the Prix de Diane, chased Speciosa throughout, eventually beaten two and a half lengths into second. Nasheej came third, a length behind Confidential Lady, with Silca's Sister fourth, Rumplestiltskin seventh, Flashy Wings eleventh and Nannina twelfth. As well as being an occasion to remember for her owners, Speciosa's victory also provided her jockey Micky Fenton with his first classic success in Britain (he had won an Oaks d'Italia in 2001).

Fenton is Irish and one of his ambitions is to win a classic in his homeland. That was never likely with Speciosa as her trainer felt that Speciosa's tendency to go left would count against her on the right-handed Guineas course at the Curragh.

Michael H. Sly, Dr T. Davies & Mrs Pam Sly's "Speciosa"

She was supplemented instead for the Oaks, connections admitting it was 'a bit of a gamble whether she will stay'. Speciosa's free-running style, coupled with her pedigree, seemed likely to be her undoing at Epsom and so it proved. In an ordinary field by the standards of the race, Speciosa and Short Skirt (who had beaten Oaks favourite Alexandrova in the Musidora) were the only contenders who had won in pattern company. Speciosa spread a plate beforehand, but it did not affect her chance. She was allowed the run of things from the front but wasn't able to sustain her effort fully after trying to stretch clear from Tattenham Corner. Alexandrova and Rising Cross swept past her over a furlong out and Short Skirt also passed her in the last few strides, though the £23,703 that Speciosa earned for fourth covered her owners' costs for running. Speciosa finished seven and three quarter lengths behind the wide-margin winner Alexandrova. Speciosa was returned to shorter distances after Epsom but didn't repeat her Oaks form, never mind approach her Guineas performance. She managed only ninth of fifteen in a strong renewal of the Coronation Stakes at Royal Ascot, beaten by five of those who had finished behind her at Newmarket, Nannina, Flashy Wings, Nasheej, Race For The Stars and Silca's Sister. Rested until the autumn, she came only sixth, more patiently ridden but still hanging, behind Iffraaj in the Park Stakes at York on her return in September and was withdrawn from the Sun Chariot Stakes at Newmarket in October on the morning of the race, reportedly lame behind. A scan revealed no break or serious injury and Speciosa is set to remain in training at four.

Breeze Up sales started as something of a novelty in Britain at Doncaster in the late-'seventies, the two-year-olds offered mostly being from the bargain basement. It was a different story in America. The sire of Speciosa's grandam the dual Arc winner Alleged was sold for 175,000 dollars at Hollywood Park in March 1976 and is probably the best horse to emerge from a two-year-old-in-training sale. The standing of such sales in America was illustrated graphically in 2006 when The Green Monkey, as yet unraced, set a thoroughbred auction record of 16m dollars at the Fasig-Tipton Calder Sale. The public perception of Breeze Ups in Britain went up when three Group 1 winners emerged from the catalogues at Newmarket and Doncaster in 2005, the Middle Park winner Amadeus Wolf and Racing Post Trophy winner Palace Episode both finding their way into training with Kevin Ryan after being led out unsold at the Newmarket Breeze Up Sale, while four-year-old Prix de l'Opera winner Kinnaird had been an 8,000-guinea graduate of the Doncaster Breeze Up Sale. Kinnaird was consigned by Mocklershill Stables, County Tipperary, which specialises in preparing horses for the Breeze Ups (the top four lots at the 2006 Newmarket Breeze Up Sale all came from Mocklershill, the top one making 625,000 guineas). Speciosa was consigned by Mocklershill and made 30,000 guineas (after changing hands for €25,000 as a yearling) at the Doncaster Breeze Up Sale in 2005.

			Danehill	Danzig
	Danehill Dancer (IRE)	Danehill	(b 1986)	Razyana
	(b 1993)		Mira Adonde	Sharpen Up
Speciosa (IRE)			(b or br 1986)	Lettre d'Amour
(b.f. 2003)			Sky Classic	Nijinsky
	Specifically (USA)	Sky Classic	(ch 1987)	No Class
	(b 1994)		Specificity	Alleged
			(b 1988)	Mandera

It would have been interesting to see how much Speciosa would have fetched had she been sent to the December Sales where prices for broodmares and fillies out of training went through the roof. Speciosa's dam Specifically, a two-year-old winner bought for only 17,000 dollars as a six-year-old at Keeneland and then for €50,000 (in foal to Statue of Liberty) at Goffs four years later, made 1.85m guineas, in foal to Speciosa's sire, at the latest December Sales to join Newsells Park Stud (about whose operation more can be found in the entry on Soapy Danger). Specifically's sale at Keeneland came before her second foal Major Rhythm (by Rhythm) reached the racecourse and showed himself a smart miler on turf in the States, winning at listed level and placed in Grade 3 company and still going strongly as a seven-year-old in the latest season. Specifically's half-sister Pride, winner of the Champion Stakes and second in the Arc in the latest season, has enhanced the family's reputation considerably, as obviously has Speciosa, and the filly foal that Specifically was carrying at the time of her sale at Goffs made 270,000 guineas as a yearling in 2006, when Specifically had a colt foal by Indian Haven. Specifically has bred five winners so far and more can be found about the distaff side of the family in the essay on Pride.

Speciosa's sire Danehill Dancer was a smart performer at six and seven furlongs and, at stud, has been one of the busiest stallions around, shuttling between Ireland and Australia and, as expected, proving an influence for speed with such as the high-class sprinter Choisir and Queen Elizabeth II Stakes winner Where Or When among his notable winners. The money-spinning Miss Beatrix, winner of the inaugural Goffs Million, helped Danehill Dancer to finish second to his sire Danehill in the combined sires' table for Britain and Ireland in 2006. Danehill Dancer's meteroric rise to prominence is illustrated by the fact that Speciosa was conceived at a fee of IR £9,000 and Miss Beatrix when his fee was €30,000. His fee in 2007 will be €115,000 (from €75,000), behind only those of Galileo (€150,000) and Montjeu (€125,000) among the advertised stallions on the Coolmore roster (the fee for Sadler's Wells is 'private' but is believed to be higher than for either Montjeu or Galileo). Whatever the leggy, quite good-topped Speciosa achieves as a four-year-old, her One Thousand Guineas win is sure to be recalled when discussions turn to thoroughbreds whose humble origins and their subsequent achievements have provided food for the optimist. The Speciosa story may, of course, end up having another chapter. If it does, it will probably be one recounting further front-running victories at up to a mile and a quarter, probably on going ranging from soft to good to firm. Although Speciosa can get on her toes in the preliminaries and has had to be taken quietly to post, she is a genuine racehorse who keeps on gamely despite her tendency to hang left. *Mrs P. Sly*

SPECKLED HEN (IRE) 3 b.f. Titus Livius (FR) 115 – Colouring (IRE) 79 (Catrail (USA) 123) [2006 8s⁵ 7g p8g p7.1s Dec 14] €28,000Y: second foal: dam Irish 8.5f winner: fair form in minor events at Saint-Cloud and Deauville at 2 yrs: well held in 2006 after reappearance, sold from R. Gibson in France 4,500 gns after second start: stays 7f: tried blinkered. *D. Haydn Jones* **60**

SPECTACULAR DANCER (IRE) 4 b.g. Fasliyev (USA) 120 – Committal (USA) (Chief's Crown (USA)) [2006 –: p6g Feb 18] tall, lengthy gelding: little form: tried tongue tied. *Mrs H. Dalton* **–**

SPECTACULAR JOY (IRE) 2 b.g. (Apr 25) Spectrum (IRE) 126 – Great Joy (IRE) (Grand Lodge (USA) 125) [2006 5g³ p5.1g Sep 11] modest form in maidens (third to Zanida) and Wolverhampton 3 months apart: will be suited by 6f/7f. *Mrs A. Duffield* **60**

SPECTACULAR SHOW (IRE) 3 ch.f. Spectrum (IRE) 126 – Stage Presence (IRE) 95 (Selkirk (USA) 129) [2006 79: 7v⁵ p6g⁶ 7m³ 6d³ 8.1f⁶ 6g⁴ 6m 6m⁵ 7m⁵ Aug 10] leggy, angular filly: fair performer: stays 7f: acts on good to firm going, probably on good to soft: has taken keen hold. *M. Quinn* **77**

SPECTAIT 4 b.g. Spectrum (IRE) 126 – Shanghai Girl 102 (Distant Relative 128) [2006 91: p7g* 8.1s² p8g⁵ 8f* 9d Sep 30] big, lengthy gelding: smart performer: won handicaps at Kempton (by 6 lengths from Desert Dreamer) in May and Goodwood (beat Dunelight by ½ length in totesport Mile) in August: easily best other effort when creditable fifth to Echo of Light in Summer Mile at Lingfield: stays 8.6f: acts on polytrack, best effort on turf on firm going (has won on soft). *Sir Mark Prescott* **112**

SPECTESTED (IRE) 5 ch.g. Spectrum (IRE) 126 – Nisibis (In The Wings 128) [2006 66§: p16.5g⁴ f16g Feb 9] just modest handicapper in 2006: effective at 1½m to 2½m: acts on polytrack, soft and good to firm going: usually wears headgear: often slowly away: carries head high: not one to trust. *A. W. Carroll* **55 §**

SPECTRAL STAR 4 b.f. Unfuwain (USA) 131 – Hyperspectra 91 (Rainbow Quest (USA) 134) [2006 76p: p10g 12.1s³ 11.8d* 12.6m⁴ 11s Oct 10] good-topped filly: fair handicapper: won at Leicester in August: stays 12.6f: acts on polytrack, good to firm and good to soft going. *J. R. Fanshawe* **79**

SPEED DIAL HARRY (IRE) 4 b.g. General Monash (USA) 107 – Jacobina 71 (Magic Ring (IRE) 115) [2006 68, a74: f8g* f8g* f8g² p8.6g⁴ f8g² f7g* p8g f8s³ p8g 7g³ 8.1g³ 9.8v³ 8.9m 8.3g³ 7.6g 8d 8.2s³ f8g⁴ f11g³ p9.5g⁵ f12g² Dec 27] smallish, sturdy gelding: fairly useful handicapper: won 3 times at Southwell in January/February: creditable efforts last 4 starts: seems to stay easy 1½m: acts on all-weather and any turf going: usually visored, tried in cheekpieces/blinkers: races up with pace. *K. R. Burke* **86 a90**

SPEEDFIT WORLD 2 ch.c. (Mar 23) Spinning World (USA) 130 – Petomi 75 (Presi- –
dium 124) [2006 7m 7g p8g 6d 7s Oct 14] rather leggy, quite good-topped colt: little form
in maidens/nurseries: tried blinkered: sold 9,000 gns, sent to Spain. *G. G. Margarson*

SPEEDIE ROSSINI (IRE) 4 b.g. Rossini (USA) 118 – Skatt (Caerleon (USA) 132) –
[2006 –, a50: p7.1g f8g Feb 23] strong gelding: modest maiden at 3 yrs: no form in 2006:
tried blinkered/visored. *Miss J. R. Tooth*

SPEED OF SOUND 4 ch.f. Zafonic (USA) 130 – Blue Siren 113 (Bluebird (USA) **56**
125) [2006 56: 5.5g 6f Jul 31] tall, good-topped filly: modest maiden handicapper: should
stay 6f: best efforts on good going. *A. M. Balding*

SPEEDY SAM 3 b.c. Medicean 128 – Warning Star 104 (Warning 136) [2006 78: 9v² **103**
f8g* 8d³ 9m* 10s³ 10s⁵ p8.6m² p10g* Nov 25] strong colt: useful performer: progressed
well in 2006, winning maiden at Southwell in June and handicaps at Goodwood in August
and Lingfield (by 2½ lengths from Alpine Red) in November: stays 1¼m, but not short of
speed: acts on all-weather, unraced on firm ground but acts on any other turf: tended to
wander third start. *K. R. Burke*

SPEEDY SPIRIT 4 ch.f. Wolfhound (USA) 126 – Ansellady 67 (Absalom 128) [2006
33: f7g Jan 24] sturdy filly: poor maiden: tried tongue tied/blinkered. *M. Salaman*

SPEEDY SUZANNE (USA) 2 b.f. (Mar 21) Forest Camp (USA) 114 – Gilded Image **71**
(USA) (Gilded Time (USA)) [2006 6g⁶ p6g* 8f⁶ Dec 31] $195,000Y: lengthy filly,
unfurnished at 2 yrs: first foal: dam lightly-raced US maiden: better for debut, won
maiden at Wolverhampton in November despite not clear run: sold 15,000 gns and left
B. Meehan, creditable sixth to Valbenny in non-graded event at Santa Anita following
month: seems to stay 1m. *J. M. Cassidy, USA*

Mr Edward S. A. Belcher's "Spectait"

SPELLBINDING (IRE) 2 b.f. (Feb 4) Kirkwall 118 – Ancient Secret (Warrshan –
(USA) 117) [2006 8.3d 10.1d Oct 18] half-sister to several winners, including fairly
useful 2002 2-y-o 6f winner who stayed 1m Secret Formula (by So Factual): dam unraced
half-sister to smart stayer Primitive Rising: detached in maidens: sold 4,000 gns, sent to
Spain. *J. M. P. Eustace*

SPELL CASTING (USA) 3 b.g. Kingmambo (USA) 125 – Copper Play (USA) (Fast   **90**
Play (USA)) [2006 77: 10.1g² 11.1d⁴ 12m² 12g³ 10d⁵ Sep 14] tall, quite good-topped
gelding: fairly useful maiden: best effort when second to Prowess at York third start:
below form last 2 outings: gelded after: stays 1½m: acts on good to firm and good to soft
going: not straightforward. *M. H. Tompkins*

SPENCE APPEAL (IRE) 4 b.g. Nicolotte 118 – It's All Academic (IRE) 91 (Mazaad –
106) [2006 58, a68: p12.2g Dec 6] strong gelding: fair performer at best: well held only
outing on Flat in 2006: tried in cheekpieces/blinkers. *C. Roberts*

SPENCE'S CHOICE (IRE) 2 b.g. (Feb 20) Desert Sun 120 – Late Night Lady (IRE)   **58 d**
65 (Mujadil (USA) 119) [2006 5m 6f⁴ p6g 7m⁵ 8f p8g f6g⁴ Dec 23] lengthy gelding:
modest maiden: below form in nurseries last 4 starts, leaving M. Easterby prior to final
one: should stay 1m. *G. P. Kelly*

SPHINX (FR) 8 b.g. Snurge 130 – Egyptale (Crystal Glitters (USA) 127) [2006 76:   **87**
p13g p10g 14.1s* 16g⁵ 13.9s* 14.1s* 14s⁴ 13.3g Aug 18] smallish, workmanlike gelding:
fairly useful handicapper: won at Nottingham in April, and at York and Nottingham in
May: pulled up as if amiss final outing: stays 1¾m, probably not 2m: acts on polytrack,
heavy and good to firm going: blinkered of late. *Jamie Poulton*

SPICE BAR 2 b.g. (Mar 10) Barathea (IRE) 127 – Scottish Spice 92 (Selkirk (USA)   **63**
129) [2006 7d p7g⁶ f8g⁴ Nov 20] strong, close-coupled gelding: modest form in maidens/
minor event: stays 1m: gelded after final outing. *A. M. Balding*

SPICE GARDENS (IRE) 2 ch.f. (Feb 3) Indian Ridge 123 – Lime Gardens 113   **56 p**
(Sadler's Wells (USA) 132) [2006 6d⁶ Oct 27] 80,000Y: strong, lengthy filly: first foal:
dam, 7f (in Ireland at 2 yrs) and 12.5f (Prix Minerve) winner, half-sister to champion
South African filly Kundalini out of half-sister to high-class 1m/1¼m filly Kooyonga:
14/1 and backward, sixth to Miss Lucifer in maiden at Newmarket: will benefit from
1m+: sure to improve. *W. Jarvis*

SPIDERBACK (IRE) 2 ch.g. (Apr 21) Redback 116 – Geht Schnell (Fairy King   **73**
(USA)) [2006 6g 6d p7g 8m³ 8d³ 8.3d³ 8s³ Oct 21] 26,000Y: well-made gelding: half-
brother to several winners, notably smart 6f (including at 2 yrs) winner Ruby Rocket (by
Indian Rocket) and 3-y-o Alexander Alliance: dam Irish sprint maiden: fair maiden: third
in 4 nurseries, behind Bed Fellow last 2 (wore blinkers): stays 8.3f: acts on soft and good
to firm going, probably polytrack. *R. Hannon*

SPIN DANCER 2 b.f. (Jan 28) Muhtarram (USA) 125 – Rosa Canina 91 (Bustino 136) –
[2006 6g p7.1g 7.6f Sep 23] 2,000Y: compact filly: fourth foal: half-sister to 4-y-o
Thorny Mandate: dam 1¾m to 2¼m winner: no form. *W. M. Brisbourne*

SPINETAIL RUFOUS (IRE) 8 b.g. Prince of Birds (USA) 121 – Miss Kinabalu 50   **54**
(Shirley Heights 130) [2006 54, a59: 5f 6d 5.1g 5g f6m⁶ p6g⁴ p5g³ p5.1g⁶ p5g³ p5g⁴ p6g⁵
Dec 22] modest performer: effective at 5f to easy 7f: acts on all-weather, firm and soft
going: has been tongue tied, usually wears headgear. *Miss Z. C. Davison*

SPINNING 3 ch.g. Pivotal 124 – Starring (FR) 74 (Ashkalani (IRE) 128) [2006 f6g³   **70**
6.1m⁵ 6d² 6d⁴ f6g³ 6.9f² 8m⁴ 5s 7m* Sep 11] 21,000F, 46,000Y: leggy gelding: first foal:
dam, second at 1¼m from 2 starts at 3 yrs, half-sister to smart sprinter Watching: fair
performer: won maiden at Redcar in September: stays 7f: acts on good to firm and good
to soft going: slowly away penultimate outing. *T. D. Barron*

SPINNING COIN 4 b.f. Mujahid (USA) 125 – Cointosser (IRE) 66 (Nordico (USA))   **85**
[2006 88: p12g 16g 11.7g⁶ 14.8m⁵ 11.6f³ 12f⁴ 12g² 12d³ 14.1d* 12d Oct 27] quite good-
topped, leggy filly: fairly useful handicapper: won at Salisbury in September: stays 1¾m:
acts on firm and soft going: in cheekpieces last 4 outings: has been reluctant to enter stall.
J. G. Portman

SPINNING CRYSTAL (IRE) 2 b.f. (Mar 7) Spinning World (USA) 130 – Crystal   **67**
Valkyrie (IRE) 81 (Danehill (USA) 126) [2006 5.1g 6f 6f⁵ p6g² 6f* 6d 7d Oct 19] smallish, good-bodied filly: first foal: dam, 2-y-o 6f winner who stayed 11f, out of half-sister
to Iktamal (very smart at 6f/7f) and First Magnitude (smart in France up to 7f): fair
performer: won nursery at Folkestone in September: should be suited by 7f/1m: acts on
polytrack and firm going, below form on good to soft: sold 15,000 gns. *B. W. Hills*

SPINNING DANCER (IRE) 3 b.f. Spinning World (USA) 130 – Fair McLain (IRE) –
76 (Fairy King (USA)) [2006 –: 8.3d 10m 6.1d⁶ p8.6g p8.6g f6g Dec 28] strong filly: no
form, leaving I. Williams after second start: tried visored. *J. R. Holt*

SPINNING GAME 2 b.f. (Feb 14) Mind Games 121 – Spindara (IRE) 64 (Spinning 53 §
World (USA) 130) [2006 5d 6v* 5f⁵ 6m⁶ 6f p6g p7.1f 6s 7m 5.1d f6g³ p8.6g f7g⁶
p8.6g f8g Nov 28] 2,800Y: leggy filly: first foal: dam maiden half-sister to useful 7f/1m
performer Sporting Lad: won seller at Ripon in May (then left K. Ryan): little form after:
stays 6f: acts on fibresand and any turf going: blinkered final outing: unreliable.
D. W. Chapman

SPINNING GOLD 3 ch.f. Spinning World (USA) 130 – Blue Birds Fly 78 (Rainbow –
Quest (USA) 134) [2006 45: p9.5g f12g⁶ Dec 9] poor maiden. *Miss Gay Kelleway*

SPINNING QUEEN 3 ch.f. Spinning World (USA) 130 – Our Queen of Kings 118
(Arazi (USA) 135) [2006 96: 7g² 8s⁶ 7s³ 7.1m* 7m* 7f⁵ 7g² 8d* Sep 30]
  Prices more in keeping with those at Keeneland in November saw the
Newmarket December Sales provide an unparalleled level of trade for broodmares
and fillies out of training. Records were set in both categories as Alexandrova's
close relative Magical Romance, successful in the Cheveley Park Stakes in 2004,
fetched 4.6m guineas—a European record for any thoroughbred bought at auction
—in foal to Pivotal (she produced the foal prematurely in December), and Spinning
Queen sold for three million guineas, easily breaking the 2.5m guineas record set
by Dance Design in 1997. Both prices reflected what can happen when a bidding
battle between two determined parties develops at an auction, in this instance
representatives of Lady Serena Rothschild, who secured both lots, and Sheikh
Mohammed. Spinning Queen was a very smart filly who put up an eye-catching
performance when a wide-margin winner of the Kingdom of Bahrain Sun Chariot
Stakes at Newmarket at the end of September, but she was not quite the leader of
her generation. Similarly, as might be guessed from the fact that she was retained
for only 42,000 guineas as a yearling at Newmarket, her distaff family is good
without being truly exceptional. Betting three million guineas on such a filly is an
astonishing act of faith, if only because, assuming her new owner retains her, the
time before any return is forthcoming on the investment is likely to be lengthy.
Spinning Queen will not produce a foal until 2008 at the earliest, and that foal, even

*Kingdom of Bahrain Sun Chariot Stakes, Newmarket—outsider of five Spinning Queen
takes some notable scalps as she wins by nine lengths from Soviet Song (rail),
Alexander Goldrun (quartered cap), Musicanna and Red Evie*

if good enough, will not be a classic contender until 2011. No doubt Lady Roths-child will be hoping that Spinning Queen does better at stud than Dance Design, who was resold for 4.7m dollars before producing her first offspring, but has so far had nothing of great significance from five foals to race, the best of them the fairly useful winner Sindy.

The Sun Chariot Stakes was remarkable not only for the way Spinning Queen won but for the fact that two of her ablest opponents were withdrawn and virtually all the remainder failed to reproduce anything approaching their best form. The latter isn't exactly a common occurrence in a Group 1 event at any stage of the season, though arguably it is likelier in the autumn when horses have been on the go for a long time and softer going can disadvantage some. Even with two Group 1 winners, Peeress and Speciosa, absent because of setbacks, three of Spinning Queen's remaining four opponents had also been successful at that level, two of them managing this within three months of the Sun Chariot. It was no surprise to see Spinning Queen sent off as the outsider at 12/1. The favourite Alexander Goldrun had won the Pretty Polly Stakes and finished a close second to Ouija Board in the Nassau Stakes, while Red Evie had beaten Peeress in the Matron Stakes at Leopardstown at the start of September. Soviet Song, though unable to add to her impressive tally at the top level, had landed the Windsor Forest Stakes and run second in the Sussex Stakes. The other runner, Musicanna, had finished third in the 2005 Sun Chariot Stakes and more recently in the Falmouth Stakes. All were fully effective at a mile, unlike Spinning Queen who had finished out of the frame and not shown her best at two outings over the trip. As soon as the stalls opened

Marston Stud & Cavendish Investing Ltd's "Spinning Queen"

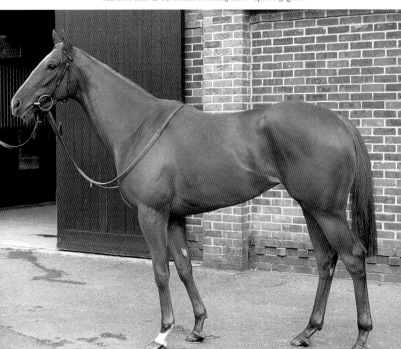

Spinning Queen went to the front, but not in tearaway fashion, and she settled down comfortably at the head of affairs followed by Alexander Goldrun. Red Evie was the first beaten, before halfway, and from three furlongs out Spinning Queen's jockey turned the screw. The writing was on the wall even at that stage as the others came under pressure and could muster no effective reply. The further they went the greater became the leader's superiority. Spinning Queen passed the post nine lengths clear of Soviet Song, who just got up to pip Alexander Goldrun. Red Evie was tailed-off last. Clearly Soviet Song, Alexander Goldrun, and particularly Red Evie, were out of form, but it would be extremely unwise to dismiss Spinning Queen's victory as an aberration not worth the paper it is written on. The time value of her performance, 0.81 fast, was well above average, marginally better than Alexandrova's in the Oaks and, among the three-year-olds, below only the one recorded by George Washington in the Two Thousand Guineas. Suffice to say this was a very smart performance and it was a shame Spinning Queen was not given the chance to run again—a crack at the Breeders' Cup Mile, an idea mooted after the Sun Chariot but abandoned, might have been worthwhile.

So much for Spinning Queen at her best. What of her earlier career? She had proved herself tough, with fourteen runs over two seasons, and smart, improving as she matured, with some rather headstrong tendencies, displayed early on, becoming less pronounced by the time she reached the mid-point of her classic campaign. At two she won a maiden race at Haydock and finished in the frame in the Albany Stakes, Cherry Hinton Stakes and Prestige Stakes, and she confirmed her well-being when a length second to Speciosa in the Nell Gwyn Stakes on her reappearance. A mile, which eventually suited her admirably, seemed too far in the Fillies' Mile in 2005 and again when she was sixth to Speciosa once more in the One Thousand Guineas, a race in which Spinning Queen was on her toes and required two handlers. Her excitability was evident again when she raced much too freely when third to Jeremy in the listed King Charles II Stakes at Newmarket, but improvement soon followed. Spinning Queen readily won the listed Planet Fashion Eternal Stakes at Warwick from Secret Night in June and then gained her first pattern victory in the Irish Stallion Farms EBF Brownstown Stakes at Leopardstown in July. In the latter she finished like a rocket, after being dropped out, to catch Wake Up Maggie on the line for a head win, the pair clear. In the Oak Tree Stakes at Goodwood later in the month Spinning Queen gave weight to the other three-year-olds and did not have any luck in running, finishing fifth to Red Evie, and in the Dubai Duty Free Cup at Newbury a fortnight before the Sun Chariot she showed good acceleration when the pace quickened and only just went down to Sleeping Indian, the margin a neck with Satchem, Polar Ben and Cesare just behind them. This was undoubtedly Spinning Queen's best run to that point, but it was still hard to envisage her demolishing her rivals in the Sun Chariot Stakes in the way that she did.

Spinning Queen (ch.f. 2003)	Spinning World (USA) (ch 1993)	Nureyev (b 1977)	Northern Dancer
			Special
		Imperfect Circle (b 1988)	Riverman
			Aviance
	Our Queen of Kings (ch 1997)	Arazi (ch 1989)	Blushing Groom
			Danseur Fabuleux
		Lady Blackfoot (b 1978)	Prince Tenderfoot
			Indian Graduate

Spinning Queen is of similar ability to her sire's only other European Group 1 winner, Ancient World, who landed the Premio Vittorio di Capua in 2004, but, overall at stud, Spinning World has not lived up the hopes engendered by his own performances over a mile and his fine pedigree. Spinning Queen's dam Our Queen of Kings never ran and has produced two other winners, notably Shannon Springs (by Darshaan), a useful gelding who won at a mile and a quarter and at a mile and a half. Her yearling filly by Cadeaux Genereux was retained for 120,000 guineas at the Newmarket October Sales and her colt foal by King's Best sold for 130,000 guineas at the same venue in November. The grandam Lady Blackfoot was smart at five and six furlongs, principally as a two-year-old, and produced seven successful progeny. The pick of these were the only other top-level scorer in the immediate family, the very smart colt Labeeb (Hollywood Derby and Woodbine

Mile), the high-class dual Grade 2 winner Fanmore, and Alrassaam, successful in the International Stakes at the Curragh. Spinning Queen's great grandam Indian Graduate won over a mile and a half in France and foaled three other winners, none of them noteworthy. Spinning Queen, a well-made filly with an unimpressive, quick action, acted on soft and good to firm going and was usually bandaged on her hind joints. *B. W. Hills*

SPINNING REEL 3 ch.f. Spinning World (USA) 130 – Glenross (IRE) (Warning 136) **62**
[2006 8.2m⁶ p8.6g² p10g⁴ p9.5g Dec 11] workmanlike filly: seventh foal: half-sister to 3 winners in Italy, including smart 7f/1m performer Scabiun (by Dolphin Street) and useful sprinter Su Tirolesu (by Tirol): dam unraced: modest maiden: stays 8.6f. *W. R. Swinburn*

SPINNING RUBY 3 b.f. Pivotal 124 – Red Rabbit 86 (Suave Dancer (USA) 136) **94**
[2006 78p: 7.6m* 8s⁴ 7m⁶ 8m 7m Aug 31] leggy filly: fairly useful performer: won minor event at Lingfield in May: below form after: should stay 1m: acts on good to firm and good to soft going: sometimes races freely: sold 25,000 gns in November. *R. M. Beckett*

SPIRITED SPEEDFIT (IRE) 2 b.c. (Mar 9) Invincible Spirit (IRE) 121 – Winsome **63**
Girl (Music Boy 124) [2006 6g 6.1m⁵ 6m 7m 7d⁵ 7s³ Oct 14] modest maiden: third in nursery at Catterick: stays 7f: acts on soft and good to firm going: sold 8,500 gns. *G. G. Margarson*

SPIRIT GUIDE (FR) 4 b.g. Anabaa (USA) 130 – Shining Molly (FR) 103 (Shining **–**
Steel 123) [2006 7d p8.6g 8m 7.1f f8g Oct 12] sold from Mme C. Head-Maarek 18,000 gns and gelded after final 3-y-o start, little form in Britain: stays 8.3f: free-going sort: withdrawn after unruly in stall intended fourth outing. *R. C. Guest*

SPIRIT OF ADJISA (IRE) 2 b.c. (Apr 17) Invincible Spirit (IRE) 121 – Adjisa (IRE) **66**
(Doyoun 124) [2006 p7g⁶ p8.6g⁴ Dec 29] €40,000F, €40,000Y: third foal: half-brother to useful Irish 1¼m/1½m winner Princess Nala (by In The Wings): dam unraced half-sister to smart Irish miler Adjareli: better effort in maidens when fourth to Alfredian Park at Wolverhampton, hanging left: slowly away both starts. *Pat Eddery*

SPIRIT OF AROSA (IRE) 3 b.f. Dansili 127 – Vettorina (IRE) (Vettori (IRE) 119) **83**
[2006 69: p6g² 6f* 7s² 7g⁴ Jun 2] sturdy filly: fairly useful performer: won handicap at Folkestone in May: creditable second to Red Evie in similar event at Newbury next time: should stay 1m: acts on firm and soft going. *J. Akehurst*

SPIRIT OF CONISTON 3 b.g. Lake Coniston (IRE) 131 – Kigema (IRE) 58 (Case **66**
Law 113) [2006 64, a55: p6g p6g³ p6g p6g⁶ p5.1g⁶ p5.1g³ 5m* p6g³ 5.3f³ 5.1g² p5g* p5g⁴ 5f³ 5.1f⁶ 5g p5.1m p5.1g p5g p5g⁴ f5g* Dec 27] stocky gelding: fair performer: left M. Wellings and rejoined former trainer after sixth start: won claimer at Folkestone in April, handicap at Kempton in June and, having been gelded after fifteenth outing, claimer at Southwell in December: raced only at 5f/6f: acts on all-weather and firm going: usually wears headgear: races up with pace. *Peter Grayson*

SPIRIT OF ECSTACY 2 b.f. (Feb 26) Val Royal (FR) 127 – Isla Negra (IRE) (Last **–**
Tycoon 131) [2006 7d⁵ 8.1g Sep 23] tall, leggy filly: fourth foal: dam 13f winner in Italy: little show in maidens. *G. M. Moore*

SPIRIT OF FRANCE (IRE) 4 b.g. Anabaa (USA) 130 – Les Planches (Tropular) **101**
[2006 101: 8m² 8m³ 7.5d⁵ 8g 8f Aug 4] tall, rather leggy gelding: useful handicapper: trained by M. Johnston in 2005: best efforts at 4 yrs when nose second to Pentecost at Nad Al Sheba and, having been off 5 months, eighth to Salinja at Newbury penultimate outing: stays 1m: acts on firm and good to soft going: usually races prominently: acts on firm and good to soft going: usually races prominently. *C. Wroe, UAE*

SPIRIT OF THE FEN (IRE) 3 b.f. Pivotal 124 – Malabarista (FR) (Assert 134) **96**
[2006 8m⁵ 8.3f⁵ 10m p10g* 10.1m p13g Oct 26] 47,000Y: small, leggy filly: sixth foal: half-sister to 3 winners, including fairly useful 7f (at 2 yrs)/1m winner Capulette (by Grand Lodge): dam French 12.5f winner: useful performer: won maiden at Lingfield in August: very stiff task, seemed to run very well when eighth to High Heel Sneakers in listed race there final outing: stays 13f: acts on polytrack. *J. H. M. Gosden*

SPIRIT OF THE MIST (IRE) 2 ch.c. (Apr 16) Trans Island 119 – Exciting (Mill **84**
Reef (USA) 141) [2006 7.1m⁴ 7d* 7d Sep 19] €55,000Y: half-brother to numerous winners, notably very smart 6f (at 2 yrs) 1m winner Almushtarak (by Fairy King) and smart 1m (including in Hong Kong) to 1¼m winner Tiber (by Titus Livius): dam ran once: much improved (fairly useful form) from debut when making all in maiden at Epsom in August: weakened final 2f when last of 28 in valuable sales race at the Curragh: will stay 1m. *T. J. Pitt*

SPIRIT OF VENUS (FR) 2 b.f. (Feb 23) Invincible Spirit (IRE) 121 – Trazando **53**
(Forzando 122) [2006 5.1m^5 p5g May 23] 18,000Y: small, good-bodied filly: first foal:
dam unraced half-sister to smart 6f/7f performer Three Points: mid-field at best in
maidens. *E. A. L. Dunlop*

SPIRIT ONE (FR) 2 b.c. (Feb 14) Anabaa Blue 122 – Lavayssiere (FR) (Sicyos (USA) **113**
126) [2006 6g^2 7d^3 7d* 8s* 8d* 8g^2 10g^4 Nov 12] second foal: half-brother to useful
French 4.5f (at 2 yrs) to 10.8f winner Salsalava (by Kingsalsa): dam French 7.6f to 10.5f
winner: smart performer: won minor event and valuable listed race (established clear
lead, unchallenged when beating Mysterious Peintre 8 lengths) at Deauville in August
and Prix des Chenes at Longchamp (by 6 lengths from San Domenico) in September:
creditable head second, rallying, to Mount Nelson in Criterium International at Saint-
Cloud, before respectable fourth to Passage of Time in Criterium de Saint-Cloud: probably stays 1¼m: acts on soft ground: front runner. *P. H. Demercastel, France*

SPIRIT RISING 2 gr.g. (Feb 12) Zilzal (USA) 137 – River's Rising (FR) 88 (Mendez **46**
(FR) 128) [2006 5.5d 5d^4 5.1f 6f^6 5.1m Aug 20] tall, close-coupled gelding: poor maiden:
bred to stay 1m. *J. M. Bradley*

SPIRITUAL PEACE (IRE) 3 b.g. Cadeaux Genereux 131 – Emerald Peace (IRE) **91**
103 (Green Desert (USA) 127) [2006 81: 6g^8 6.1s^5 p6g^5 p6g^6 6d 5g^2 5.1f 6v Oct 28]
lengthy, quite good-topped gelding: fairly useful performer: made all in maiden at Southwell in April: good second in handicap at Thirsk (gelded after), but well below form in
similar events last 2 starts: stays 6f: acts on polytrack and good to firm going: in cheekpieces last 4 outings. *K. A. Ryan*

SPIRITWIND (IRE) 3 ch.g. In The Wings 128 – Tallahassee Spirit (THA) (Presi- **54**
dential (USA)) [2006 10.2s 10d p10g 11.9d Nov 19] moderate maiden: should be suited by
1½m+: tongue tied/in cheekpieces after debut. *W. R. Swinburn*

SPITFIRE BOB (USA) 7 b.g. Mister Baileys 123 – Gulf Cyclone (USA) (Sheikh **–**
Albadou 128) [2006 –, a56: f8g f11g^2 p12g^5 p13.9g f12g^6 f12g^6 9.9g May 13] sturdy **a60**
gelding: modest performer on all-weather, little recent form on turf: stays easy 1¾m: acts
on all-weather: has worn visor/cheekpieces. *M. E. Sowersby*

SPITTAL POINT 4 b.f. Tagula (IRE) 116 – Ring Side (IRE) (Alzao (USA) 117) [2006 **–**
8m^6 Jul 10] fifth foal: half-sister to 1¼m winner Border Terrier (by Balnibarbi): dam
unraced: last in maiden at Ripon on debut. *J. J. Quinn*

SPITTING IMAGE (IRE) 6 ch.m. Spectrum (IRE) 126 – Decrescendo (IRE) (Polish **84**
Precedent (USA) 131) [2006 72: f16g* f14g^2 p16g Feb 15] close-coupled, quite attractive
mare: fairly useful handicapper: won at Southwell in January: well held final outing: will
stay beyond 17f: acts on all-weather, firm and good to soft going: tried in cheekpieces:
tends to edge right. *M. Johnston*

SPLENDIDIO 2 b.f. (Feb 25) Zamindar (USA) 116 – Diddymu (IRE) 66 (Revoque **52**
(IRE) 122) [2006 5g 5.1g^5 5.2g^4 p5g^2 6f 5m^5 f5g^3 5.2f^3 p5g^4 p5.1g^5 f5g^3 Dec 27] unfurnished filly: first foal: dam, 1¼m winner, half-sister to smart sprinter Flanders: modest
maiden: claimed from M. Channon £6,000 fourth start: best at 5f: acts on all-weather and
firm going. *D. K. Ivory*

SPLENDORED LOVE (USA) 2 gr. or ro.f. (Mar 21) Buddha (USA) 122 – Star- **66**
crossed Affair (USA) (Black Tie Affair 128) [2006 6m^5 p7g 6m 6g 8m Sep 21] $65,000F,
42,000Y: close-coupled filly: second foal: dam unraced: fair maiden: best form at 6f: sold
4,500 gns. *R. Hannon*

SPLIFF 5 b.g. Royal Applause 124 – Snipe Hall 93 (Crofthall 110) [2006 5g 6f p5.1g **–**
Oct 14] leggy, useful-looking gelding: fairly useful handicapper at 3 yrs: missed 2005 and
well held in 2006: tried blinkered. *M. S. Saunders*

SPLIT BRIEFS (IRE) 2 b.f. (Mar 13) Mull of Kintyre (USA) 114 – Jay Gee (IRE) 93 **71**
(Second Set (IRE) 127) [2006 6m 7m 7d^5 Aug 12] €21,000Y: good-bodied filly: fourth
foal: half-sister to 3-y-o Collateral Damage: dam, 2-y-o 6f winner, became unreliable:
fair form in maidens, fifth to Passage of Time at Newmarket: stays 7f. *D. J. Daly*

SPLIT THE WIND (USA) 2 ch.f. (Feb 8) Just A Cat (USA) – Maple Hill Jill (USA) **–**
(Executive Pride 127) [2006 5.1f p7g Oct 6] sixth foal: sister to 2002 2-y-o 6f/7f winner
Southampton Joe and to minor winner in USA, and half-sister to minor winner in USA by
Val de l'Orne: dam sprint winner in USA: well held in maidens. *R. F. Johnson Houghton*

SPLODGER MAC (IRE) 7 b.g. Lahib (USA) 129 – Little Love (Warrshan (USA) **58**
117) [2006 55: 7m 8.5g^2 7.9m 7.5f 10f* 9.9f 8f^5 10m^6 8g 8.5m^4 Sep 13] sturdy gelding:
modest performer: won apprentice handicap at Pontefract in July: stays 1¼m: acts on firm

and good to soft going: sometimes blinkered: usually races prominently: inconsistent.
N. Bycroft

SPOILSPORT 3 b.f. Muhtarram (USA) 125 – Spoilt Again 91 (Mummy's Pet 125) **57**
[2006 70: 8.5d 8m 10s 7.5g p7.1m⁵ p9.5g p9.5s⁴ p9.5g⁵ p8.6g Dec 27] half-sister to
several winners, including useful 1m (at 2 yrs)/9f winner Inch Again (by Inchinor): dam
9f/1¼m winner: just modest maiden in 2006: left James G. Burns in Ireland after fourth
outing: best effort at 1m: acts on good to firm going: blinkered final start. *P. D. Evans*

SPOOF MASTER (IRE) 2 b.g. (Mar 12) Invincible Spirit (IRE) 121 – Talbiya (IRE) **86**
(Mujtahid (USA) 118) [2006 p5g² 5s* 5d² 5g³ 5m³ 6g 5.1f⁴ 5s² Oct 14] €26,000F,
15,000Y: sturdy gelding: third foal: dam, well beaten only start, out of half-sister to Dante
winner Torjoun: fairly useful performer: won minor event at Redcar in March: in frame 6
of other 7 starts, second to Luscivious in minor event at Catterick final one: gelded after:
best at 5f: acts on polytrack, firm and soft going. *W. G. M. Turner*

SPORTING GESTURE 9 ch.g. Safawan 118 – Polly Packer 81 (Reform 132) [2006 **85**
93: 13.8d 12g³ 12.3d 12d 12g⁵ 12m⁶ 11.5g 12f⁴ 12.3m³ 11.7m 12m³ 13.4f⁶ 12s 12d³
Nov 3] rather leggy, close-coupled gelding: has a round action: fairly useful handicapper: stays easy 13.4f: acts on firm and good to soft going: tried blinkered in 2002.
M. W. Easterby

SPOTONCON 5 b.g. Contract Law (USA) 108 – Emma Victoria (Dominion 123) **–**
[2006 p7.1g Dec 26] of no account over hurdles: well held in claimer at Wolverhampton
on Flat debut. *A. J. Lidderdale*

SPOT THE SUBBIE (IRE) 3 b.g. Tagula (IRE) 116 – Agent Scully (IRE) 66 (Simply **61**
Great (FR) 122) [2006 47: 6d⁵ 6g² 7.5f² 7.5f³ 9m⁵ 7d⁴ 7d³ p7g³ Dec 19] modest maiden:
left A. Leahy in Ireland, good third in handicap at Lingfield (British debut) final start:
stays 7.5f: acts on polytrack, firm and good to soft going: tried in cheekpieces. *Jamie
Poulton*

SPRIGGAN 2 b.c. (Feb 20) Ishiguru (USA) 114 – Hope Chest 70 (Kris 135) [2006 6m³ **76 p**
Aug 19] half-brother to fairly useful 1m winner (including at 2 yrs) Liberty Royal (by
Ali-Royal) and 2003 2-y-o 5f/6f winner Lotto (by Nicolotte), later successful in Spain:
dam lightly-raced maiden (stayed 1½m): 25/1, 2½ lengths third of 6 to easy winner
Rahiyah in maiden at Goodwood, not knocked about once held: should do better.
C. G. Cox

SPRING DREAM (IRE) 3 gr.f. Kalanisi (IRE) 132 – Zest (USA) (Zilzal (USA) 137) **79**
[2006 67: 12.1d⁶ 12.6g* p12.2g* 11.9m³ 12m⁶ 11.6m Aug 5] leggy filly: fair handicapper: won at Warwick in May and Wolverhampton in June: stays 12.6f: acts on polytrack
and good to firm going. *M. R. Channon*

SPRING GLORY 2 b. or gr.f. (May 9) Dr Fong (USA) 128 – Doctor Bid (USA) (Spec- **66 p**
tacular Bid (USA)) [2006 p8g⁵ p8g⁴ Dec 19] half-sister to several winners, including
1¾m/2m winner On Call (by Alleged) and Irish 9f/1¼m winner Medico (by Highest
Honor), both useful: dam unraced: fair form in maidens at Lingfield, fourth to Grande
Caiman: should improve at 1¼m+. *Sir Mark Prescott*

SPRING GODDESS (IRE) 5 b.m. Daggers Drawn (USA) 114 – Easter Girl (Efisio **79**
120) [2006 89: p8g² p7g² p7g² p8g³ p7g⁵ 8f⁶ 8d 8g p9.5g p8g⁵ p8g Dec 4] good-topped **a89**
mare: fairly useful handicapper on all-weather, fair on turf: stays 1¼m: acts on poltrack
and good to firm going. *A. P. Jarvis*

SPRING IS HERE (FR) 2 ch.c. (Apr 22) King's Best (USA) 132 – Aube d'Irlande **83**
(FR) (Selkirk (USA) 129) [2006 7g² Jun 29] 42,000F, €52,000Y: well-made colt: third
foal: half-brother to French 9.5f/10.5f winner Domani (by Stravinsky): dam French 1m
winner: 8/1, neck second to Dubai Magic in maiden at Salisbury, quickening 2 lengths
clear before running green (fly-jumped one point): joined R. Collet in France. *R. Hannon*

SPRING TIME GIRL 4 b.f. Timeless Times (USA) 99 – Daira 72 (Daring March **53**
116) [2006 56: p10g 7g 10.1d 7g⁴ 8.3m 10.2m 8.2f³ 8d⁵ 8m⁴ 8d² p8g³ f8m Oct 31] modest
performer on turf, poor on all-weather: stays 1¼m: acts on polytrack, firm and good to
soft ground: usually wears headgear. *B. Ellison*

SPRINGTIME PARKES 2 ch.f. (Apr 1) Medicean 128 – Summerhill Spruce 70 **–**
(Windjammer (USA)) [2006 5g 6s 5.1g Jun 7] strong filly: half-sister to several winning
sprinters, including Lucky Parkes (by Full Extent) and Summerhill Parkes (by Zafonic),
both useful: dam 6f winner: little form in maidens. *K. A. Ryan*

SPRINGWOOD BLUES (IRE) 3 b.f. Bluebird (USA) 125 – Fun Board (FR) (Sau- **–**
marez 132) [2006 –: 11.9m 12m 9.9g Aug 27] no form: left H. Alexander after second
outing. *I. W. McInnes*

SPRINKLE 3 b.f. Selkirk (USA) 129 – Showery 76 (Rainbow Quest (USA) 134) [2006 **61**
7g p8.6g 6m³ 8.1m 8.3g 6.1g 7d p8g Dec 10] 40,000Y, 50,000 2-y-o: good-bodied filly:
sixth foal: sister to useful 1m winner (including at 2 yrs) Bestam and half-sister to 2
winners, including 2004 2 y-o 1¼m winner Louise Rayner (by Vettori), later successful
abroad: dam, 6f winner, half-sister to smart 1¼m performer Adiemus· modest maiden:
left R. Beckett 4,000 gns after seventh start: should stay 1m: acts on good to firm going:
blinkered (ran poorly) penultimate outing. *B. R. Johnson*

SPRITZA (IRE) 2 b.f. (Jan 18) Spectrum (IRE) 126 – Starlight Smile (USA) (Green **71**
Dancer (USA) 132) [2006 6s² 6f² p7g 7d Sep 19] €135,000Y: angular, workmanlike filly:
third foal: half-sister to fairly useful 1½m winner Portrait of A Lady (by Peintre Celebre):
dam unraced half-sister to dam of Irish Derby winner Grey Swallow: fair maiden:
runner-up at Haydock and Windsor (to Scarlet Runner): well beaten in sales event at the
Curragh final start: should be suited by 1m: acts on firm and soft going. *M. L. W. Bell*

SPROUSTON (FR) 3 ch.g. Grand Lodge (USA) 125 – River Fantasy (USA) (Irish **–**
River (FR) 131) [2006 66: p6g 6g 7f 5.9m p8g p7g Dec 18] tall gelding: fair maiden at
2 yrs: little form in 2006: tried blinkered/in cheekpieces: often slowly away. *J. S. Moore*

SPUME (IRE) 2 b.g. (Apr 15) Alhaarth (IRE) 126 – Sea Spray (IRE) 101 (Royal **85 p**
Academy (USA) 130) [2006 7d p8g 8d* Sep 27] strong gelding: sixth foal: dam, 7f (at
2 yrs)/1m winner who probably stayed 1¼m, out of smart performer up to 1½m Sailor's
Mate: fairly useful form: won maiden at Salisbury by ¾ length from Coeur de Lionne,
still rather green (hung left) but finishing strongly: gelded after: will stay 1¼m: should go
on improving. *Sir Michael Stoute*

SPUNGER 3 b.f. Fraam 114 – Complimentary Pass 80 (Danehill (USA) 126) [2006 68: **–**
f12g⁶ p12g Dec 15] quite attractive filly: fair performer at 2 yrs: well beaten in handicaps
in 2006. *H. J. L. Dunlop*

SPURRON (IRE) 6 b.m. Flying Spur (AUS) – The Realtour 84 (Warning 136) [2006 **54**
59: 7m⁴ 9m⁶ 9m⁴ 9.5d p8.6g Nov 20] first foal: dam, Irish maiden, best at 7f/1m: modest
maiden handicapper: stays 9f: acts on heavy and good to firm ground. *G. Keane, Ireland*

SPY GAME (IRE) 6 b.g. Definite Article 121 – Postie (Sharpo 132) [2006 p16g 15.8g **56**
11.7d May 17] ex-Irish gelding: fairly useful at best: won maiden at Listowel in 2003:
lightly raced and just modest form on Flat since: blinkered last 2 starts. *Jennie Candlish*

SPY GUN (USA) 6 ch.g. Mt Livermore (USA) – Takeover Target (USA) (Nodouble **– §**
(USA)) [2006 47§, a62§: p8.6g⁴ f7g f8g² f7g⁴ p9.5g⁵ p9.5g² p9.5g⁴ f8g⁴ 8.1g 10m Jul 29] **a55 §**
angular, useful-looking gelding: modest performer on all-weather: stays 9.5f: acts on
all-weather, little recent form on turf: tried visored: unreliable. *T. Wall*

SQUADRON 2 b.g. (Mar 8) Sakhee (USA) 136 – Machaera (Machiavellian (USA) 123) **66**
[2006 8.2s p9.5g³ p9.5g⁵ Dec 7] 55,000Y: well-made gelding: sixth foal: half-brother
to 3 winners, including fairly useful 7f winner Megec Bliss (by Soviet Star): dam
unraced half-sister to smart sprinters Russian Bond and Snaadee: gradual improvement in
maidens, fair form at Wolverhampton final start: gelded after: stays 9.5f. *Mrs A. J. Perrett*

SQUADRON LEADER (IRE) 3 b.g. Imperial Ballet (IRE) 110 – Tancholo (So **65**
Factual (USA) 120) [2006 74: p8g 6g 5.3f 6.1d⁴ 7f 7g 8f Jul 18] strong, good sort: fair
maiden: best form at 6f: acts on polytrack, soft and good to firm going: sold 10,000 gns.
R. Hannon

SQUAW DANCE 4 ch.f. Indian Ridge 123 – Likely Story (IRE) 94 (Night Shift **101**
(USA)) [2006 102?: 7s⁴ 8.3f* 8g³ 8g³ 8m Aug 20] good-topped filly: useful performer:
won minor event at Hamilton in June by 3½ lengths from Little Miss Gracie: creditable
third next 2 starts in Alice-Cup at Hamburg and listed race at Ascot: best form at 1m: acts
on firm and soft going: sold, thought to be in foal to Dubawi, 190,000 gns in November.
W. J. Haggas

SQUIFFY 3 b.g. Kylian (USA) – Cebwob 85 (Rock City 120) [2006 10m 8.3f 8.3g **59**
13.1m 10d Sep 25] modest maiden: below form in handicaps last 2 starts. *P. D. Cundell*

SQUIRREL TAIL 3 ch.c. Band On The Run 102 – Crees Sqaw (Cree Song 99) [2006 **–**
p7.1g Apr 28] well held in maiden at Wolverhampton. *E. S. McMahon*

SQUIRTLE (IRE) 3 ch.f. In The Wings 128 – Manilia (FR) (Kris 135) [2006 60: **76**
12.1d⁵ 12.6g² 12.1m² 12.1g 12g² 14m* 13.1m³ 15.9m⁵ 13.4f 15d² p12.2g³ p13.9m
Nov 9] workmanlike filly: fair handicapper: won at Haydock in August: stays 2m: acts
on polytrack, firm and good to soft going: visored last 2 starts: tends to run in snatches.
W. M. Brisbourne

betdirect.co.uk Winter Derby, Lingfield—Sri Diamond prevails in a tight finish;
runner-up Grand Passion (No.9) is followed by Nayyir, Red Spell (rail) and Cimyla

SRI DIAMOND 6 b.g. Sri Pekan (USA) 117 – Hana Marie 101§ (Formidable (USA) **114**
125) [2006 103: p12g* p10g* 12g Apr 22] good-topped gelding: smart performer: further
progress in 2006, winning handicap in February (by 3 lengths from Zonergem) and
betdirect.co.uk Winter Derby in March (beat Grand Passion by ½ length), both at Lingfield: ran as if amiss in John Porter Stakes at Newbury final outing: stays easy 1½m: acts
on polytrack, good to firm and good to soft ground: has run well sweating: held up. *S. Kirk*

SRIOLOGY (IRE) 5 b.g. Sri Pekan (USA) 117 – Sinology (Rainbow Quest (USA) **58**
134) [2006 62: p12.2g p10g f8g5 f8g2 p10g f8g6 f8g6 p8g5 8m6 8.5g2 p10g5 10d6 f8g3
p10g5 f12g Dec 12] modest performer: left G. Prodromou after twelfth start: should stay
1½m: acts on all-weather and soft going: tried visored/tongue tied: sometimes slowly
away, and often travels with little fluency. *J. Pearce*

SRI PEKAN TWO 2 b.c. (Jan 14) Montjeu (IRE) 137 – Brigadiers Bird (IRE) (Mujadil **77**
(USA) 119) [2006 6m5 6f5 p8g* 8d4 8m5 Sep 19] 105,000Y: good-bodied colt: sixth foal: **a87**
half-brother to useful 6f (at 2 yrs) to 1m winner Lady Lahar and 7-y-o Lord Lahar: dam
unraced: fairly useful form when winning maiden at Lingfield in August, only start on
all-weather: fair form on turf: will be suited by 1¼m/1½m. *P. F. I. Cole*

STACEYMAC (IRE) 3 ch.f. Elnadim (USA) 128 – Neat Shilling (IRE) (Bob Back **59**
(USA) 124) [2006 p5g2 p5g* p7g Dec 30] 6,500Y: fourth foal: half-sister to 5-y-o Mr
Jack Daniells and 6-y-o Tidy: dam unraced: modest form: won maiden at Kempton in
December: should stay 7f (raced freely when tried). *B. R. Johnson*

STAFF NURSE (IRE) 6 b.m. Night Shift (USA) – Akebia (USA) (Trempolino (USA) **–**
135) [2006 53: p13.9g f12g Dec 12] modest performer: well held mare: modest performer in 2005, well
held in 2006: usually wears headgear. *N. Wilson*

STAGBURY HILL (USA) 4 ch.g. Woodman (USA) 126 – Shalabia 84 (Fast Topaze **91**
(USA) 128) [2006 101: 7s 6m 7m 8.1m p10g 10g 7.5d* Dec 9] close-coupled gelding:
just fairly useful performer in 2006, best effort on reappearance, though won amateurs
event at Pisa in December on first outing after leaving J. Hills for £6,000: stays 1m: acts
on good to firm and good to soft going. *A. Bianco, Italy*

STAGECOACH EMERALD 4 ch.g. Spectrum (IRE) 126 – Musician 104 (Shirley **70**
Heights 130) [2006 65: p8.6g4 p12.2g 10.9s f12g2 p12.2g2 Dec 22] close-coupled gelding: fair maiden: stays 1½m: acts on all-weather and good to soft going: tongue tied (ran
well) final outing. *R. W. Price*

STAGE FLIGHT 3 b.f. In The Wings 128 – Midsummernitedream (GER) 43 (Thatching 131) [2006 94: 10s⁵ 8m 8.1m Jul 8] tall, leggy filly: useful performer at 2 yrs: well below form in listed races in 2006, including in handicap: should stay at least 1m: acts on soft and good to firm going: sent to Saudi Arabia. *B. J. Meehan* –

STAGE GIFT (IRE) 3 ch.g. Cadeaux Genereux 131 – Stage Struck (IRE) 83 (Sadler's Wells (USA) 132) [2006 77p: p10g* 10.1m* 10.1m* 12d 8.9g² 9d* Oct 14] strong, well-made gelding: fluent mover: smart performer: progressed well in 2006, winning handicaps at Kempton in April, Yarmouth in May and Epsom (beat Military Cross by 1¼ lengths in Vodafone Live! Stakes) in June, and Unicorn Asset Management Darley Stakes at Newmarket (by head from Windsor Knot) in October: stays 1¼m, may prove most effective around 1m: acts on polytrack, good to firm and good to soft going: changed hands after final outing, and joined I. Mohammed in UAE. *Sir Michael Stoute* 116

STAGEHAND (IRE) 2 b.g. (Jan 23) Lend A Hand 124 – Ridotto (Salse (USA) 128) [2006 5m 6g⁴ 7f² p7g* 7m³ 8g³ 7.1d⁶ p8g Oct 6] €11,000Y: third foal: half-brother to useful 2004 2-y-o 5f winner Salsa Brava (by Almutawakel): dam lightly raced in France: fair performer: won nursery at Kempton in July: third in nurseries won by Cesc and Sweet Lilly next 2 starts: stays 1m: acts on polytrack and firm going: gelded after final outing. *B. R. Millman* 76

STAGELIGHT (IRE) 4 b.c. Montjeu (IRE) 137 – Zivania (IRE) 101 (Shernazar 131) [2006 105: 8m 8.1m⁶ 9d Sep 30] sturdy colt: smart performer, lightly raced: reportedly suffered injury after final 3-y-o outing and off over 16 months prior to reappearance: good 3 lengths sixth to Hinterland in valuable handicap at Sandown, only form in 2006: will stay 1¼m: acts on dirt, good to firm and good to soft going: has worn crossed noseband. *J. Noseda* 108

STAGE MANAGER (IRE) 4 ch.c. In The Wings 128 – Evangola (Persian Bold 123) [2006 p10g p12g* p12.2g p12g⁴ p13g⁶ 10m⁵ May 3] 86,000F, 9,000 3-y-o: closely related to 1994 2-y-o 6f winner Scenic Heights (by Scenic), later successful in Australia, and half-brother to 3 winners, including useful Irish performer up to 7f Persian Creek (by Treasure Kay): dam unraced: fair performer: won maiden at Lingfield in January: stays 13f: raced on polytrack and good to firm going: has joined A. J. Martin, Ireland. *M. J. Wallace* 78

STAGNITE 6 ch.g. Compton Place 125 – Superspring (Superlative 118) [2006 65: p8g p7.1g⁵ p6g² p5.1g p6g p6g² 6m⁶ p6g⁶ 6d⁴ 5.1d³ p6g 6m* 6f⁶ 6f 8m 7m p7g* p6g p6g p7g⁶ Dec 19] just modest performer in 2006: claimed from K. McAuliffe £5,000 after tenth start: won ladies handicap at Salisbury in July and, having left P. Blockley after sixteenth outing, banded race at Kempton in November: stays easy 7f: acts on polytrack and firm going, probably on good to soft: usually wears headgear: often makes running. *Miss K. M. George* 62

Vodafone Live! Stakes (Handicap), Epsom—Stage Gift runs out one of the easiest handicap winners of the season; Military Cross takes second, ahead of Lake Poet and King's Head (rail)

STAINLEY (IRE) 3 b.g. Elnadim (USA) 128 – Fizz Up 77 (Alzao (USA) 117) [2006 **70**
71: 10s⁴ 10g⁴ 8g⁶ 8.2s³ 8.2g⁵ 7.6f³ 8g⁵ 10.3m Sep 9] rather leggy, close-coupled gelding:
has a round action: fair handicapper: stays 1¼m: acts on firm and soft going: usually
races prominently: sold 10,000 gns, joined Mrs S. Bradburne, and won over hurdles in
November. *J. D. Bethell*

STAKED A CLAIM (IRE) 2 ch.c. (Mar 6) Danehill Dancer (IRE) 117 – Twany **72 p**
Angel (Double Form) 130) [2006 5m⁴ Sep 13] €44,000Y: lengthy colt: has scope: closely
related to useful 1996 Irish 2-y-o 5f winner Melleray (by Danehill), later 1m winner in
USA, and half-brother to several winners, notably very smart 6f (including at 2 yrs)/7f
(including Prix de la Foret) winner Mount Abu (by Foxhound): dam French maiden: 6/1,
promising fourth in maiden at Beverley, chasing impressive winner Deserted Dane to
over 1f out: sure to improve. *T. D. Barron*

STALLONE 9 ch.g. Brief Truce (USA) 126 – Bering Honneur (USA) (Bering 136) **–**
[2006 74: p12.2g Dec 18] good-bodied gelding: fair performer in 2005: well held in seller
only outing in 2006: tried tongue tied/in cheekpieces: tends to start slowly: usually held
up. *N. Wilson*

STAMFORD BLUE 5 b.g. Bluegrass Prince (IRE) 110 – Fayre Holly (IRE) 57 (Fayruz **71**
116) [2006 71, a49: p6g 8.5d 7g 8.1d⁶ 6.1d⁴ 7m 7m³ 7.6f⁴ 6.1d³ 7.1f 6d³ 6g³ 7.1m⁴ 6.1m³ **a–**
5.1m* 5.5d 5m 7d Oct 3] workmanlike gelding: fair performer on turf, modest at best on
all-weather: won handicaps at Chepstow in May, June and September: has won over 1m,
at least as effective at 5f: acts on polytrack, firm and good to soft going: wears blinkers
(tried in cheekpieces): has run well sweating: often slowly away: usually claimer ridden.
R. A. Harris

STAMFORD STREET (IRE) 3 ch.c. Distant Music (USA) 126 – Exemplaire (FR) **57**
(Polish Precedent (USA) 131) [2006 p6g² p8g p7g⁶ p6g 7s p6g Apr 12] modest maiden:
should stay beyond 7f: acts on polytrack. *J. S. Moore*

STANCE 7 b.g. Salse (USA) 128 – De Stael (USA) 93 (Nijinsky (CAN) 138) [2006 79: **75**
p16g⁶ Mar 6] strong, well-made, attractive gelding: type to carry condition: has a quick,
fluent action: fairly-raced handicapper on Flat nowadays, fair form sole start in 2006:
stays 21f: acts on sand/polytrack, firm and good to soft going: tried in cheekpieces: useful
hurdler/chaser at best. *G. L. Moore*

STAND BY ME 3 b.g. Tomba 119 – Princess Zara (Reprimand 122) [2006 7.1m 8.1m **–**
Sep 4] good-topped gelding: well held in maidens at Warwick. *M. A. Jarvis*

ST ANDREWS (IRE) 6 b.g. Celtic Swing 138 – Viola Royale (IRE) 90 (Royal **114 d**
Academy (USA) 130) [2006 115: 7.6m³ 9m 9.7m³ 8g 8.1v⁴ 9m p8.6g³ 9d Oct 14] lengthy,
quite attractive gelding: smart performer: creditable third in listed event at Lingfield (1¾
lengths behind Stronghold) and 4-runner minor event at Folkestone (beaten 3¼ lengths
by Weightless) first/third outings: below form after: effective at 1m/1¼m: unraced on
firm going, probably acts on any other: in cheekpieces last 4 starts: has run well when
sweating: gelded after final start. *M. A. Jarvis*

STANLEY BAY (IRE) 3 ch.f. Namid 128 – Joy St Clair (IRE) (Try My Best (USA) **51**
130) [2006 53: 6f⁴ 8.1m 8f⁶ 9.3m⁵ 7.5g Aug 31] quite good-topped filly: modest maiden:
stays 1m: acts on firm going: tried blinkered/visored. *T. D. Easterby*

STANLEY GEORGE (IRE) 2 b.c. (Feb 6) Noverre (USA) 125 – Quinzey (JPN) **81**
(Carnegie (IRE) 129) [2006 7g³ 7.1d p7.1g⁵ p9.5m³ p8.6g² f8g* Dec 21] 23,000 2-y-o:
first foal: dam unraced: fairly useful performer: didn't need to be at best to land odds in
maiden at Southwell, making all: will stay 1¼m: acts on all-weather. *M. A. Jarvis*

STANLEY GOODSPEED 3 ch.g. Inchinor 119 – Flying Carpet 76 (Barathea (IRE) **101**
127) [2006 p8g 6.1m* 7.1s⁴ 7.1m⁶ 8.3m p8.6g⁴ 6g* 6s² 6g* Sep 23] 13,000Y: big,
good-topped gelding: second foal: half-brother to fairly useful 7f/1m winner Casemate
(by Efisio), later successful at 9f in Bahrain: dam 8.5f winner: developed into a useful
performer, winning maiden at Nottingham in May and handicaps at Newbury in August
and Haydock (by short head from Knot In Wood) in September: effective at 6f to 8.6f:
acts on polytrack, soft and good to firm going: tongue tied last 4 starts: has worn crossed
noseband: has hung right: held up. *J. W. Hills*

STANLEY WOLFE (IRE) 3 b.g. City On A Hill (USA) 114 – Quatredil (IRE) 67 **50**
(Mujadil (USA) 119) [2006 –: p6g 5d 5m³ p5.1g 5m⁵ 5.9g* 5.9m 5m⁶ p6g Oct 29] modest
performer: won handicap at Carlisle in May: left J. Moffatt before final outing: effective
at 5f/6f: acts on good to firm going. *Peter Grayson*

STAR BERRY 3 b.f. Mtoto 134 – Star Entry 67 (In The Wings 128) [2006 p8g 8.3f 10g⁶ **57** 10d Sep 25] fifth foal: sister to 5-y-o Star of Light: dam 9.7f winner: modest maiden: probably stays 1¼m. *B. J. Meehan*

STARBOARD LIGHT 3 b.f. Mark of Esteem (IRE) 137 – Light Ship 72 (Warning **67** 136) [2006 53: p8.6g⁵ p8.6g 8f² 8.1f⁴ 8.5g² 8m² p8.6m* 8m⁴ Sep 25] unfurnished filly: fair handicapper: won maiden event at Wolverhampton in September: stays 8.6f: acts on polytrack and firm going: sold 23,000 gns. *R. M. Beckett*

STARBOUGG 2 b.f. (Mar 7) Tobougg (IRE) 125 – Celestial Welcome 96 (Most Wel- **72** come 131) [2006 7d² 7.2d Sep 15] 52,000Y: good-topped filly: has scope: third foal: half-sister to 3-y-o Startori and 4-y-o Shekan Star: dam, 7f to 1½m winner, half-sister to smart middle-distance performer Snowstorm: fair form when second to Musical Mirage in maiden at Redcar: ran as if amiss month later: will stay at least 1m. *B. Smart*

STAR CLUSTER 3 b.f. Observatory (USA) 131 – Didicoy (USA) 104 (Danzig (USA)) **102** [2006 106p: 7d² 10g⁴ 8.1m* 8g⁵ Jul 27] leggy, useful-looking filly: useful performer: creditable efforts in frame in minor event at Leicester (behind Red Evie) and listed race at Newbury (3½ lengths fourth to Princess Nada) prior to winning listed race at Sandown (by short head from Silver Touch) in July: below form final outing: barely stayed 1¼m: acted on good to firm and good to soft going: stud. *H. R. A. Cecil*

STARCROSS MAID 4 ch.f. Zaha (CAN) 106 – Maculatus (USA) (Sharpen Up 127) **59** [2006 53: f8g³ f8g f8g⁵ p9.5g⁶ p9.5g⁵ f11g⁵ f11g⁴ f12g* 12g⁶ 11.5g² 12m 9.9f³ f12g* Jul 7] modest performer: won claimers at Southwell in May and July: stays 1½m: acts on all-weather and firm going: blinkered (raced freely) once. *J. F. Coupland*

STAR CROWNED (USA) 3 b.c. Kingmambo (USA) 125 – Fashion Star (USA) **92** (Chief's Crown (USA)) [2006 74p: p8.6g 7g² 7s⁴ 8d³ 10m⁵ 10.2g² p8g⁶ 8.3g* Aug 21] tall colt: good efforts second to fourth starts: won maiden at Windsor in August: will prove best at 7f/1m: acts on soft going: tongue tied, usually blinkered. *B. J. Meehan*

STAR DUSTER 4 gr.f. Paris House 123 – To The Stars (IRE) (Zieten (USA) 118) [2006 **75** 75: 5g 5.5d⁵ 5s 5g* Jun 10] fair handicapper: won at Lingfield in June: was best at 5f: acted on firm going: usually raced prominently: dead. *B. R. Millman*

STAR FERN 5 br.g. Young Ern 120 – Christening (IRE) (Lahib (USA) 129) [2006 61§, **– §** a38§: p9.5g 8f 8.2g 7g f7g f8g p8.6g⁴ p9.5g Dec 4] big, close-coupled gelding: modest **a56 §** performer on all-weather, little form on turf: stays 9.5f: acts on all-weather: visored once: often slowly away: unreliable. *M. J. Attwater*

STARGAZER JIM (FR) 4 br.g. Fly To The Stars 124 – L'Americaine (USA) (Verba- **89** tim (USA)) [2006 90: 10g p9.5g* p12.2g⁴ p9.5g⁴ p10g³ Dec 20] sturdy gelding: fairly useful handicapper: won at Wolverhampton in November: stays 1¼m: acts on polytrack and any turf going. *W. J. Haggas*

STARGAZY 2 b.c. (Apr 11) Observatory (USA) 131 – Romantic Myth 105 (Mind **71** Games 121) [2006 6m 5m 5m² 5.2f² p5.1g p6g p7.1g p6g⁴ Dec 28] 50,000Y, 125,000 2-y-o: sturdy, well-made colt: second foal: dam, 5f winner (including Queen Mary) at 2 yrs, half-sister to 2002 Queen Mary winner Romantic Liason: fair maiden: runner-up at Windsor and Yarmouth: best form at 5f: acts on firm going, below form on polytrack: blinkered once. *R. Charlton*

STARGEM 5 b.m. Compton Place 125 – Holy Smoke 83 (Statoblest 120) [2006 74: **–** p6g f6g Feb 7] rather leggy mare: fair handicapper in 2005: last both outings in 2006. *J. Pearce*

STAR JASMINE 3 b.f. Grand Lodge (USA) 125 – Shalimar (IRE) 95 (Indian Ridge **54** 123) [2006 9.7d⁴ 8.2m 8.2m 8.2s May 20] strong, lengthy, workmanlike filly: second foal: dam, 7f/1m winner, out of useful half-sister to very smart middle-distance stayer Gamut: modest maiden: probably stays 9.7f: sold 6,000 gns. *M. L. W. Bell*

STARK CONTRAST (USA) 2 ch.c. (Mar 9) Gulch (USA) – A Stark Is Born (USA) **79** (Graustark) [2006 7f⁴ 7m⁴ Aug 11] $75,000Y: tall, lengthy colt, unfurnished at 2 yrs: brother to smart US Grade 2 6.5f/1m winner Nasty Storm and closely related/half-brother to several winners in USA: dam 6f (at 2 yrs)/1m winner in USA: fourth in maidens won by Medicine Path at York and Furnace at Newmarket: will stay 1m. *G. A. Butler*

STARLIGHT GAZER 3 b.g. Observatory (USA) 131 – Dancing Fire (USA) (Dayjur **77** (USA) 137) [2006 79p: 6g⁵ 6g* 6g⁵ 6g⁴ 6g⁵ 7d Oct 28] tall, close-coupled gelding: fair performer: won maiden at Windsor in May, hanging badly left: should be suited by 7f+: acts on good to firm going: gelded after final outing. *J. A. Geake*

STARLING (IRE) 4 ch.f. Cadeaux Genereux 131 – Warrior Wings 81 (Indian Ridge –
123) [2006 68: f6g p9.5g Jan 13] first foal: dam, Irish 2-y-o 5f winner, out of half-sister
to smart 1m winner Killer Instinct: fair maiden at best: left D. Gillespie in Ireland, well
held both starts in 2006: stays 1¼m: acts on good to firm and good to soft going: tried
blinkered. *D. Nicholls*

STAR MAGNITUDE (USA) 5 ch.g. Distant View (USA) 126 – Stellaria (USA) 98   **83**
(Roberto (USA) 131) [2006 69: p7g p8g⁵ p8g* p10g² p10g⁵ p10g* 10g p8g² 8.1d 10f³   **a87**
9.9g³ 10m² 10.1d p10g Sep 6] good-bodied gelding: fairly useful handicapper: won at
Lingfield in February and April (apprentices): creditable efforts when placed after: effective at 1m/1¼m: acts on polytrack and firm going: often held up. *S. Dow*

STAR MEMBER (IRE) 7 b.g. Hernando (FR) 127 – Constellation (IRE) (Kaldoun –
(FR) 122) [2006 –: 16.2f Jun 10] leggy, quite good-topped, close-coupled gelding: useful
handicapper in 2004: well held on Flat since. *Ian Williams*

STARMIX 5 gr. or br.g. Linamix (FR) 127 – Danlu (USA) (Danzig (USA)) [2006 –:   –
15.8d 12.1f⁶ 12g 16.2g Aug 17] sturdy gelding: maiden: no form since 3 yrs: tried in
blinkers/cheekpieces. *G. A. Harker*

STARNEVEES (FR) 5 b.g. Kaldounevees (FR) 118 – Stadia (FR) (Star Maite (FR)   **94**
111) [2006 8f⁶ 10g² p10g Sep 6] just fairly useful handicapper in 2006: left J. Pease in
France prior to reappearance: best effort in Britain when second to Inchloch at Newbury second outing: stays 1¼m: acts on soft going: sold 9,000 gns, joined C. Mann.
L. M. Cumani

STAR OF CANTERBURY (IRE) 3 ch.g. Beckett (IRE) 116 – Villa Nova (IRE) 55   **80**
(Petardia 113) [2006 72: p10g p7g p7g f11g* 11m* 11m Jul 21] big, strong gelding: fairly
useful performer: won handicaps at Southwell (visored) in April and Goodwood in June:
stays 11f: acts on fibresand and good to firm going: somewhat wayward. *A. P. Jarvis*

STAR OF ERHAAB 3 b.g. Erhaab (USA) 127 – Star Glade (Charnwood Forest (IRE) –
125) [2006 –: 10m 14.1d May 19] last in maidens. *E. A. Wheeler*

STAR OF LIGHT 5 b.g. Mtoto 134 – Star Entry 67 (In The Wings 128) [2006 103:   **109**
9m* 10.1g³ 10m⁵ 11.9g³ 10.4f 10.5m Aug 12] good-bodied gelding: useful handicapper:
won quite valuable event at Newmarket (beat Look Again ½ length) in May: best efforts
after when good 2 lengths third to Chancellor at Epsom next time and creditable seventh
behind Fairmile in John Smith's Cup at York penultimate outing: stays 1½m: acts on
polytrack and firm going. *B. J. Meehan*

STAR OF NIGHT 2 ch.f. (Mar 10) River Falls 113 – Gemma's Choice (Beveled –
(USA)) [2006 7f 7d Aug 13] second foal: dam 5f and 7f winner in Greece: well beaten in
maidens. *C. Grant*

STAR OF RUSSIA (IRE) 4 ch.f. Soviet Star (USA) 128 – Shakanda (IRE) (Shernazar   **70**
131) [2006 69: 6v 9m 7g 6v² 7s p6g⁶ p7g Dec 10] €22,000Y: sister to 2003 2-y-o 7f
winner Hoxne Star and half-sister to 3 winners, notably smart 7f (at 2 yrs) to 1½m winner
The Glow-Worm (by Doyoun): dam Irish 1½m winner: fair handicapper: won at Bellewstown and Tralee in 2005, only successes: left C. Collins in Ireland, better effort in Britain
when creditable sixth at Lingfield: effective at 6f to 1m: acts on polytrack, heavy and
good to firm going. *V. Smith*

STAR OF SIAM (IRE) 3 ch.f. Elnadim (USA) 128 – Thoroughly (IRE) (Woodman   **45**
(USA) 126) [2006 –: 5f 7f Jul 19] leggy, close-coupled filly: poor maiden: possibly amiss
final outing. *J. D. Bethell*

STAR OF THE DESERT (IRE) 3 b. or br.g. Desert Story (IRE) 115 – Cindy's Star   **76**
(IRE) 68 (Dancing Dissident (USA) 119) [2006 p8g⁴ 8m⁴ 10.2s⁶ 9.9m⁵ 8g⁴ 8f⁴ 9m
p9.5m⁶ Oct 9] €25,000Y: close-coupled, useful-looking gelding: brother to 7f winner in
Spain and half-brother to several winners, including fairly useful Irish 2000 2-y-o 7f
winner Ducky Divey (by Elbio), later successful in Hong Kong: dam 1m winner: fair
maiden: barely stays 1¼m: acts on firm ground: didn't handle bend at Bath third outing:
sold 18,000 gns, joined Mrs K. Walton. *C. G. Cox*

STAROFTHEMORNING (IRE) 5 ch.m. Foxhound (USA) 103 – Leggagh Lady   **39**
(IRE) 76 (Doubletour (USA)) [2006 38: 12f p10g Dec 3] poor maiden: stays 1½m: acts
on firm going. *A. W. Carroll*

STARPARTY (USA) 2 gr.f. (Mar 31) Cozzene (USA) – Cherie Yvonne (USA) (Vice   **70**
Regent (CAN)) [2006 7d p8g⁴ p8g³ Nov 29] $50,000Y: lengthy filly: second foal: sister
to 2004 2-y-o 6f winner Westland: dam US 6f to 8.5f winner, including minor stakes: fair
form in maidens, twice in frame at Kempton: stays 1m. *Mrs A. J. Perrett*

STAR RISING 4 ch.f. Most Welcome 131 – My Greatest Star 93 (Great Nephew 126) **58**
[2006 59: p10g⁶ p12.2g⁴ p10g⁵ 11.8d² p12g 13.9m⁵ p13.9g² 12m⁴ p16.5f³ 14.1d² 16g
p13.9m p16g Oct 11] strong filly: modest maiden: left W. Musson after tenth start: pulled
up amiss final outing: effective at 1¼m to 1¾m: acts on polytrack, good to firm and good
to soft going: often patiently ridden. *N. B. King*

STARRY MARY 8 b.m. Deploy 131 – Darling Splodge (Elegant Air 119) [2006 f14g **–**
Jan 11] close-coupled mare: modest performer at best: unraced on Flat in 2005: in cheekpieces, well beaten only outing in 2006. *R. J. Price*

STARRY MESSENGER 2 b.f. (Mar 7) Galileo (IRE) 134 – The Faraway Tree 113 **74 p**
(Suave Dancer (USA) 136) [2006 8.3m³ 9m⁴ Sep 20] good-bodied filly: fourth foal: dam,
6f (at 2 yrs) and 1¾m winner, half-sister to very smart 9f/1¼m performer Sasuru: promise
when in frame in maidens at Leicester and Goodwood (favourite, fourth to Philanthropy),
nearest finish both times: capable of better at 1¼m/1½m. *M. P. Tregoning*

STARS ABOVE 2 b.f. (Feb 14) Observatory (USA) 131 – Skimra 91 (Hernando (FR) **48**
127) [2006 6d 6g 6s⁶ p9.5g⁴ p8.6g⁶ p9.5g³ p8.6g⁶ Dec 18] third foal: dam, 1½m winner,
out of half-sister to Petoski: poor maiden: claimed £5,000 final start: barely stays 9.5f.
Sir Mark Prescott

STARSHIP (IRE) 3 b.f. Galileo (IRE) 134 – Council Rock 74 (General Assembly **89**
(USA)) [2006 76: 8m* 8.3m* 10.4f⁵ 9m Aug 27] angular, quite attractive filly: fairly
useful performer: won handicaps at Newmarket in June and Windsor (dead-heated with
Zaafran) in July: stays 8.3f, seemingly not 9f: raced only on polytrack and ground firmer
than good. *W. J. Haggas*

STAR SIGN 4 b.f. Robellino (USA) 127 – Amid The Stars 61 (Midyan (USA) 124) **68**
[2006 –: 8v 8m⁴ 8m³ 9d* 8m⁶ 9.9m 12s Oct 24] big, workmanlike filly: fair performer:
won maiden at Redcar in August: stays 9f: acts on good to firm and good to soft going:
wore cheekpieces (looked tricky ride) final outing. *D. W. Barker*

STAR STRIDER 2 gr.c. (Feb 29) Royal Applause 124 – Onefortheditch (USA) 79 **70**
(With Approval (CAN)) [2006 5.1d 5.1f⁴ 5.1g³ 7f 6.1g³ 7f 6m⁶ p6g⁶ 5.1m³ Oct 8]
38,000F: leggy, close-coupled colt: fourth foal: brother to smart 7f/1m winner Royal
Prince, and half-brother to 4-y-o Cape Greko and fairly useful 2002 2-y-o 5.7f winner
who stayed 1m Morning After (by Emperor Jones): dam 1m/1¼m winner: fair maiden:
placed 3 times, third to Vaunt in nursery at Bath final start: effective at 5f/6f: acts on good
to firm going. *A. M. Balding*

STARTENGO (IRE) 3 ch.g. Nashwan (USA) 135 – Virgin Hawk (USA) (Silver Hawk **57**
(USA) 123) [2006 62p: p8g 12m⁶ Apr 19] workmanlike gelding: modest maiden: gelded,
flashed tail repeatedly final outing. *D. R. C. Elsworth*

START OF AUTHORITY 5 ch.g. Muhtarram (USA) 125 – Heiden's Delight (USA) **56**
(Shadeed (USA) 135) [2006 53: p7g³ p7g³ 8m 8f* 8f⁵ 8d³ 8m f7g³ p8.6g Nov 20]
workmanlike gelding: modest performer: won handicap at Brighton in July: races freely,
but stays 1m: acts on all-weather, firm and good to soft ground. *J. Gallagher*

STARTOLINI 2 ch.f. (Feb 26) Bertolini (USA) 125 – Ragged Moon 72 (Raga Navarro **72**
(ITY) 119) [2006 5d³ 5d³ 6g 5f* 5m³ 5m⁴ Aug 24] 3,200Y, resold 15,500Y: angular filly:
half-sister to several winners, including 7f/1m (including at 2 yrs) winner My Raggedy
Man and 1991 2-y-o 6f winner Misterioso (both by Forzando), both useful: dam won 1m
sellers: fair performer: won maiden at Carlisle in July: better form when third to Aahayson in nursery at Musselburgh: excuses final start: may prove best at 5f: acts on firm
going. *B. Smart*

STARTORI 3 b.f. Vettori (IRE) 119 – Celestial Welcome 96 (Most Welcome 131) [2006 **86**
85: 8.2m 8.3g⁶ 8v 10.5g f8g⁵ p7.1g p8.6g² f8g Dec 27] neat filly: fairly useful handi- **a75**
capper on turf, fair on all-weather: stays 8.6f: acts on polytrack, good to firm and good to
soft going: tried visored. *B. Smart*

STAR WELCOME 5 ch.m. Most Welcome 131 – My Greatest Star 93 (Great Nephew **–**
126) [2006 62, a59: p12.2g² p12g p10g* Feb 21] rather leggy, close-coupled mare: **a61**
modest performer: second run in 2 days, won handicap at Lingfield in February: stays
1½m: acts on polytrack, good to firm and good to soft going. *W. J. Musson*

STATE DILEMMA (IRE) 5 b.g. Green Desert (USA) 127 – Nuriva (USA) 100 **67**
(Woodman (USA) 126) [2006 76d: p6g⁵ f6g p8g⁵ p10g⁴ p6g* p8g p6g³ p6g⁶ Dec 30]
good-bodied gelding: has a quick, fluent action: fair handicapper nowadays: won at
Lingfield in November: effective at 6f to 1m: acts on polytrack, soft and good to firm
going: wears headgear: usually waited with: none too resolute. *D. Shaw*

STAY ACTIVE (USA) 2 gr.c. (Jan 28) Johannesburg (USA) 127 – Mature Miss (USA) **65** (Mi Cielo (USA)) [2006 6g⁶ 6g⁴ 6m³ 6d Sep 15] $30,000Y: quite attractive colt: first foal: dam 5f to 6.5f winner in USA: fair form in maidens, not knocked about: seemed amiss in nursery (well backed): raced at 6f. *I. Semple*

STAY QUIET (USA) 2 b.g. (Feb 12) Quiet American (USA) – Serene Nobility (USA) **–** (His Majesty (USA)) [2006 6m Sep 22] well-made gelding: backward and well beaten in maiden: sold 2,600 gns. *T. D. Barron*

STEADY AS A ROCK (FR) 2 ch.c. (Apr 6) Rock of Gibraltar (IRE) 133 – Metisse **84 p** (USA) (Kingmambo (USA)) 125 [2006 5m* May 3] €60,000Y: well-grown, good-topped colt: fluent mover: fifth foal: half-brother to 2 winners in France, including useful 6.5f winner who stayed 1m Marie Vison (by Entrepreneur): dam, French winner around 7f, closely related to Prix Marcel Boussac winner Macoumba: 5/1, not fully wound up when winning maiden at Pontefract (made most to beat Jack Rackham by ½ length): looked a useful prospect. *M. Johnston*

STEADY RAIN 4 br.f. Zafonic (USA) 130 – Love The Rain (Rainbow Quest (USA) **68** 134) [2006 p9.5g² p12.2g 10m p7.1g Jun 9] 6,000 3-y-o: leggy filly: second foal: dam, French 11f winner, sister to smart performer up to 1½m Bonash (dam of 5-y-o Day Flight): form (fair) only when runner-up in maiden at Wolverhampton on debut: left Mrs L. Featherstone after second start: visored final outing. *P. S. McEntee*

STEAM CUISINE 2 ch.f. (Jan 20) Mark of Esteem (IRE) 137 – Sauce Tartar 90 (Salse **84** (USA) 128) [2006 7.2d² p8g* 7m* 7d⁴ Sep 30] 15,000Y: tall filly: first foal: dam 7f (including at 2 yrs) winner: fairly useful form: won maiden at Lingfield in August and nursery at Yarmouth (overcame trouble) in September: good fourth to Blithe in nursery at Newmarket, again travelling strongly: will prove best up to 1m. *M. G. Quinlan*

STEEL BLUE 6 b.g. Atraf 116 – Something Blue (Petong 126) [2006 92: 6g 7.2g⁵ 6g **92** 7g⁶ 6m⁴ 6g* 6f 5m² 6d⁵ 6m 6d 5g 7g p6g p6g⁴ Nov 17] leggy, quite good-topped gelding: **a72** fairly useful handicapper on turf, fair on all-weather: made all at Epsom in July: below form last 4 starts: probably needs good test at 5f nowadays, and stays easy 7f: acts on dirt, soft and good to firm going: tried visored/in cheekpieces: usually races prominently. *R. M. Whitaker*

STEEL CITY BOY (IRE) 3 b.g. Bold Fact (USA) 116 – Balgren (IRE) (Ballad Rock **80** 122) [2006 –: 5g 5g⁵ p5.1g* p6g³ p5.1g⁵ Nov 11] lengthy, good-bodied gelding: fairly useful performer: won handicap at Wolverhampton in June: may prove best at bare 5f: acts on polytrack: withdrawn after unruly in stall intended second outing. *D. Carroll*

STEELCUT 2 b.g. (Mar 15) Iron Mask (USA) 117 – Apple Sauce 70 (Prince Sabo 123) **90** [2006 5m³ 5g* 5g³ May 31] 16,000Y: good-topped gelding: fourth foal: half-brother to 5f winner Cut And Dried (by Daggers Drawn): dam, 5f winner, half-sister to smart sprinter Sizzling Melody: fairly useful form: won minor event at Redcar in May: ran bit better again when third to Everymanforhimself in similar race at Beverley 2 days later (gelded and absent after): speedy, raced at 5f. *R. A. Fahey*

STEEL GREY 5 gr.g. Grey Desire 115 – Call Me Lucky 65 (Magic Ring (IRE) 115) **–** [2006 –: 6d f6g Nov 28] leggy gelding: lightly-raced maiden: little form. *M. Brittain*

STEEL SILK (IRE) 2 b.c. (Mar 4) Desert Style (IRE) 121 – Dear Catch (IRE) 69 **–** (Bluebird (USA) 125) [2006 8s Oct 7] sturdy colt: 20/1 and burly, last in maiden at York. *G. Woodward*

STEELY DAN 7 b.g. Danzig Connection (USA) – No Comebacks 70 (Last Tycoon **–** 131) [2006 –, a91: p6g p8g* p10g Mar 27] strong gelding: fairly useful handicapper on **a85** all-weather, fair at best on turf: won at Lingfield (ninth course success) in March: effective at 7f to easy 1½m: acts on all-weather, firm and good to soft going: best with waiting tactics: not straightforward. *J. R. Best*

STEENBERG (IRE) 7 ch.g. Flying Spur (AUS) – Kip's Sister (Cawston's Clown 113) **121** [2006 112: 6s⁵ 7s⁵ 6d* 5s 6s 6d 7g⁵ Sep 30] big, lengthy gelding: very smart performer: career-best effort when winning Duke of York Hearthstead Homes Stakes at York in May by ½ length from Quito: well below that form on his other starts in 2006: best at 6f/7f: acts on soft and good to firm going: blinkered (below form) twice: tends to carry head awkwardly/hang right. *M. H. Tompkins*

STELLENBOSCH (USA) 3 b.g. Cape Town (USA) 125 – New Account (USA) **78** (Private Account (USA)) [2006 66: p8g³ p8.6g⁴ p10g⁵ 10.2g 10m⁵ 10f⁴ 11.7f* 12g⁴ 12m⁵ 11.7f⁵ 12m⁵ Aug 27] close-coupled gelding: fair handicapper: won at Bath in June: gelded after final outing: stays 1½m: acts on polytrack and firm going: tried visored/tongue tied: tended to hang third/fourth outings: reliable: sold 22,000 gns, joined C. Mann. *J. W. Hills*

STELLITE 6 ch.g. Pivotal 124 – Donation (Generous (IRE) 139) [2006 72: 7d* 8g³ 7.2d⁴ 8g² 8p.8g⁶ 7.1m⁴ 6m² 7d* 6d 7.1s⁴ 6v⁶ p6g Nov 16] workmanlike gelding: fairly useful handicapper: won at Thirsk in April and Newcastle in August: stays 8 6f, all 5 wins at 7f: acts on all-weather, soft and good to firm going: reliable. *J. S. Goldie*   **84**

STEPASIDE (IRE) 2 gr.g. (Feb 10) Fasliyev (USA) 120 – Felicita (IRE) 97 (Catrail (USA) 123) [2006 5d⁵ 5s 5m³ Jun 5] €52,000Y: fourth foal: closely related to fairly useful 2004 2-y-o 5f winner Bunditten (by Soviet Star): dam French 2-y-o 5.5f to 7f winner: fair form when third in maiden at Carlisle (gelded after): likely to prove a sprinter. *M. Johnston*   **65**

STEPHANIE'S MIND 4 b.f. Mind Games 121 – Adorable Cherub (USA) 58 (Halo (USA)) [2006 –, a61: p6g p5.1g p5g⁶ p5g 5f 5.2f Jul 25] tall filly: modest performer on all-weather, little recent form on turf: effective at 5f/6f: acts on polytrack and good to firm going: sometimes wears headgear. *M. Quinn*   **–**
a53

STEPPE DANCER (IRE) 3 b.c. Fasliyev (USA) 120 – Exemina (USA) (Slip Anchor 136) [2006 72p: p8g* 9.9m⁴ 12m 10m* 10d³ p12.2f* 12.3m⁴ Sep 9] big, strong colt: useful performer: won maiden at Kempton in May and handicap at Wolverhampton (4 ran, beat Gandor 3 lengths) in August: seemingly very good ¾-length fourth to Foxhaven in listed race at Chester final outing: stays 1½m: acts on polytrack, good to firm and good to soft going. *D. J. Coakley*   **106**

STEP PERFECT (USA) 5 b.g. Royal Academy (USA) 130 – Gossiping (USA) (Chati (USA)) [2006 –: f14g³ f16g² 18v 15.8d 16m p16.5f⁵ 14.1m f16g⁶ Oct 12] rangy, angular gelding: modest maiden: below form after second outing: stays 2m: acts on all-weather and firm ground: often in cheekpieces in 2006: sold 3,600 gns. *G. M. Moore*   **58 d**

STEPPING STONES 3 ch.f. Selkirk (USA) 129 – Light Step (USA) 91 (Nureyev (USA) 131) [2006 8.1g³ 8.2m³ 7m* 6g Jun 30] quite good-topped filly: third foal: dam, 1¼m winner, half-sister to very smart performer up to 1½m Eltish: fairly useful performer: won maiden at Yarmouth in June: well held in minor event at Newmarket final outing: stays 1m: acts on good to firm going: has raced freely: hung markedly right on debut/final start: sold 48,000 gns in November. *H. R. A. Cecil*   **83**

STEPPING UP (IRE) 3 ch.c. Soviet Star (USA) 128 – Rise And Fall (Mill Reef (USA) 141) [2006 104p: 7g⁴ Sep 30] angular, well-made colt: useful performer: left M. Johnston, shaped as if retaining all of his ability when 4¾ lengths fourth to New Seeker in listed race at Redcar only outing in 2006: will be suited by 1m: acts on good to firm going: proved handful in preliminaries at 2 yrs. *Saeed bin Suroor*   **100 +**

STEP TO THE STARS (IRE) 2 ch.f. (Mar 13) Galileo (IRE) 134 – Tudor Loom (Sallust 134) [2006 7d 6d Oct 27] 62,000F: leggy filly: half-sister to several winners, including smart Irish/US performer up to 9f Rainbow Blues (by Bluebird): dam third at 7f in Ireland: free to post/in race when eighth in maiden at Leicester: possibly amiss 3 weeks later. *M. Johnston*   **55**

Duke of York Hearthstead Homes Stakes, York—Steenberg ends a two-year losing streak in style, beating Quito, Somnus (armlets) and Fayr Jag (halved sleeves)

STERLING MOLL 3 gr.f. Lord of Men 116 – Princess Maud (USA) (Irish River (FR) –
131) [2006 12m 9.9d⁶ 12.4s Oct 10] 1,600F, 800Y: first foal: dam unraced: well held all
starts, twice slowly away. *W. de Best-Turner*

STEVEDORE (IRE) 5 ch.g. Docksider (USA) 124 – La Belle Katherine (USA) **68**
(Lyphard (USA) 132) [2006 69, a76: p8g⁵ 8.3s p8g f8g² p8.6g⁴ f11g⁶ f8g² Dec 23] **a82**
good-topped gelding: fairly useful on all-weather, fair on turf: good second in handicap at
Southwell final outing: stays 1m: acts on all-weather and firm going, probably on soft:
tried in blinkers/cheekpieces: usually races up with pace. *J. R. Boyle*

STEVIE GEE (IRE) 2 b.c. (Mar 26) Invincible Spirit (IRE) 121 – Margaree Mary **101**
(CAN) (Seeking The Gold (USA)) [2006 6m p6g⁵ f5g* 6d* 6s* 6g Sep 30] €32,000Y:
well-made colt: fifth foal: half-brother to fairly useful Irish 1m winner Samer (by
Spinning World): dam, Canadian 8.5f winner, out of sister to Irish St Leger winner Dark
Lomond: useful performer: rapid progress in summer, won maiden at Southwell, nursery
at Redcar and listed race at Ripon, in last-named beat Everymanforhimself by 1½ lengths:
7/2, only mid-field in listed Two-Year-Old Trophy at Redcar final start: will stay 7f: acts
on fibresand and soft going. *G. A. Swinbank*

ST FRIS 3 gr.g. Silver Patriarch (IRE) 125 – Fragrance (Mtoto 134) [2006 p12g p10g **56**
p12g Nov 9] modest maiden. *J. A. R. Toller*

STICKY MINT (IRE) 3 b.f. Inchinor 119 – Creme de Menthe (IRE) (Green Desert –
(USA) 127) [2006 54?: p8g p8g p10g Dec 13] no form since debut at 2 yrs. *M. Blanshard*

STILL CALM 2 b.c. (Apr 13) Zamindar (USA) 116 – Shining Water 111 (Kalaglow **59**
132) [2006 7m Sep 9] half-brother to numerous winners, including Grand Criterium/
Dante Stakes winner Tenby (by Caerleon) and smart 1m (at 2 yrs)/1½m winner Bristol
Channel (by Generous): dam won Solario Stakes and second in Park Hill Stakes: 8/1,
seventh in maiden at Chester, pulling hard and never a threat: will be suited by 1½m: sold
25,000 gns. *B. W. Hills*

STING LIKE A BEE (IRE) 7 b.g. Ali-Royal (IRE) 127 – Hidden Agenda (FR) 55 **46**
(Machiavellian (USA) 123) [2006 60, a–: p9.5g p9.5g p9.5g Jan 28] poor performer nowadays: stays 11f: acts on fibresand, heavy and good to firm going: tried blinkered/tongue
tied: held up. *J. S. Goldie*

STINGRAY (IRE) 4 b.c. Danehill (USA) 126 – Music And Dance (USA) (Northern –
Dancer) [2006 6f 5.1d May 30] strong colt: tailed off both Flat starts. *N. I. M. Rossiter*

STIR CRAZY (IRE) 2 b.g. (Feb 16) Fath (USA) 116 – La Captive (USA) 68 (Selkirk **70**
(USA) 129) [2006 5v³ p5g* 5g 6f⁵ 5g⁴ 7m 6f³ 6f* p6g⁵ 5m 5g 6d⁴ 6m² 6d 5.1m 5.2d
p6m* p5.1g Nov 16] €18,000F, 9,000Y, resold 12,000Y: medium-sized, quite good-
bodied gelding: first foal: dam Irish 2m winner: fair performer: raced 18 times, won
maiden in April and nursery in July, both at Lingfield, and seller at Wolverhampton in
November: effective at 5f/6f: acts on polytrack and any turf going. *M. R. Channon*

ST IVIAN 6 b.g. Inchinor 119 – Lamarita 92§ (Emarati (USA) 74) [2006 50, a66: f6g⁵ **49**
f6g p6g⁴ p5.1g⁴ p6g⁴ f5g³ f6g³ p6g p6g² 5f⁵ 7f 6f Jul 19] leggy gelding: just **a59**
modest performer on all-weather, poor on turf in 2006: was effective at 5f to easy 7f:
acted on all-weather, firm and soft going: was effective with or without headgear: dead.
Mrs N. Macauley

STOCK EXCHANGE (IRE) 4 b.g. King's Best (USA) 132 – Queen's Ransom (IRE) –
70 (Last Tycoon 131) [2006 7m Apr 25] well beaten in maiden at Folkestone on Flat
debut. *P. Bowen*

STOCKHOLDER 3 b.g. Hernando (FR) 127 – Springs Welcome 86 (Blakeney 126) –
[2006 p9.5g f11g 10f⁵ 11.5m Jul 26] lightly-made gelding: little form. *C. A. Cyzer*

STOIC LEADER (IRE) 6 b.g. Danehill Dancer (IRE) 117 – Starlust 79 (Sallust 134) **87**
[2006 97, a82: p7g* p7g p7.1g² p8g⁵ p7.1g⁴ 7.1g p7.1m² 7g³ p6g⁴ p7.1g⁶ 8f⁴ p8.6g⁴ **a78**
7m 8.1m 8m⁶ 7f⁴ 7.1m* 7.1m³ 7.1s 8g p7.1m p6g³ p7.1g⁶ p7.1g Dec 6] sturdy gelding:
fairly useful handicapper on turf, fair on all-weather: won at Lingfield in January and
Musselburgh in August: creditable efforts after only when third: effective at 6f to easy
8.6f: acts on all-weather, firm and good to soft going: wore cheekpieces fourth/fifth
outings: has raced freely: tends to edge left: tough. *R. F. Fisher*

STOKESIES LUCK (IRE) 3 gr.c. King Charlemagne (USA) 120 – Lesley's Fashion –
67 (Dominion 123) [2006 –: 8m 7.1m 6d 6d Oct 2] big, leggy colt: little sign of ability:
tried in cheekpieces: refused to enter stall intended reappearance. *J. L. Spearing*

STOKESIES WISH 6 ch.m. Fumo di Londra (IRE) 108 – Jess Rebec 63 (Kala Shikari **55**
125) [2006 70: 6.1d⁶ 6f 6g 6f 6g 6.1m 5v f6g Nov 2] strong mare: just modest performer
in 2006: effective at 5f/6f: acts on firm and soft going. *J. L. Spearing*

STOLEN 4 b.g. Groom Dancer (USA) 128 – Jezyah (USA) 80 (Chief's Crown (USA)) –
[2006 47: p12g Jan 3] poor maiden: tried blinkered: has had breathing problem.
W. R. Muir

STOLEN GLANCE 3 b.f. Mujahid (USA) 125 – Stolen Melody 74 (Robellino (USA) **84**
127) [2006 49: f8g* 8m⁴ 8d* 8s² 8.5g 8g 11.5m⁶ 9.1v² 10s³ f11g⁴ f11g⁵ Dec 5] fairly
useful performer: won handicaps at Southwell (hung left) in April and Newcastle in May:
very good second in similar event at Thirsk next time, but below form after: stays 1¼m:
acts on fibresand, soft and good to firm ground. *M. W. Easterby*

STOLEN HOURS (USA) 6 b. or br.h. Silver Deputy (CAN) – Fasta (USA) (Seattle **79**
Song (USA) 130) [2006 85: 10g 12m⁴ 12g 12g 11.8m⁴ 11.5m⁴ 14.1d Sep 27] good-topped
horse: just fair handicapper in 2006: effective at 1½m/1¾m: acts on firm and good to soft
going: visored (carried head awkwardly) final 3-y-o start. *J. Akehurst*

STOLEN LIGHT (IRE) 5 ch.g. Grand Lodge (USA) 125 – Spring To Light (USA) 93 **80**
(Blushing Groom (FR) 131) [2006 68: 14m³ 14m³ 10s³ 16g² 16d f14g* f14g f14g² Dec 9]
fairly useful performer: left D. Weld in Ireland 28,000 gns after fourth start: won handicap
at Southwell in November: stays 2m: acts on fibresand, probably on soft and good to firm
going: often blinkered. *A. Crook*

STOLEN SONG 6 b.g. Sheikh Albadou 128 – Sparky's Song 63 (Electric 126) [2006 –
64: f16g⁶ p12.2g p16g f14g⁶ Jul 11] good-topped gelding: only poor performer in 2006:
effective at 1¼m to easy 2m: acts on all-weather and firm ground: wears headgear.
J. Ryan

STOLEN SUMMER (IRE) 3 ch.g. Spectrum (IRE) 126 – Touche-A-Tout (IRE) **88 d**
(Royal Academy (USA) 130) [2006 70: 7s* 7g 8.1g 8d 8.2s 7v f8g⁶ f8g Nov 15]
€14,000Y: sturdy gelding: sixth foal: brother to 4-y-o Ronsard and half-brother to 7-y-o
Quantica: dam unraced: fairly useful form when winning maiden at Limerick in April:
little show subsequently, leaving T. Stack in Ireland after next start: stays 7f: acts on soft
going. *B. S. Rothwell*

STOLT (IRE) 2 b.g. (May 2) Tagula (IRE) 116 – Cabcharge Princess (IRE) 64 (Rambo **86**
Dancer (CAN) 107) [2006 5d* 5f⁴ 5g 5m 5.1m³ 5m² Jul 22] 20,000Y: close-coupled gelding: sixth foal: brother to 2 winners, including 7-y-o Aahgowangowan, and half-brother
to 1½m winner Luz Bay (by Tenby): dam 2-y-o 5f winner: fairly useful performer: won
maiden at Musselburgh in April: ran well most subsequent starts, on last 2 placed in minor
event at Chester (third to Invincible Force) and nursery at Haydock: speedy (usually
makes running), will prove best at 5f/6f: acts on firm and good to soft going. *N. Wilson*

STONEACRE BOY (IRE) 3 ch.g. City On A Hill (USA) 114 – Sans Ceriph (IRE) 75 **79**
(Thatching 131) [2006 66: p6g³ p7.1g f5g* p6g² f5g* p6g* f5g* 5g p5g⁴ p6g p6g p5.1g
p5g p5.1m p5.1g p5g* p5.1g³ Dec 23] strong gelding: fair performer: won maiden at
Southwell in February, and handicaps there and at Lingfield in March and at Lingfield
again in December: effective at 5f/6f: acts on all-weather and good to firm ground:
blinkered nowadays: sometimes slowly away/hangs right. *Peter Grayson*

STONEACRE FRED (IRE) 3 br.g. Lend A Hand 124 – Election Special 78 (Chief **55**
Singer 131) [2006 48: f5g² p5g³ f5g³ f5g⁶ p6g 5m⁶ 6d⁴ f5m p8.6g³ f7g* p7g Dec 30]
modest performer: won banded event at Southwell in December: effective at 5f to
easy 8.6f: acts on all-weather and good to soft going: tried in cheekpieces/blinkers.
Peter Grayson

STONEACRE GARETH (IRE) 2 b.c. (Apr 4) Grand Lodge (USA) 125 – Tidal **75**
Reach (USA) 68 (Kris S (USA)) [2006 p6g⁵ f5g⁶ p7.1g⁶ p7g⁵ p7.1g* p9.5s p8g⁴ p6g⁵
Dec 28] €20,000Y: half-brother to 3 winners, including useful 2000 2-y-o 5f to 1m
winner Innit (by Distinctly North), later US Grade 2 1¼m winner: dam 2-y-o 1m winner
who stayed 10.5f: fair performer: dead-heated in nursery at Wolverhampton in November: should stay beyond 7f: acts on polytrack: blinkered last 2 starts: no easy ride. *Peter
Grayson*

STONEACRE GIRL (IRE) 3 ch.f. Rossini (USA) 118 – Ring of Light (Auction Ring **38**
(USA) 123) [2006 –: p5.1g p6g f5g⁵ f6g p6g⁴ f5g⁵ p5.1g⁴ May 5] smallish filly: poor
maiden: blinkered last 2 starts. *Peter Grayson*

STONEACRE LAD (IRE) 3 b.c. Bluebird (USA) 125 – Jay And-A (IRE) 98 (Elbio **94 §**
125) [2006 75: f5g* p5g³ p5g³ 5.1f 5s² 5.1g 5f* 5.1f 5m 5d 5s³ f5g⁶ f5g* Dec 5] good-
topped colt: fairly useful handicapper: won at Southwell in February and December and

Leicester in June: best at 5f: unraced on heavy going, acts on any other turf and all-weather: blinkered in 2006: hangs left: not one to rely on. *Peter Grayson*

STONEACRE LIL (IRE) 3 b.f. Fasliyev (USA) 120 – Lady Ounavarra (IRE) – (Simply Great (FR) 122) [2006 51: f11g Feb 9] workmanlike filly: maiden: tailed off only outing in 2006: tried in cheekpieces/blinkers. *Peter Grayson*

STONE ARCH (IRE) 6 b. or br.g. Turtle Island (IRE) 123 – Broadway Royal (Royal **51** Match 117) [2006 53: 7s⁵ 7.2d 5.8m⁶ 5s⁵ p5g² 6g⁵ 5m² 7f⁶ 6f p5.1g Dec 4] modest performer: effective at 5f to 1m: acts on polytrack and any turf going: tried blinkered/in cheekpieces/tongue tied. *Jarlath P. Fahey, Ireland*

STONECRABSTOMORROW (IRE) 3 b.g. Fasliyev (USA) 120 – Tordasia (IRE) **91** (Dr Devious (IRE) 127) [2006 76: p6g² p7g* 7f g² p6g* 6s³ p7g p7g⁴ p7.1m² Oct 9] fairly useful performer: won maiden in February and handicap (off 5 months, beat Libor by neck) in August, both at Lingfield: creditable efforts when in frame in handicaps after: stays 7f: raced mainly on all-weather, acts on soft going: hung left sixth start: sold 24,000 gns, and gelded. *P. F. I. Cole*

STONEHAUGH (IRE) 3 b.g. King Charlemagne (USA) 120 – Canary Bird (IRE) 59 **83** (Catrail (USA) 123) [2006 68: 7m* 8m⁶ 7m³ 7.5f* 7d Sep 5] good-bodied gelding: fairly useful performer: won maiden at Catterick in April and handicap at Beverley in July: best form short of 1m: acts on firm ground: tongue tied: gelded after final start. *J. Howard Johnson*

STOOP TO CONQUER 6 b.g. Polar Falcon (USA) 126 – Princess Genista 108 (Ile **93** de Bourbon (USA) 133) [2006 85: 16m³ 20s 14g 13.3g* 14v⁶ 16d⁶ Sep 23] big, leggy, lengthy gelding: fairly useful handicapper: left A. Carroll and returned to former trainer prior to reappearance: won Newbury (by length from Zurbaran) in August: creditable sixth to Peppertree Lane in Old Borough Cup at Haydock next time: stays 2¼m: acts on any turf going: sometimes races freely: rejoined A. Carroll. *J. L. Dunlop*

STORMBURST (IRE) 2 b.f. (Jan 26) Mujadil (USA) 119 – Isca 66 (Caerleon (USA) **64** 132) [2006 5d⁵ 6.1g Jun 1] €24,000F, 21,000Y: half-sister to several winners, including useful Italian performer up to 1m Sonda (by Dolphin Street) and fairly useful 5f/6f winner Type One (by Bigstone): dam maiden who should have been suited by middle distances: better run in maidens (favourite both times) when fifth at Pontefract. *M. Dods*

STORM CENTRE 4 ch.g. Pivotal 124 – Long View 68 (Persian Bold 123) [2006 72: **66** p7.1g p8g³ 7s 8m p7g 7.1m Aug 28] fair maiden handicapper: pulled up third (reportedly bled, left A. Balding £5,200 after) and final outings: takes good hold, and may prove best short of 1m: acts on polytrack and good to firm ground: tried blinkered: sold £700 in December. *Miss J. S. Davis*

STORM CHASE (USA) 4 b. or br.g. Awad (USA) 124 – Night Duja (USA) (Dayjur **65** (USA) 137) [2006 68: p7.1g⁵ p7g p7g a8g⁴ a6d⁶ Dec 17] fair handicapper: sold from A. Jarvis 3,500 gns after third start: barely stays 1m: acts on polytrack, firm and soft going: often visored: races prominently. *B. Hallencreutz, Sweden*

STORMINGMICHAELORI 3 b.g. Vettori (IRE) 119 – Stormswept (USA) 74 **46** (Storm Bird (CAN) 134) [2006 49: 8s 7g 7.5f 6m 7f⁴ 8s⁶ 7m 7m Sep 16] poor maiden: stays 7f: acts on firm ground: in cheekpieces last 4 starts. *N. Wilson*

STORM MISSION (USA) 2 b. or br.g. (Mar 20) Storm Creek (USA) – Bemissed **54** (USA) (Nijinsky (CAN) 138) [2006 6m 6m³ p6g 7f 5m 6d f6g f6g⁴ p8g Nov 24] tall, close-coupled gelding: modest maiden: should stay 1m: tried in blinkers: inconsistent. *Miss V. Haigh*

STORM OF ARABIA (IRE) 3 b.g. Intikhab (USA) 135 – Mauradell (IRE) (Mujadil **73** (USA) 119) [2006 63: p8g 10m 11.6d² 11.7g² p10g* p12g Dec 16] well-made gelding: fair handicapper: won at Lingfield in December: stays 11.7f: acts on polytrack and good to soft going. *W. R. Swinburn*

STORM ON THE RUN (IRE) 3 b.c. Desert Prince (IRE) 130 – Happy Dancer **86** (USA) 95 (Seattle Dancer (USA) 119) [2006 81: 6.1m² p6g* 7m³ 8m² 8.2m Jul 29] close-coupled colt: fairly useful performer: won maiden at Lingfield in May: creditable placed efforts in handicaps after: stays 1m: acts on polytrack, good to firm and good to soft going: raced too freely final outing: tends to hang: sold 5,000 gns in October. *R. Hannon*

STORM PATH (IRE) 2 gr.c. (Feb 2) Giant's Causeway (USA) 132 – Sianema 62 – (Persian Bold 123) [2006 7m 10d³ Oct 3] quite good-topped colt: well beaten in maiden/minor event. *C. E. Brittain*

STORM PETREL 2 b.f. (Mar 15) Xaar 132 – Vitesse (IRE) 61 (Royal Academy **64 p**
(USA) 130) [2006 7d p6g⁴ Nov 14] leggy filly: second foal: dam 1m winner: modest form
in maidens, staying-on fourth at Wolverhampton: will be suited by 1m: should improve.
N. P. Littmoden

STORM PROSPECT 3 b.g. Mujahid (USA) 125 – Bajan Blue 59 (Lycius (USA) 124) **79**
[2006 62: 8.1s 10m⁴ 13.1m* Sep 4] sturdy gelding: fair performer: won maiden handicap
at Bath in September: stays 13f: acts on good to firm going: blinkered second start: signs
of waywardness: sold 23,000 gns, joined Miss L. Russell. *C. Tinkler*

STORM TROOPER (GER) 6 ch.h. Monsun (GER) 124 – So Sedulous (USA) 102 **100**
(The Minstrel (CAN) 135) [2006 114: 9d⁶ 9d 12g⁵ 12d 11d 10s Nov 19] brother to 3
winners, notably 5-y-o Shirocco, and half-brother to 2 winners: dam 1m winner: one-time
smart performer: trained by A. Schutz prior to 2005, best efforts when third in Deutsches
Derby at 3 yrs and short-head second in Hansa-Preis at 4 yrs, both at Hamburg: won
minor event at Ovrevoll in 2005: just useful form at best since (below form in listed race
at Newmarket fourth start, final outing for R. Haugen in Norway): stays 1½m: raced only
on good ground or softer: blinkered of late. *P. Schiergen, Germany*

STORMY LOVE (IRE) 4 ch.c. Giant's Causeway (USA) 132 – Hula Angel (USA) **–**
111 (Woodman (USA) 126) [2006 65: 9.2d 8d Jun 1] angular, useful-looking colt: fair
maiden at 3 yrs: last both starts in 2006: sold 3,500 gns. *M. Johnston*

STORMY MONDAY 3 b.f. Cadeaux Genereux 131 – Hasta (USA) (Theatrical 128) **78**
[2006 68: p7g⁶ p7g² p6g p6g⁵ p7g⁶ 7g* 7m 7d 8d² 8d Oct 27] angular filly: fair
performer: won apprentice handicap at Salisbury in August: stays 7f: acts on polytrack
and good to soft going. *J. W. Hills*

STORMY RIVER (FR) 3 gr.c. Verglas (IRE) 118 – Miss Bio (FR) (River Mist **123**
(USA) 119) [2006 106: 7v* 8g* 8g³ 8m² 8d* 8s⁴ 8g² 7m⁴ Sep 30]
　　Stormy River enjoyed the biggest success of his career when winning
the Prix Jean Prat in July. Whilst he may have achieved slightly more—judged
purely on form—in finishing runner-up in the St James's Palace Stakes and Prix
du Moulin, Stormy River's half-length defeat of Kentucky Dynamite at Chantilly
confirmed him as the best three-year-old miler trained in France. Starting second
favourite behind the Prix Daphnis winner Dilek, the patiently-ridden Stormy River
found things unfolding ideally in the Jean Prat, which was run at a sound pace.
After beginning his run around two furlongs out, Stormy River still had several
horses to pass entering the last furlong, but quickened well to collar the runner-up
close home, with Dilek a length and a half further back in third. The pick of the
three foreign challengers, Ivan Denisovich, was only eighth, the fourth successive
time he'd finished behind Stormy River.
　　Stormy River started the season in promising fashion, winning at Maisons-
Laffitte and Longchamp, both in April. He won the seven-furlong Prix Djebel, run
under testing conditions, despite carrying his head rather high and wandering
under pressure, beating Marchand d'Or by three quarters of a length. In the Prix
de Fontainebleau, over a mile at Longchamp, Stormy River faced his Criterium

*Prix Jean Prat, Chantilly—a Group 1 success for Stormy River, who comes with a well-timed run
under Thierry Thulliez on this occasion; Kentucky Dynamite is second, ahead of favourite Dilek*

Ecurie Mister Ess A. S.'s "Stormy River"

International conqueror Carlotamix, as well as third-placed Porto Santo and the Aidan O'Brien-trained duo Aussie Rules and Ivan Denisovich. Stormy River gained his revenge on Carlotamix in fine style, drawing clear from two furlongs out and beating Light of Joy by four lengths. Stormy River started a warm favourite for the Poule d'Essai des Poulains, yet could do no better than finish third to two of the four O'Brien-trained three-year-olds in the race, Aussie Rules, who turned the tables after finishing fourth in the Prix de Fontainebleau, and Marcus Andronicus. Lethargic during the preliminaries, Stormy River didn't look the easiest of rides in the race itself, again showing a high head carriage once hitting the front, after racing close up and leading two furlongs from home. In the St James's Palace Stakes at Royal Ascot, Stormy River was ridden with more restraint, but Olivier Peslier, replacing the suspended Thierry Thulliez, received a deal of criticism in some quarters for giving his mount too much to do. Well in rear for a long way, seemingly racing lazily, Stormy River finished two lengths second to the impressive Araafa, doing little wrong under pressure. Thulliez was back on board for Stormy River's remaining races, and, after winning the Prix Jean Prat, the colt started a short-priced favourite on his first outing against older horses in the Prix Jacques le Marois at Deauville. However, he managed only fourth, a length and three quarters behind the winner Librettist. Stormy River's next outing, in the Prix du Moulin de Long-champ, saw him put up his best performance, ridden a bit more prominently than in his three previous starts and keeping on well to finish behind Librettist again, this time beaten half a length in second in a race in which the winner dictated a steady pace.

Stormy River (FR) (gr.c. 2003)	Verglas (IRE) (gr 1994)	Highest Honor (gr 1983)	Kenmare / High River
		Rahaam (gr 1987)	Secreto / Fager's Glory
	Miss Bio (FR) (ch 1996)	River Mist (ch 1982)	Irish River / Principle
		River Sans Retour (b 1987)	Vacarme / Riverstar

Stormy River can now be considered the best performer by Verglas, a distinction which previously went to Blackdoun, an ex-French performer who went on to show improved form when winning two Grade 2 events in the States. Verglas won the Coventry Stakes and was second to Desert King in the Irish Two Thousand Guineas. He was best at around a mile, failing for stamina when a well-held sixth behind the same rival in the Irish Derby. Verglas was unable to reproduce his smart form when moved to North America and, while he began his stud career in France, he is now a resident of the Irish National Stud. Stormy River is the second foal of Miss Bio, an unraced half-sister to Fantastic Filly, a Grade 3-winning miler in the States. Miss Bio's first foal, Norman Bio, has won at eleven and a half furlongs to two miles in France, and is by Chef de Clan II, the non-thoroughbred sire of Clan Royal, twice placed in the Grand National. Stormy River is likely to prove best at around a mile, seemingly unsuited by the test of speed when fourth to Caradak in the steadily-run Prix de la Foret at Longchamp on his final outing. The angular, heavy-topped Stormy River acts on heavy and good to firm going, tends to be languid during the preliminaries and has raced lazily and carried his head high. He seems best when produced late and has worn a crossed noseband. *N. Clement, France*

STOTSFOLD   3 b.g. Barathea (IRE) 127 – Eliza Acton 70 (Shirley Heights 130) [2006 **104** 10d 10m⁶ 8m⁵ p10g* 10.3f* 10d³ p10g* 10.3f* 12s Oct 7] good-bodied gelding: third foal: half-brother to fairly useful 8.6f and 1¾m winner Maggie Tulliver (by Spectrum): dam, 2-y-o 1m winner, sister to useful stayer Top Cees and closely related to dam of smart performer up to 10.5f Leporello: progressed into a useful performer, winning handicaps at Lingfield in June, Chester in July and Kempton and Chester (beat Salute Him by 2½ lengths) in September: should stay 1½m: acts on polytrack, firm and good to soft going (bit below form on soft final outing). *W. R. Swinburn*

ST PETERSBURG   6 ch.g. Polar Falcon (USA) 126 – First Law 57 (Primo Dominie **107** 121) [2006 107: 8s⁵ 8.1v³ 8d² 8s 8g 8d p8g³ Dec 30] strong, lengthy gelding: useful **a95** performer: off 9 months (reportedly due to growth on a hind foot) prior to reappearance: good head second to Vicious Warrior in handicap at Ayr: well below form after: stays 1m: acts on all-weather, used only on good or softer going on turf (acts on heavy): tongue tied penultimate outing. *M. H. Tompkins*

ST PHILIP (USA)   2 b.c. (Jan 6) Dance Brightly (CAN) – Tender Moment (USA) **98** (Torrential (USA) 117) [2006 6m² 6m* 7m* 7d Sep 29] $13,000F, $28,000Y, 77,000 2-y-o: tall, useful-looking colt: third foal: half-brother to Italian 2004 2-y-o 5f/6f winner Tenderlit (by Lit de Justice): dam unraced half-sister to US Grade 1 2-y-o 6.5f winner Great Navigator: useful form: won maiden at Salisbury in August and minor event at Southwell in September: further improvement when seventh of 10 to Thousand Words in Somerville Tattersall Stakes at Newmarket: likely to stay 1m. *R. M. Beckett*

STRABINIOS KING   2 b.g. (Feb 23) King's Best (USA) 132 – Strawberry Morn **63 p** (CAN) (Travelling Victor (CAN)) [2006 f8g⁴ Dec 9] fourth foal: half-brother to 3-y-o Strawberry Lolly: dam multiple stakes winner in Canada at 6.5f/8.5f, including at 2 yrs: 33/1, 5¾ lengths fourth to Mardi in maiden at Southwell, forced wide: should improve. *P. C. Haslam*

STRAFFAN (IRE)   4 b. or br.f. Shinko Forest (IRE) – Katherine Gorge (USA) (Hansel **54 §** (USA)) [2006 60§: f6g* f5g p6g f6g³ f6g* f6g f6g f6g 6m 6m⁶ 6g 6m³ 7.1m 5m 6v f6m⁴ f7g⁶ f6g³ p6g Dec 6] lengthy filly: modest performer: won banded races at Southwell in January and February: was best at 5f/6f: acted on all-weather, firm and soft going: wore cheekpieces/blinkers: sometimes slowly away: usually raced prominently: was inconsistent: dead. *J. Hetherton*

cantorspreadfair.com Stakes (Handicap), Goodwood—
Strategic Mount completes a hat-trick from Bandama; King's Head (cheekpieces) snatches third

STRAIGHT AS A DIE 3 b.f. Pyramus (USA) 78 – Tenderetta (Tender King 123) **46**
[2006 47: p5.1g⁵ p6g⁵ f8g 5g p6g Oct 23] poor maiden: raced mainly at 5f/6f.
R. J. Hodges

STRAIGHT FACE (IRE) 2 b.g. (Mar 19) Princely Heir (IRE) 111 – Dakota Sioux **73**
(IRE) 90 (College Chapel 122) [2006 6m 6g² 7m⁶ p7g³ p7g 7f⁴ 7f⁴ 6m² 6d² 6d Oct 2]
40,000Y: sturdy gelding: first foal: dam 7f/1m winner: fair maiden: made frame 6 times:
stays 7f: acts on polytrack, firm and good to soft going: visored last 4 starts: gelded after
final one: of suspect temperament. *W. J. Knight*

STRAIGHT GAL (IRE) 3 br.f. Namid 128 – Kazimiera (IRE) 77 (Polish Patriot **52**
(USA) 128) [2006 6.1g 7m Jun 29] 5,000Y: fourth foal: half-sister to 4-y-o Revien: dam,
placed up to 1m, half-sister to useful 1994 2-y-o 5f/6f winner Fallow: better effort when
seventh in maiden at Nottingham on debut. *G. A. Huffer*

STRATEGIC MOUNT 3 b.c. Montjeu (IRE) 137 – Danlu (USA) (Danzig (USA)) **99**
[2006 69p: 10d³ 11.6m⁴ 11.6g² 12.1s⁴ 11.7m* 14.1f* 12m* 13.9d Sep 8] big, strong colt:
useful performer: much improved in 2006, winning maiden at Bath in June and handicaps
at Nottingham in July and Goodwood (beat Bandama by 1¾ lengths in cantorspread-
fair.com Stakes) in August: well below form in Mallard Handicap at York final outing:
effective at 1½m/1¾m: acts on firm going: blinkered second start. *P. F. I. Cole*

STRATEGIC PRINCE 2 b.c. (May 9) Dansili 127 – Ausherra (USA) 106 (Diesis **114**
133) [2006 5g⁴ 5m⁵ 6m* 7m* 7d³ Oct 14]
On the face of it, Strategic Prince ended the season with his limitations
exposed, but he achieved a smart level of form, ahead of schedule from some points
of view, and he may yet make an even better performer at three. A late foal, on the
balance of his pedigree Strategic Prince wasn't bred to win a maiden over five
furlongs as a two-year-old; in fact, his two-year-old season as a whole bore a striking resemblance to that of his trainer's 1991 Derby winner Generous, who also won
on his debut over five furlongs, was runner-up in the Coventry Stakes at Royal
Ascot and third in the Vintage Stakes at Glorious Goodwood before winning the
Dewhurst at Newmarket. Even if it is asking a lot to expect Strategic Prince to
bridge the gap with Teofilo, for one, there should be another good prize in him at a
mile or more as a three-year-old.
Strategic Prince would have tackled the Coventry Stakes but for an admin-
istrative hiccup. After winning a maiden at Salisbury on his debut in May, he found
five furlongs too sharp kept to the trip in the Norfolk Stakes at Royal Ascot, but
showed his worth in pattern company when stepped up to six for the TNT July
Stakes at Newmarket. A 16/1-shot in a field of nine, Strategic Prince lost his position when short of room approaching the Dip, but rallied strongly when switched
right on meeting the rising ground, winning going away by a length and three
quarters from Armigerent. Strategic Prince proved even better suited by seven
furlongs on his last two starts. The only penalised runner in a field of ten, he was a
6/1-shot conceding 3 lb all round in the Veuve Clicquot Vintage Stakes at Goodwood in August, but showed further improvement. Soon prominent, he quickened
ahead two furlongs out and held on well close home from Duke of Marmalade,
winning by a neck, the pair two lengths clear of Kirklees in third. Strategic Prince
was seen out next when trying to emulate the two previous winners of the Vintage

TNT July Stakes, Newmarket—from left to right,
Strategic Prince draws away from (left to right) Armigerent, Dubai's Touch and Dazed And Amazed

Stakes, Sir Percy and Shamardal, by winning the Dewhurst Stakes at Newmarket in October. Looking in fine shape after his absence, Strategic Prince was beaten but still ran his best race, travelling as well as any for most of the way and keeping on steadily as the first two quickened away, going down by two and a half lengths to close-finishers Teofilo and Holy Roman Emperor.

Strategic Prince (b.c. May 9, 2004)	Dansili (b 1996)	Danehill (b 1986)	Danzig
			Razyana
		Hasili (b 1991)	Kahyasi
			Kerali
	Ausherra (USA) (ch 1988)	Diesis (ch 1980)	Sharpen Up
			Doubly Sure
		Princess of Man (ch 1975)	Green God
			White Legs

One element of speed on the dam's side of Strategic Prince's pedigree is his close relative Asley (by Dansili's sire Danehill), a fairly useful six/seven-furlong winner as a two-year-old. Dansili was a high-class miler, placed in the Sussex Stakes and the Breeders' Cup Mile as a four-year-old, but has been responsible for good winners over further, notably Rail Link. Strategic Prince's dam Ausherra, a

Veuve Clicquot Vintage Stakes, Goodwood—Strategic Prince follows in the hoofprints of classic winners
Sir Percy and Shamardal; Duke of Marmalade is second, ahead of Kirklees

sister to Oaks winner and St Leger runner-up Ramruma, was successful over six furlongs as a two-year-old and won the Lingfield Oaks Trial over eleven and a half furlongs at three. Ausherra was trained by Paul Cole, who was also responsible for the two best progeny of Ausherra prior to Strategic Prince, both of whom stayed very well. Yorkshire (by Generous), who later won over hurdles, was a smart performer at his best, successful at a mile to two and a quarter miles, and finished runner-up in the Queen Alexandra Stakes as a four-year-old when he was also an unlucky fifth in the Melbourne Cup. Strategic Prince's other notable half-brother Riyadh (by Caerleon) showed useful form at up to two miles as a three-year-old before being sold out of Paul Cole's stable, winning the Ascot Stakes over two and a half miles as a four-year-old. Riyadh became temperamental and another of the better progeny of Ausherra, the useful Red Admiral, a winner at a mile and a mile and a half, is none too genuine. A 150,000-guinea yearling, Strategic Prince has done nothing wrong so far, racing with enthusiasm. A tall, close-coupled, quite attractive colt, who moved poorly to post at Royal Ascot, he acts on good to firm and good to soft ground, though his trainer thought twice about allowing him to tackle the latter surface at Newmarket. *P. F. I. Cole*

STRATHAIRD (IRE) 2 b.g. (Jan 29) Medicean 128 – Heed My Warning (IRE) 102   **47**
(Second Set (IRE) 127) [2006 p7.1g p6g⁴ Dec 6] poor form in maidens at Wolverhampton. *P. C. Haslam*

STRATHCLYDE (IRE) 7 b.g. Petong 126 – It's Academic 73 (Royal Academy   **44**
(USA) 130) [2006 57: p5.1g p6g⁵ p6g Apr 12] good-topped gelding: one-time fairly useful 5f/6f winner: only poor performer in 2006: stays 6f: acts on polytrack, firm and good to soft ground: tried in cheekpieces/blinkers. *A. M. Hales*

STRATHMORE (IRE) 2 gr.g. (Apr 20) Fath (USA) 116 – In The Highlands (Petong   **70**
126) [2006 5m 7s 5m³ Aug 31] €26,000Y: sixth foal: closely related to fairly useful 2001 2-y-o 5f/6f winner Glenmorangie (by Danzig Connection) and half-brother to winner in Jersey by Missed Flight: dam well beaten: fair form: claimed from E. O'Neill £6,000 second start: much improved when third at Redcar (gelded after): should prove best at 5f/6f. *R. A. Fahey*

STRATHTAY 4 ch.f. Pivotal 124 – Cressida (Polish Precedent (USA) 131) [2006 60:   **–**
p10g p13.9g⁵ f11g Jan 29] neat filly: modest performer at 3 yrs: no form in 2006: often wears headgear. *M. Appleby*

STRAVARA 3 b.g. Kayf Tara 130 – Stravsea 65 (Handsome Sailor 125) [2006 81p: **74**
f12g³ f11g p9.5g Dec 18] good-topped gelding: fairly useful form at 2 yrs: best effort in 2006 when just fair third in handicap at Southwell: should stay 1½m: acts on heavy going, probably on fibresand. *R. Hollinshead*

STRAVINSKY'S ART (USA) 2 b.c. (Feb 7) Stravinsky (USA) 133 – Halo's Gleam   **–**
(USA) (Halo (USA)) [2006 6s May 27] lengthy, good-topped colt: tailed off in maiden. *D. R. C. Elsworth*

STRAVITA 2 b.f. (Apr 16) Weet-A-Minute (IRE) 106 – Stravsea 65 (Handsome Sailor   **74**
125) [2006 p8.6m* Nov 21] second foal: half-sister to 3-y-o Stravara: dam 7f/1m winner: 50/1, won maiden at Wolverhampton by head from Letham Island, hanging right. *R. Hollinshead*

STRAWBERRY DALE (IRE) 4 b.f. Bering 136 – Manchaca (FR) (Highest Honor   **111**
(FR) 124) [2006 103: 10.4s* 10s⁵ 10d Sep 19] tall, close-coupled filly: has a fluent action: smart performer: improved again when winning totepool Middleton Stakes at York in May by 3 lengths from Mango Mischief, dictating: creditable fifth to Satwa Queen in Prix Jean Romanet at Deauville 3 months later, but ran poorly in Blandford Stakes at the Curragh final start: stays 10.4f: has won on good to firm ground, easily best efforts on soft/heavy: free-going sort (more tractable than she used to be). *J. D. Bethell*

STRAWBERRY LEAF 4 ch.f. Unfuwain (USA) 131 – Satin Bell 99 (Midyan (USA)   **–**
124) [2006 88p: 10g Apr 26] leggy filly: fairly useful performer at 3 yrs: tailed off only start in 2006: sold 5,000 gns in November. *R. Charlton*

STRAWBERRY LOLLY 3 b.f. Lomitas 129 – Strawberry Morn (CAN) (Travelling   **89**
Victor (CAN)) [2006 68p: p9.5g⁶ p8.6g* p10g* 10.3m⁶ Aug 25] unfurnished filly: fairly useful form: won maiden at Wolverhampton in July and apprentice handicap at Kempton in August: stays 1¼m: acts on polytrack and good to firm going. *Sir Michael Stoute*

STRAWBERRY PATCH (IRE) 7 b.g. Woodborough (USA) 112 – Okino (USA) **63**
(Strawberry Road (AUS) 128) [2006 –: 5f 6m 5f⁵ 5m* 5m² 5m 5m⁴ 6m⁶ 5m² 5g² 5d 5d
5d Nov 3] strong, good-topped gelding: modest handicapper: won at Musselburgh in
July: best at 5f/6f: acts on firm going, probably on good to soft: usually wears cheekpieces. *J. S. Goldie*

STRAW BOY 2 br.g. (Apr 15) Hunting Lion (IRE) 115 – Sky Light Dreams (Dreams **57**
To Reality (USA) 113) [2006 7m 5.7f⁴ 6m 6s⁴ 7m² 8.3s Oct 2] close-coupled gelding:
modest maiden: second in selling nursery (left M. Channon £6,000): should stay 1m: acts
on soft and good to firm going. *R. Brotherton*

STREAMER 2 b.f. (Feb 29) Elnadim (USA) 128 – Noble Water (FR) 46 (Noblequest **53**
(FR) 124) [2006 6g⁶ 7v⁶ p8g Nov 8] second foal: half-sister to winner in Greece by
Gothenberg: dam 6f and (in Belgium) 7f winner: modest form: dead. *M. Johnston*

STREET LIFE (IRE) 8 ch.g. Dolphin Street (FR) 125 – Wolf Cleugh (IRE) 65 (Last **73**
Tycoon 131) [2006 76: p12g p12g⁵ 14.1s 12g 10.1m 10.1m⁴ p10g p9.5g p9.5g* Dec 29]
rather leggy, angular gelding: fair handicapper: won at Wolverhampton in December:
effective at 9.5f, barely stays 1¾m: acts on all-weather, heavy and good to firm going:
held up: sometimes edges left. *W. J. Musson*

STREETS AHEAD 2 b.c. (Feb 13) Beat Hollow 126 – Frond 85 (Alzao (USA) 117) **101**
[2006 7m⁵ 7g² 7g* 8g* 8f⁴ Sep 17] 26,000F, 20,000Y: well-made colt: fifth foal: half-
brother to 3 winners, including useful Scandinavian 1m/1¼m winner Azolla (by Cadeaux
Genereux) and 2004 2-y-o 6f winner Ridder (by Dr Fong): dam, 7f winner (ran only at
2 yrs), out of useful 1½m winner Fern: useful performer: won maiden and listed race at
Salisbury in August, in latter beating Eddie Jock by length: not discredited in Grade 3
Summer Stakes at Woodbine (8½ lengths fourth to Dreaming of Anna) final start: will
stay 1¼m: has edged right. *A. M. Balding*

STREET WARRIOR (IRE) 3 b.g. Royal Applause 124 – Anne Bonny 105 (Ajdal **86**
(USA) 130) [2006 77: 7v⁵ 7.1g² 6d³ 7m 8.3f* p10g⁴ p9.5g p8.6g p12g Dec 1] rather leggy
gelding: fairly useful performer: won handicap at Leicester in September: stays 1¼m:
acts on polytrack and firm ground. *M. Johnston*

STRENSALL 9 b.g. Beveled (USA) – Payvashooz 78 (Ballacashtal (CAN)) [2006 78, **76**
a–: 5g 5f² 5f⁶ 5f³ 5m⁶ 5m⁵ 5m* 5f⁶ 5f 5m⁴ 5f³ 5g Sep 30] sturdy gelding: fair handicapper:
won at Catterick in July: best at 5f: acts on fibresand, firm and soft going: sometimes
slowly away: often races prominently. *R. E. Barr*

STRETTON (IRE) 8 br.g. Doyoun 124 – Awayil (USA) 82 (Woodman (USA) 126) **90**
[2006 87, a77: 12.3d* p12g 12g⁶ 12d⁵ 12.3m 12d² 12m⁴ 12s⁵ p12.2m Oct 31] leggy, **a65**
close-coupled gelding: fairly useful handicapper on turf, fair on all-weather: won at
Chester in May: best effort after when good second to London Express at York: stays
1½m: unraced on heavy going, acts on any other turf and polytrack: wore cheekpieces
once: held up. *J. D. Bethell*

STRIDENT (USA) 5 ch.g. Deputy Commander (USA) 124 – Regrets Only (USA) **–**
(Black Tie Affair 128) [2006 70: p16.5g p12.2g Mar 25] maiden: no form in 2006: stays
1¼m: tried visored. *J. J. Lambe, Ireland*

STRIFE (IRE) 3 b.g. Stravinsky (USA) 133 – Fife (IRE) 95 (Lomond (USA) 128) **55**
[2006 –: 7f* 8d 8m 8f⁵ p9.5g p12.2s⁴ Dec 13] good-topped gelding: modest performer:
won handicap at Folkestone in May: left R. Hannon 11,500 gns after fourth outing: stays
1m: acts on firm ground: tried in cheekpieces. *W. M. Brisbourne*

STRIKEEN (IRE) 2 ch.c. (Apr 30) Intikhab (USA) 135 – Sheen Falls (IRE) 56 (Prince **91**
Rupert (FR) 121) [2006 8d⁴ 8.1d² p7.1g⁴ f8g* f8g² Dec 9] €21,000Y, 57,000 2-y-o:
good-bodied colt: half-brother to several winners, including useful Irish 7f to 9f winner
Provosky (by Polish Patriot) and Irish 11f winner Glandore (by Persian Bold): dam Irish
maiden half-sister to smart Irish performer up to 1¼m Noora Abu: fairly useful performer: won nursery at Southwell in November: more progress when second in similar event
there (odds on): will stay 1¼m: raced on all-weather and good to soft going. *T. G. Mills*

STRIKE FORCE 2 b.g. (May 7) Dansili 127 – Miswaki Belle (USA) 73 (Miswaki **71**
(USA) 124) [2006 6s 6g* 7m⁵ p8.6g⁵ Dec 23] well-made gelding: eighth foal: closely
related to smart 5f/6f winner Danehurst (by Danehill) and half-brother to useful 1m to
10.5f (Prix Penelope) winner Humouresque (by Pivotal): dam, second at 7f on only start,
closely related to smart performer up to 1m Dazzle: fair performer: won maiden at Lingfield in June: gelded, left J. Gosden 6,000 gns and off over 4 months prior to final outing:
will prove best up to 7f. *M. Wellings*

Merbury Catering Consultants Supreme Stakes, Goodwood—Stronghold (centre) edges out Byron (left); fifth-placed Daniella is also in the picture

STRIKE UP THE BAND 3 b.c. Cyrano de Bergerac 120 – Green Supreme (Primo **114** Dominie 121) [2006 104: 7g 6m³ 6d³ 6m 5.1m⁴ 5f 5g³ 5m² 5.5d* Oct 5] strong, good-topped colt: smart performer: won listed race at Chantilly in October by 2 lengths from One Putra: placed earlier in similar contests at Lingfield, Newbury and York and minor event at Beverley (neck second to Philharmonic): best at 5f/6f: acts on firm and good to soft going. *D. Nicholls*

STRING SERENADE (IRE) 5 b.m. Key of Luck (USA) 126 – Bubbly Dancer **53** (USA) 67 (Crafty Prospector (USA)) [2006 –: p7.1g p9.5g⁶ p8g 10m* 10m³ 11.5f⁵ 11.9f³ 11.5f p10g f11g Oct 12] first foal: dam, Irish maiden, stayed 1½m: modest performer: left G. O'Leary in Ireland prior to reappearance: won seller at Brighton in June: stays 11.5f: acts on polytrack and firm going. *V. Smith*

STRINGSOFMYHEART 2 b.f. (Apr 25) Halling (USA) 133 – Heart's Harmony **–** (Blushing Groom (FR) 131) [2006 7d Aug 12] big, rangy filly, unfurnished at 2 yrs: sister to useful 6f (at 2 yrs) and 1¼m winner Tug of Love and half-sister to several winners, including smart 1m to 1¼m winner National Anthem (including in USA, by Royal Academy) and 4-y-o Celtique: dam second from 2 starts at 1m in France: 12/1, last in maiden at Newmarket, slowly away and never on bridle. *Sir Michael Stoute*

STRIVING STORM (USA) 2 b.c. (Apr 22) Stormin Fever (USA) 116 – Sugars For **103** Nanny (USA) (Brocco (USA) 124) [2006 7g³ 7s² 8.1v* 7s³ Oct 21] 50,000Y: big, lengthy colt: has plenty of scope: second foal: half-brother to winner in USA by Elusive Quality: dam, 6f/7f winner in USA, half-sister to very smart performer up to 1¼m Cruachan: useful performer: won maiden at Haydock in September: better form starts either side, second to Visionario in listed event at Deauville and third to Dijeerr in Horris Hill Stakes (hung left) at Newbury: stays 1m: raced on good going or softer. *P. W. Chapple-Hyam*

STROBE 2 ch.g. (Feb 17) Fantastic Light (USA) 134 – Sadaka (USA) 77 (Kingmambo **59** (USA) 125) [2006 6m 5.7m 5d Sep 29] good-bodied gelding: modest form second start in maidens: gelded after final one: will stay at least 1m. *J. A. Osborne*

STROBILUS 2 b.c. (Mar 5) Mark of Esteem (IRE) 137 – Mount Elbrus 106 (Barathea **107** (IRE) 127) [2006 7d² 7.1s* p8g* 8g² Oct 15] first foal: dam, 1¼m to 13f (in France) winner, out of sister to Prix de Diane winner Rafha: useful form: progressed well, winning maiden at Haydock in September and nursery at Lingfield (impressively by 3 lengths from Brainy Benny) in October: short-head second to Kirklees in Gran Criterium at Milan final outing, making much of running: will probably stay 1¼m/1½m: joined Godolphin. *M. A. Jarvis*

STROBINIA (IRE) 4 b.f. Soviet Star (USA) 128 – Robinia (USA) 90 (Roberto (USA) **–** 131) [2006 45: f6g⁶ Jan 2] poor maiden. *R. M. Beckett*

STROLL IN THE PARK (IRE) 3 b.g. Galileo (IRE) 134 – Highshaan (Pistolet Bleu **–** (IRE) 133) [2006 8g 7m⁶ May 31] strong, stocky gelding: well held in maidens: sold 2,500 gns in October. *D. R. C. Elsworth*

STRONG APPROACH (IRE) 3 ch.g. Fruits of Love (USA) 127 – Shragraddy Lass **69** (IRE) 73 (Jareer (USA) 115) [2006 72: 7m 7g⁶ 8g 6f⁴ f6g³ 7f⁴ 9d Aug 2] strong gelding: fair maiden: needs test at 6f, and stays 1m: acts on fibresand and good to firm going: tried blinkered: joined S. Clark. *T. D. Barron*

STRONGHOLD 4 b.c. Danehill (USA) 126 – Insinuate (USA) 99 (Mr Prospector **120** (USA)) [2006 108: 7.6m* 8s 8g² 8m² p8g⁴ 7d* 7d Oct 14] strong, lengthy, attractive colt: very smart performer: won listed race at Lingfield (by 1½ lengths from Vortex) in May and Merbury Catering Consultants Supreme Stakes at Goodwood (beat Byron by length) in September: also very good efforts when runner-up in listed event at Goodwood (beaten short head by Satchem) and Royal Hunt Cup at Royal Ascot (beaten neck by Cesare): well held in Challenge Stakes at Newmarket final outing: effective at 7f/1m: acts on good to firm and good to soft going (seemingly not on soft), probably on polytrack. *J. H. M. Gosden*

STRONG SURVIVOR (USA) 3 b.g. Kingmambo (USA) 125 – Summer Solstice **64** (IRE) (Caerleon (USA) 132) [2006 8m⁶ 10m 8.1s⁶ Sep 7] big, rangy gelding: first foal: dam, useful 9f (in USA) to 12.5f (in France) winner, half-sister to Prix du Jockey Club runner-up Act One: modest form at best in maidens. *L. M. Cumani*

STRUT 3 ch.f. Danehill Dancer (IRE) 117 – Boast 99 (Most Welcome 131) [2006 97: **103** 7m⁴ 7m³ 6s⁶ 6f 7d⁵ Sep 8] strong, lengthy filly: has quick action: useful performer: mainly creditable efforts in 2006, best effort when sixth to Borehan in Coral Sprint (Handicap) at Newmarket: 1¼ lengths third to Echelon in Chartwell Fillies' Stakes at Lingfield on second start: stays 7f: acts on soft and good to firm going: found little when visored fourth start. *R. Charlton*

ST SAVARIN (FR) 5 ch.g. Highest Honor (FR) 124 – Sacara (GER) (Monsagem **96** (USA) 117) [2006 86: p8g p9.5g⁴ p10g³ p12g² 12d³ 11.9s* 11m² 14g 12s² 11.6d f11g* **a90** f12g³ Dec 2] sturdy gelding: useful handicapper: won at Haydock (by length from Juniper Girl) in September and Southwell (by ¾ length from Heathyards Pride) in November: seems to stay 1¾m: acts on all-weather, firm and soft ground: reliable. *R. A. Fahey*

STUMPED 3 b.g. Bertolini (USA) 125 – So Saucy 59 (Teenoso (USA) 135) [2006 8m⁵ **76** 8m p8.6g⁵ 8.3g⁵ p12g² Sep 5] 31,000Y: lengthy, good-topped gelding: half-brother to several winners, including 7f to 2m winner Most-Saucy (by Most Welcome) and 1¼m/ 1½m winner Tidal (by Bin Ajwaad), both fairly useful: dam 1¼m and 17f winner: fair maiden: stays 1½m: raced only on polytrack and good/good to firm going: tongue tied first 3 starts: joined H. Daly. *W. J. Haggas*

STUNNINGJO 2 gr.f. (Mar 31) Pursuit of Love 124 – Dolly Bevan 53 (Another Realm **46** 118) [2006 5.1d 5d 5.1g⁵ 7s 6d Aug 21] 10,000Y: compact filly: half-sister to 3 winners, including useful 6f winner (including at 2 yrs) Oggi and fairly useful 6f (at 2 yrs) to 1m winner Pengamon (both by Efisio): dam, 2-y-o 6f seller winner who stayed 1m, half-sister to smart sprinter Pips Pride: poor maiden: should stay 1m: blinkered after second start. *J. L. Spearing*

STYLE SUNDAY (IRE) 2 b.c. (Feb 16) Alhaarth (IRE) 126 – March Star (IRE) 109 **66** (Mac's Imp (USA) 116) [2006 7m 7d 6.1m⁵ Sep 15] 42,000Y: angular, workmanlike colt: fourth foal: half-brother to 5-y-o Kensington and 4-y-o Scuba: dam 6f winner, including at 2 yrs: fair form in maidens: will stay 1m: sold 10,000 gns, sent to USA. *B. W. Hills*

STYLISH SUNRISE (IRE) 5 b.g. Desert Style (IRE) 121 – Anita At Dawn (IRE) 77 — §
(Anita's Prince 126) [2006 48§: f12g⁶ May 9] lengthy gelding: poor and inconsistent
performer nowadays. *A. J. Chamberlain*

STYLISTIC (IRE) 5 b.m. Daggers Drawn (USA) 114 – Treasure (IRE) 72 (Treasure — **67**
Kay 114) [2006 69: f6g⁵ p6g⁵ p7g 6m 6v p7.1g Nov 25] fair maiden: trained by P. Morris
first 3 starts in 2006 before rejoining former stable: stays 9.3f: acts on polytrack, firm and
soft going: tried blinkered/in cheekpieces. *J. J. Lambe, Ireland*

SUALDA (IRE) 7 b.g. Idris (IRE) 118 – Winning Heart 98 (Horage 124) [2006 84: **85**
13.9s 12g² 12.1m* 11.5g 11.9g⁴ 11.5f* 12g Aug 19] tall gelding: fairly useful performer:
won handicap at Hamilton in June and 4-runner claimer at Carlisle (claimed from
R. Fahey £15,000) in July: stays 2m: acts on firm and good to soft going: tried in blinkers/
cheekpieces/tongue tie, though not in recent seasons: often held up: reliable: successful
over hurdles in September. *D. Carroll*

SUBADAR 2 b.c. (Jan 22) Zamindar (USA) 116 – Valencia 79 (Kenmare (FR) 125) **73 p**
[2006 p7g³ p7g⁴ Oct 20] fifth foal: half-brother to several winners, including smart
sprinter Deportivo (by Night Shift) and 3-y-o Cantabria: dam, second at 1m at 2 yrs only
start, half-sister to very smart performers Wandesta (up to 13.5f in Britain/USA) and De
Quest (up to 12.5f in France): promise in maidens at Lingfield, third to Ekhtiaar on debut:
likely to prove best up to 7f: should do better. *R. Charlton*

SUBSIDISE (IRE) 3 br.g. Key of Luck (USA) 126 – Haysong (IRE) (Ballad Rock 122) **60 d**
[2006 55?: p9.5g f8g² f8g* f12g⁴ 10g 10g 11g 7.9m f8g Jul 31] modest performer on
all-weather, little solid form on turf: won handicap at Southwell in February: below form
after, leaving J. Given following fourth outing: should stay 1¼m: acts on fibresand:
usually blinkered/visored: unseated rider seventh appearance. *F. P. Murtagh*

SUCCEED (IRE) 3 b.f. Elnadim (USA) 128 – Pico 71 (Piccolo 121) [2006 63: p5g⁴ **64**
p5g⁴ p6g⁴ f5g² 5.7g p5g 5m 5m p5.1m⁶ p5.1g² p5g p5g² p5.1g* p5g³ Dec 20] modest
performer: won handicap at Wolverhampton in December: will prove best at 5f/6f: acts
on all-weather and firm ground: has shown signs of temperament. *Mrs H. Sweeting*

SUCCESSOR 6 ch.g. Entrepreneur 123 – Petralona (USA) (Alleged (USA) 138) [2006 **56**
58: p10g³ p10g Feb 6] lengthy gelding: modest performer: stayed 1¼m: acted on polytrack, good to firm and good to soft ground: usually tongue tied: dead. *M. D. I. Usher*

SUDAN (IRE) 3 ch.c. Peintre Celebre (USA) 137 – Sarabande (USA) (Woodman **117**
(USA) 126) [2006 10.5d* 11d³ 12g² 12g2 12m³ 10s⁶ 12m³ 9.8m⁴ Sep 30] leggy, close-
coupled colt: first foal: dam useful French 1¼m/12.5f winner: smart performer: won
newcomers race at Saint-Cloud in April: placed 5 times at Longchamp, 3 times behind
Rail Link, notably when third in Grand Prix de Paris (beaten 2¼ lengths) and Prix Niel
(beaten 2½ lengths) fifth/seventh starts: respectable fourth to Soldier Hollow in Prix
Dollar there final start: ideally suited by 1½m: acts on good to firm and good to soft
ground. *E. Lellouche, France*

SUDDEN EDGE 4 b.g. Bold Edge 123 – Surprise Surprise 91 (Robellino (USA) 127) —
[2006 66: 6.1m 6m Jul 1] fair maiden at 3 yrs: well held in 2006. *H. Candy*

SUDDEN IMPULSE 5 b.m. Silver Patriarch (IRE) 125 – Sanshang (FR) (Astronef **69**
116) [2006 –: f11g⁴ p12.2g² f11g⁶ p10g³ p12g 12f² 12g* 12m² 12g⁴ 14.1d 10g* 9.9g*
12d² 10.1s² 10s 12d Nov 3] strong mare: fair handicapper: won at Musselburgh in July
and Leicester and Beverley in August: effective at 1¼m/1½m: acts on polytrack, firm and
soft ground: tried in cheekpieces. *A. D. Brown*

SU DOKU (USA) 2 ch.f. (Mar 4) Lemon Drop Kid (USA) 131 – Bellehop (USA) **66 ?**
(Hennessy (USA) 122) [2006 5v³ 5m 6.1m⁵ 8d p6g p6g Nov 11] $10,000Y, 50,000 2-y-o:
sturdy filly: second foal: dam, 6f winner in USA, half-sister to useful Irish sprinter Check
The Band): modest maiden on balance: sometimes highly tried (possibly flattered second
outing): blinkered (well beaten in nursery) final start. *N. P. Littmoden*

SUDOOR 2 b.f. (Feb 26) Fantastic Light (USA) 134 – Wissal (USA) (Woodman (USA) **98**
126) [2006 7m⁷ 7.1m* 8g⁵ 7d Oct 14] smallish, unfurnished filly: first foal: dam unraced
sister to very smart performer up to 1¼m Bahhare and half-sister to high-class 1m/1¼m
performer Bahri: useful performer: won maiden at Newbury in June and listed event at
Sandown (idled, beat Precocious Star by length) in July: better form again when 2¼
lengths fifth of 9 to Simply Perfect in May Hill Stakes at York, found little: well held in
Rockfel Stakes at Newmarket: stays 1m: acts on good to firm going. *J. L. Dunlop*

SUESAM 3 b.f. Piccolo 121 – Barnacla (IRE) 83 (Bluebird (USA) 125) [2006 73: 8.3m **67**
8m 8.3g⁵ 6.1g⁶ 8m Sep 25] leggy filly: fair performer: stays 8.3f: acts on good to firm
going: has looked none too straightforward: tried blinkered. *B. R. Millman*

SUES SURPRISE (IRE) 2 b.f. (Apr 3) Montjeu (IRE) 137 – My Micheline (Lion **91 p**
Cavern (USA) 117) [2006 7g⁴ 8d² Oct 28] €82,000Y: lengthy filly: has scope: third foal:
half-sister to 4-y-o Kova Hall: dam unraced out of sister to dam of Zafonic: shaped well
in minor event at Newbury and listed race at Newmarket, in latter 5 lengths second
(boxed in briefly) of 12 to Passage of Time: will be suited by 1¼m/1½m: useful prospect,
sure to win races. *B. W. Hills*

SUFFOLK HOUSE 4 b.g. Paris House 123 – Suffolk Girl (Statoblest 120) [2006 –: **46**
f8g f6g f7g⁴ f8g⁵ p9.5g⁵ f11g Dec 28] poor performer: left K. Ryan after second outing:
stays 7f: acts on fibresand: tried in cheekpieces. *M. Brittain*

SUGAR RAY (IRE) 2 b.c. (Feb 15) Danehill (USA) 126 – Akuna Bay (USA) 88 (Mr **70 p**
Prospector (USA)) [2006 7g Sep 15] 290,000Y: well-made colt: third foal: half-brother
to winner in Greece by King of Kings: dam, Irish 2-y-o 7f winner, out of Irish St Leger
winner Dark Lomond: 10/1, needed experience when seventh to Opera Music in maiden
at Newbury: will do better. *Sir Michael Stoute*

SUGGESTIVE 8 b.g. Reprimand 122 – Pleasuring 68 (Good Times (ITY)) [2006 117, **114**
a119: 7.5m² 6.5m⁴ 7.1g⁶ 7f* p8g⁶ 7m 7g⁵ 7g² 7d Oct 14] big gelding: smart performer:
won Woodford Reserve Criterion Stakes at Newmarket in July by a head from Mac Love:
creditable efforts after when 1½ lengths fifth to Price Tag in Prix du Pin at Longchamp
and 2½ lengths second to New Seeker in listed race at Redcar: winner at 1m, best at 7f:
acts on polytrack, firm and soft going: visored/blinkered: not straightforward: usually
held up. *W. J. Haggas*

SUGITANI (USA) 4 b.g. Kingmambo (USA) 125 – Lady Reiko (IRE) (Sadler's Wells **81**
(USA) 132) [2006 68: f11g² f12g⁴ p12g⁶ p16g⁴ f14g⁵* p13g² p13.9g* f12g⁴ 15s Apr 4]
sturdy gelding: fairly useful handicapper: won at Southwell and Wolverhampton (amateur event), both in March: stays easy 2m: acts on all-weather and good to firm going:
tongue tied at 2 yrs: sometimes blinkered: held up. *N. B. King*

SUHAYL STAR (IRE) 2 b.g. (Mar 31) Trans Island 119 – Miss Odlum (IRE) 81 **72**
(Mtoto 134) [2006 p5g² 5.2m⁵ 5g 7m⁴ 6f 7f⁶ 7m⁶ 7g* 7m² 7d 7d Oct 19] €13,000F,
€54,000Y: close-coupled, useful-looking gelding: first foal: dam Irish 1¼m winner: fair
performer: won claimer at Thirsk (left M. Channon £10,000) in August: best effort in
nurseries after when second at Chester: stays 7f: acts on polytrack and good to firm going:
visored (below form) once: often forces pace. *W. J. Musson*

SUHEZY (IRE) 3 b.f. Orpen (USA) 116 – Ervedya (IRE) (Doyoun 124) [2006 54: **56**
p6g f7g⁴ f6g f6g 5d⁴ 5m⁵ 6m² 6g 5.9m² 5f⁵ 7.5f 6.1f⁴ 7.2f² 5.9m⁶ 7s³ 7.1m⁴ 7.5g
Aug 31] plain, leggy filly: modest performer: left P. Midgley after eighth outing: effective
at 5f to 7f: acts on fibresand, firm and soft going: tried in cheekpieces (below form).
J. S. Wainwright

SUITS ME 3 ch.g. Bertolini (USA) 125 – Fancier Bit (Lion Cavern (USA) 117) [2006 **73**
80: p8g⁶ 6d 8m³ 9.9f 10f³ 8.9f⁵ 7d Aug 12] tall, close-coupled gelding: fair performer:
stays 9f (probably not 1¼m): acts on firm going: sometimes starts slowly: sold 17,000
gns, joined T. Tate. *J. J. Quinn*

SUIVEZ MOI (IRE) 4 ch.g. Daggers Drawn (USA) 114 – Pamiers (Huntercombe **–**
133) [2006 75: 8m 10.1g Aug 3] lengthy gelding: fair maiden at best: stayed 1¼m: acted
on polytrack and good to firm going: tried visored: dead. *M. F. Harris*

SUJANA (USA) 3 b.f. Grand Slam (USA) 120 – Indian Fashion (USA) 71 (General **–**
Holme (USA) 128) [2006 7g 8.2m May 3] $130,000Y: leggy, quite attractive filly: half-
sister to several winners, including smart 7f (at 2 yrs) and 11.4f winner Solaia (by
Miswaki): dam, second at 1m in Britain at 2 yrs, later won in USA and second in Grade 2
1½m event: well held in maidens: sold 36,000 gns in July, resold $82,000 in November.
B. J. Meehan

SUKI BEAR 2 br.f. (Jan 27) Xaar 132 – Dominion Rose (USA) 65 (Spinning World **73**
(USA) 130) [2006 6g* 6m 6.5s Sep 22] 22,000Y: close-coupled filly: first foal: dam, 7f
winner, closely related to smart Irish/US winner up to 9f Castledale: 50/1, fair form when
winning maiden at Windsor in August: no impact in better company after: will be suited
by 1m. *W. R. Muir*

SULARINA (IRE) 3 br.f. Alhaarth (IRE) 126 – Quiet Counsel (IRE) 81 (Law Society **74**
(USA) 130) [2006 8m⁴ Jul 30] 110,000F, 150,000Y: fifth foal: half-sister to French 1½m
winner Alithini and smart 1¼m/14.6f winner Discreet Brief (both by Darshaan): dam,
Irish 1½m winner, half-sister to Yorkshire Oaks winner Key Change: 14/1, shaped well
when 2½ lengths fourth to Pearl's Girl in maiden at Ascot, nearest finish not knocked
about: will be suited by 1¼m/1½m: looked sure to improve. *L. M. Cumani*

SULARNO 2 ch.c. (Apr 19) Medicean 128 – Star Precision 103 (Shavian 125) [2006 8s **79 p**
p7g f7g* Nov 13] strong, good-bodied colt: second foal: dam 1m to 13f winner: progressive in maidens, winning at Southwell: should be suited by 1m/1¼m: type to thrive at
3 yrs. *H. Morrison*

SULLIVAN'S CASCADE (IRE) 8 b.g. Spectrum (IRE) 126 – Sombre Lady (Shar- **–**
pen Up 127) [2006 p16.5g Jan 6] ex-Irish gelding: poor maiden handicapper: trained by
T. O'Mara in Ireland in 2003: unraced on Flat in 2004/5: no show only start at 8 yrs: stays
1¼m: acts on soft and good to firm ground: tried blinkered/tongue tied/in cheekpieces.
E. G. Bevan

SUMI GIRL (IRE) 2 b.f. (Apr 23) Tiger Hill (IRE) 127 – Allonia (GER) (Surumu **73**
(GER)) [2006 6s* Sep 4] fifth foal: half-sister to German 1¼m winner Amangani (by
Goofalik): dam 8.5f winner in Germany: 50/1, won maiden at Newcastle by 2½ lengths
from Love Dubai, patiently ridden. *R. A. Fahey*

SUMMER BOUNTY 10 b.g. Lugana Beach 116 – Tender Moment (IRE) 78 (Caerleon **71 §**
(USA) 132) [2006 81d, a53: p9.5g p12.2g⁵ 10.9s* 10.2d⁴ 10.2d p12g 10.2m 10.2m⁴ **a50 §**
12.6g 10m 10.9d³ 10d Oct 19] leggy, close-coupled gelding: fair handicapper on turf,
modest on all-weather: won at Warwick in April: effective at 1m to 1½m: acts on
all-weather and any turf going: tried blinkered/tongue tied: sometimes starts slowly (has
virtually refused to race): held up. *F. Jordan*

SUMMER CELEBRITY (IRE) 3 ch.f. Spinning World (USA) 130 – Summer Style **59**
(IRE) 70 (Indian Ridge 123) [2006 7g 6m² 6d³ Oct 2] €22,000Y: quite good-topped filly:
fourth foal: dam, second at 9f in Ireland, sister to very smart performer up to 1½m
Definite Article: modest form in maidens: sold 22,000 gns. *D. R. C. Elsworth*

SUMMER CHARM 4 b.f. Dansili 127 – Regent's Folly (IRE) 101 (Touching Wood **80**
(USA) 127) [2006 80, a76: p12.2g⁶ p13g 11g* 11.5m² 10s* 10m⁶ p10g 12m 11s Oct 10] **a73**
sturdy, close-coupled filly: fairly useful handicapper on turf, fair on all-weather: won at
Redcar in April and Sandown in May: stays 12.6f: acts on all-weather, soft and firm
going: waited with: unreliable: sold 58,000 gns, sent to Saudi Arabia. *W. Jarvis*

SUMMER DANCER (IRE) 2 br.g. (Mar 29) Fasliyev (USA) 120 – Summer Style **72 p**
(IRE) 70 (Indian Ridge 123) [2006 7m 7g⁴ 7d p8g* Dec 8] €26,000Y: tall gelding: fifth
foal: dam, second at 9f in Ireland, sister to very smart performer up to 1½m Definite
Article: fair form in maidens, winning easily at Kempton: gelded after: stays 1m: open to
improvement. *D. R. C. Elsworth*

SUMMER FORCE 4 ch.g. Tina's Pet 121 – Hustle An Bustle (USA) 59 (Lomond **–**
(USA) 128) [2006 –: 9.9g⁶ Aug 27] no form. *C. N. Kellett*

SUMMER LODGE 3 b.g. Indian Lodge (IRE) 127 – Summer Siren (FR) (Saint Cyrien **76**
(FR) 128) [2006 74: 8.3g 8m⁵ 10v³ 9m² 9.9m² 10m³ 10f² 10.3g³ p12.2m³ 12.4s³ p9.5g⁶
p9.5g⁴ f12g⁴ Dec 23] small, sturdy gelding: fair maiden: left M. Tompkins £30,000 after
eighth start: stays 1½m: acts on all-weather, firm and soft going: blinkered/visored
nowadays: hung left into runner-up and demoted fourth outing. *A. J. McCabe*

SUMMER OF LOVE (IRE) 2 b.f. (Feb 16) Fasliyev (USA) 120 – Overboard (IRE) **67**
73 (Rainbow Quest (USA) 134) [2006 7m p8.6g p8.6g⁵ p9.5g² Nov 16] big, rangy filly:
first foal: dam, maiden (placed at 1½m), half-sister to smart performer up to 1½m Red
Sea out of smart winner up to 1½m Up Anchor: fair maiden: gradual progress, second to
New Beginning at Wolverhampton: will stay 1½m. *P. F. I. Cole*

SUMMER RECLUSE (USA) 7 gr.g. Cozzene (USA) – Summer Retreat (USA) 78 **78**
(Gone West (USA)) [2006 79: 6d p5g² 6g³ 6m 6.1m³ 5.7m⁴ 6g⁵ 6f 6f³ 5.7m* 6.1m⁶ 5.7m
5.7f⁴ 5m 5.3d² p6g 5.3g⁶ p6g p6g⁴ p6g Nov 24] fair handicapper: won at Bath in August:
effective at 5.5f to 1m: acts on polytrack, firm and soft going: tried in cheekpieces:
usually tongue tied: sometimes slowly away: tough. *J. M. Bradley*

SUMMER'S EVE 3 gr.f. Singspiel (IRE) 133 – Early Rising (USA) (Grey Dawn II **104**
132) [2006 61p: 10g² 12m² 11.5m³ 9s* 9g³ 10d⁴ 9.9m²ᵈ 10.1m⁶ 10g³ Oct 12] lengthy
filly: useful performer: first past post in maidens at Folkestone (second start, demoted)
in April and Goodwood in May: good efforts when in frame after, in Prix Chloe at
Maisons-Laffitte (promoted third to disqualified Mandesha), Prix de Psyche at Deauville
(3¾ lengths fourth to Chaibia) and listed races at Salisbury (failed dope test and
disqualified after 4 lengths second behind Pictavia) and Newmarket (third to Innocent
Air): stays 1½m: acts on soft and good to firm going: has hung left. *H. Candy*

SUMMER SHADES 8 b.m. Green Desert (USA) 127 – Sally Slade 80 (Dowsing (USA) 124) [2006 67, a62: p8.6g⁴ f8g Mar 16] small mare: fair performer at best: well held in 2006: sometimes blinkered at 3 yrs: usually waited with: sold 5,000 gns in March. *W. M. Brisbourne* –

SUMMERTIME PARKES 3 ch.f. Silver Patriarch (IRE) 125 – Summerhill Spruce 70 (Windjammer (USA)) [2006 70p: 7s May 25] rangy filly: twice-raced maiden: well held only outing in 2006. *H. Candy* –

SUMMERVILLE STAR (IRE) 2 b.f. (Mar 31) Fruits of Love (USA) 127 – Alexandra Fair (USA) 104 (Green Dancer (USA) 132) [2006 7s p7g Nov 25] €4,500Y: half-sister to several winners, including useful French 1¼m to 12.5f winner Anticles (by Barathea) and Irish 13f winner Le-Monde (by Anabaa): dam French 1m (at 2 yrs) to 11f winner: little impact in maidens, including at Kempton. *Michael McElhone, Ireland* –

SUMNER (IRE) 2 b.c. (Mar 27) Xaar 132 – Black Jack Girl (IRE) (Ridgewood Ben 113) [2006 7d 7g p7g Nov 1] €5,000Y: big, workmanlike colt: third foal: dam well beaten both starts: not knocked about in mid-field in maidens, still backward second start: will stay 1m: type to do better in handicaps at 3 yrs. *M. H. Tompkins* **65 p**

SUN BIAN 4 b.c. Makbul 104 – Silken Dalliance 91 (Rambo Dancer (CAN) 107) [2006 71: 8.2s Apr 12] fair maiden at 3 yrs: well held only start in 2006. *L. P. Grassick*

SUNBOLT (IRE) 3 b.g. Barathea (IRE) 127 – Sunset (IRE) (Polish Precedent (USA) 131) [2006 65: 9v³ 9.9f 9.8g 12v⁵ p12.2g⁶ 8.3m f8g 9.3f 16g Aug 4] big, strong gelding: fair maiden: well below form after third outing: probably stays 1¼m: acts on heavy and good to firm going: tried blinkered: sold 7,000 gns. *T. D. Barron* **67 d**

SUNBURN (IRE) 2 b.g. (Jan 25) Mark of Esteem (IRE) 137 – Sundrenched (IRE) 99 (Desert King (IRE) 129) [2006 7g Oct 12] good-bodied gelding: 50/1 and backward, well beaten in maiden at Newmarket: subsequently gelded. *Mrs A. J. Perrett* –

SUN CATCHER (IRE) 3 b.g. Cape Cross (IRE) 129 – Taalluf (USA) 82 (Hansel (USA)) [2006 78: 8.1m p7g⁶ 6g* p6g 7d p7g⁶ p6g⁴ p6g Dec 20] good-topped gelding: fairly useful handicapper: won at Epsom in August: may prove best at 5f/6f: acts on polytrack and good to firm going: usually races prominently. *R. Hannon* **82**

SUNDAE 2 b.g. (Mar 23) Bahamian Bounty 116 – Merry Rous 66 (Rousillon (USA) 133) [2006 p6g⁶ Jul 13] 50,000Y: brother to 5-y-o Paradise Isle and 3-y-o Murfreesboro, and half-brother to several winners: dam, 2-y-o 6f winner, half-sister to very smart sprinter Tina's Pet: 25/1, sixth to Al Khaleej in maiden at Wolverhampton, racing prominently from wide draw: will prove best at 5f/6f: open to improvement. *C. F. Wall* **65 p**

SUNDANCE (IRE) 4 ch.g. Namid 128 – Titchwell Lass 57 (Lead On Time (USA) 123) [2006 84: 5m 7.1m 5s 6.1s p6g Nov 24] strong, lengthy gelding: has a round action: fairly useful performer: well below form after reappearance: needs to settle to stay beyond 5f: acts on polytrack and good to soft going: tried visored. *H. J. Collingridge* **81 d**

SUNDAY SYMPHONY 4 br.g. Sunday Silence (USA) – Darrery 98 (Darshaan 133) [2006 104: 13.4g² 13.9d* 14.1g Sep 14] big, useful-looking gelding: smart handicapper: won Ladbrokes Mallard Stakes at York in September easily by 5 lengths from Zurbaran: better other effort in 2006 when creditable 2 lengths second to New Guinea at Chester: stays 1¾m: acts on good to firm and good to soft going: blinkered last 2 starts at 3 yrs: usually wears crossed noseband: has hung left/carried head awkwardly: joined S. Seemar in UAE. *Saeed bin Suroor* **111**

SUNDERLAND ECHO (IRE) 3 ch.f. Tagula (IRE) 116 – La Alla Wa Asa (IRE) 60 (Alzao (USA) 117) [2006 60: f12g 8m 6v² 6d* 6g 6.1d* 6s⁴ 6d⁵ 6d⁶ 6s³ Aug 26] strong, lengthy filly: fairly useful performer: won maiden at Pontefract in April and handicap at Nottingham in May: seemingly good efforts in listed races 3 of last 4 starts, including when 2½ lengths third to Appalachian Trail at Newmarket: should stay 7f: acts well on soft/heavy ground: races prominently: has flashed tail. *B. Ellison* **87**

SUNDRIED TOMATO 7 b.g. Lugana Beach 116 – Little Scarlett 54 (Mazilier (USA) 107) [2006 70d: f7g p6g f7g⁶ f6g* p6g p6g f6g³ 6m⁶ 5.9m 5d 6m⁵ 6g 5d Oct 8] good-topped gelding: modest performer nowadays, better on all-weather than turf: won banded race at Southwell in March: effective at 5f to easy 7f: acts on all-weather, heavy and good to firm going: usually wears blinkers/cheekpieces: has bled: often races prominently. *D. W. Chapman* **50 a59**

SUNDRIVE (IRE) 2 ch.f. (Mar 30) Dr Fong (USA) 128 – Wood Sorrel (IRE) (Woodman (USA) 126) [2006 8d p8.6g⁶ Nov 18] €11,500F: first foal: dam unraced half-sister **50**

to useful winner up to 1¼m in France/Italy Relais d'Aumale: mid-field in maidens at Navan and Wolverhampton, sixth to Peregrine Falcon at latter. *E. Tyrrell, Ireland*

SUNGIO 8 b.g. Halling (USA) 133 – Time Or Never (FR) (Dowsing (USA) 124) [2006 63: p16g⁴ p12.2g f16g p12g 14.5d 12.5g a14g⁴ Oct 21] poor performer nowadays: left B. Baugh after fourth start: stays 16.5f: acts on all-weather, soft and good to firm going: sometimes slowly away: tried visored, usually blinkered nowadays. *R. Verheye, Belgium* — **49**

SUN HILL 6 b.g. Robellino (USA) 127 – Manhattan Sunset (USA) 76 (El Gran Senor (USA) 136) [2006 69§, a73§: f14g³ f14g⁴ f14g f14s* Mar 7] sturdy, close-coupled gelding: fair performer: won claimer at Southwell (claimed £6,000) in March: stays 2m: acts on all-weather and soft going: tried visored: has carried head awkwardly: unreliable. *C. W. Fairhurst* — **– §** / **a73 §**

SUNISA (IRE) 5 b.m. Daggers Drawn (USA) 114 – Winged Victory (IRE) 93 (Dancing Brave (USA) 140) [2006 81: 10.5g⁵ 12g²² 12d 10d⁵ Oct 4] robust, close-coupled mare: fairly useful handicapper: won at Salisbury in May: stays 1½m: acts on all-weather, soft and good to firm going: tongue tied in 2005. *J. Mackie* — **87**

SUNKEN RAGS 2 b.f. (Mar 14) Superior Premium 122 – Mise En Scene 85 (Lugana Beach 116) [2006 5g³ p5.1g* 5g 5m³ p5.1g⁶ Sep 30] 4,500Y: good-quartered filly: second foal: half-sister to 3-y-o Ace Baby: dam, 5f winner, raced only at 2 yrs: modest performer: won maiden at Wolverhampton in May: below form after in listed race and sellers: raced at 5f. *K. R. Burke* — **64 d**

SUN KING 9 ch.g. Zilzal (USA) 137 – Opus One 63 (Slip Anchor 136) [2006 57: 15.8g 12.4m⁵ 14.1d⁴ 14.1m⁴ 14.1m⁶ Sep 11] modest maiden on balance: should be suited by 2m+: acts on good to firm and good to soft going: tongue tied nowadays: won twice over hurdles in 2006. *K. G. Reveley* — **60**

SUNLEY GIFT 2 b.f. (Mar 24) Cadeaux Genereux 131 – Thracian 92 (Green Desert (USA) 127) [2006 5.2d* 5m 6f Sep 18] 56,000F: quite attractive filly: sixth foal: half-sister to several winners, including fairly useful 2001 2-y-o 7f winner Thrasher (by Hector Protector) and 2m winner Trilemma (by Slip Anchor): dam, 2-y-o 6f/7f winner, half-sister to very smart performers up to 1½m Maysoon, Richard of York and Three Tails: fair form: won minor event at Newbury in May: well beaten in Queen Mary Stakes and nursery 3 months apart: should be suited by 6f/7f. *M. R. Channon* — **70**

SUNLEY PEACE 2 ch.c. (Feb 22) Lomitas 129 – Messila Rose (Darshaan 133) [2006 8m 8g⁵ 8s³ 8s⁴ Oct 21] 25,000Y: strong, lengthy colt: has a quick action: fourth foal: dam unraced out of half-sister to US Grade 1 winners Musical Lark (7f at 2 yrs) and Spark of Life (1¼m): fairly useful form: promise all starts, in frame at Newbury last 2, third to Go On Be A Tiger in maiden and fourth to Bed Fellow in nursery (hampered/rallied): will stay 1¼m/1½m: type to do better in handicaps as 3-y-o. *D. R. C. Elsworth* — **80 p**

SUNLEY SONG 3 b.f. Fleetwood (IRE) 107 – Sunley Sinner 93 (Try My Best (USA) 130) [2006 p10g 10.9m p10g 12d⁶ Aug 23] half-sister to several winners, including sprinter Garnock Valley (by Dowsing) and 7f (at 2 yrs)/1m winner Sunley Seeker (by Elmaamul), both fairly useful: dam 2-y-o 7f winner: well held on Flat: won juvenile hurdle in September. *B. G. Powell* — **–**

SUNLEY SOVEREIGN 2 b.g. (Mar 15) Josr Algarhoud (IRE) 118 – Pharsical 80 (Pharly (FR) 130) [2006 6f 5f⁵ 7f³ 7.1d p6g⁶ Sep 30] modest maiden: stays 7f: acts on firm going. *M. R. Channon* — **64**

SUNLIGHT (IRE) 2 ch.f. (Mar 5) Sinndar (IRE) 134 – Church Light 88 (Caerleon (USA) 132) [2006 8m² p8g* Oct 20] tall, attractive filly, unfurnished at 2 yrs: half-sister to several winners, including useful Irish 7f (at 2 yrs)/9f winner Right Honorable (by Rainbows For Life) and fairly useful Irish 1½m winner Crested Pochard (by Desert King): dam 6f (at 2 yrs)/1m winner who stayed 1¼m: good impression in maidens, second to Light Shift at Newmarket prior to winning at Lingfield (odds on, made all) by 1¼ lengths from Gold Hush with bit in hand: will be suited by 1¼m/1½m: sure to make mark in higher grade. *M. A. Jarvis* — **92 p**

SUNNY AFTERNOON 6 ch.m. Atraf 116 – Pinup 44 (Risk Me (FR) 127) [2006 61: p7g p6g p6g² p7g Feb 25] modest performer nowadays: stays 1m: acts on polytrack, raced mainly on good going or firmer on turf: visored of late. *Miss E. C. Lavelle* — **61**

SUNNY DISPOSITION (IRE) 3 b.c. Desert Sun 120 – Madam Waajib (IRE) (Waajib 121) [2006 –: p10g 14.1m 16g Aug 4] big colt: little form. *E. F. Vaughan* — **–**

SUNNY HAZE 3 ch.f. Compton Place 125 – Sunrise Girl 62 (King's Signet (USA) 110) [2006 –: f6g⁴ 7g 6m 6d f6g f8g Nov 28] poor maiden: tried visored. *Mrs P. N. Dutfield* — **33**

SUNNY PARKES 3 ch.f. Arkadian Hero (USA) 123 – Janette Parkes 39 (Pursuit of **48**
Love 124) [2006 56: p8.6g⁶ p9.5g 8.1m 14m⁵ 14.1g 12d 16.1g Sep 27] tall filly: poor
maiden: has wandered under pressure. *M. Mullineaux*

SUNNYSIDE TOM (IRE) 2 b.g. (Apr 22) Danetime (IRE) 121 – So Kind 90 (Kind **82 p**
of Hush 118) [2006 6f⁶ 5f* Aug 15] 4,500Y: big, strong gelding: has plenty of scope:
half-brother to useful 1994 2-y-o 5f/6f winner Princely Hush (by Prince Sabo) and 1995
2-y-o 6f winner Sweet Nature (by Classic Secret): dam 6f winner who stayed 7f: much
improved from debut when winning maiden at Carlisle: should prove best at 5f/6f: type
to make a useful 3-y-o. *R. A. Fahey*

SUN OF THE GLEN (IRE) 4 b.f. Key of Luck (USA) 126 – Gaelic Foray (IRE) 63 **–**
(Unblest 117) [2006 p8.6g f8g 7g May 29] first foal: dam 7f winner: no sign of ability.
B. D. Leavy

SUN OF THE SEA 2 b.g. (Mar 6) Best of The Bests (IRE) 122 – Gem 58 (Most Wel- **58**
come 131) [2006 5f 5.1s p5.1g Oct 30] leggy gelding: modest form in maidens: gelded
after final outing. *N. P. Littmoden*

SUNOVERREGUN 2 b.c. (Feb 17) Noverre (USA) 125 – Jumairah Sun (IRE) 98 **81 p**
(Scenic 128) [2006 6g³ 6d* Nov 4] half-brother to several winners, including 4-y-o
Chrysander and 8-y-o Millennium Force: dam 1¼m winner who stayed 1½m: fairly
useful form: confirmed debut promise when winning maiden at Windsor (beat Kyle by ½
length): bred to be suited by 1m: likely to progress again. *J. R. Boyle*

SUN QUEST 2 b.c. (Jan 28) Groom Dancer (USA) 128 – Icaressa 56 (Anabaa (USA) **58**
130) [2006 6m⁴ 7f⁶ Aug 15] modest form when fourth in maiden at Windsor on debut:
seemed unsuited by track at Brighton: will stay at least 1m. *R. Hannon*

SUNRISE SAFARI (IRE) 3 b.g. Mozart (IRE) 131 – Lady Scarlett (Woodman (USA) **81**
126) [2006 97: 7.1g³ 6m* 6m Jun 17] lengthy gelding: won maiden at Hamilton in May:
stays 6f: acts on soft and good to firm going: visored last 2 starts. *I. Semple*

SUNSET BOULEVARD (IRE) 3 b.g. Montjeu (IRE) 137 – Lucy In The Sky (IRE) **67**
59 (Lycius (USA) 124) [2006 12d⁶ p12g⁵ 10d⁶ Oct 9] 140,000Y: leggy, useful-looking
gelding: third foal: dam 5f/6f winner: fair form in maidens: visored final start: sold 18,500
gns, and gelded. *J. Noseda*

SUNSET DREAMER (USA) 5 ch.m. Boundary (USA) 117 – Quaff (USA) 115 **48**
(Raise A Cup (USA)) [2006 48: p8g p7g p7g 10m³ 10f f11g p11g⁵ Nov 6] quite good-
topped mare: poor maiden: stays easy 11f: acts on polytrack and firm going: often wears
headgear. *P. Mitchell*

SUNSET RIDGE (IRE) 3 b.f. Indian Ridge 123 – Barbara Frietchie (IRE) (Try My **56 §**
Best (USA) 130) [2006 64: 6g 5.1g⁵ 5m⁴ 7f³ 7f³ 7m⁶ Sep 12] lengthy filly: modest
maiden: should stay 7f: acts on good to firm and good to soft going: tried in cheekpieces:
ungenuine: sold 5,000 gns. *Rae Guest*

SUNSHINE KID (USA) 2 b.c. (Feb 21) Lemon Drop Kid (USA) 131 – Nepenthe **94 p**
(USA) (Broad Brush (USA)) [2006 8m² 8s* 8s⁶ Oct 21] rather leggy, useful-looking colt:
first foal: dam 8.5f to 1½m (minor stakes winner) in USA: fairly useful form: second to
Empire Day at Newmarket, then won maiden at Newbury readily by 3½ lengths from
Ajhar in October: 10¼ lengths sixth of 14 to Authorized in Racing Post Trophy at latter
course, disputing lead over 1f out: will probably stay 1¼m/1½m: probably still capable
of better. *J. H. M. Gosden*

SUNSTROKE (IRE) 2 b.f. (Mar 4) Raphane (USA) 102 – Wish List (IRE) 98 (Mujadil **59**
(USA) 119) [2006 p5.1g 5f 5m⁴ 7f* 6f⁴ 7m³ 7.1m* 8m 8f⁵ 7.1d p8.6g⁶ Nov 18] 2,000F:
close-coupled filly: fourth foal: sister to winner in Greece: dam Irish 2-y-o 5f winner:
modest performer: won sellers at Brighton in July and Musselburgh in August: best short
of 1m: acts on firm going: blinkered (ran to form) once: sold 4,500 gns. *M. G. Quinlan*

SUNTAN LADY (IRE) 2 b.f. (Feb 16) Redback 116 – Scarletta (USA) 79 (Red **46**
Ransom (USA)) [2006 5d 5.1m f5g p6g⁴ 5d⁴ 5m 5.3m p5.1g f5g⁴ p6s² f5g⁴ p7.1g⁵
f6g⁶ Dec 23] strong, close-coupled filly: third foal: dam maiden should have stayed 1¼m:
poor maiden: in frame in nurseries 3 times: stays 7f: acts on all-weather and good to soft
going: in cheekpieces/visor last 5 starts. *Miss V. Haigh*

SUPA SAL 2 b.f. (Mar 18) King's Best (USA) 132 – Supamova (USA) 88 (Seattle Slew **73 p**
(USA)) [2006 p7.1g* Jul 11] seventh foal: half-sister to 1¼m/1½m winner Swellmova
(by Sadler's Wells) and 3-y-o Supaseus: dam, 8.5f winner, sister to very smart French 7f
to 9f performer Septieme Ciel: 7/1, promising start when winning maiden at Wolverhampton by 3 lengths, just pushed out: will be suited by 1m: sure to improve. *P. F. I. Cole*

SUPASEUS 3 b.g. Spinning World (USA) 130 – Supamova (USA) 88 (Seattle Slew **102**
(USA)) [2006 96: 8m* 8m 8m 8d* 8d⁵ 8d Oct 28] big, good-bodied gelding: useful performer: won maiden at Newmarket in May and handicap at Ascot (beat South Cape
by 2 lengths) in September: below form in handicaps at Pontefract and Newmarket after:
should stay 1¼m: acts on good to firm and good to soft going: tends to race lazily.
H. Morrison

SUPA TRAMP 3 b.g. Kayf Tara 130 – Shirley Superstar 94 (Shirley Heights 130) [2006 **67**
–p: p8.6g⁵ 11g³ Apr 25] well-made gelding: fair form in maidens: will be suited by
1½m+: sold 11,000 gns in July, joined G. L. Moore. *J. R. Fanshawe*

SUPER CANYON 8 ch.g. Gulch (USA) – Marina Park 112 (Local Suitor (USA) 128) **–**
[2006 48d: f7g p7.1g f8g May 16] poor performer: well held in 2006: tried visored/in
cheekpieces: tongue tied of late. *J. Pearce*

SUPERCAST (IRE) 3 b.g. Alhaarth (IRE) 126 – Al Euro (FR) 57 (Mujtahid (USA) **81**
118) [2006 85: p5g 5g 5d⁴ 5g 5g⁴ 5g 5g³ 5g⁵ 6d 5.3g p6g⁴ p7.1g⁵ p7.1g³ Dec 27] lengthy
gelding: fairly useful performer: left J. S. Moore 5,000 gns after tenth outing: probably
stays 7f: acts on polytrack, firm and good to soft going: tried in cheekpieces/blinkers: has
reared leaving stall: none too reliable. *W. M. Brisbourne*

SUPER CROSS (IRE) 2 b.c. (Mar 3) Cape Cross (IRE) 129 – Super Trouper (FR) 64 **77**
(Nashwan (USA) 135) [2006 7m 8.1g³ Sep 23] €100,000F, 52,000Y: good-topped colt:
first foal: dam, maiden who should have stayed 1¼m+, sister to useful performer up to
1½m Flamboyant Lad: better run in maidens when third to Petara Bay at Haydock, again
taking good hold. *E. A. L. Dunlop*

SUPER DOMINION 9 ch.g. Superpower 113 – Smartie Lee 66 (Dominion 123) [2006 **– §**
–§, a57§: p9.5g³ f8g p8.6g⁵ p10g p9.5g p9.5g⁴ p9.5g p8.6g 8f f8g Dec 12] sturdy gelding: **a53 §**
modest performer: effective at 7f to 1¼m: acts on all-weather, firm and soft going: tried in
visor, usually wears cheekpieces: tongue tied earlier in career: unreliable. *R. Hollinshead*

SUPERFLING 5 ch.g. Superpower 113 – Jobiska (Dunbeath (USA) 127) [2006 p9.5g **–**
12.1d May 30] lengthy gelding: modest maiden: well beaten in 2006. *H. J. Manners*

SUPER FRANK (IRE) 3 b.g. Cape Cross (IRE) 129 – Lady Joshua (IRE) 88 (Royal **71**
Academy (USA) 130) [2006 57p: p7g* p8g⁴ 9.7m 8m p7g p10g p10g 10.2m p7g* Dec
19] rather leggy gelding: fair handicapper: won at Lingfield in January and December
(first start after leaving G. Butler): stays 1m: acts on polytrack: has been blinkered/tongue
tied. *J. Akehurst*

SUPERIOR DREAM 4 b.g. Superpower 113 – California Dreamin (Slip Anchor 136) **–**
[2006 p8.6g Jan 20] tailed off in bumper at Huntingdon for J. Panvert and maiden at
Wolverhampton. *J. W. Unett*

SUPERIOR POINT 3 b.f. Superior Premium 122 – Raisa Point 60 (Raised Socially **–**
(USA)) [2006 p6g Jan 29] 800Y: fourth foal: dam 5f maiden: 66/1, well held in maiden at
Lingfield: sold £1,300 in April. *P. Howling*

SUPERIOR STAR 3 b.g. Superior Premium 122 – Lindfield Belle (IRE) 78 (Fairy **73**
King (USA)) [2006 68: 5v⁵ 8g² 7m 8.5f⁶ 8.1m² 9d* 8m Aug 9] quite good-topped gelding: fair handicapper: won at Musselburgh in August: stays 9f: acts on firm and good to
soft going: often blinkered/visored. *R. A. Fahey*

SUPERJAIN 2 b.f. (Mar 27) Lujain (USA) 119 – Plie 75 (Superlative 118) [2006 p6g⁵ **60**
5.1d³ f5g⁵ p6g Dec 8] 3,500Y: leggy, quite attractive filly: half-sister to several winners,
including 4-y-o Bahamian Ballet and 6-y-o Dispol Peto: dam, 2-y-o 6f winner, stayed
1m: modest maiden: third to Kompete at Nottingham, only turf start: raced at 5f/6f.
J. M. Jefferson

SUPER NEBULA 2 b.c. (Jan 25) Fantastic Light (USA) 134 – It Girl 60 (Robellino **–**
(USA) 127) [2006 p7.1g Oct 8] 100/1, well held in maiden at Wolverhampton.
P. L. Gilligan

SUPERSHOT (IRE) 8 b.g. Son of Sharp Shot (IRE) 105 – One To Two (IRE) (Astro- **–**
nef 116) [2006 61: 9s Sep 24] strong, workmanlike gelding: modest maiden: well beaten
only start in 2006. *O. Brennan*

SUPER SIFTED (GER) 2 b.f. (Apr 14) Saddlers' Hall (IRE) 126 – Sun Moon Stars **–**
(IRE) (Shahrastani (USA) 135) [2006 p8.6m Nov 21] €12,000Y: fifth foal: half-sister to
German 9.5f to 12.5f winner Sunmoon Island (by Turtle Island): dam German 1m winner:
16/1, eighth in maiden at Wolverhampton. *H. R. A. Cecil*

SUPERSONIC DAVE (USA) 2 b. or br.c. (Apr 21) Swain (IRE) 134 – Vickey's Echo **89 p**
(CAN) (Clever Trick (USA)) [2006 7d* Sep 29] $55,000Y, 70,000 2-y-o: workmanlike
colt: brother to 2 winners in USA and half-brother to smart US winner up to 1½m French
Braids (by Personal Flag): dam maiden: 8/1, won maiden at Newmarket by ¾ length from
Kirk Michael, bit unbalanced when driven ahead: likely to stay 1½m: should improve.
B. J. Meehan

SUPPORT FUND (IRE) 2 ch.f. (Mar 4) Intikhab (USA) 135 – Almost A Lady (IRE) **67 p**
70 (Entitled 126) [2006 6m³ 5.7m³ Sep 25] 13,000Y: eighth foal: closely related to useful
2001 2-y-o 6f and 1m winner Henri Lebasque (by Sri Pekan) and half-sister to 2 winners,
including fairly useful 2005 2-y-o 1m winner Almost Spinning (by Spinning World):
dam, second at 1m at 2 yrs in Ireland, half-sister to very smart 1¼m performer Insatiable:
encouraging third in maidens at Lingfield and Bath (beaten 1¾ lengths by Maker's
Mark): will be suited by 1m: likely to improve. *R. F. Johnson Houghton*

SUPPOSE (USA) 2 b.f. (Jan 22) Danehill (USA) 126 – Sophisticat (USA) 117 (Storm **76**
Cat (USA)) [2006 7m 6m⁵ 5m⁶ Aug 10] smallish, well-made filly: first foal: dam, 6f (at
2 yrs) and 1m (including Coronation Stakes) winner, out of multiple US Grade 1 winner
Serena's Song: best run (fair form) in maidens when fifth to Sacre Coeur at Goodwood:
should stay 1m. *A. P. O'Brien, Ireland*

SUPPOSITION 2 b.f. (Mar 20) Dansili 127 – Topicality (USA) (Topsider (USA)) **103 p**
[2006 7g² 7d* 7m³ 7g Sep 16] seventh live foal: half-sister to smart 6f to 1m winner
Border Subject (by Selkirk) and 6f and 1m winner Toppling (by Cadeaux Genereux):
dam, French 1m winner, sister to smart performer up to 1m Top Socialite and half-sister
to 2000 Guineas runner-up/US Grade 1 1¼m winner Exbourne: useful form: runner-up to
Duke of Marmalade at the Curragh before winning maiden at Galway by 7 lengths in
August: more progress when length third of 12 to Miss Beatrix in Moyglare Stud Stakes
at the Curragh: odds on, badly hampered and eased in C. L. Weld Park Stakes at the
Curragh: will stay 1m: capable of better yet. *D. K. Weld, Ireland*

SUPREME CHARTER 3 b.g. Diktat 126 – Alchi (USA) 112 (Alleged (USA) 138) **81**
[2006 81: 10.5g p12g 10d p12.2m⁶ p9.5g Nov 28] leggy gelding: fairly useful performer **a71**
on turf, fair on all-weather: stays 1¼m: acts on firm and good to soft going: blinkered
final outing: carries head high. *M. Johnston*

SUPREME KISS 3 b.f. Barathea Guest 117 – Kiss Me Again (IRE) 80 (Cyrano de **66**
Bergerac 120) [2006 67: p5g 5.1g⁴ 5m⁵ 5m 5m⁴ 5d 5.1m³ 5.7m⁵ p6g² p5g p6g² p6g³
Nov 28] good-topped filly: fair maiden handicapper: left Miss B. Sanders after seventh
start: raced only at 5f/6f: acts on polytrack and good to firm going: tried blinkered/tongue
tied: often slowly away: held up. *Mrs N. Smith*

SUPREME SALUTATION 10 ch.g. Most Welcome 131 – Cardinal Press (Sharrood **–**
(USA) 124) [2006 66, a63: f8g⁵ p8g³ f8g⁵ f8g f8g p7.1g 10.2g p10g May 15] leggy, **a60**
sparely-made gelding: modest performer: effective at 7f to 11f: acts on all-weather and
any turf going: tried blinkered (not since 2001): sometimes slowly away. *D. K. Ivory*

SUPREME SPEEDSTER 2 br.c. (Apr 4) Superior Premium 122 – Effervescent 89 **82**
(Efisio 120) [2006 5g* 5g 5g Aug 19] 6,000Y, resold 28,000Y: rather leggy, close-
coupled colt: first foal: dam 6f winner who stayed 7f: fairly useful form when winning
maiden at Beverley in May: weakened as if amiss in minor event and nursery, off 3
months/left K. Ryan in between. *T. R. George*

SURDOUE 6 b.g. Bishop of Cashel 122 – Chatter's Princess (Cadeaux Genereux 131) **60**
[2006 60: f12g⁶ f11g² f11g* f11g* f11g p10g Mar 22] leggy gelding: modest performer
nowadays: won banded races at Southwell in January and February: stays easy 1½m: acts
on fibresand and good to firm ground: tried in cheekpieces. *P. Howling*

SURELY TRULY (IRE) 3 b.f. Trans Island 119 – Londubh (Tumble Wind) [2006 82: **65**
6d p7g 6d⁶ 6m p8g² p6g p6s Dec 15] rather leggy filly: just fair form in 2006: claimed
from K. Burke £12,000 after fifth start: stays easy 1m: acts on polytrack, good to firm and
good to soft going: in cheekpieces/visored last 6 starts. *A. E. Jones*

SURF CITY 3 ch.c. Distant Music (USA) 126 – Tolyatti (Green Desert (USA) 127) **–**
[2006 73d: 7.5d Apr 19] tall colt: maiden: well held only start at 3 yrs: should stay 1m:
has worn blinkers/cheekpieces last 4 starts: sold 500 gns, sent to Sweden. *R. A. Harris*

SURPRISE PENSION (IRE) 2 b.g. (Feb 16) Fruits of Love (USA) 127 – Sheryl **52**
Lynn (Miller's Mate 116) [2006 6s 6m 7s Oct 10] stocky gelding: modest form second
start in maidens. *J. J. Quinn*

SURREY SPINNER 2 ch.c. (Apr 23) Intikhab (USA) 135 – Markievicz (IRE) 73   **53 p**
(Doyoun 124) [2006 6g Jun 15] 45,000Y: strong, good-bodied colt: half-brother to unreliable 6f (including at 2 yrs) winner Oases (by Zilzal) and 1¼m to 2m winner Paarl Rock
(by Common Grounds): dam Irish 6.5f winner: 7/2, green and soon behind in maiden at
Newbury: will be better for experience. *Mrs A. J. Perrett*

SURWAKI (USA) 4 b.g. Miswaki (USA) 124 – Quinella (Generous (IRE) 139) [2006   **84**
–: p8g 7m² 8g³ 7m 7g 7m⁴ 8.3d* 8d p7g Nov 24] close-coupled gelding: fairly useful
handicapper: fractured pelvis only 3-y-o start: won at Leicester in August: left C. Cox
15,000 gns after eighth outing: stays 1m: acts on good to firm and soft going.
R. M. H. Cowell

SUSANNA'S PROSPECT (IRE) 2 ch.f. (Feb 2) Namid 128 – Substantive (USA)   **64**
(Distant View (USA) 126) [2006 6g 6d p7g 6g⁴ 6d⁴ p8g Nov 8] 7,000Y: first foal: dam,
last on only outing, half-sister to smart 6f/7f winner Demonstrate: modest maiden: best
run when fourth in nursery at Catterick fifth start: better at 6f than further: acts on polytrack and good to soft ground. *B. J. Meehan*

SUSIEDIL (IRE) 5 b.m. Mujadil (USA) 119 – Don't Take Me (IRE) (Don't Forget Me   **37 §**
127) [2006 49§: f8g f8g Mar 8] close-coupled mare: poor performer: stays 1½m: acts on
fibresand and firm ground: tried visored: sometimes hangs: unreliable. *D. Nicholls*

SUSIE MAY 2 ch.f. (Feb 17) Hernando (FR) 127 – Mohican Girl 112 (Dancing Brave   **51**
(USA) 140) [2006 p8g p8g Nov 5] 3,500Y: half-sister to 3 winners, including useful 7.6f
to 9f winner The Prince (by Machiavellian): dam, 1¼m/11.4f winner, half-sister to Yorkshire Oaks winners Untold and Sally Brown: green in maidens at Lingfield: bred to stay
1¼m+. *C. A. Cyzer*

SUZIEBLUE (IRE) 2 b.f. (Apr 14) Redback 116 – Blue Holly (IRE) 83 (Blues Travel-   **50**
ler (IRE) 119) [2006 5g 5f 6f⁶ 5.1d* 5.1g 5.2f⁶ 5.1f⁴ p5.1g² p5.1g Sep 30] 7,500Y: first
foal: dam, 5f (including at 2 yrs)/6f winner, half-sister to smart 7f/1m performer Rockets
'N Rollers: modest performer: raced mainly in sellers, winning at Chepstow in June: best
at 5f: acts on polytrack, firm and good to soft going: usually in cheekpieces/blinkers.
J. S. Moore

SUZUKI (IRE) 3 ch.f. Barathea (IRE) 127 – Nishan (Nashwan (USA) 135) [2006 10m   **55**
f11g 10g 16.2m⁶ 11.9m Sep 19] 77,000Y: sister to 1½m winner Molomo and 1m to 1¾m
winner Pepperwood (both useful, in Ireland) and half-sister to 2 winners: dam French
maiden: modest maiden: sold 32,000 gns. *H. Morrison*

SUZY BLISS 3 b.f. Spinning World (USA) 130 – Poppy Carew (IRE) 110 (Danehill   **105**
(USA) 126) [2006 95: p8g⁴ 9.9g⁴ 8.5g 12m Jun 22] small, close-coupled filly: has a
quick, unimpressive action: useful performer: fourth in listed races at Kempton and
Goodwood (3¾ lengths behind dead-heaters Rising Cross and Soft Centre): best effort
when 3½ lengths seventh to Mont Etoile in Ribblesdale Stakes at Royal Ascot final start:
stays 1½m: acts on polytrack, good to firm and good to soft going. *W. R. Swinburn*

SVENSON 5 ch.h. Dancing Spree (USA) – Bella Bambola (IRE) 42 (Tate Gallery   **–**
(USA) 117) [2006 7g May 29] strong, workmanlike horse: little form (missed 2005).
J. S. Wainwright

SVEN (SWE) 2 b.g. (Apr 5) Duty Time 104 – Last Romance (IRE) (Last Tycoon 131)   **–**
[2006 8.2s Oct 18] strong, sturdy gelding: well held in maiden at Nottingham: bred to
stay 1½m. *B. I. Case*

SWAINS BRIDGE (USA) 4 b.c. Swain (IRE) 134 – Saraa Ree (USA) 102 (Caro 133)   **79**
[2006 75+: 7m⁶ 10.1f* 10f⁵ 10d⁵ Aug 13] strong colt: fair performer: won handicap at
Yarmouth in July: stays 1¼m: acts on firm going: sold 13,000 gns. *L. M. Cumani*

SWAINSON (USA) 5 br.g. Swain (IRE) 134 – Lyphard's Delta (USA) 112 (Lyphard   **72**
(USA) 132) [2006 79: p13g⁴ p12.2g p12g⁵ p12g³ 15.4m³ p12g p16g⁶ Dec 15] sturdy
gelding: fair handicapper: stays 13f: acts on polytrack and good to firm going: tried
blinkered/in cheekpieces: sometimes races freely. *P. Mitchell*

SWALLOW SENORA (IRE) 4 b.f. Entrepreneur 123 – Sangra (USA) 69 (El Gran   **46**
Senor (USA) 136) [2006 50: 6f 6m 5g 5d 6d f6g⁴ f6g⁵ f6g Dec 28] lightly-made filly:
poor maiden: tried blinkered. *M. C. Chapman*

SWAN OF RAUNDS 2 b.g. (Apr 3) Fraam 114 – Persian Fortune 53 (Forzando 122)   **–**
[2006 p7.1g 7d 8.1g Sep 23] tailed off in maidens. *J. R. Norton*

SWAN QUEEN 3 br.f. In The Wings 128 – Bronzewing 103 (Beldale Flutter (USA)   **85**
130) [2006 –p: 10d⁴ 12m* 12s* p11g Sep 1] lengthy, angular filly: fairly useful perfor-

mer: won maiden at Folkestone (awarded race) in April and handicap at York in May: tailed off final outing: will stay 1¾m: acts on soft and good to firm going. *J. L. Dunlop*

SWAYZE (IRE) 3 b.g. Marju (IRE) 127 – Dance of Love (IRE) 99 (Pursuit of Love **69** 124) [2006 62: 8.2s 10d* p12.2g 10m Jul 30] good-topped gelding: fair performer: won handicap at Redcar in May: stays 1¼m: acts on polytrack and heavy going. *N. P. Littmoden*

SWEENEY (IRE) 2 ch.c. (Jan 15) Jade Robbery (USA) 121 – Arduine 79 (Diesis 133) **95 p** [2006 p8g* p8g* Dec 16] third foal: half-brother to French 1¼m/17f winner Country Fair (by Timber Country): dam, maiden who stayed 1¼m, out of half-sister to Oaks winner Ramruma: created very good impression when winning maiden and minor event at Lingfield in December: odds on, beat Nordic Affair by 1¼ lengths for latter success, merely pushed out: will stay 1¼m: loose in paddock and troublesome at stall on debut: sure to improve further. *M. A. Jarvis*

SWEET AFTON (IRE) 3 b.f. Mujadil (USA) 119 – Victory Peak (Shirley Heights **98** 130) [2006 96: 5.1g 6f⁵ 8m 6f* 6m⁴ 6g⁶ 6g 7.5g Aug 24] lengthy filly: poor mover: useful performer: won minor event at Fairyhouse in July: creditable efforts in listed races at Fairyhouse and Leopardstown next 2 starts: below form in Britain on 4 occasions: stays 6f: raced only on good going or firmer (acts on firm): sweating final start at 2 yrs: sold 35,000 gns. *E. Tyrrell, Ireland*

SWEET BOULANGERE 3 ch.f. Grand Lodge (USA) 125 – Cybinka 107 (Selkirk **64** 129) [2006 70: p8g p10g 10.5g⁵ p10g 11.5m 10f Jul 18] good-bodied filly: just modest maiden handicapper in 2006: best efforts at 6f: acts on firm going: sold 3,500 gns in August, resold €5,000 in November. *R. Hannon*

SWEET CANDY 2 ch.f. (Mar 26) Cadeaux Genereux 131 – Hajat 64 (Mujtahid (USA) **67** 118) [2006 5g⁴ 5g p7g⁵ p6g* p6g⁵ 6d 6m 6.5s 6v³ Oct 9] 18,000Y: tall filly: fifth foal: **a76** half-sister to 2001 2-y-o 7f winner Desert Royal (by Ali-Royal) and 3-y-o Imperial Sword: dam 5f winner: fair performer: won nursery at Wolverhampton in July: best at 5f/ 6f: acts on polytrack and heavy going: well held in cheekpieces (stiff task): sold 10,000 gns, sent to USA. *K. A. Ryan*

SWEET CHEROKEE 3 b.f. Mind Games 121 – Sioux Lady (Petong 126) [2006 –: **41** p5.1g⁴ p6g⁴ p6g⁶ f7g p6g f7g⁵ f5g Apr 10] smallish filly: poor maiden: stays 6f: acts on polytrack: blinkered last 2 starts. *C. N. Kellett*

SWEET EMILY 4 ch.f. Inchinor 119 – Thamud (IRE) (Lahib (USA) 129) [2006 84p: **72** 7m p7.1g 7m⁴ 7g⁵ 7m 7s³ 8.5s 7s Oct 30] fair handicapper: sold from J. Fanshawe 10,000 gns after third start: stays 7f: acts on soft ground: hung right/found little third outing. *P. J. Flynn, Ireland*

SWEETEST REVENGE (IRE) 5 ch.m. Daggers Drawn (USA) 114 – Joza 90 (Mar- **60** ju (IRE) 127) [2006 72: p7.1g p6g³ p6g² p6g p6g* p6g* p6g⁵ p5g⁶ p5g 7.1m 7m 6m 6m **a78** 6f 5.1g⁶ 6.1m⁵ 5m p6m³ p6g* Oct 15] leggy mare: fair handicapper on all-weather, modest on turf: won at Lingfield in February, Wolverhampton in March and Lingfield in October: effective at 5f to easy 7f: acts on polytrack, firm and good to soft going: tried in cheekpieces/visor. *M. D. I. Usher*

SWEET GEORGIE BEE (IRE) 2 b.c. (Feb 29) Titus Livius (FR) 115 – Duck Over **63** 72 (Warning 136) [2006 5g⁶ Jun 2] sixth in minor event at Catterick: dead. *R. A. Fahey*

SWEETHEART 2 b.f. (Mar 8) Sinndar (IRE) 134 – Love And Adventure (USA) **62** (Halling (USA) 133) [2006 p8g⁶ p9.5g⁴ Dec 7] second foal: half-sister to French 2005 2-y-o 9f winner Love Knot (by Lomitas): dam useful French 7f (at 2 yrs) and 1m winner: modest form in maidens: will stay 1¼m. *M. A. Jarvis*

SWEET INDULGENCE (IRE) 5 ch.g. Inchinor 119 – Silent Indulgence (USA) **102** (Woodman (USA) 126) [2006 86: 12d⁶ 10g³ 12m⁶ 12g* 14v 12d 12s³ p12g* p12g* p12.2s* Dec 15] lengthy gelding: useful handicapper: improved at 5 yrs, winning at Newmarket in August, Lingfield (twice, beating Cold Turkey by 1¾ lengths in latter) in November and Wolverhampton (by neck from Millville) in December: stays 1¾m, seemed to find stamina stretched at 2¼m (2005 Cesarewitch): acts on polytrack, soft and good to firm going, possibly not on heavy: tends to race freely/carry head awkwardly: consistent. *W. J. Musson*

SWEET LAVINIA 3 ch.f. Lomitas 129 – Latch Key Lady (USA) 48 (Tejano (USA)) **51** [2006 8m 9.8m⁴ 9.9m⁶ 10m⁶ 16.1g⁵ 13.8s f14g Nov 2] 6,500Y: sparely-made filly: sixth living foal: half-sister to 1999 2-y-o 5f seller winner Foxkey (by Foxhound): dam well beaten after debut: modest maiden: stays 2m: acts on good to firm going. *J. D. Bethell*

totesport.com Silver Tankard Stakes, Pontefract—Sweet Lilly makes it four wins in five starts, seeing off the favourite Champlain with a swish of her tail

SWEET LILLY 2 b.f. (Mar 4) Tobougg (IRE) 125 – Maristax 74 (Reprimand 122) **100** [2006 6m p7g³ 7m³ 7f* 7m* 8g* 8g⁴ 8s* Oct 16] 12,000Y: big, rangy filly: fourth foal: half-sister to 6-y-o Ofaraby: dam 2-y-o 7f winner: useful performer: improved right through season, winning maiden and minor event at Yarmouth, nursery at Salisbury and listed race at Pontefract, last-named by 1¾ lengths from Champlain and Empire Day: also ran well when 2¼ lengths fourth of 9 to Simply Perfect in May Hill Stakes at York: likely to stay 1¼m: acts on polytrack, firm and soft going: not straightforward (tail flasher). *M. R. Channon*

SWEETLY SHARP (IRE) 3 ch.f. Daggers Drawn (USA) 114 – Pecan Pie (IRE) (Sri **47** Pekan (USA) 117) [2006 53: 5d 6m 5.9g³ 5g 6m 5v f6g Dec 5] lightly-made filly: poor performer: stays 6f: acts on soft going: tried in cheekpieces. *A. Berry*

SWEET MEDICINE 4 ch.f. Dr Devious (IRE) 127 – Crimley Crumb (Rainbow Quest **78 d** (USA) 134) [2006 p12.2g² p8g³ p12.2g³ 15.4m⁴ 11.5f⁴ 12m p8.6g p12.2g⁶ Dec 28] first foal: dam ran twice in Irish bumpers: fourth in bumper on debut: fair maiden: stays 15.4f: raced only on polytrack and firm/good to firm going. *P. Howling*

SWEET NAMIBIA (IRE) 4 ch.f. Namid 128 – Almond Flower (IRE) (Alzao (USA) **58** 117) [2006 67: p6g p7.1g p8g Feb 7] good-quartered filly: just modest performer in 2006: effective at 5f/6f: acts on good to soft going: sold 23,000 gns. *J. W. Hills*

SWEET PICKLE 5 b.m. Piccolo 121 – Sweet Wilhelmina 87 (Indian Ridge 123) **74** [2006 65: p6g¹ f7g⁵ p6g p6g⁴ p6g f6g* f6s* f6g⁶ p6g⁴ f7g³ 6f³ 6f² 6g f6g² 7g* 6f² 6m⁴ 6m⁶ 6m f6g² f6g³ f6g Dec 23] leggy mare: fair performer: won 2 handicaps at Southwell in March and claimer at Epsom in August: stays 7f: acts on all-weather and firm going: visored first 3 starts in 2005, wears eyeshields nowadays: often held up. *J. R. Boyle*

SWEET REQUEST 2 ch.f. (Apr 8) Best of The Bests (IRE) 122 – Sweet Revival 41 **63 p** (Claude Monet (USA) 121) [2006 p7g⁶ Sep 18] tall, good-topped filly: half-sister to several winners, notably very smart US Grade 1 9f/1¼m winner Sweet Return (by Elmaamul), 7.5f winner in Britain at 2 yrs: dam 1¼m winner: 25/1, sixth to Regal Quest in maiden at Kempton, soon lot to do: capable of better. *R. M. Beckett*

SWEET ROSELLA 3 b.f. Alhaarth (IRE) 126 – Thamud (IRE) (Lahib (USA) 129) **–** [2006 42: f7g⁶ f6g Feb 23] maiden: well held in 2006. *G. M. Moore*

SWEET SEVILLE (FR) 2 b.f. (Mar 25) Agnes World (USA) 123 – Hispalis (IRE) **55** (Barathea (IRE) 127) [2006 6m Aug 11] smallish filly: first foal: dam, French 11f winner, sister to smart French 9f/1¼m performer Hidalguia: backward, eighth in maiden at Haydock. *Mrs G. S. Rees*

SWEET SOUL DIVA 2 b.f. (Apr 6) Cadeaux Genereux 131 – Alarming Motown **42** (Warning 136) [2006 p7g 6g 6d⁵ 8g a8g a6d Dec 17] rather leggy filly: fourth foal: half-sister to 5-y-o Mr Belvedere: dam, ran twice, out of half-sister to top-class sprinter Committed: poor maiden: sold from Miss V. Haigh 8,500 gns after fourth start. *Mrs S. Dysell, Sweden*

SWEET SPOT 3 ch.f. Generous (IRE) 139 – Cutting Glance (USA) (Woodman (USA) **91** 126) [2006 60: 7m⁴ 10.2g² 10m² 10g 8m* 9.5m² 8d Aug 16] 6,000Y: leggy filly: second foal: dam ran twice in France: fairly useful performer: won maiden at Bellewstown in July· better effort in Britain when second in similar event at Bath second start: stays 1¼m: acts on good to firm going: sold 38,000 gns, sent to USA. *E. Tyrrell, Ireland*

SWEET STREAM (ITY) 6 b.m. Shantou (USA) 125 – Snug Dinner (IRE) (Jareer **117** (USA) 115) [2006 117: 10s² 12g⁵ Oct 15] tall mare: smart performer: reportedly suffered fractured hind foot early in year but still as good as ever when making eye-catching belated reappearance over inadequate trip when 1½ lengths second to Satwa Queen in Prix Jean Romanet at Deauville: creditable 2¼ lengths fifth to Cherry Mix in Gran Premio del Jockey Club Italiano at Milan only other start: ideally needs further than 1¼m and stays 14.6f: unraced on firm ground, acts on any other: tried blinkered/tongue tied. *J. E. Hammond, France*

SWEET TRAVEL (IRE) 3 b.f. Danzig (USA) – Raise A Beauty (USA) (Alydar **101** (USA)) [2006 99: 7g⁴ 7d³ 6d³ 5m Sep 10] leggy, angular filly: has a quick action: sister to 2 winners, notably smart French 5f (at 2 yrs) to 7f winner Iron Mask, and half-sister to 2 winners, including French 1998 2-y-o 1m winner Beautimix (by Linamix): dam, French 9f winner, half-sister to dam of Dayjur (by Danzig): useful maiden: runner-up all 3 starts in 2005, including in Prix d'Arenberg at Chantilly and Prix Eclipse at Maisons-Laffitte: good efforts first 2 outings on return when 2 lengths fourth to Speciosa in Nell Gwyn Stakes at Newmarket and length third to Sabasha in listed race at Deauville: below best last 2 starts, in Prix du Petit Couvert at Longchamp final one: needs further than 5f and stays 7f: acts on good to soft going. *A. Fabre, France*

SWEET TREAT (IRE) 4 b.f. Orpen (USA) 116 – Canton Lightning 102 (Rheingold **102** 137) [2006 107: 8g² 8v⁵ 8m² 7d 8d Sep 23] €110,000Y: attractive filly: half-sister to several winners, including Irish 1m winner Attalicus (by Lake Coniston) and Irish 1997 2-y-o 1m/9f winner Chenille (by Tenby), later successful in USA, both fairly useful: dam 1¼m winner: useful performer: won maiden at Cork in 2005: left J. Oxx in Ireland, best effort in 2006 when 1¼ lengths second to Nantyglo in listed race at Goodwood on reappearance: not discredited when neck second to Three Wrens in similar event at Bath, then repeatedly hampered when eighth in listed handicap at Ascot: stays 1m: acts on soft going: below form in blinkers final start at 3 yrs. *J. R. Fanshawe*

SWEET WORLD 2 b.g. (Apr 2) Agnes World (USA) 123 – Douce Maison (IRE) 67 **63** (Fools Holme (USA)) [2006 p7g⁴ p7g p8.6g p7g³ p8g p6g³ Dec 5] 16,000Y, resold 10,000Y: closely related to useful German miler Montestefano and 6-y-o Zariano (both by Emperor Jones), and half-brother to 2 winners by Distant Relative: dam 1m winner who stayed 1½m: modest maiden: third in 2 nurseries at Kempton: effective at 6f, seems to stay 8.6f: raced on polytrack. *A. P. Jarvis*

SWELL LAD 4 b.g. Sadler's Wells (USA) 132 – Lydara (USA) (Alydar (USA)) [2006 **59 §** 51§: p8.6g⁶ p10g p16g p9.5g Mar 20] lengthy gelding: modest maiden nowadays: stays 1m: acts on firm going: tried blinkered/in cheekpieces: unreliable. *S. Gollings*

SWIFT CUT (IRE) 2 ch.c. (Apr 26) Daggers Drawn (USA) 114 – Jugendliebe (IRE) **76** (Persian Bold 123) [2006 6m 6m² 6g² p7g* p6g Oct 23] 20,000Y: compact colt: half-brother to 3 winners, including useful 2002 2-y-o 6f winner All Nines (later 9f/1¼m winner in Hong Kong) and 2004 2-y-o 5f winner Alvarinho Lady (both by Royal Applause): dam German 1¼m winner: fair performer: twice runner-up before winning maiden at Lingfield in October: stays 7f. *A. P. Jarvis*

SWIFT IMAGE 2 gr.f. (Apr 1) Act One 124 – Swift Dispersal 87 (Shareef Dancer **83 p** (USA) 135) [2006 6m² 7.1m* Sep 4] close-coupled, good-bodied filly: second foal: dam 6f/7f winner: shaped promisingly in maidens, second to Winged Flight at Yarmouth prior to winning at Warwick decisively by 2½ lengths from Sophia Gardens: will stay 1m: useful performer in the making. *S. C. Williams*

SWIFTLY ADDICTED (IRE) 2 ch.f. (Mar 19) King's Best (USA) 132 – Swiftly 73 **60 p** (Cadeaux Genereux 131) [2006 6m 7f p6g 5g² p5g Sep 30] 26,000Y: unfurnished filly: first foal: dam 2-y-o 5f winner: fair maiden: shaped well in nurseries last 2 starts, second at Sandown and eighth at Kempton (stopped in run): should prove suited to 6f/7f: still unexposed. *A. King*

SWIFT OSCAR 4 b.g. Mark of Esteem (IRE) 137 – Surf Bird (Shareef Dancer (USA) **88** 135) [2006 87: p8g⁴ p8g⁴ p8g⁴ Feb 1] close-coupled, useful-looking gelding: has a quick action: fairly useful handicapper, better on all-weather than turf: good efforts in frame all 3 starts in 2006: effective at 7f to 8.6f: acts on polytrack and firm ground: swerved left third start at 3 yrs: sent to Macau. *J. W. Hills*

SWIFT PRINCESS (IRE) 2 b.f. (Feb 16) Namid 128 – Swift Chorus (Music Boy –
124) [2006 6.1d Oct 4] 21,000Y: good-bodied filly: half-sister to several winners, notably
5-y-o Presto Shinko: dam Irish 2-y-o 6f winner: needed experience (tended to hang left)
in minor event at Nottingham. *K. R. Burke*

SWIFT SAILOR 5 gr.g. Slip Anchor 136 – New Wind (GER) (Windwurf (GER)) –
[2006 105: 12g Apr 22] rangy gelding: has rather round action: useful performer at best:
well beaten in John Porter Stakes at Newbury only Flat outing in 2006: fair hurdler,
successful in October/November. *G. L. Moore*

SWINBROOK (USA) 5 ch.g. Stravinsky (USA) 133 – Dance Diane (USA) (Affirmed 98
(USA)) [2006 91: 6g⁴ 6g* 5s 6m 6m⁶ 7m⁴ 6m 6f⁴ p7g⁴ Oct 6] workmanlike gelding:
useful handicapper on turf: won at Leicester (beat Zidane 2½ lengths) in April: best
at 6f/7f: acts on firm and soft ground, below form both starts on all-weather: visored.
J. A. R. Toller

SWINDON (USA) 4 b.f. Kingmambo (USA) 125 – Dance Design (IRE) 119 (Sadler's 71
Wells (USA) 132) [2006 73: 11.8m⁵ 11m⁴ 14.1m p10g Nov 15] fair maiden, lightly raced:
stays 1½m: raced only on good to firm going on turf, well held on all-weather: tongue
tied final start. *P. F. I. Cole*

SWING ON A STAR (IRE) 2 br.f. (Feb 6) Celtic Swing 138 – Lady Stalker 57 (Primo 64 p
Dominie 121) [2006 p7g⁴ Nov 1] €18,000F, 15,000Y: second foal: dam, sprint mai-
den, half-sister to Middle Park Stakes winner Stalker: 20/1, encouraging fourth to
Hanbrin Bhoy in steadily-run maiden at Kempton, closing from rear: sure to improve.
W. R. Swinburn

SWING THE RING (IRE) 3 b.c. Rossini (USA) 118 – Sharkiyah (IRE) 75 (Polish 98
Precedent (USA) 131) [2006 96: 8d 6g² 6g⁴ 6.5g⁴ 8g⁵ 7s 6g⁵ 6.5g⁵ 7d Oct 20] close-
coupled colt: useful performer: best efforts when promoted second behind Raptor in
listed race at Baden-Baden second start and when fifth to Poseidon's Bride in minor event
at Chantilly and to Santiago Atitlan in listed race at Cologne seventh/eighth starts: seems
best around 6f: acts on good to firm going (below form on soft in listed race at York sixth
start): blinkered last 3 starts. *Bruce Hellier, Germany*

SWING WING 7 b.g. In The Wings 128 – Swift Spring (FR) 56 (Bluebird (USA) 125) 106
[2006 16.1m Jul 1] good-topped gelding: has a quick, fluent action: smart performer in
2004, winning listed race at Milan: off nearly 2 years, shaped as if retaining plenty of
ability when thirteenth of 20 to Toldo in Northumberland Plate (Handicap) at Newcastle
only outing in 2006: stays 2m: acts on heavy and good to firm going: tried blinkered:
races prominently. *P. F. I. Cole*

SWINTON 5 gr.g. Grey Desire 115 – Portite Sophie 54 (Doulab (USA) 115) [2006 –: –
12g f11m Oct 31] no sign of ability: tried tongue tied. *M. Brittain*

SWIPER HILL (IRE) 3 b.g. City On A Hill (USA) 114 – Alkariyh (USA) 79 (Alydar 70
(USA)) [2006 p6g* p7.1g 5g May 8] €16,000F, 36,000Y, 16,000 2-y-o: half-brother to
several winners, including smart 6f (including at 2 yrs)/7f (in France) winner Jarn (by
Green Desert) and 6-y-o Yomalo: dam 2-y-o 6f winner: 5/1 and green, won maiden at
Kempton (hung left) in March: disappointing in handicaps after, veering left as stall
opened in latter: should stay 7f. *B. Ellison*

SWISS ACT 2 ch.c. (Mar 5) Act One 124 – Dancing Mirage (IRE) 83 (Machiavellian 81 p
(USA) 123) [2006 8v⁴ 8g³ 8.3d* Sep 25] 32,000Y: lengthy, good-topped colt: third
foal: half-brother to 4-y-o Foxhaven and a winner in South Africa by Danehill: dam 2-y-o
7f winner who stayed 1m: fairly useful form in maidens, winning at Hamilton by 1¼
lengths from Hohlethelonely: will probably stay 1¼m/1½m: likely to improve as 3-y-o.
M. Johnston

SWORDS 4 b.g. Vettori (IRE) 119 – Pomorie (IRE) 67§ (Be My Guest (USA) 126) 68
[2006 61: p10g p9.5g² f8g⁶ f12g² p16.5f* 16d⁵ p12g* p12.2g⁴ p16.5m p12.2g³ Nov 10]
sturdy gelding: fair handicapper: claimed from P. Howling £5,000 after reportedly finishing lame on third start: won at Wolverhampton in August and Kempton in September:
effective at 1½m to 2m: acts on all-weather, unraced on extremes of going on turf.
Mrs H. Dalton

SWORD'S EDGE (IRE) 5 b.g. Pennekamp (USA) 130 – Scimitarra 115 (Kris 135) –
[2006 65: 7s p9.5m p12.2m p12.2g Nov 18] fair form when fourth in maiden at Wexford
on Flat debut at 4 yrs (left P. Nolan after next start): well held since, including in handicaps at Wolverhampton last 3 outings (reportedly finished lame final one). *W. A. Murphy,
Ireland*

SWORDSMAN (GER) 4 b.c. Acatenango (GER) 127 – Saiga (Windwurf (GER))   **97**
[2006 12g³ 14m⁵ 16g 12d 14g⁴ 11.8g* Nov 11] good-topped colt: second foal: dam
German 1m winner: won allowance race at Belmont when trained by D. W. Lukas in USA
in 2005: trained by Dr A. Bolte in Germany on reappearance only: useful form at best in
handicaps in Britain for M. Bell subsequently: won minor event at Machecoul in November on debut for new stable: stays 1¾m: acts on firm going: often blinkered. *R. Gibson,
France*

SWORN IN (USA) 5 ch.h. Kingmambo (USA) 125 – Under Oath (USA) (Deputed   **–**
Testamony (USA)) [2006 –: 14.1s 16m⁶ May 3] lengthy horse: bumper winner: stiff tasks
and highly tried in 3 starts on Flat, finished lame when sixth of 7 in Sagaro Stakes at
Lingfield final one. *N. I. M. Rossiter*

SYBELLA 3 ch.f. In The Wings 128 – Samara (IRE) 108 (Polish Patriot (USA) 128)   **84**
[2006 12f³ 11.8m⁴ 11.6f² 14.1f⁵ 12.1m³ 16g⁴ 16d p12g Nov 9] tall, close-coupled filly:
fifth foal: half-sister to 3 winners, including useful 1¼m/1½m winner Santa Sophia (by
Linamix) and 4-y-o Sanchi: dam, 1m/8.5f winner, half-sister to smart middle-distance
stayer Lille Hammer: fairly useful maiden: stays 2m: acts on firm ground: sold 40,000
gns. *J. L. Dunlop*

SYLVAN (IRE) 2 b. or br.f. (Feb 23) Shinko Forest (IRE) – Auriga 73 (Belmez (USA)   **79**
131) [2006 6m 6g* 6m Sep 16] €7,000F, 8,000Y: leggy filly: sixth foal: sister to 5-y-o
Morse and half-sister to 3 winners, including 6-y-o Forest Air: dam, maiden, half-sister
to smart middle-distance performer Beldale Star and useful sprinter Moon Drop: fair
form: won maiden at Salisbury (beat Maker's Mark by ½ length) in August: not clear run
when in mid-field in nursery at Newbury: likely to stay 1m. *S. Kirk*

SYMBOL OF PEACE (IRE) 3 b.f. Desert Sun 120 – Rosy Lydgate 53 (Last Tycoon   **79**
131) [2006 10f² 10m⁴ 9.5d 8f⁴ 10f 10s 9s p8.6g⁶ p9.5g p9.5g* p9.5g³ Dec 26] €5,500F:
half-sister to 3 winners, including 8-y-o Loyal Tycoon and fairly useful Irish 6f to 1m
winner Peace Angel (by Goldmark): dam maiden half-sister to smart performer up to 11f
Supreme Sound and useful stayer Top Cees: fair performer: left S. Slevin in Ireland after
seventh start: won maiden at Wolverhampton in December: stays 1¼m: acts on polytrack
and firm going, probably on soft. *J. W. Unett*

SYNONYMY 3 b.g. Sinndar (IRE) 134 – Peony 108 (Lion Cavern (USA) 117) [2006   **77**
65: p12g³ 12d³ 12.6g 10m⁶ p12g 11.7g 16g³ 14m⁴ 16g⁴ 17.2m² p16.5g* 17.2g⁶ p16.5m²
Nov 21] good-bodied gelding: fair handicapper: won at Wolverhampton in October: stays
17f: acts on polytrack, yet to race on extremes of going on turf. *M. Blanshard*

T

TABADUL (IRE) 5 b.g. Cadeaux Genereux 131 – Amaniy (USA) 96 (Dayjur (USA)   **97**
137) [2006 94: p10g* 9m p10g² 9.9m² 9m⁴ 10s Sep 22] leggy gelding: smart handicapper   **a110**
on all-weather, useful on turf: won at Kempton (impressively by 5 lengths from Desert
Cristal) in May: excellent 1¼ lengths second to Fairmile at same track third start: respectable efforts at Goodwood next 2 outings: will prove best up to 1¼m: acts on polytrack,
soft and good to firm ground: none too genuine. *E. A. L. Dunlop*

TABARET 3 ch.c. Bertolini (USA) 125 – Luanshya 78 (First Trump 118) [2006 104: 5m   **105**
5m 5m Jul 8] smallish, good-bodied colt: fluent mover: useful performer: good ninth to
Dandy Man in Palace House Stakes at Newmarket on reappearance: already fading when
clipping heels and falling heavily in King's Stand Stakes at Royal Ascot next time: tailed
off in Sprint Stakes at Sandown final start: raced only at 5f: acts on firm going, below
form on good to soft. *R. M. Whitaker*

TABOOR (IRE) 8 b.g. Mujadil (USA) 119 – Christoph's Girl 50 (Efisio 120) [2006   **79**
62: p6g⁴ p5.1g³ p5.1g² p5.1g³ p6g³ p5g 6m² 5d* 5.2g* p5g⁶ 5d p5g⁴ p5.1g p6g Dec 1]
heavy-topped gelding: fair handicapper: won at Hamilton in May and Yarmouth in June:
best at 5f/easy 6f: acts on all-weather, firm and good to soft ground: has worn cheek-
pieces/blinkers/tongue tie (not for current stable). *R. M. H. Cowell*

TABULATE 3 b.f. Dansili 127 – Let Alone 78 (Warning 136) [2006 –: p8.6g⁵ f8g⁵   **64**
p8.6g⁵ p7g³ 6g p7.1g f8g² p9.5g² 10.2g⁴ Oct 17] close-coupled filly: modest maiden:
stays 9.5f: acts on all-weather: reportedly in season fifth outing. *P. L. Gilligan*

TACID 4 b.f. Diktat 126 – Defined Feature (IRE) 91 (Nabeel Dancer (USA) 120) [2006   **59**
51: f8g* f8g f8g* f8g³ p8g f7g⁶ f8g³ 10.1g f8m⁴ f8g² f8g⁵ Dec 28] workmanlike filly:

modest performer: won banded race in January and handicap in February, both at South-well: stays 8.6f: acts on all-weather, soft and good to firm ground: visored final start. *Dr J. D. Scargill*

TACKCOAT (IRE) 6 b.g. Sesaro (USA) 81 – Damaslin (Camden Town 125) [2006 **61** 42: 8v 7s 8d f7g⁶ p8g³ f7g f8g* Dec 29] modest performer: won banded event at South-well in December: stays 1m: acts on fibresand, heavy and good to firm going: tried tongue tied, often wears cheekpieces. *Eoin Doyle, Ireland*

TADLIL 4 b.g. Pivotal 124 – Pretty Poppy 67 (Song 132) [2006 55: 5.1m⁴ 5.2m 5.7s **84** 6.1m 6g* 6d 6m* 6.1m³ 6m* Aug 31] well-made gelding: fairly useful handicapper, lightly raced: improved to win at Ripon (maiden event) in July and Haydock and Redcar in August: best at 5f/6f: acts on good to firm going, almost certainly not on softer than good. *J. M. Bradley*

TAFILAH 3 b.f. Foxhound (USA) 103 – Petra Nova 51 (First Trump 118) [2006 60: **56** p8g⁴ p7g² f7g⁴ p8g* Feb 7] modest performer: won seller at Lingfield in February: stays 8.6f: acts on all-weather and soft ground: visored last 5 starts: has looked wayward: sold 6,000 gns. *P. W. D'Arcy*

TAFIS BEACH 2 b.f. (Apr 2) Lugana Beach 116 – Sifat 77 (Marju (IRE) 127) [2006 **–** 5m 6m p6g f5g Nov 13] close-coupled filly: first foal: dam 1m/1¼m winner: no form in maidens: tried in visor/blinkers. *J. R. Jenkins*

TAFIYA 3 b.f. Bahri (USA) 125 – Fickle 95 (Danehill (USA) 126) [2006 83p: p8g² p10g **74** 8m² 10.2f³ 9m 10.3m⁵ p9.5g⁴ Oct 28] tall, leggy filly: fair maiden on turf, modest on all- **a62** weather: in frame 5 times: stays 1¼m: acts on polytrack and firm going: sold 15,000 gns. *G. A. Butler*

TAGART 3 b.g. Triple Hay 103 – Clancassie (Clantime 101) [2006 8m⁵ 8m⁶ 7m⁴ Sep **47** 16] poor maiden: stays 7f: raced only on good to firm ground. *J. J. Quinn*

TAG TEAM (IRE) 5 ch.g. Tagula (IRE) 116 – Okay Baby (IRE) 67 (Treasure Kay 114) **–** [2006 63, a78: f5g⁶ p5.1g⁴ f5g² f5s f5g 5.2m p6m² p6m* p5.1g⁶ p6g f6g² Dec 23] **a75** tall gelding: fair handicapper: won at Wolverhampton in October: effective at 5f/sharp 6f: acts on all-weather and firm going: tried blinkered/visored: races up with pace. *John A. Harris*

TAGULA BAY (IRE) 4 b.f. Tagula (IRE) 116 – Nezool Almatar (IRE) (Last Tycoon **59** 131) [2006 73: 6v 6.1m³ 6d⁶ 6g⁴ 6g⁶ 5s 7m 5g 6.1d² f5m Oct 31] quite good-topped filly: modest maiden: effective at 5f/6f, seemingly doesn't stay 7f: acts on heavy and good to firm going: blinkered last 2 outings: flashed tail and looked none too keen ninth start. *T. D. Easterby*

TAGULA BLUE (IRE) 6 b.g. Tagula (IRE) 116 – Palace Blue (IRE) (Dara Monarch **73** 128) [2006 57§: 10.9s³ 10d* 10g* 10d 10d⁵ May 30] good-bodied gelding: has a round action: fair handicapper: won at Pontefract (apprentices) and Leicester in April: stays 10.6f: acts on heavy ground: tried visored/blinkered: has been tongue tied: usually slowly away (has unseated rider/refused to race): fairly useful hurdler, successful in June and December. *Ian Williams*

TAGULA MUSIC (IRE) 2 ch.f. (Feb 5) Tagula (IRE) 116 – Mandolin (IRE) 69 **41** (Sabrehill (USA) 120) [2006 5.1d 5g 5.1d⁵ 5.1g 6m 7m 5g] leggy filly: first foal: dam, ran once, sister to useful performer up to 1¼m Alboostan and half-sister to smart performer up to 1½m Crown of Light: poor maiden. *B. Palling*

TAGULA SUNRISE (IRE) 3 ch.f. Tagula (IRE) 116 – Lady From Limerick (IRE) 61 **101** (Rainbows For Life (CAN)) [2006 93: 7g 7.2g³ 7m 6v* 7g 7.2g* 6f⁵ 6g⁴ 6s 6s⁴ 7d Sep 8] good-topped filly: fluent mover: useful performer: won handicaps at Ripon in May and Ayr (beat Dispol Katie 2½ lengths) in June: best efforts after at York, when good fifth to La Chunga in Summer Stakes and respectable seventh in listed event final outing: probably needs good test at 6f nowadays, and stays 7f: acts on any going: usually held up. *R. A. Fahey*

TAHAFUT 2 b.f. (Feb 16) Marju (IRE) 127 – Farha (USA) 85 (Nureyev (USA) 131) **52** [2006 5m 6m Sep 19] smallish, unfurnished filly: second foal: half-sister to German 6f winner Naqi (by Cadeaux Genereux): dam, 6f winner (including at 2 yrs), granddaughter of Arc winner All Along: modest form in maidens at Sandown and Newmarket: sold 4,000 gns. *W. J. Haggas*

TAILI 5 b.m. Taipan (IRE) 124 – Doubtfire 71 (Jalmood (USA) 126) [2006 –: 16m **–** 11.1g⁵ 11.1m 15m 11.1d Sep 25] of no account: tried blinkered/visored. *D. A. Nolan*

TAJAATHUB (USA) 4 ch.f. Aljabr (USA) 125 – Tajannub (USA) 104 (Dixieland **84**
Band (USA)) [2006 6v³ 7.1m 7.2g 7.1m⁴ 8.5d 7.1s Sep 24] sturdy filly: fairly useful
performer: won minor event at Compiegne for J. Hammond in France final start in 2005,
then sold 18,000 gns: best effort in 2006 when fourth in handicap at Musselburgh: likely
to prove best at 1m+: acts on good to firm ground. *M. Johnston*

TAJJREE 3 b.f. Lujain (USA) 119 – Rateeba (IRE) (Green Desert (USA) 127) [2006 **59**
p6g⁶ 7.1m p6g p5.1g² p5g Nov 11] 800 2-y-o: first foal: dam well held all 3 starts: modest
maiden: best effort at 5f: acts on polytrack: in cheekpieces all starts, tongue tied last 2.
Miss K. B. Boutflower

TAKAFU (USA) 4 b.g. Lemon Drop Kid (USA) 131 – Proper Protocol (USA) (Deputy **87**
Minister (CAN)) [2006 89: 11.7d 10g 10s 12g⁵ 14.1g² 15m* 14m⁴ 16.1d⁶ 17.2m³ p16g
Oct 20] tall, leggy, useful-looking gelding: fairly useful handicapper: won at Warwick in
July: barely stays 17f: acts on good to firm going. *W. S. Kittow*

TAKANEWA (IRE) 3 b.f. Danetime (IRE) 121 – Lady Ingabelle (IRE) 71 (Catrail **72 d**
(USA) 123) [2006 50: 9.8g³ 7.5g³ 6.9m 6f⁵ 7.5f 8d⁶ 7m Sep 16] tall filly: fair maiden:
stays 9.8f: best efforts on good going. *J. Howard Johnson*

TAKE A BOW 5 b.h. Royal Applause 124 – Giant Nipper (Nashwan (USA) 135) [2006 **107**
113: 8.1m⁵ 8.3m³ 9.7m² 8g³ 10m³ 9.9m⁴ 9d⁴ 10d⁴ 11.6d⁴ Nov 4] rather leggy, lengthy
horse: useful performer: several creditable efforts in 2006, including when fourth in
listed race at Goodwood (behind Imperial Stride) and 33-runner Cambridgeshire (Handicap) at Newmarket (better than bare result when beaten 5 lengths by Formal Decree,
hampered 2f out) sixth/seventh outings: stays 1¼m: acts on firm and soft going: consistent. *P. R. Chamings*

TAKE A MILE (IRE) 4 ch.g. Inchinor 119 – Bu Hagab (IRE) (Royal Academy (USA) **67**
130) [2006 70: 10f 10.1g³ 10f⁶ 9.7f⁴ Sep 18] tall gelding: fair performer: stays 1¼m:
acts on polytrack, firm and soft going: fairly useful hurdler, successful in October and
December. *B. G. Powell*

TAKE IT THERE 4 ch.f. Cadeaux Genereux 131 – Feel Free (IRE) 86 (Generous **64**
(IRE) 139) [2006 69: p8.6g 6d p7g p7.1m 8g* f8g* Nov 28] lengthy filly: modest
performer nowadays: won handicap (amateurs) at Southwell in November: stays 1m: acts
on fibresand and firm ground. *A. J. Lidderdale*

TAKE MY TURN 2 b.c. (Feb 13) Josr Algarhoud (IRE) 118 – Swizzle (Efisio 120) **47**
[2006 5g p6g 6g⁶ 7m 7g 5g Aug 26] neat colt: poor maiden: tried in blinkers: joined
G. Bridgwater. *M. Blanshard*

TAKE NO NOTICE (IRE) 3 b.f. Imperial Ballet (IRE) 110 – North Telstar 104 **–**
(Sallust 134) [2006 –: f8g f8g⁶ Jan 29] little sign of ability: tried visored. *K. R. Burke*

TAKEOVER TARGET (AUS) 7 b.g. Celtic Swing 138 – Shady Stream (AUS) **126**
(Archregent (CAN)) [2006 122: 5g* 5.5v³ 6g* 5m* 6m³ 6m 6g² 6f* Oct 1]
    Ginger McCain has long been the most celebrated taxi-driver-turned
racehorse-trainer but Red Rum's trainer, who retired in 2006, had some competition
for media attention in the latest season from another cabbie, Joe Janiak, whose
Takeover Target became the latest Australian horse to challenge successfully for
top sprinting honours in Britain. Choisir's historic Royal Ascot double in the King's
Stand Stakes and Golden Jubilee Stakes in 2003 inspired similar ventures from
Exceed And Excel in 2004 and Fastnet Rock in 2005, but the fact that neither of

King's Stand Stakes, Royal Ascot—the prize goes to Australia for the second time in four years
as Takeover Target (noseband) beats Benbaun (visor) and Pivotal Point (right)

those Australian sprinters even lined up at Royal Ascot served as a reminder that travelling halfway round the world to compete at the top level, let alone win, is not always so straightforward as Choisir made it look. Fastnet Rock reportedly failed to recover from travel sickness on arrival in Britain, while Exceed And Excel, another who came with high-class form in Australia, had to miss Royal Ascot the year before with a viral infection; he only beat one home when favourite for the July Cup at Newmarket. Hong Kong sprinter Cape of Good Hope had better luck at the Royal meeting at York in 2005 when his win in the Golden Jubilee Stakes, adding to an earlier success in the Australia Stakes, clinched him the inaugural Global Sprint Challenge.

The Global Sprint Challenge was made a more enticing target in 2006 with the addition of a million-dollar bonus for a horse successful in different countries in any three of the five Group 1 races in the seven-race series. The Hong Kong Sprint was added as the seventh and final leg of the Challenge in 2006 after the two races in Australia early in the year, Royal Ascot's two big sprints, and two contests in Japan in the autumn. Newmarket is trying to secure a place for the July Cup in future. Royal Ascot's sprints were also made more attractive to would-be foreign runners with boosts in prize money, the Group 2 King's Stand Stakes going to £113,560 to the winner and the Group 1 Golden Jubilee Stakes to £198,730. Recruitment by the Ascot executive was rewarded when three Australian sprinters made the journey for the Royal meeting.

Falkirk and Glamour Puss were smart pattern winners themselves, but Takeover Target was acknowledged as the best of the trio in Australia where his record prior to Royal Ascot stood at eleven wins from eighteen starts. Takeover Target began the year just as Choisir had done three years earlier by winning the Lightning Stakes at Flemington before finishing third in the Oakleigh Plate at Caulfield. In the Lightning (the first leg of the Global Sprint Challenge) he had Cape of Good Hope back in third, while in the Oakleigh Plate, a handicap, he was below his best on heavy ground. Like Choisir, Takeover Target contested the Newmarket Handicap at Flemington in March on his final start before Royal Ascot but, whereas Choisir had finished only sixth, Takeover Target defied top weight in a tight finish, beating the Oakleigh Plate winner Snitzel into second, with Glamour Puss dead-heating for fourth close behind.

Choisir started at 25/1 when winning the King's Stand but Takeover Target was afforded more respect despite having to shoulder a penalty like his predecessor. In the twenty-eight-runner field, Takeover Target was sent off the 7/1 joint-second favourite with the previous year's Nunthorpe winner La Cucaracha behind 5/1 market leader Moss Vale, winner of pattern races at the Curragh and Chantilly on his last two starts. Falkirk (ridden by Johnny Murtagh, who had partnered Choisir) was at 14/1, with Glamour Puss on 16/1. In what proved a rather muddling contest, Takeover Target from stall seventeen was among the highest drawn of those who raced in the larger stand-side group, racing towards the centre of the track and away from the main focus of the race. He showed prominently though, and by the closing stages had edged left towards his main rivals, leading outright on his side from under two furlongs out. At the line, Takeover Target had only a short head to spare from Benbaun, with Pivotal Point half a length back in third. Falkirk was another who flashed home just a neck behind to dead heat for fourth with Dandy Man who was clear on the opposite side of the track from halfway. Heads and necks separated the remainder of the first dozen home, with Glamour Puss finishing seventh just in front of Moss Vale and La Cucaracha. The 100/1-shots Tabaret and Orientor came down as a result of clipping the heels of other runners inside the final furlong.

Joe Janiak was of the firm opinion that Takeover Target was better at six furlongs than five, which augured well for his attempt to follow up in the Golden Jubilee Stakes four days later; indeed, Janiak had joked beforehand about using the King's Stand as a 'barrier trial' for the Group 1 contest. Takeover Target was made favourite to emulate Choisir's double, taking on five horses in the eighteen-runner field who had finished behind him earlier at the meeting. The fact that Takeover Target could finish only third behind one of those, Les Arcs (eleventh in the King's Stand), took nothing away from his performance earlier in the week. Some jumped to the conclusion that Takeover Target's failure to win both races, as Choisir had, made him inferior, but, in truth, there was precious little between the two in terms

Sprinters Stakes, Nakayama—Takeover Target adds Japan's premier sprint race to his haul and secures victory in the Global Sprint Challenge

of form. Takeover Target ran below his best in the Golden Jubilee, beaten just over two lengths, giving the impression his earlier exertions had left him a little flat. There were certainly those prepared to overlook the Golden Jubilee form when Takeover Target and Les Arcs met for a third time in the July Cup at Newmarket, where Takeover Target started the 9/2 favourite. He wasn't discredited but faded to finish behind Les Arcs again, coming a close seventh after being drawn one in a race dominated by those from high-numbered stalls.

The July Cup had marked the final start for Choisir before his retirement to stud, as it did for Falkirk (who was down the field at Newmarket) in the latest season. The mare Glamour Puss had already been retired to the paddocks after her tenth place in the Golden Jubilee. However, for gelding Takeover Target the remaining legs of the Global Sprint Challenge beckoned, starting with the two races in Japan. In the Group 2 Centaur Stakes at Chukyo in September he was beaten three lengths into second by the Japanese mare She Is Tosho, but three weeks later Takeover Target came right back to his best when decisively winning the Group 1 Sprinters Stakes at Nakayama over a field that included Benbaun (fifth) and Les Arcs (seventh), with She Is Tosho only eighth.

So far so good. Takeover Target had already done enough to take an unassailable lead in the Global Sprint Challenge, and victory in Hong Kong would have brought him a third Group 1 in the series and the million-dollar bonus which went with it. But a lot of the gloss was taken off his excellent international campaign by events in Hong Kong which led to his effectively being banned from the final leg of the series. Drugs were again the issue in a year when a number of top international races were tarnished by horses testing positive either before or after the race. A common thread to the incidents was that all the horses involved were from outside the country they were competing in. Brass Hat from the States and Deep Impact from Japan were disqualified after being placed in the Dubai World Cup and Prix de l'Arc de Triomphe respectively after banned substances were found in their systems, despite connections in both cases claiming that they had allowed enough time for the medication to pass through their horses' systems before race day. Another American gelding to fall foul of a foreign country's drug rules was Honor In War who was voluntarily withdrawn by connections from the

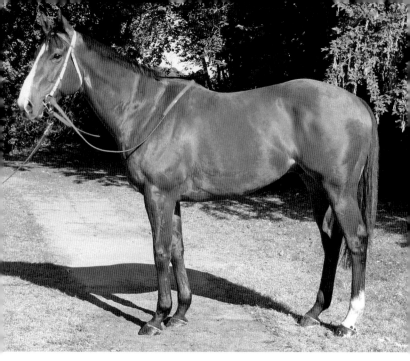

Messrs J. & B. Janiak's "Takeover Target"

Cox Plate in Australia after pre-race tests taken in quarantine showed steroid levels which were likely to have resulted in his disqualification had he raced.

Takeover Target's case in Hong Kong bore some similarity to that of Honor In War. His trainer reported that Takeover Target had been given a 'mild steroid' in Japan to help him overcome the stress of travel to Hong Kong. Since then, five tests in quarantine in Hong Kong had revealed traces of a banned substance known (though presumably only to those with a degree in chemistry) as 17-alpha-hydroxy-progesterone hexanoate. Janiak had until the day of the Hong Kong Sprint to withdraw Takeover Target of his own volition but, having failed to do so, and with the horse still testing positive, the stewards took the decision for him under Hong Kong Jockey Club rules and withdrew Takeover Target on the morning of the race. An inquiry, which resulted in a HK $200,000 fine (around £13,000) for Janiak, was delayed so that an independent test on the horse's B sample could be carried out. Janiak claimed that he had used the same medication before and that it normally cleared a horse's system in a couple of weeks at most, but that on this occasion the steroid had been accidentally injected into a ligament rather than a muscle, resulting in the substance not being released so quickly. Some experts were reportedly of the opinion that the steroid could stay there permanently, which would have repercussions for the remainder of Takeover Target's career, particularly for his future overseas. In the wake of the year's various infringements there were calls for the global standardisation of rules and regulations covering drugs. Even a world-wide policy of zero tolerance would not address the problem which all these cases highlighted, namely that trainers are free to use substances which are effectively illegal on race day but can be used with impunity at any other time.

Combined with driving his taxi, Joe Janiak (also part-owner of the horse with his sons) has always had a very small-scale training operation, one which had yielded only around a hundred winners in the course of thirty years or so. Takeover Target was typical of the horses he had operated with, bought as an unraced four-year-old with knee problems for just A$1,250 (about £500). But Takeover Target made remarkable progress once put into training and was unbeaten in seven starts in 2004, starting with a maiden at his local track of Queanbeyan and completing the sequence at Wagga Wagga, Kensington, Rosehill, Gosford, Grafton and Flemington, his final win that year coming in the Group 1 Salinger Stakes. Takeover Target ended the following year with wins in a Group 3 and a listed race at Doomben before embarking on his international campaign in 2006.

Few would have expected a high-class sprinter to be the best of Celtic Swing's offspring so far. He was never raced at shorter than seven furlongs, came from a family of stayers, won the Prix du Jockey Club and would have probably contested the St Leger had he stayed sound. Celtic Swing's best horse before Takeover Target was the French-trained Breeders' Cup Mile winner Six Perfections but there is another sprinter among his leading progeny, Celtic Mill, a smart gelding who was also in the King's Stand field. Celtic Swing has been kept on the move at stud. He began his stallion career at the National Stud at Newmarket and currently stands at the Irish National Stud. In between, he had a spell in France, and Takeover Target is the result of one of his spells on shuttle duty in Australia. Takeover Target's unraced dam Shady Stream has only two other living foals of racing age, Shady Henrietta and Saskarla, both by a once-raced son of Mr Prospector (Celtic Swing's grandsire), Mr Henrysee, and both minor sprint winners (including over just four furlongs) in Australia. Grandam Merry Shade, one of nine winners out of the twice-raced Parasol, won listed races over five and seven furlongs and was third at the latter trip in the Group 1 AJC Sires' Produce Stakes to that season's top Australian two-year-old Burst, showing useful form.

Takeover Target (AUS) (b.g. 1999)	Celtic Swing (br 1992)	Damister (b 1982)	Mr Prospector
			Batucada
		Celtic Ring (b 1984)	Welsh Pageant
			Pencuik Jewel
	Shady Stream (AUS) (ch 1994)	Archregent (b 1981)	Vice Regent
			Respond
		Merry Shade (gr 1989)	Spectacular Spy
			Parasol

Takeover Target is a sturdy, good-bodied gelding who was woolly in his coat on all his starts in Britain in the summer, mid-winter in southern hemisphere time. He has won at seven furlongs but is best at shorter and acts on firm and good to soft ground. Takeover Target races prominently and has been ridden in all bar one of his starts by Jay Ford. His wins have netted the Janiaks the equivalent of nearly £1.5 million (or a good few taxi fares), and in addition to the Global Sprint Challenge title, Takeover Target was also voted champion sprinter and best international performer for the Australian 2005/6 season. Another European campaign is on the cards in 2007, all being well, with the possibility of the Nunthorpe Stakes also forming part of his programme. *J. Janiak, Australia*

TAKES TUTU (USA) 7 b.g. Afternoon Deelites (USA) 122 – Lady Affirmed (USA) **82 d** (Affirmed (USA)) [2006 84: f8g⁶ p8.6g⁶ p9.5g⁶ p8.6g³ p10g⁵ p10g² p8g⁶ 9.9d 8m* 8m³ 8.1m* 8m 8f³ 8.1g⁶ 7.1f⁵ p8g² p8g⁵ 8f 8.1m 8.3f p7.1g p7g p10g⁴ Dec 22] tall, useful-looking gelding: fairly useful handicappper: claimed from K. Burke after sixth start: won at Brighton in April and Haydock (Flat/Jump jockeys event) in May: below form after sixteenth outing: effective at 7f to easy 10.5f: acts on all-weather and firm going: sometimes wears headgear: can race freely/idle. *C. R. Dore*

TAKE TO THE SKIES (IRE) 2 b.c. (Mar 22) Lujain (USA) 119 – To The Skies **–** (USA) 89 (Sky Classic (CAN)) [2006 5m Jun 22] well-grown, rather leggy colt: burly and green, always behind in Norfolk Stakes at Royal Ascot. *A. P. Jarvis*

TAKITWO 3 b.g. Delta Dancer – Tiama (IRE) 50 (Last Tycoon 131) [2006 49: 7g* 8m **74** p7g 7f* 7f* 7d⁴ 7m 8m Sep 25] fair handicapper: won at Salisbury in June and Folkestone in July and August: stays 7f: acts on firm ground, probably on good to soft: has looked less than straightforward. *P. D. Cundell*

totesport.com Winter Hill Stakes, Windsor—a fourth win in five starts for Tam Lin;
Reunite (left) runs him close, while Kandidate is third

TALBOT AVENUE 8 b.g. Puissance 110 – Dancing Daughter 79 (Dance In Time **105**
(CAN)) [2006 108: 6.5m⁴ 6m⁴ 6.5g 5m² 5.1m 6m 5m p5g² p6g Dec 16] compact gelding: **a100**
useful performer: on long losing run: ran at Nad Al Sheba first 3 starts in 2006: off nearly
4 months, good 1¼ lengths second to Golden Dixie in handicap at York (not clear run):
left M. Mullineaux, creditable ¾-length second to Harry Up in similar event at Kempton
penultimate start: effective at 5f/easy 6.5f: acts on polytrack, firm and soft going: blinkered (ran well) once in 2005: sometimes bandaged on joints: often wanders. *M. Blanshard*

TALBOT STREET 3 ch.c. Compton Place 125 – Roxy (Rock City 120) [2006 7g 7.9m –
Jul 8] tongue tied, tailed off in maiden and seller. *Robert Gray*

TALCEN GWYN (IRE) 4 b.g. Fayruz 116 – Cheerful Knight (IRE) (Mac's Imp **69**
(USA) 116) [2006 78: 9p5g³ a5.5g⁴ a5.5g⁶ p5.1g 5m⁴ 5.1g² 5m³ 5m³ 5.3m² 5.1m* 5.7f*
5.5d⁴ 5f⁵ 5.3d Sep 25] workmanlike gelding: fair handicapper: made all at Chepstow
in August and Bath in September: seemed to go amiss final start: effective at 5f/6f: acts
on polytrack, firm and good to soft going: usually visored: sometimes hangs right.
M. F. Harris

TALISKER ROCK (IRE) 6 gr.g. Tagula (IRE) 116 – Hallatte (USA) (Trempolino –
(USA) 135) [2006 12f⁶ 8g Aug 4] strong gelding: has shown little in bumpers/over
hurdles, and well held in maidens at Catterick and Thirsk. *B. Storey*

TALLYHOBYE 3 b.g. Foxhound (USA) 103 – Bebe de Cham 75 (Tragic Role (USA)) **57**
[2006 62: f8g p7.1g 9v⁵ 8.1g 6m 11g* 12.1f 10f⁵ 10m 12m 11s Aug 13] modest
performer: won claimer at Redcar (claimed from J. Weymes) in May: stayed 11f: acted
on firm going: raced freely third outing: tried blinkered: dead. *M. E. Sowersby*

TALLY (IRE) 6 ch.g. Tagula (IRE) 116 – Sally Chase 101 (Sallust 134) [2006 60: f7g **46**
f7g f7g p8g p7.1g p10g 7m 8f Jul 18] close-coupled gelding: poor performer: stays 7.6f:
acts on all-weather, firm and soft going: tried in headgear. *D. G. Bridgwater*

TALPOUR (IRE) 6 ch.g. Ashkalani (IRE) 128 – Talwara (USA) (Diesis 133) [2006 –
12m⁶ 9.9g f8g Oct 12] workmanlike gelding: poor form in bumpers: well held in 2
maidens and a maiden claimer (reportedly finished lame). *M. C. Chapman*

TAMAGIN (USA) 3 b.c. Stravinsky (USA) 133 – Luia (USA) (Forty Niner (USA)) **96**
[2006 68: p7.1g⁵ p7g* p7.1g p8g² p8.6g⁵ p8g* p7g² p8g* 8d⁵ p7g⁴ p8g⁶ p7g* p7g p7g³
p7g p7g⁴ p7g⁴ p8g² p8g Dec 30] tall, close-coupled colt: useful performer: won maiden

in February and handicaps in March, April and May, all at Lingfield: good ½-length second to Mina A Salem in handicap there penultimate outing: stays easy 1m: acts on polytrack: wears cheekpieces nowadays: free-going front runner. *P. D. Evans*

TAMATAVE (IRE) 4 b.g. Darshaan 133 – Manuetti (IRE) 86 (Sadler's Wells (USA) 132) [2006 7.1g 12f³ 9.8v 8.1g⁵ 7.1f p7.1g⁵ f7g² p8.6g Dec 29] quite attractive gelding: has a quick action: fair maiden nowadays: unraced in 2005: sold from Saeed bin Suroor 26,000 gns and gelded prior to reappearance: stays 1m: acts on fibresand and good to firm ground: tongue tied at 2 yrs: looked ungenuine second start. *K. A. Ryan*   **72**

TAMINO (IRE) 3 b.c. Mozart (IRE) 131 – Stop Out 89 (Rudimentary (USA) 118) [2006 59: 6g 6.1m³ 5f⁶ 5g* 5m² 5.5d² p6g Oct 15] fair handicapper: won at Sandown in August: good second next 2 starts: effective at 5f/6f: acts on good to firm and good to soft ground: races up with pace. *H. Morrison*   **72**

TAMINOULA (IRE) 5 b.m. Tagula (IRE) 116 – Taormina (IRE) (Ela-Mana-Mou 132) [2006 70, a74: p7.1g p6g⁴ p8g p7g³ p9.5g⁴ p8g 8.1g 7.9m Jun 5] strong mare: modest performer: left P. Mitchell 7,000 gns after fourth start: has form at easy 13f, but best efforts of late up to 1m: acts on polytrack and firm ground, well beaten on soft: tried blinkered. *J. G. Given*   **–**
a63

TAM LIN 3 b.c. Selkirk (USA) 129 – La Nuit Rose (FR) 109 (Rainbow Quest (USA) 134) [2006 10g* 11.1d* 12m⁵ 10g* 10g* 11g² Sep 15] tall colt: has a fluent, round action: brother to 6f/7f winner Finders Keepers and half-brother to 2002 2-y-o 7f winner Finger of Fate (by Machiavellian), both fairly useful: dam, 2-y-o 7f winner, out of Prix de Diane winner Caerlina: very smart form: progressive, but hasn't impressed with attitude: won maiden at Leicester in April, listed races at Hamilton in May and Newbury (beat Windsor Knot by head) in July and totesport.com Winter Hill Stakes at Windsor (beat Reunite by ½ length) in August: good ¾-length second to Blue Monday in Arc Trial at Newbury after: stays 11f (pulled hard in King Edward VII Stakes at Royal Ascot at 1½m): unraced on extremes of going: tends to flash tail/carry head high: joined Godolphin. *Sir Michael Stoute*   **120**

Gainsborough Stud's "Tam Lin"

TAMMY 3 b.f. Tamure (IRE) 125 – Heather Honey (Insan (USA) 119) [2006 9.8m 9.8g   –
12s 11g 15.8m Aug 8] angular filly: sixth foal: sister to 5-y-o Big Bradford and half-sister
to 2001 2-y-o 5f/6f winner Dusty Bankes (by Greensmith): dam unraced: little form:
slowly away and hung sharply left on debut. *C. W. Thornton*

TAMORA 4 ch.f. Dr Fong (USA) 128 – Tahara (IRE) (Caerleon (USA) 132) [2006 52:   –
p8g p8.6g³ p7g* p7g p7.1g⁶ 8f Jul 9] modest performer on all-weather, poor on turf: won   **a58**
banded event at Kempton in May: effective at 7f, probably at 1¼m: acts on polytrack,
probably on good to firm going: often visored: has looked difficult ride. *A. P. Jarvis*

TAMWORTH (IRE) 4 b.g. Perugino (USA) 84 – Faiblesse (Welsh Saint 126) [2006   **61**
77: 8g a8.3s⁴ a8.3g 8d⁶ p7g² p7g f6g⁵ f7g p7g⁶ p7.1g Dec 26] fair performer in Ireland at
3 yrs, winning maiden at Gowran on final outing for K. Condon: ran in Spain for current
stable early in 2006: just modest form in handicaps/claimer in Britain: stays 1m: acts on
sand/polytrack and good to firm going, probably on heavy: tried blinkered/tongue tied.
E. J. Creighton

TANCREDI (SWE) 4 b.g. Rossini (USA) 118 – Begine (IRE) (Germany (USA) 124)   –
[2006 p8.6g Dec 29] won maiden at Ovrevoll at 2 yrs: sixth in handicap and fifth in minor
event (turf debut) at same course in 2005 (left R. Haugen in Norway after): well held in
handicap at Wolverhampton only Flat outing in 2006. *N. B. King*

TANCRED TIMES 11 ch.m. Clantime 101 – Mischievous Miss 73 (Niniski (USA)   –
125) [2006 64: 5d f6g f6g p5g Dec 18] small mare: modest performer: well beaten in
2006: tried blinkered: usually races up with pace. *D. W. Barker*

TANFORAN 4 b.g. Mujahid (USA) 125 – Florentynna Bay 61 (Aragon 118) [2006 84:   **88**
p8g⁶ p7g⁴ p8g⁶ p7.1g p7g² 6g² 7m 6g² 6m 6d 7.6m 7d 7m 7m 7.1s 10g⁵ p6g² p6g p7g
Nov 29] quite attractive gelding: fairly useful handicapper: good efforts in 2006 when
runner-up: left K. McAuliffe after tenth outing, K. Reveley after sixteenth: effective at 6f
to 1m: acts on polytrack, firm and soft going: sometimes wears blinkers (including last 3
starts). *Ms J. S. Doyle*

TANG 2 ch.f. (Apr 3) Bahamian Bounty 116 – Hymne (FR) (Saumarez 132) [2006 5.1m⁴   **63**
p5.1g⁵ p5.1g³ f5g Dec 5] 3,000 2-y-o: third foal: half-sister to fairly useful 2004 2-y-o 5f
winner Arabian Dancer (by Dansili): dam French 9f winner who stayed 1½m: modest
maiden: likely to prove best at 5f/6f. *W. G. M. Turner*

TANGARITA 3 b.f. Tagula (IRE) 116 – Santa Isobel 94 (Nashwan (USA) 135) [2006   **65**
53: 10.2g² 10m² p10g 10.2f 9.9f³ 10.1f² 9.9s 10.9m⁶ Sep 4] lengthy filly: fair maiden
handicapper: placed 4 times in 2006: stays 1¼m: acts on firm ground: tongue tied on
debut: sold 9,500 gns, sent to Qatar. *A. M. Balding*

TANMEYA 5 gr.m. Linamix (FR) 127 – Ta Awun (USA) 99 (Housebuster (USA)) [2006   **47**
10.9m⁶ 12f Jul 11] poor maiden: slowly away both outings in 2006. *R. C. Guest*

TANNENBERG (IRE) 5 b.g. Polish Precedent (USA) 131 – Upper Strata 109 (Shirley   **90**
Heights 130) [2006 73: 12.4d⁴ 12d* 14g⁵ Jun 1] sturdy gelding: fairly useful performer:
much improved when winning handicap at Pontefract (by 6 lengths) in May: slowly away
when below final start: stays 13f: acts on firm and good to soft ground: suffered heart
problem fourth outing at 4 yrs. *G. A. Swinbank*

TANNING 4 b.f. Atraf 116 – Gerundive (USA) (Twilight Agenda (USA) 126) [2006 52:   **50**
p10g⁴ p12.2g Jul 17] modest performer: left A. Carroll after reappearance: stays 12.6f:
acts on polytrack and any turf going: tried in cheekpieces/blinkered, visored last 3 starts:
has raced freely: won over hurdles in October. *M. Appleby*

TANTIEN 4 b.f. Diktat 126 – Tahilla 112 (Moorestyle 137) [2006 46: f8g⁶ 8.2s 7f 8.2f   **44**
6d p7g p10g f11g Dec 29] rather leggy filly: poor maiden: left J. Harris after fourth start:
seems to stay 11f: acts on fibresand, good to firm and good to soft ground: tried in
cheekpieces/blinkered. *T. Keddy*

TANZANITE (IRE) 4 b.f. Revoque (IRE) 122 – Resume (IRE) 69 (Lahib (USA) 129)   **100**
[2006 94: 8.1m³ 9m 8g³ 8.1s* 8g 9.9m⁵ 8.1g 8.1v⁵ 9d Sep 30] leggy, close-coupled filly:
useful performer: won handicap at Sandown (by 3½ lengths from Spectait) in May:
creditable effort after only when fifth to Portal in listed handicap at Goodwood sixth start:
effective at 1m to 10.5f: acts on any going. *D. W. P. Arbuthnot*

TAPA 4 b.f. Tagula (IRE) 116 – Tweed Mill 88 (Selkirk (USA) 129) [2006 67: p6g p6g   **67**
p8g³ p8g p7.1g p8g Mar 17] sturdy filly: fair performer: left A. Balding after second
start: barely stays 1m: acts on polytrack, heavy and good to firm ground: usually visored/
blinkered: none too consistent: sold 3,000 gns in November. *C. A. Dwyer*

TAPAU (IRE) 8 b.m. Nicolotte 118 – Urtica (IRE) (Cyrano de Bergerac 120) [2006 –: 6g² 6m² 7m 7m 5.7m⁶ Sep 25] lengthy mare: modest performer nowadays: best at 6f/7f: acts on all-weather and firm going: tried in cheekpieces. *J. M. Bradley*   **56**

TAPPING TOES (IRE) 3 b.f. Danehill Dancer (IRE) 117 – It's A Gift (IRE) (Brief Truce (USA) 126) [2006 p6g a7g⁵ Dec 1⁷] 11,000 2-y-o: second foal: half-sister to German 6f/7f winner Italian Night (by Monashee Mountain): dam maiden in Germany: well held both starts, in latter for J. Best on debut. *S. Hernandez, Spain*   **–**

TAPPIT (IRE) 7 b.g. Mujadil (USA) 119 – Green Life 63 (Green Desert (USA) 127) [2006 44: 6m May 11] neat gelding: poor performer nowadays: tried in headgear/tongue tied. *L. R. James*   **–**

TAPSALTEERIE 3 b.f. Tipsy Creek (USA) 115 – Croft Sally (Crofthall 110) [2006 p7.1g p9.5g p8.6g f6g Nov 15] fifth living foal: dam unraced: no sign of ability. *M. J. Attwater*   **–**

TARABUT 4 b.f. Green Desert (USA) 127 – Nabadhaat (USA) 72 (Mr Prospector (USA)) [2006 87: 12g⁴ 20m 13.8m Aug 8] tall filly: fairly useful handicapper: easily best effort in 2006 on reappearance: may prove best short of 17f: raced only on good/good to firm going: sold 33,000 gns in November. *E. A. L. Dunlop*   **84**

TARA KING 4 b.f. Deploy 131 – Trinity Hall 67 (Hallgate 127) [2006 –: p12.2g³ p12.2g Apr 13] modest maiden: raced only around 1½m on polytrack. *A. B. Haynes*   **57**

TARANAKI 8 b.g. Delta Dancer – Miss Ticklepenny (Distant Relative 128) [2006 76: p7.1g p6g⁶ p7.1g² p7g 7s 6m³ p7.1g² 7m p7.1g² 7f³ 7m⁴ p7.1g² 8.3m⁵ p7.1g² 7m⁵ 7.6d* 8f 7g* 7m* 7m³ 7d³ 7s⁵ Oct 10] rather leggy gelding: fairly useful handicapper on turf, fair on all-weather: won at Lingfield and Goodwood in August and Lingfield in September: effective at 6f to 7.6f: acts on all-weather, firm and good to soft going: blinkered (raced freely) once: sometimes slowly away: consistent. *P. D. Cundell*   **80 a69**

TARANDOT (IRE) 5 b.m. Singspiel (IRE) 133 – Rifada 103 (Ela-Mana-Mou 132) [2006 104: 10.4s⁶ 11.9s⁴ 16.1m⁵ 14f 16g 18d Oct 14] tall, good-topped mare: useful performer: only creditable effort in 2006 when fifth to Toldo in Northumberland Plate (Handicap) at Newcastle: visored when tailed off in Cesarewitch final start: stays 2m: acts on soft and good to firm ground. *G. G. Margarson*   **100**

TARANIS 3 b.g. Lomitas 129 – Woodbeck 90 (Terimon 124) [2006 –p: 10f p12g⁵ 8f² 7.1m 8s⁴ 8g⁵ 11.9d⁴ Oct 19] modest maiden: stays 1½m: acts on firm and good to soft going: has looked hard ride. *Sir Mark Prescott*   **58**

TARANTO 3 b.f. Machiavellian (USA) 123 – Magna Graecia (IRE) 112 (Warning 136) [2006 p13g² 10d⁵ Nov 4] leggy, angular filly: first foal: dam, French 9f to 15.5f winner, out of useful half-sister to Dubai World Cup winner Street Cry (by Machiavellian) and to dam of Shamardal: successful at 2 yrs in newcomers race at Maisons-Laffitte and minor event at Longchamp (when left A. Fabre in France): off 12 months, much improved (smart form) when head second to High Heel Sneakers in listed race at Lingfield on belated reappearance: bit below that level when fifth to Lake Toya in similar event at Windsor 9 days later: should prove best at 1¼m/1½m: raced only on polytrack and ground softer than good on turf: has left Godolphin. *Saeed bin Suroor*   **111**

TARAN TREGARTH 2 b.f. (Apr 14) Tobougg (IRE) 125 – Little Change 70 (Grundy 137) [2006 5f p6g p7.1g⁶ 7m 10d 8.2s f7g² f7g p8.6g p9.5g Dec 9] 11,500Y: workmanlike filly: closely related to fairly useful 2000 2-y-o 7f winner Harmony Row (by Barathea), later 1m and 10.5f winner in Spain, and half-sister to several winners, including 7f and 1½m winner Spring Sixpence (by Dowsing): dam best at 2 yrs when third at 5f: poor maiden: wore blinkers/cheekpieces last 5 outings. *A. Bailey*   **41**

TARAS TORNADO 3 b.f. Distant Music (USA) 126 – Yellow Ribbon (IRE) 72 (Hamas (IRE) 125§) [2006 56: p6g 6d* 7f⁶ 5.9g⁶ 5.9m 7d Oct 10] unfurnished filly: modest performer: won seller at Leicester in April: stayed 7f: acted on polytrack and any turf going: dead. *J. J. Quinn*   **56**

TARA TOO (IRE) 3 b.f. Danetime (IRE) 121 – Gone With The Wind (IRE) (Common Grounds 118) [2006 85: 7s⁴ 7g 7.1m 7.1m⁴ 8.1m⁵ 7.1m 6m* 6m 7d 6g Oct 12] leggy, close-coupled filly: useful performer: won handicap at Goodwood (by 2 lengths from Aahgowangowan) in August: below form in listed races last 2 starts: probably stays 1m: acts on soft and good to firm going: not straightforward. *D. W. P. Arbuthnot*   **97**

TARFAH (USA) 5 b.m. Kingmambo (USA) 125 – Fickle 95 (Danehill (USA) 126) [2006 108: 8.5g Jun 2] tall, good-topped mare: useful performer: some way below best behind Echelon in Princess Elizabeth Stakes at Epsom only start in 2006, weakening   **95**

inside final 1f: stays 9f (raced freely at 1¼m): acts on firm and good to soft ground: has worn crossed noseband/gone early to post. *G. A. Butler*

TARGER PLACE 3 ch.g. Compton Place 125 – Floral Spark 69 (Forzando 122) [2006 **57** 64p: 5g⁶ 5s⁵ p5.1g Oct 14] good-bodied gelding: modest maiden: raced only at 5f: acts on polytrack: reportedly finished lame final outing. *T. T. Clement*

TARIF (IRE) 2 b.c. (Feb 12) Fath (USA) 116 – Tarrifa (IRE) (Mujtahid (USA) 118) **62** [2006 5g⁶ f6g⁴ 7f⁵ f7g³ 7.5g⁵ Aug 17] compact colt: modest maiden: will stay 1m: quirky. *Mrs P. Sly*

TARIQ 2 ch.c. (Feb 27) Kyllachy 129 – Tatora (Selkirk (USA) 129) [2006 6s* 6m³ **101** Jun 20] 32,000F, 65,000Y: close-coupled colt: good walker: second foal: dam unraced: useful form: impressive winning debut in maiden at Newmarket (beat Ebn Reem by 3½ lengths) in May: 1¾ lengths third of 21 to Hellvelyn in Coventry Stakes at Royal Ascot, staying on well despite drifting right: likely to prove best at 5f/6f. *P. W. Chapple-Hyam*

TARKAMARA (IRE) 2 ch.f. (Feb 20) Medicean 128 – Tarakana (USA) 101 (Shah- **80** rastani (USA) 135) [2006 5g² 5m⁴ 5m Jun 21] 75,000Y: big, useful-looking filly: has a round action: half-sister to several winners, including 7f/1m winner Tarakan (by Doyoun) and 1m (at 2 yrs) to 1½m winner Tarakala (by Dr Fong), both useful in Ireland: dam Irish 9f winner who stayed 1½m: fairly useful form: in frame in maidens at Newmarket (second to Silk Blossom on debut) then eighth to Gilded in Queen Mary Stakes at Royal Ascot: looked speedy, but should stay at least 1m. *P. F. I. Cole*

TARRABURN (USA) 2 ch.g. (Feb 13) Eltish (USA) 120 – Rahy's Wish (USA) (Rahy **75** (USA) 115) [2006 5f 6m⁴ 6s³ 6d* Oct 2] 60,000 2-y-o: rather leggy, useful-looking gelding: first foal: dam, ran twice in USA, half-sister to US Grade 3 2-y-o 6.5f winner Bully Bones: steady improvement, fair form when winning nursery at Pontefract: will be suited by 7f/1m. *J. Howard Johnson*

TARRJOO 2 b.f. (Apr 18) Diktat 126 – Maid of Kashmir (IRE) 94 (Dancing Brave **?** (USA) 140) [2006 7m a6d* Dec 17] eighth foal: half-sister to 3 winners, including use- ful 1¼m winner Bezzaaf (by Machiavellian) and fairly useful UAE 1m to 2m winner Shaalayn (by In The Wings): dam Irish 1¼m winner who stayed 1½m: last in maiden at Salisbury for M. Channon: sold 3,500 gns, won similar event at Taby in December. *M. Kahn, Sweden*

TARTAN SPECIAL 4 b.g. Fasliyev (USA) 120 – Colchica (Machiavellian (USA) **54** 123) [2006 56: p5.1g⁶ 6g 6m 6g³ 6g p8g* f8m⁶ p8.6g³ p8g⁴ Dec 6] leggy gelding: modest performer: won banded race at Kempton in October: stays easy 1m: acts on all-weather and good to firm ground: tried in headgear. *K. R. Burke*

TARTAN TIE 2 b.c. (May 21) Grand Lodge (USA) 125 – Trois Graces (USA) **69** (Alysheba (USA)) [2006 7.2m³ 7.2g⁴ Aug 21] 40,000Y: sixth foal: half-brother to smart 7f (at 2 yrs)/1m winner Flat Spin (by Spinning World) and fairly useful 2002 2-y-o 7f winner Goodness Gracious (by Green Desert): dam, French 1m winner, half-sister to smart French sprinter/miler Crack Regiment and to Prix de l'Abbaye second La Grande Epoque: green, in frame in maidens at Ayr won by Valbenny and Massive: will stay 1m. *M. Johnston*

TARTATARTUFATA 4 b.f. Tagula (IRE) 116 – It's So Easy 63 (Shaadi (USA) 126) **87** [2006 85: f5g p5g p5g 5.2d 5g 5s⁶ 5d³ p5.1m* p5.1g* p5.1g² p5g Dec 10] strong filly: fairly useful handicapper: won twice at Wolverhampton in November: good second there following month: speedy and best at 5f: acts on all-weather, firm and soft going: visored nowadays: sometimes hangs: front runner. *D. Shaw*

TARTEEL (USA) 2 b.f. (Feb 16) Bahri (USA) 125 – Elrehaan 96 (Sadler's Wells **91** (USA) 132) [2006 7m 7m⁴ 8.1g* 8d⁶ Oct 28] tall, rather leggy filly: on weak side at 2 yrs: second foal: dam, 7f (at 2 yrs) and 12.6f winner, out of half-sister to high-class sprinter Committed: fairly useful form: progressive in maidens, and won in good style at Haydock (beat Malyana by 6 lengths) in September: favourite, well-held sixth on softer ground to Passage of Time in listed race at Newmarket: will stay 1¼m. *J. L. Dunlop*

TARTOUCHE 5 b.m. Pursuit of Love 124 – Megan's Flight 74 (Welsh Pageant 132) **110** [2006 110: 12s* 16d⁴ 14f* 12.5s 12s⁴ Oct 7] leggy, quite good-topped mare: smart performer: won handicap at Newmarket (beat by 3½ lengths from Camrose) in May and Lillie Langtry Stakes at Goodwood (for second successive year, beat Art Eyes a neck) in August: below form otherwise in 2006 (reportedly pulled a muscle in her quarters final start): best at 1½m/1¾m: acts on firm and soft going: game: sold 150,000 gns. *Lady Herries*

TASHKANDI (IRE) 6 gr.g. Polish Precedent (USA) 131 – Tashiriya (IRE) 106 **87**
(Kenmare (FR) 125) [2006 99: p9.5g 10.2d* 10m Jul 7] sturdy, lengthy gelding: smart
performer at best, lightly raced in recent years: gelded, fairly useful form when winning
handicap at Chepstow in June: last both other starts in 2006: stays easy 1¼m: acts on
good to firm and good to soft going: won over hurdles in August and November (twice).
P. Bowen

TASJEEL (USA) 3 b.f. Aljabr (USA) 125 – Siyadah (USA) 106 (Mr Prospector **88**
(USA)) [2006 63: 9.8g² 8g* 10.4m³ 11.8m⁴ Jul 8] sturdy filly: fairly useful performer:
won maiden at Bath in June: on toes and unseated rider in paddock (taken straight to
post), good third in handicap at York penultimate start: stays 10.4f (seemingly not 1½m):
acts on good to firm ground. *W. J. Haggas*

TASK COMPLETE 3 ch.f. Bahamian Bounty 116 – Taskone (Be My Chief (USA) **55**
122) [2006 49: 6f 7g 6.1f 7.1m⁵ 5.1m p6g² p7g⁶ Dec 6] modest maiden: left J. Osborne
after third start: stays 6f: acts on polytrack and good to firm ground: blinkered last 4
starts: fractious beforehand and unseated rider behind stall at Warwick third outing: held
up. *Jean-Rene Auvray*

TASLEEM (IRE) 2 b.f. (Feb 21) Alhaarth (IRE) 126 – Almurooj 54 (Zafonic (USA) **59**
130) [2006 6g⁶ 5.1g Oct 17] medium-sized, quite attractive filly: fifth foal: sister to useful
6f (including at 2 yrs) winner Judhoor, closely related to 2003 2-y-o 6f winner Al Sifaat
(by Unfuwain) and half-sister to 3-y-o Muzher: dam, ran 4 times (best effort at 6f),
half-sister to Haafhd out of Irish 1000 Guineas winner Al Bahathri: mid-division at best
in maidens at Newmarket (very free) and Bath. *B. W. Hills*

TASTAHIL (IRE) 2 ch.c. (Feb 22) Singspiel (IRE) 133 – Luana 101 (Shaadi (USA) **84**
126) [2006 7g⁶ p8g²* 8g⁶ Sep 15] 330,000Y: strong, good sort: has scope: seventh foal:
half-brother to 4-y-o Hattan and UAE 7.5f winner Luzern (by Selkirk): dam, 6f winner,
half-sister to Luso, Needle Gun, Cloud Castle and Warrsan: fairly useful form: promising
debut in listed race at Newbury (sixth to Dubai's Touch), then made all in maiden at
Kempton in September: found little in minor event at Newbury following week: will
probably stay 1½m. *B. W. Hills*

TASWEET (IRE) 2 b.g. (Apr 23) Mujahid (USA) 125 – Injaad (Machiavellian (USA) **71 p**
123) [2006 7d 7g⁵ p7g Dec 3] deep-girthed gelding: third foal: closely related to 3-y-o
Mutamarres and 4-y-o Molem: dam unraced half-sister to smart 1¼m winner Bull Run:
fair form when fifth to Perfect Star in maiden at Newmarket: left J. Gosden 43,000 gns,
not knocked about final start: will be suited by 1m: remains capable of better. *T. G. Mills*

TATA NAKA 6 ch.m. Nashwan (USA) 135 – Overcast (IRE) 72 (Caerleon (USA) 132) **63**
[2006 67d: 10.1m 11.5m p10g 11.5m⁵ 10s 10.1g⁵ 10g* 10m⁶ 11.5f 10.1f 10.1f² 10m⁶
10g⁵ 10g 10.1m Sep 13] workmanlike, angular mare: modest performer nowadays: won
apprentice handicap at Nottingham in June: flattered in listed events tenth/final outings:
best efforts at 1¼m: acts on soft and firm going: tried in headgear. *Mrs C. A. Dunnett*

TATILLIUS (IRE) 3 ch.g. King Charlemagne (USA) 120 – Aunty Eileen (Ahonoora **–**
122) [2006 5.7m 6s 6.1d Oct 13] good-topped gelding: well beaten in maidens, saddle
reportedly slipped on first occasion. *J. M. Bradley*

Lillie Langtry Fillies' Stakes, Goodwood—a second successive win in the race for Tartouche,
who beats Art Eyes, Sirce (visor), Cresta Gold (quartered cap) and Scottish Stage (blaze)

TATSTHETICKET 3 b.g. Diktat 126 – Dekelsmary 61 (Komaite (USA)) [2006 50: p5.1g² f5g f5g 6.1f p6g⁶ Jul 28] stocky gelding: modest maiden on all-weather, no form on turf: likely to prove best at 5f: acts on all-weather: blinkered/visored last 6 starts, tried tongue tied. *J. Balding*   **– a50**

TAU CETI 7 b.h. Hernando (FR) 127 – Napoli 108 (Baillamont (USA) 124) [2006 116: 10g 9.9s⁵ 10g⁴ 9d 10d Oct 27] sturdy horse: useful performer in 2006: creditable 3 lengths fourth to Tam Lin in Winter Hill Stakes at Windsor: below form in Darley Stakes and listed race, both at Newmarket, after: will stay 1½m: has won on good to firm ground, though raced mostly on good/good to soft: blinkered last 2 outings in 2003: has worn crossed noseband: held up. *R. M. Beckett*   **109**

TAVALU (USA) 4 b.g. Kingmambo (USA) 125 – Larrocha (IRE) 116 (Sadler's Wells (USA) 132) [2006 66: 17.2s³ 12f⁵ 12m³ Jul 20] fair maiden handicapper, lightly raced: effective at 1½m to 17f: acts on firm and soft going. *G. L. Moore*   **68**

TAWAAF 3 b.c. Medicean 128 – Yasalam (IRE) (Fairy King (USA)) [2006 74p: p7.1g³ Jan 28] fair form: good third in handicap at Wolverhampton only start in 2006: will be suited by 1m: raced only on polytrack. *P. W. Chapple-Hyam*   **76**

TAWAAFUD 3 b.f. Nashwan (USA) 135 – Intimaa (IRE) 104 (Caerleon (USA) 132) [2006 85: 8.2m 8m⁴ 8m* 10m³ 10.3m⁵ Aug 25] quite attractive filly: fair performer: won maiden at Ripon in July: should stay 1½m: acts on good to firm and good to soft going: sold 6,000 gns. *B. W. Hills*   **77**

TAWAAGG 2 b.g. (Apr 25) Kyllachy 129 – Ascendancy (Sadler's Wells (USA) 132) [2006 p7g Oct 26] 84,000F, 110,000Y: third foal: half-brother to Irish 11f winner Enamoured (by Groom Dancer): dam unraced half-sister to smart 7f/1m performer Polar Bear: 8/1, ninth in maiden at Lingfield won by Cabinet: gelded after: should improve. *M. A. Jarvis*   **58 p**

TAWAAJUD (USA) 3 ch.f. Dixieland Band (USA) – Tabheej (IRE) 100 (Mujtahid (USA) 118) [2006 7m⁶ 7d* 8g⁶ 8.1d⁵ p8g Nov 5] good-topped filly: second foal: dam, 2-y-o 5f/6f winner, sister to useful 1995 2-y-o 5f winner Mubhij: fair performer: won maiden at Chester in May: may prove best short of 1m: acts on good to firm and good to soft ground. *B. W. Hills*   **77**

TAWAASSOL (USA) 3 b.c. War Chant (USA) 126 – Montecito (USA) (Seeking The Gold (USA)) [2006 79: 6m* 7m² 6g* 6m² 5m⁴ 6g³ 6s 6g Oct 13] strong, close-coupled colt: smart performer: won maiden at Yarmouth in April and handicap at Haydock (beat Imperial Sword by ½ length) in June: further progress after, fourth to Pivotal Point in Sprint Stakes at Sandown and close third to Fayr Jag in Hackwood Stakes at Newbury (wide throughout) fifth/sixth starts: below form in listed race and Bentinck Stakes (warm) at Newmarket last 2 outings: effective at 5f/6f: acts on good to firm going (well below form on soft penultimate outing): tongue tied last 6 starts. *Sir Michael Stoute*   **111**

TAWNYBRACK (IRE) 2 b.g. (Mar 27) Rossini (USA) 118 – Ceannanas (IRE) 77 (Magical Wonder (USA) 125) [2006 6m⁴ Aug 9] €40,000Y: fourth foal: brother to winner in Holland, and half-brother to 2003 2-y-o 6f winner Chauvinism (later smart 5f to 7f winner in Hong Kong) and 6-y-o Hilltime (both by Danetime): dam, Irish maiden, stayed 1m: 7/2, fourth to Flying Valentino in maiden at Newcastle, weaving through having missed break/met trouble: sold 8,500 gns, joined Jane Chapple-Hyam, and gelded. *E. J. O'Neill*   **68**

TAX FREE (IRE) 4 b.g. Tagula (IRE) 116 – Grandel (Owington 123) [2006 112p: 5m³ 5m³ 5m 6m⁵ 5g⁴ 5m* 6m* 6g³ Oct 13] strong gelding: smart performer: won minor event at Leicester (by 3 lengths from Dixie Belle) and listed race at Goodwood (by neck from Ashdown Express) 4 days apart in September: also good efforts in 2006 when 1¾ lengths third to Dandy Man in Palace House Stakes at Newmarket (clear of stand-side group), 2½ lengths third to Moss Vale in Prix du Gros-Chene at Chantilly, close fifth to Borderlescott in Stewards' Cup (Handicap) at Goodwood and ¾-length third to Bygone Days in Bentinck Stakes at Newmarket: will prove best at 5f/6f: yet to race on heavy ground, acts on any other turf: races up with pace. *D. Nicholls*   **117**

TAXMAN (IRE) 4 ch.g. Singspiel (IRE) 133 – Love of Silver (USA) 110 (Arctic Tern (USA) 126) [2006 71: p12g²* p16g p12g² p16g³ p13.9g² 14s 11.5m* 13.3m² p13.9g* 14.8m⁵ 11.8d⁴ 11.5m⁵ p12g⁵ p16.5g³ p13.9g⁵ p13g Nov 25] close-coupled gelding: fair handicapper: won at Lingfield in February, Yarmouth in May and Wolverhampton in July: stays 2m, at least when emphasis is on speed, and effective at 11.5f: acts on all-weather, firm and soft going: wears cheekpieces nowadays: consistent. *C. E. Brittain*   **79**

TAY BRIDGE (IRE) 3 ch.g. Tagula (IRE) 116 – Wild Liffey (USA) (Irish River (FR) – 131) [2006 54: 11g 8.3d⁵ 10.9g 7d 6.1d f7g p12.2g Nov 24] lengthy gelding: maiden: well held in 2006, left M. Bell after second start: tried blinkered/tongue tied. *G. F. Bridgwater*

TAYLOR MAID 4 b.f. First Trump 118 – Island Maid (Forzando 122) [2006 51: f7g – p9.5g Mar 29] maiden: well held in 2006 (left R. Cowell after reappearance): usually wears headgear. *G. A. Ham*

TAYMAN (IRE) 4 b. or br.g. Sinndar (IRE) 134 – Sweet Emotion (IRE) 97 (Bering **71** 136) [2006 58: 11.8d⁶ p10g 12m³ 12m 12d* 11.5m p12.2g⁵ Sep 30] quite good-topped gelding: fair handicapper: won at Folkestone in August: stays 1½m: acts on polytrack, good to firm and good to soft going: sold 20,000 gns, joined C. Mann. *G. Wragg*

TCHERINA (IRE) 4 b.f. Danehill Dancer (IRE) 117 – Forget Paris (Broken **88 d** Hearted 124) [2006 90: 13.8d⁴ 12d³ 12d⁴ 11.5g 12m 10.5g⁴ 12s 12d Oct 27] leggy, useful-looking filly: fairly useful handicapper: below form after third start: stays 1½m: acts on soft and good to firm ground. *T. D. Easterby*

TEACH TO PREACH (USA) 3 ch.c. Pulpit (USA) 117 – Chateaubaby (USA) 62 **77** (Nureyev (USA) 131) [2006 72p: 8d* 9.8m 12.3m⁵ Jul 1] good-topped colt: good mover: fair performer: won maiden at Bath in April: ran as if amiss final outing: stays 1m: acts on good to soft ground: sold 15,000 gns in October, joined B. De Haan. *B. W. Hills*

TEAM-MATE (IRE) 8 b.g. Nashwan (USA) 135 – Ustka 60 (Lomond (USA) 128) – [2006 –: p16.5g p12.2g Jan 20] leggy gelding: lightly raced and little solid form since 2004: tried tongue tied/in cheekpieces. *Miss J. Feilden*

TEARS OF A CLOWN (IRE) 3 b.g. Galileo (IRE) 134 – Mood Swings (IRE) 77 **91** (Shirley Heights 130) [2006 76p: f8g* 10.4d³ May 17] tall, good-bodied gelding: fairly useful performer: won maiden at Southwell (by 10 lengths) in May: upped in trip, better form when third to Reem Three in handicap at York (hung left) next time: gelded after: stays 10.4f: acts on polytrack and good to soft going. *J. A. Osborne*

TEASING 2 b.f. (Feb 23) Lujain (USA) 119 – Movieland (USA) 109 (Nureyev (USA) **76** 131) [2006 6g 6d p6g* p6g³ p6g² Dec 1] 16,000Y: leggy filly: half-sister to 3 winners, including useful 1m/9f winner Diamond Lodge (by Grand Lodge): dam French 2-y-o 1m (Prix des Reservoirs) winner: fair performer: won maiden at Wolverhampton in November: placed behind Hurricane Spirit in minor event/nursery at Lingfield: raced at 6f: on edge first 2 starts. *J. Pearce*

TEBEE 2 ch.f. (Mar 26) Selkirk (USA) 129 – Massarra 99 (Danehill (USA) 126) [2006 **76 P** p8g⁵ Oct 20] 110,000Y: first foal: dam, 6f winner (including at 2 yrs) who stayed 7f, closely related to very smart sprinter Invincible Spirit out of Prix de Diane winner Rafha: 3/1, highly-promising fifth to Fragrancy in maiden at Lingfield, going strongly in rear before eye-catching headway in straight, not knocked about: will improve considerably, and sure to win races. *J. H. M. Gosden*

TECKTAL (FR) 3 ch.f. Pivotal 124 – Wenge (USA) (Housebuster (USA)) [2006 61: 8f **62** p10g Dec 10] leggy filly: modest maiden: left L. Cumani 4,000 gns after reappearance: should be suited by 7f+. *P. M. Phelan*

TEDDY MONTY (IRE) 3 b.g. Bold Fact (USA) 116 – Mount Soufriere (IRE) **50** (Maledetto (IRE) 103) [2006 53: p8g⁴ f8g p7.1g p7g f6g* f7g 6d 6m 5.7g f5g 5f 10.1m f7g f6g Dec 28] leggy gelding: modest performer: won banded race at Southwell in March: left M. Quinn after twelfth start: effective at 6f, probably stays easy 1m: acts on all-weather and good to firm going: often wears headgear. *R. E. Barr*

TEDSDALE MAC 7 ch.g. Presidium 124 – Stilvella (Camden Town 125) [2006 68: **71 d** 8.9m⁴ 7.9m⁵ 9.9f² 12.1f⁵ 7f 9.8d⁶ 8.9f 9.3f⁶ 12.1d 10g⁶ 9.9m Sep 19] close-coupled, quite good-topped gelding: fair handicapper: below form after third start: stays 1¼m: acts on firm and soft ground: tried in cheekpieces/blinkers. *N. Bycroft*

TEDSTALE (USA) 8 ch.g. Irish River (FR) 131 – Carefree Kate (USA) (Lyphard **78** (USA) 132) [2006 89, a85: f16g³ p12.2g 11.5g 11.8f* 12m⁶ 8.3m⁴ 12s⁵ Oct 14] smallish, sturdy, close-coupled gelding: unimpressive mover: fair performer: won claimers at Leicester in July and Catterick in August: barely stays 2m: acts on all-weather, firm and good to soft going: wears blinkers/cheekpieces: sometimes slowly away: usually waited with: sometimes finds little. *K. A. Ryan*

TEE JAY KASSIDY 6 b.g. Petong 126 – Priceless Fantasy (Dunbeath (USA) 127) **62** [2006 60: p7g f8g f7g* f8g⁶ Dec 27] smallish gelding: modest performer nowadays: won banded race at Southwell in December: stays 8.5f: acts on all-weather and firm going: sometimes wears headgear (visored for latest win). *P. S. McEntee*

TEENAGE RAMPAGE 4 b.g. Prince Sabo 123 – Sorridar 77 (Puissance 110) [2006 – 39: f6g p8.6g p8.6g p7.1g p9.5g Mar 29] leggy, lengthy gelding: poor performer at 3 yrs: little form in 2006. *W. M. Brisbourne*

TEEN AGER (FR) 2 b.c. (Mar 22) Invincible Spirit (IRE) 121 – Tarwiya (IRE) 103 – (Dominion 123) [2006 6m⁶ Jun 29] very green when sixth of 8 in maiden at Leicester. *J. S. Moore*

TEE OFF (IRE) 2 ch.f. (Jan 28) Barathea (IRE) 127 – Forget Me Not (IRE) (Danehill **75** Dancer (IRE) 117) [2006 6g⁵ 6m³ 6g 6f 6.1d² 6v³ p7g⁴ Nov 25] €75,000F, €140,000Y: lengthy filly: first foal: dam unraced half-sister to Irish 2000 Guineas/Poule d'Essai des Poulains winner Bachir: fair maiden: in frame 4 times, twice in nurseries: likely to stay 1m: acts on polytrack, good to firm and good to soft going: tongue tied last 4 starts: sold 15,000 gns, sent to USA. *B. W. Hills*

TEES COMPONENTS 11 b.g. Risk Me (FR) 127 – Lady Warninglid (Ela-Mana- **102** Mou 132) [2006 95: 14g* 18s² Oct 7] tall, well-made gelding: useful on Flat and over hurdles, lightly raced: off 9 months, won handicap at Haydock (50/1, beat Candle ¾ length) in September: creditable second in similar event at York only other outing in 2006: stays 2¼m: acts on polytrack, soft and good to firm going: tongue tied: held up. *K. G. Reveley*

TEIDE LADY 3 ch.f. Nashwan (USA) 135 – Oshiponga 72 (Barathea (IRE) 127) [2006 **75** 66: 12.1d 8d p9.5g³ f8g⁴ p10g² 9m* 9g 12s 8d p9.5m³ p9.5g³ Nov 11] angular filly: fair performer: awarded maiden at Newcastle (hampered when beaten neck by Summer Lodge) in August: good placed efforts in handicaps last 2 starts: stays 1¼m: acts on polytrack and good to firm going. *Rae Guest*

TEJAREB (IRE) 3 b.f. Sadler's Wells (USA) 132 – La Pepite (USA) (Mr Prospector – (USA)) [2006 8.2m May 12] leggy, close-coupled filly: half-sister to several winners, including 7f (at 2 yrs)/1m winner Soldera (by Polish Numbers) and 1m/1¼m winner Asly (by Riverman), both useful: dam, placed in USA, out of champion Canadian filly Fanfre-luche: 80/1, well held in maiden at Nottingham. *C. E. Brittain*

TELEGONUS 3 b.g. Fantastic Light (USA) 134 – Circe's Isle (Be My Guest (USA) **73** 126) [2006 –: p10g⁶ p12g Sep 18] leggy, close-coupled gelding: fair maiden: left G. Wragg 20,000 gns and gelded after reappearance: should be suited by 1½m: acts on polytrack. *C. E. Longsdon*

TELEPATHIC (IRE) 6 b.g. Mind Games 121 – Madrina 70 (Waajib 121) [2006 61: **56** 5m⁵ 5d 6g⁶ 5.9g 6m Aug 12] big, good-bodied gelding: modest performer: stays 6f: acts on firm and soft ground: tried tongue tied/blinkered/in cheekpieces: has reared leaving stall/been slowly away. *A. Berry*

TELL 3 b.c. Green Desert (USA) 127 – Cephalonie (USA) (Kris S (USA)) [2006 88: **106** 8.1g² 10s⁶ 10m 10f⁴ 8g³ Aug 5] well-made colt: useful performer: best efforts when placed in minor event at Sandown (beaten a head by Ivy Creek) and listed race at Deau-ville (beaten 2 short heads by Kersimon): better at 1m than 1¼m: acts on good to firm and good to soft going: has worn crossed noseband: joined E. Charpy in UAE. *J. L. Dunlop*

TELLING 2 b.g. (Apr 5) Josr Algarhoud (IRE) 118 – Crystal Canyon 59 (Efisio 120) **55** [2006 5g³ 5d 6s Oct 16] sturdy gelding: went wrong way after third in maiden at Ponte-fract: bred to prove best up to 7f: gelded after final start. *Mrs A. Duffield*

TELLITLIKEITIS 5 b.g. Defacto (USA) – Chimes of Peace 64 (Magic Ring (IRE) – 115) [2006 f8g Dec 14] well beaten in 3 bumpers: last of 11 in seller on Flat debut. *Miss Kariana Key*

TELLTIME (IRE) 2 b.f. (Apr 6) Danetime (IRE) 121 – Tesla (IRE) 42 (Fayruz 116) **66 p** [2006 p5g² Dec 16] first foal: dam, lightly-raced Irish maiden, closely related to very smart US performer up to 9f The Deputy and half-sister to high-class Japanese performer up to 1½m King Kamehameha: 14/1, head second of 7 to Rocker in maiden at Kempton, staying on well: will stay 6f: sure to improve. *A. M. Balding*

TEMBANEE (IRE) 2 b.c. (Feb 5) Selkirk (USA) 129 – Rivana 79 (Green Desert **89 p** (USA) 127) [2006 8.1m* 7d⁴ Sep 27] 20,000Y: third foal: brother to 6f winner in Aust-ralia/Hong Kong and half-brother to useful 2004 2-y-o 1m winner Bayeux de Moi (by Barathea): dam, Irish maiden (stayed 9f), half-sister to Irish Oaks winner Winona: won both starts, maiden at Chepstow and minor event at Salisbury, in latter good attitude to beat Aqmaar by 1¼ lengths: will stay 1¼m: sent to Hong Kong, where renamed Conti-casta: useful prospect. *R. Hannon*

TEMBLADORA (IRE) 3 b.f. Docksider (USA) 124 – Oiche Mhaith 74 (Night Shift (USA)) [2006 6v 6.1g⁵ p6m³ p6g Dec 20] €4,000F, €6,000Y: sister to 4-y-o Clinet and half-sister to 2 winners in Italy: dam Irish 6f winner: modest maiden: trained on debut by E. Lynam in Ireland: will stay 7f. *J. W. Hills*   **64**

TEMPELSTERN (GER) 2 gr c (Apr 24) Sternkoenig (IRE) 122 – Temple Esprit (Esprit du Nord (USA) 126) [2006 8.5g³ 8m³ Sep 21] €24,000Y: brother to German winners Telramund (at 10.5f to 11.7f) and Temple Magic (1½m), and half-brother to 2 winners in Germany: dam German 1¼m to 2m winner: fair form in maidens, third to Regime at Beverley and Ommraan at Pontefract: will be suited by 1¼m/1½m. *H. R. A. Cecil*   **78**

TEMPERANCE (IRE) 3 b.f. Orpen (USA) 116 – Alberjas (IRE) (Sure Blade (USA) 130) [2006 60: 10g⁵ 8.2m⁴ 8.3m² 8.2m⁴ 10d² 8.5f* 9f⁴ Oct 5] rather leggy filly: fair performer: left S. Kirk, won maiden at Del Mar in September: stays 1¼m: acts on firm and good to soft going. *D. Vienna, USA*   **76**

TEMPER TANTRUM 8 b.g. Pursuit of Love 124 – Queenbird 90 (Warning 136) [2006 61, a69: p8g⁵ p10g⁵ p10g p7g⁶ Feb 13] strong, good-bodied gelding: modest performer: effective at 7f to easy 1¼m: acts on all-weather, firm and good to soft ground: tried tongue tied (not since 2002): usually wears headgear: held up. *J. R. Best*   **57**

TEMPESTUOUS SEA (IRE) 3 ch.f. Tagula (IRE) 116 – Mrs Siddons (IRE) 82 (Royal Academy (USA) 130) [2006 60: 6g Aug 4] well-grown filly: maiden: tailed off only outing in 2006: unruly and unseated at stall once at 2 yrs. *T. D. Barron*   **–**

TEMPLE AIR (IRE) 2 ch.g. (Feb 18) Abou Zouz (USA) 109 – Regal Air (IRE) 68 (Distinctly North (USA) 115) [2006 5.1g p5.1g p6m Nov 8] well beaten in sellers. *W. G. M. Turner*   **–**

TEMPLE BELLE XPRES 4 b.f. Overbury (IRE) 116 – Kustom Kit Xpres 69 (Absalom 128) [2006 36: f12g p8.6g f5g⁶ Apr 4] close-coupled filly: maiden: no form in 2006: tried blinkered. *S. R. Bowring*   **–**

TEMPLE PLACE (IRE) 5 b.g. Sadler's Wells (USA) 132 – Puzzled Look (USA) (Gulch (USA)) [2006 101: 10.3m 12m Jun 24] good-topped gelding: useful handicapper at best: better effort in 2006 on reappearance: effective at 1m to 1½m: acts on good to firm and good to soft going: tried blinkered: fair winning hurdler. *D. McCain Jnr*   **93**

TEMPLET (USA) 6 b.g. Souvenir Copy (USA) 113 – Two Step Trudy (USA) (Capote (USA)) [2006 82d: 9.2m⁴ 16g⁶ 8d 11.1m⁵ p9.5g⁴ p12.2g⁴ f13.9g² p12.2g⁵ Dec 18] stocky gelding: modest performer: effective at 7.2f, seemingly at 2m: acts on all-weather and any turf going: wears headgear: ungenuine. *W. G. Harrison*   **57 §**

TEMPSFORD FLYER (IRE) 3 b.g. Fasliyev (USA) 120 – Castellane (FR) (Danehill (USA) 126) [2006 74: p8.6g* p8g² 8s⁶ 8g* 8m⁵ 8m p8g p8.6g Nov 16] neat gelding: fairly useful performer: won maiden at Wolverhampton in April and handicap at Newbury in June: stays 8.6f: acts on polytrack and good to firm ground: gelded after final outing. *J. W. Hills*   **88**

TEMTATION (IRE) 2 b.f. (Jan 12) Trans Island 119 – Ish (IRE) (Danehill (USA) 126) [2006 5g⁶ p6g³ 6g⁴ 5d² 5.1m⁴ 6d Sep 29] 4,000Y: first foal: dam unraced out of half-sister to high-class French 7f to 1¼m performer Bigstone: fair maiden: stiff task final outing: stays 6f: acts on good to soft going, probably polytrack. *J. R. Boyle*   **68**

TENANCY (IRE) 2 b.c. (Mar 15) Rock of Gibraltar (IRE) 133 – Brush Strokes (Cadeaux Genereux 131) [2006 7.1d³ 8s p8.6g⁴ p7.1g⁴ Nov 28] 80,000Y: close-coupled colt: has round action: closely related to French 10.5f winner Craft Fair (by Danehill) and half-brother to 3-y-o Kassiopeia, both useful: dam, unraced, out of half-sister to Irish Oaks winner Colorspin, herself dam of Opera House and Kayf Tara: fair maiden: should stay 1¼m: acts on polytrack and soft ground: free-going sort. *J. A. Osborne*   **69**

TEN BLACK 2 ch.g. (Mar 14) Dr Fong (USA) 128 – Pulau Pinang (IRE) 101 (Dolphin Street (FR) 125) [2006 6.1g 7f⁵ p6g⁶ p7.1g⁵ p8g³ Dec 2] modest maiden: left J. Osborne before final start (third in nursery): stays 1m: acts on polytrack and firm going. *R. Brotherton*   **55**

TEN CARAT 6 b.g. Grand Lodge (USA) 125 – Emerald (USA) (El Gran Senor (USA) 136) [2006 101: 16m 16d 18m⁴ 16.1m 15.8m³ 21m 18s Oct 7] big, strong gelding: fairly useful handicapper: stays 21f: acts on soft and good to firm going: tried in visor/blinkers: got very warm before third start: often front runner. *M. Todhunter*   **81**

TENCENDUR (IRE) 2 ch.c. (May 4) King Charlemagne (USA) 120 – Jallaissine (IRE) (College Chapel 122) [2006 5.1d⁴ 5m² 5d² 7f* 7m² 7f⁴ 7.5g³ 8s* Sep 14] 26,000Y: **81**

lengthy colt: second foal: half-brother to 3-y-o Campbeltown: dam French maiden half-sister to smart 1½m winner Riyafa: fairly useful performer: won maiden at Brighton in July (then left M. Johnston 12,000 gns) and minor event at Ayr in September, in latter made all to beat Massive by head: in frame all other starts, including 3 nurseries: stays 1m: acts on firm and soft going: usually front runner. *D. Nicholls*

TEN CENTS 4 b.f. Dansili 127 – Daylight Dreams 77 (Indian Ridge 123) [2006 66: **67** p9.5g⁴ p10g* p10g³ 11.9g² 11.9m³ 12m 10.1f² Jul 6] close-coupled filly: fair performer: won banded race at Lingfield in February: stays 1½m: acts on polytrack and firm going: sometimes races freely: usually patiently ridden: sold 21,000 gns, sent to Qatar. *C. F. Wall*

TEN COMMANDMENTS (IRE) 3 br.f. Key of Luck (USA) 126 – Zoudie 79 **41** (Ezzoud (IRE) 126) [2006 40: p8.6g f7g⁶ f6g p12.2g⁶ p12g⁶ p12g 10f³ Jul 4] leggy filly: poor maiden: left J. Balding after third start: probably stays easy 1½m: acts on polytrack and firm going: tried blinkered: upset in stall final outing. *K. J. Burke*

TENDER FALCON 6 br.g. Polar Falcon (USA) 126 – Tendresse (IRE) 60 (Tender **87** King 123) [2006 98: 12g⁴ 14.1f⁶ May 7] tall, good-topped gelding: useful handicapper at 6 yrs: fairly useful form on reappearance: ran as if amiss subsequent outing: effective at 1¼m/1½m: acts on firm and good to soft going: game. *R. J. Hodges*

TENDER MOMENTS 2 br.f. (Jan 22) Tomba 119 – Cherish Me 88 (Polar Falcon **77** (USA) 126) [2006 6s* 6m³ 8d Sep 16] 30,000Y: tall, workmanlike filly: third foal: sister to 4-y-o Golden Square: dam 6f winner: fair form: won maiden at Haydock in May: last in nursery final start (sweated): should stay 7f/1m: sold 5,500 gns. *K. A. Ryan*

TENDER PROCESS (IRE) 3 b.g. Monashee Mountain (USA) 115 – Appledorn 99 **83** (Doulab (USA) 115) [2006 6.1m⁶ 6.1m⁵ 5.1s² 5g* 5m 5v* Oct 9] 8,000 2-y-o: big, strong gelding: half-brother to several winners, including fairly useful 7f winner Lady Pahia (by Pivotal) and 4-y-o Dorn Dancer: dam 6f/7f winner, latter including at 2 yrs: fairly useful performer: won handicaps at Thirsk in August and Ayr (comfortably) in October: should prove as effective at 6f as 5f: acts on heavy going: slowly away first 3 outings. *E. S. McMahon*

TENDER THE GREAT (IRE) 3 br.f. Indian Lodge (IRE) 127 – Tender Guest (IRE) **75** (Be My Guest (USA) 126) [2006 61: 9.8g 8.5g² 8m⁶ 8m* 8m 10g 8d⁶ p8.6g² p9.5g³ p8.6g² p9.5g⁴ p8.6g⁶ Dec 8] big, close-coupled filly: fair handicapper: won apprentice event at Newmarket in June: stays 9.5f: acts on polytrack and good to firm going: in cheekpieces (tended to flash tail)/visor last 4 outings: has pulled hard. *V. Smith*

TENDER TRAP (IRE) 8 b.g. Sadler's Wells (USA) 132 – Shamiyda (USA) 83 (Sir **88** Ivor (USA) 135) [2006 90: p16g⁶ p16.5g 14m² 14.1g Jun 29] useful-looking gelding: fairly useful handicapper, lightly raced: stays 2m: acts on all-weather, soft and good to firm going: suspect temperament nowadays: sold 6,000 gns, joined Miss J. Foster. *T. G. Mills*

TEN DOLLARS MORE (IRE) 2 b.c. (Apr 15) Elnadim (USA) 128 – Saltaire (IRE) **80** (Idris (IRE) 118) [2006 5f⁵ 6m³ 6d³ f6g* 7.1g⁴ 7.1g² p7g⁵ 7m³ p8.6m⁴ 7m⁵ 7.1d 6d⁵ Sep 29] €10,000F, €15,000Y: quite good-topped colt: second foal: half-brother to Italian 5f (at 2 yrs) and 1m winner by Second Empire: dam well beaten only start: fairly useful performer: won maiden at Southwell in May: mostly ran creditably in minor events/nurseries after: stays 7f: acts on all-weather and firm going: blinkered last 3 outings. *J. A. Osborne*

TEN FOR TOSCA (IRE) 2 b.c. (Apr 28) Distant Music (USA) 126 – Errazuriz (IRE) **59** 94 (Classic Music (USA) 125) [2006 5g⁵ 5f 5.1f³ 5.1m⁴ 5g⁴ 5.3m⁵ Sep 19] modest maiden: speedy, raced at 5f (bred to stay 1m): acts on firm going. *J. A. Osborne*

TENINI 3 ch.g. Bertolini (USA) 125 – River Abouali (Bluebird (USA) 125) [2006 f8g³ **52** 10g⁵ 8g a8g² 12.5s Oct 27] third in maiden at Southwell on debut: sold from J. Osborne 9,000 gns afterwards and left C. Von Der Recke after third start: second in minor event at Mons, only other form: best efforts at 1m. *W. Beetens, Belgium*

TENNESSEE BELLE (IRE) 4 b.f. Lahib (USA) 129 – Spirito Libro (USA) 89 (Lear **49** Fan (USA) 130) [2006 45: p6g⁶ p7g p7.1g 11.5g⁴ 10m p12g p12.2g² f12g p12.2g Jul 13] poor maiden: stays 12.2f: acts on polytrack: tried blinkered. *C. N. Allen*

TENNIS STAR (IRE) 3 b.g. Montjeu (IRE) 137 – Fabled Lifestyle (Kings Lake **79** (USA) 133) [2006 78p: 10.2g⁴ p8g⁵ 10d⁶ 8.3g² Oct 16] compact gelding: fair maiden: stays 1¼m: raced only on polytrack and good/good to soft ground: tends to find little/hang: sold 20,000 gns. *R. Charlton*

TEN PROPHETS (IRE) 3 b.g. Namid 128 – Mrs Evans (IRE) 97 (College Chapel **70**
122) [2006 p6g⁵ f6g a5g* 7g a6g* Jun 17] €26,000F, €40,000Y: third foal: half-brother
to 6f winner Wendy's Girl (by Ashkalani): dam Irish 7f winner, including at 2 yrs: better
effort in maidens for J. Osborne first 2 starts when fifth at Wolverhampton on debut
(reportedly lost action next time): won minor event at Mijas in March and handicap there
in June: stays 6f: acts on sand: returned to Britain, joined D. Nicholls. *P. Haley, Spain*

TEN SHUN 3 ch.g. Pivotal 124 – Mint Royale (IRE) 44 (Cadeaux Genereux 131) [2006 **83**
59: p8g² p8.6g* p8.6g⁵ f7g² p8g p8g³ 6.1d³ 8g⁵ 7.1f⁵ 7.1m 6.1m* 5s* 6d² 6v² p6g p6g³
p7.1g Dec 23] fairly useful performer: won seller at Wolverhampton in January and,
having left M. Polglase after fourth start, handicaps at Chepstow and Ayr in September:
effective at 5f to 8.6f: acts on all-weather, heavy and good to firm going: tried in blinkers/
visor (better without). *P. D. Evans*

TENSION POINT 2 b.g. (Feb 8) Hernando (FR) 127 – Blessed (IRE) (Jurado (USA)) **71**
[2006 7.1m³ 7m p7g⁶ 8g p8.6g⁴ 10.2m³ Sep 25] 16,000F, 62,000Y: medium-sized, quite
attractive gelding: seventh foal: half-brother to 3 winners in Italy, including one at 9f by
Dolphin Street: dam Italian 8.5f to 1¼m (including 9f at 2 yrs) winner: fair maiden: will
stay 1½m: gelded after final start. *J. A. Osborne*

TEN TENORS (IRE) 3 b.f. Rossini (USA) 118 – Prima 76 (Primo Dominie 121) **59**
[2006 p7.1g f6g² p6g⁶ p6g Mar 15] €45,000Y: second foal: half-sister to useful Italian
winner up to 9.5f Bond Deal (by Pivotal): dam sprint maiden (best at 2 yrs): modest
maiden: sold 5,500 gns, sent to USA. *J. A. Osborne*

TENTERHOOKS (IRE) 2 b.f. (Jan 18) Orpen (USA) 116 – Punta Gorda (IRE) (Roi **55**
Danzig (USA)) [2006 p6g p7g² p6g⁶ Jul 1] 36,000Y, resold 20,000Y: fifth foal: half-sister
to fairly useful 1½m winner Man At Arms (by Daggers Drawn): dam second at 11f in
France: modest form when runner-up in maiden at Lingfield: will stay at least 1m: raced
on polytrack. *J. A. Osborne*

TEN TO THE DOZEN 3 b. or ch.g. Royal Applause 124 – Almost Amber (USA) 88 **70**
(Mt Livermore (USA)) [2006 77p: 9.8m 7.5f⁴ p8.6g p7.1m p6g p8.6g f7g Dec 2] strong,
close-coupled gelding: fair maiden: stays 7.5f: acts on firm and good to soft going: has
twice been withdrawn at start, including when breaking out of stall prior to intended
reappearance. *P. W. Hiatt*

TEODORA ADIVINA 2 b.f. (Mar 19) Fantastic Light (USA) 134 – Omara (USA) 87 **68 p**
(Storm Cat (USA)) [2006 8.2s⁴ Oct 18] tall, close-coupled filly: fourth foal: half-sister
to French 1m winner (including at 2 yrs) Monte Real (by Royal Academy): dam, won
around 1¼m, half-sister to smart performer up to 1½m Etizaaz, out of half-sister to
Swain: 20/1, under 4 lengths fourth to Metaphoric in maiden at Nottingham, hampered
briefly: will probably stay 1½m: sure to improve. *H. R. A. Cecil*

TEOFILO (IRE) 2 b.c. (Feb 9) Galileo (IRE) 134 – Speirbhean (IRE) 111 **126**
(Danehill (USA) 126) [2006 7m* 7g* 7g* 7g* 7d* Oct 14]
　　　There is no shortage of two-word combinations which have resonance
in the world of racing, including, at random, King George, Rowley Mile, Royal
Ascot, dead heat, short head and starting price, but none excites the racing public
and media to quite the extent of this one—triple crown. The term is of historical
importance and implies superlative excellence and versatility and, in addition to the
modern era, virtual impossibility of attainment. Given that only one colt has won
the Two Thousand Guineas, Derby and St Leger in the last seventy years—Nijinsky
in 1970—even trying for the triple crown, let alone winning it, has become an
equine version of the search for the Holy Grail. Mentioning the words in connection
with a two-year-old might be seen as preposterous hubris deserving only ridicule.
Despite this, Jim Bolger's almost throwaway line about Teofilo in September—'If
he wants to be the next triple crown horse, I'm not going to stand in his way'—was
taken up and analysed at length by pundits with a surprising degree of tolerance
and sobriety. This probably reflected the esteem in which Bolger is held, and the
acceptance that he is not prone to exaggeration, but it was also a reflection of the
ability and enormous potential of the colt the trainer was discussing.
　　　Like Nijinsky after his juvenile campaign, Teofilo is unbeaten against the
best of his age, and in gaining Group 1 victories in two countries, in the National
Stakes and the Dewhurst Stakes, he went one better than his illustrious predecessor
whose principal success in Ireland came in the Beresford Stakes. Teofilo is also like
Nijinsky in the sense that he fulfils these remarks in *Racehorses of 1970*: 'For a

Galileo EBF Futurity Stakes, the Curragh—
Teofilo idles and has only a head to spare over Eagle Mountain (striped sleeves)

two-year-old with pretension to stay he had a record unusual by present-day standards in that it had come through a succession of important races unblemished.'
Teofilo isn't so good as Nijinsky was at two. The latter was rated 131 after being
extended only once in five races and winning the Dewhurst Stakes without coming
off the bit, whereas Teofilo had to work hard to gain his Dewhurst success in
particular. In the past ten years, only two juveniles have been rated higher than
Teofilo, namely Xaar (132 in 1997) and Johannesburg (127 in 2001), though
Alhaarth and Shamardal were also rated 126. Furthermore, Teofilo has a timefigure
from the Dewhurst (0.98 fast) which equates to a timerating of 125 and was the best
by any horse of any age in Britain in the latest season and the best by a juvenile
since Xaar. He is, in short, a first-rate prospect. Bolger has stated that Teofilo is
the best he has trained, which means he believes him superior to the champion
three-year-old of 1992 St Jovite, who was rated 135 after winning the Irish Derby
by twelve lengths and the King George VI and Queen Elizabeth Stakes by six. If
Teofilo proves capable of that level of form, the triple crown may yet be a possibility, providing everything else goes according to plan, which it rarely does.
Nothing can ever be certain with thoroughbreds and the 12/1 odds about his landing
the treble look ridiculously cramped. Asked how he would cope with the pressure
of training the champion juvenile colt (owned and bred, incidentally, by his wife)
and juvenile filly (Finsceal Beo) in the run up to the classics, Bolger quipped
'I don't do pressure. Pressure is for tyres and footballs, not me.' With luck he will
be given the chance to prove the point, not just in the period up to the classics but
through the whole season.

Teofilo's first three races take little describing. He made his debut in a
ten-runner maiden at the Curragh on Irish Oaks day in July and, starting fourth
favourite, beat the Aidan O'Brien-trained odds-on favourite Red Rock Canyon by
a neck. Later in the month at Leopardstown Teofilo followed up as favourite in the
Korean Racing Association Tyros Stakes, beating Chesham Stakes third Middle-

ham in good style by a length and three quarters, before emulating such top-class colts as Giant's Causeway, Hawk Wing, Oratorio and Horatio Nelson by landing the Galileo E.B.F. Futurity Stakes at the Curragh. In the latter, facing six opponents including Anglesey Stakes winner Regional Counsel and three O'Brien-trained maiden winners, Teofilo looked like justifying favouritism emphatically when quickening to lead over a furlong out after racing a bit freely early on. However, he idled in front before producing a willing response under pressure to get the better of Eagle Mountain by a head. The Laing O'Rourke National Stakes on the same course in mid-September was the next target and, for once, the race lacked strength in depth, four of the six runners, including Teofilo's pacemaker Slaney Time, being maidens and there being no challengers from Britain. Holy Roman Emperor, fresh from his victory in the Phoenix Stakes a month before, was 9/4-on, odds which rather overstated his claims, with Teofilo at 2/1 and the rest at 25/1 or longer. Slaney Time did his job effectively and two furlongs out Teofilo, in second virtually from the outset, showed fine acceleration to take it up and go clear. Holy Roman Emperor, not devoid of speed by any means, could do nothing about cutting back the leader, who maintained his run in great style to pass the post a length and a quarter to the good.

Bolger was reportedly in two minds where to run Teofilo next, eventually deciding to bypass the Prix Jean-Luc Lagardere, won in his absence by Holy Roman Emperor, in favour of the Darley Dewhurst Stakes at Newmarket later in October. The National Stakes-Dewhurst Stakes double is not achieved that often, no colt having managed it since Dashing Blade in 1989 (Vincent O'Brien had done it with Cellini in 1973 and with Monteverdi, Storm Bird and El Gran Senor between 1979 and 1983). The Dewhurst was a much stronger race than the National Stakes, with six pattern winners among the fifteen contenders. Besides Teofilo, who was sent off 11/8 favourite, and Holy Roman Emperor, these were Strategic Prince (July Stakes and Vintage Stakes), Halicarnassus (Superlative Stakes), Hamoody (Richmond Stakes) and Vital Equine (Champagne Stakes and third behind Holy Roman Emperor in France). With such promising maiden and/or minor winners as Adagio, Haatef and Rallying Cry also in the field, this was pretty clearly the most competitive juvenile event of the year. It provided a fine spectacle, too, as Teofilo and Holy Roman Emperor confirmed their standing. After a rather tardy start, Teofilo soon took closer order on the stand side, racing in fourth place with his customary enthusiasm while Holy Roman Emperor was held up. Inside the three-furlong marker the favourite was switched slightly right and asked to make ground. He didn't show instant acceleration, but quite sufficient to take up the running, galloping on strongly until, as previously, he began to idle a little. All the others were under strong driving, and only one danger remained—Holy Roman Emperor,

Laing O'Rourke National Stakes, the Curragh—Teofilo starts to live up to the high opinion his trainer holds of him by beating odds-on Holy Roman Emperor; Eyshal (virtually obscured) and Slaney Time (rail) are third and fourth

Darley Dewhurst Stakes, Newmarket—
closer between the pair this time as Teofilo has only a head to spare over Holy Roman Emperor

who was producing a strong finish on the outside after having had to weave his way through. Holy Roman Emperor's run took him in front of Teofilo momentarily, before the latter, who towered over his rival, rallied to snatch the lead again on the line, having to cope with Holy Roman Emperor's edging left into him. The margin was a head, with Strategic Prince two and a half lengths away third just ahead of the strong-finishing Haatef and the always prominent Vital Equine. Hamoody and Halicarnassus both ran below form.

Kevin Manning on Teofilo received a one-day suspension for his use of the whip in the Dewhurst. Some argued that Holy Roman Emperor was unlucky, and there is no denying he had to be extricated to obtain a clear passage but, unlike Horatio Nelson the previous year, he got through in plenty of time to launch his challenge. Not that Holy Roman Emperor needed any excuses. Teofilo's performance was as good as any in the Dewhurst, apart from Xaar's, in the last twenty years, and the form looks rock solid. As usual, the outcome encouraged all sorts of thoughts about the future. Winners of the Dewhurst Stakes who have proved fully effective at a mile and a half as three-year-olds have a fine record. They do not form a majority in the last twenty years. In fact just nine have run at the distance and only five of those got the trip well, but that quintet were Derby winners Generous, Dr Devious and Sir Percy, Derby third Tobougg and Dashing Blade, who picked up a Group 1 on his only attempt at the distance. With confidence in Teofilo's ability to stay the distance at Epsom, it was no surprise to see his Derby odds tumble from 10/1 to 4/1. He was also cut to 5/2 favourite for the Two Thousand Guineas. The Dewhurst provided the last piece of information available to punters, though Bolger apparently toyed with the idea of giving Teofilo another run, in the Criterium International, the plan abandoned when the ground came up soft. Teofilo has yet to race on extremes of going and it remains to be seen whether he is raced on very soft. As a long-striding sort, he may not be seen to best advantage on such a surface. Teofilo should look the part at three, being a tall, rather leggy, good-topped colt and a good walker. He has the scope to develop into an imposing individual. For the record, Bolger's achievement of training both the top two-year-old colt and filly matched that of Aidan O'Brien in 2005 with Horatio Nelson and Rumplestiltskin; Etienne Pollet had been the last to do so with Le Mesnil and Hula Dancer in 1962, two years after Paddy Prendergast with Floribunda and Kathy Too.

The raising of Galileo's fee at Coolmore for 2007 from €37,500 to €150,000 indicates the remarkable season he enjoyed. From just two crops of racing age he was responsible not only for Teofilo but also for the best three-year-old stayer Sixties Icon, Breeders' Cup Turf winner Red Rocks, Irish One Thousand

Guineas winner Nightime, and Group 2 winners Allegretto and Vendangeur. No surprise, then, that he will not be shuttling to Australia, where he covered for A\$55,000 in the latest season. Galileo was a first-rate Derby winner who followed up his easy Epsom success with similar emphatic victories in the Irish Derby and King George VI and Queen Elizabeth Stakes before narrowly losing to Fantastic Light in the Irish Champion Stakes. Galileo is by Sadler's Wells, the most successful sire in European history, out of Urban Sea who won the Prix de l'Arc de Triomphe, making him among the best-bred champion three-year-olds in the history of the turf. Predictably he was strongly patronised at Coolmore, where his books have grown over the last three years from one hundred and three to one hundred and ninety-five, with plenty of the mares bred in the purple. With Sadler's Wells in his twenties and covering slightly smaller books, the success of Galileo, following that of Montjeu, must have seemed like manna from heaven for Coolmore. Unlike some of Montjeu's progeny, Galileo's seem pretty unflappable and they also seem to have plenty of stamina, as witnessed by the fact that he sired the first three home in the St Leger, and that none of his two-year-old winners has scored over shorter than seven furlongs. These also include Soldier of Fortune, who came out the best horse at the weights when second in the Criterium de Saint-Cloud over a mile and a quarter. On the sire's side there is certainly no reason to doubt Teofilo's staying the Derby trip, and maybe further.

However, there are two sides to every pedigree, so what about his dam Speirbhean? A minor point is that she is by Danehill, which means Teofilo, in keeping with an increasing number of thoroughbreds in Europe, is inbred to Northern Dancer. Speirbhean was a smart but unlucky filly who raced only four times, win-

Mrs J. S. Bolger's "Teofilo"

ning the Derrinstown Stud One Thousand Guineas Trial over a mile only to injure herself in the classic itself and never reappear. Her first foal, also by Galileo, is the useful three-year-old Senora Galilei, trained by Bolger and an eight-length winner of a handicap over a mile and a quarter at the Curragh in June. She ran once more, when a good second in a similar event the following month, but wasn't seen out again. She looked as if a mile and a half would be within her compass. Speirbhean's dam Saviour, trained by Bolger, was no stakes performer on the racecourse but she won three of her nine starts from nine furlongs to eleven furlongs, including handicaps at Dundalk and Killarney. On her only outing over a mile and a half, she was nineteenth of twenty-two when humping 10-2 in another handicap at Galway, beaten only six lengths. Saviour produced six other winners including Cornwall, who ran three times at two including when second in a listed race over seven furlongs. Saviour's other progeny included Graduated, a versatile sort successful in a bumper, a maiden race at a mile and three quarters and, dropped back in trip afterwards, six handicaps at a mile to nine furlongs, one of them listed. Saviour is also the dam of Mise Eire, winner of a two-mile maiden, and Citizen Edward, who scored at seven furlongs to a mile and a half. Saviour came from a fine family since her brother War won the Grade 1 Blue Grass Stakes over nine furlongs and two of her half-brothers, Judge Angelucci and Peace, also won at that level over the same trip, Judge Angelucci coming third in the Breeders' Cup Classic. Saviour's sire Majestic Light won at up to a mile and a half and her dam Victorian Queen, officially champion older filly in Canada in 1975, won at up to eleven furlongs.

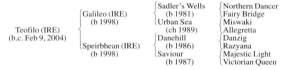

		Sadler's Wells (b 1981)	Northern Dancer Fairy Bridge
	Galileo (IRE) (b 1998)	Urban Sea (ch 1989)	Miswaki Allegretta
Teofilo (IRE) (b.c. Feb 9, 2004)		Danehill (b 1986)	Danzig Razyana
	Speirbhean (IRE) (b 1998)	Saviour (b 1987)	Majestic Light Victorian Queen

Teofilo's pedigree is very much a middle-distance one, which makes his achievements in his first season all the more meritorious. His sire Galileo ran only once at two, when landing a maiden over a mile by fourteen lengths. On the face of it, the Derby distance should suit Teofilo better than the mile of the Two Thousand Guineas, but stamina can sometimes depend nearly as much on temperament and style of racing as on pedigree. Teofilo showed a tendency to race fairly keenly on most of his starts and that is not usually encouraging for a horse with pretensions to staying a mile and half, let alone further. However, there is no sign of Teofilo's being a highly-strung sort—he handled the preliminaries in the Dewhurst with aplomb—and he is by no means headstrong. In all probability his style of racing in his first season can be put down to exuberance that can flow from immaturity, a trait which in theory ought to become less noticeable as he matures. Providing this is so, the Two Thousand Guineas promises to be a pretty tough assignment for Teofilo. The trip may be on the sharp side at that stage of his development, and he will be facing at least one high-class colt trained specifically for the race—his old rival Holy Roman Emperor, who will not get the Derby trip. Also to take into consideration is Bolger's remarks about Teofilo's fitness and the fact that he has stated the colt will not be asked to carry a Group 1 penalty in any trial for the first classic on unsuitable ground, preferring a racecourse gallop: 'He's a great "grubber"; it's something we'll have to deal with to get him to Newmarket fit and ready.' Bolger knows his job, though, and he will not saddle Teofilo at Newmarket without making sure he is fit enough for the job in hand. Suffice to say that the clash of Teofilo and Holy Roman Emperor in the Two Thousand Guineas promises to be an intriguing encounter, a race which, at the time of writing, and bearing in mind the odds available, looks one to watch closely rather than bet on. Be that as it may, provided he comes through this initial test having performed well, even if he fails to win, Teofilo should still be a very tough nut to crack at Epsom. *J. S. Bolger, Ireland*

TEORBAN (POL) 7 b.g. Don Corleone 115 – Tabaka (POL) (Pyjama Hunt 126) [2006 **62** 62: p16.5g p16g p16g p16.5g⁵ Dec 29] modest handicapper: left D. ffrench Davis after second start: stays 17f: acts on all-weather and good to firm going: tried in cheekpieces. *Mrs N. S. Evans*

TE QUIERO 8 gr.g. Bering 136 – Ma Lumiere (FR) (Niniski (USA) 125) [2006 –, a99d: f8g⁵ f7g f8g² f8s² p7g p7g May 24] good-topped gelding: fairly useful handicapper on all-weather, fair on turf: effective at 7f to 9.4f: acts on fibresand (well held on polytrack), soft and good to firm going: usually tongue tied/in headgear: often makes running. *Miss Gay Kelleway* — **a90**

TEQUILA ROSE (IRE) 3 b.f. Danehill Dancer (IRE) 117 – Enthrone (USA) (Diesis 133) [2006 52: p6g⁵ f6g⁴ f7g⁴ p6g Mar 29] sparely-made filly: poor maiden: raced mainly at 5f/6f: acts on all-weather, good to firm and good to soft ground. *A. Bailey* — **47**

TEQUILA SHEILA (IRE) 4 ch.f. Raise A Grand (IRE) 114 – Hever Rosina 63 (Efisio 120) [2006 77d: f7g⁶ p7.1g 6g² 8d 6m 7.2g 6.9g⁶ 8g* 7s* 7m³ 8.1m³ 7.2s⁴ 7.2v⁶ Oct 28] quite attractive filly: modest handicapper nowadays: won at Thirsk (selling event) and Catterick in August: stays 1m: acts on polytrack, soft and good to firm going: sometimes wanders: has worn visor/cheekpieces. *K. R. Burke* — **60**

TERATAI (IRE) 2 b.f. (May 5) Shinko Forest (IRE) – London Pride (USA) 106 (Lear Fan (USA) 130) [2006 7g Aug 18] half-sister to 3 winners, including 5-y-o Bukit Fraser and 1999 2-y-o 7f winner Pekan's Pride (both by Sri Pekan): dam, 1m winner and third in Fred Darling on only starts in Britain, ran 3 times in USA: well held in maiden at Folkestone. *M. A. Jarvis* — **–**

TERENTIA 3 br.f. Diktat 126 – Agrippina 99 (Timeless Times (USA) 99) [2006 74p: 5g* 5d* 5f⁵ 5f* 5d² 5g 6g Oct 12] strong, lengthy filly: useful performer: won handicaps at Haydock in April, Windsor in May and Goodwood (beat unlucky Buachaill Dona by neck) in August: poor effort in listed race at Newmarket final outing: will prove best at 5f/6f: acts on firm and good to soft going. *E. S. McMahon* — **103**

TERENZIUM (IRE) 4 b.g. Cape Cross (IRE) 129 – Tatanka (ITY) (Luge 113) [2006 65: p8.6g³ p8g* 8.1f⁵ p8g² p8g⁶ 8f Aug 15] leggy gelding: modest performer: won apprentice banded race at Kempton in May: should stay 1¼m: best efforts on polytrack/good ground: tried visored: said to have finished lame final outing: sold 9,000 gns, joined M. D. Hammond, and gelded. *L. M. Cumani* — **62**

TERLAN (GER) 8 b.g. Medicus (GER) – Taxodium (GER) (Blakeney 126) [2006 57: 8v⁵ Oct 28] leggy gelding: well held in 3 handicaps in Britain: fair winning hurdler/chaser. *P. Monteith* — **–**

TERMINATE (GER) 4 ch.g. Acatenango (GER) 127 – Taghareed (USA) 93 (Shadeed (USA) 135) [2006 80: 10.9g 10g 10d 8g 10m 9.9m* 10m 10g p10g Sep 3] leggy gelding: fair handicapper: won 4-runner event at Beverley in July: best at 1¼m: acts on polytrack, good to firm and good to soft going: in cheekpieces/blinkers last 5 starts: often slowly away: none too reliable. *N. P. Littmoden* — **70**

TERRAQUIN (IRE) 6 b.g. Turtle Island (IRE) 123 – Play The Queen (IRE) (King of Clubs 124) [2006 56§: p12g Apr 5] good-bodied gelding: one-time fairly useful performer: modest and inconsistent latterly, and reportedly lame only outing in 2006: usually wore headgear: dead. *J. J. Bridger* — **– §**

TERRY MOLLOY (IRE) 2 b.g. (Jan 29) Xaar 132 – Pile (USA) 62 (Shadeed (USA) 135) [2006 6g 5.9g* 7.1g⁶ 7m⁶ Sep 16] €13,000F, 12,500Y: good-topped gelding: third foal: dam lightly-raced Irish maiden (third at 8.5f): fair performer: made all in maiden at Carlisle in August: stamina seemingly stretched in 2 nurseries (then gelded): likely to prove best at 5f/6f. *K. R. Burke* — **75**

TERRYS ALFIE 3 b.g. Compton Place 125 – Loveless Carla (Pursuit of Love 124) [2006 p12.2g p8.6g p6g p6g Jun 15] well held in maidens/handicap: tried blinkered, *N. P. Littmoden* — **–**

TESLIN (IRE) 2 b.c. (Feb 11) In The Wings 128 – Yukon Hope (USA) 75 (Forty Niner (USA)) [2006 8.1g² 8.1m² 8g* 8s 8g Oct 29] 50,000Y, resold 44,000Y: strong, well-made colt: fifth foal: half-brother to smart 7f/1m winner Independence (by Selkirk), dam of 2-y-o Mount Nelson: dam, maiden who would have stayed 1¼m, out of half-sister to Reference Point: fairly useful performer: runner-up in 2 maidens prior to winning minor event at Newbury (by 1¼ lengths and head from Aqaleem and newcomer Authorized) in September: stiff task in Racing Post Trophy at Newbury and Criterium International at Saint-Cloud: likely to stay 1¼m/1½m. *M. Johnston* — **89**

TESORO 3 b.g. Compton Place 125 – Zenita (IRE) (Zieten (USA) 118) [2006 –: p7.1g f8g⁵ f7g⁶ 9.9g May 13] poor maiden, lightly-raced: dead. *P. A. Blockley* — **42**

TETOUAN 2 b.c. (Apr 27) Danehill Dancer (IRE) 117 – Souk (IRE) 98 (Ahonoora 122) **61 p**
[2006 7.1m 7d Sep 29] 120,000Y: smallish, sturdy colt: half-brother to numerous winners, including 5-y-o Golden Quest, smart 1¼m/1½m winner Puce (by Darshaan) and to
dam of 3-y-o Alexandrova: dam 7f winner (including at 2 yrs): some promise in maidens
at Warwick and Newmarket, staying on after hampered: likely to do better, especially at
1¼m/1½m. *R. Charlton*

TETRAGON (IRE) 6 b.g. Octagonal (NZ) 126 – Viva Verdi (IRE) 70 (Green Desert **67**
(USA) 127) [2006 72: 10.3m⁶ 11.6m⁴ 9.2m⁴ 12.1m² 10g⁴ 11.8g f11g Oct 12] good-
topped gelding: fair performer: stays 1½m: acts on fibresand, good to firm and good to
soft ground: ran well in visor/blinkers earlier in career: has raced freely/wandered: best
ridden up with pace. *D. Carroll*

TETRODE (USA) 4 b.g. Quiet American (USA) – Mother Courage 67 (Busted 134) **61 d**
[2006 f6g⁶ 6f⁴ 6d⁴ 6d 6d Sep 25] form only in maiden at Lingfield second outing.
R. M. H. Cowell

TEUTONIC (IRE) 5 b.m. Revoque (IRE) 122 – Classic Ring (IRE) 50 (Auction Ring **50**
(USA) 123) [2006 41: p12.2g⁴ f11g² 16g⁴ 16g Jul 3] tall, quite good-topped mare: modest **a55**
maiden: stays 2m: acts on all-weather, best turf effort on good going: often slowly away
(has refused to race over hurdles). *R. F. Fisher*

TEXAS GOLD 8 ch.g. Cadeaux Genereux 131 – Star Tulip 99 (Night Shift (USA)) **107**
[2006 110: 5m 5m 5m 6m p5g² 5m 6m 5m³ 5d⁵ 6m 5.4g⁴ 6m⁵ 5g p6g⁵ p5g* p5.1g p6g
Nov 11] sturdy, close-coupled gelding: useful handicapper: won at Lingfield in October
by 1½ lengths from Intrepid Jack: below form last 2 starts: effective at 5f/easy 6f: acts on
polytrack (well beaten on fibresand), firm and good to soft going: has been early to post:
waited with: none too consistent. *W. R. Muir*

TEYAAR 10 b.g. Polar Falcon (USA) 126 – Music In My Life (IRE) 59 (Law Society **48 §**
(USA) 130) [2006 –, a50: f6g³ f6g p6g p5.1g⁴ f6g p6g p5.1g f6g⁵ 6m⁴ 6m p6g³ p7g **a51 §**
p7.1g⁴ p6g⁴ p6g⁴ Dec 13] strong gelding: modest on all-weather, poor on turf: stays easy
7f, best at 5f/6f: acts on all-weather, best turf form on good going or softer: has worn
blinkers/visor: sometimes hangs: unreliable. *M. Wellings*

THABAAT 2 ch.c. (Feb 10) Pivotal 124 – Maraatib (IRE) 93 (Green Desert (USA) 127) **89**
[2006 7g² 7.1m² Sep 4] smallish, sturdy colt: half-brother to several winners, including
5f/6f (including at 2 yrs) winner Khasayl (by Lycius) and 2001 2-y-o 7f winner Muklah
(by Singspiel), both useful: dam 5f (including at 2 yrs)/6f winner: second in maidens,
fairly useful form when beaten 1¼ lengths by Prince Forever at Newbury on debut: hung
right at Warwick (odds on) 2 weeks later: not sure to stay much beyond 7f. *B. W. Hills*

THALBERG 3 gr.g. Highest Honor (FR) 124 – Stage Manner 104 (In The Wings 128) **81**
[2006 –p: 10g² 9.8m² 9m³ Jun 23] tall, close-coupled gelding: fairly useful maiden,
lightly raced: stays 1¼m: raced only on good/good to firm going: on edge penultimate
start, found little final one: gelded after. *M. A. Jarvis*

THARUA (IRE) 4 b.f. Indian Danehill (IRE) 124 – Peig Sayers (IRE) 58 (Royal Aca- **–**
demy (USA) 130) [2006 53, a59: f14g² p16.5g⁶ f14g³ p16.5g Jul 28] leggy, lengthy filly: **a56**
modest performer: stays 2m: acts on all-weather, firm and good to soft ground: often
visored/in cheekpieces. *E. R. Oertel*

THAT LOOK 3 b.g. Compton Admiral 121 – Mudflap 82 (Slip Anchor 136) [2006 57: **62**
6m 11.5m 14.1g² p16.5g³ Dec 29] modest maiden on Flat: stays 2m: raced only on polytrack and good/good to firm going: fair juvenile hurdler. *D. E. Cantillon*

THAT'S BLUE CHIP 3 b.g. Namid 128 – Star Cast (IRE) 82 (In The Wings 128) **68**
[2006 58: 5f 5m* Aug 5] sturdy gelding: fair performer, lightly raced: won handicap at
Windsor in August, carried markedly left then hanging right: raced only at 5f: acts on
good to firm going. *P. W. D'Arcy*

THAT'S RACING 6 ch.g. Classic Cliche (IRE) 128 – All On 68 (Dunbeath (USA) **–**
127) [2006 f14g Apr 10] rather lengthy, good-topped gelding: lightly-raced maiden on
Flat: poor hurdler, winner in December. *J. Hetherton*

THE ALDBURY FLYER 3 b.g. Royal Applause 124 – Fantasy Ridge 92 (Indian **77**
Ridge 123) [2006 10m⁶ 8.2m³ 10d⁵ p10g Oct 20] 15,000Y: lengthy, unfurnished gelding:
first foal: dam, 2-y-o 7f winner, granddaughter of top-class miler Milligram: fair maiden:
virtually pulled up final outing: stays 1¼m: acts on good to firm and good to soft going:
has been bandaged in front. *W. R. Swinburn*

THEANN 2 b.f. (Mar 31) Rock of Gibraltar (IRE) 133 – Cassandra Go (IRE) 119 (Indian **101**
Ridge 123) [2006 6m² 6m² 7d⁵ 6d⁵ 6s² 6d* Oct 15] €400,000Y: close-coupled filly: half-
sister to 4-y-o Neverletme Go and 3-y-o Mannikko: dam, 5f (including Temple/King's
Stand Stakes) to 7f winner, half-sister to Irish 2000 Guineas second Verglas: useful
performer: odds-on winner of maiden at Naas in October: best form previous 2 starts, 3
lengths fifth of 11 to Indian Ink in Cheveley Park Stakes at Newmarket and 5 lengths
second of 12 to Evening Time in listed race at the Curragh: probably best at 6f: acts on
soft and good to firm going. *A. P. O'Brien, Ireland*

THEATRE GROOM (USA) 7 ch.g. Theatrical 128 – Model Bride (USA) (Blushing **–**
Groom (FR) 131) [2006 p12g Aug 30] bumper winner/modest novice hurdler: well
beaten in maiden at Lingfield only Flat start. *M. R. Bosley*

THEATRE ROYAL 3 b.f. Royal Applause 124 – Rada's Daughter 107 (Robellino **67**
(USA) 127) [2006 71: 7d⁶ 8.3d³ p10g⁵ 10.2f² 10m⁵ 8m³ 9m Aug 27] unfurnished filly:
fair maiden handicapper: stays 1¼m: acts on firm and good to soft ground. *A. M. Balding*

THEATRE TINKA (IRE) 7 b.g. King's Theatre (IRE) 128 – Orange Grouse (IRE) **56**
105 (Taufan (USA) 119) [2006 59: p12.2g⁴ Feb 20] close-coupled gelding: modest
performer: effective at 1¼m to 1¾m: acts on all-weather, firm and good to soft going:
usually wears cheekpieces: consistent: modest winning hurdler. *R. Hollinshead*

THEATRE (USA) 7 b.g. Theatrical 128 – Fasta (USA) (Seattle Song (USA) 130) **88**
[2006 81: 16s⁶ 18m⁵ 16g⁴ p16g³ 21m² 16m² 16d* 18d Oct 14] close-coupled gelding:
fairly useful handicapper: won at Ascot in September: creditable seventh in Cesarewitch
at Newmarket (looked none too keen) final outing: stays 21f: acts on polytrack, firm and
soft going: blinkered (ran to form) twice at 3 yrs: usually held up. *Jamie Poulton*

THE BEAR 3 ch.g. Rambling Bear 115 – Precious Girl 76 (Precious Metal 106) [2006 **–**
91: 6m⁶ May 12] well-grown, angular gelding: fairly useful performer at 2 yrs: stiff task,
well held in minor event at Hamilton on only outing in 2006: will prove best at 5f/6f: acts
on firm and soft going: joined G. A. Swinbank. *I. Semple*

THE BEDUTH NAVI 6 b.g. Forzando 122 – Sweets (IRE) (Persian Heights 129) **–**
[2006 52: f12g p16.5g p13.9g Mar 6] angular, heavy-topped gelding: modest performer:
no form in 2006: blinkered once (ran poorly). *D. G. Bridgwater*

THEBESTISYETTOCOME 4 b.g. Montjeu (IRE) 137 – French Quartet (IRE) **59**
(Lycius (USA) 124) [2006 61: p10g⁴ p12g p10g⁵ 10m p12g 10.9d³ p12g⁴ Sep 29] rather **a66**
leggy gelding: fair handicapper on all-weather, modest on turf: should stay 1½m: acts on
polytrack, firm and good to soft ground: visored (ran creditably) third start. *T. G. Mills*

THE BONUS KING 6 b.g. Royal Applause 124 – Selvi (Mummy's Pet 125) [2006 75: **67**
p8g p7.1g³ 8d⁵ p8.6g* 8.5g⁶ 8d 7f p8.6g 8.2m Jul 29] strong, angular, good-topped
gelding: has a fluent action: fair handicapper: won at Wolverhampton in April: best at 7f/
1m: acts on all-weather and any turf going: tried blinkered: won over hurdles in August/
September. *J. Jay*

THE BRAT 2 b.f. (Mar 4) Perryston View 114 – Kalarram (Muhtarram (USA) 125) **44**
[2006 5m 5m⁵ 6m⁵ 5m⁵ 5f⁶ 7s 5m⁵ Sep 11] good-bodied filly: first foal: dam well held in
3 starts: poor maiden: tried visored. *James Moffatt*

THE BRONX 2 b.c. (Mar 20) Dansili 127 – Carradale 73 (Pursuit of Love 124) [2006 **66 p**
p7g 5.1d³ p5g Dec 16] 23,000Y, 85,000 2-y-o: quite good-topped colt: first foal: dam,
2-y-o 5f winner, out of half-sister to smart middle-distance stayers Applecross and Coig-
ach: fair form in maiden on debut: inadequate test both other starts: will be suited by 1m+:
probably capable of better. *M. J. Wallace*

THE CARLTON CANNES 2 b.c. (Feb 10) Grand Lodge (USA) 125 – Miss Riviera **73 p**
Golf 106 (Hernando (FR) 127) [2006 7d⁶ 7d⁶ Oct 28] compact colt: third foal: brother to
3-y-o Hotel du Cap: dam, 1m winner, sister to useful 1¼m performer Miss Corniche:
encouragement when sixth in maidens at Leicester and Newmarket, 4 lengths behind
Mr Napper Tandy at latter, rallying: will improve, particularly at 1¼m+. *G. Wragg*

THE CAYTERERS 4 b.g. Cayman Kai (IRE) 114 – Silky Smooth (IRE) (Thatching **81**
131) [2006 55: 5.1s⁵ 7f* 6d* 6g 5.7m* 6m* Sep 19] fairly useful handicapper: won at
Leicester in July and August, and Bath and Brighton (readily, despite hanging left) in
September: effective at 5.7f to 7f: acts on firm and good to soft going. *J. M. Bradley*

THE CITY KID (IRE) 3 b.f. Danetime (IRE) 121 – Unfortunate 55§ (Komaite **66**
(USA)) [2006 76: f7g³ 7g 6.1s⁶ f6g⁵ f6g 7.2s f6g² f6g⁴ f7g⁶ p8.6g* Dec 30] leggy

filly: fair performer: won claimer at Wolverhampton in December: stays 8.6f: acts on all-weather and heavy ground: wears headgear. *P. D. Evans*

THE COMBO 3 gr.c. Selkirk (USA) 129 – Snowing 88 (Tate Gallery (USA) 117) [2006 – p9.5g 9.9g Aug 25] well held in maidens at Wolverhampton and Salisbury. *M. Blanshard*

THE COMPOSER 4 b.g. Royal Applause 124 – Superspring (Superlative 118) [2006 77 82: p12g 16g 10.5s* 9.9g⁶ 11.9g³ 11.9m 11.9s⁴ 10g 10d⁶ Oct 10] good-bodied gelding: fair handicapper: won at Haydock in May: stays 1½m: acts on soft and good to firm ground. *M. Blanshard*

THE COOL SANDPIPER 2 ch.g. (Mar 22) Piccolo 121 – The Dark Eider (Super- 65 p lative 118) [2006 5.1m² Aug 20] first foal: dam unraced out of half-sister to 10-y-o The Whistling Teal: 10/1, length second to Cuppacocoa in maiden at Bath: gelded after: should progress. *P. Winkworth*

THE CROOKED RING 4 b.g. Magic Ring (IRE) 115 – My Bonus 79 (Cyrano de 68 Bergerac 120) [2006 94: 7g 5.1m 6m 6g p7.1f 6.1m⁵ p6m⁶ 7d p7g⁴ p7g Nov 8] leggy, workmanlike gelding: fair handicapper: seems to stay 7f: acts on polytrack, firm and soft ground: often wears headgear. *P. D. Evans*

THE CRUNCH (IRE) 5 b.m. College Chapel 122 – Lady Tristram (Miami Springs 49 121) [2006 –: 7s³ 7.2d⁴ 7.5s² 8.5d 7d⁴ 8.2v⁶ 8g f8g Nov 14] poor maiden: stays 7.5f: acts on soft going: tongue tied nowadays. *D. Loughnane, Ireland*

THE CUTE WON (USA) 8 b.g. Defensive Play (USA) 118 – Alzabella (USA) (Top 55 Command (USA)) [2006 –: 12g⁴ 13m⁶ p12.2g⁵ Dec 23] modest performer nowadays: lightly raced of late: probably stays 13f: acts on polytrack, firm and good to soft going: tried in cheekpieces, often blinkered. *N. Dooly, Ireland*

THE DAGGER 2 ch.g. (Mar 12) Daggers Drawn (USA) 114 – Highland Blue 55 – (Never So Bold 135) [2006 p6g Oct 17] last in maiden at Lingfield. *J. R. Best*

THE DANDY FOX 2 b.f. (Mar 26) Foxhound (USA) 103 – Classic Storm 73 (Belfort 52 (FR) 89) [2006 5d 5m⁵ 7m 7m³ 7g⁴ 6s 6s p5.1g 6s⁵ Oct 16] 3,300Y: well-grown, close- coupled filly: seventh foal: dam 2-y-o 5f/6f winner: modest maiden: claimed from D. Nicholls £3,000 fifth outing: stays 7f: acts on soft and good to firm going: tried blink- ered. *R. Bastiman*

THE DIAMOND BOND 2 bl.g. (Feb 28) Josr Algarhoud (IRE) 118 – Alsiba 68 50 (Northfields (USA)) [2006 7d⁴ 7d⁶ Aug 28] never nearer in maidens at Newcastle, modest form on debut: bred to be suited by 1¼m+. *G. R. Oldroyd*

THE DUNION 3 br.g. Beckett (IRE) 116 – Dacian (USA) (Diesis 133) [2006 –: 9.2m 47 7.2v 9m 8.3g 11.1m 12.1m⁶ 14g⁶ Aug 31] good-bodied gelding: poor maiden: seems to stay 1¾m. *Miss L. A. Perratt*

THE FIFTH MEMBER (IRE) 2 b.c. (Apr 17) Bishop of Cashel 122 – Palace Soy 66 (IRE) (Tagula (IRE) 116) [2006 p8g⁵ p8g⁴ p8g Nov 29] €3,000F, €10,000 2-y-o: first foal: dam unraced: fair form second start in maidens, fourth to Mafeking at Kempton: raced at 1m on polytrack. *R. M. Flower*

THE FISIO 6 b.g. Efisio 120 – Misellina (FR) 57 (Polish Precedent (USA) 131) [2006 63 76: p5g p5.1g⁵ 5s p5g p5g³ p5g Dec 20] smallish, strong gelding: modest handicapper nowadays: best at 5f/easy 6f: acts on all-weather, soft and good to firm going: usually visored: often races prominently. *S. Gollings*

THE FLYING COWBOY (IRE) 2 b.g. (Feb 16) Tagula (IRE) 116 – Sesame Heights – (IRE) 63 (High Estate 127) [2006 8m Sep 19] compact gelding: last (reportedly lost action) in maiden at Newmarket: gelded after. *N. P. Littmoden*

THE FLYING PEACH 3 ch.f. Observatory (USA) 131 – Taffeta (IRE) 69 (Barathea 41 (IRE) 127) [2006 –: 8.1g p8g 8.3d 7.9m⁶ 8.3m² 8f 8.1m Aug 10] strong filly: poor maiden: stays 1m: acts on good to firm going. *W. M. Brisbourne*

THE FONZE (IRE) 5 br.g. Desert Sun 120 – Ultimate Beat (USA) (Go And Go) [2006 74 52: 10.2m² p10g* p10g* 12s² Aug 10] fair handicapper: won twice at Lingfield in June: stays 1½m: acts on polytrack, soft and good to firm going: fairly useful hurdler. *Eoin Doyle, Ireland*

THE GAIKWAR (IRE) 7 b.g. Indian Ridge 123 – Broadmara (IRE) 91 (Thatching 79 131) [2006 83, a72: p10g p8.6g⁶ 9.7f⁵ 8d 8.1d 10.2g⁵ 8f 8m³ 8.1g³ 8.1f* 8m⁶ 8.1m³ 9m³ **a63** 8.3d⁵ 8.1m⁴ 9.7m 8d⁶ p8.6m p8.6g⁴ f8g⁵ 8.6g p8.6g Dec 11] lengthy gelding: fair handi- capper on turf, modest on all-weather nowadays: won at Chepstow in July: effective at

1m, stays easy 9.7f: acts on polytrack, firm and soft going: tried in cheekpieces, blinkered nowadays: sometimes slowly away. *R. A. Harris*

THE GEESTER 2 b.c. (Apr 4) Rambling Bear 115 – Cledeschamps 46 (Doc Marten 104) [2006 6g 7.5m⁵ 7g f7g⁵ f5g³ f5g⁵ p6s f5g² Dec 23] strong colt: modest maiden: seems suited by 5f/6f: acts on fibresand: best efforts in blinkers, also tried in cheekpieces: tongue tied final start. *S. R. Bowring*   **60**

THE GEEZER 4 ch.c. Halling (USA) 133 – Polygueza (FR) 78 (Be My Guest (USA) 126) [2006 122: 13.9s⁵ May 19] big, lengthy colt: very smart performer at 3 yrs for D. Elsworth: in excellent shape, well below form in Yorkshire Cup at York only start in 2006: suffered suspensory injury after: stays 14.6f: acts on soft going: tended to edge left fifth/ninth outings at 3 yrs, flashed tail for one of 3-y-o wins. *Saeed bin Suroor*   **–**

THE GRAIG 2 b.c. (Apr 20) Josr Algarhoud (IRE) 118 – Souadah (USA) (General Holme (USA) 128) [2006 6f⁶ 6m 6m⁶ Aug 19] little impact in maidens. *C. Drew*   **–**

THE GREAT DELANEY 3 b.g. Inchinor 119 – Top 74 (Shirley Heights 130) [2006 –: f8g p10g 8.1s* 9m⁶ 9d⁴ 8s 8.1m p10g⁶ Dec 19] modest handicapper: left Miss D. McHale after reappearance: 150/1, won at Chepstow in May: left K. McAuliffe after fourth outing: stays 1¼m: acts on polytrack and soft going: tried in cheekpieces/blinkers. *Ms J. S. Doyle*   **64 a56**

THE GREY BAM BAM 2 gr.f. (Mar 4) Baryshnikov (AUS) – Leonie Samual 50 (Safawan 118) [2006 5g 6m 7.1m Aug 16] tall filly: first foal: dam 1m winner: last in maidens. *R. J. Hodges*   **–**

THE GREY BERRY 2 gr.c. (May 1) Observatory (USA) 131 – Elderberry (Bin Ajwaad (IRE) 119) [2006 6m³ 6s⁵ 6s⁵ Sep 28] modest form in maidens: likely to prove best at 5f/6f. *C. Grant*   **64**

THE GREY MAN 5 gr.g. Muhtarram (USA) 125 – Lavender Della (IRE) 66 (Shernazar 131) [2006 f12g⁴ 10g⁶ 12f⁴ 14.1s 14.1g⁶ 16.2f⁴ 16m² 16.2m² 16.2d Sep 16] angular gelding: won bumper in 2005: fair maiden handicapper on Flat: left E. McMahon after eighth outing: stays 2m: acts on firm going: won over hurdles in November. *J. W. Mullins*   **73**

THE GREY ONE (IRE) 3 gr.g. Dansili 127 – Marie Dora (FR) 86 (Kendor (FR) 122) [2006 58: 7.1s 7f³ 6.1d² 8s 5.9m 7f⁵ 6m 6.1d² 8.2v² 8.2d Nov 1] tall, close-coupled gelding: modest maiden: stays 1m: acts on any going: in cheekpieces after reappearance: has hung. *J. M. Bradley*   **64**

THE HISTORY MAN (IRE) 3 b.g. Titus Livius (FR) 115 – Handsome Anna (IRE) 67 (Bigstone (IRE) 126) [2006 78: 6d 6d⁴ 6s.1d² 5g⁵ 6g 6f 6f² 6g 6s⁵ 6g 5v³ Oct 9] workmanlike gelding: fair handicapper: raced only at 5f/6f: acts on heavy and good to firm going: blinkered: quirky and unreliable. *M. W. Easterby*   **77 §**

THE ILLIES (IRE) 2 b.c. (Apr 19) Fasliyev (USA) 120 – Velvet Appeal (IRE) 101 (Petorius 117) [2006 5.2m⁶ 5s⁵ 6f 8m* 8g* 8g Oct 12] 36,000F, 70,000Y: strong, good sort: sixth foal: half-brother to 3 winners, including useful 7f winner Craiova (by Turtle Island) and 5-y-o Nephetriti Way: dam Irish 1m winner: fairly useful performer: much improved in nurseries, winning at Bath and Yarmouth in September: pulled too hard final start: stays 1m: acts on good to firm going: patiently ridden. *B. W. Hills*   **84**

THE IRON GIANT (IRE) 4 b.g. Giant's Causeway (USA) 132 – Shalimar (IRE) 95 (Indian Ridge 123) [2006 59: 10.9m 14.1m⁶ 14.1g p12g³ p12g⁵ 11.9m³ 10.2m p12g p10g³ p12.2g⁶ Dec 9] lengthy, good-topped gelding: modest maiden handicapper: left A. O'Brien in Ireland after 3 yrs: stays 1¾m: raced on polytrack and good/good to firm going. *B. G. Powell*   **64**

THE ITALIAN JOB 2 b.f. (Apr 16) Bertolini (USA) 125 – Charming Lotte 80 (Nicolotte 118) [2006 5d 5g² 5f⁵ 5m 5m⁶ 5g⁴ 5m³ 6v p5.1g² Nov 10] 12,000Y: leggy, workmanlike filly: second foal: dam 6f winner, including at 2 yrs: fair performer: placed 3 times (including 2 nurseries), and won maiden at Southwell in November: best at 5f: acts on all-weather and good to firm going: keen sort, often front runner. *T. D. Easterby*   **73**

THE JAILER 3 b.f. Mujahid (USA) 125 – Once Removed 65 (Distant Relative 128) [2006 41: p8.6g⁵ f8g² p10g³ 10g⁶ p8.6g² 8.3d⁴ p8g³ 8m³ 7.1g⁶ Jul 5] leggy filly: poor maiden: stays 1m: acts on all-weather, good to firm and good to soft going: tried in cheekpieces/visor. *J. G. M. O'Shea*   **47**

THE JAY FACTOR (IRE) 2 b.c. (Mar 31) Bold Fact (USA) 116 – Corn Futures 78 (Nomination 125) [2006 5g⁵ 5m p6g⁴ Nov 22] modest form in maidens: off 4 months between last 2: may prove best at 5f/6f. *Pat Eddery*   **61**

THE JOB 5 ch.g. Dancing Spree (USA) – Bay Bianca (IRE) (Law Society (USA) 130) **59**
[2006 54: f7g² f8g⁶ f7g⁶ f7g p8g p8g⁴ 8m³ Aug 19] workmanlike gelding: modest performer: stays 9.4f: acts on all-weather and firm going: visored: reportedly bled fourth
start. *A. D. Smith*

THE JOBBER (IRE) 5 b.g. Foxhound (USA) 103 – Clairification (IRE) 57 (Sher- **108**
nazar 131) [2006 94: p5g p5g* 5g 5m 6m 5m⁶ 5m⁶ 5f 5.2m* 5m* 5.4g 5f* Sep 18] strong
gelding: made up into a useful handicapper in 2006 and won at Lingfield in May,
Newbury and Haydock in August, and Leicester (best effort, beat Cape Royal by 1¼
lengths) in September: effective at 5f/6f: acts on polytrack, firm and good to soft going.
M. Blanshard

THE KEEP 4 ch.f. Shinko Forest (IRE) – Poyle Amber 55 (Sharrood (USA) 124) [2006 **55**
52: 6f⁴ 6f 6m⁶ 6g 5s⁴ 6g 5v⁵ f6g Nov 15] leggy filly: modest and inconsistent maiden:
stays 6f: acts on polytrack and any turf going: blinkered/visored. *R. E. Barr*

THE KIDDYKID (IRE) 6 b.g. Danetime (IRE) 121 – Mezzanine (Sadler's Wells **113**
(USA) 132) [2006 114: 6s 6d 6m⁶ 6m² 6.1m* 6d 6s Oct 7] tall, lengthy gelding: smart
performer: won listed event at Chester in August by ½ length from Beckermet: only other
placing in 2006 (ran as if amiss final outing) when head second to One More Round in
handicap at Windsor: best at 6f: acts on any going: races up with pace. *P. D. Evans*

THE KING AND I (IRE) 2 b.g. (Mar 20) Monashee Mountain (USA) 115 – Scrim- **68**
shaw (Selkirk (USA) 129) [2006 5g³ 6m⁶ Sep 22] €24,000F, 33,000Y: quite attractive
gelding: sixth foal: half-brother to 4-y-o Bronze Dancer and 2003 2-y-o 1m winner Messe
de Minuit (by Grand Lodge): dam unraced: promising third to Grand Prix in maiden at
Sandown: found little at Haydock 3½ months later (gelded after). *Miss E. C. Lavelle*

THE LADY CASTER 3 ch.f. City On A Hill (USA) 114 – Cinnamon Lady 77 (Ema- **52**
rati (USA) 74) [2006 61d: p5g⁶ 6.1s 6.1f³ 5.5g 6f 5g Aug 23] sturdy filly: modest maiden:
left D. Morris after reappearance: stays 6f: acts on firm going: usually wears headgear:
sometimes races freely. *R. M. Beckett*

THE LADY ERMYN 3 b.f. Mull of Kintyre (USA) 114 – Corniche Quest (IRE) 74 **–**
(Salt Dome (USA)) [2006 p8g p10g Feb 8] 10,500Y: fifth foal: half-sister to 3 winners,
including 5-y-o Black Oval and 6-y-o winner Blakeshall Quest: dam 5f to 1m winner: last
in maidens at Lingfield. *T. G. Mills*

THE LADY MANDARIN 3 b.f. Groom Dancer (USA) 128 – Lonely Shore (Blake- **–**
ney 126) [2006 –: p10g 10m p12g Aug 23] smallish, leggy, close-coupled filly: well
beaten in maidens: bred to be suited by 1½m+. *G. Wragg*

THE LAST DROP (IRE) 3 b.c. Galileo (IRE) 134 – Epping 81 (Charnwood Forest **118**
(IRE) 125) [2006 80p: 10g* 10m² 10.4s⁵ 12m 12d⁴ 13.9g² 12s Oct 22] tall, good-bodied
colt: won maiden at Windsor in April by 1¼ lengths from Summer's Eve, looking ill at
ease on track: in frame after at Sandown in Classic Trial (neck second to Primary) and at
York in both Great Voltigeur Stakes (100/1, 4¼ lengths fourth to Youmzain, coming from
fair way back despite finding a little trouble inside final 1f) and St Leger (best effort, 2½
lengths second to Sixties Icon, leading 2f out): below form when seventh behind Collier
Hill in Canadian International at Woodbine final start: suited by 1¾m, will probably stay
2m: acts on good to firm and good to soft going (well held in Dante Stakes on first
occasion on soft going): ran poorly in King George V Handicap at Royal Ascot fourth
outing, tongue tied after. *B. W. Hills*

THE LEATHER WEDGE (IRE) 7 b.g. Hamas (IRE) 125§ – Wallflower (Polar **78**
Falcon (USA) 126) [2006 78: 5d 5f 5d³ 5m 5m⁴ 5m 5g⁴ 5f² 5g 5g 5s 5d p5.1g p5.1g
Nov 27] good-topped gelding: fair handicapper: best at 5f: acts on fibresand, firm and
good to soft going: tried blinkered/in cheekpieces/tongue tied: front runner: inconsistent.
R. Johnson

THE LIGHT FANDANGO 2 ch.f. (Jan 19) Kyllachy 129 – Alifandango (IRE) 78 **50**
(Alzao (USA) 117) [2006 5.1f 6g⁴ 6g 6d f7g³ p8.6g⁴ p8.6g² Dec 31] 16,000Y, 25,000
2-y-o: fourth foal: half-sister to 6f winner Miss Poppets (by Polar Falcon): dam 1m
winner: modest maiden: stays 8.6f: acts on all-weather. *R. A. Harris*

THE LONDON GANG 3 b.c. Mind Games 121 – Nom Francais 39§ (First Trump **70 §**
118) [2006 81: f5g p7g³ p6g⁶ p7g p6g p6g p6g p6g 7m⁴ 6d² 7f f6g 6m* 7f⁶ 5.9g 6s⁵ 7.1d³ f7g
f6g p6s* p7g⁵ p7.1g* Dec 26] leggy, angular colt: fair performer: won handicap at Ayr in
July, and seller and claimer at Wolverhampton in December: stays 7f: acts on all-weather,
heavy and good to firm going: usually wears headgear: often slowly away, and usually
soon off bridle: tends to hang/wander: unreliable. *P. D. Evans*

Red Corner Events Queensferry Stakes, Chester—the most valuable win of the season for champion apprentice in the turf season Stephen Donohoe, who is unable to claim his allowance on board The Kiddykid (right) in this listed race; Beckermet (check sleeves) is second as Indian Maiden (out of shot) finishes strongly on the outside to take third off Moone Cross (noseband)

THE LOOSE SCREW (IRE) 8 b.g. Bigstone (IRE) 126 – Princess of Dance (IRE) (Dancing Dissident (USA) 119) [2006 46: 12d p7g p8.6g⁶ Dec 30] good-bodied gelding: maiden: well held in 2006: tried blinkered, usually wears cheekpieces (not in 2006). *C. W. Thornton* —

THE LORD 6 b.g. Averti (IRE) 117 – Lady Longmead (Crimson Beau 124) [2006 98, a89: f5g* f5g 5.1s³ 5.2m 5.1f 5s* 5s* 5f 5g 5s p5g⁶ p5.1g Oct 29] close-coupled, quite good-topped gelding: has a quick action: useful performer on turf, fairly useful on all-weather: won handicap at Southwell in January, and handicap and 4-runner listed race at Goodwood (beat Green Manalishi by 1¼ lengths) on consecutive days in May: best at 5f: acts on all-weather, firm and soft going: tried in cheekpieces/visor: often races prominently: sometimes slowly away. *W. G. M. Turner* **108 a94**

THEME TIME (USA) 10 b.g. Stop The Music (USA) – Ranales (USA) (Majestic Light (USA)) [2006 8d f8g f7g Dec 9] poor performer in 2002: no form on belated return: wears tongue tie. *D. Morris* —

THE MIGHTY OGMORE 2 ch.f. (Apr 21) Dr Fong (USA) 128 – Welsh Dawn (Zafonic (USA) 130) [2006 5g 5g⁴ 5m² 5m* 5g³ 6f⁶ 6m⁴ 6s 7d Oct 3] 7,000Y: fourth foal: half-sister to unreliable 2004 2-y-o 6f seller winner Jay (by Bluebird) and useful Italian 1¼m performer Vigata (by Orpen): dam ran 3 times in Italy: modest performer: won seller at Musselburgh in June: effective at 5f/6f: acts on good to firm going: in cheekpieces last 2 starts: temperamental. *R. C. Guest* **63 §**

THE MUSIC QUEEN 5 ch.m. Halling (USA) 133 – Sadly Sober (IRE) 70 (Roi Danzig (USA)) [2006 12s⁵ Aug 18] 55,000Y, 7,000 3-y-o: fifth foal: half-sister to 7-y-o Ettrick Water and winner in Hong Kong by Charnwood Forest: dam, maiden who stayed 1¼m well, half-sister to smart winner up to 11f Overbury: fairly useful bumper winner: 14/1, well held in maiden at Catterick on Flat debut, not knocked about. *G. A. Swinbank* —

THE NAWAB (IRE) 4 ch.c. Almutawakel 126 – Eschasse (USA) (Zilzal (USA) 137) [2006 99: p16g² 18.7m 18m² Jun 16] lengthy, quite attractive colt: useful handicapper: creditable second to Sirce at Kempton and Ski Jump at York: stays 2½m: acts on polytrack, firm and good to soft going: said to have had breathing problem final 3-y-o start: sold 10,000gns. *J. L. Dunlop* **99**

THE NIFTY FOX 2 b.g. (Mar 4) Foxhound (USA) 103 – Nifty Alice 80 (First Trump 118) [2006 5d⁴ 5g⁶ 5m⁵ 5m³ 5f⁶ 5m 6s⁵ 5m² 5d⁴ 5d⁶ 5d* 5s³ Oct 1] 10,000Y: big, lengthy gelding: has a rather round action: first foal: dam 5f winner at 2 yrs: fairly useful performer: won maiden at Catterick: good third to Luscivious in minor event there later in October (gelded after): suited by 5f: acts on soft and good to firm going: visored (ran respectably) once. *T. D. Easterby* **82**

THE OLD FELLA 2 ch.c. (Mar 24) Compton Place 125 – Centre Court 74 (Second Set (IRE) 127) [2006 6g⁴ 5m³ 7g* 6m⁵ 6d² 6s p6g⁵ 5d Oct 7] 25,000F, 75,000Y: tall, leggy, close-coupled colt: fifth foal: half-brother to unreliable 2002 2-y-o 5f seller winner **96**

1089

Service (by College Chapel): dam 2-y-o 5f winner: useful performer: third to Elhamri in listed race at Royal Ascot prior to winning maiden at Epsom (didn't handle track that well) in July: ran creditably in minor events next 2 starts, but none too keen in Group 3s last 2: likely to prove best up to 7f: acts on good to firm and good to soft going, probably polytrack: hard ride: sold 67,000 gns. *R. Hannon*

THE OLD SOLDIER 8 b.g. Magic Ring (IRE) 115 – Grecian Belle 53 (Ilium 121) **61**
[2006 60: 5.9m⁴ 7f³ 6f* 7m⁴ Aug 8] tall gelding: modest performer: won seller at Catterick in July: stays 7f: acts on polytrack, firm and good to soft going. *A. Dickman*

THEOLOGICUM 3 b.f. King's Best (USA) 132 – Valnerina (IRE) (Caerleon (USA) **67 d**
132) [2006 p10g⁵ 9.9g 9.9g 10.9d p12g⁶ p10g p12g Dec 22] angular filly: second foal: dam, unraced half-sister to high-class Irish performer up to 1¼m Entitled and National Stakes winner El Prado, out of Irish 1000 Guineas winner Lady Capulet: fair form on debut: failed to progress: stays 1¼m: acts on polytrack. *Miss J. R. Gibney*

THEORETICAL 2 b.f. (Feb 23) Marju (IRE) 127 – Relativity (IRE) (Distant Relative **66**
128) [2006 5s 6.1m⁴ 6.5s p7.1g⁶ p6g* f6g Dec 23] 16,000Y: smallish, workmanlike filly: first foal: dam French 1m winner out of Lupe Stakes winner Scimitarra: fair performer: off 4 months after debut (trained by M. Polglase): won nursery at Kempton in December: bred to stay at least 1m: acts on polytrack: free-going type. *A. J. McCabe*

THE OSTEOPATH (IRE) 3 ch.g. Danehill Dancer (IRE) 117 – Miss Margate (IRE) **78**
60 (Don't Forget Me 127) [2006 70: 8s³ 7.2d* 8.1m⁶ 8g⁵ 7s 9.1v 8d Oct 27] leggy gelding: fair handicapper: won at Ayr in June: stays 1m: acts on soft going: in cheekpieces after reappearance: carries head awkwardly: tricky ride. *M. Dods*

THE PEN 4 ch.f. Lake Coniston (IRE) 131 – Come To The Point (Pursuit of Love 124) **65**
[2006 56: 9.9f* 10f* 11.1g* 12m 12g³ 12.1m Aug 16] workmanlike filly: fair handicapper: won apprentice events at Beverley in June and Hamilton in July: stays 1½m: acts on firm and good to soft going, respectable efforts on all-weather. *C. W. Fairhurst*

THE PERFECT PLAN (IRE) 3 b.g. Kalanisi (IRE) 132 – Talbiya (IRE) (Mujtahid **–**
(USA) 118) [2006 –p: 6v 5v 8g 10m p9.5g Dec 29] well held in Ireland for D. Weld, and in handicap on British debut final outing: tried blinkered. *T. G. Dascombe*

THE PLAINSMAN 4 b.g. Atraf 116 – Mylania 70 (Midyan (USA) 124) [2006 55: **45**
f11g p16g f8g f11g⁵ f11g f12g⁵ f8g Mar 14] leggy gelding: poor maiden: stays 1½m: acts on all-weather and good to firm ground: tried in cheekpieces. *P. W. Hiatt*

THE POWER OF PHIL 2 b.c. (Feb 24) Komaite (USA) – Starboard Tack (FR) 76 **–**
(Saddlers' Hall (IRE) 126) [2006 5.7f Jul 27] well held in maiden at Bath. *R. Brotherton*

THE PREACHER 3 b.g. Namaqualand (USA) – Bustling Around (Bustino 136) [2006 **54**
47: 10v 10d 10f 12.1g³ 12.1m⁵ Sep 19] stocky gelding: modest maiden: left J. Given after fourth start: stays 1½m: tried in cheekpieces. *J. S. Wainwright*

THE QUANTUM KID 2 b.c. (Feb 24) Desert Prince (IRE) 130 – Al Hasnaa (Zafonic **–**
(USA) 130) [2006 9m⁵ Sep 11] good-topped colt: 33/1, fifth in maiden at Redcar. *T. J. Etherington*

THE REBOUND KID 4 b.g. Royal Applause 124 – Hayhurst (Sandhurst Prince 128) **66**
[2006 53: p8g³ p7.1g⁵ p8.6g 10d⁶ 7m 8m Apr 27] fair maiden: stays 1¼m: acts on polytrack and good to soft going: tried blinkered. *G. A. Huffer*

THE RIP 5 ch.g. Definite Article 121 – Polgwynne 48 (Forzando 122) [2006 66: 10m **–**
9.9m p10g Dec 22] strong gelding: modest maiden at 4 yrs: well held in 2006: tried blinkered. *R. M. Stronge*

THE SALWICK FLYER (IRE) 3 b.g. Tagula (IRE) 116 – Shimla (IRE) 55 (Rudi- **60**
mentary (USA) 118) [2006 48: 6d⁴ p5.1g⁶ 5m³ 6m 6g⁵ 5s² 5g 6d* 6g 6d 6s⁴ p5.1g Nov 18] small, leggy gelding: modest performer: won maiden at Catterick in September: stays 6f: acts on soft and good to firm going. *A. Berry*

THE SKERRET 2 ch.c. (May 11) Loup Sauvage (USA) 125 – Cosmic Star 58 (Sibe- **57**
rian Express (USA) 125) [2006 7f⁴ 8g⁶ 7f Sep 18] leggy, lengthy colt: modest form in maidens: barely stays 1m. *P. Winkworth*

THE SLIDER 2 b.f. (Mar 7) Erhaab (USA) 127 – Cottage Maid (Inchinor 119) [2006 **54**
p7.1g⁴ 7.5f* 7f p1.1g² Jul 28] 1,300Y: quite good-topped filly: second foal: half-sister to fairly useful 7f winner Actuality (by So Factual): dam little worthwhile form: modest performer: raced in sellers, winning at Beverley in July: will stay 1¼m: acts on polytrack and firm going. *P. A. Blockley*

THE SNATCHER (IRE) 3 b.c. Indian Danehill (IRE) 124 – Saninka (IRE) 82 (Doyoun 124) [2006 93: 7g⁶ 7s³ 7s³ 6g⁶ 7.1m* 7m⁵ 6g³ 6d Sep 22] rather leggy, attractive colt: useful handicapper: won at Sandown in July by ¾ length from Ans Bach: stays 7f: acts on heavy and good to firm going. *R. Hannon* — **98**

THE SPREAD 3 ch.f. Alhaarth (IRE) 126 – Evie Hone (IRE) 69 (Royal Academy (USA) 130) [2006 54: 10.2m p12g⁵ 12f⁵ 14.1g⁶ 16.2m² 16g⁵ Sep 14] rather leggy, close-coupled filly: modest maiden handicapper: stays 2m: acts on polytrack and good to firm going. *M. Blanshard* — **58**

THE STAFFORD (IRE) 5 b.g. Selkirk (USA) 129 – Bint Zamayem (IRE) 95 (Rainbow Quest (USA) 134) [2006 p7g 7s Mar 28] no form. *L. Wells* — –

THE STRUIE 3 b.f. Observatory (USA) 131 – My Way (IRE) (Marju (IRE) 127) [2006 67?: 8.3g p10g p12g Jun 29] leggy filly: maiden: well held in 2006, leaving Miss J. Gibney after second start: tried in cheekpieces: sold 1,000 gns, sent to Spain. *E. F. Vaughan* — –

THETA 2 b.f. (Feb 24) Rainbow Quest (USA) 134 – Self Esteem (Suave Dancer (USA) 136) [2006 p7.1g Nov 14] first foal: dam unraced out of smart 1¼m winner Maidment: 10/1, well held in maiden at Wolverhampton, slowly away: should do better at 1¼m+. *H. R. A. Cecil* — – p

THE TATLING (IRE) 9 b.g. Perugino (USA) 84 – Aunty Eileen (Ahonoora 122) [2006 121: 6g 5m⁵ 5g⁴ 5d 5m 6m⁶ 5m⁶ 5f⁴ 5s⁶ 5g⁶ 5.2m 5g⁶ 5g Oct 12] strong, lengthy gelding: very smart performer at best: not quite so good in 2006, pick of efforts when beaten around 1¾ lengths in Palace House Stakes at Newmarket (fifth behind Dandy Man), Sprint Stakes at Sandown (sixth behind Pivotal Point) and Audi Stakes (King George) at Goodwood (fourth behind La Cucaracha) second/seventh/eighth outings: has won at 6f, probably best at 5f: acts on firm and soft going: tried tongue tied earlier in career: held up, and best in strongly-run race: sometimes early to post. *J. M. Bradley* — **118 d**

THE TERMINATOR (IRE) 4 b.g. Night Shift (USA) – Surmise (USA) 75 (Alleged (USA) 138) [2006 46: 8m 9m⁶ p6g p7g p8.6g⁶ f8g Dec 27] good-topped gelding: poor maiden on balance: left R. Johnson after second start: stays at least 7f: acts on polytrack and good to firm ground: tried blinkered/in cheekpieces. *M. Mullineaux* — –

THE TERRIER 3 b.f. Foxhound 103 – Branston Gem 59 (So Factual (USA) 120) [2006 75: 6f³ 6d 7m³ 6f³ 6d³ 6m 7d Sep 5] sturdy filly: fair handicapper: ran as if amiss last 2 starts: stays 7f: acts on firm and soft going. *G. A. Swinbank* — **76**

THE THRIFTY BEAR 4 ch.g. Rambling Bear 115 – Prudent Pet 65 (Distant Relative 128) [2006 74: 6d 6f 6g 5m 7m 5.9g 5d⁴ p5.1g 8d Oct 8] big, workmanlike gelding: fair performer: regressed in 2006: best at 5f/6f: acts on good to firm going, probably on good to soft: tried blinkered. *C. W. Fairhurst* — **68 d**

THE TRADER (IRE) 8 ch.g. Selkirk (USA) 129 – Snowing 88 (Tate Gallery (USA) 117) [2006 119: 5m 5d² 5m 5m³ 5m³ 6m⁴ 5s⁴ 5m⁵ Sep 5] sturdy, close-coupled gelding: usually impresses in appearance: poor mover: smart performer: best efforts in 2006 in Temple Stakes at Sandown (1¼ lengths second to Reverence), Sprint Stakes on same course (1½ lengths third to Pivotal Point) and Nunthorpe Stakes at York (2 lengths fourth to Reverence) second/fourth/seventh starts: reportedly finished distressed final outing: effective at 5f to 6.5f: acts on firm and soft going: blinkered: sometimes slowly into stride: held up, and usually travels strongly: tough. *M. Blanshard* — **115**

THE TYKE 3 gr.g. Cloudings (IRE) 112 – Vonispet (Cotation) [2006 p7.1m² p6g⁵ Dec 7] first foal: dam well beaten both starts: better effort in maidens at Wolverhampton when ½-length second to Ours on debut, making most: folded tamely next time: should stay 1m. *C. G. Cox* — **67**

THE VIOLIN PLAYER (USA) 5 b.g. King of Kings (IRE) 125 – Silk Masque (USA) 91 (Woodman (USA) 126) [2006 88, a93: p12g⁵ p10g p12g* p12.2g⁵ p12g² p13g⁴ p16g 11g p12g 12g⁵ 12m 11.9f⁵ p12.2f p12g p13.9m² Oct 9] stocky gelding: fairly useful handicapper on all-weather, fair on turf: won at Lingfield in February: largely below form in second half of season: probably stays easy 1¾m: acts on polytrack, best turf efforts on good to firm/firm ground: tried visored/sometimes wears cheekpieces: sometimes idles in front. *H. J. Collingridge* — **69 a92 d**

THEWHIRLINGDERVISH (IRE) 8 ch.g. Definite Article 121 – Nomadic Dancer (IRE) 52 (Nabeel Dancer (USA) 120) [2006 84: 13.8g 16f 16.2f³ 14m² 18f 16m⁴ 14.1f² 17.1d 15.8d³ 17.5d² 17.1d* 18s 15.8s² 16d⁶ Nov 3] lengthy, good-topped gelding: fair handicapper: won at Pontefract in October: stays 2¼m: acts on firm and soft going: sometimes finds little. *T. D. Easterby* — **74**

Blue Square Ormonde Stakes, Chester—
The Whistling Teal belies his years to become the joint oldest horse to win a pattern race in Europe;
the temperamental Orcadian (rail) runs a remarkable race in second

THE WHISTLING TEAL 10 b.g. Rudimentary (USA) 118 – Lonely Shore (Blakeney 126) [2006 119: 12g⁵ 13.4d* 14m⁶ 15.9d³ 14g³ 12s⁴ Oct 21] strong gelding: carries condition: smart performer: won Ormonde Stakes at Chester in May by ½ length from Orcadian: not discredited when third behind Sergeant Cecil in Lonsdale Cup at York (warm beforehand, stamina stretched) and Kastoria in Irish St Leger at the Curragh: reluctant to enter stall, below form in St Simon Stakes at Newbury final outing: stays 1¾m: acts on fibresand, firm and soft going: held up: genuine. *G. Wragg* **116**

THE WILY WOODCOCK 2 b.c. (May 26) Mark of Esteem (IRE) 137 – Lonely Shore (Blakeney 126) [2006 6g p7g Nov 22] useful-looking colt, unfurnished at 2 yrs: half-brother to 2 winners, notably 10-y-o The Whistling Teal: dam Italian 13.5f winner: green and little impression in maidens: will benefit from 1¼m+. *G. Wragg* **60 p**

THE WIZARD MUL 6 br.g. Wizard King 122 – Longden Pride (Superpower 113) [2006 56: 12g f8g 9.2g Aug 23] leggy gelding: modest performer at best: well held in 2006: tried blinkered: tongue tied last 4 starts. *W. Storey* **–**

THE WIZENED APPLE (USA) 2 b.g. (Mar 31) Gulch (USA) – Lakabi (USA) 63 (Nureyev (USA) 131) [2006 7g² Aug 23] $40,000Y, 30,000 2-y-o: third foal: half-brother to winner in USA by Coronado's Quest: dam ran once: 40/1, ¾-length second of 17 to Cold Quest in maiden at Leicester: sent to USA: should progress. *N. A. Callaghan* **88 p**

THEY ALL LAUGHED 3 ch.g. Zafonic (USA) 130 – Royal Future (IRE) (Royal Academy (USA) 130) [2006 61: p9.5g⁶ p7g p7g p6g 8.1g⁵ 10m⁵ p8.6g* 8f 8m⁴ 8g 7.9g⁵ 8.5g⁵ 9m⁶ 10m⁵ Sep 19] tall, useful-looking gelding: modest handicapper: trained by T. Mills until after third outing, by Karen George for fourth start only: won at Wolverhampton (hung left) in June: barely stays easy 1¼m: acts on polytrack, good to firm and good to soft ground: tried blinkered (ran poorly). *P. W. Hiatt* **60**

THINKING POSITIVE 2 b.f. (Feb 12) Rainbow Quest (USA) 134 – Midnight Air (USA) 111 (Green Dancer (USA) 132) [2006 8m⁴ Sep 19] tall, leggy, quite attractive filly: half-sister to several winners, including useful 1m winner Midnight Line (by Gone West) and smart 7f (at 2 yrs) to 1½m winner Midnight Line (by Kris S): dam won May Hill Stakes and first past post in Fillies' Mile: 7/1, 6 lengths fourth to Light Shift in maiden at Newmarket, considerably handicapped: will be suited by 1¼m/1½m: sure to improve. *J. H. M. Gosden* **76 p**

THIRD SET (IRE) 3 b.g. Royal Applause 124 – Khamseh 85 (Thatching 131) [2006 7s² p7g* p7g⁵ 6m² Jul 30] 95,000F, 55,000Y: tall, good-topped gelding: fourth foal: half-brother to 6-y-o Bonus and 5-y-o Corky: dam, 7f winner, half-sister to high-class performer up to 1½m Predappio: fairly useful form: won maiden at Kempton in June: tongue tied, good neck second to Charles Darwin in handicap at Ascot final outing: suffered a few minor problems after: effective at 6f, will probably stay 1m. *R. Charlton* **92**

THISTIMESFORGOOD (IRE) 3 ch.g. Rossini (USA) 118 – Midsummer Night (IRE) 69 (Fairy King (USA)) [2006 12s p6g p7.1m* p9.5g Dec 9] third foal: dam sprint maiden: 66/1, only form when winning maiden at Wolverhampton in November: well held on handicap debut final start: should stay at least 1m: acts on polytrack. *Adrian Sexton, Ireland* **67**

THISTLE 5 ch.g. Selkirk (USA) 129 – Ardisia (USA) 87 (Affirmed (USA)) [2006 80: 12m⁵ 9.8m⁵ 8.5f⁶ 8m Aug 5] good-topped gelding: fair handicapper: stays 11f: acts on good to firm ground, probably on firm: gelded after final start. *J. Howard Johnson* **66**

THOMAS A BECKETT (IRE) 3 b.g. Beckett (IRE) 116 – Kenema (IRE) 88 (Petardia 113) [2006 64: 8.2m 8.1s p9.5g 8.1m 10d⁴ p9.5g Nov 20] unfurnished gelding: modest maiden: barely stays 1¼m: acts on good to firm and good to soft going. *P. R. Chamings* **55**

THOMAS OF BATHWICK 3 b.g. Beckett (IRE) 116 – Bathwick Babe (IRE) 71 (Sri Pekan (USA) 117) [2006 65: p10g 8d Oct 27] smallish, sturdy gelding: fair maiden at 2 yrs for B. R. Millman: well held in handicaps in 2006. *B. G. Powell* **–**

THORNABY GREEN 5 ch.g. Whittingham 104 – Dona Filipa 51 (Precocious 126) [2006 67d: f7g³ 8v⁴ 7.9m 8f⁴ 8.3g² 9f³ 10.1f* 9.1m 10.1d 10.1s 10m 10f² 11g f7g³ f8g⁴ p9.5g* p8.6g p9.5g⁴ Dec 21] tall, quite good-topped gelding: modest performer: won apprentice handicap at Newcastle in July and banded race at Wolverhampton in November: stays 1¼m, effective at much shorter: acts on all-weather, firm and soft going: tried in cheekpieces/visor: sometimes makes running. *T. D. Barron* **61**

THORNBILL 3 ch.g. Gorse 116 – Red Hot Dancer (USA) (Seattle Dancer (USA) 119) [2006 6.1d p7.1m Nov 8] big, strong gelding: well held in maidens at Warwick (slowly away) and Wolverhampton. *H. Candy* **–**

THORNFIELD CLO (IRE) 3 gr.f. Zafonic (USA) 130 – Flounce 74 (Unfuwain (USA) 131) [2006 –: 8m* 9.7f⁴ 8.3m 7f 8.1m³ Aug 10] tall filly: modest performer: won selling handicap at Bath in June: stays 9.7f: acts on firm ground: flashed tail penultimate start: joined Ms Joanna Morgan in Ireland. *R. Hannon* **58**

THORNTON PRINCESS 3 b.f. Most Welcome 131 – Princess Emily (IRE) 68 (Dolphin Street (FR) 125) [2006 69d: 6g⁴ 7.5f 7.1g 9.8m 8.3m⁴ Jul 15] leggy filly: modest maiden: should stay 7f: acts on firm going: tried in cheekpieces. *B. S. Rothwell* **55**

THORNTON WELCOME 3 ch.g. Most Welcome 131 – Lindrick Lady (IRE) 70 (Broken Hearted 124) [2006 7f May 6] well beaten in maiden at Thirsk. *B. S. Rothwell* **–**

THORNYLEE 2 b.c. (Jan 17) Selkirk (USA) 129 – Sound Asleep (USA) (Woodman (USA) 126) [2006 7.2v Oct 28] 32,000Y: first foal: dam unraced out of US Grade 1 9f winner Sleep Easy, herself closely related to US Grade 1 1¼m winner Aptitude: 7/2, green and tailed off in maiden at Ayr. *M. Johnston* **–**

THORNY MANDATE 4 b.g. Diktat 126 – Rosa Canina 91 (Bustino 136) [2006 69: 10.2d 10m* p10g 10m 10.9f⁴ 9.9g⁴ 12g Aug 7] strong, close-coupled gelding: fair handicapper: won at Pontefract in May: stays 10.9f: acts on polytrack, firm and good to soft going: sometimes races freely. *R. F. Johnson Houghton* **68**

THORPENESS (IRE) 7 b.g. Barathea (IRE) 127 – Brisighella (IRE) (Al Hareb (USA) 123) [2006 55: p13.9g⁶ Jan 4] strong, good-topped gelding: lightly-raced maiden: modest at best. *P. D. Cundell* **–**

THOUGHTSOFSTARDOM 3 b.g. Mind Games 121 – Alustar 71 (Emarati (USA) 74) [2006 64: p5.1g* p6g² p6g⁵ p7.1g⁴ p7g⁶ p6g 5.1s⁴ 5m³ p5.1g⁵ 5.3f p5g 5.3m⁵ 6f⁶ 5m⁵ 5.3f³ 6m³ 6f 6m p6g p6g p6g⁶ Dec 20] lengthy gelding: modest performer: won seller at Wolverhampton (left W. M. Brisbourne) in January: stays 6f: acts on polytrack, firm and soft going: tried visored/blinkered (hung very badly and virtually unrideable), often wears cheekpieces nowadays: jinked and unseated rider once at 2 yrs. *P. S. McEntee* **63**

THOUSAND WORDS 2 b.c. (Mar 2) Dansili 127 – Verbose (USA) 97 (Storm Bird (CAN) 134) [2006 6g* 7g* 7g⁶ 7d* 8s⁵ Oct 21] big, good-topped colt: second foal: dam, 1m winner, closely related to 3-y-o Acrobatic, out of half-sister to dam of Poule d'Essai **112**

Somerville Tattersall Stakes, Newmarket—
Thousand Words is a convincing winner from Dijeerr and Ferneley (noseband)

des Pouliches winner Matiara: smart performer: won maiden and minor event (beat Drumfire by neck) at Newbury in summer and 10-runner Somerville Tattersall Stakes at Newmarket in September, in last-named positively ridden when beating Dijeerr by 2½ lengths (sweated up beforehand): found less than looked likely when 5¼ lengths fifth of 14 to Authorized in Racing Post Trophy at Newbury: should stay 1m: raced on good going or softer. *B. W. Hills*

THOU SHALT NOT 3 b. or br.g. Commands (AUS) – Soyalang (FR) (Alydeed – (CAN) 120) [2006 8.2g 10d 8.2v Oct 25] strong gelding: no form in maidens at Nottingham. *P. S. Felgate*

THOUTMOSIS (USA) 7 ch.g. Woodman (USA) 126 – Toujours Elle (USA) (Lyphard 57 (USA) 132) [2006 14m⁴ 16.1d⁵ May 16] fairly useful maiden when trained in France by F. Head in 2001/2002: modest form at best on return to Flat in 2006: stays 1¾m: acts on heavy and good to firm ground: fair winning hurdler. *L. Lungo*

THREE BOARS 4 ch.g. Most Welcome 131 – Precious Poppy 70 (Polish Precedent 69 (USA) 131) [2006 61§: p16.5g² p16g p16.5g p10g⁵ 14m 12f⁴ 11.8f⁵ 14.1d 15.8d³ p12g³ p11g* p13.9g* p10g² Dec 19] quite good-topped gelding: fair performer: won banded races at Kempton and Wolverhampton in November: overly-confident ride when short-head second in handicap at Lingfield final start: effective at 1¼m to 16.5f: acts on polytrack, firm and good to soft ground: effective blinkered or not: has looked far from keen. *S. Gollings*

THREE COUNTIES (IRE) 5 b.h. Danehill (USA) 126 – Royal Show (IRE) 63 – (Sadler's Wells (USA) 132) [2006 –: 12m 21.7m 16.2m 12g⁵ Jul 28] close-coupled horse: fair form in bumpers: well held on Flat: tried blinkered. *N. I. M. Rossiter*

THREE DECADES (IRE) 2 b.f. (Jan 12) Invincible Spirit (IRE) 121 – Parvenue 83 (FR) 79 (Ezzoud (IRE) 126) [2006 p5g³ 5g p5g³ p6g* 6f⁴ 6m p6g⁵ p6g³ p6g⁵ Oct 21] 24,000F, 24,000Y: close-coupled filly: second foal: half-sister to Italian 2005 2-y-o 5f winner by Fasliyev: dam, 2-y-o 6f winner, out of sister to Middle Park Stakes winner/ 2000 Guineas runner-up Lycius: fairly useful performer: won maiden at Wolverhampton in June: better form after, including when in frame in listed race at Newmarket and minor event at Lingfield (third to Resplendent Alpha): effective at 5f/6f: acts on polytrack and firm going: not straightforward: sold 30,000 gns, joined S. Seemar in UAE. *C. A. Cyzer*

THREE FEATHERS 3 b.g. Averti (IRE) 117 – Jane Grey 64 (Tragic Role (USA)) 49 [2006 –: p6g⁶ p7.1g³ f8g 7s⁴ p6g p8g⁴ 6m⁴ 6f³ 7m⁶ 7.1g³ 8f⁶ 7f² Aug 15] leggy gelding: poor maiden: stays 7f: acts on polytrack and firm ground. *M. Salaman*

THREE HALF CROWNS (IRE) 2 b.c. (Mar 26) Barathea (IRE) 127 – My-Lorraine (IRE) 77 (Mac's Imp (USA) 116) [2006 p7g Oct 20] well held in maiden at Lingfield. *P. Howling*

THREE MATES 2 b.f. (Apr 30) Auction House (USA) 120 – Great Aim (Great – Nephew 126) [2006 5s 5g p5g⁶ May 2] half-sister to winners abroad by Formidable and Statoblest: dam maiden who seemed to stay 1m: little form. *W. G. M. Turner*

THREE NO TRUMPS 2 ch.f. (Jan 23) First Trump 118 – Renaissance Lady (IRE) 65 45 (Imp Society (USA)) [2006 7m⁵ 7f⁴ 7f⁴ 8g f7g⁴ 8.2s p9.5g p8g⁴ Nov 18] 2,000Y: good-topped filly: first foal: dam 11.5f to 2m and hurdles winner: poor maiden: should stay 1¼m+: tongue tied once. *D. Morris*

THREE SHIPS 5 ch.g. Dr Fong (USA) 128 – River Lullaby (USA) (Riverman (USA) 60 131) [2006 61: p12.2g f11g* 11.5f 11.6g⁶ Aug 7] leggy, quite good-topped gelding: modest performer: won amateur handicap at Southwell in February: stays 11f: acts on all-weather: tried in blinkers/cheekpieces: often races up with pace. *Miss J. Feilden*

THREE STRINGS (USA) 3 b.g. Stravinsky (USA) 133 – Just Cause (Law Society 62 (USA) 130) [2006 –: 8d⁵ f7g 10f⁴ 8d³ 9m* 8f 9.9m² 9.9m 12d⁵ Sep 5] modest handicapper: won at Musselburgh in July: stays 1¼m: acts on firm and good to soft going: in cheekpieces after second start. *P. D. Niven*

THREE THIEVES (UAE) 3 ch.g. Jade Robbery (USA) 121 – Melisendra (FR) 70 (Highest Honor (FR) 124) [2006 81p: 10.2f 11m p10g p9.5g⁵ p12.2s⁵ p12.2g⁵ Dec 27] tall gelding: fairly useful form at 2 yrs for M. Johnston: fair at best in handicaps in 2006: stays 1¼m: acts on polytrack, has best turf efforts on good going. *M. S. Saunders*

THREE WELSHMEN 5 b.g. Muhtarram (USA) 125 – Merch Rhyd-Y-Grug (Sabre- 59 hill (USA) 120) [2006 10.9s 10.2d 8s⁴ p10g Jun 17] modest handicapper: stays 1m: acts on polytrack and soft ground: sometimes slowly away: sometimes blinkered/in cheekpieces in 2004. *D. Burchell*

THREE WRENS (IRE) 4 b.f. Second Empire (IRE) 124 – Three Terns (USA) (Arctic **99**
Tern (USA) 126) [2006 93: p8g⁴ 7.6m⁵ 8s 8m* 7d⁶ p8g⁵ Oct 26] tall, sparely-made filly:
useful performer: contested listed races in 2006, winning at Bath in August by neck from
Sweet Treat: best other effort when good fourth to Royal Alchemist at Kempton: effective
at 7f/1m: acts on polytrack, firm and soft going. *D. J. Daly*

THREEZEDZZ 8 ch.g. Emarati (USA) 74 – Exotic Forest 66 (Dominion 123) [2006 **–**
76: 8.1m 7g 8.1d 7m 8d 7d Oct 3] tall, useful-looking gelding: well held in 2006 (left
P. D. Evans after third start): tried blinkered: usually tongue tied: withdrawn after unseating rider and bolting once. *R. A. Harris*

THROW THE DICE 4 b.g. Lujain (USA) 119 – Euridice (IRE) 66 (Woodman (USA) **77 d**
126) [2006 88: 7.1g 5f 6s 6m 6m 6f⁶ 6m³ 5d² 5g⁶ 5m 6v 5s³ 5v 5d Nov 3] strong, lengthy
gelding: on downgrade and just fair handicapper in 2006: free-going sort, probably
stays 7f: acts on firm and soft going: sometimes in cheekpieces: none too consistent.
D. W. Barker

THUMPERS DREAM 3 b.f. Cape Cross (IRE) 129 – Perfect Peach 100 (Lycius **86**
(USA) 124) [2006 73p: 10d⁴ 10m⁴ 10f³ 12g 10.3m* 10.3f⁵ 10s⁶ Oct 10] neat filly: fairly
useful performer: won maiden at Chester in August: best effort in handicap there next
time: likely to prove best up to 1¼m: acts on firm and soft going. *H. R. A. Cecil*

THUNDEROUSAPPLAUSE 2 b.f. (Mar 30) Royal Applause 124 – Trustthunder 87 **81**
(Selkirk (USA) 129) [2006 7g² p7g⁶ Oct 21] second foal: dam, 6f (including at 2 yrs)
winner, half-sister to smart German sprinter Raffelberger: much better effort in maidens when second to Ransom Captive at Redcar: will be at least as effective at 5f/6f as 7f.
K. A. Ryan

THUNDER ROCK (IRE) 4 b.g. King's Best (USA) 132 – Park Express 123 (Aho- **97**
noora 122) [2006 98p: 10m³ 12m⁵ 11.9g 10.4d⁶ 12d⁴ 12g⁵ Oct 12] tall, useful-looking
gelding: useful handicapper, lightly raced: ran creditably in 2006 on first 2 starts, and
when fourth to Pevensey in valuable event at Ascot: likely to stay 1¾m: acts on good to
firm and good to soft going: gelded, and joined Jonjo O'Neill. *Sir Michael Stoute*

THUNDER STORM CAT (USA) 2 b.c. (May 5) Storm Cat (USA) – Tenga (USA) **95 p**
(Mr Prospector (USA)) [2006 p7.1f² 6m* Sep 16] $350,000 2-y-o: compact colt: eighth
foal: half-brother to smart US 1¼m/1½m performer Startac (by Theatrical): dam, French
2-y-o 5f winner, closely related to US Grade 2 8.5f winner Jade Flush: stirred up in
paddock but confirmed debut promise when winning maiden at Newbury by 1¼ lengths
from Longquan: shapes as if will prove best up to 7f: likely to go on progressing.
P. F. I. Cole

THUNDER S (USA) 3 ch.f. Kris S (USA) – Thunder Maid (USA) (Alydar (USA)) **–**
[2006 p8.6g 10.5m⁵ Aug 10] tall filly: half-sister to several winners abroad: dam, 1½m
winner in USA, sister to champion US older horse Turkoman: well held in maidens at
Wolverhampton and Haydock: sold 6,000 gns in November. *L. M. Cumani*

THUNDERWING (IRE) 4 b. or br.g. Indian Danehill (IRE) 124 – Scandisk (IRE) 88 **75**
(Kenmare (FR) 125) [2006 95: 8v 8g 7.9g 6f p8.6g⁶ p7.1f 7.5g³ p8.6g⁶ p8.6g Sep 30]
good-topped gelding: just fair form in handicaps in 2006: effective at 1m/1¼m: acts on
heavy going: tried visored/in cheekpieces. *K. R. Burke*

THURLESTONE ROCK 6 ch.g. Sheikh Albadou 128 – Don't Smile 76 (Sizzling **75**
Melody 117) [2006 90?, a77: p6g³ p6g 6g⁴ 6m Jun 5] compact gelding: fair handicapper:
ran as though amiss final outing: barely stays easy 7f: acts on all-weather, good to firm
and good to soft going: sometimes races freely: tried in blinkers/cheekpieces, tongue tied
last 2 starts. *B. J. Meehan*

THYOLO (IRE) 5 ch.g. Bering 136 – Topline (GER) (Acatenango (GER) 127) [2006 **90**
103: p7g 10g 8.5g 10.5g 12m² 11.6m 11.7m³ 11g Sep 15] big, useful-looking gelding:
fairly useful handicapper: stays 1½m: acts on firm ground, below form on softer than
good: tried in headgear: edgy sort (has run well when sweating). *C. G. Cox*

TI ADORA (IRE) 4 b.f. Montjeu (IRE) 137 – Wavy Up (IRE) (Brustolon 117) [2006 **98**
82: 12g⁶ 14.1g* 14m* 14m² 16.1m³ 12m³ 12g² 12d³ 14v 12d² 12s³ p13g Oct 26] leggy
filly: useful performer: won handicaps at Nottingham and Sandown in June: good seventh
to High Heel Sneakers in listed event at Lingfield final outing: effective at 1½m to 2m:
acts on polytrack and any turf going: has worn crossed noseband: tends to go freely: tough
and consistent. *P. W. D'Arcy*

TIANA 3 b.f. Diktat 126 – Hill Welcome 52 (Most Welcome 131) [2006 98: 8.1g⁵ 8d⁵ **94**
Sep 23] strong filly: just useful performer in 2006, better effort when fifth to Wagtail in

listed handicap at Ascot final outing, short of room until over 1f out: stays 1m: yet to race on extremes of going: tongue tied twice at 2 yrs: sold 75,000 gns. *J. H. M. Gosden*

TIARA BOOM DE AY (IRE) 2 b.f. (May 15) Fasliyev (USA) 120 – Fez 94 (Mujtahid (USA) 118) [2006 5g⁵ May 1] second foal: dam, 5f winner, ran only at 2 yrs: 14/1, fifth to Nina Blini in maiden at Warwick. *R. Hannon* **54**

TIBER TIGER (IRE) 6 b.g. Titus Livius (FR) 115 – Genetta (Green Desert (USA) 127) [2006 82, a–: 7g 7m⁴ 8d⁴ 8m² 8m 8m 8.1m² 6.9f³ 8.1m⁵ Sep 7] rather angular gelding: fair handicapper: effective at 7f/1m: acts on firm and good to soft going, lightly raced on polytrack: usually wears headgear: ungenuine. *N. P. Littmoden* **74 §**

TIBER TILLY 3 b.f. King Charlemagne (USA) 120 – Clarice Orsini (Common Grounds 118) [2006 78, a71: 5m 6d 6g 8.1g⁴ 6.9g 7m⁴ 6g³ 7.1m p8.6m Oct 14] leggy, lengthy filly: fair handicapper: won at Yarmouth in August: stays 1m: acts on fibresand, good to firm and good to soft going: sometimes makes running. *N. P. Littmoden* **68**

TIBINTA 2 b.f. (Jan 31) Averti (IRE) 117 – Bint Albadou (IRE) 91 (Green Desert (USA) 127) [2006 6g⁶ 5g³ 6m² 7m p7.1m p8g Nov 24] 4,000Y: sixth foal: sister to 6-y-o Badou and half-sister to 3 winners, including 8.5f/1¼m winner Monduru (by Lion Cavern): dam Irish 2-y-o 6f winner: modest maiden: placed in 2 sellers, claimed in second from Rae Guest £6,000: left J. O'Keeffe 6,000 gns after next start: best effort at 6f. *P. D. Evans* **57**

TIBURON 2 b.c. (Mar 25) Xaar 132 – Sahara Rose (Green Desert (USA) 127) [2006 6m 7g⁶ 5m⁴ p6g⁴ Sep 10] modest maiden: staying-on fourth in nursery final start: should be suited by 1m: sold 16,000 gns, sent to Belgium. *H. Morrison* **62**

TICKING 3 ch.g. Barathea (IRE) 127 – Tuning 114 (Rainbow Quest (USA) 134) [2006 p7g 8.3d p9.5g Oct 28] well held in maidens. *T. Keddy* **–**

TICKI TORI (IRE) 4 b.f. Vettori (IRE) 119 – Lamees (USA) (Lomond (USA) 128) [2006 77: 10d 12d May 28] tall, quite good-topped filly: lightly-raced maiden: well held in 2006. *G. C. H. Chung* **–**

TIDAL CHORUS 3 ch.f. Singspiel (IRE) 133 – South Shore 102 (Caerleon (USA) 132) [2006 10m⁵ 10m Sep 5] big, strong filly: half-sister to several winners, including useful 7f/1m winner South Rock (by Rock City) and fairly useful 1m winner Leonica (by Lion Cavern): dam, 1¼m/1½m winner, half-sister to very smart 7f/1m performer Soviet Line: 2½ lengths fifth to Early Evening in maiden at Nottingham: bandaged behind, dropped out tamely next time: bred to stay 1½m: sold 8,000 gns. *J. G. Given* **72**

TIDY (IRE) 6 b.g. Mujadil (USA) 119 – Neat Shilling (IRE) (Bob Back (USA) 124) [2006 82: f8s 8m 8d 8d* 8g³ 8m 8g⁶ 9.8d⁵ 10d³ 10.1s 10s Oct 16] smallish gelding: fair handicapper: won at Ayr in June: stays 1¼m: acts on all-weather and heavy going. *M. D. Hammond* **74**

TIE BLACK (IRE) 3 b.f. Machiavellian (USA) 123 – Tender Is Thenight (IRE) (Barathea (IRE) 127) [2006 7g* 9s³ 8g* 8g* 8d³ Jul 30] **110**

Fillies have continued to be the mainstay of the Francois Rohaut stable in recent seasons. In 2002, the Pau-based trainer sent out Pearly Shells to win the Prix de Malleret, Prix de la Nonette and Prix Vermeille, and Turtle Bow the Prix Cleopatre and Prix d'Astarte. The Prix Minerve, Premio Lydia Tesio and Prix Jean Romanet winner Whortleberry kept the ball rolling, and then, to put the icing on the cake, along came Torrestrella and Tie Black, both of whom won the Poule d'Essai de Pouliches, the latter in controversial circumstances.

Going into the Gainsborough Poule d'Essai des Pouliches, run at Longchamp in May, Tie Black had one more run and one more win to her name than Torrestrella at the same stage. Unlike Torrestrella, Tie Black had been successful at two, at Toulouse where she won again in March and April, in listed company on the latter occasion. Earlier in April she had failed where Torrestrella had succeeded, finishing only third in a listed race at Longchamp, the nine-furlong Prix Finlande. Tie Black's form was no more than useful, a remark which applied to the majority of her twelve rivals in the Poule d'Essai des Pouliches, the exception being the smart New Girlfriend, though she hadn't won in Group 1 company either and was having her first start since disappointing in the Prix Morny as a two-year-old. New Girlfriend failed to stay, but she did set a good gallop before weakening in the last furlong, which benefited those held up well off the pace, among them Price Tag, Tie Black and Impressionnante. They were the first three to pass the post, in that order, a length and a half and a short neck the distances between them. No sooner had they done so, however, than a stewards' inquiry was announced. This was to investigate interference which occurred well inside the final furlong, caused by Price Tag who made her run widest of all but edged right as she came through to lead, which resulted in Impressionnante being checked momentarily. Tie Black, who made her effort towards the rail and led briefly inside the last furlong, was beaten on merit by Price Tag, and would have finished third if Impressionnante had had a trouble-free run. The rules are stricter in France than in Britain and the stewards decided that the interference had prevented Impressionnante from obtaining the best possible placing, and they disqualified Price Tag and placed her third, also giving a two-day ban to her rider Thierry Thulliez. Price Tag's trainer Pascal Bary was very unhappy about the stewards' decision—'she was the best filly in the race'—and with some justification. Had the race taken place in Britain the result would have been allowed to stand. Compare the case with that of Ad Valorem in the Queen Anne at Royal Ascot. Ad Valorem's rider caused considerable interference but 'the interference had not improved Ad Valorem's placing' and the placings remained unaltered, Fallon receiving a four-day suspension. The outcome in the Poule d'Essai des Pouliches, however, was that the filly who was probably only third best on the day was awarded first prize, Tie Black's promotion giving her rider Jean-Bernard Eyquem his first Group 1 victory. The inquiry added to the problems at Longchamp on that particular day, a wildcat strike called by on-course tote operators just before racing having threatened to result in the meeting being abandoned. The first race finally got under way almost two and a half hours after the original start time. With connections of Price Tag lodging an appeal, the result of the Poule d'Essai des Pouliches wasn't officially confirmed until ten days later, when the appeal was rejected. Torrestrella showed markedly better form in the Poule d'Essai des Pouliches than Tie Black did, but failed by a long way to reproduce it in four subsequent starts, the last three of which took place in the States, including one the following year. Tie Black, on the other hand, reproduced her form on what turned out to be her only appearance after Longchamp, when third behind Mandesha and Impressionnante (with Price Tag fifth) in the Prix d'Astarte at Deauville, beaten half a length and a length and a half.

Tie Black (IRE) (b.f. 2003)	Machiavellian (USA) (b 1987)	Mr Prospector (b 1970)	Raise A Native
			Gold Digger
		Coup de Folie (b 1982)	Halo
			Raise The Standard
	Tender Is Thenight (IRE) (b 1996)	Barathea (b 1990)	Sadler's Wells
			Brocade
		Mill Princess (b 1977)	Mill Reef
			Irish Lass II

Tie Black, who cost €330,000 as a yearling, is the third foal of Tender Is Thenight. Successful over an extended mile and a quarter in the French Provinces as a three-year-old, Tender Is Thenight is a half-sister to numerous winners. They include Last Tycoon, top-class winner of the King's Stand Stakes and William Hill Sprint Championship before becoming Europe's first winner of the Breeders' Cup Mile, the smart sprinter Astronef, the Prix du Bois winner The Perfect Life

Gainsborough Poule d'Essai des Pouliches, Longchamp—Tie Black (rail) is awarded the race after Price Tag is demoted for causing interference to Impressionnante (No.13); Daltaya is fourth as New Girlfriend (right) weakens into sixth

(dam of Gordon Stakes dead-heater Rabah), Save Me The Waltz, dam of the 1999 Poule d'Essai des Pouliches winner Valentine Waltz, and Zelda, dam of the 2001 Prix Robert Papin winner Zipping. Their dam Mill Princess, a mile-and-a-quarter winner in France, is a half-sister to the Irish Derby winner Irish Ball, and to the top-class broodmare Irish Bird, responsible for the Prix du Jockey Club winners Assert and Bikala and the Irish St Leger winner Eurobird. Tie Black, a big, good sort who stays a mile, has raced only on good ground or softer and she acts on soft. *F. Rohaut, France*

TIEGS (IRE) 4 ch.f. Desert Prince (IRE) 130 – Helianthus (Groom Dancer (USA) 128) **55** [2006 55: f14g⁴ f12g f12g* f12g⁴ f11g Dec 28] modest performer: won apprentice handicap at Southwell in March: best efforts around 1½m: acts on fibresand and good to soft ground: tried in cheekpieces. *P. W. Hiatt*

TIFERNATI 2 b.g. (Apr 13) Dansili 127 – Pain Perdu (IRE) (Waajib 121) [2006 6m⁶ **66 p** Jul 30] 26,000F, 32,000Y, 42,000 2-y-o: fifth foal: half-brother to fairly useful 2002 2-y-o 7f winner Sister Bluebird (by Bluebird): dam, French 1¼m winner, half-sister to smart French miler Fine Fellow: shaped as if needed run when sixth to Bid For Glory in maiden at Newmarket: gelded after: should improve. *W. J. Haggas*

TIFFIN DEANO (IRE) 4 b.g. Mujadil (USA) 119 – Xania 32 (Mujtahid (USA) 118) **–** [2006 61d: 5.1d 6g Jun 13] good-topped gelding: modest performer at best: no form on Flat in 2006: tried blinkered. *H. J. Manners*

TIGER FROG (USA) 7 b.g. French Deputy (USA) 118 – Woodyoubelieveit (USA) **–** (Woodman (USA) 126) [2006 54: 12m Apr 26] strong, lengthy gelding: lightly-raced handicapper on Flat: well held only start in 2006: tried blinkered/in cheekpieces. *J. Mackie*

TIGER HUNTER 4 b.g. Lake Coniston (IRE) 131 – Daynabee 61 (Common Grounds **–** 118) [2006 43, a57: f7g f8g Jan 24] poor performer: well held in 2006. *P. Howling*

TIGER KING (GER) 5 b.g. Tiger Hill (IRE) 127 – Tennessee Girl (GER) (Big Shuffle **–** (USA) 122) [2006 –: 13.8d Apr 12] winner in Germany in 2004: well beaten in handicaps on Flat in Britain. *P. Monteith*

TIGER TANGO (USA) 2 b.f. (Apr 13) Johannesburg (USA) 127 – Sweet Little Lies **53 p** (USA) (Raise A Native) [2006 6.1f⁶ Jul 15] 10,000Y, 40,000 2-y-o: leggy filly: looked weak at 2 yrs: half-sister to numerous winners in USA: dam unraced: 8/1, sixth to Boreal Applause in maiden at Nottingham, green and never nearer: likely to improve. *W. J. Haggas*

TIGER TIGER (FR) 5 b.h. Tiger Hill (IRE) 127 – Adorable Emilie (FR) (Iron Duke **100** (FR) 122) [2006 100: p10g* p10g p12g⁵ 10.3m 10.4d 9.9s⁴ 12d 12d 12s Oct 7] close-coupled horse: useful performer: won handicap at Lingfield in March from Boo: creditable fourth to Blue Monday in listed event at Goodwood after: stays easy 1½m: acts on polytrack, heavy and good to firm ground: usually held up: none too consistent. *Jamie Poulton*

TIGNASSE (FR) 5 b.m. Double Bed (FR) 121 – Off Guard (FR) (Bakharoff (USA) **53** 130) [2006 –: p13g* p12g p13.9g p12g Apr 5] modest performer: won claimer at Lingfield in February: left G. L. Moore after next outing: stays 13f: acts on polytrack and soft going: tried blinkered/in cheekpieces. *Miss K. M. George*

TIKRAM 9 ch.g. Lycius (USA) 124 – Black Fighter (USA) 79 (Secretariat (USA)) **78** [2006 20m Jun 20] tall, close-coupled gelding: very lightly-raced handicapper on Flat: blinkered, well held in Ascot Stakes only outing in 2006: smart chaser. *G. L. Moore*

TILAPIA (IRE) 2 ch.c. (Apr 16) Daggers Drawn (USA) 114 – Mrs Fisher (IRE) 94 **64 p** (Salmon Leap (USA) 131) [2006 p6g⁴ p6g² p6g Dec 26] half-brother to several winners, including useful 1m to 13f winner Masafi (by Desert King) and fairly useful 5f to 7f (at 2 yrs) winner Grandma Lily (by Bigstone): dam 7f winner, including at 2 yrs: modest form in maidens: very green on debut: will stay 1m: raced on polytrack: likely to improve. *Sir Mark Prescott*

TILBURY 3 ch.f. Peintre Celebre (USA) 137 – Dockage (CAN) (Riverman (USA) 131) **66** [2006 7g⁴ 7f Jul 15] €220,000 2-y-o: angular filly: half-sister to numerous winners, notably smart performer up to 9f in Britain and USA Wharf (by Storm Bird) and to dam of 3-y-o Rail Link: dam, French 1m (at 2 yrs) and 9f winner, out of close relation of Dahlia: 3 lengths fourth to Usk Poppy in maiden at Salisbury, finishing well: well held in similar event at York following month. *H. R. A. Cecil*

TILEN (IRE) 3 ch.g. Bluebird (USA) 125 – New Sensitive (Wattlefield 117) [2006 –: **50 d**
f8g p7.1g* p7.1g⁶ p8.6g 7m 7.1m 12.1f 10.9m 7.1d f8m f7g⁶ p10g⁶ p16.5g Dec 29]
strong gelding: modest performer: won banded race at Wolverhampton in January, hanging: little form after next start, leaving S. Parr prior to penultimate one: stays 7f: acts on
polytrack: often blinkered. *V. Smith*

TILLA 6 b.m. Bin Ajwaad (IRE) 119 – Tosca (Be My Guest (USA) 126) [2006 –: p16g **–**
p16.5g 12d p12.2g 14.1g Aug 17] workmanlike mare: fair handicapper in 2004, little
form since: tried blinkered and visored. *Mrs A. J. Hamilton-Fairley*

TILLY'S DREAM 3 ch.f. Arkadian Hero (USA) 123 – Dunloe (IRE) 54 (Shaadi **75**
(USA) 126) [2006 69, a62: 6d⁵ 6.1g p7g f6g² f6g⁶ 6g² 5d* Aug 23] tall filly: fair handicapper: won at Folkestone in August: best at 5f/6f: acts on fibresand, good to firm and
good to soft going. *G. C. H. Chung*

TILSWORTH CHARLIE 3 bl.f. Dansili 127 – Glossary (Reference Point 139) **54**
[2006 p7g p8g p7g⁴ 8.1g 8m 8.5m 10.2f 7f² 5.7m* 6d⁵ p5.1g Nov 3] eighth foal: half-
sister to several winners, including 4-y-o Polish Index and 1½m winner Fifth Edition (by
Rock Hopper): dam unraced close relation to smart middle-distance filly Valley of Gold:
modest performer: won maiden at Bath in September: best around 6f: acts on polytrack,
firm and good to soft going: visored last 4 starts: signs of temperament. *J. R. Jenkins*

TILT 4 b.g. Daylami (IRE) 138 – Tromond 94 (Lomond (USA) 128) [2006 82: 13.8d⁵ **95**
13d* 12.4d³ 14g³ 16.1m 13d³ 14d⁶ Nov 3] useful-looking gelding: useful handicapper:
won at Hamilton in May by 3 lengths from First Look: rare poor effort final outing:
effective at 13f, needs to settle to stay 2m: acts on polytrack, soft and good to firm going.
B. Ellison

TILTILI (IRE) 3 ch.f. Spectrum (IRE) 126 – Alexander Confranc (IRE) 73 (Magical **51**
Wonder (USA) 125) [2006 –: 9v 16.2m⁶ 13.8m⁴ Sep 16] strong filly: modest maiden,
lightly raced: seems to stay 2m: acts on good to firm going. *P. C. Haslam*

TIMBERLAKE 4 b.f. Bluegrass Prince (IRE) 110 – Ambience Lady (Batshoof 122) **–**
[2006 63: p10g Nov 15] maiden: well held only outing in 2006. *Miss E. C. Lavelle*

TIMBER TREASURE (USA) 2 b. or br.c. (Mar 5) Forest Wildcat (USA) 120 – Lady **65 p**
Ilsley (USA) (Trempolino (USA) 135) [2006 6m⁶ Jun 23] $340,000 2-y-o: strong, well-
made colt: third foal: half-brother to 5-y-o Lord Admiral: dam useful French 1m (at
2 yrs)/8.5f winner, sister to dam of Breeders' Cup Juvenile winner Action This Day: 7/1,
7¾ lengths sixth of 9 to Charlie Farnsbarns in maiden at Newmarket: will do better.
H. R. A. Cecil

TIME DANCER (IRE) 2 ch.g. (Mar 27) Desert Sun 120 – With Finesse (Be My Guest **–**
(USA) 126) [2006 6s 8.2d p7.1g p8.6g p8.6g Dec 31] stocky gelding: no form: tried
blinkered. *A. Berry*

TIME FOR CHANGE (IRE) 2 ch.g. (Jan 31) Elnadim (USA) 128 – Dance Lesson **50**
47 (In The Wings 128) [2006 5f 6g 5.1f Sep 9] modest form in maidens, then gelded.
B. W. Hills

TIME FOR LIFE (USA) 3 br. or b.c. Woodman (USA) 126 – Marie's Star (USA) **85**
(Risen Star (USA)) [2006 89: p10g² p10g⁴ p8.6g² 8.1d³ 8s⁶ 9.9m 8m Sep 13] quite good-
topped colt: fairly useful handicapper: stays 1¼m: acts on polytrack and good to soft
going: tried visored, effective with/without cheekpieces: sold 24,000 gns. *H. J. Collingridge*

TIME FOR YOU 4 b.f. Vettori (IRE) 119 – La Fija (USA) 49 (Dixieland Band (USA)) **–**
[2006 44: 11.9m 10.9f Jun 19] workmanlike filly: poor performer: well held in 2006: tried
blinkered/in cheekpieces. *J. M. Bradley*

TIME MARCHES ON 8 b.g. Timeless Times (USA) 99 – Tees Gazette Girl 42 (Kala- **45**
glow 132) [2006 59: 9d 10.1d 14g Aug 31] leggy gelding: poor performer on Flat
nowadays: stays easy 2m: acts on firm and soft going: tried tongue tied: sometimes looks
none too keen: fair winning hurdler. *K. G. Reveley*

TIME N TIME AGAIN 8 b.g. Timeless Times (USA) 99 – Primum Tempus 49 **62 d**
(Primo Dominie 121) [2006 64, a74: p7g p7.1g p6g f6g p6g p6g p6g f6g f5g Dec 29]
leggy, useful-looking gelding: modest performer, on downgrade: best at 5f/6f: acts on
all-weather, firm and good to soft going: usually wears cheekpieces/blinkers: has looked
temperamental. *Peter Grayson*

Weatherbys Bank Cheshire Oaks, Chester—Time On makes light of the step up from maiden company; Mont Etoile (left), Prowess (right) and Kaylianni are next

TIME ON 3 b.f. Sadler's Wells (USA) 132 – Time Away (IRE) 114 (Darshaan 133) **114** [2006 79p: 9.7d* 11.4m* 12g⁶ 12d* 12.5g 12m 10s⁴ Oct 22] sturdy, close-coupled filly: smart performer: won maiden at Folkestone in April, listed Cheshire Oaks at Chester (beat Mont Etoile readily by 3 lengths) in May and Prix de Malleret at Saint-Cloud (clear in straight before eased to beat Lahudood 1½ lengths) in June: on toes, not discredited when 11 lengths sixth to Alexandrova in Oaks at Epsom third start: respectable efforts last 3 outings, fourth to Floriot in Premio Lydia Tesio at Rome final one: stayed 1½m: acted on soft and good to firm going: raced prominently: stud. *J. L. Dunlop*

TIME OUT (IRE) 3 b.g. Alhaarth (IRE) 126 – Waif (Groom Dancer (USA) 128) [2006 **–** 74: 8m 10s 11.6g 8g Jun 29] workmanlike gelding: maiden handicapper: well held in 2006: sold £13,000, joined Miss M. Bragg. *A. M. Balding*

TIMES REVIEW (USA) 5 b.g. Crafty Prospector (USA) – Previewed (USA) (Ogy- **55** gian (USA)) [2006 68, a76: p6g p6g p5.1g* f5g⁶ p6g⁶ p5g² p5.1g⁶ p5g² p5g p6g⁵ 5.2g 5m **a70** Jun 12] quite good-topped gelding: fair handicapper on all-weather, just modest form on turf in 2006: won at Wolverhampton in January: best at 5f/6f: acts on all-weather, firm and good to soft going: tried visored, usually blinkered: races prominently: sold 5,000 gns in July. *C. A. Dwyer*

TIME TO REGRET 6 b.g. Presidium 124 – Scoffera 63 (Scottish Reel 123) [2006 **60** 59: 8d² 8m⁶ 8.1m³ 8v 9g 8.1m⁶ 8m 9.1v Oct 28] tall gelding: modest handicapper: left J. Wainwright prior to sixth outing: stays 9.3f: acts on polytrack and any turf going: tried in cheekpieces: tends to hang: races up with pace. *I. W. McInnes*

TIME TO SHINE 7 b.m. Pivotal 124 – Sweet Jaffa 73§ (Never So Bold 135) [2006 12s **–** Oct 21] fair handicapper at 4 yrs: well held only outing on Flat since: tried blinkered: won over fences in October. *Mrs L. J. Mongan*

TIME UPON TIME 2 b.f. (Mar 4) Groom Dancer (USA) 128 – Watchkeeper (IRE) 86 **–** (Rudimentary (USA) 118) [2006 p8g Oct 20] compact filly: second foal: dam, 1¼m winner, out of Ribblesdale winner Third Watch: looked none too keen when beating 2 in maiden: had refused to enter stall intended debut. *W. J. Knight*

TINA'S MAGIC 3 ch.f. Primitive Rising (USA) 113 – Night Transaction 59 (Tina's Pet 121) [2006 –: 10d May 15] no sign of ability. *Mrs G. S. Rees*   **–**

TINIAN 8 b.g. Mtoto 134 – Housefull 81 (Habitat 134) [2006 –, a44: f12g 7d⁵ 8.5d 8d Aug 2] short-backed gelding: poor performer: stays 1¼m: acts on all-weather and any turf going: sometimes wears headgear: none too resolute. *Miss Tracy Waggott*   **46 a–**

TINNARINKA 2 ch.f. (Apr 27) Observatory (USA) 131 – Dancing Fire (USA) (Dayjur (USA) 137) [2006 p7g⁵ p7g² 7s⁴ Oct 10] 27,000Y: sturdy, good-bodied filly: sister to 3-y-o Starlight Gazer and half-sister to fairly useful 1m (in USA) and 1½m winner Montecito (by Montjeu): dam unraced out of Poule d'Essai des Pouliches winner Danseuse du Soir: fair form in maidens: second at Kempton and fourth (to Mythical Kid) at Newbury: will stay 1m. *R. Hannon*   **72**

TINTAC 5 b.m. Intikhab (USA) 135 – Susquehanna Days (USA) 68 (Chief's Crown (USA)) [2006 45, a53: p9.5g p16.5g Jan 23] poor maiden: stays 9.5f: acts on polytrack: withdrawn after refusing to enter stall twice in 2005. *E. J. O'Neill*   **a43**

TINTAWN GOLD (IRE) 6 b.m. Rudimentary (USA) 118 – Clear Ahead (Primo Dominie 121) [2006 51: p16g Jan 18] sturdy mare: poor maiden: effective at 1¼m/ 1½m: acts on polytrack, firm and good to soft going: has worn blinkers/cheekpieces. *S. Woodman*   **–**

TINTED VIEW (USA) 2 ch.f. (Feb 15) Distant View (USA) 126 – Gombeen (USA) (Private Account (USA)) [2006 6m⁶ p7.1g⁶ Nov 2] fourth foal: half-sister to 4-y-o Ground Rules: dam, placed in USA, half-sister to Danehill: mid-field in maidens at Goodwood and Wolverhampton: will stay 1m. *B. W. Hills*   **55**

TINY TIM (IRE) 8 b.g. Brief Truce (USA) 126 – Nonnita 71 (Welsh Saint 126) [2006 48: f6g 6f² 7m p6g⁵ Dec 13] leggy, sparely-made gelding: poor performer: effective at 6f to 1m: acts on all-weather, firm and good to soft going: tried tongue tied: usually blinkered: claimer ridden. *A. M. Balding*   **47**

TIOGA GOLD (IRE) 7 b.g. Goldmark (USA) 113 – Coffee Bean (Doulab (USA) 115) [2006 –: f12g⁵ 17.1d Oct 2] leggy gelding: modest at best: no form since 2003: tried blinkered/tongue tied/in cheekpieces. *L. R. James*   **–**

TIPSY LAD 4 b.g. Tipsy Creek (USA) 115 – Perfidy (FR) (Persian Bold 123) [2006 53, a66: p7g p8g⁶ p6g⁸ p8g p7.1g Jul 11] poor performer nowadays: stays 7f: acts on all-weather: usually tongue tied/in headgear: has been slowly away: unruly in stall and withdrawn Jul 12. *D. J. S. ffrench Davis*   **49**

TIPSY LILLIE 4 ch.f. Tipsy Creek (USA) 115 – Belle de Nuit (IRE) 85 (Statoblest 120) [2006 61, a49: 6g² 5v f6g f7g⁴ p8g⁵ f8g Dec 29] modest performer: stays easy 1m: acts on all-weather, heavy and good to firm ground: tried blinkered, visored final start. *P. S. McEntee*   **54**

TIPSY ME 3 b.f. Selkirk (USA) 129 – Time Saved 89 (Green Desert (USA) 127) [2006 8.3g 8.1s⁴ 8.2g³ p8.6m⁴ p9.5g p7.1g⁵ Dec 1] 55,000Y: leggy filly: second foal: half-sister to smart 7f (at 2 yrs) to 1½m (King Edward VII Stakes) winner Plea Bargain (by Machiavellian): dam, 1¼m winner, half-sister to smart performers Time Allowed (at 1½m) and Zinaad (stayer) out of Time Charter: fair maiden: will stay 1¼m: acts on polytrack. *M. L. W. Bell*   **70**

TIPSY PRINCE 2 b.g. (Feb 14) Tipsy Creek (USA) 115 – Princess of Garda 79 (Komaite (USA)) [2006 p6g² 5f³ p6f⁴ 5.5m⁶ 6.1g⁵ 6d* 6v* Oct 9] 5,500Y: sturdy gelding: first foal: dam, 2-y-o 5f winner, sister to useful sprinter Castelletto: fair performer: progressed to win nurseries at Catterick and Ayr in October: should prove best at 5f/6f: acts on polytrack and heavy going. *Mrs G. S. Rees*   **75**

TIPTOEING 3 b.f. Tipsy Creek (USA) 115 – Grove Dancer 61 (Reprimand 122) [2006 67: 8.2m 7.2v p7g 11.5f 11.5f 12.1g p10g² 10.1m² 10s⁵ Oct 2] useful-looking filly: modest maiden: reportedly struck into final start: stays 1¼m: acts on polytrack, good to firm and good to soft going: blinkered last 3 outings. *M. H. Tompkins*   **57**

TIP TOES (IRE) 4 b.f. Bianconi (USA) 123 – Tip Tap Toe (USA) (Pleasant Tap (USA)) [2006 42: 7m p12g⁴ p12g³ 11.6m² 16.2f² 14m⁶ p16g⁵ 16g⁴ p13.9g³ f16g p13.9g Dec 31] plain, close-coupled filly: modest maiden: stays 2m: acts on polytrack and firm ground: has carried head high. *P. Howling*   **55**

TIP TOP STYLE 3 b.g. Tipsy Creek (USA) 115 – Eliza Jane (Mistertopogigo (IRE) 118) [2006 f8g⁶ f8g⁶ p9.5g 7.9g 10d p8.6g f8g⁶ f8g² Dec 29] modest maiden: best effort at 1m: acts on fibresand: tried tongue tied/in cheekpieces. *J. Mackie*   **62**

TIPU SULTAN 6 ch.g. Kris 135 – Eye Witness (IRE) 72 (Don't Forget Me 127) [2006 **56** 8.3d 13.8f² 17.2m 12f 14.1g Aug 3] big, angular gelding: has a markedly round action: left P. Haley in Spain after final 5-y-o start: modest form at best in 2006: seems to stay 1¾m: best effort on good going, probably acts on firm. *M. D. Hammond*

TIRADE 2 b.g. (Jan 27) Vettori (IRE) 119 – Elfin Laughter 76 (Alzao (USA) 117) [2006 **– p** 7d Oct 28] 52,000Y: well-made gelding: eighth foal: half-brother to several winners, including 7f/1m winner Smirk (by Selkirk) and 6f (including at 2 yrs) and 7.5f (in UAE) winner Stetchworth Prince (by Cadeaux Genereux), both smart: dam 2-y-o 7.5f/ 1m winner: 20/1, raced wide and given considerate introduction in 19-runner maiden at Newmarket: gelded after: will improve. *J. H. M. Gosden*

TIRAILLEUR (IRE) 6 b.m. Eagle Eyed (USA) 111 – Tiralle (IRE) 71 (Tirol 127) **48** [2006 55: f8g p9.5g f8g⁴ f8g f11g Apr 10] sturdy mare: poor performer: stays 1¼m: acts on all-weather, good to firm and good to soft going: tried in headgear (visored last 3 starts)/tongue tied: joined M. Gingell, won over hurdles in August. *J. R. Boyle*

TIROL LIVIT (IRE) 3 ch.g. Titus Livius (FR) 115 – Orange Royale (IRE) (Exit To **54** Nowhere (USA) 122) [2006 41: f8g⁵ f8g⁴ 7v⁴ 11g 10g⁴ f11g⁵ Jul 7] close-coupled, good-topped gelding: modest maiden: stays 1¼m: acts on heavy going. *N. Wilson*

TITAN TRIUMPH 2 b.c. (Mar 19) Zamindar (USA) 116 – Triple Green 69 (Green **81** Desert (USA) 127) [2006 7m 7m⁴ Aug 30] fourth foal: half-brother to 5-y-o Burning Moon: dam, maiden who stayed 1m, half-sister to smart 1¼m/1½m performer Talented: improved third (backward) when fourth to My Learned Friend in minor event at Lingfield, not clear run: will be suited by 1m. *W. J. Knight*

TITIAN DANCER 3 ch.c. Danehill Dancer (IRE) 117 – La Limite (IRE) (Dr Devious **82** (IRE) 127) [2006 p7g³ 7m p6g³ p7g⁴ 8g² 8.1g 10d Sep 16] €32,000F: big, good-topped colt: first foal: dam fairly useful French 7f (at 2 yrs)/1m winner: fairly useful maiden: below form final start: effective at 7f/1m (raced freely at 1¼m): acts on polytrack: tongue tied last 3 starts: sold 12,000 gns. *W. R. Swinburn*

TITIAN SAGA (IRE) 3 ch.f. Titus Livius (FR) 115 – Nordic Living (IRE) 53 (Nor- **59** dico (USA)) [2006 74: 6d 5m 6f 7m 6m p6g 5d 5d⁵ Oct 3] smallish, sturdy filly: just modest performer in 2006, leaving C. Allen after sixth start: stays 6f: acts on good to firm ground: tried blinkered. *D. Nicholls*

TITINIUS (IRE) 6 ch.g. Titus Livius (FR) 115 – Maiyria (IRE) 68 (Shernazar 131) **78** [2006 82: 6g³ 7d⁵ 7g⁴ 7g³ 6g⁵ 6f⁶ 6m⁴ 6m² 6d⁶ 7s⁵ 7v Oct 31] good-bodied gelding: fair handicapper: should stay 1m: acts on any turf going: wore cheekpieces final start. *M. D. Hammond*

TITUS ALONE (IRE) 3 ch.g. Titus Livius (FR) 115 – Swan Sea (USA) (Sea Hero **91** (USA) 124) [2006 102: 6m⁵ 5m 5.1f⁶ 6f Jul 23] good-topped gelding: just fairly useful at best in 2006: will prove best at 5f/6f: raced mainly on good to firm/firm going, ran poorly in Flying Childers Stakes on soft: edgy sort, has been very free to post and reluctant to enter stall on reappearance: gelded, and sent to South Africa. *B. Smart*

TITUS LUMPUS (IRE) 3 b.g. Titus Livius (FR) 115 – Carabosse 52 (Salse (USA) **68** 128) [2006 51: p7g p8g p8g⁵ p8g² p8g* p8g p7g⁶ 8.3f⁶ 7f⁶ p8g² Sep 3] fair performer: won handicap at Lingfield in April: stays 8.3f: raced mostly on polytrack, acts on firm going: races prominently. *R. M. Flower*

TITUS MAXIMUS (IRE) 3 ch.g. Titus Livius (FR) 115 – Haraabah (USA) 99 (Top- **63** sider (USA)) [2006 74: p5g⁵ 5d 5.3m⁶ 5m p6g Nov 5] close-coupled, quite attractive gelding: just modest form in 2006: left G. Butler £1,600 after fourth start: will prove best at 5f: best effort on good going: tried tongue tied: carried head high third outing. *H. J. Manners*

TITUS WONDER (IRE) 3 ch.f. Titus Livius (FR) 115 – Morcote (IRE) 109 (Magical **54** Wonder (USA) 125) [2006 57: p6g p6g² p7g p6g⁶ p6g⁵ f5g* p5.1g⁵ 6g Aug 18] modest performer: won banded event at Southwell in April: effective at 5f/6f: acts on all-weather: tried in cheekpieces: often makes running. *P. A. Blockley*

TIVERS JEWEL (USA) 2 b. or br.g. (Feb 1) Tiznow (USA) 133 – Box of Jewels **68** (USA) (Half A Year (USA) 130) [2006 6m 7s Oct 10] $165,000Y: very big gelding: third foal: half-brother to a winner in USA by Cherokee Run: dam, 5f (at 2 yrs) to 6.5f winner in USA, half-sister to US Grade 1 1m/8.5f winner Golden Ballet: fair form on first of 2 starts in maidens at Newbury, very green: gelded after second one. *Mrs A. J. Perrett*

TIVERS SONG (USA) 2 gr.c. (Mar 24) Buddha (USA) 122 – Rousing (USA) (Alydar **74** (USA)) [2006 7s p7.1g⁶ p8.6g³ p8.6g Nov 23] $110,000Y: close-coupled, workmanlike colt: half-brother to several winners in USA, notably Grade 3 6f and 7.5f winner Chindi (by El Prado)· dam 6f winner in USA: fair form in maidens, third to Maraca at Wolverhampton: well held in nursery. will be suited by 1¼m. *Mrs A. J. Perrett*

TIVISKI (IRE) 4 b.f. Desert Style (IRE) 121 – Mummys Best (Bustino 136) [2006 67, a58: p6g³ p6g² p6g³ p6g⁵ p6g⁴ p6g⁵ p6g p8g p6g p6g³ 6m⁵ 7.1g 6g 6g p6g p6m p6g f6g⁵ f6g Dec 29] lengthy, leggy filly: has quick action: fair performer on all-weather, modest on turf: claimed from E. Alston £6,000 after third start: won handicap at Lingfield in February: left G. Margarson after eleventh outing: stays 6f: acts on polytrack, good to firm and good to soft going: tried in cheekpieces/visor: has hung left. *Miss Gay Kelleway* **54 a71 d**

TIYOUN (IRE) 8 b.g. Kahyasi 130 – Taysala (IRE) (Akarad (FR) 130) [2006 88: 16.1m 14.8m³ Jul 22] leggy, lengthy gelding: fairly useful handicapper: better effort in 2006 when third to Mersey Sound at Newmarket: stays 2m: acts on firm and soft going: tried visored earlier in career: raced freely on reappearance. *Jedd O'Keeffe* **83**

TIZI OUZOU (IRE) 5 ch.m. Desert Prince (IRE) 130 – Tresor (USA) (Pleasant Tap (USA)) [2006 p12g Feb 20] good-bodied mare: very lightly-raced maiden on Flat: winning hurdler. *M. C. Pipe* **–**

TIZ TIMELY (USA) 3 b.f. Tiznow (USA) 133 – Delivery Day (USA) (Dayjur (USA) 137) [2006 9.9g p8.6g⁴ p8g⁵ p8g p8d Oct 19] $50,000Y: half-sister to 3 winners in USA: dam US maiden half-sister to US Grade 1 1m/1¼m winner Lite Light: modest maiden: probably stays 1¼m, will be effective at 7f: raced only on polytrack and good/good to soft ground: raced freely second start, visored final one. *A. M. Balding* **60**

TIZZYDORE (IRE) 2 b.f. (Mar 6) Shinko Forest (IRE) – Shannon Dore (IRE) 81 (Turtle Island (IRE) 123) [2006 p7g 7d Oct 3] 20,000Y: sturdy filly: second foal: closely related to smart 2004 2-y-o 6f winner Borthwick Girl (by Cape Cross) who stayed 1m: dam 2-y-o 6f winner: no show in maidens. *A. M. Balding* **–**

TO ARMS 4 b.g. Mujahid (USA) 125 – Toffee 66 (Midyan (USA) 124) [2006 66: 10m³ 10d⁶ 10m 12m⁵ Jun 21] tall gelding: modest maiden handicapper: stays 1½m: unraced on extremes of going: sold 4,200 gns. *T. D. Easterby* **64**

TOBAGO REEF 2 b.g. (Mar 27) Tobougg (IRE) 125 – Silly Mid-On (Midyan (USA) 124) [2006 m3 5g 6g⁵ 8g⁶ 5m p7.1m³ p7.1m² p6g² p7.1g⁸ p7.1g⁸ Dec 30] 4,200Y: good-topped gelding: fifth foal: dam once-raced half-sister to smart 1¼m to 2m winner Sarangani: fair performer: improved to win nurseries at Wolverhampton (2) in December: stays 7f: acts on polytrack: tried blinkered, wore cheekpieces last 4 starts: races prominently. *Mrs L. Stubbs* **75**

TO BE FARE (IRE) 6 ch.g. Eagle Eyed (USA) 111 – Petrolea Girl (Connaught 130) [2006 43: f8g² f8g⁵ f11g² f11g² f14g Mar 14] sturdy gelding: has a quick action: modest performer: free-going sort, but stays 11f: acts on fibresand: tried blinkered. *J. Pearce* **59**

TOBERMORY (IRE) 2 b.f. (Feb 8) Green Desert (USA) 127 – Kerrera 115 (Diesis 133) [2006 6.1m* 5s⁵ Oct 2] small, compact filly: closely related to 2 winners in France by Danehill, including smart miler Firth of Lorne, and half-sister to several winners, including fairly useful 7f winner (stayed 1¼m) Kerry Ring (by Sadler's Wells): dam, second in 1000 Guineas but at least as effective at 5f/6f, half-sister to very smart 6f to 1m performer Rock City: fairly useful form when winning maiden at Nottingham, always in control and beating Cape Velvet by 2 lengths: again favourite, once fifth behind Oldjoe-said in nursery at Windsor on much softer ground: should prove best at 5f/6f. *M. A. Jarvis* **86**

TOBEROGAN (IRE) 5 b.g. Docksider (USA) 124 – Beltisaal (FR) (Belmez (USA) 131) [2006 73: 6d 7g 7m 6g 6v Oct 9] modest handicapper: well below par at Ayr final outing: best at 6f: acts on firm and soft going, below form only start on polytrack. *W. A. Murphy, Ireland* **63**

TOBOGGAN LADY 2 b.f. (Apr 2) Tobougg (IRE) 125 – Northbend (Shirley Heights 130) [2006 p9.5g p8g⁶ Dec 4] 800R, 800Y, €12,000 2-y-o: fifth foal: half-sister to Italian 7.5f/9f winner Polishnow (by Polish Precedent): dam French maiden: towards rear in polytrack maidens. *Mrs A. Duffield* **–**

TOBOSA 2 b.c. (Apr 29) Tobougg (IRE) 125 – Sovereign Abbey (IRE) 68 (Royal Academy (USA) 130) [2006 6m 7f* 7m* 7m* 6d² 7s⁶ Oct 21] 34,000Y: good-bodied, attractive colt: third living foal: half-brother to Italian 1¼m to 11.5f winner by First Trump: dam, 9.4f winner, half-sister to useful sprinter Espartero: useful performer: won maiden at Yarmouth in July, and minor event (by 8 lengths) and nursery at Newmarket in August: improved form and better attitude when ½-length second of 28 to Caldra (pair clear) in valuable sales race at Newmarket: below form in Horris Hill Stakes (reportedly **107**

lost shoe going down) final start: will be suited by 1m: acts on firm and good to soft ground: swishes tail in paddock, and has seemed lazy when racing. *W. Jarvis*

TOBOUGG WELCOME (IRE) 2 ch.c. (Apr 13) Tobougg (IRE) 125 – Three White Sox 73 (Most Welcome 131) [2006 p7g Dec 15] well held in maiden at Kempton. *S. C. Williams* —

TOCCATA (IRE) 2 b.f. (Feb 11) Cape Cross (IRE) 129 – Sopran Marida (IRE) (Darshaan 133) [2006 p7g 8.2s² Oct 18] €65,000Y: leggy, close-coupled filly: half-sister to several winners, including fairly useful 2000 2-y-o 6f winner Millenium Princess (by Eagle Eyed), later successful in USA: dam Italian 7f and 9f winner: better effort in maidens when neck second to Metaphoric at Nottingham: stays 1m. *D. M. Simcock* 74

TODLEA (IRE) 6 b.g. Desert Prince (IRE) 130 – Imelda (USA) (Manila (USA)) [2006 8.1m* 8m 9m* 8.3f⁶ p8.6g⁵ Nov 7] smallish, quite good-topped gelding: has reportedly had wind operation: fairly useful handicapper in 2004: unraced at 5 yrs: fair form in 2006: won seller at Chepstow (left J. Osborne 10,500 gns) in August and amateur handicap at Goodwood in September: effective at 1m/1¼m: acts on polytrack, firm and good to soft going: tried tongue tied (including last 4 starts). *Jean-Rene Auvray* 77

TOD SLOAN (IRE) 4 ch.g. Titus Livius (FR) 115 – Poscimur (IRE) (Prince Rupert (FR) 121) [2006 48: p7g⁴ p8g⁴ f8g p9.5g⁶ p9.5g 8.2s 8m⁶ Jun 15] modest maiden: trained at 3 yrs by T. Hogan in Ireland: seems to stay 9.5f: acts on polytrack and soft going: tried blinkered: returned to Ireland, and joined D. Cullen. *I. M. Bradley* 51

TO DUBAI 3 b.f. Daylami (IRE) 138 – Albertville (USA) 108 (Polish Precedent (USA) 131) [2006 11.8d 12m⁵ a7.3g² a11.5g a12.5g⁴ a11.5g⁵ Dec 31] lengthy filly: seventh foal: sister to winner in Denmark and half-sister to 1¼m winner Alnahda (by Mark of Esteem): dam French listed 1¼m winner: modest maiden: sold from M. Jarvis 3,500 gns after second start: stays 1½m. *C. Von Der Recke, Germany* 58

TODWICK OWL 2 b.g. (Feb 20) Namid 128 – Blinding Mission (IRE) 70 (Marju (IRE) 127) [2006 6v p6g⁵ 6m p6g⁵ 7d³ Sep 29] good-topped gelding: modest maiden: best efforts in nurseries last 2 starts, then gelded: stays 7f: acts on polytrack and good to soft going. *J. G. Given* 63

TOFFEE VODKA (IRE) 4 b.f. Danehill Dancer (IRE) 117 – Vieux Carre (Pas de Seul 133) [2006 84: 7m 8g⁴ 7m 7g 7.1m⁴ p7.1g² 8.5g⁵ 7f² 7f* 7m⁵ p8g Sep 18] lengthy filly: fairly useful handicapper: won at Brighton (by 5 lengths) in August: effective at 7f to 8.6f: acts on polytrack and firm going (no form on softer than good). *J. W. Hills* 83 a86

TOFTA TILLY 6 ch.m. Muhtarram (USA) 125 – Budding Prospect (Rudimentary (USA) 118) [2006 f8g Apr 10] second foal: dam ran once: tailed off in bumper: 100/1, well beaten in maiden claimer at Southwell on Flat debut. *L. R. James* —

TOGGLE 2 b.g. (Apr 9) Tobougg (IRE) 125 – Niggle 65 (Night Shift (USA)) [2006 7m 7f⁵ 7.1m⁶ p7g Oct 6] 25,000Y: strong, compact gelding: fifth foal: half-brother to fairly useful 1999 2-y-o 5f winner Punctuate (by Distant Relative) and 4-y-o Faithisflying: dam ran twice: fair maiden: sixth to Buccellati at Warwick, hampered but easily best effort: may prove better at 5f/6f than 7f. *R. Hannon* 76

TO HATTA (IRE) 2 b.g. (Mar 24) Shinko Forest (IRE) – Monarchy (IRE) (Common Grounds 118) [2006 7d Aug 28] badly needed experience in maiden at Newcastle. *M. R. Channon* —

TOJONESKI 7 b.g. Emperor Jones (USA) 119 – Sampower Lady 55 (Rock City 120) [2006 54: 12f 12f 12f⁶ 13m⁵ 15m Aug 12] compact gelding: poor performer nowadays: stays easy 13f: acts on all-weather and any turf going: tried in headgear. *I. W. McInnes* 45

TOKEWANNA 6 b.m. Danehill (USA) 126 – High Atlas 65 (Shirley Heights 130) [2006 61, a71: p12.2g⁵ Jan 13] good-bodied mare: fair handicapper on all-weather, modest on turf: not discredited (very slowly away) only outing in 2006: stays 12.2f: acts on polytrack and firm ground: tried visored/in cheekpieces (found little): usually tongue tied: races freely: sold 4,500 gns in March. *W. M. Brisbourne* — a63

TOKYO JO (IRE) 2 b.f. (Mar 29) Raise A Grand (IRE) 114 – Wakayi 87 (Persian Bold 123) [2006 5v⁵ 5g² 5f⁴ 6v² 6g* 5.2g² 6m³ f7g 6s⁶ p6g² p7.1g² p7.1g p7g² Dec 10] €3,000Y: half-sister to several winners, including 7-y-o Royal Storm and fairly useful 5f (at 2 yrs)/7f winner Arruhan (by Mujtahid): dam, 2-y-o 5f winner, half-sister to smart sprinter Reesh: modest performer: won seller at Catterick in May: claimed from K. Burke £6,000 eleventh start: stays 7f: acts on polytrack and any turf going: effective with or without visor. *T. T. Clement* 57

TOKYO ROSE 2 b.f. (Mar 7) Agnes World (USA) 123 – Wildwood Flower 107 **80** (Distant Relative 128) [2006 6m⁶ 5m³ 6d³ Sep 26] 25,000Y: closely related to UAE 5f to 7.5f winner Wilde (by Polish Precedent) and half-sister to 3 winners, including 6f winner (including at 2 yrs) Bandit Queen (by Desert Prince): dam 6f winner, including at 2 yrs: progressive form in maidens, third to Lorena Wood at Goodwood: likely to prove best at 5f/6f. *R. Hannon*

TOLDO (IRE) 4 gr.g. Tagula (IRE) 116 – Mystic Belle (IRE) 88 (Thatching 131) [2006 **101** 94: 10v 16m⁴ 16d⁵ 16d⁴* 16.2f⁵ 16.1m* Jul 1] strong, close-coupled gelding: useful handicapper: won at Ascot (by ¾ length from Elusive Dream) in May and John Smith's Northumberland Plate at Newcastle (by neck from River Alhaarth) in July: reported in August to have suffered minor injury: stays 16.5f: acts on any going: blinkered twice at 2 yrs: tough and reliable. *G. M. Moore*

TOLINIS GIRL 3 b.f. Bertolini (USA) 125 – Skiddaw Bird (Bold Owl 101) [2006 56: **?** f7g a6g⁵ a6g³ a6g⁴ 8m² 8g 8g a8.7g⁵ Aug 24] smallish filly: modest maiden: sold from B. Smart 1,200 gns after reappearance (blinkered): stays 1m: acts on dirt and good to firm ground. *Charlotte Sjogren, Sweden*

TOLPUDDLE (IRE) 6 b.g. College Chapel 122 – Tabdea (USA) 106 (Topsider **112** (USA)) [2006 112: 8v⁴ 10s² 9g³ 8d⁶ 8g Sep 17] big, close-coupled gelding: smart performer: good efforts at the Curragh first 2 starts when fourth to Bawaader in Irish Lincolnshire (Handicap) and 4½ lengths second to Arch Rebel in listed race: respectable third to Notnowcato in Earl of Sefton Stakes at Newmarket next time, but below form in listed races last 2 starts: effective at 1m/1¼m: acts on good to firm ground, but goes particularly well (all his wins) on soft/heavy: has had tongue tied. *T. Stack, Ireland*

TOMBALINA 3 ch.f. Tomba 119 – Ashkernazy (IRE) 60 (Salt Dome (USA)) [2006 46, **54** a61: f5g⁵ f5s f5g 5d⁵ 5.1d 5m 5m Aug 8] smallish, close-coupled filly: modest performer: best efforts at 5f: acts on all-weather and good to soft ground. *C. J. Teague*

TOM BELL (IRE) 6 b.g. King's Theatre (IRE) 128 – Nordic Display (IRE) 77 (Nor- **–** dico (USA)) [2006 12.1d 13f Jun 29] leggy gelding: no form on Flat in 2006: tried visored, better form when not: fair hurdler, successful in June. *J. G. M. O'Shea*

TOMBI (USA) 2 b.g. (Mar 5) Johannesburg (USA) 127 – Tune In To The Cat (USA) **90** (Tunerup (USA)) [2006 6d³ 6m⁴ 7m⁵ 6g Sep 30] $260,000F, €475,000Y: rangy gelding: half-brother to several winners in USA, including smart performer up to 9f Tour of The Cat (by Tour d'Or): dam 6f (at 2 yrs)/7f winner in USA: fairly useful maiden: tongue tied, improved form when seventh of 24 to Danum Dancer in listed Two-Year-Old Trophy at Redcar: gelded after: shapes like a sprinter. *J. Howard Johnson*

TOM FOREST 4 b.g. Forest Wildcat (USA) 120 – Silk Masque (USA) 91 (Woodman **60** (USA) 126) [2006 78: 8.2d 7m⁶ 7g 7.2m³ 9.9m Sep 19] smallish, lengthy gelding: just modest performer in 2006: stays 7f: acts on soft and good to firm going: in cheekpieces last 2 starts: races prominently: reared over and injured rider when withdrawn on intended third outing. *K. A. Ryan*

John Smith's Northumberland Plate, Newcastle—Toldo gains the biggest prize of his career from River Alhaarth (left), who finishes strongly to take second off Greenwich Meantime

TOMMY TOBOUGG 2 ch.g. (Apr 30) Tobougg (IRE) 125 – Celebrate (IRE) 77 **61 p**
(Generous (IRE) 139) [2006 8d⁵ Nov 3] fourth foal: half-brother to 2 winners in Germany, including 1m/1¼m winner Caesarina (by Hernando): dam maiden who should have stayed 1m: 50/1, fifth to Hohlethelonely in maiden at Musselburgh, late headway: should do better. *I. Semple*

TOMMY TOOGOOD (IRE) 3 b.c. Danehill (USA) 126 – On The Nile (IRE) 103 **89**
(Sadler's Wells (USA) 132) [2006 61p: p8g* 8.3m² p8g⁴ 8g⁵ p10g* Oct 20] strong colt: fairly useful performer: won maiden in March and handicap (dead-heated) in October, both at Lingfield: stays 1¼m: acts on polytrack and good to firm going. *B. W. Hills*

TOMMYTYLER (IRE) 7 b.g. Goldmark (USA) 113 – John's Ballad (IRE) (Ballad **–**
Rock 122) [2006 56: f8g f8g² f8g⁵ f8g f7g² f8g² p8.6g f8g² f8g⁴ 8.2s f8g f8g Dec 28] **a54**
modest maiden: stays 1m: acts on fibresand: tongue tied in 2006: reportedly bled final outing. *D. Carroll*

TOMORROW'S DANCER 2 b.g. (Jan 31) Danehill Dancer (IRE) 117 – Today **64 p**
(IRE) (Royal Academy (USA) 130) [2006 6d 6g⁴ 6d Oct 27] €8,000Y, 55,000 2-y-o: rangy, angular gelding: first foal: dam French maiden sister to smart German 1997 2-y-o El Maimoun: modest form in maidens: caught the eye when fourth to Chief Operator at Newcastle, soon lot to do (boxed in) and finishing strongly for hands and heels: gelded after well held next time: likely to stay 1m: probably still capable of better, and one to look out for in handicaps. *K. A. Ryan*

TOM PARIS 2 b.g. (Mar 12) Bertolini (USA) 125 – Nom Francais 39§ (First Trump **78**
118) [2006 5d 5g⁴ 5f 6f³ p6g³ 6m* 6.1m⁵ 6d 5g⁶ 6m³ p6g⁶ p8.6m* p8g⁴ Nov 13] 13,000F, 22,000Y: good-topped gelding: third foal: half-brother to 2004 2-y-o 6f winner Monsieur Mirasol (by Mind Games) and 3-y-o The London Gang: dam, maiden who seemed to stay 2m (probably ungenuine), closely related to smart sprinter Perryston View: fair performer: won nurseries at Leicester in July and Wolverhampton in October: stays 8.6f: acts on polytrack and firm going: usually blinkered (effective when not). *W. R. Muir*

TOMTHEVIC 8 ch.g. Emarati (USA) 74 – Madame Bovary 82 (Ile de Bourbon (USA) **54**
133) [2006 50: 5.3m⁴ 5m⁵ 5.1g³ 5f⁵ 5.1f⁴ 5.7f⁵ 5g⁵ 5.3m⁴ Aug 22] strong-quartered gelding: modest performer: has form at 6f, but probably best at 5f: acts on polytrack and firm going: tried tongue tied (not since 2001): wears headgear nowadays: usually races prominently: none too consistent. *J. M. Bradley*

TOM TOWER (IRE) 2 b.g. (Mar 21) Cape Cross (IRE) 129 – La Belle Katherine **72**
(USA) (Lyphard (USA) 132) [2006 5.1d 5m⁵ 5.1d* 6.1m³ 7m 6m Sep 22] 110,000F: tall, good-topped gelding: has scope: fifth foal: half-brother to 3 winners, including 5-y-o Stevedore and 6-y-o Aventura: dam ran twice in France: fair performer: won maiden at Chepstow in May: good third in minor event there: off 3 months, well held in nurseries: effective at 5f/6f: sold 10,000 gns. *M. R. Channon*

TOM TUN 11 b.g. Bold Arrangement 127 – B Grade 59 (Lucky Wednesday 124) [2006 **–**
101: 6s 6g Apr 22] workmanlike gelding: has a round action: useful performer at best: well held in 2006: blinkered: tongue tied earlier in career: races prominently. *J. Balding*

TONI ALCALA 7 b.g. Ezzoud (IRE) 126 – Etourdie (USA) (Arctic Tern (USA) 126) **53**
[2006 72d: p13.9g⁵ p13.9g⁴ Dec 4] close-coupled gelding: just modest form in 2006: effective at 13f to 17f: acts on all-weather and any turf going: tried in cheekpieces: edgy sort: held up: none too resolute nowadays. *R. F. Fisher*

TONIGHT (IRE) 4 b.g. Imperial Ballet (IRE) 110 – No Tomorrow (IRE) (Night Shift **–**
(USA)) [2006 51: p9.5g p8.6g p8.6g 10d May 29] stocky gelding: maiden: no form in 2006: tried blinkered/tongue tied. *W. M. Brisbourne*

TONNANTE 2 b.f. (Jan 22) Hernando (FR) 127 – Thunder Queen (USA) (Thunder **63 p**
Gulch (USA) 129) [2006 p7g⁶ 7.5m 8.3d⁴ Sep 25] good-topped filly: second foal: dam, Brazilian Group 3 1m/1¼m winner, out of half-sister to 1000 Guineas winner Ravinella: mid-field at best in maidens (all in September), green and not knocked about: will be suited by 1¼m/1½m: type to flourish as 3-y-o. *Sir Mark Prescott*

TONY THE TAP 5 b.g. Most Welcome 131 – Laleston 73 (Junius (USA) 124) [2006 **91**
96: 6m⁶ 6m 6.1f⁵ 5m⁵ 6d 6f Sep 18] smallish gelding: fairly useful handicapper, on long losing run: below form last 2 starts: effective at 5f to 7f: acts on polytrack, firm and good to soft going: effective visored or not. *B. Palling*

TOO KEEN 5 ch.m. Keen 116 – Janie-O 62 (Hittite Glory 125) [2006 p8.6g Feb 6] little **–**
sign of ability. *J. M. Jefferson*

TO PARTY (IRE) 2 ch.f. (Apr 24) Elusive Quality (USA) – Magongo 103 (Be My **76** Chief (USA) 122) [2006 p6g² 6m⁴ 6m⁵ Sep 10] close-coupled filly: sixth foal: dam, 5f (at 2 yrs) and 9f (in UAE) winner, half-sister to Irish 1000 Guineas winner Classic Park, herself dam of Derby runner-up Walk In The Park: fair form in maidens, in frame at Kempton and Goodwood (fourth to Sacre Coeur): will probably stay 1m. *M. P. Tregoning*

TOPARUDI 5 b.g. Rudimentary (USA) 118 – Topatori (IRE) 89 (Topanoora 118) [2006 **–** 83: p10g Jan 4] big, good-topped gelding: fairly useful handicapper at best: all-weather debut when well held only start in 2006: won over hurdles in March. *M. H. Tompkins*

TOPATOO 4 ch.f. Bahamian Bounty 116 – Topatori (IRE) 89 (Topanoora 118) [2006 **108** 85: 8d² 8.2d⁴ 8.9m* 8g 10.4d* 10.4g² 10.4s² 10g Oct 12] leggy, angular filly: useful performer: much improved form in 2006, winning at York (by 2½ lengths from She's Our Lass) in June and August (beat Dunaskin readily by 1¼ lengths): good second there next 2 starts, notably when beaten 1½ lengths by Scriptwriter (pair clear) seventh outing: sweating, below par in listed event at Newmarket final start: stays 1¼m: acts on soft and good to firm ground: tough and reliable. *M. H. Tompkins*

TOP AWARD 3 b.g. Mark of Esteem (IRE) 137 – First Fantasy 97 (Be My Chief (USA) **–** 122) [2006 10m 10d May 26] big, good-topped gelding: well held in maidens at Windsor and Newmarket: dead. *J. R. Fanshawe*

TOPAZLEO (IRE) 2 ch.g. (Jan 20) Peintre Celebre (USA) 137 – Mer Noire (IRE) **69 p** (Marju (IRE) 127) [2006 8s⁶ Oct 7] 40,000F, 50,000Y: strong, angular gelding: has quick action: second foal: half-brother to 5.5f/6f winner in Italy by Mull of Kintyre: dam ran twice in France: 20/1, sixth to Victorian Prince in maiden at York, free early: should do better. *J. Howard Johnson*

TOP BID 2 b.c. (Mar 18) Auction House (USA) 120 – Trump Street 77 (First Trump **84** 118) [2006 6m⁴ 5d* 6m⁴ 6g⁵ Aug 7] 24,000Y: smallish, lengthy colt: has a quick action: third foal: half-brother to 2004 2-y-o 6f winner Street Cred (by Bold Edge) and 3-y-o Trumpita: dam 6f winner: fairly useful form: won maiden at Leicester (by 8 lengths) in May: fourth to Hamoody in minor event at Newmarket: disappointing final start: should prove best at 5f/6f. *T. D. Easterby*

TOP DIRHAM 8 ch.g. Night Shift (USA) – Miller's Melody 86 (Chief Singer 131) **84 d** [2006 88: 7g 7m⁴ 7.9g 8f 7.6m 7.2m⁶ 8d 8g 7.2v Oct 9] good-topped gelding: fairly useful performer: creditable fourth in handicap at York: below form otherwise in 2006: stays 1m: acts on any turf going: tried blinkered/tongue tied/in cheekpieces: waited with. *M. W. Easterby*

TOPFLIGHT WILDBIRD 3 br.f. Diktat 126 – Jamarj 113 (Tyrnavos 129) [2006 45: **67** p8g f8g 8.1m⁶ 9.2g* 11.9m⁴ 10.3m Sep 9] big, strong filly: fair handicapper: won at Hamilton (7 lb out of weights) in June: stays 9f: blinkered first 4 starts. *Mrs G. S. Rees*

TOPIARY TED 4 ch.g. Zafonic (USA) 130 – Lovely Lyca 76 (Night Shift (USA)) **70 §** [2006 76d: 8.2d f6g⁶ p8.6g* p8.6g p8.6g* Dec 23] useful-looking gelding: fair performer: won seller in November and handicap in December, both at Wolverhampton: stays easy 8.6f: acts on polytrack, good to firm and good to soft ground: tried tongue tied/ blinkered: looks temperamental. *H. Morrison*

TOPIC (IRE) 2 b.f. (Apr 23) Stravinsky (USA) 133 – Lyric Fantasy (IRE) 115 (Tate **–** Gallery (USA) 117) [2006 5g Jun 1] €40,000Y: half-sister to 3 winners abroad, including German 5.5f winner Moon God (by Thunder Gulch): dam, won Nunthorpe Stakes at 2 yrs and best up to 6f, closely related to Dewhurst winner In Command and half-sister to very smart sprinter Royal Applause: behind in maiden at Sandown. *J. W. Hills*

TOP JARO (FR) 3 b.g. Marathon (USA) 116 – Shammy (USA) (Lear Fan (USA) 130) **85** [2006 73: 8d² 8g 10d² 10g 10s⁶ 9.1v* Oct 28] sturdy gelding: fairly useful performer: won handicap at Ayr in October: stays 1¼m: acts on heavy going, yet to race on firmer than good: very free to post on reappearance: makes running: sold 20,000 gns, joined Jennie Candlish. *T. P. Tate*

TOPJEU (IRE) 3 b.c. Montjeu (IRE) 137 – Arabian Lass (SAF) (Al Mufti (USA) 112) **95** [2006 10d⁵ 12g² 11.7m* 12g Oct 12] 125,000Y: big, strong, close-coupled colt: third living foal: dam champion 2-y-o filly/Group 1 1m winner in South Africa: useful form: shaped with plenty of promise in maidens prior to winning similar event at Bath (by 5 lengths from Fisher Bridge) in August: below form on handicap debut at Newmarket final start: stays 11.7f: acts on good to firm ground. *L. M. Cumani*

TOP LEVEL (IRE) 3 b.f. Fasliyev (USA) 120 – Aiming Upwards (Blushing Flame **50** (USA) 109) [2006 p9.5g 7g³ 8.1m 10.1g⁵ 10d 10d f8m³ f7g* f7g⁵ Nov 21] €82,000F, **a55** 35,000Y: neat filly: first foal: dam unraced out of half-sister to dam of Derby winner

Oath: modest performer: won banded event at Southwell in November: stays 1m: acts on fibresand and good to firm going. *M. G. Quinlan*

TOP MAN TEE 4 gr.g. Vettori (IRE) 119 – Etienne Lady (IRE) 67 (Imperial Frontier (USA) 112) [2006 82: 13.9s May 18] smallish gelding: fairly useful performer at 3 yrs: well beaten only Flat start in 2006. *D. J. Daly* —

TOP MARK 4 b.g. Mark of Esteem (IRE) 137 – Red White And Blue (Zafonic (USA) 130) [2006 86: p7g 7.1m* 7m p8g⁴ p7g p7g⁴ p7g² p7.1g f8g⁴ p8.6g* Dec 21] tall, short-backed gelding: fairly useful performer: won handicap at Chepstow in June and, having been claimed from H. Morrison £12,000 after seventh start, claimer at Wolverhampton in December: stays 8.6f: acts on polytrack and good to firm ground: visored penultimate outing. *J. R. Boyle* **83**

TOPPLE 5 b.m. Master Willie 129 – Top Cover (High Top 131) [2006 –: p9.5g Jan 4] compact mare: no sign of ability: tried in cheekpieces. *P. W. Hiatt* —

TOP ROYELLE 2 b.f. (Feb 3) Royal Applause 124 – Colchica (Machiavellian (USA) 123) [2006 5g⁵ 5d² 5d* 6g 6s² 6f 6.1d p7g Oct 21] 17,000Y: rather leggy, good-topped filly: third foal: half-sister to 2 winners by Fasliyev, including 4-y-o Tartan Special: dam French 1¼m/11.5f winner: fair performer: won maiden at Leicester in May: off 3 months, below form after except when second in nursery at Newmarket: should stay 7f/1m: acts on soft going: sold 6,000 gns, sent to USA. *R. Hannon* **79**

TOP SEED (IRE) 5 b.g. Cadeaux Genereux 131 – Midnight Heights 104 (Persian Heights 129) [2006 94d: 11.5m⁵ 11.7d* 11g* 12d 12m 11.6m⁴ 12m² 12d 14m 12g 12d 11.7f 12m⁴ p12g² p12g p13g f14g⁵ p12g⁶ Dec 20] quite good-topped gelding: fairly useful handicapper: won at Bath in April and Goodwood in May: left M. Channon 20,000 gns, well below form last 4 starts: should stay 1¾m: acts on polytrack, firm and soft going: tried visored/tongue tied: sometimes edgy, and has been early to post: has looked ungenuine. *A. J. Chamberlain* **93 d**

TOP SHOT 3 ch.g. College Chapel 122 – Topatori (IRE) 89 (Topanoora 118) [2006 p6g⁶ p7.1g p7g⁴ p8.6g⁵ 8.2s* 8d* Apr 21] angular gelding: third foal: half-brother to 5-y-o Toparudi and 4-y-o Topatoo: dam 7f to 10.5f winner: fairly useful form: won handicaps at Nottingham and Thirsk in April: stayed 1m: acted on polytrack and soft going: dead. *M. H. Tompkins* **82**

TOP SPEC (IRE) 5 b.g. Spectrum (IRE) 126 – Pearl Marine (IRE) (Bluebird (USA) 125) [2006 83: p12.2g⁴ p12.2g⁵ 9.7f⁴ 10d⁵ 9.8m² 12m⁴ 11.8m² 10m⁵ 10m 11.8g⁴ 14.1m 11.9g⁴ 12g** 10d² p12g⁴ Dec 2] small gelding: has a quick action: fairly useful performer: won claimer at Newmarket (easily by 6 lengths) in October: stays 1½m: acts on polytrack, firm and soft ground: tried visored (looked unwilling): usually slowly away: held up: consistent. *J. Pearce* **81**

TOP STYLE (IRE) 8 ch.g. Topanoora 118 – Kept In Style 49 (Castle Keep 121) [2006 70: p13.9g 15.8d Apr 12] fair handicapper at 7 yrs: well held (in cheekpieces) in 2006: tried blinkered. *G. A. Harker* —

TOPSY MAITE 2 b.f. (Apr 1) Komaite (USA) – Noble Soul 67 (Sayf El Arab (USA) 127) [2006 5.1d Apr 11] half-sister to 1m winner Jessinca (by Minshaanshu Amad) and 3-y-o Noble Edge: dam 1m winner: last in maiden at Bath. *R. Curtis* —

TOP THE CHARTS 4 b.g. Singspiel (IRE) 133 – On The Tide 72 (Slip Anchor 136) [2006 90: 20m² 10v Oct 25] tall, lengthy, good-topped gelding: good walker: useful performer: good 5 lengths second to Baddam in Ascot Stakes (Handicap) at Royal Ascot on reappearance: inadequate trip in similar event at Navan only other Flat start in 2006: stays 2½m: acts on firm and soft ground: sometimes gives trouble at stall (refused to enter once): consistent: successful over hurdles in June. *A. J. Martin, Ireland* **100**

TOP TIER 2 gr.f. (Mar 9) Best of The Bests (IRE) 122 – Ladycake (IRE) 71 (Perugino (USA) 84) [2006 5d⁶ 5d⁴ 6f³ 5f* 5g* p5g p5g 5m⁵ 5.2g⁴ 5m p5.1g p7.1g f5g⁶ Dec 27] 1,200Y: third foal: dam 2-y-o 5f winner: modest performer: won seller and nursery (left I. Semple in between) at Musselburgh in summer: lost form after (tried blinkered): best at 5f/6f: acts on firm going: once unseated to post. *Peter Grayson* **61 d**

TOP TIGER 2 b.c. (Apr 16) Mtoto 134 – Topatori (IRE) 89 (Topanoora 118) [2006 8s⁴ Oct 7] small colt: fourth foal: half-brother to 5-y-o Toparudi, 4-y-o Topatoo and 3-y-o Top Shot: dam 7f to 10.5f winner: 20/1, fourth to Victorian Prince in maiden at York, finishing well after running green: should do better, particularly at 1¼m+. *M. H. Tompkins* **76 p**

TOP TREES 8 b.g. Charnwood Forest (IRE) 125 – Low Line 66 (High Line 125) [2006 **61 §** 61§, a52§: p12g 15m⁶ 16m⁵ Sep 10] modest performer, better on turf than all-weather: **a– §** stays 16.5f: acts on all-weather and firm ground: has been slowly away/reluctant to race: untrustworthy: modest hurdler (won in July/August). *W. S. Kittow*

TORA PETCHA (IRE) 3 b.g. Bahhare (USA) 122 – Magdalene (FR) (College **77 d** Chapel 122) [2006 81: 7.1g⁴ 7.2d⁴ 7f 10m⁵ 10m p12.2g Sep 11] quite attractive gelding: fairly useful performer at 2 yrs: fair at best in 2006: below form last 5 starts: stays 7f: acts on good to firm going: fair winner over hurdles. *R. Hollinshead*

TORA WARNING 2 b.c. (Mar 19) Warningford 119 – Torrecilla 68 (General Monash **–** (USA) 107) [2006 5f Jul 20] lengthy colt: well beaten in seller at Leicester. *John A. Harris*

TORGIANO (IRE) 5 b.g. Cadeaux Genereux 131 – Delimara (IRE) (In The Wings **60** 128) [2006 –: 7.1g² 10.1g 9.2m May 12] well held in bumpers: form on Flat only when fourth in maiden at Musselburgh: dead. *P. Monteith*

TORNADODANCER (IRE) 3 b.g. Princely Heir (IRE) 111 – Purty Dancer (IRE) 71 **67** (Foxhound (USA) 103) [2006 7d 5m⁵ 7f⁵ 6g 6s³ 7s⁶ p7.1m Oct 31] €15,000F, €15,000Y: second foal: half-brother to 4-y-o Send Me Home: dam Irish 7f/1m winner: fair maiden: below form at Wolverhampton final start: best effort at 6f on soft going. *T. G. McCourt, Ireland*

TORQUEMADA (IRE) 5 ch.g. Desert Sun 120 – Gaelic's Fantasy (IRE) (Statoblest **73** 120) [2006 72: p8g³ p8g⁶ 8.5g³ 8m 7m* 7f 7f⁴ 7g² 7m* 7.5m p7g Nov 15] compact gelding: fair handicapper: won at Lingfield in June and Leicester in September: stays easy 1m: acts on polytrack and good to firm going: tried in cheekpieces: races freely: has shown signs of temperament. *W. Jarvis*

TORRENS (IRE) 4 b.g. Royal Anthem (USA) 135 – Azure Lake (USA) (Lac Ouimet **88** (USA)) [2006 89: 10.4d 10g⁴ 10.3g⁵ 9.8g⁵ 10g² 9.8d 12m⁶ 12s Oct 6] good-bodied gelding: fairly useful handicapper: creditable efforts when in frame in 2006: stays 1½m: acts on firm and soft ground: reportedly had breathing problem sixth start: tried tongue tied. *R. A. Fahey*

TORRENT 11 ch.g. Prince Sabo 123 – Maiden Pool 85 (Sharpen Up 127) [2006 61§, **36 §** a55§: f5g f5g p5.1g p5.1g 6g 6f 5m 5s⁶ f5g Dec 29] strong, lengthy gelding: poor performer nowadays: left D. Chapman after fourth start: best at 5f/6f: acts on all-weather and any turf going: wears headgear: tried tongue tied: has bled, and reportedly can't be subjected to strong pressure: carries head high: unreliable. *J. M. Saville*

TORRID KENTAVR (USA) 9 b.g. Trempolino (USA) 135 – Torrid Tango (USA) **81** (Green Dancer (USA) 132) [2006 84: f12g p12.2g³ p12.2g 12g 12g³ 12s Sep 30] close-coupled gelding: fairly useful handicapper on all-weather, fair on turf: left B. Ellison 15,000 gns after third start: effective at 1m to 1½m: acts on all-weather and any turf ground: tried blinkered: free-going sort, usually held up: has hung: fair hurdler/chaser nowadays. *J. J. Lambe, Ireland*

TORVER 2 br.f. (Apr 20) Lake Coniston (IRE) 131 – Billie Blue 63 (Ballad Rock 122) **58** [2006 6m 7d 6m⁴ 6f p7.1m Nov 9] good-topped filly: half-sister to several winners, including smart 5f (at 2 yrs) and 7f winner Tumbleweed Ridge (by Indian Ridge) and useful 6f winner (including at 2 yrs) Tumbleweed Pearl (by Aragon): dam runner-up at 7f only outing: modest maiden: should stay 7f. *Dr J. D. Scargill*

TOSHI (USA) 4 b.g. Kingmambo (USA) 125 – Majestic Role (FR) 107 (Theatrical 128) **88** [2006 88, a82: 8.3m² 10f³ 8m 12.3m 9.2m 9m⁴ 8.3g p9.5g⁶ Oct 29] close-coupled **a–** gelding: fairly useful performer: placed in handicaps first 2 starts in 2006: largely below form after, claimed £8,000 final outing: stays 1¼m: acts on polytrack, firm and good to soft going: tried in cheekpieces/visored: sometimes looks none too keen. *I. Semple*

TOSS THE CABER (IRE) 4 ch.g. Dr Devious (IRE) 127 – Celtic Fling 77 (Lion **67** Cavern (USA) 117) [2006 63: 11g 14m² 12g³ 12f 14.1f⁴ 14.1g 10.1d Aug 18] tall, useful-looking gelding: has a quick, fluent action: fair handicapper: stays 1¾m: acts on firm ground: wore cheekpieces final outing at 3 yrs, tongue tied in 2006: fair hurdler. *K. G. Reveley*

TOTAL IMPACT 3 ch.g. Pivotal 124 – Rise 'n Shine 67 (Night Shift (USA)) [2006 57: **96** p5g² p6g* p5g* p7g⁵ p7g⁴ 5m⁴ 6m 5f⁶ m Sep 10] close-coupled gelding: has a short, scratchy action: won maiden at Wolverhampton in March and handicap at Kempton in April: good efforts in handicaps at Newmarket and Goodwood sixth/eighth starts: very best form at 5f: raced only on polytrack and good going or firmer on turf. *C. A. Cyzer*

TOTALLY FREE 2 ch.g. (Apr 30) Woodborough (USA) 112 – Barefooted Flyer **55** (USA) 67 (Fly So Free (USA) 122) [2006 p6g 5.7m⁵ 6g 5f² 5g p5.1g⁵ p6g p7g⁶ p6g² p6s⁶ p6g* p7.1g Dec 27] good-topped gelding: modest performer: won seller at Lingfield in December: best at 5f/6f: acts on polytrack and firm going: usually visored, wore cheek-pieces final start. *M. D. I. Usher*

TOTALLY SCOTTISH 10 b.g. Mtoto 134 – Glenfinlass (Lomond (USA) 128) [2006 **56** 55: 18v⁵ 15.8d⁴ 21.6d⁴ 17.2m⁵ 14d³ 18s Oct 16] sturdy gelding: modest maiden on Flat: stays 21.6f: acts on heavy and good to firm going: tried blinkered/tongue tied: held up: fairly useful hurdler, won in May and June. *K. G. Reveley*

TO THE MAX (IRE) 2 b.c. (Jan 19) Spectrum (IRE) 126 – Pray (IRE) (Priolo (USA) **93 +** 127) [2006 6g* 7m Oct 1] €42,000Y: rather leggy, attractive colt: fifth foal: half-brother to 3 winners, including 4-y-o Bon Nuit and useful 6f (at 2 yrs) to 1¼m winner In A Silent Way (by Desert Prince): dam unraced half-sister to smart performer up to 9f Anshan: fairly useful form when winning newcomers event at Ascot (beat Dijeerr by ¾ length) in July: out of depth in Prix Jean-Luc Lagardere at Longchamp: will be suited by 1m. *R. Hannon*

TO TIGER (GER) 5 b.g. Tiger Hill (IRE) 127 – The Mood (GER) (Mondrian (GER) **75** 125) [2006 17.5d* Sep 15] ex-German gelding: won maiden at Cologne in 2004, well held in 2005: successful British debut in handicap at Ayr (by 6 lengths) in September: stays 17f: raced on good going or softer. *P. Monteith*

TOUCANTINI 2 b.f. (Apr 12) Inchinor 119 – French Quartet (IRE) (Lycius (USA) **65** 124) [2006 p7g² p7g Nov 1] 11,000Y: fourth foal: half-sister to 4-y-o Thebestisyettocome and 1¼m winner Silver Palace (by Night Shift): dam Irish maiden half-sister to smart dam of Luso, Warrsan and Needle Gun: fair form when second to Diamond Diva in maiden at Lingfield: only eighth when favourite for similar event at Kempton, still green under pressure: will stay 1m/1¼m. *R. Charlton*

TOUCH OF IVORY (IRE) 3 b.f. Rossini (USA) 118 – Windomen (IRE) (Forest **69** Wind (USA) 111) [2006 60: 8m⁶ 8g⁵ 9m³ 10f* 8.3m* 9.9f⁴ 7.5f* 9d² 10m² 9.2m 7.2v Oct 28] leggy filly: fair performer: won handicap at Redcar in June, and handicap at Hamilton and claimer at Beverley (left R. Fahey £10,000) in July: effective at 7.5f to 1¼m: acts on firm and good to soft going: usually wears cheekpieces: often held up. *P. Monteith*

TOUCH OF LAND (FR) 6 b.h. Lando (GER) 128 – Touch of Class (GER) (Be My **118** Guest (USA) 126) [2006 119: 8.9m* 8.9m 10d* 10f 9.8m⁶ Sep 30] big, good-topped horse: smart performer: won Derrinstown Stud Jebel Hatta at Nad Al Sheba (by 1¼ lengths from Lord Admiral) in March and Grand Prix de Vichy-Auvergne (for second year, by 1½ lengths from Ruwi) in July: mid-division in Dubai Duty Free at Nad Al Sheba in between (off 4 months afterwards): not discredited in Arlington Million penultimate start, but last of 6 when seeking hat-trick in Prix Dollar at Longchamp final outing: effective at 8.9f to 1¼m: acts on firm and good going: held up. *H-A. Pantall, France*

TOUCH OF STYLE (IRE) 2 b.g. (Apr 2) Desert Style (IRE) 121 – No Hard Feelings **82** (IRE) 86 (Alzao (USA) 117) [2006 6g⁴ 6m Jun 27] €52,000Y: good-bodied gelding: brother to 7f (at 2 yrs) and 1m (in USA) winner Si Si Amiga and half-brother to several winners, including 1½m winner Athletic Sam (by Definite Article): dam 5f (at 2 yrs) to 1½m winner: fairly useful form both starts at Newbury, fourth to Thousand Words in maiden and seventh to Dazed And Amazed in listed race: gelded after: bred to stay 1m. *J. R. Boyle*

TOUGH LOVE 7 ch.g. Pursuit of Love 124 – Food of Love 109 (Music Boy 124) **79** [2006 87: 7g⁵ 7f 8g⁶ 7m⁶ 7m* 7.9g 7f³ 7f 8f³ 7.5m 8m⁶ 8g 6m 7.2v⁵ 7.5m⁶ Sep 19] strong, lengthy gelding: fair handicapper: won at Thirsk in June: effective at 7f to 8.5f: acts on firm and soft going: has worn cheekpieces, including of late: tongue tied last 2 starts: waited with: none too resolute. *T. D. Easterby*

TOUR D'AMOUR (IRE) 3 b.f. Fruits of Love (USA) 127 – Touraneena (Robellino **74** (USA) 127) [2006 67: f7g* 7.5d³ p7.1g³ 7d² 8m³ 6.9g³ 8d² 8g³ 8v 8v⁵ 10f 8g Nov 15] **a59** sparely-made filly: fair performer, better on turf than all-weather: left Stef Liddiard, won seller at Southwell in March: stays 1m: acts on all-weather and any turf going: reliable. *R. Craggs*

TOURNEDOS (IRE) 4 b.c. Rossini (USA) 118 – Don't Care (IRE) 93 (Nordico **114** (USA)) [2006 108: 5.2m 5g⁵ 5.1m* 5f 5m⁵ 5m⁴ 5.2m Sep 16] sturdy colt: good walker: has a quick action: smart performer: best efforts on second/third starts in 2006, fifth to Dandy Man in listed race at the Curragh then winning listed Chester City Wall Stakes (for second successive year) at Chester (by ½ length from Desert Lord) in July: just respectable efforts at best after, including when 3¼ lengths fourth to Majestic Missile in Prix du Petit Couvert at Longchamp: best at 5f: acts on any going: sometimes sweats: has worn crossed noseband: joined D. Nicholls. *R. Charlton*

TOUS LES DEUX 3 b.g. Efisio 120 – Caerosa 70 (Caerleon (USA) 132) [2006 79: 5.7d³ p6g² 6g 5f⁵ 6g⁶ p7g⁵ 7.1m p6g 6d p8.6m² p9.5g² p8.6g³ p9.5g* p9.5g⁴ p8.6g⁵ p12.2g⁴ Dec 26] rather leggy gelding: fairly useful performer: left F. J. Houghton 12,000 gns after ninth start: won handicap at Wolverhampton in November: tends to race freely, but stays easy 9.5f: acts on polytrack and good to soft ground, probably on firm: held up. *Peter Grayson* **80**

TOWER HILL (IRE) 3 b.g. Grand Lodge (USA) 125 – Champaka (IRE) (Caerleon (USA) 132) [2006 71: 11.6m⁶ Apr 24] smallish gelding: has a quick action: fair maiden: gelded, below par in handicap at Windsor only start on Flat in 2006 (reluctant at stall): sold 16,000 gns in May, joined Mrs L. Jewell. *M. A. Jarvis* **66**

TOWEROFCHARLEMAGNE (IRE) 3 ch.c. King Charlemagne (USA) 120 – Nozet (Nishapour (FR) 125) [2006 –: 7s 8.3g⁴ 8.3g Aug 23] big, workmanlike colt: has scope: fair maiden: best effort on second outing: stays 8.3f. *Miss Gay Kelleway* **73**

TOWN HOUSE 4 gr.f. Paris House 123 – Avondale Girl (IRE) 73 (Case Law 113) [2006 60, a53: p5.1g³ f5g⁵ p5.1g p5.1g p5.1g⁶ p5.1g 5m⁵ 5g⁶ 5.1g Aug 4] close-coupled filly: modest performer: best at 5f: acts on all-weather, good to firm and good to soft going: races prominently. *B. P. J. Baugh* **54**

TOWNSVILLE (IRE) 4 b.g. Soviet Star (USA) 128 – Valmarana (USA) 51 (Danzig Connection (USA)) [2006 63: p13g p16.5g Mar 15] maiden: no form in 2006. *E. J. O'Neill* **–**

TOWY GIRL (IRE) 2 b.f. (Mar 28) Second Empire (IRE) 124 – Solar Flare (IRE) (Danehill (USA) 126) [2006 8m p8g³ p8g² p8g³ Dec 4] third foal: half-sister to 4-y-o She's My Outsider: dam injured only outing: fair maiden: placed all starts after debut (only run on turf): stays 1m: carries head high. *I. A. Wood* **77**

TOY TOP (USA) 3 gr. or ro.f. Tactical Cat (USA) 116 – I'll Flutter By (USA) (Concorde's Tune (USA)) [2006 46: 5d² 5.1d² 5m* 5m³ 5d⁴ 5m³ 5m* 5g* 5f² 5f⁴ 5g 5g⁵ 5.1f 6d Oct 3] leggy, angular filly: fairly useful handicapper: won at Catterick in April, Newcastle in June and Warwick in July: best at 5f/easy 6f: acts on firm and good to soft going: blinkered. *M. Dods* **86**

TRACE CLIP 8 b.g. Zafonic (USA) 130 – Illusory 81 (Kings Lake (USA) 133) [2006 62: 5.5d⁴ 7g 5s 5.7f³ 6m 5.2m 5f⁶ 6f Jul 22] neat, quite attractive gelding: modest handicapper nowadays: best at 5f/6f: acts on polytrack, firm and good to soft going: tongue tied earlier in career: often slowly away, markedly so last 2 starts: headstrong: has found little. *N. I. M. Rossiter* **58**

TRACER 2 b.c. (Feb 14) Kyllachy 129 – Western Sal 75 (Salse (USA) 128) [2006 5f⁶ 6g⁵ 6g Oct 12] 92,000Y: tall, close-coupled colt: half-brother to 3 winners, including useful German performer up to 2m Western Devil (by Dr Devious) and 2003 2-y-o 6f winner Just One Look (by Barathea): dam 1¼m/1½m winner who stayed 15f: fair form when fifth to Traffic Guard in maiden at Newbury: hung left both other starts. *R. Hannon* **72**

TRACKATTACK 4 ch.g. Atraf 116 – Verbena (IRE) (Don't Forget Me 127) [2006 50: f11g f11s⁶ f11g 11.6m Jul 17] modest performer in 2005: no form in 2006: tried blinkered. *P. Howling* **–**

TRADITIONALIST (IRE) 2 ch.c. (Feb 26) Traditionally (USA) 117 – Rouberia (IRE) 64 (Alhaarth (IRE) 126) [2006 7g⁵ p7g Sep 2] €70,000Y: quite good-topped colt: first foal: dam, maiden, should have been suited by 1m+, half-sister to smart performer up to 1¾m I'm Supposin': fair form when fifth to Prince Forever in maiden at Newbury: sweating/edgy, found little in minor event at Kempton. *G. A. Butler* **75**

TRAFALGAR BAY (IRE) 3 b.g. Fruits of Love (USA) 127 – Chatsworth Bay (IRE) (Fairy King (USA)) [2006 90: 6f³ 6g* 6m⁵ 6m 7g⁶ 7m⁶ 6d⁵ 7g Oct 13] compact gelding: useful handicapper: won at Ascot (by ½ length from Pearly Way) in May: creditable fifth to Prince Tamino in William Hill Trophy at York next start: will prove best at 6f/7f: acts on firm and good to soft going: edgy sort, often early to post (withdrawn after bolting intended reappearance): sold 110,000 gns, joined K. Burke, and gelded. *S. Kirk* **100**

TRAFALGAR DAY 3 b.g. Mark of Esteem (IRE) 137 – Rosy Sunset (IRE) (Red Sunset 120) [2006 71p: 12.3m³ 12m³ 12.4d⁵ Aug 28] tall, attractive gelding: has a quick action: fair maiden: stays 12.4f: acts on good to firm and good to soft going. *W. M. Brisbourne* **65**

TRAFALGAR SQUARE 4 b.c. King's Best (USA) 132 – Pat Or Else 72 (Alzao **96** (USA) 117) [2006 86: 8.3g⁶ 7m⁵ 7m⁶ 8s* 8.5g 7m 7d Sep 23] strong, compact colt: useful handicapper: comfortably best effort when winning by 4 lengths from Davenport at Goodwood in May: reportedly finished lame next start: effective at 7f/1m: acts on heavy and good to firm going: sometimes hangs left: held up. *J. Akehurst*

TRAFFIC GUARD (USA) 2 b.c. (Mar 23) More Than Ready (USA) 120 – Street **100** Scene (IRE) (Zafonic (USA) 130) [2006 6g* 6m* 7d Oct 14] $60,000Y, 42,000 2-y-o: strong, lengthy colt: has scope: second foal: dam, lightly-raced US maiden, half-sister to South African Group 1 1½m winner Chief Advocate: useful form: won maiden at Newbury (beat Prime Defender by length) in July and minor event at Newmarket in September, in latter not all out to hold Resignation by neck: stiff task in Dewhurst Stakes (ninth of 15 to Teofilo) at Newmarket: will probably stay 1m. *J. S. Moore*

TRAILMIX (FR) 3 gr.g. Linamix (FR) 127 – Yield To Maturity (USA) (Conquistador **68** Cielo (USA)) [2006 10s⁵ p9.5g⁴ Nov 24] tall, leggy gelding: second foal: dam 2-y-o 7f winner in USA, out of sister to US Grade 1 winner to 1½m winner Bounding Basque: similar form in maidens at Nottingham and Wolverhampton (still green): stays 1¼m: very slowly away on debut. *D. R. C. Elsworth*

TRANCE (IRE) 6 ch.g. Bahhare (USA) 122 – Lady of Dreams (IRE) 84 (Prince Rupert **88 §** (FR) 121) [2006 92d, a83: p12.2g f12g³ f14g² 16v 14g² 16g* 18.7m 14s³ 20m 16f² 16.1m 16g⁶ 14g⁴ 16g² 18s³ 18d⁵ 16d Oct 27] strong, lengthy gelding: fairly useful handicapper: won at Newbury in April: several other creditable efforts: stays 2¼m: acts on all-weather, firm and soft going: blinkered (well held) twice at 3 yrs, often wears cheekpieces: usually held up: moody. *T. D. Barron*

TRANOS (USA) 3 b.c. Bahri (USA) 125 – Balancoire (USA) (Diesis 133) [2006 p7.1g **68** 7m⁴ 8.1s⁶ 9.9g 8.1m p10g⁶ 12.4d 10m³ Sep 19] $70,000F, 72,000Y: good-topped colt: second foal: dam unraced out of Oaks/Irish Oaks runner-up Royal Ballerina: fair maiden: stays easy 1¼m: acts on polytrack and good to firm ground: visored sixth/seventh starts: sold 20,000 gns. *L. M. Cumani*

TRANQUILITY 2 b.f. (Mar 6) Barathea (IRE) 127 – Immortelle (Arazi (USA) 135) **–** [2006 6f p7g p6g Dec 2] 14,000Y: fourth foal: half-sister to 1½m winner Corker (by Grand Lodge) and winner in Greece by Generous: dam unraced half-sister to Poule d'Essai des Pouliches winner Danseuse du Soir: well held in maidens. *J. Pearce*

TRANQUILIZER 4 b.f. Dr Fong (USA) 128 – Tranquillity 70 (Night Shift (USA)) **–** [2006 61, a73: p12.2g² p12.2g² p16.5g² p16g⁵ p12g p13.9g³ p13.9g² p12.2g* Dec 26] **a83** big, good-bodied filly: fairly useful handicapper on all-weather, modest at best on turf: won at Wolverhampton in December: stays 2m: acts on polytrack, best turf run on good going: tongue tied. *D. J. Coakley*

TRANQUIL TIGER 2 ch.c. (Mar 17) Selkirk (USA) 129 – Serene View (USA) 105 **72 p** (Distant View (USA) 126) [2006 8s⁶ Oct 10] strong, good-bodied colt: third foal: dam, French 1m winner, out of half-sister to dam of 1000 Guineas winner Wince: 16/1, needed race when sixth to Sunshine Kid in maiden at Newbury: will progress. *H. R. A. Cecil*

TRANSACTION (IRE) 4 ch.g. Trans Island 119 – Meranie Girl (IRE) 52 (Mujadil **61 d** (USA) 119) [2006 72d: p6g⁵ p7.1g p6g p6g 8g 6g⁶ 6.8g⁵ 7d 10f³ 8v a9.5g⁵ a7.5g² a6g² a5.5g Dec 31] well-made gelding: only modest performer nowadays: sold from J. Eustace 1,300 gns after fourth start: second in handicaps at Neuss and Dortmund late in year: probably best up to 1m: acts on polytrack/sand and firm ground: tried blinkered/visored/tongue tied. *C. Speiser, Germany*

TRANSCEND 2 ch.c. (Feb 6) Beat Hollow 126 – Pleasuring 68 (Good Times (ITY)) **85** [2006 7g 7d⁴ Oct 28] 52,000F, 190,000Y: smallish, sturdy colt: half-brother to several winners, including 8-y-o Suggestive and useful French 7.5f to 9f winner (latter at 2 yrs) Rashbag (both by Reprimand): dam sprint maiden: much better effort in maidens at Newmarket when fourth to Spanish Moon, racing wide. *J. H. M. Gosden*

TRANSIT 7 b.g. Lion Cavern (USA) 117 – Black Fighter (USA) 79 (Secretariat (USA)) **57** [2006 –: f16g⁴ p16.5g⁴ 13.9m 14.1f⁶ 16g³ 16m⁵ p16.5g⁴ 13m⁴ 14.1f 14m⁶ Aug 24] tall, leggy gelding: has a fluent, round action: modest maiden handicapper: stays 2m: acts on all-weather and any turf going: often wears cheekpieces, tried in blinkers/tongue tie final start: successful over fences in December. *B. Ellison*

TRANSPIQUE (IRE) 2 b.c. (Mar 26) Trans Island 119 – Repique (USA) 88 (Sharpen **77** Up 127) [2006 6d⁴ 6g³ 5m² 6s Aug 24] 29,000Y: strong colt: half-brother to useful Irish 5f winner Give A Whistle (by Mujadil) and 5f winner (including at 2 yrs) Roman Mistress (by Titus Livius): dam, 6f/7f winner, half-sister to high-class 7f to 9f performer Indian

Lodge: fair form: in frame in maidens, second to Prime Defender at Sandown: creditable eighth of 19 behind Doctor Brown in valuable nursery race at York: should prove best at 5f/6f: acts on soft and good to firm going. *C. G. Cox*

TRANSPONDER 3 b.g. Piccolo 121 – Miletrian Cares (IRE) 67 (Hamas (IRE) 125§) – [2006 p7g Apr 12] 66/1, slowly away and always behind in maiden at Lingfield: sold 1,200 gns, sent to Spain. *W. R. Muir*

TRANS SONIC 3 ch.g. Trans Island 119 – Sankaty Light (USA) 55 (Summer Squall (USA)) [2006 86d: p6g² p7g* p8g* p8g 8m 7.6f⁶ 8m 7.1m p7g p6g⁴ 8g⁶ 10s⁴ p12g⁶ Nov 5] big, workmanlike gelding: has plenty of scope: fairly useful on all-weather, fair on turf: made all in maiden at Lingfield in February and handicap at Kempton in April: stays 1½m: acts on polytrack and soft going: visored last 3 starts. *A. P. Jarvis* — **74 a86**

TRANSVESTITE (IRE) 4 b.g. Trans Island 119 – Christoph's Girl 50 (Efisio 120) [2006 82: 10g⁴ 10g⁵ 10d³ 10.3g 10.2d 10.1g³ 10m* 10.1g³ 11.9f² 12d⁵ 11g³ p12g² p12g⁴ 11.6d⁵ Nov 4] quite good-topped gelding: fairly useful handicapper: won apprentice event at Sandown in July: mostly creditable efforts after: stays 1½m: acts on polytrack, firm and good to soft going: has been visored: hung left tenth outing. *J. W. Hills* — **92**

TRAPPETO (IRE) 4 b.c. Barathea (IRE) 127 – Campiglia (IRE) (Fairy King (USA)) [2006 62: f12g³ Jan 3] modest maiden: stayed easy 1½m: raced only on all-weather and good/good to firm ground on turf: dead. *C. Smith* — **52**

TRAVELLING BAND (IRE) 8 b.g. Blues Traveller (IRE) 119 – Kind of Cute 52 (Prince Sabo 123) [2006 p9.5g 8m May 3] leggy, quite attractive gelding: well held both starts on Flat since 2004: tried visored/blinkered. *J. Mackie*

TRAVELLING FOX 3 b.g. Slip Anchor 136 – Lola Mora (Nearly A Hand 115) [2006 10m 10.1d May 16] well held in maidens at Windsor and Newcastle: gelded after. *H. Morrison*

TRAVOLTA 3 b.g. Dansili 127 – Generous Diana 90 (Generous (IRE) 139) [2006 62p: 8.1s 10d 11.5m² p12g⁶ 16.2m Jul 24] modest maiden: stays 11.5f: acts on good to firm going: wore cheekpieces final start: joined C. Egerton. *C. G. Cox* — **59**

TRAYTONIC 5 b.g. Botanic (USA) – Lady Parker (IRE) (Nordico (USA)) [2006 109§: p7g 9.8d 8f 8s 7m 7m 6f 7d* 6s 7g⁶ 7.2d Sep 16] tall, useful-looking gelding: useful performer: won handicap at Redcar in August: well below form most other starts in 2006: stays 7f: acts on firm and good to soft ground, probably on polytrack: sometimes reluctant to post/in early stages: tried visored: temperamental, and needs treating with caution: sold 10,000 gns. *D. Nicholls* — **95 §**

TREASON TRIAL 5 b.g. Peintre Celebre (USA) 137 – Pampabella (IRE) (High Estate 127) [2006 77: 14.1s 15d f12g Dec 29] good-bodied gelding: fair performer at 4 yrs: well beaten in 2006, leaving Stef Liddiard after reappearance. *W. M. Brisbourne* — **–**

TREASURE CAY 5 ch.h. Bahamian Bounty 116 – Madame Sisu 47 (Emarati (USA) 74) [2006 105, a95: 6m p6g⁴ 5.2m³ 5m 5g² 5.1m 5m 5.4g⁶ 5f p5g Oct 21] strong horse: useful performer: several creditable efforts in 2006, including when third to Green Manalishi in handicap at Newbury and ¾-length second to Tycoon's Hill in listed race at Chantilly: effective at 5f/easy 6f: acts on all-weather and good to firm going: tried blinkered, visored sixth start: often wears tongue strap: sometimes slowly away: has refused to enter stall on 3 occasions (banned from running in Britain briefly in 2006). *P. W. D'Arcy* — **101**

TREASURE HOUSE (IRE) 5 b.g. Grand Lodge (USA) 125 – Royal Wolff (Prince Tenderfoot (USA) 126) [2006 62+: p6g 7g² 7g p7.1g⁴ p8.6g³ p8.6g p7.1g⁴ 8.1m³ 8m 7.1m⁵ 7.5m* Sep 19] well-made gelding: fairly useful handicapper: won at Beverley in September: stays 8.6f: acts on polytrack and firm ground: has looked none too keen. *M. Blanshard* — **80**

TREAT 2 b.f. (Jan 19) Barathea (IRE) 127 – Cream Tease 99 (Pursuit of Love 124) [2006 7m 8.2m* 8d² Sep 23] 39,000F, 80,000Y: tall filly: has scope: second foal: dam, 7f winner (including at 2 yrs), half-sister to smart winner up to 8.5f Enharmonic: off 3 months after debut, won maiden at Nottingham in September: further marked improvement 8 days later when 1½ lengths second of 8 to Simply Perfect in Fillies' Mile at Ascot, hampered as headed late on: likely to stay 1¼m: smart prospect, will win more races. *M. R. Channon* — **108 p**

TREBELLO 5 b.g. Robellino (USA) 127 – Trempkate (USA) (Trempolino (USA) 135) [2006 55: f16g* p16g Nov 6] modest performer: won banded race at Southwell in March: stays 2m: acts on all-weather and soft ground: wore cheekpieces last 2 starts at 4 yrs. *J. R. Boyle* — **56**

TREDEGAR 2 ch.c. (Mar 16) Inchinor 119 – Ffestiniog (IRE) 96 (Efisio 120) [2006   **99 p**
6m⁵ p7g² 7g* p7.1g* Nov 6] good-bodied colt: fifth foal: half-brother to several winners,
including smart performer up to 1½m Brecon Beacon (by Spectrum), 5f to 7f winner at
2 yrs, and 5-y-o Eisteddfod: dam 6f (at 2 yrs) to 1m winner: useful form: trained on debut
by C. Cox: progressed well, winning maiden at Newmarket in October and minor event
at Wolverhampton (beat Sagredo by 1¼ lengths) in November: will stay 1m: should go
on improving. *P. F. I. Cole*

TREETOPS HOTEL (IRE) 7 ch.g. Grand Lodge (USA) 125 – Rousinette (Rousil-   **74**
lon (USA) 133) [2006 61: p10g⁶ p10g* p9.5g⁶ p10g⁶ p10g⁴ 10g³ 10m 10.9f² 7m p12g*
p16g* p12g⁴ p12g⁵ Dec 8] quite attractive gelding: fair handicapper: won at Lingfield
in February, September (apprentices) and October: stays easy 2m: acts on polytrack, firm
and good to soft going: tried in headgear/tongue strap: held up: has carried head
awkwardly. *B. R. Johnson*

TREGARRON 5 br.g. Efisio 120 – Language of Love 63 (Rock City 120) [2006 77:   **64**
p8g⁴ p8.6g⁶ p9.5g p7g⁵ p10g⁵ p7g p9.5g p9.5g 7.1m 8.1m Sep 1] leggy, quite good-
topped gelding: modest performer: claimed from R. Hannon £6,000 after fourth start:
stays 1¼m: acts on polytrack, firm and good to soft going: tried in cheekpieces: none
too consistent: sold 2,500 gns. *P. A. Blockley*

TREPA (USA) 2 ch.c. (May 1) Hennessy (USA) 122 – Ball Gown (USA) (Silver Hawk   **76 p**
(USA) 123) [2006 6m* Sep 6] 105,000 2-y-o: sturdy, close-coupled colt: fifth foal:
half-brother to several winners, including 4-y-o Palomar and fairly useful 9f (in France)
and 1½m winner Hayhaat (by Irish River): dam unraced out of sister to top-class 1982
2-y-o 7f winner Gorytus: 4/1, overcame greenness to win maiden at Southwell by neck
from Malaaq: will be suited by 1m+: sure to improve. *W. Jarvis*

TRES HOMBRES 2 ch.g. (Mar 26) Tobougg (IRE) 125 – Duena (Grand Lodge (USA)   **59 d**
125) [2006 5s 6m³ 7.1g⁵ 7g⁵ 7m p8g⁵ Dec 8] compact, deep-girthed gelding: modest
maiden: best effort on debut: probably stays 7f. *T. G. Dascombe*

TRESOR SECRET (FR) 6 b.g. Green Desert (USA) 127 – Tresor (USA) (Pleasant   **– §**
Tap (USA)) [2006 66§: p12.2g Dec 27] close-coupled gelding: fair performer at 5 yrs:
well held only outing in 2006: tried blinkered: reportedly resents whip: tail flasher.
J. Gallagher

TREVIAN 5 ch.g. Atraf 116 – Ascend (IRE) (Glint of Gold 128) [2006 63: 8s 7m⁵ 7.9m⁴   **61**
8f³ 8f* 8.1g⁴ 8.1g 8.3f 7.6g 8m* p8g⁵ p8g Nov 24] big gelding: modest handicapper: won
at Ripon in June and Brighton in September: stays 1m: acts on polytrack and firm going.
J. M. Bradley

TREW FLIGHT (USA) 4 b.g. Rahy (USA) 115 – Magdala (IRE) (Sadler's Wells   **50**
(USA) 132) [2006 55: p10g f6g 11.5m⁶ 9.8m 10.2g May 2] modest maiden: bred to stay
at least 1m (seemed not to stay 11.5f): tried blinkered. *M. H. Tompkins*

TREW STYLE 4 ch.g. Desert King (IRE) 129 – Southern Psychic (USA) (Alwasmi   **89**
(USA) 115) [2006 77: f14g⁴ f11g⁶ 15.4m* Apr 25] big, workmanlike gelding: fairly useful performer: won handicap at Folkestone (by 6 lengths) in April: stays 15.4f: acts on
polytrack, good to firm and good to soft going. *M. H. Tompkins*

TRIALS 'N TRIBS 4 b.f. Rainbow Quest (USA) 134 – Seasonal Splendour (IRE) 95   **53**
(Prince Rupert (FR) 121) [2006 62: 11.5m p16g p12g⁴ 16.2g² 16f p16.5f⁶ 16.2m⁶ 16m   **a47**
p8.6g⁵ 10d Nov 4] angular filly: modest maiden on turf, poor on all-weather: stays 2m:
acts on polytrack and firm ground: none too genuine. *C. A. Cyzer*

TRIBE 4 b.g. Danehill (USA) 126 – Leo Girl (USA) 100 (Seattle Slew (USA)) [2006 74:   **77**
11.7d 10m⁵ 10d⁵ 14.1g⁴ Jun 7] very big gelding: fair maiden: lightly raced: ran creditably
in handicaps in 2006: stays 1¾m: acts on good to firm and good to soft ground: sold
27,000 gns in October. *Sir Michael Stoute*

TRIBUTE (IRE) 5 b.g. Green Desert (USA) 127 – Zooming (IRE) (Indian Ridge 123)   **69 d**
[2006 76: 5m³ 5.7s 5m 5f p7.1g f5g⁴ Dec 28] quite attractive gelding: fair handicapper:
well below form after reappearance, leaving P. Blockley prior to final outing: effective at
5f/6f: acts on firm going: tried in headgear: has worn tongue tie: sometimes early to post.
John A. Harris

TRICK CYCLIST 5 b.g. Mind Games 121 – Sabonis (USA) 68 (The Minstrel (CAN)   **73 §**
135) [2006 79: 6m 5d 5m 6g 5m² 5g⁴ 5f⁶ 5m 5d 5m 5g³ 5d² a7g² Dec 17] leggy gelding:
fair handicapper: sold from M. Easterby 6,000 gns before final start: best at 5f: acts on
polytrack, firm and good to soft going: tried in headgear (best efforts in 2006 in blinkers):
often slowly away: unreliable. *P. Diaz, Spain*

TRICKLE (USA) 2 ch.f. (Jan 22) Rahy (USA) 115 – Avitrix (USA) (Storm Bird **69** (CAN) 134) [2006 6g 6d⁶ p6g⁵ p8g⁶ p7.1g³ p7.1g² Dec 27] neat filly: second foal: dam unraced sister to smart French/UAE miler Grazalema: fair maiden: left E. Dunlop 7,000 gns after fourth start: placed in nurseries last 2 outings: should stay 1m: tried tongue tied. *Miss D. Mountain*

TRICK OR TREAT 3 b.f. Lomitas 129 – Trick of Ace (USA) (Clever Trick (USA)) **100** [2006 51: f11g⁴ 9.9f* 12f* 12g* 12g* 13.9s* 12m² 11.8d² 12s² p13g⁶ Oct 26] lengthy filly, unfurnished at 3 yrs: progressed into useful performer in 2006, winning handicaps at Beverley and Pontefract in July, and Thirsk, Salisbury and York (beat Ask by short head in Melrose Stakes) in August: good efforts after, 5 lengths second to Anna Pavlova at Ascot and 6¼ lengths sixth to High Heel Sneakers at Lingfield in listed races on last 2 outings: stays 1¾m: acts on all-weather, firm and soft going: waited with, and usually travels strongly. *J. G. Given*

TRICKSTEP 5 b.g. Imperial Ballet (IRE) 110 – Trick of Ace (USA) (Clever Trick **–** (USA)) [2006 –, a51: 15.8m Aug 8] modest performer: well beaten only outing on Flat in 2006: stayed 13f: acted on all-weather and soft going: often blinkered/in cheekpieces: dead. *D. McCain Jnr*

TRICKY VENTURE 6 gr.g. Linamix (FR) 127 – Ukraine Venture 96 (Slip Anchor **–** 136) [2006 77, a69: p9.5g p10g p8g p10g p10g Aug 5] leggy gelding: fair performer at best: well held in 2006: tried in cheekpieces (raced freely). *Mrs L. C. Jewell*

TRIFFID 4 b.g. Dracula (AUS) 121 – Rockfest (USA) 104 (Stage Door Johnny (USA)) **–** [2006 46: f11g Jan 11] poor maiden: stayed 7f: raced solely on all-weather: tried in cheekpieces: dead. *R. A. Fahey*

TRIFTI 5 b.g. Vettori (IRE) 119 – Time For Tea (IRE) 73 (Imperial Frontier (USA) 112) **62** [2006 62, a91: p8.6g² p8.6g p10g⁶ p8.6g² p8g p8g² p7g p8g p8g⁶ p8g 10m⁵ p8g⁵ p12.2f⁴ **a92** 10g p8.6m p8.6g p8g² p8g⁵ Dec 30] medium-sized gelding: fairly useful performer on all-weather, modest on turf: creditable efforts when runner-up in minor event/handicaps in 2006: best form at 1m/1¼m: acts on polytrack and good to firm going: hung left penultimate outing. *C. A. Cyzer*

TRIM IMAGE 4 br.f. Averti (IRE) 117 – Altizaf 66 (Zafonic (USA) 130) [2006 75: 5d **–** 5g Sep 30] rather leggy filly: fair performer at best: well held in handicaps in 2006 (very upset in stall on latter occasion). *K. R. Burke*

TRIMLESTOWN (IRE) 3 b.g. Orpen (USA) 116 – Courtier (Saddlers' Hall (IRE) **94** 126) [2006 62: 8m⁵ 8m 7m³ 7m* 7d³ 7m² 7m* 7d* Oct 28] strong, good-topped gelding: fairly useful performer: won maiden at Lingfield in July, and handicaps at Newbury in September and Newmarket (beat Resplendent Nova by 1¾ lengths) in October: probably stays 1m: acts on good to firm and good to soft going: races prominently. *H. Candy*

TRINCULO (IRE) 9 b.g. Anita's Prince 126 – Fandangerina (USA) (Grey Dawn II **95** 132) [2006 94: f5g³ p6g⁵ f5g f5g 5d* p5g² 5.1f 5s* 5s p5g³ 5m 5s* 5v* p5.1m⁴ p6g² Dec 2] good-bodied gelding: has a long, round action: useful performer: won handicaps at Beverley in April and York (by ¾ length from Orientor) in May: below that form after tenth start, though still won claimers at Catterick in August and October: races mainly at 5f nowadays: acts on all-weather and any turf going: has been blinkered/in cheekpieces: often forces pace: sometimes finds little. *D. Nicholls*

TRINITY COLLEGE (USA) 2 ch.c. (Mar 8) Giant's Causeway (USA) 132 – City **100** College (USA) (Carson City (USA)) [2006 7m* 7g⁴ 7m Oct 1] $650,000Y: big, good-topped colt: has plenty of scope: fourth foal: half-brother to minor winners in USA by Boston Harbor and Skip Away: dam, 5.5f (at 2 yrs)/6.5f winner in USA, out of half-sister to Kentucky Derby/Belmont Stakes winner Bold Forbes: landed odds in maiden at Cork in August by length from Sweet Peak: still green, improved when 5 lengths fourth of 7 to Teofilo in Futurity Stakes at the Curragh: took good hold and folded tamely when seventh of 9 in Prix Jean-Luc Lagardere at Longchamp: raced at 7f. *A. P. O'Brien, Ireland*

TRINITY ROSE 3 ch.f. Generous (IRE) 139 – Stylish Rose (IRE) 65 (Don't Forget **87** Me 127) [2006 –: 12g² 12m⁴ 11.8d² 16d p13g⁴ f16g² p16g⁴ Nov 29] fairly useful handicapper: won at Southwell in November: respectable efforts last 2 starts: stays 2m: acts on all-weather and good to soft going. *M. Johnston*

TRIPLE BEND 3 b.c. Singspiel (IRE) 133 – Triple Green 69 (Green Desert (USA) **54** 127) [2006 10m Jun 17] close-coupled colt: modest form in maiden at Sandown only outing: dead. *Mrs A. J. Perrett*

TRIPLE BLUFF 3 b.c. Medicean 128 – Trinity Reef 80 (Bustino 136) [2006 10d **66** 11.9m 9m 10m 12m p10g Oct 11] tall, quite good-topped colt: fourth foal: half-brother to fairly useful 1¾m winner Tangible (by Hernando): dam, 1½m winner, sister to smart 1¼m/1½m performer Talented: fair maiden: should stay 1½m: tongue tied (below form) final outing: raced freely third start: sold 17,000 gns. *Mrs A. J. Perrett*

TRIPLE JUMP 5 ch.g. Inchinor 119 – Meteoric 102 (High Line 125) [2006 60: f8g⁵ 55 p8.6g f7s p9.5g Mar 20] angular, useful-looking gelding: modest performer, lightly raced: stays 1¼m: acts on fibresand, soft and good to firm going: tried blinkered/in cheek-pieces/tongue tied. *K. A. Ryan*

TRIPLE POINT (IRE) 4 b.g. Perugino (USA) 84 – Quench The Lamp (IRE) (Glow – (USA)) [2006 p5g Nov 11] tailed off in maiden at Lingfield on debut. *J. M. Plasschaert, Belgium*

TRIPLE SHADOW 2 ch.g. (Feb 29) Compton Place 125 – Arctic High 62 (Polar 74 Falcon (USA) 126) [2006 5m 5g* 6g 6g Sep 30] 15,000Y: first foal: dam 8.5f winner: fair performer: won maiden at Hamilton in August: stiff task in listed Two-Year-Old Trophy at Redcar final outing: free-going sort, likely to prove best at 5f. *T. D. Barron*

TRIPLE ZERO (IRE) 4 b.f. Raise A Grand (IRE) 114 – Locorotondo (IRE) 83 – (Broken Hearted 124) [2006 67: p7.1g³ p6g³ p7g p6g⁵ p7g³ p7g 7g May 1] lengthy filly: **a66** fair performer: effective at 6f to 1m: acts on polytrack and firm ground: has worn visor: sold 3,800 gns in August. *A. P. Jarvis*

TRISKAIDEKAPHOBIA 3 b.g. Bertolini (USA) 125 – Seren Teg 80 (Timeless 81 d Times (USA) 99) [2006 93: 5.1f 5.1g 5f⁵ 5m 5f 6g 5m 5m p5g p5.1g Dec 31] small, sturdy gelding: fairly useful handicapper at best in 2006: reportedly finished distressed final outing: best at 5f: acts on good to firm going: tried visored/blinkered (below form). *Miss J. R. Tooth*

TROIALINI 2 b.c. (Mar 22) Bertolini (USA) 125 – Troia (IRE) 54 (Last Tycoon 131) 89 [2006 7g p9.5g* p9.5s² Dec 14] 9,500Y: tall colt: fourth foal: dam lightly-raced half-sister to smart performer up to 1½m Ela-Aristokrati: fairly useful form: better for debut, won maiden at Wolverhampton in November by 6 lengths from Miss Fancy Pants: further progress when length second to Love Dubai in nursery there: will stay 1¼m. *S. W. Hall*

TROJAN FLIGHT 5 ch.g. Hector Protector (USA) 124 – Fairywings 85 (Kris 135) 82 [2006 90: 6g⁶ 5m 7f 7g 6g³ 6g³ 6f⁵ 6m 6m 5f 6f 7.5m³ 6g 6m³ 7.5g 6d* 6d⁶ 7s Oct 24] good-topped gelding: fairly useful handicapper: won at Catterick in September: probably best at 5f/6f: acts on any going: often in cheekpieces of late: held up. *D. W. Chapman*

TROMBONE TOM 3 b.g. Superior Premium 122 – Nine To Five 64 (Imp Society 65 (USA)) [2006 67: p6g³ p6g⁶ 6g⁶ 5g³ 6f p6g⁵ 5f³ 5d³ 5m⁵ 5f 5g f5m⁶ Oct 31] fair performer: effective at 5f/6f: acts on polytrack, firm and good to soft going. *J. R. Norton*

TROMP 5 ch.g. Zilzal (USA) 137 – Sulitelma (USA) 63 (The Minstrel (CAN) 135) 80 [2006 82: p12.2g² p13g⁵ p12g³ p12g⁵ p12.2g⁶ Nov 10] fairly useful handicapper: creditable efforts first 3 starts off over 7 months, below form on return: stays 13f: acts on polytrack and good to soft going. *D. J. Coakley*

TROMPETTE (USA) 4 b.f. Bahri (USA) 125 – Bold Bold (IRE) (Sadler's Wells 82 (USA) 132) [2006 12g⁴ 12.1s⁵ May 29] fifth foal: half-sister to fairly useful French 12.5f winner/smart hurdler Ambobo (by Kingmambo) and fairly useful French 10.5f winner True Wooman (by Capote): dam, French 1¼m winner, sister to smart 1¼m (in UAE)/1½m winner Sabadilla: fairly useful performer: won maiden at Argentan and minor event at Lyon-Parilly in 2005: left F. Head in France 50,000 gns, much better effort in handicaps on Flat in Britain when fourth at Salisbury: stays 1½m: acts on soft going: fairly useful hurdler. *N. J. Henderson*

TROODOS JET 5 b.g. Atraf 116 – Costa Verde 77 (King of Spain 121) [2006 –: 7.1g – Jul 3] big, good-topped gelding: modest performer at 3 yrs: no form on Flat since: won over hurdles in August. *K. W. Hogg, Isle of Man*

TROPICAL CLIMATE (USA) 3 b.f. Lear Fan (USA) 130 – Navarene (USA) 59 (Known Fact (USA) 135) [2006 8g⁶ 7.1g Jul 7] fluent mover: sixth foal: half-sister to 3 winners, including useful French 1m winner Serene View (by Distant View) and French 1¼m winner Never Regret (by Quest For Fame): dam, third at 9f in France, half-sister to US Grade 1 2-y-o 1m winner Contredance and to dam of 1000 Guineas winner Wince: modest form when sixth to Petrovich in newcomers race at Newmarket: reportedly bled next time: sold 7,500 gns. *B. W. Hills*

TROPICAL LADY (IRE) 6 b.m. Sri Pekan (USA) 117 – Tropical Lake (IRE) 100 **117** (Lomond (USA) 128) [2006 115: 10d⁶ 10g⁴ 12m Aug 7] smart performer: good 2¼ lengths fourth to stable-companion Alexander Goldrun in Pretty Polly Stakes at the

Curragh second start: well below form both other outings: finds 7f a minimum and stays 1¼m (not beaten by longer trip final outing): acts on any turf going: held up. *J. S. Bolger, Ireland*

TROUBLE MAKER 5 b.g. Green Desert (USA) 127 – River Abouali (Bluebird **61** (USA) 125) [2006 59: p6g2 p6g* p7g5 p7g3 p8g p6g May 23] well-made gelding: modest performer: won banded race at Wolverhampton in January: stays easy 7f: acts on polytrack, good to firm and good to soft going: tried blinkered/visored. *A. M. Balding*

TROUBLE MOUNTAIN (USA) 9 br.g. Mt Livermore (USA) – Trouble Free (USA) **82** (Nodouble (USA)) [2006 82: 11g 10.1m3 10s* 10.2d2 10d2 10.5g4 10.1m3 10.5f6 9.8g4 10.1d5 10g* 10d2 10g4 10d5 Nov 1] small, sparely-made gelding: fairly useful handicapper: won at Nottingham in May, Haydock in June and Redcar in September: effective at 1m to 1½m: acts on fibresand and any turf going: tried blinkered, tongue tied nowadays: has worn crossed noseband: tends to race in snatches. *M. W. Easterby*

TROUVILLE (IRE) 7 b.m. Mukaddamah (USA) 125 – Trouville Lass (IRE) 77 (Be **60** My Native (USA) 122) [2006 65: 11.9g5 12f 13f3 12.9f 12m6 13f2 p13.9m Oct 2] just modest handicapper in 2006: stays 13f: acts on firm going, probably on soft: sold €900 in December. *G. O'Leary, Ireland*

TRUCKLE 4 b.g. Vettori (IRE) 119 – Proud Titania (IRE) 103 (Fairy King (USA)) **–** [2006 70: f11g Dec 19] lengthy, angular gelding: fair performer at best: well held only outing on Flat in 2006. *C. W. Fairhurst*

TRUE CAUSE (USA) 3 ch.c. Storm Cat (USA) – Dearly 107 (Rahy (USA) 115) [2006 **104** 104: 10.1g2 8m5 Aug 5] well-made, attractive colt: has scope: has a powerful round action: useful performer: visored, creditable efforts both starts in 2006, second to Impeller in minor event at Epsom, then 2½ lengths fifth to Prince of Light in listed race at Goodwood: will prove suited by 1¼m: unraced on extremes of going: tends to hang. *Saeed bin Suroor*

TRUE COMPANION 7 b.g. Brief Truce (USA) 126 – Comanche Companion 88 **84** (Commanche Run 133) [2006 93: p12g4 p12g 10d4 11.9s3 p10g Oct 6] fairly useful handicapper: stays 1½m: acts on polytrack, firm and soft going: usually held up: sometimes races freely/wanders. *N. P. Littmoden*

TRUE (IRE) 5 ch.m. Barathea (IRE) 127 – Bibliotheque (USA) 79 (Woodman (USA) **55** 126) [2006 55: f8g6 12f3 10f* 11.5f 10m 15.8m* 17.1d3 15.8d4 15.8m5 15.8d4 f16g4 15.8s4 f14g p13.9g Dec 11] lengthy mare: modest performer: won claimer at Redcar in June and seller at Catterick in August: stays 17f: acts on fibresand, firm and good to soft going: tried in cheekpieces: has carried head awkwardly. *Mrs S. Lamyman*

TRUE MAGIC 5 b.m. Magic Ring (IRE) 115 – True Precision 84 (Presidium 124) **77** [2006 75: p6g* p5.1g4 5m5 6d 5g 6f4 p6g 5m2 5f2 6f 5f4 6m p6g2 p6g p6g3 Dec 28] compact mare: fair handicapper: won at Wolverhampton in March: effective at 5f/easy 6f: acts on polytrack, firm and good to soft going: tried blinkered (ran poorly). *J. D. Bethell*

TRUE NIGHT 9 b.g. Night Shift (USA) – Dead Certain 123§ (Absalom 128) [2006 **75** 91d: f8g4 f8g p7.1g6 p8.6g p7g4 p7g2 p10g p8.6g5 7d* 7d6 7g 6f5 7.1m6 7.9m3 7d3 7g4 8d 10s Sep 14] smallish, attractive gelding: just fair performer in 2006: won handicap at Catterick in April: best at 7f/1m: acts on all-weather, firm and good to soft going: tried visored: sometimes races freely: none too reliable. *D. Nicholls*

TRUE RUBY 3 b.f. Josr Algarhoud (IRE) 118 – St James's Antigua (IRE) 79 (Law **–** Society (USA) 130) [2006 –: 8.3f Jul 31] well held in maidens. *S. Kirk*

TRUE TO YOURSELF (USA) 5 b.g. Royal Academy (USA) 130 – Romilly (Mach- **59** iavellian (USA) 123) [2006 55: f14g f11g* f11g4 Mar 14] tall gelding: modest performer: won banded race at Southwell in February: stayed 1¾m: acted on all-weather: visored of late: sold 5,400 gns later in March, joined T. O'Mara in Ireland: dead. *J. G. Given*

TRUE VALENTINE 3 br.f. Primo Valentino (IRE) 116 – Prim N Proper (Tragic Role **–** (USA)) [2006 47: f5g 5.9g 6.9m Jul 8] close-coupled filly: poor maiden. *A. Berry*

TRUE WEST (USA) 3 b.f. Gulch (USA) – True Life (USA) 66 (El Gran Senor (USA) **64** 136) [2006 8.2m5 8d 8f3 10m 10m p8g p7.1g p8g5 Dec 5] 40,000Y: quite good-topped filly: first foal: dam, placed up to 9f in Ireland, out of sister to dam of outstanding broodmare Toussaud: modest maiden: left J. Noseda after third start and G. Chung after sixth: stays 1m: acts on polytrack and firm going: visored last 2 appearances: very slowly away sixth outing. *Miss Gay Kelleway*

TRULY FRUITFUL (IRE) 3 ch.g. Fruits of Love (USA) 127 – Truly Flattering **77** (Hard Fought 125) [2006 72: p9.5g6 p12g4 9.8m 10m4 10f2 10m4 11m3 10g 10g5 Sep 26] good-topped gelding: fair handicapper: first past post at Pontefract in July, demoted to second after hanging markedly right: stays 11f: acts on polytrack and firm going: sold 25,000 gns, joined R. Fahey. *K. R. Burke*

TRULY GENUINE (IRE) 2 ch.f. (Mar 11) Hernando (FR) 127 – Truly Generous – (IRE) 104 (Generous (IRE) 139) [2006 p8.6s⁵ Dec 15] sixth foal: half-sister to 3 winners, including 4-y-o Antique and 8-y-o Nawamees: dam, French 1¼m winner who stayed 12.5f, half-sister to very smart French middle-distance performer Modhish: 50/1 and very green, soon lost touch in maiden at Wolverhampton. *K. A. Ryan*

TRULY ROYAL 2 b.c. (Mar 20) Noverre (USA) 125 – Her Ladyship 119 (Polish **96 P** Precedent (USA) 131) [2006 6g* Oct 12]

Godolphin's most expensive yearling of 2005, Jalil, who cost 9.7m dollars, may have fallen well short of expectations when making his debut at Newmarket in October, but the stable can take plenty of consolation from the performance of the home-bred Truly Royal who had his first outing at the same venue twenty-four hours earlier. Although not odds on like Jalil, Truly Royal came with a reputation, opening up at 13/8 before drifting to 2/1 for the Anglo Hibernian Bloodstock Insurance EBF Maiden over six furlongs. He faced fourteen rivals, including Danny Templeton, a promising second at Yarmouth on his debut, and another well-fancied newcomer in Land's End, but he made short work of them all. Soon prominent, Truly Royal sprinted clear in no time at all late on, racing exuberantly and really stretching out as he neared the line, winning by three lengths from Danny Templeton. There were few more impressive debuts all season and Truly Royal was quoted at as short as 20/1 for the Two Thousand Guineas afterwards.

		Rahy	Blushing Groom
Truly Royal	Noverre (USA)	(ch 1985)	Glorious Song
(b.c. Mar 20, 2004)	(b 1998)	Danseur Fabuleux	Northern Dancer
		(b 1982)	Fabuleux Jane
	Her Ladyship	Polish Precedent	Danzig
	(b 1991)	(b 1986)	Past Example
		Upper Strata	Shirley Heights
		(b 1985)	Bright Landing

Truly Royal is bred to be anything. His dam, Her Ladyship, a winner over ten and a half furlongs, was a smart filly, beaten only a head for Andre Fabre in the Prix de Diane in the colours of Sheikh Mohammed. She is a half-sister to the equally smart middle-distance performer Lord of Men out of the useful stayer Upper Strata. Her Ladyship has bred several other winners, none so far as good as herself but including the useful French two-year-old seven-furlong/mile (Prix d'Aumale) winner Dignify (by Rainbow Quest) and the fairly useful winners at around a mile and a half House of Bourbon (also by Rainbow Quest) and Attorney General (by Sadler's Wells), the latter also a useful staying hurdler when in the mood. Truly Royal's sire Noverre was among the leading first-season sires for wins and prize money earned in 2006. As a racehorse, Noverre had a much busier first season than Truly Royal, winning four of his seven starts under the Godolphin banner when trained in France by David Loder, his successes including the July Stakes over six furlongs and the Champagne Stakes over seven. Noverre was even better for Godolphin as a three-year-old, proving high-class as well as tough, finishing first past the post in the Poule d'Essai des Poulains, from which he was disqualified for failing a dope test, and in the Sussex Stakes, a race in which he was also placed as a four-year-old, alongside the International Stakes at York and the Champion Stakes at Newmarket. Noverre's best representative from his first crop was the speedy Elhamri, but, on balance, Truly Royal should be well suited by seven furlongs and a mile at three. On breeding, he should have little difficulty in staying a mile and a quarter, though he is a well-made sort, muscular already, and on looks appears built for speed. He is one to follow. *Saeed bin Suroor*

TRUMAN 5 b.g. Entrepreneur 123 – Sabria (USA) (Miswaki (USA) 124) [2006 63: – 10.9m Jul 2] quite attractive gelding: fair maiden: stayed 1¼m: acted on polytrack and good to firm ground: dead. *John A. Harris*

TRUMP CALL (IRE) 2 b.c. (Feb 6) Mull of Kintyre (USA) 114 – Trumped (IRE) 50 **70** (Last Tycoon 131) [2006 p7g³ p8g Dec 19] €13,000F, 30,000Y: sixth foal: half-brother to 2 winners, including fairly useful Irish 1m (at 2 yrs) and 11f winner Hurricane Alley (by

Ali-Royal): dam 13f seller winner: reportedly split off-hind pastern in April: better effort in maidens when third at Kempton: not knocked about next time. *R. M. Beckett*

TRUMPITA 3 b.g. Bertolini (USA) 125 – Trump Street 77 (First Trump 118) [2006 7v² **55** 6d 6d 8m 8.3m 6.1f 5.9m 5g* 5s⁵ 5d Oct 8] tall, leggy gelding: modest performer: won handicap at Ayr in August: effective at 5f to 7f: acts on heavy going. *T. D. Easterby*

TRUMPS (IRE) 2 ch.c. (Apr 19) Raise A Grand (IRE) 114 – Manuka Too (IRE) 68 – (First Trump 118) [2006 6f Jun 12] 66/1, last in maiden at Windsor. *M. Blanshard*

TRUSTED MOLE (IRE) 8 b.g. Eagle Eyed (USA) 111 – Orient Air 74 (Prince Sabo – 123) [2006 52: p9.5f 10.9m Sep 4] deep-girthed gelding: modest handicapper in 2005: well held in 2006: tried blinkered. *W. M. Brisbourne*

TRYSTING GROVE (IRE) 5 b.m. Cape Cross (IRE) 129 – Elton Grove (IRE) **50** (Astronef 116) [2006 –: f11g² p12g f11g f11m Oct 31] leggy, unfurnished mare: modest performer: stays 1½m: acts on fibresand and good to soft going. *E. G. Bevan*

TSAROXY (IRE) 4 b.g. Xaar 132 – Belsay 68 (Belmez (USA) 131) [2006 90: 8m³ 8g⁶ **81** 8m 9.8d⁴ 10g⁶ Sep 16] quite good-topped gelding: fairly useful handicapper: creditable efforts when in frame twice at Ripon: stays 1¼m: acts on good to firm and good to soft going: blinkered (well held) once. *J. Howard Johnson*

TUCKER 4 b.g. Inchinor 119 – Tender Moment (IRE) 78 (Caerleon (USA) 132) [2006 **109** 113: 9g⁵ 8s 8m³ 8m 8g² 9m² 10s Oct 7] big, close-coupled gelding: has a round action: just useful performer in 2006: creditable second in handicaps at Ascot (beaten short head by Prince of Thebes) and Goodwood (beaten neck by Illustrious Blue): ran poorly final outing: stays 9f: has won on soft going, but best form on good or firmer: visored (well below form) fourth outing: in cheekpieces last 3 starts: gelded after final outing. *W. R. Swinburn*

TUCKERMAN 5 b.g. Gulch (USA) – Remuria (USA) 93 (Theatrical 128) [2006 47: – p9.5g 8d a7g 9s Oct 20] maiden: no form in 2006: tried blinkered/tongue tied. *Frederick John Bowles, Ireland*

TUCKERS POINT (IRE) 3 b.f. Mujadil (USA) 119 – Romanovna (Mummy's Pet **59** 125) [2006 67: f6g⁴ p7g⁵ f7g³ Feb 14] leggy filly: fair maiden on turf at 2 yrs, modest on all-weather in 2006: stays 7f: acts on fibresand and good to soft going: sold 2,000 gns in November. *J. A. Osborne*

TUDOR BELL (IRE) 5 b.g. Definite Article 121 – Late Night Lady (IRE) 65 (Mujadil **67** (USA) 119) [2006 10.5s³ 10f 12.3m 16.2m Sep 4] useful-looking gelding: unraced on Flat in 2005: just fair form at best in 2006: pulled up (reportedly lame) final outing: stays 1¾m: acts on heavy and good to firm going. *J. G. M. O'Shea*

TUDOR PRINCE (IRE) 2 b. or br.c. (Feb 29) Cape Cross (IRE) 129 – Savona (IRE) **94** 70 (Cyrano de Bergerac 120) [2006 6s 6s³ 6m 7g² p7g² 6m² 6s* 6d⁶ Sep 29] 30,000F: well-made colt: fifth foal: half-brother to 2001 2-y-o 6f winner London Follies (by Danehill Dancer): dam, maiden, should have stayed 7f: fairly useful performer: runner-up 3 times (including nursery) prior to winning maiden at Newmarket in August by 5 lengths from We'll Come: not at best when sixth of 28 to Caldra in sales race there final start: effective at 6f/7f: acts on polytrack, soft and good to firm going. *B. J. Meehan*

TULLOCHROME 3 b.f. Foxhound (USA) 103 – Choire Mhor 100 (Dominion 123) **50** [2006 a6.5g a7.5g p10g⁴ 8.5d f8g Apr 27] good-topped filly: half-sister to several winners, including smart 5f winner Cathedral (by Prince Sabo) and 9f and 1⅓m winner Plutocrat (by Polar Falcon): dam, 6f winner, ran only at 2 yrs: maiden: left R. Pritchard-Gordon in France after second start: just modest form at best in Britain: tried blinkered: sold 5,000 gns in July. *E. J. O'Neill*

TULLYTHERED (IRE) 2 ch.c. (Feb 29) Docksider (USA) 124 – Marjie (IRE) – (Desert Style (IRE) 121) [2006 5s 7m Aug 6] tailed off in maidens. *A. Berry*

TUMBELINI 2 b.f. (Apr 30) Pivotal 124 – Kundalini (USA) (El Gran Senor (USA) – 136) [2006 6.1g Sep 26] eighth foal: half-sister to fairly useful French 1½m winner Vijanti (by Rainbow Quest) and French 11f winner Vivianna (by Indian Ridge): dam, champion 3-y-o filly in South Africa, out of half-sister to high-class 1m/1¼m performer Kooyonga: 14/1, very green in maiden at Nottingham. *C. F. Wall*

TUMBLE JILL (IRE) 2 b.f. (Mar 15) Dilshaan 119 – Jack-N-Jilly (IRE) 43 (Anita's **50** Prince 126) [2006 6m 7m² 7f⁵ 7.5f³ 7f⁵ 7g 8.3s p7g p7g p8g⁵ p8g³ Dec 18] good-bodied filly: sixth foal: half-sister to 2001 2-y-o 5f and 7f winner Strandiam (by Darnay): dam, placed in 5f/6f sellers, ran only at 2 yrs: modest and exposed maiden: left J. S. Moore after fifth start: stays 1m: acts on polytrack and firm going. *J. J. Bridger*

TUMBLEWEED GLORY (IRE) 3 b.g. Marju (IRE) 127 – Tathkara (USA) (Alydar **90**
(USA)) [2006 74: p10g⁵ 10g³ 9s 9m⁵ 10m² p8g* 8g⁶ 8.3g⁴ Aug 7] rangy gelding: fairly
useful handicapper: won at Kempton in July: stays 1¼m: acts on polytrack and good
to firm going: blinkered (pulled hard, tailed off and dismounted after line) third start.
B. J. Meehan

TUMBLIN ROSIE 2 ch.f. (Apr 28) Tumbleweed Ridge 117 – Myhat 71 (Factual **52**
(USA) 108) [2006 6.1g p6g⁵ p6g⁵ Dec 5] third foal: half-sister to 2004 2-y-o 7f winner
Lojo (by Pivotal): dam 2-y-o 6f winner who probably stayed 7f: modest maiden: off 5
months after debut: will stay 7f. *M. Blanshard*

TUMBY LAWN (USA) 2 ch.g. (May 2) Rahy (USA) 115 – Dharma (USA) (Zilzal **62**
(USA) 137) [2006 7m Jul 30] fourth foal: dam, ran 3 times in France, half-sister to very
smart German performer up to 1m Royal Abjar: 33/1 and green, mid-field in maiden at
Newmarket won by Safe Investment. *E. A. L. Dunlop*

TUMPULUNA (IRE) 3 b.f. Marju (IRE) 127 – Tarhhib 95 (Danzig (USA)) [2006 6f³ **62**
7f 7d Oct 3] half-sister to winners abroad by Linamix and Indian Ridge: dam 7f winner:
modest maiden: broke a leg final outing: should have been suited by 7f+. *G. Prodromou*

TUNE UP THE BAND 2 b.c. (Mar 8) Bandmaster (USA) 97 – Name That Tune 40 **69**
(Fayruz 116) [2006 5.1d³ Apr 11] 500 2-y-o: brother to 5f to 7f winner Chorus: dam sprint
maiden: 9/1, third to Carson's Spirit in maiden at Bath in April (reportedly lame, absent
after). *R. J. Hodges*

TUNGSTEN STRIKE (USA) 5 ch.g. Smart Strike (CAN) 121 – Bathilde (IRE) 102 **118**
(Generous (IRE) 139) [2006 113: 16m² 16.4s* 20m 16f³ 15.9d 18d Sep 8] good-bodied
gelding: smart performer: career-best effort when winning wbx.com World Bet Exchange
Henry II Stakes at Sandown in May by 5 lengths from Winged d'Argent: easily best run
after when creditable 8½ lengths third to Yeats in Goodwood Cup: stays 2m (below-form
eighth in Gold Cup at Royal Ascot at 2½m): acts on firm and soft going: usually races
prominently. *A. J. Perrett*

TUNING FORK 6 b.g. Alzao (USA) 117 – Tuning 114 (Rainbow Quest (USA) 134) **61**
[2006 67d: 8.1g² 8m² 9m 8m⁵ 8f 7.6m 8.1m Sep 12] strong, lengthy, attractive gelding:
just modest performer in 2006: effective at 1m/1¼m: acts on good to firm going, only
win on good to soft: tried visored/in cheekpieces/tongue tied: makes running: sometimes
looks ungenuine. *T. M. Jones*

TURIBIUS 7 b.g. Puissance 110 – Compact Disc (IRE) 48 (Royal Academy (USA) 130) **66**
[2006 75: p5g 5.3m 5m 6d* p6g⁶ p6g⁴ p5g⁴ p6g⁵ Dec 22] compact gelding: fair handicapper: won at Brighton in September (only outing for G. L. Moore): rejoined former
trainer after: effective at 5f/easy 6f: acts on polytrack, firm and good to soft going: sometimes wears headgear. *T. E. Powell*

TURKISH SULTAN (IRE) 3 b.g. Anabaa (USA) 130 – Odalisque (IRE) (Mach- **66**
iavellian (USA) 123) [2006 76: 7f² 6v² 6d⁵ 7d³ 7.1d Oct 13] good-topped gelding: fair
maiden: should stay 1m: acts on heavy and good to firm going: sold 10,000 gns.
T. D. Easterby

TURKUS QUERCUS (USA) 2 gr. or ro.f. (Feb 9) Tactical Cat (USA) 116 – Anti- **76**
podes (USA) 76 (Pleasant Colony (USA)) [2006 5.1g² Jun 7] tall filly: unfurnished at
2 yrs: first foal: dam, maiden (would have proved best around 1m), out of very smart
French sprinter La Grande Epoque: 7/1, second to Bridge It Jo in maiden at Nottingham,
needing experience (hung left): withdrawn (unruly/unseated) later in month: sold 18,000
gns in October, sent to USA. *J. L. Dunlop*

TURN AROUND 6 b.g. Pivotal 124 – Bemuse 89 (Forzando 122) [2006 59, a74: p7.1g **–**
f6g 6g p8.6g Sep 11] well-made gelding: fair performer in 2005: no form in 2006: signs
of temperament. *J. Pearce*

TURNER 5 gr.g. El Prado (IRE) 119 – Gaily Royal (IRE) (Royal Academy (USA) 130) **61 §**
[2006 72§: p12.2g 10.2g 12.3g⁵ 12.6m 16.2m⁵ 15.9m⁴ 12m 12.3m 12.3m⁶ 16.2m⁵ 10.9d
14d⁴ Oct 8] compact gelding: just modest performer in 2006: stays 2m: acts on good to
firm going: visored (tailed off) once: not to be trusted: sold 5,600 gns. *W. M. Brisbourne*

TURNER'S TOUCH 4 ch.g. Compton Place 125 – Chairmans Daughter 68 (Unfu- **80 §**
wain (USA) 131) [2006 70§: p9.5g³ p10g* p10g* 10.2d⁶ p12g* p12g⁴ p13g p11g p12g*
p12g² Dec 20] fairly useful handicapper: won at Lingfield in February and March, and
Kempton in April and December: good second in terms of form at Lingfield final start,
though carried head awkwardly and refused to go past: stays easy 1½m: acts on polytrack and good to firm ground: tried visored, usually blinkered nowadays: ungenuine.
G. L. Moore

wbx.com World Bet Exchange Henry II Stakes, Sandown—
Tungsten Strike stakes his Gold Cup claims in beating Winged d'Argent

TURNKEY 4 br.g. Pivotal 124 – Persian Air (Persian Bold 123) [2006 107: 7s³ 6d 7s² May 26] rather leggy, close-coupled gelding: has a quick action: useful performer: below form in Gladness Stakes at the Curragh and listed race at Cork before creditable 2 lengths second of 4 to Polar Ben in minor event at Goodwood: stays 7f: seems to act on any going: often blinkered of late: sold 40,000 gns in July, joined D. Nicholls. *M. R. Channon* **104**

TURN ME ON (IRE) 3 b.g. Tagula (IRE) 116 – Jacobina 71 (Magic Ring (IRE) 115) [2006 82: p7g 6f⁴ 6f³ 5g⁵ Aug 7] tall gelding: just modest maiden in 2006: gelded and off over 12 months before reappearance: probably stays 6f: raced only on polytrack and good ground or firmer: tongue tied last 3 starts: tended to hang second outing. *M. L. W. Bell* **57**

TURN 'N BURN 5 b.g. Unfuwain (USA) 131 – Seasonal Splendour (IRE) 95 (Prince Rupert (FR) 121) [2006 81§: 10d p10g⁵ p16g³ p11g⁴ p13g³ p16g Dec 15] sturdy gelding: just fair performer in 2006: stays 2m: acts on polytrack, good to firm and good to soft ground: sometimes slowly away: ungenuine. *C. A. Cyzer* **77 §**

TURN OF PHRASE (IRE) 7 b.g. Cadeaux Genereux 131 – Token Gesture (IRE) 113 (Alzao (USA) 117) [2006 68: 12.1m 12.1d³ 10.1s* p12.2g³ 10f² 10.1s Oct 10] fair handicapper: won at Newcastle in September: effective at 1¼m to 1¾m: acts on polytrack, firm and soft ground: usually wears headgear. *B. Ellison* **68**

TURN ON THE STYLE 4 ch.g. Pivotal 124 – Elegant Rose 72 (Noalto 120) [2006 87: p6g⁶ p6g⁶ f5g Nov 15] good-topped gelding: just fair handicapper in 2006: effective at 5f/6f: acts on polytrack, soft and good to firm going: blinkered nowadays: sometimes slowly away: refused to enter stall once at 3 yrs. *J. Balding* **79**

TURTLE MAGIC (IRE) 4 b.f. Turtle Island (IRE) 123 – Theda 61 (Mummy's Pet 125) [2006 –§: p5.1g p8.6g Feb 27] maiden: no recent form: often wears headgear: weak finisher. *Miss J. S. Davis* **– §**

TURTLE SOUP (IRE) 10 b.g. Turtle Island (IRE) 123 – Lisa's Favourite (Gorytus (USA) 132) [2006 78: 18v² Apr 4] sturdy gelding: fair handicapper, lightly raced on Flat in recent years: stays 2¼m: acts on heavy and good to firm going: useful hurdler. *T. R. George* **78**

TUSCAN FLYER 8 b.g. Clantime 101 – Excavator Lady 65 (Most Secret 119) [2006 **52** 58, a52: p6g f6g p7g 6f⁶ 6m² 6g 6f* f6g f7g Dec 21] deep-bodied gelding: modest performer: won selling handicap at Brighton in August: effective at 5f/6f: acts on polytrack, firm and good to soft going: often blinkered: tends to hang: races up with pace. *R. Bastiman*

TUSCAN TREATY 6 b.m. Brief Truce (USA) 126 – Fiorenz (USA) (Chromite **53** (USA)) [2006 55: p9.5g p10g⁴ p10g³ p9.5g⁵ p9.5g⁴ p10g p8.6g² p9.5g May 2] quite good-topped mare: modest performer: stays easy 1¼m: acts on all-weather and firm going: tried visored, often in cheekpieces of late: tongue tied nowadays: held up. *P. J. McBride*

TUSCANY QUEEN (IRE) 3 b.f. Titus Livius (FR) 115 – Queen Molly 53 (Emarati **60** (USA) 74) [2006 49: p7g⁵ 6m 7f 7g⁵ 6d p7g* p7g p7g Aug 11] modest performer: won seller at Lingfield in June: stays easy 7f, may prove best at shorter: acts on polytrack: sold 2,500 gns. *R. Hannon*

TUSCANY ROSE 3 ch.f. Medicean 128 – Rosewood Belle (USA) 70 (Woodman **53** (USA) 126) [2006 –: 10.2f 8.1m 8.3m⁵ 11.9f⁵ p12.2f³ 12.1m⁴ 13.8m* 16.1g Sep 27] modest performer: won seller at Catterick in September: stays 13.8f: acts on polytrack and good to firm ground: sold 10,000 gns. *W. R. Muir*

TUSCARORA (IRE) 7 b.m. Revoque (IRE) 122 – Fresh Look (IRE) 64 (Alzao (USA) **70** 117) [2006 74: p7g p7.1g* f6g p7.1g 8.1g⁵ 7.1f⁴ 8.1m² 8m* 8.1m 8d p7.1g p8.6g p7.1g p9.5g⁵ Dec 9] smallish mare: fair handicapper: won at Wolverhampton in January and Bath in August: effective at 7f to 9.5f: acts on polytrack (seemingly not fibresand), firm and good to soft going: sometimes races freely. *A. W. Carroll*

TUSCULUM (IRE) 3 b.c. Sadler's Wells (USA) 132 – Turbaine (USA) (Trempolino **115** (USA) 135) [2006 88p: 10g⁴ 14m* 13.9g⁵ Sep 9] leggy, close-coupled colt: smart performer: won listed race at the Curragh in August by 2½ lengths from Good Surprise: creditable 4¾ lengths fifth to Sixties Icon in St Leger at York final outing: stays 1¾m: acts on soft and good to firm going: has hung, and is rather awkward: sold 440,000 gns, joined A. Fabre in France. *A. P. O'Brien, Ireland*

TU SEI ROMANTICA (IRE) 2 b.f. (Apr 19) Agnes World (USA) 123 – Akamantis **–** 97 (Kris 135) [2006 6m⁶ p6g p7.1g Dec 1] half-sister to several winners, including smart Irish 6f to 9f winner Theano (by Thatching): dam, 2-y-o 1m winner later placed up to 1½m, half-sister to smart 7f/1m performer Thourios and St Leger runner-up Demophilos: well held in maidens (at Milan on debut). *K. A. Ryan*

TWENTYFIRST DANSAR 3 b.g. Zahran (IRE) 77 – Jokers Luck (Desert Splendour **–** 97) [2006 59: f8g 8.1g 7g May 18] modest performer at 2 yrs: little form in 2006: visored last 5 starts, tongue tied on final one. *A. D. Smith*

TWENTY PERCENT 2 ch.g. (Apr 23) Auction House (USA) 120 – Truly Madly **–** Deeply (Most Welcome 131) [2006 7g Aug 17] smallish, sturdy gelding: 50/1, detached throughout in maiden at Salisbury (gelded after). *P. R. Chamings*

TWENTYTWOSILVER (IRE) 6 ro.g. Emarati (USA) 74 – St Louis Lady 71 (Absa- **60** lom 128) [2006 56: p13g² p12g p12.2g² p13.9g³ p12g³ p16g³ p12g* p12g 11.9f Jul 18] modest performer nowadays: won banded race at Kempton in May: stays 2m: acts on all-weather and good to firm going: blinkered (went too freely): held up of late: sold 11,500 gns in October, joined L. Corcoran: winning chaser. *D. B. Feek*

TWILIGHT AVENGER (IRE) 3 b.g. Dr Fong (USA) 128 – Asterita 103 (Rainbow **55** Quest (USA) 134) [2006 56, a47: p7g⁴ p6g⁵ f7g³ p7g p7.1g⁴ p6g⁴ f7g⁴ p7g⁴ p7.1g⁵ p6g p7g 7g 8.5f⁴ 9d³ 10.1m⁶ 9.8s Aug 28] strong, compact gelding: modest maiden: left M. Polglase after twelfth start: probably stays 9f: acts on all-weather and firm going, probably on good to soft: tried in blinkers/cheekpieces. *W. M. Brisbourne*

TWILIGHT DAWN 2 ch.f. (Mar 17) Muhtarram (USA) 125 – Indigo Dawn 78 **–** (Rainbow Quest (USA) 134) [2006 8.1v⁵ 8.2g Sep 26] strong, useful-looking filly: fourth foal: half-sister to 1¾m winner St Jerome (by Danzig Connection): dam, 13f to 2m winner, half-sister to smart middle-distance stayer Fight Your Corner: no show in maidens: sold 8,000 gns. *M. Johnston*

TWILL (IRE) 3 ch.g. Barathea (IRE) 127 – Khafaya 68 (Unfuwain (USA) 131) [2006 **87** 81: 10d⁴ 10.4d 12g 14m² 14.1d 15.9g 16m* 13d⁴ 18s Oct 7] big, good-bodied gelding: fairly useful handicapper: won 3-runner event at Goodwood in September: ran poorly final outing: stays easy 2m: acts on fibresand, good to firm and good to soft going: visored sixth start: would probably have won but for wandering fourth outing: not a straightforward ride/none too resolute. *H. Morrison*

TWINDEGO 3 b.g. Komaite (USA) – On The Wagon (Then Again 126) [2006 70: 6d **60** Apr 20] good-topped gelding: fair maiden: off almost 10 months, gelded and not right in coat, well held in handicap at Ripon only outing in 2006: will stay 7f: acts on good to firm going: sold 1,000 gns in October, sent to Sweden. *T. D. Barron*

TWINNED (IRE) 3 ch.g. Soviet Star (USA) 128 – Identical (IRE) (Machiavellian **63** (USA) 123) [2006 68: p5.1g* p5.1g⁶ p5g⁴ 5.1g p5.1g p5.1g⁴ 5.1f⁵ 5.1m⁶ p6g⁶ p5.1m* p5g p5g⁴ p5g p5.1g Dec 31] leggy, well-grown gelding: just modest performer in 2006: won seller at Wolverhampton in April, and having left J. S. Moore after seventh outing, claimer there in November: raced mainly at 5f: acts on polytrack, good to firm and good to soft going: tried blinkered, usually wears cheekpieces: often makes running. *Miss K. M. George*

TWIST BOOKIE (IRE) 6 b. or br.g. Perugino (USA) 84 – Twist Scarlett (GER) **60** (Lagunas) [2006 54: 10m 8m p13.9g³ p13.9g³ p12.2g* Dec 23] modest performer: left J. S. Moore after second start: won handicap at Wolverhampton in December: stays 1¾m: acts on polytrack and soft going: tried blinkered. *S. Lycett*

TWITCH HILL 2 ch.f. (Feb 2) Piccolo 121 – Whittle Woods Girl 80 (Emarati (USA) **64** 74) [2006 5s² 5m⁵ 6.1d⁴ Oct 13] strong filly: half-sister to 3 winners, including 5f/6f winner High Esteem (by Common Grounds) and 7f winner Zagala (by Polar Falcon): dam, 6f winner, sister to useful 6f/7f performer Emerging Market and half-sister to smart performer up to 7f Atraf: modest form in maidens: may prove best kept to 5f/6f. *H. Candy*

TWO ACRES (IRE) 3 b.g. Danetime (IRE) 121 – Raise-A-Secret (IRE) (Classic Sec- **57** ret (USA) 91) [2006 p7g 6g 6.1m 5f* 5.1m Aug 25] sturdy gelding: modest performer: won on handicap debut at Leicester in July: best efforts at 5f/6f on ground firmer than good. *A. G. Newcombe*

TWO CHIMNEYS (USA) 4 b.f. Deputy Commander (USA) 124 – Take Heart (USA) **–** (Secretariat (USA)) [2006 58: f14g a6f⁵ Mar 18] modest maiden at best: well held in 2006, leaving K. Ryan after reappearance: tried blinkered/tongue tied. *G. Fox, USA*

TWO DREAMERS 2 ch.f. (Mar 12) Best of The Bests (IRE) 122 – Mossy Rose 78 **–** (King of Spain 121) [2006 6m 8.1g Sep 23] 800Y: good-topped filly: half-sister to fairly useful 11.6f to 1¾m winner Browning (by Warrshan) and 5-y-o Bienvenue: dam 6f and 1m winner: behind in maidens. *A. Crook*

TWO SIPS SUE 2 b.f. (Apr 23) Zamindar (USA) 116 – Miss Waterline 77 (Rock City **50** 120) [2006 5g 5g² 5.8g⁵ 5.8g⁶ a6g² a8g⁴ a6s² a6g² a6d⁶ Dec 17] 500Y: close-coupled filly: fourth foal: half-sister to 5-y-o Ligne d'Eau and 2004 2-y-o 6f winner On The Wat- erline (by Compton Place): dam, 2-y-o 6f winner, half-sister to smart sprinters Double Action and Sir Nicholas: modest maiden: second in claiming event at Haydock second start (left P. D. Evans £10,000) and 3 times subsequently at Taby: effective at 5f/6f: acts on dirt, raced on good going on turf. *C. Bjorling, Sweden*

TYBALT (USA) 2 b.c. (Mar 19) Storm Cat (USA) – Tuzla (FR) 121 (Panoramic 120) **97 p** [2006 7m² p7g* Oct 11] smallish, good-topped colt: third foal: half-brother to 3-y-o Desert Authority and fairly useful 9.7f and 1½m (in USA) winner Mambo Princess (by Kingmambo): dam US Grade 1 9f winner at 5 yrs: useful form: confirmed promise shown in maiden at Newmarket in September (short-head second to Adagio) when readily landing odds in similar event at Lingfield, merely pushed out: will stay 1m/1¼m: sure to go on to better things. *J. H. M. Gosden*

TYCHEROS 4 b.g. Polar Falcon (USA) 126 – Marie de Flandre (FR) 109 (Crystal **68** Palace (FR) 132) [2006 62: p16.5g² p16g* p16g* p16g² 18v p16g Jul 29] fair handi- capper on all-weather, lightly raced on turf: won twice (latter apprentices) at Lingfield in February: stays 16.5f: acts on polytrack: ridden prominently: sold 11,000 gns in October. *S. C. Williams*

TYCOON HALL (IRE) 6 ch.g. Halling (USA) 133 – Tycooness (IRE) 80§ (Last **65** Tycoon 131) [2006 89: 14m 12.3m Aug 6] good-topped gelding: lightly-raced handi- capper on Flat, just fair form in 2006: stays 1¾m: acts on good to firm and good to soft going: fairly useful hurdler, winner in July. *P. Bowen*

TYKIE TWO 2 ch.f. (Apr 21) Primo Valentino (IRE) 116 – Tycoon's Last 64 (Nalchik **–** (USA)) [2006 6m Sep 11] first foal: dam 10.5f and 1½m winner: 14/1, outpaced in maiden at Folkestone. *E. J. O'Neill*

TYPHOON GINGER (IRE) 11 ch.m. Archway (IRE) 115 – Pallas Viking (Viking **68** (USA)) [2006 70: 9.8v 8.9m 8m 10.9m 8f 8.9f 8s* 8g⁵ 8v⁵ 8d³ 10m Sep 15] close-coupled mare: fair handicapper: won at Redcar in August: stays 1¼m: probably acts on any going: sometimes slowly away: held up. *G. Woodward*

TYPHOON TILLY 9 b.g. Hernando (FR) 127 – Meavy 86 (Kalaglow 132) [2006 76: p12.2g Jan 5] quite good-topped gelding: fair performer in 2005: well held only outing in 2006: tried blinkered: races freely: sometimes finds little. *C. R. Egerton* —

TYRONE LADY (IRE) 3 b.f. Key of Luck (USA) 126 – Kutaisi (IRE) (Soviet Star (USA) 128) [2006 5s Aug 19] fifth foal: dam unraced: green, last in maiden at Ripon. *J. J. Quinn* —

TYRONE SAM 4 b.g. Mind Games 121 – Crystal Sand (GER) (Forzando 122) [2006 74, a69: p6g⁴ f8g p7.1g p7.1g f8g f8g Dec 21] fair handicapper: stays 7f: acts on all-weather and good to firm going: tried in cheekpieces, wears blinkers: no easy ride, though has looked more straightforward of late. *K. A. Ryan* **67**

TYSPANE 3 b. or br.f. Zilzal (USA) 137 – Simply Sooty 78 (Absalom 128) [2006 8g Jun 2] 19,000Y: half-sister to several winners, notably smart 6f (at 2 yrs) to 9f winner Umistim (by Inchinor): dam 2-y-o 5f winner: reluctant at stall, tailed off in maiden at Bath. *S. Kirk* —

TYZACK (IRE) 5 b.g. Fasliyev (USA) 120 – Rabea (USA) 61 (Devil's Bag (USA)) [2006 63§: f7s* f7g* f7g* f8g* 8.1s 8.1f² 8.1m⁴ 8m 7m Jul 29] good-topped gelding: fairly useful handicapper: much improved when winning 4 times at Southwell in March/April, beating Exit Smiling by 1½ lengths on final occasion: below form after other than when creditable second at Haydock: stays 1m: acts on fibresand and firm going: has been troublesome to post: has joined W. M. Brisbourne. *Stef Liddiard* **91**

U

UACE MAC 2 b.f. (Mar 4) Compton Place 125 – Umbrian Gold (IRE) 83 (Perugino (USA) 84) [2006 5m Aug 7] 800F, 3,500Y: third foal: sister to Italian 5f to 7f winner and half-sister to 4-y-o Kudbeme: dam 7f winner: last in maiden at Carlisle. *N. Bycroft* —

UGENIUS 2 b.c. (Apr 20) Killer Instinct 111 – I'm Sophie (IRE) 64 (Shalford (IRE) 124§) [2006 f6g⁴ p9.5g p8.6g Dec 31] little sign of ability in sellers/claimer. *R. A. Harris* —

UGO FIRE (IRE) 3 b.f. Bluebird (USA) 125 – Quiet Mouse (USA) (Quiet American (USA)) [2006 100: 7s³ 8v 7m⁵ 7.5g³ 8m⁶ 8g⁶ 7.5v² 6s* 7d² Nov 5] lengthy filly: smart performer: creditable neck second to Noelani in Concorde Stakes at Tipperary before winning listed race at the Curragh in October by 3½ lengths from Senor Benny: stays 1m: acts on heavy and good to firm ground: tough. *K. Prendergast, Ireland* **114**

UHOOMAGOO 8 b.g. Namaqualand (USA) – Point of Law (Law Society (USA) 130) [2006 104: p7g p7g p8g⁵ 8f 8.5g 7m* 7m² 7g⁴ p8g Sep 2] leggy gelding: useful handicapper, better than ever in 2006: won 27-runner Buckingham Palace Stakes at Royal Ascot in June by neck from Appalachian Trail: good efforts in frame there (neck second to Dabbers Ridge in totesport International) and at Galway (fourth to Bolodenka in quite valuable event) next 2 starts: effective at 7f to 8.5f: acts on all-weather and any turf going: usually blinkered, has worn cheekpieces/visor: sometimes takes long time to warm up/wanders, and best in strongly-run race. *K. A. Ryan* **109 a94**

UHURU PEAK 5 ch.g. Bal Harbour 113 – Catherines Well 99 (Junius (USA) 124) [2006 64: 7.5f³ 8.1g 8.5g 7.5f 8.1g 6.9f⁴ 7.9m* 10m⁵ p9.5g² f8g⁴ p9.5s⁴ p9.5g Dec 29] lengthy gelding: fair handicapper: won at Carlisle (ladies) in August: stays 1¼m: acts on polytrack, firm and good to soft going: often blinkered nowadays: tongue tied in 2006. *M. W. Easterby* **65**

UIG 5 ch.m. Bien Bien (USA) 125 – Madam Zando 51 (Forzando 122) [2006 80: p10g p10g⁵ p10g 12.1s⁶ 10m 9m Aug 2] compact mare: just fair handicapper in 2006: stays 1¼m: acts on polytrack, soft and good to firm going: usually makes running. *H. S. Howe* **69**

UIMHIR A HAON (IRE) 2 b.f. (Mar 31) Montjeu (IRE) 137 – Vallee Des Reves (USA) (Kingmambo (USA) 125) [2006 8g 8v⁴ 7s* Oct 30] 825,000Y: fifth foal: closely related to 1¼m winner Corum (by Galileo) and half-sister to smart 7f (at 2 yrs)/1m winner Maids Causeway (by Giant's Causeway): dam unraced half-sister to very smart French performers Vetheuil (miler) and Verveine (up to 1½m), latter dam of very smart winner up to 13.5f Vallee Enchantee: progressive form in maidens: made all in 17-runner event at Leopardstown in October, staying on gamely to beat Truly Mine 1¾ lengths: bred to be well suited by 1¼m+: sure to progress further. *A. P. O'Brien, Ireland* **87 p**

ULLAH PENDRAGON (IRE) 3 gr.g. Beckett (IRE) 116 – Marathon Maid 82 (Kala- **49** glow 132) [2006 60?: p10g⁶ p10g p12g 12s p10g Nov 27] tall, leggy gelding: poor maiden: left M. Polglase after third start: tried in cheekpieces. *A. J. McCabe*

ULSHAW 9 ch.g. Salse (USA) 128 – Kintail 76 (Kris 135) [2006 59: p12.2g⁶ 11.9m³ **57** p16g 11.8d 11.7f⁴ 11.9f 12.1m⁶ p16.5g p12.2g⁶ p13.9g f12g³ Dec 12] quite good-topped gelding: modest performer: stays 21f, but effective at 1½m: acts on all-weather and any turf going: tried visored at 3 yrs. *J. M. Bradley*

ULYSEES (IRE) 7 b.g. Turtle Island (IRE) 123 – Tamasriya (IRE) (Doyoun 124) [2006 **76** 76, a–: 7.1m⁴ 9.2m* 7.1g⁴ 8m* 8.3m* 9.1g⁶ 9.2m⁶ 9.2m⁴ 9.2m⁶ 8.3m⁵ 9s³ 9.2d⁴ 10.1s⁴ **a53** 9.1v⁵ 12d p12.2m Nov 8] quite good-topped gelding: fair performer: won handicap at Hamilton in May and sellers at Musselburgh and Hamilton in June: stays 1¼m: acts on heavy and good to firm going, lightly raced and little form on all-weather: tried in cheek-pieces/visor: has looked none too keen/carried head high. *I. Semple*

UMLILO 4 b.f. Mtoto 134 – Ingozi 91 (Warning 136) [2006 64: 10.2g 8f⁴ 9.7f⁵ Jun 30] **59** modest maiden: should be suited by 1¼m+: acts on firm going. *Mrs A. J. Perrett*

UMPA LOOMPA (IRE) 2 ch.c. (Feb 15) Indian Lodge (IRE) 127 – Bold Fashion **57** (FR) (Nashwan (USA) 135) [2006 6g 6f 7m 6g⁵ Sep 27] close-coupled colt: modest maiden: best efforts at 6f (including in visor final start). *D. Nicholls*

UMTHOULAH (IRE) 4 br.f. Unfuwain (USA) 131 – Susquehanna Days (USA) 68 **–** (Chief's Crown (USA)) [2006 81p: 10.4s May 18] good-bodied filly: unraced at 2 yrs, fairly useful winner only outing at 3 yrs: tailed off in Middleton Stakes at York sole start in 2006: stays 1½m: acts on good to firm going. *K. R. Burke*

UNASUMING (IRE) 3 b.f. Orpen (USA) 116 – Untold 124 (Final Straw 127) [2006 **59** 58: p9.5g 10m* 11.5m 10f 11.9d p13.9g p13.9g Dec 4] strong filly: modest performer: 100/1, won handicap at Nottingham in May: should stay 1½m: acts on fibresand and good to firm going: tongue tied final outing (said to have had breathing problem). *J. Pearce*

UNBRIDLED STORM (IRE) 3 b.g. Aljabr (USA) 125 – Afkaar (USA) 68 (Unbrid- **58** led (USA) 128) [2006 10g⁶ May 30] 10½ lengths sixth to Hopeful Purchase in maiden at Redcar, racing freely and carrying head high. *G. A. Swinbank*

UNCLE MAX (IRE) 6 b.g. Victory Note (USA) 120 – Sunset Park (IRE) 61 (Red **–** Sunset 120) [2006 10.2d p13.9g May 15] fair maiden at 3 yrs: well held both starts on Flat since (won over fences in August): tried blinkered. *N. A. Twiston-Davies*

UNDER FIRE (IRE) 3 b.g. Lear Spear (USA) 124 – Kahyasi Moll (IRE) 35 (Brief **62** Truce (USA) 126) [2006 55?: p7.1g 8.1g 8.3d 8.1m⁴ 11g 6.1f 8.3m⁴ 7g⁴ 8m* 8g* p8g p8.6g³ f8g Dec 21] sturdy gelding: modest performer: won handicaps at Bath in August and Brighton in October: stays 8.6f: acts on all-weather and good to firm ground. *A. W. Carroll*

Buckingham Palace Stakes (Handicap), Royal Ascot—a good result for the bookmakers as Uhoomagoo (25/1) gains his seventeenth career victory; Appalachian Trail (50/1), Binanti (33/1) and Bayeaux (14/1, noseband) complete the frame

UNDERSCORE (USA) 4 ch.g. Spinning World (USA) 130 – Speed Dialer (USA) **75**
(Phone Trick (USA)) [2006 83+: 10g 7.1f⁴ 8.1m⁶ 7m p8.6g³ p7.1f 9m Sep 10] well-made
gelding: just fair performer in 2006: stays 8.6f: acts on polytrack, firm and good to soft
going: in cheekpieces (below form) last 2 starts: signs of waywardness: sold 1,500 gns,
joined Miss A. Stokell and gelded. *R. A. Harris*

UNDERTHEMISTLETOE (IRE) 4 b.f. Lujain (USA) 119 – Christmas Kiss 82 **43 §**
(Taufan (USA) 119) [2006 49: 6d 6g 6f³ 6m 7m⁵ 6m 6f⁴ 6m 6v Sep 2] compact filly: poor
maiden: best form at 6f: acts on fibresand and firm ground: tried in cheekpieces/visor:
sometimes flashes tail: unreliable. *R. E. Barr*

UNDER THE RAINBOW 3 gr.f. Fantastic Light (USA) 134 – Farfala (FR) 106 (Lin- **107**
amix (FR) 127) [2006 91p: 10s⁶ 12s⁵ 12s⁵ 10d³ 10.5v⁶ Dec 5] big, good-bodied filly:
useful performer: reportedly banged head on knee leaving stall and fractured nose on
reappearance (off over 4 months after): much improved when 1½ lengths third to Lake
Toya in listed race at Windsor in November: well below form in similar event at Saint-
Cloud final outing: stays 1½m: raced only on good ground or softer. *P. W. Chapple-Hyam*

UNDERTONE (IRE) 2 ch.f. (Feb 20) Noverre (USA) 125 – Shadow Roll (USA) 79 **84 p**
(Mark of Esteem (IRE) 137) [2006 6d* Oct 18] leggy, lengthy filly: first foal: dam,
maiden best at 6f/7f at 2 yrs, out of smart performer up to 1¼m Warning Shadows: 25/1,
winning debut in maiden at Yarmouth (beat Atlantic Light by ½ length), always prominent: refused to enter stall later in October: will probably stay 1m: should improve.
C. E. Brittain

UNDETERRED 10 ch.g. Zafonic (USA) 130 – Mint Crisp (IRE) 108 (Green Desert **80**
(USA) 127) [2006 85: p5.1g³ p5g p6g⁴ p7.1g p6g⁴ 8s p8.6g* 8.1m² 7m 8.3m⁴ 11.5g³
8.1m⁶ 8m² 11.6g* 12s p12g Sep 30] lengthy, deep-girthed gelding: has a quick action:
fairly useful performer: won amateur claimer at Wolverhampton in April and amateur
handicap at Windsor in August: effective at 6f to easy 11.6f: acts on polytrack, firm and
soft going: has been blinkered/visored: edgy sort: sometimes early/reluctant to post.
K. J. Burke

UNICORN REWARD (IRE) 6 b.g. Turtle Island (IRE) 123 – Kingdom Pearl 57 **80**
(Statoblest 120) [2006 9d³ 10m⁶ 8.5m⁵ a7g p10g p8.6g f8g p10g Dec 8] neat gelding: **a–**
fairly useful performer: left D. Hughes in Ireland after fourth outing: well below form
after: stays 9f: acts on polytrack, good to firm and good to soft going: blinkered/visored
last 3 starts. *Mrs L. C. Jewell*

UNION JACK JACKSON (IRE) 4 b.g. Daggers Drawn (USA) 114 – Beechwood **63**
Quest (IRE) 65 (River Falls 113) [2006 65: f8g f8g p8.6g f7g⁶ f6g² f6g² f6g* p6g⁵ f6g*
f7g 6m³ f6g p5.1g p8.6g f6g³ Dec 29] good-topped gelding: just modest performer in
2006: won banded races at Southwell in April and May: has won over 8.6f, effective at
6f: acts on all-weather and good to soft ground: often blinkered: sometimes slowly away.
J. G. Given

UNIQUE MOMENT 3 ch.f. Vettori (IRE) 119 – Lonesome 60 (Night Shift (USA)) **82 d**
[2006 72: 12d* 12.1d⁴ 12s 11.6f³ 11.1m* 12.1f¹ 12m 12g 16g Sep 14] lengthy, leggy
filly: fairly useful performer: won handicap at Catterick in April and claimers at Hamilton and Beverley (claimed from M. Johnston £15,000) in June: well below form after, in
blinkers final outing: stays 1½m: acts on firm and good to soft going: looked awkward
fourth start: sold 12,000 gns, joined K. O'Brien in Ireland. *D. J. S. ffrench Davis*

UNITED NATIONS 5 ch.g. Halling (USA) 133 – Congress (IRE) 86 (Dancing Brave **81**
(USA) 140) [2006 –: p8.6g³ p8.6g⁵ 10.5m² 8g² p8.6g* p8.6g⁶ 8.9s Oct 7] sturdy, lengthy
gelding: fairly useful handicapper: mostly at least respectable efforts in 2006, winning at
Wolverhampton in September: effective at 1m, barely stays 10.5f: acts on polytrack, good
to firm and good to soft going (possibly unsuited by soft). *N. Wilson*

UNITED SPIRIT (IRE) 5 b.m. Fasliyev (USA) 120 – Atlantic Desire (IRE) 100 (Ela- **–**
Mana-Mou 120) [2006 63, a72: 11.1m⁴ Jul 15] rather leggy, lengthy mare: fair performer
at best: well held only Flat outing in 2006: has worn blinkers/cheekpieces: sold 5,000 gns,
joined P. Rothwell in Ireland. *Jedd O'Keeffe*

UNLEASH (USA) 7 ch.g. Benny The Dip (USA) 127 – Lemhi Go (USA) (Lemhi Gold **–**
(USA) 123) [2006 –: p16g Jul 15] strong, close-coupled gelding: useful handicapper at
best: well beaten only Flat outing in 2006: tried blinkered: has idled: useful hurdler/
chaser. *P. J. Hobbs*

UNLIMITED 4 b.g. Bold Edge 123 – Cabcharge Blue 81 (Midyan (USA) 124) [2006 **68**
75: 5d f6g⁵ 6d 5g 5s 5f 5g² 6f⁴ 7.1m² 8.1m⁶ 7.1m⁴ p6g⁴ p7g⁴ Oct 26] big, leggy gelding:

fair performer: left Mrs A. Duffield after eighth start: effective at 5f to 7f: acts on all-weather, soft and good to firm going: tried blinkered/visored. *R. Simpson*

UNO 3 b.f. Efisio 120 – Glen Falls (Commanche Run 133) [2006 7g⁶ 8s² 8m³ 8.2g² 7.1m²   **81** 8.1s* 8.1g⁵ p8.6m³ Oct 2] quite good-topped filly: sixth living foal: half-sister to 4-y-o Gringo and winners in France by Alzao and Vettori: dam, useful French 1m winner, half-sister to smart 1¼m performer Port Vila: fairly useful performer: won maiden at Haydock in September: creditable efforts in handicaps after: stays 1m: acts on polytrack, soft and good to firm going: has run well when sweating: often makes running. *B. W. Hills*

UNPRECEDENTED (IRE) 5 br.g. Primo Dominie 121 – Misellina (FR) 57 (Polish   **–** Precedent (USA) 131) [2006 37: f5g p6g⁶ p6g⁶ p7g 8d Aug 18] quite good-topped gelding: poor maiden: tried blinkered/visored. *T. T. Clement*

UNQUENCHABLE (USA) 3 b.f. Kingmambo (USA) 125 – First Night (IRE) 102   **64** (Sadler's Wells (USA) 132) [2006 p10g Nov 13] $550,000Y: second foal: dam, 1m (in Britain)/9f (in USA) winner, closely related to Oaks and Irish Derby winner Balanchine: 7/2, 4¾ lengths seventh of 10 to Majestic Halo in maiden at Lingfield, green, slowly away and running on late: looked likely to improve, but left Godolphin shortly after. *Saeed bin Suroor*

UNREACHABLE STAR 2 ch.f. (Mar 19) Halling (USA) 133 – Spinning The Yarn   **70 p** 70 (Barathea (IRE) 127) [2006 7m Aug 31] 200,000Y: fourth foal: half-sister to smart 2003 2-y-o 7f (including Moyglare Stud Stakes) winner Necklace (by Darshaan), who stayed 9.5f: dam, ran once, closely related to Kayf Tara and Opera House: 25/1, mid-division behind Puggy in maiden at Salisbury: should do better over further (will stay 1¼m/1½m). *Mrs A. J. Perrett*

UNRESTRICTED 4 ch.f. Mark of Esteem (IRE) 137 – Generous Lady 98 (Generous   **66** (IRE) 139) [2006 60: p10g³ p10g p10g p9.5g p9.5g Nov 6] small filly: fair maiden handicapper: bred to stay beyond 1¼m: acts on polytrack, raced only on good/good to firm ground on turf: not straightforward. *C. F. Wall*

UNSHAKABLE (IRE) 7 b.g. Eagle Eyed (USA) 111 – Pepper And Salt (IRE)   **97** (Double Schwartz 128) [2006 98: 8m 7.1g⁶ 8.1g³ 9m 8d 8s⁶ 8d Oct 28] good-bodied gelding: useful handicapper: best effort of 2006 when creditable ¾-length third to Killena Boy at Sandown: effective at 1m/9f: acts on soft and good to firm going. *Bob Jones*

UNSUITED 7 b.m. Revoque (IRE) 122 – Nagnagnag (IRE) 103 (Red Sunset 120) [2006   **–** 66: 10s 10d Oct 14] strong mare: fair handicapper in 2005: well beaten in 2006. *J. E. Long*

UNTIL WHEN (USA) 2 b.g. (Mar 17) Grand Slam (USA) 120 – Chez Cherie 108   **75** (Wolfhound (USA) 126) [2006 7.5d 6m⁴ 7f³ 7s⁴ p7.1g⁴ Nov 18] $50,000Y, 62,000 2-y-o: good-topped gelding: first foal: dam 7f (at 2 yrs) and 11f (in USA) winner who stayed 1½m: fair maiden: made frame all starts after debut, best when third to Karoo Blue at Redcar: will stay at least 1m: acts on polytrack and firm going: has been gelded. *B. Smart*

UP AT DAWN 3 b.f. Inchinor 119 – Up And About 77 (Barathea (IRE) 127) [2006 –:   **51** 8.3g p10g Oct 23] modest maiden: tongue tied final outing. *C. F. Wall*

UP IN ARMS (IRE) 2 b.c. (Mar 10) Daggers Drawn (USA) 114 – Queenliness (Exit   **74** To Nowhere (USA) 122) [2006 5g 6.1g 7f² 7d⁴ 7.1m 8d Sep 26] €21,000F, €31,000Y: second foal: dam French 2-y-o 1m winner: fair maiden: easily best efforts when in frame at Lingfield and Folkestone in summer: should stay 1m: acts on firm and good to soft going. *P. Winkworth*

UPPER HAND 3 ch.c. Mark of Esteem (IRE) 137 – Pelagia (IRE) 77 (Lycius (USA)   **107 §** 124) [2006 99: 7g⁴ 8.3g* 7d³ 8m³ Jun 22] big colt: has a quick action: useful performer: won 4-runner minor event at Windsor (by 1¼ lengths from Chief Commander) in May: sweating, good 2¼ lengths third of 30 to Sir Gerard in Britannia Stakes (Handicap) at Royal Ascot final start: stays 1m: acts on good to firm and good to soft going: temperamental (blanketed, withdrawn after unruly at stall intended fourth outing): sent to Hong Kong, renamed Royal Prince. *M. R. Channon*

UP TEMPO (IRE) 8 b.g. Flying Spur (AUS) – Musical Essence 65 (Song 132) [2006   **79** 77: f6g² p6g* p7.1g f6g² p6g² 6v 6m* 7g* 7.1d* 8d³ p6g p6g² p7g² 7.5g p6g 7s 6.1s⁶ 7v⁶ p8g⁵ p8.6g p7.1s Dec 14] useful-looking gelding: fair performer: won claimers at Wolverhampton in February, Yarmouth in April and Newcastle (apprentices, claimed from K. Ryan £10,000) in May, and handicap at Chepstow later in May: effective at 6f to 1m: acts on all-weather and any turf going: wears headgear: sometimes soon off bridle. *C. R. Dore*

UPTHEDOWNS (IRE) 3 b.g. Beckett (IRE) 116 – Golden Charm (IRE) 63 (Common – Grounds 118) [2006 64: f7g Jan 26] close-coupled, workmanlike gelding: has a quick, unimpressive action: modest performer at 2 yrs: well held in seller only outing in 2006: effective at 6f/7f: acts on good to firm ground: in headgear nowadays: sold 2,500 gns. *T. D. Barron*

UP THE POLE 2 ch.f. (Feb 11) Polish Precedent (USA) 131 – Arletty 63 (Rainbow **48** Quest (USA) 134) [2006 6g p6g 7m 7m⁵ f8g p8.6g Dec 18] 3,000Y: sixth foal: half-sister to 11f winner in Switzerland by Zafonic: dam, maiden who stayed 1½m, half-sister to high-class miler Shavian and Gold Cup winner Paean: poor maiden: will stay 1¼m+: blinkered once. *M. W. Easterby*

UPTOWN ROSIE (IRE) 3 ch.f. Desert Sun 120 – Downtown Rosie (IRE) (Good – Thyne (USA) 98) [2006 10g p7.1g Dec 21] second foal: dam poor Irish maiden hurdler: well held in claimer/maiden. *John Monroe, Ireland*

URBAN CALM 5 b.m. Cadeaux Genereux 131 – Silver Sun 83 (Green Desert (USA) – 127) [2006 61, a55: p6g p7.1g Nov 20] compact mare: modest performer at best: well held in 2006: blinkered once. *J. W. Unett*

URBAN FREEWAY (IRE) 7 b. or br.g. Dr Devious (IRE) 127 – Coupe d'Hebe 87 – (Ile de Bourbon (USA) 133) [2006 8.5g 15.8m 15.8d 14d Oct 8] fair performer at best: unraced on Flat from 2003-5: no form in 2006: blinkered/tongue tied final outing. *Robert Gray*

URBAN ROSE 5 b.m. Piccolo 121 – Blue Lamp (USA) 68 (Shadeed (USA) 135) [2006 **45** 58: p6g Jan 4] leggy, close-coupled mare: modest performer in 2005: poor form only start in 2006: effective at 5f/6f: acts on firm ground: tried tongue tied/in cheekpieces: sold 1,400 gns, sent to Saudi Arabia. *J. W. Unett*

URBAN SPIRIT 2 b.c. (May 2) Dansili 127 – Tenuous 111 (Generous (IRE) 139) **90 p** [2006 7d² Sep 29] angular, useful-looking colt: sixth foal: closely related to 11.6f winner Rarefied (by Danehill) and half-brother to a winner in Greece by Grand Lodge: dam French 1¼m (Prix de Psyche) and 1½m winner: 33/1, shaped well when second to Desert Dew in maiden at Newmarket, staying on from rear (free early): will be suited by 1m/ 1¼m: should make a useful 3-y-o. *B. W. Hills*

URBAN TIGER (GER) 3 b.g. Marju (IRE) 127 – Ukraine Venture 96 (Slip Anchor **87** 136) [2006 80: 8.3m⁶ 7g 11.6g³ 10m* 10f³ 10m* Aug 5] tall, useful-looking gelding: fluent mover: useful performer: won handicaps at Sandown in June and Windsor (by 1¼ lengths from Krugerrand, edging markedly right) in August: stays 11.6f: acts on firm going: sometimes slowly away: joined C. Llewellyn. *A. King*

URBAN WARRIOR 2 b.g. (Apr 7) Zilzal (USA) 137 – Perfect Poppy 73 (Shareef **73 d** Dancer (USA) 135) [2006 p5g² p5g² f5g² 5g* 5g⁵ 6d⁴ 5v⁴ 7m 6f⁴ f7g 8m⁶ 8m 7.1d³ 8d p7g⁶ Oct 15] 800F, 3,000Y: leggy gelding: has a markedly round action: sixth foal: half-brother to 7f/1m winner (latter at 2 yrs) Armentieres (by Robellino): dam 1¼m winner: fair performer: won maiden at Folkestone in April: not so good in autumn (left J. Best after tenth start): should stay 1m: acts on all-weather and heavy going: tried in visor. *Mrs Norma Pook*

URBE CONDITA (IRE) 3 b.g. Titus Livius (FR) 115 – Kayanga (Green Desert **90** (USA) 127) [2006 5f² 5.1g* 5m* 5m Dec 26] €7,500Y: good-topped gelding: fourth foal: half-brother to 4-y-o Desertina and 6-y-o Nevada Desert: dam Italian maiden out of half-sister to Prix du Jockey Club winner Natroun: fairly useful performer: won maiden at Nottingham in June and handicap at Hamilton (beat Rothesay Dancer by 5 lengths) in July: left T. Etherington, off over 5 months and renamed Pacific Advantage, below form in handicap at Sha Tin final start: raced only at 5f: acts on firm going. *S. Woods, Hong Kong*

URSIS (FR) 5 b.g. Trempolino (USA) 135 – Bold Virgin (USA) (Sadler's Wells (USA) – 132) [2006 11.6d Nov 4] useful form in France at 2/3 yrs when trained by J. Boisnard, winning 3 of 11 starts: mid-field in November Stakes at Windsor only Flat outing since: stays 1½m: acts on soft and good to firm going: tried blinkered: fairly useful hurdler. *Jonjo O'Neill*

USEFUL 3 ch.f. Nashwan (USA) 135 – Tarf (USA) 92 (Diesis 133) [2006 8m 7g 8m **52** p8g p8.6g⁶ Dec 9] sparely-made filly: fifth foal: dam, 2-y-o 5f winner, half-sister to 8-y-o Musadif: modest maiden: may prove best beyond 1m: signs of temperament. *A. W. Carroll*

USK MELODY 2 ch.f. (Apr 7) Singspiel (IRE) 133 – One of The Family 73 (Alzao **74** (USA) 117) [2006 7d p7g³ p8.6g³ Oct 29] smallish, workmanlike filly: fourth foal: half-sister to 5-y-o Pass The Port and 3-y-o Som Tala: dam, maiden who stayed 9f, half-sister to Juddmonte International winner One So Wonderful and Dante winner Alnasr Alwasheek: fair form in maidens, third at Lingfield and Wolverhampton: will be suited by 1¼m/1½m. *B. J. Meehan*

USK POPPY 3 b.f. Mark of Esteem (IRE) 137 – Wars (IRE) 60 (Green Desert (USA) 127) [2006 56p: 7s² 8m³ 7g* 8m² 8d³ 7m Aug 27] unfurnished filly: fairly useful performer: won maiden at Salisbury in June. at least creditable placed efforts in handicaps there and Newmarket after: stays 1m: acts on soft and good to firm going: sent to USA. *D. R. C. Elsworth* **85**

US RANGER (USA) 2 b.c. (Apr 22) Danzig (USA) – My Annette (USA) 78 (Red Ransom (USA)) [2006 8d* 8g* 8v* Dec 10] third foal: half-brother to winner in USA by Hennessy: dam, maiden (raced only at around 1¼m), closely related to smart US winner up to 1½m Dynaformer: unbeaten in newcomers race at Bordeaux (by 8 lengths) in September and minor events at Toulouse in November/December, taking strong hold final start before drawing clear impressively to beat Dona 5 lengths: should stay 1¼m: type to make his mark in much better company at 3 yrs. *J-C. Rouget, France* **97 P**

UTMOST RESPECT 2 b.c. (Apr 12) Danetime (IRE) 121 – Utmost (IRE) 30 (Most Welcome 131) [2006 5s* 6d* Sep 15] good-bodied colt: second foal: dam maiden who seemed to stay 11f: useful form: unbeaten in 2 starts, 2 weeks apart, namely maiden at Haydock (by 7 lengths) and nursery at Ayr, in latter beating Aahayson by length (pair clear): will stay 7f: raced on going softer than good: smart prospect. *R. A. Fahey* **104 p**

V

VACATION (IRE) 3 b.c. King Charlemagne (USA) 120 – Lady Peculiar (CAN) (Sunshine Forever (USA)) [2006 65p: p9.5g³ 7s⁵ 7.5g⁵ 7s 7d⁵ 8.2s³ 8d³ p8.6g* p9.5g² p8g* p8g³ p9.5g² Dec 31] lengthy, good-topped colt: useful performer: improved late in year, winning maiden at Wolverhampton (hung left) in November and handicap at Kempton in December: good short-head second to Bahar Shumaal in similar event at Wolverhampton final outing: stays 9.5f: acts on polytrack and soft going. *V. Smith* **97**

VADINKA 2 b.c. (Mar 15) Averti (IRE) 117 – Inchalong 80 (Inchinor 119) [2006 5.1g⁴ 5f⁵ 5.3f⁵ p7g⁶ p6g² p7g³ p6g² 6d³ p6g² p7.1g p6g³ f7g² f5g³ Dec 23] 4,000Y, resold €12,000Y: first foal: dam 6f/7f winner (including at 2 yrs): fair maiden: placed 8 times (left P. Winkworth after eighth start): effective at 5f to 7f: acts on all-weather, firm and good to soft going: once in cheekpieces. *N. Tinkler* **73**

VAGUE STAR (ITY) 4 b.c. Soviet Star (USA) 128 – Simova (USA) (Vaguely Noble 140) [2006 75: p5.1g f5g³ 5.1m 6d 5g Jun 1] sturdy colt: fair performer: effective at 5f/6f: acts on all-weather, firm and good to soft ground: tongue tied once at 2 yrs: blinkered of late. *R. Ingram* **65**

VAGUE (USA) 3 b.f. Elusive Quality (USA) – April In Kentucky (USA) (Palace Music (USA) 129) [2006 98: a7f* a8f* 8m a10s 9f a8.5f a7f⁶ Dec 30] sturdy, quite attractive filly: useful performer: successful at Nad Al Sheba in minor event in January and Gulf News UAE 1000 Guineas in February, latter by 5¼ lengths from Imperial Ice (reportedly suffered stress fracture of a cannon bone): off 4 months, creditable 4¾ lengths seventh to Nannina in Coronation Stakes at Royal Ascot next time: just respectable efforts at best in US after (left J. Noseda before penultimate start), blinkered when sixth to Downthedustyroad in La Brea Stakes at Santa Anita final outing: should stay 1¼m: acts on dirt and good to firm going, yet to race on softer than good on turf. *D. F. O'Neill, USA* **106**

VALANCE (IRE) 6 br.g. Bahhare (USA) 122 – Glowlamp (IRE) 93 (Glow (USA)) [2006 86: p16g² 16.2f 13.8m⁴ p13.9f* p16g² Nov 29] lengthy gelding: fairly useful handicapper, better on all-weather than turf: won at Wolverhampton in August: creditable second at Kempton final outing: stays 2m: acts on polytrack and firm going: tongue tied last 3 starts: consistent. *C. R. Egerton* **90**

VALART 3 ch.f. Bien Bien (USA) 125 – Riverine (Risk Me (FR) 127) [2006 9.9g⁵ 11.5m³ 11.7m⁴ 11.7m² 10.2m⁵ p12g Nov 25] smallish filly: half-sister to useful 7f/1m winner Pango (by Bluegrass Prince): dam, ran twice, out of half-sister to Yorkshire Oaks winner/excellent broodmare Hellenic: fair maiden: left C. Tinkler after third start: should be suited by 1½m: acts on good to firm going. *Ms J. S. Doyle* **72**

VALBENNY (IRE) 2 b.f. (Apr 12) Val Royal (FR) 127 – Dark Indian (IRE) (Indian **103 p** Ridge 123) [2006 5m⁶ 5g² 7.2m* 8f* 8f* Dec 31] €10,500Y, resold €16,000Y: third foal: half-sister to Italian 1m to 9f winner by Entrepreneur: dam Italian 1m/9f winner: useful form: most progressive, winning maiden at Ayr in July (then left G. A. Swinbank), Grade 3 Miesque Stakes at Hollywood (strong run from rear to beat Mystic Soul by ¾ length) in November and non-graded event at Santa Anita (by a length from Courtwood) in December: will stay at least 9f: acts on firm going: capable of better still. *P. Gallagher, USA*

VALDAN (IRE) 2 b.g. (Mar 23) Val Royal (FR) 127 – Danedrop (IRE) (Danehill **95 p** (USA) 126) [2006 6g⁴ 6f* 7g 6m² Sep 7] €20,000F, €6,000Y: leggy, close-coupled gelding: second foal: dam unraced: useful form: won maiden at York in July: continued progress, seventh in listed race at Newbury and second to Abunai (plenty to do) in nursery at Southwell: will stay 1m: raced on good or firmer going: should improve further. *P. D. Evans*

VAL DE MAAL (IRE) 6 ch.g. Eagle Eyed (USA) 111 – Miss Bojangles (Gay Fan- **68** dango (USA) 132) [2006 70, a64: f6g³ 6.1m p6g p6g³ 6g 5.9g² 6d p6g⁵ p6m⁴ p6m⁶ f6g p6g⁶ Dec 22] quite good-topped gelding: fair performer: best at 6f/7f: acts on all-weather, good to firm and good to soft going: wears headgear: has hung left. *Miss J. A. Camacho*

VALDEMOSA 3 ch.f. Mark of Esteem (IRE) 137 – Valagalore 91 (Generous (IRE) **61** 139) [2006 8.3d⁴ 8m p12g Aug 23] fourth foal: half-sister to 1¾m winner The Varlet (by Groom Dancer): dam, 1¾m winner, half-sister to top-class sprinter Mozart: modest maiden: said to have finished distressed final outing: should stay at least 1¼m. *B. I. Case*

VALE DE LOBO 4 b.f. Loup Sauvage (USA) 125 – Frog 84 (Akarad (FR) 130) [2006 **82** 82: 10.3m* 12g⁵ p10g³ 10d⁶ 10g p10g Nov 11] sturdy, close-coupled filly: fairly useful performer: won claimer at Chester (left W. Haggas £25,000) in July: creditable efforts in handicaps next 2 starts but below form last 3: effective at 1¼m/1½m: acts on all-weather, good to firm and good to soft going. *B. R. Millman*

VALEESHA 2 b.f. (Mar 30) Erhaab (USA) 127 – Miss Laetitia (IRE) (Entitled 126) **47** [2006 7f³ 7g p7g Sep 10] half-sister to 1¼m seller winner Diletia (by Dilum): dam of little account: poor form in maidens: bred for middle distances. *W. G. M. Turner*

VALENTINA GUEST (IRE) 5 b.m. Be My Guest (USA) 126 – Karamiyna (IRE) **100** (Shernazar 131) [2006 102: 10m* 13m³ 12d 14g⁶ 9g 10g⁵ 12s 12m 8d 10v Oct 25] lengthy, good-bodied mare: fourth foal: half-sister to French 1¼m/13f winner Kariyfi (by Doyoun): dam, French 1m to 11f (listed race) winner, sister to very smart 1¼m performer Kartajana: useful performer: all 4 wins at Leopardstown, beat Bush Maiden by length in handicap in April: creditable 3 lengths third to Kastoria in listed race at Navan a week later: below form last 4 starts, in listed race at York on first occasion: stays 1¾m: acts on any going. *Peter Casey, Ireland*

VALENTINE'S PET 6 b.m. My Best Valentine 122 – Fabulous Pet (Something- **–** fabulous (USA)) [2006 36: f8g Jan 3] quite good-topped mare: maiden: no recent form: tried visored. *A. W. Carroll*

VALENTINO SWING (IRE) 3 ch.g. Titus Livius (FR) 115 – Farmers Swing (IRE) **80** (River Falls 113) [2006 74: 5.7d 6.1g⁴ 6g 6d² 6g 6m⁵ 6.1m 7f³ 7g p7.1m⁴ 8m⁵ 7.1d* p7.1g p7.1m⁴ p7g Nov 15] sturdy gelding: fairly useful handicapper: won at Warwick in October: stays 1m: acts on polytrack and good to soft going, probably on firm: tried in cheekpieces/blinkers/visor. *J. L. Spearing*

VALENTINO TAFFI 3 b.g. Primo Valentino (IRE) 116 – Drudwen (Sayf El Arab **57 d** (USA) 127) [2006 –: p7.1g⁵ p7.1g p7g 10d 9.9g May 13] form only on reappearance: should be suited by 1m+: acts on polytrack: blinkered/visored last 2 starts. *S. C. Williams*

VALE OF BELVOIR (IRE) 2 b.f. (Mar 24) Mull of Kintyre (USA) 114 – Sunrise **96** (IRE) 58 (Sri Pekan (USA) 117) [2006 5d² 5f* 5.1f* 5g* 5.2g² Aug 19] 20,000, 2-y-o: rather leggy, attractive filly: fourth foal: half-sister to 3-y-o Mystified: dam, maiden (best effort at 5f at 2 yrs), half-sister to useful sprinter March Star: useful form: completed hat-trick in summer, comprising maiden at Catterick and nurseries at Chester and Thirsk: more improvement when second to Abby Road (Alzerra third) in listed event at Newbury: speedy, raced at 5f: acts on firm and good to soft going. *K. R. Burke*

VALERIE 3 b.f. Sadler's Wells (USA) 132 – Horatia (IRE) 106 (Machiavellian (USA) **59** 123) [2006 57p: 8.2m p12.2g⁵ 14.1m⁵ Jun 15] well-made filly: modest maiden: stays 1½m: acts on polytrack. *L. M. Cumani*

VALERY BORZOV (IRE) 2 b.c. (Mar 12) Iron Mask (USA) 117 – Fay's Song (IRE) **76 p** 84 (Fayruz 116) [2006 6s* Oct 24] €13,500F, 26,000Y: sixth foal: half-brother to 6-y-o

Craic Sa Ceili: dam 5f (at 2 yrs) and 6f winner: 7/2, won weak maiden at Catterick (beat Onatopp by neck) in October, field well strung out: will progress. *D. Nicholls*

VALET 4 b.g. Kayf Tara 130 – Val de Fleurie (GER) 64 (Mondrian (GER) 125) [2006 –: – p16g f14g May 16] good-topped gelding: of no account. *J. G. M. O'Shea*

VALEUREUX 8 ch.g. Cadeaux Genereux 131 – La Strada (Niniski (USA) 125) [2006 60 –, a54: p12.2g⁵ f14g p13.9g² p13.9g² 14.1s⁴ p12.2g⁵ 14.1m 15.8d 14d Oct 8] big gelding: modest performer: stays 1¾m: acts on polytrack, heavy and good to firm ground: tried visored/in cheekpieces/tongue tied: twice reportedly suffered from breathing problem in 2006. *J. Hetherton*

VALHAR 3 b.f. Diktat 126 – Diamond Jayne (IRE) (Royal Abjar (USA) 121) [2006 54: 48 7m 7.1s 5m⁵ 7g 5.9g Aug 3] only poor maiden in 2006: left J. Jenkins prior to final outing: tried visored. *D. W. Thompson*

VALIANCE (USA) 2 ch.c. (Feb 16) Horse Chestnut (SAF) 119 – Victoria Cross (IRE) 94 101 (Mark of Esteem (IRE) 137) [2006 p7g* 7g² p8g³ Nov 11] 130,000Y: compact, well-made colt: first foal: dam, 7f winner who probably stayed 1¼m, out of smart performer up to 10.5f Glowing With Pride: fairly useful form: won maiden at Lingfield in July: good 1¼ lengths second to Dubai's Touch in listed race at Newbury next time: odds on, below form in minor event at Lingfield final outing: should be suited by 1m+. *J. H. M. Gosden*

VALIANT ROMEO 6 b.g. Primo Dominie 121 – Desert Lynx (IRE) 79 (Green Desert 46 (USA) 127) [2006 65: f5g p5.1g f5g 5f 5.1m f5g Nov 21] sturdy gelding: only poor performer in 2006: best at 5f: acts on firm and good to soft ground: usually wears headgear. *R. Bastiman*

VALIANT SHADOW (GER) 4 b.g. Winged Love (IRE) 121 – Vangelis (Gorytus – (USA) 132) [2006 61: 12v⁵ p16g Nov 8] well-made gelding: lightly-raced maiden: well held in 2006. *W. Jarvis*

VALIXIR (IRE) 5 b.h. Trempolino (USA) 135 – Vadlamixa (FR) 114 (Linamix (FR) 111 127) [2006 127: 8.9m 8.9m 10d May 14] big, good-topped horse: had an unimpressive action: high-class performer in 2005, when won Prix d'Ispahan at Longchamp and Queen Anne Stakes at Royal Ascot (at York): left A. Fabre in France, form in 2006 only when seventh to Touch of Land in Derrinstown Stud Jebel Hatta at Nad Al Sheba on reappearance: well held after in Dubai Duty Free there and Singapore International Cup (visored, looked unenthusiastic) at Kranji: had form up to 1½m but best at 1m/9f: acted on soft and good to firm going: tended to carry head awkwardly/wander: to stand at Lomar Park Stud, New South Wales, Australia. *Saeed bin Suroor*

VALLEMELDEE (IRE) 2 b.f. (Mar 15) Bering 136 – Vassiana (FR) (Anabaa (USA) 68 130) [2006 p7g⁴ 8.1d Oct 13] good-bodied: first foal: dam, French 1m winner, sister to French sprinters Victorieux (smart) and Villadolide (useful): better effort in maidens when 5½ lengths fourth to Regal Quest at Kempton: reportedly lost action next time: should stay 1m. *P. W. D'Arcy*

VALLEY OBSERVER (FR) 2 ch.c. (May 3) Observatory (USA) 131 – Valleyrose – (IRE) (Royal Academy (USA) 130) [2006 6m Jun 5] well held in maiden at Leicester. *W. R. Swinburn*

VALLEY OF THE MOON (IRE) 2 b.f. (May 11) Monashee Mountain (USA) 115 75 – Unaria (Prince Tenderfoot (USA) 126) [2006 6g 5m⁴ 5f* 5f⁴ 6d³ 6d 6s⁶ Sep 7] 20,000Y: useful-looking filly: half-sister to several winners, including useful 6f winner (including at 2 yrs) Mujado (by Mujadil), later successful in USA: dam, French maiden, sister to dam of smart sprinter Chookie Heiton: fair performer: won maiden at Catterick in July: creditable effort in nurseries after only when third at Redcar: will probably stay 7f: acts on firm and good to soft going: sometimes takes strong hold. *R. A. Fahey*

VALRHONA (IRE) 2 b. or br.f. (Feb 13) Spectrum (IRE) 126 – Minerva (IRE) (Caer- 72 p leon (USA) 132) [2006 7d⁶ Oct 28] leggy filly: third foal: half-sister to winner in USA by Machiavellian: dam, unraced, closely related to US Grade 2 11f winner Sword Dance out of half-sister to smart Irish miler Fatherland: 7½ lengths sixth to Measured Tempo in maiden at Newmarket, going on strongly at finish: will be suited by 1m/1¼m: sure to improve. *J. Noseda*

VALUE PLUS (IRE) 4 b.f. Mujadil (USA) 119 – Brittas Blues (IRE) 52 (Blues Travel- – ler (IRE) 119) [2006 –: f6g p6g⁵ p6g f7s 6d 6g 5f 6.1m Jul 2] fair maiden at 2 yrs: no form after, leaving C. Teague prior to seventh start in 2006: stayed 6f: acted on firm and good to soft going: tried visored/in cheekpieces/tongue tied: dead. *S. Parr*

VALUTA (USA) 3 gr. or ro.c. Silver Charm (USA) 132 – Misleadingmiss (USA) (Miswaki (USA) 124) [2006 9m⁴ 12g 11.5m² a8.7g 10g p10g³ p12g⁵ p10g⁵ p12g⁴ Dec 5] $80,000F: first foal: dam, 1m winner in USA, out of half-sister to smart performer up to 1m Firm Pledge: fair maiden: stays 1½m: acts on polytrack and good to firm going: usually tongue tied: visored (sweated badly) fifth start. *R. A. Kvisla* **76 a71**

VALVERDE (IRE) 3 b.c. Sinndar (IRE) 134 – Vert Val (USA) 103 (Septieme Ciel (USA) 123) [2006 8g⁴ 10d² 10g² 10s⁵ Oct 18] quite attractive colt, unfurnished at 3 yrs: fourth foal: half-brother to 3 winners, including smart 2003 2-y-o 5f (including Norfolk Stakes) winner Russian Valour (by Fasliyev) and 5f to 7f winner Come Away With Me (by Machiavellian): dam French 6.5f to 9f (at 2 yrs) winner: fair maiden: will probably stay beyond 1¼m: sold 27,000 gns. *J. L. Dunlop* **76**

VAMPYRUS 3 ch.g. Dracula (AUS) 121 – Anna Karietta 82 (Precocious 126) [2006 8.1s² p8.6g 8s⁵ 8d 8.2v Oct 25] tall gelding: half-brother to several winners, including 2004 2-y-o 5f winner Moscow Music (by Piccolo) and German 6f/7f performer Just Heaven's Gate (by Slip Anchor), both useful: dam 6f/7f winner: maiden: fair form on debut: well below that level after. *H. Candy* **73 d**

VANADIUM 4 b.g. Dansili 127 – Musianica 92 (Music Boy 124) [2006 88: 8m 7f 6g 6d* 7.1s⁴ 6d⁵ 6.1d p6g³ p6g⁶ p6g⁴ Dec 9] tall, good-topped gelding: fairly useful handicapper: won at Newcastle in August: mainly creditable efforts after: effective at 6f to 1m: acts on polytrack, soft and good to firm going: in cheekpieces final outing: often races freely. *J. G. Given* **84**

VANATINA (IRE) 2 b.f. (Apr 29) Tagula (IRE) 116 – Final Trick (Primo Dominie 121) [2006 5g 6g p6g 5s³ Sep 1] 16,000Y: third foal: half-sister to fairly useful 2004 2-y-o 6f winner Imperial Sound (by Efisio): dam ran twice: modest maiden: best effort at 5f: acts on soft going: hung left final outing. *A. Bailey* **55**

VANCOUVER GOLD (IRE) 4 b.f. Monashee Mountain (USA) 115 – Forest Berries (IRE) (Thatching 131) [2006 76: p7.1g* p7.1g³ f7g² f8g* f8g* f8g* 7.1v³ p8.6g² p8.6g⁵ Apr 13] sparely-made filly: fair performer: off almost 9 months (reportedly broke pelvis) before reappearance: won sellers at Wolverhampton in January and Southwell in February, and claimer and handicap at Southwell in March: stays 8.6f: acts on all-weather, heavy and good to firm going. *K. R. Burke* **72**

VANDAL 6 b.g. Entrepreneur 123 – Vax Star 96 (Petong 126) [2006 p7.1g p7.1g p7.1g p8.6g p6g 10.2g p10g 10g 11.7f⁶ 10.2f Jun 17] sturdy, attractive gelding: unraced on Flat in 2004/5: modest performer at best in 2006: stays easy 1¼m: acts on polytrack and firm going. *M. Appleby* **52**

VANDERLIN 7 ch.g. Halling (USA) 133 – Massorah (FR) 108 (Habitat 134) [2006 118: p8g* 8m⁵ 7m² 8m 8f Sep 17] strong gelding: usually impresses in appearance: smart performer: as good as ever in 2006, dead-heating with Kandidate in listed race at Lingfield in March: creditable efforts in Champions Mile at Sha Tin (2½ lengths fifth to Bullish Luck) and minor event at Chester (1¼ lengths second to Prince of Light) next 2 starts: well below form in Sussex Stakes at Goodwood (reportedly returned stiff behind) and Woodbine Mile only subsequent outings: probably best at 7f/1m: acts on polytrack, firm and soft going: tried visored earlier in career. *A. M. Balding* **118**

VANILLA DELIGHT (IRE) 3 b.f. Orpen (USA) 116 – Fantastic Bid (USA) (Auction Ring (USA) 123) [2006 75: 7.5g 8m 8.1s² 7s⁴ Oct 14] workmanlike filly: fair handicapper: stays 1m: acts on soft and good to firm ground. *J. Howard Johnson* **74**

VANISHING DANCER (SWI) 9 ch.g. Llandaff (USA) – Vanishing Prairie (USA) 93 (Alysheba (USA)) [2006 60: p16.5g⁶ Feb 17] lengthy, workmanlike gelding: modest handicapper: stays easy 2m: acts on all-weather and firm going, not on soft: tried visored (pulled too hard): has been blinkered/tongue tied: sold £1,400, joined Mrs O. Thomas. *B. Ellison* **61**

VANQUISHER (IRE) 2 b.g. (Mar 23) Xaar 132 – Naziriya (FR) (Darshaan 133) [2006 7d⁵ 8m⁵ 8.3s² Oct 2] 30,000Y: leggy, useful-looking gelding: half-brother to several winners, including smart US Grade 2 1½m winner Nazirali (by Kahyasi) and useful Irish 1¼m winner Nasafar (by Cape Cross): dam, French 10.5f winner, half-sister to Prix du Jockey Club winner Natroun: fairly useful form: best effort in maidens when 1¼ lengths second to Ajaan at Windsor final outing, still green: will stay at least 1¼m: gelded. *W. J. Haggas* **84 +**

VAUDEVIRE 5 b.g. Dancing Spree (USA) – Approved Quality (IRE) 66 (Persian Heights 129) [2006 47: f5g p5.1g Jan 16] tall gelding: poor performer: well held in 2006: wears blinkers/cheekpieces. *Peter Grayson* **–**

VAUNT 2 b.g. (Mar 10) Averti (IRE) 117 – Boast 99 (Most Welcome 131) [2006 5.7g⁵ **87**
6f⁴ 5.7m² 6.1g² 5.1f* 5.1m* 8f⁴ Nov 24] third foal: half-brother to useful 2005 2-y-o 5f
winner Strut (by Danehill Dancer) and 5f (at 2 yrs) to 9f (in USA) winner Brag (by Mujadil): dam 5f (at 2 yrs)/6f winner: fairly useful performer: won maiden in September and
nursery (beat Another True Story by ½ length) in October, both at Bath: left R. Charlton
100,000 gns, creditable 3¾ lengths fourth to Whatsthescript in Grade 3 Generous Stakes
(Div 2) at Hollywood final outing: effective at 5f to 1m: acts on firm going: blinkered last
4 starts. *D. L. Hendricks, USA*

VAUQUELIN (IRE) 2 b.c. (Apr 22) Xaar 132 – Beryl 77 (Bering 136) [2006 6m² 6m² **95**
6f² 8f* 8f² Nov 24] 14,000F, 28,000Y: well-made colt: fourth foal: half-brother to 3-y-o
Glenmuir and 6f winner Juniper Banks (by Night Shift): dam 1½m winner: useful performer: runner-up all 3 starts in Britain, best effort when beaten a neck by Dazed And
Amazed in listed race at Newbury second outing: left E. McMahon after next appearance:
won maiden at Hollywood in October, then good ½-length second to Whatsthescript in
Grade 3 Generous Stakes (Div 2) at Hollywood: stays 1m: raced only on firm/good to
firm going. *Kathy Walsh, USA*

VEBA (USA) 3 ch.g. Black Minnaloushe (USA) 123 – Make Over (USA) (Time For A **–**
Change (USA)) [2006 66p: f8g 6m⁶ p8g p8g Dec 5] fair maiden at 2 yrs: gelded, little
form in 2006: left B. Hills 2,000 gns after second outing. *M. D. I. Usher*

VEENWOUDEN 2 b.f. (Jan 27) Desert Prince (IRE) 130 – Delauncy (Machiavellian **80**
(USA) 123) [2006 p6g⁴ 7g* 7m³ 6d Sep 29] 97,000Y: neat filly: third foal: half-sister to
smart 1¼m winner who stayed 13.4f Delsarte (by Theatrical) and 3-y-o Peppertree: dam,
useful French 2-y-o 1m winner who stayed 1¼m, daughter of Park Hill winner Casey:
fairly useful performer: won maiden at Folkestone in August: better effort after when
third in nursery at Lingfield: will stay 1m/1¼m. *J. R. Fanshawe*

VEGAS BOYS 3 b.g. Royal Applause 124 – Brief Glimpse (IRE) 108 (Taufan (USA) **77**
119) [2006 78: p7g 6f⁵ 6g⁶ 6f⁶ 7g 6m 5g 5.3g 5d p6g* p6g² Dec 30] angular gelding: has
a markedly round action: fair performer: fairly backed, won handicap at Wolverhampton
December: good second there final start: should stay 7f: acts on polytrack and firm going. *M. Wigham*

VEHARI 3 ch.g. Tomba 119 – Nannie Annie 60 (Persian Bold 123) [2006 –: p9.5g **77**
11.8d² 12.1s² May 29] sturdy gelding: fair maiden: stays 1½m: acts on soft going.
M. Scudamore

VEILED APPLAUSE 3 b.g. Royal Applause 124 – Scarlet Veil 75 (Tyrnavos 129) **77**
[2006 65: 8.3f⁵ 8m² 8.1m* 8.1m⁴ p9.5m⁴ p10g⁴ Oct 26] fair handicapper: won at Chepstow in August: stays easy 1¼m: acts on polytrack and good to firm going: tends to hang.
R. M. Beckett

VEILS OF SALOME 2 ch.f. (Apr 5) Arkadian Hero (USA) 123 – Helen Bradley **–**
(IRE) 85 (Indian Ridge 123) [2006 7s p6s f7g Dec 23] first foal: dam, 2-y-o 6f winner
who stayed 1m, half-sister to Norfolk Stakes winner Blue Dakota: well held in maidens.
A. J. McCabe

VELVET HEIGHTS (IRE) 4 b.c. Barathea (IRE) 127 – Height of Fantasy (IRE) 101 **104**
(Shirley Heights 130) [2006 87: p16g* 13.9s 14g⁶ p16g² 15.9g² 16g⁴ 13.1s⁴ p12g² f14g*
f12g* p12.2s³ Dec 15] sturdy, close-coupled colt: useful handicapper: improved further
in 2006, winning at Kempton in April, and Southwell in November and December (beat
Mighty Moon by 4 lengths): good 2¾ lengths third to Sweet Indulgence at Wolverhampton final outing: effective at 1½m to 2m: acts on all-weather and soft going. *J. L. Dunlop*

VELVET TOUCH 5 b.m. Danzig Connection (USA) – Soft Touch (GER) (Horst- **38 §**
Herbert) [2006 51, a46: f6g³ 7g⁴ Jan 24] workmanlike mare: poor maiden: stays 6f:
acts on all-weather, firm and soft ground: tried visored: tongue tied of late: unreliable.
D. M. Simcock

VELVET VALLEY (USA) 3 ch.g. Gone West (USA) – Velvet Morning (USA) **73**
(Broad Brush (USA)) [2006 67: p7g⁶ 8.5f³ 9m 10g p10g⁶ Dec 30] rangy, good-topped
gelding: fair maiden: left Sir Michael Stoute 12,000 gns and gelded after fourth start:
stays 8.5f: acts on firm going: free-going sort. *C. E. Longsdon*

VELVET WATERS 5 b.m. Unfuwain (USA) 131 – Gleaming Water 81 (Kalaglow **77**
132) [2006 80: 11.5m⁴ 10.2g 11.6m³ 12g² 12m³ 11.8m³ 11.6f Jul 10] leggy mare: fair
handicapper in 2006: possibly amiss final outing: effective at 11.5f to 1¾m: acts on
polytrack, firm and good to soft going: wore cheekpieces final start at 4 yrs: usually races
prominently. *R. F. Johnson Houghton*

VENEER (IRE) 4 b.g. Woodborough (USA) 112 – Sweet Lass (Belmez (USA) 131) **59**
[2006 70d: p8.6g f12g 9.7d⁶ 8.5d⁴ 7g⁶ f8g³ p7g² f8g p7g² May 23] lengthy gelding: just
modest performer in 2006: stays 9.7f: acts on all-weather and good to soft going: usually
blinkered/in cheekpieces. *Miss Gay Kelleway*

VENERABLE 2 b.c. (Feb 17) Danehill (USA) 126 – Fragrant View (USA) 99 (Distant **56 p**
View (USA) 126) [2006 7d Oct 28] well-made colt: first foal: dam, 1¼m winner, sister to
high-class performer up to 1¼m Distant Music (also Dewhurst Stakes winner at 2 yrs):
40/1, coltish and green, mid-field in maiden at Newmarket, never going pace: likely to do
better. *J. H. M. Gosden*

VENETIAN DANCER (IRE) 2 gr.c. (Jan 24) Danehill Dancer (IRE) 117 – Venize **74**
(IRE) 110 (Kaldoun (FR) 122) [2006 f5g³ 7g⁶ 6m⁶ a6.5g⁶ Dec 29] 90,000F, 70,000Y:
third foal: half-brother to useful 7f (at 2 yrs) to 1¼m winner Fenice (by Woodman) and
1¼m to 1½m winner Le Byzantin (by Dynaformer), both in France: dam, French 7.5f (at
2 yrs) and 1m (Prix de la Grotte) winner, sister to smart French miler Simon du Desert:
fair form in maidens: left M. Wallace 18,000 gns before final outing: will be suited by
1m. *N. Minner, Belgium*

VENETIAN PRINCESS (IRE) 4 b.f. Desert Style (IRE) 121 – Dance With Care **47**
(Arazi (USA) 135) [2006 53: f8g f8g f8g⁶ f8g⁵ f7g Mar 14] lengthy filly: only poor
performer in 2006: stays 1m: acts on fibresand. *P. Howling*

VENETIAN ROMANCE (IRE) 5 ch.m. Desert Story (IRE) 115 – Cipriani 102 **55**
(Habitat 134) [2006 –: p12.2g⁴ p12.2g p12.2g Apr 28] smallish mare: poor maiden: left
D. ffrench Davies after reappearance: stays 1½m: acts on polytrack and good to soft
ground: tried in headgear/tongue tied. *M. R. Bosley*

VENETO (IRE) 3 ch.g. Spinning World (USA) 130 – Padua (IRE) (Cadeaux Genereux **–**
131) [2006 48: f11g Apr 3] modest maiden: tongue tied, virtually pulled up only outing
in 2006: will be suited by 1m+: raced only on fibresand and good to firm going.
K. G. Reveley

VENGEANCE 6 b.g. Fleetwood (IRE) 107 – Lady Isabell 62 (Rambo Dancer (CAN) **102**
107) [2006 12g* 12m 12m 11.9g⁵ Jul 8] tall gelding: useful handicapper: unraced on Flat
in 2005: virtually as good as ever when winning at Epsom in April by length from Red
Racketeer: best other effort in 2006 when creditable eighth behind Alfie Noakes there
next time: stays 1½m: acts on soft and good to firm going. *S. Dow*

VENIR ROUGE 2 ch.c. (Apr 17) Dancing Spree (USA) – Al Awaalah 52 (Mukadda- **73**
mah (USA) 125) [2006 6s 6g 7.1m 7f 7f⁴ 7.1m 8s p8g² Nov 8] big, lengthy colt: first foal:
dam maiden who barely stayed 9.4f: fair maiden: good second in nursery at Kempton
final start: stays 1m: acts on polytrack and firm going: has run well sweating. *M. Salaman*

VENTURA (USA) 2 b. or br.f. (Jan 31) Chester House (USA) 123 – Estala (Be My **74 p**
Guest (USA) 126) [2006 p7g⁶ Oct 26] half-sister to 3 winners, including useful 7f/1m
winner Entail (by Riverman) and fairly useful 1¼m winner Latest Moment (by Quest For
Fame): dam, useful French 2-y-o 9f winner who stayed 10.5f, half-sister to 7-y-o Vortex:
25/1, 3¼ lengths sixth to Dalvina in maiden at Lingfield: should be suited by 1m+: should
improve. *Mrs A. J. Perrett*

VERACITY 2 ch.c. (May 2) Lomitas 129 – Vituisa (Bering 136) [2006 8.3s Oct 2] third **69 p**
foal: half-brother to 3-y-o Shoshoni and useful French 7.5f/1m winner Terra Verde (by
Indian Ridge): dam, French 11.5f winner, out of smart 1m/1¼m winner (Sun Chariot
Stakes) La Confederation: 8/1 and green, never dangerous when seventh to Ajaan at
Windsor: will be suited by 1¼m+: open to improvement. *M. A. Jarvis*

VERBATIM 2 b.f. (Feb 3) Vettori (IRE) 119 – Brand (Shareef Dancer (USA) 135) **– p**
[2006 p7g⁵ Sep 10] half-sister to several winners, including 6f (at 2 yrs) and 1m winner
Royal Warrant (by Royal Applause) and 4-y-o Banknote, both useful: dam, unraced half-
sister to useful winner up to 1½m Clever Cliche, out of sister to Height of Fashion, herself
the dam of Nashwan, Unfuwain and Nayef: 12/1, 11½ lengths fifth to Lady Grace in
maiden at Kempton, late headway: will do better at 1m+. *A. M. Balding*

VERONICA'S GIRL 3 b.f. Desert Prince (IRE) 130 – Veronica Franco 90 (Darshaan **75**
133) [2006 66: p8g⁵ p6g³ p8g³ p10g⁶ 11.5m 7.6d Aug 13] fair handicapper: left P. Hedger
after third start: bred to stay 1¼m, though not short of speed and effective at 6f: acts on
polytrack. *W. J. Knight*

VERSATILE 3 b.g. Vettori (IRE) 119 – Direcvil (Top Ville 129) [2006 10.5d⁴ 9.5v² **?**
9.5v p8g 10g p13g Sep 29] good-topped gelding: maiden: second at Bordeaux both starts
at 2 yrs and at Mont-de-Marsan (blinkered) in March: left J-C. Rouget in France after

next outing: little form in Britain: stays 9.5f: raced only on polytrack and good or softer ground. *G. A. Ham*

VERSTONE (IRE) 4 b.f. Brave Act 119 – Golden Charm (IRE) 63 (Common Grounds 118) [2006 44: f14g May 16] leggy filly: poor maiden on Flat: poor winner over hurdles in August. *R. F. Fisher* –

VERY AGREEABLE 3 b.f. Pursuit of Love 124 – Oomph 83 (Shareef Dancer (USA) 135) [2006 60p: p10g² 12g* Jul 28] quite good-topped filly: fairly useful performer, lightly raced: best effort in maidens when winning at Newmarket in July by ½ length from Topjeu: stays 1½m: raced only on polytrack and good going. *W. R. Swinburn* 87

VERY CLEAR 4 b.f. Loup Sauvage (USA) 125 – Shoot Clear 111 (Bay Express 132) [2006 p7g p6g f7g⁶ p7.1g Jun 9] half-sister to several winners, including 2002 2-y-o 1m winner Famous Grouse (by Selkirk) and 1½m winner Shoot Ahead (by Shirley Heights), both useful: dam, 5f to 7f winner at 2 yrs and fourth in 1000 Guineas, half-sister to Yorkshire Oaks winners Untold and Sally Brown: poor maiden: tried in cheekpieces. *R. M. H. Cowell* 47

VERY FAR (USA) 3 br.c. Forestry (USA) 121 – Hail Atlantis (USA) (Seattle Slew (USA)) [2006 8.3g* 8m² 8.1m Sep 8] $575,000Y: closely related to US minor stakes-winning sprinter Stormy Atlantic (by Storm Cat), and half-brother to 3 winners in USA, including dam of very smart US Grade 1 9f winner Bandini: dam US Grade 1 8.5f winner: fairly useful performer: won maiden at Windsor in August: creditable efforts in handicaps next 2 starts: stays 1m: acts on good to firm going: tongue tied: possibly temperamental: joined S. Seemar in UAE. *Saeed bin Suroor* 89

VERY WISE 4 b.g. Pursuit of Love 124 – With Care 78 (Warning 136) [2006 93: 8.1f 8.9m 8.1m³ p8.6g* Dec 8] tall, good sort: fairly useful handicapper, lightly raced: off 5 months, won at Wolverhampton in December by head from Atlantic Quest: may stay 1¼m: acts on polytrack, soft and good to firm going: has worn crossed noseband: saddle slipped on reappearance: held up. *W. J. Haggas* 92

VESUVIO 2 br.c. (Mar 19) Efisio 120 – Polo 83 (Warning 136) [2006 6g³ p7.1g Nov 3] fourth foal: brother to 3 winners, including 3-y-o Vino: dam, 1¼m winner, out of unraced sister to Prix du Jockey Club winner Polytain: better effort in maidens when 3 lengths third to Vitznau at Windsor on debut: should be suited by 7f/1m. *B. W. Hills* 70

VETTORI DANCER 3 b.f. Vettori (IRE) 119 – Assertive Dancer (USA) (Assert 134) [2006 8.1g 11.5m p12g 14.1m Jun 15] fourth foal: dam 8.5f to 11f winner in North America: little form. *G. G. Margarson* –

VEVERKA 5 b.m. King's Theatre (IRE) 128 – Once Smitten (IRE) 58 (Caerleon (USA) 132) [2006 –: p10g 10.2g Jun 2] small mare: fair maiden at 2 yrs: no form on Flat since, but won over hurdles in July and September. *J. C. Fox* –

VIABLE 4 b.g. Vettori (IRE) 119 – Danseuse Davis (FR) (Glow (USA)) [2006 74: p10g 10d³ 9.9f 10f 10d⁴ 10m² 10m Sep 21] fair maiden handicapper: barely stays 11.8f: acts on good to firm and good to soft going: ungenuine. *Mrs P. Sly* 69 §

VIBE 5 gr.g. Danzero (AUS) – Courting 108 (Pursuit of Love 124) [2006 65, a54: 8m 6.1m* 6.1d⁴ p7g³ 6f⁶ 6g 7.1m⁶ Sep 1] leggy, useful-looking gelding: modest handicapper: won maiden event at Chepstow in June: best at 6f to 1m: acts on polytrack and firm going: tried in cheekpieces. *A. W. Carroll* 52

VIBRATO (USA) 4 b.g. Stravinsky (USA) 133 – She's Fine (USA) (Private Account (USA)) [2006 f6g f6m⁵ 5s 5d 6v⁴ 7.1d² 6.1d f8m* f7g⁴ f8g⁵ p8.6g⁶ p9.5g f8g* Dec 27] tall gelding: modest performer: won banded race in December and handicap in December (visored), both at Southwell: stays 8.6f: acts on all-weather and heavy ground: tried in cheekpieces. *C. J. Teague* 62

VICE ADMIRAL 3 ch.g. Vettori (IRE) 119 – Queen of Scotland (IRE) 75 (Mujadil (USA) 119) [2006 –: 10d 12.6g 10f 12f² 12f⁵ 16.2m² 16g² 14.1d 14.1m* 16.1s* 14.1m 17.1d p16.5m 15.8s Oct 24] workmanlike gelding: fair handicapper: won at Redcar in August and Newcastle in September: stays 2m: acts on firm and soft going: tried blinkered. *M. W. Easterby* 70

VICIOUS KNIGHT 8 b.g. Night Shift (USA) – Myth 89 (Troy 137) [2006 95§: p9.5g* 7d 7.1m a5g⁴ a6g a8.8g a6.5g³ a6.5g³ 7g* 8s 8g Dec 3] robust, good sort: good walker: fairly useful performer at best: won claimer at Wolverhampton on all-weather debut in March and (having left D. Nicholls after third start) handicap at Madrid in October: effective at 7f to easy 9.5f: acts on polytrack, soft and good to firm ground: sometimes visored, including for win in 2005: sometimes finds little: unreliable. *P. Haley, Spain* 84 §

VICIOUS PRINCE (IRE) 7 b.g. Sadler's Wells (USA) 132 – Sunny Flower (FR) – (Dom Racine (FR) 121) [2006 77: p12.2g 16v 16.2m⁶ Aug 16] strong, lengthy gelding: has a fluent, round action: fair handicapper in 2005, no form in 2006. *R. M. Whitaker*

VICIOUS WARRIOR 7 b.g. Elmaamul (USA) 125 – Ling Lane (Slip Anchor 136) **95** [2006 93, a85: 8g⁴ 8m 7.9g⁴ 7.9m³ 9.8d² 10.1f⁵ 10g³ 8s⁶ 8d* 8s p10g Dec 20] big, strong **a–** gelding: useful handicapper: won at Ayr in May and September, best effort of season when beating St Petersburg a head in latter: stays 1¼m: acts on polytrack, good to firm and good to soft going: free-going sort: usually races prominently. *R. M. Whitaker*

VICKY POLLARD 3 b.f. King Charlemagne (USA) 120 – Day Star 77 (Dayjur **50** (USA) 137) [2006 57: 6f 5f⁴ f5g³ 5m³ p5.1g p5.1g⁵ p6g p5g³ f5g Dec 29] modest maiden: may prove best at 5f: acts on all-weather and firm going. *P. Howling*

VICTIMISED (IRE) 4 b.g. Victory Note (USA) 120 – Eurolink Virago (Charmer 123) – [2006 36: p6g p9.5g f6g p6g Apr 10] tall gelding: maiden: no form in 2006: tried in cheekpieces/blinkers. *R. J. Price*

VICTOR BUCKWELL 4 br.g. Pivotal 124 – Lonely Shore (Blakeney 126) [2006 **43** 47: 11.9m⁵ p16g 11.6m Jul 17] close-coupled gelding: poor maiden: stays 1½m: acts on polytrack and good to firm going: tried blinkered. *G. L. Moore*

VICTORIANA 5 b.m. Wolfhound (USA) 126 – Silk St James (Pas de Seul 133) [2006 **43** 32: p6g⁴ p5.1g p5g 5.2m 6f Jun 22] neat mare: poor maiden: should stay 7f: acts on polytrack and soft going: wears cheekpieces. *H. J. Collingridge*

VICTORIAN PRINCE (IRE) 2 b.c. (Feb 8) Desert Prince (IRE) 130 – Miss Lorilaw **87 p** (FR) 104 (Homme de Loi (IRE) 120) [2006 8s* Oct 7] 26,000Y, 21,000 2-y-o: good-topped colt: second foal: dam 1m (at 2 yrs) and 1½m winner: 12/1, won maiden at York by 3 lengths from Cut The Cake, green having led over 1f out: will stay 1¼m+: sent to USA: sure to improve. *E. J. O'Neill*

VICTORS PRIZE (IRE) 4 b.f. Dr Devious (IRE) 127 – Spoken Word (IRE) (Peru- – gino (USA) 84) [2006 57: 9.1v Oct 28] modest maiden: well beaten sole outing in 2006: wore cheekpieces last 2 starts at 3 yrs. *T. J. Pitt*

VICTOR TRUMPER 2 b.g. (Feb 9) First Trump 118 – Not So Generous (IRE) 68 **83** (Fayruz 116) [2006 7.1m 7.1d* 8.3g⁵ p8g² p7.1g² p7.1g⁴ f8g² Dec 2] 12,000Y: close-coupled gelding: half-brother to 2001 2-y-o 5f winner Neptune's Gift (by Lugana Beach): dam 5f winner, including at 2 yrs: fairly useful performer: won maiden at Warwick in September: ran creditably in frame in minor events/nurseries after, though hung and found little last 2 starts: stays 1m: acts on all-weather and good to soft going: blinkered sixth start: gelded after final outing. *P. W. Chapple-Hyam*

VICTORY QUEST (IRE) 6 b.g. Victory Note (USA) 120 – Marade (USA) (Dahar **71 §** (USA) 125) [2006 71: f16g⁵ f14g f14g⁵ f16g* f14g p16.5g f16g² f16g⁶ p16.5g⁴ f14g f16g² Dec 19] fair handicapper: won at Southwell in February: will stay beyond 2m: acts on fibresand and good to firm going: visored: unreliable. *Mrs S. Lamyman*

VICTORY SPIRIT 2 b.c. (Mar 5) Invincible Spirit (IRE) 121 – Tanouma (USA) 114 **75** (Miswaki (USA) 124) [2006 6g⁴ 6m 6m² 6m* 7d Sep 29] 9,000Y: closely related to 6f winner (including at 2 yrs) Medeena and 1995 2-y-o 6f/7f winner Tamnia (both useful, by Green Desert), and half-brother to several winners, including 1m (at 2 yrs) to 13f winner Azzilfi (by Ardross) and 1¼m to 15f winner Khamaseen (by Slip Anchor), both smart: dam 6f (at 2 yrs)/7f winner: fair form: won maiden at Folkestone in September: well held in nursery: will prove best at 5f/6f: acts on good to firm going: ran as if amiss second start: has joined H. Dunlop. *J. L. Dunlop*

VIENNA'S BOY (IRE) 5 b.g. Victory Note (USA) 120 – Shinkoh Rose (FR) 67 **78** (Warning 136) [2006 75: p7g p7.1g³ p7g f6g² 7.1m⁴ p7.1g* p7.1g p7.1f³ 7g⁵ 7m⁴ Sep 5] tall, leggy gelding: fair handicapper: won at Wolverhampton in June: best at 6f/7f: acts on polytrack, unraced on heavy going but acts on any other turf: often slowly away: tends to hang: sold 7,000 gns. *W. J. Musson*

VIETNAM 2 ch.g. (Mar 4) Compton Place 125 – Mosca 83 (Most Welcome 131) [2006 **57** 6f p8g p8.6g⁵ 10g Sep 26] compact gelding: modest maiden: stays 8.6f, seemingly not 1¼m: acts on polytrack. *S. Kirk*

VIEWFORTH 8 b.g. Emarati (USA) 74 – Miriam 59 (Forzando 122) [2006 76, a69: 6d **70** 5d 5g 5d² 6m³ 6g* 5m³ 6m³ 6g 6d 6s² 5s⁴ 5v⁶ p6g⁵ p6g⁵ p7g⁴ Dec 19] good-bodied **a63** gelding: fair performer on turf, just modest on all-weather in 2006: won handicap at Hamilton in July: claimed from I. Semple after fourteenth outing: effective at 5f to easy 7f: acts on all-weather and any turf going: usually visored/blinkered. *M. A. Buckley*

VIEW FROM THE TOP 2 b.c. (Mar 1) Mujahid (USA) 125 – Aethra (USA) 89 **69** (Trempolino (USA) 135) [2006 7m⁴ 7.1m 7f p8.6g Dec 23] useful-looking colt: closely related to useful French 6f (at 2 yrs)/1m winner Kane Ore (by Green Desert) and half-brother to 3 winners, including 8.5f (at 2 yrs) and 1¼m winner Alphaeus (by Sillery) and 3-y-o Ogee, both useful: dam, maiden who should have stayed at least 1¼m, out of half-sister to Prix de Diane winner Lacovia: fair form when fourth to Hanging On at Newmarket, easily best effort in maidens: reportedly lost a shoe third start (left W. Knight 57,000 gns after): raced too freely on nursery debut: should stay 1m. *Sir Mark Prescott*

VIJAY (IRE) 7 ch.g. Eagle Eyed (USA) 111 – Foolish Fun (Fools Holme (USA)) [2006 – § 54§: 5m May 11] fair performer at best: was effective at 5f to 7f: acted on fibresand, firm and good to soft going: often wore headgear: was unreliable: dead. *Mrs J. C. McGregor*

VIKING SPIRIT 4 b.g. Mind Games 121 – Dane Dancing (IRE) 68 (Danehill (USA) **108** 126) [2006 104: p6g⁵ 6d p6g³ p7g² p6g² Nov 11] tall, quite attractive gelding: useful handicapper: reportedly injured and off nearly 5 months after reappearance: placed last 3 starts, career-best effort when 1½ lengths second to Maltese Falcon at Lingfield final one: effective at 6f/7f: acts on polytrack, good to firm and good to soft going, probably on firm: below form in cheekpieces. *W. R. Swinburn*

VIKING STAR (IRE) 5 b.g. Indian Rocket 115 – Nordic Flavour (IRE) 84 (Nordico – (USA)) [2006 46: p12.2g Jan 28] poor maiden: tried blinkered. *A. D. Brown*

VILLA BIANCA'S (IRE) 3 ch.f. Priolo (USA) 127 – Ostrusa (AUT) (Rustan (HUN)) **52** [2006 f6g⁵ p6g² Dec 6] €24,000Y: sister to 4-y-o Riolo and half-sister to 3 winners, notably 7-y-o Osterhase: dam won in Austria: better effort in maidens when third at Wolverhampton, flashing tail. *J. A. Osborne*

VILLA CHIGI (IRE) 4 ch.g. Pistolet Bleu (IRE) 133 – Musical Refrain (IRE) (Danc- – ing Dissident (USA) 119) [2006 6f⁶ f6g 9d Aug 12] little form: tried in cheekpieces. *G. R. Oldroyd*

VILLAGE STORM (IRE) 3 b.g. Mujadil (USA) 119 – First Nadia (Auction Ring – (USA) 123) [2006 –: p9.5g Dec 11] no form in maidens: tried blinkered. *C. J. Teague*

VILLAGO (GER) 6 b.g. Laroche (GER) 123 – Village (GER) (Acatenango (GER) **67** 127) [2006 69: 15.8d 21.6d* 20s May 18] good-topped gelding: fair handicapper: won at Pontefract in April: stayed 21.6f: acted on good to firm and good to soft going: tried blinkered: held up: dead. *E. W. Tuer*

VILLAROSI (IRE) 4 b.f. Rossini (USA) 118 – Trinida (Jaazeiro (USA) 127) [2006 **77 d** 59: 7m² 7m⁶ 8m 9.7m 10g 7d Oct 3] workmanlike filly: fair maiden: below form after reappearance: may prove best at 6f/7f: acts on good to firm going: visored final start. *J. R. Best*

VILLA SONATA 3 b.f. Mozart (IRE) 131 – Villa Carlotta 110 (Rainbow Quest (USA) **77** 134) [2006 66p: 7d² 8.2m⁴ 8.3m 10m⁵ 10g* 11m 11.6s⁴ 12g⁵ Oct 13] rather leggy, attractive filly: fair performer: won handicap at Windsor in August: stays 11.6f: acts on soft and good to firm going: reportedly lost action sixth outing. *J. R. Fanshawe*

VINANDO 5 ch.h. Hernando (FR) 127 – Sirena (GER) (Tejano (USA)) [2006 108: **109** 18.7m² 16.4s⁵ 21.7m³ 16.4m⁵ 13.9f⁶ 18d Oct 14] leggy, close-coupled horse: useful performer: good 1¼ lengths second to Admiral in Chester Cup (Handicap) on reappearance: creditable efforts next 2 starts, including third to Baddam in Queen Alexandra Stakes at Royal Ascot, and when ninth to Detroit City in Cesarewitch (Handicap) at Newmarket final one: stays 2¾m: acts on soft and good to firm going: blinkered/tongue tied: went in snatches third outing at 4 yrs/looked none too keen fifth outing in 2006. *C. R. Egerton*

VINCENNES 2 b. or br.f. (May 10) King's Best (USA) 132 – Park Appeal 122 (Aho- **74** noora 122) [2006 p7.1g⁵ p8g² Dec 20] half-sister to several winners, including high-class miler Cape Cross (by Green Desert) and the dams of Diktat and Iffraaj: dam, won Cheveley Park Stakes and 8.5f winner in USA at 4 yrs, half-sister to Desirable, Alydaress and to dam of Russian Rhythm: better effort in maidens when length second to Algarade at Kempton. *M. A. Jarvis*

VINCENT VEGAS 3 b.g. Foxhound (USA) 103 – Annie's Song 69 (Farfelu 103) – [2006 –: f6g 11.9s⁶ 7.5f 15.8m Aug 8] close-coupled gelding: no form: tried in cheekpieces. *Mrs S. Lamyman*

VINDICATION 6 ch.g. Compton Place 125 – Prince's Feather (IRE) 77 (Cadeaux **70 d** Genereux 131) [2006 79: p6g³ 7m⁴ 7m⁶ 6m⁴ 7f p6g³ 5.2f⁴ 6m 7m⁴ 6g 7d⁶ p6g Oct 23] smallish, well-made gelding: fair handicapper, on downgrade: effective at 6f/7f: acts on polytrack and firm going, probably on soft: usually in headgear/tongue tie: very slowly away third start: finds little. *R. M. H. Cowell*

VINIYOGA 4 b.g. Cadeaux Genereux 131 – Optimistic 90 (Reprimand 122) [2006 –: – f16g Jan 17] smallish, close-coupled gelding: no sign of ability: tried blinkered. *M. H. Tompkins*

VINO 3 b.f. Efisio 120 – Polo 83 (Warning 136) [2006 –p: 8.1g⁴ 7g³ 7g* p7.1g⁵ p8g   **73** Nov 9] sturdy, good-topped filly: fair performer: won maiden at Salisbury in August: respectable efforts in handicaps both starts after: bred to stay 1¼m: raced only on polytrack and good going. *B. W. Hills*

VINSKA (USA) 3 br.f. Stravinsky (USA) 133 – Konvincha (USA) (Cormorant (USA))   **60** [2006 45: 10m 9.9m p10g 9.7f 10m³ Aug 6] modest maiden: stays 1¼m: acts on good to firm going: wore cheekpieces final start. *J. W. Hills*

VINTAGE (IRE) 2 b.c. (Feb 4) Danetime (IRE) 121 – Katherine Gorge (USA) (Hansel   **67** (USA)) [2006 p6g May 25] €10,000Y, 14,000 2-y-o: sixth foal: half-brother to 3 winners, including fairly useful 6f (at 2 yrs) to 1m winner Miss Champers (by Grand Lodge) and 4-y-o Straffan: dam unraced daughter of useful sprinter Katies First, herself out of Irish 1000 Guineas winner Katies: 40/1, 5½ lengths seventh to We'll Confer in maiden at Lingfield, slowly away. *P. Mitchell*

VINTAGE TIMES (IRE) 4 b.g. Namid 128 – Vintage Escape (IRE) 84 (Cyrano de   – Bergerac 120) [2006 –: f8g Jan 11] leggy gelding: little form: dead. *R. A. Fahey*

VIOLENT VELOCITY (IRE) 3 b.c. Namid 128 – Lear's Crown (USA) 82 (Lear   **77** Fan (USA) 130) [2006 71: p7.1g* 6g 6d 5s p6g f6g Dec 21] neat colt: fair performer: readily won maiden at Wolverhampton in February: below form in handicaps after: stays 7f: acts on polytrack and good to firm ground. *J. J. Quinn*

VIOLET BALLERINA (IRE) 3 b.f. Namid 128 – Violet Spring (IRE) 32 (Exactly   **85** Sharp (USA) 121) [2006 72: 7s p6g⁵ p6g⁴ p6g³ p6g* 6d Oct 19] leggy, attractive filly: fairly useful performer: best effort when winning handicap at Kempton in September by 1½ lengths from Calypso King: effective at 6f/7f: acts on polytrack, soft and good to firm going: blinkered last 3 starts: sometimes starts slowly. *B. J. Meehan*

VIOLET PARK 5 b.m. Pivotal 124 – Petonellajill 73 (Petong 126) [2006 99+: p8g² 9s*   **105** 8m⁶ Jun 21] rangy mare: useful performer: benefited from exaggerated waiting tactics when winning Stan James Dahlia Stakes at Newmarket in May by ½ length from Royal Alchemist: respectable sixth to Soviet Song in Windsor Forest Stakes at Royal Ascot subsequent start: stays 9f: acts on polytrack, firm and soft going: seems quirky, at least under pressure (has carried head awkwardly/jinked sharply left). *B. J. Meehan*

VIOLET'S PRIDE 2 b.f. (Apr 25) Kyllachy 129 – Majalis 79 (Mujadil (USA) 119)   **62** [2006 5m⁵ 5m 6.1f⁴ 5f² 5m 5d² 5.2d⁶ p5.1g Oct 30] 1,500Y: compact filly: fourth foal: dam 5f winner who stayed 1m: modest maiden: second at Leicester and Musselburgh: may prove best at 5f: acts on firm ground: tends to hang right, and crashed through rail at Warwick second start. *S. Parr*

VIOLETTE 3 b.f. Observatory (USA) 131 – Odette 72 (Pursuit of Love 124) [2006 106:   **100** 8v⁶ 7m p7g⁵ 6d⁶ p8.6m Nov 21] neat filly: useful performer: best effort in 2006 when sixth to Rising Shadow in listed race at Windsor penultimate outing, forcing pace: well below form in minor event at Wolverhampton final start: should stay 1m: acts on firm and good to soft going: tried blinkered: has hung left/flashed tail. *Sir Mark Prescott*

VIRGINIA PLAIN 3 ch.f. Vettori (IRE) 119 – Iyavaya (USA) 85 (Valiant Nature   **43** (USA) 118) [2006 10d 9s 12.1m⁵ 10.9m 10.1f 11.5f 8f⁶ 7f⁶ 7m⁴ 7d f8g Oct 12] 2,800Y: tall filly: first foal: dam, 5f winner, became one to treat with caution: poor maiden: blinkered last 4 starts. *Miss Diana Weeden*

VIRGINIA REEL 2 b.f. (Jan 18) King's Best (USA) 132 – Golden Dancer (IRE)   **55** (Sadler's Wells (USA) 132) [2006 7.1m 7d⁴ p7g f8g Nov 28] strong, lengthy filly: fourth foal: half-sister to 3-y-o Expert Witness: dam unraced sister to smart Irish 1¼m/1½m winner Briolette and half-sister to top-class 1¼m/1½m performer Pilsudski: modest maiden: form only on first 2 starts: should be suited by 1m+. *M. Johnston*

VIRGINIA ROSE (IRE) 3 b.f. Galileo (IRE) 134 – Rispoto 58 (Mtoto 134) [2006   **70** 55p: 8d⁶ 8.1s⁶ p9.5g 12.1m² 16.2m 14m⁶ 14.1g⁶ 9.9m 14d* 12d* p12g³ f14g⁴ Nov 20] big filly: fair performer: won banded race in October (by 6 lengths) and handicap in November, both at Musselburgh: stays 1¾m: acts on all-weather, good to firm and good to soft going: sold 95,000 gns. *J. G. Given*

VIRGIN ISLANDS (IRE) 3 b.f. Sadler's Wells (USA) 132 – Antiguan Jane 71 **79** (Shirley Heights 130) [2006 p10g² 9.7d² 12s³ May 20] 110,000Y: fourth foal: half-sister to winner in USA by Crafty Prospector: dam, easily best effort at 1¼m, sister to useful performer up to 1¾m (also US Grade 3 11f winner) Party Season: placed in 3 maidens, best effort when 2 lengths second to Time On at Folkestone on second outing: should be suited by 1½m: sent to Australia. *M. A. Jarvis*

VIRTUOSITY 3 ch.f. Pivotal 124 – Virtuous 92 (Exit To Nowhere (USA) 122) [2006 **88** 10f* 10.4f⁶ 10.2f 10d p8g Nov 5] strong, rangy filly: has scope: fourth foal: closely related to 4-y-o Iceman and half-sister to 2 winners, including fairly useful 1¼m winner Peace (by Sadler's Wells): dam, 2-y-o 1m winner who stayed 11.5f, out of half-sister to 2000 Guineas winner Entrepreneur: fairly useful performer: won maiden at Pontefract (by 5 lengths) in July: went wrong way in handicaps after: stays 1¼m: acts on firm ground: withdrawn after unruly in stall on intended debut at 2 yrs (blanketed for stall entry and attended by stable representative at start at Pontefract). *Sir Michael Stoute*

VI'S BOY 3 b.g. Almushtarak (IRE) 122 – Risk The Witch (Risk Me (FR) 127) [2006 **–** p7.1g p9.5g p8.6g Feb 27] well held in maidens. *W. M. Brisbourne*

VISCOUNT ROSSINI 4 b. or br.g. Rossini (USA) 118 – Spain 62 (Polar Falcon **43** (USA) 126) [2006 –: p16.5g p9.5g⁵ p8.6g⁴ p8.6g⁶ 12f 10m 8m 10.2m⁵ Sep 7] poor maiden: trained by E. McMahon on reappearance only: stays 1¼m: acts on polytrack and good to firm ground: tried in visor/cheekpieces. *A. W. Carroll*

VISINDAR 3 ch.c. Sinndar (IRE) 134 – Visor (USA) (Mr Prospector (USA)) [2006 **118** 96P: 9g* 10m⁵ Jun 3]
　　To paraphrase Senator Bentsen, 'Shergar won the Guardian Classic Trial by ten lengths. Shergar won the Chester Vase by twelve lengths. Shergar won the Derby by ten lengths. Visindar, you are no Shergar.' Derby Day brought the same withering response to the comparisons widely drawn between Visindar and his owner's legendary 1981 Derby winner as the put-down delivered by the late Lloyd Bentsen to Vice President Dan Quayle before the 1988 US Election after Quayle likened himself to President Jack Kennedy. 'Senator, I served with Jack Kennedy. I knew Jack Kennedy. Jack Kennedy was a friend of mine. Senator, you are no Jack Kennedy,' said Bentsen to the widespread approval of the studio audience to the live television debate.
　　Hindsight is one thing. Few people bristled before Epsom about the parallels being drawn with Visindar's potential, or with those being drawn with his sire, the 2000 Derby winner Sinndar, also owned by the Aga Khan. Visindar was cut to 8/1 favourite for Epsom even before he made his reappearance, the hype surrounding him fuelled partly by the comments of stable jockey Christophe Soumillon, quoted in the spring as saying of Visindar's recent work: 'On only two previous occasions has a horse given me such a feeling. Those were Dalakhani and Hurricane Run.' The winning distances recorded by Visindar on his first two outings as a three-year-old couldn't quite compare with Shergar's, but the style of Visindar's performances was enough to keep the bandwagon rolling. A four-length winner of a newcomers race over a mile at Saint-Cloud in November on his only

Prix Greffulhe Mitsubishi Motors, Saint-Cloud—Visindar consolidates his position as Derby favourite; Onerous (left), Hello Sunday and the grey Zatonic chase him home

start as a juvenile, he barely came off the bridle when landing the odds by two and a half lengths in a minor event at Longchamp in April. Visindar was just as impressive when maintaining his unbeaten record in front of an unusually large travelling contingent of the British media on his final appearance before the Derby back at Saint-Cloud in May. Opposed by five rivals, he started at 5/1-on, coupled with his pacemaker, in the Group 2 Prix Greffulhe Mitsubishi Motors, scoring by a long-looking four lengths without being hard ridden.

Visindar showed himself to be a fine mover as well as a relaxed sort at Saint-Cloud, all of which looked sure to stand him in good stead at Epsom. However, despite looking in excellent shape again and taking the preliminaries with aplomb, the bubble was burst in the Derby. Possibly significantly, he moved far less fluently to post on his second run on firmish ground, and, starting at 2/1, the shortest-priced favourite in the race since Entrepreneur was beaten at 6/4-on in 1997, he was never travelling smoothly. Set a fair bit to do by Soumillon, Visindar edged left down the camber under pressure, making things difficult for his jockey. Eased a little once held, he finished only fifth to Sir Percy, two lengths behind the four horses involved in the photo. Visindar was reportedly very jarred up afterwards, suffering a sesamoid problem, and wasn't seen out again.

			Grand Lodge	Chief's Crown
	Sinndar (IRE)		(ch 1991)	La Papagena
	(b 1997)		Sinntara	Lashkari
Visindar			(b 1989)	Sidama
(ch.c. 2003)			Mr Prospector	Raise A Native
	Visor (USA)		(b 1970)	Gold Digger
	(b 1989)		Look	Spectacular Bid
			(b 1984)	Tuerta

Visindar's sire Sinndar was a fair way behind the prodigious Shergar in terms of his performance on Derby Day, but he improved as the season went on, adding the Irish Derby and the Arc de Triomphe as well as the Prix Niel. Visindar might never have got his chance at Epsom but for the death of his breeder Jean-Luc Lagardere, whose bloodstock interests were sold to the Aga Khan in 2005. Visindar's dam Visor was a six-furlong winner in the States out of a half-sister to the Kentucky Derby/Belmont winner Swale, and she has produced several other good performers. Visionary, Visionnaire and Visorama (all by Linamix), and Visorhill (by Danehill), were all smart winners between a mile and ten and a half furlongs in France. Visionnaire has since produced Visionario, winner of his first three races as a two-year-old for the Aga Khan in 2006, including the Prix La Rochette, before finishing only sixth when favourite for the Prix Jean-Luc Lagardere. Visionario still looks a good prospect for 2007, but it remains to be seen if the Derby experience has left a lasting mark on Visindar. A tall, angular colt, who had a skin rash, reportedly due to an allergy, on his last two starts, Visindar is still lightly raced and well worth another chance to confirm the promise of his first three runs. He acts on soft and good to firm ground. *A. Fabre, France*

VISIONARIO (IRE) 2 b.c. (Mar 28) Spinning World (USA) 130 – Visionnaire (FR) **109 p**
112 (Linamix (FR) 127) [2006 6g* 7s* 7g* 7m⁶ Oct 1] leggy, attractive colt: third foal: closely related to French 11f winner Vison Celebre (by Peintre Celebre): dam, French 1m winner who stayed 10.5f, half-sister to 3-y-o Visindar: impressed in winning his first 3 races, newcomers event at Maisons-Laffitte (by 4 lengths) in July, listed race at Deauville (by 2½ lengths from Striving Storm) in August and Prix La Rochette at Longchamp (comfortably by length from Holocene) in September: favourite but just beginning to go in coat when only sixth of 9 to Holy Roman Emperor in Prix Jean-Luc Lagardere at Longchamp final start, keeping on steadily: will stay 1m: acts on soft going: worth another chance to confirm earlier potential. *A. Fabre, France*

VISIONIST (IRE) 4 b.g. Orpen (USA) 116 – Lady Taufan (IRE) (Taufan (USA) 119) **108**
[2006 98: p7g* 7m 7g Oct 13] big, lengthy, good-topped gelding: good walker: has a quick action: useful handicapper: chipped a bone final 2-y-o start: left J. Osborne after final start at 3 yrs and gelded: lightly raced in 2006, but better than ever when winning at Kempton in April by 2½ lengths from Presumptive, despite losing off-fore shoe: eased as if amiss both starts after (5 months apart): raced at 6f/7f: acts on polytrack and good to firm ground: free-going sort, usually waited with: sold 25,000 gns, joined M. Al Muhairi in UAE. *Pat Eddery*

The Sportsman Newspaper Champagne Stakes, York—Vital Equine (right) makes it three from three and gives trainer Eoghan O'Neill a second successive win in the race; Eagle Mountain (left) gets up to deprive Cockney Rebel (centre) of second place

VITAL EQUINE (IRE) 2 b.c. (Feb 24) Danetime (IRE) 121 – Bayalika (IRE) (Selkirk (USA) 129) [2006 6m* 6m* 7g* 7m³ 7d⁵ 8g Oct 29] 18,000F, 24,000Y: big, strong colt: second foal: dam unraced granddaughter of Arc runner-up Behera: smart performer: won maiden at Newcastle in May, minor event at Yarmouth in June and The Sportsman Newspaper Champagne Stakes at York (by ½ length from Eagle Mountain, taking strong hold but finding extra) in September: good efforts next 2 starts, when 2¾ lengths third to Holy Roman Emperor in Prix Jean-Luc Lagardere at Longchamp and 3 lengths fifth to Teofilo in Dewhurst Stakes at Newmarket: below form in Criterium International at Saint-Cloud final outing, fading from over 1f out: may prove best at 7f: acts on good to firm and good to soft going: often tongue tied. *E. J. O'Neill* **113**

VITAL STATISTICS 2 br.f. (Apr 19) Indian Ridge 123 – Emerald Peace (IRE) 103 (Green Desert (USA) 127) [2006 5g⁴ 5d² 5m⁶ 6g⁴ 6m* 6m² 6m* 6d Sep 29] 54,000Y: good-bodied filly: third foal: half-sister to 6f (including at 2 yrs) winner Emerald Lodge (by Grand Lodge) and 3-y-o Spiritual Peace, both fairly useful: dam, 5f (including at 2 yrs) winner, out of half-sister to Cheveley Park winner Embassy: useful performer: won maiden at Newbury in July and listed race at Salisbury (best effort when beating Wid by ½ length, held up and getting on top close home despite again edging left) in August: also ran well when ½-length second to Scarlet Runner in Princess Margaret Stakes at Ascot in between: below form in Cheveley Park Stakes at Newmarket final outing: likely to prove best at 5f/6f: acts on good to firm going, probably on good to soft: has been bandaged fore joints: nervy sort, though has run well when sweating. *D. R. C. Elsworth* **102**

VITAL TRYST 2 ch.g. (Apr 20) Pivotal 124 – Splicing 82 (Sharpo 132) [2006 7d Oct 10] 40/1, always behind in maiden at Leicester: subsequently gelded. *J. G. Given* **–**

VITZNAU (IRE) 2 b.c. (Apr 5) Val Royal (FR) 127 – Neat Dish (CAN) 90 (Stalwart (USA)) [2006 p6g⁴ 6d 6f³ 6d⁶ 5m⁴ 6g* Oct 16] €29,000F, €32,000Y: tall, useful-looking colt: has scope: half-brother to several winners, including 1m (at 2 yrs) to 1¾m winner Riddlesdown (by Common Grounds) and useful Irish 7f (at 2 yrs) and 1¼m winner Fill The Bill (by Bob Back): dam, Irish 2-y-o 6f winner, stayed 7f: fair performer: often shaped well prior to winning maiden at Windsor in October by short head: will be suited by 7f: acts on firm going. *R. Hannon* **79 +**

VIVA VOLTA 3 b.g. Superior Premium 122 – La Volta 86 (Komaite (USA)) [2006 74: 7.5d* 8g⁶ 6d³ 7g⁵ 7m² 7m³ 7s Oct 14] strong, lengthy gelding: fair handicapper: won at Beverley in April: stays 7.5f: acts on good to firm and good to soft going: blinkered once at 2 yrs. *T. D. Easterby* **77**

VIVI BELLE 2 b.f. (Jan 10) Cadeaux Genereux 131 – Locharia 91 (Wolfhound (USA) 126) [2006 p6s Dec 14] 35,000Y: first foal: dam, 2-y-o 5f winner, out of half-sister to **–**

Nunthorpe winners Lochsong and Lochangel: green, 10½ lengths eighth to Pixie Ring in maiden at Wolverhampton. *M. L. W. Bell*

VIXEN VIRAGO 3 ch.f. Foxhound (USA) 103 – Le Pin 59 (Persian Bold 123) [2006 –: 6.1s p7g 10.2g p13.9g⁵ p8g p8g Dec 10] quite good-topped filly: little form. *Jane Southcombe*

VIZIONARY 2 b.f. (Mar 18) Observatory (USA) 131 – Zietunzeen (IRE) 99 (Zieten (USA) 118) [2006 5g 5.1g 6.1g 5g⁶ 5d f6g⁶ Nov 15] 15,000Y: compact filly: first foal: dam 2-y-o 6f winner: poor maiden: probably stays 6f: sweating/on edge fourth start. *Mrs P. Sly*

VIZULIZE 7 b.m. Robellino (USA) 127 – Euridice (IRE) 66 (Woodman (USA) 126) [2006 –, a66: p9.5g⁵ p8.6g⁶ p7.1g p10g May 8] good-topped mare: modest performer: effective at 8.6f to easy 1½m: acts on all-weather, firm and good to soft going: tried blinkered/visored: sometimes finds little. *A. W. Carroll*

VLASTA WEINER 6 b.g. Magic Ring (IRE) 115 – Armaiti 78 (Sayf El Arab (USA) 127) [2006 –, a66: p7.1g 5g p7.1g p6m p6g p6g f6g p6g³ f6g⁵ Dec 29] fair performer at 5 yrs, modest in 2006: stays 7f: acts on all-weather, raced mainly on good ground or firmer on turf: blinkered. *J. M. Bradley*

VODKA LUGE 2 ch.f. (Mar 1) Inchinor 119 – Turn To Vodka (FR) (Polish Precedent (USA) 131) [2006 p7g 7g⁵ p8g 8g⁶ p7g⁴ a8g⁴ Dec 10] 10,000Y: lengthy, workmanlike filly: third foal: dam unraced half-sister to smart French performer up to 12.5f Fabulous Hostess: modest maiden: sold from J. Hills 1,200 gns before final start: stays 1m: acts on polytrack/dirt. *Annika Kallse, Sweden*

VODKAT 2 ch.f. (Feb 16) Kyllachy 129 – Ebba 88 (Elmaamul (USA) 125) [2006 5m 5s 5g 6g⁵ 6s Aug 28] 11,000F, 13,000Y: useful-looking filly: third foal: dam 2-y-o 5f/6f winner: little form: blinkered final start. *N. Tinkler*

VODKATINI 3 b.g. Bertolini (USA) 125 – Cold Blow 67 (Posse (USA) 130) [2006 73: p7.1g⁶ 8.3g⁶ 8.2d⁵ 8.3m⁴ 8.1m 10f⁵ p10g p8.6f Aug 30] big, close-coupled gelding: fair maiden handicapper: should stay 1¼m: acts on polytrack, good to firm and good to soft ground: blinkered/visored: sold 10,000 gns. *P. J. Makin*

VOICE 2 b.f. (Mar 23) Zamindar (USA) 116 – Seven Sing (USA) 83 (Machiavellian (USA) 123) [2006 p6m⁴ Nov 9] second foal: half-sister to winner in Hungary by Dansili: dam, 2-y-o 6f winner, closely related to high-class miler Distant View: 11/1, encouraging 2¾ lengths fourth to Golden Desert in maiden at Wolverhampton, taking strong hold in rear after sluggish start and not knocked about to close up in straight: should do better. *H. R. A. Cecil*

VOICE MAIL 7 b.g. So Factual (USA) 120 – Wizardry 83 (Shirley Heights 130) [2006 84, a–: p8g 8d 10.2g² 8f⁵ 10f 8m 10f⁴ 10.5f 10m⁴ 8f³ 9.9m⁵ 10m p8.6g p12g Dec 20] useful-looking gelding: fairly useful handicapper on turf, modest on all-weather: left A. Balding 5,500 gns after twelfth outing: seems to stay 11.7f: acts on polytrack and firm going, probably on soft: usually visored/blinkered: held up. *P. Howling*

VOLAIRE 4 b.f. Zaha (CAN) 106 – Appelania 63 (Star Appeal 133) [2006 p9.5g⁴ 10m 9.9g p12g Jun 6] 12,000Y: leggy filly: seventh foal: half-sister to 2 winners, including fairly useful 1m (at 2 yrs) to 1½m winner Domappel (by Domynsky): dam 1m winner: well held in bumper: modest maiden: easily best effort on debut: tongue tied final start. *A. J. Lidderdale*

VOL DE NUIT 5 gr.h. Linamix (FR) 127 – Bedside Story 104 (Mtoto 134) [2006 114: 9.9s³ 12m³ 10.5m 10m⁵ Nov 5] tall horse: smart performer: trained by L. Brogi in Italy prior to 2006: third in listed race at Goodwood (behind Blue Monday) and Gran Premio di Milano (behind Shamdala) first 2 starts: below form both subsequent outings, in Rose of Lancaster Stakes at Haydock (visored, hung badly on bend) and Premio Roma at Rome: stays 1½m: acts on firm and good to soft ground, probably on soft. *L. M. Cumani*

VOLERIS PEARL 2 b.f. (Mar 10) Voleris (FR) 121 – Maureen's Hope (USA) (Northern Baby (CAN) 127) [2006 p7g Nov 22] third foal: half-sister to 3-y-o Medfae: dam 1m to 11f (minor stakes) winner in USA: 20/1, seventh to Boscobel in maiden at Kempton: likely to be suited by 1m. *C. F. Wall*

VONDOVA 4 b.f. Efisio 120 – Well Proud (IRE) (Sadler's Wells (USA) 132) [2006 –: 8.3f⁴ 5d 6m⁶ 5m 6m 5m Aug 16] tall, leggy filly: fairly useful performer at 2 yrs: little form since: tried in cheekpieces: has shown signs of temperament. *D. A. Nolan*

VONNIES NIGHT OUT 3 ch.c. Night Shift (USA) – Mountain Bluebird (USA) 79 – (Clever Trick (USA)) [2006 6v f11g Dec 29] no sign of ability, again tailed off when pulled up second start. *C. J. Teague*

VON WESSEX 4 b.g. Wizard King 122 – Gay Da Cheen (IRE) (Tenby 125) [2006 60§: 51 § 5.1d 6m² p6g 5.7f 6f 6.1f Jul 8] compact gelding: modest performer: effective at 5f/easy 6f: acts on good to firm and good to soft going: tried tongue tied/in cheekpieces: slowly away on reappearance: tends to hang: unreliable. *W. G. M. Turner*

VOODOO MOON 2 b.f. (Feb 11) Efisio 120 – Lunasa (IRE) 82 (Don't Forget Me 127) 89 [2006 5d⁵ 5m² 6v⁶ 6m* 6m³ 6d² 7m³ 7d² 6.5s Sep 22] 8,500Y: tall, close-coupled, quite good-topped filly: fourth foal: half-sister to 9.7f winner Moonfleet (by Entrepreneur) and a winner in Greece by In The Wings: dam, Irish 1¾m winner, out of half-sister to St Leger winner Moon Madness: fairly useful performer: won maiden at Ayr in July: placed in nurseries after, good second to Ronaldsay at York penultimate outing: effective at 6f/7f: acts on good to firm and good to soft going, well held on soft/heavy: races prominently. *M. Johnston*

VORTEX 7 b.g. Danehill (USA) 126 – Roupala (USA) 75 (Vaguely Noble 140) [2006 114 119: 7.6m² 8m⁵ a7f⁶ 8f⁵ 6m² 7g p7g p7g⁴ p7g³ p8g* p7g* Dec 22] big, good-bodied gelding: smart performer: reportedly suffered from back injury after fourth outing: won 2 minor events at Lingfield in December, both by a head from Red Spell: stays 1m: acts on all-weather/dirt and good to firm going (possibly not firm): usually tongue tied: sometimes blinkered/visored: often wears bandages: travels strongly, and tends to idle. *Miss Gay Kelleway*

VOSS 2 b.f. (Apr 28) Halling (USA) 133 – Valdara (Darshaan 133) [2006 8v⁶ 8.2d p8g – Dec 19] leggy filly: half-sister to 3 winners, including smart winner around 1¼m Musha Merr (by Sadler's Wells) and useful Irish 1¼m/11f winner Queen's Colours (by Rainbow Quest): dam useful French 2-y-o 1m winner: little form in maidens. *M. Johnston*

VOTIVE DANIEL (IRE) 3 b.c. Dansili 127 – Volte Face 61 (Polar Falcon (USA) 50 126) [2006 5.7m 6s p8g p10g Oct 23] form only when 6¼ lengths eighth to Dab Hand in maiden at Lingfield third start. *Simon Earle*

VRUBEL (IRE) 7 ch.g. Entrepreneur 123 – Renzola (Dragonara Palace (USA) 115) – [2006 –, a51: p16.5g f11g Feb 7] well-made gelding: modest performer: no form since 6-y-o reappearance: has worn headgear, tried tongue tied. *J. R. Holt*

W

WABRA (USA) 3 ch.f. Diesis 133 – Min Elreeh (USA) 68 (Danzig (USA)) [2006 8g 84 ? 11.5m May 13] $75,000Y: strong filly: sixth foal: half-sister to several winners, including fairly useful 2000 2-y-o 5f winner Golden Hind (by Seeking The Gold) and useful French 9f to 15.5f winner Allodial Land (by Woodman): dam once-raced daughter of Yorkshire Oaks winner Roseate Tern: better effort (possibly flattered) when 8½ lengths seventh of 10 to Sindirana in listed race at Lingfield second outing. *C. E. Brittain*

WACHIWI (IRE) 2 ch.f. (Jan 31) Namid 128 – Carpet Lady (IRE) 70 (Night Shift 67 (USA)) [2006 p6g 5m³ 5.7m⁴ p6g* Sep 10] 10,000Y, resold 18,000Y: second foal: dam, maiden who should have stayed at least 7f, out of sister to smart middle-distance stayer Shambo: fair form: further improvement when winning nursery at Kempton in September by ½ length from Spinning Crystal: stays 6f: acts on polytrack. *A. P. Jarvis*

WADDON (IRE) 3 b.g. Green Desert (USA) 127 – Baldemara (FR) (Sanglamore 67 (USA) 126) [2006 72: 5.7d⁴ 6m 7d⁵ 7f p7g Oct 15] fair maiden: below form after reappearance in 2006: may prove best at 5f/6f: acts on firm ground: wore cheekpieces/blinkers in 2006: signs of waywardness: sold 11,500 gns. *C. G. Cox*

WADNAGIN (IRE) 2 b.f. (Jan 20) Princely Heir (IRE) 111 – Band of Colour (IRE) 59 (Spectrum (IRE) 126) [2006 6m⁶ p6m⁶ p7.1g⁶ p6s⁴ p5g⁵ Dec 16] €20,000Y: second foal: dam once-raced daughter of useful 5f performer Regal Scintilla: modest maiden: probably stays 7f. *I. A. Wood*

WAGGLEDANCE (IRE) 4 b.g. Mujadil (USA) 119 – Assertive Lass (USA) (Assert 52 134) [2006 58: f6g p6g 6.1m 5f⁴ 5f 5m⁶ 5m 5d p5g p5.1m Nov 8] tall, lengthy gelding: modest maiden: should stay 6f: acts on firm going: tried in cheekpieces/blinkers: usually races prominently. *D. Carroll*

WAGTAIL 3 b.f. Cape Cross (IRE) 129 – Dancing Feather 72 (Suave Dancer (USA)   **101**
136) [2006 p8g* 10m³ p8g 8.3m* 8.5g* 8m⁴ p8g 8d* Sep 23] 120,000Y: leggy, attractive
filly: fourth foal: half-sister to 3 winners, including useful performer up to 1¼m Feathers
Flying (by Royal Applause), 7f winner at 2 yrs, and fairly useful 1m (at 2 yrs)/9.5f winner
Kings Empire (by Second Empire): dam, 1m winner who stayed 1½m, half-sister to smart
1¼m performer Spring Oak: useful performer: won maiden at Lingfield in March and
handicaps at Windsor in July, Epsom (hung left again) in August and Ascot (listed event,
by length from Grain of Truth, hampered 2f out before quickening well) in September:
stays 8.5f: acts on polytrack, good to firm and good to soft going: tongue tied last 5 outings: has worn crossed noseband. *E. A. L. Dunlop*

WAHCHI (IRE) 7 ch.g. Nashwan (USA) 135 – Nafhaat (USA) 91 (Roberto (USA)   **–**
131) [2006 69: 10f 9.9s 7.9m 10.1m 10g p8.6g Dec 1] strong, lengthy gelding: fair
handicapper in 2005: well held in 2006: tongue tied fourth outing: blinkered last 3 starts:
sometimes slowly away. *M. W. Easterby*

WAHOO SAM (USA) 6 ch.g. Sandpit (BRZ) 129 – Good Reputation (USA) (Gran   **86**
Zar (MEX)) [2006 80: p7.1g* p8.6g⁵ f8s 7.9g 8.3m³ 8m 8m² 8.3g 7.1s p9.5m⁴ p9.5g
p7.1g Dec 26] lengthy, good-topped gelding: fairly useful performer: won handicap at
Wolverhampton in January: effective at 7f to 9.8f: acts on all-weather, firm and good to
soft going: tried blinkered/in cheekpieces: front runner: inconsistent. *K. A. Ryan*

WAIHEKE ISLAND 2 b.f. (Mar 22) Winged Love (IRE) 121 – West of Warsaw (Dan-   **69 ?**
zig Connection (USA)) [2006 6d² 7.2g⁶ 6m 6s⁶ Sep 28] first foal: dam unraced: maiden:
second at Ayr on debut: poor form after: should stay 1m+. *B. Mactaggart*

WAINWRIGHT (IRE) 6 b.g. Victory Note (USA) 120 – Double Opus (IRE) (Petorius   **71**
117) [2006 75: p6g³ p6g 6m⁶ 7.1m p6m⁴ 6d p7.1g p6m f6g⁴ Nov 28] quite attractive
gelding: fair handicapper: effective at 5f to 7f: acts on all-weather, firm and soft going:
tried tongue tied/in cheekpieces/blinkered. *P. A. Blockley*

WAIT FOR THE LIGHT 2 b.c. (May 20) Fantastic Light (USA) 134 – Lady In Wait-   **80 p**
ing 113 (Kylian (USA)) [2006 8.3d⁶ p7.1g* Oct 30] 65,000Y: third foal: dam, 5f (at 2 yrs)
to 10.4f winner, closely related to smart stayer Savannah Bay: fairly useful form: much
improved from debut to win maiden at Lingfield, still learning but getting up close home
to beat Royal Rationale by neck: will benefit from 1¼m+: should continue to progress.
E. A. L. Dunlop

WAIT FOR THE WILL (USA) 10 ch.g. Seeking The Gold (USA) – You'd Be Sur-   **–**
prised (USA) 117 (Blushing Groom (FR) 131) [2006 82, a77: p16g p12g p12g p16g²   **a72**
p13.9g* p12g⁵ Nov 13] tall gelding: fair handicapper: won amateur event at Wolverhampton in November: stays easy 2m: acts on polytrack, firm and good to soft going:
tongue tied/visored once, usually blinkered: held up: sometimes finds little. *G. L. Moore*

WAITING FOR MARY (IRE) 3 b.f. Tagula (IRE) 116 – Lady Abigail (IRE) (Royal   **51**
Academy (USA) 130) [2006 65: 8.2d 6.1d 7g 7.1f⁵ 8.1m 8m⁶ Sep 4] small, workmanlike
filly: just modest form in 2006: stays 7f: acts on good to firm ground. *J. G. M. O'Shea*

WAIT WATCHER (IRE) 2 b.f. (May 16) Fath (USA) 116 – Campestral (USA) 97   **96**
(Alleged (USA) 138) [2006 6g² 7f³ 6g* 7d² Sep 19] €30,000Y: half-sister to several
winners, including smart winner around 11f Camporese (stayed 13.5f, by Sadler's Wells)
and 4-y-o Desert Move: dam 2-y-o 7f winner who stayed 11.5f: useful form: developed
well, won maiden at Newmarket in August and first past post in 27-runner Shelbourne
Hotel Goffs Fillies Five Hundred at the Curragh in September, latter by 1¼ lengths but
demoted having edged left and hampered Silk Blossom: will stay 1m. *P. A. Blockley*

WAKE UP MAGGIE (IRE) 3 b.f. Xaar 132 – Kalagold (IRE) 81 (Magical Strike   **110**
(USA) 114) [2006 108: 8s⁵ 7s² 8m 7m² 7d² Sep 8] medium-sized, close-coupled filly:
smart performer: good efforts in 2006 when runner-up in listed race at Newmarket
(beaten neck by Jeremy), Brownstown Stakes at Leopardstown (went down by a head to
Spinning Queen) and listed event at York (beaten 1¼ lengths by Silver Touch): stays 7f:
acts on soft and good to firm going: genuine. *C. F. Wall*

WAKEYS WIZZARD 2 ch.f. (Jan 30) Piccolo 121 – Golden Ciel (USA) (Septieme   **–**
Ciel (USA) 123) [2006 6m 7.5f⁴ 7.5f⁵ 7m⁵ 6d Aug 12] 2,500Y: big, workmanlike filly:
fourth foal: half-sister to 3 winners, including 1m (at 2 yrs) and 1½m winner Bold Blade
(by Sure Blade): dam 2-y-o 7f winner in Italy: little form. *M. E. Sowersby*

WALKING TALKING 2 b.c. (Jan 19) Rainbow Quest (USA) 134 – Wooden Doll   **83 p**
(USA) 98 (Woodman (USA) 126) [2006 7d² Oct 28] big, strong colt: second foal: dam,
French 2-y-o 6f winner, closely related to smart 6f/7f performer Welcome Friend and

half-sister to Poule d'Essai des Poulains second Rainbow Corner, out of Lowther Stakes winner Kingscote: 15/2, promising ½-length second to Mr Napper Tandy in maiden at Newmarket, soon prominent, sustaining challenge: useful prospect. *H. R. A. Cecil*

WALK IN THE PARK (IRE) 4 b.c. Montjeu (IRE) 137 – Classic Park 115 (Robellino (USA) 127) [2006 123: 10g 12d³ May 8] huge, rather leggy, good-topped colt: very smart performer at 3 yrs, 5 lengths second to Motivator in Derby at Epsom (reportedly jarred up in Irish Derby at the Curragh only outing afterwards): below best at Longchamp in 2006, faring better than on reappearance when 1¾ lengths third to Bellamy Cay in Prix d'Hedouville, more amenable than usual and finishing well: stays 1½m: acts on soft going: has had tongue tied: tends to pull hard. *J. E. Hammond, France* **107**

WALLY BARGE 3 b.g. Reprimand 122 – Linda's Schoolgirl (IRE) (Grand Lodge (USA) 125) [2006 p8g p8g p7g 8m p8g Sep 10] modest form: best effort on third outing. *D. K. Ivory* **61**

WALNUT GROVE 3 b.f. Forzando 122 – Final Rush 66 (Final Straw 127) [2006 52: 8s 7.5f* 8.3m³ 7.2m 7.1m³ 7m² Sep 16] strong, workmanlike filly: has a moderate, round action: modest handicapper: won at Beverley in June: should stay 1m: acts on firm going. *T. D. Barron* **65**

WALTZING WIZARD 7 b.g. Magic Ring (IRE) 115 – Legendary Dancer 90 (Shareef Dancer (USA) 135) [2006 –, a55: f7g Jan 17] tall, leggy gelding: modest performer: well held sole outing in 2006: tried tongue tied: usually wears cheekpieces: reportedly bled final start at 6 yrs. *A. Berry* **–**

WANCHAI LAD 5 b.g. Danzero (AUS) – Frisson (Slip Anchor 136) [2006 92§: 5d³ 5g 5.1f 5s 5m 5f 5m 5m⁵ 5d 6.1g* 6.1d* 5s⁵ 6v Oct 28] good-topped gelding: fairly useful handicapper: left D. Nicholls after seventh start: won in large fields at Nottingham in September and October: effective at 5f/6f: acts on firm and soft going: tongue tied last 4 starts. *T. D. Easterby* **88**

WANCHAI NIGHT 2 b.g. (Mar 1) Night Shift (USA) – Hot Tin Roof (IRE) 112 (Thatching 131) [2006 5f⁶ 5.9g⁵ 5f³ 5m 5m 7m³ 7m Sep 6] strong, good-bodied gelding: modest maiden: stays 7f: acts on firm going. *T. D. Easterby* **57**

WANDLE 2 b.c. (Apr 2) Galileo (IRE) 134 – Artistic Blue (USA) 109 (Diesis 133) [2006 7d⁵ Oct 28] 56,000F, 90,000Y: compact colt: third foal: half-brother to winner in Japan by Machiavellian: dam Irish 2-y-o 7f winner: 25/1 and green, fifth to Spanish Moon in maiden at Newmarket, nearest finish: will be suited by 1m+: should do better. *T. G. Mills* **79 p**

WANESSA TIGER (IRE) 2 ch.f. (Mar 27) Titus Livius (FR) 115 – Lominda (IRE) 80 (Lomond (USA) 128) [2006 7d p7g⁶ 8.3d³ Sep 25] 70,000Y: sixth living foal: half-sister to 2002 2-y-o 7f winner Skehana (by Mukaddamah) and 7-y-o Fayr Jag: dam 2-y-o 6f winner: modest form in maidens, all over 7f/1m (has sprinting pedigree). *M. R. Channon* **58**

WANNABE POSH (IRE) 3 b.f. Grand Lodge (USA) 125 – Wannabe 84 (Shirley Heights 130) [2006 64: 8.2s⁶ 10.2g 11.6g* 12g³ 11.8m* 11.9s³ 12m² 11.6s² 12d² Oct 27] well-made filly: fairly useful handicapper: won at Windsor in June and Leicester (by 5 lengths, despite hanging right and flashing tail) in July: good second last 3 starts: will stay 1¾m: acts on soft and good to firm going. *J. L. Dunlop* **94**

WANNA SHOUT 8 b.m. Missed Flight 123 – Lulu (Polar Falcon (USA) 126) [2006 49, a57: 8.6g f8g p8.6g* p8.6g p8.6g² p8.6g* p8g p9.5g 8m⁶ 8f p8g⁵ p8.6g p8.6g p8.6g p8g Dec 18] modest performer: won banded races at Wolverhampton in March and Kempton in May: below form after: stays 1¼m: acts on all-weather, firm and soft ground: tried in headgear/tongue tied: sometimes slowly away/wayward. *R. Dickin* **60 d**

WAR AT SEA (IRE) 4 b.g. Bering 136 – Naval Affair (IRE) 101 (Last Tycoon 131) [2006 86: 11.8d* p12.2g p12g⁶ p9.5g Dec 18] well-made gelding: just fair performer in 2006: won claimer at Leicester (claimed from P. Hobbs £12,000) in October: stays 1½m: acts on polytrack, good to firm and good to soft going: tried visored/tongue tied: has found little. *A. W. Carroll* **67**

WAR DANCER 4 b.g. Wolfhound (USA) 126 – Batchworth Dancer 67 (Ballacashtal (CAN)) [2006 –: p8g p5g Mar 2] well held in maidens. *E. A. Wheeler* **–**

WARDEN ROSE 3 ch.f. Compton Place 125 – Miss Rimex (IRE) 84 (Ezzoud (IRE) 126) [2006 7g 8.3f 7m 7g⁵ 8.3g⁶ Aug 26] lengthy, leggy filly: third foal: sister to useful 7f winner Warden Complex (later successful at up to 9f in Hong Kong) and half-sister to Irish 1m winner Baileys Best (by Mister Baileys): dam 6f (at 2 yrs) and 1m winner: **61**

modest maiden: probably stays 8.3f: acts on firm ground: raced freely last 3 starts. *D. R. C. Elsworth*

WARDEN WARREN 8 b.g. Petong 126 – Silver Spell 54 (Aragon 118) [2006 78§: **55 §** p7g p10g f8g 7f f7g 7f 7f⁶ 7m 7g 7d p8g⁴ p7g* f6g p8.6g³ p8g p7.1g p7g Dec 18] sparely-made gelding: modest performer nowadays: won banded race at Kempton in October: best around 7f: unraced on heavy going, acts on any other turf/all-weather: wears headgear: tends to start slowly/carry head awkwardly: sometimes races alone (reportedly unsuited by being crowded): unreliable. *Mrs C. A. Dunnett*

WAR FEATHER 4 b.c. Selkirk (USA) 129 – Sit Alkul (USA) 73 (Mr Prospector **52** (USA)) [2006 52: p10g p12g p16g⁵ p13g p16g p12g p12g⁵ p12g Dec 6] tall colt: modest maiden: stays 2m: raced mostly on polytrack. *T. D. McCarthy*

WARLINGHAM (IRE) 8 b.g. Catrail (USA) 123 – Tadjnama (USA) (Exceller (USA) **–** 129) [2006 59, a53: f7s p7.1g p8g Apr 3] strong gelding: modest performer: well held in 2006: blinkered once: tends to carry head awkwardly: sometimes races freely: reportedly bled fourth 7-y-o start. *P. Howling*

WARM TRIBUTE (USA) 2 ch.c. (Jan 28) Royal Anthem (USA) 135 – Gentle Mind **58 ?** (USA) (Seattle Slew (USA)) [2006 5d⁴ 7s Oct 10] better run in maidens when fourth at Catterick, possibly flattered: bred to stay 1m+. *W. G. Harrison*

WARNE'S WAY (IRE) 3 ch.g. Spinning World (USA) 130 – Kafayef (USA) 46 **70** (Secreto (USA) 128) [2006 p8g 10g 11g 11m Jun 10] 20,000F, 35,000Y: sturdy gelding: eighth foal: half-brother to several winners, including fairly useful 2002 2-y-o 7f winner Almaviva (by Grand Lodge) and useful French 2004 2-y-o 5.5f/7f winner Ascot Dream (by Pennekamp): dam, ran 3 times, half-sister to smart performer up to 2m Melrose Avenue: fair maiden on Flat: probably stays 11f: sold 5,000 gns and joined B. Powell, fair winner over hurdles. *R. Hannon*

WAR OF THE ROSES (IRE) 3 b.c. Singspiel (IRE) 133 – Calvia Rose (Sharpo 132) **–** [2006 p9.5g Nov 24] 25/1, last of 9 in maiden at Wolverhampton. *R. Brotherton*

WAR PENNANT 4 b.g. Selkirk (USA) 129 – Bunting 102 (Shaadi (USA) 126) [2006 **–** 70, a75: 11.6g Aug 7] fair performer at 3 yrs: well held only outing on Flat in 2006: visored/blinkered (looked none too keen) last 2 starts. *G. L. Moore*

WARREN PLACE 6 ch.g. Presidium 124 – Coney Hills 35 (Beverley Boy 99) [2006 **–** 48: 6d p7.1g f6g 7g p6g 6.9f Jul 21] leggy, sparely-made gelding: poor maiden: no form in 2006: often blinkered/visored. *A. D. Brown*

WARSAW PACT (IRE) 3 b.g. Polish Precedent (USA) 131 – Always Friendly 111 **95** (High Line 125) [2006 53p: 11.8d⁴ p12.2g² p12.2g* p12g* p12.2g* 14.8m² p13.9f² p11g⁴ Sep 1] lengthy gelding: has scope: developed into a useful handicapper, winning at Leicester in May and Wolverhampton, Lingfield and Wolverhampton again (by 5 lengths) in July: stays 1¾m: acts on polytrack, good to firm and good to soft going: sold 200,000 gns, joined P. Hobbs. *Sir Mark Prescott*

WASALAT (USA) 4 b.f. Bahri (USA) 125 – Saabga (USA) 83 (Woodman (USA) 126) **79** [2006 77: 16d⁶ 13.8g 9.2m⁵ 9.8s 10.3m⁴ 10f⁴ 10g⁶ p8.6m⁶ p8.6g² p9.5g* p9.5g² Dec 2] smallish, strong filly: fair handicapper: won at Wolverhampton in November: stays at least 10.3f: acts on polytrack and firm going: tried blinkered/in cheekpieces at 3 yrs: often starts slowly, sometimes markedly so. *D. W. Barker*

WASSEEMA (USA) 3 br.f. Danzig (USA) – Vantive (USA) (Mr Prospector (USA)) **111** [2006 77p: 7g 8m* 8g* 8.1g* 7g³ Sep 9] tall filly: improved into a smart performer, winning maiden at Goodwood in June and listed races at Ascot (worked up in preliminaries, beat Highway To Glory impressively by 7 lengths) in July and Sandown (beat Bahia Breeze convincingly by 1¼ lengths) in August: on edge, good length third to Iffraaj in Park Stakes at York final start: reportedly split pastern on gallops later in month and had 2 screws inserted: not sure to stay much beyond 1m: raced only on good/good to firm going: front runner (raced too freely on reappearance): stays in training. *Sir Michael Stoute*

WASSFA 3 b.f. Mark of Esteem (IRE) 137 – Mistle Song 112 (Nashwan (USA) 135) **76** [2006 72: 11.4m p12g⁶ 10m⁴ 12m 8.1d p8g⁵ p9.5m 8d² p8g⁵ p10g⁴ p12.2g Dec 27] tall, leggy filly: fair maiden: effective at 1m, seems to stay easy 1½m: acts on polytrack, good to firm and good to soft ground: races prominently. *C. E. Brittain*

WATAMU (IRE) 5 b.g. Groom Dancer (USA) 128 – Miss Golden Sands 80 (Kris 135) **91** [2006 p10g² Dec 20] strong, lengthy gelding: fairly useful handicapper: off over 2 years, good second at Lingfield only outing in 2006: stays 1½m: acts on polytrack and good to firm going: tried visored: has run in snatches. *P. J. Makin*

WATCHING 9 ch.g. Indian Ridge 123 – Sweeping 104 (Indian King (USA) 128) [2006 **59**
7g 6g p7g² Jun 15] neat gelding: modest performer nowadays: missed 2005: effective at
5f to 7f: acts on polytrack, heavy and good to firm going: tried in visor/cheekpieces:
sometimes early to post. *R. A. Fahey*

WATCHMAKER 3 b.g. Bering 136 – Watchkeeper (IRE) 86 (Rudimentary (USA) **–**
118) [2006 11m Sep 10] 20/1, last of 9 in maiden at Goodwood, slowly away and soon off
bridle. *W. J. Knight*

WATCH OUT 2 b.g. (Mar 3) Observatory (USA) 131 – Ballet Fame (USA) 79 (Quest **46 ?**
For Fame 127) [2006 6m 8m² 9m 7s Oct 10] neat gelding: form only when second in
claimer at Musselburgh: stays 1m. *M. W. Easterby*

WATCH OUT JESS 3 gr.f. Averti (IRE) 117 – Out Line 98 (Beveled (USA)) [2006 57: **54**
5.3f⁶ 6f 6f⁴ 5.3f 5.1m Sep 7] modest maiden: stays 6f: raced only on good ground or
firmer: once withdrawn at 2 yrs (unruly at start). *M. Madgwick*

WATEERA (IRE) 2 b.f. (Mar 24) Sakhee (USA) 136 – Azdihaar (USA) 81 (Mr Pros- **74**
pector (USA)) [2006 7d 8.3m⁵ 8.2g² Sep 26] big, lengthy filly: half-sister to several
winners, including 7f/1m winner (including at 2 yrs, and in UAE) Alshawameq (by Green
Desert) and 3-y-o Bunood, all useful: dam, 7f winner, half-sister to 1000 Guineas winner
Shadayid and smart performer up to 7f Fath: progressive in maidens, second to Kayah at
Nottingham: will stay 1¼m: has shown quirks. *J. L. Dunlop*

WATERLINE TWENTY (IRE) 3 b.f. Indian Danehill (IRE) 124 – Taisho (IRE) 96 **89**
(Namaqualand (USA)) [2006 85: p5g 5.1g 6.1f⁵ 6g⁶ 7m⁶ 7m* 6f⁴ 7m³ 7.6m² 8m⁵ 7.6g 8f⁶
p8g⁵ Dec 19] leggy filly: fairly useful performer: won handicap at Chester in July: several
creditable efforts after: stays 1m: acts on polytrack and firm going. *P. D. Evans*

WATERLOO CORNER 4 b.g. Cayman Kai (IRE) 114 – Rasin Luck (Primitive **73**
Rising (USA) 113) [2006 69: f11g⁶ 9.8m⁶ 11f³ 11.5g Jun 28] smallish, close-coupled
gelding: fair maiden: will probably prove best up to 1¼m: acts on all-weather and firm
going: tried blinkered. *R. Craggs*

WATER MARGIN (IRE) 2 b.c. (Feb 8) Shinko Forest (IRE) – Tribal Rite 95 (Be My **–**
Native (USA) 122) [2006 p7g Sep 27] behind in maiden at Lingfield (stumbled halfway).
T. G. Mills

WATERMILL (IRE) 3 b.g. Daylami (IRE) 138 – Brogan's Well (IRE) (Caerleon **–**
(USA) 132) [2006 f12g f11g⁴ Dec 14] never dangerous in 2 bumpers, and well held both
Flat starts. *D. W. Chapman*

WATER MILL (USA) 2 gr.c. (Mar 22) Unbridled's Song (USA) 125 – Capote Miss **88 p**
(USA) (Capote (USA)) [2006 p7g* Sep 2] $330,000Y: leggy, close-coupled colt: fifth
foal: half-brother to 3 winners in USA, including smart performer up to 8.5f Bull Market
(by Holy Bull): dam unraced half-sister to US Grade 1 1982 2-y-o 6f winner Share
The Fantasy: 7/1 and very fit, won minor event at Kempton by short head from Black
Rock, dictating pace and holding on all out: likely to stay 1m: open to improvement.
A. M. Balding

WATER PISTOL 4 b.g. Double Trigger (IRE) 123 – Water Flower 79 (Environment **–**
Friend 128) [2006 65: 16g Apr 25] leggy gelding: fair maiden at 3 yrs: fit from hurdling,
well beaten in handicap at Southwell only Flat start in 2006: probably stays 2m: best
efforts on good ground: has wandered. *M. C. Chapman*

WATERSIDE (IRE) 7 b.g. Lake Coniston (IRE) 131 – Classic Ring (IRE) 50 (Auction **97**
Ring (USA) 123) [2006 91: f8g² f6g⁵ 10g p8g f7g p8g⁴ 8s* p7g p8g⁴ p8g* 7m* 7.1m²
8m* 9m⁵ 7.1g* p8g 8d Sep 16] strong gelding: has a round action: useful handicapper:
won at Southwell in March, Kempton in May, Goodwood (2) in June and Sandown in
August: not at best last 2 starts: best at 7f/1m: acts on all-weather and any turf going:
tried tongue tied: sometimes slowly away: usually races up with pace: tough and reliable.
G. L. Moore

WATERWAYS (IRE) 3 b.f. Alhaarth (IRE) 126 – Buckle (IRE) 77 (Common Grounds **93**
118) [2006 99: 6d 5m⁶ 6f* 5m⁶ 5g⁵ 5v⁵ Oct 1] sparely-made filly: useful performer: didn't
need to be at best to win minor event at Cork in June: creditable fifth in listed races last 2
starts, behind Angus Newz at Hamilton and Peace Offering at Tipperary: speedy, raced
only at 5f/6f: acts on any going: game and consistent. *P. J. Prendergast, Ireland*

WAVERTREE BOY (IRE) 6 ch.g. Hector Protector (USA) 124 – Lust (Pursuit of **–**
Love 124) [2006 12d 14.1g Jun 29] rather leggy, good-topped gelding: useful performer
in 2003: well held both outings on Flat since. *D. R. C. Elsworth*

WAVERTREE ONE OFF 4 b.g. Diktat 126 – Miss Clarinet (Pharly (FR) 130) [2006 — 59: p10g Jan 4] quite good-topped gelding: maiden: well held only outing in 2006: blinkered last 4 starts. *D. R. C. Elsworth*

WAVERTREE WARRIOR (IRE) 4 br.g. Indian Lodge (IRE) 127 – Karamana **99** (Habitat 134) [2006 85: p7.1g p8g³ p8g⁴ p7g³ 8s 8.3g* 8d² 7s* 8.5g⁶ 7.1m* 7m 8s² 7g p8g⁴ p7g² p8g⁴ Dec 22] leggy gelding: useful handicapper: further improvement in 2006, winning at Windsor in April, Goodwood in May and Sandown (by 1½ lengths from Waterside) in June: good second to Army of Angels at York twelfth start: best at 7f/ 1m: acts on polytrack, soft and good to firm going: tried in cheekpieces (well held). *N. P. Littmoden*

WAX ELOQUENT 3 ch.f. Zaha (CAN) 106 – Wax Lyrical 94 (Safawan 118) [2006 **67** 7g⁵ Aug 18] lengthy filly: first foal: dam 2-y-o 6f winner: 22/1, green and wearing crossed noseband, 5¼ lengths fifth to Lady Stardust in maiden at Newbury, niggled along after slow start and fading. *C. G. Cox*

WAYMARK (IRE) 2 ch.c. (Apr 8) Halling (USA) 133 – Uncharted Haven (Turtle **71 p** Island (IRE) 123) [2006 8.3d² Oct 10] €260,000Y: second foal: dam useful French/ US 1m (including at 2 yrs) and 9f winner: 9/1, promising ¾-length second to Maid To Believe in maiden at Leicester, travelling strongly: likely to stay 1¼m: should improve. *M. A. Jarvis*

WAY TO THE STARS 3 gr.f. Dansili 127 – Reason To Dance 96 (Damister (USA) **75** 123) [2006 59p: 6g 7s 7m² 8m⁵ 7m⁴ 8m 7d² 7.1d p7g Nov 25] close-coupled filly, unfurnished at 3 yrs: fair maiden: should stay 1m: acts on good to firm and good to soft going: visored final start. *A. M. Balding*

WAYWARD SHOT (IRE) 4 b.g. Desert Prince (IRE) 130 – Style Parade (USA) 78 **63** (Diesis 133) [2006 68: 7.1v 7g⁶ 8m 8g 8f 8m 8.5m p8g³ f7g⁶ Dec 9] lengthy gelding: modest handicapper: left M. Easterby after seventh start: stays 8.5f: acts on polytrack, soft and good to firm going: front runner. *G. P. Kelly*

WAZIR (USA) 4 b. or br.c. Pulpit (USA) 117 – Top Order (USA) 94 (Dayjur (USA) **92** 137) [2006 99: 8m 6.5m⁴ a8s a8g* a8g* Nov 19] tall, leggy colt: fairly useful performer: respectable fourth to Kodiac, best of 3 starts in handicaps at Nad Al Sheba early in year: sold from J. Gosden 22,000 gns, won minor event at Jagersro and handicap at Taby in November: stays 1m: acts on polytrack/dirt and good to firm going. *L. Reuterskiold, jnr, Sweden*

WEAKEST LINK 5 b.g. Mind Games 121 – Sky Music 85 (Absalom 128) [2006 58, **56** a50: p6g³ f6g p6g³ 6g² 6m 6m 5.9g⁶ 6m² 5s² 5d 5f p5.1g f7m Oct 31] useful-looking gelding: modest maiden: effective at 5f to 7f: acts on all-weather, soft and good to firm going: usually wears headgear. *E. J. Alston*

WEBBOW (IRE) 4 b.g. Dr Devious (IRE) 127 – Ower (IRE) 71 (Lomond (USA) 128) **77** [2006 p8.6g² f7g* 8.2s³ 8d 9.8v⁵ May 21] tailed off in bumper: fair performer: won maiden at Southwell in March: stays 1m: acts on all-weather and soft going: made running first 3 starts. *T. D. Easterby*

WEBBSWOOD LAD (IRE) 5 b.g. Robellino (USA) 127 – Poleaxe (Selkirk (USA) **65** 129) [2006 65: p12g² p10g⁴ p10g⁵ p12.2g Mar 6] fair maiden: stays 16.5f: acts on polytrack, best turf run on good going: wore cheekpieces last 4 starts: has joined M. Bosley. *Stef Liddiard*

WEDNESDAYS BOY (IRE) 3 b.g. Alhaarth (IRE) 126 – Sheen Falls (IRE) 56 **62** (Prince Rupert (FR) 121) [2006 56?: p6g² 7.2v² p9.5g 8.3g³ 8.3m⁴ 10g* 10.1s⁶ Sep 4] modest handicapper: won at Ayr in August: stays 1¼m: acts on polytrack and heavy going: wore cheekpieces last 2 starts: hung left on reappearance. *P. D. Niven*

WEE CHARLIE CASTLE (IRE) 3 b.g. Sinndar (IRE) 134 – Seasonal Blossom **74** (IRE) (Fairy King (USA)) [2006 71, a60: p9.5g² 7d⁵ p9.5g⁵ 8m² 8g⁵ p10g* p12g 8m⁵ **a71** p9.5m p12g* p12g⁵ Dec 16] rangy gelding: fair performer: won handicaps at Kempton in August and November: stays 1½m: acts on polytrack, firm and good to soft going: tried visored at 2 yrs: reportedly lost a shoe eighth start: of suspect temperament. *G. C. H. Chung*

WEE ELLIE COBURN 2 ch.f. (Mar 27) Bold Edge 123 – Wathbat Mtoto 88 (Mtoto **57** 134) [2006 8g⁵ 8g 8.2s f6g² p6g² f7g⁵ Dec 23] sparely-made filly: seventh foal: half-sister to 3 winners, including fairly useful 1m winner Saladin (by Lahib) and UAE 6f winner Wathbat Mujtahid (by Mujtahid): dam 1¼m winner who stayed 1½m: modest maiden: left I. Semple after second start: runner-up at Southwell (nursery) and Wolverhampton: effective at 6f, probably stays 1m: acts on all-weather: hung badly third start. *A. Bailey*

WEEKEND FLING (USA) 2 b. or br.f. (Mar 23) Forest Wildcat (USA) 120 – Woodman's Dancer (USA) (Woodman (USA) 126) [2006 6m² 6m³ Jul 4] $120,000Y: second foal: half-sister to winner in Canada by Dixieland Band: dam, US 6f/7f winner, out of US Grade 1 9f winner Pattern Step: fair form when placed in maidens at Pontefract and Thirsk: will stay 7f. *M. Johnston* **67**

WEET A HEAD (IRE) 5 b.g. Foxhound (USA) 103 – Morale (Bluebird (USA) 125) [2006 74, a70: p12.2g p9.5g⁶ p9.5g 14.1s 10.2d³ 10.2m 10.2m Sep 7] quite good-topped gelding: modest performer: on downgrade: stays 1½m: acts on all-weather, firm and soft going: tried in cheekpieces/blinkers: won over hurdles in October. *R. Hollinshead* **67 d**

WEET AN HAUL 5 b.g. Danzero (AUS) – Island Ruler 79 (Ile de Bourbon (USA) 133) [2006 –: 7m Jun 4] sturdy gelding: no form since 2004: tried visored/in cheekpieces/tongue tied. *T. Wall* **–**

WEET FOR EVER (USA) 3 br. or b.g. High Yield (USA) 121 – Wild Classy Lady (USA) (Wild Again (USA)) [2006 9v 7.1m⁶ 8.1m⁴ 8.1m 7.1m p8.6g⁴ p7.1m⁵ p8.6g⁶ f12g³ p13.9g f12g³ p9.5g Dec 29] modest maiden: stays 1½m: acts on all-weather and good to firm ground. *P. A. Blockley* **59**

WEET IN LINE 2 gr.f. (May 4) Weet-A-Minute (IRE) 106 – Weet Ees Girl (IRE) 75 (Common Grounds 118) [2006 p5.1g⁵ p5.1g⁴ 6g Oct 16] half-sister to 6-y-o Weet Watchers: dam 2-y-o 5f winner: poor maiden: claimed from R. Hollinshead £6,000 second start: should stay 6f/7f. *K. J. Burke* **49**

WEET N MEASURES 4 b.g. Weet-A-Minute (IRE) 106 – Weet Ees Girl (IRE) 75 (Common Grounds 118) [2006 –: p6g f6g f6g p9.5g Feb 11] no form since 2 yrs. *T. Wall* **–**

WEET WATCHERS 6 b.g. Polar Prince (IRE) 117 – Weet Ees Girl (IRE) 75 (Common Grounds 118) [2006 49: p12.2g 7m⁵ 5.7f Jun 17] rather leggy, workmanlike gelding: poor performer nowadays: tried in headgear: usually races prominently. *T. Wall* **41**

WEET YER TERN (IRE) 4 b.g. Brave Act 119 – Maxime (IRE) 60 (Mac's Imp (USA) 116) [2006 61: f6g⁴ p6g f8g⁴ p9.5g⁴ p9.5g³ p12.2g p8.6g⁵ p7.1g⁶ p10g² p9.5g² p10g⁴ f8g p8.6g⁶ Dec 29] tall gelding: modest maiden: left P. Blockley after sixth start: stays 1¼m: acts on all-weather and good to firm ground: has worn headgear: tried tongue tied. *W. M. Brisbourne* **58**

WEE ZIGGY 3 b.g. Ziggy's Dancer (USA) 97 – Midnight Arrow 81 (Robellino (USA) 127) [2006 6d 7m 6.9f Jul 21] compact gelding: well held in maidens: unseated rider to post and troublesome at stall on debut. *D. Nicholls* **–**

WEIGHTLESS 6 ch.g. In The Wings 128 – Orford Ness 107 (Selkirk (USA) 129) [2006 116: 10g⁵ 9.9s⁶ 9.7m* 10d⁴ 10m⁶ 9d p10g p8.6m⁵ p9.5g Dec 31] sturdy, lengthy gelding: useful performer nowadays: won minor event at Folkestone (by 1¼ lengths from Take A Bow, having run of things) in June: also creditable efforts in Gordon Richards Stakes at Sandown (fifth to Day Flight) and La Coupe at Longchamp (promoted fourth behind Blue Monday): below form last 5 starts, leaving Mrs A. Perrett 46,000 gns after second of those: stays 10.5f: acts on good to firm and good to soft going: usually free-going front runner: hung right penultimate outing. *N. P. Littmoden* **109 d**

WELCOME APPROACH 3 b.g. Most Welcome 131 – Lucky Thing (Green Desert (USA) 127) [2006 73: 5d⁴ 5m* 5g² 5m⁶ 5g² 6m⁶ 5g² 5m⁶ 6.1g 6s Oct 24] sturdy, angular gelding: fair handicapper: won at Musselburgh in May: creditable second after: effective at 5f/6f: acts on good to firm going: tried blinkered (ran poorly). *J. R. Weymes* **75**

WELCOME RELEAF 3 ch.g. Most Welcome 131 – Mint Leaf (IRE) 78 (Sri Pekan (USA) 117) [2006 53: p9.5g p8.6g² p9.5g⁵ p8g 7m 6m⁵ 6f f8g² f8g⁶ Jul 31] close-coupled gelding: modest maiden, better on all-weather than turf: left Mrs L. Featherstone after third start: stays 8.6f: acts on all-weather: visored last 3 starts: has missed break/raced freely. *G. C. H. Chung* **52 a64**

WELCOME SPIRIT 3 b.g. Most Welcome 131 – Valadon 72 (High Line 125) [2006 –: 10f 12d Oct 8] quite good-topped gelding: no sign of ability. *J. S. Haldane* **–**

WELD IL BALAD (IRE) 2 b.c. (Jan 18) Alhaarth (IRE) 126 – Claustra (FR) 91 (Green Desert (USA) 127) [2006 7.5d* 8g⁶ Oct 12] 100,000F, 150,000Y: good-topped colt: good walker: second foal: dam, Irish 9f winner, half-sister to smart French sprinter Wessam Prince: fairly useful form: won maiden at Beverley in August: off 2 months, free to post and in race but improvement when sixth of Ladies Best in well-contested nursery at Newmarket: stays 1m: type to go on thriving as 3-y-o. *M. Johnston* **78 p**

WELL ARMED (USA) 3 b.c. Tiznow (USA) 133 – Well Dressed (USA) (Notebook (USA)) [2006 99: a7f* a8f a9g Mar 25] big, strong colt: useful performer: won minor **102**

event at Nad Al Sheba (by 3½ lengths from Testimony, making most) in January: well below that form on same course after, in UAE 2000 Guineas (reportedly lost a shoe) and UAE Derby: stays 1¼m: acts on polytrack/dirt and good to firm ground: blinkered once at 2 yrs: sent to USA. *C. E. Brittain*

WE'LL COME 2 b.g. (Mar 1) Elnadim (USA) 128 – Off The Blocks 55 (Salse (USA) 128) [2006 6s² 6d 7g² Oct 12] 15,500F, 60,000Y: big, heavy-bodied gelding: has a quick action: seventh foal: brother to 3-y-o Jaad and half-brother to 3 winners in Italy: dam maiden who stayed 1¼m: fairly useful form: shaped well all starts, at Newmarket, second in maidens (to Tudor Prince then Tredegar) either side of seventh of 28 to Caldra in sales race: will prove best up to 7f: gelded after final start: has plenty of scope, and will continue to progress. *M. A. Jarvis*   **93 p**

WE'LL CONFER 2 b.c. (Apr 18) Piccolo 121 – Medina de Rioseco 70 (Puissance 110) [2006 5f² p6g* 5m⁶ 5.2g³ 6s⁴ p6g³ 5d⁴ 6d Oct 28] 30,000Y: quite good-topped colt: third foal: half-brother to 6f winner Crown of Medina (by Fraam): dam, maiden, best efforts at 5f: useful performer: won maiden at Lingfield in May: better form when in frame in Super Sprint at Newbury (third to Elhamri), St Leger Yearling Stakes at York (fourth to Doctor Brown) and Sirenia Stakes at Kempton (third to Dhanyata) fourth to sixth starts: changed hands 100,000 gns, stiff task in Criterium de Maisons-Laffitte final start: will be best kept to 5f/6f: acts on polytrack and soft ground: promise on firm: tends to edge left: sent to Spain. *K. A. Ryan*   **96**

WELL ESTABLISHED (IRE) 4 b.g. Sadler's Wells (USA) 132 – Riveryev (USA) (Irish River (FR) 131) [2006 88: 10.1d⁴ 10.1m p12g⁵ 12g⁶ 11g Dec 17] sturdy, quite attractive gelding: fairly useful performer, lightly raced: creditable efforts first/third starts: left M. Jarvis 17,000 gns before final outing: stays 1½m: acts on polytrack and good to soft ground. *F. Turner, Italy*   **88**

WELL GUARDED (IRE) 3 b.g. Sadler's Wells (USA) 132 – En Garde (USA) 82 (Irish River (FR) 131) [2006 78p: 8.3g⁵ Aug 14] fair form in just 2 races, short of room when fifth to Very Far in maiden at Windsor only outing in 2006: dead. *C. R. Egerton*   **72**

WELL HIDDEN 3 b.f. Sadler's Wells (USA) 132 – Phantom Gold 119 (Machiavellian (USA) 123) [2006 11.9m³ 12g⁵ 12d* 12s Aug 24] big, raw-boned filly: sister to Oaks runner-up Flight of Fancy, 7f winner at 2 yrs, and half-sister to useful 2002 2-y-o 7f winner Dexter Star (by Green Desert) and fairly useful 1½m winner Daring Aim (by Daylami): dam 1m (at 2 yrs) to 13.3f (Geoffrey Freer Stakes) winner, also won Ribblesdale Stakes: fairly useful performer: still green, best effort when making virtually all in maiden at Newmarket in August: stays 1½m: acts on good to soft ground. *Sir Michael Stoute*   **92**

WELLINGTON HALL (GER) 8 b.g. Halling (USA) 133 – Wells Whisper (FR) 71 (Sadler's Wells (USA) 132) [2006 89: p12g⁶ 10m² 10g⁵ 12m 10m 12m 12s² 10g Oct 16] leggy gelding: fairly useful handicapper: effective at 1¼m to 1¾m: acts on polytrack and any turf going: tried in headgear: has run well when sweating. *P. W. Chapple-Hyam*   **87**

WELL VERSED 3 b.f. Most Welcome 131 – Versatility 61 (Teenoso (USA) 135) [2006 9.9g p12g 9.9d Sep 26] leggy filly: first foal: dam winner around 15f: modest form in maidens only on debut: pulled up at Goodwood final start (reportedly lame). *C. F. Wall*   **53**

WELSH AUCTION 2 ch.c. (Mar 28) Auction House (USA) 120 – Anneli Rose 56 (Superlative 118) [2006 6m 5d Sep 29] sturdy colt: no show in maidens. *G. A. Huffer*   **–**

WELSH CAKE 3 b.f. Fantastic Light (USA) 134 – Khubza 86 (Green Desert (USA) 127) [2006 60: p8.6g⁴ 8m 7g 7f² 7f* 8m² Sep 25] close-coupled filly: fair performer: improved in 2006, winning handicap at Folkestone in September: stays 8.6f: acts on polytrack and firm ground: blinkered/tongue tied of late. *Mrs A. J. Perrett*   **76**

WELSH DRAGON 3 b.g. Cape Cross (IRE) 129 – Blorenge (Prince Sabo 123) [2006 –: p7g³ p7g² p7g³ p8g³ 7d 8f a8g 8d² a8g² 8g⁶ a8s⁵ a8g⁶ a12g⁶ Dec 10] small, close-coupled gelding: fair handicapper: won at Lingfield in January: placed after on same course (3 times) (left A. Balding 8,000 gns after sixth start) and at Övrevoll and Taby for new stable: stays 1m: acts on polytrack/dirt and soft ground: wore cheekpieces on fourth start. *O. Stenstrom, Sweden*   **66**

WELSH EMPEROR (IRE) 7 b.g. Emperor Jones (USA) 119 – Simply Times (USA) 64 (Dodge (USA)) [2006 116: 6g* 6d 7d* 7g 7m² 7d Oct 14] tall gelding: very smart performer: better than ever in 2006 (though not so reliable) and won minor event at Thirsk (by 2½ lengths from River Falcon) in April and Hungerford Stakes at Newbury (held on to beat Jeremy by ½ length) in August: ran well when dead-heating for second with Linngari, short neck behind Caradak, in steadily-run Prix de la Foret at Longchamp: dropped away tamely in Challenge Stakes at Newmarket final outing: effective at 6f/7f: **120**

The Sportsman Newspaper Hungerford Stakes, Newbury—seven-year-old Welsh Emperor shows the way home to his younger rivals; Jeremy (blaze), Caradak, Mac Love (right) and Royal Power are next

acts on good to firm going, raced mainly on good or softer (winner on heavy) since 2 yrs: formerly blinkered: often front runner. *T. P. Tate*

WELSH WHISPER 7 b.m. Overbury (IRE) 116 – Grugiar (Red Sunset 120) [2006 47: p7.1g p6g p8.6g⁴ p9.5g⁵ p8.6g⁵ p8.6g* 8.1d 8.1f p8.6g p12.2g⁶ Jul 17] modest performer: won banded race at Wolverhampton in April: seems to stay 9.5f: acts on all-weather and soft going: sometimes slowly away. *S. A. Brookshaw* **50**

WELSH WIND (IRE) 10 b.g. Tenby 125 – Bavaria 80 (Top Ville 129) [2006 68: p8g³ p8g Feb 4] strong, lengthy gelding: modest performer: stays easy 1¼m: acts on polytrack, firm and good to soft going: wears cheekpieces: usually tongue tied: sold 800 gns in March. *M. Wigham* **60**

WENDALS 3 br.f. Xaar 132 – Runelia (Runnett 125) [2006 68p: 6.1m 6.1g 8m 6g⁵ 5.1m Aug 28] quite good-topped filly: just modest maiden at 3 yrs: bred to be suited by 1m+: wore blinkers final start. *Rae Guest* **51**

WENDY'S BOY 2 b.c. (Apr 11) Elnadim (USA) 128 – Tatouma (USA) 79 (The Minstrel (CAN) 135) [2006 5.5d May 13] 5/1, better than result when well held in maiden at Warwick, chasing leaders from wide draw to past halfway (reportedly lost action). *R. Hannon* **–**

WENSLEYDALE STAR 3 b.g. Alzao (USA) 117 – Janiceland (IRE) 75 (Foxhound (USA) 103) [2006 64: f7g⁵ f8g⁶ 7f 10d⁵ 11g⁴ 11.1f 7.9m 9.8m³ 10m⁴ 12.1g⁴ Aug 1] smallish, strong gelding: poor maiden: stays 1½m: acts on good to firm going: wore cheekpieces third outing: joined B. Llewellyn. *T. D. Barron* **44**

WESSEX (USA) 6 ch.g. Gone West (USA) – Satin Velvet (USA) 103 (El Gran Senor (USA) 136) [2006 85, a96: p7.1g⁵ f6g² f7g² f6g* p8.6g p6g⁶ f8g² Dec 2] big, rather leggy gelding: useful handicapper, better on all-weather than turf: won at Southwell (by 3½ lengths from Glaramara, hanging right) in February: good second there third/final outings: effective at 6f to 1m: acts on all-weather, firm and good to soft ground: tried visored/tongue tied: sometimes slowly away. *P. A. Blockley* **100**

WESTBROOK BLUE 4 b.c. Kingsinger (IRE) 94 – Gold And Blue (IRE) (Bluebird (USA) 125) [2006 95: 5d⁴ 5d 5.2d 5.1g 5s 5v² p5.1g Dec 2] big, good-topped colt: fairly useful handicapper nowadays, better on turf than all-weather: should stay 6f: acts on all-weather, heavy and good to firm going: wore cheekpieces/tongue tied last 2 starts: inconsistent. *W. G. M. Turner* **87**

WESTCOURT DREAM 6 ch.m. Bal Harbour 113 – Katie's Kitty 42 (Noble Patriarch 115) [2006 63: 9.9f⁴ 9.8m⁴ 10.5m 8m² 8f⁴ 7.9f² Aug 15] workmanlike mare: modest handicapper: stays 1¼m: acts on polytrack, firm and good to soft going: blinkered second 5-y-o start: sometimes races freely: often races prominently. *M. W. Easterby* **58**

WESTCOURT PHOENIX 3 b.f. Josr Algarhoud (IRE) 118 – Boulevard Rouge –
(USA) 71 (Red Ransom (USA)) [2006 f11g 9.3m 7m f11g Dec 9] lengthy filly: third foal:
half-sister to 5-y-o Ego Trip: dam maiden who barely stayed 11f: no form: very mulish on
second outing (unseated rider on way to start): tried blinkered. *M. W. Easterby*

WESTERING HOME (IRE) 3 b.f. Mull of Kintyre (USA) 114 – Glympse (IRE) 59 **69**
(Spectrum (IRE) 126) [2006 71: 8.3m⁶ 8.1g 10f³ 12g⁴ 9.9m⁴ 10f p9.5g⁵ Dec 26]
€46,000F: good-topped filly: first foal: dam, maiden who stayed 9f, out of sister to dam
of Irish Derby winner Grey Swallow: fair performer: trained by D. Weld in Ireland in
2005, winning nursery at Gowran: several creditable efforts in handicaps in 2006: stays
1½m: acts on polytrack and firm going: has worn blinkers, including for win. *J. Mackie*

WESTER LODGE (IRE) 4 ch.g. Fraam 114 – Reamzafonic 46 (Grand Lodge (USA) **77**
125) [2006 79: 8g⁵ 10.3g³ 9.8m⁴ 10.1m 11.8m⁶ 10f² 10m p10g⁵ p12g p10g p13.9g Oct **a70**
30] big, close-coupled gelding: fair handicapper, better on turf than all-weather: should
stay 1¾m: acts on polytrack and firm going: tried blinkered/visored. *J. M. P. Eustace*

WESTERN ADVENTURE (USA) 2 b.c. (May 11) Gone West (USA) – Larrocha **83 p**
(IRE) 116 (Sadler's Wells (USA) 132) [2006 7m² Sep 5] sturdy, good-bodied colt: sixth
foal: closely related to fairly useful 1½m winner Golden Lariat (by Mr Prospector) and
half-brother to very smart 9f to 1½m winner Razkalla (by Caerleon): dam, 1¼m and 1½m
(Galtres Stakes) winner and third in Prix Vermeille, half-sister to Ardross: 14/1, encouraging second to Celtic Step in maiden at Leicester, soon niggled but going on well at
finish: will be suited by 1¼m/1½m: sure to improve and win races. *E. A. L. Dunlop*

WESTERN ROOTS 5 ch.g. Dr Fong (USA) 128 – Chrysalis 66 (Soviet Star (USA) **58**
128) [2006 64, a76: p10g³ p9.5g⁵ p9.5g³ p8.6g⁵ p12g 10.5f 8.3f p8.6g p7g p12.2g⁶ 10.9d⁶ **a76**
p9.5m³ p9.5m⁶ p8.6m⁸ p8.6g³ p9.5g⁶ p8.6g⁴ Dec 6] lengthy gelding: fair on all-weather,
modest on turf: won handicap at Wolverhampton in November: barely stays 10.8f: best
efforts on polytrack/good ground: wore cheekpieces 3 of last 4 starts, including when
successful: has run well when sweating. *M. Appleby*

WESTERN SKY 3 ch.f. Barathea (IRE) 127 – Western Heights (Shirley Heights 130) **56**
[2006 p6g⁴ p10g Feb 20] sister to smart 6f (at 2 yrs)/7f winner who stayed 1m Barathea
Guest, and half-sister to several winners, including useful 1m (at 2 yrs)/1¼m winner
Pinchincha (by Priolo): dam unraced half-sister to useful performer up to 1½m Startino:
better effort in maidens at Lingfield when fourth on debut: should be suited by 7f+: sold
17,000 gns in November. *J. Noseda*

WESTER ROSS (IRE) 2 b.c. (Feb 13) Fruits of Love (USA) 127 – Diabaig 76 (Preco- **77**
cious 126) [2006 7d⁴ Oct 28] 25,000Y: compact, close-coupled colt: sixth foal: half-
brother to fairly useful 1m winner Ailincala (by Pursuit of Love): dam 1m winner: 100/1,
looked fit and knew his job (always prominent) when fourth to Mr Napper Tandy in
maiden at Newmarket: will stay 1m. *J. M. P. Eustace*

WEST HIGHLAND WAY (IRE) 5 b.g. Foxhound (USA) 103 – Gilding The Lily –
(IRE) 58 (High Estate 127) [2006 10g 10.1s Oct 10] good-bodied gelding: fairly useful
performer at 3 yrs: unraced in 2005: well held both starts in 2006. *Mrs H. O. Graham*

WESTLAKE BOND (IRE) 4 b.f. Josr Algarhoud (IRE) 118 – Rania (Aragon 118) **43**
[2006 –: p7.1g p6g f8g 6f⁵ 5g f6g Nov 15] workmanlike filly: poor maiden: left B. Smart
after reappearance: stays 6f: wore cheekpieces last 3 starts. *G. R. Oldroyd*

WEST OF AMARILLO (USA) 3 b.g. Gone West (USA) – Navarra (USA) 68 (El **113**
Gran Senor (USA) 136) [2006 95: 8.1g³ 8g⁴ May 14] strong, attractive gelding: smart
performer: in need of race when close third to Ivy Creek in minor event at Sandown on
reappearance: best effort when 1¾ lengths fourth to Aussie Rules in Poule d'Essai des
Poulains at Longchamp following month: met with recurrence of a previous injury while
being prepared for St James's Palace Stakes and missed rest of season (also gelded): stays
1m: raced only on good/good to firm going: raced too freely second 2-y-o outing: stays
in training. *J. H. M. Gosden*

WESTPORT 3 b.g. Xaar 132 – Connemara (IRE) 100 (Mujadil (USA) 119) [2006 p8g⁴ **85**
f8g⁸ p7g⁴ 6d² 6g* 6g 6m⁵ 6g⁶ 6g 5d² Nov 3] €75,000Y: strong gelding: half-brother to
winning sprinter in Italy by Pursuit of Love: dam 2-y-o 5f winner: fairly useful performer:
won maiden at Southwell in February (left J. Gosden 35,000 gns after) and handicap at
Redcar in May: good short-head second to Blazing Heights in handicap at Musselburgh
final start: gelded after: winner at 1m, but has plenty of speed and will prove best at 5f/6f:
acts on all-weather and good to soft going. *K. A. Ryan*

WEST WARNING 2 b.g. (Apr 30) Warningford 119 – Westcourt Pearl 46 (Emarati –
(USA) 74) [2006 5g 5m 5d Oct 3] compact gelding: well held in maidens/claimer: blinkered: dead. *M. W. Easterby*

WEYBA DOWNS (IRE) 2 b.g. (Mar 4) Daggers Drawn (USA) 114 – Jarmar Moon **67**
(Unfuwain (USA) 131) [2006 p5g⁵ p5g⁴ 5g 5f p5g² 5m⁴ p5g⁵ p7.1g Nov 2] 25,000Y:
seventh foal: half-brother to fairly useful 2000 2-y-o 5f/6f winner who stayed 1½m Ash
Moon (by General Monash): dam ran 3 times: fair maiden: second in nursery at Kempton,
clear best effort: should be suited by 6f/7f: acts on polytrack. *J. R. Best*

WHALEEF 8 b.g. Darshaan 133 – Wilayif (USA) 75 (Danzig (USA)) [2006 12.1f Jun **–**
27] lightly raced on Flat nowadays and well beaten only start in 2006: wore cheekpieces/
tongue tie last 2 starts: fair chaser. *B. J. Llewellyn*

WHAT-A-DANCER (IRE) 9 b.g. Dancing Dissident (USA) 119 – Cool Gales 85 **77 §**
(Lord Gayle (USA) 124) [2006 80, a88: p7.1g⁵ 7m p7g⁶ 7.1m p7g⁶ 8.1g⁵ 8.1f⁵ 8.3f⁶ 7.1f*
p7g 7m³ 8.1m 8.1m 7.1m p7g p7g f7g Nov 15] sparely-made gelding: fair performer: left
D. ffrench Davis after fifth start: won handicap at Chepstow in July: stays 1m: acts on
polytrack, seems best on good going or firmer on turf: wears blinkers/cheekpieces:
sometimes slowly away: held up: sometimes finds little, and not one to trust. *R. A. Harris*

WHATATODO 4 b.f. Compton Place 125 – Emerald Dream (IRE) 47 (Vision (USA)) **60 d**
[2006 62: 8m² 7m 8f⁴ 8f 7f 8m Aug 9] angular, quite good-topped filly: modest handicapper: below form after reappearance: stays 1m: acts on firm going: visored final start:
usually races up with pace: none too reliable: sold 800 gns in October. *M. L. W. Bell*

WHAT A TREASURE (IRE) 2 ch.f. (Feb 23) Cadeaux Genereux 131 – Treasure **73**
Trove (USA) 62 (The Minstrel (CAN) 135) [2006 6.1f 6m⁴ 5.1m⁶ p6g Sep 27] 26,000Y:
unfurnished filly: seventh foal: sister to smart German 6f/7f winner Toylsome and half-
sister to 8-y-o Zhitomir: dam, maiden who stayed 7f, half-sister to useful 5f (Queen
Mary Stakes) to 1m (US Grade 2 event) winner Dance Parade: fair maiden: best effort
when fourth to Blue Rocket at Haydock: awkward leaving stall in nursery: will stay 7f.
L. M. Cumani

WHAT BUDGET 2 br.f. (Apr 27) Halling (USA) 133 – Baked Alaska 93 (Green Desert **55**
(USA) 127) [2006 6g 7g p7g Oct 11] strong filly: sixth foal: half-sister to 3 winners,
including useful 6f/7f winner Aleutian (by Zafonic) and fairly useful 2004 2-y-o 7f
winner Royal Jelly (by King's Best): dam 2-y-o 6f winner: modest form in maidens: sold
4,000 gns, sent to Norway. *B. J. Meehan*

WHAT DO YOU KNOW 3 b.g. Compton Place 125 – How Do I Know 91 (Petong **76**
126) [2006 78p: 6m p6g⁴ 5m⁶ p6g 8m 7.5g⁵ p6g⁵ Nov 5] sturdy gelding: fair performer:
stays 6f, probably not 7.5f: acts on polytrack: wore cheekpieces penultimate start, tongue
tied final outing: wandered third outing: sold £800. *G. A. Butler*

WHATIZZIT 3 b.f. Galileo (IRE) 134 – Wosaita 70 (Generous (IRE) 139) [2006 76p: **88**
p10g⁴ 10m² 10m² p12g² Sep 6] fairly useful handicapper: good second last 3 starts: stays
1½m: raced only on polytrack and good to firm going. *E. A. L. Dunlop*

WHATS YOUR GAME (IRE) 2 ch.g. (Mar 10) Namid 128 – Tahlil 46 (Cadeaux **–**
Genereux 131) [2006 6g Jul 7] neat gelding: last in maiden at Haydock.. *A. Berry*

WHAXAAR (IRE) 2 b.c. (Mar 27) Xaar 132 – Sheriyna (FR) (Darshaan 133) [2006 **–**
8.1m p8g p8g⁶ Nov 29] no solid form in maidens, continuing to look green: will stay
1¼m. *S. Kirk*

WHAZZAT 4 b.f. Daylami (IRE) 138 – Wosaita 70 (Generous (IRE) 139) [2006 101: **97**
10m a12s 10.1m⁴ Jun 29] quite good-topped filly: useful performer: reportedly suffered
stress fracture of foreleg after winning listed race at Royal Ascot at 2 yrs, and lightly
raced since: trained by D. Selvaratnam at Nad Al Sheba first 2 starts in 2006: below form
in listed event at Newcastle only other outing: bred to be suited by 1¼m/1½m: acts on
any turf going, well held on dirt. *P. W. Chapple-Hyam*

WHAZZIS 2 br.f. (Feb 7) Desert Prince (IRE) 130 – Wosaita 70 (Generous (IRE) 139) **78**
[2006 6.1m³ 6.5s⁴ p7g² p7.1g* Nov 14] 50,000Y: useful-looking filly: fifth foal: half-
sister to 3 winners, including 4-y-o Whazzat and 3-y-o Whatizzit: dam, third at 1½m from
3 starts, half-sister to Prix de Diane winner Rafha, herself dam of very smart sprinter
Invincible Spirit: fair form: in frame 3 times, including sales race at Ascot (fourth of 22 to
Indian Ink) before winning maiden at Wolverhampton by length from Scarlet Ibis: will
stay at least 1m: acts on polytrack, soft and good to firm going. *W. J. Haggas*

WHEELAVIT (IRE) 3 b.g. Elnadim (USA) 128 – Storm River (USA) 81 (Riverman **75**
(USA) 131) [2006 p7g 7g 8.3d⁶ 6.1f* 6g³ 7m p8g Dec 30] close-coupled gelding: third
foal: half-brother to French 2003 2-y-o 4.5f/5.5f winner Belle Entreprise (by Entrepreneur): dam, ran twice (runner-up at 1m), out of useful 6f/7f winner Storm Dove: fair
performer: won handicap at Nottingham in July: best efforts at 6f: acts on firm ground.
B. G. Powell

WHEELS IN MOTION (IRE) 2 b.c. (Apr 21) Daylami (IRE) 138 – Tarziyana 83 + (USA) 76 (Danzig (USA)) [2006 7d* 8s³ Sep 14] sixth living foal: half-brother to useful Irish 1¼m/1½m winner Taraza (by Darshaan) and winner in Italy by Bluebird: dam, Irish 7f winner, half-sister to Dante Stakes winner Torjoun: fairly useful form: won maiden at Newcastle in August by short head from Arena's Dream (pair 10 lengths clear): some improvement when third of 4 behind Tencendur and Massive in minor event at Ayr: will stay 1¼m. *T. P. Tate*

WHENWILLITWIN 5 b.g. Bluegrass Prince (IRE) 110 – Madam Marash (IRE) 51 56 (Astronef 116) [2006 56: p10g* p10g⁵ f11g p9.5g Apr 24] modest performer: won seller at Lingfield in January: stays 1¼m: acts on polytrack: in cheekpieces/blinkers 6 of last 7 starts. *J. S. Moore*

WHERE'S BROUGHTON 3 ch.f. Cadeaux Genereux 131 – Tuxford Hideaway 102 77 (Cawston's Clown 113) [2006 70p: p9.5g* p9.5g⁴ Dec 18] useful-looking filly: fair performer: won maiden at Wolverhampton in November: still green, good fourth on handicap debut there (hung left) final start: should stay 1¼m: acts on polytrack. *W. J. Musson*

WHERE'S SALLY 6 b.m. Polar Prince (IRE) 117 – Mustang Scally (Makbul 104) – [2006 p9.5g f8g p9.5g⁶ Mar 29] first foal: dam well beaten in 3 sellers: well held in bumpers, looking headstrong: no form in seller/maiden claimers. *J. Mackie*

WHIFFLE (USA) 2 b.f. (Feb 12) Red Ransom (USA) – Whist (Mr Prospector (USA)) 70 [2006 5g⁴ 6.1m* Jun 16] fourth foal: half-sister to winners in USA by Capote and A P Indy: dam, French 11.5f winner, sister to smart performer up to 1½m Wall Street and half-sister to St Leger winner Nedawi: fair form: better effort when winning maiden at Nottingham by ¾ length from Gazboolou: bred to be suited by 1¼m+. *M. Johnston*

WHINHILL HOUSE 6 ch.g. Paris House 123 – Darussalam 78 (Tina's Pet 121) [2006 77 d 93: f5g f5g p6g 5d⁵ 5d 5f 6d 5m² 5m⁵ 5m 6f⁵ 5m 5f³ 5d 6m 6f 5g Sep 27] strong gelding: fair handicapper: below form last 4 starts: best at 5f/easy 6f: acts on all-weather, firm and good to soft ground: usually wears cheekpieces: races up with pace. *D. W. Barker*

WHIPCHORD (IRE) 2 ch.f. (Apr 6) Distant Music (USA) 126 – Spanker 71§ (Suave 64 Dancer (USA) 136) [2006 5g⁵ 6.1g 5.1f 7f⁴ 6g² 6f Sep 18] 10,000Y: third foal: half-sister to 2004 2-y-o 7.5f winner Mastman (by Intikhab) and Irish 1m to 1¼m winner Skerries (by Dr Fong), both fairly useful: dam, irresolute maiden (stayed 1½m), out of smart performer up to 1¼m Yawl: modest maiden: second in nursery at Windsor: will stay 1m: acts on firm ground: has flashed tail. *R. Hannon*

WHIPPER IN 3 ch.f. Foxhound (USA) 103 – Come To The Point (Pursuit of Love 124) 45 [2006 62: p6g⁶ f5g Feb 7] sturdy, close-coupled filly: maiden: just poor form in 2006: stays 6f: acts on soft and good to firm going: visored final start: races prominently: hung right on reappearance. *P. C. Haslam*

WHISKEY JUNCTION 2 b.g. (Apr 22) Bold Edge 123 – Victoria Mill 59 (Free State 72 125) [2006 p5g³ p6g² 5m p5g⁴ p6g Jul 28] closely related to 7.5f winner Victory Spin (by Beveled), later 4.5f to 8.5f winner in USA, and half-brother to several winners, including 1m/1¼m winner Lara Falana (by Tagula): dam, maiden, best at 1¼m: fair maiden: stays 6f: acts on polytrack: has raced freely. *A. M. Balding*

WHISPERING DEATH 4 br.g. Pivotal 124 – Lucky Arrow 60 (Indian Ridge 123) 91 + [2006 76p: 12.4d 14s 14.1g 13.9m² 16f* 15m² 18f* 14.8d⁴ 12d 18d⁶ Oct 14] tall, good-topped gelding: fairly useful handicapper: won at Thirsk (by 5 lengths) and York (beat Lodgician 3½ lengths) in July: not clear run when good sixth of 31 to Detroit City in Cesarewitch at Newmarket final start: stays 2¼m: acts on firm and good to soft going: visored nowadays: tended to run in snatches sixth outing. *W. J. Haggas*

WHISPER INTHE WIND (IRE) 3 ch.f. King Charlemagne (USA) 120 – Persian 56 Mistress (IRE) (Persian Bold 123) [2006 64: 6f 6f 7g⁵ 7m f8g⁴ 8.5m⁶ 7m 6g 6m f7g Oct 12] neat filly: modest maiden: stays 7f: raced only on good going or firmer on turf: tongue tied final start. *Miss J. Feilden*

WHIST DRIVE 6 ch.g. First Trump 118 – Fine Quill (Unfuwain (USA) 131) [2006 – p16g Nov 8] big, lengthy gelding: maiden: well held only outing on Flat since 2004: tried blinkered. *Mrs N. Smith*

WHISTLE AWAY 3 b.g. Piccolo 121 – Miss Dangerous 70 (Komaite (USA)) [2006 62 p6g p6g² 7g⁶ Aug 17] strong, close-coupled gelding: modest maiden: likely to prove just as effective at 5f as 6f, didn't seem to stay 7f: acts on polytrack. *W. R. Swinburn*

WHISTLER 9 ch.g. Selkirk (USA) 129 – French Gift 99 (Cadeaux Genereux 131) 68 [2006 100: 5g 5g 5m 5g 5g 5.1s 5s⁵ 5.3m⁴ 5m 5m 5m⁶ 5g 5.1g⁵ 5.5m 5d 5.2m 5.1g*

5g 5m[6] 5.1m 5m 5.5d 5m Sep 21] angular, workmanlike gelding: has a quick action: fair handicapper: won at Nottingham in August: best at 5f: acts on any turf going: wears cheekpieces/blinkers: sometimes hangs left: often gets behind: none too consistent. *Miss J. R. Tooth*

WHISTLEUPTHEWIND 3 b.f. Piccolo 121 – The Frog Queen 64 (Bin Ajwaad (IRE) 119) [2006 –: 6v p6g 9s 7g[4] 8f[2] 8m* 7m* 8.1g 8f[5] 7m[2] 7g[2] p7.1g p6g[5] p7g Dec 19] neat filly: modest handicapper: won at Yarmouth in June and Lingfield (hung left) in July: stays 1m: acts on polytrack and firm going: usually blinkered: usually races prominently. *J. M. P. Eustace* **64**

WHISTON LAD (IRE) 3 b.g. Barathea (IRE) 127 – Fille de Bucheron (USA) 83 (Woodman (USA) 126) [2006 10g 10g 8.2m 16.2m Jul 24] big gelding: poor maiden. *S. R. Bowring* **47**

WHITBARROW (IRE) 7 b.g. Royal Abjar (USA) 121 – Danccini (IRE) 78 (Dancing Dissident (USA) 119) [2006 88: p7g[6] p7.1g p6g[2] p6g p5g 5g 6m[6] 5m[2] 5g 5.1g 5.1f[2] 6g[3] 6m[6] 5m 5.5d 7d[5] p7g[6] Oct 26] strong, good sort: fair handicapper, on long losing run: left A. Carroll after fifth start: best at 5f/6f: acts on all-weather, firm and soft going: tried in headgear: races prominently: inconsistent. *B. R. Millman* **76**

WHITBY ECHO (IRE) 4 b.g. Entrepreneur 123 – Nom de Plume (USA) 116 (No-double (USA)) [2006 65: p13.9g p9.5g[2] p12g 12g Jun 21] compact gelding: modest maiden: stayed 1½m: acted on good to firm going, probably on polytrack: dead. *R. Hollinshead* **60**

WHITE BEAR (FR) 4 ch.g. Gold Away (IRE) 125 – Danaide (FR) (Polish Precedent (USA) 131) [2006 73: f8g[3] p7g* p7g* p7g[2] p7g[3] p8g[3] p7.1g p8g Jul 12] leggy gelding: fair handicapper: won twice at Lingfield in February: reportedly bled final start: effective at 6f to 1m: acts on all-weather and good to firm going: often blinkered/visored: has shown signs of temperament, but generally consistent. *C. R. Dore* **76**

WHITE DEER (USA) 2 b. or br.c. (Feb 28) Stravinsky (USA) 133 – Brookshield Baby (IRE) (Sadler's Wells (USA) 132) [2006 5.9g[4] 7f[2] 7g[4] Sep 16] fourth live foal: dam, French 1½m winner, half-sister to dam of Breeders' Cup Sprint winner Lit de Justice, Racing Post Trophy winner Commander Collins and Derby third Colonel Collins: fairly useful performer: won maiden at Epsom in August despite not looking comfortable on track, making all: creditable third in nursery at Ayr final start: stays 1m: acts on firm and good to soft going. *M. Johnston* **85**

WHITE HEATHER 3 br.f. Selkirk (USA) 129 – Durrah Green 79 (Green Desert (USA) 127) [2006 p8g 8d Apr 11] fifth living foal: half-sister to fairly useful 2000 2-y-o 6f winner Strike The Green (by Smart Strike) and winner in USA by Slew City Slew: dam Irish 5f winner: last in maidens at Lingfield and Bath. *A. M. Balding* **–**

WHITE LADDER (IRE) 3 br.c. Marju (IRE) 127 – Lady Rachel (IRE) 75 (Priolo (USA) 127) [2006 68: p6g[4] 7d p7.1m p6g Sep 27] good-topped colt: fair maiden at 2 yrs: well beaten after reappearance in 2006: should stay 7f: acts on good to firm ground: tried blinkered. *P. F. I. Cole* **62**

WHITE LEDGER (IRE) 7 ch.g. Ali-Royal (IRE) 127 – Boranwood (IRE) (Exhibitioner 111) [2006 –: p5.1g p6g p6g p6g p5.1g p6g[5] Dec 22] useful-looking gelding: modest performer nowadays: best at 5f/6f: acts on all-weather, firm and soft going: tried visored, wore cheekpieces last 2 starts: sometimes slowly away. *R. E. Peacock* **54**

WHITE LIGHTENING (IRE) 3 ch.g. Indian Ridge 123 – Mille Miglia (IRE) 96 (Caerleon (USA) 132) [2006 55: 9.2f[2] 8s[5] Sep 4] easily best effort in maidens (fair form) when neck second at Hamilton on reappearance: well below form next time: stays 9f: acts on firm ground. *J. Howard Johnson* **79**

WHITE ON BLACK (GER) 5 b.h. Lomitas 129 – White On Red (GER) (Konigs-stuhl (GER)) [2006 p12g Apr 12] successful in maiden at Cologne (for A. Schutz) at 3 yrs and minor event at Mons (for Mme S. Braem) in 2005: well held in handicap at Lingfield only outing in 2006: stays 11.5f: acts on dirt. *G. L. Moore* **–**

WHITETHORNE 4 b.f. Mujadil (USA) 119 – Sharpthorne (USA) 91 (Sharpen Up 127) [2006 74: 7m* 7.1f[2] 7.2g 7.9m* 8g Jul 28] rather leggy, lengthy filly: fairly useful performer: won handicaps at Leicester in June and Carlisle (successful all 4 starts there) in July: pulled up final start: stayed 1m: acted on firm and good to soft going: dead. *R. A. Fahey* **84**

WHITE WINGO (SAF) 6 gr.g. Al Mufti (USA) 112 – Glib Talk (SAF) (Mr Justice (USA)) [2006 a11f[4] a11f[6] 11.7m 10.3d[4] Sep 30] modest form in maidens/handicaps when **53**

trained by D. Watson in UAE: tailed off only outing in Britain (for R. Simpson) before fourth in minor event at Krefeld final start: stays 11f: tried blinkered/visored. *A. Wohler, Germany*

WHITGIFT ROCK 5 b.g. Piccolo 121 – Fly South (Polar Falcon (USA) 126) [2006 **69** 79: p8g p8g⁶ p10g p10g May 23] good-topped gelding: fair performer: barely stays 1½m: acts on polytrack, firm and soft going: below form in visor/cheekpieces. *S. Dow*

WHITSBURY COMMON 4 b.f. Lujain (USA) 119 – Vallauris 94 (Faustus (USA) – 118) [2006 63: p10g p12g p8g Apr 8] good-topped filly: modest maiden at 3 yrs: no impact in 2006: blinkered final outing. *D. R. C. Elsworth*

WHITTINGHAMVILLAGE 5 b.m. Whittingham (IRE) 104 – Shaa Spin 63 **65** (Shaadi (USA) 126) [2006 8d² 7.9m⁶ 9.2g 7.1g⁶ 6m 8m⁶ 9.1m³ 7.1m 8s³ 8.5m 8d³ Oct 8] leggy, workmanlike mare: fair maiden: unraced in 2005: below form after reappearance: stays 9f: acts on firm and good to soft going: wore cheekpieces fifth start. *D. W. Whillans*

WHOLE GRAIN 5 b.m. Polish Precedent (USA) 131 – Mill Line 71 (Mill Reef (USA) – 141) [2006 ?: f12g Jan 2] rangy mare: lightly-raced maiden: blinkered, well beaten only outing in 2006. *B. R. Millman*

WHOOPEE (USA) 3 b. or br.f. Mozart (IRE) 131 – Time For A Wedding (USA) **42** (Manila (USA)) [2006 –: 7f 7f⁵ 6m⁴ 9.9g Aug 31] leggy, quite good-topped filly: poor performer: should be suited by further than 6f: sold 4,000 gns. *M. Johnston*

WHOOPSIE 4 b.f. Unfuwain (USA) 131 – Oops Pettie 93 (Machiavellian (USA) 123) **58** [2006 62: 14.1d 14m⁴ 16.2g³ 14.1g 16m⁶ 16g 15.8d p16g³ p16g⁶ p12g Nov 27] stocky **a54** filly: modest performer: won handicap at Musselburgh (made all, hung left) in May: stays 17f: acts on polytrack, firm and soft ground. *S. Parr*

WHOS COUNTING 2 ch.f. (Apr 28) Woodborough (USA) 112 – Hard To Follow **44** (Dilum (USA) 115) [2006 p7.1g p8g⁵ p6g³ Dec 4] first foal: dam no form: poor form, including in sellers. *R. J. Hodges*

WHO'S WINNING (IRE) 5 ch.g. Docksider (USA) 124 – Quintellina 83 (Robellino **87** (USA) 127) [2006 92: p6g p7g p6g² p7g 6g p7g⁶ 6g⁶ 6g 5.7f⁶ 6f⁴ 6f* 5f³ 6m⁵ 5m⁴ 5.7m² 5m 5.3d³ 6d⁶ p6g p6g⁴ p6s³ p6g³ Dec 30] sturdy gelding: fairly useful performer: won handicap at Brighton in July: several creditable efforts after: best at 5f/6f: acts on polytrack, firm and good to soft going: tried blinkered/in cheekpieces/tongue tied: free-going sort: has reportedly bled. *B. G. Powell*

WHOZART (IRE) 3 b.g. Mozart (IRE) 131 – Hertford Castle (Reference Point 139) – [2006 p6g p7.1g Dec 9] well beaten in maidens at Wolverhampton. *A. Dickman*

WHY HARRY 4 b.g. Cyrano de Bergerac 120 – Golden Ciel (USA) (Septieme Ciel – (USA) 123) [2006 –: p6g Jan 5] sturdy gelding: modest performer at 2 yrs: no show both starts since. *J. J. Quinn*

WHY NOW 4 b.f. Dansili 127 – Questionable (Rainbow Quest (USA) 134) [2006 81: – f6g Jan 29] lengthy filly: fairly useful performer at 3 yrs: well beaten only start in 2006: races prominently. *K. A. Ryan*

WIBBADUNE (IRE) 2 ch.f. (Mar 28) Daggers Drawn (USA) 114 – Becada (GER) **58** (Cadeaux Genereux 131) [2006 p6g p5g p5g⁵ p5.1g p5.1g⁴ p5.1g³ p5g² p5.1g² p5.1g² Dec 29] second foal: dam, lightly-raced German maiden, half-sister to smart German 7f/1m winner Bear King: modest maiden: raced mainly at 5f: acts on polytrack. *Peter Grayson*

WICKEDISH 2 b.f. (Jan 21) Medicean 128 – Sleave Silk (IRE) 58 (Unfuwain (USA) – 131) [2006 6g 7m 7m 7m⁵ Sep 12] 20,000Y, 32,000 2-y-o: sturdy, good-bodied filly: third foal: dam 1½m and 2m winner: well held in maidens and a nursery. *P. Howling*

WICKED LADY (UAE) 3 b.f. Jade Robbery (USA) 121 – Kinsfolk (Distant Relative **59** 128) [2006 p10g Dec 30] 800 3-y-o, resold 2,700 3-y-o: second foal: dam, ran once in Ireland, out of sister to multiple US Grade 1 winner Chief's Crown: 33/1, 5¾ lengths seventh to Samarinda in maiden at Lingfield. *B. R. Johnson*

WICKED UNCLE 7 b.g. Distant Relative 128 – The Kings Daughter 79 (Indian King **68** (USA) 128) [2006 81: p5g³ p5g² p5g⁴ p5g⁴ p5g* 5g p5g* 5g p5g⁵ 5f 5f Jul 8] smallish, **a89** sturdy gelding: impresses in appearance: fairly useful performer on all-weather, fair on turf: won handicaps at Lingfield in April and Kempton in May: best at 5f: acts on all-weather and firm going: wears headgear: sold 3,500 gns in August. *S. Gollings*

WICKED WILMA (IRE) 2 b.f. (Jan 15) Tagula (IRE) 116 – Wicked 40 (Common **59** Grounds 118) [2006 5m³ 5.1m³ 5g³ 5m* Aug 3] €9,000Y: second foal: half-sister to 2-y-o sprint winner in Sweden by Revoque: dam lightly raced: modest performer: won maiden at Musselburgh in August by length from Almora Guru: raced only at 5f: acts on good to firm ground: has looked hard ride. *A. Berry*

WI DUD 2 b.c. (Apr 14) Elnadim (USA) 128 – Hopesay 84 (Warning 136) [2006 **116**
5m* 5m² 6d² 5g* 6d² Sep 29]

Wi Dud had a good first season, finishing in the first two on all his five starts, four of them in pattern company, and progressing with every outing. His trainer Kevin Ryan obviously knew Wi Dud's capabilities at an early stage, nominating the Gimcrack Stakes as his long-term target immediately after he overcame a slow start to win a maiden at York on his debut.

Wi Dud was sent off favourite in a field of thirteen on his debut and the race had already thrown up a couple of winners by the time Wi Dud contested the Molecomb Stakes at Goodwood in early-August, when he confirmed his promise, beaten a short head by Enticing, despite being drawn wide, challenging strongly from two furlongs out. Later that month, Wi Dud sought to emulate the success enjoyed by his stable in the previous year's renewal of the Gimcrack with Amadeus Wolf. The smallest field since the millennium did not attract a single runner who had been successful in pattern company. Wi Dud was running at six furlongs for the first time and was passed over by stable jockey Neil Callan, who instead rode He's A Humbug, leaving the stable's second jockey Daragh O'Donohoe on Wi Dud. Wi Dud looked sure to land the spoils when nosing ahead over a furlong out, but was collared close home by Conquest, who needed every yard and all of his rider Jimmy Fortune's renowned strength to get up and win by three quarters of a length. The first two pulled two and a half lengths clear of Bodes Galaxy, with He's A Humbug a disappointing fifth.

Wi Dud's progression didn't stop there, as he landed the Group 2 Persimmon Homes Flying Childers Stakes back at York (usually at Doncaster) in September. In an above-average renewal of what is usually the season's best five-furlong event for two-year-olds, the Norfolk form was represented by the second Hoh Mike (the winner Dutch Art had gone on to win the Prix Morny) while Wi Dud represented the Molecomb and Gimcrack form. Sent off the 11/4 favourite, Wi Dud beat Bahama Mama by a length and a half under a confident Callan ride. Wi Dud's best effort, however, came when stepped back up to six furlongs for the Middle Park Stakes, a race the Ryan stable had taken in 2005 with Amadeus Wolf. Wi Dud faced five rivals, including Dutch Art, Conquest, and Coventry winner Hellvelyn. Wi Dud was behind all three of those named in the betting as well as Ballydoyle's listed winner Brave Tin Soldier, but he improved again to finish two lengths second to Dutch Art, on the heels of the winner going into the Dip, before finding him too good.

Persimmon Homes Flying Childers Stakes, York—Wi Dud (left) is given a confident ride by Neil Callan; Bahama Mama (dark colours), Hoh Mike (right) and Siren's Gift (behind winner) are next

J. Duddy, L. Duddy, P. McBride & E. Duffy's "Wi Dud"

		Danzig	Northern Dancer
	Elnadim (USA)	(b 1977)	Pas de Nom
	(b 1994)	Elle Seule	Exclusive Native
Wi Dud		(ch 1983)	Fall Aspen
(b.c. Apr 14, 2004)		Warning	Known Fact
	Hopesay	(b 1985)	Slightly Dangerous
	(b 1994)	Tatouma	The Minstrel
		(ch 1986)	Sheer Fantasy

    Wi Dud is by Elnadim, a son of Danzig who progressed with age, his biggest success coming in the 1998 July Cup as a four-year-old. Elnadim has only three crops of racing age, but seems to be passing on plenty of speed, and is also responsible for another smart two-year-old in the latest season in Caldra. Wi Dud's dam Hopesay was a fairly useful maiden for John Gosden who stayed six furlongs. She made it to the racecourse only seven times, racing only on good ground or firmer. Wi Dud is her fifth foal and she has produced three other winners, notably the useful Sailing Through (by Bahhare) who completed a four-timer in handicaps at eight and a half furlongs to a mile and a quarter in the summer of 2003. Wi Dud is only smallish, but he's sturdy and quite attractive and, having gone through the sales ring unsold as a yearling, he made 25,000 guineas as a two-year-old. Wi Dud progressed well, improving with each run, and will probably have a campaign which will see him taking on his stablemate Amadeus Wolf in 2007 in some of the top sprints. Wi Dud showed in the Middle Park that he stays six furlongs, and he is effective on ground ranging from good to firm to good to soft (yet to encounter extremes). *K. A. Ryan*

WID (USA) 2 gr.f. (Mar 24) Elusive Quality (USA) – Alshadiyah (USA) 102 (Danzig **100** (USA)) [2006 6g* 6m* 6m² 6d Sep 29] lengthy, good-bodied filly: first foal: dam, 2-y-o 6f winner, out of 1000 Guineas winner Shadayid: useful form: successful on first 2 starts in maiden at Newmarket (from Light Shift) in June and minor event at Haydock (from La Presse) in August, having ½ length to spare each time: good ½-length second to Vital Statistics (pair clear) in listed race at Salisbury: below form in Cheveley Park Stakes at Newmarket final outing, racing freely: will probably stay 7f: acts on good to firm ground (possibly not good to soft). *J. L. Dunlop*

WIGGY SMITH 7 ch.g. Master Willie 129 – Monsoon 66 (Royal Palace 131) [2006 **90** 93: 12d 10g⁶ Jun 1] angular gelding: fairly useful handicapper: better effort in 2006 when sixth at Nottingham: may prove best short of 1½m: acts on polytrack, soft and good to firm going: fair hurdler, won in June/July: sold 14,500 gns in November. *O. Sherwood*

WIG WAM BAM (IRE) 3 b.f. Indian Rocket 115 – Almasa 83 (Faustus (USA) 118) **–** [2006 57: 6.1f Jun 19] useful-looking filly: modest maiden: well held in handicap only outing in 2006: raced only on good or firmer going. *R. A. Fahey*

WIGWAM WILLIE (IRE) 4 b.g. Indian Rocket 115 – Sweet Nature (IRE) 71 **89** (Classic Secret (USA) 91) [2006 90: 8v⁵ 7g 8m⁵ 10d⁴ 7.9g⁶ 8d* 8g 8v⁴ Oct 28] quite good-topped gelding: fairly useful handicapper: won at Ayr in September: likely to prove best around 1m: acts on heavy and good to firm going: blinkered/in cheekpieces last 6 starts: looked wayward last 2 outings. *K. A. Ryan*

WILD ACADEMY (IRE) 3 b.f. Royal Academy (USA) 130 – Wild Vintage (USA) **72** (Alysheba (USA)) [2006 7m³ 7m 7g p8g 8.3s p8g Oct 23] 40,000Y: workmanlike filly: seventh foal: sister to very smart Hong Kong 1m/1¼m performer Bullish Luck (formerly 2-y-o 6f/7.3f winner in Britain as Al Moughazel): dam, French 1¼m winner, half-sister to very smart French miler In Extremis and Prix Marcel Boussac winner Juvenia: third in maiden at Yarmouth on debut: failed to progress: should stay beyond 7f: blinkered final outing: reportedly lame second start: sold 84,000 gns in November. *G. C. Bravery*

WILDE JASMINE (IRE) 2 ch.f. (Apr 21) Daggers Drawn (USA) 114 – No Tomor- **–** row (IRE) (Night Shift (USA)) [2006 5g 5m 6m 5g⁵ p7.1g Oct 30] quite good-topped filly: third foal: dam, ran 4 times, out of half-sister to dam of dual Breeders' Cup Mile winner Da Hoss: little form. *J. R. Weymes*

WILDERNESS BAY (IRE) 4 b.f. Fasliyev (USA) 120 – Pleine Lune (IRE) (Alzao **67 d** (USA) 117) [2006 75: 10.2m 9.7f p10g 11.6f 10.2m Oct 8] 65,000Y: first foal: dam, French 2-y-o 6f/1m winner, half-sister to top-class French middle-distance performer Pistolet Bleu: fair performer: won maiden at Fairyhouse in 2005: left D. Weld in Ireland and off over 10 months, regressive form in handicaps in 2006: stays 1¼m: acts on firm ground. *M. R. Bosley*

WILDE THING 2 b.f. (May 4) Muhtarram (USA) 125 – Lochbelle 70 (Robellino **–** (USA) 127) [2006 8.1d 8.2d p8.6g Nov 23] 900Y: smallish filly: sixth foal: half-sister to fairly useful 2001 2-y-o 5f winner Locharia (by Wolfhound): dam, 1¼m winner who stayed 1½m, half-sister to Nunthorpe winners Lochsong and Lochangel: well held in maidens. *S. Curran*

WILD FELL HALL (IRE) 3 ch.c. Grand Lodge (USA) 125 – Genoa 96 (Zafonic **–** (USA) 130) [2006 71: 9v May 21] smallish, workmanlike colt: sixth in maiden at Salisbury on debut at 2 yrs: no form in 2 runs since. *W. R. Swinburn*

WILD GARDENIA 2 b.f. (Feb 21) Alhaarth (IRE) 126 – Frappe (IRE) 93 (Inchinor **57 p** 119) [2006 p8g Nov 15] third foal: sister to 3-y-o Quantum and closely related to use- ful 7f (at 2 yrs) to 1½m (Ribblesdale Stakes) winner Thakafaat (by Unfuwain): dam, 2-y-o 6f winner, half-sister to 2000 Guineas winner Footstepsinthesand: seventh to Flower of Kent in maiden at Kempton, weakening as if race needed: should improve. *J. H. M. Gosden*

WILD LASS 5 ch.m. Bluegrass Prince (IRE) 110 – Pink Pumpkin 52 (Tickled Pink 114) **52** [2006 p7g 8d 8.1g 10m 7g* 8.1g⁶ 7f 10m 8d⁵ 8d p8g p8g p8g p10g Dec 22] fifth foal: dam 5f winner, including at 2 yrs: modest performer: 100/1, best effort when winning claimer at Salisbury in June: stays 7f: best effort on good going: blinkered/in cheekpieces after fourth start. *J. C. Fox*

WILD PITCH 5 ch.g. Piccolo 121 – Western Horizon (USA) 58 (Gone West (USA)) **66** [2006 74, a67: p10g* 10d⁴ p12g* 10g⁵ p13g p12g⁵ Dec 20] leggy, close-coupled gelding: **a77** fair performer: won handicaps at Kempton in May and June (apprentices): stays easy 1½m: acts on polytrack, good to firm and good to soft going: blinkered. *P. Mitchell*

WILD SAVANNAH 4 b.c. Singspiel (IRE) 133 – Apache Star 96 (Arazi (USA) 135) **111**
[2006 108: 10m* 10m² Jun 23] strong, quite attractive colt: impresses in appearance:
smart handicapper: further improvement when winning at Newmarket in May by neck
from Chantaco: good 1¼ lengths second to I'm So Lucky in Wolferton Handicap at
Royal Ascot only other start in 2006: stays easy 1½m, but may prove best at 1¼m: acts
on polytrack and good to firm going: effective visored or not: sold privately, and joined
I. Mohammed in UAE. *J. H. M. Gosden*

WILD THYME 2 ch.f. (Apr 4) Desert Prince (IRE) 130 – Once Upon A Time 77 **74**
(Teenoso (USA) 135) [2006 8.1m² 8.2m⁴ 8.1g⁵ Sep 23] lengthy filly: half-sister to several
winners, including smart performer up to 1½m Arabian Story (by Sharrood) and fairly
useful 1¼m winner Island Story (by Shirley Heights), both of whom stayed 2m: dam, 8.5f
(at 2 yrs) and 1½m winner, sister to smart 1¼m performer Starlet: fair form in maidens all
3 starts, in frame at Chepstow and Nottingham: will stay at least 1¼m: sold 15,000 gns.
R. Hannon

WILFORD MAVERICK (IRE) 4 b.g. Fasliyev (USA) 120 – Lioness 74 (Lion **56**
Cavern (USA) 117) [2006 54: p8.6g⁵ p7.1g p8.6g p7.1g⁴ p7.1g f6g f7g* p6g³ f7g⁵ f8g f7g
f7g p8g² p8.6g⁶ f7g f7g Dec 28] close-coupled gelding: modest performer: won banded
race at Southwell in March: stays 8.6f: acts on all-weather and soft ground: effective with/
without visor: inconsistent. *M. J. Attwater*

WILKO (USA) 4 ch.c. Awesome Again (CAN) 133 – Native Roots (IRE) (Indian Ridge **–**
123) [2006 –, a118: a9f³ a10f³ a10g² a8f⁵ a10f a9f⁶ Jul 31] well-made, attractive colt: has **a120**
a quick action: very smart performer on dirt: won Breeders' Cup Juvenile at Lone Star
Park in 2004 (left J. Noseda afterwards): best effort in 2005 when creditable third in Santa
Anita Derby on second outing (underwent surgery for chipped bone in off-fore ankle after
fourth start): creditable length third to Spellbinder in Grade 2 San Antonio Handicap at
Santa Anita on reappearance and (having left C. Dollase after next start) ran well when
4½ lengths third (promoted to second) to Electrocutionist in Dubai World Cup at Nad Al
Sheba, leading 2f out until inside last: below form at Belmont after in Metropolitan
Handicap (left J. Noseda again afterwards) and Suburban Handicap (blinkered) and at
Saratoga in allowance optional claimer: stays 1¼m: acts on dirt, firm and good to soft
going: has reportedly suffered from quarter cracks, and has bled (in Kentucky Derby).
M. A. Hennig, USA

WILL BE (IRE) 3 b. or br.f. In The Wings 128 – Bintalshaati 95 (Kris 135) [2006 8f⁴ **83 ?**
a12g⁶ 11.5m⁶ 10f³ p10g² p12.2g³ 11.6d⁴ a12g* Dec 30] 9,000 2-y-o: sixth foal: half-sister
to fairly useful 1¼m winner Munadil (by Nashwan): dam 1m winner out of half-sister to
Kentucky Derby winner Winning Colors: won maiden at Taby on debut in 2005: seemingly good efforts in Swedish 1000 Guineas at Taby and Oaks at Jagersro first 2 starts:
just fair form in handicaps in Britain before winning similar event at Taby in December
(first start after leaving R. Kvisla): stays 1½m: acts on dirt, polytrack, firm and good to
soft going: often in cheekpieces/tongue tie. *B. Bo, Sweden*

WILL DOO 2 b.c. (Apr 8) Elmaamul (USA) 125 – Perpetuo 81 (Mtoto 134) [2006 7.5d **–**
8.5g p7.1g Sep 16] no form, including in seller. *M. E. Sowersby*

WILLHECONQUERTOO 6 ch.g. Primo Dominie 121 – Sure Care 62 (Caerleon **79**
(USA) 132) [2006 80: p6g⁵ p7g p6g³ p6g⁶ p6g p6g Mar 3] sturdy gelding: fair handicapper: pulled up final start: races mainly at 5f/6f nowadays: acts on polytrack and firm
going: usually tongue tied/in cheekpieces/visored: often races prominently. *I. W. McInnes*

WILLHEGO 5 ch.g. Pivotal 124 – Woodrising 64 (Nomination 125) [2006 79: p10g⁴ **93**
p12g* p10g* p10g² p12g p10g Feb 11] plain gelding: fairly useful handicapper: won
twice at Lingfield in January: reportedly lame final outing: effective at 1m to 1½m: acts
on polytrack, good to firm and good to soft going. *J. R. Best*

WILL HE ROCK (IRE) 5 b.g. Diesis 133 – Recoleta (USA) (Wild Again (USA)) **77**
[2006 82: p13.9g³ Mar 31] fair performer: ran creditably in apprentice handicap at
Wolverhampton only outing in 2006: effective at 9.5f to 1¾m: acts on polytrack, good to
firm and good to soft going: sold 18,000 gns in May. *John A. Quinn, Ireland*

WILL HE WISH 10 b.g. Winning Gallery 94 – More To Life (Northern Tempest **95**
(USA) 120) [2006 94: p7g³ 7.1m* 7m⁵ 7.1m 8.3f⁶ 7m⁵ 7.6m 7.1g p7g p6g⁶ p7.1g⁴ p8g⁶
Dec 19] good-bodied gelding: useful performer: won handicap at Musselburgh (beat
Stoic Leader by neck) in May: stiff tasks, flattered when last of 5 in minor events at Leic-
ester and Chester: effective at 6f to easy 1m: acts on polytrack, firm and good to soft
going: effective blinkered earlier in career. *S. Gollings*

WILLHEWIZ 6 b.g. Wizard King 122 – Leave It To Lib 66 (Tender King 123) [2006 **86**
85, a81: f5g⁴ f5g 5.1s² 6g 5.7g 6g⁴ 5.7f² 5g⁵ 5.3f³ 6m 5f 6f⁶ 5.7m Aug 20] good-topped

gelding: fairly useful handicapper: below form after seventh outing: best at 5f/6f: acts on all-weather, firm and soft going: tried in headgear: races prominently. *M. S. Saunders*

WILLIAM JOHN 3 b.g. Foxhound (USA) 103 – Classy Relation (Puissance 110) **66** [2006 61: 12d[6] 8g[3] 10g[3] 10f[3] 12f 7.9g* 9.3f[3] 8m Aug 27] tall, workmanlike gelding: fair handicapper: won at Carlisle in August: probably stays 9.3f: acts on polytrack and firm going: tried in cheekpieces, tongue tied last 3 starts. *B. Ellison*

WILLIAM'S WAY 4 b.g. Fraam 114 – Silk Daisy 74 (Barathea (IRE) 127) [2006 11.6f **80** p8.6g[3] p8g[5] 10f* 11m[6] 10g[2] 10d[5] 10g p10g[4] 10d p12.2g f12g[2] f11g[2] Dec 5] fairly useful handicapper: won at Windsor in July: good second at Southwell last 2 starts, hanging left in latter: stays 1½m: acts on all-weather and firm going. *I. A. Wood*

WILLIAM TELL (IRE) 4 b.g. Rossini (USA) 118 – Livry (USA) (Lyphard (USA) **67** 132) [2006 72: p13.9g 11g 15.8g 14.1d 15.8m Sep 16] leggy, angular gelding: fair performer: seems to stay easy 1¾m: acts on polytrack and soft going: sold 1,500 gns, sent to Israel. *M. D. Hammond*

WILLOFCOURSE 5 b.g. Aragon 118 – Willyet (Nicholas Bill 125) [2006 –: 5.5d **55** 7.1m 6.1m[4] 6.1d p6g Jul 11] modest maiden, lightly raced: stays 6f: acts on good to firm ground: tried visored. *H. Candy*

WILL THE TILL 4 b.g. Fraam 114 – Prim Ajwaad (Bin Ajwaad (IRE) 119) [2006 66: **65** 8.1d 8d[3] 8s 7.1m 10.2m 8.2f 8m[3] 8.1m[4] 10.2m 10.2f[5] 10.9d Sep 16] leggy, good-topped gelding: modest handicapper: stays 1m: acts on good to firm and good to soft going: in cheekpieces/blinkers last 3 outings: sometimes slowly away, and temperament under suspicion: has joined Evan Williams. *J. M. Bradley*

WILLY (SWE) 4 ch.g. Heart of Oak (USA) 103 – Kawa-Ib (IRE) 78 (Nashwan (USA) **52** 135) [2006 a12s 11s p12.2g[3] f11g[2] p12.2g Dec 23] Swedish-bred gelding: won 4 handicaps at Taby in 2005: modest form in 2006, leaving R. Kvisla after third start: stays 1½m: raced mainly on dirt, probably acts on all-weather: tried blinkered/tongue tied. *R. Brotherton*

WILMAS GAL 3 ch.f. Compton Place 125 – Malthouse Girl (IRE) (Barathea (IRE) **–** 127) [2006 8.3d 9v 6m 7m f6g 8f Jul 28] 1,800Y: first foal: dam unraced: no sign of ability: tongue tied. *R. Bastiman*

WILMINGTON 2 ch.g. (Apr 12) Compton Place 125 – Bahawir Pour (USA) (Green **72** Dancer (USA) 132) [2006 6f p7g 6m[2] 6d p7g[6] 7d[3] f7g[5] Nov 14] 43,000F, 30,000Y: strong, useful-looking gelding: sixth foal: brother to useful 2002 2-y-o 7f winner Captain Saif and half-brother to 3-y-o Future's Dream and winner abroad by Mister Baileys: dam unraced: left R. Hannon 14,000 gns after penultimate start (blinkered), and gelded: stays 7f: acts on polytrack, good to firm and good to soft ground. *N. P. Littmoden*

WILTSHIRE (IRE) 4 br.g. Spectrum (IRE) 126 – Mary Magdalene 78 (Night Shift **66** (USA)) [2006 55, a63: p8.6g p8g p7g[4] p8g[4] p7.1g[3] p7g[2] p7.1g 8.3m[2] 8f 7d p8.6g[3] p8g **a62** p8.6g[4] p8.6g Dec 27] leggy gelding: fair performer on turf, modest on all-weather: left P. Blockley after ninth outing: stays easy 8.6f: acts on polytrack and firm ground: usually wears headgear: none too consistent. *P. T. Midgley*

WINDBENEATHMYWINGS (IRE) 2 b.f. (Feb 7) In The Wings 128 – Moneefa **65** 73 (Darshaan 133) [2006 p7g 8.3s[6] p9.5g[5] Nov 11] sturdy filly: sixth foal: half-sister to smart 1m winner Dandoun (by Halling) and useful 1m and 9.4f winner Zyzania (by Zafonic): dam 1¼m winner: fair form in maidens only on second start: should stay 1¼m+. *J. W. Hills*

WIND CHIME (IRE) 9 ch.h. Arazi (USA) 135 – Shamisen 86 (Diesis 133) [2006 77, **61** a56: p9.5g 10.2g[4] 8f 8m 8.3f 8.1m* 7g 10.2f p10g[5] p10g[6] p10g* Dec 18] smallish horse: **a51** just modest performer in 2006, better on turf than all-weather: won ladies handicap at Chepstow in August and banded race at Kempton in December: effective at 1m/1¼m: acts on all-weather, firm and good to soft going: tried in cheekpieces. *A. G. Newcombe*

WIND FLOW 2 b.c. (May 5) Dr Fong (USA) 128 – Spring 112 (Sadler's Wells (USA) **72 p** 132) [2006 p7g 7d[6] Aug 13] 52,000Y: brother to fairly useful 1¼m winner Double Aspect and half-brother to several winners, including smart 1m/1¼m winner Inglenook (by Cadeaux Genereux): dam, 1½m/1¾m winner, closely related to Pentire: fair form in maidens, again never dangerous and not knocked about when sixth to Nightinshining at Leicester: should be suited by 1m+: capable of better. *E. A. L. Dunlop*

WINDJAMMER 2 b.g. (Jan 9) Kyllachy 129 – Absolve (USA) (Diesis 133) [2006 5s[6] **48** 6f[6] f5g Jul 31] poor form second start in maidens. *T. D. Easterby*

WIN

WIND SHUFFLE (GER) 3 b.g. Big Shuffle (USA) 122 – Wiesensturmerin (GER) **66**
(Lagunas) [2006 56p: 7g² 7d⁴ Oct 3] big, leggy gelding: lightly-raced maiden: easily best
effort when second to Sir Orpen at Catterick on reppearance, hanging left: off 5 months
after: has got upset in stall and gave deal of trouble before withdrawn prior to second
intended start: sold 4,200 gns. *T. P. Tate*

WINDS OF CHANGE 3 gr.f. King's Best (USA) 132 – New Wind (GER) (Windwurf **80**
(GER)) [2006 60p: 8m³ p10g 12.1m* 12.1g² 11.7f² 12g³ 11.8m² 16m 12g Aug 29]
good-topped filly: fairly useful handicapper: won at Hamilton in May: left M. Johnston
24,000 gns prior to well held last 2 starts: should stay at least 1¾m: acts on firm going:
reportedly resented kickback at Lingfield second outing: usually raced prominently. *H. de*
Bromhead, Ireland

WINDSOR KNOT (IRE) 4 ch.c. Pivotal 124 – Triple Tie (USA) 81 (The Minstrel **115**
(CAN) 135) [2006 101: 10m² 10g² 10m* 11.6g⁴ 9d² Oct 14] big, rangy colt: good walker:
fluent mover: has been fired on near-hock: smart performer: ran only once in 2005: back
to best in 2006, winning minor event at Newmarket in August by ½ length from Khyber
Kim, drifting left: also ran well when head second to Tam Lin in listed event at Newbury
and to Stage Gift in Darley Stakes at Newmarket second/final starts: stays 11.6f: acts on
good to firm and good to soft going. *Saeed bin Suroor*

WIND STAR 3 ch.g. Piccolo 121 – Starfleet 66 (Inchinor 119) [2006 8m⁶ 8m⁴ 7m² **95**
8.3m² 8m* 9.2m* 8.1m 9.2d³ Sep 25] 2,000F, €14,000Y: angular gelding: first foal: dam,
maiden who may have proved best around 1m, half-sister to useful performers Pool
Music (stayed 8.5f) and Russian Music (stayed 1¼m): useful handicapper: won in small
fields at Ayr and Hamilton in July/August: stays 9.2f: acts on good to firm and good to
soft going. *G. A. Swinbank*

WINDY PROSPECT 4 ch.g. Intikhab (USA) 135 – Yellow Ribbon (IRE) 72 (Hamas **54**
(IRE) 125§) [2006 75d: f12g⁵ f11g 7f 7.5f 7m 8f⁵ p9.5f 8.1m f6g* f7g⁴ f7g² f7g⁴ f8g⁴ **a71**
Dec 27] smart leggy gelding: fair performer on all-weather, modest on turf: left C. Dore
after second start, Miss S. West after sixth: won apprentice handicap at Southwell in November: effective at 6f to 1m: acts on fibresand, firm and good to soft going: tried blinkered
(raced freely): often races prominently. *P. A. Blockley*

WING COLLAR 5 b.g. In The Wings 128 – Riyoom (USA) 83 (Vaguely Noble 140) **94**
[2006 91: 13.9s² 16.2f³ 16.1m Jul 1] tall, quite good-topped gelding: fairly useful handicapper: effective from 1½m to 2m: acts on any going: in cheekpieces 5 of last 6 starts:
usually held up: sometimes races freely: consistent. *T. D. Easterby*

WING COMMANDER 7 b.g. Royal Applause 124 – Southern Psychic (USA) (Al- **80**
wasmi (USA) 115) [2006 94: 8s 8g 8.1m 10m 9g⁵ 9.8m³ 8.9m⁵ 9.9f³ 8f⁵ 8.5f⁵ 8f 10m*
9.3f* 10g⁶ Aug 21] strong, lengthy gelding: fairly useful handicapper: won at Ayr and
Carlisle within 4 days in August: probably best at 1m/1¼m on good going or firmer:
usually wears headgear: has been bandaged. *I. W. McInnes*

WINGED D'ARGENT (IRE) 5 b.g. In The Wings 128 – Petite-D-Argent 91 (Noalto **115 d**
120) [2006 118: 15.5d 18.7m⁵ 13.9s 16.4s² 20m 16.4m³ 16f 15.9d 18d 16d³ Sep 23]
sturdy gelding: smart performer on his day: creditable efforts in 2006 only when close
fifth to Admiral in Chester Cup (Handicap) and 5 lengths second to Tungsten Strike in
Henry II Stakes at Sandown on second/fourth starts: stays 2½m: acts on soft and good to
firm going, probably on heavy: occasionally blinkered/visored tends to race lazily: none
too genuine. *M. Johnston*

WINGED FARASI 2 b.c. (Feb 17) Desert Style (IRE) 121 – Clara Vale (IRE) (In The **68**
Wings 128) [2006 6m⁵ 7d⁴ Aug 23] 800 2-y-o: first foal: dam, lightly-raced Irish maiden,
half-sister to smart performer up to 7f My Branch, herself dam of high-class sprinter
Tante Rose: better effort in maidens when third to Big Player at Folkestone: should stay
1m. *Miss J. Feilden*

WINGED FLIGHT (USA) 2 b.c. (Jan 19) Fusaichi Pegasus (USA) 130 – Tobara- **88**
nama (IRE) 94 (Sadler's Wells (USA) 132) [2006 6g³ 6m* 7d Aug 2] $95,000Y: rangy,
good-topped colt: second foal: dam, Irish 9f winner who stayed 1¾m, closely related
to smart sprinter Pharaoh's Delight (grandam of 3-y-o Red Rocks): fairly useful form:
promising third in newcomers event at Ascot, then landed odds in maiden at Yarmouth in
August by 3½ lengths from Swift Image, soon in front and quickening clear impressively:
last behind Big Timer in Acomb Stakes on softer ground at York final start: bred to be
suited by 7f+, but isn't short of speed. *M. Johnston*

WINGMAN (IRE) 4 b.g. In The Wings 128 – Precedence (IRE) 88 (Polish Precedent **94**
(USA) 131) [2006 95: 12g³ 10.4d⁴ 12m⁵ 14m⁵ p12g⁴ 12g 12g p12g⁶ Sep 30] big, strong

gelding: fairly useful handicapper: better at 1½m than 1¼m: acts on any turf going: wore cheekpieces penultimate start: has joined G. L. Moore. *J. W. Hills*

WINGSINMOTION (IRE) 2 b.f. (Feb 21) Indian Lodge (IRE) 127 – Coulisse (IRE) (In The Wings 128) [2006 p7.1g 7.1m Aug 24] first foal: dam unraced: well beaten in sellers. *K. R. Burke* —

WINGS OF DAWN 3 b.f. In The Wings 128 – Petit Point (IRE) 78 (Petorius 117) [2006 58: 10m 11m⁶ 12f³ 13.1m* 16d Sep 26] close-coupled filly: modest handicapper: won at Bath in August: stays 13f: raced mostly on good going or firmer: sold 23,000 gns. *M. P. Tregoning* **63**

WINGS OF MORNING (IRE) 5 ch.g. Fumo di Londra (IRE) 108 – Hay Knot (Main Reef 126) [2006 49: f7g* f8g f7g⁴ p7.1g⁵ f7g³ f7g* p6g p7.1g² p8.6g p7.1g f7g p7g Dec 30] sturdy gelding: modest performer: won banded races at Southwell in January and May: stays 7.5f: acts on all-weather and good to soft ground: tried blinkered, usually visored: sometimes slowly away: none too consistent. *D. Carroll* **58**

WINNERS DELIGHT 5 ch.g. First Trump 118 – Real Popcorn (IRE) 52 (Jareer (USA) 115) [2006 85, a88: p8g 10d⁶ 10f* 10g 11.6f 10g p10g³ Oct 6] compact gelding: fairly useful handicapper: left A. Jarvis after reappearance: won at Windsor in June: stays 1½m, not 1¾m: acts on polytrack, firm and good to soft going: usually held up, though ridden prominently at Windsor: sold 10,000 gns. *C. F. Wall* **83**

WINNING CONNECTION (IRE) 3 b.g. Beckett (IRE) 116 – Schiranna (Seymour Hicks (FR) 125) [2006 7.1m 10.2g 8.2g Aug 4] well held in maidens. *P. A. Blockley* —

WINNING PLEASURE (IRE) 8 b.g. Ashkalani (IRE) 128 – Karamana (Habitat 134) [2006 f6g p6g f6g* f6g* f6g³ f6g* p6g f6g⁵ Dec 21] leggy, sparely-made gelding: fairly useful performer: off 2 years before reappearance: won seller and claimer at Southwell in February and handicap there in March: probably best at 6f: acts on fibresand, best runs on turf on good/good to firm ground: tried visored/in cheekpieces, effective blinkered or not. *J. Balding* **a82**

WINNING SMILE (USA) 2 ch.f. (Mar 24) With Approval (CAN) – Acquiesce (Generous (IRE) 139) [2006 6.1d Oct 13] close-coupled, quite attractive filly: unfurnished at present: sixth foal: half-sister to 3 winners, including useful 2002 2-y-o 7f winner Oblige (by Robellino) and 3-y-o Moi Aussi: dam, unraced, out of sister to Dewhurst winner Scenic: 14/1 and wintry in coat, well held in maiden at Warwick. *P. W. Chapple-Hyam* —

WINNING SPIRIT (IRE) 2 b.g. (Feb 2) Invincible Spirit (IRE) 121 – Taisho (IRE) 96 (Namaqualand (USA)) [2006 5s³ 6m² 5f³ 5f* 5m 5d⁵ Aug 29] 50,000Y: strong, good-quartered gelding: third foal: half-brother to 4-y-o Mulberry Lad and 3-y-o Waterline Twenty: dam Irish 6f/7f winner, including at 2 yrs: fairly useful performer: won maiden at Redcar in June: dropped away tamely in Molecomb Stakes at Goodwood and minor event at Ripon afterwards: best efforts at 5f: acts on firm and soft going: tends to carry head awkwardly: best treated with caution: sold 12,000 gns, and gelded. *J. Noseda* **82 §**

WINNING VENTURE 9 b.g. Owington 123 – Push A Button (Bold Lad (IRE) 133) [2006 67: p6g p5.1g p7.1g* f8g p7.1g⁵ p6g⁴ p6g⁴ p7.1g May 8] lengthy, good-topped gelding: unimpressive mover: useful on turf in his prime: modest performer on all-weather nowadays: won handicap at Wolverhampton in February: stays 1m: acts on polytrack, firm and soft going: tried in blinkers/cheekpieces: often tongue tied at 4 yrs: usually races prominently: none too consistent. *A. W. Carroll* **60**

WINSLOW BOY (USA) 5 b. or br.g. Expelled (USA) 116 – Acusteal (USA) (Acaroid (USA)) [2006 59: 10f⁶ Jul 17] fair handicapper at 3 yrs: lightly raced since, well held only outing on Flat in 2006. *P. Monteith* —

WINTHORPE (IRE) 6 b.g. Tagula (IRE) 116 – Zazu 58 (Cure The Blues (USA)) [2006 75: p7.1g³ f6g³ f6g* f6g* f6g* p7.1g⁵ f6g³ 5.1s⁴ p6g² 6d 6f⁵ 5d⁴ 6g² 6d 5m⁴ p6g p7.1g Dec 1] leggy gelding: fair handicapper: won twice at Southwell in February: effective at 5f to easy 7f: acts on all-weather and any turf going: tried in cheekpieces at 4yrs: sometimes carries head high, but is consistent. *J. J. Quinn* **75**

WISDOM'S KISS 2 b.g. (Feb 18) Ocean of Wisdom (USA) 106 – April Magic (Magic Ring (IRE) 115) [2006 p7g Nov 1] 50/1, well held in maiden at Kempton. *J. D. Bethell* —

WISE CHOICE 3 b.g. Green Desert (USA) 127 – Ballykett Lady (USA) 105 (Sir Ivor (USA) 135) [2006 54: f12g p9.5g⁵ p12g⁴ 12d⁴ 12.6g⁵ 14.1m³ 14.1g² 11.5m p12g⁶ 16.2m⁵ 12g* p12.2g³ Sep 11] angular, good-topped gelding: modest handicapper: won at Folkestone in August: stays 1¾m: acts on polytrack, raced mainly on good/good to firm ground on turf: modest winning hurdler. *N. P. Littmoden* **63**

WISE DECISION (IRE) 2 b.f. (Feb 12) Redback 116 – Eleanor Rigby (IRE) (Turtle   –
Island (IRE) 123) [2006 p7g Oct 6] 15,000Y: first foal: dam little sign of ability: tailed off
in maiden. *E. J. O'Neill*

WISE DENNIS 4 b.g. Polar Falcon (USA) 126 – Bowden Rose 100 (Dashing Blade   **101**
117) [2006 108: 8m 8f 8.1m⁴ 8s 8d⁴ 9d Sep 30] tall, leggy gelding: useful handicapper:
creditable efforts in 2006 at Newbury on reappearance, and when fourth to Audience at
Haydock and Supaseus at Ascot: well below form in Cambridgeshire at Newmarket final
start: stays 1m: acts on soft and good to firm going: sometimes races freely: held up.
A. P. Jarvis

WISE KID 3 b.g. Cloudings (IRE) 112 – Samana Cay 52 (Pharly (FR) 130) [2006 –: f5g   –
f5g Feb 7] of no account. *P. T. Midgley*

WISE OWL 4 b.g. Danehill (USA) 126 – Mistle Thrush (USA) 90 (Storm Bird (CAN)   **92**
134) [2006 90: p12g⁵ p12g⁶ p10g⁶ p16.5g* p16g² p13.9g⁶ 16.1m⁵ 16g⁴ 16g⁵ p13.9f⁴ 12s⁴
12d p13g³ Oct 15] angular gelding: fairly useful handicapper: won at Wolverhampton in
March: stays 2m: acts on polytrack and firm going: blinkered once at 3 yrs: has hung left/
raced freely: consistent: has joined D. Pipe. *J. Pearce*

WISE TALE 7 b.g. Nashwan (USA) 135 – Wilayif (USA) 75 (Danzig (USA)) [2006 56:   –
15.8g May 9] well-made gelding: modest maiden: well held only Flat outing in 2006:
wears headgear. *P. D. Niven*

WISETON DANCER (IRE) 2 b.c. (Apr 23) Danehill Dancer (IRE) 117 – Your   –
Village (IRE) 64 (Be My Guest (USA) 126) [2006 5s⁶ p7.1g Dec 31] leggy colt: well held
in minor event at Redcar and maiden at Wolverhampton 9 months apart. *Miss V. Haigh*

WISE WAGER (IRE) 4 b.f. Titus Livius (FR) 115 – Londubh (Tumble Wind) [2006   **65**
76: p5g 5.3m⁶ 5m 5f Jun 24] rather plain, unfurnished filly: fair handicapper: raced only
at 5f: acted on fibresand and firm going: tended to start slowly: usually raced prom-
inently/carried head awkwardly: dead. *Miss Z. C. Davison*

WISHING ON A STAR 2 b.f. (Feb 10) Fantastic Light (USA) 134 – Sephala (USA)   **78**
(Mr Prospector (USA)) [2006 7d⁴ 7.5m Sep 13] €60,000Y: close-coupled filly: half-sister
to 3 winners abroad, including UAE 9f winner Septette (by Indian Ridge): dam, French
2-y-o 7f/1m winner, sister to dams of very smart performer up to 7f One Cool Cat and
high-class US 1m/9f winner Aragorn: 2½ lengths fourth to Golden Dagger in maiden at
Newmarket in August: well held in similar event at Beverley following month: should be
suited by 1m+. *E. J. O'Neill*

WISTMAN (UAE) 5 br.g. Woodman (USA) 126 – Saik (USA) (Riverman (USA) 131)   **55**
[2006 73: f8g p8.6g 7d 7m 8d Apr 21] tall, close-coupled gelding: modest handicapper,
lightly raced: should stay 1m: acts on soft ground: visored (raced freely, well held) final
start: inconsistent. *D. Nicholls*

WITCHELLE 5 br.m. Wizard King 122 – Tachelle (IRE) (Elbio 125) [2006 66: f6g⁵   **65**
6v⁶ 7f² 6f⁶ 8f 7m f6g Nov 14] sturdy mare: fair handicapper: effective at 6f to 1m: acts on
fibresand and firm going: often makes running. *R. Craggs*

WITCHRY 4 gr.g. Green Desert (USA) 127 – Indian Skimmer (USA) 133 (Storm Bird   **80**
(CAN) 134) [2006 79: p6g 5.7f⁴ 6g⁶ 5.7m³ 5f* 5m 5.7m 5g² 5v³ p6g² p5.1m⁵ p6g⁵
Dec 20] compact gelding: fairly useful handicapper: won at Folkestone in July: effective
at 5f/6f: acts on polytrack and any turf going. *A. G. Newcombe*

WITH ADMIRATION 3 ch.g. Whittingham (IRE) 104 – Admire 77 (Last Tycoon   –
131) [2006 10g 7d May 28] tall, leggy gelding: last in maidens at Windsor and Newmarket: dead. *C. Drew*

WITH INTEREST 3 b.c. Selkirk (USA) 129 – With Fascination (USA) 111 (Dayjur   **111 p**
(USA) 137) [2006 95p: 8.2d* Nov 1] good-topped colt: has scope: smart form: successful in maiden at Newbury for A. Balding on only 2-y-o outing: off over a year, much
improved when winning 5-runner minor event at Nottingham in November readily by a
length from Babodana, confidently ridden: stays 8.2f: open to further improvement, and
likely to make mark at higher level. *Saeed bin Suroor*

WITHOUT A PADDLE 3 ch.g. Woodborough (USA) 112 – Sandra Dee (IRE) 60 (Be   **65 d**
My Guest (USA) 126) [2006 69: 5v⁵ 5.8m 6d 6v 6m⁴ 6m 5f 5m 5f³ 6m 5f⁵ 6m 6m 5f 5d⁵
5d Oct 17] fair maiden at best: fifth in banded race at Musselburgh penultimate outing:
effective at 5f/6f: acts on firm going: usually blinkered: inconsistent. *D. Loughnane,
Ireland*

WITH STYLE 3 b.f. Grand Lodge (USA) 125 – Coyote 91 (Indian Ridge 123) [2006   **65**
78p: 10m⁶ 8f⁴ 8.1m⁴ Aug 10] sturdy, close-coupled filly: fair maiden, lightly raced:

should be suited by 1¼m: raced only on good ground or firmer: sold 34,000 gns, sent to Qatar. *E. A. L. Dunlop*

WIZARD LOOKING 5 b.g. Wizard King 122 – High Stepping (IRE) (Taufan (USA)   **60**
119) [2006 73: 10m 11.5m 10m Jun 16] tall, close-coupled gelding: modest handicapper:
stays 1½m: acts on polytrack, firm and good to soft going: tried blinkered/tongue tied
earlier in career: sold 9,500 gns in November. *J. S. Wainwright*

WIZARDMICKTEE (IRE) 4 b.g. Monashee Mountain (USA) 115 – Epsilon 62   **–**
(Environment Friend 128) [2006 –: 7.5f Jul 7] leggy gelding: maiden: well held since
2 yrs. *A. Bailey*

WIZARD OF US 6 b.g. Wizard King 122 – Sian's Girl (Mystiko (USA) 124) [2006 –:   **63**
8.1s² 10.5m 8.5g² 7.1s 8g 8.2d³ Nov 1] smallish, workmanlike gelding: modest handicapper: stays 8.5f: acts on heavy going. *M. Mullineaux*

WIZARD PRINCE 3 b.g. Wizard King 122 – Choral Dancer (USA) (Night Shift   **–**
(USA)) [2006 53: p5.1g 7.1g Jul 5] maiden: well held in sellers in 2006, leaving R. Harris
after reappearance: stays 6f: in cheekpieces/blinkers nowadays. *J. G. M. O'Shea*

WIZARD QUAY 3 b.g. Wizard King 122 – Roonah Quay (IRE) (Soviet Lad (USA))   **45**
[2006 50: 7.1m 6m 6.1d Jun 26] workmanlike gelding: poor maiden: stays 7f: acts
on firm and good to soft going: tried in cheekpieces/blinkers: somewhat wayward.
W. K. Goldsworthy

WIZARDS DREAM 3 b.c. Silver Wizard (USA) 117 – Last Dream (IRE) 80 (Alzao   **72**
(USA) 117) [2006 8d 10f⁵ 8.2g⁴ 11.6d⁶ Oct 9] sturdy, well-made colt: fifth foal: half-
brother to 3 winners in France, including 1m (including at 2 yrs)/1¼m winner Landslide
(by Bigstone) and 8.5f winner Last Cry (by Peintre Celebre), both useful: dam, Irish 1½m
winner, half-sister to Grand Criterium winners Lost World and Fijar Tango: fair maiden:
will stay 1½m: acts on firm and good to soft ground. *D. R. C. Elsworth*

WIZBY 3 b.f. Wizard King 122 – Diamond Vanessa (IRE) (Distinctly North (USA) 115)   **57**
[2006 59: 7.1s 6.1d³ 6.1s³ 6.1d⁴ 6f⁴ 7m 8.1d* 8.1g 8.1f 8s⁶ 9.1v³ 8.2d f8g Dec 9] compact
filly: has a quick action: modest handicapper: won at Chepstow in June: stays 9f: acts on
any turf going: effective tongue tied or not: sometimes slowly away. *P. D. Evans*

WODHILL BE 6 b.m. Danzig Connection (USA) – Muarij (Star Appeal 133) [2006 49:   **53**
f7g³ f7g p7.1g³ p7g p7.1g p7g f7g 7f⁵ 7m 7m⁴ 7d f8g⁶ f7g p7.1g³ f7g⁴ Dec 28] modest
performer: stays 1m: acts on all-weather, good to firm and good to soft going: has taken
strong hold: inconsistent. *D. Morris*

WODHILL GOLD 5 ch.g. Dancing Spree (USA) – Golden Filigree 48 (Faustus   **59**
(USA) 118) [2006 53: p9.5g p10g f8g* 8m 10.1f⁵ 8m p8.6g⁵ f7g² f8g³ p8.6g² p8g⁶ Dec
18] sturdy gelding: modest performer: won banded race at Southwell in May: probably
stays 1¼m: acts on all-weather: tried blinkered, often visored. *D. Morris*

WODHILL SCHNAPS 5 b.g. Danzig Connection (USA) – Muarij (Star Appeal 133)   **58**
[2006 7m 8.2m 7f⁴ p8g 7m 7m 7d⁶ p7g f8g² f8g⁵ f8g³ Dec 28] sturdy gelding: modest
maiden: stays 1m: acts on fibresand and firm going: tried in cheekpieces, blinkered last 4
starts: has looked far from keen. *D. Morris*

WOLDS DANCER 4 b.f. Fraam 114 – Dancing Em 60 (Rambo Dancer (CAN) 107)   **53**
[2006 58: 10d⁴ 12g 9.9m Sep 19] lengthy filly: modest maiden handicapper: stays 1¼m:
acts on good to firm and good to soft going: usually blinkered. *T. D. Easterby*

WOLFMAN 4 ch.g. Wolfhound (USA) 126 – Madam Millie 99 (Milford 119) [2006 –:   **54**
p6g⁶ f6g⁶ p6g 5f 6m 5m 6v⁶ 6d 7m² Sep 16] leggy, workmanlike gelding: modest maiden:
stays 7f: acts on all-weather and good to firm going: in cheekpieces after reappearance.
D. W. Barker

WOLF PACK 4 b.g. Green Desert (USA) 127 – Warning Shadows (IRE) 113 (Cadeaux   **–**
Genereux 131) [2006 –: 6m f6g⁵ f8g 10d 8d Oct 18] good-bodied gelding: little form.
R. W. Price

WOLF RIVER (USA) 2 b.c. (Mar 30) Mr Greeley (USA) 122 – Beal Street Blues   **76**
(USA) (Dixieland Band (USA)) [2006 p7.1f³ p7g Sep 27] closely related/half-brother to
several winners in USA: dam US Grade 2 2-y-o 1m winner, sister to US Grade 2 8.5f
winner Dixieland Brass: better effort in steadily-run maidens when 6 lengths third to
Manchurian at Wolverhampton: will stay 1m. *D. M. Simcock*

WONDERFUL DESERT 3 b.f. Green Desert (USA) 127 – One So Wonderful 121   **–**
(Nashwan (USA) 135) [2006 57: 7f⁶ Jul 4] modest maiden at 2 yrs: well held in handicap
only outing in 2006: stays 6.9f: acts on good to firm going. *L. M. Cumani*

WONDERFUL ONE (IRE) 3 ch.f. Nashwan (USA) 135 – Ring The Relatives 75 **66**
(Bering 136) [2006 57p: p8g⁶ 10.2g² p9.5g Nov 11] leggy filly: fair maiden, lightly raced:
easily best effort when 4 lengths second to Mowazana at Bath (made running): stays
1¼m. *J. H. M. Gosden*

WOODCOTE (IRE) 4 b.g. Monashee Mountain (USA) 115 – Tootle (Main Reef 126) **102**
[2006 102: 6m 6m³ 5f⁶ 6m² 6.1f² 6m 6g⁴ 5.4g⁵ 6d 5d* Oct 7] strong, lengthy gelding:
useful handicapper: several creditable efforts prior to winning at Ascot by neck from
Godfrey Street, racing alone much of way: effective at 5f/6f: acts on firm and good to
soft going: usually in cheekpieces nowadays: races prominently: formerly headstrong.
C. G. Cox

WOODCOTE PLACE 3 b.c. Lujain (USA) 119 – Giant Nipper (Nashwan (USA) **99**
135) [2006 81p: 7s⁶ 7f 8.3m² 8.3f² 7.1m 7.1m⁶ 7.1m* 7d* p7g 7g² Oct 13] well-made,
attractive colt: useful performer: progressed well in 2006, winning maiden at Warwick
in August and handicap at Goodwood in September: very good neck second to King's
Caprice in handicap at Newmarket final outing: stays 8.3f: acts on polytrack, firm and
good to soft going: held up. *P. R. Chamings*

WOOD DALLING (USA) 8 b.g. Woodman (USA) 126 – Cloelia (USA) (Lyphard **– §**
(USA) 132) [2006 –§: 9.2m 7.1g 8m 8d 7.2m 8.3m⁶ Aug 16] small, sturdy gelding: ungenuine performer: no form since 2004: tried in headgear/tongue tie. *Mrs J. C. McGregor*

WOOD FERN (UAE) 6 b.g. Green Desert (USA) 127 – Woodsia 97 (Woodman **60**
(USA) 126) [2006 54§: f8g⁴ p12.2g* p9.5g² p12.2g⁴ 11.8d⁵ 10m⁴ p9.5g⁶ 12.3g⁶ 10.2f⁴
10.2m² 10f⁶ 9.9f⁶ 10.1g 10.2f³ p10g³ p9.5g³ p10g⁵ p10g² p10g² p10g² Dec 22] strong,
close-coupled gelding: modest performer: won banded race at Wolverhampton in
April: best at 1¼m/1½m: acts on polytrack, firm and soft going: effective visored or not.
W. M. Brisbourne

WOODFORD CONSULT 4 b.f. Benny The Dip (USA) 127 – Chicodove 91 (In The **52**
Wings 128) [2006 62: 16g⁶ 16v⁶ Oct 25] big, workmanlike filly: modest handicapper:
stays 2m: acts on fibresand, firm and good to soft going: has run well sweating: reluctant
to enter/leave stall once at 3 yrs. *M. W. Easterby*

WOODLANDS BELLE 3 ch.f. Woodborough (USA) 112 – Blushing Belle 74 (Local **–**
Suitor (USA) 128) [2006 –: 11.9f Aug 10] strong filly: no form. *B. G. Powell*

WOODLAND SYMPHONY 2 b.g. (Apr 26) Auction House (USA) 120 – Red Sym- **–**
phony 64 (Merdon Melody 98) [2006 5d 6m 5.1d p6m Nov 8] angular gelding: little
form: visored final start. *N. Tinkler*

WOODLAND TRAVELLER (USA) 2 b.g. (Mar 6) Gone West (USA) – Iftiraas **64**
114 (Distant Relative 128) [2006 6m 6s³ 7.5m⁶ Sep 13] tall, close-coupled gelding: best
effort in maidens when 2½ lengths third to Lafontaine Bleu at Ripon in August: should
stay beyond 6f: tongue tied last 2 outings. *N. Tinkler*

WOODNOOK 3 b.f. Cadeaux Genereux 131 – Corndavon (USA) 95 (Sheikh Albadou **96**
128) [2006 73: 5.2m⁴ 5m² 6d p6g³ p6g³ 5m² 5g⁴ 5.2m⁴ p6g* p6g³ p6g² p6g⁶ Dec 16]
rather leggy, lengthy filly: useful handicapper: won at Lingfield in October: good neck
second to Maltese Falcon there penultimate outing: free-going sort, will prove best at 5f/
6f: acts on polytrack and good to firm going: consistent. *J. A. R. Toller*

WOODSLEY HOUSE (IRE) 4 b.g. Orpen (USA) 116 – Flame And Shadow (IRE) **79**
(Turtle Island (IRE) 123) [2006 81: 8g 8g 6g* p6g p7g Dec 10] tall gelding: fair
performer: showed little in 3 starts for D. Hall in Hong Kong under name Avoidance of
Doubt in 2005/6: won maiden at Goodwood in August on return to Britain: well held in
handicaps last 2 outings, leaving W. Muir 7,000 gns in between: probably best at 6f/7f:
acts on soft and good to firm going. *Miss Gay Kelleway*

WOODWEE 3 ch.g. Woodborough (USA) 112 – Evaporate 51 (Insan (USA) 119) **61**
[2006 65: f7g⁴ f8g³ p7.1g⁵ f6g⁶ f7g³ 5v³ 6d³ 6g 6f7g f7g f6g⁴ f6g f7g Dec 28] big,
plain gelding: just modest performer in 2006: probably stays 1m: acts on fibresand, firm
and good to soft going: tried in cheekpieces/blinkered. *J. R. Weymes*

WOODWOOL 4 br.f. Benny The Dip (USA) 127 – Woodcrest 82 (Niniski (USA) 125) **64**
[2006 54p: p10g p10g Feb 1] modest maiden: barely stays 1¼m: raced only on polytrack.
H. Candy

WOOLFALL BLUE (IRE) 3 gr.c. Bluebird (USA) 125 – Diamond Waltz (IRE) **87**
(Linamix (FR) 127) [2006 86: 7.1g 10g⁴ 7m a9.5g² 9m³ p10g* p9.5g³ p9.5g p10g⁴ Dec 8]
leggy colt: fairly useful performer: won maiden at Kempton in September: good fourth in

handicap there final start: stays 1¼m: acts on polytrack and soft going: bit slipped on reappearance. *G. G. Margarson*

WOOLFALL KING (IRE) 3 b.g. King Charlemagne (USA) 120 – Bazaar Promise 58 (Native Bazaar 122) [2006 –: 7m 6m 11.5m 10.1f 7g 8m 9.8d Aug 29] useful-looking gelding: little form: tried visored. *G. G. Margarson* – **–**

WOOLLY BACK (IRE) 5 b.g. Alzao (USA) 117 – Hopping Higgins (IRE) 103 (Brief Truce (USA) 126) [2006 64: 10.1m 10g⁵ p8.6g² p12.2f² 10.1s 9s Sep 24] sturdy gelding: modest maiden: stays 1½m: acts on polytrack, good to firm and good to soft going on turf: wore cheekpieces final start: carries head high: sold 2,500 gns. *A. C. Whillans* **64**

WOOLLY BULLY 3 b.c. Robellino (USA) 127 – Belle Ile (USA) 67 (Diesis 133) [2006 70p: 8m² 8.3g² 8d* 10s⁴ 8d Oct 27] good-bodied colt: fairly useful performer: didn't need to be anywhere near best to win maiden at Pontefract in October: good fourth in handicap at Nottingham after: stays 1¼m: acts on soft and good to firm going. *G. A. Huffer* **85**

WOOL MART 2 ch.g. (Mar 29) Auction House (USA) 120 – Worsted 70 (Whittingham (IRE) 104) [2006 6d p6g 6m⁴ 6s⁶ 6.1g Sep 15] good-topped gelding: third foal: dam, sprint maiden, out of sister to dam of very smart sprinter Cape of Good Hope: fair maiden: easily best effort when fourth at Haydock: well held in nurseries last 2 outings: raced only at 6f: acts on good to firm going. *M. Blanshard* **70**

WOOLSEY 3 b.g. Kingsinger (IRE) 94 – Worsted 70 (Whittingham (IRE) 104) [2006 10g 8.1s 9.9g 8.1m 11.7m Aug 25] workmanlike gelding: modest maiden: stays 1m: acts on good to firm ground. *M. Blanshard* **58**

WOOLSTONE BOY (USA) 5 ch.g. Will's Way (USA) 125 – My Pleasure (USA) (Marfa (USA)) [2006 63: f14g Jul 11] modest performer: well beaten only Flat outing in 2006: tongue tied: has carried head high/hung left. *K. C. Bailey* **–**

WOQOODD 2 b.g. (Mar 30) Royal Applause 124 – Intervene (Zafonic (USA) 130) [2006 6g 6m³ 5.1d⁴ Oct 4] 75,000Y: well-made gelding: fourth foal: dam unraced half-sister to smart French performer up to 1¾m Short Pause and to dam of July Cup winner Continent: best effort in maidens when 4¼ lengths third to Longquan at Haydock: possibly unsuited by softer ground next time: stays 6f: acts on good to firm ground: sold 37,000 gns, and gelded. *M. A. Jarvis* **72**

WORCESTER LODGE 5 ch.g. Grand Lodge (USA) 125 – Borgia 91 (Machiavellian (USA) 123) [2006 p12g Apr 2] strong, good sort: fair handicapper at best: unraced at 4 yrs: well below form only outing in 2006. *Mrs L. Richards* **–**

WORD PERFECT 4 b.f. Diktat 126 – Better Still (IRE) (Glenstal (USA) 118) [2006 82: 6v³ 7d 5.9g³ 6.1d⁶ 9.8s⁵ 7.1s 6s* 6d² 6g⁶ 6v Oct 28] tall, useful-looking filly: fair handicapper: won at Ayr in September: best at 6f/7f: acts on heavy and good to firm going: blinkered last 4 starts. *M. W. Easterby* **79**

WORLABY DALE 10 b.g. Terimon 124 – Restandbethankful (Random Shot 116) [2006 –, a43: p16.5g f14g Dec 5] workmanlike gelding: maiden: no recent form. *Mrs S. Lamyman* **–**

WORLD AT MY FEET 4 b.f. Wolfhound (USA) 126 – Rehaab 72 (Mtoto 134) [2006 58: 9.9f 5f 6m 5d 5g 9.9g 10m 10f⁶ Sep 20] small, close-coupled filly: has a short action: modest performer: seemingly effective at 5f to 1¼m: acts on firm and good to soft going: tried blinkered/tongue tied (including last 5 starts). *N. Bycroft* **48**

WORLD IN ACTION (IRE) 3 br.g. Spinning World (USA) 130 – Pretty Procida (USA) (Procida (USA) 129) [2006 70: 8d 9.9m 10.5s a9.5g Nov 23] leggy, lengthy gelding: fair maiden at 2 yrs: below form in 2006, sold from A. Jarvis 1,200 gns after second start: stays 1m: blinkered final outing. *Mme D. U. Smith, Germany* **–**

WORLDLY 2 gr.g. (Mar 14) Selkirk (USA) 129 – Miss Universe (IRE) 99 (Warning 136) [2006 7g² p8.6f* 8m Sep 19] 10,000Y: tall gelding: third foal: half-brother to useful 2004 2-y-o 7f winner Tasdeed (by Cadeaux Genereux) and 5-y-o Day To Remember: dam 2-y-o 6f winner: confirmed debut promise (slowly away and green) when winning maiden at Wolverhampton in August by 3½ lengths from Grand Lucre: reportedly bled when tailed off in nursery final start: stays 8.6f: sent to USA. *S. Kirk* **82**

WORLDLY PURSUIT 3 ch.f. Spinning World (USA) 130 – Final Pursuit 92§ (Pursuit of Love 124) [2006 52: p7.1g 7f Apr 26] rather leggy filly: seemingly modest maiden: well held in handicaps both starts in 2006. *B. Smart* **–**

WORLD'S HEROINE (IRE) 2 ch.f. (Feb 26) Spinning World (USA) 130 – Meta- **83** phor (USA) (Woodman (USA)) 126) [2006 6m 6f⁴ 7f* 7d Sep 30] 40,000Y: angular, good-topped filly: sixth foal: half-sister to fairly useful French 2001 2-y-o 7f winner Celestial Lagoon (by Sunday Silence): dam, French 2-y-o 1m winner, half-sister to smart miler King of Happiness (by Spinning World): won maiden at York in July (sweating/ edgy) by 2½ lengths from Dancing Granny: creditable seventh in nursery at Newmarket final start: should stay 1m. *G. A. Butler*

WORLD SPIRIT 2 b.f. (Apr 6) Agnes World (USA) 123 – Belle Esprit (Warning 136) **73 p** [2006 6s 7g² p8g* Nov 29] 3,500Y: close-coupled filly: fifth foal: half-sister to fairly useful 1½m winner All Business (by Entrepreneur) and 4-y-o Reluctant Suitor: dam unraced sister to smart performer up to 1¼m Torch Rouge: fair form in maidens: won at Kempton in November by 1¼ lengths from First Buddy: 2 lengths second to Milligait at Newcastle previous start: will stay 1¼m: acts on polytrack: should do better still. *Rae Guest*

WORLD SUPREMACY (IRE) 3 b.g. Spinning World (USA) 130 – Cream Jug **–** (IRE) (Spectrum (IRE) 126) [2006 63: 10m 7d 8v p12.2g Nov 24] modest maiden at 2 yrs: little form in 2006. *G. O'Leary, Ireland*

WORTH ABBEY 4 b.g. Mujadil (USA) 119 – Housefull 81 (Habitat 134) [2006 49, **–** a64: p8.6g p8.6g p9.5g Mar 15] modest performer at 3 yrs: well beaten in 2006. *M. Appleby*

WOTAVADUN (IRE) 3 ch.g. King of Kings (IRE) 125 – Blush With Love (USA) (Mt **39** Livermore (USA)) [2006 –: p5g f5g⁶ p6g 5.3f⁶ p5.1g p5g⁶ p5g⁶ Dec 13] strong, work-manlike gelding: poor maiden: left K. McAuliffe after third outing and C. Dore after fifth: often blinkered: hung badly left fourth start: reportedly bled fifth outing. *Ms J. S. Doyle*

WOTCHALIKE (IRE) 4 ch.c. Spectrum (IRE) 126 – Juno Madonna (IRE) (Sadler's **53** Wells (USA) 132) [2006 70, a80: p12.2g 8.3d⁶ 8m p12g⁴ p12g⁶ p12.2g⁶ p16.5g⁵ Oct 8] **a67** strong, good-topped colt: fair handicapper on all-weather, modest on turf nowadays: seems to stay easy 2m: acts on polytrack, soft and good to firm ground: sometimes visor-ed: usually races up with pace: won over hurdles in October. *R. J. Price*

WOVOKA (IRE) 3 b.g. Mujadil (USA) 119 – Common Cause 87 (Polish Patriot **100** (USA) 128) [2006 101: a7f⁴ a8f a9f 7.5m⁵ 8m³ 10s 10d 10m⁶ Jul 21] workmanlike gelding: useful performer: easily best effort in 2006 when third to Dunelight in handicap at Newmarket on fifth outing: should stay 1¼m: acts on dirt, soft and good to firm going: tried visored: usually held up: has run well when sweating. *M. R. Channon*

WRAITH 2 b.c. (Apr 25) Maria's Mon (USA) 121 – Really Polish (USA) (Polish **58 p** Numbers (USA)) [2006 8.1g Sep 23] 24,000Y: big colt: second foal: dam won 9 races in USA, including Grade 3 8.5f event: 10/1, hampered start when never-nearer seventh to Petara Bay in maiden at Haydock: will do better. *H. R. A. Cecil*

Skybet Dash (Handicap), York—not quite the OK Corral,
but Wyatt Earp comes out best in a fight also involving Ice Planet (check cap) and Blue Tomato

WRECKING CREW (IRE) 2 b.c. (Feb 15) Invincible Spirit (IRE) 121 – Rushing **71**
(Deploy 131) [2006 p5g⁶ 5d⁶ 5m³ 6.1m Jun 3] €16,000F, €17,000Y: compact colt: first
foal: dam, French maiden who stayed 1½m, out of sister to Lancashire Oaks winner
Andaleeb: easily best effort (fair form) when 3 lengths third to King's Bastion in maiden
at Lingfield: should stay 1m. *B. R. Millman*

WRENLANE 5 ch.g. Fraam 114 – Hi Hoh (IRE) (Fayruz 116) [2006 67: f8g³ p8.6g **62**
p8.6g p9.5g⁴ 9g 7.9m 16d² 14.1m Sep 11] compact gelding: modest handicapper: left
R. Fahey after fourth start: stays 2m: acts on polytrack, good to firm and good to soft
going: tried in cheekpieces/blinkers: won over hurdles in August. *J. J. Quinn*

WRIGHTY ALMIGHTY (IRE) 4 b.g. Danehill Dancer (IRE) 117 – Persian Emp- **79 d**
ress (IRE) 51 (Persian Bold 123) [2006 89: 6d p7g p8g 7.1f⁴ 7g⁴ 7m 6m p8g Oct 23] tall,
useful-looking gelding: fair performer nowadays: below form last 4 starts: stays 7f: acts
on firm going, probably on polytrack: tried in cheekpieces/blinkers. *P. R. Chamings*

WRIT (IRE) 4 ch.g. Indian Lodge (IRE) 127 – Carnelly (IRE) 101 (Priolo (USA) 127) **–**
[2006 63: p8g p7.1g⁴ p8g* p8g² p10g³ 10s 7.2s⁶ p8.6m* p8.6g* p8.6g⁴ p9.5g⁵ p7.1g* **a82**
Dec 23] quite good-topped gelding: fairly useful performer: won handicaps at Lingfield in June and, having left Ernst Oertel after fifth start, Wolverhampton in October (2)
and December: effective at 7f, barely stays easy 1¼m: acts on polytrack, no form on turf.
I. Semple

WRYNOES PASS (IRE) 2 b.g. (Mar 29) Bold Fact (USA) 116 – Home To Reality **–**
(IRE) (Imperial Frontier (USA) 112) [2006 5f 7f Jul 23] tailed off in seller and maiden.
R. F. Fisher

WUJOOD 4 b.g. Alzao (USA) 117 – Rahayeb 79 (Arazi (USA) 135) [2006 80, a69: 8.3g **–**
10.2g⁶ May 2] small, good-topped gelding: fairly useful performer at best: well held in
2006, in cheekpieces final start. *H. Morrison*

WULIMASTER (USA) 3 b. or br.g. Silver Hawk (USA) 123 – Kamaina (USA) (Mr **75**
Prospector (USA)) [2006 7p: 10.2s³ 8.3d² Jun 26] close-coupled gelding: fair form in
maidens: stays 1¼m: acts on soft and good to firm ground: sold 25,000 gns in October,
and gelded. *Sir Michael Stoute*

WUNDERWOOD (USA) 7 b.g. Faltaat (USA) – Jasoorah (IRE) 98 (Sadler's Wells **115**
(USA) 132) [2006 115: p10g⁶ 12s 12m³ 14m* 14m² 14.1m* Aug 31] well-made gelding:
smart performer: won handicap at Goodwood (beat Solent by 2½ lengths) in June and,
having left Lady Herries after fourth start, minor event at Salisbury (by neck from Collier
Hill) in August: also ran well when 1¼ lengths second to Soulacroix in handicap at
Goodwood in between: was effective at 1½m to 1¾m: acted on polytrack, firm and good
to soft going: put down after fracturing near-fore in November while being prepared in
Australia for Melbourne Cup. *D. R. C. Elsworth*

WYATT EARP (IRE) 5 b.g. Piccolo 121 – Tribal Lady 80 (Absalom 128) [2006 93: **100**
5f⁴ 6f² 6f* 6f* 6d 7d⁵ 6s Oct 7] smallish, sturdy gelding: useful handicapper: won twice
at York in July, beating Ice Planet by ¾ length in fairly valuable event second occasion:
also ran creditably when ½-length second to Fantasy Believer at Pontefract and fifth to
All Ivory in totesport.com Stakes at Ascot: has form at easy 1m, barely stays 7f when
conditions are testing: acts on polytrack, soft and firm going: blinkered (ran poorly) once
at 4 yrs: consistent. *R. A. Fahey*

WYETH 2 ch.c. (Apr 23) Grand Lodge (USA) 125 – Bordighera (USA) 104 (Alysheba **58 p**
(USA)) [2006 8.2s⁶ Oct 25] good-topped colt: brother to 2 winners, notably high-class
but quirky 7f (at 2 yrs) to 11f winner Grandera and half-brother to 2 winners, notably
3-y-o George Washington: dam useful French 13f winner: 5/1 and green, 11 lengths sixth
to Sahrati in maiden at Nottingham, nearest finish and learning all while: will stay at least
1¼m: sure to do better. *J. R. Fanshawe*

X

XAAR BREEZE 3 b.f. Xaar 132 – Dicentra (Rambo Dancer (CAN) 107) [2006 –: f7g **51**
f8g⁴ 5f 5.7f³ 6f 5.1g 6f Jul 27] modest maiden: left Rae Guest after second outing: stays
6f: acts on firm going: withdrawn after bolting before start intended final outing in
October. *Mrs P. Townsley*

XAARETTA (IRE) 2 b.f. (Mar 15) Xaar 132 – Hello Mary (IRE) (Dolphin Street (FR) **–**
125) [2006 6g Jul 6] 45,000Y: second foal: half-sister to Irish 2005 2-y-o 1m winner
Crosshaven (by Cape Cross): dam, Italian 5f winner (including at 2 yrs), half-sister to

dam of 5-y-o Moss Vale: 33/1, behind when breaking leg 2f out in maiden at Newbury: dead. *R. Hannon*

XAAR TOO BUSY 2 b.f. (Apr 19) Xaar 132 – Desert Serenade (USA) (Green Desert (USA) 127) [2006 6f 7d 6g³ 7d Oct 3] €22,000Y: seventh foal: half-sister to 3 winners, including 4-y-o Muscari and fairly useful French 1m (at 2 yrs) to 13f winner Major Performance (by Celtic Swing): dam, ran twice, sister to high-class sprinter Sheikh Albadou: modest maiden: should prove suited by 7f+: visored last 2 outings, slowly away on former. *Mrs A. Duffield* **54**

XACOBEO (IRE) 4 b.g. Montjeu (IRE) 137 – Afisiak 60 (Efisio 120) [2006 66: 10.2d p12.2g 12.1g Jul 5] big gelding: modest maiden at 3 yrs: well beaten in 2006, saddle slipped final outing: sold 4,000 gns in July, and gelded. *R. Hannon* **–**

XALOC BAY (IRE) 8 br.g. Charnwood Forest (IRE) 125 – Royal Jade 82 (Last Tycoon 131) [2006 36: p8.6g f7g³ f8g⁴ f8g f8g f6g⁴ p7.1g⁴ Mar 27] sturdy gelding: poor mover: poor performer: stays 8.6f: acts on all-weather, soft and good to firm ground: tried in headgear: usually races prominently. *R. A. Harris* **53**

XALTED 2 b.f. (Mar 24) Xaar 132 – Joonayh 81 (Warning 136) [2006 6m 6s 5m Sep 13] 12,000F, 3,000Y: good-bodied filly: third foal: half-sister to 4-y-o Majehar: dam, 2-y-o 6f winner, half-sister to smart 7f performer Millennium Force: backward, behind in maidens: slowly away first 2 outings: will be suited by 7f+: may well improve. *S. C. Williams* **– p**

XALUNA BAY (IRE) 3 br.f. Xaar 132 – Lunadine (FR) (Bering 136) [2006 77: 5.7d 5m 6d 6f² p6g* p6g² 7m³ p6g⁶ 6m³ 6d³ 5m⁴ p6g⁴ p6g² p5g⁴ Oct 17] tall, rather leggy filly: fairly useful handicapper: won at Kempton in June: probably needs good test at 5f, barely stays 7f: acts on polytrack and firm going: raced freely seventh start: reportedly bled eleventh outing: consistent. *W. R. Muir* **87**

XENIA 3 b.f. Labeeb 124 – Known Class (USA) (Known Fact (USA) 135) [2006 –: f8g⁵ 10f 9d⁶ 12d Sep 5] close-coupled filly: little form: left J. Given after reappearance: tried blinkered. *T. J. Etherington* **–**

XENIAM (IRE) 3 b.g. Rossini (USA) 118 – Rose Tint (IRE) (Salse (USA) 128) [2006 9.9g 11m Sep 10] well held in maidens at Salisbury and Goodwood. *A. King* **–**

XENOPHILE 3 ch.g. Elnadim (USA) 128 – Femme Femme (USA) (Lyphard (USA) 132) [2006 –: 8s⁶ 7g Jun 13] lengthy gelding: well held in maidens: sold 800 gns, sent to Sweden. *J. L. Dunlop* **–**

XOCOLATL 3 b.f. Elnadim (USA) 128 – Chocolate (IRE) 77 (Brief Truce (USA) 126) [2006 p6g⁴ Dec 7] first foal: dam maiden at 2 yrs in Britain (later 6f and 1m winner in France/Belgium): well held in maiden at Wolverhampton. *Peter Grayson* **–**

XPRES BOY (IRE) 3 b.g. Tagula (IRE) 116 – Highly Motivated 84 (Midyan (USA) 124) [2006 63: p6g p7.1g⁵ 10d 6.1d 8.1m f8g f7g f5g Dec 22] modest performer on all-weather: stays 7f: acts on all-weather, no form on turf: tongue tied final outing. *S. R. Bowring* **– a58**

XPRES DIGITAL 5 b.g. Komaite (USA) – Kustom Kit Xpres 69 (Absalom 128) [2006 74, a81: f6g Jan 1] good-topped gelding: fairly useful on all-weather, fair on turf in 2005: well held only outing in 2006: tried tongue tied. *S. R. Bowring* **–**

XPRES MAITE 3 b.g. Komaite (USA) – Antonias Melody 86 (Rambo Dancer (CAN) 107) [2006 7m⁶ f8g⁵ 7.5f⁵ p6g* f6g* 7.5f⁵ 6.1m⁴ 8g p7.1m⁶ Nov 9] sturdy, compact gelding: third foal: brother to 5-y-o Kingsmaite: dam 6f (including at 2 yrs)/7f winner: fair performer: won handicaps at Wolverhampton and Kempton in July: effective at 6f to 7.5f: acts on all-weather and firm ground: in cheekpieces/blinkered last 2 starts. *S. R. Bowring* **77**

XTRA TORRENTIAL (USA) 4 b.g. Torrential (USA) 117 – Offering (USA) (Majestic Light (USA)) [2006 101, a–: 7g⁶ 8s p7g p7g p8g Dec 22] tall, leggy gelding: useful performer, better on turf than all-weather: lightly raced: best effort in 2006 when 4¼ lengths sixth of 7 to Etlaala in listed race at Leicester: stays 1m: acts on polytrack and good to soft going. *D. M. Simcock* **105 a98**

Y

YAKIMOV (USA) 7 ch.g. Affirmed (USA) – Ballet Troupe (USA) (Nureyev (USA) 131) [2006 91: 8s 10.9g* 11.7d⁶ 10.3m 10.5g 12m² 10m Jul 7] strong, lengthy gelding: fairly useful handicapper: won at Warwick in April: effective at 7f to 1½m: acts on fibresand, soft and good to firm going. *D. J. Wintle* **91**

YA LATE MAITE 3 ch.f. Komaite (USA) – Plentitude (FR) (Ela-Mana-Mou 132) **55**
[2006 51: 7g³ 7g² Jun 2] good-bodied filly: modest maiden: should stay 1m.
E. S. McMahon

YANDINA (IRE) 3 b.f. Danehill (USA) 126 – Lughz (USA) (Housebuster (USA)) **74**
[2006 7g³ 7f* p7g Sep 29] €250,000Y: sturdy filly: second foal: dam unraced half-sister
to Falmouth Stakes winner Alshakr and to dam of 1000 Guineas winner Harayir, out of
Irish Oaks winner Give Thanks: fair form: won maiden at Lingfield in September: raced
only at 7f: acts on firm going: very slowly away and hung left on debut. *B. W. Hills*

YANKEEDOODLEDANDY (IRE) 5 b.g. Orpen (USA) 116 – Laura Margaret **–**
(Persian Bold 123) [2006 83: p12g 14g p16g Aug 2] compact gelding: fairly useful
handicapper at best: well held in 2006: sometimes wears cheekpieces. *C. Roberts*

YAQEEN 2 b.f. (May 2) Green Desert (USA) 127 – Lady Elgar (IRE) (Sadler's Wells **90 p**
(USA) 132) [2006 6g³ Jun 30] $400,000Y: good-topped filly: fourth foal: half-sister to
fairly useful 1¼m winner Sir Edward Elgar (by King's Best) and smart French 9f (at
2 yrs) to 1½m winner Grand Couturier (by Grand Lodge): dam, well beaten in France
only start, sister to smart Irish performer up to 1½m Desert Fox: 5/2, ½-length third to
Wid in maiden at Newmarket, slowly away before running on well: should stay 1m:
should progress. *M. A. Jarvis*

YARQUS 3 b.g. Diktat 126 – Will You Dance 83 (Shareef Dancer (USA) 135) [2006 **101**
87: p8g⁶ 8.1g* 12.3f⁴ 12g⁶ 8m 8g 8m⁶ 8s p8g p8g Dec 22] good-topped gelding: useful
performer: dead-heated with King's Head in handicap at Sandown in April: mostly
highly tried after, seeming to run well when 3 lengths fourth to Papal Bull in Chester Vase
(probably flattered) and sixth to Prince of Light in listed race at Goodwood seventh
outing: below form in handicaps last 3 starts: stays 1½m: acts on polytrack, firm and good
to soft going. *C. E. Brittain*

YASHIN (IRE) 5 b.g. Soviet Star (USA) 128 – My Mariam 79 (Salse (USA) 128) [2006 **59**
67: f11g⁴ f11g³ p9.5g² p9.5g f11g* p10g⁵ May 23] sturdy gelding: modest performer:
won banded race at Southwell in May: stays 11f: acts on all-weather, unraced on extremes
of going on turf: tried blinkered. *P. A. Blockley*

YASOODD 3 br.c. Inchinor 119 – Needwood Epic 61 (Midyan (USA) 124) [2006 103: **111**
8s* 8g 8v⁴ 8m⁶ 10.4f⁴ Jul 29] tall colt: smart performer: won Leopardstown 2000 Guineas
Trial Stakes in April by neck from Heliostatic: best effort after when 4 lengths fourth to
Araafa in Irish 2000 Guineas at the Curragh: increasingly agitated in preliminaries in
St James's Palace Stakes at Royal Ascot (ran creditably) and York Stakes at York after:
stays 1m: acts on heavy going: tends to get on toes, and has been early to post: held up:
joined D. Selvaratnam in UAE. *M. R. Channon*

YASSOOMA (IRE) 3 b.g. King of Kings (IRE) 125 – Statistic (USA) (Mr Prospector **40**
(USA)) [2006 –: f7g f8g⁵ f6g⁴ f7g p6g 7d Apr 12] tall gelding: poor maiden: best efforts
at 6f: tried blinkered/visored. *T. J. Pitt*

YAWMI 6 ch.h. Zafonic (USA) 130 – Reine Wells (IRE) 107 (Sadler's Wells (USA) 132) **72**
[2006 77: p12.2g⁴ Jan 16] angular, good-topped horse: fair performer: stays 1½m: acts on
polytrack and good to firm going: races prominently. *B. D. Leavy*

YAZAMAAN 2 b.c. (Feb 8) Galileo (IRE) 134 – Moon's Whisper (USA) (Storm Cat **107 p**
(USA)) [2006 8d* 8m* Aug 31] first foal: dam unraced out of very smart French 1m and
10.5f winner East of The Moon, herself half-sister to Kingmambo out of Miesque:
created good impression in winning both starts in small fields in August, namely slowly-
run maiden at Newmarket (by 3 lengths) and 3-runner minor event at Salisbury (beat
Princeton by 6 lengths, again edging left): should stay at least 1¼m: smart performer in
the making. *J. H. M. Gosden*

YEAMAN'S HALL 2 b.c. (Apr 26) Galileo (IRE) 134 – Rimba (USA) 82 (Dayjur **89 p**
(USA) 137) [2006 8s² Oct 10] big, close-coupled colt: fourth foal: half-brother to 4-y-o
Elkhorn: dam, maiden best at 6f at 2 yrs, daughter of very smart 1m/1¼m (Sun Chariot)
winner Ristna: 28/1, 1½ lengths second to Go On Be A Tiger in maiden at Newbury,
travelling strongly up with pace and leading briefly after 2f out: open to improvement,
and sure to win races. *A. M. Balding*

YEARNING (IRE) 2 b.f. (Apr 17) Danetime (IRE) 121 – Hiraeth 76 (Petong 126) **53**
[2006 5.7f 5.1m⁵ 5.1m 7.1d Oct 13] 8,800Y: leggy, close-coupled filly: second foal: dam,
6f winner, half-sister to smart sprinter Ringmoor Down: modest maiden: has been slowly
away/flashed tail. *J. G. Portman*

YEATS (IRE) 5 b.h. Sadler's Wells (USA) 132 – Lyndonville (IRE) (Top Ville **128** 129) [2006 125: 20m* 16f* 14g² 16g Nov 7]

The notion of a 'race of the season' has a long tradition, with votes on the subject invariably tending to come up with the finish of the season, which is not necessarily the same thing. There were some superb finishes to big races in the latest season to thrill racegoers, among them the Derby, the Nassau Stakes and the Dewhurst Stakes. These were magnificent climaxes, epitomising the best of thoroughbred racing as a spectator sport. But would anyone have voted for the Gold Cup as the race of the season? Probably not, yet in the sense of a contest revealing exceptional merit—in the Shergar Derby tradition, as it were—Yeats's display in what is the top race for out-and-out stayers in Europe was a revelation and just as exciting for discerning racegoers as any nip-and-tuck finish. Make no mistake, Yeats is well up to the standard of champion stayers in the modern era and it is excellent news that he stays in training. Aidan O'Brien is on record as saying 'We want him around for the next couple of years'. In the form he showed at Ascot and, more particularly, when trouncing his rivals in the Goodwood Cup, it will take an exceptional opponent to prevent his winning the showpiece of the Royal meeting again.

O'Brien had runners in the Gold Cup each year from 2003 to 2005, with Wolfe Tone finishing fourth and Group 1 winners Brian Boru and Black Sam Bellamy out of the frame. He had earmarked Yeats for the race from the start of the season and the fact that the horse started only 7/1 fourth favourite in a field of twelve takes a little explaining, given his connections and the fact that he had already proved himself a high-class horse when making all to win the Coronation Cup just over a year previously. However, Yeats had failed to reproduce that form when ninth in the Grand Prix de Saint-Cloud, or when a fairly close fourth in the Irish St Leger and sixth in the Canadian International. After ending his four-year-old campaign under something of a cloud, a hind-joint infection kept him out of the Yorkshire Cup in May, which meant the Gold Cup was his first start of the year as well as being his first over an extreme trip. Distinction, runner-up in 2005, started favourite, ahead of the smart French stayer Reefscape and Sergeant Cecil, second in the Yorkshire Cup. The other runners included the first three in the Henry II Stakes (Tungsten Strike, Winged d'Argent and Barolo), 2002 Melbourne Cup winner Media Puzzle who had won a listed event at Leopardstown in May, and smart ex-French mare Guadalajara representing Godolphin. The gallop set by 100/1-shot High Action was far from breakneck, which played into the hands of the speedier types. After travelling strongly within reach of the leader for most of the race, Yeats quickened to take up the running soon after entering the straight. He galloped on strongly to pass the post with four lengths to spare over Reefscape, who rallied after being pushed wide on the turn. Distinction was a head away third—he could have done with a stronger pace—followed by High Action and Sergeant Cecil; Media Puzzle unfortunately broke his near-fore on the line and was put down.

Allowing Reefscape something for the problems he encountered, this was still a good performance from Yeats, one which should perhaps be placed in historical context. Yeats was the first Coronation Cup winner to win the Gold Cup since Solario seventy years before—there had been three in the period 1905-1913, Zinfandel, The White Knight and Prince Palatine. The Gold Cup has not changed

Gold Cup, Royal Ascot—a high-class performance from Yeats on his reappearance;
the grey Reefscape takes second from the previous year's runner-up Distinction (dark cap);
High Action (partially hidden by Distinction), Sergeant Cecil (right) and Guadalajara are next

ABN Amro Goodwood Cup, Goodwood—Yeats again proves a class apart; Geordieland is revitalised by his new trainer, finishing a fine second; Tungsten Strike is third

dramatically in character over the years, and is no more the preserve of specialist stayers than formerly. Yeats was, however, the first since Botticelli in 1955 and Zarathustra in 1957 to have notched a top-flight middle-distance event earlier—those two respectively won the Derby Italiano and Irish Derby. In the inter-war years, only two besides Solario had managed this, Oaks winner Quashed in 1936 and Champion Stakes winner Flares in 1939, though Buchan, successful in the Eclipse Stakes and Champion Stakes, was disqualified from first in the 1920 Gold Cup, and Felicitation, successful in 1934, had won the Middle Park Stakes. By far the most significant change in the Gold Cup, as noted in the comments on Westerner in *Racehorses of 2005*, is the way winners are regarded by the breeding industry nowadays.

Even with a 5-lb penalty Yeats looked a good bet to land the Gold Cup-Goodwood Cup double last achieved in the same season by Double Trigger in 1995. Distinction, who was injured, Percussionist and Alcazar were absentees from the ABN Amro-sponsored event but there were still fifteen runners, including all the other leading stayers. Yeats started at 11/10-on followed by Reefscape, Golden Quest, having his first run since finishing second in the event in 2005, and Sergeant Cecil. The rest, including Tungsten Strike and 2005 Grand Prix de Chantilly winner Geordieland, were at 16/1 or longer. The gallop, set by Foreign Affairs, who was unproven at the trip, was much stronger than at Ascot but Yeats was still able to travel sweetly in mid-division before cruising into contention three furlongs out and blinding his rivals for speed when asked to go on with a quarter of a mile left. Yeats was merely pushed out to beat Geordieland by five lengths with Tungsten Strike three and a half lengths back in third. The time of 3m 21.55sec on firm going was a course record, beating that of 2002 winner Jardines Lookout by .08sec, and the form was even better than in the Gold Cup, marking the winner down as a high-class stayer.

The Irish St Leger is the only classic (if the all-aged race still qualifies for the title) in Britain and Ireland to have eluded Aidan O'Brien and Yeats started at 7/2-on in a field which had little strength in depth and just two other runners at odds shorter than 20/1, the smart and in-form mare Kastoria and Yorkshire Cup victor Percussionist. Despite taking up the running still going well six furlongs out, Yeats could not shake off Kastoria. Ridden along in the straight, he failed to show his customary turn of foot and was a sitting duck when Kastoria challenged inside the last furlong, battling on but going down by half a length. Kastoria is a very smart mare and Yeats came out the better horse at the weights, but this run didn't quite match the form of his Goodwood victory. The idea of running Yeats in the Melbourne Cup had been mooted in 2005 but abandoned, and, as soon as the Gold Cup had been run, his participation in the latest edition became the subject of much speculation. When the weights were announced early in September Yeats was at the top on 59 kg (9-4), 5 lb more than Gold Cup winner Enzeli carried in 2000. By the time of the Irish St Leger, Yeats was ante-post favourite at around 6/1 after being heavily backed, according to bookmakers in Australia, whose liabilities reportedly included one bet of A\$166,000 (£66,000) each way at 12/1. Yeats's defeat at the

Mrs John Magnier's "Yeats"

hands of Kastoria led to something approaching farce regarding his appearance at Flemington, with the governing authority in the state, Racing Victoria Limited, stating boldly on their website two days after the race that they had received 'official confirmation from connections' that Yeats would not run in Australia. O'Brien denied any such thing, saying that although Yeats had been a bit stiff when ridden out that morning—a comment similar to those issued when Yeats missed most of his three-year-old season—connections would wait a week before a final decision. Nine days later, Yeats was announced as a definite and he duly became O'Brien's first runner in Australia. Kieren Fallon had the mount, having just finished a ten-meeting ban incurred at Moonee Valley for causing interference.

In a field of twenty-three, Yeats was third favourite at Flemington behind the Japanese five-year-old Pop Rock and ex-British Tawqeet, successful in the Caulfield Cup. Yeats was sent on half a mile out but was soon swallowed up and finished seventh behind the other Japanese contender Delta Blues, beaten around eight lengths. Fallon stated afterwards that 'We thought we had the right horse for the race, but we were wrong. What's needed is a good-class mile and a half horse, or maybe even a mile and a quarter horse. You have to have speed for this race and Yeats, at this stage of his career, didn't have the kick to stay with them when they quickened.' The assessment takes some believing. A horse who had won a tactical Group 1 event over a mile and a half and shown a fine turn of foot after racing strongly throughout the Gold Cup and Goodwood Cup should not have been outpaced so readily over two miles. Anyway, the theory that there is some ideal make-up for a horse capable of running well in the Melbourne Cup doesn't hold good, at least with the European challengers. Central Park, runner-up in 1999, had never raced beyond a mile and a half but Vintage Crop, successful in 1993, was suited by a test of stamina, while the 2002 winner Media Puzzle was effective at a mile and a half but stayed two miles. Give The Slip, second in 2001, was a front runner without a notable turn of foot who had made all in the Ebor, and Vinnie Roe, fourth in 2002 and runner-up in 2004, was suited by a mile and three quarters or more, having already finished second in the Gold Cup. Persian Punch, a close third in 1998 and a slightly more distant third in 2001, and Jardines Lookout, third in 2003, were out-and-out stayers. In all probability, Yeats was simply not at his best for some reason. Whatever the reason, he seems difficult to keep in top trim for a campaign lasting four or five months. Preparing him for both the Gold Cup and the Melbourne Cup in 2007 may not prove straightforward for his trainer.

Yeats (IRE) (b.h. 2001)	Sadler's Wells (USA) (b 1981)	Northern Dancer (b 1961)	Nearctic
			Natalma
		Fairy Bridge (b 1975)	Bold Reason
			Special
	Lyndonville (IRE) (b 1988)	Top Ville (b 1976)	High Top
			Sega Ville
		Diamond Land (br 1978)	Sparkler
			Canaan

Yeats's pedigree has been dealt with in detail previously but it is worth repeating facts relevant to his ability to stay long distances. Following Kayf Tara, successful at Royal Ascot in 2000 and 2002, he is the second Gold Cup winner for his sire Sadler's Wells. The dam Lyndonville, by another stamina influence in Top Ville, was successful at a mile and three quarters and was out of Diamond Land, who won over thirteen and a half furlongs and hailed from the family of St Leger winner Cantelo. With this background and his relaxed style of racing, Yeats's ability to stay two and a half miles is not exactly surprising. Another development with the family is that one of Lyndonville's other offspring, the very smart mile- to mile-and-a-quarter horse Solskjaer (by Danehill), has been retired to stud in South Africa because of a recurring hock injury at a fee equivalent to around £1,800. Yeats is a tall, good-topped horse and a good walker with a powerful, round action of the sort often associated in the public mind with runners who are not suited by firm going. At both Ascot and Goodwood, Yeats showed he is at home under such conditions—it was particularly firm on the latter course—and he acts on soft as well. He has worn a crossed noseband. *A. P. O'Brien, Ireland*

YELDHAM LADY 4 b.f. Mujahid (USA) 125 – Future Options 71 (Lomond (USA) 128) [2006 52: p12.2g 8m p12g p10g Dec 18] quite attractive filly: modest performer at best: no form in 2006: tried blinkered/in cheekpieces. *A. J. Chamberlain* —

YELLOW CARD 3 ch.g. Inchinor 119 – Tranquillity 70 (Night Shift (USA)) [2006 73: 5m⁵ 5.3f² 5m* 6f² 5m³ 5m⁶ Jun 23] rangy gelding: fairly useful performer: won maiden at Folkestone in June, despite not looking quite straightforward: stays 6f: acts on polytrack and firm going: sold 10,500 gns in July. *N. A. Callaghan* **80**

YELLOW MANE (IRE) 3 ch.c. On The Ridge (IRE) 115 – Mother Nellie (USA) (Al Nasr (FR) 126) [2006 8g 6f⁶ 12m 7d 16m f8g p6g Dec 20] little form. *Luke Comer, Ireland* —

YELLOW RIDGE (IRE) 3 ch.c. On The Ridge (IRE) 115 – Jonathan's Rose (IRE) (Law Society (USA) 130) [2006 10g 10m 12m⁴ 12d⁴ 7d* 7m 7.5v 12s 7d p8g Dec 30] sixth foal: dam Irish maiden half-sister to very smart stayer Tyrone Bridge: fair performer: dropped significantly in trip, won maiden at Galway in August: well beaten after: seems effective at 7f to 1½m: acts on good to firm and good to soft going. *Luke Comer, Ireland* **73**

YELLOWSTONE (IRE) 2 b.c. (Apr 13) Rock of Gibraltar (IRE) 133 – Love And Affection (USA) (Exclusive Era (USA)) [2006 8f* 7g 8g³ Oct 29] 60,000Y: closely related to 2005 2-y-o 8.6f winner Danamour (by Dansili) and half-brother to several winners, including useful 7f (including at 2 yrs)/1m winner Londoner (by Sky Classic) and fairly useful 1¼m winner Grooms Affection (by Groom Dancer): dam, US 5f to 1m winner (second in Grade 1 6f event at 2 yrs), closely related to very smart 1¼m performer Zoman: landed odds in maiden at Cork in July: much the better effort afterwards when 1¾ lengths third to stable-companion Mount Nelson in Criterium International at Saint-Cloud, staying on well from rear: shapes as though he'll be suited by further than 1m. *A. P. O'Brien, Ireland* **110**

YEMEN DESERT (IRE) 3 b.f. Sadler's Wells (USA) 132 – Humble Fifteen (USA) (Feather Ridge (USA)) [2006 12m² 10f⁵ Jul 3] fourth foal: half-sister to 7f winner in USA **73**

by Stravinsky: dam, 2-y-o 6f winner in USA, out of half-sister to Oaks and Irish Derby winner Balanchine (by Sadler's Wells): easily better effort in maidens at Pontefract when 2½ lengths second of 10 to Fyvie. *M. Johnston*

YENALED 9 gr.g. Rambo Dancer (CAN) 107 – Fancy Flight (FR) 74 (Arctic Tern (USA) 126) [2006 62, a73: f12g³ p9.5g p12g 11.5m 10.2m⁶ p10g 11.6m² 12.1f 10.2m 12.1m² 10.9d² 12d 12s p12.2g Nov 6] leggy, sparely-made gelding: fair performer on all-weather, modest on turf: left P. McEntee prior to fifth outing: stays 13f: acts on all-weather and any turf going: tried in visor/cheekpieces: held up: quirky. *J. M. Bradley*   **61 a67**

YEOMAN LEAP 2 b.c. (Feb 29) Val Royal (FR) 127 – Chandni (IRE) (Ahonoora 122) [2006 8g Oct 17] 15,000Y: half-brother to fairly useful Irish 9f/1½m winner Chanoud (by Ezzoud) and 2001 2-y-o 5f winner Arctic Falcon (by Polar Falcon): dam, of no account, sister to smart 1m/1¼m performer Visto Si Stampi: 40/1 and green, slowly away and not knocked about in maiden at Bath: should improve. *A. M. Balding*   **58 p**

YEOMAN SPIRIT (IRE) 3 ch.c. Soviet Star (USA) 128 – Hollywood Pearl (USA) (Phone Trick (USA)) [2006 p8g 8d² 10d³ 10.5g Sep 22] €36,000Y: big colt: second foal: dam unraced: fair form: placed in maidens at Bath and Nottingham: stays 1¼m: acts on polytrack and good to soft ground. *A. M. Balding*   **76**

YEREVAN 2 b.f. (Mar 30) Iron Mask (USA) 117 – Unfuwaanah 74 (Unfuwain (USA) 131) [2006 5.2d⁵ 6.1g* p6g⁴ 6m³ 6g² 5m⁴ 6.1m³ 6g* 6.1m⁵ 5g* 5m⁶ Sep 10] 16,000Y: unfurnished filly: half-sister to several winners, including 6f (at 2 yrs) to 9.4f winner Marjurita (by Marju) and 7f to 1¼m (in Italy) winner Donegal Dancer (by Spectrum), both fairly useful: fair performer: won maiden at Nottingham (by 5 lengths, flattered) in June and, having been claimed from M. Channon £14,000 fifth start, nurseries at Windsor and Leicester in August: last in nursery final start: will prove best at 5f/6f: acts on good to firm going: usually races prominently: game. *R. T. Phillips*   **73**

YES DEAR 3 ch.f. Fantastic Light (USA) 134 – Abeyr 106 (Unfuwain (USA) 131) [2006 68: 10.3f May 11] quite good-topped filly: has a quick action: maiden: well held only outing in 2006. *W. M. Brisbourne*   **–**

YOMALO (IRE) 6 ch.m. Woodborough (USA) 112 – Alkariyh (USA) 79 (Alydar (USA)) [2006 102: f5g² 5.1g⁶ 6m⁵ 6m⁵ 6f⁴ 6f⁶ Jul 29] angular mare: smart performer: better than ever in 2006, winning Ballyogan Stakes at Leopardstown (beat Noelani ½ length) in June: creditable efforts when ¾-length second to Fyodor in handicap at Southwell and fourth to La Chunga in Summer Stakes at York: stays 6f: acts on all-weather, firm and good to soft going: comes from behind, usually soon off bridle: sold 45,000 gns in November. *Rae Guest*   **110**

YO PEDRO (IRE) 4 b.g. Mark of Esteem (IRE) 137 – Morina (USA) (Lyphard (USA) 132) [2006 88: 9.7f⁶ 10f⁴ 8.1m³ 7g 11.9d⁵ 7s Sep 20] leggy gelding: fairly useful performer: well held after third outing: sold from J. Fanshawe 22,000 gns after fourth: effective at 1m/1¼m: acts on polytrack and firm going. *B. Potts, Ireland*   **85 d**

YORK CLIFF 8 b.g. Marju (IRE) 127 – Azm (Unfuwain (USA) 131) [2006 70, a65: p12.2g⁴ p13.9g⁶ p12.2g⁵ p12.2g⁴ p12.2g³ p12.2g* p12.2g p9.5g⁴ p16.5g⁵ f12g* f11g⁴ f14g² p12.2g² p12.2g² p12.2g⁵ p13.9g³ 12.3g³ 13.1g* 13f³ 14m⁴ 12.3m² 14.1m⁶ 13.4f Sep 23] good-bodied gelding: modest performer: won seller at Wolverhampton in February, banded race at Southwell in March and apprentice handicap at Ayr in June: stays 1¾m: acts on all-weather and any turf going: tried in cheekpieces/visor: lazy, but generally reliable. *W. M. Brisbourne*   **64**

YORKE'S FOLLY (USA) 5 b.m. Stravinsky (USA) 133 – Tommelise (USA) (Dayjur (USA) 137) [2006 53: 6d⁴ 5f 5f² 5m⁶ 6m⁵ 6f² 6m 5d² Aug 31] big, lengthy mare: modest maiden: stays 6f: acts on fibresand and firm going: tried visored, usually blinkered nowadays. *C. W. Fairhurst*   **54**

YORKIE 7 b.g. Aragon 118 – Light The Way 72 (Nicholas Bill 125) [2006 57, a68: 6g 6d p7.1g 6.1m⁶ 7.2g 7f 7m f7g p6g Nov 6] tall, quite good-topped gelding: modest performer on turf, poor on all-weather nowadays: effective at 5f to 1m: acts on all-weather and any turf going: tried blinkered/visored: formerly tongue tied. *J. Pearce*   **59 a41**

YORKIES BOY 11 gr.g. Clantime 101 – Slipperose 72 (Persepolis (FR) 127) [2006 57: 7g p7g 6m 7g Aug 17] good-bodied gelding: one-time smart performer: very much on downgrade, and no form in 2006: tried blinkered, usually wears cheekpieces. *N. E. Berry*   **–**

YORKSHIRE BLUE 7 b.g. Atraf 116 – Something Blue (Petong 126) [2006 73: 7.1v 7d 6d 6f² 6g* 6f* 6m² 6d* 6m³ 6f⁵ 7d 6d 7.2d⁴ 6v* Oct 28] close-coupled gelding: fairly   **90**

useful handicapper: better than ever in 2006, winning twice at Hamilton in June, and at Ayr in July and October: effective at 6f/7f: acts on all-weather and any turf going: twice blinkered (below form): has been slowly away: held up. *J. S. Goldie*

YORKSHIRE LAD (IRE) 4 b.g. Second Empire (IRE) 124 – Villaminta (IRE) 59 (Grand Lodge (USA) 125) [2006 76, a69: 6m 6m 6m 6m Apr 30] lengthy, quite attractive gelding: modest performer nowadays: stays 6f, possibly not 7f: acts on all-weather and firm ground: tried visored/tongue tied. *Miss Gay Kelleway*

YOSSI (IRE) 2 b.c. (May 19) Montjeu (IRE) 137 – Raindancing (IRE) 94 (Tirol 127) 81 [2006 8.1d² 10d³ 10.1d⁴ Oct 18] €65,000Y: good-bodied colt: sixth foal: half-brother to 3 winners, including 7f winner Dash For Cover (by Sesaro) and 2000 2-y-o 5f winner Jack Spratt (by So Factual), both fairly useful: dam 2-y-o 6f winner who became untrustworthy: fairly useful form when placed in maidens at Sandown (second to Kid Mambo) and Pontefract (third to Eglevski): never a threat final outing: will stay 1½m: raced on good to soft going. *M. H. Tompkins*

YOUBETTERBEGOOD (IRE) 2 b.g. (Apr 29) Indian Rocket 115 – Milain (IRE) – (Unfuwain (USA) 131) [2006 7s p7.1g⁵ p8.6g Nov 7] well held in maidens/minor event. *Adrian Sexton, Ireland*

YOU CALL THAT ART (USA) 3 b.f. Royal Academy (USA) 130 – Support The 75 Arts (USA) (Taylor's Falls (USA)) [2006 83: 7g⁵ 6f⁴ 6m p7g 8f⁵ Aug 8] leggy, useful-looking filly: fair maiden: may prove best at 6f: acts on good to soft ground (below form on firmer than good): blinkered last 2 starts: sent to USA. *R. Hannon*

YOU LIVE AND LEARN 3 ch.f. Galileo (IRE) 134 – Anniversary 101 (Salse (USA) 64 128) [2006 10m 10g⁵ 8.3g 11.9m Sep 19] first foal: dam, 1½m winner who stayed 2m, half-sister to very smart performers Craigsteel (best at 1½m/1¾m) and Invermark (stayer): modest maiden: bred to be suited by 1½m+. *H. Morrison*

YOUMZAIN (IRE) 3 b.c. Sinndar (IRE) 134 – Sadima (IRE) 103 (Sadler's Wells 125 (USA) 132) [2006 88p: 12m* 10d³ 12m 13m* 12d* 12m² 12g* Sep 24]

Youmzain's owner Jaber Abdullah had the last word—as he was fully entitled to do—and turned down his trainer's plea to run the colt in the St Leger. Youmzain was second favourite in the ante-post betting after winning the most significant trial for the final classic, the Ladbrokes Great Voltigeur Stakes at York. The St Leger, switched to York from Doncaster, was run over a distance one hundred and fifty-five yards shorter than at its traditional home, and Youmzain would have had to run only one hundred and ninety-seven yards further than when successful over thirteen furlongs in the Bahrain Trophy at Newmarket in July, when he was not hard pressed to hold off another St Leger entry Jadalee by a length. Whether Youmzain would have beaten the impressive Sixties Icon in the St Leger will never be known. By the end of the season there was precious little between the pair on their best form, though Youmzain's owner might point to the fact that

Ladbrokes Great Voltigeur Stakes, York—
Youmzain comes from a poor position to overhaul Red Rocks (left)

IVG - Preis von Europa, Cologne—Youmzain makes his first start against older horses a winning one;
Egerton runs his best race for over two years to be second,
with Enforcer (stripes) third and Oriental Tiger fourth

Jadalee was beaten much further by Sixties Icon when sixth in the St Leger and that the Great Voltigeur runner-up Red Rocks, only a head behind Youmzain, finished three and a half lengths behind Sixties Icon when third in the St Leger.

Concerns over Youmzain's stamina were reportedly at the root of his owner's decision to bypass the St Leger and he was sent instead for the Prix Niel at Longchamp on the same weekend. His performance in running Rail Link to half a length was made to look even better when Rail Link went on to win the Prix de l'Arc de Triomphe, a race for which there was briefly talk of supplementing Youmzain. Youmzain was sent instead for Germany's final Group 1 of the season, the IVG - Preis von Europa at Cologne the weekend before the Arc, when he also advertised the Prix Niel form. The Preis von Europa, about a quarter of the value of the St Leger, attracted seven runners, Youmzain and Enforcer from Britain taking on five home-trained runners including the Deutsches Derby third Oriental Tiger, runner-up in the Grosser Preis von Baden on his previous outing. Youmzain started at 5/4-on for his first start against older horses and came through to lead inside the final furlong, winning by half a length from the five-year-old Egerton, a very smart performer who had finished in the frame in the same race behind Albanova in 2004 before missing the whole of 2005 (he had been fourth in the Grosser Preis von Baden on his most recent outing). With Enforcer third and Oriental Tiger fourth, the form of the latest Preis von Europa represented a little more improvement by the progressive Youmzain, who stays in training and should do well as a four-year-old.

Youmzain had started the latest season in much more modest surroundings with victory in a minor event at Catterick in April, improving on that when third to Dylan Thomas in the Derrinstown Stud Derby Trial at Leopardstown in May and, after losing his footing and nearly coming down when unplaced in the King Edward VII Stakes at Royal Ascot, winning the Bahrain Trophy and the Great Voltigeur. The winner of the King Edward VII Stakes, Papal Bull, started favourite for the Voltigeur but ran poorly. Youmzain's trainer would have preferred him to run in the

Geoffrey Freer at Newbury the previous weekend and he was a 12/1-chance in a good field at York. Youmzain continued his improvement, showing a good turn of foot to overhaul King Edward VII Stakes runner-up Red Rocks, who had since finished second to Rail Link in the Grand Prix de Paris. Six of the nine previous St Leger winners had run in the Voltigeur and, although he needed to improve again to win, Youmzain made plenty of appeal at the time in what was shaping up into just an average St Leger.

Youmzain (IRE) (b.c. 2003)	Sinndar (IRE) (b 1997)	Grand Lodge (ch 1991)	Chief's Crown
			La Papagena
		Sinntara (b 1989)	Lashkari
			Sidama
	Sadima (IRE) (b 1998)	Sadler's Wells (b 1981)	Northern Dancer
			Fairy Bridge
		Anima (b 1989)	Ajdal
			Cocotte

The St Leger trip would almost certainly have proved within Youmzain's compass judged on his pedigree. It is early days for Youmzain's sire Sinndar, winner of the Derby, Irish Derby and Prix de l'Arc, but he always looked like proving an influence for stamina (his dam won the Irish Cesarewitch), and the average distance of races won by his first two crops of three-year-olds to reach the racecourse is around a mile and a half. Sinndar had ninety-four mares in his first year and seventy-three in his second at the Aga Khan's Gilltown Stud in Ireland, but his popularity waned and he received only twenty-nine in his fifth year, 2005, ironically the year that Shawanda provided him with his first Group 1 victories as a sire when winning the Irish Oaks and Prix Vermeille. Youmzain, from Sinndar's second crop, is his first Group 1-winning colt, though his success came too late for his sire who has now been lost to British and Irish breeders, switched to the Aga Khan's Haras de Bonneval in France in 2006. Youmzain, who cost 30,000 guineas as a yearling, is the first foal out of Sadima, successful in a maiden at a mile and a quarter in Ireland, her only win. Her two-year-old Creachadoir (by King's Best) had a couple of runs at the Curragh for Jim Bolger, finishing a good fourth in the Railway Stakes. Sadima is a daughter of Sadler's Wells, another influence for stamina in Youmzain's pedigree, and is the best of three winners out of the twice-raced maiden Anima. Anima is a half-sister to Pilsudski who enjoyed a brilliant international career on the track, his victories including the Breeders' Cup Turf, the Japan Cup, the Champion Stakes and the Irish Champion, as well as being runner-up in two Arcs and a King George. Youmzain's great grandam Cocotte, a smart mile and a quarter winner and granddaughter of Irish One Thousand Guineas winner Gaily, had a very successful career at stud, Pilsudski not the only champion she produced. Cocotte's Danehill filly Fine Motion was the champion three-year-old filly of her year in Japan and Cocotte was also responsible for a Group 3 winner in Glowing Ardour and for three listed winners, two of whom, Peach Out of Reach and Briolette won at a mile and a half and were daughters of Sadler's Wells and therefore closely related to Sadima. Youmzain, a strong colt who has run well when sweating, acts on good to firm and good to soft going. He has a good turn of foot. One cautionary note is that he didn't look an entirely straightforward ride at York, carrying his head high and soon starting to pull himself up once he hit the front (Kieren Fallon's services were enlisted for the Preis von Europa). *M. R. Channon*

YOUNG BERTIE 3 ch.g. Bertolini (USA) 125 – Urania 66 (Most Welcome 131) [2006 **74** 70?: 6m³ 6f⁴ p7g² 7m³ 7f² p7g* 7m⁵ p6g³ p6g Oct 17] strong gelding: fair handicapper: won at Lingfield in August: stays 7f: acts on polytrack and firm going: tried in cheekpieces: visored last 4 starts. *H. Morrison*

YOUNG EMMA 3 b.f. Vettori (IRE) 119 – Just Warning (Warning 136) [2006 p12.2g – Nov 14] second foal: half-sister to 4-y-o Young Mick: dam, well beaten only start, half-sister to very smart 6f to 1m performer Young Ern: well beaten in bumper: tailed off in maiden at Wolverhampton. *G. G. Margarson*

YOUNG FLAVIO 3 b.g. Mark of Esteem (IRE) 137 – Flavian 94 (Catrail (USA) 123) – [2006 70, a53: 6f 7.1g 6.1f 5f 6d 7m Sep 12] leggy gelding: fair performer at best: no form in 2006: usually wears cheekpieces: tried blinkered: none too genuine. *J. M. Bradley*

YOUNG KATE 5 b.m. Desert King (IRE) 129 – Stardyn (Star Appeal 133) [2006 56: **56**
f8g³ p8.6g⁴ p8g* p8g⁵ p9.5g Mar 20] sturdy mare: modest performer: won banded race at
Lingfield in February: stays 1¼m: acts on all-weather and good to soft ground. *J. R. Best*

YOUNG MICK 4 br.g. King's Theatre (IRE) 128 – Just Warning (Warning 136) **118 +**
[2006 62: p8.6g p9.5g* p10g* p9.5g* p10g² p9.5g² p12.2g* 11.5m* p12g²
p10g³ 10m⁴ p10g⁶ 12m* 11.9g⁶ 12g* 12g* 13.9d³ 12d* Sep 24]
    'Modest maiden' was how *Racehorses of 2005* summed up the seemingly-
exposed Young Mick, who completed a memorable rags-to-riches story in the latest
season. He began 2006 beaten over fourteen lengths into ninth in a maiden on the
all-weather at Wolverhampton and ended it winning in pattern company, the Cumberland Lodge Stakes at Ascot providing him with his tenth win of a remarkable
campaign. Young Mick gained his first win, on the fourteenth start of his career, at
one of the year's quota of fifty regional meetings (a three-year experiment with
what came to be known as 'banded racing', catering for lowly-rated horses, has
now ended with the class 7 races being integrated into standard fixtures from 2007).
Young Mick got off the mark in a maiden claimer at the regional meeting at Wolverhampton in January, a race in which he could have been claimed for £5,000. Modest
handicaps at Lingfield and Wolverhampton (two) were also in the bag before the
turf season got under way, by which time Young Mick's record would have looked
even better but for going down in a photo-finish in two other handicaps, in one of
which he met trouble and was most unlucky.
    Young Mick improved again, recording his fifth win towards the end of
March in a handicap on the all-weather at Kempton, and a sixth with another
impressive victory in a fairly useful handicap at Yarmouth four days later, showing
further improvement switched to turf. Young Mick's BHB mark went up in the
region of 30 lb in the first three and a half months of the year but he continued to
thrive and had a couple of good placed efforts in better handicaps to his name when
lining up for the well-contested Duke of Edinburgh at Royal Ascot. Typically
travelling well under a patient ride, Young Mick pulled off a surprise win, sent on
over a furlong out and scoring at 28/1 in a blanket finish from Glistening and
Palomar, both of whom finished strongly. Young Mick was ridden at Royal Ascot
by Richard Quinn who, apparently, had decided beforehand that the horse would be
his last ride. News of Quinn's retirement—'You have to move on in life'—was not
given, however, until early-July, the announcement made to general surprise while
he was serving a six-day ban for careless riding and excessive use of the whip on
Young Mick at the Royal meeting. Quinn rode over two thousand winners, his
highest seasonal score in Britain being one hundred and fifty-one in 1999, one of
three occasions that he finished runner-up in the jockeys' championship (each time
to a different champion). Quinn won British classics on Snurge and Millenary (both
successful in the St Leger) and Love Divine (Oaks), and was also associated, for
part of their careers, with Generous (on whom he won the Dewhurst) and Persian
Punch.

*Duke of Edinburgh Stakes (Handicap), Royal Ascot—Young Mick (visor) provides Richard Quinn
with a win in what proves to be his last ride; they hold on from Glistening (right), Palomar (left),
Polygonal (noseband), Thunder Rock (on Young Mick's left), Rehearsal (black cap),
Consular (third right) and Chantaco (diamonds on sleeves)*

National Bank of Dubai Cup (Handicap), Ascot—Young Mick continues his improvement;
Consular is about to be run out of second place by both Royal Jet (white cap) and Glistening (right)

After being raised again in the handicap for winning the Duke of Edinburgh, Young Mick managed only sixth in the Old Newton Cup at Haydock in July and looked to have come to the end of his improvement. Remarkably, however, he won two more handicaps, returned to Ascot, taking the valuable National Bank of Dubai Cup in July, when Glistening and Old Newton Cup winner Consular were in the frame behind him, and the Michael Page International Shergar Cup Challenge in August. Those victories earned him a 7-lb penalty for the Ebor at York, where he ran another cracker, going down by a head and a short head to the 100/1-winner Mudawin and Glistening (8 lb better off with Young Mick compared to the Duke of Edinburgh). Young Mick met Glistening again in the Grosvenor Casinos Cumberland Lodge Stakes, both running in pattern company for the first time. Though the Group 3 Cumberland Lodge was not so well contested as it sometimes has been, Young Mick still had to improve again to win. He added to his reputation as the most improved horse in training, landing his fourth win of the season from as many starts at Ascot. Young Mick won decisively by a length and three quarters and the same from the favourite Munsef and Glistening. The Melbourne Cup and the Japan Cup were both mentioned as possible further targets for Young Mick, but he wasn't seen out again, connections said to be planning a Cup campaign in Britain for him as a five-year-old. Who is to say that the irrepressible Young Mick has finished improving yet? His trainer is a Yorkshireman and blamed himself for Young Mick's narrow defeat in the Ebor, saying he should not have risked incurring the double penalty. Perhaps Young Mick will gain consolation in the Yorkshire Cup as a five-year-old.

Grosvenor Casinos Cumberland Lodge Stakes, Ascot—a tenth win of the year for Young Mick;
behind him are Munsef, Glistening (No.6) and Foxhaven

Mr M. F. Kentish's "Young Mick"

Young Mick (br.g. 2002)	King's Theatre (IRE) (b 1991)	Sadler's Wells (b 1981)	Northern Dancer
			Fairy Bridge
		Regal Beauty (b or br 1981)	Princely Native
			Dennis Belle
	Just Warning (br 1997)	Warning (b 1985)	Known Fact
			Slightly Dangerous
		Stardyn (br 1982)	Star Appeal
			Northern Dynasty

The useful-looking Young Mick is by the King George VI and Queen Elizabeth Stakes winner King's Theatre, who has now been switched to producing jumpers and is already making his mark in that sphere. Young Mick is the first foal of his dam Just Warning, who was well beaten on her only start but is a half-sister to the very smart Young Ern, who was effective at six furlongs to a mile. The distaff side of the family is largely undistinguished otherwise. Young Mick's grandam Stardyn was a poor middle-distance handicapper who never won, and his great grandam Northern Dynasty won only a mile claimer on the Flat. She did win four times over hurdles, however, and is also grandam of smart six/seven-furlong winner Nice One Clare, who was another notably game and reliable performer for one of the smaller Newmarket yards. Young Mick stays a mile and three quarters and acts on polytrack, soft and good to firm going. He wears blinkers or a visor and has been tried tongue tied. Usually patiently ridden to make the most effective use of his good turn of foot, the game and genuine Young Mick is a credit to his connections. *G. G. Margarson*

ZAB

YOUNG MR GRACE (IRE) 6 b.g. Danetime (IRE) 121 – Maid of Mourne (Fairy 55
King (USA)) [2006 88d: 8d 7d 8d 7.2g⁶ 7.1m 8f Sep 20] quite good-topped gelding:
modest performer nowadays: left T. Easterby after third start: stays 1m: acts on firm and
soft ground, well held on heavy/fibresand: tried visored: usually races prominently: none
too consistent. *B. S. Rothwell*

YOUNG SCOTTON 6 b.g. Cadeaux Genereux 131 – Broken Wave 103 (Bustino 136) 50
[2006 66: f8g⁵ 8d Apr 21] lengthy gelding: useful form in bumpers prior to losing way
over hurdles: modest form at best in maidens: should stay 1¼m. *J. Howard Johnson*

YOUNG THOMAS (IRE) 4 ch.g. Inchinor 119 – Splicing 82 (Sharpo 132) [2006 –: –
f7m Oct 31] strong, lengthy gelding: maiden: well held only start in 2006: tried visored/
in cheekpieces. *B. Storey*

YOUNG VALENTINO 4 ch.g. Komaite (USA) – Caprice (Mystiko (USA) 124) –
[2006 61d: 5.7m f6m p6g p8.6g p8g Dec 15] workmanlike gelding: little form since 3-y-o
reappearance. *A. W. Carroll*

YOURALITTLEMILLER 3 b.f. Kalanisi (IRE) 132 – Jam (IRE) (Arazi (USA) 135) 54
[2006 54: p9.5g⁴ f8g⁶ p10g Feb 28] leggy filly: modest maiden: should stay 1¼m: acts on
polytrack: tried in cheekpieces. *P. G. Murphy*

YOUR AMOUNT (IRE) 3 b.g. Beckett (IRE) 116 – Sin Lucha (USA) (Northfields 73
(USA)) [2006 77: 7.1g 8.2d⁶ 10m p10g 10g 11.6d p13.9g* p13.9g³ Dec 8] smallish,
useful-looking gelding: has a quick action: fair handicapper: left A. King after fourth
start: won at Wolverhampton in November: stays 1¾m: acts on polytrack, soft and good
to firm going. *W. J. Musson*

YOU'RE MY SON 4 b.g. Bold Edge 123 – Sheer Nectar 72 (Piaffer (USA) 113) [2006 60
–: p10g⁵ 10m p7g⁶ p8g p8.6g Dec 11] workmanlike gelding: modest maiden: likely to
prove best at 1m+: form only on polytrack: has looked wayward. *A. B. Haynes*

YOU TOO 4 b.f. Monsun (GER) 124 – You Are The One 85 (Unfuwain (USA) 131) –
[2006 74: 14.1g 16.2f⁴ Jul 18] lengthy, good-topped filly: fair 1¾m winner at 3 yrs: well
held in 2006. *M. Johnston*

YUNGABURRA (IRE) 2 b.g. (May 4) Fath (USA) 116 – Nordic Living (IRE) 53 100 p
(Nordico (USA)) [2006 5g 6m⁵ p6g³ p5.1g* p5.1m* p5.1g* p6g³ p5.1g* Dec 6] 14,000Y:
half-brother to several winners, including fairly useful 1999 2-y-o 5f winner Alfie Lee
(by Case Law) and 4-y-o Nova Tor: dam ran 4 times in Ireland: useful form on all-
weather: gelded and left G. A. Swinbank after third start, then won 2 nurseries and minor
event in November and nursery in December, all at Wolverhampton, last-named comfortably by 5 lengths from Dress To Impress: will prove best at 5f: acts on polytrack: capable
of further improvement. *T. J. Pitt*

YVE SAM LA CHAMP 2 b.c. (Apr 30) Tomba 119 – Dona Krista 84 (King of Spain –
121) [2006 5m 5d⁶ 6d 6g Oct 16] well beaten in maidens. *A. W. Carroll*

Z

ZAAFIRA (SPA) 2 b.f. (Feb 5) Limpid 119 – Hot Doris (IRE) (Fayruz 116) [2006 p7g 48
f7g p8g⁴ p8.6g³ Dec 31] first foal: dam Spanish 4.5f (at 2 yrs) and 1m winner: poor
maiden: looked wayward final outing. *E. J. Creighton*

ZAAFRAN 3 b.f. Singspiel (IRE) 133 – Roshani (IRE) 79 (Kris 135) [2006 61p: 8.5g² 86
8.2m⁵ 8.3m* 10g* 10.1d² Aug 28] smallish, good-bodied filly: fairly useful form: won
handicaps at Windsor (dead-heated with Starship) in July and Nottingham in August:
stays 1¼m: acts on good to firm and good to soft going: often makes running: joined
D. Selvaratnam in UAE. *M. A. Jarvis*

ZAAHID (IRE) 2 ch.c. (Feb 27) Sakhee (USA) 136 – Murjana (IRE) 80 (Pleasant 53
Colony (USA)) [2006 7m Jul 12] big, good-bodied colt: second foal: half-brother to 3-y-o
Mosharref: dam, 1¼m winner, out of US Grade 2 2-y-o 6f winner Golden Reef: 12/1,
burly and green, tenth to Kalgoorlie in maiden at Newmarket. *B. W. Hills*

ZABEEL HOUSE 3 b.g. Anabaa (USA) 130 – Divine Quest 81 (Kris 135) [2006 89: 83
10g⁵ 8m⁶ 7s⁴ 8.1m³ 8.3d 8g 8.1m p7g³ p8g⁴ Nov 28] strong, well-made gelding:
fairly useful handicapper: left E. Dunlop 33,000 gns after fifth outing: creditable efforts
at Lingfield last 3 starts: should stay 1¼m: acts on polytrack and firm ground, below form
all 3 outings on softer than good. *J. A. R. Toller*

1183

ZABEEL PALACE 4 b.g. Grand Lodge (USA) 125 – Applecross 117 (Glint of Gold **88**
128) [2006 92: a12f p12g 10g⁶ Oct 16] useful-looking gelding: fairly useful handicapper,
lightly raced: trained by I. Mohammed on reappearance: bred to be suited by 1½m+, but
may prove best at shorter: acts on polytrack and good to firm going: sold 28,000 gns,
joined B. Curley. *Saeed bin Suroor*

ZABEEL TOWER 3 b.g. Anabaa (USA) 130 – Bint Kaldoun (IRE) 82 (Kaldoun (FR) **57**
122) [2006 72: 10g⁵ 9.8m* 12.1m⁶ 8.1f 12f Jul 19] leggy, useful-looking gelding: modest
performer: won seller at Ripon (sold from M. Channon 10,200 gns) in April: stays 1¼m:
acts on good to firm and good to soft going. *James Moffatt*

ZACATECAS (GER) 6 b.g. Grand Lodge (USA) 125 – Zephyrine (IRE) (Highest **–**
Honor (FR) 124) [2006 16.2d p16.5g⁶ p16.5g f12g⁵ Dec 14] useful performer at best:
won 5 times at Ovrevoll in 2004, below form in second half of 2005 prior to leaving
R. Haugen in Norway: last all 4 Flat starts in Britain: stays 1½m: acts on dirt and soft
ground. *A. J. Chamberlain*

ZADALLA 2 b.f. (Mar 19) Zaha (CAN) 106 – Inishdalla (IRE) 103 (Green Desert **68**
(USA) 127) [2006 7m 5g⁴ 6s 6d 5.7v f5g* f5g² Dec 21] 6,000Y: seventh foal: half-sister
to 4-y-o Hearthstead Wings and 2 winners in USA: dam, Irish 6f (at 2 yrs)/7f winner, later
successful in USA: fair performer: won maiden at Southwell in December: should stay
further than 5f: acts on fibresand, best turf effort on good going. *A. Oliver, Ireland*

ZAFANTAGE 3 ch.f. Zafonic (USA) 130 – Up On Points 97 (Royal Academy (USA) **63**
130) [2006 71: 7.1g 8m 10m 8.1d⁴ 8.1f⁵ 8.3m 8m 7.1m³ 7f³ 8g Oct 13] leggy, workmanlike filly: modest performer: stays 1m: acts on firm and good to soft going: tried blinkered
(looked wayward): sold 3,500 gns. *S. Kirk*

ZAFARILLA (IRE) 3 b.f. Zafonic (USA) 130 – Claustra (FR) 91 (Green Desert **–**
(USA) 127) [2006 –: 8f 6.9m 10m Sep 19] little form. *Pat Eddery*

ZAFARSHAH (IRE) 7 b.g. Danehill (USA) 126 – Zafarana (FR) (Shernazar 131) **59 §**
[2006 65, a74: 8m 8.1d⁵ 7m 8.1d 7m 8m³ 8.1g⁴ 7f³ 8.1m² 7.6g⁴ 8f⁴ 7m⁴ 8.1m p8g p7g f7g **a– §**
Nov 15] good-bodied gelding: modest performer: best at 7f to 8.5f: acts on all-weather,
firm and soft going (unraced on heavy): tried visored/tongue tied, blinkered nowadays:
often looks none too keen. *R. A. Harris*

ZAFFEU 5 ch.g. Zafonic (USA) 130 – Leaping Flame (USA) (Trempolino (USA) 135) **65**
[2006 61: p12.2g² p12.2g³ p16.5g³ p12.2g² p12.2g² p12.2g² p12g p12.2m³ p13.9g*
p13.9g⁵ p13.9g⁵ Dec 31] leggy, useful-looking gelding: has no left eye: modest performer: claimed from N. Littmoden £6,000 after reappearance: won claimer at Wolverhampton in November: stays easy 2m: acts on polytrack, firm and soft ground: blinkered (well
held) twice: sometimes slowly away: tends to hang. *A. G. Juckes*

ZAFONICAL STORM (USA) 2 ch.c. (Mar 13) Aljabr (USA) 125 – Fonage (Zafonic **94**
(USA) 130) [2006 p5g³ 5s* 6m 6g 7m⁵ 7g 8m² 7.5v* 8s Oct 16] $5,500Y: tall, rather
leggy colt: second foal: dam, 6.5f/1m winner in USA, half-sister to smart performer up
to 9f Wharf and to dam of 3-y-o Rail Link: fairly useful performer: won maiden at
Folkestone in March and listed race at Tipperary (beat Chinese Whisper 4½ lengths) in
October: below form in listed event at Pontefract final start: stays 1m: acts on heavy
ground: tended to hang on debut: often makes running: none too consistent. *B. W. Duke*

ZAGREUS (GER) 4 gr.g. Fasliyev (USA) 120 – Zephyrine (IRE) (Highest Honor (FR) **–**
124) [2006 50: p8.6g 8.3g p13.9g Nov 6] big, leggy, workmanlike gelding: modest
maiden at 3 yrs: in cheekpieces, no form in 2006: stays 7.5f. *H. J. Manners*

ZAHARA JOY 3 ch.f. Cayman Kai (IRE) 114 – Enjoy (IRE) (Mazaad 106) [2006 65d: **–**
6.9g 8g 7.1m 13.8m Sep 16] sturdy filly: maiden: well held in 2006. *D. W. Thompson*

ZAHARATH AL BUSTAN 3 ch.f. Gulch (USA) – Cayman Sunset (IRE) 108 (Night **73**
Shift (USA)) [2006 80: 8d 9.2m² 10s 8.2g 10s Sep 30] leggy filly: fair maiden:
sold from M. Channon 35,000 gns after fourth outing: stays 9f: acts on firm going.
E. D. Delany, Ireland

ZAHOUR AL YASMEEN 2 b.f. (May 5) Cadeaux Genereux 131 – Bareilly (USA) **76 p**
(Lyphard (USA) 132) [2006 5.1g p6g* Jun 28] strong, lengthy filly: sister to 2 winners,
including useful 5f (at 2 yrs) to 7f winner Revenue and half-sister to 3-y-o La Mottie: dam
unraced out of sister to Triptych: fair form when winning maiden at Kempton in June
by 1¼ lengths from To Party, soon prominent: should stay beyond 6f: should progress.
M. R. Channon

ZAH REEF 3 b.f. Zaha (CAN) 106 – Cuban Reef 54 (Dowsing (USA) 124) [2006 **–**
12.1m⁶ Jun 16] 1,200F: fifth foal: half-sister to 1¾m/2m winner Annakita (by Unfuwain)

and 1m/8.6f winner Chief Dipper (by Benny The Dip): dam 7f and 1¼m winner: 66/1, never dangerous in maiden at Chepstow. *P. A. Blockley*

ZAIF (IRE) 3 b.g. Almutawakel 126 – Colourful (FR) 97 (Gay Mecene (USA) 128) [2006 91: 8m 8s⁴ 10m* 9.9f⁶ 10.1d⁵ 10s² 12s Oct 7] close-coupled, quite good-topped gelding: useful performer: won maiden at Newmarket in July: good second to Blue Bajan in minor event at Ascot after: stays 1¼m: acts on soft and good to firm going: has been blanketed for stall entry (refused to enter stall third intended outing): gelded after final start. *D. R. C. Elsworth* **96**

ZAIN (IRE) 2 b.c. (Mar 26) Alhaarth (IRE) 126 – Karenaragon (Aragon 118) [2006 6d 5.1d⁴ p5g p8.6g⁵ p7.1g Dec 21] good-topped colt: modest maiden: stays 8.6f: raced on polytrack and good to soft ground. *J. G. Given* **50**

ZAKFREE (IRE) 5 b.g. Danetime (IRE) 121 – Clipper Queen 66 (Balidar 133) [2006 73: 10v 10g 16m 7g 10m³ 10m 10g⁴ 9v 10s² 10v p9.5g⁴ Dec 22] rather leggy gelding: fair handicapper: won at the Curragh in 2005 (only success): stays 1¼m: acts on polytrack, heavy and good to firm going: usually blinkered: has looked no easy ride. *L. McAteer, Ireland* **75**

ZALKANI (IRE) 6 ch.g. Cadeaux Genereux 131 – Zallaka (IRE) (Shardari 134) [2006 56, a82: p10g³ p8.6g⁶ p12.2g p10g* p10g³ p10g p10g⁴ p12g² p10g* p12g p12.2g* p12.2g* p12.2g⁴ p12.2g⁴ p12g p16.5m p13.9g² p12g* p13.9g² p10g p9.5g⁶ Dec 22] fair on all-weather, modest at best on turf: won 6 times in 2006, namely handicap in February and claimer (claimed from B. Powell £12,000) in April, both at Lingfield, claimers at Wolverhampton in May (claimed from J. Boyle £10,000) and June (2) and amateur handicap at Lingfield in November: effective at 1¼m to easy 1¾m: acts on polytrack, firm and soft going: has hung left: held up. *J. Pearce* **– a79**

ZALZAAR (IRE) 4 b.g. Xaar 132 – Zalamalec (USA) (Septieme Ciel (USA) 123) [2006 58p: 7.1m⁴ 10m 8.1m 10.2m Oct 8] modest maiden: stays 7f: acts on good to firm going: sold 8,000 gns. *C. G. Cox* **60**

ZAMALA 3 b.f. King's Best (USA) 132 – Ajayib (USA) 84 (Riverman (USA) 131) [2006 72: 8.1s 8s* 8.2g⁵ 8.3m Jul 8] rather leggy filly: fairly useful performer: won handicap at Goodwood in May: stays 1m: raced mainly on good or softer going: sold 15,000 gns in November. *J. L. Dunlop* **81**

ZAMBEZI RIVER 7 ch.g. Zamindar (USA) 116 – Double River (USA) (Irish River (FR) 131) [2006 41§: p8g p7.1g p6g p7g p7g 8.2s May 20] temperamental maiden: only poor form. *J. M. Bradley* **– § a43 §**

ZAMBOOZLE (IRE) 4 ch.g. Halling (USA) 133 – Blue Sirocco (Bluebird (USA) 125) [2006 79: p9.5g⁵ p12g* p13g⁵ 12g 11g⁶ p10g Jun 7] strong gelding: fairly useful handicapper: won at Lingfield in March: stays 1½m: acts on polytrack and good to firm going: reared as stall opened on reappearance: held up: gelded after final outing. *D. R. C. Elsworth* **86**

ZAMELIANA 2 ch.f. (Apr 6) Zaha (CAN) 106 – Amelia's Field 56 (Distant Relative 128) [2006 p6g May 23] £400Y: first foal: dam, ran 3 times, should have stayed 1¼m: last in maiden at Kempton. *Dr J. R. J. Naylor* **–**

ZAMHREAR 3 b.f. Singspiel (IRE) 133 – Lunda (IRE) 60 (Soviet Star (USA) 128) [2006 8m⁴ p10g 8.2m 7d⁵ f7g* 10d p8.6g² f8g* Dec 14] lengthy filly: sixth foal: half-sister to several winners, notably 5-y-o Blue Monday and smart 1m/1¼m winner Lundy's Lane, both by Darshaan: dam maiden half-sister to very smart/high-class middle-distance performers Luso and Warrsan: fair performer: won banded race in October and handicap in December, both at Southwell: stays 8.6f: acts on all-weather. *C. E. Brittain* **73**

ZANDO 4 b.g. Forzando 122 – Rockin' Rosie 59 (Song 132) [2006 53: p9.5g p9.5g³ p8.6g⁵ p8.6g f8g p9.5g Dec 29] big, good-topped gelding: modest performer: seems to stay 9.5f: acts on all-weather, raced only on good going or firmer on turf: tried in cheekpieces/visored. *E. G. Bevan* **63**

ZANGEAL 5 ch.g. Selkirk (USA) 129 – Generous Lady 98 (Generous (IRE) 139) [2006 p8g² Jun 14] strong, rangy gelding: fairly useful maiden, lightly raced: missed 2005: gelded, good second in handicap at Kempton only start at 5 yrs: stays 1¼m: acts on all-weather: tongue tied fourth 3-y-o outing (hung badly right). *C. F. Wall* **79**

ZANIDA (IRE) 2 b.f. (May 8) Mujadil (USA) 119 – Haraabah (USA) 99 (Topsider (USA)) [2006 6.1g⁴ 5g⁵ 5d⁵ 6d⁴ 6s⁴ 6d Oct 27] 22,000Y: tall, useful-looking filly: half-sister to several winning sprinters, including 1998 2-y-o 5f winner Speedy James (by Fayruz) and 5f winner (including at 2 yrs) Double Quick (by Superpower), both useful: **91**

dam 5f (at 2 yrs) to 7f winner: fairly useful form: won maiden at Ayr in June: best effort when 1¾ lengths fourth to Princess Iris in Firth of Clyde Stakes at Ayr fourth start, making running and flashing tail: below that form in listed races at York and Newmarket (raced alone) last 2 outings: speedy, and will prove best at 5f/6f: yet to race on ground firmer than good. *K. R. Burke*

ZANTERO 4 b.g. Danzero (AUS) – Cruinn A Bhord 107 (Inchinor 119) [2006 51d: **46** p7g⁴ 6g 8.3f 7.1m 8.3m 6.9f⁴ 5.9g 6m⁴ 5m⁶ Aug 17] poor maiden nowadays: stays 7f: acts on all-weather and firm going: tried blinkered. *W. M. Brisbourne*

ZAP ATTACK 6 b.g. Zafonic (USA) 130 – Rappa Tap Tap (FR) 111 (Tap On Wood **46** 130) [2006 –: f6g 7g f5g⁶ 6d⁵ 6f 5m 5d 8f 6v Oct 9] close-coupled gelding: poor performer nowadays: seemingly stays 8.6f: tried in cheekpieces/tongue tie. *J. Parkes*

ZARABAD (IRE) 4 b.g. King's Best (USA) 132 – Zarannda (IRE) 112 (Last Tycoon **77 d** 131) [2006 84: p8g 7f⁵ 8g⁶ 7m 8d⁶ 7.2v p7.1g⁶ p7.1g⁵ Dec 27] good-topped gelding: fair handicapper, on downgrade: stays 1m: acts on polytrack and firm going. *K. R. Burke*

ZARAKASH (IRE) 6 b.g. Darshaan 133 – Zarannda (IRE) 112 (Last Tycoon 131) **80 d** [2006 –: p7g⁴ 7.1d 10d 7.5g a5g 6.5s 5v Oct 25] fairly useful form at best: well beaten after reappearance, leaving Jonjo O'Neill after third start: has looked none too keen (tends to start slowly). *N. Madden, Ireland*

ZARIANO 6 b.g. Emperor Jones (USA) 119 – Douce Maison (IRE) 67 (Fools Holme – (USA)) [2006 –, a68: f7g⁵ f6g⁶ f8g⁴ f8g⁵ p8.6g p8.6g May 2] modest performer: stays **a55** 9.5f: acts on all-weather, little form on turf since 2003: tried in cheekpieces. *T. D. Barron*

ZARNITZA (USA) 2 b.f. (Apr 28) Quiet American (USA) – Zawaahy (USA) 89 (El – Gran Senor (USA) 136) [2006 7g Sep 30] half-sister to several winners, including useful French 2001 2-y-o 1m winner Summertime Legacy (by Darshaan) and 7f and 8.5f winner Bay of Delight (by Cadeaux Genereux): dam, 1m winner, closely related to Derby winner Golden Fleece: 20/1 and green, well beaten in maiden at Redcar. *E. A. L. Dunlop*

ZAROVA (IRE) 4 gr.g. Zafonic (USA) 130 – Estarova (FR) (Saint Estephe (FR) 123) **67 d** [2006 64: 12m³ 10m 12m* 13.9m 12f⁴ 10f 12m 9.9s³ 10m⁶ 9.9m 14d Oct 8] tall, leggy gelding: fair handicapper: won at Ripon in June: mainly well below form after: stays 1½m: acts on all-weather and firm going: tried blinkered: none too genuine. *M. W. Easterby*

ZAR SOLITARIO 2 b.c. (Apr 24) Singspiel (IRE) 133 – Ginevra di Camelot (FR) **69 p** (Alzao (USA) 117) [2006 p8.6g⁴ Nov 23] €260,000Y: brother to useful 1m to 10.5f winner Solista and half-brother to several winners in Italy: dam Italian 7.5f (at 2 yrs) to 1¼m winner: favourite, 6½ lengths fourth to History Boy in maiden at Wolverhampton, hanging left: sure to improve. *M. Johnston*

ZARWALA (IRE) 3 b.f. Polish Precedent (USA) 131 – Zarlana (IRE) (Darshaan 133) **92** [2006 11v* 12s⁶ 12g 10s Oct 30] leggy, useful-looking filly: fifth foal: half-sister to 7f winner Zarandja (by King's Best) and 1½m winner Zarghari (by Groom Dancer), both fairly useful in Ireland: dam, French 1m winner, half-sister to smart French 7f/1m winner Zarannda: fairly useful form: won maiden at Limerick in May: easily best effort in listed races after when 10½ lengths sixth to Anna Pavlova at York 3 months later: stays 1½m: blinkered third outing. *J. Oxx, Ireland*

ZARZU 7 b.g. Magic Ring (IRE) 115 – Rivers Rhapsody 104 (Dominion 123) [2006 **83** 84, a92: f5g⁵ p5g p5g² p5g⁶ p5g³ 5g² p6g 5g p6g p6g p5g p6g² p6g* p6g⁴ p6g Dec 3] **a91** close-coupled, good-topped gelding: fairly useful handicapper: won at Wolverhampton in November: effective at 5f/6f: acts on all-weather, firm and good to soft ground: tried in visor/cheekpieces much earlier in career: sometimes slowly away. *C. R. Dore*

ZASTRA'S PRIDE 3 ch.f. Zaha (CAN) 106 – Strath Kitten 36 (Scottish Reel 123) – [2006 30: f8g⁵ 10.1g 10.2m Sep 7] poor maiden: tried tongue tied. *W. G. M. Turner*

ZATO (IRE) 3 ch.g. Zafonic (USA) 130 – Top Table 65 (Shirley Heights 130) [2006 **100** 103: p8g³ 7m⁵ 8m 8m⁵ 8g 8f⁵ p8g⁶ p8g* p9.5g² Oct 28] lengthy, useful-looking gelding: useful performer: creditable 2¾ lengths third behind Close To You in listed race at Lingfield on reappearance: won handicap at Lingfield in October by neck from Cross The Line: stays 9.5f: acts on polytrack, firm and soft going: genuine. *M. R. Channon*

ZAVILLE 4 gr.f. Zafonic (USA) 130 – Colleville 97 (Pharly (FR) 130) [2006 75: 13.9s **72** 11.9m² 12m 11.9g 11g p16.5m⁶ p13.9g* p13.9g* p13.9g Dec 8] leggy filly: fair handicapper: left M. Jarvis 7,000 gns after third start: won at Wolverhampton in October and November: stays 2m: acts on polytrack and good to firm going: often in cheekpieces (including for wins) of late. *J. O'Reilly*

ZAWARIQ (IRE) 2 b.f. (May 7) Marju (IRE) 127 – Alikhlas 81 (Lahib (USA) 129) **62 p**
[2006 p7g Oct 26] €68,000F, €210,000Y: fifth foal: half-sister to 3 winners, including
useful 7f winner (including at 2 yrs) Silk Fan (by Unfuwain): dam, 1m winner, half-sister
to dam of 5-y-o Maraahel: 16/1, 7 lengths ninth to Dalvina in maiden at Lingfield, slowly
away and green, not knocked about: should improve. *M. P. Tregoning*

ZAYN ZEN 4 ch.f. Singspiel (IRE) 133 – Roshani (IRE) 79 (Kris 135) [2006 107: 9s **105**
8.5g³ 8m⁴ 10.4f⁵ Jul 29] good-topped filly: has a quick action: useful performer: creditable efforts in 2006 when length third to Echelon in Princess Elizabeth Stakes at Epsom
and 4½ lengths fourth to Soviet Song in Windsor Forest Stakes at Royal Ascot: stays 11f:
acts on polytrack, firm and good to soft going. *M. A. Jarvis*

ZAYYIR (IRE) 2 b.c. (Jan 29) Indian Ridge 123 – Lurina (IRE) 111 (Lure (USA) 131) **60 p**
[2006 6d Aug 23] 78,000 2-y-o: rather leggy, lightly-made colt: second foal: dam, 7f
winner who stayed 1m, half-sister to high-class French 1¼m/1½m performer Croco
Rouge: 10/1 and on edge, ninth in maiden at York: likely to improve. *G. A. Butler*

ZAZOUS 5 b.g. Zafonic (USA) 130 – Confidentiality (USA) (Lyphard (USA) 132) **68**
[2006 63: f5g p6g* p7g⁶ p6g* p6g² p6g² 6m 5s² 6.1d 6m² 5m 5m⁴ 5.3g⁴ 6d p6g p7g³
p6g* Nov 28] well-made gelding: fair performer: won 2 banded races (first one apprentices) at Lingfield in February and handicaps at Newbury in August and Lingfield in November: effective at 5f to 7f: acts on polytrack, soft and good to firm going. *J. J. Bridger*

ZED CANDY (FR) 3 b.g. Medicean 128 – Intrum Morshaan (IRE) 95 (Darshaan 133) **71**
[2006 48p: p9.5g 9s³ 10v⁴ 10d 8.1s⁶ p12.2g 8d⁴ 10.2m 13.8s 12v³ f11g* f11g* f12g³
Dec 14] leggy, angular gelding: fair performer: won handicaps at Southwell in November
and December: stays 1½m: acts on fibresand and heavy going. *J. T. Stimpson*

ZEENA 4 b.f. Unfuwain (USA) 131 – Forest Fire (SWE) 88 (Never So Bold 135) [2006 **53**
57, a54: p12.2g p10g⁴ p10g May 15] rather leggy filly: modest maiden: stays 1½m: acts
on polytrack, soft and good to firm going: ran in cheekpieces last 2 starts. *C. A. Horgan*

ZEEUW (IRE) 2 b.g. (Feb 10) Xaar 132 – Lucky Bet (IRE) 69 (Lucky Guest 109) **70**
[2006 p6g⁶ 7.1m⁵ Jun 25] €18,000F, 30,000Y: first foal: dam Irish 9f to 10.5f winner: 5½
lengths sixth in maiden at Lingfield in May, slowly away: raced freely only subsequent
start (gelded after): should stay 7f/1m. *D. J. Coakley*

ZEFOOHA (FR) 2 ch.f. (Apr 19) Lomitas 129 – Bezzaaf 97 (Machiavellian (USA) **80 p**
123) [2006 7f⁴ 7f* Jul 27] third foal: half-sister to 3-y-o Ans Bach and a winner in Greece
by Bachir: dam 1¼m winner: fairly useful form: won maiden at Folkestone in July by
head from Ronaldsay, always close up: should stay 1m: very slowly away on debut: open
to further improvement. *M. R. Channon*

ZELL AM SEE 2 b.g. (Mar 25) Averti (IRE) 117 – Pretty Pollyanna (General Assem- **–**
bly (USA)) [2006 7m 7d Sep 29] rather leggy, close-coupled gelding: 100/1, well held in
maidens at Newmarket (tailed off final start): subsequently gelded. *M. H. Tompkins*

ZELL (IRE) 3 b.f. Lend A Hand 124 – Skisette (Malinowski (USA) 123) [2006 –p: 9d **65**
8d 8s² 7m 9.2d⁵ Sep 25] fair maiden: stays 1m: acts on soft going: stumbled and unseated
rider on reappearance. *E. J. Alston*

ZELOS (IRE) 2 b.g. (Mar 6) Mujadil (USA) 119 – First Degree 50 (Sabrehill (USA) **66**
120) [2006 7.1m p7.1g³ 7.6f⁴ Aug 5] €48,000F, 44,000Y: strong gelding: second foal:
half-brother to 3-y-o Keel: dam, maiden who should have stayed 1¼m, half-sister to
smart performers up to 1m Auditorium and Mister Cosmi: fair maiden: gelded after final
start: stays 7f: acts on polytrack and good to firm ground. *J. A. Osborne*

ZELOSO 8 b.g. Alzao (USA) 117 – Silk Petal 105 (Petorius 117) [2006 58: 16.1d³ 16g **50**
May 22] good-bodied gelding: modest performer nowadays: stays 2m: acts on all-
weather, soft and good to firm going: tried blinkered, visored nowadays: won over
hurdles in June. *M. F. Harris*

ZENDARO 4 b.g. Danzero (AUS) – Countess Maud (Mtoto 134) [2006 69: 7g⁵ 9.1g **72**
8d* 7.2m p8.6g* 8.1d p8g Oct 5] tall gelding: fair performer on turf, modest on all- **a63**
weather: won sellers at Musselburgh in August and Wolverhampton in September: stays
8.6f: acts on polytrack, firm and good to soft ground: effective held up or making running:
sold 15,000 gns. *W. M. Brisbourne*

ZENNERMAN (IRE) 3 b.g. Observatory (USA) 131 – Precocious Miss (USA) 88 **87**
(Diesis 133) [2006 85: 6.1f⁶ 8m² 7m⁴ 7.5f³ 8.2m 7.1m⁴ 7d³ 8d⁶ 7f⁵ p7g Oct 21] smallish,
strong gelding: fairly useful performer: stays 1m: acts on firm and good to soft going:
tried in cheekpieces (ran poorly): held up. *W. M. Brisbourne*

Bank of Scotland Corporate Hambleton Stakes (Handicap), York—
conditions are ideal for Zero Tolerance, who is given a well-judged ride by Jamie Spencer;
Babodana (right) is a close second, followed by Dabbers Ridge and Blythe Knight (hooped cap)

ZERO (IRE) 3 b.c. Halling (USA) 133 – Zonda 100 (Fabulous Dancer (USA) 124) **85**
[2006 74p: 10.3f³ 10.9m* Jul 13] fairly useful form: won maiden at Warwick in July by
1¾ lengths from Kibara: stays 10.9f: acts on polytrack and firm going: sold 10,000 gns in
October. *M. A. Jarvis*

ZERO TOLERANCE (IRE) 6 ch.g. Nashwan (USA) 135 – Place de L'Opera 98 **113**
(Sadler's Wells (USA) 132) [2006 113: 8s⁴ 8d 8s* 8.5m⁵ 8g 8s 8.1v* 10s⁴ 11.6d Nov 4]
lengthy, workmanlike gelding: smart performer: won listed races at York (handicap, by
head from Babodana) in May and Haydock (beat Indian Steppes by 3 lengths) in
September: creditable fourth behind Book of Music in handicap at Ascot penultimate
start: stays 1¼m: has form on fibresand and good to firm going, best efforts (including 7
of 8 wins) on softer than good: reportedly took journey poorly when well below form at
Saint-Cloud second outing: often carries head awkwardly: free-going sort, often front
runner. *T. D. Barron*

ZEYDNAA (IRE) 6 b.g. Bahhare (USA) 122 – Hadawah (USA) 68 (Riverman (USA) **57**
131) [2006 57: 13f³ 13.9m 12f⁶ 16.2f 15.8d 15.8d Oct 3] close-coupled gelding: modest
handicapper: stays 2m: acts on firm and good to soft going. *C. R. Wilson*

ZHITOMIR 8 ch.g. Lion Cavern (USA) 117 – Treasure Trove (USA) 62 (The Minstrel **70**
(CAN) 135) [2006 79, a70: 7d⁵ 7g 6g⁵ 7.1s⁶ 7.2v² 6s 7.2v 7v⁵ Oct 31] strong gelding: fair
handicapper: effective at 7f to easy 8.6f: acts on polytrack, heavy and good to firm going:
has run well when edgy/sweating. *M. Dods*

ZIBELINE (IRE) 9 b.g. Cadeaux Genereux 131 – Zia (USA) 88 (Shareef Dancer **79**
(USA) 135) [2006 13.8m 12d 12.1m³ Sep 1] tall gelding: useful performer at best:
unraced on Flat in 2005: fair form in 2006: stays 2¼m, effective at 1½m: acts on firm
going, probably not on softer than good: tried in cheekpieces/blinkers: held up. *B. Ellison*

ZIDANE 4 b.g. Danzero (AUS) – Juliet Bravo 61 (Glow (USA)) [2006 81p: 6g 6g² 6d* **99 p**
6m² 6m* 7m 6m⁴ Sep 3] lengthy gelding: useful form: impressive winner of handicaps at
Thirsk in May and Newmarket (didn't have to come under serious pressure to beat Pick
A Nice Name by 2 lengths) in June: better than bare result in Bunbury Cup (Handicap)
at Newmarket and handicap at Lingfield last 2 starts: likely to prove best short of 7f: acts
on good to firm and good to soft going: usually waited with: worth another chance to
progress. *J. R. Fanshawe*

ZILCASH 3 b.g. Mujahid (USA) 125 – Empty Purse (Pennine Walk 120) [2006 76: **79**
10.2d⁵ 10.4d 9.9m⁶ 10m⁴ 11.5m³ 11.6g⁴ 11.6s Oct 2] tall, close-coupled gelding: fair
performer: reportedly split a pastern at 2 yrs: below form last 3 starts in 2006: stays 1¼m:
acts on polytrack, good to firm and good to soft ground. *A. King*

ZILLI 2 ch.f. (Mar 27) Zilzal (USA) 137 – Zizi (IRE) 87 (Imp Society (USA)) [2006 **45**
p7.1g p6g⁶ p5.1g⁵ Dec 29] fourth foal: half-sister to 1m winner Ellesappelle (by Benny
The Dip): dam 2-y-o 5f winner: poor form in maidens. *N. P. Littmoden*

ZIMBALI 4 ch.f. Lahib (USA) 129 – Dawn 70 (Owington 123) [2006 63, a–: 5.7f 5f 5f **54** 5.5g⁶ 6f⁵ 5.1f⁴ 6g 5.3m⁶ 5.1m 5.1m Sep 7] small filly: modest handicapper: effective at 5f/6f: acts on firm and soft going, little form on all-weather: tried in cheekpieces: races up with pace. *J. M. Bradley*

ZINGBAT (IRE) 3 b.g. Rainbow Quest (USA) 134 – Shastri (USA) 73 (Alleged (USA) **–** 138) [2006 –: 8d 8.1s 12.1f 14g Jul 7] leggy gelding: little form. *J. G. Given*

ZINGING 7 b.g. Fraam 114 – Hi Hoh (IRE) (Fayruz 116) [2006 46§, a52§: p8g⁴ p10g **51 §** p10g⁵ p7g p7g 10.2d 10g* 10m⁵ 10g 8.5g 8f⁵ 8f 10.1g 8f³ 8f 8m 10d p10g p10g Dec 18] **a54 §** small gelding: modest performer: won apprentice handicap at Brighton in May: stays 1¼m: acts on all-weather, firm and soft going: often blinkered/visored: has been tongue tied: ungenuine. *J. J. Bridger*

ZIRKEL (IRE) 3 br.g. Highest Honor (FR) 124 – Mythical Creek (USA) (Pleasant Tap **73** (USA)) [2006 10g⁶ 10m⁴ 12g 10d Oct 4] 9,000Y: workmanlike gelding: fifth foal: half-brother to fairly useful 8.6f to 1½m winner Fiddlers Creek (by Danehill) and useful Irish 1¼m to 1½m winner Menwaal (by Montjeu): dam 1¼m winner in Italy at 2 yrs: fair maiden: best effort on second start. *Mrs A. L. M. King*

ZIZOU (IRE) 3 b.g. Fantastic Light (USA) 134 – Search Committee (USA) (Roberto **61 d** (USA) 131) [2006 75d: p10g³ p8g p10g p8g p10g 9.7s⁵ 7.1s 9.7m⁶ 10m 11.5m⁴ 11m 10f p12g³ 12f³ 11.6m 16g 11.5d Oct 18] neat gelding: modest maiden at best at 3 yrs, leaving P. Hedger after third start: stays 1½m: acts on polytrack, firm and soft going: tried in visor/cheekpieces/tongue tie. *J. J. Bridger*

ZOHAR (USA) 4 b.g. Aljabr (USA) 125 – Dafnah (USA) (Housebuster (USA)) [2006 **96** 95: 7g⁴ 8.1m 7g May 27] tall, lengthy gelding: useful performer: good fourth to King's Caprice in handicap at Newmarket on reappearance: stayed 9f: acted on good to firm going, below form both outings on softer than good: dead. *B. J. Meehan*

ZOLTANO (GER) 8 b.g. In The Wings 128 – Zarella (GER) (Anatas) [2006 16v 16.1d **–** May 16] tall gelding: fair winning handicapper in 2004: missed 2005: well held at 8 yrs. *M. Todhunter*

ZOMERLUST 4 b.g. Josr Algarhoud (IRE) 118 – Passiflora 75 (Night Shift (USA)) **105** [2006 97: 8s 6d* 7g 6m 6m 6g 6s 6s⁶ 6d² 7f Sep 23] good-topped gelding: useful handicapper: won by 2½ lengths from Commando Scott at Pontefract in April: good head second of 26 to Geojimali in Ayr Silver Cup: best at 6f/7f: acts on soft and good to firm going: tough. *J. J. Quinn*

ZONERGEM 8 ch.g. Zafonic (USA) 130 – Anasazi (IRE) (Sadler's Wells (USA) 132) **97** [2006 93: p12g² p13g⁶ p10g³ p12g⁴ Oct 5] good-topped gelding: useful performer: hasn't won since 2002: mostly creditable efforts in 2006: stays easy 1½m: acts on polytrack and firm going: tried blinkered, usually wore cheekpieces prior to 2006: has been slowly away/carried head high/found little: usually held up: quirky. *Lady Herries*

ZONIC BOOM (FR) 6 ch.g. Zafonic (USA) 130 – Rosi Zambotti (IRE) 104 (Law **–** Society (USA) 130) [2006 69: p9.5g p12.2g Dec 27] fair handicapper at best on turf, modest on all-weather: well held both Flat starts in 2006 (in cheekpieces/tongue tied in latter): won over hurdles in November. *Mrs H. Dalton*

ZONTA ZITKALA 2 gr.f. (Feb 18) Daylami (IRE) 138 – Sioux Chef 78 (Be My Chief **76** (USA) 122) [2006 6g 6.1f² 7m² Aug 5] lengthy filly: third foal: half-sister to 4-y-o Seyaadi: dam 2-y-o 5.7f winner: fair form in maidens: short-head second to So Sweet at Newmarket final start, making most: should stay 1m+: raced on good ground or firmer: slowly away on debut. *R. M. Beckett*

ZOOM ONE 2 ch.c. (Jan 26) In The Wings 128 – Seyooll (IRE) 78 (Danehill (USA) **82 p** 126) [2006 8.1m⁵ 9m* 8d* Sep 26] medium-sized, sturdy colt: second foal: dam, maiden (probably stayed 1½m), out of Prix de l'Opera winner Andromaque: fairly useful form: won maiden at Redcar and nursery at Goodwood in September, making most when beating Aegis by ½ length in latter: will be suited by 1¼m+: type to keep on progressing. *M. P. Tregoning*

ZOORINA 2 b.f. (Mar 18) Xaar 132 – Saeedah 75 (Bustino 136) [2006 p7g 7f 7d Oct 3] **53** big, strong filly: fourth foal: half-sister to fairly useful 2003 2-y-o 6f winner Dallaah (by Green Desert): dam twice-raced sister to smart performer up to 1¼m Bulaxie and half-sister to very smart performer up to 1½m Zimzalabim: tongue tied, modest form at best in maidens at Kempton, Goodwood and (after 2-month break) Leicester: should stay 1m+. *M. P. Tregoning*

ZORIPP (IRE) 4 b.g. Spectrum (IRE) 126 – Allspice (Alzao (USA) 117) [2006 61: **64** f12g* 12.4m 11.8d p9.5g⁴ p12g⁶ Jun 15] small, sturdy gelding: modest handicapper: won at Southwell in April: stays 1½m: acts on all-weather and good to firm going: blinkered nowadays. *J. G. Given*

ZORN 7 br.g. Dilum (USA) 115 – Very Good (Noalto 120) [2006 61, a67: p6g f7g⁴ p6g **–** f6g f6g* f6g f6g⁵ f6g⁶ f6g³ f7s* f7g² p7g f7g f6g May 2] fair handicapper: won at **a70** Southwell in February and March: best form at 6f/7f: acts on all-weather, lightly raced on turf. *P. Howling*

ZORN (GER) 7 b.g. Lavirco (GER) 125 – Zypern (GER) (Acatenango (GER) 127) **–** [2006 10m 12d Aug 23] useful form when successful twice (1m/9f) from 5 starts on Flat in Germany at 3 yrs when trained by P. Schiergen: well held in 2 handicaps in Britain. *M. F. Harris*

ZOROONI 3 b.f. Josr Algarhoud (IRE) 118 – Zeyaarah (USA) 86 (Rahy (USA) 115) **53** [2006 63: p8g⁴ Jan 28] modest maiden: stays 7f: raced only on polytrack: tongue tied only outing in 2006: sold 3,000 gns in July. *M. A. Jarvis*

ZOWINGTON 4 gr.c. Zafonic (USA) 130 – Carmela Owen (Owington 123) [2006 96: **104** 5g* 5s⁶ 5m 6m 5d 6g³ 6d f5g Nov 15] quite good-topped colt: useful performer: won handicap at Epsom in April by ¾ length from Cape Royal: best effort when very close third to Stanley Goodspeed in similar event at Haydock: well held in listed race and handicap (first run on fibresand) last 2 starts: raced at 5f/6f: acts on polytrack and good to soft going, probably on good to firm: has started slowly/hung left. *C. F. Wall*

ZUMRAH (IRE) 5 b.g. Machiavellian (USA) 123 – The Perfect Life (IRE) 106 (Try **–** My Best (USA) 130) [2006 7m Apr 25] won bumper on debut: modest form over hurdles: slowly away and well held in maiden at Folkestone. *P. Bowen*

ZURBARAN (IRE) 3 ch.c. Alhaarth (IRE) 126 – Broken Romance (IRE) (Ela-Mana- **109** Mou 132) [2006 81: 8.1s⁵ 10m⁵ 14.1d* 13.3g² 13.9d² 14g² 16d⁴ Oct 14] strong, lengthy colt: useful performer: trained by S. Keightley at 2 yrs: left K. Morgan after second start in 2006: won handicap at Nottingham in August: improved again subsequently, second in handicaps at Newbury and York (Mallard Stakes, to Sunday Symphony) then very good efforts at Newmarket last 2 starts, in listed race (short-head second to Novellara) and Jockey Club Cup (6¾ lengths fourth to Hawridge Prince, again hanging left): stays 2m: acts on heavy going: sold 210,000 gns in October, joined Godolphin. *B. J. Meehan*

The following unraced horses appeared in ante-post lists for 2007 classics or had a Group 1 entry at two years, and are included for information purposes.

AJZAL (IRE) 2 b.c. (Apr 1) Alhaarth (IRE) 126 – Alkaffeyeh (IRE) (Sadler's Wells (USA) 132) half-brother to several winners, including 7f (at 2 yrs) and 1¾m winner Tholjanah (by Darshaan), 1½m/1¾m winner Ta-Lim (by Ela-Mana-Mou) and 9f (in UAE) to 1½m (in Ireland) winner Mudaa-Eb (by Machiavellian), all 3 smart: dam unraced sister to smart 1½m filly Larrocha and half-sister to Ardross. *M. P. Tregoning*

ALADDINS CAVE 2 b.c. (Feb 19) Rainbow Quest (USA) 134 – Flight of Fancy 114 (Sadler's Wells (USA) 132) second foal: half-brother to 3-y-o Fleeting Memory: dam, 2-y-o 7f winner and runner-up in Oaks, out of Ribblesdale and Geoffrey Freer winner Phantom Gold. *Sir Michael Stoute*

BONIFACIO (IRE) 2 b.c. (Apr 6) Sadler's Wells (USA) 132 – Anaza 100 (Darshaan 133) 320,000Y: half-brother to several winners, including very smart French 1m (at 2 yrs) to 10.5f winner Astarabad (by Alleged) and to dam of top-class performer up to 1½m Azamour: dam French 2-y-o 1m/8.5f winner (only season to race). *A. P. O'Brien, Ireland*

BRAVELY (IRE) 2 b.c. (Apr 22) Rock of Gibraltar (IRE) 133 – Raghida (IRE) 102 (Nordico (USA)) €200,000Y: sixth foal: half-brother to smart 5f to 1m (latter including at 2 yrs) winner Marionnaud (by Spectrum): dam, Irish 2-y-o 5f winner, half-sister to Irish Derby and Eclipse runner-up Sholokhov. *J. S. Bolger, Ireland*

DABAWIYAH (IRE) 2 b.f. (Mar 5) Intikhab (USA) 135 – The Perfect Life (IRE) 106 (Try My Best (USA) 130) 260,000Y: half-sister to several winners, including smart 7f (at 2 yrs) to 1½m (Gordon Stakes) winner Rabah and useful 1m/1¼m winner Muhtafel (both by Nashwan): dam, French 5f (at 2 yrs) and 7f winner, sister to Last Tycoon. *L. M. Cumani*

DOUBLE DOORS 2 b.c. (Apr 11) Grand Lodge (USA) 125 – Daring Miss 113 (Sadler's Wells (USA) 132) third foal: half-brother to useful 6.5f (in USA) and 7f (at 2 yrs) winner Quickfire (by Dubai Millennium): dam, French 1½m/14.5f winner, out of Oaks runner-up Bourbon Girl. *J. H. M. Gosden*

DUSTOORI 2 b.c. (Mar 26) In The Wings 128 – Elfaslah (IRE) 107 (Green Desert (USA) 127) half-brother to several winners, including high-class 7f (at 2 yrs) to 1¼m (Dubai World Cup) winner Almutawakel, smart 1m (including UAE 1000 Guineas) winner Muwakleh and smart 1¼m/1½m (in UAE) winner Elmustanser (all by Machiavellian): dam, won around 1¼m, half-sister to high-class 1½m performer White Muzzle. *Saeed bin Suroor*

EL MORZILLO (USA) 2 b.c. (Feb 21) Green Desert (USA) 127 – Bosra Sham (USA) 132 (Woodman (USA) 126) fifth foal: half-brother to 3 winners, including useful 1¼m and 1½m winner Shami (by Rainbow Quest) and UAE 7.5f to 1¼m winner Bosra's Valentine (by Sadler's Wells): dam, won Fillies' Mile, 1000 Guineas and Champion Stakes, from an excellent family. *A. P. O'Brien, Ireland*

EZDIYAAD (IRE) 2 b.c. (May 15) Galileo (IRE) 134 – Wijdan (USA) 101 (Mr Prospector (USA)) sixth foal: closely related to 1¼m winner Mohafazaat (by Sadler's Wells) and half-brother to smart 1m winner (including at 2 yrs) Oriental Fashion (by Marju) and 3-y-o Makderah: dam, 1m and 10.4f winner, closely related to Nayef and half-sister to Nashwan and Unfuwain. *M. P. Tregoning*

FONDLED 2 b.f. (Mar 13) Selkirk (USA) 129 – Embraced 103 (Pursuit of Love 124) second foal: half-sister to 3-y-o Caressed: dam, 1m winner (including at 2 yrs), half-sister to very smart 1½m performer Nowhere To Exit. *J. R. Fanshawe*

HILLTOP HERO 2 b.c. (Jan 16) Danehill (USA) 126 – Nadia 116 (Nashwan (USA) 135) first foal: dam French 1¼m (including Prix Saint-Alary) winner. *Saeed bin Suroor*

KING'S EVENT (USA) 2 b.c. (Apr 26) Dynaformer (USA) – Magic of Love 99 (Magic Ring (IRE) 115) $150,000Y: second foal: half-brother to 3-y-o Gigs Magic: dam 2-y-o 5f/6f winner. *Sir Michael Stoute*

LION ON THE PROWL (IRE) 2 b.c. (May 25) Sadler's Wells (USA) 132 – Ballerina (IRE) 88 (Dancing Brave (USA) 140) brother to 2 winners, including very smart 1m (at 2 yrs)/1¼m winner Let The Lion Roar, and half-brother to very smart St Leger winner Millenary (successful at 11f to 2¼m) and smart 1½m winner Head In The Clouds, both by Rainbow Quest: dam, 2-y-o 7f winner, half-sister to Princess Royal winner Dancing Bloom and smart dam of Spectrum. *J. Oxx, Ireland*

LUCARNO (USA) 2 b.c. (Feb 10) Dynaformer (USA) – Vignette (USA) 93 (Diesis 133) third foal: half-brother to a minor winner in USA by Olympio: dam, 2-y-o 6f winner (later 5.5f/6.5f winner in USA), out of smart French 9f winner Be Exclusive. *J. H. M. Gosden*

MORNING CRY (USA) 2 b.f. (Mar 22) Danzig (USA) – Morning Devotion (USA) 102 (Affirmed (USA)) closely related to several winners, notably top-class Oaks/Irish Derby winner Balanchine (by Storm Bird), also 7f winner at 2 yrs, and smart 7f to 1½m winner Romanov (by Nureyev) and half-sister to useful Irish 2002 2-y-o 7f winner Some Kind of Tiger (by Storm Cat): dam, 2-y-o 6f winner, stayed 1½m. *B. J. Meehan*

PRAXITELES (IRE) 2 b.c. (Apr 30) Sadler's Wells (USA) 132 – Hellenic 125 (Darshaan 133) brother to several at least smart performers, including 1¼m winner Greek Dance and 1¼m/1½m winner Islington, both very smart, and half-brother to 7f/1m winner Desert Beauty (by Green Desert) and 4-y-o Mountain High: dam won Yorkshire Oaks and second in St Leger. *Sir Michael Stoute*

PUSS IN BOOTS (IRE) 2 b.c. (Feb 3) Storm Cat (USA) – Saganeca (USA) 120 (Sagace (FR) 135) half-brother to several winners, most at least useful, notably Arc winner Sagamix (by Linamix) and French performer up to 1½m (third in Arc) Sagacity (by Highest Honor, 9f/1¼m winner at 2 yrs), both high-class: dam won 12.5f Prix de Royallieu. *A. P. O'Brien, Ireland*

RIGGINS (IRE) 2 b.c. (Mar 18) Cape Cross (IRE) 129 – Rentless (Zafonic (USA) 130) €130,000Y: first foal: dam, Italian 7f (at 2 yrs) to 1m winner, sister to useful 1¼m/1½m winner Yawmi. *L. M. Cumani*

SALSA VERDI (USA) 2 b.f. (Apr 17) Giant's Causeway (USA) 132 – Cape Verdi (IRE) 126 (Caerleon (USA) 132) fourth foal: sister to 3-y-o Benandonner: dam, won 1000 Guineas (also 6f winner at 2 yrs), out of sister to Breeders' Cup Classic winner Arcangues. *Saeed bin Suroor*

STAND GUARD 2 b.c. (Mar 11) Danehill (USA) 126 – Protectress 110 (Hector Protector (USA) 124) first foal: dam, 2-y-o 7f winner from 2 starts (stayed 1¼m), out of useful sister to Racing Post Trophy winner/St Leger runner-up Armiger. *Sir Michael Stoute*

STREET TALK 2 b.c. (Apr 16) Machiavellian (USA) 123 – Helen Street 123 (Troy 137) brother to top-class 6.5f (at 2 yrs in US) to 1¼m (including Dubai World Cup) winner Street Cry and to dam of high-class 1m to 10.5f performer Shamardal, and half-brother to several winners: dam won Irish Oaks. *Saeed bin Suroor*

TOP CLASS (USA) 2 b.c. (Feb 3) Storm Cat (USA) – Simadartha (USA) (Gone West (USA)) $1,600,000Y: third foal: dam, French 1¼m winner, closely related to smart French performer up to 1½m Way of Light from excellent family. *A. P. O'Brien, Ireland*

WAR AND PEACE (IRE) 2 b.c. (Mar 20) Danehill (USA) 126 – Pipalong (IRE) 121 (Pips Pride 117) second foal: dam 5f/6f winner (including at 2 yrs). *A. P. O'Brien, Ireland*

ERRATA & ADDENDA

'Racehorses of 1954'

p315   picture caption should be: wins from Darius (noseband) and Landau

'Racehorses of 1965'

Aureate   failed to win a race in **1965**

Derring-Do   form figures for 1965: 8f* 8g³ 8v³ 8s* **8s*** 10g

'Racehorses of 1966'

p343   line 7: Hill Rise won the Santa Anita **Derby**

'Racehorses of 2003'

Rosacara   has no **near-side** eye: **second** foal

'Racehorses of 2004'

Wilko   was trained until after the Breeders' Cup Juvenile by Jeremy Noseda in Britain

Notnowcato   **third** foal

PROMISING HORSES

Selected British-trained horses (plus those trained by Aidan O'Brien) with either a p or P in *Racehorses of 2006* are listed under their trainers for 2007.

A. M. BALDING
Water Mill (USA) 2 gr.c   88p
Yeaman's Hall 2 b.c   89p

M. L. W. BELL
Hohlethelonely 2 ch.c   86p
Metaphoric (IRE) 2 b.c   85P

J. R. BEST
Hurricane Spirit (IRE) 2 b.c   103p

J. R. BOYLE
Sunoverregun 2 b.c   81p

C. E. BRITTAIN
Undertone (IRE) 2 ch.f   84p

H. R. A. CECIL
Ajaan 2 br.c   87p
Passage of Time 2 b.f   113p
Phoenix Tower (USA) 2 b.c   85p
Walking Talking 2 b.c   83p
Multidimensional (IRE) 3 b.c   115p

M. R. CHANNON
Bateleur 2 b.g   85p
Go On Be A Tiger (USA) 2 br.c   98p
Lakshmi (IRE) 2 b.f   87p
Majestic Roi (USA) 2 ch.f   86p
Mr Napper Tandy 2 ch.c   84p
Treat 2 b.f   108p
Zefooha (FR) 2 ch.f   80p

P. W. CHAPPLE-HYAM
Authorized (IRE) 2 b.c   118p
Cat de Mille (USA) 2 b.c   86p
Hamoody (USA) 2 ch.c   106p
Al Qasi (IRE) 3 b.c   117p

R. CHARLTON
Farley Star 2 b.f   82p
Fifty Cents 2 ch.c   88p
Monzante (USA) 2 gr.g   110p
Proponent 2 b.c   100P

P. F. I. COLE
Circus Polka (USA) 2 br.c   82p
Thunder Storm Cat (USA) 2 b.c   95p
Tredegar 2 ch.c   99p

C. G. COX
Perfect Star 2 b.f   84p

L. M. CUMANI
Furmigadelagiusta 2 ch.c   80p
Lion Sands 2 b.c   80p
Monte Alto (IRE) 2 b.c   83p
Sanbuch 2 b.c   83p
Bauer (IRE) 3 gr.c   98p
Mail Express (IRE) 3 b.f   82p
Manipulate 3 b.c   85p
Pentatonic 3 b.f   86p

E. A. L. DUNLOP
Al Khaleej 2 b.c   85p
Broomielaw 2 ch.c   86p
Dalvina 2 ch.f   90p
Dream Scheme 2 b.f   91p
Fort Amhurst (IRE) 2 ch.c   81p
King Charles 2 b.g   94p
Silmi 2 gr.c   81p
Wait For The Light 2 b.c   80p
Western Adventure (USA) 2 b.c   83p

J. L. DUNLOP
Mutadarrej (IRE) 2 ch.c   91p
Sacre Coeur 2 b.f   90p
Mount Kilimanjaro (IRE) 3 b.c   96p

D. R. C. ELSWORTH
Barshiba (IRE) 2 ch.f   73P
Salford Mill (IRE) 2 b.c   80p
Sunley Peace 2 ch.c   80p

P. D. EVANS
Valdan (IRE) 2 b.g   95p

R. A. FAHEY
Sunnyside Tom (IRE) 2 b.g   82p
Utmost Respect 2 b.c   104p

J. R. FANSHAWE
Artimino 2 b.c   90p
Cape 3 b.f   101p
Font 3 b.g   94p
Lady Stardust 3 b.f   90p
Riotous Applause 3 b.f   100p
Zidane 4 b.g   99p

J. H. M. GOSDEN
Asperity (USA) 2 b.c   104P
Bergonzi (IRE) 2 ch.c   80p
Broghill 2 ch.c   93p
Ekhtiaar 2 b.g   89p
Escape Route (USA) 2 b.c   87p
Maraca (IRE) 2 b.c   82p
Raincoat 2 b.c   91p
Safe Investment (USA) 2 b.c   94p
Sunshine Kid (USA) 2 b.c   94p
Tebee 2 ch.f   76P
Tybalt (USA) 2 b.c   97p
Yazamaan 2 b.c   107p

W. J. HAGGAS
Blithe 2 b.f   91p
Eco Centrism 2 ch.c   81p
Mutajarred 2 ch.g   73P
Abandon (USA) 3 ch.f   90p
Heaven Knows 3 ch.c   97p

R. HANNON
Aegean Prince 2 b.c   80p
Athar (IRE) 2 ch.c   83p
Baroness Richter (IRE) 2 b.f   88p
Grande Caiman (IRE) 2 ch.c   85p
Lazy Darren 2 b.g   80p

Mr Aviator (USA) 2 b.c 80p
Tembanee (IRE) 2 b.c 89p

B. W. HILLS
Apache Dawn 2 ch.g 83p
Celestial Halo (IRE) 2 b.c 86p
Hollow Ridge 2 b.f 91p
Miss Lucifer (FR) 2 b.f 86p
Princess Valerina 2 ch.f 94p
Rhaam 2 b.c 90p
Sues Surprise (IRE) 2 b.f 91p
Urban Spirit 2 b.c 90p
Mosharref (IRE) 3 b.g 99p

P. HOWLING
Resplendent Ace (IRE) 2 b.c 88p

M. A. JARVIS
Black Rock (IRE) 2 ch.c 91p
Folk Opera (IRE) 2 ch.f 80p
Fragrancy (IRE) 2 ch.f 83p
Marozi (USA) 2 ch.c 81p
Mutanaseb (USA) 2 b.c 87p
Ommraan (IRE) 2 ch.c 83p
Prince Forever (IRE) 2 b.c 96p
Sunlight (IRE) 2 ch.f 92p
Sweeney (IRE) 2 ch.c 95p
We'll Come 2 b.g 93p
Yaqeen 2 b.f 90p
Hala Bek (IRE) 3 b.c 121p

J. HOWARD JOHNSON
Fushe Jo 2 gr.c 83p
Musca (IRE) 2 b.g 88p

M. JOHNSTON
Aureate 2 ch.c 81p
Boscobel 2 ch.c 91p
Colorado Rapid (IRE) 2 b.c 84p
Dollar Chick (IRE) 2 b.f 82p
Five A Side 2 b.c 84p
Hearthstead Maison (IRE) 2 b.c 89p
Legend House (FR) 2 b.f 70p
Penny Post (IRE) 2 b.f 93p
Record Breaker (IRE) 2 b.c 81p
Salaasa (USA) 2 ch.c 79p
Serengeti 2 b.c 80p
Steady As A Rock (FR) 2 ch.c 84p
Swiss Act 2 ch.c 81p

M. A. MAGNUSSON
Ransom Captive (USA) 2 b.f 85p

P. J. MAKIN
Sharpazmax (IRE) 2 b.c 86p

E. S. MCMAHON
Cartimandua 2 b.f 81p

B. J. MEEHAN
American Spin 2 ch.c 81p
Benfleet Boy 2 gr.g 82p
Day By Day 2 ch.f —P
Diamond Tycoon (USA) 2 b.c 84p
Rainbow Promises (USA) 2 b.f 99P
Roshanak (IRE) 2 b.f 91p
Supersonic Dave (USA) 2 b.c 89p

T. G. MILLS
Petara Bay (IRE) 2 b.c 89p

H. MORRISON
Sakhee's Secret 2 ch.c 104p
Salsa Steps (USA) 2 ch.f 80p

W. R. MUIR
Big Robert 2 b.c 106p

D. NICHOLLS
Buachaill Dona (IRE) 3 b.g 101p

J. NOSEDA
Kafuu (IRE) 2 b.c 84P
Life (IRE) 2 b.c 87p
Loulwa (IRE) 2 b.f 82p
Rahiyah (USA) 2 ch.f 105p
Sander Camillo (USA) 2 b.f 116p
Shevchenko (IRE) 2 b.c 85p
Petrovich (USA) 3 ch.c 111p

A. P. O'BRIEN, IRELAND
Abraham Lincoln (IRE) 2 b.c 98p
Admiralofthefleet (USA) 2 b.c 116p
Albert Einstein (IRE) 2 b.c 94p
Anton Chekhov 2 b.c 98p
Archipenko (USA) 2 b.c 97p
Astronomer Royal (USA) 2 b.c 90p
Duke of Marmalade (IRE) 2 b.c 110p
Gstaad (USA) 2 b.c 88p
Macarthur 2 b.c 95P
Mount Nelson 2 b.c 114p
Soldier of Fortune (IRE) 2 b.c 114p
Spanish Harlem (IRE) 2 br.c 98p
Uimhir A Haon (IRE) 2 b.f 87p

MRS A. J. PERRETT
Dramatic Turn 2 b.f 87p
Russki (IRE) 2 b.c 88p
Sharp Dresser (USA) 2 ch.f 80p
Nosferatu (IRE) 3 b.g 84p

T. J. PITT
Yungaburra (IRE) 2 b.g 100p

SIR MARK PRESCOTT
Pixie Ring 2 b.f 85p
Sagredo (USA) 2 b.g 95p

K. A. RYAN
Fantasy Parkes 2 ch.f 82p

SIR MICHAEL STOUTE
Adagio 2 br.c 109p
Al Shemali 2 ch.c 97p
Al Tharib (USA) 2 b.c 87p
Cabinet (IRE) 2 b.c 96p
Cliche (IRE) 2 b.f 92p
Dance of Light (USA) 2 b.f 73P
Eternal Path (USA) 2 ch.f 83p
Gold Hush (USA) 2 ch.f 80p
Hi Calypso (IRE) 2 b.f 80p
Kaseema (USA) 2 b.f 88p
Ladies Best 2 b.c 99p
Lang Shining (IRE) 2 ch.c 84p
Lost In Wonder (USA) 2 b.f 82p
Manaal (USA) 2 b.f 88p
Ravarino (USA) 2 ch.f 57P
Regal Flush 2 b.c 83p

Shorthand 2 b.f 95p
Spanish Moon (USA) 2 b.c 97p
Spume (IRE) 2 b.g 85p
Galactic Star 3 ch.c 81p
Great Hawk (USA) 3 b.c 108p

SAEED BIN SUROOR
Eastern Anthem (IRE) 2 b.c 97P
Empire Day (UAE) 2 ch.c 107p
Gemology (USA) 2 b.c 90p
Mariotto (USA) 2 b.c 96p
Measured Tempo 2 b.f 100P
Mofarij 2 ch.c 92p
Mythical Kid (USA) 2 b.c 111p
Shane (GER) 2 ch.f 106p
Truly Royal 2 b.c 96P
Counterpunch 3 ch.g 115p
Desert Authority (USA) 3 b.c 117p
Discreet Cat (USA) 3 b.c 127p
Green Coast (IRE) 3 b.c 82p
New Guinea 3 b.g 110p
Rampallion 3 b.c 106p
Seabow (USA) 3 b.c 91p
With Interest 3 b.c 111p

G. A. SWINBANK
Deserted Dane (USA) 2 b.c 97p
Flying Valentino 2 b.f 83p
Prince Evelith (GER) 3 b.g 82p

W. R. SWINBURN
Count Ceprano (IRE) 2 b.c 94p
Happy Go Lily 2 b.f 83p

T. P. TATE
Raucous (GER) 3 b.g 89p

J. A. R. TOLLER
Barney McGrew (IRE) 3 b.g 84p

M. H. TOMPKINS
Marvo 2 b.c 82p

M. P. TREGONING
Basaata (USA) 2 b.f 85p
Zoom One 2 ch.c 82p
Majaales (USA) 3 b.g 90p

C. F. WALL
Curzon Prince (IRE) 2 b.c 84p

M. J. WALLACE
Les Fazzani (IRE) 2 b.f 83p

S. C. WILLIAMS
Swift Image 2 gr.f 83p

SELECTED BIG RACES 2006

Prize money for racing abroad has been converted to £ sterling at the exchange rate current at the time of the race. The figures are correct to the nearest £. The Timeform ratings (TR) recorded by the principals in each race appear on the last line.

NAD AL SHEBA Saturday, Mar 25
Turf course: GOOD to FIRM, Dirt course: STANDARD

1 **Dubai Sheema Classic Sponsored By Nakheel (Gr 1) (4yo+)** £1,714,286 — 1½m (Turf)

HEART'S CRY (JPN) *KHashiguchi,Japan* 5-8-11 CPLemaire (13)	11/4		1
COLLIER HILL *GASwinbank,GB* 8-8-11 DeanMcKeown (3)	22/1	4¼	2
FALSTAFF (IRE) *MFdeKock,SouthAfrica* 4-8-11 (b) JMurtagh (2)	25/1	1¼	3
Ouija Board *EALDunlop,GB* 5-8-7 KFallon (8)	9/4f	3½	4
Alexander Goldrun (IRE) *JSBolger,Ireland* 5-8-7 KJManning (7)	10/1	5¾	5
Alayan (IRE) *JOxx,Ireland* 4-8-11 MJKinane (12)	20/1	2¼	6
Layman (USA) *IMohammed,UAE* 4-8-11 (t) KerrinMcEvoy (1)	50/1	½	7
Norse Dancer (IRE) *DRCElsworth,GB* 6-8-11 JohnEgan (10)	25/1	¾	8
Mustanfar (USA) *KPMcLaughlin,USA* 5-8-11 (v) RHills (5)	50/1	3¾	9
Punch Punch (BRZ) *CMorgado,Brazil* 5-8-11 (v) MAlmeida (6)	40/1	½	10
Oracle West (SAF) *MFdeKock,SouthAfrica* 5-8-11 KShea (4)	12/1	2¾	11
Relaxed Gesture (IRE) *CClement,USA* 5-8-11 (t) CNakatani (14)	7/1	2½	12
Greys Inn (USA) *MFdeKock,SouthAfrica* 6-8-11 WCMarwing (9)	15/2	3¼	13
Shanty Star (IRE) *RBouresly,UAE* 6-8-11 GAvranche (11)	66/1	dist	14

Shadai Race Horse Co Ltd 14ran 2m31.89 — TR: 127/119/119/106+

2 **Dubai Duty Free Sponsored By Dubai Duty Free (Gr 1) (3yo+)** £1,714,286 — 1m195y (Turf)

DAVID JUNIOR (USA) *BJMeehan,GB* 4-9-0 JamieSpencer (1)	9/2f		1
THE TIN MAN (USA) *REMandella,USA* 8-9-0 VEspinoza (2)	14/1	3½	2
SEIHALI (IRE) *DJSelvaratnam,UAE* 7-9-0 JMurtagh (5)	25/1	1¼	3
Host (CHI) *TAPletcher,USA* 6-9-0 JVelazquez (7)	20/1	1¾	4
Bullish Luck (USA) *ASCruz,HongKong* 7-9-0 (b) CSoumillon (15)	12/1	nk	5
Perfect Promise (SAF) *DLFreedman,Australia* 7-8-10 KerrinMcEvoy (8)	22/1	nk	6
Fields of Omagh (AUS) *DHayes,Australia* 9-9-0 (s) SKing (3)	16/1	nk	7
Touch of Land (FR) *H-APantall,France* 6-9-0 CPLemaire (10)	6/1	1½	8
Russian Pearl (NZ) *ASCruz,HongKong* 6-9-0 (t) FCoetzee (16)	18/1	2¼	9
Tyson (SAF) *MFdeKock,SouthAfrica* 6-9-0 MJKinane (14)	22/1	¾	10
Whilly (IRE) *DFO'Neill,USA* 5-9-0 (t) FMartinez (11)	20/1	½	11
Hat Trick (JPN) *KSumii,Japan* 5-9-0 OPeslier (13)	6/1	¾	12
Linngari (IRE) *HBrown,SouthAfrica* 4-9-0 KShea (4)	10/1	2¾	13
Valixir (IRE) *SaeedbinSuroor,UAE* 5-9-0 LDettori (12)	6/1	8½	14
Asakusa Den'en *MKono,Japan* 7-9-0 (s) YTake (9)	12/1	14	15

Roldvale Limited 15ran 1m49.65 — TR: 132/122/119/115/114/109/113

3 **Dubai World Cup Sponsored By Emirates Airline (Gr 1) (3yo+)** £2,057,143 — 1¼m (Dirt)

Order as they passed the post: Brass Hat finished second, but was disqualified after failing a dope test.

ELECTROCUTIONIST (USA) *SaeedbinSuroor,UAE* 5-9-0 LDettori (1)	5/4f		1
BRASS HAT (USA) *WBradley,USA* 5-9-0 (b+t) WMartinez (7)	11/2	1½	2
WILKO (USA) *JNoseda,GB* 4-9-0 GGomez (9)	33/1	3	3
Magna Graduate (USA) *TAPletcher,USA* 4-9-0 (b) JVelazquez (8)	12/1	2¾	4
Kane Hekili (JPN) *KSumii,Japan* 4-9-0 YTake (3)	7/2	2¾	5
Chiquitin (ARG) *IPDJory,SaudiArabia* 6-9-0 (t) MJKinane (5)	50/1	1½	6
Maraahel (IRE) *SirMichaelStoute,GB* 5-9-0 (v) RHills (6)	9/1	3½	7
Star King Man (USA) *HMori,Japan* 7-9-0 OPeslier (10)	40/1	nk	8
Super Frolic (USA) *VCerin,USA* 6-9-0 (t) CNakatani (11)	16/1	1¾	9
Choctaw Nation (USA) *JMullins,USA* 6-9-0 (v+t) VEspinoza (4)	16/1	nk	10
Shakis (IRE) *DWatson,UAE* 6-9-0 (v+t) WilliamSupple (2)	66/1	4¾	11

Godolphin 11ran 2m01.32 — TR: 127/124/120/116/112+/108

SHA TIN Sunday, Apr 23 GOOD to FIRM

4 **Audemars Piguet Queen Elizabeth II Cup (Gr 1) (3yo+)** £578,871 — 1¼m

	IRRIDESCENCE (SAF) *MFdeKock,SouthAfrica* 5-8-10 WCMarwing	485/100		1
	BEST GIFT (NZ) *JMoore,HongKong* 5-9-0 (t) ESaint-Martin	11/1	hd	2
1	OUIJA BOARD *EALDunlop,GB* 5-8-10 LDettori	8/5f	sh	3
	Super Kid (NZ) *JMoore,HongKong* 7-9-0 SDye	14/1	1½	4

2	Bullish Luck (USA) *ASCruz,HongKong* 7-9-0 (b) BPrebble	17/1	1¾	5
	Viva Pataca *JMoore,HongKong* 4-9-0 GMosse	5/2	1¼	6
	Bowman's Crossing (IRE) *CFownes,HongKong* 7-9-0 DDunn	24/1	1¼	7
	Green Treasure (AUS) *DCruz,HongKong* 5-9-0 YTCheng	46/1	nk	8
2	Russian Pearl (NZ) *ASCruz,HongKong* 6-9-0 (t) FCoetzee	24/1	1¼	9
	River Dancer (IRE) *JSize,HongKong* 7-9-0 GSchofield	61/1	sh	10
1	Falstaff (IRE) *MFdeKock,SouthAfrica* 4-9-0 (b) DJWhyte	50/1	6	11
	Laverock (IRE) *CLaffon-Parias,France* 4-9-0 MBlancpain	60/1	1½	12
1	Norse Dancer (IRE) *DRCElsworth,GB* 6-9-0 DarryllHolland	50/1	7¾	13

Team Valor 13ran 2m02.00   TR: 118/122/117+/118/114+/112+

LONGCHAMP Sunday, Apr 30   GOOD to SOFT

5   **Prix Ganay - Grand Prix Air Mauritius (Gr 1) (4yo+)** £119,042   1¼m110y

CORRE CAMINOS (FR) *MDelzangles,France* 4-9-2 TJarnet	28/10			1
ROYAL HIGHNESS (GER) *PBary,France* 4-8-13 TThulliez	9/1		5	2
MANDURO (GER) *AFabre,France* 4-9-2 CSoumillon	11/10cpf		¾	3
Pride (FR) *AdeRoyerDupre,France* 6-8-13 CPLemaire	3/1		1	4
Montare (IRE) *JEPease,France* 4-8-13 (s) TGillet	10/1		4	5
Vatori (FR) *PHDemercastel,France* 4-9-2 SPasquier	18/1		sn	6
Near Honor (GER) *PVovcenko,Germany* 8-9-2 MSautjeau	11/10cpf		¾	7

Marquesa de Moratalla 7ran 2m17.10   TR: 124/113/107+

NEWMARKET Saturday, May 6   GOOD to FIRM (Rowley Mile Course)

6   **Stan James 2000 Guineas Stks (Gr 1)** (3yo c+f) £187,374   1m

GEORGE WASHINGTON (IRE) *APO'Brien,Ireland* 3-9-0 KFallon (6)	6/4f		1
SIR PERCY *MPTregoning* 3-9-0 MartinDwyer (4)	4/1	2½	2
OLYMPIAN ODYSSEY *BWHills* 3-9-0 JamieSpencer (2)	33/1	1½	3
Araafa (IRE) *JNoseda* 3-9-0 AlanMunro (1)	66/1	¾	4
Misu Bond (IRE) *BSmart* 3-9-0 TonyCulhane (14)	66/1	½	5
Final Verse *SirMichaelStoute* 3-9-0 RobertWinston (5)	50/1	½	6
Amadeus Wolf *KARyan* 3-9-0 NCallan (12)	9/1	¾	7
Horatio Nelson (IRE) *APO'Brien,Ireland* 3-9-0 MJKinane (11)	6/1	nk	8
Asset (IRE) *RHannon* 3-9-0 RichardHughes (9)	10/1	sh	9
Close To You (IRE) *TGMills* 3-9-0 IanMongan (7)	80/1	hd	10
Killybegs (IRE) *BWHills* 3-9-0 MichaelHills (8)	16/1	1	11
Red Clubs (IRE) *BWHills* 3-9-0 RHills (3)	25/1	¾	12
Frost Giant (USA) *APO'Brien,Ireland* 3-9-0 JMurtagh (10)	50/1	9	13
Opera Cape *SaeedbinSuroor* 3-9-0 (t) LDettori (13)	16/1	1½	14

Mrs John Magnier,Mr M.Tabor & Mr D.Smith 14ran 1m36.86
       TR: 129/+/122+/118/116/114/113/111

NEWMARKET Sunday, May 7   SOFT (Rowley Mile Course)

7   **Stanjamesuk.com Jockey Club Stks (Gr 2) (4yo+)** £51,102   1½m

SHIROCCO (GER) *AFabre,France* 5-9-3 CSoumillon (6)	10/11f		1
MUNSEF *JLDunlop* 4-8-12 RHills (2)	7/2	3½	2
BANDARI (IRE) *MJohnston* 7-9-1 KDarley (5)	11/1	1½	3
Self Defense *MissECLavelle* 9-8-12 AlanMunro (7)	16/1	½	4
Enforcer *WRMuir* 4-8-12 LDettori (4)	12/1	sh	5
Gulf (IRE) *DRCElsworth* 7-8-12 (t) LPKeniry (1)	100/1	17	6
Hard Top (IRE) *SirMichaelStoute* 4-9-1 MJKinane (3)	11/2	4	7

Baron G. von Ullmann 7ran 2m36.25   TR: 129/119/118/114/115

8   **Stan James 1000 Guineas Stks (Gr 1)** (3yo f) £187,374   1m

SPECIOSA (IRE) *MrsPSly* 3-9-0 MickyFenton (3)	10/1		1
CONFIDENTIAL LADY *SirMarkPrescott* 3-9-0 SebSanders (5)	12/1	2½	2
NASHEEJ (USA) *RHannon* 3-9-0 RyanMoore (11)	16/1	1	3
Silca's Sister *SaeedbinSuroor* 3-9-0 LDettori (4)	13/2	1½	4
Wake Up Maggie (IRE) *CFWall* 3-9-0 AlanMunro (1)	25/1	1½	5
Spinning Queen *BWHills* 3-9-0 MichaelHills (13)	50/1	2	6
Rumplestiltskin (IRE) *APO'Brien,Ireland* 3-9-0 KFallon (7)	3/1f	2½	7
Race For The Stars (USA) *APO'Brien,Ireland* 3-9-0 JMurtagh (12)	12/1	1½	8
La Chunga (USA) *JNoseda* 3-9-0 DarryllHolland (9)	33/1	3½	9
Alexander Alliance (IRE) *TStack,Ireland* 3-9-0 WMLordan (8)	9/1	5	10
Flashy Wings *MRChannon* 3-9-0 JamieSpencer (2)	7/1	sh	11
Nannina *JHMGosden* 3-9-0 JimmyFortune (6)	7/1	3	12
Donna Blini *BJMeehan* 3-9-0 MJKinane (10)	16/1	10	13

Michael H. Sly Dr T. Davies Mrs Pam Sly 13ran 1m40.53   TR: 115/109/106+/102+/98+

LONGCHAMP Sunday, May 14

9   **Gainsborough Poule d'Essai des Poulains (Gr 1) (3yo c)** £156,548   1m

AUSSIE RULES (USA) *APO'Brien,Ireland* 3-9-2 KFallon (5)	27/10cp		1

MARCUS ANDRONICUS (USA) *APO'Brien,Ireland* 3-9-2 ½ 2
   CSoumillon (2) 27/10cp
STORMY RIVER (FR) *NClement,France* 3-9-2 TThulliez (7)....................... 4/5f hd 3
West of Amarillo (USA) *JHMGosden,GB* 3-9-2 JimmyFortune (6).............. 59/1 1 4
Garnica (FR) *J-CRouget,France* 3-9-2 IMendizabal (9) 6/1 1 5
Porto Santo (FR) *PHDemercastel,France* 3-9-2 SPasquier (10)................ 11/1 nk 6
Ivan Denisovich (IRE) *APO'Brien,Ireland* 3-9-2 OPeslier (8) 27/10cp 1½ 7
Dream In Blue (FR) *RCollet,France* 3-9-2 JAuge (3).................................... 23/1 hd 8
Yasoodd *MRChannon,GB* 3-9-2 TedDurcan (4) .... 17/2 hd 9
Fenice (IRE) *RCollet,France* 3-9-2 CPLemaire (11).................................... 51/1 ¾ 10
James Joyce (IRE) *APO'Brien,Ireland* 3-9-2 DavidMcCabe (1) 27/10cp 15 11

Mrs J. Magnier, Mr M. Tabor, Mr F. Salman 11ran 1m37.00

TR: 118/117/116/113/111/110

10   **Gainsborough Poule d'Essai des Pouliches (Gr 1) (3yo f) £156,548**   1m

   Order as they passed the post: Price Tag was demoted to third for causing
   interference to Impressionnante.

PRICE TAG *PBary,France* 3-9-0 TThulliez (10).. 28/1 1
TIE BLACK (IRE) *FRohaut,France* 3-9-0 J-BEyquem (1)........................ 87/10 1½ 2
IMPRESSIONNANTE *CLaffon-Parias,France* 3-9-0 OPeslier (11)............. 11/1 sn 3
Daltaya (FR) *AdeRoyerDupre,France* 3-9-0 CSoumillon (2).................. 24/10f ½ 4
Mauralakana (FR) *J-CRouget,France* 3-9-0 IMendizabal (12)................... 11/2 1½ 5
New Girlfriend (IRE) *RCollet,France* 3-9-0 CPLemaire (3) 57/10 4 6
Damoiselle (FR) *FHead,France* 3-9-0 DBonilla (5)................................. 10/1 ¾ 7
Beauty Bright (IRE) *APO'Brien,Ireland* 3-9-0 TJarnet (13)..................... 8/1 2 8
Daaly Babet (FR) *CScandella,France* 3-9-0 DBoeuf (8).......................... 10/1 3 9
Dama'a (IRE) *JHMGosden,GB* 3-9-0 JimmyFortune (6)............................ 46/1 6 10
Kamarinskaya (USA) *APO'Brien,Ireland* 3-9-0 KFallon (4)..................... 8/1 1½ 11
Silva (FR) *CLaffon-Parias,France* 3-9-0 MBlancpain (7)........................ 10/1 2½ 12
Silver Touch (IRE) *MRChannon,GB* 3-9-0 TedDurcan (9) .... 12/1 dist 13

Mr J. Gispert 13ran 1m36.60   TR: 114/110/109+/108/104

NEWBURY Saturday, May 20   SOFT

11   **Juddmonte Lockinge Stks (Gr 1) (4yo+) £113,560**   1m

PEERESS *SirMichaelStoute* 5-8-11 KFallon (10) 4/1 1
MAJORS CAST (IRE) *JNoseda* 5-9-0 LDettori (2)................................. 9/2 1¾ 2
COURT MASTERPIECE *EALDunlop* 6-9-0 GMosse (3) 7/1 3½ 3
Soviet Song (IRE) *JRFanshawe* 6-8-11 JamieSpencer (4)...................... 7/2f 1½ 4
Kandidate *CEBrittain* 4-9-0 (t) SebSanders (9)................................... 33/1 1¼ 5
Rob Roy (USA) *SirMichaelStoute* 4-9-0 MJKinane (6)........................... 9/2 5 6
Common World (USA) *THogan,Ireland* 7-9-0 FMBerry (8).................... 12/1 3 7
New Seeker *CGCox* 6-9-0 (v) PhilipRobinson (5)................................. 25/1 9 8
Rocamadour *MRChannon* 4-9-0 TedDurcan (7) 14/1 11 9

Cheveley Park Stud 9ran 1m44.57   TR: 124/123/115/108+/108

LONGCHAMP Sunday, May 21   GOOD to SOFT

12   **Prix d'Ispahan (Gr 1) (4yo+) £85,034**   1m1f55y

4 LAVEROCK (IRE) *CLaffon-Parias,France* 4-9-2 DBonilla (5)............... 266/10 1
5 MANDURO (GER) *AFabre,France* 4-9-2 OPeslier (9)........................ 77/10 sn 2
  KRATAIOS (FR) *CLaffon-Parias,France* 6-9-2 MBlancpain (2)............. 77/10 ½ 3
  Archange d'Or (IRE) *AFabre,France* 4-9-2 CSoumillon (3).................. 51/10 3 4
5 Corre Caminos (FR) *MDelzangles,France* 4-9-2 TJarnet (8) 4/5cpf 2 5
5 Vatori (FR) *PHDemercastel,France* 4-9-2 SPasquier (4)...................... 33/1 ¾ 6
  Turtle Bowl (IRE) *FRohaut,France* 4-9-2 CPLemaire (1)..................... 69/10 ½ 7
  Helios Quercus (FR) *CDiard,France* 4-9-2 IMendizabal (11) .... 24/1 sn 8
  Special Kaldoun (IRE) *DSmaga,France* 7-9-2 DBoeuf (7) 33/1 2 9
  Kendor Dine (FR) *YdeNicolay,France* 4-9-2 TThulliez (10) 49/1 3 10
  Thistle Suite *MCheno,France* 8-9-2 TGillet (6) 4/5cpf 11

Maktoum Al Maktoum 11ran 1m52.20   TR: 123/123/121/114/109/108

CURRAGH Saturday, May 27   HEAVY

13   **Boylesports Irish 2000 Guineas (Gr 1) (3yo c+f) £152,721**   1m

6 ARAAFA (IRE) *JNoseda,GB* 3-9-0 AlanMunro (8) 12/1 1
6 GEORGE WASHINGTON (IRE) *APO'Brien* 3-9-0 KFallon (2).................. 4/7f 2 2
  DECADO (IRE) *KPrendergast* 3-9-0 DPMcDonogh (6)........................ 4/1 1 3
9 Yasoodd *MRChannon,GB* 3-9-0 ChrisCatlin (3) 25/1 1 4
  Golden Arrow (IRE) *DKWeld* 3-9-0 (b) PJSmullen (1) .... 33/1 nk 5
  Heliostatic (IRE) *JSBolger* 3-9-0 KJManning (9).............................. 40/1 3 6
  Hurricane Cat (USA) *APO'Brien* 3-9-0 JAHeffernan (5) .... 13/2 nk 7
  Crookhaven *JohnJosephMurphy* 3-9-0 DMGrant (4).......................... 200/1 sh 8
  Caribbean *JOxx* 3-9-0 FMBerry (10)... 50/1 1½ 9

River Tiber *APO'Brien* 3-9-0 DavidMcCabe (7) 50/1 9 10
Arabian Prince (USA) *APO'Brien* 3-9-0 CO'Donoghue (11) 66/1 25 11
Saleh Al Homaizi & Imad Al Sagar 11ran 1m49.80 TR: 119+/115+/113/111/110/104

CURRAGH Sunday, May 28 HEAVY

14 **Tattersalls Gold Cup (Gr 1) (4yo+)** £105,442 1¼m110y
HURRICANE RUN (IRE) *AFabre,France* 4-9-0 KFallon (3) 1/4f 1
1 ALEXANDER GOLDRUN (IRE) *JSBolger* 5-8-11 KJManning (1) 7/2 7 2
LORD ADMIRAL (USA) *CharlesO'Brien* 5-9-0 FMBerry (2) 25/1 12 3
Mr Michael Tabor 3ran 2m26.42 TR: 130/114+

15 **Boylesports Irish 1000 Guineas (Gr 1) (3yo f)** £152,721 1m
NIGHTIME (IRE) *DKWeld* 3-9-0 PJSmullen (15) 12/1 1
ARDBRAE LADY *JGMurphy* 3-9-0 FMBerry (8) 50/1 6 2
QUEEN CLEOPATRA (IRE) *APO'Brien* 3-9-0 JAHeffernan (10) 11/1 1½ 3
8 Race For The Stars (USA) *APO'Brien* 3-9-0 KFallon (9) 7/1 3 4
Abigail Pett *JSBolger* 3-9-0 (b) KJManning (11) 14/1 3½ 5
8 Confidential Lady *SirMarkPrescott,GB* 3-9-0 SebSanders (13) .... 5/2f ¾ 6
Be My Queen (IRE) *APO'Brien* 3-9-0 CO'Donoghue (5) 40/1 2 7
Talwin (IRE) *KPrendergast* 3-9-0 WilliamSupple (6) 33/1 1 8
Gist (IRE) *WJMartin* 3-9-0 TPO'Shea (3) 200/1 1 9
10 Kamarinskaya (USA) *APO'Brien* 3-9-0 DavidMcCabe (12) 25/1 3 10
Ugo Fire (IRE) *KPrendergast* 3-9-0 DPMcDonogh (7) 10/1 3 11
Dont Dili Dali *JSMoore,GB* 3-9-0 JohnEgan (14) 20/1 4½ 12
Short Dance (USA) *BWHills,GB* 3-9-0 RichardHughes (4) .... 5/1 ¾ 13
8 Nasheej (USA) *RHannon,GB* 3-9-0 RyanMoore (1) .... 7/1 ½ 14
10 Beauty Bright (IRE) *APO'Brien* 3-9-0 SMLevey (2) .... 66/1 ½ 15
Mrs C. L. Weld 15ran 1m48.37 TR: 113/100/97/91/83

EPSOM DOWNS Friday, Jun 2 GOOD

16 **Vodafone Coronation Cup (Gr 1) (4yo+)** £141,950 1½m10y
7 SHIROCCO (GER) *AFabre,France* 5-9-0 CSoumillon (5) 8/11f 1
4 OUIJA BOARD *EALDunlop* 5-8-11 LDettori (2) 11/4 1¾ 2
7 ENFORCER *WRMuir* 4-9-0 MartinDwyer (3) .... 66/1 ½ 3
Ace (IRE) *APO'Brien,Ireland* 5-9-0 KFallon (1) 11/2 2½ 4
Notable Guest (USA) *SirMichaelStoute* 5-9-0 RichardHughes (6) 14/1 2½ 5
Something Exciting *DRCElsworth* 4-8-11 TQuinn (4) 50/1 9 6
Baron G. von Ullmann 6ran 2m37.64 TR: 126+/120+/123/118/113

17 **Vodafone Oaks (Gr 1) (3yo f)** £250,627 1½m10y
ALEXANDROVA (IRE) *APO'Brien,Ireland* 3-9-0 KFallon (5) 9/4f 1
RISING CROSS *JRBest* 3-9-0 GeorgeBaker (3) 33/1 6 2
SHORT SKIRT *SirMichaelStoute* 3-9-0 MJKinane (10) 9/2 1¼ 3
8 Speciosa (IRE) *MrsPSly* 3-9-0 MickyFenton (4) .... 5/1 ½ 4
Guilia *RaeGuest* 3-9-0 AlanMunro (6) 8/1 2 5
Time On *JLDunlop* 3-9-0 LDettori (9) 7/1 1¼ 6
Kassiopeia (IRE) *MRChannon* 3-9-0 TonyCulhane (7) .... 66/1 nk 7
Kaylianni *MRChannon* 3-9-0 TedDurcan (11) 100/1 1½ 8
Prowess (IRE) *BWHills* 3-9-0 MichaelHills (2) 33/1 1¼ 9
Riyalma (IRE) *SirMichaelStoute* 3-9-0 CSoumillon (8) 9/2 5 10
Mrs John Magnier, Mr M.Tabor & Mr D.Smith 10ran 2m37.71
TR: 123/112/110/109/106/104

EPSOM DOWNS Saturday, Jun 3 GOOD to FIRM

18 **Vodafone Derby Stks (Gr 1) (3yo c+f)** £740,695 1½m10y
6 SIR PERCY *MPTregoning* 3-9-0 MartinDwyer (10) 6/1 1
DRAGON DANCER *GWragg* 3-9-0 DarryllHolland (11) .... 66/1 sh 2
DYLAN THOMAS (IRE) *APO'Brien,Ireland* 3-9-0 JMurtagh (18) .... 25/1 hd 3
Hala Bek (IRE) *MAJarvis* 3-9-0 PhilipRobinson (5) .... 9/1 sh 4
Visindar *AFabre,France* 3-9-0 CSoumillon (8) 2/1f 2 5
Best Alibi (IRE) *SirMichaelStoute* 3-9-0 RyanMoore (17) 33/1 1 6
Sixties Icon *JNoseda* 3-9-0 ShaneKelly (4) 66/1 2 7
Mountain (IRE) *APO'Brien,Ireland* 3-9-0 JAHeffernan (13) 50/1 1¼ 8
Linda's Lad *AFabre,France* 3-9-0 LDettori (16) 9/1 1¼ 9
Papal Bull *SirMichaelStoute* 3-9-0 RobertWinston (14) .... 11/1 ¾ 10
Championship Point (IRE) *MRChannon* 3-9-0 TedDurcan (7) 12/1 1½ 11
Septimus (IRE) *APO'Brien,Ireland* 3-9-0 MJKinane (9) 17/2 1¼ 12
Before You Go (IRE) *TGMills* 3-9-0 IanMongan (3) 100/1 1¾ 13
Sienna Storm (IRE) *MHTompkins* 3-9-0 (b) MichaelHills (6) .... 200/1 ½ 14
Atlantic Waves (IRE) *MJohnston* 3-9-0 JoeFanning (1) 25/1 4 15
Snoqualmie Boy *DRCElsworth* 3-9-0 JohnEgan (2) 150/1 2½ 16

Noddies Way *JFPanvert* 3-9-0 RobertMiles (12)..500/1   10 17
6 Horatio Nelson (IRE) *APO'Brien,Ireland* 3-9-0 KFallon (15).......................11/2   pu

Mr A. E. Pakenham 18ran 2m35.23   TR: 119+/119/118+/118+/115+/113+

CHANTILLY Sunday, Jun 4   GOOD to FIRM

19   **Prix du Gros-Chene Mitsubishi Motors (Gr 2) (3yo+) £50,753**   5f

MOSS VALE (IRE) *DNicholls,GB* 5-9-2 KFallon (7) 6/1   1
BENBAUN (IRE) *MJWallace,GB* 5-9-2 (v) JamieSpencer (6)..................... 87/10   2 2
TAX FREE (IRE) *DNicholls,GB* 4-9-2 AdrianTNicholls (9)......................... 44/10   ½ 3
Balthazaar's Gift (IRE) *KARyan,GB* 3-9-0 NCallan (2)............................... 18/1   ¾ 4
Pivotal Flame *ESMcMahon,GB* 4-9-2 (s) GrahamGibbons (11).................. 15/1   sn 5
Pivotal Point *PJMakin,GB* 6-8-13 SebSanders (1).................................... 29/1   sh 6
Tycoon's Hill (IRE) *RCollet,France* 7-8-13 OPeslier (5)............................ 46/10   1½ 7
Mister Chocolate (IRE) *RCollet,France* 3-8-9 JAuge (3) .... 46/10   hd 8
Biniou (IRE) *RCollet,France* 3-8-9 CSoumillon (8) .... 46/10   ½ 9
Latona (FR) *JEPease,France* 4-8-13 TGillet (2) 43/10f   3 10
Alyzea (IRE) *CLaffon-Parias,France* 3-8-6 (b) MBlancpain (12) 10/1   6 11
Ajigolo *MRChannon,GB* 3-9-0 TedDurcan (10)....................................... 28/1   2 12

Lady O'Reilly 12ran 56.90secs   TR: 126/119/117/117/114/111

20   **Prix du Jockey Club Mitsubishi Motors (Gr 1) (3yo c+f) £587,055**   1¼m110y

DARSI (FR) *AdeRoyerDupre,France* 3-9-2 CSoumillon (7)........................ 76/10   1
BEST NAME *RCollet,France* 3-9-2 CPLemaire (12)................................... 72/10   ¾ 2
ARRAS (GER) *AFabre,France* 3-9-2 OPeslier (13).................................... 49/10   sn 3
Art Deco (IRE) *CREgerton,GB* 3-9-2 LDettori (9) .... 13/1   sh 4
Numide (FR) *J-CRouget,France* 3-9-2 IMendizabal (2)............................. 73/10   sh 5
Irish Wells (FR) *FRohaut,France* 3-9-2 DBoeuf (8).................................. 29/1   ½ 6
9 Aussie Rules (USA) *APO'Brien,Ireland* 3-9-2 KFallon (1)..................... 36/10cpf   1½ 7
Hazeymm (IRE) *MRChannon,GB* 3-9-2 TedDurcan (11) 34/1   1 8
Hello Sunday (FR) *MmeCHead-Maarek,France* 3-9-2 TJarnet (14) .... 48/1   ¾ 9
Champs Elysees *AFabre,France* 3-9-2 SPasquier (3) 13/1   1 10
Barastraight *J-CRouget,France* 3-9-2 MJKinane (4)................................. 11/1   2 11
6 Olympian Odyssey *BWHills,GB* 3-9-2 JamieSpencer (6) .... 69/10   sh 12
Aspectus (GER) *HBlume,Germany* 3-9-2 AdeVries (10) 26/1   6 13
9 Fenice (IRE) *RCollet,France* 3-9-2 JAuge (5) 72/10   1½ 14
13 Hurricane Cat (USA) *APO'Brien,Ireland* 3-9-2 DavidMcCabe (15)......... 36/10jf   8 15

H.H. Aga Khan 15ran 2m05.80   TR: 118/116/116/116/116/114

CHANTILLY Sunday, Jun 11   GOOD to FIRM

21   **Prix de Diane Hermes (Gr 1) (3yo f) £257,534**   1¼m110y

15 CONFIDENTIAL LADY *SirMarkPrescott,GB* 3-9-0 SebSanders (3) 433/10   1
GERMANCE (USA) *J-CRouget,France* 3-9-0 IMendizabal (15) 17/10cpf   1½ 2
15 QUEEN CLEOPATRA (IRE) *APO'Brien,Ireland* 3-9-0 KFallon (4)............ 18/1   ns 3
Mussoorie (FR) *RGibson,France* 3-9-0 TJarnet (8)................................... 26/1   2 4
Alix Road (FR) *MmeMBollack-Badel,France* 3-9-0 (h) OPeslier (5)......... 77/10   ¾ 5
10 Mauralakana (FR) *J-CRouget,France* 3-9-0 TGillet (16)......................... 51/1   nk 6
Heaven's Cause (USA) *NClement,France* 3-9-0 TThulliez (1) 30/1   3 7
Chaibia (IRE) *DSmaga,France* 3-9-0 DBoeuf (2).................................... 20/1   ½ 8
Grande Melody (IRE) *PBary,France* 3-9-0 CPLemaire (12) .... 17/1   ½ 9
Alloway *AFabre,France* 3-9-0 SPasquier (10) 9/2   2½ 10
Pearl Sky (FR) *YdeNicolay,France* 3-9-0 (b) DBonilla (13)...................... 48/1   1½ 11
Sanaya (IRE) *AdeRoyerDupre,France* 3-9-0 (s) MJKinane (11) 42/10   10 12
Sirene Doloise (FR) *ABonin,France* 3-9-0 J-BEyquem (9) 34/1   2½ 13
10 Daltaya (FR) *AdeRoyerDupre,France* 3-9-0 CSoumillon (14)................. 42/10   ¾ 14
Danzon (USA) *J-CRouget,France* 3-9-0 MBlancpain (7).......................... 21/1   dist 15
Keladora (USA) *J-CRouget,France* 3-9-0 J-RDubosc (2) .... 17/10cpf dist 16

Cheveley Park Stud 16ran 2m05.90   TR: 116/112/112/108/106/106

ASCOT Tuesday, Jun 20   GOOD to FIRM

22   **King's Stand Stks (Gr 2) (3yo+) £113,560**   5f

TAKEOVER TARGET (AUS) *JJaniak,Australia* 7-9-7 JFord (17) 7/1   1
19 BENBAUN (IRE) *MJWallace,GB* 5-9-2 (v) JamieSpencer (12)................... 16/1   sh 2
19 PIVOTAL POINT *PJMakin,GB* 6-9-2 LDettori (5) .... 25/1   ½ 3
Falkirk (NZ) *LeeFreedman,Australia* 6-9-2 (b+t) JMurtagh (9) .... 14/1   nk 4
Dandy Man (IRE) *CCollins,Ireland* 3-8-10 NGMcCullagh (22) .... 10/1   dh 4
Baltic King *HMorrison,GB* 6-9-2 (t) JimmyFortune (4)............................. 16/1   hd 6
Glamour Puss (NZ) *DO'Brien,Australia* 6-9-4 (b) SKing (18).................... 16/1   hd 7
19 Moss Vale (IRE) *DNicholls,GB* 5-9-5 KFallon (7)..................................... 5/1f   hd 8
La Cucaracha *BWHills,GB* 5-8-13 MichaelHills (25)............................... 7/1   nk 9
The Tatling (IRE) *JMBradley,GB* 9-9-2 RyanMoore (26)........................... 20/1   hd 10
Les Arcs (USA) *TJPitt,GB* 6-9-2 JohnEgan (15) .... 33/1   sh 11

	Ashdown Express (IRE) *CFWall* 7-9-2 AlanMunro (14)	50/1	nk 12
8	La Chunga (USA) *JNoseda* 3-8-7 DarrylHolland (16)	33/1	¾ 13
	Mecca's Mate *DWBarker* 5-8-13 NCallan (11)	100/1	1¼ 14
19	Tax Free (IRE) *DNicholls* 4-9-2 AdrianTNicholls (19)	12/1	1 15
	Reverence *EJAlston* 5-9-5 KDarley (27)	16/1	hd 16
	Resplendent Glory (IRE) *TGMills* 4-9-2 IanMongan (1)	40/1	½ 17
	Majestic Missile (IRE) *WJHaggas* 5-9-2 (v+t) TonyCulhane (4)	20/1	2 18
	Texas Gold *WRMuir* 8-9-2 MartinDwyer (24)	100/1	sh 19
	Celtic Mill *DWBarker* 8-9-2 (s) EddieAhern (23)	100/1	½ 20
	Corridor Creeper (FR) *JMBradley* 9-9-2 (s) ShaneKelly (28)	66/1	sh 21
	The Trader (IRE) *MBlanshard* 8-9-2 (b) TedDurcan (20)	33/1	1½ 22
	Godfrey Street *RHannon* 3-8-13 PatDobbs (21)	100/1	1 23
	Fire Up The Band *DNicholls* 7-9-2 WilliamSupple (13)	100/1	nk 24
	Bond City (IRE) *BSmart* 4-9-2 RobertWinston (8)	100/1	6 25
	Boogie Street *RHannon* 5-9-2 RichardHughes (3)	22/1	5 26
	Tabaret *RMWhitaker* 3-8-10 DeanMcKeown (10)	100/1	f
	Orientor *JSGoldie* 8-9-2 ChrisCatlin (6)	100/1	bd

Messrs J. & B. Janiak 28ran 59.79secs　　TR: 126/121/119/118/115+/117/119/119+

23　St James's Palace Stks (Gr 1) (3yo c) £141,950　　1m (Rnd)

13	ARAAFA (IRE) *JNoseda* 3-9-0 AlanMunro (2)	2/1f	1
9	STORMY RIVER (FR) *NClement,France* 3-9-0 OPeslier (4)	7/2	2 2
9	IVAN DENISOVICH (IRE) *APO'Brien,Ireland* 3-9-0 KFallon (9)	13/2	1¾ 3
9	Marcus Andronicus (USA) *APO'Brien,Ireland* 3-9-0 JMurtagh (10)	9/1	¾ 4
	Metropolitan Man *DMSimcock* 3-9-0 KerrinMcEvoy (3)	40/1	1½ 5
13	Yasoodd *MRChannon* 3-9-0 ChrisCatlin (5)	16/1	hd 6
	Royal Power (IRE) *MRChannon* 3-9-0 LDettori (8)	12/1	1 7
	Yarqus *CEBrittain* 3-9-0 RyanMoore (11)	66/1	7 8
13	Decado (IRE) *KPrendergast,Ireland* 3-9-0 DPMcDonogh (7)	7/1	nk 9
	Aeroplane *PWChapple-Hyam* 3-9-0 EddieAhern (6)	16/1	4 10
13	Arabian Prince (USA) *APO'Brien,Ireland* 3-9-0 CO'Donoghue (1)	66/1	5 11

Saleh Al Homaizi & Imad Al Sagar 11ran 1m39.59　TR: 125/120+/115/113/109/109/106

24　Queen Anne Stks (Gr 1) (4yo+) £141,950　　1m (Str.)

	AD VALOREM (USA) *APO'Brien,Ireland* 4-9-0 KFallon (2)	13/2	1
11	COURT MASTERPIECE *EALDunlop* 6-9-0 JamieSpencer (3)	11/2	1½ 2
	PROCLAMATION (IRE) *SaeedbinSuroor* 4-9-0 LDettori (9)	2/1	nk 3
11	Peeress *SirMichaelStoute* 5-8-11 MJKinane (8)	7/4f	1¾ 4
	Vortex *MissGayKelleway* 7-9-0 (es+t) MartinDwyer (5)	20/1	7 5
11	Kandidate *CEBrittain* 4-9-0 (t) RyanMoore (6)	16/1	4 6
	Akimbo (USA) *JamesLeavy,Ireland* 5-9-0 WilliamSupple (4)	66/1	4 7

Mrs John Magnier & Mr R. W. Ingham 7ran 1m40.00　　TR: 125/121+/120/113+

ASCOT Wednesday, Jun 21　GOOD to FIRM

25　Prince of Wales's Stks (Gr 1) (4yo+) £211,207　　1¼m

16	OUIJA BOARD *EALDunlop* 5-8-11 OPeslier (5)	8/1	1
3	ELECTROCUTIONIST (USA) *SaeedbinSuroor* 5-9-0 LDettori (4)	9/4	½ 2
12	MANDURO (GER) *AFabre,France* 4-9-0 CSoumillon (6)	12/1	¾ 3
2	David Junior (USA) *BJMeehan* 4-9-0 JamieSpencer (3)	11/8f	¾ 4
	Notnowcato *SirMichaelStoute* 4-9-0 MJKinane (1)	12/1	sh 5
12	Corre Caminos (FR) *MDelzangles,France* 4-9-0 TJarnet (2)	33/1	1 6
16	Ace (IRE) *APO'Brien,Ireland* 5-9-0 (v) KFallon (7)	9/1	1¼ 7

Lord Derby 7ran 2m06.92　　TR: 123+/125+/123/122/121/119/117

ASCOT Thursday, Jun 22　GOOD to FIRM

26　Gold Cup (Gr 1) (4yo+) £136,953　　2½m

	YEATS (IRE) *APO'Brien,Ireland* 5-9-2 KFallon (8)	7/1	1
	REEFSCAPE *AFabre,France* 5-9-2 CSoumillon (2)	10/3	4 2
	DISTINCTION (IRE) *SirMichaelStoute* 7-9-2 MJKinane (4)	5/2f	hd 3
	High Action (USA) *IanWilliams* 6-9-2 RichardHughes (3)	100/1	3 4
	Sergeant Cecil *BRMillman* 7-9-2 AlanMunro (11)	5/1	1½ 5
	Guadalajara (GER) *SaeedbinSuroor* 5-8-13 LDettori (12)	12/1	¾ 6
	Barolo *WRSwinburn* 7-9-2 JMurtagh (7)	25/1	5 7
	Tungsten Strike (USA) *MrsAJPerrett* 5-9-2 RyanMoore (6)	8/1	nk 8
	Winged d'Argent (IRE) *MJohnston* 5-9-2 JoeFanning (5)	33/1	19 9
	Akarem *KRBurke* 5-9-2 PatCosgrave (10)	40/1	3 10
	Motafarred (IRE) *MDHammond* 4-9-0 NCallan (9)	200/1	dist 11
	Media Puzzle (USA) *DKWeld,Ireland* 9-9-2 (b) PJSmullen (1)	16/1	pu

Mrs John Magnier & Mrs David Nagle 12ran 4m20.45　TR: 122+/118/117/114/112/109

ASCOT Friday, Jun 23   GOOD to FIRM

27   **Coronation Stks (Gr 1) (3yo f)** £152,170   1m (Rnd)

8	NANNINA *JHMGosden* 3-9-0 JimmyFortune (13)	6/1jf	1
8	FLASHY WINGS *MRChannon* 3-9-0 JamieSpencer (9)	13/2	2 2
15	NASHEEJ (USA) *RHannon* 3-9-0 RyanMoore (15)	20/1	¾ 3
15	Race For The Stars (USA) *APO'Brien,Ireland* 3-9-0 KFallon (5)	7/1	sh 4
	Rajeem *CEBrittain* 3-9-0 KerrinMcEvoy (14)	150/1	1 5
8	Silca's Sister *SaeedbinSuroor* 3-9-0 LDettori (7)	7/1	sh 6
	Vague (USA) *JNoseda* 3-9-0 MJKinane (11)	20/1	1 7
10	Price Tag *PBary,France* 3-9-0 TThulliez (12)	6/1jf	¾ 8
17	Speciosa (IRE) *MrsPSly* 3-9-0 MickyFenton (1)	9/1	½ 9
8	Wake Up Maggie (IRE) *CFWall* 3-9-0 AlanMunro (10)	14/1	½ 10
	Lolita (GER) *ALowe,Germany* 3-9-0 OPeslier (8)	12/1	2 11
	Nantyglo *MLWBell* 3-9-0 TQuinn (2)	150/1	1¼ 12
8	Donna Blini *BJMeehan* 3-9-0 RichardHughes (6)	33/1	1¾ 13
	Mostaqeleh (USA) *JLDunlop* 3-9-0 RHills (4)	50/1	2 14
15	Nightime (IRE) *DKWeld,Ireland* 3-9-0 PJSmullen (3)	7/1	9 15

Cheveley Park Stud 15ran 1m39.14

TR: 119/114/112/111/109+/108/106

ASCOT Saturday, Jun 24   GOOD to FIRM

28   **Hardwicke Stks (Gr 2) (4yo+)** £79,492   1½m

3	MARAAHEL (IRE) *SirMichaelStoute* 5-9-0 (v) RHills (6)	9/2	1
	MOUNTAIN HIGH (IRE) *SirMichaelStoute* 4-9-0 KFallon (8)	7/2f	hd 2
16	ENFORCER *WRMuir* 4-9-0 KerrinMcEvoy (1)	8/1	1½ 3
	Day Flight *JHMGosden* 5-9-0 RichardHughes (9)	5/1	¾ 4
7	Hard Top (IRE) *SirMichaelStoute* 4-9-0 MJKinane (5)	4/1	2 5
7	Self Defense *MissECLavelle* 9-9-0 AlanMunro (2)	50/1	½ 6
1	Collier Hill *GASwinbank* 8-9-5 DeanMcKeown (7)	9/1	nk 7
7	Bandari (IRE) *MJohnston* 7-9-0 MartinDwyer (3)	17/2	3 8

Mr Hamdan Al Maktoum 8ran 2m29.25

TR: 123+/124/121/118+/115/113/118

29   **Golden Jubilee Stks (Gr 1) (3yo+)** £198,730   6f

22	LES ARCS (USA) *TJPitt* 6-9-4 JohnEgan (4)	33/1	1
19	BALTHAZAAR'S GIFT (IRE) *KARyan* 3-8-11 JamieSpencer (14)	50/1	nk 2
22	TAKEOVER TARGET (AUS) *JJaniak,Australia* 7-9-4 JFord (13)	7/2f	2 3
22	Ashdown Express (IRE) *CFWall* 7-9-4 AlanMunro (5)	50/1	½ 4
6	Amadeus Wolf *KARyan* 3-8-11 NCallan (9)	7/1	nk 5
22	The Tatling (IRE) *JMBradley* 9-9-4 RyanMoore (2)	20/1	1¼ 6
	Iffraaj *SaeedbinSuroor* 5-9-4 LDettori (15)	6/1	hd 7
	Eisteddfod *PFICole* 5-9-4 JimmyFortune (1)	33/1	1 8
	Noelani (IRE) *JOxx,Ireland* 4-9-1 MJKinane (6)	33/1	sh 9
22	Glamour Puss (NZ) *DO'Brien,Australia* 6-9-1 SKing (10)	13/2	¾ 10
22	Pivotal Point *PJMakin* 6-9-4 DarrylHolland (11)	16/1	½ 11
19	Ajigolo *MRChannon* 3-8-11 SamHitchcott (8)	100/1	1¼ 12
	Gift Horse *DNicholls* 6-9-4 KFallon (3)	7/1	2 13
	Etlaala *BWHills* 4-9-4 RHills (19)	14/1	1½ 14
	Fayr Jag (IRE) *TDEasterby* 7-9-4 TQuinn (7)	14/1	½ 15
	Royal Storm (IRE) *MrsAJPerrett* 7-9-4 RichardHughes (12)	150/1	5 16
	Quito (IRE) *DWChapman* 9-9-4 (b) TonyCulhane (18)	20/1	1¼ 17
	Beckermet (IRE) *RFFisher* 4-9-4 MartinDwyer (16)	125/1	3 18

Mr Willie McKay 18ran 1m13.12

TR: 126/123/119/117/114/112

SAINT-CLOUD Sunday, Jun 25   GOOD to SOFT

30   **Grand Prix de Saint-Cloud (Gr 1) (4yo+)** £156,548   1½m

5	PRIDE (FR) *AdeRoyerDupre,France* 6-8-13 CPLemaire	66/10	1
14	HURRICANE RUN (IRE) *AFabre,France* 4-9-2 KFallon	1/5cpf	hd 2
12	LAVEROCK (IRE) *CLaffon-Parias,France* 4-9-2 DBonilla	11/1	2 3
	Policy Maker (IRE) *ELellouche,France* 6-9-2 SPasquier	49/10	2 4
	Petrograd (IRE) *ELellouche,France* 5-9-2 (b) GFaucon	49/10	20 5
5	Near Honor (GER) *AFabre,France* 8-9-2 MSautjeau	1/5cpf	8 6

N P Bloodstock 6ran 2m35.90

TR: 123+/127+/123/119

CURRAGH Saturday, Jul 1   GOOD

31   **Audi Pretty Polly Stks (Gr 1) (3yo+)** £103,448   1¼m

14	ALEXANDER GOLDRUN (IRE) *JSBolger* 5-9-8 KJManning (1)	11/8f	1
	CHELSEA ROSE (IRE) *CCollins* 4-9-8 PShanahan (4)	6/1	nk 2
	RED BLOOM *SirMichaelStoute,GB* 5-9-8 JMurtagh (2)	7/2	2 3
	Tropical Lady (IRE) *JSBolger* 6-9-8 DJMoran (3)	16/1	sh 4
21	Queen Cleopatra (IRE) *APO'Brien* 3-8-11 KFallon (5)	11/2	6 5
15	Ardbrae Lady *JGMurphy* 3-8-11 FMBerry (7)	20/1	3½ 6

1202

Perfect Hedge *JOxx* 4-9-8 MJKinane (6).. 50/1   9 7

Mrs N. O'Callaghan 7ran 2m04.80   TR: 122/121/117/117

CURRAGH Sunday, Jul 2   GOOD

32   **Budweiser Irish Derby (Gr 1) (3yo c+f) £584,483**   1½m

18	DYLAN THOMAS (IRE) *APO'Brien* 3-9-0 KFallon (9) 9/2f	1
	GENTLEWAVE (IRE) *AFabre,France* 3-9-0 JMurtagh (8)...................... 11/2	3½ 2
18	BEST ALIBI (IRE) *SirMichaelStoute,GB* 3-9-0 MJKinane (7)............... 9/1	1½ 3
18	Dragon Dancer *GWragg,GB* 3-9-0 DarryllHolland (12) 7/1	1½ 4
20	Darsi (FR) *AdeRoyerDupre,France* 3-9-0 CSoumillon (2) 5/1	½ 5
18	Mountain (IRE) *APO'Brien* 3-9-0 JAHeffernan (11) 14/1	sh 6
13	Heliostatic (IRE) *JSBolger* 3-9-0 KJManning (10) 25/1	sh 7
20	Best Name *RCollet,France* 3-9-0 CPLemaire (4)............................... 13/2	1 8
	Classic Punch (IRE) *DRCElsworth,GB* 3-9-0 JohnEgan (5)................. 22/1	4 9
	Puerto Rico (IRE) *APO'Brien* 3-9-0 CO'Donoghue (1) 12/1	2 10
	Monsieur Henri (USA) *JCHayden* 3-9-0 NGMcCullagh (13) 400/1	¾ 11
	Cougar Bay (IRE) *DWachman* 3-9-0 (b) WMLordan (3) 28/1	2½ 12
	Land Before Time (IRE) *RJOsborne* 3-9-0 RMBurke (6) 200/1	20 13

Mrs John Magnier 13ran 2m29.70   TR: 127+/120/117/114/113/113+

SANDOWN Saturday, Jul 8   GOOD to FIRM

33   **Coral-Eclipse Stks (Gr 1) (3yo+) £260,620**   1¼m7y

25	DAVID JUNIOR (USA) *BJMeehan* 4-9-7 JamieSpencer (2) 9/4	1
25	NOTNOWCATO *SirMichaelStoute* 4-9-7 MJKinane (6) 9/1	1½ 2
25	BLUE MONDAY *RCharlton* 5-9-7 SteveDrowne (8)............................ 8/1	nk 3
20	Aussie Rules (USA) *APO'Brien,Ireland* 3-8-10 AlanMunro (3) 11/2	sh 4
25	Ouija Board *EALDunlop* 5-9-4 CSoumillon (7) 2/1f	2 5
18	Snoqualmie Boy *DRCElsworth* 3-8-10 JohnEgan (5) 22/1	1 6
	Royal Alchemist *BJMeehan* 4-9-4 MichaelTebbutt (9)....................... 100/1	1¾ 7
	Hattan (IRE) *CEBrittain* 4-9-7 KerrinMcEvoy (1)............................ 66/1	¾ 8
16	Notable Guest (USA) *SirMichaelStoute* 5-9-7 RichardHughes (4)........ 16/1	7 9

Roldvale Limited 9ran 2m07.31   TR: 124+/121+/120+/118/112+/111

NEWMARKET Wednesday, Jul 12   GOOD to FIRM (July Course)

34   **Chippenham Lodge Stud Cherry Hinton Stks (Gr 2) (2yo f) £39,746**   6f

	SANDER CAMILLO (USA) *JNoseda* 2-8-12 LDettori (4)...................... 11/8f	1
	ALZERRA (UAE) *MRChannon* 2-8-12 TedDurcan (8).......................... 12/1	5 2
	GILDED (IRE) *RHannon* 2-9-1 RichardHughes (10) 11/1	nk 3
	Hope'n'charity (USA) *CGCox* 2-8-12 AdamKirby (9)......................... 12/1	1½ 4
	Alderney (USA) *MAJarvis* 2-8-12 PhilipRobinson (1)......................... 10/3	sh 5
	Silk Blossom (IRE) *BWHills* 2-8-12 MichaelHills (3) 5/1	hd 6
	Divine Right *BJMeehan* 2-8-12 JimmyFortune (6).......................... 28/1	2½ 7
	Slipasearcher (IRE) *PDEvans* 2-8-12 SteveDrowne (5)..................... 66/1	nk 8
	Nina Blini *BJMeehan* 2-8-12 JamieSpencer (2) 25/1	¾ 9
	Three Decades (IRE) *CACyzer* 2-8-12 EddieAhern (7) 100/1	6 10

Sir Robert Ogden 10ran 1m12.12   TR: 115+/99/101/93/93/92

NEWMARKET Thursday, Jul 13   GOOD to FIRM

35   **Princess of Wales's wbx.com Stks (Gr 2) (3yo+) £51,102**   1½m

	SOAPY DANGER *MJohnston* 3-8-3 KDarley (1) 5/1	1
28	MOUNTAIN HIGH (IRE) *SirMichaelStoute* 4-9-2 RyanMoore (2)............... 4/7f	¾ 2
28	ENFORCER *WRMuir* 4-9-2 MartinDwyer (3)................................... 9/2	¾ 3
28	Bandari (IRE) *MJohnston* 7-9-2 RHills (4) 10/1	2 4

Mrs R. J. Jacobs 4ran 2m32.82   TR: 120/120+/118/114

NEWMARKET Friday, Jul 14   GOOD to FIRM (July Course)

36   **Darley July Cup (Gr 1) (3yo+) £204,408**   6f

29	LES ARCS (USA) *TJPitt* 6-9-5 JohnEgan (15) 10/1	1
29	IFFRAAJ *SaeedbinSuroor* 5-9-5 LDettori (12) 11/2	hd 2
29	ASHDOWN EXPRESS (IRE) *CFWall* 7-9-5 AlanMunro (16) 20/1	¾ 3
29	Amadeus Wolf *KARyan* 3-8-13 NCallan (13).................................. 10/1	sh 4
22	Moss Vale (IRE) *DNicholls* 5-9-5 AdrianTNicholls (9) 14/1	¾ 5
29	Quito (IRE) *DWChapman* 9-9-5 (b) TonyCulhane (17)..................... 25/1	sh 6
29	Takeover Target (AUS) *JJaniak,Australia* 7-9-5 JFord (3) 9/2f	sh 7
29	Pivotal Point *PJMakin* 6-9-5 SebSanders (6) 16/1	1¼ 8
29	Gift Horse *DNicholls* 6-9-5 EddieAhern (8) 16/1	1¼ 9
29	Fayr Jag (IRE) *TDEasterby* 7-9-5 DavidAllan (14) 33/1	½ 10
22	La Cucaracha *BWHills* 5-9-2 MichaelHills (7)................................ 9/1	nk 11
6	Red Clubs (IRE) *BWHills* 3-8-13 RyanMoore (2)............................ 10/1	3½ 12
22	Falkirk (NZ) *LeeFreedman,Australia* 6-9-5 (b+t) JMurtagh (10) 13/2	1½ 13

```
23  Marcus Andronicus (USA) APO'Brien,Ireland 3-8-13 MJKinane (4) .......... 20/1    sh 14
    Murfreesboro JHMGosden 3-8-13 JimmyFortune (11)................................. 66/1   2½ 15
    Mr Willie McKay 15ran 1m11.16                      TR: 125+/125+/122/120/119+/119/119
```

LONGCHAMP Friday, Jul 14   GOOD to FIRM

37   Juddmonte Grand Prix de Paris (Gr 1) (3yo c+g) £198,403   1½m

```
    RAIL LINK AFabre,France 3-9-2 CSoumillon ............................................. 1/1f      1
    RED ROCKS (IRE) BJMeehan,GB 3-9-2 LDettori ...................................... 4/1    2  2
    SUDAN (IRE) ELellouche,France 3-9-2 TThulliez.................................... 22/1   hd 3
    Grand Couturier J-CRouget,France 3-9-2 TJarnet.................................. 19/1   sn 4
20  Art Deco (IRE) CREgerton,GB 3-9-2 OPeslier ...................................... 12/1    1  5
    Gravitas AFabre,France 3-9-2 KerrinMcEvoy ...................................... 24/1   1½ 6
32  Mountain (IRE) APO'Brien,Ireland 3-9-2 KFallon.................................. 25/1   hd 7
20  Numide (FR) J-CRouget,France 3-9-2 (s) IMendizabal ........................... 3/1    2½ 8
32  Puerto Rico (IRE) APO'Brien,Ireland 3-9-2 CO'Donoghue....................... 50/1   ¾  9
    Mr K. Abdulla 9ran 2m26.40                        TR: 121+/117/117/117/115/112/112
```

LINGFIELD Saturday, Jul 15   STANDARD

38   Ladbrokes Summer Mile Stks (Gr 3) (4yo+) £56,780   1m (Polytrack)

```
    ECHO OF LIGHT SaeedbinSuroor 4-9-1 KerrinMcEvoy (5) ...................... 7/1      1
    SATCHEM (IRE) SaeedbinSuroor 4-9-1 (t) LDettori (12).......................... 3/1    2½ 2
    NOTABILITY (IRE) MAJarvis 4-9-1 PhilipRobinson (8)............................. 11/1   1¼ 3
    Stronghold JHMGosden 4-9-1 RichardHughes (3)................................. 7/4f    ½  4
    Spectait SirMarkPrescott 4-9-1 SebSanders (11)................................... 8/1    hd 5
    Suggestive WJHaggas 8-9-1 (b) NickyMackay (7).................................. 12/1    1  6
33  Royal Alchemist BJMeehan 4-8-12 MichaelTebbutt (9)........................... 20/1   1½ 7
    Boule d'Or (IRE) JAkehurst 5-9-1 DeanCorby (2)................................. 20/1    1  8
    Babodana MHTompkins 6-9-1 JimmyFortune (4).................................. 16/1   1¾ 9
    Cesare JRFanshawe 5-9-1 JamieSpencer (10)...................................... 5/1     1 10
    Gig Harbor MissECLavelle 7-9-1 DavidKinsella (6) .............................. 66/1   23 11
    Godolphin 11ran 1m36.23                           TR: 125/118+/114/113/112/110
```

CURRAGH Sunday, Jul 16   GOOD to FIRM

39   Darley Irish Oaks (Gr 1) (3yo f) £167,014   1½m

```
17  ALEXANDROVA (IRE) APO'Brien 3-9-0 KFallon (2)............................. 8/15f     1
    SCOTTISH STAGE (IRE) SirMichaelStoute,GB 3-9-0 MJKinane (4) ......... 13/2    4  2
17  RISING CROSS (IRE) JRBest,GB 3-9-0 MDwyer (1).............................. 20/1    1  3
    Mont Etoile (IRE) WJHaggas,GB 3-9-0 MichaelHills (3)......................... 11/1   hd 4
21  Confidential Lady SirMarkPrescott,GB 3-9-0 SebSanders (6)................... 5/1    2½ 5
    Flyingit (USA) ThomasMullins 3-9-0 JMurtagh (5)............................... 200/1   10 6
    Mrs John Magnier 6ran 2m29.60                     TR: 120+/112/110/110/105
```

ASCOT Saturday, Jul 29   GOOD to FIRM

40   King George VI and Queen Elizabeth Diamond Stks (Gr 1) (3yo+) £425,850   1½m

```
30  HURRICANE RUN (IRE) AFabre,France 4-9-7 CSoumillon (4) ................. 5/6f     1
25  ELECTROCUTIONIST (USA) SaeedbinSuroor 5-9-7 LDettori (1).............. 4/1    ½  2
 1  HEART'S CRY (JPN) KHashiguchi,Japan 5-9-7 CPLemaire (3)............... 3/1    ½  3
35  Enforcer WRMuir 4-9-7 MartinDwyer (2).......................................... 50/1   1¾ 4
28  Maraahel SirMichaelStoute 5-9-7 (v) RHills (6)................................... 14/1   1½ 5
    Cherry Mix (FR) SaeedbinSuroor 5-9-7 (t) KerrinMcEvoy (5)................... 50/1   ½  6
    Mr M. Tabor 6ran 2m30.29                          TR: 128+/127/126/123/120/119
```

GOODWOOD Tuesday, Aug 1   GOOD to FIRM

41   Betfair Cup (Lennox) (Gr 2) (3yo+) £85,170   7f

```
36  IFFRAAJ SaeedbinSuroor 5-9-4 LDettori (10) ................................... 6/4f     1
    JEDBURGH JLDunlop 5-9-0 (b) TedDurcan (1)..................................... 40/1   4  2
    ASSERTIVE RHannon 3-8-8 RyanMoore (2).......................................... 33/1   hd 3
    Nayyir GAButler 8-9-0 JohnEgan (6) ................................................. 7/1    nk 4
29  Etlaala BWHills 4-9-0 RHills (3)...................................................... 11/1   ¾  5
    Jeremy (USA) SirMichaelStoute 3-8-8 MJKinane (9)............................. 5/2    sh 6
    Mac Love RCharlton 5-9-0 SteveDrowne (8)....................................... 25/1   ½  7
38  Suggestive WJHaggas 8-9-0 (b) NickyMackay (4)................................ 66/1   1¾ 8
    Prince of Light (IRE) MJohnston 3-8-8 JoeFanning (5) ......................... 9/1    sh 9
36  Quito (IRE) DWChapman 9-9-0 (b) TonyCulhane (7)........................... 20/1   3½ 10
    Godolphin 10ran 1m25.58                           TR: 127/111/109/110+/108+/105
```

GOODWOOD Wednesday, Aug 2   GOOD to FIRM

42   Cantor Spreadfair Sussex Stks (Gr 1) (3yo+) £180,135   1m

```
24  COURT MASTERPIECE EALDunlop 6-9-7 JimmyFortune (5) .................. 15/2     1
11  SOVIET SONG (IRE) JRFanshawe 6-9-4 JMurtagh (1)............................ 11/2   2  2
```

11	ROB ROY (USA) *SirMichaelStoute* 4-9-7 RyanMoore (6)	12/1	½ 3
33	Aussie Rules (USA) *APO'Brien,Ireland* 3-9-0 MJKinane (7)	8/1	½ 4
23	Araafa (IRE) *JNoseda* 3-9-0 AlanMunro (2)	11/10f	½ 5
38	Echo of Light *SaeedbinSuroor* 4-9-7 LDettori (4)	9/2	4 6
	Vanderlin *AMBalding* 7-9-7 MartinDwyer (3)	100/1	18 7

Gainsborough Stud 7ran 1m36.10 TR: 126+/117/119/116/115

GOODWOOD Thursday, Aug 3 FIRM

43 ABN Amro Goodwood Cup (Gr 2) (3yo+) £56,780 2m

26	YEATS (IRE) *APO'Brien,Ireland* 5-9-10 MJKinane (8)	10/11f	1
	GEORDIELAND (FR) *JAOsborne* 5-9-5 LDettori (6)	16/1	5 2
26	TUNGSTEN STRIKE (USA) *MrsAJPerrett* 5-9-8 MartinDwyer (1)	25/1	3½ 3
26	Sergeant Cecil *BRMillman* 7-9-5 AlanMunro (3)	10/1	1½ 4
	Baddam *MRChannon* 4-9-5 IanMongan (9)	33/1	nk 5
	Land 'n Stars *JamiePoulton* 6-9-5 PaulDoe (12)	25/1	hd 6
26	Reefscape *AFabre,France* 5-9-10 RichardHughes (2)	11/2	¾ 7
	Bulwark (IRE) *MrsAJPerrett* 4-9-5 (b+es) KerrinMcEvoy (7)	25/1	sh 8
	Balkan Knight *DRCElsworth* 6-9-5 JohnEgan (15)	20/1	3 9
	Cover Up (IRE) *SirMichaelStoute* 9-9-5 RyanMoore (13)	20/1	3 10
	Golden Quest *MJohnston* 5-9-5 JoeFanning (14)	9/1	3½ 11
26	High Action (USA) *IanWilliams* 6-9-5 EddieAhern (11)	50/1	1 12
	Ebtikaar (IRE) *JLDunlop* 4-9-5 RHills (16)	25/1	2½ 13
26	Winged d'Argent (IRE) *MJohnston* 5-9-5 KDarley (10)	66/1	1½ 14
	Foreign Affairs *SirMarkPrescott* 8-9-5 SebSanders (5)	16/1	20 15

Mrs John Magnier & Mrs David Nagle 15ran 3m21.55 TR: 128/116+/114/108+/109/108

GOODWOOD Saturday, Aug 5 GOOD to FIRM

44 Vodafone Nassau Stks (Gr 1) (3yo+ f+m) £113,560 1m1f192y

33	OUIJA BOARD *EALDunlop* 5-9-5 LDettori (7)	1/1f	1
31	ALEXANDER GOLDRUN (IRE) *JSBolger,Ireland* 5-9-5 KJManning (5)	9/2	sh 2
27	NANNINA *JHMGosden* 3-8-10 JimmyFortune (4)	4/1	2 3
31	Chelsea Rose (IRE) *CCollins,Ireland* 4-9-5 PShanahan (1)	12/1	2½ 4
	Echelon *SirMichaelStoute* 4-9-5 KDarley (3)	16/1	2 5
27	Race For The Stars (USA) *APO'Brien,Ireland* 3-8-10 MJKinane (2)	10/1	1½ 6
27	Nasheej (USA) *RHannon* 3-8-10 RyanMoore (6)	20/1	5 7

Lord Derby 7ran 2m04.47 TR: 125/125/119/115/110/106

ARLINGTON Saturday, Aug 12 FIRM

45 Arlington Million (Gr 1) (3yo+) £314,136 1¼m

2	THE TIN MAN (USA) *REMandella,USA* 8-9-0 VEspinoza	55/10	1
	CACIQUE (IRE) *RJFrankel,USA* 5-9-0 EPrado	39/10	1 2
	SOLDIER HOLLOW *PSchiergen,Germany* 6-9-0 RDouglas	139/10	1¼ 3
	English Channel (USA) *TAPletcher,USA* 4-9-0 JVelazquez	21/10f	hd 4
	Cosmonaut (USA) *PLBiancone,USA* 4-9-0 JLeparoux	224/10	nk 5
25	Ace (IRE) *APO'Brien,Ireland* 5-9-0 GGomez	37/10	nk 6
	Better Talk Now (USA) *HGMotion,USA* 7-9-0 (b) RADominguez	94/10	1 7
2	Touch of Land (FR) *H-APantall,France* 6-9-0 CPLemaire	25/1	ns 8
	Major Rhythm (USA) *EBeam,USA* 7-9-0 (b) EFires	39/1	1¾ 9
	Phoenix Reach (IRE) *AMBalding,GB* 6-9-0 MartinDwyer	16/1	6 10

Aury & Ralph E. Todd 10ran 2m01.35 TR: 124/122+/119/118/117/117

CURRAGH Sunday, Aug 13 GOOD to FIRM

46 Independent Waterford Wedgwood Phoenix Stks (Gr 1) (2yo c+f) £112,568 6f

	HOLY ROMAN EMPEROR (IRE) *APO'Brien* 2-9-1 KFallon (4)	13/8jf	1
	HELLVELYN *BSmart,GB* 2-9-1 TedDurcan (6)	13/8jf	1¾ 2
	MISS BEATRIX (IRE) *KPrendergast* 2-8-12 WilliamSupple (3)	50/1	½ 3
	Brazilian Bride (IRE) *KPrendergast* 2-8-12 DPMcDonogh (7)	7/1	hd 4
	Drayton (IRE) *TStack* 2-9-1 WMLordan (5)	7/1	sh 5
	Rabatash (USA) *DWachman* 2-9-1 MJKinane (1)	14/1	1¼ 6
	King of Swords (IRE) *CCollins* 2-9-1 PShanahan (2)	100/1	6 7

Mrs John Magnier 7ran 1m11.53 TR: 114+/108/103/103/106/101

47 Patrick P. O'Leary Memorial Phoenix Sprint Stks (Gr 3) (3yo+) £32,939 6f

36	MOSS VALE (IRE) *DNicholls,GB* 5-9-10 KFallon (5)	7/4f	1
36	RED CLUBS (IRE) *BWHills,GB* 3-9-4 MichaelHills (8)	6/1	1¾ 2
36	PIVOTAL POINT *PJMakin,GB* 6-9-8 SebSanders (1)	9/2	1½ 3
22	The Trader (IRE) *MBlanshard,GB* 8-9-5 (b) TedDurcan (3)	12/1	nk 4
36	Fayr Jag (IRE) *TDEasterby,GB* 7-9-10 DavidAllan (7)	11/1	1½ 5
	Miss Sally (IRE) *MHalford* 4-9-5 (t) JMurtagh (4)	7/1	hd 6
29	Beckermet (IRE) *RFFisher,GB* 4-9-5 DPMcDonogh (2)	8/1	sh 7

Indian Maiden (IRE) *MSSaunders,GB* 6-9-2 FMBerry (6) 14/1   1¾ 8
Lady O'Reilly 8ran 1m10.84   TR: 126/117/113/109/109

COLOGNE Sunday, Aug 13   GOOD

48 **Rheinland-Pokal der Sparkasse KolnBonn (Gr 1) (3yo+) £64,189**   1½m
40   CHERRY MIX (FR) *SaeedbinSuroor,GB* 5-9-6 KerrinMcEvoy 38/10   1
     FRACAS (IRE) *DWachman,Ireland* 4-9-6 JimmyFortune 71/10   4 2
28   COLLIER HILL *GASwinbank,GB* 8-9-6 DeanMcKeown........................... 22/10f   sh 3
     Egerton (GER) *PRau,Germany* 5-9-6 THellier 25/10   2 4
     Song Writer (GER) *FrauCBocskai,Switzerland* 6-9-6 ABoschert 99/10   1¼ 5
     All Spirit (GER) *NSauer,Germany* 4-9-6 EPedroza 263/10   6 6
     Donaldson (GER) *PRau,Germany* 4-9-6 TMundry 64/10   1¼ 7
     El Tango (GER) *PSchiergen,Germany* 4-9-6 WMongil 139/10   1 8
     Academy Reward (IRE) *MHofer,Germany* 6-9-6 AStarke...................... 203/10   3½ 9
     Godolphin 9ran 2m28.25   TR: 123/115/115/111/108

DEAUVILLE Sunday, Aug 13   SOFT

49 **Prix du Haras de Fresnay-Le-Buffard Jacques le Marois (Gr 1) (3yo+ c+f)**   1m
     £231,649
     LIBRETTIST (USA) *SaeedbinSuroor,GB* 4-9-4 LDettori........................... 29/10   1
25   MANDURO (GER) *AFabre,France* 4-9-4 OPeslier .... 19/4   nk 2
24   PEERESS *SirMichaelStoute,GB* 5-9-1 RyanMoore.................................... 8/1   hd 3
23   Stormy River (FR) *NClement,France* 3-8-11 TThullier............................. 6/4f   1½ 4
24   Ad Valorem (USA) *APO'Brien,Ireland* 4-9-4 JamieSpencer 12/1   2½ 5
12   Special Kaldoun (IRE) *DSmaga,France* 7-9-4 DBoeuf 30/1   2 6
     Ramonti (FR) *A&GBotti,Italy* 4-9-4 EBotti 18/1   1½ 7
10   New Girlfriend (IRE) *RCollet,France* 3-8-8 JAuge 43/1   2½ 8
12   Helios Quercus (FR) *CDiard,France* 4-9-4 IMendizabal............................ 14/1   sn 9
     Kendargent (FR) *YFouin,France* 3-8-11 RMarchelli................................ 22/1   15 10
     Godolphin 10ran 1m43.10   TR: 124/123/120/119/114/110

DEAUVILLE Sunday, Aug 20   SOFT

50 **Darley Prix Morny (Gr 1) (2yo) £134,221**   6f
     DUTCH ART *PWChapple-Hyam,GB* 2-9-0 CSoumillon................................ 9/2   1
     MAGIC AMERICA (USA) *MmeCHead-Maarek,France* 2-8-11 CPLemaire 11/1   1 2
     EXCELLENT ART *NACallaghan,GB* 2-9-0 LDettori .... 11/4   hd 3
     Sandwaki (USA) *CLaffon-Parias,France* 2-9-0 OPeslier 5/4f   3 4
     Golden Titus (IRE) *ARenzoni,Italy* 2-9-0 SLandi..................................... 13/1   ns 5
     Beauty Is Truth *RCollet,France* 2-8-11 (b) TThullier.............................. 17/1   sn 6
     Boccassini (GER) *MRulec,Germany* 2-8-11 DBonilla 27/4   2 7
     Mrs Susan Roy 7ran 1m13.60   TR: 118/112/114/104/104/100

YORK Tuesday, Aug 22   GOOD to SOFT

51 **Ladbrokes Great Voltigeur Stks (Gr 2) (3yo c+g) £76,653**   1½m
     YOUMZAIN (IRE) *MRChannon* 3-8-12 RichardHughes (3)...................... 12/1   1
37   RED ROCKS (IRE) *BJMeehan* 3-8-12 LDettori (2)................................. 10/3   hd 2
37   PUERTO RICO (IRE) *APO'Brien,Ireland* 3-8-12 JAHeffernan (1)............. 40/1   3 3
     The Last Drop (IRE) *BWHills* 3-8-12 (t) MichaelHills (10)...................... 100/1   1 4
35   Soapy Danger *MJohnston* 3-9-1 KDarley (4).. 4/1   hd 5
     Fire And Rain (FR) *APO'Brien,Ireland* 3-8-12 MJKinane (6) 8/1   2½ 6
     Stage Gift (IRE) *SirMichaelStoute* 3-8-12 RobertWinston (9)................... 8/1   10 7
18   Papal Bull *SirMichaelStoute* 3-9-1 RyanMoore (7)............................... 11/4f   4 8
18   Championship Point (IRE) *MRChannon* 3-8-12 TedDurcan (5).............. 8/1   10 9
18   Sienna Storm (IRE) *MHTompkins* 3-8-12 NCallan (8).......................... 100/1   16 10
     Mr Jaber Abdullah 10ran 2m34.93   TR: 120+/119+/113/111/114/107

52 **Juddmonte International Stks (Gr 1) (3yo+) £283,900**   1¼m88y
33   NOTNOWCATO *SirMichaelStoute* 4-9-5 RyanMoore (5).......................... 8/1   1
40   MARAAHEL (IRE) *SirMichaelStoute* 5-9-5 (v) RHills (3) .... 9/1   sh 2
33   BLUE MONDAY *RCharlton* 5-9-5 SteveDrowne (8)................................. 11/2   3 3
32   Dylan Thomas (IRE) *APO'Brien,Ireland* 3-8-11 MJKinane (2) .... 5/6f   ¾ 4
30   Laverock (IRE) *CLaffon-Parias,France* 4-9-5 (t) DBonilla (4)................... 12/1   ½ 5
48   Cherry Mix (FR) *SaeedbinSuroor* 5-9-5 (t) LDettori (1) .... 7/1   ½ 6
33   Snoqualmie Boy *DRCElsworth* 3-8-11 JohnEgan (6) 66/1   8 7
     Anthony & David De Rothschild 7ran 2m12.32   TR: 126/126/119/117/117+/116

YORK Wednesday, Aug 23   GOOD to SOFT

53 **Darley Yorkshire Oaks (Gr 1) (3yo+ f+m) £156,145**   1½m
39   ALEXANDROVA (IRE) *APO'Brien,Ireland* 3-8-11 MJKinane (4)............... 4/9f   1
17   SHORT SKIRT *SirMichaelStoute* 3-8-11 RobertWinston (5) 11/2   3½ 2
     ALLEGRETTO (IRE) *SirMichaelStoute* 3-8-11 RyanMoore (6).................. 12/1   ¾ 3

1206

Exhibit One (USA) *VValiani,Italy* 4-9-7 EBotti (2) .... 66/1 nk 4
Sina Cova (IRE) *PeterCasey,Ireland* 4-9-7 JMurtagh (1) 50/1 9 5
Shamdala (IRE) *AdeRoyerDupre,France* 4-9-7 CSoumillon (3)..................... 6/1 27 6

Mrs John Magnier, Mr M. Tabor & Mr D. Smith 6ran 2m32.41   TR: 123/116/115/114

YORK Thursday, Aug 24   SOFT

54   **VC Bet Nunthorpe Stks (Gr 1) (2yo+) £147,401**   5f

22 REVERENCE *EJAlston* 5-9-11 KDarley (6).. 5/1   1
36 AMADEUS WOLF *KARyan* 3-9-9 NCallan (16)... 5/1   2 2
19 PIVOTAL FLAME *ESMcMahon* 4-9-11 (t) SebSanders (2) .... 14/1   hd 3
47 The Trader (IRE) *MBlanshard* 8-9-11 (b) TedDurcan (4) .... 33/1   ¾ 4
47 Red Clubs (IRE) *BWHills* 3-9-9 MichaelHills (17)................................... 25/1   ¾ 5
29 The Tatling (IRE) *JMBradley* 9-9-11 RyanMoore (8) 20/1   1¼ 6
    Steenberg (IRE) *MHTompkins* 7-9-11 TPQueally (11)............................... 16/1   sh 7
22 Orientor *JSGoldie* 8-9-11 JohnEgan (15).. 33/1   sh 8
47 Fayr Jag (IRE) *TDEasterby* 7-9-11 DavidAllan (10) .... 50/1   nk 9
22 Mecca's Mate *DWBarker* 5-9-8 RobertWinston (13) .... 50/1   nk 10
36 Gift Horse *DNicholls* 6-9-11 EddieAhern (3)... 14/1   ½ 11
22 Dandy Man (IRE) *CCollins,Ireland* 3-9-9 PShanahan (14) 4/1f   1 12
    Enticing (IRE) *WJHaggas* 2-7-12 NickyMackay (9) 11/1   1 13
47 Moss Vale (IRE) *DNicholls* 5-9-11 AdrianTNicholls (12)........................... 9/2   ½ 14

Mr & Mrs G. Middlebrook 14ran 1m00.68   TR: 125+/118/118/115/112+/108

GOODWOOD Sunday, Aug 27   GOOD to FIRM

55   **totesport Celebration Mile (Gr 2) (3yo+) £56,780**   1m

    CARADAK (IRE) *SaeedbinSuroor* 5-9-1 LDettori (5)................................... 6/1   1
6   KILLYBEGS (IRE) *BWHills* 3-8-9 RHills (4)... 50/1   sh 2
13 GEORGE WASHINGTON (IRE) *APO'Brien,Ireland* 3-9-1 MJKinane (2)... 5/6f   1¼ 3
13 River Tiber *APO'Brien,Ireland* 3-8-9 DavidMcCabe (6) 100/1 1½ 4
42 Soviet Song *JRFanshawe* 6-9-1 JamieSpencer (1)................................... 3/1   hd 5
42 Rob Roy (USA) *SirMichaelStoute* 4-9-4 RyanMoore (3) .... 7/1   nk 6

Godolphin 6ran 1m37.26   TR: 121/120/122+/112?/113/115

HAYDOCK Saturday, Sep 2   SOFT

56   **Betfred Sprint Cup (Gr 1) (3yo+) £170,340**   6f

54 REVERENCE *EJAlston* 5-9-3 KDarley (10).. 11/4f 1
41 QUITO (IRE) *DWChapman* 9-9-3 (b) RobertWinston (3)............................ 9/1   nk 2
54 AMADEUS WOLF *KARyan* 3-9-1 NCallan (4) 4/1   1¼ 3
    Somnus *TDEasterby* 6-9-3 JohnEgan (1) 8/1   1 4
54 Red Clubs (IRE) *BWHills* 3-9-1 MichaelHills (9)..................................... 16/1   2 5
    Excusez Moi (USA) *CEBrittain* 4-9-3 KerrinMcEvoy (5)............................ 11/1   3 6
29 Balthazaar's Gift (IRE) *TRGeorge* 3-9-1 JamieSpencer (7)...................... 14/1   4 7
47 Miss Sally (IRE) *MHalford,Ireland* 4-9-0 (t) JMurtagh (2) .... 10/1   nk 8
    Kodiac *JLDunlop* 5-9-3 (b) LDettori (11) 28/1   6 9
    Philharmonic *RAFahey* 5-9-3 PaulHanagan (6)....................................... 25/1   7 10
54 Steenberg (IRE) *MHTompkins* 7-9-3 TPQueally (8) 12/1   7 11

Mr & Mrs G. Middlebrook 11ran 1m15.78   TR: 122+/121/117+114/109

LONGCHAMP Sunday, Sep 3   GOOD

57   **Prix du Moulin de Longchamp (Gr 1) (3yo+) £115,824**   1m

49 LIBRETTIST (USA) *SaeedbinSuroor,GB* 4-9-2 LDettori............................. 1/1f   1
49 STORMY RIVER (FR) *NClement,France* 3-8-12 TThulliez .... 13/2   ½ 2
49 MANDURO (GER) *AFabre,France* 4-9-2 CSoumillon .... 21/4   ½ 3
42 Aussie Rules (USA) *APO'Brien,Ireland* 3-8-12 KFallon............................. 8/1   2 4
4   Irridescence (SAF) *JEHammond,France* 5-8-13 FSpanu 12/1   2 5
    Kentucky Dynamite (USA) *AdeRoyerDupre,France* 3-8-12 CPLemaire 7/1   2 6
    Quiet Royal (USA) *CLaffon-Parias,France* 3-8-8 OPeslier 33/4   1½ 7
    Indesatchel (IRE) *DWachman,Ireland* 4-9-2 NCallan 55/1   4 8

Godolphin 8ran 1m38.10   TR: 123/123/120+/117/107/106

YORK Saturday, Sep 9   GOOD

58   **Ladbrokes St Leger Stks (Gr 1) (3yo c+f) £269,705**   1m5f197y

18 SIXTIES ICON *JNoseda* 3-9-0 LDettori (11) 11/8f 1
51 THE LAST DROP (IRE) *BWHills* 3-9-0 (t) RHills (5) 50/1   2½ 2
51 RED ROCKS (IRE) *BJMeehan* 3-9-0 RichardHughes (7)........................... 4/1   1 3
    Ask *SirMichaelStoute* 3-9-0 (t) RobertWinston (4) .... 16/1   hd 4
    Tusculum (IRE) *APO'Brien,Ireland* 3-9-0 JAHeffernan (12) 17/2   1 5
    Jadalee (IRE) *MPTregoning* 3-9-0 MartinDwyer (6) .... 15/2   sh 6
37 Mountain (IRE) *APO'Brien,Ireland* 3-9-0 KDarley (9) .... 16/1   ½ 7
39 Mont Etoile (IRE) *WJHaggas* 3-8-11 MichaelHills (4) 18/1   4 8

	51	Championship Point (IRE) *MRChannon* 3-9-0 TonyCulhane (10)	20/1	nk 9
	51	Fire And Rain (FR) *APO'Brien,Ireland* 3-9-0 CO'Donoghue (2)	20/1	1½ 10
		Galient (IRE) *MAJarvis* 3-9-0 PhilipRobinson (3)	18/1	25 11

Mrs Susan Roy 11ran 2m57.29
TR: 123+/118/117/116/115/115/114

LEOPARDSTOWN Saturday, Sep 9 GOOD to FIRM

59 Coolmore Fusaichi Pegasus Matron Stks (Gr 1) (3yo+ f+m) £109,060 1m

		RED EVIE (IRE) *MLWBell,GB* 3-8-12 JamieSpencer (8)	6/1	1
	49	PEERESS *SirMichaelStoute,GB* 5-9-3 RyanMoore (2)	7/2	sh 2
	27	FLASHY WINGS *MRChannon,GB* 3-8-12 MJKinane (6)	7/2	¾ 3
	44	Nannina *JHMGosden,GB* 3-8-12 JimmyFortune (4)	9/4f	hd 4
	44	Race For The Stars (USA) *APO'Brien* 3-8-12 KFallon (9)	7/1	½ 5
	15	Ugo Fire (IRE) *KPrendergast* 3-8-12 DPMcDonogh (3)	33/1	1 6
		Bahia Breeze *RaeGuest,GB* 4-9-3 FMBerry (1)	40/1	1½ 7
	31	Ardbrae Lady *JGMurphy* 3-8-12 PJSmullen (5)	50/1	6 8

Mr Terry Neill 8ran 1m38.70
TR: 117/117+/115/114/113/110/106

60 Baileys Irish Champion Stks (Gr 1) (3yo+) £402,013 1¼m

	52	DYLAN THOMAS (IRE) *APO'Brien* 3-9-0 KFallon (2)	13/8f	1
	44	OUIJA BOARD *EALDunlop,GB* 5-9-4 JamieSpencer (5)	11/4	nk 2
	44	ALEXANDER GOLDRUN (IRE) *JSBolger* 5-8-9 KJManning (3)	3/1	2½ 3
		Mustameet (USA) *KPrendergast* 5-9-7 DPMcDonogh (6)	8/1	1½ 4
	45	Ace (IRE) *APO'Brien* 5-9-7 MJKinane (4)	12/1	2½ 5

Mrs John Magnier 5ran 2m02.90
TR: 129/125/119/119/113

LONGCHAMP Sunday, Sep 10 GOOD to FIRM

61 Prix Foy Gray d'Albion Barriere (Gr 2) (4yo+) £49,732 1½m

	16	SHIROCCO (GER) *AFabre,France* 5-9-2 CSoumillon	22/10	1
	40	HURRICANE RUN (IRE) *AFabre,France* 4-9-2 KFallon	7/10f	nk 2
	30	PRIDE (FR) *AdeRoyerDupre,France* 6-8-13 CPLemaire	15/4	nk 3
		Divine Story (FR) *RPritchard-Gordon,France* 5-8-13 DBonilla	22/1	5 4
	30	Near Honor (GER) *AFabre,France* 8-9-2 MSautjeau	13/1	8 5

Baron G. von Ullmann 5ran 2m32.90
TR: 128+/127+/124+/115?/105

62 Prix Vermeille Lucien Barriere (Gr 1) (3yo+ f+m) £115,047 1½m

		MANDESHA (FR) *AdeRoyerDupre,France* 3-8-7 CSoumillon	26/10	1
	5	MONTARE (FR) *JEPease,France* 4-9-2 (s) OPeslier	9/2	1½ 2
	5	ROYAL HIGHNESS (GER) *PBary,France* 4-9-2 TThulliez	11/2	½ 3
		Freedonia *JEHammond,France* 4-9-2 TGillet	9/4f	1½ 4
	21	Alix Road (FR) *MmeMBollack-Badel,France* 3-8-7 DBoeuf	25/1	nk 5
		Fermion (IRE) *APO'Brien,Ireland* 3-8-7 KFallon	9/1	¾ 6
	17	Time On *JLDunlop,GB* 3-8-7 RichardHughes	27/1	1 7
		Ponte Tresa (FR) *YdeNicolay,France* 3-8-7 CPLemaire	43/1	¾ 8
		Mysterious Lina (FR) *PHDemercastel,France* 3-8-7 SPasquier	15/1	hd 9
		Mary Louhana *MDelzangles,France* 3-8-7 SMaillot	62/1	¾ 10
		Wurfscheibe (GER) *PRau,Germany* 4-9-2 TMundry	30/1	11

Princess Zahra Aga Khan 11ran 2m29.20
TR: 118+/115+/114/110+/110/108

63 Prix Niel Casino Barriere d'Enghien Les Bains (Gr 2) (3yo c+f) £49,732 1½m

	37	RAIL LINK *AFabre,France* 3-9-2 CSoumillon	1/2f	1
	51	YOUMZAIN (IRE) *MRChannon,GB* 3-9-2 RichardHughes	23/4	½ 2
	37	SUDAN (IRE) *ELellouche,France* 3-9-2 SPasquier	12/1	2 3
	32	Dragon Dancer *GWragg,GB* 3-9-2 DarrylHolland	7/1	¾ 4
	51	Papal Bull *SirMichaelStoute,GB* 3-9-2 KFallon	6/1	2 5
		Bremen *AFabre,France* 3-9-2 OPeslier	18/1	8 6

Mr K. Abdulla 6ran 2m31.90
TR: 122+/121/117/115/111

CURRAGH Saturday, Sep 16 GOOD

64 Irish Field St Leger (Gr 1) (3yo+) £118,776 1¾m

		KASTORIA (IRE) *JOxx* 5-9-7 (t) MJKinane (8)	6/1	1
	43	YEATS (IRE) *APO'Brien* 5-9-10 KFallon (5)	2/7f	½ 2
		THE WHISTLING TEAL *GWragg,GB* 10-9-10 WilliamSupple (2)	20/1	10 3
	48	Fracas (IRE) *DWachman* 4-9-10 WMLordan (3)	20/1	1¾ 4
	26	Akarem *KRBurke,GB* 5-9-10 PatCosgrave (1)	33/1	sh 5
		Frank Sonata *MGQuinlan,GB* 5-9-10 PJSmullen (7)	33/1	2 6
		Percussionist (IRE) *JHowardJohnson,GB* 5-9-10 DPMcDonogh (4)	12/1	1¼ 7
		Chimes At Midnight (USA) *LukeComer* 9-9-10 (b) FFDaSilva (6)	300/1	5 8

H. H. Aga Khan 8ran 3m01.00
TR: 124/126/110/107/107/104

CURRAGH Sunday, Sep 17 GOOD

65 Laing O'Rourke National Stks (Gr 1) (2yo c+f) £122,721 7f

| | | TEOFILO (IRE) *JSBolger* 2-9-1 KJManning (5) | 2/1 | 1 |

46 HOLY ROMAN EMPEROR (IRE) *APO'Brien* 2-9-1 KFallon (6) 4/9f 1¼ 2
EYSHAL (IRE) *JOxx* 2-9-1 (t) MJKinane (1) 25/1 4½ 3
Slaney Time (IRE) *JSBolger* 2-9-1 (b) DJMoran (2) 100/1 1 4
Davidii (IRE) *KJCondon* 2-9-1 JMurtagh (3) 33/1 2½ 5
Flash Harry *JohnJosephMurphy* 2-9-1 DMGrant (4) 100/1 13 6
Mrs J. S. Bolger 6ran 1m26.40 TR: 120+/116/103?/100?/93

ASCOT Saturday, Sep 23 GOOD to SOFT

66 Meon Valley Stud Fillies' Mile (Gr 1) (2yo f) £134,324 1m (Rnd)

SIMPLY PERFECT *JNoseda* 2-8-12 DarryllHolland (5) 11/4 1
TREAT *MRChannon* 2-8-12 JamieSpencer (2) 16/1 1½ 2
ENGLISH BALLET (IRE) *BWHills* 2-8-12 MichaelHills (8) .... 5/2f ¾ 3
Satulagi (USA) *JSMoore* 2-8-12 JohnEgan (6) 25/1 2½ 4
Gaudeamus (USA) *JSBolger,Ireland* 2-8-12 KJManning (4) 12/1 1¾ 5
Sesmen *MBotti* 2-8-12 OscarUrbina (7) 3/1 2 6
Alexander Tango (IRE) *TStack,Ireland* 2-8-12 WMLordan (3) .... 9/1 nk 7
Lost In Wonder (USA) *SirMichaelStoute* 2-8-12 RyanMoore (1) 8/1 2½ 8
Mr D Smith, Mr M Tabor & Mrs J Magnier 8ran 1m41.89 TR: 110/106+/104/98/94

67 Queen Elizabeth II Stks (Gr 1) (3yo+) £141,950 1m (Rnd)

55 GEORGE WASHINGTON (IRE) *APO'Brien,Ireland* 3-8-13 MJKinane (7) 13/8f 1
42 ARAAFA (IRE) *JNoseda* 3-8-13 CSoumillon (3) 7/1 1¼ 2
42 COURT MASTERPIECE *EALDunlop* 6-9-3 JamieSpencer (8) 13/2 2 3
55 Killybegs (IRE) *BWHills* 3-8-13 MichaelHills (6) 33/1 1¼ 4
24 Proclamation (IRE) *SaeedbinSuroor* 4-9-3 KerrinMcEvoy (2) 5/1 3½ 5
57 Librettist (USA) *SaeedbinSuroor* 4-9-3 LDettori (1) 3/1 2 6
55 River Tiber *APO'Brien,Ireland* 3-8-13 DavidMcCabe (5) 100/1 10 7
23 Ivan Denisovich (IRE) *APO'Brien,Ireland* 3-8-13 (v) JAHeffernan (4) .... 28/1 ¾ 8
Mrs John Magnier, Mr M. Tabor & Mr D. Smith 8ran 1m40.06
TR: 132+/128/123+/120/110/105

COLOGNE Sunday, Sep 24 GOOD

68 IVG - Preis von Europa (Gr 1) (3yo+) £67,568 1½m

63 YOUMZAIN (IRE) *MRChannon,GB* 3-8-11 KFallon 4/5f 1
48 EGERTON (GER) *PRau,Germany* 5-9-6 TMundry .... 61/10 ½ 2
40 ENFORCER *WRMuir,GB* 4-9-6 MartinDwyer 34/10 1¾ 3
Oriental Tiger (GER) *UOstmann,Germany* 3-8-10 ABoschert .... 38/10 ½ 4
Brisant (GER) *MTrybuhl,Germany* 4-9-6 AHelfenbein 21/1 5 5
Quelle Amore (GER) *AWohler,Germany* 3-8-6 ASuborics .... 119/10 ½ 6
48 All Spirit (GER) *NSauer,Germany* 4-9-6 EPedroza 20/1 4½ 7
Mr Jaber Abdullah 7ran 2m28.51 TR: 123+/122/118/116/107/101

NEWMARKET Friday, Sep 29 GOOD to SOFT (Rowley Course)

69 Sky Bet Cheveley Park Stks (Gr 1) (2yo f) £96,526 6f

INDIAN INK (IRE) *RHannon* 2-8-12 RichardHughes (7) 3/1jf 1
DHANYATA (IRE) *BJMeehan* 2-8-12 JimmyFortune (1) .... 16/1 nk 2
SILCA CHIAVE *MRChannon* 2-8-12 TedDurcan (4) 11/2 1¼ 3
La Presse (USA) *BWHills* 2-8-12 MichaelHills (8) .... 18/1 hd 4
Theann *APO'Brien,Ireland* 2-8-12 MJKinane (12) 12/1 1¼ 5
50 Magic America (USA) *MmeCHead-Maarek,France* 2-8-12 CPLemaire (10) .... 3/1jf hd 6
50 Beauty Is Truth *RCollet,France* 2-8-12 (b) TThulliez (5) .... 14/1 hd 7
Scarlet Runner *JLDunlop* 2-8-12 KerrinMcEvoy (3) 20/1 2 8
Blue Rocket (IRE) *TJPitt* 2-8-12 NCallan (2) .... 33/1 ¾ 9
Vital Statistics *DRCElsworth* 2-8-12 JohnEgan (6) .... 12/1 sh 10
Wid (USA) *JLDunlop* 2-8-12 RHills (11) 16/1 3 11
Mr Raymond Tooth 11ran 1m14.81 TR: 110/109/105+/105/101/101/100

70 Shadwell Middle Park Stks (Gr 1) (2yo c) £96,526 6f

50 DUTCH ART *PWChapple-Hyam* 2-8-12 LDettori (2) 6/5f 1
WI DUD *KARyan* 2-8-12 NCallan (1) 10/1 2 2
CAPTAIN MARVELOUS (IRE) *BWHills* 2-8-12 MichaelHills (6) 33/1 1¼ 3
46 Hellvelyn *BSmart* 2-8-12 TedDurcan (5) 11/2 1¼ 4
Brave Tin Soldier (USA) *APO'Brien,Ireland* 2-8-12 MJKinane (4) 9/2 1¼ 5
Conquest (IRE) *WJHaggas* 2-8-12 (b) JimmyFortune (3) 5/1 16 6
Mrs Susan Roy 6ran 1m14.07 TR: 122+/116/112/108/104

LONGCHAMP Sunday, Oct 1 GOOD to FIRM

71 Prix du Cadran Casino Les Princes Barriere de Cannes (Gr 1) (4yo+) £95,872 2½m

43 SERGEANT CECIL *BRMillman,GB* 7-9-2 LDettori (5) 6/5f 1

53	SHAMDALA (IRE) *AdeRoyerDupre,France* 4-8-13 CSoumillon (2)	21/4	¾	2
	LE MIRACLE (GER) *WBaltromei,Germany* 5-9-2 DBoeuf (1)	7/2	½	3
43	Reefscape *AFabre,France* 5-9-2 KFallon (3)	7/2	1½	4
	Petite Speciale (IRE) *ELecoiffier,France* 7-8-13 CPLemaire (4)	34/1	5	5
	Alcazar (IRE) *HMorrison,GB* 11-9-2 MickyFenton (7)	11/1	¾	6
43	Baddam *MRChannon,GB* 4-9-2 IanMongan (6)	20/1	1½	7

Mr Terry Cooper 7ran 4m20.90   TR: 118+/115/117/115/108/111/110

72   **Prix de l'Abbaye de Longchamp Majestic Barriere (Gr 1) (2yo+) £95,872**   5f

	DESERT LORD *KARyan,GB* 6-9-11 (b) JamieSpencer (12)	231/10		1
56	REVERENCE *EJAlston,GB* 5-9-11 KDarley (13)	7/4f	nk	2
54	MOSS VALE (IRE) *DNicholls,GB* 5-9-11 KFallon (11)	5/1	sn	3
19	Biniou (IRE) *RCollet,France* 3-9-11 TThulliez (5)	34/1	1½	4
56	Amadeus Wolf *KARyan,GB* 3-9-11 NCallan (9)	23/4	nk	5
15	Beauty Bright (IRE) *APO'Brien,Ireland* 3-9-8 PJSmullen (2)	41/1	nk	6
22	Majestic Missile (IRE) *WJHaggas,GB* 5-9-11 (t) CSoumillon (14)	27/4	1½	7
54	Pivotal Flame *ESMcMahon,GB* 4-9-11 (s) SebSanders (4)	29/1	sn	8
56	Red Clubs (IRE) *BWHills,GB* 3-9-11 MichaelHills (3)	15/2	2	9
54	Gift Horse *DNicholls,GB* 6-9-11 JohnEgan (10)	34/1	½	10
	Meliksah (IRE) *MmeDUSmith,Germany* 12-9-11 TRicher (6)	144/1	1½	11
56	Excusez Moi (USA) *CEBrittain,GB* 4-9-11 KerrinMcEvoy (3)	13/1	hd	12
19	Mister Chocolate (IRE) *RCollet,France* 3-9-11 OPeslier (8)	41/1	¾	13
56	Kodiac *JLDunlop,GB* 5-9-11 (b) MJKinane (1)	31/1	hd	14

Bull & Bell Partnership 14ran 54.80secs   TR: 124/123/122/118/117/113

73   **Prix de l'Opera Casino Barriere d'Enghien Les Bains (Gr 1) (3yo+ f+m)**   1¼m
     £95,872

62	MANDESHA (FR) *AdeRoyerDupre,France* 3-8-12 CSoumillon (6)	6/5		1
53	SATWA QUEEN (FR) *JdeRoualle,France* 3-8-12 TThulliez (5)	17/1	¾	2
53	ALEXANDROVA (IRE) *APO'Brien,Ireland* 3-8-12 KFallon (3)	9/10f	2½	3
57	Irridescence (SAF) *JEHammond,France* 5-9-2 WCMarwing (2)	33/4	1½	4
59	Nannina *JHMGosden,GB* 3-8-12 JimmyFortune (1)	23/1	½	5
	Dionisia (USA) *LMCumani,GB* 3-8-12 CPLemaire (4)	17/1	10	6

Princess Zahra Aga Khan 6ran 2m00.90   TR: 124/120/116+/110/111

74   **Prix Marcel Boussac-Criterium des Pouliches Royal Barriere Deauville**   1m
     (Gr 1) (2yo f) £115,047

	FINSCEAL BEO (IRE) *JSBolger,Ireland* 2-8-11 KJManning (9)	192/10		1
	DARRFONAH (IRE) *CEBrittain,GB* 2-8-11 KerrinMcEvoy (10)	22/1	5	2
	LEGERETE (USA) *AFabre,France* 2-8-11 OPeslier (11)	19/4	nk	3
	Poltava (FR) *DSmaga,France* 2-8-11 DBoeuf (8)	3/1f	1	4
	Bicoastal (USA) *BJMeehan,GB* 2-8-11 (b) LDettori (12)	7/1	nk	5
	Ikat (IRE) *DSepulchre,France* 2-8-11 CPLemaire (13)	12/1	sn	6
	Bal de La Rose (IRE) *FRohaut,France* 2-8-11 CSoumillon (5)	5/1	½	7
	Impetious *ETyrrell,Ireland* 2-8-11 NCallan (3)	59/1	nk	8
	Cumin (USA) *BWHills,GB* 2-8-11 MichaelHills (2)	11/1	3	9
	Sismix (IRE) *CLaffon-Parias,France* 2-8-11 SPasquier (7)	35/1	5	10
	Sugar Baby Love (GER) *MHofer,Germany* 2-8-11 WCMarwing (6)	15/1	1½	11
	Nell Gwyn (IRE) *APO'Brien,Ireland* 2-8-11 KFallon (1)	31/4	6	12
	Princess Taise (USA) *MJohnston,GB* 2-8-11 JoeFanning (4)	51/1	5	13

Mr M. A. Ryan 13ran 1m34.90   TR: 118/106/105+/102/101/100

75   **Prix Jean-Luc Lagardere (Grand Criterium) (Gr 1) (2yo c+f) £134,221**   7f

65	HOLY ROMAN EMPEROR (IRE) *APO'Brien,Ireland* 2-9-0 KFallon (5).	18/10		1
	BATTLE PAINT (USA) *J-CRouget,France* 2-9-0 IMendizabal (7)	63/10	2	2
	VITAL EQUINE (IRE) *EJO'Neill,GB* 2-9-0 (t) RichardMullen (8)	87/10	¾	3
	He's A Decoy (IRE) *DWachman,Ireland* 2-9-0 MJKinane (7)	23/1	nk	4
	Fleeting Shadow (IRE) *DKWeld,Ireland* 2-9-0 PJSmullen (1)	23/1	1½	5
	Visionario (IRE) *AFabre,France* 2-9-0 CSoumillon (4)	14/10f	1½	6
	Trinity College (USA) *APO'Brien,Ireland* 2-9-0 JamieSpencer (10)	18/10cp	5	7
50	Sandwaki (IRE) *CLaffon-Parias,France* 2-9-0 OPeslier (9)	11/1	3	8
	To The Max (IRE) *RHannon,GB* 2-9-0 CPLemaire (6)	25/1	2½	9

Mrs John Magnier 9ran 1m18.60   TR: 119+/112+/110+/109/104/100+

76   **Prix de l'Arc de Triomphe Lucien Barriere (Gr 1) (3yo+ c+f) £766,980**   1½m

Order as they passed the post: Deep Impact finished third, but was disqualified after
failing a dope test.

63	RAIL LINK *AFabre,France* 3-8-11 SPasquier (4)	236/10		1
61	PRIDE (FR) *AdeRoyerDupre,France* 6-9-2 CPLemaire (5)	22/1	nk	2
	DEEP IMPACT (JPN) *YIkee,Japan* 4-9-5 YTake (2)	1/2f	½	3
61	Hurricane Run (IRE) *AFabre,France* 4-9-5 KFallon (1)	4/1	2½	4
32	Best Name *RCollet,France* 3-8-11 OPeslier (3)	99/1	2	5
20	Irish Wells (FR) *FRohaut,France* 3-8-11 DBoeuf (7)	92/1	sn	6

58	Sixties Icon *JNoseda,GB* 3-8-11 LDettori (8)	17/1	4	7
61	Shirocco (GER) *AFabre,France* 5-9-5 CSoumillon (6)	41/10	1½	8

Mr K. Abdulla 8ran 2m26.38   TR: 132/128/130/125+/122+/122/114/111

NAKAYAMA Sunday, Oct 1   FIRM

77   **Sprinters Stks (Gr 1) (3yo+)** £446,452   6f

36	TAKEOVER TARGET (AUS) *JJaniak,Australia* 7-9-0 JFord	32/10f		1
	MEISHO BOWLER (JPN) *TShirai,Japan* 5-9-0 YFukunaga	196/10	2½	2
	TAGANO BASTILLE (JPN) *KIkezoe,Japan* 3-8-10 MKatsuura	168/1	nk	3
	Silent Witness (AUS) *ASCruz,HongKong* 7-9-0 FCoetzee	53/10	hd	4
22	Benbaun (IRE) *MJWallace,GB* 5-9-0 DJO'Donohoe	271/10	nk	5
	Cheerful Smile (JPN) *YIkee,Japan* 6-8-10 YIwata	86/10	½	6
36	Les Arcs (USA) *TJPitt,GB* 6-9-0 ESaint-Martin	6/1	hd	7
	She Is Tosho (JPN) *ATsurudome,Iapan* 6-8-10 KIkezoe	53/10	nk	8
	Orewa Matteruze (JPN) *HOtonashi,Japan* 6-9-0 YShibata	64/10	hd	9
	Blue Shotgun (JPN) *KTake,Japan* 7-9-0 YFujioka	43/1	hd	10
	Venus Line (JPN) *NHori,Japan* 5-8-10 SAkiyama	161/10	nk	11
	Golden Cast (JPN) *KHashiguchi,Japan* 6-9-0 FKomaki	97/1	ns	12
	Symboli Escape (JPN) *TKubota,Japan* 5-9-0 MEbina	153/10	1¼	13
	Keeneland Swan (USA) *HMori,Japan* 7-9-0 LInnes	137/1	nk	14
	Tamamo Hot Play (JPN) *KMinai,Japan* 5-9-0 KWatanabe	48/1	2½	15
	Suteki Shinsukekun (USA) *HMori,Japan* 3-8-10 HGoto	189/10	1½	16

Messrs J. & B. Janiak 16ran 1m08.10   TR: 126/117/114/116/115/109/113

KEENELAND Saturday, Oct 7   FIRM

78   **Shadwell Turf Mile Stks (Gr 1) (3yo+)** £198,930   1m

57	AUSSIE RULES (USA) *APO'Brien,Ireland* 3-8-11 (v) GGomez	49/10		1
	REMARKABLE NEWS (VEN) *APennajnr,USA* 4-9-0 RDouglas	53/10	1¾	2
	OLD DODGE (BRZ) *RAHorgan,USA* 5-9-0 RAlbarado	50/1	ns	3
	Miesque's Approval (USA) *MDWolfson,USA* 7-9-0 ECastro	29/10	hd	4
45	Cosmonaut (USA) *PLBiancone,USA* 4-9-0 JLeparoux	83/10	dh	4
	Three Valleys (USA) *RJFrankel,USA* 5-9-0 RBejarano	58/10	ns	6
	Silent Name (JPN) *GMandella,USA* 4-9-0 VEspinoza	26/10f	¾	7
	Hendrix (USA) *CDollase,USA* 5-9-0 DFlores	19/1	3½	8
	British Blue (USA) *JRuvalcaba,USA* 6-9-0 CMejia	716/10	nk	9

Mrs J. Magnier, Mr M. Tabor, Mr F. Salman 9ran 1m34.23

TR: 123/117/117/117/117

NEWMARKET Saturday, Oct 14   GOOD to SOFT (Rowley Mile Course)

79   **VC Bet Challenge Stks (Gr 2) (3yo+)** £51,102   7f

	SLEEPING INDIAN *JHMGosden* 5-9-3 JimmyFortune (11)	9/2f		1
67	KILLYBEGS (IRE) *BWHills* 3-9-1 MichaelHills (3)	7/1	1	2
38	SATCHEM (IRE) *SaeedbinSuroor* 4-9-3 (t) KerrinMcEvoy (8)	8/1	hd	3
56	Somnus *TDEasterby* 6-9-3 KDarley (13)	28/1	2	4
10	Silver Touch (IRE) *MRChannon* 3-8-12 RyanMoore (16)	12/1	¾	5
	Polar Ben *JRFanshawe* 7-9-3 JamieSpencer (14)	25/1	1	6
	Art Museum (IRE) *APO'Brien,Ireland* 3-9-1 JAHeffernan (10)	7/1	2½	7
56	Quito (IRE) *DWChapman* 9-9-3 (b) TonyCulhane (15)	50/1	½	8
41	Jedburgh *JLDunlop* 5-9-3 (b) SebSanders (6)	100/1	sh	9
	Welsh Emperor (IRE) *TPTate* 7-9-7 DarrylHolland (9)	22/1	nk	10
41	Suggestive *WJHaggas* 8-9-3 (b) NickyMackay (2)	66/1	4	11
41	Jeremy (USA) *SirMichaelStoute* 3-9-1 MJKinane (5)	8/1	1¾	12
23	Aeroplane *PWChapple-Hyam* 3-9-1 EddieAhern (4)	16/1	2	13
38	Stronghold *JHMGosden* 4-9-3 RichardHughes (7)	17/2	¾	14
	Makderah (IRE) *MPTregoning* 3-8-12 (b) RHills (1)	14/1	2	15
	Byron *SaeedbinSuroor* 3-9-3 (t) LDettori (12)	8/1	dist	16

Mr George Strawbridge 16ran 1m26.16   TR: 122/120/119/113/109/108+

80   **Emirates Airline Champion Stks (Gr 1) (3yo+)** £198,730   1¼m

76	PRIDE (FR) *AdeRoyerDupre,France* 6-9-0 CPLemaire (2)	7/2		1
55	ROB ROY (USA) *SirMichaelStoute* 4-9-3 KerrinMcEvoy (4)	20/1	3	2
76	HURRICANE RUN (IRE) *AFabre,France* 4-9-3 MJKinane (6)	9/4f	hd	3
20	Olympian Odyssey *BWHills* 3-8-12 JamieSpencer (5)	33/1	1½	4
39	Confidential Lady *SirMarkPrescott* 3-8-9 SebSanders (8)	14/1	2½	5
52	Maraahel (IRE) *SirMichaelStoute* 5-9-3 (v) RHills (7)	11/1	sh	6
18	Sir Percy *MPTregoning* 3-8-12 MartinDwyer (1)	11/4	½	7
52	Notnowcato *SirMichaelStoute* 4-9-3 RyanMoore (3)	7/1	1¾	8

N P Bloodstock 8ran 2m06.81   TR: 126+/122/122/120/111/113

81   **Darley Dewhurst Stks (Gr 1) (2yo c+f)** £141,950   7f

65	TEOFILO (IRE) *JSBolger,Ireland* 2-9-1 KJManning (4)	11/8f		1

75 HOLY ROMAN EMPEROR (IRE) *APO'Brien,Ireland* 2-9-1 MJKinane (9). 3/1   hd 2
    STRATEGIC PRINCE *PFICole* 2-9-1 EddieAhern (5) 9/1   2½ 3
    Haatef (USA) *KPrendergast,Ireland* 2-9-1 DPMcDonogh (7)...................... 22/1   nk 4
75 Vital Equine (IRE) *EJO'Neill* 2-9-1 (t) RichardMullen (3) .... 20/1   hd 5
    Rallying Cry (USA) *JHMGosden* 2-9-1 JimmyFortune (1) 40/1   1 6
    Adagio *SirMichaelStoute* 2-9-1 KerrinMcEvoy (11)................................... 25/1   nk 7
75 He's A Decoy (IRE) *DWachman* 2-9-1 RyanMoore (8).................. 40/1   3½ 8
    Traffic Guard (USA) *JSMoore* 2-9-1 JohnEgan (10) 40/1   2½ 9
    Dubai Builder *JSMoore* 2-9-1 MartinDwyer (2) .... 100/1   sh 10
    Prime Defender *BWHills* 2-9-1 MichaelHills (13) .... 20/1   sh 11
    Mount Parnassus *APO'Brien,Ireland* 2-9-1 JAHeffernan (12).................... 200/1   1¾ 12
    Hamoody (USA) *PWChapple-Hyam* 2-9-1 LDettori (6)........................... 9/1   nk 13
    Halicarnassus (IRE) *MRChannon* 2-9-1 TonyCulhane (15).................. 20/1   2½ 14
    Naigani (USA) *APO'Brien,Ireland* 2-9-1 DavidMcCabe (14)..................... 200/1   3 15
    Mrs J. S. Bolger 15ran 1m26.12   TR: 122+/122+/114/113/113/110/109

82   **'In The Pink' Rockfel Stks (Sponsored By Owen Brown) (Gr 2) (2yo f)**   7f
    £39,746

74 FINSCEAL BEO (IRE) *JSBolger,Ireland* 2-9-2 KJManning (1) 9/4f   1
    RAHIYAH (USA) *JNoseda* 2-8-12 LDettori (14)...................................... 7/1   3 2
    PUGGY (IRE) *RAKvisla* 2-8-12 (t) FJohansson (9)................................ 25/1   3½ 3
    Shorthand *SirMichaelStoute* 2-8-12 KerrinMcEvoy (7)........................... 8/1   nk 4
66 English Ballet (IRE) *BWHills* 2-8-12 MichaelHills (8)............................. 4/1   1 5
69 Dhanyata (IRE) *BJMeehan* 2-8-12 JimmyFortune (10) 7/1   1¼ 6
    Kaseema (USA) *SirMichaelStoute* 2-8-12 MartinDwyer (13) .... 12/1   sh 7
    Passified *DRCElsworth* 2-8-12 JohnEgan (11).................................... 25/1   2½ 8
74 Impetious *ETyrrell,Ireland* 2-8-12 DPMcDonogh (2) .... 66/1   sh 9
    Queen of France (USA) *DWachman,Ireland* 2-8-12 WMLordan (5) .... 16/1   nk 10
    Sudoor *JLDunlop* 2-8-12 RHills (3) .... 18/1   ½ 11
    Awwal Malika (USA) *CEBrittain* 2-8-12 RyanMoore (12) 66/1   1¾ 12
    Onida (IRE) *CGCox* 2-8-12 MJKinane (6)... 50/1   5 13
    Fontana Amorosa *KARyan* 2-8-12 KDarley (4)...................................... 33/1   4 14
    M. A. Ryan 14ran 1m27.12   TR: 118/105/95/95

MILAN Sunday, Oct 15   GOOD

83   **Gran Premio del Jockey Club Italiano (Gr 1) (3yo+)** £158,503   1½m

52 LAVEROCK (IRE) *CLaffon-Parias,France* 4-9-5 DBonilla 84/100cpf   1
    FAIR NASHWAN *BGrizzetti,Italy* 4-9-2 DVargiu .... 161/10   hd 2
52 CHERRY MIX (FR) *SaeedbinSuroor,GB* 5-9-5 LDettori 84/100cpf   1½ 3
68 Egerton (GER) *PRau,Germany* 5-9-5 TMundry.................................. 546/100   nk 4
    Sweet Stream (ITY) *JEHammond,France* 6-9-2 TGillet .... 278/100   nk 5
    Dickens (GER) *HBlume,Germany* 3-8-12 ASuborics 97/10   5 6
    Groom Tesse *LCamici,Italy* 5-9-5 (b) SLandi 496/100   1½ 7
    Miles Gloriosus (USA) *RMenichetti,Italy* 3-8-12 MDemuro 566/10   10 8
    Sheikh Mohammed 8ran 2m29.80   TR: 123/120/120/119/115/109

NEWBURY Saturday, Oct 21   SOFT

84   **Racing Post Trophy (Gr 1) (2yo c+f)** £93,687   1m

    AUTHORIZED (IRE) *PWChapple-Hyam* 2-9-0 LDettori (8) 25/1   1
    CHARLIE FARNSBARNS (IRE) *BJMeehan* 2-9-0 RyanMoore (7)............. 33/1   1¼ 2
    MEDICINE PATH *EJO'Neill* 2-9-0 RichardMullen (11)........................... 20/1   2 3
    Eagle Mountain *APO'Brien,Ireland* 2-9-0 MJKinane (9) .... 8/11f   nk 4
    Thousand Words *BWHills* 2-9-0 RichardHughes (14)............................. 7/1   1¾ 5
    Sunshine Kid (USA) *JHMGosden* 2-9-0 JimmyFortune (10) 11/1   5 6
    Regime (IRE) *MLWBell* 2-9-0 JamieSpencer (5) 15/2   1¾ 7
    Red Rock Canyon (IRE) *APO'Brien,Ireland* 2-9-0 JAHeffernan (4) .... 25/1   hd 8
    Teslin (IRE) *MJohnston* 2-9-0 KDarley (2)... 40/1   hd 9
    Petara Bay (IRE) *TGMills* 2-9-0 DaneO'Neill (6) .... 16/1   nk 10
    Drumfire (IRE) *MJohnston* 2-9-0 JoeFanning (3)................................. 25/1   17 11
    Great Sphinx (USA) *APO'Brien,Ireland* 2-9-0 DavidMcCabe (1) 100/1   2 12
    Malacara *APO'Brien,Ireland* 2-9-0 CO'Donoghue (12) 100/1   13 13
    Prince Golan (IRE) *KARyan* 2-9-0 NCallan (13) 100/1   3 14
    Saleh Al Homaizi & Imad Al Sagar 14ran 1m43.74   TR: 118/115/110/110+/105

LONGCHAMP Sunday, Oct 22   GOOD

85   **Prix Royal-Oak (Gr 1) (3yo+)** £83,893   1m7f110y

62 MONTARE (IRE) *JEPease,France* 4-9-4 (s) OPeslier 58/10   1
    BELLAMY CAY *AFabre,France* 4-9-4 SPasquier .... 27/4   sn 2
71 SERGEANT CECIL *BRMillman,GB* 7-9-4 RyanMoore 11/4   1 3
    Lord du Sud (FR) *J-CRouget,France* 5-9-4 IMendizabal .... 2/1f   ¾ 4
39 Rising Cross *JRBest,GB* 3-8-6 MartinDwyer .... 37/1   ½ 5

Loup de Mer (GER) *WBaltromei,Germany* 4-9-4 DBoeuf 25/4 2 6
71 Shamdala (IRE) *AdeRoyerDupre,France* 4-9-1 CSoumillon .... 17/4 hd 7
Soledad (IRE) *GCherel,France* 6-9-4 FSpanu.. 35/1 ¾ 8
71 Petite Speciale (USA) *ELecoiffier,France* 7-9-1 TJarnet 30/1 4 9
64 Frank Sonata *MGQuinlan,GB* 5-9-4 TPQueally.. 29/1 15 10
Mr George Strawbridge 10ran 3m20.30 TR: 116/118/117+/116/115/113

WOODBINE Sunday, Oct 22 SOFT

86 Pattison Canadian International Stks (Gr 1) (3yo+) £645,161 1½m

48 COLLIER HILL *GASwinbank,GB* 8-9-0 DeanMcKeown.......................... 108/10 1
GO DEPUTY (USA) *TAPletcher,USA* 6-9-0 JVelazquez .... 35/10 ns 2
SKY CONQUEROR (USA) *DDBanach,Canada* 4-9-0 TKabel................. 84/10 3½ 3
52 Blue Monday *RCharlton,GB* 5-9-0 SJDrowne .... 57/10 ½ 4
Meteor Storm *WDollase,USA* 7-9-0 (b) JCastellano .... 11/1 ½ 5
Last Answer (USA) *MichaelKeogh,USA* 6-9-0 ERamsammy .... 31/1 ¾ 6
58 The Last Drop (IRE) *BWHills,GB* 3-8-7 RHills... 26/1 1¼ 7
64 Kastoria (IRE) *JOxx,Ireland* 5-8-11 MJKinane 24/10f 2 8
Jambalaya (CAN) *CatherineDayPhillips,Canada* 4-9-0 JCJones 27/1 4½ 9
1 Relaxed Gesture (IRE) *CClement,USA* 5-9-0 GGomez 5/1 1 10
R H Hall J D Abell R Crowe 10ran 2m37.34 TR: 122/122/116+/115/114/113

SAINT-CLOUD Sunday, Oct 29 GOOD

87 Criterium International (Gr 1) (2yo c+g) £95,872 1m

MOUNT NELSON *APO'Brien,Ireland* 2-9-0 JAHeffernan 109/10 1
SPIRIT ONE (FR) *PHDemercastel,France* 2-9-0 DBoeuf .... 3/5f hd 2
YELLOWSTONE (IRE) *APO'Brien,Ireland* 2-9-0 CO'Donoghue 109/10 1½ 3
Friston Forest (IRE) *AFabre,France* 2-9-0 CSoumillon................................ 17/2 ¾ 4
81 Rallying Cry (USA) *JHMGosden,GB* 2-9-0 OPeslier .... 19/1 sh 5
Makaan (USA) *FHead,France* 2-9-0 DBonilla .... 82/10 sn 6
Holocene (USA) *PBary,France* 2-9-0 CPLemaire .... 9/1 ¾ 7
81 Vital Equine (IRE) *EJO'Neill,GB* 2-9-0 RichardMullen................................. 9/1 ¾ 8
Beltanus (GER) *TGibson,Germany* 2-9-0 SPasquier...................................... 30/1 4 9
84 Teslin (IRE) *MJohnston,GB* 2-9-0 KDarley 56/1 3 10
Mr Derrick Smith 10ran 1m41.30 TR: 114/113/110/108/108/108

CHURCHILL DOWNS Saturday, Nov 4 Turf course: FIRM, Dirt course: FAST

88 Emirates Airline Breeders' Cup Filly & Mare Turf (Gr 1) (3yo+ f+m) 1m3f (Turf)
£625,263

60 OUIJA BOARD *EALDunlop,GB* 5-8-11 LDettori (2)................................ 14/10f 1
FILM MAKER (USA) *HGMotion,USA* 6-8-11 (b) EPrado (4) 83/10 2¼ 2
HONEY RYDER (USA) *TAPletcher,USA* 5-8-11 (b) JVelazquez (5).......... 88/10 nk 3
Wait A While (USA) *TAPletcher,USA* 3-8-7 GGomez (7).......................... 23/10 1¾ 4
73 Satwa Queen (FR) *JdeRoualle,France* 4-8-11 TThulliez (9)...................... 95/10 1 5
My Typhoon (IRE) *WIMott,USA* 4-8-11 RAlbarado (8) .... 30/1 nk 6
21 Mauralakana (FR) *PLBiancone,USA* 3-8-7 JLeparoux (3)......................... 208/10 4½ 7
Dancing Edie (USA) *CDollase,USA* 4-8-11 CNakatani (1)...................... 365/10 2¼ 8
57 Quiet Royal (USA) *TAPletcher,USA* 3-8-7 OPeslier (6) 422/10 6½ 9
21 Germance (USA) *J-CRouget,France* 3-8-7 CSoumillon (10) 173/10 12 10
Lord Derby 10ran 2m14.55 TR: 124+/118/118/115/111/110

89 NetJets Breeders' Cup Mile (Gr 1) (3yo+) £616,737 1m (Turf)

78 MIESQUE'S APPROVAL (USA) *MDWolfson,USA* 7-9-0 ECastro (10) .. 243/10 1
ARAGORN (IRE) *NDDrysdale,USA* 4-9-0 CNakatani (7).............................. 4/1 2¾ 2
BADGE OF SILVER (USA) *RJFrankel,USA* 6-9-0 EPrado (8)............... 146/10 hd 3
79 Sleeping Indian *JHMGosden,GB* 5-9-0 ASolis (4).................................... 215/10 nk 4
80 Rob Roy (USA) *SirMichaelStoute,GB* 4-9-0 RADominguez (9).............. 235/10 nk 5
78 Silent Name (JPN) *GMandella,USA* 4-9-0 VEspinoza (2)........................ 318/10 hd 6
Gorella (FR) *PLBiancone,USA* 4-8-11 JLeparoux (12)............................... 36/10 hd 7
78 Aussie Rules (USA) *APO'Brien,Ireland* 3-8-11 (v) GGomez (14)................. 11/1 1¼ 8
67 Araafa (IRE) *JNoseda,GB* 3-8-11 JVelazquez (3) .... 3/1f nk 9
67 Librettist (USA) *SaeedbinSuroor,GB* 4-9-0 CSoumillon (13).................... 162/10 1¼ 10
Free Thinking (USA) *DWDanner,USA* 5-9-0 JSantos (5)......................... 367/10 4¼ 11
3 Super Frolic (USA) *SBlasi,USA* 6-9-0 SBridgmohan (11)......................... 659/10 nk 12
49 Ad Valorem (USA) *APO'Brien,Ireland* 4-9-0 JamieSpencer (1) 254/10 1 13
42 Echo of Light *SaeedbinSuroor,GB* 4-9-0 LDettori (6).................................. 97/10 hd 14
Live Oak Plantation 14ran 1m34.75 TR: 126/118/117/117+/116+/115

90 John Deere Breeders' Cup Turf (Gr 1) (3yo+) £852,632 1½m (Turf)

58 RED ROCKS (IRE) *BJMeehan,GB* 3-8-10 LDettori (9) 108/10 1
45 BETTER TALK NOW (USA) *HGMotion,USA* 7-9-0 (b) ½ 2
RADominguez (8) 186/10

```
     45  ENGLISH CHANNEL (USA) TAPletcher,USA 4-9-0 JVelazquez (10) ...... 37/10      2¼  3
         Rush Bay (USA) TMAmoss,USA 4-9-0 RBejarano (5) ............................ 326/10     1½  4
         Scorpion (IRE) APO'Brien,Ireland 4-9-0 MJKinane (4) ..................... 59/10     ¾  5
     80  Hurricane Run (IRE) AFabre,France 4-9-0 CSoumillon (7) ................... 29/10f     ½  6
     86  Go Deputy (USA) TAPletcher,USA 6-9-0 OPeslier (1) ......................... 98/10     ¾  7
         T. H. Approval (USA) EInda,USA 5-9-0 (b) ASolis (2) ....................... 115/10     ¾  8
         Silverfoot (USA) DStewart,USA 4-9-0 MGuidry (11) ......................... 393/10    1¾  9
     45  Cacique (IRE) RJFrankel,USA 5-9-0 EPrado (6) ................................. 38/10    2¾ 10
         Icy Atlantic (USA) TAPletcher,USA 5-9-0 MJLuzzi (3) ...................... 773/10    28 11
         Mr J. Paul Reddam 11ran 2m27.32           TR: 124/120/115/112/111/110
```

91 Breeders' Cup Classic - Powered By Dodge (Gr 1) (3yo+) £1,421,053   1¼m (Dirt)

```
         INVASOR (ARG) KPMcLaughlin,USA 4-9-0 FJara (11) ........................... 67/10      1
         BERNARDINI (USA) TAlbertrani,USA 3-8-10 JCastellano (3)................ 11/10f     1  2
         PREMIUM TAP (USA) JCKimmel,USA 4-9-0 EPrado (2) ...................... 278/10     2½  3
         Giacomo (USA) JAShirreffs,USA 4-9-0 MESmith (9)........................... 214/10     1  4
         Brother Derek (USA) DLHendricks,USA 3-8-10 ASolis (1).................. 225/10     ½  5
     67  George Washington (IRE) APO'Brien,Ireland 3-8-10 MJKinane (4).......... 94/10     2  6
         Lava Man (USA) DFO'Neill,USA 5-9-0 (b) CNakatani (8) ..................... 61/10    8¾  7
         Perfect Drift (USA) MWJohnson,USA 7-9-0 GGomez (6)...................... 343/10    hd  8
         Lawyer Ron (USA) TAPletcher,USA 3-8-10 PValenzuela (5)................. 202/10     ½  9
         Sun King (USA) NPZito,USA 4-9-0 (v) RBejarano (13) ....................... 197/10     ¾ 10
         Flower Alley (USA) TAPletcher,USA 4-9-0 (b) JVelazquez (10) .......... 355/10    1½ 11
         Suave (USA) PJMcGee,USA 5-9-0 (v) KDesormeaux (12)...................... 59/1    25 12
     33  David Junior (USA) BJMeehan,GB 4-9-0 JamieSpencer (7)................... 143/10    pu
         Mr Hamdan Al Maktoum 13ran 2m02.18      TR: 128+/127+/123/121/121/118
```

ROME Sunday, Nov 5   GOOD to FIRM

92 Premio Roma (Gr 1) (3yo+) £109,204   1¼m

```
     83  CHERRY MIX (FR) SaeedbinSuroor,GB 5-9-2 (t) TedDurcan ............... 336/100     1
     33  HATTAN (IRE) CEBrittain,GB 4-9-2 SebSanders.................................. 98/10     4  2
         DISTANT WAY (USA) FBrogi,Italy 5-9-2 MDemuro ......................... 281/100    1¾  3
     45  Soldier Hollow PSchiergen,Germany 6-9-2 SPasquier ........................ 17/10f    sn  4
         Vol de Nuit LMCumani,GB 5-9-2 FBranca ....................................... 281/100    1¼  5
     48  Donaldson (GER) PRau,Germany 4-9-2 TMundry ............................... 13/2     1½  6
     83  Fair Nashwan BGrizzetti,Italy 4-8-13 (t) DVargiu............................... 429/100    nk  7
         Lauro (GER) PSchiergen,Germany 3-9-0 AStarke................................ 13/2    1¾  8
         Cocodrail (IRE) FBrogi,Italy 5-9-2 (t) TJarnet.................................... 42/1     ½  9
         Emily Bronte SaeedbinSuroor,GB 3-8-10 TPQueally............................ 336/100    20 10
         Godolphin 10ran 1m59.40                     TR: 123/113/109/108/105/102
```

FLEMINGTON Tuesday, Nov 7   GOOD

93 Emirates Melbourne Cup (Hcap) (Gr 1) (3yo+) £1,255,060   2m

```
         DELTA BLUES (JPN) KSumii,Japan 5-8-11 YIwata ........................... 17/1      1
         POP ROCK (JPN) KSumii,Japan 5-8-5 DMOliver................................ 5/1jf    sh  2
         MAYBE BETTER (AUS) BMayfield-Smith,Australia 4-7-12 CMunce ......... 9/1    4½  3
         Zipping (AUS) GARogerson,Australia 5-8-4 GBoss................................ 9/1    1½  4
     43  Land 'n Stars JamiePoulton,GB 6-8-5 JohnEgan................................ 200/1    1½  5
         Mahtoun (AUS) MsKWaugh,Australia 7-8-5 CoreyBrown..................... 200/1    sn  6
     64  Yeats (IRE) APO'Brien,Ireland 5-9-4 KFallon.................................. 11/2    nk  7
         Activation (NZ) GARogerson,Australia 5-8-5 MRodd...................... 20/1     ½  8
         Mandela (NZ) RYuill,NewZealand 5-8-0 CraigWilliams ..................... 20/1     1  9
         Glistening LMCumani,GB 4-8-0 SSeamer........................................ 80/1     ¾ 10
         Kerry O'Reilly (NZ) JGibbs,NewZealand 6-8-3 CELammas ................ 50/1     3 11
         Railings (AUS) JHawkes,Australia 5-8-10 DBeadman........................ 50/1    3½ 12
         Headturner (AUS) JHawkes,Australia 4-8-7 GChilds......................... 70/1    2¾ 13
         Short Pause DHayes,Australia 7-8-6 NCallow .................................. 200/1    ns 14
         Dolphin Jo (AUS) T&KO'Sullivan,Australia 4-7-12 (b) ASpiteri............... 80/1     2 15
         Art Success (NZ) JCollins,NewZealand 5-8-2 APatti ........................ 40/1    3¼ 16
         Dizelle (AUS) JHawkes,Australia 5-8-8 BShinn.............................. 25/1     2 17
     43  Geordieland (FR) JAOsborne,GB 5-8-7 LDettori.............................. 15/1    1¾ 18
         Tawqeet (AUS) DHayes,Australia 5-8-5 DDunn................................ 5/1jf    ¾ 19
         On A Jeune (AUS) PMontgomerie,Australia 6-8-5 DGauci................... 20/1    nk 20
         Demerger (AUS) DTO'Brien,Australia 6-8-1 (b) SBaster..................... 100/1    sh 21
         Ice Chariot (AUS) REMaund,Australia 4-8-3 JByrne........................ 200/1     ¾ 22
         Zabeat (NZ) DonnaLogan,NewZealand 7-8-3 ODoleuze...................... 200/1    15 23
         Sunday Racing Co Ltd 23ran 3m21.42     TR: 125/119+/109/110/109/108/121
```

SAINT-CLOUD Sunday, Nov 12   GOOD

94 Criterium de Saint-Cloud (Gr 1) (2yo c+f) £95,233   1¼m

```
         PASSAGE OF TIME HRACecil,GB 2-8-11 RichardHughes ................. 32/10     1
```

SOLDIER OF FORTUNE (IRE) *APO'Brien,Ireland* 2-9-0 KFallon............ 64/10   ¾ 2
EMPIRE DAY (UAE) *MJohnston,GB* 2-9-0 KDarley.................................... 17/2   3 3
87 Spirit One (FR) *PHDemercastel,France* 2-9-0 DBoeuf............................ 13/10f   ¾ 4
84 Red Rock Canyon (IRE) *APO'Brien,Ireland* 2-9-0 JAHeffernan .... 64/10   sn 5
    Meridia (GER) *MHofer,Germany* 2-8-11 SPasquier..................................... 18/1   5 6
    Consul General *DKWeld,Ireland* 2-9-0 PJSmullen...................................... 32/10   hd 7
    Aaim To Prosper (IRE) *MRChannon,GB* 2-9-0 JohnEgan........................... 60/1   sh 8
    Nommo (FR) *RMartens,Belgium* 2-9-0 TJarnet.. 80/1   ¾ 9
    Perdono (USA) *AWohler,Germany* 2-9-0 EPedroza................................... 74/1   ½ 10
    Dilshaan's Prize (IRE) *RPritchard-Gordon,France* 2-9-0 DBonilla........... 56/1   1½ 11
    Ailton (GER) *WBaltromei,Germany* 2-9-0 JVictoire................................. 38/1   8 12
    Massive (IRE) *MRChannon,GB* 2-9-0 CSoumillon..................................... 49/10   ½ 13
Mr K. Abdulla 13ran 2m08.90   TR: 113/114/107/105/105

TOKYO Sunday, Nov 26   FIRM

95   **Japan Cup (Gr 1) (3yo+) £1,121,428**   1½m

76 DEEP IMPACT (JPN) *YIkee,Japan* 4-9-0 YTake.. 3/10f
    DREAM PASSPORT (JPN) *HMatsuda,Japan* 3-8-10 YIwata.............. 152/10   2 2
88 OUIJA BOARD *EALDunlop,GB* 5-8-10 LDettori................................... 17/2   ½ 3
    Cosmo Bulk (JPN) *KTabe,Japan* 5-9-0 FIgarashi.. 40/1   1 4
    Fusaichi Pandora (JPN) *TShirai,Japan* 3-8-6 YFukunaga 52/1   1½ 5
    Meisho Samson (JPN) *TSetoguchi,Japan* 3-8-10 MIshibashi .... 15/1   ns 6
62 Freedonia *JEHammond,France* 4-8-10 TGillet.. 89/1   ½ 7
    Swift Current (JPN) *HMori,Japan* 5-9-0 NYokoyama................................ 42/1   ¾ 8
    Tosen Shana O (JPN) *HMori,Japan* 3-8-10 HGoto.................................. 150/1   3½ 9
40 Heart's Cry (JPN) *KHashiguchi,Japan* 5-9-0 CPLemaire 58/10   6 10
    Yukino Sun Royal (JPN) *SMasuzawa,Japan* 5-9-0 KTanaka.................... 216/1   3½ 11
Kaneko Makoto Holdings Co. Ltd 11ran 2m25.10   TR: 128+/126/119/121/115/119

SHA TIN Sunday, Dec 10   GOOD to FIRM

96   **Cathay Pacific Hong Kong Vase (Gr 1) (3yo+) £521,910**   1½m

86 COLLIER HILL *GASwinbank,GB* 8-9-0 DeanMcKeown (10)..................... 11/1   1
86 KASTORIA (IRE) *JOxx,Ireland* 5-8-10 (t) MJKinane (1) .... 69/10   ns 2
85 SHAMDALA (IRE) *AdeRoyerDupre,France* 4-9-0 10 CSoumillon (3)........... 11/1   1 3
    Song of Wind (JPN) *HAsami,Japan* 3-8-9 KTake (6)................................... 7/2   ¾ 4
80 Maraahel (IRE) *SirMichaelStoute,GB* 5-9-0 (v) RHills (9)...................... 10/1   1½ 5
83 Egerton (GER) *PRau,Germany* 5-9-0 TMundry (7)................................... 56/1   1½ 6
90 Scorpion (IRE) *APO'Brien,Ireland* 4-9-0 JAHeffernan (5) .... 78/10   ¾ 7
    Admire Main (JPN) *MHashida,Japan* 3-8-9 YTake (4)............................. 13/10f   7½ 8
    Saturn (IRE) *CFownes,HongKong* 6-9-0 DNikolic (8)............................... 21/1   6¾ 9
R H Hall J D Abell R Crowe 9ran 2m27.10   TR: 121/117+/115/117/114/111

97   **Cathay Pacific Hong Kong Sprint (Gr 1) (3yo+) £447,351**   6f

    ABSOLUTE CHAMPION (AUS) *DJHall,HongKong* 5-9-0 (s)
    BPrebble (5).. 54/10   1
77 SILENT WITNESS (AUS) *ASCruz,HongKong* 7-9-0 FCoetzee (2) 6/1   4¼ 2
77 BENBAUN (IRE) *MJWallace,GB* 5-9-0 (v) JamieSpencer (3)...................... 38/1   ¾ 3
    Down Town (AUS) *CHYip,HongKong* 3-9-0 ODoleuze (13) 39/10   1¼ 4
    Sunny Sing (IRE) *JMoore,HongKong* 4-9-0 (t) CSoumillon (8) 8/5f   1 5
    Billet Express (AUS) *JMoore,HongKong* 5-9-0 DJWhyte (10).................. 48/1   ¾ 6
    Able Prince (AUS) *JMoore,HongKong* 6-9-0 (b+t) MNunes (9)................. 30/1   1¾ 7
    Scintillation (AUS) *CSShum,HongKong* 6-9-0 (h) GMosse (6)................... 17/1   sh 8
    Red Oog (AUS) *JPride,Australia* 7-9-0 (h) HBowman (14) 34/1   2¾ 9
77 She Is Tosho (JPN) *ATsurudome,Japan* 6-8-10 KIkezoe (11)..................... 22/1   nk 10
    Natural Blitz I (AUS) *DCruz,HongKong* 4-9-0 ADelpech (1)..................... 40/1   3½ 11
72 Desert Lord *KARyan,GB* 6-9-0 (b) NCallan (4) .... 30/1   ns 12
77 Meisho Bowler (JPN) *TShirai,Japan* 5-9-0 (h) YFukunaga (7)................... 12/1   rtr
Mr & Mrs Eddie Wong Ming Chak 13ran 1m07.80   TR: 129/114/111+/107/103

98   **Cathay Pacific Hong Kong Mile (Gr 1) (3yo+) £596,468**   1m

    THE DUKE (AUS) *CFownes,HongKong* 7-9-0 ODoleuze (4).................. 142/10   1
    ARMADA (NZ) *JSize,HongKong* 5-9-0 DJWhyte (5)............................... 6/5f   hd 2
49 RAMONTI (FR) *A&GBotti,Italy* 4-9-0 (t) EBotti (12)................................ 16/1   1¼ 3
4 Bullish Luck (USA) *ASCruz,HongKong* 7-9-0 (b) BPrebble (7)................. 16/1   ½ 4
2 Linngari (IRE) *HBrown,SouthAfrica* 4-9-0 GSchofield (13).................... 66/1   sh 5
    Joyful Winner (AUS) *JMoore,HongKong* 6-9-0 (t) CSoumillon (2) .... 14/1   hd 6
    Floral Pegasus (AUS) *ASCruz,HongKong* 4-9-0 (t) LDettori (6) .... 5/1   sh 7
    Rebel Rebel (IRE) *REDutrow,jnr,USA* 4-9-0 (b+t) EPrado (3)................... 44/1   2½ 8
    Sir Ernesto (AUS) *DCruz,HongKong* 4-9-0 FCoetzee (1)......................... 16/1   nk 9
4 Russian Pearl (NZ) *ASCruz,HongKong* 6-9-0 (t) ESaint-Martin (10)......... 37/1   ½ 10
4 Bowman's Crossing (IRE) *CFownes,HongKong* 7-9-0 GMosse (8)............. 40/1   ¾ 11
    Dance In The Mood (JPN) *KFujisawa,Japan* 5-8-10 YTake (14)............... 9/1   sh 12

Dave's Best *CHYip,HongKong* 6-9-0 MJKinane (9) 55/1 1¾ 13
60 Mustameet (USA) *KPrendergast,Ireland* 5-9-0 DPMcDonogh (11) 29/1 1¼ 14
Mr E. Yau jnr 14ran 1m33.40 TR: 123/123+/119/117+/117+/117

99 Cathay Pacific Hong Kong Cup (Gr 1) (3yo+) £745,585 1¼m

80 PRIDE (FR) *AdeRoyerDupre,France* 6-8-10 CPLemaire (9) 51/20 1
ADMIRE MOON (JPN) *HMatsuda,Japan* 3-8-11 (t) YTake (4) ..... 10/1 sh 2
VENGEANCE OF RAIN (NZ) *DEFerraris,HongKong* 6-9-0 (t) ADelpech (2) 4/1 1¾ 3
4 Viva Pataca *JMoore,HongKong* 4-9-0 CSoumillon (8) 73/10 1½ 4
Art Trader (USA) *JMoore,HongKong* 5-9-0 (t) ESaint-Martin (12) ..... 73/1 ¾ 5
88 Satwa Queen (FR) *JdeRoualle,France* 4-8-10 LDettori (5) ..... 26/1 hd 6
Dia de La Novia (JPN) *KSumii,Japan* 4-8-10 YFukunaga (11) ..... 37/1 nk 7
Hello Pretty (AUS) *ASCruz,HongKong* 4-9-0 (t) BPrebble (6) ..... 23/10f nk 8
60 Alexander Goldrun (IRE) *JSBolger,Ireland* 5-8-10 KJManning (10) 9/1 2½ 9
Musical Way (FR) *PVandePoele,France* 4-8-10 RonanThomas (3) 100/1 1½ 10
Growl (NZ) *DHayes,Australia* 4-9-0 (t) CraigWilliams (7) 28/1 4 11
High Intelligent (AUS) *JSize,HongKong* 6-9-0 (b) DJWhyte (1) 50/1 4 12
N P Bloodstock 12ran 2m01.60 TR: 118/123+/118/114/112/108

NAKAYAMA Sunday, Dec 24 FIRM

100 Arima Kinen (Gr 1) (3yo+) £796,553 1½m110y

95 DEEP IMPACT (JPN) *YIkee,Japan* 4-9-0 YTake 1/5f 1
93 POP ROCK (JPN) *KSumii,Japan* 5-9-0 OPeslier 30/1 3 2
DAIWA MAJOR (JPN) *HUehara,Japan* 5-9-0 KAndo ..... 141/10 ¾ 3
95 Dream Passport (JPN) *HMatsuda,Japan* 3-8-10 HUchida ..... 121/10 ns 4
95 Meisho Samson (JPN) *TSetoguchi,Japan* 3-8-10 MIshibashi 20/1 1¼ 5
93 Delta Blues (JPN) *KSumii,Japan* 5-9-0 YIwata ..... 38/1 nk 6
Tosho Knight (JPN) *KYasuda,Japan* 5-9-0 TBushizawa ..... 73/1 ¾ 7
Admire Fuji (JPN) *MHashida,Japan* 4-9-0 KTake ..... 130/1 nk 8
96 Admire Main (JPN) *MHashida,Japan* 3-8-10 YShibata ..... 34/1 ns 9
Sweep Tosho (JPN) *ATsurudome,Japan* 5-8-10 KIkezoe ..... 29/1 nk 10
95 Cosmo Bulk (JPN) *KTabe,Japan* 5-9-0 FIgarashi 35/1 2 11
95 Swift Current (JPN) *HMori,Japan* 5-9-0 NYokoyama ..... 91/1 nk 12
Win Generale (JPN) *SKunieda,Japan* 6-9-0 MEbina 209/1 1¾ 13
95 Tosen Shana O (JPN) *HMori,Japan* 3-8-10 MKatsuura 217/1 2½ 14
Kaneko Makoto Holdings Co. Ltd 14ran 2m31.90 TR: 131+/125/123/125+/123/120

INDEX TO SELECTED BIG RACES

Aaim To Prosper (IRE) 94
Abigail Pett 15^{5}
Able Prince (AUS) 97
Absolute Champion (AUS) 97*
Academy Reward (IRE) 48
Ace (IRE) 16^{4}, 25, 45^{6}, 60^{5}
Activation (NZ) 93
Adagio 81
Admire Fuji (JPN) 100
Admire Main (JPN) 96, 100
Admire Moon (JPN) 99^{2}
Ad Valorem (USA) 24*, 49^{5}, 89
Aeroplane 23, 79
Ailton (GER) 94
Ajigolo 19, 29
Akarem 26, 64^{5}
Akimbo (USA) 24
Alayan (IRE) 1^{6}
Alcazar (IRE) 71^{6}
Alderney (USA) 34^{5}
Alexander Alliance (IRE) 8
Alexander Goldrun (IRE) 1^{5}, 14^{2}, 31*, 44^{2}, 60^{3}, 99
Alexander Tango (IRE) 66
Alexandrova (IRE) 17*, 39*, 53*, 73^{3}
Alix Road (FR) 21^{5}, 62^{5}
Allegretto (IRE) 53^{3}
Alloway 21
All Spirit (GER) 48^{6}, 68
Alyzea (IRE) 19
Alzerra (UAE) 34^{2}
Amadeus Wolf 6, 29^{5}, 36^{4}, 54^{2}, 56^{3}, 72^{5}
Araafa (IRE) 6^{4}, 13*, 23*, 42^{5}, 67^{2}, 89
Arabian Prince (USA) 13, 23
Aragorn (IRE) 89^{2}
Archange d'Or (IRE) 12^{4}
Ardbrae Lady 15^{2}, 31^{6}, 59
Armada (NZ) 98^{2}
Arras (GER) 20^{3}
Art Deco (IRE) 20^{4}, 37^{5}
Art Museum (USA) 79
Art Success (NZ) 93
Art Trader (USA) 99^{5}
Asakusa Den'en 2
Ashdown Express (IRE) 22, 29^{4}, 36^{3}
Ask 58^{4}
Aspectus (IRE) 20
Assertive 41^{3}
Asset (IRE) 6
Atlantic Waves (IRE) 18
Aussie Rules (USA) 9*, 20, 33^{4}, 42^{4}, 57^{4}, 78*, 89
Authorized (IRE) 84*
Awwal Malika (USA) 82
Babodana p38
Baddam 43^{5}, 71
Badge of Silver (USA) 89^{3}
Bahia Breeze 59
Bal de La Rose (IRE) 74
Balkan Knight 43
Balthazaar's Gift (IRE) 19^{4}, 29^{2}, 56
Baltic King 22^{6}
Bandari (IRE) 7^{3}, 28, 35^{4}
Barastraight 20
Barolo 26
Battle Paint (USA) 75^{2}
Beauty Bright (IRE) 10, 15, 72^{6}
Beauty Is Truth 50^{6}, 69
Beckermet (IRE) 29, 47
Before You Go (IRE) 18
Bellamy Cay 85^{2}
Beltanus (GER) 87
Be My Queen (IRE) 15
Benbaun (IRE) 19^{2}, 22^{2}, 77^{5}, 97^{3}
Bernardini (USA) $a91^{2}$
Best Alibi (IRE) 18^{6}, 32^{3}
Best Gift (NZ) 4^{2}
Best Name 20^{2}, 32, 76^{4}
Better Talk Now (USA) 45, 90^{2}
Bicoastal (USA) 74^{5}

Billet Express (AUS) 97[6]
Biniou (IRE) 19, 72[4]
Blue Monday 33[3], 52[3], 86[4]
Blue Rocket (IRE) 69
Blue Shotgun (JPN) 77
Boccassini (GER) 50
Bond City (IRE) 22
Boogie Street 22
Boule d'Or (IRE) p38
Bowman's Crossing (IRE) 4, 98
Brass Hat (USA) a3[2d]
Brave Tin Soldier (USA) 70[5]
Brazilian Bride (IRE) 46[4]
Bremen 63[6]
Brisant (GER) 68[5]
British Blue (USA) 78
Brother Derek (USA) a91[5]
Bullish Luck (USA) 2[5], 4[5], 98[4]
Bulwark (IRE) 43
Byron 79

Cacique (IRE) 45[2], 90
Captain Marvelous (IRE) 70[3]
Caradak (IRE) 55*
Caribbean 13
Celtic Mill 22
Cesare p38
Chaibia (IRE) 21
Championship Point (IRE) 18, 51, 58
Champs Elysees 20
Charlie Farnsbarns (IRE) 84[2]
Cheerful Smile (JPN) 77[6]
Chelsea Rose (IRE) 31[2], 44[4]
Cherry Mix (FR) 40[6], 48*, 52[6], 83[3], 92*
Chimes At Midnight (USA) 64
Chiquitin (ARG) a3[5]
Choctaw Nation (USA) a3
Classic Punch (IRE) 32
Close To You (IRE) 6
Cocodrail (IRE) 92
Collier Hill 1[2], 28, 48[3], 86*, 96*
Common World (USA) 11
Confidential Lady 8[2], 15[6], 21*, 39[5], 80[5]
Conquest (IRE) 70[6]
Consul General 94
Corre Caminos (FR) 5*, 12[5], 25[6]
Corridor Creeper (FR) 22
Cosmo Bulk (JPN) 95[4], 100
Cosmonaut (USA) 45[5], 78[4]
Cougar Bay (IRE) 32
Court Masterpiece 11[3], 24[2], 42*, 67[3]
Cover Up (IRE) 43
Crookhaven 13
Cumin (USA) 74

Daaly Babet (FR) 10
Daiwa Major (JPN) 100[3]
Daltaya (FR) 10[4], 21
Dama'a (IRE) 10
Damoiselle (USA) 10
Dance In The Mood (JPN) 98
Dancing Edie (USA) 88
Dandy Man (IRE) 22[4], 54
Danzon (USA) 21
Darrfonah (IRE) 74[2]

Darsi (FR) 20*, 32[5]
Dave's Best 98
Davidii (IRE) 65[5]
David Junior (USA) 2*, 25[4], 33*, a91
Day Flight 28[4]
Decado (IRE) 13[3], 23
Deep Impact (JPN) 76[3d], 95*, 100*
Delta Blues (JPN) 93*, 100[6]
Demerger (AUS) 93
Desert Lord 72*, 97
Dhanyata (IRE) 69[2], 82[6]
Dia de La Novia (JPN) 99
Dickens (GER) 83[6]
Dilshaan's Prize (IRE) 94
Dionisia (IRE) 73[6]
Distant Way (USA) 92[3]
Distinction (IRE) 26[3]
Divine Right 34
Divine Story (FR) 61[4]
Dizelle (AUS) 93
Dolphin Jo (AUS) 93
Donaldson (GER) 48, 92[6]
Donna Blini 8, 27
Dont Dili Dali 15
Down Town (AUS) 97[4]
Dragon Dancer 18[2], 32[4], 63[4]
Drayton (IRE) 46[5]
Dream In Blue (FR) 9
Dream Passport (JPN) 95[2], 100[4]
Drumfire (IRE) 84
Dubai Builder 81
Dutch Art 50*, 70*
Dylan Thomas (IRE) 18[3], 32*, 52[4], 60*

Eagle Mountain 84[4]
Ebtikaar (IRE) 43
Echelon 44[5]
Echo of Light p38*, 42[6], 89
Egerton (GER) 48[4], 68[2], 83[4], 96[6]
Eisteddfod 29
Electrocutionist (USA) a3*, 25[2], 40[2]
El Tango (GER) 48
Emily Bronte 92
Empire Day (UAE) 94[3]
Enforcer 7[5], 16[3], 28[3], 35[3], 40[4], 68[3]
English Ballet (IRE) 66[3], 82[5]
English Channel (USA) 45[4], 90[3]
Enticing (USA) 54
Etlaala 29, 41[5]
Excellent Art 50[3]
Excusez Moi (USA) 56[6], 72
Exhibit One (USA) 53[4]
Eyshal (IRE) 65[3]

Fair Nashwan 83[2], 92
Falkirk (NZ) 22[4], 36
Falstaff (IRE) 1[3], 4
Fayr Jag (IRE) 29, 36, 47[5], 54
Fenice (IRE) 9, 20
Fermion (IRE) 62[6]
Fields of Omagh (AUS) 2
Film Maker (USA) 88[2]
Final Verse 6[6]
Finsceal Beo (IRE) 74*, 82*

Fire And Rain (FR) 51[6], 58
Fire Up The Band 22
Flash Harry 65[6]
Flashy Wings 8, 27[2], 59[3]
Fleeting Shadow (IRE) 75[5]
Floral Pegasus (AUS) 98
Flower Alley (USA) a91
Flyingit (USA) 39[6]
Fontana Amorosa 82
Foreign Affairs 43
Fracas (IRE) 48[2], 64[4]
Frank Sonata 64[6], 85
Freedonia 62[4], 95
Free Thinking (USA) 89
Friston Forest (IRE) 87[4]
Frost Giant (USA) 6
Fusaichi Pandora (JPN) 95[5]

Galient (IRE) 58
Garnica (FR) 9[5]
Gaudeamus (USA) 66[5]
Gentlewave (IRE) 32[2]
Geordieland (FR) 43[2], 93
George Washington (IRE) 6*, 13[5], 55[3], 67*, a91[6]
Germance (USA) 21[2], 88
Giacomo (USA) a91[4]
Gift Horse 29, 36, 54, 72
Gig Harbor p38
Gilded (IRE) 34[3]
Gist (IRE) 15
Glamour Puss (NZ) 22, 29
Glistening 93
Go Deputy (USA) 86[2], 90
Godfrey Street 22
Golden Arrow (IRE) 13[5]
Golden Cast (JPN) 77
Golden Quest 43
Golden Titus (IRE) 50[5]
Gorella (FR) 89
Grand Couturier 37[4]
Grande Melody (IRE) 21
Gravitas 37[6]
Great Sphinx (USA) 84
Green Treasure (AUS) 4
Greys Inn (USA) 1
Groom Tesse 83
Growl (NZ) 99
Guadalajara (GER) 26[6]
Guilia 17[5]
Gulf (IRE) 7[6]

Haatef (USA) 81[4]
Hala Bek (IRE) 18[4]
Halicarnassus (IRE) 81
Hamoody (USA) 81
Hard Top (IRE) 7, 28[5]
Hattan (IRE) 33, 92[2]
Hat Trick (JPN) 2
Hazeymm (IRE) 20
Headturner (AUS) 93
Heart's Cry (JPN) 1*, 40[3], 95
Heaven's Cause (USA) 21
Helios Quercus (FR) 12, 49
Heliostatic (IRE) 13[6], 32
Hello Pretty (AUS) 99
Hello Sunday (FR) 20
Hellvelyn 46[2], 70[4]
Hendrix (USA) 78
He's A Decoy (IRE) 75[4], 81
High Action (USA) 26[4], 43
High Intelligent (AUS) 99

Holocene (USA) 87
Holy Roman Emperor (IRE) 46*, 65², 75*, 81²
Honey Ryder (USA) 88³
Hope'n'charity (USA) 34⁴
Horatio Nelson (IRE) 6, 18
Host (CHI) 2⁴
Hurricane Cat (USA) 13, 20
Hurricane Run (IRE) 14*, 30², 40³, 61², 76³, 80³, 90⁶

Ice Chariot (AUS) 93
Icy Atlantic (USA) 90
Iffraaj 29, 36², 41*
Ikat (IRE) 74⁶
Impetious 74, 82
Impressionnante 10²
Indesatchel (IRE) 57
Indian Ink (IRE) 69*
Indian Maiden (IRE) 47
Invasor (ARG) a91*
Irish Wells (FR) 20⁶, 76⁵
Irridescence (SAF) 4*, 57⁵, 73⁴
Ivan Denisovich (IRE) 9, 23³, 67

Jadalee (IRE) 58⁶
Jambalaya (CAN) 86
James Joyce (IRE) 9
Jedburgh 41², 79
Jeremy (USA) 41⁶, 79
Joyful Winner (AUS) 98⁶

Kamarinskaya (USA) 10, 15
Kandidate 11⁵, 24⁶
Kane Hekili (JPN) a3⁴
Kaseema (USA) 82
Kassiopeia (IRE) 17
Kastoria (IRE) 64*, 86, 96²
Kaylianni 17
Keeneland Swan (USA) 77
Keladora (USA) 21
Kendargent (FR) 49
Kendor Dine (FR) 12
Kentucky Dynamite (USA) 57⁶
Kerry O'Reilly (NZ) 91
Killybegs (IRE) 6, 55², 67⁴, 79²
King of Swords (IRE) 46
Kodiac 56, 72
Krataios (FR) 12³

La Chunga (USA) 8, 22
La Cucaracha 22, 36
Land Before Time (IRE) 32
Land 'n Stars 43⁶, 93⁵
La Presse (USA) 69⁴
Last Answer (USA) 86⁶
Latona (IRE) 19
Lauro (GER) 92
Lava Man (USA) a91
Laverock (IRE) 4, 12*, 30³, 52⁵, 83*
Lawyer Ron (USA) a91
Layman (USA) 1
Legerete (USA) 74³
Le Miracle (GER) 71³
Les Arcs (USA) 22, 29*, 36*, 77

Librettist (USA) 49*, 57*, 67⁶, 89
Linda's Lad 18
Linngari (IRE) 2, 98⁵
Lolita (GER) 27
Lord Admiral (USA) 14³
Lord du Sud (FR) 85⁴
Lost In Wonder (USA) 66
Loup de Mer (GER) 85⁶

Mac Love 41
Magic America (USA) 50², 69⁶
Magna Graduate (USA) a3³
Mahtoum (AUS) 93⁶
Majestic Missile (IRE) 22, 72
Major Rhythm (USA) 45
Majors Cast (IRE) 11²
Makaan (USA) 87⁶
Makderah (IRE) 79
Malacara 84
Mandela (NZ) 93
Mandesha (FR) 62*, 73*
Manduro (GER) 5³, 12², 25³, 49², 57³
Maraahel (IRE) a3⁶, 28*, 40⁵, 52², 80⁶, 96⁵
Marcus Andronicus (USA) 9², 23⁴, 36
Mary Louhana 62
Massive (IRE) 94
Mauralakana (FR) 10⁵, 21⁶, 88
Maybe Better (AUS) 93³
Mecca's Mate 22, 54
Media Puzzle (USA) 26
Medicine Path 84³
Meisho Bowler (JPN) 77², 97
Meisho Samson (JPN) 95⁶, 100⁵
Meliksah (IRE) 72
Meridia (GER) 94⁶
Meteor Storm 86⁵
Metropolitan Man 23⁵
Miesque's Approval (USA) 78⁴, 89*
Miles Gloriosus (USA) 83
Miss Beatrix (IRE) 46³
Miss Sally (IRE) 47⁶, 56
Mister Chocolate (IRE) 19, 72
Misu Bond (IRE) 6⁵
Monsieur Henri (USA) 32
Montare (IRE) 5⁵, 62², 85*
Mont Etoile (IRE) 39⁴, 58
Moss Vale (IRE) 19*, 22, 36⁵, 47*, 54, 72³
Mostaqeleh (USA) 27
Motafarred (IRE) 26
Mountain High (IRE) 28², 35²
Mountain (IRE) 18, 32⁶, 37, 58
Mount Nelson 87*
Mount Parnassus 81
Munsef 7²
Murfreesboro 36
Musical Way (FR) 99
Mussoorie (FR) 21⁴
Mustameet (USA) 60⁴, 98
Mustanfar (USA) 1
Mysterious Lina (FR) 62
My Typhoon (IRE) 88⁶

Naigani (USA) 81

Nannina 8, 27*, 44³, 59⁴, 73⁵
Nantyglo 27
Nasheej (USA) 8³, 15, 27³, 44
Natural Blitz I (AUS) 97
Nayyir 41⁴
Near Honor (GER) 5, 30⁶, 61⁵
Nell Gwyn (FR) 74
New Girlfriend (IRE) 10⁶, 49
New Seeker 11
Nightime (IRE) 15*, 27
Nina Blini 34
Noddies Way 18
Noelani (IRE) 29
Nommo (FR) 94
Norse Dancer (IRE) 1, 4
Notability (IRE) p38³
Notable Guest (USA) 16⁵, 33
Notnowcato 25⁵, 33², 52*, 80
Numide (FR) 20⁵, 37

Old Dodge (BRZ) 78³
Olympian Odyssey 6³, 20, 80⁴
On A Jeune (AUS) 93
Onida (IRE) 82
Opera Cape 6
Oracle West (SAF) 1
Orewa Matteruze (JPN) 77
Oriental Tiger (GER) 68⁴
Orientor 22, 54
Ouija Board 1⁴, 4³, 16², 25*, 33⁵, 44*, 60², 88*, 95³

Papal Bull 18, 51, 63⁵
Passage of Time 94*
Passified 82
Pearl Sky (FR) 21
Peeress 11*, 24⁴, 49³, 59²
Percussionist (IRE) 64
Perdono (FR) 94
Perfect Drift (USA) a91
Perfect Hedge 31
Perfect Promise (SAF) 2⁶
Petara Bay (IRE) 84
Petite Speciale (USA) 71⁵, 85
Petrograd (IRE) 30⁵
Philharmonic 56
Phoenix Reach (IRE) 45
Pivotal Flame 19⁵, 54³, 72
Pivotal Point 19⁶, 22³, 29, 36, 47³
Polar Ben 79⁶
Policy Maker (IRE) 30⁴
Poltava (FR) 74⁴
Ponte Tresa (FR) 62
Pop Rock (JPN) 93², 100²
Porto Santo (FR) 9⁶
Premium Tap (USA) a91³
Price Tag 10³, 27
Pride (FR) 5⁴, 30*, 61³, 76², 80*, 99*
Prime Defender 81
Prince Golan (IRE) 84
Prince of Light (IRE) 41
Princess Taise (USA) 74
Proclamation (IRE) 24³, 67⁵
Prowess (IRE) 17
Puerto Rico (IRE) 32, 37, 51³
Puggy (IRE) 82³
Punch Punch (BRZ) 1

Queen Cleopatra (IRE) 15³, 21³, 31⁵

Queen of France (USA) 82[6]
Quelle Amore (GER) 68[6]
Quiet Royal (USA) 57, 88
Quito (IRE) 29, 36[6], 41, 56[2], 79

Rabatash (USA) 46[6]
Race For The Stars (USA) 8, 15[4], 27[4], 44[6], 59[5]
Rahiyah (USA) 82[2]
Railings (AUS) 93
Rail Link 37*, 63*, 76*
Rajeem 27[5]
Rallying Cry (USA) 81[6], 87[5]
Ramonti (FR) 49, 98[3]
Rebel Rebel (IRE) 98
Red Bloom 31[3]
Red Clubs (IRE) 6, 36, 47[2], 54[5], 56[5], 72
Red Evie (IRE) 59*
Red Oog (AUS) 97
Red Rock Canyon (IRE) 84, 94[5]
Red Rocks (IRE) 37[2], 51[2], 58[3], 90*
Reefscape 26[2], 43, 71[4]
Regime (IRE) 84
Relaxed Gesture (IRE) 1, 86
Remarkable News (VEN) 78[2]
Resplendent Glory (IRE) 22
Reverence 22, 54*, 56*, 72[2]
Rising Cross 17[2], 39[3], 85[5]
River Dancer (IRE) 4
River Tiber 13, 55[4], 67
Riyalma (IRE) 17
Rob Roy (USA) 11[6], 42[3], 55[6], 80[2], 89[5]
Rocamadour 11
Royal Alchemist 33, p38
Royal Highness (Argentine) 5[2], 62[3]
Royal Power (IRE) 23
Royal Storm (IRE) 29
Rumplestiltskin (IRE) 8
Rush Bay (USA) 90[4]
Russian Pearl (NZ) 2, 4, 98

Sanaya (IRE) 21
Sander Camillo (USA) 34*
Sandwaki (USA) 50[4], 75
Satchem (IRE) p38[2], 79[3]
Satulagi (USA) 66[4]
Saturn (IRE) 96
Satwa Queen (FR) 73[2], 88[5], 99[6]
Scarlet Runner 69
Scintillation (AUS) 97
Scorpion (IRE) 90[5], 96
Scottish Stage (IRE) 39[2]
Seihali (IRE) 2[3]
Self Defense 7[4], 28[6]
Septimus (IRE) 18
Sergeant Cecil 26[5], 43[4], 71*, 85[3]
Sesmen 66[6]
Shakis (IRE) a3
Shamdala (IRE) 53[6], 71[2], 85, 96[3]
Shanty Star (IRE) 1
She Is Tosho (JPN) 77, 97
Shirocco (GER) 7*, 16*, 61*, 76
Short Dance (USA) 15

Shorthand 82[4]
Short Pause 93
Short Skirt 17[3], 53[2]
Sienna Storm (IRE) 18, 51
Silca Chiave 69[3]
Silca's Sister 8[4], 27[6]
Silent Name (JPN) 78, 89[6]
Silent Witness (AUS) 77[4], 97[2]
Silk Blossom (IRE) 34[6]
Silva (FR) 10
Silverfoot (USA) 90
Silver Touch (IRE) 10, 79[5]
Simply Perfect 66*
Sina Cova (IRE) 53[5]
Sirene Doloise (FR) 21
Sir Ernesto (AUS) 98
Sir Percy 6[2], 18*, 80
Sismix (IRE) 74
Sixties Icon 18, 58*, 76
Sky Conqueror (USA) 86[3]
Slaney Time (IRE) 65[4]
Sleeping Indian 79*, 89[4]
Slipasearcher (IRE) 34
Snoqualmie Boy 18, 33[6], 52
Soapy Danger 35*, 51[5]
Soldier Hollow 45[3], 92[4]
Soldier of Fortune (IRE) 94[2]
Soledad (IRE) 85
Something Exciting 16[6]
Somnus 56[4], 79[4]
Song of Wind (JPN) 96[4]
Song Writer (GER) 48[5]
Soviet Song (IRE) 11[4], 42[2], 55[5]
Special Kaldoun (IRE) 12, 49[6]
Speciosa (IRE) 8*, 17[4], 27
Spectait p38[5]
Spinning Queen 8[6]
Spirit One (FR) 87[2], 94[4]
Stage Gift (IRE) 51
Star King Man (USA) a3
Steenberg (IRE) 54, 56
Stormy River (FR) 9[3], 23[2], 49[4], 57[2]
Strategic Prince 81[3]
Stronghold p38[4], 79
Suave (USA) a91
Sudan (IRE) 37[3], 63[3]
Sudoor 82
Sugar Baby Love (GER) 74
Suggestive p38[6], 41, 79
Sun King (USA) a91
Sunny Sing (IRE) 97[5]
Sunshine Kid (USA) 84[6]
Super Frolic (USA) a3, 89
Super Kid (NZ) 4[4]
Suteki Shinsukekun (USA) 77
Sweep Tosho (JPN) 100
Sweet Stream (ITY) 83[5]
Swift Current (JPN) 95, 100
Symboli Escape (JPN) 77

T. H. Approval (USA) 90
Tabaret 22
Tagano Bastille (JPN) 77[3]
Takeover Target (AUS) 22*, 29[3], 36, 77*
Talwin (IRE) 15
Tamamo Hot Play (JPN) 77
Tawqeet (USA) 93
Tax Free (IRE) 19[3], 22
Teofilo (IRE) 65*, 81*

Teslin (IRE) 84, 87
Texas Gold 22
Theann 69[5]
The Duke (AUS) 98*
The Last Drop (IRE) 51[4], 58[2], 86
The Tatling (IRE) 22, 29[6], 54[6]
The Tin Man (USA) 2[2], 45*
The Trader (IRE) 22, 47[4], 54[4]
The Whistling Teal 64[3]
Thistle Suite 12
Thousand Words 84[5]
Three Decades (IRE) 34
Three Valleys (USA) 78[6]
Tie Black (IRE) 10*
Time On 17[6], 62
Tosen Shana O (JPN) 95, 100
Tosho Knight (JPN) 100
To The Max (IRE) 75
Touch of Land (FR) 2, 45
Traffic Guard (USA) 81
Treat 66[2]
Trinity College (USA) 75
Tropical Lady (IRE) 31[4]
Tungsten Strike (USA) 26, 43[3]
Turtle Bowl (FR) 12
Tusculum (IRE) 58[5]
Tycoon's Hill (IRE) 19
Tyson (SAF) 2
Ugo Fire (IRE) 15, 59[6]

Vague (USA) 27
Valixir (IRE) 2
Vanderlin 42
Vatori (FR) 5[6], 12[6]
Vengeance of Rain (NZ) 99[3]
Venus Line (JPN) 77
Visindar 18[5]
Visionario (IRE) 75[6]
Vital Equine (IRE) 75[3], 81[5], 87
Vital Statistics 69
Viva Pataca 4[6], 99[4]
Vol de Nuit 92[5]
Vortex 24[5]

Wait A While (USA) 88[4]
Wake Up Maggie (IRE) 8[5], 27
Welsh Emperor (IRE) 79
West of Amarillo (USA) 9[4]
Whilly (IRE) 2
Wi Dud 70[2]
Wid (USA) 69
Wilko (USA) a3[2]
Winged d'Argent (IRE) 26, 43
Win Generale (JPN) 100
Wurfscheibe (GER) 62

Yarqus 23
Yasoodd 9, 13[4], 23[6]
Yeats (IRE) 26*, 43*, 64[2], 93
Yellowstone (IRE) 87[3]
Youmzain (IRE) 51*, 63[2], 68*
Yukino Sun Royal (JPN) 95

Zabeat (NZ) 93
Zipping (AUS) 93[4]

THE TIMEFORM 'TOP HORSES ABROAD'

This review of the year covers the major racing countries outside Britain. It includes Timeform Ratings for the top two-year-olds, three-year-olds and older horses. Horses not rated highly enough to be included in the main lists, but which finished in the first three in a European pattern race, or, in the sections on Japan and North America, won a Grade 1 during the season are included below the cut-off line. Fillies and mares are denoted by (f); * denotes the horse was trained for only a part of the season in the country concerned; † against a horse in the sections outside Europe and the UAE indicates the horse has a commentary in the main section of *Racehorses*. Overseas customers wishing to keep in touch with Timeform's coverage of racing through the year can subscribe to Computer Timeform, Timeform Perspective or our internet site (http://www.timeform.com) for reports on all the important races. It is also possible to obtain up-to-date Timeform commentaries (including many not published in the weekly Timeform Black Book), undertake progeny research and access daily form guides on the internet site. Race Cards for many Group 1 races in France and Ireland, plus major races in several other countries, including the Dubai World Cup, the Breeders' Cup and the Hong Kong International meeting, are also available.

IRELAND   Though it has long been an important racing nation, in recent years Ireland has arguably produced a disproportionately high number of good-class horses compared with the size and scope of its racing programme. Take the latest year. Ireland staged only 52 pattern races, compared with 138 such contests in Britain and 107 in France, yet once again it was home to the highest-rated horse in Europe, namely **George Washington**, and the champion two-year-old, **Teofilo**. Though there are other factors involved, it is undeniable that much of Ireland's success can be attributed to the dominance of the Coolmore breeding operation whose influence is now felt throughout the world-wide racing industry, not just Ireland. Driven by John Magnier and his associates, Coolmore has gone a long way towards realising the vision of Magnier's father-in-law, the legendary trainer Vincent O'Brien. O'Brien had most of his success in the 'seventies and 'eighties with a succession of US-bred champions, but he envisaged a day when such champion racehorses would instead be bred in Ireland, a dream which lately has started to become a reality on a regular basis.

Teofilo, by the Coolmore sire Galileo and trained by Jim Bolger, showed high-class form when unbeaten in five starts, his biggest successes coming in the National Stakes and the Dewhurst Stakes on his last two outings, beating the Aidan O'Brien-trained **Holy Roman Emperor** into second both times. Holy Roman Emperor finished only a head behind Teofilo in the Dewhurst, showing form at least as good as most champion two-year-olds of recent seasons, having previously been successful in the Railway Stakes and the Phoenix Stakes. O'Brien, who is the principal trainer for Coolmore, also handled the enigmatic George Washington. He was beaten more times than he was successful, showing some temperamental shortcomings along the way, but there was no doubting his brilliance when he was at the top of his game in the Two Thousand Guineas and the Queen Elizabeth II Stakes. He was retired after failing to stay in the Breeders' Cup Classic on his final outing.

Four of the five Irish classics stayed at home. **Nightime**, trained by Dermot Weld, won the Irish One Thousand Guineas, while **Dylan Thomas** and **Alexandrova**, in the care of O'Brien, won the Irish Derby and Irish Oaks respectively. Alexandrova had already been successful in the Oaks at Epsom, and she went on to win the Yorkshire Oaks. The high-class Dylan Thomas also won two other starts, namely the Derrinstown Stud Derby Trial and the Irish Champion Stakes, but he failed to show his best form outside Ireland, including when tried on dirt in the USA on his final outing. He did, though, fare best of his stable's four runners in the Derby when a narrowly-beaten third, **Horatio Nelson** sadly breaking down fatally in the closing stages and the wide-margin Dante winner **Septimus** also finishing with an injury. Both Dylan Thomas and Septimus, as well as Alexandrova, are set to stay in training as four-year-olds. The five-year-old **Kastoria** was a late starter to racing, not making her debut until she was four, but she progressed further in 2006 and won four races, including the Curragh Cup and the Irish St Leger, in the latter beating the hot favourite **Yeats**. Yeats had started a short price by virtue of his high-class wins in Britain in the Gold Cup and the Goodwood Cup, and he was also a bit below par in the Melbourne Cup on his final outing.

There were five other Irish-trained Group 1 winners in 2006. In addition to the leading two-year-old colt, Bolger also had the distinction of training Europe's highest-rated juvenile filly (and ante-post One Thousand Guineas favourite), **Finsceal Beo**, successful in the Prix Marcel Boussac and the Rockfel Stakes. **Alexander Goldrun**'s only success came in the Pretty Polly Stakes (which she won for the second year), but she was involved in one of the races of the season when losing out to Ouija Board on a bob of the head in a thrilling renewal of the Nassau Stakes. **Aussie Rules** won twice at the top level, firstly in the Poule d'Essai des Poulains (beating stable-companion **Marcus Andronicus** into second) then in the US Grade 1 Shadwell Turf Mile at Keeneland. Kevin Prendergast's two-year-old filly **Miss Beatrix** proved a real money spinner for connections. Not only did she achieve Group 1 success in the Moyglare Stud Stakes, she also won the inaugural running of the Goffs Million, a sales race worth almost £670,000 to the winner. The other Group 1 winner was O'Brien's two-year-old **Mount Nelson**. Successful in the Criterium International, Mount Nelson has shown smart form in only three starts and is open to further progress, while similar comments apply to his stable-companion **Soldier of Fortune**, runner-up in the Criterium de Saint-Cloud.

A couple of other O'Brien two-year-olds who achieved pattern success were **Eagle Mountain** and **Admiralofthefleet**. Eagle Mountain ran away with the Beresford Stakes before disappointing in the Racing Post Trophy at Newbury, while the lightly-raced Admiralofthefleet won the Royal Lodge Stakes at Ascot with something in hand on his final outing. Another O'Brien inmate, **Duke of Marmalade**, looked capable of better after finishing second in the Vintage Stakes at Goodwood, but he wasn't seen out again. Interestingly, O'Brien's two-year-olds won only 19 % of the races they contested, a good figure by most trainers' standards, but well below the outstanding 28%, 30% and 32% he recorded in 2003, 2004 and 2005 respectively. Several other two-year-olds are worthy of mention. **Arch Swing** was unbeaten in two starts for John Oxx, the second of them the C. L. Weld Park Stakes, and she looks capable of better, while Prendergast's **Evening Time** looks a good prospect for 2007 after winning both her starts in impressive fashion, the second of them a listed event at the Curragh by five lengths. Her stable-companion **Haatef** was another Irish colt to show plenty of promise in the Dewhurst Stakes when staying on strongly for fourth. The other two-year-old pattern winners were **Regional Counsel** (Anglesey Stakes), **Confuchias** (Killavullan Stakes), **Rabatash** (Round Tower Stakes), **Brazilian Bride** (Swordlestown Stud Sprint Stakes) and **Gaudeamus**, the last-named recording one of the lowest ratings for a Group 2 winner in recent years when successful in the Debutante Stakes.

Dandy Man and **Mustameet** made up into very smart performers. Dandy Man won twice, namely the Palace House Stakes at Newmarket and a well-contested listed race at the Curragh, while Mustameet won five times including the International Stakes and the Royal Whip Stakes. **Alayan** showed he was better than ever too when winning the Mooresbridge Stakes, but he had to be retired after fracturing a sesamoid on the gallops shortly afterwards. **Frost Giant** showed smart form when winning the Kilternan Stakes, as did **Heliostatic** when successful in the Meld Stakes. **Ivan Denisovich** and **Mountain** had only a listed win each to their names, but they ran in good company for much of the year. **Galatee** looked a live Oaks prospect when successful in the Blue Wind Stakes in May, but met with a setback and could not repeat the form in a couple of starts on her return to action late in the season. **An Tadh** and **Sina Cova** established themselves as smart performers, winning the Ballycorus Stakes and the Noblesse Stakes respectively, but the veteran **Common World** regressed after winning the Gladness Stakes early in the season. **Noelani** won the Concorde Stakes, her final outing before retiring to stud, while **Decado**, who won the Tetrarch Stakes before finishing third in the Irish Two Thousand Guineas, was not seen out again after finishing well beaten next time in the St James's Palace Stakes. **Puerto Rico** won the Gallinule Stakes early in the year, but he ran his best race when third in the Great Voltigeur Stakes at York on his final outing. **Cougar Bay** ran well in good company without adding to his win, and **Fermion** progressed well to win a listed race at Newbury in the summer. **Danak** made a very promising start to his career, winning all three of his starts before meeting with a setback.

Others worth mentioning are the pattern winners **King Jock** (Desmond Stakes), **Queen Cleopatra** (Derrinstown Stud 1000 Guineas Trial), **Kamarinskaya** (Dimitrova 1000 Guineas Trial), **Jazz Princess** (Athasi Stakes), **Rhythm'n Roots** (Ballysax Stakes), **Race For The Stars** (Denny Cordell Stakes), **Danehill Music** (Park Express Stakes) and **Beauty Bright** (Renaissance Stakes). The handicap performance of the year once again belonged to **Osterhase** who carried top weight (10-3) to victory in the Rockingham Handicap at the Curragh, a feat he also achieved in 2004.

Two-Year-Olds

126	Teofilo
125	Holy Roman Emperor
118	Eagle Mountain
118	Finsceal Beo (f)
116p	Admiralofthefleet
114p	Evening Time (f)
114p	Mount Nelson
114p	Soldier of Fortune
113p	Haatef
110p	Duke of Marmalade
110	Yellowstone
109	He's A Decoy
107	Drayton
106	Miss Beatrix (f)
105	Brave Tin Soldier
105	Red Rock Canyon
104p	Arch Swing (f)
104p	Consul General
104+	Fleeting Shadow
104	Chinese Whisper
104	Ferneley
104	Rabatash
103p	Chanting (f)
103p	Supposition (f)
103p	Thiella (f)
103	Brazilian Bride (f)
102	Creachadoir
102	Hammers Boy
102?	*Whatsthescript
101	Alexander Tango (f)
101	Emerald Hill
101	Facchetti
101	Newgate Lodge (f)
101	Theann (f)
100	Trinity College
99p	Capital Exposure
99	Regional Counsel
98p	Abraham Lincoln
98p	Anton Chekhov
98p	Spanish Harlem
98	Country Song
98	Dimenticata (f)
97p	Archipenko
97	Chivalrous
97	Howya Now Kid
97	Smarty Socks
96p	Boca Dancer (f)
96p	Finicius
96	Confuchias
96	Flash McGahon
96	Star Inside
95P	Macarthur

95	Fabrigas
95	Gaudeamus (f)
94p	Albert Einstein
92	Frederick Ozanam
91	Gee Kel (f)
91	Impetious (f)
91	Silk Dress (f)
90	Dushinka (f)
82	Eyshal

Three-Year-Olds

133	George Washington
129	Dylan Thomas
123	Alexandrova (f)
123	Aussie Rules
123	Dandy Man
121	Septimus
117	Marcus Andronicus
116	Cougar Bay
116	*Frost Giant
116	Soar With Eagles
115	An Tadh
115	Galatee (f)
115	Heliostatic
115	Ivan Denisovich
115	Tusculum
114p	Danak
114	Mountain
114	Ugo Fire (f)
113	Beauty Bright (f)
113	Decado
113	Fermion (f)
113	Lounaos (f)
113	Nightime (f)
113	Puerto Rico
113	Race For The Stars (f)
113	Rumplestiltskin (f)
112	Arabian Prince
112	Modeeroch (f)
112	Queen Cleopatra (f)
112	Reform Act (f)
112?	Road To Mandalay
111	Hurricane Cat
110	Golden Arrow
110	Horatio Nelson
110	Paris Winds (f)
109	Anna Karenina (f)
109	Taqseem
107	Art Museum
107	*Caribbean
107	Cool Touch
107	Duff

107	Farinelli
107	Fire And Rain
107	Kempes
107	Leitra (f)
107	Royal Intrigue
106	Albertinelli
106	Cheyenne Star (f)
106	Dynamo Dancer
106	*Medico
106	Rhythm'N Roots
106	Senora Galilei (f)
105	Abigail Pett (f)
105	Kamarinskaya (f)
105	Poseidon Adventure
105	Rekaab
105	Rockall Blizzard
104+	Hitchcock
104	Artist's Tale
104	Be My Queen (f)
104	Laywaan (f)
104	Mon Michel
104d	Savannah
103	Chief Crazy Horse
103	Cousteau
103	King In Waiting
103	Kingsdale Ocean
103	Miss Donovan (f)
102	Altius
102	Ardbrae Lady (f)
102	Jioconda (f)
102	Moone Cross (f)
102	Rockie
101	Ayla (f)
101	Danehill Music (f)
101	Ice Princess (f)
101	Kerdem
101	Kushnarenkovo (f)
101	Nick's Nikita (f)
101	Tamazug (f)
101	Worldly Wise
100	Hovering (f)
100	James Joyce
100	Lady Orpen (f)
100	*Sable d'Olonne
99	Eastern Appeal (f)
99	Karawana (f)
99	Mrs Snaffles (f)
99	Sacrosanct (f)
99	Talwin (f)
99	That's Hot (f)
98	Absolutelyfabulous (f)
98	Dancing Sky (f)
98	House of Bourbon

98 Missisipi Star (f)	116d Common World	104 Princess Nala (f)
98 Moon Mix	115 Fracas	103 Al Eile
98 Noplacelikehome	115 Lord Admiral	103 Benwith Breeze
98 Sandton City	115 Luas Line (f)	103 Jazz Princess (f)
98 Sweet Afton (f)	115 Miss Sally (f)	103 Only Make Believe
98 Zanderi	115 Mkuzi	103 Swiss Cottage
97 Arosa (f)	114 Arch Rebel	102 Bon Nuit (f)
97 Dapple Grey (f)	114 Latino Magic	102 Redstone Dancer (f)
97 De Roberto	114 Noelani (f)	101 Rathgowney Lad
97 Film Festival	114§ Democratic Deficit	101 Saintly Rachel (f)
97 Gemini Gold (f)	113 Media Puzzle	101 The Carbon Unit
97 Michikabu (f)	113 Quinmaster	101 Utterly Heaven (f)
97 Monsieur Henri	112 Good Surprise	100 Crooked Throw
97 Nasafar	112 Mutakarrim	100 Fairy of The Night (f)
97 Shehira (f)	112 Senor Benny	100 Fit The Cove
97 Tajneed	112 Tolpuddle	100 Fontanally Springs (f)
96 Chenchikova (f)	112d Simple Exchange	100 Hoffman
96 Free Roses (f)	111 Allexina (f)	100 Mombassa
96 Glitter Baby (f)	111 Hard Rock City	100 Nakiska (f)
96 Kalmez	111 Kalderon	100 Top The Charts
96 Marsam	111 Scorpion	100 Valentina Guest (f)
96 Mist And Stone (f)	110 Cairdeas	99+ Catch Me
96 The God of Love	108 Bush Maiden (f)	99 Adoration
95 Basra	108 Perfect Hedge (f)	99 Baggio
95 Crookhaven	108 Slip Dance (f)	99 Belleinga (f)
	107 Blessyourpinksox (f)	99 Bricks And Porter
93 Sandie (f)	107 Bobs Pride	99 Davorin
	107 Mister Hight	99 Ireland's Call
Older Horses	106 Absolute Image	99 Victram
128 Yeats	106 Bawaader	98 Emmpat
125 Ad Valorem	106 Clara Allen (f)	98 Kevkat
125 Alexander Goldrun (f)	106 Jazz Messenger	98 King of Tory
124 Kastoria (f)	106 Menwaal	98 Sister Sox (f)
123 *Grey Swallow	106 Pout (f)	97 Deerpark
123 Mustameet	106d Arturius	97 Rockazar
122 Alayan	105 Cheddar Island	96 Christavelli
121 Chelsea Rose (f)	105 Gift Range (f)	96 Dashing Home
120 Osterhase	105 Helena Molony (f)	96 Mrs Gillow (f)
119 Moon Unit (f)	105 Shersha (f)	96 Orbit O'Gold
118 *Ace	105 Virginia Woolf (f)	96 Subtle Affair (f)
117 *King Jock	105? Ask Carol (f)	96 Telemachus
117 Tropical Lady (f)	104 Akimbo	96 The Last Hurrah
116 *Kendor Dine	104 Back To Paris	95 Tipperary All Star
116 Majestic Times	104 Chained Emotion	95 Visit Wexford
116 Sina Cova (f)	104 Orpailleur	95 Yaria (f)

FRANCE   It was a measure of the sort of strength in Andre Fabre's stable that his seventh winner of the Prix de l'Arc de Triomphe, **Rail Link**, should have been generally regarded beforehand as the stable's third string. That was despite the progressive Rail Link sharing the typical profile of recent Arc winners (ten of the previous twelve Arc winners were three-year-old colts) and he had the classic Arc winner's preparation too, winning the Prix Niel as Carnegie, Helissio, Sagamix, Montjeu, Sinndar, Dalakhani and Hurricane Run had all done in the previous dozen years. The Prix du Jockey Club came too soon for Rail Link, who was unraced at two, but he was ready for Group 1 competition by the time of the Grand Prix de Paris in July. His defeat of the future Breeders' Cup Turf winner Red Rocks maintained the upturn in fortunes of the Grand Prix in its second running as a mile and a half event. Rail Link's Arc win was rather overshadowed by the defeats of his better-fancied stable-companions and Japanese favourite Deep Impact, but he was entitled to more credit than he received and looks sure to enjoy further top-level success as a four-year-old.

    Two more Andre Fabre colts, **Carlotamix** and **Linda's Lad**, had both already won Group 1 events in the autumn of their two-year-old campaigns, but the former proved disappointing at three and Linda's Lad's narrow win in the Derby Trial at Lingfield preceded a tame effort in the Derby itself. By then, a stronger Derby candidate had emerged from the same stable in the form of **Visindar**, who started 2/1 favourite at Epsom after being unbeaten in three starts in France, including the Prix Greffulhe. Visindar fared better than Linda's Lad but was still only fifth in the Derby and was not seen out again after reportedly finishing very jarred up. The Fabre stable's main contender for the Prix du Jockey Club was **Arras**, he too unbeaten beforehand but not seen out again after finishing third at Chantilly. Out of luck in the Derbys at both Epsom and Chantilly, Fabre had better luck in the Italian version with **Gentlewave**, who went on to finish a good second in the Irish Derby before injury prompted his retirement. Gentlewave was unfortunate not to be unbeaten prior to the Curragh, his only defeat beforehand coming in the Prix Hocquart, when his rider lost his whip, going down narrowly to **Numide**. As well as Rail Link and Visindar, another good four-year-old prospect for the Fabre stable is **Getaway** who had looked a most progressive stayer until finishing third to **Vendangeur** (whom he had beaten in the Prix de Lutece the time before) in the Prix Chaudenay on Arc weekend.

The Prix du Jockey Club went to the Aga Khan's **Darsi** in course-record time. That was his pattern-race debut, but he failed to build on it when fifth in the Irish Derby next time before being retired to stud. The Prix du Jockey Club runner-up **Best Name** and sixth-placed **Irish Wells** made more of a name for themselves afterwards. They lined up as rank outsiders in the Prix de l'Arc de Triomphe (neither discredited in finishing fifth and sixth past the post respectively), but not before winning pattern races, Best Name taking the Prix du Prince d'Orange in good style and Irish Wells beating older horses in the Grand Prix de Deauville. Still lightly raced, Best Name was bought by Godolphin after the Arc. While Darsi fell by the wayside, another Aga Khan-owned, Alain de Royer-Dupre-trained colt emerged as a smart replacement in the autumn. **Daramsar** won five of his seven starts, including the Prix du Conseil de Paris, and he should win more good races at four. **Sudan** and **Grand Couturier**, third and fourth respectively in the Grand Prix de Paris, showed smart form without a big win to show for it. Sudan regularly found Rail Link in his way (including when also third in the Prix Niel), while Grand Couturier ran well against older horses in the USA when third in the Sword Dancer Invitational at Saratoga.

There were fewer three-year-old colts of note over shorter trips, among whom **Stormy River** and **Marchand d'Or** were the leading pair. Miler Stormy River gained Group 1 success in the Prix Jean Prat over the Royer-Dupre pair **Kentucky Dynamite** and **Dilek** (both Group 3 winners beforehand) in July. Prior to that, Stormy River had been placed in the Poule d'Essai des Poulains and St James's Palace Stakes, and he went on to run well against older horses later in the year, notably when second to Librettist in the Prix du Moulin. Gelding Marchand d'Or had been beaten in a claimer on his only two-year-old start but progressed into a very smart six/seven-furlong performer and provided his trainer Freddie Head with a first Group 1 winner as a trainer in the Prix Maurice de Gheest. **Passager**'s win in the Prix Perth in the autumn suggests he'll win again in pattern company over a mile at four, and **Garnica** was another to end the year with his best effort, winning the Badener Sprint-Cup over seven furlongs at Baden-Baden. **Biniou** ran in a number of the top French sprints and was a good fourth in a typical Prix de l'Abbaye—one dominated by British-trained sprinters—though he too will count as British-trained from now on having been sold on the eve of the race to join Robert Cowell from Robert Collet.

Mandesha, who stays in training at four with the Arc as her target, stood out as much the best three-year-old filly. She showed rare versatility too, her Group 1 wins coming at a mile, ten furlongs, and twelve furlongs, in the Prix d'Astarte, Prix Vermeille and Prix de l'Opera. Unraced at two and beaten first time out, she was then first past the post in her six remaining starts. Campaigned principally over middle distances, Mandesha's best effort came in the Prix de l'Opera, while when dropped in trip for the Prix d'Astarte she proved too good for what proved a substandard group of miling fillies, with **Impressionnante** (second), **Tie Black** (third) and **Price Tag** (fifth) among those behind her at Deauville. This trio had already met in a controversial Poule d'Essai des Pouliches at Longchamp where Price Tag was demoted from first place to third after causing interference to the subsequent Prix de Sandringham winner Impressionnante, with Tie Black awarded the race. Price Tag gained compensation at the top level when winning the Matriarch Stakes on her US debut for Bobby Frankel. Prix Saint-Alary winner **Germance** fared best of the French-trained fillies in the Prix de Diane, taking second place behind Confidential Lady, while second places in the Prix de Malleret, Prix de Psyche and Prix de Royallieu showed **Lahudood** to be another of the better middle-distance fillies. The previous season's Prix Robert Papin winner **New Girlfriend** proved best when dropped back to sprinting from a mile, winning the Prix de Seine-et-Oise in the autumn.

Rail Link owed his third-string status in Andre Fabre's Arc team to the presence of top-class older horses **Hurricane Run** and **Shirocco**, winners of the Arc and Breeders' Cup Turf respectively in 2005. The pair were kept apart for much of the latest season. Hurricane Run's four-year-old season followed an identical path to that of Montjeu six years earlier. Things went less smoothly than they had for his sire though, and while he emulated Montjeu by winning the Tattersalls Gold Cup and King George VI and Queen Elizabeth Stakes, he suffered a surprise defeat in the Grand Prix de Saint-Cloud and went down by a neck to Shirocco when their paths crossed in what proved a less than full-blooded encounter in the Prix Foy. Hurricane Run's form tailed off in the autumn, much as Montjeu's had done, though he took third place in the Arc (albeit on Deep Impact's disqualification) and Champion Stakes. Shirocco proved even more disappointing in the Arc than Hurricane Run but that was his only defeat of the year. Prior to the Foy, Shirocco had won both his starts in Britain, the Jockey Club Stakes and Coronation Cup, giving his trainer a sixth win in the latter race. Six-year-old mare **Pride** ensured that the Fabre pair did not have a monopoly on top-level middle-distance success among France's older horses. As well as getting up late to beat Hurricane Run in the Grand Prix de Saint-Cloud, she too gained a Group 1 success in Britain when winning the Champion Stakes, and bowed out with a narrow win in the Hong Kong Cup, going one better than her second places at both Newmarket and Sha Tin the year before. After finishing third in the Prix Foy, Pride also improved greatly on her two previous efforts in the Arc when failing by just a neck to overhaul Rail Link.

The Baron von Ullmann-owned Shirocco had begun his career in Germany, and **Manduro**, in the same ownership, was among several German horses to move to Andre Fabre prior to the latest season. He made a winning debut in France, getting first run on the subsequent five-length Prix Ganay winner **Corre Caminos** in the Prix d'Harcourt. The rest of Manduro's season resulted in a frustrating series of placed efforts, including when second to **Laverock** in the Prix d'Ispahan and third in the Prince of Wales's Stakes, and Manduro gave the impression a mile was barely enough of a test for him later in the year despite good runs in the Jacques le Marois and Prix du Moulin. Laverock was not seen to best effect on his visit to Britain in the Juddmonte International, but had been third in the Grand Prix de Saint-Cloud earlier in the summer and he won a second Group 1 when successful in the Gran Premio del Jockey Club Italiano at Milan. Also contributing to a good year for trainer Carlos Laffon-Parias was **Krataios**, winner of the Prix du Muguet before finishing third to his stable-companion in the Ispahan. Unusually, there were few other older milers of real note, though **Svedov** and **Apsis** beat smart fields in the Prix Edmond Blanc and Prix du Chemin de Fer du Nord respectively.

Among others over middle distances, **Touch of Land** won the Grand Prix de Vichy for the second year running (he also won the Group 2 Jebel Hatta at Nad Al Sheba early in the year), while another to gain a repeat win was **Policy Maker** who added to his 2004 success in the Grand Prix de Chantilly. Policy Maker was stepped up in trip later in the year but failed to fill the gap left by his former stable-companion Westerner at the top of the staying tree. **Reefscape** looked a good candidate to be France's top stayer at the start of the season, and while he failed to win, his second to Yeats in the Gold Cup was a good effort. Reefscape's relative **Bellamy Cay** has been a steadily progressive type for the same connections (Andre Fabre/Khalid Abdulla) and he looks set for a good season in staying events in 2007 after ending the year with second place in the Prix Royal-Oak. A creditable fourth in the same race was front-runner **Lord du Sud** who had Policy Maker and Reefscape among his victims when successful in the Prix Kergorlay on his favoured soft ground at Deauville.

In contrast to the three-year-old fillies, there was more strength in the older fillies/mares division behind clear leader Pride. Among them, **Montare** and **Shamdala** were two more of the leading stayers. Shamdala beat Montare a nose in the Prix Vicomtesse Vigier, and after dropping back to a mile and a half to win the Gran Premio di Milano (and running poorly in the Yorkshire Oaks for the second year running), Shamdala was returned to longer trips in the autumn, running a good second to Sergeant Cecil in the Prix du Cadran and looking unlucky not to make the frame behind Montare in the Prix Royal-Oak, before taking third place in the Hong Kong Vase. After her narrow defeat to Shamdala, Montare was second in three more pattern races, behind Bellamy Cay in the Maurice de Nieuil, **Freedonia** in the Prix de Pomone, and Mandesha in the Vermeille, but as in her three-year-old season, Montare came good in the autumn when re-fitted with cheekpieces, winning the Prix de Royallieu before following up in the Royal-Oak. **Satwa Queen** showed improved form as a four-year-old, finishing runner-up twice in Dubai, then winning the Prix Jean Romanet at Deauville from **Sweet Stream** before finding only Mandesha too good in the Prix de l'Opera.

France's older sprinters were headed by **Linngari**, a surprise perhaps to those who remembered him as a smart mile/nine-furlong winner for Sir Michael Stoute in 2005. Linngari was successful over similar trips in Dubai early in the year but did well back over shorter distances when moved to Diego Lowther in France in the summer, winning Germany's top sprint, the Goldene Peitsche at Baden-Baden, before dead-heating for second in the Prix de la Foret and coming out the best horse at the weights when fourth in the Prix de Seine-et-Oise at Maisons-Laffitte. **Satri** was another to do well when dropped in trip, winning the Prix du Palais-Royal over seven furlongs and finishing second in the Maurice de Gheest.

French two-year-olds struggled in their top juvenile events, failing to win any of their five Group 1 events or either of the Group 2 races. There were still some smart youngsters in evidence though, and in any case, lack of success at pattern level at two does not entail a poor crop of three-year-olds the following season given that those who excel at three (Rail Link and Mandesha good examples in the latest season) have often not even raced as juveniles. Confirmed front-runner **Spirit One** ran away with a listed race at Deauville and the Prix des Chenes at Longchamp by a combined total of fourteen lengths but had his limitations exposed in two tries in Group 1 company at Saint-Cloud, running his better race there when beaten a head by Mount Nelson in the Criterium International. **Battle Paint** was another to find a Ballydoyle colt too strong when second to Holy Roman Emperor in the Prix Jean-Luc Lagardere, for which the previously-unbeaten Prix La Rochette winner **Visionario** (out of a half-sister to Visindar) started favourite but finished only sixth. The same race saw **Sandwaki** finishing well beaten; he had been the speediest of the early-season juveniles, winning the Prix du Bois. **Magic America** had the best form among the fillies. She was placed in the Prix Robert Papin and Prix Morny and shaped better than the bare result when sixth in the Cheveley Park Stakes, but looked much better suited by the step up to seven furlongs when winning the Prix Miesque at Maisons-Laffitte on her final start. **Legerete** fared best of the French-trained fillies when third in the Prix Marcel Boussac and she looks capable of progressing further at three. Outside pattern company, Royal And Regal (rated 97P) caught the eye in no uncertain terms on his debut before winning a minor event at Saint-Cloud in smooth fashion, and he looks an excellent three-year-old prospect for Andre Fabre, while US Ranger (also 97P) was unbeaten in three starts in the south-west for Jean-Claude Rouget and looks another capable of making his mark in pattern company.

Two-Year-Olds				
114	Battle Paint	103	Cicerole (f)	
113	Spirit One	103	Nuqoosh (f)	
112	Magic America (f)	102p	Law Lord	
109p	Visionario	102p	Spycrawler	
109	Sandwaki	102	Finikas	
108	Friston Forest	102	*Optari	
108	Makaan	102	Poltava (f)	
107p	Legerete (f)	101	Beta (f)	
106	Charlotte O Fraise (f)	101	Damdam	
106	Holocene	101	Kahyasola (f)	
105p	Chinandega (f)	101	Out of Time (f)	
105p	Just Little (f)	101	Russian Desert	
105	Beauty Is Truth (f)	101	San Domenico	
104	Iron Lips (f)	101	Vadapolina (f)	
103p	Calbuco (f)	100p	Prairie Spirit	
103p	Literato	100	Ikat (f)	

98	Zut Alors (f)		
98	Mpumalanga (f)		
97	Sismix (f)		
95	Cervinio		

Three-Year-Olds	
132	Rail Link
124	Mandesha (f)
123	Best Name
123	Stormy River
122	Irish Wells
121	Marchand d'Or
120	Gentlewave
118	Biniou
118	Darsi
118	Kentucky Dynamite
118	Visindar

117	*Dilek	
117	*Grand Couturier	
117	Passager	
117	Sudan	
116p	Daramsar	
116	Arras	
116	Garnica	
116	Linda's Lad	
116§	Numide	
115	Luisant	
115	New Girlfriend (f)	
115	*Price Tag (f)	
114	Baby First	
114	Boris de Deauville	
114	Hello Sunday	
114	Impressionnante (f)	
114	Lahudood (f)	
113	Barastraight	
113	Germance (f)	
113	Gwenseb (f)	
113	*Mauralakana (f)	
113	Vendangeur	
112	Alix Road (f)	
112	Alloway (f)	
112	Getaway	
112	Gravitas	
112	Kendargent	
112	Poquelin	
112	*Porto Santo	
112	Racinger	
112	Sanaya (f)	
111	*Chaibia (f)	
111	Histoire de Moeurs (f)	
111	Wingspan (f)	
110	Blue Damask	
110	Champs Elysees	
110	Miss Salvador (f)	
110	Ponte Tresa (f)	
110	*Quiet Royal (f)	
110	Tie Black (f)	
109	Aigle D'Or	
109	*Grande Melody (f)	
109	*Oh So Awesome	
109	Princesse Dansante (f)	
108	Carlotamix	
108	Daltaya (f)	
108	Dynaforce (f)	
108	Epatha (f)	
108	Headache	
108	Kachgai	
108	Mary Louhana (f)	
108	Minatlya (f)	
108	Multiplex	
108	Mussoorie (f)	
108	On A Cloud (f)	
108	Riche Americaine (f)	
108	Silva (f)	
107	Danzon (f)	
107	Grey Mystique (f)	
107	Indianski	
107	Mednaya (f)	

107	Penchee (f)	
107	*Phantom Rose (f)	
107	The West's Awake	
107?	*Light of Joy	
106	Dream In Blue	
106	Fauvelia (f)	
106	Fenice	
106	Grigorieva (f)	
106	Kersimon	
106	Onerous	
106	Sabasha (f)	
106	Young Poli	
105	Armand	
105	Balius	
105	Bremen	
105	Britannic	
105	Grand Vadla (f)	
105	Heaven's Cause (f)	
105	Mysterious Lina (f)	
105	Nordic Thunder	
105	Rhenus	
105	Sirene Doloise (f)	
105	Sister Trouble (f)	

104	*Ballet Pacifica (f)	
104	Echoes Rock	
103	Anna Mona (f)	

Older Horses

130	Hurricane Run	
129	Shirocco	
128	Pride (f)	
124	Corre Caminos	
123	Laverock	
123	Manduro	
121	Krataios	
120	*Linngari	
120	Satwa Queen (f)	
119	*Geordieland	
119	*Irridescence (f)	
119	Policy Maker	
118	Bellamy Cay	
118	Reefscape	
118	Touch of Land	
117	Apsis	
117	Freedonia (f)	
117	Sweet Stream (f)	
116	Archange d'Or	
116	*Kendor Dine	
116	Lord du Sud	
116	Montare (f)	
116	*Oracle West	
116	Salutino	
116	Satri	
116	Svedov	
115	Advice	
115	*Art Master	
115	Helios Quercus	
115	Magadino	
115	Ostankino	
115	Paita (f)	
115	Reve de Paix	
115	Shamdala (f)	

115	Turtle Bowl	
114	Early March	
114	Ratio	
114	*Royal Highness (f)	
114	Valentino	
113	Doctor Dino	
113	Gharir	
113	Marend	
113	Ruwi	
112	Afaf (f)	
112	Kocab	
112	Latona (f)	
112	Musical Way (f)	
112	Petite Speciale (f)	
112	Willywell	
111	Abundance (f)	
111	In Clover (f)	
111	Mister Conway	
111	Runaway	
111	Soledad	
111	Tycoon's Hill	
110	Annenkov	
110	Bastet (f)	
110	Rageman	
110	Special Kaldoun	
110	Ysoldina (f)	
109	Billy Allen	
109	Blip	
109	Breath Of Love (f)	
109	Goetot	
109	Gold Sound	
109	*Jersey Bounce	
109	*Karlo Guitar	
109	Le Carre	
109	Mister Charm	
109	Poly Dance	
109	Ricine (f)	
109d	Silver Cross	
108	Atlantic Air	
108	Mosaic	
108	Musketier	
108	Sendalam	
108	Vatori	
107	Elasos	
107	Kalahari King	
107	Kavafi	
107	Mullins Bay	
107	Nid d'Abeilles	
107	*Quinquin The King	
107	Ridaar	
107	Special Envoy	
107	Walk In The Park	
106	Howard Le Canard	
105	Chopastair	
105	Macleya (f)	
105	Malikhan	
105	My Man	
105	Solsiste	

104	Together (f)	
102	Chantilly Beauty (f)	

GERMANY   Unusually, it was a miler rather than a middle-distance horse who proved Germany's best three-year-old colt. **Lateral** had been unbeaten at two, when his wins included the Gran Criterium, a race which proved a much stronger contest than the four-runner field looked at the time. After being returned to a mile in the summer, Lateral won three pattern races, one at Hamburg and two at Cologne, his six-length win in the Grosse Europa-Meile at the latter track in September the best performance of the year by a German-trained three-year-old. The Gran Criterium third **Lord of England** also developed into a leading three-year-old, though the more important of his two pattern wins came in a slowly-run and substandard renewal of the Grosser Dallmayr-Preis, against older horses, over a mile and a quarter at Munich. A tendon injury prompted his retirement to stud.

Germany's hosting of the football World Cup caused the rescheduling of several races, notably the Deutsches Derby, which was put back three weeks from its usual early-July date. That enabled the Derby winner **Schiaparelli** to have an unorthodox prep race against older horses by finishing second in the Group 1 Deutschland-Preis. Schiaparelli was maintaining a fine family tradition when winning the Deutsches Derby, being a brother to the 2000 winner Samum and the 2002 runner-up Salve Regina. Neither Schiaparelli nor runner-up **Dickens** repeated their Derby form afterwards, both disappointing in the Grosser Preis von Baden, but Schiaparelli ended the season by winning the Deutsches St Leger. The now Group 3 event rarely figures in the schedule of German Derby winners these days, and Schiaparelli was the first to win both classics since Ordos in 1983. A substandard Grosser Preis von Baden was dominated by three-year-olds who had finished behind Schiaparelli in the Derby. Victory went to outsider **Prince Flori**, who had been well beaten at Hamburg, over **Oriental Tiger** and **Saddex**, third and fourth respectively in the Deutsches Derby.

Flashing Numbers was another leading German-trained colt, though he has never raced in his own country, and after starting the year in Dubai, put up his best effort when winning the Prix Eugene Adam at Maisons-Laffitte from Epsom Derby runner-up Dragon Dancer. **Aspectus** had been Germany's top two-year-old, and whilst only sixth in the Deutsches Derby, he too trained on well, finishing second in the Mehl-Mulhens-Rennen (2000 Guineas) to the British-trained Royal Power and winning the main Derby trial, the Union-Rennen at Cologne. **Wiesenpfad** was one of the more progressive colts later in the year, winning Group 3 events at Dusseldorf and Frankfurt on his last two starts.

Germany's three-year-old fillies lacked a clear leader and none made much of an impression on a wider stage. **Lolita** beat the subsequent Preis der Diana (Oaks) winner **Almerita** in the German 1000 Guineas, while the placed horses from the Diana, **Karavel** and **Nordtanzerin**, each won lesser pattern races against older horses in the autumn at Hoppegarten and Frankfurt respectively. **La Dancia** was a later developer and won four of her five starts, beating Nordtanzerin in a Group 3 event at Frankfurt to end the season.

There was little strength in depth among Germany's leading older middle-distance performers. Five-year-old **Egerton** was still Europe's best maiden on his return from

BMW Deutsches Derby, Hamburg—a later date than usual to avoid clashing with football's World Cup; Schiaparelli maintains his family's fine record in the race, winning from Dickens, Oriental Tiger and Saddex (rail)

Grosser Volkswagen Preis von Baden, Baden-Baden—Prince Flori overturns Deutsches Derby form with Oriental Tiger (rail) and Saddex (Schiaparelli managed only sixth)

missing all of 2005, but soon shed that tag before going on to win Hamburg's Hansa-Preis in July. His best effort came when second to the British-trained three-year-old Youmzain in the Preis von Europa at Cologne, almost matching the form he had shown when second, splitting Warrsan and Shirocco, in the Grosser Preis von Baden two years earlier. **Soldier Hollow** failed in his attempt to win a third successive Premio Roma, but typically for him, still hit top form in the second half of the year, finishing third in the Arlington Million before a defeat of his former-stable companion Manduro in the Prix Dollar at Longchamp. **Arcadio**, like Soldier Hollow trained by Peter Schiergen, won the Grosser Mercedes-Benz-Preis at Baden-Baden's May meeting over eleven furlongs. He did not show the same level of form over shorter trips subsequently, even when beating Soldier Hollow into second over a mile in the pferdewetten.de-Trophy at Cologne. **Donaldson** was the only German-trained older male horse to win a Group 1 event, when beating Schiaparelli in the Deutschland-Preis, but he did so setting a slow pace and failed by a long way to repeat the form. Unusually for a Group 1 winner, he was gelded later in the season.

Lucky Strike had dominated Germany's top sprints in 2005, but he was less of a force in the latest season. **Soave** and **Donatello** beat him into third in the Benazet-Rennen at Baden-Baden in May, and the same pair were placed (Donatello coming out the better both times) behind French-trained horses in both the Goldene Peitsche and Badener Sprint-Cup at the same course later in the year. Both Soave and Donatello ended the year winning in listed company. Donatello was trained by Werner Baltromei who also had Germany's best stayer in his stable, **Le Miracle**. There are few opportunities for good stayers in Germany, and Le Miracle was campaigned entirely in France, where progressed from claimers to win the Prix Gladiateur and finish third in the Prix du Cadran. Another to do well outside Germany was the leading older filly **Floriot**. She did all her winning in Italy, culminating in a defeat of the Prix de Diane winner Confidential Lady in the Premio Lydia Tesio at Rome. Incidentally, Floriot, along with the above-mentioned Schiaparelli, Arcadio, Le Miracle and Karavel, plus the likes of Shirocco, Manduro, Gentlewave and Getaway elsewhere in Europe, were among those to contribute to a tremendously successful season for their sire Monsun, champion for the year in both Germany and Italy.

Germany's top two-year-old races went to **Molly Max** and **Shane**, the former a colt and the latter a filly despite their names. Molly Max defeated the Maurice-Lacroix Trophy winner **Global Dream** in the Preis des Winterfavoriten, while Shane, a sister to the 2004 German 1000 Guineas winner Shapira, was bought by Godolphin after her win in the Preis der Winterkonigin. Two more German youngsters, both fillies, were successful in pattern company abroad, with **Scoubidou** taking the Premio Dormello at Milan and **Boccassini** gaining a noteworthy success in the Prix Robert Papin at Maisons-Laffitte.

Two-Year-Olds
106p	Shane (f)
105	Boccassini (f)
103p	Molly Max
102p	Lowenherz
102	Global Dream
102	Scoubidou (f)
101p	Next Style
100	Carolines Secret (f)
100	Chantra (f)
100	Touch My Soul (f)
99+	Kaleo
99	Lucky It Is
99	Sugar Baby Love (f)
99	Sybilia (f)
98	Adamantinos
98	Ailton
97	Forthe Millionkiss
97	Persian Storm
95	Hashbrown (f)

Three-Year-Olds
123	Lateral
119	Lord Of England
119	Prince Flori
116	Flashing Numbers
116	Oriental Tiger
116	Schiaparelli
115	Dickens
114	Aspectus
114	Wiesenpfad
113	Electric Beat
113	Saddex
112	Lauro
112	Lucidor
111	Lolita (f)
110p	Art Attack
110	Almerita (f)
110	Imonso
110	La Dancia (f)
110	*Proudinsky (f)
110	Silex
109	Dark Dancer
109	Karavel (f)

109	Waleria (f)
108	Mannico
108	N'Oubliez Jamais
108	Turning Light (f)
107	Nordtanzerin (f)
107	Quelle Amore (f)
107	Sexy Lady (f)
107	Signum
106	Fantastica (f)
105	Dwilano
105	Fair Breeze (f)
105	Inter Mondo
105	Sommertag
105	Ticinella (f)
105	Vega's Lord

104	Elcanos
103	Litalia (f)
101	Rovana Jowe (f)
100	Ioannina (f)
100	Mrs Snow (f)
100	Mharadono
91	Lasira (f)

Older Horses
122	Arcadio
122	Egerton
119	Soldier Hollow
118	Floriot (f)
117	Le Miracle
116	Konig Turf
115	Donatello
115	Fight Club
115	Soave
114	Donaldson
114	Wurfscheibe (f)
113	Lucky Strike
113	Proudance
113?	Loup de Mer
112p	Quijano
112	All Spirit
112	Idealist
112	Lazio
111	Bussoni

111	Matrix
111	Mohandas
111	Ryono
111	Simonas
111	Toylsome
111	Willingly
110	Apeiron
110	Cliffrose (f)
110	Expensive Dream
110	Kiton
110	Sacho
109	Delora (f)
109	Encinas
109	Madresal
109	Molly Art (f)
109	White Lightning
108	Bailamos
107	Brisant
107	Chiron
107	Laredo Sound
107	Omasheriff
107	Sculpted (f)
107	*Tirwanako
106	Alpacco
106	Anatola (f)
106	El Tango
106	Fulminant
106	Gandolfino
106	Santiago Atitlan
106	Shinko's Best
106	The Spring Flower (f)
106d	Glad To Be Fast
105	Carus
105	Diable
105	Grantley
105	*Near Honor
105	Senex
105	Soterio
105?	Evinado

104	Wellola (f)
103	Apollo Star
102	Lord Areion
101	Golden Rose (f)

ITALY At the start of the season it was hard to know where Italy's best horse was going to come from. Of the leading horses from 2005, Electrocutionist had joined Godolphin and Altieri had retired to stud, while the three-year-old crop from the previous season promised little. However, the Premio Parioli (2000 Guineas) winner and Derby Italiano runner-up **Ramonti** improved into a very smart miler as a four-year-old, winning five races. They included the Premio Emilio Turati at Milan in June, and the Premio Vittorio di Capua (his best effort) and the Premio Ribot at Rome in the autumn. The front-running Ramonti was below form in the Prix Jacques le Marois on his first start outside Italy, but fared better when filling third place in the Hong Kong Mile at the end of the year. On home turf he is yet to finish worse than second. Ramonti's record attracted the attention of Godolphin, for whom he will be racing in 2007. **Distant Way** had been Italy's top miler in 2005 and returned better than ever to complete a hat-trick at Rome, which included a defeat of Ramonti in a nine-furlong listed race (giving that rival 7 lb) and a Group 1 win in the Premio Presidente della Repubblica. Distant Way was not in the same form in the autumn however, finishing only fourth to Ramonti in the Vittorio di Capua and then third in the Premio Roma.

Premio Vittorio di Capua, Milan—the previous year's Premio Parioli winner Ramonti gets the better of British-trained challengers Notability and Caradak (right)

Fair Nashwan, third in the Oaks d'Italia in 2005, looked no better than useful on most of her form, including when beating **Groom Tesse**, who gave her 7 lb, in the Premio Federico Tesio at Milan in October. But on her next start, she excelled herself in the Gran Premio del Jockey Club Italiano, going down by a head to the French-trained Laverock. The subsequent Premio Roma winner Cherry Mix was behind her in third, but Fair Nashwan could finish only seventh in that race herself on her final start. The Federico Tesio runner-up Groom Tesse returned to the sort of form which had won him the Derby Italiano in 2004. He was also third in the Presidente della Repubblica and runner-up in the Gran Premio di Milano and Grand Prix de Deauville, as well as successful in the Premio Carlo d'Alessio at Rome in May. **Exhibit One** had won only a Catterick maiden for Sir Michael Stoute in 2005 but made into a smart filly for her new trainer Valfredo Valiani. She won the Premio Paolo Mezzanotte at Milan (from Germany's subsequent Premio Lydia Tesio winner Floriot) and made the frame in the Prix de Pomone at Deauville and the Yorkshire Oaks, the latter a race her stable had won with Super Tassa in 2001.

Italy's sprinting honours were evenly spread, with all three pattern races kept at home. **Kuaicoss** defeated **Krisman** in the Premio Tudini in May and Krisman was also runner-up to the three-year-old filly **Champion Place** in the Premio Omenoni later in the year, but the first two from the Omenoni were below form behind **Patapan** in the Premio Umbria in November.

The three-year-olds were headed by the tough filly **Dionisia**. Already successful four times in listed company as a two-year-old, she won four of her five starts on her return at three, meeting her only defeat in the Premio Regina Elena (1000 Guineas) won by **Windhuk**, but putting up much her best effort to win the Oaks d'Italia by six lengths. She subsequently joined Luca Cumani but finished last in the Prix de l'Opera on her only start afterwards. The Premio Parioli winner **Rattle And Hum** failed to stay in the Derby Italiano, in which **Storm Mountain** fared best of the home-trained colts behind impressive French-trained winner Gentlewave. Italy's classics generally struggle to attract quality fields, and the downgrading for 2007 of both Guineas from Group 2 to Group 3 and the Oaks from Group 1 to Group 2 is a move which better reflects the status of those races.

The early-season form of **Golden Titus** still made him the leading two-year-old by the end of the year. He won his first three starts, including the Premio Primi Passi at

Premio Parioli ABN Amro Bank, Rome—
the Italian version of the Two Thousand Guineas goes to the smart Rattle And Hum (noseband),
with the only overseas challenger Royal Power (striped sleeves) taking second

Milan, and lost out by just a head to the German filly Boccassini in the Prix Robert Papin. Golden Titus was not discredited later in either the Prix Morny or the Gran Criterium; in the latter event he fared best of the Italian colts in fourth place despite the mile trip stretching his stamina. **Palin** was another to run well in France, finishing third in the Prix du Bois, and he later won a five-furlong listed event at Rome in the autumn. The most interesting prospect among the Italian two-year-olds looks to be **Il Cadetto**. He was first past the post in his only two starts at Rome, both by five lengths or so, though was reported to have tested positive after the Premio Guido Berardelli, which he won from **Rob's Love**, who had himself been a four-length winner of a listed race on his previous outing.

Two-Year-Olds					
107	Golden Titus	92	Project Dane	99	Wickwing (f)
106p	Il Cadetto				
102	Palin	91	Amante Latino	**Older Horses**	
102	Rob's Love			122	Ramonti
100	Donoma (f)			120	Fair Nashwan (f)
99	Titus Shadow	**Three-Year-Olds**		119	Distant Way
97	Golden Dynamic	114	*Dionisia (f)	114	Exhibit One (f)
97	Moriwood	112	Storm Mountain	114	Groom Tesse
95	Muccia (f)	111	Rattle And Hum	111	Krisman
94p	Men's Magazine	109	Champion Place (f)	111	Kuaicoss (f)
94	Iuturna (f)	107	Agata Laguna (f)	110	Bening
94	Walharer	107	Great Uncle Ted	110	Patapan
94	Xenes	107	Miles Gloriosus	109	Crucial
93	Depp	107	Windhuk (f)	109	Dream Impact
93	Docksil (f)	106	Golden West	108	Cocodrail
93	Next King	106	*Sabana Perdida (f)	107	Desert Quiet (f)
93	Polar Wind	106	Sound of Desert	107	Urgente
93	Troppo Bello (f)	105	Rockmaster	106	Los Bonitos
92	Ancus Martius	105	Velvet Revolver (f)	106	Mister Fasliyev
92	Joybee			105	Montalegre
92	Noble Hero (f)	104	Musa Golosa (f)		
92	Notturno di Chopin	104	*Rumsfeld	103	Kykuit (f)
		104	Twardowska (f)	101	La Vriga (f)
		102	Adorabile Fong	97	Mary Pekan (f)

SCANDINAVIA A sixth race was added to Scandinavia's pattern-race programme in 2006, with the promotion of the Stockholms Stora Pris from listed to Group 3 status. Run at Taby in May over almost ten furlongs, it was won by Scandinavia's top-rated horse of the year **Jubilation** from **Fly Society**. Jubilation was also first past the post in a listed race over a mile at Ovrevoll but subsequently disqualified. He had won Scandinavia's other pattern race over an intermediate trip, the Marit Sveaas Minnelop at Ovrevoll, in 2005, but was a disappointing favourite for the latest renewal which went to the Danish-trained **Binary File** ahead of the ex-French-trained colt **Crimson And Gold**. Binary File also won in listed company earlier in the year on both turf and dirt, including the valuable Pramms Memorial at Jagersro, the final leg of the European All-Weather Series, by five lengths from the Richard Hannon-trained Red Spell. In addition to her third place in the Stora Pris, the mare **Funny Legend** went one better than in 2005 by winning four listed races at a mile/extended nine furlongs, including repeating her successes at Taby (twice) and Ovrevoll in the autumn. Mainly a dirt performer, **Maybach** has won over longer distances in the past but gained his two wins for the year over a mile at Taby, including in a listed event, before finishing six lengths second to the leading Scandinavian three-year-old **Highway** in a similar race at Jagersro, where Svenskt Derby winner Mad Dog Slew (101) was only fourth.

Traditionally, Scandinavia has had a number of smart performers over a mile and a half, but that was a notably weak division in 2006. That was evident from Collier Hill's nine-length win in the Stockholm Cup International (a race he also won in 2004) in which Binary File still managed to finish second despite running below form over a trip beyond his best. The other mile and a half Group 3 event, the Scandinavian Open Championship at Copenhagen, failed to attract foreign interest and went to the mare **Halfsong** (winning her twelfth race) from **Zenato** and **Alpino Chileno**, who had finished third and first respectively in the same race twelve months earlier.

Over sprint trips, the Norwegian-trained filly **Solvana** had the best record in the two Group 3 contests, beaten half a length into second in both the Polar Cup at Ovrevoll (behind French filly Ricine) and in the Taby Open Sprint Championship. However, several male rivals had better form, including the ten-year-old winner of the Taby Open Sprint, **Bellamont Forest**. Another ten-year-old still going strong was the remarkable **Waquaas**, who took his win tally to seventeen in the latest season, adding two more listed races at Taby and Ovrevoll to his record and finishing third in the Polar Cup. The previous season's Taby Open Sprint winner **Pipoldchap** proved disappointing in both the Group 3 sprints but he won two listed races on dirt at Jagersro, chased home on the second occasion by his stable-companions **Media Hora** and **Aramus**.

Three-Year-Old			109	Maybach	106	Salt Track
110	Highway		109	Media Hora	106	Sibelius
			109	Zenato	106	Solvana (f)
Older Horses			108	Fly Society	106	Xstase (f)
114	Jubilation		108	Muskateer Steel	105	Danish Shopping (f)
112	Bellamont Forest		107	Alpino Chileno	105	Halfsong (f)
112	Binary File		107	Aramus	105	Tiberius Caesar
110	Pipoldchap		107	Funny Legend (f)		
110	Waquaas		107	Mambo King	102	Day Walker
109	Crimson And Gold		106	Hide And Seek		

The following European-trained horses also achieved significant ratings in major races

Two-Year-Olds		115	Ribella (f) (Turkey)	105	Polish Magic
105p	Midnight Beauty (Spain)	114	Champs To Champs (Turkey)		(Slovakia)
104	Stoneside (Spain)	114	Song Writer (Switzerland)		
		113	Win River Win (Turkey)		
Three-Year-Olds					
111	Scarface (Turkey)	112	Sabirli (Turkey)		
110	Kurtiniadis (Turkey)	110	Grand Ekinoks (Turkey)		
Older Horses					
116	Kaneko (Turkey)	107	Tunduru (Spain)		

UNITED ARAB EMIRATES   Whilst the Dubai World Cup started out as easily the most valuable and important race at the world's richest race meeting, the two turf events on the same card, the Dubai Sheema Classic over a mile and a half and the Dubai Duty

Dubai Golden Shaheen Sponsored By Gulf News, Nad Al Sheba—
Proud Tower Too leads home a 1,2,3,4,5 for American-trained sprinters
ahead of subsequent Breeders' Cup Sprint winner Thor's Echo

Free over almost nine furlongs, have quickly grown in stature to the extent that they can no longer be viewed as mere supporting acts. Increased prize money for the latest World Cup meeting made them the richest turf races ever run (each worth more than £1.7m to the winner) and judged both on level of form required to win and strength in depth of the fields behind the winner, neither race could be considered a lesser event than the World Cup itself. Heart's Cry's defeat of Collier Hill (placed for the second year running, with Ouija Board fourth) in the Sheema Classic was every bit as good a performance as Electrocutionist's win in the World Cup, while David Junior put up a top-class effort (the best by a British-trained horse anywhere in the world in 2006) in the Duty Free to beat the subsequent Arlington Million winner The Tin Man.

The UAE Derby proved another highly significant contest on World Cup night, with **Discreet Cat** coasting home by six lengths from stable-companion **Testimony** over a field which included the subsequent Breeders' Cup Classic winner Invasor back in fourth. Neither colt met with defeat subsequently in American campaigns as they both developed into top performers on dirt, and an intriguing rematch looks on the cards in the 2007 Dubai World Cup. Another subsequent Breeders' Cup winner on show at the latest World Cup meeting was Sprint winner Thor's Echo, runner-up to Proud Tower Too in an all-American finish to the Dubai Golden Shaheen, six of the last seven runnings of that contest going to a US-trained sprinter. The other race on World Cup night, the Godolphin Mile, went to Heart's Cry's stable-companion Utopia, who subsequently joined Godolphin, but didn't race for them.

Godolphin's two winners on World Cup night, **Electrocutionist** and Discreet Cat, had each been successful in prep races earlier at the Dubai International Racing Carnival (Electrocutionist impressive on his dirt debut in Round III of the Maktoum Challenge), but in general, horses that had been competing successfully earlier at the Carnival found the stronger competition of the races on World Cup night beyond them.

In its third year in 2006, the Carnival retained much the same format as previous years, though with some of the non-handicap events upgraded. British stables again fared well, winning sixteen races in addition to David Junior's Dubai Duty Free. Clive Brittain, Mick Channon and Jeremy Noseda won three races apiece, Noseda's Vague winning twice, including the listed UAE 1000 Guineas. Other notable British-trained winners were the John Hills-trained Clinet, successful twice, including in the listed Cape Verdi for older fillies, and Gerard Butler's Jack Sullivan who won Round II of the Maktoum Challenge for the second year running before finishing third in the Godolphin Mile.

South African Mike de Kock again brought the strongest team of horses among the international trainers present in Dubai. They included **Oracle West**, the only horse to win three races at the Carnival and who completed a hat-trick in the Group 3 Dubai City of Gold before finishing down the field in the Sheema Classic, in which stablemate **Falstaff**, a handicap winner earlier at the Carnival, finished a good third. His other smart stable-companions included the mare **Irridescence** (winner of a listed event before injuring herself in the paddock prior to her intended run in the Duty Free) and handicap winners **Candidato Roy** (sprinter), **Tyson** (who won twice in taking style, and later joined Venetia Williams) and **Evil Knievel**. Another South African-trained horse to do well was **Linngari** from the Herman Brown stable. The former Sir Michael Stoute-trained colt disappointed in the Duty Free but had won two group races prior to that, the Al Rashidiya (from Mike de Kock's **Greys Inn**) and the Al Fahidi Fort. Brown was also responsible for the listed UAE Oaks winner Imperial Ice (rated 98).

One of the best performances at the Carnival outside World Cup night came from Brazilian sprinter **Heart Alone** who gave weight and a sound beating to his rivals in the Group 3 Al Shindagha Sprint on dirt, though he proved a big disappointment in the Golden Shaheen on his first start for local trainer Ismail Mohammed. Two more South American imports to do well were stable-companions **Gold For Sale** and **Simpatico Bribon** representing Saudi-based trainer Ian Jory. Gold For Sale earned his place in the UAE Derby by winning the UAE 2000 Guineas, while Simpatico Bribon joined him in the Derby after winning the main trial, the Al Bastikiya, impressively. However, neither colt gave his running in the Derby itself. Turkey was again represented by some smart horses, with Sabirli and Win River Win both successful in handicaps, the latter going on to finish second in the Godolphin Mile.

Locally-trained horses had their share of success at the Carnival too. Mile/nine-furlong turf performer **Seihali** was better than ever in the latest season, winning at the Carnival for the third year running before taking a good third place in the Dubai Duty Free. Another Carnival regular is dirt specialist **Tropical Star** whose two wins included the Group 3 Mahab Al Shimaal over six furlongs. Other important winners for Dubai stables were **Blatant**, a former Godolphin pacemaker, successful in Round I of the Maktoum Challenge and second in Round II (with **Eccentric** third behind the British-trained Jack Sullivan), and **Marbush**, who was a wide-margin winner of the main trial for the Godolphin Mile, the Group 3 Burj Nahaar. **Caesar Beware** and **Shakis** put up a couple of the best performances in handicaps at the Carnival when winning turf events over seven and a half and ten furlongs respectively. Smart seven-furlong/mile performer **King Jock** was in the care of Erwan Charpy when winning the opening race of the 2006 Carnival, and also won two listed races at Abu Dhabi late in the year at the beginning of the new Emirates season for Irish trainer Robbie Osborne.

Godolphin Mile Sponsored By Jebel Ali International Hotels, Nad Al Sheba—with six countries represented, victory goes to front-running Japanese challenger Utopia

The performances reviewed here are those that took place in the calendar year 2006. Horses which were trained and raced in the UAE but showed significantly better form elsewhere are not included in the list below.

Three-Year-Olds

127p	*Discreet Cat
109	*Where's That Tiger
108	*Testimony

Older Horses

127	*Electrocutionist
120	*Heart Alone
120	*Linngari
119	Caesar Beware
119	*Falstaff
119	*Irridescence (f)
119	Seihali
119	Shakis
117	Blatant
117	*Eccentric
117	*Greys Inn
117	*King Jock
117	*Tyson
116	*Oracle West
116	*Simpatico Bribon
116	Tropical Star
115	*Candidato Roy
115	*Chiquitin
115	*Etesaal
115	*Evil Knievel
115	Marbush
114	*Excalibur
114	Iqte Saab

114	National Captain
114	Parole Board
114	Shanty Star
114	Winisk River
113	Brunel
113	Go For Gold
112	Blue On Blues
112	Elmustanser
112	*Kodiac
112	Remaadd
111	Botanical
111	Dubai Honor
111	Royal Prince
111	Singing Poet
111	T-Bird
111	*Valixir
111?	Holiday Camp
110	Cartography
110	*Gold For Sale
110	Howick Falls
110	Trademark
109	*Desert Destiny
109	*Jersey Bounce
109	Le Prince Charmant
109	Little Jim
109	Morshdi
109	Parnassus
109	*Punch Punch
109	*Safe Structure
109	So Will I

109	Thajja
109	*Tiger Shark
108	*Azul da Guanabara
108	Corriolanus
108	Doctor Hilary
108	Earl's Court
108	Lundy's Lane
108	Mutafanen
108	Mutasallil
108	Parasol
108	Raging Creek
108	Sabbeeh
108	Stetchworth Prince
107	*Key of Destiny
107	Mandobi
107	Rock Music
106	Mogaamer
106	Sea Hunter
106	Sevillano
106	*Sir Edwin Landseer
105	Attilius
105	Bo Bid
105	*Brahminy Kite
105	Conroy
105	*Happy Pearl
105	*Lundy's Liability
105	*My Royal Captain
105	Rock Opera (f)
105	Three Graces

NORTH AMERICA   Since its inception with the equitrack surface at Lingfield in 1989, all-weather racing has become firmly established in Britain, to the extent that more than one in three races will take place on all-weather tracks in 2007. The notion that one day all-weather racing might also be successfully exported to the USA, home of racing on dirt, would have long been considered akin to taking coals to Newcastle. But 2006 will go down as the year in which the switch from traditional dirt tracks to what the Americans call 'synthetic' surfaces began to gather momentum. Dirt and all-weather surfaces might appear similar but they have different properties and are as distinct from each other as each is from turf. This is best appreciated after heavy rain, when a dirt track, unlike an all-weather one, will turn sloppy.

Polytrack was the first all-weather surface to gain a foothold in North America when it was installed on Keeneland's training track in September 2004. Twelve months later, Turfway Park became the first to adopt it as a racing surface, and in the autumn of 2006 Woodbine and then Keeneland followed suit. Keeneland staged the first Grade 1 event on Polytrack, the Lane's End Breeders' Futurity, in which the first three home went on to take the first three places in the Breeders' Cup Juvenile. Later in the year, Hollywood became the first of California's tracks to turn 'synthetic' when adopting Cushion Track. The California Horse Racing Board has decreed that all of the state's tracks must be synthetic by 2008, to which end Del Mar has announced its change to Polytrack and Golden Gate Fields to Tapeta, a surface originally perfected by Michael Dickinson at his own training establishment. Arlington is also due to install Polytrack in 2007 and the New York circuits are also expected to replace their dirt tracks in due course. The main motive for scrapping dirt in favour of all-weather surfaces is that the latter are already proving their worth in reducing greatly the incidences of horses breaking down in work or in races, an issue which was sadly highlighted twice in the latest season.

The serious leg injury sustained by the Kentucky Derby winner **Barbaro** in the early stages of the Preakness Stakes was a high-profile and unwelcome example of the sort of demands which dirt racing can place on its competitors. Barbaro survived lengthy surgery to mend multiple fractures to his off-hind and for a while looked on his way to making a recovery but ultimately was unable to overcome complications, including laminitis, and finally had to be put down in January 2007. Barbaro was a hot favourite for the Preakness after maintaining his unbeaten record in the Kentucky Derby in which his winning margin of six and a half lengths was the widest since Assault's eight-length victory in 1946. Barbaro recorded a top-class effort, a big improvement on his half-length defeat of **Sharp Humor** in the Florida Derby on his previous start.

After Churchill Downs, Barbaro was naturally seen as a potential Triple Crown winner, but while the Preakness saw the end of one top-class colt's career, it also marked the emergence of another at least as good. **Bernardini** didn't contest the Kentucky Derby but ran out a decisive winner of the Preakness from the gelding who had started favourite at Churchill Downs (after a nine and a quarter length win in the Grade 2 Illinois Derby), **Sweetnorthernsaint**. Given a break until Saratoga in the summer, Bernardini recorded wide-margin wins in the Grade 2 Jim Dandy Stakes and then the Travers Stakes, in the latter giving a seven and a half length beating to the Kentucky Derby and Belmont Stakes runner-up **Bluegrass Cat**, who had himself been a seven-length winner of the Haskell Invitational in the meantime. Going from strength to strength, Bernardini was left with two just smart older rivals to beat when Irish Derby/Champion Stakes winner Dylan Thomas failed comprehensively to take to the dirt in the Jockey Club Gold Cup at Belmont in October. Having now completed a six-timer, Bernardini started a short-priced favourite for the Breeders' Cup Classic but possibly took up the running too soon in a strongly-run race, having no answer to the length winner Invasor.

Subsequently retired to stud, the Sheikh Mohammed-owned Bernardini played a leading part in a particularly successful year in the USA for the Maktoum family. After finishing second to **Bob And John** in the Wood Memorial Stakes and dead-heating for fourth in the Kentucky Derby, Sheikh Hamdan's **Jazil** appreciated the greater test of stamina provided by the Belmont Stakes, in which the Florida Derby third **Sunriver** and Kentucky Derby third Steppenwolfer (rated 116) completed the frame behind Bluegrass

Kentucky Derby (Presented By Yum! Brands), Churchill Downs—
In a race sponsored for the first time, Barbaro wins easily, scoring by six and a half lengths,
the widest margin of victory in the race since 1946

Cat. Incidentally, no horse contested all three legs of the Triple Crown for the first time since 1983, while for the first time since 2000, each Triple Crown race was won by a different horse.

Jazil missed the remainder of the year due to injury, but stays in training along with **Discreet Cat**, who ran under the Godolphin banner at three. Unbeaten in six starts, Discreet Cat was given a light campaign but is yet to be extended, has already shown high-class form, and looks a most exciting prospect. Two wins in Dubai early in the year, including a six-length win in the UAE Derby, fuelled speculation that Discreet Cat might be aimed at the Kentucky Derby or Preakness Stakes, but he was rested instead for an autumn campaign which featured a ten and a quarter length win (giving between 8 and 10 lb to his rivals) in the Grade 2 Jerome Breeders' Cup Handicap at Belmont and a decisive beating of older rivals (again giving weight all round) in the Cigar Mile Handicap at Aqueduct.

Yet another leading colt in Maktoum ownership (like Jazil, trained by Kiaran McLaughlin) was high-class sprinter **Henny Hughes**. The 2005 Breeders' Cup Juvenile runner-up started favourite for the Breeders' Cup Sprint after being unbeaten for the year in three outings, including the King's Bishop Stakes at Saratoga and, against older horses, the Vosburgh Stakes at Belmont. However, he failed to travel with his usual fluency at Churchill Downs and trailed home on what proved to be his final start before retirement.

Three colts who emerged in the spring as leading Kentucky Derby contenders but failed to varying degrees at Churchill Downs were **Brother Derek**, **Lawyer Ron** and **Sinister Minister**. Brother Derek fared best of the trio, dead-heating for fourth in the Derby and running up to his best later in the year when fifth in the Breeders' Cup Classic. He had been ante-post favourite for the Kentucky Derby early in the year, when completing a hat-trick at Santa Anita, including a defeat of the Breeders' Cup Juvenile winner **Stevie Wonderboy** in a Grade 2 event and an all-the-way win in the Santa Anita Derby. Lawyer Ron, who had had a busy two-year-old campaign, had won his last six starts prior to the Kentucky Derby but was found to be injured after the race. Although well held in the Breeders' Cup Classic as well, he had returned to his best earlier in the autumn when second to **Strong Contender** in the Grade 2 Super Derby at Louisiana Downs. Strong Contender missed the Triple Crown races and the Breeders' Cup but he had won another

Preakness Stakes, Pimlico—Bernardini gives Sheikh Mohammed his first success in an American classic, though the race is marred by a serious injury to Barbaro

Grade 2 event in the summer, the Dwyer Stakes by almost eight lengths. Sinister Minister put up the most spectacular trial for the Kentucky Derby when making all for a near thirteen-length win in the Blue Grass Stakes at Keeneland (Strong Contender and Bluegrass Cat among those he ran off their feet) but finished well in rear at Churchill Downs.

The year's other high-profile accident which did no favours for the image of racing on dirt occurred on the even wider stage of the Breeders' Cup, leading three-year-old dirt filly **Pine Island** suffering fatal injuries in a fall in the Distaff. Out of a sister to the previous year's Distaff winner Pleasant Home, Pine Island had not finished worse than second in her six other starts. She showed promise when runner-up in the Mother Goose Stakes and Coaching Club American Oaks before defeating **Teammate** (the pair finishing clear both times) in the Alabama Stakes and Gazelle Stakes, performances which had her vying for favouritism in the Distaff. Tough front-runner **Bushfire** was below her best later in the year in the Gazelle Stakes and Breeders' Cup Distaff, but her defeat of Pine Island, with **Ready To Please** third, in the Mother Goose at Belmont in July was her third Grade 1 success of the year. She had earlier won the Ashland Stakes at Keeneland and the Acorn Stakes at Belmont (gamely, from **Hello Liberty**), with a third-place finish (demoted to sixth for causing interference) in the Kentucky Oaks in between.

The Kentucky Oaks had its longest-priced winner in the history of the race when 47/1-shot **Lemons Forever** came off a strong pace, but she was beaten in five more Grade 1s, her best efforts when fifth against older rivals in the Spinster Stakes and Breeders' Cup Distaff. Favourite **Balance** reportedly returned with a cut in the Kentucky Oaks, though she had also been a below-form favourite when third in the Ashland Stakes after early-season wins at Santa Anita in the Las Virgenes Stakes and Santa Anita Oaks. **Wonder Lady Anne L** was promoted to fourth in the Kentucky Oaks prior to her best effort when beating Pine Island in muddy conditions in the Coaching Club American Oaks, though that form was turned around substantially in the Alabama Stakes next time. Neither of the first two from the previous season's Breeders' Cup Juvenile Fillies made much of an impact at three. Winner Folklore was beaten in a Grade 2 at Santa Anita on her only appearance, while runner-up **Wild Fit** was placed behind Balance in her two Grade 1 wins at the same track.

Wait A While began the year in the company of the best dirt fillies, finishing second in the Ashland Stakes and promoted third in the Kentucky Oaks. But when switched to turf she was a clear-cut winner of all three of her starts prior to the Breeders' Cup and proved the best US-trained three-year-old filly on turf for some time. In the American Oaks at Hollywood she routed her rivals, who were headed by the Japanese filly Asahi Rising, and after a Grade 2 win at Saratoga, Wait A While impressed again when beating older fillies in the Yellow Ribbon Stakes. In the Breeders' Cup Filly & Mare Turf she looked like proving a big threat to the older mares but finished only fourth, lacking her usual turn of foot. As well as Wait A While, the Todd Pletcher stable also housed two more leading three-year-old fillies on turf. **Magnificent Song** had her stable-companion **Jade Queen** behind her in third in the Garden City Breeders' Cup Handicap at Belmont, with the latter going on to run well against older mares when filling the same position in the Flower Bowl Invitational. Canadian Horse of The Year **Arravale**, third in the American Oaks, went on to Grade 1 success in the Del Mar Oaks and E. P. Taylor Stakes, beating older rivals at Woodbine. Other fillies successful in Grade 1 company on turf were the unbeaten Queen Elizabeth II Challenge Cup winner **Vacare** and the Matriarch Stakes winner **Price Tag** who gave Bobby Frankel his seventh winner of the Hollywood contest in the last ten runnings on her first outing after leaving Pascal Bary in France.

Compared to the fillies, the three-year-old males on turf had fewer names of note but had a clear leader in **Showing Up** who raced in the same colours as Barbaro. He finished sixth to that colt in the Kentucky Derby, his first defeat, but like Wait A While, Showing Up improved a good deal for the switch to turf. His only defeat in five starts on turf came against older horses when a good third in the Man o'War Stakes. Showing Up's final win came in the Hollywood Derby from the ex-French gelding **Obrigado**, with the Aidan O'Brien-trained Ivan Denisovich, whom he had already beaten in the Secretariat Stakes at Arlington in the summer, in third. Showing Up looks sure to do well again at four. Ivan Denisovich's stable-companion **Aussie Rules** enjoyed better luck on the first of his two starts in the USA, winning the Shadwell Turf Mile, while **Red Rocks** was the sole

Breeders' Cup Classic - Powered By Dodge, Churchill Downs—a 1,2 for the Maktoum family with Invasor (striped cap) getting the better of Bernardini (rail); George Washington (white face) manages only sixth

representative of the three-year-old generation when keeping up the good recent record of European-trained horses in the Breeders' Cup Turf.

In addition to several of the leading three-year-olds, the best older horse on dirt, **Invasor**, was also in Maktoum ownership. Sheikh Hamdan's colt began his career in Uruguay where he had been unbeaten champion three-year-old in 2005. His fourth place behind Discreet Cat in the UAE Derby on his reappearance turned out to be his only defeat so far in ten starts, as he went on to win all four of his Grade 1 races in the USA, culminating in the Breeders' Cup Classic. Along the way, Invasor took the Pimlico Special Handicap (a race that won't be run in 2007 due to a lack of funds), the Suburban Handicap at Belmont and the Whitney Handicap at Saratoga in a stirring finish by a nose from **Sun King**. None of those wins had required a high-class performance, but, having been supplemented for the Breeders' Cup, Invasor put up an improved effort in the Classic, coming from off a strong pace under his eighteen-year-old rider Fernando Jara, who had also partnered the same connections' Jazil in the Belmont. Invasor, who was voted Horse of The Year at the Eclipse awards, is due to be aimed at the Dubai World Cup in 2007.

While Invasor dominated in the East, the tough gelding **Lava Man** swept the board in California where he won all seven of his races prior to the Breeders' Cup. Lava Man became the first horse to win California's three biggest dirt races for older horses in the same year; the Santa Anita Handicap, the Hollywood Gold Cup (which he had also won in 2005) and the Pacific Classic, the last-named from the very smart **Good Reward** (who is equally effective on turf) and the Hollywood Gold Cup third **Super Frolic**. However, none were particularly well-contested given their status. Lava Man also took a Grade 1 on turf, the Charles Whittingham Memorial at Hollywood, in his winning sequence, but his best effort came in Grade 2 company on his final start before the Breeders' Cup when giving weight and a beating to three-year-old Brother Derek and the previous year's Kentucky Derby winner **Giacomo** in the Goodwood Breeders' Cup Handicap. Lava Man failed to repeat the form in the Breeders' Cup Classic (in which Giacomo was a creditable fourth), fading into seventh and not for the first time underperforming outside California.

Premium Tap finished only fifth behind Invasor on his Grade 1 debut in the Whitney Handicap, but he thrived in the autumn, gaining a surprise win in the Woodward Stakes at its new venue of Saratoga (formerly run at Belmont) and finishing third in the Breeders' Cup Classic before routing his field by more than seven lengths in the Clark Handicap back at Churchill Downs later in November. Premium Tap, who has been sold to Saudi Arabian interests but who is to remain with trainer John Kimmel, will be one of the best older horses around in 2007 and could meet Invasor again in the Dubai World Cup. The latest running of that contest ended in controversy from an American point of view. The

Donn Handicap winner **Brass Hat** fared best of the US-trained runners when second past the post behind Electrocutionist, but he was subsequently disqualified (losing more than a million dollars in prize money) after failing a drugs test, despite connections being adamant that they had complied with local rules governing the administering of medication. As a result, **Wilko** and **Magna Graduate** were promoted to the places in the Dubai World Cup, Wilko at that time briefly back in the care of Jeremy Noseda for whom he had won the Breeders' Cup Juvenile. Brass Hat went on to dead-heat for fifth in the Stephen Foster Handicap at Churchill Downs behind the 92/1 winner **Seek Gold**, who caught the idling **Perfect Drift** to win by a nose, with favourite **Buzzards Bay** (a Grade 2 winner at Oaklawn at the time before) in fourth. That was Perfect Drift's third placing in the Stephen Foster since he won the race in 2003, while he contested his fifth Breeders' Cup Classic later in the year, albeit unable to match his good efforts to reach the frame in the previous two runnings.

Whilst three-year-old sprinter Henny Hughes disappointed in the Breeders' Cup Sprint, it proved a competitive renewal among the older runners and was contested by most of those who had shared top honours through the year. **Bordonaro**, who had won nine of his twelve career starts before the Breeders' Cup, notably the Ancient Title Breeders' Cup Stakes at Santa Anita in October, looked the best of them, but was unable to dominate in the Breeders' Cup Sprint, finishing fourth behind the Ancient Title runner-up **Thor's Echo**. A four-length winner at Churchill Downs, Thor's Echo went on to win the Frank J. de Francis Memorial at Laurel Park later in November without having to repeat his Breeders' Cup form. Earlier in the year, Thor's Echo had been runner-up to **Proud Tower Too** in the Dubai Golden Shaheen at Nad Al Sheba, where American sprinters dominated as usual, taking the first five places. No doubt with that race in mind for him again, Thor's Echo was bought by Sheikh Rashid at the end of the year. The placed horses in the Breeders' Cup Sprint were **Friendly Island** (earlier third in the Forego Handicap at

TVG Breeders' Cup Sprint, Churchill Downs—
Thor's Echo takes it up on the outside rounding the home turn before drawing clear

Saratoga behind **Pomeroy** and **War Front**) and **Nightmare Affair**, winner of the Grade 2 Smile Sprint Handicap at Calder from Pomeroy, who was below form in the Breeders' Cup Sprint. **Siren Lure** was another with some of the best form over shorter distances but disappointed in the Breeders' Cup Sprint after wins under top weight over seven furlongs in the Triple Bend Handicap at Hollywood and the Grade 2 Pat O'Brien Breeders' Cup Handicap at Del Mar. The 2005 Breeders' Cup Sprint winner **Silver Train** ran his best races over seven furlongs and a mile in the latest season, winning the Metropolitan Handicap at Belmont from Sun King and the Grade 2 Tom Fool Handicap at Belmont (from War Front) and finishing third to Discreet Cat in the Cigar Mile Handicap. Barbaro was not the only horse whose fight for life made the headlines. The previous year's champion sprinter **Lost In The Fog** won a Grade 3 at Churchill Downs in June but ran just three times before succumbing to cancer of the spine and spleen in September. Lost In The Fog's regular rider Russell Baze broke Lafitt Pincay's world record for career wins when registering his 9,531st success in December, though for all his success, Baze has had few opportunities in Grade 1 company and most of his wins have been gained at a modest level on the California circuit.

There was a muddling picture among the older fillies and mares on dirt, the Breeders' Cup Distaff raising more questions than it answered in determining a clear leader to the division. As well as Pine Island, the mare who shaded her for favouritism, **Fleet Indian**, also failed to finish, pulling up with a fetlock injury, though hers at least did not have fatal consequences. In addition, it was not certain that the Distaff winner **Round Pond** was the best horse on the day, despite winning by over four lengths, as **Asi Siempre**, second past the post, looked unlucky in having to switch twice in the straight before finishing strongly. However, she was judged to have been the culprit rather than the victim and was demoted to fourth, with **Happy Ticket** and **Balletto** promoted to second and third respectively.

Fleet Indian had built an impressive record prior to the Distaff, having won her last eight starts, six of them since joining Todd Pletcher at the start of the year. They included Grade 1 wins over Balletto in the Personal Ensign Stakes at Saratoga in clear-cut fashion and a more hard-won head success in the Beldame Stakes at Saratoga (in the process breaking Pletcher's own record for prize money earned in a season) where they pulled clear of Round Pond in third. Asi Siempre, who began her career in France, started the year on turf and was making her dirt debut in the Distaff after putting up an improved effort on Keeneland's Polytrack to win the Spinster Stakes. Balletto had been second in the 2004 Breeders' Cup Juvenile Fillies, but failed to run for Godolphin in her three-year-old season and had even been retired at one point. However, while a win eluded her, she showed she had lost none of her ability back with Tom Albertrani in 2006. As well as her two defeats by Fleet Indian, she was placed earlier in the year in the Ogden Phipps Handicap (beaten a long way when third to **Take d'Tour**) at Belmont and when losing out on the nod to **Spun Sugar** in the Go For Wand Handicap at Saratoga. Spun Sugar was below form in the Distaff but the Go For Wand was her second Grade 1 success of the year after her defeat of Happy Ticket in the Apple Blossom Handicap at Oaklawn, while Happy Ticket ran a much better race in the Distaff than twelve months earlier, having been unlucky not to have finished second when a badly hampered sixth in the Spinster Stakes beforehand. **Hollywood Story** and **Healthy Addiction** were both well held in the Distaff for the second year running, but they were as good as ever as five-year-olds, taking the first two places in the Vanity Handicap at Hollywood, with Healthy Addiction having made all to beat **Dream of Summer** in the Santa Margarita Handicap at Santa Anita earlier in the year. The best race over shorter distances in the older fillies/mares division turned out to be the Humana Distaff Handicap on the Kentucky Derby card in which **Pussycat Doll** beat the Santa Monica Handicap winner **Behaving Badly**.

European horses made up half the field in the Breeders' Cup Mile, but of those, Sleeping Indian and Rob Roy suffered problems in running in finishing fourth and fifth respectively, while the remainder disappointed. Victory went instead to the oldest horse in the race, **Miesque's Approval**, a seven-year-old who had been beaten in a claimer twelve months earlier and who was winning his first Grade 1. Miesque's Approval's defeat of the 2005 Breeders' Cup Mile winner **Artie Schiller** (by a nose, in receipt of 6 lb) in the Grade 2 Maker's Mark Mile at Keeneland in April was an indication of his improve-

NetJets Breeders' Cup Mile, Churchill Downs—
Miesque's Approval wins his first Grade 1 at the age of seven

ment, but his Grade 1 debut, when dead-heating for fourth with **Cosmonaut** in a tight finish behind placed horses **Remarkable News** and **Old Dodge** in the Shadwell Turf Mile won by three-year-old Aussie Rules was still some way short of Breeders' Cup-winning form. Miesque's Approval (a grandson of the 1987/1988 winner Miesque through her son Miesque's Son) came from well off the pace at Churchill Downs to beat **Aragorn**, who had looked a much stronger contender as the winner of his last four starts in California. Those wins included two Grade 2 events, and prior to that, the Shoemaker Breeders' Cup Mile at Hollywood, and the Eddie Read Handicap at Del Mar in which he had been impressive in smashing the track record under top weight. Aragorn lacked his usual turn of foot in the Breeders' Cup Mile but was retired to stud afterwards having finished first or second in all nine of his starts in the USA after leaving David Loder in Britain during his three-year-old season.

As well as Aragorn, two more leading milers on turf (neither of whom contested the Breeders' Cup Mile) who were British imports were **Ashkal Way** and **Milk It Mick**. Ashkal Way had been a useful handicapper for Brian Ellison and was gradually raised in class to win six of his seven starts in the USA for Godolphin, notably the Grade 2 Kelso Breeders' Cup Handicap at Belmont (from **Free Thinking**, who was also second to Miesque's Approval in a similar event at Churchill Downs) and a competitive Citation Handicap at Hollywood. **Milk It Mick** was winning for the first time since the 2003 Dewhurst Stakes (for Jamie Osborne) when beating Aragorn a head in a tight finish to the Frank E. Kilroe Mile Handicap at Santa Anita in March. Milk It Mick ran his best race afterwards when third in the nine-furlong Woodford Reserve Turf Classic at Churchill Downs behind **English Channel** and **Cacique** who were the leading pair of older middle-distance performers on turf throughout the year.

English Channel, the top three-year-old on turf in 2005, and the ex-French miler Cacique met four times in all prior to the Breeders' Cup Turf, with English Channel

Arlington Million—a triumph for eight-year-old The Tin Man;
ex-European Cacique (left) keeps on for second ahead of Soldier Hollow

beating Cacique into second place in the United Nations Stakes at Monmouth as well as in the Turf Classic at Churchill Downs. In between, Cacique had English Channel back in a close fourth when dictating a slow pace to win the Manhattan Handicap, and Cacique emerged the better in another slowly-run race when they finished second and fourth respectively behind **The Tin Man** in the Arlington Million. The pair went their separate ways prior to the Breeders' Cup, with English Channel impressing in winning the Joe Hirsch Turf Classic and Cacique successfully stepping up to eleven furlongs to beat the Sword Dancer Invitational winner **Go Deputy** in the Man o'War Stakes. While the normally reliable Cacique proved disappointing at Churchill Downs, English Channel bettered his effort in the Turf from the previous year (whilst still seeming a shade reluctant) in taking third to Red Rocks, a place behind the 2004 winner **Better Talk Now**.

Arlington Million winner The Tin Man made an unlikely comeback at the age of eight but proved better than ever after being restricted by injury to just one start in 2005. He began the year by beating Milk It Mick in a Grade 2 at Santa Anita before finishing second in the Dubai Duty Free, and after the Arlington Million was allowed another uncontested lead to repeat his success of 2002 in the Clement L. Hirsch Memorial Turf Championship at Santa Anita. Former stable-companions **Relaxed Gesture** and **Grey Swallow** finished close behind Cacique in a good renewal of the Manhattan Handicap in June. That was Grey Swallow's final start for Dermot Weld before his transfer to Australia, and prior to that he had made a winning reappearance in the Grade 2 Jim Murray Memorial Handicap at Hollywood. Relaxed Gesture was second in the Manhattan for the second year running and also took third in the United Nations, but he was less successful later in the year than he had been in 2005, finishing last in his attempt at a repeat win in the Canadian International. The Woodbine race resulted in a thrilling finish, with British-trained **Collier Hill** gamely holding on by a nose from Go Deputy.

Ouija Board became the seventh dual winner of a Breeders' Cup race and only the second after Da Hoss to regain a Breeders' Cup title when repeating her 2004 success in the Filly & Mare Turf. She proved too good again for the Americans at Churchill Downs, but **Film Maker** has an admirable record in the same event too, and finished runner-up to Ouija Board as she had done in 2004, having also been a place behind her when third a year later. Film Maker also made the frame in the Flower Bowl Invitational at Belmont for the third year running, losing out by only a nose to another tough and consistent mare **Honey Ryder**, who was later third in the Filly & Mare Turf. Film Maker and Honey

Ryder also finished second and fourth respectively behind **Gorella** in the Beverly D Stakes at Arlington. That represented a step up in trip for the 2005 Breeders' Cup Mile third, but Gorella was aimed at the Mile again at the latest Breeders' Cup rather than the Filly & Mare Turf, starting second favourite after winning four of her five starts beforehand, but finished only seventh.

Both two-year-old races at the Breeders' Cup, as well as the Sprint and Distaff, were won by horses drawn in stall 1, leading to criticism of the apparent bias on the dirt track in favour of those who raced nearest the rail. Another feature of several races at the meeting was an overly-strong pace, something particularly evident in the Breeders' Cup Juvenile, which was won by ten lengths—a record margin for the race—by **Street Sense**, who sliced through the field from the rear as the pace-setters gave way and coasted home after getting a run up the rail to beat favourite **Circular Quay** (who also came from well off the pace) and **Great Hunter**. The first three had already met in the Breeders' Futurity on the Polytrack at Keeneland where they had finished in reverse order, Great Hunter getting the better of Circular Quay, who had started favourite on that occasion as well following his defeat of stable-companion **Scat Daddy** in the Hopeful Stakes at Saratoga. Scat Daddy went on to win the Champagne Stakes at Belmont, providing his trainer Todd Pletcher with a record ninety-third stakes success of the year, but, despite saddling seventeen runners at the Breeders' Cup (another record), Pletcher had to settle for place money at best, with Scat Daddy finishing fourth at Churchill Downs. Street Sense's connections will be hoping he fares better than the five previous winners of the Breeders' Cup Juvenile, none of whom won a race of any sort afterwards, still less the Kentucky Derby which continues to elude the Juvenile winner. **Nobiz Like Shobiz** didn't contest the Breeders' Cup, but looks capable of making more of a name for himself as a three-year-old. He finished second to Scat Daddy in the Champagne (after being badly hampered at the start) in between a facile maiden win at Belmont and a six and a half length win in the Grade 2 Remsen Stakes at Aqueduct. **Tiz Wonderful** is unbeaten in three starts and was twice successful in graded company at Churchill Downs, including a defeat of **Any Given Saturday** in the Grade 2 Kentucky Jockey Club Stakes, but reportedly suffered a tendon injury in January 2007 and will be sidelined for a while. An ankle injury sustained in the Grade 2 Norfolk Stakes at Santa Anita (won by subsequent Breeders' Cup Juvenile fifth and Hollywood Futurity winner **Stormello**) prevented **Horse Greeley** from taking his chance at the Breeders' Cup, but he would have been well worth his place in the line-up judged on his defeat of Great Hunter and Stormello in the Grade 2 Del Mar Futurity.

The Breeders' Cup Juvenile Fillies was won by the favourite for the fifth year running, with **Dreaming of Anna** making all to extend her unbeaten record to four in beating the

Bessemer Trust Breeders' Cup Juvenile, Churchill Downs—the biggest winning margin in the race's history, ten lengths, as Street Sense puts up a scarcely believable performance

Todd Pletcher-trained pair **Octave** and **Cotton Blossom**. The winner may return to turf at some stage as her pedigree is oriented that way (by Rahy out of a half-sister to champion turf horse Kitten's Joy) and she has already won twice on the grass, including a Grade 3 event at Woodbine. The placed horses both ran their best races in the Juvenile Fillies. Octave was suited by the longer trip after dead-heating for second behind **Meadow Breeze** in the Matron Stakes at Belmont, while Cotton Blossom had finished second to **Appealing Zophie** in her other start in Grade 1 company in the Spinaway Stakes at Saratoga. Appealing Zophie was a creditable fourth in the Juvenile Fillies and, like Cotton Blossom, turned the form round with **Bel Air Beauty**, who was a long-priced winner of the Grade 2 Alcibiades Stakes at Keeneland, where Cotton Blossom and Appealing Zophie had finished only fourth and sixth respectively. **Cash Included** was a leading contender for the Breeders' Cup Juvenile Fillies after an impressive defeat of the Del Mar Debutante winner **Point Ashley** in the Oak Leaf Stakes, but she was a never-dangerous fifth at Churchill Downs. The other Grade 1 winner in the Juvenile Fillies line-up was **Sutra**, but she had won only a modest renewal of the Frizette Stakes and was well held at the Breeders' Cup. **Romance Is Diane** showed a good attitude when completing a hat-trick in the Hollywood Starlet Stakes from the Juvenile Fillies' also-ran **Quick Little Miss**, but it was third-placed Down (rated 108p) who really caught the eye (on just her second start) and looks a good prospect for Bobby Frankel.

European-trained horses who showed or reproduced their best form in North America are included in this list

Two-Year-Olds

124+	Street Sense
119	Dreaming of Anna (f)
118	Great Hunter
116	Cash Included (f)
116	Circular Quay
116	Octave (f)
115p	Nobiz Like Shobiz
115	Scat Daddy
115	Tiz Wonderful
114	Any Given Saturday
114	Chace City
114	Horse Greeley
113	Cotton Blossom (f)
113	Miss Atlantic City (f)
113	Pegasus Wind
113	Stormello
113	U D Ghetto
112	Appealing Zophie (f)
112	Bel Air Beauty (f)
112	Dilemma
112	King of The Roxy
112	Liquidity
112	Principle Secret
112	Romance Is Diane (f)
111	E Z Warrior
111	Featherbed (f)
111	Meadow Breeze (f)
111	Point Ashley (f)
111	Sutra (f)
110	C P West
110	Lady Joanne (f)
110	Skip Code
110	Untouched Talent (f)
109p	Day Pass
109	Belgravia
109	Quick Little Miss (f)
109	Roman Commander
109	Shermanesque

DIRT/ARTIFICIAL SURFACES

Three-Year-Olds

132	Bernardini
130	Barbaro
127p	†Discreet Cat
125	Henny Hughes
122	Jazil
122	Pine Island (f)
121	Brother Derek
120	Bluegrass Cat
120	Bushfire (f)
120	Sinister Minister
119	Balance (f)
119	Lemons Forever (f)
119	Strong Contender
119	Wonder Lady Anne L (f)
118	First Samurai
118	Lawyer Ron
118	Ready To Please (f)
118	Sharp Humor
118	Stevie Wonderboy
118	Sweetnorthernsaint
117	Bob And John
117	Hello Liberty (f)
117	Sunriver
117	Teammate (f)
117	Wild Fit (f)

116	Downthedustyroad (f)
116	Latent Heat
115	Swap Fliparoo (f)

Older Horses

133	†Invasor
130	†Lava Man
126	Thor's Echo
125	Brass Hat
124	Fleet Indian (f)
124	Round Pond (f)
123	Asi Siempre (f)
123	Balletto (f)
123	Perfect Drift
123	Premium Tap
123	Spun Sugar (f)
122	Lost In The Fog
122	Siren Lure
121	Behaving Badly (f)
121	Bordonaro
121	Buzzards Bay
121	Giacomo
121	Happy Ticket (f)
121	Proud Tower Too
121	Seek Gold
121	Take d'Tour (f)
120	Good Reward
120	Pomeroy
120	Pussycat Doll (f)
120	Silver Train
120	†Wilko
119	Dream of Summer (f)
119	Magna Graduate
119	Nightmare Affair (f)
119	Suave
119	Super Frolic
119	War Front
118	Healthy Addiction (f)
118	Oonagh Maccool (f)
118	Second of June
118	Sun King
118	Wanderin Boy
117	Attila's Storm
117	Dubai Escapade (f)
117	Friendly Island
117	High Limit
117	Hollywood Story (f)
117	Magnum
117	Master Command
117	Pool Land (f)
117	Proposed (f)

117	Silver Wagon
117	Star Parade (f)
117	Surf Cat

116	Bishop Court Hill
115	Pure As Gold
114	Malibu Mint (f)

TURF

Three-Year-Olds

124	†Red Rocks
123	†Aussie Rules
123	Showing Up
123	Wait A While (f)
119	Magnificent Song (f)
118	Fast Parade
118	Get Funky
117	†Grand Couturier
117	Jade Queen (f)
117	Obrigado

116	Arravale (f)
115	†Price Tag (f)
114p	Vacare (f)

Older Horses

126	Miesque's Approval
125	Aragorn
125	English Channel
125	†Ouija Board
124	Artie Schiller
124	Cacique
124	The Tin Man
123	†Collier Hill
123	†Grey Swallow
122	Go Deputy
122	Gorella (f)
121	Relaxed Gesture
120	*Ashkal Way
120	Better Talk Now
119	Boboman
119	*Dance In The Mood (f)
119	Einstein
119	King's Drama

119	Milk It Mick
119	†Soldier Hollow
118	†Ace
118	Film Maker (f)
118	Free Thinking
118	Honey Ryder (f)
118	Remarkable News
117	Badge of Silver
117	Cosmonaut
117	Hotstufanthensome
117	Old Dodge
117	Rebel Rebel
117	Runaway Dancer
117	Silver Tree
117	Three Valleys
117	Whilly

116	Angara (f)
116	Becrux
116	Shining Energy (f)
115	Dancing Edie (f)

JAPAN The success of Japanese-trained horses outside their own country hit new heights in 2006 with several notable performances worldwide. Ironically, **Deep Impact**, Japan's champion for the second year running and considered by many in Japan the best horse the nation has produced, was not part of that international success, failing a drugs test and disqualified after finishing only third past the post in the Prix de l'Arc de Triomphe on what was his only appearance abroad. But that took little gloss off a year of international success which began with stable-companions **Heart's Cry** and **Utopia** winning the Dubai

Emirates Melbourne Cup, Flemington—a first Group 1 win for Japan in Australia as Delta Blues (right) just holds off stablemate Pop Rock

Sheema Classic and Godolphin Mile respectively on World Cup night at Nad Al Sheba in March, with Heart's Cry going on to finish a close third in the King George VI and Queen Elizabeth Stakes at Ascot. Their successes were followed by **Cosmo Bulk**'s win in the Singapore Airlines International Cup, and then by top mare **Dance In The Mood** winning the valuable Grade 3 Cashcall Invitational Stakes at Hollywood, where Japanese Oaks third **Asahi Rising** took second in the American Oaks. Highlight of the year for Japanese success abroad came in Australia though, when stable-companions **Delta Blues** and **Pop Rock** took the first two places in the Melbourne Cup, the pair having finished third and seventh respectively in the Caulfield Cup beforehand. Other good efforts in defeat abroad came from Deep Impact's travelling companion **Picaresque Coat**, who finished second in the Prix Daniel Wildenstein at Longchamp, and from three-year-old colt **Admire Moon**, who was beaten just a short head by Pride in the Hong Kong Cup. Inevitably, not all those sent abroad were as successful. The previous year's top dirt performer (and winner of the February Stakes beforehand) **Kane Hekili** started second favourite for the Dubai World Cup but wasn't at his best, promoted from fifth to fourth.

Domestically though, the year belonged once again to Deep Impact. He won all five of his starts in Japan and rounded off his career with easy wins in the Japan Cup (a race he had side-stepped in 2005) and the Arima Kinen, the race in which he met with his only defeat at home when losing out to Heart's Cry the year before. Whilst the latest Japan Cup attracted its smallest ever field, and was weakened further by a poor showing from Heart's Cry, the Arima Kinen was the strongest contest in Japan all year, and by our reckoning, Deep Impact's defeat of Pop Rock, eased down by three lengths, was a career-best effort. The manner and ease of his victories in Japan made it hard to quantify exactly how good Deep Impact was, but a rating 7 lb lower than the 1999 Arc runner-up El Condor Pasa in the World Thoroughbred Rankings seemed to underestimate his overall standing.

Third place in the extended twelve-furlong Arima Kinen went to the versatile **Daiwa Major**, who had established himself as the top older performer over a mile/ten furlongs. As well as the Tenno Sho (Autumn), which he won from **Swift Current**, Daiwa Major won three other group races, with Dance In The Mood finishing second to him each time, notably in the Mile Championship, in which **Symboli Gran** took third place. Dance In

The Mood enjoyed top-level success as well though, winning the new Group 1 for older fillies/mares in the spring, the Victoria Mile at Tokyo. Singapore winner Cosmo Bulk found success harder to come by at home, though he did finish fourth in both the Tenno Sho (Autumn) and the Japan Cup. Most of the other leading older performers at middle distances and beyond came up against Deep Impact at some stage, with **Lincoln** proving no match for him in the two-mile Tenno Sho (Spring) and **Narita Century** and **Balance of Game** filling the places behind him in his other Group 1 win, the Takarazuka Kinen.

Unusually, there were few Japanese sprinters of real note and Australia's Takeover Target proved too good for the locals in the Sprinters Stakes at Nakayama in October. Among those behind him there were the mare **She Is Tosho**, who had beaten Takeover Target in Japan's other leg of the Global Sprint Challenge, the Group 2 Centaur Stakes, and **Orewa Matteruze**, winner of the Group 1 sprint in the spring, the Takamatsunomiya Kinen, in which She Is Tosho finished third. **Meisho Bowler** took second place in the Sprinters Stakes, but his overall record is inconsistent and he disgraced himself by refusing to race in the Hong Kong Sprint.

It looked for a while as though Japan might have a triple crown winner for the second year running after Deep Impact had taken all three classics in 2005. **Meisho Samson** won the first two legs, the Satsuki Sho and Tokyo Yushun, but could finish only fourth to **Song of Wind** in the Japanese St Leger, the Kikuka Sho. Meisho Samson acquitted himself well against older horses back over shorter trips when sixth in the Japan Cup and fifth in the Arima Kinen, as did Song of Wind, a creditable fourth in the Hong Kong Vase. The top three-year-old though was **Dream Passport** who was placed in each of the triple crown races (second in the Guineas and St Leger, third in the Derby) but showed his best form later in the year against Deep Impact, finishing second in the Japan Cup and fourth in the Arima Kinen. With Deep Impact and Heart's Cry retired to stud, Dream Passport looks in a good position to win his first Group 1 in 2007. His stable-companion Admire Moon should also be challenging for top honours as a four-year-old. Prior to his narrow defeat by Pride in Hong Kong, he'd run a good third against older rivals in the Tenno Sho (Autumn). The leading three-year-old colts on turf were completed by the Derby runner-up **Admire Main**, who also ran third in the St Leger and wasn't discredited in ninth place in the Arima Kinen. **Alondite**'s win in the Japan Cup Dirt, his fifth win in a row, made him the top three-year-old on dirt.

The three-year-old fillies had a clear leader in the form of Yushun Himba (Oaks) winner **Kawakami Princess**. She also took the Shuka Sho (from Asahi Rising) in the autumn and would have been unbeaten in six races had she not been disqualified for causing interference when first past the post in the Queen Elizabeth II Commemorative Cup on her final start. That race was awarded instead to **Fusaichi Pandora** who had been second in the Oaks and third in the Shuka Sho and who went on to finish fifth in the Japan Cup. The Oka Sho (1000 Guineas) winner **Kiss To Heaven** failed to make much of an impact in the top fillies races afterwards.

The ongoing process of opening up Japan's stakes races to foreign competition will reach a significant stage in 2007 when half of all such races will be open to horses from abroad. In addition, Japan has now been promoted to Part I of the International Cataloguing Standards book. In practice, this will mean that around sixty Japanese group races will have internationally-recognised Group 1, 2 or 3 status, which will be labelled as such in sales catalogues, and will be subject to the same sort of standards (based on the quality of runners) which govern the grading of stakes races in other leading racing countries such as those in the European pattern.

Three-Year-Olds

126	Dream Passport	116	Fine Grain	127	†Heart's Cry
124	Admire Moon	116	Maruka Shenck	125	†Delta Blues
123	Meisho Samson	116	Meiner Scherzi	125	Pop Rock
122	Song of Wind	115	Asahi Rising (f)	124	Daiwa Major
120	Admire Main	115	Friendship	123	Kane Hekili
119	Alondite	115	Fusaichi Pandora (f)	121	Balance of Game
118	Kawakami Princess (f)	115	Kinshasa No Kiseki	121	Cosmo Bulk
117	Fusaichi Richard			121	Swift Current
117	Logic	113	Kiss To Heaven (f)	121	Utopia
117	Sakura Mega Wonder			120	Adjudi Mitsuo
117	Tosen Shana O	**Older Horses**		120	Lincoln
		134	†Deep Impact	119	Dance In The Mood (f)

1249

119	Orewa Matteruze	117	Fast Tateyama	116	Sweep Tosho (f)
119	Symboli Gran	117	Precise Machine	116	Telegnosis
119	Tosho Knight	117§	Meisho Bowler	115	Air Messiah (f)
118	Admire Fuji	116	Blue Concorde	115	Bonneville Record
118	Eye Popper	116	Company	115	Hishi Atlas
118	Narita Century	116	Picaresque Coat	115	Rhein Kraft (f)
118	Time Paradox	116	Seeking The Dia	115	Sakura Century
117	Asakusa Den'en	116	She Is Tosho (f)		

HONG KONG   The Hong Kong Sprint, one of the four Group 1 races at Sha Tin's international meeting in December, saw the emergence of a new champion sprinter to overthrow the former dual winner of the race **Silent Witness**, who had missed the Hong Kong Sprint through illness twelve months earlier and looked a shadow of his former self in 2006. **Absolute Champion** struggled to live up to his new name in Hong Kong at first, winning only one of his first thirteen starts (only seventh in the 2005 Hong Kong Sprint), but he had smart form in his native Australia where he raced as Genius And Evil, as a two-year-old once beating subsequent high-class sprinter Fastnet Rock. With a new trainer in 2006, Absolute Champion improved to win his two starts prior to the Hong Kong Sprint, including when breaking the track record with a narrow defeat of **Sunny Sing** in a Group 3 handicap in October, but he only made the line-up for the Hong Kong Sprint as a reserve when British entry Red Clubs dropped out. Sunny Sing, switched back to sprinting when the new season started after winning the Hong Kong Classic Mile early in the year, was favourite to turn the tables on better terms in the Hong Kong Sprint but finished only fifth behind an impressive Absolute Champion, who came off a very strong pace to pull more than four lengths clear, lowering the track record for a second time. Although not the force of old, Silent Witness still managed to take second place in the Hong Kong Sprint, with other leading sprinters **Billet Express** and **Scintillation** (winners of the Chairman's Sprint Prize and Centenary Sprint Cup respectively early in the year) down the field, along with the surprise 2005 Hong Kong Sprint winner **Natural Blitz**, he more inconvenienced than most by the race being run over six furlongs (on the round

Cathay Pacific Hong Kong Sprint, Sha Tin—
Absolute Champion is a clear-cut winner in course-record time

*Cathay Pacific Hong Kong Mile, Sha Tin—in a close finish with Armada,
The Duke (No.10) finally prevails after being placed in the two previous runnings*

course) for the first time rather than the straight five. Hong Kong's other former star sprinter **Cape of Good Hope** managed just one outing all year, sustaining an injury when third in the Lightning Stakes in Australia.

Whilst Absolute Champion's emergence was rather sudden, **Armada** was one who made constant progress, meeting his only defeat in his first seven starts in Hong Kong when fourth behind Absolute Champion and Sunny Sing over six furlongs in October. Better over further, Armada won the International Mile Trial before starting a hot favourite for the Hong Kong Mile itself, finishing strongly but going down by a head to **The Duke**. The winner had been placed twice in the race before but was without a win previously in 2006, having finished second to Armada in the Mile Trial. **Bullish Luck** finished fourth in the Hong Kong Mile for the second year running. His form peaked earlier in the year when wins in the Champions Mile at home (from the subsequently injured **Danacourt**) and the Yasuda Kinen in Japan earned him a US million-dollar bonus for winning two legs of the Asian Mile Challenge (he was also fifth in an earlier leg, the Dubai Duty Free) and went a long way towards securing him the title of Hong Kong Horse of the Year for the 2005/6 season. **Joyful Winner**, sixth in the Hong Kong Mile, was another in better form earlier on, finishing third to Bullish Luck in both the Champions Mile and Yasuda Kinen after a defeat of Silent Witness in the Queen's Silver Jubilee Cup in April. **Floral Pegasus**, like Armada, made significant progress in seven furlong/mile handicaps without quite reaching the same heights, finishing third nonetheless in the International Mile Trial but only seventh in the Hong Kong Mile itself.

Very smart performer **Vengeance of Rain** had looked all set to dominate the middle-distance scene again after his win in the Hong Kong Cup at the end of 2005 but setbacks kept him out of action until late-October. He had two starts over inadequate trips on his return before running third to the previous year's runner-up Pride in the Hong Kong Cup, showing he retained much of his ability. Just behind him in fourth was **Viva Pataca** who had been among the most progressive newcomers to racing in Hong Kong in the first half of the year. A formerly smart two-year-old for Sir Mark Prescott (when named Comic Strip), Viva Pataca landed the odds in a substandard Hong Kong Derby, but beat a stronger field of older rivals in the Champions & Chater Cup over a mile and a half in May from **Best Gift**, **Super Combed** and **Super Kid**, none of whom were seen out in the second half of the year. Best Gift had also finished second in a tight finish to a tactical Audemars Piguet Queen Elizabeth II Cup against foreign rivals, splitting the mares Irridescence and Ouija Board. Super Kid was fourth in the same contest after a narrow defeat of Bullish Luck and **Bowman's Crossing** in the Hong Kong Gold Cup in February.

129	Absolute Champion	121	Cape of Good Hope	117	Helene Pillaging
124	Armada	120	Danacourt	117	Joyful Winner
124	Bullish Luck	120	Viva Pataca	117	Russian Pearl
123	Scintillation	119	Super Combed	117?	Sir Ernesto
123	The Duke	118	Art Trader	116	Bowman's Crossing
122	Best Gift	118	Sunny Sing	116	Dave's Best
122	*Super Kid	117	Billet Express	116	Silent Witness
122	Vengeance of Rain	117	Floral Pegasus	115	Natural Blitz

AUSTRALIA AND NEW ZEALAND   While the 2006 Australian and New Zealand domestic racing year lacked a household name champion, it did provide several fine performances from an emerging group of horses. It was always going to be hard to find a replacement for retired champion mare Makybe Diva, but the depth across the younger age groups coming into 2006 looked stronger than in the previous couple of years. The year also saw Australian racing highlighted abroad through the deeds in Britain and Japan of champion sprinter **Takeover Target**, who won three legs of the Global Sprint Challenge. His sterling performances in those countries did much to focus attention on the strength of the Australian and New Zealand industry internationally.

Takeover Target was bought as an unraced four-year-old by trainer Joe Janiak at a disposal sale in Sydney for the equivalent of a mere £500 but made rapid progress through the sprinting ranks. His first win in 2006 came in the Lightning Stakes which he took narrowly from up-and-coming three-year-old **God's Own** and Hong Kong's 2005 Global Sprint Challenge winner Cape of Good Hope. The win stamped Takeover Target as the leading sprinter in Australia. However in the second leg of the Autumn Sprinting Triple Crown, the Oakleigh Plate, Takeover Target was handicapped by racing on the worst of the rain-softened ground, but, under top weight, still finished a game third to the smart **Snitzel** and **Virage de Fortune**. Back on better ground in the Newmarket Handicap at Flemington, Takeover Target returned to form, beating Snitzel and 2005 Golden Slipper winner **Stratum**. A full account of Takeover Target's subsequent international campaign, which for all its success ended in controversy in Hong Kong, can be found in his extended entry in the main part of the annual.

Takeover Target shared top spot in the ratings with **Racing To Win**, who won six of his ten appearances, four at Group 1 level and two at Group 2. As well as Randwick's Doncaster and Epsom Handicaps, his other Group 1 wins came in the George Main Stakes, also at Randwick, and the George Ryder Stakes at Rosehill. The Epsom Handicap form subsequently proved to be strong with runner-up Desert War winning the Mackinnon Stakes and third-placed **Malcolm** winning at Group 3 level during the Flemington Melbourne Cup carnival on their next appearances. Racing To Win's last run of the year was in the Cox Plate at Moonee Valley. On the strength of his excellent Sydney form he started a warm favourite, but was injured in the race and failed to produce his best.

The leading middle-distance performers were **Desert War** and **Eremein** ahead of **El Segundo** and **Fields of Omagh**. Desert War gained his Group 1 wins in the Chipping Norton Stakes at Warwick Farm and when making all in the Mackinnon Stakes at Flemington to win from **Growl** and Caulfield Cup runner-up **Aqua d'Amore**. In addition he took the Group 2 Hill Stakes for the second successive year at Rosehill, defeating a strong line-up including Eremein and **Grand Zulu**. However, his best run was when beaten a short neck by Racing To Win in the Epsom Handicap, carrying top weight in a race he had won for the last two years. Eremein, the 2005 AJC Derby winner, had his campaign cut short by injury but was in sparkling form earlier in the year, winning at Group 1 level on three consecutive occasions. The sequence started with the Ranvet Stakes at Rosehill, where he defeated **Our Smoking Joe** and Desert War in decisive fashion. A fortnight later at the same track he came off a strong pace in the BMW Stakes to gather in 2005 Caulfield Cup winner **Railings** with Our Smoking Joe in third, and he completed his hat-trick with a defeat of Aqua d'Amore in the Queen Elizabeth Stakes at Randwick.

Prior to going amiss in the autumn Eremein also won the Group 2 Chelmsford Stakes and was second to Desert War in the Hill Stakes.

Australia's feature weight-for-age race, the Cox Plate at Moonee Valley, assembled a balanced field that provided a fairytale ending to the career of one of the most popular horses to race in Australia, nine-year-old Fields of Omagh. Fields of Omagh lined up for a record-equalling fifth straight run in the Cox Plate having won the race in 2003 and finishing second in 2004 and third in 2005. He was fifth behind Northerly in 2002. Fields of Omagh had also won the Futurity Stakes run for the first time over a mile at Caulfield as part of the Asian Mile Challenge Series back in March. Despite being pushed wide on the home turn at Moonee Valley, Fields of Omagh got up in the last stride to gain a nose decision over El Segundo with **Pompeii Ruler** close up in third place. Immediately after the race, connections announced the gelding's retirement from racing. His career spanned 45 runs for 13 wins and prize money earnings of A$6,496,240.

Already successful with 1986 and 1994 Melbourne Cup winners At Talaq and Jeune, who both began their careers in Britain, Sheikh Hamdan Al Maktoum sent 2005 St Leger third **Tawqeet** to Australia to be prepared for the Caulfield and Melbourne Cups. Following preparatory runs over shorter trips, Tawqeet won the AJC Metropolitan at Randwick from **Activation** and Vanquished. Two weeks later, Tawqeet followed up in the Caulfield Cup, coming from well back to beat Aqua d'Amore on the line with Japan's subsequent Melbourne Cup winner Delta Blues in third. Tawqeet was sent off joint-favourite for the Melbourne Cup, but on the eve of the race pulled a shoe which took part of his hoof off. Although passed fit to run, Tawqeet was never comfortable and finished well back.

The highest-rated older mares were up-and-coming sprinter **Miss Andretti** and proven Group 1 performer Glamour Puss. Miss Andretti won her first Group 1 race when she took the Manikato Stakes at Moonee Valley in course record time, defeating subsequent Salinger Stakes winner **Dance Hero** and Sassbee. She was subsequently unluckily beaten in the Sir Rupert Clarke Stakes at Caulfield behind **Rewaaya** and on her last run for the year was third to Dance Hero in the Salinger Stakes at Flemington. **Glamour Puss**, a dual Group 1 winner in 2005, did not have the same degree of success during 2006, finishing

Tattersall's Cox Plate, Moonee Valley—Fields of Omagh (blinkers) gets up to record his second win in Australia's most prestigious weight-for-age event; El Segundo (centre) and Pompeii Ruler fill the places

a close-up fourth behind Takeover Target in the Newmarket Handicap and then going down narrowly to **Red Oog** in the T J Smith Stakes at Randwick. In her two races in Britain, she ran well to be seventh in the King's Stand Stakes, but was below form in the Golden Jubilee Stakes.

As well as Racing To Win, the four-year-old age group included a number of other Group 1 winners. **Paratroopers** gained a hard fought win over **Niconero** in the All-Aged Stakes at Randwick during the Easter Racing Carnival. Paratroopers had previously won the Group 2 Canterbury Stakes and was beaten a nose by Racing To Win in the George Ryder Stakes at Rosehill. AJC Australian Derby winner **Headturner** looked to be a major Cup contender after one of the most impressive victories in the race in the last decade, winning by two and a half lengths from Rosehill Guineas winner **De Beers** with subsequent South Australian Derby winner Testafiable in third place, but failed to reproduce the same level of form and was well held in both the Caulfield and Melbourne Cups. **Red Dazzler** and Pompeii Ruler both made rapid improvement throughout 2006. Red Dazzler ran his best races at a mile, running Fields of Omagh to a head in the Futurity Stakes at Caulfield and Racing To Win to a length in the George Main Stakes at Randwick in September. He followed this with a narrow win in the Toorak Handicap at Caulfield where he defeated Rewaaya and Niconero. The lightly-raced **Pompeii Ruler** upset many big names in the Group 2 J J Liston Stakes over seven furlongs at Caulfield when resuming from a break and then took another Group 2 event, the Craiglee Stakes over a mile at Flemington. Also a narrow second in the Yalumba Stakes behind **Casual Pass** and a gallant third in the Cox Plate behind Fields of Omagh, Pompeii Ruler finished the year with a career record of five wins from just nine starts and showed versatility, being competitive from seven to ten furlongs. Formerly trained in New Zealand, older horse **Sphenophyta** showed enough during a limited campaign to indicate he has a big future in Australia. He was runner-up in the Craiglee Stakes behind Pompeii Ruler before adding the Turnbull Stakes to his already good record.

Smart sprinter **Natural Destiny** came to the fore following a similar campaign to Takeover Target the year before. Like that horse, Natural Destiny won the first two legs of the Summer Triple Crown in Brisbane, the Summer Stakes and the Doomben Stakes, both in emphatic fashion, in the latter breaking Takeover Target's course record. Unlike Takeover Target, Natural Destiny will attempt the third leg of the series over a mile early in 2007. **Fast 'n' Famous** was another sprinter to make sharp improvement, ultimately defeating a strong line-up, including subsequent Salinger winner Dance Hero, in the Group 3 Gilgai Stakes at Flemington. Fast 'n' Famous looks certain to be a major sprinting force in 2007. Western Australia has an up-and-coming four-year-old in the shape of **Marasco**. He has raced just ten times for six wins, notably the Group 2 Winter-bottom Stakes and Group 3 A J Scahill Stakes over six and seven furlongs respectively.

Two very smart fillies in Miss Finland and Gold Edition sit at the top of the three-year-old handicap. 2006 looked like being an excellent year for this age group but several promising types failed to deliver and the year ended with just seven horses rated 120 or higher, compared to twenty the previous year. A Group 1 winner from six to twelve and a half furlongs, **Miss Finland** was one of the most exciting horses all year. She was campaigned early in the year for the A$3 million Golden Slipper Stakes, the richest juvenile race in the world. Fitted with blinkers for the Golden Slipper, Miss Finland won going away by four-and-a-half lengths—the third biggest winning margin in the fifty-year history of the race. After running second to **Mentality** in the AJC Champagne Stakes over a mile at Randwick, Miss Finland was rested before a successful return in September. The following month she came from last to win the Thousand Guineas at Caulfield, defeating **Permaiscuous** and Flight Stakes winner **Cheeky Choice**. After a luckless sixth in the Cox Plate, Miss Finland took her place in the VRC Oaks over twelve-and-a-half furlongs during the Melbourne Cup Carnival in which she beat Wakeful Stakes winner **Tuesday Joy** by just over two lengths with stablemate **Anamato** in third place. Miss Finland became the first filly to win both the Golden Slipper and VRC Oaks and is also the highest-rated winner of the latter race in the last fifteen years. Connections have not ruled out an overseas campaign for Miss Finland in 2007.

The other leading three-year-old filly **Gold Edition** earned her rating in sprints against the best of her age group. Early in the year Gold Edition won the Group 2 Magic Night

Stakes at Rosehill, one of the major lead-up races to the Golden Slipper. During the Brisbane Winter Carnival she won the Group 2 Champagne Classic at Doomben and ran second to **Danleigh** in the QTC Sires' Produce Stakes at Eagle Farm. After returning from a break she was a convincing winner of two more Group 3 contests at Randwick. During the Melbourne Cup Carnival Gold Edition improved again with a four-length win in the Group 1 Ascot Vale Stakes at Flemington and just five days later she romped home again over the same course and distance in listed company, winning pulling up by seven lengths.

The three-year-old males were headed by Victoria Derby winner **Efficient**. He was all set to start in the Melbourne Cup but did not recover from his hard Derby win the previous Saturday and was scratched on the morning of the race. On his way to the Victoria Derby, Efficient won the Group 2 AAMI Vase over ten furlongs at Moonee Valley, with the Derby being just his sixth start. On Derby day, when most horses had found it hard to make headway from the rear, Efficient came from near last on the turn to run out the winner by just over two lengths from **Gorky Park**. **Court Command** impressed with some good efforts from a limited campaign, including when winning the Group 3 Golden Rose over seven furlongs at Rosehill. His other wins were gained in the Group 3 Up And Coming Stakes and Group 2 Stan Fox Stakes, both at Randwick, and he was a good third in the Caulfield Guineas on his first attempt at a mile. With just six outings to his name much can be expected from him in 2007.

Haradasun, a half-brother to 2005 Dubai Duty Free winner Elvstroem, is another exciting prospect, but he suffered a hairline fracture after running Miss Finland to a head in the McNeil Stakes when failing to get a clear run. He wasn't seen out again, but has reportedly made a full recovery. His prevous two appearances yielded impressive wins, including in the listed Vain Stakes over five and a half furlongs at Caulfield. **Nadeem** beat Miss Finland and subsequent Caulfield Guineas winner **Wonderful World** in the Blue Diamond Stakes in February on just his fourth start, but he suffered a leg injury soon after, and his absence was felt in the second half of the year.

From a limited number of races, the leading two-year-olds to emerge by the end of the year were **Murtajill** and **Husson Lightning**. The Group 3 Maribyrnong Plate at Flemington during Cup week won by Husson Lightning from **Deferential** confirmed Murtajill's standing as top juvenile. Previously Husson Lightning had been soundly beaten by Murtajill at Randwick in the listed Breeders Plate, when both horses were making their debut.

Ratings and text for Australia and New Zealand are supplied courtesy of Gary Crispe (www.racingandsports.com.au). The ages listed below are as at 31st December 2006.

Two-Year-Olds

118p	Murtajill
117	Husson Lightning
114p	Solo Flyer
114	Deferential
114	Royal Asscher (f)
113p	Mimi Lebrock (f)
113	Zizou
112	Hurried Choice (f)
111	Meurice
111	Miss Argyle (f)
111	Miss Watagan (f)

Three-Year-Olds

123	Miss Finland (f)
122	Gold Edition (f)
121p	Efficient
120p	Court Command
120	Haradasun

120	Nadeem
120	Wonderful World
119	Tuesday Joy (f)
118p	Reigning To Win
118	Mentality
118	Permaiscuous (f)
118?	Sender
117	Cheeky Choice (f)
117	Danleigh
117	Diego Garcia
117	Due Sasso
117	Excites
117	Plagiarize (f)
117	Teranaba
116	Anamato (f)
116	Churchill Downs
116	*Down The Wicket
116	The One
116?	Gorky Park
116?	Green Birdie
115p	Mearas
115	Casino Prince
115	Danever
115	Tarleton
115?	Mirror Mirror (f)

Four-Year-Olds

126	Racing To Win
125	Paratroopers
124	God's Own
124?	Headturner
123	Red Dazzler
123	Snitzel
122p	Pompeii Ruler
122	Apache Cat
122	California Dane
122	Mnemosyne (f)
121	Rewaaya (f)
121	Virage de Fortune (f)
120p	Natural Destiny
120	Perfectly Ready
120?	Stratum
119	Darci Brahma
119	Hotel Grand
119?	De Beers
119?	Growl
118	Maybe Better
118	Primus
118	Regal Cheer (f)
118?	Spinney
117p	Fast 'n' Famous
117	Al Samer
117	Divine Madonna (f)

117	Jet Spur	124	Eremein	118	Miss Andretti (f)
117	Media (f)	123	El Segundo	118	Utzon
117	Oh Oklahoma	123	Fields of Omagh	118?	Newton's Rings
117	Serenade Rose (f)	122	Casual Pass	117	Activation
117	Wasp	122	Court's In Session	117	Johan's Toy (f)
116	Magnus	122	Dance Hero	117	Men At Work
116	Shadoways	122	Malcolm	117	Roman Arch
116	Tesbury Jack	122	Patezza	117	Spark of Life
116	Written Tycoon	122	*Super Kid	117	Undue
115p	Marasco	120p	Tawqeet	117	Vroom Vroom
115	*Flying Pegasus	120	Lad of The Manor	117?	Dizelle (f)
115	Minson	120	Our Smoking Joe	116	Aqua d'Amore (f)
115	The Free Stater	120	Red Oog	116	Bentley Biscuit
115	Wahid	119	Above Deck	116	County Tyrone
115?	Ice Chariot	119	†Glamour Puss (f)	116	Zipping
		119	Niconero	116?	Grand Zulu
Older Horses		119	Railings	115	Stormhill
126	†Takeover Target	118p	Sphenophyta		
124	Desert War	118	†Falkirk		

INDEX TO PHOTOGRAPHS

PORTRAITS & SNAPSHOTS

Horse	Age & Breeding	Copyright	Page
Admiral's Cruise	4 b.c A P Indy – Ladies Cruise	John Crofts	33
Ad Valorem	4 b.c Danzig – Classy Women	Caroline Norris	35
Alcazar	11 b.g Alzao – Sahara Breeze	John Crofts	43
Amadeus Wolf	3 b.c Mozart – Rachelle	Alec Russell	60
Appalachian Trail ...	5 b.g Indian Ridge – Karinski	Alec Russell	68
Araafa	3 b.c Mull of Kintyre – Resurgence	John Crofts	72
Ashdown Express	7 ch.g Ashkalani – Indian Express	Clare Williams	83
Atlantic Waves	3 b.c Sadler's Wells – Highest Accolade	Alec Russell	90
Aussie Rules	3 gr.c Danehill – Last Second	Caroline Norris	94
Baltic King	6 b.h Danetime – Lindfield Belle	John Crofts	110
Benbaun	5 b.g Stravinsky – Escape To Victory	Clare Williams	124
Big Timer	2 ch.g Street Cry – Moonflute	Alec Russell	133
Borderlescott	4 b.g Compton Place – Jeewan	Alec Russell	153
Caradak	5 b.h Desert Style – Caraiyma	John Crofts	180
Cesare	5 b.g Machiavellian – Tromond	Clare Williams	191
Cockney Rebel	2 b.c Val Royal – Factice	Clare Williams	211
Confidential Lady ...	3 b.f Singspiel – Confidante	John Crofts	222
Conquest	2 b.c Invincible Spirit – Aguinaga	Clare Williams	225
Court Masterpiece ...	6 b.h Polish Precedent – Easy Option	John Crofts	237
Crosspeace	4 b.c Cape Cross – Announcing Peace	Alec Russell	243
Dandy Man	3 b.c Mozart – Lady Alexander	Peter Mooney	254
David Junior	4 ch.c Pleasant Tap – Paradise River	John Crofts	268
Desert Lord	6 b.g Green Desert – Red Carnival	Alec Russell	286
Dhanyata	2 b.f Danetime – Preponderance	John Crofts	290
Dixie Belle	3 b.f Diktat – Inspiring	Clare Williams	300
Dragon Dancer	3 b.c Sadler's Wells – Alakananda	Clare Williams	309
Dutch Art	2 ch.c Medicean – Halland Park Lass	John Crofts	321
Dylan Thomas	3 b.c Danehill – Lagrion	Caroline Norris	326
Echo of Light	4 b.c Dubai Millennium – Spirit of Tara	John Crofts	334
Enforcer	4 b.c Efisio – Tarneem	John Crofts	349
English Ballet	2 ch.f Danehill Dancer – Stage Presence	John Crofts	351
Enticing	2 b.f Pivotal – Superstar Leo	Clare Williams	352
Excellent Art	2 b.c Pivotal – Obsessive	Clare Williams	360
Finsceal Beo	2 ch.f Mr Greeley – Musical Treat	Peter Mooney	381
Firenze	5 ch.m Efisio – Juliet Bravo	Clare Williams	383
Fonthill Road	6 ch.g Royal Abjar – Hannah Huxtable	Alec Russell	393
Galatee	3 b.f Galileo – Altana	Peter Mooney	407
George Washington .	3 b.c Danehill – Bordighera	Caroline Norris	421
Hamoody	2 ch.c Johannesburg – Northern Gulch	John Crofts	456
Hawridge Prince	6 b.g Polar Falcon – Zahwa	Bill Selwyn	462
Hellvelyn	2 gr.c Ishiguru – Cumbrian Melody	Alec Russell	470
Iffraaj	5 b.h Zafonic – Pastorale	John Crofts	499
Indian Ink	2 ch.f Indian Ridge – Maid of Killeen	Clare Williams	508
Jadalee	3 b.c Desert Prince – Lionne	John Crofts	524
Jeremy	3 b.c Danehill Dancer – Glint In Her Eye	John Crofts	529
Kandidate	4 b.c Kabool – Valleyrose	John Crofts	543
Kastoria	5 ch.m Selkirk – Kassana	Peter Mooney	547
Killybegs	3 b.c Orpen – Belsay	John Crofts	555
Kirklees	2 b.c Jade Robbery – Moyesii	Alec Russell	563
Les Arcs	6 br.g Arch – La Sarto	Clare Williams	592
Librettist	4 b.c Danzig – Mysterial	John Crofts	598
Linas Selection	3 ch.c Selkirk – Lines of Beauty	Alec Russell	602
Majestic Missile	5 b.h Royal Applause – Tshusick	Clare Williams	627
Mandesha	3 b.f Desert Style – Mandalara	Bertrand	636
Mine	8 b.h Primo Dominie – Ellebanna	Alec Russell	667
Miss Beatrix	2 b.f Danehill Dancer – Miss Beabea	Caroline Norris	673
Misu Bond	3 b.c Danehill Dancer – Hawala	Alec Russell	681
Mulaqat	3 b.c Singspiel – Samana	John Crofts	708
Multidimensional	3 b.c Danehill – Sacred Song	Clare Williams	709
Mutamared	6 ch.g Nureyev – Alydariel	Alec Russell	515

1257

Nannina	3 b.f Medicean – Hill Hopper	*John Crofts*	726
Nightime	3 ch.f Galileo – Caumshinaun	*Peter Mooney*	738
Noelani	4 b.f Indian Ridge – Dawnsio	*Peter Mooney*	742
Notnowcato	4 ch.c Inchinor – Rambling Rose	*John Crofts*	748
Olympian Odyssey	3 b.c Sadler's Wells – Field of Hope	*John Crofts*	756
Ouija Board	5 b.m Cape Cross – Selection Board	*John Crofts*	770
Papal Bull	3 b.c Montjeu – Mialuna	*John Crofts*	780
Paradise Isle	5 b.m Bahamian Bounty – Merry Rous	*Clare Williams*	783
Presto Shinko	5 b.g Shinko Forest – Swift Chorus	*Clare Williams*	821
Pride	6 b.m Peintre Celebre – Specificity	*Bertrand*	825
Primary	3 b.c Giant's Causeway – Prospective	*Clare Williams*	827
Prince of Light	3 ch.c Fantastic Light – Miss Queen	*Alec Russell*	830
Prince Tamino	3 b.g Mozart – Premiere Dance	*John Crofts*	835
Rail Link	3 b.c Dansili – Docklands	*Bertrand*	854
Rajeem	3 b.f Diktat – Magic Sister	*John Crofts*	859
Red Evie	3 b.f Intikhab – Malafemmena	*John Crofts*	870
Red Rocks	3 b.c Galileo – Pharmacist	*John Crofts*	875
Reunite	3 ch.f Kingmambo – Allez Les Trois	*Clare Williams*	883
Reverence	5 ch.g Mark of Esteem – Imperial Bailiwick	*Alec Russell*	886
Road To Love	3 ch.g Fruits of Love – Alpine Flair	*Alec Russell*	897
Sander Camillo	2 b.f Dixie Union – Staraway	*John Crofts*	923
Satchem	4 br.c Inchinor – Mohican Princess	*John Crofts*	927
Sergeant Cecil	7 ch.g King's Signet – Jadidh	*Bill Selwyn*	943
Sesmen	2 br.f Inchinor – Poetry In Motion	*Clare Williams*	945
Shirocco	5 b.h Monsun – So Sedulous	*John Crofts*	956
Silk Blossom	2 ch.f Barathea – Lovely Blossom	*John Crofts*	964
Simply Perfect	2 gr.f Danehill – Hotelgenie Dot Com	*John Crofts*	971
Sir Gerard	3 b.c Marju – Chapeau	*Clare Williams*	975
Sir Percy	3 b.c Mark of Esteem – Percy's Lass	*John Crofts*	981
Snoqualmie Boy	3 b.c Montjeu – Seattle Ribbon	*Clare Williams*	994
Soviet Song	6 b.m Marju – Kalinka	*Clare Williams*	1009
Speciosa	3 b.f Danehill Dancer – Specifically	*Clare Williams*	1014
Spectait	4 b.g Spectrum – Shanghai Girl	*John Crofts*	1017
Spinning Queen	3 ch.f Spinning World – Our Queen of Kings	*John Crofts*	1020
Stormy River	3 gr.c Verglas – Miss Bio	*Bertrand*	1038
Takeover Target	7 b.g Celtic Swing – Shady Stream	*Clare Williams*	1064
Tam Lin	3 b.c Selkirk – La Nuit Rose	*John Crofts*	1067
Teofilo	2 b.c Galileo – Speirbhean	*Peter Mooney*	1081
Wi Dud	2 b.c Elnadim – Hopesay	*Alec Russell*	1158
Yeats	5 b.h Sadler's Wells – Lyndonville	*Caroline Norris*	1174
Young Mick	4 br.g King's Theatre – Just Warning	*Clare Williams*	1182

RACE PHOTOGRAPHS

Race and Meeting	Copyright	Page
Abergwaun Stakes (Tipperary)	*Caroline Norris*	790
ABN Amro Goodwood Cup (Goodwood)	*John Crofts*	1173
Addleshaw Goddard Stakes (Esher) (Sandown)	*John Crofts*	578
Addleshaw Goddard Stakes (Handicap) (York)	*Alec Russell*	992
Anheuser-Busch Adventure Parks Railway Stakes (the Curragh)	*Peter Mooney*	482
Arima Kinen (Nakayama)	*Keiba Books*	277
Ascot Stakes (Handicap) (Royal Ascot)	*John Crofts*	102
Audi Pretty Polly Stakes (the Curragh)	*George Selwyn*	45
Audi Stakes (King George) (Goodwood)	*John Crofts*	570
Baileys Irish Champion Stakes (Leopardstown)	*Frank Sorge*	325
Bank of Scotland Corporate Hambleton Stakes (Handicap) (York)	*John Crofts*	1188
betdirect.co.uk Winter Derby (Lingfield)	*Lesley Sampson*	1026
Betfair Cup (Lennox) (Goodwood)	*John Crofts*	498
betfred.com Mile (Sandown)	*Ed Byrne*	898
betfredpoker.com Old Borough Cup Stakes (Handicap) (Haydock)	*Bill Selwyn*	797
Betfred Sprint Cup (Haydock)	*Bill Selwyn*	885
bet365.com EBF Maiden Fillies Stakes (Newmarket)	*Lesley Sampson*	653
bet365 Lancashire Oaks (Haydock)	*Alec Russell*	53
bet365 Old Newton Cup (Handicap) (Haydock)	*Alec Russell*	226
BGC Stakes (Gordon) (Goodwood)	*John Crofts*	984
Blue Square Ormonde Stakes (Chester)	*John Crofts*	1092
Boylesports Irish 1000 Guineas (the Curragh)	*Caroline Norris*	737

Boylesports Irish 2000 Guineas (the Curragh)	*Peter Mooney*	71
Britannia Stakes (Handicap) (Royal Ascot)	*John Crofts*	974
Buckingham Palace Stakes (Handicap) (Royal Ascot)	*John Crofts*	1125
Budweiser Irish Derby (the Curragh)	*Caroline Norris*	323
cantorspreadfair.com Stakes (Handicap) (Goodwood)	*Bill Selwyn*	1040
Cantor Spreadfair Sussex Stakes (Goodwood)	*John Crofts*	236
Cathay Pacific Hong Kong Cup (Sha Tin)	*George Selwyn*	824
Cathay Pacific Hong Kong Vase (Sha Tin)	*George Selwyn*	215
Celebrated Artist Piran Strange Paints For Sparks Stakes (Serlby) (Windsor)	*John Crofts*	51
Cervoglass Fortune Stakes (Haydock)	*Alec Russell*	846
Cheshire Regiment Dee Stakes (sponsored by the Elifar Foundation) (Chester)	*John Crofts*	79
Chippenham Lodge Stud Cherry Hinton Stakes (Newmarket)	*Ed Byrne*	922
Coolmore Fusaichi Pegasus Matron Stakes (Leopardstown)	*Frank Sorge*	869
Coral-Eclipse Stakes (Sandown)	*John Crofts*	267
Coral Sprint Trophy (York)	*Alec Russell*	893
Coronation Stakes (Royal Ascot)	*Alec Russell*	725
Coventry Stakes (Royal Ascot)	*Ed Byrne*	469
Criterium de Maisons-Laffitte (Maisons-Laffitte)	*John Crofts*	177
Criterium de Saint-Cloud (Saint-Cloud)	*John Crofts*	786
Criterium International (Saint-Cloud)	*Ed Byrne*	699
Darley Dewhurst Stakes (Newmarket)	*Alec Russell*	1080
Darley Irish Oaks (the Curragh)	*Peter Mooney*	48
Darley July Cup (Newmarket)	*John Crofts*	590
Darley Prix Jean Romanet (Deauville)	*Bertrand*	928
Darley Prix Morny (Deauville)	*Bill Selwyn*	319
Darley Yorkshire Oaks (York)	*John Crofts*	49
David Wilson Homes Jockey Club Cup (Newmarket)	*John Crofts*	461
Derby Italiano (Rome)	*Stefano Grasso*	414
Doonside Cup Stakes (Sponsored By Easy-Breaks.com) (Ayr)	*Alec Russell*	647
Dubai Duty Free Arc Trial (Newbury)	*John Crofts*	141
Dubai Duty Free Mill Reef Stakes (Newbury)	*Bill Selwyn*	359
Dubai Duty Free Sponsored By Dubai Duty Free (Nad Al Sheba)	*George Selwyn*	266
Dubai Sheema Classic Sponsored By Nakheel (Nad Al Sheba)	*Bill Selwyn*	466
Dubai Tennis Championships Stakes (John Porter) (Newbury)	*John Crofts*	705
Dubai World Cup Sponsored By Emirates Airline (Nad Al Sheba)	*George Selwyn*	340
Duke of Edinburgh Stakes (Handicap) (Royal Ascot)	*John Crofts*	1180
Duke of York Hearthstead Homes Stakes (York)	*Ed Byrne*	1033
EBF Dubai Tennis Championships Maiden Stakes (Newbury)	*John Crofts*	837
EBF Galtres Stakes (York)	*John Crofts*	65
Emirates Airline Breeders' Cup Filly & Mare Turf (Churchill Downs)	*George Selwyn*	769
Emirates Airline Champion Stakes (Newmarket)	*Alec Russell*	823
Emirates Airline Yorkshire Cup (York)	*Alec Russell*	798
Gainsborough Poule d'Essai des Poulains (Longchamp)	*Bertrand*	93
Gainsborough Poule d'Essai des Pouliches (Longchamp)	*Ed Byrne*	1097
Galileo EBF Futurity Stakes (the Curragh)	*Peter Mooney*	1078
GNER Doncaster Cup (York)	*Alec Russell*	942
Gold Cup (Royal Ascot)	*Alec Russell*	1172
Golden Jubilee Stakes (Royal Ascot)	*Alec Russell*	589
Gran Criterium (Milan)	*Stefano Grasso*	562
Grand Prix de Deauville Lucien Barriere (Deauville)	*Bertrand*	517
Grand Prix de Saint-Cloud (Saint-Cloud)	*Bertrand*	823
Gran Premio del Jockey Club Italiano (Milan)	*Stefano Grasso*	583
Grosvenor Casinos Cumberland Lodge Stakes (Ascot)	*Ed Byrne*	1181
Hardwicke Stakes (Royal Ascot)	*John Crofts*	640
Hong Kong Jockey Club Sprint (Handicap) (Ascot)	*Bill Selwyn*	621
Igloos Bentinck Stakes (Newmarket)	*Bill Selwyn*	166
Independent Waterford Wedgwood Phoenix Stakes (the Curragh)	*Peter Mooney*	483
intercasino.co.uk Easter Stakes (Kempton)	*John Crofts*	87
'In The Pink' Rockfel Stakes (Sponsored By Owen Brown) (Newmarket)	*John Crofts*	379
Invesco Perpetual Goodwood Stakes (Handicap) (Goodwood)	*John Crofts*	552
Irish Field St Leger (the Curragh)	*Peter Mooney*	546
Irish National Stud Blandford Stakes (the Curragh)	*Caroline Norris*	866
Irish Thoroughbred Marketing Park Hill Stakes (York)	*George Selwyn*	891

Iveco Daily Solario Stakes (Sandown)	*John Crofts*	314
IVG - Preis von Europa (Cologne)	*Frank Sorge*	1178
Jaguar Cars Lowther Stakes (York)	*Alec Russell*	963
Japan Cup (Tokyo)	*Bill Selwyn*	275
Jardine Lloyd Thompson Huxley Stakes (Chester)	*Alec Russell*	639
John Deere Breeders' Cup Turf (Churchill Downs)	*George Selwyn*	874
John Guest Diadem Stakes (Ascot)	*George Selwyn*	867
John Smith's Cup (Handicap) (York)	*Alec Russell*	365
John Smith's 'Extra Cold' Chipchase Stakes (Newcastle)	*Bill Selwyn*	372
John Smith's Northumberland Plate (Newcastle)	*Alec Russell*	1105
John Smith's Stakes (Handicap) (Newbury)	*Ed Byrne*	809
Juddmonte Beresford Stakes (the Curragh)	*Caroline Norris*	328
Juddmonte Grand Prix de Paris (Longchamp)	*Bertrand*	850
Juddmonte International Stakes (York)	*John Crofts*	747
Juddmonte Lockinge Stakes (Newbury)	*George Selwyn*	793
Juddmonte Royal Lodge Stakes (Ascot)	*Ed Byrne*	31
Keepmoat May Hill Stakes (York)	*John Crofts*	969
Killavullan Stakes (Leopardstown)	*Peter Mooney*	223
Kingdom of Bahrain Sun Chariot Stakes (Newmarket)	*Ed Byrne*	1019
King Edward VII Stakes (Royal Ascot)	*John Crofts*	779
King George V Stakes (Handicap) (Royal Ascot)	*John Crofts*	601
King George VI and Queen Elizabeth Diamond Stakes (Ascot)	*Frank Sorge*	493
King of Beers Stakes (Richard H. Faught Memorial) (the Curragh)	*Peter Mooney*	253
King's Stand Stakes (Royal Ascot)	*George Selwyn*	1061
Ladbrokes Bunbury Cup (Handicap) (Newmarket)	*Ed Byrne*	666
ladbrokes.com Stakes (Handicap) (Ascot)	*John Crofts*	798
ladbrokes.com Stakes (Handicap) (Goodwood)	*John Crofts*	896
Ladbrokes Great Voltigeur Stakes (York)	*John Crofts*	1177
Ladbrokes Portland (Handicap) (York)	*Alec Russell*	368
Ladbrokes Rockingham Handicap (the Curragh)	*Caroline Norris*	765
Ladbrokes St Leger Stakes (York)	*George Selwyn*	985
Ladbrokes Summer Mile Stakes (Lingfield)	*Lesley Sampson*	333
Laing O'Rourke National Stakes (the Curragh)	*Peter Mooney*	1079
Laing O'Rourke Solonaway Stakes (the Curragh)	*Caroline Norris*	521
Laurent-Perrier Champagne Sprint Stakes (Sandown)	*George Selwyn*	811
Lillie Langtry Fillies' Stakes (Goodwood)	*John Crofts*	1071
London Paddy Power Gold Cup (Handicap) (Newbury)	*John Crofts*	792
Mehl-Mulhens-Rennen - German 2000 Guineas (Cologne)	*Frank Sorge*	908
Meon Valley Stud Fillies' Mile (Ascot)	*John Crofts*	970
Merbury Catering Consultants Supreme Stakes (Goodwood)	*Bill Selwyn*	1044
Montjeu Coolmore Prix Saint-Alary (Longchamp)	*Bertrand*	423
Moyglare Stud Stakes (the Curragh)	*Peter Mooney*	671
National Bank of Dubai Cup (Handicap) (Ascot)	*Ed Byrne*	1181
NGK Spark Plugs Maiden Stakes (Newmarket)	*Ed Byrne*	86
Patrick P. O'Leary Memorial Phoenix Sprint Stakes (the Curragh)	*Caroline Norris*	695
Pattison Canadian International Stakes (Woodbine)	*Michael Burns*	214
Persimmon Homes Flying Childers Stakes (York)	*John Crofts*	1157
Phil Bull Trophy Conditions Stakes (Pontefract)	*Alec Russell*	1002
Prince of Wales's Stakes (Royal Ascot)	*John Crofts*	767
Princess Elizabeth Stakes (Sponsored By Vodafone) (Epsom)	*Alec Russell*	332
Princess of Wales's wbx.com Stakes (Newmarket)	*Ed Byrne*	997
Prix Daniel Wildenstein Castel Marie-Louise de la Baule (Longchamp)	*Bertrand*	333
Prix d'Astarte (Deauville)	*Bertrand*	633
Prix de Diane Hermes (Chantilly)	*Bertrand*	221
Prix de l'Abbaye de Longchamp Majestic Barriere (Longchamp)	*Ed Byrne*	285
Prix de la Foret Casino Barriere de Biarritz (Longchamp)	*John Crofts*	179
Prix de l'Arc de Triomphe Lucien Barriere (Longchamp)	*Bertrand*	852
Prix de l'Opera Casino Barriere d'Enghien Les Bains (Longchamp)	*Bertrand*	635
Prix de Meautry Lucien Barriere (Deauville)	*Bertrand*	509
Prix d'Ispahan (Longchamp)	*Bertrand*	583
Prix du Cadran Casino Les Princes Barriere de Cannes (Longchamp)	*Frank Sorge*	942
Prix du Gros-Chene Mitsubishi Motors (Chantilly)	*John Crofts*	694
Prix du Haras de Fresnay-le-Buffard Jacques le Marois (Deauville)	*John Crofts*	596

Prix du Jockey Club Mitsubishi Motors (Chantilly)	*Ed Byrne*	263
Prix du Moulin de Longchamp (Longchamp)	*Bill Selwyn*	597
Prix Foy Gray d'Albion Barriere (Longchamp)	*Bertrand*	955
Prix Ganay - Grand Prix Air Mauritius (Longchamp)	*John Crofts*	231
Prix Greffulhe Mitsubishi Motors (Saint-Cloud)	*Bertrand*	1139
Prix Jean-Luc Lagardere (Grand Criterium) (Longchamp)	*Bertrand*	484
Prix Jean Prat (Chantilly)	*Bertrand*	1037
Prix Maurice de Gheest (Deauville)	*Bertrand*	642
Prix Marcel Boussac-Criterium des Pouliches Royal Barriere Deauville (Longchamp)	*Bertrand*	378
Prix Niel Casino Barriere d'Enghien Les Bains (Longchamp)	*Ed Byrne*	851
Prix Royal-Oak (Longchamp)	*Bertrand*	687
Prix Vermeille Lucien Barriere (Longchamp)	*John Crofts*	634
Queen Alexandra Stakes (Royal Ascot)	*Bill Selwyn*	103
Queen Anne Stakes (Royal Ascot)	*John Crofts*	34
Queen Elizabeth II Stakes (Ascot)	*John Crofts*	419
Queen Mary Stakes (Royal Ascot)	*Alec Russell*	425
Queen's Vase (Royal Ascot)	*John Crofts*	996
Racing Post Trophy (Newbury)	*John Crofts*	96
Red Corner Events Queensferry Stakes (Chester)	*Alan Wright*	1089
Rheinland-Pokal der Sparkasse KolnBonn (Cologne)	*Frank Sorge*	199
Ribblesdale Stakes (Royal Ascot)	*Alec Russell*	688
Royal Hunt Cup (Handicap) (Royal Ascot)	*John Crofts*	190
Scottish Equitable Gimcrack Stakes (York)	*John Crofts*	224
Shadwell Middle Park Stakes (Newmarket)	*John Crofts*	320
Shelbourne Hotel Goffs Fillies Five Hundred (the Curragh)	*Caroline Norris*	964
Shelbourne Hotel Goffs Million (the Curragh)	*Bill Selwyn*	672
Sky Bet Cheveley Park Stakes (Newmarket)	*Ed Byrne*	507
Skybet Dash (Handicap) (York)	*Alec Russell*	1168
Skybet York Stakes (York)	*Alec Russell*	129
Snap On Equipment Solutions EBF Maiden Stakes (Newmarket)	*Ed Byrne*	29
Somerville Tattersall Stakes (Newmarket)	*Ed Byrne*	1093
Sony Shergar Cup Mile (Handicap) (Ascot)	*George Selwyn*	831
Sprinters Stakes (Nakayama)	*Keiba Books*	1063
Stan James Horris Hill Stakes (Newbury)	*John Crofts*	294
Stan James 1000 Guineas Stakes (Newmarket)	*George Selwyn*	1013
Stan James 2000 Guineas Stakes (Newmarket)	*Ed Byrne*	417
Stanscasino.co.uk Conditions Stakes (Newmarket)	*Bill Selwyn*	697
Sterling Insurance Richmond Stakes (Goodwood)	*Bill Selwyn*	455
St James's Palace Stakes (Royal Ascot)	*John Crofts*	71
Swettenham Stud Fillies' Trial Stakes (Newbury)	*John Crofts*	933
Takarazuka Kinen (Kyoto)	*Keiba Books*	274
Tatler Summer Season Stakes (Handicap) (Goodwood)	*Bill Selwyn*	1005
Tattersalls Gold Cup (the Curragh)	*Peter Mooney*	491
Tattersalls Ireland Sale Stakes (the Curragh)	*Caroline Norris*	516
Tattersalls Musidora Stakes (York)	*Ed Byrne*	958
The Sportsman Newspaper Champagne Stakes (York)	*John Crofts*	1141
The Sportsman Newspaper Geoffrey Freer Stakes (Newbury)	*John Crofts*	32
The Sportsman Newspaper Hungerford Stakes (Newbury)	*John Crofts*	1151
£300000 St Leger Yearling Stakes (York)	*George Selwyn*	302
Timeform Silver Salver (Cecil Frail) (Haydock)	*Alec Russell*	782
TNT July Stakes (Newmarket)	*Ed Byrne*	1041
totepool Silver Bowl (Handicap) (Haydock)	*Alec Russell*	64
totepool Two-Year-Old Trophy (Redcar)	*Alec Russell*	259
totescoop6 Stakes (Handicap) (Sandown)	*Ed Byrne*	478
totesport Ayr Gold Cup (Handicap) (Ayr)	*Empics*	392
totesport Cambridgeshire (Handicap) (Newmarket)	*Ed Byrne*	396
totesport Celebration Mile (Goodwood)	*George Selwyn*	178
totesport Cesarewitch (Handicap) (Newmarket)	*John Crofts*	288
totesport Chester Cup (Handicap) (Chester)	*Alec Russell*	30
totesport.com Derby Trial Stakes (Lingfield)	*John Crofts*	603
totesport.com Heritage Handicap (Beverley)	*Alec Russell*	192
totesport.com November Stakes (Handicap) (Windsor)	*John Crofts*	448
totesport.com September Stakes (Kempton)	*John Crofts*	542
totesport.com Silver Tankard Stakes (Pontefract)	*Alec Russell*	1056
totesport.com Stakes (Handicap) (Ascot)	*Ed Byrne*	54
totesport.com Stakes (Handicap) (Haydock)	*Alec Russell*	258

totesport.com Stakes (Handicap) (Newmarket)	*Bill Selwyn*	262
totesport.com Winter Hill Stakes (Windsor)	*George Selwyn*	1066
totesport Dante Stakes (York)	*John Crofts*	940
totesport Ebor (Handicap) (York)	*Alec Russell*	706
totesport International Stakes (Handicap) (Ascot)	*Ed Byrne*	248
totesport 0800 221 221 Stakes (Handicap) (Ascot)	*Ed Byrne*	804
totesport 0800 221 221 Stakes (Handicap) (Lingfield)	*George Selwyn*	567
£250000 Tattersalls October Auction Stakes (Newmarket)	*John Crofts*	170
UAE Derby Sponsored by S & M Al Naboodah Group (Nad Al Sheba)	*Frank Sorge*	296
UAE Equestrian And Racing Federation Falmouth Stakes (Newmarket)	*John Crofts*	858
United Arab Emirates Racing And Equestrian Federation Royal Whip Stakes (the Curragh)	*Caroline Norris*	714
VC Bet Challenge Stakes (Newmarket)	*Alec Russell*	989
VC Bet Nunthorpe Stakes (York)	*Bill Selwyn*	884
Veuve Clicquot Vintage Stakes (Goodwood)	*John Crofts*	1041
Vodafone Coronation Cup (Epsom)	*Ed Byrne*	955
Vodafone 'Dash' Stakes (Handicap) (Epsom)	*Alec Russell*	285
Vodafone Derby Stakes (Epsom)	*George Selwyn*	977
Vodafone Derby Stakes (Epsom)	*John Crofts*	978
Vodafone Derby Stakes (Epsom)	*John Crofts*	979
Vodafone Diomed Stakes (Epsom)	*John Crofts*	730
Vodafone Live! Stakes (Handicap) (Epsom)	*Alec Russell*	1027
Vodafone Nassau Stakes (Goodwood)	*John Crofts*	768
Vodafone Oaks (Epsom)	*Ed Byrne*	47
Vodafone Rose Bowl (Handicap) (Epsom)	*John Crofts*	193
Vodafone Stewards' Cup (Handicap) (Goodwood)	*Ed Byrne*	152
Watership Down Stud Sales Race (Ascot)	*Steven Cargill*	506
wbx.com World Bet Exchange Henry II Stakes (Sandown)	*George Selwyn*	1121
Weatherbys Bank Cheshire Oaks (Chester)	*Alec Russell*	1100
Weatherbys Superlative Stakes (Newmarket)	*John Crofts*	454
Weatherbys Super Sprint (Newbury)	*John Crofts*	341
William Hill Great St Wilfrid Stakes (Ripon)	*Alec Russell*	361
William Hill Lincoln (Handicap) (Redcar)	*Alec Russell*	143
William Hill Trophy (Handicap) (York)	*Alec Russell*	834
Windsor Forest Stakes (Royal Ascot)	*Alec Russell*	1008
Wokingham Stakes (Handicap) (Royal Ascot)	*John Crofts*	109

ADDITIONAL PHOTOGRAPHS

The following photographs appear in the Introduction:– Sir Michael Stoute (photo taken by Bill Selwyn), Ryan Moore (John Crofts), Royal Ascot returns home (Ed Byrne), the Derby finish (Alec Russell), the One Thousand Guineas (George Selwyn), Frankie Dettori dismounts from Ouija Board (Bill Selwyn), Fulke Johnson Houghton and Richard Quinn (both Bill Selwyn).

Credits for the photographs in 'Top Horses Abroad' are as follows:– Deutsches Derby and Grosser Preis von Baden (both Frank Sorge), Premio Vittorio di Capua and Premio Parioli (Stefano Grasso), Dubai Golden Shaheen and Godolphin Mile (Frank Sorge), Kentucky Derby and Preakness Stakes (International Racing Photos), Breeders' Cup Classic, Breeders' Cup Sprint and Breeders' Cup Mile (all George Selwyn), Arlington Million (International Racing Photos), Breeders' Cup Juvenile (George Selwyn), Melbourne Cup (Bronwen Healy), Japan Cup Dirt (Bill Selwyn), Hong Kong Sprint and Hong Kong Mile (George Selwyn), Cox Plate (Bronwen Healy).

by Baillamont

ACT ONE

**Highest Rated French-trained Two Year Old
Timeform: 124**

GROUP 1 WINNER AT 2 AND 3

**Successful FIRST CROP SIRE in 2006
with a host of eye-catching youngsters
scoring at Grade 1 racecourses in the last
months of the Turf Season**

By INDIAN RIDGE - NOSEY
by Nebbiolo

COMPTON PLACE

CHAMPION EUROPEAN
3-Y-O SPRINTER
THE LEADING BRITISH SIRE OF
2-Y-O's in 2006 *(% winners to runners)*

*Yearlings sold for 120,000gns, 105,000gns, €105,000,
100,000gns, etc, in 2006*

UP TO 24x HIS 2004 FEE

FREE OF NORTHERN DANCER BLOOD

By GROOM DANCER -
DANCE QUEST
by Green Dancer

PURSUIT OF LOVE

SIRE OF THE WINNERS OF

748 RACES and **OVER £7.5 million (60% W/R)**

In 2006 Sire of **dual Gr.3 winner TARTOUCHE**

(Lillie Langtry Fillies' Stakes at Goodwood in 2005 and 2006)
and Stakes-placed **Lasika** *(2nd Winter Stakes in USA)*

Broodmare Sire of

**ATTRACTION (Gr.1), ANTONIUS PIUS (Gr.2,) WINDHUK
(Gr.2), SILCA'S GIFT (Gr.3), VIOLETTE (Gr.3)**

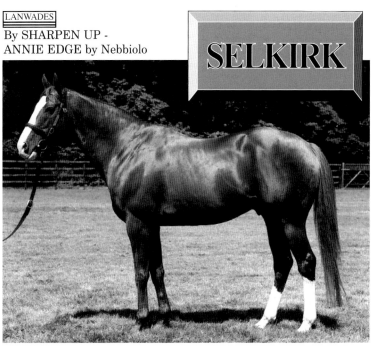

By FORZANDO -
DEVIL'S DIRGE by Song

THE CHAMPIONS

Timeform's 'Racehorses' series stretches back to 1948 when the first prototype Annual—the 'Timeform Supplement'—was produced covering the 1947 season. The selecting of a 'horse of the year' began in the 'sixties.

Horse of the Year

The title has usually been awarded to the highest rated horse, except in 1969 (when Habitat was rated higher at 134), 1984 (El Gran Senor 136), 1985 (Slip Anchor 136) and 2003 (Hawk Wing 136).

1960	Charlottesville	**135**
	Floribunda	**135**
1961	Molvedo	**137**
1962	Match	**135**
1963	Exbury	**138**
1964	Relko	**136**
1965	Sea Bird	**145**
1966	Danseur	**134**
1967	Petingo	**135**
1968	Vaguely Noble	**140**
1969	Levmoss	**133**
1970	Nijinsky	**138**
1971	Brigadier Gerard	**141**
	Mill Reef	**141**
1972	Brigadier Gerard	**144**
1973	Apalachee	**137**
	Rheingold	**137**
1974	Allez France	**136**
1975	Grundy	**137**
1976	Youth	**135**
1977	Alleged	**137**
1978	Alleged	**138**
1979	Troy	**137**
1980	Moorestyle	**137**
1981	Shergar	**140**
1982	Ardross	**134**
1983	Habibti	**136**
1984	Provideo	**112**

1985	Pebbles	**135**
1986	Dancing Brave	**140**
1987	Reference Point	**139**
1988	Warning	**136**
1989	Zilzal	**137**
1990	Dayjur	**137**
1991	Generous	**139**
1992	St Jovite	**135**
1993	Opera House	**131**
1994	Celtic Swing	**138**
1995	Lammtarra	**134**
1996	Mark of Esteem	**137**
1997	Peintre Celebre	**137**
1998	Intikhab	**135**
1999	Daylami	**138**
2000	Dubai Millennium	**140**
2001	Sakhee	**136**
2002	Rock of Gibraltar	**133**
2003	Falbrav	**133**
2004	Doyen	**132**
2005	Hurricane Run	**134**
2006	George Washington	**133**

Best Two-Year-Old Colt

Year	Horse	Rating	Year	Horse	Rating
1960	Floribunda	**135**	1979	Monteverdi	**129**
1961	Abdos	**134 p**	1980	Storm Bird	**134**
1962	Le Mesnil	**131 ?**	1981	Wind And Wuthering	**132**
1963	Santa Claus	**133 +**	1982	Diesis	**133**
	Showdown	**133**	1983	El Gran Senor	**131**
1964	Grey Dawn	**132**	1984	Kala Dancer	**129**
1965	Soleil	**133**	1985	Huntingdale	**132**
	Young Emperor	**133**	1986	Reference Point	**132**
1966	Bold Lad (Ire)	**133**	1987	Warning	**127 p**
1967	Petingo	**135**	1988	Prince of Dance	**128**
1968	Ribofilio	**130**		Scenic	**128**
	Yelapa	**130**	1989	Be My Chief	**123 p**
1969	Nijinsky	**131**	1990	Hector Protector	**122 p**
1970	My Swallow	**134**	1991	Arazi	**135**
1971	Deep Diver	**134**	1992	Armiger	**131 p**
1972	Simbir	**130**	1993	Grand Lodge	**120 p**
	Targowice	**130**	1994	Celtic Swing	**138**
1973	Apalachee	**137**	1995	Alhaarth	**126 p**
1974	Grundy	**134**	1996	Bahhare	**122 p**
1975	Manado	**130**		Revoque	**122 p**
1976	Blushing Groom	**131**	1997	Xaar	**132**
1977	Try My Best	**130 p**	1998	Mujahid	**125 p**
1978	Tromos	**134**	1999	Distant Music	**121 p**

2000	Nayef	**123 p**	2004	Shamardal	**126 p**
2001	Johannesburg	**127**	2005	Horatio Nelson	**123 +**
2002	Oasis Dream	**122**	2006	Teofilo	**126**
2003	Bago	**121 p**			

Best Two-Year-Old Filly

1960	Kathy Too	**131**	1985	Femme Elite	**124**
1961	La Tendresse	**135**	1986	Forest Flower	**127**
1962	Hula Dancer	**133**	1987	Ravinella	**121 p**
1963	Texanita	**128**	1988	Pass The Peace	**116 p**
1964	Fall In Love	**126**		Tessla	**116 p**
1965	Soft Angels	**124**	1989	Negligent	**118 p**
1966	Silver Cloud	**125**	1990	Shadayid	**117 p**
1967	Sovereign	**129**	1991	Midnight Air	**111 p**
1968	Saraca	**125**	1992	Sayyedati	**116 p**
1969	Mange Tout	**125**	1993	Lemon Souffle	**115**
1970	Cawston's Pride	**131**	1994	Gay Gallanta	**112**
1971	First Bloom	**129**	1995	Blue Duster	**116 p**
1972	Jacinth	**133**	1996	Dazzle	**116 d**
1973	Hippodamia	**130**		Red Camellia	**116**
1974	Broadway Dancer	**131**	1997	Embassy	**114**
1975	Theia	**128**	1998	Bint Allayl	**114 p**
1976	Cloonlara	**130**	1999	Morning Pride	**113 p**
1977	Cherry Hinton	**125**	2000	Superstar Leo	**114**
1978	Sigy	**132**	2001	Queen's Logic	**125**
1979	Aryenne	**120**	2002	Six Perfections	**120 p**
1980	Marwell	**124**	2003	Attraction	**118**
1981	Circus Ring	**122**	2004	Divine Proportions	**119**
1982	Ma Biche	**123**	2005	Rumplestiltskin	**116**
1983	Treizieme	**121**	2006	Finsceal Bio	**118**
1984	Triptych	**125**			

Best Sprinter

1960	Bleep Bleep	**134**	1987	Ajdal	**130**
1961	Floribunda	**136**	1988	Soviet Star	**128**
1962	Gay Mairi	**131**	1989	Cadeaux Genereux	**131**
	Secret Step	**131**	1990	Dayjur	**137**
1963	Matatina	**132**	1991	Polish Patriot	**128**
1964	Althrey Don	**130**	1992	Sheikh Albadou	**128**
1965	Majority Blue	**126**	1993	Lochsong	**129**
	Port Merion	**126**	1994	Lochsong	**129**
1966	Caterina	**124**	1995	Lake Coniston	**131**
1967	Be Friendly	**126**	1996	Anabaa	**130**
1968	Be Friendly	**130**	1997	Elnadim	**126 p**
	So Blessed	**130**	1998	Elnadim	**128**
1969	Song	**132**	1999	Stravinsky	**133**
1970	Amber Rama	**133**	2000	Namid	**128**
	Balidar	**133**	2001	Mozart	**131**
	Huntercombe	**133**	2002	Kyllachy	**129**
1971	Joshua	**129**	2003	Oasis Dream	**129**
1972	Deep Diver	**134**	2004	Somnus	**126**
1973	Sandford Lad	**133**		Tante Rose	**126**
1974	Saritamer	**130**	2005	Pastoral Pursuits	**127**
1975	Flirting Around	**134**	2006	Reverence	**127**
1976	Lochnager	**132**			
1977	Gentilhombre	**131**			
1978	Solinus	**130**			
1979	Thatching	**131**			
1980	Moorestyle	**137**			
1981	Marwell	**133**			
1982	Sharpo	**130**			
1983	Habibti	**136**			
1984	Chief Singer	**131**			
1985	Never So Bold	**135**			
1986	Last Tycoon	**131**			

Best Miler

Year	Horse	Rating	Year	Horse	Rating
1960	Martial	131	1986	Dancing Brave	140
1961	Petite Etoile	131	1987	Miesque	131
1962	Romulus	129	1988	Warning	136
1963	Hula Dancer	133	1989	Zilzal	137
1964	Baldric	131	1990	Markofdistinction	130
1965	Carlemont	132		Royal Academy	130
1966	Silver Shark	129	1991	Selkirk	129
1967	Reform	132	1992	Lahib	129
1968	Sir Ivor	135		Selkirk	129
1969	Habitat	134	1993	Zafonic	130
1970	Nijinsky	138	1994	Barathea	127
1971	Brigadier Gerard	141	1995	Pennekamp	130
1972	Brigadier Gerard	144	1996	Mark of Esteem	137
1973	Thatch	136	1997	Spinning World	130
1974	Nonoalco	131	1998	Intikhab	135
1975	Bolkonski	134	1999	Dubai Millennium	132
1976	Wollow	132	2000	King's Best	132
1977	Blushing Groom	131	2001	Medicean	128
1978	Homing	130		Slickly	128
1979	Kris	135	2002	Rock of Gibraltar	133
1980	Known Fact	135	2003	Hawk Wing	136
1981	Northjet	136	2004	Haafhd	129
1982	Green Forest	134		Rakti	129
1983	Luth Enchantee	130	2005	Proclamation	130
1984	El Gran Senor	136		Rakti	130
1985	Shadeed	135	2006	George Washington	133

Best Middle-Distance Horse

Year	Horse	Rating	Year	Horse	Rating
1960	Charlottesville	135	1993	Opera House	131
1961	Molvedo	137	1994	Balanchine	131
1962	Match	135	1995	Lammtarra	134
1963	Exbury	138	1996	Helissio	136
1964	Relko	136	1997	Peintre Celebre	137
1965	Sea Bird	145	1998	Swain	132
1966	Nelcius	133	1999	Daylami	138
1967	Busted	134	2000	Dubai Millennium	140
1968	Vaguely Noble	140	2001	Sakhee	136
1969	Levmoss	133	2002	High Chaparral	130
1970	Nijinsky	138		Sulamani	130
1971	Mill Reef	141	2003	Alamshar	133
1972	Mill Reef	141		Dalakhani	133
1973	Rheingold	137		Falbrav	133
1974	Allez France	136	2004	Doyen	132
1975	Grundy	137	2005	Hurricane Run	134
1976	Youth	135	2006	Rail Link	132
1977	Alleged	137			
1978	Alleged	138			
1979	Troy	137			
1980	Argument	133			
1981	Shergar	140			
1982	Ardross	134			
	Assert	134			
1983	Shareef Dancer	135			
1984	Sagace	135			
	Teenoso	135			
1985	Slip Anchor	136			
1986	Dancing Brave	140			
1987	Reference Point	139			
1988	Mtoto	134			
	Tony Bin	134			
1989	Old Vic	136			
1990	Saumarez	132			
1991	Generous	139			
1992	St Jovite	135			

Best Stayer/Best Performance In A Staying Race

Year	Horse	Rating		Year	Horse	Rating
1960	Charlottesville	135		1985	Lanfranco	123
1961	Pandofell	132			Phardante	123
	St Paddy	132		1986	Moon Madness	128
1962	Hethersett	134		1987	Reference Point	127 *
1963	Ragusa	137		1988	Minster Son	130
1964	Prince Royal	134		1989	Michelozzo	127 p
1965	Reliance	137		1990	Snurge	130
1966	Danseur	134		1991	Toulon	125
1967	Ribocco	129		1992	Mashaallah	123
1968	Dhaudevi	127		1993	Vintage Crop	125
	Samos	127		1994	Moonax	121
1969	Levmoss	133			Vintage Crop	121
1970	Hallez	130		1995	Double Trigger	122
	Roll of Honour	130			Moonax	122
1971	Ramsin	130			Strategic Choice	122
1972	Rock Roi	127		1996	Classic Cliche	124 *
1973	Parnell	130			Oscar Schindler	124 *
1974	Sagaro	131			Shantou	124
1975	Bruni	132		1997	Classic Cliche	126
1976	Crow	131 *		1998	Kayf Tara	126
1977	Alleged	135 *		1999	Kayf Tara	130
1978	Buckskin	133		2000	Kayf Tara	130
1979	Buckskin	131		2001	Milan	129
	Le Moss	131		2002	Vinnie Roe	126
1980	Le Moss	135		2003	Vinnie Roe	125
1981	Ardross	131		2004	Vinnie Roe	128
1982	Ardross	134		2005	Westerner	126 *
1983	Little Wolf	127		2006	Yeats	128
1984	Commanche Run	129				

achieved higher rating at middle distances

Best Three-Year-Old Colt

Year	Horse	Rating		Year	Horse	Rating
1960	Charlottesville	135		1985	Slip Anchor	136
1961	Molvedo	137		1986	Dancing Brave	140
1962	Arctic Storm	134		1987	Reference Point	139
	Hethersett	134		1988	Warning	136
1963	Ragusa	137		1989	Zilzal	137
1964	Prince Royal	134		1990	Dayjur	137
1965	Sea Bird	145		1991	Generous	139
1966	Danseur	134		1992	St Jovite	135
1967	Reform	132		1993	Zafonic	130
1968	Vaguely Noble	140		1994	Tikkanen	130
1969	Habitat	134		1995	Lammtarra	134
1970	Nijinsky	138		1996	Mark of Esteem	137
1971	Brigadier Gerard	141		1997	Peintre Celebre	137
	Mill Reef	141		1998	Desert Prince	130
1972	Deep Diver	134			High-Rise	130
	Sallust	134		1999	Montjeu	137
1973	Thatch	136		2000	Sinndar	134
1974	Caracolero	131		2001	Galileo	134
	Dankaro	131		2002	Rock of Gibraltar	133
	Nonoalco	131		2003	Alamshar	133
	Sagaro	131			Dalakhani	133
1975	Grundy	137		2004	Bago	130
1976	Youth	135		2005	Hurricane Run	134
1977	Alleged	137		2006	George Washington	133
1978	Ile de Bourbon	133				
1979	Troy	137				
1980	Moorestyle	137				
1981	Shergar	140				
1982	Assert	134				
	Green Forest	134				
1983	Shareef Dancer	135				
1984	El Gran Senor	136				

Best Three-Year-Old Filly

Year	Horse	Rating	Year	Horse	Rating
1960	Marguerite Vernaut	**129**	1983	Habibti	**136**
1961	Crisper	**127**	1984	Northern Trick	**131**
	Sweet Solera	**127**	1985	Oh So Sharp	**131**
1962	Gay Mairi	**131**	1986	Darara	**129**
	Secret Step	**131**		Sonic Lady	**129**
1963	Hula Dancer	**133**	1987	Indian Skimmer	**132**
	Noblesse	**133**	1988	Diminuendo	**126**
1964	La Bamba	**129**	1989	Behera	**129**
1965	Aunt Edith	**128**		Sierra Roberta	**129**
1966	Caterina	**124**	1990	Salsabil	**130**
1967	Casaque Grise	**126**	1991	Magic Night	**128**
1968	Roseliere	**127**	1992	User Friendly	**128**
1969	Flossy	**129**	1993	Intrepidity	**124**
1970	Highest Hopes	**129**	1994	Balanchine	**131**
	Miss Dan	**129**	1995	Ridgewood Pearl	**125**
1971	Pistol Packer	**133**	1996	Bosra Sham	**132**
1972	San San	**133**	1997	Borgia	**124**
1973	Allez France	**132**	1998	Cape Verdi	**126**
	Dahlia	**132**	1999	Ramruma	**123**
1974	Comtesse de Loir	**131**	2000	Egyptband	**128**
1975	Rose Bowl	**133**	2001	Banks Hill	**128**
1976	Pawneese	**131**	2002	Bright Sky	**124**
1977	Dunfermline	**133**	2003	Six Perfections	**124**
1978	Swiss Maid	**129**	2004	Attraction	**125**
1979	Three Troikas	**133**		Ouija Board	**125**
1980	Detroit	**131**	2005	Divine Proportions	**125**
1981	Marwell	**133**	2006	Mandesha	**124**
1982	Akiyda	**131**			
	Time Charter	**131**			

Best Older Male

Year	Horse	Rating	Year	Horse	Rating
1960	Bleep-Bleep	**134**	1985	Rainbow Quest	**134**
1961	Pandofell	**132**		Sagace	**134**
	St Paddy	**132**	1986	Shardari	**134**
1962	Match	**135**	1987	Mtoto	**134**
1963	Exbury	**138**	1988	Mtoto	**134**
1964	Relko	**136**		Tony Bin	**134**
1965	Free Ride	**129**	1989	Carroll House	**132**
	Indiana	**129**	1990	Markofdistinction	**130**
1966	Diatome	**132**		Old Vic	**130**
1967	Busted	**134**	1991	Epervier Bleu	**129**
1968	Royal Palace	**131**	1992	Pistolet Bleu	**133**
1969	Levmoss	**133**	1993	Opera House	**131**
1970	Balidar	**133**	1994	Barathea	**127**
1971	Caro	**133**		Hernando	**127**
1972	Brigadier Gerard	**144**	1995	Freedom Cry	**132**
1973	Rheingold	**137**	1996	Halling	**133**
1974	Admetus	**133**	1997	Pilsudski	**134**
	Margouillat	**133**		Swain	**134**
1975	Bustino	**136**	1998	Intikhab	**135**
1976	Trepan	**133** ?	1999	Daylami	**138**
	Lochnager	**132**	2000	Dubai Millennium	**140**
1977	Balmerino	**133**	2001	Sakhee	**136**
	Sagaro	**133**	2002	Keltos	**132**
1978	Alleged	**138**	2003	Hawk Wing	**136**
1979	Ile de Bourbon	**133**	2004	Doyen	**132**
1980	Le Moss	**135**	2005	Azamour	**130**
1981	Northjet	**136**		Rakti	**130**
1982	Ardross	**134**		Westerner	**130**
1983	Diamond Shoal	**130**	2006	David Junior	**132**
1984	Sagace	**135**			
	Teenoso	**135**			

Best Older Female

Year	Horse	Rating	Year	Horse	Rating
1960	Petite Etoile	134	1986	Triptych	132
1961	Petite Etoile	131	1987	Triptych	133
1962	Crisper	126	1988	Indian Skimmer	133
1963	Secret Step	128		Miesque	133
1964	Matatina	124	1989	Gabina	121
1965	Astaria	123		Indian Skimmer	121
1966	Aunt Edith	126		Royal Touch	121
1967	Parthian Glance	119	1990	Lady Winner	121
1968	Bamboozle	114		Ode	121
	Park Top	114	1991	Miss Alleged	125
	Secret Ray	114	1992	Kooyonga	125
1969	Park Top	131	1993	Lochsong	129
1970	Park Top	129	1994	Lochsong	129
1971	Miss Dan	124	1995	Hever Golf Rose	123
1972	Abergwaun	128	1996	Timarida	125
1973	Attica Meli	125	1997	Bosra Sham	130
1974	Allez France	136	1998	One So Wonderful	121
1975	Lianga	133		Seeking The Pearl	121
1976	Ivanjica	132	1999	Alborada	122
1977	Flying Water	132		Susu	122
1978	Sanedtki	129	2000	Shiva	127
	Trillion	129	2001	Pipalong	121
1979	Trillion	124	2002	Banks Hill	126
1980	Three Troikas	128	2003	Islington	124
1981	Gold River	132	2004	Soviet Song	126
1982	April Run	130		Tante Rose	126
1983	All Along	134	2005	Soviet Song	126
1984	Cormorant Wood	130	2006	Pride	128
1985	Pebbles	135			

Timeform Race Cards

Price £6 each

Availability

Timeform Race Cards are available for every meeting every day from www.timeform.com.

They are also available by post for major Flat meetings Wed-Sat (posted at the 48-hour stage), and are on sale on the day at most of Britain's racecourses.

Features

The Timeform Race Card is indispensable to the serious backer. It presents everything you need for profitable betting in a clear and concise form. Each individual entry includes

➤ a Timeform commentary packed with winner-finding details

➤ a Timeform rating adjusted to the weight allocated

➤ ratings summary for up to the last six starts

➤ Timeform Computer Timefigures (Flat cards only)

Available to download for every meeting every day from www.timeform.com

For mail order sales please call 01422 330540
or write to 19 Timeform House, Halifax HX1 1XF

Timeform Black Book

Price £19 each

Availability

New issue posted every
Wednesday [Flat issues Apr-Oct;
Jumps issues Oct-Apr]. Available
only by post and through selected
trade agents.

Features

The Timeform Black Book is the weekly A-to-Z of British
racing. It's an invaluable reference for professionals and is also
ideal for backers who concentrate their betting around the
weekend's racing as each issue contains the Timeform Briefing
for Thursday, Friday, Saturday and Sunday, with race-card
style coverage of selected big races.

➤ an individual rating and commentary for every horse that
   has run during the season to date

➤ the complete Timeform Briefing for the weekend's racing

➤ the current Timeform top 100s

➤ the previous week's 'Horses In Focus'

Order online at www.timeform.com/shop

Timeform Perspective

Price For current season subscriptions please see www.timeform.com/shop or call 01422 330540

Availability

Published in Flat and Jumps versions, either as a full service (sent three times a week) or as Perspective Weekend, posted every Wed.

Features

Timeform Perspective presents analysis race by race rather than horse by horse.

What sets Perspective apart as a form-book is the quality of the analysis it contains. The penetrating observations of Timeform's racereaders are supplemented by those of our handicappers and comment writers to make a thoroughly rewarding read and a magnificent guide to winner-finding.

➤ the full result of every race in Britain and Ireland

➤ analysis of thousands of individual performances

➤ a comprehensive Timeform Briefing service, with ratings for forthcoming meetings

Order online at www.timeform.com/shop

AGE, WEIGHT & DISTANCE TABLE

Timeform's scale of weight-for-age for the flat

Dist	Age	July 1-16	July 17-31	Aug 1-16	Aug 17-31	Sept 1-16	Sept 17-30	Oct 1-16	Oct 17-31	Nov 1-16	Nov 17-30	Dec 1-16	Dec 17-31
5f	4	10–0	10–0	10–0	10–0	10–0	10–0	10–0	10–0	10–0	10–0	10–0	10–0
	3	9–11	9–12	9–12	9–12	9–13	9–13	9–13	9–13	10–0	10–0	10–0	10–0
	2	8–8	8–9	8–10	8–11	8–12	8–13	9–0	9–1	9–2	9–2	9–3	9–4
6f	4	10–0	10–0	10–0	10–0	10–0	10–0	10–0	10–0	10–0	10–0	10–0	10–0
	3	9–10	9–10	9–11	9–11	9–12	9–12	9–12	9–13	9–13	9–13	9–13	10–0
	2	8–5	8–6	8–7	8–8	8–9	8–10	8–11	8–12	8–13	9–0	9–1	9–2
7f	4	10–0	10–0	10–0	10–0	10–0	10–0	10–0	10–0	10–0	10–0	10–0	10–0
	3	9–9	9–9	9–10	9–10	9–11	9–11	9–11	9–12	9–12	9–12	9–13	9–13
	2	8–2	8–3	8–4	8–5	8–6	8–7	8–9	8–10	8–11	8–12	8–13	9–0
1m	4	10–0	10–0	10–0	10–0	10–0	10–0	10–0	10–0	10–0	10–0	10–0	10–0
	3	9–7	9–8	9–8	9–9	9–9	9–10	9–10	9–11	9–11	9–12	9–12	9–12
	2			8–2	8–3	8–4	8–5	8–6	8–7	8–8	8–9	8–10	8–11
9f	4	10–0	10–0	10–0	10–0	10–0	10–0	10–0	10–0	10–0	10–0	10–0	10–0
	3	9–6	9–7	9–7	9–8	9–8	9–9	9–9	9–10	9–10	9–11	9–11	9–12
	2					8–1	8–3	8–4	8–5	8–6	8–7	8–8	8–9
1¼m	4	10–0	10–0	10–0	10–0	10–0	10–0	10–0	10–0	10–0	10–0	10–0	10–0
	3	9–5	9–5	9–6	9–7	9–7	9–8	9–8	9–9	9–9	9–10	9–10	9–11
	2						8–0	8–1	8–2	8–4	8–5	8–6	8–7
11f	4	10–0	10–0	10–0	10–0	10–0	10–0	10–0	10–0	10–0	10–0	10–0	10–0
	3	9–3	9–4	9–5	9–5	9–6	9–7	9–7	9–8	9–8	9–9	9–9	9–10
1½m	4	10–0	10–0	10–0	10–0	10–0	10–0	10–0	10–0	10–0	10–0	10–0	10–0
	3	9–2	9–2	9–3	9–4	9–5	9–5	9–6	9–7	9–7	9–8	9–9	9–9
13f	4	9–13	9–13	10–0	10–0	10–0	10–0	10–0	10–0	10–0	10–0	10–0	10–0
	3	9–0	9–1	9–2	9–3	9–4	9–4	9–5	9–6	9–6	9–7	9–8	9–8
1¾m	4	9–13	9–13	9–13	10–0	10–0	10–0	10–0	10–0	10–0	10–0	10–0	10–0
	3	8–13	9–0	9–1	9–2	9–3	9–3	9–4	9–5	9–5	9–6	9–7	9–7
15f	4	9–12	9–13	9–13	9–13	9–13	10–0	10–0	10–0	10–0	10–0	10–0	10–0
	3	8–12	8–13	9–0	9–1	9–1	9–2	9–3	9–4	9–4	9–5	9–6	9–6
2m	4	9–12	9–12	9–13	9–13	9–13	9–13	10–0	10–0	10–0	10–0	10–0	10–0
	3	8–10	8–11	8–12	8–13	9–0	9–1	9–2	9–3	9–3	9–4	9–5	9–5
2¼m	4	9–11	9–12	9–12	9–12	9–13	9–13	9–13	9–13	10–0	10–0	10–0	10–0
	3	8–8	8–9	8–10	8–11	8–12	8–13	9–0	9–1	9–2	9–2	9–3	9–4
2½m	4	9–10	9–11	9–11	9–12	9–12	9–12	9–13	9–13	9–13	9–13	10–0	10–0
	3	8–6	8–7	8–8	8–9	8–10	8–11	8–12	8–13	9–0	9–1	9–2	9–3

For 5-y-o's and older, use 10-0 in all cases
Race distances in the above tables are shown only at 1 furlong intervals.
For races over odd distances, the nearest distance shown in the table should be used:
thus for races of 1m to 1m 109 yards, use the table weights for 1m;
for 1m 110 yards to 1m 219 yards use the 9f table

**The age, weight and distance table covering January to June
appears on the end paper at the front of the book**